Corporate Information Systems Management
Text and Cases

Corporate Information
Systems Management
Text and Cases

James I. Cash, Jr.

F. Warren McFarlan

James L. McKenney

Michael R. Vitale

All of the
Graduate School of Business Administration
Harvard University

Second Edition
1988

Homewood, Illinois 60430

To Clemmie, Karen, and Mary

This book was set in Century Schoolbook by Carlisle Communications, Ltd.
The editors were Lawrence E. Alexander, Paula M. Buschman, Joan A. Hopkins.
The production manager was Carma W. Fazio.
The drawings were done by John Foote.
The Maple-Vail Book Manufacturing Group was the printer and binder.

ISBN 0-256-03626-8

Library of Congress Catalog Card No. 87—81572

Printed in the United States of America

1 2 3 4 5 6 7 8 9 0 V 5 4 3 2 1 0 9 8

Preface

This book of text and cases is aimed at students and managers interested in contemporary information technology (IT)—computer communication and office systems—management. It is intended to communicate the relevant issues in effectively managing the information services activity. No assumptions are made in the book concerning the prior background of the readers with regard to the details of IT technology. It is, however, assumed that the reader has a basic background of either administrative experience or management training.

Our purpose is to provide perspective and advice for coping with the information explosion. This expansion is best characterized by the doubling of the number of volumes in the Library of Congress from 1933 to 1966 and the doubling again from 1967 to 1979; the collection is expected to double a third time before the end of 1987. At the same time, acceleration in the growth of knowledge in science is stimulating a dramatic increase in the number of new products based on new technology. This growth, coupled with the increasing international nature of many businesses, puts an enormous burden on the individual to keep abreast of events. It is a sound scientific conjecture that a human can retain 25 billion characters of information.[1] However, it has proven impossible to retrieve and use everything one knows, let alone keep the knowledge up to date.

As Peter Keen and Michael Scott-Morton[2] have suggested, man-machine systems can assist the individual in coping with this information overload. We feel the broader issue is to help organizations adapt the new technology to better compete in their industry segments. Since the first edition of this book appeared, there has been a significant increase in awareness of how IT impacts a firm's competitiveness and how to search for competitive advantage. This edition of the book incorporates this material. Its treatment of organizational issues has also been modified to deal with the new challenges posed by the latest

---

[1]Carl Sagan, *The Dragons in Eden* (New York: Random House, 1971).

[2]Peter F. Keen and Michael S. Scott-Morton, *Decision Support Systems* (Reading, Mass.: Addison-Wesley Publishing, 1978).

technologies. This book is designed to help present and future managers prepare their organizations for better information services management.

Conceptually the book is organized around a management audit of the information services activity. We have combined text and cases to convey and illustrate key conceptual frameworks. Chapter 1 begins with an overview of the key questions to resolve in assessing the health of an IT activity. Chapter 2 then presents a series of frameworks that the authors have found useful in analyzing and structuring the problems in this field. Subsequent chapters address issues relating to how the IT activity can best be organized, planned, and controlled.

The material in this book is the outgrowth of a series of research projects conducted by the authors at the Harvard Business School over the past several years. We are indebted to both former Dean Lawrence E. Fouraker and Dean John H. McArthur for making the time available for this work.

We are particularly indebted to the many firms and government organizations that provided us with so much time and insight during the course of our research. All the cases and concepts in this book are based on observation of real practice. Without the cooperation of these organizations, it would have been impossible to prepare this manuscript.

We are especially grateful for the many valued suggestions and insights provided us by our colleagues David Goldstein, Melissa Mead, John Sviokla, and Shoshanah Zuboff. In addition we acknowledge the valuable work done by Jane Linder, Poppy McLeod, Donna Stoddard, Phillip Pyburn, and Kathleen Curley during their time as doctoral students. Lynn Salerno, in her editorial capacity at the *Harvard Business Review,* provided valuable assistance. We would also like to express our appreciation to our office staff, Judith Tully, Maureen Donovan, Lillian Braudis, and Diane Shapiro, who typed and edited numerous versions of the work.

James I. Cash, Jr.
F. Warren McFarlan
James L. McKenney
Michael R. Vitale

Contents

1 Introduction *1*

The Challenge of IT Technology. Complexity of the IT Management Task: *A Young Technology. Technological Growth. IT-User Coordination. Specialization. A Shift in Focus.* Senior-Management Questions. Issues in Information Technology: *The IT Environment. Organization. Management Control. Project Management. Multinational Issues. Planning. The IT Business.*

Case 1–1   **Frontier Airlines, Inc.**   *17*

Case 1–2   **Hercules Incorporated**   *42*

2 Manageable Trends *71*

Introduction. Theme 1: Strategic Impact. Theme 2: Merging Technologies. Theme 3: Organizational Learning: *Phase 1. Technology Identification and Investment. Phase 2. Technological Learning and Adaptation. Phase 3. Rationalization/Management Control. Phase 4. Maturity/Widespread Technology Transfer.* Theme 4: Make or Buy: *Make. Buy.* Theme 5: Systems Life Cycle: *Design. Construction. Implementation. Operation. Maintenance. Summary.* Theme 6: Power Balance among Three Constituencies: *IT Management. User Management. General Management.*

Case 2–1   **Mark Twain Bancshares, Inc. (1980) (A) (Condensed)**   *92*

Case 2–2   **Mark Twain Bancshares, Inc. (1980) (B) (Condensed)**   *107*

Case 2–3   **Mark Twain Bancshares, Inc. (1980) (C) (Condensed)**   *110*

3 Information Technology Changes the Way You Compete 119

Analyzing Impact: *Forces that Shape Strategy. Search for Opportunity.* Value Chain Analysis: *Inbound Logistics. Operations and Product Structure. Outbound Logistics. Marketing and Sales. After-Sales Service. Corporate Infrastructure. Human Resources. Technology Development. Procurement.* The Risks of Information Systems Success: *1. Systems that Change the Basis of Competition to a Company's Disadvantage. 2. Systems that Lower Entry Barriers. 3. Systems that Bring On Litigation or Regulation. 4. Systems that Increase the Power of Customers or Suppliers, Perhaps to the Point of Encouraging Them to Bypass the Innovator Entirely.* Assessing Competitor Risk. The Challenge. A New Point of View: *Planning Issues. Confidentiality and Competition. Evaluating Expenditures. The IT-Management Partnership. Opening Questions.* A Final Thought.

Case 3–1 OTISLINE 146

Case 3–2 Manufacturers Hanover Corporation: Worldwide Network 163

4 IT Redraws Competitive Boundaries 201

IOS Development. IOS versus DDP. Analyzing IOS's Impact. IOS and Generic Strategy: *1. Overall Cost Leadership. 2. Differentiation. 3. Focus.* Influence on Industry Structure. Organizational Impact IOS Participation Profiles: *Information Entry and Receipt. Software Development and Maintenance. Network and Processing Management.* Control and Influence.

Case 4–1 American Hospital Supply Corporation: The ASAP System 217

Case 4–2 Jet Age Travel (Condensed) 235

5 IT Organization Issues 251

The IT Challenge to Organizational Structure: *Technological Change. Environmental Factors.* Merging the Islands of Information Technology. Managing the Assimilation of Emerging Information Technology: *The Four Phases of IT Assimilation. Innovation Management Study. The Emerging Technology (ET) Group.* Patterns of Hardware/Data Distribution: *Pressures toward a Large Central Hub of a Distributed Network. Pressures toward a Small Hub and Primary Distributed Environment.*

Case 5-1   General Foods: Information Services
           Department   *282*
Case 5-2   PlanPower: The Financial Planning Expert
           System   *301*

6   Organizational Issues and IT   *319*

Organization Issues in IT Development: *1. A Short-Term User-Need Situation—Strategically Important.   2. User Control to Achieve Automation.   3. Step-by-Step Innovation of a New Technology. 4. User Innovation as a Source of Productivity.*   Pressures toward User Dominance: *Pent-Up User Demand.   Competitive and Service Growth in the IT Market.   User Control.   Fit to Organization. User Learning.*   Pressures toward IT Control: *Staff Professionalism.   Feasibility Study Concerns.   Corporate Data Base System.   Fit to Corporate Structure and Strategy.   Cost Analysis.   IT Responsibilities.   User Responsibilities. General Management Support and Policy Overview.*

Case 6-1   Alcon Laboratories: Information Technology
           Group   *338*
Case 6-2   Mishawaka Industries, Inc.   *357*

7   IT Management Control   *373*

IT Evolution and Management Control: *Software Issues. Operations Issues.   Corporate Culture Forces.   Corporate Planning and Control Process.   Strategic Impact of IT on the Corporation.   Looking Ahead: Other Aspects of Control.*   Control Architecture: *Unallocated Cost Center.   Allocated Cost Center and Chargeout.   Profit Center.   Investment Center.   Transfer Pricing.*   Control Process (Financial and Nonfinancial): *Financial Reporting Process.   Nonfinancial Reporting Process.*   IT Audit Function.

Case 7-1   Frito-Lay, Inc.: Funding for Information Systems   *399*
Case 7-2   Intercontrol Chemical Corporation   *411*

8   A Portfolio Approach to IT Development   *429*

Project Risk: *Elements of Project Implementation Risk.   Project Categories and Degree of Risk.   Assessing Risk in Individual Projects.*   Portfolio Risk.   Project Management: A Contingency Approach (By Project Type): *Management Tools.   Influences on Tool Selection.   Relative Contribution of Management Tools.*

Case 8-1   Rogers Automotive Company   447

Case 8-2   Concordia Casting Company   469

9   Operations Management   483

Changing Operations Environment.   Developing an Operations Strategy: *The Role of IT Architecture.   System Design and Operations.   Externally Sourced Services—Pressures and Challenges.   Service Sourcing—Decision Authority.   Examples of Different Organization Approaches to Life-Cycle Control.* Technology Planning.   Measuring and Managing Capacity. Managing the IT Operations Work Force: *Selection of Operations Manager and Staff.   Human Issues in Managing the Work Force.* Production Planning and Control: *Resolving Priorities. Implementing Production Control and Measurement.*   Security.

Case 9-1   IBM Europe Headquarters   515

Case 9-2   Air Products and Chemicals, Inc.: Local Area Network (A)   535

Case 9-3   Air Products and Chemicals, Inc.: Local Area Network (B)   557

10   Multinational IT Issues   567

Diversity between Countries: *Sociopolitical.   Language.   Local Constraints.   Economic.   Currency.   Autonomy.   National Infrastructure.*   National IT Environments: *Availability of IT Professional Staff.   Central Telecommunications.   National IT Strategy.   General Level of IT Sophistication.   Size of Local Market.   Data Export Control.   Technological Awareness. Trade Union Environment.   Border Opportunities.*   Corporate Factors Affecting IT Requirements: *Nature of Firm's Business. Strategic Impact of IT.   Corporate Organization.   Company Technical and Control Characteristics.   Effects of Geography and Size of Companies.   Economic Analysis.   Other Considerations.* Multinational IT Policy Issues: *Communication and Data Management Standards.   Central Hardware/Software Concurrence or Approval.   Central Approval of Software Standards and Feasibility Studies.   Central Software Development.   IT Communications.   Staff Planning.   Consulting Services. Central IT Processing Support.   Technology Appraisal Program.*

Case 10-1   Finnpap/Finnboard   587

11 IT Planning: A Contingent Focus   *615*

Pressures toward IT Planning: *External (Corporate) Pressures.*
Internal (IT Process) Pressures.   Limitation of Planning Benefits:
Planning as a Resource Drain.   Fit to Corporate Culture.
Strategic Impact of IT Activities.   IT Management Climate.
IT Planning and Corporate Strategy: *Strategy 1: Be the Low-Cost*
Producer.   Strategy 2: Produce a Unique, Differentiated Product.
Strategy 3: Identify and Fill the Needs of Specialized Markets.
Corporate Environmental Factors Influencing Planning: *1. Perceived*
Importance and Status of the Systems Manager.   2. Physical
Proximity of Systems Group and General Management Team.
3. Corporate Culture and Management Style.   4. Organizational Size
and Complexity.   Example.

Case 11-1   Corning Glass Works: Information Systems
**   Planning   *639***

12 The IT Business   *659*

The IT Marketing Mix: *Product.   IT Consumer.   Cost.*
Channels of Distribution.   Competition.   Promotion.   Price.
Role of the Board of Directors.   Role of IT Chief Executive Officer.

General Management Library for the IT Manager   *677*

IT Library for the General Manager   *681*

Case Index   *683*

Index   *685*

Chapter 1

Introduction

The Challenge of IT Technology

Over the past 30 years, a major new set of managerial challenges has been created by the rapid evolution and spread of information systems technology (IT), which in this book will include the technologies of computers, telecommunications, and office automation. Attempting to deal with these changes has resulted in creation of new departments, massive recruiting of staff, major investments in computer hardware and software, and installation of systems that have profoundly affected both how the firm operates and how it chooses to compete. The impact of IT has not been confined to the large corporations; in its current form, it influences the very small (i.e., under $1 million sales) firms as well. Further, in the large corporations its influence is now very pervasive, reaching both into the smallest departments of the company and into managerial decision-making processes to an extent not even visualized 10 years ago.

Facing these challenges is complex because many members of corporate senior management received both their education and early work experience prior to the wide-scale introduction of computer technology. Consequently many feel somewhat uneasy about the subject and lack confidence that they have sufficient grasp to provide managerial oversight. Many IT managers face similar problems, since their first-hand technical experience was with technologies so different from those of the 1980s as to pose seemingly unrecognizable problems. Understanding the programming challenges of the rotational delay of the drum of an IBM 650 (a popular machine in the late 1950s) has no value in dealing with the challenges posed by today's sophisticated computer operating systems.

Further, the understanding of what makes acceptable management practice in the IT field has changed dramatically since 1971. Virtually all major, currently accepted conceptual frameworks for theories of management in this field have been developed since 1971. Therefore, a special burden has been placed on IT management, not just to meet day-to-day operating problems and new technologies but to assimilate and implement quite different methods for managing the activity. If IT managers are not committed to a process of self-renewal, they very quickly become obsolete.

This book is aimed at two quite different audiences in a firm. The first is the general corporation management, collectively responsible for providing general guidance for all activity, including IT. For these readers, this book offers a set of frameworks for looking at the IT activity in their firm, defines the policies they are responsible for executing, and provides insights on how they can be executed. It attempts to do this by helping them integrate the IT forest and its management challenge into the overall activities of the firm.

The second audience is senior IT management. For these readers, we have developed an integrated view of the totality of IT management for the 1980s. We identify key patterns that organize and make sense out of a bewildering cluster of operational detail. The focus for these senior managers moves from analysis of bark composition on individual trees to an overall perspective of the IT forest and its management challenge. The book thus integrates the needs of two quite different audiences (who are operationally very interdependent) and provides them with a common set of perspectives and a language system for communicating with each other.

It would be a serious mistake, of course, to consider the problems of IT management as being totally unique and separate from those of general management. While the authors freely admit to having spent most of their professional lives dealing with IT technical and managerial issues, much of our thinking has been shaped by literature dealing with general business. The issues of IT organization, for example, are best thought of as special applications of the work on integration and differentiation first started by the behaviorists Paul Lawrence and Jay Lorsch. Issues of IT planning and strategy are influenced on the one hand by the work of Michael Porter and Alfred Chandler in business policy and on the other hand by Kirby Warren and Richard Vancil in the area of planning. Notions of budgeting, zero-based budgeting, transfer pricing, profit centers, and so forth from the general field of management control are relevant here. The work of Wickham Skinner and Richard Rosenbloom in the area of factory management and transfer of technology has shed light on how the computer operations function can be better managed.

Many individual aspects of the IT management problems thus are not unique. What is unique is the peculiar confluence of these notions in running an efficient and evolving IT function. In thinking about this, some authors have found it useful to regard IT as a business within a business. Integrating the IT business into the rest of a firm may then have special organizational, strategy-formulating challenges. This book is organized around four concepts of how this kind of business can be better managed.

Strategic Relevance. An efficiently and effectively managed IT activity's strategic relevance to the firm is not a constant; rather, it varies between industries and firms and, over time, for an individual firm. It is also more significant to some operating units and functions of a company than to others. This notion of differing strategic relevance is critical in understanding the wide diversity of potential practices for managing and integrating the IT function.

Corporate Culture. "Within a business" is a very important phrase in understanding how the IT business itself should be managed. The values of senior management, the approaches to corporate planning, the corporate philosophy of control, and the speed of technological change in the company constitute one set of determinants. The other set is composed of the variables of the external marketplaces. Both sets of factors have a major influence on what is appropriate management practice both in managing IT internally and in integrating it with the rest of the firm. What works in one corporate environment may fail abysmally in another one.

Contingency. IT management in the 1980s is much more influenced by notions of contingency than it was in the 1970s. In the 1970s, as IT management systems were being implemented where chaos existed before, simplistic and mechanistic approaches to management control, planning, and so forth were a great improvement over what was there before. As these systems were assimilated into the firm, the initial surge of value from their introduction gave way to frustration in many cases because of their inherent rigidity. They answered some challenges well and others not at all. Dealing with this rigidity has required introduction of more complexity and flexibility in the approaches used to adapt them to a continually changing environment.

Technology Transfer. The diffusion of information technology can and must be managed. If poorly managed, it will evolve not into a well-functioning support system but instead into a collection of disjointed islands of technology. Although the general work in technology transfer forms the basis for our thinking, we have expanded that experience because of the unique aspects of a technology that deals with information. What makes the introduction and evolution of IT so challenging is that, in many of its applications, success comes only when people have changed their thinking processes. Hence we will refer to it as an "intellectual technology." Without this concomitant change in thinking, we too frequently have a technical success but an administrative failure.

Complexity of the IT Management Task

A number of factors make the assimilation of IT technology a particularly challenging task. An understanding of these factors is essential if a sensible IT management strategy is to be developed. The more important of these factors are enumerated here.

A Young Technology

IT, at least in its modern form (with high-speed computers), has had a very short life. Its earliest commercial application occurred in 1952. Thirty-five years is a very short time for the distilled outline of a new management profession to develop. Fields like marketing, accounting, finance, and production had a thriving body of literature and know-how in place in 1920. An incredible amount of knowledge and changes in thinking has occurred in these fields in this century, but it could be assimilated within an organized field of thought. Evolution, not revolution, has been the challenge in these fields. The challenge in IT has been to develop from a zero base during a period where applications grew from being very narrow and specialized to being quite broad and integrated, with budgets and staffs exploding in size.

In this environment, not surprisingly, the half-life of administrative knowledge has been quite short. Not a framework or avenue of thinking in this book predates 1973 in a published form, with most theories developing in the late 1970s and early 1980s. Indeed, this second edition differs markedly from its predecessor, published only four years ago. (We are under no illusion that this will be the last word on the subject but still hope to contribute to better insights through further research.)

Technological Growth

Another source of administrative challenge lies in the fact that the field has undergone sustained and dramatic growth in the cost/performance of its technologies. Over a 10^6 improvement in processing and storage capacity has occurred since 1953, and the rate of change is expected to continue at the same pace at least through the 1980s and early 1990s. (As in all technologies, a point of maturity will come, but we are not yet there.)

This technical explosion has continuously cast up new families of profitable applications as well as permitting old ones to be done in different ways. One painful aspect of this has been that yesterday's strategic coup often becomes today's high-overhead, inefficient liability. The natural tendency to utilize a particular approach too long has been exacerbated by the prevailing accounting practice of writing off software expense as incurred rather than capitalizing it and then amortizing it over a period of years. These practices conceal both the fact that the organization has an asset and the fact that it is becoming an aging asset.

IT-User Coordination

The complexities of developing IT systems has forced the creation of specialized departments, resulting in a series of strained relationships with the users of their service. This has been an enduring headache from the start of IT, and there is probably not a better example of C. P. Snow's two-culture problem in existence in the 1980s than the relationship between IT and general management.

IT has specialized in order to harness the various necessary technical skills to get the job done. The specialists have appropriately developed their own language systems. To communicate among each other, they speak of bits, bytes, DOS, CICS, and so on. General management, however, has a quite different language, featuring words such as sales growth, return on investment, and productivity. While it is clear that some of the newer technologies (such as user-oriented programming languages and microcomputers) have helped users, substantial problems still remain. Indeed, the coordination issues are more complex. A long-term need will exist for continually developing new integrating devices, such as steering committees and user department analysts, to help handle the problem.

This problem is not remarkably different from that faced by the accounting profession with its special language. Despite 6,000 years of accounting history, substantial friction and misunderstanding still exist between accounting departments and users of accounting information. It is surprising to the authors that significant numbers of people who enter general management have only a sketchy ability to handle accounting information.

For numerous reasons, education will continue only partially to address these problems. The experience that students have in colleges and high schools in writing one-time, problem-solving programs—

while useful and confidence expanding—develops a very different set of skills than those skills necessary to generate programs for processing business transactions reliably on a day-in, day-out basis. Neither does experience in preparing spreadsheet programs as a staff analyst provide necessary perspective. Unfortunately, education often does not address the existence of these differences, and it produces graduates who are ill trained for these tasks but don't know it and thus have excessive self-confidence. Another educational issue is that some individuals are cognitively better equipped to assimilate information technology than others. One of our colleagues has colorfully described this as the world being divided into "poets" and "engineers" (roughly equally prevalent in general management).

Specialization

The increased specialization of contemporary technology and the explosion of skills needed to staff it have posed a fourth major managerial challenge. As IT has evolved, it has created a proliferation of languages, data base management needs, operating systems support staff needs, and so on, all of which have increased significantly the complexity of the IT management job from an internal perspective.

A Shift in Focus

A fifth challenge has been a significant shift in the types of applications being automated. Early applications were heavily focused on highly structured problems, such as hard transaction processing, where one could usually be quite precise about the potential stream of benefits. These applications involved automation of a number of clerical functions and operational control functions, such as inventory management, airline seat reservations, and credit extension. In the case of airline seat reservations, it was able to bring to the activity a level of structure and decision rules not previously present.

Increasingly, today's applications are providing new types of decision support information for both management control and strategic planning decisions. Evaluation of the payout of these expenditures on an objective basis either before, during, or after they are expended is almost impossible. Individuals may have opinions about these values, but quantification turns out to be very elusive. Also, the best way to develop these decision support applications is quite different from the conventional wisdom for the transaction-driven systems.[1] The detailed

---

[1]Michael Scott-Morton and Peter Keen, *Decision Support Systems* (Reading, Mass.: Addison-Wesley Publishing, 1980).

systems study, with its documentation and controls prior to programming, is often too rigid. For these systems, prototyping or doing it "rough and dirty" is proving to be the best approach. In short, the new types of application are forcing a shift both in the ways to evaluate projects and in the best ways to manage them. This is not an argument for a more permissive approach to system design and evaluation but rather a cry to be tough minded in a positive way.

In combination, these factors create a very complex and challenging managerial environment. They form the backdrop in the discussions of specific managerial approaches in the succeeding chapters.

Senior-Management Questions

In viewing the health of an organization's IT activity, our research indicated that a series of six critical questions repeatedly emerge in senior management's minds. We will not argue at this stage that these are the questions that *should* be raised but rather note that they are the questions that *are* raised. Four of these questions are essentially diagnostic in nature, while the remaining two are clearly action oriented.

1. Is my firm being affected *competitively* either by omissions in work being done or by poor execution of this work? Am I missing bets that, if properly executed, would give me a competitive edge? Conversely, maybe I am not doing so well in IT, but I don't have to do well in IT in my industry to be a success. Failure to do well in a competitively important area is a significant problem. Failure to perform well in a nonstrategic area is something that should be dealt with more calmly.

2. Is my development portfolio *effective*? Am I spending the right amount of money, and is it focused at the appropriate applications? This question is one that is often inappropriately raised. Scenario: An industry survey calculating IT expenditures as a percent of something or other for 15 industry competitors is circulated among the firm's senior management. On one dimension or another, it is observed that their firm is distinctly different from the others, which causes great excitement (normally, when their firm's figures are on the high side). After much investigation, one of two findings often emerges: (*a*) Our company has a different accounting system for IT than our competitors, and therefore the results are not meaningful. (*b*) Our company has a different strategy, geographical location, and/or mix of management strengths and weaknesses than our competitors, and therefore, on this dimension also, the results are not meaningful.

In short, raising the question of effectiveness is appropriate in our judgment, but attempting to identify it simplistically through industry surveys of competitors is not.

3. Is my firm spending *efficiently*? Maybe I have the right expenditure level, but am I getting the productivity out of my hardware and staff resources that I should get? This is a particularly relevant question in the 1980s, a decade that is being dominated both by extreme levels of professional staff shortages and by intensified international competition.

4. Is my firm's IT activity insulated well enough against the *risks* of a major *operational disaster*? There is no general-purpose answer as to what an appropriate level of protection is. Rather, it varies by organization, relating to the current dependence on smoothly operating existing systems.

5. Is the *leadership* of the IT activity appropriate for the role it now plays in our organization and the special challenges now in front of it? Historically, senior management has used the mechanisms of changing IT management as one of its main tools in dealing with frustrating IT performance shortfalls. (This high turnover has continued in the 1980s.) One key reason for this is that it represents the quickest and apparently easiest step for senior management to take when uneasy about departmental performance. Also, as you will read in Chapter 2, the nature of the job and its requisite skills tend to evolve over time, and a set of leadership skills and perspectives for one environment may not be appropriate for another. Further, in many situations, the problem is compounded by lack of suitable explicit performance measurement standards (metrics) and data to assess performance objectively. As will be discussed in subsequent chapters, we believe the development and installation of these metrics is absolutely vital. In their absence a 50 percent improvement in ability to meet service schedules, for example, may be totally overlooked, with the concern about remaining problems simply being heightened so the managerial situation is judged not to have changed.

6. Are the IT resources *appropriately placed* in the firm? Organizational issues—such as where the IT resource should report, how development and hardware resources should be distributed within the company, and existence and potential role of an executive steering committee—are examples of topics of intense interest to senior management. They not only are actionable but are similar in breadth to decisions made by general management in other aspects of the firm's operations.

These questions are intuitive from the viewpoint of general management and flow naturally from its perspective and experience in dealing with other areas of the firm. We have not found all of them as stated to be easily researchable or answerable in specific situations and have consequently neither selected them as the basic framework of the book

FIGURE 1-1   The IT Environment

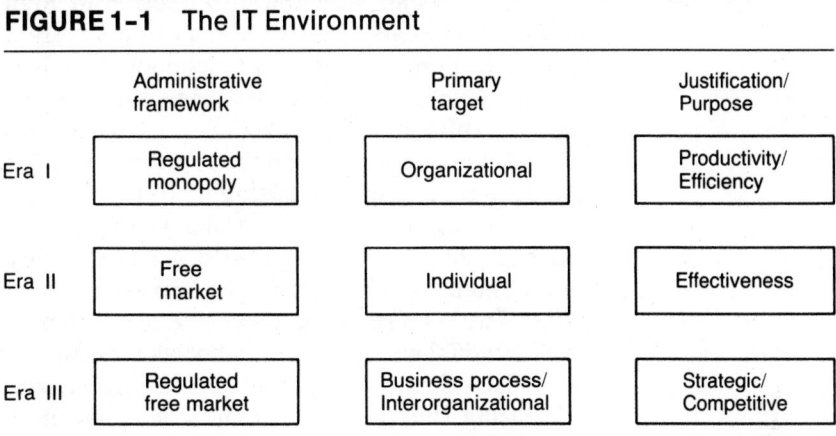

	Administrative framework	Primary target	Justification/ Purpose
Era I	Regulated monopoly	Organizational	Productivity/ Efficiency
Era II	Free market	Individual	Effectiveness
Era III	Regulated free market	Business process/ Interorganizational	Strategic/ Competitive

nor attempted to describe specifically how each can be answered. Rather, we selected a complementary set of questions that not only form the outline of the book, but whose answers will give insight into the earlier questions. The following paragraphs summarize these questions, and Chapters 3 through 12 deal with them in far greater depth. Together they form the outline of a "management audit" of the IT activity that can produce an agenda for action.

Issues in Information Technology

The IT Environment

The text of Chapters 2, 3, and 4 defines a very different role for IT, compared to its early uses. One way of describing the new role is illustrated in Figure 1-1. This chart explains the changing environment by focusing on three items: the administrative framework in place to facilitate and control the assimilation of information technology, the primary target of IT applications, and the way IT applications have been justified.

From the 50s to the early 70s the data processing manager was the single source of computing cycles and technology expertise. To use an industrial analogy, IT operated as a "regulated monopoly." If someone wanted access to computing cycles and technology expertise, they had to go to the data processing manager. There was no alternative. The primary focus of applications was organizationwide (payroll, accounting, production scheduling, order entry). New applications were justified on either a cost elimination or cost displacement basis. This IT management environment we call Era I.

Era II began with the introduction of minicomputers and time sharing in the early 1970s. It was dramatically accelerated in the late 70s by the personal computer. Suddenly a wide range of new channels was introduced for users to pursue technology expertise, processing cycles, and software. This introduced a "free market" (at least relatively; users no longer had to go to the IT manager to gain access to computer and communications technology). Today's M.B.A. graduates may enter a company bringing with them a computer which has 20 times the capability of an early computer at .5 percent the price. In Era II's free-market arena, the rigid top-down controls developed and implemented in Era I were no longer applicable. At this point for many applications, the individual was the primary decision maker and now often had sufficient discretionary resources to reinforce that independence.

During this period a dramatic shift occurred in project justification. Individual and corporate *effectiveness* became the key justification measure. Era I applications and their administrative systems could not and did not disappear. Rather, the IT management environment was made more complex with the additional challenge of managing easily accessible, individually exploited technology concurrently with Era I technology.

In what we will call the third era of information technology, management again did not preempt prior applications, although it has forced important changes in administrative processes. Era III is best described on the basis of the justification/purpose column in Figure 1–1. A growing number of companies have used IT to cause significant shifts in market share or competitive positioning. As we examine the administrative framework for these companies, it becomes clear they are not at one end of this regulated versus free-market spectrum or the other. They have attempted to create a "regulated free-market environment" where the primary objective is exploiting the awareness, knowledge, and expertise generated during Era II, to innovate and create dramatically different approaches to the conduct of business, based on the capability of IT. Frequently these uses of technology transcend traditional company or industry boundaries and/or facilitate restructuring internal organizations and functions.

Organization

Chapters 5 and 6 are most closely aligned to the senior management questions 5 and 6 listed earlier in this chapter. Several main themes are important in this material. First and foremost, what is an appropriate pattern for distributing hardware and software development resources within the corporation? The issues of patterns of distributed resources (including stand-alone mini- and microcomputers) have been well studied, and appropriate ways of thinking about them have been developed. These ways are heavily contingent on such influences as corporate organization, corporate culture, leadership style of the chief executive officer (CEO), importance of IT to achievement of corporate goals, and current sophistication of IT management. Within any pattern of distributed resources, there is need for appropriate policies administered centrally to ensure that suitable overall direction is being given.

A second complicating issue is ensuring that IT is broadly enough defined and that the converging and increasingly integrated technologies of computing, telecommunications, and word processing are in fact being adequately integrated. When dealing with international coordination, these issues are more complicated than in the domestic arena. Chapter 10 is devoted to the issues posed by different national infrastructures: staff availability, level of telecommunications sophistication, specific vendor support, great geographic distance, different spoken languages, transborder data flows, national culture and sensitivity, and so forth.

Finally, issues of organization reporting chains, level of reporting, IT leadership style, and steering committees are also of concern. In the mid-1980s, we believe there are better ways to think about these issues. Although common questions and methods of analysis exist, very different answers will emerge in different organizational settings.

Appropriate controls over daily IT operations as described in Chapter 9 ensure that both cost efficiency and operations reliability are important parts of the IT activity. The IT operations activity represents a very specialized form of manufacturing environment, with some unique problems. First, operations are completing a significant transition from a batch, job-shop style to a continuous-process manufacturing or utility style. Not only has this changed the way they can best be organized, but it has dramatically altered the types of controls that are appropriate. Second, in a number of firms, the IT activity has embedded itself so deeply in the heart of the firm's operations that unevenness in its performance causes immediate operating problems. These firms need significantly greater controls and backup arrangements than firms that have less dependence.

The performance of operations can be measured on a number of dimensions. Cost control, ability to meet batch report deadlines, peak-load response time, and speed of response to complaints or unexpected requests are examples of these dimensions. To optimize all of these simultaneously is impossible. Each firm needs a clear identification and prioritization of these items before it can come up with a coherent operations strategy. Different firms will have quite different priorities; hence, a search for a universal operations strategy and set of management tools represents a fruitless quest.

Management Control

The questions of efficiency and, to a lesser degree, those of effectiveness are best addressed by ensuring that an appropriate IT management control structure and process, as discussed in Chapter 7, are in place. Planning's role is to ensure that long-term direction is spelled out and that steps are taken to acquire the necessary hardware/staff resources to implement it. The role of management control is to ensure that the appropriate short-term resource allocation decisions are made and that acquired resources are being utilized efficiently. The key issues in this field include the following:

1. Establishing an appropriate (for the organization) balance between user and IT responsibility for costs. Establishment of IT as a managed cost center, profit center, investment center, and so on is a critical strategic decision for an organization, as is the election of an appropriate IT transfer-pricing policy to go along with it. Again, not only does this policy appropriately change over time but it varies by type of organization as well.

2. Identification of an appropriate budgeting policy for IT. While many components of the IT budget are either fixed or transaction driven, others are discretionary. These discretionary components need to be examined to ensure both that they are still being allocated to essential missions and that an appropriate balance is struck between the needs of many legitimate end users. This balance is necessary in a world of limited financial resources for projects and where project benefits in many cases are not easily quantifiable. Zero-based budgeting has proven to be a useful tool in some IT settings (albeit with some operational difficulties, as will be discussed in Chapter 7).

3. A need for a regular weekly and monthly performance reporting cycle, not just against goals but against objective standards where possible. Unfortunately, the move of IT operations from a primarily batch to an on-line activity not only reduces the territory for objective standard setting but has made many of the older approaches obsolete.

Project Management

The questions of efficiency and effectiveness are also addressed through analysis of the project management process in Chapter 8. The 1980s have seen a proliferation of so-called project management processes and methodologies that have helped to rationalize a formerly very diverse area. The installation of these methodologies, an obvious improvement, has created a new set of opportunities.

The first opportunity lies in the area of implementation risk. The advocates of these methodologies have implied that by utilizing their approach, implementation risk will be eliminated. A careful examination of the long list of partial and major project fiascoes in the past four to five years suggests clearly that this is not the case. As described in Chapter 8, our contention is that project risk not only exists but can be measured, and a decision can be made regarding its acceptability long before the majority of funds have to be committed to a project development effort. In the same vein, it is possible and appropriate to talk about the aggregate-implementation-risk profile of the development and maintenance portfolio of projects. Not only does risk information provide a better language between general management, user management, and IT management during the project planning phase (where many options can be considered) but it provides a firmer and more valid context for after-the-fact performance assessment.

The second opportunity comes from the recognition that different types of projects can best be attacked by quite different kinds of project management methodologies. A single methodology is better than the anarchy and chaos that often precede its introduction. Several years of its use, however, can create a straitjacket environment. The approach will normally fit one kind of project very well and others considerably less well. Different organization structures within a project team, different types of user interfaces, and different planning and control approaches are suitable for different types of projects. In the mid-1980s it is clear that the most appropriate project management approach for any project should flow out of the project's innate characteristics.

Multinational Issues

International operations, discussed in Chapter 10, pose special problems in dealing with IT activity. Geographic separation, different cultures, and availability of IT staff skills vary widely from one country to another. When combined with differing cost and availability of telecommunications gear, different vendor support from one country to another, and issues related to transborder data flows, execution of an international IT strategy clearly is much more complex than when one is operating primarily within the borders of one country.

Planning

"Is my firm competitive and effectively focused on the right questions?" We believe the question is best answered by looking carefully at the IT planning process covered in Chapter 11. The design and evolution of this process has turned out to be much more complicated than anticipated in the early 1970s, when some fairly prescriptive ways of dealing with it were identified. Elements creating this complexity can be classified in three general categories.

The first is an increased recognition that, at any time, IT plays very different strategic roles in different companies. Strategic roles significantly influence both the structure of the planning process (who should be involved, the level of time and financial resources to be devoted to it, etc.) and its interconnection to the corporate planning process. Where new developments are critical to the introduction of new products and to achievement of major operating efficiencies or speeded-up competitive response times, firms must devote significantly more senior management time to planning than in settings where this is not the case.

The second category of issues relates to both IT and user familiarity with the nuances of the specific technologies being planned. Applications of technologies with which both IT and user staffs have extensive experience can be planned in considerable detail and with great confidence. To IT and/or the users, the newer technologies pose very different planning problems, both as to why planning is being done and how it can best be done. In any individual year, a company will be dealing with a mix of older and newer technologies that complicates the planning task tremendously.

The third category of issues relates to the matter of the specific corporate culture. The nature of the corporate planning process, formality versus informality of organizational decision making and planning, geographic and organizational distance of IT management from senior management—all influence how IT planning can best be done. These issues suggest that, as important as IT planning is, it must be evolutionary and highly individualistic to fit the specific corporation.

The IT Business

Chapter 12 integrates this discussion by considering the challenge of managing IT development and diffusion from the perspective of a business within a business. In that chapter, we emphasize the present marketing posture of the IT business.

We see the early years of IT as unavoidably captured by the term *R&D*: "Could it work, and could we learn to make it work?" Subsequent years were characterized by start-up production: "Could large projects be managed in a way which would create useful, reliable services in a high period of growth when technology was new and changing?" We learned to manage a service organization with a rapidly evolving technology, and applications proliferated. Today's environment is one characterized by marketing. The challenge is to blend, in a thoughtful manner, new product opportunities posed by new technologies with their new customers.

Conclusion

This chapter has identified, from a managerial viewpoint, the key forces shaping the IT environment, senior management's most frequent questions in assessing the activity, and the questions that we think are most useful in diagnosing the situation and taking corrective action. In this final section, we would like to leave you with a set of questions that we believe both IT management and general management should ask on a periodic basis (once every six months or so). They are a distillation of the previous analysis and, we believe, a useful managerial shorthand.

1. Do the perspective and skills of my IT and general management team fit the firm's changing applications, operations, user environment, and strategic relevance? There are no absolute, for-all-time answers to these questions, only transitional ones.
2. Is the firm organized to identify, evaluate, and assimilate new information technologies? In this fast-moving field an internally focused, low-quality staff can generate severe problems. Unprofitable, unwitting obsolescence (which is hard to recover from) is terribly easy here. There is no need for a firm to adopt leading-edge technology (indeed, many are ill equipped to do so), but it is inexcusable not to be aware of what the possibilities are.
3. Are the three main management systems for integrating the IT environment to the firm as a whole in place and architected? These are the planning system, the management control system, and the project management system.
4. Are the security, priority setting, manufacturing procedure, and change control systems in the IT operations function appropriate for the role it now plays in your firm?
5. Are appropriate organization structures and linking mechanisms in place to ensure both appropriate senior management guidance of the IT activity and appropriate user dialogue?

To answer these questions, we have developed a framework based upon four organizing concepts: strategic relevance, corporate culture, contingent action planning, and technology transfer. In each of the areas of organization, planning, management control, project management, and operations, we will be examining the concepts' implications for action. Realistically, we are moving today in a complicated milieu of people, differing organization strategies, different cultures, and changing technologies. We have taken as our task the identification of a sequence of frameworks that allow better analysis of the problems and issues facing organizations in relation to IT. We rely upon readers to apply this discussion to their own business situation to formulate a realistic action plan.

Frontier Airlines, Inc.

"I'm not a programmer, and in fact I've never written a line of code in my life." Lowell R. Shirley, senior director–information services of Frontier Airlines, was discussing his background with a visitor in mid-1983. "My previous experience was designing aircraft, and then project management in a rocket manufacturing company and a large construction firm. I've always been a user of information services, of course, but before I joined Frontier two years ago my only direct responsibility for DP had been 12 years earlier. Ironically, at that time I was helping Frontier's management dismantle their in-house data processing operation."

Shirley's initial mandate from the airline's president was to provide him with the tools necessary for competing more effectively in the newly-deregulated and rapidly-changing airline industry. In the ensuing two years, Frontier had spent more than $10 million on new computer hardware and facilities to house it. The information services (I/S) staff had grown from 9 technical personnel to 55, with an annual operating budget of $11 million. In July 1983, following the only new construction which Frontier had done for many years, I/S personnel and equipment moved into a freshly remodeled building.

This case was prepared by Michael R. Vitale.

Copyright © 1983 by the President and Fellows of Harvard College
Harvard Business School case 9–184–041.

EXHIBIT 1 Corporate Organization

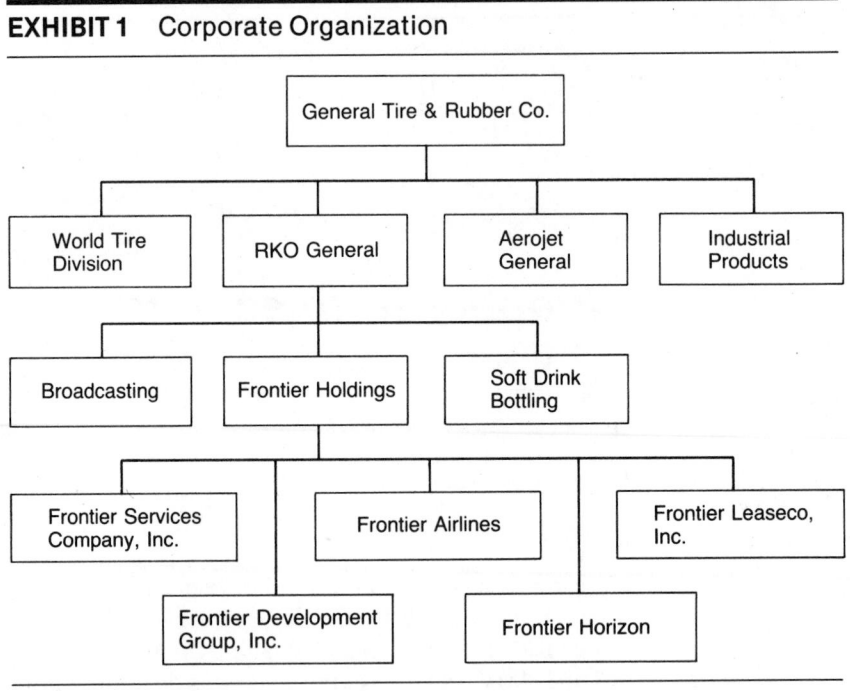

Company Background

Founded in 1946 and later expanded through merger with two local carriers that operated DC–3s to communities in the Rocky Mountains, Frontier added steadily to its route structure and equipment as the Denver area developed. In 1964, RKO General, a subsidiary of General Tire & Rubber Company, purchased a controlling interest in the airline (see Exhibit 1). Frontier's growth was accelerated by its 1967 merger with Texas-based Central Airlines. By the mid-1970s, Frontier served almost 100 cities, more than any other carrier in the country. Under the federal regulations then in effect, airlines required government permission to begin or end service on a given route. Carriers flying to certain small cities were paid a government subsidy in order to maintain minimum essential services. Thirteen of Frontier's 100 cities accounted for 70 percent of the airline's profits; the 55 subsidy-eligible cities generated 8 percent. Frontier's stops included almost 30 Rocky Mountain ski towns, and the airline promoted itself heavily to vacationers. Its jet flights offered one-class service, with the rows of seats separated by as much space as was ordinarily found in first class. Frontier also sought and gained a reputation for superior food service.

EXHIBIT 2

General Tire & Rubber and Subsidiaries
1982 Revenue and Income
($000)
General Tire and Rubber

Segment	Revenue	Operating Income
World Tire	$ 999,246	$ 39,167
Industrial Products	498,247	18,033
Aerojet General	564,166	51,525
Total	2,061,659	108,725

Loss before tax and income of RKO General	$(1,931)
Income before income of RKO General	6,507
RKO General net income	20,929
Income from continuing operations	27,436
Loss on disposal of discontinued operations	(8,000)
Net income	$19,436

RKO General

Segment	Revenue	Operating Income
Broadcasting	$164,030	$14,607
Soft Drink Bottling	117,800	14,781
Other	9,988	1,047
Total	291,818	30,435

Net income after tax from continuing operations	$ 8,097
Equity in net income of Frontier Holdings, Inc.	12,832
Net income after tax	$ 20,929

Frontier Holdings, Inc.

Revenue	$548,846
Net income after tax	$ 24,140

SOURCE: 1982 Annual Report.

Frontier had often been a technical leader; it was an early user of Boeing 727 and 737 aircraft, and was one of the first airlines to handle its passenger reservations completely with a computerized system. Financial returns did not improve as fast as the airline's technology (see Exhibit 3), and in 1971 Frontier's parent company installed new

EXHIBIT 3

FRONTIER AIRLINES
General Statistics

| Year | RPM* | ASM† | Load Factor‡ | Operating Expenses§ | | Yield‖ |
				Per RPM	Per ASM	
1982	3,571 miles	5,852 miles	61.0%	14.87 cents	9.07 cents	13.71 cents
1981	3,502	5,642	62.1	15.03	9.33	14.78
1980	2,972	5,009	59.3	14.55	8.63	13.91
1979	3,012	4,944	60.9	11.86	7.23	11.32
1978	2,398	3,771	63.6	11.34	7.21	10.52
1977	1,902	3,235	58.8	11.00	6.46	10.66
1976	1,690	2,951	57.3	10.75	6.16	10.27
1975	1,460	2,617	55.8	10.67	5.96	9.76
1974	1,392	2,491	55.9	9.87	5.52	9.16
1973	1,308	2,473	52.9	9.04	4.78	8.00
1972	1,102	2,123	51.9	8.96	4.65	7.88
1971	1,066	2,306	46.2	4.65	4.16	7.65
1970	1,075	2,427	44.3	8.52	3.77	7.38
1969	988	2,179	45.3	8.32	3.77	7.26
1968	910	2,052	44.3	8.11	3.61	6.55
1967	658	1,512	43.6	8.37	3.64	6.84
1966	466	1,042	44.7	8.89	3.97	7.10
1965	310	776	39.9	11.03	4.40	7.58
1964	274	674	40.6	11.43	4.64	7.16
1963	233	597	39.0	12.22	4.76	7.08

*Revenue passenger miles, in millions. One revenue-paying passenger flown one mile generates one RPM.
†Available seat miles, in millions. One seat available for passengers flown one mile on scheduled service generates one ASM.
‡Load factor = RPM divided by ASM, expressed as a percentage.
§In cents.
‖Passenger revenue per RPM, in cents (scheduled service only).
SOURCE: Company reports.

FRONTIER AIRLINES
Operating Results
($ millions)

Year	Operating Revenues			Operating Expenses			Income	
	Passenger	Subsidy	Total	Depreciation	Total		Operating	Net
1982	$489.6	$ 9.9	$539.8	$30.7	$530.9		$ 9.0	$17.2
1981	517.6	22.8	577.4	24.1	526.5		50.9	32.0
1980	413.4	18.0	468.9	20.9	432.5		36.4	23.2
1979	340.9	20.8	389.7	18.2	357.3		32.3	21.1
1978	251.9	17.1	290.8	14.3	271.9		18.9	16.2
1977	202.6	11.5	234.3	11.4	209.1		25.2	12.7
1976	173.5	11.1	201.0	11.3	181.7		19.3	9.9
1975	142.5	11.8	168.8	9.4	155.9		12.9	6.7
1974	127.5	11.4	153.0	8.8	137.4		15.7	10.6
1973	104.7	11.8	129.1	8.8	118.3		10.8	7.2
1972	86.6	14.3	108.9	6.6	98.7		10.1	7.1
1971	79.6	9.6	97.4	6.6	96.0		1.3	(2.5)
1970	75.5	6.6	91.8	6.7	91.5		.3	(3.6)
1969	66.8	6.7	82.7	6.8	82.2		.5	(11.9)
1968	56.8	7.6	71.8	7.1	74.0		(2.2)	(6.1)
1967	41.7	8.7	57.0	4.6	55.1		1.9	1.6
1966	31.9	9.6	45.6	2.6	41.4		4.2	2.0
1965	23.4	9.6	35.4	1.2	34.1		1.3	0.5
1964	19.5	11.0	32.6	1.2	31.3		1.3	0.6
1963	16.1	12.3	30.4	1.1	28.4		1.9	0.9

SOURCE: Company reports.

management from Aerojet General, another subsidiary of General Tire & Rubber. The team included Alvin Lindbergh Feldman, president and chief executive officer, and Glen L. Ryland, vice president–finance.

The new managers brought with them "management by commitment," a system developed at Aerojet General, and it soon spread throughout the airline. In the commitment system, the chief executive officer announced a set of goals—profits, return on investment, market share, etc.—in the fall of each year. Each division, and then each organization within each division, put together its own plan for meeting one or more of the goals. For example, marketing might target a certain load factor, catering a maximum number of complaints per 10,000 meals, and so on. This process, which extended down to the individual level, resulted in formal "commitments" against which performance would be measured. Commitments were expected to be met exactly: there was no reward for gross overachievement, since the rest of the organization was typically not prepared to take full advantage of it; missing by a small amount was still regarded as failure. For 1983, Lowell Shirley's commitments included reducing maintenance of certain old applications from five person-years to three; reducing the cost of Frontier's voice communications network by $30,000 per month; relocating data entry to user departments; relocating hardware to the new facility; and completing a set of new applications. These commitments were supported by more detailed commitments from each of the four I/S directors, who got commitments from their staff. The commitments, in turn, supported the annual I/S budget.

One intended outcome of the commitment system was a renewed focus by managers on the specific areas for which they were responsible. The resulting environment was described within the airline as "brick walls" surrounding the operating divisions, focusing managers' attention on the areas for which they were directly responsible. Implementation of I/S applications had tended to put "windows" in the brick walls through the use of common systems, data, and equipment.

The Airline Deregulation Act of 1978 allowed air carriers to change routes simply by giving 90 days' notice, and between 1978 and early 1982 Frontier dropped 39 cities, added 29 others, and expanded operations at its Denver hub. In March 1978, Frontier served 490 city-pairs; by March 1983, this number was 231, including only 90 of those served five years earlier. Frontier was joined in Denver by seven new competitors, including American, Eastern, Northwest, Piedmont, and Southwest. Both of its traditional competitors, United and Continental, added flights to Denver, giving them 145 and 108 daily by early 1983. Frontier, which started, ended, or connected each of its flights through Denver (see Exhibit 4), offered 114. The airline served 84 cities in 27 states, Canada, and Mexico, operating more than 50 aircraft. Its

EXHIBIT 4 Route System: Boeing 737 and McDonnell Douglas Super 80 Jet Service

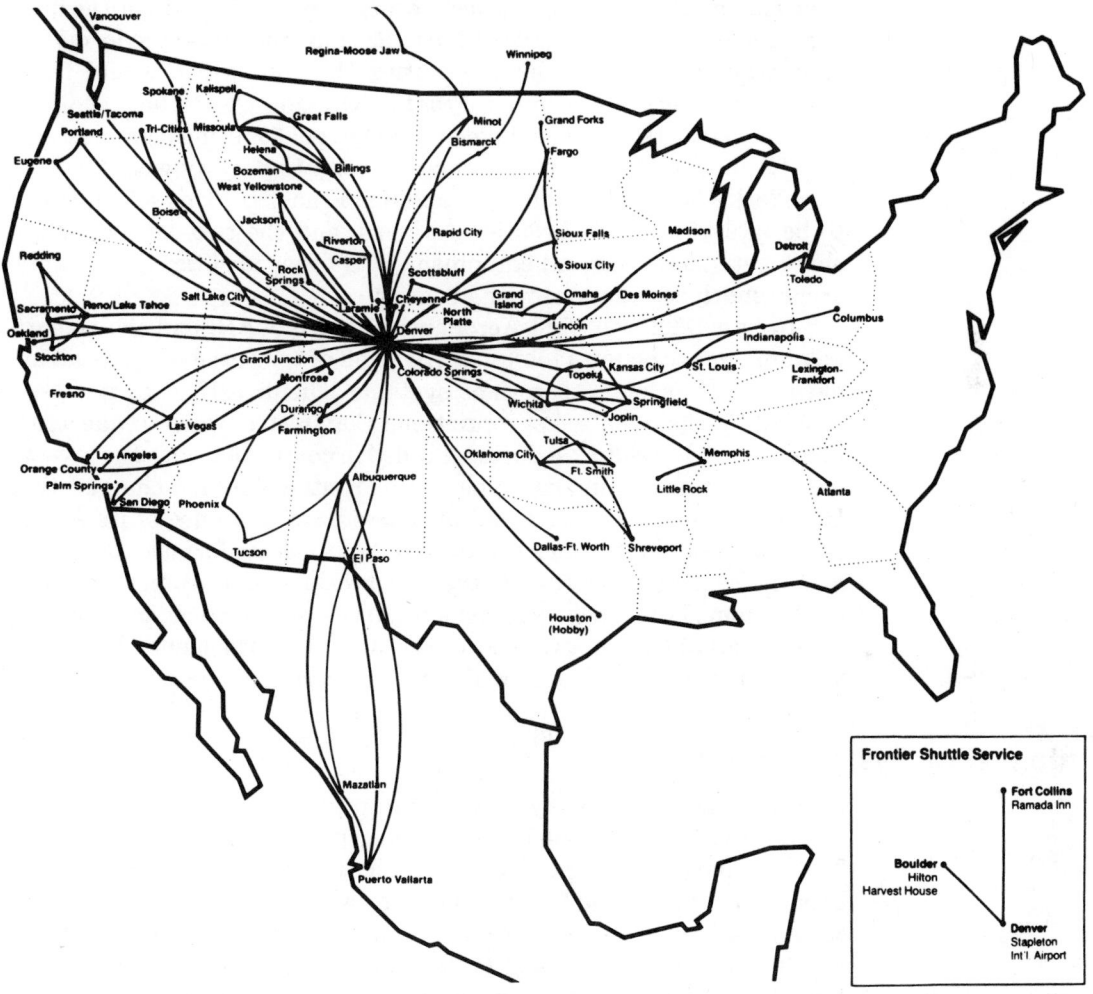

passengers were roughly evenly divided between business and pleasure travellers. Frontier competed with United on 34 routes, up from 8 at the time of deregulation. "I assume United will survive in Denver, and I assume there will be room for one other major carrier," Frontier's president commented.

In May 1982, Frontier Airlines became a subsidiary of the newly formed Frontier Holdings, Inc. Other subsidiaries included Frontier

Services, which offered training, maintenance, ground handling, and ground transportation in Denver and other cities. Glen Ryland, by then chairman and president of the airline, assumed those posts at the holding company as well. In August 1983, Ryland announced the formation of another airline subsidiary, Frontier Horizon, which would begin flight operations in December. Frontier Horizon was to be a separate company with its own management and the goal of being a low-cost carrier. Its initial schedule of 10 round-trip flights per day would include New York, Chicago, Washington, and San Francisco. This schedule was to be integrated with Frontier Airline's, and the two carriers would share gate space, ground equipment, and other facilities, based upon arm's-length negotiations with Frontier.

In late 1982, the Civil Aeronautics Board (CAB) and the Department of Justice began a joint investigation of the possible antitrust implications of airline reservations systems. The investigation had been ordered by the Senate Appropriations Committee, which requested a report by early 1983. In a document filed in connection with the investigation (reproduced in the Appendix), Frontier Airlines charged that United Airlines was unfair and uncompetitive in its use of its Apollo computerized reservations system. United made no formal response to Frontier's charges, but it and other reservations system operators generally claimed that their systems were developed independently as part of long-range strategies to sell tickets through travel agents. Participation in these systems by other airlines was permitted for a fee.

Information Systems

Frontier had been an early user of data processing, automating its accounting systems by 1965 and passenger reservations a few years later. The new management group from Aerojet General, believing that some Frontier managers had begun paying closer attention to printouts than to operations, determined to de-emphasize data processing; in the words of one veteran, "They fired the computers." It was in this context that Shirley, who had worked for Ryland at Aerojet General, was brought briefly to Frontier to, along with other assignments, study the dismantling of in-house data processing. The DP staff was reduced to nine programmers, and applications programs were run at service bureaus. In September 1972, after a brief experiment with a manual system, Frontier decided to purchase computerized reservations service from Greenwich Data Systems, a subsidiary of Planning Research Corporation. In 1974, Frontier's reservations software was moved to hardware operated by Control Data Corporation. Finally, in 1976, Frontier began to purchase reservations services from Continental Airlines. Shirley viewed this decision as the most important one Frontier had ever made regarding information systems. "At most airlines, the res [ervations] system drives the information systems strategy," he noted. "Frontier decided that it made economic sense to share the overhead of a res system. Supposedly there are some marketing advantages to owning your res system, but those advantages had never happened in Frontier's experience."

With all of Frontier's centrally maintained information systems running in batch mode on a variety of outside computers, I/S users were, in one manager's words, "surly but not rebellious." Nevertheless, in 1978 a number of them obtained stand-alone minicomputers for marketing, crew scheduling, and other applications. "Each minicomputer application was an uphill battle," one manager said of the period, "but each represented a significant stride as well. In aircraft scheduling, for example, turnaround dropped from two days with the batch system to a few minutes with the minicomputer. We were not concerned about a uniform data base—we wanted to maintain the manager's ability to innovate." The use of outside time-sharing had also increased. President Ryland, feeling he did not have adequate decision support tools, brought in outside consultants to evaluate Frontier's information systems. The consultants found a large backlog of desired applications, many of which had never been proposed formally. They recommended that Frontier take advantage of new technology by consolidating data processing and telecommunications within a single in-house organization, which would use IBM mainframes and purchased software. "The most important impact of the study," Shirley noted, "was probably the message that the airline had to do *something*." In the summer of 1981, shortly after receiving the consultant's report, Frontier recruited Shirley from the major engineering and construction company where he was then working.

Hardware

"My first decision," Shirley said later, "was that we would not ever run a res system. Then I started to address everything else. When I first spoke to users, they all said they needed 'real time data.' It turned out, though, that they really meant 'yesterday's data.' Compared to the batch environment, yesterday was 'real time'! I estimated that only 5 percent of the applications—for example, flight dispatching—really required real time data.

"I next asked how much data sharing was required. About 90 percent of our data is used within a single division—only about 10 percent is ever shared. Finally, I investigated the source of our data. About 5 percent comes from the Official Airline Guide, the Airline Tariff Publishing Company, the weather bureau, and other outside organizations. The great majority, however, is generated inside Frontier.

"Based on this survey of our data needs, I thought about what hardware would be most suitable. At my previous employer I had seen tremendous gains in programmer productivity when a mainframe computer was replaced with several 'super-minicomputers.' You don't save a lot on hardware by buying multiple small machines instead of one big one, but overall system reliability is higher, and overhead—for example, systems programmers and facilities—is lower. Another advantage of using smaller boxes is that you can start small and grow.

"There were some disadvantages to the super-mini approach, of course. At the time there were not good systems for integrating several machines, so each application had to fit entirely on one super-mini. There was little packaged software available—in evaluating the super-mini alternative, I assumed that we would not be able to buy anything from the outside. And using a distributed system instead of a central mainframe was a unique approach in the airline industry.

"I was familiar with the IBM System 38," Shirley continued, "and I believed that IBM would continue to expand and develop that line. I liked the System 38 architecture, particularly the built-in data base features, and our largest application would just fit on the biggest System 38 available at the time. I therefore decided to use the 38, and our first machine was delivered in November 1981. By February of 1982 we had our initial applications up and running."

By mid-1983 Frontier was using three System 38s, with a fourth due in early 1984. One machine was used for production, one for software development, and one for remote job entry to those applications still running outside. A task force on station computing had recommended IBM Series 1s to handle remote computing and communications routing on Frontier's distributed network, and the first such machine had been installed. The network itself, which would eventually link all of Frontier's outlying stations to Denver, would use the X.25 packet-switching protocol. X.25 was widely used by public and private data networks, but was unusual in the airline industry, which almost universally relied on a protocol designed in the early days of computer reservations systems. X.25 would result in somewhat slower response time but greatly improved reliability.

Frontier's use of distributed processing was also unusual in its industry, but fit in with the airline's super-mini choice. "Trying to do all the processing in Denver would have buried the System 38s," Shirley commented. In addition, there were a number of applications—aircraft weight and balance, air cargo tracing, cash drawer reconciliation, etc.—which affected only a single station, and doing them locally reduced network traffic. The Series 1 was capable of controlling ticket and boarding pass printers, credit card readers, and other devices in addition to terminals, and was also good at message routing. Like the System 38, the Series 1 was modular and could be expanded to meet growth.

Several Frontier managers had become interested in microcomputers, and Shirley felt that the introduction of micros was an important issue. "I decided to initiate the move to micros, not fight it," he said. By Frontier policy, all purchases of computer hardware had to be approved by Shirley, and he had elected to standardize on the IBM Personal Computer. Once a division was allowed to obtain a PC, all applications had to be approved by a technical specialist in Shirley's group. Only BASIC, one spreadsheet analysis package, and qualified third-party applications were permitted, and only divisional data could be used. It was possible to draw data from one of the System 38s, but data could not be sent in the opposite direction. Violators risked the loss of their machine. One of the earliest owners of a PC was marketing, which used the micro to keep track of expenditures. Other micro applications in Denver included budgeting, personnel records, and flight attendant domiciling.

Software

The largest single application under development at Frontier was revenue accounting, which was being converted from a largely manual system. Frontier handled about 600,000 ticket coupons a month; each had to be scanned, microfilmed, and sorted to determine whether the coupon represented an asset or a liability. The increasing complexity and rate of change of airline fares had made the job more difficult. "Without adequate controls, only bad things can happen," said Robert G. Oatley, Frontier's vice president–finance and chief financial officer. "You underbill, overpay, or both." The automated system, justified on the basis of manpower replacement and revenue recovery, was expected to pay back its development costs in less than 18 months. The current accounting system produced some reports on yield, fare usage, and so on, which were supplemented by manual reports. "We really should correlate revenue accounting with ticket lift data," Oatley said, "but it's better to take the information from revenue accounting and feed it to other systems than to try to keep one big data base. We're aiming for compatibility, not integration."

Oatley believed that Frontier needed several additional applications in the accounting area. Accounts payable and general ledger were both automated, but were not linked. The airline's computerized payroll system was also in need of replacement. "The question," Oatley said, "is what to do first. None of these accounting systems are critical to our daily operations, and it's more important to give the operating guys their data first."

Although Oatley noted that Frontier users were generally unsophisticated and could be somewhat impatient, he felt that their general attitude towards information systems was healthy. "They had to learn about their responsibilities for specifying their own systems," he said, "and that they had to commit manpower and time to the job." When a new project was approved, a technical specialist was assigned to it as project manager and was assigned a project team of programmer/analysts. The team worked in a matrix arrangement with its own department and the user; it was expected that each team member would come to understand the user's job well enough to perform it. The user organization paid the technical specialists' salaries during project development.

Shortly after arriving at Frontier, Shirley had agreed with top management on how many people were required to complete certain critical applications within a given time. Frontier had then hired more than 30 technical personnel, only two of whom had previous airline experience. "Airline people would have wanted to use airline methods," Shirley said. "It's key that our technical specialists establish with the user that they both understand the user's problem and can help solve it." Thereafter, users who wanted new applications proposed them to their vice president. It was that vice president's job to sell each new project to Shirley's boss, and to convince him to obtain whatever additional people and equipment were needed. The general basis for project approval was an evaluation of information systems costs versus benefits to the user.

Shirley noted that in his two years at Frontier he had not seen a proposal for a project with a payback of more than 18 months; despite efforts by Shirley, Ryland, and others to convince users that there were other reasons for proposing a project, most users apparently felt that direct cost savings were the only allowable justification. "We could double our staff and still work only on systems with a payback of less than two years," Shirley commented. "I want to focus on the high-leverage items."

Frontier used a structured development methodology for generating requirements, external specifications, and then internal technical specifications. All software development was done in-house. Frontier built new applications on-line, using a data base approach and a heuristic design philosophy. " 'Heuristic' does not mean 'free wheeling,' " Bob Oatley noted. "We have specifications, including screen designs and reports, at the outset. It does mean that we don't consider an application finished when it's first released. In fact, if it's any good it will continue to be changed." Frontier estimated that its programmers were able to complete an application in about half the time required in other development environments. The System 38 included a query facility which

EXHIBIT 5   Partial Organization Chart, August 1983

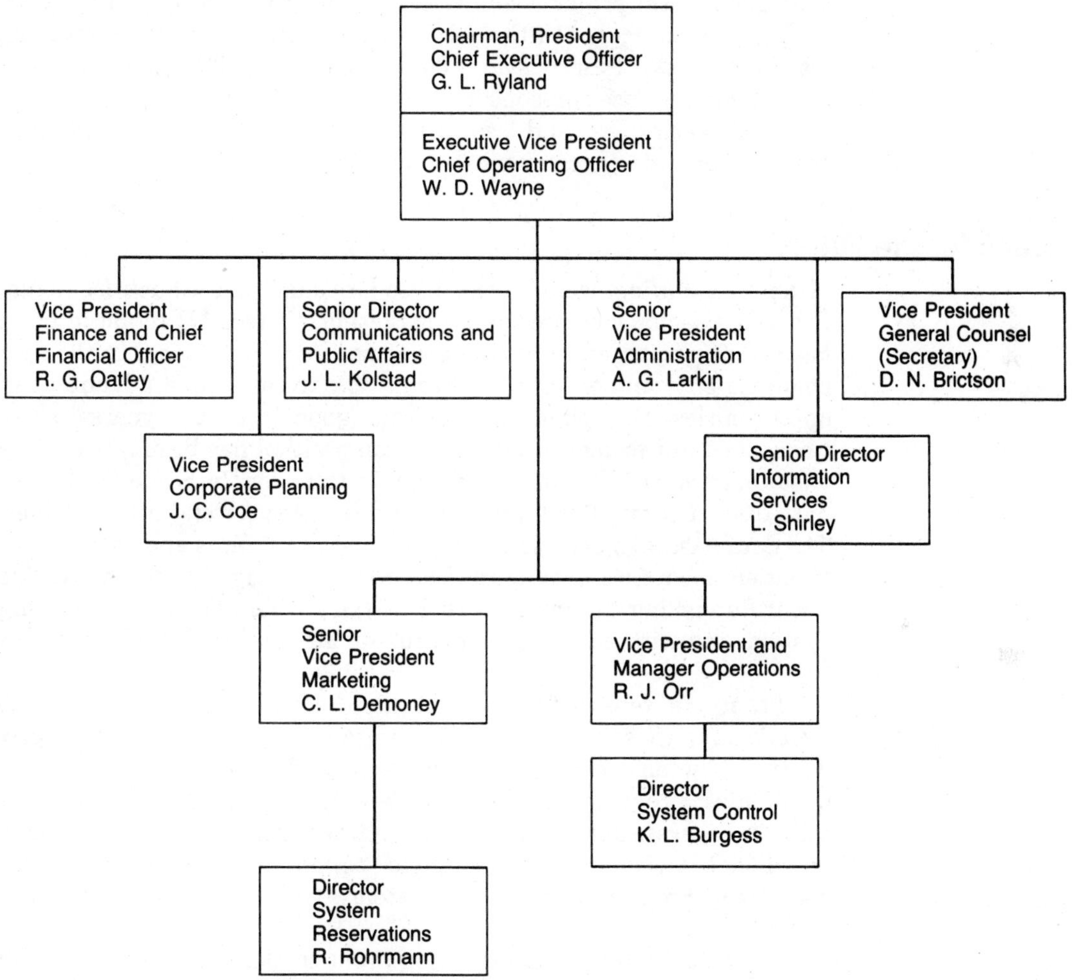

```
                    Chairman, President
                    Chief Executive Officer
                    G. L. Ryland

                    Executive Vice President
                    Chief Operating Officer
                    W. D. Wayne
```

| Vice President Finance and Chief Financial Officer R. G. Oatley | Senior Director Communications and Public Affairs J. L. Kolstad | Senior Vice President Administration A. G. Larkin | Vice President General Counsel (Secretary) D. N. Brictson |

Vice President
Corporate Planning
J. C. Coe

Senior Director
Information
Services
L. Shirley

Senior
Vice President
Marketing
C. L. Demoney

Vice President and
Manager Operations
R. J. Orr

Director
System Control
K. L. Burgess

Director
System
Reservations
R. Rohrmann

allowed users to create their own one-time reports, but users were not permitted to change their programs.

Frontier departments were charged for terminals and other hardware and for the cost of running their applications. Time on the System 38 was billed at $5.00 per terminal hour, paper reports at 50 cents a page. The hourly rate was intended to recover the out-of-pocket cost of operating the in-house machines. There was no charge for any software maintenance needed to bring an application up to specifications, but users had to pay for enhancements. "I want to draw attention to the fact that fixing old things also uses resources," Shirley said. Large, interdepartmental projects and telecommunications were funded from corporate resources. "In the service bureau environment, everything was billed back," Shirley said. "The attitude was, 'This must be worth something, because someone is willing to pay for it.' We're moving towards allocating less and less cost to the user—we charge only when the act of charging accomplishes some goal."

Issues for the Future

"Under regulation, we had very little latitude," said Chuck Demoney, Frontier's senior vice president–marketing. "The CAB required us to keep certain data, and timeliness was not very important. In the new, changing environment, it's vital to be able to take rapid advantage of opportunities. Our planning cycle has gone from 4–5 years to 4–5 weeks, and our former awareness of competition has been replaced by vast uncertainty." One of the first applications for the System 38 was a data base of some 70,000 fares charged by Frontier and other airlines. The data base was used to monitor competitors' fares and to maintain Frontier's own fare data. Fare data were exchanged with the Airline Tariff Publishing Company, with Frontier's reservation and ticketing system, and with a pricing model run on an outside time-sharing system.

Frontier's reservation system had recently been enhanced to include advance seat selection and assignment and boarding pass production. The airline had also become part of American Airline's frequent flyer program, AAdvantage (see Exhibit 6); American maintained a separate data base on these Frontier passengers, but Demoney noted that it was "nearly impossible" to manipulate the data in any useful way. Frontier used its own System 38 data base for analysis purposes.

Of all the I/S-related issues facing Frontier, Demoney felt that travel agency use of reservations systems was most important. "We have mounted a vocal campaign to let the CAB, the Department of Justice, and others know about biases in these systems," Demoney said, "and we believe we may have seen some softening recently. It's a very critical issue, but maybe not one on which our in-house information systems can help much." At one time Frontier had marketed its reservations system, SENTRY, to travel agents, but had not been able to compete with the large carriers (United and American) for travel agent acceptance.

EXHIBIT 6

Frequent fliers...

don't forget, Frontier has the
American Airlines A'Advantage®
Program that can earn you Travel
Awards to over 150 cities in more
than a dozen countries!*

Ask your Ticket Agent how you
can qualify.

*AAdvantage rules, regulations and special offers are
subject to change without notice.

A'A AmericanAirlines

Appendix: *Comments of Frontier Airlines, Inc. before the Civil Aeronautics Board, Washington, D.C.*

At the present time about 80 percent of the nation's travel agencies have automated reservations systems.[1] Computerized agencies tend to be the high volume operators, with mostly the smaller (often rural)

Source: Report to Congress on Computer Reservation Systems, Docket 41207.

[1]This is Frontier's current best estimate. According to the Louis Harris study in *Travel Weekly*, May 1982, p. 46, 68 percent of the travel agencies were automated in 1981, and Frontier knows the growth has continued since then.

agencies remaining unautomated. In 1981, computerized agencies accounted for $24.5 *billion* of airline ticket sales![2] Sales through travel agencies are critically important to Frontier's business since they account for 65 percent of our total sales volume.

While American Airlines' SABRE system and United Airlines' Apollo system are the largest in use throughout the nation, Frontier's comments focus primarily on United's Apollo system because of its impact upon Frontier and the Denver hub. Frontier is United's chief competitor at Denver, with United enplaning 3.6 million passengers versus 2.5 million by Frontier in 1982. United and Frontier now compete head to head on 31 routes out of Denver, versus only 8 when the Deregulation Act of 1978 was implemented. United's January 1983 Denver departures are 141 a day, up 40 percent from one year ago.

The combined effect of United's leverage through the Apollo system and its other extraordinary measures at Denver have had a serious impact on the competitive airline picture at this important hub:[3]

- United enplaned 1,013,975 passengers at Denver in the fourth quarter of 1982, a 40.2 percent increase over the fourth quarter of 1981. This translates into a 36.9 percent share of Denver enplanements for United at the end of 1982 versus 26.8 percent for the fourth quarter of 1981.
- The growth of United's domination at Denver is more clearly reflected by comparing quarterly increases during 1982 with one year earlier. United's percentage share of enplaned Denver passengers increased 1.5 percent, 4.6 percent, 17.6 percent, and 28.1 percent during each of the four quarters of 1982 over the same periods in 1981, while Frontier's quarterly share of enplaned Denver passengers *decreased* 9.2 percent, 6.5 percent, 8.3 percent, and 9.8 percent versus the same periods last year.

The ability of United to significantly affect the Denver hub through its Apollo system is shown by the following section.

1. United Dominates the Computerized Reservations System Market at the Denver Hub

At Denver, the dominance of United's Apollo system among agencies is particularly strong:

- 148 out of 198 (75 percent) automated travel agencies in the Denver area subscribe to Apollo.

---

[2]Ibid.

[3]Based on preliminary fourth quarter 1982 data.

- Apollo has automated four times more travel agencies in the Denver area than its next largest competitor.
- Apollo travel agencies in the Denver area account for about $250 million in airline revenues, or about 82 percent of total airline revenues generated by Denver's automated agencies.[4]

Frontier believes that United has used its control over one market, i.e., the Denver travel agents' automated reservations systems, as an unfair and anticompetitive means to further United's goals in another market, i.e., that sale of air transportation, where it competes with Frontier and other carriers.

2. Normal Market Forces Have Not Disciplined the Travel Agency Computer Reservation Systems Market

Normally, competition between United's Apollo system, American's SABRE system, TWA's PARS system, and other lesser competitors for placement of computer reservation systems at travel agencies would discipline this market. However, this has not been the case as demonstrated by abuses which have occurred. Set forth below are examples of past practices, as well as future prospects, of the anticompetitive impact of United's control of the Apollo system.

3. United Uses Apollo in an Unfair and Uncompetitive Manner

A. United Has Discriminatorily Excluded Carriers from Apollo

For over two years United refused to allow Frontier to become an Apollo co-host for "competitive" reasons. Although Frontier was finally allowed to become a co-host in July of 1982, our prior efforts to join Apollo were stalled by United's claim that its Apollo system did not have the capacity to handle Frontier. However, during the same time period at least three other major carriers were granted co-host status. After repeated inquiries, Frontier was finally told in August of 1981 by a United vice president that it was to be excluded for "competitive" reasons. Further entreaties by Frontier were similarly rebuffed, until soon after the Department of Justice and the CAB began their investigative efforts into anticompetitive aspects of automated reservation systems.

Frontier also understands that Midway Airlines' complete schedules—direct and connecting—were expunged from Apollo for a period

---

[4]As of March 1982: Apollo 148; SABRE 37; PARS 12; EA 1. Denver metro area includes Boulder, Longmont, Loveland, and several other front-range communities. Estimated annual revenues of $1.8 million per agency, which was the average annual revenue figure of 47 Denver Apollo travel agencies as of June 1981.

of time. (During the period Frontier was denied co-host status, its direct flights remained in the Apollo system.) United therefore has the power to completely eliminate smaller carriers' schedules from Apollo unless a fee is paid, regardless of the impact on the carrier, the public, or travel agents. Air California now pays such a fee for inclusion of its direct flights, and had Frontier not become a co-host, United threatened complete expulsion of all our flights from Apollo unless a fee were paid.

B. "Tying" Arrangements under Apollo

In order to become a co-host under United's Apollo system, Frontier was forced to also agree on a "net ticketing arrangement" with United. Under the "net ticketing arrangement," Frontier pays United a dollar amount for tickets written by United on Frontier, and United pays Frontier a dollar amount for tickets written by Frontier on United. However, Frontier did not want this agreement, since United writes more tickets on Frontier, and we asked that separate negotiations be held on this subject. United refused, saying it was a package deal. Frontier estimates that the ticketing "tying" arrangement will cost the company about $350,000 in 1983. Thus, United used its power in the "tying" product—co-host status in the Apollo system—to impose its will with respect to a separate agreement—net ticketing. Interestingly, in Frontier's negotiations with TWA, a similar package deal was presented to Frontier, i.e., membership in PARS coupled with net ticketing, but TWA agreed to sever the two products and negotiate each separately.

C. Bias Problems Continue Even after Achieving Co-Host Status

Even after Frontier achieved co-host status under Apollo, and during Frontier's long-standing co-host status under SABRE, bias problems continue to exist which give host carriers such as United and American an unfair competitive advantage.

Host carriers continue to maintain a super-bias which displays their schedules in a superior manner to that afforded co-host carriers. For example, when a travel agent requests flight information from Apollo, the system will display schedules of co-hosts from the desired time *forward*, while United alone will display backwards in time (about two hours) in addition to displaying schedules after the desired time. More comprehensive and complicated rules are employed to display connecting schedules—always designed to give United a leg up on its co-hosts.

In addition to the super-bias enjoyed by United as a host carrier, some co-hosts are more equal than other co-hosts in the tradition of Orwell's *Animal Farm*. Thus, Delta is accorded a special display on Apollo. Host carriers also retain the right to create new categories of co-hosts such as that United has accorded to Delta and thereby create new echelons of bias among co-hosts for which differentiated (and higher) rates can be charged.

To date, host carriers have concentrated on biasing schedule displays in their travel agent systems, but Frontier expects that bias will play a greater role in reservation systems' *fare* displays in the future. Even now the fare categorization/classification program employed by United in the Apollo system can result in a competitively inferior display for a carrier desiring to improvise with new fares. A host carrier such as United also enjoys a competitive advantage in institution of a new fare, since United can plan and control the display of its new fares in Apollo, whereas Frontier and other co-hosts must hope that the display accorded the new fare in Apollo is a good one (or a co-host must conform his new fare within existing fare display formats, which is not always possible or desirable). If such a new and innovative fare by a co-host does not receive a favorable Apollo display, its acceptance by travel agents can be drastically affected.

D. Host Carriers Have an Unfair Advantage by Their Computerized Access to Confidential Information of the Competitors

United and American have *exclusive* and *immediate* access on their respective Apollo and SABRE systems to highly sensitive sales data which they can use to their competitive advantage. United, for example, generates reports for each Apollo travel agency identifying by market the total number of passengers carried in the period, and the amount and percentage of traffic carried by each competitive carrier in the market. This information is not available to co-hosts such as Frontier. The only information United will give Frontier is the total number of passengers carried by Frontier, and currently even this limited information (which does not indicate Frontier's share of the total market, or other carriers' shares) is available about one month in arrears.

Access to this information gives United/American a tremendous and unfair competitive advantage. United sales representatives have immediate knowledge whether United and its competitors are losing/gaining market share, and United can promptly take measures (e.g., bonus incentives, lower fares, more schedules) to rectify the developing situation. The *immediate* access of United sales representatives to this data allows United sales representatives to contact travel agents long before Frontier knows of market changes. At several travel agencies where Frontier has made inroads into United market shares, the agents have mentioned "pressure" from United sales representatives to increase United market shares, as reflected in a recent article appearing in *Travel Agent*:

> Agents are also becoming accustomed to receiving printouts of their reservation histories with little comments, sometimes nasty at that, asking why some other carrier was used instead of them.[5]

E. United Coerces Agents into Exclusive Use of Apollo

While Frontier has finally attained co-host status in Apollo, United still maintains its schedule bias over Frontier in the system, and Frontier's schedules enjoy a superior display vis-á-vis United in American's SABRE system. Therefore United's efforts to maintain exclusivity with travel agents using Apollo—particularly in the crucial Denver market—harms Frontier (not to mention travel agencies and the public). United uses several means to preclude competition by SABRE and other automated systems.

The 95 Percent Rule.

> Over the last year, United has added a clause to its Apollo contract requiring the travel agent to "process 95 percent of its tickets containing at least one United segment through the Apollo equipment." To assure compliance, United has the right to audit the agency's books and records without notice. The admitted purpose of this provision, according to United's senior vice president in charge of marketing (John Zeeman), is to prevent agencies from maintaining two systems.
>
> He agreed that this section would have the effect of forcing agents to make a choice between two or more systems, but he said the written document is only a manifestation of a continuing policy of pushing agents to make such choices. . . . It is clear that any agency with two airline systems could not possibly satisfy the 95 percent rule, but Zeeman said United would not let such an agency have the option of signing the contract anyway. The agency would be asked to choose between Apollo and the second system.[6]

---

[5]*Travel Agent*, October 11, 1982, p. 19.

[6]*Travel Weekly*, November 15, 1982.

The December issue of *Frequent Flyer* speaks of the same subject:

> But to American and United, second automated res systems are pure anathema. Reportedly, both carriers have threatened to pull their computer terminals out of agencies that install a competitor's hardware.
>
> United admits that it discourages Apollo users from using another system, particularly SABRE: "We feel that it is not an effective way to do business," says Zeeman.[7]

Other Coercive Efforts. The September 13, 1982 issue of the *Aviation Daily* contains another example of United pressure to preclude a Colorado Springs travel agency from using two systems:

> Myers originally wanted two systems in order to get boarding passes and last-seat availability for both carriers. He said a succession of meetings between Ambassador Travel and each airline made it clear that United prefers an exclusive arrangement so that it can look at any agency's business and determine if it is delivering to United a share of business that reflects the carrier's market share in the area.

F. The Pending "Boarding Pass" Enhancement to Apollo

United is currently seeking to add a new feature to Apollo which would allow travel agencies to automatically issue boarding passes to United passengers. This feature, we understand, will not be allowed for Frontier passengers, nor will United permit SABRE users to issue United boarding passes, whether manually or otherwise. This seems to be yet another means to be used by United to enhance its airline market position, by way of its control over the Apollo system.

G. Host Carriers Can Also Control the Content of Data Reaching Travel Agents

Host carriers have the ability to control the content of information reaching travel agencies. This control has adverse competitive implications to Frontier and other outsiders. For example, Frontier recently instituted a $99 one-way fare in many markets on its system. While United did insert the Frontier fare information into Apollo, United used the same system to undermine Frontier in the eyes of the travel

---

[7]"New Reservations about Airlines Computers," *Frequent Flyer*, December 1982, pp. 45, 49.

agents using Apollo. Thus, United inserted a "sales message" to agents informing them that it was matching Frontier fares, but gratuitously added that "Because these fares are *nongenerative*, we have planned a 3/3/83 travel expiration date *to try to minimize dilution of your commission*" (Wednesday, 1/12/83 message to Apollo users).

The clear message by United to the travel agents was that Frontier's new fares would not produce any new passengers, and that all they would do was reduce travel agents' commissions. Standing alone, this may not seem earth-shaking, but how many other messages have been sent which Frontier has not seen?

Other examples of potential anticompetitive effects of hosts' control of information in their automated systems include:

- The host carrier alone knows the intricate details of the bias system program. The host also controls when changes are made, as well as variations to bias that are implemented from time to time in "special" markets, where a host may perceive a lower usage of its service or an opportunity to improve market penetration. Despite continuous efforts, Frontier has not been able to effectively monitor its schedules in the Apollo and SABRE systems.

- At times, Frontier schedules are "dropped" from Apollo/ SABRE, or fares are delayed in their entry. Frontier's monitoring catches some of these problems, but not all of them. The host always explains these problems as attributable to a computer mistake or other rational vagary of the system, and Frontier is in no position to contest these explanations. However, with a prime competitor controlling the system, a co-host's doubts are never really satisfied.

- From time to time, Frontier receives reports from travel agents that Apollo/SABRE sets reflect Frontier flights as being fully booked, whereas in fact seats remain to be sold. Again, these occurrences may be unintentional breakdowns, but a co-host never really knows.

H. Other Means Host Carriers Use to Maintain Exclusivity or to Proselytize Travel Agents

- According to the October 1982 *Michigan Travel Bulletin*, a tour wholesaler in the Detroit area was told by United that its Winter Hawaii Program was in jeopardy ostensibly because of unavailability of aircraft. In an open letter to United, the publication asked: "Why no airplanes? They don't happen to use Apollo computers. We're told that you (United) advised this wholesaler, in so many words, switch to Apollo or else. . . . Has it really come to this?"

• United discriminates against non-Apollo agencies by withholding information. For example, we understand United has informed travel agents that only Apollo users will be able to sell special "last-minute" fares based on seat availability, and that these fares will be denied to SABRE travel agencies. In a similar vein, United has threatened to steer commercial accounts to/ from travel agencies depending upon their usage of the Apollo system.

• Large bonuses paid to travel agencies to switch automated systems, e.g.:

— the July 29, 1982 issue of the *Travel Agent* refers to an allegation that "one Midwestern travel agent was offered $100,000 to switch reservation systems."

— Another periodical claims that "United has agreed to provide Apollo free of charge if they drop SABRE. . . . United has even gone a step further, offering not only cash payments to some agencies of as much as $500,000 to make such a switch, but also to override commissions . . . and installation givebacks."[8]

— *Business Week* of August 23, 1982 confirms these practices:

To compete, United this spring began offering what one agent calls "convenience money" as well as bonuses on increases in United sales, contract buyouts, and free installation to tempt agencies—and not just SABRE users—to take Apollo.[9]

Some agents resent United's pressure tactics, says one: "Using power and money to buy market share may be a wise move for United from an airline point of view. But its insistence on getting rid of other airline systems, and *the thinly veiled threat that it will give us rotten service if we don't*, has dire implications for an agent's independence."[10]

I. Concerns about Charges

Exclusion from either Apollo or SABRE can have devastating results because of the number of agencies they serve, and this is particularly true with respect to hub and spoke carriers who rely heavily on a favorable display of connecting flights. In the context, a host carrier can charge just about all it pleases. Since Frontier initially negotiated to become an Apollo co-host, segment charges imposed by United have increased 5 to 10 times the originally quoted rates. Frontier is very

---

[8]Ibid., pp. 45–46.

[9]*Business Week*, August 23, 1982, p. 68.

[10]Ibid., p. 69.

concerned that United's leverage on the Apollo system will enable it to extract excessive fees in the future.

Conclusion

Frontier and the other smaller airlines are not the only ones hurt by the giant host carriers' control over this distribution system. The travel agent industry and the public at large are also ill-served by the current situation.

The American Society of Travel Agents (ASTA) has passed a resolution warning carriers that " 'any attempt, either subtle or blatant, to pervert or undermine the impartiality of travel agent system subscribers will henceforth be resisted whenever possible,' and that the 'deliberate suppression' of computerized information on competing carriers' schedules is 'not in the best interest' of either the public or the agency community."[11] An official of the Travel Agent's Computer Society has likewise stated: "Most agents see themselves as professionals—able to present unbiased information to clients. They resent a 'dealership' relationship. They feel it would jeopardize their integrity."[12] So also the members of Associated Travel Nationwide (ATN) issued a press release on August 2, 1982 proclaiming: "As responsible travel agents, ATN members recognize their primary obligations to the consumer, and in order to meet their needs, full and complete unprejudiced information about air transportation must be available at all times."

The initial adverse effects of giant carriers' control of this distribution system upon their smaller competitors, upon travel agencies, and upon the public has already been felt. The future impact augurs to be even more pervasive. Smaller carriers such as Frontier, even with the help of the travel agencies, have not been able to avoid the consequences of the current situation. Frontier strongly believes that legislative relief is necessary, as suggested below.

Frontier's Proposed Remedy

Frontier recommends that the CAB and the DOJ recommend to Congress that legislation be enacted to remedy the anticompetitive evils resulting from host airlines controlling these automated reservations systems. The law should require nondiscriminatory treatment of all airlines, including hosts and co-hosts, and schedules, fares, and other information should be displayed on the basis of objective standards. There should be no host or co-host levels, and all airlines should have

---

[11]*Travel Management Daily*, August 18, 1982.

[12]"Bias, Dealerships' Top Concerns," *Travel Agent*, October 11, 1982, p. 94.

access to the systems on an impartial basis and for a fee, graduated according to their relative inputs into the system. Each airline owner of a computer display system should also be required to form a separate subsidiary which would operate the computerized display and reservation systems independently of the airline parent.

Respectfully submitted,

Frontier Airlines, Inc.

By   /s/David N. Brictson

             David N. Brictson

             Vice President–General Counsel

Case 1-2

Hercules Incorporated
Anatomy of a Vision

Computer technology is allowing us as managers—I should say forcing us—to move to new and different organization types so that we can better meet competitive needs. And the people who can best harness these new technologies in the future will be the most successful. Information becomes the key to success only with a management and information system that causes information to flow up to top management where we can make decisions . . . and where we can effectively communicate back down so our decisions can quickly be put into action.

Alexander Giacco
President and CEO
Hercules Incorporated
Paris, September 1984

Al Giacco was impatient. He had been working for his entire tenure as CEO of Hercules to motivate the company to embrace information technology. To Giacco's way of thinking, not enough progress had been made. He could point to state-of-the-art video-conferencing facilities, a fiber optic telecommunications network, and sophisticated process control systems, but these did not address Giacco's most important objective. He believed that information technology would allow the company to significantly reduce management staff and, at the same time, improve managerial effectiveness. Despite his efforts to convey this message to his staff, including an expensive study by Nolan, Norton &

This case was prepared by Jane Linder under the direction of Robert Eccles.

Company, Giacco did not see much headway being made. He was considering making an organizational change that would simply remove a layer of management.

Company Background: 1913–1977

In 1913, Hercules Incorporated emerged from the mating of E. I. du Pont de Nemours Chemical Company and the Sherman anti-trust law. Teddy Roosevelt's trust-busting administration ruled that Du Pont's total monopoly of the explosives market in the United States was unfairly restraining trade. Hercules was created around several of the existing Du Pont plants.

In its early days, Hercules was a single-department, single-technology, single-concept company. By 1928, it broadened its technological base by branching off from explosives into cellulosics and naval stores. To administer the more complex company, Hercules formed three operating departments, one for each business. This basic structure, with minor modifications, remained in place for 50 years.

In the mid-50s, Hercules moved into petrochemical-based plastics products. Markets were growing and globalizing, and Hercules had adopted a posture of buying inexpensive Middle East oil. Their prices reflected their lower costs, and their sales and market share grew accordingly. At this point in the firm's history, 43 percent of its gross fixed assets were devoted to oil-based commodity chemicals.

The 1973–74 oil crisis brought Hercules to its knees. Its cost advantage relative to other U.S. firms turned quickly and increasingly into a disadvantage. The company's financial structure shuddered under the additional debt they sought to maintain positive cash flow. Both the board of directors and Hercules management realized that strong measures would be needed to make the company viable again. In 1977, Giacco was named president and CEO, with a charter to put the struggling company back on its feet.

Giacco's story at Hercules was reminiscent of Horatio Alger. Born in San Giovanni, a picturesque town in rugged Italy, Giacco emigrated to America with his family as a baby. He entered grade school in Meriden, Connecticut speaking no English. By the time he was 21, he had completed his B.S. in chemical engineering at Virginia Polytechnic Institute. That summer, 1942, he joined Hercules in operations at the Radford army ammunition plant.

Giacco's rise through the ranks at Hercules was rapid and steady. Before being called to the CEO's chair in 1977, he held management positions in research, production, marketing, planning, and international groups. Although Giacco's background included all of the business centers (see descriptions below), most of his experience was in Aerospace and polypropylene. (In 1986, the polypropylene resins business was assigned to HIMONT. The polypropylene Fiber and Film business became a part of Hercules Engineered and Fabricated Products. There is more description of these units below.)

The Strategic Restructuring 1977–1985

Giacco's primary strategic objective as he assumed the lead at Hercules was to reduce the company's dependence on petrochemical-based commodity products. In the short term, he had to find enough cash to keep the firm on the right side of its debt covenants. As a start, Giacco announced the first major reorganization since 1928. (See Exhibit 1.)

> When I became CEO, we started a complete top to bottom management restructuring, dissolving the old departments and converting the company to a modified functional matrix system. Functional activities such as marketing, manufacturing, and R&D were put under the direction of corporate vice presidents reporting to the CEO—to give the effective control we felt we needed. Meanwhile, profit and loss responsibility and strategic planning of each business were vested in business center directors—who cut across functional lines, and who also reported to me. This gave us the flexibility and quick response we felt we needed.[1]

Ross Watson, vice president of information resources, commented on the organizational change, "Al was frustrated by a pyramid he could not get beneath. He always wanted to reach down into the organization and rattle people's chains." Another executive suggested that the reorganization was Giacco's way of dissolving the entrenched power bases in the company to make room for some new ways of thinking.

Through divestitures, acquisitions, geographic expansion, and just plain "squeezing" internal costs, Hercules improved its financial and competitive profile. As a result of the restructuring and other productivity emphases, staff was reduced by more than 1,600 people between 1978 and 1981, a period that saw a $800 million increase in sales.

In the years that followed the reorganization, several more major shifts were made. Some of the moves decentralized decision making; others centralized it. Some interpreted the constant reshuffling as Giacco's attempt to import the organizational fluidity of the Aerospace business into the commercial side of the house. Another executive characterized it as a "diversion so Al could move the guys he wanted up and the guys he didn't sideways."

---

[1] Alexander Giacco, Address to the Chemical Industry Society, September 1984.

EXHIBIT 1 Organization Chart

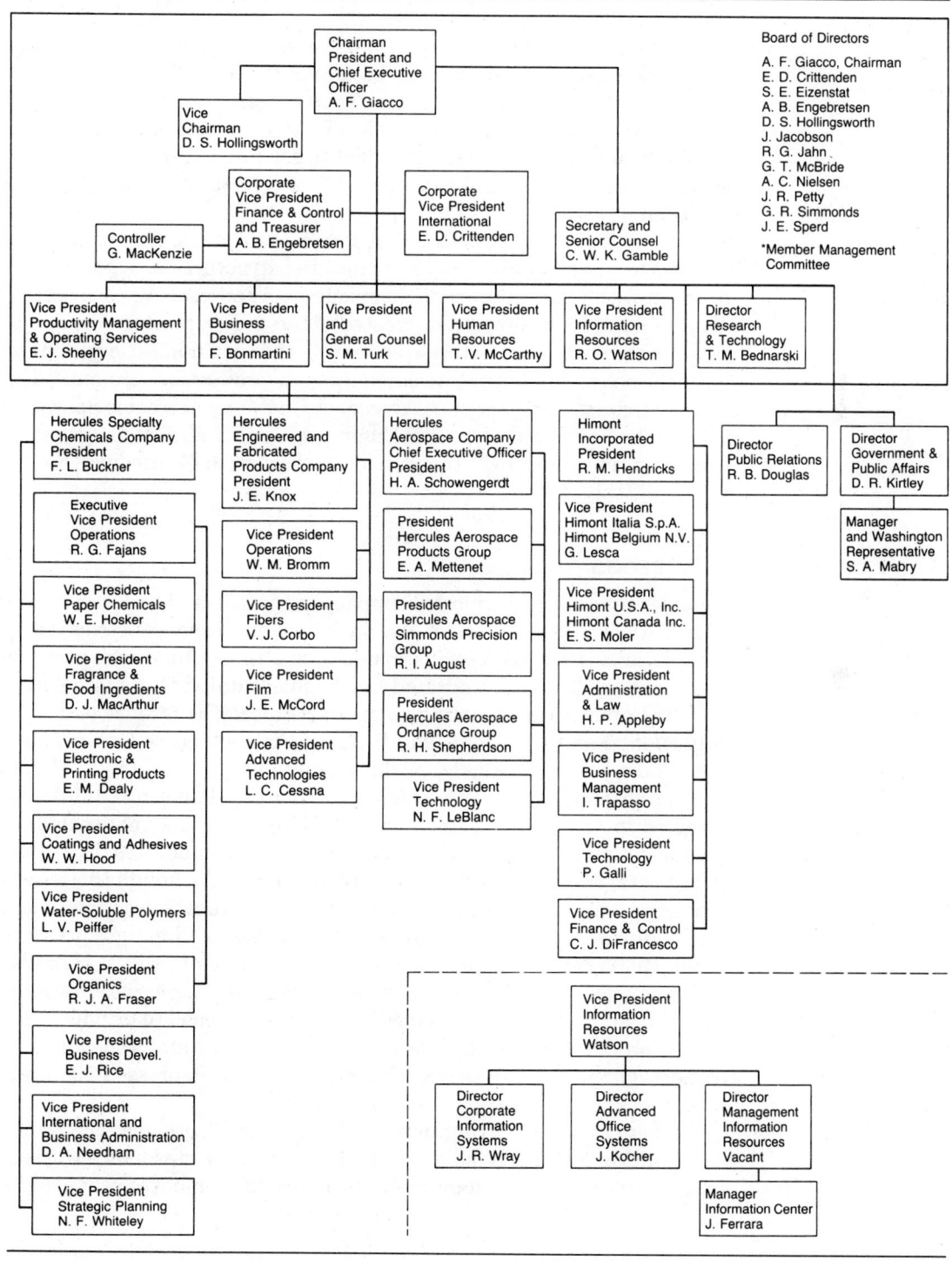

Although he was one year from the mandatory retirement age, Giacco was asked to continue as chairman and CEO in late 1983. "In view of the recent changes in the makeup of Hercules . . . it was felt by the full Hercules board that since Mr. Giacco was the architect of the corporate strategy, it would be prudent to ask him to remain until these strategic moves were implemented."[2] Giacco's service was extended until January 1987.

The organization structure that was in force at the time of the case was put in place in July 1984. Hercules was structured as a parent corporation with four major world companies. As *Hercules News* reported, "Each of the four companies, created along major product lines, will have its own president, advisory review board, and domestic and international sales, marketing, technology, and production groups." The four companies were Hercules Aerospace Company, Hercules Specialty Chemicals Company, Hercules Engineered and Fabricated Products Company, and HIMONT, Inc., a joint venture with Montedison S.p.A. of Milan, Italy.

The Company's Businesses

Hercules Specialty Chemicals Company manufactured and marketed a wide variety of products for use in industries from construction to graphic arts, from electronics manufacture to perfume and personal care. This business incorporated five business units: Organics; Water-Soluble Polymers and Coatings; Paper Chemicals; Fragrance and Food Ingredients; and Electronic and Printing Products. (See Exhibit 2 for sales and return statistics by business group.)

The Organics and Water-Soluble Polymers and Coatings units were involved in converting petrochemical and organic raw materials into chemicals for the industrial market. Products included resins, rosins, elastomers, and others for a variety of industries. Although these business segments accounted for a great deal of Hercules' sales growth and profits during the 1970s, the intense competition and margin pressure of the 1980s had made them a less reliable source of profits. Hercules had struggled to maintain adequate returns on a large, international capital base. In 1985, new overseas plants were opened to provide a European production base with access to low-cost raw materials and protection against the currency exchange losses that depressed 1985 revenues.

Paper Chemicals, Fragrance and Food Ingredients, and Electronic and Printing Products had a record of consistent performance with excellent profitability. Both marketing and production bases provided in-

---

[2]*Hercules News*, September 9, 1983.

EXHIBIT 2

HERCULES INCORPORATED
Selected Financial Statistics by Business Group
($ millions)

	1983	1984	1985
Specialty Chemicals			
Net sales	$1,056	$1,151	$1,156
Profit from operations	86	101	37
Capital expenditures	97	136	110
Aerospace			
Net sales	662	748	844
Profit from operations	62	81	84
Capital expenditures	38	50	94
Engineered and Fabricated Products			
Net sales	653†	368	389
Profit from operations	35	23	25
Capital expenditures	20	17	24
HIMONT*			
Net sales	—	533	498
Profit from operations	—	75	53
Hercules' equity (at 50 percent) . .	—	37.5	26.5

---

*HIMONT sales and profit are not included in Hercules' consolidated financial results.

†Includes HIMONT sales for 10 months.

ternational scope for product penetration and coordinated acquisition activity. In the Paper and Electronic businesses, management continued to leverage its strong position in chemicals to move into related value-added areas such as process control equipment for the paper industry.

Hercules Aerospace Company manufactured products such as rocket motors, graphite fiber, electromechanical and electronic equipment, and smokeless powders for the defense, aerospace, military, and sport shooting markets. In 1985, the Aerospace Company posted record sales and earnings, with more than 80 percent of its business coming from defense contracts. In comparison to the other three business groups, Aerospace earned far higher returns on both sales and assets. As one of the world's leading producers of solid propellant rocket motors, the company's Propulsion Systems unit was involved in more than 25 ongoing strategic and tactical missile and space programs. Through its Materials and Structures unit, it provided graphite fiber for lightweight aircraft, missile, and space applications. The Subsystems and Components segment manufactured a variety of electronic and electromechanical fuel, ignition, and flight control systems for military and commercial aircraft. The Ordnance and Services business, through the sale in 1985 of the Industrial Explosives unit, was repositioned to concentrate on the growth segments of the military and sport powder markets.

In 1983, Hercules acquired Simmonds Precision Products and merged it with the Aerospace division. According to Giacco's announcement at the time,

> Simmonds brings to Hercules proven management and technological excellence that will augment and strengthen our existing aerospace activities. . . . The merger is a fitting first step as we begin Phase II of our strategic plan for growth and expansion. The commercialization of space is just beginning, and we see Hercules as a key player in this emerging growth industry. Simmonds affords us an opportunity to expand our commitment to aerospace technology and value-added products.

Hercules Engineered and Fabricated Products Company (E&FP) sold what they called "tailored properties: coverage, aesthetics, and structural performance." The Fibers business produced and marketed polypropylene fibers for applications such as disposable diaper liners, carpeting, and furniture fabrics. Research and development had identified a polypropylene-based substitute for the traditional cigarette filter that was intended to allow selective filtration. For the most part, the Film business marketed packaging to the food, confectionary, soft drink, and tobacco industries. Advanced Technologies was formed to develop growth businesses in materials and structures for commercial application. It was composed of a commercial venture (synthetic pulp), a venture nearing commercialization (METTON high-performance structural plastic), and several potential applications based on aerospace technology and Hercules R&D. In the 1985 strategic planning conference, company president, Fred Buckner, described the situation as "two divisions operating in the red and two divisions scaling up from investments made in 1980 to 1982." His strategic mission for the company involved increasing the value-added in the product lines and solidifying the international presence. (In early 1986, Fred Buckner moved to Specialty Chemicals as the company president, and Jim Knox took his place as president of Hercules Engineered and Fabricated Products.)

In addition to its consolidated subsidiaries, Hercules held equity positions in a number of important ventures. It joined Montedison in Milan, Italy on several endeavors, the largest of which was HIMONT. Through Montedison's contribution of product technology and Hercules' addition of process technology, HIMONT became the most economical producer of polypropylene in the world. With approximately a

20 percent worldwide market share in 1985, HIMONT was poised to source and ship from the lowest cost areas of the world through a well-dispersed, global marketing organization.

1986—A Strategic Consolidation

Since the trauma of the oil embargo, Hercules' restructuring effort had made major changes in the firm's asset portfolio and geographic reach. By 1985, consolidated sales had flattened out at about $2.6 billion and the company was repositioned in higher value-added products with major capital expenditures behind them. In addition, Hercules' share of the profits from affiliated companies had continued to grow. (Exhibit 3 shows financial statistics for the years 1976 through 1985.) Nineteen eighty-six was to be the beginning of a new strategic phase. The emphasis moved to consolidating the competitive position of each business unit and concentrating on earnings improvement. Giacco described Hercules as a "world company." In his words, the corporate mission was "meeting the world's needs through materials and performance chemicals, through world class technology and manufacturing economics."

In the most recent strategic planning conference, Dr. Larry Cessna, then director of planning and acquisitions, outlined 1986–1990's targets as improved operating margins, better return on assets, and improved asset turnover. He identified four key strategic issues: (1) finding the cash to finance growth; (2) determining how big the Aerospace Company should be; (3) balancing international and domestic growth to become a world company; and (4) human resources development. Arden Engebretson, corporate VP of finance and treasurer, described the corporation's challenge: "We have to be clever as well as hard-nosed." He cautioned that they would not be able to afford their aggressive growth plans unless they could squeeze more cash out of their current assets.

There was some concern that they had "eaten the seed corn" of the corporation. George MacKenzie, corporate controller, explained that the finance department had risen in stature over the past few years because it had made major contributions to the bottom line. "Hercules is full of technical people, not financiers. They used to think of us as a necessary evil; now they know we're part of the team." MacKenzie indicated that finance had discovered "financial windfalls" through deals, changes in the pension plan assumptions, and in "just taking a very critical look at the dollars." He felt uncomfortable about the fact that, since most of the easy opportunities had been exploited, the company would have to find a new source of cash for the coming years.

EXHIBIT 3

HERCULES INCORPORATED
Selected Financial Statistics

	1976	1977	1978
Operating review ($ millions)			
Net sales	$1,646	$1,764	$2,029
Profit from operations	166	131	196
Equity in net income of affiliated companies	13	15	20
Net income	110	62	108
Research and development	37	40	43
Capital expenditures	153	132	119
Stockholders' statistics			
Income per share	$2.22	$1.27	$2.17
Dividends per share	.85	1.00	1.00
Return on average stockholders' equity .	15%	8%	13%
Average stock price	$31.00	$21.63	$15.44
Employee statistics			
Number of employees	25,678	26,344	27,077

Includes extraordinary gain of $11.6 million from an exchange of common stock for debentures.

SOURCE: Hercules Incorporated, 1985 Annual Report.

Giacco outlined his scheme for sustaining the growth and vitality of the corporation:

Although we have hired like mad in R&D, we don't expect any fundamental breakthroughs. We can't afford the *really* new. We are more development oriented. Our approach is to acquire small companies that bring us new technology, then use our development and marketing skills to exploit it globally. After we have exhausted the penetration potential, we will sell off the business to someone who is content with lower growth. I know a lot of companies that enter joint ventures, but I don't know very many that carve off pieces of their own organization to get better leverage. We were successful doing this with HIMONT and we're ready to do it again with water solubles.

Hercules had recently announced a joint venture with Henkel KGaA, a privately held German firm, to pursue the market for water-soluble polymers (thickeners found in a variety of products from whipped topping and shampoo to oil field mud). The venture would start with about $350 million in annual sales and concentrate on the European market initially. Part of the implementation effort for Hercules included isolating the corporate indirect expenses associated with the business and either transferring them to the new venture or elimi-

1979	1980	1981	1982	1983	1984	1985
$2,453	$2,617	$2,857	$2,622	$2,629	$2,571	$2,587
226	169	233	136	183	210	131
21	23	7	24	25	72	51
179	114	146	110*	174	197	133
50	57	65	74	74	72	76
190	236	172	174	168	218	234
$3.49	$2.24	$2.81	$2.10	$3.17	$3.54	$2.40
1.075	1.20	1.26	1.32	1.38	1.48	1.60
20%	11%	14%	10%	14%	15%	9%
$19.44	$20.06	$22.56	$22.81	$35.19	$32.63	$35.94
27,418	26,089	25,893	24,450	24,221	25,262	25,448

nating them. (In Hercules' terminology, "indirect" included all expenses except those directly attributable to manufacturing. About 6,500 employees were in this category in 1986.)

Giacco had named Ed Sheehy the "Czar of Indirect" to help accomplish this. Reporting directly to Giacco, Sheehy had the authority to do whatever was necessary to achieve his goal of cutting indirect expenses down to 16 percent, from 20 percent of sales. "The Commander," as he had been known since his navy days, pegged his target at a $100 million reduction. He was working with the human resources department to structure a "golden door" program to offer incentives for early retirement. Although the specifics were yet to be worked out, Sheehy anticipated moving out about 200 people by the end of the second quarter of 1986 through this and other means. "We'll use the joint venture to trigger everything. We can make a lot of changes under its umbrella. We have done this kind of thing before at Hercules and it has helped people accept the changes." An executive commented, "Al has been a master at doing one thing and promoting another. It's the way he gets people ready for what is to come."

During Giacco's tenure, both the skills mix and the average seniority in the company had changed dramatically. Tom McCarthy, vice president of human resources, noted, "In 1977 half of our professionals had greater than 15 years of service. Today, half have less than six years' seniority. In addition, the chemists and chemical engineers no longer dominate the company's thinking." Along with this shift came a revitalized reward system. "Ten years ago, tenure drove pay. Since the early 80s, however, we have paid for performance."

About 200 of Hercules' top managers participated in a structured bonus system. The board annually approved a bonus pool which Giacco allocated among the companies based on performance. This was divided among the eligible managers in proportion to Hay points (a measure of job size created by Hay Associates). Bonuses for the most senior executives were determined separately by Giacco. According to the assessment of one executive in this category, a year of solid performance could be destroyed, bonuswise, by a stupid decision in December. In McCarthy's opinion, Hercules' culture and decision-making style were much more pervasive and powerful influences on management than the bonus system.

The Hercules Culture

When Hercules' executives talked of the culture, they mentioned characteristics such as "inbred," "defensive," and "risk-averse." One manager described what he called "the whale syndrome. When you stick your head up and spout off, you get harpooned." Another manager indicated that people spent an inordinate amount of time building numerical cases to protect themselves from inquisitions. Others clearly disagreed. One VP remarked, "Our company thrives on confrontation. Conflict brings important problems to light." "My job," Giacco explained, "is to innovate and pull the organization with me—even when they are not willing to listen. I have to take the risk myself."

In the opinion of another executive, the culture was driven by the preponderance of engineers in the professional ranks. "This is a highly technical company. Most of the managers think there is a technical solution to every problem." (Exhibit 4 shows the background of the senior executives.)

Giacco had shaped the Hercules culture in his tenure. He said, "I get involved in a lot of things, but I don't make any decisions. That's what my company presidents do. For the most part, I just stir up the pot. I am a 'floor walker.' People will talk to me in their own environment and complain about the things they don't like."

There were some differences of opinion among the management ranks about whether Giacco really made decisions. One executive stated, "Al doesn't make any decisions. The way he manages makes decisions." Another remarked, "Al's organizational moves are masterful. He taught Machiavelli how to write the book." In describing Giacco's intuitive management style, a third executive noted, "Al isn't an implementer, he's a conceptualizer. He fixes on a vision then screams and

EXHIBIT 4 Executive Profiles

Name	Title	Degree	School
Alexander Giacco	Chairman, president, and CEO	B.S. Chemical Engineering	Virginia Polytechnic Institute
		Doctor of Business (honorary)	William Carey College
		Doctor of Laws (honorary)	Widener University
		Doctor of Business Administration (honorary)	Goldey Beacom College
David S. Hollingsworth	Vice chairman of the board of directors	B.S. Chemical Engineering	Lehigh University
Fred Buckner	President, Hercules Specialty Chemicals Company	B.S. Mechanical Engineering	University of Utah
R. Michael Hendricks	President and CEO, HIMONT Inc.	B.S. Industrial Management	MIT
George MacKenzie, Jr.	Controller	B.S. Chemical Engineering	University of Delaware
		M.B.A.	University of Chicago
James Knox	President, Hercules Engineering and Fabricated Products Company	B.S.E. Chemical Engineering	University of Michigan
Henry Schowengerdt	President and CEO, Hercules Aerospace Company	B.S. Electrical Engineering	University of Illinois
		M.S. Electrical Engineering	University of Illinois
Thomas McCarthy	Vice president, human resources	B.A. Economics	Cornell University
Edward Sheehy	Vice president, productivity management and operating services	B.S. Naval Engineering	U.S. Naval Academy
		M.S. Chemistry	Lehigh University
Ross Watson	Vice President, information resources	B.S. Chemical Engineering	MIT
D. James MacArthur	Vice President, Fragrances and Food Ingredients, Hercules Specialty Chemicals Company	B.S. Chemical Engineering	University of Michigan
Walter Bromm	Vice president, operations, Hercules Engineered and Fabricated Products Company	B.S. Chemistry and Physics	Geneva College
Dominick DiDonna	Director, finance and control, Hercules Specialty Chemicals Company	B.B.A. Accounting	Temple University
Clark Kingery	Director, information and services, Hercules Specialty Chemicals Company	B.A. Physics	Grinnell College
James Wray	Director, corporate information systems (east & west), information resources	B.S. Mathematics	University of Wyoming
		M.S. Mathematics	University of Wyoming
Barry J. Kocher	Director, advanced office systems	B.A. Mathematics	University of Delaware

Note: Among 6,800 exempt Hercules employees in 1986 (excludes foreign, Simmonds, and GOco employees), there were 905 chemical engineering degrees, 706 chemistry degrees, and 748 mechanical engineering degrees.

yells until someone makes it happen. He runs the company like an Italian family; he's a patriarch." Describing Giacco as a "Vince Lombardi type," a vice president remarked, "He wants to kick you in the butt and put his arm around you all at once." Another noted, "It takes a strong leader to move down the cost curve in a low-growth situation. When you are not growing, innovation means getting rid of people."

In the words of one middle manager, "This is a one-man company. The culture is moving toward inaction and indecision because everyone is trying to please 'Dad.' We have extra layers in the hierarchy because no one trusts us. Whenever a mistake is made, another manager is inserted in the organization to watch over you." Another manager suggested that Giacco had changed during his term in office. "In the beginning, we were ready to follow him anywhere. Now, some of us wonder whether he has lost touch." There was some feeling that Giacco would use his considerable power over the board of directors to keep his position indefinitely. Giacco said, "I feel bad for the people who are intimidated by me. All I want is what's best for the company."

To Giacco, middle management at Hercules was a "filtration system. Middle management passes orders down and passes information up, and every layer takes something out. Often, that something is innovation. It's like permafrost. No matter how enthusiastic the top management is, the energy just can't penetrate through to the people that have to make it happen."

Although Hercules was accustomed to making bets that didn't pay off for 12 or 15 years, stories about two of Giacco's decisions had reached almost heroic proportions. The first "epic" spun the tale of the polypropylene fiber plant in Oxford, Georgia. Based on some very uncertain market forecasts, Giacco had committed to a $30 million investment in a plant to manufacture polypropylene staple fiber—100 million pounds annual capacity. Through the construction cycle, when the wisdom of the decision came under fire, Giacco was steadfast in his support. When the plant was finished, there was virtually no market for the size and type of fiber it produced. Hercules management scrambled and found that they could modify the plant to manufacture a fiber that would make an inexpensive liner for disposable diapers. This and subsequent investments made them the world's leading producer of polypropylene staple fiber.

Dave Hollingsworth, vice chairman of the board, recounted a similar experience with the cigarette filter business. "For four or five years, the Hercules system has been fighting Giacco on the applicability of polypropylene for cigarette filters. He believes that our fibers can be used to make filters that can selectively remove materials from the cigarette smoke. Both the cigarette industry and our internal analysts have been skeptical, but Al has insisted on pursuing it. He may be right!"

Giacco described the role of the CEO as that of an integrator. "The CEO presumably has the best brains and the most experience in the company, and he has got to know what's going on. He should have the ability to bring together talent to get the best decisions made. The CEO's number one problem is the future of the company. He should be ahead of his people."

Giacco's Information Technology Vision

Almost from the beginning of his tenure as CEO, Giacco had been promoting information technology (I/T). In his mind, it was one way to "innovate in the management process. Information technology makes a big company seem like a small one. It means that each manager can do more, but not lose touch with his people. The technology to achieve this exists, but the organizational concepts do not." After declaring his intentions within the company, Giacco sought help in defining new concepts to begin to implement his vision.

In 1984, Giacco and some of his staff began talking in earnest about the idea of using computing to increase span of control. One since-retired vice president had been thinking about an "executive robot" to replace some of his less productive staff members. Giacco's specific question was, "How can we use computing to cut out layers of management?" During 1984 and early 1985, they solicited advice from experts from Wharton, University of Virginia, and MIT. Giacco did not receive an answer that satisfied him, so, in mid-1985, he commissioned a $350,000 study by Nolan, Norton & Company to explore the issue further.

The consultants spent about six months studying the Fiber and Film group of Hercules Engineered and Fabricated Products Company. At the outset, they articulated their assumption that management staffing levels would look like a "fat-waisted" hierarchy. They reported that, in most firms they studied, middle management had bulged to about 60 percent of the total staff. In their view, 35 percent was a more appropriate proportion.

Among their other results and conclusions, Nolan, Norton was somewhat surprised to find that Fiber and Film was atypical. The business center's middle *and* senior management ranks were far less populated than in other companies. (See Exhibit 5.) Watson grinned, "We knew we were lean and mean." The consultants also found that Film and Fiber fit their definition of a "break-away" company. Its I/T spending as a percent of sales far exceeded that of other firms in its industry.

Giacco's reaction was, "They did a very nice job for us, but they didn't answer my question." Giacco had seen the impact of computer-aided design (CAD) in Aerospace and of simple control systems in the commercial business. When Watson was supervising U.S. production,

EXHIBIT 5 Hercules Seems to Have Embarked upon a Computer Strategy that Has Impacted the Top and Middle Levels

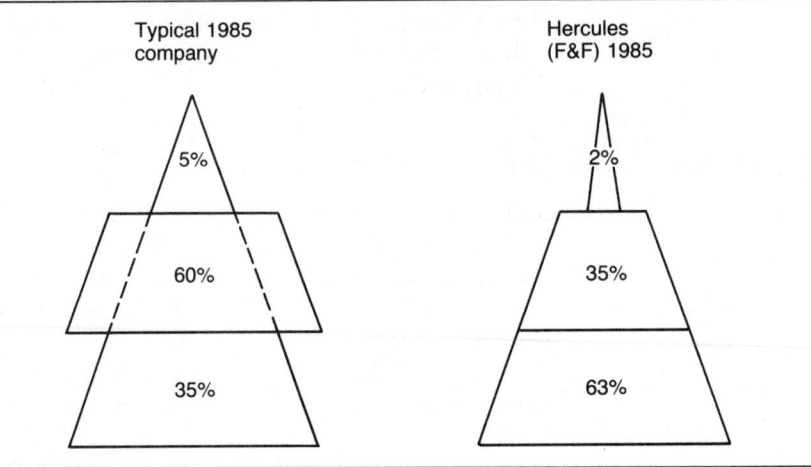

Typical 1985 company

Hercules (F&F) 1985

SOURCE: Nolan, Norton 1985 study.

he and Giacco had cut the hierarchy from 14 layers to 6. Watson noted, "We moved a large number of staff people back to the field." Giacco was certain that there were more improvements of this kind to be made through computing. He said, "If this were my company, I would run it with half of the corporate staff we have today."

History of Information Technology

Hercules entered the computer revolution in the 1960s, with corporate financial systems for closing the books and stand-alone plant systems to help control inventory. By 1977, the centralized group had subsumed plant computing and reported directly to the CEO. One executive remarked, "The data flowed in one direction. It was sent from the plant to tell the corporate office what they wanted to know. We kept little green books for ourselves at the plant. The centralization did give us standard accounting systems, but it did not provide better access to data."

As a part of the company reorganization to the "matrix structure" in 1978, the Management Information Department (MID) was broken into three pieces: Business Information Department, Advanced Office Systems, and Computer Systems Department. The Business Information Department (BID) was formed to represent the users' interest by initiating and managing development projects. It was also responsible for business planning at Hercules. The change was intended to reestablish the credibility of the DP function.

The former MID director was given a small group called Advanced Office Systems (AOS), with a charter to investigate new technologies such as word processing, video conferencing, and satellite communications to determine their importance to Hercules. The remainder of MID was renamed the Computer Systems Department (CSD) and charged with running the computer center and providing systems analysis and programming functions.

By 1982, BID had been dissolved, but the distributed computing effort it had spawned in the plants was firmly under way. AOS was making plans to wire the new corporate headquarters for modern office technology, and a nucleus of two people had formed an information center within CSD.

In 1983, Watson was named vice president, Information Resources Department (IRD), reporting to the CEO, with CSD and the AOS group under his aegis. Shortly thereafter, the information center was brought out from under CSD, resulting in the organization shown in Exhibit 1. Exhibit 6 shows the staffing levels through the years 1977 to 1985.

Watson brought a wealth of operating experience to the information systems activity at Hercules. A freshly minted chemical engineer from MIT in 1949, he started his career at the research center just like 99 percent of all Hercules' professional hires at that time. From there, he had held a variety of technical and supervisory positions, working his way up to plant manager by 1963. He served as president of Hystron Fibers, Inc., a joint venture he helped engineer, from its inception in 1966 until it was sold in 1970. He worked in general management positions, directed production control, and served as corporate controller before assuming the lead at IRD.

Watson believed it was important for IRD to "have something the user wants. We have to develop skill in the way the company runs and then be able to translate that into systems. In the three or four hours a month I get to spend with Al, I have to convey to him where we are going with all this."

Computer Systems Department (CSD)

CSD supported a corporate computer center in Wilmington with the "image" of a single large computer. In addition, an auxiliary computer center in Bacchus, Utah handled the computing requirements for the Aerospace Company and was targeted as a disaster backup site in the future. Jim Wray, director of CSD, stated, "We are responsible for data collection, data processing, data management, and data network control. We design, program, and maintain all the corporate and plant systems."

EXHIBIT 6 Information Resources Department Personnel and Spending*

	1977	1978	1979	1980	1981	1982	1983	1984	1985
Personnel									
Management Information Department (MID)	140								
Computer Systems Department (CSD)		114	119	150	145	143	142	147	143
Business Information Department (BID)		20/50	29/50						
Advanced Office Systems (AOS)		1	6	11	12	13	15	21	20
Information Center (Management Information Resources—MIR)						2	4	6	7
Vice president and secretary							2	2	2
Total	140	135/165	154/175	161	157	158	163	176	172
Spending ($000)	140					$20,023	$26,203	$25,495	$22,611†

*Excludes CSD West costs, which are zeroed out each year, as they are billed to government work orders.
†1986 budget was set at $21,416,000.

Watson described the essence of the task at CSD. "Hardware is no problem for us. Our 3090 mainframe is double the MIPS of a 3081 and $600,000 per year cheaper. But software drives us up a tree. The major systems Hercules uses were invented by the Egyptians—they haven't changed that much—but it's still impossible to buy modern software. We really don't want to develop software ourselves, but most of the time we have to."

The list of systems implemented by CSD since 1977 was a source of pride. Recent major projects included a manufacturing cost system, corporate human resources system, domestic pricing system, and sales forecasting system. (Exhibit 7 shows the 1985 accomplishments and 1986 I/T plans.) Hewlett-Packard computers had been installed in 20 plants, and a generic set of applications had been tailored to the specific requirements of each.

Advanced Office Systems

Jay Kocher, director of AOS, described the group's mission as "addressing personal productivity. The original AOS 'missionaries' started pilots in clerical and managerial technologies, and we have some pretty amazing results today."

The backbone of Hercules' voice, video, and data communications was a satellite-based network with seven earth stations. Other locations were tied to the earth stations through terrestrial links. Kocher commented, "This network handles about 1.5 million minutes of voice traffic per month and about 250,000 minutes of calls on our 800 lines. In addition, we use satellite services to handle our European data transmission. In November 1985, we were the first company in the United States to use an on-premise earth station for this purpose. We

---

EXHIBIT 7   1985 Accomplishments and 1986 Plans:
Computer Systems Department

1985 accomplishments
  (estimated return on investment—35.8 percent)

- Manufacturing cost—What if III
- Human resources

Long-term disability	Actuary system
Group life	Pension history
Loan feature	Savings plan recording
PAYSOP	and reporting system

- Credit management
- Customer specifications
- Domestic pricing

EXHIBIT 7 *(concluded)*

1985 accomplishments
- Sales forecasting
- WMC salesmen compensation
- Computer resource portfolio
- Appropriations and facilities control
- Material safety data sheets
- Security

1986 projects
   (carried over from 1985)

Development	*Sponsor*
Corporate inventory	Controller's
Corporate procurement	Purchasing
Disbursement management	Treasurer's
Human resources	
Treasurer's/salary area	Treasurer's
Human resources area	Human Resources
Plant wage payroll	Controller's
Essential material	
Inventory	Controller's
Specifications	Purchasing
Ledger	Controller's
Safety reporting	Safety and Loss
Tax reporting (federal, state, local)	Treasurer's
Financial Practices Codebook—gross profit	Controller's
Hercules lab manual	Research Center
Sales index	Controller's

New 1986 projects

Development	*Sponsor*
Worldwide product pricing	Marketing
Product directory	Controller's
Credit management systems enhancements	Treasurer's
Late payment finance charges	
CPV generation from credit balances	
Customer specifications enhancements	Production and Quality
Interface with order entry	
Extract—focus	
Interface with HP	
Miscellaneous codebook	Controller's
Hercalpha codebook	Controller's
Quality-related losses by product	Production and Quality
Freight payment interface enhancements	Transportation
Material safety data sheets—samples	Health and Environment

Strategies	
Sales/marketing	Marketing
Financial system strategy	Controller's

Strategic enhancements	
Relational databases	Computer Systems

EXHIBIT 8   Telecommunications Network

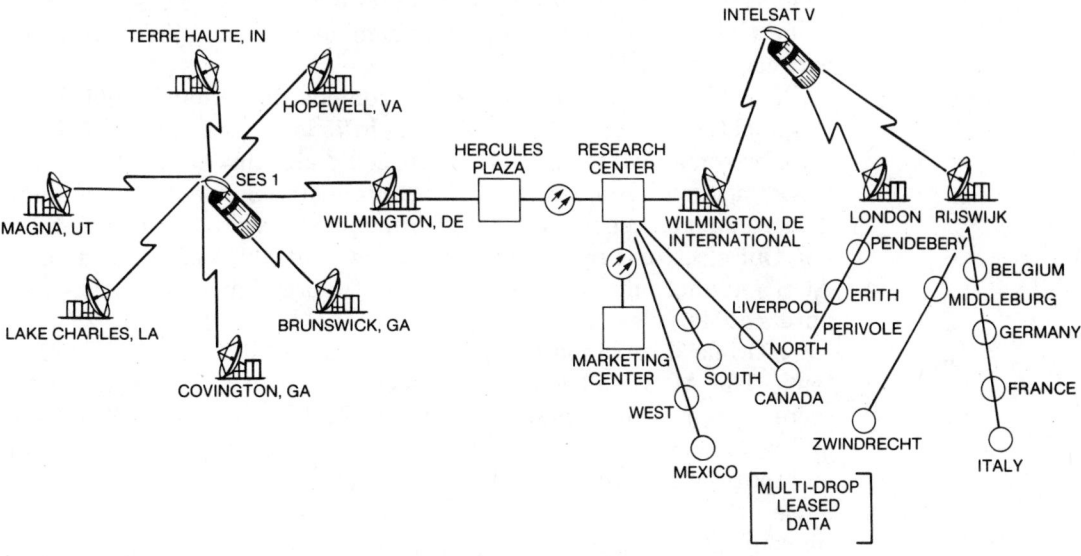

have installed Delaware's first private fiber optics network to connect our home office, marketing center, and research center in Wilmington." (See Exhibit 8.)

It was Hercules' video conferencing technology that had drawn significant attention in the press. At a capital cost of $1 million, Hercules had installed 24 freeze frame video conference rooms at major locations in the U.S., Canada, and England. Giacco remarked in a 1984 speech to a chemical industry association in Paris, "Thanks to satellite communications, the number of vice-presidential positions has been cut by half, while satellite conferences have reduced travel costs dramatically."

Aerospace was the first and largest video conference user. Hank Schowengerdt, company president, said, "It saved travel time from Wilmington to Bacchus, Utah, and let us get more people involved in project decisions. We scheduled everything from routine staff meetings to company board meetings through the video conference rooms." Most managers agreed that the most important benefit from the technology was in flexibility, speed, and "wear and tear on people," rather than in tangible cost savings.

Hercules was also a leader in voice messaging. In December 1980, AOS installed the second store-and-forward voice messaging system in the world. In 1985, the system handled more than 1.1 million messages at about $.25 each. Knox commented, "VMS makes me at least 10 percent more efficient. I couldn't live without it. It is a marvelous tool that changes the way I do my job." Another executive remarked, "I don't make a lot of calls out, but I get a lot coming in. Often I just need a one-way conversation."

The Hercules office network was composed of almost 2,000 Wang terminals connected to 100 controllers in 75 locations. All could dial up the electronic mail facility, and most could also link to the mainframe (SNA) network. Kocher said, "The administrative people have documented an increase in the ratio of principals to secretaries from 4.0 to 4.9. Our electronic mail volume is almost 150,000 documents a year." AOS's 1985 equipment census showed more than 1,600 microcomputers at Hercules.

AOS used a unique training concept to implement the office systems. The AOS staff identified a coordinator—usually an interested secretary—in each administrative unit. The coordinators were trained and were then, in turn, responsible for training the other secretaries and the principals in their groups. They also became the "first line of defense" when problems arose. AOS got involved only when the coordinator could not answer the user's question.

Information Center

Through the information center (I/C), Joan Ferrara and her small staff of six analysts marketed end-user computing throughout Hercules. Her domain included a series of sponsored applications and technologies including personal computer, mainframe, and office system capabilities. The I/C supported six mainframe packages: Report Management and Distribution System, STorage And Information Retrieval System, FOCUS, IFPS, the Executive Information System, and the Presentation Graphics Facility. (Exhibit 9 lists and describes these products.)

Most of the I/C's products were well received, but reactions to the Executive Information System (EIS) were mixed. One executive termed it "useless." Another reported that he used it daily for quick status checks. A third remarked that it gave "misinformation," because it could disagree substantially from the corporate financial records. Based on the invoice data base rather than the general ledger system, the information was available faster, but it was not as well "scrubbed."

One of the most popular I/C activities was its support of personal computing. Ferrara described the I/C's role, "We help the users configure their systems. We train them. We help them get started." As of the end of 1985, 578 people had received the beginning LOTUS seminar

---

EXHIBIT 9   Applications Sponsored by the Information Center

- Report Management and Distribution System—RMDS is an IBM package which makes paper reports available on-line. In 1985, Hercules was loading 300,000 report pages a month onto this system.
- Storage and Information Retrieval System—STAIRS is a software package that maintains a large body of literature and allows the user to search through it by assorted indices. Although the package itself was not especially "friendly," it was used by the Research Center to maintain a large library of journal abstracts. The system enabled users to search the entire text file for a particular word or set of words.
- FOCUS—A "user-approachable" fourth generation language, FOCUS was heavily used throughout Hercules. About 600 active users worked with extracts of corporate data bases to create their own reports and analyses. The I/C was extremely active in providing training and in working with CSD to make the extract files available. Although a PC version of FOCUS was on the market, it was not supported by the I/C.
- Interactive Financial Planning System—IFPS is a financial modeling language with some data management capabilities. In 1982, about the same time FOCUS was bought, the Controller's department surveyed the vendors and recommended that the corporation buy IFPS. The I/C agreed and began to support it for use in building models that required more detail and sophistication than LOTUS could provide.
- Executive Information System—EIS was the only custom developed system in the I/C's list of supported software. The system was designed to allow a small number of senior executives in the company to access key operating statistics through their PC's. Using simple menus, an executive could review the prior day's results such as sales, orders booked, inventory, and backlog.
- The Presentation Graphics Facility—Through timesharing, a user could create graphs, then draw them on the plotter connected to his or her PC terminal.

---

and 886 had been to the intermediate and advanced seminars. (Additionally, more than 1,000 had been trained in FOCUS.)

The process for purchasing a PC was fairly informal. The user called the I/C for help in defining the right configuration, then wrote a letter describing the need to the purchasing agent and Wray (director of CSD). Neither Ferrara nor Watson could remember any requests having been refused. Watson remarked, "At this point, almost everyone who needs a PC has one. All the major groups have developed general spreadsheet applications. Now we want the specific systems problems."

Because of the size of her staff, Ferrara had to develop some innovative approaches for dealing with the demand for her group's services. Forty individuals throughout the corporation were identified as FOCUS and/or PC coordinators. "These are liaison people in each functional area who act as the first line of defense. New users can go to them with questions, and the coordinators do some informal training. It's like a 'buddy system.' " Ferrara stated she was trying to make the users self-sufficient, "to put myself out of business if I can."

Use of Personal Computers

Both the operations and the finance organizations had gravitated to PCs. Dom DiDonna, controller of Specialty Chemicals reported that, on average, he spent two hours a day with his company's president and an equal amount of time with the computer. His uses included calendar and time management, correspondence filing, electronic mail, and FOCUS, LOTUS, and IFPS applications. "About 75 percent of my work is on acquisitions and divestitures. We have three or four home-grown LOTUS models that give us a good overview. When we want more details, we go into IFPS. It's a lot easier to justify an acquisition when the numbers work. When they don't we sometimes go ahead anyway for 'strategic' reasons."

DiDonna talked about the benefits of PCs to the company: "Computing is still in its infancy; we're just getting to the point where we don't get hard copy. Today it doesn't really save us time, it just gives us more information. PCs have proliferated to provide some individualism to the corporate reports."

Regarding the operations groups' fascinations with models, DiDonna cautioned, "A bell doesn't ring when you get the right model. Somewhere you have to make a decision."

When asked about their own use of computing, Hercules executives were remarkably consistent. Knox said, "I use my PC about two hours a week. I have two staff members who prepare the spreadsheets for me, and I do the 'what if's.' " Buckner agreed, "Making spreadsheets is a waste of my time. I can get someone who can do it 15 times faster, to do it for 15 times less money. We went through a period of overspending on PCs two or three years ago. Now we're getting more specific about what we want to do. We may not have been able to get where we are any other way, though."

Not all users were as sanguine. One executive complained, "We're three generations behind. Software is in the dark ages. The reason we have so many PCs is that no one can get anything out of the mainframe." Another manager described IRD generally as "mismanaged and understaffed. They don't have the resources to sit with the users and ask how to use the technology. They get defensive and drop into 'hyper-techno-speak.' "

Computing for Operations

Some of the most active PC users were in the operations function. Clark Kingery, director of information and services for Hercules Specialty Chemicals Company, described the impetus for the explosion of LOTUS modeling. "In 1978, all of the computers were controlled centrally by MID. The driving force was accounting. When operational information was brought to the top of the company, the accounting systems organized it in ways that distorted it for operational decisions. We had a lot of problems with senior management making decisions based on distorted numbers.

"Now we have distributed processing. Each plant has systems that let it look at its information in its own way, not the way the accountants want to look at it." Having been an operations director himself, Watson added, "Forget the accounting system; we need engineering accuracy. We have to go down to the accounting data molecules and strip out their assumptions."

Kingery indicated that they had learned a great deal in the process of developing and using more than 60 product/profit and scheduling models. Prior to PCs the operations staff had concentrated on capturing every detail of the logistical situation in linear models. The results were complex, intricate models that the operations management didn't trust. They had since discovered that simple, powerful LOTUS models that managers could understand were far more helpful in making decisions. Kingery noted, "It's a tool that helps us focus people's attention. The models let us look at many more alternatives, rule out the fruitless ones sooner, and optimize the best. The model enforces a discipline. It gives us an analytical answer unencumbered by individual enthusiasm or opinions."

Walt Bromm, vice president of operations for E&FP, described two other important uses of models in project management.

> During the construction period on a new facility, we use the models to check ourselves. Because our building cycles are so long, we need to keep looking to make sure our assumptions are still true. After a project is finished, we use them for post audit. We can look at the model to analyze why our predictions were off. In our experience, the operations side of the models have been right on. Where we have trouble is in the marketing side. Projects fail because we don't make what the market wants.

In Bromm's opinion, "We are not pushing far enough or fast enough in process control and information systems. As our volume grows over the next five years, we need to be able to continue to reduce people. Some of the improvement will come from incremental savings, and some will come from ground-breaking notions. It will depend on how far down we can push decisions." Kingery agreed, "The first thrust is to do what you have been doing more efficiently. But operating labor is only 9 percent of our total plant costs; total people costs are only 22 percent. We need to look for lower cost curves on other dimensions, too. Al talks about people because you can count them; people reductions are more grippable than reductions in inventory, improvements in yield, or better customer service. But if you do a good job in all those areas, you can take out layers of management and staff."

Bromm continued, "Management had enough foresight five years ago to bet on the come—to make some serious investments in information technology. Al has been our umbrella to do a lot. As we grow with it, we begin to think in a different way. We think in LOTUS."

Computing at Aerospace

Intensive computing was not a choice at Hercules Aerospace Company, it was a requirement. Hank Schowengerdt, company president, remarked, "We are much more technically oriented than the commercial businesses. Our computers are not only administrative, they are part of our products. All of the major competitors in this business are computerized. We can't afford not to be."

The Utah data center, a part of Watson's organization, held more than twice as much computing power as Wilmington, including an extensive CAD system. The I/T staff, not including the Simmonds Precision group, consisted of 190 people with skills ranging from technical and scientific programming to telecommunications and commercial systems development.

As an example of the importance of computing, Schowengerdt described the process of designing and developing a missile. "In the early 60s, we would fire 25 or 30 missiles as a part of the design process. It was enormously expensive. Today, our CAD system has cut that down to 4 or 5." Computing had helped Aerospace improve professional productivity as well. Schowengerdt remembered, "In the 60s, we had 6,000 people in Bacchus [Utah] developing two rocket motors. Today we have 5,000 for nine motors. Computers have taken the drudgery away and allowed our people to be more innovative." Another executive added, "It takes about 10 minutes to get a new computer approved for Aerospace." Because of his focus on strategic direction and competitors' plans, Schowengerdt reported that he personally devoted little time to information technology.

Computing at Fragrance and Food Ingredients

Jim MacArthur, vice president of the Fragrance and Food Ingredients group (part of Hercules Specialty Chemicals Company), was not only computer literate, but was articulate about his vision of the technology direction. Having spent a year in Watson's organization promoting end-user computing, MacArthur had packaged his view into a four-step process for building a "brotherhood of professionals using computing." As a first step, he advocated a general uplifting of the literacy of the group. "The entire 'society' must come up a level in understanding the use of the tool. The way you do this is find people who have problems, select a good solution, like LOTUS 1–2–3, then lock on that and never waver. In the beginning, you force people into learning by example or through intimidation at the highest level. You start from the top and you 'force train' the organization."

In his second step, MacArthur suggested people would

clean off their desks. They will use the computer to do just what they used to do on paper. They will do it faster and neater, but none of this is *really* useful to the organization. No savings accrue; no one walks out the door, and the organization begins to worry because it saw this phase as the goal.

By the third step, people begin to work smarter. They do productive things that could not have been done before, like modeling their business. They make new kinds of decisions. For example, with Hercules' high fixed cost structure, contribution is often more relevant to a decision than profit. The accountants keep their numbers fully burdened when the decision maker needs an incremental view. We developed some models that let sales, marketing, and production management collaborate on incremental pricing decisions. The results were more business, more profit, and a smarter bunch of managers.

The fourth step is that rare case where a sharp person will find an opportunity to totally change the way the game is played—to give strategic advantage. This is what we should be driving the technology toward.

When I first took this job about a year ago, the district offices of the Specialty Chemicals field sales group had just been eliminated in response to a call for reduced indirect expenses. In the Flavors business, we were worried that the change would hurt our revenue stream. I put my entire U.S. sales force in a room and asked them to help me make two lists: what is absolutely essential to every sale of a flavor; and what supervisors have traditionally requested. Hours later, the second list was long, but the first had only one item:

"obtain a brief." A brief is a statement of what the customer wants—for example, a smoky, mesquite flavor with a certain water solubility, heat stability, etc. Now, no one really knows what "smoky mesquite" tastes like, so the first sample in the door sets the standard. You've got to be fast, and you've got to be close.

We started working on a system that will change the way this business is conducted. The sales rep carries a GRid portable computer and enters the information for the brief right in the customer's office. It is sent over the telephone line to a dedicated PC at our lab, which has access to a data base of all the flavors we have ever produced—there are about 30,000 of them. For most requests, we will have a flavor sample and a nice letter in the mail to the customer that day.

This system is just being introduced; we are in the prototype stage. Although the Information Center isn't supposed to work on applications, Ross Watson loaned us one person to help us build the system and I eventually hired her as a permanent member of my business team. I consider information at the same level of importance as manufacturing, marketing, operations, and sales.

MacArthur described himself as a "change agent." Speaking about his direct subordinates, he noted, "Their job is to operate the business; my job is to change the business. I give them more responsibility than they are used to because I don't want to duplicate their efforts. Growth is different; that's my job. Growth is change, change means complexity, and that means the computer. I want to build a showcase for the use of computing to run a corporation."

The Future of Computing at Hercules

Most executives agreed that computing would be useful for the company. Buckner said, "Al knows that this gets more important every year. We have to get our feet in the water." A more cynical manager stated, "We have overspent on technology. It is mostly hype, but if hype increases the stock price, it's worth it." In Hollingsworth's view:

There's a great gulf between the PC movement and the concept that Giacco has. For that growing core of people who use the PC as a tool, their lives are never the same. The impact is profound. But our indirect overhead costs are going up, not down. Giacco's notion of streamlining the organization through information systems is a bunch of poppycock. Although the system can move information faster and help us make faster and perhaps better decisions, I don't believe it will enable us to reduce people significantly.

According to Dick Douglas, a member of Giacco's staff:

We are in the midst of a major change in our corporate culture. Obviously not everyone will totally agree on the merits of such a change. You'll find there are basically three reactions to this kind of thing. There are those who enthusiastically embrace new management techniques, and there are those who accept change slowly, and, of course, there are the laggards who never accept change or, at best, accept it slowly and painfully. The third group is reminiscent of those people who ran along the beach at Kitty Hawk during man's first flight yelling up to the pilot, "I tell you, Orville, the damn thing won't fly." Hercules and every large company has a few of these "progress impeders."

As Giacco looked over the Wilmington skyline from his well-appointed office in Hercules Plaza, he weighed the alternatives. He could follow the Nolan, Norton recommendation and turn IRD's attention toward operations and marketing applications. He could keep promoting the vision and try to penetrate the "permafrost." As he watched the afternoon shadows play on the waters of the Brandywine Creek, however, he felt rather inclined to act. He wondered what would happen if he just ordered an organizational change that would leave the hierarchy one level flatter.

Chapter 2

Manageable Trends

Introduction

In the first chapter, we identified key issues that make the assimilation of information technology (IT) so challenging. We then discussed the implications of these issues for management practice. The major headings in this book were selected to provide a comprehensive treatment of these issues. Analysis of these areas in a firm's situation, complete with appropriate recommendations, is normally called an IT management audit.

Underlying our treatment of each of these headings is a cluster of six themes that reflect both changing insight into management practice and guidance for administrative action. A discussion of the nature and implications of each theme is presented here, as well as our identification of its future. These themes, which form within each chapter the organizational basis of our discussion on an aspect of management, represent in our opinion the most useful ways to think about the forces driving transition in the IT unit in the mid-1980s. Our expectation, as mentioned in Chapter 1, is that additional experience, research, and evolving technology will inevitably produce new formulation of these and other themes in subsequent years.

In outline form, these six themes include:

1. IT impacts different industries and the firms within them in different ways strategically. The thrust of this impact strongly influences the appropriate selection of IT management tools and approaches.
2. Office technology, telecommunications, and information processing technologies are evolving. Formerly disparate areas of

technologies now require coordination, minimally at a policy level and most frequently at a line control level.

3. Organizational learning about IT is a dominant fact of life. The type of management approaches appropriate for assimilating a technology change sharply as the organization gains familiarity with it.

4. Environmental forces are shifting the balance of make-or-buy decisions on IT services in the direction of buy, which profoundly impacts the kind and quality of IT support an organization can receive.

5. While the functions of the system life cycle remain, the best approaches to executing them and the problems of implementation have both changed significantly, with a wide diversity of approaches being appropriate for different systems.

6. Effective IT policy and responsibility involve a continuous reshifting and rebalancing of power between general management, IT management, and user management. Each group has a legitimate and important role to play in ensuring an appropriate level of IT support to the firm.

Theme 1: Strategic Impact

Increasingly, it is clear that different industries are being affected in fundamentally different ways by information technology. In some industries, IT has enabled massive transformation of the various operational aspects of the value chain. Imbedding technology in the product, computer-aided design and manufacturing (CAD/CAM), automation of factories and inbound logistics, increased quality, and massive cost shocks have all profoundly changed the industry's standards of competition as industry leaders put great pressure on competitors to meet new standards. In other industries, the new technology has more strongly affected marketing and distribution. New channels of distribution have been set up, prior methods outmoded, new customer service features introduced, and new promotion and market research methods developed. In such areas as product formulation and service response time, operational and marketing impacts are double counted; this separation permits us to make a useful distinction between the role of technology in different industry settings.

Table 2–1 is a series of questions for managers trying to place their firm and industry in the marketing axis. If the answers to most of the questions posed are *no*, IT probably will play a rather limited role in transforming the marketing function. Conversely, if the answer to most is *yes*, the technology has or will play a major role in transforming the firm's marketing organization. Table 2–2 provides a similar series of questions for managers trying to place firms on the operational axis.

TABLE 2-1   Marketing Questions for Managers

- Does the business require a large number of routine customer interactions per day with vendor for either ordering or information?
- Is product choice complex?
- Do customers need to compare competitors' product/service/price configurations simultaneously?
- Is a quick customer decision time necessary?
- Is accurate, quick customer confirmation essential?
- Would an increase in multiple ordering or service sites provide value to customer?
- Are consumer tastes potentially volatile?
- Do significant possibilities exist for product customization?
- Is pricing volatile (can/should salesman set price at point of sale)?
- Is the business heavily regulated?
- Can the product be surrounded by value-added information to customer?
- Is the real customer two or more levels removed from the manufacturer?

TABLE 2-2   Production Questions for Managers

- Is there large geographic dispersion in sourcing?
- Is high technology embedded in the product?
- Does the product require a long complex design process?
- Is the process of administering quality control standards complex?
- Is the design integration between customer and supplier across company boundaries complex?
- Are there large buffer inventories in the manufacturing process?
- Does the product require complex manufacturing schedule integration? Are time and cost savings possible?
- Does potential for major inventories reductions exist?
- Are direct and indirect labor levels high?

Figure 2–1 shows how industry leaders in several industries have competitively used this technology very differently. In the airline industry, the reservation system, which heavily controls the travel agencies, has given leading developers American Airlines and United Air Lines a major marketing advantage and has been the foundation for new services such as "frequent flyer" programs and joint incentive programs for hotels, car rental agencies, and the airlines. The ongoing operations of the airline—seat allocation, crew scheduling, maintenance, etc.—have also been profoundly impacted. When the systems fail, almost immediately the overall operations of the airline are unfavorably affected, as Figure 2–2 illustrates. Second-tier airlines, however, have invested much less and consequently have paid a significant penalty in terms of their ability to differentiate their services in the eyes of the

FIGURE 2-1 IT Impact: Current Position of Industry Leader

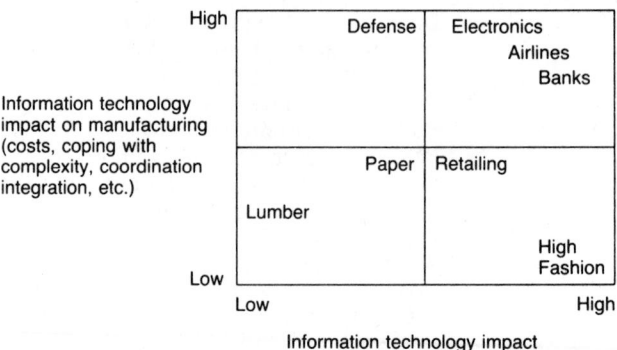

FIGURE 2-2 IT Impact: Position of Key Players in Airlines and Banks

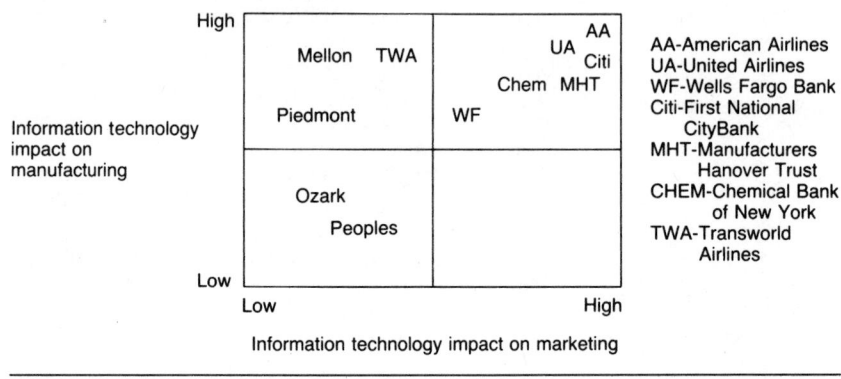

buying public (marketing) and in their ability to coordinate and cost-effectively transform the delivery of their product (manufacturing).

A similar analysis of the banking industry shows, for example, that Chase Manhattan, Citibank, Chemical, and Manufacturers Hanover have aggressively moved to distinguish their product and services through effective use of information technology. Other banks have used it primarily to transform the back office and have been unable to significantly change the front office (to ultimate competitive disadvantage). The problem is further complicated because the large players have made major (and successful) investments that have created very high entry barriers for their successors, who are smaller and who find such investments prohibitive.

Figure 2–1 shows the impact of information technology on several other industries. Defense, for example, with CAD/CAM robotics and imbedded technology has been deeply affected by this technology on the manufacturing side. The marketing impact on defense, however, has been markedly less significant, partly because of the much lower transaction rate, but also because the much higher value of the transaction brings into play a very different set of marketing forces that are less sensitive to the technology's impact.

Lumber is an industry where both the manufacturing and the marketing impacts of the technology have been relatively limited. While there is solid use of technology in the most sophisticated lumber mills, it is much less significant than in the specialty paper mills. Similarly, the delivery of logs and board does not have the same potential for marketing electronic value added, for example, as does the delivery of specialty papers or a wide range of papers to a major customer. Consequently, while the major paper manufacturers have paid heavy attention to this area in the past several years (as opposed to the major airlines 20 years ago and the banks 10 years ago), the lumber IT activities have occurred at a much slower pace.

By comparison, retailing operations have been significantly altered by the technology (but not to the same extent as airlines or banks). With display management, computer-assisted cosmetics analysis, and point-of-sales terminals, retailers are now experimenting with marketing applications. The results to date, however, have been mixed.

Figure 2–3 identifies the different competitive investment selections facing players. First are those firms that have already made dramatic transformations in the marketing and operations areas. They have normally been facilitated by leadership and structure. (At Manufacturers Hanover the vice chairman is responsible for this technology; at American Airlines the reservation system reports to the senior vice president of marketing. The trick is to *maintain advantage,* and current management approaches are usually adequate.)

Another group is in settings where the marketing component is relatively unimportant but where major investments are needed in manufacturing to increase integration and to control costs. These organizations require work that cuts across many organizational boundaries and that cannot be easily implemented by a highly decentralized IT organization. Strong IT and senior management linkage is needed to increase the firm's integrative capacity.

A third group faces a primary challenge mostly on the marketing side and must increase capacity to adapt to change. These firms need to invest in R&D and strong marketing control.

FIGURE 2-3 Competitive Investment Selection: Task vis-à-vis Industry Leader

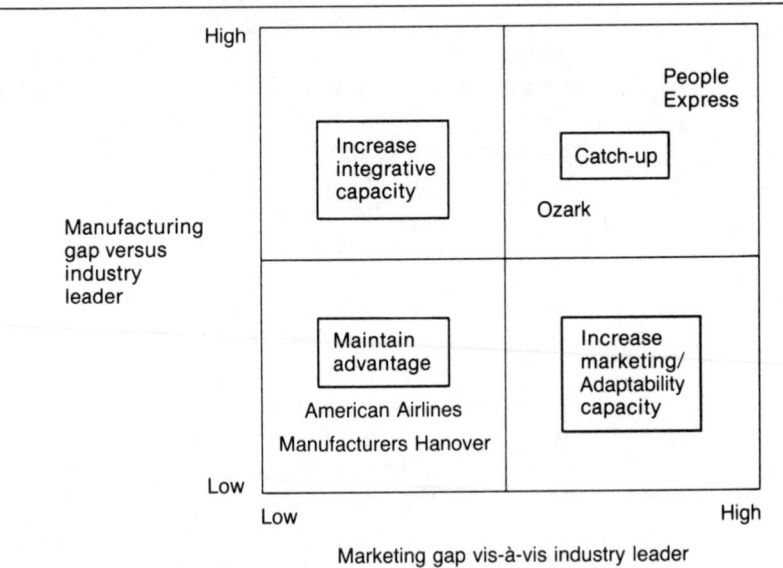

Finally, there are the firms that are in a deep catch-up situation, having been outmaneuvered on both dimensions. Strong coordinated efforts are needed by both the CEO and IT management to enable organizational adaptation to the new environment. The combination of being outmaneuvered by competitors, the long lead times required to develop a competitive response, and the high capital investment costs of a new response have in some cases created a situation so serious that the very corporate survival is at stake. (This figure was prepared before People Express lost its independence.)

In short, information technology plays very different roles in various industry settings. For some firms it has played a predominantly operational role, while for others its impact has been on marketing. In many of these settings, industry leaders have been so aggressive as to transform the rules of competition and to put followers under great pressure. Leadership, structure, and other changes, as mentioned in the previous chapter, are all part of this adaptation.

Within this industry context it is increasingly clear that good management of IT varies widely in different settings. For some organizations, IT activities represent an area of great strategic importance; for other organizations, they play and appropriately will continue to play a cost-effective and useful role but one distinctly supportive in nature.

FIGURE 2-4 Categories of Strategic Relevance and Impact

		Low	High
Strategic impact of existing systems	High	Factory	Strategic
	Low	Support	Turnaround

Strategic impact of
applications development portfolio

Organizations of this latter type require less senior management strategic thinking to be devoted to their IT organization.

A complicating element in some organizations is that while today's existing IT applications are not critical to the firm in meeting its goals, the thrust of its new systems applications portfolio has great significance for the future. The opposite, of course, is also true. In other settings, IT plays a strategic operational role in the company's day-to-day operations, but future development applications do not offer the same payoff. Understanding an organization's position on these issues is critical to developing an appropriate management strategy.

Figure 2–4 summarizes these points by identifying four quite different IT environments.

Strategic. There are companies for whom smooth functioning of the IT activity is critical to their operation on a daily basis and whose applications under development are critical for their future competitive success. Banks, insurance companies, and heavy-equipment manufacturing companies are examples of firms that frequently fall into this category. Appropriately managed, not only do these firms require considerable planning but the organizational relationship between IT and senior management is very close. In fact, in some firms the head of the IT function, broadly defined, sits on the board of directors.

Turnaround. Some firms may receive considerable amounts of IT operational support, but the company is not absolutely dependent on the uninterrupted cost-effective functioning of this support to achieve either short-term or long-term objectives. The applications under development, however, are absolutely vital for the firm to reach its strategic objectives. A good example of this is a rapidly growing manufacturing firm. The information technology embedded in its factories and accounting processes, while important, is not absolutely vital to their effectiveness. However, the rapid growth of the firm's domestic and international installations in number of products, number of sites, number of staff, and so on, has severely strained its management control systems and made its improvement of critical strategic interest to the company. Enhanced IT leadership, new organizational placement of IT, and an increased commitment to planning are all steps being taken to resolve the situation. Another firm may systematically stunt the IT development function for a period of years—until existing systems are dangerously obsolete. Retrieving this situation becomes a matter of high corporate priority.

Factory.   For smooth operations, some firms are heavily dependent on cost-effective, totally reliable IT operational support. Their applications portfolios, however, are dominated by maintenance work and applications that, while profitable and important in their own right, are not fundamental to the firm's ability to compete. Some manufacturing, airline, and retailing firms fit into this category very nicely. In these organizations, even a one-hour disruption in service from existing systems has severe operational consequences on the performance of the business unit.

Support.   There are firms, some of which may have very large IT budgets, that are not fundamentally operationally dependent on the smooth functioning of the IT activity nor are their applications portfolios aimed at the critical strategic needs of the company. A recently studied large manufacturing company spent nearly $30 million per year on IT activities, with more than 500 employees involved. Without a doubt, this sum was being well spent, and the firm was getting a good return on its investment. But clearly the firm could operate, albeit unevenly, in the event of major operational difficulties, and the strategic impact of the application portfolio under development was limited. IT was at a significantly lower organizational level than in other settings, and the commitment to planning—particularly at the senior management level—was quite low. Our research has uncovered a surprisingly large number of companies in this category.

In attempting to diagnose where a firm or business unit should be on the dimension of the strategic impact of the applications development portfolio, examination of the business strategy of the corporation as a whole provides useful context. Subsequent chapters describe several currently widely used frameworks of competitive analysis and suggest how the bridge can be built between their frameworks and the identification of the strategic impact of the IT development portfolio.

Theme 2: Merging Technologies

Management of data processing or computing can no longer be considered as a useful concept around which to organize a program of management focus. Rather, the technologies of computing (DP), telecommunications (TP), and office automation (OA) must be thought of as providing in aggregate a common cluster of policies and management focus. When we refer to information technology departments or policies, we include all three of these technologies under this umbrella. At present the coordination and, indeed, integrated management of these technologies have been accomplished in most firms.

For at least two major reasons, the three technologies must be viewed and managed (at least at a policy level) as a totality. The first is the enormous number of physical interconnections that increasingly must take place between the three. On-line inquiry systems, electronic mail, and end-user programming terminals are a few examples of the type of applications requiring the physical integration of two or more of the technologies. The second major reason is that, today, execution of many projects utilizing any one of these technologies poses very similar management problems. Each technology tends to involve large projects in terms of expenditures, rapidly changing technology, substantial disruptions to people's work styles, and often the development of complex computer programs.

Integration has been complicated by the fact that 15 years ago, not only were these technologies not integrated but they had come from vastly different managerial traditions. These traditions made them independent and, unless actively managed toward integration, they tended to remain apart. In dealing with the three technologies as a totality, they need at least to be integrated at a policy-setting level and, in many settings, should have a common line management for all three.

Over the past four years, integration has advanced from a largely speculative idea to one overwhelmingly embedded in management practice. Consequently we will spend little time defending it, focusing rather on the managerial implications of this ongoing integration, particularly on which decisions must be guided by central policies and which are better distributed to end users.

Theme 3: Organizational Learning

Throughout the development of IT there has been an ongoing effort to understand the managerial issues associated with implementing and evolving automated systems in an organization. Starting from Thomas Whisler and Harold Leavitt's article[1] on the demise of middle manage-

---

[1]Thomas L. Whisler and Harold J. Leavitt, "Management in the 1980s," *Harvard Business Review,* November–December 1958.

ment and going on to Dick Nolan's and Cyrus Gibson's stages[2] and Chris Argyris' espoused theory versus theories in actions,[3] there has been a range of concepts on how to deal with the problem of getting individuals to use automated systems appropriately. After field studies on 28 organizations over a seven-year period, we have concluded that the managerial situation can be best framed as one of managing technological diffusion. Successful implementation of a technology requires that individuals learn new ways of performing intellectual tasks. As this learning takes place, changes occur in information flows as well as in individual roles. Often this results in organization changes substantiating Leavitt's and Whisler's conjecture and reinforcing Nolan's and Gibson's original four stages.

We consider this process to be closely akin to the problems of organizational change identified by Kurt Lewin[4] and described in action form by Ed Schein[5] as unfreezing, moving, and then refreezing again. The process can best be summarized by rephrasing Nolan's and Gibson's original four stages (called phases here) and considering the process as ongoing, with a new start for each new technology, be it data base, office automation, or CAD/CAM. This approach usefully emphasizes the enduring tension that exists between efficiency and effectiveness in the use of IT. At one time it is necessary to relax and let the organization search for effectiveness, while at another it is necessary to test for efficiency to maintain control.

Phase 1. Technology Identification and Investment

This phase involves identifying a technology of potential interest to the company and funding a pilot project, which may be considered akin to R&D. The key outputs of the project should be seen as expertise on technical problems involved in using the technology and a first cut at identifying the types of applications where it might be most useful. It is generally inappropriate to demand any hard profit and loss payoff identification either before or after the implementation of this pilot project.

---

[2]Cyrus F. Gibson and Richard L. Nolan, "Managing the Four Stages of EDP Growth," *Harvard Business Review,* January–February 1974.

[3]Chris Argyris, "Double Loop Learning in Organizations," *Harvard Business Review,* September–October 1977, p. 115.

[4]Kurt Lewin, "Group Decision and Social Change," in *Readings in Social Psychology,* ed. G. E. Swanson, T. M. Newcomb, and E. L. Hartley (New York: Holt, Rinehart & Winston, 1952).

[5]Ed Schein, "Management Development as a Process of Influence," *Industrial Management Review,* Second Issue (1961), pp. 59–77.

Phase 2. Technological Learning and Adaptation

The objective during this phase is to take the newly identified technology of interest to an organization where a first level of technical expertise has been developed and to encourage user-oriented experimentation with it through a series of pilot projects. The primary purpose of these pilot projects is to develop user-oriented insights into the potential profitable applications of this technology and to stimulate user awareness of the existence of the technology. In the past, what the IT department thought were going to be implications of a technology repeatedly turned out to be quite different in reality. As is true of Phase 1, there is a strong effectiveness thrust to Phase 2.

Phase 3. Rationalization/Management Control

Phase 3 technologies are those whose end applications are reasonably understood by both IT personnel and key user personnel. The basic challenge in this phase is the development of appropriate tools and controls to ensure that IT is being utilized efficiently. In earlier phases, basic concerns revolve around stimulating awareness and experimentation. In this phase, the primary attention turns to development of controls to ensure that the applications are done economically and can be maintained over a long period of time. Formal standards, cost-benefit studies, and user chargeout mechanisms are all appropriate for technologies in this phase.

Phase 4. Maturity/Widespread Technology Transfer

Technologies in this phase have essentially passed through the gauntlet of organizational learning, with technological skills, user awareness, and management controls in place. Often the initiating organization will move on to new technologies and spend no energy on transferring the expertise. If not managed, organizational rigidity may slow the process of adaption to the new technology.

Technologies in all four phases exist simultaneously in an organization at any point in time. The art of management in the 1980s is to bring the appropriate perspectives to bear on each technology simultaneously (that is, supporting IT Phase 1 research, IT Phase 2 aggressive selling to the end user, and intensive IT Phase 3 generation of controls). This calls for a subtlety and flexibility from IT management and general management that too often they do not possess or see the need for. A monolithic IT management approach, however, will not do the job. This will be discussed further in Chapters 5 and 6.

Theme 4: Make or Buy

A source of great tension and repositioning of IT in the 1980s is the acceleration of the pressures pushing firms toward greater reliance on external sources for software and computing support as opposed to the internal delivery of these services. Escalating costs of large-system development, limited staff, availability of proprietary industry data bases, and a dramatic increase in the number of potential applications are some of the factors driving this trend to buy from outside sources rather than make systems internally.

Make

Key factors pointing in the direction of the make decision include the following:

1. Potential for firm to develop a customized product totally responsive to its very specific needs. This is true not only for initial development but for necessary system enhancements and maintenance throughout its life. Further, one has the psychological comfort gained by having key elements of one's firm under one's supervision (corollary of "not invented here").

2. Ability to maintain confidentiality about data and type of business practices being implemented. This is particularly important in situations where IT types of services are at the core of how the firm chooses to compete.

3. Ability to avoid vulnerability to the fluctuating business fortunes of outside software or data services suppliers.

4. Increased ease in developing systems, due to the growth of user-oriented programming language, data base management systems, online debugging aids, and other user-oriented pieces of software.

5. Ease of adapting made software to rapidly changing business needs without having to coordinate your requirement with other firms.

Buy

Key forces pushing in the direction of the buy decision include the following:

1. Ability to gain access to specialized skills either that cannot be retained or where there is insufficient need to have them continuously available. These include skills in end-use application, in programming and system construction, in system operation, and in system maintenance. Both demographic trends (in reduced work force entrants) and increased end-use specialization needs are making this a more important rather than less important item.

2. Cost. The ability to leverage a portion of the development cost over a number of firms can drive the costs down for everyone and make the in-house development alternative unattractive. This is particularly significant for standard accounting applications and data base systems.

3. Staff utilization. Scarce in-house resources can be saved for applications that are so company specific or so confidential that they cannot safely be subcontracted. Saving these resources may involve buying into a set of systems specifications for the common applications that are less than optimal.

4. Ability to make a short-term commitment for IT processing support instead of having to make a major investment in facilities.

5. Immediate access to the high standards of internal control and security offered by the large, well-run service organization.

6. Proliferation in the types of information services that can be bought; also the active marketing of those services. Key categories include:

- Programmer availability (contract programmers, etc.).
- Proprietary data bases.
- Access to service bureau computer processing.

The change in balance of these pressures in favor of the buy alternative has significantly impacted IT management practice as internally supplied services lose market share. Care must be taken to ensure that adequate management procedures are in place. For example, the management control system must be checked to ensure it is not, through excess charges, tilting the balance too much in favor of buy. Another example is that as project management for software is being delegated more to the outside, procedures must be developed to ensure that these suppliers have suitable project management systems. Finally, implementation risk on a fixed-price contract becomes strongly related to vendor viability. A good price is no good if the supplier goes under before completion.

Managing this shift toward buy is a dominant concern in planning the necessary IT human resource. A critical factor in implementing new programs to complement existing activities (which must be maintained), this shift is discussed further in Chapter 9.

Theme 5: Systems Life Cycle

The activities necessary to provide a specific information service can be characterized classically as the following series of steps:

DESIGN/CONSTRUCT/IMPLEMENT/OPERATE/MAINTAIN

Since the first edition of this book was published, the practical shape of this theme has been dramatically impacted by the emergence of two very different types of projects. The first is the traditional project that used to be the mainstay of the industry. Characteristics of these projects include being large, requiring extensive development periods (often well in excess of six months), changing the nature of work in several departments, being functionally complex, and involving at the outset both unknown data structures and processing. Production scheduling, airline reservation systems, and demand deposit accounting systems are all examples of projects that lie in this area. The traditional system life cycle continues to be appropriate for these projects. On the other hand, the second type of project involves the construction of a decision support system (DSS) on a department minicomputer or personal computer, often using data from a central data base. Here a heuristic approach using prototyping and other tools is most appropriate; the rigid sequencing of steps implied in the traditional development cycle is simply inappropriate. As a practical matter, well more than half of a firm's computing today is associated with DSS.

The following paragraphs define the life cycle of the traditional project and also identify those aspects most likely to be mismanaged in current approaches to the development of decision support systems. The test of the appropriateness of an IT organization and its project management policies is how successful they are in encouraging and controlling each of the steps below for multiple large projects. While changing technology and improved managerial insights have significantly altered the way each of these steps can be implemented, their functions have remained relatively unchanged for a considerable period. However, with an increasing shift to buy (versus make) decisions occurring, significant changes may be needed in many of these steps, with IT management in many cases becoming more like a broker.

Design

The objectives of the design step are:

A definition of the information service desired and the important criteria for selection of the service.

Identification of the users, the initial tasks to be implemented, and if relevant the long-run form of service and support. The first step has traditionally been either a user request or a joint IT department–user proposal based on the IT plan. More and more it is being initiated by a user request, often stimulated by the marketing effort of an IT hardware/software/service supplier. The design step is a critical activity that demands careful attention to short- and long-term information service requirements as well as to ensuring the delivery of reliable service. This step was traditionally dominated by the IT staff but is more and more being assumed by the user. The shift should be managed carefully.

The substance of the design work normally begins with an analysis to determine the feasibility and potential costs and benefits of the proposed system. If the results of the analysis are favorable an explicit decision to proceed is made. This is followed by substantive joint work by the potential user and an IT professional to develop a working approach to a systems design. Depending on the systems scope, these design efforts may range from formal systematic analysis to informal discussions and a flowchart.

The end product of design is both a definition of the desired service and identification of a means (including in-house or purchased) of providing it. Prototyping is proving to be an indispensable tool today in speeding up the design process, improving the quality of the design, and reducing the possibility of major misunderstandings.

Construction

A highly specialized activity, the structuring of automatic procedures to perform a timely, errorless information service is a combination of art and logic. Professional judgment is needed in the areas of:

1. Selection of firm, brand of equipment, and/or service bureau.
2. Selection of programming language, data base system, and so on.
3. Documentation of operating procedures and content of software.
4. Identification and implementation of appropriate testing procedures.
5. Review of adequacy or long-term viability of purchased software service.

Very technical in content, this work depends on both good professional and good IT management skills. In the past it was very dependent upon good organization linkage to the users. As more services are purchased, this phase may be eliminated entirely, although often a portion exists to adopt a standard system to the specific details of the situation. As in IT, this phase, the design phase, and the implementation phase are often inextricably intertwined in decision support systems.

Implementation

Implementation still involves extensive user-IT coordination as the transition is made from the predominantly technical IT-driven tasks of the construction step to its completed installation and operation in the user environment. Whether the system is bought or made, implementation is still a joint effort. Establishment and testing of necessary communication links, bringing new skills and an assortment of intrusions into the normal habits of the organization, are critical. During implementation a key general management concern is to ensure adequate technical support to a user of a purchased system.

Operation

In most settings the operation of systems has received the least amount of attention during the systems development process and consequently enormous frustration and ill will has been created when the system is installed. Further, as more users become operators the subtleties of operations shortfalls become familiar to all managers. A significant amount of the difficulty, as will be discussed later, stems from inadequate attention to clear definition of the critical performance specifications to be met by the new system and from failure to recognize the often inherent conflicts between specific service goals.

At the front end of the systems development process is the need for specific procedures to test and document services, including a formal procedure for approval of the operations department. This clearly separates responsibility for construction of a service from responsibility for its operation, a role separation particularly important when the same department (or even individual) is responsible for both construction and operation of the system. In addition, operations approval procedures are needed for systems enhancement and maintenance.

After the system is built and installed, measures must be developed to assess the actual delivery of the service and its quality. This is a real point of weakness in user-designed decision support systems, as many of them are so idiosyncratically designed that they cannot easily be transferred to other appropriate users, when the initial user is promoted.

Maintenance

Ongoing design, construction, and implementation activities on existing services are labeled as maintenance. When action is desired on a steadily growing need, normally caused by an outside change or user desire, it requires some technical support. (The word *maintenance* is a complete misnomer because it implies an element of deferrability that does not exist. Modernization is a better label.) Much of maintenance stems from real-world changes in tax laws, organization shifts such as new offices or unit mergers, business changes such as new product line creation or elimination, new technology, and so on. It can be as simple as changing a number in a data base of depreciation rates or as complex as rewriting the tax portion of the payroll. Effective maintenance faces three serious problems:

1. Most professionals consider it to be dull and noncreative, as it involves working on systems created by someone else.
2. In actuality, it is very complex for older systems, requiring competent professionals to safely perform necessary changes.
3. Accounting procedures do not recognize that software is an asset or that it tends to age over time, making eventual conversion vastly more complex and, in extreme cases, putting the entire organization at risk as it struggles to free itself from obsolete hardware and software.

Newer systems permit users to develop their own adaptations by including report writers or editors. Because these complex systems require more CPU cycles, however, a cost comes with the benefit. Managing maintenance continues to be a troublesome problem, but organization, planning, and management control all provide critical context to ensure that these issues are resolved appropriately. For the user-designed decision support applications, this has been an area of particular concern.

Summary

The description of the systems life cycle helps capture much of the complexity of IT management. At any point in time an organization has hundreds of systems, all in different positions along this life-cycle line. Of necessity, the IT management system in the overwhelming majority of cases must be organized by IT function rather than by specific application system. This inevitably creates significant friction because the IT organization forces the passing of responsibility for an application system from one unit to another as it passes through these steps. The user is often the only link (although changes often take place here also) as the system's responsibility is passed from one group of technical specialists to another.

To further complicate the situation, the execution of the life-cycle process (and the dividing line between the steps) varies widely from one type of application system to another. For example, a structured, transaction-oriented system requires an intensive, up-front design effort to get firm specifications that can then be programmed. A decision support system as described above, however, involves more a process of user learning. An appropriate methodology here is often a crude design followed by a simple program. Use of the program by the user leads to successively different and more comprehensive designs as its performance is analyzed and then to a series of new programs. Interactively, one cycles through this sequence a number of times. Such a design process (pragmatically useful) flies in the face of many generally held nostrums about good development practices.

In Chapter 9 we deal with the issues of operations management and the impact of buy decisions on the systems life cycle.

Theme 6: Power Balance among Three Constituencies

Much of the complexity of IT management problems stems from managing the conflicting pressures of three different and vitally concerned constituencies: IT management, user management, and the general management of the organization. The relationship between these groups quite appropriately varies over time as the organization's familiarity with different technologies evolves, as the strategic impact of IT shifts, and as the company's overall IT management skills grow. Chapters five through nine are largely devoted to identifying the various aspects of managing this relationship.

IT Management

A number of forces drive the creation of an IT department and ensure its existence. IT provides a pool of technical skills that can be developed and deployed to meet complex problems facing the firm. Appropriately staffed, an important part of its mission is to scan leading-edge technologies and make sure that the organization is aware of their existence. It is responsible for conveying knowledge of the existence of a technology, and of how to use it, to appropriate clusters of potential users. By virtue of its central location IT can conceive where potential interconnection between the needs of different user groups exists, and it can help to facilitate their connection. In a world of changing and merging technologies, this unit is under continued pressure to modernize if it is to remain relevant. Basically, the reason the unit exists is that its specialization permits implementation of otherwise undoable tasks.

As information technology has evolved the problem has become more complex because IT staff members themselves have become users of the system (through development of operating systems, etc.). Further complicating the situation is the growing availability of user-friendly systems and experienced users who do not feel the need to call on IT for help. Inadequate involvement of IT skills in the development of new systems comes at the peril of the organization. Great fiascoes can occur when management vision overlooks the realities of implementation.

User Management

Specialization of the IT function has taken place at a cost: erosion of some of the tasks of the user department while not relieving users of responsibility for ensuring that ultimately the tasks are well done. In the past, requirements of the technology served to disenfranchise users in the designing of services. This was coupled with a complicated charge-out system that further estranged the user from IT.

Also complicating matters is the aggressively marketed availability of outside services that go directly to the user. As the ultimate customer of IT service, the user best understands and has internalized the key operating problems. If the existing service is poor, the user feels the full impact in terms of inability to execute the corporate mission and wants to buy without IT help.

The term *user* often implies a narrower definition than exists in a real situation: the user may be many individuals at different levels scattered across multiple departments. Particularly in the early stages of a technology, the user is a specialist in living with the problem and not a specialist in the technologies that can be brought to solve the problem. As the user becomes more sophisticated through experience with the older IT technologies and as the technologies become more user friendly, some (not all) of the reasons for having a specialized IT organization disappear. User management, through increased experience with personal computing, is gaining more confidence (unwarranted) in its ability to manage all stages of the project life cycle. (The same is true of general management. See below.) Thus the level of services between the specialist department and the user is appropriately being reappraised continuously.

General Management

The task of general management in the IT environment is to ensure that the appropriate structure and management processes are in place to monitor the balance between user and IT to fulfill the overall needs of the organization. (This task is complicated in these executive decision support systems when general management becomes the user.) The ability and enthusiasm of executives for playing this role vary widely, both as a function of their comfort with IT and their perception as to its strategic importance to the firm as a whole. Since many have reached their positions with little exposure to IT issues early in their careers or with exposure to radically different types of IT issues, discomfort is often extreme. Much of this book is aimed at helping this group to feel more comfortable about its grasp of this activity.

As the years have passed, however, this group, through its experience with personal computing and earlier encounters with different (now obsolete) IT technologies, has gained confidence (often misplaced) in its ability to handle the policy issues implicit in information systems technology. Indeed, in many of the most successful strategic companies, the IT units are headed by general managers who had early and mid-career jobs in quite different parts of the organization.

In brief, each group's perspective and confidence is evolving. These changes, however, while solving some problems are creating new ones.

Summary

In this chapter we have identified the manageable trends that are intimate to all aspects of managing information services in the 1980s. Figure 2–5 maps the remaining chapters and identifies each chapter's emphasis in relation to these organizing themes.

Chapter 3 describes how IT is changing the way companies compete. It suggests a set of five diagnostic questions to get an overview of the likely impact of technology in a firm. It then introduces value chain analysis and shows how each element of the chain is permeated by information opportunities in different settings. Finally, the chapter concludes by identifying some of the strategic risks posed by this technology. Chapter 4 focuses on the particular role of interorganizational IT systems and how they have changed the boundaries of firms and industries.

Chapter 5 describes new technology assimilation as an organization learning problem that requires a series of contingent actions in order to manage the diffusion of technology effectively. It then proposes a new organizational unit to focus on this issue. Chapter 6 describes in depth the special management issues posed by the new, fast-moving evolution in technology and the necessary modification in organization structure.

In Chapter 7 the emphasis is on how corporate cultures influence the managerial roles and on how to integrate the services. Chapter 8 on project management focuses on developing a set of contingent actions for IT, users, and general management for different types of projects. Chapter 9 focuses on the special issues and challenges of delivering reliable day-to-day service. In Chapter 10 we extend the culture concept to include the range of complexities present in international situations. The planning discussion in Chapter 11 focuses on how planning is influenced by the strategic relevance of IT and on its potential impact on the organization. This includes both corporate culture and the type of contingent actions needed to assimilate the technology. Chapter 12 uses the marketing mix model to synthesize the overall issues in order to interface IT activity with the company as a whole.

FIGURE 2-5 Map of Chapters and Themes

Manageable Trend / Chapter	Strategic Impact	DP/TP/OA	Organization Learning	Make/Buy Decisions	Life Cycle	Power Balance
Information Technology Changes the Way You Compete **Chapter 3**	•	•				
IT Redraws Competitive Boundaries **Chapter 4**	•	•				
IS Technology Organization Issues **Chapter 5**		•	•			•
Organizational Issues and IT **Chapter 6**	•		•	•		•
IT Management Control **Chapter 7**	•		•	•		•
A Portfolio Approach to Information Systems Development **Chapter 8**	•				•	•
Operations Management **Chapter 9**	•			•	•	•
Multinational IT Issues **Chapter 10**		•				•
Planning— A Contingent Focus **Chapter 11**	•		•			•
The IT Business **Chapter 12**	•		•	•		•

Mark Twain Bancshares, Inc. (1980) (A) (Condensed)

In early 1980 Tony Guerrerio, the vice president of operations of Mark Twain Bancshares, Inc. and president of Mark Twain Services, a service subsidiary to the bank holding company, faced a difficult decision. Currently, Mark Twain got most of its data processing services from a computer service company. Recent incidents, however, had made this relationship seem too dangerous to continue. Less than one year with the bank, Mr. Guerrerio saw several alternative approaches for serving the bank's data processing needs.

Mark Twain Bancshares, Inc. (MTB) was a multibank holding company located in St. Louis, Missouri. The organization was started in 1963 as the South County Bank in St. Louis by Adam Aronson, who became chairman of MTB. After the acquisition and start-up of additional banks in the St. Louis area, the Mark Twain Bancshares Corporation was formed in 1969. MTB was the fastest growing St. Louis bank in the years 1974–1979, and by 1980 totaled 11 banking locations, all in the St. Louis area, controlling nearly $500 million in assets. (See Exhibits 1, 2, 3, and 4 for organization charts and financial results of the past five years.) Five more banks were expected to be added to MTB in the next two years, including two in Kansas City, Missouri.

This case was prepared by Michael R. Vitale.

Copyright © 1985 by the President and Fellows of Harvard College
Harvard Business School case 9–186–009

EXHIBIT 1 Mark Twain Bancshares, Inc.

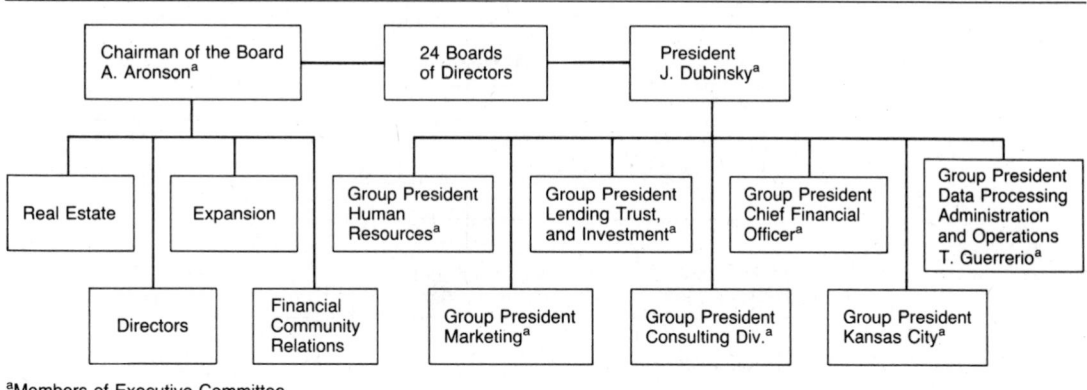

[a]Members of Executive Committee.

EXHIBIT 2 Operations, MTB

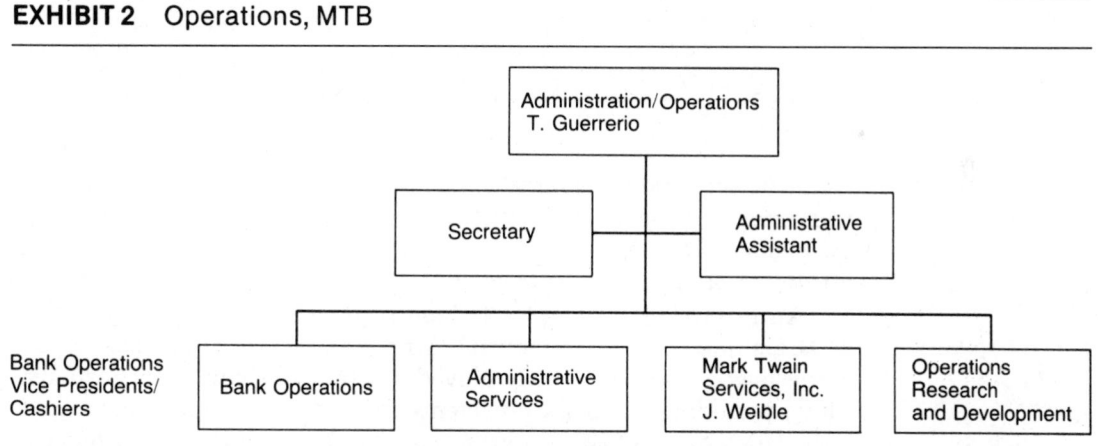

In 1980, MTB had 500 full-time employees and was the fifth largest banking organization in St. Louis. MTB's target market consisted of entrepreneurs, family-owned businesses, and independent professionals such as doctors and lawyers. MTB had grown in these markets both through acquisition and through aggressive marketing to lure customers away from other St. Louis banks. The St. Louis market for financial services had been characterized as "stodgy."

The company's goal for the future was rapid growth, with targets of $1 billion of assets in 1983, $2 billion in 1986, and a total of 26 bank locations by 1986. It was anticipated that half of this asset growth

EXHIBIT 3 Mark Twain Services

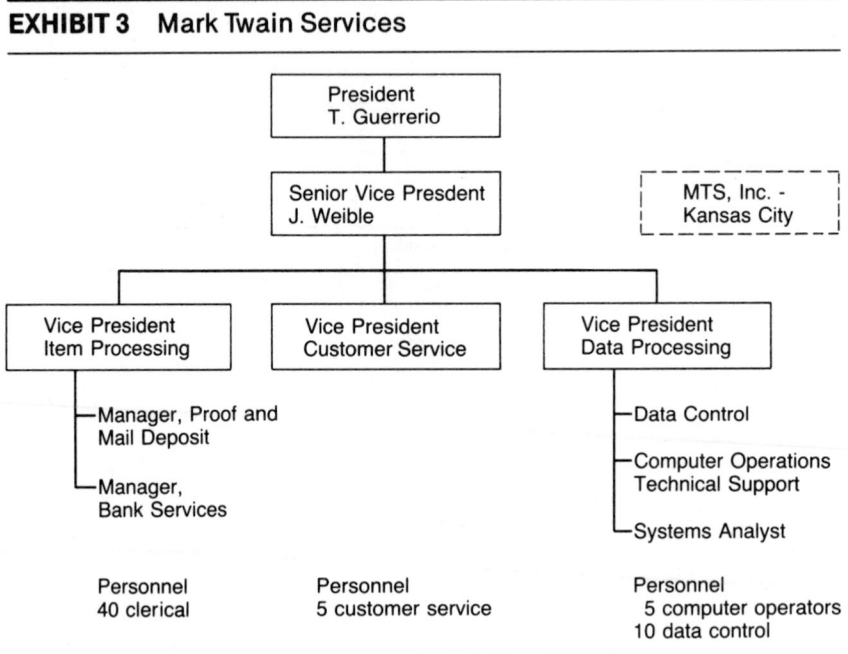

would be acquired and half would be internally generated. Profitability was expected to be maintained at the current 20 percent return on equity. To achieve the dual goals of growth and profitability, MTB developed strategies based on marketing and managerial innovation.

An example of the MTB unique approach was its hiring of new M.B.A.s into the bank's internal management development program. These new hires were quickly moved into areas of significant responsibility, sometimes as bank presidents under senior management guidance. One upshot of this program was that many of the senior officials in the MTB banking organization were under 40 years of age. John Dubinsky, president of MTB, had stated that he wanted every member of the organization, even down to the clerk level, to have the capabilities to become a bank president.

Mark Twain Services

Responsibility for both bank operations and data processing rested with Tony Guerrerio. Mr. Guerrerio, age 31, a Harvard M.B.A. of 1977, came to MTB from Salomon Brothers in 1979 with no data processing experience and no formal banking experience. To provide more effective data processing for the banks a separate subsidiary, Mark Twain

EXHIBIT 4

MARK TWAIN BANCSHARES, INC.
Selected Financial Data
($000 except per share data)

	Year ended December 31			
	1979	*1978*	*1977*	*1976*
Interest income	$ 47,160	$ 32,147	$ 22,583	$ 18,126
Interest expense	26,157	16,679	11,725	9,494
Net interest income	21,003	15,468	10,858	8,632
Provision for loan losses	828	797	740	230
Other income	1,989	1,292	1,278	1,091
Other expenses	13,980	11,282	8,974	7,327
Income before income taxes and securities transactions	8,184	4,681	2,422	2,166
Applicable income taxes	2,584	1,227	194	245
Income before securities transactions .	5,600	3,454	2,228	1,921
Net securities gains (losses)	(224)	(35)	190	149
Net income	$ 5,376	$ 3,419	$ 2,418	$ 2,070
Primary earnings per share:				
Income before securities transactions	$2.99	$1.87	$1.22	$1.05
Net income	$2.87	$1.85	$1.32	$1.13
Total average assets	$459,109	$381,663	$313,573	$260,252

Services Inc., had been established; Mr. Guerrerio served as president. (See Exhibit 3 for the subsidiary organization.) Mark Twain Services had an operating budget of approximately $3 million per year and employed 60 people. The average age of the Mark Twain Services employee was 27 compared to the average age of 31 for the rest of MTB. Nearly all of the personnel in the Mark Twain Services organization were involved in the check processing function; this included one technical person and one contract programmer who would enhance the basic check processing package. The remainder of the staff had mainly clerical functions (see Exhibit 3).

Commenting upon the situation which he took over, Mr. Guerrerio noted,

From very early on, I saw that data processing resources of the bank were not sufficient to support the business strategy of the corporation. When I joined MTB, the bank was receiving all the data processing service for checking accounts, savings deposits, loans, and saving certificates from Computer Services Inc. (CSI) out of Pittsburgh. MTB had an on-line Bunker-Ramo terminal system which tied directly into the service bureau in Pittsburgh. The teller terminal system hardware was MTB's but all the network software and application software was from the service bureau. At the time (1979), MTB was processing about 50,000 transactions a day through CSI and this represented over 50 percent of the total volume of that data center in Pittsburgh. We were having severe problems getting an acceptable level of service. MTB member banks were complaining about timeliness of reports and slow on-line response times. Many times reports were a day or more late. I couldn't imagine what would happen as we continued to grow.

The CSI Pittsburgh data center was small, it had poor management, poor operating procedures, and no support from the CSI corporate headquarters. CSI had purchased the center, along with a number of other data centers, a few years earlier during a growth by acquisition phase. The Pittsburgh center was out of the mainstream of CSI banking development because it had Honeywell hardware while the rest of the CSI banking division was being standardized on IBM hardware.

The straw that broke the camel's back was a small bank in Nebraska, Westown Bank, with $15 million in assets. This bank was not affiliated with MTB. The Pittsburgh center tried to convert that bank onto their system in their usual fashion, "on the fly," and the whole center blew up. I didn't get reports for a week. I got upset and demanded some answers, that's how I found out about the situation in Nebraska. The regulators almost closed the doors on Westown. At this time I had been on the job 30 days.

I began to develop a data processing strategy which would accomplish three objectives: one, it would give us reliable service on a current basis as well as potential to grow with the business, obviously this meant a move away from CSI, Pittsburgh; two, it would give us an opportunity to exploit profitable opportunities in bank operations, this was important since Mark Twain Services is reponsible for insuring profitable bank operations for the group as a whole; and, three, it would have to happen very quickly since the bank was moving aggressively in the marketplace, and it didn't appear that the service bureau center could survive it. To begin with we conceptually split bank data processing into two functions, the item processing function and the account processing function.

Item Processing at Mark Twain Bancshares

Item processing involved the physical movement of checks, deposit slips, and other similar paper through the banking system. Both the checks written by MTB customers and checks cashed by MTB customers were collected, the data captured off the checks, the physical checks sorted, and finally, either filed at MTB or sent to the bank upon which the check was drawn.

MTB saw the checks flowing through its 11 locations as a very valuable, fast-moving inventory, coming from many locations and traveling to many locations. This situation created opportunities for creative use of data processing in two ways. One was reducing the cost of processing the checks. A second opportunity was to speed up the check clearing process and thus make more money available to the bank. Because of these opportunities MTB had decided that it would handle its own check processing. MTB was implementing a new item processing system that would greatly improve the effectiveness and efficiency of check processing. The only interface between the item processing system and the service bureau was a transaction file which was stored on disks at Mark Twain Services as items were processed. A number of times during the day, this file was dumped through two 9600-baud lines to the Pittsburgh data center to become part of the customer account systems (discussed below).

The new item processing would use a medium-scale Burroughs computer and Burroughs check processing software. This system was scheduled to be implemented in May of 1980 at a cost of about $160,000 and was expected to save approximately $15,000/month in check processing costs in addition to increasing the availability of money to the bank.

Account Processing: Front and Back Office

The second area of bank data processing was account processing, an entirely separate set of systems that included checking accounts, savings accounts, NOW accounts, savings certificates, commercial loans, and installment loans. General ledger processing for the bank was also included in this category. All of MTB's account processing was tied to the CSI processing center in Pittsburgh through MTB's Bunker-Ramo terminal system.

Tony Guerrerio then spoke of his work in the account processing area:

> The Monetary Control Act of 1980 will have a substantial influence on all of banking, especially on the operations side. We are expecting a great deal less regulation, specifically in the area of lids on interest rates that can be paid to depositors and also in restriction, against inter- and intrastate banking. Missouri is a unit banking state, that is, banks are prohibited from having more than two facilities within a municipal area. We have 11 locations in the St. Louis area because of the large number of independent municipalities surrounding the city of St. Louis. Our locations form a ring

around the city. However, the whole industry is in a state of flux both in products, markets, and locations. We on the operations side have to be able to supply products on shorter notice in response to regulations and competition; convert new banks to our systems regardless of physical location; and basically provide a complete product/service line to our customers whose financial service needs are escalating rapidly. Our competition right now is primarily the downtown St. Louis banks, but our future competition will most certainly be Merrill Lynch, American Express, and even Sears, Roebuck as they offer financial services in our target markets.

In the year that I've been with MTB, I've considered the alternative of bringing the account processing functions in-house but three issues force me to realize that continuing to buy account processing on the outside is the only real option at this point in time. The first issue is the necessity to make our move very soon. We cannot afford to stay one day longer than necessary on the Pittsburgh system; we are risking disaster. It simply would take too long to begin building a hardware and software facility from scratch even if we could purchase software packages. The second issue is that I don't believe that we currently have the management resources and corporate discipline to bite off both check processing and account processing at the same time. The third issue involves the economics of in-house processing. I think that in-house processing is significantly more costly than a service bureau if you can get adequate service on the outside. My feeling is that many banks sincerely wish they didn't have to administer data processing in-house. They're really caught in a crush of user demands, rising costs, and personnel shortages. I personally hope never to be put in a position of competing with Anheuser-Busch, Monsanto, and McAuto [all St. Louis area companies] for "propeller-heads," that is, data processing professionals who don't know a thing about their own business . . . in this case banking. Maybe this is going beyond the issue of relative economics into my own views of data processing, but while I'll spend plenty for good bank operations people, we have no need or desire for "rocket scientists." My current staff of two technicians was hired on the mutual goal of being quickly assimilated into the mainstream of bank operations where they could use their talents to make money for the bank.

As a result of these factors we have begun an intensive search for an alternative service bureau for our applications processing. After an initial screening of 12 service bureaus, only three have the abilities to fill our current and future needs.

These three were Western Information Systems Inc. (WIS), Bank Data Corp. (BDC), and Computer Services Inc. in Cincinnati

(CSI). We had a great deal of hesitancy about including CSI on our list again after our negative association with the Pittsburgh operation but when we investigated it we found the CSI Cincinnati operation to be totally different. The center had been set up to fit the CSI standards of IBM hardware and much larger capacity; they had developed reasonably good services and a good set of operating procedures. Most of all we were impressed with the job the general manager of the Cincinnati operation was doing. He appeared to be a real taskmaster.

The evaluation procedure of the alternatives is being conducted under conditions of mitigated haste. We are on a day-to-day basis with the current operations in Pittsburgh, and we have to make the best choice for the future since, to my mind, we are tying the future of MTB to the service company. The choice is essentially mine as the VP of operations and the president of Mark Twain Services. No other MTB executives are involved in this process.

To assess the alternatives, I think there are basically three important considerations. First, it is critical to us that the service bureau be able to deliver products and services to MTB on time with a high degree of reliability. The bank and, in turn, my operations are completely exposed in the event of a computer service delay. The second factor is the product/programming flexibility that can be expected by the service bureau. This aspect of the service bureau is critical to our continued success in banking because of the increasingly competitive nature of the banking industry and the aggressive marketing strategy of MTB. MTB wants to be an innovator and requires an innovative data processing service. Cost is the third consideration in the evaluation process, but considering the relative importance of the first two criteria a premium will be paid if necessary.

Herein [Exhibits 5 through 9] are the data that have been compiled to help with this decision. First we looked at the products each of the companies offered and rated them on a 1 to 4 basis, 1 being good and 4 being poor [the results are shown in Exhibit 5]. The specific product offerings from each of the companies are shown and rated. The key items for MTB are checking (DDA), savings, loans, general ledger, and the customer information file. It was also important that they could accept our POD [proof of deposit] file. Basically all three companies offered a sufficient range of products at an acceptable level of quality for MTB's needs. But, as can be seen from the table, they vary from product to product in the quality. Then we contacted other users of each of these companies and tried to assess how MTB fit the current customer base. [This is shown in Exhibit 6.] Next [in Exhibit 7] we identified the hardware

---

EXHIBIT 5   Product Evaluation

	Computer Services (Cincinnati)	Bank Data Corp.	Western Information Systems Inc.
Checking	2	2	1
Savings certificate	1	2	3
Cash reserve	2	1	2
Installment loan	2	1	2
Commercial loan	4—slightly better than current system	1	2
General ledger	2	1—generated entries available	3
Customer information file as link of application	Household oriented; history available on deposit accounts only	Household oriented; history available; demographic reports	Individual oriented; history available; demographic reports
Proof of deposit (POD)	Available on Burroughs; we support IBM[a]	Learning experience on IBM	Good
NOW accounts	Current software can handle NOW environment	Running in New York	Will be available 10/80
ATM support	Not currently supporting but can support Diebold	Not currently supporting ATMs	Extensive shared network; can support Diebold, IBM, and DOCutel ATMs
Single statement	No	Yes	Scheduled for 10/80
Bulk filing technical requirements	Yes	Yes	Yes
Alpha inquiry	Yes	Yes	Yes
Branch reporting	No—but must develop for Atlanta	Yes	No—and would find it difficult to change
Programming flexibility	Some	A good deal	Virtually none

Scale: 1 good—4 poor.
[a]CSI would provide software support for a Burroughs remote item processing center. However, if MTB chooses IBM hardware for its item processing work then MTB will have to support the entire POD application.

and service performance levels of the companies. We also tried to evaluate the entire company in several areas such as financial viability and size [Exhibit 8]. Finally [Exhibit 9], we estimated the costs associated with each of the alternatives on a cumulative basis and also by individual product.

To my knowledge we've covered all the bases and now the only thing left is to make the choice and get started with the conversion.

EXHIBIT 6   Primary Characteristics of Users

Bank Data Corp. California Users
1.   Most of the banks are relatively small, with assets in the $30–40 million range. Two exceptions are Sumitomo Bank ($1 billion plus) and Union Safe Deposit ($200 million). But both of these banks are in-house users rather than service-bureau clients.
     The largest user in a service-bureau relationship is First Trust Bank of Ontario ($250 million).
2.   Most of the banks are new and began their operation with BDC rather than converting from another service bureau.
3.   All banks use NCR equipment, including NCR terminals, with the exception of First Trust of Ontario, which uses Bunker-Ramo terminals.

Bank Data Corp. Indiana Users
1.   These banks are brand new users. Some of them are not even converted to BDC. As a result, they cannot provide much information on the quality of service level.
2.   The banks are of moderate size. They range from $35 million to $118 million in assets.
3.   They use Burroughs or NCR hardware.

Western Information Systems Inc.
Description of Users: WIS has perhaps the largest network of user banks of any service bureau in the country. More than 500 banks have more than one WIS application system and more than 2,000 banks have at least one application.

All WISCO affiliates use WIS as do many WISCO correspondents. WISCO correspondents, in fact, market the service to other banks and provide the remote capture centers which communicate with the WIS host computer in Chicago. The WIS network extends throughout Minnesota, Michigan, Montana, Wyoming, Nebraska, North Dakota, South Dakota, and Iowa. User size ranges from $20 million in assets to $420 million.

A large percentage of users merely use batch processing and are not on-line. This is particularly true of users located outside the Chicago area.

Computer Services Inc.—Cincinnati
Description of Users: There are currently nine banks using CSI in Cincinnati. Most are relatively small banks ($20–30 million in assets), but two have assets that exceed $100 million.

Most of these banks were using Continental's data processing service and converted to CSI when Continental decided to leave the business. Also, most of the banks are still in the process of converting various applications to CSI, the CSI Center being less than a year old.

SOURCE: Phone calls to Service Bureau's client list.

EXHIBIT 7 Hardware/Service Level Evaluation

	Computer Services, Inc. (Cincinnati)	*Bank Data Corp.*	*Western Information Systems, Inc.*
Visits to data center	IBM configuration. New data center, but apparently organized well.	NCR mainframe	IBM configuation with complete redundancy. No computer operators, rather controllers. Sophisticated trouble-shooting equipment.
Review of third-party/FDIC audits	FDIC audit being conducted December 1979.	None available, too new	Very favorable.
Contact all system users	Service/delivery problems typical of a start-up operation. Weak customer service area.	Delivery excellent. Weak customer service area.	Delivery excellent. Little customer service contact.
History	Have overcommitted themselves in the part. Digging out of "strategic" hole.	Greenfield, Ind. data center has no operating history to speak of. San Francisco and Winston-Salem data centers have excellent operating histories.	Solid record of performance.

Operating philosophy	Multiple data centers with remote capture/transmission.	Multiple data centers with remote capture/transmission.	Centralized CPU with remote capture/transmission. They will never be in St. Louis with a data center: the best we can hope for is satellite communications or as close as Iowa.
Operating flexibility	Mark Twain will be processed stand-alone on an IBM 370/135 or /145.	Same as CSI, only NCR equipment.	Individual bank processing by application/complete flexibility in scheduling.
Conversion capabilities	Same as we have experienced; however most of MTB's[a] previous efforts will not be wasted.	Tape to tape. Team leader/extensive program checklist.	Could require extensive manual effort.
Remote item-processing centers being supported	None being supported yet; have chosen Burroughs as their recommended configuration but can support IBM.	NCR, Burroughs.	IBM, Burroughs.
Compatibility with Bunker-Ramo	Yes, their system has been developed around Bunker-Ramo terminals.	1 bank in California (1,920 characters per screen); will cost MTB dollars.	A problem; will cost MTB dollars.

[a]MTB—Mark Twain Bancshares, Inc.
Note: Mark Twain's on-line operations use Bunker-Ramo's BCS190 terminal system (3270 protocol); currently there are (140) terminals at the bank's locations.

EXHIBIT 8 Overall Company Posture

	Computer Services, Inc. (Cincinnati)	Bank Data Corp.	Western Information Systems, Inc.
Basic business	Service bureau.	Service bureau (75 percent of revenues in government/financial industries).	Wholly owned subsidiary of a $13 billion bank holding company.
Revenues FY 1979 (projected FY 1980)	$250 million total company; $10 million in bank services business.	$38 million ($75 million).	$38 million.
"Staying power"	Demonstrated in other computer services areas.	Yes?	Yes.
Product development staff	20 programmers at year-end 1979 in bank services business.	103 systems personnel in Atlanta, Georgia.	195 systems personnel in Chicago, Illinois.
Depth/banking expertise	Very thin; building.	Growing organization, but much banking expertise.	Solid.
"In a nutshell"	Well established in the computer processing field; feeling its way into a new business.	Young, aggressive, dynamic service organization which will become a leader in its field.	Large, steady computer processor delivering a good product day in and day out.
Costs/contracts: Length of time	x years: 60 days' termination notice.	x years; 90 days' termination notice.	3 years; 6 months' termination notice.

Price protection	4th year, from time to time; 60 days' notice.	4th year, ± Indianapolis CPI.	90 days' notice.
Hardware	Arrangement between MT and hardware vendor or CSI to obtain Burroughs price advantage.	Arrangement between MT and hardware vendor.	Arrangement between MT and hardware vendor.
Cost: Application[a] Processing On-line			
Conversion costs	None.	$43,247 + $3,300 per month for 18 months (receive 10 percent free volume — $40K per year over initial contract term). $3,358.80 per month.	$50,000; however, $12,100 have been waived; application conversion training applies to first bank only. $1,925.56 per month.
Communication costs	$1,643.08 per month for two 9,600-baud lines.		
Other		(Optional) $12,600 (10 percent of $126,000) to lock in price of licensing software on NCR $X for ARP and POD capability.	
Performance guarantees	Yes, but only to the extent that we can get out of the contract if service level does not meet our "specs."	They will guarantee both conversions and subsequent performance with substantial financial penalties.	No.

[a]Please refer to Exhibit 9.

EXHIBIT 9   Comparative Pricing: Monthly Charges

	Computer Services Inc. (Cincinnati)	Bank Data Corp.	Western Information Systems, Inc.
Per individual account			
DDA (account)	$.1365	$ .36	$ .208[a]
SAV (account)	.0780	.13	.0875[a]
CD (certificate)	.250	.13	.0850[a]
ISL (loan)	.2145	.27	.1750
CML (loan)	.3375	.33	1.350
Mortgage loan (loan)	N/A	.33	.310
G/L	.1040	.40	.750 (account)
			.006 (item)
Cumulative, by application ($000)[b]			
DDA	$12.4	$15.1	$ 6.2
CRC	2.0	2.0	—
SAV	3.0	5.2	2.6
ATA	1.4	.8	—
CD	2.6	1.7	0.8
ISL	2.0	2.5	1.4
CML	2.7	2.0	7.0
GL	2.2	1.5	2.0
Miscellaneous	1.3	1.8	7.1
	$29.6	$32.6	$28.1

[a]Based upon 28 items per account.
[b]Based upon July 1979 volumes.

Case 2–2

Mark Twain Bancshares, Inc. (1980) (B) (Condensed)

In February 1980, Mark Twain Services decided to contract for data processing services from the Cincinnati operation of Computer Services Inc. (CSI). Tony Guerrerio, vice president of operations and president of Mark Twain Services, was responsible for both the evaluation and the decision. He stated that the basis for his decision boiled down to a trade-off along two dimensions (shown in Exhibit 1). The first dimension had to do with the service bureau's ability to deliver products and services on time with high reliability. Along that dimension, Western Information Systems Inc. (WIS) was rated much higher than either CSI or Bank Data Corp. (BDC). CSI was evaluated on this dimension to be superior to BDC. The second critical dimension was the product/programming flexibility offered by the service bureaus. This dimension was also deemed to be very critical because of the increasingly competitive nature of the banking industry and Mark Twain's aggressive marketing strategy. On this dimension, the ranking of the service bureaus reversed, with BDC having superior flexibility and development potential to CSI and especially to WIS, which was said to have a very structured and somewhat inflexible approach. "WIS has a superior delivery system. . . . They take the 'assembly line' approach," said Mr. Guerrerio. Cost was a third consideration in the evaluation process, but

This case was prepared by Michael R. Vitale.

Copyright © 1985 by the President and Fellows of Harvard College
Harvard Business School case 9-186-010.

EXHIBIT 1 Overall Assessment of Competing Value

	BDC	CSI (Cincinnati)	WIS
	Low	Delivery system reliability	High
	High	Product/programming flexibility	Low

Risky areas			
Commerical loan system ($) Proof of deposit (POD) ($) Bunker-Ramo terminal system ($) IBM mainframe development process Licensing Not supporting remote item processing (RIPS)	Meeting product development needs	Commercial loan system Branch reporting Bunker-Ramo ($) terminal system Conversions Meeting product development needs	

Costs over initial contract term*			
	$1,375,000	$1,250,000	$1,187,500
	x + 10%	x	x − 5%
Year 1:	490,000	375,000	355,000
Year 2:	420,000	425,000	405,500
Year 3:	465,000	450,000	427,500

*Costs include application costs, conversion costs, communication costs, plus "other," but do not include "soft" costs such as retraining or "scrubbing" Central Information File. In that area, CSI has a distinct advantage.

considering the relative importance of the first two criteria, a premium would have been paid if necessary. As it turned out, the costs with CSI were relatively moderate. "We are paying significantly less than what it would cost to have the computing horsepower in-house," said Tony Guerrerio. "Our costs with CSI are approximately $500,000 for 1981."

Since the original decision to go ahead was made, the seven St. Louis banks of Mark Twain Bancshares, Inc. (MTB) had been converted to the CSI system. Speaking of the conversion process and the future, Mr. Guerrerio said,

This is not a passive sort of relationship for us with CSI. We've had significant problems in getting them up to speed with our needs. The main problem is not that they're not trying, it's really a lack of experience in the banking industry. We started out assuming that they would have the technical know-how to handle the bank conversion, but we ended up spending a lot of time having to pick up the details that were somehow overlooked by their people. For example, we set up a checklist of critical items that had to be done before the conversion would be successful. We had anticipated using the checklist to verify CSI's work. When they first saw our checklist, they were quite excited and wanted to adapt it for their own use since they didn't have anything like that.

We were also quite concerned about CSI's pricing of services as specified in our contract. Mark Twain had hammered the price down so low during the original negotiation process that I didn't see any way they could make money on the deal. Since a "good" business deal must be good for both parties, I began to get worried that corporate CSI might not be interested in a loss leader. We settled that issue recently by renegotiating certain items in the contract.

The decision to go with CSI had been only the first part of a continuing evaluation process on how to fill Mark Twain's data processing needs. Mr. Guerrerio was content to use computer services for the bank's application processing as long as three things were maintained. The first was that the service must be reliable and not degrade as the bank grew. The second was that an innovative approach to using automation in banking must be demonstrated. Since the financial services marketplace was creating new products daily, MTB needed the ability to lead the market and respond immediately. The third was that the price must be right.

Right now, the key issue was the ability to innovate. It would take approximately three years to build a sufficient in-house capability, forcing the bank constantly to estimate where CSI would be in three years. In speaking of managing the relationship with CSI, Mr. Guerrerio said,

> We've tried to deal with this issue by using our position as the largest of CSI's banking customers to influence the direction of CSI's banking product development. For example, we have some input on priority setting for various application systems. We have many top level meetings with CSI's management, and we've formalized both performance monitoring and request procedures.
>
> The only way this relationship can work is if it is actively managed from both sides. Fortunately, but not coincidentally, the motivation for making this relationship work is very strong from both sides. MTB gets cost-effective data processing without the headaches of in-house DP, and by being an early, large customer, we have significant influence with the development work that CSI does. CSI gets its first real hands-on experience with a large bank that is willing to help it develop competitive products. CSI currently has all the pieces for a truly national banking product, but it remains to be seen if and when they will put it all together.

Case 2-3

Mark Twain Bancshares, Inc. (1980) (C) (Condensed)

Of course data processing is strategic for us—it could have closed us down in 1979! I know what corner of the grid we're in and so forth. But that doesn't mean we have to own it! There is nothing proprietary about our DP as a basis on which we compete, nothing so unique that we need to have hordes of rocket scientists. We actively manage DP, but we don't do it ourselves.

Tony Guerrerio, executive vice president of Mark Twain Bancshares and president of its subsidiary, Mark Twain Services, was speaking to a visitor in mid-1985. Since 1978 Mark Twain had been buying data processing services from Computer Systems, Inc. (CSI). Problems at one of CSI's data centers had led to a 1980 reevaluation of the use of outside services and Mark Twain's eventual decision to switch to another CSI center.

By 1985 Mark Twain was spending about $1 million a year with CSI, representing about 8 percent of the vendor's revenues from banking services and making Mark Twain by far its largest banking customer. A 1984 study by a well-known financial services consulting group reported, "It is apparent that Mark Twain is receiving effective support from CSI at this time," and Guerrerio was generally satisfied with both

This case was prepared by Michael R. Vitale.

Copyright © 1985 by the President and Fellows of Harvard College
Harvard Business School case 9-186-023.

EXHIBIT 1 Mark Twain Facilities and Retail Transaction Accounts (June 30, 1984)

Market/Facility	Percent of Total Accounts
St. Louis	
St. Louis Bank	1.0%
South County Bank	12.2
Bank 21	3.8
State Bank	11.6
Bank 70	2.6
Northland Bank	15.4
Parkway Bank	6.3
Chesterfield Village	3.7
Harvester	5.1
O'Fallon	5.0
St. Peter	0.9
National Bank	6.2
Frontenac	1.8
Progress	3.2
Fenton	2.6
St. Louis total	81.1
Kansas City	
Bank South	2.5
Empire (Tower)	4.5
Plaza	8.5
Noland	3.4
Kansas City total	18.9
System total	100.0%

the service and its cost. Nevertheless, he was considering the bank's options for the future. "If this could go on forever, it would be wonderful," Guerrerio said, "but it won't. We categorically will not have to bring DP inside merely because of growth. But if you define 'in-house DP' as a system that ties together all the separate applications that are currently being provided by a host of vendors, then we will have to come in-house—not because of growth in volume, but because of the proliferation of relationships with customers."

Company Background and Strategy

Founded in 1963, Mark Twain had grown rapidly to comprise by mid-1984 some 19 separate facilities in and around St. Louis and Kansas City, Missouri (see Exhibit 1). Earnings and assets had not risen as rapidly in 1984 as in the past (see Exhibit 2) but Mark Twain remained solidly profitable and was steadily expanding its range of services.

Mark Twain aimed its retail services at households with an annual income of $50,000 or more and its commercial services at a "middle market" of firms with annual sales of up to $50 million, though some of its customers had sales in excess of $1 billion. Mark Twain saw its industry expertise and its general experience in the middle market as being important competitive strengths. "It's difficult to lend to companies that don't have certified financials," Guerrerio noted. "Most large banks don't want to do it, and most small banks can't."

On the retail side, Mark Twain relied heavily on its personalized service and delivery system. "We offer convenience," Guerrerio said, "like being able to pick up the phone and tell the bank to move $50,000 from one account to another. People do business with us because they like us and because we give them good service, not because we have a fancy computer." The bank priced its services to discourage the mass market while at the same time attracting upscale customers. Mark Twain's pricing of retail checking accounts, for example, was the highest of any commercial bank in St. Louis. Installment loans were priced higher than the competition and were not promoted, again a deliberate attempt to keep users of those services from banking at Mark Twain. At the same time, the bank's interest rates on savings and time deposits were consistently better than the market, resulting in the attraction of considerable deposits from upscale customers.

Mark Twain, alone among the large St. Louis and Kansas City banks, did not offer automatic teller machines (ATMs) (see Exhibit 3). ATMs were somewhat discouraged by Missouri's modified unit banking law, which classified off-site machines in the same way as full-service facilities and limited the number of facilities that each bank could have. Impeded by state law, shared ATM networks had not penetrated Missouri to any great extent.

EXHIBIT 2

MARK TWAIN BANCSHARES, INC.
Income Statement
($ millions)

	1984	1983	1982	1981	1980	1979
Interest income:						
Interest and fees on loans . .	$ 86.5	$68.6	$ 64.1	$66.1	$50.0	$37.4
Interest on securities . . .	20.5	19.3	23.8	19.6	9.8	7.4
Other interest income . . .	2.9	6.0	24.2	13.5	4.9	2.4
Total interest income . .	109.9	93.9	112.1	99.2	64.7	47.2

EXHIBIT 2   *(concluded)*

	1984	1983	1982	1981	1980	1979
Interest expense:						
Interest on deposits	63.4	52.3	52.5	52.8	32.8	22.4
Other interest expense . . .	8.8	10.1	30.1	16.4	6.6	3.7
Total interest expense .	72.2	62.3	82.6	69.1	39.4	26.2
Net interest income	37.7	31.6	29.5	30.1	25.3	21.0
Less: Loan loss provision . . .	3.2	1.8	2.0	2.0	1.1	0.8
Other income	9.5	7.9	5.2	4.0	2.7	2.0
Other expenses:						
Salaries and benefits . . .	18.4	16.5	15.5	12.9	9.3	7.6
Other	17.7	15.9	14.0	11.6	8.8	6.4
Total	36.1	32.4	29.5	24.5	18.1	14.0
Income before securities . .	7.9	5.3	3.2	7.5	8.8	8.2
Transactions and taxes:						
Income taxes	.4	(1.0)	(2.5)	0.2	2.5	2.6
Securities losses (net) . . .	—	.4	—	0.1	0.0	0.2
Net income	$ 7.5	$ 6.7	$ 5.7	$ 7.3	$ 6.3	$ 5.4
Return on common stockholders' equity . . .	15.2%	15.0%	13.1%	19.1%	19.1%	19.7%

MARK TWAIN BANCSHARES, INC.
Balance Sheet
December 31
($ millions)

	1984	1983	1982	1981	1980	1979
Assets						
Cash and due from banks . .	$ 66.4	$ 49.4	$ 51.3	$ 46.5	$ 31.9	$ 37.1
Investment securities	254.3	194.9	217.1	259.9	159.5	93.6
Federal funds sold and other short term	73.4	51.7	90.8	112.1	44.7	53.0
Loans (net of loss allowance) .	655.5	571.2	457.8	362.6	332.1	270.9
Premises and equipment . . .	15.8	15.6	18.7	14.5	5.9	5.4
Other assets	50.3	49.6	29.8	54.4	52.2	11.6
Total assets	$1,055.7	$932.5	$865.5	$850.3	$626.3	$471.6
Liabilities						
Noninterest bearing	$ 181.1	$166.4	$153.0	$165.9	$139.7	$146.3
Interest bearing	703.9	623.3	506.9	450.5	363.9	249.0
Total deposits	885.0	789.7	659.9	607.4	503.6	395.3
Federal funds purchased and other short-term debt . . .	73.3	50.1	110.7	165.9	65.1	25.7
Long-term debt	31.0	33.5	36.2	21.5	15.7	14.2
Other liabilities	14.0	11.3	13.5	12.9	8.5	7.4
Total liabilities	$1,003.3	$884.6	$820.3	$807.7	$589.3	$442.6
Shareholders' Equity						
Preferred stock	$ 3.0	$ 3.0	$ 3.0	$ 3.0	$ 3.0	$ 3.0
Common stock	14.4	14.2	15.2	15.3	14.5	3.6
Retained earnings	35.1	30.7	27.0	24.0	19.6	22.4
Total equity	$ 52.5	$ 47.9	$ 45.2	$ 42.6	$ 37.1	$ 29.0

EXHIBIT 3 Major Commercial Banks—Facilities and ATMs
(June 30, 1984)

Bank	Facilities	ATMs
St. Louis		
Mark Twain	15	0
Centerre	8	6
Boatmen's	9	9
Mercantile	9	7
Commerce	19	20
Landmark	12	12
United Missouri	3	3
CharterBank	6	2
Major independents	17	3
Total	98	62
Kansas City		
Mark Twain	3	0
Centerre	10	10
Boatmen's	8	8
Mercantile	8	8
Commerce	11	11
United Missouri	11	13
CharterBank	4	3
Major independents	19	2
Total	76	55

Guerrerio felt that Mark Twain should watch its competitors' moves in the ATM arena but not necessarily be aggressive in placing the machines. Mark Twain already had an excellent retail distribution system. Mark Twain's offices were attractive, modern, and located in upscale trade areas. Almost 50 percent of the banks were large facilities located in or adjacent to office park complexes. These facilities had been designed to appeal to owners/operators, entrepreneurs, and professionals. This network was believed to provide considerable marketing advantage to the bank as well as potential for significant future growth in both corporate and retail banking.

In addition, Guerrerio did not believe that ATMs were a particularly important means of competing in Mark Twain's market. He noted:

In St. Louis, you can cash a check in any supermarket. Supermarkets are in fact the biggest branch banking network we have. Nevertheless, I am concerned about being shut out, and I am still intrigued with the thought of employing our excellent location strategy with today's technology, i.e., financial service centers in malls, shopping centers, etc., where we could offer all our products:

investments and insurance (via sales reps) and transaction accounts (via ATMs). The relative economics are 10–15 financial service centers for every one new bank we could establish.

If Mark Twain decided to install ATMs, on-line support for them was available from CSI. The bank estimated that it would take at least nine months after a decision to use ATMs to get the first machines and the necessary systems in place.

Tony Guerrerio and Mark Twain Services

Guerrerio, who had joined the bank in 1979 at age 31 as senior vice president for operations, was by 1985 a member of Mark Twain's executive committee and one of the bank's top officers. He had come to Mark Twain from a Wall Street investment bank with no previous work experience in either data processing or commercial bank operations. "I spent the first three months trying to figure out what bank operations was all about," Guerrerio said later. "At first I didn't know enough to know there were problems." He found an operations group of 60 clerks working in makeshift facilities and a small data processing group reporting to an assistant treasurer. Later he concluded that operational weaknesses were limiting the bank's ability to grow. "If we had achieved our growth goals for 1979, we would have blown up the bank from the inside."

During his first two years, Guerrerio worked to understand operations and data processing. He was able to communicate effectively with top management and relate his area to the company's strategy. In the past, management had typically heard about data processing only when there was a problem.

After becoming familiar with operations, Guerrerio began to restructure the group's work. By 1985 a transaction volume three times that of 1979 was being handled by 35 clerks and 20 professionals who had been promoted from other bank jobs. A data processing liaison staff of eight worked with users and with CSI. "The staff knows the applications and what they can do even better than the vendor," Guerrerio said. "If you know the software and how it works you can figure out ways to offer the products you want."

Organizationally, both operations and data processing were handled by Mark Twain Services (MTS), of which Guerrerio was president (see Exhibit 4). MTS was run as an expense center, with its officers receiving bonuses for spending less than budgeted expenses. MTS paid CSI and charged the individual banks on a per-item basis. The banks communicated directly with Guerrerio about desired changes to services and reports, and Guerrerio passed along the requests to CSI for time and cost estimates. Based on these estimates, he decided whether

EXHIBIT 4   Mark Twain Services—St. Louis

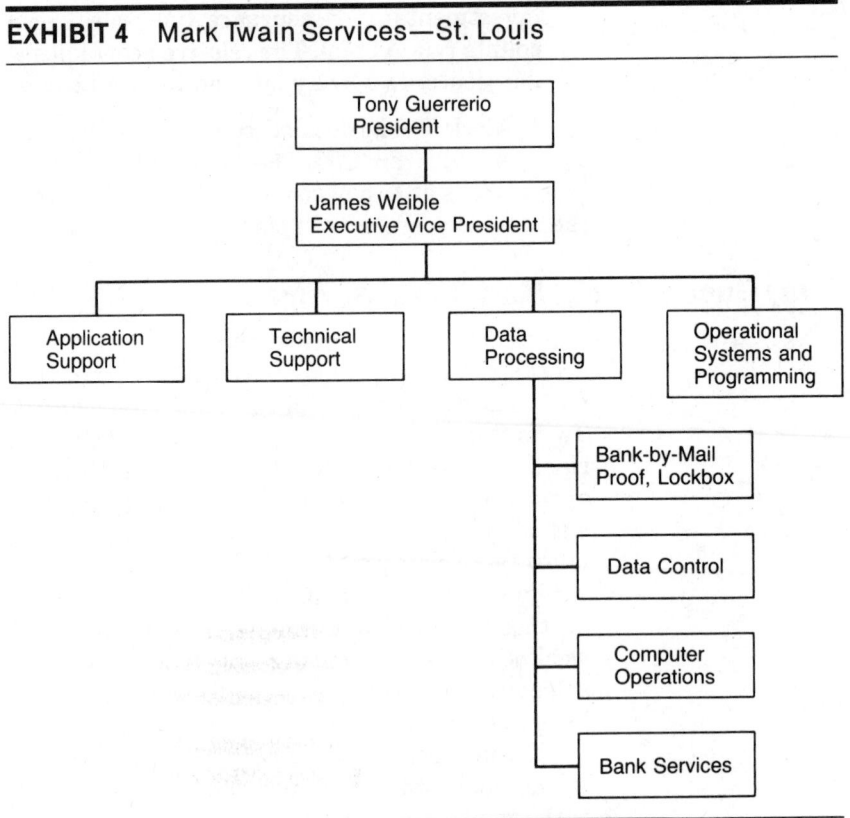

to go ahead with the changes. All changes suggested by MTS were also available to CSI's other customers, and theoretically CSI could refuse to make alterations that other customers did not want. In fact, CSI and MTS had never disagreed about changing the system. "We realize that they have to have generic software, and we can't have everything tailored for us," Guerrerio reported. "But banks don't compete on an extra bell or whistle in their demand deposit system. The traditional ways of competing in banking—convenience, location, and service—are still valid."

Decisions about the Future

At the time of Mark Twain's 1980 decision to remain with CSI, the bank considered two other vendors, BDC and WIS. Since that time, BDC had left the services business and was nearly bankrupt. WIS had grown by about 50 percent; its customers were primarily banks considerably larger than Mark Twain. Guerrerio felt strongly that CSI had been the correct choice. "We view our vendor as our own," he said. "We have one with whom we have some clout."

Mark Twain's major concerns regarding CSI's present level of service involved data communications response time and report customization. Mark Twain personnel indicated there was sometimes a severe deterioration in response time during the period of month-end processing. While response time in excess of 60 seconds had been documented in single incidents, Mark Twain personnel estimated that 97 percent of all transactions had a response time of less than 15 seconds.

CSI was also somewhat slow to respond to Mark Twain's requests for changes to the banking software. This was seen as more frustrating than anything else, and was not believed to have put the bank at a competitive disadvantage. With regard to report customization, Mark Twain personnel indicated that the reports generally contained the necessary data elements, but were not formatted to provide the most effective utilization.

Mark Twain's other concern was that CSI would leave the banking business. At the time of the 1980 agreement, the bank had negotiated the right to license CSI's software in the future at a fixed price. This gave Mark Twain the option to build up its own operations area, get the software, and run it internally. Alternatively, the bank could find a facilities management firm to run the software for them. Guerrerio met every six months with the president of CSI to determine the vendor's view of its business in the future. "It's a concern," Guerrerio said, "and we watch it all the time. If CSI doesn't make money on banking, they'll be out of it. We had that experience with our original data processing vendor, who left the business in the early 1970s. Mark Twain was forced to move to another vendor, and chose its regional clearinghouse bank."

In many ways, Guerrerio felt that Mark Twain was ahead of its time in understanding that it did not need to have data processing in-house. "At many large banks," he said, "it takes three years to get anything done. This was certainly true of the clearinghouse bank that was providing us with 'service' before we moved to CSI. That's not 'control'! You can't take the data processing area and tell them, 'Develop the best of everything.' Your own DP shop can't handle it all. You've got to look at purchased systems. I learned on Wall Street that the DP shops that were the worst disaster areas were those that took technical people and tried to teach them the business."

Mark Twain did not as yet offer its customers integrated statements showing all their transactions with the bank—banking, brokerage, credit cards, mortgage, trust, etc.—on one piece of paper. "It would be nicer to have it all tied together," Guerrerio said, "but I'm not a pioneer. So we have great people instead." Mark Twain had a "terminal strategy," not yet implemented, in which all data on a given customer would be available on-line to customer service representatives in the banks. "We can't have the best of all systems," Guerrerio noted, "so the key is putting the information together on an account basis. We are not the biggest bank around here, so we have to be the deepest."

Mark Twain was making limited use of microcomputers, having placed one in each bank. Other divisions could get micros only by cost-justifying them. A microcomputer steering committee, chaired by Guerrerio, evaluated all requests for systems development. "I want to encourage people to develop things," Guerrerio said, "but we have to control it. Otherwise these yuppies and technofreaks develop applications and walk out the door with their data bases. Three times people have gone around me to get micros, and three times we have had disasters. The last time a person left the bank with his data base we had to get the police and the FBI involved. I envision having micros on people's desks, but I don't want everybody sitting around playing with their personal computers—I want them out selling."

Chapter 3

Information Technology
Changes the Way You Compete

To solve customer service problems, a major distributor installs an on-line network to its key customers so that they can directly enter orders into its computer. The computer's main purpose is to cut order-entry costs and to provide more flexibility to customers in the order submission process. The system yields a large competitive advantage, adding value for customers and generating a substantial rise in the distributor's sales. The resulting sharp increase in the company's market share forces a primary competitor into a corporate reorganization and a massive systems development effort to contain the damage, but these corrective actions have gained only partial success.

A regional airline testifies before the U.S. Congress that it has been badly hurt by the reservation system of a national carrier. It claims that the larger airline, through access to the reservation levels on every one of the smaller line's flights, can pinpoint all mutually competitive routes where the regional is performing well and take competitive pricing and service action. Since the regional airline lacks access to the bigger carrier's data, it alleges a decided competitive disadvantage.

A large aerospace company has required major suppliers to acquire CAD (computer-aided design) equipment to link directly to its CAD installation. It claims this has dramatically reduced total cost and time of design changes, parts acquisition, and inventory, making it more competitive.

The above examples are not unusual. With great speed the sharp reduction in the cost of information systems technology (IT) has allowed computer systems to move from applications for back-office support to those offering significant competitive advantage. Particularly outstanding are systems that link customer and supplier (discussed at length in Chapter 4).

Though such links offer an opportunity for a competitive edge, they also bring a risk of strategic vulnerability. In the case of the aerospace manufacturer, operating procedures have shown much improvement. But this has been at the cost of vastly greater dependence, since it is now much harder for the manufacturer to change suppliers.

In many cases the new technology has opened up a singular, one-time opportunity for a company to redeploy its assets and rethink its strategy, giving the organization the potential for forging sharp new tools that can produce lasting gains in market share. Of course, such opportunities vary widely from one company to another, just as the intensity and the rules of competition vary widely from one industry to another. Similarly, a company's location, size, and basic product technology also shape potential IT applications. Computer advances have affected even the smallest companies. (Recently, for example, a $6 million manufacturer of electronic components profitably acquired CAD technology.) Further, in different situations, a company may appropriately attempt to be either a leader or an alert follower. The stakes can be so high, however, that this must be an explicit, well-planned decision.

Analyzing Impact

Forces that Shape Strategy

The variety of existing competitive and strategic uses of IT is as broad and complex as the industries within which they have evolved. To facilitate planning, general managers need a comprehensive framework. The framework must view use of computer and communications technology from a strategic rather than a tactical perspective. Michael Porter's industry and competitive analysis (ICA) framework,[1] augmented with potential technological uses, has proven very effective in this respect.

Porter's work was directed at strategic business planners and general managers. He argued that many of the contemporary strategic

---

[1]Porter, Michael E., *Competitive Strategy: Techniques for Analyzing Industries and Competitors,* New York: The Free Press, 1980.

FIGURE 3-1   Competitive Forces

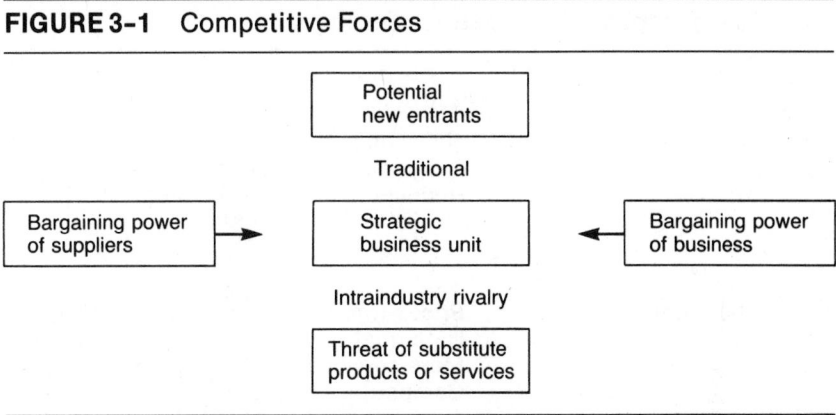

---

planning frameworks viewed competition too narrowly and pessimistically because they were primarily based on projections of market share and market growth. He asserted that the economic and competitive forces in an industry segment were the result of a broader range of factors than the established combatants in a particular industry. According to him, the state of competition in an industry depends on five basic forces: (1) bargaining power of suppliers, (2) bargaining power of buyers, (3) threat of new entrants into the industry segment, (4) threat of substitute products or services, and (5) positioning of traditional intraindustry rivals. Figure 3–1 lists the five competitive forces and illustrates the ICA framework.

Although Porter's initial work did not include information systems as part of the company's resource pool for ICA, it has proven very useful in considering the business and industry impact of IT. Table 3–1 puts the basic ICA model in the context of implications for industry and potential technology impact.

Column 1 lists the key competitive forces that shape competition in a given industry segment. In a specific industry, not all forces are of equal importance (Figure 3–2). Some industries are dominated by suppliers (for example, the impact of OPEC on the petroleum industry), while other industries are preoccupied with the threat of new entrants and/or substitute products (such as the banking and insurance industries).

Column 2 of Table 3–1 lists key implications of each competitive force. For example, when new entrants move into an established industry segment, they generally introduce significant additional capacity. They frequently have allocated substantial resources to establish a beachhead in the new industry. The result of new entrants typically is reduced product prices or increased costs for incumbents.

TABLE 3-1   Impact of Competitive Forces

Force	Implication	Potential Uses of IT to Combat Force
Threat of new entrants	New capacity Substantial resources Reduced prices or inflation of incumbents' costs	Provide entry barriers: Economies of scale Switching costs Product differentiation Access to distribution channels
Buyers' bargaining power	Prices forced down High quality More services Competition encouraged	Buyer selection Switching costs Differentiation Entry barriers
Suppliers' bargaining power	Prices raised Reduced quality and services (labor)	Selection Threat of backward integration
Threat of substitute products or services	Potential returns limited Ceiling on prices	Improve price/performance Redefine products and services
Traditional intraindustry rivals	Competition: Price Product Distribution and service	Cost effectiveness Market access Differentiation: Product Services Firm

---

Column 3 lists uses of IT to combat the implications of the given competitive force. For example, the establishment of entry barriers can be implemented with IT that generates significant economies of scale or builds switching costs that reduce the ability of suppliers and buyers to move to new entrants, or differentiates product or company, or limits access to key markets or distribution channels.

Two basic types of competitive advantage, combined with the scope of activities for a firm seeking to achieve them, lead to three *generic strategies* for achieving above-average performance in an industry: cost leadership, differentiation, and focus. (See Figure 3–3.) The focus strategy has two variants: cost advantage, and differentiation.

Each generic strategy involves a fundamentally different route to competitive advantage, combining a choice about the type of competitive advantage sought with the scope of the strategic target in which competitive advantage is to be achieved. The cost leadership and differentiation strategies seek competitive advantage in a broad range of

FIGURE 3–2 Elements of Industry Structure

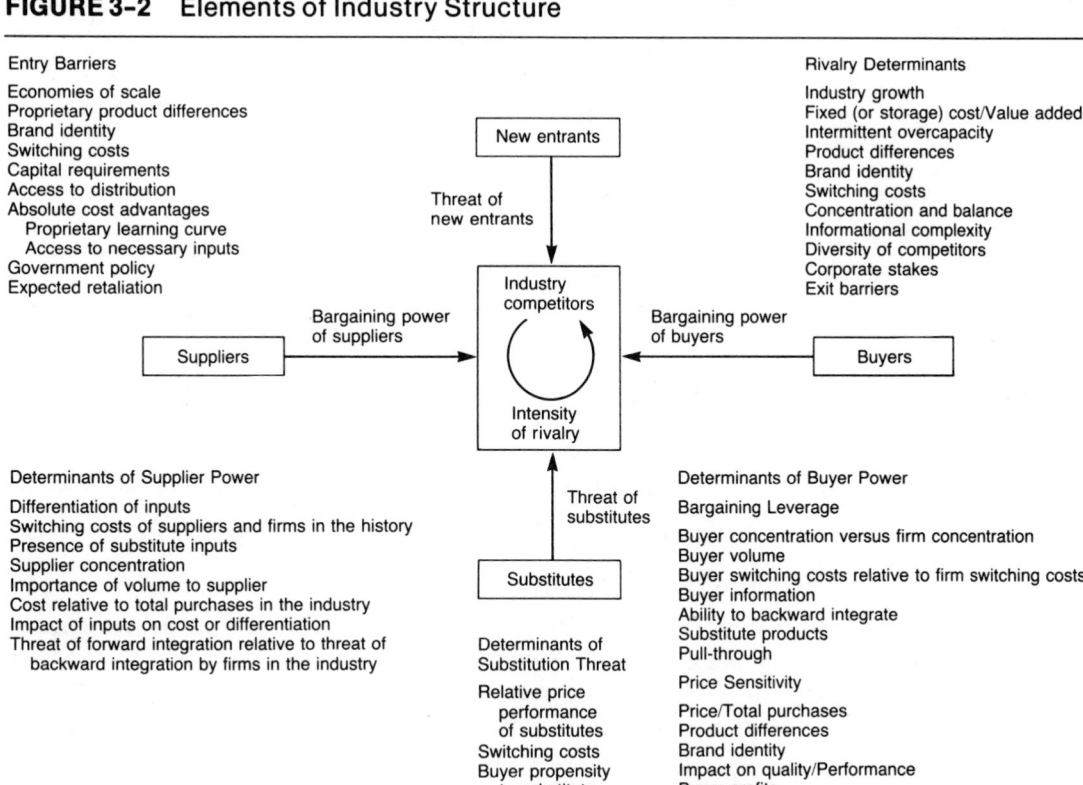

Entry Barriers

Economies of scale
Proprietary product differences
Brand identity
Switching costs
Capital requirements
Access to distribution
Absolute cost advantages
   Proprietary learning curve
   Access to necessary inputs
Government policy
Expected retaliation

Rivalry Determinants

Industry growth
Fixed (or storage) cost/Value added
Intermittent overcapacity
Product differences
Brand identity
Switching costs
Concentration and balance
Informational complexity
Diversity of competitors
Corporate stakes
Exit barriers

Threat of new entrants

New entrants

Bargaining power of suppliers

Suppliers

Industry competitors

Intensity of rivalry

Bargaining power of buyers

Buyers

Determinants of Supplier Power

Differentiation of inputs
Switching costs of suppliers and firms in the history
Presence of substitute inputs
Supplier concentration
Importance of volume to supplier
Cost relative to total purchases in the industry
Impact of inputs on cost or differentiation
Threat of forward integration relative to threat of
   backward integration by firms in the industry

Threat of substitutes

Substitutes

Determinants of Substitution Threat

Relative price
   performance
   of substitutes
Switching costs
Buyer propensity
   to substitute

Determinants of Buyer Power

Bargaining Leverage

Buyer concentration versus firm concentration
Buyer volume
Buyer switching costs relative to firm switching costs
Buyer information
Ability to backward integrate
Substitute products
Pull-through

Price Sensitivity

Price/Total purchases
Product differences
Brand identity
Impact on quality/Performance
Buyer profits
Decisionmakers' incentives

industry segments, while focus strategies aim at cost advantage (cost focus) or differentiation (differentiation focus) in a narrow segment. The specific actions required to implement each generic strategy vary widely from industry to industry, as do feasible generic strategies in a particular industry. While selecting and implementing generic strategies is far from simple, however, they are the logical routes to competitive advantage that must be probed in any industry.

Underlying the concept of generic strategies is the notion that competitive advantage is at the heart of any strategy, and achieving competitive advantage requires a firm to make a choice about the type of competitive advantage it seeks to attain and the scope within which it will attain it. Being "all things to all people" is a recipe for strategic mediocrity and below-average performance, because it often means that a firm has no competitive advantage at all.

FIGURE 3-3   Three Generic Strategies Related to Competitive
Advantage and Scope

		Competitive Advantage	
		Lower Cost	*Differentiation*
Competitive Scope	*Broad Target*	Cost leadership	Differentiation
	Narrow Target	Cost focus	Differentiation focus

Search for Opportunity

In assessing the ultimate impact of IT for planning purposes, companies can begin by addressing the following five questions. If the answer
to one or more of these questions is yes, information technology may
represent a strategic resource that requires attention at the highest
level. Those questions operationalize the competitive IT analysis implicit in the previous section.

Can IT Build Barriers to Entry?   In the earlier example of the distributor, the company was able to open up a new electronic channel to its
customers. Not only was the move highly successful but other companies could not replicate. Customers did not want devices from different
vendors on their premises.

A successful entry barrier not only offers a new service to appeal to
customers but also offers features that keep the customers "hooked."
The harder the service is to emulate, the higher the barrier for the competition. An example of such a defensible barrier is the development of
a complex software package that adds value and is capable of evolution
and refinement. A large financial service firm used this approach to
launch a different and highly attractive financial product that depended
on sophisticated software. Because of the complexity of the concept
and its software, competitors lagged behind, giving the firm valuable
time to establish market position. Further, the firm has been able to enhance its original product significantly, thus making itself a moving
target.

The payoff from value-added features that increase both sales and market share is particularly noteworthy for industries in which there are great economies of scale and where price is important to the customer. By moving first down the learning curve, a company can gain a cost advantage that enables it to put great pressure on its competitors.

Electronic tools that increase the scope and speed of price quotes for salespeople represent another kind of barrier. By permitting the sales force to prepare complex quotations on the customers' premises, portable microcomputers not only give better support but also make the sales force feel more confident and hence sell more aggressively. The sophisticated financial planning packages being used by sales forces of major insurance companies build similar barriers.

Conversely these projects require large capital investments and have uncertain ultimate benefits. Further, in difficult economic times, investment in these electronic systems may create both serious cost rigidity and exit barriers against an orderly withdrawal from the industry. It is difficult, for example, for a large airline to scale its computing activity down sharply to deal with reduced operations or great cost pressures.

While a company may have difficulty in maintaining an advantage, it can parlay a series of innovations into a valuable image as a company that is at the leading edge. This image can help maintain market position, especially in periods when a line of products is not successfully competitive.

Can IT Build In Switching Costs?   Are there ways to encourage customer reliance on the supplier's electronic support, to build it into their operations so that increased operational dependence and normal human inertia make switching to a competitor unattractive? In the ideal case, the electronic support system is simple to get started with but contains a series of increasingly complex and useful procedures that insinuate themselves into the customer's routines. Finally, the customer will have to spend too much time and money to change suppliers. Electronic home banking is a good example of this. When customers have learned to use such a system and have coded all monthly creditors for the system, they will be much more reluctant to change banks than before.

A heavy-machine manufacturer provides another example of electronic services and features that add value to and support a company's basic product line while increasing the switching cost. The company has attached electronic devices to its machinery installed on customer premises. In case of mechanical failure, the device signals over the telecom network to a computer program at corporate headquarters. The program analyzes the data, diagnoses the problem, and either suggests changes in the machine's control settings or pinpoints the cause of the failure and identifies the defective parts. In the same vein, another manufacturer has supplemented such a service with immediate dispatching of spare parts.

In some industries dominated by cost-based competition, IT has permitted development of product features that are so different that they cause the basis of competition to change radically. For example, in the mid-1970s, a major distributor of magazines to newsstands and stores was in an industry segment dominated by cost-based competition. For years it had used electronic technology to drive costs down by developing cheaper methods of sorting and distributing magazines. While using less staff and lower inventory, it had achieved the position of low-cost producer.

In 1977 the distributor decided to build on the fact that its customers were small, unsophisticated, and unaware of their profit structures. By using its records of weekly shipments and returns from a newsstand, the distributor could identify what was selling on the newsstand. It developed programs that calculated profit per square foot for every magazine and compared these data with information from newsstands operating in economically and ethnically similar neighborhoods and often carrying very different mixes of merchandise. The distributor could thus tell each newsstand every month how it could improve the product mix. Instead of just distributing magazines, the company used technology to add a valuable inventory management feature that permitted it to raise prices substantially and changed the basis of competition from cost to differentiation.

Other companies have used IT the same way. For example, the suppliers to the aerospace manufacturer described earlier used to compete on the basis of quality, speedy handling of rush orders, and ability to meet customized requests, as well as cost. The CAD-to-CAD link and the move to numerically controlled machine tools have negated the value of many of these elements of differentiation and made overall cost more important.

Dramatic cost reduction can significantly alter the old ground rules of competition. In a low-cost competitive environment, companies should look for a strategic opportunity from IT, either through sharp cost reduction (for example, staff reduction or ability to grow without hiring staff, improved material use, increased machine efficiency through better scheduling or more cost-effective maintenance, and lower inventories) or by adding value to their products that will permit a change to competing on the basis of product differentiation. In the airline industry in the 1960s, American Airlines pioneered a new kind of reservation service, which brought a large increase in market share and competition. For the past decade in the industry, airlines have been fighting to get their on-line reservation systems into travel agencies and, through positioning of flight recommendations on a CRT screen, influence the travel agent's purchase recommendation. In another example, relentless competition is taking place in the diversified financial services industry as insurance companies, banks, and brokerage houses merge and companies jockey for position.

A large insurance carrier recently identified systems development as its biggest bottleneck in the introduction of new insurance products. It is therefore heavily investing in software packages and outside staff to complement its large (500-person) development organization. A cost-cutting activity in the 1960s and 1970s, the carrier's IT organization has become vital to the implementation of a product differentiation strategy in the 1980s. This company, which is cutting staff and financial expenditures overall, is increasing IT expenditures and staff as a strategic investment.

A future challenge is the risks and opportunities that will come with the timing and packaging of videotex and cable services as a new way of retailing, particularly to the upscale market. In many cases these changes could in a short time dramatically alter old processes and structures. No example is more striking than the situation confronting libraries. They have a 1,000-year-plus tradition of storing books made of parchment and wood pulp. Soaring materials costs, the advent of cheap microfiche and microfilm, expansion of computer data bases, CD–ROM (compact disk read-only memory), and electronic links between libraries will make the research facility of the year 2000 unrecognizable from the large library of today. Those libraries that persist in spending 65 percent of their budget to keep aged wood pulp warm (and cool) will be irrelevant to the needs of their readers.

Though in the early stages it is difficult to distinguish the intriguing (but ephemeral) from an important structural innovation, the consequences can be devastating if managers misread the issues in either direction.

Can IT Change the Balance of Power in Supplier Relationships?   The development of interorganizational systems can be a powerful asset. For example, just-in-time delivery systems can drastically reduce inventory levels in the automotive and other industries, thus permitting big cost savings. Since companies in these industries are uncertain about what they will need downstream or when they will be cut off from their suppliers, they used to keep enormous safety stocks of components and ready-to-ship subassemblies. Increasingly, they are taking up slack by using electronic links between suppliers and dealers, in essence substituting information for surplus inventory, capital, and production facilities.

Similarly, electronic CAD links from one organization to another permit faster response, smaller inventory, and better service to the final consumer. In one case, a large retailer has linked its materials-ordering system electronically to the suppliers' order-entry systems. If 100 sofas are needed for a particular region, the retailer's computer automatically checks the order-entry system of its primary sofa suppliers, and the one with the lowest cost gets the order.

Equally important, the retailer's computer continually monitors the suppliers' finished-goods inventories, factory scheduling, and commitments against its schedule to make sure enough inventory will be available to meet unexpected demand. If inventories are inadequate, the retailer alerts the supplier. If suppliers are unwilling to go along with this system, they may find their overall share of business dropping until they are replaced by others.

Such interorganizational systems can redistribute power between buyer and supplier. In the case of the aerospace manufacturer, the CAD–CAD systems increased dependence on an individual supplier, became hard to replace, and left the company vulnerable to major price increases. The retailer, on the other hand, was in a much stronger position to dictate the terms of its relationship to its suppliers.

Can IT Technology Generate New Products? As described earlier, IT can lead to products that are of higher quality, can be delivered faster, or are cheaper. Similarly, at little extra cost, existing products can be tailored to customers' needs. Some companies may be able to combine one or more of these advantages. They should ask themselves if they can join an electronic support service with a product in order to increase the value in the consumer's eyes. Sometimes this can be done at little additional cost, as in the case of the on-line diagnostic system for machine failure described earlier.

Sometimes a company's existing data can be bundled or packaged to generate revenue. Data Resources, Inc. (DRI), the large econometrics subsidiary of McGraw-Hill, introduced a product called VISI-LINK that for the first time permitted owners of personal computers to use DRI's econometrics data base and to extract desired information. This service significantly broadened DRI's appeal and allowed it to reach many small companies and individuals who either were unaware of DRI or who previously could not afford DRI's service. Similarly, the software developed to support a product may have commercial value.

Value Chain Analysis

An effective formal way to think about IT opportunities is to analyze a company's value chain—the series of interdependent activities that

FIGURE 3-4 The Value Chain

Support activities	Corporate infrastructure					
	Human resource management					
	Technology development					
	Procurement					
		Inbound logistics	Operations	Outbound logistics	Marketing and sales	Service
		Primary activities				Margin

Activity	Definition*
Inbound logistics	Materials receiving, storing, and distribution to manufacturing premises.
Operations	Transforming inputs into finished products.
Outbound logistics	Storing and distributing products.
Marketing and sales	Promotion and sales force.
Service	Service to maintain or enhance product value.
Corporate infrastructure	Support of entire value chain, such as general management, planning, finance, accounting, legal services, government affairs, and quality management.
Human resource management	Recruiting, hiring, training, and development.
Technology development	Improving product and manufacturing process.
Procurement	Function or purchasing input.

*Abstracted from Michael E. Porter, *Competitive Advantage* (New York: Free Press, 1985), pp. 39–43.
SOURCE: Michael E. Porter and Victor E. Millar, "How Information Gives You Competitive Advantage," *Harvard Business Review,* July–August 1985, p. 151.

brings a product or a service to the customer. Figure 3–4 shows a typical value chain, drawn from Michael Porter's analysis, and briefly defines the meaning of each company's activities. IT can profoundly affect each one of these activities, sometimes simply by improving effectiveness and sometimes by fundamentally changing the activity. In the process, the value chains of key customers and of competitors may change as well.

Inbound Logistics

IT has already shown its important effects in expediting materials to the point of manufacture. One major distribution company, for example, has installed a sophisticated series of terminals on supplier premises to permit implementation of just-in-time, on-line ordering. The company requires its suppliers to keep adequate inventory and to make the figures on available stock accessible to the distribution company's computerized purchasing system.

This system has cut down on warehousing needs for incoming materials and has reduced disruptions due to inventory shortfalls. The need to maintain inventory safety stocks, and the associated holding costs, have been passed along to the suppliers. The purchaser's computer can also rapidly scan several suppliers' data bases and order from the one offering the lowest price. This new efficiency has sharply eroded suppliers' margins. Because the distribution company just mentioned has great purchasing power, it has reaped most of the system's benefits. To change vendors has, however, become more difficult for the distributor.

A large department store chain is hooked directly to several of its textile suppliers. This hookup not only has improved delivery and permitted inventory reduction but has also provided flexibility to meet changing demand almost immediately, which in turn has offset the price differentials by making it easier to deal with local American suppliers rather than remote foreign suppliers.

Operations and Product Structure

Information systems technologies affect a manufacturer's operations and its product offerings. When one financial services firm, for example, wanted to go after more small private investors (with portfolios of about $25,000), it introduced a flexible financial instrument. It gave investors immediate on-line ability to move their funds among stocks or out of stocks, and it provided money market rates on idle funds as well as liquidity equal to that of a checking account.

This company, the first to introduce this service, captured huge initial market share. Continued product enhancement has ensured that investors have no incentive to switch services. In the first two years, this original provider achieved six times the volume of its nearest competitor. Five years later it retains a 70 percent share of the market.

A newswire service company reconceptualized its business as being essentially a bit-moving operation (getting data from one place to another). This new concept led it to offer a new line of financial services, such as instantaneous financial information (up-to-the-second foreign exchange rates, for example) and was the key to development of new services. The company had to make no important changes in its technology. With growing sales and profits from the new product line, the company recently went public, and the offering was very successful.

A major insurance company thought of its business as being a diversified financial services and bit-moving company. It improved services to policyholders by allowing immediate on-line checking of status for claims and claims processing. The company also provided on-line access to new services and products for customers. These included modeling packages that enabled corporate benefits officers to determine the costs of various benefit packages so as to tailor them to costs and employee requests. It responded to clients' needs by selling either software for claims processing or claims processing services to corporate clients who elect to be self-insured. The company credits these initiatives with keeping it firmly in place at the top of its industry despite tremendous competition from other diversified financial services companies.

Outbound Logistics

IT has a great impact on the way services and products are delivered to customers. As mentioned earlier, the reservations system links to travel agents, provided chiefly by United Air Lines and American Airlines, have affected their business relationships so profoundly that the smaller airlines that do not furnish this service have found it difficult to match. For example, in December 1984 prominent screen placement, which has strongly influenced purchasing behavior, prompted the Civil Aeronautics Board to issue a cease-and-desist order against the practice.

Further, such close cooperation with travel agents allows faster pricing and scheduling adjustment (they have lower priority access to scarce flights) as well as disciplinary action against uncooperative agents. The arrangement also contributes to revenues through the ability to charge the competition for listings, reservations, and tickets written. Obviously, each of the examples just cited as inbound logistics for one company represents outbound logistics for the other partner.

Marketing and Sales

A large pharmaceutical company offers on-line order-entry services to pharmacies for itself and a consortium of allied but not competing companies. Not only has it increased market share but it has also derived sizable added revenues from its consortium partners. Some companies excluded from the bundle have threatened legal action because of damage to their market shares.

In the industrial air-conditioning industry a major corporation built a microcomputer-based modeling system to help architects model the heating and cooling system requirements for commercial properties, measurably reducing design time. The system often leads architects to consider this company's products more favorably than others.

A competing corporation subsequently made a similar model available to remote users via communications links, providing rapid support and allowing the architect to get detailed costs and parts listings quickly to complete the design. Because the system is on-line, this company was able to neutralize the damage produced by the competitor's earlier product.

An agricultural chemicals company has obtained similar results through a sophisticated on-line crop-planning service for its chief agricultural customers. From a personal computer, using a standard telephone connection, farmers can call up agricultural data bases containing prices of various crops, necessary growing conditions, and the costs of various chemicals. They can then call up various models and decision support systems and can tailor them to their fields' requirements, after which they can experiment with the models and examine the implications of various crop rotations and timing for planting. The model then helps the farmers to select fertilizer and chemical applications and to group purchases to achieve maximum discounts. Finally, farmers can place orders for future delivery by hitting a few keys.

In a different vein, a major bank trying to strengthen its marketing of agricultural loans has offered a similar crop-planning service. Two previously noncompetitive companies are now competing in the same software arena. Marketing, the functional area most often bypassed in the first three decades of IT, is the area of highest impact in a number of firms.

After-Sales Service

On its new line of elevators, an elevator company has installed flight-recording devices such as airlines use. It has done so because customers often place service calls without indicating how the elevators have malfunctioned. The recording device permits the service representative to connect it to the elevator company's computer, discover the cause of the malfunction of two hours before, and then do the necessary repairs on the spot, reducing repair costs and increasing customer satisfaction by correcting problems right the first time.

A large manufacturer of industrial machinery has installed an expert maintenance system in its home office computer. When a machine failure occurs on the customer's premises, the machine is connected over a telephone line to the manufacturer's computer, which does the fault analysis and issues instructions to the machine operator. Not only are direct service visits down by 90 percent but customer satisfaction is also up markedly.

Corporate Infrastructure

A major travel agency uses an on-line link to provide support to small, outlying offices. Because the travel industry still needs to deliver paper documents—passports, visas, tickets, itineraries—satellite or remote offices near big corporate customers are highly useful for pickup and delivery. These offices must have the full support capabilities of the home office. The on-line links have changed the organizational structure from a large, central office to many small, full-service offices. This change appears to have produced a 27 percent growth in sales.

Management Control.   A major financial services firm used to pay a sales commission on each product sold by its sales force. The result was that the sales force had maximum incentive to make the initial sale of a product and no incentive for the salesman to make sure the customer was happy and did not take his money elsewhere (a matter of intense concern to the management of the financial services firm). With its new integrated customer data base in place, the company has reduced the commission paid on the initial sale of products and pays a new commission for maintaining and expanding the customer assets managed by the financial services firm. This new approach (only made possible by new technology) has aligned the company strategy and its sales force incentive system much more effectively.

In some instances the use of IT to enhance coordination is fairly informal—voice mail for messages to officers or consultants when they are out of the office, videotex to update instructions to sales personnel in the field. But means of increasing coordination are often much more formal, making extensive use of data retrieval and computer processing.

For example, at least one U.S. air carrier uses a network to monitor the location of all its aircraft. By knowing its planes' locations and passenger lists, the passengers' connections, and the connection schedules, it can instantaneously make decisions about speeding up late flights or delaying connecting departures. The opportunities for controlling fuel costs and preventing revenue loss (because passengers continue on competitors' flights after missing connections) amounts to tens of millions of dollars a year. Trucking companies and trains use similar methods to track cargoes and optimize schedules.

Human Resources

An oil company has given desk terminals to all its corporate management committee members. Through these machines the committee has full on-line access to the detailed personnel files of the 400 most senior members in the corporation, complete with such data as five-year performance appraisals and lists of positions each person is backing up. The company believes this capability has facilitated its important personnel decisions.

Technology Development

On-line access to large computing facilities inside and outside the company has allowed a heavy industrial manufacturer to increase technical productivity by more than half. Senior technical management now would not want to operate without this support.

To guide its drilling decisions, a large oil company processes large amounts of infrared data gathered from an overhead satellite. The company believes this information, which is used in all aspects of the search for petroleum deposits, is essential to its operations, from deciding on which tracts to bid to determining where to drill. Similarly, CAD/CAM (computer-aided design and manufacturing) technology has fundamentally changed the quality and speed with which the company can manufacture its drilling platforms.

Procurement

With a series of on-line electronic bulletin boards that make latest spot prices instantly available around the country, a manufacturing company directs its nationwide purchasing effort. The boards have led to a tremendous improvement in purchasing price effectiveness.

A retailer, by virtue of its large size, has succeeded in its demand for on-line access to the inventory files and production schedules of its smaller suppliers. This access permits the company to manage its inventories more tightly than before and to pressure suppliers on price and product availability. This is another dimension of the earlier cited inbound logistics example.

We have found systematic examination of a company's value chain an effective way to search for profitable IT applications. This analysis requires keen administrative insight, awareness of industry structure, and familiarity with the rules of competition. Companies need to understand their value chains and those of key customers and suppliers in order to uncover potential new service areas. Similarly, understanding competitors' value chains provides insight on the likely source of competitive attack. Finally, careful thought is needed to identify potential new entrants to an industry. These are companies whose value chains make expansion into a particular area attractive.

The Risks of Information Systems Success[2]

An insidious danger for the would-be developers of strategic information systems is that they will succeed in the narrow technical sense but have unintended disastrous organizational and competitive consequences. The following paragraphs describe the risks of information systems "success" and suggest some management policies and procedures to ensure that potentially high-risk projects are appropriately evaluated.

Examples gathered from fieldwork, the trade and business press, and consulting suggest that the catalog of Pyrrhic victories in IT includes at least the following entries:

1. Systems that Change the Basis of Competition to a Company's Disadvantage

Once information systems are used to gain competitive advantage in a given industry, their use may become obligatory for continued competitive viability. An organization that is not prepared to stay the course with continued investments in information systems may be better off not firing the first salvo. "If the other side has bigger guns, don't start a gunfight" is sound advice in locations outside the Old West.

This lesson was learned, through experience, by an American manufacturer of commercial appliances. The company's products were typically purchased and installed by building contractors who worked from a set of technical specifications for size, capacity, and so on. Historically the company had offered contractors a mail-in consulting service that could translate specifications into products and instructions for the wiring, plumbing, and other site preparation work required.

In early 1981 the company built this consulting expertise into programs for a mainframe and an early model microcomputer. Contractors could continue to send specifications by mail; the company would feed the requirements through the mainframe and mail back a neatly printed list of products and instructions. (As would be expected, most of the products were manufactured by the company itself.) The relatively few contractors who at that time owned that particular microcomputer could, using company-supplied software, enter their specifications onto a diskette and mail that instead of written data. The micro itself

---

[2]The material for this section has been adapted from Michael R. Vitale, "The Growing Risks of Information Systems Success," *MIS Quarterly*, December 1986.

was not powerful enough to analyze the specifications, although it could check them for completeness and consistency.

Over time, the appliance market evolved, as did the microcomputer industry. The company, having achieved success with its initial development, reaped a harvest of increased market share but did no further development. One of its competitors—larger, older, and equipped with a bigger and more progressive information systems staff—developed a similar system. This system, however, ran on the more powerful and more readily available IBM personal computer. Software was provided to contractors at no charge, as were electronic connections to the company's mainframe. Analysis could be performed immediately, and the required products—made almost exclusively by the new system's owner—could be ordered at the push of a key. As IBM began to dominate the business microcomputer use, the second company recaptured its lost market share and more.

By introducing customers—and competitors—to the use of information systems, then failing to track or adapt to changes in the technology, the first company turned an initial IT success into a competitive failure.

2. Systems that Lower Entry Barriers

As described earlier, information systems can be used to raise and/or maintain barriers to entry in many industries. In some situations an extensive investment in hardware and software has become necessary for all participants, increasing the investment required for entry. In other circumstances information systems have been used to capture distribution channels, again increasing the cost and difficulty of entrance.

On the other hand, by making information systems the major vehicle for producing, selling, distributing, or servicing its product, a company may in fact be facilitating competition by established organizations with large and perhaps underutilized IT resources.

A major seller of health and casualty insurance recently faced this type of decision about the increased use of information systems. The company does the majority of its business on a payroll deduction basis with very small employers who do not offer insurance as a fringe benefit. These employers often do their payrolls by hand, making bookkeepers a major target for the insurer's field sales force. The primary competition is not so much from other insurers as from the bookkeeper's lack of time and willingness to be involved with handling another deduction.

To help overcome this obstacle, the insurer considered offering a computerized payroll preparation package for small companies. The development of such software was considered to be well within the capabilities of its IT group, and its sales force was already in contact with many potential customers for the new service. Pricing was to be designed to provide some profit, but the main intent was to create tighter links to small insurance customers.

Before much work had been done on the new payroll system, the vice president for IT recognized a danger. Although it might well be possible to convince customers to do their payrolls by computer, there was a chance that the business would go not to the insurer but to one of the large, experienced firms that dominate the payroll business. Any of these organizations could, if they chose, offer health and casualty insurance as well through a relationship with an insurer. The link to customers might well be tighter, but it was not clear who would be at the other end! The idea of offering payroll service was postponed until such time as the insurer's small customers began to show some interest in doing their payroll by computer. To continue the project would, in the company's opinion, have risked opening its primary line of business to new competitors.

3. Systems that Bring On Litigation or Regulation

These systems are in the category of things that work too well for their own good. They achieve their initial objectives and then continue to grow in size and effectiveness, eventually giving rise to claims of unfair competition and cries for government regulation. Other possible outcomes are forced divestiture of the system or an agreement to share it with competitors.

The airline reservations systems used by travel agents are a clear example of this danger. The United and American reservation systems control the offices of nearly 80 percent of U.S. travel agents. Some of the two carriers' competitors have claimed that this level of penetration allows the two big airlines to effectively control the industry's channels of distribution. Examples of such alleged domination include biased display of data, close monitoring and control of travel agents, and inaccurate data on competitors' flights.

After a lengthy investigation of these claims, the Civil Aeronautics Board (CAB) ordered changes in the operation and pricing of computer reservations systems. Nevertheless, United and American were sued by 11 competitors, who demanded that the two carriers spin off their reservations systems into separate subsidiaries. United and American opposed the suit but did agree, along with TWA, to provide unbiased displays.

Although they deny unfair practices, United and American have never denied using their reservations systems to gain competitive advantage. Indeed, the two airlines claim that the systems are not economically viable on the basis of usage fee income alone—they were *intended* to generate increased sales. United and American may in fact already have recovered their investments in the reservation systems. The precedent of government intervention suggests, however, that future developers of competitively effective systems may find their returns limited by law or regulation.

4. Systems that Increase the Power of Customers or Suppliers, Perhaps to the Point of Encouraging Them to Bypass the Innovator Entirely

Strengthening relationships with customers and suppliers is one of the areas in which information systems have been used most effectively. In some circumstances, however, companies appear to be giving their customers or suppliers the tools and expertise to get along without them. This change may be inevitable over the long run, but there is no reason to hasten its onset.

An overnight delivery company, for example, recently began offering very fast delivery of messages transmitted electronically between its offices. The original is picked up from the sender and put through a facsimile machine at a nearby office; the transmitted image is received at an office near the recipient and delivered by hand. Although the new service has not yet made money, its usage continues to grow.

More recently the delivery company has announced that it will place facsimile machines on its customers' premises and act as a switch among the installed machines. Delivery promises to be even quicker, since there will be no need to take the original copy to the sending office or to deliver the received copy. How much value the delivery company can add to off-the-shelf facsimile technology is questionable. There is little to prevent its customers from installing similar equipment directly; indeed, the manufacturer of the facsimile machines advertises its products prominently as the ones supporting the delivery company's system.

A somewhat similar risk is created by systems that unintentionally lower switching costs in an attempt to make the customer's life easier. American Hospital Supply Corporation provides an interesting example of steps taken to avoid this danger. American's ASAP system, installed in over 3,000 U.S. hospitals, allows on-line ordering of medical and surgical supplies from American's extensive product line. Substitutes are suggested for out-of-stock items, and the hospital can specify several options for delivery time, depending on how urgently each item is needed. ASAP is generally felt to have contributed heavily to the steady growth that has made American the largest company in its field.

Some of American's competitors have developed similar systems of their own but have found it difficult to overcome American's lead—hospitals, like travel agents, are generally reluctant to install more than one on-line system. The extensive use of computerized order-entry systems might, however, offer another sort of competitive opportunity. Why not develop a "master system" that would take data from hospitals and pass it to suppliers' systems? The hospitals could retain the advantages of a single system and might get lower prices as well, since the master system could "shop" among suppliers for the best price.

If American had not continued to develop and enhance ASAP, this danger might be very real today. In fact, the company has taken the system well beyond the order-entry stage. Later versions of ASAP allow the hospital to order, based on its own stock numbers as well as American's, to create and store files of frequently ordered items, and in other ways to "personalize" ASAP to the hospital's own environment. It would be extremely difficult for any master system to keep up with these ongoing developments. By continually adapting ASAP to its customers' needs, American preserves the competitive advantages of the system and minimizes the risk of being bypassed.

Assessing Competitor Risk

Understanding risks is the first step to managing them. Understanding is, in turn, a two-phase process: (1) describing in advance and in detail the industry-level changes that may be brought about by development and implementation of a given information system and (2) determining the potential impact of these changes on the company. These views of the future are likely to be cloudy and their probabilities are likely to be rough estimates. But together with estimates of project costs and benefits, they must be considered before a decision is made on whether to proceed.

The increasing use of information systems is often viewed as inevitable. Certainly there are situations in which firms must invest in and adapt to the use of IT in order to remain viable—even if the increase in technological intensity causes a complete reevaluation and reformulation of the firm's strategy. Yet there are some technological "advances" that have remained in an embryonic stage for years. Home banking and home shopping are two examples. Sometimes these developments are waiting for improvements in cost, IT capability, or consumer acceptance. Other changes are held back by a lack of support from established industry participants. Rather than uniformly criticizing these firms for technological backwardness, we should consider the possibility that they understand the technology completely, are prepared to utilize it when that becomes necessary, but are unwilling to precipitate an unfavorable change in their competitive environment.

The logical place to start in considering the potential impact of a new strategic use of information systems is with the motivation for the new system. Potential justifications include raising entry barriers, increasing switching costs, reducing the power of buyers or suppliers, deterring substitute products, lowering costs, and increasing differentiation. The outcome over time will be a change in the competitive forces affecting the industry. It is tempting but dangerous to consider these forces as impacting only current industry participants—suppliers, buyers, and competitors. As the examples indicate, certain IT uses can open up an industry to new and potentially dominant players and therefore may be a reason to delay moves.

Further, a firm considering a new investment in strategic information systems should assess whether it will obtain any sustainable competitive advantage or if a more likely outcome is an extension of the current competitive situation at an increased level of cost. IT software purchased from a nonexclusive source may not confer lasting advantage. Also, many firms have difficulty retaining skilled IT personnel, who may take key ideas with them when they leave a leading company for its competitors. Thus, leading-edge developments may soon be diffused, leaving the pioneering firm relatively no better off than before. In the absence of strong first-mover advantages, investments in information systems may simply not pay off competitively.

The long-term commitment of top management must be obtained before firing the first shot on the IT battlefield. Before starting an IT effort a clear view must exist of the company's long-range strategy and how this move fits into it. Further, the resources and capabilities of competitors, both current and potential, should be considered carefully.

Most crucial is the assessment of the likely long-term consequences of a new system. Initial development cost and benefit may not be an accurate indicator of the potential effects. A positive control is the "impact statement" that lays out the competitive changes expected to result from a new information system. Substantial benefits accruing from an improved competitive situation should alert the organization to consider the risks as well. Consideration of the positive impacts of the new system on competition forces broad-gauge thinking on potential negative impacts as well.

Over time the key to managing risks will be the organization's ability to learn from its experience so it can continue to roll out strategic IT applications as and when appropriate. There must be a common understanding among general managers and senior IT executives about which pieces of software should be considered "directional"—that is, likely to have a major effect on the organization's future competitive position. A thorough review of the potential impacts should be carried out before such systems are developed and again before they are implemented.

The Challenge

Achieving these advantages while avoiding the pitfalls requires broad IT management-user dialogue plus imagination. The process is complicated by the fact that, while many IT products are strategic, the potential benefits are very subjective and not easily verified. Often a strict return-on-investment (ROI) focus by senior management may turn attention toward narrow, well-defined targets as opposed to broader strategic opportunities that are harder to analyze.

Visualizing their systems in terms of the strategic grid (see Figure 3–4), senior and IT managements in a number of organizations have concluded that their company or business unit is located in either the support or the factory quadrant. They have set up staffing, organization, and planning activities accordingly. As a result of both the sharp change in IT performance and the evolution of competitive conditions, this categorization may be wrong. For the new conditions, for example, the competitor of the distributor (described in this chapter's opening paragraph) was complacent about its position in the support box. The company never realized what was happening until it was too late. Playing catch-up can be difficult and expensive in the IT area.

A number of companies and industry groups are and will appropriately remain in the support and factory boxes. Technical changes, however, have been so sudden in the past several years that the role of a company's IT function needs reexamination to ensure its placement is still appropriate.

A New Point of View

To address the issues raised here, management will need to change the way it operates.

Planning Issues

The CEO must insist that the end products of IT planning clearly communicate the true competitive impact of the expenditures involved. Figure 3–5 shows how to accomplish this by identifying priorities for the allocation of financial and staff resources.

In this connection, managers should realize that an embarrassingly large amount of development effort must be devoted to repairing

FIGURE 3-5   Identifying Resource Allocation Priorities by Strategic Business Unit

Goal of IS expenditure	Growing, highly competitive industry	Relatively stable industry, known ground rules	Static or declining industry
Rehabilitate and maintain system	1	1	1
Experiment with new technology	2	3	3
Attain competitive advantage	2	2	3*
Maintain or regain competitive parity	2	3	4
Defined return on investment [†]	3	3	4

*Assuming the change is not so dramatic as to revolution-ize the industry's overall performance

[†]In an intensely cost-competitive environment, defined ROI is the same as gaining competitive advantage

Note:
Numbers indicate relative attractiveness or importance of the investment, with 1 having the highest priority.

worn-out systems and to maintaining them in order to meet changed business conditions.[3] Also, a vital but often unrecognized need exists for research and development to keep up with the technology and to ensure that the company knows the full range of possibilities (developed in depth in Chapter 10)—in the early phases, for appropriate investments. Distinctly separate are the areas where a company spends money to obtain pure competitive advantage (very exciting) or to regain or maintain competitive parity (not so exciting, because the company is trying to recover from its shortsightedness). Finally, projects where the investment is defined for measurable return on investment (ROI) are also separate.

The aim of the ranking process is to allocate resources to areas with the most growth potential. Each company should have an IT plan summary, about three pages long, that vividly communicates to the CEO the data derived from Figure 3–5, why IT expenditures are allocated as they are, and what explicit types of competitive business benefits the company might expect from its IT expenditures. Today many companies fall short of this goal.

Confidentiality and Competition

Until now it has been the industry norm for organizations and individuals to share widely data about information systems technology and plans, on the grounds that no lasting competitive advantage would emerge from IT and that collaboration would allow all to reduce administrative headaches. But managers today should take appropriate steps to ensure the confidentiality of strategic IT plans and thinking. Great care should be taken in choosing the attendees at industry meetings and in determining what they can talk about and what information they can share with vendors and competitors.

Evaluating Expenditures

Executives should not permit the use of simplistic rules to calculate desirable IT expense levels. Judging an IT budget as a percentage of something, such as sales, has always been an easy way to compare the performance of different companies. In today's more volatile competitive arena, such comparisons are very dangerous. We have observed some companies that are spending 6 percent of their total sales in this area and that are clearly underinvesting. We have seen others making an outlay of 1 percent of their sales volume that are overspending.

---

[3]See Martin D. J. Buss, "Penny-Wise Approach to Data Processing," *Harvard Business Review,* July–August 1981, p. 111.

The IT–Management Partnership

To make full use of the opportunities that IT presents, managers need close partnership with technical experts. Bridging the gap between IT specialists and general management for purposes of strategic planning is, however, an enduring problem. Often uncomfortable with technology, many general managers are unaware of new options IT provides and the ways in which it can support strategy. On their part, IT professionals are often not attuned to the complexities and subtleties of strategy formulation. They are generally not part of the strategy development process (discussed further in Chapter 11).

Partnership is necessary. IT experts understand the economies of the technology and know its limits. They can also help move the organization toward the potential of tomorrow's technology. A change that is clumsy and inefficient in today's technology sometimes may eliminate the need to redesign in the next generation. For example, very rich, interrelated data bases today may be so slow to access as to present a serious cost (and possibly response time) problem. Tomorrow's technology may remove the speed problem and highlight the usefulness of the data.

General managers bring insight to overall business priorities. They have detailed knowledge of the various value chains and their potential in the real world and can help identify the paths of least staff resistance in implementation. Synthesis of the two worlds is essential.

Opening Questions

Finally, as a way of starting the process, establishment of joint task forces to address the following questions has proved a valuable way to get started.

What business are we really in? To answer that question, the task force may ask: What value do we provide to our customer? Do widespread, cheap, high-volume data communications and computer technology change this? Are we an insurance company, or should we think of ourselves as a provider of diversified financial services? A newswire service or a mover of electronic bits? A provider of spare parts or of parts and parts status reporting?

Who are our biggest competitors? What new competitors in the future does this technology make possible? Who else does, or can, provide the same products or services? If we see ourselves in the future as an insurance company, our competitors will be companies such as Aetna and Travelers. If we see ourselves as a financial services company, our competitors will be firms such as American Express/Shearson Lehman, Merrill Lynch, Sears Financial Services, and Citicorp.

Can we integrate our clients' operations with our own through telecommunications and offer them faster, easier, or cheaper service? In particular, how can we lock them in? By introducing significant switching costs?

Can we permanently lock competitors out through aggressive use of telecommunications and other electronic services?

Has our operating environment been changed by deregulation of our industry? Can technology help us compete for marketing, scheduling, control, and coordination in this new setting?

Has our environment changed due to deregulation of a related industry? Again, can technology help us compete? How can we add new products and services to retain our existing customer base?

Can we get there first? Should we attempt to make this move? These two may be the most difficult questions of all. They require foreseeing what's going to happen to the marketplace and to relationships with clients, customers, competitors, and regulators. Also, the company must determine which innovations will provide sustainable advantage and which competitors can readily copy, adding to the costs of all industry participants or shaving all margins.

A Final Thought

At resource allocation time, the difference between an effective strategic initiative and a harebrained scheme is razor thin. Only after the passage of money and time is the answer obvious.

Case 3-1

_____

OTISLINE

When elevators are running really well, people do not notice them. . . .
Our objective is to go unnoticed.

> Bob Smith
> *Executive Vice President and*
> *Chief Operating Officer*
> *Otis Elevator*

In late November 1985, Mr. John Miller, director of Information Systems for Otis Elevator North American Operations, was contemplating the future of OTISLINE, an application developed to enhance Otis Elevator's responsiveness to elevator maintenance customers. The nationwide rollout of OTISLINE was underway and several other applications that could use the infrastructure of OTISLINE were being considered.

Company Overview

Otis Elevator, a subsidiary of United Technologies Corporation, was the world leader in elevator sales and service (i.e., maintenance). Its 1984 revenue of $2 billion[1] represented 13 percent of United Technologies' total revenue. Otis Elevator was organized into four geographic divisions: North American Operations, Latin American Operations, Pacific Area Operations, and European Transcontinental Operations.

_____

[1] 1984 Annual Report, United Technologies Corporation.

This case was prepared by Donna Stoddard under the supervision of Warren McFarlan. The names of Otis Elevator employees have been disguised.

Otis Elevator described its business as the design, manufacture, installation, and service of elevators and related products (e.g., escalators and moving sidewalks). The company name was taken from its founder Elisha Graves Otis. By the end of the 19th century, Otis' name was known worldwide and had become synonymous with one of the most useful and dramatic inventions of the century, the passenger elevator.[2] Exhibit 1, an excerpt from *Going Up*, describes the events leading to the installation of the first passenger elevator.

The Otis name connoted technological leadership, reliability, and quality. Since Otis Elevator was perceived to be the best, customers were willing to pay a premium for its products.

Otis marketed three elevator lines: Otis Hydraulics were installed in low-rise buildings (up to six stories), Otis Geared were installed in mid-rise buildings (up to 24 stories), and Otis Gearless were installed in high-rise buildings. Since customers were more price sensitive when purchasing elevators for small building projects, Otis had been most successful selling elevators for large projects, for projects that required highly customized elevators (e.g., atrium elevators) or for projects where the customer was interested in installing the state-of-the-art in elevator technology. Additionally, the fact that Otis Elevator had a large, highly regarded service organization often led a customer to choose an Otis elevator instead of another manufacturer's product.

In the late 1970s microprocessor technology transformed the design of elevators. Mechanical elevator control systems were replaced by microprocessor-based control systems. One of the most advanced elevator systems was Otis Elevator's Elevonic[3] 401, which contained three microcomputer-based control units all of which were under software control. Exhibit 2 contains a description of Elevonic 401. The exploitation of microcomputer technology enabled Otis Elevator North American Operations (NAO) to significantly increase market share between 1980 and 1984. Management believed that equivalent technological change would similarly impact the service business in the future.

Elevator Industry Overview

By 1985 North American elevator new equipment sales and service represented approximately $1 billion and $2 billion markets respectively. The industry was very competitive. Otis, Westinghouse, Dover, Montgomery, Schindler, US Elevator, and Fujitec were the major manufacturers.

---

[2]Jean Gavois, *Going Up* (Otis Elevator, 1983), p. 74.

[3]Elevonic is a registered trademark of Otis Elevator.

EXHIBIT 1*

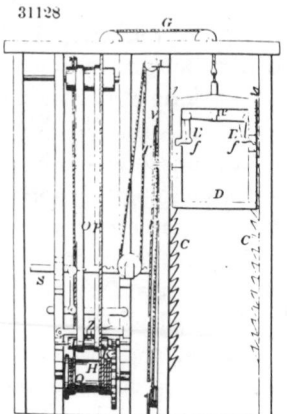

31128

The story of Elisha Graves Otis is a textbook tale of inventiveness, opportunity and enterprise. Along with other folk heroes of Victorian America, Otis took his place in books of precept and example. Imagine the scene: a small factory in Yonkers, making cheap iron bedsteads. The young Elisha Otis, master mechanic and inventor of a system for raising and lowering beds, contemplates the arid prospect of his future. Then in comes Mr. Newhouse from Hudson Street, New York, to ask if Mr. Otis could adapt his safety elevator to the problem of shifting merchandise. Could he, in fact, build him two elevators for hauling goods rather than lifting bedsteads. Two years later there were 27 Otis elevators in service in New York, and the foundations had been laid for enduring fame and fortune. Otis demonstrated his safety elevator in characteristically dramatic fashion at the New York Crystal Palace exhibition in 1853. He had himself hoisted up on the elevator platform, in full view of alarmed spectators and delighted journalists, and promptly cut the suspension cord. Nothing happened; the rack and pinion safety lock ensured that he was *All safe, Gentlemen!* The first passenger elevator was installed in E. V. Haughwout and Co.'s store on Broadway in 1857; it was the talk, and envy, of the town, attracting thousands of visitors.
Otis Collection.

BROADWAY: THE STORE OF MESSRS. E. V. HAUGHWOUT AND CO.

*Reprinted with permission of Otis Elevator.

EXHIBIT 2 Description of Elevonic 401*

SYSTEM HARDWARE

The advent of microprocessor technology has enabled Otis to reassign elevator control strategies from hardware to microcomputer software

Elevonic 401 control hardware is an integrated network of three microcomputer-based control units; a

Group Controller (in the machine room) to make dispatching decisions and call assignments; :

Car Controller (one per car in the machine room) to govern the operation and motion of the car; and a

Cab Controller (mounted behind the car operating panel) to interface with control hardware on the car, communicate cab data (e.g. passenger load, car calls) with the car controller, and control car-operating panel speech systhesis, visual display functions and coded secure entry.

Transducers, the sensors of the system, together with the car controller, form the closed loop structure that provides feedback that enables corrections to be made within milliseconds.

The group and car controllers employ the latest microprocessor technology. They differ in the number of cards in their card files and in the resident software. Although control hardware is standard for all Otis high-rise duties, and designed to suit practically all building specifications, custom software is added to personalize the controllers for each building's specific requirements.

The cab controller serves as a bi-directional information link between the cab mounted devices (car call buttons, load weighing transducers, speech synthesizer, secure entry modules) and the car controller. Multiplexing (transmitting hundreds of signals back and forth over a single pair of wires) between controllers significantly reduces the number of wires required for communicatior between controllers and peripheral devices. For example, while previous systems required an average of three traveling cables, the new Elevonic 401 system utilized just one.

System hardware determines the quantity and quality of input received by the control system permitting control decisions and corrective actions to be made and implemented within milliseconds. Digital measurement yields such benefits as the precise control knowledge of car velocity, acceleration and position.

Transducer feedback, obtained as digital numbers is compared by the controller with the prescribed specifications. The difference, or error, is driven toward zero to enforce the specified flight pattern programmed in the computer.

The hardware components of the new Elevonic 401 system permit placing total operating authority under software cotrol. Minimum physical or mechanical adjustments are required to maintain control. Changes in strategy and performance requirements are implemented in the software. The result is more precise, more efficient control, with the capacity to control a greater number of functions with much greater flexibility — making instantaneous decisions based on real time conditions.

*Reprinted with permission of Otis Elevator.

Elevator sales were cyclical since they were highly correlated to the building cycle. Conversely, the elevator service market was very stable. Elevator manufacturers often accepted a low margin on the sale of an elevator in order to obtain the elevator service contract since a significantly higher portion of their profit was attributable to service.

The elevator service market was fragmented. There were thousands of elevator service companies which included the elevator manufacturers and many small companies which provided only elevator service. The service market was attractive to many because of its stable demand and high profitability. Also, an elevator service company could service multiple manufacturers' elevators since, prior to the introduction of microprocessor-based elevator control systems, all elevators were electromechanical devices utilizing similar technologies.

For a small building project the elevator manufacturer was selected by the contractor, architect, or building owner. For larger projects, all three parties were often involved in the decision process. The manufacturer was selected based on its ability to satisfy the elevator performance specifications and architectural requirements, its price, and the reputation of its products (elevators and service).

The elevator service company was selected based on its responsiveness, quality, and price. An elevator manufacturer was typically awarded 60 percent to 80 percent of the service contracts for newly installed elevators. As the building aged and competition for tenants increased, the cost of service often became the major consideration and the service contract was awarded to the lowest bidder. The diagnostics of elevators with microprocessor-based control systems often required proprietary maintenance devices. Thus the manufacturer was more likely to maintain the service contract for these elevators. Many elevator manufacturers also offered discounts for long-term service contracts in an effort to attract and maintain service customers.

North American Operations Overview

The second largest division of Otis Elevator was North American Operations. At the end of 1985 it employed 8,000 people. The nature of its business necessitated a large geographically dispersed field organization. Exhibit 3 shows the NAO organization chart.

District offices had profit and loss responsibility and represented the entity to which branch offices and smaller field offices reported. (Hereafter, district, branch, and smaller field offices will be referred to as "field" offices.) Field offices handled both sales and service and varied in size from one to two people in outlying areas to very large offices of 100 people in large metropolitan areas.

EXHIBIT 3 NAO Organization Chart

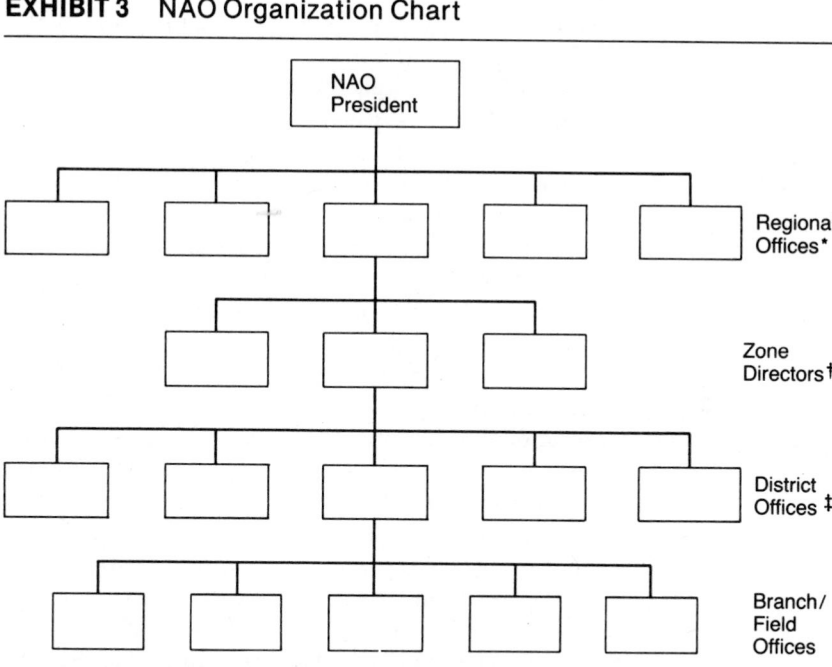

*Regional offices are geographically dispersed throughout North America.
†A zone director has three to five district managers reporting to him or her.
‡A district manager has two to six branch/field offices reporting to him or her.

Otis was the leader in the North American elevator sales and service markets. Its customer base ranged from installations with elevators installed in 2- to 5-story buildings to the elevators installed in the World Trade Center in New York City, a 110-story building.

NAO Information Services

NAO installed its first computer, an IBM 1401, in 1965. The 1401 was acquired to automate maintenance billing. From 1965 until 1978, all applications were batch and related to production control or accounting. The early online applications, installed from 1978 to 1981, provided data entry and inquiry capabilities for the factory control and accounting systems.

In 1981 a corporatewide cost reduction drive was implemented to enhance NAO's profitability. Bob Smith, then president of NAO, asked John Miller to suspend all efforts in the area of new systems development until the applications development course could be recharted.

There was considerable concern that the applications development resources were being spent to automate old, tired, manual procedures rather than new, helpful systems. As a result, 60 percent of the programmers were laid off, no hardware upgrades were allowed, and no new applications were implemented. A workload elimination project was started in the information services department to "keep the ship afloat," since the system (an IBM 370/158) was often running at 100 percent utilization.

The year 1982 was one of transition for NAO's information services area. With the cost reduction program completed, management began to assess the ability of information services to enhance the quality of its maintenance service offerings.

In late 1981, NAO began to assess the feasibility of using information technology to establish a central customer service center (on either a regional or a divisionwide basis) to accept nonprime-time callbacks (a callback is a customer request for elevator maintenance). At the time, Otis and other elevator service companies used commercial answering services to accept nonprime-time callback requests. A local commercial answering service was given a duty roster from which it selected the service mechanic to dispatch to the customer. In small cities it was not uncommon for the same answering service to be used by multiple elevator service companies. During prime time the customer called the local NAO field office to make a callback request. An Otis employee accepted the call and dispatched the appropriate service mechanic.

Responsiveness to callbacks was one of the criteria used by service customers to assess the quality of an elevator company's service offerings. The callback response time was defined as the time it took for the service mechanic to arrive at the building from the time that the customer reached Otis Elevator (or its answering service). Whereas Otis had received assurances from the local, commercial answering services that Otis would be promptly notified of a customer callback, the quality of service provided by the answering services varied greatly. In a videotape that described the need for the central customer service center, Bob Smith stated, "A commercial answering service does not have the same interest that we have to get service to the customer as fast as possible."

By August 1982 the central customer service center concept had been successfully piloted in a major eastern market. The decision was made to implement a North American customer service center to dispatch service mechanics in response to callbacks, 24 hours a day. A project team, composed of individuals from many functional areas, including information services, was selected to implement this concept which was called OTISLINE.

The 1985 NAO information services budget was more than double the 1982 level. An IBM 3083 was installed in early 1983 to replace the IBM 370/158 and by 1985 the installed peripheral equipment included the state-of-the-art in direct access storage devices, tape drives, and telecommunications equipment. The primary justification for these additional information services resources was OTISLINE.

NAO Service Organization

In 1985 NAO employed approximately 2,300 service mechanics. Most service mechanics were assigned to routes. The route service mechanic had responsibility for both callbacks and preventive maintenance of elevators on the route.

NAO strove to minimize callbacks. It had calculated that, if callbacks were reduced by one per year per installed elevator, it would save $5 million annually. Additionally, an out-of-service elevator irritated the customer, impacted a customer's business, and affected the customer's perception of the quality of an Otis elevator.

OTISLINE Overview

Brad Robertson, director, Service Operations, was the leader of the OTISLINE development team. He also had responsibility for the implementation and management of the OTISLINE customer service center. During the development of OTISLINE, Brad reported to the VP of finance. In August 1985 a reorganization occurred which resulted in Brad reporting to the VP of marketing.

In describing OTISLINE Brad stated,

> OTISLINE improved the visibility of our service business and helps management and local office personnel to more effectively provide quality service to our customers. Our responsiveness to customer callback requests has been greatly enhanced. OTISLINE's reporting functions have provided district, regional, and NAO headquarters management with a significant amount of information on the quality of service rendered to our customers. Prior to OTISLINE, management became aware of many service problems only if there was a customer complaint. OTISLINE has allowed us to produce "excess" callback reports for various levels of management. For example, elevators receiving three or more callbacks in a month are reported to the district manager; those receiving eight or more in 90 days are reported to the regional vice president. Critical situations are reported to the president.

The excess callback reports highlight problem installations and have enhanced our ability to quickly diagnose problems that may be due to a specific component malfunction. With this information local office management (or engineering management if the problem is with a component malfunction) can focus resources on key problem areas.

The success of OTISLINE is attributable to the top management support of the project which fostered cooperation among functional areas and provided the resources and motivation required to "make it happen."

OTISLINE has changed the way NAO does business. The OTISLINE system impacted many of NAO's business functions including information services, customer service, service mechanic dispatching and control, service marketing, and engineering. Additionally, its infrastructure has been used to support applications that enhance the productivity of elevator sales representatives and service mechanics. In the future, OTISLINE could interface directly with installed elevators through the use of remote diagnostic technology.

Following is a description of OTISLINE's impact on these areas.

Information Services

The OTISLINE application was a part of NAO's Service Management System (SMS), an integrated database management system (Exhibit 4). Prior to OTISLINE the SMS database contained the customer master file (customer name, building location, contract information) and other information that was used to monitor and control the service business (route information, service price estimating, etc.). With OTISLINE the SMS has been expanded to include *all* maintenance activity for elevators under service contracts, applications have been enhanced (e.g., service price estimating), and new applications will be added (e.g., billing). The SMS database is accessed and updated by an OTISLINE dispatcher (or one supporting another application) through a display that is attached to the IBM 3083 host.

The system was designed to provide the OTISLINE dispatcher with subsecond response time. This was achieved by giving the OTISLINE dispatcher a local display and by ensuring that short database paths existed to the data needed by the OTISLINE dispatcher when a customer is on the telephone. Subsecond response time was an important design element. Experience showed that when more than 2 percent of the transactions had greater than a five-second response time, the length of time to handle a customer's service request became unacceptable.

EXHIBIT 4 Service Management System*

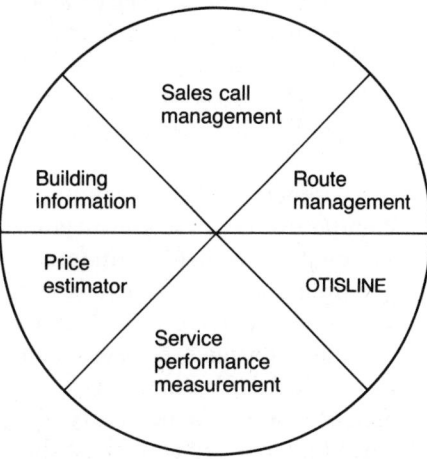

*Reprinted with permission of Otis Elevator.

The SMS database was designed in the late 1970s. Its existence significantly shortened the time it took to develop OTISLINE. According to Tim Clark, manager of Systems Development, it would have taken four to five years to develop the OTISLINE application if the SMS database had not been in place.

Because of the strategic nature of the OTISLINE application, a large portion of the information services budget was earmarked for its support. The data center operations budget was increased significantly to support OTISLINE's stringent response time and performance requirements. In the systems development area, OTISLINE resulted in the introduction of new systems development methodologies that are being used to develop future strategic systems.

At the end of 1985 there were 37 local terminals installed at the OTISLINE Service Center to support OTISLINE. By the end of 1986, 150 personal computers located in field offices would also have OTISLINE inquiry capability.

Customer Service

The OTISLINE Service Center was staffed with 60 OTISLINE dispatchers. These dispatchers were highly skilled. About half had college degrees, and many spoke two languages. New hires received from four to six weeks of in-house training which covered the following:

- The OTISLINE software (i.e., the dispatching system).
- The IBM display.
- Operation of the phone system.
- Appropriate telephone salutations and courtesies.
- Listening and customer satisfaction skills.
- Overview of Otis Elevator organization structure.
- Elevator terminology and possible systems problems.

The objective of the training was to ensure that the dispatcher could handle a customer call in an efficient and effective manner. Periodic seminars were held to update the dispatchers on system changes, sample dialogues for situations that were likely to be encountered (e.g., an irritated customer or a trapped-in-an-elevator scenario), and the criteria that was used to assess dispatcher performance.

OTISLINE dispatchers were trained to be courteous, sensitive, efficient, and to speak clearly. They were required to update the database with information that they obtained during a call which would shorten the amount of time to identify the building and elevator the next time the customer called for service. Periodically, a supervisor or manager listened in as a dispatcher answered a call. A dispatcher evaluation form was completed by the supervisor or manager and reviewed with the dispatcher.

Customers accessed OTISLINE by calling an 800 number which connected them to the North American customer service center. Incoming calls were distributed to either the next available dispatcher or to a specific dispatcher (e.g., calls from a French-speaking province in Canada are routed to a French-speaking dispatcher). Calls coming in on specific lines could be moved to the head of the queue.

The telephone system produced a variety of statistics. Reports showed dispatcher availability, i.e., the amount of time the dispatcher was available to accept calls during the shift. Dispatcher performance was measured against department standards and averages. The system also produced statistics on the length of time that customers had to wait for an available dispatcher. This information helped management determine when additional staff was needed to ensure that a high level of responsiveness was maintained.

The OTISLINE application display screens were designed to quickly lead the dispatcher and the customer through a series of questions to identify the building and elevator needing service. The OTISLINE dispatcher filled in the display screen shown in Exhibit 5 when a customer call was received. OTISLINE was implemented with four ways for the building and elevator to be recognized: (1) the building identification number; (2) the telephone number; (3) the building name, city, and state; or, (4) the building address, city, and state. If the build-

---

EXHIBIT 5 Otis—Customer Call Recording

	Type:	Call MSG
	Phone:	
	Name of Caller:	
	Building ID:	
Request		
	Building Name:	
	Address:	
	City:	
	State:	
If Message, Phone Number Customer Called:		Next Function:

Reprinted with permission of Otis Elevator

ing and elevator needing service could not be identified using one of the above-mentioned criteria, a "no hit" situation was encountered. The dispatcher was expected to assure the customer that a service mechanic would be dispatched, terminate the call, and use manual procedures to find the information on the building and elevator.

If a "hit" was made, the dispatcher verified the building address and elevator identification number. The call was terminated, and the fact that a situation had been opened was logged by the dispatcher. Another dispatcher who was serving as a pager then took the call and paged the mechanic (all mechanics carry small pagers).

The OTISLINE Service Center was functionally organized to promote dispatcher efficiency. During a shift, a dispatcher was typically assigned to perform one function, that is, accept calls, page service mechanics, or handle New Equipment Sales (described below). Thus, a callback request often involved four OTISLINE dispatchers: the dispatcher that logged the service request, the dispatcher that paged the service mechanic, the dispatcher that received the call from the service mechanic that resulted in dispatching him to the customer, and the dispatcher that logged the situation resolution data when the service mechanic called in to "close" the call.

By the end of 1985, 11 of the 47 districts were using OTISLINE for 24-hour dispatch of service mechanics. The service center received 4,300 calls on an average weekday. The center was expected to handle 10,000 incoming calls per day when the system was implemented for all of the districts. Customer calls accounted for one-third of the total. Of the customer calls, 75 percent were for service requests. Customers also called to leave messages for service mechanics and sales representatives.

Service Mechanic Dispatching and Control

Prior to OTISLINE, the field office handled the dispatching of service mechanics during normal working hours. Answering services dispatched service mechanics after hours and on weekends and holidays. Service mechanics were required to complete a written report for each callback. These reports provided the data for a callback and repair history log that was manually maintained by the field office's service desk representative. This log was used by the local office in support of daily operations and by engineering to flag problems and determine preventive maintenance procedures. Since these logs were maintained manually, it was very time-consuming to prepare summary reports. Thus, callback data were reported to district, region, or NAO headquarters *only* when requested.

With OTISLINE, the service mechanic was relieved of the requirement to file a written report for each callback. Rather, the service mechanic placed a phone call to OTISLINE, described the situation that was noted when he or she arrived at the building, and reported the actions taken to repair the elevator. The service mechanics were supplied with a pocket notebook that they used to record information on the service call. This notebook also showed them the questions that they needed to answer for the OTISLINE dispatcher to complete the callback report.

The quality and timeliness of information available to district, region, and NAO management increased significantly. One measure of performance in field offices was the number of callbacks received. Prior to OTISLINE the level of accuracy and consistency in the reporting of callbacks varied from office to office. It was difficult to pinpoint problems that might have been attributable to a malfunctioning component or recurring problem since the data were recorded by elevator in the field office and the detail data were not stored in a central database.

With OTISLINE, all customers (including those large installations that have on-site service mechanics) were requested to call OTISLINE to request service. The OTISLINE dispatcher then paged the service mechanic to request service on a particular elevator. All data about service calls were stored in a central computer (see Exhibit 6). Thus, the local office no longer needed to keep manual elevator maintenance history logs.

Some field offices were initially skeptical of the OTISLINE concept. They felt the system would decrease the control that local management had to dispatch service mechanics for callbacks and therefore know the location of the service mechanics throughout the day. OTISLINE is being enhanced to address these concerns. Personal computers with OTISLINE inquiry were installed in field offices in 1986 to enable local management to track callback activity in their territories.

EXHIBIT 6 Callback Data Stored Online

Elevator identification
Date/time service requested
Requestor of service
Time service mechanic notified
Time service mechanic arrived on site
Condition of elevator on arrival
Repair action taken
Service mechanic responding to request
Maintenance supervisor
Cause of malfunction or problem

Bob Smith noted that, while centralization of service mechanic dispatching was contrary to NAO's decentralized organization, the *quality* and *reliability* of Otis products (i.e., elevators and service) was what differentiated Otis from its competitors. With OTISLINE Otis had the information that service and engineering management needed to continue to enhance the quality and reliability of Otis products.

Marketing—New Equipment Sales

OTISLINE was also used to support the elevator sales function. The New Equipment Sales (NES) application could be accessed by New Equipment Sales representatives by calling OTISLINE. NES was an integrated database management system designed to automate the process of reporting the status of elevator sales prospects. It had three primary components: negotiation, estimating, and disposition:

Negotiation provided a vehicle for the New Equipment Sales representative to organize data regarding new equipment projects and communicate the status of those projects to responsible managers.

Estimation provided cost estimates and configurations for certain new equipment products. These cost estimates were used by the New Equipment Sales representative and local office to determine the elevator sales price.

Disposition provided the mechanism to convert a negotiation to a customer decision to purchase the elevator from Otis; to record it as a competitive loss; or to place it in an abandoned status.

NES made data about competitive losses and New Equipment Sales representative performance easily accessible to management. In the future, when a negotiation becomes a sale, the information that had been entered into NES will be used to establish a record in SMS.

Marketing—Service

In a brochure published in 1984 to describe OTISLINE to the NAO service mechanics, six factors were described as Otis Elevator's philosophy of service: responsiveness, reliability, innovation, communication, teamwork, and customer satisfaction. OTISLINE addressed all of these factors:

Responsiveness. OTISLINE dramatically improved NAO's responsiveness to customer maintenance requests. The system kept track of whether a service mechanic had been dispatched in response to the customer's call. If the service mechanic assigned to the route was unavailable to take the call either an alternate service mechanic or the service supervisor was paged. The system produced reports that could be reviewed with customers that show response time statistics.

Response time was critical to some customers, e.g., hospitals and one-elevator installations. OTISLINE provided the opportunity to offer a guaranteed response time to these customers.

Reliability. OTISLINE dispatchers updated the SMS to reflect actions that were necessary to repair out-of-service elevators. This data could be used by management to allocate resources to locations that had recurring problems. This data could also be used by engineering to spot trends that indicated elevator design problems.

Innovation. As the leader in the industry, customers expected more from Otis. NAO was the first to offer a customer service center staffed with professionals.

Communication. OTISLINE enhanced customer to service and sales representative communication. Additionally it provided a more effective way for service and sales to submit reports to management.

Teamwork. The OTISLINE dispatcher was an additional member of the team that was concerned with providing a high level of service to the customer.

Customer Satisfaction. Customer satisfaction improved as a result of the implementation of OTISLINE.

The United Technologies 1985 Annual Report noted that in North America, Otis strengthened its number one share of the service market. OTISLINE contributed to NAO's ability to improve service quality and compete successfully with lower-priced independent service companies.

Future Applications

Bob Smith noted that information technology could be utilized in a number of ways to impact Otis Elevator's service marketing in the future.

Remote Elevator Monitoring (REM). Otis Elevator had been testing REM where a microprocessor-based elevator had the capability to monitor the elevator's control system and log performance statistics. The elevator was also equipped with communications capability. In the pilot installations, the elevator communicated its problems to a personal computer located at the NAO headquarters. The personal computer analyzed the problems and produced trouble reports that were used to dispatch service mechanics before the elevator went out of service.

REM could be enhanced by having the elevator communicate to a central computer that would interpret the problems being experienced by the elevator, determine the cause of the problem, transmit a message to the OTISLINE system, and result in the dispatch of the service mechanic.

The advantage of REM was that it would allow NAO to dispatch a service mechanic to the customer location before the elevator is out of service. Additionally the service mechanic could make adjustments to running elevators to keep them operating at maximum performance levels.

In-Car Phones. The most sensitive kind of callback that Otis received was a "trapped-in-an-elevator" scenario. Many Otis elevators had a telephone installed in the cab (i.e., in-car phones). The passenger could use this phone which would be equipped with an autodialer to notify the OTISLINE dispatcher of the situation. Since the OTISLINE phone system recognized calls coming in on priority lines, it could move the call to the head of the queue and alert the OTISLINE dispatcher that an emergency call had been received via a message on the telephone display or an audible beep. The dispatcher would then be prepared to work with the passenger to identify the location of the elevator and dispatch a service mechanic immediately.

Replace Service Mechanic Pagers with Hand-Held Terminals. Field service mechanics were contacted using pagers. These could eventually be replaced with hand-held terminals thus enabling the OTISLINE dispatcher to send a message to the service mechanic and eliminating the requirement for the service mechanic to call in for messages. Additionally, the service mechanic could use the hand-held terminal to complete callback reports and to order parts for out-of-service elevators.

New Equipment Ordering.   NES could be expanded to include new equipment ordering. Thus when the New Equipment Sales representative called in to report that a project had resulted in a sale, the order for the elevator could be placed. This information could be transmitted to the plant and thus shorten the lead time to complete the manufacture of an elevator. Also by reducing the amount of time that it took to notify the plant of an order, management of the plant's raw material inventory level could be improved.

Contract Management.   When a sale was recorded, it was important for Otis to manage to the customer's installation schedule. Slippages in the installation schedule could be caused by building contractor delays, technical problems encountered by the Otis superintendent at the construction site, or elevator manufacturing delays. Clearly the building was unusable until the elevator was installed!

It was important for Otis and building management to be aware of problems that affected the installation of the elevator. A personal computer could be installed at the construction site to be used by the construction superintendent to document slippages that may be encountered in the schedule. This information could be communicated to the factory and others involved in the installation and used to keep both Otis management and the building owner aware of the reasons for changes that occur in the installation schedule.

Telemarketing of Service.   The SMS database contained information on all installed Otis elevators in North America. The OTISLINE facility could be used to contact those customers that do not have a service contract with Otis. The OTISLINE dispatcher could find out when the current elevator maintenance contracts expire. A prospect list could be produced and distributed to the service sales representatives monthly.

In a 1985 NAO management newsletter, Bob Smith stated:

> The real significance of OTISLINE is its ability to collapse both distance and time, resulting in faster responses to customer problems, better maintenance procedures, and ultimately more reliable elevators. . . . This can translate into real competitive advantage. We're confident that it will, and we are investing accordingly.

Case 3-2

Manufacturers Hanover
Corporation
Worldwide Network

Ed Nyce, senior vice president and deputy general manager for Technical Support Services at Manufacturers Hanover Bank, was reflecting in late 1983 on the status of GEONET, the bank's worldwide communications network:

> To sell GEONET to other parts of operations, we have to address three major issues: technology, economics, and control. We need to put a good solid argument down on paper and take a hard look at both sides of the ledger, because 1984 will be the year that we begin to assess charges to the users for GEONET, and 1984 will be the year the rubber will hit the road. We must lay the technical concerns on the table.

Nyce, Roberta Frackman, vice president of corporate telecommunications, and Gunther Kempin, vice president of data communications, had been working toward a corporatewide communications net since 1976. After an initial period of responding to individual product communication needs, they had decided the only reasonable way to deliver quality communication service was through an internally designed and

This case was prepared by James L. McKenney and John Sviokla.

managed network. The company's global business had the volume of transactions to support such a net, but to obtain economies of scale most applications would be obliged to use it.

The goal was to develop a net that could serve all the business needs of the corporation in a transparent manner. That is, users would be unaware of the net, and systems designers and builders could easily adapt to the net standards. Further, the net should be able to operate in all countries in which the bank had markets. Starting with a general concept of corporate network, the three had worked to design and build GEONET. The original intention had been to convert all existing networks to the one system to obtain economies of scale.

During the development process, the telecommunications group began spending more time providing support for new and better products and for geographic expansion. This, combined with a few technical implementation problems and rapid change in communication technology, slowed the progress of converting existing applications to GEONET. Consequently the network had not attained the volume of traffic that Roberta Frackman had planned to achieve by 1984. The costly duplication was getting worse as business expanded.

Manufacturers Hanover Corporation

With 1983 earnings of $337 million and total assets of $64 billion, Manufacturers Hanover Trust (MHT) was the fourth largest bank in the United States. Despite the volatile economy and changing banking environment, 1983 was the 11th consecutive year of increased earnings. The bank was a subsidiary of Manufacturers Hanover Corporation (MHC), a bank holding company that owned many banking and non-banking companies, the largest of which was MHT.

In MHT, the most basic client distinctions were between those with large transactions (usually $100,000 or more per transaction), known as wholesale clients, and those with small amounts (usually $100 per transaction), known as retail clients. MHT was organized in four main groups: wholesale, retail, trust (which had to be separate by law), and corporate.

Within these major areas, MHT had various banking divisions focused on particular target markets, such as the North American Banking division (NAD) which serviced large corporate clients and correspondent banks throughout the United States and Canada, the energy division, and the international wholesale division. These divisions were usually set up as profit centers and the division management reviewed on profit performance.

Reorganization Issues in the 70s

Starting in the 1970s there was increasing competition and volatility in traditional banking businesses due to deregulation, large swings in the economy, and a changing customer base. The most dramatic shift was away from the traditional sheltered source—interest income. Competition from many sources reduced the spread between what a bank had to pay in interest and what it could charge. This led banks to seek income from fees for services.

A second force that had influenced MHT was the growth of multinational business and global financial markets. For the largest money center banks like MHC, banking had become globalized. In the past decade, MHC's international business had grown so rapidly that, by 1983, 51 percent of its profits were earned offshore.

Shrinking interest income forced banks to pursue noninterest income sources. Typically these sources were a service around financial information aimed either at reducing the cost of obtaining funds or of facilitating the timing of transactions. At MHT, as at other banks, the cost of operations was rising, partly as a result of the number of new services and the global complexity of the market, placing intense focus on cost control and on meeting competition with new products to attain market share. This new competitiveness in banking came at a time when banking itself was changing because of deregulation. Now MHC was competing not just with other banks but with insurance companies, brokers, and other financial service organizations as well.

One MHC response was to appraise the potential competitive advantage their computer systems could provide. In evaluating the role of operations, which managed a large central data processing activity, management became convinced information systems had to change: it was no longer a large factory where the sole objective was minimizing costs, but a critical factor in the bank's strategy. This was particularly true in the international arena, where competition was changing from one of long-term relationships to one of available services and costs.

Jack Evans, vice chairman of MHC, commented on the key issues of that time.

> Our present focus on competitive information services goes back to the early 70s. In the process of reviewing our DP support we became convinced that we should develop our systems on the needs of the business, not the technology. We had allowed our technology to become obsolete and were therefore not competitive in information support. However, upon analysis of our business needs we became

convinced we could use the need to redo the DDA[1] system to better our competitive position.

Wholesale had fundamentally different requirements from retail. It was relatively small volume with large dollar transactions in a global market, compared to a high-volume, small dollar transaction in a domestic market. Further the wholesale market was becoming more competitive and growing. It was increasingly clear a bank had to be able to provide a worldwide relationship to expanding international corporations. It was an information-rich environment that required extracting information from each transaction and storing this information so it could be made available on demand to customers. This included both customer and account information, requiring most information to be moved to New York and then back to the customer. The new system would be very dependent upon communication.

The first step was to reorganize to provide distinctly different data processing support for each major business. What emerged were vertically integrated operations centers with separate divisions for wholesale and retail. These had responsibility for all system development and maintenance as well as independent data center operation. This may have cost a bit more for some redundancy, but the gain from better understanding of the business needs and more responsiveness would far outweigh the costs.

The result of the reorganization was four data support groups referred to as Vertically Integrated Operating Centers (VIOCs) (see Exhibit 1). The managers of the VIOCs were formally within the operations department, but their primary responsibility was to serve the needs of their user community. This reorganization placed the responsibility for operations with the business that needed this information. Exhibit 2 is an organization chart of the operations department.

Each VIOC was a cost center, with costs absorbed by the division they served. Within the four VIOCs there were a total of nine data centers that operated a varied base of data processing and communications equipment. Most of the computer hardware in trust was IBM; in retail it was NCR; corporate and wholesale had IBM. There was also a large variety of minicomputers scattered throughout the data centers.

The VIOCs responded to the changing market and increased competitiveness by generating a rash of new products. The period from 1970 to 1975 saw a fourfold increase in the number of MHC electronic-based products, a majority of which relied upon some form of telecommunications. The trend at MHC, as was true of many competitors in

---

[1]DDA is demand deposit accounts—usually money in checking accounts.

EXHIBIT 1   Schematic of Vertically Integrated Operating Centers

Operations Division Management

Policies/Procedures

Staff Support Groups

Vertically Integrated Operations Centers

Wholesale	Retail	Trust	Corporate
Computer Hardware	Computer Hardware	Computer Hardware	Computer Hardware
Systems & Programming	Systems & Programming	Systems & Programming	Systems & Programming
Staff Support Groups	Staff Support Groups	Staff Support Groups	Staff Support Groups

General Administration Board

Senior Automation Steering Committee (Projects less than $500,000)

Local Steering Committee (Projects less than $150,000)

this industry, was to provide a better telecommunication link to the customer's office or their home. Before the VIOCs were created, communication costs were relatively unnoticed, as they were mixed with several aspects of data processing. Communication costs due to the new products grew in excess of 25 percent per year from 1970 to 1975.

Jack Evans commented on the emergence of communications as a specific concern.

EXHIBIT 2 Operations and Support Services

Operations Department Organization Chart

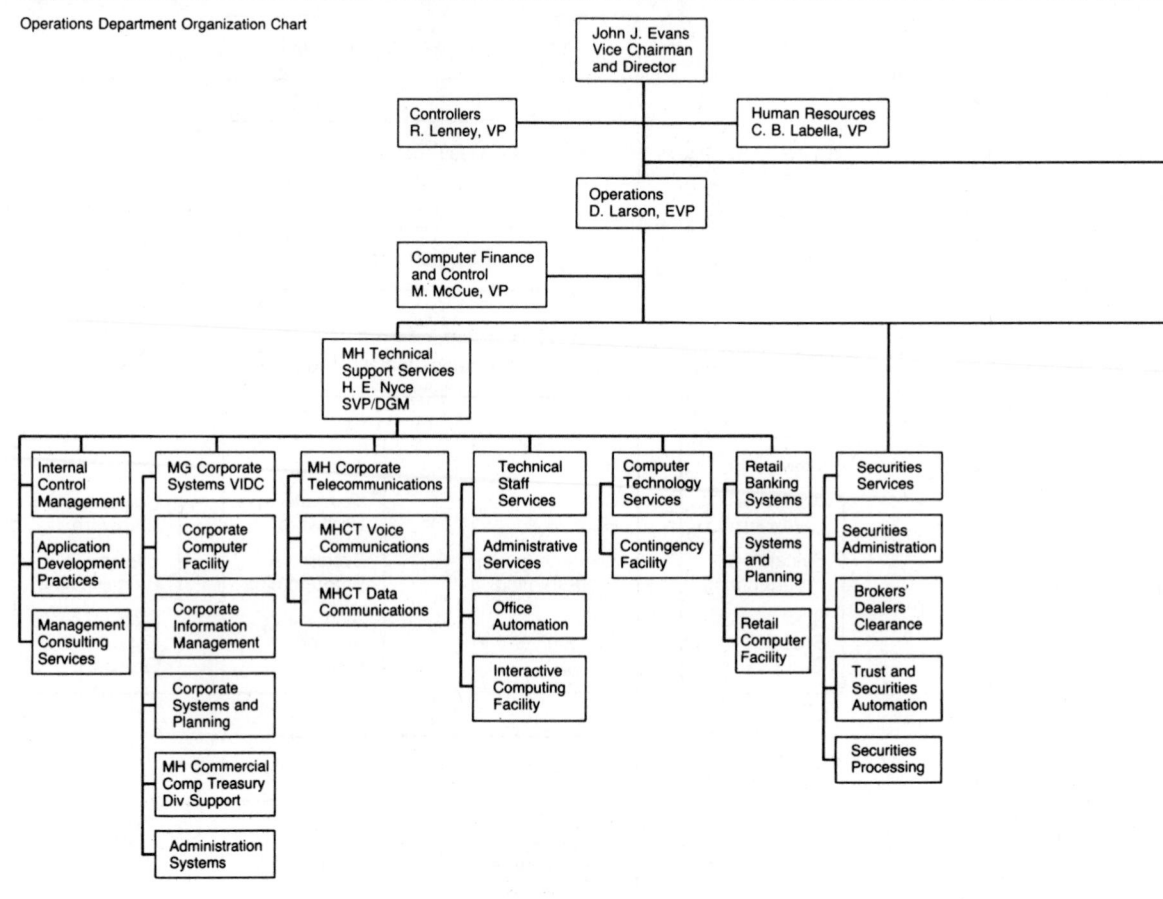

The business-driven plan that emerged in the 1976–77 era initiated the new organization and also developed a guiding philosophy that has strongly influenced our management of communication. First, information was going to become more important and would be a basis for pricing for services as we moved to gain more noninterest income. To make income, costs have to be controlled and one of the costs that was growing in an uncontrolled fashion was communications. We saw this as a prime opportunity to be managed into a competitive advantage.

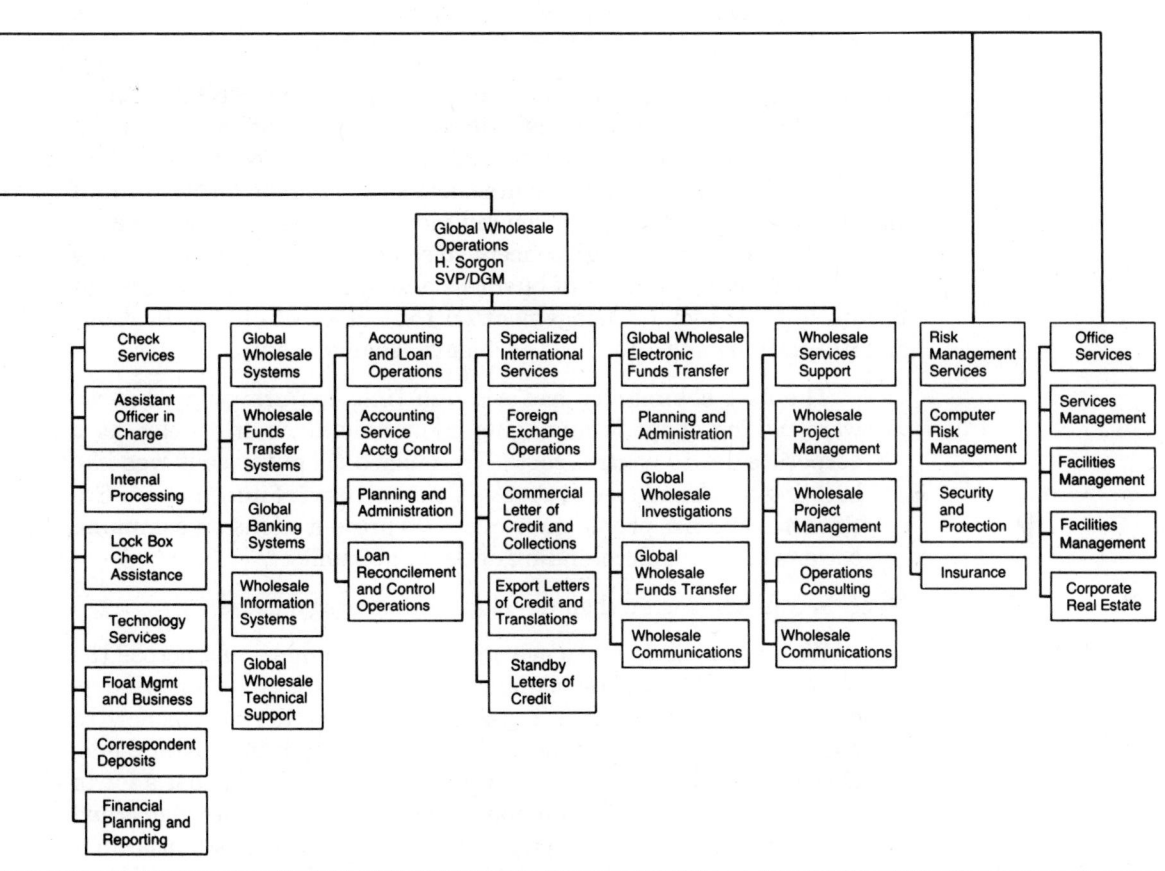

One of the key users of systems that participated in these discussions, Merrill Burns, senior vice president and deputy general manager of the North American division, commented on the competitiveness of the era:

> At MHC we were out of phase with the rest of the industry. For example, in wholesale banking, Chemical had announced its Chemlink package, Morgan had MARS, Chase had Infocash, all aimed at

the wholesale client.[2] . . . We began to see that the transaction was an important information event. The customer wanted quick access to the status and implications of transactions, so did the bank. We also saw that we had decentralized information systems transactions, but had a centralized need for data—a single point where the customer could come to MHC for current status. When we began to view the problem in that context, we began to see that we needed a telecommunications strategy of some sort.

Although seemingly counter to the independent VIOC concept, Jack Evans and Ed Nyce thought it would be prudent to manage the development of telecommunications from a corporate perspective. The economics dictated a shared resource, and the technology would permit this with little interference in the individual businesses. They also assumed this would be a tough concept to sell because it seemed to imply putting technology in front of business needs. In 1975–76 they set out to inform their senior management on the nature of communications and its relationship to business problems. Evans noted:

The user community had a tough time conjuring up what we were talking about in managing communications or developing a corporate net to control costs. We pushed them to see it was like building a railroad track to move their box cars of information. Ed, Roberta, and her people gave over 100 presentations on communications to gain understanding of the opportunity.

Nyce, in commenting on their development strategy, noted:

We decided early on to sell the project top down and across the organization. The net development had to be driven by business requirements, not technical considerations. Further it was new to management and took time and effort to make it understandable. Our estimates at the time showed that the net would cost a lot in the long run, and in 1976 management was much more concerned with cost than potential. Our role was to show the potential in a manner understandable to bankers. We likened it to the building of a highway and how we were starting with two-lane roads, building to superhighways. I felt transmission was the crux of the opportunity—a true adaptive delivery system that did not care about the contents; a complicated idea to sell.

Key to gaining confidence was a series of projects that came in on time and on budget. We developed a sequence of one-year pro-

---

[2]Chemical Bank (Chemical), Morgan Guaranty Trust (Morgan), and Chase Manhattan Bank (Chase) were major New York City banks.

grams to design and build a network. These provided the basis for discussion and an ongoing education of the opportunities.

Telecommunications Management at MHC 1972–1976

Manufacturers Hanover's customer-oriented data communications effort began in 1972 with the installation of their first on-line system—a Passbook Savings system with about 200 terminals in the retail branches. (See Appendix for a chronology of significant communication developments.) Two men developed the communications requirements and installed the network. One of them, Gunther Kempin, the manager of telecommunications, was part of a technical support group that was staff to the emerging VIOCs. Because of increased demand, Kempin had to double his staff almost every year. Between 1970 and 1975, 22 new products that provided information directly to the customer's premises were developed. By 1976 Gunther had run out of resources to install new systems and was devoting most of his energy to maintain and adapt existing services to changing demands.

In 1976, as the VIOCs emerged as operating entities, Nyce and Evans gave the responsibility for corporatewide communications to Roberta Frackman, with Gunther Kempin as technical manager. A study team was organized to analyze the existing data communication services and costs.

The team found that data communications needs were served through no fewer than 28 teleprocessing networks that supported various MHC business products. These networks emanated from the nine data centers, each responsible for supporting its networks. Different mainframes—IBM, DEC, and NCR—hosted the networks, with additional minicomputers in use at various locations.

As the telecommunications staff began to analyze existing systems' costs and operations, the deficiencies of MHC's telecommunications approach became clearer. The proliferation of specialized networks was a prime cause of the skyrocketing costs; none of the networks could communicate with any other; duplication of facilities was rampant—each of 200 retail branches housed two separate networks and their unique equipment. The networks provided no volume information and no diagnostics. Further, the networks were highly labor-intensive at a time of increasing competitiveness in the applicable labor market. Finally, the initial networks were short-lived—an average of 18–24 months—and enhancements and expansions inevitably required extensive physical replacement of equipment, with accompanying disruption of banking activities.

Toward an Integrated Solution

In 1976, management developed and approved a two-pronged program to initiate an integrated approach to communications:

1. A top-down sell to gain understanding of the issues of communication investment and operation.
2. A network planning study to establish a managed communication program for MHC that would include:
   a. A feasibility study of present and planned business needs for communications.
   b. A network design to meet the communication needs of MHC.
   c. A network implementation plan, with implementation in distinct phases and geared toward corporate business needs.

Implementation of a corporate managed network would require top management support right from the beginning. The network would ultimately affect almost every part of the corporation and the costs of full installation would need budgetary approval from the top. Further, without the support of top management, the bank would not be able to convert the main body of users to a common net, which was essential in obtaining economies of scale. Hence Nyce, Frackman, and Kempin adopted an approach of starting small, implementing a series of projects with set deadlines and budgets, meeting obligations, and discussing each step as often as possible.

They designed the network study to be carried out in three sequential stages. The feasibility study (Part 2.*a*) was to define the scope of communications at MHC in business terms and translate these into communication requirements. Its three main goals were to minimize cost by integrating voice, data, and graphic communication services; to create flexibility by allowing any terminal or host to communicate; and to develop the ability to manage communication services as a competitive asset. In implementing the study a working relationship between the data centers and the network planning effort would be generated. The study would also produce the base line information needed for network design.

The network design stage (2.*b*) would define alternatives and evaluate them on the basis of technical/economic performance and business requirements. The result would be a network architecture for meeting the communication needs of MHC.

The network implementation plan (2.*c*) was a sequence of activities with a variety of objectives: to meet business needs, to build an experience base, and to establish creditability. It was to be a phased approach that would start with a pilot study to test and to demonstrate the network design in parallel with the development of a functional specification of the network. Next a production stage would convert an existing net to the common net, ideally demonstrating cost and quality improvements. Finally there would be a conversion of existing nets and support of new services.

The Feasibility Study

The feasibility study was begun in March of 1978 and was completed in the fourth quarter of the same year, on time and within its budget of $96,000. Two parallel activities were carried out: defining the business requirements and organizing information about existing communication systems.

To define business requirements, each business unit filled out a questionnaire on its planned growth of product offerings, enhancements, new services, etc., and what communications volume each item would produce. For example, the user would specify the needed response time and requirements for availability of service, as well as type and number of transactions per customer.

The job of describing existing information systems was relatively technical and involved acquiring specific information for each terminal and each type of message or transaction. The key dimensions were the geographical distribution and the nature of traffic.

These two sets of data together gave a projection of likely future communication demand. Kempin developed a computer model that related performance requirements and capacity needs to evaluate the impact of changing assumptions or different technologies. This model aided considerably in generating a discussion on real needs and feasible communication support. Seven cut-and-try efforts working with the users were needed to develop a set of requirements that seemed workable and affordable. Exhibits 3A and 3B show the traffic summaries.

The matrix of business and communications requirements confirmed that the existing traffic of over 800,000 transactions per day was sufficient to justify an integrated corporate network if all the traffic were on the network. It provided a factual basis for proceeding with the next phase of the network development of what was then called the Corporate Networking Study.

Network Design

The feasibility matrix served as the basis for the network design by Kempin's team. The team, in discussions with Nyce, Frackman, and senior managers, developed criteria that included: meeting business

EXHIBIT 3A Corporate Network Summary, January 1979

Traffic Type Summary

Traffic Type	Total Number of Transactions		Percent of Total		Average Message Length
Nonmanual traffic	837,205		55.7%		—
Interactive		335,015		22.3	434 characters
Bulk transmission		502,190		33.4	149
Manual traffic	664,600		44.3		138
	1,501,805		100.0%		

Geographic Traffic Summary

Geographic Breakdown	Total Number of Transactions		Percent of Total	
A. Interactive traffic				
Metropolitan	103,100		31%	
Domestic (excludes Metro)	193,380		57	
Trust		129,870		39
Wholesale		28,600		9
Securities		19,910		6
Retail upstate		15,000		3
International	38,535		12	
Total interactive traffic	335,015		100%	
B. Bulk traffic				
Metropolitan	7,000		2%	
Domestic (excludes Metro)	474,190		94	
Retail control system		430,000		86
All other		44,190		8
International	21,000		4	
Total bulk traffic	502,190		100%	

needs, containing the growth in communication costs, the use of established technologies that could be built upon in 1979, and a set of standards that were both worldwide and relatively permanent. They defined five generic networks as feasible alternatives:

1. Specialized networks (adaptation of existing facilities).
2. Public networks (offered by common carriers).
3. Vendor networks (architectures and interfaces).
4. Third-party designed networks.
5. Internally designed and managed networks.

As a first step in designing the proposed net, the team met with three major vendors to evaluate their network support: IBM for whole-

EXHIBIT 3B Worldwide Network

Networks/ Systems	Applications	Hardware	Software	Total Number of Transactions per Interactive
International				
Midas	An on-line accounting system which transfers funds between International Division and its clients.	IBM370/168, IBM3705 IBM SYS/7, IBMSA18080	MVS, TCAM, CICS	17,510/275
Cabex	A store and forward message switching system which provides for sending cables to overseas branches and common carriers.	PDPSE (Dual)	IBM2740 Emulation	7,600/650 1,250/650 700/650 375/300
Swift/DSL	A store and forward message switching system which speeds transfer of transactions.	IBM370/168 IBM 3705	MVS, TCAM, CICS, DSL (IBM PBM PROD)	1,250/250
Mars	An on-line minicomputer application providing reimbursement letters of credit for correspondent bank customers, where MHC is to be the paying agent.	PDP11/70VA		1,900/660
RJE/RTSO	Remote job-entry and time-sharing option.	IBM370/168	MVS, JES, TSO	N/A/100
Wholesale				
WDDA Inquire	An on-line system that provides on-line transaction processing, on-line command processing, and off-line reporting for wholesale, demand depositing.	IBM370/168 IBM3705	MVS, TCAM, JES, Inquire (Infodata) being replaced by CICS	7,000/870
CLS (Corporate Banking Center)	An on-line system that provides on-line transactions processing, on-line command processing, and off-line reporting for commercial loans.	IBM370/168 IBM 3705	MVS, TCAM, JES3, Inquire (Infodata)	3,600/900
DMTS	A funds transfer system which processes FED-IN and FED-OUT messages via a message collection and transfer processing system.	NCR8550 PDP 11/70 (Dual) (FES)	VPX (Virtual Processing Exec) COBOL, NEAT/VS	9,450/2,000

EXHIBIT 3B *(concluded)*

Networks/ Systems	Applications	Hardware	Software	Total Number of Transactions per Interactive
TRANSEND	A communications-based cash management service which provides corporate customers with demand deposit account reporting.	IBM 370/168 SYCOR 340 Mohawk/2402 (temporary)	TCAM, 2780 Emulation	—
Securities DCS (BOE)	An on-line system to maintain accounting information for government securities traded by customers, with a communications link to the FRB.	PDP 11/70's PDP 11/34's	RSX 11-M MHS-11 Fortran Four Plus MACRO-11	2,000/272
BTS	An on-line system which provides the PIB Dept. with capability to perform trade capture, report generation, fanfolds, and data base inquiry.	PDP 11/70	RSTS/E Basic Interpretor DMS-500 (D.B.)	TXNS: 3,510/200 Rpt. Lines 10,000
Trust SM&C	An on-line personal trust system which provides various MHC departments with securities movement and control functions.	IBM 370/158 IBM 3705 IV Phase Paradyne Pix II	MVS/JES2, BTAM, CICS	28,000/200
Transifac	An on-line stock transfer and shareholder record-keeping system which supports ticket flow, production, inquiry, account maintenance, and system control for corporate trust.	IBM 370/158 IBM 3705 IV Phase MPX Channel Adapter	MVS/JES2 GAM 2260 Emulation	100,000/350 (200,000 input and output screens)
Ostroll	A time-sharing system which provides the Trust Department with a market and financial analysis modeling capability.	IBM 370/158	MVS/JES2, BTAM, TSO EP/NCP	Small/100
IMPAC	An on-line reporting, processing, and settlement system, which allows customers to receive confirmations and confirm trades.	IBM 370/158	—	1,870/60/line
RJE and TSO	Remote job-entry and time-sharing option systems which support the Trust Department.	IBM 370/158	MVS/JES2, BTAM, BRAM TSO	N/A/100

	Description	Hardware	Software	
Retail				
CI/RF	An on-line system that provides a customer reference file capability for all retail demand deposit accounts for the metropolitan branch offices.	NCR/8570	IPC, NEAT/3	49,100/400 42,300 remote 6,800 local
Upstate network	A CI/RF-type network for the central, capital, and western region branches which supports on-line demand deposit accounting, savings, account inquiry, and account holds.	NCR/8570	NEAT/3	15,000/500 (estimate)
Retail Olivetti	An on-line system that provides the metropolitan region branches with passbook savings support such as passbook updates, monetary transactions, inquire and file maintenance.	IBM 370/168 IBM 3705	MVS, TCAM CICS	41,000/60
Security	A telemetry-based network which monitors various events at all metropolitan region branches for security purposes, and uses a subchannel of the retail savings net lines.	IBM 370/168 General Automation CPU, Diabold Transponders	Turnkey software by DELCO for G/A CPU	N/A/7
PS	An on-line personal loan, data entry, and inquiry system serving the metropolitan region and operating on local lines only.	NCR/8570	NEAT/3	13,000/950
Affiliates				
MR Leasing	A time-sharing system which provides the MHC Leasing Corp. with financial analysis modeling for clients requiring equipment leasing for financing.	DEC 20/40 Varian/77, MPX	BASIC	(27,500/N/A share/day)
Ritter	An on-line system which piggybacks on the Beneficial Finance Cos. BVENCOM System, and provides for loan entry, payment, inquiries, and reports.	IBM 370/168, IBM 3705 IBM SYS/7 Concentrators	PARS, NCP Beneficial developed software	N/A/N/A
Total internal				314,115/442

EXHIBIT 4 Summary of NAC Analysis: Manufacturers Hanover Telecommunications Architecture Evaluation Matrix, December 1978

Technical Criteria	SNA	DECNET II	DNA	MHC–Built, X.25–Based Net
Heterogeneity	Good	Fair	Good	Good
Internetworking	Fair	Poor	Superior	Superior
Addressing	Superior	Superior	Superior	Superior
Functionality	Good	Fair	Superior	Superior
Performance	Fair	Good	Unknown	Good
Expandability	Good	Superior	Superior	Superior
Topology	Fair	Good	Good	Superior
Special features	Fair	Fair	Good	Good

EXHIBIT 5 Comparison of Network Alternatives—I: Management Criteria

Type of Networks	User Interface	Management Control	Technical Performance Monitoring	Size of Internal Management Group
A. Specialized networks	Ideal, direct	No centralized control	Little monitoring	Many small groups
B. Public networks	Second-hand through internal support group	Little control	Excellent control of network	One small group
C. Vendor interfaces	Second-hand	Little control	Excellent control of software	One small group
D. Third-party designed networks	Second-hand	Indirect through internal group	Indirect control through internal group	One moderate group
E. Internal design and management	Good, single internal group	Ideal, direct, internal, centralized	Good monitoring of both network and software through internal NCC	One large group

sale, NCR for retail, and DEC for corporate. Initial appraisal indicated no one supplier had a system that would accommodate other communication systems. Needing an independent view of these alternatives, the team contracted with Network Analysis Corporation (NAC) to review the networks solutions offered by IBM, NCR, and DEC, and to advise which approach could best serve their needs. Exhibit 4 is a summary of NAC's evaluations. Their report noted that in 1978 each vendor required the almost exclusive use of its own equipment; none offered flexibility or international communication presence.

NAC recommended a packet switched network with X.25 as the communication protocol. Kempin, working with the consulting team, developed an X.25 trial configuration for comparative analysis. Exhibit 5 shows the criteria and the evaluation. A MHC-developed net, based on X.25 packet switching technology, was indicated.

Major Responsibility for Network Maintenance	Ability to Respond to Change	Simplicity	Risk	Fragmentation of Approach	Consistency of Approach with MHC Goals
Directly with application	Very low	Excellent	Moderate	High	Low
Outside	Low	Good	Low	Moderate	Low
Outside	Low	Good	Low	Moderate	Low
Shared between third party and internal group	Moderate	Fair	Moderate	None	High
Directly with internal group	High	Fair	Moderate	None	Total

Nyce, Frackman, and Kempin concluded that packet switching was really the only viable option to use in its international operations and that it would be the best long-term solution for the bank as a whole. Of all the alternatives it was consistently best on all the management criteria, and average or good on other dimensions. It could support many suppliers and was accepted as an international standard, and its use in Europe and the Far East proved it a workable communication means. The other major alternative was to wait for IBM to make its communications systems available. IBM had announced that their Systems Network Architecture (SNA) would enable a customer to establish a complex, privately owned, communications network, but that was at least three years away.

The final step in the analysis was a cost/benefit study that compared the MHC-managed, X.25-based network with the projected costs of continuing the current approach of specialized networks. This comparison was especially difficult because no reliable figures existed for current telecommunications costs. Expenses and capital equipment associated with communications were buried in many different accounts such as equipment, data processing, and miscellaneous. By painstakingly going through the chart of accounts for the different departments and conservatively assessing which costs should be associated with communications, the team was able to estimate current and future communication expenses. Exhibit 6 gives the projected cash flows associated with the two options.

The economic analysis of an X.25 net produced a sobering reality. An investment analysis of the net with only the money saved on telecommunications costs as income and a 15 percent hurdle rate produced a negative discounted cash flow. In the short run the integrated net would be a cost avoidance investment and not a source of cost savings. Furthermore, most of the returns would probably come from increased revenues and more customers, but no one wanted to attempt to project those numbers.

The Corporate Network Development Phase I

Frackman and Kempin proposed implementing a pilot net and developing the functional specifications for an integrated network in the fall of 1978. The projects were planned to complement each other, with the functional spec team identifying which uncertainties to test and the pilot team testing as well as defining the nature of the network design problem. They envisioned this net as a worldwide utility that would provide the lowest cost communications service to the bank. The proposal was approved by the Automation Steering Committee to continue the networking study with a budget of $336,000 for 1979. In approving

EXHIBIT 6   Corporate Network Facility (CNF): Cash Flow Analysis

Data Transmission		Cash Expenditures					
	1981	1982	1983	1984	1985	1986	1987
I. With CNF							
1. CNF direct expense	$(9,130)	$(8,727)	$(9,084)	$(9,722)	$(10,351)	$(11,227)	$(12,435)
2. Tax benefit—59.05 percent	5,391	5,153	5,364	5,741	6,112	6,630	7,343
3. Depreciation	1,647	2,066	1,869	1,651	1,417	1,166	896
4. CNF after-tax cash expenses	(2,092)	(1,508)	(1,851)	(2,330)	(2,822)	(3,431)	(4,196)
5. Add: Equipment purchases, net of investment tax credit	(5,273)	(450)	(450)	(450)	(450)	(450)	(450)
6. CNF after-tax cash flow	(7,365)	(1,958)	(2,301)	(2,780)	(3,272)	(3,881)	(4,646)
7. Add: Data transmission expenses from existing networks	(8,836)	(6,729)	(8,074)	(9,689)	(11,627)	(13,952)	(16,743)
8. Tax benefit—59.05 percent	5,218	3,973	4,768	5,721	6,866	8,239	9,887
9. Cash flow with CNF	(10,983)	(4,714)	(5,607)	(6,748)	(8,033)	(9,594)	(11,502)
II. Without CNF							
10. Data transmission expenses	(11,214)	(13,457)	(16,148)	(19,378)	(23,253)	(27,904)	(33,485)
11. Associated maintenance staff	(474)	(694)	(954)	(1,259)	(1,617)	(2,032)	(2,516)
12. Tax benefit—59.05 percent	6,902	8,356	10,099	12,186	14,686	17,677	21,259
13. Cash flow without CNF	(4,786)	(5,785)	(7,003)	(8,451)	(10,184)	(12,259)	(14,742)
14. Net cash flow with CNF (line 9 minus line 13)	(6,197)	1,081	1,396	1,703	2,151	2,665	3,240
15. Present value of net cash flow, discounted at 15 percent	$(5,391)	$ 817	$ 919	$ 974	$ 1,069	$ 1,151	$ 1,218

16. Net present value of future cash flows . . . . $ 757
17. Add: 1979 and 1980 CNF cash flow, after tax, in current dollars . . . . (3,717)
18. Net present value with CNF . $(2,960)

EXHIBIT 7   MHC Pilot Network

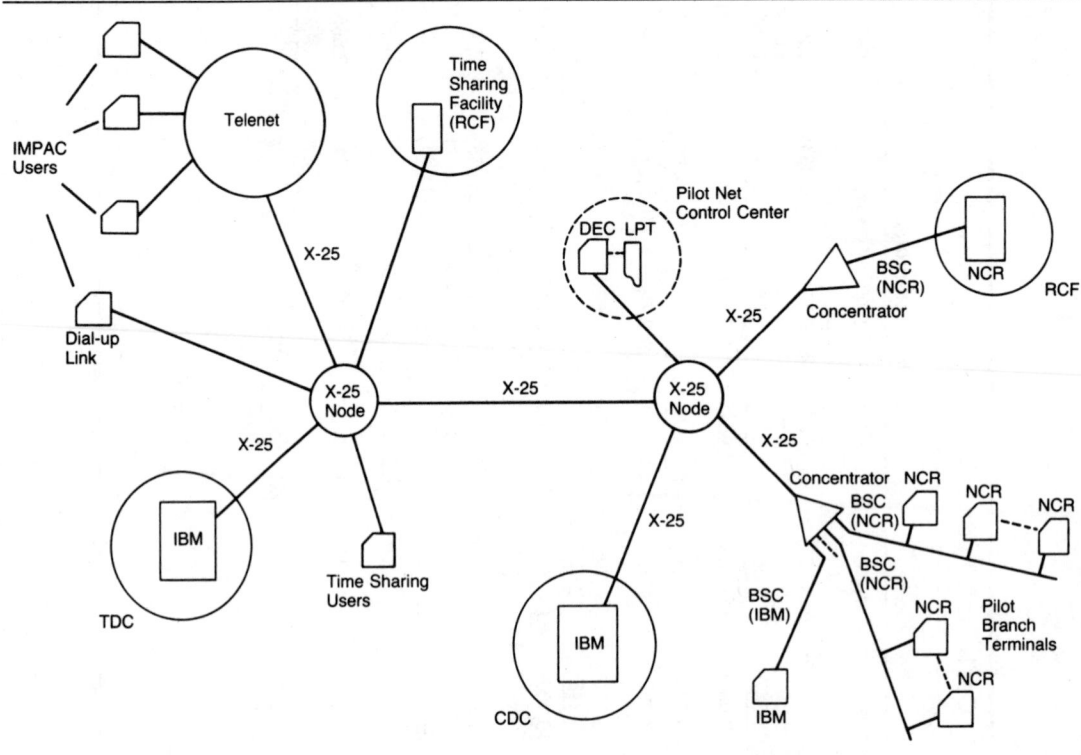

the budget, senior management concluded that an internal group would be more responsive to the business needs of the bank and that control of the network would insulate the corporation from some of the uncertainty that could come from depending on multiple vendors.

The pilot study objectives were (1) to gain an understanding of how to develop and to manage an X.25 net; and (2) to prove to the organization the versatility and performance of the system. The team that developed the pilot worked closely with the team defining the functional specifications to clarify MHC needs. The pilot network consisted of a small scale X.25 network with sufficient components (nodes, concentrators, and control center) and links (communication lines with different protocols), schematically shown in Exhibit 7. Two nodes and concentrators were linked to five different communication services:

1.   Interfacing the Trust Data Center IBM computer to a public network using the X.25 communications standard.

2. Interfacing the Retail NCR system via a communication processor using NCR's 796 protocol, and the Corporate Data Center IBM system via available 370X software to an X.25 network. In this way the wholesale and the retail systems were accessible to one another.
3. Integrating a time-sharing connection to the MHC Remote Computing Facility (RCF) from one of the test nodes. This permitted testing of the routing capability of an X.25 network between nodes and the time-sharing service.
4. Simulating a network control center to capture and report performance and status information.
5. Interfacing a terminal concentrator to the X.25 network to demonstrate the ability of a single network to support different terminals such as the IBM 3270 and the NCR 796–501.

The first and third links were existing services that were using leased specialized nets. The second link was between two applications that presently were running in different systems with a demonstrated need to communicate to each other. The fifth was to test the ability of X.25 to link to different terminals and different systems.

The pilot came up in the summer of 1979 and after a few implementation glitches achieved all its technical goals. The X.25 net had demonstrated its ability to link a wide range of MHC applications, on different equipment, in a transparent fashion. In fact the trust department decided to put their new IMPAC system up on the corporate network as soon as possible. IMPAC allowed customers to have on-line access to their securities trading information. A second application, TRANSEND, was added shortly thereafter. TRANSEND gave wholesale customers on-line information on their DDA transactions. Before the corporate net, TRANSEND had been serviced by the GE Timesharing System, which involved a cumbersome transfer of files between systems. The prime reason for using GE was the need for broad access to customers. The corporate net provided the necessary coverage at a savings of $1 million per year. Soon after, the MHC time-sharing service adopted the corporate net as its communication support, allowing the bank to bring this application in-house also.

The Implementation of a Full Scale GEONET

Following the successful pilot and completion of the functional specifications, Frackman was provided funds in the fall of 1979 for the first phase of the net's full scale implementation, which was to officially be called GEONET. The implementation was more complicated than originally anticipated. Frackman and her staff already had two applications shifting to GEONET, which they had not initially planned for; a third, electronic mail, was to start in the first quarter of 1980. As a result it was necessary to continue to operate the pilot equipment while planning and implementing the full-blown network.

The specifications for the full scale net were sent to five qualified suppliers. Three responded seriously and Telenet was selected as the main supplier. By December of 1980 GEONET was supporting TRANSEND, IMPAC, the time-sharing data center, and electronic mail, domestically and internationally. Competition and new product development had shifted some focus from conversion to supporting the introduction of new products on the network. A second diversion was the planning of local area networks for buildings within New York City, a pressing issue for the telecommunications staff as MHC space needs grew. In 1981, top management reaffirmed their commitment to the implementation of GEONET through completion in late 1982.

By the end of 1981 the net linked New York, London, Hong Kong, Singapore, Bangkok, Kuala Lumpur, Djakarta, Tokyo, Seoul, and Caracas with a private X.25 net. The net had access via pubic networks throughout the United States and 40 other countries on six continents. The telecommunications group continued to support the four initial applications while adding six new services. The experience of the first two years made them aware of the complexities and time lags in dealing with overseas communication agencies. For Frackman, this reinforced the need to have business planning to guide the net's development. Meetings were held to involve the responsible managers in building the net in the correct locations and with adequate capacity. The expansion included 10 switching nodes and 15 concentrators for a total of about $4 million. A prime rationale for this investment was controlling communication costs through the purchase of equipment and volume use of the owned system.

In 1982/1983 the net continued to expand in geographic coverage and new services. In reviewing the budget for a two-year program, Frackman emphasized that one of the advantages of the existing net was its quick response to new products or facilities. There had also been a noticeable flattening of the growth of communication costs. Projected total expense of data transmissions for 1983 was expected to increase 18.9 percent, down from the 22.7 percent in 1982. Unfortunately, however, traffic volume was not up to plan by a significant margin. Traffic growth was lower than predicted due to lower than expected conversion of high-volume specialty nets and some optimistic projections on the part of users. Nevertheless, in general the converted users were using more traffic than planned, particularly for electronic mail and time-sharing. The conversion of existing nets to GEONET was lagging primarily due to the support of products in development and new services coming on-line.

Frackman introduced a new planning approach based upon a "location analysis form," for 1983–84, to capture business inputs by site from users. The form covered market profitability, operational needs, telecommunication alternatives, and GEONET cost projections. This evaluation resulted in a three-level approach for 1983–84; to push forward with the connection of subsidiary and affiliate offices located in or near domestic nodes; to complete 11 overseas cities already in progress; and to expand the net to an additional 11 cities which should be the last big push. This would allow 1984 to be the year for converting existing nets and building up traffic volume.

Frackman pointed out the difference between the 1980 plan and the 1982 network plan in a budget review meeting. The startling fact was the net as of December 1982 was more than twice as large as planned in December of 1980: two overseas nodes planned versus five existing nodes and six planned versus 12 actual domestic nodes. The basic cause was new product development to meet or lead competition in the wholesale and the expanding global market. This expansion had had the strong support of senior management and had been included in the normal budget process. The result was a capital investment through 1984 of almost three times the amount planned. The critical cost increase was recurring expense growth, in large part because the net was bigger than planned. A second reason for the variance in recurring expenses was the large number of parallel circuits that were not on GEONET. This delivered a strong message on the importance of converting users to GEONET in order to achieve economies of scale and be more cost competitive.

The expansions planned for 1983 were completed toward the end of that year (Exhibit 8). The traffic volume estimate for 4.8 million packets by December was not achieved. Although no new conversions were made, seven new products were added to the net. One of the largest uses of the network was the office automation application, providing electronic mail, spreadsheet analysis, word processing, data retrieval, etc. Electronic mail alone produced one of the highest volumes of any application; it had expanded geographically so that in 1984 there was equipment in 33 cities in 20 countries, plus 17 domestic locations. The plans for 1984 were to expand into over 30 more locations. Those areas that were not directly on the network usually had access to GEONET through public networks.

When the network was first installed, the approach had been to support only packet switched communications. Since that time the telecommunications staff realized that the network would also need to support circuit switched communications capability. In addition there was a pilot program testing the ability to connect Local Area Nets (LANs) to GEONET in the fourth quarter.

EXHIBIT 8 The List of Current Installations as Reported by March 8 and Planned GEONET Implementation (March 31, 1984)

CURRENT INT'L LOCATIONS	EQUIP
Hong Kong Branch MH Leasing	M C T
Singapore Branch	M C
Kuala Lumpur Malaysia, Rep	T
Tokyo Branch Japan	C
Seoul Branch MH Leasing	C T
Jakarta, Rep MHLC	C T
Bangkok, Rep Thailand	C
Taipei Branch	C
Manila, Branch Philippines	C
U.K., London: Queens B. HSE Boardman HSE	M C C
Guernsey, Br.	C
Switzerland Berne Zurich Br.	M C
Bahrain Branch	W C
Caracas, Rep MHLC	T C
Bogota, Rep Colombia	C
W. Germany Frankfurt, Br. Dusseldorf, Br. Hamburg, Br. Hanover, Br.	C C C C
Buenos Aires Br., Argentina	C
Cairo, Branch Rep, Egypt	C T
Bank Nordique Paris	C

CURRENT DOMESTIC LOCATIONS	EQUIP
U.S.A. Los Angeles California MHCC Office	M C
Denver, COLO	M
Dallas, TX	M
Chicago, ILL MHIBC	M C
New York City	
4NYP, NYC	NCC 4M
55 Water 270 Park Hicksville	M M M
Cleveland, OH	M
Atlanta, GA MHCC Office MHIBC	M T C
Boston, Mass. MHIBC	C
Wilmington, Delaware MHBA	C

1984 INTL. IN PROGRESS LOCATIONS	EQUIP	TARGET DATE
Rio, Sao Paulo Rep, MHLC Brazil	C T	4Q/84
Bucharest, Br. Bucharest	C	2Q/84
Italy: Milan Branch Rome Branch Milan Leasing	C C T	2Q/84
Spain: Madrid, Branch Madrid, Rep. Barcelona, Br.	C T C	4Q/84
Belgium Antwerp Brussels	C C	2Q/84
Bnk MendesCans Amsterdam	C	3Q/84
Luxembourg	C	Hold
Bombay, Rep India	C	3Q/84
Osaka, Rep Tokyo	C	3Q/84
Istanbul, Br Turkey	C	3Q/84
Lisbon, Br Portugal	C	4Q/84
Sydney, Rep Australia	C	Hold
Beijing, Rep P.R. China	C	Hold

Legend: C–Concentrator   M–Mode
         T–Terminal   NCC–Network control

1984 DOMESTIC PLANNED LOCATIONS	EQUIP	TARGET DATE
Chicago, Ill		
MHCC	T	2Q/84
MHMC	T	Hold
National LPO	T	Hold
Oaklawn, Ill		
MHMC	T	Hold
Schaumburg, Ill		
MHMC	T	|
MICHIGAN Farmington, Mich.		H
MHMC	T	
Detroit, Mich.		O
MHMC	T	
Grand Rapids, Mich.		L
MHMC	T	
Lansing, Mich. MHMC	T	D
Warren, Mich. MHMC	T	|
Cleveland, OH MHMC	T	Hold
San Francisco MHIBC	C	2Q/84
Dallas, TX MHCC Office	T	4Q/84
Houston, TX MHIBC	C	2Q/84
VIRGINIA Danville, Vir. MHCC	T	2Q/84
ARIZONA Phoenix MHMC	T	Hold
Los Angeles, CA MHIBC	C	
National LPO	T	2Q/84
Miami, Fl. MHIBC	C	2Q/84

1984 NYC PLANNED LOCATIONS	EQUIP	TARGET DATE
New York, USA Wholesale, CBC		|
4 NYP	8C	
270 Park	C	|
Empire Station	C	
CBC, 1460 Bway	C	|
CBC, 40 Wall	C	
CBC, 530 Fifth	C	3Q/84
CBC, Plaza	C	
CBC, Chrysler Bldg.	C	|
CBC, Time/Life Bldg.	C	|
CBC, Queens	C	|
CBC, Long Island	C	|
CBC, White Plains	C	
MHCC—Mac	C	2Q/84

The Management Control Issue of Charge Out

The GEONET project was carried as a development project through 1983 and all associated costs had been absorbed into corporate overhead. Although there had been some discussions of future chargeback, no charges were actually assessed in order to encourage use of the system and to absorb the typical start-up costs of a new development. As Ed Nyce pointed out: "We had to learn all over again the complexities of how to equitably charge for a resource that has high fixed costs regardless of usage, as well as an ongoing developmental expense—it was DP circa 1968."

The major objectives in setting the charge-out rates were to reach break-even between recovery and expenses by the fourth quarter of 1984, and to charge in accordance with varying levels of performance and usage.

For financial statements and external reporting purposes, MHC expensed all development and operations expenses associated with GEONET as incurred, as they did with all data processing and communications applications. However, the MHC management control system used a different procedure. There were two major types of expenses: direct charges, a manager can usually control, and for which he or she is held responsible, and indirect charges, generally out of the manager's control but allocated both to inform the manager of the indirect costs associated with business and to enable the company to see the return from each area on a fully allocated basis.

In early 1983, Frackman asked Greg Ward, deputy controller, for help in developing a chargeback algorithm to use for GEONET within the management control system. MHC adopted a usage-sensitive method (measured in packets) similar to that used by public data networks. These charges included traffic charges, connect charges, access port charges, host concentrator charges, and installation charges. The prices for the latter two were derived from standard MHC, full absorption costing. For traffic and connect charges the policy was to set prices as an average over five years, intended to be slightly below current market prices. The kilopacket (1,000 packets) charge was set to recover the costs of the backbone network, including the computerized switching nodes and leased lines, by the end of the period.

Greg Ward commented in a discussion paper on this set of pricing policies for GEONET:

> Although corporate policy normally requires that transfer prices provide for full recovery of all expenses each year, it is reasonable in this case to allow for underabsorption of expenses initially, coupled with the intent to eventually fully recover this amount within a reasonable time frame. The underabsorptions for 1983 and

1984 should be charged to a newly established R&D department. Overabsorptions in the future should be credited to the R&D department. An updated forecast of recovery and expenses should be made each year to determine whether or not rates should be revised in order to attain the goal of full recovery over the five-year period.

Ward also commented,

> Essentially, we are looking for two break-even points. The first one will come when GEONET's quarterly costs are fully recovered within the same quarter. The second one will come when all the costs from 1984 forward will have been recovered.
>
> If we had based prices on costs and used fully absorbed costing, essentially all users would have been substantially discouraged from using the network due to the high prices.

Implementation of the cost system was to begin in the summer of 1984 with full implementation in 1985. Users were to see the actual price list for the first time in August 1984. Beginning in the third quarter of 1984 the managers would be assessed the costs of GEONET on an indirect basis, and in 1985 they would probably be billed on a direct basis. Use of Telenet or other public network services telecommunications would be billed on a direct basis starting in 1984.

Exhibit 9 shows a comparison of GEONET and Telenet rates. In every category, GEONET prices were less than the corresponding service from Telenet. Attaining complete absorption of costs, at those prices, was heavily dependent on sufficient volumes of traffic passing through the network.

The Opportunities in Spring 1984

The biggest problem for the managers of GEONET in 1984 was to increase the network's volume: traffic estimates for the network were much higher than actual volume. In July 1984 the average usage was about 3 million packets per day, where the plan had indicated 4.8 million by December of 1983. Frackman noted:

> We had been very conservative in the growth rates we assumed in predicting our usage figures. In fact usage has been much greater than we expected in the applications now up and running. We ran into problems with the conversions. Those took longer than expected.

Ed Nyce commented on some of the issues surrounding the process of implementation of GEONET:

> The overseas people wanted GEONET right away. It gave them more access, better service, etc., than they could get from the local

EXHIBIT 9 Comparison of Telenet and GEONET Rates: Proposed
GEONET Rates (1983)

Description	GEONET	Telenet[1]	Units
Traffic charges:			
Domestic	$ 1.40	$ 1.55	Kilopackets
International	13.50	15.00[2]	"
Connect charges (for dial-up):			
Domestic	3.51	3.90/6.90[4]	Hours
International	16.20	18.00[2]	"
Access concentrator port charges:			
Domestic—stand alone			
300/1,200 baud	115	550[3]	Port/month
2,400 baud	210	925	"
4,800 baud	315	925	"
9,600 baud	625	1,400	"
Domestic—redundant			
300/1,200 baud	275	N.A.	Port/month
2,400 baud	365	N.A.	"
4,800 baud	550	N.A.	"
9,600 baud	1,100	N.A.	"

Description	GEONET	Telenet[1]	Units
International—redundant			
300/1,200 baud	$ 475	N.A.	Port/month
2,400 baud	630	N.A.	"
4,800 baud	945	N.A.	"
9,600 baud	1,890	N.A.	"
One-time installation charges			
Domestic—stand alone			
300/1,200 baud	530	1,000	Port
Other speeds	770	1,000	"
Domestic—redundant			
300/1,200 baud	830	N.A.	"
Other speeds	1,330	N.A.	"
International—redundant			
300/1,200 baud	1,000	N.A.	"
Other speeds	1,600	N.A.	"
Host concentrator charges:			
Domestic TP3010 system			
Stand alone			
rental	1,800	N.A.	Concentrator/month
Redundant			
rental	3,200	N.A.	"

[1]List price.
[2]U.K. rates used as average.
[3]Within 100 miles of Telenet access facilities.
 Add $125/month for each additional 100 miles.
[4]High density $3.90, low density cities $6.90 per hour.

EXHIBIT 9   *(concluded)*

Description	GEONET	Telenet[1]	Units
One-time installation			
Stand alone	5,000	N.A.	"
Redundant	7,500	N.A.	"

Description	GEONET	Telenet[1]	Units
International TP3010 system			
Stand alone			
rental	$ 3,100	N.A.	Concentrator/month
Redundant rental	5,500	N.A.	"
One-time installation			
Stand alone	7,500	N.A.	"
Redundant	10,000	N.A.	"
TP4000 dual system			
Domestic rental	10,100	N.A.	Concentrator/month
International rental	*	N.A.	"
One-time installation	*	N.A.	Concentrator
TP4000 quad system			
Domestic rental	13,100	N.A.	Concentrator/month
International	*	N.A.	"
One-time installation	*	N.A.	Concentrator
X.25 link			
Domestic	1,200	N.A.	Month
International	1,500	N.A.	"

*Rates by arrangement with MHCT.
[1]List price.

facilities. The domestic U.S. people also wanted GEONET, at least those who have dial-up facilities. The security in that environment is poor and GEONET helps them with that. In New York City, where you deal with big data centers of 1,000 terminals, you begin to get into another set of problems. They are accustomed to very fast telecommunications and response time. They are worried that GEONET will degrade performance of their system, that it will make the communications remote instead of local, and that it will give the control of communications to someone else.

Since GEONET's implementation, IBM had begun to offer better telecommunications support; SNA was becoming more standardized and satisfying more communications needs. A fully compatible SNA for all IBM products was promised by 1986. Further, a recent product announced by IBM would provide a gateway to connect the SNA and X.25 environments. This led some of the operating groups to want to wait for an IBM communications solution, a point of view continually sold by the IBM sales force.

Senior Management Views of GEONET

Dick Groppa, vice president of technical staff services, was responsible for office automation and other support of professionals and staff in MHC. Frackman had hired Dick as a long-range technology planner for the operations division, but as the bank moved to VIOCs this function was decentralized and Groppa moved into a new position as head of office automation. His area was born at about the same time as was GEONET, 1976–1977.

Groppa's responsibility was to provide computer and communications support for the professionals and clerical personnel in MHC and to survey the marketplace to determine which products and services might be added. Groppa reflected on GEONET's development:

> Currently we have 5,000–6,000 electronic mail users. Over half of the professionals in this organization, worldwide, use some portion of the bundle of tools we provide every day. This could not have happened without GEONET. Some people would say that it is a chicken and egg question: did the GEONET highway create the usage or did the usage cause the spread of the highway? In our case I think it was the former.
>
> GEONET has allowed us to provide one type of asynchronous application after another. This has given us much greater flexibility than if we had to offer a fully integrated, tightly coupled solution like PROFS.[3] What I like about GEONET is that, by design, it can take advantage of all the different technologies.

Howard Sorgan, senior vice president and deputy general manager of global wholesale activities, gave his impressions.

> We have to be a low-cost producer and GEONET is cost effective, reliable, flexible, and secure.
>
> Today our profit from credit-based businesses is going down, but noncredit profits are going up. GEONET is the delivery mechanism. From this point of view, investment in technology is important. The system will surely reduce costs in the long term; however,

---

[3]PROFS was IBM's integrated office productivity product that included electronic mail, analysis capabilities, and data management.

the advantages are invisible to the user. Explaining the value of GEONET to the customer is very difficult.

As a vice president for global wholesale, Wendy Richman was in a staff role with responsibility for talking with the systems people and the users of the systems for all products in her area. In her current role she had considerable contact with users of GEONET, both inside and outside the bank. Commenting on how GEONET was received by her staff, Richman said:

> It is innovative, leading edge, and has taken us ahead of the competition. I am convinced of its strategic necessity. The network decision is whether centralized or decentralized is better for the corporate purpose. The latter approach allows more adaptations and customized products, but the former gives more centralized information access for the customer, which is obviously more economical. We want a mix of the two—the only way this is workable is through GEONET.

John Reynolds, vice president in the national accounts division, was in charge of correspondent bank relationships. He shared some of his experiences with GEONET and its implementation at MHC:

> Our area has over 2,200 relationships in 48 states and we cover this territory with less than 12 people. We could not do that kind of business without the use of GEONET. The economics of our products are driven by the telecommunications support we have. We are continually competing for funds at attractive rates. With a good telecommunications network, with low transaction costs and good service, it makes that job easier to accomplish.

Richard Matteis, senior vice president of cash management services, one of MHC's largest nonfunds-based businesses, was responsible for the cash management services the bank offered its corporate clients. Matteis reflected on his impressions of GEONET:

> When I came here last year, after 12 years at Citibank, I was pleasantly surprised to find MHC had done what Citi was currently planning—a truly global interactive communications network. GEONET allows me to develop and deliver cash management products worldwide with no worry about communications. A key planning assumption is the availability of a link. This reduces market entry by months and allows a faster rate of product introduction. I couldn't understand why they do not market their system to their advantage; it was as if they had a technological inferiority complex. Now I am beginning to understand it is the culture of MHC to talk about business and customer relationships first and then

technology. Perhaps with time they will be more aggressive as they see the two integrating more.

We are very close to the point where we are connected electronically to all of our major wholesale customers. This will be reinforced as we merge data and voice together to provide a common link. The latter is a part of the present challenge for telecommunication processing: to integrate all the systems into common links, in a standardized process. The challenge is to get all systems to talk to each other and be hardware independent. It is a common objective for all banks but a complicated engineering and management problem. The upcoming conversion is going to be tough when we start shifting more to high-volume work in retail. However, the payoff for a common net is great.

The availability of the net is key, as it allows me to accommodate my different markets as they change. For example, in Latin America GEONET links to correspondent banks are a competitive advantage, which they are not in Europe. However, in Europe GEONET is a strong lever with international corporations. The availability allows me to tailor my services and prices in accordance with particular markets. For the 1985 plan I have been working with Jack Evans on how to invest in new products on the basis of what I need and what he can deliver at what price. A major advantage we have is a product costing system that allows a basis for deciding what products to introduce where.

Because of the effort to add high-volume internal applications to the network, the network's performance concerned many potential users. Gunther Kempin discussed three major areas in which his group was working to better support the bank's user community.

A major concern is the 1.0–1.5 seconds added delay to on-line systems when these systems are shifted to an X.25-based packet switching system. I feel that user cooperation in fine tuning the on-line systems could result in the elimination of most, if not all, of the added delay, and that a good, average 3–5 second on-line response time could be maintained.

A second area of concern in the network's performance is the modification of the network to better handle the volume of data it must support. The original Telenet equipment did not have the throughput capacity required, but improvements to the equipment hardware and software were being implemented so that the volume requirements could be met. It is going to be a challenge to convince some early users that the system will perform as promised.

The third area of work involves linking local area networks to the packet switching network. Early efforts in this area have resulted in a new interface design, which is currently being developed. When completed, it will provide transparent linking between users on the local area network and users on the packet switching network. A key issue in this development is the appropriate addressing scheme that would maintain security yet allow broad access among users.

Frackman commented on telecommunications personnel's relationship with other people in the operations department and how it might affect further implementation of GEONET:

> We have not been able to spend a great deal of time dealing with the technical staff because of time pressures. We sold top-down because of business concerns and expediency. We did not seek their advice perhaps as much as we might have when we decided on technical alternatives, particularly on the X.25 decision and then the choice of supplier, but we had a tight time schedule and strong competitive pressure.
>
> Understandably, they are a bit unhappy, as all technical people have a point of view and want to be consulted. This has generated a bit of latent animosity in that all glitches are quickly pointed out and genuine cooperative efforts are difficult to initiate. However, to move forward we really need their active participation. I just wish they did not have such narrow perspectives—always worrying about system idiosyncrasies and never the overall corporate view.

Steve Sheinheit, vice president of computer technology services, Stan Wine, a senior technical officer in trust, and Nick Sziklai, a vice president of global wholesale technical support, were discussing some of the issues surrounding the implementation and use of GEONET in their respective departments.

Among Steve's responsibilities was strategic planning and review of technical research for the operations department. He was in a staff role that supported the line operations groups. Steve reflected on the early days of GEONET:

> The original plan was visionary. Not many large institutions were doing this sort of planning at all. . . . The original selling of GEONET was like evangelistic preaching. That was probably necessary to get it off the ground, but now we are in a period of mending fences that were broken in the early implementation and planning of the system.

Stan Wine discussed some of the implications of GEONET for trust, where he was responsible for keeping the data center in his department operating successfully.

One major concern we have with GEONET is that it might present problems with software and hardware upgrades. IBM is continually announcing new communications capabilities for our software and hardware. If IBM announces a new feature or capability that would be desirable in our environment, we would be quite concerned if we were not able to adopt it because of some incompatibility it might have with GEONET.

Nick Sziklai coordinated the activities of the different global wholesale data centers around the world. He added:

We have been discussing many issues, but I feel that there is one central issue—change. We are introducing change and we all want to know where the management control will be. The technical problems we can deal with. The diagnostics, communication, etc., can be solved and there will still be a reluctance to give up control of communications when your user still expects you to handle it. . . . A certain level of service must be provided, your users expect that. Communications, from the point of view of running a service business, must be a utility. A key question is who has responsibility for that utility.

In wholesale, we have an absolute dependence on GEONET to transport information for our business. We need an IBM mainframe connection both in the United States and worldwide. Our biggest worry is that the IBM support has been coming on last and we need that one the most.

Stan Wine responded:

I agree with Nick, we need to know where the control will be. We have optimized our system, and trained our people to identify problems and diagnostic methods. We will need to know how those resources will be affected by GEONET.

Leigh Ahrens, vice president of trust and securities automation, was responsible for the trust operations, which handled millions of transactions for both individuals and institutions. There were some implementation problems when the trust department first started using GEONET. The trust staff had difficulty with the equipment and access to the network. The telecommunications staff realized, with hindsight, that they had attempted to make this conversion before they had the necessary manpower available for the job. Ahrens reflected on his operation and its relationship to GEONET:

It has taken our technicians a long time to tune our system and build up our expertise and diagnostic capabilities to the point where they are today. In the majority of our applications we don't have need for a packet switched network. We have over 4 million customers for whom we handle stock transfer. All the data is transferred locally. We simply need a big, reliable pipe to ship that data from one place to another. Any change to our existing, reliable network must be made with great care. In some of our other applications we have had reliability and performance problems with GEONET. . . .

We cannot afford any degradation of performance due to the high transaction volumes processed and critical nature of the work.

We'll get there eventually but a big issue is who will control it? Who will provide the support and diagnostics?

Carl Morales, senior vice president of retail banking systems, had joined MHC in the operations division. In 1970, he had been the manager who hired Gunther Kempin to aid in the technical problems they had at the time. As head of retail operations, Carl was responsible for all retail systems at MHC. Most of these were clustered in and around the metropolitan New York City area, but with increasing deregulation, retail would probably expand to a much wider geographic area in the United States. Carl expressed some concerns about GEONET:

In the past I had three basic problems with our telecommunications folks. First, at the beginning of this process it was not properly sold to the end users. The DP people were the primary "end users" and they were not involved correctly. The issue of who will control the network and who will be responsible if something goes wrong was never fully addressed.

Second, Roberta and her folks have not been able to present cost saving numbers that I can compare with my current budget to see if GEONET will save me money. I need to know what the costs and associated charges will be. Also packet switching may not be the best service for a tight geographical environment, like metropolitan New York.

Third, they have yet to demonstrate the capability of the network in an environment like mine. I have huge volumes of transactions and I am not yet sure what it will do to my response time, error rates, security, etc.

Even though we have these disagreements, we are continually working to fix them. We have already started some very fruitful discussions. In fact Roberta and I have a very good relationship. The friction on these issues is at the day-to-day working level in the organization.

Jack Evans, commenting on the current state of GEONET, noted:

It is now time to get on with the conversion. In the beginning there was no time to convert because of new business needs and

---

EXHIBIT 10   Manufacturers Hanover Trust Telecommunications: Available GEONET Services (1984)

Functionality supported: Interface software

- Most of the computer and terminal devices in the following environments: IBM, DEC, Honeywell, Prime, Tandem, NCR.
- Telex.
- Wide variety of asynchronous equipment at speeds up to 9,600 baud per second.
- Wide variety of synchronous equipment at speeds up to 9,600 baud per second.
- Host interfaces at speeds up to 9,600 baud per second.
- Plans to convert to 56,000 baud per second or more, where needed.

Applications supported for both internal and external customers

- GEOTELX—interactive telex service allowing access to MHT services and databases worldwide.
- Advanced Information Services Office Automation System—an integrated system which provides several computer-based services including: management communications, single terminal access to other bank systems, word processing, data processing, financial planning packages, and remote networking.
- TRANSEND—Wholesale Demand Deposit Accounting Information which provides balance and transaction information, and funds transfer capabilities—on line.
- FACTS Expanded Inquiry Service—gives clients immediate access to their security records.
- GEO-FX—Foreign Exchange Advisory Service assists clients in assessing current and potential FX trades.
- Global Exposure System (GES)—gives management and account officers information on MHT's exposure in each country, region, and market segment.
- Interactive Computer Facility (ICF)—MHT's in-house time-sharing facility. Its functions include: IFPS (financial modeling), IDA (conversational statistics), Tell-a-Graf/Cuechart (graphics), DPL (data management).
- GEOPAC Total Securities Services—provides processing, inquiries, messages, instructions, and immediate information exchange between MHT and the security holders.
- Trade Account System—an automated system to handle the trading activity of recognized securities dealers and larger banks.
- BDAS—Broker and Dealer Automation System—the primary function of BDAS is to send and receive trades (messages) for customers (brokers and dealers) in order that they may buy and sell government securities.
- MH COMET—worldwide electronic mail package.

---

getting on top of the system. Now it is essential to convert to establish the volume base. It will be difficult because now we have to deal with peers, and the transition to VIOCs has made them turf-conscious. It will take time in meetings and establishing joint efforts to ensure it works. We will just have to get it done.

Appendix   *Time Line of MHC Communication Developments* —————

1972   Communication specialists hired, first customer communication product (passbook saving) on-line.

1974   Jack Evans and senior management began review of bank data processing technology and operational support.

1975   Move to Vertically Integrated Operations Centers to develop stronger ties to the business units.

1976   Communication management organized under Roberta Frackman. Gunther Kempin formed the Network Study Project.

1977   Analysis of existing systems identified 23 specialized nets and rapidly rising costs; a Corporate Network Study was proposed.

1978   Feasibility study completed: a corporate managed and developed X.25 packet switched net recommended; pilot study and functional specifications budget approved.

1979   Functional specifications completed and put out for bid; pilot study implemented connecting major users on X.25; first stage implementation of GEONET approved for 1980.

1980   Telenet selected as main supplier of hardware and software for GEONET; implementation planning completed and initial nodes and concentrators of the X.25 net installed; two products and two internal services supported by the net.

1981   Implemented worldwide net of 5 nodes and 15 concentrators supporting 6 new products; strong push to finish the implementation by the end of 1983.

1982   New planning approach to define needs introduced; net expanded to include LANs.

1983   Received two-year budget to complete net and to convert existing specialized nets to GEONET; GEONET expanded to include 19 nodes worldwide and to complete the basic design of the network; design study to include circuit switching as part of GEONET initiated; management control system study team formed to develop costing/chargeback system.

Chapter 4

IT Redraws Competitive Boundaries

In a 1966 *Harvard Business Review* article, Felix Kaufman implored general managers to think beyond their own organizational boundaries to the possibilities of extracorporate systems.[1] His was a visionary argument about newly introduced computer time-sharing and networking capabilities. In the nearly 20 years since that article was written, as noted in Chapter 3, developments in information technology (IT) have made feasible many new applications of strategic importance.

Today many of the most dramatic and potentially powerful uses of IT involve networks that transcend company boundaries. These interorganizational systems (IOS's)—defined as automated information systems shared by two or more companies—will significantly contribute to enhanced productivity, flexibility, and competitiveness of many companies. However, current examples illustrate that some IOS's will radically change the balance of power in buyer-supplier relationships, provide entry and exit barriers in industry segments, and in most instances shift the competitive position of intraindustry competitors.

For example, a major automotive manufacturer has established computer-to-computer communication with its primary suppliers to implement just-in-time inventory systems. As an extension, the automotive manufacturer could add instructions to scan the computers of its primary suppliers and place an order with the company's computer

---

[1]Felix Kaufman, "Data Systems that Cross Company Boundaries," *Harvard Business Review,* January–February 1966, p. 141.

that contained the lowest bid or price for the desired product (assuming that other things such as product quality are equal).

Such a system would encourage competition among the vendors, and this rivalry would enhance the manufacturer's bargaining power with them. Unfortunately, companies are making the decision whether to participate in these systems without an appreciation of the broader strategic implications; in some cases such decisions are made at the production clerk level. Approximately half the time, under the guise of faster information flow and greater data integrity, the new system suddenly shifts inventory holding costs and business risk to a supplier. Such an imbalance would clearly far outweigh any advantages that the more efficient information system might bring to the supplier.

Some IOS's already have 10- to 15-year histories that clearly illustrate the economic impact and the social and public policy implications that such systems may have. The most dramatic and best-documented example is the airline industry's reservation systems, a class of IOS shared by intraindustry competitors and organizations that have a buyer-supplier relationship, as noted in Chapter 3 and the Frontier Airlines case. In testimony before the Civil Aeronautics Board (CAB), Frontier Airlines alleged that United Air Lines, developer-owner of the widely used APOLLO reservation system, was enjoying unfair competitive advantage by monitoring loading factors of competitors and then using the system to either lower prices or broadcast special messages to travel agents. Since two major carriers, American and United, own reservation systems that provide the primary market access for almost two thirds of the travelers who make reservations through U.S. travel agents, this issue generated a great deal of public interest.

The CAB's airline reservation system inquiry showed the necessity for participants to anticipate the effects of an IOS. Further, it illustrated a need for social, regulatory, and strategic business perspectives in this rapidly evolving area. Given the rapid diffusion of computer and communications technology into most organizations, the potential is great for similar IOS growth and impact in a broad range of industries. In the following discussion, we will describe the trends contributing to IOS development; show what an IOS is and how it works; describe frameworks for analyzing business, industry, and organizational impact; and suggest a way to think about the alternative forms of participation in these systems.

IOS Development

The growth of interorganizational systems is due to various technological, economic, and organizational changes:

The Need for Fast, Reliable Information Exchange in Response to Rapidly Changing Markets, Products, and Services.   This trend is mainly based on increasing international competition, shrinking geographic separation, and deregulation with more open competition.

The shift in world economics is shown by the change in the world aggregate GNPs. Shortly after World War II, the U.S. GNP was about half the world GNP. By 1986 it was about a fourth of world GNP. This shift has greatly stepped up international competition.

The new international competitors often have different cost structures (for example, the relative labor component of total costs), manufacturing, production processes, and so on. In many industries the injection of these new competitors has changed fundamental characteristics of products (cars, for example), reduced the time span of product life cycles, and added much new productive capacity (which generally limits prices and margins and/or increases costs).

Increased deregulation in industries that range from trucking to petroleum to airline and financial services has accompanied the shifts already mentioned. Together these changes foster redefinition of products, of the relationships between buyers and suppliers in a product-service delivery chain, and of ancillary services to the end consumer. Some industry segments that are still heavily regulated, such as the insurance industry, are also affected by this trend.

The Evolution of Guidelines, Standards, and Protocols.   As a response to the need for better and faster information exchange, interest has grown in developing standard definitions, protocols, and product encoding. Historically, government regulation was the primary impetus for establishing standards. But now organizations such as industry associations and industry groups are also introducing standards. Two examples are the universal product code (UPC) in the grocery industry and magnetic ink character (MICR) sets and magnetic strips on credit cards and cards for automatic teller machines in retail banking. By forcing consistency of message content and product form, such standards make it much easier to establish and participate in interorganizational systems.

Penetration of Information Technology into Internal Business Processes.   The combination of decreasing IT costs and increasing capability has resulted in a broader range of internal computer applications. As more and more data are stored in computers, the natural next step is to transmit these data in machine-readable form to wherever they are needed. This prevents redundant encoding of data and makes information readily accessible. Both the money and the time saved easily justify such data and resource sharing. The combination of more internal company data on computers, standards for intercompany exchange of information, and clear economic justification makes participation in interorganizational systems very attractive.

Technical Quality and Capability of Information Technology. As IT has become increasingly reliable, companies can use IOS's in business-sensitive areas, such as in dealing with customers. For example, with automatic teller machines (ATMs) the customer's perception of a bank's service is tested at each use of the machine. Too frequent problems may cause users to change banks.

Favorable experience with internal computer and communications systems has led companies to explore external applications of these technologies.

Use of IT to Distinguish Product and/or Company. An example of such use is a large construction company that first developed, for its own internal use, a program for more efficient project management. Next the company gave "dumb" terminals (those that have no independent processing ability) to its clients so that they could track progress of the project, analyze changes in specifications, and forecast maintenance schedules and costs. In this second step, the company sought to distinguish itself from its competitors, who lacked such computer backup.

Finally the company gave "intelligent" terminals to customers to use primarily for special maintenance management programs that originate with the construction company's computer. In competitive bidding, this IT service differentiates the construction company from competitors. Further, it links the customer in a manner that encourages a continuing relationship with the company after the project is completed.

IOS versus DDP

In the broadest terms, an IOS consists of a computer and communication infrastructure that permits the sharing of an application, such as programs for making reservations or for ordering supplies. The players in a system are either participants or facilitators.[2] An IOS *participant* is an organization that develops, operates, or utilizes an IOS to ex-

---

[2]The definitions in this section are partially based on S. Barrett and Benn R. Konsynski, "Inter-Organizational Information Sharing Systems," *MIS Quarterly,* Special Issue, Fall 1982, p. 93.

change information that supports a primary business process. Participants can be competitors, organizations in the buyer-supplier chain, or a combination of these. An IOS *facilitator* is an organization that aids in the development, operation, or use of such a network for exchange of information among participants. The supporting products or services are a part of the primary business of the facilitator.

Although some larger companies have well-established IOS's, many executives barely understand the concept of such a system. The most frequent response to a general description of an interorganizational system is "What's different about it? Isn't it a special form of distributed data processing (DDP)?"

It is possible to distinguish an IOS from distributed data processing in four important ways:

1. Whereas DDP is under the control of a single company, an IOS crosses company boundaries. Thus an employee in one company can directly allocate resources and initiate business processes in another company. This capability introduces very different challenges for a company's internal control, planning, and resource allocation systems. As a result, most companies need to revise these management control systems to permit the requisite coordination across organization boundaries.

2. With an IOS, in contrast to DDP, the question of government regulation arises as a result of the information exchange across the boundaries of separate organizations and hence across separate legal entities. Among the numerous potential issues are questions of legal liability. For example, when does the electronic message passing over communication lines in an IOS actually become an order? When an IOS involves competitors, as illustrated by airline reservation systems, what constitutes unfair business practice? When an IOS involves participants engaged in interstate commerce, are current regulations sufficient to protect consumer interests?

3. The IOS facilitator is a player that doesn't exist in DDP. Although intermediaries are not new in most industry segments, their role in interorganizational electronic communication is new. An example of an IOS facilitator is the CIRRUS nationwide network of automated teller machines. CIRRUS, which is not a bank, permits subscribing banks to give their customers 24-hour, coast-to-coast access to their ATM system. The home banking system network offered by CompuServe is another example of an IOS facilitator.

4. An IOS frequently has a broader and more significant potential competitive impact than the traditional internal uses of IT. For example, a major bank has developed an application it calls the treasury decision support system (TDSS). TDSS is a microcomputer-based system

that the bank makes available to its largest corporate customers for use by their company treasurers. The system communicates with the bank's host computer and will accept input from a range of other systems. TDSS permits a treasurer to track, report, analyze, and perform simple manipulation of data concerning the company's funds. Data for TDSS can be transferred from several sources, including the company's computer or computers owned by competitive banks. The company may ask other banks or repositories to transfer data on company funds under their control to TDSS, in machine-readable form. Currently, the bank that developed TDSS is the only organization, in addition to the (customer) company, that can examine all the data in the microcomputer. This examination would yield a complete profile of the company's funds management and would (the bank hopes) provide an excellent basis for developing a new (and tailored) product offering for the customer.

Analyzing IOS's Impact

The variety and use of existing IOS's are as broad and complex as the industries in which they have evolved. To facilitate planning, analyzing, and deciding whether to develop or participate in an IOS, companies need a comprehensive framework. The framework must show use of computer and communications technology from a strategic rather than a tactical perspective.

Michael Porter's industry and competitive analysis (ICA) framework (described in Chapter 3) can be used in this manner. Porter argues that many strategic planning frameworks view competition too narrowly and pessimistically because they are primarily based on projections of market share and market growth.[3] He asserts that the economy and competitive forces in an industry segment result from a broader range of factors than the established combatants in a particular industry. According to him, the state of competition in an industry depends on five forces; (1) bargaining power of suppliers, (2) bargaining power of buyers, (3) threat of new entrants into the industry segment, (4) threat of substitute products or services, and (5) positioning of traditional intraindustry rivals.

Figure 4-1 shows the potential effect of an IOS, using the ICA framework of the five competitive forces. Note that in a given industry segment not all forces are equal. Suppliers dominate some industries

---

[3]Michael E. Porter, *Competitive Strategy: Techniques for Analyzing Industries and Competitors* (New York: Free Press, 1980); "How Competitive Forces Shape Strategy," *Harvard Business Review,* March–April 1979, p. 137.

FIGURE 4-1 Competitive Forces

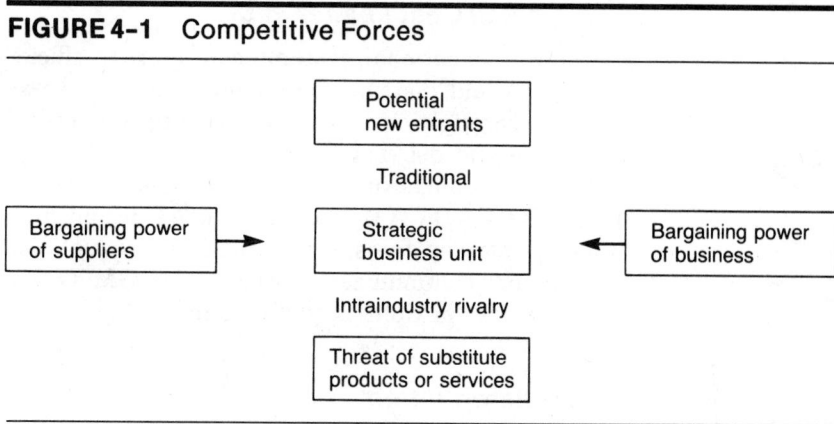

(as OPEC and the petroleum industry in the 1970s), and others are preoccupied with the threat of new entrants and/or substitute products (as in the banking industry). This model describes possible strategic uses of IOS's and thus helps in planning.

Implementation of an IOS is not guaranteed to demonstrably improve return on investment, productivity, or operational efficiency. The impact of such systems may be more subtle.

IOS and Generic Strategy

Companies that have a strategic planning process formulate their competitive strategy in two steps. The first step involves using some kind of framework to describe their competitive environment (such as Michael Porter's ICA). In the next step, managers consider the resources available to derive and implement company strategy. Traditionally most companies have not explicitly considered the potential uses of IT resources as part of this process. Chapter 3 showed how companies could use information technology to implement one of Porter's three generic competitive strategies—overall cost leadership, product differentiation, and special market focus—and cited companies in which the technology has changed the basis of competition.

As part of the two-step strategic planning process, managers should consider the IOS's potential impact on the competitive environment and on the implementation of competitive strategy. Following are examples of how a company can use an IOS to implement competitive strategy.

1. Overall Cost Leadership

Interorganizational systems can improve efficiency and scale in production and distribution. A number of these systems have reduced costs through electronic purchasing and ordering. The fashionable just-in-time delivery systems are examples of such electronic links among organizations. In one plant, General Motors has experimentally tied its CAD/CAM (computer-aided design and manufacturing) and order-entry systems to its suppliers' production systems. A supplier's computer communicates directly with GM's robot-based assembly line to provide "flexible" manufacturing.

2. Differentiation

In support of a differentiation strategy, an IOS can be used to add value to products and services. It may be coupled with a special service that differentiates the product or company. For example, a company that manufactures maintenance chemicals gave its largest customers microcomputers linked to its host computers. Customers could thus use an application that helped them make decisions on product mix, order frequency, and maintenance schedules (as well as the obligatory direct order-entry capability). Over time, the chemical company changed the basis of competition from price alone to a range of services. And once its customers had accepted the microcomputers, they were unwilling to take similar systems from the chemical company's competitors.

An IOS may serve as a means of differentiation by a radical modification of access and distribution channels. American Airlines' SABRE and United's APOLLO reservation systems, developed from the late 1960s to 1986, illustrate interorganizational links that control market access in their industry. Travel agencies that use automated reservations systems will, on average, use one of these two systems in 65 percent of the reservations they make.[4]

3. Focus

This strategy usually combines low cost and differentiation. In addition, the business entity chooses to address a particular niche of one industry. An example of this strategy is a consortium of small stock brokerage and investment firms with various specialties. They are sponsoring the development of an application similar to Merrill

---

[4]*Report to Congress on Airlines Computer Reservation Systems* and addendum to the report, prepared by the Civil Aeronautics Board in consultation with the Department of Justice, Spring 1983.

Lynch's Cash Management Account. Access to the system will be by a home banking network offered by a major West Coast bank. The target customer for this product is the investor with a portfolio of $40,000 or more. The consortium will attempt to offer a flexible range of integrated services at a much lower cost than its competitors.

Influence on Industry Structure

When the basis for competition changes, restructuring can occur. Shifts in buyer, supplier, and intraindustry rivalries take place together with the introduction of new or substitute products and new entrants. Good examples of this can be found in the financial services industry, where IOS's have permitted small savings and loan companies to provide insurance and discount brokerage services.

Heavy-equipment manufacturers have required their major suppliers to link directly into their CAD/CAM systems while also providing their customers with ancillary IOS services such as order tracking. In this case the IOS sets the stage for redefinition of organizational boundaries and competition patterns in their industry segments.

Organizations may unite under a common set of standards and protocols, which can set up entry or exit (mobility) barriers. For example, General Motors now requires its primary suppliers to adhere to computer hardware standards and communication protocols recommended by the Automotive Industry Action Group, of which GM is a part.

In other instances the IOS stimulates new entrants, as happened when small savings and loan institutions started providing insurance and brokerage services as mentioned above.

Similarly an IOS may protect or amplify the status of a given market as in the several consortiums for nationwide networks of ATMs. Some industry observers believe participation in this system for some banks is a defensive maneuver to protect their retail banking markets from potential new entrants (for example, Sears) that already have in place computer and communication infrastructures to offer interstate banking services.

Clearly, interorganizational links have brought and will continue to bring changes in the pattern of competition within industries. Further, we can expect that industry boundaries will adjust and reshape themselves as new relationships emerge and traditional organizational boundaries become blurred.

Organizational Impact

Interorganizational systems can have a range of impacts on participants. The order of internal change triggered by an IOS appears to vary depending on whether an organization is reacting to an IOS implemented by another company or whether it is the initiator or implementer of the IOS.

If a company joins in an IOS proposed by another organization, general management frequently does not participate in the decision-making process, and it neither explicitly plans nor considers the implications of the system. Thus changes will occur in business process (first-order impact), skills and staff requirements (second-order impact), and then organization structure and business strategy (third-order impacts).

First changes generally occur in business processes. The particular process (such as order entry and production) must change to conform with the standards of the IOS or to take into account various procedures in internal control, report formats, planning systems, and communication patterns. This shift in the underlying business process and communication pattern then brings changes in the skills of employees and in some cases even new employee categories. Examples are independent insurance agencies that now illustrate products through a computer network and do their back-office accounting through links to the home offices of large insurance companies. This has enabled brokers to become "estate planners" and to sell much more complex but customized products than were feasible a decade ago. Similarly, the customer service representative in large travel agencies has evolved from the clerk who simply flipped pages in airline guidebooks to the sophisticated computer user who can access numerous data bases on hotels and car rental agencies. When an IOS is used for a key business function such as market access systems (for example, shared ATMs in retail banking), the IOS may force changes not only in business processes, required skills, and organization structure but even in business strategy.

When an organization is the initiator or implementer of an IOS, the order of these impacts changes, due primarily to more effective planning for the system. The IOS is the enabling vehicle for changes in organization structure and strategy. Skill and staff level changes are next with changes in the business process occurring last because of the planning for the introduction.

The 7–S framework, popularized in a contemporary book[5] has proven useful to categorize these observations. Table 4–1 briefly describes each S. Figure 4–2 is a schematic of the S's and emphasizes the need for appropriate balance between them. The term *fit* is frequently used to describe the objective of choosing appropriate alternatives for each S, which addresses their interdependence.

---

[5]A. Athos and R. J. Pascale, *The Art of Japanese Management,* Warner Books, 1982.

TABLE 4-1   The Seven S's

Strategy	Plan or course of action leading to the allocation of a firm's scarce resources, over time, to reach identified goals.
Structure	Characterization of the organization chart (e.g., functional, decentralized, etc.)
Systems	Proceduralized reports and routinized processes such as meeting formats.
Staff	"Demographic" description of important personnel categories within the firm (e.g., engineers, entrepreneurs, M.B.A.'s, etc.). "Staff" is *not* meant in line-staff terms.
Style	Characterization of how key managers behave in achieving the organization's goals; also, the cultural style of the organization.
Skills	Distinctive capabilities of key personnel or the firm as a whole.
Superordinate goals	The significant meanings or guiding concepts that an organization imbues in its members.

SOURCE: A. Athos and R. J. Pascale, *The Art of Japanese Management*, Warner Books, 1982.

Using this framework, the initial changes mentioned above that occur in an organization participating in an IOS occur in the *systems* category. This shift in the underlying business process and communication pattern frequently precipitates changes in the *skills* that are needed by associated employees and causes, in some cases, the emergence of a new *staff* category. Third-order effects include the development of new or changed *style, structure,* and *strategy*. The key concern related to these changes is the impact on the balance, or fit, between the S's.

FIGURE 4-2   A Schematic of the S's: Emphasizing the Need for Appropriate Balance (Fit) between Them

Shifts in systems, skills, and so on, without compensating shifts in the other elements, generate unplanned conflict, contention, and in some cases dysfunctional behavior.

As discussed, the order of change among the elements appears to vary based on whether the organization is in a participant role, reacting to an IOS implemented by another organization, or is the proactive initiator/implementer of the IOS. In the first case, where there is usually no general management participation and thus no explicit planning or broad thinking about implications of the system, the pattern of evolution is:

- First-order impact: systems.
- Second-order impact: skills, staff.
- Third- and higher-order impacts: style, structure, strategy.

In the second case, an organization implementing a strategic IOS, the order changes because explicit planning of desired impact and requisite resources precedes implementation of the IOS:

- First-order impact: strategy, structure.
- Second-order impact: staff, skills.
- Third- and higher-order impacts: systems.

Although the IOS was the enabling vehicle for changes in structure and strategy, the actual changes in the systems category occurred last because of the explicit planning for the introduction.

In the cases examined to this point we have not discussed changes in *superordinate goals* that could be attributed to an IOS. The degree of change in style, structure, and strategy appears to be directly related to the significance of competitive forces that the IOS impacts. In some instances where IOS is involved the overall pattern of behavior among key managers in the organization has to change because of competitive pressure. In such cases, although the IOS addresses key competitive forces, it is very difficult to relate the changes directly to the IOS. Clearly, however, the IOS becomes a critical part of the infrastructure that is frequently evaluated to make key decisions on structure and strategy. General managers must ensure that the organization makes an appropriate commitment to such change and that the commitment is incorporated into the superordinate goals of the firm.

IOS Participation Profiles

Managers reacting to or contemplating the implementation of an IOS should also understand the range of involvement alternatives. They must first consider the extent of investment and management of information technology in which they want to be involved. A second consideration is how much influence they want over access to and design of the IOS. Technologically, participation in IOS's falls into three levels:

1. Information entry and receipt.
2. Software development and maintenance.
3. Network and processing management.

As the level of involvement increases, responsibility, cost commitment, and organizational and technical complexity also increase.

Information Entry and Receipt

At the first level, the IOS participant performs no application processing and merely acts as an information entry-receipt node. The user generally has access only through restricted protocols. The IOS simply provides standard messages, as when an independent travel agency uses one of the major airline reservation systems with no additional in-house processing capability. The majority of current IOS participants are operating at this entry level. Employees using these systems include shipping clerks, order clerks, salespersons, and fund and credit managers—all of whom are involved in information retrieval, authorization, and validations activities.

At this first level of participation, higher-level participants determine the standards and procedures and retain control of the application. For example, in the airline reservation system just mentioned, the travel agent must follow the policies and procedures embedded in the computer programs written and maintained by the major carrier. At this stage, interconnections exist only at the basic data-exchange level, and the switching cost (for example, the cost of moving from one automated reservation or home banking system to another if simple inquiry is the only use) is low.

Compatibility requirements generally exist, but exact protocols are rarely needed initially. In some situations, the higher-level participant will increase the dependence of lower-level participants. (Some home banking systems, for example, permit automatic payment systems after the customer keys in a large amount of data, which dramatically increases the cost of changing to another system.) The Level 1 participant can become increasingly dependent on the higher-level participant, as tasks or processes require more coordination across organizational boundaries. Although Level 1 participation is not complex, the relationships established with other organizations over time can help restructure the industrial marketplace in which the participant operates. This restructuring is driven by the provider of the IOS.

For example, IOS brokerage networks have permitted savings and loan (S&L) organizations to offer discount brokerage services. This innovation has given the larger S&Ls a new customer segment, and the resulting increased transaction volume has forced improvements in the software and communications systems. This improvement in turn has had the effect of bringing about economies of scale, driving unit costs down, and introducing other products and services (such as insurance). This chain of events illustrates why the distinctions among brokerage houses, insurance agencies, and banks have become blurred from a consumer perspective and how structural change in one element of an industry can cause industry or marketplace changes. Changes are not isolated; when one element changes, changes occur in other areas.

Software Development and Maintenance

Companies participating at Level 2 develop and maintain software used by other IOS participants. Usually, the developer of the IOS has absorbed the cost of this development and of maintenance to gain exclusive control over decisions on access, price, and design of the application and the network. In the airline reservation system examples already mentioned, American and United are Level 2 participants; they are primarily responsible for developing their SABRE and APOLLO systems, respectively. Data Resources, Inc., an economic modeling and information resource firm that permits customers to access its data and applications, is another example.

Administrative overhead increases for Level 2 participants as coordination across organizational boundaries becomes necessary. For example, in planning the system, an organization may need input (such as estimates of transaction volume for capacity planning) from other participant or facilitator organizations, which generally increases the time required to develop the plan.

Network and Processing Management

The Level 3 participant serves as a utility and usually owns or manages all the network facilities as well as the computer processing resources. Examples include public information networks such as the Bell operating companies, The Source, and CompuServe. Costs increase dramatically at this level.

In addition to network development and maintenance costs, the Level 3 participant accepts considerable internal control responsibility for the integrity of information exchanged. For example, consider the CIRRUS network that permits ATM transactions nationwide. CIRRUS must accept a great deal of responsibility for the reliability, availability, integrity, security, and privacy of its system.

Control and Influence

Following the technology involvement question, the major consideration in IOS participation is the degree of control or influence a Level 1, 2, or 3 participant or a facilitator exerts over key management decisions about the IOS. The chief control lies in access and participation—that is, in determining who can or cannot participate in the IOS and under what conditions.

Owners of major airline reservation systems were able to exclude schedules of regional carriers and other airlines from their systems until forced by legal and regulatory pressures to include them. Likewise, some airlines have established guidelines that require travel agents to execute minimum numbers of transactions on their systems to remain "qualified" to use them. Companies also determine entrance and exit guidelines that include timing and characteristics of use.

The pressures are so intense in the airline industry, as noted in Chapter 3, that United Air Lines and American Airlines are at present fighting an antitrust suit that 11 other U.S. airlines have filed against them for limiting competition. United and American are accused of charging inordinate fees for competing airlines' participation in information systems, stringently limiting that participation, and displaying competitors' flights in an unfavorable light on the computer screen.[6]

Pricing and cost decisions are also a critical part of exploiting the system. In many instances companies have used pricing to erect access barriers. One major air carrier, for example, prices the use of its reservation system high enough that low-cost, long-haul carriers would find participation impractical. The specification of transaction pricing to achieve cost recovery is also an important consideration in IOS's. From the perspective of an IOS participant, the cost of using an IOS should be directly related to the amount of use.

The final category of control involves the mechanism for establishing, maintaining, and changing the application, standards, protocols, and internal control procedures. Some companies at Levels 2 and 3 have found that although higher investments in technology can result in great expense, they also bring greater control.

Summary

In considering IOS's as a strategic possibility, managers should weigh internal and industry aspects, participation issues, and social impact and public policy.

---

[6]"Rivals Sue United, American," *New York Times,* November 11, 1984.

The key internal issue is the readiness of the organization to deal with changes in business process, personnel, and structure it may face as a result of IOS participation. It must also have the ability to adapt to the competitive pressures that may arise.

The industry issues involve the strategy and position of the organization in its market. The Porter framework for assessing the potential impact of an IOS in an industry provides a perspective for this analysis. Companies must also determine the appropriate level of technology investment and the level of control they expect to exert over an IOS. The organization becomes a participant in a new entity that presents new problems as well as opportunities.

The social impact and public policy issues, though not always obvious, are critical. What impact will the continued rapid introduction of IOS systems in the buyer-supplier chain, for example, have on the large portion of our work force involved in direct sales? At what point is the consumer paying an inappropriate price because of biases built into dominant systems, such as those in the airline industry? When should regulatory guidelines be introduced so they do not discourage creativity, innovation, and risk taking but do prevent unfair business practices via these systems?

To assess the potential impact of an IOS, managers should first identify and assess key competitive forces for given strategic business units. Next they should explore potential uses and the impact of an IOS on these forces. Since a short-run, return-on-investment focus may obscure opportunities for adding value through electronic links, managers must think broadly. Next they should develop a plan for evaluating the possible current and future effects of an IOS. Finally the company should monitor and track IOS's generally, especially in regard to public responses to these systems, such as the congressional hearings on airline reservation systems, so that they will be in a position to adapt to and perhaps even influence the trends.

Case 4–1

American Hospital Supply Corporation
(A) The ASAP System

"The computer is at the heart of our success," said Karl D. Bays, chairman and chief executive officer of American Hospital Supply Corporation (AHSC) in early 1985, describing the importance of information systems to the company. AHSC had 1984 sales of $3.5 billion and net earnings of $238 million. Virtually all of the 7,500 short-term general hospitals in the United States bought at least some of their supplies from AHSC's list of over 135,000 products. Some 5,400 of these hospitals entered their orders through AHSC's on-line purchasing system, ASAP.

With an estimated 25–30 percent share of the fragmented hospital supply market, AHSC had increased its sales an average of 13 percent per year from 1978 to 1983; profits after tax rose an average of 18 percent per year over the same period (see Exhibit 1). By 1984, however, the health care industry was in the midst of dramatic changes that impacted AHSC. Fixed-rate reimbursement from the government-sponsored Medicare program, which paid for 40 percent of all hospital patient days, had made hospitals much more cost-conscious. Businesses and insurers also were exerting pressure to cut health care expenditures, which by 1984 had risen to some $360 billion, more than 10 percent of the nation's GNP. Hospital admissions fell to 36.2 million in 1984 from their 1982 peak of 37.9 million, while the average hospital stay shortened from 7.2 to 6.7 days. The total number of hospitals had declined from its peak in 1980, although the number of beds had increased slightly.

This case was prepared by Michael R. Vitale.

Copyright © 1985 by the President and Fellows of Harvard College
Harvard Business School case 9–186–005 (Rev 4/86)

EXHIBIT 1

AMERICAN HOSPITAL SUPPLY CORPORATION
Financial Comparison 1974–1984
($ and shares in millions, except per share amounts)

	1984	1983	1982	1981
Operating statistics for continuing operations:				
Net sales	$3,448.5	$3,310.5	$2,965.8	$2,660.0
Earnings from continuing operations	237.8	211.9	170.0	133.5
Increase over previous year (percent):				
Net sales	4.2%	11.6%	11.5%	17.6%
Earnings	12.2	24.6	27.4	14.0
Ratios to net sales:				
Gross profit	33.4	34.6	34.3	33.5
Operating expenses	24.8	24.8	25.1	25.1
Operating earnings	8.6	9.8	9.2	8.4
Earnings	6.9	6.4	5.7	5.0
Effective income tax rate	14.7	30.9	31.0	33.9
Investments in continuing operations:				
Capital expenditures	$141.2	$129.4	$125.3	$123.3
Research and development	$ 90.0	$ 81.2	$ 57.3	$ 49.6
Asset statistics for continuing operations:				
Accounts receivable days	56	54	53	55
Inventory days	111	108	103	105
Net sales per dollar of average net working assets	$ 2.18	$ 2.35	$ 2.46	$ 2.51
Capital structure statistics:				
Long-term debt	$ 169.0	$ 135.4	$ 164.0	$ 195.4
Total debt	$ 399.9	$ 327.5	$ 303.2	$ 297.9
Total debt as a percent of total capital	21.1%	19.0%	20.4%	22.5%
Shareholders' investment	$1,497.3	$1,396.8	$1,185.5	$1,026.0
Total capital	$1,897.2	$1,724.3	$1,488.7	$1,323.9
Total assets	$2,461.4	$2,280.0	$2,018.4	$1,770.2
Return on average shareholder's investment	16.4%	16.3%	15.8%[c]	15.0%
Return on net working assets[b]	15.2%	15.2%	14.5%[c]	13.2%
Common share statistics:				
Earnings per share from continuing operations	$3.23	$2.86	$2.36	$1.87
Increase over previous year	12.9%	21.2%	26.2%	12.7%
Dividends per share	$1.09	$ .96	$ .81	$ .69
Increase over previous year	13.5%	18.5%	17.4%	16.9%
Average number of common shares outstanding and equivalents	73.6	74.2	72.1	71.3
Other statistics:				
Number of employees at year-end	31,300	33,600	32,800	30,100
Number of shareholders at year-end	33,800	34,600	34,500	33,500

[a]In 1980, American changed to the last-in, first-out method of determining cost for substantially all U.S. inventories.

[b]An internal measurement that is substantially equivalent to the return on total capital.

[c]Excludes gains on sale of operations discontinued in 1982 and early retirement of debt.

1980[a]	1979	1978	1977	1976	1975	1974
$2,261.9	$1,928.1	$1,619.5	$1,364.4	$1,238.2	$1,065.3	$915.3
117.1	100.0	81.3	70.1	58.5	50.2	42.4
17.3%	19.1%	18.7%	10.2%	16.2%	16.4%	18.7%
17.1	22.9	16.1	19.9	16.4	18.5	12.4
33.1	33.0	33.0	34.1	33.5	33.6	33.9
25.0	24.7	24.3	24.7	24.7	25.1	24.8
8.1	8.3	8.7	9.4	8.8	8.5	9.1
5.2	5.2	5.0	5.1	4.7	4.7	4.6
35.2	29.5	36.4	41.6	44.1	42.5	45.4
$104.7	$63.2	$66.8	$63.7	$37.2	$41.4	$53.4
$ 39.2	$34.8	$30.5	$23.1	$17.5	$12.2	$10.6
58	60	61	59	60	62	64
108	111	114	116	112	108	117
$ 2.38	$2.22	$2.16	$2.12	$2.13	$2.05	$2.09
$ 200.3	$ 247.4	$ 226.6	$ 220.4	$ 93.9	$ 92.7	$ 94.3
$ 232.6	$ 276.5	$ 294.0	$ 246.9	$153.2	$128.2	$109.0
20.1%	26.9%	30.7%	29.3%	22.3%	21.1%	20.1%
$ 927.0	$ 752.8	$ 663.9	$ 595.2	$534.4	$480.3	$432.6
$1,159.6	$1,029.3	$ 957.9	$ 842.1	$687.6	$608.5	$541.6
$1,551.1	$1,348.6	$1,230.7	$1,077.2	$884.9	$763.1	$676.8
14.6%	14.6%	13.5%	12.9%	12.0%	12.2%	11.9%
13.0%	12.8%	11.8%	11.8%	10.8%	10.4%	10.6%
$1.66	$1.47	$1.23	$1.06	$ .89	$ .77	$ .66
12.9%	19.5%	16.0%	19.1%	15.6%	16.7%	11.9%
$ .59	$ .51	$ .43	$ .35	$ .26	$ .21	$ .20
15.7%	18.6%	22.9%	34.6%	23.8%	5.0%	5.3%
70.8	69.2	67.9	67.9	67.9	67.8	64.2
27,600	26,900	25,300	23,600	22,400	21,200	19,800
34,700	35,600	38,000	39,800	38,800	41,800	43,100

EXHIBIT 1   *(continued)*

AMERICAN HOSPITAL SUPPLY CORPORATION AND SUBSIDIARIES
Years ended December 31
($ millions except per share amounts)
Statement of Earnings

	1984	1983	1982
Net sales	$3,448.5	$3,310.5	$2,965.8
Cost of products sold	2,296.2	2,166.5	1,948.7
Gross profit	1,152.3	1,144.0	1,017.1
Selling, distribution and administrative expenses	855.7	820.7	743.5
Operating earnings	296.6	323.3	273.6
Other income	13.8	24.5	12.9
Interest income	(31.6)	(41.2)	(40.3)
Earnings before income taxes	278.8	306.6	246.2
Income taxes	41.0	94.7	76.2
Earnings from continuing operations	237.8	211.9	170.0
Operations discontinued in 1982	—	—	34.0
Gain on early retirement of debt	—	—	25.5
Net earnings	$ 237.8	$ 211.9	$ 229.5
Earnings per share:			
Continuing operations	$3.23	$2.86	$2.36
Discontinued operations	—	—	.47
Gain on early retirement of debt	—	—	.35
Net earnings per share	$3.23	$2.86	$3.18

AMERICAN HOSPITAL SUPPLY CORPORATION AND SUBSIDIARIES
Years ended December 31
($ millions)
Balance Sheet

	1984	1983
Assets		
Current assets:		
Cash	$ 28.9	$ 16.9
Marketable securities, at cost (approximates market)	259.7	232.6
Receivables, less allowances—$12.4 (1984), $10.6 (1983)	522.0	513.3
Inventories	586.2	544.4
Prepaid expenses	89.0	52.7
Total current assets	1,485.8	1,359.9

EXHIBIT 1 (*continued*)

	1984	1983
Assets		
Other assets:		
Investments in affiliates and unconsolidated subsidiary	126.0	18.8
Long-term receivables	17.1	29.3
Investments in securities, at cost	21.1	22.0
Miscellaneous	15.4	12.8
Total other assets	179.6	82.9
Property, plant, and equipment, at cost:		
Land	43.2	54.9
Buildings	427.7	413.7
Machinery and equipment	507.5	465.5
Furniture and fixtures	87.3	85.4
	1,065.7	1,019.5
Less: Accumulated depreciation	(349.6)	(300.6)
Total property, plant, and equipment	716.1	718.9
Intangibles, less amortization—$14.7 (1984), $16.7 (1983)	79.9	118.3
Total assets	$2,461.4	$2,280.0
Liabilities		
Current liabilities:		
Notes payable to banks	$ 7.5	$ 10.0
Commercial paper	218.3	156.6
Current maturities on long-term obligations	5.1	25.5
Accounts payable	345.9	340.7
Commissions, salaries, and withholdings	74.8	72.3
Retirement and other benefit plans	16.5	19.1
Taxes other than federal income taxes	16.6	21.9
Federal income taxes	20.5	27.2
Total current liabilities	705.2	673.3
Long-term obligations, less current maturities	169.0	135.4
Deferred income taxes	89.9	74.5
Shareholders' investment:		
Common stock	271.7	320.0
Earnings reinvested in the business	1,254.1	1,095.9
Foreign currency translation adjustment	(28.5)	(19.1)
Total shareholders' investment	1,497.3	1,396.8
Total liabilities	$2,461.4	$2,280.0

EXHIBIT 1   *(concluded)*

AMERICAN HOSPITAL SUPPLY CORPORATION
Market Segment Information
($ millions)

	1984	1983	1982
Net sales:			
Hospital	$2,862.8	$2,717.6	$2,444.2
Medical	625.4	627.9	552.9
	(39.7)	(35.0)	(31.3)
Total	$3,448.5	$3,310.5	$2,965.8
Operating earnings:			
Hospital	$269.2	$296.4	$258.1
Medical	76.4	74.7	60.1
Less: Intersegment transactions, unallocated interest, corporate overhead, and other	(66.8)	(64.5)	(72.0)
Earnings before income taxes .	$278.8	$306.6	$246.2
Identifiable assets:			
Hospital	$1,495.0	$1,505.3	$1,334.3
Medical	651.4	536.3	471.3
Corporate and other	315.0	238.4	212.8
Total	$2,461.4	$2,280.0	$2,018.4
Capital expenditures:			
Hospital	$ 83.0	$ 84.2	$ 89.5
Medical	41.7	27.2	20.0
Corporate and other	16.5	18.0	15.8
Total	$141.2	$129.4	$125.3
Depreciation and amortization:			
Hospital	$ 55.5	$ 52.8	$ 35.4
Medical	21.3	15.2	11.8
Corporate and other	10.4	8.0	6.0
Total	$ 87.2	$ 76.0	$ 53.2

Supplies were receiving considerably more attention than in the past; they made up an estimated 10–15 percent of hospital costs, while the logistical expenses associated with supplies made up another 20–30 percent. In this difficult environment, AHSC had been able to increase 1984 sales only 4 percent over 1983. After-tax earnings rose 12 percent, due largely to a lower tax rate, while operating earnings fell 8 percent.

For the future, AHSC expected continued change in the health care system. Aggregate demand for care would likely increase, but more slowly than in the past, and consumers would exert more choice. More and more care would be moved outside of hospitals to "alternate sites," such as doctors' offices and walk-in emergency and surgical centers, and health maintenance organizations (HMOs) would continue to proliferate. At the same time, hospitals would enter into less traditional markets, such as occupational health and "wellness" programs, sometimes in partnership with physicians, nurses, and other providers. AHSC intended to focus on reducing its operating expenses and on increasing its sales, particularly of products that it manufactured inhouse. Research and development and an active acquisition program were important links in the company's competitive strategy.

The future role of information systems was somewhat less clear. Could ASAP, which had contributed so much to the company's progress over the past 20 years, continue to play a leading part? Could the company build other strategically important systems for the new competitive environment? Or were information systems now to be primarily support for AHSC's other activities?

Company Background and Strategy

After its founding in 1922 by Foster G. McGaw, AHSC grew slowly, expanding from its original base near Chicago to include a few regional offices by the end of World War II. In the postwar era AHSC began for the first time to manufacture supplies as well as to distribute them. The company also expanded into the sale of prepared intravenous (IV) solutions and products and other similar patient care items. During the rapid expansion of the health care industry in the initial years of Medicare, AHSC grew as well; its sales reached $1 billion in 1975 and $2 billion in 1979, partially due to the acquisition of other distributors and manufacturers. By 1984 the company had more than 4 million square feet of manufacturing space and almost 150 distribution centers worldwide. AHSC-manufactured items made up some 46 percent of sales and 83 percent of net profits. The company was organized into sectors according to type of customer: hospital and laboratory, medical specialty, and international.

The hospital and laboratory sector provided products for general and specialized patient care, including IV solutions, surgical drapes and gowns, gloves, syringes, and other items, and instruments, chemical reagents, and other products and services for biomedical and industrial laboratories. Hospitals accounted for about two-thirds of AHSC's sales; the company could provide virtually everything a hospital needed except pharmaceuticals, X-ray gear, and other heavy medical equipment. AHSC made about 25 percent of its sales to laboratories. Medical specialties developed, manufactured, and marketed devices and drugs to physicians and related specialists, primarily in surgery and critical-care medicine. Medical specialty products included diagnostic equipment, surgical instruments, heart valves, and blood-collection systems. AHSC served international markets through wholly owned subsidiaries, joint ventures, and independent distributors. International business accounted for roughly 10 percent of sales.

AHSC faced competition from other broad-line manufacturers, including Johnson & Johnson and Baxter Travenol, from hundreds of local and regional distributors, and from specialist firms such as Baxter Labs, Pfizer, and SmithKline Beckman. AHSC promoted its nationwide coverage, broad product line, high service level, and the local presence provided by a 2,700-person field sales force. The company's employees tended to be relatively young—Bays himself had become president of the company at age 36—and well educated. AHSC's culture was characterized by promotion from within, a willingness to take risks, and a strong emphasis on ethical behavior.

AHSC's strategy for the future included increased emphasis on self-manufactured products, on the alternate-site market, and on sales to corporate accounts. Some $700 million was to be invested between 1983 and 1989 on research and development, primarily for products that promoted more cost-effective health care. Almost $1 billion would be spent over the same period on improved facilities for manufacturing and distribution. Acquisitions reflected the key strategy of more manufacturing as well as moving AHSC into the physicians' office and home care markets. Corporate agreements with large hospitals and large multihospital chains gave customers competitive pricing, limits on price increases, and cash bonuses in return for purchasing certain volumes of products. These corporate agreement customers were also eligible for consulting services designed to help them control their costs. With some observers predicting that consolidation would soon sweep through the hospital industry, leaving the survivors combined into groups and allied with insurers, physicians, and home health care agencies, AHSC's corporate buying program was expected to play an increasingly important role.

The Role of Information Systems

Traditionally, AHSC's products had been sold by its field salespeople, who worked from their homes and called directly on hospitals and other organizations. Until 1964, orders were generally taken in person by the salesperson, who would then mail the orders to company headquarters. Bays, who joined AHSC in 1958 as a salesman, recalled that upon arrival in a town he would immediately find out when the last mail of the day went out. "When I had made my calls," Bays continued, "I would rush back to my hotel room and write out all my orders and customer inquiries and get to the post office in time to make the last mail. That was an imperative." The paperwork could be formidable: an 800-bed hospital might easily stock 30,000 items and generate 50,000 purchase orders per year, at an estimated preparation cost of $25–30 each.

Within a single hospital there might be as many as 10 different buyers—the pharmacy, food service, anesthesiology, etc.—and even in hospitals that had adopted centralized purchasing, individual department heads often remained powerful buying influences. The price of each item was negotiated by the customer and the sales representative, making billing a complex process.

In 1957 AHSC had begun to automate its order-entry and billing procedures by installing IBM 632 tab-card billing machines in its distribution centers. Orders received at the centers would be keypunched, and the cards fed through the 632. A packing list for the warehouse was produced, as was a summary card for the accounts receivable system. The line item cards from the order were sent on to the home office for sales analysis.

In the early 1960s one of AHSC's West Coast offices began having difficulty servicing a large hospital customer. Orders were frequently delivered late and incomplete, creating problems for both the customer and AHSC. The West Coast office manager put an IBM 1001 Dataphone in the hospital's purchasing department and attached an IBM 026 card punch in the AHSC distribution center to a phone line. The hospital was given a box of prepunched cards, one for each item purchased from AHSC. The cards were physically placed on the shelves of the hospital's stockroom, each card stuck between boxes of supplies at the point where more should be ordered. When the box above the card was taken from the stockroom, the prepunched card was added to the pile of items to be ordered. On a regular schedule the hospital connected the 1001 to the 026 via telephone. Each card was fed through the 1001, causing a duplicate to be punched by the 026 at the AHSC distribution center. The result was a duplicate deck representing the hospital's order. This deck was fed through the 632 and the order process continued as usual. The hospital was able to speed up communications and thus could reduce its inventory. Orders were more accurate and more timely. AHSC benefited as well, and decided to offer the 1001-based service to other customers. More than 200 agreed immediately, and the system, named Tel-American, was extended to other West Coast customers, then to Chicago, and then to other areas. A similar service, Telephone American, worked in somewhat the same way but without the 1001. Instead, the prepunched cards were kept in a box at the AHSC office, and customers called in their orders. The cards were taken from the box manually by the telephone order-entry clerk.

Tel-American was well in place by 1969, when Gary Nei was hired as product manager for systems marketing and asked to identify additional customer benefits of the system. "The 1001 was the nucleus but not magic," Nei said later. "The customers could just as easily phone in their orders, and many did. The question was how to bundle additional services." Nei read the relatively small amount of material then available on materials management and wrote a document translating the general theory to the hospital environment. He began to advocate a "prime vendor" approach, in which hospitals would contract to obtain a major portion of their supplies from AHSC. In return, the hospital would get the benefits of lower inventory, reduced paper handling, lower "shrinkage" due to loss, spoilage, and theft, fewer purchase orders and deliveries to handle, and guaranteed service. Tel-American was promoted as part of an overall hospital materials management system. Nei worked with the field sales force to bring home to hospitals the benefits of materials management and to obtain commitments to implement the required disciplines and procedures. In some cases Nei and his staff swept stockroom floors and physically rearranged inventory in order to get a customer started. Later, as rising interest rates made holding inventory more expensive and as hospital purchasing agents began to understand their ability to become more professional through the use of modern techniques, the concepts promoted by AHSC became widely adopted. "We changed the industry," Nei noted, "we really did."

By the mid-1970s some of the novelty of Tel-American had worn off, and IBM had decided to drop support for the 1001. In response, AHSC's laboratory manufacturing division, TekPro, designed and built a much faster device to read and transmit data from cards. AHSC had by this time installed a mainframe computer system that kept track of orders and inventory, and the TekPro device was attached to this system rather than to a reproducing card punch. The TekPro unit also allowed the hospital to enter some data, for example, order quantities, by hand, and more importantly it acknowledged that each line of data had been received correctly. The new order-entry system, with mainframe computer support, was called Analytic Systems Automatic Purchasing (ASAP).

Both the Tel-American system and its successor, ASAP, were essentially one way: although special inventories were reserved for Tel-American and TekPro users, the customers could find out for certain when the ordered items would be delivered and in what quantity only by phoning the AHSC office or by waiting until the AHSC truck arrived. The TekPro unit was highly reliable—some were still in use in

1985—but customers' need for a printed response led to the adoption of the Bell 43 terminal as a standard input and output device in 1977.

The printing device and steady improvements in its central computer software gave AHSC the ability to respond to customer orders by verifying the item number and showing the availability and price of each item. Items could be ordered using AHSC's catalog numbers or those of its competitors, and orders could be edited for accuracy and completeness before they were transmitted. For items that were not currently in stock, the system could often recommend a substitute but did not make any substitutions automatically. The enhanced system, called ASAP 2, also allowed messages to be transmitted electronically among AHSC, the sales representatives, and customers. As with the earlier systems, customers who used ASAP 2 paid for the terminal themselves; AHSC paid the telephone line charges.

In 1980 AHSC announced ASAP 3, which allowed customers to enter orders using the hospital's own internal stock numbers. Customers could also build electronic files for standing orders and for repetitive orders. These files shortened the customer's order-entry time and improved ordering accuracy. ASAP 3 produced output to customer specifications as well, including inventory lists, purchase orders, and requisition forms. The customer could inquire on-line into pending back orders, prices, and delivery dates. Like its predecessors, ASAP 3 was intended to be used as part of an overall materials management program. The system did not, however, actually manage the hospital's inventory. An enhancement, ASAP 3 PLUS, incorported bar code scanning of shelf labels, requisition forms, or a catalog to facilitate order entry. Over the next few years, teletypes, CRTs, and other "dumb" terminals were added to the list of devices supported by ASAP.

ASAP 4, a computer-to-computer order-entry system, was released in 1983. It simplified the hospital's purchasing process by eliminating all the manual steps except actual approval. The customer's internal computer system produced recommended orders that, once approved, were automatically transmitted through a high-speed phone connection to AHSC's mainframe. Order confirmations were sent directly to the customer's computer system to update the hospital's files. Hospital size did not always correlate with informations systems capability, with some small hospitals being relatively sophisticated and some very big hospitals relying almost totally on manual systems. Nevertheless, it was expected that ASAP 4 would be used initially by the major multihospital groups who had corporate agreements with AHSC. (See Exhibit 2.)

Each hospital placed its ASAP 4 orders at prearranged times of the day; the system was not designed for emergency orders. Customers did

---

EXHIBIT 2   The ASAP System

Fast, Easy
Order Communication

Keeps Control at Your Fingertips

Today's environment calls for utilizing all your resources to their full capacity. With ASAP 1, you can apply systems technology to automate the order entry process. You gain increased productivity and ensure prompt order processing. Choose Touch-Tone order entry for the convenience of ordering from any location in your facility. Or, you may prefer the portability, accuracy and speed inherent in bar code order entry. Whichever method you choose, you'll receive a monthly management report of all your purchases.

Bar code order entry using SCAN gives you:
- **Flexibility**—Bar code information is available in label or catalog form. You also can manually enter items using the AHSC catalog number, ASAP number, manufacturers' number or another distributor's number (S/P division only). The SCAN unit works with both UPC and Code 39 bar codes.
- **Time Savings**—Rapid order entry and order communication reduce ordering time. Bar code scanning is quick—a 50-line order can be sent in only ten seconds.
- **Increased Accuracy**—Bar code scanning reduces ordering errors significantly.

Touch-Tone order entry turns any Touch-Tone phone into a rapid order communication device. You'll find this system:
- **Easy to Use**—A computer-synthesized voice is available to prompt you through your order.
- **Timely**—7-digit ASAP numbers and "menu" order messages keep entry time to a minimum.

Printback Confirmation Option
By using the printback option available with ASAP 2, you can receive hard copy documentation to confirm price and availability of your SCAN or Touch-Tone orders.

---

not pay for the use of ASAP or for any necessary software customization, which could take up to eight work hours.

ASAP 5, which went into pilot use in December of 1984, promised to extend the capabilities of ASAP 3 by using an IBM Personal Computer (PC) as the customer's input and output device. Customers could build and edit order files on the PC instead of on-line, thus reducing telephone expenses. The PC would also be equipped with extensive tutorial software, allowing a new user to learn in about 15 minutes how to enter ASAP orders. The new system would be menu-driven and would

EXHIBIT 2   *(continued)*

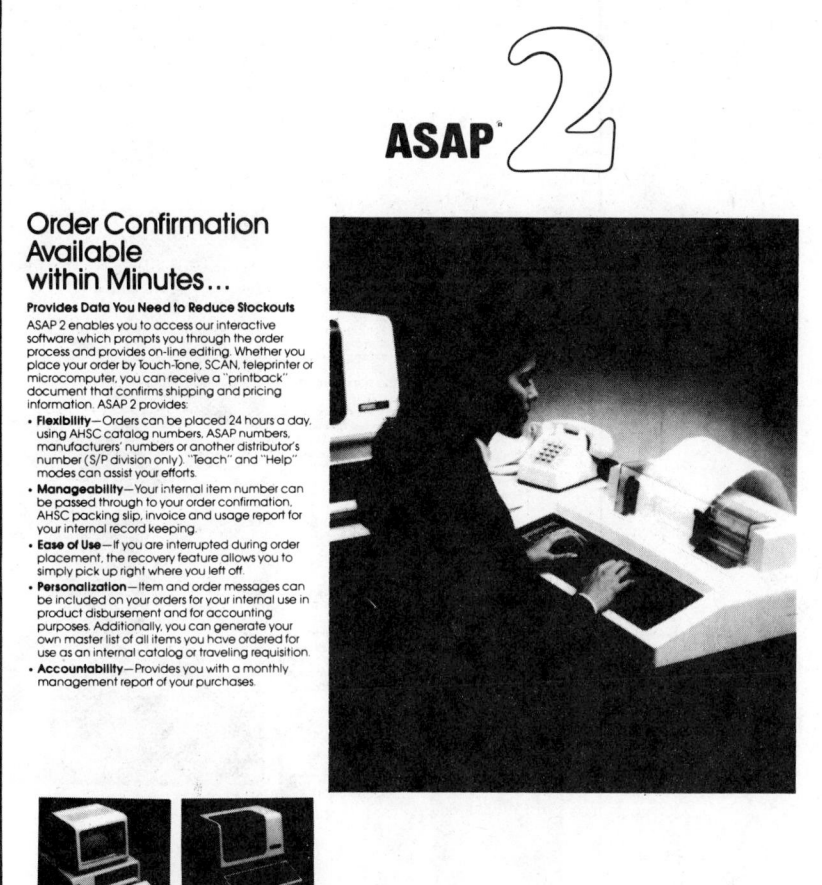

include a HELP facility that could be accessed while entering an order. As in the past, the hardware would be supplied by the customer.

AHSC's competitors had responded to ASAP, but it had taken them some time to do so; the first response came two years after the introduction of ASAP. Initial response was difficult in part because the competitors had to computerize their own inventories in order to offer a computerized system to customers.

By late 1984 ASAP and a few AHSC financial applications were running on five Burroughs mainframes, three B7800s and two B7700s.

EXHIBIT 2 *(continued)*

The ASAP software, which had been written totally by AHSC, was in a mixture of ALGOL and COBOL. A program to convert ASAP to IBM hardware had been underway for a year and had another 18 months to go. Looking back, AHSC estimated that it had spent about $30 million to build ASAP. Ongoing maintenance required six to nine full-time people. Annual operating costs for the 9,000-terminal system were about $3 million.

The Information Services Division (ISD), responsible for maintaining and enhancing ASAP and other corporate applications, had a staff

EXHIBIT 2 *(concluded)*

The Ultimate in Paperless Purchasing

Now Your Computer Can Talk Directly with Ours

ASAP 4 offers you the ability to fully automate the purchasing cycle except for one step—your actual approval. Here's how it works. Your mini or mainframe computer provides a recommended purchase order generated on the basis of stored information. Once you've reviewed and approved it, your computer can automatically communicate your needs to our mainframe. We'll return data to you in a flexible format to update your internal informational systems.

Computer-to-computer interface:

- **Provides "missing link" in the transaction process**—The automation you're utilizing internally now can be extended to include order communication and confirmation activities.
- **Maximizes your internal system**—This is accomplished through immediate routing of information from our computer to any location served by your internal system, such as purchasing, receiving, accounting and end user departments.
- **Allows easier access to decision-making information**—The data we communicate can be used in your internal system to keep you up-to-date on issues such as open order status.
- **Simplifies the monitoring of conformance with your purchasing policies**—Whether you're interested in a particular department or an entire facility, ASAP 4 makes your task easier.
- **Eliminates time-consuming duplicate entry**—Now there's no need to re-key order status information into your system as this occurs automatically.

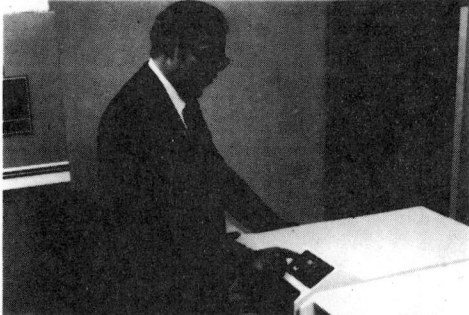

of about 400. ASAP was not static; a systems review board met four–six times per year with key users to set priorities for changes to ASAP and other systems as well as for new development. Review board meetings were coordinated by Carl Steiner, director of information systems planning, who was also responsible for putting together a strategic I/S plan for AHSC. Steiner also promoted information systems planning by AHSC's divisions and helped newly acquired divisions analyze their needs for information systems. ISD was judged on the basis of net expense, that is, on spending less chargeouts to divisions.

Customer Benefits

Although no quantitative cost-benefit study had ever been performed on ASAP, customers seemed to feel intuitively that using the system paid off. Through ASAP, hospitals were able to move towards more effective materials management, which was generally perceived as a step forward. Ordering was easier and more fun, and the cost of using the system was very low. Overall, about 50 percent of AHSC's hospital orders came through ASAP.

At Emerson Hospital, a 250-bed community hospital in Concord, Massachusetts, purchasing administrator Coco Richardson discussed ASAP from a customer's point of view. In 1984, Emerson spent some $9.3 million, almost 30 percent of its overall operating budget, on supplies and related expenses. The hospital purchased supplies from AHSC, Johnson & Johnson, two regional distributors, and a number of small local distributors. AHSC was the dominant supplier, accounting for over half of Emerson's annual purchases.

Richardson explained that ASAP had been the first order-entry system installed at the hospital. Since then, the hospital's other three major suppliers had developed similar systems. All four systems used the same terminal, which Emerson leased. Some suppliers, such as American, paid the telephone charges, while others did not. Each system worked differently, and to Richardson, each had some strengths and some weaknesses. She did not regard ASAP as a particularly outstanding system in itself, but ASAP combined with AHSC's excellent service record was enough for Richardson to order from the company even if its prices were 1–2 percent higher than the competition. The stock room clerk, who did the actual order input based on instructions from Richardson, noted that it had taken him about a week to learn each new system and that he had little trouble keeping them apart. He, too, regarded ASAP as a good, but not outstanding, system.

In Richardson's office, she and AHSC account manager Tom Ingles discussed some items that Emerson was ordering for the first time. The price of each item was negotiated between the two; Ingles worked within broad company pricing guidelines, and was compensated entirely on the basis of account profitability. When he returned to his office at AHSC's New England Operations Center, Ingles would have the new prices entered into ASAP. The cost of storing this pricing, like the cost of his automobile, was borne by Ingles out of his gross commissions.

Later, in the smoke-filled hospital cafeteria, Ingles recalled that when he first joined AHSC he had spent a good deal of time dealing with order problems. He sometimes felt that he saw problems on every order, from every account, every day. Now Ingles was able to spend more time selling. While he noted that ASAP was no longer the unique selling proposition that it once had been, Ingles still regarded the system as an important part of AHSC's service. From a personal point of view, he also appreciated the ability to retrieve order data from his home computer, allowing him to be better prepared for sales calls.

AHSC's sales representatives were able to spend less time handling paperwork and more time selling product features and benefits. (The additional focus was evident in the company's sales performance: sales more than tripled from 1975 to 1984 with little increase in the field sales staff and no increase in the sales support staff.) The ability to send and receive messages from customers and the home office made the sales representatives more effective account managers who were thereby able to achieve greater account penetration.

The off-loading of order entry, order status checking, and price and availability queries to customers saved AHSC time and money, as did error checking on input. Customers using ASAP tended to be more disciplined buyers who got more items on each order, thus lowering the costs of packing, shipping, billing, and collecting. Finally, AHSC received important but difficult to measure benefits from analyzing ASAP data to determine order history, usage patterns, economic order quantities, pricing and service levels, and other useful information.

AHSC had also implemented VIP, a "reverse ASAP" that linked the company to its suppliers. Purchase orders were transmitted to suppliers electronically, as were messages about inventory levels, prices, etc. VIP was not mandatory, but the benefits of faster communications were sufficient to convince most suppliers to use the system.

As important as it was, however, ASAP was viewed by at least some within AHSC as a mature order processing system. It could, of course, be enhanced to reduce costs, to provide additional reports, and to include such technical features as voice recognition and a video catalog. The system's ability to enhance ordering convenience was, however, clearly decreasing. AHSC had accordingly evaluated other areas of hospital software and hardware, looking for ways to bundle its products with services that would create an incentive to order from the company. The American Data Services division, which reported to Corporate Marketing, distributed materials management software and consulting services. The American Annson Company, acquired in 1983, sold practice-management software for physicians' offices; the package included inventory management but not ordering. AHSC also offered ADMIS, a microcomputer software package used in operating rooms and radiology departments to identify and monitor the supplies, labor, and time that go into a service or procedure, and STRAPCOE, a hospital admissions forecasting and analysis software package.

As it looked to the future, AHSC saw potentially large changes coming in the ordering and use of supplies. Hospitals were banding to-

---

EXHIBIT 3   AHSC Organization Chart

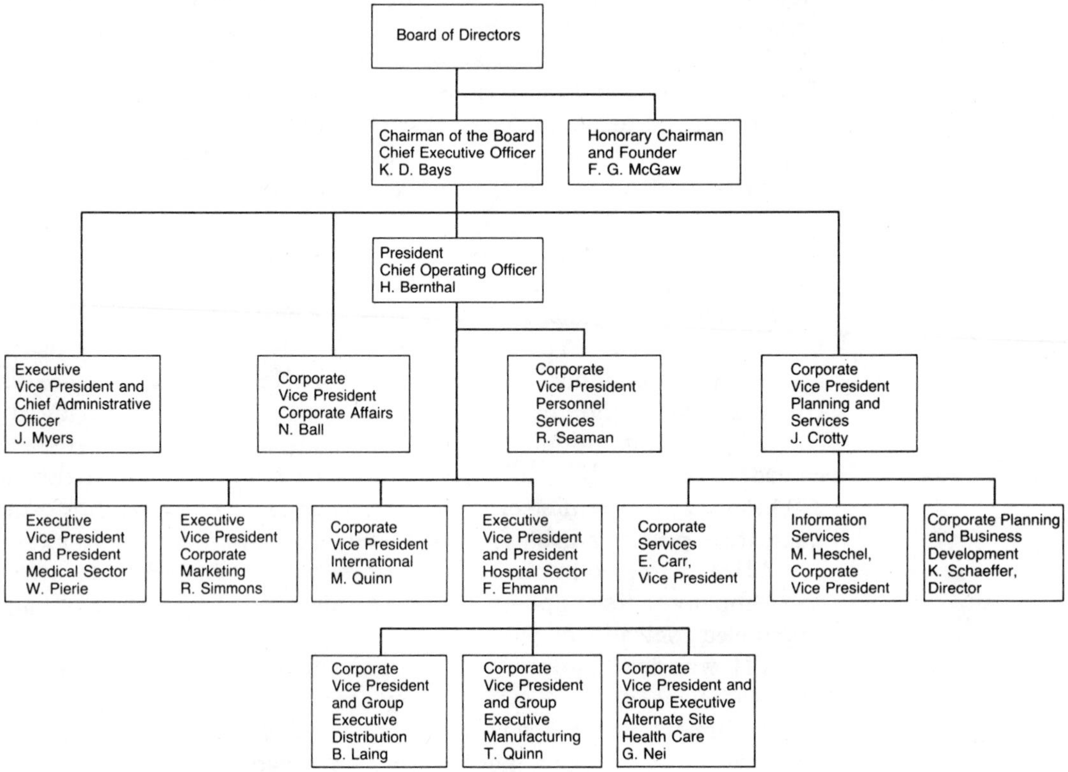

```
                          ┌─────────────────┐
                          │ Board of Directors │
                          └─────────────────┘
                                   │
              ┌────────────────────┴──────────────────┐
   ┌──────────────────────┐              ┌──────────────────────┐
   │ Chairman of the Board │              │ Honorary Chairman     │
   │ Chief Executive Officer│             │ and Founder           │
   │ K. D. Bays            │              │ F. G. McGaw           │
   └──────────────────────┘              └──────────────────────┘
                                   │
                          ┌─────────────────────┐
                          │ President            │
                          │ Chief Operating Officer│
                          │ H. Bernthal          │
                          └─────────────────────┘
```

Executive Vice President and Chief Administrative Officer — J. Myers

Corporate Vice President Corporate Affairs — N. Ball

Corporate Vice President Personnel Services — R. Seaman

Corporate Vice President Planning and Services — J. Crotty

Executive Vice President and President Medical Sector — W. Pierie

Executive Vice President Corporate Marketing — R. Simmons

Corporate Vice President International — M. Quinn

Executive Vice President and President Hospital Sector — F. Ehmann

Corporate Services — E. Carr, Vice President

Information Services — M. Heschel, Corporate Vice President

Corporate Planning and Business Development — K. Schaeffer, Director

Corporate Vice President and Group Executive Distribution — B. Laing

Corporate Vice President and Group Executive Manufacturing — T. Quinn

Corporate Vice President and Group Executive Alternate Site Health Care — G. Nei

---

gether into chains and voluntary buying groups, increasing their leverage and sophistication. Alternate care sites such as physicians' offices, surgical and emergency centers, and nursing homes kept much smaller inventories than hospitals and tended to stock relatively low-cost items. In the home care market, where AHSC faced at least 8,000 suppliers of durable medical equipment, ordering could be done by health care providers or by patients themselves. None of these alternate sites faced a materials management problem as extensive as that of the hospitals, and thus they could probably not make effective use of the more sophisticated versions of ASAP. Alternate sites had provided only $200 million of AHSC's 1984 sales, including $60 million from the $2 billion physicians' office market. (The typical physician in private practice spent about $9,200 on medical supplies and $5,100 on medical equipment in 1984.) The key seemed to be a coordinated approach leveraging American Hospital Supply's skills in technology, distribution, and information systems.

Case 4-2

Jet Age Travel (Condensed)

"At first glance it may appear impossible for us to do a better job at selling airline tickets than the airlines themselves can do, but that's what happens." Harry Jonat, founder, owner, and president of Jet Age Travel, explained. "We've made Jet Age into an absolutely first-rate organization that provides a most useful link between the airlines and their passengers. We provide improved service, including full information and hand-delivered tickets, at not one penny of extra cost to the passenger. The ticket that costs you $103.40 if purchased direct from the airline, also costs you exactly $103.40 if purchased from Jet Age. Not one mil of difference in price—but a vast difference in service."

In January 1983, Jonat was considering strategies for the further growth and development of the firm. One important question in this regard was how the travel agency (TA) industry would change as a result of the Airline Deregulation Act of 1978. There was considerable uncertainty about airline fare structures, TA commissions, and the relationship between the airlines, TAs, and TA customers. Jonat had several alternatives—going public to finance growth, merging with other TAs, or developing "in-plants," Jet Age branch offices on customer sites. Since Jet Age owed much of its past success to information technology (IT),

This case was prepared by Michael R. Vitale and Gregory L. Parsons. Names, locations, and financial data have been disguised.

Copyright © 1984 by the President and Fellows of Harvard College
Harvard Business School case 9-184-184

Jonat believed that future strategies should be based also on the extensive use of IT.

The Travel Agency Industry and Competition

The 1970s had been a period of unprecedented growth for the U.S. travel agency industry. Over the period 1970–81, the number of U.S. agencies had grown from 6,700 to roughly 19,400, and industry revenues increased from $5 billion to almost $30 billion. In large part, industry growth reflected expanded use of air transportation. From 1956 to 1977, per capita expenditures for air travel grew 12.8 percent per year on average compared to 7.7 percent for all forms of transportation. In terms of passenger miles traveled by air, the North American market had increased 67 percent from 1975 to 1983. Travel agents accounted for about 60 percent of annual passenger airline ticket sales in the U.S., and such sales represented 70 percent of agency revenues. In 1980, U.S. airlines paid TAs $1.5 billion in commissions.

However, there was much uncertainty in the industry as it entered the 1980s. Because of changing travel habits, continuing changes in the regulatory environment, shifting agency-supplier and agency-client relationships, new forms of competition, and rising costs, all agencies had to evaluate the effectiveness and efficiency of their operations.

Under prevailing law, accredited travel agents and the airlines themselves had the exclusive right to sell airline tickets. Virtually all U.S. airlines paid TAs a nominal 10 percent commission on tickets sold. It was common, however, for airlines to pay overrides—extra commissions—to some agents, while other airlines sold a high proportion of tickets through their own offices. Commissions paid thus varied by airline from less than 5 percent to more than 17 percent of passenger revenues. Although each airline was free to set any commission rate it wished, periodic efforts by some carriers to pay less than 10 percent failed when competition refused to go along.

In 1981 the Civil Aeronautics Board (CAB) ruled that as of January 1985, other retail outlets—banks, supermarkets, department stores, and so on—would also be allowed to sell airline tickets. Some observers anticipated a move towards "bulk ticketing," in which carriers would sell blocks of tickets to TAs and others who could then resell the tickets at whatever price they chose. Although this change from the traditional fixed-price fare environment was allowed for the first time by the Airline Deregulation Act of 1978, airlines and agents had thus far maintained the status quo.

Another challenge to the TAs came from one of their long-time suppliers, the publisher of the *Official Airline Guide* (OAG). A new, "electronic OAG" was available for a fee to anyone with a computer terminal or microcomputer. The electronic edition contained the same schedule and fare data as did the printed OAG used by travel agents. The computer version could display flight information in order of cost as well as by departure time. The electronic OAG did not initially include any provisions for making a reservation or getting a ticket—these tasks still had to be carried out via a phone call or trip to a travel agency. One airline, TWA, had made its reservation system available to users of a teletext information service.

TA customers were also applying pressure to some agents. More than 350 major corporations already had "in-plant" agencies. Before deregulation, airlines were allowed to pay only 3 percent commission to such agencies, and even after regulation ended most carriers stuck to the 3 percent. Corporations were thought to be able to arrange for commission rebates; some in-plants, in turn, were said to be able to use their large volume to negotiate higher commissions from the airlines. A few corporations had asked the CAB to allow their travel departments to receive compensation directly from the airlines.

Given the likely changes in the commission structure, the president of one agency estimated that the late 1970s benchmark of $200,000 to $250,000 sales per agency employee necessary for profitability had to grow to $400,000 or more in the future. Among the likely sources of productivity improvements were increased automation; more sophisticated management and personnel practices; increased attention to market selection and other marketing activities; and more efficient organizational forms. The president of the advertising agency that led the ad industry in travel account billings suggested, "There is still plenty of money to be made in travel, but only those who keep up with the times will enjoy the rewards.... Of today's (1980) 17,000 travel agencies, only 10,000 are likely to be in business by the end of the 1980s."

The TA industry contained a large number of firms, most of them small; more than two-thirds were single office locations. In the Jet Age area, there were branch offices of two international firms, American Express and Thomas Cook, and four other local firms. Two of the local firms, each slightly smaller than Jet Age, served only corporate clients and were therefore "commercial" agencies like Jet Age. The other two local firms did about half of their business on the "retail" side (pleasure travel) and had commercial activities of about the same size and scope as Jet Age.

Thomas Cook and American Express had many more offices than the local agencies and therefore had larger, more sophisticated telecommunications systems. However, each office of each agency had about the same amount of electronic technology. TAs such as Jet Age typically had much better market penetration in their local areas than the larger

EXHIBIT 1 Estimated Population Statistics in Jet Age's Market Area

	1965	1970	1975	1982
Total population (millions)	1.2	1.6	1.8	2.2
Percent of population that has used air travel	42%	49%	56%	70%
Percent of population that takes one flight per year	11	14	18	21
Percent of population that takes two or more flights per year	5	6	6	7

firms. This suggested, according to Jonat, only that the local agencies had historically done a better job in the local areas. He did not believe that there were any structural prohibitions in the industry which would prevent this situation from changing.

History and Growth of Jet Age

In the spring of 1964, Harry Jonat, who had an M.B.A. from a leading West Coast school and a Ph.D. in business from another major university, read a *Wall Street Journal* article describing the travel requirements of major enterprises. The article stated that significant numbers of firms were establishing their own in-house travel departments or were seeking travel agencies that could handle their needs. Over the next several months, Jonat and two friends explored the viability of establishing a travel agency to serve the greater Atlanta area (see Exhibit 1 for details). This area included some 6,000 organizations with more than 25 employees (see Exhibits 2 and 3).

EXHIBIT 2 Estimated Number of Corporations and Nonprofit Organizations with More than 25 Employees in Jet Age's Marketing Area

Travel Budget	Number of Organizations			
	1965	1970	1975	1982
Above $500,000	600	775	1,100	1,500
$250,000–$500,000	1,150	1,200	1,450	1,625
$100,000–$250,000	1,500	1,750	2,250	2,300
$25,000–$100,000	1,900	2,100	2,600	2,800
Below $25,000	1,150	1,575	1,500	1,875
Total	6,300	7,400	8,900	10,100

EXHIBIT 3   Estimated Market Statistics for Jet Age in 1982

	Number of Organizations that Use:				
Travel Budget	Jet Age	Major JA Competitors	Other TAs	In-House Office	Mixed* (In-House/TA)
Above $500,000	35	160	75	935	295
$250,000–$500,000	80	270	125	1,200	350
$100,000–$250,000	120	520	170	1,115	375
$25,000–$100,000	90	340	400	1,220	750
Below $25,000	75	290	275	235	600
Total	400	1580	1045	4705	2370

*A very small number of in-house offices were actually in-plant offices of TAs.

On April 19, 1965, Jet Age Travel opened for business with a staff of two people, the manager and a secretary/clerk. Initially the agency did not specialize in any one sector of the travel industry. Instead, Jet Age accepted any kind of travel business that "walked in the door." Over the next two and one-half years, as Jet Age Travel grew "slowly and painfully," Jonat found his own management involvement expanding "almost day-to-day." This process climaxed in early 1968 when he assumed the duties of president on a full-time basis; the employment of the original manager was terminated at this time. Beginning in 1968 Jet Age's marketing efforts emphasized airline reservations for businesses located in the immediate vicinity of Jet Age's office. In fiscal 1975, these clients accounted for almost 90 percent of Jet Age's clients' bookings.

Airlines preferred travel agents to concentrate on pleasure travel, particularly packaged tours. At the time, airlines paid an 11 percent commission for domestic tours and 10 percent for international tours, but only a 7 percent commission on regular ticket sales, which usually were simple and straightforward. To encourage direct booking, most airlines issued their own air travel credit cards. No commission was earned by a travel agent if its clients used an airline credit card to pay for domestic tickets obtained through an agency. Most travel agencies focused on the higher commission sales even though more work and time were required by each sale. Jonat believed that the trade-off between the work required of the TA and the commission received was about equal but chose the lower commission alternative because there was generally less "hassle" with regular ticket sales.

Jet Age's specialization thus meant that some of its heaviest competition came from the airlines themselves. Jonat justified Jet Age's atypical strategy partly on the grounds that he simply did not like, nor feel comfortable with, the tour business. "My theory," Jonat said, "is that a substantial portion of the people who take tours really don't want to leave home, and are miserable if they do. Such individuals are conned into taking a tour by their wife or husband, or by some well-meaning relative, or by some organization they belong to, or because of some desire to keep up with the Joneses. But they're ill at ease and uncomfortable with the whole idea. With some, it's a case of actual fear of strange surroundings. As a result, while on tour, such individuals constantly are looking for reasons to be unhappy, and they usually find them. And what better whipping boy to pour out your unhappiness on than the travel agent through whom you booked?"

By following his strategy, Jonat could say, "By 1975 we were one of the biggest agencies in town; in the entire state, for that matter. Clearly, we were the biggest of the agencies that specialized in regular airline bookings. We're committed to one thing, service. Our customer must get the best reservation service available and at not one penny's additional price. We are seen as an innovator in the agency business. When the 'brass' from many of the airlines are in town, they're frequently brought to Jet Age to see a model travel agency at work." In 1975, Jet Age had earned commissions of $997,000, up from $665,000 in 1973, on sales in excess of $13 million. Net profit after tax was $45,000. In 1982, Jet Age got commissions of $3.5 million on sales in excess of $35 million and had a net profit after tax of $106,000. (See Exhibit 4 for financial details.) Jet Age had 112 employees, up from 59 in 1970 and 83 in 1975. The number of commercial client accounts was 185 in 1970, 270 in 1975, and nearly 400 in 1982. The number of tickets issued increased from 47,000 in 1970 to 76,000 in 1975 and 110,000 in 1982. Jonat estimated that Jet Age had grown 15–20 percent faster than its competitors.

Closely related through the years to Jet Age's strategy and operations, and reflective of Jonat's personal penchant for technological innovation, was the company's emphasis upon the most up-to-date techniques of data handling, including the processing of reservations. Jonat was convinced that such capabilities were essential to assuring Jet Age's customers of superior service and to differentiating Jet Age from competing agencies. He thus responded quickly when, in 1969, a major trunk airline announced its intention to install computer terminals in a few carefully selected travel agencies throughout the U.S. These terminals were to be identical to those employed at airport ticket offices. With their use, information on schedules and seat availability for most U.S. airlines could be ascertained, and reservations could be booked and confirmed, almost immediately. The rental charge was to be $220 per terminal per month.

Jonat's desire to be one of the agencies selected for the new terminals was increased since Jet Age had just launched a major campaign

---

EXHIBIT 4

Jet Age Travel
Consolidated Statement of Income and Expenses
Fiscal years ending October 31
($000)

	1970	1975	1982
Income			
Airline commissions	$365	$883	$3,040
Hotel commissions	14	53	205
Other commissions and retainers	11	54	229
Other income	0	7	26
Total income	$390	$997	$3,500
Expenses			
Employee salaries and payroll taxes	$231	$561	$2,085
Interest	23	57	150
Rent	17	41	145
Telephone/telegraph/cable	21	40	130
Depreciation and amortization	14	35	125
Office expenses	13	32	112
Consulting	13	31	64
Printing and stationery	11	28	99
Reservation equipment rental and information systems	2	25	100
Accident and health insurance	5	13	21
Dues and subscriptions	4	11	53
Automobile expense	4	9	37
Advertising and sales promotion	3	8	24
Travel and entertainment	3	8	16
Postage	3	7	18
Electricity	2	6	14
Legal and accounting	2	6	19
Officer life insurance	1	2	8
Bad debts	1	1	3
Other expenses (office cleaning/ commissions/insurance/adjustments/ delivery expenses, etc.)	7	19	51
Total expenses	$380	$940	$3,274
Pretax profit	$ 10	$ 57	$ 226
Posttax profit*	$ 7	$ 45	$ 126

---

*i.e., after federal and state income taxes. Reflects effects of certain investment credit carry-over for current and prior years.

to increase its share of the $75,000 per year of travel business generated by a nearby university. Through considerable hard work and help from friends, Jet Age received a terminal. Jonat said, "This was a major victory for us. As a result, we got something like 85 percent of the airline bookings generated by the university. We completely eclipsed the competition. The terminals permitted us to gain a number of additional clients as well. I would guess that at least 10 percent of our business is directly related to our use of terminals."

Shortly after the first airline's decision, two other carriers announced their intention to make their computer terminal systems available to selected travel agencies. One airline promptly chose 5 travel bureaus (not including Jet Age), while the other stated that it would choose 10 agencies. In exploring the possibility of including Jet Age among these 10 agencies, this carrier stated that they "assumed" Jet Age would abandon its use of the first system if its system were made available instead. This carrier, a worldwide airline, offered greater travel coverage, and its terminal system was less expensive as well. Jonat had worked closely with the domestic airline's local management over the years and had received many favors from them, including their help in Jet Age's selection for one of the first terminal installations. He therefore refused to abandon the already installed system. After some delay, the second airline agreed to make its terminals available to Jet Age, even though the agency retained its initial system.

In 1974, Jet Age installed a specially designed automated system that printed tickets and provided each customer with a detailed itinerary for every trip. Jonat believed that this move into clerical automation typified the technological innovation necessary to keep Jet Age ahead of the ever-mounting volume of paperwork generated by growth in the company's volume of business.

Jet Age Operations

Marketing

Jet Age's market included all organizations within 30 miles of the home office, and was segmented by travel budget. Jet Age preferred clients with larger travel budgets, since its return on sales declined from about .7 percent for larger accounts to about .4 percent for the smaller clients. The percentage commission earned was the same for all clients, so the difference in earnings resulted from the nearly fixed level of administrative cost.

Marketing was the responsibility of six marketing people, up from three in 1975 and one in 1970 (see Exhibit 5 for organizational details). The people acted on referrals, requests for proposals from organizations, and general word-of-mouth information, making approximately 2,500 sales contacts each year. The majority were made by phone, with Jet Age initiating more than half. Through an exchange of phone conversations, letters, and sometimes trial services, Jet Age would win an

EXHIBIT 5 Organization Chart, January 1983

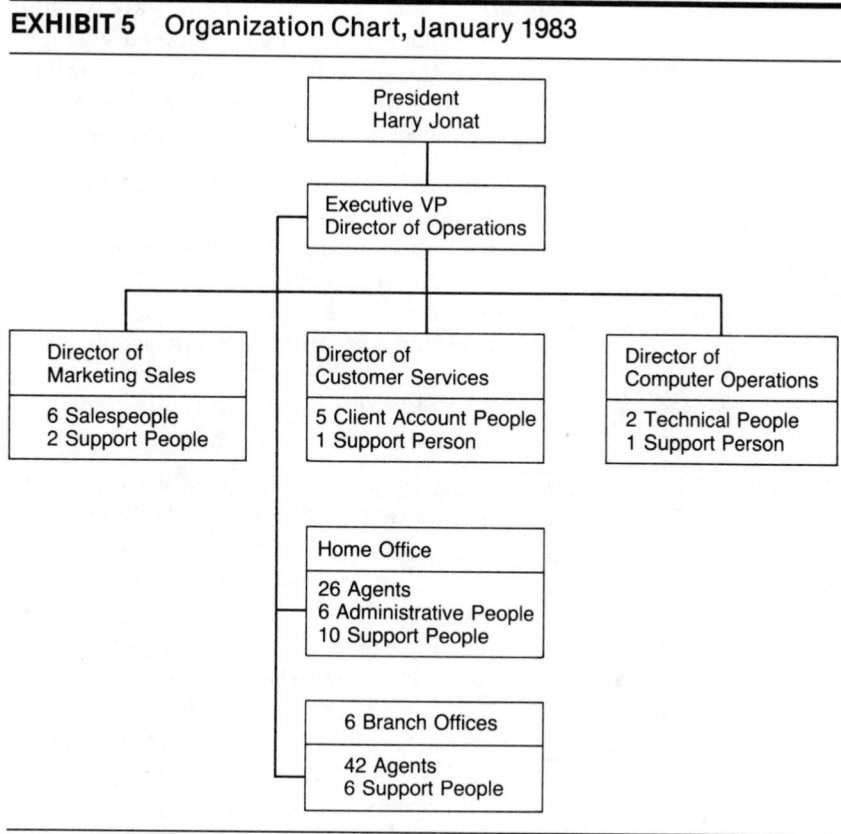

average of 80 smaller accounts per year. To obtain larger accounts, Jet Age made some 700 initial sales calls on an average of 500 firms per year. Following a sales call, Jet Age would screen the prospective client according to the potential volume of sales and commissions versus the expected services and associated costs. If a quick estimate did not yield an approximate .5 percent return on sales, Jet Age would not pursue the prospect any further. On average, about 20 percent of the prospects were screened out. Good prospects were pursued with additional sales calls, letters, short proposals outlining Jet Age's services and qualifications, and more fully developed proposals which included sample formats for invoices, accounting data, and travel history analysis reports along with a list of references. Each year, Jet Age submitted 40 or 50 fully developed proposals and about 150 letter proposals.

Often two or three competing TAs would be invited to make a presentation to an organization looking for a new agent. At this point, a preliminary client needs analysis would be conducted, and Jonat or another senior person would get involved with prospects having annual travel budgets over $300,000. The presentation would stress the benefits of working with Jet Age by pointing out how well the firm could meet five criteria for measuring TA effectiveness:

1. Accuracy and thoroughness in making itineraries, schedules, and reservations.
2. Providing prompt, efficient service.
3. Making the transactions promised and physically delivering tickets on time.
4. Providing accurate, prompt billing in a format that was compatible with the client's accounting system.
5. As needed by clients, providing analysis and reports of travel history and associated costs.

While competitors made essentially the same presentation, Jet Age, according to Jonat, could better demonstrate that its services were special. Jonat believed, based on clients' comments, that Jet Age won at least 25 percent of its accounts because of its ability to deliver data, analysis, and reports.

Jet Age also promoted its use of information technology. In particular, Jet Age claimed that its use of many reservation systems—six airlines, two rental car and two hotel chains—assured accuracy and thoroughness. Since major airline reservation systems provided access to most airlines, hotels, and rental car agencies, it was possible for a TA to get by with only one system. And although 80 percent of TAs used one or another of the airline systems, it was unusual to have more than one. Indeed, United Air Lines had instituted a "95 percent rule" which stated that agencies having its APOLLO system must book at least 95 percent of trips containing any United flight entirely through the United computer system. Some large, long-time APOLLO users, including Jet Age, were able to avoid the rule. Since airlines updated prices and schedules in their own systems directly, but sent data to other airlines on tapes, data could be a week or more out of date. Agencies with more than one system could therefore keep better track of prices. Jet Age had one person who checked all reservation systems as well as newspapers each morning for price changes and then updated the "price change sheet"[1] which was used by Jet Age agents to provide the latest prices.

---

[1] The "price change sheet" was actually a typed sheet which was photocopied and distributed to home office agents. For branch offices it was a series of "electronic mail" messages sent via a reservation system (see Exhibit 6).

Multiple reservation systems also permitted Jet Age to get around seat availability calculations. With the objective of filling all seats on each flight, airline systems had to protect against overbooking as well as "no-shows." Depending on the particular circumstances, the systems would display one number for seat availability to its own users and other numbers (usually smaller) to other systems. If several reservations were made from a particular outside system, the system might cut it off by showing no seats available. Without access to an airline's own system, a TA could not tell how many seats were actually available on a flight; with a number of systems, a TA could provide much better service to its clients.

An associated problem had to do with seat cancellations and the seat/fare structure for a particular flight, which depended on historical use factors, elasticity calculations, and promotional activities. The least expensive seats were reserved first. A particular airline's system would not only display differing seat availability to various other systems, but would also reserve more of the less expensive seats for itself and would not always show seat cancellations on a timely basis. The TA without access to multiple systems could be at a significant disadvantage.

Not all major airline systems carried schedules or seat availability for local, regional, and so-called "upstart" carriers such as People Express. Some of these smaller or newer airlines had refused to pay the major airlines to have their flights listed. Thus, not all reservation systems were able to schedule all flights, and the use of several systems assisted TAs in providing a more comprehensive service.

Reservation systems generally had a certain amount of "display bias" in that an airline's system showed its own flights in an advantageous manner. While this bias could make scheduling difficult and frustrating, a well-trained TA could get around the bias of a given system. However, problems could occur when an agent was trying to work out a complicated schedule within the parameters of lower cost and shorter time. In these cases, it was simply easier for an agent to consult several different host systems. Its own "back office" computer permitted Jet Age to provide more data, more analysis, and more reports in more different custom-designed formats than any of the competitors could. While client comments suggested that Jet Age did provide superior service and that most other agencies did not attempt to compete with Jet Age in this area, only about half the clients considered these analyses and reporting services to be important, and even those clients assigned only about 20 percent of the TA selection decision to them.

Jet Age won 20 or so large accounts annually with approximately 5 being included among its top 25 clients. These results were approximately double what they were in 1975 and triple those of 1970.

Once an account was established, Jet Age conducted a more extensive analysis of the client's travel needs and practices. Based on this analysis, Jet Age offered advice on travel policies and procedures to meet expressed client objectives. Jet Age would also offer special cost-saving deals such as reduced hotel rates. And Jet Age would, through discussion, develop a set of working relationships and a detailed base line of expectations on the part of both the client and the agency. When the inevitable problems and differences of opinion arose, the agreed-upon expectations facilitated the work of the client account representatives, who were responsible for keeping accounts once the marketing people won them. For example, a client employee might become angry because she was routed from Chicago to Atlanta through Cleveland, Ohio and Birmingham, Alabama. The client account representative might respond with, "Yes, there was a direct Chicago to Atlanta flight that cost $257, but your firm's policy is to save money, therefore, we booked you on the 'milk run' that cost $178." While Jet Age was sorry for the inconvenience, it was acting according to previously arranged policies and expectations.

A second reason for taking particular care in working out policies and relationships was that it suggested to Jonat how Jet Age's business was changing and how he was adding value for various clients. By keeping close track of such trends, Jet Age could adjust ongoing operations and predict how things might continue to change in the future. For example, Jonat believed that in 1975 most of the value added by Jet Age had come from providing accurate information and from completing ticketing and reservation transactions efficiently. The "front office" reservation aspect of the business was more important than the "back office" aspects. By 1982, clients expected Jet Age to provide advice in addition to information and to broker more cost-saving deals. The back office had become more important and Jet Age responded by hiring a computer programmer to design and implement back office services such as better analysis and reports in custom-designed formats. Jonat reasoned that Jet Age was in the "reduction of corporate travel cost" business. He was spending much more time brokering special deals and maintaining relations with suppliers such as airlines and hotels, and less time on marketing and general management.

In 1970, Jet Age's average client account life was approximately six years; in that year Jet Age still had most of the clients it started with. In 1975, the average account tenure was a little over five years. By 1980, approximately 25 percent of the accounts at Jet Age were new each year, about 20 percent due to turnover, and 5 percent from newly-founded organizations.

One reason clients changed was to keep TAs "honest and on their toes"; a number of firms had a policy of switching TAs every three or four years. Other clients "went shopping" for better services from TAs, and would switch if another TA were willing to offer a larger range of services or appeared to have higher quality services. A number of firms also regularly compared the costs and benefits of using a TA to the use of an in-house travel office. These firms tended to switch between the alternatives every five to seven years. Harry Jonat believed, in the final analysis, that TA clients behaved according to the "tea cup theory." Every time a TA made a mistake—late delivery of a ticket, inaccurate invoice, wrong size rental car, booking in a second class hotel—the client would put a rather large marble into a rather small tea cup. When the cup was full the client would switch travel agencies.

Advice for Suppliers

Jet Age constantly assessed the match between sellers' offerings and its clients' needs. The agency then advised the suppliers on the need for new products and for changes in pricing. In this way Jet Age assisted in shaping the suppliers' operations and offerings. For example, Jet Age was often asked by airlines to estimate the price/convenience/time trade-off for flights between well-traveled points. By analyzing the data base it had developed to serve its clients, Jet Age could provide this and other valuable marketing information. And when Jet Age needed a favor, such as getting a seat on a fully booked flight, the suppliers often responded to the benefit of the agency and its clients.

Operations

In general, clients phoned Jet Age with requests for tickets and other travel arrangements. Jet Age personnel handled the requests, produced and delivered the necessary tickets and documents, generated billing and accounting data, and updated customer records. These same records would be used later when Jet Age offered its clients analysis, reports, and additional advice.

Jonat believed that Jet Age made particularly effective use of its branch offices. Even though it was technically possible to handle all clients from the home office, many clients still believed that TAs which were physically closer could better meet their needs. Moreover, TAs generally felt that smaller offices were more efficient and productive because the working groups were more cohesive and the individual agents took more pride in their work. Jet Age had thus established six branch offices with an average of eight people per office, and used a telecommunication link to permit the branches to share the computer power of the home office. Jonat believed that at least 10–15 percent of Jet Age's business was directly due to its use of branch offices.

While Jonat thought that Jet Age conducted day-to-day operations at least as well as its competitors, there were two problems that he guarded against. The first was "bonus" tickets offered by the airlines to agents who produced well for the carrier. This practice could bias agents against providing the lowest cost alternatives for clients. Jonat did not allow his agents to participate directly in the bonus and "give-away" activities of the airlines. Jonat would personally take tickets provided for past performance and distribute them to employees as he decided. The second problem affected Jonat more personally: the more Jet Age lowered its clients' travel costs, the more Jet Age lowered its own revenues. Jonat responded to this dilemma by honestly striving for low-cost solutions to client needs, on the assumption that his virtue would be rewarded with more accounts and larger volume.

Other Services

Jonat used Jet Age's electronic technology, expertise, and relatively larger size to make it function as a service bureau for smaller agencies around the country. For example, although a small agency closed its doors at 6 P.M., it somehow needed to respond to an 11 P.M. call from a client who wanted a hotel room that night. The client could call a toll-free number and ask Jet Age to find the room. By assisting smaller agencies around the clock, Jet Age made better use of its own fixed costs and provided better service for its own clients as well. An added benefit was that Jet Age had begun to develop a national network of travel service suppliers and buyers.

Jet Age's Information Technology

Jet Age used a Data General Nova 3 minicomputer with 300 megabytes of disk storage space. This machine kept customer records and produced tickets, itineraries, invoices, accounting data, and travel history analysis reports. Twelve ticketing machines, located in branch offices, were also driven by the minicomputer, which also handled Jet Age's accounts receivable, accounts payable, and the "ATC report." (The Air Traffic Conference [ATC] served as a financial clearinghouse for airlines and travel agencies, and each week the TAs would transfer to the ATC a report of ticket sales along with payment. The ATC distributed the payments among the airlines and handled refunds due the agents. Most commercial TAs ran on a 7-day accounts payable cycle and a 30-day accounts receivable cycle.)

Jet Age had some 112 terminals that permitted company personnel to check flight availabilities and schedules, make reservations, instruct the ticketing machines, and update customer records. At the other elec-

---

EXHIBIT 6 Jet Age's Information Technology System

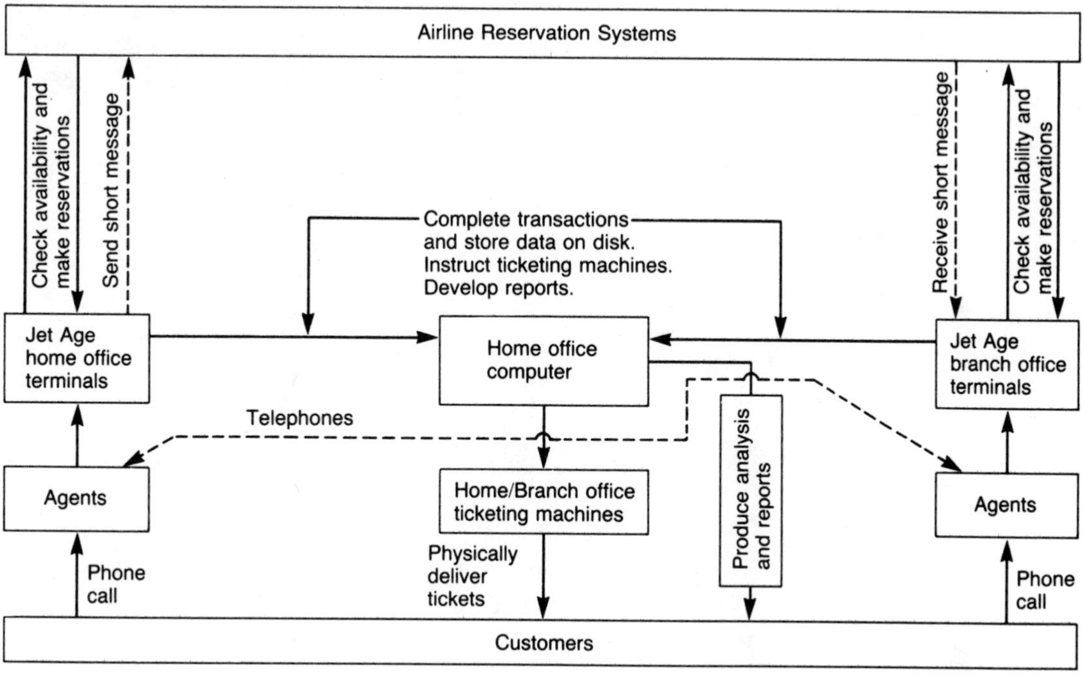

Airline reservation systems permit individual travel agency offices to send short messages to other offices. This is how Jet Age sometimes delivered price change information to branch offices. Price information was also distributed by telephone. Jet Age could have used its central computer for all electronic mail but the volume did not justify the cost.

---

tronic end, the terminals were tied into various airline reservation systems (see Exhibit 6).

The Future

Jonat noted that at various times he had "toyed with" such possibilities as opening additional Jet Age offices in new geographic areas; operating "captive" in-house travel departments for major clients; broadening Jet Age's product line to include additional facets of the travel business; acquiring other established agencies; or diversifying into entirely different services. In the "heat of battle," none of these alternatives had yet received serious, sustained study. However, Jonat remained committed to developing a new strategy based on information technology.

Chapter 5

IT Organization Issues

The IT Challenge to Organizational Structure

Organizational instability has been an enduring feature of the information technology (IT) environment. In the past decade technological changes have repeatedly challenged existing IT organizational structures in many companies, raising the possibility of major reorganization. Several key reasons lie behind this.

Technological Change

First, both for efficiency and for effectiveness, IT in the 1980s must include office automation, data and voice communications, and data processing, all managed in a coordinated and (in many situations) an integrated manner. Developing this coordination has not always been easy. In many organizations in the 1960s and 1970s each of these activities had different technical bases, was marketed to the company quite separately, and was usually managed independently. Quite different internal organizational structures and practices for handling them developed. Frequently these organizations included neither the necessary staff levels nor the required mix of skills for the new technology. The varied managerial histories and decision processes associated with each of these technologies in the past has made their integration exceptionally difficult.

Second, ensuring the success of information technologies new to the organization requires approaches that are quite different from those used with technologies that the organization has had more experience with. New organization structures have emerged to facilitate this.

TABLE 5-1 Costs and Performance of Electronics

Technology	1958 Vacuum Tube	1966 Transistor	1972 IC*	1980 LSI†
Dollars per unit	$ 8.00	$ 0.25	$ 0.02	$0.001
Dollars per logic	160.00	12.00	200.00	.05
Operation time	16×10^{-3}	4×10^{-6}	40×10^{-9}	200×10^{-12}

*Integrated circuit.
†Large-scale integrated circuit.
SOURCE: W. D. Frazer, "Potential Technology Implications for Computers and Telecommunications in the 1980's," *IBM Systems Journal* 18, no. 2, pp. 333–36.

Third, where the firm's data and computer hardware resources should be located organizationally requires rethinking. The dramatic hardware performance improvements (in all three technologies) in the past decade allows very different solutions today than it did in the early 1970s. These improvements have been facilitated by the technology shift from the vacuum tube to the very large-scale integrated circuits with their vastly improved cost-performance ratios. Equally significant, integrated circuits have permitted development of stand-alone minicomputer systems or office automation systems that can be tailored to provide specific service for any desired location.

Technological change, then, has permitted a dramatic shift in both the type of information services being delivered to users and the best organizational structure for delivering them. This structure involves not only the coordination of data processing, teleprocessing, and office automation but also change in both the physical and the organizational placement of the firm's technical and staff resources that provide IT services. Technical resources include items such as computers, word processors, private telephone exchanges, and intelligent terminals. Staff resources consist of all the individuals responsible for either operating these technologies, developing new applications, or maintaining them.

Productivity changes are continuing as still smaller, more reliable, useful circuits are being developed. Table 5–1 shows the cost trends per individual unit and circuit over the past 20 years, trends that will continue for the next decade. The cost reduction and capacity increase caused by these changes have reduced computer hardware cost to below 30 percent of total departmental cost in most large IT environments. Today computer cost often does not exceed corporate telecommunications expense and for many firms is significantly less than software development and maintenance charges.

Environmental Factors

In addition to technology changes, several nontechnological factors have prompted the reexamination of the most effective way to organize IT services inside the firm.

Human Resources. The United States has a significant shortage of competent, skilled people to translate this technology into ongoing systems and processes within organizations. These shortages, severe in 1986, will continue in the coming decade for the following reasons:

1. The number of individuals reaching their 18th birthday in the 15 years between 1986 and 2000 is estimated to plunge by more than 20 percent. Because the technical side of this field has historically been dominated by young people, a decrease in the flow of new entrants to the work force is of concern.
2. The decline in Scholastic Aptitude Test scores in the past 15 years and the necessary reworking and simplification of college freshman curricula indicate problems of quality in the entrants to the labor pool.
3. The limited availability of professional-level IT curricula, as potential faculty choose industry over university careers. In the spring of 1986, over 200 unfilled teaching openings in information technology courses existed in major universities.

Telecommunications Environment. Highly reliable, cheap digital telecommunications systems have been developed in the United States, and the explosion of optical fibre cable installation in Europe is helping to expand telecommunication growth there. The economics and reliability of worldwide telecommunications, however, differ from those in the United States and Canada, which presents unique environments for the immediate future.

In Western Europe, excessive tariffs (often an order of magnitude higher than the United States and Canada), coupled with inordinate delays once an installation is planned, create additional challenges. However, as European countries better coordinate their government-owned systems, more cost-effective environments may emerge.

In Latin America and other parts of the globe, reliability problems further compound these general problems. For example, because of unplanned, unacceptable communication breakdowns (sometimes more than 24 hours in duration), one South American company was forced to shut down a sophisticated on-line system supporting multiple branches. In another situation, a company was able to achieve acceptable reliability only by gaining permission to construct and maintain its own network of microwave towers. For multinationals this poses important problems in development of international networks and common standards.

Supply-Demand Imbalances.   Legitimate user demand for IT support continues to vastly exceed the supply available from an IT organization. Cost-justified applications waiting to be implemented and exceeding available IT staff resources by three or more years—the norm rather than the exception—lead to a perception of unsatisfactory support and to unhappy interpersonal contacts with the central IT organization.

Widespread user frustration provides additional momentum for end-user computing, personal computers, and so on, as alternative ways to meet legitimate needs. As discussed later this is not allowed. The new personal computer technologies increasingly permit users to bypass central IT control and relieve these frustrations. In addition, users' confidence in their ability to run a computer (sometimes unwarranted) because of personal experience has not only grown but is likely to continue to grow.

Systems Design Philosophy.   A fundamental shift has occurred in computer-based systems design philosophy. The prevailing practice in the 1960s and early 1970s involved writing computer programs that intermixed data processing instructions and data elements within the computer program structure. In the 1980s world, the management of data elements is clearly separated from the computer program instructions. Implementing this shift, plus coping with legitimate changes in business processing needs, has placed enormous pressures on IT organizations. They must balance investing human resources in new systems developments against redesigning old systems to increase their relevance, while ensuring reliable operation of the old systems until the updated ones can be installed.

The above factors combined with changing computer hardware economics have meant that organization structures correctly designed in the early 1970s may be seriously flawed for the mid-1980s and that a major reappraisal is in order for many firms. Succeeding sections of this chapter will cover the need for and challenges in merging the disparate technologies, the different approaches to assimilating IT (depending on the organization's familiarity with it), and the issues involved in selecting an appropriate centralization/decentralization balance of data and hardware.

Merging the Islands of Information Technology

Problems in the speedy integration of data processing, telecommunications, and office automation are largely a result of the very different management practices relating to these technologies (as shown in Table 5–2). The following paragraphs analyze these differences in more depth.

In 1920, an operational style of information services—elements of which continue to this day—was in place in most corporations. The manager and his secretary were supported by three forms of information services, each using different technologies. For word processing, the typewriter was the main engine for generating legible words for distribution. A file cabinet served as the main storage device for output, and the various organization units were linked by secretaries moving paper from one unit to another. Data processing, if automated at all, was dependent upon card-sorting machines to develop sums and balances, using as input punched cards that served as memory for this system. The telecommunications system involved wires and messages that were manipulated by operator control of electromechanical switches to connect parties. The telecommunications system had no storage capacity.

Also, in 1920 (as shown in Table 5–3) the designer of each of the three islands (office technology, data processing, and telecommunications) had significantly different roles. For word processing, the office manager directed the design, heavily influenced by the whim of his or her manager. Although office system studies were emerging, word processing was primarily a means of facilitating secretarial work. The prime means of obtaining new equipment was through purchasing agents and involved selecting typewriters, dictaphones, and file cabinets from a wide variety of medium-sized companies. Standardization was not critical. Data processing was the domain of the controller-accountant, and the systems design activity was carried out by either the chief accountant or a card systems manager whose job it was to design the protocols for processing information. Both data processing and teleprocessing were sufficiently complex and expensive that they required that managers develop an explicit plan of action.

A key difference between data processing and telephones, starting in the 1920s, was that the service of data processing was normally purchased and maintained as a system from one supplier. Thus, from the beginning, a systems relationship existed between buyer and seller. Teleprocessing, however, evolved as a purchased service. As AT&T had made available a network of cheaper inner-city telephones, companies

TABLE 5-2 Information Technology: Equipment Used

	1920			1965			1986		
Functions of the Technology	Word Processing	Data Processing	Communication	Word Processing	Data Processing	Communication	Word Processing	Data Processing	Communication
Human-to-machine translation	Shorthand Dictaphone	Form Keypunch	Phone	Shorthand Dictaphone	Form Keypunch	Phone	Shorthand Dictaphone Terminal	Terminal	Phone Terminal
Manipulation of data	Typewriter	Card sort	Switch	Typewriter	Computer	Computer	Computer	Computer	Computer
Memory	File cabinet	Cards	None	File cabinet	Computer	None	Computer	Computer	Computer
Linkage	Secretary	Operator	Operator	Secretary	Computer	Computer	Computer	Computer	Computer

Islands of Technology

TABLE 5-3 Information Technology: Human Roles

| | Islands of Technology | | | | | | | | |
| | 1920 | | | 1965 | | | 1986 | | |
Roles	Word Processing	Data Processing	Communication	Word Processing	Data Processing	Communication	Word Processing	Data Processing	Communication
Designer	Office manager	Card designer	AT&T	Office system analyst	System analyst	AT&T	System analyst	System analyst	System analyst
Operator	Secretary	Machine operator	AT&T	Secretary	Operator	AT&T	Manager Secretary Editor	Manager Secretary Operator	Manager Secretary Multiple suppliers
Maintainer	Many companies	Single supplier	AT&T	Many companies	Single supplier	AT&T	Many companies or single supplier	Multiple suppliers	Multiple suppliers Other
User	Manager	Accountant	Manager	Manager	Manager Accountant	Everybody	Everybody	Everybody	Everybody

responded by ordering the phones, and the utility developed a monopoly of the phone system. All three islands, therefore, were served in a different manner in 1920: one by many companies, one by a single systems supplier, and one by a public utility.

In 1965 the servicing and management of all three islands were still institutionalized in the 1920s pattern. Word processing had a design content but was still very much influenced by the manager and centered around the secretary. Services, such as typewriters and reproducing systems, were purchased as independent units from a range of competitors offering similar technology. There was little long-term planning, with designs and systems evolving in response to new available technical units. Data processing, however, had emerged as an ever more complex management process, requiring serious evaluation of major capital investments in computers and software as well as multiyear project management of the design and development of systems support. In addition all employees and users needed extensive training sessions to take full advantage of the productivity of the new system. At times even the corporate organization was changed to accommodate both the problems and the new potential caused by computer technology. In 1965 AT&T completely dominated the provision of communications service; from a user's perspective, management of communications was a passive purchase problem. In some organizations, managing communications implied placing three-minute hourglasses by phones to reduce length of calls.

Today, however, the management concerns for word processing and telecommunications have become integrated with those of data processing for three important reasons. First, all three areas now require large capital investments, large projects, complex implementation, and extensive user training. Further, significant portions of all three services increasingly may be purchased from a single supplier. The managers of these activities, however, have often had no significant prior expertise in handling this type of situation. A special problem for office automation is the move from multiple vendors with small, individual dollar purchases to a single vendor that will provide integrated support. The size of the purchase decisions and the complexity of the applications are several orders of magnitude larger and more complex than those faced a decade ago. For telecommunications the problem revolves around breaking the psychology of relying on a purchased service decision from a public utility and instead looking at multiple sources for large capital investment decisions. Both cases involve a sharp departure from past practices and require a type of management skill that was added to the data processing function 15 years ago.

The second link to data processing is that, to an increasing extent, key sectors of all three components are physically linked together in a network. For example, in one manufacturing company the same WATS line is used over a 24-hour period to support on-line data communications, normal voice communication, and an electronic mail message-switching system. The problems of one component therefore cannot be addressed independently of the problems of the other two.

To complicate the situation today, a dominant supplier for each of the three islands will attempt to market his product as the natural technological base for coordinated automation of the other islands. For example, IBM is attempting to extend its data processing base into products supporting office automation and communications; AT&T is attempting to extend its communications base into products supporting data processing and office automation; Xerox is attempting to expand its office automation effort into communications and data processing.

Failure to address these management issues constructively poses great risk to an organization. In the past several years most U.S.A. organizations have consolidated at least policy control and, in the majority of cases, management of the islands in a single IT unit. The key reasons for this include:

1. Decisions in each area now involve large amounts of money and complex technical/cost evaluations. Similar staff backgrounds are needed in each case to do the appropriate analysis.
2. Great similarity exists in the type of project management skills and staff needed to implement applications of these three technologies.
3. Many applications require integrated technological networks to handle computing, telecommunications, and office automation.

Managing the Assimilation of Emerging Information Technology

Chapters 3 and 4 focused on how developments in information technology have facilitated many new strategic applications. Indeed, as noted, many companies depend heavily on this technology to operationalize and implement their competitive business strategy. For them, relevant new technology (e.g., expert systems) must be identified and exploited as quickly as possible. A sustained rate of product innovation, new vendors, and technology options pose significant organizational challenges as these firms balance the need to run day-to-day operations smoothly while appropriately investigating and assimilating new technologies.

Two key steps must be taken to address this problem. First, corporate management needs to take a contingency approach to administrative systems for managing technology assimilation. Each technology requires different management approaches at various points of its life cycle. Introducing technologies to a firm requires an organizational learning perspective as opposed to considering only cost and efficiency. (These concepts are well grounded in organizational theory research. For example, the work of Chris Argyris and Donald Schon[1] describing how organizations successfully exploit new technologies has been particularly helpful.)

The second step is careful consideration of the establishment of a new unit in the IT structure called "emerging technologies." This unit, successfully installed in a number of settings, manages the identification and introduction of new technology with high payoff potential. The experience of British and Scottish firms entering the post-World War II electronics industry, as described later in this chapter, provides additional support for the potential effectiveness of this unit.[2]

The Four Phases of IT Assimilation

For nearly 15 years the notion of information technology being assimilated in stages has been discussed. The pivotal work was introduced by Cyrus Gibson and Richard Nolan.[3] Focusing on large-scale computer technology and the development of centralized data processing departments during the late 60s and early 70s, they described four stages of assimilating data processing (essentially batch oriented) technology.

Today, as described in Chapter 2, we have refined this to talk about a company having a portfolio of different information technologies. Each technology goes through a set of phases that relate to Nolan and Gibson's original stages and are also consistent with organizational change concepts developed by Edgar Schein.[4] These phases are characterized in Figure 5-1 as investment/project initiation, technology learning and adaptation, rationalization/management control, and maturity/widespread technology transfer.

---

[1]C. Argyris and D. A. Schon, *Organizational Learning: A Theory of Action Perspective* (Reading, Mass.: Addison-Wesley Publishing, 1978).

[2]T. Burns and G. M. Stalker, *The Management of Innovation* (London: Tavistock Publishing, 1979).

[3]R. L. Nolan and C. F. Gibson, "Managing the Four Stages of EDP Growth," *Harvard Business Review*, January-February 1974, pp. 76-88.

[4]Edgar Schein, "Management Development as a Process of Influence," *Industrial Management Review* 2 (1961), pp. 59-77.

FIGURE 5-1   Phases of Technological Use

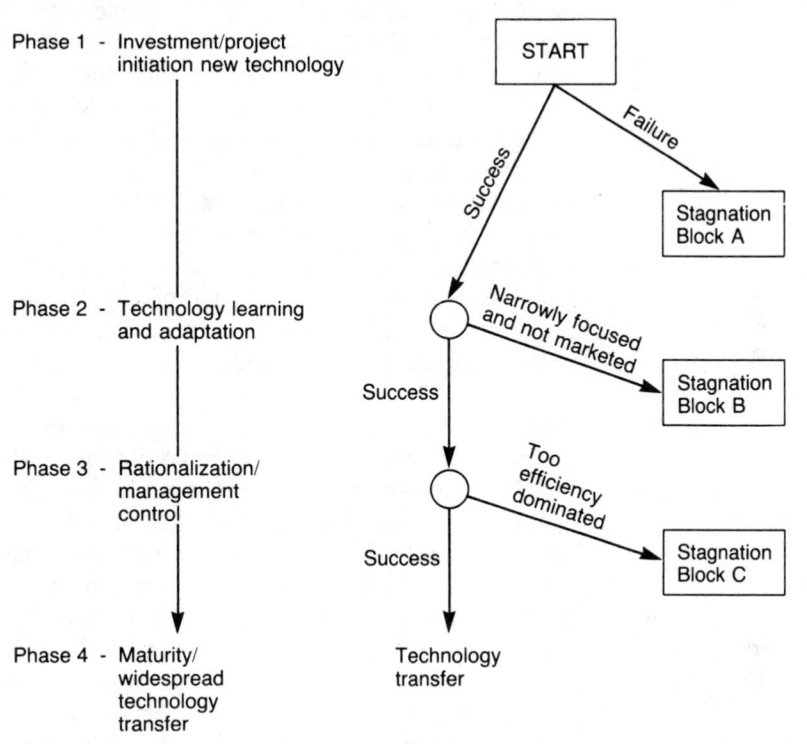

Phase 1 - Investment/project
            initiation new technology

Phase 2 - Technology learning
            and adaptation

Phase 3 - Rationalization/
            management
            control

Phase 4 - Maturity/
            widespread
            technology
            transfer

START

Failure

Success

Stagnation
Block A

Narrowly focused
and not marketed

Success

Stagnation
Block B

Too
efficiency
dominated

Success

Stagnation
Block C

Technology
transfer

Phase 1.   The first phase is initiated by a decision to invest in a new (to the organization) information-processing technology: it involves one or more complementary project development efforts and initial individual training. These projects are characterized by impreciseness in both their costs and ultimate stream of benefits. The resulting systems when looked at retrospectively often seem quite clumsy. Each step of the project life cycle is characterized by much uncertainty, and considerable learning takes place. The second phase seems to follow unless there is a disaster in Phase 1, such as vendor failure, discovery that the technology is inappropriate to the firm, or poor user involvement, resulting in Stagnation Block A.

Stagnation Block A typically generates a two-year lag before new investments in this technology are tried again—normally along with a complete change of personnel. The decision to disinvest is normally a result of there being increased work and little benefit from the system.

Sources of these problems may be vendor failure, lack of real management attention, incompetent project management, poor fit of technology to organizations, or merely bad choice. Rarely are the causes recognized quickly. The complexity and time requirements of implementing new information technology normally hide perception of the developing failure for 18 to 36 months. The project typically is not a clear technological disaster but rather an ambiguous situation that is perceived as adding more work to the organization with little perceived benefit. Rejection of the system follows. All projects studied of this type that aborted had significant cost overruns. Each failure created anxieties and prevented development of coordinated momentum. Typically organizations frozen in this state end up purchasing more services of a familiar technology. They become relatively adept at adapting this technology to their use but become vulnerable to obsolescence.

Phase 2. The second phase involves learning how to adapt the new technology to particular tasks beyond those identified in the initial proposal. As learning takes place the actual benefits coming from the projects in this phase also are often quite different from those anticipated. Again retrospectively the resulting systems look clumsy. The project life cycles in this phase, although not characterized by great technical problems, tend to be hard to plan. A study of 37 office automation sites showed that in none of them was the first utilization of technology implemented as originally planned.[5] In each case significant learning took place during implementation. If the second phase is managed in an adaptive manner that permits managers to capture, develop, and refine new understanding of how this technology could be more helpful, the organization moves to Phase 3. Failure to learn from the first applications and to effectively disseminate this learning leads to Stagnation Block B.

A typical Stagnation Block B situation occurred in a large manufacturing company and involved automation of clerical word processing activities that were under the control of a very cost-conscious accounting function. Highly conservative in its approach to data processing technology, the firm had developed automated accounting systems centrally controlled in a relatively outmoded computer operating system and had yet to enter into data base systems. Focusing on word processing only to do mass mailing in order to save costs, it forfeited additional benefits. After three years of use, mass mailing is the only activity on its system. The company is presently reviewing a proposal

---

[5]Kathleen Curley, *Word Processing—First Step to the Office of the Future* (New York: Praeger Publishers, 1983).

for microcomputers as executive aids for activities that could be done by the word processors. But the organization is frozen into their use for mass mailing only.

Phase 3. This phase typically involves a change in the organization, continued evolution of the uses of technology to ones not originally considered, and, most important, development of precise controls guiding the design and implementation of systems that use these technologies (to ensure that later applications can be done more cost efficiently than the earlier one). In this phase the various aspects of the project life cycle are analyzed, with the roles of IT and user becoming clearer and the results more predictable.

If, in Phase 3, control for efficiency does not excessively dominate and room is left for broader objectives of effectiveness, then the organization moves into a Phase 4, which involves broad-based communication and implementation of technology to other groups in the organization. Stagnation Block C is reached when excessive controls are developed that are so onerous as to inhibit the legitimate profitable expansion of the use of technology. An example of Stagnation Block C with respect to data processing is the case of a manufacturing company that entered into large-scale centralization with distributed input systems. To justify the expense of the new operating system, it focused on gaining all the benefits of a very standardized, highly efficient production shop. In the process of gaining this efficiency, the organization became so focused on standard procedures and efficiency that it lost its ability and enthusiasm for innovation and change with respect to this technology, and it began to actively discourage users. Further, the rigorous protocols of these standard programs irritated users and helped set the stage for surreptitious local office automation experimentation (Phase 1 in a different technology). Too rigorous an emphasis on control prevented logical growth.

Phase 4. This final phase can be characterized as a program of technological diffusion. Here firms take experience gained in one operating division and expand its use throughout the corporation.

Quite naturally, as time passes, new technologies will emerge that offer the opportunity either to move into new applications areas or to restructure old ones. Each of the three components (islands) of IT is thus confronted over time with a series of waves of new technologies and at any point in time must adapt different approaches to managing and assimilating each, as each is in a different phase (see Figure 5–1). For example, a manufacturing company studied in 1986 was in Phase 4 in terms of its ability to conceptualize and utilize enhancements to its finished-goods inventory systems over a multiyear period. At the same time, it was in Phase 3 in terms of organizing protocols to solidify control over the efficiencies of MRPII, its on-line inquiry and data systems, whose growth had exploded in the past several years. It had recently made an investment in several laptop computers for the marketing organization and was clearly in Phase 1 with respect to this technology. Finally, it had just been decided that CAD (computer-aided design) was an important technology to deal with and was at the beginning of Phase 1 in terms of planning how to use it as both an engineering and a marketing support tool.

For organizational structure planning, these four phases can be grouped into two broader categories. Phases 1 and 2 comprise a category called *innovation phases*, Phases 3 and 4 will be grouped as *control phases*. The differences between them can be described as *forecasting, assessing, learning, creating, and testing* (innovation) versus *general usage, acceptance, and support* (control).

Work in this area suggests that different parts of the organization will (or should) be responsible for these different functions. Keeping innovation phase activities separate from control phase activities helps ensure that the efficiency goals of one do not blunt the effectiveness goals of the other. This idea initially emerged from the organizational behavior literature. For example, James March and Herbert Simon, in their classic book on organizations,[6] referred to the innovation versus control phases as unprogrammed versus programmed activity. To enable and encourage unprogrammed or innovative activity, they recommended that organizations make special and separate provisions for it. Frequently this would involve the creation of special units for the innovative purpose.

Innovation Management Study

The earlier mentioned study of the electronics industry in the United Kingdom[7] also discussed separating the innovative and creative functions from the implementation and control functions in organizations. Twenty post-World War II manufacturing firms in Scotland and England were closely examined. In diverse businesses ranging from textiles to television and radio, all the firms were interested in exploring the fledgling electronics industry. Their success and problems in moving new technology from testing and piloting stages to distribution,

---

[6]J. S. March and H. A. Simon, *Organizations* (New York: John Wiley & Sons, 1958).

[7]Burns and Stalker, *Management of Innovation*.

implementation, and control stages were studied. The analogy between their experience and the issues facing the IT area today is striking and is discussed in some depth here. Particularly for firms strategically dependent on IT, the stakes are very high as they try to balance efforts between requisite innovation based on new information technology and maintenance of more established, production-oriented applications of IT.

Burns and Stalker's study noted significant cultural differences between the electronics research and development laboratories and the production workshops. Within today's IT organizations analogous cultural differences exist between the units responsible for Innovation phase aspects of IT assimilation versus Control phase aspects (e.g., information center versus traditional applications development). These differences must be managed. The study suggested that linguistic differences accounted for much of the cultural incompatibility between the two types of organizational departments. The engineers and scientists of the development laboratories spoke a different language and had different norms of interaction from those of the personnel in the production divisions. The critical challenge to the management of these companies was to find ways of translating the language of the laboratory into the language of production. Ironically the problem was aggravated by the fact that most companies separated the R&D labs as much as possible (physically in most cases) from the rest of the organization in order to avoid cultural clashes. We find similar linguistic differences between effective managers of the Innovation phase and Control phase categories of IT. The languages of expert systems and COBOL are very different.

The most successful companies in the electronics industry were those firms that adopted an "organic" organizational structure for innovation. They were characterized by informal supervisor-subordinate relationships and considerable flexibility in the assignment of tasks between function. The organizations more established in the electronics industry sustained their competitive advantage by effective use of a "mechanistic" organizational structure featuring more formality in relationship and structure. These two styles of management can be seen as two endpoints on a continuum. Organizations that fell somewhere between these two endpoints on the continuum delivered conflicting messages to employees and appeared less effective in handling the organic-mechanistic/innovation-control distinction in IT. Innovation phase activities flourish best under an organic structure while control phase activities require a mechanistic structure. Many IT units have constructed very mechanistic structures to deal with daily operations and, in so doing, have erected major barriers to effective innovation.

TABLE 5-4 Effective Management Characteristics Needed for Each Phase Category

Management Issues	Characteristic	
	Innovation Phase Effectiveness	Control Phase Efficiency
Organization	Organic (ET)	Mechanistic (traditional IT)
Management control	Loose, informal	Tight
Leadership	Participating	Directive (telling to delegating)

The Emerging Technology (ET) Group

Increasingly, a new, explicitly separate organization unit to address innovation phase technology exploitation and management appears to be a promising approach. Called the emerging technology (ET) group, it often resides initially in the IT organization on an equal level with applications development and operations departments. In some large, strategic IT organizations, the ET unit has been placed outside the IT department to ensure that it is not swamped by the IT control philosophy.

Key Management Issues. Three issues must be dealt with by general management in structuring the ET group: organization, management control, and leadership (Table 5–4). The following paragraphs address the three issues in relation to the innovation and control phases. Because the innovation phase is the major problem in most organizations, it is somewhat more fully discussed.

Innovation Phase. The atmosphere within the emerging technology group should be exploratory and experimental. Examples of current technologies that such a group might be exploring are laser disks and local area networks. The organizational structures and management controls are loose and informal. Cost accounting and reporting are flexible (though accuracy is essential), and little or no requirement exists for pro forma project cost-benefit analysis. The leadership style resembles what Hersey et al refers to as "participating"; that is, the distinctions between leaders and subordinates are somewhat clouded, and the lines of communication are shortened. The level of attention to relationships is high compared to that of task orientation. As noted earlier, this informality is key to innovation and organizational learning. The electronics industry study, for example, clearly identified the importance of informality in the R&D departments.

A recent study of the tobacco industry[8] referred to such informality as organizational slack and stated that "the creation or utilization of slack normally requires the temporary relaxation of performance standards." In the effective companies standards of efficiency must be greatly reduced during the early testing phases of a new IT innovation. Organizations strategically dependent on information technology should view innovation phase activities as an integral part of their ongoing response to pressures to adapt to their changing environments and should appropriately fund them.

Illustrative of the pressure and responses that lead to establishment of a separate department is the dramatic growth of "information centers" in response to end-user computing. These facilities are generally staffed with nontraditional data processing professionals and have very different accounting, justification, and cost-benefit systems. Firms strategically dependent on IT cannot afford to establish such centers reactively. They must proactively forecast, assess, and test appropriate technology to introduce it at an early stage. These activities are unlikely to occur without specific responsibility being assigned to a person or an organizational unit. The role of this unit may be seen as being similar to that of a corporate R&D department. In the Appendix to this chapter, excerpts from a sample position analysis more fully illustrate the scope of this department.

Two key features contained in this position analysis for ET are noteworthy because of their variation from the general corporate R&D model. The first is that the manager of ET and the department staff are primarily given the role of facilitator as opposed to guru. This implies the use of professionals outside the ET organization to forecast, track, and assess specific technology evolution. For example, a person in the data base administrator's organization might be partially funded by ET to forecast, track, and test new data base management system products. The second feature is that ET is responsible for what we call intraorganizational technology transfer. This refers to the role of designing and managing the Phase 2 introduction and diffusion of the targeted technology in the company. This is the key role of an ET group when contributing to the broad-based learning in a company. ET must first facilitate the development of user-oriented, creative pilot applications of the new technology. They then participate in discussions about how the new applications could best be developed and implemented; education and training of appropriate users and IT professionals using the new technology; and changes in strategy or structure that may result from implementing the new technology and associated applications.

---

[8]R. Miles, *Coffin Nails and Corporate Strategies* (Englewood Cliffs, N.J.: Prentice-Hall, 1982).

After the personnel directly involved with the new technology (e.g., the emerging technology group) develop the ability to support it, general management then decides whether or not to provide additional resources to continue the diffusion of the technology throughout the organization (Phase 2). With requisite support of senior management, the emerging technology group begins to teach others throughout the organization how to utilize it and to encourage experimentation. A chief concern of the ET manager at this point becomes how to market IT effectively to the rest of the organization. (In some organizations the job of selling IT will be easy because the organizational culture encourages innovation and experimentation.) In the words of March and Simon, innovation in such companies is "institutionalized."[9]

Again the cultural differences between laboratory and workshop noted in the electronics industry study are important. Part of the task of successfully selling this technology to other parts of the organization is finding a way to translate the unique language associated with the technology to a language compatible with the larger organizational culture. It was noted in the study that these cultural differences existed more in the minds of the organizational participants than in any objective reality. The "artifacts" resulted from the natural tendency for people, "when faced with problems in human organizations of an intractable nature, to find relief in attributing the difficulties to the wrongheadedness, stupidity, or delinquency of the others with whom they had to deal."[10]

The issue is not whether or not the cultural differences exist only in the minds of the participants but rather, given that they do exist somewhere, what can be done about them. The study identified two useful solutions employed by the sample companies. One solution was assigning members of the design department to supervise the production of the new design, and vice versa. For IT this means assigning responsibility for user implementation work to ET staff, as well as putting the user in charge of ET group projects. To be effective this solution must be implemented with consideration for the wide gaps between subordinates and their managers in level of technical expertise. (Usually the subordinates will know more about the technology or business process than the manager does.) However, if the key individuals are chosen carefully this has proven to be a viable approach.

A second approach used effectively by the electronics firms was the creation of special intermediaries to serve as liaison between the design and production shops in the organizations. IT steering committees,

---

[9]March and Simon, *Organizations.*
[10]Burns and Stalker, *Management of Innovation*, p. 53.

user department analysts, etc., are examples where this has worked effectively in the IT environment. This strategy increases the bureaucracy of the organization structure, but for many organizations it is an effective solution to the language problem.

ET managers must analyze existing or potential resistance by the organization members to the change brought about by the new technology. The study noted that a high percentage of resistance to change stemmed from the reluctance of organization members to disturb delicately balanced power and status structures. ET managers should adopt a "selling" leadership style, characterized by high task orientation and high levels of interpersonal interaction. Major organizational changes threaten long-established positions and open up opportunities for new ones. The advocate of a new technology who is insensitive to the political ramifications of the new system will face unpleasant, unanticipated consequences.

Once the range of potential uses of the new technology has been generated and appropriate users are acquainted with the new technology, management must make a decision about putting the technology permanently into place. At this juncture the assimilation project moves away from the innovative phases to the control stages via Phase 3.

Control Phase.   The focus of the control phase is the development and installation of controls for the new technology. While the main concern during the innovation phase was the effectiveness of the technology, control phase management is concerned with efficiency. In installing the necessary controls over the technology, management's task is to define the goals and criteria for technology utilization. The leadership style here is more one of "telling," with lower interpersonal involvement relative to task orientation. During this phase the organizational users (non-IT staff) are better able to judge the appropriateness and feasibility of the new technology to their tasks than they were during the innovation phase. The traditional IT organization and associated administrative systems are generally appropriate for this task.

For technologies in the later aspects of the control phase, IT managers typically exhibit a "delegating" leadership style. Interpersonal involvement and task orientation are low. With operation procedures well understood and awareness high the managers let subordinates run the show.

Patterns of Hardware/Data Distribution

As technology capabilities evolve (apart from the issues in handling emerging technology), another key organizational issue concerns the physical location of the data and hardware elements. (The issues associated with the location of the development staff will be dealt with in the next chapter.) At one extreme is the organization form that has a large centralized hub connected by telecommunications links to remote input/ output devices. At the other extreme is a small or nonexistent hub with most or all data and hardware distributed to users. In between these two extremes lies a rich variety of intermediate alternatives.

The early resolution to this organizational structure was heavily influenced by technology. The higher per computation cost of hardware in the early 1960s (when the first large investments in computing began) made consolidation of processing power into large data centers very attractive (large machines having a much lower cost per computation than smaller machines). In contrast, the technology of the mid-1980s permits but does not demand cost-effective organizational alternatives. (In the 1980s technological efficiency of hardware per se is not a prime reason for having a large central data center.)

Pressures toward a Large Central Hub of a Distributed Network

To retain market share, the vendors of large computers are suggesting (as the comparative difference in efficiency of large computers versus small ones is eroded) that many members of an organization have a critical need to access the same large data files; hence the ideal structure of an information service is a large central processing unit with massive data files connected by a telecommunications network to a wide array of intelligent devices (often at great distance). While this is certainly true in many situations, the problem unfortunately is more complex, as is discussed below.

Resolution of the organizational structure problem depends on the key factors of management control, technology, data, professional services, and organizational fit. The impact of each of these factors is discussed here, with Table 5–5 presenting a summary.

Management Control. The ability to attract, develop, maintain, and manage staffs and controls to assure high-quality, cost-effective operation of existing systems is a key reason for a strong central processing unit (CPU). The argument is that a more professional, cheaper, and higher-quality operation (from the user's perspective) can be put together in a single large unit than through the operation of a series of much smaller units. This administrative skill caused one major decentralized company to decide not to eliminate its corporate data center and move to regional centers. In the final analysis, it was unconvinced that eight small data centers could be run as efficiently in aggregate or that even if they could it was worth the cost and trauma to make the

TABLE 5–5 Summary of Pressures on Balancing the Hub

Pressures	Toward Increasing the Hub	Toward Increasing Distribution
Management control	More professional operation. Flexible backup. Efficient use of personnel.	User control. User responsiveness. Simpler control. Local reliability improved.
Technology	Access large-scale capacity. Efficient use of capacity.	Small is efficient. Telecommunications costs reduced.
Data	Multiple access to common data. Assurance of data standards. Security control.	Easier access. Fit with field needs. Data only relevant to one branch.
Professional services	Specialized staff. Reduced vulnerability to turnover. Richer career paths.	Stability of work force. User career paths.
Organizational fit	Corporate style—central. Corporate style—functional. IT centralized from the beginning.	Corporate style—decentralized. Business need—multinationals.

transition. The company felt that through its critical mass, the corporate data center permitted retention of skills for corporatewide use that could not be attracted or retained if the company had a series of smaller data centers. They decided instead to keep the operation and maintenance of all three technologies central, while emphasizing user input to projects in the design and construction phases through development departments in the several divisions.

Further, provision of better backup occurs through the ability to have multiple CPUs in a single site. When hardware failure occurs in one CPU, switching the network from one machine to another can take place by simply pushing a button. Obviously this does not address the problem of a major environmental disaster that impacts the entire center.

Technology. Another strong reason for a large hub is the ability to provide very large-scale processing capacity for users who need it but whose need is insufficient to justify their own independent processing system. In a day of rapid explosion in the power of cheap computing, it has become easier for users to visualize doing some of their computing on their own personal computers, such as IBM PCs or stand-alone minis. At the same time, however, some users have other problems, such as large linear programming models and petroleum geological reservoir mapping programs that require the largest available computing capacity. The larger the computer capacity available, the more detail they can profitably build into the infrastructure of their computer programs.

Many firms see consolidation (a large hub) as an opportunity to better manage aggregate computing capacity in the company, thus reducing total hardware expenditures. When many machines are present in an organization and each is loaded to 70 percent, the perception is that there are a vast number of wasted CPU cycles that could be eliminated if the processing was consolidated. An important issue in the technology economics of the 1960s, the significance of this as a decision element in the 1980s, however, has largely disappeared.

Data. Another pressure for the large central hub is the ability to provide controlled, multiple-user access to common corporate data files on a need-to-know basis. An absolutely essential need from the early days for organizations such as airlines and railroads, with sharp reductions in storage and processing costs, this access has become economically desirable for additional applications in many other settings, such as financial services. Management of data at the hub can also be a very effective way to control access and thus security.

Professional Services. Development of the sizable staff that accompanies the large IT data center provides an opportunity to attract and keep challenged a specialized technical staff. The ability to work on challenging problems and share expertise with other professionals provides a necessary air of excitement, not only attracting IT specialists to the firms but keeping them focused on key issues. Having these skills in the organization permits individual units to undertake complex tasks as needed without incurring undue risks. Furthermore, when staff and/or skills are limited, consolidation in a single unit permits better deployment from a corporate perspective. Further, having the large staff resources at a hub permits more comfortable adaptation to inevitable turnover problems. Resignation of one person in a distributed three-person group is normally more disruptive than five persons leaving a group of 100 professionals.

For the technically ambitious individual who doesn't want to leave the IT field, the large unit provides more opportunity to find alternative stimuli and avenues of personal development. (Perceived technical and professional growth has proven to be a key element in reduced turnover.) This is a critical weapon in battling the so-called burnout problem.

Organizational Fit. In a centralized organization, the above-mentioned set of factors takes on particular weight since they lead to congruency between IT structure and overall corporate structure and help eliminate friction. This point is particularly important for organizations where IT hardware was introduced in a centralized fashion and the company as a whole adapted its management practices to IT's location in this way. Reversal of such a structure can be tumultuous.

Pressures toward a Small Hub and Primary Distributed Environment

Today important pressures push toward placing significant processing capacity and data in the hands of the users and only limited or nonexistent processing power at the hub of the network.

Management Control.   Most important among these pressures, such a structure better satisfies the user's expectation of control. The ability to handle the majority of transactions locally is consistent with users' desires to maintain a firm grip on their operation. The concept of locally managed data files suggests that the user will be the first person to hear about deviations from planned performance of the unit and hence have an opportunity to analyze and communicate on a planned basis his or her understanding of what has transpired. Further, there now exist a greater number of user-managers with long experience in IT activities who have an understanding of systems and their management needs. These individuals are justifiably confident in their ability to manage IT hardware and data.

The user is offered better guarantees of stability in response time by being removed from the hourly fluctuations in demand on the corporate network. The ability to implement a guaranteed response time on certain applications has turned out to be a very important feature from the user's perspective.

Distribution of hardware provides a way to remove or insulate the user from the more volatile elements of the corporate chargeout system. It permits the user to predict in advance more accurately what the costs are likely to be (therefore reducing the danger of embarrassing negative variances); not infrequently it appears to offer the possibility of lower costs.

Distribution of processing power to the user offers a potential for reduction of user and overall corporate vulnerability to a massive failure in the corporate data center. A network of local minis can keep key aspects for an operation going during a service interruption at the main location. A large forest products company decentralized to local fabricators all raw material and product decisions through installation of a mini system. This reduced the volatility of on-line demand at the corporate computer center and permitted the service levels to both corporate and distributed users to rise.

From the user's perspective the distributed network offers a simpler operating environment both in terms of feeding work into the system and in terms of the construction of the operating system. The red tape of routing work to a data entry department is eliminated, and the procedures can be built right into the ongoing operation of the user department. (Surprisingly, in some cases regaining this control has been viewed with trepidation by the user.) Similarly, with the selection of the right type of software the problems in interfacing with the basic operating system can be dramatically simplified. (To use the jargon of the trade, they are "user friendly.")

Technology.   In the early days large central processing units did have efficiency superior to that of much smaller units. Today, however, several important changes have occurred:

1. The economics of CPUs and memories in relation to their size have altered. The rule (commonly called Grosch's law) that the power of computers rises as the square of the price no longer applies.[11]
2. The economics of Grosch's law never applied to peripheral units and other elements of the network. The CPU and internal memory costs are a much smaller percentage of the total hardware expenditures today than they were in 1970.
3. The percentage of hardware costs as a part of the total IT budget has dropped dramatically over the past decade as personnel, telecommunications, and other operating and development costs have risen. Efficiency of hardware utilization consequently is not the burning issue it was a decade ago. Considering these factors, including the much slower improvement in telecommunications costs (11 percent per year) and the explosion of user needs for on-line access to data files that can be generated and stored locally, the economic case for a large hub has totally reversed itself in many cases.
4. As more systems are purchased rather than made, the users are better informed in the procedures of how to select and manage a local system.

Data.   Universal access by users to all data files is not a uniformly desired goal. Telecommunications costs and users' only occasional needs to access some data files (other than at the site where the data is generated) mean that in many settings it is uneconomical or undesirable to provide central access to all data. Further, the inability to relate data from different segments of the firm may be part of corporate strategy.

---

[11]Edward G. Gale, Lee L. Gremillion, James L. McKenney, "Price/Performance Patterns of U.S. Computer Systems," *Communication of the ACM* (April 1979).

As a case in point consider a large decentralized company with a central corporate computing center that is a service bureau for its eight major divisions (all development staff resides in the divisions). No common application or data file exists between even two of the divisions in the company (not even payroll). If survival depended on it, the company could not identify in under 24 hours what its total relationship as a company was with any individual customer. In senior management's judgment, this lack of data relationships between divisions appropriately reinforces the company's highly decentralized structure. No pressure exists anywhere in the organization for change. The corporate computing center, an organizational anomaly, was conceived simply as a cost-efficient way of permitting each division to develop its network of individual systems, and it is not worth the organizational turmoil to change it.

Technicians can easily suggest interesting approaches for providing information that has no practical use, and the suggestion may even threaten soundly conceived organizational structures.

Professional Services. Moving functions away from the urban environment toward more rural settings offers the opportunity to reduce employee turnover, the bane of metropolitan-area IT departments. The recruiting and training process is very complicated to administer in these settings. But once the employees are there and if they are sensitively managed, the relative lack of headhunters and nearby attractive employers reduces turnover pressures.

When the IT staff is closely linked to the user organization, it becomes easier to plan employee promotions that may take technical personnel out of the IT organization and put them into other user departments. This is critical for the department with low employee turnover, as the former change agents begin to develop middle-age spread and burnout symptoms. Two-way staff transfers between user and IT are one way to deal with this problem and to facilitate closer user-IT relations.

Organizational Fit. In many settings the controls implicit in the distributed approach better fit the corporation's organization structure and general leadership style. This is particularly true for highly decentralized structures (or organizations that wish to evolve in this fashion) and/ or organizations that are geographically very diverse.

Finally, widely distributed facilities fit the needs of many multinational structures. While airline reservation data, shipping container operations, and certain kinds of banking transactions must flow through a central location, the overwhelming amount of work in many settings is more effectively managed in the local country, with communication to corporate headquarters either by telex, mailing tapes, transmitting bursts of data over a telecommunications link, or some other way, depending on the organization's management style, size of unit, and so on.

Assessing the appropriateness of a particular hardware-data configuration for an organization is very challenging. For all but the most decentralized of organizations, there is a strong need for central control over standards and operating procedures. The changes in technology, however, both permit and make desirable in some settings the distribution of significant amounts of the hardware operations and data handling.

Conclusion

The trend to merge technologies and the ability to distribute data and hardware must be carefully managed in combination because they are interdependent. Since firms come from different positions in use of IT, history, culture, and business strategy, they may appropriately develop radically different structures. For firms where IT is strategic (such as banking or insurance) and new needs arise for central integrated files, there is a strong tendency to accelerate the merging of all services into single-site support systems. (Support industries can move more slowly.) On the other hand, some banks will have distributed stand-alone systems providing similar support. Key reasons for these differences will lie in the bank's culture, geography, and other factors relating to its business practices.

Reexamination of the deployment of hardware and software resources for the information technology function is a priority item if not recently addressed. Changing technology economics, merging of formerly disparate technologies with different managerial traditions, and the problems of managing each technology innovation have obsolesced many organizational structure decisions appropriate in 1970. To ensure that these issues are being properly addressed, five steps must be taken:

1. Establish, as part of the objectives of a permanent corporate policy group, the development of a program to manage change. This policy group must assess the current program of merging the technology islands, guide the process of balancing the desires for a strong hub against the advantage of a strongly distributed approach, and ensure that different technologies are being guided in an appropriate way.

2. The policy group must ensure that uniformity in management practice is not pushed too far and that appropriate diversity is accom-

modated. Even within a company it is entirely appropriate for different parts of the organization to develop and continue different patterns of distributed support for hardware and data. Different phases of development of specific technologies, geographical distance from potential central service support, and so on, are valid reasons for different approaches.

3. The policy group must show particular sensitivity to the needs of international activities. Great care is necessary. What works in the United States often will not work in Thailand. Either for companies operating primarily in a single country or for the multinational that operates in many countries, enforcing common approaches internationally may be inappropriate. Each country has different cost and quality structures of telecommunications, different levels of IT achievement, different reservoirs of technical skills, different cultures, and so on. These differences are likely to endure for the foreseeable future.

4. The policy group must address its issues in a broad strategic fashion. The arguments and reasoning leading to a set of solutions are more complex than simply the current economics of hardware or deciding which persons should have access to certain data files. Corporate organization structure, corporate strategy and direction, availability of human resources, and current operating administrative processes are all additional critical inputs. Both in practice and in writing, the technicians and information theorists have tended to oversimplify a very complex set of problems and options. A critical function of the group is to ensure adequate innovation phase investment (in Phases 1 and 2). A special effort must be made to ensure that appropriate investment occurs in experimental studies, pilot studies, and development of prototypes. Similarly the group must ensure that proven expertise is being distributed appropriately within the firm, often to places that are unaware of the technology's existence or potential. The establishment of an ET group is a highly effective approach, particularly for firms that have high strategic dependence on information technology. Firms that have strong commitments to R&D in non-IT areas have found it easier to deal with these issues.

5. The policy group must ensure an appropriate balance between long-term and short-term needs. A distributed structure optimally designed for the technology and economics of 1986 may fit the world of 1994 rather poorly. Often it makes sense to postpone feature development or to design an approach that is clumsy in today's technology but will be quite efficient in the anticipated technologies of the early 1990s. As a practical matter, the group will work on these issues in a continuous, iterative fashion rather than implement a revolutionary change.

Appendix _____

Air Products & Chemicals, Inc.: Position Analysis

POSITION: Manager
TITLE: Emerging Technologies
GROUP: Corporate MIS

Position Summary

This position is accountable for organizing and managing the introduction of new and emerging leading-edge information technologies into the Air Products environment. After first researching new state-of-the-art computing technologies, the incumbent provides the leadership necessary for selection and assimilation of appropriate technologies that will significantly impact company productivity and competitive position. Identification and preliminary evaluation of these technologies could also occur in other MIS departments and satellite locations.

Nature and Scope

Environment/Challenges

Advances in information technology are occurring at an accelerated pace. Breakthroughs in both computing and telecommunications technologies continue to enable new hardware and software products to be introduced daily. This environment creates a great opportunity for corporations that know how to take advantage of these emerging technologies to increase productivity and gain a competitive edge. However, the options are mind boggling because of the number of vendors, the number of products, and the number of different implementation approaches now available.

Corporations that sit back and wait for a vendor shakeout to occur before making their choices, rather than exploiting the new technologies, will lose out. Many vendors and existing products will not survive, but new vendors, products, and capabilities will continue to be introduced at a rapid pace, at least until the end of the century. Companies who act without proper planning and management of risks associated with the introduction of new technology will also fail. It is therefore necessary for the management information systems (MIS) department to provide leadership by establishing its own defacto standards of interrelationships for the corporation.

The challenge of this position is to work within this dynamic environment to select and ensure the rapid introduction and assimilation of appropriate technologies having high payoff potential. This leadership is required to enable Air Products to take full advantage of information technology in order to gain a significant advantage over competitors. Decisions made by Emerging Technologies will have a significant impact on the productivity of the firm in the 80s and upon the ability of the corporation to survive and prosper as society makes the transition from the industrial age to the service-oriented information age of the 90s.

A significant challenge of this position will be to continue the development of an organization of highly competent professionals that can sustain the knowledge base required to ensure appropriate introduction and use of emerging technologies within the company. The organization will be required to blend research and experimentation with full-scale practical implementation of delivery systems with various hardware and software products having complexity transparent to the end user. Appropriate and different management frameworks will be required to carry the technology from an entrepreneurial to a formalized structure.

Organization

This position reports to the assistant director of MIS, who provides broad policy and guidelines regarding the introduction of information technologies. Reporting to this position are the managers of technical assessment, office systems, information center, development center, and training. Although each organization is oriented towards the common goal of the management of Emerging Technologies, they have diverse activities in different stages of evolution, which sometimes leads to organizational conflict.

Office systems was formed in 1978 to promote application of advanced office automation throughout Air Products, with special attention to increased professional productivity. This organization is shifting from a solely research and development mode to include managing the proliferation throughout the corporation of selected technologies such as text processing, electronic mail, message switching, information retrieval, and professional support tools.

The information center is responsible for facilitating the use of end-user personal computing both through direct access to central computing systems and through the use of personal microcomputers. This relatively new organizational concept has now achieved wide recognition as a key ingredient to successful use of computing technologies in a modern corporation and has already had a dramatic effect upon Air Products. Also reporting to the information center is the training department.

The training group's services is being expanded for educating all levels of end users and MIS professionals on all aspects of computing technologies. Executive training for personal computing has become an important new thrust for this activity.

The development center is a newer organizational concept, just now gaining significant recognition. Its role is geared towards selecting and promoting the best available techniques to support MIS professionals in the development of complex, highly integrated computing applications within the firm.

The technology assessment group is a newly formed organization responsible for researching and evaluating newly introduced hardware and software products. This function will then manage the experimentation and assimilation of selected products that can significantly benefit the company.

The incumbent is also responsible for administering the MIS R&D fund to be utilized throughout all MIS activities. This new and very important activity enables the proper focus to be applied in the allocation of scarce discretionary resources used for MIS R&D. This coordination ensures that R&D take place to maximize results rather than occurring either in a vacuum or in a dispersed, unorganized fashion.

Job Activities

Recruiting, retention, and staff development are necessary to ensure the effective use of this group of highly competent professionals. A key objective of the incumbent is to develop a highly qualified organization of experts that can provide leadership and support to all MIS organizations and to several thousand MIS end users within the company.

A significant contribution is being made to the MIS long-range plan. The work of Emerging Technologies greatly impacts the long-term future of all other MIS organizations as well as the use of computers by end users throughout the corporation. Close coordination with MIS department heads and senior corporate management is required. Emerging Technologies provide leadership affecting worldwide use of new technologies. The incumbent devotes a lot of attention to interfacing with MIS directors at satellite locations including the European and Engineering Services Group Operations. As a senior member of the MIS management team the incumbent significantly influences strategic and operational decisions made by MIS.

Interfaces with top management, including the MIS policy committee, are routinely required. The incumbent must have external links to other companies in our industry in order to gain competitive assessments and to share information where appropriate. The incumbent should be an active participant in professional societies and will be called upon to enhance the image of Air Products in this field. Also required are strong ongoing links to the latest academic thinking in the management and assimilation of new technologies.

Principal Accountabilities

1. Assimilate, integrate, and manage the introduction of emerging information technologies within the corporation to significantly impact company productivity and competitive position.
2. Assess brand-new computing technologies to determine potential value for Air Products. Provide a source of specialized expertise that can serve the needs of other MIS activities.
3. Ensure the rapid introduction of selected technologies within the corporation to maximize benefit flow. Establish a proactive organizational framework that supports both end-user computing and MIS professional computing with a proper balance to maximize benefit for the company.
4. Manage a diverse group of information technology specialists, utilizing management styles appropriate for each activity.
5. Provide worldwide direction on the use of emerging technologies for MIS satellite operations, including Europe and engineering services.
6. Administer and control the MIS R&D fund to gain the best possible return through innovation programs.
7. Establish programs to measure benefits, particularly productivity-related, in order to ensure value is being added consistent with corporate productivity goals.
8. Interface with external industrial and academic organizations in order to maintain state-of-the-art knowledge in emerging technologies and to enhance Air Products' image as a first-class corporation utilizing the latest thinking in this field.

Case 5–1

General Foods
Information Services
Department

Ed Schefer, vice president of information services (ISD) at General Foods, looked back at the accomplishments of his department over the past year with considerable satisfaction. Since June 1981 the number of personal computers had increased from 10—authorized on an ad hoc, informal basis—to more than 70 acquired under the new policy on personal computers.

Schefer realized that the success of the new policy depended on striking an appropriate balance between encouraging managers to find profitable uses for personal computers and discouraging too rapid growth of what could be an expensive passing fad. ISD had taken specific steps to achieve this balance: (1) set up the personal computer placement advisory council, with the unanimous support of all functional units, to help the various departments find advantageous ways to use personal computers to their best advantage; (2) launched the executive development program to acquaint senior managers with the potential of these new tools; and (3) opened a computer store where managers and other employees of General Food's functional units could familiarize themselves with personal computers before deciding to acquire one. The computer store also offered classes for interested employees in how to use the computer. Although these achievements were substantial, Ed Schefer knew there was much left to do.

This case was prepared by Leslie R. Porter.

Company Background

Several food processing firms, notably Maxwell House coffee and Jell-O, joined forces with the Post cereals business in the early 1920s to form General Foods (GF). By 1982, with net annual sales well past the $8 billion dollar mark, GF was one of the world's leading producers of packaged grocery products, such as Sanka, Bird's Eye, Tang, Shake 'n Bake, and Gaine's among others. Seventy percent of GF sales came from the U.S. market, but the international market was increasingly important.

In the 1970s, after an abortive attempt at diversification, General Foods settled into a period of slow, steady growth. By the end of the decade the company was losing market share in its leading products, such as coffee, and faced a need to develop a more aggressive growth strategy to maintain its position of dominance for the future. In 1980 General Foods reorganized into four sectors, giving increased responsibility and authority to sector management (see Exhibit 1).

Packaged Convenience Foods

Net sales here, the largest of the four sectors, accounted for 40 percent of GF total net sales. The sector had six product groups and four functional support groups organized as a matrix. The functional support groups serviced not only the product divisions of Packaged Convenience Foods but also the two divisions of the Coffee and Food Services sector. Thus all the products sold by these two sectors as well as many of the products sold by the International Operations sector were produced in the 20 GF plants that reported functionally through this sector. Each plant was operated as a cost center and might have produced several GF products.

Coffee and Food Services

Coffee was viewed at GF as its flagship product and the company took great pride in the fact that Maxwell House was the nation's largest selling coffee. This sector was also responsible for the Food Service Products Division, which dealt with institutional clients who purchased many of GF's products.

International Operations

This sector was becoming increasingly important as GF tried to increase its sales volume. It was broken down into four geographical regions, with each region responsible for profits in the area it served. In addition to the products GF manufactured in the United States, the

EXHIBIT 1　Corporate Management Organization Chart, July 1982

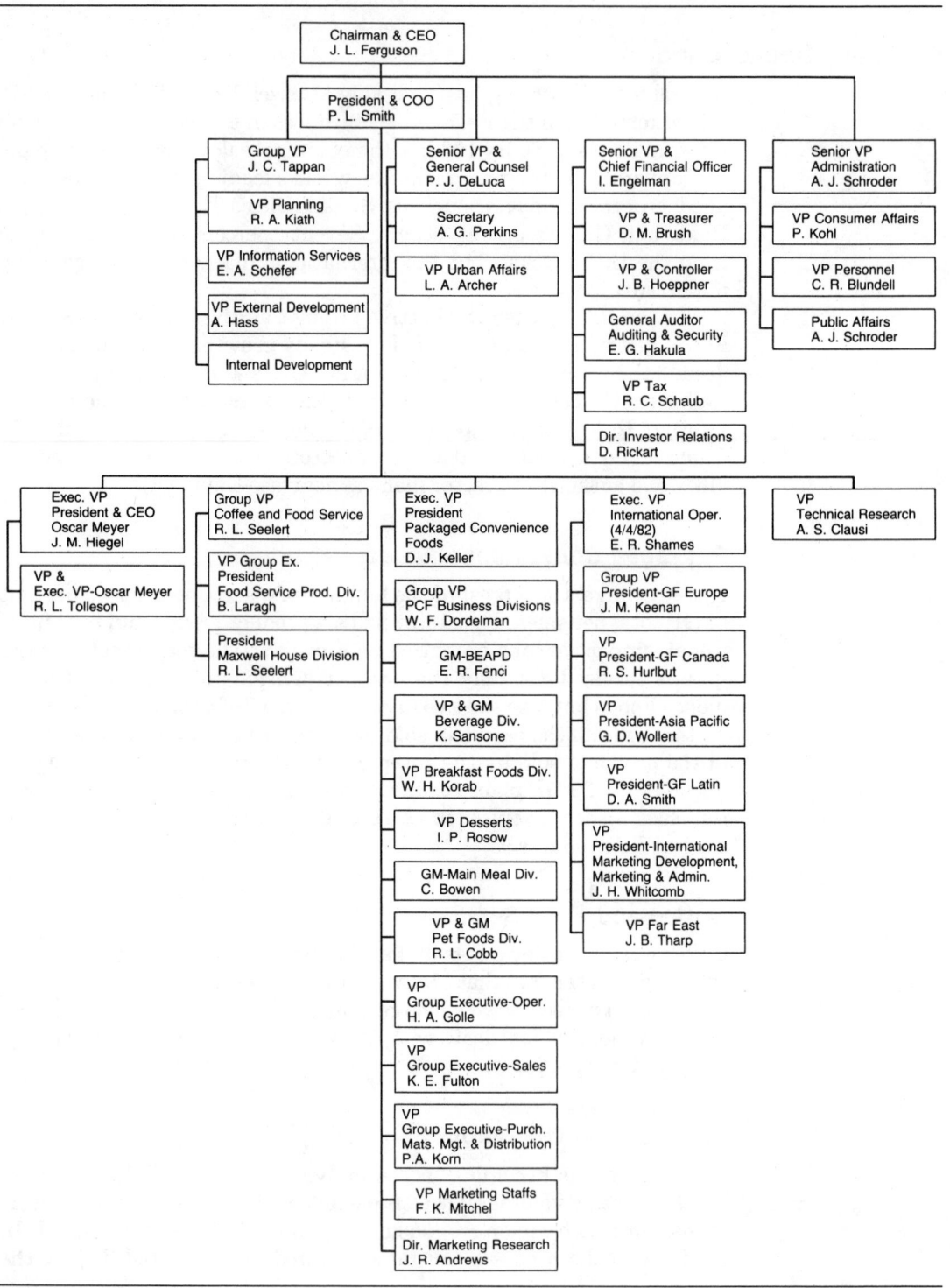

international operation manufactured and sold products that were unique to the region served. Although the regions shared a marketing and development function, each region had its own administrative support function, such as personnel. The heads of these had dotted-line relationships to their functional counterparts in the United States.

Oscar Mayer

Of the four sectors, Oscar Mayer was the most autonomous and least integrated into the GF corporation. With its headquarters in Madison, Wisconsin, Oscar Mayer was left pretty much intact since it was acquired in May 1981. To date, it shared none of the corporate functional support resources, though the heads of its functional support units had a dotted-line relationship with their counterparts at corporate headquarters in White Plains.

GF's corporate management was aware that changing its orientation toward growth would require more than a change in organizational structure. As James Ferguson, chairman and CEO, asserted:

> We are encouraging managers to take an aggressive stance, one that's oriented toward growth. All of us must be willing to take prudent risks to attain it.
>
> It boils down to what you might call the "culture" of a company. And we are changing our corporate culture by articulating goals, increasing risk levels. By doing so, we have established the kind of environment in which aggressiveness and risk will be rewarded, recognizing that people may fail once in a while.
>
> The ultimate responsibility lies with the people running the business. We have told our various sectors: "You tell us how you can do your job better, and we'll support you." We find we are gaining their whole-hearted commitment to this cultural change, because it's fun and rewarding to build a business.

To emphasize this change away from cost control to growth, GF added two new operating goals. First, each sector was to meet its own specific growth targets to generate volume growth that was greater than the growth of the aggregate market. Second, each sector was to accelerate its investments in new and existing businesses. These investments were to add value to GF through incremental cash returns and growth in earnings.

Information Services Division

In the late 1970s GF became concerned about the effectiveness of its information services function. A review by external consultants reported:

To a considerable extent, the facilities planning responsibility is fragmented throughout the various information services organizations within the corporation. As is frequently the case when facilities planning is performed and controlled on a decentralized basis by people who have other full-time responsibilities, facilities decisions appear to be made on a reactive rather than on a carefully planned basis. The overall result of the decentralized planning process is a diverse picture of hardware, facilities plans of varying quality, unnecessarily high costs to satisfy processing requirements, and significant barriers to the use of common systems. As was found in the project team's review of the existing systems plans, there is no comprehensive corporate facilities plan which defines the long-range strategic direction that the company plans to follow in providing operational support for its future information requirements.

The study concluded that GF ranked relatively low in its adoption of information systems technology when compared with other major consumer goods companies of similar size and sophistication.

In 1978 GF had 16 data centers located throughout the country. Two were in the corporate offices, one at Battle Creek (IBM 360/65) and the other in White Plains (IBM 360/65, 370/158). In addition, each of the strategic business units (SBUs) and plants had some data processing capability. The Distribution, Sales, and Service Division had four regional centers, each with either an IBM 370/138 or 370/125. The Food Products Division had a 370/138 in Dover and the plants had System 34s. Pet Foods, Beverage and Breakfast Foods, and Maxwell House all had some degree of data processing support in their plants.

Along with the proliferation of equipment throughout GF went a proliferation of applications and approaches to the applications. The marketing function had 26 different systems for sales tracking and analysis, 13 systems related to call reporting, and 10 systems for sales forecasting. The main reasons given for this proliferation of duplicate systems were incompatibility of hardware and a general lack of communication about what other divisions were doing.

Despite this large number of installed systems, few aids were provided to managers to help them increase sales or reduce costs. Interviews with users indicated that the information they received was often neither timely nor useful:

- I know the information is available in our current systems but I can't get it in the format (or within the time frame) that I need it.
- This report has information which I consider critical, but it is so difficult to dig it out from the details, that it's not worth the effort.

- Yes, I get that voluminous report once a month. My secretary files the new one, throws away the old one, and I seldom, if ever, reference it.
- We collect the data on a daily basis, but when I see it in a report, it's 10 days old and no longer actionable.
- If we could state plant costs on a comparable basis, we could make those decisions with more confidence.
- That other function collects the information at the level of detail we need it, but we don't have access to the detail.

Expenditures for data processing had grown to over $35 million by 1978. The report on the information services function concluded that a real need existed for more centralized control of this resource and anticipated three primary advantages. First, large savings could accrue from centralizing the hardware in White Plains and distributing the processing capability only to those plants that had unique needs for local processing. Further, those plants that required local processing capability should all use the same hardware to facilitate the sharing of software. Second, centralized control of software development would bring significant savings by eliminating duplication in projects and providing more cost effectiveness through a larger development group. Third, centralizing would allow those responsible for information resources to focus on software that would support the strategic objectives of the corporation as a whole. Jim Tappan, group vice president with responsibility for planning and development as well as information services, saw ISD supporting the corporate strategic objectives in two ways: (1) by providing better and more timely information, ISD would support the goal of building GF's base businesses, and (2) ISD needed to take an active role in helping the divisions and functional departments meet their strategic objective of controlling and reducing corporate administrative costs.

By 1982 the ISD budget had grown to over $50 million, and most of the recommendations arising from the 1978 report had been implemented. Information Services Department was now a centrally directed function, with a corporate staff that managed business information systems for the Coffee and Food Services sector, Packaged Convenience Foods sector, the domestic divisions, and all corporate functions. It was also responsible for coordinating the International Operations' systems activities worldwide. At that time Oscar Mayer still had its own MIS function.

ISD was responsible not only for data processing but also for management science and telecommunications support. To provide this as well as the systems development support, ISD was divided into five groups (see Exhibit 2).

EXHIBIT 2   Information Services Department Organization Chart, March 12, 1981

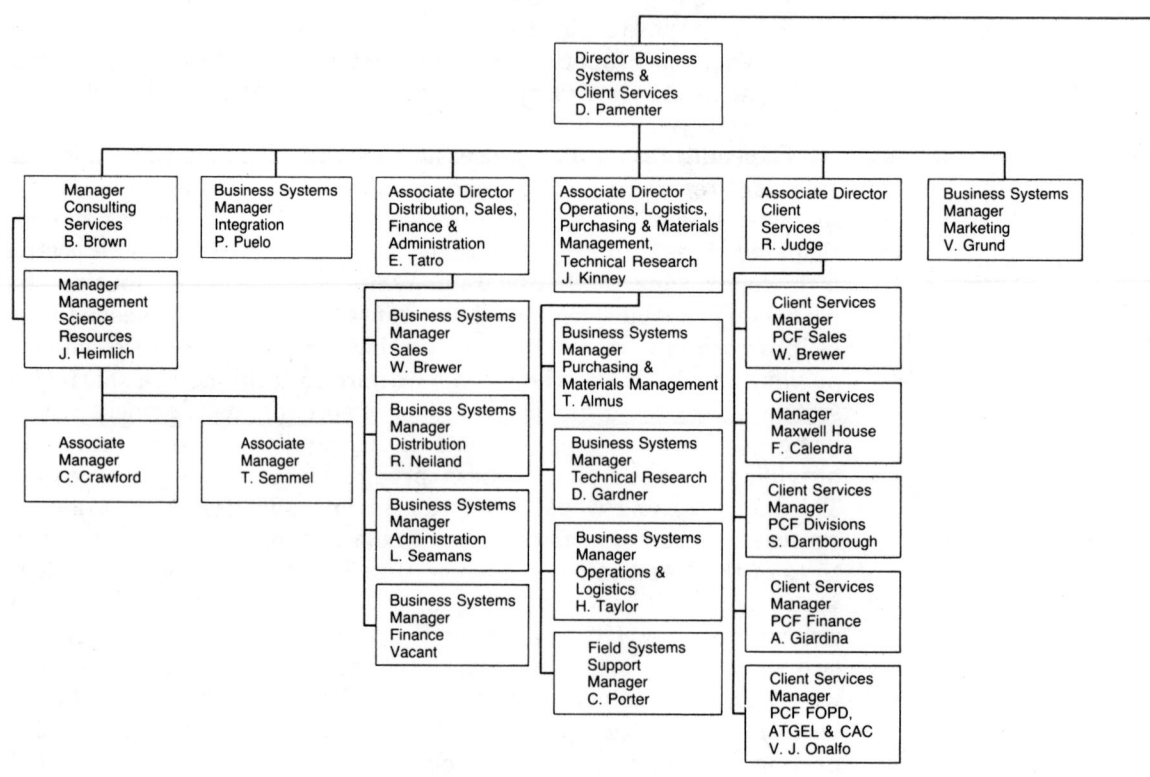

Business Systems and Client Service

This group was the focal point for ISD's support of clients. It was composed of two units—business systems and client services. Business systems was responsible for identifying opportunities to improve business performance by strengthening the business systems, for developing an integrated portfolio of strategic systems and a practical implementation plan for that portfolio, and for satisfying division and sector system needs.

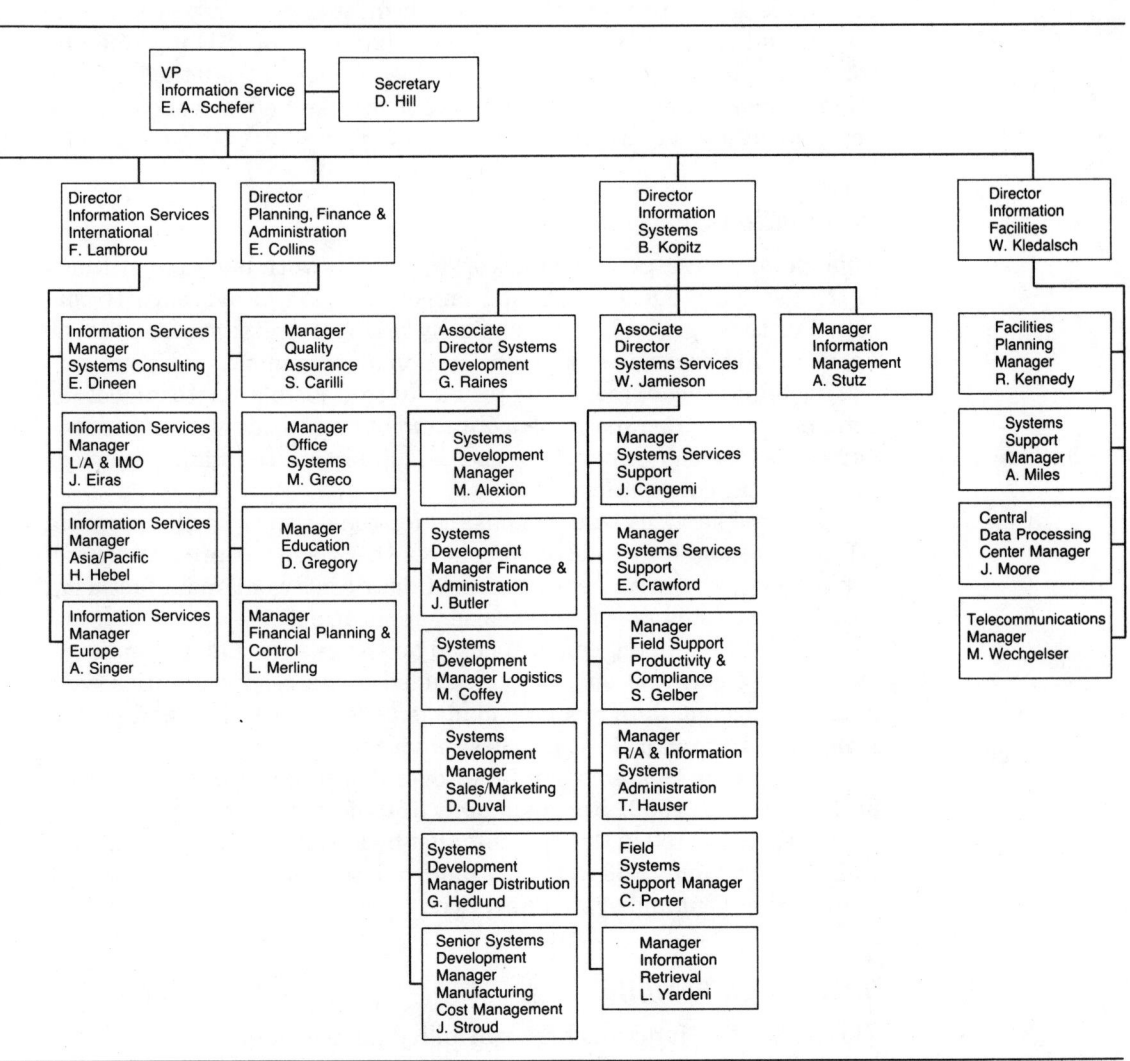

Business systems staff included the following among their roles: assuring commonality of business information, translating business solutions into data processing designs, determining the feasibility and economic practicality of systems solutions to business problems, and providing overall project management to most systems projects.

Client services was staffed by client service managers, each assigned to a sector or a division and each responsible for assisting the client in developing and executing systems plans. The client services manager helped his or her client identify business problems, explore alternatives, and determine which were the most appropriate systems solutions and arranged for support from other areas of ISD in achieving solutions. The client services unit provided feedback from the business units, which helped to insure the practicality and effectiveness of the department's services.

Information Systems

This group was responsible for working closely with business systems in the design, programming, and implementation of systems. It consisted of three professional technically oriented units: systems development, system services, and information management.

Systems development was primarily responsible for technical design, programming, and implementation of large-scale systems identified as strategically important and as supporting the major business thrusts of the corporation.

Systems services was responsible for the support of all operating GF systems and for the development of others, such as process control applications, the management of field data centers at manufacturing locations, and support of time-sharing applications.

Information management focused on the integration and management of the corporation's data. Included in its responsibilities were data base design, data resource management, and support and performance monitoring of GF's data base environment.

Information Systems employed over 300 programmers and other professionals in 1982. Approximately 150 of these professionals were permanently located in the 17 plants that had data processing capability, while the remaining 150 were split more or less evenly between new system development and systems services.

Information Facilities

This group had functional responsibility for GF information processing facilities and provided a service-oriented operation across the corporation. The group managed the corporate data processing center and all voice and data network facilities. Specialists in hardware, systems software, and telecommunications were located within this group.

In 1982 this equipment at GF included an IBM 370/158 and a 3033 operating in an MVS environment supporting its transaction-oriented systems. GF's general purpose time-sharing needs were met with two IBM 4300s running CMS. At that time 17 of GF's 23 plants supported local processing and the sending and receiving of data with System 34s which were to be replaced with System 38s. While these machines were owned by the plants, the staff (seven to nine supporting operations, data entry and programming), reported to information services.

In addition, 18 of the 20 distribution centers had IBM Model 34s for order entry. These machines had no support staff at all. Four regional centers were also in operation—one with an IBM 370/138 and the remaining three had IBM 370/135s. These machines were scheduled to be replaced with System 34s.

Finance, Planning, and Administration

This group was responsible for developing the department's strategic and financial plans, operating policies and procedures, and standards; for assuring that all systems developed conformed to standards; and for training and development programs to help increase the skills of all information services people.

It was also in charge of developing office systems for the corporation (automating secretarial/clerical activities, electronic mail communications, work simplification studies, and other projects).

International

This was a complete systems management function responsible for coordinating all international operations systems activities and for integrating international operations plans and objectives into an overall information services strategy. It also assisted in the transfer of technology and applications between the systems organizations of GF's domestic operations and GF's various international companies.

Personal Computers

Although the recommendations for centralizing information services were being implemented, Schefer had become increasingly concerned about determining the appropriate role for personal computers within GF. To help define this role, he participated in numerous discussions with the research board as well as other industry groups. In summer 1980, Schefer acquired a Radio Shack Model III to be used and experimented with by the ISD staff. By the following summer significant interest in personal computers was clearly evident within GF's user departments. ISD had installed one as an experiment six months earlier in the Food Service Products Division which had already achieved productivity gains through the use of its spreadsheet program. In June, Sal Andreoli had returned from a tax conference where he met an old friend who had an Apple computer. Andreoli knew that his system, which ISD had charged him $11,000 for development and was costing him $300 to $400 per month to run, was not meeting his needs. Rather than spend another $13,000 estimated by ISD to redo the system, Andreoli believed he should spend only $7,000 to try an Apple computer. His friend had assured him that the applications were straightforward and even offered to come and set them up for him in one afternoon. After ISD had received Andreoli's proposal to forgo the new system in favor of acquiring an Apple, ISD staff had numerous meetings with him to make absolutely certain he understood both the Apple's limitations as well as the potential problems he could expect.

To date, ISD had hesitated about taking a position on personal computers because it was not clear how they would fit in. With the success of the food services experiment, however, and pressures from other departments, Schefer decided it was time for ISD to develop its policy on this issue. The first problem he faced was where to assign responsibility for personal computers. Bill Kiedaisch, director of information facilities (see Exhibit 2), believed that personal computers were primarily pieces of hardware and that information facilities should be responsible for their dissemination and control. Bernie Kopitz, director of information systems, believed that since the use of these devices was primarily software driven, responsibility for them should fall under his group. Schefer felt strongly, however, that the approach taken should focus on the users rather than the technology; consequently he believed the responsibility for personal computers should be located in the ISD marketing area (client services). He asked Bob Judge, associate director of client services, to synthesize the information collected and come up with a proposal for General Foods.

Proposal on Personal Computer Use

Judge's proposal stated that ISD should aggressively support the introduction of personal computers for three reasons. First, they were useful as stand-alone productivity tools to help people do their jobs better. Second, as prototyping tools, they could be used to develop working models of large systems. ISD could work with users to create the models of a desired system, get the bugs out, and make certain that the system met the users' needs, thus having a beneficial impact both in the user departments and in ISD. Third, a personal computer could serve as an intelligent terminal to access data on the mainframe. Judge felt that the concern should not be on the number of personal computers placed but where they were placed. They could be counterproductive in an inappropriate location because of all the distraction. For this reason Judge felt that it was important to have top management involved in their placement. He also proposed setting up an area in GF where the potential user could come and work with personal computers to gain a better understanding of what they could and could not do.

Schefer agreed with Judge's proposals and authorized him to implement them.

Judge first involved senior management by meeting with the heads of every functional unit and division to explain what ISD was doing and to get from each of them the name of a representative to serve on the personal computer placement advisory council (PCPAC). PCPAC would meet once a quarter to recommend policies on personal computers, thus providing a forum for dissemination of information back to the individual units and divisions. The signature of the unit's representative on PCPAC would also be required for any placement request submitted to ISD for a personal computer; this would assure the unit head or division president that the acquisition program in his or her area was being controlled. All the unit heads and division presidents agreed, and within a week each had provided the name of the appropriate individual. In some cases this individual was the unit head or division president himself; in other cases the person nominated was in a responsible management position, usually on the staff of the unit head or division president.

Along with the creation of PCPAC, Judge felt that it was very important to raise the overall level of understanding at GF on the capabilities of personal computers. It was generally accepted that there was a growing gap in senior management's awareness of the potentials of system technology. Judge felt that it was especially important to GF's future that the company's top management understand not only the capabilities of these machines but also how these systems could have an impact on the functions they managed. To facilitate this goal, Judge proposed establishing the executive development program in which each function head and division head would be loaned a personal computer for 120 days and given a structured set of exercises to follow, thus building their confidence with the device. The final project required the participant to put up two applications; one from the job, and one from home.

Finally, Judge proposed creating a computer store within GF that would provide interested employees hands-on experience in working with one of three personal computers. He decided that the store should stock Apple IIs, IBM personal computers, and Radio Shack Model IIIs. It would also stock a wide array of software to support business functions. The store would provide classes in the morning for employees interested in using these devices. GF negotiated favorable purchasing contracts at computer stores in the area and also arranged for GF's employees to purchase personal computers for their own use at the same discount.

In October Andreoli's tax department received its Apple Computer, and by the following spring every group within the tax department had some applications on the Apple, using either Visicalc or DB Master (a data base package). The Apple was being used over 160 hours a month and it was usually necessary to reserve it in advance. Andreoli pointed out: "These things are really cost efficient because they remove all that grunt work from a person's job. I feel I'm using my job time better. I look at it as job enrichment for those who work for me, for their jobs are becoming more meaningful. People are staying late or coming in early just to get access to the computer because it means that much to them."

Executive's Response to Personal Computers

By the end of June the proposals defined in General Foods' strategy statement for implementing GF/ISD's policy on personal computers were almost completely implemented (see Exhibit 3). PCPAC's representatives had approved the purchase of over 70 personal computers. Twenty of GF's senior managers were involved in the executive development program and each had a personal computer at home. All were enthusiastic about the opportunity this new technology provided and they were convinced that it had many applications for the various functions that reported to them. Andrew Schroder, senior vice president-administration, believed that the personal computer helped address a number of issues:

> I'm not a financial executive. My responsibilities are government relations, consumer affairs, public relations, and corporate personnel. I picked up my computer last Friday and have only worked on it over this past weekend. So far I'm halfway through the chicken farm exercise which involves setting up tables for dealing with inventory issues. I'm about at the point where I wonder whether this is really what I, in my particular capacity, need. However, I'm beginning to get some feel for how one goes about interacting with a computer and I think that will be helpful. Whether I need to get very much further with the chicken farm exercise is another question.
>
> There are some principles here which I would certainly support. One of the issues I've felt strongly about is what we in General Foods are doing about making certain that the learning experience doesn't stop when an individual enters the workplace. So in the broadest form, this is an opportunity for us to continue learning. This would avoid putting ourselves in the unfortunate situation where massive learning has been acquired by our newer entries but is not being understood by the more senior levels of our organization.
>
> A second issue which is applicable to my function, is learning firsthand what are the capabilities of personal computers in terms

---

EXHIBIT 3 Strategy for Implementing FG/ISD Policy

Personal Computing

I. Top Down Direction

GF management will set the direction on placement of personal computers in their respective units. Information services will support all unit heads in this process by implementing and managing the ongoing aspects of our executive development program on personal computing.

Executive Development Program

Designed to:

A. Inform Unit Heads of the current technology, capabilities, and trends from a business perspective.
B. Review the GF/ISD process for providing appropriate guidance and support to assist users in the effective use of this technology.
C. Involve senior management in determining the extent to which their organizations should pursue the personal computing option.
D. Assist Unit Heads in selecting an appropriate delegate to act as that Unit's representation on the Advisory and Placement Council.

Placement Advisory Council

The Personal Computer Advisory Council will meet on a quarterly basis for the purposes of constructively reviewing and discussing policies, activities, and uses of personal computers across GF. The activities of this group will result in periodic reports to senior management on the status of personal computers in the company.

The council is a forum to foster understanding within GF and to insure consistent communication of policies, progress, and plans. The makeup of the group will consist of representatives from each functional area and division appointed by the unit head.

II. Facility Support

Information Services will maintain a support facility that will assist Units in the placement and use of personal computers. The facility will consist essentially of the following:

EXHIBIT 3 *(continued)*

A. *Personal Computer Center*

1. A facility designed to serve the units' educational needs, demonstrate equipment (current Apple, IBM, TRS–80), software and selected applications, and counsel users and potential users on the myriad of tools and packages available.
2. This center will provide GF Units with a single contact and coordinating point for obtaining purchases at the best possible price, insuring maintenance and service contracts are in order, and provide troubleshooting/problem solving service to the Units.

B. *Loan Program*

Accompanying the Executive Development Program is a loan program of personal computers for up to 120 days. This program is managed through the computer center and is designed to increase management's awareness and understanding of how technology-based information processing and tools can impact their operation, via hands-on activity.

GF Policy on Personal Business Computers

Policy Statement

It is the policy of General Foods to promote the effective use of technology-based productivity tools—namely, personal computers through an active program of coordination and support. This responsibility resides in Corporate Information Services and:

1. Recommends policy and strategy to senior GF management.
2. Supports all GF Units in identifying the appropriateness of personal computers for specific needs.

It is also the policy of General Foods that each Unit is responsible for determining the business justification for personal computers in their organization.

Definition

Personal computers are technology-based information tools, sometimes referred to as "micro" computers which are usually desk top sized and cost less than $7,500 to purchase.

EXHIBIT 3 *(continued)*

Corporate Information Services

A. Consulting and Advisory Role

Corporate Information Services will maintain a current knowledge of the state-of-the-art technology and developing trends relating to personal computers, and will help potential or current users by:

1. Assisting GF Business Units and functions in determining the appropriate use of personal computers as productivity and decision-making aids.
2. Assisting clients in the actual use of these tools through education and training programs appropriate to individual area needs.
3. Providing support in determining the appropriate hardware and software to meet needs at minimum cost.

B. Concurrence Role

Corporate Information Services Personal Computer Center will be the central facility for concurring on the purchase and placement of personal computers to ensure that:

1. Hardware and software are obtained at the lowest cost.
2. Adequate service is negotiated and provided when required.
3. Users of personal computers are informed of new developments.
4. Information Services overall strategies and support resources remain tuned to the developing activity in the individual Units.

This will enable ISD to maintain a central inventory of equipment and software in order to facilitate sharing of experience, software developments, etc.

User Area Responsibility

Decision authority on use and placement of personal computers resides with the Unit Head and is based on the Unit's assessment of business justification and assurance that its usage is consistent with the Unit's mission. The user will be responsible for equipment operation and physical security.

EXHIBIT 3 *(concluded)*

Accounting Considerations

Accounting Financial Policy No. 28 requires that all costs related to the purchase of Personal Computers be expensed at the time of purchase. Control of these expenditures will be through the normal budget process.

SOURCE: Company document.

---

of managing the knowledge mass that we have got to handle in our part of the business. I can't think of any more interesting issue of technology, new technology, busting onto the scene than the notion of the personal computer which provides the capability in the office or in one's home of keeping pace with this information. Again, a chicken farm exercise must not be an end in itself but a means to something else. I see the exercises as a means to understanding the computer as a tool for monitoring more effectively the news, either media or congressional events. I'm going to be increasingly interested in ways that it can be harnessed for my particular purposes. Putting together a P&L for hypothetical business again had better be a means to some other more appropriate end, for as an end in and of itself it is going to grow old very quickly.

June 7 was the opening day of Bob's Byte Boutique, as Judge's computer store had become affectionately known. The store had a classroom with 10 Radio Shack Model IIIs and a large screen TV. Because Judge had chosen to restrict the class size so that each student had a machine to work with, plus two for instructors, each class could accommodate only eight students. The classes were so successful that they quickly became booked up for two months in advance. Judge charged each sponsoring department $25 per student thereby limiting, it was hoped, the enrollment to those who had a serious interest. Further, it was hoped that those who enrolled in the class would feel obliged to attend, give that their department was going to be charged whether they came or not. The computer store was open from 12 noon to 4:30 P.M. for anyone to come and experiment at no charge.

Although everyone in ISD management was supportive of Judge's effort to raise the general level of computer literacy within GF, there was some disagreement on the potential benefits. Bernie Kopitz and Bill Kiedaisch, for instance, both felt that the interest in personal computing was based, to a large extent, on a general misunderstanding of the machines' capabilities and that this alone provided an excellent educational opportunity justifying the expense. Ed Collins, director of planning, finance, and administration, said: "The installation of these 70 or so personal computers provided an excellent cost-effective opportunity which was well worth the investment of $350,000. Even if you assumed $2 of personal time for $1 of computer cost, the cost to GF was only .01 percent of GF's net revenue. Besides, very few new individual systems could be developed for under $350,000."

Bill Kiedaisch emphasized the importance of this educational aspect of GF's personal computer policy:

> The person coming in the door who says "Gee, I've never had a computer before but now I can use it," sees a lot of potential benefit that probably will not materialize. People like CMS with its broad range of software; capability to share data; and this is what they need to solve their problem. They can use vehicles like Visicalc but eventually they are going to say "How do I get the general ledger data into my Visicalc model, massage it, and put it back?" This opens up the whole broad issue of centralized data management. Further, there is just as much discipline required in programming a personal computer as there is in programming a Cray computer. As people bump against these limitations they are going to take a different point of view and eventually these things are going to collect dust. However, we have to let the people get hands-on experience if they are going to begin to understand the benefits and the limitations of personal computers. That's what we are looking to achieve.

For emphasis Bernie Kopitz added:

> A minority of these computers will stick to the ribs but the majority will fall off and collect dust. That's what is really underlying our basic philosophy in setting up the computer store. Let them try it and get it out of their systems rather than going out and buying a computer for anyone who is interested. Just because their sixth grade child can sit at a micro and program it, they come in here and say, "I can do everything for myself with only a one-time cost of a few thousand dollars. I don't have to pay you to do what I need. I'm going to try it." We give them one of these things to try for awhile and most of them will come back. They will realize they can't do everything that they want.

In discussions with ISD's senior management several concerns were raised on the introduction of personal computers. First, Kiedaisch felt that rather than being a productivity aid the personal computer could actually be counterproductive: "As far as productivity is concerned, this is where I feel we have the biggest trap. Unless you have a vehicle like Visicalc where a person sits down and becomes productive immediately, who knows how much time managers waste trying to program these things. You can't take a guy who is supposed to be forecasting sales and let him get enamored with the hardware and software. He's not going to be doing his job."

Another problem of concern often expressed was the potential for departments to become operationally dependent on systems developed on their personal computers. These systems were not likely to be adequately documented, thus when the person who developed them was promoted or worse left GF, there was the danger that the department could not fully function. Although ISD strongly discouraged the development of such systems, once the user had the machine, ISD's managers believed it was out of their hands. As Kopitz stressed: "Let him not back up his system, let him not document it, that's his prerogative. That's how he saves his money. If he wants all those things, he may as well pay us to do it."

As Kiedaisch pointed out earlier, there were problems concerning data security and access. To cope with the problem of data access, ISD had already formed the data access center as part of the information management group. This center was staffed with people who were responsible for providing data from any of GF's data bases in whatever form the user needed it. Data could be provided in printed reports or in files in the data interchange format (DIF) which could be accessed by personal computers. The data access center, with its extensive data dictionary, provided the interface between the data and the users. Here, ISD managers felt that they could control access to data. Further, it was ISD's policy that all updates to such data were to be done on GF's mainframe. Thus, a user who needed to work with the most recent data could simply download the data from the mainframe to the personal computer. This approach limited the user's responsibility for the security of the data, as the files of record were the data files stored on the mainframe.

Schefer was well aware of potential problems, such as data and program security, inappropriate use of management and employee time, and excessive expenditure of corporate funds for something that ultimately would not be used. But he believed that the potential for productivity gains made it essential to pursue the opportunities presented by personal computers. Schefer hoped that this policy would serve to strengthen the relationship between users and ISD, thus giving ISD the credibility necessary to help users avoid potential pitfalls.

PlanPower: The Financial Planning Expert System

Bill Myers, president of Financial Designs, was reflecting on Plan-Power, a financial planning expert system.

> We know exactly where we want this company to be in five years. We want to know exactly how PlanPower helps get us there. The amount of expertise it contains is impressive—its planning approach first rate—the question is: How should we use it?

Financial Designs (FD) prided itself on being a top financial planning firm—one of New England's best. Located in an elegant office townhouse off Lexington Green,[1] FD had the air of "new-tech rich," where personal computers and mahogany desks blended in an elegant ambiance. The office helped communicate FD's philosophy of quality, professionalism, and managed growth to their wealthy clientele.

Applied Expert Systems (APEX) of Cambridge, Massachusetts had created the PlanPower system. The product of over 40 man-years

---

[1]Lexington Green is an exclusive part of Lexington, Massachusetts, a wealthy Boston suburb.

This case was prepared by John J. Sviokla under the supervision of James L. McKenney.

Copyright © 1986 by the President and Fellows of Harvard College

Harvard Business School case 9-186-293 (Rev 7/86)

of work, PlanPower represented one of the most complex expert systems in the world. It was designed to take the rules of thumb of many expert financial planners (also called the "logic") and codify them in a flexible software package. FD was a test-site ("beta-site" in software jargon) for PlanPower. In exchange for helping APEX with the design and de-bugging of the system, FD had use of PlanPower at no charge.

By February 1986, FD had successfully used PlanPower to analyze and create three financial plans. There was no doubt in Myers's mind that the plans were first rate, yet the use of PlanPower was straining the FD organization. They continued to run their existing analyses on each case along with the PlanPower plan. The double work was necessary to verify the numbers and augment the PlanPower formats. In addition, FD staff had invested hours learning the workings of Plan-Power's logic so that when a client pointed to a part of a plan and asked: "Where does that come from?" the FD staff member could explain the reasoning behind the number or the recommendation.

Overall, Myers was trying to assess the incremental benefit of using PlanPower to FD and to think through his alternatives.

Financial Planning

Broadly defined, financial planning is the creation of a systematic set of financial objectives and action plans for an individual or family. The interest in financial planning increased dramatically in the 1980s. From 1980 to 1986 the membership of the Institute of Certified Financial Planners, a trade organization, grew from 1,108 to 17,637.[2] It was felt that deregulation of the financial markets, along with a new consumer awareness of financial concerns, was fueling expansion. A study conducted by SRI International, a research firm based in Menlo Park, California, estimated that by 1990 there would be 12 million people in the United States who would be wealthy enough to warrant financial planning. Further, SRI estimated that over 25,000 professional financial planners would be needed to service that market.[3]

There are many possible components in a comprehensive financial plan. Ideally it begins with an analysis of the client's financial and estate goals. This set of desires is tempered by the reality of the person's income and net worth. The analysis often has many facets, including:

---

[2]"Financial Planning," *The Wall Street Journal*, Special Section, December 2, 1985, p. 4D.

[3]PlanPower press kit.

- Tax planning.
- Investment advice.
- Education planning.
- Retirement planning.
- Estate planning.
- Insurance.
- The necessary legal documents—wills, trusts, etc.

For many people, a well executed financial plan can make a significant difference in their long term net worth by lowering taxes, marshalling expenses, and providing sound investment advice.

There was no general consensus on how to do financial planning. Philosophies, techniques, and content varied widely. Generally, the backgrounds of the firm's principals influenced their planning focus. For example, insurance agents often emphasized the issues of estate planning, where many insurance needs can be found. Tax attorneys, on the other hand, might focus on tax reduction strategies and investment in tax shelters. Moreover, there were many hucksters in the field who used the term *financial planning* simply to open doors and cover schemes. Periodically, Congress considered regulating the industry, but progress on such action was uncertain. Standards would be difficult to create because there were no objective measures for planning performance, requisite content, or approach. Furthermore, each business constituency, such as brokerage firms or insurance companies, might have a different slant on what constituted "reasonable financial planning." Issues such as these slowed any movement on standards.

Suppliers

There were many suppliers in the market. Companies which offered financial planning services ranged in size from one person operations to large, multinational firms. All of them fell into one of three categories: fee-only planners, fee-and-commission planners, and commission-only planners. Fee-based firms were paid on a fee for service basis. Commission-only planners often marketed a particular product or set of products and used financial planning as an umbrella for their selling strategy. Fee-and-commission planners had a mix of both.

A planning firm's revenue mix had many implications. For example, those firms which had a fee-based planning practice generally developed a client base by building long-term relationships and providing quality service. A significant portion of their income might come from client retainers. At the other extreme, product-based firms strove for large volumes of customers and focused on transactions—with many clients coming and going.

Financial Designs

Financial Designs was incorporated in 1980. Bill Myers related FD's strategy:

> Financial Designs was founded on one concept—quality. We aim to become the "trusted financial advisor" of individuals with high net worth and income—preferably $2 million or above in net worth and $300,000 plus in income. We have other clients, but we perform best for a person with complex finances.

To achieve this end, FD was founded with a team of five financial experts with at least one individual with experience in each of the important areas of financial planning. Bill Myers had experience in estates, trust, and administration. Marshall March had over 20 years of experience as a portfolio manager and investment advisor. John Whistler was an insurance agent with over 10 years' experience in investments and tax shelters. Mike Harvey had an extensive background in personal estate planning and real estate, and Peter Ward was an attorney with a degree and practice in tax law.

The five principals each owned 20 percent of the firm. They hoped to grow FD's client base to between 110 and 140 individuals with high net worth. Each principal hoped to be able to receive about $100,000–150,000 in compensation from FD each year. In terms of reputation, they wanted to be known as one of the premier planning firms in the Northeast. Myers expounded on their strategy:

> Our marketing is "word of mouth." It may cause us to grow slower, but we think it allows us to grow better. An advertisement in a magazine is not going to attract the person we want into the type of relationship we prefer. A recommendation from a satisfied customer is our best advertisement.

Since 1980, their client base grew to 83 clients; the average net worth was $2.5 million. In 1985, FD had revenue of $320,000—two-thirds from fees, one-third from commissions.

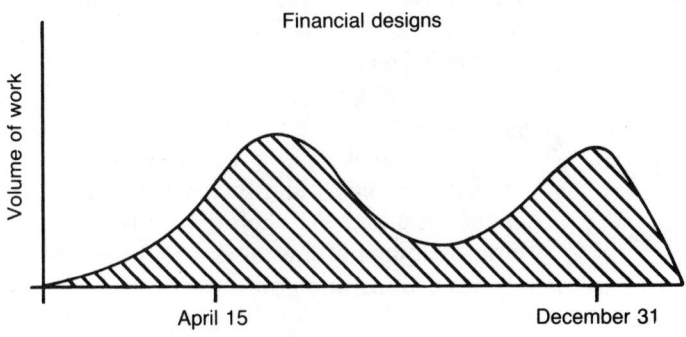

EXHIBIT 1   Financial Designs Organization Chart

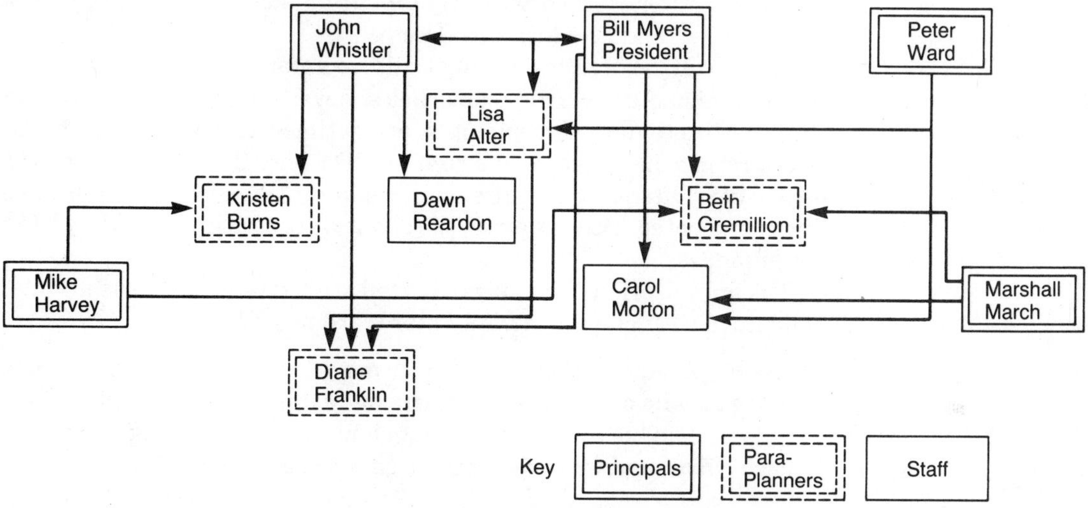

The workload at FD varied widely through the year. The most active times were immediately after tax time, when repentant clients reached out for help, and just before year end when clients scrambled to make final adjustments. (See diagram on the previous page.)

Capacity

At any given time, FD had 3–5 new client plans "in the works," with a 7–10 client backlog. Each year they added 10–15 new clients, and their renewal rate on existing clients was about 95 percent. Myers estimated that they created between 12 and 15 new plans per year. The average fee per client for the initial plan was approximately $6,000–8,000 with wide variation ($500–25,000). The retainer fee was customarily 50 percent of the initial plan cost—renewed yearly.

Roles and Responsibilities of FD Personnel before PlanPower

By 1985 there were 11 people in FD—5 professionals, 4 para-planners, 1 data administrator, and a secretary. See the organization chart, Exhibit 1. Myers, as president of the firm, was responsible for day-to-day management. He and John Whistler were the most active in FD. The other three principals spent two or more days a week at FD, but they also pursued outside interests. Lisa Alter, Beth Gremillion, Kristen Burns, and Diane Franklin were all "para-planners," which meant that they worked to support one of the five principals in managing and servicing his clients. Alter worked with Myers, Gremillion with March, Burns with Whistler, and Franklin with Harvey.

Carol Morton was receptionist and secretary. Dawn Reardon was data administrator, which meant that she was responsible for keeping client files up to date. For example, every time a client filled out his or her tax return, he would send a copy to FD where Reardon updated the client's file. Often she found errors made by the client's accountant. When confronted with the error, the client was often impressed by FD's thoroughness.

The organization was especially well staffed relative to the number of clients in their client base. As Peter Ward noted:

> Compared to other planning firms we are "top heavy." I know one guy who calls himself a financial planner and has over 700 clients—all on his own. We have much more talent coming to bear on each client, and we perform more comprehensive service.

Systems at Financial Designs

FD used many systems to help them in pursuit of their business goals. Myers developed a number of administrative systems designed to assure consistent, quality contact with the entire client base.

Whistler had taken the lead in developing personal computer-based systems for the preparation of plans, creation of exhibits, and client tracking. There were three primary systems in his design. One helped in the management of text documents. The second was a group of Lotus 1–2–3 templates for financial planning, product tracking, and client fee estimation. The third was a set of small database files used for tracking client status. Whistler had established procedures to keep them up to date.

Financial Design's Processes

If one were to look at the work processes at FD, one would find four important, interrelated business tasks: (1) transactions, (2) creation of new plans for new clients, (3) review of existing clients, and (4) product review and inventory.

Transactions. Clients came to FD in different states of financial repair. As is evidenced by the peak demands for FD services, many clients came to FD with specific questions about taxes. Clients also consulted FD before performing a major transaction, such as buying a house. FD always serviced these short-term needs; after all, they charged high prices for first rate service. Yet, they tried to tie any advice into a larger plan. Because every financial maneuver affects the overall picture, FD believed it was wrong to do any planning, tax or otherwise, in isolation. In practice they honored customers' requests for "one time service" but avoided being only a transaction service for their clients.

New Clients.   The FD relationship usually began with the client sitting down and discussing his or her planning needs with one of FD's principals. Then the client filled out a two page data form which gave some basic family facts, financial goals, and information.

After this initial contact, Myers and Whistler met to determine the fee and the "fit." There was an art to determining which clients would be "a good fit," that is, clients who would be willing to give accurate, timely data and who would seriously consider FD's recommendations. FD did turn some clients over to other planning firms due to "poor fit."

Once Myers and Whistler "accepted" the client, they decided which of the five FD principals should become the senior person responsible for the client, known at FD as the "client administrator." The client administrator was to stay informed of all client activity and shepherd the client through FD's planning process to assure good service. If the client signed on, he or she paid one-half the fee up-front, with one-half to be paid at delivery of the final plan.

New Client Financial Planning Process.   Many different inputs went into the creation of a financial plan: client data, expert opinion, planning, and research. (See Exhibits 2 and 3 for a description of the entire process.) Data accuracy was critical to the entire process. The more comprehensive and current the data were, the more reasonable the plan would be. After signing the contract, the client was given a data booklet with an extensive questionnaire on goals and desires as well as questions on income, expenses, assets, and liabilities. Some clients gave data promptly, but for many it was the most grueling part of the entire planning process.

The para-planners collected most of the data. Lisa Alter recounted an extreme case:

> When I asked one of our clients to provide the data for the plan, he gave me three phone numbers—one for his attorney, one for his banker, and one for his accountant. That one took a lot of digging.

Most of the FD staff identified "getting client data" as one of the worst bottlenecks in the planning process. Many aspects of the data collection required an understanding of planning. For example, the

---

EXHIBIT 2   Financial Designs Process Flow: New Clients

Initial client contact
and commitment

↓

Data collection/Verification

↓

Plan creation*

↓

Presentation to client

---

*Detail in Exhibit 3.

client might give the para-planners a series of financial documents, full of jargon and complexities which were only decipherable by a knowledgeable reader.

When sufficient data was collected to attain a reasonably complete picture of a person's financial situation, the client administrator, the para-planners, and Dawn and Carol put together a one-two page client profile. It included a balance sheet containing all assets and liabilities, funds flow statement, and a synopsis of the client's goals and personal issues—the building blocks for a plan.

The Planners' Meeting.   FD's philosophy of integrated financial planning was embodied in the firm's organization and processes. Every Wednesday all five principals gathered around an oblong conference table to convene the "Wednesday Meeting," as it was known at FD. At this meeting they designed and reviewed the cases of the day. They worked on one or occasionally two new plans, along with existing client reviews, product reviews, and general business. Mike Harvey noted the importance of the Wednesday meeting to the firm:

> Our distinctive competence is that every client is reviewed by the entire team of experts at our Wednesday meetings. The knowledge that comes to bear at the time, on that person's financial affairs, is as good as, or better than, any planning firm.

It was at the Wednesday meeting that the interconnection between planners occurred. Each perspective was informed by the others—a team effort. It also served as an efficient use of the principals' time because all could examine and interact on the plan together and quickly. Further, the Wednesday meeting allowed firm members to share new planning information and keep in regular contact.

EXHIBIT 3   Plan Creation—Before PlanPower

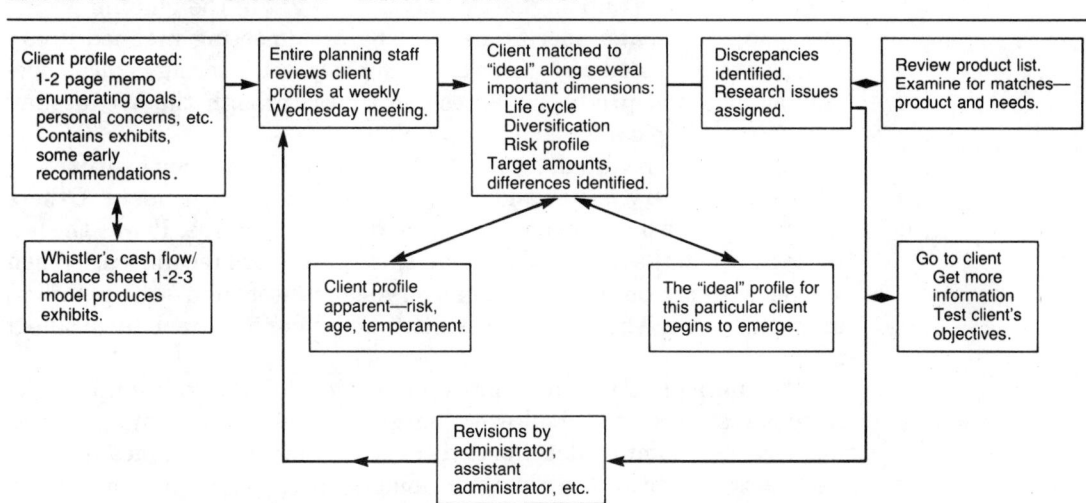

There were some "guiding principles" which the planners used for each client: asset diversification, risk tolerance, and life-cycle phase. The asset diversification model was based on the notion that wealthy individuals should diversify their holdings in counter-cyclical investments—thus reducing investment risk. The categories in FD's model were: fixed income (bonds); American (American equities); international (international equities); natural resources (oil, agriculture, etc.); real estate; and tangibles (gold, stamps, antiques, etc.). Most individuals were heavily invested in one or two categories (often real estate and American equities) and light on others. FD often suggested a re-diversification of assets to achieve portfolio balance. Further, they believed in buying professionally managed mutual funds—again diversifying risk.

The aggressiveness of the investments depended on the client's attitude toward risk and his or her "life-cycle phase." Generally, people age 30–50 were in the acquisition stage where they were trying to build their net worth. Those in the 50–70 age group were generally trying to conserve their assets and live off the income from the assets. Those in the 70 and over age group were often preparing for dissipation of assets and passing their wealth on to the next generation with fewest taxes. These categories served as a guide for the planning goals. However, they were often modified. For example, there were young individuals in the conservation stage and older individuals still aggressively acquiring, with no thought of dissipation.

At the Wednesday meeting all planners would review the one-two page client profile and suggest changes—in light of the guiding principles and the client's specific needs. The first meeting mapped broad changes to be tested and researched. Subsequent meetings traced specific actions and products. Three-five times through the Wednesday meeting was typical for a new client plan.

Client needs varied. Some had very simple financial situations where the primary issues and actions were almost self-evident. Others had finances with many interrelated and complex issues. It was the latter type which the principals enjoyed most. As Ward recounted, "When we get working on a tough case everyone is interested—the planning most enjoyable. The challenge of a new and different financing problem is fun."

The para-planners took notes and performed the follow-up on the planners' suggestions. Follow-up entailed running the numbers, making sure all recommendations tied together. Sometimes it meant going back to the client for new data or doing research on important issues. Lisa Alter noted, "I love figuring out how to do a complex financial plan. To develop the numbers, do the analysis, and design the solution—that's challenging."

When the plan had progressed through the Wednesday meeting enough times, the written plan was begun. Often the report could be as long as 100 pages, covering a wide range of client issues. The text usually served two purposes: on one hand, it explained basic concepts of asset diversification, life-cycle, risk, etc. On the other hand, it gave a precise accounting of the individual's financial situation, FD's recommendations, and rationale.

From the founding of the firm until September of 1985, the plan writing had been done by one person—Susan Most. Most had been skillful in assembling the plan parts into a coherent whole. Her prose was concise—her style businesslike. Often she had been the contact point for the client, and her dual role as plan writer and client contact person had kept her on top of the issues and the plan current.

When Most had the report completed, all the principals presented the plan to the client. Generally, Myers began the presentation, and he was followed by the other four principals, each explaining his own area of expertise. It took two to four hours in all.

It was a challenge to keep the plan current. Often, clients made changes between the date they gave their data to FD and the date of the presentation. Changes caused FD to make adjustments up to the last minute to reflect current status. In extreme cases, one of the para-planners might be modifying and proofing text and exhibits outside the presentation room, during a presentation. Whistler's Lotus® 1-2-3® systems were instrumental in allowing rapid update of client's exhibits and text. Sometimes, Whistler used a personal computer during the presentation to generate new numbers, although this was infrequent.

By early 1985 two things had changed. First, the volume of clients had been straining Most's capacity to generate plans. Second and more importantly, Most left in July 1985 to become a full-time mother. Since Most's departure, FD had shifted to generating "mini-plans" around specific issues. Client presentations were targeted on specific topics and only 30–60 minutes long. FD scheduled three to five presentations for each client, to deliver the entire plan.

Whistler and Myers did not know exactly what the capacity of the "mini-plan system" was. They felt that the mini-plans had been effective but at the same time they wanted to get back to complete plans and single presentations.

Old Client Update. On a weekly basis, Whistler and Myers reviewed the status of every client. Whistler had a "tickler file" on a database package which allowed him to track a few lines of information on every FD customer. The file included the last meeting date, current pending issues, people responsible, etc. He, Myers, and Lisa Alter reviewed this weekly.

Product Review. Another service FD offered was investment advice. FD kept track of many categories of investments, and investigated their past performance. Tax shelters and mutual funds were two important categories, for these were recommended often. FD kept a list of approved deals so that when they suggested a solution, they might have the product ready to sell to the client.

In sum, the four processes at FD—transactions, new client planning, old client update, and product review—worked together to provide service. Overall, FD attempted to match clients' goals, risk profile, and life-cycle stage with the least expected risk by suggesting diversification of assets and professional investment management.

APEX and PlanPower

PlanPower is the name of an expert system which was designed and built by Applied Expert Systems. APEX was founded in 1983 by a group of executives and academics with experience in financial planning services, artificial intelligence (AI), and management information systems consulting.

Dr. Fred Luconi, a Ph.D. from the Massachusetts Institute of Technology in computer science, was one of the founders. Before founding APEX, Luconi had 15 years' experience with INDEX systems, a provider of information systems consulting and decision support software. Jim Joslin, another one of the co-founders, had over 20 years' experience in management of personal and tax-qualified investment portfolios. Other people involved in the company included Dr. Randall Davis, a professor at MIT's Sloan School of Management, and a Ph.D. in Artificial Intelligence from Stanford University, and Richard Karash, a co-founder of another software company called Management Decision Systems, which had successfully marketed decision support software.

APEX was a privately held company, and there were no financial reports publicly available. It was known that there were a number of institutional investors backing the company, including Travelers Insurance. Since its founding, APEX had offered financial planning products and services, including a personal computer-based planning aid. PlanPower was their first expert systems product and its success in the marketplace was clearly of strategic importance to APEX. In the period from 1984 to 1986, the company had grown from a core group of 20 to a staff of over 70. It was speculated that many of the new employees were hired to support the rollout of PlanPower.

PlanPower was designed to be a comprehensive financial planning system. With over 6,000 rules it was one of the largest expert systems tools in the world. APEX saw it serving two different markets. On the one hand, PlanPower would provide the conduit for financial products from the large institutions to the world at large. It had the potential to contain data on over 125 different types of financial products. When such products were in the system (a service to be added early in 1986) the APEX financial plan would be able to make recommendations and name specific products to execute those recommendations. This feature was expected to be particularly appealing to large institutional clients who might be able to leverage their existing sales force by giving the salespeople expert support. To these clients the cost of purchasing the hardware and software, bundled together, would be $50,000 per unit. The renewal cost of the software license was expected to be approximately $10,000 per year.

The other major market was the independent financial planners. The Travelers Insurance company was to distribute PlanPower through their First Financial Planner Services (FFPS) subsidiary. FFPS was to sell PlanPower bundled with a set of other financial services including product review, regulatory support, managerial assistance, and marketing support. All together, including PlanPower software, the FFPS service would cost approximately $15,000 per year. There was also a cost of about $7,500 per year to lease computer hardware.

In both arrangements, PlanPower was part product and part service. APEX wanted to ensure quality plans based on the most up-to-date tax laws and financial data. The question of liability for poor planning advice had yet to be settled in the courts, but it was almost certain that all parties to the investment transaction, including the software vendor, would be named in the event of a suit by an unhappy plan recipient. APEX wanted to be responsible and prudent in this regard. Consequently, the product was never to be sold without ongoing service and updates.

Due to the fact that there were no standards in financial planning, the APEX system "took a stand" on the "correct approach" to the task. The core philosophy of the system was similar to that of FD—that is, asset diversification, and the investment pattern that the asset diversification model implied, was the driving force behind the logic of the system.

PlanPower provided coverage of all the areas involved in the creation of a financial plan: estate planning, insurance, tax advice, etc. It was broad and detailed in its knowledge, but in any one area it was not as knowledgeable as an expert in that area. Overall, it performed well for most planning situations which it was expected to encounter. Yet, because there were no standards in the field nor were there any figures on the number of people who had "standard" financial situations, the specific applicability of the PlanPower system to all the possible types of planning situations was unknown.

The PlanPower software ran on a Xerox 1186 workstation, a computer specially built to run LISP, a language common to expert systems software. Physically, the Xerox 1186 had a large screen with very high resolution. Many "windows" could be opened to view different client data or perform different tasks on the clients' data simultaneously.

The Xerox 1186 did have the capability to run IBM personal computer software, but there was no compatibility between PlanPower data and any other data. For example, one could run Lotus 1-2-3 on the 1186, but PlanPower could not read the data residing in existing Lotus 1-2-3 spreadsheets. In anticipation of high customer demand, APEX had announced an agreement with Xerox to buy 1,000 of the 1186 workstations.

There were three basic components to the APEX system: the knowledge representation system, the expert framework, and the computed text. In the knowledge framework, information was represented in terms of objects and their financial characteristics. Bonds, stocks, employment criteria, and descriptions of family members were examples. The system contained over 200 classes of objects and accessed nearly 2,000 characteristics associated with the objects. The multiple attributes allowed the system to take many factors into account when choosing tools to meet a particular financial objective.

In the expert framework, the rules of analysis, which had been derived from a panel of experts, were encoded to analyze and manipulate the data objects and make trade-offs to create solutions. As a product release stated:

> The APEX framework does real planning, not just diagnosis. It simulates and tests its recommendations in a consistent and integrated way, i.e., it will model all the buy-and-sell transactions required to implement its recommendations.[4]

The third component, computed text, generated prose which was "ready to be viewed by the client."

Using PlanPower

To do financial planning with PlanPower, one began by entering the data into the system. Depending on the level of detail, this process could take from 30 minutes to 3 hours per client. There were many default values, and few required data, so even a complex plan could be sketched quickly for a preliminary analysis.

After data entry, one could ask for the "observations," a process which usually took 10 to 20 minutes. In this analysis, the system provided observations on the client's position, such as "Mr. Mulcahey's leverage is low, with a debt to equity ratio of 1.0 to 1.1." There were no recommendations in this "pre-planning scenario," as it was called.

Next the user could ask for "recommendations." This process could take anywhere from 10 minutes to an hour or more, depending on the complexity of the plan. In this stage, the system went through a person's entire financial situation and generated a series of specific recommendations—known as the "after-plan scenario." The observations and recommendations, or "obs and recs" as they were called, gave an overview of what the plan would look like and where the recommendations came from.

Often, after the obs and recs had been created, some "what-iffing" was done on the plan. The planner could go in and simulate client transactions, such as buying stock or selling land. This would create a new pre-plan case from which new obs and recs could be generated.

Four types of documents could be made from the after-plan scenario:[5] summary, presentation, complete, and custom. The summary plan,

---

[4]Ibid., Technical Overview, p. 7-7-7.

[5]The documents mentioned here are the most commonly used in creating a new plan. There were many other document options.

Schematic of PlanPower Planning Activity

```
Enter data → Observations → Recommen-    → What-if   →  Summary
                            dations          scenarios    plan

                                                          Presentation
                                                          plan

                                                          Complete
                                                          plan

                              Custom      →  Custom
                              template       plan
```

which gave a brief overview of the summary exhibits and text, was intended for use by the planner. Its wording and appearance were not designed for customer viewing. The presentation plan, as its name indicated, was designed to be used as the basis for a client presentation. The complete plan, which had 40 to 100 or more pages of text, graphics, and tables integrated together, was the most complete standard plan.

If the users desired, they could create a custom plan by assembling the plan components into a "template," as it was called. In a template, one chose the exhibits, text, and charts to include. However, the effort to create such a template was warranted only if it could be used for a number of clients. Otherwise, it was easier to make changes to the text in a word processor, also integrated as part of PlanPower.

Any of the four documents could be edited in the PlanPower word processor. This method was often faster than making changes and rerunning a plan. However, one had to be careful to check the consistency of the plan because when a number or recommendation was changed in the word processor the implications of that change were not reflected in the other planning exhibits or recommendations. These other changes had to be done by hand. The overall flow of creating the four basic documents is sketched above.

The user had considerable flexibility in inputting assumptions about the economy, the planning parameters, and the client. The assumed inflation rate and the yield on different investment categories were two of the many assumptions which could be specified by the user. There were also a number of "influence points" where the planner could "turn-off" or "turn-on" certain recommendations by entering the appropriate data. A simple example was client's preferences. Every investment category had a data item which recorded the client's "preference" toward the investment. More specifically, each investment had a rating of "APPROVED" or "DISAPPROVED." If the planner marked oil and gas tax shelters DISAPPROVED for a particular client, then the plan would never recommend that type of investment for that client. After using PlanPower for a number of plans, a planner could learn the interactions of the influence points and their effects on recommendations.

As in most software purchases, the price allowed the client to have a copy of the software which would run on the machine, but it did not give the client a copy of the software code itself. In an expert system, this traditional approach to selling software added a new wrinkle. The client did not have access to view or change the rules of thumb which the system used. If the user wanted to change the recommendations of the system, he or she would have to work within the available variables.

In effect, PlanPower brought two things to the financial planning market simultaneously. First, it provided support for financial planners at a level never before experienced in the industry. Second, it was pushing a standard set of solutions which were prudent, backed by experts, but not yet standard in the industry.

FD's Expectations of PlanPower

The principals at FD hoped that PlanPower would allow them more time for client contact—this was of primary concern. In addition, they hoped it would help them write the actual financial plans.

When PlanPower came to FD, John Whistler worked closely with Dawn Reardon and Carol Morton to learn the system, its strengths, and limitations. Whistler expressed his feelings in November 1985:

> I think PlanPower will allow better Wednesday meetings. Now, planning meetings begins with data. After PlanPower, the meetings will begin with the PlanPower plan as the base line—an improvement. Yet, we will need to invest a considerable amount of time and effort with the system before we can tell if it's a success for us.

The FD Experience

The PlanPower machine arrived at FD on November 25, 1985. The first step in adopting PlanPower was the training. Carol Morton and Dawn Reardon were given eight one-hour tutorials designed to familiarize them with the machine and its functions before they began training. John Whistler, Carol Morton, and Dawn Reardon all participated in a two and one-half day program which covered data entry, plan generation, scenario planning, client management, customization of plan, office management, and system maintenance. This training provided a basic understanding of the system and its use.

FD had an aggressive schedule for using the system. First FD had intended to put all new clients through PlanPower immediately—for real planning, not just test cases. Second, they wanted to put their existing clients onto the system as each client came up for his or her annual review.

The first two plans to go through PlanPower were a resounding success. Each passed through the Wednesday meetings without major changes and the clients liked the results. The turn around time was shortened dramatically. Only four weeks transpired between the date when FD received each client's data and the complete plan was delivered. Before, it took six weeks or more to process a plan.

Whistler's third client presented a significant challenge. The client had many stock options—a category of assets which PlanPower did not have in its repertoire. Whistler, Alter, and Morton spent a day and a half on the phone with APEX customer support discussing the program's logic. APEX was continually enhancing the software, but they did not yet have a method to input a complex stock option plan. To enter the stock options the trio had to simulate the stock option plan by creating an asset under the heading "another asset." This artificial asset was constructed to have the same cash flow and tax characteristics of the stock option plan. This jerry-rigged financial instrument worked, and the PlanPower logic was able to take account of the client's stock option in the planning process.

Whistler felt that there might be five or six other financial categories which PlanPower did not cover and which he might have to "simulate." However, he was not sure of this number. If many "special assets" were necessary, for FD's clients, it might be difficult to use PlanPower on a regular basis. On the other hand, if most of the clients fit into the PlanPower mold and only needed minor customization, the benefits from PlanPower use could be substantial.

After the first few plans, the FD staff realized that it was unrealistic to put every existing client onto the system on his or her renewal date. With one machine, it took all the available time to enter data and run the plans for the new clients—existing clients would have to wait. Myers and Whistler had to be careful about scheduling use of the workstation to assure that the highest priority items were done on time.

There were a number of bottlenecks in the PlanPower approach. Data entry was exacting and often slow. Waiting for the system to generate the plan sometimes slowed things up even more. For example, if a mistake was found or a new set of numbers was added, an entire new plan might have to be run—a two to four hour task. APEX was aware of the delays, and they were working to speed up the software before its final release in April 1986.

During this trial period for PlanPower, the existing systems at FD were maintained. Every client's data was entered into Whistler's models and filing systems. When necessary, the PlanPower plan was supplemented with 1–2–3 exhibits, especially when FD staff made last minute adjustments. In doing this, compatibility between the systems was an issue. Creating supplemental exhibits took time because the para-planners had to match the supplemental exhibits to the PlanPower exhibits—exactly. The PlanPower system provided significant detail but in a slightly different format than the detail in Whistler's systems.

Changing Process and Roles

Use of PlanPower was changing the planning process at FD. There seemed to be more emphasis on data entry, because PlanPower was so exacting in its use of the data. Carol Morton's role was expanding significantly because, in order to enter the data and understand the data's effects on the recommendations, she had to understand more about financial planning. She worked closely with the APEX customer support representatives and with Whistler. The experience was an education for her and something she would not have delved into as FD's secretary and receptionist.

The roles of other individuals shifted as well. Wednesday meetings centered on review and critique of the PlanPower plan as opposed to active plan design. Much of the meeting time was spent figuring out how PlanPower arrived at its recommendations. Whistler was usually the one who informed the other principals about the workings of the APEX system. He had gladly taken on the responsibility of making PlanPower work at FD, but Myers was concerned that Whistler might be overworked. If this situation was temporary, then everything would be all right. Yet Myers was trying to estimate if and when FD's investment in learning PlanPower would level off.

In reviewing the initial experience with PlanPower, the principals felt it was a success, but questions remained. Every principal agreed that client contact was the most important part of the business and they wondered if PlanPower was allowing more client contact. They wondered if PlanPower could be used to pursue more clients and to grow the business faster or bigger, however such a strategy might necessitate fundamental changes in their business approach.

There were many options. Marshall March summed up a concern which all the principals shared when considering PlanPower's role:

> As investors in our own business, we want to know: Where is the leverage in this business? Is it in the products, or in the service? What is the long-term profit potential of planning, and how should we configure ourselves to realize those possibilities?

Chapter 6

Organizational Issues and IT

In the preceding chapter we noted that the management structures needed for guiding new technologies into the organization are quite different from those for the older technologies. The corporation must encourage innovation, by both information technology (IT) staff and users, in the newer ones while focusing on control and efficiency in the more mature ones. In this chapter we will discuss two aspects of IT management that are rapidly changing: first, the range of organizational alternatives for assigning responsibility for IT development; second, coordination and the integration of word processing, telecommunications, and data processing.

Organization Issues in IT Development

Policies for guiding the deployment of information technology development staff and activity in the future must deal with two sets of tensions. The first is the balance between *innovation* and *control*. (This follows from our discussion of the phases of technology assimilation in the previous chapter.) The relative emphasis a firm should place on the aggressive innovation phase will vary widely, depending on a broad assessment of the potential strategic impact of information technology on the firm, corporate willingness to take risk, and so on. If IT is perceived to be of great impact in helping the firm reach its strategic objectives, significantly greater investment is called for than if it is seen to be merely helpful.

The second set is the tension between *IT dominance* and *user dominance* in the retention of development skills and in the active selection

---

TABLE 6-1 Possible Implications of Excess Dominance of Systems Life Cycle

---

IT Dominance	*User Dominance*
Too much emphasis on data base hygiene.	Too much emphasis on problem focus.
No recent new supplier or new distinct services (too busy with maintenance).	IT says out of control.
New systems always must fit data structure of existing system.	Explosive growth in number of new systems and supporting staff.
All requests for service require system study with benefit identification.	Multiple suppliers delivering services. Frequent change in supplier of specific service.
Standardization dominates—few exceptions.	Lack of standardization and control over data hygiene and system.
IT designs/constructs everything.	Hard evidence of benefits nonexistent.
Benefits of user control over development discussed but never implemented.	Soft evidence of benefits not organized.
Study always shows construction costs less than outside purchase.	Few measurements/objectives for new systems.
Head count of distributed minis and development staff growing surreptitiously.	Technical advice of IT not sought or, if received, considered irrelevant.
IT specializing in technical frontiers, not user-oriented markets.	User buying design/construction/maintenance services and even operations from outside.
IT spending 80 percent on maintenance, 20 percent on development.	User building networks to own unique needs (not corporate need).
IT thinks they are in control of all.	While some users are growing rapidly in experience and use, other users feel nothing is relevant because they do not understand.
Users express unhappiness.	
Portfolio of development opportunities firmly under IT control.	No coordinated effort for technology transfer or learning from experience between users.
No strong user group exists.	Growth in duplication of technical staffs.
General management not involved but concerned.	Communications costs are rising dramatically through redundancy.

---

of priorities. The user often tends toward short-term need fulfillment (at the expense of long-term IT hygiene and orderly development). IT, on the other hand, can become preoccupied with the mastery of technology and an orderly development plan at the risk of slow response to legitimate user needs. Effectively balancing the roles of these two groups is a complex task, which must be dealt with in the context of the corporate culture and the potential strategic IT role and in a contingent manner.

Table 6-1 illustrates some environmental consequences of excessive domination by either IT or user. It shows clearly that very different application portfolios and operating problems will emerge in each setting. This chapter focuses strongly on the need for experimentation because of the repeated inability of organizations to foresee the real implications of launching into a new technology. The following four incidents are typical of this problem.

1. A Short-Term User-Need Situation—Strategically Important

The present number one priority in a large machine tool manufacturer's engineering department is computer-aided design (CAD). Early success has led to a major expansion of the effort. Department personnel are modifying the digital information design output to enable them to control computer-driven machine tools directly. This work has deliberately been kept independent of their bill of materials/cost system, which is in a data base format and is maintained by the IT unit.

Short of staff to integrate the new system in their data base structure, immediately, the user department decided to go ahead despite major future system integration problems. The work was done over the objection of IT management, but the engineering department has received full support from senior management because of the project's potential major impact on shortening the product development life cycle.

The engineers are enthusiastically working on the CAD project to make it work; the IT team is lukewarm. Early results appear to have justified the decision.

2. User Control to Achieve Automation

At a division of a large consumer products manufacturer, a substantial investment in office automation was undertaken with modest, up-front cost-benefit justification. Managers and administrative support personnel were encouraged by IT to "use" the systems with only modest direction and some introductory training on a Wang word processor that was made available to them. In four months, three product managers had developed independent networks to support sales force activities; two had automated portions of their word processing, with substantial savings; two others did little but encourage their administrative support staff to "try it out." The users gained confidence and were pursuing new programs with enthusiasm.

The challenge to the IT management now, after only six months, is to develop and evolve an efficient program with these seven different "experienced" users. The IT manager currently estimates it will take roughly two years to achieve this efficient integration. However, both he and divisional management feel, retrospectively, that it would have been impossible to implement office automation (OA) with a standard IT-dominated systems study and that the expense of the after-the-fact rationalization is an acceptable price for these benefits. This word processing program was in sharp contrast to the strong central control IT was exerting over its mature data processing technologies.

3. Step-by-Step Innovation of a New Technology

A third example is the experience of a large grocery chain that acquired a system of point-of-sales terminals. These terminals were initially purchased by the retail division (with the support of the IT manager) to assist store managers in controlling inventory. They were to be used exclusively within individual stores to accumulate daily sales totals of individual items. These totals would permit individual stores to trigger reorders in case lots at a given point in time.

Once installed, however, these isolated systems evolved quickly into links to central headquarters. These links were established to supply data to new computer programs that provided a better measurement of advertising effectiveness and the ability to manage warehouse stock levels on a chainwide level.

Implementation of this nonplanned linkage involved significant extra expense because the communication protocols in the selected terminals were incompatible with those in the computer at headquarters. However, the possibilities and benefits of the resulting system would have been difficult to define in advance, as this eventual use was not considered important when the initial point-of-sale terminals were being installed. Further, in management's opinion, even if the organization had considered it, the ultimate costs of the resulting system would have been seen as prohibitive in relation to benefits (in retrospect, *incorrectly* prohibitive).

4. User Innovation as a Source of Productivity

A final example concerns a large bank's separate introductions of an electronic mail system and a word processor system strictly to facilitate preparation of bank loan paperwork. The two systems soon evolved to link the loan managers (initially not planned to be customers of either system) to a series of analytical programs. This evolution developed as a result of conversations between a loan officer and a consultant. They discovered that the word processor loan system included a powerful analytical tool that could be used for analyzing loan performance. Because of the bank's electronic mail system, the analysis could be easily accessed by loan personnel (both at headquarters and in branches). After three months of use, the bank was faced with a series of internal tensions as the costs of both the electronic mail and the word processing systems unexpectedly rose. Further, there was no formal means to review "experiments" or evaluate this unexpected use of the systems by participants not initially involved. Eventually a senior management review committee supported the project, and it was permitted to continue, with substantial enhancements made to the word processing software.

These examples are typical of emerging new services that support professionals and managers in doing work. They form the underpinning of our conviction that it is impossible to foresee in advance the full range of consequences of introducing information technology. Excessive control and focus on quick results in the early stages can deflect important learning. Neither IT nor users have had outstanding records in predicting all the consequences of new technology in terms of its impact on the organization; consequently a necessary general management role is to help facilitate this assimilation.

This chapter is divided into three main sections. The first focuses on the pressures that are on users to gain control, not only over development but, when possible, to have the resulting product run on stand-alone mini or micro systems operating in their departments. The second section identifies both the advantages that come from a strong IT development coordination effort and the potential pitfalls of uncontrolled proliferation of user-developed systems. The third section identifies the core policies that must be implemented by IT management, user management, and general management, respectively, in order to ensure a good result. In our judgment, the general management role is critical in facilitating technological change and organizational adaptation.

Pressures toward User Dominance

The intense pressures toward user dominance, which encourage stronger control by users over their development resources and the acquisition of independent IT resources, can be clustered into four main categories: pent-up user demand, competitive and service growth in the IT market, user control, and fit to organization.

Pent-Up User Demand

The backlog of development work facing an IT department is frequently very large in relation to its staff resources. (Three- to five-year backlogs tend to be the norm.) The sources of these staffing crunches are multiple, and the problems are not easily solved. First, existing systems require sustained maintenance to deal with changing regulatory and other business requirements. As more systems are automated, the maintenance needs continue to rise, forcing either increases in development staff or the postponement of new work. This problem has been intensified by the shift in systems design philosophy (in the early 1970s) from one that incorporated data into programs to one that clearly separates data base management from processing procedures. Effecting this one-time conversion of data systems is expensive in terms of staff resources.

Further, the most challenging, high-status jobs tend to be with computer vendors and software houses, which puts great pressure on the in-company IT department. Its most talented staff is tempted to move into more challenging (and often more financially remunerative) assignments. Frequently it is easier for the IT development unit to get the budget allocations than to find the staff resources to use them.

There are strong reasons for users to develop their own expertise. Systems people linked to the user organization make it easier to plan employee promotions that move IT personnel to other functional jobs, enhancing user-IT coordination. Combining IT experience with user responsibilities creates a knowledgeable IT user. Some care must be taken on local development, however, as user groups often tend to buy or develop systems tailored to their very specific situations, and this may lead to long-term maintenance problems. In an environment characterized by local development, there often is also poor technology transfer between similar users and thus consequent lack of corporate leverage, issues of low importance to the local unit. A large forest products company, organized geographically, combined a regional system-minded manager with an aggressive growth-oriented IT manager who was promoted to be in charge of all administrative support. In three years their budget for IT was double that of a comparable region, but only one application was exported. Subsequent review of this unit's work indicated that nearly half of their developments had focused on problems of potentially general interest to the company which could have been exported.

Finally, the protocols of interfacing with a network and of meeting corporate control standards can be very time consuming and complex. A stand-alone system purchased by a user that is independent of the network can simplify the job and permit less-skilled staff resources to be utilized. It may require no major changes, particularly if it is a system familiar to one or more employees from prior experience.

For reasons beyond IT management control, these items collectively make IT *appear* to be unresponsive to users' demands. These perceived IT management shortcomings (in responsiveness and excessive focus on detail) make user-developed systems and stand-alone minis attractive to users as a nonconfrontational way of getting work done. Using either their own staffs or outside software houses, users significantly speed up the process of obtaining "needed" service.

Competitive and Service Growth in the IT Market

Thousands of stand-alone computer systems are available for specific applications ranging from simple accounts payable systems to complete office automation products. Their existence makes them beguilingly easy solutions to short-term problems. Marketed by hardware or software vendors to end-user managers, the systems' functional features are emphasized, with technical and software problems being soft-pedaled. This is particularly true of standard word processing systems; most are marketed with no mention of their computer foundation.

A stand-alone solution seems particularly attractive because on-line response times given are faster and more consistent than those which depend on a central unit. The stand-alone provides easy access to on-line systems; it also permits the user to avoid the problems associated with being only one of multiple users of a system who in aggregate, over the hours of the day and the weeks, provide a highly variable volume of transactions. Also, the system appears operationally simple, needing only an operator to run it when developed. Air conditioning, physical maintenance, and power availability are not seen as issues.

Frequently the local solution *appears* to be more cost effective than work done or purchased by the controlling IT development group. Not only is there no cumbersome project proposal to be written and defended in front of IT technicians who have their own special agendas but often a simple up-front price is quoted. Developed under user control, the project is perceived to be both simple and relatively free of red tape.

User Control

The idea of regaining control over a part of their operations, particularly if information technology is a critical part of their units' operations, is very important to users—often reversing a trend that began 20 years ago in a very different technology. Control in this context has at least three different dimensions.

First is the ability to exert direct control over systems development priorities. By using either their own staffs or self-selected software houses, users often believe they can get a system functioning in less time than it would take to navigate the priority-setting process in the corporate IT department, let alone get staff assigned to projects. The systems also will be closer and more responsive to user needs. Development mistakes made by a local group are often more easily accepted than those made by a remote group and are rarely discussed; successes are often topics of conversation.

The second dimension is that users see themselves gaining control over the maintenance priorities. This is done either by themselves or by contracting with suppliers that are dependent upon the users for income. Quite often the promotional message is that the maintenance can be performed by a clerk following a manual. A rare occurrence!

The third dimension of importance for stand-alone computer systems is that users see themselves as gaining control over day-to-day operations. Insulated from the vicissitudes of corporate computer scheduling, users believe they will be able to exert firmer control over the pace of their departments' operations. This is particularly important to small, marginal users of heavily utilized data centers with volatile loads. Today these points are intensified in many users' minds because of previous experiences with service degradation at month-end in large computer systems or with jobs not run because of corporate priorities. Additionally, as a result of home computers, managers are becoming more confident in their ability to manage a computer project successfully. Clever computer-vendor marketing has helped to increase their confidence. Sometimes, however, this experience is of insufficient depth, and the user has more confidence than is warranted.

Fit to Organization

As the company becomes more decentralized in structure and geographically diverse, a distributed development function becomes a much better fit and avoids heavy marketing and coordination expenses. In conglomerates, for example, only a few have tried to centralize development, with most leaving it with the original units. Another advantage of distributed development is that if you have any intention of divesting the corporation of a unit, the less integrated its IT activities are with the rest of the company, the easier it is to implement the divestiture.

User Learning

As suggested in the four examples at the beginning of the chapter, predicting the full ramifications of the introduction of a new technology is very hard. Firsthand, enthusiastic experimentation by the user can unlock creativity and stimulate new approaches to troublesome problems. Systems developed by an IT unit have to overcome more user resistance in adoption. This is a special case in the IT field that reflects broader work done in the fields of organization development and control, where this factor of organization learning has been identified as one of the principal forces in favor of organizing in multiple profit centers, as opposed to functionally. As noted in Chapter 5, this is increasingly evident in office automation and new professional support such as CAD.

Summary

In aggregate, these four items represent a powerful set of arguments in favor of a strong user role in systems development and suggest when that role might be the dominant one. They further suggest a summary statement of the pressures driving users toward purchase, development, and/or use of stand-alone, mini-based, and local systems and software: *short-term user driven.* Stand-alones, minis, and local development offer users more immediate solutions to their problems, under their control and in a perceived enjoyable fashion. While benefits associated with Phase 1 and 2 learning can be achieved, these are often gained with little regard for information hygiene, as discussed below.

Pressures toward IT Control

Heavy internal pressures exist to consolidate the development resource or keep it consolidated in one or more large clusters. The principal pressures are discussed here.

Staff Professionalism

A large support staff provides an opportunity to attract, and keep challenged, specialized technical personnel. Such a central unit also provides useful support for a small division or function that does not have its own information technology staff but needs occasional access to information technology skills. As the average age of some IT development staffs continues to rise (graying of IT), these opportunities become a critical element in trying to increase productivity. Their importance is intensified by the fact that salary levels, individual interests, and perceived interpersonal communication problems make lateral movement out of the department unfeasible for some individuals.

Developing and enforcing better standards of IT management practice is also easier in a large group. Documentation procedures, project management skills, and disciplined maintenance approaches are examples of critical infrastructure items in development departments. In 1971 a large financial service organization faced with a deteriorating relationship between its central development department and key users was forced to split the development department into a number of smaller units distributed around the company, thereby changing both reporting responsibility and office location. Although the change was initially successful in stimulating new ideas and better relationships with users (many development people came to identify better with users than with technical development issues), by 1977 the quality of IT staff professionalism had dropped so low through neglect that several major project fiascoes occurred that required assistance from an outside service organization. Today significant parts of the development function have been recentralized, with much tighter controls installed over management practices in the remaining distributed development groups.

A central staff quality and/or expertise is particularly important to support user-designed or user-selected computer-based systems. Lacking practical systems design experience and purchased software standards, the user often ignores normal data control procedures, documentation standards, and conventional costing practices. Consequently, purchasing from several suppliers or incrementally from one results in a clumsy system design that is hard to maintain. For example, one large financial organization discovered that all those people had left who were involved in the design and purchase of software for three of their stand-alone computer systems used to process data on a daily basis, no formal documentation or operating instructions had been prepared, and all source programs had been lost. All that remained were disk files with object programs on them. The system ran, but why it ran no one knew; and even if the company's survival depended on it, changes were very difficult and time consuming to execute.

Feasibility Study Concerns

A user-driven feasibility study may contain some major technical mistakes, an important problem resulting in the computer system being inadequate to handle growing processing requirements. Because of inexperienced staff, such a feasibility study may underestimate both the complexity of the software needed to do the job and the growth in the number of transactions to be handled by the system. (The risk increases if there were limited technical inputs to the feasibility study or if the real business needs were not well understood.)

Often users organize a feasibility study to focus on a specific service and fail to recognize that a successful first application leads to the generation of an unexpected second application, then a third, and so forth. Each application appears to require only a modest incremental purchase price and therefore may not receive a comprehensive full-cost review. The result may be that the hardware configuration or software approach selected is unable to handle the necessary work. Unless great care was taken in the initial hardware selection and system design process to allow for growth, expansion can result both in major business disruptions and in very expensive software modifications.

User-driven feasibility studies are more susceptible to acquiring an unstable vendor. In this rapidly growing industry sector it is unlikely that all the current vendors will remain viable over the next five years. The same trends to hit the pocket calculator and the digital watch industry in the late 1970s will hit this industry sector as it reaches a point of maturity. Stability is critical because many of these systems insinuate themselves into the heart of a department's operations. With software-intensive investments, failure of a vendor will mean both expensive disruption in service provided by the department and intensive, crisis spending efforts to convert the software to another machine. These concerns apply not just to hardware suppliers but also to the packages and services provided by software suppliers. A single experience with a product from a failed software vendor provides painful learning.

Corporate Data Base System

Development of corporate data base strategy includes collection of files at a central location for reference by multiple users. The availability of staff in a central unit provides a focal point for both conceptualizing and developing systems that can serve multiple users. The need for this varies widely with the nature of the corporation's activities. A conglomerate often has less need for this data than does a functionally organized, one-product company. If such needs exist, a central department can best develop and distribute such systems to users or at least coordinate the development process in a company where systems development is farmed out to local development units.

Inevitably the first concern raised in discussing stand-alone islands of automation is that the company is losing the opportunity to manage and control its data flows, that data of significance to many people beyond those in the originating unit will be locked up in a nonstandardized format in inaccessible locations. Without denying the validity of this concern (there is substantial truth in it), several mitigating factors demand that such objections be carefully examined in any specific situation.

One factor is the issue of timing. In many cases the argument raised against a stand-alone system is the erosion of data as a corporate resource. Allegedly, in order to preserve flexibility for future data base design, this stand-alone computer should not be acquired. However, it frequently turns out that this flexibility is not needed for three or more years in the future. In this context a well-designed stand-alone system may be an equally good (if not better) starting point for these long-term systems as jumping directly from the present set of manual procedures would be. This possibility must be pragmatically assessed.

Another mitigating factor, often overlooked, is the capability that data can be abstracted, if necessary, from a locally managed system at planned frequent intervals and sent directly to a central computer. This is assisted by the fact that ordinarily not all information in a stand-alone file is relevant to other users (indeed, often only a small percentage is).

On the other hand, uniquely designed data-handling systems can prove expensive to maintain and link. A clear need exists to identify in operational terms the data requirements of the central files and, if relevant, to suggest guidelines for what data can be stored locally. This problem is exemplified by the typical word and data processing systems, which generate voluminous records in electronic format. Unless well designed these files may be bulky, lock up key data from potential users, and pose potential security problems. For example, a mail-order house recently discovered that each customer representative was using over 200 disks per day and storing them in boxes by date of order receipt, making aggregate customer information impossible to obtain in a timely manner. A new procedure reduced the number of disks to five.

The organization of and access to electronic files may require central storage to maintain the availability of data and ensure appropriate security. Maintaining good security is often easier when all files are in a single location than when scattered around a number of locations.

Fit to Corporate Structure and Strategy

Centralized IT development's role is clearest in organizations where there is centrally directed planning and operational control. A large farm equipment manufacturer that has a tradition of central functional control from corporate headquarters had successfully implemented a program where all software for factories and distribution units worldwide was developed by their corporate systems group. Now, as these groups are growing in size, the company's structure is becoming more decentralized. The cost of running effective central systems development is consequently escalating, and the firm is having to implement a marketing function to educate users on the virtues of using central services and decentralize some functions. It is becoming increasingly common for centralized development groups to have an explicitly defined and staffed internal marketing activity.

Cost Analysis

A significant edge that a centralized IT group has, through its practical experience in other systems efforts, is the ability to produce a realistic software development estimate (subject to all the problems discussed in Chapter 8) that takes into account the interests of the company as a whole. Software development estimates have turned out to be a real problem in user feasibility studies. There are two contributing factors to this. The first is that in most cases a new system turns out to be more software intensive than hardware intensive. Typically software costs run from 75 percent to 85 percent of the total costs for a customized system. Since the user often has had little or no experience in estimating software development costs, an order-of-magnitude mistake in a feasibility study (particularly if it is an individually developed system and not a "turnkey" i.e., general purpose, package) is not unknown.

The second factor is the lack of experience with true costs of service because of complicated chargeout systems. Many corporate chargeout systems present calculations in terms of utilization of computer resource units that are completely unintelligible to the user. The result is that each month or quarter an unintelligible and unpredictable bill arrives. (In management control environments where the user is held responsible for variance from budget, this causes intense frustration.) A locally developed system, particularly if it is for a mini, is perceived as a solution to this. Further, many chargeout systems are designed on a full-cost basis; therefore, the charges from the corporate center often seem high to the user.

Since particularly in the short run there are significant fixed-cost elements to a corporate information systems center, what appears a cost reduction opportunity to the user may be a cost increase for the company. Policies for ensuring that appropriate cost analyses are prepared must be established.

Summary

A phrase capturing the spirit of these pressures would be *long-term information hygiene*. In many respects they are not immediately evident at the time of system installation but tend to grow in importance with the passage of time. Policies to manage the trade-offs between the obvious short-term benefits and long-term risks are delicate to administer but necessary.

The tension over control can be managed by establishing clear core policies as to what makes up the user domain, what makes up the IT domain, and what is senior management's role. Senior management must play a significant role in ensuring both that these policies are developed and that they evolve appropriately over time. Both IT and users must understand the implications of these roles and the possible conflicts.

IT Responsibilities

The following items comprise the central core of IT responsibilities, the irreducible minimum needed to manage the long-term information hygiene needs of an organization:

1. Development of procedures to ensure that, for potential IT projects of any size, a comparison is made of internal development versus purchase. If the projects are implemented outside the

firm or by the user, this must include establishment of the appropriate professional standards for project control and documentation. These standards need to be flexible, since user-developed systems for micros pose demands quite different from systems to be run on large mainframe computers. Further, a process for forcing adherence to the selected standards must be defined.

2. Maintenance of an inventory of installed or planned-to-be-installed information services.

3. Development and maintenance of a set of standards that establishes:

    a. Mandatory telecommunication standards.

    b. Standard languages for classes of acquired equipment.

    c. Documentation procedures for different types of systems.

    d. Corporate data dictionary with clear definitions for when elements must be included. Identification of file maintenance standards and procedure.

    e. Examination procedure for systems developed as independent islands to ensure that they do not conflict with corporate needs and that any necessary interfaces are constructed.

4. Identification and provision of appropriate IT development staff career paths throughout the organization. These include sideways transfers within and between IT units, upward movements within IT, and appropriate outward movement to other functional units. (More difficult in distributed units, it is still possible.)

5. Establishment of appropriate internal marketing efforts for IT support activities. These should exert pressure to speed up and to coach the units that are lagging, while slowing down the units that are exceeding technological prudence.

6. Preparation of a detailed checklist of questions to be answered in any hardware/software acquisition to ensure that relevant technical and managerial issues are raised. These questions should concern:

    a. How the proposed system meets corporate communication standards (Item 3).

    b. For word processing systems, questions on upward growth potential and built-in communication and data processing capability.

    c. For data processing systems, availability of languages that support systems growth potential, available word processing features, and so on.

    d. For communication systems, the types of data-transfer capabilities, list of available services, storage capacity, and so forth.

7. Identification of preferred systems suppliers and the conditions for entertaining exceptions to the list of standards to be met by vendors before a business relationship is established. For example, size, number of systems in place, and financial structure requirements should be clearly spelled out.

8. Establishment of education programs for potential users, to communicate both the potential and the pitfalls of new technology and to define the users' roles in ensuring its successful introduction in their departments.

9. An ongoing review of which systems are not feasible to manage and which should be redesigned.

These comments apply with particular force to the design of systems that embed themselves operationally in the company. Decision support systems do not pose nearly the same problems.

These responsibilities, of course, can be significantly expanded with much tighter and more formal controls if the situation warrants it. In this regard, a diagnostic framework presented in 1980 in the *Harvard Business Review* is particularly useful in assessing both the current position of an organization and where it should move.[1]

User Responsibilities

To assist in the orderly implementation of new IT services and grow in an understanding of their use, cost, and impact on the organization, the following responsibilities should be fulfilled by the user of IT service:

1. Maintain a financial control system of all user-IT types of activities. Increasingly in the more experienced organizations a user-understandable IT chargeout system has been installed.

2. Make an appraisal of the user personnel investment for each new project, in both the short term and the long term, to ensure a satisfactory service.

3. Develop a comprehensive user support plan for projects that will support vital aspects of the business or that will grow in use. This includes inputs to networks' architecture, data base policies, filing policies for word processors, and user training programs at both the staff and managerial levels.

---

[1] Jack R. Buchanan and Richard G. Linowes, "Understanding Distributed Processing," *Harvard Business Review,* July–August 1980, pp. 143–53.

4. Manage the IT-user interface consistent with its strategic relevance, as an integral aspect of the business. The mix of central site, prepackaged programs, outside contracts, and all new-services expenditure should be approved by the user.
5. Perform periodic audits on the appropriateness of system reliability standards, communications services, and security requirement documentation.

These represent the very minimum sets of policies that the users should develop and manage. Depending on the firm's geography, corporate management style, stage of IT development, and mix of technology phases of development, expanded levels of user involvement may be appropriate, including acquisition of their own staff. As these facets evolve over time, the appropriateness of certain policies will also evolve.

General Management Support and Policy Overview

Distinct from the issues involved in the distribution of IT services is a cluster of broad policy and direction activities that require *senior management perspective*. In the past these activities were built into the structure of a central IT organization. Now, because of the need to link IT to business planning, they are frequently separated. A major oil company reorganized to produce a 300-person systems and operations department reporting directly to the head of administrative services. This department does the implementation and operational IT work of the company on a month-to-month, year-to-year basis. At the same time, an 8- to 10-person IT policy group reports directly to the head of corporate planning, which works on overall policy and long-range strategy formulation. A major conglomerate that has all its developments and hardware distributed to key users has, at the same time, a three- to four-person group at headquarters level.

Key functions of any corporate policy group should include:

1. Ensuring that there is an appropriate balance between IT and user inputs across the different technologies and that one side is not dominating the other inappropriately; initiating appropriate personnel and organizational moves if the situation is out of balance. Executive steering committees, for example, are a common response to a user imbalance.

2. Through its broad overview and perspective on the total role of IT in the company, ensuring that a comprehensive IT corporate strategy is developed. In particular, in an environment where the resources are widely distributed it is critical that a comprehensive overview of tech-

nology, corporate use thereof, and linkage to overall corporate goals be put together. The relative amount of resources to be devoted to this will appropriately vary widely from organization to organization as the perceived contribution to corporate strategy, among other things, changes. (This will be discussed in more depth in Chapter 11.)

3. Auditing the inventory of hardware/software resources to assure that the corporate view is provided in the establishment of purchasing relationships and contracts. In certain settings the corporate group will be the appropriate place to initiate standard vendor policies.

4. Ensuring development and evolution of appropriate sets of standards for both development and operations activities and ensuring that those standards are being applied appropriately. In this regard, the corporate policy group plays a combined role of consultant on the one hand and auditor (particularly if there is a weak or nonexistent IT auditing function) on the other hand. The implementation of this role requires staff that is both technically competent and interpersonally sensitive.

5. Acting as the facilitating authority in managing the transfer of technology from one unit to another. This will occur through recognizing common systems needs between units and the stimulation of joint projects. Actual transfer will require a combination of sustained visits to the different operating units, organizing of periodic corporate MIS conferences, development of a corporate information systems newsletter, and other means.

6. Acting as an initiative center to identify and encourage appropriate forms of technical experimentation. A limited program of research is a very appropriate part of the IT function; an important role of the corporate policy group is to ensure that it does not get swept away in the press of urgent operational issues. Further, the corporate function is in a position to encourage patterns of experimentation that smaller units might feel pose undue risk if they were the sole beneficiary.

7. Assuming responsibility for the development of an appropriate planning and control system to link IT firmly and appropriately to the company's goals. Planning, system appraisal, chargeout, and project management processes should be monitored and (if necessary) encouraged to develop by the policy group. In this context, the group should work closely with the corporate steering committee.

These roles suggest the group needs to be staffed heavily with individuals who in aggregate represent both broad technical backgrounds and extensive practical IT administrative experience. Except in very limited numbers, it is not a very good entry-level department for new staff members.

Summary

Chapters 5 and 6 have focused on the key issues surrounding organization of the information technology activity for the next decade. There has been a significant revolution in what is regarded as good managerial practice in this field. Since conventional wisdom has changed considerably and seems likely to continue its evolution, many IT organization structures effectively put together in the 1970s are inappropriate for the mid-1980s. A significant contributing component of this change has been the development of new hardware and software technologies. These technologies not only permit quite different types of services to be delivered but also offer the potential for quite different ways of delivering these services.

The subject of determining the appropriate pattern of distribution of IT resources within the organization is both complex and multifaceted. The general manager should develop a program to encourage innovation and to maintain overall control to manage the distribution of services.

The final resolution of these organization and planning issues is inextricably tied to non-IT oriented aspects of the corporate environment. Current leadership style at the top of the organization and that person's view of the future provide one important thrust for redirection. A vision of tighter central control sets a different context for these decisions than one that emphasizes the autonomy of operating units. Closely associated and linked to this is the broad corporate organizational structure and culture and the trends occurring there. Also, the realities of geographical spread of the business units heavily impact on IT possibilities. The large corporate headquarters of an insurance company poses different constraints than the multiple international plants and markets of an automobile manufacturer.

On a less global scale are the realities of quality and location of current IT resources (organizationally and physically). Equally important is how responsive and competent current users perceive these resources to be. The unit that is seen (no matter how unfairly or inaccurately) as unresponsive has different organization challenges than the well-regarded unit. Similarly the current and perceived appropriate strategic role of IT on the dimensions of applications portfolio and operations has important organizational implications. The support unit, for example, must be placed to deal with its perceived lack of relevance to corporate strategy.

In dealing with all of these forces, one is trying to find an appropriate balance between innovation and control and between the input of the IT specialist and the user. Not only do appropriate answers to these questions vary between companies but different answers and structures are often appropriate for individual units in an organization. In short there is a right series of questions to ask and an identifiable but a very complex series of forces that, appropriately analyzed, determine for each organizational unit what the direction of the right answer is— for now.

Case 6–1

Alcon Laboratories
Information Technology Group

In April 1985, Dennis Beikman was concluding his third year as manager of the Information Technology (IT) group at Alcon Labs in Fort Worth, Texas. He had supervised a major turnaround in the IT group, creating a state-of-the-art information systems shop. The 1970s vintage batch COBOL systems had been replaced by a combination of online COBOL systems, software packages, and systems developed in RAMIS—a fourth-generation language.

Beikman's success, however, had become a source of concern to him. Users who previously had relied on the IT group to develop information systems to meet their needs, were now using RAMIS to develop the systems themselves. Hence, the backlog for new information systems had almost disappeared. Since Beikman's current organization was designed to develop and maintain application systems effectively, he became concerned that these tasks might no longer require IT professionals. If this were the case, he would have to decide what the IT organization's role should be in this new systems development environment. As he saw it, the key question was: How does the successful exploitation of software packages and fourth-generation languages affect the role and structure of Alcon's IT organization?

This case was prepared by David K. Goldstein.

EXHIBIT 1   Alcon Sales 1973–1984 ($ millions)

Year	Sales
1973[a]	$ 40
1974	49
1975	58
1976	68
1977	82
1978[b]	116
1979	166
1980	205
1981	250
1982	274
1983	289
1984	375

---

[a]1973–1977 sales from Alcon Laboratories Annual Reports.
[b]1978–1984 sales in Swiss francs converted to U.S. dollars. (From Nestle, S.A. Annual Reports.)

Alcon Laboratories

In 1947, two Texas pharmacists, Robert D. Alexander and William C. Conner, had founded Alcon Laboratories in order to develop in a large-scale manufacturing facility more accurate, sterile, and stable specialty pharmaceutical entities than could be developed in a retail drug store. In its early years, Alcon concentrated on manufacturing and marketing ophthalmological drugs (drugs used in the treatment of diseases of the eye). At the time the company was founded, 85 percent of all eye-care drugs were being compounded in drug stores.

As doctors became familiar with the company's products and their quality, they prescribed them more frequently, and Alcon prospered. Its sales grew from $1.3 million in 1958 to $68 million in 1976. In 1976, Alcon manufactured pharmaceuticals in 22 plants in the United States, Puerto Rico, and overseas, and sold them in 100 countries. Although over 50 percent of Alcon's sales were ophthalmic pharmaceutical products, the company also sold ophthalmic surgical products and dermatological, urological, and pediatric products.

In 1978, Alcon was acquired by Nestle, S.A., the $12.7 billion Swiss-based food company. This acquisition allowed Alcon to expand its research and marketing efforts, and by 1984 sales had risen to $375 million (see Exhibit 1).

EXHIBIT 2   Organization Chart for Alcon Labs

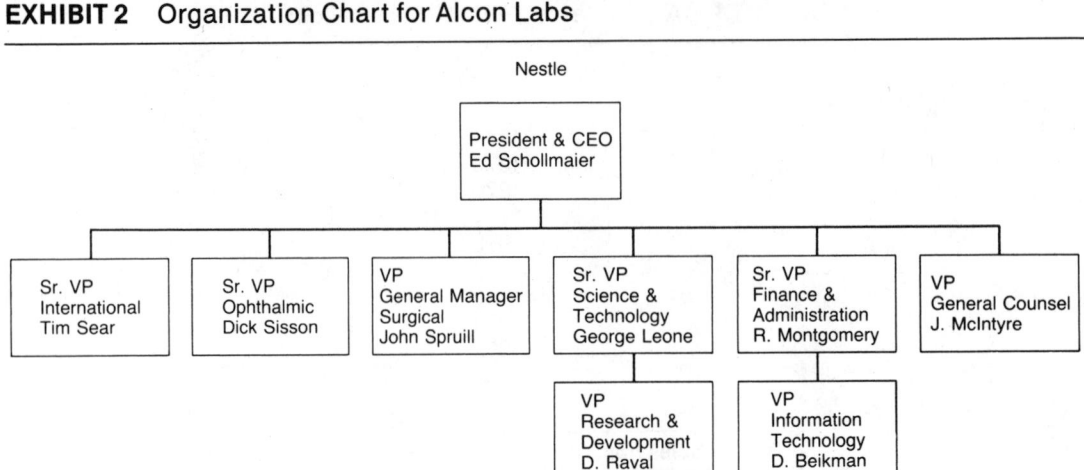

Organization and Corporate Culture

In spite of its rapid growth, Alcon still had the feel of a small company: it was not uncommon to see Ed Schollmaier (the current president) and several of Alcon's vice presidents having lunch together, alongside research scientists and factory workers, in the company cafeteria. The friendliness of the employees, coupled with the large amount of research that took place at the company, created a collegial corporate culture.

Alcon was organized into three product divisions—ophthalmic, surgical, and international. The three division senior vice presidents, and the senior vice presidents in charge of finance and administration, legal, and science and technology activities reported to Ed Schollmaier (see Exhibit 2). Most of the senior managers were in their early 50s, with over 20 years' experience at Alcon. The majority had started out as salespeople and had worked their way up through sales and marketing. Ed Schollmaier had joined Alcon as a salesperson directly after receiving his M.B.A. from Harvard in 1958, and had moved up through the marketing ranks to assume the corporate presidency in 1972.

Marketing

One key to Alcon's success was its marketing efforts. The company continued to focus its efforts in the prescription ophthalmic-drug market. Alcon controlled about 20 percent of the $650 million U.S. ophthalmic-drug and contact lens–care market. It also sold dermatological drugs and contact lenses. It faced competition from other specialty pharmaceutical companies, such as Allergan (a subsidiary of Smith-Kline Beckman), Barnes Hines (a subsidiary of Revlon), Coopervision, and, to a lesser extent, from the larger pharmaceutical companies (e.g., Merck and Pfizer).

Alcon's strategy with respect to prescription ophthalmic drugs was to develop and market a broad range of high-quality products that met the needs of ophthalmologists. Individually, the products did not account for large sales volume, but in aggregate, they created Alcon's significant market share. Product quality was essential for maintaining the company's favorable reputation among ophthalmologists.

The direct sales force was Alcon's principal tool for marketing its prescription pharmaceutical products, and its two distinct activities were *creating demand and distribution.* To create demand the salesperson called directly on the ophthalmologist to "detail" (describe) a few of Alcon's products and to try to convince the doctor to prescribe them. The detailing of products involved a great deal of nonproductive time since the salesperson might wait half an hour to see an ophthalmologist for five minutes between appointments. The products being detailed by the sales force would also be featured in advertisements in medical journals and at conventions.

The distribution effort involved sales calls on pharmacies, hospitals, and wholesalers. Salespeople visited the 10 percent of pharmacies that sold a large amount of prescription ophthalmic drugs. In their distribution-related sales calls, the salespeople mentioned the products they were detailing and tried to ensure that a sufficient supply of all Alcon products was in stock.

Alcon sold its nonprescription products through optical retail, drug, supermarket, and discount chains, and through wholesalers. These sales efforts were supplemented by selective mass media advertising and special promotions.

Research and Development

The showpiece of Alcon's corporate headquarters was the new $30 million research and development facility, one of the largest ophthalmological research facilities in the world. It housed 300 employees, including 78 Ph.D. chemists, biologists, and statisticians, who developed and tested new ophthalmic drugs.

The development of new products was important for ensuring the future profitability of Alcon since new products usually are very profitable once they get to market. Within the pharmaceutical industry, only one in 10,000 compounds makes it through the development process, which typically lasts between ten and fifteen years. Approximately 27 percent of Alcon's 1984 sales came from products released in the past five years.

The Management Information Services Group in Early 1982

In early 1982, just prior to Dennis Beikman's arrival, the Management Information Services (MIS) group consisted of 48 people involved in systems development, data entry, data center operations, and technical services. It was responsible for Alcon's corporate data center in Fort Worth. The group operated an IBM 4341 computer that was running at approximately 40 percent of its capacity. The major systems developed by the group were accounting systems (e.g., accounts payable, accounts receivable, and general ledger), a domestic and an international order entry system, and a sales analysis system. These applications were all batch COBOL systems developed by the MIS group.

The systems under the control of the MIS group were not, however, the only computer systems at Alcon. The research and development area had several of Digital Equipment's PDP 11 series computers used for statistical analysis and laboratory data gathering. In addition, each of Alcon's four major manufacturing plants had an IBM System/34 computer. There were six programmer/analysts and operators in R&D and three operators in manufacturing. Several users developed their own systems using time-sharing service bureaus.

There was a great deal of dissatisfaction with the systems development and operations functions among information system users and their managers. Robert Montgomery, then the controller in the International Division, summed up the user attitude toward the MIS group in 1981: "If you wanted to do something, you did it yourself. The MIS group couldn't meet the company's changing technological needs. They were ready to go under." Nick Tsumpis, then manager of technical services in the MIS group, expressed similar sentiments: "The MIS group wasn't supplying the services that the users wanted. That was why we were losing end users to time-sharing."

Changes Made between 1982 and 1985

Dennis Beikman came to Alcon in February 1982 with a background in chemistry and 20 years of experience working in information systems groups at pharmaceutical companies, starting out as a programmer on an IBM 1401. In his previous job, he had been the information systems manager for the division of a large pharmaceutical company.

Beikman's first task was to assess the state of affairs in the MIS group. He asked Tom Caraway, who had just been made manager of systems development, to bring him up-to-date on the problems he

EXHIBIT 3

Date: March 8, 1982

From: Tom Caraway

Dept. or Terr: MIS

Subject: Daily Billing, Sales, and Quota Systems

To: Dennis Beikman

During the past few weeks we have, as you know, lost all of our personnel with expertise in the Daily Billing and Sales Systems. It has been a priority for us to re-establish this knowledge quickly. In doing this we have discovered several deficiencies in the systems highlighted by the following points.

A. The systems contain no edit programs. Editing is by data entry verification. This is a very inefficient and dangerous practice. I have no idea why this was allowed. It must be corrected with the addition of edit programs in the systems.

B. There are no reliable audit trails in any of these systems.

C. There are no control reports in these systems.

D. The systems design is very poor. I feel that no real overall design was followed, rather a series of programs were produced following a disjointed (if any) plan.

E. Interface with other systems i.e., inventory was very poorly planned. An example of this is the creation of an additional perpetual inventory file. The sole purpose of this file is to report inventory quantities. It, however, is an exact duplicate of the perpetual inventory master and appears to have been created for the same purpose. I can only guess that no interface took place with the inventory programmer/analyst at design time. This file will be eliminated.

F. The systems are very inefficient, requiring an average of three hours a night for each processing cycle.

In short this newly developed series of programs are the most unreliable, ineffectual, and costly I have ever seen. It is in Alcon's best interest that we repair or replace as soon as practical.

---

faced. Caraway reported that the systems development group had lost all its personnel with expertise in the billing, sales, and quota systems. Moreover, these systems were poorly designed and needed to be replaced (see Exhibit 3). The problems described by Caraway were not limited to those three systems. Of the 11 major applications supported by the MIS group, Beikman rated 4 as acceptable, 1 as marginal, and 6 as unacceptable in a presentation he made to senior management shortly after his arrival.

EXHIBIT 4

Date: February 8, 1982

From: Dennis Beikman

Dept. or Terr: MIS

Subject: Management Information Services Update Status

To: R. R. Montgomery

It has been one month today since assuming responsibilities of Director, Management Information Services. My assessment of the department's overall status is essentially optimistic but with a few, serious reservations. Namely:

- The billing, sales, and quota systems are in a catastrophic state. See Attachment A. (Exhibit 3)
- The MVS conversion has not been properly managed or controlled. We are still facing an estimated three months full time effort of nine Programmer/Analysts to complete this task. The justification or rationale to convert to MVS seems to me to have been very poorly thought out, if at all. The only basis that I can determine for this decision is that "future growth and capability" mandated the conversion. It will be a costly effort for Alcon. However, in the long run Alcon should be able to recover this cost by providing user oriented support capabilities that would not otherwise have been available under DOS/VS. I believe that it is in Alcon's best interest to continue with the conversion effort despite the lack of planning and the cost incurred to date.
- No backup exists for the Manager of Software Systems. All of the conversion support expertise rests with one individual. Alcon is at great risk with its dependence on one individual.
- All applications software is being converted as is from DOS/VS to OS/MVS. Therefore, if the design quality was poor under DOS it will remain equally poor under OS/MVS.

I have taken the following measures to address these problems as well as other issues not mentioned . . . .

The group faced problems in one other area. It was converting its operating system from DOS/VS (a system designed for smaller IBM installations) to the more powerful OS/MVS operating system. This conversion was behind schedule, a problem documented in the memo from Beikman to Montgomery (who had by this time been promoted to vice president for finance and was Beikman's boss) found in Exhibit 4.

After assessing the situation at Alcon, Beikman developed a plan, and he discussed his proposed changes in a presentation to Ed Schollmaier and several senior vice presidents in June 1982:

1. Accelerate the implementation of on-line interactive application systems to replace old batch-oriented operational systems, utilizing packaged software whenever possible.
2. Increase user personnel awareness and direct participation in systems development, by providing direct access to appropriate databases utilizing advanced "user friendly" software.
3. Decentralize the data entry function to user departments by providing on-line, interactive data entry capability.
4. Provide appropriate software capability and ongoing training and support to user personnel to begin addressing decision support applications.
5. Integrate more fully MIS applications development personnel into Alcon's business operations.

Over the next three years, Beikman acted on his five points. His first priority was to replace the unacceptable batch applications with on-line systems that met the needs of Alcon.

The first application that the MIS group replaced was the accounts receivable system: Alcon was collecting its receivables up to nine months late. A project team led by the credit manager, with participants from both the accounting and MIS areas, developed the systems requirements and considered alternative systems development approaches: an Alcon-developed accounts receivable system and several software packages. Rejecting an in-house systems-development effort, the team selected a system from a major software vendor. The development process, from requirements definition to package installation, took six months. The implementation was a success, and receivables were brought down to a more reasonable level.

A similar process was used to purchase packaged software for accounts payable and purchasing. The MIS group is currently installing a general ledger package and will be installing a centralized manufacturing package later this year. The only major system that was rewritten in-house was the order entry system.

The MIS group, in an effort led by Beikman and Tom Caraway, selected RAMIS as its "user friendly" software to increase direct access to information by end users. RAMIS is a fourth-generation language that can be used by trained users and MIS personnel to answer database queries and to write reports.

The major application for RAMIS involves sales data analysis. Data on customer orders is taken from the order entry system each night and is placed in a RAMIS database that contains sales data for all the company's products and customers. Both scheduled (e.g., weekly or monthly) and ad hoc reports are then written using RAMIS. To insure the success of RAMIS, a major user training effort was implemented.

Another major change made by Beikman was the introduction of Business Systems managers (BSMs). The BSMs act as liaisons between user groups and the Information Technology group. They have a matrix reporting relationship and report to both Beikman and to the controller of the user group for which they work. The BSMs work with users and MIS personnel in defining systems requirements, in systems design, and in providing support for existing systems. In describing his strategy for hiring BSMs, Dennis Beikman stated, "I was not looking for traditional information systems people. I wanted people with a general business background and an interest in technology."

Status of the Information Technology Group in 1985

The Information Technology group contained 48 people who reported directly to Beikman or to one of his subordinates and 9 people who had a matrix reporting relationship to Beikman (Exhibit 5). The 48 direct reports were divided into two groups: the Corporate Communications and Technical Services group, and the Systems Development and Administration group.

The Corporate Communications and Technical Services group was headed by Nick Tsumpis, who joined Alcon in 1978 as a programmer/analyst after four years in technical services. The group performed three main functions—technical services, computer operations, and communications. Nick Tsumpis described the major responsibilities of the group:

> The group has a strong service orientation. Availability of the computer is very important. The technical services people work with both the applications area and with the operations area in diagnosing and resolving systems problems. The group is also responsible for hardware capacity planning, installing and maintaining the current operating system, operating the voice and data communication network, and administering the data security function.

The Systems Development and Administrative group was managed by Tom Caraway, who had a degree in computer science and worked as a programmer and project leader before joining Alcon in 1976. The group had two main functions: systems development and maintenance, and user training.

The systems development and maintenance function was performed by 13 programmers and systems analysts and three project leaders. They had the responsibility for developing new interactive COBOL systems and for supporting the COBOL systems, the RAMIS systems, and the software packages. They worked with users to define

EXHIBIT 5

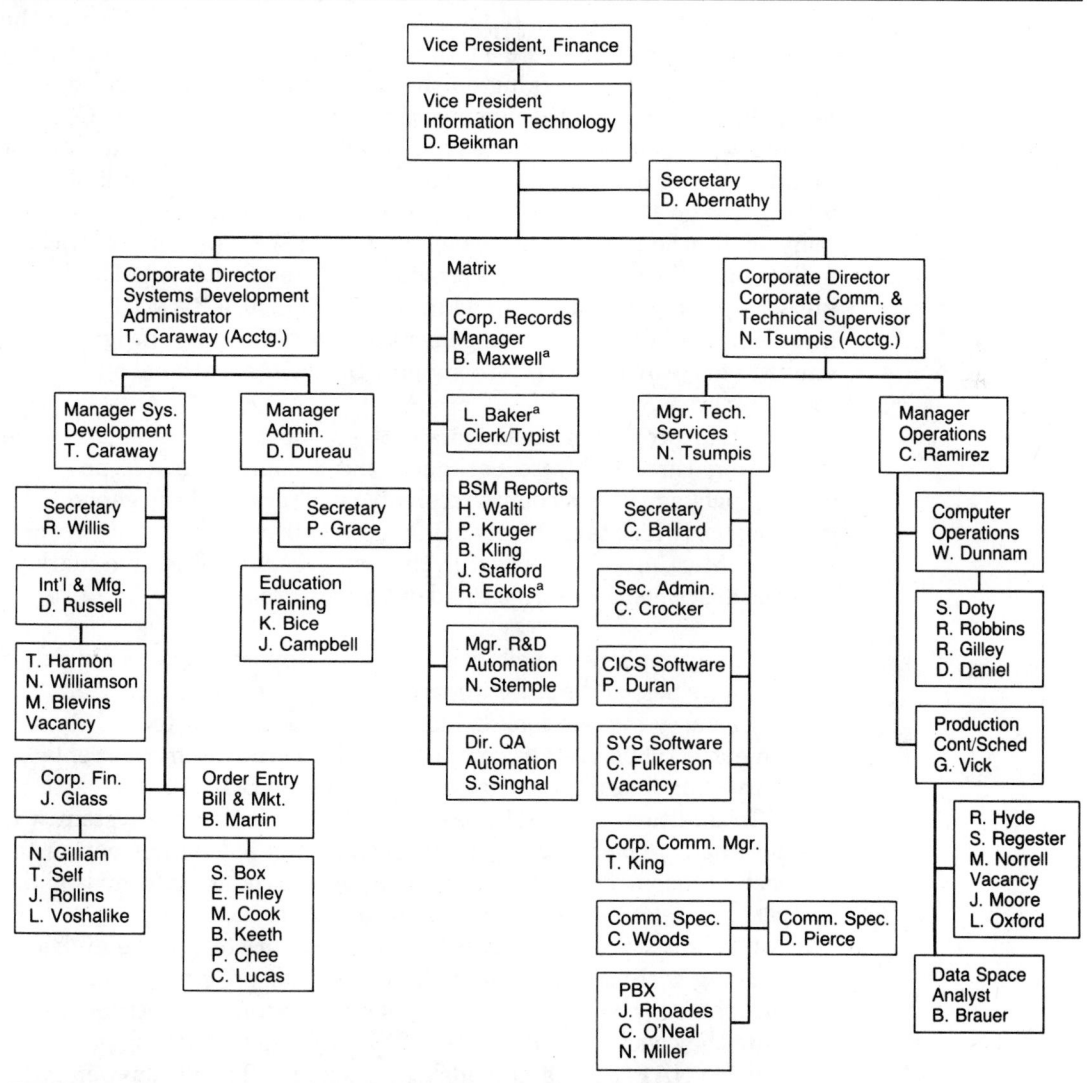

[a]Included in VP Information Technology Headcount and Expense Budget.

systems requirements, to choose new software packages, and to develop RAMIS databases and write reports. Four of the programmer/analysts were working primarily on COBOL applications, three were supporting software packages, four were supporting RAMIS applications, and two were working on both COBOL and RAMIS applications.

The systems development area was divided into three project groups—international and manufacturing systems, corporate financial systems, and order entry, billing, and marketing systems. Two of the three programmer/analysts in the international and manufacturing systems group were working on the development of a centralized on-line COBOL system in the manufacturing area. The centralized COBOL system will replace the System/34-based system in the four largest manufacturing plants. This system, in turn, will be replaced by a software package being developed by Martin Marietta (the parent company of Mathematica—the maker of RAMIS) to be run on Alcon's mainframe. This package will provide easy links with RAMIS for inquiries and report writing. In addition, it will utilize RAMIS' new and more powerful database management system. The third programmer/analyst was providing RAMIS support to the international and manufacturing areas.

The four programmer/analysts in the corporate financial area were supporting three software packages: the accounts/payable and purchasing package, the accounts/receivable package, and the general ledger package (which is currently being installed).

B. J. Martin, project leader in the order entry, billing, and marketing area described the work carried out by his group:

The group's responsibilities are the support of the order entry, billing, sales, and marketing areas. When I took over in 1982, the order entry system looked like it contained converted IBM 1401 [an early 1960s vintage computer] code. This system was replaced with an on-line order entry system written in COBOL.

In addition, a RAMIS-based sales and marketing system was developed. The system's databases contain sales information for each division. They also contain customer product information, inventory, sales quota, and sales forecast data.

Of the six people who work for me, two are out in the divisions working with users. [Almost all of the other programmer/analysts are located in the IT area.] They support people in getting the results they want with RAMIS, IFPS [a financial modeling package], and DYNAPLAN [a spreadsheet package]. They'll answer questions from users and work with users to develop new programs. Some of the users are very good at RAMIS. Users come from many areas including Science and Technology and corporate accounting. A third person supports sales and marketing applications that use both RAMIS and COBOL.

The three other programmer/analysts work on order entry, customer service, and billing applications. They develop and maintain on-line COBOL applications and RAMIS reports. The applications themselves are written in COBOL. Each night the data files from the applications are added to the RAMIS database. All reports are then written in RAMIS.

The order entry process had recently changed with Alcon's participation in the ORDERNET system. The system was operated by a time-sharing service bureau and was used by pharmaceutical wholesalers and distributors to place orders with their suppliers. Wholesalers and distributors, using computer terminals, dialed up the ORDERNET system and simultaneously placed orders with all their suppliers. All orders for Alcon were stored in computer-readable form in an Alcon "mailbox." These orders were transferred daily to Alcon's order entry system. About 40 percent of Alcon's dollar volume of orders, mostly those for consumer products, was received through ORDERNET.

The second major function carried out by the Systems Development and Administration group was user training. Two trainers have taught the basic RAMIS course to 215 Alcon employees. The nine-hour class developed by Mathematica has been given to personnel ranging from clerks to middle managers. Of those trained in RAMIS, about 45 percent used it at least once in the third quarter of 1984. Tom Caraway estimated that between 20 and 30 of those are "hard-core users"—people who use RAMIS several times a week.

There were also four advanced RAMIS courses that have had a combined attendance of 104 employees. The most popular of these was a records management course designed for workers who want to build their own databases. According to Kathylin Bice, one of the trainers, Alcon employees were using RAMIS to build many small databases that were previously handled manually. These included databases of doctors' names and addresses, project control information, mailing lists, distribution lists for internal reports, and the Alcon internal phone book. Two other popular courses taught DYNAPLAN (a spreadsheet package) and GDDM (a graphics package). Both packages were available on the mainframe.

Another function of the IT group was technology assessment. This task was carried out by Nick Tsumpis and Tom Caraway. Tsumpis estimated that they each spent seven or eight days a month examining new technologies and assessing the feasibility of introducing the technologies at Alcon. The latest outcome of this endeavor was a voice mailbox system used by the field sales force.

The Role of the Business Systems Managers

There were five Business Systems managers at Alcon. Each reported both to Dennis Beikman and to the controller of the user division for whom he worked. All five were located in the user area. Four of the five were part of the headcount for the user division.

Brad Kling, the BSM for the ophthalmic products division, was one of the first BSMs, having been hired in August 1982. His previous work was with a public accounting firm and as a controller in a small company. He had an interest in personal computing, but no formal information systems background. He described his role at Alcon:

I view my role as primarily one of providing direction by working with the Information Technology group and with users in information systems planning and in application definition.

Currently, I spend about 70 percent of my time on planned projects and 30 percent handling ad hoc requests from users. During the past year, I have spent three-fourths of my planned time working on the new manufacturing system. The manufacturing plants were using IBM System/34 computers, but they had difficulty integrating the manufacturing systems with other systems that were run on our mainframe.

Our first step in this process involved reassessing manufacturing systems requirements. We found that inventory concepts used by other companies, such as "just-in-time," were not used at Alcon. We decided to look for a centralized system to fill our needs. A project team was formed that was led by me and made up of members of the Information Technology group and one person from each plant. We made plant visits, developed a requirements document, and selected Martin Marietta's MAS–E system.

This system will not be available until later this year. In the meantime, we have converted the decentralized system to a centralized system written in COBOL and RAMIS. This was completed in mid-March. Manufacturing has traditionally lagged behind in end user computing and now, with access to RAMIS databases, they have the opportunity to catch up.

The other planned projects that I'm working on are a sales forecasting system, an office automation equipment upgrade, and the billing and order entry systems. My nonplanned time consists of answering user questions and working on administrative items, such as obtaining users IDs.

One problem I have found is that there is some confusion as to who is the primary user contact. Now if users have a question or want information, they can go to their BSM, a programmer/analyst or their project manager. I would like the IT group to formalize their support role with respect to users and BSMs. The BSMs need a central source of technical assistance on a variety of issues.

I found that the job offers lots of opportunities and lots of freedom to pursue my own direction. Sometimes, however, I ask myself, "Am I spending my time productively?"

Rick Eckols provided another perspective on the role of the BSM. Before becoming a BSM in October 1984, he had been a senior programmer/analyst, working on the development of the order entry, pricing, and customer service systems (all interactive COBOL-based applications). Eckols was the BSM working with the corporate staff functions—human resources, corporate accounting, treasurer, tax, legal, and auditing. He described his role:

> Two of my tasks are writing RAMIS procedures and designing RAMIS databases. I made some enhancements to our RAMIS-based executive compensation system and transferred the Science and Technology compensation system to RAMIS. I am also working on writing reports in RAMIS for our new general ledger system. The system has a poor report writer. It would take about 500,000 lines of code to produce the reports we wanted using the general ledger's report writer. Only 100 to 200 lines are needed to write the reports using RAMIS.
>
> Currently, my main responsibility is getting users in the human resources group started using RAMIS. They have RAMIS databases, but few end users are producing their own reports. If they want to do something in RAMIS, I do it. My goal is to train them so they can do it themselves. The human resources users were all trained in RAMIS, but they had the training before they had data to work with. Of the 11 RAMIS users whom I work with, 4 can write their own reports.
>
> I also have a role as a technical reference for users. I help them understand what technology they should use. In addition, I help coordinate and make recommendations for computer terminals, personal computers, and workstations, etc. I also work with users to develop hardware and software plans and serve as a liaison between users and the IT group.
>
> The users see me as their advisor. I have always viewed myself as a user advocate.
>
> This job is very different from my previous job as a senior programmer/analyst. I work more on my own with much less direction from management.

End User Perspective

User satisfaction with the work of the Information Technology group can be examined in two ways. The questionnaire results in Exhibit 6 indicate a high degree of user satisfaction with the projects on which the IT group worked in 1984.

EXHIBIT 6 User Evaluation of 1984 IT Projects

	Excellent (4)	Good (3)	Fair (2)	Poor (1)	No Response	Mean
Overall satisfaction with project	76	64	3	0	16	3.5
Quality of documentation	54	46	4	0	55	3.5
Satisfaction with assigned MIS personnel	87	53	0	1	18	3.6
Satisfaction with requested deliverable	73	59	1	0	26	3.6

Another perspective on user attitude to the changes made in the IT group was obtained from Dick Hedlund, manager of sales services for the lens care and ophthalmic division. Hedlund, a pharmacist by training who became a salesperson for Alcon, moved into his current job in 1977. He reported to the national sales manager for the ophthalmic division.

The sales services group consisted of 27 people who provided sales district managers with reports, and with information on customer bids and on government contracts. They also provided sales management with summary reports on sales data.

Hedlund, who had no previous computer experience or training, was an experienced and knowledgeable RAMIS user. He described the use of RAMIS in his group:

At first users were very reluctant to use RAMIS to create their own reports. Once the users understood the advantages of creating their own reports and controlling their own data, their attitude completely turned around. Now the users are using RAMIS extensively. Of the 27 people who work for me, 15 are RAMIS users and 8 have their own RAMIS databases. Further, we plan to add four more individual databases in the near future.

About 25 percent of my time involves working with RAMIS—10 percent answering ad hoc queries from management or field sales and 15 percent writing RAMIS programs. We are working to get all the sales service production programs converted to RAMIS. We are working closely with four people in the IT group to convert these programs. They provide help mostly in converting external files to RAMIS databases and in writing the file descriptions in RAMIS. We write our own reports and modify existing reports.

We are now working on converting our bid system to RAMIS. It was a mixture of COBOL and RAMIS. We are getting advice from the IT group, but we are writing and testing the programs ourselves.

The IT group estimated it would take them 9 to 10 months to convert the bid system. We can do it in 60–90 days. Knowing the system, I have a much better feel for what I want and how I want it to look. If the IT group was developing the system, I would have to explain to them what I wanted and we would go through a lengthy trial and error period. Being able to adjust the results immediately is a real plus for me.

Using RAMIS has allowed us to take on additional responsibilities without hiring more people. We get more and better reports, better data, and we have more control over our data. I have no idea how many people we'd need if we didn't have RAMIS.

We currently have 15 people handling customer service and hospital chargebacks (transactions between Alcon, the wholesaler, and the hospital). When all the changes have been made, we'll only need 10 to 11 people to handle chargebacks and customer services.

Our goal is to get all applicable data in our RAMIS system so that we can have control of our reporting.

Computing in Research and Development

Among the organizational changes that have occurred since 1982, both the R&D and the Quality Assurance computing facilities reported to Dennis Beikman (and also to the directors of the R&D and QA functions, respectively).

The R&D computing facility was managed by Norm Stemple, a Ph.D. chemist, who joined Alcon R&D in 1975 with 15 years' experience in laboratory automation. Six people worked for him—two in operations and four in systems development and maintenance. R&D had systematically upgraded its hardware between 1975 and 1985 and had added some new packaged software. In addition to two PDP 11 series computers used for data gathering, there were three of DEC's VAX series computers in R&D. One was used for statistical analysis of data from drug tests; the second was used for centralized word processing, serving 30 secretaries and word processing specialists; the third was used for drug design.

Interactive computing had always been the key objective in R&D computing systems. In 1985 there were about 170 terminals serving the 300 R&D scientists and staff. Almost all employees used the computer for part of their daily work. The digital data network in R&D permitted any user (given proper password authorization) to access any of Alcon's computers (including the corporate IBM system).

To accommodate special reporting and file storage and retrieval needs the fourth-generation language DATATRIEVE was installed in 1982. It has provided R&D users with capabilities similar to those provided to corporate users through RAMIS. For some applications, data were transferred between RAMIS and DATATRIEVE. DATATRIEVE was only one of several software packages used by R&D personnel. At the request of the chemists, the R&D organization purchased a large software package to do chemical modeling to aid in drug design. The system was developed by a company that specializes in software for the chemical and pharmaceutical industries. The request was reviewed by Stemple's group before the purchase was approved.

Stemple's group was examining other software packages including a system that facilitated the presentation of data from the testing of drugs on animals. Norm Stemple commented on the changes in R&D computing:

> Originally (1976) most of our software consisted of small systems developed in-house. Now the emphasis is on purchased software. The push for this software is coming from the users. They know what's out there (through going to conferences and talking with their colleagues) better than us. The growth in computer usage has been phenomenal, from 15 terminals in 1981 to the current 170.

Future Directions for the IT Group

One of the major short-term problems facing the Information Technology group was the shrinking backlog of new systems projects. The systems development group was working on three major products—the manufacturing system, the general ledger system, and the order entry system. These three projects employed 6 of the 13 programmer/analysts. When these were completed (later in 1985) there would be no new major projects on which the programmer/analysts could work. Much of the demand for new applications was being satisfied by the users themselves with the aid of RAMIS.

There were, however, two technological changes that would be introduced into Alcon through the IT group. A new more user friendly version of RAMIS called RAMIS/ENGLISH was being tested at Alcon. This language should make the RAMIS databases more easily accessible to users. Alcon was also planning to upgrade its RAMIS database manager. The upgraded system would have more capabilities than the current system, and would permit Alcon to write more of its applications in RAMIS and further reduce its dependence on COBOL.

Several of the people at Alcon had ideas about the future role of the IT group:

Tom Caraway: The systems development staff should shrink in size over the next three years. By that time it should be split into two groups. A development group that supports the packaged software and does maintenance and small development requests in

COBOL, and an information resource center that supports end user software (e.g., RAMIS and IFPS), personal computer software, training, and database administration.

There will have to be a change in outlook on the part of our managers. While the number of people who report to them is important now, in the future, the number of functions they support should be important.

We have a staff that's done a great job, but they will have to be retrained. We will need more product specialists than we have now.

Nick Tsumpis: There are several big issues that we will have to handle in the future. We are growing in CPU usage at 100 percent per year. Our biggest challenge is to handle the growth by insuring that new CPUs perform properly and are cost effective. We will also need to install a local area network and a digital PBX in the next few years. People are also starting to get personal computers and I'm starting to hear them say, "If I only had the data on my PC." Data access and security is an issue now and will be a bigger issue in the future.

I don't think there will be any growth in either the data center or in technical services. I would like to set up a help desk so that there is a central place for users to call if they have a problem. There's a need to supply better services to the end user.

Bob Montgomery: Alcon's strategy for the future is to be the most successful specialty pharmaceutical company we can be. Our success will depend on our ability to develop significantly technologically advanced products in the ophthalmological area. We must also successfully manufacture and market these products in the U.S. and worldwide. With larger companies entering the ophthalmic market, we must be preemptive in our development of new products.

The IT group must become more user oriented so that it can provide the best tools to aid the company in implementing its strategy. We need people with a high degree of product sensitivity who are able to interface with operations managers. The members of the IT group need to have a better sense of where Alcon makes its money.

One area where an information system could be used is the improvement of our relationships with ophthalmologists. Each year we sponsor a visit to Alcon by ophthalmological interns from several leading hospitals. The purpose of the visit is to familiarize the interns with our products and our research efforts. Providing a database system containing our latest research and product information would allow us to maintain contact with the doctors. This type of system could provide Alcon with an important strategic advantage over our competitors.

Dennis Beikman was aware that his organization was designed to develop and maintain application systems. It appeared that these tasks might not be the responsibility of the IT group in the future. He wanted to set new goals for the IT group and to reorganize the group to meet these goals. As he contemplated *how* he would do this, he decided the best starting point would be to develop a vision for the future. What functions would the IT group at a typical company perform in 1990? How would that group be structured? Determining the answers to these questions would help Beikman decide what actions he should take between 1985 and 1990 to prepare for these future requirements.

Case 6-2

Mishawaka Industries, Inc.

On January 10, 1984, Gary Templeton anxiously awaited a response from his new boss, Ken Bogart, corporate controller, concerning his proposal for achieving better corporatewide coordination of DP activities. Templeton had been with Mishawaka Industries for three years. In his previous role as manager of corporate systems planning he had been asked to develop an overall plan for information systems—both corporate and divisional—so that data processing resources and activities would be better coordinated. However, work on this task had been severely constrained due to excessive demands on his time as a "fire-fighter." Assisting divisions with the details of their MIS operations, he was left with no time for developing the much-needed corporatewide plans.

Ken Bogart was particularly anxious to get better coordination between data processing operations throughout the company, and lessen the divergence of various divisional efforts in this area. For several years he had pressed for progress in this direction. Ultimately, Templeton's former boss was fired and Templeton was put in his place in October 1983. This management action startled Gary, since, after all, development of the plan was his specific responsibility. Later, though, he realized that the dismissal was consistent with the prevailing philosophy at Mishawaka: managers operated autonomously, and each alone

This case was prepared by Janis L. Gogan under the direction of Leslie R. Porter.

Copyright © 1984 by the President and Fellows of Harvard College
Harvard Business School case 9–184–183 (Rev 6/86)

was responsible for their unit's performance. Templeton interpreted his promotion as a clear message to move ahead quickly with the development of DP plans. He recalled all too clearly the announcement of his promotion to a meeting of corporate officers: "Gentlemen, this is Gary Templeton, the most recent occupant of the position of director of management information systems."

Within a few months, Templeton had prepared a position paper addressing both structure and management control processes for corporatewide data processing. He identified problems in the current situation and suggested a more centralized approach to MIS development. "In the past," he noted, "the corporate MIS function as a whole has seemed to lack direction and thrust, and the data processing effort at Mishawaka in toto has fallen short of its true potential, while spending more money than necessary to do so." In the future, Templeton proposed that "the corporate data processing organization will have overall responsibility for providing the total spectrum of data processing services required by the divisions. This includes planning computer hardware acquisition, operating computer centers, and all systems development."

Bogart had to approve the basic plan before Templeton could proceed. Templeton foresaw a very busy few months enlisting the support of the division's data processing managers for the new plan.

History of Mishawaka Industries

In 1906 the Owens family of Mishawaka, Indiana, established the Mishawaka Wet Mill in the rolling countryside just outside their hometown. The company thrived in those early years, transforming the corn and wheat of nearby farms into meal that was shipped to bakers and grocers in Indianapolis. When one of the founders' sons moved to Indianapolis during the 1920s, the company branched into other lines of business. First the company moved into baked goods, using their own grain products. Later, after daughter Cathi married a manager from Eli Lilly, the company opened up its own pharmaceutical operation. Both ventures went well, and during the next 20 years, Mishawaka Wet Mill expanded its activities in both food processing and pharmaceuticals.

In 1953, a group of well-financed bankers from Chicago purchased the business and renamed it Mishawaka Industries. The new president, Thomas Bruner, adopted a strategy of growth through acquisition.

A careful acquisition strategy yielded tremendous growth over the next three decades. More than 40 different companies were purchased. From profits of $1,252,000 in 1953, earnings grew to $113,992,000 in 1983. The excitement of those two decades of growth inspired a retiring corporate executive to rhyme; Exhibit 1 presents his poetic review of

EXHIBIT 1

Ten-year income growth ($ millions)

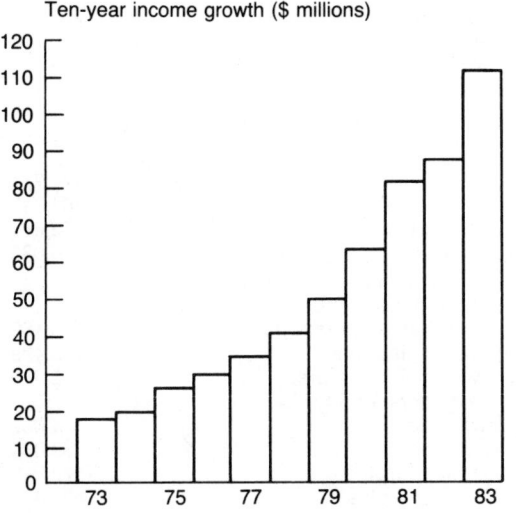

Ten-year revenue ($ millions)

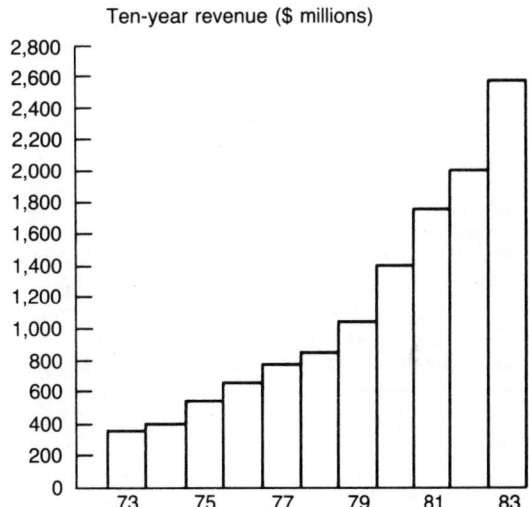

Ballad of Mishawaka Industries   by Robert M. Brown   December 17, 1983

'Twas early in the year of fifty-three
When four swashbucklers set forth on a spree;
Established a company for profits to make,
Come hell or highwater, their fortunes at stake.

No money at hand, they signed up for debt,
Hocking their total, all they did bet
That somehow or other they'd favorably cope
With swings of the market to fulfill their hope.

The pressure was on them relentlessly
To keep the cash flowing for solvency.
The goals in those days were clear without doubt;
Take our full swings—but do not strike out!

With our debt to equity at twenty-eight to one,
Some bankers were pale if not downright wan
At the thought of advancing more working lucre
To a fledgling which had a secureless future.

But they did; and we did; to our future we rolled,
Rationalizing capital which in excesses untold
Was tied up in industry by barons of old;
Their monuments full of inventory which couldn't be sold.

We merged; we acquired—*their* common for our preferred.
At times we paid cash but stoutly demurred
From issuing our common (to avoid dilution);
'Cause the assets we acquired really begged for solution!

Catastrophe avoidance was the first priority;
Maintain operations came secondly.
If energy were were left, after meeting these two;
Improvements were in order if confined to a few!

Diversification served us quite well
To dampen the swings of the pell and the mell.
Joint ventures we tried and liked very much;
Developed good deals and patterns for such.

Instructions to divisions were considerate—not rash;
Run it your way, but send corporate all cash.
As long as there're profits, you'll have a full say;
But start losing money, you'll lose it our way!

We scratched in our markets for meaningful shares;
And watched competition for treacherous snares.
Our view towards inventory was cautious—not bold;
It's a liability—not an asset—until it is sold!

Then came the day with capital abundant;
Other people's problems looked repulsively redundant.
So, earnings of quality with vigor we sought;
We issued our common for some that we bought.

The torch has been passed to a new generation,
Whose competence commands new heights of veneration.
The journey's been great for me and for mine;
Godspeed and success for thee and for thine!

EXHIBIT 2

MISHAWAKA INDUSTRIES, INC.
Consolidated Balance Sheet
December 31, 1983
($000)

Assets		Liabilities and Stockholders' Equity	
Current assets		Current liabilities	
Cash	$ 56,043	Accounts payable	$ 176,771
Accounts receivable	397,062	Accrued expenses	163,715
Inventory	454,959	Income taxes	53,673
Prepaid expenses	11,371	Other	18,086
Other	36,974	Total current liabilities	432,245
Total current assets	956,409	Reserve for divestiture of marginally	
Plant, property and equipment	1,163,426	profitable operations	29,159
Less: Accumulated depreciation	495,234	Long-term liabilities	435,499
		Convertible debentures	72,310
Net plant investment	668,192	Stockholders' equity	
Other assets	200,680	Preferred	14,657
		Common	33,084
		Capital surplus	172,919
		Earned surplus	635,408
		Total stockholders' equity	856,068
		Total liabilities and stockholders'	
Total assets	$1,825,281	equity	$1,825,281

MISHAWAKA INDUSTRIES, INC.
Consolidated Income Statement, 1983
($000)

Sales	$2,606,193
Operating costs	
Cost of sales	1,999,721
Depreciation	70,503
Selling and administration	273,859
Total operating costs	2,344,083
Operating profit	262,110
Other deductions	
Interest expense	34,553
Other expenses	6,187
Income before taxes	221,370
Taxes	107,378
Net income	$ 113,992

the firm's history as well as 10 years' sales and profit figures, highlighting steady and dramatic growth. By 1984, Mishawaka had expanded well beyond its base in foodstuffs and pharmaceuticals. Recent acquisitions included businesses in heavy machinery, construction materials, and data communications. Financial statements for 1983 appear in Exhibit 2.

Philosophy of Mishawaka Industries

The company grew by acquiring going concerns in a broad spectrum of industries, much as an investor would build a diversified portfolio. The new acquisitions were usually left to operate fairly autonomously. A desirable candidate was a well-run company that complemented the existing collection of divisions, either by (1) rounding out some divisions' product lines; or (2) exploiting fundamentally different business cycles than other businesses in the firm. Companies were bought—and sometimes sold—the way a shrewd investor might buy and sell stocks. This philosophy was emphasized in the company's formal statement of goals:

> To build a strong, highly diversified operating company with consistent growth in earnings per share year after year and to build a strong base for continued growth. Accomplishment of this goal requires continually increasing operating profits while maintaining satisfactory return on investment.
>
> Of paramount importance in achieving the long-term company goal is the increasingly successful operation of the individual divisions of the company.

Company Organization

The company consisted of 16 operating divisions in five industry groups. The organization chart in Exhibit 3 illustrates how the divisions were grouped as of January 1984. Dealings across industry groups were rare, but within each group there existed some synergy. The groups were characterized by the products they manufactured:

a. Pharmaceuticals—three divisions that manufactured drugs, medicines, ointments, and medical supplies, some under nationally recognized brand names sold directly to consumers, others aimed at institutions and private-label retailers.

b. Foodstuffs—seven divisions that processed meat and other foods. Meat sold in local markets, whereas baked goods, frozen foods, and baking mixes were sold regionally.

c. Heavy Machinery—four capital-intensive divisions that manufactured heavy-duty equipment for construction, agriculture, and shipbuilding. The fire engines and amphibious landers were well known, but most of the products were production equipment and factory material-transfer machines for sale to other manufacturing firms.

d. Keydisk Systems—a young, promising division which manufactured key-to-disk systems, OCR scanners, MICR reader-sorters and other automatic input devices.

EXHIBIT 3 Organization Chart

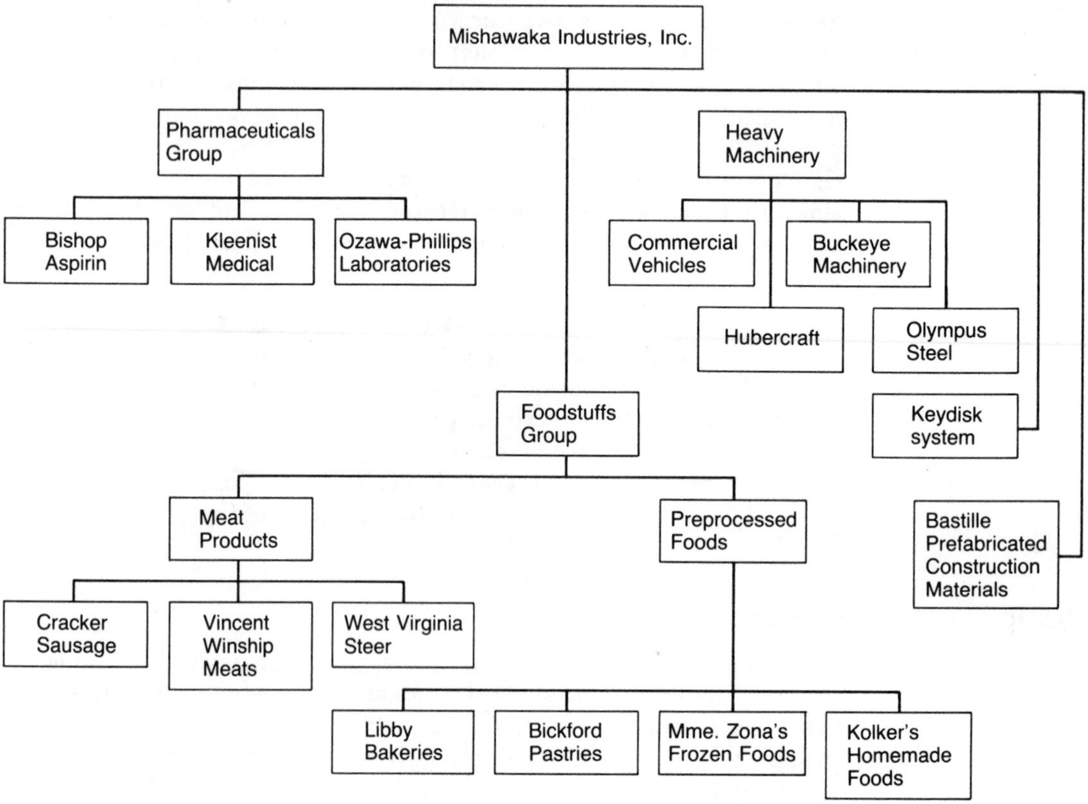

```
                        Mishawaka Industries, Inc.
          ┌──────────────────────┬──────────────────────────────┐
     Pharmaceuticals                                        Heavy
     Group                                                  Machinery
   ┌──────┬──────────┬──────────┐              ┌────────────┬──────────────┐
 Bishop   Kleenist   Ozawa-Phillips        Commercial        Buckeye
 Aspirin  Medical    Laboratories          Vehicles          Machinery
                                                     Hubercraft    Olympus
                                                                   Steel
                          Foodstuffs                               Keydisk
                          Group                                    system
              ┌─────────────────────────┐
         Meat                      Preprocessed
         Products                  Foods                      Bastille
   ┌────────┬──────────┬──────────┐                           Prefabricated
 Cracker   Vincent    West Virginia                           Construction
 Sausage   Winship    Steer                                   Materials
           Meats
                    ┌─────────┬──────────┬──────────┐
                 Libby      Bickford   Mme. Zona's  Kolker's
                 Bakeries   Pastries   Frozen Foods Homemade
                                                    Foods
```

    e. Construction Materials—a single division that manufactured prefabricated materials for housing, office buildings, and hotels all over the world. They also offered construction supervision services for major projects.

Group level staff typically consisted of a group president, controller, and no more than four staff assistants. As shown in Exhibit 4 the group controllers reported directly to Bogart, although they physically resided at the same location as the group president. Corporate headquarters were in Chicago, but the industry group president and divisional presidents were located near their operating locations around the country. Mishawaka employed 20,400 people and operated plants, warehouses, and administrative offices in 27 states, Canada, Europe, and Brazil.

EXHIBIT 4 Corporate Staff Organization

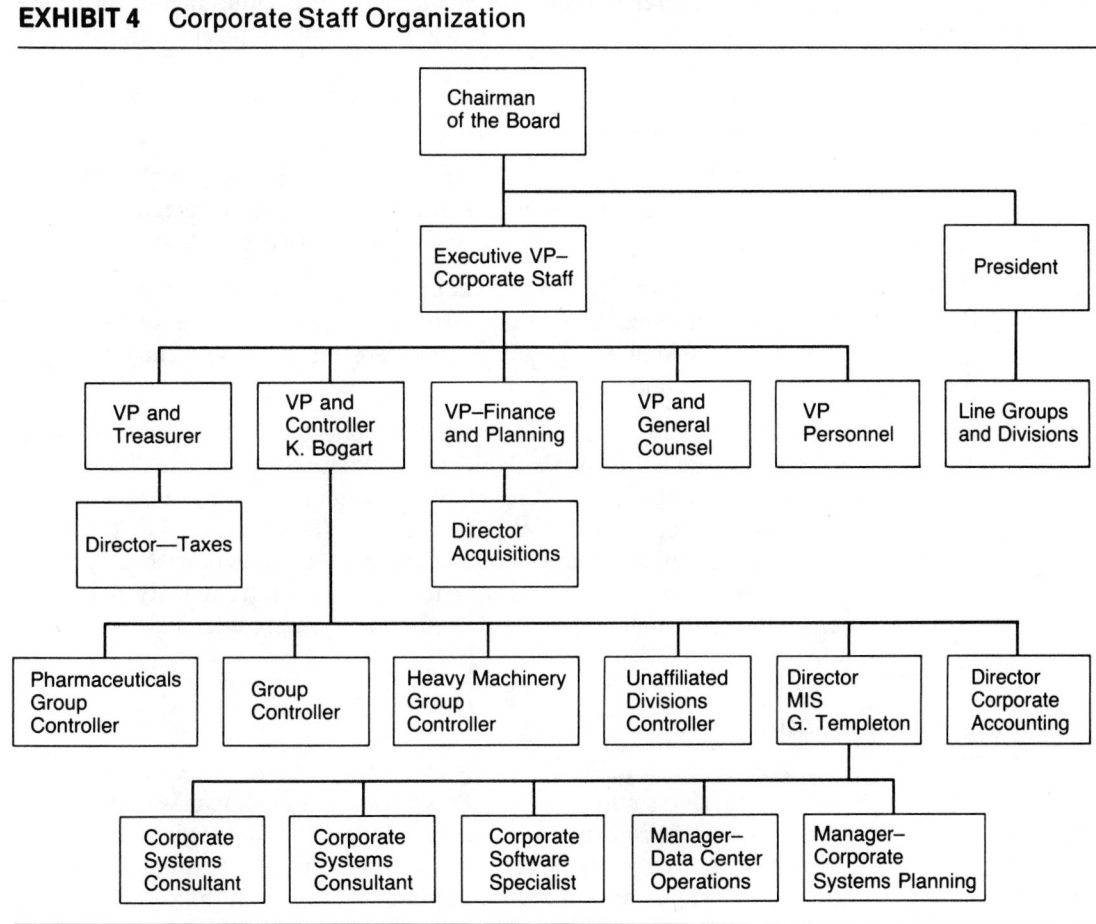

Corporate-Level Activities

Though the divisions were profit centers operating as independent businesses, corporate headquarters assisted the divisions and monitored and evaluated their performance. The 90 corporate staff employees served as an extension of the president's office and were charged with the following roles:

- Support and assist operations management.
- Maintain systematic surveillance and administer systems of control.
- Evaluate operational performance and trends.

- Administer corporate housekeeping functions including financial, legal, tax, communications, personnel, public and investor relations.
- Provide leadership, planning, and implementation for the company to grow in new areas.

Corporate staff could and often did get involved in divisional activities, but usually only to provide assistance or review plans, decisions, and financial performance. According to the corporate policy manual:

> Staff personnel at all levels provide in-house consulting, task force assistance, and administration of systems, but make no operating decisions. Staff effectiveness is rooted solely in the powers of persuasion and expertise.

Some divisions actively sought corporate-level expertise, while other divisions kept interactions at an absolute minimum. The type of relationship varied, depending on the division president. Some who had established their divisions as entrepreneurs (and remained at the helm after selling out to Mishawaka) resented involvement with corporate staff. Capital allocations and division plans were frequently points of contention between corporate staff and division presidents.

Business Planning and Control

A major effort to make planning and control procedures more useful and informative to divisional and corporate management was currently under way. The procedures called for a long-term strategic plan and an annual operating plan. Monthly and quarterly performance reports tracked divisional activity against plan.

Long-range planning was the responsibility of each operating division. Each division president established objectives based on anticipated business opportunities over a reasonable planning horizon for that industry, ranging from at least 3 years to as long as 10 years. Long-range plans were reviewed and approved by the presidents of industry groups and top management at corporate headquarters.

Yearly operating plans were also the responsibility of each operating division, but preparation of these plans usually required the participation of many individuals. The operating plan called for detailed estimates of revenues and costs. These figures were to be consistent with the division's long-term strategic plan.

Operating reports tracked performance against operating plan. The corporate accounting office received its data over the telephone from division controllers 10 days after the close of every month. Corporate staff then prepared the monthly Operating Highlights Report, showing sales and expense data, balance sheets, inventory status, ROI, and a three-month forecast of anticipated revenues and expenses, compared to the year's operating plan. Quarterly reports highlighted changes in debt position and capital expenditures.

Top management wanted these formal planning and control activities to receive greater attention than they had in the past. A significant level of corporate-level staff work was now committed to improving planning and control throughout the company.

Information Systems

Each division managed data processing in a highly decentralized fashion. There were no data processing personnel at the group level. DP personnel and equipment had been reflected directly in each division's budget since computers were introduced into the company (see Exhibit 5). This had resulted in numerous problems and inefficiencies. Templeton reflected on the status of MIS throughout the company:

The 1983 data processing budget is $27,390,000, and in 1984 is projected to be $33,350,000, a 20 percent increase. With few exceptions, neither the quality nor quantity of DP output has increased at a commensurate rate. Mishawaka cannot afford to allocate time, money, and people to information systems which do not have a significant, coherent impact on performance. We need information systems which help identify potential business problems earlier (analysis), help develop alternative solutions (simulation), and insure proper execution of the chosen solutions (control). In a rapidly changing competitive and technological environment, Mishawaka must *plan ahead.*

MIS efforts at Mishawaka are handicapped by the present organizational structure, which does not encourage divisional managers to consider the best interests of the corporation. Sharing of personnel or equipment resources is difficult to arrange. Joint development of applications with multi-divisional utilization is not occurring.

To improve this situation, in mid-1981 two positions were authorized: manager of corporate systems planning and corporate software specialist. This was meant to provide for (1) closer assistance and guidance for divisional MIS efforts; and (2) better coordination and planning of companywide data processing efforts. While some of those objectives have been achieved, the manager of corporate systems planning was overused in the consultant function. A coordinated corporate MIS development plan was not formulated. The corporate MIS function has lacked direction and thrust, and has fallen short of its true potential. The primary reasons are:

EXHIBIT 5 Mishawaka Data Processing Installations

	Division	Location	Primary Equipment	DP Personnel*			Total Group DP** Budget 1983 ($000)	Percent Group Sales Revenues
				SYS	PRG	OPN		
Bastille	PCM	Passaic	IBM 4341/2	11	17	15	$ 2,820	1.1%
Keydisk Systems	KS	East St. Louis	DEC—1090 SMP	7	15	8	3,600	3.7
Foodstuffs	CS	Peoria	Burroughs B1885	7	11	7		
	VWM	Skokie	DEC PDP–11/23 DS336	13	25	3		
	WVS	Lewisburg	Hewlett-Packard 3000/44	6	12	6		
	LB	Chicago	IBM 3081	9	17	31		
	BP	Gary	Datapoint 8600	7	21	3		
	ZFF	Boston	Data General Eclipse S/140	5	9	5		
	KHF	Madison	Burroughs B1900	8	13	8	8,600	1.0
Heavy Machinery	CV	Detroit	Honeywell 6600	15	28	12		
	BM	Diablo	DEC 2040	7	15	9		
	OS	Pittsburgh	DEC PDP 11/44	7	11	7		
	Huber	San Diego	DCE PDP 11/23 PLUS	4	6	6	5,440	0.9
Pharmaceuticals	BA	Providence	Honeywell DPS 6/48	7	9	6		
	KM	Medfield	Honeywell DPS 6/38	4	6	4		
	OPL	Corvallis	IBM 3033/S4	12	21	27	6,930	2.2
Total							$27,390	1.0%

*SYS includes Jr. and Sr. systems analysts; PRG includes all levels of programmers except trainees; OPN includes technical systems and operations personnel but does not include data entry.

**Average major DP budget items for total corporation are:

Hardware	35%	Average budget increase 1983 over 1982:	
Personnel	57	In hardware	35%
Lease/purchase software	6	In software	30
Supplies and other	2	In personnel	20

1. Development efforts are fragmented—divisions are reinventing similar wheels.
2. Small divisional staff which:
   a. Spend too much time on maintenance or minor enhancements.
   b. Lack strong experience in analyzing business problems and devising comprehensive, integrated, effective systems solutions.
   c. Therefore do not develop the major systems which can have significant, positive impact.
3. Many small, underutilized computers instead of larger, more fully utilized computers.

In 1980, when several divisions of the foodstuffs group simultaneously needed to upgrade their computing capability, corporate staff recognized that several divisions had similar DP needs. A centralized facility was established on the premises of Libby Bakeries. Its users were nearby food divisions (Libby Bakeries, Vincent Winship Meats, Bickford Pastries) and Mishawaka corporate staff. Initially, the center was run by its "home" division, although each division employed its own systems and programming personnel and operations team for use of the system during scheduled production hours. Administrative squabbles between divisions occurred with such frequency that corporate was brought in—as resident arbiter—to manage operations of the center in 1981. The facility was renamed Corporate Data Center. Each division still retained its own systems and programming team. At this point corporate MIS staff was increased to the six positions shown in Exhibit 4, with the manager of data center operations reporting to Templeton. Operations staff were listed as Foodstuffs Group employees. Costs for the operations staff and center were charged back to users. Currently neither operations nor the chargeout system were issues of management contention.

Proposed Restructuring

Templeton believed that the company's DP problems would best be met by reorganization. Following the pattern set by the Foodstuffs Group data center, the company should establish regional data centers to perform all DP operations, consolidating the disjointed and costly activity of separate divisions. Each industry group would form a control board to oversee and set priorities for MIS development work at the data centers. Each DP project would report in matrix fashion to both the regional data center and the group control board.

Templeton, a 45-year-old ex-Coast Guard officer with 20 years of data processing experience (6 with the Coast Guard, 5 with a large computer manufacturer as a salesman, 3 as an independent consultant, 3 with a public accounting firm, and the last 3 with Mishawaka) wrote up these suggestions in the MIS plan now awaiting Bogart's review. He argued as follows:

Many multi-divisional corporations, such as Mishawaka, have allowed their subsidiaries to manage their own EDP activities. Recently, however, there has been a trend toward consolidation of EDP activities into a corporatewide function. Such consolidation can result in lower costs, less duplication of systems and development efforts, and improved corporate control. Against this must be weighed possible disadvantages such as reduced divisional autonomy, disruption of services during conversion, and greater performance demands on EDP personnel due to more complex multi-access systems. It is important that top management be involved at the feasibility plan stage, long before consolidation occurs.

The following consolidation strategy should be examined, tested, and developed in a feasibility study:

- Establish a separate organization with corporatewide responsibility for administrative and operating control of all systems development and computer operations.
- Consolidate computer operations centers into regional data centers, supplemented as required by outside vendor time-sharing and/or remote batch processing services.
- Combine all computer operations at these centers.
- Combine the divisional business system development groups at regional data centers.
- Reduce the number of computer manufacturers represented to a single vendor within three years.
- Standardize the approach to computer systems development, maintenance, and operations.

(Exhibit 6 contains details of the proposed MIS Reorganization.)

Many companies of Mishawaka's size, structure, and philosophy have successfully implemented similar plans. This proposal poses many difficult decisions, and will require a good deal of effort over at least a two- to three-year period; but change is long overdue. Halfway measures and personal efforts, however well-intentioned and well-performed, have not had a significant impact. Now is the time to fully examine alternatives, make a rational decision, and proceed to implement it.

Due to the import of this subject, I would like to discuss it thoroughly with you at your earliest convenience.

G. L. Templeton

EXHIBIT 6 Proposed Restructuring of MIS

I. **Statement of Objectives for MIS**

   A. Advise corporate, group, and divisional management on the adequacy of existing automated and manual systems, and feasible alternatives.

   B. Formulate short- and long-range plans to identify, develop, and implement cost-effective solutions at plant, divisional, group, or corporate levels.

   C. Assure that approved plans are implemented in a cost-effective manner, from systems definition to acquisition and utilization of DP equipment.

   D. Audit information systems to ensure that they continue to be cost-effective.

Although the current corporate MIS department staffing and organizational relationship with divisional systems staff and management are compatible with the above charter, the four objectives have not all been fulfilled.

Even with a larger planning, auditing, and consulting staff, we will not achieve corporatewide effective data processing given the current organization structure.

II. **Reorganization**

In order to maximize the benefits of consolidation and minimize potential disadvantages, the functions listed below are suggested:

   A. Corporate Services and Regional/Group Data Centers

The *corporate data processing* organization will have overall responsibility for the total spectrum of corporate and divisional data processing services. This includes planning for hardware acquisition, computer centers operations, and all systems development. Control and budgeting of the total expenditure for data processing is a major assignment, as is promotion of corporatewide use of common software and systems. Regional systems and computing centers would report directly to this level. Specific responsibilities of this level are:

- *Information systems consulting*—advise corporate, group, and divisional management.
- *Equipment planning and acquisition*—plan computer requirements for the entire corporation, and negotiate purchase/rental/lease agreements.
- *Purchasing evaluation and audit*—evaluate the performance of regional/group systems and computing centers, and assess existing systems in terms of user satisfaction, corporate requirements, production costs, etc.
- *Corporate systems development*—study the feasibility of companywide systems, review existing systems to determine transferability between divisions, review divisional/group systems development projects to avoid duplicate efforts.

EXHIBIT 6 *(continued)*

- *Technical services*—coordinate technical services throughout the corporation in terms of software development, standards, evaluation and planning of hardware usage, and communications.

The primary responsibilities of *regional/group centers* would include actual operation of the computers and detailed design and programming of systems. Divisional sites would report to this level. Functions of the regional/group center would include:

- *Detailed systems design and development*—coordination, short-range planning, and application programming support.
- *Technical services*—evaluate and plan hardware and operating systems software usage, provide systems programming support, maintain systems software at the regional/group center, and provide teleprocessing and communication hardware and software support.
- *Data center*—operate production programs, test programs being developed, control input data and output reports, control and operate computer file libraries, schedule computer installation, and control and operate data communications equipment.
- *Administration and accounting*—develop and train regional personnel, operate a mechanized project control system, maintain regional budget and accounting records, prepare budget comparisons, and enforce corporate standards and procedures.

B. Information Systems Control Board

In order to ensure that consolidated information systems functions (1) remain responsive to the legitimate systems development needs of division/group business operations; and (2) provide consistently high quality service in daily operations, control boards would be established. This structure would clearly define the responsibilities of management for assessment of overall systems performance, and aid users in formulating their requirements and achieving their needs.

The *corporate information systems control board* would ensure sound planning and control of the development of management information systems throughout Mishawaka. The board would insure utilization of data processing equipment and personnel in a manner that would improve the quality and timeliness of information reporting, at a cost commensurate with improvement in operating results.

Membership would consist of the chairman of the board, corporate president, group presidents, corporate vice president/controller, vice president/finance and planning, and corporate director of management information systems. Meetings would be held quarterly, but could be less frequent once group computer

EXHIBIT 6 *(concluded)*

boards are well-established and new computer centers are fully operational.

The board would establish corporate computer policies and procedures, assess and approve group/divisional plans, and assess the overall effectiveness of services provided by the regional/ group systems and computing centers.

Membership of the *group boards* would consist of the group president, plus division presidents, corporate director of MIS, and head of the regional/group computer center. Meetings of these boards should be held monthly, or more often if warranted by the number of projects.

Through the use of both regional centers and control boards, Mishawaka would attain a higher degree of control over data processing activities. Reorganization would eliminate many inefficiencies and open the door to innovative applications that would enable divisions to compete more effectively in their markets.

Proposed Management Information Systems Organization

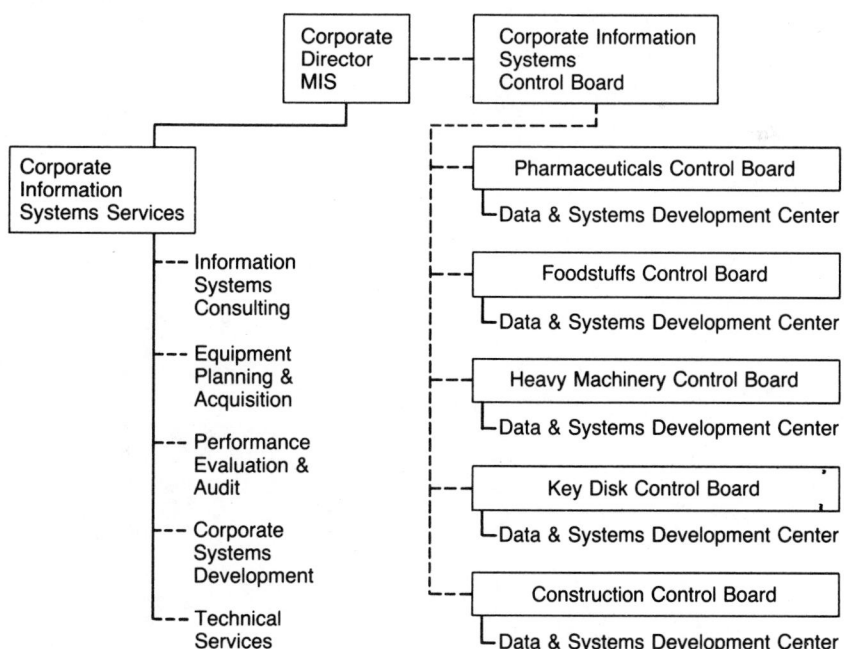

Chapter 7

IT Management Control

The IT management control system is a critical network that integrates IT activities with the rest of the firm's operations. Whereas the project management system *guides* the life cycle of individual projects (which often last more than a year) and the planning process takes a multiyear view in assimilating technologies and systems to match the company's evolving needs and strategies, the IT management control system focuses primarily on guiding the entirety of the information technology department on a year-to-year basis. The management control system builds on the output of the planning process to develop a portfolio of projects, hardware/software enhancements and additions, facilities plans, and staffing levels for the year. It then monitors their progress, raising red flags for action when appropriate. The broad objectives an effective IT management control system must meet include the following:

1. Facilitate appropriate communication between the user and deliverer of IT services and provide motivational incentives for them to work together on a day-to-day, month-to-month basis. The management control system must encourage users and IT to act in the best interests of the organization as a whole. It must motivate users to use IT resources appropriately and help them balance investments in this area against those in other areas.

2. Encourage the effective utilization of the IT department's resources and ensure that users are educated on the potential of existing and evolving technology. In so doing, it must guide the transfer of technology consistent with strategic needs.

3. Provide the means for efficient management of IT resources and give necessary information for investment decisions. This requires development both of standards of performance measures and of the means to evaluate performance against those measures to ensure that productivity is being achieved. It should help facilitate make or buy decisions.

Early IT management control systems tended to be very cost focused, relying heavily, for example, upon return-on-investment (ROI) evaluations of capital investments. These systems proved workable in situations where the technology was installed on a cost displacement justification basis. However, in firms where the computer was a competitive wedge (CAD/CAM, or industrial robotics, today) or the technology was pervasively influencing the industry's structure of operations (such as in banking and financial services), cost analysis and displacement alone were not an appropriate measurement standard. Development of additional management control techniques has been necessary. For example, a large metropolitan bank several years ago instituted an expensive, complex chargeout system to improve user awareness of costs. Poorly thought out in broad context, the system generated a surge in demand for "cheap" minicomputers, triggered an overall decline in quality of central IT support, and ultimately created market image and sales difficulties for the bank as a whole. Recently the system was abandoned.

Four special inputs now appear to be critical to an appropriate IT management control system structure for an organization:

1. The control system must be adapted to a very different software and operations technology in the 1980s than was present in the 1970s. An important part of this adaptation is development of appropriate sensitivity to the mix of phases of information technologies in the company. The more mature technologies must be managed and controlled in a tighter, more efficient way than ones in an early start-up phase that need protective treatment appropriate to a research development activity.

2. Specific aspects of the corporate environment influence the appropriate IT management control system. Key issues here include IT sophistication of users, geographic dispersion of the organization, stability of the management team, the firm's overall size and structure, nature of the relationship between line and staff departments, and so on. These items influence what is workable.

3. The general architecture of the organization's overall corporate management control system and the philosophy underlying it influence IT control systems.

4. The system is affected by the perceived strategic significance of IT, in both the thrust of its applications portfolio and the role played by currently automated systems.

IT Evolution and Management Control

Software Issues

The management control problem posed by software development has become more complex. Because an increasing percentage of central data processing software support is for maintenance while most office automation (OA) software is bought, necessary operational changes to keep the business running have become intermixed with a stream of small, long-term, service-improving capital investments. Since these two streams are not easily merged in many organizations, controls on operating expense maintenance are often inappropriately applied to stimulate or choke off systems enhancements that are really capital investments.

A second software issue arises with outside software sourcing. As the percentage of development money devoted to outside software acquisition grows, management control systems designed for an environment where all sourcing was done internally may be inappropriate for environments now dominated by software make/buy alternatives.

Operations Issues

For IT operations, management control is complex because of the difficulty in measuring and allocating costs in a way that will encourage appropriate behavior in a situation where short-term costs are relatively fixed and there is considerable volatility in the mix of uses of the IT resource. The operations cost control problem has been further complicated by the cost behavior of IT over time. Technical change has created a world where the replacement for a previous computer generally has 4 to 10 times more capacity than the existing one while costing somewhat less than the purchase price of the original one. This has created an interesting control issue: Should the cost per unit of IT processing be lower in the early years (to reflect the lower load factor) so that it can be held flat over the life of the gear while permitting full (but not excessive) recovery of costs? Conversely, as utilization grows over the years, should the user's cost per unit of IT processing decline?

An example of coping with this problem is provided by a large insurance company that replaced an IBM 370/158 several years ago with an Amdahl V5, gaining four times the computing capacity at 15 percent less cost. Because the machine, after conversion, was loaded to barely 30 percent capacity, the managers were faced with the choice of spreading all the present costs among their current users or forecasting future costs (assuming future volume activity) and setting a three-year average that would recover costs at the period's end. The first approach would have covered expenses from the start but through its higher prices would inhibit the initiation of useful work that was economically justified long term. They therefore chose the three-year average cost as the price basis to encourage use and to pass on the immediate productivity improvement to their current users. The unabsorbed costs became part of corporate overhead.

The selection of a particular method of cost allocation varies with the firm's experience with technology. Many organizations' current control system gives to the user complete management of office automation, while giving the same authority to IT for communications. As we have noted, however, office automation and telecommunications are so interrelated as to make such a separation of management highly suspect. A critical contemporary problem is to ensure that IT control systems evolve along with changes in an organization's technical environment. For example, a large industrial organization gave free OA support to stimulate users while simultaneously charging for its traditional data base time-sharing decision support system. Very quickly users started creating their own data bases on the micro OA equipment, which both limited their OA experimentation and underutilized the time-sharing, thereby undercutting the firm's objectives. Our discussion of control structure, while recognizing these issues, does not attempt to definitely resolve them.

Corporate Culture Forces

The User Growth in Influence.   A major stimulant to growth in IT usage has been the emergence of a group of experienced IT users familiar with how to solve problems with information technology. After 20 years it is clear that effective applications by users generate additional ideas for use on their part. This is desirable and healthy, provided a control system exists to encourage appropriate appraisal of the new use's potential costs and benefits to the organization. The absence of such controls may result in explosive growth (often unprofitable and poorly managed), with new capacity required every one or two years, or alternatively little growth with frustrated users obtaining necessary services surreptitiously (and more expensively). Both events cause confidence in the IT department and its management control system to erode. Also, for many of the new generation of user demands, articulating benefits is more difficult than determining costs of provision. In repeated situations the control system has given the hard cost of an applications implementation undue weight against the soft but often very strategic management benefits.

The preceding discussion suggests a paradoxical aspect of controlling information services; namely that while the area is technologically complex, most of the critical success factors for its effective and efficient use are *highly* human dependent; thus posing very familiar management control challenges from a corporate perspective. A complicating element is that since both technology and user sophistication are continually changing, the types of applications are also changing. Many individuals are sufficiently set in their ways (reinforced by a control approach) that they find change difficult to implement and attempt to resist it. As a by-product, the user perceptions of the change agent (IT department) are often unnecessarily poor. For example, users attribute all sorts of spurious effects to the introduction of new computer systems, word processors, and so on.

External and Internal Factors. In addition to technology and user learning, hidden forces of change also exist in external items such as new tax laws and in internal strategic items such as adding customers or products, moving offices, and modifying the organization. Recognition and appropriate handling of these changes can be facilitated by a well-designed management control system.

Geographic and Organizational Structure. Other important control aspects relate to the organization's geographic dispersion and size. As the number of business sites grows and staff levels increase, often substantial changes are needed in organizational structure, corporate management control, and IT management control. Informal personnel supervision and control that fit the more limited setting will fall apart in the larger and more dispersed ones. Similarly the nature of relationships between line and staff departments within the company in general influences what relationship between the IT department and its users can be reasonably expected to evolve and thus the type of IT management control that is appropriate.

The organizational structure of the firm plays an important role in the IT management control architecture. Firms that have a strong functional organization with the central services function maintained as an unallocated cost center often find it appropriate to keep IT as an unallocated cost center. On the other hand, firms that are heavily decentralized into profit or investment centers or that have a tradition of charging out for corporate services are propelled down the path of charging for corporate IT activities, often going as far as setting it up as a profit or investment center. Over time it becomes increasingly difficult to manage with good results an IT organization where the control architecture is sharply different from that of the rest of the firm.

Corporate Planning and Control Process

In concept an appropriate IT planning and management control system should be similar to the corporate planning and control system. Ideally in both cases there should be a multiyear plan linked appropriately to the overall business strategy, which is also linked to a budget process that allows the responsible managers to negotiate an operating budget. As such, IT planning/budgeting should be compatible with overall business planning/budgeting. However, if business planning primarily consists of an annual budget with periodic follow-up of performance during the year, a very difficult environment exists for IT management control. In IT, implementation of any sizable change can easily take two or more years from beginning to end, including as much as a year to formulate, select, and refine the appropriate design approach. Thus an IT organization often must maintain at least a three-year view of its activities to ensure that resources are available to meet these demands. In many cases, this extends the IT planning horizon beyond the organization's planning horizon.

To be useful, IT project plans must systematically and precisely identify alternative steps for providing necessary service. For example, to upgrade reservation service in a large hotel chain the IT department, in concert with key hotel managers, had to project the type of service the hotels would need four years out. This was necessary in order to select the correct terminals and provide an orderly transition from the present situation to the new one over a 30-month period. A key bottleneck in this massive, one-time, 600-terminal installation was the total lack of a corporate planning and control approach that extended more than a year into the future.

This combination of short corporate time horizons, long IT time horizons, and technical innovation generates corporate conflict concerning management control. These conflicts, which can only be resolved by repeated judgments over time, involve two major clusters of managerial issues. First, how congruent/similar should the IT management control architecture and process be to that present in other parts of the organization? Where differences do exist, how can this dissonance be best managed? Should they be allowed to exist long term? Second, how can the tension between sound control and timely innovation best be balanced? Control typically depends on measuring costs against budgets, actual achievements versus predictions, and returns against investments. Innovation involves risk taking, gaining trial experience with emerging technologies, relying on faith, and at times moving forward despite a lack of clear objectives. A portfolio excessively balanced in either direction poses grave risks. (As will be discussed in Chapter 8, different companies will appropriately balance their portfolios quite differently.)

Strategic Impact of IT on the Corporation

An important input into how closely the IT control system should be matched to the business planning/control process is the strategic importance of IT for the next three years. If very strategic for the firm to achieve its goals, then development of a close linkage between corporate planning and control and IT planning and control is important, and differences between the two will cause great difficulty. Additionally IT investment decisions and key product development innovations must be subject to periodic top management review.

The control system for these strategic environments must encourage value-based innovations even though perhaps as few as one out of three will produce payoff. Often in this situation the key challenge is to encourage the generation, evaluation, and management of multiple and unplanned sources of suggestions for new services, while maintaining adequate control. Several now defunct brokerage houses and soon-to-be-merged banks were unable to do this.

If IT is not strategically core to the business but is more a factory or support-type effort, congruency of links to the rest of the business planning and control activities is not as critical. IT can more appropriately develop an independent planning and control process to deal with its need to manage a changing user demand and an evolving technology. A factory environment, for example, must emphasize efficiency controls, while a turnaround should focus upon effective utilization of new technology.

Looking Ahead: Other Aspects of Control

To achieve appropriate results the specific approach to IT management control must vary widely by organization, its specific context based on one or more of the dimensions discussed above and evolving over time. The rest of the chapter describes the key factors, beyond these contextual items, that influence selection of different forms of control architecture (financial), control process (financial and nonfinancial), and audit. Each aspect of control is briefly defined here and discussed in depth later in the chapter.

1. Control Architecture. Should the IT function be set up as an unallocated cost center, an allocated cost center, a profit center, or an investment or residual income center? Further, if costs are allocated from the IT function to the users, should the transfer price be market based, cost based, cost plus, split level, or negotiated? Each of these alternatives generates quite different behavior and motivation and is a fundamental decision that once made is not lightly changed. Finally, what nonfinancial measurements should be designed to facilitate effective use of IT?

2. Control Process (Financial and Nonfinancial). What form of action plan is most appropriate? Typically this is represented by the annual budget and drives both operations and project development. Particular attention will be given here to the issues surrounding zero-based budgeting. What forms of periodic reporting instruments and exception (against budget targets) reporting tools during the year are appropriate? These forms change much more frequently than architectural forms.

3. Audit Function. Issues here include ensuring that an IT audit function exists, that it is focused on appropriate problems, and that it has suitable staff.

Control Architecture

Unallocated Cost Center

Establishment of the IT department as an unallocated cost center is a widely used approach and has many advantages associated with it. As an essentially free resource to the users, it stimulates user requests and creates a climate conducive to user experimentation. This is particularly good for technologies in Phase 1 or 2 of their assimilation into the firm. The lack of red tape makes it easier for the IT department to sell its services. All the controversy and acrimony over the IT chargeout process is avoided, since no chargeout system exists. Further, very low expenditures need to be made on development and operations of IT accounting procedures.

In aggregate these factors make this a good alternative for situations where a small IT budget is present. Innovation is facilitated by settings where financial resource allocation is not a high-tension activity. A large western bank, operating as an unallocated cost center, has been introducing electronic mail and word processing for two years. Its intent is to build a network and establish standard procedures. The firm sees the short-run value of encouraging a growing network as outweighing the cost savings from a standard systems development.

On the other hand, significant problems exist when IT is treated as an unallocated cost center. With no financial pressure, the user can quickly perceive IT as a free resource where each user should be sure to get a piece of the action. This can rapidly generate a series of irresponsible user requests for service that may be difficult to turn down. Further, in a situation where staff or financial resources are short, the absence of a chargeout framework increases the possibility of excessive politicization around IT resource allocation decisions. The unallocated cost center also insulates the IT department from competitive pressures and external measures of performance, permitting the hiding of operational inefficiencies. Further, this approach fits the management control structure of some firms poorly (i.e., firms that have a strong tradition of charging out corporate staff services to users). Finally, an unallocated cost center poses particular problems for organizations where IT charges are perceived to be both large and strategic. In combination these pressures explain why, although many firms start with an unallocated cost center approach, they often evolve forward to another approach, at least for their more mature technologies and users.

One approach widely followed is to keep IT as an unallocated cost center but inform users through memos of what their development and operations charges would have been if a chargeout system was in place. Without raising the friction (described below) associated with chargeout procedures, this approach stimulates awareness by users that they are not using a free resource of the corporation and gives them a feel for the general magnitude of their charges. The approach is often adopted as a transitional measure when a firm is moving IT from an unallocated cost center to some other organizational form. Unfortunately, however, a memo about a charge does not have the same bite as the actual assignment of the charge.

Allocated Cost Center and Chargeout

Establishing the IT department as an allocated cost center has the immediate virtue, from a corporate perspective, of helping to stimulate honesty in user requests. This approach fits rather well the later phases of technology assimilation, where the usefulness of the technology has been widely communicated within the firm. While it opens up a debate about costs, it avoids controversy about whether an internal IT department should be perceived as a profit-making entity. An allocated approach particularly fits environments that have a strong tradition of corporate services charges.

Allocation Problems.   Inevitably the allocated cost center introduces a series of complexities and frictions, since such a system necessarily has arbitrary elements in it. The following paragraphs suggest some of the practical problems that come from allocating IT department costs to users (whether in a cost center or using some other approach).

The first problem is that the IT charges will be compared to IT charges prepared both by other companies in the same industry and by outside service organizations, raising the possibility of misleading and invidious conclusions. The words *misleading* and *invidious* are related because the prices prepared by other organizations often have one or more of the following characteristics:

1. The service being priced out is being treated as a by-product rather than as a joint costing problem.
2. IT is being treated under a different management control system from that present in the company making the evaluation. Thus cost comparison is highly misleading.
3. An independent IT services firm or an in-house operation selling services to outside customers may deliberately produce an artificially low price as a way of buying market share over a short-term horizon. Thus their prices may be perceived as fair market when in fact they are nothing of the sort.

Since the prices produced by other companies are not the result of an efficient market, comparing them to in-house prices may produce misleading data for management decisions.

Another issue of concern is innovation. Unless carefully managed, the chargeout system tends to discourage Phase 1 and Phase 2 research projects. These activities must be segregated and managed differently from projects utilizing the more mature technologies. In our view 100 percent of IT costs need not be charged to the users. Segregating as much as 15 percent to 25 percent as a separately managed R&D function to be included in corporate overhead is a sound strategy.

This is particularly important in the technology of the 1980s to ensure that artificial and inappropriate incentives are not stimulating improperly the installation of mini- and microcomputers. Repeatedly minicomputer systems have looked good to the user when their estimated costs were compared with the full-cost charges of a central IT installation. From the corporate perspective, however, when an incremental analysis of costs is done, a quite different picture may emerge.

On a more technical note today, in the majority of companies that are charging out IT costs two major concepts underlie the chargeout process. First, the chargeout system for IT operations costs uses a very complex formula (based on use of computer technology by an application) that spreads the costs in a supposedly equitable fashion to the ultimate users. Featuring terms such as EXCPs, the concept is that users should bear computer costs in relation to their pro rata use of the underlying resource. The second concept is that the chargeout system ensures that *all* costs of the activity are passed to consumers of the service. Not infrequently this involves reimbursement of all IT costs each month and certainly by year-end.

Rigorous application of these concepts has led to a number of unsatisfactory consequences from the user's perspective. Most important, the charges are absolutely *unintelligible* and *unpredictable* to the end user, as they are clothed in technical jargon and highly affected by whether it has been a heavy or light month in the IT department. There is no way for the user to predict or control them short of disengaging from the IT activity (hence the explosion of stand-alone minis).

Not infrequently the charges are highly *unstable*. The same application processing the same amount of data, run at the same time of the week or month will cost very different amounts depending on what else happens to be scheduled in the IT department during the month. In addition, if all unallocated costs are charged out to the users at the end of the year, they may be hit with an entirely unwelcome and unanticipated surprise, generating considerable hostility.

The charges tend to be *artificially high* in relation to incremental costs. As mentioned earlier, this can cause considerable IT-user friction and encourage examination of alternatives that optimize short-term cost behavior at the expense of the long-term strategic interests of the firm.

In addition, in both operations and development this approach makes no attempt to hold IT uniquely responsible for variances in IT efficiency. Rather, all efficiency variances are directly assigned to the ultimate users, creating additional friction and allegations of IT irresponsibility and mismanagement. Finally, administration of a chargeout system of this type frequently turns out to be very expensive.

These factors in combination have generated chargeout systems that do not satisfactorily meet the needs of many organizations. We believe this is a direct result of the technical and accounting foundations of the system. For most situations, technology and accounting are the wrong disciplines to bring to the problem. The task can be better approached as a problem in applied social psychology: What type of behavior do you want to trigger on the part of the IT organization and the users? What incentives can be provided to them to assure that as they move to meet their individual goals, they are moving in a more or less congruent fashion with the overall goals of the corporation?[1]

---

[1]Robert N. Anthony and James S. Reece, *Accounting: Text and Cases,* 6th ed. (Homewood, Ill.: Richard D. Irwin, 1979), pp. 778–79.

The design of such a system is a very complex task requiring trade-offs along multiple dimensions. As the corporation's needs change, the structures of the chargeout system will also appropriately change. Critical issues to be dealt with include:

1. Should the system be designed to encourage use of IT services (or components thereof) or should it set high barriers for potential investments? The answer for Phase 1 and Phase 2 technology projects will be different from that for Phase 3 and Phase 4 technology projects.
2. Should the system encourage IT to adopt an efficiency or an effectiveness focus? The answer may evolve over time.
3. Should the system favor use of IT department resources or encourage outside IT service sourcing decisions?
4. What steps must be taken to ensure that the system is congruent with the general control architecture in the organization or, if not congruent, to ensure an acceptable deviation?

Desirable Characteristics.   While the answers to these questions will dictate different solutions for different settings, some generalizations that fit most settings and represent the next step in the evolution of a chargeout system are possible. First of all, for an IT chargeout system to be effective in this environment it is critical that the users understand it. The corollary of understandability is that the system be simple. Again and again, evidence suggests that an IT operations chargeout system that is a gross distortion of the underlying electronics but that the user can understand is vastly preferable to a technically accurate system that no one can comprehend. User understanding encouraging even partial motivation and goal congruence is better than nothing. In this context systems that are based on an agreed-upon standard cost per unit are better than those that allocate all costs to whoever happened to use the system. Even better (and a clear trend today) is designing these standards not in IT resource units but in transactions that users understand (e.g., so much per paycheck, so much per order line, so much per inquiry).

A second desirable characteristic is that the IT operations chargeout system should be *perceived* as being fair and reasonable on all sides. In an absolute technical sense it doesn't have to be fair. It is enough that all involved believe that it is a fair and reasonable system. In this vein the IT operations chargeout system should produce replicable results. A job processing a certain level of transactions at 10 A.M. every Tuesday morning should cost the same thing week after week.

When it does not, an air of skepticism sets in that undermines the system's credibility.

A third desirable characteristic of an IT operations chargeout system is that it should separate IT efficiency issues from user utilization of the system. IT should be held responsible for its inefficiencies. Charging month-end or year-end cost variances to the user usually accomplishes no useful purpose. (It only raises the emotional temperature.) After appropriate analysis of the causes for the variance, it should properly be closed directly to corporate overhead.

IT Maintenance and Development Charges.　The issues involved in charging for IT maintenance and systems development are fundamentally different from those of IT operations and must be dealt with separately. In advance of development and maintenance expenditures of any size, a professional contract must be prepared between IT and the users (as though it were a relationship with an outside software company). Elements of a good contract include:

1. Estimates of the job costs are prepared by IT, and IT is held responsible for all costs in excess of this.
2. Procedures are established for reestimating and, if necessary, killing the job if changes in job scope occur.
3. If a job is bid on a time and materials basis (very frequent in the software industry), a clear understanding must be developed in advance with the user as to what represents such a change in scope that the contract should be reviewed.

For many systems, such as data base systems, the most challenging (sometimes impossible) task is to identify the definable user (or group thereof) with which to write the contract. Further, if the contract is written with one group of users and others subsequently join, are they charged at incremental cost, full cost, or full cost plus (because they have none of the development risks and are buying into a sure thing)? Neither easy nor general-purpose answers to these questions are possible.

A recently studied company provided computer services to 14 user groups, many of which had very similar needs. Operations expenses were spread in the following ways:

1. Every time a piece of data was inputted or extracted on a computer screen, a standard charge was levied on the user, irrespective of the type of processing system involved. This was understandable by the user.

2. Since all costs from the modems out (terminal, line) could be directly associated with a user in a completely understandable fashion, these charges were passed directly to the end user.

3. All report and other paper costs were charged to the user on a standard cost per ton basis, irrespective of the complexity of the system that generated them.

4. All over- or underrecovered variances were analyzed for indications of IT efficiency and then closed directly to a corporate overhead account, bypassing the users.

With respect to maintenance and development cost the following procedures were used:

1. Items budgeted for less than 40 hours were charged directly to the users at a standard rate per hour times the number of hours spent.

2. Projects budgeted to take more than 40 hours were estimated by the IT organization. If the estimate was acceptable to the user, work would be done. Any variances in relation to budget were debited or credited to the IT organization, with the user being billed only budget.

3. A job reestimating process was created to handle potential changes in job specification, with the users having the option of accepting the new costs, using the old specifications, or aborting the job.

4. Research and development projects were budgeted separately by the IT organization. IT was accountable to corporate for the costs of these jobs, and the users were not charged for them.

The combination of these items over a several-year period did a remarkable job of defusing the tensions in user-IT relationships, enabling them to work together more easily.

Profit Center

A third frequently discussed and used method of management control is the establishment of the IT department as a profit center. Advocates of this approach note that this puts the inside service on the same footing as an outside one and brings the pressures of the marketplace to bear on it. It consequently encourages the IT function to hold costs down through efficiency and to market itself more aggressively inside the company. This structure hastens the emergence of the IT marketing function, which if well managed will improve relationships with users. Further, excess IT capacity tends to be dealt with promptly by IT management, and they are willing to run more risks on the user service side.

Excess capacity also encourages sales of services by the IT department to outside firms, which has frequently turned out to be a mixed blessing. Often priced as incremental sales (rather than on a full-cost basis), not only are these sales unprofitable but many IT departments—excited by the volatile *hard* outside dollars as opposed to the captive *soft* inside ones—begin to give preferential treatment to these outside customers, with a resulting erosion of service to inside users.

Establishing IT as a profit center has other problems. First, significant concern is often raised inside the firm as to whether it is appropriate for an inside *service* department to establish itself as a profit center, particularly when it does not sell any products outside the company. "Profits come from outside sales, not service department practices" is the dominant complaint. The problem is further complicated by the fact that, because of geography, shared data files, and privacy and security reasons, many users do not have a legitimate alternative of going outside. Therefore the argument that the profit center is subject to normal market forces is widely perceived by many users to be a spurious one.

Setting up the IT activity as a profit center leads, at least in the short run, to higher user costs because a profit figure is added to the user costs. Not only can this create user hostility but in many settings it prevents the user from having legitimate full-cost data from the corporation for external pricing decisions.

In summary all of these issues must be addressed before an organization moves to install a profit center approach. A deceptively intriguing approach on the surface, it has many pitfalls underneath.

Investment Center

Many of the issues involved in establishing the IT activity as an investment center or residual income center (where a carrying charge for net assets employed is subtracted from the profit figure for both budget and actual performance) are similar to those involved in the establishment of IT as a profit center. The critical reason for moving in this direction (as opposed to a profit center) is to make the IT department fully responsible for the assets employed and force them to make appropriate trade-offs of investment versus additional profits. In a nonstrategic support role this may work well.

An IT department run as an investment center or residual income center must be managed very sensitively because it produces strong motivations to delay capacity expansion and to run close to the margin on service. Close monitoring is needed because it is easy to make a good short-term residual income through serious erosion in service levels. Another problem is that for these purposes almost no one worries about software as an asset, but the focus is only on hardware. This can result in serious misunderstanding about the real assets of the company and the amount of maintenance necessary to service them.

In general, if IT is to be held responsible for the profit–net asset trade-off, it is better to do it on residual income than on an ROI basis. When return on investment is used, high-ROI units are reluctant to make investments that would be to the overall benefit of the firm; conversely, low-ROI units are willing to make some marginal investments that would improve their ROI but are not in the best interest of the company. Residual income has every unit of a company thinking in the same way about the attractiveness of new investment.

An additional advantage of the IT unit being a stand-alone investment or residual income center is that it can be perceived as being fully neutral organizationally instead of being the captive of a particular business unit. Several years ago a multibank holding company found it attractive for this reason to spin the IT activity out of the lead bank and put it as a stand-alone unit (measured on residual income) in the holding company. Over the years the IT department's relationships with other member banks improved markedly as a result of this move, which allowed the department to be perceived as independent.

Transfer Pricing

When an IT activity is set up as a profit, investment, or residual income center, establishment of the IT transfer price becomes a critical issue. At least four different conceptual approaches are possible, each with specific strengths and weaknesses. (The issues involved are very similar in nature to those found in transfer pricing situations in general.)

For the purpose of this discussion we will assume that IT operations are being priced in end-user transaction terms (e.g., so much per paycheck, so much per invoice line, etc.), while for IT development and maintenance a fixed-price contract is being written. As described in our earlier discussion on chargeout issues, many other ways exist to approach these items. However, these assumptions are useful in order to introduce the different cluster of issues described in these paragraphs:

Cost-Based Price.   Assuming a full-cost method is used, this method has the advantage of producing the lowest cost from the user's perspective and is thus most likely to produce minimal user complaints. In this setting, establishing IT as a profit center is largely similar to making it a cost center, since profits can be earned only on internal sales by generating positive efficiency variances (obviously sales outside the company can be priced to generate a profit). This approach does not permit one to sidestep the previously mentioned issue as to what constitutes cost and how it should be determined (joint versus by-product, etc.).

A variant of this approach is a cost-plus basis. On the positive side this makes IT generate profits and at the same time provides an understandable number for users to deal with. On the negative side the users raise both the narrow issue of capriciousness in how the "plus" was selected and the broader issue of the general inappropriateness of an internal service department earning profits.

Market-Based Price. A key alternative, this method is used in many companies, particularly since the availability of outside services has grown. Its implementation, however, poses several problems similar to creating profit centers. The first is the near impossibility in many settings of finding comparable products and services to establish the market. Unique data bases or process control systems are examples of items where it is impossible to find them. Even so-called standardized services such as payroll and accounting turn out to have so many special ramifications and alternative designs as to make identification of a market price very elusive. Also, suppliers of IT services treat some IT products as a by-product. Still other organizations calculate prices for in-house use; they make no attempt at rigor but only attempt to achieve ballpark figures. Using these figures as market price surrogates invites difficulty.

Split-Level Price. This approach is designed to satisfy the motivational needs of the IT department and the key users simultaneously. As long as a single transfer price is used it is impossible to come up with a price that will both allow IT to feel that it is earning a fair profit and allow the users to be given prices that will permit them to manage aggregate costs in line with the company's overall interests. The pain can be spread around, but in the end it is reallocation of a finite amount of pain as opposed to its elimination. Split-level transfer pricing in IT works as follows:

1. The users are charged items at either direct or full cost, depending on the company's overall management control philosophy.
2. The IT department is allocated revenue based on a standard cost of services delivered, plus a standard fixed markup (or at a market price if a good one happens to exist). Improvements in actual profits vis-à-vis plan come either from selling more services than planned or from gaining unanticipated cost efficiencies.
3. The difference between the revenue of the IT department and the cost figure charged to the user is posted to an overhead expense account, which on a monthly basis is closed to corporate overhead.

This method, at least in theory, allows both the IT department and users to be simultaneously motivated to behave in the best overall corporate interest. Users are given appropriate economic trade-offs to consider, while IT is provided incentives both to operate efficiently and to sell extra services.

Split-level pricing has worked satisfactorily in a number of settings and has dramatically changed the tenor and quality of relationships where the accounting system now permits IT group and user to work together instead of against each other. Its Achilles' heel is that careful attention must be paid to the establishment of the cost target to ensure that the IT group is being asked to stretch enough and is not building excess slack into its budget. Also, implementation involves some additional accounting work.

Negotiated Price. This is quite difficult to execute in the IT business environment because the two parties often bring quite different strengths to the negotiating table. For example, systems that interface directly with other systems or that share proprietary data bases must be run by the central IT department, hence the negotiating positions of the two parties cannot be considered equal.

Summary

Many potential IT control architectures are possible. None represents a perfect general-purpose solution. The challenge is to pick the one that fits well enough the company's general management control culture, present user-IT relationships, and current state of IT sophistication. The typical firm has approached these issues in an evolutionary fashion rather than being able to get it "right" the first time.

Control Process (Financial and Nonfinancial)

Financial Reporting Process

The foundation of the IT management control process is the budgeting system. Put together under a very complex set of trade-offs and interlocked with the corporate budgeting process, its first objective is to provide a mechanism for appropriately allocating scarce financial resources. While the planning effort sets the broad framework for the IT activity, the budgeting process ensures fine-tuning in relation to staffing, hardware, and resource levels. A second important objective of budgeting is to set a dialogue in motion to ensure that organizational consensus is reached on the specific goals and possible short-term achievements of the IT activity. This is particularly important in organizations where the planning process is not well formed. Finally, the budget establishes a framework around which an early warning system for negative deviations can be built. Without a budget it is difficult to spot deviations in a deteriorating cost situation in time to take appropriate corrective action.

The budget system must involve senior management, IT management, and user groups. Its key outputs include establishing the planned service levels and costs of central operations, the amount of internal development and maintenance support to be implemented, and the amount and form of external services to be acquired. The planned central IT department service levels and their associated costs must flow from review of existing services and the approved application development portfolio as well as user desire for new services and the degree of available purchased service. In addition these planned service levels must take into account long-term systems maintenance needs. This ensures that appropriate controls are in place on purchased services (software and hardware, such as minis) as opposed to being focused only on the activities of the central IT department. The dialogue between users and the IT department on their forecast of needs and usage for the budget year helps generate an understanding of the IT department's goals and constraints that iteratively leads to a better IT plan as well as to clarification of what the user intends to provide.

To ensure that this happens, for example, a leading chemical company asks both the user and the IT department to develop two budgets, one for the same amount of dollars and headcount as last year and one for 10 percent more dollars and 2 percent more headcount. Typically the IT department's proposals involve an expansion of distributed services. To ensure communication the main descriptions of key items are all in user terms, such as the number of personnel records and types of pension planning support, with all the jargon relating to technical support issues being confined to appendixes. Both groups are asked in this process to rank services of critical importance as well as to identify those that are of lower priority or that are likely to be superseded. A senior management group then spends one day reviewing a joint presentation that "scopes" the budget in terms of probable levels of expenditure and develops a tentative ranking of priority. This meeting allows senior management to provide overall direction to the final budget negotiations between the two groups. The priorities coming out of these discussions are then consolidated by the IT manager for final approval. This modified, zero-based budgeting approach is judged to have provided good results in this setting.

The IT budget must establish benchmark dates for project progress, clarify type and timing of technical changeovers, and identify needed levels and mixes of personnel, as well as fix spending levels. A further mission is identifying key milestones and completion dates and tying them to the budget to ensure that periodic review and early detection of variance from plan can take place. Budgeting the key staff head count and levels is a particularly important management decision. A major cause for project overruns and delays in many situations is lack of talent available to support multiple projects in a timely manner. Shortage of personnel must be dealt with realistically in fitting projects together. (This needs to be done not just in the budget process but periodically through the year as well.)

An important benefit of involving both users and suppliers in the budget is the joint educational process. On the one hand, it helps the IT department to truly understand the particular needs of each business and to assess their real needs for IT support vis-à-vis other programs. On the other hand, the users develop an awareness of what is possible with available technology and better define their potential needs. For example, in one financial institution the budget process is used heavily as a stimulus for innovation. During budget preparation both user and IT unit take many trips to other installations and receive information from their hardware/software suppliers to generate thinking on potential new banking services. Over a several-year period this has significantly improved the relationship between the two groups.

Zero-Based Budgeting.   One of the dangers of the budgeting process is that it can become too routinized and incorporate successive layers of fat in the discretionary costs. An effective tool for separating out this fat in many organizations has been zero-based budgeting (ZBB). In practice most firms do not realize zero-based budgeting, because building a department's budget up from scratch would be prohibitively expensive. Rather each staff (as opposed to line) department begins by taking a 15 to 20 percent reduction in budget from the previous year and then identifies the services it can deliver for this amount of money that would best support the organization. This is called the base increment. The staff department then identifies in descending priority a series of discretionary increments of services, each with a price tag attached to it. (If it gets more money, here is how it will be spent, and here are the benefits.) This base increment and the associated sequence of prioritized discretionary increments then ascend through the various levels in the organizations. At each level they are reviewed for appropriateness and blended with increments from other departments. Finally, at the very top of the organization, the overall list of priorities is reviewed, and a line is drawn through the sheet of prioritized discretionary increments. Items above the line are funded, and those below the line are not funded. All departments do not have equally favorable outcomes in this process. A department whose mission is perceived to be vital in the coming year might have its budget increased by 51 percent, while two other departments, whose missions are decreasing in perceived significance, might have their budgets decreased.

ZBB is a reallocation process for marginal (optional) expenditures, not an aggregate budget reduction tool. Under ZBB it is perfectly appropriate for discretionary expenditures to rise in aggregate. This process has turned out to be very appropriate for the discretionary-level IT staff departments such as technical support, development, and planning. It is not so appropriate for manufacturing departments whose staffing is driven by the physical volume of work passing through it, such as computer operations, data entry, or maintenance.

Zero-based budgeting is attractive to IT organizations (particularly when it is also being done elsewhere in the firm) because it forces careful examination of all expenditures and should identify redundant or obsolete services. All too often in companies, realistic budgeting starts with last year's budget, and attempts are then made to add extra items to it. However, staffing and expenditure levels that made sense at one point in time may unfortunately have been obsolesced by later developments. Zero-based budgeting is an important discipline for ensuring that the layers of fat are exposed and peeled away.

Often ZBB's most important benefit is that it is a sharp change from the past. People are forced to budget in a very different way, with the positive by-product being that old ways of thinking are challenged and creativity is stimulated.

The theory behind ZBB is conceptually clean and sound. However, resolving the many problems of practical administration has been the key to whether it has been successful in specific situations. These problems are real, and failure to resolve them has turned ZBB into a very expensive game in some organizations.

First, effective ZBB is heavily dependent on good top-down communication within the corporation during planning. This is because ZBB is fundamentally a bottom-up process. If a clear understanding of corporate mission and departmental goals is not communicated to the department head who prepares the initial ZBB materials, the formation of the base package and discretionary increments may be so flawed as to prevent effective review and action when the package reaches senior level.

Further, since the priorities of different increments are reviewed in the organization chain of command, not until very late in the review process is general management input provided to the reviewers. By that time so much detail often is present that it is hard for management to gain the perspective needed to spot trends and meaningfully influence overall direction. Additionally, because the ranking process works up the organization hierarchy there is a substantial possibility of gamesmanship in the establishment of priorities.

The ZBB process takes place independent of the personnel system. Consequently a series of adjustments between different programs of activities may be suggested that turn out to be impossible from a personnel viewpoint. People are not infinitely retrainable, and simultaneous layoffs and hirings often have their hidden pitfalls, if indeed they are possible.

Critical to successful ZBB is the establishment of integrity in the base increment. In reality, the process of reviewing the priority of the discretionary increments at the senior level is often so time consuming that inadequate attention is paid to the base increments' contents. It therefore becomes an attractive hiding place for departmental pet projects that cannot stand the light of day.

Zero-based budgeting in its full-blown form is very time consuming and expensive. During a company turnaround year it is very useful and can produce significant benefits by finding layers of fat and stimulating creative ideas as to how they should be dealt with. Often, however, the same payoff is not present in immediately subsequent years, and a number of firms have moved to doing it only every three to four years (or conversely only a few departments each year).

Finally, ZBB with its one-year departmental focus runs directly contrary to the thrust of multiyear programs (which cut across a number of departments) and therefore poses dangers through bringing a nonintegrated short-term focus to the overall IT function. Related to this is the problem of how to develop a satisfactory approach for projects and service relationships between departments, where the service being offered is relatively low priority to the generating department but very high priority to the receiving department.

In combination these factors have tended to make ZBB a more useful ad hoc tool for the technical services and development groups than for the IT operations groups. The red tape and complexity associated with it make utilization every three to four years more attractive than annually. To get a payoff, however, requires that careful attention be paid to multiple administrative dimensions. Unassailable in logic, in reality it can be very frail.

Periodic Reporting.   Effective monitoring of the department's financial performance requires a variety of tools, most of which are common to other settings. These normally include a series of reports that highlight actual performance versus plan on a monthly basis; often this includes the generation of exception reports. Design and operation of these systems are rather routine. Obvious issues include the following: Are budget targets readjusted during the year through a forecasting mechanism? If so, is the key performance target actual versus budget or actual versus forecast? Are budgets modified for seasonal factors, or are they prepared on a basis of one-twelfth of the annual expense each month?

The IT financial reporting task is complicated by the fact that an IT organization requires a matrix cost reporting system as it grows in size. One side of the matrix is represented by the IT department structure and the need to track costs and variances by IT organizational unit; the other side of the matrix involves keeping track of costs and variances by programs or projects.

An issue that will be identified but not discussed in this book is whether budget numbers and actual results should be reported in nominal dollars or in inflation-adjusted dollars. Today this is an issue of major importance for corporate management control systems in general.

Nonfinancial Reporting Process

At least in an operational sense the nonfinancial controls are of more importance than financial ones in assuring management that the day-to-day and month-to-month aspects of the IT function remain on target. Critical items here include preparation of regular six-month surveys of user attitudes toward the IT support they are receiving. Not only do such surveys identify problems but they provide a benchmark against which progress can be measured over time. Their distribution to the users for completion also clearly communicates that IT is concerned about user perception of service. Problems surfacing in such a survey need to be acted on promptly if the survey is to be an effective control.

Another important set of controls is those relating to staff. Reports that monitor personnel turnover trends provide a critical early insight into the problems of this notoriously unstable group. These data allow timely action to be taken on items such as sensitivity of leadership, adequacy of salary levels, and working climate conditions. In the same vein, development of formal training plans and periodic measurement of progress toward their implementation is an important management tool in both ensuring a professionally relevant group and maintaining morale.

In IT operations, reports and other procedures for generating absolute measures of operational service levels are very important. These include data on items such as trends in network uptime, ability to meet schedules on batch jobs, average transaction response time by type of system, number of missends and other operational errors, and a customer complaint log. Critical to the effectiveness of these systems is that they be maintained and adhered to on a constant basis. It is easy to allow quality control errors to creep in and show better performance than is actually present. Those issues are discussed further in Chapter 9, with a particular emphasis on the fact that all dimensions of service cannot be simultaneously optimized. Additionally, reliable records concerning installed equipment and its location are important infrastructure data. Lack of sound, fact-based registers of equipment opens the possibility of excess equipment and inadequate and excessive payments of bills.

In relation to systems development the reports on development projects in terms of elapsed time and work-months expended (vis-à-vis budget) are a critical early warning system in assessing overall performance. The type of data needed and appropriately available varies widely by company. The company's maturity in dealing with information technology, the relative strategic role of IT development and operations, and the corporation's general approach to managerial control also influence both the form of these issues and the detail with which they are approached.

IT Audit Function[2]

Located as a part of the office of the general auditor, this function provides a vital check and balance on IT activity as it moves to meet cost and service goals. The elements of its basic mission are threefold. The first is to ensure that appropriate standards for IT development and operations have been developed and installed consistent with the control architecture. With changes in both technology and the organization's familiarity with it, development of these standards is not a one-time job but requires continuous effort.

The second element is to ensure that these standards are being adhered to by the various operating units. This includes both regular progress reviews and the conduct of surprise audits. Such audits should reduce exposure to fraud and loss. Ensuring adherence to these standards should help reduce operations errors and omissions and increase user confidence and satisfaction. Audits also act as a prod toward improving operating efficiency.

The third element is active involvement in both the systems' design and their maintenance functions to ensure that systems are designed to be easily auditable and that maintenance changes do not create unintended problems. This clearly compromises the supposedly independent mission of the auditor but is a necessary accommodation to the real world. Such involvement helps ensure the smooth running of

---

[2]This is an introductory discussion to emphasize the role and importance of auditing. For a fuller treatment see B. Allen, "Embezzler's Guide to the Computer," *Harvard Business Review,* July–August 1975.

the final system. Successful execution of all three mission elements helps to reduce the amount of outside assistance needed by the firm.

These apparently straightforward tasks have turned out to be very hard to implement in the real world. The three main causes of this IT auditing difficulty are discussed here.

1. The most important block is the difficulty in maintaining necessary auditing staff skills. Operating at the intersection of two disciplines (IT and auditing), good practice demands thorough mastery of both. In fact, because IT auditing frequently turns out to be a dead-end career path, staff members who can be retained are often sufficiently deficient in both disciplines to be ineligible as practitioners in either. Better salaries and visibly attractive career paths are essential preconditions to reversing this situation.

2. The art of IT auditing continually lags behind the challenges posed by new technologies. Today, understanding methodologies for controlling batch systems for computers is not very relevant for a world dominated by complex operating systems, networks, and on-line technologies. Managing catch-up for these lags poses a key IT auditing challenge for the foreseeable future.

3. There has been an unevenness of senior management support for IT auditing, due in part to the lack of formally defined requirements from an outside authority. Support for a strong IT auditing function tends to be very episodic, with periods of strong interest following conspicuous internal or external failure. This interest, however, tends to erode rapidly as time passes and the calamity is over.

The IT auditing function at this time has a poorly defined role in most organizations. Typically part of the internal auditing organization and often not reporting to senior management, this is a function that deserves serious consideration at that management level.

Summary

Many of these IT management control issues are clearly similar to the general issues of management control that face an organization. Several dimensions, however, do make them especially interesting. The first is posed by the rapid changes in the underlying technology and the long time span required for users to adapt to new technologies. The Phase 1 and Phase 2 technologies require a commitment to R&D and user learning that is in direct conflict with the chargeout techniques appropriate for the Phase 3 and Phase 4 technologies. It is very easy for an organization to become too uniform in its control system and to try to standardize in order to use systems "efficiently," stamping out appropriate innovation as a by-product. In most organizations today, different divisions (at separate stages of learning and using varying mixes of technologies) require quite different control approaches. Further, as organizational learning occurs, different types of control approaches become appropriate. Thus, quite apart from any breakthroughs in the general area of IT control approaches, their practice in an organization undergoes a continual process of evolution. In most organizations what constitutes good IT control practice changes continually.

As IT buries itself deeper into the fabric of an organization's operation, the penalties of uneven performance of technology may impose very severe consequences for the organization as a whole. As a company, department, or system evolves from turnaround to factory to support, very different control philosophies become appropriate.

When these thoughts are added to the issues discussed at the beginning of the chapter concerning the changing corporate environment and evolving corporate planning and control processes (in a world shifting from make to buy in software), the full complexity of the IT management control problem is apparent. Different organizations must adopt quite different control approaches, which must evolve over time to deal with a changing corporate environment, changing strategic role of IT, and changing technologies.

Case 7–1

Frito-Lay, Inc.
Funding for Information Systems

"In order to optimize our overall system, we may need to suboptimize some of the individual components. The trick is to get out in front and take a leadership position, even if you're not sure. There's disaster, which is not taking a position, and there's 'good enough,' which is using technology that does the job." Charles S. Feld, vice president–Management Services at Frito-Lay, Inc., was speaking in early 1986 about his approach to managing information systems at the Dallas-based snack food company. One of the major changes during Feld's five years as head of Management Services had been the design and implementation of a system for funding certain information systems activities through charges to users. The funding method appeared to Feld to be working well, and the company as a whole was prospering. Some users, however, were questioning the fairness of the system, one describing Feld in jest as "a crook—not only does he get other people to help negotiate his budget, but he's running the only overhead function in the company that shows a positive bottom line."

Feld himself was aware that the funding system might now require some adjustment to keep pace with the evolution of the business and technical environments it had been designed to match. "Whenever anybody tries to lay too much logic on this," he said of his approach to funding, "it falls apart. Nobody ever claimed it was fair—it is primarily a pragmatic approach that made reasonable sense to senior management."

This case was prepared by Michael R. Vitale.

399

EXHIBIT 1

PEPSICO, INC.
Financial Results
1983–1985
($ millions)

	1985	1984	1983
Net sales			
Soft drinks	$3,128.5	$2,908.4	$2,940.4
Snack foods[a]	2,847.1	2,709.2	2,430.1
Restaurants	2,081.1	1,833.5	1,529.4
Total	8,056.7	7,451.1	6,899.9
Foreign portion	951.9	963.9	1,128.6
Operating profits			
Soft drinks	263.9	246.4	126.2
Snack foods	401.0	393.9	347.7
Restaurants	194.0	175.2	154.3
Total	858.9	815.5	628.2
Foreign portion	66.7	35.5	(99.1)
Net income	$ 543.7	$ 212.5	$ 284.1

---

[a]The snack foods business segment included Frito-Lay and PepsiCo Foods International.
SOURCE: PepsiCo, Inc. Annual Report.

Company Background and Strategy

Frito-Lay, a division of PepsiCo, Inc. (see Exhibit 1), produced salty snacks (potato chips, corn chips, tortilla chips, pretzels, etc.), cookies, and other snack foods. The company had 35 manufacturing plants and six regional distribution centers. Frito-Lay products were delivered directly to more than 300,000 retailers by a sales force of some 10,000 route drivers. The company had doubled the number of items in its product line during 1985 and expected similar growth in the future. As snack foods, Frito-Lay products were characterized by perishable raw materials and a limited shelf life. The average selling price of these products was 70 cents. The company had 1985 sales of $2.5 billion and a 1990 revenue goal of $5 billion.

Frito-Lay characterized itself as having a lean staff—of the company's 26,000 employees, more than 24,000 were directly involved with making or selling products—and a bias for action. Frito-Lay headquarters employees tended to be relatively young, and were described by Feld as "positive, enthusiastic, and nondefensive."

Frito-Lay's sales had increased rapidly during the 1970s, but by 1982 growth had slowed. The company's routes had finally covered the entire country, and lower inflation meant fewer price increases. Moreover, other companies, including some very large tobacco, brewing, and consumer products firms, had started to produce snack foods that competed with Frito-Lay's products. In response, Frito-Lay adopted a more complex organizational structure that included a field marketing force, distribution directly from plants to large stores, and a regional focus for products and promotion. The company also gave increased attention to productivity and to new product development. In Feld's view, the keys to Frito-Lay's future success were research and development, which would create new products and new packaging techniques; process engineering, which would lower costs; and information technology, which would allow the company to collect, analyze, and use information about its increasingly competitive environment.

Management Services

Until 1970, Frito-Lay had relied entirely on an outside service bureau to perform its data processing chores. In that year, Charlie Feld, then an IBM systems engineer and later a sales representative, was assigned to the Frito-Lay account after the company bought its first in-house computer. Over the next 11 years Feld continued to work with the organization as it brought existing applications in-house and then began to develop new ones. Management Services, as the information systems group was called, reported to the chief financial officer, and one Frito-Lay manager recalled that as late as 1978 the company's applications were "99 percent accounting." Around that time, however, the first on-line applications were installed, and user demand began to grow rapidly. The company purchased its first personal computers in 1982, and the use of time-sharing increased dramatically.

Feld, who during his time at IBM had seen four data processing managers come and go at Frito-Lay, was hired by his former customer in 1981. As he later described the situation, "We were doing important stuff, but we weren't doing it consistently well." Management Services was experiencing 40 percent staff turnover per year and was making heavy use of contract programmers. Many users were dissatisfied with the time it took to get an application developed and with the quality of the resulting software. The general development approach at the time was for users to define systems, which were then designed and built by Management Services staff. Disagreements over whether a given application actually met its specifications were common, largely due to high employee turnover within Management Services.

In late 1981, Feld hired an outside consulting firm to assess Frito-Lay's use of information systems. The consultants found that the company had developed several significant applications of information

EXHIBIT 2 Management Services Headcount and Budget, 1980–1987 ($ millions)

Year	Headcount	Budget
1980	144	$12
1981	166	16
1982	222	19
1983	252	22
1984	282	26
1985	312	31
1986	325	36
1987	345 (projected)	51 (projected)

systems, and felt that Frito-Lay's overall technology position was strong. The firm, however, found weaknesses in the company's processes and controls for information systems, and criticized underfunding and the lack of organizational stability within Management Services. Most important, the consultants found no clear link between information systems and corporate strategy. "We were staff-driven, not business-driven," Feld said.

Feld and others felt that Frito-Lay's approach to funding was responsible for part of the discrepancy. At that time, the company's functional groups (sales, marketing, manufacturing, and distribution) outlined systems projects as part of their annual plans. These systems outlines were submitted to Management Services, which then set development priorities. The user groups had no central contact point with Management Services. The information systems budget (see Exhibit 2) was negotiated with top management by Management Services, which then allocated staff to the various functions. Users were not charged for systems development or operation.

Ernest W. Harris, who as director of Distribution Services had designed a vehicle scheduling system that became the company's first on-line application, recalled those earlier days as "a constant struggle to get things onto the data processing queue. It was every man for himself to get the available dollars. We never got firm commitments. The interface tended to be adversarial, with lots of finger-pointing and not much understanding." Harris felt that on-line systems tended to receive relatively low priority. "We had all these batch applications that required maintenance—and who is willing to take a risk and not fix the payroll system?" Harris himself had been able to get what he wanted from Management Services; he described himself as "hard nosed" and said, "I just intimidated my way through that organization. I find that this technique doesn't work so well anymore."

Funding for information systems received increased attention after a 1982 corporate edict limiting the growth of general and administrative expenses. The initial cap, 15 percent per year, was quickly reduced to 8 percent. As part of the general and administrative area, Management Services could not continue to increase its spending at the current rate of 35–40 percent per year and at the same time have the area comply with the expense limit. Either the company would have to cut back on information systems development, or it would be necessary to find another way to fund part of the cost.

To address the funding issue, Feld hired Dori Reap, then a member of the corporate planning staff, into a newly created Management Services position, manager of planning and control. As part of this job, Reap was asked to gather data and make recommendations for a new funding system. Reap began by identifying some objectives. First, users should be charged only for things over which they had control, for example, systems development. Second, the funding system should not require a large investment of people or money to develop and administer. Third, it was desirable to move quickly during a "window of opportunity"—personal computers and time-sharing were not yet in heavy use, and it would be some time before the new applications being conceived for sales and manufacturing would require large amounts of money to implement. The immediate impact on user budgets would therefore be relatively small. Finally, Feld wanted to achieve central control over information systems. At a meeting of Frito-Lay directors, Feld presented his philosophy on this point in a single slide:

Integration is the key to Economics.

Control is the key to Integration.

Leadership is the key to Control.

Vision and Execution are the keys to Leadership.

Given these objectives and the data she had gathered, Reap developed three funding alternatives. The corporation could do nothing, that is, it could continue to live with the current method. The corporation could charge users at the "micro level," that is, for specific use of hardware, staff time, and so on, meanwhile limiting the growth of the Management Services budget and restricting the functional groups with respect to end-user computing. Or the corporation could aim somewhere in between these options, with some services charged directly to users and others treated as overhead.

System Design and Implementation

The scheme chosen by Management Services, and approved by top management, charged the operating functions (sales, manufacturing, and distribution) directly for system development, and all users for data communications and for end-user hardware (terminals, personal computers, printers, modems, etc.) and software (Lotus 1–2–3, word processing packages, etc.). There were, however, no charges for use of the "central complex"—mainframe hardware and software, operations personnel, etc. In particular, there was no charge for running an applications program. Management Services also took on, as part of its budget, software development for the general and administrative area and all applications maintenance. On this basis, the 1982 budget would have broken down into roughly 20 percent direct user charges and 80 percent overhead.

When the new approach was announced in June 1982, users were told that they would have to include information systems expenses as part of their 1983 budget. As a starting point, users were given a 1983 budget equal to Management Services' budget expenses for 1982 on items that would be charged to users in the future ($3.3 million), plus the additional spending that had already been approved for the second half of that year ($1.5 million). Additions to this initial budget would have to be approved as part of the annual budget review process. Management Services offered to purchase at book value the several hundred personal computers that were already within the company and put them under the same nationwide service agreement that would cover new units purchased centrally. Virtually all of the existing personal computers were transferred to Management Services.

Charging for Equipment and Communications

By the end of 1985, the funding system had gone through its initial shakedown and was operating smoothly. Mary Cass, who with her staff of five was responsible for acquisition, installation, maintenance, and charging for data communications and end-user equipment, described that part of the system. "Our attitude about equipment is, if you want to own it, fine," Cass said, "but if it's not ours, we can't maintain the hardware or software, provide training, or offer network support." There were nearly 1,300 personal computers within Frito-Lay, plus thousands of terminals, printers, plotters, and other peripherals. About 20 units were owned directly by users, the rest by Management Services.

Users who wanted to buy equipment filled out an order form (see Exhibit 3) and got whatever approvals were required by their particular

EXHIBIT 3   Network Administration Equipment/Software
Order Form

GENERAL INFORMATION Please fill in all requested information
Contact Name_____
Function _____
Mailing Address(Field)_____
City_____ State_____ Zip_____
Office #/Floor(Hdqs)_____
Phone(   )_____ Date of Order_____

ORDER DESCRIPTION
Briefly describe the intent of the order_____

Is host connection desired? YES_____ NO_____ What systems will you need to access?_____
If a host connection is requested, what is the printer node name you want the device to print to?_____

SPECIAL INSTRUCTIONS
_____
_____
_____

CROSS CHARGE APPROVAL
User agrees to retain hardware for two years. Budget pricing will be determined and announced in July of each year for the following year. Beginning 1/1/86, Field Communications costs are fixed for the year and charged separately from the hardware costs.

For software purchases, user agrees to read and comply with software licensing agreements. Questions should be referred to the Law Department.

_____   _____
_____   _____
_____   _____   _____
AUTHORIZED SIGNATURES   DATE   CHARGE DIVLOC

TOTAL ONE-TIME CHARGES   _____(From Pg. 2)

TOTAL PERIOD CHARGES   _____(From Pg. 2)

If you have any questions, call (214) 353-5764

Return Completed Forms To: Network Administration
Plano Headquarters-4th floor

FOR NETWORK ADMINISTRATION USE ONLY

PROJECT #   _____
DATE ORDER RECEIVED   _____
TARGET COMPLETION DATE   _____

order(1)

EXHIBIT 3   Equipment List and Pricing

	QTY	ONE-TIME CHARGE	ONE-TIME TOTAL	PERIOD CHARGE HDQS	FIELD	PERIOD TOTAL
HOST TERMINALS						
IBM 3179	____	50	_____	91	64	____
IBM 3278 W/LIGHTPEN	____	60	_____	176	149	____
3270-XT W/MONITOR	____	160	_____	234	207	____
HOST PRINTERS						
MEDIUM SPEED IBM 3268	____	195	_____	412	385	____
HIGH SPEED IBM 3262	____	300	_____	464	437	____
STANDALONE PC DEVICES						
PC W/MONITOR	____	65	_____		110	____
XT W/MONITOR	____	65	_____		175	____
COMPAQ	____	50	_____		76	____
PC PRINTERS						
DIABLO 630	____	65	_____		67	____
IBM QUIETWRITER	____	65	_____		67	____
HP LASERJET PLUS	____	90	_____		115	____
EPSON FX85 (80 COLUMN)	____	25	_____		26	____
EPSON FX286 (132 COLUMN)	____	25	_____		28	____
HP THINKJET	____	450	_____			____
HP 6-PEN PLOTTER	____	50	_____		52	____
SOFTWARE *						
LOTUS 123	____	325	_____			
OFFICEWRITER W/SPELLER	____	290	_____			
GRAPHWRITER	____	425	_____			
OPTIONS AVAILABLE ON 3270-XT *						
PC GRAPHICS	____	450	_____	or	17	____
HOST GRAPHICS	____	650	_____			
2ND HALF-HEIGHT FLOPPY	____	333	_____			
2ND HALF-HEIGHT HARD	____	700	_____			
AST CARD	____	575	_____			
OTHER OPTIONS						
PC TERMINAL FURNITURE	____	250	_____			
MODEM	____	500	_____			
POWER STRIP	____	25	_____			
AB SWITCH	____	110	_____			
OTHER	____	____	_____		_____	____
TOTAL CHARGES (Record on Page 1)			━━━━			━━━━

*   If ordering for existing device, please provide the serial number of the system unit in the "Special Instructions" section. In addition, if ordering drives or software, provide the current drive configuration (i.e. full-height hard drive and two half-height floppy drives).

order(2)

group. The list of standard items was relatively short, but users were free to order any equipment or software they wanted. There was, however, no education, training, user assistance, or other support for items not on Management Services' standard list. Frito-Lay had negotiated volume purchase agreements with a number of suppliers, including IBM, that gave discounts of about 30 percent from retail prices. User prices were set at a level intended to make Cass's group break even each year.

Equipment purchased through Management Services was assembled and tested in Dallas. At that time, special menu-driven software and additional memory were installed on personal computers. The equipment was then delivered directly to the user and set up in its chosen location. Service requests were telephoned to a help desk in Dallas; if the problem appeared to be hardware-related then an employee of an outside contract maintenance firm would be dispatched to the user's site. Problems not related to hardware were handled directly by the help desk staff.

Data communications was charged at a fixed cost per location, based on the number of units in use and the telephone line charges. (Voice communications was run by a different part of Management Services and was charged for separately.) Cass's group also sent out bills for in-house time-sharing, which had about 150 user accounts. This service cost $4,000 per account per year for unlimited access to the mainframe and a large amount of disk storage. End-user tools, including the statistical package SAS and the report generator FOCUS, were available. There was no charge for using Frito-Lay's electronic mail system, which could be used to send messages, documents, and data files, or for the use of other on-line systems.

Asked to assess her group's impact on Frito-Lay's use of information systems, Cass replied, "In a way we stimulate demand, because we make it very easy. Without us the user has to locate a vendor, get three bids, fill out a capital appropriation request, and then worry about service." There had been relatively few complaints about equipment and communications charges, although some users were irritated by the amount of initial paperwork that had to be done, the lack of clear explanation of bills, and the length of time required to fill an order. (On the last point, Dori Reap commented, "We ask for 30 days, but in fact we can do anything in a week.")

Cass foresaw a potential problem as purchased equipment became fully depreciated. Terminals, for example, were on a three-year depreciation schedule with a 3 percent scrap value. "As users see this equipment coming off depreciation," she said, "they may expect to get it for free. We have continually explained that we work on a pooled average cost basis, under which we reduce *everybody's* expense by an appropriate amount as the equipment in the pool becomes fully depreciated. Also, maintenance and communications costs are continually incurred, and we provide lots of service, which is not free." All equipment of the same kind was billed at the same price, regardless of age; the price was adjusted to account for the steady downward trend of equipment costs.

Regarding the equipment policy, Ernest Harris commented, "Charlie Feld has done an extremely good job. He has always let user need drive acquisition—he has tried to coordinate, but never control. Of course, he couldn't have stopped users anyway, and he never could have met the demand for mainframe applications."

Charging for Applications Development

The funding process for applications development was also running smoothly, although with something less than total agreement from users. "I compare it to democracy," Feld said. "It's not perfect, but nobody has come up with anything better."

Under the new process, each functional group had a coordinator who served as the area's key contact with Management Services. The functional coordinator worked with the group during the annual planning process, which began in June, to develop a "wish list" of preliminary designs for desired applications. This list was sent to the group's applications development manager, a member of the Management Services staff who was responsible for liaison with that particular functional group. The applications development manager added to the wish list any projects that Management Services, based on its work with the group, thought the group should have, then prepared a staffing estimate for each project. The project specifications were typically quite vague at this point. "We try to talk with the users," noted Wayne Hyde, the systems development manager for manufacturing, "but a conversation of two hours is really a luxury. We expect ourselves to know enough about the business to know where to go for more information. We may try to sell a preliminary evaluation, two to three months long, for a particularly large or complicated project. Often we can't even get to the preliminary evaluation until the following year, but the eventual result is a better project list and clearer priorities."

After receiving the staffing estimates, users did a benefits assessment and assigned priorities to the projects. The user groups then negotiated with Management Services for staff. There was a fixed pool of developers assigned to each area (see Exhibit 4), and if more were needed, the users and Management Services negotiated jointly for the additional budget required. All development expenses were charged back to users at about $55,000 per person per year. Such charges were essen-

EXHIBIT 4 Management Services Organization Chart (1986)

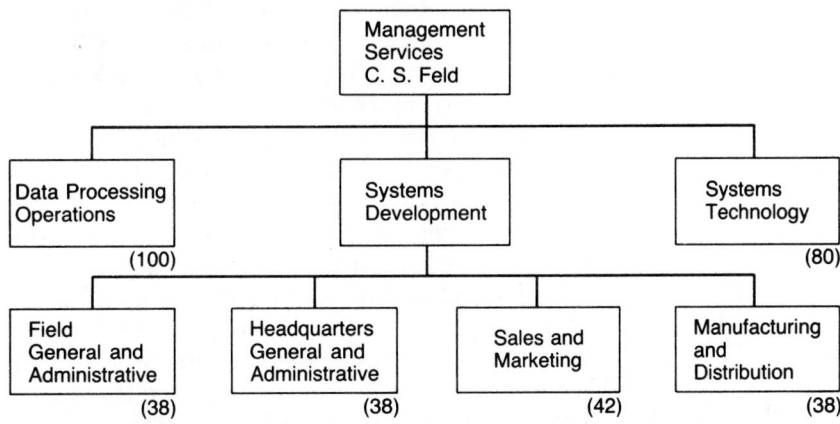

Figures in parentheses indicate the approximate number of personnel in each area.

SOURCE: Company records.

tially fixed once a project had been agreed upon; Charlie Feld noted, "We deliver the project for the estimate, unless the scope changes."

Some negative comments about the new funding system came from managers in the general and administrative area, which was considered "poor" since it had to live within the 8 percent corporate growth guidelines. Mike Miller, the director of accounting, said that it was difficult to get any attention for accounting systems until there was a crisis. Miller noted that in 1985 the clerks in the accounting function had worked almost 90,000 hours of overtime to meet processing and reporting deadlines. Much of this time was spent on tasks that could readily be automated or streamlined. As a result, Miller felt, some staff in his department were becoming frustrated, and morale was dropping. Miller also pointed out that a hand-held computer project now under way in the sales area was consuming a tremendous amount of programming resource. It was more difficult than ever to get approval for upgrading or replacing such "routine" systems as accounts payable or general ledger. Yet precisely these areas were beginning to feel the strain of all the changes under way.

Miller recognized that even the potential automation of the entire accounting group of 600 clerks would not make as large an economic impact on the company as would some of the other development projects that Management Services had under way. Nevertheless, he couldn't help but worry that one of the "routine" systems might become a serious financial or operating control weakness in the future.

Feld, who had been listening to Miller's remarks, added, "It's gotten to the point where Management Services is not working on the important things at all—there isn't time. All we work on are the crucial things."

From her new perspective in strategic planning to which she had moved in late 1985, Dori Reap looked back on the funding systems she had helped to create and said, "I think chargeback works great in general, but now it's time to tweak it a bit." Reap's 10-person staff shared a number of personal computers and terminals. By 7 A.M., Reap noted, every device was in use and there were lines waiting. "Some of my people are working very long hours and wasting a lot of their $50,000-per-year time. Others are being badly affected by stress. Our accounting system is inadequate, so we have to do lots of work and rework. I only have 10 people on my staff, and I can't afford to let one go so I can afford another computer. What's the solution—do less analysis?"

Another Frito-Lay manager noted that small staff groups without a clearly defined client tended to suffer under the new system. He recalled, for example, that the quality assurance group had wanted a system costing $150,000, about 15 percent of their annual budget. The group could not fit the new system into their annual plan, so they went to the vice president for manufacturing and got his support in asking for more money. The manager continued, "But the more esoteric groups—strategic planning, for instance—have no natural constituency, hence tend not to get much support."

Users generally felt that systems quality had improved markedly under the new funding scheme, as had their relationship with Management Services. From the Management Services perspective, the new system increased central control over development and was an incentive to do good systems planning. There were, however, some complaints. "The system involves a fixed charge for people," one manager noted, "even if there are vacancies. Basically, the user is agreeing to pay for headcount, not for outcomes. Users get no good day-to-day descriptions of the work being done. Systems will say this isn't happening, but trust me—it's exactly what's going on. I'm willing to go on trust over the short term because quality has gotten so much better. But my confidence is based more on the management of the Management Services function than on their control systems. Some people in the company don't have the trust level I do."

Case 7-2

Intercontrol Chemical Corporation

Cyrus Meredith, Assistant Vice President of Data Processing for Intercontrol Chemical Corporation (ICC), was engaged in a heated discussion concerning the establishment and role of a data processing internal audit function. Other major participants in the discussion were Gary Waters, ICC's newly appointed internal auditor, and Jerome Hart, a data processing management consultant. It was mid-June 1987, and Meredith had spent the last two years implementing changes recommended by Hart to ICC senior management. Some of the recommendations were contrary to proposals made by Meredith himself, but senior management had requested that he follow the consultant's strategy.

The meeting, scheduled to last one hour, was originally convened at 9 A.M. in the ICC board room on the top floor of ICC's plush 14-floor headquarters building overlooking the Wabash River in West Lafayette, Indiana. By 12:15, it had become apparent to Barry Loughton, Chairman of the ICC Board of Directors (see Exhibit 1), that Waters and Meredith needed to resolve substantial philosophical differences before a presentation could be made to the ICC Board's audit subcommittee. Loughton instructed Waters, Meredith, and Hart to continue their discussions in the office of ICC's Vice President for Finance, Doug

This case was prepared by James I. Cash, Jr.

Copyright © 1987 by the President and Fellows of Harvard College
Harvard Business School case 9–187–116 (Rev 2/87)

EXHIBIT 1 ICC Organization Chart

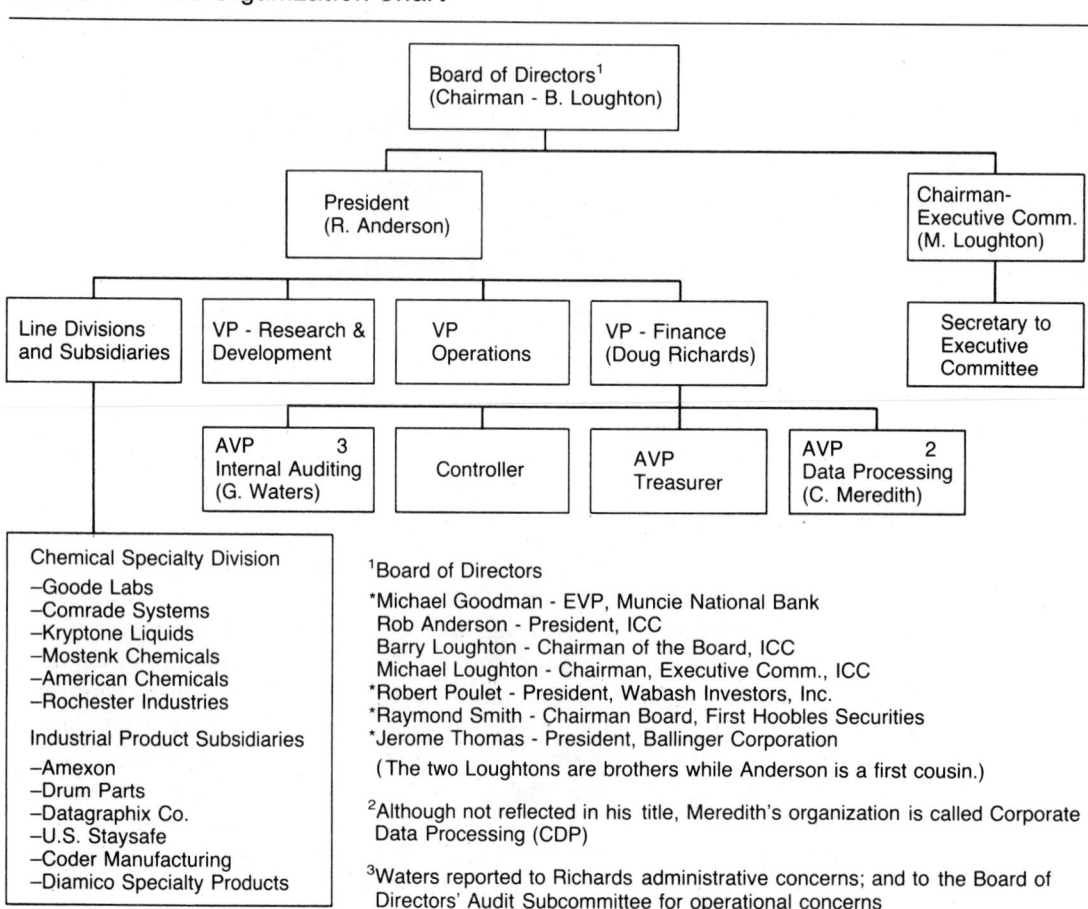

Chemical Specialty Division

–Goode Labs
–Comrade Systems
–Kryptone Liquids
–Mostenk Chemicals
–American Chemicals
–Rochester Industries

Industrial Product Subsidiaries

–Amexon
–Drum Parts
–Datagraphix Co.
–U.S. Staysafe
–Coder Manufacturing
–Diamico Specialty Products

[1]Board of Directors

*Michael Goodman - EVP, Muncie National Bank
 Rob Anderson - President, ICC
 Barry Loughton - Chairman of the Board, ICC
 Michael Loughton - Chairman, Executive Comm., ICC
*Robert Poulet - President, Wabash Investors, Inc.
*Raymond Smith - Chairman Board, First Hoobles Securities
*Jerome Thomas - President, Ballinger Corporation

(The two Loughtons are brothers while Anderson is a first cousin.)

[2]Although not reflected in his title, Meredith's organization is called Corporate Data Processing (CDP)

[3]Waters reported to Richards administrative concerns; and to the Board of Directors' Audit Subcommittee for operational concerns

---

*Audit committee.

Richards. Richards, who had been in the board room during the initial meeting, had direct management responsibility for both Waters and Meredith. Loughton stated he would regard Richards' recommendations on these matters as a final decision. As the meeting ended, Loughton made clear that it was an acceptable alternative *not* to establish the internal audit group.

As Meredith walked to the second meeting location, he reflected on the past two years. He felt that Hart's study had precipitated numerous unnecessary changes. Surely a small shop like his, in a very informal company, didn't need all the administrative systems of the larger companies with whom Hart spent most of his time. Meredith had considered leaving ICC in the past but had never been able to match the

ICC compensation package. He therefore dismissed any thoughts of pursuing that course of action and began preparing his arguments on issues related to the auditing group.

Company Background

Intercontrol Chemical Corporation was founded in 1948 by Barry Loughton to manufacture and distribute chemical products used in the maintenance of industrial equipment. After a very successful period with chemical maintenance products, ICC added new nonchemical products to its product line. Through an aggressive acquisitions program, ICC entered the business of replacement plumbing parts and maintenance tools. The most recent acquisition had been made in August 1986, with two potential acquisitions being considered for 1987. Additional growth was achieved by expanding into international markets. Foreign sales were conducted through wholly owned subsidiaries throughout the world, including Latin America and the Far East. The company operated 5 domestic and approximately 70 foreign subsidiaries; the latter provided approximately 50 percent of sales and profits.

At fiscal year-end (May 31, 1987) ICC employed approximately 8,375 people worldwide. As shown in Exhibit 2, net sales grew 24 percent to $402,901,040. Net income was up 23 percent to $34,934,200, and earnings per share were $3.25, as compared with $2.50 reported for fiscal 1986.

Competition in the industry was based primarily on price, service, and product performance. No one company or group of companies dominated the market. ICC emphasized service and product performance rather than price. Many ICC products were part of total maintenance systems that included equipment and tools to apply chemicals properly or to install and repair equipment. ICC's successful marketing/advertising strategy argued that customers could extend the life of

---

EXHIBIT 2

ICC HIGHLIGHTS
Years ended May 31

	1987	*1986*
Net sales	$402,901,040	$325,753,938
Net income	34,954,220	28,374,896
Earnings per share	3.25	2.50
Average number of shares outstanding	13,467,143	14,212,848
Treasury shares acquired:		
Number of shares	294,000	808,000
Cost of shares	$ 5,584,534	$ 12,999,210

EXHIBIT 2   *(concluded)*

Working capital	$121,597,250	$107,425,740
Total assets	269,692,561	221,097,142
Net capital expenditures	16,316,069	7,412,564
Long-term indebtedness	5,393,848	2,648,299
Stockholders' equity	173,541,384	149,919,654
Number of employees	8,375	7,541

HISTORICAL TREND

NET SALES in millions of dollars

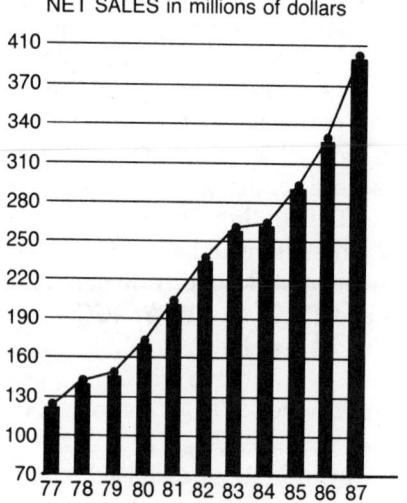

NET INCOME in millions of dollars

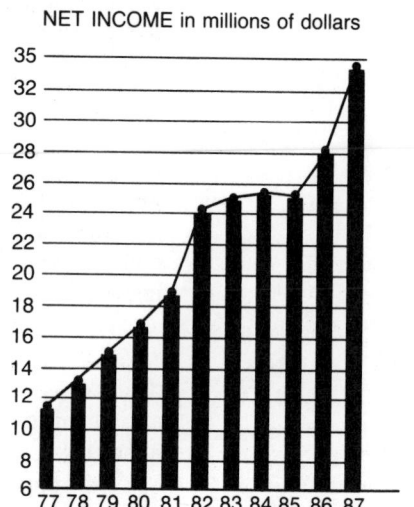

EARNINGS PER SHARE in dollars

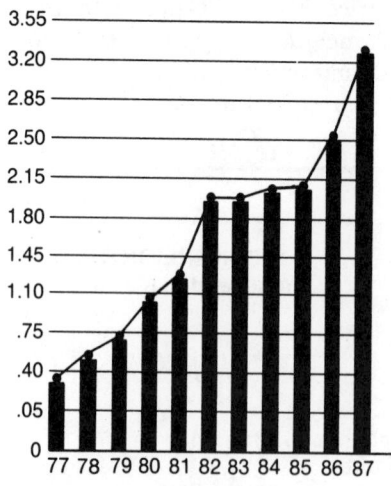

ANNUAL RATE
PER SHARE DIVIDEND
(at year end)

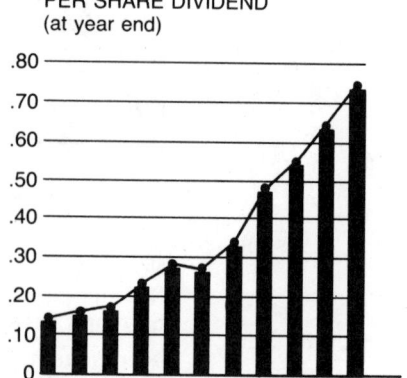

their facilities and equipment, thus delaying or avoiding costly purchases, if they used high-quality ICC products for scheduled preventive maintenance and repairs. ICC sales were not dependent upon a limited number of customers, with no particular customer accounting for even as much as 1 percent of total sales.

The company did not have a formal planning process but all executive committee members agreed that diversification and acquisition programs were expected to increase. This posed major challenges to the corporate organization, and specifically to the data processing group. Meredith suggested that this business strategy would require greater flexibility, application effectiveness, and technical proficiency than had been required in the past."

The Data Processing Department

Data processing activity in ICC had evolved as a highly centralized function. The Corporate Data Processing (CDP) Group (see Exhibit 3) supported both domestic and international operations. CDP, located in West Lafayette, maintained IBM 370/158 and 4381 mainframes that supported an extensive communication network. CDP also supported remote DEC VAX computers at seven branch facilities and at subsidiaries in Tucson, Arizona; Columbus, Ohio; and Austin, Texas. (Exhibit 4 illustrates the equipment configuration and communications network.) ICC corporatewide data processing costs totaled approximately $4.9 million and were distributed as shown below:

DP management staff and education	$ 171,364
Computer services	2,497,991
Domestic systems development	761,170
International data processing	
United States	526,680
Europe	627,625
Other	268,919

The CDP manager, Cyrus Meredith, was about 50 years of age and had never worked for another firm during his professional career. He joined ICC in 1958 after graduating from Purdue University with an engineering degree. During 1969 Meredith became the first, and thus far the only, director of data processing ever employed by ICC. During the late 1960s Meredith went to business school on a part-time basis and received an M.B.A. degree from Ball State.

EXHIBIT 3 CDP Organization Chart*

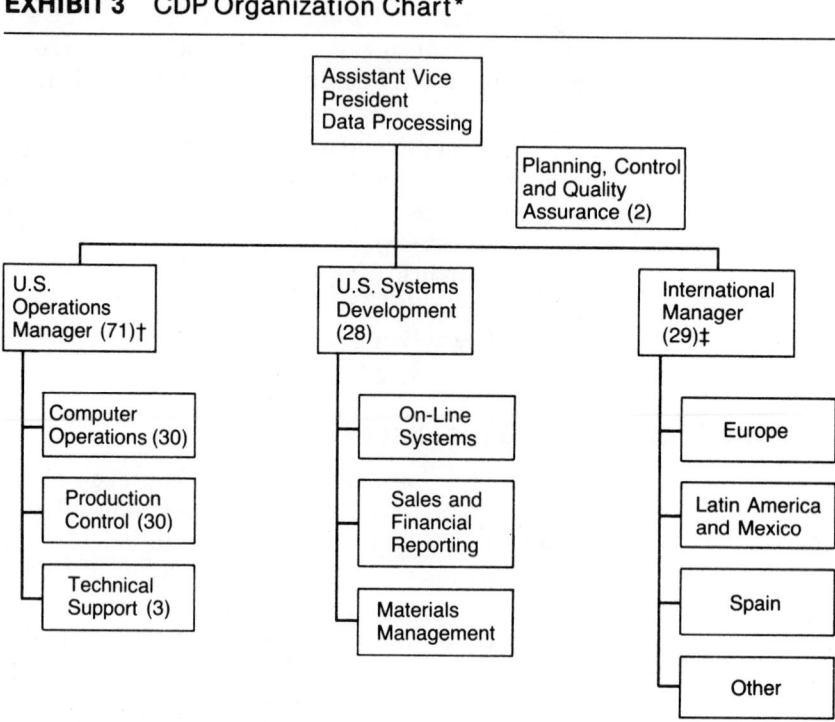

*Numbers in parentheses indicate size of workforce.
†Includes 26 data entry personnel.
‡International manager resides in England. Includes operations staff in Europe (5), Latin America (3), and Spain (2).

The Corporate Data Processing Group had developed various application systems to support the functional requirements of ICC. These applications fell into four classes:

- Order processing:
    Entry.
    Shipping.
    Credit.
    Collection.
    Invoices.
    Receivables.
- Sales reporting:
    Sales management performance reports.
    Statistical sales reports.
    Weekly and monthly sales comparisons.

EXHIBIT 4 ICC DP Equipment and Communications Network

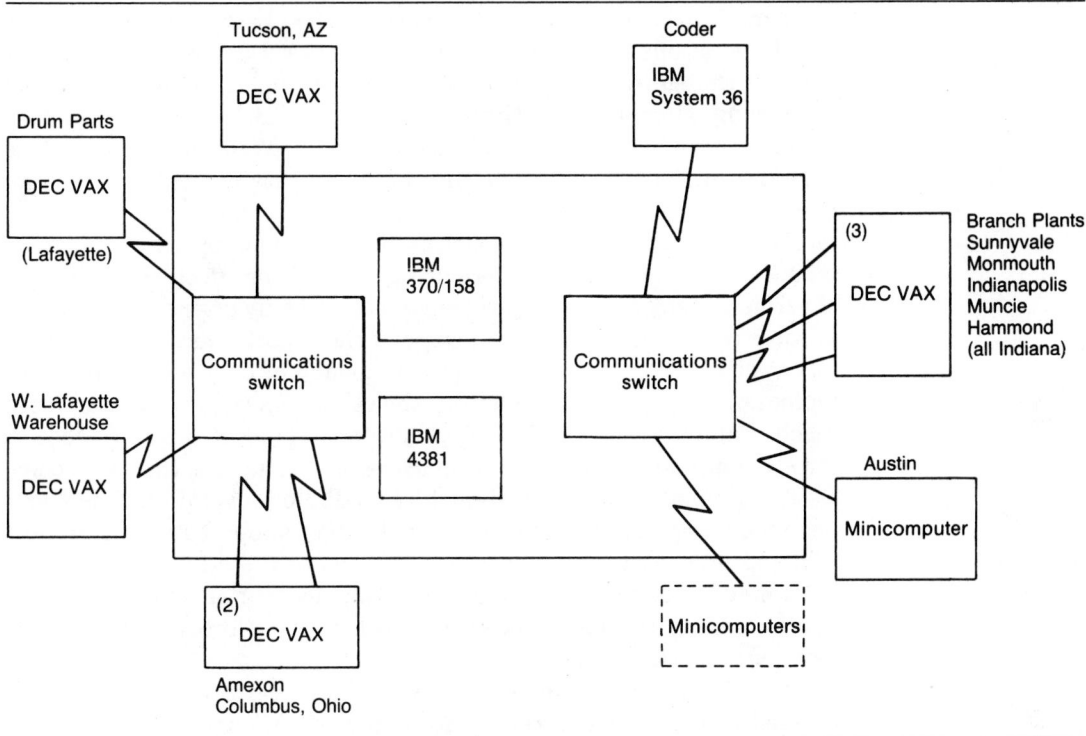

- Financial:
    General ledger.
    Payroll.
    Sales commissions.
- Manual control:
    Purchasing.
    Inventory.
    Work-order processing.

All of these systems had been developed internally by corporate data processing to support the information processing requirements of the chemicals business. Subsequently, as the diversification strategy of the company was implemented, these systems were extended to support the nonchemical business.

CDP managed most computing activity required by ICC's international divisions and subsidiaries. An international application development group (29 persons), located in England, provided programming support for most of Europe. The U.K.-based group operated an IBM 4341 computer that processed sales, commission, financial, and accounting information for the European offices. In some countries with small operations, the subsidiaries used local service bureaus. Finally, some of the subsidiaries operated their own minicomputers for order processing. Computing activities in Mexico and Latin America were overseen by a system designer who resided in West Lafayette but reported administratively to the International Data Processing Manager in England.

In early 1985, after the installation of a new operating system, mainframe users started experiencing a significant decline in the level of service. Many critical reports were received only after delays of three or more days; and, even worse, some of the reports were received with incorrect results. The number and frequency of operational mistakes increased while the turnover in the Data Processing Department reached an unprecedented level. Senior management began to receive strong complaints from European users, who criticized the service levels and project priorities assigned by CDP. For several months European managers had been requesting stronger support in their production and inventory control system. Instead of providing that service, data processing was planning and implementing the installation of minicomputers in some of the smaller countries of Europe and in several locations in Latin America.

Under a constant barrage of complaints, ICC upper management decided to hire a data processing management consulting firm. The consultants were asked to perform both management and operational audits of the data processing function, and to provide guidance for solving the service level problem.

The Consulting Study

The consultants confirmed the deteriorating level of service, and informed management that inadequate data processing policies and practices were the main cause of the ineffective delivery of computing support to users. The lack of a system development methodology and formal project management practices reduced responsiveness of programming services and increased the cost and time devoted to system maintenance. Operations management procedures were considered inadequate to support ongoing production needs. Other deficiencies mentioned were the lack of budget control, the limited use of cost-benefit analysis, and the insufficient monitoring of companywide EDP costs.

The consultants' report recommended the development of an operational plan to improve the data processing service levels. The main components of this plan suggested establishment of the following policies:

- Machine loading and job scheduling.
- Operating errors and procedure controls.
- Quality control assurance.
- Tape and disk management.
- Back-up and security.
- Disaster planning.
- User and internal coordination forums.
- Senior management steering committee.
- Formal acceptance testing and change control.
- Documentation maintenance and procedures.
- Resource management and performance monitoring.
- Strategic planning.

The CDP management team was not pleased with the report. In addition to its very negative tone, the proposals set forth a totally different strategic direction than CDP had been pursuing, for example with respect to the installation of minicomputers in smaller countries. CDP management worried that their credibility with top management had declined as a result of the report.

Events Leading to the Meeting

During 1985 and 1986 most of the consultants' recommendations were implemented. Jerome Hart or another member of the original consulting team made follow-up reviews every six months during this two year period. The reviews indicated that CDP was making substantial progress in addressing concerns listed in the study. In early 1987, the consultants recommended that an EDP audit function was imperative to monitor the performance of the data processing function on a continuing basis.

Coincidentally, the current internal audit staff manager was retiring, and Doug Richards thought this was an opportunity to hire a person capable of managing both financial and data processing auditors.

In explaining why he desired that his lead internal auditor have the ability to manage data processing auditors, Richards replied:

A number of forces have focused my attention on this skill mix. First, our management team has become increasingly dependent on data processing for controlling activities in their functional areas. As we have geographically expanded our business, data that has a high degree of integrity is critical to provide for consistent corporatewide planning, evaluation, and control decisions. I think EDP internal auditing is one mechanism to protect the integrity of our data. Second, there have been some spectacular losses reported in companies that didn't pay enough attention to adequate internal controls and Q/C [quality control] in their EDP systems. The one case that comes to mind immediately is the Equity Funding scandal. Finally, and most important to me, is the Foreign Corrupt Practices Act (FCPA). FCPA, as a matter of law, now mandates that companies subject to the securities laws maintain a system of internal accounting control sufficient to provide reasonable assurance that:

- Transactions are executed in accordance with management's authorization.
- Transactions are recorded so as to permit preparation of financial statements in accordance with GAAP (generally accepted accounting principles) or other criteria applicable to such statements and to maintain accountability for assets.
- Access to assets is permitted only in accordance with management's authorization.
- Recorded assets are compared with existing assets at reasonable intervals and appropriate action is taken with respect to any differences.

Many attributes of our internal control system that address these requirements are buried in our EDP systems. Therefore we need a verification and compliance checking mechanism for EDP, which most logically should reside in the internal audit department.

Recruiting a new lead internal auditor with the skill mix he wanted was more difficult than Richards initially anticipated, and salaries for such persons seemed excessive. Finally, with help from the management consulting firm that employed Jerome Hart, Richards located and hired Gary Waters for the position.

Waters, 42 years of age, had extensive formal business education. He acquired both undergraduate and graduate business degrees in accounting. He was a CPA and had worked as a financial auditor with three different public accounting firms during the first nine years of his career. In the next five-year period (age 33–37) he worked as Controller and Information Systems Director for a small ($110 million in sales) manufacturing company. During the five years prior to joining ICC, Waters was Director of Operations for a medium-sized insurance company ($300 million annual premium income) where the lead data processing manager reported to him. Waters described his decisions for major career changes as follows:

My decision to leave public accounting was because financial auditing became boring. I was one year from becoming a senior manager and five or six years from becoming a partner, but couldn't see myself doing that type of work for the remainder of my career. Because EDP was having a dramatic effect on my profession, and on business in general, I decided a job involving EDP would be the most challenging and interesting. After a couple of jobs in which I had responsibility for the EDP organization, I began to miss some of the challenges and rewards obtainable when working in an auditing role. The ICC job presented me with an opportunity to bring these two worlds together.

Waters joined ICC May 1, 1987. During his first six weeks in the new job Waters spent most of his time trying to develop a plan for establishment of a data processing auditing capability in the internal auditing department. Waters' initial assessment of the financial operational audit area of his department was very positive, and thus he decided there was almost no need for work in that area. However, there was no prior activity or concentrated expertise for EDP auditing. Any need to review or verify data processing results was handled by "auditing around the computer."

Waters followed an outline (shown in Exhibit 5) as he pulled together a proposal for establishing the new area in his department. His initial thoughts on an appropriate organization structure for the new area are shown in Exhibit 6. Waters used Jerome Hart to help refine his thinking on these matters and in early June arranged a meeting with Cyrus Meredith to share his current thoughts on role, scope, organization, and implementation of the new area. Forty-five minutes into the discussion, Meredith called Richards (Waters remained in Meredith's office) to convey his "total disagreement" with Waters on almost every key issue—especially the implementation time frame Waters planned to adopt. Meredith told Richards in part:

> Although I think Gary developed an excellent framework for thinking about this area, I'm afraid he's been contaminated by Hart's big company perspective and insensitivity to the ICC culture. With all the changes implemented in the last two years, it would be devastating to hit CDP with internal auditors. As you know, we've lost a number of programmers as a result of formalizing system development and introducing formal project management that requires them to log their activity. Many of them interpret introduction of those administrative systems as an expression of senior management's lack of confidence in our organization. If Gary brings half-cocked auditors into our shops before the end of

---

EXHIBIT 5 Waters' Approach to Establishing the EDP Internal Audit Function

---

I. Define objective [done—May 6].

   To work with other members of the internal audit department, and to assist all members of management who use computer facilities or provide computer services, in the effective and efficient discharge of their responsibilities by furnishing them with analyses, appraisals, recommendations, and pertinent comments on all activities of the data processing department.

II. Obtain mandate from management [done—May 13].

   Make formal presentation to management addressing following issues: objective, need, projected cost, risks, and benefits.

III. Identify key issues [done—May 19].
   A. Establishing the area.
       1. Initial staffing, career management, and training.
       2. Internal organization.
       3. External organization.
       4. Development of policies, standards, and procedures.
       5. Salary base (auditing or data processing).
   B. Role and scope of activity.
       1. Systems development.
       2. Operations.
       3. Existing application systems.
       4. DP administration and control.
       5. Assist function (financial and external auditors).
   C. Process issues.
       1. Audit planning.   4. Developing findings.
       2. Initial surveys.   5. Reporting.
       3. Communication.   6. Follow-up.

IV. Discuss key issues with interested managers [in progress].

V. Present proposal to audit subcommittee [scheduled for July 2].

VI. Hire/move personnel [following July 2 audit approval].

VII. Implement [end of year].

---

the year, as he currently plans, I may lose my entire programming team.

Unknown to Waters or Meredith, Richards took the call over his speaker phone. Barry Loughton, who was sitting in Richards' office during the conversation, overheard Meredith's concerns. Loughton had planned to have Waters present his proposal in the July 2 audit subcommittee meeting. The audit subcommittee was very eager to have an EDP auditing capability inside the company.

EXHIBIT 6 Gary Waters' Proposed Organization for ICC's Internal Audit Function

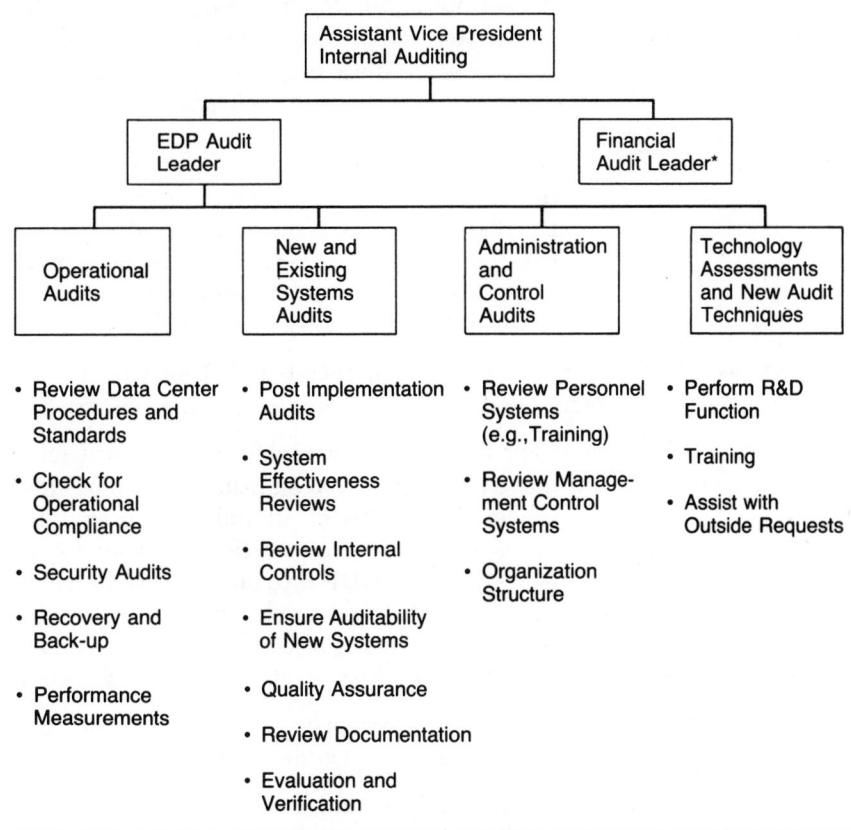

*There are currently six people in the Financial Audit Group (including the audit leader).

Loughton's first thought was to take Waters' proposal off the agenda for the subcommittee meeting. Richards suggested that a brief meeting involving Loughton, Waters, Meredith, Hart, and Richards might resolve the differences. The meeting was initially scheduled for June 17, and then rescheduled for June 20.

Other Views

Stan Newlin, partner in charge of the account for ICC's public accounting firm, was supportive of the move to establish the data processing internal audit function:

We [the CPA firm] have listed the lack of such a function as a glaring weakness of the overall ICC internal control system in our last three audits. I think everyone concerned would benefit. ICC's bill for our audit would be reduced; top management and the audit committee could attach greater credibility to their overall control mechanisms; data processing would get more frequent and less contentious reviews of their activities; we [CPA firm] would have a well defined entry point for our review of data processing controls; and finally, we could use this group [DP internal audit] in some phases of our "processing results" review and gathering of evidential matter. . . . The issues of role and scope of the group must be decided within the company. There are no general guidelines. However, a significant trend to "operational auditing," which ICC has followed, impacts this decision as well.

John Conrad, financial audit leader in ICC's internal audit department, also supported establishing the new function:

to provide better service for the corporation. Our financial staff has moved to operational auditing. We define this approach as the comprehensive review of administrative systems practice and procedures, in addition to traditional financial systems reviews. . . . The penetration of EDP into our operational systems requires that we have the capability to review data processing functions. We have been totally inadequate in the EDP area and cannot profess to thoroughly examine our systems without such expertise.

When asked how receptive managers around the corporation had been to the new operational auditing role, Conrad replied:

There is inherent contention between auditee and auditor regardless of any specific context you may want to examine. ICC managers, in general, have not been receptive to our expanded role. They generally seem to think that "bean counters" cannot and/or should not become general management consultants. However, we were commissioned in June 1979 by the audit subcommittee of our Board to pursue the expanded role and, I guess, ICC management will have to learn to live with us!

The Meeting

Although most participants arrived about 8:45, the meeting began about 9:05 when Loughton arrived. Everyone agreed that they were eager to resolve the differences and "get back to the desk." As each major issue was discussed, it became apparent to Loughton that Meredith was in virtually total opposition to Waters' proposals. (Comments during the meeting are organized by issue in Exhibit 7.) The major theme was Meredith's concern about the need for such formalism in ICC. He insisted that continued revamping of procedures and auditors would precipitate a mass resignation of CDP personnel. Waters and Hart also sounded convincing while conveying the risk of significant losses if their proposals weren't adopted. After more than three hours of discussion and minimal progress towards significant agreement, Loughton suggested they move to Richards' office.

As the second meeting convened, Jerome Hart turned to Meredith and said, "Cyrus, I think you are missing a key issue here. If the EDP audit group is successfully established, you may never see me again! They will perform the services we've been providing."

Meredith replied: "Jerome, the prospect of getting you out of my hair provides almost enough incentive for me to agree with all of Gary's suggestions!"

EXHIBIT 7 International Chemical Corporation: Excerpts from the June 20th Meeting

Issue	Description	Gary Waters	Cyrus Meredith
Staffing, career management and training	What should be the skill mix of initial staff, and what are their career path options?	"We should hire top processing professionals and provide training in audit procedures and practice. They should have keen business acumen, which will facilitate movement into line management. I expect that good people will have offers to leave IA (internal auditing) within the first two years of work on our staff. . . . I will strongly support an up-and-out process."	"Given the shortage of data processing professionals, your approach isn't viable. We're currently 10 percent under our alloted headcount. . . . Your plan to turn over employees on a two-year basis really worries me. This ensures we will have inexperienced people making redundant findings and reports. In addition, you will have significant incremental training costs, and I am willing to bet you will have low-quality work being performed."
Internal organization	How will the IA group be organized?	(Waters' proposal for an organization structure is shown in Exhibit 6.)	"Your proposal isn't consistent with the skill and experience mix your auditors will have given the decisions on career path. There is no responsibility structure for training."
External organization	Where will IA report in overall corporate structure?	To promote independence this capability should report in the IA group.	"These people should be part of my quality assurance function. This would permit their training and insight into the technology to remain current. I don't understand how you plan to evaluate these people without my input."
Developing policies, procedures, and standards	How are policies, procedures, and standards for this function developed?	"We should borrow some procedures from financial IA. . . . The best option is to engage a consulting (or 'advisory services' component of a public accounting firm) and piggy-back on their study."	"Hire an experienced individual from outside and establish a tailored (customized) version of his or her experience."

Salary basis	"Salary must be consistent with financial auditing staff since they reside in the same organization."	"This issue illustrates why your (external) organization decision is incorrect. You will not be able to recruit or retain qualified people using auditing salary ranges."
Role and scope		
1. Should auditors be members of new system development team?	"Yes. . . . This would ensure systems will be available and adhere to appropriate internal control guidelines. Furthermore, it will serve as a training mechanism for the auditors."	"Absolutely not. They slow the development process and unconsciously inhibit the use of new technological approaches as they force traditional control techniques on a new environment. We already have a backlog of activity without their help!
2. To what level of depth should IA review operations?	"We should focus primarily on security, procedure integrity (adherence to standards and controls), and performance measurement."	"My DP folks will enjoy blowing smoke at IA's! But more seriously, your staff should focus primarily on hardware and physical reviews."
3. Should IA review systems currently in production?	"Check for compliance with designed controls; and to perform application effectiveness and sunset review."	"Those reviews are part of the planning process we implemented last year. Our quality assurance group should be monitoring this."
4. Should IA review and critique DP management's administrative and control systems?	"Yes, IA should examine administrative processes (e.g., planning, personnel reviews, organization structure, charging system)."	"Absolutely not, that is the reason I report to Doug Richards.

Chapter 8

A Portfolio Approach to IT Development

A major industrial products company discovers one and a half months before the installation date for a computer system that a $15 million effort to convert from one manufacturer to another is in trouble and installation must be delayed a year. Eighteen months later the changeover has still not taken place.

A large consumer products company budgets $250,000 for a new computer-based personnel information system to be ready in nine months. Two years later $2.5 million has been spent, and an estimated $3.6 million more is needed to complete the job. The company has to stop the project.

A sizable financial institution slips $3 million over budget and has to decommit two thirds of its plan for the development of programs for a new financial systems package, vital for the new competitive systems.

Nine months after it had installed a state-of-the-art office automation system for $900,000, a Midwest mail-order house found that 50 percent of the terminals were unused and 90 percent of the work was simple word processing. Further, the communications system was incompatible with the main data processing, and system support was unobtainable. They returned the system.

Stories from the Stage 1 and Stage 2 days of the late 1960s and early 1970s?[1] Unfortunately not! Although it is almost too embarrassing to admit, the day of the big disaster on a major information technology (IT) project has not passed. Given business's more than 30 years of IT experience, the question is: Why? An analysis of these cases (these are domestic companies; we could have selected equally dramatic examples from overseas) and firsthand acquaintance with a number of IT projects in the past 10 years suggest three serious deficiencies in practice that involve both general management and IT management: (1) failure to assess the individual project implementation risk at the time a project is funded; (2) failure to consider the aggregate implementation risk of the portfolio of projects; (3) lack of recognition that different projects require different managerial approaches.

These aspects of the IT project management and development process are so important that we have chosen to deal with them here, in a separate chapter. Chapter 9 will discuss project management in terms of how differences in corporate cultures and perceived strategic relevance of the technology influence the balance of control between IT and the user over different parts of the project management life cycle. Since many projects have multiyear life cycles, these project management issues have to be dealt with separately from those of the management control system with its calendar-year focus, as discussed in Chapter 7.

Project Risk

Elements of Project Implementation Risk

In discussing risk, we are assuming that the manager has brought appropriate methods and approaches to bear on the project (mismanagement is obviously another element of risk). Implementation risk, by definition here, is what remains after application of proper tools. In our discussion, we are also not implying a correlation between the terms *risk* and *bad.* These words represent entirely different concepts, and the link between the two normally is that higher-risk projects must yield higher benefits to compensate for the increased downside exposure.

The typical project feasibility study covers exhaustively such topics as financial benefits, qualitative benefits, implementation costs, target milestone and completion dates, and necessary staffing levels.

---

[1]Richard L. Nolan and Cyrus F. Gibson, "Managing the Four Stages of EDP Growth," *Harvard Business Review,* January–February 1974, p. 76.

In precise, crisp terms the developers of these estimates provide voluminous supporting documentation. Only rarely, however, do they deal frankly with the risks of slippage in time, cost overrun, technical shortfall, or outright failure. Rather they deny the existence of such possibilities by ignoring them. They assume the appropriate human skills, controls, and so on, are in place to ensure success.

Consequences of Risk. By risk we are suggesting exposure to such consequences as:

1. Failure to obtain all or even any of the anticipated benefits because of implementation difficulties.
2. Implementation costs that are much greater than expected.
3. Implementation time that is much greater than expected.
4. Technical performance of resulting systems that turns out to be significantly below estimate.
5. Incompatibility of the system with the selected hardware and software.

In practical situations, of course, these kinds of risk are not independent of each other; rather, they are closely related.

Dimensions Influencing Inherent Risk. At least three important project dimensions influence the inherent implementation risk:

1. Project Size. The larger the project is in dollar expense, staffing levels, elapsed time, and number of departments affected by the project, the greater the risk. Multimillion dollar projects obviously carry more risk than $50,000 projects and also usually affect the company more if the risk is realized. A related concern is the size of the project relative to the normal size of an IT development group's projects. A $1 million project in a department whose average undertaking costs $2 million to $3 million usually has lower implicit risk than a $250,000 project in a department that has never ventured a project costing more than $50,000.

2. Experience with the Technology. Because of the greater likelihood of unexpected technical problems, project risk increases as the project team's and organization's familiarity with the hardware, operating systems, data base handler, and project application language decreases. Phase 1 and Phase 2 technology projects are intrinsically more risky for a company than Phase 3 and Phase 4 technology projects. A project that has a slight risk for a leading-edge, large systems development group may have a very high risk for a smaller, less technically advanced group. (The latter group can reduce risk through purchase of outside skills for an undertaking involving technology that is in general commercial use.)

3. Project Structure. In some projects the very nature of the task defines the outputs completely from the moment of conceptualization. We classify such schemes as highly structured. They carry much less risk than those whose outputs are more subject to the manager's judgment and hence are vulnerable to change. The outputs of highly structured projects are fixed and not subject to change during the life of the project.

An insurance company automating preparation of its agents' rate book is an example of such a highly structured project. At the project's beginning, planners reached total agreement on the product lines to be included, the layout of each page, and the process of generating each number. Throughout the life of the project there was no need to alter these decisions. Consequently the team organized to reach a stable, fixed output rather than to cope with a potentially mobile target.

Quite the opposite was true in the personnel information project we mentioned at the beginning of the chapter, which was a low-structure project. In that situation the users could not reach a consensus on what the outputs should be, and these decisions shifted almost weekly, crippling progress.

Project Categories and Degree of Risk

Figure 8-1, by combining in a matrix the various dimensions influencing risk, identifies eight distinct project categories, each carrying a different degree of implementation risk. Even at this gross intuitive level, such a classification is useful to separate projects for quite different types of management review. IT organizations have used it successfully to distinguish the relative implementation risk for their own understanding and as a basis for communicating these notions of implementation risk to users and senior corporate executives. A legitimate concern is how to ensure that different people viewing the same project will come to the same rough assessment of its risks. While the best way to assure this is still uncertain, several companies have made significant progress in addressing the problem.

Assessing Risk in Individual Projects

Figure 8-2 presents, in part, a method one large company developed for measuring implementation risk: a list of 42 questions that the project manager answers about a project, both prior to senior management's approval of the proposal and several times during its implementation.

FIGURE 8-1 Effect of Degree of Structure, Company-Relative Technology, and Size on Project Implementation Risk

	High Structure	Low Structure
Low Company-Relative Technology	Large size— low risk	Large size— low risk (very susceptible to mismanagement)
	Small size— very low risk	Small size— very low risk (very susceptible to mismanagement)
High Company-Relative Technology	Large size— medium risk	Large size— very high risk
	Small size— medium-low risk	Small size— high risk

This company developed the questions after carefully analyzing its experience with successful and unsuccessful projects. We include some of them as an example of how to bridge concepts and practice. No analytic framework lies behind these questions, and they may not be appropriate for all companies. However, they represent a good starting point, and several other large companies have used them.

Both the project leader and the key user answer these questions. Differences in the answers are then reconciled. (Obviously the questionnaire provides data that are no better than the quality of thinking that goes into the answers.)

FIGURE 8-2 Implementation Risk Assessment Questionnaire
(sample from a total of 42 questions)

Size Risk Assessment		*Weight*
1. Total development work-hours for system*		**5**
100 to 3,000	Low—1	
3,000 to 15,000	Medium—2	
15,000 to 30,000	Medium—3	
More than 30,000	High—4	
2. What is estimated project implementation time?		**4**
12 months or less	Low—1	
13 months to 24 months	Medium—2	
More than 24 months	High—3	
3. Number of departments (other than IT) involved with system		**4**
One	Low—1	
Two	Medium—2	
Three or more	High—3	

Structure Risk Assessment		*Weight*
1. If replacement system is proposed, what percentage of existing functions are replaced on a one-to-one basis?		**5**
0 to 25 percent	High—3	
25 to 50 percent	Medium—2	
50 to 100 percent	Low—1	
2. What is severity of procedural changes in user department caused by proposed system?		**5**
Low—1		
Medium—2		
High—3		
3. Does user organization have to change structurally to meet requirements of new system?		**5**
No	—0	
Minimal	Low—1	
Somewhat	Medium—2	
Major	High—3	

FIGURE 8-2   (*continued*)

Structure Risk Assessment		Weight
4. What is general attitude of user?		5
Poor—against IT solution	High—3	
Fair—sometimes reluctant	Medium—2	
Good—understands value of IT solution	—0	
5. How committed is upper-level user management to system?		5
Somewhat reluctant, or unknown	High—3	
Adequate	Medium—2	
Extremely enthusiastic	Low—1	
6. Has a joint IT–user team been established?		5
No	High—3	
Part-time user representative appointed	Low—1	
Full-time user representative appointed	—0	

Technology Risk Assessment		Weight
1. Which of the hardware is new to the company?†		5
None	—0	
CPU	High—3	
Peripheral and/or additional storage	High—3	
Terminals	High—3	
Mini or micro	High—3	
2. Is the system software (nonoperating system) new to IT project team?†		5
No	—0	
Programming language	High—3	
Data base	High—3	
Data communications	High—3	
Other—specify	High—3	
3. How knowledgeable is user in area of IT?		5
First exposure	High—3	
Previous exposure but limited knowledge	Medium—2	
High degree of capability	Low—1	

FIGURE 8-2 *(concluded)*

Technology Risk Assessment		Weight
4. How knowledgeable is user representative in proposed application area?		5
Limited	High—3	
Understands concept but no experience	Medium—2	
Has been involved in prior implementation efforts	Low—1	
5. How knowledgeable is IT team in proposed application area?		5
Limited	High—3	
Understands concept but no experience	Medium—2	
Has been involved in prior implementation efforts	Low—1	

*Time to develop includes systems design, programming, testing, and installation.

†The question is scored by multiplying the sum of the numbers attached to the positive response, by the weight.

Note: Since the questions vary in importance, the company assigned weights to them subjectively. The numerical answer to the questions is multiplied by the question weight to calculate the question's contribution to the project's risk. The numbers are then added together to produce a risk score number for the project. Projects with risk scores within 10 points of each other are indistinguishable, but those separated by 100 points or more are very different to even the casual observer.

SOURCE: This questionnaire is adapted from the Dallas Tire case, no. 9–180–006 (Boston, Mass.: Harvard Business School Case Services, 1980).

These questions not only highlight the implementation risks but also suggest alternative ways of conceiving of and managing the project. If the initial aggregate risk score seems high, analysis of the answers may suggest ways of lessening the risk through reduced scope, lower-level technology, multiple phases, and so on. Thus managers should not consider risk as a static descriptor; rather its presence should encourage better approaches to project management. Numbers 5 and 6 under the section on structure are particularly good examples of questions that could trigger changes.

The higher the score, the higher must be the corporate level of approval. Only the executive committee in this company approves very risky projects. Such an approach ensures that top managers are aware of significant hazards and are making appropriate trade-offs between risk and strategic benefits. Managers should ask questions such as the following:

1. Are the benefits great enough to offset the risks?
2. Can the affected parts of the organization survive if the project fails?
3. Have the planners considered appropriate alternatives?

On a periodic basis during the undertaking, these questions are answered again to reveal any major changes. If all is going well, the risk continuously declines during implementation as the size of the remaining tasks dwindle and familiarity with the technology grows.

Answers to the questions provide a common understanding among senior, IT, and user managers as to a project's relative implementation risk. Often the fiascoes occur when senior managers believe a project has low implementation risk and IT managers know it has high implementation risk. In such cases IT managers may not admit their assessment because they fear that the senior executives will not tolerate this kind of uncertainty in data processing and will cancel a project of potential benefit to the organization.

Portfolio Risk

In addition to determining relative risk for single projects, a company should develop an aggregate implementation risk profile of the portfolio of systems and programming projects. While there is no such thing as a correct implementation risk profile in the abstract, appropriate implementation risk profiles do apply to different types of companies and strategies.

For example, in an industry where IT is strategic (such as banking and insurance), managers should be concerned when there are no high-risk projects. In such a case the company may be leaving a product or service gap for competition to step into. On the other hand, a portfolio loaded with high-risk projects suggests that the company may be vulnerable to operational disruptions when projects are not completed as planned. In support companies heavy investment in high-risk projects may not be appropriate. Often, however, even those companies should have some technologically exciting ventures to ensure familiarity with leading-edge technology and to maintain staff morale and interest.

These examples suggest that the aggregate implementation risk profiles of the portfolios of two companies could legitimately differ. Table 8–1 lists the issues that influence toward or away from high-risk efforts. (The risk profile should include projects that will come from outside software houses as well as those of the internal systems development group.) As the table shows, the aggregate impact of IT on corporate strategy is an important determinant of the appropriate amount of implementation risk to undertake.

TABLE 8-1 Factors That Influence Implementation Risk Profile of Project Portfolio

---

	Portfolio Risk Focus	
Factor	Low	High
Stability of IT development group	Low	High
Perceived quality of IT development group by insiders	Low	High
IT critical to delivery of current corporate services	No	Yes
IT important decision support aid	No	Yes
Experienced IT systems development group	No	Yes
Major IT fiascoes in last two years	Yes	No
New IT management team	Yes	No
IT perceived critical to delivery of future corporate services	No	Yes
IT perceived critical to future decision support aids	No	Yes
Company perceived as backward in use of IT	No	Yes

In summary, it is both possible and useful to talk about implementation risk during the feasibility study stage. The discussion of risk can be helpful both for those working on the individual project and for the department as a whole. Not only can this systematic analysis reduce the number of failures but, equally important, its power as a communication link helps IT managers and senior executives reach agreement on the risks to be taken in line with corporate goals.

Project Management: A Contingency Approach (By Project Type)

Much of the literature and conventional wisdom suggest that there is a single right way of doing project management. A similar bias holds that managers should apply an appropriate cluster of tools, project management methods, and organizational linkages uniformly to all such ventures.

While there may indeed be a general-purpose set of tools, the contribution each device can make to planning and controlling the project varies widely according to the project's characteristics. Further, the means of involving the user—through steering committees, representation on the team, or as leader—should also vary by project type. In short there is no universally correct way to run all projects.

Management Tools

The general methods (tools) for managing projects are of four principal types:

1. *External integration tools* include organizational and other communication devices that link the project team's work to the users at both the managerial and the lower levels.
2. *Internal integration devices* ensure that the team operates as an integrated unit. These include a variety of personnel controls.
3. *Formal planning tools* help to structure the sequence of tasks in advance and to estimate the time, money, and technical resources the team will need to execute them.
4. *Formal results-control mechanisms* help managers evaluate progress and spot potential discrepancies so that corrective action can be taken.

Results controls have been particularly effective in the following settings:[2]

1. Where clear knowledge exists as to what results are desirable.
2. Where the desired result can be controlled (at least to some extent by the individuals whose actions are being influenced).
3. Where the controllable result areas can be measured effectively.

Projects with high structure and a low degree of technology satisfy these conditions very well. Formal results-control mechanisms are very effective in those settings. For low-structured projects and those with a high degree of technology, none of the above conditions apply; consequently results control can make only a limited contribution. In those settings internal integration devices (personnel controls) represent the major contributions that can be brought to bear.

Table 8–2 gives examples of the tools in each category that are commonly used by companies. The next paragraphs suggest how the degree of structure and the company-relative technology influence the selection of items from the four categories.

Influences on Tool Selection

High Structure–Low Technology. Projects that are highly structured and that present familiar technical problems are not only the lower-risk

---

[2]Kenneth A. Merchant, *Control in Business Organizations* (Marshfield, Mass.: Pitman Publishing, 1985).

TABLE 8-2   Tools of Project Management

External Integration Tools

Selection of user as project manager.

Creation of user steering committee.

Frequent and in-depth meetings of this committee.

User-managed change control process.

Frequent and detailed distribution of project team minutes to key users.

Selection of users as team members.

Formal user specification approval process.

Progress reports prepared for corporate steering committee.

Users responsible for education and installation of system.

Users manage decision on key action dates.

Internal Integration Tools

Selection of experienced IT professional to lead team.

Frequent team meetings.

Regular preparation and distribution of minutes within team on key design evolution decision.

Regular technical status reviews.

Managed low turnover of team members.

Selection of high percentage of team members with significant previous work relationships.

Participation of team members in goal setting and deadline establishment.

Outside technical assistance.

Formal Planning Tools

PERT, critical path, etc. networking.

Milestone phases selection.

Systems specification standards.

Feasibility study specifications.

Project approval processes.

Project postaudit procedures.

Formal Control Tools

Periodic formal status reports versus plan.

Change control disciplines.

Regular milestone presentation meetings.

Deviations from plan, reports.

---

projects but also the easiest to manage (see Figure 8–1). They are also the least common. High structure implies that the outputs are very well defined by the nature of the task and the possibility is essentially nonexistent that the users will change their minds as to what these outputs should be. The project leaders, therefore, do not have to develop extensive administrative processes in order to get a diverse group of users both to agree to a design structure and to keep to that structure. Such external integration devices as inclusion of analysts in user departments, heavy representation of users on the design team, formal approval of the design team by users, and formal approval of design specifications by users are cumbersome and unnecessary for this type of undertaking. Other integrating devices, such as training users in how to operate the system, remain important.

The system's concept and design stages, however, are stable. At the same time, since the technology involved is familiar to the company, the project can proceed with a high percentage of persons having only average technical backgrounds and experience. The leader does not need strong IT skills. This type of project readily gives opportunity to the department's junior managers, who can gain experience that may lead to more ambitious tasks in the future.

With their focus on defining tasks and budgeting resources against them, project life-cycle planning concepts, such as PERT (program evaluation and review technique) and critical path, force the team to develop a thorough and detailed plan (exposing areas of soft thinking in the process). Such projects are likely to meet the resulting milestone dates and keep within the target budget. Moreover the usual results-control techniques[3] for measuring progress against dates and budgets provide very reliable data for spotting discrepancies and building a desirable tension into the design team to work harder to avoid slippage.

An example of this type of highly structured project is the agent's rate book project mentioned earlier. A portfolio in which 90 percent of the projects are of this type should produce little unplanned excitement for senior and user managers. It also requires a much more limited set of skills for the IT organization than might be needed for companies with portfolios that have a quite different mixture of project types.

High Structure–High Technology. These projects, vastly more complex than the first kind, involve some significant modifications of practices outlined in project management handbooks. A good example of this type of project is the conversion of systems from one computer manufacturer to another with no enhancements (easier said than done, of course). Another example is the conversion of a set of manual procedures onto a minicomputer with the only objective being performance of the same functions more quickly.

The normal mechanisms for liaison with users are not crucial here; the outputs are so well defined by the nature of the undertaking that both the development of specifications and the need to deal with systems changes from users are sharply lower. Liaison with users is nevertheless important for two reasons: (1) to ensure coordination on any changes in input/output or other manual procedure changes necessary

---

[3]Ibid.

for project success and (2) to deal with any systems restructuring that must follow from shortcomings in the project's technology.

In this kind of project it is common to discover during implementation that the technology is inadequate, forcing a long postponement while new technology is chosen or vital features modified to make the task fit the available technology. In one such situation a major industrial products company had to convert some computerized order-entry procedures to a manual basis so that the rest of an integrated materials management system could be shifted to new hardware already purchased.

Such technological shortcomings were the main difficulty in the financial institution described at the start of this chapter. In such a case where system performance is much poorer than expected, user involvement is important both to prevent demoralization and to help implement either an alternative approach (less ambitious in design) or a mutual agreement to end the project.

The skills that lead to success in this type of project, however, are the same as for effective administration of projects involving any kind of technical complexity. Unless the project is not very large the leader needs this experience (preferably but not necessarily in an IT environment) as well as administrative experience. The leader must also be effective in relating to technicians. From talking to the project team at various times, the ideal manager will anticipate difficulties before the technicians understand that they have a problem. In dealing with larger projects in this category the manager's ability is vital to establish and maintain teamwork through meetings, a record of all key design decisions, and subproject conferences.

Project life-cycle planning methods identify tasks and suitable completion dates. Their predictive value is much more limited here, however, than in the preceding category. The team will not understand key elements of the technology in advance, and seemingly minor bugs in such projects have a curious way of becoming major financial drains.

Roughly once an hour an on-line banking system in one company generated garbage across the computer screen. Although simply hitting a release key erased this screen of zeroes and x's, four months and more than $200,000 went into eliminating the so-called ghost screen. The solution lay in uncovering a complex interaction of hardware features, operating system functions, and application traffic patterns. Correction of the problem ultimately required the vendor to redesign several chips. Formal results-control mechanisms have limits in monitoring the progress of such projects, and personnel controls become more important.

In summary, technical leadership and internal integration are the keys in this type of project, and external integration plays a distinctly secondary role. Formal planning and control tools give more subjective than concrete projections, and the great danger is that neither IT managers nor high-level executives will recognize this. They may believe they have precise planning and close control when in fact they have neither.

Low Structure–Low Technology.   When such projects are intelligently managed they have low risk. Over and over, however, such projects fail because of inadequate direction. (In this respect they differ from the first type of project, where more ordinary managerial skills could ensure success.) The key to operating this kind of project lies in an effective effort to involve the users.

Developing substantial user support for *only one* of the thousands of design options and keeping the users committed to that design are critical. Essential aspects of this process include:

1. A user either as project leader or as the number two person on the team.
2. A user steering committee to evaluate the design.
3. An effort to break the project into a sequence of very small and discrete subprojects.
4. Formal user review and approval on all key project specifications.
5. Distribution of minutes of all key design meetings to users.
6. Strong efforts to keep at least chief subproject time schedules. Low managerial and staff turnover in the user areas is vital (since a consensus on approach with the predecessor of a user manager is of dubious value).

The personnel information debacle we mentioned at the start of this chapter is an example of what can happen when this process does not take place. Soon after work started, the director of human resources decided that his senior staff's participation in the design was a waste of their time, and he made sure none of them was involved. Instead of immediately killing the undertaking, the IT manager attempted to continue work under the leadership of one of his technically oriented staff members with little experience dealing with the human resources department. Bombarded by pressures that he did not understand from the human resources staff, the project manager allowed the systems design to expand to include more and more detail of doubtful merit until the system collapsed. The changing design made much of the programming obsolete. Tough, pragmatic leadership from users in the design stages would have made all the difference in the outcome.

The importance of user leadership increases once the design is final. At that stage users almost inevitably will produce some version of "I have been thinking . . . . " Unless the desired changes are of critical strategic significance to the user (a judgment best made by a responsible, user-oriented project manager) the requests must be diverted and postponed until they can be considered in some formal change process. Unless that process is rigorously controlled (a problem intensified by the near impossibility of distinguishing between the economies of a proposed alternative and those implicit in the original design), users will make change after change, and the project will evolve rapidly to a state of permanent deferral, with completion always six months in the future.

If the project is well integrated with the user departments, the formal planning tools will be very useful in structuring tasks and helping to remove any remaining uncertainty. The target completion dates will be firm as long as the systems target remains fixed. Similarly the formal results-control devices afford clear insight into progress to date, flagging both advances and slippages. Personnel controls are also vital here. If integration with user departments is weak, for example, excessive reliance on these results controls will produce an entirely unwarranted feeling of confidence. By definition the problems of technology management are usually less difficult in this type of project than in the high-technology ventures, and a staff with a normal mixture of technical backgrounds should be adequate.

In almost every respect, in fact, management of this type of project differs from the previous two. The key to success is close, aggressive management of external integration supplemented by formal planning and control tools. Leadership must flow from the user rather than from the technical side.

Low Structure–High Technology. Because these projects are complex and carry high risk, their leaders need technical experience as well as knowledge of and ability to communicate with users. The same intensive effort toward external integration described in the previous class of projects is necessary here. Total commitment on the part of users to a particular set of design specifications is critical; and again, they must agree to *one* out of the many thousands of options.

Unfortunately, however, an option desirable from the user's perspective may turn out to be infeasible in the selected hardware/software system. In the last several years such situations have occurred, particularly with stand-alone minicomputer systems designs, and they commonly lead either to significant restructuring of the project or to elimination of it altogether; therefore users should be well represented at both the policy and the operations levels.

At the same time, technical considerations make strong technical leadership and internal project integration vital. This kind of effort requires the most experienced project leaders, and they will need whole-

---

TABLE 8-3   Relative Contribution of Tools to Ensuring Project Success

Project Type	Project Description	External Integration	Internal Integration	Formal Planning	Formal Results Control
I	High structure–low technology; large	Low	Medium	High	High
II	High structure–low technology; small	Low	Low	Medium	High
III	High structure–high technology; large	Low	High	Medium	Medium
IV	High structure–high technology; small	Low	High	Low	Low
V	Low structure–low technology; large	High	Medium	High	High
VI	Low structure–low technology; small	High	Low	Medium	High
VII	Low structure–high technology; large	High	High	Low +	Low +
VIII	Low structure–high technology; small	High	High	Low	Low

hearted support from the users. In approving such a project, managers must decide whether it can or should be divided into a series of much smaller problems or use less innovative technology.

While formal planning and results-control tools can be useful here, at the early stages they contribute little to reducing overall uncertainty and to highlighting all problems. The planning tools do allow the manager to structure the sequence of tasks. Unfortunately in this type of project new tasks crop up with monotonous regularity, and tasks that appear simple and small suddenly become complex and protracted. Time, cost, and resulting technical performance turn out to be almost impossible to predict simultaneously. In the Apollo moon project, for example, technical performance achievement was key, and cost and time simply fell out. In the private sector this all too often is an unacceptable outcome.

Relative Contribution of Management Tools

Table 8–3 shows the relative contribution that each of the four groups of project management tools makes to ensure the maximum possibility of project success. It reveals that managers need quite different styles and approaches to manage the different types of projects effectively. Although the framework could be made more complex by including more dimensions, that would only confirm this primary conclusion.

Conclusion

The usual corporate handbook on project management, with its unidimensional approach, fails to deal with the realities of the task facing today's managers, particularly those dealing with information technology. The right approach flows from the project rather than the other way around.

The need to deal with the corporate culture within which both IT and project management operate further complicates the problems. Use of formal project planning and results-control tools is much more likely to produce successful results in a highly formal environment than in one where the prevailing culture is more personal and informal. Similarly the selection and effective use of integrating mechanisms is very much a function of the corporate culture.

Thus the type of company culture further complicates our suggestions as to how different types of projects should be managed. (Too many former IT managers made the fatal assumption that they were in an ideal position to reform corporate culture from their position!)

The past decade has brought new challenges to IT project management, and experience has indicated better ways to think about the management process. Our conclusions, then, are threefold:

1. We will continue to experience major disappointments as we push into new fields. Today, however, the dimensions of implementation risk can be identified in advance and a decision made whether to proceed. If we proceed, we will sometimes fail.

2. The work of the IT development department in aggregate may be thought of as a portfolio. Other authors have discussed what the appropriate components of that portfolio should be at a particular point in time. The aggregate implementation risk profile of that portfolio, however, is a critical (though often overlooked) strategic decision.

3. Project management in the IT field is complex and multidimensional. Different types of projects require different clusters of management tools if they are to succeed.

Rogers Automotive Company

In June 1984, Bob Chairling, coordinator of Profit Improvement Projects at Rogers Automotive Company (RAC), was reviewing the past few years' efforts in the marketing project. Originally conceived in 1981, the project was expected to reduce RAC's administrative costs by $8 million, and improve the company's marketing information system. Mr. Chairling hoped a critical review would prepare him to effectively manage the production project, which was just about to begin.

Company Background

RAC ranked in the top 100 in sales, assets, and profits in *Fortune* magazine's list of U.S. industrial corporations. RAC's technical and marketing innovations made it a "Blue Chip" stock on Wall Street. During the 1970s RAC had begun efforts to strengthen financial and personnel management. A major nationwide recession in the early 1980s added an urgent note to this effort. American automobile makers were hit especially hard both by the general economic climate and the inroads made by Japanese automakers. Like their counterparts in other major auto companies, RAC managers were under enormous pressure to reduce costs. One cost reduction project was the marketing project, a collaborative effort of the marketing and accounting departments.

This case was prepared by Janis Gogan and Ramon O'Callaghan under the supervision of Leslie R. Porter.

EXHIBIT 1 Accounting Department

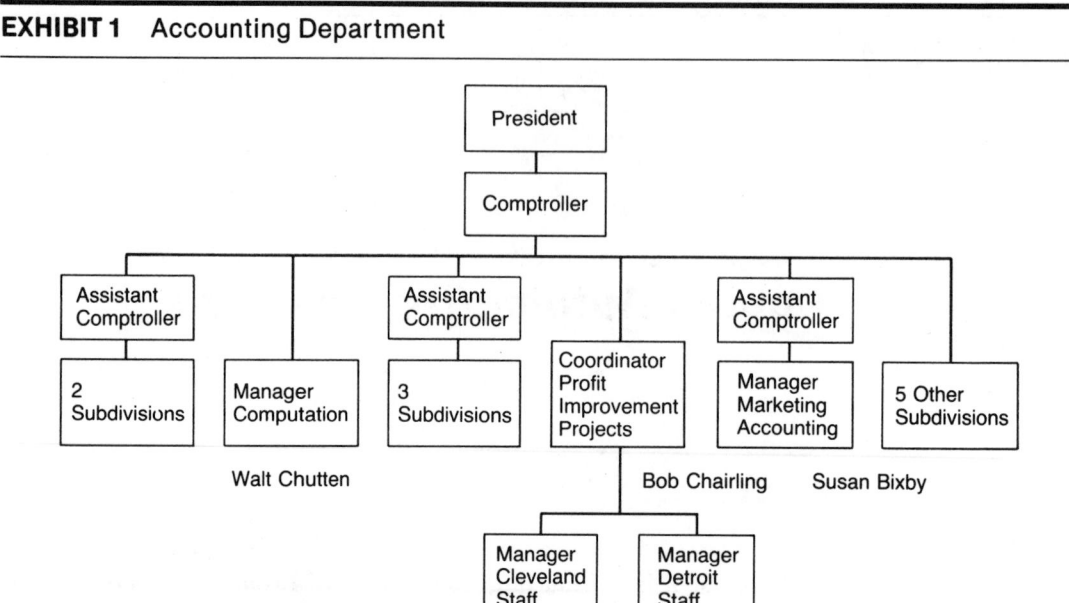

Accounting Department

Accounting was under the supervision of the comptroller. The accounting department served every company operation, and its 4,650 employees were located throughout the world (see Exhibit 1). Of the 13 accounting department subdivisions, 3 were involved in the marketing project:

1. Profit Improvement Projects, Bob Chairling

Chairling reported directly to the comptroller and indirectly to the functional executive in whose area a project was undertaken. Chairling's 105-person profit improvement department, organized in the fall of 1981, developed tools to improve corporate and divisional effectiveness. A five-step internal consulting process was employed to (1) identify the client unit's primary mission, (2) define the specific business problem, (3) gather relevant facts, (4) recommend a solution, and (5) implement the change. This internal consulting department conducted systems analysis, design, and audits and provided end-user computing support. Studies were undertaken at the departmental, divisional, or corporate levels.

2. Computation Center, Walt Chutten

The computation center provided large-scale computing facilities. Its 475 employees were organized into four divisions:

Operations. Managed the central computing facility, which operated three shifts a day. Short-run jobs were scheduled for normal working hours to minimize turnaround time for users. Longer batch jobs were run on the second and third shifts. The majority of computer resource uses consisted of on-line applications.

Systems Development. Developed new applications, including assisting users in defining problems, designing computer solutions and assessing their expected profitability, coding and testing programs, and maintaining software.

Data Control. This department was set up to establish a centralized data library and formulate a corporate data architecture. This department was organized in 1982 in response to management's recognition that data, not applications, was the driving force for RAC's information resource strategy.

Office Automation and Telecommunications. Managed a rapidly growing installed base of terminals, word processors, and workstations. One division had installed its own local area network, which was managed by this department. A long-range data, text, and voice communications plan was expected to be formulated by June 1985. By 1983 there had been some confusion over responsibility for personal computers, which were currently part of Bob Chairling's end-user area.

Mr. Chutten had been recommending for some time that the computation center be reorganized as a separate information systems division, rather than reporting to the comptroller.

3. Marketing Accounting, Susan Bixby

This, the largest group in the accounting department, was responsible for tracking the transport, storage, and delivery of goods, and billing, collection, and banking of all monies received. Susan Bixby worked closely with marketing management to define reports which would enable them to more effectively control their activities and formulate marketing strategies.

Overhauling the Marketing Accounting System

In August 1981 a consulting firm, together with Chairling's project team, presented a threefold proposal to completely overhaul the marketing accounting system at RAC. The system at that time utilized over 2,000 employees. The proposed marketing project called for a major change from semi-automated batch accounting operations carried out in 49 district offices to a highly automated distributed system. Much processing would take place on minicomputers in district offices throughout the United States, and a central mainframe computer in Detroit would receive daily inputs from all offices for updating a central data file. The project, which encompassed the collecting, processing, and preparing of financial information and related statistics bearing on RAC's marketing activities, was organized into three interrelated, concurrent parts, described below.

I. Non-Computer Cost Reduction in the Field

Part I of the marketing project called for "belt-tightening" at the seven regional and 49 district offices. Streamlining measures included work simplification, standardization, and major methods changes. Initially a reduction of 450 jobs, leading to $8 million annual savings, was forecast. By June 1982, office procedures had been changed substantially and 520 personnel relocated, saving $9.5 million. Most of the district managers felt their efforts were as effective as before.

II. Improvement of Decision Support

Part II called for identifying marketing information requirements for long-term strategic planning, and developing appropriate decision support systems for strategic planning. By December of 1982 five areas were targeted: automotive products, industrial products, spare parts, financial reporting, and operations. These new management support systems were to be in place by June of 1984. By March 1983 some prototype systems had been built, and were implemented well ahead of schedule, by November 1983. Chairling felt this phase of the marketing project was functioning well, but that the honeymoon would be over soon. Management was pleased with the results and asking for more. The initial systems were based primarily on historical data. Now managers were asking for on-line systems based on current data, and these could not be provided until Part III was completed.

III. Designing and Installing a Computerized Marketing Accounting System

Part III of the marketing project began in late 1981. Its objectives were:

- Reduce costs of field and home office marketing accounting and related systems.

- Improve quality and timeliness of management information generated from marketing accounting and related activities.
- Ease administrative burden on field management.

Target dates and milestones were formulated in management meetings during early 1982 for the four phases described below:

Phase 1, prepoint zero: During this start-up period initial staff were hired, oriented, and trained.

Phase 2, specifications development: Applications were analyzed, the scope of the system determined, and the approach for conversion selected. Equipment requirements were defined, and systems specifications submitted to manufacturers. Manufacturers' proposals were evaluated and equipment orders placed. Exhibit 2 lists the components of the marketing project. Target completion: December 1982.

Phase 3, systems and programming: During this period the detailed system was to be designed and programmed. Target completion: June 1984.

EXHIBIT 2 Components of the Marketing Project

---

1. *Accounts receivable:* Includes (a) dealer accounts, including reconciliation of checks-in-progress and credits to dealers with the verified credits by regional officers, (b) fleet accounts, (c) attorney accounts. The system should track all charges and credits made to a dealer's account, maintain current records on dealers' names, addresses, and status, and prepare accounting and credit reports as required. Aged receivables will be maintained for collection purposes and open item statements prepared at regular intervals. Accounts receivable will be updated daily and exception reports will be available, as well as full on-line inquiry.
2. *Dealer accounting:* Includes processing vehicle invoices, transportation charges, taxes, overhead allowances, rent, refunds, and other dealer data. It should help to evaluate customer, model, and location performance and develop statistical criteria for selecting future dealers and locations.
3. *Expense analysis:* Expense distribution, selling expense reports, transportation expenses, financial statements, and sales operations reports. Expense distribution includes classification and distribution of selling expenses and preparation of appropriate reports. The selling expense report function maintains the selling expense subledger by dealership, district, and region, and audits, balances, and distributes expense statements.
4. *Sales operations reports:* Although this is currently concerned with transport reports, more detailed reports will be required.

EXHIBIT 2 *(concluded)*

---

5. *Marketing statistics and analysis* includes:
   - Sales costing: The net assembly and manufacturing costs would be tracked for all vehicles and revenues and gross profits assigned to appropriate plants, models, and options.
   - Forecasting: Forecasts of sales and revisions of budgets, and analysis of the effects of pricing, advertising, and distribution. Although this area has not yet been fully defined, it is expected that additional management information needs will be identified by the project team.
   - Income: Profitability reports by product, model, option, dealer, and territory.
   - Sales statistics: Periodic sales reports for the field (districts and regions) and home office.
6. *Stock control:* Maintain stock control records for all finished vehicles. The system should capture vehicle data at physical checkpoints such as end-of-assembly line, factory parking lot, transport, intermediate storage lots, regional and district lots, and dealer locations; maintain inventory records for each location; compare book and physical inventories; generate inventory values for corporate records; determine regional and district inventory mix reorder points; and automatically restock intermediate storage locations. The stock control system should reduce accounting costs, provide more timely management information, allow for more consistent inventory policies, maintain optimum stock levels, and reduce lost sales resulting from wrong dealer mix or poor delivery.
7. *Product tax accounting:* Record, maintain, and provide information on product taxes, and prepare necessary reports. The taxes that would be processed are: state and federal excise, selected ad valorem, state and local sales and use, and others such as motor carrier and over-the-road taxes.
8. *Payroll:* Processing pay records now done in Detroit, San Jose, Springfield, and Cleveland. It would include distributing the marketing operation payroll, maintaining stock purchase plan information, processing pay records for casual employees, and preparing statistics and reports. This activity is not scheduled for conversion until late 1985.
9. *Accounts payable, purchasing:* Process and pay marketing and non-marketing vendor bills, including those now paid through the imprest fund and by the Corporate Accounting department. Includes: preparation of checks and cash disbursement records, check reconciliation, forecasting cash demand, and providing information on items purchased by vendor and commodity categories. Conversion should be completed by early 1985.
10. *Company-owned dealership accounting:* Preparation of sales and financial reports. Simplified procedures in the field have substantially reduced the economic justification for processing daily transactions on a computer system.

Although initially some of the reports would be available on a monthly basis, the goal is to have every report updated daily and available on-line to qualified users, subject to appropriate security measures.

Phase 4, conversion: This included installing equipment, parallel operations, and total conversion from existing systems to the automated on-line system. Target completion: December 1984.

Hardware

During April and May, 1982, computation center representatives met with Susan Bixby, the marketing accounting manager, several times to review preliminary systems flow charts and capacity estimates. Chairling was satisfied that the center had sufficient information to order equipment that would support the marketing project.

Chutten, manager of the computation center, planned to upgrade his existing equipment, which currently consisted of two IBM System 370/Model 168s, two newer IBM 3032s, and several less powerful older machines including an IBM 370/135 and a 370/155. All these machines had been purchased and all but the 3032s were fully depreciated. The center proposed to replace the equipment in several steps, as follows:

1. Install IBM System 3083 on December 1, 1982. Use OS/MVS operating system and IMS data base management system. Disconnect the IBM 370/135, 370/155, and 370/168s.

2. Install IBM System 34s in each of the district offices by February 1983. These standalone minicomputers would support unique needs at each district, and provide the necessary communications and data storage capabilities for the daily central file updates.

3. Install a fourth generation programming language, probably RAMIS II, by April 1, 1983 (see Exhibit 3). This would be used instead of COBOL to develop many of the new projects. It was expected that programmer productivity would increase significantly using RAMIS II. For some applications new RAMIS II data bases would be used; for others existing IMS data bases would be tapped.

4. Install second 3083 on June 1, 1983 and upgrade both 3083s to the new XA (Extended Architecture) operating system. Disconnect the two IBM 3032s and sell to used computer dealer.

Anticipated Benefits

After the initial study in late 1981 Chairling's group conducted a detailed economic study. Anticipated gross annual savings, not including the initial noncomputer field office cutbacks, would be between $6.8 million and $7.6 million. Annual operating costs would range from $2.4 million to $2.6 million, resulting in a net annual savings of $4.4 million to $5 million. The cost to develop the system was estimated at $5 million to $6 million, 84 percent of which would go to salaries of systems and programming personnel (see Exhibit 4).

EXHIBIT 3 "Fourth-Generation Language Ups Firm's Output: Replacing Cobol Programs"

Paramus, N.J.—Can 10-year Cobol programming veterans find happiness and increased productivity with a fourth-generation language?

Yes, according to personnel at the Corporate Data Center of Becton Dickinson & Co. Increases in productivity topping 10 to 1 have been realized since the installation of Mathematica, Inc.'s Ramis II fourth-generation language and data base management system at the company headquarters in 1979.

A leading manufacturer of medical, diagnostic and industrial safety products for the health care field, Becton Dickinson now completes the development of most small to average-size applications in 3 to 5 days—a far cry from the average 15 to 30 days required to develop the same kind of applications using Cobol in the pre-Ramis II days, according to Data Center manager Dave Miller. Because of this, no new programs have been written in Cobol at Becton Dickinson since Ramis II arrived on the scene.

Using Ramis II, Becton Dickinson was able to develop an automated financial reporting system to track product sales for all divisions in only four months with one person working part-time on the application, Miller said. The project was started with Ramis II on a time-sharing basis while Becton Dickinson awaited the delivery of its first CPU, an IBM 370/158. The resulting application considers market share, market penetration, product life cycles, product age and source of sales.

Data Center project manager Len Sokol and programmer/analysts Joan Seidman and Sally Ann Sposato all use Ramis II for development of applications for their specific areas of concentration at Becton Dickinson. All three employees were experienced Cobol, RPG and/or assembler programmers prior to joining the company. Each received one week of training in the use of Ramis II prior to programming with it.

"Now, it takes about three Ramis II statements to produce the same result as approximately 100 lines of Cobol code," Seidman said.

Seidman, who concentrates on applications for the human resources section of Becton Dickinson, developed Ramis II requests for 90 monthly and 40 quarterly reports required for Equal Employment Opportunity reporting over the last two years. Reports for the human resources section often require calculations on totals, text and report writing, all features enhanced with Ramis II, Seidman maintained. Most human resources department reports are done in batch using external files that were originally developed using Cobol.

Entire Cobol programs often are replaced with as few as 30 statements when using the fourth-generation language, Seidman said. As a result, over 15 old Cobol programs have been converted into Ramis II. Depending on the complexity of the program, she added, approximately 780 lines of Cobol code can be translated into a Ramis II request in one day.

We also use REF, a Ramis II component which allows [extensive] access to non-Ramis II files because of our need to generate quick reports or sample sets from existing files," Sokol added. In one instance he was required to extract a test file of a few records from the International Sales Division's sequential forecasting master file, consisting

EXHIBIT 3 (*concluded*)

of thousands of 2,193-byte production records. The user wanted to select particular records based on certain key-field or partial key-field
values.

The entire process took less than a half hour, with the resulting
completed program being a 15-line Ramis II request, Sokol said. The
request enables the user to have complete control over the selection
criteria, job submission and sample file creation for control-testing
the batch production application.

"The reports needed from those samplings were produced that
afternoon in only a few hours," Sokol said.

Because request development is done on-line with Ramis II, errors
are detected immediately and can be corrected as the program is developed, Seidman said, allowing some projects to be completed in two
to three hours. There is no longer the need to follow the time-consuming procedures of coding, compiling, testing and debugging as with
Cobol. Ramis II runs both on-line under IBM's VM/CMS and in batch
under IBM's OS/VSI at Becton Dickinson.

Documentation of new applications and programs is also easier
and faster, according to Seidman. "Because Ramis II requests use English, getting users to understand definitions of key words for the desired results is no longer a difficult task." With Cobol, she said, "documentation had to take into account the operator as well as the end
user. It was an additional strain on time to have to include information
on I/OI, operator intervention and storage."

A hidden benefit, according to Sokol, is the fact that costs for applications development are kept low and monies for the development
of applications are kept within the company.

"When we quoted estimates on applications development using
Cobol, the numbers were outlandish. With Ramis II, these figures are
one-quarter to one-fifth of the cost of developing the same program
using Cobol. This, of course, is a visible savings for the company in
general," he said.

"The hidden savings comes in the fact that we have a charge-back
system at Becton Dickinson and our users are not required to use in-
house data processing services," he added. "By using Ramis II, our estimates are quite reasonable and very competitive with application
vendors on the outside. Now, many Becton Dickinson data center customers use our in-house services not only for their speed, but for the
cost-effectiveness."

Approximately 90 percent of the gross annual savings would result
from headcount reduction; the rest would be from reduced equipment
costs. Some 275 employees would be displaced by this system; 172
from field offices and 103 from home office departments. These personnel savings would begin to accrue during the last quarter of 1984 and
maximum gross savings would begin during the third quarter of 1985.

EXHIBIT 4 Marketing Project

			Estimate of Costs and Savings ($000)			
Priority	Activities	Development Costs	Annual Gross Savings	Annual Operating Costs	Annual Net Savings	Percent of Total Gross Savings
I	Accounts receivable	$1,200	$1,400	$ 840	$ 560	21%
I	Dealer accounting	940	1,760	1,100	660	26
I	Expense analysis	360	340	40	300	5
I	Sales operations	60	260	140	120	4
I	Marketing statistics and analysis	920	920	40	880	14
I	Stock control	300	620	40	580	8
I	Product tax accounting	400	380	40	340	6
I	Nonmarketing functions	240	40	40	—	—
	Subtotal	$4,420	$5,720	$2,280	$3,440	84%
	Payroll					
II	Payroll department and casual payroll	$ 640	$ 800	$ 80	$ 720	10
II	Production and manufacturing	—	—	40	(40)	—
III	Accounts payable, purchasing	320	340	40	300	5
IV	Company-owned dealership accounting	120	80	40	40	1
	Subtotal	$1,080	$1,220	$ 200	$1,020	
	Range (total program)*	$5,000–6,000	$6,800–7,600	$2,400–2,600	$4,400–5,000	100%

*These figures apply to savings that would be a direct result of computerization.

During the development period the marketing project staff was expected to increase to 75 persons, including 6 supervisors, 35 analysts, and 34 programmers, all under the control of the marketing project leader. During conversion the staff would expand to 90: 7 supervisors, 25 analysts, 36 programmers, and 21 field analysts who would assist in implementing the computer system in the field.

Ranking of Projects

During Phase 2 (specifications development) the staff examined each application in Exhibit 2 and determined that all were technically possible and economically desirable. Projects were ranked based on economics, support for management information and field projects, manpower dislocation impact, technical sequencing, development manpower utilization, and conversion risk. Chairling's staff grouped the projects into four priorities for conversion. The fixed asset accounting project was postponed, since it was more closely related to other corporate accounting applications that were not a part of this effort and the projected savings were relatively small. As it was independent of the other systems, it could be implemented at a later date.

In early 1982, the comptroller initiated conversations with a second consulting team which specialized in corporate data base management. These consultants urged RAC management to focus on long-term data requirements. As a result of this recommendation, the Data Control division was set up within Mr. Chutten's computation center. A major data base study was initiated and conducted in parallel with the systems development effort. Chutten assigned one member of the data control team to ensure that the progress made in defining a corporate data architecture was reflected in the developing marketing projects.

First-phase computer implementation was set to begin in June 1984. Some projects identified during the specifications development phase were deferred. First to go was the dealer accounting system. The experiment in field office streamlining had improved existing procedures, with substantial savings. Since this lessened the potential impact of proposed computer-based improvements, the project could no longer be cost justified.

Next, the payroll project was deferred. Most of the payroll was already on the IBM 370/135, except casual payroll, which was not large enough to justify a computer application. The current payroll system made inefficient use of programs and equipment; however, in light of schedule requirements and resource limitations, it was felt that time could be better spent on systems with greater paybacks. Initially payroll was to be written in RAMIS II; later this was discovered to be an inappropriate use of RAMIS II's capabilities. The payroll activity could be deferred without impact on other programs. Furthermore, a payroll system could be purchased outside if necessary, since it represented a fairly standard application.

Accounts payable was also deferred, because not enough staff were available to design and implement the program. This program could be backed off without affecting completion of others.

Although programming had already begun on sales operations and nonmarketing activities, these two projects were postponed in 1983. Neither had large savings potential, both could be pulled out without affecting the remaining projects, and the hardware could still be used for some time in the future.

By December 1983 it became necessary to defer more activities. Chairling attempted to determine which projects could be pulled out to reduce the remaining workload so completion could still be achieved by June 1984. Accounts receivable was proving to be rather complex. Because the remaining projects still would not be materially affected, it was given a lower priority ranking. Further, the payoff from the accounts receivable activity depended on conversion of the data communication network, which was not scheduled for early implementation. Thus lowering the accounts receivable priority allowed some breathing room in the conversion process without seriously affecting the overall economic benefits of this project.

Organization of Computer Programming

During August of 1982 RAC management agreed to a change in the assignment of the systems and programming responsibilities: systems under Chairling's marketing project leadership and programming under the direction of Chutten's computer center. The early plan had analysts, programmers, and data management specialists all under the marketing project leader. This decision had been justified on the grounds that it clearly fixed "cradle-to-grave" responsibility and provided for effective planning, coordination, and control over the many complex, highly interrelated program projects. It would also facilitate communications with the marketing department, which had a vital interest in the project's success.

The outside consultants recommended that the computation center be given programming and data management responsibility because the computation center's programmers were more highly skilled than a small specialized programming group could be, and some synergies could be achieved with other programming work of the computation center, leading to more efficient manpower utilization. They also felt that the computation center could more easily attract and train new technical staff. Furthermore, since many programmers would be transferred to the computation center on completion of the project, it was desirable to recruit them into the center from the start. Finally, the use of a centrally trained programming team would facilitate the incorporation of a unified data architecture.

The consultants defined the broader purpose of the center: on a centralized basis, to provide the programming and data management for all applications, large and small, administrative and engineering. For the marketing project and other large-scale, discrete projects the following programming organization and relationships were set forth.

The computation center was to:

- Hire, fire, evaluate, and compensate all programming and data management personnel.
- Train staff in programming and file management techniques and operating procedures.
- Provide effective, responsive service to "customer" projects. This meant full-time assignment of technical staff to teams working on large-scale projects.

The project manager would:

- Plan project requirements and inform the computation center of significant changes in project programming needs to permit the center to effectively rebalance its workload and staffing.
- Monitor progress and consult with the center if assigned technical personnel did not meet reasonable performance standards.
- Maintain liaison with operating management and achieve project objectives in terms of cost, timetables, and benefits.

Since this division of responsibilities was new to RAC, and in light of the importance of the marketing project, RAC was encouraged to establish careful controls to ensure that this joint effort operated effectively.

Control over Analysts' Time

Systems analysis was broken down into five levels:

- Integrated system design.
- Definition of program data and processing requirements through flow charts and structured diagrams.
- Preparation of test data.
- Preparation of procedures manual.
- Publication of manuals and documentation of efforts.

A lead analyst took charge of one or more systems activities and supervised several other analysts. As activities were further broken down into the five levels, time was allocated to schedule the accomplishment of each project level (see Exhibit 5).

EXHIBIT 5 Weekly Status Report—Systems Phase

MP–22 Rev 1

Activity

Expense Distribution

Assigned to

A. Stevens

	Level 3	9/5/83 to 10/25/83						
	1—Date started	9/8	9/8	9/8	9/8	9/8	9/8	9/8
JOB PERFORMANCE	2—Original estimate of analyst-days required	28	28	28	28	28	28	28
	3—Revised estimate of analyst-days required	28	28	28	28	28	28	28
	4—Applied analyst-days	4	9	13	17.5	23	26	27
	5—Percent should be complete (4 ÷ 3)	14%	32%	46%	63%	82%	93%	96%
	6—Estimated analyst-days required to complete (3–4)	24	19	15	11	4.5	1.5	.5
	7—Current estimate of analyst-days required	28	28	28	28.5	27.5	27.5	27.5
	8—Percent actually completed (4 ÷ 7)	14%	32%	46%	62%	84%	95%	98%

TIME / STATUS							
9—Adjusted estimate of analyst-days required	28	28	28	28	28	28	28
10—Analyst-days elapsed	7	12	16	21	24	27	28
11—Percent time elapsed (10 ÷ 9)	25%	43%	57%	75%	86%	96%	100%
12—Percent ahead or behind schedule (8-11)	11%	-11%	-11%	-13%	-2%	-1%	-2%
13—Number of personnel assigned	1	1	1	1	1	1	1
14—Revised estimated completion date						10/22	10/28
15—Original estimated completion date	10/21	10/21	10/21	10/21	10/21	10/21	10/21
TODAY'S DATE	9/11	9/18	9/25	10/4	10/11	10/18	10/25

Lost time—Analyst-days	Number	Comments (include explanation of any impediments)
ACCUMULATED—LAST REPORT		
9/11	3	
9/18	3	
9/25	3	
10/4	3.5	Staff meeting
10/11	3.5	Phase II delays
10/18	3.5	
10/25	3.5	
ACCUMULATED TO DATE		Note: Phase 4 to begin 11/1/83

EXHIBIT 6 Computation Center Progress Report on Marketing
Project for Week 3/21/84 through 3/27/84

Project Number	Project Name	Start Date	Current Completion Date	REV
	Trans	12/01/83	7/31/84	0
	Dated	12/01/83	4/11/84	1
	Edit1	12/01/83	4/11/84	2
	Edit2	12/01/83	4/11/84	1
	Edit3	12/01/83	3/22/84	2
Stock control				
0401	Daily	10/15/83	4/01/84	1
0402	Month	10/15/83	6/08/84	1
Tax accounting				
0501	Month	10/15/83	5/17/84	2
0502	Daily	2/05/84	4/11/84	1
Dealer accounting				
0601	Daily	7/29/83	5/01/84	1
0602	Month	8/13/83	5/30/84	3
0605	S Proc.	1/30/84	3/29/84	0
	S Cost	12/01/83	4/09/84	1
Sales statistics				
0801	Daily	11/25/83	4/06/84	3
0802	Weekly	11/25/83	4/12/84	2
0803	Update	12/15/82	5/01/84	0
0804	C Rep	12/15/82	4/19/84	1

The analysts were provided with a terminal and a time-sharing-based productivity tool. Its graphics and word processing features enabled each analyst to prepare flowcharts and data flow diagrams on-line instead of manually. This saved some time at initial creation and was a great time-saver when charts, diagrams, and specifications had to be revised. Included in this system was a documentation facility and a specifications dictionary which greatly facilitated review, change, and verification of designs. Several other features were expected to become available some time in 1984. These included a more advanced dictionary which would be compatible with the corporate data base standards, a screen prototype facility which would enable systems designers to simulate reports for end users, and a project control system. By 1984 many of the analysts complained that the time-sharing system was slow compared with systems just becoming available on personal computers. However, no analysts requested to go back to manual procedures!

		Applied Programmer Days					
This Week	To Date	Required to Complete	Start to Finish	W.O. Estimate	REV	Percent Complete	Calculated Weeks Left
0.	6.2	63.8	70.0	70	0	8.8%	18.0
17.0	129.8	35.2	165.0	165	0	78.7	2.1
10.3	75.1	16.2	91.3	23	0	82.3	2.1
7.2	79.7	12.8	92.5	85	0	86.2	2.1
4.0	59.2	0.9	60.1	68	0	98.5	−0.7
8.4	190.5	0.6	191.2	168	1	99.7	0.7
0.	8.9	168.0	176.9	218	1	5.1	10.4
17.7	192.7	171.3	364.0	455	1	52.9	7.3
4.2	26.9	5.1	32.0	20	0	84.1	2.1
20.1	412.9	111.4	524.3	393	0	78.8	5.0
1.4	23.1	64.9	88.0	45	0	26.3	9.1
1.4	15.0	6.6	21.6	60	0	69.3	0.3
2.0	32.0	29.4	61.5	65	1	52.1	1.9
4.4	75.2	21.8	97.0	55	0	77.5	1.4
1.9	50.8	9.2	59.9	55	0	84.7	2.3
6.4	77.2	87.8	165.0	165	0	46.8	5.0
9.9	113.3	44.8	158.0	145	0	71.7	3.3

Control over Programmers' Time

Programmers also worked at terminals connected to a host computer. Several had complained that response time was slow during the middle of the day, and that the editing facility was not as useful as more recent offerings on the market. Chutten had recently instructed one of his assistants to investigate several personal computer vendors. Both the editing and response time complaints would then be eliminated, but possibly with some sacrifice of their present control systems. Currently each programmer keyed in information about his/her activity at the end of the day, and the lead programmer for each team of six or seven programmers could check on progress instantly, make schedule revisions, and communicate changes to the programmers via electronic mail.

The major difference between the method of control of analysts' and programmers' time was the lack of detailed activity breakdown by the programmers. Programs were viewed in their entirety and progress was recorded from the start date to complete date of an entire activity. Exhibit 6 shows examples of the programmers' control system. The lead programmers defined start and complete dates and the number of programmer days necessary to complete each activity.

The data management specialists worked with lead analysts and lead programmers to ensure that data in the new programs was being used in conformance with corporate standards and structured for efficient processing. In a project of this magnitude, changes were frequent and the need for close coordination was great. Each Friday, lead analysts from the marketing project, the center's lead programmers, a data specialist, management of the two organizations, and a representative from marketing accounting met at the computation center for informal discussion of "where we are and where we want to go." Projects were reviewed to determine status and possible schedule revisions (Exhibit 7).

Schedule Slippage

By early 1984, Chutten and Chairling both expressed doubts that the entire project would be completed by June 1984. During the spring of 1984 more schedule slippage occurred. Chairling guessed that full implementation would occur sometime between January and June, 1985.

Problems contributing to the schedule slippage included:

Installing RAMIS II. Although the most inexperienced programmers in the group were making dramatic productivity gains with RAMIS II, some of Chutten's best COBOL programmers actually seemed to be losing ground. Some of them complained that their long years of COBOL training were going to waste. They argued that RAMIS II's programming efficiency was bought at the cost of loss of flexibility and heavier use of machine resources. Chutten felt these complaints simply reflected temporary growing pains, but Chairling wondered whether morale was on a permanent decline.

Growth in Computer Center. The center was having growing pains hiring, introducing, and training new programmers. Hiring systems experts was especially expensive and difficult, and retaining them was even more of a problem. Six of the first eight hired left for higher paying jobs outside of Detroit. Chairling wondered also whether the current hiring strategy adequately reflected the transition to fourth generation software.

Data Management. The data management specialists complained that analysts and programmers were causing problems. One problem was the use of common terms in unauthorized ways. For example, an

---

EXHIBIT 7   Summary of Marketing Project Joint Status Meeting, 2/12/84

As of 2/6, 95 programmers were on the Marketing Project.

Dealer accounting
Daily: Coding 85–90 percent complete. Acceptance test now being run on existing part (completion date is still 4/1).
Monthly: Completion rescheduled from 4/1 to 4/30. Monthly is not needed until daily program has been run for a month.
Special processing: No problems. Should be complete by 2/29.

Expense distribution/financial reports
Subsystem 11–01 of Expense Distribution is complete and acceptance test is being run. The rest of the work is on schedule.

Sales statistics
Daily and weekly: Currently testing.
Update: Currently testing; coding 90 percent complete.
Customer history: Currently performing preliminary tests; coding 80 percent complete.

Daily stock control
Completely coded; should start acceptance testing 2/15.
Daily Stock should be ready for integration test 3/1.

Monthly stock control
Work delayed due to revisions of Daily Stock. Earliest anticipated completion date is 4/30/84.

Daily tax accounting
New space on control totals will add six programmer days. Priority given to daily at the expense of monthly. Coding 90 percent complete; testing should start next week.

Monthly tax accounting
Received additional test data. Coding progressing satisfactorily on all seven programs. Should begin testing next week on three smaller programs.

---

analyst might prepare a flow chart using the term "cash flow" in a very different way than had been defined in the corporate data dictionary. There were frequent discussions about whether the data dictionary should be changed to reflect RAC managerial vocabulary, or whether flow charts and code should be rewritten to conform with existing standards. All too often Chutten was called in as a final arbiter in these disputes.

Programmer-Analyst Communications.   Each group blamed the other for delays in their schedule. Programmers claimed that the test data prepared by the analysts was unsatisfactory because it did not test all the parameters of the program. Programmers also contended that analysts' specs were inadequate and that they could not understand some of the unfamiliar notations which the analysts were using on their new systems development tool. Some programmers grumbled that the analysts' fancy on-line system was only camouflaging sloppy specifications. Analysts countered that the programmers wanted to redesign their work. One lone analyst was repeatedly saying that the systems development methodology in use at RAC no longer made sense in the new RAMIS II environment. Whenever he encountered Chairling in the hallway he would repeatedly ask why RAC was so set on the traditional systems life cycle approach when the fourth generation language offered the opportunity to approach projects in a very different way. "We really don't even need most of those programmers," he kept arguing. "Why not let the analysts, who know what's going on, do the whole job?" Chairling had an uneasy feeling that there was a grain of truth in the analyst's continual commentary. But what could he change? Surely RAC needed its system of checks and balances to control the design process.

Poor Response Time.   During the peak middle of the day hours, response time for test and debug trials was more than a minute. This was a matter of great concern, since it was expected that the field offices would wish to make extensive use of on-line query capabilities. End users in a distributed processing environment would have little patience with a slow system. Use of personal computers or intelligent terminals for much of the data manipulation would alleviate some, but not all, of this problem. Chairling knew that once users gained experience with this system their demands for on-line access would skyrocket.

Inefficient Field Processing.   Initial tests indicated that with only 45 percent of the modules operating, the processing of the central file update from daily field input was taking approximately 11 hours. The systems design called for input of data from 56 locations starting at 5 P.M. daily with all updating complete by 8 A.M. the next day.

Looking Ahead

Bob Chairling pondered these problems of RAC's first entrance into distributed computer utilization. Each passing month cost RAC approximately $300,000 in forgone savings and benefits. Now in June of

1984 Mr. Chairling was already busy assisting the production department executives with plans for an even larger profit improvement project with a potentially very high payback. The production project was expected to take more than three years. Mr. Chairling hoped he could provide helpful guidance to production management by communicating the knowledge gained from his first large-scale project.

Chairling was acutely aware of sweeping changes in the way information systems were being managed in his own and other companies. Personal computers were popping up everywhere, and end users were demanding an ever-expanding list of services which Chairling's group was not well equipped to handle. He suspected that many microcomputer applications were being developed within the company without his knowledge (and largely beyond his control). Chairling had also been reading about new systems design methodologies, both for individual decision support systems and larger organizational information systems. One which interested him was developed at an East Coast MIS consulting firm.

These consultants used what they termed a "Top-Down, Middle-Out" approach to systems design. They started with an assessment of an organization's Critical Success Factors (CSF), gleaned from interviews with executives from both general management and MIS management. The CSF process was intended to identify those computer-based applications which would add the most value to an organization, and concentrate development effort on these applications. The systems design phase involved spending less time on detailed upfront analysis in favor of building inexpensive prototypes. This had been the approach taken in Phase II, the early decision support project. Eliciting managers' reactions to these prototypes was felt to result in higher-quality systems designs. Chairling had set a date to meet with a vice president at the consulting firm to explore whether their approach might be useful for designing future large systems at Rogers.

Chairling was also concerned about the long-run impact of fourth generation languages. Although their initial experience with RAMIS II had its rough moments, users were giving the product high marks, and some of the applications programmers were working more efficiently. Chairling worried that use of RAMIS II and other ad hoc languages would create pressure on the corporate data base, in terms of size, architecture, and security. The task of formulating a corporate data architecture was far from complete. Chairling felt that as applications shifted from highly structured, batch reports to more ad hoc, discretionary reports, the need for a clear data base architecture, a data dictionary, and security measures was increasing faster than was progress by the data control group.

Chairling would have liked to spend considerably more time investigating these and other issues related to changing technology and the changing role of his Profit Improvement Projects group. But his pressing problem was to complete the marketing project. He headed down the hallway to confer with Chutten on how to keep the project on track.

Case 8-2

Concordia Casting Company

In late October 1984, Stuart McMillen, director of Corporate Information Services (CIS) for Concordia Casting Company, was concerned about a major schedule slippage in his department's most important systems development effort, the CAPS project. After several weeks of intense investigation, some key management changes, and a major rescheduling effort, it was clear that CAPS would come on line almost a year late. This was the latest in a series of missed completion dates for CAPS.

McMillen wanted to make several additional changes within his department, but for the time being, he planned to concentrate on the CAPS project. McMillen also knew that his 1985 operating plan would have to contain longer-term proposals for managing CIS.

Background on Concordia and CIS

Concordia Casting Company, based in Fort Wayne, Indiana, was a large, multidivisional manufacturing organization with 1983 revenues of more than $1 billion. The company had four business segments. The largest and most profitable division was Automotive (engine blocks and other automobile parts). Machine Tools (lathes, power presses, drills, etc.), Precision Parts (screws, nuts, bolts, and other machined

This case was prepared by James P. Ware and F. Warren McFarlan.

Copyright © 1986 by the President and Fellows of Harvard College
Harvard Business School case 9–187–029

parts), and Fluid Controls (valves and piping for commercial applications) collectively accounted for about half of the company's revenues. Much of Concordia's growth had come through acquisition. Each division, composed of several independent companies, was treated as a separate profit center.

McMillen was hired as director of Corporate Information Services in March 1980. He had previously worked for the consulting firm of Huntington and Wells, Concordia's auditors. His contact with Concordia's Corporate Information Services department began in 1978, when he consulted on systems design for the department. McMillen had an M.B.A. from the University of Virginia and an engineering degree from Purdue. His early experience included six years in systems design for a major retailing company.

McMillen inherited a department in the midst of major organizational transition. An aggressive corporate diversification program had led to acquisition of numerous small specialty manufacturing companies, each with special data processing needs. CIS had previously served only the Automotive Division. In 1977, Jim Butler was hired as CIS director and charged with building a corporatewide information system. Butler devised a plan for a centralized corporate data utility, and recommended the company select a single hardware vendor in order to integrate the various systems.

In 1979 senior management chose IBM as prime vendor. IBM was not comfortable, however, with Butler's concept of a centralized data utility. Concordia was highly decentralized. Acquired companies retained their original names and identities, and were explicitly encouraged to operate independently. Said one senior executive: "Concordia is not inclined to get into management's shoes. We bought these companies because it made financial sense, but we repeatedly tell our division presidents that they are autonomous. Our takeovers are friendly; often they come to us and ask if they can become part of the Concordia family."

Butler's centralized data processing proposal was not well received. His boss, Bradley Sherman (former CIS director and now a corporate vice president and treasurer), hired Huntington and Wells to help develop a long-range plan for data processing. The consultant team included McMillen. In early 1980, Butler left Concordia for another job, and McMillen was hired as his replacement.

When McMillen took over CIS in 1980, the department had an operating budget of $1.8 million, and was organized into five functional groups: systems and programming; DP operations; process control; planning and control; and operations research. Of the 52 people in the department, 37 were in operations and systems.

Recognizing that a fully centralized data utility would not be appropriate at Concordia, McMillen worked with the consultants to de-

EXHIBIT 1

CIS Organization Structure, Early 1980

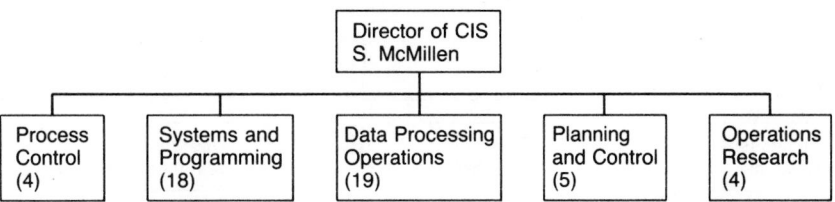

CIS Organization Established by McMillen, 1981

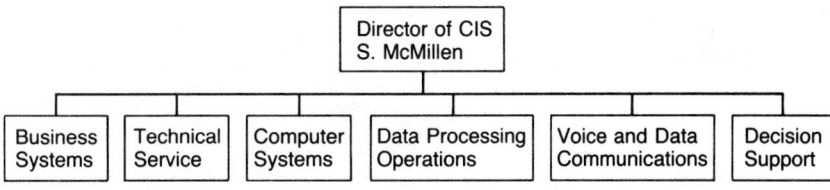

NOTE: **Numbers in parentheses indicate number of staff in each area.**

velop an alternative approach. He also needed to increase and upgrade the CIS professional staff since converting existing systems to run on IBM equipment was putting a severe strain on the department. None of the CIS staff, as of 1980, had been trained on standard IBM systems; indeed, only a few had a solid grasp of the existing systems.

In 1981 McMillen requested a budget allocation of $2.5 million, and began an aggressive recruiting program that brought to Concordia a number of systems engineers and project managers who were well-versed in IBM systems, equipment, and design methodologies.

McMillen also worked on strengthening and expanding his management team. He added a business systems manager and a voice/data communications manager to his staff, and he rearranged somewhat the existing CIS groups. By the end of 1981 seven managers reported directly to him (see Exhibit 1).

In 1982 the Huntington and Wells consultants proposed a "distributed" organization for CIS. Corporate data processing functions would be clearly separated from work done for the operating divisions. Several regional data centers would service clusters of operating divisions, while corporate staff would focus on corporate systems development, decision support, long-range planning, policy-setting, communications, corporate DP standards, database management, and business

EXHIBIT 2

CIS Organization Proposed by Huntington and Wells, 1982

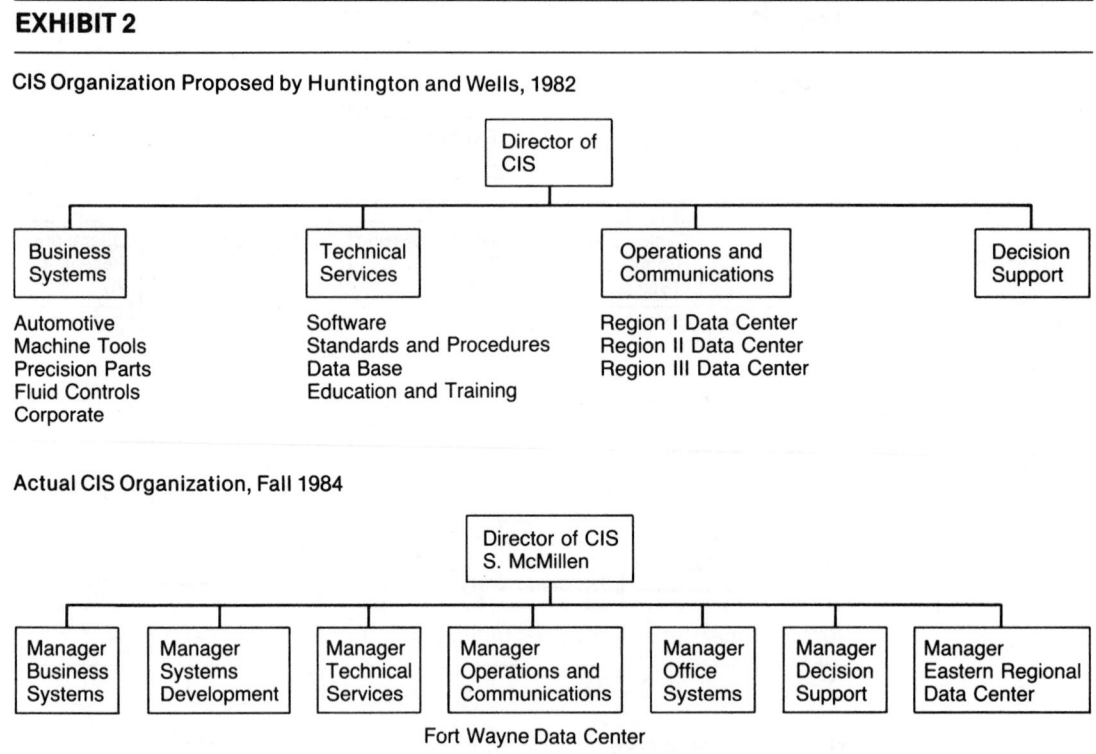

Actual CIS Organization, Fall 1984

systems consulting throughout the company. With senior management approval, much of McMillen's time over the next several years was devoted to moving CIS in that direction.

By late 1984 McMillen believed he had a strong, viable Corporate Information Services group. The staff numbered just over 100, including 22 in the Eastern Regional Data Center in Hagerstown, Maryland. The 1984 operating budget for CIS was in excess of $7 million, and the organization resembled the one the consultants had recommended in 1982 (see Exhibit 2).

McMillen reflected on the situation he had inherited five years earlier.

> First I discovered that Butler hadn't done a very good job. CIS had no basic design standards, no formal systems development methodology, no chargeout system. And there was tremendous unsatisfied user demand—almost a five-year backlog of projects—with nowhere near the staff to handle it.

To make matters worse, in 1980 the CIS staff in Fort Wayne was spread out on eight different floors in three separate buildings, in old, crowded offices. On top of that, I had a staff of about 50 people and no personnel function to speak of. No performance appraisal system, no way to measure individual development, no formal training programs.

McMillen reviewed his major accomplishments:

- Constructing a $2.3 million wing to the headquarters building, bringing the entire CIS staff together for the first time.
- Increasing the CIS staff located in Fort Wayne (from 50 in 1980 to over 80 in 1984).
- Installing an IBM 3083 and related peripheral equipment.
- Completing several new corporate and divisional applications: two on-line purchasing systems, a payroll-personnel system, and several period-end accounting systems. Combined, these projects were as big as the CAPS efforts.
- Opening an Eastern Regional Data Center in Hagerstown, Maryland, which included a new facility.
- Developing a formal college recruiting program to bring qualified systems designers into CIS.
- Improving the operation of the corporate DP steering committee.

Sherman also felt McMillen had succeeded in several areas, especially his development of a DP plan that provided a framework for future development: "Stu is a brilliant conceptual thinker, and he's had a clear vision of where he wants CIS to go. Sometimes he's tenacious to the point of being more aggressive than people around here are used to—you know: damn the torpedoes, full speed ahead. But actually, I don't see how he could have done as much as he has without being a little pushy."

McMillen knew that these impressive accomplishments counted for little in senior management's eyes as long as CAPS was not yet completed. CAPS was the driving force in the department. It consumed the most resources, was highly visible, and had the highest potential for improving operations in the heart of the Automotive Division.

The CAPS Conversion Project

The original CAPS system was developed at Concordia in the late 1960s as a state-of-the-art, on-line system. It operated on two Centronics 275s (disguised name) and comprised 12 subsystems:

1. Order entry.	7. Shipping assembly.
2. Order maintenance.	8. Shipping maintenance.
3. Production scheduling.	9. File maintenance.
4. Production maintenance.	10. Inquiry.
5. Packed production.	11. Invoicing.
6. Packing lists.	12. Accounts receivable.

In addition, 16 batch systems produced periodic and special status reports:

1. Order file reports.	9. File balance.
2. Order analysis.	10. Accounts receivable.
3. Customer allocation.	11. Physical inventory.
4. Delay notices.	12. Weekly inventory analysis.
5. Stock status.	13. Forecasting.
6. Stock usage.	14. Product history.
7. In-process report.	15. Marketing inventory.
8. Shipment report.	16. File maintenance.

The original Centronics programs were written in machine language by Concordia systems staff; the operating system was also homegrown. Although the system worked adequately in the early 1980s, a major overhaul was clearly required. Software maintenance was difficult and time-consuming, and the system required more memory storage space than the Centronics equipment could provide. The hardware was difficult to maintain, and many felt it was obsolete.

These difficulties led to a decision to replace the Centronics 275s with more powerful equipment. Upgrading the Centronics hardware would necessitate a rewrite of all existing systems. Concordia management did not want to go through a major conversion each time central processors were changed. It felt that the Centronics product line was insufficient to meet the division's processing needs. So in 1979 management decided to convert to IBM as a prime vendor.

Converting all of Concordia's systems from Centronics to IBM was a massive effort. IBM originally estimated the conversions would require 15 programmer-years. By 1981 it was evident that the initial estimate was wholly inadequate. At that time IBM and Huntington and Wells reviewed the conversion effort, and concluded that it would take a minimum of 27 programmer-years. By 1984 it was clear that the conversions would actually consume well over 75 programmer-years (of which half would be dedicated to the CAPS system). Furthermore, the hardware being installed was much more powerful than the machine initially recommended. A Huntington and Wells consultant commented: "The CAPS conversion project was consistently underestimated since Day 1. Although the functions of the system have not been changed dramatically, the software and hardware requirements turned out to be significantly greater than we realized. On the other hand, if we *had* predicted accurately what it would take, no one would have believed us."

McMillen believed several factors had contributed to the poor estimates. First, no one fully appreciated the difficulties of building a complex, interdependent system virtually from scratch. There were 420 online programs (over 750,000 lines of code) and 126 batch programs, plus over 350 user procedures to be written. Second, many enhancements had been added to the original design. McMillen estimated that the new system had 40 percent more functions than the old one. Third, the old system itself had evolved during the past four years. Hence, the conversion design was modified several times while the new system was being developed.

Meanwhile, McMillen was under pressure from Ronald Lawton, controller of the Automotive Division, to ensure uninterrupted service. Recently Lawton stopped McMillen in the hallway to remind him: "What really scares me, Stu, is how much we depend on CAPS. If that system goes down for more than a day, we have to start thinking about closing the plant. We cannot run without it."

Stu McMillen understood Lawton's concern, but he did not believe Lawton recognized how substantially the old system had been modified. Supporting changes in the old system had a double impact on CIS: modifications consumed CIS resources directly and necessitated substantial revisions in already completed portions of the new system.

Staffing Problems

"Our technical problems, horrendous as they were, were nothing compared with our personnel problems," said McMillen. Attracting new employees had been very difficult. When they arrived, management had a new set of problems. The new staff understood IBM systems and procedures, but they were not familiar with the old CAPS system, with Concordia's businesses, or with the "Concordia approach" to solving problems. Many of the experienced CIS staff resented the newcomers and were reluctant to share their knowledge. In the words of one long-time CIS manager:

> We do need these IBM-trained people, but we don't have enough Concordia people. You can't completely describe the system on paper; a programmer needs to know all the file structures, the program linkages, and so on. I offered to introduce the new staff people to the operating people, but they were always too busy. I guess they saw themselves as "professional" managers and thought that was enough. Around here, it isn't. Most of the managers in the

plant have been here a long time. I started there and fought my way up, but a lot of these college kids want to be managers overnight.

Managers outside of CIS were also concerned about the rapid influx of new technical specialists. Lawton commented:

> These newcomers have really affected the morale of the old-timers, who see new people placed above them in the organization. What's worse, the old-timers worry about losing their jobs when the conversion is complete. What role does a Centronics programmer play when we're 100 percent IBM?
>
> The newcomers have been pretty insensitive. It's getting better, but not too long ago it was: "Hi, I'm from CIS. Here's the system you're going to use." Our people won't forget being treated like that.

Sherman told a similar story, stressing how radically different the newcomers were: "In one instance, four people from CIS were visiting a division. Each one rented a separate car, and they acted like 'big-shot' representatives of corporate headquarters, making pronouncements about company policies. They don't understand our low-key, people-sensitive organization. We get things done by patient, gentle persuasion. Yet CIS has to impose change on divisions who view themselves as highly autonomous."

Over the past five years McMillen had hired close to 90 people for the Fort Wayne operations, just to achieve a growth in staffing from 50 to 80. In 1984 alone he had spent close to $350,000 in recruiting fees, travel expenses, and relocation costs to bring in 20 new people. Since almost as many had resigned to take positions elsewhere, he had just managed to stay even.

McMillen attributed the turnover problem to two primary factors: salary levels and location. A telecommunications analyst making $26,000 a year had recently left for $37,000 at another company. Qualified technical people had many other options. Salary pressures were also creating internal equity problems. New hires were making almost as much as top managers both in CIS and in other departments.

McMillen believed that Concordia's location in Fort Wayne had hampered his efforts to attract and retain quality DP personnel. He recalled one prime candidate from Philadelphia who drove through town from the airport to Concordia's headquarters, took a quick tour of the facilities, and announced he wanted to leave on the next plane.

As a short-term strategy, McMillen had made extensive use of outside contract programming personnel, budgeting over $1 million in 1984 for the purpose. But contract programmers were not very efficient. They usually traveled to Fort Wayne on Monday mornings and left on Friday afternoons. Although they put in evening hours to make up for travel time, their work pattern irritated many of the internal programmers.

Recent History of the CAPS Project

The CAPS team had had four project managers in three years; one had been fired, and two had resigned. Frank Northrup, the most recent resignee, left Concordia in April 1984. Northrup had predicted the system would be up and running before the end of 1984; the consultants agreed. McMillen wondered whether Northrup had been uneasy about CAPS and left before major problems surfaced.

Testing of the individual programs suffered because of a personality clash between two key analysts (a newcomer and an old-timer), and because of performance problems with the newly installed IBM 3083 central processor. During a two-month period in late spring, the 3083 had over 200 hours of downtime—a senior IBM executive labelled Concordia's machine "the worst-performing installation of a 3083 anywhere in the United States." IBM technicians, arriving in Fort Wayne, "by the plane-load," literally rebuilt two-thirds of the 3083 on site. By early summer, it was finally performing more reliably.

As McMillen understood it, the testing problems related primarily to the integration of CAPS' separate units. Since the project team had already tested the individual programs, it assumed the system testing would proceed smoothly. During the summer of 1984, many unexpected modifications had to be made by a short-handed project team. In addition, a test generator package had not worked as expected. The systems tests were taking much longer than expected.

The CAPS plan called for running the IBM system in parallel with the Centronics system for a day, and assessing the results before a final cutover. In late August, it became apparent that the system was not ready to run in parallel. Lawton (controller for the Automotive Division) recalled his frustration at learning of the delay:

> The stuff hit the fan at a review meeting on September 6. The project leader told me the system wouldn't be ready until late in the fourth quarter. I got pretty excited, but he told me they announced the delay several weeks earlier. That was news to me! He told me to go back and read my mail.
>
> Well, I finally found one sentence on page 3 of the monthly Executive Summary. Why hadn't they communicated it to me personally? Our manager of Production and manager of Scheduling hadn't known about it before September 6, either.
>
> When word got to our division vice president, he started asking what was going on, and got Brad Sherman to look into it pretty closely.

McMillen had initiated an intensive review of the CAPS project well before Lawton learned of the problems.

> I called the whole CAPS team into the office on Sunday, August 19. We met from 9 A.M. to 4 P.M., and by then I knew it couldn't be done until April or May 1985 at the earliest. I ordered an exhaustive review of CAPS and the other conversion projects, using new assumptions about machine downtime, program modification, programmer availability, and so on. By mid-September I realized the CAPS conversion couldn't be completed before September 1985.

> We purposely kept this information from the users until we could give them reasonable new estimates that we *knew* we could live with.

McMillen asked Len Creighton, his strongest technical manager, to take over the CAPS projects. Creighton, who had over 10 years at Concordia, had developed the company's operations research effort, and most recently had been in charge of the CIS business systems analysis group. When Creighton stepped into the CAPS project, he found: "Chaos. The team was too small, the planning was almost nonexistent. The few Gantt charts they had weren't detailed enough. The guy who had been managing the project wasn't strong enough. He's good technically, but his planning and control skills were weak."

McMillen had shuffled other assignments and added 10 new people to the project, bringing its staff up to 18. Creighton made certain that the team included a project administrator with extensive project planning and control experience. As Creighton put it:

> He's monitoring progress on a daily basis, and training others to do so. He's put up a huge magnetic board in his office, and now everyone can track their commitments, their progress, and their problems. That alone is helping the team watch interim deadlines, and rearrange activities and schedules on their own.

> The testing is already uncovering a can of worms, so there is a lot of need to constantly rearrange people and activities. But we are staying with the basic plan.

Organizational Implications

Although McMillen was confident Creighton would bring CAPS under control, he was concerned about the deeper organizational problems that the CAPS difficulties had revealed. In a memorandum written several months earlier (see box and Exhibit 3), Huntington and Wells had recommended a narrower structure for CIS. It proposed an additional level of management, with only three people reporting directly to McMillen.

EXHIBIT 3 Consultant's Proposal CIS Organization

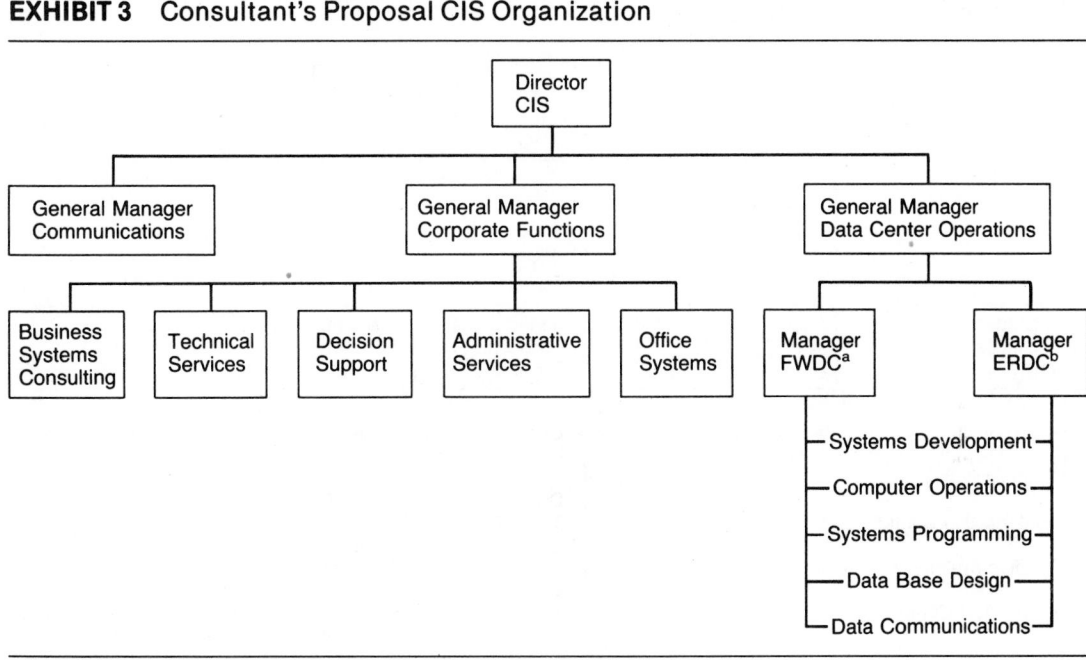

[a]Fort Wayne Data Center
[b]Eastern Regional Data Center

McMillen and the consultants subsequently developed a slightly different organizational plan (see Exhibit 4). Like the consultant's original proposal, McMillen's current plan proposed a sharper separation between CIS's two primary functions. The data centers in Hagerstown and Fort Wayne were to meet the ongoing data processing and systems development needs of individual operating divisions. In contrast, the field support function would provide corporatewide systems planning and coordination, and serve corporate headquarters' own data processing needs. McMillen believed the planned organization would help resolve many of the user relationship problems that had plagued CIS.

McMillen wondered how quickly he could implement the new structure. The Eastern Regional Data Center in Hagerstown was operating. But the situation in Fort Wayne was tenuous, due to an inadequate management team. The conversion projects were soaking up so many people that many other projects were being tabled or delayed: there was no one to work on fundamental problems like recruiting, training, performance evaluation, career planning, project planning and control systems, and user relations. And there was a tremendous backlog of

EXHIBIT 4   Proposed Organization of CIS, October 1984

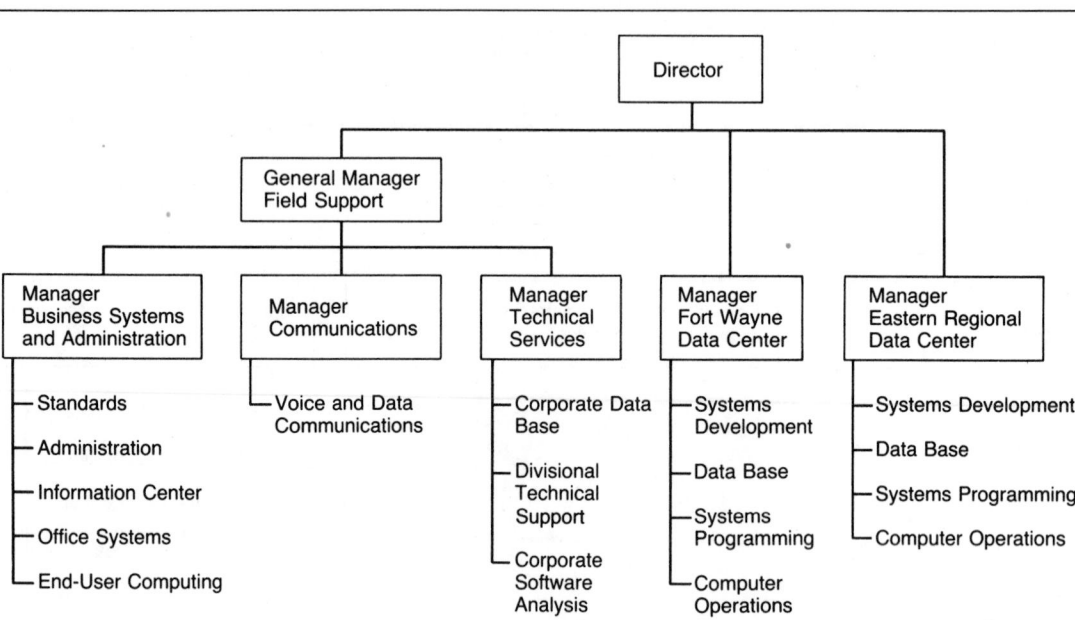

user demand for new applications. McMillen spoke: "The Automotive Division alone has requested 18 major new applications. Our other divisions have literally tens of programmer-years of work that they need done. Most of the divisions' 1985 plans assume that they will get new systems next year. They can't meet their business plans without those new systems."

As McMillen pondered these operating problems and organizational alternatives, he wondered what goals and priorities he should set for 1985. He also wondered how he should allocate his time, and what steps he should take to implement his goals.

Excerpts from Consultant's Recommendations for Reorganization of the CIS Department, June 1984

A three-tier structure (see Exhibit 3) has been proposed to replace the existing two-tier structure based on the following:

1. The director has too many people reporting to him, which limits severely the time he can spend with corporate and divisional management.

2. An increase in the size and scope of the department necessitates an increase in the number of management personnel.
3. Conversion from Centronics to IBM computers has revealed problems in the existing organization which the revised organization should address.

The new organization calls for a greater division between "line" and "staff" activities, in order to concentrate on longer-term issues affecting the company. This division will require a strong coordination effort between the two groups which should be accomplished by the general managers of corporate support and data center operations; an effective quality assurance function; and establishment of a career path which requires employees to work in both major areas.

Below are brief descriptions of the revised positions:

1. *Director*—The principal role of the director will not change, but he will have more time for liaison with corporate and divisional senior management.
2. *General Manager-Communications*—This new position would separate communications from computer operations. Presently, 90 percent to 95 percent of communications work is associated with voice transmission, although data communications requirements will increase significantly in the next few years.
3. *General Manager-Corporate Support*—Coordinate all "indirect" data processing support major functions:
   a. Coordinate activities within the "corporate" group for consistency.
   b. Ensure coordination between the two major groups by continued contact with the general manager.
   c. Screen information now going to the director and assume some of the decision making.
   d. Respond to divisional planning needs.
4. *General Manager-Data Center Operations*—Initial responsibility for two data centers (each with their respective managers). Responsibility may increase through the addition of data centers or separation from the existing regional data centers of the divisional support activities. Prime functions are:
   a. Control and coordinate activities of the regional data centers.
   b. Ensure review by line personnel of proposed policies/procedures developed by corporate group, and ensure adherence to them once they are adopted.
   c. Report to the director on all aspects of data center operations and systems development.

5. *Manager-Business Systems and Decision Support*—Little change in functions from those currently performed.
6. *Manager-Technical Services*—Combine the current decision-making functions of the existing Technical Services Department with equipment requirements determination and selections.
7. *Manager-Standards and Quality Assurance*—Combine the existing standards function with a new quality assurance function. Need for the latter will be heightened by the proposed division between line and staff positions.
8. *Manager-Administrative Services*—Responsibility for user billings and associated follow-up, and possibly training and other administrative functions.
9. *Manager-Regional Data Center*—Follow closely the role performed now by the Eastern Regional Data Center Manager, but with total unit responsibility for systems development (as indicated in Exhibit 3).

Chapter 9

Operations Management

A major North American manufacturing company has a brand-new $3.5 million underground operations center protected by four guards, nine TV cameras, and multiple levels of access security. The chief executive officer personally approved and supervised its construction. At the same time, the critical application being run in the center (an on-line order system) is 13 years old. Under tight head-count control imposed by senior management, the systems and programming staff has decreased by nearly 35 over the previous four years and is barely able to implement necessary maintenance work, let alone major systems enhancements of new projects. Senior IT management is deeply concerned about the unbalanced allocation of resources between invisible required maintenance and visible facilities.

After years of debate a major bank reluctantly has built a second data center 50 miles away from the primary data center. The source of debate focused on whether a 7 percent increase in costs was a good trade-off vis-à-vis the extra security against disaster provided by the second data center. This bank currently has over 4,000 on-line terminals and is deeply dependent on the smooth, uninterrupted, 24-hour-a-day operation of IT services to meet its daily operating performance targets.

The chief executive officer of an industrial products concern discovers that the delay in year-end financial closing is not due to reduced emphasis on close control of financial accounting but to unexpected work and personnel problems in the IT department.

Increased use (and associated problems) of an on-line query system to provide salesmen and customers with detailed delivery and cost information has absorbed all available system support personnel to keep this vital system operational. No time was left to revise the accounting system for changes in the new tax law before year-end closing.

The director of IT of a major engineering firm is pondering whether to break apart and totally reorganize his operations center. At present, a single large computer supports the company's batch and on-line system. Workloads are quite erratic. Also, in the past year long response-time delays on the on-line systems, combined with batch schedules, have put him under considerable user pressure to be more responsive.

Unusual problems? Hardly! Historically, the glamorous part of the IT function has been the technology orientation of systems development, with maintenance and operations occupying a distinctly back-seat role. In this chapter the term *operations* is defined as the running of IT hardware, data input, equipment scheduling, and work forces associated therewith. This chapter also deals with the tendency toward outside sourcing for software and the impact of such make or buy decisions on the systems life cycle. While this could have been covered in Chapter 8, the *operational* implications of this shift seemed so important that we chose to deal with it here in detail.

Changing Operations Environment

Both the type and amount of management resources devoted to operations activities and the sophistication of management practices within the operations center have often been inadequate for their growing and changing mission inside the company. A number of aspects of changing technology are now triggering major changes in the way these activities are managed.

1. Move to On-Line System. Greatly increased on-line technology applications and sophistication in operating systems in the past decade have taken what originally was a batch, job-shop environment with heavy human control and turned it first into a process manufacturing shop and at present into a largely self-scheduled and monitored 24-hour-a-day utility. This change in manufacturing work flow has precipitated a total rethinking of both what is appropriate scheduling and what is the definition of adequate service levels.

2. Diversity of Performance Measures.   There is no such thing as an ideal standard IT operations management control system or a set of performance metrics. The trade-off between quality of service, response time of on-line systems, handling of unexpected jobs, total cost, and ability to meet published schedules on batch systems varies appropriately from one organization to another.

3. Efficiency-Effectiveness Balance.   Different IT operations environments must strike different balances between efficiency (low-cost producer) and effectiveness (flexibility) in responding to unplanned, uneven flows of requests. IT operations cannot be *all things* simultaneously to *all people* but must operate on a set of priorities and trade-offs based on corporate strategy. Implementing these priorities has caused the reorganization of some large IT operations into a series of focused, single-service oriented groups, each of which can be managed to quite different user service objectives.

4. Changes in Types of Staffing Needed.   Many formerly appropriate employees are unsuited now for the new tasks. These problems have been complicated by the unionization of this function in many parts of the globe.

5. Continued Change in Technology.   Evolving technology initiates the normal problems of change and new operating procedures, while offering potential benefits of lower cost and new capabilities.

6. The Trend toward Outside Sourcing.   The major shift toward more outside sourcing in IT processing and software sourcing decisions requires changes in the procedures of both the operations and development functions of IT if they are to be handled responsibly.

These issues are similar to those involved in running a manufacturing facility characterized by the terms *highly volatile technology, specialized labor, serving dynamic markets,* and *changing industry structure.* Consequently much of the analysis in this chapter draws on work done in manufacturing management, particularly as it relates to efficiency-effectiveness trade-offs.

A key question stemming from this manufacturing analogy is how focused the department should be. Should it subdivide itself into sets of stand-alone services or be organized as a general-purpose IT service? In the example at the beginning of the chapter, the problem of the late closing of the books versus providing on-line service for query stimulated the company to review how operations were responding to the demands of new services. The review produced a conclusion similar to Skinner's plea for a focused factory:[1] They perceived it as being impossible for a single unit to respond adequately to such very different user needs.

To address the problem, the IT development and maintenance group was reorganized into four independent systems groups, each of which operated independent of the others but reported to a common boss (the IT manager). One group was to support the on-line query systems with goals to provide 10-second response, one-day change implementation, and all data refreshed hourly. The second group was devoted to the general ledger accounting system. Their goals were to keep the software up-to-date for month-end closing schedule work so as not to interfere with other systems, ensure the quality and reliability of accounting data, and operate to close the books five days after the end of the last working day of the month. The third group was to be responsible for all material-management systems. Their objectives were to ensure that all production control persons were well trained in use of the system, to provide updated data overnight, and to maintain an operation of the system in a manner consistent with material policies on inventory and customer delivery. The fourth group was to work with the systems supporting new-product development. They were responsible for identifying system requirements of new products, maintaining the availability of the capacity simulator for planning new-product developments, establishing data standards and new data files in existing systems for approved new products, and developing and performing analyses on new products as directed by the vice president of product development. Each focused group included at least one user and two to three systems professionals. All worked full time on their respective services with the exception of the new-product group, which had spurts of work as new products hit the market and lulls after the market settled down. This structure has produced happier customers and significantly better percentages of service as well as increased employee morale.

Historically IT systems were developed to be run out of an integrated IT operations unit. As noted above, some firms have reorganized IT development and construction to be more responsible to user needs. For example, many organizations have not only shifted application programmers (e.g., construction) to users but have also allowed maintenance and operations to be decentralized around the local sys-

---

[1]Wickham Skinner, "The Focused Factory," *Harvard Business Review,* May–June 1974.

tem. As IT's monopoly of system construction and make or buy decisions erodes to more and greater user control, the result is fragmentation of the factory into a series of focused services (e.g., a word processing system for customer mailing). For some users and applications this may be very effective. The services for other users, however, may be dependent upon an integrated set of data, in which case severe coordination problems can be created. The challenge is to identify where focus in operations (either within the central unit or by distributing to the user) is appropriate and then execute it in a way that provides the necessary thrust. Implementation of this will be discussed further in the section on production planning and control.

To build on this manufacturing strategy theme and develop an appropriate range of make or buy plans, our operations management discussion is organized around the following topics:

> Development of an operations strategy.
> Technology planning.
> Measuring and managing capacity.
> Managing the IT operations work force.
> Production planning and control.
> Security.

Developing an Operations Strategy

As noted earlier the management team of an IT operations activity is trying to stay on top of a utility that is radically changing its production system, customer base, and role within the company. Ten years ago the manager and his staff were monopolists running a job shop where the key issues were scheduling (with substantial human inputs), ensuring telecommunications were adequate, managing a large blue-collar staff, and planning capacity and staffing levels for future workloads of similar characteristics. Today they are operating an information utility providing a 24-hour, 7-day-a-week service that must cope cost effectively with uncertain short-term and long-term user demand; manage a work force far more highly skilled, more professional, and much smaller in numbers; and evaluate both internal and external competing services that in many cases offer the potential to solve problems more cheaply and more comprehensively. Key issues for the IT operations manager still include staff, capacity, and telecommunications. Prominent additions to this list, however, are appropriate assessment, assimilation, and integration of software and services emanating from outside the corporation.

Senior management both must assess the quality of IT operations support and, depending on how critical it is to the overall strategic mission of the corporation, must involve themselves appropriately. The central question both senior and IT management must address is whether the current IT operations organization now effectively supports the firm.

In this context an operations strategy must address the following key issues:

1. Ensuring that an architecture has been conceived and is being implemented.
2. Ensuring that each step of a system's life cycle appropriately addresses the critical long-term operating needs of the system.
3. Ensuring that the internal/external sourcing decisions are carefully thought through, both as to their outcome and as to who should primarily influence the outcome with respect to operational characteristics.
4. Resolving the extent to which IT operations should be managed as a single entity or be broken down into a series of perhaps more costly but more focused subunits that provide more customized user service than is possible from a monolithic facility.

The following paragraphs discuss these items in more detail.

The Role of IT Architecture

In today's evolving technology, managing an IT portfolio to gain a competitive advantage is akin to urban renewal. Great tensions exist between meeting today's needs and providing a platform that permits tomorrow's services to evolve. To balance these conflicting goals, many firms have developed an overall IT architecture that prescribes for the future the necessary services and critical performance needs. This architecture (1) provides an operational vision, (2) results from and is modified as an ongoing process, (3) allows concrete projects to be identified for the immediate future, (4) serves as a basis for establishing priorities and sequencing IT projects, and (5) establishes a basis for organization change.

Vision. The most celebrated operational vision was that of C. A. Smith (past CEO of American Airlines): the idea of a passenger name record for every reserved seat on American Airlines. Created in 1954 this idea drove the development of SABRE in 1968 and its subsequent modification. Such a vision encompasses the key business purpose of IT (examples: an active electronic link to every important customer for industrial wholesalers; a complete product history and potential sale for all financial service customers). The practical implications of the vision—such as seat selection, boarding passes, frequent flier programs, and personal marketing—will evolve through ongoing discussion and implementation. Both changing competitive situations and evolving technology cost and performance make this a dynamic process.

Ongoing Process.   Successful architectures are not bound in a book but rather are present in ongoing discussions among the key decision makers: architecture in action. An illustration of this process is the strategy status room of a multinational bank. On one wall are posted descriptions of the key strategy and service objectives for each decision-making unit, retail branch, and overseas office, as well as lists of new electronic-based products for each major business. In 1985 these new products include a retail branch experiment in a distributed data base, the final phase of their worldwide net, a rollout of their focused service branches, and an expert-system project. On another wall is a chart listing all sites and the services provided at each site along with planned maintenance. On the back wall is a list of all hardware and main software providing these services. Senior management meets in this room once a month to review progress and deal with new issues.

Project Identification.   A working architecture permits and encourages the planning of sound projects that can be justified and initiated within the existing organizations. These projects will originate from both business and IT staffs stimulated by the ongoing dialogue. For example, in a large chemical business the R&D group initiated an experimental local area network (LAN) as a means to improve R&D productivity (an objective of their architecture). Over time the LAN grew into a network supporting corporate headquarters. It started in R&D and was phased into IT as it became a useful general service. In a publishing company, a group of editors formed a steering committee to explore how PCs could better support the editorial process—in part stimulated by a series of architectural discussions on the role of workstations in supporting editorial work.

Priorities.   A prime purpose of IT architecture is to facilitate the establishment of priorities and the funding of new projects to meet both today's needs and tomorrow's competitive arena. The recent explosion of PC use, expansion of communication services, and massive reorganization of data structures have highlighted the contrast in time and resources needed to implement these services, which are often interdependent. A network development and implementation program may be measured in years, while new terminal systems can take only weeks. Without an architecture the short-term tactical moves can insidiously postpone the long-term projects. Further implementation complications are caused by the shift to buying software and services and the movement of the responsibility for these decisions to line managers. An IT architecture imposes a global perspective on priority setting for IT projects.

System Design and Operations

A review of IT operations organization must start with an assessment of the first step in the systems life cycle: the design phase. The key operations decisions for a system are often made early in the design phase and, unless identified as such and handled appropriately at that phase, can cause great difficulty. Proper operations input to the systems design phase is complicated by the fact that the IT operations department is a victim of history: Past decisions have shaped today's operating environment, which influences the vision of what is possible in both today's operating environment and today's design decisions.

To get their viewpoint across as well as to be educated on the reality of the existing situation, both user operational personnel and IT operational personnel need to be involved in the early design phase for significant ongoing processing systems. IT operations involvement not only guarantees the operational integrity of the new system design but ensures that existing systems operations are not adversely impacted during the design and implementation stages of the new system and that the conversion plan from the old to the new is satisfactory. Reviewing these issues is particularly important for externally sourced software, since interfacing issues are complex.

Externally Sourced Services—Pressures and Challenges

The recent shift in software construction—from a situation where the bulk of energy was devoted to in-house software construction managed by IT staff, to today's position where there is a greater reliance on purchased software and service—is not surprising. The supply of cheap hardware is growing dramatically, while the human resources to develop corresponding software have remained relatively constant—thus shrinking significantly in relation to demand. Neither user-oriented programming languages nor programmer workbench or other efficiency aids have been able to address the problem of resource shortage fully.

Consequently salaries for skilled people have increased significantly. Further, a large market has developed for software firms that can develop reliable products at significantly lower user cost by spreading these costs over multiple users. The industry started with software vendors developing complex technical software to support the operation of computers (operating systems, data base handlers, inquiry languages, etc.). Vendor software has now moved downstream to products such as standard user-oriented software services, including payroll and accounting packages, report writers, procedural languages' spreadsheet programs, and so on.

The trend toward outside services has caused the in-house system construction phase to be eliminated (or drastically shortened) for many office automation and data processing activities. The design phase continues to focus on careful definition of business operational needs, often to guide a package selection. The challenge of the system implementation phase is to understand the purchased services' key characteristics so as to train individuals to use it. Systems maintenance involves ensuring that the vendor is prepared to be responsive to long-term needs.

Purchased systems generate special problems for IT operations management. These problems are particularly sticky where the user has full authority to purchase and operate the new service while the IT operations department must maintain and operate other services and at the same time ensure their compatibility with the new service. Loss of sole control of operations poses four key challenges to IT operations management:

1. How to maintain existing services while building appropriate and necessary data bridges to the new ones.
2. How to evolve the IT operations organization from a primary integrated system of data processing to a series of services that are better focused on the specific needs of different users.
3. How to develop user understanding both of their real operational responsibility over the systems under their control and of how to interface effectively with corporate IT.
4. How to help users manage vendor relationships to protect the company against ill-advised changes to software that can hurt operations. (The 1986 announcement of Lotus 1–2–3 Release 2.0, which was incompatible with the previous versions of Lotus 1–2–3, is illustrative of this type of problem.)

Individual skill levels and perspectives of IT operations managers further complicate these problems. Many, accustomed to exercising monopoly control over operations while sharing control with users over selection and implementation of maintenance changes, must now learn to adapt to new ways of operations. Evidence of failure to adapt is provided by the many organizations that, because of senior management frustration over IT's unresponsiveness, have given users total authority for purchased services acquisition and operation.

IT operations must assume roles that include reviewing designs in the *design* phase to ensure that they are compatible with existing services; auditing documentation preparation in the *construction* phase to ensure long-term maintainability; ensuring that essential services are still being provided during the *implementation* phase; and appraising whether necessary skills are in the organization (IT and/or user) to assure effective operation in the *operations* phase. The degree to which senior management needs to get involved in this process depends on whether existing and planned services are critical for the organization to meet its day-to-day operating objectives.

Service Sourcing—Decision Authority

Senior management must provide guidance as to the company's direction on decisions about software and processing service sourcing and whether the user or IT department should have a primary voice in these decisions. Sourcing decisions can occur in all phases of the information technology life cycle, from design to maintenance, and for all three information technologies: telecommunications (TC), data processing (DP), and office automation (OA). In practice, most of these decisions will involve at least some input from both IT and user, particularly in the design and implementation phases. At the extremes, however, either group may be willing to take total responsibility.

Further, each phase of the project life cycle presents options: where in the organization the service sourcing decision should be made, whether the service should be sourced in-house or externally, and what internal work should be done by IT versus the user. For example, in the design phase in many organizations the in-house users are developing more *make* capacity (decision support systems and user programming), therefore becoming less dependent on IT departments or an outside supplier (with the risk that the organization may lose operational control over key systems). Similarly some office managers are personally purchasing and installing completely designed support systems.

What is being constructed is also changing. No one (outside of the vendor) builds internal computer operating systems any more, and only a few construct data base systems software. A shrinking percentage of data processing applications consequently are being designed and constructed by IT staff, with an even smaller percentage of OA systems software being designed and built inside the firm.

Implementation is changing from being almost the exclusive domain of IT to a situation where the user often has control over local department micro-based systems and either IT or user may have the primary relationship with an outside software vendor. Operations has moved from an exclusively IT-controlled activity to one where service bureaus and user-controlled minis and micros have considerably altered the picture. Maintenance in some of the newer technologies can be done more by the users.

The nature of the application is important in determining primary decision-making responsibility. On the one hand, implementation and operation of a customized new decision support system in a bank can be completely under the control of the portfolio manager fresh from school, because it requires neither two-way interaction with the organization's data files nor the controls implicit in day-to-day transaction processing. An office automation system implementation effort, on the other hand, may require significant IT professional support in user training to ensure that potential operating problems are avoided.

Different firms may have valid reasons for locating in quite different positions the sourcing decision for different phases of the system's life cycle for different technologies. Two concerns stand out:

1. This is an important strategic decision and should be addressed explicitly rather than be left to chance.
2. The transitional nature of the IT industry makes it hard to be specific as to what long-term sourcing policy a firm should implement for any phase of the system's life cycle or any information technology. The dynamics of change defy either simplistic or long-term solutions.

Within these general caveats, however, we find that discussion on the location of decision-making power should flow primarily around the OA and DP technologies. Communications decisions have such a pervasive influence on the ability to distribute data and other information that they demand a strong central IT policy and decision-making role. In the two other technologies, however, either the IT department or user may have the prime authority to decide, although continuous consultation with each other is strongly encouraged.

Examples of Different Organization Approaches to Life-Cycle Control

Three comparative examples are presented of how six firms have allocated decision responsibility for each phase of the product life cycle and how these vary by make or buy decisions.

Table 9–1 compares the IT sourcing decisions for two organizations in which IT plays a role of *strategic significance*. The one that emphasizes central IT decision power is a bank; the other, which emphasized decentralized decision power, is a multidivision consumer product firm. Both desire to maintain control over systems integration activity and develop expertise inside their firms while simultaneously gaining experience in purchasing services and reducing software costs. The bank, however, feels the integrated nature of its business and customer relationships dictate that it maintain central control of data and develop

Bank

	Technology	Life-Cycle Phases to Be Bought	Life-Cycle Phases to Be Made
User responsibility	Communications		I*
	Data processing		D* I* C* O*
	Office automation		D I* O*
IT responsibility	Communications	D C M	D I* O
	Data processing		D* C* I* O* M
	Office automation	D C M	I* O* M

Consumer Product Firm

	Technology	Life-Cycle Phases to Be Bought	Life-Cycle Phases to Be Made
User responsibility	Communications	C* M	D* I*
	Data processing	C*	D I
	Office automation	D C I M	D I O
IT responsibility	Communications	C* O	D* O I*
	Data processing	C*	C O M
	Office automation		

D - Design
C - Construct
I - Install
O - Operate
M - Maintain
Note: A letter appearing on same line twice means some aspects of phase are bought and others made.
*Indicates joint responsibility for phase by user and IT.

central standards compatible with its overall mode of operations. The consumer product firm, on the other hand, has traditionally decentralized profit responsibility along with all staff support to each division. It felt that integrated data files were neither critical to its operation nor appropriate to its management philosophy and structure. Although the consumer product firm has a central IT department, all development is done by divisional staff. Each company reached its decision only after careful consideration of all elements, although obviously different structures emerged. Of particular interest is that the IT-dominated bank felt more need for joint efforts in implementation than the user-oriented consumer products divisions.

Table 9–2 compares two organizations where IT's thrust is heavily oriented to marketing. Both firms have completed development of most of their transaction systems. The retailing chain, with a standard set of point-of-sale devices implemented in its five major divisions, has decentralized all applications design and operations to the divisions. These new applications systems are primarily decision support and focus on helping managers to understand markets better. Although the IT unit has primary responsibility only for communications, it also constructs special OA and DP systems and provides maintenance support for these systems as well as for the transaction systems. The distribution company has a large central marketing group and local warehouse control of operations. The warehouses require ongoing TC development and operations staff as they proceed to develop direct links to all their suppliers. This unique structure gives the local warehouse control over their TC and OA while assigning responsibility for all DP to the central group.

Table 9–3 compares two firms that rely heavily upon IT for manufacturing and technical applications. In this description we have included CAD/CAM (computer-aided design and manufacturing) in DP. In both firms, OA is completely managed by the users. The defense company's day-to-day operations are managed by the chief operating officer, who is reported to by engineering, manufacturing, and IT. In this instance the user-IT role separation is not clear, as both IT and user staffs are interchangeable in practice. The engineering function however, tends to dominate the selection of workstations for CAD and also advises manufacturing on the selection and design of CAM systems. As CAD is linked to CAM, the IT department works with both engineering and manufacturing on TC activities to ensure appropriate integration, as well as on developing planning and reporting systems. IT further manages the archiving function (i.e., tape library). The engine manufacturer has IT reporting to the vice president of engineering, with a dotted-line relationship to manufacturing. Again, the majority of IT efforts are planned and executed jointly. The unit, however,

TABLE 9-2 Systems Are Adaptive, Marketing Oriented—Two Organizational Strategies

Retail Marketing Firm

	Technology	Life-Cycle Phases to Be Bought	Life-Cycle Phases to Be Made
User responsibility	Communications	DC* I* M	D* I*
	Data processing	DC* I* M*	D* I* O*
	Office automation		D* I* O
IT responsibility	Communications	DC	D* I* OM
	Data processing	C* I*	D* CI* O* M
	Office automation	C* I* M*	D* CI* M

Distribution Company

	Technology	Life-Cycle Phases to Be Bought	Life-Cycle Phases to Be Made
User responsibility	Communications	D C I O M	D* I*
	Data processing	D C I M	I* O*
	Office automation		D I O
IT responsibility	Communications		D* I*
	Data processing		D C I* O* M
	Office automation		

D - Design
C - Construct
I - Install
O - Operate
M - Maintain

Note: A letter appearing on same line twice means some aspects of phase are bought and others made.
*Indicates joint responsibility for phase by user and IT.

TABLE 9-3 Systems Are Strategic to Manufacturing Company—Organizational Strategies

		Defense Company			Jet Engine Company	
	Technology	Life-Cycle Phases to Be Bought	Life-Cycle Phases to Be Made		Life-Cycle Phases to Be Bought	Life-Cycle Phases to Be Made
User responsibility	Communications	D*	D* I*			D* C I
	Data processing	D* C* M*	D I* O*		C* M*	D* I* O*
	Office automation	D* C	D* I O M		C M	D I O
IT responsibility	Communications	D* C O M	D* I* O M		C O M	D*
	Data processing	D* C* M*	I* O* M		C* M*	D* C I* O* M
	Office automation	D*	D*			

D - Design
C - Construct
I - Install
O - Operate
M - Maintain
Note: A letter appearing on same line twice means some aspects of phase are bought and others made.
*Indicates joint responsibility for phase by user and IT.

is the dominant authority in DP due to issues surrounding the development and maintenance of a comprehensive production planning and control system. User department managers have authority to acquire OA within hardware/software policies developed by an IT/user committee.

These examples emphasize the range of possible organizational and control structures for each phase of the system's life cycle. The final decisions rest on the nature of the business, with each organization tending to have some user and IT involvement in design/construction/implementation phases both in internally developed and in purchased systems. The scope and balance of these decisions, however, vary widely. The engine company felt that its large backlog of maintenance would preclude many inside developments, since it believed its location would make recruitment of more programmers very difficult. The bank conversely was actively recruiting systems personnel because it felt its design needs were expanding rapidly and that even withdrawing from internal construction efforts would not free up adequate resources for maintaining key systems. In an urban market, they felt they both had to and could compete for a substantial increase in staff resources.

Technology Planning

The technology planning for operations involves an ongoing audit for potential obsolescence and opportunities. The technology planning scope and effort associated with this audit depend upon the nature of the business and the state of IT: for a bank it should be across many technologies and be very extensive; a mail-order business may concentrate on OA technology; a wholesale distributor may just focus on DP and TC technologies. To be effective, the audit must involve very high-caliber, imaginative staff (the role of the emerging technologies department was discussed in Chapter 6). It should compare today's IT possibilities with the potential available two or three years from now. This potential must be based on technological forecasting.

If a company is trying to differentiate itself from competition by application of these technologies, the resources focused on technological planning should be quite extensive. If a firm is trying just to stay even and the IT activity is seen primarily as support, comparison with the operations of competitors or leaders in particular fields may be sufficient. A few firms periodically solicit bids from different vendors on the service they are providing to ensure their IT department is fully up-to-date. For example, a large insurance company whose IT department is dominated by the technology of one vendor annually asks a competitor of the vendor to bid an alternative system, even though they do not perceive a need for change. As a result of these bids, they switched to another vendor's minicomputers in the recent past and on still another occasion installed a large machine purchased from a different vendor.

The objective of the audit is to determine (relative to available and announced systems) how cost effective and adequate for growth the existing installed technologies are. It should generate an updated priority list of technologies to be considered as replacements. Such lead time is critical. Technology replacement or additions planned two years in advance cause a small fraction of the disruption of those planned only six months in advance. In order to better define the architecture of the future information service, planning should include external testing, field trips, education, and pilot studies as vehicles for obtaining an understanding of emerging technologies.

A useful approach to a technology audit is to categorize the applications portfolio of operations systems by length of time since development or last total rewrite of each system. If a significant percentage of IT systems running today were designed a decade or more ago, this is normally a strong tip-off that a major redesign and rewrite offer great opportunities for reduced maintenance and improved operational efficiency.[2] A large financial service firm recently performed such an audit and discovered that 40 percent of their systems and 75 percent of their systems effort were devoted to maintaining an accounting-like system constructed in the second era (Figure 1–1). The purchase of a general ledger package, four months of development, and a period of parallel runs permitted 28,000 lines of COBOL code to be scrapped, and almost half of their maintenance effort was freed up.

The identification and implementation of new technology can be transparent to the user when it involves hardware replacement or new systems that use existing hardware more effectively. Other replacement technology may affect users by providing different or improved service such as report writers for data bases or new terminals, but these basically support users rather than change their basic operations style. Some of these will be so integrated with user habits that it is important to obtain user leadership in the implementation. Each implementation situation requires a careful plan to ensure that service is not interrupted and relevant individuals understand how to operate with the new service. Figure 9–1 illustrates the tensions and forces that must be managed in IT innovation.

When IT planning includes an ongoing appraisal of user readiness, an inventory of use of existing technology, and an appropriate assessment of where technology is going, a program of new technology

---

[2]Martin Buss, "Penny-Wise Approach to Data Processing," *Harvard Business Review*, July–August 1981.

FIGURE 9-1 Forces to Be Managed in IT Innovation

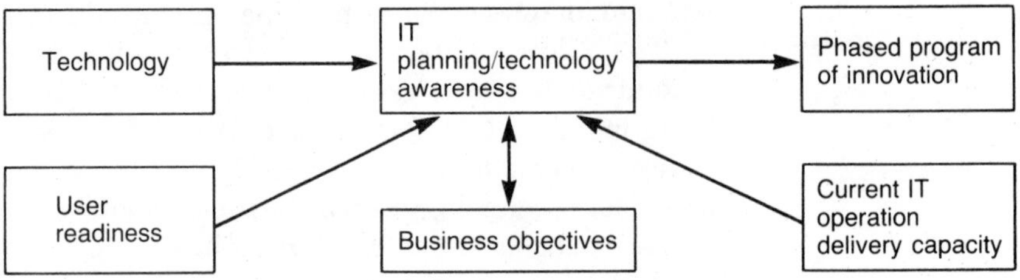

can be developed rather easily for each entity. A large consumer products company, for example, has an IT unit with a very strong emerging-technology group. As part of their activity they maintain for each division and function an updated log of services in use and an assessment of current problems. They are currently in the midst of a program of introducing OA that includes a large portfolio of different applications in a pilot division. Their detailed program for this division, scheduled over 24 months, includes benchmarks and reviews to evaluate both benefits and operating problems and progress. Such pilot testing stimulates broader organizational awareness of the opportunities and operational issues associated with new technology and permits better planning for full-scale implementation in the other divisions.

Measuring and Managing Capacity

The less one knows about computer hardware/software technology, the more certain one is of the definition of capacity. In reality the different hardware/software elements tend to interact in such a complex way that the diagnosis of bottlenecks and proper long-term planning of capacity are very important tasks requiring a high order of skill to execute. To understand capacity and its key changeability, we must consider the following key elements:

1. Capacity comes in much smaller, less expensive increments than a decade ago. In many organizations this has created an asymmetric reward structure for capacity excesses versus shortages: a shortage of capacity in critical operating periods is very expensive, while the cost of extra capacity is very low. For these organizations, carrying excess capacity is a sound decision.

2. A capacity crunch develops with devastating suddenness. During one six-month period a large financial institution operated with few

difficulties with a 77 percent load on the central processing unit (CPU) during peak demand. Senior management refused to listen to IT management, which warned that they were on the edge of a crisis, and would not permit IT management to place an order for additional equipment. During the next six months the introduction of two new minor systems and steady growth in transaction volumes brought CPU load during peak periods to 83 percent. This was accompanied by a dramatic erosion in on-line systems response time and a steady stream of missed schedules on the batch systems, and key delivery times of items to an industry clearinghouse were missed twice. The move from a satisfactory to a thoroughly unsatisfactory situation does not creep up on an organization but to the untutored eye seems to arrive dramatically.

3. There has been an explosion of diagnostic tools, such as hardware and software monitors, to assist in the identification of these problems. These tools are only analytical devices and are no better than the quality of the analyst using them and the detailed forecast of future demands to be placed on the systems. In firms where operations plays a vital role this explosion has led to significant growth in both the number and quality of technical analysts in the operations group.

4. A dramatic increase has taken place in the number of suppliers of equipment to be hooked onto a computer configuration. This is reducing the number of firms totally committed to a single vendor's gear. Additional features, coupled with attractive prices of specialist manufacturers, push many firms in the direction of IT vendor proliferation. When combined with the integration of telecommunications and office automation this phenomenon makes the task of capacity planning more complex as well as increasing the need to referee vendor disputes when the firm's network goes down.

5. Complex trade-offs have to be made in innovation (with both its risks and economic opportunities) versus conservatism (with perhaps higher operating costs but more reliability). Companies where *significant* (in terms of overall company profitability) cost reductions are offered by IT or where significant strategic competitive advantage may stem from its operation would appropriately be more adventuresome than would firms where this is not true. Similarly firms that greatly depend on the smooth operation of existing systems must be more careful about introducing new technology into a network. Unanticipated interaction with existing systems could jeopardize reliable operation of key parts of the organization.

6. The cost and disruption caused by change often outweighs the advantages associated with a particular technology, and skipping a generation of change becomes attractive. This has to be examined carefully from two perspectives:

a. The system design practices of the 1960s and early 1970s were quite different from those being employed today. Some firms anxious to postpone investment have stayed too long with these systems and exposed themselves to great operational risk by trying to implement massive change in an impossibly short period of time, with disastrous results. Software is, in every sense, like a building—it depreciates. Because industry accounting practices do not recognize this, it is consequently very easy to get into difficulty through excessive, apparently innocent postponement.

b. Some changes are critical if the firm is to be competitive, while others are nice but cannot legitimately be considered essential. Investments in this latter category are clearly eligible for postponement.

7. As increasing investments are made in the products of small software and hardware vendors, another cluster of important issues surfaces related to vendor viability and product maintainability. Over the past 15 years there has been a high mortality rate among these suppliers. In evaluating hardware vendors the issues are: If they go under, is there an acceptable alternative? Is it easy to keep existing systems going in both short term and long term? What are the likely costs of these alternatives? In evaluating software vendors, the question is: If the vendor goes out of business, has the contract provided for our having access to source programs and documentation? An additional area of complexity is the vendor's posture toward program maintenance, both the type of error correction and the systems enhancement change that may be expected and the cost-charging policy for these items. As noted earlier, experienced operations thinking is critical in these negotiations. All too often very unhappy outcomes have ensued when either the user or the systems and programming department acquired software without understanding the long-term operating implications of the decision.

8. Finally, a hidden set of capacity decisions focuses on the acquisition of appropriate infrastructure backup (such as power) and adequate building strength for the weight of the equipment. The importance of availability and reliability of these items is often easily underassessed. For example, the temperature in a large metropolitan data center suddenly went from 78 degrees to 90 degrees in a two-hour period, shutting down the entire operation. A frantic investigation finally uncovered the fact that three floors down a plumber had mistakenly cut off a valve essential to the cooling system room.

These points clearly suggest that not only is capacity planning a very complex subject but it requires as much administrative thinking as technical thinking. For most organizations in the 1980s we are not talking about building a new factory but rather implementing a continuous program of renovation and modernization on the factory floor while keeping the assembly line in full production. This is a formidable and, unfortunately, often seriously underestimated task.

Managing the IT Operations Work Force

The personnel issues in the operations function have changed significantly in the past few years. Most dramatic has been the major reduction in data input and preparation departments. The introduction of on-line data entry has not only changed the type of tasks to be done (keypunching, key verification, job-logging procedures, etc.) but has permitted much of this work to be transferred to the department that originated the transaction, indeed often to the person who first initiates the transaction. This is a desirable trend in terms of locating control firmly with the person most interested. But in some settings it has been exceptionally hard to implement, with users turning out to be less enthusiastic than anticipated about taking over this accountability. In general, however, the large centralized data entry departments have faded into history.

At the same time, the jobs in the computer operations section are being significantly altered:

1. Data base-handling jobs are being steadily automated. The mounting of tapes and disks is being reduced in frequency. Many firms have even successfully automated the entire tape library function. Further, as cathode-ray tubes (CRTs) have exploded in popularity, the amount of paper handling has been reduced.

2. Formerly manual expediting and scheduling functions have been built into the basic operating system, eliminating a class of jobs.

3. In the more sophisticated shops many of the possible economies indicated in Items 1 and 2 have already been achieved. A point of diminishing return has been reached, and past gains in economies are not a prologue to the future here.

4. The establishment of work performance standards in this environment has become less feasible or useful. As the data input function disappears and as the machine schedules itself rather than being paced by the operator's performance, the time-and-motion performance standards of the 1960s have become largely irrelevant for the 1980s. Inevitably performance evaluation of individuals has become more subjective.

As these factors indicate, the composition of the operations work force has changed dramatically. The blue-collar component is significantly reduced, with a large number of new, highly educated technologists and production planners needed instead. The issue is further complicated by continuous technological change, which requires both types of staff to upgrade skills if they are to be relevant for future needs.

In this environment career path planning is a particular challenge. At present, three major avenues are available for the professionals. Those with technical aptitude tend to move to positions in either technical support or systems development. A very common exit point for console operators is as maintenance programmers. As a result of operations experience, they have developed a keen sensitivity to the thorough testing of systems changes. The second avenue is a position as a manager in operations, particularly in large shops where a multitude of management positions ranging from shift supervisors to operations managers are filled mostly through internal promotions. Finally, in banks and insurance companies in particular there have been a number of promotions out of IT operations into other user positions in the firm. Especially in the manufacturing sector this is a neglected avenue of opportunity. All these promotion paths, if given the proper attention, make the operations environment an attractive place to work and prevent it from becoming ossified and therefore unresponsive to change.

The trade union movement has been relatively inactive in the U.S. IT environment. It has been quite active in Europe and in portions of western Canada. Organizing this department gives the union great leverage in many settings, because a strike by a small number of individuals can virtually paralyze an organization. For example, strikes of small numbers of computer operations staff in the United Kingdom's Inland Revenue Service have caused enormous disruptions in its day-to-day operations in the past.

In thinking about the potential impact of unionization, the following points are important:

1. The number of blue-collar jobs easily susceptible to being organized has been dropping. A convincing argument can be made that shops were more vulnerable to being organized in the technology of the past generation than in the current generation. One reason some companies have embraced the new technology is to reduce this unionization exposure, through job elimination.

2. The creation of multiple data centers in diverse locations makes the firm less vulnerable to a strike in any one location. Reducing this vulnerability has been a factor (although generally not the dominating one) in some moves toward distributed processing.

3. The inflexibilities of work-to-rule are enormous in this type of manufacturing organization. The dynamics of technical change in nec-

essary functions and jobs make this a particularly poor time from the firm's point of view to be organized. If technology stabilizes, the inefficiencies resulting from premature organization will be less a matter of concern.

Selection of Operations Manager and Staff

Another area of significance is the selection of the IT operations manager and his or her key staff. Several important factors generate different skill needs for different environments.

1. *Size.* Size is the most important dimension. As an IT activity grows in numbers of staff, the complexity of the management task significantly increases, requiring many more managerial skills at the top.

2. *Criticality of IT operations unit.* Firms heavily dependent on IT operations (factory or strategic) are forced to devote higher-caliber professional staff resources to this area. Uneven quality of support is very expensive for these companies, and extra effort must be made to avoid this disruption.

3. *Technical sophistication of shop.* A shop heavily devoted to batch-type operations (there are still some around) with a relatively routine, nondynamic hardware/software configuration requires less investment in leading-edge management than a shop with a rapidly changing, leading-edge environment. The latter situation requires staff who can effectively lead, efforts in upgrading operating systems, etc.

These factors suggest the impossibility of defining a general-purpose operations manager. Not only do different environments require different skills but over time the requirements in an individual unit shift. The overall trend in the last decade is to demand an ever higher quality of manager. The tape handler or console operator of 15 years ago has more and more often proven inadequate for handling this job.

Human Issues in Managing the Work Force

A series of long-term human issues must be dealt with in managing the work force effectively:

1. The problem of staff availability and quality is a long-term challenge for IT operations. In an environment of decreasing entrants to the total work force, intensified efforts are needed to attract quality individuals to the IT operations group. Career paths and salary levels require continuous reappraisal. For factory and strategic companies, IT operations can no longer be treated as a stepchild to the development group.

2. There is a critical need for IT operations to develop appropriate links to both the users and the development group. The linkage to development focuses on ensuring that appropriate standards are in place so that both new systems and enhancements are operable (without the development staff being present or on call) and no unintended interactions take place with other programs and data files. The establishment of an IT operations quality assurance function is an increasingly common way to deal with this. The user linkage is critical to ensure that when operating problems occur the user knows who in IT operations can solve them. Finally, when development and operations have their respective roles vis-à-vis one another clearly defined and separate, a minimum of confusion exists in the users' minds as to where to go for the solution when they have a problem.

3. Not only does a long-term IT staff development plan need to be generated but a specific training program must be prepared and executed for staff.

4. Issues related to quality of work life need to be addressed continuously. This includes items such as flexible time, three-day (12 hours at a time) workweeks, and shift rotation.

No clear right answer exists for these issues; rather, a continuous reassessment must occur.

Production Planning and Control

Operations production planning is complicated by the fact that a multitude of goals are possible for an IT operations function. Among the most common ones are the following:

- Ensure a high-quality, zero-defect operation. All transactions will be handled correctly, no reports lost or missent, and so forth.
- All long-term job schedules will be met (or at least within some standard).
- The system will be responsive to handling unanticipated, unscheduled jobs, processing them within x minutes or hours of receipt, providing they do not consume more than 1 percent of the resource.
- Average response time on terminals for key applications during the first shift will be x seconds. Only 1 percent of transactions will require more than y seconds.
- Day-to-day operating costs will not exceed the given levels. Capital expenditure for IT equipment will not exceed the budgeted levels.

Resolving Priorities

By and large these are mutually conflicting goals; all cannot be optimized simultaneously. For companies where IT operations support is critical to achievement of corporate missions (factory and strategic), resolution of these priorities requires senior management guidance. In environments where it is less critical they can be sorted out at a lower level. Failure to explicitly sort out the priorities in an appropriate manner (that is, to gain widespread concurrence and understanding of the trade-offs to be made) has been a primary source of the poor regard in which some operations units have been held. When goals were not prioritized, their task has been an impossible one.

The sorting out of these priorities immediately gives insight into how to address two other items:

1. *Organization of capacity.* Whether to have a *single integrated computer* configuration or a series of modular units either within a single data center or multiple data centers is an important strategic decision (assuming the nature of the workload is such that you have a choice). Setting up modular units (plants within a plant, at some cost) will allow specialized delivery of service for different types of applications and users. These multiple factories also allow for simpler operating systems, allowing quite different types of performance measures and management styles to be implemented for each. This "focused factory" concept has been too often neglected in IT operations.

2. *Ensuring consistent operating policies.* Uncoordinated management specialists, each trying to optimize his or her own function, may create a thoroughly inconsistent and ineffective environment. In one large insurance company the following policies were simultaneously operational:

   a. An operator wage and incentive system based on meeting all long-term schedules, and minimizing job setup time.
   b. A production control system that gave priority to quick turnaround, small-batch jobs meeting certain technical characteristics.
   c. A quality control system that focused on zero defects, ensuring that no reruns would have to take place.
   d. A management control system that rewarded both low operating budgets and low variances from the operating budgets. Among other things, this control incentive had helped to push the company toward a very constrained facilities layout to minimize costs.

While individually each of the policies could have made sense, collectively they were totally inconsistent and had created tension and friction within the IT operations group and a very uneven perception of service on the part of key users.

Job Shop versus Process Manufacturing.   The conflicting needs posed by a job-shop operation versus a process manufacturing operation cause significant tensions and confusion because each type of operation poses quite different production planning problems. The job shop (the predominant IT environment in 1970) involves the processing of multiple discrete jobs, each of which uses different amounts of computing capacity. Many of these jobs require different routing paths through the operation center (Inforex, check sorting, bursting, etc.) as well as within the computer.

Quality control in the job shop involves ensuring that key production deadlines are not missed, jobs and outputs are not lost, incorrect data is not processed, reports are not sent to the wrong locations, and so forth. Production scheduling is a complex task divided between a production control department and the computer's operating system.

The production control department identifies desired target times for completing job processing, establishes and schedules priorities for workstations outside the computer department's control, prepares necessary job setup instructions, and determines relative job priority. The computer operating system then does the detailed allocation of the computer resource to each job (balancing its relative priority against efficient use of the system) and shepherds it through to completion.

The production control department normally has both an expediting function for squeezing short rush jobs through the system and a tracing function to allow them to answer user questions about the status of different jobs. Human expediting is an important part of ensuring that jobs get done on schedule. In addition, since a job moves from workstation to workstation careful attention is paid to overall facilities layout to minimize congestion and confusion while ensuring that staff resources are efficiently utilized. Within limits, machine downtime and rerun problems can be effectively hidden from the customer (assuming there is some excess capacity).

In the job-shop environment it is possible to identify precisely what jobs are to be run, assess closely the volume of transactions to be processed, predict the amount of time each job would take, and write a detailed production schedule. The week's production schedule can be formalized in some detail in advance and posted on a board in a GANTT chart or some similar type of format. Long-term production planning involves forecasting increases in business volume (hence transaction levels) and identifying major new applications and their potential requirements. Both of these turn out to be relatively cut and dried. Finally, throughout the day, tactical decisions as to how to juggle the schedule have to be made on items such as unexpected machine downtime, extra reruns, and the occurrence of more or fewer transactions than planned for in programs such as order entry. Other complications include submission of unplanned small jobs or programmer test shots. Schedule changes are made by both production schedulers and machine operators. Production planning in this environment is not only well structured but has a high amount of predictive power associated with it and can be fine-tuned with considerable human input.

Process manufacturing, or utility operation (most on-line systems), poses very different problems. It involves the continuous processing and flow of transactional work through a finite resource. The arrival of work in the IT environment takes place in an unscheduled, intermittent fashion with a variety of queues to hold it during periods of excess demand.

With unscheduled work arrivals substantial control has been lost over the timing of the utilization of the computing configuration. Since it is difficult to predict the number of transactions coming from dispersed users in half-hour periods, forecasting becomes more probabilistic, and the definition of service levels in terms of response-time performance becomes more complex.

A lot of terminal use in process manufacturing turns out to be less transaction driven and more user-inquiry driven. As a result substantial organizational learning takes place, and more individuals find it attractive to use terminals in ways they could not conceive of in advance. This significantly complicates the task of capacity planning.

Quality control in process manufacturing involves ensuring that an acceptable pattern of response time exists during the day and that an acceptable level of systems downtime and machine downtime is maintained. In general, much higher absolute levels of service are required than in the job shop because failures are absolutely visible and cause great emotional strain. Day-to-day production scheduling outside the operating system's priority setting mechanism is not an important issue. Transaction volume forecasting, capacity planning, and bottleneck analysis, however, are very important. When the IT computing resource is near capacity it takes only a very small increase in volume over planned levels to go from satisfactory to intolerable response times. Human expediting is not necessary.

In the mid-1980s the problem is complicated because most organizations do not present an either/or situation but rather are a mix of both types of processing occurring simultaneously. In general the move from a heavily batch world to an extensive on-line environment that still handles batch work has resulted in the following changes:

• A pronounced shift in the number and type of staff working in IT operations. There has been a sharp decrease in the number of blue-collar workers (tape handlers, console operators, disk pack mounters, etc.) and an increase in the number of high-salary process engineers (i.e., tech support people). Not only have the maintenance and fine-tuning of the operating system become much more complex but the payoff resulting from capacity fine-tuning is more important and is having to take place on a more continuous basis than in the past.

• A move away from very detailed human production scheduling to a more macro approach, where analyzing and attempting to manage the patterns across the hours and work shifts of a week become the major role of a production control group. Expediters and schedulers for individual production jobs have become much less numerous and important.

• Hot-line troubleshooting advice on an instantaneous basis has become important. The immediate transparency of operating system glitches and users' frustration with one-minute downtimes have increased the importance of this integration.

• Much tighter quality control checks. Both systems modifications and the introduction of new systems need these in order to protect against unintentional impact on other systems running simultaneously. Similarly the problems of introducing poorly tested new technology have become much more severe.

• User priority rules built into the operating system. Such rules have been established so that in times of peak utilization the resource is allocated in accordance with some corporate priorities. The heavy loads posed by unexpected volumes of on-line transactions and inquiries make it difficult to meet batch run schedules, unless their priorities are set. Since many of the users are inputting data at locations physically remote from the operation center, priority rules must be carefully built into the operating system.

In combination these factors mean that the human scheduling on an hour-to-hour basis is much less important than in the past and that considerable attention must be devoted to the architecture of the priority system inside the basic operating system. Long-term scheduling and planning of IT are harder because of uneven and sometimes unpredictable organizational learning about the utilization of this technology. (In one bank the use of an on-line portfolio management system grew fourfold over a two-year period as individual trust officers successively became comfortable with working with this new management tool.) Even though new applications can be identified in advance the growth in their use cannot be predicted in the same way as for transaction processing systems.

In many settings this transition in management focus has not taken place smoothly but has been quite troubled because of both resistance to change and lack of explicit definition as to how corporate goals have changed.

Strategic Impact of IT Operations. The management focus brought to IT operations depends on that function's role in the firm. IT operations in the support and turnaround categories can appropriately be dominated by an orientation toward cost efficiency. Deadlines, while attractive to meet, are not absolutely critical to the organization's success. Quality control, while important on the error dimension, can be dealt with in a slightly relaxed way. It is appropriate to take more risks on the capacity dimension for both job-shop and process-type IT operations in order to reduce the financial investment. Less formal and expensive backup arrangements are also appropriate. Finally, corners can safely be cut in user-complaint response mechanisms.

The factory type of operation poses very different challenges because IT is integrally woven into the ongoing fabric of the company's operations. Quality in accuracy, response time, and schedule meeting is absolutely critical. Appropriate capacity to meet various contingencies is critical because severe competitive damage may occur otherwise. The issue of capacity not only needs to be managed more carefully but usually more reserve capacity for contingencies needs to be acquired. New operating systems and hardware enhancements must be very carefully evaluated and managed to avoid the danger and financial damage of downtime. In a budget crunch these factors cause a company to make cost reductions more carefully than in organizations less dependent on IT service.

The strategic operation, while facing all the issues of the factory, has several other facets. Capacity planning is more complicated because it involves major new services instead of just extrapolation of old services with new volume forecasts. A stronger liaison needs to be maintained with the users in order to deal with the potential service disruptions associated with both new technology and new families of applications. These factors suggest the need for more slack in both capacity and budget to protect vital corporate interests.

Implementing Production Control and Measurement

The above factors show the need for an evolutionary and adaptive control and reporting structure. The indexes, standards, and controls that fit one organization at a particular point in time will not meet their own or other organizations' needs over an extended period of time as both the technology and the organization evolve toward an on-line system and perhaps a factory organization.

Within the appropriate goals for the operations department, there is a critical need to identify both performance indexes and standards of performance. Actual data can then be compared against these standards. These indexes will normally include items in the following areas:

- Cost performance: Aggregate performance versus the standards for different types of IT services.
- Staff turnover rates.
- Average and worst 5 percent response times for different services.
- Quality of service indicators, such as amount of system downtime, by services.
- Number of user complaints, by service.
- Number of misrouted reports and incorrect outputs.
- Growth in usage of services, such as word processing, electronic mail, peak hours, and computer utilization.
- Surveys focusing on user satisfaction with service.

While the underlying detail may be quite voluminous, this data (including trends) should be summarizable in a one- to two-page report each week or month. Such quantitative data provide a framework within which qualitative assessments of performance can then take place.

Security

One of the emotional topics related to IT operations is how much security is needed to protect the site and how much actually exists. This complex subject bears mentioning here only to call attention to the nature and importance of the problem. Exhaustively covered in other sources, the breadth of the issue is defined by the following points:

1. Perfect security is unachievable at any price. The question for an organization is to understand where the point of diminishing returns is located for its particular mission and geography. Different units in the organization or different systems may have distinctly different requirements in this regard.

2. Smaller organizations where IT activity is critical have found it attractive to go to something like the SUNGUARD solution, where a consortium of users has funded the construction and equipping of an empty data center. If anyone incurs a major disaster, this site is then available for them to use.

3. Large organizations where IT activity is fundamental to the very functioning and existence of the firm appropriately will think

about this differently. Such firms will be strongly motivated toward multiple remote centers. Duplicate data files, telecommunications expense, and duplicate staff and office space all make this an expensive (although necessary) way of organizing. These firms have come to the conclusion that if they do not back themselves up, no one else will.

4. For organizations where the IT operation is less critical, appropriate steps may include arranging backup with another organization. (It always sounds better in theory than it is in reality.) Another alternative is to prepare a warehouse site with appropriate wiring, telephone lines, air-conditioning, and so on. (In a real emergency, locating and installing the computer is the easiest thing to do. It is the location and installation of all other items that consume the time.)

5. Within a single site, a number of steps can be taken to improve security. Listed below are some of the most common, each of which has a different cost associated with it.

- a. Limiting physical access to the computer room. Methods from simple buzzers to isolated "diving-chamber" entrances can be used.
- b. Surrounding the data center with chain-link fences, automatic alarms, and dogs. Access to inner areas monitored by guards using remote TV cameras.
- c. Uninterrupted power supply, including banks of batteries and stand-alone generators.
- d. Complex access codes to deny file and system entry to all but the most qualified personnel.
- e. Significant number of files stored off-site and updated with a high level of frequency.
- f. Use of a Halon inert gas system to protect the installation in case of fire.
- g. Systematic rotation of people through jobs, enforcement of mandatory vacations (no entry to building during the vacation), and physical separation of development and operations staff.

This is merely an illustrative list and in no sense is intended to be comprehensive.

Summary

IT operations management is a very complex and evolutionary field. This problem stems partly from changing technology that obsolesces existing manufacturing processes and controls, partly from technology's impact on how best to implement the system life cycle, partly from the changing profile of the work force. Major insights appear to come from applying the understanding gained in the management of technological change and manufacturing to this very special type of high-technology factory. Most large firms now know how to schedule and control multiprocessing batch computer systems working on numerical data from decentralized input stations. Building upon this base to include word processing, electronic mail, and a host of more decentralized IT activities is a challenging growth opportunity. The critical resource for operations success is the acquisition and retention of knowledgeable people to operate, maintain, and evolve IT services.

Case 9-1

IBM Europe Headquarters

Tony Braithwaite, manager of the office systems group at IBM's European headquarters (EHQ), leaned back in his chair and surveyed the Paris skyline. As of June 1985, over 90 percent of the 2,300 headquarters employees had computer terminals and access to PROFS, the electronic mail and office support system that Braithwaite's group had introduced. The system had caused changes in how staffs' and managers' work was carried out, simplifying the scheduling of meetings and facilitating communication both within EHQ and among EHQ, IBM in the United States, and the European country organizations. However, it had also changed the work of secretaries and relationship between managers and secretaries, creating uncertainty about their future role.

IBM Europe

IBM had 1984 revenue of $46 billion and net income of $6.6 billion (Exhibit 1). Revenue came from the sales, rental, and service of computers and computing equipment, telecommunications systems, office systems, typewriters, and copiers. Headquartered in Armonk, New York, IBM's products were produced and sold throughout the world.

The company set four goals for the 1980s: to grow with the information industry, to exhibit product leadership across its entire product

This case was prepared by David K. Goldstein.

Copyright © 1986 by the President and Fellows of Harvard College
Harvard Business School case 9-187-025

EXHIBIT 1

IBM EUROPE HEADQUARTERS
Financial Highlights
Year ended December 31, 1984
($ millions, except per share amounts)

	1984	1983
Highlights of the year:		
Gross income from sales, services, and rentals	$ 45,937	$ 40,180
Earnings before income taxes	11,623	9,940
Income taxes	5,041	4,455
Net earnings	6,582	5,485
Per share	10.77	9.04
Cash dividends paid	2,507	2,251
Per share	4.10	3.71
Investment in plant, rental machines, and other property	5,473	4,930
Return on stockholders' equity	26.5%	25.4%
At end of year:		
Total assets	42,808	37,461
Net investment in plant, rental machines, and other property	16,363	16,142
Working capital	10,735	8,168
Long-term debt	3,269	2,674
Stockholders' equity	26,489	23,219
Number of employees	394,930	369,545
Number of stockholders	792,506	769,979

---

line, to be the low-cost seller, producer, servicer, and administrator, and to sustain profitability.

IBM Europe coordinated operations in 83 countries in Europe, the Middle East, and Africa. These operations accounted for 28 percent of IBM's 1984 earnings. Products were manufactured and marketed through five units: four operated in the major European countries—France, Germany, the United Kingdom, and Italy—and the fifth—the Areas Division—included all the smaller European countries, the Middle East, and Africa.

IBM Europe provided "functional guidance" for the units. It was run by a five-member Executive Office Committee (EOC) chaired by Kap Cassani, president of IBM Europe (Exhibit 2). The EOC met twice a week and made major decisions for IBM's European operations. EHQ contained manufacturing, marketing, customer service, and administrative organizations that supported the country organizations and an internal administrative function.

EXHIBIT 2   IBM Europe Abbreviated Organization Chart

Executive Office:

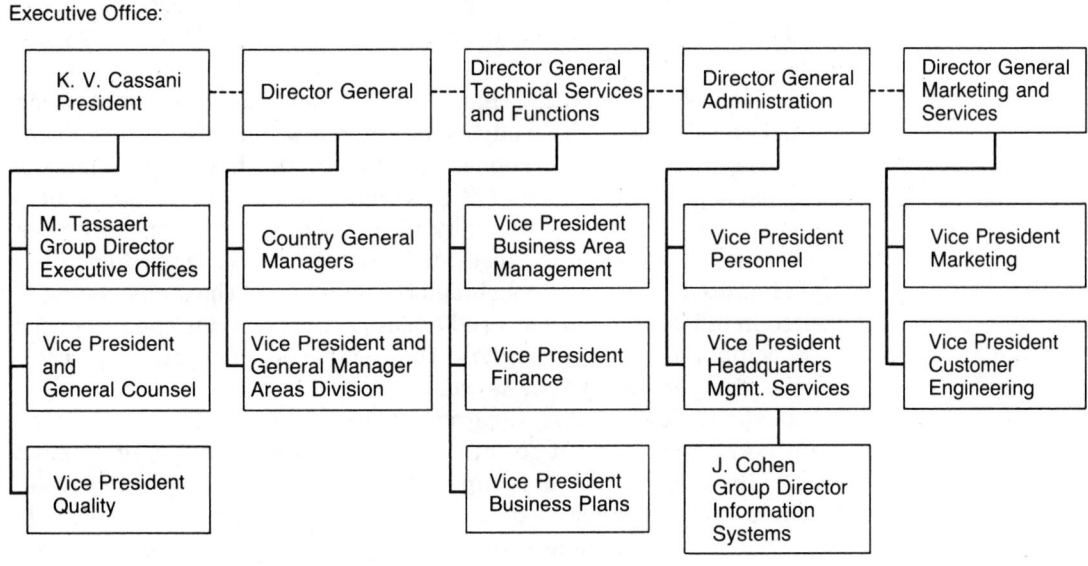

At least two-thirds of the nonclerical employees at EHQ were assignees. These employees came mostly from the European country organizations for three-year assignments. The assignees worked at all levels, from staff positions (called professionals and program managers) to senior management, including the EOC. All secretaries and many of the IS professionals were "locals."

Even though EHQ was in Paris, the language of business was English. Knowledge of French was not required among either locals or assignees. Conversation, however, took place in both languages, with much conversation among locals in French.

History of the Implementation of the PROFS Office System

Two important decisions concerning the automation of EHQ took place in 1980. The members of the EOC decided to study the implementation of an office system at EHQ and to consolidate all headquarters functions in one building. Up to that point EHQ had been housed in eight locations in and around Paris. The new building was to be a showcase for advanced office technology.

In early 1981, an office systems strategy development group was established. The group, headed by Joerg Lehmann, a German assignee, was separate from the EHQ Information Systems. It reported to Jacques Cohen, the Group Director of HQ Administration and IS. Members were chosen for the group who had an IS background, had good communication skills, and were willing to take risks and try new ideas.

In its first few months, the group took three actions. First, it conducted an office systems study, examining how much paper was generated at EHQ, how many copies were made, and how much mail was sent. Second, it installed an office system, enabling the group's members to communicate electronically, to edit text, and to keep their calendars. Third, it reviewed the results of a study carried on by Booz, Allen and Hamilton. The study concluded that almost all the money being invested in office systems was used to support secretaries and not principals. Supporting principals, however, was where the vast majority of overhead expenses could be saved.

In the middle of 1982, the group presented its findings to management and got agreement to run two pilot projects, involving 25 members of the business plans group and 35 members of the finance group. Business plans consisted of about 200 people who worked with the countries in the planning process. Many of the members of the group had worked with APL and data base applications. Finance, in contrast, had few terminals and limited computer expertise.

The forerunner of the current PROFS product was used in the pilots. The system included mail, calendar, text editing, and directory functions. Through the system, the pilot participants could communicate with others at IBM worldwide who had access to an electronic mail system. The group's objective was to introduce a system that addressed the needs of managers, professionals, and secretaries.

The pilots ran from September 1982 to March 1983. After their conclusion the Vice Presidents of Finance and Business Plans agreed that PROFS should be installed throughout EHQ. Ian Simpson, an original member of the group, and its manager at the time of the pilot, described the reaction of the Vice President of Finance and the lessons learned from the pilots:

> The Vice President of Finance commented that even though he could not quantify the savings the system provided, he saw several benefits in using the system. First, he was able to communicate rapidly with his counterparts in the United States. Second, he could access economic, exchange rate, and pricing information quickly. Third, the system allowed the finance professionals to easily generate graphs, tables, and text for overhead transparencies (a principal means of communication within IBM), and to electronically distribute the transparencies for comment by others in the

group. Their use of PROFS allowed the finance staff to reduce the amount of time spent generating the annual plan from two months to six weeks.

The information group learned two valuable lessons from the pilot. First, if top management started using the system, the rest of the people would follow. For example, a finance professional did not use the system until he received a phone call from an executive asking why he hadn't replied to an urgent message sent on the system two days prior. Second, we needed executive sponsorship to successfully introduce the system. Given that the participants in the pilot had to perform their normal workload, in addition to learning the system and a new way to work, we needed an executive to say, "You're going to participate in this, because we feel it will have long-term benefits."

In April 1983, the EOC decided to go ahead with the implementation. One of the office systems group's first projects was to give terminals to top management—the president, the members of the Executive Office, their reporting staff, and their secretaries. Before the members of the EOC were given access to the system their secretaries and reporting staff were trained and given terminals in June 1983. There was then a community of 50 people using the system when the five top executives received terminals in September.

Another important event took place in September. EHQ operations were consolidated at Tour Pascal, a modern office tower located in a district of high rises just outside of Paris.

Coinciding with the move, two changes were made that affected EHQ's 300 secretaries. First, they were grouped into offices of four to six called Administration Support Groups. Up until that time, the secretaries had been placed outside the offices of the senior person who they supported. Second, rather than reporting to their boss, they now reported to an Administrative Support manager (ASM). These individuals (many of whom were former secretaries) managed up to 20 secretaries.

Implementation of the system proceeded rather quickly after September. So quickly that the office systems group could not keep up with demand. The number of PROFS users increased from 350 in September of 1983, to 1,802 by the end of 1984, and to 2,150 by June of 1985 (Exhibit 3).

Office Systems Used at EHQ in 1985

By June 1985, there were over 2,000 users of the PROFS system at EHQ. The system provided a common front-end for several applications

EXHIBIT 3   PROFS Installations: Actual versus Plan

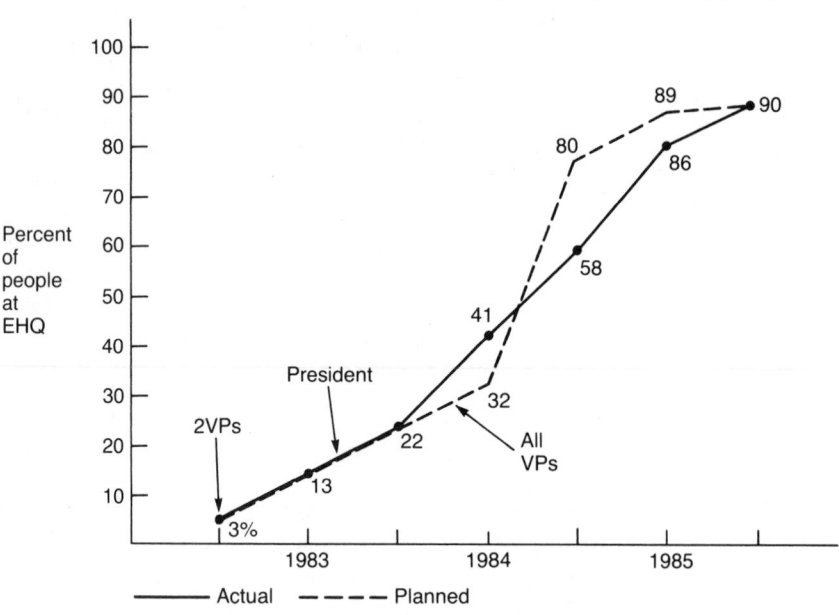

including electronic mail, calendar management, information retrieval, and text, graph, and overhead transparency production. See Appendix 1 for a further description of PROFS.

The electronic mail facility allowed employees at EHQ to communicate with over 150,000 IBM employees worldwide, who were either using PROFS or similar systems. Messages, as well as documents and transparencies, could be sent via PROFS. See Appendix 2 for an example of the dialogue used to send a PROFS message.

The calendar management function allowed principals to keep their calendar on the PROFS system. Others could be granted update or read-only facilities for their calendar. This allowed secretaries to change managers' calendars and allowed selected colleagues to read calendars, facilitating the scheduling of meetings.

The information retrieval functions were of two types. Some information was made available to all EHQ users. This included telephone directories, organization charts, and job postings. Other information was available to a group of users who accessed PROFS through the same mainframe, for example an economic data base was available to the finance staff.

PROFS ran on nine 4300 series computers (a mid-sized mainframe). Separate machines were used for different functional areas. Tony Braithwaite discussed the strategy of using several smaller computers, "We wanted to give user groups personalized service. We can work with the user group in timing maintenance and upgrades. Office systems users are much more demanding than data processing users. We can better assure an acceptable level of service with smaller machines."

Training in PROFS took place in two one-day sessions. The first session taught how to use the calendar, note sending and receiving, and directory functions. The second taught document preparations and storage. Both classes emphasized the technical aspects of using PROFS. Assignees and new hires were supposed to take the first class within two weeks of arrival and the second class six weeks later.

A help desk was set up to handle questions about PROFS. It initially received between 50 and 100 calls per day. The number tapered off as people became more familiar with the system and the help desk was subsequently folded into the EHQ information center.

Use of Office Systems at EHQ

Reaction to the introduction of PROFS had been generally favorable. The staff and managers were pleased with the productivity improvements brought about by using PROFS' calendar, transparency generation, and messaging functions. They also commented on how international communication was greatly facilitated by PROFS. The area of concern mentioned most often was the changes in the role of secretaries that occurred after the system was introduced.

Use of PROFS by Staff

The EHQ staff made use of more of PROFS' functions than either managers or secretaries. Two members of the staff, a long-time EHQ employee and a recently transferred assignee, discussed the impact of the system on their work.

Egbert Hoeferlein, a program manager in manufacturing and a heavy PROFS user, had a background in mathematics and logic. He had joined IBM Germany in 1961 and came to EHQ in 1971. He had worked in various staff positions before assuming responsibility for manufacturing functional strategies in Europe. He reported to the Controller of the Manufacturing group. Hoeferlein commented on the changes in his job due to the introduction of PROFS:

> Initially I had reservations about the value of office automation. In examining it for manufacturing, I never became convinced that

it would increase productivity. Further, I was not enthusiastic about using a keyboard or about spending time typing.

My first impression of PROFS was that it was a fantastic presentation tool—flexible and fast. A graphical transparency that previously would take me one hour to draft in a format that my secretary could work with, could now be produced by myself in five minutes. Further, the computer-generated transparencies look better than the ones produced by a secretary.

I can send a presentation via PROFS to my boss when he is visiting the States. I am producing the graphics here that he will use in his presentation later this week. I will send him a copy which will be plotted in White Plains. In addition, I keep the original files on the system and can use them in later presentations.

PROFS greatly simplified producing letters for my boss and for the Manufacturing Vice President. In the past, I would draft a letter that my secretary would type, revise it, and send it to my boss through his secretary. Now I draft it and send it to my boss through PROFS.

Today, I am one of the heaviest users of PROFS at EHQ. Between 1983 and today, my telephone bill dropped 90 percent. Before PROFS, I made 10–15 international calls per day, many to the United States. Today, I make one international call every day or two. Before, I sent three to four telexes per day and now I send none. I averaged two letters per day, which my secretary typed. Now I send none, just PROFS messages. I use the system to communicate with the United States and the European plants.

The system gave me more freedom in communicating with the plants. Previously, it was very difficult to send a message to the plants after 17:30 when the secretaries went home and the telex room closed. Now I can type a message myself and plant managers will have it when they arrive in the morning.

One problem I have now is access to data. I key in all the data I use for analysis and presentations. I would like to have automatic access to consolidated plant data that can be down loaded and stored on my workstation. The three functions—communication, data access, and graphics are all needed to produce a complete office automation system.

My other concern is my secretary. Before the introduction of PROFS, she sent memos, letters, and telexes for me. Now, I do those tasks myself and have much less work for her. The only functions she performs are covering telephones and making copies. I would prefer to replace my secretary with an office assistant, someone who could develop graphical presentations and send communications with minimal instruction from me.

Maurizio De Gregorio, an Italian assignee in the marketing staff, provided the perspective of a new PROFS user. He joined IBM in 1970 as a systems engineer and was a member of the systems engineering staff in Milan before he arrived at EHQ in April 1984 (two months prior to this interview). In Italy, he had been a user of HONE, a marketing system that provides, among other things, electronic mail and information retrieval. He commented on his introduction to PROFS:

> As soon as I arrived at EHQ, I started using PROFS—there was no way to avoid it. People were sending me messages through PROFS to my HONE account even before I received a PROFS account, which occurred about two weeks after I arrived. I learned PROFS' basic functions on my own, and didn't take the PROFS course until six weeks after I arrived. By that time, however, I had learned 75 percent of the material covered in the course.
>
> Eighty percent of my PROFS usage is sending and receiving messages, about five messages per day primarily to units within the European countries and to staff centers in the United States. I use the calendar and directory functions and send telexes through PROFS to IBMers who are in field sites and do not have access to a terminal.
>
> Walking around EHQ you can see that everyone has a terminal and is using PROFS. Using PROFS allows me to rely much less on the telephone. This is helpful for people like myself who having just started their assignment have some problems understanding English. There were times when I couldn't fully understand a person on the phone. I have no such trouble when using PROFS.

Use of PROFS by Senior Managers

The two PROFS functions used most often by senior managers were messaging and calendar management. Most typed in their own messages, although some used a secretary or a personal assistant as an intermediary. Managers stated that the messaging function simplified communication and reduced "telephone tag." They felt that having one copy of their calendar on-line improved its accuracy and facilitated the scheduling of meetings.

Maurice Tassaert, group director of the Executive Office and a 25-year veteran of EHQ, made extensive use of PROFS. He was responsible for career planning for executives, for logistics, and for representing IBM Europe to several outside groups. In addition, he was secretary to the Executive Office Committee, the IBM Europe advisory council organization, and the Board of IBM Europe. He discussed his use of PROFS in his role of EOC secretary:

The EOC meets twice a week for a half day. At each meeting a number of topics are presented for either decision or information. I keep a record of what happens at each meeting and follow up on EOC decisions.

I learned PROFS in June 1983 in one hour with the help of a tutor. The system was very easy to learn. My only problem was inexperience with typing. Initially I was neutral about the system. Little by little I became enthusiastic.

I found that I could use PROFS' calendar to keep track of EOC meetings. We receive requests from managers in many functional areas to make presentations to the EOC. The system keeps track of all the items to be covered at each meeting. If a change needs to be made, which is a common occurrence, my secretary can update the calendar immediately. We have just given access to the calendar to our functional vice presidents, allowing them to see what items are on the agenda and to better prepare for the meetings.

I also use the calendar function as a follow-up system. I have a separate calendar that tracks all items for which the EOC requested follow-up action. Vice presidents can find all the action items for which they are responsible.

I send messages through PROFS and use it to access the key marketing data base. The data base, which is available to senior managers, is a subset of our sales reporting system and contains sales volume data by type of product, by country, and by month.

Using PROFS improved my own productivity by 10–20 percent and improved my effectiveness in communicating with people. At least 50 percent of my communication is through PROFS. I do not feel that the time I now spend typing is wasted. I think while I type and I feel that the memos that I type myself are easier to read.

In addition, using the system reduced the amount of secretarial support I needed by 50 percent. Before the introduction of PROFS, I had a secretary and a scheduler. Now both functions are performed by one person. My secretary does much less typing and her task of scheduling presentations before the EOC is greatly simplified. Since not every EOC member can attend each meeting, my secretary often must find the next open meeting slot that a subset of the members will attend, so that she can schedule a certain presentation. This is easy to do using PROFS.

A former aide in the Executive Office discussed a problem caused by the use of PROFS:

The problem involves the use of letters. At IBM, letters are a more formal means of communication than memos. When I worked in Kap Cassani's office [the president of IBM Europe], there were times when he needed to get a letter on John Aker's [the president of IBM] desk when he arrived in the morning. I would draft the letter and give it to his secretary, who would type it on his letterhead and in his format. He would review and either sign it or change it. After it was signed, his secretary would send it by electronic mail to John Aker's secretary. She would print it on a blank piece of paper and put it on Aker's desk. Since Cassani's secretary could have several drafts of the letter, it is important to insure that the copy Cassani signed was the same as the one that arrived on Aker's desk.

The Use of PROFS by the Business Area Management Group

In 1984, the Business Area Management (BAM) function was established at IBM Europe. Its principal function was to provide a liaison role between the product development groups located in the United States and the marketing and manufacturing groups located in the European countries. IBM's product line was divided into 15 business areas, such as copiers, workstations, and large systems.

The key members of the BAM group were the 15 District Business Area Managers (DBAMs) and the 5 unit Business Area Managers (UBAMs). The DBAMs, located at the product sites, were responsible for insuring that IBM Europe's needs for their products were made known to the development organizations and the worldwide business area strategists. The UBAMs, located in the European units, were responsible for championing the unit's needs to each DBAM. Under each UBAM there were principals responsible for determining the unit's needs in each business area. The European Business Area Management organization was established at EHQ to manage the DBAMs and UBAMs.

Since the development organizations located in the United States were primarily concerned with the American market, the BAM group was established to insure that these groups knew the needs of European customers. Toward that end, BAM carried out competitive analyses, made pricing and product recommendations to the EOC, developed implementation plans for marketing and manufacturing, and planned for future product growth.

Members of the BAM group worked across several functions—including development, manufacturing, marketing, and service—making sure that everyone was kept informed of new product plans. This became difficult if, for example, development was done in San Jose, marketing was done in Germany, Italy, and England, and the management structure was in Paris. The work of the BAM group, therefore, involved a great deal of international communication, virtually around the clock. Someone in BAM was working 18 of the 24 hours in the day.

The PROFS system was used extensively by members of the BAM group. It facilitated clerical tasks, such as the rescheduling of the group's weekly international video conferencing meeting. Using PROFS eliminated the need for several international telephone calls. By replacing a two-way communication link (telephone) with a one-way link (PROFS messages), BAM managers found that it was less likely that someone would object to the rescheduling of the meeting. In addition, having both the message and calendar functions automated and on the same system simplified the secretary's task.

Michael O'Brien, director of BAM systems, commented on his use of PROFS and on concerns he had regarding the use of PROFS at EHQ:

> I can best illustrate how we use PROFS by telling you about a message that I received last night. (O'Brien moves over to his terminal.) The message was sent by Dorothy in Boulder. It concerns moving a person to Boulder. The shift was agreed on two months ago, but she is running into some administrative problems and wants my help in sorting them out. This morning I forwarded the message to Fred, who works for me and takes care of these things. I attached a note that said, "Fred, I thought you took care of this a month ago," and I sent a copy of this note to Dorothy. Again simple problems are handled efficiently with no phone calls.
>
> I have a concern brought on by the introduction of PROFS. First, we could be losing our ability to keep an audit trail of our decision-making process, since much of our information is being exchanged through PROFS notes. Suppose we wanted to develop a software program, did the market research studies to set the price and volume objectives, assigned the manager, hired the people, and got started. A year later the manager says that he has incremental costs and some delays, a not unusual situation in development. Top management, based on all the input, decides to proceed to announce the product, but on a different assumption basis. During each step of the development process decisions were made and the documentation for the decisions were PROFS notes. Our problem would occur if a government agency thought that we were selling the software below cost and tried to stop us. Where is our audit trail?
>
> Within PROFS there are capabilities to save notes. There are not, however, the formal procedures in place to insure that the notes are saved and the audit trail is maintained. We would have the audit trail if this scenario occurred before the introduction of PROFS—everyone sent memos and the secretaries kept chrono files.

To deal with these problems, we must develop better office procedures. We must learn what it means to file something electronically. The office systems group must design procedures that enable us to use office systems effectively, while eliminating the need to keep tons of paper.

Use of PROFS by Secretaries

The major problem that occurred after the introduction of PROFS was dissatisfaction among secretaries. Many commented on the reduction in the amount of typing, in the number of phone calls answered, and in the amount of mail being processed. Some felt that they were out of the communication loop, because managers communicated directly with each other, and not through secretaries. A former secretary with 11 years at EHQ who was appointed an ASM in June 1984, described some of the concerns secretaries had after PROFS was introduced:

The main problem faced by secretaries is determining how they will work with their boss now that the technology is in place. For example, when people are sending the boss mail, it comes through the system and the secretary might not see a copy, hence she feels that she is out of the communication loop. If someone phones the secretary regarding a piece of correspondence, she might not know about it, because it came directly to the boss through PROFS.

The magnitude of the problem varies based on the level of the boss. If you are a Vice President's secretary, you're still in the loop, because you receive your boss' PROFS notes and forward them to him. Some of the Vice Presidents do not type at all, they write their notes and either their assistant or their secretary types them onto PROFS.

At lower levels of the organization, where secretaries work for up to nine people, there is more concern that secretaries are out of the communication loop. There are some cases, for example in the IS area, where the professionals are heavy system users and the secretary has very little to do.

The magnitude of the problem also varies with the degree of comfort the manager has with PROFS. There is one junior manager who makes his secretary print out all his messages. He then makes handwritten notes on the messages and the secretary types his responses into the system. She also keeps two copies of his calendar—one on the system and another on the paper for him to reference and update.

Some secretaries, whose workload has been reduced, have taken on administrative responsibilities. For example, the secretary in the product administration area now receives all new product announcements from the States through PROFS. She logs them, updates them if needed, and forwards them to appropriate managers. She also attends the weekly product meetings with the professionals and managers in her group and produces a status report that is sent to the country organizations.

We are still going through an adjustment phase. There was an EHQ strategy for introducing the technology, but no EHQ guidance on how to use it. To address this problem, we have formed a quality team to try and develop recommended procedures for more effectively using PROFS.

Phil Kenny, an Administrative Support Operations Manager, Office Services Operations, provided his perspective on the future role of secretaries:

> While high-level managers will still need traditional secretarial support, other professionals will take over much of the work now performed by their secretaries. The secretaries, therefore, will need other things to do. To answer this problem, we are creating the job of office support specialist in my area. We have taken one secretary, who was heavily involved in technology, and are training her in our information center. She will become a technology specialist in her function.
>
> The reactions of the secretaries to the introduction of the technology has been mixed. Some, who had been at EHQ for several years, had trouble adjusting to the changes in their jobs caused by the introduction of PROFS, while others are happy with the technology. Martine Dubois, a recent graduate with a degree in secretarial studies, stated, "I find learning and using the system challenging and am looking forward to learning the PC. I wouldn't have remained at EHQ, if it weren't for the experience of learning the technology."

Outlook for the Future

Both Christian LeBreton, director of HQ Personnel, and Tony Braithwaite had suggestions for changes to be made in Office Systems:

> C. LeBreton: I feel that the secretary will have a key role to play in our organization. She will be a critical support for a manager— not someone who types, files, and answers messages. If secretaries only type, file, and answer phones for a principal, that principal does not need a secretary. The secretary should know the organization well and should know how to work within the organization. For

example, many people who have a personnel problem see my title and send me a memo. If I did not have an efficient secretary, I would be handling many problems that could be better dealt with by others. My secretary understands the personnel function and can protect my time.

Even with the changes, some people will need traditional secretarial support, which will involve less typing and more administrative assistant activities. For others, especially those who are in specialized technical jobs, no traditional secretarial support will be needed. They will, however, need other types of administrative support. For example, an office systems expert should be added to each functional area and specialized administrators should be added to handle clerical tasks.

The technology has not created problems as much as it has opened up opportunities for secretaries. These new jobs and new career paths will expand their options.

T. Braithwaite: The key will be managing the relationship among three factors—secretaries, principals, and the technology. We can manage the relationship between principals and technology, but we have to work on the principal-secretary and the secretary-technology relationships.

There are three areas that will evolve over the next five years. First, more emphasis that will be put on the role of the office systems group as the consultant to EHQ for all types of office support including evaluating and pilot testing new products, conducting surveys and running quality circles, and proposing changes to the office support environment.

Second, the role of the Administrative Support Managers should be expanded. They should coordinate the provision of office systems support at the function level. Currently, office systems support is provided for all of EHQ by my group, while the ASMs are primarily concerned with managing secretaries. Their role will become one of managing both secretaries and functional specialists, such as office systems support specialists, graphics specialists, office administrators, and so on. They will also provide support for such activities as video conferencing. This will reduce reliance on central support and provide new career opportunities for secretaries. Office Systems will provide guidance for the ASMs in these areas.

Third, Office Systems should work with the ASMs and the functional managers, to insure that EHQ remains at the leading edge in office systems technology. We should examine new options for text, voice, data, and graphics systems. Currently, we are examining the migration from terminal-based to PC-based workstations and the potential role of local area networks at EHQ. We are also looking for ways to improve our document-handling capabilities, to facilitate the development of data bases by users, to simplify the integration of graphics and text, and to move closer to a paperless office.

It is significant that new jobs have already been identified, and are starting to be filled, as a result of PROFS. I have no doubt that investigation and understanding of these new areas will, first, lead to implementation in EHQ, followed by the identification of other new jobs we don't know about today at all.

T. Braithwaite felt confident that the problems of dispersing the technology had been handled well by his group. The level of training and technical support, however, was no more than adequate to meet the needs of EHQ employees. The morale of the secretaries had been improved from the low level hit in early 1984.

Now that the technology introduction was successful, the problems of using it on a day-to-day basis were starting to surface. T. Braithwaite had to develop a strategy to handle the major changes caused by the use of office technology at EHQ.

Appendix 1

Introduction to the EHQ Professional Office System

PROFS is the Office System that is being provided to EHQ staff. It will become increasingly available to all personnel at their desks. The system you will be using includes enhancements provided to meet the requirements of the EHQ environment.

Summary of Functions

A wide range of facilities is provided by EHQ-PROFS to help you do your job. These facilities include:

Communication. (Between you and other IBMers, in your department, in your tower, or almost any other location.) You can:

- Write and send notes—a "note" is used mainly for informal communication and is sent through the IBM worldwide computer network (RSCS—Remote Spooling Communication Subsystem).

- Receive notes.
- Redistribute (forward) received notes.
- Reply to received notes.
- Send and receive data files.
- Send brief messages.

Received notes and copies of sent notes can be electronically filed by you, according to the subject.

Time Management.

- A diary, showing details of your (and others') daily schedules.
- A weekly, monthly, and quarterly calendar function.
- Meeting scheduling (and rescheduling).
- Ability (with permission) to look at or maintain diaries for others.

Letters, Documents, and Files.

- Prepare letters, documents, and files, using predefined layouts.
- Check the spelling, use of English.
- Make changes, or check/edit something passed to you for review.
- Print on various devices.

Mail, File, and Search.

- Send electronically, draft or final letters, documents or files to other PROFS users.
- File all letters and documents created on the system.
- File details about hardcopy documents, reports.
- Search quickly and accurately for electronic and hardcopy documents.

Other Aids and Information.

- Rapid lookup of telephone numbers, for EHQ and worldwide.
- Useful functions facility for defining printers, password management, delegate during absence, etc.

EHQ-PROFS is a menu-driven system. Menus are lists of functions that are displayed on the screen of your terminal. You select a particular function by pressing the PF key (Program Function key) associated with it. Behind every menu screen is a HELP facility which explains that application. Press the PF9 key for Help. Note that there may be more than one page of Help screen: by pressing the designated PF key (shown at the bottom of the screen) you can scroll forward to the next information screen. Press PF12 to return to your application screen.

Appendix 2 _____

PROFS Screens Used to Send a Note

```
                              Screen 1

        Office Systems Programs     MX _ EHQPROFS     MX Main Menu

        r------- PF01 -------¬   r------- PF02 -------¬   r------- PF03 -------¬
        |       Free         |   |    Information     |   |  Options, news,   |
        |   CP_CMS_EXEC       |   |  Asset Security    |   |  IWS and tools    |
        L-------------------┘   L-------------------┘   L-------------------┘

        r------- PF04 -------¬   r------- PF05 -------¬   r------- PF06 -------¬
        |                    |   |       File         |   |  Access to EHQ    |
        |    User menu       |   |    Handling        |   |   Data Bases      |
        L-------------------┘   L-------------------┘   L-------------------┘

        r------- PF07 -------¬   r------- PF08 -------¬   r------- PF09 -------¬
        |   3279 _ color     |   |                    |   |                    |
        |  graphic tools     |   |    EHQPROFS         |   |     HELP          |
        L-------------------┘   L-------------------┘   L-------------------┘

        r------- PF10 -------¬   r------- PF11 -------¬   r------- PF12 -------¬
        |   Use of APL       |   |  Access other      |   |                    |
        |  and APL tools     |   |     system         |   |     EXIT          |
        L-------------------┘   L-------------------┘   L-------------------┘

        Press the chosen PF key or PA2 to LOGOFF
        4A.
```

Appendix 2 (continued)— _____

```
                              Screen 2


        E H Q   P R O F E S S I O N A L   O F F I C E   S Y S T E M   A00


     Press one of the following PF keys.          Time: 11:04
     PF1  Today's diary
     PF2  Diary functions                    1986    JUNE    1986
     PF3  In-basket                       S   M   T   W   T   F   S
     PF4  Messages_notes                  1   2   3   4   5   6   7
     PF5  Directories                     8   9  10  11  12  13  14
     PF6  Prepare_Update a document      15  16  17  18  19  20  21
     PF7  Mail Log_Search a document     22  23  24  25  26  27  28
     PF8  Useful functions               29  30

     PF10 Next Function Menu                   Day of Year: 177
     PF11  Query In-basket

                                        PF9 Help     PF12 End
```

```
                              Screen 3

                         Note Management



        PF1   Send a note     ==   (     ) (      ) (      )

        PF2   Send an immediate message

        PF3   Review filed notes

        PF4   Handle postponed notes

        PF5   Archive a notebook




     Press a PF key            PF9 Help              PF12 Return

 4A.
```

Appendix 2 (concluded)— _____

```
                              Screen 4

                Send a note to the following addressee(s)


    Specify the addressee(s) after "To" and, optionally, after "cc".
    You may specify them as nicknames, as local userids,
    and_or as "userid at node"s.

    Separate addressees by at least one blank.

    Press PF1 to prepare the text of your note.



    To ==>  ian hbern at milvm1
       ==>

    cc ==>  cassani
       ==>

PF1 Prepare the text   PF4 Clear   PF5 Own Directory  PF6 Dir.update
PF7 Central Name   PF8 WW Directories   PF9 Help       PF12 Return

4A.
```

```
                              Screen 5

                           Send a Note

====>

Date:   26 June 1986, 15:54:41 EUR                        =====
From:   Tony Braithwaite              TONYB     at EHQVMDP9  =====
        Phone:4.767.7891                                   =====
        HQ Office Systems                                  =====
                                                           =====
To:     Ian Simpson                   IANS      at HPLVM2   =====
        Harry Bernhard                HBERN     at MILVM1   =====
cc:     Kaspar Cassani                CASSANI   at EHQVMDP3 =====
                                                           =====
Subject:  IBM-Harvard Case Study                           =====
                                                           =====
An update on the status of the case. . .                   =====
                                                           =====
                                                           =====
                                                           =====
                                                           =====
                                                           =====
                                                           =====
                                                           =====

PF1 Send+file PF2 Send  PF3 Proof  PF4 S_J PF5 Add a line PF6 Postpone
PF7 Diary PF8 Print  PF9 Help  PF10 Next PF11 Previous PF12 Return

4A.
```

Case 9-2

Air Products and Chemicals, Inc.
Local Area Network (A)

By April of 1983, Peter Mather, vice president of Management Information Services at Air Products and Chemicals, Inc. (APCI), knew he had to decide on the capital expenditure request on his desk. It requested $500,000 for the installation of a broadband local area network (LAN)[1] to be used by APCI's research and development (R&D) staff. While the projected internal rate of return was 43 percent, and the estimated payback only 2.3 years, all savings came from noncash productivity gains. In addition, LAN technology was new and still in a fluid state, and the proposed vendor, Sytek, was a small, privately-held company with limited installations. Major computer vendors, whose equipment Air Products used or planned to use, including DEC, Wang, and IBM, had not yet announced LAN products, and it was unclear whether baseband or broadband technology would dominate the industry (see Appendix for a discussion of the technology). Mather was faced with either attempting to exploit LAN technology early in its life cycle, or losing potential productivity gains while waiting for the technology and marketplace to solidify.

---

[1]Please see Glossary for definition of technical terms.
This case was prepared by James L. McKenney and Arthur Warbelow.

Copyright © 1987 by the President and Fellows of Harvard College
Harvard Business School case 9-187-117 (Rev 2/87)

Air Products and Chemicals, Inc., a major international company with corporate headquarters in Allentown, Pennsylvania, had fiscal 1982 sales of $1.6 billion and after-tax profits of $169 million. The company was organized into five operating groups: Industrial Gases, Chemicals, Engineering Services, Equipment and Related Services, and Air Products–Europe. All line operating groups reported to the president as did Management Information Services, while administrative staff functions reported to the vice chairman (see Exhibit 1 for organization chart).

The Air Products Research Lab

Air Products' growth and success was driven by its skill in applying chemical and mechanical technology in the engineering, manufacturing, and marketing of its diverse range of products and services. R&D expenditures in 1982 totalled $37 million, or about 2.5 percent of sales. Some of APCI's R&D efforts were exploratory and fundamental, but the focus was primarily on applied research, aimed at major product and process improvements, and on the introduction of new products. New product areas included semiconductors, where Air Products had developed a broad line of specialty gases such as tetrafluoromethane, which was used in plasma etching of silicon chips for VLSI circuits.

The R&D lab on the Trexlertown "campus" in Allentown employed 600 engineers and researchers, 300 technicians, and support personnel. The R&D labs used a wide range of electronic data processing equipment, including the corporate Amdahl V8 and IBM 3033 mainframe computers, dedicated DEC PDP 11 minicomputers, automated analytical and control instrumentation, and various data acquisition devices, terminals, and other peripherals. Starting in the late 1970s, manufacturers of many laboratory instruments began embedding intelligence within the devices through the use of internal microprocessors and software to control the equipment and capture results in digital form. Prior to this, the analog output from instruments had been transferred manually to a computer for data reduction and analysis. By 1983, many of the major pieces of lab equipment used by Air Products had the capability to output digital information, thereby opening up the possibility of communicating directly with a computer. These devices included gas chromatographs, surface spectrometers, and a scanning electron microscope, as well as smaller devices, and ranged in price from $10,000 to over $500,000, with an average cost of about $25,000.

The present style of R&D operations created several problems that the lab professionals thought could be solved by a LAN. The first involved the transfer of data between the digital data acquisition equipment in the laboratory and the computers the results of experiments

EXHIBIT 1 Corporate Organization, 1983[a]

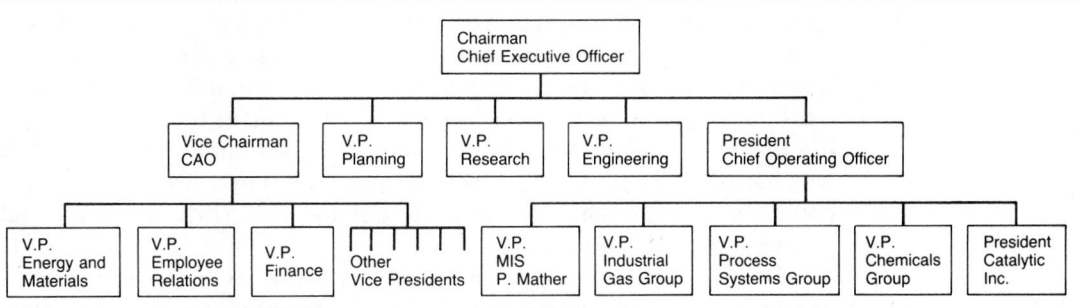

[a]Depicts reporting relationships only.

were analyzed in. In setting up an experiment, researchers would wire devices with digital output to a computer for data collection on an ad hoc basis, usually using the industry standard RS232 port as an interface. Because of the diversity of equipment required in the labs, communications protocols were seldom compatible, and as much as a week might be spent writing a program to convert the digital output to a format acceptable by the PDP 11's normally used for data capture. The mainframe architecture and operating systems were not suited to data acquisition applications. Data was therefore usually collected on the PDP 11's, and transferred to the more powerful IBM and Amdahl mainframes for data reduction and analysis. Data was sometimes transferred between machines by manual keypunching. Dial-up lines could be used in some cases, but the data transfer rates across these lines were low compared to the capacity of a LAN.

A second major problem for the lab professionals was the proliferation of different types of terminals to do different jobs. Three types of terminals were used in the laboratory to communicate with computers and intelligent instruments. IBM 3270 terminals were used with the mainframe to provide full-screen editing and processing, while ASCII terminals were used with other applications operating on a line-oriented basis. In addition, 12 Tektronix terminals, at a cost of about $10,000 each, were used for graphics and connected to the computer over phone lines. A LAN would allow one terminal to perform functionally like several different terminals.

Finally, multiple terminals of the same type were sometimes required to monitor several different computers or instruments. One experiment might result in the use of three terminals, one each to access the mainframe and the PDP 11 minicomputer, and another to monitor an intelligent laboratory device. Each terminal was custom-wired to its respective device for an experiment that might last a few days. A LAN would allow a single terminal to communicate with several different devices, and avoid the constant rewiring of terminals for specific experiments. For instance, a professional in his or her office might wish to query the status of a data acquisition device to monitor the status of work in progress, or to troubleshoot an experiment being set up by a lab technician. Now, while he or she might have an office terminal, it was hard-wired only to one of several computers available. Providing a connection to the laboratory instrument for a short duration was not practical with the available facilities.

A LAN would allow a terminal connected to the network at any location on the Trexlertown campus to access any other device or computer that was connected to the net. Connection points placed at frequent intervals in the laboratories and in offices would allow instruments to be connected quickly as needed for each experiment, and the data stream then directed to any computer connected to the LAN, or to a single terminal in the professional's office.

In summary, it was felt that the LAN would eliminate redundant terminals, increase the functionality of the remaining terminals, increase the data transfer rate, and provide access to the laboratory instrumentation from professionals' offices, thereby increasing professionals' time on experiments rather than on setting up terminals.

The Management Information Services Organization

Air Products placed considerable importance on managing its information systems resources. Peter Mather was the only staff manager who reported directly to the president. As a result, information planning, development, operation, and support activities were well represented in the corporate Management Information Services organization (MIS). For fiscal 1983, Air Products' worldwide information systems budget was about $31 million; this amount had grown about 19 percent annually for the past few years. Corporate MIS accounted for just over half this total, with most of the rest being spent by parallel I/S organizations in the Engineering Services Group and in Air Products– Europe. The MIS organization had 708 employees worldwide in 1983, of which 368 worked at the corporate headquarters in Allentown (see Exhibit 2 for the MIS organization chart).

Air Products followed a policy of multivendor sourcing for its hardware. Mather commented on this strategy:

> We are willing to accept the challenge of increased complexity from a mixed vendor environment because the rewards are greater.

EXHIBIT 2 Corporate MIS Organization, 1983

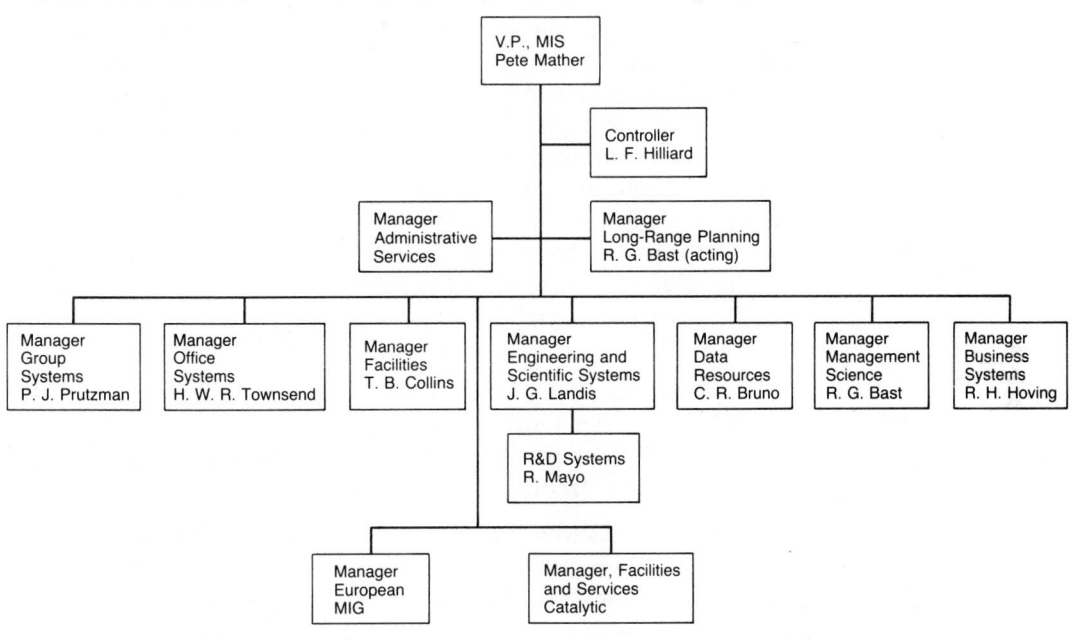

The application niches of specific vendors provide better functionality at the same or reduced cost. However, we aren't content to run these applications as islands of automation, so strategies for integration and connectivity are very important to us. The proposed LAN may help solve some of these communication issues for the R&D community.

To execute this strategy, we are willing to take managed risk with smaller emerging companies who have demonstrated product superiority with market penetration potential. We can form a good business relationship to each other's benefit, and grow with the vendor as a key user of successful product.

History of the LAN Issue

Since 1979, several organizations in Air Products had separately pursued networking as a possible solution to their communications problems. Different groups in Office Systems, Engineering and Scientific Systems, and Communications were examining the issue.

Office Systems

IBM magcard typewriters and Superwylbur, a mainframe-based text editing package, were the technologies of the day in Air Products offices in 1980 when Mather formed the Office Systems Committee. He charged the three-person committee to develop a three-year plan for office automation (OA). The committee, under Bill Townsend, manager of Office Systems, examined the possible architectures and applications, and the impact on people working in the office. Townsend felt that rapid development in OA technology offered significant opportunity for Air Products to upgrade the existing systems.

A consultant was brought in to assist in the planning, and by late 1981, the report was complete. Two main threads ran through the conclusions:

1. Wang equipment was a likely choice for the office environment.
2. Because of the multivendor equipment culture at Air Products, any LAN used would have to be capable of integrating different vendors' products.

Benchmark tests were run on the IBM 5520 office system and the Wang office system equipment during the spring of 1982, and a $78,000 capital investment was made in Wang equipment for OA in August of 1982. Wang was developing a broadband LAN called Wangnet for the office environment. By 1983 Wangnet was still being tested and would support only Wang equipment, but had the potential to be a major contender in the LAN market.

The Wang system used a central processor that supported up to 100 intelligent terminals hard-wired to the processor. These processors could then be interconnected via telephone lines or a LAN. It was not entirely clear what else the office of the future might hold. As the consultant commented, "We know precious little about the office of the future, and to design in constraints on what will undoubtedly be a critical resource is, to my way of thinking, a very, very dangerous posture." Townsend did not see the LAN issue as being driven by a need to interconnect existing or even planned equipment in the office, but rather as building for the future:

> We concluded that the office of the future would require high bandwidth and high connectivity. Having done that, we then looked at specific projects to see how that would help them. We had a vision on the LAN as "building the highways," even though we didn't have any "cars" yet.

The potential for a varied base of equipment in the OA environment because of an active vendor market made flexibility a key criterion for any solution. At the same time, the committee wanted to make the office of the future into the office of the present as soon as possible.

To them, the LAN option seemed a promising means to achieve resource-sharing and better communications, which would also lay the groundwork for greater automation.

Communications

The communications department, a staff group outside MIS, was responsible for advising the line groups on voice and audiovisual communications. Joe Prestileo, Manager of the Communications Department, reported through Phil Newman, Manager General Services, to Jerry White, Vice President of Finance. Prestileo was interested in the LAN issue for several reasons. Currently, computing and office equipment were connected to remote areas over phone lines, using modems; this method required heavy telephone use, and added to the increasing voice load on the phone system. As the number of lines on campus increased, Prestileo began to appraise the value of a Computerized Branch Exchange (CBX) to increase phone efficiency and capacity. While he thought it was too early in the life cycle of the available technologies to push data and voice communication down the same wires, Prestileo felt that eventually the use of the CBX for data would spread the fixed costs and drive down the costs of voice communications on the CBX. Then the LAN could be connected to a CBX, or the CBX would replace some functions of the LAN.

CAD/CAM

Don Seccombe, in the Engineering Scientific Systems Department, was planning to install an integrated system of software and hardware by Intergraph that would be used for CAD/CAM work for groups who were widely dispersed over the campus. The processor would be hard-wired to graphics workstations, but 50 to 100 feet was the maximum separation for the two units using this system. The CAD/CAM displays were data intensive, so coaxial cable was necessary to provide the data rate needed for good performance. Different operating groups wanted terminals in other buildings, and Seccombe was investigating the possibility of using a network to provide remote access to the system. Intergraph did not have experience operating the system over a LAN, but suggested that a dedicated coaxial cable was the best approach to networking several CAD/CAM workstations from the central processor.

Integration

Mather was concerned with how the R&D labs could better use IS technology, and discussed this with Bob Lovett, Vice President of R&D.

Lovett had asked Ralph Mayo, who was chairman of the R&D Computing Committee and had spent 13 years in the Analytical Department of R&D, to study the computing opportunities for the R&D labs in the fall of 1980. After discussing the potential uses with his own people in R&D, Mayo felt there was considerable promise that LAN technology could improve productivity in the lab. Having concluding that Air Products should implement an aggressive R&D computing capability, Mather and Lovett, with Mayo's concurrence, decided that it would be most useful for Lovett to work from the MIS side of the organization. Mayo became Manager, R&D Systems & Productivity in May 1981, in John Landis' Engineering and Scientific Systems Department (ESS).

Upon joining ESS, Mayo began developing a five-year action plan to address the use of computers in R&D, and identified a list of nine strategic activities, of which the installation of networking capability was number one. John Landis felt strongly that the R&D plan should meet the vision of "a researcher's desk with one device having access to all computing services." Mayo commented on his perception of the need for a network:

> With 13 years of working on the R&D side of the organization, I knew that the lab people needed access to the computers in the lab, not down the hall. They needed the ability to interface the lab equipment easily with computers located around the campus. And, a LAN would allow them to monitor experiments around campus, or even from home using a modem to gateways on the LAN. A LAN was of even higher priority than the new VAX minicomputer technology, and the VAX was absolutely necessary.

Shortly after joining MIS, Mayo brought Ron Crane, also from the R&D organization, to MIS to help on the R&D computing implementation issue. Crane had a strong technical background, and had been very interested in computer support of R&D. He started by collecting articles on LAN technology, and visited sites where LANs had been installed, including Brown University's large Sytek LAN.

As the three functional managers most affected by the networking issues, Mather charged Mayo, Tom Collins (who was Manager of Computer Facilities), and Bill Townsend with analyzing the LAN situation. On Townsend's recommendation, Mayo contacted an outside consultant working on the OA project in July 1981, and was impressed by his knowledge of the newly emerging LAN technology. Mayo was pleased to find that they had independently arrived at similar thoughts, that the key issue to resolve first was the baseband versus broadband issue. The consultant was engaged to provide an analysis of Air Products' LAN requirements, and a recommendation on the appropriate architecture and technology. In conjunction with the OA study, the consultant had been analyzing the potential use of Wangnet in the office environment.

With strong upper management support from Mather, the three managers began to focus on an integrated solution to Air Products' communication issues. Their analysis was driven by two concerns. First, they wanted to avoid a suboptimal solution that addressed just the R&D needs, preferring instead a flexible, general solution that could eventually extend to all functional areas of Air Products that needed LAN support. Second, they wanted to address the multivendor environment at Air Products in a manner that would allow effective support of different vendors' equipment. Over the next several months, they targeted two issues for analysis: (1) the potential of Wangnet and (2) broadband versus baseband technology.

Wangnet was a broadband technology that used two coaxial cables, one on which to send messages, and one on which to receive. A headend box on the system switched messages sent on the send cable by one device onto the receive cable, where they were intercepted by the device addressed. The system was similar to single-cable broadband systems, but avoided the use of some complex circuitry in the headend box by using the second cable. The Wang system controlled use of the entire bandwidth for the cable, making it less flexible than other broadband systems. For instance, it was not possible to piggyback a baseband network on Wangnet. Also, Wangnet could not be piggybacked on any other broadband cable, because of the unique way in which it managed bandwidth and the dual-cable system.

Because Wang equipment had been selected for the OA environment, the committee was reluctant to foreclose the possibility of using Wangnet, at least within the office. It was not clear yet what impact Wangnet would have on the market when it became available, but it appeared possible that Wangnet's dual-cable system could become a standard for LANs. It was discovered, however, that Wang had no intention of connecting to other manufacturers' protocols. Therefore, the committee decided not to consider Wangnet further.

Because of the diversity of equipment that a LAN would support within the Air Products environment, Ron Crane felt it was desirable to have a flexible system with potential for expansion. He pointed out that Xerox's Ethernet system, which used baseband technology, had a proven history. Ethernet was widely-installed, but offered data rates of only 5 megabits in 1983, although 10 megabits were promised. Others argued that broadband technology offered much greater functionality and flexibility at only slightly higher cost.

A broadband system potentially would allow logical "piggybacking" of other baseband networks, such as Ethernet, on the same physical cable, while baseband allowed only one baseband system at a time on a cable, and no voice communication. In addition, broadband technology had adequate capacity to support video transmission channels simultaneously with other data channels. While APCI had no specific need for video at the present time, the flexibility and capacity to handle it were desirable.

By December 1981, Mayo commented that he and the other managers felt that if given the go ahead by Pete Mather, the system would be a broadband LAN with a backbone cabling system to all R&D buildings on campus and to the Intergraph CAD/CAM System. The backbone would be a coaxial cable that connected a central wiring closet in each building to a main artery that ran between all the buildings. Cabling to individual offices and labs would then be made from each wiring closet, but would not have to all be made at the time of the original backbone installation. The question now was what vendor to select, how much cable to lay, and how to provide evidence to Mather that a workable and cost effective system could be installed.

The Working Committee

On December 11, 1981, a meeting was held to discuss the design of a broadband LAN. At this meeting, a formal working committee was set up that included Bud Bates from the Communications Department, Karen Crandall from Office Systems, Ron Crane from R&D Systems, Barney Cook from Computer Facilities, and two representatives from Purchasing. Crane, Crandall, and Cook had all been actively involved doing the technical leg work for their respective department managers over the previous nine months.

The committee members had diverse backgrounds and differing levels of expertise in LAN technology. Crane, as chairman, felt they had to select a vendor and test the system before presenting the proposal to Mather. In an effort to build consensus for a particular brand, the committee first educated itself about the critical issues involved in looking at a LAN. Crane attended a number of educational sessions and then shared this information with the others. The consultant made presentations to the group on the state-of-the-art in LAN technology and described his findings on Air Products' needs.

In discussing the work of the committee, Crane commented that there was a working deadline for the decision because of renovation work being done in Administration Building #1 and the construction schedule for a new R&D building. Some cost savings were expected if the wiring work could be done during the construction, but almost as important, there would be no work disruption.

Consultant's Report

On February 4, 1982, the draft report from the consultant was received, supporting the decision to use a broadband LAN system. The report stated that the motivation for wiring the Trexlertown R&D facility with a broadband LAN went far beyond eliminating the difficulties of cabling between central computers, terminals, and intelligent instrumentation:

1. Data rate: Today, many local connections are made through dial-up lines. While this may be satisfactory for current terminals, future generations of terminals will communicate at a much higher data rate. A local area network can provide transmission capacity.

2. Interconnectivity: Today, most organizations have a small number of computers, and terminals are either permanently wired to a particular computer, or dial-up lines are utilized. Future office automation systems will need to interconnect quickly and easily to a variety of devices. For example, a workstation might need to be connected to a variety of computers, printers, copiers, communication gateways, etc. We can begin to see a general architecture in which specific application and function "servers" exist on a LAN and are accessed as needed by workstations on the LAN.

3. Integration: Today, voice and data networks are, to a large extent, separate worlds. With the rapid evolution toward digital technology, we can see an integration of voice, data, text, and image into a single communications system. Already, we are beginning to see voice and text integrated in new office automation products. A LAN can provide an integrated communications backbone.

4. Compatibility: A major problem exists today in the area of communications capability between vendors. A LAN can provide a common communications base and, hence, provide a level of compatibility among vendors. The interfaces to the LAN are highly intelligent devices and can provide significant protocol translation.

In addition, hardware devices installed between a dumb terminal and the LAN would result in this terminal having the functionality of an IBM 3270 terminal as well. Since this single terminal could then connect to multiple computers as well as be used to monitor intelligent instruments, it would meet the vision of "one device for all computing services."

Cost Justification

The benefits to be derived from the LAN were mostly soft productivity savings in R&D and MIS (see Exhibit 3 for a summary of the projected

EXHIBIT 3 LAN Cost Savings

	R&D Personnel Productivity Improvement	MIS Personnel Productivity Improvement	Elimination of Need for MIS Services	Computer Resources (Capital Cost) Hardware and Software	New Capabilities
Laboratory automation	$ 60,000	$15,000			
Communication between noncompatible devices	22,500				
Minicomputer port utilization	45,000	5,000	$15,000	$ 59,000	
Minicomputer communications and software	30,000				
Multifunctional terminals	22,500	5,000		14,000	
Installation costs	45,000	5,000	15,000	35,000	
Graphics	60,000			29,000	
Computer services	45,000				
CAD/CAM	120,000				
Peripheral usage	15,000				
Subtotals	465,000	30,000	30,000	137,000	
Total	662,000				

EXHIBIT 4 Local Area Network, Trexlertown Complex ($000)

	1983	1984	1985	1986	1987	1988
Book profit before taxes	$ (21)	$178	$266	$329	$391	$443
Plus: Interest expense		65	43	27	11	
Book depreciation		100	100	100	101	101
Cash from operations before tax . .	(21)	343	409	456	503	544
Less: Tax exposure[a]	(10)	170	202	226	249	269
Plus: Tax shield from depreciation[b] .		66	53	53	53	29
Investment tax credit . . .		40				
Cash from operations after tax . . .	(11)	279	260	283	307	304
Less: Working capital investment .						
Plant investment						
Distribution equipment . . .						
Other investment	502					
Total increase (decrease) in cash . .	$(513)	$279	$260	$283	$307	$304

Internal rate of return = 46.5 percent

[a]Tax exposure = Tax rate × Cash from operations, before tax.
[b]Tax shield from depreciation = Tax rate × Tax depreciation.

cost savings). In addition, a savings was expected because minicomputers were port-bound, rather than CPU- or memory-bound. The LAN would allow more terminals to be connected to the same number of ports, thereby deferring the purchase of hardware. Also, in a LAN environment, software packages on any one computer would be available to all users, reducing the need to have multiple copies of the same software. Users could use developmental tools on one computer, transfer the task image of the program to another computer with the same operating system, and execute the program. For small R&D computers used for data acquisition, only operating system licenses would be purchased, rather than a license for the applications software for each unit.

The controller for MIS, Larry Hilliard, prepared a cashflow analysis of the projected cost and savings to justify the request for fundings being presented to Mather (Exhibit 4). Total yearly savings attributable to the LAN were estimated to be $662,000, of which $495,000 were "soft" productivity improvements, $30,000 resulted from elimination of need for MIS services, and the remaining $137,000 were savings in hardware and software. The analysis was done over a five-year period, and showed an after-tax net cash inflow of from $260,000 to $307,000 each year, with an initial capital expenditure of $513,000 in the first year. No consideration was given in the cost analysis to possible *new* capabilities that the LAN might provide. In his analysis, Hilliard noted that the savings were difficult to quantify, since Air Products had only limited experience with the use of LANs.

Vendor Selection

By late 1981, some 25 vendors were offering products to the embryonic LAN market. Many, however, were baseband technology, and some vendors were still in the beta test stage. On January 5, 1982, Mayo sent requests for general and technical information to all LAN vendors who had been identified as supplying equipment that potentially met Air Products' needs, and invited them to make presentations on their products. The field quickly narrowed to Sytek and three other companies, called here NET1, NET2, and NET3 (see Exhibit 5 for specifications).

Sytek's LAN was flexible in accommodating diverse vendors' equipment. The modems used to connect a device to the network cost $1,175 for a two-port modem, or $4,200 for an eight-port modem. The modems contained a microprocessor and 32K of RAM, and this intelligence allowed them to interface between otherwise incompatible devices on the net. The modems, for instance, could translate baud rate, stop bit, echo, and parity differences between devices on the LAN. These capabilities were not available in most LANs designed by computer vendors, since they would be redundant in environments where all equipment supported was made by the same manufacturer. While Sytek was currently one of the leaders in the broadband LAN field, it was not clear how viable the company would be once IBM, DEC, Wang, and other major players entered the market.

As Ralph Mayo and Ron Crane looked more closely at the possible vendors, the Sytek system emerged as the only viable system that met the requirements, had a track record of installations, and was available. Ron explained:

> We looked at the different vendors and talked with their users. Some of the users were very happy, others had mixed reviews, and, in a short time, we were down to a choice between the Sytek system and the NET1 system. The thing that impressed me the most about the Sytek system was that they did not exaggerate a single claim. That clarity impressed us.

The consultant also recommended Sytek as the vendor of choice to provide the broadband LAN equipment. Sytek had entered the broadband LAN market early, using its experience as a manufacturer of Cable TV equipment as a springboard. Identical equipment, coaxial cable, and frequency division were used on broadband LANs as were used on CATV.

To get actual experience with the system, and to become familiar with the Sytek system, R&D Systems bought a test kit for $11,225 in May 1982. The test kit contained a small broadband communications network. Ron Crane designed three test situations to simulate the operating environment for LAN at Air Products: a small computer environment, a laboratory environment, and a mainframe environment.

EXHIBIT 5

	NET1	NET2	Sytek	NET3
Data	All data	All data	All data	All data
Voice	Yes	Yes	Yes	Yes
Technology	Broadband	Broadband	Broadband	Broadband
Topology	Tree	Tree	Tree	Tree
Access method	Some dedicated channels, some reservation (switched)	Circuit switched and some fixed, point to point	CSMA/CD, FDM	CSMA, CSMA/CD, FDM
Transmission media	Coaxial cable	Coaxial cable	Coaxial cable	Coaxial cable
Maximum distance	50 miles	50 miles	35 miles approximate	8–9 miles approximate
Maximum number of nodes	4,090	15,000	25,000	1,500
Maximum number of end users	16,360	60,000	65,000	36,000
Total throughput	14 Mbps	5 Mbps	10 Mbps	25 Mbps
Transmission nodes	Analog/digital	Analog/digital	Analog/digital	Analog/digital
Number of current users	Over 100	Approximately 300	150	New product
Average price per end user connect	$1,300	$500–1,000	Approximately $600	$500
Price includes:	Net management and connection, hardware; net operating software documentation; technical support.	—	Net hardware, operating software applications support, installation, technical support documentation training, trouble shooting, with office connections to X.25.	Transmission, connection and network management hardware, network operation and applications support software, installation, documentation training.

In the first two tests, which lasted one month apiece, Crane performed such functions as file transfers, data retrieval, and remote connections, all without any difficulties. In the mainframe environment, however, some substantial problems arose. When terminals interacted with the IBM mainframe, they would display half a screen of data and then "go crazy." It appeared that the IBM was sending data to the network faster than the other connected equipment could receive it.

Communications with the mainframes was considered crucial and, after several months of testing and adjusting without success, the choice of vendors was opened up again to consider other broadband vendors. In February and March of 1983, analysis of broadband LAN systems by NET1, NET2, and NET3 was started anew. Considering the minimum requirements Air Products felt were necessary for LAN, these alternatives did not appear viable. In late March, Ralph commented in a memo:

> If we wait long enough, I am sure other alternatives will appear, but Sytek is the single leader at the present time. The presentation NET2 gave to Air Products was 80 percent futures. It appeared to me that they were *at least* a year away from a commercial product meeting the performance specifications of their presentation. At present, I know of no one who has a working commercial product based on a 10 MBPS (megabytes per second) CSMA/CD channel on a broadband network. NET1 folded trying to make it work. The last I heard, Xerox was having trouble getting their 10 MBPS baseband channel to work reliably. The existing Ethernet sites last spring were operating at 4 MBPS. Wang doesn't seem to be in much better shape.

Meanwhile, Crane called together technicians from IBM and Sytek, and together they worked out a solution that allowed the network to interface with the mainframe, but at a reduced data rate. Although it had taken eight months to iron out this difficulty, the system eventually met all performance objectives. The three managers concluded that Sytek was the only vendor that could meet the functional requirements. On March 18, a "show and tell" session was held in the basement of the labs where the Sytek tests had been set up. Mather commented on the two-hour test of the system: "There were wires and boxes all over the place, but the thing worked."

Cabling Decisions

The cabling plan suggested by the consultant included laying a backbone of coaxial cable between buildings on campus, some of which were labs and some administrative buildings, but all were to be used by the R&D professionals. A complete grid of wiring and connections would be installed in one building, and five others would be partially wired. Trunk lines would be installed to connect all major buildings on campus. Drops into other offices and labs would be made on an as-needed basis.

Although the wiring plan called for one Sytek CATV cable plus a backup of 1/2-inch steel sheathed cabling, the design team decided to pull five cables to meet present needs and to allow for future contingencies. Two additional cables were needed to support a Wangnet system if this became desirable in the future. In addition, although the CAD/CAM applications had been planned to be carried over the LAN network, the graphics system manufacturer was hesitant to commit to that mode of operation. Although using the LAN was technically possible, Don Seccombe requested that an additional coaxial cable be pulled for the exclusive use of the CAD/CAM system. As the system grew, it would be switched over to the Sytek LAN system if, in fact, that proved feasible. The cables were to be installed between the buildings in a 4-inch conduit. While it was possible to pull several cables through simultaneously, it was difficult, if not impossible, to pull a cable through the conduit once one or more cables had been installed. Since most of the cost was labor, the marginal cost for each additional cable was about $25,000.

The Decision

Despite the persuasive 30 pages of justification and financial analysis accompanying the $500,000 capital request for the LAN, and the pilot demonstration of the technological feasibility of the system, Peter Mather felt uneasy. It was crucial that the company support a robust and productive R&D effort, but the projected cost savings were soft. Although the consultant was a strong believer in the dominance of broadband technology, there were many proponents of the baseband technology as evidenced by the large installed base of Xerox Ethernets. Sytek was currently the only manufacturer that could provide a system that would meet Air Products' needs, but other major manufacturers had products in the works. While Sytek had a strong position in the CATV market, their long-term viability in LANs was an open question. Mather wondered if he should wait for the technology issues to be resolved and other major manufacturers to enter the market, or move decisively to take advantage of interim benefits and organizational learning.

Glossary

analog data The physical representation of information so that the relationship of information bears an exact relationship to the original information. The electrical signals on a telephone are an analog-data representation of the original voice.

ASCII terminals A line-oriented terminal that uses the American Standard Code for Information Interchange (ASCII), a standard 8-bit information code used with most computers and data terminals. Information is communicated on a line-by-line basis.

bandwidth The difference between the limiting frequencies of a continuous frequency band. The wider the bandwidth, the greater the amount of information that can be sent in a given time.

baseband See Appendix.

baud A measure of information rate of flow, interchangeable with the number of binary bits per second that can be sent over a transmission medium.

benchmark tests Various tests for assisting in measurement of product performance under expected conditions of use. Typically, a program or group of programs are run on several computers for purposes of comparing speed, throughput, ease of conversion, etc.

broadband See Appendix.

CAD/CAM Computer-aided design and computer-aided manufacturing systems. These systems usually include a cathode ray tube display, keyboard, plotter, and one or more graphic input devices. These elements comprise a user workstation that is linked to peripherals such as readers, printers, tape and disk drives, and a microcomputer. CAD/CAM systems can help design parts and machinery, generate schematics, diagram complex wiring arrangements and printed circuit boards, and create accurate art work on glass or film.

CATV Cable television, using a broadband distribution system.

CBX Computerized branch exchange—A sophisticated digital switching system that makes use of state-of-the-art electronic technology to control voice and data communications over the same transmission cable.

coaxial cable (coax) A physical transmission medium consisting of a wire core surrounded by an insulating medium which is, in turn, covered by a braided metal jacket. Very high-frequency signals can be carried.

CSMA/CD Carrier sense multiple access with collision detect. A type of protocol for communicating on a LAN.

digital data Information which is expressed in discrete or noncontinuous form. Opposite of analog data.

data terminal A terminal that does not have information processing capability of its own, but rather depends entirely upon the computer to which it is connected.

headend box   The active electronic device on a broadband LAN that receives the incoming signal, modulates it to a different frequency, and sends it back out on the cable.

local area network (LAN)   A communication system that allows devices to send data/messages directly to another device connected to the network.

megabits   A measure of information, equal to 1 million bits.

MHz   Millions of cycles per second.

modem   A device which converts data from a form compatible with data processing equipment (usually digital) to a form compatible with transmission facilities (usually analog) and vice-versa.

plug compatible   Pertaining to the capability of various devices to be interchangeable without modification to them or to the connecting or replacement devices.

port   The entry channel to which a data set is attached.

protocols   A basic procedure or set of rules that governs and controls flow of messages between computers or, in general, a set of conventions between communication processes on the format and content of messages to be exchanged.

RAM   Random access memory. Access can be made directly to any element in the memory.

stop bit   The last element of a character designed for asychronous serial transmission that defines the character space immediately to the left of the most significant character in accumulator storage.

Tektronix terminals   A particular brand of terminal designed to display graphical data.

topology   The physical or logical layer of nodes in a computer network.

VLSI circuits   Very large-scale integrated circuits.

Z80 microprocessor   A type of eight-bit microprocessor, used in many personal computers.

Appendix

Local area networks (LANs) consist of a set of independent nodes that are equipped to communicate with one another. Each node on the network might consist of a mainframe, mini- or microcomputer, terminal, or peripheral. While several terminals connected to a computer are also a network, the operative word here is *independent*. LANs do not pivot on master-slave relationships, but rather suggest a peer relationship between the nodes on the network. LANs are not central switches, but instead broadcast all messages to every node on the network. Each node monitors the appropriate channel (this is not necessary on a base-

Broadband versus Baseband

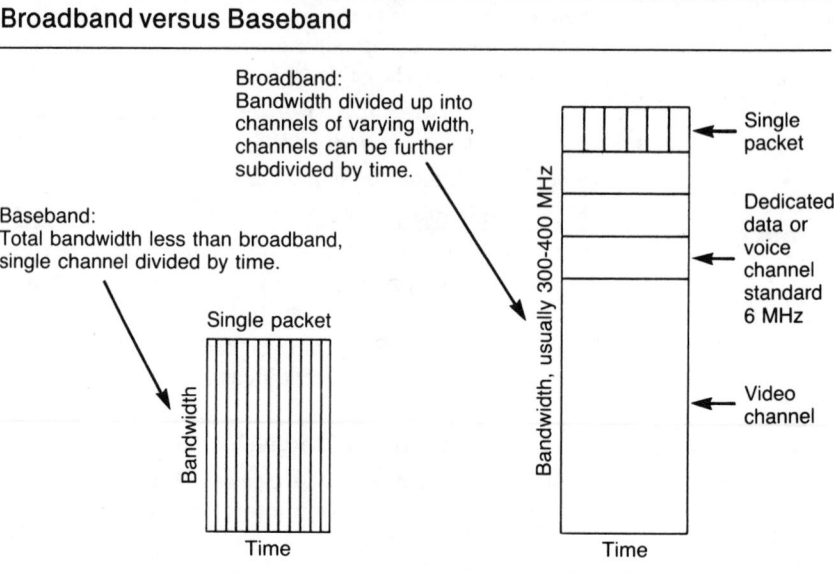

band system since there is only one channel) and checks the address of each message, pulling off only those addressed to that node. Unlike a phone, the system is not interactive. LANs, by definition, are local—the system is geographically limited, although it may extend for a distance of miles. In addition, LANs imply a high data rate and low error rate, relative to a phone line connection.

LANs generally use one of two methods to divide up the capacity of the transmission medium: frequency division multiplexing (FDM) or time division multiplexing (TDM). Broadband technology can use either or both methods to divide up the bandwidth, while baseband can use only TDM.

Baseband

Using baseband technology, one and only one signal can occupy the physical transmission medium at any one time. The frequency spectrum starts with a direct current signal, and can range up to the available bandwidth of the carrier. The transmission is sent in short bursts which utilize the entire bandwidth. The baseband network allocates the use of the shared resource, the distribution medium, through time division multiplexing or TDM.

Each node on the system gains access by one of several protocols. In a carrier sense multiple access/collision detect (CSMA/CD) system, each station listens first to determine if the line is free, in the same way as you would listen for a dial tone on the telephone. If the network is free, the station sends a message and listens to ensure that another station did not simultaneously send a message, causing a collision of the two messages. If this happens, both stations wait a random length of time, then retransmit. Token ring networks use a logical token which is passed between stations in a continuous closed logical loop. Only the station with the token is allowed to transmit a message. Less frequently used access methods include polling and time division multiple access.

Data transmitted over a TDM system is sent in small messages, rather than a continuous stream. The data file to be transmitted is broken up into small formatted messages of fixed maximum length. Each message includes a header, which contains the address of the node to which the packet is to be directed. Messages from different nodes can then be interleaved over the same physical medium, using TDM. This prevents any one node from tying up the system while it transmits a long data file.

Baseband technology tends to be simple and economical, especially for small systems. Some vendors systems can use twisted wire pairs as the physical transmission medium, although most require coaxial cable. However, baseband systems can be used only for data transmission. The network is passive, in that the actual signal is generated at each node and is placed on the network using a modem. In systems using CSMA/CD such as Ethernet, failure of any piece of equipment will remove only that node from the system. If the physical wire is cut, nodes on each segment of the wire will still be able to communicate with nodes on the same segment.

Broadband

Broadband technology allows multiple signals to use the same physical transmission medium at the same moment in time. This is possible by assigning each signal a specific frequency range, and tuning in only the desired signal, in exactly the same manner as a TV selects a single channel from a CATV network. The resource is shared through FDM. Single channels on the system can either be dedicated between two modes, or can be further shared through TDM of a single channel, with access to the channel controlled through CSMA/CD, token ring, or other control mechanism.

Because of the requirement to provide a different frequency for each signal on the network, broadband systems typically have wider bandwidth overall than baseband systems. This necessitates the use of coaxial cable as the physical transmission medium. The signal on a broadband system is generated by a headend signal generator, making the system active. Failure of the headend equipment brings down all nodes on the network. Each node on the network must have a modem to modulate the signal at the appropriate frequency.

Broadband has greater total capacity because it uses a wider bandwidth, although the capacity of a particular channel on the system is less than the capacity of the entire broadband system. A baseband system can be carried over several channels of a broadband network.

Broadband networks tend to be more expensive and to have higher maintenance costs, but offer greater functionality and flexibility than baseband. They can support data, voice, and video simultaneously.

Case 9-3

Air Products and Chemicals, Inc.
Local Area Network (B)

In February 1986, Ray Hoving, Manager of Emerging Technologies at Air Products and Chemicals, Inc. (APCI), was reviewing the options for expanding the local area network (LAN) at the company's Allentown, Pennsylvania, facilities. The planned expansion of the LAN to all buildings created the potential to provide service to all 4,000 employees on the Air Products "campus." At present the service was limited to individuals in research and development (R&D) and management information services (MIS). The LAN Committee, formed in July of 1985, had the responsibility "to assess potential opportunities to use, to develop, and to deploy LAN within the framework of the corporation's worldwide network."[1] The Committee, which Hoving chaired, was currently reviewing how to expand the R&D network in the context of a set of experiments on PC Nets and a soon to be implemented CBX.[2] Expansion of the existing LAN would be the subject of its March meeting.

---

[1] From LAN Committee Charter—see Appendix A.

[2] CBX stands for Computerized Branch Exchange. The one chosen by Air Products and Chemicals, Inc. was offered by Intecom. The specific product was called IBX, which stands for Integrated Business Exchange.

This case was prepared by James L. McKenney and Arthur Warbelow.

The initial R&D LAN, manufactured by Sytek and called AIRNET by Air Products, had repaid its $500,000 cost through productivity improvements in the first year after installation. However, the initial users had a well-defined need for high speed data transfer and were familiar with computer technology. Expansion beyond R&D would include less technically oriented users having modest need for large-volume data transfer, but an assortment of uses for reliable instantaneous communication. How AIRNET might meet these needs was not clear, and the impact of IBX on potential LAN users was unknown. Long-term cost comparisons and support issues needed to be addressed. In addition, members of the Committee were concerned about degrading LAN performance by expanding the number of users, potentially by a factor of 10.

The initial implementation of AIRNET, linking all R&D and MIS users in each building, had been a success. The system had been installed in 10 months and, after a brief debugging period, had grown as a reliable service connecting three DEC systems to two IBM systems and a myriad of laboratory instruments, automation computers, and terminals. Prior to AIRNET, researchers had had to go both to the lab and to the computer room to diagnose experimental problems and to collect the data. Now all of the data was collected automatically and most problems could be resolved from a single terminal. Researchers used AIRNET to upload information from their instruments to either the DEC or IBM systems and to do analysis by remotely managing the data transfer from a terminal in their offices. In addition, they could manage data flow among systems and easily perform file transfers.

Ralph Mayo, Manager of R&D Systems, and Ron Crane, System Manager, both former researchers, had guided the technical analysis that settled on the Sytek broadband system as the basis of AIRNET. This was the first step in their vision to allow researchers to design, conduct, and analyze experiments through a terminal in their offices. The APCI's acquisition of DEC VAX systems for data analysis was the second step, along with expanded graphics systems. The success of AIRNET had generated a strong demand for access by employees located in areas not linked to the network.

The LAN Committee had been commissioned by Peter Mather, Vice President of Management Information Services, in June of 1985 to cope with the complexities of future LAN developments. The Committee's Charter included all premise-based communication systems, such as LAN and PBX, that were geographically limited. The Committee included Roger Bast, Manager of Computing Services; Pete Bilan, Manager of Corporate MIS; John Landis, Manager of Engineering/ Scientific Systems; Ralph Mayo; Virgil W. Palmer, Telecommunication Planning; Paul Slaski, Manager of Technology Assessment; and Joe

EXHIBIT 1 MIS Organization, March 1986

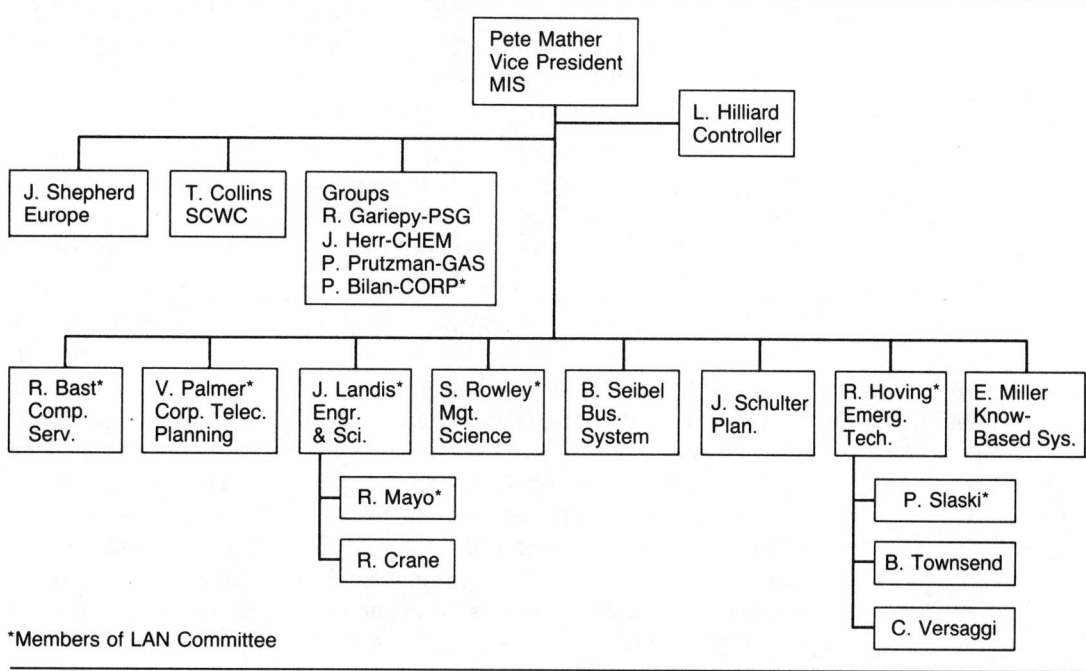

*Members of LAN Committee

Prestileo, Manager of Communication Administration. (See Organizational Chart of MIS in Exhibit 1.) The Committee had met monthly starting in July 1985 to track the evolution of the R&D AIRNET experience, to explore other technological alternatives, to assess needs for further LAN service, and to plan new developments and LAN deployments. Vital inputs on new technologies were reports of members' visits to sites using different LAN technologies as well as analyses of vendor proposals. At the initial meeting, John Landis had discussed strategies for expanding AIRNET, noting that the expansion of wiring in the building was a key factor.

During the fall of 1985, the Committee evaluated both the potential of the new IBX as a LAN support system and several new LAN technologies including IBM's Token Ring and PC Net. They frequently discussed the technical and operational uses of interconnectivity for different services for voice, data, and video. In October, the Committee asked Ralph Mayo and Roger Bast to prepare a cost analysis for an expansion of AIRNET throughout the campus to meet LAN service requirements in areas not yet wired. Their effort led to a Capital Expenditure proposal for an expansion of AIRNET cabling within all campus buildings. The proposal was reviewed and recommended by the Committee in December for implementation by August 1986. At that time, although they recommended continuing the policy of limiting AIRNET service to the R&D community, the Committee also initiated a study to review alternatives prior to the physical expansion of the AIRNET system. The review considered the following points:

1. Current costs of connecting to the AIRNET.
2. LAN service requirements throughout the campus.
3. Comparison of IBX and AIRNET capabilities.
4. Preparation of a support plan and resource requirements for the expansion.

A formal decision-making approach was outlined that called for an April deadline for a recommended plan of action for Pete Mather. This decision point would allow orderly development of a working program by mid-July, prior to completion of the recommended wiring expansion.

In January the Capital Expenditure proposal to install AIRNET cabling in all buildings by August was approved. The expansion was funded by R&D, with the stated purpose of facilitating movement of R&D people by providing a full range of R&D information services to all sites. The initial AIRNET system wired only three of the buildings completely and wired portions of other buildings where appropriate R&D and MIS staff were located. This was done to reduce the initial capital yet provide for future expansion. The productivity improvements and growing demand by R&D for AIRNET services had prompted the follow-on expansion to distribute AIRNET connectivity to all areas.

A prime concern of the Committee was how the planned implementation of the IBX system in July could supplement LAN service. Virgil Palmer had developed a campus wiring plan for the Committee in the fall and suggested alternative connections for users to either IBX or AIRNET for LAN support. This led to an overall review of the status of AIRNET, the potential of the IBM Token Ring, and the potential of the IBX system. An outcome of the meeting was the following list of alternatives to expanding AIRNET service:

1. Maintain the current policy of limiting AIRNET use to the Research and Development and MIS support staff, where the benefits are the greatest and the success has been demonstrated.
2. Form "cooperative ventures" with certain organizations within the company, such as engineering, to include them in the use of AIRNET. This would provide the best benefit, but would not endorse AIRNET as a general campus-wide connectivity option.
3. Decide that AIRNET technology is one of several appropriate long-term solutions and begin a plan for its orderly roll out,

              eventually providing full capability for the entire campus, leaving connections with the new IBX as a later decision.

4. Agree AIRNET is the clear winner for data and video transmission, and aggressively ramp up to provide full service without consideration of alternatives such as the IBX.

Discussion of the Alternatives

John Landis felt AIRNET allowed company scientists to take advantage of new instrumentation with embedded software and digital output. As the responsible manager for both R&D and engineering support, Landis wanted to expand the productivity gains in the research and scientific community to engineers and other individuals with similar data transfer needs. He had been a proponent of AIRNET expansion, and his organization provided budget support for operation of the network, although responsibility for operation and support of AIRNET were being switched from the Engineering and Scientific Services organization to Computing Services and Facilities. Landis thought that AIRNET could be of significant value to the engineering group and other departments with multiple computer access and data transfer needs. Such expansion would increase new usage and lower average cost for all users. Two-thirds of the cost of AIRNET was fixed in the design, original purchase of communications equipment, and implementation, with connection equipment, maintenance, and support costs variable with the number of users.

Bill Townsend, Manager of OA, had implemented, in parallel with AIRNET, three WANG VS and seven OIS computers to provide secretarial support throughout the campus. He had discarded Wang's LAN, Wangnet, as too expensive and rigid as a network base and simply connected the Wangs directly for word processing and electronic mail and to the IBM mainframe for document exchange with other systems. Townsend felt that AIRNET expansion could eventually link to these secretarial services.

Charlie Versaggi, Manager of the Information Center, was exploring methods of connecting the growing number of office PCs at APCI. At the outset of the LAN project in 1982, there were 40 PCs, operating largely as stand-alone terminals. By the spring of 1986 there were about 400 PCs on the campus and growing demand for linking them to each other and to other systems. One experiment was under way to test the effectiveness of PC Net, an IBM product for linking PCs. Since PC Net was manufactured by Sytek, connectivity over the LAN was technically possible. Charlie was hopeful the pilot test at six sites would demonstrate the viability of PC Net so that if linking PCs became desirable, he would have a proven alternative to individual PC Nets.

Roger Bast felt that new services on AIRNET should not be added until the expansion had stabilized and standard procedures for maintenance and trouble shooting had been developed. The Sytek system had relatively crude diagnostic facilities for locating failures and identifying probable causes. Typically one went to the location of the failure and probed with test equipment to locate the problem and its cause. Processes were still very much ad hoc, and it would take experience, time, and more support from Sytek for them to become more routine. Bast was concerned that further expansion to more users would degrade the present service.

In addition, Bast was concerned about adding new types of users who might become dependent upon the system, yet not be as understanding or tolerant of downtime as the existing clients. He felt office workers with little training in systems required a reliable, user friendly environment, whereas the present R&D users were tolerant of the occasional downtime the new system required, as they came from complex data transfer situations, and had been sympathetic participants in the introduction of AIRNET. Bast felt that system network management would be complex, especially given the need to interconnect AIRNET to other services.

Virgil Palmer was also cautious about expanding the LAN user base, but more concerned about the pending arrival of a new technology than about the riskiness of the LAN. As Manager of Corporate Telecommunications Planning, Palmer had worldwide responsibility for voice and data telecommunications planning, including Europe as well as the home office. He was also active in the implementation of the IBX that was scheduled to provide voice communication for the campus. It was to be installed in the summer and had a broad range of functions in addition to voice, including data transfer. Palmer felt there were three user groups: one similar to R&D with high data transfer needs, a second with modest needs that could be met with a twisted wire connection through the IBX system, and a middle group whose needs were ambiguous. He felt this middle group was large in number and that some of their needs might be met by the IBX. Palmer thought that connection through the IBX system would be more efficient and recommended a "wait and see" attitude toward rolling out AIRNET services. After the IBX was up and running, it would be easier to evaluate the economics of AIRNET versus IBX, as a means of data transfer.

Joe Prestileo, Manager of Communications Administration, agreed with Palmer about delaying the roll out of the LAN to all users. He was aware of the increased functionality of the IBX voice system, such as store and forward and call transfer, that was scheduled for installation in July. These new services posed both a system debugging problem and a training problem to the same individuals that were po-

EXHIBIT 2 Connectivity at APCI

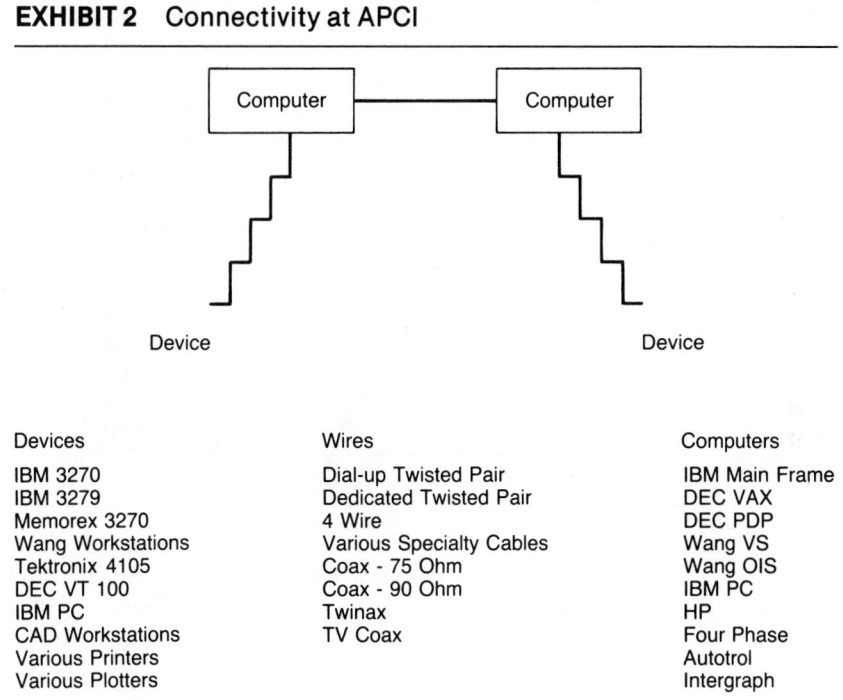

Devices	Wires	Computers
IBM 3270	Dial-up Twisted Pair	IBM Main Frame
IBM 3279	Dedicated Twisted Pair	DEC VAX
Memorex 3270	4 Wire	DEC PDP
Wang Workstations	Various Specialty Cables	Wang VS
Tektronix 4105	Coax - 75 Ohm	Wang OIS
DEC VT 100	Coax - 90 Ohm	IBM PC
IBM PC	Twinax	HP
CAD Workstations	TV Coax	Four Phase
Various Printers		Autotrol
Various Plotters		Intergraph

tential LAN users. Introducing IBX and AIRNET at the same time could create a mess that would upset the users. Prestileo preferred to sit tight until late fall and then consider expanding AIRNET service.

Further Work of the Committee

In order to better understand the needs of their clients, the LAN Committee analyzed their existing and expected communication needs. This analysis was presented to Peter Mather and Jerry White, Vice President of Finance, to obtain broader understanding of the situation and to propose a standard long-run approach. Exhibit 2 shows the salient information.

The bulk of the discussion documented the scope of the present communication system and its connectivity problems. At present, the campus had 25 types of terminals, printers, and plotters connected by eight different wiring technologies to 10 different computer systems. This required 16 different message protocols of which 7 were from IBM, 2 were from DEC and Wang, and the remainder were from public network standards. The Committee recommended that APCI standardize on the three transmission means of (1) twisted pair, (2) CATV

EXHIBIT 3 Telecommunication Technologies

	Technology	Wire	Band	Media
High	Telephone–Dial-up	Twisted pair	Base	Voice, data
	Dedicated	Various	Base	Data
Maturity	Local area network (Sytek, IBM PC)	TV coax	Broad	Data, video
	PBX (IBX)	Twisted pair Fiber optics	Base	Voice, data
Low	MAP (GM)	TV coax	Broad	Data, video
	Token Ring (IBM)	Twisted pair IBM specific Optic fiber	Base	Data
	ISDN (AT&T)	Twisted pair Optic fiber	?	All

---

cable and (3) fiber optics, to meet present and future communication needs. Their recommendations, as shown in Exhibit 3, would support the mature technologies of dial-up-phone and dedicated links, the planned IBX system, and the potential LAN technologies of ISDN (AT&T), Token Ring (IBM), and MAP (GM). Using standard CATV cable lessened APCI's total dependence on Sytek. A commitment to broadband CATV cable would enable additional LAN technologies, such as MAP, to be added by using different transmission frequencies.

Ray Hoving felt the Committee faced a very complex technological planning situation. Should they decide now on a communication architecture with a campus-wide broadband LAN that could eventually connect everything on a LAN superhighway, or should they focus on connecting nodes that would serve as distribution points for information services of IBX? Hoving knew there was a role for both a broadband LAN and a CBX on the campus because of the unique capabilities of each (video for LAN, voice for CBX). Data could go on either service with a gateway connecting the two. However, gateways were future products from vendors and the Committee had to take it on faith that the product would become available to support the desired connectivity. Also, Hoving was not sure he had enough information at this time on the economics or reliability of the alternative technologies. He knew Peter Mather wanted to provide access to all legitimate users. Yet Hoving was not sure the timing was correct for a decision on the future architecture.

The March agenda called for a review of the analyses on the LAN expansion. It included the following topics:

1. Potential communication services demand.
2. Comparison of AIRNET and IBX.
3. Cost analysis (one time and ongoing).
4. Vendor viability assessment.
5. Security assessment.

Hoving felt comfortable that the discussion would produce a firm appraisal of the art of the possible. As his mission was to maintain momentum in utilizing new technologies and testing their potential, he hoped a consensus would emerge so they could move ahead.

Appendix   LAN Committee Charter
Purpose

The ability to deliver information when and where it's needed has become an increasingly more complex challenge with the proliferation of computing technology through all levels of the organization. Local area networks (LANs) may provide opportunities to meet this critical need. While the *basic* technology of LANs is reasonably well established, their suitability in meeting the particular information transfer and availability requirement of selected business applications is less certain. Further, it is recognized that LAN* technology and the industry standards which define it are continuing to evolve.

Therefore, a committee has been organized consisting of representatives from key areas in the company having interest in the issues and concerns surrounding LANs and their use by Air Products. The purpose of this committee is to assess potential opportunities to use, develop, and deploy LANs within the framework of the corporation's worldwide information requirements. Assessment is understood to include the examination of LAN technology and the impact its use may have on the company's tactical and strategic information and telecommunication plans.

Membership

The committee will be chaired by the Manager of Emerging Technology. Committee members will be the Managers of Corporate Telecommunications Planning, Communications Administration, Engineering and Scientific Systems, and MIS Computer Services and Facilities.

---

*The term *LAN* as it relates to this charter shall mean all premise based data communications systems such as Sytek, IBM PC Net, PBX, etc. that are geographically limited in their use and deployment.

The committee meetings will be open, but the attendees should be able to provide either technical or consultation inputs that are relevant to the topic(s) and issues being discussed by the LAN Committee.

Responsibilities

The local area network committee will have the following responsibilities:

• Review all proposals involving the use of LANs. This includes evaluation and comment on the appropriateness of using LAN technology to meet the information availability and transfer requirements outlined in the proposal. All proposals for review shall be sent to the Chairman, LAN Committee.

• Review and approval of all proposals to expand use of in-place LANs. Note: Day-to-day activities associated with the operation of in-place LANs are not subject to committee review unless these activities would impact the overall LAN operational environment.

• LAN proposals either for new systems or upgrades to current technology will be reviewed and approved by the LAN Committee, along with a representative of the parent organization submitting the request.

The purpose of the review and approval of LAN requests is to ensure that APCI takes advantage of our knowledge base in LAN developments. There could be a system already in place or a vendor identified that meets the needs of the new request. This should eliminate the need for a technical evaluation and review of LAN products and service in order to meet the needs of the new request. All requests for LANs will be sent to the Chairman, LAN Committee.

• Tracking, review, and comment pertaining to LAN technological developments and potential application by Air Products. This responsibility includes review and assessment of LAN-related products (including software), inter-networking (PBX, computer to computer, etc.) and gateway or bridge services. Also opportunities to influence the development of LAN technology, through alpha or beta test agreements, will be subject to consideration by the committee.

Frequency of Meetings

Meeting frequency will be determined by the committee chairman, but shall be no less than monthly.

Chapter 10

Multinational IT Issues

The head of multinational IT (MIS) of a major European research company suddenly discovered that three of their largest foreign subsidiaries had recently ordered medium-sized computers and were planning to move their work from the corporate IT department to installations in their countries (reducing the workload in corporate IT's data center by 45 percent). The reasons cited for this decision were better control over day-to-day operations, more responsive service, and lower costs. Located in a country with a high-cost, tight labor pool, the IT head was unsure how to assess the risks this now posed to his operation and to the company as a whole.

The head of corporate IT in a large pharmaceutical company recently held a three-day international meeting of the 15 IT heads of the company's major foreign subsidiaries. A major unresolved problem raised at the meeting was what the relationship of corporate IT should be to the more than 50 smaller foreign subsidiaries that also had computing equipment. Historically the department had responded to requests for assistance (five to eight per year) but had not gone beyond that. The head of corporate IT was increasingly uncertain whether this was an appropriate level of involvement.

The chief financial officer of a major Singapore company ordered 13 APPLE II computers in his controller's department to stimulate awareness of how modern financial analysis could help the company. Five months later, with the experiment a great success, he found himself overwhelmed with requests for system support.

The company not only lacked the staff to provide the support but, even in the two- to three-year planning horizon, was likely to be unable to acquire it in the local market at any price.

These stories are representative of a major, largely unreported, unstudied IT story: namely that management of multinational IT support for any company is very complex and its issues go well beyond legislation relating to transborder information flows. These issues have become more significant in the past decade as the post-World War II explosion of multinationals, in both numbers and scope, has continued. This growth has sparked the need for development and expansion of management systems to permit appropriate coordination of geographically distant business activities.

In the past, investigation of these issues tended to be lost between two schools of thought. On the one hand the area has seemed so specialized and technical that the scholars of international business tended to ignore it. On the other hand those writing about management of information technology have seemed to be highly national in their orientation and tended to slide past the issues in this area of information technology application.

International IT represents a major management challenge today, and the resolution of its issues is likely to be even more significant in the coming years. Many companies require, for competitive reasons, far tighter linkage of their foreign operations. Managing the forces (described as six trends in Chapter 2) driving transition in IT is complicated by the diversity of national infrastructures (for example, Germany versus Sri Lanka) as well as previously discussed variations in corporate manufacturing and distribution technologies, in current scope of IT activity, and in relative sophistication in IT application. Building on our concepts of strategic relevance, culture, contingent planning, and managing diffusion of technology, we will focus on aspects of international business that influence IT.

The first section of this chapter deals with some important national characteristics that influence the type of IT support appropriate for a firm's operations in any country. The second section talks about specific IT environmental issues that influence how a firm can develop IT support in a specific country. The third section deals with company-specific issues that influence how corporations should think about IT development overseas. The final part tells about the types of policies that firms have adopted for dealing with these issues and discusses the factors that make them more or less appropriate in different settings.

Diversity between Countries

A number of important factors inherent in a country's culture, government, and economy influence which IT applications make sense, how they should be implemented, and the appropriate type of corporate guidance from an IT activity located in another country. The most important of these factors are discussed here.

Sociopolitical

The obvious factors of industrial maturity and form of government are particularly important in considering the use of information technology. Emerging countries with high birth rates have views and opportunities far different from those of mature industrial states with shrinking labor populations. Mature societies have stable bureaucracies that provide the necessary continuity for development of communications systems. In some countries investments in technical infrastructure may come only at the expense of other national priorities such as food and medical care.

Language

Common languages of Western origin provide a sound means for technical communications and relevant documentation. However, this is lacking if the local language is not based on Latin, especially for discussions of a technical nature. Frequently senior managers of the subsidiary are fluent in the parent company language, but lower-level managers and staff technicians are not. This tends to be true even in companies such as N. V. Philips (the large Dutch electronics company), which has made a major effort to develop English as a companywide language.

Local Constraints

An entire network of local cultural facets makes it difficult to develop coordinated systems and an orderly process of technology transfer. From one country to another, union agreements, timing of holidays, government tax regulations, and customs procedures all force major modifications of software for applications such as accounting and personnel. Further, differences in holidays, working hours, and so on, complicate coordination of reporting and data gathering.

Also important are issues relating to geography and demographics. For example, a large phonograph record company has found it attractive to have centralized order-entry and warehouse management located in Paris, to serve retailers around the country. It fits the structure of the French distribution system. In Germany, however, the company established multiple factories, distribution points, and a quite different order-entry system to service the market. The German structure is an appropriate response to the realities of German geography and prevailing distribution patterns. Unfortunately this also meant that the software and procedures used in the French subsidiary were inappropriate for the German situation.

Economic

A mature industrial economy normally has an available pool of well-trained, procedurally oriented individuals who typically earn high wages relative to world standards. Their economic incentive to replace clerical people with IT systems is complemented by the limited availability of talent. It is a sensible economic decision. In cultures with low wage rates, often dependent on one or two main raw material exports for currency, there is typically a lack of both talent and economic incentive toward IT. The true need is to develop a *reliable* source of available information (a noneconomic decision). Implementing this, however, may move against both economic and cultural norms. Trying to serve the interests of both cultures in a multinational IT organization is understandably complicated.

Currency

Organizing international data centers is complicated by both currency restrictions and volatility in exchange rates. Change in exchange rates may mean that a location initially cost effective for providing service to neighboring countries may suddenly become quite cost ineffective. For example, several Swiss data centers that were very cost competitive in the early 1970s became very noncompetitive in the late 1970s as a result of the heavy appreciation of the Swiss franc, even against currencies like the German mark.

Autonomy

Another point of importance is the universal drive for autonomy and feelings of nationalism. The normal drive for autonomy in units within a single country is intensified by differences in language and culture as one deals with international subsidiaries. In general, a larger integration effort is needed to coordinate foreign subsidiaries appropriately than is needed with domestic ones, not necessarily with better results.

Difficulties increase not only with the distance of the subsidiary from corporate headquarters but also as the relative economic importance of the subsidiary drops.

National Infrastructure

The availability of utilities and a transportation system is often an important constraint on feasible alternatives. On the other hand their absence also serves as an opportunity for emerging technology. For example, to overcome the unpredictable transportation and communication systems, one South American distributor developed a private microwave tower network to link the records of a remote satellite depot with the central warehouses. This system enabled him to obtain a significant competitive edge that led to rapid growth.

In one Southeast Asian country, a major multinational has made extensive use of minicomputers on its plantations. Operated by local electric generators, they can only be linked together by the monthly shipping of thousands of diskettes because of the unavailability of telecommunications in the remote areas. Further complicating matters is that, without special influence in the capitol, it takes an average of 37 months from the time an order for telecommunications gear is placed until it is delivered.

All of the above factors make international coordination of IT activities in general more complicated than coordination of domestic IT activities. Often development of special staff and organizational approaches is needed if these issues are to be effectively handled.

National IT Environments

In addition to the above, more general issues, some very specific IT issues make the coordination and transfer of IT technology particularly challenging from one country to another. These are due in part to the long lead times to build effective systems and in part to the changing nature of the technology. The most important of these issues are outlined below.

Availability of IT Professional Staff

Inadequate availability of systems and programming resources, a general worldwide problem, is much worse in some settings than others. Singapore, for example, in 1984 had only 2,500 analysts and programmers to fill a need for over 8,500. Further, as fast as people develop these skills in English-speaking countries, they become targets for recruiters from the high-wage, highly industrialized countries, a particular problem in the Philippines, for example.

This personnel shortage has led to a spurt of growth in India-based software companies that take advantage of their high skills and very low wage rates to bid effectively on overseas programming jobs. Obviously the geographic distance limits the type of work that can be bid on.

When an attempt is made to supplement local staff with individuals from headquarters the results are not always uniformly satisfactory. An initial outburst of productivity by the expatriates and the effective transfer of technology in a later phase often lead to resentment by the local staff (whose salaries and benefits are usually much lower) and broken career paths for the expatriates, who find they have become both technically and managerially obsolete when they return to corporate headquarters. Management of IT expatriates' reentry has generally been quite inadequate.

Central Telecommunications

The price and quality of telecommunications support vary widely from one country to another. On both dimensions the United States sets the standard. In many European countries the tariffs will run an order of magnitude higher than those in the United States. Also, lead times to get extra land lines, terminals, and so forth, from date of order can stretch to years instead of weeks in many countries (if indeed they are available at any price). Finally, communication quality, availability, and cost differ widely from one country to another. Varying line capacity, costs, and uptime performance mean that profitable on-line applications in the home country may be either cost ineffective or fail to meet adequate uptime or reliability standards in other countries.

National IT Strategy

In some countries development of a local computer manufacturing and software industry is a key national priority (France, Germany, Singapore, and the United Kingdom, for example). In these situations subsidiaries of foreign companies often see buying the products of the local manufacturer as good citizenship and as building credit for later dealings with the government. This may create a legitimate need for local deviation from corporate hardware/software standards.

In a related issue, some countries (such as India and Nigeria) require that computer vendors sell a majority share of their local subsidiary to local shareholders if they are to do business in the country. Some vendors (such as IBM) have preferred to withdraw from a market rather than to enter into such an arrangement. This also may force a deviation from corporate-mandated IT standards.

Finally, concern may exist about whether the country exporting the hardware will continue to be a reliable supplier in a world of turbulent national politics and shifting foreign policies. A number of South African companies, for example, uneasy about the ability to get a sustained flow of products from any one country, have moved to prevent potential disruptions of equipment delivery by dealing with vendors of several countries although they are incurring significant additional costs.

General Level of IT Sophistication

The speed and ease with which companies can either start or grow an IT activity are linked to the general level of IT activity in the country. A firm located in a country with a substantial base of installed electronic-based information systems and well-trained, mobile labor can grow more rapidly and effectively than if none of these preconditions exist. Countries with limited installed electronic-based information systems require substantially more expatriate labor to implement IT work, as well as great effort and time to educate users in the idiosyncrasies of IT and how best to interface with it. Careful investigation of the staff mobility factor is particularly important because both bonding arrangements and cultural norms may add real rigidities to what appears on the surface to be a satisfactory labor supply situation.

Size of Local Market

The size of the local market influences the number of vendors who can compete for service in it; in smaller markets a company's preferred international supplier may not have a presence. Further, the quality of service support often varies widely from one setting to another, with vendors who provide good support in one country turning out to be inadequate in another. Another important issue is the availability and quality of local software and consulting companies (or subsidiaries of large international ones). A thriving, competent local IT industry can do much to offset other differences in local support and availability of staff.

Data Export Control

A topic receiving significant publicity in the past six to seven years has been possible legislation to reduce dramatically the amount of information relating to people and finances that can be transmitted electronically across national boundaries. Increased governmental prescription concerning the types of teleprocessing services that may be offered by suppliers involves establishment of both technical standards and type of nonlocally manufactured equipment that can be used. Another factor is possible regulation of the type of data (including quality and security standards) that should be permitted to be sent abroad. Not only is individual privacy threatened but security and quality controls over these data are unacceptable, endangering the individual.

The potential scope of such legislation and the procedures for effectively monitoring compliance with it are very speculative at present. When the dust settles, its practical impact on a firm's operations may be limited, although some modifications in procedures will have to be made to accommodate problems in specific countries. Indeed, in a number of settings significantly less concern exists about the practical implications of such control than existed in 1980.

Technological Awareness

Awareness of contemporary technology spreads very rapidly around the globe because key IT magazines and journals have international distribution. This awareness poses real problems in terms of orderly development of applications in less sophisticated countries, because subsidiaries often tend to promote technologies that they neither really understand, need, nor are capable of managing. Conversely, starting with a high degree of IT awareness has advantages, as distinctly different paths may be implemented for exploiting information technology in the subsidiaries than took place in home offices.

Trade Union Environment

In the past ten years, particularly in Europe and Western Canada, there have been substantial successful efforts to organize IT departments. In 1980 and 1981, for example, serious and successful strikes by the United Kingdom's Inland Revenue Service's computer operations staff substantially interrupted its operations (as mentioned in Chapter 9). This possibility has caused some companies to do a better job of distributing their IT activities in order to minimize both the possibility of labor action and the disruption that flows from it. It has also become a factor in picking appropriate locations for regional data centers to support activities in several countries.

Border Opportunities

In periods of fluctuating exchange rates, significant discontinuities often appear in vendor prices for the same equipment in different countries. In 1980, for example, there was a period where a 15 to 20 percent savings could be achieved by buying equipment in Italy for use in Switzerland, as opposed to a direct purchase in Switzerland.

For the multinational firm the practical implication of these factors is severe restraint of the degree to which standard policies and controls can be placed on diverse international activities. Rigid policy on many of these issues cannot be dictated effectively from corporate headquarters, often located a vast distance from the subsidiary's operating management. There are many legitimate reasons for diversity, and considerable *local* know-how must be brought to the decisions.

Corporate Factors Affecting IT Requirements

Within the context of the different national cultures and the current state of the IT profession in different countries, a number of factors inside a company influence how far it must move to manage the transfer of information technology and how actively it should attempt to centrally control international IT activity. Because of the above-mentioned environmental issues, more control must be delegated internationally than in a domestic environment. However, important opportunities exist for technology transfer, and potentially important service limitations will occur if these issues are not managed. The more important company-specific factors are discussed here.

Nature of Firm's Business

Some firms' businesses demand that key data files be managed centrally to be accessible, immediately or on a short, delayed-access basis, to all units of the firm around the globe. Airline reservation files for international air carriers require such access. A United Airlines agent in Boston confirming a flight segment from Tokyo to Hong Kong needs up-to-the-minute access to the flight's loading to make a valid commitment, while other agents around the globe need to know that seat is no longer available for sale. Failure to have this information poses risks of significant loss of market share as customers perceive the firm to be both unreliable and uncompetitive.

A major shipping company has to maintain a file, updated every 24 hours, as to where its containers are around the globe, what their status is, and their availability for future commitment by regional officers in 20 countries. The absence of this data would lead to their making unfulfillable commitments, subsequently presenting an unreliable image to present and potential customers. In another example, the standards of international banking have evolved to where the leaders can provide customers with an instantaneous worldwide picture of clearances, and so on, thus opening the door for more sophisticated cash management (for which the bank generates appropriate fees). Those firms not providing such services find themselves increasingly at a competitive disadvantage.

Other firms require integration and on-line updating of only some of their files. A major European electronics firm attempts to provide its European managers with up-to-date, on-line access to various key operational files on items such as production schedules, order status, and so forth. This is done for its network of 20-plus factories in order to manage an integrated logistics system. No such integration, however, is attempted for their key marketing or accounting data, which essentially are processed on a batch basis and organized by country. While developing such integration is technically possible the firm at present sees no operational or marketing advantage in doing so.

Still other firms require essentially no integration of data, and each country can be managed on a stand-alone basis. A major U.S. conglomerate, for example, manages each division on a stand-alone basis. Eight of its divisions have operations in the United Kingdom and by corporate policy they have no formal interaction with each other in IT or any other operational matters. (A single tax specialist who files a joint tax return for them is the sole linking specialist.) The company's staff generally perceives that this is an appropriate way to operate and nothing of significance is being lost. These examples suggest the impossibility of generalized prescriptions as to how multinational IT activities should be organized.

Strategic Impact of IT

Where the IT activity is strategic to the company, tighter corporate overview of the area is needed to ensure that new technology (and hence new ways of operating) is rapidly and efficiently introduced to the outlying areas. One of the United States' largest international banks, for example, has a group staff of over 100 at corporate headquarters both to develop software for their international branches and to coordinate the orderly dissemination of this software—thus technology—to their key countries. The bank feels the successful use of IT is too critical to the firm's ultimate success to be managed without technical coordination and senior management perspective. At the other extreme is a reasonably large manufacturer of chemicals, where IT is seen as playing an important but distinctly a support role. At least twice a year the head of the European IT unit and the head of corporate IT exchange visits and share perceptions with each other. The general consensus is that there is not enough payoff to warrant further coordination.

Corporate Organization

As its international activity grows, a firm adopts different structures, each of which requires quite different levels of international IT support and coordination. In the earliest phase of an export division there are only limited numbers of overseas staff, who require little if any local IT processing and support. As the activity grows in size it tends to be reorganized as an *international* division with an increasing number of marketing, accounting, and manufacturing staff located abroad. At this stage an increasing need may arise for local IT support. A full-blown level of international activity may involve regional headquarters (in Europe, the Far East, and Latin America, for example) to coordinate the activities of the diverse countries.

Coordinating such a structure can become very complex for a company where not only are there vertical relationships between corporate IT and the national IT activities but cross-border marketing and manufacturing integration requirements create the need for relationships between individual countries' IT units. The best form of this coordination, of course, will vary widely from one organization to another. One recently studied multibillion dollar pharmaceutical firm was discovered to have very close links between corporate IT and its major national IT units (defined by the firm as those with budgets in excess of $5 million). None of the IT unit managers, however, either knew the names of their contemporaries or had visited any of the other locations. Since there was little cross-border product flow and none planned in the near future, this did not appear to present a significant problem.

At the most complex, we have firms organized in a matrix fashion—with corporate IT activity, divisional IT activities (which may or may not be located at corporate headquarters), and national IT activities. Here balancing of relationships is a major challenge. Divisions having substantial vertical supplier relationships with each other and substantial integration of activities across national borders complicate the relationships even more. In such cases the policies that work for the international divisions are likely to be too simplistic.

Company Technical and Control Characteristics

An important factor in effective IT control structures is the corporation's general level of functional control. Companies with a strong tradition of central control find it both appropriate and relatively easy to implement line IT control worldwide. A major manufacturer of farm equipment, for example, has for years implemented very strong management and operational control over its worldwide manufacturing and marketing functions. Consequently it found considerable acceptance of similar controls for the IT organization. Today the majority of software that runs their overseas plants has been developed and is being maintained by the corporate IT headquarters group.

At the other extreme is a 30-division, multibillion dollar conglomerate with a corporate staff of approximately 100 people involved mostly in financial and legal work associated with acquisitions and divestitures. This company has totally decentralized operating decisions to the divisions, and corporate head count is deliberately controlled to prevent meddling. At present a two-person corporate IT group works on only very broad policy and consulting issues. In this organizational environment effective execution of even this role is very challenging, and effective expansion is very difficult to visualize.

Another element of significance is the technology base of the company. High-technology companies with a tradition of spearheading technical change from a central research and engineering laboratory and ensuring its dissemination around the globe have successfully used a similar approach with IT. Very important is a receptivity to technical change and a base of experience with problems associated with technical change. Firms without this experience in their management teams not only have had more difficulty assimilating information technology in general but have had more problems in transplanting IT developed in one location to another setting.

Finally, corporate size is also relevant. Smaller organizations, because of the limited and specialized nature of their application, find transfer of IT packages and expertise to be particularly complex. As the scope of the operation increases, finding common applications and facilitating transfer of technology appear to become easier, perhaps because the stakes are higher.

Effects of Geography and Size of Companies

It is possible to use the company's location in different time zones creatively to take advantage of excess capacity on the firm's large computers during the second and third shifts. The savings in hardware and staff in some cases have substantially exceeded the additional telecommunications expense. One manufacturing firm located on the East Coast of the United States uses the time between 1 A.M. and 9 A.M. to process much of the manufacturing load of its European subsidiaries. Daytime hours, 9 A.M. to 5 P.M., are primarily devoted to supporting its U.S. operations, and the early evening hours are used to handle the work of its Far Eastern subsidiaries. Another East Coast insurance company has recently set up a subsidiary in Ireland to take advantage of these opportunities. Because of data transmission costs, there are limits to the extent that this can be done profitably.

The number and relative size of foreign operations are important inputs to evolving appropriate policies. Large subsidiaries provide an opportunity for effective coordination on both technical issues and staff rotation. As the relative economic significance of the foreign unit drops, the intensity of the relationship between corporate IT and the local unit appropriately lessens. Less opportunity exists for both technical coordination and meaningful staff transfers. As will be discussed below, different policies and relationships need to be established for units of different sizes.

Economic Analysis

The relevant economies of hardware/software investment overruns need to be monitored carefully on two dimensions. First, vendors often adopt different pricing strategies within countries; the financial attractiveness or unattractiveness of an investment in the home country of the parent company may not hold true in other parts of the globe. Related to this and more serious are the problems and discontinuities caused by fluctuating currency exchange rates, which can substantially change the economics of equipment/staff trade-offs inside a country. Fortunately for U.S. companies, changes in accounting regulations have eliminated some of the artificial accounting considerations as to whether it is better to buy or lease computing equipment.

Other Considerations

Other aspects in a firm's structural environment also influence IT coordination policies. Is there substantial rotation of staff between international locations? If so, is it desirable to have common reporting systems and operating procedures in place in each subsidiary to ease the assimilation of the transfers? Do the firm's operating and financial requirements essentially demand up-to-the-week reporting of overseas financial results? If not, consolidation of smaller overseas operations on a one-month, delayed-time basis is attractive.

Multinational IT Policy Issues

As the preceding sections identify, great diversity appropriately exists in the policies used to coordinate and manage international IT activities between companies and from one country to another. This section identifies the most common types of policies and relationships and briefly focuses on some of the key issues associated with the selection and implementation of each.

The scope of these policies and the size of the effort needed for their implementation are influenced by the nature of the business (degree of central control needed), corporate culture related to corporate-mandated policies, strategic impact of information technologies, and so forth.

Communication and Data Management Standards

The opportunity to transmit data electronically between countries for file updating and processing purposes has created the need for some form of corporate international data dictionary. Too often this need is not addressed, leading to both clumsy systems designs and incorrect outputs. Where data should be stored, the form in which it should be stored, and how it should be updated are all considerations that require centrally managed policy (operating, of course, within the framework of what is legally permissible).

Similarly, centrally guided coordination of communication technology acquisition is needed. At present, communication flexibility and cost vary widely from country to country and are shifting rapidly.

Effective anticipation of these changes requires a corporate view and broad design of telecommunications needs to meet growth and changing business needs over a decade. It must be specific in terms of service levels needed and the appropriate technologies to be utilized. Such a plan requires both capable technical inputs and careful management review. An important by-product of the plan is guidance for corporate negotiation and lobbying efforts on relevant items of national legislation and policies regarding the form, availability, and cost of telecommunication.

Central Hardware/Software Concurrence or Approval

The objective of a central policy is to ensure that obvious mistakes in vendor viability are avoided and economies of scale in purchasing decisions are achieved. Other benefits include the additional support leverage companies achieve by being perceived as an important customer, the reduction of potential interface problems between national systems, and the enhancement of applications software transferability between countries. Practical factors that require sensitive interpretation and execution of central policy include the following items:

- Degree of awareness at corporate headquarters of the vendor's support and servicing problems in the local country.
- Desire of the local subsidiary to exercise its autonomy and control of its operations in a *timely* way. The Korean subsidiary of a large bank wanted to buy a $25,000 word processing system. The request for approval took six months to pass through three locations and involved one senior vice president and two executive vice presidents before the process was completed. Whatever benefits standardization might have achieved for the bank in this situation seemed to be more than offset by the cost and time of the approval process.

• Need to maintain good relationships with governments locally. This may involve such items as patronizing the local vendors, not moving to eliminate certain types of staff, and using the government-controlled IT network.

• Level and skill of corporate headquarters people setting appropriate policy in both technical and managerial dimensions. A technically weak corporate staff dealing with large, well-managed foreign subsidiaries must operate quite differently from a large, technically gifted central staff dealing with many small, rather unsophisticated subsidiaries.

Central Approval of Software Standards and Feasibility Studies

Central control of software standards ensures that software is written in both a maintainable and a secure way so that the company's long-term operational position is not jeopardized. Control of feasibility studies ensures that potential applications are evaluated in a consistent and professional fashion. The problems with this policy of central approval revolve around both the level of effort and the potential erosion of corporate culture.

Implementation of such standards can be expensive and time consuming in relation to the potential benefits. The art is to be flexible with small investments while more closely reviewing the ones where there is real operational exposure. Implementation of this approach requires more sensitivity than many staffs are capable of.

Further, directly counter to central control may be a decentralized company's prevailing management control system and the location of other operating decisions. The significance of this conflict depends on the size and relative strategic impact of the investment. Relatively small, distinctly support investments in these decentralized organizations should clearly be resolved in the local country. Large, strategic investments, however, are often appropriate for central review in these organizations, even taking time delays and cost overruns into account.

Central Software Development

In the name of efficiency, reduced costs, and standard operating procedures worldwide, firms have attempted to develop software centrally or at some designated subsidiary for installation in subsidiaries in other countries. The success of this approach has definitely been mixed. Companies that have had considerable success with this have a well-established pattern of technology transfer, strong functional control over subsidiaries, substantial numbers of expatriates working in the overseas subsidiaries, and some homogeneity in manufacturing, accounting, and distribution practices. Success has also been assisted by very intensive marketing and liaison activities of the IT unit assigned responsibility for the package's development and installation.

When these preconditions have not been present, however, installation has often turned into a troubled situation. Most commonly cited reasons by IT managers for the failure include:

> The developers of the system didn't understand local need well enough. Major functions were left out, and the package required extensive and expensive enhancements.

> The package was adequate, but the efforts needed to train people to put data in and properly handle outputs were significantly underestimated or mishandled. This was complicated by extensive language difficulties and insensitivity to existing local procedures.

> The system evolution and maintenance involved a dependence on central staff that was not sustainable in the long run. We needed more flexibility and timeliness of response than was possible.

> Cost were totally underestimated by more than an order of magnitude. The overrun on the basic package was bad enough but the fat was really in the fire when it came to estimating installation costs.

In our judgment these statements emanate directly from the above structural factors. In reality, an outside software house, with its marketing orientation and existence outside of the family, often can do a better job of selling standard software than an in-house IT unit in a decentralized environment. Finally, in many settings the sheer desire on both sides to have a success is the best guarantee of that success occurring.

IT Communications

While expensive, investments in improving communications between the various national IT units have paid big benefits. Several devices have proven useful:

Regular Interunit Meetings. An annual or biannual conference of the IT directors and their key staff from the major international subsidiaries. For organizations in the turnaround or strategic categories, these meetings ought to take place at least as frequently as meetings of international controllers. The smaller countries (IT budgets under $1 million) will probably not generate enough profitable opportunities to warrant inclusion in this conference or to have a separate one.

The agenda of the conference needs to have a blend of formal planned activities, such as technical briefing, application briefings, and company directives, together with substantial blocks of unplanned time. The informal exchange of ideas, initiation of joint projects, and sharing of mutual problems are among the most important activities of a successful conference.

Corporate-Subsidiary Visits.   Regular visits of corporate IT personnel to the national organizations, as well as national IT personnel coming to corporate. These visits should take place at planned intervals rather than just when there is an operational crisis or technical problem. Less contact is needed with the smaller units than with the larger ones.

Newsletters.   Preparation and circulation of a monthly or bimonthly newsletter to communicate staffing shifts, new technical insights, major project completions, experience with software packages and vendors, and so forth.

Education.   Organization of joint education programs where possible. This may involve the creation and/or acquisition of audiovisual-based materials to be distributed around the world. A large oil company recently supplemented communication of a radically different IT organization structure with the preparation of a special film, complete with sound track in five different languages.

The fundamental issue is to build a stronger sense of organizational identity between the national IT units by encouraging the development of better links between them, rather than to have links only between a country's IT unit and the parent company's IT unit.

Staff Planning

One very important way of addressing the issue of communications, though difficult to administer, is through rotation of staff between the national IT units and corporate IT. Key advantages that stem from this include:

- Better corporate IT awareness of the problems and issues in the overseas IT units. As a corollary the local IT units have a much better perspective on the goals and thinking at corporate headquarters because one of their members has spent a tour of duty there.

- More flexibility in managing career paths and matching positions with individual development needs. Particularly in a crowded corporate IT department an overseas assignment can provide an attractive opportunity.
- Efficient dispersion of technical know-how throughout the organization.

On the negative side of staff rotation, practical problems can occur:

- Career paths of individuals moving from corporate headquarters to less IT-developed portions of the globe have frequently been very unsatisfactory. The individuals bring leading-edge expertise to the overseas installation and have a major positive impact for several years. Upon returning to corporate headquarters they find themselves totally obsolete in terms of the contemporary technologies being used. They also on occasion have been dropped out of the normal progression stream through oversight.
- Assignment of individuals overseas is not only expensive in terms of moving allowances and cost-of-living differentials but it also raises a myriad of potential personal problems. These problems, normally of a family nature, make the success of an international transfer more speculative than a domestic one.
- Transfers from corporate to smaller overseas locations may cause substantial resentment and feelings of nationalism: "Why aren't our people good enough?" Appropriate language skills and efforts on the part of the transferred executive, control over the number of transfers, and local promotions plus the clearly visible opportunity for local staff to be transferred to corporate do much to temper these problems.

Appropriately managed within reasonable limits, the positives far outweigh the negatives.

Consulting Services

Major benefits can come from a central IT group providing foreign subsidiaries with consulting services on both technical and managerial matters. In many cases corporate headquarters is not only located in a technically sophisticated country but its IT activities are bigger in scope than those of individual foreign installations. Among other things, this means that corporate IT is:

1. More aware of leading-edge hardware/software technology and has had firsthand experience with its potential strengths and weaknesses.
2. More likely to have experience with large project management systems and other management methods. Communication of such know-how and expertise can be of value.

In both cases the communication must be done with some sensitivity in order to move the company forward at an appropriate pace. All too often the corporate group pushes too fast in a culturally insensitive fashion, creating substantial problems. Movement through the phases of technology assimilation can be speeded up and smoothed. Skipping a phase, however, is very hard.

As an organization becomes more IT intensive, effective IT auditing becomes increasingly important to ensure that the organization is not exposed to excessive and unnecessary risks. As mentioned in Chapter 9, IT auditing is still a rapidly evolving profession that faces a real shortage of staff. The problem is far worse outside the United States and Europe. Accordingly the corporate audit group of a multinational is frequently forced to undertake major responsibility both for conducting international IT audits and for helping to develop national IT audit staffs and capabilities.

Central IT Processing Support

Whether it makes sense to push IT toward a central hub or a linked international network depends absolutely on both a firm's type of industry and those particular dimensions along which it chooses to compete. At one extreme is the airline industry, where significant competitive disadvantage comes from being unable to confirm seats on a global basis. Most international airlines have been driven to establish such a network—originally as an offensive weapon and now as a defensive one. At the other extreme is a company running a network of commodity paper converting operations, where transportation costs severely limit how far away from a plant orders can be profitably shipped. Consequently it handles order entry and factory management on a strictly national basis, with little interchange of data between countries.

Technology Appraisal Program

An international appraisal can put into perspective and coordinate overseas IT effort. A U.S.-based multinational company with a long history of European operations discovered that the Far East and South American operations were posing increasingly complicated information problems. A three-year program was initiated by general management to bring the overseas operation under control. The first step was to appraise the state of each national IT unit and its potential business. The appraisal, conducted by a three-person IT team with multilingual abilities, was followed by formulation of a set of policies and, where appropriate, action programs at the annual meeting of company executives.

Originally scheduled on a one-time basis in only 11 countries, the effort was considered so successful it was reorganized as an established audit function. The team learned to appraise locally available technology and to guide local management's attention to judging its potential. This required a minimum of a week and often two weeks in the field, typically in two trips. The first visit appraised existing services and generally raised concerns that could be effectively pursued by the on-site management. The second trip sought to assess problems based on:

1. Government restriction.
2. Quality and quantity of available human skills.
3. Present and planned communications services.

Alternatives to the present means of service were examined further and economic analysis of at least three standard alternatives was prepared. This included:

1. Expansion of present system.
2. Transfer of all or portions of IT work to a neighboring country.
3. Transfer of all or portions of IT work to regional headquarters.

The enthusiasm of local managers for this review was not universal, and in several countries long delays occurred between the first and second set of meetings. However, in 7 of the original 11 the appraisals succeeded in generating appropriate change through a better understanding of the potential impact of uncertainties such as changing import duties, planned market introduction of new technologies by U.S. suppliers, and a new satellite communications alternative. This organized appraisal significantly increased senior management's awareness and comfort concerning IT. It resulted in the conversion of the activity into an ongoing effort and the addition of several more members to the team.

Summary

International IT development must be actively managed if major, long-term difficulties are not to emerge both within and between national IT activities. This is complicated since, as discussed earlier, foreign assimilation of information technology may be more heavily influenced by local conditions than by the current state of the technology. Resolving these local situations is much more complex than simply keeping abreast of technology, thus a long view is required to succeed. For some firms, however, success offers the potential for a significant competitive edge.

Finnpap/Finnboard

In the London office of Finnpap, Reginald Smith looked at the screen of his computer terminal and commented: "At least the invoices arrived so we can get the rolls through customs. It's very strange that ships are faster than computer systems." The previous Thursday a shipment of paper rolls had left the Finnish loading port of Helsinki, arriving Monday at Purfleet docks, east of London on the River Thames. The shipping documents caught up with the shipment on Tuesday, one day later. "The present system must be changed," mumbled Smith, as he returned to his task of processing the customs declaration.

The Paper and Paperboard Marketing Associations

The paper and paperboard mills of Finland sold their products to the world through jointly owned marketing associations. The Finnish Paper Mills' Association—Finnpap—established in 1918, and the Finnish Board Mills' Association—Finnboard—established in 1942, together represented 45 mills. Headquartered in Helsinki, Finland, the associations shared nearly 100 sales offices, agents, and warehousing/distributing organizations throughout the world. Since the mills had the option of using other marketing channels, the associations' success depended on their being able to offer the best marketing alternative to

This case was prepared by Tapio Reponen and Duncan Copeland under the direction of F. Warren McFarlan.

Copyright © 1985 by the President and Fellows of Harvard College
Harvard Business School case 9–186–130 (Rev 10/86)

EXHIBIT 1

FINNPAP/FINNBOARD
Income Statement
Year ended December 31, 1984
(FIM 000)

	1984		1983	
	Finnpap	*Finnboard*	*Finnpap*	*Finnboard*
Turnover (commission income)	$409,136	$59,139	$376,876	$54,666
Less: Expenses				
Salaries	43,305	15,119	38,056	14,163
Social security contribution	11,999	4,327	9,769	4,407
Rents	9,027	1,580	8,757	1,351
Other	62,039	22,951	52,743	20,896
Operation margin	282,766	15,162	267,551	13,849
Depreciation and amortization				
Machinery and equipment	3,866	1,255	3,458	964
Other fixed assets	407	401	255	287
Net earnings from operations . . .	278,493	13,506	263,838	12,598
Other income				
Interest received	67,002	7,088	35,809	6,238
Dividends received	148	—	217	—
Net income	345,643	20,594	299,864	18,836
Less: Increases in reserves				
Reserve for bad debts	8,500	1,300	5,600	1,438
Interest expenses	337,207	19,343	294,313	17,396
Taxes	9,016	1,251	6,041	1,438
Loss for the period	$ 9,080	$ 1,300	$ 6,090	$ 1,436

Note: Exchange rate: 1984—U.S. dollar = FIM 6.0; 1983—U.S. dollar = FIM 5.5

their owners. At present 90 percent of the Finnish sales went through the associations. The Helsinki offices housed approximately 550 administrative employees, while the sales staff of nearly 600 was located in 50 countries, with only a small number remaining in Helsinki. (See Exhibit 1 for recent financial data for Finnpap and Finnboard.)

In the early days of the Finnish paper and paperboard industry, the mills primarily produced bulk products such as newsprint and liner board. Marketing consisted of obtaining annual contracts with customers for standard grade products. The associations' task was to negotiate with the customers and then allocate the orders among the mills. By the 1980s the mills had developed their own specialized products and brand names, making the allocation task secondary to an increasingly sophisticated marketing effort. To meet the new marketing

EXHIBIT 1 *(concluded)*

FINNPAP/FINNBOARD
Balance Sheet
December 31, 1984
(FIM 000)

	1984		1983	
	Finnpap	Finnboard	Finnpap	Finnboard
Assets				
Current assets				
Cash and bank deposits	$ 601,932	$114,351	$ 242,193	$113,373
Accounts receivable	3,648,630	418,575	2,982,497	337,529
Other current assets	197,122	8,205	70,819	6,039
Total current assets	4,447,684	541,131	3,295,509	456,941
Fixed assets				
Machinery and equipment	18,309	6,586	16,026	5,184
Securities	20,389	5,261	12,428	4,741
Other fixed assets	2,926	2,463	1,809	2,042
Total fixed assets	41,624	14,310	30,263	11,967
Less: Loss from previous years . .	23,746	3,628	17,656	2,189
Loss from financial year . .	9,080	1,300	6,090	1,438
Total losses	32,826	4,928	23,746	3,627
Total assets	$4,521,864	$560,369	$3,349,518	$472,535
Liabilities				
Current liabilities				
Bank loans	$3,265,650	$108,832	$2,615,608	$ 73,880
Accounts payable	349,886	7,963	272,568	97,663
Other current liabilities	624,905	352,483	232,572	253,828
Total current liabilities . . .	4,240,441	506,278	3,111,748	425,371
Long-term debt				
Loans from pension institutions . .	28,809	8,939	26,175	7,945
Reserves				
Reserve for bad debts	27,606	3,250	19,106	1,950
Member companies loan equity . .	225,008	41,902	192,489	37,270
Total liabilities	$4,521,864	$560,369	$3,349,518	$472,535
Guarantees/other liabilities	$ 269,592	$ 28,657	$ 275,216	$ 30,062

Note: Exchange rate: 1984—U.S. dollar = FIM 6.52; 1983—U.S. dollar = FIM 5.80

challenge, the associations decentralized their marketing efforts and initiated training programs for their salespeople to foster an attitude devoted to customer service.

The associations' primary markets were located in Central Europe and the United Kingdom, although significant sales were made to the

United States, the Soviet Union, Denmark, Australia, and Japan. (See Exhibit 2 for sales volumes by export market.)

Responsibilities connected with the sales effort included order handling and invoicing, accounting, distributing orders to the mills, export financing, handling complaints, warehousing products in domestic and foreign ports, handling deliveries from stocks in foreign ports to customers, and information processing to support the marketing and transportation functions. The associations charged the companies for the services they offered, depending on the number of orders and on sales values.

EXHIBIT 2 Finnpap and Finnboard—Deliveries per Country, 1984 (in tons)[1]

Country	Finnpap	Finnboard	Total
Austria	48,054	5,357	53,411
Iceland	2,132	1,427	3,559
Norway	43,756	5,853	49,609
Portugal	19,465	343	19,808
Sweden	46,360	10,940	57,300
Switzerland	58,668	11,891	70,558
EFTA[2]	218,436	35,810	254,246
Belgium and Luxemburg	87,851	29,507	117,358
Denmark	167,743	38,834	206,577
France	248,352	89,517	337,869
Germany, Federal Republic of	522,888	121,517	644,405
Greece	43,777	13,600	57,377
Ireland	40,240	16,108	56,348
Italy and Vatican	61,005	18,877	79,882
Netherlands	151,436	77,007	228,443
United Kingdom	1,061,915	181,630	1,243,545
EEC	2,385,207	586,597	2,971,804
Bulgaria	2,409	1,423	3,832
Czechoslovakia	329	—	329
Germany, Democratic Republic of	1,003	2,814	3,817
Hungary	13,680	5,640	19,320
Poland	3,038	150	3,188
Soviet Union	354,912	142,144	497,056
CMEA	375,371	152,171	527,542
Madeira	137	—	137
Malta	1,155	81	1,236
Spain	74,321	15,127	89,448
Turkey	3,393	—	3,393
Yugoslavia	3,174	—	3,174
Other Europe	82,179	15,208	97,387
Europe[2]	3,061,193	789,786	3,850,979

EXHIBIT 2   *(continued)*

Country	Finnpap	Finnboard	Total
Canada	29,231	3,645	32,876
United States	386,440	6,562	393,002
Canada and United States	415,671	10,207	425,878
Argentina	12,547	1	12,548
Barbados	34	235	269
Belize	77	—	77
Bolivia	—	57	57
Brazil	36,438	—	36,438
Chile	2,689	—	2,689
Colombia	15,207	5,563	20,770
Costa Rica	451	20	471
Cuba	—	702	702
Dominican Republic	10	1	11
Ecuador	551	—	551
El Salvador	587	—	587
Guatemala	43	—	43
Guyana	9	—	9
Honduras	35	—	35
Jamaica	1,198	—	1,198
Mexico	17,453	158	17,611
Nicaragua	803	—	803
Panama	156	—	156
Peru	1,328	—	1,328
Surinam	2	—	2
Trinidad and Tobago	223	—	223
Uruguay	1,399	—	1,399
Venezuela	24,869	—	24,869
Latin America	116,109	6,737	122,846
Afghanistan	14	—	14
Bahrain	1,101	—	1,101
Burma	107	—	107
China, People's Republic of	11,077	14,179	25,256
Cyprus	552	2,260	2,812
Hong Kong	4,887	5,088	9,975
India	20,945	—	20,945
Indonesia	10,901	11,282	22,183
Iran	46,997	11,674	58,671
Iraq	21,406	879	22,285
Israel	10,404	7,269	17,673
Japan	132,496	491	132,987
Jordan	9,880	970	10,850
South Korea	860	572	1,432
Kuwait	4,971	278	5,249
Lebanon	11,869	2,460	14,329
Malaysia	9,409	5,119	14,528
Mongolia	34	45	79
Nepal	295	—	295

EXHIBIT 2 (*concluded*)

Country	Finnpap	Finnboard	Total
Oman	796	—	796
Pakistan	1,296	112	1,408
Philippines	2,627	2,359	4,986
Saudi Arabia	40,485	7,444	47,929
Singapore	11,022	2,027	13,049
Sri Lanka	57	—	57
Syria	4,375	1,418	5,793
Thailand	9,201	1,344	10,545
Taiwan	6,732	114	6,846
United Arab Emirates	2,328	1,438	3,766
North Yemen	956	—	956
South Yemen	97	—	97
Asia	378,177	78,822	456,999
Algeria	3,013	—	3,013
Cameroun	142	2,164	2,306
Egypt	33,084	5,892	38,976
Ethiopia	632	—	632
Ghana	2,094	419	2,513
Ivory Coast	—	5,521	5,521
Kenya	953	2,359	3,312
Liberia	13	—	13
Libya	1,247	2,758	4,005
Malawi	10	—	10
Mauritius	20	—	20
Morocco	7,721	7,415	15,136
Mozambique	293	—	293
Nigeria	11,272	7,582	18,854
Senegal	1,642	945	2,587
Somalia	9	—	9
South Africa, Republic of	63,907	—	63,907
Sudan	89	915	1,004
Tanzania	83	—	83
Tunisia	—	4,949	4,949
Zaire	—	6,463	6,463
Zambia	9	10	19
Zimbabwe	24	—	24
Others	—	64	64
Africa	126,257	47,456	173,713
Australia	151,959	2,387	154,346
New Zealand	3,171	21	3,192
Oceania	155,130	2,408	157,538
Export Deliveries	4,252,537	935,416	5,187,953
Finland	448,812	150,859	599,671
Total Deliveries	4,701,349	1,086,275	5,787,624

[1]Excluding mills' direct deliveries and free deliveries.
[2]Excluding Finland.

Finland's mills mainly belong to privately owned, independent companies that are responsible for the manufacture of paper and paperboard products, and for ground transportation of the product to the loading ports. No mill's market share exceeded 20 percent of Finnish production. Together, the mills and the associations determined the production schedules for each product. The method of payment to the mills differed slightly for the two associations. Although both charged the mills a fee for each item sold, Finnpap paid the mills when the products left Finnish ports, thus financing sea transportation and foreign warehousing, while Finnboard made payment only upon delivery of the product to the customer.

To rationalize transportation costs, the paper and paperboard industry owned Transfennica, a company responsible for all sea transportation from Finnish loading ports to the destination ports in foreign markets. The mills handled the delivery of cargo, usually by rail, to the loading ports. The sales offices and agents, or their service companies, were in charge of foreign distribution. Transfennica coordinated the transportation schedules along the entire distribution chain. In addition, the company arranged transport for Finnish forest products other than paper and paperboard. Transfennica employed about 100 people in 1985.

Optimizing the varied demands of domestic and foreign overland routes, coupled with the many alternative sea routes that resulted from combinations of possible loading and destination ports, made for a highly complex task. Exhibit 3 contains volume statistics for the associations. Exhibit 4 illustrates the information network for paper and paperboard export. Exhibit 5 describes the order information flow through the distribution chain.

Background: The Forest Products Industry

The history of paper begins in the Imperial Court of China, in 105 A.D., where paper was first produced by combining mulberry fibres, fish nets, old rags, and hemp waste. The art of papermaking slowly drifted westward, and by the 14th century there were a number of European paper mills, particularly in Spain, Italy, France, and Germany.

With the invention of printing in the 1450s the demand for paper greatly increased. The papermaking process remained essentially unchanged until a shortage of linen and cloth rags fueled a drive to devise a papermaking process that utilized more abundant raw materials.

In the early 1800s, practical methods were developed for manufacturing paper from wood pulp and other vegetable pulps. Several major pulping processes, principally chemical and mechanical methods, were gradually developed. Now the industry was no longer dependent on

EXHIBIT 3

19 companies, which have

30 paper mills   (50 pulp mills)

16 paperboard mills   (300 sawmills, etc.)

FINNPAP FINNBOARD	TRANSFENNICA
Marketing	Transportation

24 sales offices
50 agents
5,600 customers
110,000 invoices a year
8,000,000 rolls/pallets a year
2,600 million dollars a year
5.7 million tons a year
26 loading ports
290 destination ports

EXHIBIT 4   Information Network for Paper Export

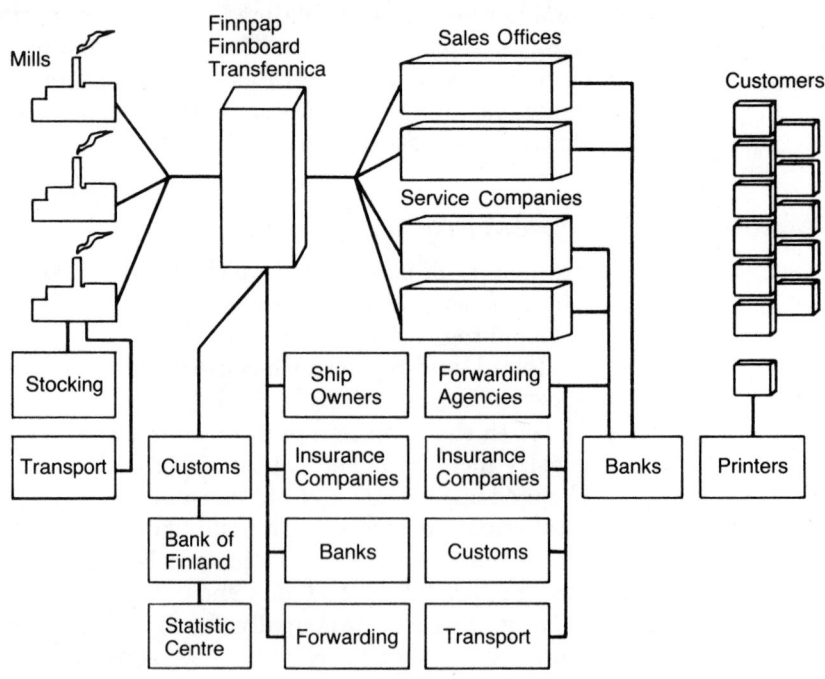

EXHIBIT 5A   Order Information Flow

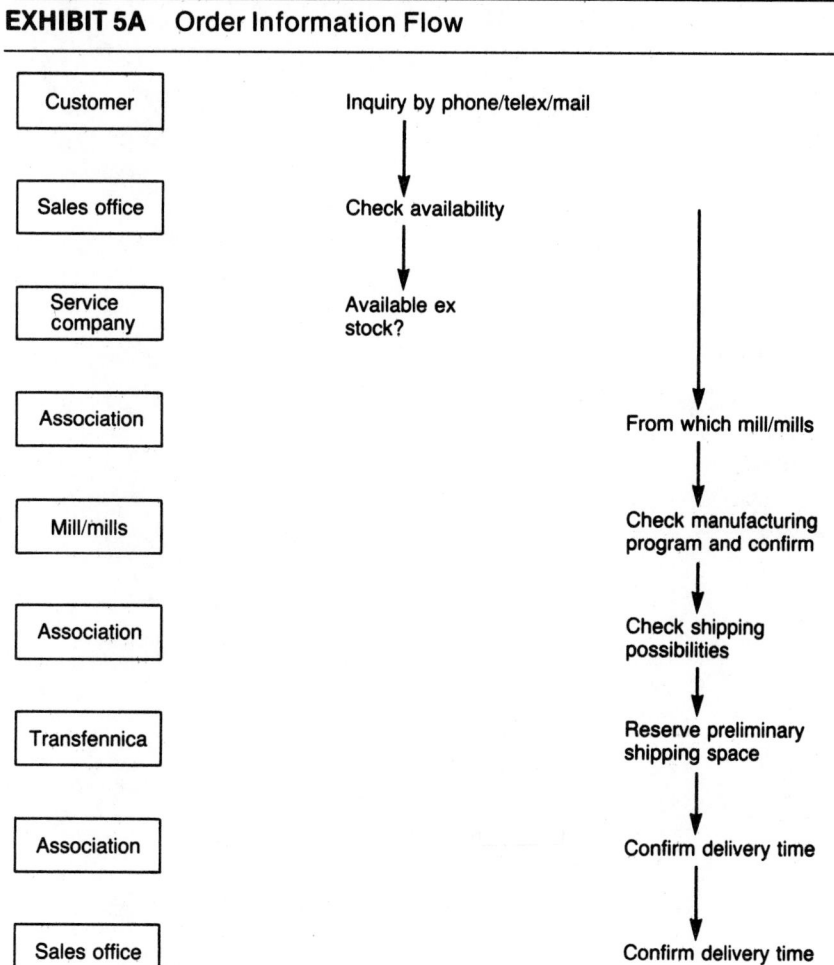

EXHIBIT 5A *(continued)*

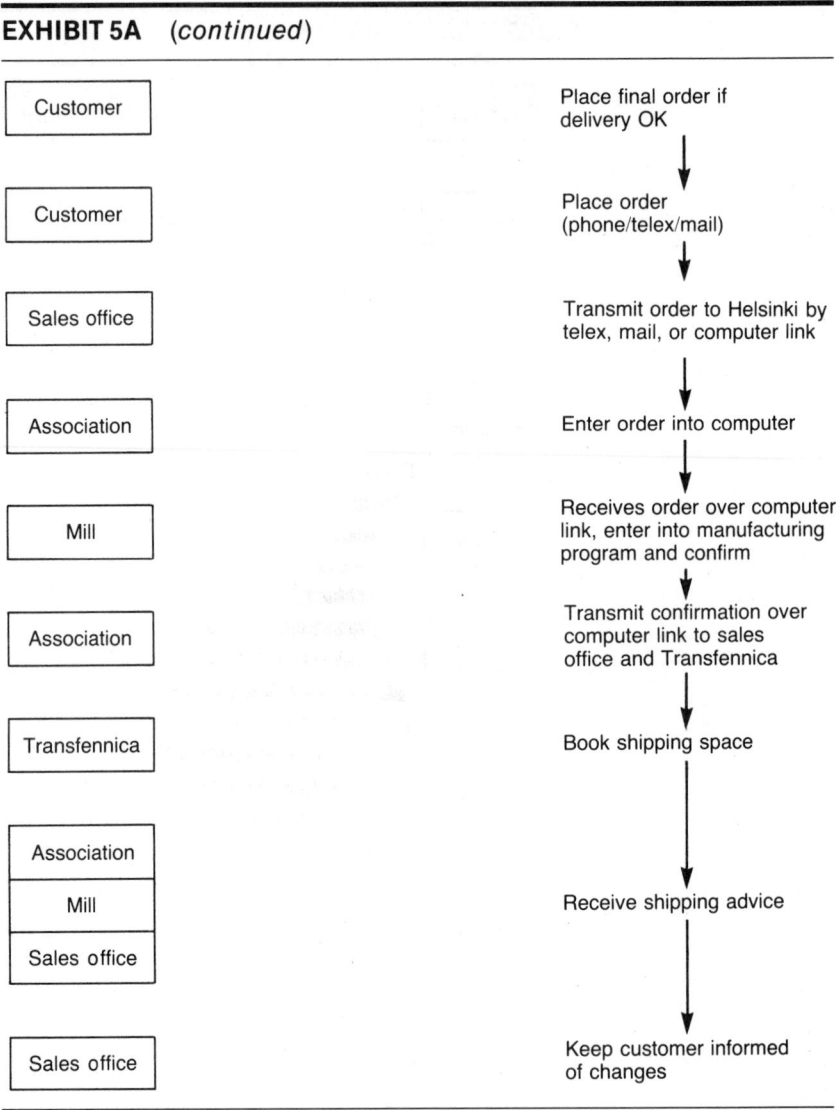

cotton and linen rags, and modern large-scale production became possible.

In 1983 world production of paper and paperboard products totalled 177.3 million metric tons (Exhibit 6). Paper products divide into four categories, according to their end use:

Newsprint—variable grades include standard, thin, telcuts (for telephone directories), and special.

EXHIBIT 5B Invoicing

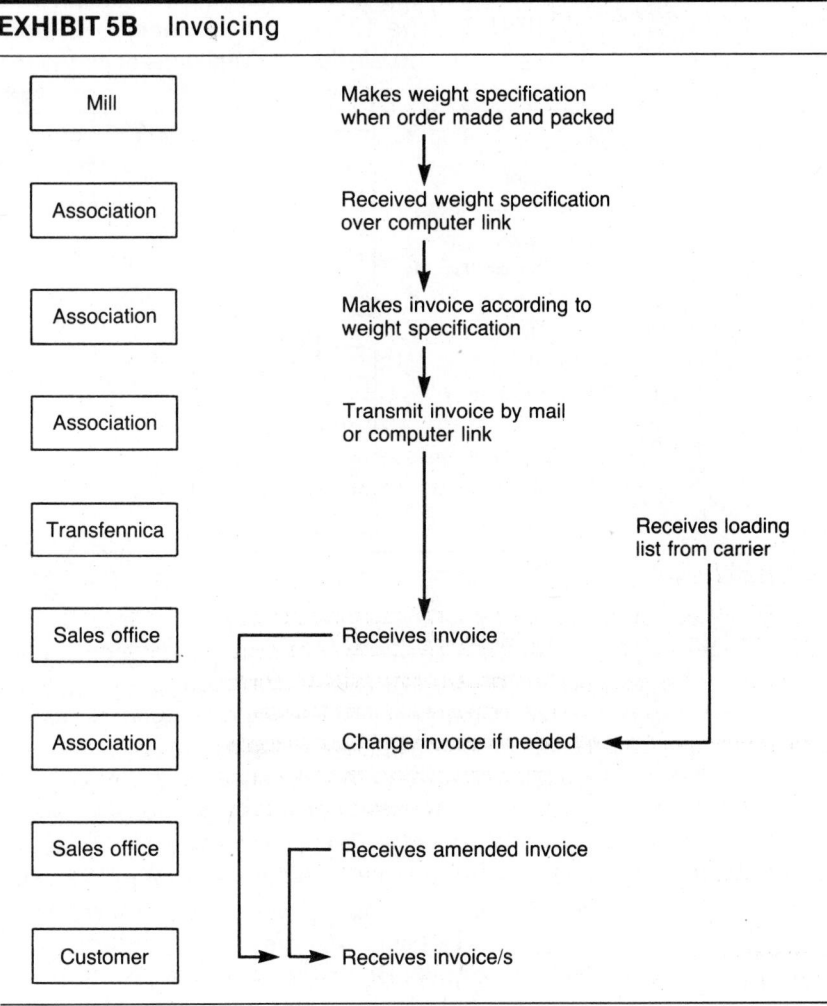

Magazine—variable grades include coated and uncoated.

Fine—includes writing paper and office-quality stationery.

Specialty—includes wallpaper, sack paper, envelopes, tissue, flexible packaging (e.g., soft-sided cigarette packs), grocery bags.

Paperboard products come in two categories:

Carton boards—used in a variety of retail packaging applications, as well as some graphic end uses like greeting cards, bookcovers, record sleeves.

Container boards—materials used as liner and corrugating medium in corrugated cases.

EXHIBIT 6 The 12 Biggest Producers of Paper and Paperboard in the World, 1983 (millions of metric tons)

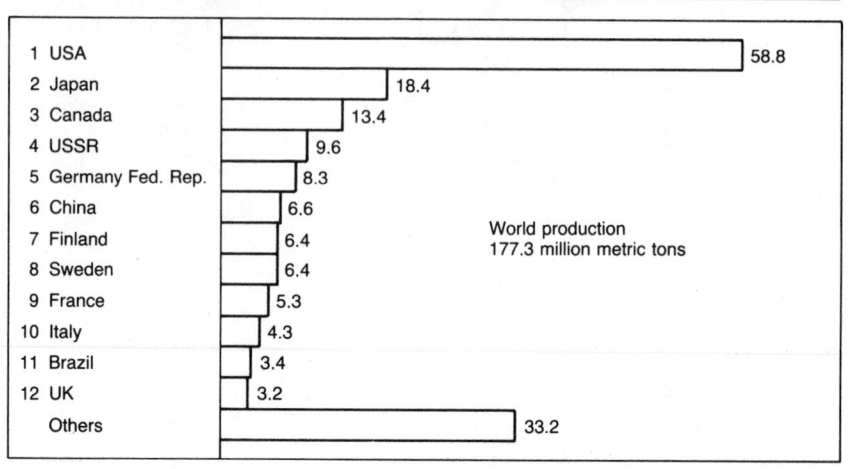

1 USA	58.8
2 Japan	18.4
3 Canada	13.4
4 USSR	9.6
5 Germany Fed. Rep.	8.3
6 China	6.6
7 Finland	6.4
8 Sweden	6.4
9 France	5.3
10 Italy	4.3
11 Brazil	3.4
12 UK	3.2
Others	33.2

World production
177.3 million metric tons

SOURCE: PPI.

Finland covers approximately 337,000 square kilometers, making it the fifth largest country in Europe, and two-thirds of Finland is forested. Not surprisingly, wood processing is the country's largest industry and the backbone of the Finnish economy, accounting for over 30 percent of manufacturing input in the Gross Domestic Product (Exhibit 7). In 1983 Finland was the seventh largest producer of paper and paperboard in the world and the second largest in Western Europe. Finland's share of total world production in 1983 was 4 percent, yet it accounted for 15 percent of the world's exports (Exhibit 8).

Finland's paper and paperboard industry had been completely rebuilt since 1960. Beginning as a bulk producer of grades like newsprint and liner board, the industry grew to become a versatile supplier of multiple grades to satisfy increasingly sophisticated market demands. During this restructuring, strategic guidelines concentrated on adding value throughout the production process, improving profitability, and developing the paper production mix to be responsive to the changing requirements of the market. As a result of the large capital investments in recent years, by 1985 Finland's paper industry was one of the most modern and efficient in the world. Exhibit 9 contains mill capacity data for Finland and several of its competitors.

One major disadvantage faced by Finland was price competitiveness. Prices for raw materials and wages were about the same as those of their main European competitors. The Finnish currency (FIM) had been very strong for many years and therefore the relative costs were high. Because of Finland's remote location, transportation of products

EXHIBIT 7 Forest-Based Industry's Share of Total Manufacturing Input in Gross Domestic Product, 1983

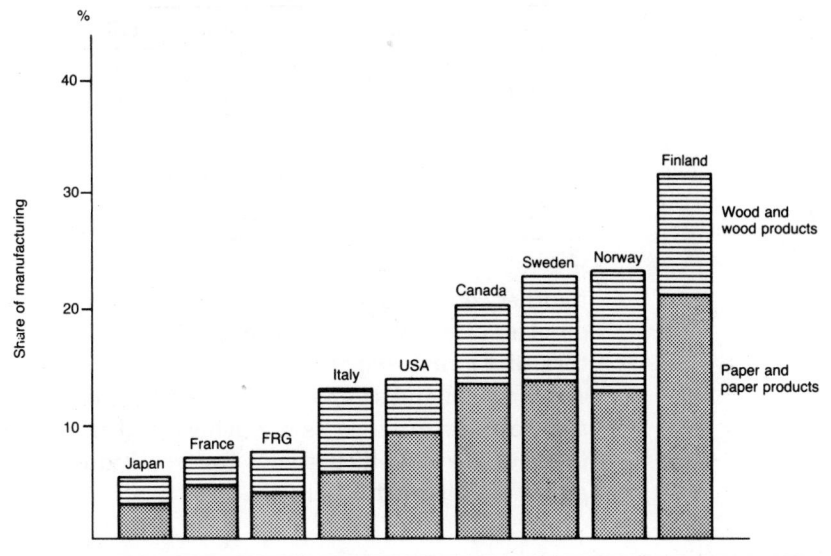

EXHIBIT 8 Exports of Paper and Paperboard, 1983 (thousands of metric tons)

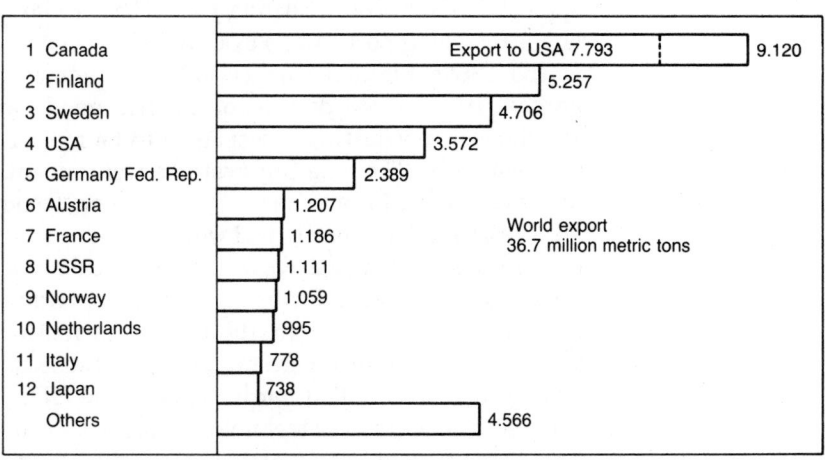

1 Canada	Export to USA 7.793	9.120
2 Finland		5.257
3 Sweden		4.706
4 USA		3.572
5 Germany Fed. Rep.		2.389
6 Austria		1.207
7 France		1.186
8 USSR		1.111
9 Norway		1.059
10 Netherlands		995
11 Italy		778
12 Japan		738
Others		4.566

World export
36.7 million metric tons

SOURCE: PPI.

EXHIBIT 9 Paper and Paperboard—Capacity per Mill, 1983 (number of mills)

Capacity tons/year	USA	Canada	FRG	France	Finland	Sweden
— 50.000	268	18	167	138	12	25
50.001 - 100.000	110	16	18	15	11	11
100.001 - 200.000	91	24	13	10	6	5
200.001 —	112	34	8	2	17	15
Total number of mills	581	92	206	165	46	56

to other countries proved very costly and required a lead time of 7 to 10 days for direct shipments from mill to customer. The principal competitors of Finnish paper goods were products produced by mills indigenous to Finland's export markets. These local companies faced neither the transportation costs nor delays, and enjoyed the additional advantages of direct mill/customer contact, reduced paperwork, and no language or cultural barriers.

Information Technology at Finnpap/Finnboard

Electronic data processing began at the associations in the late 1960s when two consultants developed a long-range information plan for Finnpap. The first applications for order-handling and invoicing were run on a service company's computer, until Finnpap purchased its own hardware in 1973.

The basic features of the current systems were planned and designed in 1974. At the time, the marketing associations took less responsibility for product delivery than they did by 1985; their job ended at the receiving port. As an example of the degree of change, at the end of the 1960s Finland's paper industry maintained negligible stocks abroad. By 1985 40 percent of finished goods were stored in foreign warehouses, permitting salespeople to be more responsive to customers' demands. The existing systems were meant to address the business needs of 1974, and as such, focused on accounting applications in an effort to reduce the clerical workload. The systems' designers could not foresee the competitive or technological climates of 1985, thus the programs were coded for batch processing and required significant effort to be modernized. In 1980, the information technology (IT) resources of Finnboard were merged with those of Finnpap. Finnboard employed Univac 90/40 hardware, and the EDP department stressed user requirements over technology. At the time of the merger, this relatively small group was starting to consider forward IT integration issues. Finnpap, on the other hand, utilized IBM equipment, with the

EXHIBIT 10

Year	Central Processing Unit	Central Memory (megabytes)	Efficiency (MIPS)	Disk Space (GB)
1973	IBM S/1130			
1974	IBM S/370–135			
1975	IBM S/370–135	0.5	0.2	0.2
1976	IBM S/370–135	0.7	0.2	0.6
1977	IBM S/370–148	2.0	0.4	2.5
1978	IBM S/370–148	3.0	0.4	3
1979	IBM S/370–148 NAS 3000	9.0	1.3	4
1980	IBM S/370–148 NAS 3000	9.0	1.3	7
1981	IBM 4341–1 NAS 3000 UNIVAC 90/40	14.6	2.3	10
1982	IBM 4341–2 IBM 4341–2 UNIVAC 90/40	24.6	3.0	12
1983	IBM 3083–B24 UNIVAC 90/40	24.6	6.2	20
1984	IBM 3083–B24 UNIVAC 90/40	24.6	6.2	35
1985 (end)	IBM 3081–K48	48.0	15.0	80

EDP department setting its own direction, emphasizing technology. Of approximately 15 Finnboard IT staffpersons that moved to Finnpap, all but the computer operators had left the company by 1985. The Finnpap data center also sold information processing services to Transfennica and two other Finnish marketing associations, Converta and Finncell.

In 1985 the systems, now grown to include nearly 8,500 programs, were supported by an EDP department of more than 75 people with an annual budget of U.S. $3 million. Personnel were divided between the computer center (30), application development (34), planning and liaison (6), and the information center (5). In the application development department there were 24 system analysts or programmers.

Qualified systems professionals were in short supply in Finland, especially in Helsinki where the demand was greatest. This had led to high salaries relative to other functional departments, and competition among employers. Turnover for EDP professionals in 1984 neared 20 percent, and among systems analysts and programmers the figure was much higher.

The mainframe computer was an IBM 3083–B24. Increases in CPU capacity were planned for the near future. An IBM Series/1 was used for telex–host connection. Exhibit 10 describes the evolution of

EXHIBIT 11   The Customers of the EDP Centre

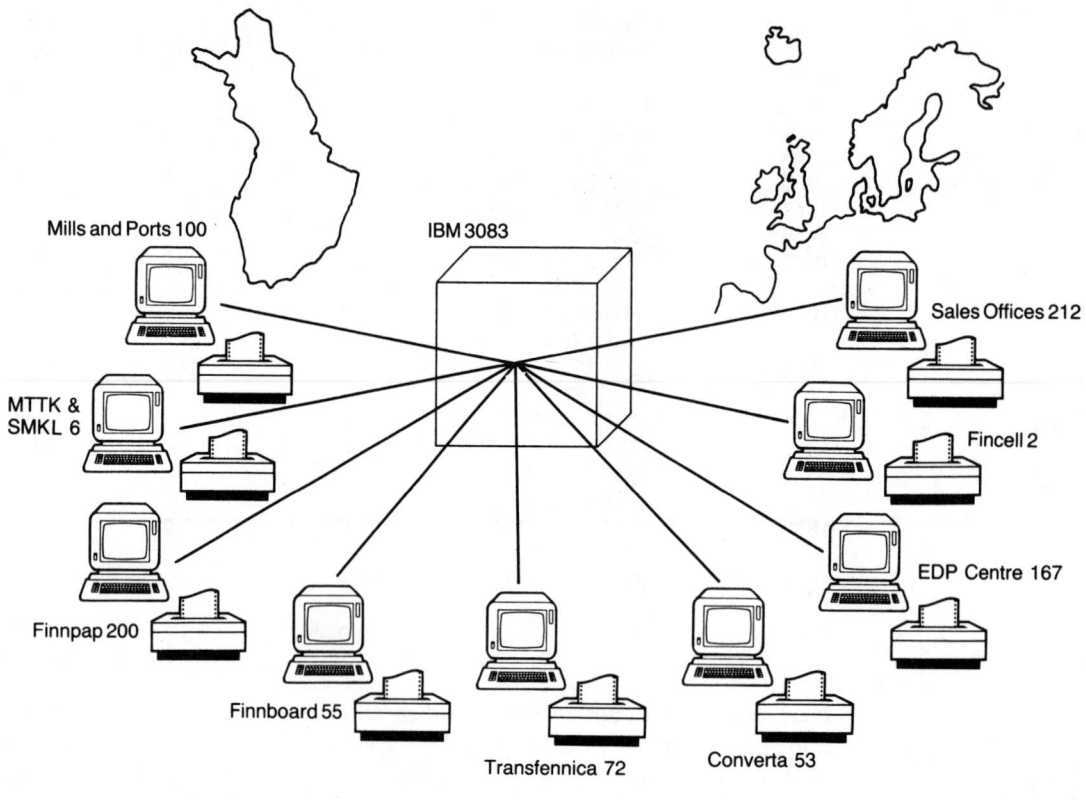

Mills and Ports 100

IBM 3083

Sales Offices 212

MTTK & SMKL 6

Fincell 2

EDP Centre 167

Finnpap 200

Finnboard 55

Transfennica 72

Converta 53

Number of Terminals About 870

computing resources. The network consisted of 870 remote terminals, used for order entry and message switching; these terminals linked headquarters with the mills, loading ports, and sales offices. Exhibit 11 describes the distribution of terminals. Exhibit 12 illustrates the communication network. In the United Kingdom there were two IBM S/38 computers and one IBM 8100. In Germany there was one IBM S/38.

The main applications included:

- Order handling and invoicing for Finnpap, Finnboard, and Converta.
- Accounting for Finnpap, Finnboard, Converta, and Transfennica.
- Sales budgeting for Finnpap and Finnboard.

EXHIBIT 12 Agency Communications Network

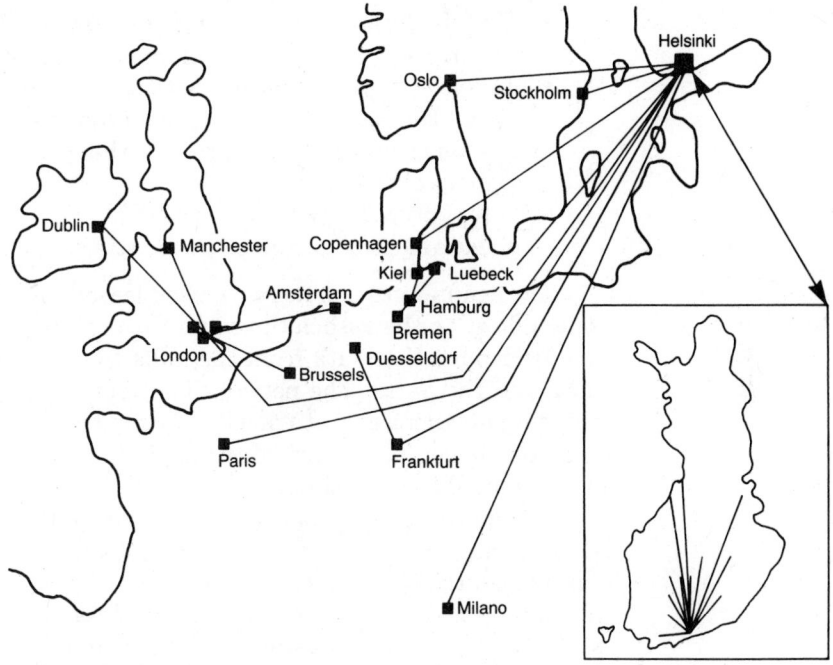

- Stock control in Germany and Denmark for Finnpap and in the United Kingdom for Finnboard.
- Sales office reporting.
- Communication links to mills for transmitting orders and weight specifications.
- Communication links to ports and sales agents for transmitting shipping documents.
- Communication links to banks, insurance companies, and customs offices.
- Loading lists for Transfennica.

Maintenance of these applications demanded considerable resources, which led to an expanding backlog of user requests for new development projects. In EDP, 12 people had worked on the conversion to IBM COBOL for over two years; these 12 amounted to 50 percent of the systems development staff. Two contract analyst programmers had also been working on the same conversion for two years. Systems development activity in the United Kingdom and Germany was devoted to stock control, sales ledger, order handling, and invoicing.

Errors and delays in the systems were due to one or more of the following:

- Ex-mill data was entered in the system at the time an order was confirmed, then not updated for subsequent changes.
- Invoices were prepared based on the mills' weight specifications. But when transportation damaged rolls and pallets, the customer received less product than invoiced, causing correction invoicing.
- Data entry delays at the ports.
- Some shipping documents were still sent by mail.

The communication network used leased lines to send orders from sales offices to the associations and then on to the mills, and to transmit transportation data from the mills to the associations, Transfennica, and the ports. The network had reduced some of the volume of shipping documents that travelled by mail, but information flow problems remained. These were due mostly to tasks that continued to require manual intervention.

The use of microcomputers was developing in 1985, although the EDP managers held a very strong opinion that they would not solve the main data processing problems of the organization. Finnboard used a small number of micros for word processing, and Finnpap had installed one in each department for word processing, statistical analysis, and budgeting. Some sales offices were beginning to work with micro-based electronic spreadsheets. For small sales offices, the EDP department had developed a stand-alone order handling and stock control package for micros. There were also plans to slowly replace the 870 existing mainframe terminals with microcomputers.

Because of the difficult competitive position of the Finnish forest industry, information processing played a very essential role in operations. The strategy of the mills was increased product differentiation with strict cost control. Differentiation meant shifting from bulk operations to a service orientation with more specialized marketing and transportation needs. Just-in-time deliveries were required, and demands were increasing for quality control and production records data with each paper roll. The successful management of this complex environment called for accurate, timely information at each phase of the marketing chain.

The managing directors of Finnpap and Finnboard, Thomas Nysten and Jarl Kohler, respectively, agreed that improved information technology was needed to strengthen their competitive position. In Nysten's words:

We have created a marketing network that enables us to gather information on markets and anticipate their future development. We are able to build a marketing database which would support our sales activities, keeping in mind that our owners, the mills, are partially competitors with one another, so data security is a strict requirement. Strategy formulation depends on collecting different signals from abroad, like end-user trends, new packaging and publishing/printing problems, prices of competing materials and packaging systems, competitor moves, customer needs, development of printing and packaging technology. Our salespeople are in a position to perform this function, but we must do it more systematically. We already have a lot of useful data in our systems, but it is virtually inaccessible.

If our information systems are to be used as a competitive weapon, we must develop a new generation of programs, which may include such applications as customer-initiated order entry, and reporting formats tailored to customers' unique needs. It will require heavy investments in both hardware and software. Since the needs of our different users vary, we need a long-range plan to prioritize this development work. We should strive to achieve an image as a modern user of information technology in our operations. We conduct business in a unique environment, however, and our plans must take this into consideration.

IT and the Marketing Associations

The Helsinki headquarters housed both marketing and administrative employees. Almost all the information flowing between customers, sales offices, and mills passed through Helsinki. Headquarters personnel negotiated annual sales budgets with the mills, prepared marketing plans, divided orders among the mills, and generally coordinated all operations. Managing information was a key component of their work.

The marketing people were not satisfied with the output from the present systems. The lack of adequate information forced them to spend a significant part of their time using the telephone to track down needed data. Their greatest need was for information on order status. Specifically, this included: when an order was scheduled for manufacture (ex-mill date); when it would be transported to a loading port; when it left the loading port; when it arrived in the destination port; and when it was transported to the customer.

The mills, transportation companies, and sales offices also wanted this information.

Tuula Virolainen, assistant sales director at Finnboard, discussed this need for information:

> In the cartonboard grades there are an increasing number of special orders, while average order size is decreasing. The customers aim for just-in-time purchasing. The number of orders has doubled in the last two years, and the many different grades and special features make each order more complex. Correct and quick information is a must in this kind of environment. However, at present even the order and invoicing system does not work very well. There are often errors and it takes a lot of time to correct them. Routine work has increased for us because of these errors as well as new tasks, such as responding to inquiries from the mills, who are much more cost sensitive than before.
>
> Getting special reports out of the existing systems is not easy. It is often faster to make manual calculations. I have a feeling that there is a lot of data in our system, but we can't get at it. This lack of flexibility has given computers a bad name in the marketing departments. I think it will be difficult to introduce any new systems without strong evidence of their usefulness. I sometimes wonder whether our needs here at Finnboard receive a low priority now that EDP has been consolidated within Finnpap.

Marketing personnel in both associations considered the order status and a good customer file to be high priorities. The existing files contained a customer's name and address, but not much more. Desired customer information included a short history of supplies, prices, competitors' supplies, inventories, order stock, and machinery. Maintaining such a file would require input from salespeople, mills, Transfennica, and the associations.

Raija Tuukkanen, assistant sales manager at Finnpap, expressed her dissatisfaction with present circumstances:

> The EDP department doesn't have any clear long-range plan, and consequently all the schedules are delayed. And there are multiple applications for the same function, like stock control. Their way of thinking must change. To be fair, though, the conversion of Finnboard's programs to our IBM standard has required a lot of work and could explain some of the delays.

Claes Ehrnrooth, Finnboard's assistant director in charge of planning and marketing research, also worried about the service he was receiving:

> We have been waiting a long time for certain customer information lists. I've developed a few of them myself using AS, our appli-

cation generator language, but they are only designed for my purposes. The program structure may not be the best possible, but the reports will satisfy our urgent needs. In my experience, end-user computing is the only way to develop the needed programs quickly enough. The EDP department is so large and the models they want to build are so comprehensive that their work will never end.

Now Finnpap and Finnboard have a common EDP organization. Sometimes I think my own computer would be a better solution. We have also been thinking about the urgency of our information needs, and we have concluded that the need for on-line transmission is quite low as far as the management information is concerned. It is possible to reduce costs with batch transmission of data and satisfy our requirements at the same time.

IT and the Sales Offices

Lamco Paper Sales Ltd., the London marketing company owned by Finnpap, sold 1.5 million tons of paper in 1984, mainly newsprint and magazine papers. For these two products, Lamco's share of the U.K. market was 30 percent and 55 percent respectively. The associations faced a marketing challenge in the United Kingdom because customers were well-informed about price levels, faced great profitability pressures, and could easily turn to alternative suppliers. Therefore customer service was critical in the British market.

Lamco sold from stock in the United Kingdom and provided customers with a weekly listing of its inventory levels. Lamco was the first supplier to offer this service, forcing other suppliers to provide similar information. Lamco had recently begun to explore the possibility of installing their terminals at some customer sites; customers were enthusiastic about the idea.

Berndt Brunow, a director of Lamco, was skeptical of the central computer system's ability to satisfy his company's needs:

> For many years we have waited for a solution to our problems, but we have been disappointed. We never get all the needed information: there are continually errors in the reports, the shipment documents come late, etc. Because of our poor experiences with the central systems, we would like to develop our own system capabilities here. We have a System 38, and qualified programmers who know our local problems and working methods. At Lamco there are nine DP professionals (DP manager, system analyst, three programmers, three operators, user coordinator) and three contract programmers. Actually, there is very little we need from the Finnpap system. We are of course willing to supply Finnpap with any

information they need, but they'll have to transform it for their own purposes.

Local systems suit us best. We currently have links to the U.K. ports from our system. Ports here have very simple systems and we cannot influence their methods of operation. We have to be able to adapt to their choices. The central systems just are not responsive enough, and I'm not confident about the communications link to Finland.

In general, the reasons for the lack of confidence in Finnpap's system were these:

- Breaks in the international communication links.
- Downtimes in computer equipment.
- Mistakes in programs and operating.
- The delays in maintenance and repairs caused by distance and time differences.

Lamco, with 200 employees, was the associations' largest marketing company. Many smaller sales offices in a number of countries also had disappointing experiences with the central systems. Although too small to acquire their own computing power, they were increasingly vocal in requesting local solutions for enhanced flexibility and uninterrupted operations.

Varma Services Ltd., a London service company that handled ground transportation in the United Kingdom, had recently bought an IBM S/38 for many of the same reasons expressed by Brunow. Kauko Pekkanen, a manager at Varma, had lately been working on the transportation process. He said:

At present we are working on reducing the number of documents required for each shipment. Some of the Finnish ports already receive loading lists from mills through our network. We've also been able to eliminate the bill of lading for some destination ports. By reducing the amount of necessary paper, we're able to save a lot of money.

Another important area is the roll identification. The volumes are very large and it is extremely time consuming to manually identify the packages in each phase of the transportation chain. One possible solution is the bar code system. Some of the mills are using them internally, and some of our customers have asked for them, but there are no international standards for codes. Because some of the mills have already invested in a certain system it is difficult to make changes. Even if we could agree on a standard we would still have the problem of identifying the great number of codes in ports and warehouses. How could we read the codes from each roll or pallet? The technology does not seem safe enough at present.

IT and Transportation

The coordinating function performed by Transfennica was more complicated than the transportation requirements that faced most of Finland's competitors. The quantities handled by Transfennica were larger, however, so their unit costs tended to be lower. These large quantities, combined with the increasingly specialized nature of the orders, created the need for an excellent information system.

Tuure Lahermaa, the managing director of Transfennica, maintained a positive attitude toward information systems of development. He commented:

> A smoothly operating information system would clearly be one source of competitive advantage. Finnish industry is not a giant—even in aggregate. Its markets are very dispersed. Only through a common solution is it possible to maintain strengths, because then the volumes are large enough for economies of scale. Common transportation is possible only when combined with common marketing.
>
> The Swedes have tried both—transportation and marketing cooperation—but they failed because of disagreements. Success also requires a good computer system; failure there means total disaster. Information is needed for decisions concerning manufacturing, transportation, and warehousing. It is currently possible to lose track of rolls or pallets for long periods of time.
>
> We in Transfennica receive many inquiries concerning transportation. A great number of working hours have been wasted responding to these questions. Mills are interested in transportation routes and order status. That information should be available to them on their terminals, but now the mills have no means to control their marketing and transportation costs. We need an open and responsible reporting system to restore everyone's trust in our operations.
>
> Transportation costs are about 15–25 percent of the sales price. These costs can be reduced with better information systems, but the investment must be in line with the benefits. There are several opportunities for reducing costs in the operating chain, but we must be able to clearly define the spheres of responsibility in this chain.

Arto Jantunen, a Transfennica transportation manager responsible for the United Kingdom and Ireland, described very clear demands for an information system:

> We need real-time information to follow up on the financial aspect of transports. Each year we should make a transportation budget based on sales budget. That exercise should include

discussions on the service level we offer to our customers. Based on that decision we can make budgets on the transportation capacity needed and sea freights. All these budgets must be in our computer system.

For everyday operations we need real-time data on ex-mill date, loading date, date of arrival, and the cost of transportation. For making effective transportation decisions, I need information on alternative routes and their budgeted costs, the actual costs of transportation, and the profitability of that route. Our present systems don't come close to these objectives. We must have one total system with linkages between subsystems. All parties now have their own systems resulting in a great deal of redundancy.

The associations and Transfennica must work together to develop the needed systems. At present our requirements have a very low priority because transportation costs are hidden by the existing systems, and if there are some mistakes in operations, the reasons should be clearly identified.

Transfennica's cargo included Finnish products other than paper and paperboard. Some producers of these other cargoes had let it be known that they could benefit from access to the associations' communications network.

IT and the Mills

Although information technology in the mills varied, in general, process control systems were very up-to-date while there was a wide range in the quality of administrative systems. Approximately 30 mills were connected to the associations' network, and that number was increasing. The mills had either Finnpap terminals or facilities for batch processing communication with the central system. In 1984 there were no CPU-to-CPU links between Finnpap and any mill system.

Some of the mills received customer orders through their terminals and then entered their weight specifications into the Finnpap system. The weight specifications included data on the manufactured products, which was used by Transfennica and agents in loading ports. In addition to this computer communication, there were numerous telephone calls between the mills and sales offices, Transfennica, and the associations. These calls concerned, among other things, negotiations, confirmations, inquiries, and complaints.

Since the mills were parts of independent companies, they had made their own decisions regarding computer hardware and software, which resulted in incompatible architectures. The mills were interested in receiving better information regarding order status, customers, and costs for transportation and marketing. As already noted, because the mills were in competition with one another, they stressed confidentiality.

Bjorn Rajalin, mill manager of A. Ahlstrom Co. Ltd., represented a high-quality producer. He said:

> The ordering process should be automated as much as possible, perhaps from customer to mill. The order should include the same data as the invoices; that way, we could rationalize the order invoicing process. There is currently duplication of effort between the mills and the associations. We have to reduce the amount of paper in these processes, and to do that we need computerized data transmission.
>
> It's very important to have close contact between the customer and the mill. We have special products with little or no warehousing. We are now developing our own EDP systems. The associations have a couple of years to show us that they are capable of designing and installing useful systems, otherwise we'll have to do it all ourselves.
>
> We need to be able to control the operation of Transfennica and the associations. The mills must have alternative ways of operating if those organizations become too bureaucratic. We are prepared to supply them with more information, but we want to control that data. We cannot have a totally open computer system. Our research work is our competitive strength, and we must protect our proprietary advantages.

This research and development work involved product development aimed at new or improved paper grades to satisfy the changing needs of the customers.

Pehr-Eric Patt was mill manager of Metsaliitto, a magazine paper manufacturer. He expressed views similar to Rajalin's. However, since warehousing was extremely important for magazine grades, Patt was concerned about inventory control:

> We should first get the existing programs in good shape. Only then will we be able to improve customer relations with customer terminals. We also have to think very carefully about the costs of our systems. Is it even possible to cover the development costs with the price we get from the market? The other problem is how to divide the development costs fairly between the different users. The value of information is very different to different people.

In general, the IT managers at the various mills would have preferred to be more informed about the central system projects. They managed their own development backlogs, and did not want to devote resources to redundant projects.

IT and the EDP Department

Jussi Berlin had been the manager of Finnpap's EDP department for only a few months, although he had been with the unit since 1975. Addressing the current situation, Berlin had these comments:

> We definitely favor a centralized solution around a database concept. We must of course insure that local operations can continue in the event of serious problems with the network. But distribution of computer centers is not practical now, for the following reasons:
>
> 1. Maintaining current, consistent data in multiple locations dramatically increases programming complexity.
> 2. We would need software for handling mistakes and for recovery.
> 3. When all the data is not stored in every location, production of summary reports is much more difficult.
> 4. Multiple computer centers increase installation, operating, and maintenance costs.
> 5. Extra costs, in both time and money, would be incurred for duplicate development tools.
> 6. Building a common database is very difficult.
> 7. We would lose flexibility in the use of our systems people.
>
> In five years' time it will be possible to implement distributed processing without significant extra work. Now we must focus on reducing the problems we have with the centralized solution. Our main problems are a lack of system reliability and an old-fashioned architecture. Given the present technology, if we want to serve all users on-line, the only realistic alternative is centralized processing. The users have legitimate problems with our systems, but the real difficulty is our shortage of resources. There is tremendous competition for qualified people in Helsinki, but despite this we have built about 8,500 programs here. We have to admit that because of their age they are batch-oriented programs, but we have plans for improving them.
>
> We have been accused in the past of not listening to the needs of end users. This attitude has changed. For example, we have a schedule to build a new order and invoice handling system that will satisfy their needs for order status information. But it is a very large system and will take two years to develop. Different users have different priorities for systems development work. We would

like to have a clear decision on these priorities, then we will be able to request the appropriate machine capacity and personnel. My staff is now kept busy maintaining the existing systems.

The Decision

Finnpap's Managing Director Thomas Nysten had now listened to all parties concerned. He knew he must resolve the intertwined issues of distributed processing, the need for new hardware, the large investments necessary to satisfy user demand, and the prioritization of that demand. Nysten also recognized that IT strategy should support overall business goals, but he was unsure of the best way to achieve this.

At the beginning of April 1985, Nysten asked Jussi Olkinuora, director of the Specialty Paper Department, to prepare a position paper on information strategy by the end of the year. At Specialty Papers there were already many marketing development activities that demanded Olkinuora's attention, but he promised to spend the coming weekend organizing an approach to his new assignment.

Chapter 11

IT Planning
A Contingent Focus

A major manufacturing company eliminates its five-person IT planning staff, reassigning three to other jobs in the IT organization and letting two go. In commenting on this the vice president–finance stated, "We just didn't seem to be getting a payoff from this. After three years of trying we thought we could find a better place to spend our money."

The executive vice president–operation of a large financial institution, in speaking of a recently completed business systems planning effort, stated that this effort has been the key to conceptualizing a new and important direction concerning both the amount of IT expenditures and where they should be directed during the next five years. "We would be lost without it," he noted.

The head of IT planning of a major financial services organization, in discussing his disillusionment with planning, noted, "When I started IT planning two years ago I was very enthusiastic about its potential for invigorating the company. It worked for a while, but now the effort seems to have gone flat."

These comments are typical of organizations that launch an IT planning effort with great hopes and apparent early results but subsequently run into difficulty. This chapter explores key managerial issues surrounding this effort that have unfolded in the past 10 years and provides guidelines for assuring success.

As information technology applications have grown in both size and complexity over the past two decades, the development of a strategy for assimilating these resources into the firm's operations has grown steadily more important. A key vehicle for strategy development is a sensitively architected planning process. To be effective such a planning process must deal simultaneously with the realities of the firm's organizational culture, corporate planning culture, different technologies, and how critical IT activities are to achieving the company's corporate goals.

Repeated studies have suggested that a clear correlation exists between effectively perceived IT activities in an organization and a focused, articulated, and appropriate planning process.[1] However, since good standards of measurement do not exist for determining the overall effectiveness of the IT activity the evidence absolutely linking effectiveness of the IT activity with planning processes is more diffuse and fragmentary.

This chapter is organized around four broad clusters of topics:

1. Identification of the external and internal pressures on the firm that generate the need for an articulated IT planning process.
2. Identification of the practical restraining pressures that limit the value to be derived from the planning process.
3. IT planning and corporate strategy.
4. Discussion of important corporate environmental factors that influence both the ultimate effectiveness of IT planning and identification of the key levers to be managed in tailoring the planning process.

Pressures toward IT Planning

External (Corporate) Pressures

A variety of critical pressures force planning ahead in the IT field. The more important are discussed here.

Rapid Changes in Technology.   Hardware/software technical and cost characteristics have and will continue to evolve rapidly, thereby offering substantially different and profitable IT applications. This requires continued meetings between IT staff and management groups to ensure that they have properly identified changes significant to the company and developed plans to manage them. It is equally important that potential users, such as office managers or analytical staffs (often quite

---

[1]Philip Pyburn, "Information Systems Planning—a Contingency Perspective," Master's thesis, Harvard Business School, 1981.

different from the traditional users of data processing systems), be made aware of the implications (as well as potential problems) of these new technologies so they can identify in their areas of responsibility appropriate profitable new applications that would not necessarily occur to the IT staff.

As the technology changes, planning becomes increasingly important to avoid proliferation of incompatible systems. Also, because the lead times for acquiring and updating equipment are often long, integration of new equipment into a company's existing technical and administrative configuration frequently extends implementation schedules up to four years.

A recently studied insurance company has a two-and-a-half year installation program to manage its transition from zero portable PCs with expert financial counseling software in them to over 5,000 being in the hands of their sales force. A detailed plan was absolutely critical to senior management's confidence in the integrity of the installation program and to the effectiveness and good morale of the sales force during the implementation.

Personnel Scarcity.   The scarcity of trained, perceptive analysts and programmers, coupled with the long training cycles needed to make them fully effective, is a major factor restraining IT development. As discussed in Chapters 5 and 6 these appear to be not cyclical problems but rather long-term difficulties that will endure throughout the 1980s. Not only are increasing amounts of software and electronic data being sourced from outside the firm but tough internal resource allocation decisions must be made. An increasing number of U.S. firms have looked overseas for English-speaking technical personnel to meet staff shortages at attractive U.S. salaries, despite the proliferation of IT productivity tools and software tools to distribute work to users.

Scarcity of Other Corporate Resources.   Another factor critical to the need for planning is the limited availability of financial and managerial resources. IT is only one of many strategic investment opportunities for a company, and the financial resources invested in it are often obtained at the expense of other areas. This problem is intensified by the overwhelming financial accounting practice in U.S. companies of charging IT expenditures directly against current year's earnings. Review of both the effectiveness and efficiency of these expenditures is of great importance, a critical limiting factor for new projects (particularly in companies under profit or cost pressures).

Scarcity of IT middle management personnel, particularly in the area of development, is also a significant constraint. The inability of companies to train sufficient project leaders and supervisors has significantly restrained IT development. This has forced either significant reductions in many applications portfolios or the undertaking of unduly high-risk projects because of inadequate human resources.

Trend to Data Base Design and Integrated Systems. An increasing and significant percentage of the applications portfolio involves the design of data bases to support a variety of different applications. A long-term view of the evolution of applications is critical in order to appropriately select both the contents of the data bases and the protocols for updating them to adequately support the systems using them.

Validation of Corporate Plan. In many organizations new marketing programs, new-product design, and introduction and implementation of organizational strategies depend on the development of IT support programs. Understanding these points of dependency is critical. If the corporate strategy is infeasible due to IT limitations this message needs to be highlighted for corporate management, and resolution of the problem must be forced while alternatives are still available.

In organizations where the IT products are integral to elements of the corporate strategy, this linkage is more important than for those organizations where IT plays an important but distinctly support function. A large paper company, for example, had to abandon major new billing discount promotions, a key part of their marketing strategy, because they were unable to translate the very complex ideas into the existing computer programs with their present level of staff skills. Advance coordination between IT and marketing management in planning sessions would have identified the problem much earlier and permitted more satisfactory solutions to be identified.

Internal (IT Process) Pressures

At different points in the evolution of an information technology the balance between these pressures shifts, and substantially different purposes are being served by planning. Reflecting upon the advent and growth of business data processing, data bases, distributed systems, telecommunications, and other new technologies, one can identify four different phases of technology assimilation, each of which poses a quite different planning challenge.

Phase 1: Technology Identification and Investment. The basic focus of planning in the initial phase of a new technology is oriented toward both technology and human resource acquisition. Key planning problems include identification of an appropriate technology for study, site preparation, development of staff skills, and managing development of the first pilot applications using this technology.

In this phase short-term technical problem resolution is so critical and experience so limited as to preclude much long-term strategic thinking about the implications of the technology. This is not bad, since those involved usually do not yet have a strong enough background in the technology and its implications for the company to think long term. As the organization gains experience, selection of appropriate applications for this technology becomes more equal to technical issues in importance, and one evolves to the second phase. As noted earlier, in some IT organizations, departments entitled "Emerging Technologies" have been established to ensure that this activity is being appropriately handled.

Phase 2: Technological Learning and Adaptation.   The basic thrust of planning in this phase is to develop potential users' consciousness of the new technology's existence and communicate the type of problems it can help solve. Sequencing projects and providing coordination between them are also important. Initiation of a series of user-supported pilot projects is key to success.

As a secondary output, the planning process focuses on numbers of staff and skills to be hired, equipment to be acquired, and generation of appropriate financial data supporting those projects. The consensus, possibly in writing, that comes out of this process is not an accurate indicator of the pace of future events, because individuals engaged in a learning process do not yet have the insight to be both concise and accurate about their real desires for this technology and how practical these desires are.

Since technology will evolve for the foreseeable future, there will usually be a Phase 2 flavor to some part of a company's IT development portfolio. Our observations of successful planning at this phase suggest clearly that:

1. Introduction of new technology is best developed by getting started with a pilot test to generate both IT and user learning rather than by years of advance introspection and design.
2. Critical to success is attracting the interest of some potential users on their terms and stimulating their understanding about adaptation of the technology. Success here leads to later requests for service.
3. Planning during this phase (and Phase 1 as well) involves a program of planned technological innovations, encouraging users to build upon past experience, and organizational receptivity to change.

Phase 2 planning has a heavy strategic focus. However, as is true in companies that are in a rapid growth phase in new industry sectors, precision suffers from both user and developer lack of familiarity with the technology and its implications. Hence planning at this stage does not have the same predictive value as planning for technology in a later phase. What the technical developer sees as the implications of the new technology often turns out to be quite different after the users have experimented.

Phase 3: Rationalization/Management Control. Effective planning for technologies in this phase has a strong efficiency focus on rationalizing the broad range of experimental operations. While technological learning and adaptation (Phase 2) planning has a long-range (if not terribly accurate) perspective, planning in Phase 3 is dominated by short-term, one- to two-year efficiency and organization considerations. These include getting applications with problems straightened away and completed, upgrading staff to acceptable knowledge levels, reorganizing to develop and implement further projects, and efficiently utilizing this new technology. During this phase planning's objective is to set appropriate limits on the types of applications that make sense with this technology and to ensure they are implemented cost efficiently. In terms of Robert Anthony's framework,[2] during this phase effective planning has a much stronger management and operational control flavor and weaker strategic planning thrust.

Phase 4: Maturity/Widespread Technology Transfer. The final phase is one of managed evolution, transferring the technology to a wider spectrum of systems applications within the organization. With organizational learning essentially complete and a technology base with appropriate controls in place, it is appropriate to look more seriously into the future and plot longer-term trends. Unfortunately, if one is not careful such planning, based on the business and technology as now understood, can become too rigid. Unexpected quirks in the business and evolution of technology often invalidate what has been done during Phase 4 planning.

Given the current dynamic state of IT, all four planning phases are present simultaneously in a typical organization. Planning for business batch data processing for most companies in 1986, for example, was in Phase 4 while electronic mail was in Phase 2. This suggests that uniformity and consistency in planning protocols are inappropriate because the organization's familiarity with particular technologies varies.

---

[2]Robert Anthony, *Planning and Control Systems: A Framework for Analysis* (Boston: Division of Research, Harvard University Graduate School of Business Administration, 1965).

Not only does the planning process style have to evolve over time for a particular family of technologies, but a consistent, uniform process for the aggregate portfolio of applications for an organizational unit is also unlikely to be appropriate. The unit is dealing with a cluster of different technologies, each of which is at a different phase of assimilation within the organization. For example, one manufacturing company studied was in Phase 4 in terms of its ability to conceptualize and deal with enhancements to its batch systems over a multiyear period. At the same time, it was in Phase 3 in terms of organizing protocols and training a broad group of individuals to solidify control over the efficiencies of its on-line inquiry and data input systems, whose growth had exploded in the past several years. Finally, the company had made an investment in several word processing systems and was beginning to examine several different methods of office automation. It was clearly in Phase 1 with respect to this technology.

In summary, planned clutter (as opposed to consistency) in the approach to IT planning for an organizational unit is a desirable rather than an undesirable feature. Similarly the approach to IT planning for different organizational units within a company should vary, since each often has quite different familiarity with specific technologies.

Limitation of Planning Benefits

As new products appear, as the competitive environment shifts, as the laws change, as corporate strategies change, and as mergers and spin-offs take place, the priorities a company assigns to its various applications appropriately evolve as well. Some previously considered low-priority or new (not even conceived of) applications may become critically important, while others that were vital will diminish in significance. This volatility places a real premium on building a flexible framework to permit orderly and consistent change management to match evolving business requirements.

In a similar vein every IT planning process must make some very specific assumptions about the nature and role of technological evolution. If this evolution occurs at a different rate from the one forecasted (as is often the case), then major segments of the plan may have to be reworked in terms of both scope and thrust of work. Suppose, for example, the present speed of access to a 100 million–character file were suddenly increased in the coming year by an order of magnitude beyond current expectations, with no change in cost. Most organizations' plans would require careful reexamination, not just of the priority of applications but, more important, of their very structure. Some individuals have used this as a reason not to plan but rather to be creatively opportunistic on a year-to-year basis. On balance we have found evidence supporting this viewpoint to be unconvincing.

Planning as a Resource Drain

Every person, or part of a person, assigned to planning diverts resources away from systems and program development. The extent to which financial resources should be devoted to planning is still very much in question. Not only will the style of planning evolve over time as parts of the organization pass through different phases with different technologies but the amount of commitment to planning will also appropriately shift. This suggests an incompatibility between the notions of stability in an IT planning process and its role of stimulating a creative view of the future. If not carefully managed, IT planning tends to evolve into a mind-numbing process of routinely changing the numbers as opposed to a sensitive focus on the company's real problems.

Fit to Corporate Culture

An important aspect of IT planning is implementation within the realities of the corporate culture. For example, when organizations have a very formal corporate planning process actively supported by senior management, an internal user-management climate supports formal approaches to IT planning. In middle management's eyes, planning is a legitimate activity, and devoting time to it is appropriate. Other organizations, however, have quite different cultures and approaches to corporate planning. These factors significantly alter both the form and the degree of commitment that can be expected from users in an IT planning process, consequently shaping the most desirable way to approach the planning task. This is discussed further later in the chapter.

Strategic Impact of IT Activities

As discussed in earlier chapters, for some organizations IT activities represent an area of great strategic importance; for other organizations they play (and appropriately will continue to play) a cost-effective, useful, but distinctly supportive role. It is inappropriate for organizations with supportive IT to expect that the same amount of senior management strategic thinking should be devoted to the IT organization as in organizations of the former type. Making the issue more complicated, the IT function that today does not have strategic importance may, because of the thrust of its applications portfolio, have great significance in the future. Thus planning is very important.

FIGURE 11–1   Information Technology Strategic Grid

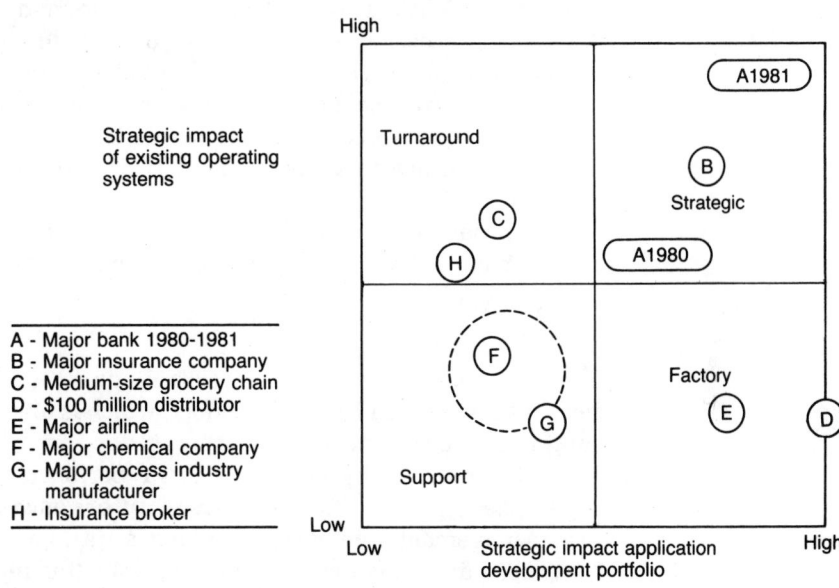

A - Major bank 1980-1981
B - Major insurance company
C - Medium-size grocery chain
D - $100 million distributor
E - Major airline
F - Major chemical company
G - Major process industry
     manufacturer
H - Insurance broker

The opposite could also be true. Where IT now plays a strategic operational role in the company's operations, future applications may not seem to offer the same payoff or significance. Here a less intensive focus on strategic planning is in order with clearly different people involved than in the previous case.

The above points (discussed first in Chapter 2) are illustrated below within four quite different IT environments. (Also see Figure 11–1.)

Strategic.   These companies are critically dependent on the smooth functioning of the IT activity. Appropriately managed, not only do such firms require considerable IT planning but IT planning needs to be closely integrated with corporate planning in a two-way dialogue. Not only does IT need the guidance of corporate goals but the achievement of these goals can be severely impacted by IT performance and capabilities (or lack thereof). The impact of IT on the firm's performance is such that significant general management guidance in IT planning is appropriate.

Comments by the chief executive officer of a large financial institution to his senior staff captured this perspective as he noted:

Most of our customer services and much of our office support for those services involve some kind of systematic information processing. Without the computer hardware and software supporting these processing efforts, we would undoubtedly drown in a sea of paper—unless we were first eliminated from the market because our costs were so high and our services so inefficient that we had no customers to generate the paper. Either way, it is abundantly clear that information systems are critical to our survival and our success.

In our businesses, the critical resources that ultimately determine our marketing and our operating performance are people and systems.

Turnaround. In a way similar to strategic companies, these firms also need a substantial IT planning effort, which is linked to corporate planning in a two-way dialogue. Corporate long-term performance can be severely impacted by shortfalls in IT performance and capabilities. Again the impact of IT on the firm's future is such that significant general management guidance in IT planning is appropriate.

These firms may receive considerable amounts of IT operational support, but the company is not absolutely dependent on the uninterrupted cost-effective functioning of this support to achieve either short-term or long-term objectives. The impact of the applications under development, however, will be absolutely vital for the firm to reach its strategic objectives. A good example of this was a rapidly growing manufacturing firm. IT embedded in its factories and accounting processes, while important, was not absolutely vital to its effectiveness. However, the rapid growth of the firm's domestic and international installations (in number of products, number of sites, number of staff, etc.) had severely strained its management control systems and had made IT improvement of critical strategic interest to the company. Enhanced IT leadership, new organizational placement of IT, and an increased commitment to planning were all steps taken to resolve the situation. Not only do companies in this block have an increased need for IT planning but frequently it takes place along with a number of other changes to enhance senior management's overview of IT.

Factory. Strategic goal setting for IT and linkage to long-term corporate strategy are not nearly as critical in this environment. IT planning can take place with appropriate guidance as to where the corporation is going; only limited feedback on IT constraints needs to go in the other direction. Senior management involvement in IT planning appropriately is much less in this environment, but detailed year-to-year operational planning and capacity planning are absolutely critical. The November 21, 1985 fiasco at the Bank of New York with its overnight loan of over $21 billion from the Federal Reserve System to keep its balance sheet balanced, as a result of the one day breakdown in a key system, gives vivid testimony to what happens when this is mismanaged.

Support. Again strategic goal setting for IT and linkage to long-term corporate strategy are not nearly as important as for the turnaround and strategic environments. IT constraints are not a critical input to corporate success, and overachievement or underachievement of IT departmental performance will not cause critical problems. Senior management involvement in the IT planning process can be much less here than in the first two situations.

Mismatches: Using the Strategic Grid. As stated above, the planning approach differs for each of the environments discussed above. The situation is further complicated when a mismatch exists between where an organization actually is on the grid (see Figure 11–1) and where senior management believes it should be. In general, more planning is needed when a firm is trying to deal with a mismatch.

A situation faced by a large financial institution illustrates the complexity of this problem. The institution's senior management was very comfortable with the company's IT performance although it came up only infrequently on their agenda. The IT management team, however, was deeply concerned that senior managers lacked the necessary conception of what the firm's goals were and what its products would be four to five years hence. They wanted to ensure that IT could provide the necessary support for the achievement of these goals.

The institution is a large international one with a very sophisticated but closely held corporate planning activity. Appropriately in a world of potential major shifts in what financial institutions can and should do, there was great concern at the top about the confidentiality of this information, and only a handful (four or five individuals) knew the full scope of this direction. Since neither the IT manager nor his boss were among this handful they were substantially in the dark about the future direction of the organization and could only crudely assess it by trying to guess why some projects were funded while others were not.

The company had a full-time IT planning manager, who had three assistants and reported to the IT manager. For the last two years the IT planners had worked closely with both middle management users and the information technologists to come up with strategies and applications portfolios that were commonly seen by both sides to be relevant to their needs. Because there was little direct linkage, either formal or informal, between the IT planning activity and the corporate planning department (repeatedly corporate planning had communicated: "Don't call us, we'll call you"), the IT staff had two overriding concerns:

1. The plans and strategies developed for IT might be technically sound and meet the needs of user management, but they could be unproductive or indeed counterproductive in terms of their ability to support the institution's corporate thrust.
2. The corporate plans were developed "at the top" by four or five executives in the know but also isolated from IT. This could unwittingly place onerous or unworkable pressures on IT in terms of future support requests.

At this stage senior management perceived IT as a factory, believed it was staffed appropriately, was being managed appropriately, and had no concerns about its planning process. IT saw itself as strategic but couldn't sell the concept to anyone. This frustration was resolved when an outside review of the institution's overall strategy convinced senior management that they had misunderstood the role of IT and that IT should be treated as strategic. Unfortunately IT management, perceived as being satisfactory to run a factory, was quickly perceived as being inadequate for this newly defined challenge and did not survive the transition.

On the surface, when one read the written plan, IT planning had looked good. In fact it had failed to come to grips with the realities of the corporate environment, and an organization for which IT activities are of significant strategic importance had been left in a state of potential unpreparedness and risk. This was fatal where IT activities on multiple dimensions were belatedly seen to be critical to the organization's achievement of its product and productivity goals.

To define the level at which IT is strategic to the company is useful, not just for talking about corporate IT planning for the company as a whole but for thinking about individual business units and functions as well. IT's impact often varies widely by unit and function, and the planning process must be adapted to deal with these differences. While making the planning's execution more complex it also makes it more useful.

Figure 11–2 contains a questionnaire used by one firm to analyze the strategic thrust of the development portfolio for each of its organi-

---

FIGURE 11–2 Portfolio Analysis

		Percent of Development Budget	Strategic Weight*
1.	Projects involved in researching impact of new technologies or anticipated new areas of applications where generation of expertise, insight, and knowledge is the main benefit.	0–5% 5–15 Over 15	−1 −2 −3
2.	Projects involved in cost displacement or cost avoidance productivity improvement.	Over 70 40–70 Under 40	−3 −2 −1

FIGURE 11–2 *(concluded)*

		Percent of Development Budget	Strategic Weight*
3.	Do estimated aggregate improvements of these projects exceed 10 percent of firm's after-tax profits or 1 percent of sales?	Yes No	-2 -0
4.	Projects focused on routine maintenance to meet evolving business needs (processing new union contract payroll data) or new regulatory or legal requirements.	Over 70 40–70 Under 40	-1 -2 -3
5.	Projects focused on existing system enhancements that do not have identifiable hard benefits.	Under 10 10–40 Over 40	-3 -2 -1
6.	Projects whose primary benefit is providing new decision support information to top three levels of management. No tangible identifiable benefits.	0–5 5–15 Over 15	-0 -2 -4
7.	Projects whose primary benefit is to offer new decision support information to middle management or clerical staff.	0–5 5–15 Over 15	-0 -1 -2
8.	Projects that allow the firm to develop and offer new products or services for sale or that enable additional significant new features to be added to existing product line.	Over 20 10–20 5–10 Under 5	-4 -3 -2 -1
9.	Projects that enable development of new administrative control and planning processes. No tangible benefit.	Over 20 10–20 5–10 0–5	-4 -3 -2 -1
10.	Projects that offer significant tangible benefits through improved operational efficiencies (reduce inventory, direct reduction in operating costs, improved credit collection, etc.)	Over 20 10–20 5–10 0–5	-4 -3 -2 -1
11.	Do tangible benefits amount to 10 percent of after-tax profit or 1 percent of gross sales?	Yes No	-2 -1
12.	Projects that appear to offer new ways for the company to compete (fast delivery, higher quality, broader array of support services).	Over 20 10–20 5–10 Under 5	-4 -3 -2 -1
13.	Do these projects offer ability to generate benefits in excess of 10 percent of after-tax earnings or 1 percent of gross sales?	Yes No	-2 -0
14.	Size of development budget as a percent of value added.	Over 4 3–4 2–3 2	-3 -2 -1 -0

*Larger numbers mean more strategic.

zational units. These questions are designed to uncover whether on balance the developmental work being done is critical to the firm's future competitive posture or whether it is useful but not strategic to competitive success. Similarly Figure 11–3 contains a questionnaire used by the firm to analyze how critical the existing systems are to an organization unit in achieving its basic operating objectives. The firm uses both exhibits as rough diagnostic tools.

Table 11–1 suggests that a firm's placement in the strategic grid not only influences how IT planning should be done but has numerous other implications in terms of the role of the executive steering committee, organizational placement of IT, appropriate type of IT management control system, and so on. Further, since different organizational units within a company may be at quite different points on the grid, the planning organization and control approaches suitable for one unit may be quite inappropriate for another. Finally, an approach suitable at one point in time may be quite inappropriate at another point in time.

IT Management Climate

In an environment of great management turmoil, turnover, and reassessment it is unlikely that the same intensity and commitment of effort to IT planning can be productively unleashed as would be possible in an environment where there is more stability in the structure and where individuals have a stronger emotional attachment to the organization. While these factors limit the benefits of planning and make the process more complex they do not eliminate the need for it. Rather they add to the multidimensional complexity of the task and restrict reasonable expectations, which appropriately vary from setting to setting.

FIGURE 11–3   Operational Dependence Questionnaire*

---

1. *Impact of a one-hour shutdown—main center.*

    Major operational disruption in customer service, plant shutdown, groups of staff totally idle.

    Inconvenient but core business activities continue unimpaired.

    Essentially negligible.

2. *Impact of total shutdown—main center—two to three weeks.*

    Almost fatal—no ready source of backup.

    Major external visibility; major revenue shortfall or additional costs.

    Expensive—core processes can be preserved at some cost and at reduced quality levels.

    Minimal—fully acceptable tested backup procedures exist; incremental costs manageable; transition costs acceptable.

FIGURE 11-3 *(concluded)*

---

3. *Costs of IT as percent of total corporate costs.*
   Over 10 percent.
   2–10 percent.
   Under 2 percent.

4. *Operating systems.*
   Operating system software totally customized and maintained internally.
   Major reliance on vendor-supplied software but significant internal enhancements.
   Almost total reliance on standard vendor packages.

5. *Labor.*
   Data center work force organized—history of strikes.
   Nonunionized work force, either inexperienced and or low morale.
   High morale—unorganized work force.

6. *Quality control—criticalness.*
   Processing errors—major external exposure.
   Processing errors—modest external exposure.
   Processing errors—irritating; modest consequence.

7. *Number of operationally critical on-line systems or batch systems.*
   10 or more.
   3–5.
   0–2.

8. *Dispersion of critical systems.*
   Critical systems—one location.
   Critical systems—two to three installations.
   Critical systems—run by multiple departments; geographic dispersion of processing.

9. *Ease of recovery after failure—six hours.*
   Three to four days—heavy workload, critical system.
   12–24 hours critical systems.
   Negligible—almost instantaneous.

10. *Recovery after quality control failure.*
    Time consuming, expensive; many interrelated systems.
    Some disruption and expense.
    Relatively quick—damage well contained.

11. *Feasibility of coping manually, 80–20 percent basis (i.e., handling 20% of the transactions that have 80% of the value).*
    Impossible.
    Somewhat possible.
    Relatively easy.

---

*First answer to each question indicates great operational vulnerability; last answer to each question indicates low operational vulnerability.

TABLE 11-1 Managerial Strategies for Companies in Support and Strategic Boxes
(assuming they are appropriately located)

Activity	Support Box	Strategic Box
Steering committee	Middle-level management membership. Existence of committee less critical.	Active senior management involvement. Committee key.
Planning	Less urgent. Mistakes in resource allocation not fatal.	Critical. Must link to corporate strategy. Careful attention to resource allocation vital.
Risk profile—project portfolio	Avoid high-risk projects because of constrained benefits. A poor place for corporate strategic gambles.	Some high-risk high-potential benefit projects appropriate if possibility exists to gain strategic advantage.
IT capacity management	Can be managed in a looser way. Operational headaches less severe.	Critical to manage. Must leave slack.
IT management reporting level	Can be low.	Should be very high.
Technical innovation	A conservative posture one to two years behind state of art is appropriate.	Critical to stay current and fund R&D. Competitor can gain advantage.
User involvement and control over system.	Lower priority—less heated debate.	Very high priority. Often emotional.
Chargeout system	Managed cost center is viable. Chargeout less critical and less emotional.	Critical they be sensitively designed.
Expense control	System modernization and development expenses postponable in time of crisis.	Effectiveness key. Must keep applications up to date. Other places to save money.
Uneven performance of IT management	Time available to resolve it.	Serious and immediately actionable.

IT Planning and Corporate Strategy

As noted in Chapters 3 and 4, in a number of organizations IT has turned into a very sharp competitive weapon capable of significantly altering the firm's competitive posture. The extent to which it can be used competitively influences how to think about and plan IT. Of particular importance is the firm's underlying basis of competitive strength.

Michael Porter's book *Competitive Strategy*[3] provides a framework for thinking about this. He suggests that there are three generic strategies a firm can adopt (described initially in Chapter 3). These are described below in a brief discussion of how they involve IT as a component of corporate strategy.

Strategy 1. Be the Low-Cost Producer

This strategy is appropriate for a standardized product. Significant profit and market share increases come from driving operating costs significantly below those of competition. IT offers strategic value in this environment if, for example, it can:

1. Permit major reduction in production and clerical staff. (This will hit labor costs, lowering cost per unit.)
2. Permit better utilization of manufacturing facilities by better scheduling, and so on. (There will be less fixed-asset expense attached to each unit of production.)
3. Allow significant reduction in inventory, accounts receivable, and so forth (that is, reduce interest costs and facilities costs).
4. Provide better utilization of materials and lower overall costs by reduction of wastage. (Better utilization of lower-grade materials is possible in settings where quality degradation is not an issue.)
5. Permit value-added differentiation to take place in the customer's eyes along one or more aspects of the value chain, thus changing the rules of competition.

If the nature of the firm's manufacturing and distribution technologies does not permit these types of savings or the major differentiation that transform the rules of competition, IT is unlikely to be of strategic importance to the firm's long-term competitive posture; consequently, close, sustained linkage between the IT and corporate planning processes is not essential. However, in this world of fast-moving technology an intense study should be undertaken every couple of years to validate this.

---

[3]Michael Porter, *Competitive Strategy: Techniques for Analyzing Industries and Competitors* (New York: Free Press, 1985).

Strategy 2. Produce a Unique, Differentiated Product

This differentiation can occur along a number of dimensions such as quality, special design features, availability, special services that offer end-consumer value. For example, IT offers strategic value to this corporate environment if:

1. IT is a significant component of the product and key aspects of its value chain; hence it is an important, differentiable feature. To compete, banks, brokerage houses, and credit card operations all use IT-based service differentiation; operations, inbound logistics, outbound logistics, and after-sales service all have strong IT components.

2. IT can significantly impact the lead time for product development, customization, and delivery. In many industries today computer-aided design/computer-aided manufacturing (CAD/CAM) provides this advantage.

3. IT can permit customization of a product to the customer's specific needs in a way not possible before (e.g., CAD/CAM in specialized textile, made-to-order operations such as men's suits).

4. IT can give a visibly higher and unique level of customer service and need satisfaction that can be built into the end price (e.g., special-order enquiry status for key items).

If IT cannot produce unique features for firms and business units competing in this way (or deliver such massive cost shocks as to change the rules of competition), it is unlikely to have strategic impact on the firm's ability to achieve long-term competitive position. Accordingly a close linkage between IT planning and corporate planning will not be essential on an ongoing basis. Again, a study should be undertaken every several years to validate this.

Strategy 3. Identify and Fill the Needs of Specialized Markets

These markets consist of special geographic regions or a cluster of very specialized end-user needs. IT plays a strategic role for a firm if:

1. IT permits better identification of special areas of customer need and various unevennesses in the market's needs. This is the ability to analyze company or industry sales data bases to spot unusual trends. Greeting card companies describe each card in a number of dimensions and can spot, for example, that three-line verses and red cards with contemporary designs are taking off in the upper plains states and thus take appropriate action.

2. Their outputs are IT-intensive products or products whose end features can be modified by IT customization to local needs.

Again, this analysis gives important inputs as to how close the link should be between corporate planning and IT.

Summary

These paragraphs suggest that:

1. The competitive position of a business unit and its generic business strategy profoundly influence the firm's thinking about potential IT investments and the contribution from existing IT systems. Key inputs to the strategic/turnaround/factory/support categorizations flow from analysis of competitive position and overall strategy.

2. Different business units in a firm often have quite different competitive positions and quite different generic competitive strategies. No common approach inside the firm is likely to be appropriate for viewing IT's contribution and role in the firm.

3. Since competitive position, generic strategy, and technology all change over time, a constant, long-term approach to IT planning may be quite inappropriate.

Corporate Environmental Factors Influencing Planning

Research has identified four clusters of corporate environmental factors that influence how IT planning must be structured to improve the likelihood of success.[4]

1. Perceived Importance and Status of the Systems Manager

The IT manager's status must align with the role IT does or should play in the overall operation and strategy formulating process of the company. In environments where IT is in a strategic or turnaround role, a low-status IT manager (in reporting level and/or compensation) has difficulty getting the necessary inputs from general management in the planning process. If the corporate communication culture at the top is heavily informal, this is apt to be fatal, as IT is outside the key communication loop. If the corporate culture is more formal, development and management of appropriate committees and other formal processes can significantly alleviate the situation.

For companies where IT is and should be in the support role, lower status is appropriate for the IT director, and less effort needs to be made to assure alignment of IT and corporate strategy. A lower level of investment (dollars and type of staff) in IT planning is also appropriate for these situations, as is illustrated by the comments of a director of strategic planning for a large process-manufacturing company: "We relate to IT by giving them insight on what the corporate goals are and what the elements and forms are of a good planning system. Because of

---

[4]Pyburn, "Information Systems Planning."

their role in the company, we do not solicit feedback from them as to what the art of the possible is. The nature of their operation is such that they can provide no useful input to the selection of corporate strategy."

2. Physical Proximity of Systems Group and General Management Team

For organizations where many important decisions are made informally in ad hoc sessions and where IT is playing a strategic or turnaround role, key IT management staff need to be physically close to the senior line manager. Regardless of the systems manager's status, being an active member of the team in this type of organization is difficult when geographically distant. According to one manager in such a company, those people who are around and easily accessible when a problem surfaces are those who solve it, and "we don't wait to round up the missing bodies." When the prevailing management culture is more formal, physical proximity becomes less important. In these situations the formal written communications and the scheduled formal meetings largely substitute for the informal give-and-take.

In informal organizations in which IT is strategic or turnaround it is critical that the IT managers, and preferably a small staff, be at corporate headquarters even if the systems groups must be located many miles away. For support and factory organizations with informal cultures, location at corporate headquarters is much less critical.

3. Corporate Culture and Management Style

In organizations where the basic management culture is characterized by the words *low key* and *informal* and where an informal personal relationship exists between the systems manager and senior management, formal IT planning procedures do not appear to be critical to systems effectiveness. Development of this relationship is assisted (as mentioned above) by geographic proximity and the IT manager's status. As an organization becomes more formal, disciplined IT planning becomes more significant as a countervailing force, even for systems environments that are not highly complex.

4. Organizational Size and Complexity

As organizations increase in both size and complexity and as IT applications grow larger and more complex, increasingly formal planning processes help to ensure the kind of broad-based dialogue essential to the development of an integrated vision of IT. This relates to the previous comments concerning management culture and style, as greater size and complexity often lead to more formal practices in general. In environments where the business unit size is small and relatively simple, formal planning approaches become less critical irrespective of the other factors. Similarly, for business units where the systems environment is not terribly complex, IT planning can safely take place in a more informal fashion. However, as the portfolio of work increases in size and in integration across user areas, more discipline and formality in the planning process become necessary.

In aggregate these corporate environmental items highlight another dimension of the complexity of selecting a planning approach and why recommendations on how to do IT planning "in general" almost always turn out to be too inflexible and prescriptive for a specific situation. Even within a company, these issues may force considerable diversity of practice between organization units.

Example

The following example shows how these issues have shaped the planning process in a billion dollar manufacturing organization. Key aspects of the corporate environment include:

1. The company has both a medium-sized corporate IT facility and stand-alone IT facilities of some significant size in each of its six major U.S. divisions. These divisional IT facilities report straight line to the divisions and dotted line to the corporate IT function. The corporate IT group is part of a cluster of corporate staff activities in an organization where considerable power traditionally has been located at the corporate level.

2. The vice president of corporate IT also has the corporate planning activity reporting to him. In addition he has had a long personal and professional relationship over a period of many years with both the chairman and the chief executive officer in a company that has an informal management culture. He was initially given responsibility for IT because the number of operational and developmental problems had reached crisis proportions. While under normal circumstances the criticality of IT might be termed support, these difficulties have pushed the firm into the turnaround category.

3. The closeness of relationships between the division general managers and their IT managers varies widely. The size of the application portfolios in relation to the overall size of the division also varies considerably, with IT activities playing a more significant role in some settings than in others.

At the divisional level of this manufacturing company, IT planning begins with some rather loose corporate guidelines concerning technological direction; it culminates in the preparation of a divisional IT plan. The planning processes and dialogues vary widely from division to division in terms of line manager involvement in developing the plans. In some settings the line managers are intimately involved in the process of developing the plan, with the division general manager investing considerable time in final review and modification. In other divisions, however, the relationship is not so close, and IT plans are developed almost entirely by the IT organization, with very limited review by the general management. The relationship of IT activities to the strategic functioning of the various units varies widely.

Critical to the IT planning process is an annual three-day meeting of the corporate IT director and his key staff, where the divisional IT managers present their plans. The director plays a major role in these sessions in critiquing and modifying plans to fit corporate objectives better. His understanding of the corporate plan (in his capacity as head of corporate planning), the thinking of the divisional general managers, and his firsthand knowledge of the thinking of the chairman and president enable him immediately to spot shortfalls in IT plans, especially in those divisions with weak IT–line management relationships.

As a result plans evolve that fit the real business needs of the organization, and the IT activity is well regarded. A set of planning processes, which in other settings might have led to disaster, has worked out well because of the special qualities of the IT director and the development of a communication approach between him and general management that is appropriate for this firm's culture.

Conclusion

Evidence continues to show a clear link between effective planning and effectively perceived IT activity for many organization settings. Effective execution of planning, however, has turned out to be far more subtle and complex than envisioned by earlier authors. Quite apart from the generation of new ideas, a major role of the IT planning process is stimulation of discussion and exchange of insights between the specialists and the users. Effectively managed it is an important element in cooling the temperature of potential conflict.

A major financial institution that we studied, for example, attempted at least four different approaches to IT planning over a six-year period. Each was started with great fanfare, with different staffs and organizations, and each limped to a halt. However, only when the firm abandoned efforts to plan did deep and ultimately irreconcilable differences arise between IT and the user organization. Communication of viewpoints and discussion of problems and potential opportunities (key to developing shared understanding) is as important as the selection of specific projects.

In this context our conclusions are:

1. Organizations where the IT activity is integral to corporate strategy implementation have a special need to build links between IT and the corporate strategy formulation process. Complex to implement, this requires dialogue and resolution along multiple dimensions. Key aspects of the dialogue are:

   a. Testing elements of corporate strategy to ensure that they are possible within IT resource constraints. On some occasions the resources needed are obtainable; in other settings resources are unavailable, and painful readjustments must be made.

   b. Transfer of planning and strategy formulating skills to the IT function.

   c. Ensuring long-term availability of appropriate IT resources.

In other support and factory settings such linkage is less critical. Over time the need for it may appropriately change as the strategic mission of IT evolves.

2. As an organization grows in size, complexity of systems, and formality, IT planning must be directly assigned to someone to avoid a lack of focus and the risk of significant pieces dropping between cracks. The job is subtle and complex, to ensure that planning occurs in an appropriate form. A strong set of enabling and communication skills is critical if the planner is to relate to all individuals and units affected by this technology and cope with their differing familiarity with it. Ensuring the involvement of IT staff and users for both inputs and conclusions is key. The great danger is that planners frequently define the task with more of a *doing* orientation than an *enabling* one and inappropriately begin to interpose their sets of priorities and understanding. To overcome this problem, many organizations have defined this job more as a transitional one than a career one.

3. Planned clutter in the planning approach is appropriate because the company is in different phases with respect to different technologies and the technologies have different strategic payouts to different organizational units at different points in time. While it is superficially attractive and orderly to conceive of planning all technologies for all business units to the same level of detail and time horizon, in reality this is an inappropriate goal.

4. IT planning must be tailored to the realities of the corporate style of doing business. Importance and status of the IT managers, geographic placement of IT in relation to general management, corporate

culture and management style, and organizational size and complexity all influence how IT planning can be best done.

5. In the range of technologies it covers, the planning process must be considerably broader than just data processing. It must deal, both separately and in an integrated fashion, with the technologies of internal and external electronic communications, data processing, office support micros, and so forth.

Case 11-1

Corning Glass Works
Information Systems Planning

Joe Malorzo, corporate manager of information systems planning for
Corning Glass Works (CGW), looked out on the gray February land-
scape from corporate headquarters in Corning, New York, as he commented on CGW's EDP planning process:

> You know, we've all come a long way in the past three years.
> When Dave Luther assigned me to the new full-time planning job in
> 1977, I couldn't understand why we even needed planning.
>
> Prior to that change, of course, I had managed the systems de-
> velopment effort in the corporate data center for a number of years.
> In that position I *knew* we were working tremendously hard to sat-
> isfy the company's needs as we saw them. My entire career had
> been concerned with systems activities, and at the time I thought I
> understood what was required.
>
> It never occurred to me that we might actually be working very
> efficiently on the wrong problems. In retrospect, though, I think
> I've learned more about systems *management,* and management in
> general, in the past 3 years than I did in the prior 12 with the com-
> pany.
>
> For a number of historical reasons, relationships between corpo-
> rate and divisional EDP groups had been deteriorating for some

---

This case was prepared by P. Pyburn under the direction of James I. Cash.

Copyright © 1980 by the President and Fellows of Harvard College
Harvard Business School case 9-181-012

time prior to 1977. The situation was so bad three years ago that the major objective of the 1978 planning cycle was simply to get divisional and corporate EDP managers talking to each other. I think we all began to see that we had common objectives and many similar problems, which was a real breakthrough. With a year of such experience under our belts, the plans submitted by the divisions and the corporate data center improved enormously in 1979. Presentations made at the annual planning session in July 1979 really began to address the critical issues such as manufacturing cost control, internationalization of our business, etc. I was really pleased with the improvement.

Not surprisingly, the plans submitted by the line divisions, staff groups, and the corporate data center in 1978 were pretty sparse and incomplete. The entire package barely filled one large looseleaf binder. In 1979, however, the plans were much more complete, reflecting, I think, a new understanding of the role of planning. That package filled two large binders with some left out. My objective for 1980 is to maintain the completeness of the plans but reduce the paper by being more concise and specific. I hope all of the plans will fit in one binder this year. It is imperative that we keep the "paper pushing" to a minimum, if only because I don't have a staff to process it.

This year we've made some changes that should finally make the plans useful for making some management decisions. Specifically, we've asked that each group concentrate on four areas as they go through the 1980 process: (1) the overall accuracy of the plans and the resource requirements expected, (2) a detailed link between the business objectives of the divisions and the systems plan, (3) an evaluation of performance on last year's plan, and (4) a management summary that can be used to communicate direction to senior divisional corporate managers. If we can get at these issues along with what we did last year, then we should be able to develop a real "no-B.S." plan for information systems companywide.

Commenting on the change in command for the Information Services Division (see Exhibit 1), Malorzo continued:

Of course, the assignment of a new Information Services Division director, John Parker, may well have an impact on the planning process. With Dave Luther [current vice president of personnel and Parker's predecessor], the planning process was primarily a communications tool. His real concern was to provide a common forum for discussion between the divisions' EDP groups, and between the corporate group and the divisional group. The content of

EXHIBIT 1   CGW Organization Chart, January 1980

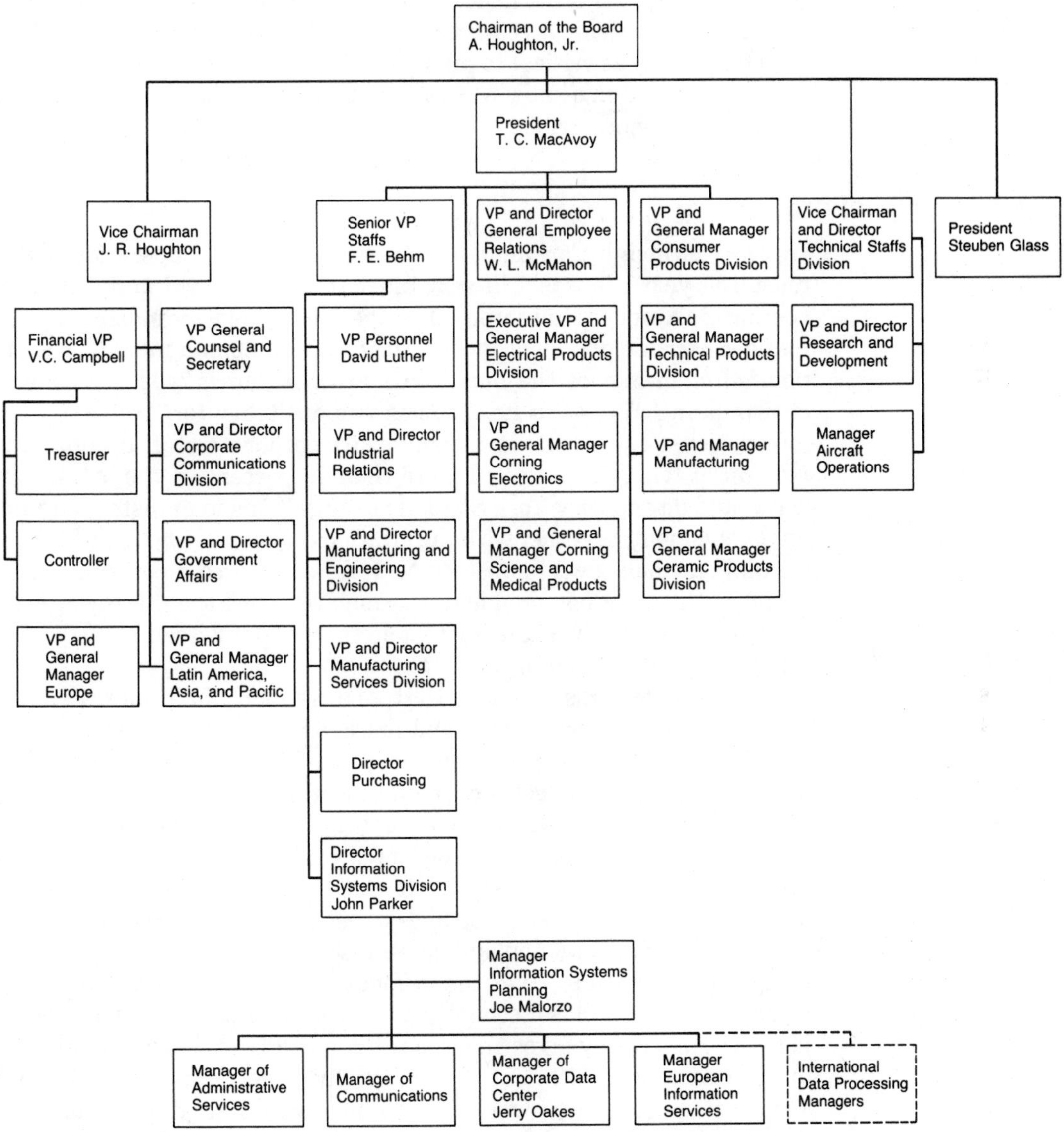

Chairman of the Board
A. Houghton, Jr.

President
T. C. MacAvoy

| Vice Chairman J. R. Houghton | Senior VP Staffs F. E. Behm | VP and Director General Employee Relations W. L. McMahon | VP and General Manager Consumer Products Division | Vice Chairman and Director Technical Staffs Division | President Steuben Glass |

Financial VP
V.C. Campbell

VP General Counsel and Secretary

VP Personnel
David Luther

Executive VP and General Manager Electrical Products Division

VP and General Manager Technical Products Division

VP and Director Research and Development

Treasurer

VP and Director Corporate Communications Division

VP and Director Industrial Relations

VP and General Manager Corning Electronics

VP and Manager Manufacturing

Manager Aircraft Operations

Controller

VP and Director Government Affairs

VP and Director Manufacturing and Engineering Division

VP and General Manager Corning Science and Medical Products

VP and General Manager Ceramic Products Division

VP and General Manager Europe

VP and General Manager Latin America, Asia, and Pacific

VP and Director Manufacturing Services Division

Director Purchasing

Director Information Systems Division John Parker

Manager Information Systems Planning Joe Malorzo

| Manager of Administrative Services | Manager of Communications | Manager of Corporate Data Center Jerry Oakes | Manager European Information Services | International Data Processing Managers |

the plans and the data that supported them were a secondary concern.

John, on the other hand, is more of a production-, output-oriented kind of guy than Dave was. I think he views the quality of the plans themselves as critical to managing this resource for the entire corporation. I don't know what this will mean for the planning process as it is now prescribed.

Company Background

In 1980, although Corning Glass Works had been in operation for almost 130 years, it was still very much a family-owned and -operated company. Amory Houghton, Jr., the great-great-grandson of the founder, became president in 1961 at the age of 35 and in 1964 was appointed chairman of the board. His brother James was named vice chairman in 1971, when he assumed responsibility for the company's international operations and many of its corporate staff groups. The Houghton family still owned more than 10 percent of the stock that was listed on the New York Stock Exchange. This long history of family involvement, together with the location of company headquarters in Corning, a small town in upstate New York, fostered a corporate environment that was personal and informal. Many of the managers were social friends after working hours, and the company itself played a major role in local civic affairs.

Since its establishment in 1851, the company had built a strong reputation as a manufacturer and marketer of specialty glasses with properties adapted to specific end uses. CGW's stated corporate objective was "to pursue excellence in glass worldwide, making this family of materials, its related products, and its corollary technologies the most unusual and useful in our civilization." This strategy, built around a material and its applications, led Corning in 1908 to become one of the country's first companies to establish a research laboratory. From that time on, technology-based research was at the center of the company's operation. Over the decades CGW's determination to become the leader in glass technology, and its willingness to back this objective with a heavy investment in research and development, resulted in the company's entry into an unusually wide range of businesses. This pattern of growth was far from a conscious strategy of product line diversification; rather it was a natural result of a management philosophy that saw application-oriented research as the company's driving force.

Thanks to expansion of existing businesses and diversification into new products, Corning's sales in 1979 exceeded $1.4 billion on total as-

---

EXHIBIT 2

CORNING GLASS WORKS AND SUBSIDIARIES
Financial Highlights
($000 except per share amounts)

	1979	*1978*
Net sales	$1,421,598	$1,251,728
Income from operations	114,350	120,574
Net income	124,943	104,363
Dividends paid	34,371	30,690
Per share of common stock		
Net income	7.05	5.89
Dividends paid	1.94	1.73
Income from operations to sales	8.0%	9.6%
Net income to sales	8.8%	8.3%
Net income to total stockholders' equity . . .	15.9%	14.8%
Additions to plant and equipment	$137,860	$103,232
Depreciation and amortization	$62,449	$57,428
Number of employees (year-end)	30,200	29,500

---

sets of the same amount. Net income after tax in that year was almost $125 million. The company had 30,200 employees worldwide and operated 90 plants in 20 countries. Exhibit 2 highlights CGW's financial status in 1978 and 1979.

Corning's Businesses

Mainly through the type of research effort described, Corning had developed over 300 different types of glass, which it converted into more than 60,000 products. These products were consolidated into six major business groupings, each of which was managed by one of CGW's product divisions in the United States.

Electrical Products. Corning got into the television bulb business after gaining experience in manufacturing radar tubes during World War II. By continually improving the product through research and development efforts, particularly on the color picture tube, Corning became one of two major U.S. suppliers to television manufacturers. When Corning started up bulb manufacturing facilities in France, Brazil, Mexico, and Taiwan, it was able to capitalize on the international purchases of major customers such as Phillips, RCA, and Sylvania. The business and its associated technologies were mature by 1980 and were not affected by the rapid developments of the 1950s and 1960s.

Electronics Products. The bulk of Corning's electronics products in 1980 consisted of resistors and capacitors for electronic equipment manufacturers, such as the OEMs of computer, communications, home entertainment, and military equipment. Most of the products were mature commodities, but the associated technology was changing rapidly and product development had to keep up with customer needs.

Consumer Products. Pyrex bakeware, Corning Ware, Centura and Corelle tableware, and flat-top glass ceramic cooking surfaces were the major products of this division. There were two broad groups of customers: the mass home market and commercial food operations. The types of retail outlets used to reach the first group varied by country, as did the distribution to the retailer. For example, in Argentina, distributors sold to independent retailers, while in the United Kingdom a direct sales force fought for shelf space in mass merchandisers' and national chains. Corning had a few global competitors, such as the popular Noritake line, but most were local or regional.

Ceramics Products. The division manufactured high-performance ceramic and glass-ceramic materials for use in diverse industrial processes involving very high temperatures and/or corrosive environments. In general, the products of the Ceramics Division were marketed directly to a relatively small number of customers.

Medical-Scientific Products. In 1980 two formerly independent divisions were merged to form the Medical-Scientific Division. The medical products included instruments such as blood-gas analyzers and white-cell analyzers and the reagents required to calibrate them, which were mainly used to determine body chemistry. In addition, the company had a line of single-test diagnostic reagent materials and kits to be used, for example, to test patients' blood for thyroid-related disorders. A direct sales force demonstrated products to potential customers in labs and hospitals.

Scientific products, on the other hand, consisted of two major businesses: scientific glassware and the chemical systems. The former was special lab glassware usually manufactured from Pyrex glass. It was an old, mature product line with competition based mainly on price and delivery. End users were small and widely dispersed, so Corning generally sold through local distributors. The second major business was chemical systems, and these consisted of process systems custom designed for specific applications.

Technical Products. Two very different businesses were included under this grouping. First there were ophthalmic products, which were principally eyeglass blanks produced to a variety of thicknesses, curvatures, and periphery specifications and made from either fixed or photochromic glass. The second part of Technical Products was known as technical materials, a highly varied business that basically involved the special application of various Corning products and technologies to a variety of industrial situations. These products were manufactured in all 22 domestic plants and were marketed through every conceivable distribution channel.

International Business Shift

As mentioned earlier, CGW began as a small, relatively local U.S. company that developed overseas branches with modest direct management involvement. The company was almost exclusively manufacturing- and technology-oriented, and it relied heavily on individuals with recognized competence in various technical and nontechnical fields. Oral communication prevailed, reinforced by the location and frequent job rotation of personnel whereby managers came to know each other personally. In the resource-rich world economy of this early growth stage, CGW systems tended to emphasize short-term results, tracking manufacturing as the prime measure of business activity. The systems were often informally built in response to local needs and were thus relatively inflexible when new demands were imposed.

Because of its significant growth during the late 1960s and early 1970s, its acquisition of majority interest in offshore subsidiaries, and increasing environmental complexity (economies, resource limitations, products, distances between locations, varying social, political, and cultural customs, etc.), CGW made some major changes. First there was a shift in emphasis from manufacturing to marketing. Next, CGW identified the need to integrate business management on a global basis. This would facilitate

- Developing fact-based data for decision making and priority setting.
- Focusing on marketplaces in addition to manufacturing concerns.
- Monitoring and reacting more quickly to social, political, and other environmental factors.
- Developing more structured reporting processes to offset the effect of geography.

A major consulting firm was hired to help specify necessary changes and to identify the appropriate administrative and organizational infrastructure to support them. As these changes were being implemented during 1975 and 1976, it became apparent that the corporation's information-processing capability would not support the new direction and emphasis. This exposure of the inadequacy of standards, uniformity of information and processes, and communication capabilities caused attention to be focused on the corporate data processing staff.

Corporate Information Systems

EDP usage at CGW began in July 1958, when an IBM RAMAC was installed. During 1962 the RAMAC was replaced by an RCA 301. Later acquisitions included an IBM 1401G in mid-1964, an IBM 360/30, and a third RCA 301 in 1966. In 1968 two RCA Spectra 70/45s replaced all older equipment. In the early 1970s a flood damaged much of CGW's corporate headquarters and accelerated a planned move to a single, large IBM mainframe in the 370 series.

Like many other large organizations, CGW initially used its EDP system in the financial area. Systems were developed for corporate financial reporting, and a centralized data center was established with computer hardware and a large development staff. The Corning Data Center (CDC) operated an IBM 3033, maintained a centralized development staff of 50 programmers and analysts, and supported administrative staff on a budget of approximately $6 million (one-quarter of corporatewide EDP costs). One division general manager noted:

> The tradition of centrally managing technology is strong in this company. Research and manufacturing developments are the key to our success, and they are very closely controlled and managed from the top. I guess it just seemed natural to manage this new technology [EDP] the same way. As recently as 1977, the director of Corporate Information Resources [CIR][1] reported to the controller, which clearly influenced the emphasis of the group. In general, CIR supported the financial and other corporate staff functions more effectively than they did the line divisions. Of course, CIR was responsible for developing and operating systems for the entire company, but most of their real effort was directed at developing corporatewide, financially oriented systems. To a large extent, this is still their focus.

Most corporate staff functions (controller, treasurer, etc.) relied exclusively on the corporate data center for systems development and operations. Their needs were usually represented by a single liaison person who reported within the staff function.

---

[1]This was the name of the corporate data processing group before a 1979 reorganization, when it was renamed the Information Services Division (ISD).

Division-Level EDP Departments

In the 1970–1977 period, most divisions established their own EDP departments, reporting directly to divisional management. In the larger, more prosperous divisions, these EDP groups created virtually independent data centers, complete with hardware and development personnel. In other divisions, the EDP department relied heavily on the corporate data center for development and operational support, though all divisions maintained some development and operational capability. For example, in the largest division, Consumer Products, 19 people were committed to systems development activity, while an additional 30 maintained an operation that included five DEC PDP 11 computers (Models 11/34–11/70), two IV Phase computers, two Data General Nova computers, a DEC IP300A, and an IBM 370/145.

The level of EDP experience and expense varied substantially from division to division. In the line divisions, for example, 1979 staffing and expenditures were:

Division	Staffing	Expenses
Ceramic	24	$ 992,000
Consumer	49	2,248,000
Electrical	22	806,000
Electronics	35	2,012,000
Medical	18	813,000
Science	31	1,478,000
Technical	24	1,531,000

Some line divisions were thus moderately sized information systems operations in their own right, while others were smaller and more dependent on CIR.

Management experience in the divisional EDP groups also varied to some extent; some managers had extensive non-EDP backgrounds and others had only EDP experience. As reflected in part by variations in expenditure and management selection, some divisions viewed EDP as a relatively low-priority activity while others saw it as essential to overall success. One general manager noted that "EDP is like the mail service or the plumbing; I only notice it when it fails." Another disagreed, suggesting that "we run on information in this division. Managing it is something we consider frequently." The quality and frequency of communication between EDP and general management thus varied substantially from division to division.

To some extent, however, all of the divisions depended on CIR for support, either for application system development or for providing EDP operations support on the IBM 3033. The continued CIR focus, primarily on staff functions, created an intolerable situation. According to Malorzo:

> It's not surprising that the communication between CIR and the divisions was poor. Because we didn't have much access to needs and business direction beyond the controller's area, it was difficult to develop comprehensive insight into the real needs of the company. As a department, we just weren't privy to the important decisions affecting the divisions. On the other hand, we controlled the largest pool of resources necessary to address many of their concerns. Without effective management direction, however, we were continually pulled from pillar to post, servicing whichever squeaky wheel was most troublesome. Naturally this created a serious credibility problem for us, and to some extent for the divisional EDP departments as well.
>
> The general perception by divisional management was that computers were a big overhead item that really didn't support many important business objectives. Senior management didn't really know what to expect, so they brought in a veritable parade of consultants to do audits, build systems, and generally be a nuisance.

Reorganization of EDP Functions

In early 1977 Dave Luther, who had moved through 14 positions in 16 years with the company, was promoted again—this time from his position as director of financial control and analysis to manager of CIR, under the controller. At this point in his career, Luther had never previously managed a data processing facility. However, he had been a very active member of a project team that focused on information systems during the internationalization of CGW. When Luther assumed responsibility for CIR, the corporate data center output was growing at an annual rate of 40 percent, and the CIR budget had been augmented by $1.6 million after several years of an average increase of $300,000 per year.

In 1977, after much discussion of perceived deficiencies in CIR information processing capabilities, information was determined to be a key strategic resource. In a presentation by the vice president of finance to a senior management committee, it was mentioned that "proper management of this resource is mandatory for a multinational corporation that is to prevail in a worldwide marketplace." In the same meeting, approval was granted for CIR to report directly to the vice president of finance.

Near the end of 1977 Luther was given responsibility for corporate planning in addition to CIR. In this new, dual-function role, Luther continued reporting to the vice president of finance, Van Campbell. He was thus at the same organizational level as the controller, reporting to the same boss.

For nearly two years Luther carried this joint planning and CIR responsibility, but in 1979 he shed his planning role when CIR was renamed the Information Services Division (ISD) and established as a division under the senior vice president–corporate staffs (Exhibit 1). The senior vice president, Forrest Behm, was a very highly regarded member of the senior management team, and he was recognized as a major force at CGW. The move was thus generally seen as strengthening the position of information systems vis-à-vis top management.

As a result of this reorganization, the director of the division had direct responsibility for the Corning data center (referred to as CDC), the Information Systems Planning staff (Joe Malorzo and a technology assessment specialist), the corporate office services function, and the corporate telecommunications function. The Corning data center continued to maintain both operations and development functions, reporting to the CDC manager, Jerry Oakes. Additionally, the director had dotted-line responsibility for the divisional EDP managers.

This dotted-line responsibility was best exemplified by the project approval process, which covered all efforts that required more than two work-years of CDC time or projects that required any additional computer hardware. For such projects, a formal appropriation request (AR) was submitted through divisional channels for approval. Before sign-off by the division general manager, however, it was standard practice to have the ISD director's signature on the AR. In most cases, moreover, large projects that would be accomplished totally within the division were also approved by the ISD director. As a practical matter, the director thus got a look at most projects costing over $100,000 and all projects requiring new computer hardware, regardless of where development took place.

Between 1977 and 1979 a flurry of activity was undertaken to improve the performance of CIR–ISD. Beyond Luther's regular contacts with members of the management committee, a number of specific organizational changes were implemented. At the corporate level a planning department, a data base function, and a technical support group were established to provide direction on critical corporatewide activities. With the realignment to divisional status, responsibility for EDP, telecommunications, and office services was consolidated under ISD. A major hiring and campus recruiting program was undertaken, and a serious personnel review and skills inventory program was started.

Additionally, a number of programs were undertaken to improve the operating performance of information systems companywide, including:

- Initiation of the project proposal and review process discussed above.
- Implementation of a worldwide planning process that included all line divisions, corporate staff functions, CIR–ISD, and the corporate data center.
- Publication of systems development standards.
- Completion of a worldwide cost study and the implementation of a standard-cost, charge-out system for CDC.
- Establishment of an EDP audit function (which reports to the internal auditing group) and initiation of security and effectiveness reviews.

With the mechanisms for an ISD turnaround in place by early 1980, the management committee named Luther vice president–personnel and replaced him with John Parker.

Of this change in command, Joe Malorzo noted:

Dave and John are very different characters, by training, background, and personality—which is not to say that one is better than the other, but they are different.

Dave's recent background includes the director of salary administration and international personnel, the director of financial analysis and control, and director of corporate planning. While Dave has certainly had his share of plant experience [as a plant controller and production superintendent], in general I think he is viewed as something of a staff person. As a result of his positions he has had regular contact with Mr. Houghton and Tom MacAvoy [the president] for some time. His credibility at the top is good.

Dave's real strengths seem to lie in his people skills—his ability to communicate and build a consensus. He's very much a word person, and he was always careful to couch everything he said about Information Systems Planning in positive terms. It was never "us" and "them," but rather "we."

John, on the other hand, is very task and product oriented. He was most recently the controller of Corning, Ltd., a wholly owned subsidiary in the United Kingdom, where EDP reported to him. Before that he was production superintendent at the Big Flats plant, where he installed a real-time shop floor reporting system in a labor-intensive, complex environment. Unlike Dave, who didn't have a strong technical background when he started, John is technically knowledgeable.

I guess if I had to summarize the difference between the two men, I'd say that Dave was very process oriented, often at the expense of the division's output, while John wants to get the job done in the most direct way possible, sometimes glossing over the process of getting there. Of course, neither is at this extreme, but the comparison does help to paint a picture of their differences.

ISD Planning Process

When asked to describe the planning process he had initiated and nurtured through two iterations, Malorzo continued:

The general philosophy behind our planning was best described by Peter Drucker, who defined planning as the process of making present risk-taking decisions systematically and with the best possible knowledge of their futurity. I think the phrase *risk-taking decisions* is key, since most people are reluctant to establish plans without detailed facts. The person doing the planning, however, will often have to make decisions with very few facts about the future and must rely upon history, professional insight, and the best available data regarding future requirements and potential impacts. Nevertheless, long-range planning is a must if we are really interested in moving out of a reactive mode into a more proactive, controlled mode regarding resource allocation, priorities, and organizational effectiveness.

The procedure we've established for the EDP strategic planning process is primarily concerned with deciding on objectives, the strategies selected to carry out objectives, and the resources required to complete the plan. The planning process thus includes all EDP resources and activities for Information Systems, Office Services, Office Systems, and Telecommunications. The Scientific and Process Control development areas have been excluded.

The EDP manager/coordinator/liaison of each CGW operating and staff division or function, and the wholly owned subsidiaries in Europe and South America are required to submit plans. In the line divisions and wholly owned foreign subsidiaries, the planning is performed by the divisional EDP managers, who all maintain some independent level of development and operations capability. In each of the staff divisions or functions, there is an information systems coordinator/liaison who is responsible for planning, though they depend entirely on the CDC for support. None of the groups, staff or line, has anyone other than the EDP manager committed to planning on even a part-time basis.

Information Systems Planning Cycle

As can be seen in Exhibits 3, 4, 5, and 6, the annual information systems planning cycle began when planning process instructions and forms

EXHIBIT 3 Information Services Planning Process

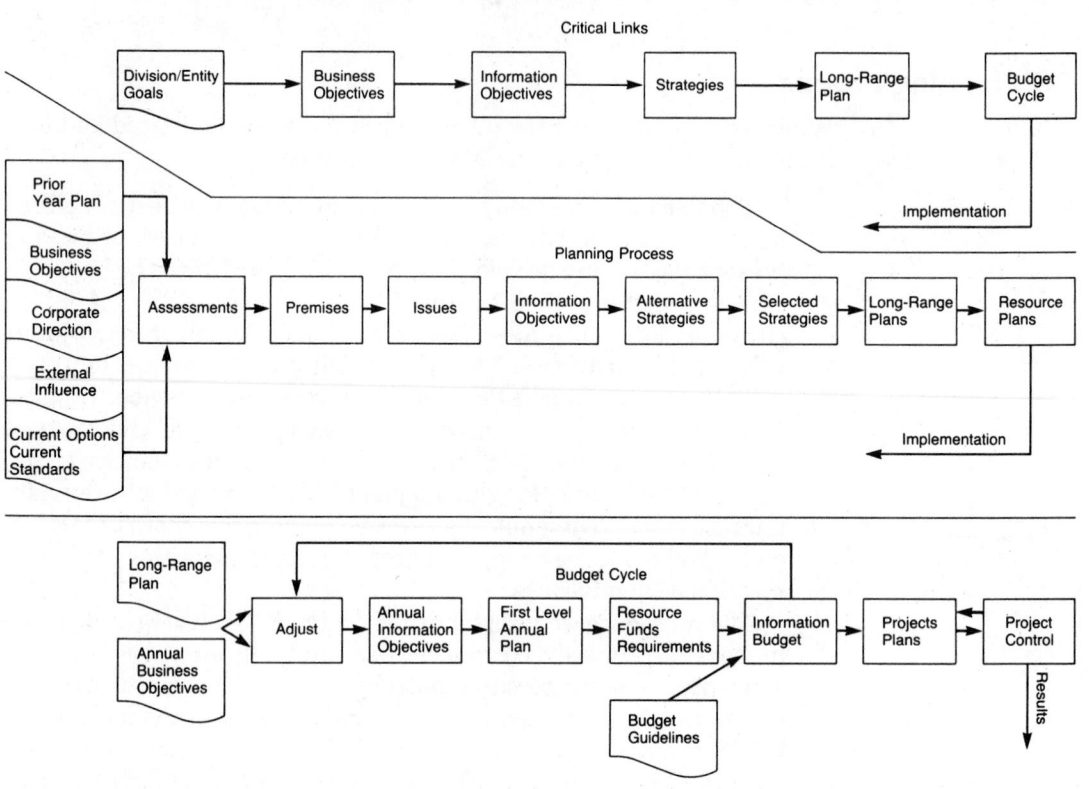

were distributed to each division. These instructions focused exclusively on completing the forms in a consistent fashion and provided only nominal guidance as to how the planning data should be gathered. On the issue of setting a strong corporate direction in the planning process, Malorzo noted:

> We provide little in the way of formal top-down guidance in the planning process for several reasons. First, the technology assessment function, which defines where we should be technically in coming years, is an ongoing responsibility of Carl Ballard, who works for me. Carl works day to day with the divisional people to come to agreement on our technological direction, so they are well aware of technical boundaries to their planning before we start. Additionally, the business constraints and objectives of each division are developed individually by the divisions as part of their annual planning. It's foolish for us to publish this kind of direction when

EXHIBIT 4 Flow and Relationships of Planning Process, Effective January 18, 1980

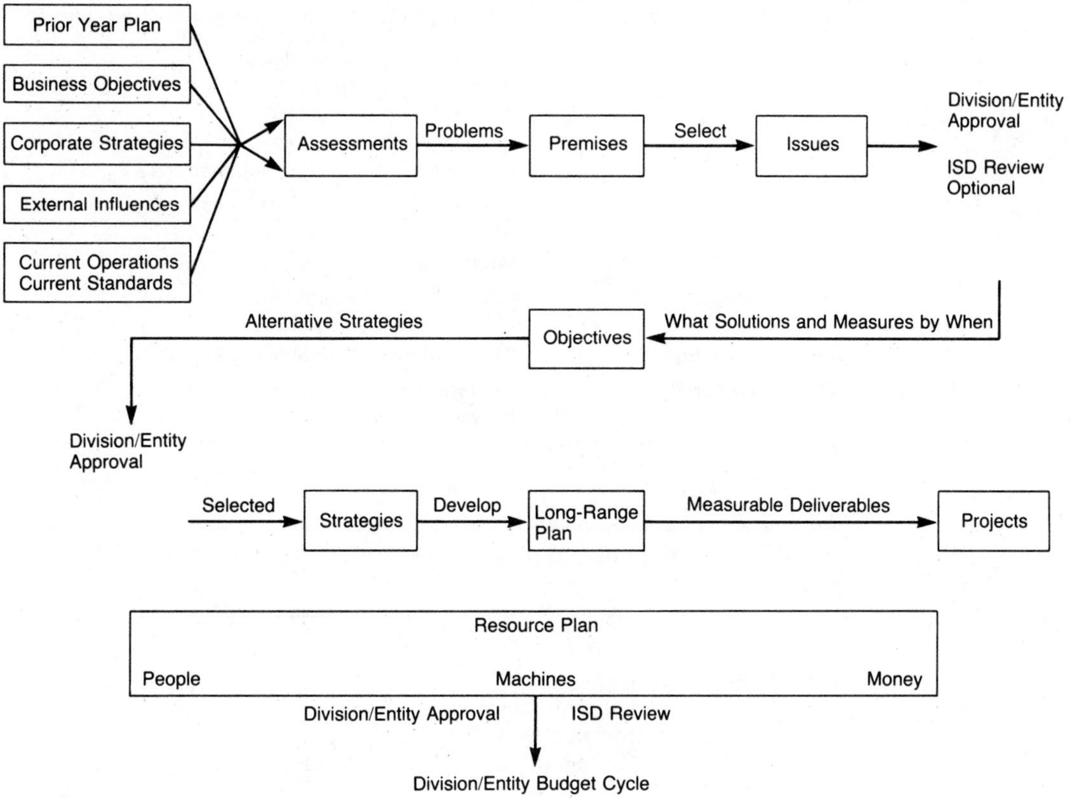

they can get it from the horse's mouth. Of course, one of my major roles is interpreting the corporate plan and direction, but I do this informally rather than as part of the planning instructions.

By mid-February each division was supposed to have assessed the EDP situation (presumably using the previous plan as a touchstone) and developed a list of premises and issues for division (and optional ISD) review. By mid-April objectives and strategies consistent with the major issues were presented to divisional management, and, based upon approval, a plan of programs and projects was submitted to ISD by June 1.

The December planning process instructions did not, however, prescribe how the information necessary for systems planning was to be gathered. To the degree that the systems manager was apprised by his

---

EXHIBIT 5   Information Systems Plan

I.	Assessments	What organizations and businesses do we support?
		What are the business objectives?
		What have we accomplished?
		What are we doing now?
		How well are we doing it?
II.	Premises	Where are the problems?
		What are the trends and assumptions?
III.	Issues	Which problems will we address?
IV.	Objectives	What solutions by when?
		What measures of success?
V.	Strategies	What are the alternatives?
		How will we approach it?
VI.	Long-Range Plan	What planned deliverables by when?
VII.	Resource Plan	How will we affect resources?
		People, machines, money?

EXHIBIT 6   Information Services Plan—Planning Process
Schedule

Task	*Submit to ISD*
Refine planning process	January 15
Distribute updated planning instruction book	January 31
1979 financial information (Schedule VI–D)	March 15
1979 through June 1980 staff movement (Schedule I–3)	March 15
Assessments	June 1
Premises	Not required
Issues	June 1
Objectives	June 1
Long-range plans	June 1
Resource plans	June 1
Executive summary	June 1
Resource allocation requests	June 1
Planning conference	Mid-June
ISD and senior management plan reviews	To be announced

---

or her division's management of the business objectives, strategies, and plans of the division, these were usually reflected in the systems planning. If, on the other hand, the line managers were not forthcoming with this business planning information, the systems manager developed the premises, issues, and so on, using his or her own experience and judgment.

Information Systems Planning Forms

The various forms to be completed by the divisional systems managers as part of the planning process are listed below. *Organizational Information* and systems *Profiles* detailed the state of the hardware, people, and applications systems and project changes in these areas over the next three years. *Assessments* of the information systems effort described the business objectives of the division and ranked applications systems relative to support of these objectives. The *Strategic Plan* detailed the premises, issues, and objectives used in the planning process and described a set of projects that were consistent with them. The *Resource Plan* detailed the financial, personnel, and computer resources necessary to achieve the plan, while the *Executive Summary* reduced the entire plan to a three- to five-page overview.

Organizational Information
 Organization chart.
 Staff summary.
 Staff movement.
Profiles
 Application systems.
 Computer.
 Telecommunications.
Resource Plan
 Financial and staff plan.
 Data center usage.
 Hardware and software.
 Telecommunications.
Assessments
 Prior year plan.
 Business objectives.
 Functional support.
 Systems effectiveness.
 Service responsiveness.
 Staff.
Strategic Plan
 Premises.
 Issues.
 Objectives.
 Long-range plans.
Executive Summary
 Resource allocation request.

In some divisions, systems managers completed most of the forms themselves, using their experience and judgment to do the assessments and develop the plans. The package was then presented to the division general management for approval. In one line division, this review lasted less than one hour.

In other cases, however, the general managers were more intimately involved in the detailed planning activity. In the Consumer Products Division, for example, an executive steering committee reviewed the systems managers' assessments and strategic plan periodically. While the systems manager generated the plan, the management review was much more thorough in this division.

Not surprisingly, therefore, there was a wide range of quality in the linkage between business plans and systems plans. Where the line managers had clearly specified *how* they were going to achieve their business strategies, and where the systems manager was aware of these plans, the systems plan was usually directly linked to business needs. Where such specification of plans was not available or where the systems manager was not aware of them, the systems manager developed his or her plan with little outside guidance.

Interestingly, the *corporate* strategic planning process specified only the broad development of strategy by business unit. The units were not required to "get under" these strategies formally to determine in more detail how they would be achieved. Some divisions continued beyond the corporate planning requirement, however, and involved line managers in the long-range planning necessary to implement strategies.

In any case, the divisional (and, in summary, the corporate) systems plans reflected the business plans of the organization only to the extent that line managers and systems managers discussed these issues. The formal corporate ISD planning process merely documented the extent of these discussions.

Corporate Planning Conference

After the divisional plans were submitted to ISD, a three-day planning conference was held in mid-July for systems managers/coordinators. Participants presented important pieces of their plans, and a set of corporatewide issues, objectives, and strategies were developed. This conference was held off site and provided a unique opportunity for the entire EDP management group of CGW to meet in an informal setting. Based on the results of this meeting, major objectives were consolidated into a corporatewide program for information systems. A budget for ISD was then developed at the corporate level to support these objectives, and a summary plan and budget were presented to the Corporate Management Committee (CMC) in September. This committee consisted of the chairman, the vice chairman, the president, the senior vice president of staffs, and the vice president of finance. Budgets for each division were developed (by the division EDP manager) in approximately the same time frame, though they were included in the divisions' individual requests to the CMC.

This annual meeting with the CMC was typically scheduled for 80 minutes and thus covered only major ISD efforts, large capital requirements, or other important issues such as significant reorganization. While this meeting was the only formal review of the information systems plan for the corporation, Dave Luther had traditionally used his informal discussions with senior management (especially in his role in corporate planning) to broach ongoing concerns. Due to the brief time allotted to ISD in the annual review meeting, it was in these informal discussions that most substantive issues were resolved. On his relationship with senior management, Luther noted, "I think it is important to 'presell' the significant points in the annual CMC presentation before that meeting. Fortunately, I had good opportunities to deal with the individual members of the CMC (especially in corporate planning), so that the major ISD issues were worked out in advance. If the planning is going to continue to work, then I think John [Parker] will have to develop a similar kind of forum."

Malorzo concurred, noting:

A lot of the real work in the planning area goes on behind the scenes with informal meetings and discussions. My role, beyond managing the formal planning apparatus, is to do the kind of "selling" of the corporate ISD strategy to the divisions that Dave talks about with the CMC. To do this, I spend most of my time in literally hundreds of meetings with systems folks throughout the company. It is here that we discuss issues like the kind of technology we expect to use in coming years, or the way we should be organized.

For example, when we decided that all of CGW's telecommunications would be SNA compatible [IBM's standard], we made this constraint known in the monthly meeting of all EDP managers [Computer Utilization Committee—CUC] rather than wait for the annual planning cycle. My role between annual planning sessions, it seems to me, is to sell the corporate position and provide guidance as the issues arise. Dave [Luther] really encouraged this kind of informal process, so that I now spend most of my effort planting seeds and selling direction. The real risk of this approach, of course, is that the formal mechanism will become little more than a rubber stamp.

Overall, though, I think the process works fairly well, but there is still a significant range in the quality of plans submitted. Some divisions have really tied their activity to the critical success factors in the division, while others seem content to address only those issues that come to their attention. To some extent I guess this is a result of the relationship the EDP manager has with his line managers. In those cases where the EDP folks are considered "part of the team," the plan seems to reflect the real needs of the division and the corporation. Where they are viewed as "second-string," this is not so true.

In general, though, the planning process is taken pretty seriously by most of the EDP managers. They typically spend several work-weeks developing their plans, discussing them with their line managers, and completing the forms. In general, it is the systems managers who individually "do" the planning, though of course they sometimes get help from others in the division.

At least in terms of budgeting *corporate* resources for division projects, we look very carefully at the divisions' plans. If it wasn't in the plan, it usually won't get into the budget. And if it's not in the budget, it's not going to get done [by the CDC]. In the more effective divisions this sort of link between planning and budgeting is also true for internal activity, though in some cases the linkage is pretty loose.

I'm sure a major contributing factor to receptivity of this process is the corporate culture of formal planning and control systems. Planning is an accepted business practice in CGW, and I tried to design the DP forms to look as similar as possible to our regular business planning forms.

In fact, the whole process mirrors the corporate planning style to a large extent by focusing on the operational implications of broad objectives. For the most part, business planning at CGW entails the divisions telling corporate how they will achieve overall corporate goals (e.g., X percent ROI). It is very much a "bottom-up" process, with the corporate plan being an aggregation of the divisions' plans. We've pretty much followed that annual bottom-up philosophy for systems planning as well.

The plans presented at the 1978 conference were really an exercise in understanding the process and developing a common language. In 1979, however, we really began to get some important issues raised that helped us all understand where we needed to head. The opportunity for 1980 and 1981 is to really get "inside the heads" of the line managers—to identify those opportunity areas that haven't even occurred to them yet. The marketing areas, for example, might be fruitful ground if we understood their needs better. I suspect there are lots of opportunities we haven't begun to address yet. In my opinion, the planning process will have succeeded if it provides a forum for this kind of line manager/EDP dialogue.

Chapter 12

The IT Business

Previous chapters laid out a series of frameworks for viewing the information technology activity and each function of IT management. In sum the book specifies in detail how one could conduct an IT management audit for the organization. This final chapter integrates these materials by highlighting the impact of our six major themes: information technology has different strategic impact on different organizations; the merging of the formerly separate technologies of computing, telecommunication, and office support into a single whole; the importance of organization learning to technology assimilation; the shift of the make or buy decision towards greater reliance on external sources of software and computing support; the continuing validity of the systems life cycle concept; and the need to balance continuously the pressures between the three constituencies of IT management, user management, and general management. We have chosen to view an organization's IT activity as a stand-alone *business within a business* and, in particular, to apply the notions of the marketing mix analysis. As described below, this view permits the development of a synthesis of the concepts of organization, planning, control, and strategy formulation for IT.

In this framework we will deal in depth with the issues of the marketing mix, strategy formulation, role of the steering committee as a board of directors, and the function of the IT director as the chief executive officer, because these items are particularly relevant in understanding the interface between the two businesses (IT and its host organization). We will not cover the operational details of operating strategy, since many of the general elements of IT operations management have already been covered in Chapter 9. Similarly not covered are issues of internal accounting and control within the IT organization, as they do not impact directly on the interface between the two businesses. For similar reasons only the IT organizational issues that deal with external relations of the IT business will be covered here.

IT is a high-technology, fast-changing business. Depending on the specific IT business one is dealing with, it may be a rapidly growing, more or less steady enterprise or (in a few cases), a declining business. Its total territory covers the development, maintenance, and operation of all IT technologies in a firm,[1] regardless of where the various parts are physically located or to whom they administratively report.

The scope of technologies to be coordinated by the IT business has expanded tremendously as computers, telecommunications, and office automation have all merged together, and its product offerings are exploding into new consumer areas, such as electronic mail, editing, and computer-aided design/computer-aided manufacturing. The complexity of implementing projects, the magnitude of work to be done, and the scarcity of human resources have forced the IT business away from primarily a product orientation to one where a significant percentage of its work involves coordinating the acquisition of outside services for use by its customers (i.e., acting as a distributor). This shift has forced major changes in its approach to planning and controls in order to deal effectively with these new products and new sources of supply.

Implicit in our view of the IT business is that, at least at a *policy* level, the overwhelming majority of firms require an integrated perspective and approach to IT. The IT activities include not just the corporate IT center and its directly linked networks but also the distributed islands of mini- and microcomputers, distributed systems development activities, outside software company contracts, computer service bureaus, and so forth. The various users of IT services are its consumers, who in many cases possess options to buy services other than directly from the central IT organization.

We believe this formulation of the IT task permits the transfer of other managerial disciplines and theories to the IT function in a way that can generate new and useful insights. Similarly we believe that for general management the analogy to the board of directors is a useful one in thinking through a realistic role for an executive steering committee and other aspects of how such a group should interface with the IT function.

Like all analogies this one can also be pushed too far, and some caution must be taken. For example, the financing of the IT business has

---

[1]Throughout this chapter the term *firm* will refer to the parent holding company of the IT business.

TABLE 12–1 IT Product Line Changes

Area	Past Focus	Future
Product obsolescence	Developing new products.	Heavy maintenance of old products meeting obsolescence challenges.
Sources	Majority of manufacturing inside.	Significant percent sourced from outside.
Dominant economic constraint	Capital intensive (hardware economy of scale).	People intensive (economy of skill).
Product mix	Mainly large, few medium, many small.	Some large, many medium, thousands small.
Profits/benefits	Strong return on investment.	Many projects have intangible benefit justification.
Technology	New technologies permit new products.	New technologies and regroupings of old ones permit new products.
Services	Structured, such as automated accounting and inventory control.	Unstructured, such as executive decision support systems and query systems.

no analogy to the corporate capital markets, since its capital support comes directly from the parent firm (with no debt analogy), and its revenues, exclusively in many cases, also come directly from the parent. The customer base in many respects is deeply interdependent on common files, and so on, so customers cannot be treated as being entirely independent. On the other hand the IT business is free from many of the inherent legal and governmental constraints that the parent company has. Other legal and governmental constraints, such as the Equal Employment Opportunity Commission (EEOC), may be placed on it primarily in the context of the firm's total corporate posture, with little possibility or need for the IT business to strike an independent posture.

The rest of this chapter deals with three main topics relating to management of the IT business:

1. The IT marketing mix and its implications for managing the IT business.
2. The role of the IT board of directors and how it can best be managed.
3 The role of the IT chief executive officer.

The IT Marketing Mix

Product

The IT product line is continuously evolving. Table 12–1 notes some of the key aspects of change. Part of the dynamism of the line stems from the enormous proliferation of opportunities afforded by the economics of new technology. The other element stems both from changing customer needs as a result of ordinary shifts in business and from new insights (Phase 2 learning) as to how this technology can be applied to specific operations.

IT products range in size from very small to enormously large (in terms of both development time and complexity to operate on a day-in, day-out basis). The large products (usually a single, one-time customized effort) can have such a long lead time (four years, not dissimilar to rebuilding automobile manufacturing processes) that significant uncertainty exists whether at the time of completion it will really meet customers' often evolving needs. For some products the possibility exists of delaying their introduction with limited damage, for other products severe damage to consumers (users) will occur if delays of any magnitude take place in development. In terms of day-to-day operations the importance of cost, good response time, quality control, and so on, varies widely.

Product obsolescence is a major headache for the IT business. The old products eventually become so clumsy that introducing the necessary enhancements (styling changes) to keep them relevant becomes more and more expensive. In due course, a major factory retooling must be implemented. Changing consumer needs (made possible by new technologies) and new manufacturing technologies for existing products offer significant opportunities for systems enhancements.

The method of delivery of IT products is shifting as the IT customer changes sourcing decisions. As an increasing percentage of IT development expenditures goes to software houses and time-sharing vendors, and production expenditures go to stand-alone minis and micros, IT's role is shifting from one of being primarily a developer and manufacturer to one where it is also a significant distributor of products manufactured by others. This distribution role involves identifying and evaluating alternate sources of supply (of both software and production) as well as professionally reviewing those identified by customers.

The products run the gamut from those where the need is clearly (and perhaps correctly) understood by customers and they are knocking down the door for the product (e.g., point-of-sales terminals) to those where there is no perceived need and where considerable and extended sales efforts must take place prior to a sale. They range from those that are absolutely essential and critical to the customers (inventory control systems) to those that are nice but whose purchase is essentially postponable. Products at the two extremes require quite different sales approaches.

Sourcing decisions are complicated by the difference in maturity in the competitive marketplaces for suppliers of different information technologies. For example, a relatively stable competitive pattern has emerged for suppliers of large mainframe computers. Conversely the supply side is very turbulent in the microcomputer and office automation markets, with considerable uncertainty as to who the winners will be and what the form of their product offerings will be five years in the future. A competitive pattern is beginning to emerge here, but in telecommunications the AT&T divestiture has contributed to making the nature of competition very murky for the foreseeable future.

Further, in the past, monopoly control over product delivery gave IT businesses considerable discretion in timing the introduction of new products to their customers. The changed pattern of competition among suppliers means that in many organizations IT has lost control over the marketing of those products.

In terms of benefits the products range from those that can be crisply summarized in a return-on-investment (ROI) framework for the customer to those with benefits more qualitative and intangible in nature. Again, products at each end of the spectrum require a different marketing approach. Some products are absolutely structured (certain types of accounting data), while others must be tailored to influence individual tastes and preferences. Further, in many instances the complexity of the product and the inherent factors that influence quality are not easily comprehended by many purchasers. Finally, some products require tailoring during field installation. These products need quite different field support and distribution staffs than the products without adaptation requirements.

The above description of IT product characteristics points to the complexity of the IT marketing task by showing the IT business as one of distributing evolving products that are differentiated by a wide range of characteristics. In other businesses a strong effort is often made to streamline the product line to permit economy of scale in manufacturing plus focus and efficiency in distribution. The inability to accomplish this in many IT businesses has contributed to the turbulence associated with their management. Too often they are trying to deliver many different types of products from their traditional monopoly-supplier position with weak promotion, surly sales, and a fixation of being a manufacturer (as opposed to a distributor, when appropriate). What works for one set of products often does not work for another. Recognizing the need for and implementing a differentiated marketing approach is very difficult, particularly for a medium-sized IT business.

IT Consumer

The IT consumer is changing in terms of both needs and sophistication. Table 12-2 captures a number of important aspects of these changes.

TABLE 12–2   IT Consumer Profile Changes

Area	Older Consumers	Younger Consumers
Older technologies	Experienced.	Inexperienced.
Newer technologies	Leery of them.	Unsophisticated with them (but they do not know it).
Visibility	Identifiable as consumers.	Often unidentifiable as consumers; many more; at all levels in organizations.
Attitude toward IT unit	Willing to accept IT business as experts.	Often hostile to IT; want to develop their own solutions.
Self-confidence	Low confidence in their own abilities (often cautious buyers because of cost).	High confidence in their abilities and judgment (often unwarranted).
Turnover rate	High.	High.

The older consumers, after 20 years of working with the mature technologies, have some sensitivity to the problems of working within their constraints. They are often quite unaware of the newer technologies and the enormous behavioral modifications they must make to use them properly. They bring their old purchasing habits to the new environment without understanding that it is new. The younger consumers, on the other hand, have close familiarity with personal computing and are more intolerant of the inability to get immediate access to it. They also are quite naive about the problems of designing and maintaining IT systems that must run on a regular basis. This generation gap suggests that both classes of consumer have major but different personal educational needs if they are to be responsible consumers.

The new user-friendly technologies have made the problem more complicated because many consumers see the opportunity to withdraw from reliance on the IT business and set up their own small business. They are often propelled in this direction by their own entrepreneurs or purchasing agents (i.e., decentralized systems analysts) who are long on hope and short on practical firsthand expertise and realistic risk assessment.

In this world of evolving technology a real challenge to the IT marketing force is to target new consumers and reach them before they begin to make their own independent decisions. New application clusters and groups of consumers keep surfacing. The ever changing composition of consumer groups sustains the need for a field sales force. An effective sales job of educating some people does no good if they move on to other assignments and their successors are unaware of both current technologies and the particular sequence of decisions that led to the present status of their organization.

Firsthand personal computing experience and a barrage of advertising have substantially raised consumers' expectations and their general level of self-confidence in making IT decisions. Unfortunately, in many cases this confidence is misplaced, with a total lack of appreciation for subtle but important nuances and for the IT control practices necessary for a significant probability of success. This again increases the need for sustained direct sales and follow-up.

In today's environment there is an explosion in the number of potential services from which customers can make a selection. As part of this diversity, cheap external market prices seem to be another source of confusion to the end consumers (as will be discussed below). Products essentially similar to those available in-house appear to be available at much lower prices. It requires great consumer sophistication (often not present) to identify correctly a real IT bargain versus an inferior product.

These facts in composite have substantially complicated the IT marketing effort. An unstable group of consumers with diversified, rapidly changing needs requires a far higher level of direct selling effort than do consumers in environments without this cluster of characteristics. The need to spend promotion money on the difficult group has been intensified by the cultural heritage of IT in many settings. These consumers, hostile about the quality of IT support, are receptive to solutions that will carry them as far away as possible from reliance on the central IT business unit. Trained to respond correctly to many of yesterday's technologies, they are inappropriately trained for today's. Underinvestment in the marketing necessary to deal with these realities has been a major cause of dissatisfaction among users.

Cost

From a marketing viewpoint significant changes are taking place both in the cost of the product and in delivery systems to get them to the users. Table 12–3 identifies some of the major shifts. On the one hand the cost of many elements of IT hardware has dropped dramatically and is likely to continue to drop significantly in the foreseeable future. On the other hand progress in reducing the cost of developing software, while positive, has been and is likely to continue to be slow for the near future. On top of this the ability to accurately estimate in advance both development and operating costs for large, high-technology, low-structure systems continues to be both limited and disappointing.

A critical component of cost explosion has been the steady increase in the cost of maintaining already installed software. These expenses are usually not carefully factored in at the time of purchase, and they tend to grow exponentially with the passage of years as the business

TABLE 12-3 Changes in Cost Profile—from Consumer Viewpoint

Area	Past Cost	Future Cost
Hardware	Very expensive.	Very inexpensive.
Economies of scale	Major in large systems; user stand-alones not feasible in most cases.	Limited in large systems; user stand-alones very attractive.
Software	Systems development expensive.	Systems development expense down but not as much as hardware.
Software acquisitions	Limited outside opportunities.	Attractive outside opportunities.
Development and production costs	Hard to estimate accurately in advance.	Still hard to estimate accurately.
Maintenance	Expense underestimated.	A soaring cost of keeping systems alive.

grows and changes. In the short term these costs can be deferred with apparently little damage. In the long term, however, their neglect can cause a virtual collapse of the product.

The proliferation of software houses and packages and cost changes have accelerated the move of a significant portion of the IT business to the distribution of services. Specialized data bases accessible to many users can be put together in a cost-effective fashion that would be utterly uneconomic if done by single users for their own purposes, and shared software development has become very attractive. For example, not long ago a major consortium of 25 regional banks funded a joint $13 million software development project (in areas such as demand deposit accounting and savings accounts) to benefit each of them. Inability to manage the project within the consortium, however, eventually doomed it to failure. A final recent change has been the large numbers of users who have acquired their own computer capacity. (At a large eastern business school 100 percent of the students and over 90 percent of the faculty now own their own micros.)

As will be discussed in the section on pricing, it is difficult to identify actual or potential total costs for any particular product or service. In part this is because a piece of data or software development may be used to support multiple products and consumers, thus generating a concern as to whether costs should be treated as joint costs or by-product costs. Another complicating issue is the extent to which previously spent R&D costs (to get to today's skill levels) should be treated as part of a product's cost.

While cost management and control are a critical component of the IT business strategy, how they are executed will vary significantly between IT settings. High-growth, very product-competitive environments appropriately take a softer line on IT efficiency and cost control

TABLE 12–4   Changes in the IT Channels of Distribution

Area	Past Profile	Future Profile
Development	Heavy development and production role by central IT.	Significant development but lower percent of total by central IT.
Purchasing	Limited direct purchase of hardware/ software by user.	Major direct purchases of hardware/ software by user.
Service source	Individual user limited to service from large shared system.	Individual user can obtain powerful independent system for use.
Service bureaus	Sell time.	Sell products and time bundled together.
External data bases	Limited use via time-sharing.	Major use via time-sharing.
Software and processing	Only crude external services available.	Large amount of external services available.
Software development by users	Limited.	Major (packages and user-friendly languages have facilitated this).
Reliance on external contract analysts/ programmers	Very significant.	Less significant; more acquisitions of applications specialists.

than environments where the IT products are more stable and where the customer mix is more concerned with cost than product quality.

In aggregate the changing cost structure of IT *products* has forced the IT *business* to reconsider its sourcing decisions and has provided distinct impetus for the IT business to take on a much stronger distribution role. Internally the relative emphasis placed on IT cost control at the expense of product line growth and quality and of responsiveness of service to consumers depends on the IT business strategy; thus wide variances exist from one setting to another.

Channels of Distribution

As described in Chapters 2, 5, and 6 the number of channels of distribution (to users) and their relative importance have been shifting rapidly. Table 12–4 shows some of the important changes in this domain. Historically, the major channel for both manufacturing and delivering the IT product has been the IT business itself; in most firms it had a complete monopoly. Changing cost factors and shifts in user preferences have put this channel under great pressure and have caused deep concern inside the IT business as it has tried to adapt to the new challenges of a competitive market—which it cannot totally serve in a cost-effective fashion from its manufacturing facility. Adapting to a new mission the IT business is now *not* the sole channel but rather one of many sources of manufacturing, with a major new role in identification of products in other channels and assessment of cost, quality, and so on. Adaptation to this new role has been very uncomfortable psychologically (involving incorrect notions of loss of power, etc.) for many IT businesses.

Successful and rapid adaptation by the IT business is critical for the health of its present and future consumers. The new channels, while offering very attractive products and cost structures, also carry with them sizable risks in many cases. The most important of these risks include:

1. Misassessment of the real development and operations costs of the products in the channel. Important elements of short-term and, more important, long-term costs may be completely overlooked.

2. Consumer vulnerability to abuse of data by failure to control access, install documentation procedures, and implement data disciplines.

3. Financial vulnerability of the supplier. Is there a possibility of failure? If so, what are the operational implications to the consumer? Is there an easy way to protect the consumer's fundamental interests if the worst occurs?

4. Obsolescence of products. Is the supplier likely to keep the products modernized (at a suitable cost) for the consumer over the years? If not, what are the safety valves for the consumer, and are safety valves important? (Obviously, a financial transaction processing system may be more vulnerable in the long term in this regard than a decision support model.)

Considerable marketing and internal adjustment of perspectives are needed by the IT business if its consumers are to feel that they can rely on the IT staff to evaluate alternate channels objectively (instead of pushing their own manufacturing facility at every opportunity). It is probable that the long-run solution will develop knowledgeable consumers. Failure to execute this mission will ultimately cripple the IT business's effectiveness in servicing consumer needs. This will occur through fragmentation of data needed by many consumers, proliferation of redundant development efforts, and an increase in poorly conceived and managed local factories.

Competition

The IT–marketing mix analogy is weakest in describing administrative practice and problems in the area of competition. The IT business appears to have two principal competitors:

1. The consumers going their own independent way to find solutions without engaging the IT business in either its manufacturing or its distribution capacity.

2. The potential consumers failing to recognize that they have problems or opportunities that can be addressed by IT.

In the first case competition has arisen by poor performance of the IT business. Its inability to formulate and implement sensible, useful guidelines to assist consumers in purchase decisions is a failure of IT to adapt its product line to meet the needs of the changing times. For the broad purposes of the firm it may be useful to run this aspect of the IT business as a loss leader. Loss of manufacturing business to other channels in a *planned* or managed way should not be seen as a competitive loss to the IT business but simply as a restructuring of its product line to meet changing consumer needs. One of the most successful IT businesses the authors have seen has recently halved its central IT manufacturing capacity. Under the heading of general policies and controls, it has created a series of smaller manufacturing centers near major clusters of users (i.e., at divisional headquarters), including an explosion of stand-alone office automation systems with all phases of the systems life cycle except the construction phase under user control.

The second type of competition—really the cost of delayed market opportunity—arises as a result of ineffective management of price, product, or distribution policies, which permits consumers in an imperfect market to allocate funds to projects that may have less payoff than IT products. The IT business has a monopoly responsibility—sometimes producing a product, in other cases stimulating consumer awareness of appropriate external sources of supply. The notion of aggressive external competition hurting the IT business through pricing, product innovation, and creative distribution is not appropriate in this setting.

Promotion

The rapid changes in information technology plus turnover in consumers make promotion one of the most important elements of the marketing mix to manage because, unlike the previous items, it is largely within the control of IT management. Phase 2 learning by consumers is at the core of a successful IT business. Even as today's mature technologies are being delivered to consumers a strong need exists to cultivate tomorrow's consumers with tomorrow's products. Price discounts (introductory offers), branch offices (decentralized analysts), and a central IT sales force are key to making this happen.

One large multinational electronics company, for example, has a 400-person central IT manufacturing facility near corporate headquarters. Included in this staff are five international marketing representatives, who constantly promote new IT products and services. Their job consists of preparation of promotional material, organization of educational seminars, and frequent trips to countries where they have a major presence to develop a close professional relationship with consumers. These relationships have permitted both effective dissemination of services and acquisition of insight into performance of existing products and need for new products. This level of expenditure was regarded as being absolutely essential to the IT business in achieving its goals. In another firm IT management distributed seven APPLE IIs with VISICALC in the controller's department at no expense to the users to help stimulate awareness of new financial analysis technology. Six months later, the controller retroactively purchased the machines and ordered four more. Today every member of the department has a PC and a LOTUS 1-2-3 spreadsheet. This type of high-profile pilot project (or test market) to spark consumer interest is another critical promotion tool.

In large part the need to adapt is due to the recent shift in the industry. From the beginning of the industry to the late 1970s the large information systems suppliers sold primarily to the IT managers. Most vendors who initially executed a strong industrial marketing approach now have added a retail marketing one. Recently, in office automation and computers the suppliers have not only opened a series of retail stores but also are attempting to sell directly to end users. This has forced the IT business to promote the validity of its guidelines within the firm to protect the users from unintentional fiascoes.

A number of IT businesses have found it attractive to organize both their development and production control activities around market structure as opposed to manufacturing technology. In other words, rather than a traditional development group, a programming group, and a maintenance group, they have designated development staffs dedicated to specific clusters of consumers. This structure permits the development of deep, long-term relationships and better understanding and action on operation problems as they arise. The extreme of this approach was McGraw-Hill's 1984 corporate reorganization away from a media-oriented structure (paper, TV, etc.) toward an end-customer structure, each of which can be served by a mix of media. Within these market units it is appropriate to fund specific integrating and liaison positions as opposed to purely technical positions. This approach is critical since, as a result of past performance and poor marketing, the IT business is often in a worse position relative to an outside software company with its large marketing staff. Money spent this way, although large, is often among the IT unit's most important expenditures and should be the last to be cut back.

IT newsletters on new services and product announcements (that is, advertising or promotional material) should be sent to key present and potential business consumers on a regular basis. Similarly a program of IT business–conducted consumer educational programs as well as identification of appropriate external educational programs can significantly assist the marketing effort. When complemented by appropriate sales calls this can accelerate Phase 2 learning.

The mix of these promotional tools will vary widely by organizational setting. Just as industrial and consumer companies have very different promotion programs, so also should different IT units. The strategic relevance of products to consumers, the sophistication level of consumers, and the consumer geographic location are examples of items that all legitimately affect the structure of an appropriate promotion process.

Price

The selection of IT prices—an emotional and rapidly changing process, as noted in Chapter 7—is a very important element in establishing a businesslike, professional relationship between the IT business and its consumers. Indeed, aggressive pricing policies with a marketing view legitimize the concept of the stand-alone IT business. Issues that make pricing a very complicated topic include:

1. Inefficient Market. The establishment of rational and competitive criteria is very complicated for the following reasons:

a. Product quality is largely hidden and is very elusive to all but the most sophisticated and meticulous consumer. Prices that on the surface appear to be widely disparate often turn out to be quite comparable when meticulously analyzed.

b. Different vendors have very different goals, product mixes, and stability. A small vendor trying to buy into a market can come up with a very attractive price to defuse questions about his financial viability.

c. Vendors may price a service as a by-product of some other necessary business and thus produce very favorable prices in relation to a system that attempts to make each user bear a proportionate share of the full cost of the manufacturing operation. This is particularly true for in-house operations trying to dispose of excess capacity for some "financial contribution." Long-term stability should be a matter of concern to the informed consumer. (What are the implications of his output becoming the main product and the other consumer's output the by-product?)

d. Excess-capacity considerations may produce attractive *short-term* marginal prices that are not sustainable on a *long-term* basis as direct costing issues evolve into full costing ones. A variant of this is a bargain entry-level price to attract the consumer. Once captured it is then easy to elevate prices significantly. This is particularly true for large, internally developed telecommunications systems.

2. Introductory Offers.   To stimulate Phase 2 learning and long-term demand, deep discounts on early business are often appropriate to generate access to long-term profits at quite different price or cost structures, once the initial learning is completed.

3. Monopoly Issues.   Review and regulation of pricing decisions by senior management is needed in many areas because of IT's de facto monopoly position. Highly confidential data and data bases needed by multiple users in geographically remote locations are examples of IT products that cannot be supplied by manufacturers other than the IT business. It is important that the prices of these services be appropriately regulated to prevent possible abuses.

4. Unbundling.   An effective pricing strategy involves two important elements not in widespread practice. The first is the unbundling of development, maintenance, operations, and special turnaround requirements into separate packages, each having its own price. The establishment of these prices at arm's length in advance is critical in ensuring a professional relationship with the consumers. The prices need to be negotiated with as much depth and care by the IT business as contracts between outside software companies and consumers. Often this negotiation can be a useful education program to alert users to the true nature of service cost.

The second element is a need to produce understandable prices for the consumers. Prices established for reports, number of customer records, price per invoice, and so on, are much easier for the consumer to relate to than prices based on utilization of IT resource units such as CPU cycles and MIPS. The added risk (if any) of a horror-struck consumer who has just been educated in the real economic facts of life tends to be more than offset by much better communication between the IT business and the consumer.

5. Profit.   A final pricing issue, which again strains the independent-business analogy, is how far notions of a profitable business should be pressed. In the short term (in some cases even in the long term), should an IT business make a profit or even break even in some settings? Environments where consumers need a lot of education and where much Phase 1 and 2 experimentation is needed may appropriately run at a deficit for a long period of time. This issue must be resolved prior to the establishment of an appropriate pricing policy.

The establishment of an appropriate IT pricing policy is one of the most complex pricing decisions to be made in industry. An appropriate resolution, critical to establishing a healthy relationship with the consumer, involves weaving a course between monopolistic and genuine competitive issues, dealing with imperfect markets, and resolving ambiguities concerning the role of profits.

Role of the Board of Directors

A question of general interest that first surfaced in Chapter 1 is what the relationship of the firm's general management to the IT business should be. We find it useful to think of its participation as being similar to the role of a board of directors for any business. (In many situations this is given de facto recognition through the creation of an executive steering committee.) Viewing its role in this way, we believe the key tasks of general management can be summarized as follows:

1. The appointment and continued assessment of the performance of the IT chief executive officer (a normal function of the nominating committee).

2. Assuring that appropriate standards are in place and are being adhered to. This includes the receipt of appropriate reports on the subject from the IT auditor and a more cursory review from the firm's external auditors (a normal function of the audit committee).

3. Ensuring that the board is constructed to provide overall guidance to the IT business from its various interested constituencies. Unlike a publicly held firm, the IT board does not need a representation of lawyers, bankers, investment bankers, and so forth. It does need senior user managers who can and are willing to provide user perspective. (As the strategic impact of the IT business on the organization as a whole drops, the level of these managers will also appropriately drop.) At the same time, R&D and technology planning and production (IT development and operations backgrounds) need to be present to ensure feasibility of suggestions.

4. Providing broad guidance for the strategic direction of the IT business, ensuring detailed planning processes are present within the IT business, and satisfying themselves that the outputs of the planning processes fit the strategic direction. Practically, this surveillance will be executed through a combination of:

   a. General presentations to the board by IT management on market development and product planning, as well as financial plans.
   b. Review by the board of summary documentation of overall direction.
   c. Formal and informal briefings of board members by other members concerning current issues as to how the IT business is supporting (or not supporting) their legitimate business needs.

    d. Request for and receipt of internal and external reviews of these issues as they seem appropriate.

This definition of the board's role is designed to deal with the realities of members' backgrounds and availability for this kind of work in relation to the other demands on their time. Focusing on operational or technical detail is unlikely to be suitable or effective. In many settings periodic (on a one- to two-year basis) education sessions for the board members have been useful both in making them more comfortable executing their responsibilities and in bringing them up to date on broad trends within the IT business as well as in the IT industry in general.

Role of IT Chief Executive Officer

Historically a high-turnover job, the IT chief executive position is very difficult and demanding, with a steadily shifting mix of skills required to be effective over time. Critical special responsibilities that must be managed by the CEO include:

1. Maintaining board relationships personally. This includes keeping the board appropriately informed about major policy issues and problems and being fully responsive to their needs and concerns. A need for a strong link between the board and the customers exists that is not present in many settings.

2. Ensuring that the strategy-formulating processes evolve adequately and that appropriate detailed action programs are developed. As in any high-technology business, high-quality technical scanning is absolutely essential. Its interpretation is crucial and may well lead to major changes in organization, product mix, and marketing strategy. Without aggressive leadership from the top the forces of cultural inertia may cause the IT business to delay far too long.

3. Paying close attention to salary, to personnel practices, and to employee quality-of-life issues. The work force in the IT business is far more mobile and less easily replaceable than an average employee.

4. Giving high priority to factory security, more important for the IT business than for most manufacturing technologies. A single, disgruntled employee can do vast amounts of damage, often undetected for long periods of time.

5. Assuring an appropriate management balance between the marketing, manufacturing, and control parts of the business. Of the three, marketing in its broadest sense is the one most often neglected. The CEO, who often comes out of the factory and has been seared by operations fiascoes, has potentially more sensitivity to these issues than to the marketing ones. Further, since this experience was at a particular time with a particular mix of technology assimilation problems and a

particular set of control responses, the CEO's perspectives in these areas may be too narrow and inappropriate for the current challenges.

6. Developing an IT esprit. A key factor in the success of the IT business is its belief in the value and potential of IT for the profit of the firm. Senior IT managers must develop team spirit and lead their organizations into new ventures with enthusiasm. At the same time, they must earn the confidence of the board by good judgment—not only taking risks but also making wise decisions on where to limit the market or when to knowingly forgo a useful technology. If they assess that the customer is not ready they must balance keeping abreast versus the receptiveness of the market.

Summary

The above discussion captures, we believe, several important complicating aspects of the IT business. Complex and shifting products, changing consumers, new major channels of distribution, and evolving cost structures have forced a major reanalysis and redirection both of IT's product offerings and its marketing efforts. This changed marketing environment is not only very complex to manage but has forced significant changes in the IT factory, organization, appropriate control systems and most fundamentally its perception of its strategic mission. Ted Levitt's great classic "Marketing Myopia"[2] best captured this as he noted that the great growth business of the 19th century—the railroads—languished because the managers saw themselves in the *railroad* rather than in the *transportation* business. The analogy here is that IT is not in the electronic-based computer, telecommunications, or office automation business. Rather it is in the business of bringing a sustained stream of innovation in information technology to change the company's internal operations and in many cases (banks, American Express, etc.) also its external products. Far too many directors of IT businesses myopically believe they are running a computer center. Failure to perceive and act on their broader role will lead to a collapse of their operations, probable loss of jobs, and great disservice to the customer base.

When IT is defined in this way the dynamism in the elements of the successful marketing mix in the late-1980s suddenly snaps into focus. Reliance on existing product structure, more efficient ways of delivering the old technology, and old organizations is a recipe for an uncontrolled dissolution of the IT business. The IT organization has been a change agent to its customers for 30 years. The change agent itself, however, must change to be relevant.

---

[2]Theodore Levitt, "Marketing Myopia," *Harvard Business Review*, September–October 1975.

General Management Library for the IT Manager

Ackoff, Russell L. *Creating the Corporate Future: Plan or Be Planned For.* New York: John Wiley & Sons, 1981.

An important book which provides a broad context for IT planning.

Anthony, Robert N. *Planning and Control Systems—A Framework for Analysis.* Boston: Division of Research, Harvard Graduate School of Business Administration, 1965.

This book introduces the framework of operational control, management control, and strategic planning that has been a major contributor to thinking about the different areas of IT application and their different management problems.

Anthony, Robert N., and James S. Reece. *Accounting Principles.* Homewood, Ill.: Richard D. Irwin, 1979.

This comprehensive treatment of current accounting and management control thinking is very relevant to a broad consideration of IT management control problems.

Beer, Michael. *Organizational Change and Development: A Systems View.* Santa Monica, Calif.: Goodyear Publishing, 1980.

A thoughtful, useful discussion by a leading practitioner/academician on managing organizational change.

Bower, Joseph L. *Managing the Resource Allocation Process—A Study of Corporate Planning and Investment.* Boston: Division of Research, Harvard Graduate School of Business Administration, 1970.

This in-depth analysis of corporate planning and capital budgeting provides critical insights relevant to both the role of steering committees and how IT planning can be effectively done.

Buzzell, Robert D., ed. *Marketing in an Electronic Age.* Boston: Harvard Business School Press, 1985.

A series of essays on how information technology will impact the marketing function.

Chandler, Alfred. *Strategy and Structure: Chapters in the History of the Industrial Enterprise.* Cambridge, Mass.: MIT Press, 1967.

This classic by the preeminent business historian examines the inexorable relationship between corporate strategy and its organization structure.

The book's insights are relevant to many facets of IT organization and planning.

Christensen, C. Roland; Kenneth R. Andrews; and Joseph L. Bower. *Business Policy: Text and Cases.* Homewood, Ill.: Richard D. Irwin, 1986.

This classic book on business policy provides important context for how IT planning should be done and its links to corporate planning.

Ennis, Ben M., and Keith Cox, eds. *Marketing Classics: A Selection of Influential Articles.* 4th ed. Boston: Allyn & Bacon, 1981.

A collection of the best of current marketing literature, it provides a series of insights on how best to market the IT business.

Heskett, James L. *Managing in the Service Economy.* Boston: Harvard Business School Press, 1986.

Practical advice on the issues in managing a service organization. Much of this advice translates directly to the IT resource.

Kimberly Miles and Associates. *The Organizational Life Cycle.* San Francisco: Jossey-Bass, 1981.

Reports, findings, and analyses of key issues concerning the creation, transformation, and decline of organizations.

Lawrence, Paul R., and Jay W. Lorsch. *Organization and Environment: Managing Integration and Differentiation.* Boston: Division of Research, Harvard Graduate School of Business Administration, 1967.

This classic presents the underlying thinking of the need for specialized departments and how they should interface with the rest of the organization. It is relevant for all IT organizational decisions.

Merchant, Kenneth A. *Control in Business Organizations.* Marshfield, Mass.: Pitman Publishing, 1986.

An excellent framework for thinking about contemporary management control issues.

Porter, Michael E. *Competitive Advantage: Creating and Sustaining Superior Performance.* New York: Free Press, 1985.

The comprehensive text on how to identify and achieve competitive advantage.

Porter, Michael E., ed. *Competition in Global Industries.* Boston: Harvard Business School Press, 1986.

A series of articles relating to competitive issues in the international environment.

Schein, Edgar H. *Organizational Psychology.* 3rd ed. Englewood Cliffs, N.J.: Prentice-Hall, 1980.

This classic book on the field focuses on how to manage the tension between the individual and the organization.

Simon, Herbert A. *Administrative Behavior: A Study of Decision-Making Processes in Administrative Organization.* New York: Free Press, 1976.

This classic destroys many of the traditional notions of administrative behavior and introduces more powerful and useful ones. Its generalizations are applicable to all aspects of the IT business.

Skinner, Wickham. *Manufacturing in the Corporate Strategy.* New York: John Wiley & Sons, 1978.

This very broad and powerful book on manufacturing strategy provides critical insights for how the IT operations function should be viewed and managed.

Vancil, Richard F. *Decentralization: Managerial Ambiguity by Design.* Homewood, Ill.: Dow Jones–Irwin, 1979.

A study of the managerial issues posed by decentralizing a firm's operations. It provides valuable context for IT organizational and management control decisions.

Warren, E. Kirby. *Long-Range Planning: The Executive Viewpoint.* Englewood Cliffs, N.J.: Prentice-Hall, 1966.

The classic in corporate planning, it provides valuable insights to how IT planning can be conducted.

IT Library for the General Manager

Ackoff, R. L. "Management Misinformation System." *Management Science,* vol. 14, no. 4 (December 1967), pp. B140–B156.

A classic, this article provides an early categorization of the real management issues in IT administration.

Blumenthal, S. *MIS—A Framework for Planning and Development.* Englewood Cliffs, N.J.: Prentice-Hall, 1969.

This is the first book on IT planning which gave the subject a comprehensive and realistic treatment.

Davis, Gordon B. *Management Information Systems: Conceptual Foundations, Structure and Development.* New York: McGraw-Hill, 1978.

A good treatment of contemporary IT technology.

Davis, William S., and McCormack, A. *The Information Age.* Reading, Mass.: Addison-Wesley Publishing, 1979.

A well-written introduction to the jargon of computer-based systems and their important issues.

Gorry, G. A., and M. S. Scott-Morton. "A Framework for Management Information Systems." *Sloan Management Review,* vol. 13, no. 1 (1971), pp. 55–70.

A classic article which lays out the domain for IT technology application. It clearly identifies why the IT applications of the 1980s provide such different problems from the 1970s.

Lucas, Henry C., Jr. *Information Systems Concepts for Management.* New York: McGraw-Hill, 1978.

A useful guide on how to think about IT management issues.

Hussain, Donna, and K. M. Hussain. *Information Processing Systems for Management.* Homewood, Ill.: Richard D. Irwin, 1985.

A good conventional treatment of what the elements of IT technology are and how to approach their management.

Maciariello, Joseph. *Program Management Control Systems.* New York: John Wiley & Sons, 1978.

A contemporary analysis of how to manage the project life cycle to ensure good results in IT projects.

"Managing and Using Computers," *Harvard Business Review,* no. 21340, reprint series, 1981.

A compendium of recent *HBR* articles on IT management, it covers from a broad perspective many of the key IT management issues.

Martin, James. Introduction to Teleprocessing. Englewood Cliffs, N.J.: Prentice-Hall, 1972.

A primer on the basics of communication technology.

McLean, Ephraim R., and John V. Soden, *Strategic Planning for MIS.* New York: John Wiley & Sons, 1977.

A comprehensive and relevant treatment of IT planning issues and how it can be done more effectively.

Nolan, Richard L. *Managing the Data Resource Function.* 2d ed. St. Paul, Minn.: West Publishing, 1982.

A collection of classics which influenced current IT management thinking.

Rodgers, William. *Think: A Biography of the Watsons and IBM.* New York: Mentor Books, 1974.

Sayles, Leonard, and Margaret Chandler. *Managing Large Systems—Organization for the Future.* New York: Harper & Row, 1971.

A comprehensive treatment of the project management insights gained in the Apollo Moon Program. It is invaluable for the manager concerned with large complex IT projects.

Scott-Morton, Michael, and Peter Keen. *Decision Support Systems.* Reading, Mass.: Addison-Wesley Publishing, 1978.

This book identifies the type of systems which have followed the large transaction-oriented ones and their special managerial issues. This has been followed by a number of working papers by the authors and others under the auspices of MIT's Center for Information Systems Research (CISR).

Synnot, William R., and William H. Gruber. *Information Resource Management—Opportunities and Strategies for the 1980s.* New York: John Wiley & Sons, 1981.

A contemporary analysis of the tactical approaches to ensuring a successful MIS operation.

Case Index

Air Products and Chemicals, Inc.: Local Area Network (A), 535
Air Products and Chemicals, Inc.: Local Area Network (B), 557
Alcon Laboratories: Information Technology Group, 338
American Hospital Supply Corporation (A): The ASAP System, 217

Concordia Casting Company, 469
Corning Glass Works: Information Systems Planning, 639

Finnpap/Finnboard, 587
Frito-Lay, Inc.: Funding for Information Systems, 399
Frontier Airlines, Inc., 17

General Foods: Information Services Department, 282

Hercules Incorporated: Anatomy of a Vision, 42

IBM Europe Headquarters, 515
Intercontrol Chemical Corporation, 411

Jet Age Travel, 235

Manufacturers Hanover Corporation: Worldwide Network, 163
Mark Twain Bancshares, Inc. (1980) (A), 92
Mark Twain Bancshares, Inc. (1980) (B), 107
Mark Twain Bancshares, Inc. (1980) (C), 110
Mishawaka Industries, Inc., 357

OTISLINE, 146

PlanPower: The Financial Planning Expert System, 301

Rogers Automotive Company, 447

Index

Administrative overhead, and IOS participation
    level, 214
After sales service, and the value chain, 132
Air Products and Chemicals, Inc.
    Local Area Network (A) (case), 535–56
    Local Area Network (B) (case), 557–66
    position analysis, 278–81
Alcon Laboratories, Information Technology Group
    (case), 338–56
Allen, B., 396 n
Allocated cost center
    allocation problems, 382–84
    desirable characteristics, 384–85
    maintenance and development charges, 386–87
American Hospital Supply Corporation (A), the
    ASAP System (case), 217–34
Analysis of IOS impact, 206–7
Anthony, Robert N., 383 n, 620 n
Apple II, 567, 670
Argyris, Chris, 80 n, 260 n
Assimilation of IT, stages of, 260–64
Athos, A., 210 n, 211 n
Audit
    audit function, 396–97
    in multinational IT, 585–86
    and planning, 498–99
    technology, 498–99

Balance
    efficiency-effectiveness, 485
    between innovation and control, 267, 319, 336, 378–
        79, 397–98
    between long- and short-term issues, 277
Balance of power
    among management groups, 72
    among suppliers, 127–28
    buyer-supplier, and IOS, 201
Barrett, S., 204 n
Base increment, 392, 394
Buchanan, Jack R., 333 n

Burns, T., 260 n, 264 n, 265 n, 268 n
Business processes, changes in response to IOS, 210
Buss, Martin D. J., 143 n, 499 n

CAD/CAM (Computer aided design and
    manufacturing), 72, 75, 495
Capacity planning, 500–503, 507, 509, 511
    in multinational IT, across time zones, 578
    and system response time, 325
Cash, James I., 639 n
CD-ROM (compact disk read-only memory), 127
Centralization
    of development function, 327–28
    of decision making in multinational IT, 580–81
Centralization of hardware
    and control of data, 272
    and technology, 271–72
Chandler, Alfred, 2
Change
    costs of, 501–2
    internal, and IOS implementation, 211–12
    rate of, and IOS, 203
    response to external forces, 377
    structural, 209, 216, 251–55
    technological, 251–52
Chargeout
    consistency and fairness, 384
    and cost analysis, 331
    critical issues in design of, 384
    predictability of, 383
    problems with, 374, 376
Competitive advantage
    forces affecting, 121, 206
    from IOS, 204–6, 209
    risks of success in using IT, 135–36
    strategic perspective on, 120
Competitive strategy, 631–33
    competitive analysis (ICA) framework, 120, 206
    and differentiation, 208
    focus, 208–9

Computing (DP), 79
Concordia Casting Company (case), 469–82
Construction
  of information systems, 491
  phase of systems life cycle, 85
Contingency approach, 3, 438–46
Control architecture, 380–90
  allocated cost center, 382–87
  and corporate culture, 377–78
  investment center, 387
  profit center, 386–87
  unallocated cost center, 380–81
Control phase of IT assimilation, 264
  new technology installation, 269
  structure for, 265
Control process, 390–96
  and budget deviations, 391
  evaluating new applications, 376
  financial reporting, 390–92
  nonfinancial reporting, 395–96
  and participation in IOS, 215
  and technology use phase, 263
Coordination of evolving technologies, 71–72
Copeland, Duncan, 587 n
Corning Glass Works, Information Systems Planning
  (case), 639–58
Corporate culture, 3
  and centralized IT, 272–73
  and intraorganizational technology transfer,
    268–69
  and IT planning, 336
  and management control, 374, 376–80
  and multinational IT, 582–83
  and phases of assimilation of IT, 265
  and planning, 14, 622, 633–34
  and project management, 446
Corporate organization; *see also* Senior management
  and General management
  infrastructure and changing technology, 133
  and multinational IT, 576–77
Cost analysis and centralized IT control, 330–31
Cost leadership
  cost reduction, 126–27
  and IOS in competitive strategy, 208
Costs
  development and maintenance for IOS, 214
  of flexible systems, 87
  hardware, 252, 274
  of IT, 665–67
  of systems as operations issue, 375
CPU (central processing unit), size and
  administration, 270–71
Critical path method, 441

Curley, Kathleen, 262 n
Customer service in value chains, 132

Data base system (DBS), 329–30
  and IT control, 329
DDP (distributed data processing), distinguishing
  from IOS, 205
Decision support systems
  contrast with operations systems, 333
  management as user, 89–90
Design of information systems, 491
  design phase of systems life cycle, 84–85
Development
  centralization of function, 327–28
  prototyping and applications focus, 7
Differentiation
  and competitive advantage, 126–27
  and IOS in competitive strategy, 208
Directional software, 141
Discretionary increment, 392
Distributed data processing (DDP), distinguishing
  from IOS, 205
Distributed IT
  and data, 274–75
  and human resources, 275
  and management control, 273–74
  and organizational fit, 275, 326
  and technology, 274
DSS (decision support systems)
  contrast with operations systems, 333
  management as user, 89–90

Efficiency and innovation, 267, 397–98
Emerging technologies (ET), 260, 266–69
Entry barriers
  and competitive advantage, 124
  lowering through systems use, 136–37
Environment, 9–10, 253–54
  categories of strategic relevance, 77–79
  and innovative phase activities, 267
  operations, 484–87
  and organization of IT, 253
ET (emerging technology), 260, 266–69
Evaluation
  of DSS, 6
  of expenditures for IT, 143–44
  performance measures, 11, 485
  questions for, 7–9, 15
  on return-on-investment (ROI) basis, 374
  of software vendors, 502
Evolution of components of ITs, 255–59

Facilitator
  role of emerging technology manager, 267
  role of IOS, 205
Factory environment, 78
Feasibility study and IT control, 328–29
Financial reporting
  periodic reporting, 394–95
  zero-based budgeting, 391, 392–94
Finnpap/Finnboard (case), 587–613
Flexibility, 81
  and innovation, 265
Flexible manufacturing, 208
Focus
  of applications, 6
  competitive strategy, 208–9
  focused factory, 507
  focused group, 486
  focused services, 487
Frito-Lay, Inc., Funding for Information Systems
    (case), 399–410
Frontier Airlines, Inc. (case), 17–41

Gale, Edward G., 274 n
GANTT chart, 508
General Foods, Information Services Department
    (case), 282–300
General management
  as board of directors for IT, 673
  emerging technology structure, 266–69
  flexibility, 81
  participation in IOS planning, 212
  partnership with IT, 144
  and power balance, 89–90
  risk assessment by, 430
  support and policy overview, 334–37
  and two-culture problem, 5
  and ZBB, 393
Generic strategies
  for competitive advantage, 122–23
  and IOS, 207
Geographic structure, and corporate culture, 377
Gibson, Cyrus F., 80 n, 260 n, 430 n
Gogan, Janis L., 357 n, 447 n
Goldstein, David K., 338 n, 515 n
Gremillion, Lee L., 274 n
Grosch's law, 274

Hardware; *see also* Centralization of hardware *and*
    Distributed IT
  costs, 252
  patterns of distribution, 269–76
Harvard Business School, 163 n

Hercules Incorporated, Anatomy of a Vision (case),
    42–69
Human resources, 324
  for the audit function, 397
  and centralized IT, 272
  changes in response to IOS, 210
  and distributed IT, 275
  human issues in managing, 505–6
  for IT, 253
  and IT control, 327–28
  managing, 503–6
  for multinational IT, 571–72
  and operations changes, 485
  selecting managers, 505
  staff rotation in multinational IT, 583–84
  and use of changing technologies, 133–34

IBM
  Europe Headquarters (case), 515–34
  and multinational market, 572
Impact statement, assessing competitor risks, 140
Implementation
  of information systems, 492
  phase of systems life cycle, 85–86
  risk and project management, 12–13
Inbound logistics in value chain, 130–31
Incremental growth of systems, 322, 328
Industry structure and IOS, 209
Information entry and receipt, 213–14
  as IOS participation level, 213
Information hygiene, 331
Information technology, and sourcing decisions, 492
Innovation
  and allocated cost center, 382
  and efficiency, 397–98
  flexibility, 265
  phase of IT assimilation, 264, 266–69
  structure for, 265
  and unallocated cost centers, 380
  by users, and productivity, 322–23
Integrated management, of information technologies,
    79
Integration
  and cost control in manufacturing, 75
  internal, and project management, 442
  of ITs, 255–59
  of technologies, 11
Intellectual technology, 4
Intercontrol Chemical Corporation (case), 411–27
Interorganizational systems (IOS), 201
Investment center, 387–88
IOS (interorganizational systems) defined, 202–4

IT as a business, 14–15
  competition, 668–69
  consumer relations, 663–65
  costs, 665–67
  distribution, 667–68
  marketing mix, 661–73
  price, 215, 375–76, 388–90, 671–73
  product, 661–63
  promotion, 669–71
  role of the board of directors, 673–74
  role of chief executive officer, 674–75
IT management
  and the budget system, 391
  control, pressures toward, 327–31
  and flexibility, 81
  and implementation risk, 437
  management audit, defined, 71
  and planning, 633
  policy issues, 660
  and power balance, 88
  risk assessment, 430
  role evaluating benefits of projects, 141
IT-user coordination, 5–6

Jet Age Travel (Condensed) (case), 235–49
Job shop, 508–9
Justification
  effectiveness as key measure, 10
  for IOS, 203–4
  new techniques for, 374
  return-on-investment (ROI), 141
Just-in-time, 130, 208
  and supplier communication, 201

Kaufman, Felix, 201 n
Keen, Peter, 6 n
Konsynski, Benn R., 204 n

Labor force; *see* Human resources
Language
  and communication in IT, 5
  and organizational structure, 265
Leadership style, for
  control phase of technology assimilation, 269
  innovation phase of emerging technology, 266
Leavitt, Harold J., 79 n
Levitt, Theodore, 675
Lewin, Kurt, 80 n
Life-cycle
  control, 493–98
  product development, 321
  project planning, 442
  systems, 261–64, 490

Linguistic differences, 5
  and organizational structure, 265
Linowes, Richard G., 333 n
Litigation, 216
  as a risk of success, 137–38
Lotus 1-2-3, 670

McFarlan, F. Warren, 469 n, 587 n
McFarlan, William, 146 n
McKenney, James L., 163 n, 274 n, 301 n
Magnetic ink character (MICR) sets, standards for, 203
Magnetic strips, standards for, 203
Maintenance
  managing, 87
  systems, and competitive advantage, 139
  user, 325, 492
Make-or-buy decisions, 72, 324–25, 328, 330–31, 375, 485–87, 490–92
  key factors affecting, 82–83
Management control, 12
  and budgeting system, 390
  of distributed IT, 273
  and evaluation of performance, 374, 485
  and hardware decisions, 270–71
  inputs for, 374–75
  objectives for, 373–74
  of risk, 436–37
Management issues
  deployment of IT resources, 276–77
  emerging technology, 267
  information hygiene, 331–33
  innovation, 264–65, 322
  integrating ITs, 259
Manufacturers Hanover Corporation, Worldwide Network (case), 163–99
March, James S., 264 n, 268 n
Marketing and distribution
  and strategic impact of IT, 72–73
  and the value chain, 131–32
Mark Twain Bancshares, Inc. (1980) (Condensed)
  (A) (case), 92–106
  (B) (case), 107–9
  (C) (case), 110–18
Merchant, Kenneth A., 439 n
Methodologies for project management, 13
MICR (magnetic ink character reader), 203
Miles, R., 267 n
Millar, Victor E., 129 n
Mishawaka Industries, Inc. (case), 357–71
Motivation for new systems, and risk management, 140

Multinational IT
  corporate factors affecting, 575–79
  corporate organization, 576–77
  data export controls, 573–74
  deployment of resources, 277
  distributed structures, 275–76
  diversity by country, 569–71
  information systems (multinational IT), 569
  national environments, 571–75
  operations, 13
  policy issues, 579–86
  staff planning, 583–84
  strategic impact, 576
  technology transfer in, 581–82
  telecommunications environment, 253–54

New technology installation, 269
Nolan, Richard L., 80 n, 260 n, 430 n
Nonfinancial reporting process, 395–96

OA (office automation), 79
Objectives, for management control system, 373–74
O'Callaghan, Ramon, 447 n
Operation of IT system
  capacity, 500–503
  human resources for, 503–6
  management control, 375
  phase of systems life cycle, 86
Operations strategy, 487–98
  decision authority, 492–93
  externally sourced services, 490–92
  focused groups, 486
  IT architecture, 488–90
  key issues in, 488
  life-cycle control, 493–98
  system design, 490
  value chain analysis, 130–31
Organizational fit
  and distributed systems, 326
  and IT control, 330
Organization issues
  flexibility, 81
  impact of IOS, 209–12
Organizational learning, 72, 79–81
  maturity/technology transfer, 81
  and new technology introduction, 260
  rationalization/management control, 81
  technological learning and adaptation, 81
  technology indentification and investment, 80
  and user control, 326

Otis Elevator Company, 146 n
OTISLINE (case), 146–62
Outbound logistics in the value chain, 131

Parsons, Gregory L., 235 n
Participants (IOS), 204–5
  costs borne by, 215
  internal changes in, 209–12
  profiles, 212–14
Pascale, R. J., 210 n, 211 n
Personal computer, 670
  IBM, 136
Performance specification, and systems success, 86
Periodic reporting, 394
Personnel; see Human resources
PERT (program evaluation and review technique)
  chart, 441
Planning, 13–14
  benefit limitations of, 621–22
  change, 616
  and competitive strategy, 631-33
  and confidentiality, 143
  and corporate culture, 622, 634
  and corporate environmental factors, 633–36
  corporate and IT horizons, 378
  data use and stand-alone systems, 329–30
  evaluating expenditures, 143–44
  and implementation risk, 13
  and management climate, 628–30
  phases of, 264
  for phases of technology assimilation, 618–21
  questions for process of, 144–45
  as resource drain, 622
  strategic impact, 621, 625–28, 637–38
  and strategic issues, 618
  and technology changes, 498–500, 616–17
  and turnaround, 624
  use of scarce resources, 617–18
PlanPower: The Financial Planning Expert System
  (case), 301–18
Policy group, corporate, key functions, 334–35
Policy issues
  in IT management, 660
  in multinational IT, 579–86
Porter, Leslie R., 282 n, 357 n, 447 n
Porter, Michael E., 2, 120 n, 129 n, 206 n, 631 n
Portfolio, risk, 437–38
Power balance, 88–90
Process manufacturing, 509–11
Product development
  and competitive advantage, 128
  life cycle and computer-aided design (CAD), 321

Production, control, 511–12
Production planning, 506–12
    job shop versus process manufacturing, 508–11
    objectives for, 506
    priorities, 507–8
Product structure in the value chain, 130–31
Profit center, 386
Program evaluation and review technique (PERT), 441
Project
    life cycle, 262, 442, 492
    types of, 84
Project management, 12–13
    contingency approach, 438–46
    high structure-high technology, 441–43
    high structure-low technology, 439–41
    low structure-high technology, 444–45
    low structure-low technology, 443–44
    tools for, 439
Prototyping, in the design process, 85
Public policy issues, 137–38, 216
Pyburn, Philip, 616 n, 639 n

Quality control, 509–11
Reece, James S., 383 n
Regulation
    and IOS, 202, 205
    as a risk of success, 137–38
Reponen, Tapio, 587 n
Resistance to change, 269, 377, 511
Response time, of
    central systems, 325
    IT and user dominance, 323–24
Retailing, strategic impact of IT, 75
Risk
    assessing competitor risk, 138–41
    assessment, 432–37
    assessment questionnaire, 434–36
    and capacity management, 501
    consequences of, 431
    implementation, 12–13
    of information systems success, 135–45
    inherent, 431–32
    of low structure-high technology projects, 444
    and multinational issues, 567
    portfolio profile, 437–38
    project implementation, 430–32
    and project structure, 432
Rogers Automotive Company (case), 447–68
Rosenbloom, Richard, 2

Schein, Edgar, 80 n, 260 n
Schon, D.A., 260 n
Scott-Morton, Michael, 6 n
Security, 512–13
Senior management
    and the budget system, 391
    and control tensions in IT, 331
    critical questions about IT, 7–9
    and direction of IT, 334
    focus for assessing strategic impact of IT, 141
    and implementation risk, 437
    and operations strategy, 487
    and strategic planning, 625–28
    support for auditing functions, 397
Simon, Herbert A., 264 n, 268 n
Skills, defined as one of Seven S's, 211
Skinner, Wickham, 2, 486 n
Smith, C. A., 488
Snow, C.P., 5
Software
    costs, 330–31
    as depreciable asset, 87, 387, 502
    development and maintenance, 214
    directional, 141
    externally developed, 490–91
    in management control, 375
Staff, defined as one of Seven S's, 211
Stagnation
    due to implementation failure, 262–63
    and excessive control, 263
    and learning failure, 262–63
Stalker, G. M., 260 n, 264 n, 265 n, 268 n
Stand-alone computer systems, 324–25
Standards
    and control, 215
    and industry structure, 209
    for information exchange, 203
    in multinational IT, 580
    software, in multinational IT, 581
Stoddard, Donna, 146 n
Strategic environment, 77
Strategic impact, 71, 72–78
    capacity planning, 511
    and corporate culture, 379
    and innovation decisions, 319
    of IOS, 202
    IT operations, 511
    of IT and planning, 637–38
    and management control, 375
    motivation for system, 140
    of multinational IT, 576

Strategic impact—*Cont.*
  of new technology use planning, 619
  and planning, 621–24, 625–28
  questions for evaluating, 124–28
  of user-need, 321
Strategic issues
  for IOS participation, 215
  and planning, 618
  for using IT resources, 277
  vulnerability and supplier links, 120
Strategic planning
  and IOS, 207
  and IT staff, 144
  relevance, 3
  roles in, 14
Strategy, defined, 211
Structural change, 214
Structure, defined, 211
Style, defined, 211
Superordinate goals, 212
  defined, 211
Supplier
  balance of power, 127
  links, risks of independence, 138
Support environment, 78–79
Sviokla, John J., 163 n, 301 n
Switching costs, 125–27
  and IOS participation level, 213
  risks of lowering through customer services,
    138–39
Systems, defined, 211
Systems life cycle, 72, 83–88, 490
  adapting a technology, 262
  construction step, 85
  design, 254
  design of traditional project, 84
  diffusion of technology, 263–64
  extending uses of technology, 263
  implementation phase, 85–86
  introducing a technology, 261
  maintenance, 86–87
  operation phase, 86

Technology
  audit, 498–99
  development, use of IT for, 134
  planning, 498–500
  and system life cycle, 261
Technology transfer, 3
  intraorganizational, 267–68
  in multinational IT, 581–82

Telecommunications (TP), 79
  worldwide environment, 213
Time horizon
  for IT management, 373
  and management control, 378–79
  of ZBB, 394
Transfer pricing
  for allocated cost center, 388
  cost-based price, 388–89
  market-based price, 389
  negotiated price, 390
  split-level price, 389–90
Turnaround
  environment, 77–78
  and planning, 624

Unallocated cost center, 380
Universal product code (UPC), standards for, 203
User
  and the budget system, 391
  and corporate culture, 376–77
  and distributed environment, 274
  dominance, 320, 323–27, 376–77
  and externally sourced services, 491
  feasibility studies, 328–29
  and low structure-low technology projects, 443
  priorities, 319–20
  responsibilities, 333–34
User control, 325–26
  and central staff support, 328
  and implementation acceptance, 321
  and organizational fit, 326
User management
  demand and supply imbalance, 254
  free market in IT, 10
  maintenance, user-designed applications, 87
  planning and user experience, 14
  and power balance, 89
  structures, 267

Value chain analysis, 128–34
Vancil, Richard, 2
Vendors, evaluating, 502
VisiCalc, 670
Vitale, Michael R., 17 n, 42 n, 92 n, 107, 110 n, 135 n,
    217 n, 235 n, 399 n, 535 n, 557 n

Ware, James P., 469 n
Warren, Kirby, 2
Whisler, Thomas L., 79 n

TABLE VI Cumulative *t*-distribution $F(t)$

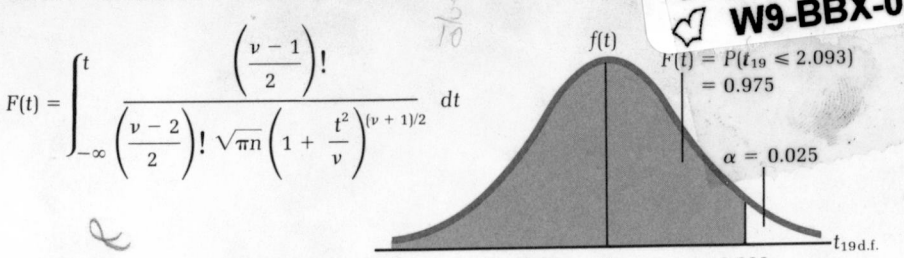

$$F(t) = \int_{-\infty}^{t} \frac{\left(\frac{v-1}{2}\right)!}{\left(\frac{v-2}{2}\right)! \sqrt{\pi n}\left(1 + \frac{t^2}{v}\right)^{(v+1)/2}}\, dt$$

$F(t) = P(t_{19} \leq 2.093)$
$= 0.975$

$\alpha = 0.025$

Example; $n = 20$, $v = 19$

$F(t)$	.75	.90	.95	.975	.99	.995	.9995
v (α)	(.25)	(.10)	(.05)	(.025)	(.01)	(.005)	(.0005)
1	1.000	3.078	6.314	12.706	31.821	63.657	636.619
2	.816	1.886	2.920	4.303	6.965	9.925	31.598
3	.765	1.638	2.353	3.182	4.541	5.841	12.941
4	.741	1.533	2.132	2.776	3.747	4.604	8.610
5	.727	1.476	2.015	2.571	3.365	4.032	6.859
6	.718	1.440	1.943	2.447	3.143	3.707	5.959
7	.711	1.415	1.895	2.365	2.998	3.499	5.405
8	.706	1.397	1.860	2.306	2.896	3.355	5.041
9	.703	1.383	1.833	2.262	2.821	3.250	4.781
10	.700	1.372	1.812	2.228	2.764	3.169	4.587
11	.697	1.363	1.796	2.201	2.718	3.106	4.437
12	.695	1.356	1.782	2.179	2.681	3.055	4.318
13	.694	1.350	1.771	2.160	2.650	3.012	4.221
14	.692	1.345	1.761	2.145	2.624	2.977	4.140
15	.691	1.341	1.753	2.131	2.602	2.947	4.073
16	.690	1.337	1.746	2.120	2.583	2.921	4.015
17	.689	1.333	1.740	2.110	2.567	2.898	3.965
18	.688	1.330	1.734	2.101	2.552	2.878	3.922
19	.688	1.328	1.729	2.093	2.539	2.861	3.883
20	.687	1.325	1.725	2.086	2.528	2.845	3.850
21	.686	1.323	1.721	2.080	2.518	2.831	3.819
22	.686	1.321	1.717	2.074	2.508	2.819	3.792
23	.685	1.319	1.714	2.069	2.500	2.807	3.767
24	.685	1.318	1.711	2.064	2.492	2.797	3.745
25	.684	1.316	1.708	2.060	2.485	2.787	3.725
26	.684	1.315	1.706	2.056	2.479	2.779	3.707
27	.684	1.314	1.703	2.052	2.473	2.771	3.690
28	.683	1.313	1.701	2.048	2.467	2.763	3.674
29	.683	1.311	1.699	2.045	2.462	2.756	3.659
30	.683	1.310	1.697	2.042	2.457	2.750	3.646
40	.681	1.303	1.684	2.021	2.423	2.704	3.551
60	.679	1.296	1.671	2.000	2.390	2.660	3.460
120	.677	1.289	1.658	1.980	2.358	2.617	3.373
$\infty(z_\alpha)$	.674	1.282	1.645	1.960	2.326	2.576	3.291

* This table is abridged from the "Statistical Tables" of R. A. Fisher and Frank Yates published by Oliver & Boyd, Ltd., Edinburgh and London, 1938. It is here published with the kind permission of the authors and their publishers.

STATISTICAL
ANALYSIS
for Business and Economics

ADDISON-WESLEY PUBLISHING COMPANY

Reading, Massachusetts ▪ Menlo Park, California ▪ Don Mills, Ontario
Wokingham, England ▪ Amsterdam ▪ Sydney ▪ Singapore
Tokyo ▪ Mexico City ▪ Bogotá ▪ Santiago ▪ San Juan

STATISTICAL ANALYSIS

for Business and Economics

THIRD EDITION

DONALD L. HARNETT

Indiana University

JAMES L. MURPHY

University of North Carolina / Chapel Hill

Cindy M. Johnson: Sponsoring Editor
ARVAK: Illustrator
Hugh Crawford: Manufacturing Supervisor
Melinda Grosser: Text and Cover Designer
Martha K. Morong: Production Manager
Michael Sklar: Developmental Editor
Joseph K. Vetere: Art Editor
West Light/Bill Ross: Cover Photographer
Barbara Willette: Production and Copy Editor

Library of Congress Cataloging in Publication Data

Harnett, Donald L.
    Statistical analysis for business
    and economics.

    Bibliography: p.
    Includes index.
    1. Economics—Statistical methods.
2. Commercial statistics.   3. Statistics.
I. Murphy, James L., 1939–
II. Title.
HB137.H376 1985   519.5′024658   84–18502
ISBN 0–201–10683–3

A B C D E F G H I J – DO – 8 9 8 7 6 5

To Jan
and Linda

PURPOSE AND APPROACH

Readability, understandability, and organization have been our major concerns throughout the writing, classroom testing, and revisions of this textbook. Designed for use in a beginning statistics course for students of business and economics, it provides a mixture of intuitive explanation, relevant examples, and mathematical rigor. Our approach avoids the verbiage of many texts in attempting to explain basic concepts. We present the single best way in which we can explain the material, and we enhance each point with numerous examples.

Although some texts include many diverse and unrelated examples that distract the reader from the statistical concepts and methodology being presented, we have selected examples that are realistic without being overly complex. Students need not have completed courses in business and economics in order to wade through our examples of how to use statistical methods. Rather we expect that students are learning statistical analysis prior to using it in their major field courses. Furthermore, we keep the numerical busywork to a minimum in ex-

PREFACE

amples (and in problems, too). Examples and problems were chosen to illustrate realistic and practical uses of the topics and thereby maintain a high level of motivation for the reader.

Throughout the presentation we have tried to avoid compromising any mathematical concepts and to provide sufficient depth for a worthwhile understanding of them. However, our presentation of the statistical methods is truly designed for the beginning student and is less mathematically demanding than that of many texts with the same prescribed entry level of college algebra. The reader is expected to be familiar with some standard mathematical symbology, including the familiar notation for summations and for functions. The material in Appendix B presents a review of these fundamentals. It is not assumed that the reader has studied calculus, although there are occasions when the explanation indicates how calculus could be used. In some instances, complementary explanations, derivations, or proofs that involve calculus or some other nonelementary mathematical concept are presented in footnotes.

We are pleased that our depth of coverage in many topics—such as expectations of random variables, statistical inference, decision theory, and econometric analysis in regression—exceeds that found in many statistics texts for business and economics students. The text may be covered consecutively, chapter by chapter, if it is used in a full-year course. For shorter courses of one semester or one quarter that emphasize specific aspects of statistical analysis, selection of chapters or of sections within chapters quite easily allows for the design of a less intensive treatment.

THIRD EDITION

The current edition represents a complete revision of our text with the addition of separate chapters on analysis of variance and nonparametric statistics and with a reworking of the descriptive statistics and regression sections of the book. Numerous examples, problems, and exercises have been added to this edition. The fresh and colorful physical design highlights clearly the important statements and formulas and helps the student to locate problem sets and end-of-book reference material.

In addition to a large increase in the use of examples, we have introduced *Study Questions* into this edition. Study Questions are presented periodically with full solutions but without extra explanation. Thus, a Study Question is an "example" of the type of analysis now expected of the reader and of the type of answer the reader might provide to similar questions encountered in the many problems or exercises in each chapter. Before most sets of problems, we again have included a list of key terms that the student should recognize and be able to define and use. At the end of each chapter is a glossary of important terms. These and the formulas or statements that are set off in boxes or in boldface type are particularly important to know in order to fully comprehend the material in later chapters. Not all formulas or definitions of new terms are given special emphasis; some are intermediate in nature rather than being final concepts.

Since problem solving is essential to learning statistical analysis, we have included problems at varied levels. Each chapter has both *Problems* and *Exercises*. The former depend quite directly on the text presentation. As many of these as possible should be worked by the reader. The latter include more challenging questions, usually because they require some extra step, mathematical expertise, or combination of concepts that were not directly illustrated in the text. Many chapters have at least one *Case Problem* as well. These longer problems, requiring more interpretation and problem formulation than end-of-chapter problems, represent situations that the student may face in later courses or in the job world.

Most chapters also have a section of problems headed *Using the Computer*. The instructor will need to select the computer problems that are most convenient given the type of computer services available and the programming or software knowledge of the students. Because of the large variability in computer usage, these computer questions may best serve as suggestions for the instructor, who can then write questions suitable for each unique situation. In a similar vein, six data sets are included in Appendix A and are often used in examples or problems throughout the text. These were designed to have enough observations for the student to realize the advantage of a computer over hand calculations but few enough observations for data entry not to be excessively tedious. Additional questions using parts or all of these data sets may be created by individual instructors, teaching assistants, or tutors. Our questions have been found to meet the appropriate level of difficulty, to help the students learn the underlying topics, and to stimulate students to seek out a data set of personal interest for special projects.

SUPPLEMENTARY MATERIALS

A *Student Workbook for Statistical Analysis* is available to accompany our text and provides brief explanations of the basic concepts and a large number of additional, fully worked examples and problems. The workbook has been evaluated as being of greatest assistance in improving the understanding and confidence of the average student.

For instructors, a complete solutions manual, a test bank of over 400 multiple-choice questions, and transparency masters are available.

ACKNOWLEDGMENTS

Special gratitude is due instructors who have used the previous two editions of this text and have made suggestions for improvements and additions for this edition, especially those instructors at the University of Illinois. The authors also express thanks to the several reviewers who carefully read the manuscript version and aided us in working toward consistency and accuracy in our presentation: Michael Sklar, University of Georgia; H. F. Williamson, University of Illinois, Urbana; Jackie Redder, Virginia Polytechnic Institute; Joseph Nordstrom, University of Houston, Central Campus; Stanley Steinkemp, University of Illinois, Urbana; Edgar Hickman, University of South Carolina; Nicholas Farnum, California State University, Fullerton; Ronald Koot, Pennsylvania State University; Paul Berger, Boston University; Terry Seaks, University of North Carolina, Greensboro; Mary Sue Younger, University of Tennessee, Knoxville; Don Robinson, Illinois State University; Jeffery Green, Ball State University; Timothy Wittig, Oklahoma State University; Nancy Carter, California State University, Chico; Jack Suyderhoud, University of Hawaii; and David Closs, Michigan State University.

Some of the exercises in this text represent actual or modified questions from old CPA exams. These exercises are the only multiple-choice questions in the book. Material from the CPA Examinations and Unofficial Answers, copyright 1971–1978 by the American Institute of Certified Public Accountants, Inc., is used with permission. Figures, tables, or data drawn from other copyrighted sources are reprinted with the permission of those sources.

We are grateful to the Literary Executor of the late Sir Ronald A. Fisher, R.F.S., to Dr. Frank Yates, F.R.S., and to Longman Group Ltd., London for permission to reprint tables from their book *Statistical Tables for Biological, Agricultural and Medical Research* (6th Edition, 1974).

Finally, we express our thanks for the understanding and help-in-kind received from our wives and children during this endeavor.

Bloomington, Indiana   **D.L.H.**
Chapel Hill, North Carolina   **J.L.M.**
October 1984

As you begin to study statistics, you should note the special features of this book designed to help you use it and learn from it. Appendix A contains six data sets that are frequently used in examples or problems. Appendix B provides a review of the notation associated with summations, variables, and functions. Appendix C contains many useful statistical tables. Since you will need to refer to these appendixes often, they are marked with a broad color band so that they will be easy to locate. Two of the most commonly used statistical tables are also reproduced inside the front cover for handy reference. Inside the back cover is a partial glossary of symbols.

Throughout the text, important formulas and definitions have been set off in boxes or in boldface type. Terms and concepts that you should be able to define are listed before problem sets, and a glossary of key definitions is included at the end of each chapter. Checking your comprehension and your ability to use these elements will help you assess your progress. Additionally, Study Questions with complete solutions appear periodically in the text. Answers to selected

TO THE
READER

odd-numbered problems follow Appendix C at the back of the book. End-of-section or end-of-chapter problems are similar to the text examples and are designed to test your knowledge of the basic concepts. We urge you to work as many of the problems as possible as a study aid. (Additional problems and examples of the basic topics and methods of analysis can be found in the workbook to accompany this text, the *Student Workbook for Statistical Analysis.* Your bookstore can order a copy for you if you do not find it on the shelf.)

The end-of-chapter Exercises involve independent work or may include some extra challenge, and there are a few multiple-choice exercises that are actual or modified questions from past CPA exams. Most chapters also include some *Using the Computer* problems and *Case Problems.* We hope these will encourage and prepare you to make use of statistical analysis outside the statistics course itself—in other course projects, term papers, and presentations or in nonclass situations of personal decision making and in your business or other career.

If you find you wish to consult additional sources, we have included a selected bibliography following Appendix C.

ONE
Introduction and Descriptive Statistics 1

1.1 Introduction 2
1.2 Statistics and Statistical Analysis 2
1.3 Describing a Population 5
1.4 Use of Samples Drawn
from a Population 10
1.5 Descriptive Statistics 15
GLOSSARY 28

TWO
Summary Measures for Populations 31

2.1 Introduction 32
2.2 Central Location 33
2.3 Measures of Dispersion 46
2.4 Other Descriptive Measures 67
2.5 Summary 71
GLOSSARY 79

CONTENTS

THREE
Probability Theory: Discrete Sample Spaces 81

3.1   Introduction 82
3.2   The Probability Model 83
3.3   Subjective and Objective Probability 86
3.4   Counting Rules 89
3.5   Permutations and Combinations 94
3.6   Probability Rules 102
3.7   Special Cases of Probability Rules 111
3.8   Marginal Probability 119
3.9   Bayes' Rule 123
3.10 Application of Probability Theory: An Example 128
      GLOSSARY 140

FOUR
Discrete Random Variables and Expectations 143

4.1   Introduction and Probability Models 144
4.2   Probability Mass Functions (p.m.f.) 151
4.3   Expected Values 160
4.4   Expectation Rules 173
4.5   Bivariate Probability Functions 178
4.6   Expectations for Combined Random Variables 184
4.7   Indicator Variable and Counting Variable 192
      GLOSSARY 201

FIVE
Discrete Probability Distributions 203

5.1   Introduction 204
5.2   The Binomial Distribution 204

5.3   Determining Binomial Probabilities 207
5.4   Characteristics and Use of the Binomial Distribution 212
5.5   Binomial Proportions 220
5.6   The Hypergeometric Distribution 226
5.7   The Poisson Distribution 231
5.8   Approximation of Discrete Random Variables by Continuous Random Variables 239
      GLOSSARY 245

SIX
Probability Theory: Continuous Random Variables 247

6.1   Introduction 248
6.2   Probability Density Functions 248
6.3   Similarities between Probability Concepts for Discrete and Continuous Random Variables 259
6.4   The Normal Distribution 266
6.5   Standardized Normal 271
6.6   Normal Approximation to the Binomial 284
6.7   Exponential Distribution 296
6.8   Probability Distributions— Summary 299
      GLOSSARY 309

SEVEN
Sampling and Sampling Distributions 311

7.1   Introduction 312
7.2   Sample Designs 312
7.3   Sample Statistics 320
7.4   Sampling Distribution of $\bar{x}$ 332
7.5   Sampling Distribution of $\bar{x}$, Normal Parent Population 340

7.6 Sampling Distribution of $\bar{x}$, Population Distribution Unknown, σ Known 343

7.7 Finite Population Correction Factor 348

7.8 Sampling Distribution of $\bar{x}$, Normal Population, σ Unknown 353

7.9 The Sampling Distribution of s^2, Normal Population 361

GLOSSARY 373

EIGHT
Estimation 377

8.1 Introduction 378

8.2 Four Properties of a "Good" Estimator 379

8.3 Estimating Unknown Parameters 385

8.4 Confidence Intervals for μ (σ Known) 392

8.5 Confidence Intervals for μ (σ Unknown) 400

8.6 Confidence Intervals for the Binomial Parameter π, Using the Normal Approximation 404

8.7 Determining the Size of the Sample (n) 408

8.8 Confidence Interval for σ^2 414

8.9 Summary 418

GLOSSARY 426

NINE
Hypothesis Testing: One-sample Tests 429

9.1 Introduction and Basic Concepts 430

9.2 The Standard Format of Hypothesis Testing 436

9.3 One-Sample Tests on μ 448

9.4 Measuring β and the Power of a Test 456

9.5 Test on the Binomial Parameter 464

9.6 Balancing the Risks and Costs of Making a Wrong Decision 470

9.7 One-Sample Test on σ^2 474

GLOSSARY 483

TEN
Hypothesis Testing: Multi-sample Tests 485

10.1 Introduction 486

10.2 Test on the Difference between Two Means (σ_1^2 and σ_2^2 Known) 486

10.3 Test on the Difference between Two Means (σ_1^2 and σ_2^2 Unknown but Assumed Equal) 488

10.4 Matched Pairs t-Test 492

10.5 Test on the Difference between Two Proportions 495

10.6 Two-sample Tests for Population Variances 497

GLOSSARY 512

ELEVEN
Analysis of Variance 515

11.1 Introduction 516

11.2 The One-Factor Model 517

11.3 The F-Test in ANOVA 523

11.4 Two-Factor Analysis of Variance 531

11.5 Testing Hypotheses in the Two-Factor Model 535

11.6 Calculating the Sums of Squares 538

11.7 Interpreting a Computer Outcome 540

GLOSSARY 548

TWELVE
Simple Regression and Correlation Analysis 549

12.1 Introduction 550
12.2 The Regression Models 551
12.3 Estimating the Values of α and β by Least Squares 558
12.4 Assumptions and Estimator Properties 571
12.5 Measures of Goodness of Fit 577
12.6 Correlation Analysis 585
12.7 Test on the Significance of the Sample Regression Line 598
12.8 Constructing a Forecast Interval 604
12.9 The *F*-Test 609
12.10 A Sample Problem 613
GLOSSARY 628

THIRTEEN
Multiple Regression and Correlation Analysis 631

13.1 Introduction to Multiple Regression 632
13.2 Multiple Least-Squares Estimation 635
13.3 Common Assumptions and Goodness-of-Fit Measures 642
13.4 Analysis-of-Variance Tests 654
13.5 Tests on Parameters 659
13.6 Dummy Variables in Regression Analysis 671
GLOSSARY 683

FOURTEEN
Econometric Analysis 685

14.1 Introduction 686
14.2 The "Common" Assumptions and Conditions 687

14.3 Multicollinearity 698
14.4 Autocorrelation 705
14.5 Heteroscedasticity 715
14.6 Use of Linear Regression for Nonlinear Relations 725
14.7 Doing a Multiple Regression Research Report 732
GLOSSARY 746

FIFTEEN
Time Series and Index Numbers 749

15.1 Introduction to Time Series 750
15.2 Linear Trend 753
15.3 Nonlinear Trends 761
15.4 Moving Averages to Smooth a Time Series 769
15.5 Estimation of Seasonal and Cyclical Components 773
15.6 Index Numbers 787
15.7 Price Index Numbers 791
15.8 Economic Indexes and Their Limitations 797
GLOSSARY 811

SIXTEEN
Statistical Decision Theory 813

16.1 Introduction to a Decision Problem 814
16.2 Expected Monetary Value Criterion 816
16.3 Perkins Plastic — An Example 818
16.4 The Revision of Probabilities 822
16.5 The Value of Information $(n = 1)$ 825
16.6 Analysis for Larger Sample Sizes 830
16.7 Utility Analysis 842
16.8 Decision Analysis for Continuous Functions 850

16.9 Bayes' Rule
       for Continuous Functions 855
16.10 Bayesian Analysis: Advantages
       and Disadvantages 861
       GLOSSARY 869

SEVENTEEN
Nonparametric Statistics 871

17.1 Introduction 872
17.2 Tests Comparable to Parametric
       t-Tests 874
17.3 Goodness-of-Fit Tests 887
17.4 Nonparametric Measures
       of Correlation 895
       GLOSSARY 907

APPENDIX A
Data Sets A-1

APPENDIX B
Subscripts, Summations,
Variables, and Functions A-15

APPENDIX C
Tables of Functions A-23

Bibliography A-69

Answers to Odd-
Numbered Problems A-71

Index I-1

Introduction and
Descriptive Statistics

ONE

1.1 INTRODUCTION

Statistical techniques are put to use in one form or another in almost all branches of modern science and in many other fields of human activity as well. As Soloman Fabricant said over 30 years ago, "The whole world now seems to hold that statistics can be useful in understanding, assessing, and controlling the operations of society." Progress in our society can be measured by a variety of numerical indexes. Statistics are used to describe, manipulate, and interpret these numbers.

One of our objectives in this chapter is to distinguish between statistics used for descriptive purposes and statistics used for making predictions and testing theories about what is called the "population." We will also begin to learn the notation and the process of relating a sample to a population. Finally, we will study various methods for describing and summarizing the information contained in either a population or a sample.

1.2 STATISTICS AND STATISTICAL ANALYSIS

Although the origins of statistics can be traced to studies of games of chance in the 1700s, it is only in the past 60 years that applications of statistical methods have been developed for use in almost all fields of science — social, behavioral, and physical. Most early applications of statistics consisted primarily of data presented in the form of tables and charts. This field, known as **descriptive statistics,** soon grew to include a large variety of methods for arranging, summarizing, or somehow conveying the characteristics of a set of numbers. Today, these techniques account for what is certainly the most visible application of statistics — the mass of quantitative information that is collected and published in our society every day. Crime rates, births and deaths, divorce rates, price indexes, the Dow-Jones average, and batting averages are but a few of the many familiar "statistics."

In addition to conveying the characteristics of quantifiable information, descriptive measures provide an important basis for analysis in almost all academic disciplines — especially in the social and behavioral sciences, where human behavior generally cannot be described with the precision possible in the physical sciences. Statistical measures of satisfaction, intelligence, job aptitude, and leadership, for example, serve to expand our knowledge of human motivation and performance. In the same fashion, indexes of prices, productivity, gross national product, employment, free reserves, and net exports serve as the tools of management and government in considering policies directed toward promoting long-term growth and economic stability.

The Use of Statistics in Decision-making

Despite the enlarging scope and increasing importance of descriptive methods over the past several hundred years, these methods now represent only a minor, relatively unimportant portion of the body of statistical literature. The phenomenal growth in statistics since the turn of the century has taken place mainly in the field called **statistical inference** or **inductive statistics.** This field is concerned with the formulation and testing of generalizations, as well as the prediction and estimation of relationships between two or more variables. The terms *inferential* and *inductive analysis* are used here because this aspect of statistics involves drawing conclusions (or "inferences") about the unknown characteristics of certain phenomena on the basis of only limited or imperfect information. Generally, this involves drawing conclusions about a set of data (called a population) based on values observed in a sample drawn from that population. From this sample information, statistical inference can often derive the quantitative information necessary for deciding among alternative courses of action when it is impossible to predict exactly what the consequence of each of these will be.

The process of drawing conclusions from limited information is one familiar to all of us, for almost every decision we face must be made without knowing with certainty the consequences. In deciding to watch television tomorrow rather than study, you may, at least subconsciously, be inferring that your grades will not suffer as a result of this decision. You probably have given considerable time and thought to your choice of a major in college, but here again your decision must be made on the basis of the limited amount of information that can be provided by aptitude tests, guidance counselors, and the advice of your parents and friends. If you make a poor choice, you may suffer the loss of considerable time and money. Similar problems are faced in business. Should a new product be introduced? What about plant expansion? How much should be spent on advertising? The economic advisor to government policy-makers must choose among various alternative recommendations for preventing unemployment, improving the trade balance, dampening inflationary spirals, and increasing production and income. In general the best choices can only be "inferred" from less-than-perfect information about future events. As a result, such decisions often are made under conditions that expose the decision-maker to considerable risk. The process of making decisions under these circumstances is usually referred to as **decision-making under uncertainty.**

Statistics as a decision-making tool plays an important role in the areas of research and development and in prediction and control in a wide variety of fields. Both government and industry, for instance, participate in the development, testing, and certification of new drugs and medicines, a process that often requires a large number of statistical tests (and decisions) concerning the safety and effectiveness of these drugs for public use. Similarly, the psychologist, the lawyer, and any person who makes decisions involving uncertain factors such as human behavior often will base decisions on data of a statistical nature. Since complex decision situations almost always call for some type of statistical analysis — formal or informal, explicit or implicit — it is difficult to overemphasize the importance of inferential statistics to the decision-maker. In fact, *statistics is often defined as the set of methods for making decisions under uncertainty.*

Definition of the Statistical Population

In statistical inference problems the set of all values under consideration — that is, all pertinent data — is customarily referred to as a **population** or **universe**.

> In general, any set of quantifiable data can be referred to as a population if that set of data consists of *all* values of interest.

For example, in deciding on the choice of a major you may want to make inferences about the set of grades you can expect to receive in the courses in a certain field; or perhaps you may want to estimate the salaries being earned by people with degrees in this field. Similarly, a business manager may want to know how many customers might buy a new product considered for possible production or what increase in sales to expect from the implementation of a particular advertising campaign. A government policy-maker may want to estimate the changes in demand for food that would result from increased welfare payments to the handicapped or a relaxation of restrictions on imported products. A legislator may need to infer the level of state revenue available from a special excise tax on tobacco products or a sales tax so that a reliable budget can be prepared. In each of these cases the set of *all relevant values* constitutes a population. The income of all CPA's in Indiana could represent a population. Or the income of CPA's in Indiana could represent a sample, the population being the income of all CPA's in the United States. Other examples of populations might include the profits of all companies in the United States, the GPA (grade point average) of all students at your university, or the monthly level of energy consumed by households with incomes near $15,000.

In making decisions we naturally would prefer to have access to as much information as possible about the relevant population or populations. One can avoid the possibility of making an incorrect inference only when all the information about a population is available. Unfortunately, it is usually impossible and much too costly to collect all the information concerning the population *associated with a practical problem*. Consequently, inferences (and the resulting decisions) must be made on the basis of limited or imperfect information about the population. The function of statistics as an aid to the decision-maker is to help him or her decide:

1. what information about a population is needed for a particular type of decision and
2. how this information can best be collected and analyzed for use in making decisions.

In trying to decide what information about a population is necessary for making a decision, we shall be referring to certain numerical characteristics that distinguish that population. These numerical characteristics, called **parameters**, describe specific properties of the population.

Numerical characteristics of populations are referred to as population parameters, or simply parameters.

For instance, one parameter of the population "executive salaries in the steel industry" is the average salary in that industry, since this measure describes the *central tendency* of all salaries in that population. The personnel director of any firm in that industry would certainly like to know the value of this parameter: such information would be valuable in setting salaries for new executives and for determining raises from one year to the next. Another population parameter involves *proportions*. For example, a number of recent court cases have centered on the proportion of workers in a company or industry who belong to a minority group. Discrimination has been charged in some situations because of the low proportion of minority workers.

1.3 DESCRIBING A POPULATION

Example 1.1 Assume that you are the mayor of Cedar Rapids, Iowa, a city of 169,775 according to the 1980 census. You have decided on a nationwide advertising campaign to try to attract new business and industry to your city. In order to advertise the relative advantages of

Cedar Rapids you decide to collect economic information for all cities in the United States whose size is roughly comparable to that of Cedar Rapids. Using information readily available from a number of sources,* you compile the data shown in **Data Set 1** in Appendix A. (Hereafter, Appendix data sets will not be cross-referenced.) These data are for the 78 cities in the United States with populations between 100,000 and 200,000 people. The first column of this table shows the income for a "typical" household in each city. The second column gives the Moody's Bond Rating (a measure of each city's credit risk, with Aaa the highest rating, followed by Aa, A1, A, and Baa). The third column indicates how vulnerable a city is to recession (a cyclical threat of unemployment that is high, moderate, or low), and the final column gives the state and local taxes a "typical" household would expect to pay.

We first note that you, as mayor of Cedar Rapids, made a decision about the relevant population when you selected data for all cities with 100,000–200,000 people. You might have gathered information for all cities in the United States or you could have decided to use data on only those cities having between 150,000 and 190,000 people (remember, Cedar Rapids has 169,775 people). This decision is a subjective one; hence, you are free to make your own choice. For the present we also assume that you have decided to focus only on the income column from **Data Set 1** (we will return to other columns later). The data from the income and tax columns are reproduced in Table 1.1.

The first step in working with any set of data is to present the information in some sort of summary form so that we can get a "feel" for the data. (Looking at Table 1.1 certainly does not give one much of a "feel" for how Cedar Rapids compares to other cities.) One way to summarize data is to group them into classes. For the first class, suppose you decide to count the number of cities with incomes above $17,000 and less than or equal to $21,000. This class is written as

$$\$17,000 < x \leq \$21,000,$$

where x represents the income of a city. Similarly, the second class might be all cities with incomes above $21,000 and less than or equal to $25,000, which would be written as $\$21,000 < x \leq \$25,000$. This process continues until enough classes are defined to include all the cities in this population. The number of cities in each class is the frequency of that class, and the set of all such frequencies is called a **frequency distribution**. The frequency

---

* These sources include The Bureau of Economic Analysis, *Regional Economic Projections, 1981.* "County and Metropolitan Area Personal Income," *Survey of Current Business, 1981*; Commerce Clearing House, *Tax Handbook*; Moody's Investors Service, *Moody's Bond Record, April, 1981.*

TABLE 1.1 **Household income and taxes for all cities with a population between 100,000 and 200,000 people.**

City, State	Income	Taxes	City, State	Income	Taxes
Abilene, TX	$24,985	$192	Lafayette, LA	$30,119	$982
Albany, GA	20,009	931	Lake Charles, LA	24,154	716
Alexandria, LA	18,878	475	Lawton, OK	17,531	520
Altoona, PA	20,104	625	Lincoln, NE	26,922	997
Amarillo, TX	28,388	214	Lynchburg, VA	22,683	1,224
Anchorage, AK	44,175	2,844	Manchester, NH	25,456	0
Anderson, IN	24,349	688	Mansfield, OH	23,369	524
Anniston, AL	18,168	920	Monroe, LA	20,920	567
Asheville, NC	20,966	1,301	Muncie, IN	21,457	604
Atlantic City, NJ	23,525	680	Muskegon, MI	21,346	986
Battle Creek, MI	25,048	1,238	Nashua, NH	25,032	314
Bay City, MI	24,379	1,151	New Bedford, MA	21,314	1,152
Billings, MT	26,943	1,954	New Britain, CT	25,344	361
Biloxi–Gulfport, MS	19,305	761	Norwalk, CT	33,518	420
Bloomington–Normal, IL	25,040	870	Odessa, TX	29,209	214
Boise City, ID	30,691	2,207	Portland, ME	23,906	1,572
Bradenton, FL	25,291	200	Pueblo, CO	24,316	1,623
Brockton, MA	26,090	1,441	Racine, WI	25,977	2,512
Cedar Rapids, IA	28,412	1,977	Reno, NV	38,686	230
Champaign–Urbana, IL	22,721	797	St. Cloud, MN	19,661	2,209
Columbia, MO	23,695	1,244	St. Joseph, MO	21,746	1,103
Danbury, CT	33,518	420	Santa Cruz, CA	26,414	2,386
Decatur, IL	26,749	928	Sioux City, IA	25,612	1,677
Eau Claire, WI	20,493	1,860	Sioux Falls, SD	26,436	364
Fall River, MA/RI	21,295	1,151	Springfield, IL	28,669	990
Fayette–Springdale, AR	22,035	1,069	Springfield, OH	22,901	772
Florence, AL	21,884	918	Stamford, CT	33,518	420
Fort Collins, CO	24,905	1,670	Terre Haute, IN	22,073	629
Gadsden, AL	20,928	991	Texarkana, TX/AR	21,354	170
Gainesville, FL	22,991	189	Topeka, KS	25,620	1,880
Galveston–Texas City, TX	27,146	203	Tuscaloosa, AL	20,820	1,030
Grand Forks, ND/MN	22,010	1,618	Tyler, TX	27,383	203
Greenbay, WI	23,614	2,230	Waco, TX	24,168	192
Greenley, CO	23,325	1,535	Waterloo–Cedar Falls, IA	26,430	1,769
Jackson, MI	24,176	1,193	Wheeling, WV	24,370	1,105
Kankakee, IL	25,699	886	Wichita Falls, TX	26,606	203
Kenosha, WI	26,568	2,593	Williamsport, PA	22,680	695
Kokomo, IN	28,793	803	Wilmington, NC	21,060	1,308
Lafayette, IN	23,115	651	Yakima, WA	25,380	277

distribution for the population of incomes in Table 1.1 is shown in Table 1.2. This frequency distribution was generated by a computer. We must be careful in interpreting the data in Table 1.2. The first line has class limits of $17,000 and $21,000. This means that a city is included in this category if its income is *larger than* $17,000, and *less than or equal to* $21,000. In other words, the lower number ($17,000) is *not* included in the interval, but the higher number ($21,000) *is* included. By counting from Table 1.1 we find that there are 12 cities with incomes greater than $17,000 and less than or equal to $21,000. Twelve cities represent 15.38% of the population of 78 cities. Similarly, 32 of the 78 cities (41.03%) had incomes greater than $21,000 and less than or equal to $25,000. The rest of the categories in Table 1.2 are interpreted in the same manner.

Calculating population parameters. As mayor, suppose you decide to calculate the average household income for all 78 cities. To do this, you merely add all the incomes and divide the sum by the number of observations (cities). The number of observations in a population is denoted by the letter N. In our example, N = 78. The average of a population is called the **population mean**, the *arithmetic mean*, or just the *mean*, and is denoted by the Greek letter μ (mu). *Generally, population parameters will be denoted by Greek characters.*

Formula (1.1) is used to calculate the mean of a population. In this formula the first value in the population is denoted as x_1, the second value as x_2, and the last value as x_N.

Formula for μ, the population mean:

$$\mu = \frac{1}{N}(x_1 + x_2 + \cdots + x_N) = \frac{1}{N}\sum_{i=1}^{N} x_i \tag{1.1}$$

Now let's use this formula to find the mean μ (mu) for the income data in Table 1.1. Note that $x_1 = 24{,}985$ (Abilene, TX), $x_2 = 20{,}009$ (Albany, GA), and $x_N = x_{78}$ (Yakima, WA) = 25,380. Thus,

$$\mu = \frac{1}{78}(24{,}985 + 20{,}009 + \cdots + 25{,}380) = \frac{1}{78}(1{,}934{,}566) = 24{,}802.13.$$

The average household income in this population is $24,802.13. Notice how much higher the Cedar Rapids household income ($28,412) is than the average for the population, a fact you as mayor may wish to emphasize in advertising for new business and industry.

Proportions may also be population parameters, and there are often many different proportions one could calculate from the same population.

[handwritten: n = # of obs. in a sample]

[handwritten: N = # of observations in a pop'n]

[handwritten: avg. of a pop'n is called the μ]

TABLE 1.2 **Frequency distribution for income.**   *[handwritten: μ = look at box on p.8]*

Class Limits	Frequency	Percent
$17000.00 < x \le 21000.00$	12	*[handwritten: 12 ÷ 78 =]* 15.38
$21000.00 < x \le 25000.00$	32	41.03
$25000.00 < x \le 29000.00$	26	33.33
$29000.00 < x \le 33000.00$	3	3.85
$33000.00 < x \le 37000.00$	3	3.85
$37000.00 < x \le 41000.00$	1	1.28
$41000.00 < x \le 45000.00$	1	1.28
	78	100.00

For example, suppose you wish to determine the proportion of the 78 cities whose tax value (given in **Data Set 1**) is over $1700 (Cedar Rapids has a tax value of $1977). (We could calculate the proportion of cities with taxes over $1900, or the proportion under $2500, or any other proportion we wanted.) A population proportion is usually denoted by the Greek letter π (pi). Since there are 12 cities, including Cedar Rapids, with taxes over $1700, π in this example is:

Proportion of cities with taxes over $1700: $\pi = \dfrac{12}{78} = 0.154.$

This result says that 15.4 percent of the cities in this population have taxes over $1700.

When dealing with proportions, we will let the symbol x represent the number of items in the population that satisfy the characteristic we wish to determine. Thus, x in the example above would be the number of cities with taxes over $1700. If N is the number of items in the population, then a **population proportion** is defined as follows.

> Population proportion:
>
> *[handwritten: π = proportion]*
>
> $$\pi = \frac{x}{N}.$$
>
> **(1.2)**

Let us use this definition to calculate the proportion of cities in our population of 78 that have a Moody Rating of Aaa. Recall that Cedar Rapids has a Moody rating of Aaa, which is the highest rating. Looking at the values in **Data Set 1,** we see that there are only four cities with this Moody rating. Hence, $x = 4$, and the proportion with a rating of Aaa is

$$\pi = \frac{4}{78} = 0.051.$$

This means that only 5.1% of the cities have a rating of Aaa. As mayor, you may wish to advertise the fact that Cedar Rapids is among the top cities in terms of bond rating.

There are numerous population parameters other than μ and π that can be used to describe a population. We will discuss some of these parameters in subsequent chapters.

It is important to note that the task of determining the exact value of a population parameter may be quite difficult. This may be due to the inconvenience or impracticality of collecting the necessary data. If we are interested in the parameter "average executive salary," it may not be possible even to identify all the executives in a given industry, much less find out their salaries. Similarly, the proportion of minority workers in an industry may be difficult to determine because of a reluctance of companies to provide such information, even if they keep records on it.

1.4   USE OF SAMPLES DRAWN FROM A POPULATION

Since it is often impossible or impractical to determine the exact value of the parameters of a population, the characteristics of a given population are commonly judged by observing a **sample** drawn from all possible values.

A sample is a subset of a population.

The individual values contained in a sample are often referred to as *observations*, and the population from which they come is sometimes called the *parent population*. We may, for example, take a sample of 100 executives, determine their current salaries, and, on the basis of these observations, make statements about different characteristics (parameters) of the population of all executive salaries — such as the average salary, or the variability of salaries in a certain industry, or perhaps the average salary in that industry a year from now.

As another example, suppose a quality-control engineer is responsible for ensuring the reliability of electrical components produced in some production process. Testing each and every item may be prohibitively expensive. Or it may be impossible if the inspection process destroys the components. Consider the problem of producing a stereo cartridge designed to last 1000 hours of playing time. An inspector might test each cartridge for 1000 hours or until it becomes defective; but then what would be left for the manufacturer to sell? The solution to this problem lies in determining the reliability of all items produced (a population parameter) by inspecting only a subset (i.e., a sample) of the items. In order to make decisions about a population on the basis of a sample, we will calculate certain numerical characteristics of a sample called **sample statistics.**

> Numerical characteristics of samples are referred to as *sample statistics* or simply *statistics*.

The mean of a sample is a sample statistic. A proportion calculated from a sample is a sample statistic.

Thus, when a numerical characteristic applies to a population, it is called a parameter. A numerical characteristic describing a sample is called a *statistic*. The usefulness of such measures is obvious if one considers the difficulty of making a logical presentation of the meaning and interpretation of a given data set. Simple intuitive or "naked-eye" analysis of the values can be misleading and may easily miss some important implications. Furthermore, presenting such analysis of large data sets is tedious for the presenter and boring for the listener or reader. If the important and most useful information in a data set can be condensed into a few summary measures, then comprehension and comparison of different populations or samples becomes much easier. In decision-making problems (for example, in statistical analysis of pollution-abatement systems or of a welfare program), summary presentation of this nature is called data reduction. All the information in a data set that is useful for a particular purpose is "reduced" into a single measure (such as a reliability measure or an average payment).

Example 1.2. Assume again that you are mayor of Cedar Rapids, but now assume that you do not have access to the census data in **Data Set 1.** Typically, census figures are not available for most populations. Furthermore, let us assume that it is quite expensive for you to collect data on the 78 cities in the population, so you have decided to take a sample. You decide to take a "random" sample of ten, where random means that all the cities have the same chance of being included in the sample. In general, a sample larger than ten would be taken. Using one of the sampling methods presented in Chapter 7, the mayor could select the sample of ten cities shown in Table 1.3.

Calculating a sample mean. The mean of a sample is found by adding all of the numbers in the sample and dividing the sum by the number of values in the sample. Generally, we let the letter n denote the number of sample values and let $\bar{x}$ (read as "x-bar") denote the **sample mean.** Thus, if $x_1, x_2, \ldots, x_n$ represent the values in a sample, then x-bar is

Mean of a sample:

$$\bar{x} = \frac{1}{n} \sum_{i=1}^{n} x_i.$$

(1.3)

To calculate the mean income for the sample data in Table 1.3, we let $x_1 = \$19,305$, $x_2 = \$25,291, \ldots$, and $x_n = x_{10} = \$21,060$. Adding these ten numbers together and then dividing the sum by 10 gives the sample mean:

$$\bar{x} = \frac{1}{10} (258, 512) = \$25,851.10.$$

Thus, if we had only this sample to use, we might estimate the average income for all cities (the population mean) to be $25,851.10. Recall from page 8 that the actual population mean is $24,802.13. The estimate is about $1050 too high.

We must emphasize at this point that sometimes a sample statistic will be a good estimate of the population parameter, and other times it may not be a good estimate. You might imagine that each student in your statistics class takes a sample of ten to estimate the mean income for the

TABLE 1.3 **Random sample of 10 cities from population of 78 cities.**

City, State	Income	Taxes	City, State	Income	Taxes
Biloxi–Gulfport, MS	$19,305	$761	Reno, NV	$38,686	$230
Bradenton, FL	25,291	200	St. Joseph, MO	21,746	1,103
Brockton, MA	26,090	1,441	Texarkana, TX/AR	21,354	170
Danbury, CT	33,518	420	Waterloo–Cedar Falls, IA	26,430	1,769
Nashua, NH	25,032	314	Wilmington, NC	21,060	1,308

population of 78 cities in Table 1.1. The cities included in each sample of size 10 may differ from student to student. Some students will get sample means quite close to the population mean of $24,802.13, while others may have sample means quite far away. Unfortunately, when the population mean is unknown (which is why we take a sample), we have no way of knowing which samples give estimates that are close and which do not.

Now let us use the sample to estimate π, the proportion of cities with taxes greater than $1700. The **sample proportion** will be denoted by the symbol p, where p is defined as follows.

Sample proportion:

$$p = \frac{x}{n}.$$ **(1.4)**

In this formula, x is the number of items in the sample satisfying the characteristic to be determined, and n is the sample size. Looking at our sample in Table 1.3 of ten cities, we see that only one city has taxes over $1700; hence, an estimate of π based on this sample would be

$$p = \frac{1}{10} = 0.10.$$

Since $\pi = 0.154$, this sample estimate is lower than the population value. The reason why sample estimates differ from population values is that a sample does not provide full information. A sample is only a part of the whole and thus provides only partial information. Also, samples generally differ from one another because each one depends on the particular part of the population selected for that sample. This introduces what statisticians call **sampling error.**

Sampling errors are the differences between sample estimates and population parameters caused by the fact that samples are merely a part of the population.

The reason large samples are preferred is because we want to keep the sampling error small — in order to have more confidence in the reliability of the estimate. Of course, larger samples cost more money, so there is a trade-off between more reliability and more expense. Perfect accuracy is obtained only when n = N, which means that we sample the whole

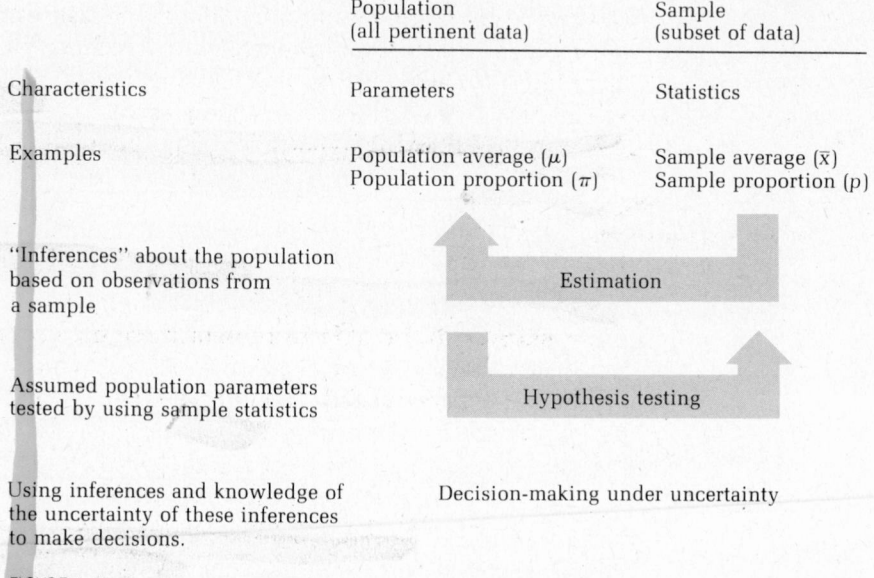

	Population (all pertinent data)	Sample (subset of data)
Characteristics	Parameters	Statistics
Examples	Population average (μ) Population proportion (π)	Sample average ($\bar{x}$) Sample proportion (p)
"Inferences" about the population based on observations from a sample		Estimation
Assumed population parameters tested by using sample statistics		Hypothesis testing
Using inferences and knowledge of the uncertainty of these inferences to make decisions.	Decision-making under uncertainty	

FIGURE 1.1 Statistical terms.

population (this is a **census** and is not really a sample). Sample statistics are used most often to:

1. make estimates about certain population parameters, or
2. test hypotheses (or assumptions) about certain population parameters, or
3. determine the optimal decision in a situation of uncertainty.

Figure 1.1 illustrates the relationships between population parameters and sample statistics.

In Fig. 1.1 the upper arrow represents the process of estimating population parameters. The lower arrow represents hypothesis testing.

The methods for relating populations and samples will be described in greater detail beginning in Chapter 7. For now we merely wish to establish the major purpose for which these concepts will be used.

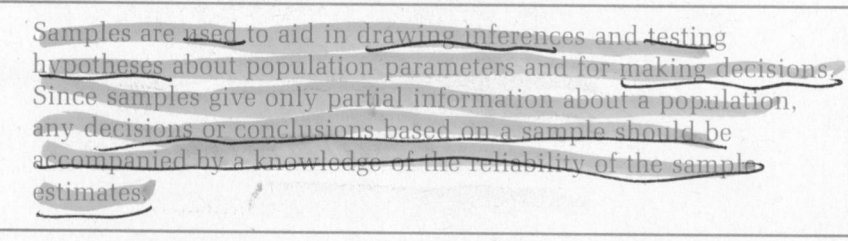

> Samples are used to aid in drawing inferences and testing hypotheses about population parameters and for making decisions. Since samples give only partial information about a population, any decisions or conclusions based on a sample should be accompanied by a knowledge of the reliability of the sample estimates.

Chapter 2 discusses additional summary measures useful in describing populations. The study of probability in Chapters 3–6 develops skills and techniques for assessing the reliability of sample information. Beginning in Chapter 7, we present sample measures that are useful in drawing inferences and testing hypotheses about population parameters.

1.5 DESCRIPTIVE STATISTICS

Once we have all the population values, or the information from a sample, it is important to be able to present these data in an efficient manner. Graphs and charts, the most popular and most convenient means for such presentations, are usually employed when a visual representation is desired. Although there are many alternative methods for presenting data in this form, only a few will be discussed here. The "pie chart," for example, is a familiar device for describing how a given quantity is subdivided. In Fig. 1.2 the relevant quantity is the 1984 U.S. federal budget dollar, and the subsets represent where the dollar comes from and where it goes. Consider the 42 cents in the lower figure, representing "Direct Benefit Payments for Individuals." This 42 cents is denoted by 42 percent of the 360 degrees in the circle (or an angle of 151.2°).

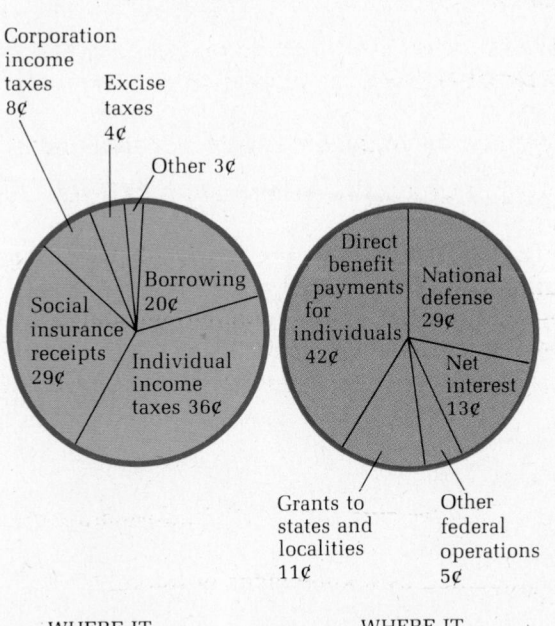

FIGURE 1.2 **The 1985 U.S. federal budget dollar.**

Corporation income taxes 8¢

Excise taxes 4¢

Other 3¢

Borrowing 20¢

Social insurance receipts 29¢

Individual income taxes 36¢

Direct benefit payments for individuals 42¢

National defense 29¢

Net interest 13¢

Grants to states and localities 11¢

Other federal operations 5¢

WHERE IT COMES FROM . . .

WHERE IT GOES . . .

Another popular descriptive device is the chart measuring levels over time in some index, such as the consumer price indexes for all items shown in Fig. 1.3. Our final illustration of a graphical form (Fig. 1.4) is derived from an example in Darrell Huff's delightful book *How To Lie With Statistics* (Norton, 1954). This example depicts the increase in the number of cows between 1860 (eight million) and 1936 (24 million). In drawing pictures of cows to represent this growth, one naturally would be inclined to draw the 1936 cow three times as long as the 1860 cow. Of course, a cow three times as long looks rather peculiar unless it is also three times as high. But if the 1936 cow is three times as high and three times as wide, it is *nine* times as large as the 1860 cow in terms of area. Such a figure would seriously misrepresent the true growth.

Business journals and news magazines often adopt a somewhat whimsical device to avoid this difficulty. Interested primarily in presenting information in a form understandable to the layman (not the

FIGURE 1.3 **Changes in the consumer price index.**

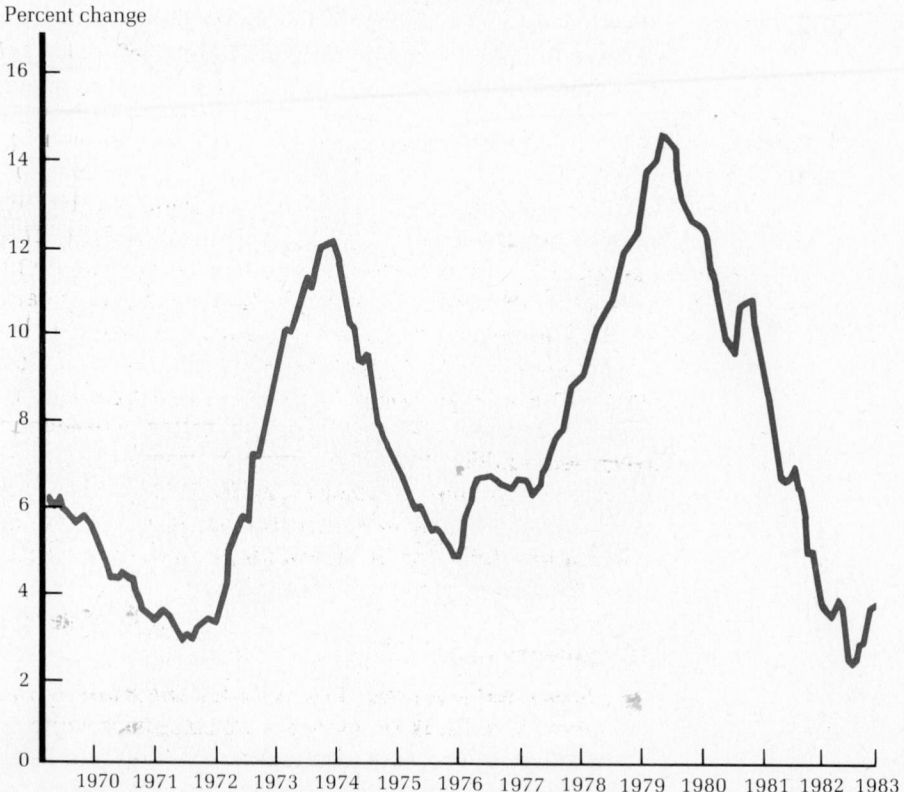

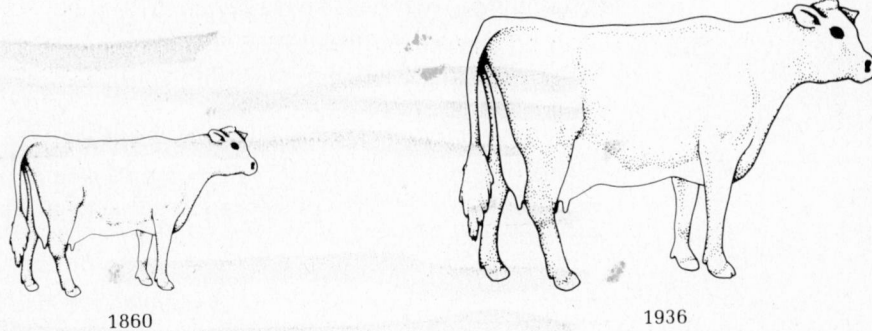

1860   1936

FIGURE 1.4 **A threefold increase.**

statistician), such journals would depict growth in the number of cows by showing one cow to represent 1860 and three cows to represent 1936 — thus, each would represent eight million animals. Similarly, growth in auto production from, let's say, ten million to 27 million cars could be indicated by lopping off the motor and front wheels of the third car. This truncation is less gruesome in the case of the car than in the case of the cow.

Frequency Distributions Although graphs and charts such as those shown in Figs. 1.2 and 1.3 often serve a very useful function, they are not appropriate for most purposes of statistical analysis and decision-making because they provide only a representation of the information and not the actual data themselves. Statistical purposes usually require that the data be presented in a form that gives a more precise indication of the information at hand. Some method is needed that will summarize or describe large masses of data without loss or distortion of the essential characteristics of the information and will also make the data easier to interpret. One such method is the arrangement of data into what is called a **frequency distribution** or **frequency table.** In constructing a frequency distribution it is first necessary to divide the data into a limited number of different categories or classes and then to record the number of times (the frequency) an observation falls (or is distributed) into each class. Table 1.2 is an illustration of a frequency distribution.

Statisticians have developed certain guidelines for the construction of frequency distributions.

1. Classes are generally chosen so that the width of each class, called the *class interval*, is the same for all categories. Otherwise, interpretation of the frequency distribution may be difficult. For example, grouping the incomes in Table 1.1 into unequal classes such as $15,000 <

x ≤ $20,000, $20,000 < x ≤ $30,000, 30,000 < x ≤ $40,000, and $40,000 < x ≤ $45,000 is ill-advised. Comparisons between the number of observations in different categories would be misleading, since the size of the categories is not consistent.

2. The number of classes should probably be _fewer than 15_ (for ease of handling and to ensure sufficient compacting of the information) and _at least 6_ (to avoid loss of information due to grouping together widely diverse data).

3. _Open-ended intervals_ should be avoided. Too much information is lost if categories such as "≤ $15,000" are used. If a few extreme values do not conveniently fit into frequency categories, they should be listed separately.

4. Categories should be defined so that no single observation could fall into more than one _overlapping_ category. For example, categories such as $17,000–$21,000 and $21,000–$25,000 are ambiguous, since it is not clear in which category to place a value of exactly $21,000. If we use our convention for denoting the categories, $17,000 < x ≤ $21,000, and $21,000 < x ≤ $25,000, there is no overlap, and it is clear that $21,000 falls in the first category.

5. The _midpoint_ of each category should be made to be representative of the values assigned to that category. This is important because these midpoints are often used as proxies for all the values in their respective classes. Such proxies or representative values are called **class marks.**

Example 1.3. Consider a group of sales items in a clothing store where many such items are priced as $9.98, $14.99, $19.95, etc. To set up classes such as $5.00 < x ≤ $10.00, $10.00 < x ≤ 15.00, $15.00 < x ≤ $20.00 would betray poor judgment, since most of the data fall near the end of each class. A better choice might be to use the classes $7.50 < x ≤ $12.50, $12.50 < x ≤ $17.50, $17.50, < x ≤ $22.50. For these classes the midpoints are $10.00, $15.00, and $20.00, which more closely represent the typical values within the classes.

Let us use these rules to determine a frequency distribution for the tax data in Table 1.1, using categories $0 < x ≤ $400, $400 < x ≤ 800, etc. Table 1.4 shows the frequency distribution of taxes in these classes and also gives the **relative frequency** of each class.

> Relative frequency is determined by dividing the frequency of each class by the total number of observations and expressing the result as a decimal.

fewer than 15
& greater than 6

TABLE 1.4 **Frequency distribution for taxes in Table 1.1.**

frequency or

class interval

Class	Frequency Distribution	Relative Frequency *can also be a percentage*
$\$0 < x \le \$400$	16	0.205 $\rightarrow \dfrac{16}{78} \rightarrow$ *ex.* 20.5%
$\$400 < x \le \$800$	18	0.231 *(.205×100)*
$\$800 < x \le \$1200$	20	0.256
$\$1200 < x \le \$1600$	8	0.103
$\$1600 < x \le \$2000$	9	0.115
$\$2000 < x \le \$2400$	4	0.051 $\dfrac{F_i}{N} = $ *Rel. Freqs.*
$\$2400 < x \le \$2800$	2	0.026
$\$2800 < x \le \$3200$	1	0.013
	$N = 78$	1.000

Thus, the first relative frequency in Table 1.4 is $f_1/N = 16/78 = 0.205$, where f denotes frequency and the subscript 1 indicates that this is the first frequency in the sample. The second relative frequency in the sample is $f_2/N = 18/78 = 0.231$, and so forth. Note that the sum of all relative frequencies must equal 1.00, since $\Sigma f_i = N$ and $N/N = 1.0$. Calculation and tabulation of these measures makes it clear that taxes between \$800 and \$1200 occurred with the greatest frequency.

While it is often useful to arrange the values in a data set into a frequency distribution (as in Table 1.4), many analysts prefer a pictorial presentation. Perhaps the most common type is the graph in which the classes are plotted on the horizontal axis and the frequency of each class is plotted on the vertical axis. This type of graph is called a **histogram** or *bar graph*. Figure 1.5 represents the histogram for the frequency distribution in Table 1.4.

A helpful addition to the histogram is a **frequency polygon,** which is constructed by drawing a straight line between the midpoints (class marks) of adjacent class intervals. The frequency polygon for the data in Fig. 1.5, indicated by the line through the class marks, serves to smooth a set of values. The reader should verify at this point that in Fig. 1.5 the graph of the *relative* frequencies is the same as that of the *absolute* frequencies except that the values for the vertical scale are different (relative frequencies are shown on the right-hand side of Fig. 1.5).

Another important method of presenting a data set is the table of *cumulative frequencies,* or table of *cumulative relative frequencies.* Table 1.5 applies this method to the tax data in Table 1.4. A **cumulative**

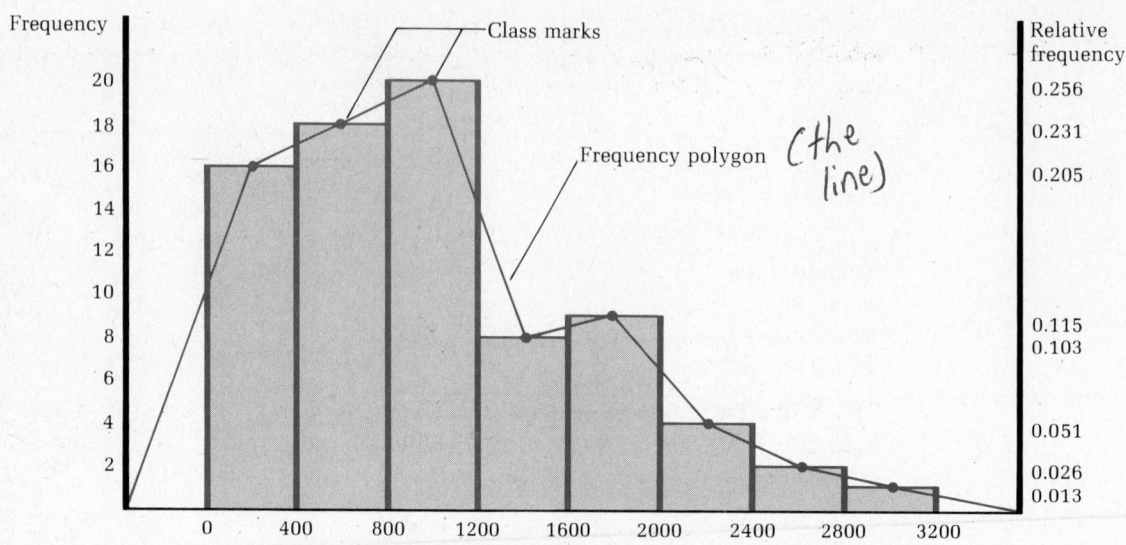

FIGURE 1.5 **Histogram and frequency polygon for data in Table 1.4.**

frequency is the *sum* of the *absolute* frequencies, from the lowest class to the highest class considered. Thus,

$$\sum_{i=1}^{k} f_i = \text{cumulative frequency of kth class.}$$

For example, by the end of the second class in Table 1.5 (at $800) the cumulative frequency for taxes is 16 + 18 = 34. Similarly, by $1200 the

TABLE 1.5

Class	Frequency	Cumulative Frequency	Cumulative Relative Frequency
$0 < x ≤ $400	16	16	0.205
$400 < x ≤ $800	18	34	0.436
$800 < x ≤ $1200	20	54	0.692
$1200 < x ≤ $1600	8	62	0.795
$1600 < x ≤ $2000	9	71	0.910
$2000 < x ≤ $2400	4	75	0.962
$2400 < x ≤ $2800	2	77	0.987
$2800 < x ≤ $3200	1	78	1.000

cumulative frequency is 54 (the sum of $16 + 18 + 20$). A **cumulative relative frequency** is the sum of the *relative* frequencies from the lowest class to the highest class considered. Thus,

$$\text{Cumulative relative frequency at class } k = \sum_{i=1}^{k} \frac{f_i}{N}.$$

At the value \$1200 for the end of the third class, the cumulative relative frequency is

$$\sum_{i=1}^{3} \frac{f_i}{N} = 0.692.$$

This value indicates that 69.2% of the taxes for this population were less than or equal to \$1200. Note that the cumulative frequency for the highest class (\$2800 $< x \le$ \$3200 in this case) must equal 1.00, since

$$\sum_{\text{all } i} \frac{f_i}{N} = \frac{N}{N}.$$

Just as a graph of the frequencies of a set of values provides a visual description of the original data, so a graph of the cumulative relative frequencies provides visual information about cumulative values. Note in Fig. 1.6 that cumulative relative frequencies can be plotted in the same fashion as relative frequencies and that this **cumulative histogram** can be smoothed by a line similar to the frequency-polygon used in Fig. 1.5. In this case the smoothing line is called an **ogive**, and the ogive connects the corner points of the cumulative histogram.

The distributions in Tables 1.4 and 1.5 might lead the mayor of Cedar Rapids to ask other questions requiring further statistical analysis. For example, what proportion of the cities have lower taxes than Cedar Rapids? Would more business and industry be attracted to the city if taxes were lower? Are taxes related to the size or the income of the city? Perhaps the Moody rating is related to the size of the tax.

Although these questions concerning Cedar Rapids do not call for earth-shattering decisions, it is evident that statistical analysis of available data can be useful in finding answers. However, if the data represent compound portfolio yields by the 40 largest insurance companies, similar kinds of questions could be very important to the financial management of a single company or to stockbrokers, bankers, and brokers in general. The same kind of statistical analysis developed in this text using simple examples also applies to a wide range of very important managerial and governmental decision-making problems.

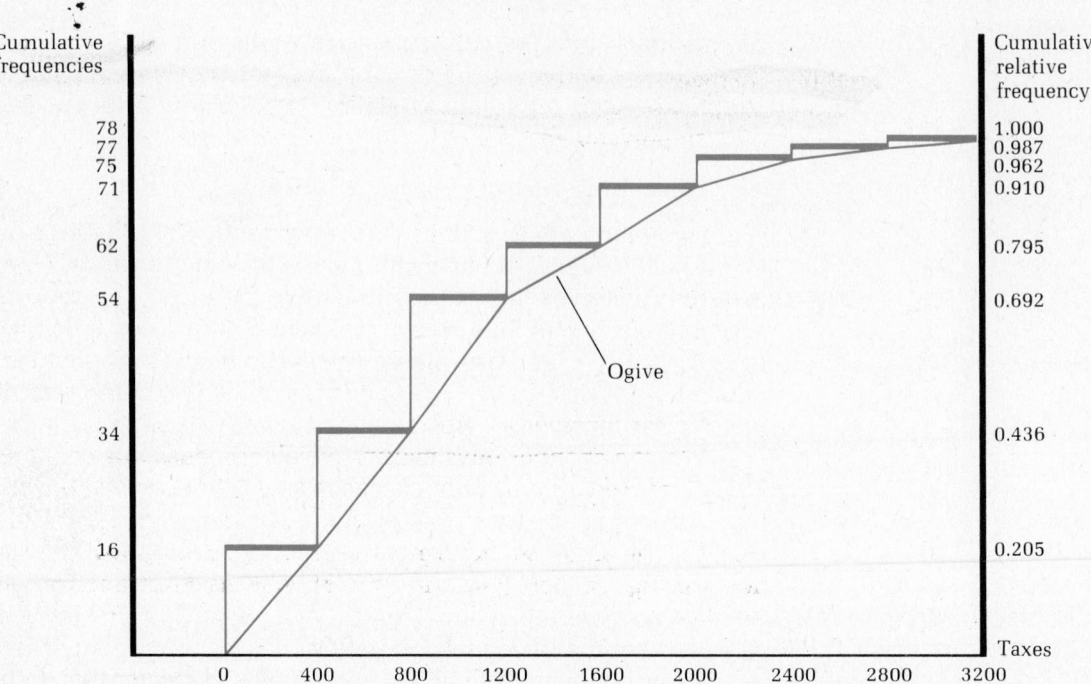

FIGURE 1.6 Cumulative frequencies and cumulative relative frequencies.

Study Question 1.1: Grocery Bills at Kroger's

A study at Kroger was designed to determine the average grocery bill paid by Kroger shoppers. The study recorded the amount paid by every tenth shopper in checkout lane number 5 over a period of five consecutive days in September. Assume that the first 20 customers in this study had the following bills (rounded to the nearest dollar):

$102 $58 $14 $89 $44 $123 $63
$75 $90 $97 $52 $84 $114 $77
$110 $99 $61 $88 $49 $63

1. What is the population in this study? Does it appear that this study will provide a sample that is representative of the population? Comment on any difficulties with the sample design. From a statistical point of view, do you see any problems in using bills that are rounded to the nearest dollar?
2. On the basis of the first 20 customers, what value would you estimate for μ? What value would you estimate for π, the

population proportion of shoppers with bills over $100?

3. Construct the frequency distribution and the histograms of relative frequencies and cumulative relative frequencies. Add the frequency polygon and the ogive to your histograms.

Answer

1. The population appears to be the "grocery bills for all shoppers at Kroger." There could be many problems with the study. First, the study involves only five consecutive days, and the store is probably open seven days a week. There is thus a possible bias in omitting two days. Also, the study was conducted in September, which may or may not be representative of the rest of the year. It is not clear whether a "grocery bill" includes other items — for example, if a shopper buys mailing envelopes, does this count as groceries? And should only checkout lane 5 be used? This lane may have different characteristics from other lanes, such as being closer to the entrance, having more efficient, friendly workers, or not catering to people with only one or two items. From a statistical viewpoint, rounding to the nearest dollar should not cause any problems because it is probably safe to assume the cents portion of a bill will be less than 0.50 half the time and greater than 0.50 half the time.

2. $\bar{x} = (102 + 58 + \cdots + 63)/20 = 1552/20 = \$77.60$
   (best estimate of μ).

   $p = \text{(no. of bills} > 100)/20 = 4/20 = 0.20$ (best estimate of π).

3. Let's pick classes of $10 in width, starting with $40 and considering the $14 bill to be an outlier (see Fig. 1.7).

FIGURE 1.7 **Relative frequencies for grocery bills.**

Class Limits	Frequency	Percent	Cumm. Freq.	Cum. Rel. Freq.
14	1	0.05	1	.05
$40 < x \le 50$	2	0.10	3	.115
$50 < x \le 60$	2	0.10	5	.25
$60 < x \le 70$	3	0.15	8	.4
$70 < x \le 80$	2	0.10	10	.5
$80 < x \le 90$	3	0.15	13	.65
$90 < x \le 100$	3	0.15	16	.8
$100 < x \le 110$	1	0.05	17	.85
$110 < x \le 120$	2	0.10	19	.95
$120 < x \le 130$	1	0.05	20	1.00

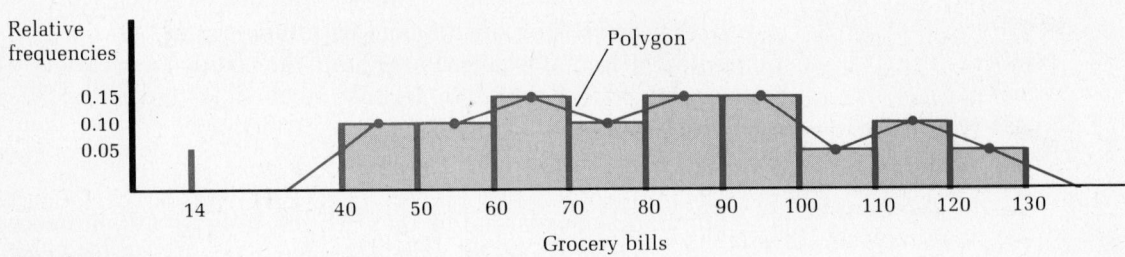

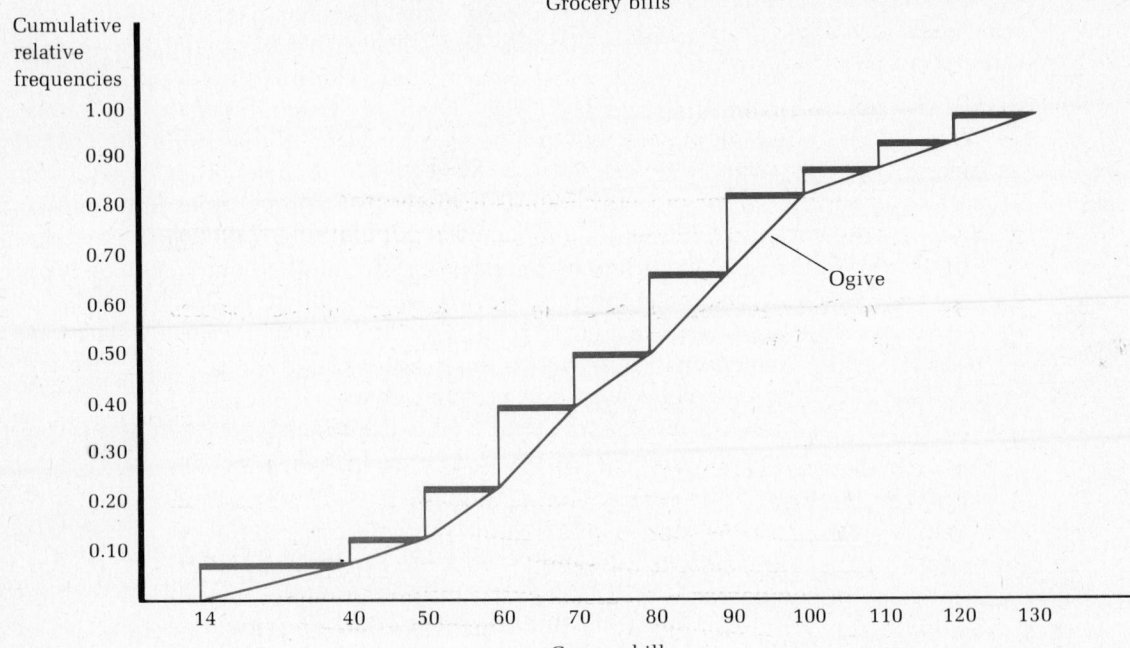

FIGURE 1.7 **(Continued)**

PROBLEMS

1.1   If you are given a set of numbers, how can you tell whether these numbers represent a population of a sample? If you are given a mean or a proportion, how can you tell whether the value is a sample estimate or a population parameter?

1.2   Use Table 1.1 in the following:
a)   Devise your own plan for taking a "random" sample of size 10 from the incomes in Table 1.1. Take the sample.
b)   Is your sample mean fairly close to the population mean?

c) Take a random sample of size 30 from the incomes in Table 1.1. Is your sample mean of size 30 closer to μ than the mean of your sample of size 10? Did you expect it to be? (Explain why.)

d) Would you guess that the mean of a sample of size 30 will always be closer to μ than the mean of a sample of size 10? Explain.

1.3 Take a random sample of size 15 from the 78 cities in **Data Set 1**. What proportion of the cities in your sample have a cyclical threat that is either "moderate" or "high"? How close an estimate is your sample proportion to the population value of π?

1.4 Answer the following questions:

a) What is the population proportion of cities in Table 1.1 having incomes greater than $27,000? Would this be a good population parameter for the mayor of Cedar Rapids to advertise?

b) If you are the mayor of Lawton, Oklahoma, what population parameter from **Data Set 1** would you advertise? Explain.

1.5 **Data Set 2** gives the sales and assets of the 50 largest retailing companies (from *Fortune* magazine).

a) Find the mean sales for this population. What proportion of the 50 companies had assets exceeding a million dollars?

b) By using a computer the following numbers were generated randomly from numbers between 1 and 50: 29, 43, 49, 11, 35, 15, 30, 3, 22, 19, 41, 8. Use the companies corresponding to these 12 numbers to form a random sample. How close is the sample mean to the population mean for sales? How close is the sample proportion to the population proportion of companies with assets over a million dollars?

c) Generate your own randomly selected numbers to take a sample of $n = 15$. Answer the same questions as in part (b).

1.6 Answer the following questions:

a) A classmate of yours has suggested that the first ten cities in **Data Set 1** would constitute a perfectly reasonable random sample of size $n = 10$. Another classmate suggests picking every fifth city until you have a sample of 10 (starting at a randomly selected place in the table). What do you think of these two methods for taking a random sample? Is one plan better than the other? Explain.

b) Repeat the questions in part (a) using **Data Set 2** and picking companies rather than cities.

1.7 Use Table 1.1 in the following:

a) Construct the frequency distribution, the histogram, and the frequency polygon using the same data as in Table 1.4 (the tax values from Table 1.1) but now using classes of width $300 rather than $400 (i.e.,

0 < x ≤ $300, $300 < x ≤ $600, etc.). Do you see much difference in using a width of $300 rather than $400? Which one seems better to you? (Explain.)

b) Construct the cumulative frequency distribution and the cumulative histogram for the tax data in Table 1.1 using the class intervals in part (a). Add the ogive to your cumulative histogram.

1.8 Construct a frequency distribution similar to Table 1.5 for the sales column in **Data Set 2.** Use the following classes: 1,000,000 < x ≤ 5,000,000, 5,000,000 < x ≤ 10,000,000, etc. (in thousands of dollars). Use your table to determine the population proportion of companies with sales less than $15,000,000 (in thousands of dollars).

1.9 For Problem 1.8, construct the histogram and the cumulative histogram. Add the frequency polygon and the ogive.

1.10 The following annual starting salaries were offered to 16 accounting majors about to receive their college degrees:

$27,500 $24,900 $26,200 $26,500 $26,400 $25,400 $25,800 $25,500
24,600 27,600 26,800 26,000 25,600 26,400 24,400 24,100

a) Is this data set a population or a sample? How do you know?
b) Find the mean of the 16 starting salaries.
c) Use classes of 24,000 < x ≤ 24,500, 24,500 < x ≤ 25,000, etc. to construct a frequency distribution similar to Table 1.2.
d) What percent of these accounting majors will earn more than $25,000? What percent will earn $26,000 or less?

1.11 Construct a pie chart using the following data on the use of spreadsheet computer programs.

VisiCalc 44.7%   SuperCalc 24.1%   Multiplan 11.7%   1-2-3 7.2%
PerfectCal 5.3%   VisiCalc Advanced 2.7%   Calcstar 2.6%   LogicCalc 1.7%

1.12 Write a brief report concerning incomes and tax in 1972 compared with 1982, using Fig. 1.8.

1.13 Using the data in **Data Set 1,** construct a pie chart showing the percent of Moody ratings falling in each of the following five categories: Aaa, Aa, A1, A, Baa.

1.14 What is statistical inference? Why is statistical inference important in business and the social and behavioral sciences? Give several examples of the use of statistical inference in your major field of study in college.

1.15 Find an example (from a newspaper, magazine, etc.) of a data set used to report business or economic data. Is the data set a population or a sample? Explain how this data set can be (or was) used in decision-making.

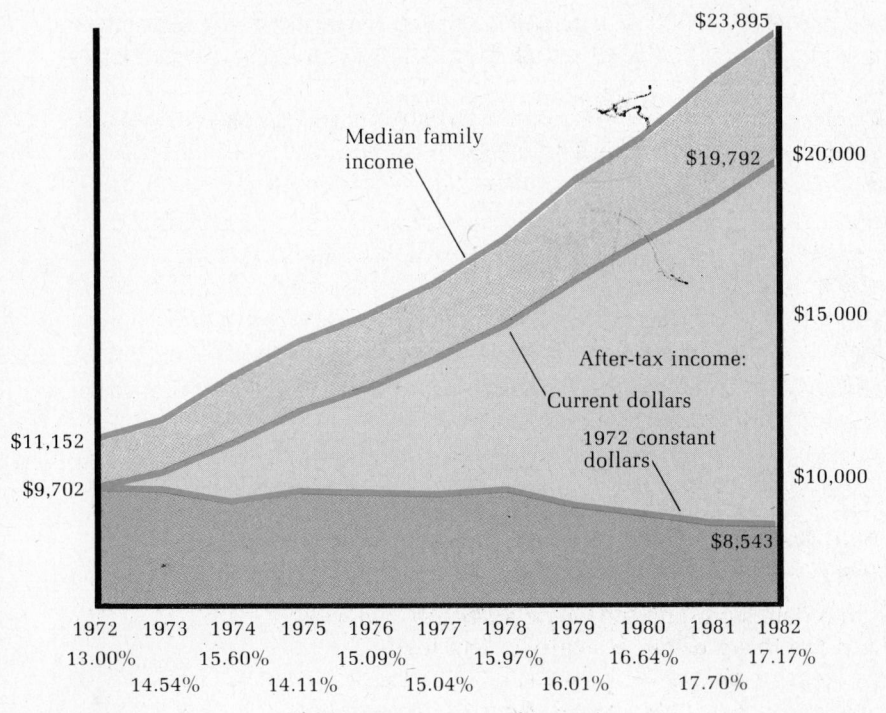

Median family income

$23,895

$19,792

$20,000

$15,000

After-tax income:

Current dollars

1972 constant dollars

$11,152

$9,702

$10,000

$8,543

1972	1973	1974	1975	1976	1977	1978	1979	1980	1981	1982
13.00%		15.60%		15.09%		15.97%		16.64%		17.17%
	14.54%		14.11%		15.04%		16.01%		17.70%	

Total taxes as percent of income

SOURCE: Tax Foundation Inc.

FIGURE 1.8 **Cumulative relative frequencies for grocery bills.**

USING THE COMPUTER

1.16 Use a computer package at your university (such as MINITAB, Microstat, Interactive Data Analysis [IDA], Statistical Package for the Social Sciences [SPSS], or Statistical Analysis System [SAS] to calculate the mean and the frequency distribution for the tax information in **Data Set 1.** If possible, use this program to generate the histogram and the cumulative histogram. Add your own frequency polygon and ogive.

1.17 Use a computer package at your university to calculate the mean and the frequency distribution for assets in **Data Set 2.**

1.18 Solve Problem 1.5 using a computer package.

1.19 Solve parts (b) and (c) of Problem 1.10 using a computer package.

1.20 Answer parts (a) and (b) of Problem 1.7 using a computer package.

1.21 **Data Set 6** represents data from a U.S. Department of Agriculture Survey on food consumption for the elderly (55 or over).
   a) Construct a histogram for monthly income, using the data in column 5.
   b) Summarize all the data presented in some convenient manner.

CASE PROBLEM

1.22 The Indiana University Memorial Union recently completed a large survey designed to study usage of the Union. This study surveyed the student population of approximately 30,000 students, plus approximately 6000 faculty and staff. Primarily, the university union wanted to know who was using the union, how often they used it, and what parts of the union they used. They were willing to send out 1000 sample questionnaires to get these data. Design a procedure for collecting and analyzing the 1000 sample questionnaires for this particular situation (or your own union, if appropriate). Be as specific as possible as to whom the questionnaires will be sent and any problems you would anticipate. (*Note:* We will return to this same case in Chapter 7 after studying more about sample designs.)

GLOSSARY

Descriptive statistics: Methods concerned with arranging, summarizing, or somehow conveying the characteristics of a set of numbers.

Statistical inference: Making generalizations, predictions, or conclusions about characteristics of a population based on the characteristics of a sample assumed to have been drawn from that population.

Decision-making under uncertainty (or risk): A decision-making process in which there is uncertainty about what outcome will result from a particular action.

Population: All relevant values of interest in a particular context.

Parameters: Certain numerical characteristics of a population such as its mean or a particular proportion.

Frequency distribution: The arranging of a data set into classes and the recording of the number (frequency) of values in each class.

Population mean: The average of a population of N values:

$$\mu = \frac{1}{N} \sum_{i=1}^{N} x_i.$$

Population proportion: The proportion of values in the population meeting some specified condition:

$$\pi = \frac{x}{N}.$$

Sample: A subset of a population.

Sample statistic: A numerical characteristic of a sample.

Sample mean: The average of a sample of n values:

$$\bar{x} = \frac{1}{n} \sum_{i=1}^{n} x_i.$$

Sample proportion: The proportion of values in the sample meeting some specified condition or characteristic:

$$p = \frac{x}{n}.$$

Sampling error: The difference between a sample estimate and the actual value of the population parameter, which occurs because a sample is only a part of the population.

Census: An enumeration or listing of the entire set of values in the population.

Class mark: The representative value for a class in a frequency distribution — often the midpoint of the class interval.

Relative frequency: The frequency of a class divided by the total number of observations and expressed as a decimal.

Histogram: A graph (or "bar chart") showing the classes on the horizontal axis and the frequency (or relative frequency) of each class on the vertical axis.

Frequency polygon: A series of straight lines connecting the midpoints (class marks) of adjacent classes on a histogram.

Cumulative frequency: The sum of the number of occurrences of all values in a specified class plus the frequencies in all preceding classes.

Cumulative relative frequency: The sum of the relative frequency in a specified class plus the relative frequencies in all preceding classes.

Cumulative histogram: A histogram showing cumulative frequencies (or cumulative relative frequencies) on the vertical axis.

Ogive: A series of straight lines connecting the lower corner points of a cumulative histogram.

Summary Measures
for Populations

TWO

2.1   INTRODUCTION

In Chapter 1 the concepts of a population and a sample were introduced. Also, some descriptive measures were presented for a population and for a sample, as were some types of charts and graphs that are useful for describing the numbers in a data set. In this chapter, the emphasis is less on the comparison between populations and samples and more on the important descriptive measures that summarize the data in quantitative form. In particular, the topics of this chapter include the meaning, the calculation techniques, and the use of summary measures for a *population*. As was mentioned before, these summary measures are called *parameters*.

The most commonly used parameters for interpreting and understanding the meaning of the values in a population are the measures of *central location* (or *central tendency*) and of *variability*. Their use in summarizing the information in a data set is invaluable for giving a logical presentation or for making an argument based on the set of facts implied by the data set.

Example 2.1. Think of the task of presenting to an economics class some information on the price of textbooks in the campus book store. Assume that you have a listing of all the retail prices for each text now in stock. Your first statements would probably be something like, "The typical price of textbooks is about $19.95," or "Textbook prices vary from a low of $5.95 to a high of $46.95." In the first statement you are trying to present the central tendency of the text prices, and in the second you are groping for a way to describe the variability.

Example 2.2. A student in your class collects data on the monthly changes in sales of durable goods for each of the past 30 months. When asked to summarize what the data show, the student may say, "The average change in sales is 0.8%, but in 17 of the months the change has been greater than 1%." The first part of the statement gives information on the central location, and the second part helps to interpret the degree of consistency or the variability of the data.

Summary measures permit us to do more than merely duplicate the entire set of observations (preferably in some convenient format, such as a chart or diagram). The two types of summary measures most often used in statistical inference and decision-making are the central location and the variability of the data. There are a number of different ways of measuring these two characteristics, as shown in Table 2.1. Some of these terms are perhaps already familiar to you, while others may be new,

TABLE 2.1 **Common summary measures.**

Central Location:	Arithmetic mean
	Median
	Mode
	Geometric mean
Variability:	Standard deviation
	Variance
	Range
	Percentiles

technical terms. Although each is useful for certain purposes, this text will emphasize the two most common and useful measures in statistical inference, namely, the *arithmetic mean* and the *standard deviation*.

2.2 CENTRAL LOCATION

The single most important measure describing numerical information is the location of the center of the data. The term *central location* may refer to any one of a number of different measures including the *mean*, the *median*, and the *mode*. As the examples in this section will illustrate, each of these measures is appropriate for certain descriptive purposes, but not for others.

Example 2.3. A city transportation office hires a college student during the summer to do traffic counts on some specific streets. A monitoring device counts the number of times a vehicle rolls over a trip wire. However, a breakdown is also desired of vehicles in terms of cars, trucks, buses and any kind of trailer, including those pulled by a truck cab. Over a randomly selected set of ten hours, the student records 14,000 vehicles, including 9200 cars, 2840 trucks, 510 buses, and 1450 trailers. What is the central location of this data set? All that can be reported is that the vehicle type most frequently observed was cars. Clearly, there is no such thing as the "average" vehicle across these categories.

Example 2.4. Suppose that all of the 2840 trucks in Example 2.3 had to pass through a weighing station and the listing of all the gross vehicle weights is available. All 2840 weights in this population might have been different, but let us assume that nine of them were the same (to the nearest ten pounds). If this weight is the most frequently occurring weight, would it be the best measure of central location for this data set? Not necessarily! This most frequently occurring weight might be near the extremes of the distribution of weights, not near the center at all.

The Mode

most often

> The **mode** is defined as the value that occurs most often or, equivalently, the point (or class mark) corresponding to the value with the highest frequency.

Note that the mode may be a poor measure of central location, since the most frequently occurring value may not appear near the center of the data. Furthermore, the mode need not even be unique. Consider the frequency distributions shown in Fig. 2.1.

The first distribution in Fig. 2.1 shows the age of persons purchasing tape decks from a stereo equipment store during a sale. The ages are recorded to the nearest five years. The mode of this distribution is located at the lowest age level, 25 years. However, this mode certainly cannot be considered representative of the central location of this distribution of ages. The second distribution classifies sales at a fast food outlet into dollar intervals. This distribution has two modes, one at sales between $1 and $2 (perhaps for a hamburger, soft drink, and small order of fries) and one at sales between $4 and $5 (such as for two double cheeseburgers, large fries, milk shake, and dessert). Neither of these modes is especially useful for decision-making applications, since neither appears to be representative of the central location.

For purely descriptive purposes the mode can be useful in representing the most frequently occurring value. Consider the distributions in Fig. 2.2, which are the same distributions shown in Fig. 2.1, except that they now represent different data.

FIGURE 2.1 **Examples of the mode for two distributions.**

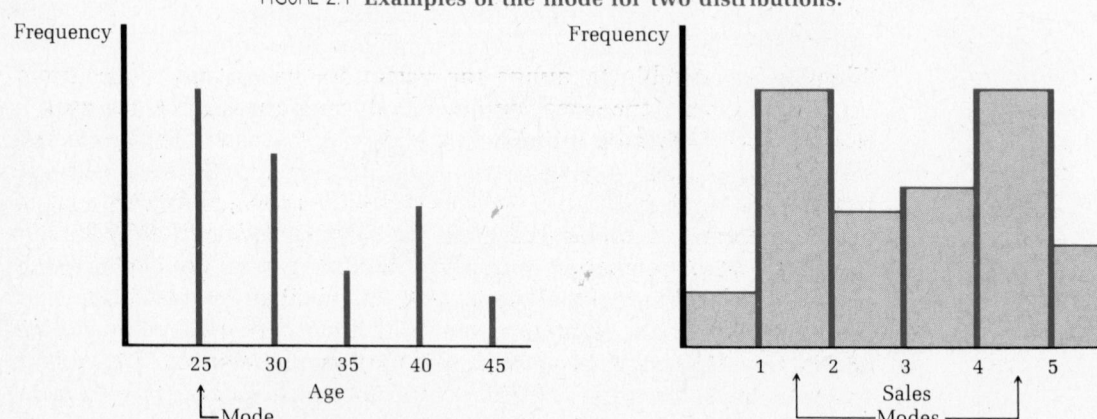

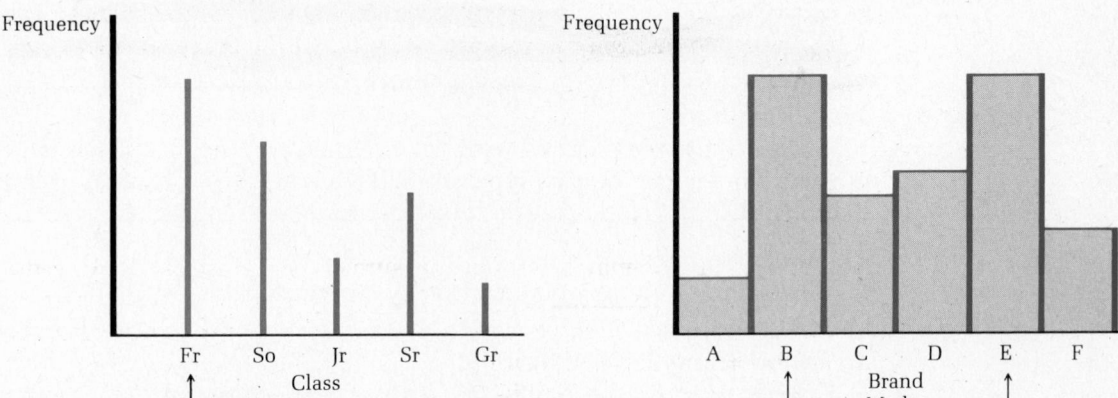

FIGURE 2.2 **Examples of the mode for two distributions.**

mode is useful if you cant find the avg. val.

The first distribution now describes the class distribution of students at a certain university. The modal class is the freshman class. There are more freshman than students of any other class. In the second distribution the groups indicate the brands of television that consumers selected as best in a recent survey. Two brands, B and E, tied for being selected most often as the best television. In such cases the mode is the appropriate measure, since the data measure only frequencies and it is not possible to find the average of these values (as we could with the "ages" or "dollars" in Fig. 2.1).

The Median Another measure of the central tendency of a data set is the **median.**

> The median is the middle value in a set of numbers arranged in order of magnitude.

When it is desirable to divide the data into two groups, each group containing exactly the same number of values, the median is the appropriate point of division. Finding the median of a set of numbers is not difficult when these numbers are arranged in ascending or descending order. If the number of values in the data set (N) is odd, the middle value can be determined by counting off, from either the highest or lowest value, (N + 1)/2 numbers; the resulting number divides the data into the two desired groups and thus represents the median. For example, in a list of five values the median is found by counting down (or up) three values, (5 + 1)/2 = 3; in a list of seven values the median is found by counting down (or up) (7 + 1)/2 = 4 values, so the median is the fourth value from either end.

*odd
1 middle value*

[handwritten: $(N+1)/2$ average of the 2 middle = median]

When N is even, there are two middle values, N/2 and N/2 + 1, and the median is usually defined as the number halfway between these two values. The median of six values is thus halfway between the third and fourth numbers.

Consider the populations with values listed in Table 2.2. Each data set gives the number of each type of small business that is located in the suburban districts of a city. The types of businesses reported are

A number of taxi companies,
B number of swimming pool contractors/service dealers,
C number of home computer sales stores,
D number of food supermarkets.

Note that in these cases (and for any data set), no matter how many items there are, the median always has a value such that the *number of values* on each side of the median *is equal* when all the values are arranged in numerical order. The only time this rule causes some confusion (but, technically, still holds) is when there are several values equal to the median, as in Data Sets C and D in Table 2.2. In Data Set D we have not arranged the data in numerical order, to emphasize that the data do not always come in order.

For population A with an odd number of values, the median number of taxi companies is the middle value of seven values. It is the fourth value in the ordering. For the other populations with an even number of values the median is the average of the third and fourth ordered values, as these are the two middle values.

Also, Table 2.2 gives the mode for each of these populations. The mode may be lower, higher, or the same as the median. No general rule applies, since the median and the mode depend on the particular population studied.

A third summary measure shown in the table is the simple *arithmetic mean,* commonly referred to as the *average.* The mean of a data set may be thought of as the *point of balance* of the data, analogous to the center of gravity for a distribution of mass in physics.

TABLE 2.2 **Central location measures.**

	Data Set A	Data Set B	Data Set C	Data Set D
Observations	2,2,3,7,8,9,11	5,7,8,10,10,14	2,3,4,4,4,7	11,9,26,11,10,11
Median	7	9	4	11
Mode	2	10	4	11
Mean	6	9	4	13

As presented in Chapter 1, this average is designated by the symbol μ for a population mean and by the symbol $\bar{x}$ for the sample mean. Note from the data sets in Table 2.2 that the mean may be less than, greater than, or equal to the median. For the populations A, B, C, and D the **population mean** is calculated by using Formula (2.1), which repeats Formula (1.1).

Population mean:

$$\mu = \frac{x_1 + x_2 + \cdots + x_N}{N} = \frac{1}{N} \sum_{i=1}^{N} x_i \qquad (2.1)$$

Comparison of the Mode, Median, and Mean

The arithmetic mean is the most widely used measure of central location. Its disadvantage for descriptive purposes is that it is affected more by extreme values than the median or the mode because it takes into account the differences among all values, not merely their rank order (as does the median) or their frequency (as does the mode). A recent cartoon illustrated this problem quite well by depicting a small-town worker commenting to a reporter that "the average yearly income in this town is $100,000 — there's one person making a million, and ten of us workers making $10,000."

Use of the median requires knowledge not only of the frequency of the values in a data set, as in determining the mode, but also of their ranking, so that these values can be ordered and the middle value obtained.

Example 2.5. Consider **Data Set 1,** containing data on cities with populations of 100,000–200,000. For each of the 78 cities reported there we have tabulated the Moody bond ratings. The table below gives the resulting frequencies, in order, from the highest bond rating (Aaa) to the lowest (Baa).

Ratings of Company Bonds

Rating	Frequency
Aaa	4
Aa	23
A1	26
A	14
Baa	11

The mode for these data is rating A1; the median also occurs at rating A1 (since the 39th and 40th values both lie in this class). It would be inappropriate to calculate a mean, since the differences between ratings are not precisely known, nor can these differences be assumed to be equal.

In contrast to this example, economic and business problems generally involve data in which the differences among values are known — income measures, output quantities, retained profits, prices, and interest rates. The same factor that makes the mean inappropriate for frequency data and ranked data is its special advantage in these cases; it is a more reliable measure of central location because it requires more knowledge about the population, namely, the difference between each value in the data set.

It should be pointed out that the mean, median, and mode are *not* the only measures of central location. Another type of mean, the geometric mean, is especially useful in certain types of problems in business and economics. It is a particularly appropriate measure of the central location of data expressed in relative terms, such as rates of change or ratios (e.g., change in the Consumer or Producer Price Indexes or in yields on stocks and bonds). The geometric mean gives equal weight to changes of equal relative importance. For example, if an index is doubled in value, this change is weighted equally to a change that halves the value of this index. One primary difficulty with the use of the geometric mean generally is that it cannot be used if any value in the data set is zero (no change). We will not present this measure or other special cases of means, since we wish to emphasize the use of the arithmetic mean.

Weighted Average

In some applications the form of the arithmetic mean presented in Formula (2.1) is not appropriate, since it weights each given value equally. For situations in which some values are more important than others, a weighted average should be used.

Example 2.6. A retired couple has three types of savings: an annuity A, some long term treasury bonds B, and a savings certificate C. The principal and yield in each type investment are:

	A	B	C
Principal	$15,000	30,000	5,000
Yield	9%	13%	8%

If this couple wishes to determine its average percentage yield, the use of the arithmetic mean given by Formula (2.1) would be inappropriate. Adding the three yields and dividing by 3 would give (9 + 13 + 8)/3 = 30/3 = 10 percent. A yield of 10% on this total savings of $50,000 would mean $5,000 per year return. Obviously, the couple is doing better than this. The actual return on the annuity is ($15,000)(0.09) = $1350. For the bonds it is ($30,000)(0.13) = $3900; and for the certificate it is ($5,000)(0.08) = $400.

The total return is $1350 + $3900 + $400 = $5650.

The correct average yield is ($5650/$50,000)100 = 11.3%.

In this example (and in many applications), a *weighted average* provides the correct mean value. If the values $x_1, x_2, \cdots, x_k$ have weights $w_1, w_2, \cdots, w_k$, a weighted average is defined as follows.

Weighted average:

$$\mu = \frac{\sum_{i=1}^{k} (w_i x_i)}{\sum_{i=1}^{k} w_i}$$ (2.2)

Each value of x_i is weighted by how often it occurs or by how important it is, and this product is divided by the sum of the weights. In Example 2.6 the x_i values are the three yields 9%, 13%, and 8%. The weights are the number of dollars invested (the principal amount) at each yield. Using the weighted average formula, the mean yield is:

$$\mu = \frac{\sum_{i=1}^{3} (principal)_i (yield)_i}{\sum_{i=1}^{3} (principal)_i}$$

$$\mu = \frac{15,000(9) + 30,000(13) + 5,000(8)}{15,000 + 30,000 + 5,000}$$

$$\mu = \frac{565,000}{50,000} = 11.3\%$$

The simple arithmetic average given in Formula (2.1) is a special case of the weighted average given in Formula (2.2) in which all the weights are equal to 1, since each value in the population is listed separately. If each $w_i = 1.0$ in Formula (2.2), then

$$\left[\sum_{i=1}^{k} (1)x_i \right] \bigg/ \sum_{i=1}^{k=N} (1) = \sum_{i=1}^{N} \frac{x_i}{N}.$$

In other cases that we will consider, the weights in Formula (2.2) may be frequencies, probabilities, or other measures. We return now to the use of the weighted average in finding a measure of central location for a population.

The Mean of a Frequency Distribution

The formula presented for the mean [Formula (2.1)] is based on the assumption that each value of the data set is given separately. Often, however, it is much easier to manipulate large amounts of data by grouping them into a frequency distribution. Columns 1 and 2 of Table 2.3 give an example of such a distribution: the monthly salaries (reported to the nearest 100 dollars) of the population of nonmedical staff in a hospital.

One way to find the mean of this population would be to sum all 250 values separately (8 values of $700 + 23 values of $800 + \cdots + 11 values of $1200), and then divide by 250. This is the procedure presented earlier in Formula (2.1). But most of us learned long ago that multiplication is easier than repeated addition; hence, we should take advantage of the fact that there are only six *different* values in Table 2.3, not 250. In other words, instead of adding $700 eight times, we can use the product 8($700). Similar products are used for every value of x_i, as shown in column (3) of Table 2.3. The sum of these products for all six values divided by 250 yields μ.

$$\mu = \frac{242,000}{250} = \$968.$$

The mean or average salary is thus $968.

TABLE 2.3 **Calculating the mean for a frequency distribution of monthly salaries.**

(1)	(2)	(3)	(4)	(5)
Salary (x_i)	Frequency (f_i)	$x_i f_i$	Relative Frequency $\left(\dfrac{f_i}{N}\right)$	$x_i \left(\dfrac{f_i}{N}\right)$
$700	8	5,600	0.032	22.4
800	23	18,400	0.092	73.6
900	75	67,500	0.300	270.0
1000	90	90,000	0.360	360.0
1100	43	47,300	0.172	189.2
1200	11	13,200	0.044	52.8
Sum	250	242,000	1.000	968.0

In this case a weighted average is used for $k = 6$ classes of values: $x_1 = 700$, $x_2 = 800$, $\cdots$, $x_6 = 1200$. The weights are the frequency f_i of occurrence of each x_i. Thus, the mean is as follows.

Population mean for frequency distribution:

$$\mu = \frac{1}{N} \sum_{i=1}^{k} x_i f_i.$$

(2.3)

Formula (2.3) is a special case of a weighted average for which the weights are the frequencies. It is sometimes convenient to rewrite Formula (2.3) in a slightly different (but equivalent) form, placing N inside the sum sign. In this application of a weighted average the values are again x_i, but the weights are now relative frequencies, $w_i = (f_i/N)$. These are shown in column (4) of Table 2.3 and (as always) these relative frequencies sum to unity. Thus, another formula for finding the mean of a frequency distribution using relative frequencies is as follows.

Population mean for frequency distribution:

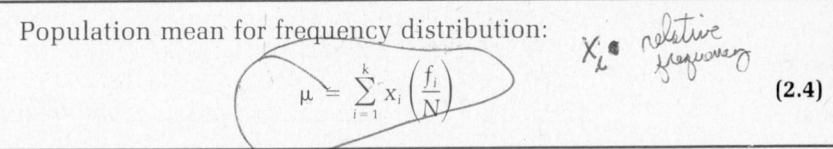

$$\mu = \sum_{i=1}^{k} x_i \left(\frac{f_i}{N} \right)$$

(2.4)

The use of Formula (2.4) is demonstrated by column (5) of Table 2.3. Note that the sum of this column yields $\mu = 968$, the same value we calculated above by using Formula (2.3).

We must point out here that it is quite common in frequency tables for the values of x to be given as class intervals rather than as specific numbers. In such cases the mean can still be calculated by using either Formula (2.3) or Formula (2.4). The value of x_i that should be used in the formula is the class mark for the ith interval. The usual class mark is the midpoint of the class interval. This selection is based on the assumption that the midpoint is the average of all occurrences of values of x within the interval. Since this assumption may not be exactly true, it is usually not worthwhile to determine exact midvalues. A rounded-off value may be used because the calculation of summary measures for a data set given in class interval form always involves a grouping error. This error tends to be small if the number of observations in each class is large. If several classes have frequencies of less than 5, it is desirable to combine some of the categories. The best strategy for small data sets (or if a computer is to be used for calculations) is to avoid grouping errors and to list all the separate values.

Study Question 2.1: Average Number of City Swimming Pools
In a selected state, there are 20 cities with approximately 50,000 people. A phone call was made to the government offices in each of these towns to determine the number of public swimming pools in the town. Table 2.4 presents the values reported for this population (source: City Parks and Recreation Departments).
a) Find the mean of this population.
b) Arrange the population values into a frequency distribution and find the mean.

Answer

a) $\mu = \dfrac{1}{N} \sum\limits_{i=1}^{N} x_i = \dfrac{1}{20} \sum\limits_{i=1}^{20} x_i$

$= \dfrac{1}{20}(3 + 3 + 1 + 0 + \cdots + 2 + 2 + 1) = \dfrac{40}{20} = 2.0$

b) value

x	0	1	2	3	4	Sum
frequency f	2	5	7	3	3	20

$\mu = \left[\sum\limits_{i=1}^{k} f_i x_i \right] \bigg/ \sum\limits_{i=1}^{k} f_i = \sum\limits_{i=1}^{5} \dfrac{f_i x_i}{N}$

$= [2(0) + 5(1) + 7(2) + 3(3) + 3(4)]/20$

$= \dfrac{40}{20} = 2.0.$

The average number of public swimming pools in cities of this state with a population of 50,000 is 2.

Study Question 2.2: Mean of Motor Assembly Times
Each of 30 trainees learning to repair small electric motors was given a test to complete an assembly of a 28-piece model of a motor. The number of minutes to complete the task was recorded for each trainee. This population of values is given in Table 2.5. Find the mean number

TABLE 2.4 **Number of public swimming pools.**

3	3	1	0	2
2	4	0	1	4
3	2	1	2	2
4	1	2	2	1

TABLE 2.5 **Minutes to complete motor assembly for 30 trainees.**

Minutes	Frequency
$3.5 < x \leq 4.5$	5
$4.5 < x \leq 5.5$	4
$5.5 < x \leq 6.5$	6
$6.5 < x \leq 7.5$	9
$7.5 < x \leq 8.5$	1
$8.5 < x \leq 9.5$	3
$9.5 < x \leq 10.5$	1
$10.5 < x \leq 11.5$	1

of minutes to complete the assembly, using frequencies as weights [as in Formula (2.3)].

Answer. A representative value (class mark) must be selected for each interval of minutes. Choose the rounded-off values of the midpoints of each interval, $x_i = 4, 5, 6, \cdots, 11$.

$$\mu = \left[\sum_{i=1}^{8} f_i x_i \right] \Big/ N$$

$$= [5(4) + 4(5) + 6(6) + 9(7) + 1(8) + 3(9) + 1(10) + 1(11)]/30$$

$$= 195/30 = 6.5.$$

The average number of minutes for trainees to complete assembly of the model of the motor is 6.5.

Two items are worth attention from these Study Questions. First, in finding the answer to a statistical problem the solution and final interpretation should always be clearly stated in a sentence. Second, the methodology and formula used should be made clear.

Define. *Mean, median, mode, central location.*

PROBLEMS

2.1 Explain what is meant by a measure of central location. Give an example from a recent newspaper or magazine of some use of a central location measure.

2.2 Refer to **Data Set 2** and find the median for the values of assets for those 50 firms.

2.3 Five $45 sweaters are on sale for $35, and three $85 coats are on sale for $60. Find the average percent decrease in price for these sale items.

2.4 The number of customers in a rural post office for 16 working days was: 68, 83, 47, 51, 91, 89, 99, 73, 62, 58, 91, 66, 75, 84, 77, 69.
a) Find the mean and the median.
b) Does this population have a unique mode? If so, is this mode a good measure of central location?

2.5 The owner of a local movie theater showing art films has tabulated the ages of customers attending the last two showings:

Age:	18–22	23–27	28–32	33–37
Number:	60	80	50	40

Age:	38–42	43–47	48–52
Number:	30	20	20

a) In which class does the median fall? Would the midpoint of this class be a good guess for the median? If not, what age would you use as an approximation to the median?
b) What is the mode of this distribution?
c) Calculate the mean for this population. Use the midpoints 20, 25, $\cdots$, 50 to represent all values in a class.

2.6 On the basis of Fig. 2.3, find the mean unemployment rate in the United States for the seven months indicated (source: Bureau of Labor Statistics). What must you assume in order for this measure to have a meaningful interpretation?

2.7 The distribution of the number of out-of-state phone calls made in a month by 100 students in a certain dormitory is indicated by the following frequencies:

Number of calls per student	0	1	2	3	4
Frequency (f)	47	33	14	5	1

a) What are the median and the mode of this population?
b) Find the mean of this population.

2.8 Suppose that a certain gasoline producer sponsors a mileage economy test involving a population of 30 cars. The frequencies of the number of miles per gallon, x, recorded to the nearest gallon, are given on page 45.

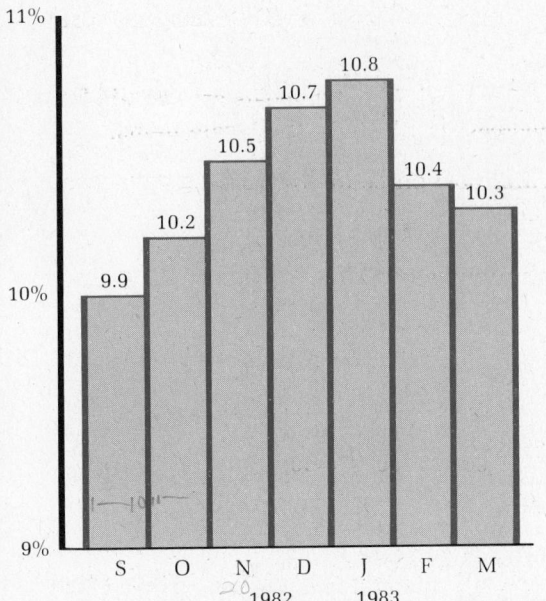

FIGURE 2.3 **United States unemployment rate.**

x	f
25	8
26	9
28	7
30	6

Find the average miles per gallon for this population by using Formula (2.3).

2.9 Twenty communities provide information on the vacancy rate in local apartments. Find the mean of the following population of vacancy rates, using Formula (2.4). (*Hint:* Use the middle value for each vacancy rate.)

Relative frequency	Vacancy Rate
0.5	3–7%
0.3	8–12%
0.2	13–17%

2.10 Refer to **Data Set 4** and consider the values for "incomes of doctors," as a population.

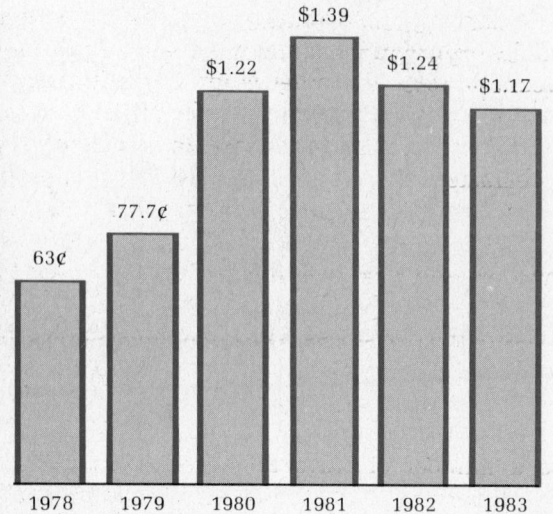

FIGURE 2.4 **Average gas prices in North Carolina at Easter.**

a) Find the median and the mean for income. Explain the difference between these two measures of central location.
b) Group the values of income into class intervals of $10,000 in width, beginning with the interval

$$\$45,000 < \text{income} \leq \$55,000.$$

Use Formula (2.3) to find μ. Explain the difference between this outcome and the mean found in part (a).

2.11 Repeat Problem 2.10 using the values for "expenses." In part (b), use intervals of $10,000, beginning at $25,000.

2.12 Using the information in Fig. 2.4, find the mean price of gas on Easter for the six years represented (source: AAA–Carolina Motor Club).

2.3 MEASURES OF DISPERSION

Measures of central location usually do not give enough information to provide an adequate description of the data because variability or spread is ignored. An individual who bases a judgment on the mean alone may be compared to the person whose head is in a freezer and whose feet are in an oven declaring, "On the average, I feel fine." Another measure is needed, one that indicates how spread out or *dispersed* the data are.

Example 2.7. A broker suggests two different stocks to a client. One is for a microelectronics firm that has an average annual rate of growth over the past five years of 16%. The other is for an electric utility firm that has a growth rate of 8%. Which one would the client choose? Is the mean growth rate sufficient information to make an intelligent choice? It may be if all other characteristics are similar. However, suppose that it is also true that the first firm has had growth in one year as large as 30% and as low as −50% (a decline). The growth rate of the utility firm has always been between 7.5% and 8.5% over this period. How does this new information on variability affect the client's choice? It might be used as an indication of the risk of the two stocks. The client must choose between stocks with a relatively sure 8% growth rate and a riskier 16% growth rate.

Since there are a number of ways to measure variability, let us consider some of the properties that a good measure should have. A good index of spread should be independent of the central location of the observations, that is, independent of the mean of the data. This property implies, in effect, that if a constant were added to (or subtracted from) each value in a set of observations, this transformation would not influence the measure of spread. In addition, to be most useful, a measure of spread should take into account *all* observations in its calculation, rather than just a few selected values such as the highest and lowest. Finally, a good measure should reflect the typical spread of the data, and it should be convenient to manipulate mathematically.

The Range   One simple example of a measure of spread is the **range.**

> The range is the *absolute* difference between the highest and lowest values in the data set.

The ranges of the four data sets in Table 2.2 are

$$|11 - 2| = 9, \quad |14 - 5] = 9, \quad |7 - 2] = 5, \quad \text{and} \quad |26 - 9| = 17.$$

The range has the advantages of being independent of the measure of central location and being easy to calculate. It has the *disadvantages of* ignoring all but two values of the data set and not necessarily giving a *typical* measure of the dispersion, since a single extreme value changes the range radically.

The Mid-range One way to help reduce the disadvantage of the range being highly sensitive to one extreme value is to throw out the outliers or extreme values by calculating a measure of the spread of the innermost concentrated portion of the data. Such a measure is called a **mid-range** and is obtained by excluding a specified proportion of the extreme values at both ends of the ordered values in the data set. Some common mid-ranges used are the 80% mid-range and the 50% mid-range.

Example 2.8. **Data Set 2** has the values of the retail sales of the top 50 companies listed in order. The range of the sales is the largest value minus the smallest.

$$R = (\text{maximum sales}) - (\text{minimum sales})$$
$$= 27,357,400 - 1,027,093 = \$26,330,307.$$

For this same population the 80% mid-range would exclude the top 10% and the bottom 10% of the values of sales. The difference between the largest and the smallest of the remaining 80% of the values is found. Since the number of items in this population is 50, the top 10% of the values is the set of the largest five values. Excluding these and excluding the smallest five values gives the middle 40 values, those ranked 6th through 45th in sales:

$$80\% \text{ mid-range} = (\text{sales of 6th firm}) - (\text{sales of 45th firm})$$
$$= 7,223,404 - 1,193,961 = \$6,029,443.$$

A mid-range uses more information than the range, since it involves the number of cases (N), the ranking of the values, the exclusion of a set percentage of the values, and the maximum and minimum of the remaining values. Since it is still quite easy to calculate, a mid-range is somewhat more desirable than the range in having the good properties for a measure of spread or variability.

Deviations There is an even better measure of variability that meets all the desirable properties. First, recall that we want our measure to be independent of the mean of the data. In other words, the value of μ should have no influence on the value of our measure of variability. This objective is accomplished by working always with data sets that have the *same* mean. That is, if all the populations that we wish to describe have the same mean, then the value of μ cannot influence our measure of variability. It is obvious, of course, that not all data sets have the same mean to begin with. We have to *transform* the values in each set in such a way that the transformed means are all equal.

The transformation used in statistics is designed to yield a data set always having $\mu = 0$. To make $\mu = 0$ is quite simple: Merely subtract the mean of the original data set from each value in that set. Each resulting number, called a *deviation* and denoted $(x - \mu)$, indicates how far and in which direction the original number lies from the mean. For example, the deviation $(x - \mu) = 5$ reflects a value of x five units above the mean, and the deviation $(x - \mu) = -7$ indicates a value of x seven units below the mean.

The sum of the deviations $(x - \mu)$ will always equal zero; and so the average of the deviations $(x - \mu)/N$ will always equal zero. Consider, for example, a data set consisting of the five values of x shown in Table 2.6, which gives the number of cars towed per day (Monday–Friday) for illegal parking in a university "permit only" lot.

If we subtract the mean of these five numbers (which is $\mu = 10$) from each value of x, the mean of the new set of values, labeled $x - \mu$, must equal zero. Any set of numbers can be transformed in this fashion into a set of deviations with a mean of zero.

To formalize the above process, consider a population with N values x_i, $i = 1, 2, \cdots, N$, and mean μ. When these N values are transformed into deviations from the mean, the new values are $x_i - \mu$ for $i = 1, 2, \cdots, N$, and the sum of these deviations must be zero. That is,

$$\sum_{i=1}^{N} (x_i - \mu) = 0.$$

Since the transformation $(x_i - \mu)$ gives all sets of data a common central location (i.e., they all have means of zero), measures of dispersion

TABLE 2.6 **Observations and deviations.**

Number of Cars Towed (x)	Deviations $(x - \mu)$
4	−6
8	−2
10	0
13	+3
15	+5
Sum 50	0
Mean 10	0

defined in terms of deviations about the mean have the desirable property of being independent of central location.

While the sum of the deviations about μ is advantageous because it takes into account *all* the observations and is independent of the mean, this sum clearly cannot be our measure of variability, since its value always equals zero. We will see in the following section that if we square each deviation before we sum, the resulting measure no longer equals zero and is relatively easy to manipulate mathematically. If we take the average of these squared deviations (i.e., divide their sum by N), our measure also will reflect the typical spread of the data.*

Variance

Consider the *average squared deviations* about the mean. Squaring the deviations avoids the problem inherent in ordinary deviations about the mean (namely, that their sum always equals zero). Indeed, as we indicated above, this index meets all the properties of a good measure of spread; *thus the average squared deviation is the traditional basis for measuring the variability of a data set.* Since it uses the deviations about the mean, it is independent of central location. It uses every value in the data set and is reasonably easy to compute mathematically. Furthermore, it is very sensitive to any change in the values; even a single change of one value in a set of 100 would result in a different measure of variability.

This "average squared deviation" measure is called the *variance* and is denoted for a population by the symbol σ^2, which is the square of the lower case Greek letter *sigma*. The **population variance (σ^2)** is defined as follows:

Population variance:

$$\sigma^2 = \frac{1}{N} \sum_{i=1}^{N} (x_i - \mu)^2. \tag{2.5}$$

In calculating a variance by using Formula (2.5), one first calculates each deviation; these deviations are squared, the squared deviations are then summed, and finally the sum is divided by N.

---

* Another possibility for measuring variability is to average the sum of the absolute deviations about the mean, which is

$$\frac{1}{N} \sum |x_i - \mu| = \text{mean absolute deviation} = \text{MAD}.$$

This MAD measure has all of the desirable properties described above, except for the fact that it is not convenient to manipulate mathematically.

μ

Example 2.9. We calculate a population variance using the values of x in Table 2.7 that represent the number of tape recorders assembled by ten different workers on an assembly line over the past month. That is, worker 1 assembled 115 recorders, worker 2 assembled 122 recorders, etc. The mean number of recorders assembled, at the bottom of the first column, is

$$\mu = \frac{1200}{10} = 120 \text{ (recorders)}.$$

The deviations about the mean are shown in the second column. Note that the sum of these deviations equals zero, as it must. The third column of values gives the *squared* deviations about the mean, the sum of which is 436. Hence, the *average squared deviation* (the variance) of this population is:

$$Recorders\ variance:\quad \sigma^2 = \frac{1}{N} \sum_{i=1}^{N} (x_i - \mu)^2 = \frac{436}{10}$$

$$= 43.6 \text{ (recorders)}^2.$$

Since we have squared the values of x in this process, the units for x have also been squared.

Computational Formula for Variance

Statisticians, like most of us, really do not enjoy performing a lot of burdensome calculations. Perhaps that is one reason why a computational formula was developed for calculating variances. Formula (2.6) is merely

TABLE 2.7 **Data for Example 2.9.**

Number of Recorders	x	$x - \mu$	$(x - \mu)^2$	x^2
	115	−5	25	13,225
	122	+2	4	14,884
	129	+9	81	16,641
	113	−7	49	12,769
	119	−1	1	14,161
	124	+4	16	15,376
	132	+12	144	17,424
mean →	120	0	0	14,400
	110	−10	100	12,100
	116	−4	16	13,456
Sum	1200	0	436	144,436
Mean	120 = μ	0	43.6 = σ^2	

$$\sigma^2 = \frac{\sum x^2}{N} - \mu^2 = \frac{144,436}{10} - 120^2 = 43.6$$

the result of manipulating Formula (2.5) algebraically. It will always give the same value of σ^2 as Formula (2.5) (except for rounding errors).*

Computational formula for variance:

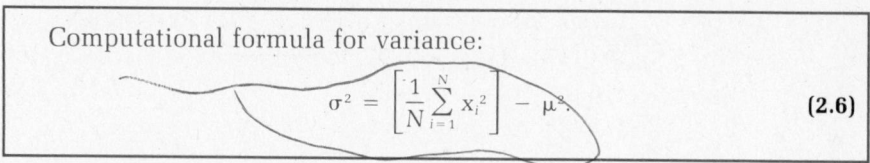

$$\sigma^2 = \left[\frac{1}{N}\sum_{i=1}^{N}x_i^2\right] - \mu^2 \qquad\qquad (2.6)$$

This computational formula for the variance is illustrated in Table 2.7. Column 4 of the table provides the sum of the squares of the x_i values: $\Sigma x_i^2 = 144{,}436$. Since the population size is $N = 10$ and the mean has been found to be $\mu = 120$, the variance using Formula (2.6) is

(handwritten: can be a time saver if these numbers aren't large.)

$$\sigma^2 = \frac{1}{10}(144{,}436) - (120)^2$$

$$= 14{,}443.6 - 14{,}400 = 43.6 \text{ (recorders)}^2$$

When the number of different values of x_i is not large and the values of the observations and of the mean are integers, the calculation of the variance is often just as easy with the use of Formula (2.5) as with this computational formula. Indeed, the computational formula in this case involved calculations with larger numbers than did the definitional Formula (2.5) using squared deviations. However, for cases in which the values of the observations and of the mean are not integers or the number of different values of x_i is large, then Formula (2.6) is a real computational time-saver. In such cases, Formula (2.5) would involve a large number of subtractions (involving decimals) and then the squaring of the resulting deviations; therefore, the computational formula would be much easier. Notice that the first term in Formula (2.6) is simply the average of the

---

* The derivation is obtained by expanding Formula (2.5), applying the definition of the mean, and simplifying:

$$\frac{1}{N}\sum_{i=1}^{N}(x_i - \mu)^2 = \frac{1}{N}\sum(x_i^2 - 2x_i\mu + \mu^2)$$

$$= \frac{1}{N}[\sum x_i^2 - 2\mu\sum x_i + \sum \mu^2]$$

$$= \frac{1}{N}\sum x_i^2 - 2\mu[\frac{1}{N}\sum x_i] + \frac{1}{N}N\mu^2$$

$$= \frac{1}{N}\sum x_i^2 - 2\mu(\mu) + \mu^2$$

$$= \frac{1}{N}\sum x_i^2 - \mu^2.$$

squares of the values of x_i. The second term is the square of the previously calculated mean. In general, the mean is calculated first (to obtain a good measure of central location), and then the mean is used to calculate the variance (as a measure of the variability of the data set). In words, Formula (2.6) can be expressed as follows.

> The variance is the average of the squares minus the square of the average.

Example 2.10. Referring to Study Question 2.1 on page 42, the variance can be determined for the data in Table 2.4 on the number of public swimming pools. The mean number of pools per city is 2.0. The actual values for the x_i are:

$$
\begin{array}{cccccccccc}
3 & 3 & 1 & 0 & 2 & 2 & 4 & 0 & 1 & 4 \\
3 & 2 & 1 & 2 & 2 & 4 & 1 & 2 & 2 & 1
\end{array}
$$

By using Formula (2.5) the variance is found as follows:

$$
\sigma^2 = \frac{1}{N} \sum_{i=1}^{N} (x_i - \mu)^2
$$

$$
= \frac{1}{20}[(3-2)^2 + (3-2)^2 + (1-2)^2 + \cdots + (2-2)^2 + (1-2)^2]
$$

$$
= \frac{1}{20}(28) = 1.4 \text{ (pools)}^2.
$$

By using the computational Formula (2.6) the variance is

$$
\sigma^2 = \left[\frac{1}{N} \sum_{i=1}^{N} x_i^2\right] - \mu^2
$$

$$
= \frac{1}{20}[3^2 + 3^2 + 1^2 + \cdots + 1^2] - 2^2
$$

$$
= \frac{1}{20}(108) - 4 = 5.4 - 4 = 1.4 \text{ (pools)}^2.
$$

Two features of these calculations are probably now apparent. First, either of the methods for finding the variance ought to be easily adapted for solution by a computer, since the same type of operation is simply repeated across all the values of the population. Indeed, it is very common to use a packaged program that begins by finding the sum of the values and the sum of the squares of the values and then computes various summary measures. Figure 2.5 shows a computer printout using a program named SPSS, which was used to compute the mean, variance, range, and sum for the variables in **Data Set 2.**

```
         RETAIL SALES AND ASSETS FOR 50 FIRMS

VARIABLE SALES

MEAN                                     4.419
VARIANCE                                23.642
RANGE                                   26.330
SUM                                    220.942

VALID OBSERVATIONS -                            50
- - - - - - - - - - - - - - - - - - - - - - - - - - - - - - - - - -
VARIABLE ASSETS

MEAN                                     2.132
VARIANCE                                23.409
RANGE                                   34.314
SUM                                    106.600

VALID OBSERVATIONS -                            50
```

FIGURE 2.5 **Summary measures for variables in Data Set 2.**

A second feature observed in the above calculations is that the same terms repeat themselves in the sum whenever the same values occur for x_i. This means that the *use of frequencies as weights* could be applied to the calculation of a variance, just as it was in calculating the mean. We will show how this is done shortly.

Study Question 2.3: Variance of Canoe Rentals
The data in Table 2.8 show the weekly number of canoes rented at the New River Camp Station for 40 weeks during the 1983 season. Find the variance of this population, first using Formula (2.5) and then using the computational Formula (2.6).

Answer. Using Formula (2.5) and the mean value of 78.2,

$$\sigma^2 = \frac{1}{40} \sum_{i=1}^{40} (x_i - 78.2)^2$$

$$= \frac{1}{40}[(63 - 78.2)^2 + (68 - 78.2)^2 + \cdots + (94 - 78.2)^2]$$

$$= \frac{1}{40}(231.04 + 201.64 + \cdots + 249.64)$$

$$= \frac{1}{40}(2214.40) = 55.36 \ (canoes)^2.$$

TABLE 2.8 **Weekly canoe rentals.**

63	68	71	74	76	78	81	84	85	89
66	70	73	75	76	79	82	84	85	90
67	71	73	75	76	79	82	85	86	92
68	71	74	75	77	79	84	85	86	94

Using Formula (2.6),

$$\sigma^2 = \left[\frac{1}{40} \sum_{i=1}^{40} x_i^2 \right] - (78.2)^2$$

$$= \frac{1}{40}(63^2 + 68^2 + \cdots + 94^2) - 6115.24$$

$$= \frac{1}{40}(246,824) - 6115.24 = 55.36 \text{ (canoes)}^2.$$

A computer printout of the variance and other measures for the population in Table 2.8 is shown in Fig. 2.6. The results are obtained from the SPSS program.

The arithmetic average is shown in the printout as the mean, 78.200. The variance shown is 56.779, which differs from the value of 55.36

FIGURE 2.6 **Frequency distribution and summary measures for the data in Table 2.8.**

```
CANOE           WEEKLY CANOE RENTALS

                ADJ CUM                ADJ CUM                ADJ CUM
        CODE FREQ PCT PCT CODE FREQ PCT PCT CODE FREQ PCT PCT
        63.   1    2    2  75.   3    7   40  85.   4   10   85
        66.   1    2    5  76.   3    7   47  86.   2    5   90
        67.   1    2    7  77.   1    2   50  89.   1    2   92
        68.   2    5   13  78.   1    2   52  90.   1    2   95
        70.   1    2   15  79.   3    7   60  92.   1    2   97
        71.   3    7   22  81.   1    2   63  94.   1    2  100
        73.   2    5   27  82.   2    5   67
        74.   2    5   32  84.   3    7   75

MEAN         78.200    MEDIAN       77.500    MODE    85.000
STD DEV       7.535    VARIANCE     56.779    RANGE   31.000
MINIMUM      63.000    MAXIMUM      94.000
VALID CASES     40    MISSING CASES     0
```

calculated above by using Formulas (2.5) and (2.6). The difference is due to the calculational method used by the SPSS program. It computes the variance as if it were a *sample* variance [as we will present in Chapter 7, Formula (7.5)], rather than a *population* variance. To adjust the computer value, we need to multiply the variance in the printout (Fig. 2.6) by $(N - 1)/N = 39/40$. The result is $56.779(39/40) = 55.360$.

This comparison of the computer output in Fig. 2.6 with our hand calculations illustrates one *disadvantage* of using preprogrammed statistical computer packages. *They do not always calculate the exact statistic that is desired.* Their *advantage* is clear: The user does not have to write the entire computer program. Remember that whenever you use someone else's computer program, you must know how the output measures are defined and calculated, or you might use them inappropriately. For example, look at Fig. 2.6 for the computer printout for percentage frequency (ADJ PCT) and cumulative frequency (CUM PCT). The printing format of the program used only integer values, so these frequencies are rounded off and could be misunderstood. The first value of 63 occurs once and should have a percentage frequency of $(1/40)100 = 2.5$, rather than 2. In the second line, for the value 66, the percentage frequency should again be 2.5. Note that the cumulative frequency is now 5 (2.5 + 2.5), although it appears that the computer has obtained 5 by adding 2 + 2.

In the margin: computers quicker but not accurate

The Standard Deviation Very often, the positive square root of the variance, denoted σ and called the **population standard deviation**, is used in place of (or in conjunction with) the population variance to describe variability. The standard deviation is usually more convenient than the variance for *interpreting* the variability of a data set, since σ^2 is in squared units while σ is in the same units as the original data. The population standard deviation is defined as follows:

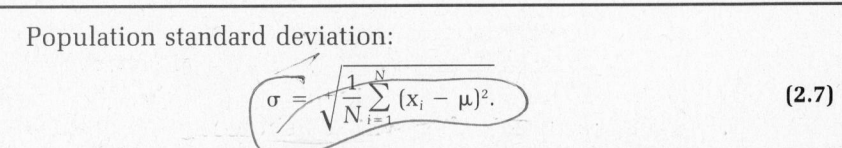

Population standard deviation:

$$\sigma = \sqrt{\frac{1}{N}\sum_{i=1}^{N}(x_i - \mu)^2}.$$

(2.7)

While the variance has the desired criteria for a good measure of dispersion, the standard deviation is a better measure of the typical size of a deviation from the mean because this measure is in the same units as the original data (while, as mentioned, the variance is in squared units). For the data in Table 2.7 the standard deviation is

$$\sigma = \sqrt{\text{Variance}} = \sqrt{43.6} = 6.60 \text{ (recorders)}.$$

TABLE 2.9 **Use of the rule of thumb for interpreting variability.**

Interval	Values within Interval	Actual Percent of Population within Interval	Rule of Thumb
$\mu \pm 1\sigma = 120 \pm 6.60$ $= \begin{cases} 113.4 \text{ to} \\ 126.6 \end{cases}$	115,116,119,120,122,124	60%	68%
$\mu \pm 2\sigma = 120 \pm 2(6.60)$ $= \begin{cases} 106.80 \text{ to} \\ 133.20 \end{cases}$	110,113,115,116,119 120,122,124,129,132	100%	95%

In general, a precise interpretation of values of σ and σ^2 is difficult because variability depends so highly on the unit of measurement. For instance, variability of income in the United States is certainly larger when measured in dollars than when measured in thousands of dollars. Nevertheless, these variability measures are very useful. In all cases, as the spread of a population increases, the values of σ^2 (and σ) will also increase. On the other hand, if $\sigma^2 = \sigma = 0$, this means that there is no variability at all to the data (all x-values are the same and equal to their mean; that is, x is a constant).

One **rule of thumb** that often provides a good *approximation* to the spread of a set of observations states:

> *About 68 percent* of all values will fall within *one* standard deviation to either side of the mean, and *about 95 percent* of all values will fall within *two* standard deviations to either side of the mean.*

In other words, the interval from $(\mu - 1\sigma)$ to $(\mu + 1\sigma)$, which we will write as $(\mu \pm 1\sigma)$, often will contain about 68 percent (or about $\frac{2}{3}$) of all population values. Similarly, the interval $(\mu - 2\sigma)$ to $(\mu + 2\sigma)$, that is $(\mu \pm 2\sigma)$, often will contain about 95% of all the population values. We must emphasize that these rules are only approximations and do not necessarily hold for any one discrete example. It is not difficult, for example, to show for the data on tape recorders (Table 2.7) that 60% of the population (six of the ten values) fall in the interval $(\mu \pm 1\sigma)$ and 100 percent of the data fall in the interval $(\mu \pm 2\sigma)$. These intervals are shown in Table 2.9. Recall that $\mu = 120.0$ and $\sigma = 6.60$.

* In Chapter 6 we will show that this rule of thumb is based on the assumption that the population has a symmetrical bell-shaped distribution called the *normal distribution*.

Example 2.11. Consider once again the canoe rental data in Table 2.8. In Study Question 2.3 we determined that the mean of this population is $\mu = 78.2$ canoes and that the variance is $\sigma^2 = 55.36$ (canoes)^2. Because the variance is in squared units, it is often more appropriate to use the value of the standard deviation:

$$\sigma = \sqrt{55.36} = 7.44 \text{ canoes.}$$

If the rule of thumb described earlier holds, then $\mu \pm 1\sigma$ should contain about 68% of the canoe rental data values, and $\mu \pm 2\sigma$ should contain about 95% of all these values. Checking these intervals against the values in Table 2.8 gives the following results:

Interval	Percent of Values
$\mu \pm 1\sigma = 78.20 \pm 7.44 \quad = 70.76$ to 85.64	70%
$\mu \pm 2\sigma = 78.20 \pm 2(7.44) = 63.32$ to 93.08	95%

These percent of values within the specified intervals are consistent with the rule of thumb. Such comparisons serve as a check on the reasonableness of the calculated values for μ and σ. If we had found that the interval $\mu \pm 1\sigma$ included more than 90% of the values of the population (too many) or that it included only 30% (too few), we would have known to recheck the calculations or reexamine the population for unusual values.

Also, understanding this rule of thumb enables us to picture mentally the distribution of the population. The mean μ gives the central location. The standard deviation σ gives a "standard" unit of spread around the mean that includes about $\frac{2}{3}$ of the values of the population. Hence, had we known only that $\sigma = 7.44$ and $\mu = 78.20$ canoes and had never seen the list of values for the population, we still could have given a good description of this particular set of values.

Considering all the measures of central location and dispersion that we have presented, the two measures most often useful in statistical inference and decision-making are the mean and the standard deviation. These are common everyday terms to any statistician, as they are used daily in helping to make decisions based on statistical analysis of data sets. The mean is precisely the balance point of all the values. The standard deviation is the typical (or standard) size of the difference (deviation) between the individual values of the population and the mean of the population. As such, it provides a good insight into the extent of variability in the data set, especially when the rule of thumb applies. The reader should keep in mind that the variance and the standard deviation do not represent two different ways of measuring the variability of a population. Since σ is merely the positive square root of σ^2, these two measures reflect the *same information* about variability but are expressed in different units. The standard deviation is easier to interpret because it is not in squared units, but it is more difficult than the variance to manipulate mathematically because of the square-root sign.

Population Variance for a Frequency Distribution

In Formulas 2.5 and 2.6 we calculated the variance of a population, assuming that all frequency values were equal to 1 (i.e., $f_1 = 1$). These formulas can be generalized to take into account frequencies other than 1 in exactly the same manner in which the formula for the mean μ was generalized. Again, we assume that there are k different values of x. A squared deviation $(x_i - \mu)^2$ is calculated for every observation. Each squared deviation is then weighted by its frequency. Dividing the sum of the products by N we get the following.

Population variance for a frequency distribution:

$$\sigma^2 = \frac{1}{N} \sum_{i=1}^{k} (x_i - \mu)^2 f_i. \qquad (2.8)$$

Formula (2.8) is illustrated by the first four columns of Table 2.10 for our salary example, which originated in Table 2.3. The mean salary was

TABLE 2.10 **Calculating the variance for a frequency distribution of monthly salaries.**

(1) Salary (x_i)	(2) Frequency (f)	(3) $(x_i - \mu)$ $(x_i - 968)$	(4) $(x_i - \mu)^2 f_i$	(5) Relative Frequency (f_i/N)	(6) $(x_i - \mu)^2 \left(\dfrac{f_i}{N}\right)$
$700	8	−268	574,592	0.032	2,298.368
800	23	−168	649,152	0.092	2,596.608
900	75	−68	346,800	0.300	1,387.200
1000	90	32	92,160	0.360	368.640
1100	43	132	749,232	0.172	2,996.928
1200	11	232	592,064	0.044	2,368.256
Sum	250 = N		3,004,000	1.000	12,016.000

found to be $\mu = \$968.$* Using Formula (2.8) and the sum in column 4, we get

$$\sigma^2 = \frac{1}{250}(3,004,000) = 12,016 \text{ (dollars)}^2.$$

As in the case of the formula for computing the mean, it is also possible to modify Formula (2.8) by moving the value (1/N) inside the sum sign and using relative frequencies as the weights. This yields the following (equivalent) formula.

Population variance for a relative frequency distribution:

$$\sigma^2 = \sum_{i=1}^{k} (x_i - \mu)^2 \left(\frac{f_i}{N}\right) \qquad \textbf{(2.9)}$$

The fact that Formula (2.9) is equivalent to Formula (2.8) can be seen by examining the sum of the values in column (6) in Table 2.10.

$$\sigma^2 = \sum_{i=1}^{k} (x_i - \mu)^2 \left(\frac{f_i}{N}\right) = 12,016 \text{ (dollars)}^2.$$

This is the same value obtained previously by using Formula (2.8). The standard deviation is the square root of this value, $\sigma = 109.6$, and it is measured in the original units (dollars).

As with the unweighted formulas for variance, there is also a computational formula for calculating the variance of a frequency distribution. Formula (2.10) gives the same value for σ^2 as Formula (2.8) or Formula (2.9), except for differences due to rounding.† The advantage of the computational formula is that in many problems it makes the process of calculating σ^2 somewhat easier (especially when μ is not an integer), since it does not require finding each deviation and squaring it. This computational formula is as follows.

Computational weighted formula for variance:

$$\sigma^2 = \left[\frac{1}{N}\sum_{i=1}^{k} x_i^2 f_i\right] - \mu^2. \qquad \textbf{(2.10)}$$

---

* The inquisitive reader may wonder why the sum of column (3) [$(x_i - \mu)$] in Table 2.10 does not equal zero. The reason is that each deviation occurs according to the frequencies in column (2). If each deviation is multiplied by its frequency and the products are summed, their total will be zero.

† Proof of this fact is left as an exercise for the reader in Problem 2.42.

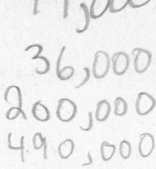

Example 2.12 Consider again the salary data in Table 2.10. The values of x_i in column (1) and the frequencies f_i in column (2) are used to illustrate Formula (2.10). We also recall the information for this case that $N = 250$ and the mean is $\mu = 968$. The new terms to calculate are the weighted squares of x_i, denoted $x_i^2 f_i$:

$$\sigma^2 = [\frac{1}{N} \Sigma x_i^2 f_i] - \mu^2$$

$$= \frac{1}{250}[(700)^2 8 + (800)^2 23 + (900)^2 75$$

$$+ (1000)^2 90 + (1100)^2 43 + (1200)^2 11] - (968)^2$$

$$= \frac{1}{250}(237{,}260{,}000) - 937{,}024 = 12{,}016 \text{ (dollars)}^2.$$

Formula (2.10) is also easily remembered by stating its meaning term by term as *"the weighted average of the squares minus the square of the average."*

Study Question 2.4: Dispersion of the Number of City Swimming Pools

a) Find the variance and standard deviation for the frequency distribution of the swimming pool data in Study Question 2.1.
b) What percentage of the population values lie within one standard deviation of the mean?

Answer

a) The calculations are easily organized by using a tabular format. If we remember that the mean is an integer, $\mu = 2$, Formula (2.8) is the easiest to apply.

x_i	f_i	$x_i - \mu$	$(x_i - \mu)^2$	$(x_i - \mu)^2 f_i$
0	2	-2	4	8
1	5	-1	1	5
2	7	0	0	0
3	3	$+1$	1	3
4	3	$+2$	4	12
	$N = 20$			Sum $= 28$

The variance is

$$\sigma^2 = \frac{1}{N}\sum_{i=1}^{k} (x_i - \mu)^2 f_i = \frac{1}{20}(28) = 1.4 \text{ (pools)}^2.$$

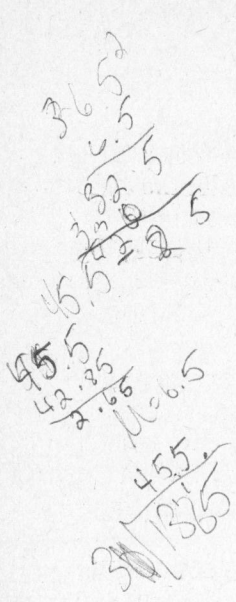

The standard deviation is

$$\sigma = \sqrt{1.4} = 1.18 \text{ pools.}$$

b) $\mu \pm 1\sigma = 2 \pm 1.18$ is the interval (0.82, 3.18), which includes the population values, 1, 2, and 3. These occur with frequencies 5, 7, and 3, respectively. Thus, $5 + 7 + 3 = 15$ of the 20 population values are in this interval $\mu \pm 1\sigma$. The percentage within the interval $\mu \pm 1\sigma$ is $(15/20) \times 100 = 75\%$.

Study Question 2.5: Dispersion of Motor Assembly Times

For the data on minutes to complete assembly of a model of a motor as given in Study Question 2.2, find the variance, the standard deviation, and the percentage of population values within the interval $\mu \pm 1\sigma$.

Answer. The data on minutes is given by a grouped frequency distribution. Class marks are used to represent the values within each group. Since the mean was found to be 6.5, not an integer, the computational Formula (2.10) is probably easiest to use. A tabular arrangement is convenient for organizing the computations.

Class Mark (x_i)	f_i	x_i^2	$x_i^2 f_i$
4	5	16	80
5	4	25	100
6	6	36	216
7	9	49	441
8	1	64	64
9	3	81	243
10	1	100	100
11	1	121	121
	$N = 30$		Sum $= 1365$

The variance is

$$\sigma^2 = \left[\frac{1}{N} \sum_{i=1}^{k} x_i^2 f_i \right] - \mu^2$$

$$= \frac{1}{30}(1365) - (6.5)^2$$

$$= 45.50 - 42.25 = 3.25 \text{ (minutes)}^2.$$

The standard deviation is $\sigma = \sqrt{3.25} = 1.80$ minutes.

The interval $\mu \pm 1\sigma$ includes values from $(6.5 - 1.80)$ to $(6.5 + 1.80)$. That is, the interval is $[4.7, 8.3]$. This interval includes the class marks of 5, 6, 7, and 8; and the frequencies of these class marks are 4, 6, 9, and 1, respectively. Thus, the approximate (due to the grouping error and the use of the class marks) percentage of population values within the interval $[4.7, 8.3]$ is $100[(4 + 6 + 9 + 1)/30] = 66.7\%$.

Three Important Measures of a Data Set

Before we present some other descriptive and summary measures of populations, it is important to recognize that we have already discussed the three most important measures of data sets. These are *size*, *central location*, and *variability*. For further study in statistics and for use in decision problems it is necessary to master the calculation of these measures and to understand their meaning.

Size, determined by counting the number of items in the population, is denoted by N. The mean (denoted by μ) is often the best measure of central location, especially for most business and economics applications. When each separate value of the population is listed, the mean is determined by using Formula (2.1). If the population values are given in a frequency listing, Formula (2.3) is most often used. If the values are grouped in class intervals, the class mark is substituted for x_i in this formula.

Variability is best measured by the variance or the standard deviation. When the mean is an integer and the number of different values is relatively small, Formula (2.5) is appropriate when the individual values are available; Formula (2.8) is appropriate when a frequency listing of values is available. When the mean is not an integer or when the number of different values of x_i is large, all the subtractions used in these formulas become tedious. The computational Formulas (2.6) and (2.10) are then recommended, the choice between them again depending on whether all the values are listed [Formula (2.6)] or whether a frequency distribution of values is used as the starting point [Formula (2.10)].

Why are these three measures so important? They are the summary measures to which most persons refer when presenting results of a study or when using quantitative data to support some argument. They are the measures to use in writing a report based on data collected or found in a reference. They are the measures that will command our attention throughout this text. It must be noted that many times one or the other of these measures is used alone by a spokesperson, whether he or she is a politician, manager, teacher, or scientist. Look in a newspaper to find some examples of the use of size, mean, or standard deviation of a data set without reference to one of the others. However, be wary in making conclusions or decisions based on fewer than all three of these measures. Data may be misrepresented for the sake of an argument by using one or two of these measures while omitting the third.

Inadequacy of Central Location Measures Alone

Consider the case in which a person must choose between two sales jobs, each having potential earnings of $25,000 a year. One company representative says that their salespeople earning $25,000 work an average of 30 hours per week. The other prospective employer says the average for similar employees is 50 hours. One might decide on this basis to work for the first company with the "average" work week of 30 hours. Be careful! The average hours worked per week to earn $25,000 in the first company may be as low as 30 because the company president has hired some relatives who hardly work at all each week while the typical salesperson is working 65 hours per week. Or the first company may have only two such salespeople who share all the mail orders. A third new person would split the total pot significantly or, perhaps, not share at all. In the other company the average may be based on 800 salespeople. The measures for the second company would give a much more reliable value for the time and salary expected to occur for the 801st person. It is necessary to know more about the distribution of the data than merely the mean before this measure can be used intelligently in making a decision.

Inadequacy of Variability Measures Alone

Consider the decision process when you ask a special friend out to dinner to celebrate your A-grade in statistical analysis. Two restaurants are suggested as very suitable, and you are told that the variability in the price of a dinner is $10 in the first and $3 in the second. Is this enough information to make a sound decision? Suppose that the mean price for a dinner in the first restaurant is $12, while in the second it is $30. Or suppose that the first restaurant has only three dinner selections—squid, shark, and eel—while the data for the second restaurant are based on 20 different specialties of the house, including meat, fish, and fowl. Again, it is obvious that while the variability is an important consideration, this measure by itself (without knowledge of the mean and the number of cases) is often insufficient for decision-making and may even be misleading.

The same consideration would apply to an investment decision between two managed funds. Information on the variability in the annual rate of return for each fund would be important to know but not sufficient. You should want to know the average as well; and you should want to know the number of years on which these measures are based.

Study Question 2.6: Analyzing Advertising Programs of Competitors
A marketing consultant for a beverage producer reviews the advertising programs of its competitors and notes that two of these competitors

are preparing for a new promotional program during which the price of a six-pack will be dropped 20%. Should the consultant try to devise a new marketing strategy that would be equally effective in offsetting the price reduction of each competitor?

Answer. The summary measure given is a central location measure. The consultant should try to learn something about the standard deviation as well. One competitor may be planning to drop the price 5–30%, depending on the location of the market throughout the country. The other competitor may be planning a 20% drop nationwide with no variability. Two different reactions may be appropriate. Also, the total market share or the number of cases of beverage sold by each of these competitors may be relevant. One may be a very small and specialized beverage producer distributing only 1000 cases per week. The other may be one of the largest producers, distributing millions of cases per day. Obviously, the beverage producer might have different levels of concern over the two planned advertising programs. In summary, the single measure of 20% does not provide enough information, although it may be a very good summary measure for indicating central location.

Define. *Dispersion, range, mid-range, deviation, variance, standard deviation.*

PROBLEMS

2.13 A recruiter for a certain company claims that advancement opportunities are great in the company because present salaries of five-year employees range from 20% to 200% more than their corresponding beginning salaries. Explain why this statistical information might be inadequate for a prospective employee who is trying to decide whether or not to take a job with this company.

2.14 Find the variance for the population described in Problem 2.4.

2.15 Find the variance for the population described in Problem 2.5.

2.16 Use the information in Problem 2.7 to do the following:
a) Find the variance of the number of calls per student using Formula (2.8).
b) Verify your answer to part (a) by using Formula (2.10).
c) What percent of the population falls within the interval $\mu \pm 1\sigma$? Within the interval $\mu \pm 2\sigma$?

2.17 Use the information in Problem 2.8 to do the following:
a) Find the standard deviation for the population.
b) Find the percent of the population that falls within the $\mu \pm 1\sigma$ and $\mu \pm 2\sigma$ intervals.

2.18 Consider the following frequency distribution:

Class	Frequency	Class Mark	fx	fx^2
1–5	4	3	12	36
6–10	8	8	—	—
11–15	3	—	—	—
16–20	5	—	90	—

a) Find the mean of this population by completing the table above.
b) Find the variance, using Formula (2.10).

2.19 Find the variance for the population in Problem 2.9 using Formula (2.9).

 2.20 A bank has 156 branch offices. The age (x) of the branch managers is given in the following frequency distribution:

Age	Frequency
$30 < x \leq 34$	8
$35 < x \leq 39$	21
$40 < x \leq 44$	24
$45 < x \leq 49$	32
$50 < x \leq 54$	40
$55 < x \leq 59$	23
$60 < x \leq 64$	8

Find the mean and standard deviation of the ages of the branch managers.

2.21 Use the information in Problem 2.12 to do the following:
a) Find the variance of the gas prices.
b) What proportion of the observed years have gas prices within one standard deviation of the mean?

2.22 Use the information in Problem 2.6 to do the following:
a) Find the standard deviation of the unemployment rates.
b) What proportion of the months have unemployment rates within one standard deviation of the mean?

2.4 OTHER DESCRIPTIVE MEASURES

While the mean and the standard deviation are the most common descriptive measures, there are a number of other measures that give additional information about the characteristics of a data set. This section is devoted to describing, rather briefly, a few of these measures.

Percentiles, Deciles, and Quartiles

The summary measures described thus far all use just a single number to describe certain characteristics of a population. In some circumstances it may be helpful to use more than one number to describe a data set. For example, a company recruiter visiting a college campus may be interested in learning more than just the mean or median grade point average for all graduating seniors. This person may want to know the average of those members of the graduating class who form the upper 10%, the upper 20%, and so forth. Percentiles, deciles, and quartiles are useful in this circumstance in that they divide a data set into a specified number of groups, each containing the same number of values. **Percentiles** divide the data into 100 equal parts, each representing one percent of all values. The 90th percentile, for example, is that value which has 90% of all values below it and 10% above it. Thus, a student scoring higher than 95% and lower than 5% of all students on the college board exams is said to have scored in the 95th percentile. Percentiles can be *determined exactly* from a table of cumulative relative frequencies of ungrouped data and *approximated* from a table of grouped data.

Quartiles and deciles are defined in much the same fashion as percentiles: **quartiles** divide the data into four equal parts, while **deciles** divide the data into ten equal parts. The *first* quartile value is that point which exceeds one-fourth and is exceeded by three-fourths of the observations. Only three quartile values are necessary to divide the data into four parts. Likewise, nine decile values divide a set of observations into ten equal parts. The *fifth decile* and the *second* quartile values are equivalent to the *median.* as is 50th percentile

Some other percentile or quartile measures are already familiar to us in terms of other measures. The 50% mid-range is equivalent to the range between the first and third quartiles, called the **interquartile range.** The range between the first and ninth decile is the 80% mid-range. The range between the 16th and the 84th percentile would include the middle 68% of the values of the population. Therefore, in accord with our rule of thumb, one-half of this 68% mid-range could be used to approximate the size of the standard deviation, especially if the distribution is symmetric and has a single mode.

Shapes of Distributions   Having a method for describing the *shape* of a frequency distribution is often more helpful than just being able to describe the central location or spread of a set of values. Most of the distributions representing real-world problems are called *unimodal distributions*, implying that they have only one peak, or mode. A distribution with two peaks is called a **bimodal distribution.** Often, distributions with more than one mode actually reflect the merging of two or more *separate* kinds of data into a single set of values.

Consider, for example, the frequency distribution shown in Fig. 2.7 representing the frequency of sales of television sets for a large department store, in intervals of $100. What Fig. 2.7 actually represents is *two* unimodal distributions: one reflecting the sales of black-and-white television sets and the other representing the sales of color television sets. If we make this distinction and plot the resulting frequency distributions, the two distributions in Fig. 2.8 are obtained. Note that the distribution in Fig. 2.8(a) has a fairly long "tail" to the right, a characteristic common to many distributions representing data in the behavioral and social sciences, especially income distributions.

A distribution is a **symmetric distribution** if it has the same shape on both sides of its median. Imagine folding the picture of a distribution in half at its median. To be symmetric, the two halves must match perfectly — they must be "mirror images" of one another. For all symmetric distributions the median equals the mean. The mode will also equal the median if the distribution is unimodal. Figure 2.9 shows three symmetric distributions.

A distribution that is not symmetric, but rather has most of its values either to the right or to the left of the mode, is said to be a **skewed**

FIGURE 2.7 **Combined television set sales.**

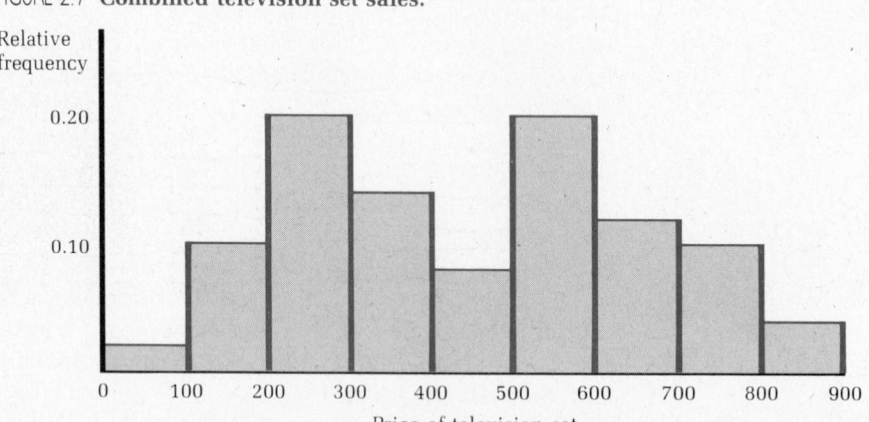

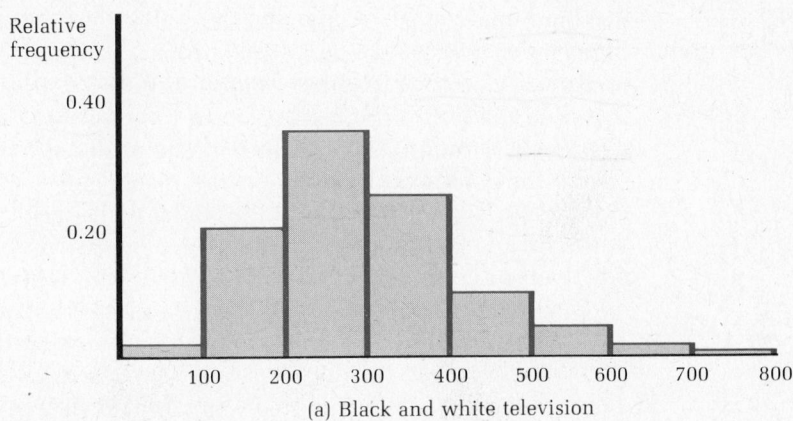

(a) Black and white television

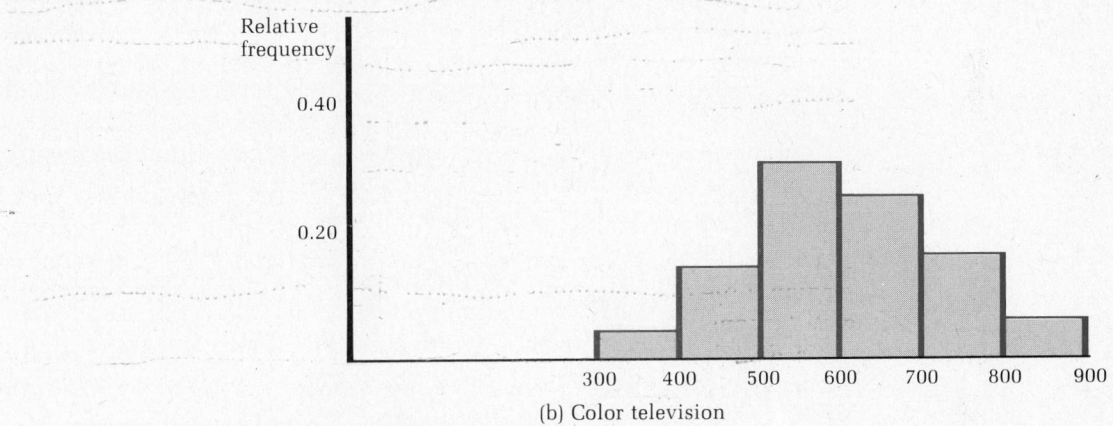

(b) Color television

FIGURE 2.8 **Television set sales.**

FIGURE 2.9 **Symmetric distributions.**

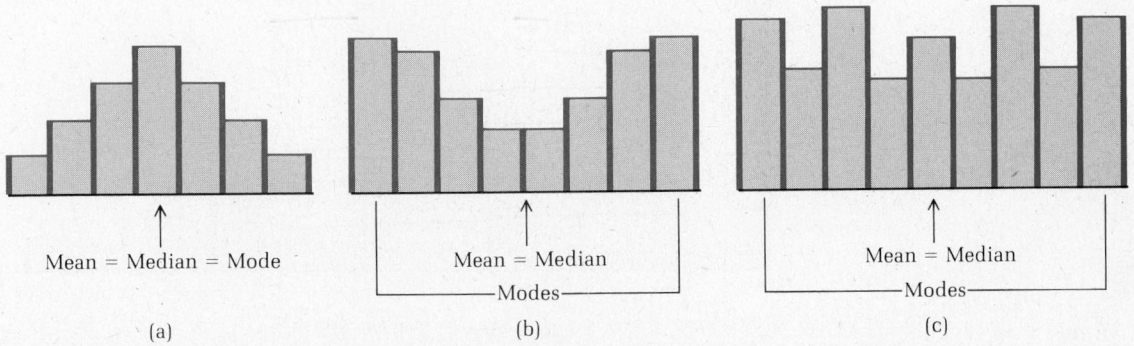

distribution. If most of the values of a distribution fall to the *right* of the mode, as in Fig. 2.8(a), this distribution is said to be skewed to the right or *skewed positively*. A distribution with the opposite shape, with most values to the *left* of the mode, is said to be skewed to the left, or *skewed negatively*. Note in Fig. 2.10 how the lack of symmetry in a distribution affects the relationship between the mean, the median, and the mode. For a completely symmetrical unimodal distribution, such as Fig. 2.9(a), these three values must all be equal. As the distribution becomes skewed positively, the mode remains at the value representing the highest frequency, but the median and the mean move to the right.

Various memory aids make it easy to remember the direction and the effect of skewness on the measures of central location in a unimodal distribution. Two useful ones are the following:

1. The order of magnitude of the central location measures is *alphabetical* in a *negatively* skewed distribution (mean < median < mode) and *reversed* in a *positively* skewed distribution (such as Fig. 2.10).
2. If a distribution is stretched sideways, the direction of stretch is the direction of skewness. A distribution with its right-hand side stretched out in the positive (increasing numerical value) direction has positive skewness. A distribution with its left tail stretched out in the negative (decreasing numerical value) direction is negatively skewed.

Kurtosis   Another descriptive measure of the shape of a distribution relates to its flatness or peakedness. The term applied to this characteristic of shape is **kurtosis.** The flat distribution with short broad tails illustrated in Fig.

FIGURE 2.10 **The relationship between the mean, the median, and the mode for a distribution with positive skewness.**

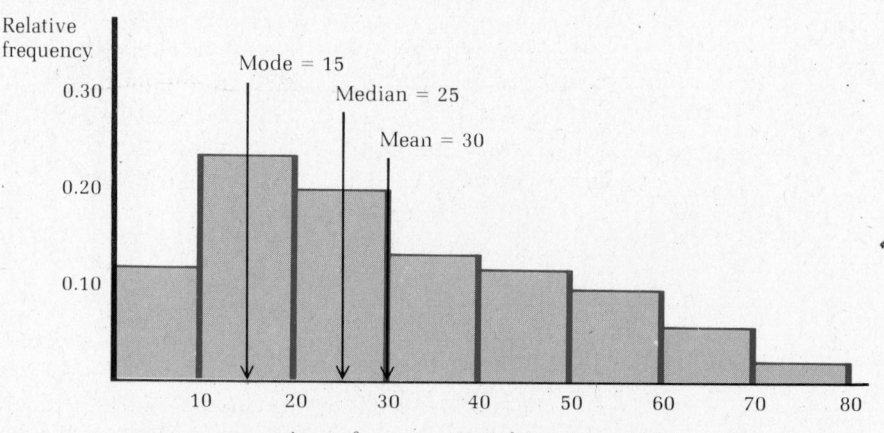

Ages of persons injured in auto accidents

FIGURE 2.11 **Platykurtic curves have short tails like a platypus, while leptokurtic curves have long tails like kangaroos, noted for "lepping" (after W. S. Gosset).**

2.11 is called *platykurtic*. A very peaked distribution with long thin tails is called *leptokurtic*. Measures of kurtosis (and skewness) are important to mathematical statisticians in their study of the theoretical properties of distributions. Although summary measures for kurtosis exist, we will not present them in this text, since measures of kurtosis are of relatively little use in elementary applications of statistics.

2.5 SUMMARY

In this chapter we have focused on describing the central location and variability of populations as aids to decision-making. The two measures that are of greatest importance are the mean and the standard deviation. The population mean μ is the most important measure of central location, and the standard deviation σ is the most important measure of variability. The primary formula for calculating the mean is

$$\mu = \frac{1}{N} \sum_{i=1}^{k} x_i f_i.$$

When all the values are listed separately and each is given equal weight, each value of f_i is 1, and $k = N$. When the data are arranged in a grouped distribution, the values of x_i are the class marks for each class.

The standard deviation is calculated as the *square root* of the variance. The definitional formula for the variance is *the average of the squared* deviations. The computational formula for the variance is *the average of the squares minus the square of the average*. The common formulas are

$$\sigma^2 = \frac{1}{N} \sum_{i=1}^{k} (x_i - \mu)^2 f_i$$

and

$$\sigma^2 = \left[\frac{1}{N} \sum_{i=1}^{k} x_i^2 f_i \right] - \mu^2.$$

Again, f_i are the frequencies, and x_i are the values or the class marks of specified groups of values.

Define. *Percentile, interquartile range, symmetry, skewness, kurtosis.*

PROBLEMS

2.23 Answer parts (a), (b), and (c).
a) A financial management company operates ten mutual funds. For each of the past five months, the number of their funds that have increased in value per share has been 3, 5, 1, 8, and 3. Show that the mean and standard deviation for this population of five numbers are 4.0 and 2.37, respectively.
b) Suppose that in the next two months the number of managed funds that increase in value per share are 2 and 6. Include these observations with those in part (a) and find the mean of this population of seven numbers. Show that it has a smaller standard deviation than in part (a).
c) Suppose that a different company also manages ten funds and had the same experience as the company in part (a). However, in the next two months the number of its funds that increased in value per share are 0 and 8. Find the mean and explain why the standard deviation is larger in this population than in part (a).

2.24 One hundred families are registered in a regional welfare office for financial assistance under the Aid for Dependent Children program. The number of children per family is given as:

Number of children:	0	1	2	3	4	5	6–10
Number of families:	2	3	15	35	20	15	10

a) What is the median number of children per family? What is the modal number? Find the mean number of children.

b) What is the 60% mid-range for the number of children per family? What is the standard deviation?

c) What proportion of the families have a number of children within one standard deviation of the mean?

2.25 Given the following values for the number of rooms reserved in a population of ten motels, find the mean, mode, median, 60% mid-range, and standard deviation:

35, 14, 6, 18, 14, 27, 19, 7, 12, 14.

2.26 The population "kitchen employees in seven local restaurants" is 2, 9, 1, 3, 10, 3, and 2.
a) Find the mean, median, and mode.
b) Calculate σ^2 for these values.
c) Is this population symmetric, or is it skewed positively or negatively?

2.27 Answer the following questions about percentiles, quartiles, and deciles:
a) What does it mean if a math score on the SAT is reported as being in the "85th percentile"?
b) If your college grades are in the "third quartile," what does this mean?
c) If the sales growth of a franchise is in the "eighth decile" among all outlets in its region, what does this mean?

2.28 Using **Data Set 1**, find the mean and standard deviation of income. Then determine the percentage of the population values in the intervals $\mu \pm 1\sigma$ and $\mu \pm 2\sigma$.

2.29 Given the following distribution on the rate (x) of capacity utilized by a population of 32 steel-producing plants, find the mean and variance of x. Use the midvalue of each class (the class mark) as the value of x.

Utilization Rate	Frequency	Class Mark
96–100	4	98
91–95	5	93
86–90	6	.
81–85	5	.
76–80	1	.
71–75	4	
66–70	2	
61–65	5	

2.30 The following frequency distribution shows the weekly sales of a pizza restaurant for its first year of operation.

Sales	Number of Weeks
0–$5,999	4
$6,000–11,999	6
12,000–17,999	10
18,000–23,999	16
24,000–29,999	12
30,000–35,999	4
	52

a) Compute the mean and the mode.
b) Compute the variance.

2.31 Return to Problem 1.10, which gives the starting salaries for 16 accounting majors after receiving their college degrees.
a) Find the median and the mode.
b) Using the classes suggested in Problem 1.10(c), find the mean of these data. Explain any difference between this mean and the one calculated in Problem 1.10(b).

2.32 Assume that the data listed in Problem 1.10 are for a population and compute
a) the range and the 75% mid-range;
b) the variance and the standard deviation;
c) the percent of the observations falling within one standard deviation from the mean and the percent falling within two standard deviations from the mean.
d) Repeat part (b) using the grouped data in Problem 1.10(c).

2.33 The ten households in Oldberry, N.C., report the following incomes:

$20,500 $14,150 $12,505 $16,245 $15,570
$16,600 $24,800 $21,325 $19,170 $29,000

a) Find the mean, standard deviation, and median of these data.
b) Compare the variability and skewness of this distribution with a regional income distribution that reports a mean of $20,000, standard deviation of $3,000, and median of $18,000.

2.34 How are the mean, the median, and the mode related in a completely symmetrical and unimodal frequency distribution? How are they related in positively skewed and in negatively skewed unimodal distributions? Sketch several distributions to illustrate your answer.

EXERCISES

2.35 Find an example (from a newspaper, magazine, etc.) of using only "means" to draw some conclusion. Examine the argument closely and explain the need to know the "size" of the populations and how this could strengthen or weaken the argument.

2.36 Find an example (from a newspaper, magazine, etc.) of using only "means" to draw some conclusions. Examine the argument closely and explain the inadequacy of it, or explain how knowledge of a variability measure could strengthen or change the argument.

2.37 Acquire 50 observations on a variable of interest to you and your fellow students (e.g., wage rates, apartment rental rates). Find the mean and the standard deviation of your data. Use these to present a summary statement of the information provided by your data.

2.38 Make up two sets of eight values each, with the following characteristics:
a) Same average but different variability;
b) Same range but different averages;
c) Same average and same range, but different 50% mid-range.

2.39 A movie producer holds a preview of a new movie and asks viewers for their reaction. By age groups the following results are obtained:

	Age Group			
	Under 20	20–39	40–49	60 and over
Liked the movie	140	75	50	10
Disliked the movie	60	50	50	20

Summarize these results using means and standard deviations.

2.40 T. M. Jones, manager of Shark Loan, Inc., has kept a record of the frequency of the *time between arrivals* of customers at his loan office. These data, shown below, indicate that the time interval between consecutive arrivals was between zero and 20 minutes on 50 occasions, between 20 and 40 minutes on 33 different occasions, etc. Since there were 150 customers during this period, there are 150 interarrival times (the time to the first customer is counted as one interarrival time).

Minutes between Customers (t)	Frequency (f)
$0 < t \le 20$	50
$20 < t \le 40$	33
$40 < t \le 60$	22
$60 < t \le 80$	15
$80 < t \le 100$	11
$100 < t \le 120$	8
$120 < t \le 140$	5
$140 < t \le 160$	3
$160 < t \le 180$	2
$180 < t \le 200$	1
	150

a) Construct a histogram of relative frequencies and a cumulative relative frequency distribution for the interarrival times. Draw the polygon for these distributions.

b) Find the mode, the median, the mean, and the standard deviation (use class marks of 10, 30, 50, · · ·).

c) What percent of the observations fall within $\mu \pm 1\sigma$? What percent fall within $\mu \pm 2\sigma$?

d) Based on these data, how many customers would you estimate for Shark Loan next week if the office is open five days a week, ten hours a day?

2.41 Assume that you are responsible for auditing last month's accounts receivable for the 10,000 credit accounts on the Easy Charge Company. The company has furnished you with the following summary data for this population (this is a slight abstraction of 12,223 actual credit balances).

Balance Due	Frequency	Balance Due	Frequency
$0–99.99	3123	$600–699.99	180
100–199.99	2085	700–799.99	90
200–299.99	1927	800–899.99	53
300–399.99	1355	900–999.99	25
400–499.99	743	$1000 and	
500–599.99	400	over	19

a) Draw the histogram and frequency polygon for these data.

b) As an auditor, are you satisfied with the manner in which the company summarized the data?

c) Use the midpoint of each class and the associated frequencies to calculate the mean of this population. Assume that the 19 values in the eleventh class average $1050.

d) Calculate σ and σ^2 for this population. What percent of the population lies within $\mu \pm 1\sigma$ and $\mu \pm 2\sigma$?

e) Is this distribution skewed to the right or the left?

2.42 Prove that Formula (2.10) is mathematically equivalent to Formula (2.8).

2.43 An important statistic to consider when using a statistical sampling audit plan is the population variability. The population variability is measured by the:
a) sample mean
b) standard deviation
c) kurtosis
d) estimated population total minus the actual population total.

2.44 The frequency distribution of employee years of service for Henry Enterprises is positively skewed (i.e., it is not symmetrical). If a CPA wishes to describe the years of service of the typical Henry employee in a special report, the measure of central tendency that the CPA should use is the:
a) standard deviation
b) arithmetic mean
c) mode
d) median.

USING THE COMPUTER

2.45 Refer to **Data Set 4** in Appendix C and find the variance and standard deviation of a doctor's income and expenses. Also, determine the percentage of the population values that lie within one standard deviation of the mean (found in Problems 2.10 and 2.11).

2.46 Refer to **Data Set 1** and find the variance and standard deviation of the taxes reported for 78 cities. Determine the proportion of the cities with taxes within the intervals $\mu \pm 1\sigma$ and $\mu \pm 2\sigma$.

2.47 The weekly wages in September 1984 of 105 employees in a textile mill are given in the following table. Find the mean and standard deviation of the weekly wages.

Weekly Wages (x)	Employees
160 < x ≤ 170	4
170 < x ≤ 180	14
180 < x ≤ 190	18
190 < x ≤ 200	28
200 < x ≤ 210	20
210 < x ≤ 220	12
220 < x ≤ 230	9

CASE PROBLEM

2.48 A number of investment services and brokerage houses regularly publish recommendations on which common stocks to purchase for various investment goals. Based on these opinions, a list is compiled of the 300 stocks that were most recommended for purchase in 1983. The subsequent total return on these stocks over a 12-month period is given below. Using summary measures, describe the total return for this population.

Total Return	f	Total Return	f
−3 < x ≤ −2	3	17 < x ≤ 18	13
−2 < x ≤ −1	1	18 < x ≤ 19	12
−1 < x ≤ 0	1	19 < x ≤ 20	10
0 < x ≤ 1	1	20 < x ≤ 21	8
1 < x ≤ 2	2	21 < x ≤ 22	6
2 < x ≤ 3	6	22 < x ≤ 23	3
3 < x ≤ 4	10	23 < x ≤ 24	2
4 < x ≤ 5	2	24 < x ≤ 25	7
5 < x ≤ 6	6	25 < x ≤ 26	2
6 < x ≤ 7	16	26 < x ≤ 27	8
7 < x ≤ 8	11	27 < x ≤ 28	2
8 < x ≤ 9	8	28 < x ≤ 29	2
9 < x ≤ 10	18	29 < x ≤ 30	1
10 < x ≤ 11	22	30 < x ≤ 31	1
11 < x ≤ 12	23	31 < x ≤ 32	1
12 < x ≤ 13	22	32 < x ≤ 33	0
13 < x ≤ 14	19	33 < x ≤ 34	1
14 < x ≤ 15	21	34 < x ≤ 35	1
15 < x ≤ 16	16	35 < x ≤ 36	0
16 < x ≤ 17	11	36 < x ≤ 37	1

GLOSSARY

Mode: The value that occurs most frequently.

Median: The middle value in a set of values (population or a sample).

Population mean: The average of a set of N values:

$$\mu = \frac{1}{N}\sum_{i=1}^{N} x_i \quad \text{or} \quad \mu = \frac{1}{N}\sum_{i=1}^{k} x_i f_i.$$

Range: The absolute value of the difference between the maximum and minimum values in a data set.

A% mid-range: The absolute value of the difference between the highest and lowest of the middle A% of the values in the data set, excluding $[(100 - A)/2]\%$ of the extreme values at each end of the distribution.

Population variance (σ^2): The average of the squared deviations of values of x from their mean:

$$\sigma^2 = \frac{1}{N}\sum_{i=1}^{k} (x_i - \mu)^2 f_i.$$

$$\sigma^2 = \left(\frac{1}{N}\sum_{i=1}^{k} x_i^2 f_i\right) - \mu^2.$$

Population standard deviation (σ): The square root of the variance:

$$\sigma = +\sqrt{\text{variance}} = +\sqrt{\sigma^2}.$$

Rule of thumb: $\mu \pm 1\sigma$ includes about 68% of the values;
$\mu \pm 2\sigma$ includes about 95% of the values.

Percentiles: Those values that separate a data set into 100 equal parts.

Quartiles: Three values that separate a data set into four equal parts.

Deciles: Nine values that separate a data set into ten equal parts.

Interquartile range: The absolute value of the difference between the third quartile value and the first quartile value, equivalent to the 50% mid-range.

Bimodal distribution: A distribution with two distinct modes.

Symmetric distribution: A distribution with the same shape on both sides of the median.

Skewed distribution: Any distribution that is not symmetric. Skewed to the right (positively) means that the mean is to the right of the median. Skewed negatively is the opposite.

Kurtosis: A measure of the shape of a distribution, depicting its degree of flatness or peakedness.

Probability
Theory: Discrete
Sample Spaces

THREE

Before we can progress further in discussing the use of statistics in making decisions or reaching conclusions, it is important to present some of the fundamental concepts necessary for statistical analysis, particularly those relating to probability. Chapters 3–6 are devoted to probability. Then in Chapter 7 we will begin to combine these probability concepts with the summary measures of Chapters 1 and 2 in order to develop methods for estimation, hypothesis-testing, and decision-making.

3.1 INTRODUCTION

Any analytical approach to statistical problems involves evaluations of just how likely it is that certain events have occurred or will occur.

> An event is defined as some subset of the possible outcomes in a decision-making situation under conditions of uncertainty.

Example 3.1. Suppose you are the owner of a large Chevrolet dealership in Champaign, Illinois. You are currently faced with the annual problem of placing the January/February order for new cars, a time when new car sales are usually quite slow. If you order too many, the cars sit on the lot, you pay interest on the money borrowed, and you may have to pay property tax on the unsold cars. An order for too few, however, may lead to lost sales for customers who want to buy from inventory. You are wondering what the probability is that you will run out of stock of the new four-door Chevrolet sedans if you order only ten cars.

> A probability is a number between 0 and 1 that indicates how likely it is that an event will occur. If an event has a probability of zero, then its occurrence is impossible. If an event has a probability of 1.0, then its occurrence is certain.

A fundamental part of almost all types of statistical analysis includes finding the value between 0 and 1 that represents how likely to occur an event is; and probability theory provides the foundation for the methods of this analysis.

The origins of probability theory date back to the 1600's when mathematicians Blaise Pascal and Pierre Fermat became interested in games of chance. Although Pascal and Fermat corresponded regularly about problems involving elements of chance, not until over 100 years later did this new branch of mathematics find many applications beyond the French gambling houses of the seventeenth century. The work of Karl Gauss and Pierre Laplace was instrumental during the later 1700's in extending probability theory to problems of the social sciences and actuarial mathematics. Laplace commented, "It is remarkable that a science that began with the consideration of games of chance could have become the most important object of human knowledge." Despite the contributions made in the seventeenth through the nineteenth centuries, the bulk of modern statistics has developed in the past 60 years. R. A. Fisher, J. Neyman, E. S. Pearson, and A. Wald are among the more prominent researchers who have contributed to the phenomenal growth of statistics in recent years.

3.2 THE PROBABILITY MODEL

In statistics we often wish to specify the probability of some event. For example, we may wish to determine the probability that an automobile accident will occur in a given location during a specified length of time, or the probability that the price of dairy products will decrease, or the probability that candidate X will be elected senator. To specify the probability associated with a given situation, it is extremely important to define what experiment underlies this situation and what outcomes can result from this experiment. As we will demonstrate in this chapter and in Chapter 4, making probability assessments is simplified by using a probability model as a framework for the mental construction of the problem. Such a probability model provides the foundation for using certain probability laws and formulas.

The Experiment   The first component in a probability model is the definition of the experiment.

> An experiment is any situation capable of replication under essentially stable conditions.

A replication is a repeat of the experiment. Replications need not actually be performed but must be at least theoretically conceivable. For example, investing $1000 in the stock market could be an experiment, even though the investor intends to do it only once. We can imagine repeating such an investment many times and consider theoretically the probability of making capital gains or losses or of earning some specified yield, such as 10%.

Example 3.2. For an experiment that would be repeated over and over, consider a manufacturing process making child-proof lids for plastic jars (containing medicine). If the lids are too loose, a child may be able to open the jar. If the lid is too tight, some people (particularly the elderly) may have difficulty opening it. Given a production process that does not always produce lids with exactly the same interior dimensions, what is the probability that a lid will be too loose or too tight?

Testing a computer program for errors might be an experiment. You might be interested in the theoretical chances that the program runs perfectly. Clearly, an experiment is defined very broadly to correspond to any situation involving uncertainty, whether it actually recurs many times or whether the replications are hypothetical.

When an experiment is defined, it is necessary to specify *all* the procedures associated with the experiment. For example, in Chapter 1 we drew a random sample from the 78 cities in **Data Set 1.** Such an experiment (it *is* an experiment!) can be conducted either with replacement or without replacement. Think of picking the cities to be included in the sample one at a time. If sampling is with replacement, after a city is picked it is put back on the list, and this same city can be picked again. Thus, the same city could appear more than once in a given sample. For sampling without replacement a city picked is not replaced on the list; hence a given city can occur at most once in the sample. Although most samples are taken without replacement, the probability analysis is easier if replacement occurs, or if we assume that it does.

Sample Spaces Once an experiment is defined, it becomes obvious that not all replications of the experiment will result in the same outcomes. For instance, suppose the experiment is to count the number of defective child-proof lids. The lids and jars are packed in boxes, where each box contains 100 child-proof jars and lids. Each time a box is inspected, this can be thought of as a replication of the experiment. The number of defective lids in each box can be any number from 0 to 100.

The different outcomes of an experiment are often referred to as sample points, and the set of all possible outcomes is called the **sample space.** In the case of child-proof lids, the sample points are *discrete* and *finite,* where discrete means that the outcomes can be separated from one another and finite means that the number of outcomes is limited. If the experiment had been "count the number of lids until you find the first defective," then the sample space would be discrete and infinite (since there is no limit to the number of lids before the first defective, assuming production continues indefinitely). Other examples of a discrete sample space include the number of errors in a computer program and the dollar amount an investor could lose in the stock market.

In contrast to a discrete sample space is the concept of a continuous sample space. A sample space is continuous if the number of possible outcomes is infinite and uncountable. The number of hours it takes a certain light bulb to burn out represents a continuous sample space because the outcome of this experiment could be *any* real number from zero up to some upper bound, say, 10,000 hours. There is obviously an infinite number of outcomes possible here and no way to separate and count them. The net weight of a box of packaged cereal, the length of fish caught in a trout stream, and the distance a car can travel on a gallon of gas are all examples of outcomes in a continuous sample space.

> Generally, the sample space is continuous if the data are obtained by measurement and discrete if the data are obtained by counting.

We must hasten to add that it is not always clear from the statement of an experiment exactly what outcomes are relevant. For example, the outcome of a $1000 investment in the stock market might be classified in any number of ways, including any one of the following:

1. Investment earns money, loses money, or breaks even;
2. investment earns some specific rate of return; or
3. investment (x) earns either $0 < x \le 2\%$, $-2\% < x \le 0$, $2\% < x \le 4\%$, $-4\% < x \le -2\%$, etc.

> In defining the sample space of an experiment, one must be sure that the outcomes are mutually exclusive and exhaustive.

Mutually exclusive outcomes are those that have no overlap. Thus, we could not define the outcomes of an investment in the stock market as 0–2%, 2%–4%, 4%–6%, etc. because these categories overlap at 2%, 4%, and so forth. **Exhaustive outcomes** mean that no possible outcome is left off the list. For example, we could not define the possible outcomes of a

$1000 investment as "earns money" or "loses money" because this sample space omits the outcome "breaks even."

Any subset of the outcomes of an experiment is called an **event.** For example, the set of outcomes $-10\% < x \leq 10\%$ could be considered an event in our investment example, as could the set of outcomes "do not lose money." Events do not need to be mutually exclusive and exhaustive.

To summarize briefly, we have defined the following terms and their role in every probability model.

1. An experiment: Situation capable of replication under stable conditions.
2. Outcome of an experiment (sample space):
   a. Discrete (separable and countable outcomes)
      - Finite (an upper limit on number)
      - Infinite (no upper limit on number)
   b. Continuous (nonseparable): The number of outcomes is infinite.
3. Event: Some subset of the outcomes of an experiment.
4. Mutually exclusive and exhaustive events: Events that do not overlap (are mutually exclusive) and account for (exhaust) all possible outcomes of the experiment.

There are two additional components of every probability model: (1) a random variable and (2) a probability function. These two additional components of the model are important in describing the probability of the entire set of events of interest in a given experiment. They will be discussed in detail in Chapter 4.

3.3 SUBJECTIVE AND OBJECTIVE PROBABILITY

There is some disagreement, even among authorities, about the definition of the **probability of an event.** The first and more traditional viewpoint uses the following definition.

> Probability is the relative frequency with which an event occurs over time.

Under this definition, a probability is usually referred to as a *frequency probability* or an **objective probability** (since it is determined by objective evidence and would have the same value regardless of who did the interpretation).

The second interpretation of probability assigns probabilities based on the decision-maker's subjective estimates, using prior knowledge, information, and experience as a guide. This approach, in which a probability is referred to as a **subjective probability,** recently has gained considerable importance in statistical theory, largely because of the influence of such statisticians as L. J. Savage, R. Schlaifer, and H. Raiffa.

Suppose you estimate the probability to be 0.25 that General Motors sells more than 80,000 cars this week. Or you might believe that there is a 0.90 chance the local Kroger store will sell more than 300 loaves of bread today. These are subjective evaluations in which your personal opinion about the probability of these events need not agree with that of the President of GM or the manager of Kroger, or anyone else.

The problem with the "frequency" approach to estimating probabilities is that in many real-world settings there may be little or no historical data available on which to base an estimate of the probability of an event. In such cases, only a *subjective* probability can be determined, and this probability may differ even among experts who have similar technical knowledge and identical information. For example, various scientists in 1960 gave different estimates of the probability that humans would walk on the moon within that decade. Similarly, investment brokers differ substantially in their opinion on how the stock market will behave over the next several months.

Much of the historical development of probability can be traced to an analysis of problems in which only a finite number of outcomes may take place and in which each of these outcomes is assumed to have the same chance of occurring. In such situations, if any one of the N "equally likely" outcomes can take place, then the probability of any one outcome occurring is $1/N$.

Example 3.3. Suppose that *Reader's Digest* mails out announcements of a contest to 50,000 different people, stating that the "grand-prize winner" will be selected "at random" from the list of 50,000 people. Random selection in this context means that each person is equally likely to be selected; the probability of being the grand-prize winner is thus $P(\text{grand-prize winner}) = 1/50{,}000 = 0.00002$.*

When the number of equally likely outcomes in a given problem is relatively small, it is often possible to determine the probability of each outcome by counting the total number of outcomes (N), and then

---

* Probability values can be stated as either fractions or decimals. For the most part, in this chapter the fractional form will be more convenient.

calculating 1/N. In Section 3.4 we will discuss several rules which aid in this counting process. Before doing so, we can now present a rule for finding the probability of an event when this event is composed of a number of equally likely outcomes.

The probability of an event is the ratio of the number of outcomes comprising this event to the total number of equally likely outcomes in the sample space.

$$P(\text{event}) = \frac{\text{No. of outcomes comprising the event}}{\text{Total no. of equally likely}} .$$
$$\text{outcomes in the sample space.}$$

We give numerous examples of this rule throughout the chapter.

Example 3.4. Assume that you are going to pick one company from the 50 shown in **Data Set 2.** You want to know the probability of picking a company with sales greater than $5,000,000,000. In this case the total number of equally likely outcomes is 50. There are 15 companies with sales over $5 billion; hence,

$$P(\text{sales} > \$5 \text{ billion}) = \frac{\text{No. of companies with sales} > \$5 \text{ billion}}{\text{No. of equally likely outcomes in the}}$$
$$\text{experiment "select one company"}$$

$$= \frac{15}{50} = 0.30.$$

Before continuing, we must present formally the two basic properties necessary for defining the probability of an event. If an event E_i is a subset of a discrete sample space denoted by S, and $P(E_i)$ is the probability of that event, then the following **two basic properties** must hold:

Property 1. $0 \leq P(E_i) \leq 1.0$ for every subset E_i of S.
Property 2. $P(S) = \sum_i P(E_i) = 1.0$.

It is easy to recognize that these properties are consistent with our previous examples. The first one says that the probability of an event can never be less than zero (which represents an impossibility) nor greater than one (which represents a certainty). The second one says that the events E_i comprising the sample space must be exhaustive—it must be a certainty that one of the mutually exclusive events in the sample space will take place in each replication of the experiment.

We have emphasized in this section that one often wants to know the total number of possible outcomes in an experiment. Since in many situations it is not immediately obvious how many different outcomes there are for a given experiment, various rules have been developed for calculating this number. These rules, called *counting rules*, are discussed in Section 3.4.

3.4 COUNTING RULES

Many probability experiments involve two or more steps, each of which can result in one of a number of different outcomes. To calculate probabilities in such experiments, we often first determine the total number of possible outcomes.

Example 3.5. Three people are asked whether or not they own stock. Here are three steps (interviewing three people), and each step has two outcomes [stock owner (S) or not a stock owner (NS)]. There are eight different outcomes to this experiment, as shown in Fig. 3.1.

FIGURE 3.1 **Tree diagram for stock ownership experiment.**

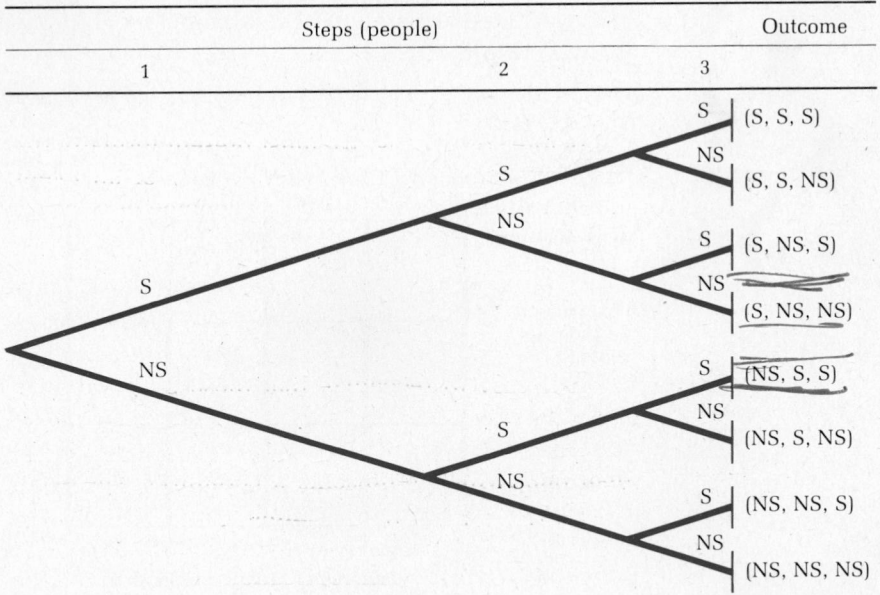

Basic Counting Rules

In the stock ownership example above, there are only three steps (people), and each step has two possible outcomes (S or NS). The total number of outcomes (N) in this experiment is

$$N = (2)(2)(2) = 8.$$

To generalize this type of calculation, suppose we denote the number of outcomes in the first step of an experiment as n_1, the number of outcomes in the second step as n_2, and so forth, with n_k denoting the number of outcomes in the last (or kth) step. The **basic counting rule** states that the total number of outcomes (N) equals the product of the number of outcomes in each step.

Basic counting rule:

$$\text{Total number of sample points } N = n_1, \cdot n_2 \cdots n_k. \qquad \textbf{(3.1)}$$

In our stock-ownership example, $n_1 = 2$, $n_2 = 2$, and $n_3 = 2$; hence, $N = n_1 \cdot n_2 \cdot n_3 = 2 \cdot 2 \cdot 2 = 8$.

Example 3.6. To illustrate Formula (3.1), consider a company that is going to select one of four different pricing policies and then select one of three different advertising packages. In this example, $n_1 = 4$ (pricing) and $n_2 = 3$ (advertising). The total number of outcomes of this experiment is (by Formula 3.1)

$$N = n_1 \cdot n_2 = 4 \cdot 3 = 12.$$

FIGURE 3.2 **Sample space for policy decisions.**

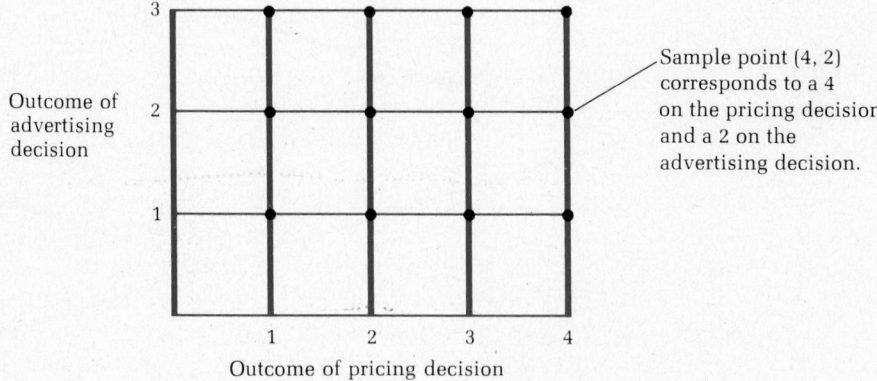

Outcome of advertising decision

Sample point (4, 2) corresponds to a 4 on the pricing decision and a 2 on the advertising decision.

Outcome of pricing decision

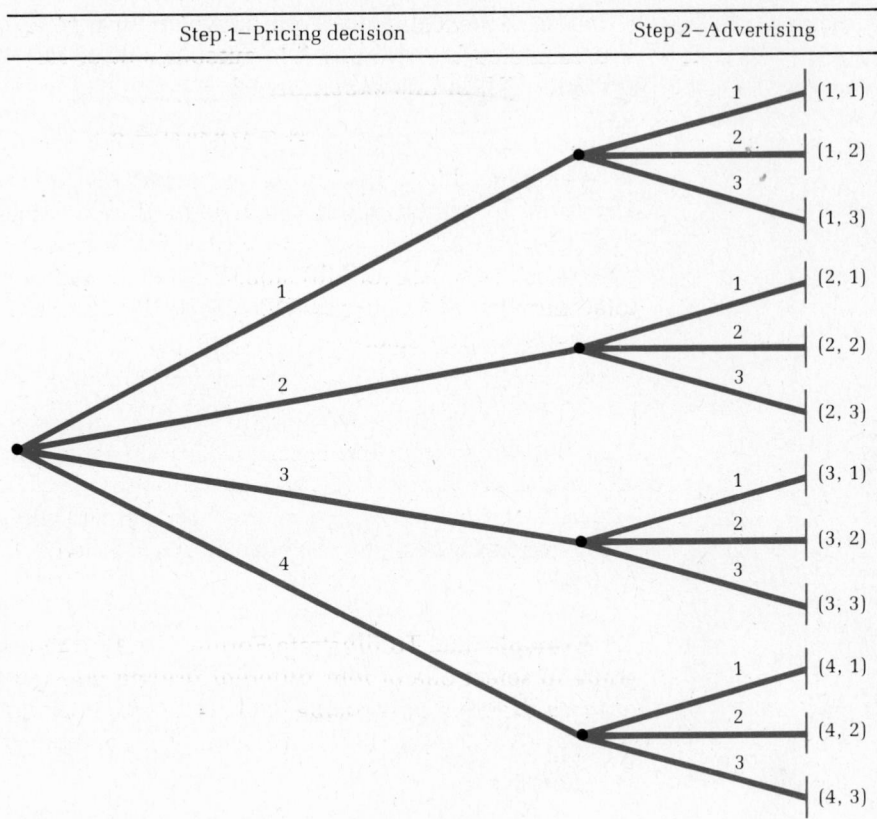

FIGURE 3.3 **Tree diagram for pricing policy decisions.**

The twelve different sample points (outcomes) in the sample space for this experiment are shown in the grid in Fig. 3.2. If all 12 sample points are assumed to be equally likely (which they may not be), then the probability of any one occurring is $1/N = \frac{1}{12}$.

As with our stock-ownership example, the sample space can be described by the use of a tree diagram (Fig. 3.3). Note that, as before, the order of outcomes is important [outcome (2, 3) differs from outcome (3, 2)].

More Basic Probability   Up to this point we have focused on determining the total number of sample points in the sample space and using this information to calculate the probability of each equally likely sample point. We now turn to the situation that occurs in most practical problems, where the event of interest includes more than one sample point. In these circumstances the **probability of an event** can be determined by *adding* the probabilities of each of the sample points that are a part of the event of interest. Since in this chapter all of the sample points we will illustrate can be assumed to be equally likely, the equivalent of adding their probabilities can be expressed by a multiplication as in the following equation.

$$P(\text{event}) = P(1 \text{ sample point}) \times \begin{pmatrix} \text{No. of relevant} \\ \text{sample points} \end{pmatrix}. \tag{3.2}$$

To illustrate this rule, we return to our marketing-policy decisions of Fig. 3.2 and assume that someone is interested in the probability that *either* the pricing strategy equals 1 *or* the advertising strategy is 2 or larger. From Fig. 3.3 we know that there are 12 different sample points; if they are all assumed to be equally likely, then

$$P(\text{one sample point}) = \frac{1}{12}.$$

The tree diagram in Fig. 3.3 can be used to determine how many different sample points have a 1 in the first position (pricing) or a 2 or more in the second position (advertising). The following nine points have those characteristics:

$$(1,1), \quad (1,2), \quad (1,3), \quad (2,2) \quad (2,3) \quad (3,2) \quad (3,3) \quad (4,2), \quad (4,3).$$

Hence, the number of relevant sample points equals 9, and

$$P(\text{price} = 1 \text{ or advertising} \geq 2) = (\tfrac{1}{12})(9) = \tfrac{9}{12} = \tfrac{3}{4}.$$

In other words, we would expect, assuming equally likely outcomes, three of every four such decisions would either have price $= 1$ or have 2 or more for advertising (or both).

Example 3.7. As another illustration of Formula (3.2), suppose that in our stock-ownership survey of three people we want to determine the probability of the outcome "two owners, one nonowner." Recall from Fig. 3.1 that the probability of each sample point, assuming equally likely outcomes, is $\tfrac{1}{8}$. Hence,

$$P(\text{one sample point}) = \tfrac{1}{8}.$$

The relevant sample points in this example are the three outcomes (S, S, NS), (S, NS, S), and (NS, S, S). Thus,

$$\text{Number of relevant sample points} = 3.$$

The probability of the event (2 stock owners, 1 nonowner) is therefore

$$P(2\ S, 1\ NS) = (\tfrac{1}{8})(3) = \tfrac{3}{8}.$$

Using this same approach, the reader should verify each of the probabilities below and note that they satisfy the two basic properties of all probabilities (described on page 88).

$$P(\text{3 stock owners}) = \tfrac{1}{8}$$
$$P(\text{2 stock owners, 1 nonowner}) = \tfrac{3}{8}$$
$$P(\text{1 stock owner, 2 nonowners}) = \tfrac{3}{8}$$
$$P(\text{3 nonowners}) = \tfrac{1}{8}$$
$$\text{Sum} = \tfrac{8}{8}$$

The above examples involved such a small number of outcomes that we could readily list the entire sample space and count the number of relevant sample points. In problems with larger sample spaces, this approach is impractical, if not impossible. The remaining sections in this chapter are devoted to presenting rules and formulas designed to help calculate probabilities without going through a cumbersome enumeration process. As we progress through these rules, however, the reader should bear in mind that, at least for finite sample spaces, the formulas still represent what are essentially counting rules.

Study Question 3.1: Assignment of OSHA Inspectors

An important task of certain business and governmental agencies involves assigning workers to specific tasks (or machines). For example, the Department of Labor assigns OSHA (Occupational Safety and Health Act) specialists to inspect employer locations for safety. Suppose a city has three inspectors (A, B, and C) and two "first-priority locations" (where a catastrophe or fatality has occurred) and must now assign one inspector to one of the two locations. Draw the tree diagram for this problem and find the probability that A is given the assignment or that the location is number 2. Use the counting rule to determine the total number of outcomes.

Answer. As shown in Fig. 3.4, there are (3)(2) = 6 outcomes, each with probability $\tfrac{1}{6}$.

$$P(A\ or\ 2) = (\text{number of relevant sample points})P(\text{one such point}) = (4)(\tfrac{1}{6}) = \tfrac{2}{3}$$

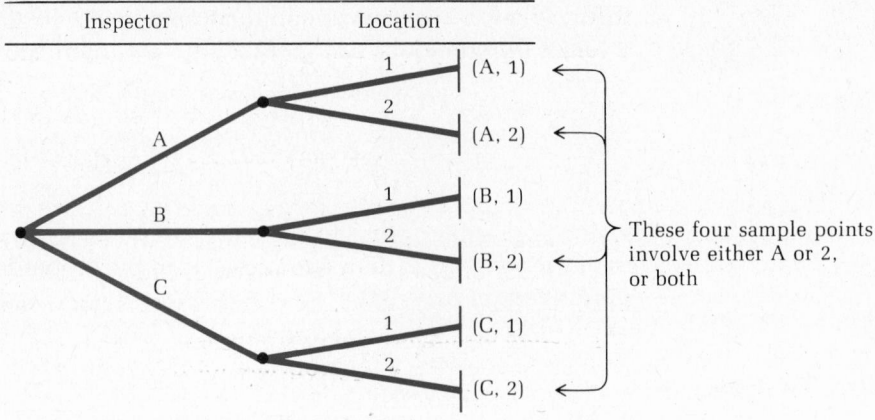

FIGURE 3.4 **Tree diagram for Study Question 3.1.**

3.5 **PERMUTATIONS AND COMBINATIONS**

In some probability problems, one has a set of objects, all distinguishable from one another, and wants to know how many different ways there are of ordering these objects. This may happen when a number of different jobs are waiting to be finished in a business which handles customizing orders. Or we might want to know the number of different cities a sales representative could visit in one week.

Example 3.8. Suppose we want to determine the number of different ways the top three candidates for the new dean of a business school can be ranked by the search and screen committee. Suppose, for example, we label the three candidates for the dean's position as A, B, and C. In this case it is quite simple to list all six different ways that the three candidates can be ordered:

$$
\begin{array}{ccc}
\text{A B C} & \text{B A C} & \text{C A B} \\
\text{A C B} & \text{B C A} & \text{C B A}
\end{array}
$$

We might think of these six orderings as all possible points in a sample space. If all six points are equally likely to occur in an experiment, then the probability of any *one* ordering is $\frac{1}{6}$.

The number of ways of ordering n objects (where n is any number) can be determined by using Formula (3.1).

Example 3.9. Suppose that a job-shop foreman has eight jobs in line and they can be completed only one at a time. Step 1 can be thought of as completing one of the jobs, step 2 as completing a second job, and so forth, step 8 being the last job to be completed. In this experiment, $n_1 =$ 8 (eight different jobs can go first), $n_2 = 7$ (there are only seven jobs left after one job is taken first), $n_3 = 6, \ldots, n_8 = 1$, so that the total number of possible outcomes (orderings) is, by Formula (3.1),

$$8(7)(6)(5)(4)(3)(2)(1) = 40,320.$$

The product of the numbers on the left-hand side is usually written in a shorthand notation as 8!, which is read as "eight factorial." In general, if the number of objects to be ranked or ordered is n (where n is a positive integer), then the symbol $n!$ (read "**n factorial**") represents the number of possible arrangements (orderings) of these n objects. Thus, the special case of Formula (3.1) appropriate for determining the number of ways of ordering n objects is:

Number of orderings of n objects:

$$n \text{ factorial: } \quad n! = n(n-1)(n-2) \cdots (3)(2)(1) \qquad \textbf{(3.3)}$$

Formula (3.3) is used to determine the number of possible orderings of n different objects.* In such cases the experiment will consist of n steps, and each step will have one fewer possible outcomes than the prior step.

Example 3.10. Consider the number of ways a corporate vice-president in charge of systems might rank four different brands of computers (A, B, C, D) being considered for purchase. In this situation the number of objects to be arranged is $n = 4$. Hence, the number of orderings is

$$n! = 4! = 4(3)(2)(1) = 24.$$

If these 24 orderings are all equally likely, then the probability that any one will occur is $\frac{1}{24}$.

Permutations Each different ordering of a set of objects is called a permutation. Thus, Formula (3.3) is one way of determining the number of permutations of n objects. In many probability problems, we are not interested in the number of permutations of *all* n objects, but rather of some *subset* of these objects.

Example 3.11. The job-shop foreman in Example 3.9 has eight jobs waiting to be finished, but only three of these jobs can be placed on tomorrow's schedule. The foreman wants to know how many orderings

---

* The value of 0! is defined as 1.

there are if three jobs are picked out of the eight. In this experiment there are three steps: The first step has eight possible outcomes (eight different jobs can be the one to be scheduled first), the second step has seven possible outcomes, and the third step has six possible outcomes. By the basic counting rate [Formula (3.1)], the number of permutations is

$$n_1(n_2)(n_3) = 8(7)(6) = 336.$$

The number 336 gives the number of permutations of 8 objects taken 3 at a time, which is denoted by the symbol $_8P_3$.

In general, we will denote the number of objects in the subset by the letter x, and the total number of objects by the letter n (where $x \le n$). Thus, $_nP_x$ denotes the number of **permutations of n objects taken x at a time**.

Permutations of n objects taken x at a time:

$$_nP_x = \frac{n!}{(n-x)!}. \qquad (3.4)$$

A good exercise for the reader would be to verify that $_8P_3 = 336$, using Formula (3.4).

To illustrate the use of Formula (3.4), suppose a list of four investments (A, B, C, D) for a business firm is presented to the board of directors, and the board is asked to rank the two projects they consider to be the best opportunities. To answer the question "How many different orderings are possible of two investment opportunities out of a total of four?", we need to calculate the number of permutations of $n = 4$ objects taken $x = 2$ at a time, or $_4P_2$:

$$_4P_2 = \frac{4!}{(4-2)!} = \frac{4!}{2!} = \frac{4 \cdot 3 \cdot 2 \cdot 1}{2 \cdot 1} = 12.$$

The 12 permutations in this example are shown in Table 3.1. If all 12 of these permutations are equally likely, then the probability of any one occurring is $\frac{1}{12}$.

TABLE 3.1 **Permutations example**

Rank	1	2	3	4	5	6	7	8	9	10	11	12
1	A	A	A	B	B	B	C	C	C	D	D	D
2	B	C	D	A	C	D	A	B	D	A	B	C

By the basic counting rule, the value of $_nP_x$ is the product of the number of outcomes of step 1 ($= n$) times the number of outcomes of step 2 ($= n - 1$), and so forth, until all x steps are included. This product is

$$_nP_x = n(n - 1)(n - 2) \cdots (n - x + 1). \qquad \textbf{(3.5)}$$

This formula for $_nP_x$ is equivalent to Formula (3.4).*

Combinations The number of permutations of a set of objects represents the number of ways the objects can be ordered. But in many circumstances, one cannot or does not want to be concerned with order. For instance, the order in which voters are surveyed on public issues generally is assumed to be unimportant, as is the order in which cards are received in a bridge hand, or the order in which bids are received in a sealed-bid competition. In these cases, interest usually centers on the number of *combinations* of objects that can occur, where two sets of objects are considered to be identical if they contain exactly the same elements, no matter how these objects are arranged. *A combination is thus a set of objects where order is unimportant.* The symbol $_nC_x$ is used to denote the number of **combinations of n objects taken x at a time.**

There are always *fewer* combinations than permutations for a given n and x, since different orderings do not count as combinations, but do count as permutations. Thus, $_nP_x$ will always be larger than $_nC_x$ by a factor of $x!$; that is,

$$_nC_x = \frac{_nP_x}{x!}.$$

By substituting for $_nP_x$ from Formula (3.5), we can write:

Combinations of n objects taken x at a time:

$$_nC_x = \frac{n!}{x!\,(n - x)!} \qquad \textbf{(3.6)}$$

---

* To prove this relationship, we first rewrite the numerator of (3.4) as

$$n! = n(n - 1)\,(n - 2) \cdots (n - x + 1)(n - x)!$$

Dividing the right-hand side of this expression by $(n - x)!$ yields

$$n(n - 1)(n - 2) \cdots (n - x + 1),$$

which is identical to the right-hand side of Formula (3.5).

Example 3.12. To illustrate (3.6), suppose the Air Force has decided to award software contracts (for $500 million worth of new computer equipment) to two of the six companies submitting bids. The number of different ways that two winning firms (x = 2) can be selected out of n = 6 is

$$_6C_2 = \frac{6!}{2!(6-2)!} = \frac{6 \cdot 5 \cdot 4 \cdot 3 \cdot 2 \cdot 1}{(2 \cdot 1)(4 \cdot 3 \cdot 2 \cdot 1)} = 15.$$

If these 15 combinations are all equally likely, then the probability that any one combination occurs is $\frac{1}{15}$.

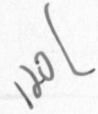

As n gets larger, the number of combinations can become very large. For example, suppose a bridge player wants to determine how many different bridge hands are possible. The number of hands in this case is the number of combinations of n = 52 objects (cards) taken x = 13 at a time (13 cards to a hand), or

$$_{52}C_{13} = \frac{52!}{13! \, (52-13)!}.$$

Even with an electronic calculator, these factorials are not much fun to evaluate; hence, they are often merely left in the factorial form shown above. Our bridge player, however, was determined enough to calculate that 635,013,559,620 different bridge hands are possible (and they are all equally likely).

Define. *Basic counting rules, factorials, permutations, combinations, P(event).*

PROBLEMS

3.1 Consider the experiment "General Motors picks a new president out of candidates A, B, C, and D."
a) Describe the outcomes of the experiment. Is this sample space finite or infinite, discrete or continuous?
b) Your present thoughts are that candidates A, B, and C are equally likely, and candidate D is three times as likely as A. What probability values should you assign to A, B, C, and D? Are these values subjective or objective probabilities?
c) Show that the probabilities you determined in part (b) meet the two basic probability properties.

3.2 Describe an experiment for each of the following situations (use business-oriented examples not mentioned in the text).
a) The sample space is discrete and finite.
b) The sample space is discrete and infinite.
c) The sample space is continuous.

3.3 Indicate whether the sample space is finite or infinite, discrete or continuous, if the experiment involves:
a) The amount of money General Motors earns this year.
b) The number of years before a woman is first elected President of the United States.
c) The percent by which the price of a stock might decrease, if percents are restricted to integer values.
d) The percent by which the price of a stock might decrease, if percents can be any decimal value.
e) The miles per gallon a new car achieves.

3.4 Indicate whether the following events are (1) mutually exclusive and/or (2) exhaustive:
a) The events "stock market goes up" and "stock market does not go up."
b) The events "Federal Government reduces taxes" and "consumer prices decline."
c) The events "make dean's list" and "earn an A in statistics."

3.5 Suppose the *Reader's Digest* contest mentioned in Section 3.3 is giving out one grand prize, 500 second prizes, and 1000 third prizes. There are 50,000 people who might win, and no one can win more than one prize. What is the probability that you will win if you are one of the 50,000 people?

3.6 NASA is testing four new space suits for future shuttle flights. For this test, each suit will be classified as either "pass" or "fail."
a) Describe the sample space for this experiment. Draw the tree diagram.
b) How many different outcomes are there? How many outcomes are there if one is interested only in the number of passes and failures?
c) If "pass" and "fail" are considered equally likely, what are $P(0$ pass$)$, $P(1$ pass$)$, $P(2$ pass$)$, $P(3$ pass$)$, and $P(4$ pass$)$? Do these values sum to one?

3.7 Use the information in **Data Set 1** to determine the probability that a randomly selected city will have a low cyclical threat and a Moody rating of Aa or better.

3.8 Suppose you are planning on taking a survey of two out of five local retail establishments.

a) Describe the sample space for the experiment "select two establishments without replacement." (*Hint:* Label the establishments 1, 2, 3, 4, 5, and list all pairs — note that order is *not* important here.)
b) What is the probability that establishment 1 will be included in the survey?
c) What is the probability that either establishment 1 or establishment 2 will be included in the survey?

3.9 The following data describe certain characteristics of the assembly-line workers for an RCA plant.

	Men	Women	Over 50
White	120	140	75
Black	40	30	10
Oriental	10	20	10

a) How many people are employed on this assembly line?
b) If a worker is selected randomly, what is the probability that this person will be black?
c) What is the probability that a person selected at random will be over 50?

3.10 The common stocks listed by a certain investing service are rated 1–5 according to return and 1–3 according to risk.
a) Draw the tree diagram representing the different ways a given stock can be classified.
b) If each stock is equally likely to be classified into each point in the sample space, what is the probability of each sample point?
c) How many sample points have either a return rating of <4 or a risk rating of <3? Use Formula (3.2) to determine P(return <4 or risk <3).
d) Use your tree diagram to determine the probability that both return <4 and risk <3.

3.11 Sears advertises that the customer can select one of the possible frequency codes on an automatic garage-door opener by selecting nine switches in one of two positions (e.g., + or −).
a) How many different codes might a person who has forgotten the code have to try before being assured of finding the correct one (the answer "all of them" is not sufficient). What is the probability that this person will be right on one randomly selected try?
b) Suppose the person knows that eight of the nine switches are set on + and one on −. What is the probability that the person will be correct on one randomly selected try?

3.12 A job-shop operation has seven possible jobs it should complete today. Unfortunately, on any one day, only four jobs can be completed.
  a) If the order in which the jobs are completed is not important, how many different schedules might the shop have today?
  b) Assume that the order is important today. How many different schedules are there now?
  c) Job 1 is for the owner of the job shop. How many of the schedules in part (a) include job 1? How many of the schedules in part (b) include job 1?

3.13 Wendy's fast food chain advertises that you can order a hamburger with any one or more of eight toppings (such as a tomato). As the manager of Wendy's, you want to advertise the number of different combinations of toppings that are possible. What is this number (including no toppings)?

3.14 The president of ARVO Industries is scheduled to visit the company plants located in the Midwest.
  a) In how many different orders can three plants be visited? Draw the tree diagram.
  b) In how many different orders can the ARVO president visit three plants if there are ten possible plants that could be visited?
  c) How many different combinations of three plants could be visited if there are ten plants?

3.15 A computer program has failed to work in the middle of an important production-scheduling operation. The head of the systems department has decided that one of three possible programming errors has caused the problem. If the three possible errors are labeled as A, B, and C, how many different orders (permutations) are there for examining the possible errors, one at a time?

3.16 Five candidates remain for the position of vice-president of finance for Datacomp Company. The personnel committee has been asked to submit three names to the company president.
  a) How many different combinations of three people are possible? (Assume that the president wants the names unranked.)
  b) How many different orderings are possible? (Assume that the president wants the names ranked.)
  c) If the candidates are listed alphabetically and three are picked randomly, what is the probability that the first three names will be picked?

3.17 The EPA (Environmental Protection Agency) director has to decide on the priorities among U.S. cities for the spending of Federal money for pollution cleanup. Ten areas are under consideration for money.

a) How many different ways can the ten areas be ranked if ties are not permitted?
b) How many different combinations are possible if only three areas will receive money for cleanups?

3.18 A CPA certification committee has announced a list of five essay questions, two of which will be selected randomly to be on the next CPA exam. Assume that in studying for the CPA exam you find time to prepare for only two of the five. You know you will pass this portion of the exam *only* if at least one of the two questions you select to study is on the exam.
a) List the sample space for the experiment "CPA committee picks two questions without replacement."
b) What is the probability that you will pass?

USING THE COMPUTER

3.19 Use a computer package to calculate the following:
a) The number of different ways all 50 U.S. states could be ranked (e.g., 1, 2, . . . , 50) in terms of the amount spent on education (per capita, before you know the dollar amounts).
b) The number of different combinations if a portfolio is to be composed of 25 stocks selected out of 100 possible stocks.
c) The number of permutations of 12 candidates for the new dean of the business school when there are 82 applicants.

3.20 Many business firms are reluctant to transmit internal data from one computer terminal to another without proper security procedures. One method for securing data has been to code the data at its entry point, the decoding method being known only to receiving personnel. Suppose a coding scheme is suggested in which the customer can select different codes by specifying each of 56 transmittable characters as either "on" or "off." As president of this company, would you consider this enough codes, knowing that a "spy" could use a computer program capable of trying (randomly) 1000 codes a second in an effort to break your code?

3.6 PROBABILITY RULES

One can often determine the probability of an event from knowledge about the probability of one or more other events in the sample space. In this section we will discuss rules for finding the probability of complementary and conditional events, the probability of the union of two events, and the joint probability of two events.

Basic Definitions. Before describing these rules, we present a few definitions. If we designate A and B as two events of interest in a particular experiment, then the following definitions hold:

1. $P(\overline{A})$ = Probability that A does *not* occur in one replication of the experiment.
   $P(\overline{A})$ is called the probability of the *complement* of A.
2. $P(A|B)$ = Probability that A occurs *given that B* has taken place (or will take place).
   $P(A|B)$ is called the *conditional probability* of A given B.
3. $P(A \cap B)$ = Probability that *both A and B* occur in one replication of the experiment.
   $P(A \cap B)$ is called the probability of the *intersection* of A and B or the *joint* probability of A and B.
4. $P(A \cup B)$ = Probability that *either A or B or both* occur in one replication of the experiment.
   $P(A \cup B)$ is called the probability of the *union* of A and B.

Elaboration of these definitions follows.

Probability of the Complement

Perhaps the simplest way to form a new event from a given event is to take the *complement* of that event. For example, the *complement* of the sample space A, which is denoted by $\overline{A}$ (read A-bar), contains all the points in the sample space that are *not part* of A. If S denotes the total sample space, then

$$\overline{A} = S - A \quad \text{or} \quad \overline{A} = \{\text{All sample points } not \text{ in } A\}.$$

Suppose that the sample space S is the set of all students in a given university and A is the subset containing sophomores; then the event $\overline{A}$ includes all students in that university who are *not* sophomores. As another example, if we define set A to represent companies with sales less than or equal to 300,000 units, which we write as

$$A = \{\text{Companies with sales} \le 300{,}000 \text{ units}\},$$

then

$$\overline{A} \{\text{Companies with sales} > 300{,}000 \text{ units}\}.$$

Using the basic properties of a probability model, from the probability of an event we can determine the probability of the complement of that event. Suppose a sample space contains N sample points and some event

A contains a of these points; that is, $P(A) = a/N$. Then $\overline{A}$ must contain $(N - a)$ sample points. Thus, we can write the **probability of the complement** of the event $P(\overline{A})$ as follows:

$$P(\overline{A}) = \frac{(N - a)}{N} = \frac{N}{N} - \frac{a}{N} = 1.0 - \frac{a}{N}.$$

Probability rule for complements:

$$P(\overline{A}) = 1.0 - P(A). \tag{3.7}$$

Let us apply this rule to our marketing-policy decision example of Section 3.4. Suppose that we label $P(A)$ as follows:

$$P(A) = P(\text{price} = 1 \text{ or advertising} \geq 2).$$

From Section 3.4 we know that this probability equals $\frac{9}{12}$. The probability of the complement of (A) is the probability that price exceeds 1 and advertising equals 1:

$$P(\overline{A}) = P(\text{price} > 1 \text{ and advertising} = 1)$$
$$= 1 - P(\text{price} = 1 \text{ or advertising} \geq 2)$$
$$= 1 - \tfrac{9}{12} = \tfrac{3}{12}.$$

As a further illustration of the probability rule for complements, if the probability that long-term interest rates will fall below 10% in the next year is 0.25, then the probability that rates will *not* fall below 10% is

$$1.00 - 0.25 = 0.75.$$

Two complementary events must be exhaustive because they take into account (or exhaust) all possible events. In addition, complementary events must always be mutually exclusive because none of the sample points in A can be a sample point in the complement of A.

Conditional Probability

In some probability problems we are interested in determining whether some event A occurs "given that" or "on the condition that" some other event B has already taken place (or will take place in the future). Such a conditional event is read as "A given B" and is usually written as $(A|B)$, where the vertical line is read as "given." Consider the following example.

Example 3.13. The Indiana University Student Union recently conducted a survey of undergraduate students in order to gather information about usage of the Union. The population for this study included all

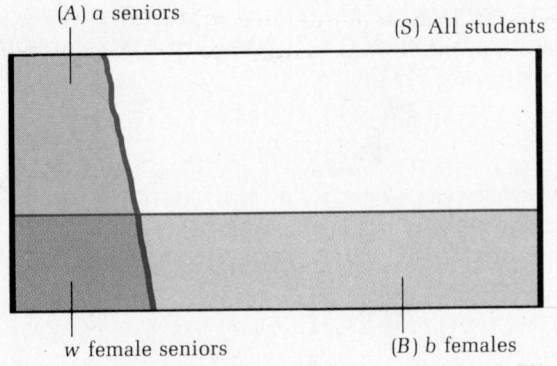

(A) a seniors

(S) All students

w female seniors

(B) b females

FIGURE 3.5 **Venn diagram of overlapping events.**

30,000 undergraduate students enrolled in the university. The Union is interested in increasing usage, particularly among females and seniors at the university. The survey is sent to a random sample of the 30,000 students. The Venn diagram* (Fig. 3.5) can be useful in illustrating probabilities. Assume that the sample space under consideration is all 30,000 undergraduate students at Indiana University, event A represents the $a = 6000$ students who are seniors, and event B represents the $b = 13,500$ students who are females. Suppose also that 2500 of the 13,500 females are seniors.

The conditional event $A|B$ represents those students who are seniors selected from those who satisfy the condition of being *female*. The probability of conditional events of this nature is often of interest in specific sampling problems. For example, if a student is selected at random, and given that the selected student is female, what is the probability that the student is also a senior? We denote this probability by $P(A|B)$ and determine its value by calculating the frequency (w) of students who are female and seniors relative to the total number of females (b). This relative frequency is

$$P(A|B) = \frac{w}{b} = \frac{2500}{13,500} = 0.185.$$

Similarly, $P(B|A)$ can be expressed as the question, "given that a selected student is a senior, what is the probability that the student is female?" The answer is,

$$P(B|A) = \frac{w}{a} = \frac{2500}{6000} = 0.417.$$

* Named after logician J. Venn (1834–1923).

Let us now write $P(A|B)$ in a slightly more convenient form. By dividing w and b by N (the total number of sample points) we obtain

$$P(A|B) = \frac{w}{b} = \frac{w/N}{b/N}.$$

Another way of writing b/N is $P(B)$. Similarly, w/N can be written as $P(W)$. Recall from our earlier definition that an event W, which represents the occurrence of "both a senior (A) and a female (B)," is the *intersection of A and B*; thus, $P(W) = P(A \cap B)$. Putting these facts together, the probability that a randomly selected student is a senior, *given that* this person is a female, is:

$$P(A|B) = P(\text{Senior}|\text{Female}) = \frac{P(A \cap B)}{P(B)} = \frac{w/N}{b/N} = \frac{w}{b} = \frac{2500}{13{,}500} = 0.185.$$

Similarly, the probability that a randomly selected student is a female *given that* this person is a senior is

$$P(B|A) = \frac{P(A \cap B)}{P(A)} = \frac{w/N}{a/N} = \frac{2500}{6000} = \frac{w}{b} = 0.417.$$

We can now formalize the definition of a **conditional probability.**

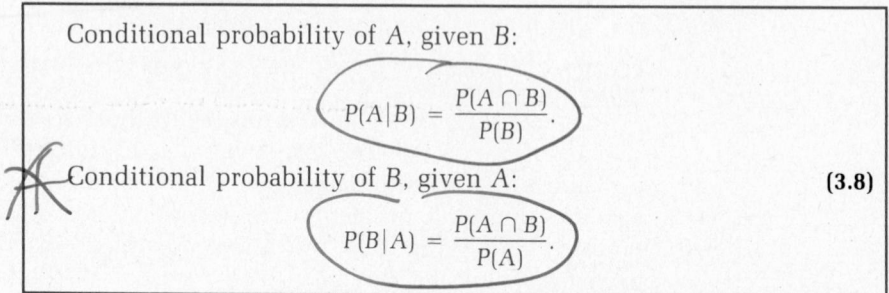

Conditional probability of A, given B:

$$P(A|B) = \frac{P(A \cap B)}{P(B)}.$$

Conditional probability of B, given A:

(3.8)

$$P(B|A) = \frac{P(A \cap B)}{P(A)}$$

To illustrate Formula (3.8), let us reconsider the marketing-policy example of Fig. 3.2 and define the following two events:

$$A = \text{ad decision is} \geq 2. \qquad B = \text{price decision is 1};$$

From the tree diagram for this example (Fig. 3.3) we know that $N = 12$ and $P(\text{price is 1}) = \frac{3}{12}$. There are two sample points for which the price $= 1$ and the ad decision is ≥ 2 [that is, $(1, 2)$ and $(1, 3)$]; hence $P(A \cap B) = \frac{2}{12}$. The conditional probability $P(A|B)$ is thus

$$P(\text{ad} \geq 2|\text{price is 1}) = \frac{P(\text{ad} \geq 2 \cap \text{price is 1})}{P(\text{price is 1})}$$

$$= \frac{\frac{2}{12}}{\frac{3}{12}} = \frac{2}{3}.$$

This result is easily verified by the tree diagram in Fig. 3.3, as we can follow the "price = 1" branch and see that two-thirds of the endpoints on this branch yield ad $\geq$ 2.

In our next example of conditional probabilities, we emphasize that it is necessary to know the total number of sample points (N) in order to use Formula (3.8), and the given condition need not occur first. Indeed, it is possible for the conditional event to occur later. For example, it is legitimate to determine the probability

P(stock market goes up today | prime interest rate will be raised tomorrow),

even though the given condition (prime interest rate will be raised tomorrow) does not occur first.

Example 3.14. Suppose that in a production process, two parts of a particular product are produced simultaneously. Let D_1 denote the fact that the first part is defective and D_2 denote the fact that the second part is defective. From past production records it is known that the probability that part 1 is defective is $P(D_1) = 0.15$. Also, it is known from these records that the probability that *both* parts are defective is

$$P(D_1 \cap D_2) = 0.05.$$

The conditional probability that part 2 is defective, *given that* the first part is defective, can be determined by using Formula (3.8):

$$P(D_2 | D_1) = \frac{P(D_1 \cap D_2)}{P(D_1)} = \frac{0.05}{0.15} = \frac{1}{3}.$$

$P(D_1 | D_2)$ cannot be calculated in this example unless we know the value of $P(D_2)$.

Probability of an Intersection　In studying conditional probabilities in the last section, we indicated that $P(A \cap B)$ represents the probability of the intersection of A and B — that is, the probability that both A and B take place in one replication of an experiment. For example, the crosshatched area in Fig. 3.5 represents the probability that a student is both a senior and a female. Since there are 2500 female seniors, $P(\text{senior} \cap \text{female}) = 2500/30{,}000 = 0.083$. Several additional intersections were presented in the last section, namely,

$$P(D_1 \cap D_2) = 0.05 \quad \text{and} \quad P(\text{ad} \geq 2 \cap \text{price} = 1) = \tfrac{2}{12}.$$

We now want to develop a formula for the probability of an intersection. To do so, one merely has to solve Formula (3.8) for $P(A \cap B)$. The resulting formula is called the *general rule of multiplication* and provides a method for finding the probability of an intersection.

General rule of multiplication:

$$P(A \cap B) = P(A)P(B|A) = P(B)P(A|B).$$ (3.9)

The first part of Formula (3.9) can be interpreted as follows: The probability that *both* A and B take place is given by two occurrences — event A takes place, with probability $P(A)$, and event B takes place on the condition that A occurs, with probability $P(B|A)$. The probability that both occurrences take place is the *product* of these two probabilities, or $P(A)P(B|A)$. For example, let us again consider the production problem previously presented, where we assumed that the probability of the first component being defective is $P(D_1) = 0.15$. Suppose that we also know from past records (as in Example 3.14) that the conditional probability $P(D_2|D_1) = \frac{1}{3}$. These two probabilities can be used to determine $P(D_2 \cap D_1)$, as follows:

$$P(D_2 \cap D_1) = P(D_1)P(D_2|D_1) = (0.15)(\tfrac{1}{3}) = 0.05.^*$$

The probability that the intersection of two (or more) events occurs in a given experiment is often referred to as the **joint probability** of these events. The term "joint probability" implies that the events under consideration take place in the same replication of an experiment. Depending on the nature of the experiment, events that occur jointly do not necessarily take place at identical points in calendar or clock time. For example, in our marketing policy problem the result of the pricing and advertising decision may be considered a joint occurrence even though the two decisions are not made simultaneously.

Because the expressions $P(E_1 \cap E_2)$ and $P(E_2 \cap E_1)$ for any events E_1 and E_2 do not imply any ordering over time,

$$P(E_1 \cap E_2) = P(E_2 \cap E_1).$$

To illustrate graphically the intersection of two events, we let A and B in the Venn diagram shown in Fig. 3.6 represent events within some sample space S. The intersection of A and B is represented by the shaded portion of these two events, labeled $A \cap B$.

Probability of a Union   The **additive probability**, or probability of the union of two events A and B, written $P(A \cup B)$, is the probability that either A occurs, or B occurs, or both A and B occur. The union of events A and B is illustrated by Fig.

---

* If the values of $P(D_2)$ and $P(D_1|D_2)$ are known, then we can calculate $P(D_2 \cap D_1)$ as follows:

$$P(D_2 \cap D_1) = P(D_2)P(D_1|D_2).$$

This approach must also yield $P(D_2 \cap D_1) = 0.05$.

Event *A*   Sample space

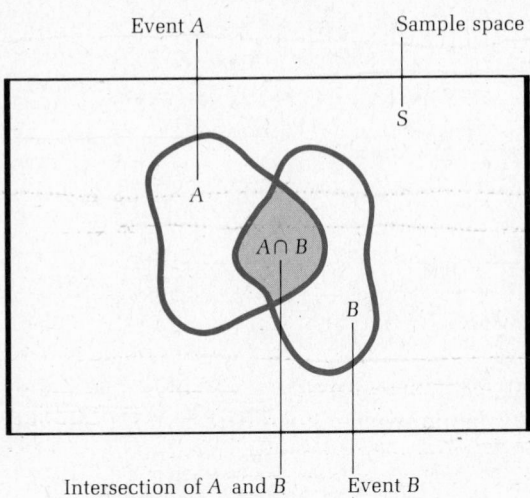

FIGURE 3.6 **The intersection of *A* and *B* (shaded portion).**

Intersection of *A* and *B*   Event *B*

3.7. The probability $P(A \cup B)$ is found by identifying the proportion of sample points that are included either in *A* or in *B*, or in the intersection of *A* and *B*.

The dark shaded area in Fig. 3.5 on page 105 also represents a union — in this case the union of the events *senior* and *female*. Recall from that example that there were a = 6000 seniors, b = 13,500 females, w = 2500 female seniors, and N = 30,000 students. To determine the

Event *A*   Sample space

FIGURE 3.7 **The union of *A* and *B* (shaded portion).**

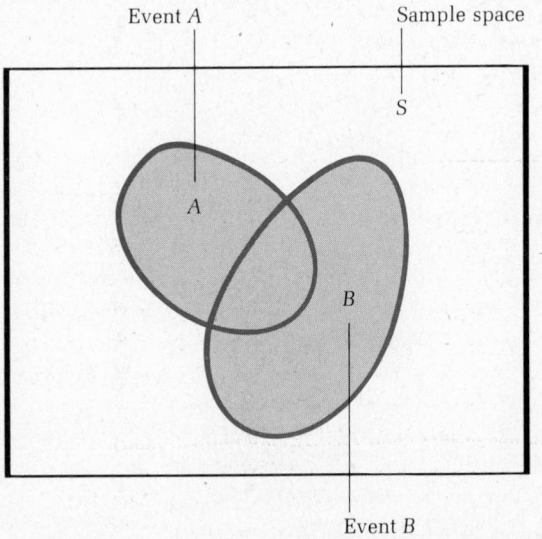

Event *B*

probability that a randomly selected student is either a senior or a female (or both), we cannot merely add

$$\frac{a}{N} + \frac{b}{N} = \frac{6000}{30,000} + \frac{13,500}{30,000}$$

because this sum *double-counts* the females who are seniors. In other words, that sum is too large by the amount

$$\frac{w}{N} = \frac{2500}{30,000},$$

and the correct probability is

$$P(\text{senior} \cup \text{female}) = P(\text{senior}) + P(\text{female}) - P(\text{senior} \cap \text{female}).$$

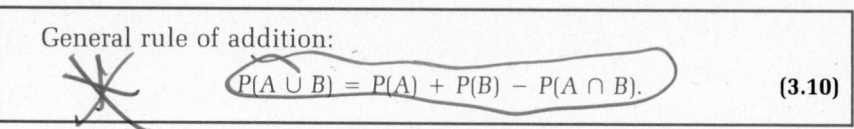

$$= \frac{a}{N} + \frac{b}{N} - \frac{w}{N}$$

$$= \frac{6000}{30,000} + \frac{13,500}{30,000} - \frac{2500}{30,000}$$

$$= 0.200 + 0.450 - 0.083 = 0.567.$$

This example demonstrates what is called the *general rule of addition*. If we substitute the letter A for senior and B for female in the formulation above, then the general rule of addition can be written as follows:

> General rule of addition:
> $$P(A \cup B) = P(A) + P(B) - P(A \cap B). \qquad \textbf{(3.10)}$$

Formula (3.10) can be used to find the probability of the union of A and B in our marketing policy problem, where

$$A = (\text{ad} \geq 2); \qquad B = (\text{price} = 1);$$

$$P(A \cup B) = P(A) + P(B) - P(A \cap B);$$

$$P(\text{ad} \geq 2 \cup \text{price} = 1) = P(\text{ad} \geq 2) + P(\text{price} = 1) - P(\text{ad} \geq 2 \cap \text{price} = 1).$$

In this example we assumed four equally likely prices and three equally likely ad decisions, and so $P(\text{ad} \geq 2) = \frac{8}{12} = \frac{2}{3}$ and $P(\text{price} = 1) = \frac{3}{12} = \frac{1}{4}$; also, we calculated $P(\text{ad} \geq 2 \cap \text{price} = 1) = \frac{2}{12}$. Thus,

$$P(\text{ad} \geq 2 \cup \text{price} = 1) = \frac{8}{12} + \frac{3}{12} - \frac{2}{12} = \frac{9}{12}.$$

This agrees with the result that we calculated (less formally) in Section 3.4. You should be able to count in Fig. 3.3 the nine sample points where either price = 1 or ad $\geq$ 2 or both.

In our production process example, suppose that we now assume that $P(D_2) = 0.10$, in addition to the values we previously assumed, namely $P(D_1 \cap D_2) = 0.05$ and $P(D_1) = 0.15$. These values can be used to calculate $P(D_1 \cup D_2)$:

$$P(D_1 \cup D_2) = P(D_1) + P(D_2) - P(D_1 \cap D_2)$$
$$= 0.15 + 0.10 - 0.05 = 0.20.$$

3.7 SPECIAL CASES OF PROBABILITY RULES

Formulas (3.9) and (3.10) are *general* formulas that are appropriate for all types of events. There are, however, special cases of these formulas that can make calculating certain probabilities easier. We will examine these special rules for the case of mutually exclusive events and for independent events.

Mutually Exclusive Events

When the events A and B are mutually exclusive, the danger of double-counting is eliminated. That is, if A and B are mutually exclusive events, then there is *no overlap* of sample points in A and B that can be counted twice. The intersection $A \cap B$ in this special case has probability zero, $P(A \cap B) = 0$. We can thus rewrite Formula (3.10) as shown next.

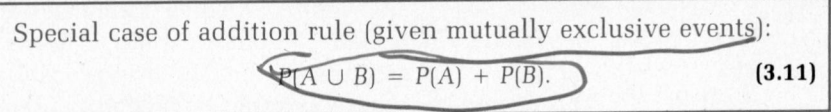

Special case of addition rule (given mutually exclusive events):
$$P(A \cup B) = P(A) + P(B). \qquad \textbf{(3.11)}$$

The Venn diagram in Fig. 3.8 illustrates the relationship between the sets A and B when these sets are mutually exclusive.

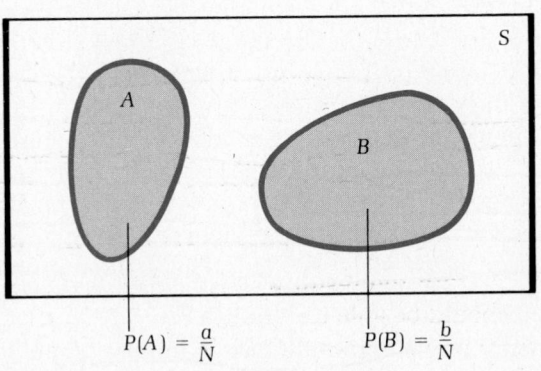

$$P(A) = \frac{a}{N} \qquad P(B) = \frac{b}{N}$$

FIGURE 3.8 **Illustration of the special rule of addition for mutually exclusive events:** $P(A \cap B) = 0$, so $P(A \cup B) = P(A) + P(B)$.

Example 3.15. Determining the probability that either the Mets or the Cubs win the National League pennant this year is an example of the type of problem that involves Formula (3.11). These events are mutually exclusive (it is not possible for both teams to win); hence,

$$P(\text{Mets win} \cup \text{Cubs win}) = P(\text{Mets win}) + P(\text{Cubs win}).$$

(Some people would say the probability *either* would win is too low to worry about, but that is only their subjective opinion.)

Special Case of Independence. Two events are said to be **independent** if what happens with one event does not influence (or is not influenced by) what happens with some other event. Suppose the two events are A and B. To be independent, the probability that A occurs cannot influence, or be influenced by, any knowledge of the event B. Dependence implies just the opposite — that the occurrence of one event is influenced by the occurrence of some other event.

Example 3.16. Most airlines use two separate computer systems to handle reservations, one system acting as a backup for the other. Let A = the event that the first system fails and B = the event that the second system fails. If A and B are independent, then the probability that the second system fails, $P(B)$, cannot be influenced by the fact that the first system has failed (event A). Medical scientists are continually conducting research to determine whether certain diseases are independent of, or dependent on, a variety of factors. The probability of getting cancer, for instance, has been reported to be related to (dependent on) whether one smokes, the quality of the air one breathes, and the food one eats.

In many problems it may be difficult to determine whether two events are independent or dependent. Note, for example, the controversy generated by the question of whether or not the presence of the artificial sweetener saccharine in soft drinks is independent of the occurrence of cancer in humans. In many statistical problems it may not be clear whether the events of interest are independent or dependent. In such cases, either: (1) it is not important or it is impossible to determine whether the events are independent or dependent, (2) one is trying to prove whether the events are independent or dependent, or (3) the experimenter can assume that the events are independent because of the way the experiment is defined. These three situations are considered below.

1. When it is not important or it is impossible to determine whether the events are independent or dependent, then the formulas derived thus

far — (3.8), (3.9), and (3.10) — should be used. *These formulas hold for both independent and dependent events*.

2. In some problems it is important to attempt to prove whether events are independent or dependent. In real-world problems, this occurs when one is trying to establish the relationship between events (such as cigarette smoking and cancer). From a statistical point of view it is more convenient to work with events that are independent, because we can use simplified versions of Formulas (3.8), (3.9), and (3.10). If A and B are independent, then P(A) must be unaffected by whether or not B occurs, and P(B) must be unaffected by whether or not A occurs. The rule for proving the independence of two events A and B is as follows.

> A and B are independent if either one of the following two relationships holds true:
>
> $$P(A|B) = P(A) \quad \text{or} \quad P(B|A) = P(B). \tag{3.12}$$

If $P(A|B) = P(A)$ then it must be true that $P(B|A) = P(B)$, and conversely.*

Since independence is the complement of dependence, to verify that two events are dependent, we need only show that one of the two relationships in (3.12) does *not* hold true; that is,

> A and B are dependent if either one of the following two relationships holds true:
>
> $$P(A|B) \neq P(A) \quad \text{or} \quad P(B|A) \neq P(B).$$

Suppose we use the rules described above to determine whether or not independence exists in our production-process example. To determine whether D_1 and D_2 are independent or dependent, we must look at one or both of the following relationships:

$$P(D_1|D_2) \text{ versus } P(D_1) \quad \text{and/or} \quad P(D_2|D_1) \text{ versus } P(D_2).$$

If *either* relationship can be shown to be an equality, then D_1 and D_2 are independent. Similarly, if either relationship can be shown *not* to be an equality, then D_1 and D_2 must be dependent. Remember from page 111 that the value of $P(D_2)$ was $P(D_2) = 0.10$. Also remember that in Example 3.14 we found the conditional probability, $P(D_2|D_1) = \frac{1}{3}$. Since

$$P(D_2|D_1) = \tfrac{1}{3} \text{ does not equal } P(D_2) = 0.10,$$

---

* Proof of this is for the reader in Exercise 3.51.

the events D_1 and D_2 cannot be independent; in other words, they must be dependent.

3. In some experiments the events are *assumed* to be independent. For instance, a bank might safely assume that the amount of loan requested is independent among loan applicants. In Chapter 7, we will discuss a procedure that assures that sample observations are taken "randomly" (independently), meaning that the outcome of one sample observation cannot influence the outcome of any other sample observation.

Probability Rules for Independent Events   The most important effect of assuming independence is that it simplifies the calculation of joint probabilities. This can be shown by substituting Formula (3.12) into the general rule of multiplication [Formula (3.9)]. The result is the special case of the multiplication rule. If A and B are independent, then the joint probability of A and B can be determined by using the following formula:

Special case of multiplication rule for A and B independent:

$$P(A \cap B) = P(A)P(B) = P(B)P(A) \tag{3.13}$$

Let's assume that one of the airlines mentioned previously, with a computer reservation system and an independent backup computer, would like to determine the probability that both systems fail. Assume that the probability that the first computer fails on any given day is 0.01 and the probability that the backup computer fails is also 0.01. Then the probability that they both fail is

$$P(\text{1st fails} \cap \text{2nd fails}) = P(\text{1st fails})P(\text{2nd fails})$$
$$= (0.01)(0.01) = 0.0001.$$

Example 3.17. Suppose a soft-drink manufacturer uses two machines in its capping process. Defective caps result from one machine with probability $P(M_1) = 0.001$, and defective caps result from the second machine with probability $P(M_2) = 0.003$. Assuming independence, the probability of a defective cap being found on both of two randomly selected bottles, each from a different machine, is

$$P(M_1 \cap M_2) = P(M_1)P(M_2) = (0.001)(0.003) = 0.000003.$$

There are thus three chances in a million that both selected bottles have defective caps.

The Distinction between Mutually Exclusive Events and Independence

Beginning students of statistics often confuse the concepts of independence and mutually exclusive events. It is important that the reader understand the difference between these concepts and the implications of each in probability theory. Thus, we present the following two general statements.

1. Events that are mutually exclusive must be dependent, but dependent events need not be mutually exclusive.
2. Events that are not mutually exclusive may be either independent or dependent. However, events that are independent cannot be mutually exclusive.

Example 3.18. To illustrate these two statements, we will consider the following four events:

A = interest rates decline in the next month.
B = interest rates do not decline in the next month.
C = the sale of homes increases in the next month.
D = the weather next year is very mild.

The events A and B are clearly mutually exclusive — if one occurs, the other cannot. Because the occurrence of either A or B influences the occurrence of the other (it *precludes* the other from taking place), A and B are dependent. Events A and C are also dependent (the sales of homes depends on the interest rate), but they are certainly not mutually exclusive (they can both happen). Thus, we have illustrated statement 1.

Events A and C are not mutually exclusive and are dependent. Events A and D are not mutually exclusive and are independent. This illustrates the first part of statement 2.

Events A and D also illustrate the second part of statement 2. These two events are independent, but they are not (and cannot be) mutually exclusive. To summarize,

Mutually exclusive implies dependence, and independence implies not mutually exclusive, but no other simple implications among these conditions hold true.

Define. *Intersection, union, conditional probability, complementary probability, joint probability, general rule of multiplication, general rule of addition, independence, dependence, mutually exclusive events.*

PROBLEMS

3.21 As an exercise to test your understanding of the concepts discussed in this chapter, answer the following questions about your perception of how prices on the New York Stock Exchange (use the Dow-Jones average) will change over the next month.
a) Estimate the probability that the Dow-Jones average will increase over the next month [denote this as P(DJ up)].
b) What is the probability of the complement of (DJ up)?
c) Estimate the probability that the unemployment rate will decline next month [denoted as P(UR down)].
d) Estimate P(DJ up|UR down). Are the two events independent or dependent? Explain.
e) Estimate P(UR down|DJ up). Must this probability be the same as P(DJ up|UR down)? Explain.
f) Determine P(DJ up ∩ UR down) and P(DJ up ∪ UR down) based on your answers to parts (a) through (e).
g) Draw a Venn diagram representing the events (DJ up) and (UR down).

3.22 The Easy Charge Company is being audited by the Internal Revenue Service (IRS). The company comptroller presents the following table to the IRS, showing the amount owed by each customer and whether or not a cash advance has been made.

Amount Owed (x) By Customers	Customers Receiving Cash Advance	Customers Not Receiving Cash Advance
$0 < x ≤ 100	229	2894
$100 < x ≤ 200	378	1707
$200 < x ≤ 300	501	1426
$300 < x ≤ 400	416	939
$400 < x ≤ 500	260	483
$500 < x	289	478
Total customers	2073 +	7927 = 10,000

a) Find P(cash advance) and P($\overline{\text{cash advance}}$)
b) Find P(cash advance|amount owed < $100)
c) Find P(amount owned < $100|cash advance)
d) Are the events "amount owed < $100" and "cash advance" independent or dependent?
e) Find P($100 < x ≤ $200 ∪ $\overline{\text{cash advance}}$)
f) Find P($100 < x ≤ $200 ∩ $\overline{\text{cash advance}}$)

3.23 The personnel manager for B.F Goodrich has kept careful records on the age (either age ≤ 30, or $30 <$ age ≤ 50, or age >50) and sex of the people applying for jobs at their Bloomington (IN) plant. Half of the applicants were 30 years old or younger, and half of these people were females.

a) Find the probability that a randomly selected applicant is 30 or under and is a female.

b) If $P(\text{female}|\text{age} \leq 30) = \frac{1}{2}$, and $P(\text{female}) = \frac{7}{16}$, does this indicate independence or dependence of the events "female" and "age ≤ 30"?

c) Use the following table to find $P(\text{female} \cap \text{age} \leq 30)$, $P(\text{age} \leq 50)$, and $P(\text{age} \leq 30|\text{female})$.

	Age		
	Age ≤ 30	$30 <$ age ≤ 50	Age > 50	
Female	$\frac{1}{4}$	$\frac{1}{16}$	$\frac{1}{8}$	$\frac{7}{16}$
Male	$\frac{1}{4}$	$\frac{3}{16}$	$\frac{1}{8}$	$\frac{9}{16}$
	$\frac{1}{2}$	$\frac{1}{4}$	$\frac{1}{4}$	

d) Find $P(\text{female} \cup \text{age} > 50)$ using $P(\text{age} > 50) = \frac{1}{4}$.

3.24 The following data describe certain characteristics of the students enrolled at a university.

	Men	Women	Over 21	
Freshmen	1325	1100	125	
Sophomores	1200	900	175	
Juniors	900	850	325	10,000
Seniors	725	775	950	
Graduates	1350	875	2225	

5500 + 4500
10,000   3800

⌀2100

Calculate:

a) $P(\text{sophomore} \cap \text{male})$ and $P(\text{sophomore}|\text{male})$.

b) The probability that a randomly selected student is over 21.

c) The probability that a randomly selected male is over 21, if age and sex are assumed to be independent.

3.25 A group of investors is about to build an indoor tennis facility in Champaign, Illinois. Their choice of heat for the facility is between gas and electricity. The investors' assessment as to the probability that each of the two methods is the better depends on the weather over the next three years, as follows.

1707

			Winters	
Heat	P	Mild (M)	Normal (N)	Cold (C)
Gas (G)	0.60	$P(G \cap M)$ = ?	$P(G \cap N)$ = ?	$P(G \cap C)$ = ?
Electricity (E)	0.40	$P(E \cap M)$ = 0.18	$P(E \cap N)$ = ?	$P(E \cap C)$ = ?
	1.00	$P(M)$ = ?	$P(N)$ = ?	$P(C)$ = 0.30

a) If $P(M|G) = 0.20$, find $P(G \cap M)$.
b) Find $P(G \cup M)$.
c) Using your prior results and assuming $P(N|G) = 0.50$, complete the table shown above.
d) Determine whether or not M and G are independent.

3.26 You have decided to conduct an in-depth study of one of ten accounting firms. Three of the firms (1, 2, and 3) are located in the Chicago area (event A). Six of the firms (2, 3, 4, 5, 6, and 7) have over 200 employees (event B), and five of the firms (2, 4, 6, 8, and 10) had revenues over one million dollars last year (event C). You decide to pick at random from among the ten firms.
a) Find $P(A)$ and $P(A \cup B)$.
b) Find $P(B|C)$ and $P(C|B)$.
c) Are the events A, B, and C mutually exclusive? Are they exhaustive? Explain.
d) Are the events A and B independent or dependent?

3.27 You have 12 employees, six males and six females, who had perfect attendance records over the past year. One of the males and one of the females are to be picked, at random, and each one wins a free trip to Hawaii. The males are numbered 1–6, and the females are also numbered 1–6.
a) What is the probability that the male and the female whose numbers are 6 will be selected?
b) What is the probability that one or both persons with the number 6 will be selected?
c) What is the probability that the two numbers selected will be different? (*Hint:* Use the rule of complements.)

3.28 Assume that the U.S. Senate is composed of 48 Republicans and 52 Democrats. Twelve of the Republicans are women, and 13 of the Democrats are women. You decide to pick senators, at random, and interview them. Selection is without replacement.

a) What is the probability that the first person you interview is a Republican and the second is a Democrat?

b) What is the probability of a Republican on either the first or second interview, or on both interviews?

c) What is the probability of interviewing a Republican on the first interview or a woman on the second interview or both?

d) Are the events "Republican on the first interview" and "woman on the second interview" independent or dependent?

e) Repeat each of the questions above, assuming that the senators are picked with replacement (i.e., a person could be interviewed twice).

3.29 A company is trying to design new chairs for the 250 employees who sit in front of a machine all day. One hundred of these employees are females, and 130 weigh over 150 pounds. Also, 30 women and 140 men are taller than 67 inches. If one of these employees is selected at random to test a new chair, what is the probability that the person:

a) is a male.

b) weighs over 150 pounds.

c) is taller than 67 inches.

d) is a male not taller than 67 inches.

e) is a female, given that the person is taller than 67 inches.

3.8 MARGINAL PROBABILITY

In a number of circumstances it is convenient to assume that a single event always occurs jointly with other events. For instance, it may be helpful not only to identify defective items resulting from a production process, but also to specify exactly *which* machines (or which workers) produced these defectives. Insurance companies are interested not only in the amount of damage associated with each automobile accident but, among other things, the city in which the accident took place and the age and sex of the driver. Similarly, students in a university are classified not only as males and females, but also according to class standing and major. An applicant for a loan may be classified not only by the dollar amount requested, but also by how long this person has been employed, the person's income, the amount of other debts, etc. In such situations the probability of the event in question (e.g., the probability of producing a defective item across all machines and all workers or the probability of an accident involving at least $1000 of damage across all cities and all drivers) may not be known directly but can be calculated by summing its chance of occurrence in combination with the other relevant factors identified in the problem.

Example 3.19. Consider the problem of producing a certain type of battery in three different plants with different equipment and employees. Suppose the weekly average of the number of batteries produced in these three plants, denoted by E_1, E_2, and E_3, is 500, 2000, and 1500, respectively. Further, let's assume that the probability that a defective (D) is produced in *each* of the three plants is

$$P(D|E_1) = 0.020, \qquad P(D|E_2) = 0.015, \qquad \text{and} \qquad P(D|E_2) = 0.030.$$

Suppose that the batteries produced by the three plants supply one automaker. That is, the automaker receives 4000 batteries weekly and the probability that a randomly selected battery would have originated in each plant is

$$P(E_1) = \tfrac{500}{4000}, \qquad P(E_2) = \tfrac{2000}{4000}, \qquad \text{and} \qquad P(E_3) = \tfrac{1500}{4000}$$

What is the probability that the battery used by the automaker in a randomly selected car is defective? This probability, P(D), is a *marginal probability*, and its value can be determined by the special rules for marginal probabilities. It may clarify the concept of a marginal probability if we express the values for this example in the form of a table (Table 3.2). Note that the values in Table 3.2 can be used to calculate the three conditional probabilities given previously, $P(D|E_1) = \tfrac{10}{500} = 0.020$, $P(D|E_2) = \tfrac{30}{2000} = 0.015$, and $P(D|E_3) = \tfrac{45}{1500} = 0.030$.

The probability of a defective in this context is called a **marginal probability** since its value can be read directly from the right-hand margin of Table 3.2; $P(D) = \tfrac{85}{4000} = 0.02125$. Slightly more than 2% of the batteries are defective. Rather than find $P(D)$ via the frequencies in Table 3.2, we often calculate such values from a list of the corresponding joint probabilities, as shown in Table 3.3. The proportion of defectives in this problem is illustrated in Fig. 3.9.

TABLE 3.2

	Plants			Total
	E_1	E_2	E_3	
Good (G)	490	1970	1455	3915
Defective (D)	10	30	45	85
Total	500	2000	1500	4000

TABLE 3.3 **Joint probabilities.**

	Plants			Total
	E_1	E_2	E_3	
Good (G)	490/4000	1970/4000	1455/4000	3915/4000
Defective (D)	10/4000	30/4000	45/4000	85/4000
Total	500/4000	2000/4000	1500/4000	$\frac{4000}{4000} = 1.00$

The circle labeled D in Fig. 3.9 represents the proportion of defectives in the sample space S. There are three shaded areas in this circle, representing the intersecton of D with $E_1, E_2,$ and E_3. The probabilities that a given battery will be in one of these three intersections are $P(D \cap E_1)$, $P(D \cap E_2)$, and $P(D \cap E_3)$. Finally, since there is no overlap among the three intersections, the probability $P(D) = \frac{85}{4000}$ is now easily seen to be the sum of three joint probabilities:

$$P(D) = P(D \cap E_1) + P(D \cap E_2) + P(D \cap E_3)$$
$$= \tfrac{10}{4000} + \tfrac{30}{4000} + \tfrac{45}{4000} = 0.02125.$$

By now it should be fairly clear that if one has a table of joint probabilities such as Table 3.3, then calculating marginal probabilities is

FIGURE 3.9 **Illustration of a marginal probability.**

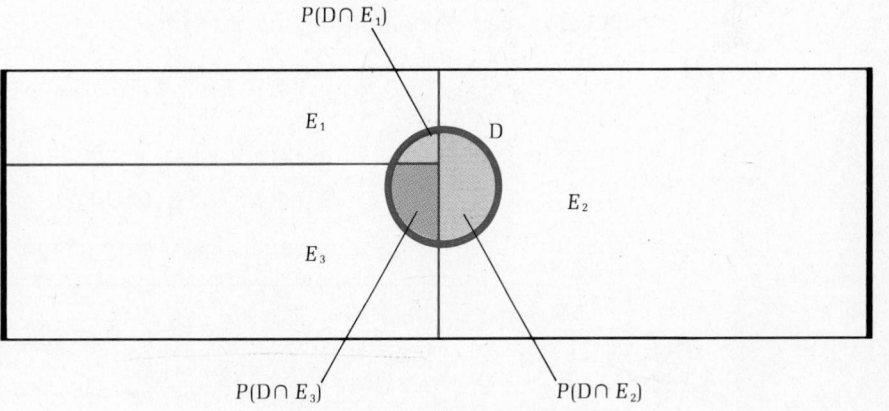

$P(D \cap E_1)$

E_1 D

E_2

E_3

$P(D \cap E_3)$ $P(D \cap E_2)$

S

Marginal probability: $P(D) = \sum_{i=1}^{3} P(D \cap E_i)$

not very difficult. Constructing a joint-probability table, however, usually involves considerably more effort than it takes to calculate the marginal probability directly by using a formula.

Let us develop our formula for a marginal probability in the context of calculating $P(D)$ for the battery example. Recall that $P(D)$ was written as the sum of three joint probabilities,

$$P(D \cap E_1) + P(D \cap E_2) + P(D \cap E_3).$$

We know from Formula (3.9) that a joint probability can always be written as the product of two probabilities, one of which is a conditional probability. Using Formula (3.9) to rewrite our expression for $P(D)$, we obtain

$$P(D) = P(E_1)P(D|E_1) + P(E_2)P(D|E_2) + P(E_3)P(D|E_3).$$

Each of the probabilities on the right-hand side are known values and can be substituted to get

$$P(D) = \tfrac{500}{4000}(0.020) + \tfrac{2000}{4000}(0.015) + \tfrac{1500}{4000}(0.030) = 0.02125.$$

This result agrees with that calculated previously. The generalization of this example leads to the following definition of $P(D)$.

> If D represents an event such that one of the mutually exclusive events $E_1, E_2, \ldots, E_k$ always must occurs jointly with any occurrence of D, then the probability of D is called a marginal (or unconditional) probability.

Its value may be determined by the rule

$$P(D) = \sum_{i=1}^{k} P(D \cap E_i) = P(D \cap E_1) + P(D \cap E_2) + \cdots + P(D \cap E_k).$$

From the general rule of multiplication, Formula (3.9), we know that

$$P(D \cap E_i) = P(E_i)P(D|E_i).$$

Thus, the formula for a marginal probability can be written as:

> Marginal probability:
> $$P(D) = \sum_{i=1}^{k} P(D \cap E_i) = \sum_{i=1}^{k} P(E_i)P(D|E_i)$$
> $$= P(E_1)P(D|E_1) + P(E_2)P(D|E_2) + \cdots + P(E_k)P(D|E_k).$$

(3.14)

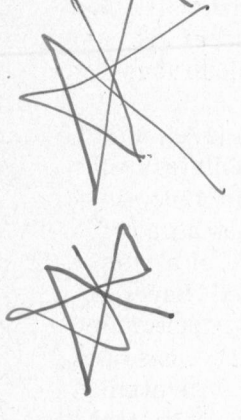

Example 3.20. Consider the problem of estimating the probability that Carl Yastrzemski (former Boston Red Sox player) gets a hit on a randomly selected turn at bat, if it is known that his relative frequency of hits was 0.315 when the pitcher was right-handed and 0.262 when the pitcher was left-handed.* If 0.315 is taken as the probability of a hit given a right-handed pitcher (i.e., $P(H|R) = 0.315$) and 0.262 as the probability of a hit given a left-handed pitcher (i.e., $P(H|L) = 0.262$), and if we assume that the probabilities that Yastrzemski faced right-handed and left-handed pitchers were $P(R) = 0.75$ and $P(L) = 0.25$, respectively, then

$$P(\text{Hit}) = P(R)P(H|R) + P(L)P(H|L)$$
$$= 0.75(0.315) + 0.25(0.262) = 0.302.$$

3.9 BAYES' RULE

One of the most interesting (and controversial) applications of the rules of probability theory involves estimating unknown probabilities and making decisions on the basis of new (sample) information. Statistical decision theory is a new field of study that has its foundations in just such problems. Chapter 16 investigates the area of statistical decision theory in some detail; this section describes one of the basic formulas of the area, **Bayes' rule.**

An English philosopher, the Reverend Thomas Bayes (1702–1761), was one of the first to work with rules for revising probabilities in the light of sample information. Bayes' research, published in 1763, went largely unnoticed for over a century and only recently has attracted a great deal of attention. His contribution consists primarily of a unique method for calculating conditional probabilities. The so-called "Bayesian" approach to this problem addresses itself to the question of determining the probability of some event, E_i, given *that* another event, A, has been (or will be) observed; i.e., determining the value of $P(E_i|A)$. The event A is usually thought of as new information. Thus, Bayes' rule is concerned with determining the probability of an event given certain new information, such as that obtained from a sample, a survey, or a pilot study. For example, a sample output of three defectives in 20 trials (event A) might be used to estimate the probability that a machine is not working correctly (event E_i).

Probabilities prior to revision by Bayes' rule are called *a priori*, or simply *prior* probabilities, because they are determined before the new

---

* Data based on Yastrzemski's major-league career record.

information is taken into account. Prior probabilities may be either objective or subjective values. A probability that has undergone revision in the light of new information (via Bayes' rule) is called a *posterior probability*, since it represents a probability calculated *after* this information is taken into account. Posterior probabilities are always conditional probabilities, the conditional event being the new information. Thus, by the use of Bayes' rule a prior probability, which is an unconditional probability, becomes a posterior probability, which is a conditional probability. In order to calculate such posterior probabilities we will first derive Bayes' rule for the general problem of determining $P(E_i|A)$.

Recall that earlier in this chapter the order of events was shown to be immaterial in calculating joint probabilities. The implication is that $P(E_i \cap A)$ must be equivalent to $P(A \cap E_i)$; therefore, the following relationships must hold true [see Formula (3.9)]:

$$P(E_i \cap A) = P(A)P(E_i|A),$$

$$P(E_i \cap A) = P(E_i)P(A|E_i).$$

If the above two formulas hold, then it must also be true that the two right-hand side representations must be equal to each other.

$$P(A)P(E_i|A) = P(E_i)P(A|E_i).$$

We can now solve for $P(E_i|A)$ directly by dividing both sides by $P(A)$:

$$P(E_i|A) = \frac{P(E_i)P(A|E_i)}{P(A)}. \tag{3.15}$$

The numerator of Formula (3.15) represents the probability that A and E_i both will occur, while the denominator is the probability that A alone will occur. If both these probabilities are calculable, then the conditional probability of the event E_i, given some new information A, can be determined.

The relationship that Bayes developed for calculating posterior probabilities uses Formula (3.14) as a substitute way to calculate the marginal probability in the denominator of (3.15).

Bayes' rule:

$$P(E_i|A) = \frac{P(E_i)P(A|E_i)}{\sum\limits_{j=1}^{k} P(E_j)P(A|E_j)}$$

$$= \frac{P(E_1)P(A|E_1)}{P(E_1)P(A|E_1) + P(E_2)P(A|E_2) + \cdots + P(E_k)P(A|E_k)}. \tag{3.16}$$

Just as in Formula (3.15), the numerator of Formula (3.16) represents the probability that both A and E_i will occur, while the denominator is the probability that A alone will occur.

To illustrate Bayes' rule using our battery example, suppose we want to calculate the probability that a battery came from Plant 2 (E_2) *given that* the battery is defective (D). In this example the event of interest is E_2 and the information is (D). By Bayes' rule we can write the following.

$$P(E_2|D) = \frac{P(E_2)P(D|E_2)}{P(E_1)P(D|E_1) + P(E_2)P(D|E_2) + P(E_3)P(D|E_3)}.$$

All the values necessary to calculate $P(E_2|D)$ were given in our previous discussion of this problem. The substitutions are shown below.

$$P(E_2|D) = \frac{(\frac{2000}{4000})(0.015)}{(\frac{500}{4000})(0.020) + (\frac{2000}{4000})(0.015) + (\frac{1500}{4000})(0.030)} = 0.353.$$

The posterior probability of E_2 after observing a defective battery is 0.353. This same value can be verified from Table 3.2 — the proportion of defectives in E_2 to the total number of defectives is $\frac{30}{85} = 0.353$. Bayes' rule allows us to calculate such probabilities without constructing such a table.

Example 3.21. Suppose that a questionnaire is sent to rural households with probability $P(R) = 0.50$ and to urban households with probability $P(U) = 0.50$, where R stands for "rural" and U for "urban." Households are divided into low-income (L) and high-income (H). Furthermore, the following conditional probabilities are known:

$$P(H|R) = 0.20, P(L|R) = 0.80,$$
$$P(H|U) = 0.40, P(L|U) = 0.60.$$

These probabilities are shown in the tree diagram of Fig. 3.10. Now suppose that the location code has been omitted on one of the questionnaires received so that it is not known whether it is from a rural or urban household. Our prior probabilities suggest that the probability is 0.50 that

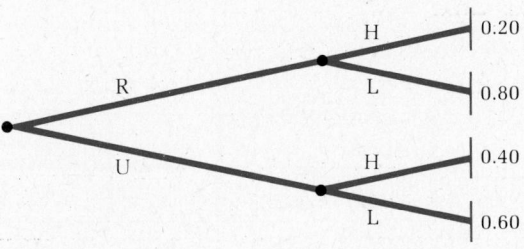

FIGURE 3.10 **Tree diagram for Example 3.21.**

it comes from a rural household and 0.50 that it comes from an urban household. Suppose that analysis of the responses in the questionnaire shows that it was obviously completed by a high-income household. How does this new information affect our probabilistic knowledge of whether it came from a rural or an urban household?

Formula (3.16) can be used to find the revised (posterior) probability that the questionnaire came from a rural household, given the information that it came from a high-income household, $P(R|H)$:

$$P(R|H) = \frac{P(R)P(H|R)}{P(R)P(H|R) + P(U)P(H|U)}$$

$$= \frac{(0.50)(0.20)}{(0.50)(0.20) + (0.50)(0.40)} = \frac{1}{3}.$$

The posterior probability that a randomly selected household is rural, given that the family is known to have a high income, is $\frac{1}{3}$. This value is illustrated in Fig. 3.11 as the ratio of the one heavily shaded rectangle to all three shaded (high-income) rectangles.

We end this section by writing Bayes' rule in a slightly different form, one that will be especially convenient in Chapter 16 when we study the use of Bayes' rule in the context of statistical decision theory.

$$P(event_i | sample\ info.) = \frac{P(event_i)P(sample\ info.|event_i)}{\sum_j P(event_j)P(sample\ info.|event_j)}.$$

Study Question 3.2: Probability of an IRS Audit

A *Time* article reported the data in Fig. 3.12 on the chances a taxpayer in the United States has of being audited by the IRS (Internal Revenue Service).

a) Rewrite these data as a 2×6 table, where the six categories are the incomes/forms and the two categories are the experiences of being audited and not being audited. In the body of the table, put the number of taxpayers (in millions). Label the six income categories C1–C6 and the two audit categories A and $\overline{A}$.

FIGURE 3.11 **Illustration for Bayes' rule.**

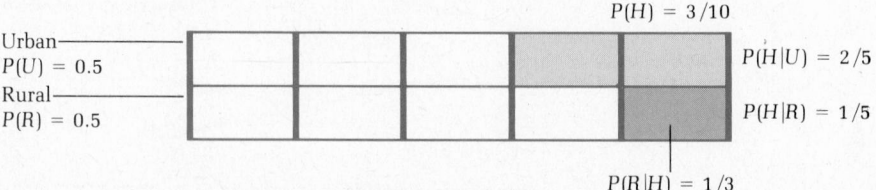

$P(H) = 3/10$

Urban —
$P(U) = 0.5$

Rural —
$P(R) = 0.5$

$P(H|U) = 2/5$

$P(H|R) = 1/5$

$P(R|H) = 1/3$

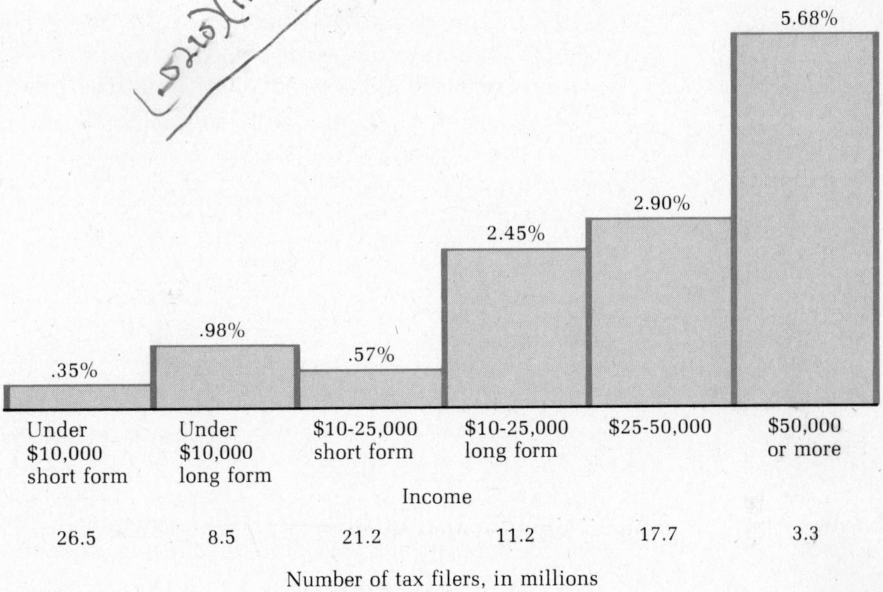

FIGURE 3.12 **Taxpayers and IRS audit. Chances of an audit. (Copyright 1983 Time Inc. All rights reserved. Reprinted by permission from TIME.)**

b) What is the probability a taxpayer will have an income in the range $25,000–$50,000?

c) What is the probability that a taxpayer with income of $25,000–$50,000 will be audited?

d) What is the probability that a randomly selected taxpayer will be audited?

e) Given that a person has been selected for an audit, what is the probability that this person had an income between $25,000 and $50,000? Use Bayes' rule.

f) Are the events "audited" and "income $25,000–$50,000" independent or dependent?

Answer

a)

Incomes/Forms							Totals
	C1	C2	C3	C4	C5	C6	
A	0.09	0.08	0.12	0.27	0.51	0.19	1.26
$\overline{A}$	26.41	8.42	21.08	10.93	17.19	3.11	87.14
Totals	26.50	8.50	21.20	11.20	17.70	3.30	88.40

b) $P(\text{income }\$25,000-50,000) = 17.70/88.40 = 0.2002$, where 88.40 is the total number of taxpayers.

c) $P(\text{audited} | \$25,000-\$50,000) = 0.0290$ (read directly from data).

d) $P(\text{audited}) = P(C1)P(A|C1) + P(C2)P(A|C2) + \cdots + P(C6)P(A|C6)$

$$= (0.0035)(26.50/88.40) + (0.0098)(8.50/88.40)$$

$$+ \cdots + (0.0568)(3.30/88.40) = 0.0144.$$

e) $$P(C5|A) = \frac{P(C5)P(A|C5)}{P(C1)P(A|C1) + P(C2)P(A|C2) + \cdots + P(C6)P(A|C6)}$$

$$= \frac{(0.0290)(17.70/88.40)}{(0.0035)(26.50/88.40) + (0.0098)(8.50/88.40)}$$
$$ + \cdots + (0.0568)(3.30/88.40)$$

$$= \frac{0.0058}{0.0144} = 0.4028.$$

f) $P(C5|A) = 0.4028$ and $P(C5) = 0.2002$. Since these two probabilities are not equal, the events are dependent.

3.10   APPLICATION OF PROBABILITY THEORY: AN EXAMPLE

Suppose that a contractor who produces delicate electronic components essential to the manufacturing of certain computer equipment cannot determine whether the component part produced has been assembled correctly without tearing the component apart and, in the process, destroying the usefulness of that component. It is possible, however, to purchase a machine that, according to its makers' claim, will help detect defective components. This machine, which indicates only that the component appears to be good ($+$) or that it appears to be defective ($-$), is not infallible — sometimes it will indicate positive when the component is defective or negative when the component is good. To determine the ability of the machine to distinguish between good and defective items, 400 randomly selected components were first tested by the machine and then torn apart to see whether they were good or defective. The results of this research are given in Table 3.4. In this case the sample space is discrete and finite. The values in Table 3.4 can be used to calculate a number of probabilities concerning the machine's reliability and the quality state of the components.

Intersections   The joint probabilities of the two component states (good or defective) with the results of the test (positive or negative) are shown in Table 3.5.

TABLE 3.4

State of Component	Results of Test		Sum across Row
	Positive	Negative	
Good	342	18	360
Defective	8	32	40
Sum of column	350	50	400

Marginals The sums across rows or down columns in Table 3.5 are marginal probabilities. Although the marginal (unconditional) probability of a good item can be determined directly (from Table 3.4) to be

$$P(\text{Good}) = \tfrac{360}{400} = 0.90,$$

its value can also be determined via Formula (3.14) as follows:

$$P(\text{Good}) = P(\text{Good} \cap \text{Pos.}) + P(\text{Good} \cap \text{Neg.})$$
$$= 0.855 + 0.045 = 0.90.$$

Similarly, the probability that the test reads positive is

$$P(\text{Pos.}) = P(\text{Good} \cap \text{Pos.}) + P(\text{Def.} \cap \text{Pos.})$$
$$= 0.855 + 0.020 = 0.875.$$

Unions The probability of the union of two events can be determined by using the general rule of addition, Formula (3.10). For example, the probability of *either* a good component *or* a positive test is

$$P(\text{Good} \cup \text{Pos.}) = P(\text{Good}) + P(\text{Pos.}) - P(\text{Good} \cap \text{Pos.})$$
$$= 0.90 + 0.875 - 0.855 = 0.92.$$

TABLE 3.5 **Joint probabilities associated with Table 3.4**

State of component	Results of test		Sum across Row
	Positive	Negative	
Good	0.855	0.045	0.900
Defective	0.020	0.080	0.100
Sum of column	0.875	0.125	1.000

Conditionals The manufacturer in our problem is primarily interested in the probability that a particular component is good given the condition that the machine indicates positive or negative. This can be determined from Table 3.4 by noting that out of 350 components that tested positive, 342 were good, and of the 50 that tested negative, 18 were good; therefore,

$$P(\text{Good}|\text{Pos.}) = \frac{342}{350} = 0.977,$$

and

$$P(\text{Good}|\text{Neg.}) = \frac{18}{50} = 0.36.$$

Note that these two probabilities do not add up to one, since they are based on different conditional events. However, the value of $P(\text{Def.}|\text{Neg.})$ must equal

$$1 - P(\text{Good}|\text{Neg.}) = 1 - 0.36 = 0.64,$$

since these events are complementary.

The conditional probability $P(\text{Good}|\text{Pos.})$ is the type of probability that can be (and often is) calculated by using Bayes' rule. To use Bayes' rule in this example, we need to know the probabilities $P(\text{Pos.}|\text{Good})$ and $P(\text{Pos.}|\text{Def.})$, which from Table 3.4 are easily seen to be $P(\text{Pos.}|\text{Good}) = \frac{342}{360} = 0.95$ and $P(\text{Pos.}|\text{Def.}) = \frac{8}{40} = 0.20$.

The Bayesian calculation of $P(\text{Good}|\text{Pos.})$ is:

$$P(\text{Good}|\text{Pos.}) = \frac{P(\text{Good})P(\text{Pos.}|\text{Good})}{P(\text{Good})P(\text{Pos.}|\text{Good}) + P(\text{Def.})P(\text{Pos.}|\text{Def.})}$$

$$= \frac{(0.90)(0.95)}{(0.90)(0.95) + (0.10)(0.20)} = \frac{0.855}{0.875} = 0.977.$$

The result agrees with the $\frac{342}{350} = 0.977$ calculated above.

The results of the machine test in this problem are obviously not independent of the state of the component. If they were independent, $P(\text{Good}|\text{Pos.})$ would have to equal $P(\text{Good})$, and $P(\text{Def.}|\text{Neg.})$ would have to equal $P(\text{Def.})$, which is not the case. But how much better off is the manufacturer by knowing the results of the test? The manufacturer is in good shape if the test is positive, as the guess can then be made that the component is good, and the guess will be correct 97.7% of the time. After a negative indication, however, by guessing the component to be defective the manufacturer will be correct only 64% of the time. Fortunately, a positive test will occur most often (87.5%) and a negative test relatively infrequently (12.5%).

Multiplying 97.7 by 0.875 and 64.0 by 0.125 gives the total percent of the time a correct assessment may be made, assuming that the manufacturer always accepts the results of the machine test. This process is just a common-sense use of the formal rule for adding up all the joint occurrences of those events. Using the formal rule, we find that the test indicates the correct state of the component 93.5% of the time.

$$P(\text{Correct}) = P(\text{Good} \cap \text{Pos.}) + P(\text{Def.} \cap \text{Neg.})$$
$$= P(\text{Pos.})P(\text{Good}|\text{Pos.}) + P(\text{Neg.})P(\text{Def.}|\text{Neg.})$$
$$= 0.875(0.977) + 0.125(0.64)$$
$$= 0.855 + 0.080 = 0.935.$$

Without this machine, if the manufacturer always presumes that all components are good, the percent of correct decisions will be 90%, since the prior probability is $P(\text{Good}) = \frac{360}{400} = 0.90$. If we knew how much this machine costs (to buy and operate) and how much the firm's revenue would increase as a result of the machine's superior ability to distinguish between good and defective components, then we could determine whether the machine is worth purchasing.

Table 3.6 provides a summary of many of the probability rules presented in this chapter and their relationships to the different conditions that may be present in statistics problems.

Define. *Marginal probability, prior and posterior probabilities, Bayes' rule.*

TABLE 3.6 **Summary of probability rules**

Rule Name	Formula	General Rule	Rule for Mutually Exclusive Events	Rule for Independence
Complements	(3.7)	$P(\overline{A}) = 1 - P(A)$	——	——
Conditional probability	(3.8)	$P(A|B) = \dfrac{P(A \cap B)}{P(B)}$	$P(A|B) = 0$	$P(A|B) = P(A)$
Joint probability	(3.9)	$P(A \cap B) = P(B)P(A|B)$ $= P(A)P(B|A)$	$P(A \cap B) = 0$	$P(A \cap B) = P(A)P(B)$
Probability of a union	(3.10)	$P(A \cup B) = P(A) + P(B)$ $- P(A \cap B)$	$P(A \cup B) = P(A) + P(B)$	$P(A \cup B) = P(A)$ $+ P(B) - P(A)P(B)$
Marginal probability	(3.14)	$P(D) = \sum_i P(D \cap E_i)$ $= \sum_i P(E_i)P(D|E_i)$	——	——
Bayes' rule	(3.16)	$P(E_i|A) = \dfrac{P(E_i)P(A|E_i)}{\sum_j P(E_j)P(A|E_j)}$	——	——

PROBLEMS

3.30 Two hundred marketing strategies were classified as "very effective," "moderately effective," or "not effective" in conjunction with three pricing strategies (I, II, III) as shown below:

	Pricing strategies			
Marketing strategies	I	II	III	Totals
Very effective	20	50	30	100
Moderately effective	20	20	20	60
Not effective	20	10	10	40
Totals	60	80	60	200

a) Convert these data into a table showing a joint probability in each cell.

b) Use Formula (3.14) to calculate the marginal probability P(Very effective).

c) Use Bayes' rule to calculate the posterior probability P(Pricing strategy II|Very effective).

3.31 Use Bayes' rule to calculate the following.

a) In Problem 3.25 find the probability that gas heat will be best given that the winters will be mild.

b) In Problem 3.23 calculate the probability that a randomly selected applicant is a female, given that this person is 30 years old or younger.

3.32 Suppose you are now the part owner of Ski World, a ski resort in Nashville, IN. Over the past several winters, January weather has been very unpredictable. Your biggest profit comes from the weekends. On some weekends it was actually too cold for skiing. Other weekends have been relatively warm, or perhaps rainy. You determine that the probability that you make a profit on a given weekend is $\frac{3}{4}$ if the weather is "favorable." If the weather is "unfavorable," the probability that you make a profit is $\frac{1}{8}$. Assume that the forecast is for a $\frac{2}{3}$ chance of "favorable" weather.

a) What is the probability that you will make a profit from the weekend operation?

b) Suppose on Monday you find that you have made a profit. What is the probability that the weather on the preceding weekend was "favorable?"

3.33 You have decided to invest in the stock market for the first time and are considering three investment strategies. You want to earn at least a 10%

return on your money. The probability of a 10% return if you pick the best of the three strategies is $\frac{1}{3}$. If you do not pick the best of the three strategies, your chances of a 10% return are $\frac{1}{5}$.

a) What is the probability that you will earn a return of 10% if you pick randomly among the strategies?

b) Given that you find at the end of six months that you have earned a 10% return, what is the probability that you picked the best of the three strategies?

3.34 One-fourth of the customers entering a certain Radio Shack store are less than 25 years old. One percent of the customers less than 25 years old make a major purchase (over $100), and 5% of the customers 25 or older make a major purchase. What is the probability that if a major purchase is made, it was by a person 25 or older?

3.35 A candidate studying for the CPA exam recognizes five potential essay questions that might be the one asked on the exam. Unfortunately, this person has time to study for only one of the essay questions. The candidate picks, at random, one of the questions to study. If the candidate studies the right question, the probability of passing the exam is 0.90. If one of the other four questions is on the exam, the probability of passing is 0.30. The exam does, in fact, contain one of the five questions.

a) What is the probability the candidate will pass the test?

b) Suppose the candidate passes. What is the probability that this person picked the correct question to study?

3.36 The Easy-Charge Company described in Exercise 3.22 has released the following data on the number of customers who were given cash advances last month.

Amounts Owed (x) by Customers	Customers Receiving a Cash Advance	Customers Not Receiving a Cash Advance
$0 < x \leq 100$	229	2894
$100 < x \leq 200$	378	1707
$200 < x \leq 300$	501	1426
$300 < x \leq 400$	416	939
$400 < x \leq 500$	260	483
$500 < x$	289	478
Total customers	2073	7927

a) Use Formula (3.14) to calculate the marginal probability $P($Cash advance$)$.

b) Use Bayes' rule to calculate the posterior probability P(Amount Owed ≤ $100|Cash advance).

3.37 A Gallup survey in the *Wall Street Journal* reported on hours worked by chief executives as shown in Fig. 3.13.

a) Among large firms, what is the probability that a randomly selected executive will be working more than 60 hours per week?

b) If an executive works 70 hours or more, what is the probability that this person is associated with a small firm? Use Bayes' rule. Assume 50% of the executives were from large firms, 25% from medium firms, and 25% from small firms.

c) Complete the following table, showing in each cell the appropriate joint probability for a randomly selected executive.

	Hours Worked				
Firm Size	Less Than 50	50–59	60–69	70 or more	Marginals
Large	0.030				0.500
Medium					
Small					
Marginals	0.115				

3.38 Given the following table of survey information:

	Years of College	
Salary ($000)	At Least 2	None
16 < s ≤ 19	30	50
19 < s ≤ 21	50	40
21 < s ≤ 24	20	10
	100	100

a) Illustrate the use of Bayes' rule by finding the probability of selecting a noncollege respondent, presuming that the one selected is in the highest salary bracket indicated.

b) Are salary and years of college independent in this problem?

3.39 Consider two types of economic stabilization policies — fiscal (controlled by Congress) and monetary policy (controlled by the Federal Reserve Board). Assume that the policy decisions made by these two institutions

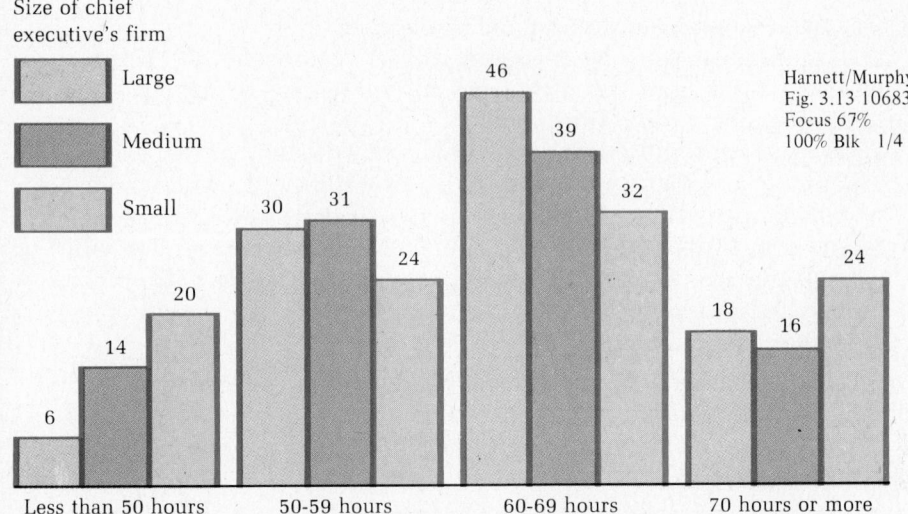

How long chief executives work each week (In percent)

Size of chief executive's firm

FIGURE 3.13 **Executive work week. (Reprinted by permission of *Wall Street Journal*. © Jones & Company, Inc., 1980. All rights reserved.)**

are independent of one another and that the action of either group is correct 80% of the time. Finally, assume that the probabilities that the economy follows a generally stable growth pattern due to (or in spite of) these policy actions are:

P(Stable growth | Neither acting correctly) = 0.40,

P(Stable growth | Both acting correctly) = 0.99,

P(Stable growth | Only 1 acting correctly) = 0.70.

a)   Use the independence assumption to calculate:

P(Neither acting correctly),

P(Both acting correctly),

P(Only 1 acting correctly).

b)   You are given the sample information that growth is stable for a particular period. Use Bayes' rule to calculate:

P(Only 1 acting correctly | Stable growth),

P(Both acting correctly | Stable growth),

P(Neither acting correctly | Stable growth).

Check to see whether these three probabilities sum to 1.0.

EXERCISES

3.40 Answer the following questions about probability.

a) Distinguish between objective and subjective probability. Describe what you think to be the advantages and limitations of each of these interpretations of probabilities.

b) What is the probability that the real GNP growth this year will exceed 4%? Is this a subjective or an objective probability? At what "odds" would you be indifferent between the two sides of a $1 bet, one side saying growth will be less than 4%, the other side saying growth will exceed 4%? Are these odds consistent with your answer about the probability of more than a 4% growth in real GNP? Explain why they are or are not consistent.

3.41 In defining probability, what is meant by the terms "experiment" and "event"? How are these terms related to the limit of relative frequency? How does one go about determining the limit of relative frequency in practical problems?

3.42 A local business has been talked into buying a number of raffle tickets. The prize is a $500 color television set. If 4000 tickets are sold, how much is each ticket worth?

3.43 Four employees have been selected to take a written test for possible promotion to supervisor. Two of the employees are women. The maximum test score is 100 points. Three of the employees scored above 90 on the test, and every employee either exceeded 90, or is a woman, or both.

a) What is the probability that an employee exceeded 90 and is a woman?

b) Given that an employee is a woman, what is the probability that she scored above 90?

c) Given that an employee scored above 90, what is the probability that this person is a woman?

3.44 Suppose your instructor in statistics announces that the final exam will consist of five questions, which will be randomly selected from a list of ten questions handed out one week before the exam. In order to pass the exam, a student must be able to answer at least four of the exam questions selected. What is the probability that a student who can answer eight of the ten questions will pass the exam?

3.45 Given the following set of weekly wages in dollars for six employees: 372, 400, 288, 395, 389, 378. If two of these employees are to be selected at random to serve as labor representatives, what is the probability that at least one will have a wage lower than the average?

3.46 Two different types of questionnaires were used during the 1980 Census of Population, a short form (asking only names, ages, and incomes of each household) and a long form (asking for considerably more information). In Town A, 30% of the houses received the long form; in Town B, 20% received the long form; and in Town C, 10% received the long form. Town A has 50,000 houses, Town B has 100,000 houses, and Town C has 40,000 houses.

a) Considering all three towns as one group, what is the probability that a house will receive the long form?

b) Given that a house received the long form, what is the probability that the house is in Town A? What is this probability for B? For C?

c) Complete the following 2 × 3 table (two forms × three towns) by placing a joint probability in each cell and five marginal probabilities around the outside. Assume that one house is randomly selected.

	Town A	Town B	Town C	Marginals
Long form	.079	.105	.021	.205
Short form	.184	.421	.19	.795
Marginals	.263	.526	.211	1.00

3.47 A bank has studied its checking accounts and found that 1% of all checks are returned for insufficient funds. For checking accounts that have been open less than one year, the percent of returned checks is 5%. Ninety-six percent of all accounts have been open for more than one year. Student accounts represent 6% of the bank's checking accounts, and one-third of the student accounts have been open for less than one year.

a) What is the probability that a randomly selected account will be for a student and will have been open for less than one year?

b) If a check is returned for insufficient funds, what is the probability that the account has been open for less than one year?

c) Is the event "check returned" independent of the event "open less than one year"? Is the event "open for less than one year" independent of the event "student"?

3.48 An automobile insurance company has examined its records and compiled the following probability table representing how likely it is that each one of their policyholders has an accident in a one-year period. The number of policyholders in each category is given in parentheses.

a) Explain the meaning of the probability 0.10 in the upper-left cell.

b) How many accidents should the company expect in a year?

c) If an accident occurs, what is the probability that it involved someone less than 25? What is the probability that a male was the driver?

d) Are the events "male is the driver" and "less than 25" independent?

Sex	Age		
	Less than 25	25–65	More than 65
Female	0.10 (10,000)	0.04 (50,000)	0.08 (20,000)
Male	0.20 (8,000)	0.05 (60,000)	0.06 (20,000)

3.49 The probability that an individual has Type O blood is 0.45, the probability of Type A blood is 0.40, the probability of Type B blood is 0.10, and the probability of Type AB blood is 0.05. Two randomly selected individuals agree to donate blood. What is the probability that both have the same blood type or that at least one of the two has Type O blood?

3.50 Credit-Wise loan company has recorded both the activity level of the local economy (either Hi, Med, or Low) and the mean interarrival times $(0 < \text{time} \le 20 \text{ min}, 20 < \text{time} \le 60 \text{ min}, 60 < \text{time} \le 200 \text{ min})$ for its customers over the past 150 weeks.

Time Interval (t) between Customers	State of Economy		
	Hi	Med	Low
A $0 < t \le 20$	30	12	8
B $20 < t \le 60$	30	21	4
C $60 < t \le 200$	30	12	3

a) Find $P(\text{Hi})$, $P(\text{Med})$, $P(\text{Low})$, $P(A)$, $P(B)$, and $P(C)$.
b) Find $P(A|\text{Hi})$, $P(A|\text{Med})$, $P(A|\text{Low})$.
c) Use Formula (3.14) to find $P(A)$.
d) Are the events A, B, C independent of the state of the economy?
e) Suppose Credit-Wise would like to revise the probabilities $P(\text{Hi})$, $P(\text{Med})$, $P(\text{Low})$ in the light of the sample evidence S. Find $P(\text{Hi}|S)$, $P(\text{Med}|S)$ and $P(\text{Low}|S)$ given that $P(S|\text{Hi}) = 0.05$, $P(S|\text{Med}) = 0.10$, and $P(S|\text{Low}) = 0.40$.

3.51 Prove that if $P(A|B) = P(A)$, then $P(B|A) = P(B)$.

3.52 The pie chart pictured in Fig. 3.14 was featured in *Time* magazine.
a) According to this chart, what is the probability that a randomly selected person who is unemployed will be both adult and white, $P(A \cap W)$? What is $P(A \cup W)$?

.36 + .25 + .08 + .095 + .08 + .095

36 + 25

.25
.36
.08
.095

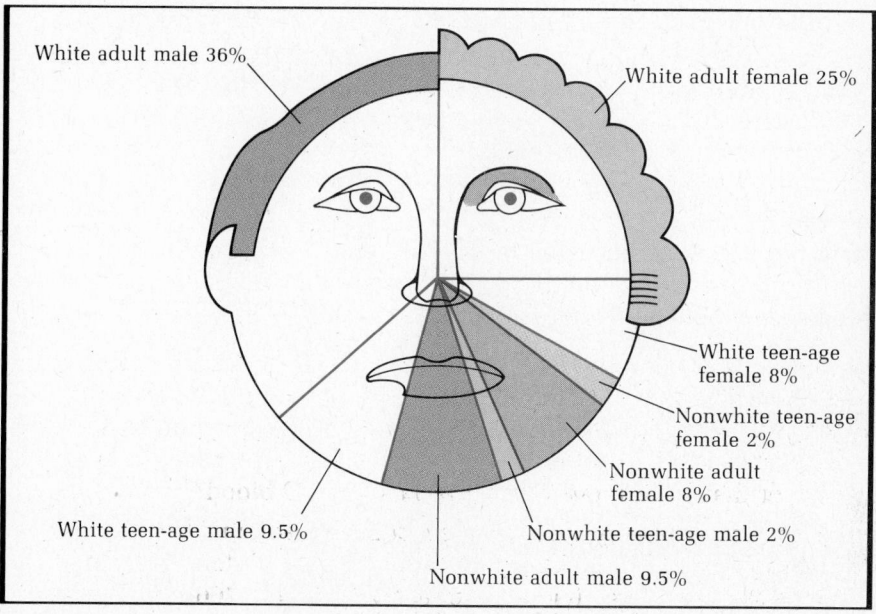

White adult male 36%

White adult female 25%

White teen-age female 8%

Nonwhite teen-age female 2%

Nonwhite adult female 8%

White teen-age male 9.5%

Nonwhite teen-age male 2%

Nonwhite adult male 9.5%

FIGURE 3.14 **Portrait of a recession: Percent share of the unemployed in July 1980. (Copyright 1980 Time Inc. All rights reserved. Reprinted by permission from TIME.)**

.785

.36 + .25 + .095 + .08

b) If the unemployed person is an adult, what is the probability that person is white? What is $P(W)$?

c) Is the event W independent of the event A? Explain, using your answer to part (b).

d) Find the value of $P(A)P(W)$. Use this value and your results from part (a) to determine whether A and W are independent.

e) Use Bayes' rule to determine the probability $P(A|W)$.

f) Place joint probabilities in the following table.

.095
.08
.36
.25

	Adult M	Adult F	Teen-age M	Teen-age F
White				
Nonwhite				

3.53 Consider the information in **Data Set 1** as a population. For a randomly selected city:

a) Find the probability of an income of at least $25,000 or a Moody Rating of Aa or higher (Aaa is the only rating higher than Aa).

.215

b) Find the probability of an income of at least $25,000 and a Moody Rating of at least Aa.

c) Find the probability of a low cyclical threat given that the Moody Rating is at least Aa. (Solve by counting cities.)

d) Solve part (c) using Bayes' rule.

e) Determine whether a city's Moody Rating is independent of that city's cyclical threat.

3.54 Use **Data Set 2** to determine the probability that a company randomly selected (from this population of 50) will be both above the median in sales and above the median in assets.

CASE PROBLEM

3.55 Culver, Inc. has advertised in numerous Sunday papers that they will sell one million new push-button telephones for $10 each plus mailing costs. Suppose Culver has had these phones made in Taiwan for a net cost of $9 each and they expect to sell all one million. They guarantee that each customer must be satisfied or money will be refunded. Culver estimates the probability to be 0.05 that a customer will receive a defective phone (they do not test the phones in advance). The probability that a defective phone will be returned is estimated to be 0.50. Culver also estimates the probability to be 0.01 that a nondefective phone will be returned. A returned defective phone costs Culver an extra $20 (the defective phone is thrown away, and Culver replaces it with a phone purchased locally). A returned phone that is not defective costs them an extra $3 (mailing and handling charges). What is the probability that a randomly selected phone is returned? If a phone is returned, what is the probability that it was defective? How much profit can Culver expect to make assuming that all one million phones are sold?

GLOSSARY

Experiment: Any operation capable of replication under essentially stable circumstances. A situation involving uncertainty.

Sample space: Outcomes of an experiment — may be discrete and finite, discrete and infinite, or continuous (infinite).

Mutually exclusive outcomes: Two or more possible results of an experiment any one of which, if it occurs, rules out the occurrence of any other.

Exhaustive outcomes: Outcomes that account for ("exhaust") the entire sample space.

Event: A subset of the outcomes of an experiment.

Probability: A number greater than or equal to 0 and less than or equal to 1 that indicates how likely an event is to occur.

Probability of an event (using equally likely outcomes): Ratio of the number of outcomes comprising the event to the total number of outcomes in the sample space.

Objective probability: A probability value determined by "objective" evidence, often relative frequencies.

Subjective probability: A probability value determined by an individual based on this person's knowledge, information, and experience.

Two basic properties: 1. $0 \leq P(E_i) \leq 1.0$ for every subset E_i of S.

2. $P(S) = \sum_i P(E_i) = 1.0$.

Basic counting rule: Total number of sample points

$$N = n_1(n_2)(n_3) \cdots (n_k).$$

n factorial: $n! = n(n - 1)(n - 2) \cdots (3)(2)(1)$.

Permutations of *n* objects taken *x* at a time:

$$_nP_x = \frac{n!}{(n - x)!}.$$

Combinations of *n* objects taken *x* at a time:

$$_nC_x = \frac{n!}{x! \, (n - x)!}$$

Probability of an event:

$P(\text{event}) = (\text{number of relevant sample points})P(\text{one relevant sample point})$

Probability of the complement: The probability that A will not take place in one replication of an experiment.

$$P(\overline{A}) = 1 - P(A).$$

Conditional probability of *A* given that *B* has taken (or will take) place:

$$P(A|B) = \frac{P(A \cap B)}{P(B)}.$$

Joint probability (intersection): Both A and B occur in one replication of an experiment: $P(A \cap B) = P(A|B)P(B) = P(B|A)P(A)$.

Additive probability (union): Either A or B or both occur in one replication of an experiment: $P(A \cup B) = P(A) + P(B) - P(A \cap B)$.

Independence: One event does not influence the probability of another.

If independent, $P(A|B) = P(A)$ and $P(A \cap B) = P(A)P(B)$.

Marginal probability: $P(A) = \sum\limits_i P(E_i)P(A|E_i)$

Bayes' rule:

$$P(E_i|A) = \frac{P(E_i)P(A|E_i)}{\sum\limits_j P(E_j)P(A|E_j)} = \frac{P(event_i)P(sample\ info\ |\ event_i)}{\sum\limits_j P(event_j)P(sample\ info\ |\ event_j)}$$

Discrete Random Variables and Expectations

FOUR

4.1 INTRODUCTION AND PROBABILITY MODELS

In Chapter 3 we studied rules for associating a probability value with a single event or with a subset of events in an experiment. Now we are ready to expand the scope of our analysis and consider *all* possible events in an experiment. A slightly more formal notation will also be introduced. We begin by examining one of the most important concepts in probability, the *random variable*.

Random Variable Given an experiment and a set of *mutually exclusive* and *exhaustive* outcomes, it is common to consider questions about the probability of the occurrence of any one or more of these outcomes by use of the **random variable** concept.

> A *random variable* is a well-defined rule for assigning a numerical value to all possible outcomes of an experiment.

This means that the symbols used in Chapter 3 to designate the outcomes of an experiment — "not defective" or "defective," etc. — are now going to be replaced with numbers. A random variable is a rule designating a number to be associated with each outcome of the experiment.

The outcomes of some experiments readily meet this definition of a random variable because they are already well-defined numbers. For example, the number of hours that a given light bulb might last is a well-defined number, the number of defectives that could occur in a lot of transistors is a well-defined number; and the potential yield on an investment of $1000 is a well-defined number. In other cases the outcomes of an experiment may be qualitative. For example, the outcome of a single ballot on a bond election is "For" or "Against," and the outcome of taking a course could be a grade of A, B, C, D, or F. In these instances the probability model must specify exactly what numerical value corresponds to each qualitative outcome. Registrars at many colleges do this for grades by letting A = 4, B = 3, C = 2, D = 1, and F = 0. In the case of the ballot, one common way to define a random variable is to let "For" = 1 and "Against" = 0. There may be less agreement in attempting to define a random variable for the experiment "drive from New York to Phoenix." In this case the sample space would need to be converted to some consistent measure, such as the *number of dollars* required for automobile repairs.

In working with *continuous* sample spaces, it is sometimes convenient to reduce the sample space to just a few discrete points. For example, the yield on a $1000 investment might be classified as falling into one of just a small number of intervals (such as 0 to 2.0, 2.1 to 4.0, etc.); and the dollar amount of repairs on a trip to Phoenix could be classified as either less than $50, between $50 and $100, or over $100. In all these examples we have a random variable only when numerical values are assigned to the outcomes of the experiment by a well-defined rule.

The rule is often expressed as a formula; it is the *general* statement defining the random variable relative to all conceivable outcomes of the experiment. When specific outcomes of the experiment are substituted into the formula, the result is a value of the random variable. The value is a *specific* result relating to a particular outcome.

In making the assignment of numerical values to the outcomes of an experiment, we will denote random variables by letters in *boldface* type, such as x, y, z, or sometimes by subscripted boldface letters such as x_1, x_2, x_3. *Specific* values of such random variables will be denoted by letters in lightface type, such as x, y, z, or perhaps x_1, x_2, x_3. Thus, the designation $\{x = x\}$ is read as "the random variable x takes on the value x." The following examples will illustrate this notation.

Example 4.1. *Experiment:* Survey a wage earner and ask whether the person bought a new car during the previous year.

Outcomes: Two discrete outcomes, bought a car or not.
Sample space: Discrete and finite.
Random variable: Define $\{x = 1\}$ if the person bought a car and $\{x = 0\}$ if not.

Although any values may be used to give numerical labels to the outcomes in an experiment such as this one, zero and one are especially convenient mathematically in many situations involving just two outcomes. Such a random variable may be called an **indicator variable,** since its value of 0 or 1 *indicates* whether or not a specific characteristic occurred. Since the variable x in this case gives a well-defined rule for assigning numerical values to the experiment, x is a random variable.

Example 4.2. *Experiment:* Taking an exam.

Outcomes: Grades A, B, C, D, F.
Sample space: Discrete and finite.
Random variable: Define $\{y = 4\}$ if the grade is A,
$\{y = 3\}$ if the grade is B,
$\{y = 2\}$ if the grade is C,
$\{y = 1\}$ if the grade is D, and
$\{y = 0\}$ if the grade is F.

The familiar four-point grade system is simply an assignment of numbers to a grade measure. Since the variable y gives a well-defined rule for assigning numbers to the outcomes of this experiment, y is a random variable.

Example 4.3. *Experiment:* Driving a car from New York to Phoenix.

Outcomes: Various car troubles that might be encountered on trip.
Sample space: Discrete (infinite but countable).
Random variable: Define z = nearest number of dollars paid for repairs, $\{z = 0, 1, 2, 3, \ldots\}$.

The random variable z in this case is discrete, and it is also infinite, since there is no limit on the amount of repairs. Realistically, however, there is some upper bound to the value of z, perhaps equal to the cost of the car if it is a total loss due to an accident. Also, this probability model assumes no negative values for z, since we doubt that anyone can find a "Tom Sawyer" mechanic willing to pay for the chance to do the needed repairs.

Example 4.4. *Experiment:* Investing \$1000 in a common stock.

Outcomes: Values of yield or rate of return.
Sample space: Continuous (always infinite).
Random variable: Define x = value of yield, $\{-\infty < x < +\infty\}$.

A *continuous random variable* is obtained from a continuous sample space whenever a single value of x is assigned to each outcome in the sample space. Thus, since a yield can be *any* positive number (or a negative number), x must be continuous.

Example 4.5. *Experiment:* Investing \$1000 in a common stock.
In this example we simplify Experiment 4 somewhat by grouping the various yields into different classes. For example, we might let one class represent all yields between 0 and 2%, another represent 2.1–4.0%, etc. This simplification results in the following probability model:

Outcomes: Class intervals of yields.
Sample space: Discrete and infinite (there is no limit on the number of classes).
Random variable: Define x = the midpoint or some representative value (the class mark) of the yields in each class interval.

We should point out that the numerical value assigned to an outcome in an experiment need not be unique to that outcome. That is, several different outcomes may be assigned the same numerical value. This fact is easily seen in the experiment about driving to Phoenix, for in this case there are certainly many different outcomes (car troubles) that would lead to the same value of the random variable (that is, lead to the same dollar value of cost).

Probability Distributions Once an experiment and its outcomes have been clearly stated and the random variable of interest has been defined, then the probability of the occurrence of any value of the random variable can be specified. Let us present some new examples.

Example 4.6. Suppose 140 salespeople are assigned to a certain region and they are to be divided randomly into four sections of this region. The number of persons assigned to each section is determined by the population and area of the sections as follows:

Section	Assignments
1	25
2	45
3	40
4	30
Total	140

If you are one of the salespeople involved in this assignment, you could view this process as an experiment with *four outcomes*. The sample space is discrete and finite; a random variable x may be defined to have values equal to the section number, $x = \{1, 2, 3, \text{ or } 4\}$. The probability that you will be assigned to any one section can be determined and denoted by the symbol $P(x)$. For example, the probability of your being assigned to Section 1 is denoted $P(x = 1)$ or $P(1)$. The probability that you will be assigned to Section 1 is simply the proportion of assignments that are made to Section 1 relative to the total number of persons, which is

$$P(1) = \tfrac{25}{140} = 0.179.$$

This is the *least probable* outcome of the experiment. What value of x has the highest probability? That is, what section assignment is the most probable outcome? Clearly, you have the highest chance of being assigned to Section 2, since this section will have the most persons. We find

$$P(2) = \tfrac{45}{140} = 0.321.$$

Continuing in this manner, we can find the probability of each possible value for the random variable **x**. When this is done, we have obtained the **probability distribution** for **x**. Table 4.1 and Fig. 4.1 depict the probability distribution for the random variable in this assignment problem.

In this example, only four discrete values of **x** have a positive probability. All other values of **x** have a probability of occurring equal to zero, indicating that they are impossible. Also, the sum of the probabilities of all values of **x** is equal to 1.0, indicating that these four are the only possible outcomes; we know with certainty that one of them will occur in each assignment.

The construction of a probability distribution is not always as simple as in the previous example (where the random variable had a unique value for each section).

To illustrate a slightly more involved experiment in which the random variable is not as directly related to the outcomes, we present a somewhat simplified version of a two-car accident problem.

Example 4.7. Suppose a highway safety consultant studies the flow of cars on a particular stretch of roadway. For simplification we will consider only two-car accidents. Also, assume that each car may contain from one to six persons and that each of these cases is equally likely. For this situation we examine the total number of persons involved in a two-car accident.

Since the number of persons in each car may be 1, 2, 3, 4, 5, or 6 (six outcomes), there are $6 \times 6 = 36$ possible outcomes if we count the number of people in two cars. The sample space of 36 outcomes is discrete and finite as illustrated in Fig. 4.2. The random variable **x** is equal to the sum of the persons in two cars involved in an accident. That is, **x** can assume any integer value from 2 to 12, depending on the number of persons in each of the cars. Note that in this case the number of

TABLE 4.1 **Probability distribution for x in the section assignment example.**

Outcome	Value of **x**	$P(x)$
Section 1	1	$(25/140) = 0.179$
Section 2	2	$(45/140) = 0.321$
Section 3	3	$(40/140) = 0.286$
Section 4	4	$(30/140) = 0.214$
Sum		1.000

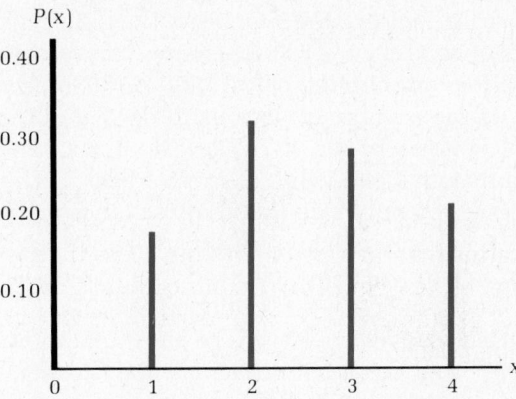

FIGURE 4.1 **Graph of the discrete probability distribution for *x* given in Table 4.1.**

different values for ***x*** is only 11, even though the number of possible outcomes in the experiment is 36. Some of the outcomes result in the same value for ***x.*** Since we have assumed that the number of persons per car, 1, 2, 3, 4, 5, or 6, is each equally likely, the probability of any value of ***x*** is given by the number of sample points for which the number of persons equals x, divided by the *total number* of sample points. For example, let us find P(***x*** = 9), which is usually shortened to P(9). We

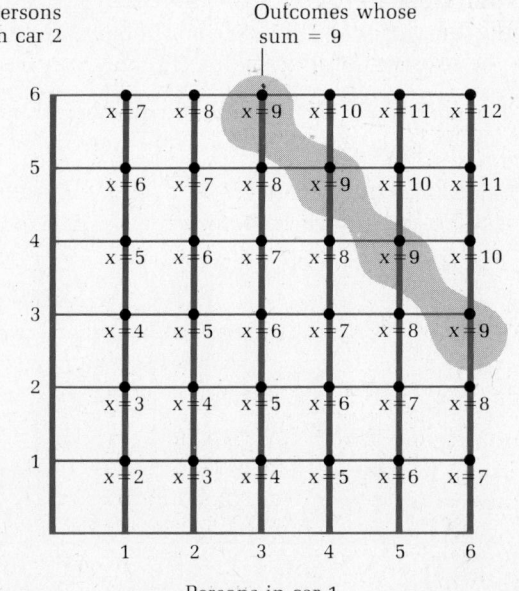

FIGURE 4.2 **Sample space for a two-car accident.**

can observe in Fig. 4.2 the number of sample points corresponding to this value of **x.** Out of all 36 outcomes, those satisfying the condition $\{x = 9\}$ are the four ordered pairs (3, 6), (4, 5), (5, 4), and (6, 3), where the first entry is the number of persons in car 1 and the second entry is the number of persons in car 2. Thus, $P(9) = \frac{4}{36}$. Similarly, we could find the probability that the value of **x** would be 3. The ordered pairs (1, 2) and (2, 1) are the only sample points satisfying $\{x = 3\}$, and so $P(3) = \frac{2}{36}$. Fig. 4.3 is a graph of the probability distribution of the random variable **x** = the number of persons involved in a two-car accident.

Once the probability distribution of a random variable is determined, it can be used to answer all types of questions about the outcomes of the experiment. From Fig. 4.3 it is obvious that the most common occurrence would be seven persons involved in a two-car accident (given our simplifying conditions). The probability that the number of persons exceeds eight could be found by summing together the probabilities for the values of **x** above eight. That is,

$$P(x > 8) = P(9) + P(10) + P(11) + P(12).$$

Once a probability distribution is obtained for a random variable, it can also be analyzed and used in decision-making or in presenting an argument. As with any distribution of values, two very important summary characteristics should be determined. These summary measures are

the population mean (to describe the central location) and
the population variance (to describe the spread of the distribution).

FIGURE 4.3 **Probability distribution of x, the number of persons involved in a two-car accident.**

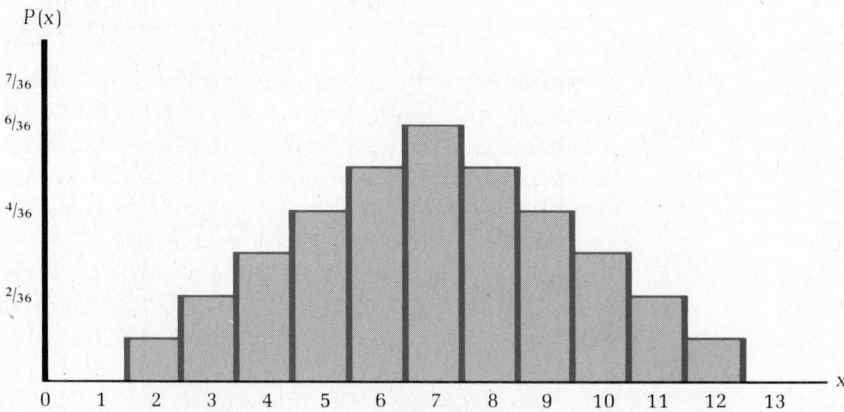

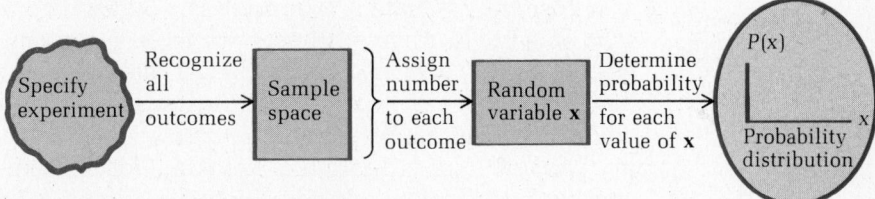

FIGURE 4.4 **The probability model.**

After we have formalized the concept of a probability distribution a little more, we will return to the task of determining methods for calculating such measures. For now, what matters is the understanding of the relation between a specific experiment and the induced probability distribution resulting from it. Fig. 4.4 illustrates this relationship and completes the process of describing the probability model. First, the experiment must be clearly stated so that all the conceivable outcomes can be understood. A random variable is then formulated to assign a value to each possible outcome of the experiment. By using probability rules the probability of each value of the random variable can be determined. The probability distribution $P(x)$ is a table, a formula, or a graph of the random variable x and the associated probabilities.

4.2 PROBABILITY MASS FUNCTIONS (p.m.f.)

> A probability distribution involving only discrete values of x is usually called a *probability mass function.*

A **probability mass function (p.m.f.)** is usually described in one of three ways: (1) by a graph, such as Fig. 4.3, (2) by a table of values, such as Table 4.1, or (3) by a formula.* The name "mass function" derives from the fact that all outcomes associated with the value of a discrete random variable can be represented on a graph by a vertical line whose height (or *mass*) indicates the probability of that value.

To illustrate the concept of describing a mass function by graph, table, and formula, consider the problem of determining how long a certain grocery item might sit on the shelf before being sold. For a package

---

* The reader is referred to the review of functions in Appendix A.

of cheese the estimate is that there is a 50:50 chance the cheese will be sold on any given day. Suppose we let x = the day on which the item is sold. Since there is a 50:50 chance that the item is sold on the first day, $P(x = 1) = \frac{1}{2}$. If $\{x = 2\}$, this means the item was not sold on day one and *is* sold on day two. Thus, $P(x = 2) = \frac{1}{2} \cdot \frac{1}{2} = \frac{1}{4}$. Similarly, $P(x = 3) = \frac{1}{2} \cdot \frac{1}{2} \cdot \frac{1}{2} = \frac{1}{8}$. A graph of the p.m.f. for this experiment, and a table of its values are shown in Fig. 4.5 and Table 4.2, respectively.

Using a graph and/or a table in this problem is inconvenient because of the fact that although x is discrete, an infinite number of x values is possible. That is, the cheese might not be sold for a very large number of days. In reality, after a certain number of days, it should be removed from the shelf and not sold. Thus, Fig. 4.5 and Table 4.2 are somewhat unsatisfactory because they present only a series of dots to indicate the values of x and their probability after five days. $\{x = 5\}$. A formula, on the other hand, can be used to *explicitly* specify how $P(x)$ and x are related for *all* values of x. In this case the relationship is easily found to be:

$$P(x) = \begin{cases} (\frac{1}{2})^x & \text{for } x = 1, 2, 3, \ldots, \infty. \\ 0 & \text{otherwise.} \end{cases}$$

By substituting $x = 1$, $x = 2$, $\ldots$, $x = 5$ into this formula the reader can verify the values in Table 4.2 and Fig. 4.5.

By now the reader should recognize the similarity between the concept of probabilities of events in Chapter 3 and the probabilities of certain values of a random variable. The same properties defined in Chapter 3 for probabilities of events can now be specified in terms of a random variable. The first property is that all probabilities associated with values of the random variable x must be nonnegative and cannot exceed 1.0.

Property 1: $0 \leq P(x = x) \leq 1$.

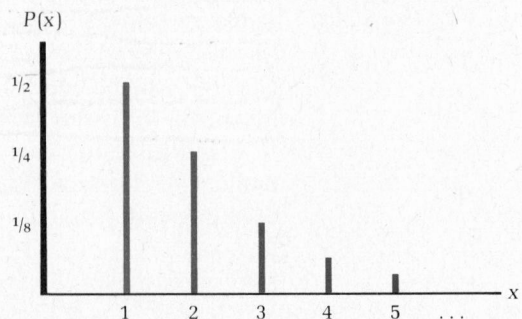

FIGURE 4.5 **Probability mass function for day of sale of cheese.**

TABLE 4.2 **The p.m.f for cheese sales**

x	P(x)
1	1/2
2	1/4
3	1/8
4	1/16
5	1/32
.	.
.	.
.	.

Second, we know that the sum of the probabilities of all values of the random variable must equal 1.0.

Property 2: $\sum_{\text{All } x} P(x) = 1.0$.

These properties repeat the fundamental concepts about probability. For any value of a random variable the probability measure is an index with a *minimum of zero* (representing impossibility) and a *maximum of one* (representing certainty). Also, since every outcome possible in an experiment must lead to some value of **x** according to a well-defined rule, Property 2 says that every time the experiment occurs, it is a certainty that some outcome and associated value of **x** occurs.

Cumulative Mass Function (c.m.f.)

The concept of *cumulative* relative frequency and the graphical representations thereof, which were introduced in Chapter 1, also have their counterparts in the study of probability. A **cumulative mass function (c.m.f.)** describes how probability accumulates in exactly the same fashion as column four in Table 1.5 describes how relative frequency accumulates — by *summing* all the relative frequency values. The value of the cumulative mass function at any given point x is usually denoted by the symbol $F(x)$, where $F(x)$ is the *sum of all values* of the probability mass function for all values of the random variable **x** that are *less than or equal* to x. That is,

Cumulative mass function at the point x_0:

$$F(x_0) = P(x \le x_0) = \sum_{x \le x_0} P(x).$$

(4.1)

TABLE 4.3 **The c.m.f for cheese sales**

x	F(x)
1	0.500
2	0.750
3	0.875
4	0.938
5	0.969
.	.
.	.
.	.

For our cheese example the value of $F(x)$ when $x = 1$ is $F(1) = 0.50$ because $P(x \leq 1) = 0.50$. Similarly, $F(2) = 0.75$ because $P(x \leq 2) = 0.50 + 0.25 = 0.75$. As with a probability mass function, a cumulative mass function must be defined for *all* values of the random variable. This is usually accomplished by means of either a graph, a table, or a formula. The table and graph for the cheese example are shown below in Table 4.3 and Fig. 4.6. A c.m.f. graph will always look like a series of steps (a "step-function") going up from zero to one as the value of *x* increases.

Figure 4.6 is perhaps a better way to illustrate the c.m.f. than Table 4.3, for the former emphasizes the fact that $F(x)$ is defined for *all* values of *x* from negative infinity to positive infinity. That is, the cumulative mass function $F(x)$ is defined for any value of *x* between positive and negative infinity, not just the integer values listed in Table 4.3. As should be clear from Fig. 4.6, $F(x) = 0$ for all values of x from minus infinity up to $x = 1$. At $x = 1$ the value of $F(x)$ becomes 0.50. Similarly, at $x = 2$ the value of the function becomes 0.75. Note that for *any* number between $x = 2$ and $x = 3$, $F(x) = 0.75$. Suppose that we arbitrarily pick a number, say $x = 2.45$. From Fig. 4.6, $F(2.45)$ can easily be seen to be

$$F(2.45) = 0.750.$$

The value $F(3) = 0.875$ is interpreted as meaning that there is a probability of 0.875 that the cheese will be sold in three days or less.

Example 4.8. Three college graduates (probably English and history majors) go into business in a little bakery shop near campus. From experience they know that students love to get a package of homemade brownies. They decide to specialize in homemade brownie squares, and they serve them in sizes from one-inch squares to a super-large foot

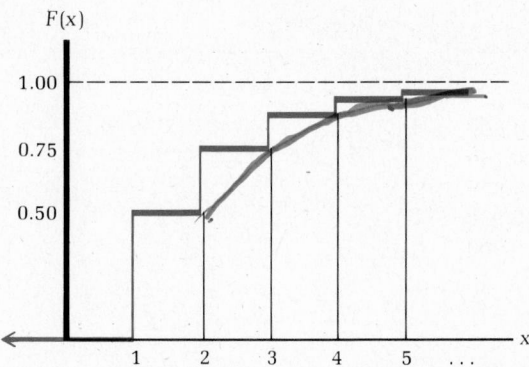

FIGURE 4.6 **The cumulative mass function for day of sale of cheese.**

square, which is their best bargain, since no special cutting and packaging is needed. Table 4.4 gives the sizes of brownie squares (x) in inches and the relative frequencies of their sales over the long run. The relative frequencies are interpreted as probabilities, P(x). We see that for this discrete set of values, $0 \leq P(x) \leq 1.0$ for each x, and

$$\sum_{\text{all } x} P(x) = 1.0,$$

so that the two properties of a probability mass function are satisfied.

The cumulative relative frequencies are given by the values in the row designated $F(x)$. In this situation the outcomes are discrete and finite. The graph of the cumulative probability distribution is shown in Fig. 4.7. Either function, the p.m.f. [P(x)] or the c.m.f. [F(x)], may be used to determine the probability of any event defined in terms of the values of x. Also, there is often more than one correct approach to logically find the probability using either the table or the graph.

For example, to find the probability of selling a brownie larger than two inches, $P(x > 2)$, we might use the p.m.f. directly:

$$P(x > 2) = P(4) + P(6) + P(12)$$
$$= 0.10 + 0.33 + 0.22 = 0.65.$$

TABLE 4.4 **The p.m.f. and c.m.f. for Example 4.8.**

x	1	2	4	6	12
P(x = x)	0.08	0.27	0.10	0.33	0.22
F(x) = P(x ≤ x)	0.08	0.35	0.45	0.78	1.00

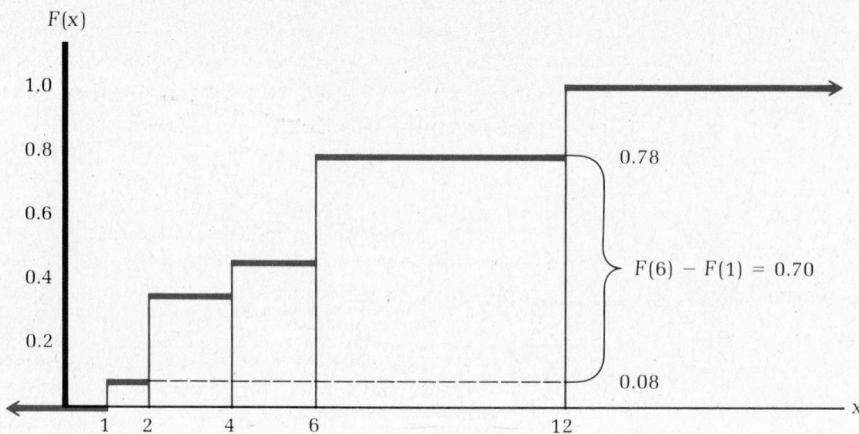

FIGURE 4.7 **A c.m.f. sketch based on Table 4.5.**

This probability can also be easily determined by using the complementary law of probability,

$$P(x > 2) = 1 - P(x \le 2).$$

With use of the p.m.f. the result is

$$P(x > 2) = 1 - P(1) - P(2)$$
$$= 1 - 0.08 - 0.27 = 0.65.$$

Since $P(x \le 2) = F(2)$, the solution could be quickly found by using the cumulative mass function:

$$P(x > 2) = 1 - F(2) = 1.0 - 0.35 = 0.65.$$

To illustrate a slightly more difficult case, let us find the probability of selling a brownie that is neither the smallest nor the largest size. This event *excludes* sizes $x = 1$ and $x = 12$; and so the event could be written $\{1 < x \le 6\}$. With use of the c.m.f., $F(x)$, as shown in Table 4.4,

$$P(x \le 6) = F(6) = 0.78.$$

But since $F(6)$ *includes* the probability $P(x \le 1) = F(1)$, we must *subtract* this value from $F(6)$. Hence,

$$P(1 < x \le 6) = F(6) - F(1) = 0.78 - 0.08 = 0.70.$$

To check this logic, the same probability may be found by summing the appropriate values of the p.m.f.,

$$P(1 < x \le 6) = P(2) + P(4) + P(6)$$
$$= 0.27 + 0.10 + 0.33 = 0.70.$$

As seen from the above examples, the cumulative mass function is useful in determining probability values for various types of events. Since this function will be used frequently in problems of statistical inference, the student should thoroughly understand this concept and all of the above examples before proceeding.

Study Question 4.1: Receipt of Registered Mail Items

A self-employed accountant receives materials, forms, and signed documents from his clients in the mail. Each day the accountant must sign for a number of "registered" mail items. In the following probability mass function, x represents the number of registered mail items received per day.

Number of items, x	0	1	2	3	4	5	6	7	8	9
P(x)	0.07	0.14	0.18	0.24	0.12	0.10	0.08	0.04	0.02	0.01

a) Sketch the p.m.f. and the c.m.f.
b) Use each sketch to find the probability that the number of registered mail items received on a given day would exceed two but not be more than seven.

Answer

a) Figure 4.8 on following page.
b) Using the p.m.f. sketch,

$$P(2 < x \le 7) = \sum_{x=3}^{7} P(x) = P(3) + P(4) + P(5) + P(6) + P(7)$$

$$= 0.24 + 0.12 + 0.10 + 0.08 + 0.04 = 0.58.$$

Or, using the c.m.f.,

$$P(2 < x \le 7) = F(7) - F(2) = 0.97 - 0.39 = 0.58.$$

Study Question 4.2: Teacher Salary Supplements

All the public school teachers in a certain rural school district receive an annual salary supplement from the local school funds depending on their experience, education, certification level, and teaching fields. There are six levels of supplements for all 970 teachers as shown below.

$ supplement, x	200	500	1000	1500	2000	3000
Number of teachers	109	204	324	186	102	45

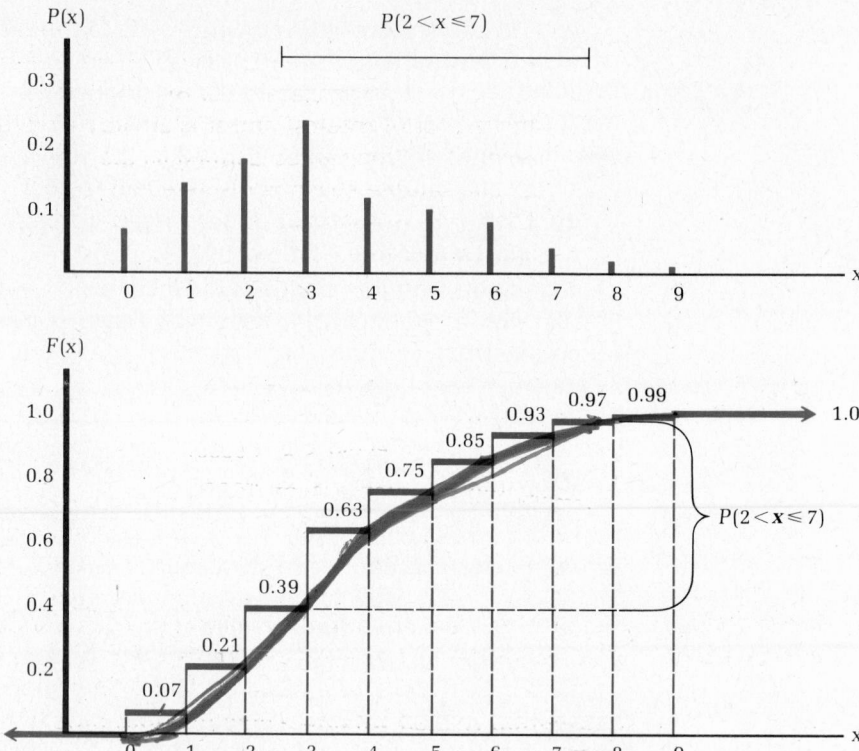

FIGURE 4.8 **The p.m.f. and c.m.f. for Study Question 4.1.**

a) If a teacher were selected at random, explain how **x** can be interpreted as a random variable.

b) Find the probability mass function and the cumulative mass function for **x**.

c) Use each of the functions in part (b) to determine the probability that a teacher selected at random would have a local salary supplement between $750 and $3000.

Answer

a) Selecting a teacher at random is a situation involving uncertainty because we do not know which one would be selected from among the total of 970. This experiment could conceivably be replicated again and again, each time selecting a teacher at random, then replacing that person into the total pool and selecting one again, then replacing and selecting, replacing and selecting, etc.

Thus, the long-run frequencies of the number of teachers with each supplement relative to the total number $N = 970$ can be interpreted as probabilities. Since the size of the supplement is the matter of interest and it is already a quantitative measure, its level of dollars can be defined as the values of a random variable **x**. The sample space is discrete and finite.

b) Each $P(x)$ is obtained as the long-run relative frequency, f_i/N, as shown in Table 4.5.

c) Using the p.m.f. (column 2) in Table 4.5,

$$P(750 < x < 3000) = P(1000) + P(1500) + P(2000)$$

$$= 0.334 + 0.192 + 0.105 = 0.631.$$

Using the c.m.f. (column 3),

$$P(750 < x < 3000) = F(2999) - F(750),$$

since the supplement of \$3000 is *not* to be included. Also, the probability accumulated at \$750 is the same as at \$500:

$$P(750 < x < 3000) = 0.953 - 0.322 = 0.631.$$

Some Further Considerations   We must next consider the parameters of a given probability distribution, such as those in the earlier examples for two-car accidents or salary supplements. Recall from Chapter 2 that the important features of *any* distribution (which we now know includes probability distributions) are the measures of *central location and dispersion*. Knowing the mean salary supplement per teacher, for example, would be of value in setting the school budget. A measure of the variability of supplements is also important when one is interested in deviations from the expected supplement. In the next section the measures of central location and dispersion for a probability distribution are presented. It is very important to be able to determine these measures for any probability distribution of interest.

TABLE 4.5 **The p.m.f. and c.m.f. for salary supplement (x)**

x	P(x)	F(x)
200	109/970 = 0.112	0.112
500	204/970 = 0.210	0.112 + 0.210 = 0.322
1000	0.334	0.322 + 0.334 = 0.656
1500	0.192	0.848
2000	0.105	0.953
3000	0.047	1.000

4.3 EXPECTED VALUES

Using the material presented thus far, we can now determine the probability of a single event of an experiment or describe the probability of the entire set of outcomes associated with a given random variable. This information, however, may not be concise enough for most decision-making contexts. Recall that we had the same problem in Chapter 2, when it was not sufficient merely to present all the data; in that situation, several characteristics of these data were also given (the most important of which were the *mean* and the *variance*). The same types of measures are also useful in describing probability distributions. However, in this case we must speak not of an *observed* mean or an *observed* variance, but of the mean or variance that would be *expected* to result (on the average) for the random variable under consideration. These summary measures are thus given the name *expectations* or *expected values*.

Expected Value

> The expected value of a discrete random variable **x** is found by multiplying each value of the random variable by its probability and then summing all these products.

The letter *E* usually denotes an expected value, and this symbol is followed by brackets enclosing the random variable of interest. Thus, the symbol *E*[**x**] represents the expected value of the random variable **x**. The expected value of **x** is the "balancing point" for the probability mass function. It is simply a *weighted average* of the population of x-values where the weights are probabilities. Recall Formula (2.2) for a weighted average, $\mu = [\Sigma_i x_i w_i]/\Sigma_i w_i$. For the mean or expected value of a probability distribution, the probability $P(x)$ is the weight used to describe how often each value of **x** should be included in the summation. In the denominator the sum of the weights is the sum of the probabilities, $\Sigma_{\text{all } x} P(x)$. However, from Property 2 on page 153, we know that the sum of the probabilities must always equal 1.0. Thus, the general formula for an **expected value** is:

expected value of **x**:

$$\mu = E[\textbf{x}] = \sum_{\text{all } x} xP(x) \tag{4.2}$$

Example 4.9. School enrollments by age group are reported for the United States in the *Current Population Reports* (series H442–448)

TABLE 4.6 **Calculating $E[x]$ for the age (x) of students**

Age Class	x	P(x)	xP(x)
5–6	5.5	0.119	0.655
7–13	10.0	0.492	4.920
14–17	15.5	0.251	3.891
18–19	18.5	0.056	1.036
20–24	22.0	0.057	1.254
25–34	29.5	0.025	0.738
	Sum	1.000	12.494

published by the Bureau of the Census. From these reports the probability $P(x)$ that a student selected from the population of all students with ages from 5 to 34 is given in column 3 in Table 4.6. We find the expected value of the age of a student by using Formula (4.2). Each age class is represented by a class mark (x). In the sum, each value of x is weighted by the probability of its occurrence, $P(x)$:

$$E[x] = 5.5(0.119) + 10(0.492) + \cdots + 29.5(0.025)$$
$$= 12.494 \text{ years.}$$

Example 4.10. A broker studies the possible return over the next year from a treasury bill fund. The interest rates fluctuate weekly, but predictions on the possible annual returns can be made. If the annual yield is 7%, then the value of an investment at the end of one year is 1.07 times its starting balance. Let the random variable x denote the investment return factor and let $P(x)$ be the (subjective) probabilities assigned by the broker (to a set of feasible factors) as shown in Table 4.7. The broker wishes to know what value to expect for x, on the average, in this experiment. In other words, if we repeated this experiment many times, what would be the average of all the x values? What we want to determine is the *expected value* of x, or $E[x]$.

One method to *approximate* the mean value in any experiment is to replicate the experiment many times, add up the observed numbers, and divide by the number of observations; but such a procedure is often

TABLE 4.7 **Investment return factors**

x = factor	1.06	1.07	1.08	1.09	1.10	1.11	1.12
P(x)	0.04	0.15	0.20	0.25	0.22	0.11	0.03

impractical, if not impossible, and gives only an approximation of the desired value.

Fortunately, there is no need to replicate an experiment if the probability mass function is known, for we then already have all the information needed. For instance, since $P(x = 1.08) = 0.20$, we would expect the factor of $x = 1.08$ to occur in 20% of all potential replications. The "weight" we assign to $x = 1.08$ is thus 0.20. Similarly, the weight for $x = 1.09$ is 0.25. By substituting the values from Table 4.7 into Formula (4.2), we can calculate the expected investment return factor next year as follows:

$$E[x] = \sum_{\text{all } x} xP(x)$$

$$= 1.06(0.04) + 1.07(0.15) + 1.08(0.20) + 1.09(0.25)$$
$$+ 1.10(0.22) + 1.11(0.11) + 1.12(0.03)$$
$$= 1.089.$$

The expected factor is 1.089, or the expected yield is 8.9%.

Study Question 4.3: Expected Value of Product Size
Find the expected size of a brownie square sold to a given customer if the probability distribution is as given in Table 4.4.

Answer. By Formula (4.2) the expected size is

$$E[x] = \sum_{\text{all } x} xP(x)$$

$$= 1(0.08) + 2(0.27) + 4(0.10) + 6(0.33) + 12(0.22)$$
$$= 5.64 \text{ inches.}$$

Expected Value of a Function of a Random Variable

The previous uses of Formula (4.2) were concerned with finding the expectation or expected value of a random variable. We can also find the expectation of any function of a random variable. For instance, instead of finding the mean of the random variable x, we might be interested in determining the expected value of x^2, or of log x, or of e^x. If x is a random variable, then these functions of x are also random variables, and their expected values can be determined. Suppose we let $g(x)$ represent the random variable whose value is $g(x)$ when the value of x is x. The expected value of $g(x)$ is defined as follows:

Expected value of $g(x)$:

$$E[g(x)] = \sum_{\text{All } x} g(x)P(x). \qquad \textbf{(4.3)}$$

The only difference between Formulas (4.3) and (4.2) is that in (4.3), $P(x)$ are the weights of values of $g(x)$ rather than values of x.

One of the most important expectations to calculate in statistics is the one in which $g(x) = x^2$; that is, $E[x^2]$. This expectation is often used to make the calculation of the variance of x much easier. We will use $E[x^2]$ for this task later. Now, we will simply use it to illustrate the application of Formula (4.3). Recalling Example 4.8 of the small student bakery making brownie squares, it would be necessary to find $E[x^2]$ if we wanted to determine the expected amount of square inches of brownies. This would help the managers decide on the quantity of raw ingredients needed for an "average" day. For this case, we let $g(x) = x^2$ and apply Formula (4.3) to the values below.

x^2	1^2	2^2	4^2	6^2	12^2
$P(x)$	0.08	0.27	0.10	0.33	0.22

$$E[x^2] = \sum_{\text{All } x} x^2 P(x)$$

$$= (1^2)(0.08) + (2^2)(0.27) + (4^2)(0.10) + (6^2)(0.33) + (12^2)(0.22)$$

$$= 46.32 \text{ (inches squared)}.$$

Note that this value of $E[x^2]$ differs from the square of $E[x]$, which is $\mu^2 = (5.64)^2 = 31.81$. In general, $E[x^2] \neq (E[x])^2$; *they have different meanings (the mean of the squares versus the square of the mean)*.

Study Question 4.4: Expected Return over Two Years
Suppose the broker in Example 4.10 had a two-year time horizon in mind. Then the broker would be interested in the compound return over two years. If the broker assumes that the same annual rates of return hold with the same probabilities, find the expected compound yield for two years.

Answer. For this problem we let x^2 represent the return for two years, where x is the one-year factor. For example, if the return factor each year is (1.08), then the return for two years would be $(1.08)^2$. Using Table 4.7 and Formula (4.3), we obtain

$$E[x^2] = \sum_{\text{all } x} x^2 P(x)$$

$$= (1.06)^2(0.04) + (1.07)^2(0.15) + (1.08)^2(0.20)$$
$$+ (1.09)^2(0.25) + (1.10)^2(0.22) + (1.11)^2(0.11)$$
$$+ (1.12)^2(0.03)$$

$$= 1.186.$$

The expected two-year factor is 1.186; the expected two-year return is 18.6%.

The Variance of a Random Variable

In the same way that the variance of a population is defined as the average squared deviation of the population values from their mean (μ), so the *variance of a random variable* can be defined in terms of the expected squared deviation of the values of **x** around their expected value $E[x]$. We denote this **variance of the random variable x** by the symbol $V[x]$, which is defined as follows:

$$V[x] = \sigma^2 = E[(x - \mu)^2].$$

Since the squared-deviation term within the brackets $[(x - \mu)^2]$ is a function of the random variable x, it can be written as $g(x) = (x - \mu)^2$. Since we know how to find $E[g(x)]$ from Formula (4.3), this means that we already know how to find $E[g(x)] = E[(x - \mu)^2]$. Making the substitution for $g(x) = [(x - \mu)^2]$ in Formula (4.3), we obtain:

Variance of **x**:
$$V[x] = \sigma^2 = E[(x - \mu)^2] = \sum_{\text{All } x} (x - \mu)^2 P(x). \qquad \textbf{(4.4)}$$

Again, the variance is simply the weighted average of the squared deviations, where the weights here are probabilities. Because the sum of the weights is $\Sigma P(x) = 1.0$, the denominator portion of the formula disappears (division by the value 1.0 is unnecessary). Formula (4.4) is the traditional way of defining the variance of a discrete random variable. It can also be used to compute a standard deviation, since the standard deviation, denoted by σ, is always the positive square root of the variance:

standard deviation of **x**: $\qquad \sigma = +\sqrt{V[x]}.$ $\qquad \textbf{(4.5)}$

While Formula (4.4) is theoretically correct, it has a major disadvantage for computational purposes. Specifically, if the mean μ is not an integer but has three or more decimals, then subtraction of μ from each value of **x** can be tedious. Also, squaring the deviations then gives numbers with at least six decimals. Finally, if the number of values taken on by **x** is quite large, all these subtractions, squares, and the ultimate summation require many steps that can lead to computational errors.

We encountered this same computational problem for finding a variance in Chapter 2. Fortunately, there is a solution using a computational formula for the variance of a probability distribution that is very similar to the computational formula for σ^2 in Chapter 2.

Computational formula for the variance of x:
$$V[x] = \sigma^2 = E[x^2] - (E[x])^2 \qquad (4.6)$$

This formula is equivalent to Formula (4.4).* Instead of finding the expected squared deviation, it requires that we first find the mean and the expected square of the values. Formula (4.6) might be remembered as *the mean of the squares minus the square of the mean.* This is a general formula that applies to any random variable, discrete or continuous. It will be used again many times throughout this book.

Example 4.11. We will use both Formula (4.4) and the computational Formula (4.6) to find the variance of the number of registered mail items received per day by an accountant as introduced in Study Question 4.1. (The p.m.f. is repeated below.)

Number of items, x	0	1	2	3	4	5	6	7	8	9
P(x)	0.07	0.14	0.18	0.24	0.12	0.10	0.08	0.04	0.02	0.01

A tabular format is convenient for demonstrating the necessary calculations. In Table 4.8, column (3) shows the product terms from columns (1) and (2). These are used in Formula (4.2) to find the expected number of registered mail items:

$$\mu = E[x] = \sum_{\text{all } x} xP(x) = 3.21 \text{ mail items.}$$

The variance using Formula (4.4) is

$$V[x] = E[x - \mu]^2 = \sum_{\text{all } x} (x - 3.21)^2 P(x).$$

* The equality between Formulas (4.4) and (4.6) is easily demonstrated as follows:

$$
\begin{aligned}
E[(x - \mu)^2] &= \Sigma(x - \mu)^2 P(x) \\
&= \Sigma(x^2 - 2x\mu + \mu^2)P(x) && \text{(by expansion)} \\
&= \Sigma x^2 P(x) - 2\mu\Sigma x P(x) + \mu^2 \Sigma P(x) && \text{(by summing each term)} \\
&= E[x^2] - 2\mu E[x] + \mu^2 && (\Sigma P(x) = 1 \text{ by definition)} \\
&= E[x^2] + (-2 + 1)(E[x])^2 && \text{(since } \mu = E(x)) \\
&= E[x^2] - (E[x])^2.
\end{aligned}
$$

TABLE 4.8 **Calculational format to find $E[x]$ and $V[x]$**

(1)	(2)	(3)	(4)	(5)	(6)	(7)
x	$P(x)$	$xP(x)$	$x - \mu$	$(x - \mu)^2 P(x)$	x^2	$x^2 P(x)$
0	0.07	0.00	-3.21	0.7213	0	0.00
1	0.14	0.14	-2.21	0.6838	1	0.14
2	0.18	0.36	-1.21	0.2635	4	0.72
3	0.24	0.72	-0.21	0.0106	9	2.16
4	0.12	0.48	0.79	0.0749	16	1.92
5	0.10	0.50	1.79	0.3204	25	2.50
6	0.08	0.48	2.79	0.6227	36	2.88
7	0.04	0.28	3.79	0.5746	49	1.96
8	0.02	0.16	4.79	0.4589	64	1.28
9	0.01	0.09	5.79	0.3352	81	0.81
Sum	1.00	3.21		4.0659		14.37

These terms involve some tedious calculations, as shown in columns (4) and (5) of Table 4.8. The result of summing column (5) gives

$$V[x] = 4.0659 \text{ (mail items)}^2.$$

Since the variance is in squared units, the more easily interpreted measure is the standard deviation,

$$\sigma = \sqrt{V[x]} = \sqrt{4.0659} = 2.016 \text{ mail items.}$$

For these data the variance is easier to compute by using Formula (4.6), since it avoids the squared deviations. The sum of the products in column (7) of Table 4.8 is used as follows:

$$V[x] = E[x^2] - \mu^2$$

$$= \left[\sum_{\text{all } x} x^2 P(x) \right] - (3.21)^2$$

$$= 14.3700 - 10.3041 = 4.0659 \text{ (items)}^2.$$

The standard deviation is

$$\sigma = \sqrt{V[x]} = \sqrt{4.0659} = 2.016 \text{ items.}$$

It is important to emphasize at this point that the reader should always check the reasonableness of calculations such as $E[x]$ and $V[x]$. For instance, if $E[x]$ is not near where you would expect the center of gravity to be, then you should double-check your calculations. A good way to check the reasonableness of $V[x]$ is to use the rule of thumb for dispersion presented in Chapter 2. This rule says that if the probability distribution is fairly symmetrical and unimodal, then 68% and 95% represent good approximations to the percent of the distribution falling in the intervals $\mu \pm 1\sigma$ and $\mu \pm 2\sigma$, respectively. For probability distributions, these rules mean that approximately 68% and 95% of the *probability* should be within $\mu \pm 1\sigma$ and $\mu \pm 2\sigma$, respectively.

Example 4.12. For the data in Table 4.8 and $E[x]$ and $V[x]$ shown in Example 4.11, the interval $\mu \pm 1\sigma$ has a lower limit of

$$(\mu - 1\sigma) = 3.210 - 2.016 = 1.194$$

and an upper limit of

$$(\mu + 1\sigma) = 3.210 + 2.016 = 5.226.$$

The interval $(1.194 < x < 5.226)$ includes values of x of 2, 3, 4, and 5 for which the sum of associated probabilities is

$$P(2) + P(3) + P(4) + P(5) = 0.18 + 0.24 + 0.12 + 0.10 = 0.64.$$

Thus, the interval $\mu \pm 1\sigma$ includes 64% of the probability distribution, which agrees with the 68% approximation using our rule of thumb.

The interval $(\mu \pm 2\sigma)$ has endpoints $[3.210 - 4.032, 3.210 + 4.032]$, which can be simplified to $[-0.822, 7.242]$. Values of x included in this interval are all those shown in Table 4.8 *except* the top two values, $x = 8$ and $x = 9$. Since $P(8) = 0.02$ and $P(9) = 0.01$, the rule of complements may be used to find

$$P(x \le 7) = 1.00 - 0.02 - 0.01 = 0.97.$$

Again, this result is reasonably close to the value suggested by our rule of thumb.

Define. *Random variable, probability mass function (p.m.f.), cumulative mass function (c.m.f.), expected value, probability model, variance.*

PROBLEMS

4.1 Sketch the probability and cumulative mass functions for the random variable x representing the size of salary supplement in Study Question 4.2. Explain their differences and the relationship between them.

4.2 Distinguish between the p.m.f. and the c.m.f. for a discrete random variable x.

4.3 Five different technologies are commonly used for preventing air pollution in coal-burning industries. The age of the technology is measured by the number of years since its introduction, denoted by **x**. The proportion of use of the technology is given by the fractions denoted by p.

x	7	17	16	8	2
p	1/3	1/4	1/6	1/12	1/6

a) Compute the expected value of the age of the technology currently in use.

b) Find $E[x^2]$ and use this result to find $V[x]$.

4.4 Use Problem 4.3 to answer the following.

a) Sketch the probability mass function for this population.

b) Sketch the cumulative mass function. What probability corresponds to $F(2.0)$, $F(9.5)$, and $F(17.0)$?

c) Does the p.m.f. graphed in part (a) meet the two conditions required of all probability functions?

4.5 Five service repair technicians for an appliance dealer handle from one to five repair jobs per hour. Suppose that the number of jobs done per hour is equally likely to be any of these values: 1, 2, 3, 4, or 5. Also, each technician does a different number of jobs. A supervisor selects at random two of the five hourly repair records of the technicians and finds the value of **x**, the *sum* of the number of repairs on the two hourly reports.

a) Sketch the probability distribution of this random variable.

b) Find the expected value of **x**.

c) Find the standard deviation of **x**.

d) Suppose the above experiment is done without the assumption that each technician does a different number of jobs. Sketch the new probability distribution.

4.6 A statistics professor announces that final grades will consist of 20% A's, 30% B's, 30% C's, 10% D's, and 10% F's.

a) If **x** is a random variable that is 4 for an A, 3 for a B, etc., what would be the expected grade point in the class?

b) Calculate $V[x]$ for this class.

c) Calculate $\mu \pm 1\sigma$ and $\mu \pm 2\sigma$ for this problem. Is the percent of values of **x** within these intervals close to the rule of thumb?

4.7 Reconsider the cheese sale example using the probability distribution in Table 4.2 and limiting x to $x \le 6$.

a) Find $E[x]$.

b) Find $V[x]$ first by using Formula (4.4) and then by using Formula (4.6).

4.8   Hospital records indicate that the need for treatment of broken legs occurs from one to seven times per day. Assume that each of these values is equally likely to occur on a given day.

   a) Suppose that you have to guess the number of such cases that will occur next Thursday. What is the probability that you will be correct?

   b) Construct the probability mass function for the number of broken-leg cases treated per day.

   c) What is the mean of the random variable?

   d) What is the variance? What percent of the days will have a number of such cases that lies within the intervals $\mu \pm 1\sigma$ and $\mu \pm 2\sigma$?

4.9   The dollar values of daily sales by a certain small store for the first ten days of the month are 175, 188, 196, 202, 194, 215, 188, 194, 196, 202.

   a) Find the mean of this population. [Each value has probability $\frac{1}{10}$.]

   b) Find σ^2 and σ.

   c) What percent of the observations falls within $\mu \pm 1\sigma$ and $\mu \pm 2\sigma$?

4.10 Weekly sales of dogwood trees at a nursery are $\{x = 1, 2, 3,$ or $4\}$ according to the following function:

$$P(x) = \begin{cases} \frac{1}{10}x & \text{for } x = 1, 2, 3, 4, \\ 0 & \text{otherwise.} \end{cases}$$

   a) Sketch this function and show that it satisfies the two properties necessary if $P(x)$ is to be a p.m.f.

   b) Find the expected number of sales.

   c) Find the variance of sales.

   d) Calculate the percent of x values falling within $\mu \pm 1\sigma$. Speculate on why this percent is not as close to 68% as in most problems thus far. Does $\mu \pm 2\sigma$ contain close to 95% of the values?

4.11 Suppose that the number of explosion levels built into skyrockets for a Fourth of July fireworks display is unknown for any particular item. However, the probability distribution is given by the following probability mass function:

$$P(x) = \begin{cases} \frac{1}{14}x^2 & \text{for } x = 1, 2, \text{ or } 3, \\ 0 & \text{otherwise.} \end{cases}$$

   a) Graph both the probability mass function and the cumulative mass function for this experiment.

   b) Show that this p.m.f. satisfies the two properties described in Section 4.2.

   c) Find the mean and the variance of this distribution.

4.12 A candy bar marketing promotion for a new 35¢ bar includes a coupon printed on the inside of the label, which gives the purchasers an immediate cash rebate. The coupons are distributed as follows:

40% have value of 5¢,   20% have value of 25¢,
30% have value of 10¢,   10% have value of $1.00.

What is the expected value of the net returns on sales of 500 bars if all the coupons are redeemed?

4.13 A manufacturer can ship either 4000 or 12,000 boxes of spark plugs to an automotive outlet in Germany. Suppose that we let x = sales of spark plugs, in units of 1000 boxes. The manufacturer estimates that the following p.m.f. accurately describes sales:

$$P(x) = \begin{cases} \dfrac{3}{x} & \text{for } x = 4 \text{ or } 12, \\ 0 & \text{otherwise} \end{cases}$$

a) Sketch this p.m.f., verifying that it meets the two necessary conditions for a mass function.
b) Find $E[x]$ and $V[x]$.

4.14 An oil company makes four brands of motor oil. Each is the same product marketed with a different label. For example, one is the label for the oil company brand and is sold at a higher price than another that uses the label of an auto parts distributor. The other two labels are marketed as Montgomery Ward oil and a generic No-Name. The prices are discounted lower and lower across these different labels so that the profits on these items are 50¢, 25¢, 10¢, and 5¢, respectively. The distribution of sales is 30% each for the brands of the oil company and auto parts distributor and 20% each for the Montgomery Ward and No-Name brands.
a) What is the probability that a randomly selected sale would earn exactly 10¢ profit?
b) What is the probability that two randomly selected sales will earn a total of 50¢ or more profit?
c) What is the average profit earned per quart of motor oil sales?

4.15 A publisher offers students a selling position to sell a series of "How To ... Books" to predetermined potential customers. The offer is unusual, owing to the sales commission rule. The payment is $2 if no sale is made to the first contact, and the work day is over. The payment is $4 if a sale is made with the first customer but not with the second. It is $8 if the first two contacts result in sales but the third does not, $16 if three consecutive sales are made but the fourth contact results in no sale, etc. That is, the commission rule is a starting payment of $2, which is increased by a factor of 2 for each consecutive contact until the string of sales is broken.

The special arrangement is offered because the publisher provides the names (sequentially) of potential customers who have already purchased the first book in the series and have returned a card indicating an interest in buying the rest of the books. On the basis of the records of other sales representatives, assume that the probability of a sales contract with any potential customer is $\frac{1}{2}$. The publishing company protects its own interests in enlisting only dedicated salespeople by charging an initial fee for the privilege of selling its books.

a) How much would you be willing to pay for the opportunity to sell? (If you said less than $2, you do not understand the problem.)

b) If a student can do this as a summer job with a fresh start every day, what is the probability on a given day that $65 or less would be earned (about the same wages as an alternate eight-hour per day job at $8 per hour).

c) If it is agreed that a run of consecutive sales can be carried over day after day until broken, what is the expected value for a one-time opportunity to participate in this scheme? Would anyone be willing to pay a participation fee equal to this expected value?

4.16 A large computer equipment firm with 13,000 employees started ten years ago and enlarged its operation for the first time seven years ago. It more than doubled its size two years ago and doubled that again last year. As a result, the distribution of the completed years of employment of workers with this company is:

Years of employment	10	7	2	1	0
Number of employees	1000	2000	3250	6500	250

a) Find the probability distribution for x = years of employment, and find the expected value of x.

b) Find the standard deviation of the years of employment x.

4.17 An entrepreneur is faced with two investment opportunities that each require an initial outlay of $10,000. The estimated return on investment x will be either $40,000, $20,000, or $0, with probabilities of 0.25, 0.50, and 0.25, respectively. For investment y the returns should be $30,000, $20,000, or $10,000, with probabilities of one third in each case.

a) Compute $E[x]$ and $E[y]$.

b) Check your calculations in (a) by first dividing all values by 10,000, determining $E[x]$ and $E[y]$, and then multiplying the results by 10,000.

c) Compute $V[x]$ and $V[y]$. Try to check your answer by again dividing by 10,000. What is the relationship between $V[x]$ and $V[x/10,000]$ and $V[x]/10,000$?

4.18 Use the p.m.f. on the age of students given in Table 4.6. Find the variance and the standard deviation of age (x).

USING THE COMPUTER

4.19 Answer parts (a) and (b).
a) Write a computer program to calculate the expected value and the standard deviation of a frequency distribution if the input data are class marks and probabilities.
b) Use your program to find the mean and standard deviation of income in 1980 for families in the United States given the following distribution (based on Series G1–15 from the U.S. Bureau of the Census). Note the problem of having an *open-ended* interval (over 15,000). Assume that the average income for all families in this group is $35,000.

Income ($)	P(x)
$0 < x \leq 3{,}000$	0.089
$3{,}000 < x \leq 5{,}000$	0.103
$5{,}000 < x \leq 7{,}000$	0.118
$7{,}000 < x \leq 10{,}000$	0.199
$10{,}000 < x \leq 12{,}000$	0.127
$12{,}000 < x \leq 15{,}000$	0.141
Over 15,000	0.223

CASE PROBLEM

4.20 The United States population according to the 1980 Census of Population was 226,545,805. The age distribution of the population is given below.

Age	P(x)	Age	P(x)
0–4	0.072	45–49	0.048
5–9	0.074	50–54	0.052
10–14	0.081	55–59	0.050
15–19	0.093	60–64	0.045
20–24	0.094	65–69	0.039
25–29	0.086	70–74	0.030
30–34	0.078	75–79	0.021
35–39	0.062	80–84	0.013
40–44	0.052	Over 84	0.010

a) If you randomly selected a person from this population, what is the probability that the age of the person would exceed 59?
b) What is the median age?
c) Find the proportion of the population with age within one standard deviation of the expected value. Assume that 90 is a representative value for the eldest age group.

4.4 EXPECTATION RULES

The concept of mathematical expectation, or expected value, will prove so useful in the coming chapters that the consideration of a few of the important properties of expectations will be beneficial at this time. In most cases these rules will be presented without formal proof, and it is not necessary that they be memorized. They will, however, be referred to in subsequent sections and be useful in solving problems.

Rule 1. $E[k] = k$ — The expected value of a constant is the constant itself.

Rule 2. $V[k] = 0$ — The variance of a constant is zero.

Rule 3. $E[kx] = kE[x]$ — The expected value of the product of a constant times a variable is the product of the constant times the expected value of the variable.

Rule 4. $V[kx] = k^2V[x]$ — The variance of the product of a constant times a variable is the product of the *square* of the constant times the variance of the variable.

Rule 5. $E[a \pm bx] = a \pm bE[x]$ — The expected value of the quantity $(a + bx)$ [or $(a - bx)$] is a plus (or minus) b times the expectation of **x**.

Rule 6. $V[a \pm bx] = b^2V[x]$ — The variance of the quantity $(a + bx)$ [or $(a - bx)$] equals b^2 times the variance of **x**.

Note in Rules 4 and 6 that the constant is squared on the right-hand side. This result occurs because variances involve squared deviations, and any constant times **x** will itself be squared in calculating the variance. Also, the addition of a constant to a random term does not affect the variance of that term.

Let us discuss these rules briefly. Rules 1 and 2 give the expected value and variance of a constant. A constant by definition always has the same value, say, $k = 3$. Each time k is observed, $k = 3$. The average of a set of the same values, $\{3, 3, 3, \ldots, 3\}$ is, of course, the constant value

3. Also, since each observation of k equals the average value of k, then any measure of squared deviations between the observations and the average will be zero. To state the obvious, the variance of a constant is zero because a constant does not vary.

Rules 3 and 4 are simple derivations based on the definitions of expected values. Consider the function $g[x] = kx$; then $E[kx] = \Sigma_{all\ x}$ $(kx)P(x)$. Since k is constant, it may be removed from the sum as a common factor. This gives $E[kx] = k\, \Sigma_{all\ x}\, xP(x)$. Since $\Sigma_{all\ x}\, xP(x) = E[x]$ by definition, we obtain $E[kx] = kE[x]$. Just as easily, we define the variance of kx in terms of the *mean of the squares minus the square of the mean* and write

$$V[kx] = E[(kx)^2] - (E[kx])^2.$$

Now we apply the rule shown above for expectation of a constant times a random variable, realizing that k^2 is a constant also, and obtain

$$V[kx] = E[k^2x^2] - (kE[x])^2$$
$$= k^2[E[x^2] - (E[x])^2] = k^2V[x],$$

by the definition of the variance $V[x]$. Rules 5 and 6 are combinations of the previous four rules. Let us practice using these rules.

Example 4.13. Suppose a time–work study shows that x, the quantity of chairs upholstered per day on a work line in a furniture factory, averages 24 with a variance of 9. If there are a total of five comparable work lines in the factory, then it is easy to find the summary measures for the total production T by applying Rules 3 and 4 with $k = 5$.

$$E[T] = E[5x] = 5E[x] = 5 \times 24 = 120 = \mu_T.$$
$$V[T] = V[5x] = 5^2V[x] = 25 \times 9 = 225 = \sigma_T^2.$$

The standard deviation for the total is $\sqrt{225} = 15 = \sigma_T$. Using our rule of thumb, we can guess that on approximately $\frac{2}{3}$ of all days the total number of chairs upholstered will be between $\mu_T - 1\sigma_T$ and $\mu_T + 1\sigma_T$; that is, between $120 - 15 = 105$ and $120 + 15 = 135$.

Example 4.14. Continuing Example 4.13, suppose management knows that the fixed cost of running the factory for a day is $2000 and the variable cost for a chair being upholstered on any work line is $140. Can we determine the important summary measures of the distribution of the daily cost when we are given the daily total number of chairs T? One way would be to use the original definitions and recompute the probability distribution for costs (C). Alternatively, we can apply Rules 5 and 6 with $a = 2000$ and $b = 140$.

$$\mu_C = E[C] = E[2000 + 140T] = 2000 + 140E[T]$$
$$= 2000 + 140(120) = \$18{,}800.$$
$$\sigma_C^2 = V[C] = V[2000 + 140T] = 0 + (140)^2 V[T]$$
$$= 19{,}600(225) = 4{,}410{,}000 \text{ (dollars)}^2.$$

To return to a measure of variability *not* in squared units, we find the standard deviation, $\sigma_C = \sqrt{V[C]} = \$2100$.

As mathematicians like to say after a long proof, Q.E.D., which stands for the Latin phrase, *quod erat demonstrandum*, which means "which was to be demonstrated" and indicates completion. In our case, Q.E.D. might mean "Quite Easily Done."

The reader can verify Rules 5 and 6 algebraically by completing Exercise 4.21 or arithmetically by working Exercise 4.31. It should be noted from the above examples that the standard deviations were obtained as multiples of the original ones:

$$\sigma_T = 5\sigma_x \quad \text{and} \quad \sigma_C = 140\sigma_T.$$

The standard deviation is not affected by adding or subtracting a constant. Such an operation has the effect only of moving the central location of a distribution but not changing its spread. Two widely used applications of Rules 1–6 are now presented for practice in understanding the rules.

Expectations of Linear Transformations

The changing from one variable into another according to a formula as we did in Examples 4.13 and 4.14 is called a *transformation*. If the formula used is $y = a + bx$ (where a and b are constants), it is called a *linear transformation*. A graph of the relation $y = a + bx$ is a straight line (i.e., linear, as opposed to quadratic, exponential, logarithmic, etc.). When $y = a + bx$, it is not necessary to derive a new probability distribution for y if the one for x is already known. Similarly, it is not necessary to recompute the mean and variance from basic definitions. Remember to use Rules 5 and 6 to find

$$E[y] = a + bE[x] \quad \text{and} \quad V[y] = b^2 V[x].$$

Expectations of a Standardized Variable

Another common transformation is one that changes the central location and the scale of a variable to "standardized units." The standardized variable is often used in scaling test scores and in making comparisons among measures with different units. In statistics, **standardization** is used extensively for simplifying distributions and variables so that solutions to problems are easier.

For a random variable x with expected value μ and standard deviation σ, we denote the standardized variable as z and define it as

$$\text{Standardized variable} = z = \frac{x - \mu}{\sigma}.$$

We can apply Rules 5 and 6 to find the expected value and variance of a standardized variable. Rewriting z as

$$z = \frac{1}{\sigma}x - \frac{1}{\sigma}\mu,$$

and remembering that μ and σ are constants (parameters of the distribution of x), we can identify the values of a and b in Rules 5 and 6 as $a = (-1/\sigma)\mu$ and $b = (1/\sigma)$. Thus,

$$E[z] = E\left[\frac{-1}{\sigma}\mu + \frac{1}{\sigma}x\right] = \frac{-1}{\sigma}\mu + \frac{1}{\sigma}E[X].$$

Since $E[x] = \mu$, $E[z] = (-\mu/\sigma) + (\mu/\sigma) = 0$. Thus, the mean of the standardized variable equals zero.

Now, let us consider the variance of a standardized variable.

$$V[z] = V\left[\frac{-1}{\sigma}\mu + \frac{1}{\sigma}x\right] = 0 + \frac{1}{\sigma^2}V[x].$$

Since $V[x] = \sigma^2$, then $V[z] = (\sigma^2/\sigma^2) = 1.0$. Thus, $\sigma_z = \sqrt{V[z]} = 1.0$ also.

The variance and the standard deviation of the standardized variable are both equal to one.

The importance of this result is that any variable may be *standardized* by subtracting its mean (to move the central location to zero) and then dividing by its standard deviation (to adjust the variability of the distribution so that it always has a standard deviation of 1).

Example 4.15. Recall the distribution used earlier (Example 4.11) of x, the number of registered mail items requiring a signature by the accountant. The p.m.f. for this distribution (plus its previously calculated mean and standard deviation) are shown in Fig. 4.9.

The first part of this standardization involves subtracting the mean μ = 3.21 from each value of x. This moves the entire distribution of x in Fig. 4.9 to one located at a mean of zero, since every value is reduced by

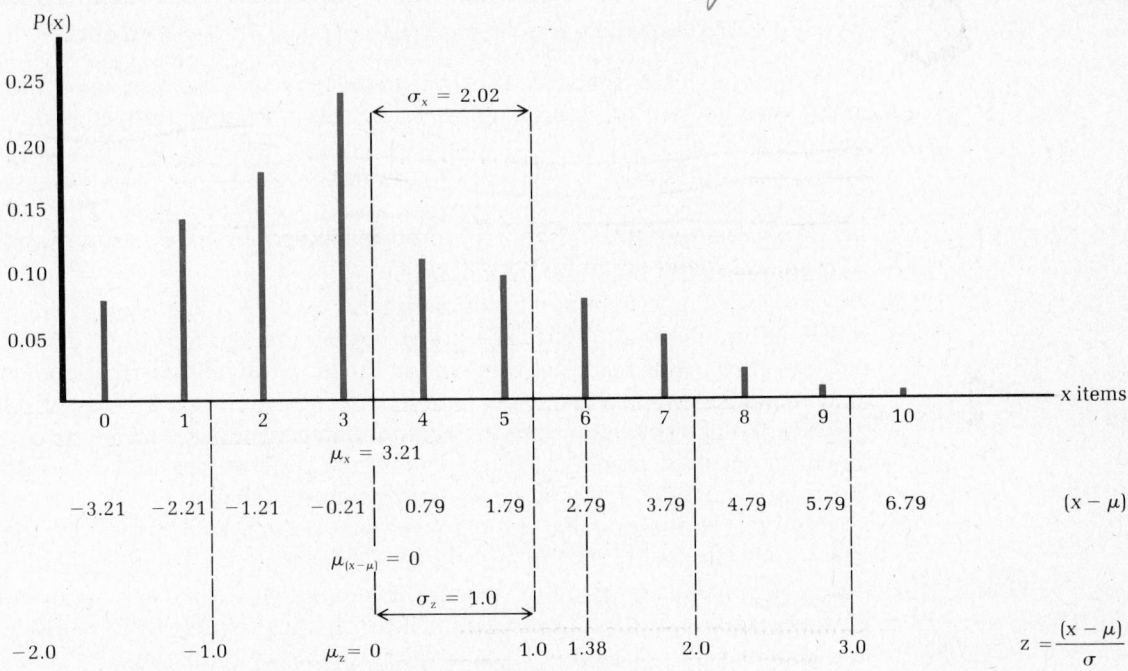

FIGURE 4.9 **Effect of a standardization.**

3.21. (See the scale for $(x - \mu)$ in Fig. 4.9.) A previous value of $x = 4$ is changed to $(4 - 3.21) = 0.79$; the value of $x = 2$ is changed to $(2 - 3.21) = -1.21$, and so on. The shape or spread of the distribution is unchanged, but the distribution now has a central location (a mean) of zero.

The final step in a standardization is the conversion of the scale of the variable from one that had a standard deviation of σ to a new scale that has a standard deviation of 1. This is accomplished by dividing all values of $(x - \mu)$ by σ. The value of $x = 6$ now becomes $(6 - 3.21)/2.016 = 1.384$. This means that the value $x = 6$ is 1.384 standard deviations above the mean of $\mu = 3.21$. Any other values for x can be transformed similarly. The new scale for z has a mean of 0 at the same point that the original scale for x had a mean of 3.21. A one-unit change on the new scale for z is equivalent to a change of 2.016 units for x. The new scale is in dimensionless standard deviation units, not in units of the number of registered mail items.

BIVARIATE PROBABILITY FUNCTIONS*

In many practical situations an experiment may involve outcomes that are related to two (or more) random variables. This section considers probability functions that involve more than one variable; such functions are called *multivariate* probability functions. In this book, only the case of *bivariate* (two variables) probability functions is presented. The distributions discussed so far in this text represent *univariate* probability functions, as only one random variable was involved.

A case of a univariate function might involve a manager who is interested in the productivity of a group of workers. Perhaps the workers' output varies per hour (or per week). If so, the long-run relative frequencies of these different productivities could be formulated as the probability distribution of a single random variable. The expected value and standard deviation of this random variable could be determined and used in discussions about pay packages, working conditions, etc.

Now, let us assume that the manager goes a step further to determine why productivity differs among workers. The manager might consider differences among workers in size, skill, training, experience, education, hours of sleep, nutrition, and so on. These characteristics of the workers are also random variables. Each or any combination of these random variables might be important in affecting the productivity of the workers. To find out which ones are and which ones are not important, joint analysis (of two or more random variables) is necessary. Given such an analysis, it might be possible to formulate policies for rest breaks, retraining seminars, exercise periods, food service, etc., to improve the expected productivity or to reduce its standard deviation.

Another illustration might involve the owner of a taxi company (assuming a nonregulated market) who is trying to decide whether to increase his rates. There is uncertainty in this situation as to what the owner's competitors intend to do and what the public will demand. The random variable x might be defined as the price changes of the competitors, and the random variable y might represent the demand levels for taxi services. If the owner can assign probabilities to the different potential price changes and demand levels, the owner will have a standard statistical decision problem involving **combined random variables.** The reader can probably begin to see some real potential for complexity in the application of combined random variables in real-life problems. In this beginning study of statistics we limit our discussion to simpler examples in order to present the basic concepts.

* Sections 4.5 and 4.6 may be omitted without loss of continuity.

| The Joint Probability Function | When a sample space involves two or more random variables, the function describing their combined probability is called a joint probability function. |

> The joint probability function for two discrete random variables **x** and **y** is denoted by the symbol $P(x, y)$, where $P(x, y) = P(x = x$ and $y = y)$. That is, $P(x, y)$ represents the probability that **x** assumes the value x and **y** assumes the value y.

As we will show, most of the probability rules discussed thus far have analogous rules for the case of two or more random variables. For example, the two properties of all probability functions presented in Section 4.2 have direct counterparts for joint probability functions, as shown below:

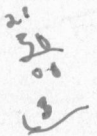

> Property 1. $0 \leq P(x, y) \leq 1$.
> Property 2. $\sum_{\text{All } y} \sum_{\text{All } x} P(x, y) = 1$.

Example 4.16. Consider the results of a study investigating the relationship between the number of jobs a college graduate holds in the first five years after graduation (**x**) and the number of promotions (**y**). Based on the experience of a large number of recent college graduates, the joint probability distribution is shown in Table 4.9. The values in Table 4.9 are the joint probabilities that **x**, the number of jobs, occurs in conjunction with **y**, the number of promotions. For example, $P(x = 2$ and $y = 3) = P(2, 3)$ is the probability that a randomly selected college graduate from this population would have had two jobs and been promoted

TABLE 4.9 **Probabilities for job-promotion study**

	No. of promotions (y)				Marginal total
	1	2	3	4	
No. of jobs (x) 1	0.10	0.15	0.12	0.06	0.43
2	0.05	0.07	0.10	0.05	0.27
3	0.04	0.02	0.14	0.10	0.30
Marginal total	0.19	0.24	0.36	0.21	$1.00 = \Sigma\Sigma\, P(x, y)$

three times in the first five years after graduation. From Table 4.9, $P(2, 3) = 0.10$. This is a relatively common occurrence based on this population, since it happens in one out of ten cases on the average.

Marginal Probability

Table 4.9 presents not only joint probabilities, but also the **marginal probabilities** for x and for y. The concept of marginal probability is the same as that used in Chapter 3. To find a marginal probability for a specific value of a combined random variable, it is necessary only to add together the probabilities of all the intersections involving that specific value. For example, the marginal probability for $x = 2$ jobs is the sum of all the joint probabilities involving $x = 2$. These are shown in Table 4.9 as the values in the second row. The sum across the columns is given in the right "margin" of the table, $P(x = 2) = 0.27$. Similarly, a marginal probability for any value of y may be found by summing all the joint probabilities involving that value of y. If you want to know the probability that a graduate will have had two promotions, then you sum all the values in the column for $y = 2$, obtaining $P(y = 2) = 0.24$. Thus, the values in the "margin" of a joint probability table give the values of the marginal probabilities for the corresponding values of x and y.*

Conditional Probability

A **conditional probability** is also defined for combined random variables in the same way that it was for events in Chapter 3. In words,

$$P(\text{event}|\text{condition}) = \frac{P(\text{intersection})}{P(\text{condition})}.$$

The relationship among the three types of probabilities — joint, marginal, and conditional — is the same as that first expressed in the multiplication law for intersections. It is always true that

Joint probability = (marginal probability)(conditional probability).

Thus, the definition for a conditional probability is

$$\text{Conditional probability} = \frac{\text{joint probability}}{\text{marginal probability}}.$$

---

* The formulas for computing such marginal probabilities for combined random variables x and y are

$$\text{Marginal probability of } x = \sum_{\text{all } y} P(x, y)$$

$$\text{Marginal probability of } y = \sum_{\text{all } x} P(x, y)$$

For example, to find the conditional probability of a value x given a conditional value y for the two random variables x and y, one computes

$$P(x|y) = \frac{P(x, y)}{P(y)}.$$

In terms of Table 4.9, such computations are quite obvious and result in the correct common-sense solution. If we wish to determine the probability that a graduate will have had three jobs given that the graduate is one of those having had two promotions, then we find

$$P(x = 3|y = 2) = \frac{P(3, 2)}{P(y = 2)} = \frac{0.02}{0.24} = \frac{1}{12}.$$

The denominator for this probability ratio does not pertain to all values that may occur in the original survey, but only that set of outcomes which satisfies the given condition (two promotions). One out of twelve such cases of two promotions, on the average, will also be a case in which the number of jobs is three.

It is also possible to find conditional probabilities for a particular number of promotions given the pool of cases for a certain number of jobs. To find the probability that the number of promotions would be four from among all those cases in which the number of jobs is one, we use

$$P(y = 4|x = 1) = \frac{P(1, 4)}{P(x = 1)} = \frac{0.06}{0.43} = 0.14.$$

Be sure always to use, in the denominator, the probability of the given condition.

Independence   Just as we were able (in Chapter 3) to determine whether two events are independent, we can, in the present context, determine whether two random variables are independent. If the knowledge of a certain condition on one variable does not affect the probability of the occurrence of values of the other random variable, then the two variables are independent. That is, x and y are independent if the conditional probability of x given y is the same as the marginal probability of x. If x and y are independent, it also follows that the conditional probability is the same as the marginal probability. Thus, for two independent random variables, their joint probability values must equal the product of the two corresponding marginal probability values.

> If x and y are independent, then $P(x, y) = P(x)P(y)$.

If the above relationship does *not* hold for *all* possible combinations of *x* and *y*, then these random variables are *dependent*. Only one violation of the condition is necessary to demonstrate dependence. For the data in Table 4.9 it is easily shown that *none* of the pairs of *x* and *y* satisfies the condition for independence. For example, the joint probability of one job and two promotions is $P(1, 2) = 0.15$, but this value is not equal to the product of the marginal probabilities,

$$P(x = 1)P(y = 2) = 0.43(0.24) = 0.1032.$$

Alternatively, we could examine any or all comparisons between marginal probabilities and their corresponding conditional probabilities. For one example, $P(x = 3) = 0.30$, but we have seen that $P(x = 3 | y = 2) = (\frac{1}{12})$. Clearly, the given condition on the number of promotions ($y = 2$) does affect the probability of the number of jobs held ($x = 3$). Thus, we can conclude that the number of jobs and number of promotions are *not* independent, but *dependent* random variables.

> **Study Question 4.5: Size and Depth of Buried Utility Cable**
> A contracting firm is bidding on a project to repair some old cable conduits for a city. The cable size *y* is either 4 cm or 9 cm in diameter and is buried at a depth *x* of either 1, 2, or 4 feet below ground. Based on city records the overall joint distribution of the size and depth of cable can be determined and is shown in Table 4.10.
> a) Find the marginal probabilities for size of cable y and depth of cable x.
> b) Find the conditional probability that a randomly selected section of cable needing repair will be buried two feet deep given that it is 9 cm cable.
> c) Determine whether the size and depth of cable are independent or dependent.

TABLE 4.10 **Joint probability distribution for size and depth of cable**

		Size (cm), y	
		4	9
	1	0.24	0.16
Depth (feet), x	2	0.12	0.08
	4	0.24	0.16

Answer

a) The marginal probability of y, P(y), equals $\sum\limits_{x} P(x, y)$ for a given y.

$$P(y = 4) = \sum\limits_{x} P(x, 4) = \begin{array}{r} 0.24 \\ +0.12 \\ +0.24 \\ \hline 0.60 \end{array}$$

and

$$P(y = 9) = \sum\limits_{x} P(x, 9) = \begin{array}{r} 0.16 \\ +0.08 \\ +0.16 \\ \hline 0.40. \end{array}$$

The marginal probability of **x**, P(x), equals $\sum\limits_{y} P(x, y)$ for a given x.

$$P(x = 1) = \sum\limits_{y} P(1, y) = 0.24 + 0.16 = 0.40.$$

$$P(x = 2) = \sum\limits_{y} P(2, y) = 0.12 + 0.08 = 0.20.$$

$$P(x = 4) = \sum\limits_{y} P(4, y) = 0.24 + 0.16 = 0.40.$$

b) The conditional probability, P(depth = 2|size = 9), is found by the definitional rule relating conditional, joint, and marginal probabilities:

$$P(x = 2 | y = 9) = \frac{P(2, 9)}{P(y = 9)} = \frac{0.08}{0.40} = \frac{1}{5}.$$

c) If **x** and **y** are independent, P(x, y) = P(x)P(y). Let's try some values of **x** and **y**.

$$P(1, 4) = 0.24; \quad P(x = 1)P(y = 4) = 0.40(0.60) = 0.24.$$
$$P(2, 4) = 0.12; \quad P(x = 2)P(y = 4) = 0.20(0.60) = 0.12.$$
$$P(4, 9) = 0.16; \quad P(x = 4)P(y = 9) = 0.40(0.40) = 0.16.$$

So far they all satisfy the condition. To prove independence, *all* values must be checked. Let us try one more combination using the alternate rule for independence that *the conditional probability must equal the marginal probability,* P(x|y) = P(x). From part (b) above, P(x = 2|y = 9) = $\frac{1}{5}$. From part (a) the marginal probability is the same, P(x = 2) = 0.20, and so independence is indicated. If we continue checking, we would find no cases of dependence. Therefore, the depth and size of cable are independent.

4.6 EXPECTATIONS FOR COMBINED RANDOM VARIABLES

As we have seen, there are three relevant probability distributions when we have situations involving more than one characteristic of interest. If we have a random variable x and another random variable y, the three relevant distributions are the *joint, marginal, and conditional* probability distributions. As with any distribution, it is important to find the summary measures of central location and variability for these distributions. The marginal and conditional distributions obtained for one of the combined random variables are simply distributions of one variable. The computation of expected values for marginal probability distributions is exactly the same as for a single random variable. For example, consider the marginal distribution of the depth of cable given in Study Question 4.5, where

x	1	2	4
$P(x)$	0.4	0.2	0.4

The formulas for finding $E[x]$ and $V[x]$ are the same as those presented in Section 4.3.

When dealing with the *joint* probability distribution of x and y, the rule for finding expectations is very similar to Formula (4.3). Suppose that we write any function of the two random variables x and y as $g(x, y)$. Then, the direct extension of Formula (4.3) gives

Expected value of $g(x, y)$:

$$E[g(x, y)] = \sum_{\text{All } y} \sum_{\text{All } x} g(x, y)P(x, y). \qquad (4.7)$$

For example, we may want to find the expected value of the product of x times y, in which case

$$g(x, y) = x \cdot y, \quad \text{and} \quad E[x \cdot y] = \sum_y \sum_x (x \cdot y)P(x, y).$$

Similarly, if $g(x, y) = x + y$, then

$$E[x + y] = \sum_y \sum_x (x + y)P(x, y).$$

We will return to investigate these two specific cases of Formula (4.7) after we consider one new concept relating to variability.

Covariance of x and y

A very important function for which we will want to apply Formula (4.7) is the function of the *cross-production of deviations*, $g(x, y) = (x - \mu_x)(y - \mu_y)$. The expected value of this function is called the **covariance of x and y** and is denoted by $C[x, y]$. The covariance measures how much the two random variables vary with each other (how they "co-vary").

Covariance of x and y:

$$C[x, y] = E[(x - \mu_x)(y - \mu_y)].$$

       (4.8)

If high values of x (relative to μ_x) tend to be associated with high values of y (relative to μ_y) and low x-values tend to be associated with low y-values, then $C[x, y]$ will be a large positive number.* If low values of one variable tend to be associated with high values of the other, and vice versa, this makes $C[x, y]$ a large negative number. If the two variables have no systematic relation to each other, but move higher or lower independently, then $C[x, y] = 0$. This is a two-variable counterpart to the concept of a variance for one variable. If each y in Formula (4.8) is replaced by an x, the result is the expectation of deviations of x squared, which is the variance, $E[(x - \mu_x)(x - \mu_x)] = E[(x - \mu_x)]^2 = V[x]$.

As in the case of computing a variance, there is a computational method for finding the covariance.

Computational formula for covariance of x and y:

$$C[x, y] = E[x \cdot y] - E[x]E[y].$$

       (4.9)

The reader may recognize this formula as just a variation of the "mean of squares minus the squared mean" relationship given in Formula (4.6). If x were identical to y, $C[x, y]$ would become $C[x, x]$, which is exactly the same as $V[x] = E[x^2] - (E[x])^2$.

In order to compute a covariance using Formula (4.9), we need to practice finding the expected value of the product, $E[x \cdot y]$. We apply Formula (4.7) using $g(x, y) = x \cdot y$. Since the same method also applies to another function, $g(x, y) = x + y$, we will give an example of both of these.

---

* This occurs because when $(x - \mu_x)$ is positive, $(y - \mu_y)$ is also positive, and when $(x - \mu_x)$ is negative, $(y - \mu_y)$ will also be negative; hence, the sign of $(x - \mu_x)(y - \mu_y)$ will be positive for such pairs of values of x and y. The sum of all these cross-products of deviations will then tend to be large and positive.

TABLE 4.11(a) Joint distribution for length and width of plywood

		Width (feet), y			
		2	4	6	P(x)
Length (feet), x	4	0.05	0.05	0.10	0.20
	8	0.10	0.50	0.20	0.80
P(y)		0.15	0.55	0.30	1.00 = ΣΣ P(x, y)

Example 4.17. As an illustration of Formula (4.7) when $g(x, y) =$ $x \cdot y$, consider a lumberyard that sells plywood paneling in two lengths, 4 ft and 8 ft, and in three different widths, 2 ft, 4 ft, and 6 ft. The owners of the lumberyard are interested in determining the average amount of paneling sold, in terms of area (square feet). That is, they want to determine $E[x \cdot y]$, where $x =$ length and $y =$ width. By the basic counting rule of Section 3.2, there are $n_1 = 2$ times $n_2 = 3$, or $n_1 \cdot n_2 = 6$, different arrangements of widths and lengths sold. The distributions $P(x)$, $P(y)$, and $P(x, y)$ for the sale of these six combinations, based on company records, are given in Table 4.11(a).

The determination of $E[x \cdot y]$ for these data is conveniently arranged in the Table 4.11(b).

The second column gives the probability for each product of x times y shown in the third column. The multiplication of these two columns

TABLE 4.11(b) Calculation of E[x] using Table 4.11(a)

(x, y)	P(x, y)	Area x · y	(x · y)P(x, y)
(4, 2)	0.05	8	0.40
(4, 4)	0.05	16	0.80
(4, 6)	0.10	24	2.40
(8, 2)	0.10	16	1.60
(8, 4)	0.50	32	16.00
(8, 6)	0.20	48	9.60
Sum = 1.00			E[x · y] = 30.80

yields the products $[(x \cdot y) \cdot P(x, y)]$ in the far right column, whose sum is the expected number of square feet of paneling sold,

$$E[\boldsymbol{x} \cdot \boldsymbol{y}] = \sum_{\text{all } x}\sum_{\text{all } y} (x \cdot y)P(x_j y)$$

$$E[\boldsymbol{x} \cdot \boldsymbol{y}] = 30.80.$$

Expectation of $x \cdot y$ when x and y are Independent

One special case of the expectation of $\boldsymbol{x} \cdot \boldsymbol{y}$ is worth noting — the case in which the variables $\boldsymbol{x}$ and $\boldsymbol{y}$ are independent.

Expectation of $\boldsymbol{x} \cdot \boldsymbol{y}$, assuming independence:

$$E[\boldsymbol{x} \cdot \boldsymbol{y}] = E[\boldsymbol{x}]E[\boldsymbol{y}]. \qquad \textbf{(4.10)}$$

Thus, if a check of the **independence** condition shows that $\boldsymbol{x}$ and $\boldsymbol{y}$ are independent, Formula (4.10) can be applied to quickly obtain $E[\boldsymbol{x} \cdot \boldsymbol{y}]$. This would not work in the above case for area of plywood since a check on any pair of values of $\boldsymbol{x}$ and $\boldsymbol{y}$ shows that they are *dependent*. Referring to Table 4.11(a), consider $x = 8$ and $y = 6$. We find $P(8, 6) = 0.20$, but $P(\boldsymbol{x} = 8)P(\boldsymbol{y} = 6) = (0.80)(0.30) = 0.24$. The length and width are dependent random variables since certain combinations are more commonly sold than others.

Example 4.18. We can illustrate Formula (4.10) for the case of the joint distribution of the size and depth of cable given in Table 4.10. Again, it is convenient to arrange the relevant computations in a tabular format as shown in Table 4.12.

TABLE 4.12 **Calculations for demonstrating Formula (4.10)**

(1)	(2)	(3)	(4)	(5)	(6)	(7)	(8)	(9)
x	$P(x)$	$xP(x)$	y	$P(y)$	$yP(y)$	(x, y)	$P(x, y)$	$(x \cdot y)P(x, y)$
1	0.40	0.40	4	0.60	2.40	(1, 4)	0.24	(4)(0.24) = 0.96
2	0.20	0.40	9	0.40	3.60	(1, 9)	0.16	(9)(0.16) = 1.44
4	0.40	1.60				(2, 4)	0.12	(8)(0.12) = 0.96
						(2, 9)	0.08	(18)(0.08) = 1.44
						(4, 4)	0.24	(16)(0.24) = 3.84
						(4, 9)	0.16	(36)(0.16) = 5.76
Sum	1.00	2.40		1.00	6.00		1.00	14.40

From the sum of columns (3) and (6) we see that $E[x] = \sum_x xP(X) = 2.40$ and $E[y] = \sum_y yP(y) = 6.0$. Thus,

$$E[x]E[y] = 2.40(6.0) = 14.40.$$

The sum of column (9) gives

$$E[x \cdot y] = \sum_x \sum_y (x \cdot y)P(x, y) = 14.40.$$

This result illustrates Formula (4.10) for a case in which x and y are independent. Substitution of the independence result of Formula (4.10) into the computational Formula (4.9) for covariance yields a result that has already been stated; namely, *when x and y are independent, the covariance is zero.* Substituting $E[x]E[y]$ for $E[x \cdot y]$, Formula (4.9) becomes

$$C[x, y] = E[x]E[y] - E[x]E[y] = 0.$$

It is important to note that even though independence implies a zero covariance, it is not necessarily true that a zero covariance implies independence. Independence must be determined by fully checking the necessary condition according to its definition, not by simply showing that the covariance is zero.

Expectations of
$ax + by$

Another special case of $E[g(x, y)]$ that has practical importance is when

$$g(x, y) = ax + by,$$

where a and b are constants. The important summary measures of this function are the **expectation of the weighted sum** $ax + bx$ and the **variance of the weighted sum** $ax + bx$.

Expected value of $(ax + by)$:

$$E[ax + by] = \sum_{\text{All } y} \sum_{\text{All } x} (ax + by)P(x, y)$$

$$= aE[x] + bE[y].$$

(4.11)

Variance of $(ax + by)$:

$$V[ax + by] = a^2V[x] + b^2V[y] + 2abC[x, y].$$

(4.12)

The derivation and proof of these formulas follow directly from the definitions of expected values already presented. These formulas are very useful for finding the summary measures for distributions of random variables that are linear combinations of previously defined random variables. By using Formulas (4.11) and (4.12), the mean and standard deviation of the new variables can be found without excessive calculation.

Example 4.19. Consider the plywood paneling example with probability distribution for x = width and y = length of plywood as given in Table 4.11(a). Table 4.13 helps us to determine the means of x and y.

The expected values are $E[x] = 7.20$ and $E[y] = 4.30$. In Exercise 4.37 the reader has been asked to practice Formula (4.6) for variances to find $V[x] = 2.56$ and $V[y] = 1.71$. Also, in Exercise 4.37 the covariance of x and y is found to be $C[x, y] = -0.16$ by using Formula (4.9).

Now, since these plywood panels are sold with a protective tape all around to protect the edges from moisture or chipping, we might be interested in the amount of protective taping used. Let us denote this by $T = 2x + 2y$, since the amount of tape depends on the perimeter of a given panel. What are the expected value and variance for the distribution of the random variable T?

It would be very tedious to recompute all possible values of the perimeter, weight these values by the appropriate probabilities, and find $E[T]$ and $V[T]$ by use of the calculational formulas. Instead, Formulas (4.11) and (4.12) can be used directly, where a and b each equal 2.

$$E[T] = E[2x + 2y] = 2E[x] + 2E[y]$$
$$= 2(7.20) + 2(4.30) = 23 \text{ feet.}$$

The average amount of tape used per panel is 23 feet.

$$V[T] = V[2x + 2y] = 2^2V[x] + 2^2V[y] + 2(2)(2)C[x, y]$$
$$= 4(2.56) + 4(1.71) + 8(-0.16)$$
$$= 15.80 \text{ (feet)}^2.$$

TABLE 4.13 **Calculation of expected values**

(1)	(2)	(3)	(4)	(5)	(6)
x	$P(x)$	$xP(x)$	y	$P(y)$	$yP(y)$
4	0.20	0.80	2	0.15	0.30
8	0.80	6.40	4	0.55	2.20
			6	0.30	1.80
Sum	1.00	7.20		1.00	4.30

The standard deviation for the amount of tape used per panel is

$$\sigma_T = \sqrt{V[T]} = 3.97 \text{ feet.}$$

Special Cases. There are two special cases in our use of Formulas (4.11) and (4.12) that are simplifications of the general rule. First, if the random variables x and y are independent, the covariance term, $C[x, y]$, equals zero. This simplifies Formula (4.12), since the final term drops out.

Another simplification occurs when both the constants, a and b, are equal to 1. This is the situation mentioned earlier when we were interested in $E[x + y]$, the sum of two random variables.

Example 4.20. Recall Example 4.7 on page 148 dealing with a two-car accident. The number of persons per car may be denoted as x for car 1 and y for car 2. The number of persons per car is independent, so the values of x do not affect the probability of a value for y. The sum of x and y equals the total number of persons involved in a two-car accident. Let us find the expected value and variance of this sum. By simplification of Formulas (4.11) and (4.12), using $a = 1$, $b = 1$, and $C[x, y] = 0$, we have

$$E[x + y] = E[x] + E[y];$$
$$V[x + y] = V[x] + V[y] + 0.$$

These measures can be calculated by using the formulas already presented (see Exercise 4.42).

A common problem in statistical applications involves finding the difference between two random variables. In this special case of Formulas (4.11) and (4.12), the values of the constants are $a = 1$ and $b = -1$. Again, if the variables x and y are independent, the expected value and the variance of the difference between x and y are given by

$$E[x - y] = E[x] + (-1)E[y]$$
$$= E[x] - E[y].$$
$$V[x - y] = V[x] + (-1)^2 V[y]$$
$$= V[x] + V[y].$$

Note that the variance of the difference between two random variables is the sum of their variances. The sum or difference of more than two independent random variables is merely an extension of the above examples for x and y. The formulas for this extension are presented below.

Expectations of sums or differences of a finite number of combined random variables, $x_1, x_2, \cdots, x_n$:

$$E[x_1 \pm x_2 \pm \cdots \pm x_n] = E[x_1] \pm E[x_2] \pm \cdots \pm E[x_n]. \qquad \textbf{(4.13)}$$

And if x and y are independent:

$$V[x_1 \pm x_2 \pm \cdots \pm x_n] = V[x_1] + V[x_2] + \cdots + V[x_n].$$

The formula for the mean of sums (or differences) of random variables holds whether or not the variables are independent. The formula for variance holds only when the variables are independent (so that all the covariance terms are zero.) Finally, note that the variance *of a sum OR of a difference* is always the *sum of the variances*. This follows because the value of $(+1)^2$ or of $(-1)^2$ is always $+1$.

Example 4.21. The number of orders written by a salesperson per week is described by a random variable x with expected value $\mu_x = 25$ and variance $V[x] = 9$. The number of these orders that are not shipped and not received within 10 days is described by a random variable y with expected value $\mu_y = 6$ and variance $V[y] = 4$. Let us find the expected value and variance of the number of "good" orders per week. Call this variable G, denoting a case in which an order is taken and then filled within 10 days (so that the customer is satisfied and likely to reorder in the future). First, we assume that the number of orders is independent of the number of orders unfilled within 10 days. This assumption means that the unfilled orders are not systematically related to the actions of this one salesperson. Then, we assign $a = 1$ and $b = -1$ to find the difference $G = x - y$, the number of successful contacts, and to find its expected value and variance according to Formulas (4.11) and (4.12):

$$E[G] = E[x] - E[y] = 25 - 6 = 19;$$
$$V[G] = V[x] + V[y] = 9 + 4 = 13.$$

Again, note that the mean of a difference is the *difference* of the means, but the variance of a difference is the *sum* of the variances.

A summary of the bivariate expectation formulas from this section is provided in Table 4.14.

TABLE 4.14 **Bivariate expectation formulas**

Function	Formulas	Special Case of Independence
Mean of $(x \cdot y)$	$E[x \cdot y] = \sum_x \sum_y (x \cdot y)P(x, y)$	$E[x] \cdot E[y]$
Covariance of $(x$ and $y)$	$C[x, y] = E[x \cdot y] - E[x]E[y]$	0
Mean of $(ax \pm by)$	$E[ax \pm by] = aE[x] \pm bE[y]$	No change
Variance of $(ax \pm by)$	$V[ax \pm by] = a^2V[x] + b^2V[y] \pm 2abC[x, y]$	$a^2V[x] + b^2V[y]$

4.7 INDICATOR VARIABLE AND COUNTING VARIABLE

A particularly interesting application of sums of random variables, which uses Formula (4.13), concerns the so-called *indicator variable* and the *counting variable*. These are used frequently in business and economics applications of combined random variables. Their probability distribution functions will be discussed in depth in the next chapter.

> An indicator variable is one used to denote numerically whether or not a certain characteristic or outcome occurred in one trial of an experiment.

For example, did a high school graduate go on to college or not? Is the head of a household male or not? Does the juror know the defendant or not? Did the Federal Reserve decide this month to expand the money supply or not? In such cases we define a random variable y for which $y = 1$ if the characteristic is observed and $y = 0$ if not. The sample space is finite and discrete as there are only two values for y. Suppose the probability that the characteristic occurs on any trial of the experiment is denoted by the lowercase Greek letter "pi," π. The probability that it does not occur is $(1 - \pi)$. The definitions for expected value and variance can be applied to this distribution as follows.

Indicator Variable	
y	$P(y)$
1	π
0	$1 - \pi$

$$\mu = E[y] = \sum_{\text{all } y} yP(y) = 1\pi + 0(1 - \pi) = \pi;$$

$$E[y^2] = \sum_{\text{all } y} y^2P(y) = 1^2\pi + 0^2(1 - \pi) = \pi;$$

$$V[y] = E[y^2] - \mu^2 = \pi - \pi^2;$$

$$V[y] = \pi(1 - \pi).$$

Now if more than one trial of the experiment occurs (as in a survey of high school graduates, wage-earners, etc), a **counting variable** can be defined to record the number of total times that the characteristic occurs in n trials.

The counting variable is given as $x = \sum_{i=1}^{n} y_i$, where y_i is the indicator variable for trial i.

Suppose that among n = 12 jurors, two have served on juries before. In order of seating in the jury, they are numbered 3 and 8. To describe the jurors with or without previous jury experience, the values of y_i are {0, 0, 1, 0, 0, 0, 0, 1, 0, 0, 0, 0}. The variable y_i equals 1 for the third and eighth jurors; otherwise, it is zero. The counting variable is $x = \sum_i y_i = 2$.

Example 4.22. Seven telecommunications ports are checked by a central monitor to see if they are currently in use. If so, $y_i = 1$; if not, $y_i = 0$. The results are coded numerically as $y_i = \{0, 1, 1, 0, 1, 1, 1\}$. Each of us can decode this information and know that the first and fourth ports are *not* in use, while all the others are. Also, the number of ports in use is $x = \sum_i y_i = 5$.

Since the value and distribution of the counting variables are often of critical importance in interpreting the results of a survey, or the status of a process, or the repeated trial of an experiment, we must be able to find the mean and variance of the counting variable **x**.

$$E[x] = E[\sum_i y_i] = E[y_1 + y_2 + y_3 + \cdots + y_n];$$

$$V[x] = V[\sum_i y_i] = V[y_1 + y_2 + y_3 + \cdots + y_n].$$

These are solvable as a direct application of Formula (4.13).

$$E[x] = E[\sum_i y_i] = \sum_i E[y_i]$$

$$= E[y_1] + E[y_2] + \cdots + E[y_n]$$

$$= \pi + \pi + \cdots + \pi = n\pi.$$

This result agrees with our common sense or intuition. Since the indicator variable has expected value of π on each trial, the counting variable for n trials has expected value, $E[x] = n\pi$.

Next, to find the variance of the counting variable, we impose the condition (which is often appropriate) that the repeated trials are independent. In this case the random variables y_i are independent and Formula (4.13) is used to find

$$V[x] = V[\sum_{i=1}^{n} y_i] = \sum_i V[y_i]$$

$$= V[y_1] + V[y_2] + \cdots + V[y_n]$$

$$= \pi(1 - \pi) + \pi(1 - \pi) + \cdots + \pi(1 - \pi)$$

$$= n\pi(1 - \pi).$$

Since each indicator variable has an identical distribution, each with the same variance [shown above to be $\pi(1 - \pi)$], it makes sense that for n trials the counting variable has variance $V[x] = n\pi(1 - \pi)$.

Define. *Expectation rules, linear transformations, joint probability function, bivariate expectations, covariance, independence, conditional probability function, marginal probability function, indicator variable, counting variable.*

PROBLEMS

4.21 Using the definitions for expected value and variance, show algebraically that
a) $E[a + bx] = a + bE[x]$.
b) $V[a + bx] = b^2 V[x]$.

4.22 Use the information about flight arrivals to answer the following.
a) The number of flight arrivals per hour at the Denver airport is described by a random variable x with mean 10 and variance 9. Find the expected value and variance of the random variable y describing the number of airline workers employed per hour in this airport where $y = 12 + 2x$.
b) Let the number of flight arrivals per hour at the Ogden, Utah, airport be a random variable x and the number at the Tampa airport be a

random variable y. Also, $E[x] = 5$, $V[x] = 9$, $E[y] = 10$, and $V[y] = 25$. The variables x and y are independent.

  i) Find $E[x \cdot y]$, $E[x + 2y]$, and $E[13 - 2x]$.
  ii) Find $V[x - y]$, $V[x + 2y]$, and $V[13 - 2x]$.
  iii) What is the value of $C[x, y]$?

4.23 The data in the following table represent the sales of cars by one of the major automobile companies for each of four recent years.

$P(x)$	x
0.250	2,483,000
0.250	2,519,000
0.250	2,511,000
0.250	2,495,000
1.000	$E[x] = ?$

a) Calculate the four values of $y = a + bx$, where $a = -2500$ and $b = 0.001$.

b) Calculate $E[x]$ by calculating $E[y] = E[a + bx]$. The value of $E[x]$ is then derived by solving Rule 5 of Section 4.4 for $E[x]$:

$$E[x] = \frac{E[a + bx] - a}{b}.$$

c) Calculate $V[x]$ by finding $V[a + bx]$ first and then by solving Rule 6 for $V[x]$:

$$V[x] = \frac{V[a + bx]}{b^2}.$$

4.24 Managers of a television manufacturing firm believe that more errors can be corrected in the products of the company if the circuits of the televisions are tested several times. A study of the values of the tests is made where y = number of tests and x = number of errors found. The following joint probability table reflects the results.

	Errors, x			
	1	2	3	Sum
1	0.10	0.05	0.05	0.20
Tests, y 2	0.10	0.20	0.10	0.40
3	0.05	0.15	0.20	0.40
Sum	0.25	0.40	0.35	

a) Find $P(x = 2)$, $P(y = 2)$, $P(x = 3 | y = 2)$.
b) Would you conclude that x and y are independent or dependent from the data? Explain.
c) Find $E[x]$ and $E[y]$.
d) Find $E[x \cdot y]$ and $E[x + y]$.
e) Find $C[x, y]$.
f) Find $E[5x - 3y]$.
g) Find $V[5x - 3y]$.

4.25 A recent study involving 46,000 women of child-bearing age in the United Kingdom suggested that women who both smoke and use birth control pills run a higher risk of death from diseases of the circulatory system. The following table indicates the annual mortality rate per 100,000 women from such diseases based on this study.

	Number of Deaths	
	Pill Users	Nonusers
Nonsmokers	13.5	3.0
Smokers	39.5	8.9

a) How many variables are there in this study? Name them.
b) What kinds of probabilities would you want to consider to determine whether smoking increases the risk of death for pill users?
c) What can one conclude from the data in this table about the relationship between using the pill, smoking, and the mortality rate? [Be careful!]
d) What additional data or analysis would you suggest to supplement this data?

Use the tabulated data to answer each of the following.

4.26 a) Assume that the values of x and y shown below occur with equal probability.

x	5	2	3	6
y	6	6	6	6

i) Find $E[x]$, $E[y]$, $V[x]$, and $V[y]$.
ii) Find $E[x + y]$ and $E[x - y]$.
iii) Are x and y independent or dependent? Explain.
iv) Find $V[x + y]$ and $C[x, y]$.

b)   Repeat the above question for the following data:

x	5	2	3	6
y	8	4	5	7

Explain (intuitively) why $C[x, y]$ is larger for part (b) than for part (a).

4.27   For the data of Table 4.12, show that
a) $E[x + y] = 8.40 = E[x] + E[y]$.
b) $V[x - y] \doteq 7.84 = V[x] + V[y]$.

4.28   In a firm it seems that a large number of high-tech positions are being filled by the younger employees. A study is done to determine the relation between the number of years of employment (x) and the number of high-tech-related job promotions (y) of those employees. The results are shown in this joint probability table.

		Employment, x		
		1	5	10
	1	1/20	2/20	3 20
Promotions, y	2	4/20	0	3/20
	3	2/20	4/20	1/20

a)   Find the marginal probability functions for x and y. What is the value of $P(y = 2)$?
b)   Find $E[x]$ and $E[y]$.
c)   Calculate $P(x = 10 | y = 1)$.
d)   Determine whether x and y are independent.

4.29   Refer to the information in Problem 4.28. Salaries, fringe benefits, and other employee matters (such as overtime opportunities) are related to both the years of employment and the number of high-tech-related job promotions of the workers. In order to establish some workable rules, the managers need to know the characteristics of the distributions of some functions of these random variables. Find
a) $E[x \cdot y]$.
b) $E[x + y]$ and $E[x - y]$.
c) $C[x, y]$.
d) $V[x + y]$ and $V[x - y]$.

EXERCISES

4.30 The table below shows the joint probability distribution for the length of want ads in a newspaper and the number of times the ad is repeated by the customer. Find
a) $V[x]$.
b) $V[y]$.
c) $C[x, y]$ using Formula (4.9).

		Length (inches), x		
		1	2	3
	0	0.10	0.05	0.05
Number of repeats, y	1	0.20	0.25	0.15
	2	0.10	0.10	0.0

4.31 A firm has a toll-free phone service for inquiries about the status of orders, shipments, etc. The total phone cost is estimated to be $4. However, if the result of the inquiry is better customer relations and good will, the benefit is estimated to be $2. Assume that half of the inquiries result in this benefit and the others are neutral (benefit of zero). Each inquiry is independent of any other. Let x denote the number of inquiries out of the next four calls that result in this positive benefit. Let the value to the firm for these next four calls be $y = 2x - 4$.
a) Is y a random variable? If so, describe it.
b) Find $E[x]$ and $V[x]$.
c) Using the probability distribution for y described in part (a), find $E[y]$ and $V[y]$.
d) Using the results in part (b) and the expectation rules, find $E[y]$ and $V[y]$. Compare your answers here to your results in part (c).

4.32 Prove that a random variable y and a constant k are always statistically independent.

4.33 Given: x is a discrete random variable with values chosen at random from the set {1, 2, 3, 4, 5, and 6}; y is a random variable with values of integers at least as large as x and not greater than 6.
a) Determine the joint probability function of x and y.
b) Find the conditional probabilities $g(y|x = 3)$.
c) Find the expected value of y.

4.34 Refer to the p.m.f. for sales of brownies (x) in Table 4.4. The cost of a sale is determined to be 5¢ per transaction plus 10¢ per inch of brownie size, that is $c = 5 + 10x$.

a) Find the p.m.f. for cost c. Then find $E[c]$ and $V[c]$ using Formulas (4.2) and (4.6).

b) Substitute the values of $E[x]$ and $V[x]$ into the expectation Rules 5 and 6 of Section 4.4 to find $E[5 + 10x]$ and $V[5 + 10x]$.

4.35 Prove that $V[ax + by] = a^2V[x] + b^2V[y] + 2abC[x, y]$.

4.36 Prove the following.
a) Expectation Rule 5 in Section 4.4 is a special case of Formula (4.11).
b) Rule 6 is a special case of Formula (4.12).

4.37 For $P(x, y)$ on the length and width of plywood panels in Table 4.11(a), find $V[x]$ and $V[y]$. Use Formula (4.9) to verify that $C[x, y] = -0.16$.

4.38 Prove that $C[x, y] = E[x, y] - E[x]E[y]$.

4.39 Refer to the ten observations in Problem 4.9. Subtract 175 from each observation. Find μ and σ^2 for the new set of values. Compare these to the values found in Problem 4.9, parts (a) and (b).

4.40 Refer to the ten observations in Problem 4.9. Subtract 195 from each observation and divide each of these differences by 10. Find μ and σ^2 for the transformed set of values. Explain your results by comparing them to the expected value and the variance of the standardized variable for these ten observations.

4.41 Consider the distribution for sales of brownie squares given in Table 4.4. Suppose the profit on these items is 3¢ per square inch of brownie. Find the expected profit per sale and the standard deviation of this profit.

4.42 Find the values for the mean and variance of the number of persons involved in two-car accidents as described in Example 4.20.

4.43 Referring to the two-car accident problem in Example 4.7, let us drop the simplifying assumption of equal probabilities for each value of x. A more realistic distribution of the number of persons per car can be determined from records of a Highway Safety Research Center.

x	1	2	3	4	5	6
P(x)	0.35	0.30	0.10	0.15	0.08	0.02

Using this p.m.f., find the mean and standard deviation of the number of persons involved in a two-car accident.

4.44 Refer to Study Question 4.2 concerning salary supplements for teachers. Suppose that the p.m.f. determined in part (b) of that question also applies to a group of teachers in a more urban school district. However, their salary supplements y are always $100 higher than double the salary supplements x. That is, $y = 100 + 2x$.

a) Find the mean and standard deviation of the salary supplement x for teachers in the rural district.
b) Find the mean and standard deviation of the salary supplement y for teachers in the urban district.

4.45 Using the data on jobs x and promotions y in Table 4.9, find
a) $V[x]$ and $V[y]$.
b) $C[x, y]$.
c) whether or not jobs and promotions are independent random variables.

4.46 With reference to Table 4.10 concerning the size x and depth y of cable, find $C[x, y]$.

4.47 Refer to Problem 4.13 for the p.m.f. of sales of boxes of spark plugs. If the net profit per box sold is $10, find the total expected profit and the variance of total expected profit.

CASE PROBLEM

4.48 Air-Overnight handles packet delivery for a large section of the country. We can simplify the description of their service by the joint probability distribution below. The distance that packets are shipped is categorized in three levels of x (miles). The weight of packets shipped is also categorized in three levels of y (pounds).

	Weight, y		
	2	5	10
500	0.02	0.18	0.17
Distance, x 1500	0.10	0.20	0.10
2500	0.03	0.12	0.08

a) Sketch the marginal p.m.f. for distance x. Find its expected value and variance.
b) Find $V[x]$, $V[y]$, and $C[x, y]$.
c) Determine whether distance and weight are independent or dependent.
d) Suppose the rate schedule for packets is 30¢ per pound plus 1¢ per mile. Find the expected value and standard deviation of the revenue per packet shipped.

GLOSSARY

Random variable: A well-defined rule for assigning a numerical value to all possible outcomes of an experiment.

Indicator variable: A variable that takes on the value one if a specific characteristic occurs and the value zero if it does not.

Probability distribution: A specification (usually by a graph, a table, or a function) of the probability associated with each value of a random variable.

Probability mass function (p.m.f.): A discrete probability distribution.

Cumulative mass function (c.m.f.): A summation of the values of a p.m.f., starting at the lower limit and going up to and including a specified value of the random variable. $F(x) = P(x \leq x)$.

Expected value of x or $E[x]$: The weighted mean or average of the random variable x. $E[x] = \sum_{\text{all } x} xP(x)$.

Variance of x or $V[x]$: The expectation of the squared deviations of a random variable about its mean μ.

$$V[x] = E[(x - \mu)^2] \text{ or } V[x] = E[x^2] - \mu^2.$$

Standardization of x: The transformation $z = (x - \mu)/\sigma$.

Combined random variables x and y: Variables having a joint probability distribution $P(x, y)$ for the probability of the intersection of specific values of x and y.

Marginal probability for one of the combined random variables, $P(x)$: The sum of all the joint probabilities for which the specific value x occurs.

Conditional probability for one of the combined random variables, $P(x|y)$: The ratio of the joint probability over the marginal probability of the given condition, $P(x|y) = \dfrac{P(x, y)}{P(y)}$.

Covariance of x and y: $C[x, y] = E[x \cdot y] - E[x]E[y]$.

Independence: $E[x \cdot y] = E[x] \cdot E[y]$; this implies a special case of $C[x, y] = 0$, $V[ax + by] = a^2V[x] + b^2V[y]$.

Expectation of a weighted sum of combined random variables:

$$E[ax + by] = aE[x] + bE[y].$$

Variance of a weighted sum of combined random variables: $V[ax + by] = a^2V[x] + b^2V[y] + 2abC[x, y]$.

Counting variable: The sum of an indicator variable over n occurrences.

Discrete Probability Distributions

FIVE

5.1 INTRODUCTION

While it is often useful to determine probabilities for a specific discrete random variable or combined random variables, there are many situations in statistical inference and decision-making that involve the same type of probability functions. In such instances, it is useful to apply the theory of probability functions from the previous chapters to obtain *general* results about the mean, the variance, independence, and other characteristics of the random variables. Then it is not necessary to derive such results over and over again in each special case using different numbers. It would be quite discouraging to know all these concepts of probability and still have to go through the process of formulating a new probability function and deriving its characteristics every time we are concerned with a slightly different experiment. Fortunately, we can avoid this difficulty by recognizing the similarities between certain types, or families, of apparently unique experiments and then merely matching a given case to the general formulas. Some of these families of discrete probability distributions are discussed in this chapter.

5.2 THE BINOMIAL DISTRIBUTION

Many experiments share the common trait that their outcomes can be classified into one of two events. For instance, a car salesperson talking to a customer might view the outcomes as either "sale" or "no sale." Similarly, a Sears bill could be classified as either "paid" or "due," a production process may turn out items that are either good or defective, and stock market indexes go either up or do not go up on a given day. In fact, it is often possible to describe the outcomes of many of life's ventures in this fashion merely by distinguishing only two events, which may for convenience be labeled "success" and "failure." (These terms do not imply good or bad.) Experiments involving repeated independent trials, each with just *two* possible outcomes, form the basis for the most widely used discrete probability distribution, the **binomial distribution**.

Bernoulli Trials
(2 outcomes)

Several generations of the Bernoulli family, Swiss mathematicians of the 1700's, usually receive credit as the originators of the early research on probability theory, especially on problems involving the binomial distribution. In fact, each replication of an experiment involving only two outcomes is called a *Bernoulli trial*. For the purposes of probability theory, interest centers not on a single Bernoulli trial, but rather on a series of independent, repeated Bernoulli trials. That is, we are interested in more than one trial. The fact that these trials must be "independent" means that the results of any one trial cannot influence the results of any other trial. In addition, when a Bernoulli trial is "repeated," it means that the conditions under which each trial is held should be an exact replication of the conditions underlying all other trials. This implies that the probability of the two possible outcomes cannot change from trial to trial.

Example 5.1. Suppose four shoppers in a supermarket are randomly selected and asked whether they prefer brand A or brand B of peanut butter. If the response of one shopper does not influence the response of any other, then the trials are independent. The trials are repeated if each shopper is asked the questions in exactly the same manner. When these conditions are met, the probability that the first shopper questioned will pick brand B will be the same as the probability that the second shopper will pick brand B or that a shopper questioned third or fourth picks it. This experiment involves four trials. Before we pick the four shoppers, we might assume, for example, that 0.70 is the probability of a success (let's call the selection of brand B a success). The assumption of 0.70 might be reasonable if a previous study had found that 70% of the shoppers preferred brand B. Before we take the sample, a typical question might be to ask what the probability is of exactly three successes in the four trials given that $\pi = 0.70$ (i.e., what the probability is that three of the four shoppers pick brand B and one picks brand A).

The binomial distribution is completely characterized by n (the number of trials) and π (the probability of a "success" on one trial). The values of n and π are referred to as the "parameters" of this distribution. The word *parameter* in this context has the same meaning as it did in Chapter 1 — it refers to a characteristic of a population.* Given specific values of n and π, one can calculate the probability of any specified number of successes.

> In a binomial distribution the probabilities of interest are those of receiving a certain number (x) of successes in n independent trials, each trial having the same probability (π) of success.

---

* Since it is common in discussing the binomial distribution to refer to the number of trials as the "sample size," we will use a lowercase n to denote this number. Technically, however, the number of trials is a population parameter and hence could be denoted by capital N. We use the Greek letter pi (π) to denote the probability of a success on a single trial, and use $p = x/n$ to denote the *sample* proportion of successes. This follows our convention of using Roman letters for sample measures and Greek letters for population measures. In some statistical texts and papers the symbol p is used to denote the probability of a success on a single trial.

The Binomial Formula

The probability rules of Chapter 3 can be used to calculate binomial probabilities. To determine the probability of exactly x successes in n repeated Bernoulli trials, each with a constant probability of success equal to π, it is necessary to find the probability of any one ordering of outcomes where there are x successes. [If there are x successes in n trials, there must, of course, be $(n - x)$ failures.] This probability is then multiplied by the number of possible occurrences. This is exactly the same process we followed in Chapter 2 using the following formula:

$$P(\text{event}) = (\text{No. of relevant sample points})P(\text{one such sample point}).$$

The number of relevant sample points is given by the combination formula from Chapter 3, for n objects taken x at a time.

$$\text{No. of relevant sample points:} \quad {}_nC_x = \frac{n!}{x!\,(n - x)!}.$$

The probability of one relevant sample point is:*

$$P(\text{one sample point}) = \pi^x(1 - \pi)^{n-x}$$

Putting these together gives the probability mass function (p.m.f.) for a random variable **x** from an experiment involving independent repeated Bernoulli trials, each having the same probability, π, of success. This p.m.f. is called the *binomial distribution*.

> Binomial formula:
>
> P(exactly x successes in n trials)
> $$= \frac{n!}{x!\,(n - x)!}\,\pi^x(1 - \pi)^{n-x} \quad \text{for} \quad \begin{array}{l} x = 0, 1, 2, \ldots, n \\ n = 1, 2, 3, \ldots \end{array} \qquad \textbf{(5.1)}$$

Example 5.2. We can illustrate the process described above via the stock owner–nonowner example from Chapter 3. In that example there were $n = 3$ trials (i.e., three interviews), and for each trial (interview)

---

* Assume that the x successes come first, followed by the $(n - x)$ failures, where π is the probability of success and $1 - \pi$ is the probability of failure.

$$\underbrace{\pi(\pi)(\pi)\cdots(\pi)}_{x \text{ successes}} \underbrace{(1 - \pi)(1 - \pi)(1 - \pi)\cdots(1 - \pi)}_{(n - x) \text{ failures}} = \pi^x(1 - \pi)^{n-x}.$$

Recall from Chapter 3 that the joint probability of a series of independent events does not depend on the *order* in which they are arranged. Hence, the value of

$$\pi^x(1 - \pi)^{n-x}$$

represents the probability of *any* possible arrangement of x successes and $(n - x)$ failures.

the probability of interviewing a stock owner was 0.50. Now suppose that we are interested in determining the probability that, in three trials (interviews), we find two stock owners and one nonowner — that is, we want to calculate $P(x = 2)$, where there are 2 stock owners and $(n - x) = (3 - 2) = 1$ nonowner. Substituting $n = 3$, $x = 2$ and $\pi = 0.50$ into Formula (5.1), we get

$$P(x = 2) = \frac{3!}{2!\,(3 - 2)!}\,(0.50)^2(0.50)^1 = \frac{6}{2(1)}\,(0.25)(0.50) = 0.375.$$

This is the same result as shown on page 93.

5.3 DETERMINING BINOMIAL PROBABILITIES

The binomial probability distribution is a *discrete distribution, since we can separately itemize the possible values of **x**.* Each probability value must be nonnegative, and the sum of these probabilities over all values of **x** must equal 1.0 — that is, the properties of a probability mass function are satisfied.

To illustrate the use of the binomial distribution, let's use the peanut butter taste test presented earlier, where $n = 4$ and $\pi = 0.70$. Recall in this case that a success is defined to be someone who picks brand B (maybe the company is sponsoring the study). Earlier we indicated that one might want to determine the probability that three shoppers will pick brand B and one will pick brand A. This is the probability of three successes and one failure in four trials and can be calculated from Formula (5.1) as follows:

$$P(x_{\text{binomial}} = 3) = \frac{4!}{3!\,(4 - 3)!}\,0.70^3(1 - 0.70)^1 = \frac{24}{6(1)}\,(0.1029) = 0.4116.$$

The probability that there will be four successes in four trials is calculated in the same manner.

$$P(x_{\text{binomial}} = 4) = \frac{4!}{4!\,(4 - 4)!}\,0.70^4(1 - 0.70)^0 = \frac{24}{24}\,(0.2401) = 0.2401.$$

Indeed, the probability of any number of successes from 0 to 4 can be determined in the same way. Table 5.1 organizes the necessary calculations for all these values, and Fig. 5.1 illustrates the resulting probability function. Notice in Column (2) of Table 5.1 that the number of combinations, $_nC_x$, has a symmetrical pattern — both the smallest value of **x** ($x = 0$) and the largest value of **x** ($x = n$) give $_nC_x = 1$. The largest values of $_nC_x$ are in the middle. This symmetry is a characteristic of $_nC_x$ no matter what values n and x assume. The values of the binomial distribution in Table 5.1 are plotted in Fig. 5.1.

TABLE 5.1 **Finding binomial probabilities for $n = 4$, $\pi = 0.70$**

(1)	(2)	(3)	(4) = (2) × (3)
x	$_nC_x$	$\pi^x(1 - \pi)^{n-x}$	$P(x) = {_nC_x}\pi^x(1 - \pi)^{n-x}$
0	$\dfrac{4!}{0!4!} = 1$	$(0.70)^0(0.30)^4 = 0.0081$	$P(0) = 0.0081$
1	$\dfrac{4!}{1!3!} = 4$	$(0.70)^1(0.30)^3 = 0.0189$	$P(1) = 0.0756$
2	$\dfrac{4!}{2!2!} = 6$	$(0.70)^2(0.30)^2 = 0.0441$	$P(2) = 0.2646$
3	$\dfrac{4!}{3!1!} = 4$	$(0.70)^3(0.30)^1 = 0.1029$	$P(3) = 0.4116$
4	$\dfrac{4!}{4!0!} = 1$	$(0.70)^4(0.30)^0 = 0.2401$	$P(4) = 0.2401$
			Sum = 1.0000

Using a Binomial Table

Although calculating the binomial probabilities in Table 5.1 was not very complex, if n becomes much larger, the difficulty of making such calculations could become tedious. In such cases we may wish to employ a binomial table.

Example 5.3. Assume that $n = 20$ items are sampled from a production process that produces either good or defective contact lenses. What is the probability of finding four defective lenses if $n = 20$ and $\pi = 0.10$? We label a defective lens as a "success" and use Formula (5.1):

FIGURE 5.1 **Binomial distribution for $n = 4$, $\pi = 0.70$.**

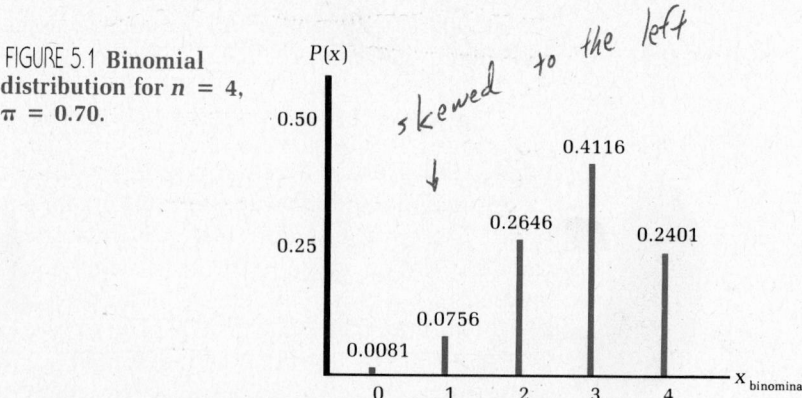

$$P(x_{\text{binomial}} = 4) = {}_nC_x\pi^x(1 - \pi)^{n-x} = {}_{20}C_4(0.10)^4(0.90)^{20-4}$$

$$= \frac{20!}{(4!)(20 - 4)} (0.10)(0.10)(0.10)(0.10)\overbrace{(0.90)(0.90) \cdots (0.90)}^{16 \text{ terms}}.$$

Only the foolish would desire to calculate such a number more than once, and only those with a computer may wish to do it once. Fortunately, computers can be used to perform such tasks and tabulate the results. The answer to this problem and many others similar to it are readily available in tables similar to Table I at the end of the book. This table gives the probability of x successes for a number of the more commonly used values of n and for values of π from 0.01 to 0.99. Figure 5.2 is an example of a binomial table — specifically, it is taken from Table I in Appendix C. This page gives the binomial probabilities for n = 20 and selected values of π.

To find the value of $P(x = 4)$ given that n = 20 and $\pi = 0.10$, look for the column whose heading is 10 (it is on the right of page 210). This column represents 0.10, as all decimals have been omitted. Now look along the *left-hand* margin until you find x = 4. At the row and column intersection of $\pi = 0.10$ and x = 4 is the probability $P(x = 4) = 0.0898$. This value is circled. If we had wanted the probability $P(x = 15)$ when n = 20 and $\pi = 0.44$, this number (also circled) could be found in the same manner and is seen in Fig. 5.2 to be $P(x = 15) = 0.0038$.

The entire probability distribution for values of *x* when n = 20 and $\pi = 0.10$ can be read from Table I. *When the probability values become smaller than 0.00005, the table ends. Thus, if an event cannot be found in the binomial table, such as 18 defectives in 20 items when $\pi = 0.10$, it should be apparent from the table that this value is very small and, for most practical purposes (certainly for any use in this text), can be considered zero, even though theoretically it is not an impossibility.* If all the probabilities for $\pi = 0.10$ and n = 20 (or any other combination of n and π) are summed, the total must equal 1.0000. Some columns in Table I do not sum to 1.0000 because of rounding errors.

An important part of Table I is its symmetry. Values of π up to 0.50 (found across the top of each set of numbers) always use the *x*-values in the *left-hand* margin. The values of π that are greater than 0.50 are found across the *bottom* of the table. When π is greater than 0.50, the appropriate *x*-values are read from the *right-hand* margin. In our example about defective lenses, we could have focused attention on good lenses rather than defective ones. That is, we might have posed our question to be "What is the probability of 16 good lenses if n = 20 and $\pi = 0.90$?" The answer to this question is the same probability we determined above, 0.0898. Refer again to Fig. 5.2. In this case the appropriate probability is

* decimal pts. aren't shown

FIGURE 5.2 **Binomial probabilities for $n = 20$ (from Table I, Appendix C).**

$n = 20$

x \ π	01	02	03	04	05	06	07	08	09	10	
0	.8179	6676	5438	4420	3585	2901	2342	1887	1516	.1216	20
1	1652	2725	3364	3683	3774	3703	3526	3282	3000	.2702	19
2	0159	0528	0988	1458	1887	2246	2521	2711	2828	.2852	18
3	0010	0065	0183	0364	0596	0860	1139	1414	1672	1901	17
4	0000	0006	0024	0065	0133	0233	0364	0523	0703	0898	16
5	0000	0000	0002	0009	0022	0048	0088	0145	0222	0319	15
6	0000	0000	0000	0001	0003	0008	0017	0032	0055	0089	14
7	0000	0000	0000	0000	0000	0001	0002	0005	0011	0020	13
8	0000	0000	0000	0000	0000	0000	0000	0001	0002	0004	12
9	0000	0000	0000	0000	0000	0000	0000	0000	0000	0001	11
	99	98	97	96	95	94	93	92	91	90	π x

x \ π	11	12	13	14	15	16	17	18	19	20	
0	0972	0776	0617	0490	0388	0306	0241	0189	0148	0115	20
1	2403	2115	1844	1595	1368	1165	0986	0829	0693	0576	19
2	2822	2740	2618	2466	2293	2109	1919	1730	1545	1369	18
3	2093	2242	2347	2409	2428	2410	2358	2278	2175	2054	17
4	1099	1299	1491	1666	1821	1951	2053	2125	2168	2182	16
5	0435	0567	0713	0868	1028	1189	1345	1493	1627	1746	15
6	0134	0193	0266	0353	0454	0566	0689	0819	0954	1091	14
7	0033	0053	0080	0115	0160	0216	0282	0360	0448	0545	13
8	0007	0012	0019	0030	0046	0067	0094	0128	0171	0222	12
9	0001	0002	0004	0007	0011	0017	0026	0038	0053	0074	11
10	0000	0000	0001	0001	0002	0004	0006	0009	0014	0020	10
11	0000	0000	0000	0000	0000	0001	0001	0002	0003	0005	9
12	0000	0000	0000	0000	0000	0000	0000	0000	0001	0001	8
	89	88	87	86	85	84	83	82	81	80	π x

x \ π	21	22	23	24	25	26	27	28	29	30	
0	0090	0069	0054	0041	0032	0024	0016	0014	0011	0008	20
1	0477	0392	0321	0261	0211	0170	0137	0109	0087	0068	19
2	1204	1050	0910	0783	0669	0569	0480	0403	0336	0278	18
3	1920	1777	1631	1484	1339	1199	1065	0940	0823	0716	17
4	2169	2131	2070	1991	1897	1790	1675	1553	1429	1304	16
5	1845	1923	1979	2012	2023	2013	1982	1933	1868	1789	15
6	1226	1356	1478	1589	1686	1768	1833	1879	1907	1916	14
7	0652	0765	0883	1003	1124	1242	1356	1462	1558	1643	13
8	0282	0351	0429	0515	0609	0709	0815	0924	1034	1144	12
9	0100	0132	0171	0217	0271	0332	0402	0479	0563	0654	11
10	0029	0041	0056	0075	0099	0128	0163	0205	0253	0308	10
11	0007	0010	0015	0022	0030	0041	0055	0072	0094	0120	9
12	0001	0002	0003	0005	0008	0011	0015	0021	0029	0039	8
13	0000	0000	0001	0001	0002	0002	0003	0005	0007	0010	7
14	0000	0000	0000	0000	0000	0000	0001	0001	0001	0002	6
	79	78	77	76	75	74	73	72	71	70	π x

x	π	31	32	33	34	35	36	37	38	39	40	
0		0006	0004	0003	0002	0002	0001	0001	0001	0001	0000	20
1		0054	0042	0033	0025	0020	0015	0011	0009	0007	0005	19
2		0229	0188	0153	0124	0100	0080	0064	0050	0040	0031	18
3		0619	0531	0453	0383	0323	0270	0224	0185	0152	0123	17
4		1181	1062	0947	0839	0738	0645	0559	0482	0412	0350	16
5		1698	1599	1493	1384	1272	1161	1051	0945	0843	0746	15
6		1907	1881	1839	1782	1712	1632	1543	1447	1347	1244	14
7		1714	1770	1811	1836	1844	1836	1812	1774	1722	1659	13
8		1251	1354	1450	1537	1614	1678	1730	1767	1790	1797	12
9		0750	0849	0952	1056	1158	1259	1354	1444	1526	1597	11
10		0370	0440	0516	0598	0686	0779	0875	0974	1073	1171	10
11		0151	0188	0231	0280	0336	0398	0467	0542	0624	0710	9
12		0051	0066	0085	0108	0136	0168	0206	0249	0299	0355	8
13		0014	0019	0026	0034	0045	0058	0074	0094	0118	0146	7
14		0003	0005	0006	0009	0012	0016	0022	0029	0038	0049	6
15		0001	0001	0001	0002	0003	0004	0005	0007	0010	0013	5
16		0000	0000	0000	0000	0000	0001	0001	0001	0002	0003	4
		69	68	67	66	65	64	63	62	61	60	π x

x	π	41	42	43	44	45	46	47	48	49	50	
1		0004	0003	0002	0001	0001	0001	0001	0000	0000	0000	19
2		0024	0018	0014	0011	0008	0006	0005	0003	0002	0002	18
3		0100	0080	0064	0051	0040	0031	0024	0019	0014	0011	17
4		0295	0247	0206	0170	0139	0113	0092	0074	0059	0046	16
5		0656	0573	0496	0427	0365	0309	0260	0217	0180	0148	15
6		1140	1037	0936	0839	0746	0658	0577	0501	0432	0370	14
7		1585	1502	1413	1318	1221	1122	1023	0925	0830	0739	13
8		1790	1768	1732	1683	1623	1553	1474	1388	1296	1201	12
9		1658	1707	1742	1763	1771	1763	1742	1708	1661	1602	11
10		1268	1359	1446	1524	1593	1652	1700	1734	1755	1762	10
11		0801	0895	0991	1089	1185	1280	1370	1455	1533	1602	9
12		0417	0486	0561	0642	0727	0818	0911	1007	1105	1201	8
13		0178	0217	0260	0310	0366	0429	0497	0572	0653	0739	7
14		0062	0078	0098	0122	0150	0183	0221	0264	0314	0370	6
15		0017	0023	0030	(0038)	0049	0062	0078	0098	0121	0148	5
16		0004	0005	0007	0009	0013	0017	0022	0028	0036	0046	4
17		0001	0001	0001	0002	0002	0003	0005	0006	0008	0011	3
18		0000	0000	0000	0000	0000	0000	0001	0001	0001	0002	2
		59	58	57	56	55	54	53	52	51	50	π x

found by looking for $\pi = 0.90$ across the bottom of each set of numbers, and then reading up the right-hand side of the table until reaching $x = 16$. Note that both methods end up at exactly the same (circled) point in Fig. 5.2. This is because the event "16 good lenses" is the same as the event "4 bad lenses." The reader should use Table I in Appendix C (for $n = 4$, $\pi = 0.70$) to verify the probabilities shown in Fig. 5.1 in this chapter.

Cumulative probabilities can also be obtained from Table I by summing the probabilities of interest. For example, the probability that two or fewer defective lenses will appear in a sample of n items is written as $P(x \leq 2) = F(2)$. If $n = 20$ and $\pi = 0.10$, this value is

$$F(2) = P(x \leq 2) = P(0) + P(1) + P(2)$$
$$= 0.1216 + 0.2702 + 0.2852$$
$$= 0.6770.$$

5.4 CHARACTERISTICS AND USE OF THE BINOMIAL DISTRIBUTION

The shape of the binomial distribution depends on both n and π. It will be useful to consider different combinations of n and π:

1. When n is small and π is less than 0.50.
2. When n is small and π is greater than 0.50.
3. When n is large and/or $\pi = 0.50$.

1. Small n and $\pi < 0.50$. Whenever $\pi < 0.50$, the binomial distribution is skewed to the right. The smaller the values of both n and π, the more pronounced will be the skewed appearance of the distribution. An illustration of a highly skewed (to the right) binomial distribution is given in Fig. 5.3, where $n = 4$ and $\pi = 0.10$.

2. Small n and $\pi > 0.50$. Whenever $\pi > 0.50$, the binomial distribution is skewed to the left. The smaller the value of n and the larger the value of π, the more pronounced will be the skewness. Figure 5.1 illustrates the skewness to the left when $n = 4$ and $\pi = 0.70$.

3. Large n and/or $\pi = 0.50$. When $\pi = 0.50$, the binomial distribution will always be symmetrical, no matter what size n assumes. The reader might try to sketch $n = 4$, $\pi = 0.50$ to verify that this distribution is, indeed, symmetrical. More important, however, is that when π is not

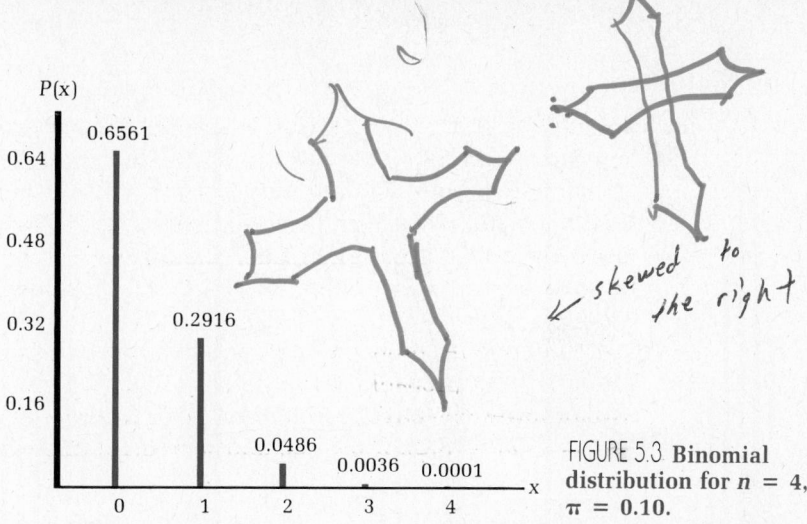

FIGURE 5.3 **Binomial distribution for** $n = 4$, $\pi = 0.10$.

equal to 0.50, the shape of the binomial becomes more and more symmetrical as the value of n increases. Figure 5.4 illustrates this fact. Note in parts (a) and (b) of this figure that even though n is as small as 20, the distributions for $\pi = 0.20$ and $\pi = 0.40$ are fairly symmetrical in appearance. For $n = 100$ and $\pi = 0.30$, as shown in part (c) of Fig. 5.4, the distribution is very symmetrical and bell-shaped. One rule of thumb is that the distribution will be fairly symmetrical if $n\pi(1 - \pi)$ is larger than 3.0. For Fig. 5.4(a), $n\pi(1 - \pi) = 20(0.20)(0.80) = 3.2$. For Fig. 5.4(b), $n\pi(1 - \pi) = 20(0.40)(0.60) = 4.8$, and for Fig. 5.4(c), $n\pi(1 - \pi) = 100(0.30)(0.70) = 21.0$. Thus, by the rule of thumb, all three of these distributions should be fairly symmetrical in appearance, especially part (c), and they are.

Mean of the Binomial Distribution

Since the binomial distribution is characterized by the value of the two parameters, n and π, one might anticipate that the summary measures of the mean and standard deviation also can be determined in terms of n and π. It should appear reasonable that the mean number of successes in any given experiment must equal the number of trials (n) times the probability of a success on each trial (π). If, for example, the probability that a process produces a defective item is $\pi = 0.10$, then the mean number of defectives in 20 trials is $20(0.10) = 2$; the mean number in 50 trials is $50(0.10) = 5$, and the mean number in 100 trials is $100(0.10) = 10$. Thus, the mean number of successes in n trials is $n\pi$:

$$\text{Binomial mean:} \quad E[x_{\text{binomial}}] = \mu = n\pi. \tag{5.2}$$

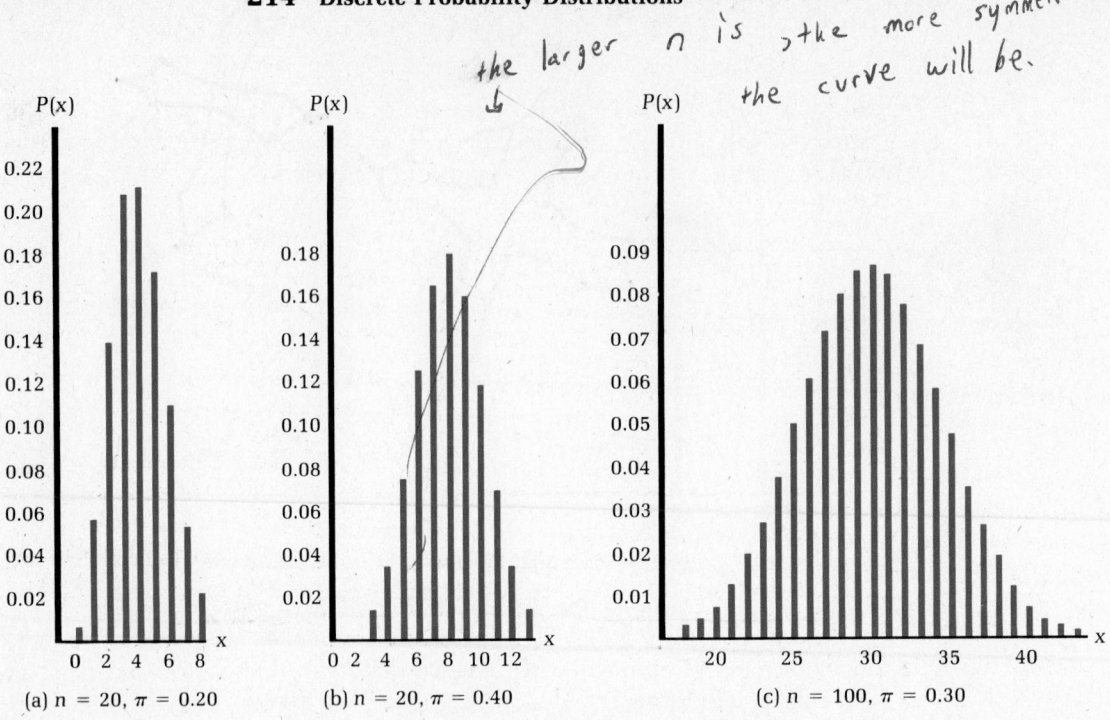

the larger n is, the more symmetric the curve will be.

(a) n = 20, π = 0.20

(b) n = 20, π = 0.40

(c) n = 100, π = 0.30

FIGURE 5.4 **The binomial distribution:** $P(x) = {}_nC_x\pi^x(1 - \pi)^{n-x}$.

Variance and Standard Deviation of the Binomial Distribution

The variance and standard deviation of the binomial distribution, the **binomial parameters,** are also quite easily derived and can be shown to be equal to:*

> Binomial variance: $V[x_{binomial}] = \sigma^2 = n\pi(1 - \pi)$;
>
> Binomial standard deviation: $\sigma = \sqrt{n\pi(1 - \pi)}$.   **(5.3)**

The variance in 20 Bernoulli trials of a process with probability $\pi = 0.10$ of producing defectives is thus

$$n\pi(1 - \pi) = 20(0.10)(0.90)$$
$$V(x) = 1.80;$$

the standard deviation is

$$\sqrt{n\pi(1 - \pi)} = \sqrt{1.80}$$
$$= 1.34.$$

---

* The explanation and derivation of these formulas is the same as for the counting variable in Section 4.7.

Note from the table below that the intervals ($\mu \pm 1\sigma$) and ($\mu \pm 2\sigma$) for this problem contain slightly more of the total probability (obtained from Table I) than the rule of thumb given in Chapter 1 (68% and 95%) would indicate.

Interval	Percent of Probability (from Table I)
$\mu \pm 1\sigma = 2.00 \pm 1.34 = 0.66$ to 3.34	$100 \sum_{x=1}^{3} P(x) = 75\%$
$\mu \pm 2\sigma = 2.00 \pm 2(1.34) = 0$ to 4.68	$100 \sum_{x=0}^{4} P(x) = 97\%$

[handwritten in margin: 68%, 95%]

The mean and standard deviation of the binomial distribution in Figs. 5.1 and 5.2 can also be found by using Formulas (5.2) and (5.3). For the former example, where $n = 4$ and $\pi = 0.5$, the mean is

$$n\pi = 4(0.5) = 2.0;$$

the variance is

$$n\pi(1 - \pi) = 4(0.5)(0.5)$$
$$= 1.0;$$

and the standard deviation is

$$\sqrt{V[x]} = \sqrt{1.0} = 1.0.$$

For the latter case of $n = 4$ and $\pi = 0.10$, the mean is $n\pi = 4(0.10) = 0.4$, the variance is $n\pi(1 - \pi) = 4(0.10)(0.90) = 0.36$, and the standard deviation is $\sqrt{V[x]} = \sqrt{0.36} = 0.60$.

Application of the Binomial Distribution

The binomial distribution is useful for investigating a number of special decision problems. One particular problem is that of determining whether the outcomes resulting from repeated trials form a sequence that has a systematic pattern, or whether the different outcomes occur randomly in an unpredictable pattern. For example, stockbrokers have various theories about whether fluctuations in the stock market occur in a random sequence. As another illustration, concern often exists about whether defectives in a production process are random or follow a systematic pattern. One popular belief is that defectives from assembly-line production occur more often on Mondays and Fridays and immediately before and after rest breaks. One test for randomness in a sequence of outcomes (called a "runs test") is based on the binomial distribution.

Study Question 5.1: Concern about Inflation/Unemployment

Assume that the President of the United States is concerned with both inflation and unemployment. The President is undecided as to which problem is viewed as more serious by the voting public. One group of presidential advisors claims that 90% of the public views unemployment as more serious. Another group of advisors suggests that the two problems are viewed as equally serious. Obviously, the President cannot learn the preferences of the entire population of U.S. voters; but suppose a decision is made to sample households at random, asking voters which problem is more serious. To illustrate the process, we will assume that a sample of $n = 20$ is taken, knowing that a much larger sample would be reasonable in this situation. The results are:

Unemployment more serious	Inflation/unemployment equally serious	Total
14	6	20

Which of the advisors would appear to be more correct on the basis of this sample? The view of the unemployment group is that $\pi = 0.90$, while the view of the other group is that $\pi = 0.50$. On the basis of $n = 20$ (the number of presumably independent trials), we can calculate the expected value (or mean) by using Formula (5.2). If $\pi = 0.90$, then

$$E[x] = n\pi = 20(0.90) = 18.$$

If $\pi = 0.50$, then

$$E[x] = n\pi = 20(0.50) = 10.$$

These values do not help the President a lot, because the observed number of voters answering "unemployment" (14) is exactly halfway between these two means. But now let's calculate the *probability* that 14 answer "inflation" when $n = 20$ and π is either 0.90 or 0.50. Using Table I in Appendix C (or Fig. 5.2), we find:

1. When $\pi = 0.90$,

$$P(x = 14) = 0.0089.$$

2. When $\pi = 0.50$,

$$P(x = 14) = 0.0370.$$

The probability of 14 voters answering "unemployment" when $\pi = 0.50$ is more than four times larger than when $\pi = 0.90$. On the basis of this survey we would thus tend to agree more with the advisors who say that unemployment and inflation are viewed as equally serious.

When examining the reasonableness of a hypothesis (such as $\pi = 0.90$) in the light of a sample result (such as x = 14), the usual procedure is to calculate the probability of the observed outcome or any more extreme outcomes. To find this type of union of outcomes, the "more extreme" outcomes are included by using the appropriate inequality (either $\leq$ or $\geq$). That is, we use $P(x \leq 14)$ or $P(x \geq 14)$ rather than the probability that x exactly equals 14. The direction of the inequality is chosen to include the "more extreme" values, meaning those farther away from the mean of the distribution. Thus, for $\pi = 0.90$ we wish to find the probability that $x \leq 14$, since the observed result ($x = 14$) is less than the expected value [which is $n\pi = 20(0.90) = 18$]. If the hypothesis is $\pi = 0.50$, then the procedure is to calculate the probability of 14 or more because the observed result (14) exceeds the expected value [which is $n\pi = 20(0.50) = 10$]. These two probabilities are:

1. When $\pi = 0.90$,

$$P(x \leq 14) = 0.0114.$$

2. When $\pi = 0.50$,

$$P(x \geq 14) = 0.0577.$$

The higher probability for $\pi = 0.50$ supports the second group of advisors who suggest that voters believe the problems are equally serious. The following procedure is appropriate in determining probabilities for decision-making.

If the observed value is less than the expected value, calculate the probability that x is *less than or equal to* the observed value:

$$P(x \leq \text{observed value}).$$

If the observed value exceeds the expected value, calculate the probability that x is *greater than or equal to* the observed value:

$$P(x \geq \text{observed value}).$$

Example 5.4. Another way of using a binomial probability distribution is to reverse the sense of the question and ask what value of π would be most compatible with the survey result. This process of examining a sample to make a statement about a population parameter is the basis of *statistical inference*. If we examine Table I (or Fig. 5.2) for $n = 20$, we see that the probability of $x = 14$ is the greatest when $\pi = 0.70$. That is, when $\pi = 0.70$ and $n = 20$, $P(x = 14) = 0.1916$, and no other value of $P(x = 14)$ is larger than 0.1916. Thus, we might conclude that a true value of $\pi = 0.70$ for the population seems most reasonable or likely. If the survey had resulted in 15 voters answering "unemployment," then the most likely value for π would have been $\pi = 0.75$.

Using probabilities in decision-mking or statistical inference can be better understood if we can determine the degree of sensitivity, or more precisely, the chances of error, in our conclusion. Such errors are discussed in detail in Chapters 9 and 10. At this point we hope merely to give some illustrations and thus a motivation for studying probability distributions. The following example is an illustration of the use of the binomial distribution in a decision process where the chances of making errors are determined.

Example 5.5. Assume that a production process for making picture frames is malfunctioning and will require a minor or a major adjustment. If the defective rate is 10% ($\pi = 0.10$), then only a minor adjustment is necessary; if the rate of defectives has jumped to 25.0% ($\pi = 0.25$), then a major adjustment is necessary. The problem at this point is how to decide, on the basis of a random sample of size $n = 20$, whether the process requires a minor or a major adjustment. This decision is not without risks, however, for we assume it to be costly to make the wrong decision — i.e., to make a minor adjustment to a process needing a major adjustment or to make a major adjustment to a process needing only minor adjustments.

In this circumstance we need to know how probable it is that x defectives will occur in a sample of $n = 20$ when $\pi = 0.10$ and how probable x defectives are when $\pi = 0.25$. Table 5.2 provides these values taken from the columns in Fig. 5.2 for $\pi = 0.10$ and $\pi = 0.25$.

Suppose, for the moment, that "four defectives" is established as the decision point between a major and minor adjustment: if there are four or more defectives, then major adjustments are made; with three or fewer defectives in the sample, minor repairs are made. This decision rule will lead to an *incorrect* decision if x (the number of defectives sampled) is greater than or equal to 4 when $\pi = 0.10$; that is, the correct decision would be a minor adjustment since the true π still equals 0.10, but our decision rule leads us to make a major adjustment (since $x \geq 4$). Similarly, if $x < 4$ when the true π has really changed to 0.25, then an incorrect decision is also made. We would make a minor adjustment (since $x < 4$) when a major adjustment is really needed (since $\pi = 0.25$). From Table 5.2 we see that the probability of making these two types of error is as follows:

TABLE 5.2 Using the binomial distribution in decision-making

x	Decision	If $\pi = 0.10$ $_{20}C_x(0.10)^x(0.90)^{20-x}$		If $\pi = 0.25$ $_{20}C_x(0.25)^x(0.75)^{20-x}$	
0			⎧0.1216		⎧0.0032
1	Minor	Correct	⎨0.2702	Error	⎨0.0211
2	adjustment	decision	⎬0.2852		⎬0.0669 ⎫ 0.2251
3	↓		⎩0.1901		⎩0.1339
			— Decision value —		
4	↑		⎧0.0898		⎧0.1897
5			0.0319		0.2023
6			0.0089		0.1686
7			0.0020		0.1124
8			0.0004		0.0609
9	Major	Error	⎨0.0001 ⎬ 0.1331	Correct	⎨0.0271
10	adjustment		0.0000	decision	0.0099
11			0.0000		0.0030
12			0.0000		0.0008
13			0.0000		0.0002
14–20	↓		⎩0.0000		⎩0.0000
Sum			1.0000		1.0000

1. Making a major adjustment when only minor adjustment is necessary:

$$P(x \geq 4 | \pi = 0.10) = 0.1331.$$

2. Making a minor adjustment when a major adjustment is necessary:

$$P(x < 4 | \pi = 0.25) = 0.2251.$$

The analysis thus far has been based on using x = 4 as a decision point. The probabilities in the analysis will, of course, change if a decision point other than x = 4 is used. Suppose the choice between a major and a minor adjustment is set to depend on the critical value of x = 3 defectives; then the probability of the two types of error can be calculated from Table 5.2 to be

1. $$P(x \geq 3 | \pi = 0.10) = 0.3232.$$

2. $$P(x < 3 | \pi = 0.25) = 0.0912.$$

For a given value of n, one of these types of errors (e.g., making a major adjustment when a minor adjustment is necessary, or vice versa) can be made smaller only if the other is allowed to become larger. Just what decision rule (such as using x = 3 or x = 4 as the critical value) is "best" in a given circumstance depends largely on the costs associated with making these errors. We shall examine this subject in more detail in Chapters 9, 10, and 16.

5.5 BINOMIAL PROPORTIONS

All the binomial problems studied thus far involved the random variable **x,** where **x** represents the *number* of successes in n Bernoulli trials. In this section we will show that any one of these problems could have been solved by using the variable x/n, where **x**/n represents the *proportion* of successes in n Bernoulli trials. For simplicity of notation, the sample proportion will be called p. For all practical purposes, *it makes no difference in solving a problem whether* **x** *is used, or* **x**/n = p *is used.*

To illustrate the statement above, suppose we redo Fig. 5.1, which shows the binomial distribution for n = 4, π = 0.70. Instead of using x on our horizontal axis, this time (in Fig. 5.5) we use p on the horizontal axis.

The important aspect of Fig. 5.5 is that it looks identical to Fig. 5.1 except for the values on the horizontal axis. In other words, dividing each value of **x** by n does not change any of the probability values. The mean and variance of p = **x**/n will be different from μ = nπ and σ^2 = n(1 − π), but we can easily derive the new values using the algebra of expectations.* The **expectations of a binomial proportion** are:

$$\text{Mean of } \boldsymbol{p} = E[\boldsymbol{p}] = \pi$$

$$\text{Variance of } \boldsymbol{p} = V[\boldsymbol{p}] = \frac{\pi(1 - \pi)}{n} \tag{5.4}$$

---

* The proofs are:

$$E[\boldsymbol{p}] = E[\boldsymbol{x}/n] = \frac{1}{n} E[\boldsymbol{x}] \qquad \text{by Rule 3 of Section 4.4}$$

$$= \frac{1}{n}(n\pi) \qquad \text{since } E[\boldsymbol{x}] = n\pi$$

$$= \pi.$$

$$V[\boldsymbol{p}] = V[\boldsymbol{x}/n] = \frac{1}{n^2} V[\boldsymbol{x}] \qquad \text{by Rule 4 of Section 4.4}$$

$$= \frac{1}{n^2} n\pi(1 - \pi) \qquad \text{since } V[\boldsymbol{x}] = n\pi(1 - \pi)$$

$$= \frac{\pi(1 - \pi)}{n}.$$

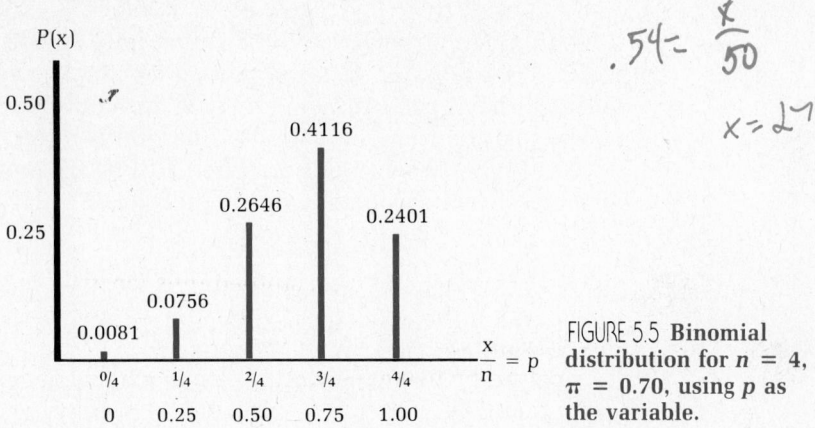

FIGURE 5.5 **Binomial distribution for n = 4, $\pi = 0.70$, using p as the variable.**

Example 5.6. A newspaper article has suggested that only 40% of the small businesses in Houston follow accepted auditing procedures. To test this assertion, a CPA takes a random sample of 50 small businesses in Houston. Should the CPA doubt the article's suggestion if 54% of these 50 small businesses are following accepted auditing procedures?

Since Table I is presented in terms of the *number* of successes (*x*), rather than the *proportion* of successes (*x*/n), a problem involving *x*/n is usually solved by transforming it to the comparable problem involving *x*.

Remember from Section 5.3 that in problems of this nature we generally do not calculate the probability of one specific value, but rather the probability that *x* is greater than or equal to the observed value when the observed value exceeds the expected value. In this example we want to calculate the proportion

$$P(p \geq 0.54)$$

because the observed value of 54% exceeds the expected value of 40%. Since n = 50, $p \geq 0.54$ is equivalent to $x \geq 50 (0.54)$, or $x \geq 27$. Thus

$$P(p \geq 0.54) = P(x \geq 27).$$

This problem is easily solved by using Table I for n = 50, $\pi = 0.40$, and $x \geq 27$. Be sure to recognize that π in this problem is 0.40 (and not 0.54), because 0.40 is the population proportion (π) that we are considering. From Table I,

$$P(x \geq 27) = 0.0154 + \cdots + 0.0001 = 0.0314.$$

Thus, in random samples of this nature, only a little over 3% of the time would one expect 27 or more "successes" in 50 trials. The CPA would appear to have good reason to doubt the newspaper's assertion and to believe that the true population proportion is larger than 0.40.

Would the newspaper's assertion still be in doubt if, say, 48% of 50 businesses used accepted auditing procedures? In this case

$$P(p \geq 0.48) = P(x \geq 24) = 0.0978,$$

which means there is almost a 10% chance that this result (48%) could occur if the newspaper is correct. Perhaps 0.10 is too high a probability for the CPA to risk criticizing the newspaper for its 40% assertion. In Chapter 9 we will study the process of trying to decide how low a probability has to be before one can reject the assertion on which this probability was calculated. One quite arbitrary rule often used is that the probability must be less than 0.05 in order to reject the assertion.

In our CPA example, the result could have been in the opposite direction — perhaps only 22% of the businesses sampled use accepted auditing procedures. The appropriate calculation now is for the probability that p will be 0.22 or less because 0.22 is less than the expected value of $\pi = 0.40$. From Table I, $n = 50$ and $\pi = 0.40$,

$$P(p \leq 0.22) = P(x \leq 11) = 0.0057.$$

There is thus less than a 1% chance of having 11 or fewer businesses using accepted practices in a sample of 50 when the true population proportion is 0.40. Since this probability is quite low (much less than the 5% rule mentioned above), a sample result of 22% would again give the CPA cause to doubt the newspaper's assertion and to worry that the true percentage of businesses using accepted procedures in the population may even be less than 40%.

Define. *Bernoulli' trial, independent trials, binomial parameters, binomial proportion.*

PROBLEMS

5.1   Six Chevy Vans are being tested by *Consumer Reports* for quality control. In the past, 40% of the vans tested have had some safety problems on delivery (such as a headlight out or a seatbelt not working).

a)   Construct a sketch of the binomial distribution for $n = 6$, $\pi = 0.40$. Is this distribution skewed right or left?

b) What is the expected number of defectives for the distribution in part (a)? What are the variance and standard deviation?

c) What is the probability of four or more defectives in part (a)?

5.2 Texas Instruments has been producing the 256K dynamic RAM memory chips for computers. In the past, about 55% of the RAM chips have been defective. Fifty new chips are being tested.

a) How many chips would you expect to be defective out of 50?

b) Draw a rough sketch of the binomial distribution. Is the distribution skewed right, skewed left, or approximately symmetrical?

c) Would you be surprised if only 20 of the chips were defective? [Hint: Calculate $P(p \leq 20 | n = 50, \pi = 0.55)$.]

5.3 Suppose that a plumbing contractor submits bids on construction projects and that there are always other plumbing companies bidding on the same projects. Assume that the long-run chances of this contractor's bid being the one selected are one of five. What is the probability that this contractor's bid will be selected in exactly two of the next four projects? Explain.

5.4 Thirty percent of the applicants for a certain job are from minority groups. What is the probability that five applicants, selected at random, will include exactly two people from a minority group?

5.5 Use Table I in Appendix C for the following:

a) Sketch the binomial p.m.f. and the binomial c.m.f. for $n = 8$ and $\pi = 0.40$.

b) What is the probability $P(x = 7)$ for the above parameters? What is the probability $P(x \geq 7)$?

c) Find the mean and the variance of this distribution.

5.6 Use Formula (5.1) to determine the binomial mass function for the parameters $n = 5$, $\pi = 0.50$. Check your answer with Table I. Sketch both the mass function and the cumulative function for these parameters.

5.7 An audit was conducted by the IRS of 22,395 invoices belonging to Anco Industries, Inc. The IRS looked at Anco invoices to determine whether the correct excise tax had been paid on a new product, for the period 1981–1984. A sample of 165 invoices indicated that Anco had underpaid on 28 of the invoices and had overpaid on 15.

a) How many of the population of 22,395 would you estimate were underpaid? How many would you estimate were overpaid?

b) If the average underpayment was $10.20 and the average overpayment was $1.81, what does Anco owe the IRS (excluding interest and penalties)?

5.8 A direct-mailing marketing approach has, in the past, resulted in sales to 1% of the customers receiving the mailing.

a) If 99,000 ads are mailed, how many sales would be expected?

b) What is the lowest number and highest number of sales you would expect? (*Hint:* Use $\mu \pm 2\sigma$.)

5.9 Important business decisions sometimes rest on the flip of a coin. In 1983, for example, the Indiana Pacers (of the NBA) lost the rights to draft Ralph Sampson (from the University of Virginia) to the Houston Rockets on the flip of a coin. Prior to this flip, heads had come up 12 times and tails eight times since 1963.

a) What is the probability of 12 or more heads in 20 tosses, assuming random flips? Would you have recommended that the Pacers call "heads" or "tails" if given the choice? (Actually, a flip is made to see who gets to make the call on the "real" flip. The Rockets chose heads and won the call. They chose heads again and won the first draft pick.)

b) From 1977 to 1981 there were five straight tails. What is the probability of five straight tails if flips are random? If you were picking in 1982, would you pick heads or tails? Explain.

5.10 Five products are selected from a very large group of a certain kind. If 40% of the products are defective, what is the probability that fewer than two or more than three of the five selected will be defective?

5.11 The Penn State Credit Union estimates that one customer in four who visits the main office will require services lasting more than four minutes. A line at the main office has six customers. What is the probability, for this line, that

a) exactly three customers will take longer than four minutes?

b) at least three customers will take longer than four minutes?

c) at most three customers will take longer than four minutes?

d) two, three, and four customers take longer?

e) What is the expected number of customers taking longer than four minutes? What is the variance?

5.12 If a manufacturing process is working properly, only 10% of the items produced will be defective.

a) You take a random sample of five items. What is the probability that exactly two of these will be defective?

b) Suppose you select 25 items at random. What is the expected number of defectives?

5.13 A certain corporation claims that, on the basis of past trends, four of every five of their new employees will remain with the company at least five years. Would you dispute this claim if only 13 of 20 new employees last five years or longer? [*Hint:* Calculate $P(x \le 13 | \pi = 0.80)$ using Table I.]

to get the total number of combinations of *both* x_1 out of N_1 *and* x_2 out of N_2. The denominator is the total number of combinations of $(N_1 + N_2)$ objects taken $(x_1 + x_2)$ at a time.

Example of the Hypergeometric Distribution

Example 5.7. Let's apply the hypergeometric distribution to a production process in which electrical components are produced in lots of 50. If this process is working correctly, there will be no defective items among the 50 produced. Let us assume, however, that at random intervals the process begins to malfunction, so that some of the components produced thereafter are defective. Since inspecting each and every one of the 50 items in a lot is relatively expensive, the hypergeometric distribution can be used to assess the probability that a random sample will detect defective components. Suppose, for example, that the process has, in fact, been malfunctioning, and exactly five components in a particular lot are defective. What is the probability that exactly one of these five defectives will appear in a sample of four randomly selected components? That is, what is the probability that a sample of four contains exactly one defective and three good components? This probability, that the sample contains $x_1 = 1$ of the $N_1 = 5$ defective components and $x_2 = 3$ of the $N_2 = 45$ good components, is given by the hypergeometric p.m.f.:

$$P(1 \text{ defective and } 3 \text{ good}) = \frac{(_5C_1) \cdot (_{45}C_3)}{_{(5+45)}C_{(1+3)}} = \frac{(_5C_1) \cdot (_{45}C_3)}{_{50}C_4}$$

$$= \frac{(5!/1!4!) \times (45!/3!42!)}{50!/4!46!} = 0.308.$$

Similarly, one might want to calculate the probability of encountering two or fewer defectives in a random sample of four components:

$P(2 \text{ or fewer defectives})$

$= P(0 \text{ defectives}) + P(1 \text{ defective}) + P(2 \text{ defectives})$

$$= \frac{(_5C_0) \cdot (_{45}C_4)}{_{50}C_4} + \frac{(_5C_1) \cdot (_{45}C_3)}{_{50}C_4} + \frac{(_5C_2) \cdot (_{45}C_2)}{_{50}C_4}$$

$$= \frac{(5!/0!5!) \cdot (45!/4!41!) + (5!/1!4!) \cdot (45!3!42!) + (5!/2!3!) \cdot (45!/2!43!)}{50!/4!46!}$$

$= 0.998.$

Similarities of the Hypergeometric and the Binomial Distributions

We should emphasize once more that the critical assumption implied by the way probabilities are calculated in the hypergeometric distribution is that *sampling takes place from a finite population, without replacement.* In terms of the present example, this means that the probability of finding a defective *changes* after each one of the four items is inspected. For instance, the probability that the first item selected is defective, assuming a random sample, is 5/50, or 0.10. If this item is, in fact, defective, then there are only four defectives remaining, so that on the second draw the probability of receiving a defective is 4/49, or 0.082. In this way, the experimental situation differs from the binomial situation, where the trials are independent — that is, where the probabilities π and $1 - \pi$ do not change during the trials.

Since calculating hypergeometric probabilities involves tedious arithmetic, sampling experiments are generally devised, whenever possible, so that the binomial distribution can be used instead. That is, experiments involve either infinite populations, or sampling with replacement, or sample sizes of 5% or less of the population (see Table 5.3). In the latter case it makes little difference whether the binomial or hypergeometric distribution is used, although the hypergeometric always gives the exact answer.

Example 5.8. Consider a hypergeometric problem in which the size of the population is fairly large, say, $N = 100$ life insurance policies written by a salesperson, and where there are two different kinds of policies, whole life (1) and term (2), with $N_1 = 40$ and $N_2 = 60$. Suppose that we are interested in the probability of drawing from this population a sample that contains $x_1 = 2$ out of $N_1 = 40$ whole life policies and $x_2 = 3$ out of $N_2 = 60$ term policies. The total sample size is thus $x_1 + x_2 = 5$. The probability of drawing this sample is given by Formula (5.5) as:

$$P(x_1 = 2 \text{ out of } N_1 = 40, \quad \text{and} \quad x_2 = 3 \text{ out of } N_2 = 60)$$

$$= \frac{(_{40}C_2) \cdot (_{60}C_3)}{_{100}C_5} = \frac{(40!/2!38!)(60!/3!57!)}{100!/5!95!} = 0.3545.$$

We can approximate the probability for this same event by using the binomial distribution. First, we denote as x (a success) the drawing of an

TABLE 5.3 **Summary of hypergeometric vs. binomial distribution**

Distribution	Assumptions	Formula
Binomial	Sampling with replacement or from an infinite population (for practical purposes, $n \leq 5\%$ of N). π is a constant.	$_nC_x\pi^x(1 - \pi)^{n-x}$
Hypergeometric	Sampling without replacement from a finite population. π changes with each sample observation.	$\dfrac{(_{N_1}C_{x_1}) \cdot (_{N_2}C_{x_2})}{_{(N_1+N_2)}C_{(x_1+x_2)}}$

object of the first kind (a whole life policy); since there are 40 objects of the first kind out of a total of 100 objects, the probability of a success on the first draw is $\pi = 0.40$. This π will change on every draw after the first, since we assume sampling without replacement. For example, if a success is received on the first draw, then the probability of a success on the second draw is $\frac{39}{99} = 0.3939$. Notice that because the population size is fairly large, the probability does not change too much from the first to the second draw. Hence, it is not unreasonable for us to assume, as we must for the binomial, that π is a constant (which in this case is $\pi = 0.40$). Under this assumption, and where the sample size is n = 5 (remember, $x_1 + x_2 = 5$), the probability of exactly two successes $P(x = 2)$ is given by the binomial distribution [Formula (5.1) and Table I] as:

$$P(x = 2 \text{ successes in } n = 5 \text{ trials}) = {}_5C_2(0.40)^2(0.60)^3 = 0.3456.$$

The binomial value of 0.3456 is seen to be a fairly good approximation to the correct value from the hypergeometric, 0.3545. Because the binomial probabilities are easier to determine, and often approximate the hypergeometric quite well, the binomial is more widely used than the hypergeometric distribution in statistical decision-making and inference. Care must be taken not to misuse this binomial approximation, for if the sample size $(x_1 + x_2)$ is large relative to the population size N = $(N_1 + N_2)$, the approximation generally will not be a good one. For example, if we change N_1 and N_2 in the hypergeometric problem above to $N_1 = 4$ and $N_2 = 6$, then Formula (5.5) yields the following value:

$$P(x_1 = 2 \text{ out of } N_1 = 4 \quad \text{and} \quad x_2 = 3 \text{ out of } N_2 = 6)$$

$$= \frac{({}_4C_2) \cdot ({}_6C_3)}{{}_{10}C_5} = \frac{(4!/2!2!)(6!/3!3!)}{10!/5!5!} = 0.4762.$$

The binomial approximation to this value is the same value calculated above, namely, 0.3456. In this case the approximation is not a good one (0.4762 vs. 0.3456) because the sample size (n = 5) is very large in relation to the population size (N = 10). Consequently, the probability of a success changes too much among trials. The binomial assumption of independence is violated since on the first draw, P(success) = 0.40, but on the second draw P(success given a success on the first draw) is $\frac{3}{9} = 0.33$.

PROBLEMS

5.20 The Dean at the Harvard Business School has been asked to select three students for a certain committee. Twenty first-year students volunteer to be on this committee, as do 30 second-year students. If the dean selects the three students randomly from the total group of 50 volunteers, what is the probability that one first-year and two second-year students will be selected?

5.21 In Las Vegas, gambling is "big business." One of the popular games is poker, in which it is possible to calculate certain probabilities when the number of decks being used is known. Assuming that only a single deck is used, calculate the following probabilities.
  a) A "full house" consisting of three aces and two kings.
  b) "Four of a kind" consisting of four aces and one king.
  c) "Four of a kind" consisting of four aces and any other card.

5.22 A university department has three assistant professors, two associate professors, and four full professors. The student newspaper randomly picks five of these professors to interview. What is the probability that they will select two assistant professors, one associate professor, and two full professors? (*Hint:* Use an extension of the hypergeometric Formula (5.5) to three categories.)

5.23 Suppose a committee of six is to be chosen from ten people, five of whom are Republicans and five of whom are Democrats.
  a) If the committee is to be chosen by random selection, what is the probability that there will be three Democrats and three Republicans on the committee?
  b) What is the probability that a majority of the committee members will be Democrats?

5.24 Brand B Aspirin Company decides to randomly select 10 out of 100 doctors working in a large hospital. If 50% of the 100 doctors actually prefer brand B, what is the probability that the results of the sample will find that "9 out of 10 doctors surveyed prefer brand B"?

5.25 The Department of Transportation (DOT) has announced that it will award a grant for the study of traffic accidents to each of four different universities. Twenty universities have applied for such a grant. If Stanford, Indiana University, and the University of North Carolina are among the 20 applicants, what is the probability that these three universities will all be winners, assuming that the selection is made randomly and each is equally likely to be selected?

5.26 A company selling magazine subscriptions has offered numerous prizes to people who return a special envelope, with either a "yes" sticker (indicating they want to subscribe) or a "no" sticker (they do not want to subscribe). Thirty percent of several thousand respondents use the "yes" sticker. In a list of the ten top prizes, you later find that eight of these people had returned the "yes" sticker. Does it appear that the

[handwritten margin notes: $N_1 = 3$ $N_2 = 7$ $X_1 = 1$ out of $N_1 = 3$ $X_2 = 2$ out of $N_1 = 7$ $3C_1 \cdot {}_6 3$]

selection of winners was random? (*Hint:* Determine the probability of eight *or more* "yes" stickers among 10 winners.]

5.27   How does the hypergeometric distribution differ from the binomial distribution? Under what circumstances is the hypergeometric appropriate? Under what circumstances is the binomial appropriate?

5.28   Suppose that in a production run of ten home air-conditioning units, three are defective. A sample of three units is to be randomly drawn from the ten. What is the probability of receiving *at least* one defective if the samples are drawn: (a) with replacement, (b) without replacement?

5.29   Redo Problem 5.20 using a binomial approximation. In this case, let the probability that a first-year student will be selected be $\pi = 20/50$, and let $1 - \pi = 30/50$ represent the probability that a second-year student is selected. There are $n = 3$ trials, and you need to calculate $P(x = 1)$. Compare this value with your answer to Problem 5.20.

5.30   Redo Problem 5.24 using a binomial approximation. Let the probability that a doctor prefers brand B be $\pi = 0.50$, and calculate $P(x = 9)$ assuming $n = 10$.

5.31   Redo Problem 5.25 using the binomial distribution.

5.32   Assume that 2073 of the 10,000 customers of the Easy Charge Company from Problem 3.22 received a cash advance during September. You take a random sample of 100 of their 10,000 customers.
   a)   Write down the hypergeometric expression representing the probability that 21% of the sample will be customers who received a cash advance.
   b)   Find the binomial probability that best approximates the hypergeometric probability represented in part (a).

5.7   THE POISSON DISTRIBUTION*

Another important discrete distribution, the **Poisson distribution**, has recently been found to have a fairly wide range of applications, especially in the area of operations research. This distribution was named for its originator, the French mathematician S. D. Poisson (1781–1840), who described its use in a paper written in 1837. Its rather morbid first applications indicated that the Poisson distribution quite accurately described the probability of deaths in the Prussian army resulting from the kick of a horse, as well as the number of suicides among women and

---

* This section may be omitted without loss of continuity.

children. More recent and useful applications involve the rates of arrivals at a service facility or requests for service at that facility, as well as the rate at which this service is provided. Examples of such successful applications of the Poisson distribution include problems concerning the number of arrivals or requests for service per unit time at tollbooths on an expressway, checkout counters in a supermarket, teller windows in a bank, and runways in an airport.

In examples of the above nature the Poisson distribution can be used to determine the probability of **x** occurrences (arrivals or service completions) per unit time if four basic assumptions are met. First, it must be possible to divide the time interval being used into a large number of small subintervals in such a manner that the probability of an occurrence in each of these subintervals is very small. Second, the probability of an occurrence in each of the subintervals must remain constant throughout the time period being considered. Third, the probability of two or more occurrences in each subinterval must be small enough to be ignored. Fourth, an occurrence (or nonoccurrence) in one subinterval must not affect the occurrence (or nonoccurrence) in any other subinterval — i.e., the occurrences must be independent.

Example 5.9. Consider the number of arrivals per hour at a bank, and assume that we divide a given hour into intervals of one second. Assume also that the *probability* that a customer will arrive during any given second is very small and remains constant throughout the one-hour period. Furthermore, assume that only one customer can arrive in a given second and that the number of arrivals in a given time period is independent of the number of arrivals in any *other* time period (e.g., customers do not turn away because of long lines). Under these circumstances the number of arrivals in the one-hour period follows the Poisson distribution. These four assumptions and how they fit the bank example are summarized below.

Assumption	Bank Example
1. Possible to divide time interval of interest into many small subintervals.	1. Can divide the hour into subintervals of one second each.
2. Probability of an occurrence remains constant throughout the time intervals.	2. The hour is one in which the most reasonable anticipation is a steady flow of customers.
3. Probability of two or more occurrences in a subinterval is small enough to be ignored.	3. Impossible for two people to enter the bank simultaneously (i.,e., in the same second).
4. Independence of occurrences.	4. Arrivals at the bank are not influenced by the length of the lines.

Of these four assumptions, numbers (1) and (3) are general enough to apply to almost any setting involving arrivals over time. However, the assumptions that occurrences are constant over time and independent are much less likely to be met in potential applications of the Poisson distribution. Nevertheless, the Poisson distribution does not seem to apply in a surprisingly large variety of different situations.

Parameters of the Poisson Distribution

Examples of the Poisson distribution such as those given above pertain to the probability of x occurrences (arrivals or service completions) per unit of time.* The only parameter necessary to characterize a population described by the Poisson distribution is the *mean rate* at which events occur. We shall use the Greek letter lambda, λ, for this parameter. Lambda can be defined as the mean rate of occurrence for any convenient unit of time — one minute, ten minutes, an hour, a day, or even a year. A value of $\lambda = 2.3$, for example, could indicate that there are, on the average, 2.3 requests for service in a particular bank every minute, or 2.3 customers arriving at a restaurant every 10 minutes. For practical applications the mean rate at which events occur must be determined empirically. That is, λ must be known in advance, perhaps on the basis of a previous study of the situation. Once λ is known, the **probability mass function for the Poisson distribution** can be used to determine the probability that exactly x occurrences, or events, take place in the specified time interval. The value of λ must be positive, and x can assume any integer value from 0 to infinity.

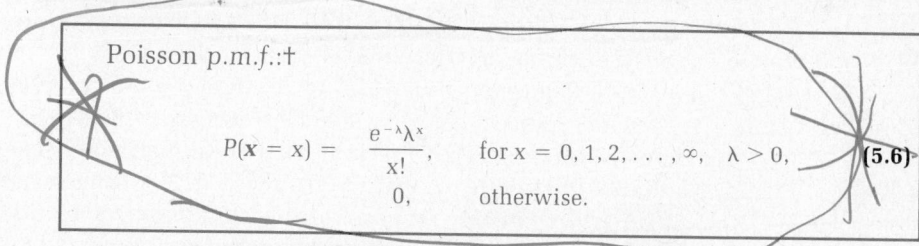

Poisson *p.m.f.*:†

$$P(\pmb{x} = x) = \begin{cases} \dfrac{e^{-\lambda}\lambda^x}{x!}, & \text{for } x = 0, 1, 2, \ldots, \infty, \quad \lambda > 0, \\ 0, & \text{otherwise.} \end{cases} \qquad \textbf{(5.6)}$$

* The Poisson distribution can also be applied to problems involving the number of occurrences of a random variable for a given unit of *area*, such as the number of typographical errors on a page, the number of white blood cells in a blood suspension, the number of flaws in a fabric, or the number of imperfections in a surface of wood, metal, or paint. In fact, the Poisson distribution can be derived from the binomial distribution by letting the number of trials (n) go to infinity and holding $n \cdot \pi$ constant. When π is small, the Poisson distribution often provides a good approximation to the binomial.

† The symbol e in this formula stands for a *constant*, the value of which is a nonrepeating, nonterminating decimal. It is the sum of the infinite series $1 + \dfrac{1}{1} + \dfrac{1}{2!} + \dfrac{1}{3!} + \dfrac{1}{4!}$ $+ \cdots$, which we will approximate with the value 2.71828.

Example 5.10. Assume that the bank discussed previously knows from past experience that between 10 and 11 A.M. of each day the mean arrival rate is $\lambda = 60$ customers per hour. Suppose that the bank wants to determine the probability that exactly two customers will arrive in a given one-minute time interval between 10 and 11 A.M. Since arrivals are assumed to be constant over a given time interval, the rate of 60 per hour is equivalent to an arrival rate of $\lambda = 1$ customer per minute. Substituting $\lambda = 1$ and $x = 2$ into Formula (5.6) yields

$$P(2 \text{ arrivals}) = \frac{e^{-1}(1)^2}{2!} = \frac{1}{2e}.$$

Since e equals (approximately) 2.71828, we obtain

$$P(2 \text{ arrivals}) = \frac{1}{2(2.71828)} = 0.1839.$$

Similarly, the bank might want to calculate $P(2 \text{ or fewer arrivals})$:

$$P(2 \text{ or fewer arrivals}) = P(0) + P(1) + P(2)$$
$$= \frac{e^{-1}(1)^0}{0!} + \frac{e^{-1}(1)^1}{1!} + \frac{e^{-1}(1)^2}{2!}$$
$$= 0.3679 + 0.3679 + 0.1839 = 0.9197.$$

As was the case for the binomial, Poisson probabilities have been extensively tabulated, so that the task of calculating probabilities using Formula (5.6) can be avoided. Table II gives the probabilities for selected values of λ from $\lambda = 0.01$ to $\lambda = 20.0$. The probability values for the above example are shown in Table II under the heading $\lambda = 1.0$. These values are graphed in part (a) of Fig. 5.6.

Each value of the parameter λ represents a different member of the family of Poisson distributions. In a supermarket, for example, the mean number of arrivals per minute may be $\lambda = 3.8$. In this case the probability of observing exactly one arrival in a randomly selected minute would be 0.0850 (determined from Table II, using $x = 1$ and $\lambda = 3.8$) as shown in Fig. 5.6(b). As a final example, the mean number of arrivals per minute might be $\lambda = 10$ at a city subway station during rush hour. The probability of observing two or fewer arrivals in a randomly selected minute during this period would be found by summing the values for $x = 0$, 1, and 2 in Table II under $\lambda = 10$. This probability is 0.0028, indicating quite a rare event (see part (c) of Fig. 5.6).

Note that in Fig. 5.6 all probabilities are nonzero, and only a discrete number of values of x have positive probabilities. Thus, x_{Poisson} is an example of a discrete random variable having an infinite number of outcomes. As for all discrete mass functions, the sum of the probabilities

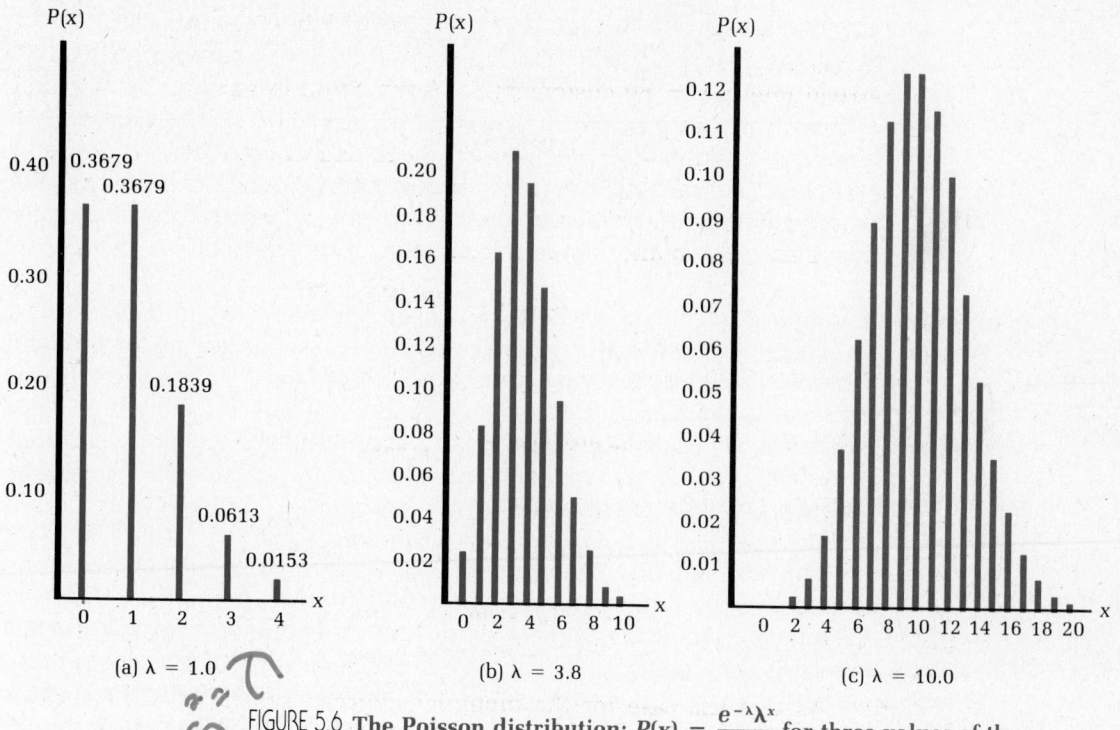

FIGURE 5.6 **The Poisson distribution:** $P(x) = \dfrac{e^{-\lambda}\lambda^x}{x!}$ **for three values of the parameter.**

(a) $\lambda = 1.0$ (b) $\lambda = 3.8$ (c) $\lambda = 10.0$

variance $= \sigma^2 = \lambda$
mean $\mu = \lambda$

over all values of **x** must be 1.0. The graphs in Fig. 5.6 demonstrate that this distribution has positive skewness, since x cannot be lower than zero but may be any positive integer. However, Fig. 5.6(c) also indicates that when λ is not too close to zero, the shape of the Poisson distribution appears to be fairly symmetrical.

Mean and Variance of the Poisson Distribution

The Poisson distribution has only one parameter (λ), so the mean and variance of the distribution must be functions of this parameter. Indeed, λ is defined as the *mean* number of occurrences of the particular event per time or space unit. Therefore, the **mean of the Poisson distribution is λ.** What is not obvious at all, but is proven in many statistics books, is that **the variance of the Poisson distribution** *is also identically equal to* λ.* That is,

* See for example, D. L. Harnett, *Statistical Methods*, 3rd edition, Section 4.7 (Reading, Mass.: Addison-Wesley, 1982).

$$
\begin{array}{ll}
\text{Poisson mean:} & \mu = \lambda; \\
\text{Poisson variance:} & \sigma^2 = V(x_{\text{Poisson}}) = \lambda.
\end{array}
\qquad \textbf{(5.7)}
$$

Thus, if a value of $\lambda = 1.0$ indicates that customers are arriving at a bank according to a Poisson probability law at an average rate of 1.0 customer every minute, then the variance of these arrivals is also 1.0.

Determining a Poisson Distribution in a Practical Situation

Example 5.11. Suppose that is has been suggested to the manager of a large supermarket that arrivals at the checkout counters might follow a Poisson distribution during certain periods of time. The manager investigates this probability by checking the reasonableness of the four basic assumptions listed earlier, especially assumptions number 2 (constant probability) and 4 (independence). After careful consideration the time interval 4–6 P.M., Monday–Friday, is selected as an appropriate period during which all four assumptions seem reasonable.

The next step this manager might take is the collection of observations concerning the number of arrivals within the two hours from 4–6 P.M. Rather than count the number of customers arriving for many different *two-hour* time periods, arrivals are recorded in each of 100 *one-minute* periods, randomly selected over several days, between 4 and 6 P.M. This procedure is reasonable, since arrivals are assumed to be constant over the two-hour period; hence it makes no difference, theoretically at least, what time unit is used. The number (x) of customers arriving per minute in this study ranged from 0 to 10, as shown in Table 5.4. For example, the third line of Table 5.4 indicates that on 19 different occasions there were exactly two arrivals in the one-minute period. The fourth row indicates that there were exactly three arrivals on 23 different occasions.

Recall that, for the Poisson distribution, both μ and σ^2 are equal. Hence, in checking to see if the data in Table 5.4 follow a Poisson distribution, the manager might first wish to see if $\mu = \sigma^2$. Column (4) in this table gives the appropriate values for calculating μ. Using Formula (2.4), the calculated value of μ is

$$
\mu = \sum_{i=1}^{k} x_i \left(\frac{f_i}{N} \right) = 3.79.
$$

The variance of the data in Table 5.4 can be calculated by using the mean-square-minus-the-square-mean relationship presented in Formula (4.6). Substituting the appropriate values [from column (6) of Table 5.4],

$$
E[x] = 3.79 \quad \text{and} \quad E[x^2] = \sum_{i=1}^{k} x^2 \frac{f_i}{n} = 18.27
$$

TABLE 5.4

(1)	(2)	(3)	(4)	(5)	(6)
Arrivals (x)	Observed Frequency	$\dfrac{f}{n}$	$x\,\dfrac{f}{n}$	x^2	$x^2\,\dfrac{f}{n}$
0	1	0.01	0.00	0	0.00
1	8	0.08	0.08	1	0.08
2	19	0.19	0.38	4	0.76
3	23	0.23	0.69	9	2.07
4	17	0.17	0.68	16	2.72
5	15	0.15	0.75	25	3.75
6	8	0.08	0.48	36	2.88
7	3	0.03	0.21	49	1.47
8	3	0.03	0.24	64	1.92
9	2	0.02	0.18	81	1.62
10	1	0.01	0.10	100	1.00
Sum	100	1.00	3.79		18.27

we obtain

$$V[\boldsymbol{x}] = \sigma^2 = E[\boldsymbol{x}^2] - (E[\boldsymbol{x}])^2$$
$$= 18.27 - (3.79)^2 = 3.91.$$

We see that for these data, μ and σ^2 are very nearly equal in value (3.79 vs. 3.91). Theoretically, they are supposed to be *exactly* equal, but in a sample of just 100 time periods we would not expect the observed value of either μ or σ^2 to *exactly* equal the population parameter λ. The closeness of μ to σ^2 in this case is encouraging enough for the store manager to make the most important test, namely, to see whether the observed relative frequencies correspond to the theoretical frequencies for the Poisson distribution. To make this comparison, suppose we assume that $\lambda = 3.8$. (Note that it is not known from the data in Table 5.4 whether $\lambda = 3.79$ or 3.91, or some other value, and so the choice of $\lambda = 3.8$ is somewhat arbitrary.) Now, if the number of arrivals in these 100 one-minute periods does follow a Poisson distribution with $\lambda = 3.8$, we would expect the observed frequencies in column (3) of Table 5.4 to closely correspond to the probabilities of the following Poisson distribution

$$P(x) = \frac{e^{-3.8}(3.8)^x}{x!}.$$

These values, from Table II under the heading $\lambda = 3.8$, are reproduced in Table 5.5. We see in Table 5.5 that the observed relative frequencies

TABLE 5.5

(1)	(2)	(3)
Arrivals	Observed Relative Frequency	Poisson Value $P(x) = e^{-3.8}(3.8)^x/x!$
0	0.010	0.0224
1	0.080	0.0850
2	0.190	0.1615
3	0.230	0.2046
4	0.170	0.1944
5	0.150	0.1477
6	0.080	0.0936
7	0.030	0.0508
8	0.030	0.0241
9	0.020	0.0102
10	0.010	0.0039
11	0.000	0.0013
12	0.000	0.0004
13	0.000	0.0001
Sum	1.000	1.0000

correspond quite well to the Poisson values for $\lambda = 3.8$. A good exercise for the reader at this point would be to verify, for the probabilities shown in the last column of Table 5.5, that the mean and variance are equal — i.e., that $\mu = \sigma^2 = 3.8$. To determine the probability within intervals about the mean, we need the standard deviation. The standard deviation of the Poisson distribution when $\lambda = 3.8$ is

$$\sigma = \sqrt{3.8} = 1.95.$$

Using Table 5.5, column (3), the intervals

$$\mu \pm 1\sigma = 3.8 \pm 1.95 \quad \text{and} \quad \mu \pm 2\sigma = 3.8 \pm 2(1.95)$$

are shown below to contain 71% and 96% of the probability, respectively. These are again close to our rule of thumb values of 0.68 and 0.95 for interpreting the meaning of the standard deviation.

Interval	Probability Included
$\mu \pm 1\sigma = 3.80 \pm (1.95) = 1.85 \text{ to } 5.75$	$\sum\limits_{x=2}^{5} P(x) = 0.7082$
$\mu \pm 2\sigma = 3.80 \pm 2(1.95) = 0 \text{ to } 7.70$	$\sum\limits_{x=0}^{7} P(x) = 0.9600$

5.8 APPROXIMATION OF DISCRETE RANDOM VARIABLES BY CONTINUOUS RANDOM VARIABLES

The use of discrete random variables, especially the binomial random variable, is very important and applies to many experimental situations. Although calculation of the probabilities of discrete random variables is often a tedious task, we are fortunate in that such probabilities are already tabulated for many mass functions. A glance at Tables I and II, however, indicates that not all values of n and π in the binomial or of λ in the Poisson, are specified. One might ask what is done in those cases for which no tabulated value exists, such as $n = 126$ or $\pi = 0.618$ in a binomial distribution, or $\lambda = 12.55$ in a Poisson distribution. It is always possible to calculate probabilities directly, using the formulas given in this chapter. However, this approach is often impractical when a computer can be used. Another approach, which is appropriate in certain cases, is to use a continuous approximation to a discrete distribution. This is one reason why we study continuous random variables (although not the only one, since there are many instances where the random variable in an experiment may actually assume a continuous form). Our point is that a study of *only* discrete probability distributions is not sufficient to enable us to proceed to more relevant and interesting problems in decision-making and statistical inference. Therefore, we will proceed in Chapter 6 to discuss continuous probability distributions.

PROBLEMS

5.33 In an airport, an average of 8.5 pieces of baggage per minute are handled, in accordance with a Poisson distribution. Find the probability that ten pieces of baggage are handled in a selected minute of time.

5.34 Suppose that in a textile manufacturing process, an average of two flaws per ten running yards of material have appeared. What is the probability that a given ten-yard segment will have 0 or 1 defects, if the number of flaws follows a Poisson distribution?

5.35 On the average, 2.3 telephone calls per minute are made through a central switchboard, following a Poisson distribution. What is the probability that during a given minute exactly two calls will be made?

5.36 Use Formula (5.6) to determine the probabilities associated with the Poisson distribution for $\lambda = 2.0$. Sketch both the mass and the cumulative distributions. Check your answers by using Table II of Appendix C. What are the mean and variance of this distribution?

5.37 For the Poisson distribution:
    a) Find what percent lies within $\mu \pm 1\sigma$ and $\mu \pm 2\sigma$ when $\lambda = 1$. How do these values compare with the rule of thumb given in Chapter 1?
    b) Repeat part (a) for $\lambda = 4$ and $\lambda = 9$, and comment on why you think the percents are getting closer to the rule of thumb.

5.38 A barbershop has, on the average, ten customers between 8:00 and 9:00 each morning that it is open. Customers arrive according to a Poisson distribution.
    a) What is the probability that the barbershop will have exactly ten customers between these times on a given morning?
    b) What is the probability that the barbershop will have more than 12 customers in this time period?
    c) What is the probability that the barbershop will have fewer than six customers?

5.39 Airplanes arrive at a small airport at the rate of three per hour, according to a Poisson distribution.
    a) What is the probability that there will be exactly three arrivals in a given one-hour period?
    b) What is the probability that there will be exactly six arrivals in a *two-hour* period?
    c) Explain, in words, why it is more probable to have exactly three arrivals in one hour than it is to have exactly six arrivals in two hours.

5.40 Consider the values of $P(x)$ for $\lambda = 1$ in Table II.
    a) Show for these values that $E[x] = \lambda = 1$.
    b) Show that $V[x] = \lambda = 1$.

EXERCISES

5.41 It is possible to generalize the binomial distribution to include the class of problems where there are more than just two outcomes. Suppose that there are k different (i.e., distinguishable) outcomes, and the probabilities of occurrence of these outcomes are $\pi_1, \pi_2, \ldots, \pi_k$. Assuming these k outcomes to be mutually exclusive and exhaustive, it must be true that $\pi_1 + \pi_2 + \cdots + \pi_k = 1$. Now, assume that we want to determine the (joint) probability of n_1 outcomes of the first kind, n_2 outcomes of the second kind, up to n_k outcomes of the kth kind, where $n = n_1 + n_2 + \cdots + n_k$. An extension of Formula (3.6) for combinations ($_nC_x$) gives the number of ways these objects could occur in n trials, where $n = n_1 + n_2$

$+ \cdots + n_k$. Multiplying this formula by the appropriate probabilities results in a probability distribution called the *multinomial distribution*.

Multinomial distribution:

$$P(n_1, n_2, \ldots n_k) = \frac{n!}{n_1! n_2! \cdots n_k!} \pi_1^{n_1} \pi_2^{n_2} \cdots \pi_k^{n_k}.$$

a) Use the multinomial distribution to determine the probability of receiving, in seven random draws (with replacement) from an inventory of spare parts, two units of Part A, four units of Part B, and one unit of Part C. Inventory consists of 20 units of Part A, 10 units of Part B, and 5 units of Part C.

b) Suppose the probability that an individual has type O blood is 0.45, the probability of type A is 0.40, the probability of type B is 0.10, and the probability of type AB is 0.05. For six randomly selected donors at a blood bank, what is the probability that three people will have type O, two will have type A, and one will have type AB blood?

5.42 The Pascal (or negative binomial) distribution is appropriate when one is interested in determining the probability that n Bernoulli trials will be required to produce r successes. This probability is

$$P(n) = \frac{(n-1)!}{(r-1)!(n-r)!} \pi^r (1 - \pi)^{n-r} \qquad \text{for } n \geq r.$$

For example, suppose an advertising agency is trying to evaluate the effects of a television commercial advertising swimming pool chlorine. A caller is assigned to randomly contact residential dwellings in Phoenix, where 40% of the homes have pools.

a) What is the probability that it will take ten or fewer calls to find exactly five homes with pools? (Assume that all calls are answered politely.)

b) What is the average number of calls required in order to have five successes if $E[n] = r/\pi$?

c) What is the variance of the number of calls required in part (a) if $V[n] = r(1 - \pi)/\pi^2$?

5.43 A company hiring systems analysts has found that, on the average, they hire one person out of every 12 who come for a second interview. On the basis of these data, what is the probability that they will hire at least one of the next four people who come for a second interview? Are the assumptions of the binomial reasonable for this application? Explain.

5.44 If the two baseball teams playing in the World Series are exactly evenly matched for each game in the series:

a) What is the most likely number of games to be played in a best-out-of-seven series?

b) What is the most likely number of games if one team is always a 3:1 favorite?

5.45 The expected value of x in a series of repeated Bernoulli trials is defined as follows:

$$E[x] = \sum_{x=0}^{n} x({}_nC_x)\pi^x(1 - \pi)^{n-x}.$$

a) Use the above relationship to prove that the mean of the binomial distribution equals $n\pi$.

b) In the same manner, prove that the variance of the binomial distribution equals $n\pi(1 - \pi)$.

5.46 A classical example of the Poisson distribution resulted from a study of the number of deaths from horse kicks in the Prussian Army from 1875 to 1894. The data for this example are:

Deaths per Corps (per Year)	Observed Frequency
0	144
1	91
2	32
3	11
4	2
5 and over	0
Total	280

a) Fit a Poisson distribution to this data. (*Hint:* Note that there were 196 deaths from the 280 observations; hence the mean death rate was $196/280 = 0.700$.) How good does the Poisson approximation appear to be?

b) Do the assumptions of the Poisson distribution seem reasonable in this problem? Explain.

5.47 Use Table I to determine the binomial probabilities for $n = 10$ and $\pi = 0.20$, and then use Table II to find the Poisson approximation to these probabilities. Comment on how good the Poisson approximation is in this case. Graph both distributions on the same sheet of paper.

5.48   Using the Poisson distribution in the third column of Table 5.5, show by calculation that its mean and variance are both equal to 3.8.

5.49   Assume that the customers of the Shark Loan Company (Exercise 2.40) arrive at the loan office at a rate of $\lambda = 12$ customers per day.
   a) Graph the probability mass function for all values of x between 5 and 18, inclusive.
   b) Suppose the people at Shark have noticed that approximately 50 people walk by their office each day. If we assume [from part (a)] that there is a constant probability that each of these people will enter, the binomial distribution can be used to describe the arrival rate.
      i) What is the appropriate value of π if we assume 12 of the 50 people enter? What will μ and σ^2 be for this binomial distribution?
      ii) Superimpose on your graph from part (a) the probability mass function of the binomial for values of x between 5 and 18.

5.50   Out of 10 salespeople, seven (call them group A) make sales on 20% of their calls. The other three (call them group B) make sales on 50% of their calls.
   a) What is the average percentage of sales to calls for all ten salespeople?
   b) Suppose the sales manager selects three of these salespeople at random to assign to a new territory. What is the probability that exactly two of them will be from group A?
   c) Suppose we follow one of the salespeople in group A on the next five calls, each of which is considered independent of any of the others. What is the probability that this person makes more than one but fewer than four sales in those five calls?

5.51   Sears has tested ten Die Hard batteries, each five years old, to see whether each battery will start a car after sitting out in zero degree weather for 24 hours. On the basis of past experience, Sears estimates the probability to be 0.08 that a battery will not start the car. Find the binomial probability that five of the ten will fail. Use a Poisson approximation to solve this problem. Compare the variance of the binomial distribution for this problem with the variance of the Poisson distribution.

5.52   The following bridge hand almost broke up the 1955 world championship tournament because it occurred twice in the space of a few hours.

Spades:	A, K, 9, 5	Hearts:	Q, 8, 4
Diamonds:	J, 7, 3	Clubs:	10, 6, 2

   a) Write down an expression representing the probability of the occurrence of this hand, assuming the cards are dealt randomly.

b) Determine a nonprobabilistic explanation as to why such a bridge hand might have occurred twice in the 1955 world championship.

5.53 The following proofs are not easy. The reader interested in them may wish to consult a more mathematically oriented text.

a) Prove $E[x] = \sum_{x=0}^{\infty} x \dfrac{e^{-\lambda}\lambda^x}{x!} = \lambda$ (for the Poisson distribution).

b) Prove $V[x] = \lambda$ (for the Poisson distribution).

c) Prove $\lim_{n \to \infty} {}_nC_x \pi^x (1 - \pi)^{n-x} = \dfrac{e^{-\lambda}\lambda^x}{x!}$ (for $\lambda = n\pi$ a constant).

d) Prove that $\sum_{\text{all } x} P(x) = 1.0$ for the binomial distribution.

5.54 A Certified Public Accountant has been asked by a client, a department store, to assist in determining the effects on customer service of eliminating a clerk in one department. The probability of a customer's arriving for service is the same at all moments in time regardless of what has happened in previous moments. If the Certified Public Accountant analyzes this queueing (waiting-line) problem mathematically, the frequency distribution generally used would be the
a) normal   b) binomial
c) hypergeometric   d) Poisson

USING THE COMPUTER

5.55 A university library has 2000 fluorescent lights that fail at random times, independently of one another. The library custodian estimates the probability that each light fails on any given day to be 0.001. It takes the custodian 30 minutes to change a light. What is the probability that it will take the custodian longer than 2 hours to change all the lights that fail on any given day? Use the binomial distribution.

5.56 Repeat Problem 5.55 using a Poisson approximation.

5.57 The marketing department of Procter and Gamble mailed 1000 questionnaires, one half to randomly selected low-income households, and one half to middle-income households. Out of the first 100 questionnaires returned, 65 were from the middle-income households, and 35 were from the low-income households. What is the probability of 65 or more questionnaires returned from the middle-income families if the two types of households have the same response rate?

CASE PROBLEM

5.58 The First National Bank is deciding on the amount of money to place in their MONEY MOVER machine each weekend. They obviously do not want to run short and have unhappy customers. On the other hand, they do not want to have too much, as they earn a considerable amount of interest each day by investing their "float" (uncommitted money). Customers of the bank can withdraw either $25 or $50 once during the weekend. The bank's vice president estimates that the probability is 0.01 that each of their 15,200 customers will use the machine. About half of the customers withdraw $25, and half withdraw $50. The money is placed in the machine in packets of $25, so that a customer who wants $50 gets two packets of $25. The bank vice president decides to place in the machine enough money so that the probability of running short is less than 0.001. How much should be placed in the machine?

GLOSSARY

Binomial distribution: Discrete probability mass function (p.m.f.) involving independent, repeated, Bernoulli trials. (A Bernoulli trial is a replication of an experiment in which one of two mutually exclusive and exhaustive outcomes must take place.)

Binomial formula: $P(x) = {}_nC_x \pi^x (1 - \pi)^{n-x}$.

Binomial parameters:

$$\mu = E[x] = n\pi;$$
$$\sigma^2 = V[x] = n\pi(1 - \pi)$$

Expectations for a binomial proportion:

$$p = \frac{x}{n}; \ E[p] = \pi, \ V[p] = \frac{\pi(1 - \pi)}{n}.$$

Hypergeometric distribution: Discrete probability mass function (p.m.f.) involving sampling without replacement from a finite population. Involved with calculating probabilities such as x_1 out of N_1 *and* x_2 out of N_2.

Hypergeometric p.m.f.:

$$P(x_1 \text{ out of } N_1 \text{ and } x_2 \text{ out of } N_2) = \frac{({}_{N_1}C_{x_1}) \cdot ({}_{N_2}C_{x_2})}{{}_{(N_1 + N_2)}C_{(x_1 + x_2)}}.$$

Poisson distribution: Discrete p.m.f. involving events which take place relatively infrequently when only a small subinterval of time is being considered.

Poisson p.m.f.:

$$P(x) = \begin{cases} \dfrac{e^{-\lambda}\lambda^x}{x!} & x = 0, 1, 2, \ldots; \\ 0 & \text{otherwise.} \end{cases}$$

Mean and variance of the Poisson distribution:

$$\mu = E[x] = \lambda;$$
$$\sigma^2 = V[x] = \lambda.$$

Probability Theory: Continuous Random Variables

SIX

6.1 INTRODUCTION

Thus far, we have examined experiments involving only a discrete set of outcomes and limited ourselves to discrete probability values. As we indicated earlier, however, an outcome set can be continuous as well as discrete, which implies that the random variable in an experiment must be able to assume a continuous form. Fortunately, most probability theory is basically the same for discrete and continuous random variables, and the formulas presented in Chapters 3 and 4 hold for both cases.

Probability functions defined in terms of a continuous random variable are usually referred to as **probability density functions** (abbreviated **p.d.f.**), or *density functions*. In this chapter we will discuss the similarities and differences between density functions for continuous random variables and the probability mass functions described in Chapters 4 and 5. Some of the more useful density functions, those used in applications dealing with a wide range of experimental situations and decision problems, will then be introduced.

6.2 PROBABILITY DENSITY FUNCTIONS

If an experiment can result in an infinite, noncountable number of outcomes, then the random variable defined must be continuous. Typically, whenever the value of a random variable is "measured" rather than "counted," a continuous random variable is defined. Examples in which outcomes are measured rather than counted include the water level in a lake, the pressure in a steam boiler, the distance between two points, and the number of ounces in a cereal box. The values of the random variables in these examples can be any of an infinite number of values within a defined interval, (a, b). If we redefine these examples as the errors (i.e., deviations from the mean) in measuring water level, pressure, distances, or ounces, then such a random variable could be any number from minus b to plus b (b could be infinity in some cases).

When we say a random variable can be *any* number between two limits, we mean any value is at least *theoretically* possible. For practical purposes we usually cannot measure such variables with very great accuracy. For example, the length of long-distance business phone calls can, theoretically, be any number from zero to infinity. However, the time is usually recorded in minutes or in minutes and seconds. With electronic timing devices the length of a long-distance call might be recorded to the nearest millisecond, but this degree of accuracy is usually not warranted. Hence, while such a variable is theoretically continuous, for measurement purposes it is more nearly discrete. We will see in this chapter that in such applications, continuous variables are often more convenient to manipulate than discrete variables.

Recall that for a probability mass function the value of $P(\mathbf{x} = x)$ was represented by the *height* of the spike at the point $\mathbf{x} = x$. One of the major differences between discrete and continuous probability distributions is that this representation no longer holds. As we will elaborate more thoroughly in this chapter, *probability for a continuous p.d.f. is represented by the area between the x-axis and the density function.*

To better understand the concept of a probability density function, consider the case of a business person who is trying to estimate the probabilities of various levels of sales for a new product to be marketed. In order to estimate the probability of sales as high as 7000 units, this person decides to assess probabilities using seven different intervals of 1000 units each. Let us assume that Table 6.1 shows this probability assessment, where $\mathbf{x}$ = number of possible sales of the new product.

This probability distribution can be represented in a histogram, just as was done in Chapter 1, and smoothed with a frequency polygon by connecting the class marks of the intervals. The resulting histogram is shown in Fig. 6.1.

The choice of a class interval of size 1000 for this problem was quite arbitrary. Almost any size interval could have been used. For example, suppose that we now decrease the width of the classes to an interval of, say, 500, or 250, or even to a class interval of 1. Figure 6.2 illustrates how the frequency polygon for these data changes as the width of the interval decreases (and, correspondingly, as the *number* of intervals increases). Let us denote the width of the class interval in a histogram as Δx (read "delta-x"), where $\Delta x = 1000$ for Fig. 6.1, $\Delta x = 500$ for Fig. 6.2(a), and $\Delta x = 250$ for Fig. 6.2(b). In these three figures *the height of*

TABLE 6.1 **Probabilities of sales**

Interval (a, b)	Midpoint; Class Mark	Probability
$0 < x \leq 1000$	500	0.00
$1000 < x \leq 2000$	1500	0.05
$2000 < x \leq 3000$	2500	0.25
$3000 < x \leq 4000$	3500	0.30
$4000 < x \leq 5000$	4500	0.25
$5000 < x \leq 6000$	5500	0.10
$6000 < x \leq 7000$	6500	0.05
	Sum = 1.00	

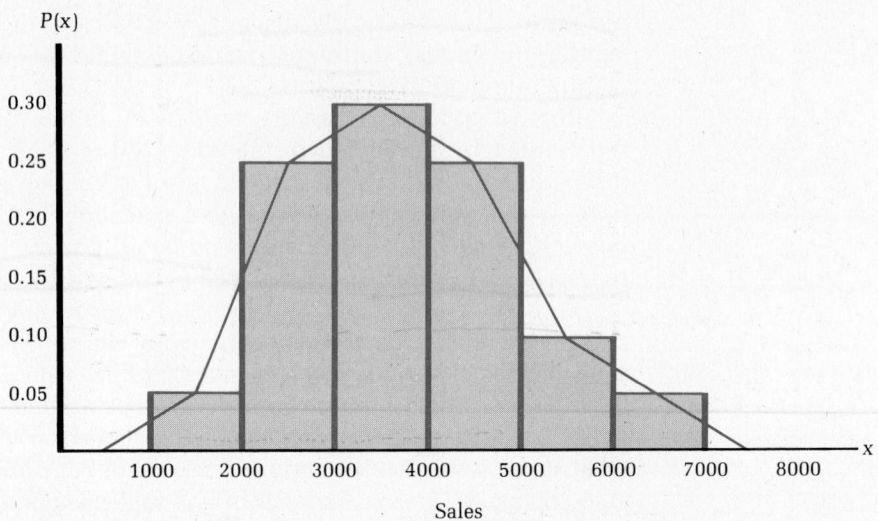

FIGURE 6.1 **Frequency polygon and histogram based on Table 6.1.**

the histogram indicates the probability that **x** *falls in the interval.* Thus, we can determine a probability such as $P(a \leq x \leq b)$ by summing the heights corresponding to each of the events that satisfy $\{a \leq x \leq b\}$.

Probability as Note what happens as $\Delta x \rightarrow 0$ (compare Figs. 6.1, 6.2, and 6.3). As the
an Area size of the intervals gets smaller and smaller, the frequency polygon begins to look more and more like a continuous function. Note particularly in Fig. 6.3 that the sum of the *heights* of the histograms begins to closely

FIGURE 6.2 **The frequency polygon for two different class sizes.**

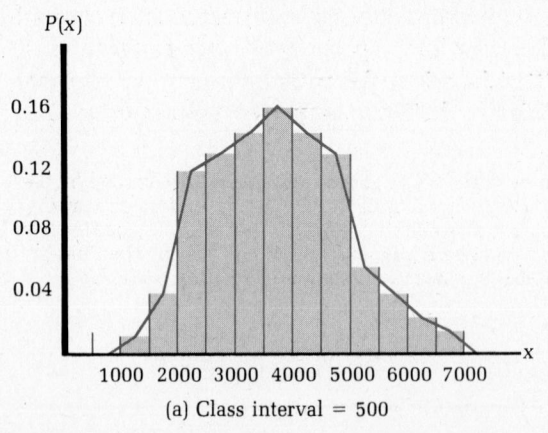

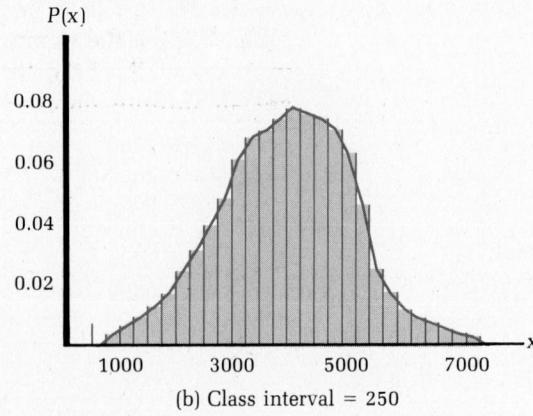

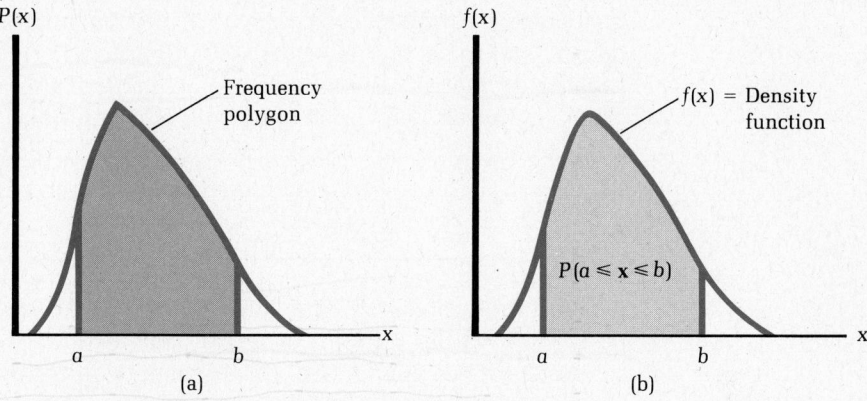

FIGURE 6.3 **(a) Discrete p.m.f. (b) Continuous p.d.f.**

approximate the *area* under the frequency polygon. Using calculus, it can be shown that at the limit, as $\Delta x \to 0$ (i.e., when the variable becomes continuous),

> The probability that the random variable x falls between the two values a and b, $P(a \leq x \leq b)$, exactly equals the area under the frequency polygon between a and b.*

Figure 6.3 illustrates the transition from a discrete p.m.f. to a continuous probability density function (p.d.f.). In order to maintain a clear distinction between them we will label the vertical axis for the mass function $P(x)$ and the vertical axis for the density function $f(x)$. The value of $f(x)$ is thus the height of the continuous function at a specific point $x = x$.

As the width of the class interval decreases and becomes closer and closer to zero, the number of classes (or events) under consideration must increase until, at the limit (that is, when the interval size $\to$ zero) there are an *infinite* number of classes between any two values of x. The

---

* More formally, at the limit, as $\Delta x \to 0$, the width of the class interval is denoted by the symbol dx instead of Δx. The frequency polygon is now called a density function, and the height of the density function at $x = x$ is denoted as $f(x)$. Finally, the summation sign becomes an integral sign, $\int_a^b$, where this integral sign is interpreted to mean "the limit of summation as $\Delta x \to 0$." Putting all this together, we obtain the following result for continuous random variables:

$$P(a \leq x \leq b) = \lim_{\Delta x \to 0} \sum_a^b P(x)\Delta x = \int_a^b f(x)dx$$

$$= \text{Area under the curve from } a \text{ to } b.$$

histogram in this case becomes an *infinite* number of infinitesimally narrow spikes set side by side. According to the rules of probability, the probability that any one of these spikes will occur is $(1/\infty)$, which is zero. Thus, an important fundamental rule of continuous random variables is:

> The probability that any one specific value takes place is zero when the random variable is continuous.

Because the probability of a single point is now zero, we can determine probability values only for intervals, such as $P(a \leq x \leq b)$.

Note in Fig. 6.3(b) that the frequency polygon is called a *density function* when the variable x is continuous. As we have indicated, the probability that x falls in the interval $a \leq x \leq b$ is given by the **area under the density function**, and not by the height of the density function. It is very important *not* to make the mistake of thinking that $f(x)$ represents probability. The value of $f(x)$ merely represents how high (or "dense") the function is at any specified value of x. It cannot represent probability, for we already pointed out that $P(x = x) = 0$ in the continuous case. To repeat what we said earlier,

> For continuous random variables:
> $$P(a \leq x \leq b) = \text{Area under } f(x) \text{ from } a \text{ to } b. \qquad \textbf{(6.1)}$$

For a continuous random variable it makes no difference whether the endpoints a and b are included in the interval or not, since the probability of observing any one specific point, such as exactly a or exactly b, equals zero. Thus, for a continuous random variable,

$$P(a < x < b) = P(a \leq x < b) = P(a < x \leq b) = P(a \leq x \leq b).$$

A probability density function (p.d.f.) is thus the description of a population (an experiment) when the variable x is continuous (just as a probability mass function is the description when x is discrete). The description of the population in the case of a p.d.f. must indicate the value of $f(x)$ for all possible values of x. Since there are an infinite number of values of x, a p.d.f. is usually not described by a table, but either by a graph [such as Fig. 6.3(b)] or by a formula. Let us give an example of a function representing a p.d.f. Then, we specify the two properties that all probability density functions must satisfy.

Example 6.1. The number of tons of crushed stone used by a state highway department each week varies, depending on the type of road

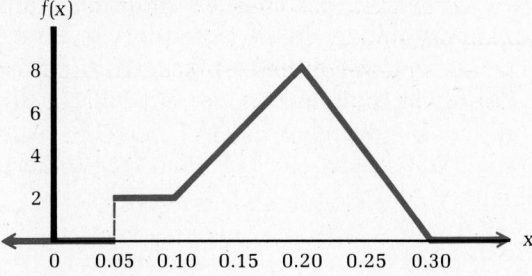

FIGURE 6.4 **Probability density function for Example 6.1.**

projects underway and the weather during that week. Fig. 6.4 shows a probability density function for the tons of crushed stone used per week, **x**, in units of 1000 tons.

The probability that values of **x** will occur is measured by the area under the probability density function, $f(x)$. The probability that **x** equals a specific value, say, $P(x = 0.15)$, is zero. Since a single point has no mathematical width, the area (height × width) above it is zero regardless of the height. Thus, the probability that the highway department will use exactly 0.15(1000) = 150 tons in a given week is zero.

Also, it is obvious in Fig. 6.4 that probability is not measured by the height of $f(x)$ alone. At the point x = 0.20 (200 tons), the height of $f(x)$ is 8.0. This cannot measure probability, since a probability value must always lie between zero and one.

A probability density function must satisfy two basic properties that are similar to those for a probability mass function. The major difference between the two is that, while neither $f(x)$ nor $P(x)$ can be negative, the values of $f(x)$ do not necessarily have to be less than or equal to 1.0. On the other hand, it must be true that the total area under $f(x)$, from $-\infty$ to $+\infty$, has to equal 1.0 (for the same reason that $\Sigma P(x) = 1$ in the case of a discrete random variable).

Properties of all probability density functions:

1. $f(x) \geq 0$:   The density function is never negative.
2. $P(-\infty \leq x \leq \infty) = 1$:   The total area under the density function always equals 1.0.*

* This property can be expressed, using calculus, as follows:

$$\int_{-\infty}^{\infty} f(x)dx = 1.0$$

Let us examine Fig. 6.5 to show how these properties hold for the probability density function of Example 6.1. First, the function $f(x)$ is always positive. It never drops below the x-axis. Next, using geometry to find the area under the function, we see that the sum is 1.0 for the areas of the subdivided rectangles and triangles. For example, the area under $f(x)$ between the values x = 0.10 and x = 0.20 is subdivided into a rectangle with

$$\text{area} = (\text{height} \times \text{width}) = (2 \times 0.10) = 0.20$$

and a triangle with

$$\text{area} = \frac{1}{2}(\text{base} \times \text{height}) = \frac{1}{2}(0.10 \times 6) = 0.30.$$

The same type of calculation gives all the other subdivided areas under the probability density function $f(x)$ in Fig. 6.5. The sum of these areas is 1.0. Note that the function $f(x)$ equals zero beyond the bounds of x < 0.05 and x > 0.30. There can be no area under the curve beyond these bounds.

Also, we can apply Formula (6.1) to find the probability of any *interval* of values for **x**. Referring to Fig. 6.5, we find,

$$P(0.10 < \mathbf{x} < 0.20) = 0.20 + 0.30 = 0.50;$$
$$P(0.20 \leq \mathbf{x} \leq 0.25) = 0.20 + 0.10 = 0.30.$$

For a continuous random variable, it does not matter whether the endpoint is included in the interval or not. The addition of the endpoint changes the probability only by the value of $\left(\dfrac{1}{\infty}\right) = 0$; and so it has no effect.

Example 6.2. Consider a mail-order book club that is interested in the pattern of its subscribers' payments for the books they order. At the time when their order is filled, the members of this club are sent a bill which states that payment is due within five weeks of the shipping date.

FIGURE 6.5 **Probability measures based on Fig. 6.4.**

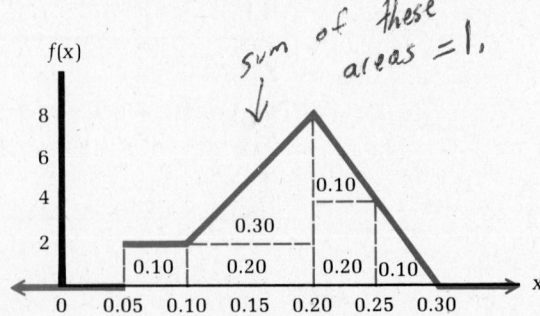

TABLE 6.2 **Example distribution of book club payments**

(1)	(2)	(3)	(4)	(5)
Week Payment was Received x	Number of Payments Received f	Relative Frequency $\dfrac{f}{N} = P(x)$	Cumultative Relative Frequency F(x)	0.08x − 0.04
1	3,940	0.039	0.039	0.040
2	12,012	0.120	0.159	0.120
3	20,133	0.201	0.360	0.200
4	27,852	0.279	0.639	0.280
5	36,063	0.361	1.000	0.360
Sum	100,000	1.000		1.000

In analyzing recent records of this book club, it was found that only about 16% of all customers remit their payment within the first two weeks; most people wait until week four or five to send in their money. Column (2) of Table 6.2 shows the number of payments received in each of the five weeks for the past 100,000 orders; the relative frequency of each value of *x* is shown in column (3).

Discrete case. Suppose we now plot the mass and cumulative functions describing the probability, for each of the five weeks, that a randomly selected customer will pay his or her bill. Figure 6.6 shows the graph of these functions. The tops of the probability lines in Fig. 6.6(a) form a fairly straight line that has a slope of 0.08 and a vertical intercept of − 0.04. This relation is shown by the dotted line in the figure. An equation for P(x) represented by a curve connecting the tops of the probability values can thus be written as $f(x) = 0.08x - 0.04$. The fact that this equation quite accurately describes P(x) for the discrete values x = 1, 2, 3, 4, and 5 is shown by comparing columns (3) and (5) in Table 6.2.

Continuous Case The probabilities shown in Table 6.2 assume that the book club can distinguish only which week (*x* = {1, 2, 3, 4, or 5}) a customer's payment was received. But suppose we want a continuous approximation based on the assumption that a payment can be received at *any* value of *x* between 0 and 5 (that is, x need not be an integer).

To find this approximation, we need a function that yields a probability of $P(0 \le x \le 1) = 0.039$ (or 0.04 when rounded) that the payment was

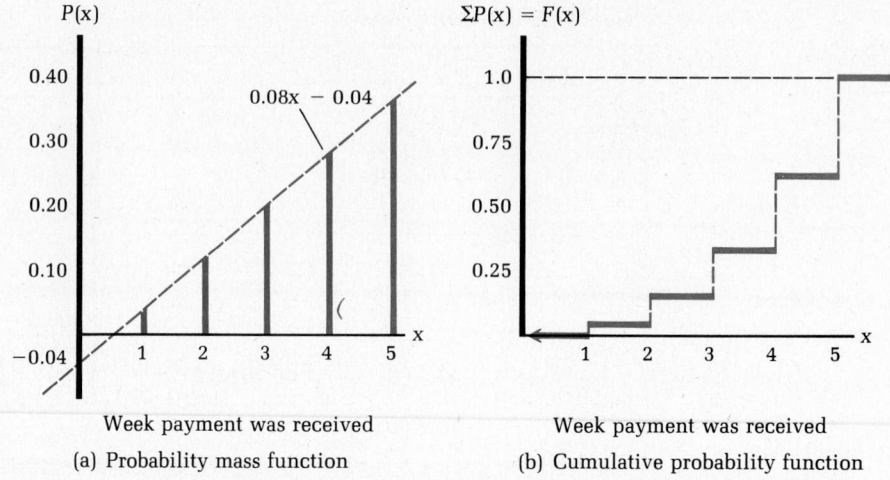

(a) Probability mass function

(b) Cumulative probability function

FIGURE 6.6 **Probability functions representing mail-order payments from Table 6.2, columns (3) and (4).**

received *between* the shipping date and the end of the first week, a probability of $P(1 < x \le 2) = 0.12$ that the payment was received in the second week, and so forth, with the last probability [$P(4 < x \le 5)$] equal to 0.361 (or 0.36 when rounded). Although we will not present the process, it is not hard to determine that the function that yields these probabilities is 0.08x. All values of **x** that do not fall between 0 and 5 must have a probability of zero (since payments are received only between $x = 0$ and $x = 5$). Hence, our formal definition of the probability density function for this example is the following:

Density function:
$$f(x) = \begin{cases} 0.08x & 0 \le x \le 5; \\ 0 & \text{otherwise.} \end{cases}$$

This continuous approximation is graphed in Fig. 6.7.

In the discrete case, the probability $P(x = 1) = 0.039$ represents the probability that a payment was received *during* the first week, meaning from 0 to 1 week. In the continuous case we approximate this value by $P(0 \le x \le 1)$. Because *area* is interpreted as probability in the continuous case, $P(0 \le x \le 1)$ is given by the area of the small triangle in the lower left-hand corner of Fig. 6.7. This triangle has a width of $w = 1.0$ and a height of $h = 0.08$. Since the area of a triangle is $A = \frac{1}{2}wh$, this area is $\frac{1}{2}(1.0)(0.08) = 0.04$. That is, $P(0 \le x \le 1) = 0.04$, which agrees very closely with the probability for the discrete case 0.039. To take another example, consider $P(2 \leq x \leq 3)$. The total area in this case consists of a triangle with area $\frac{1}{2}wh = \frac{1}{2}(1.0)(0.08) = 0.04$, plus a rectangle with area $wh = (1.0)(0.16) = 0.160$. The sum of these two areas is $P(2 \leq x \leq 3) = 0.200$, which again agrees very closely with the discrete case, $P(x = 3) = 0.201$. The remaining probabilities can be determined similarly.

Now, let us see if this density function satisfies the two properties of all probability density functions. First, as shown by Fig. 6.7, the function never goes below the x-axis; hence, the condition $f(x) \geq 0$ is satisfied. Second, we can show that the total area under the function and above the x-axis equals 1.0 by summing the areas of the individual triangles and rectangles in Fig. 6.7. Or we can find the area under the large triangle; this triangle has width $w = 5$ and height $h = 0.40$; hence, the total area is $\frac{1}{2}(5.0)(0.40) = 1.0$.

Although we have limited ourselves to integer values in assessing probabilities in this example, it is not necessary to do so. The probability $P(1.7 < x < 3.5)$, for instance, can be determined by the same methods of geometry applied above. The reader should realize that using geometry is possible in our book-club example because the function $f(x)$ is a simple one (a straight line), for which we know how to find areas. For other more complex density functions, geometry cannot be used. In such cases, the methods of integral calculus can sometimes be used to find the appropriate area under $f(x)$, although this approach usually is not very

FIGURE 6.7 **Continuous density function for example of book-club weekly payments.**

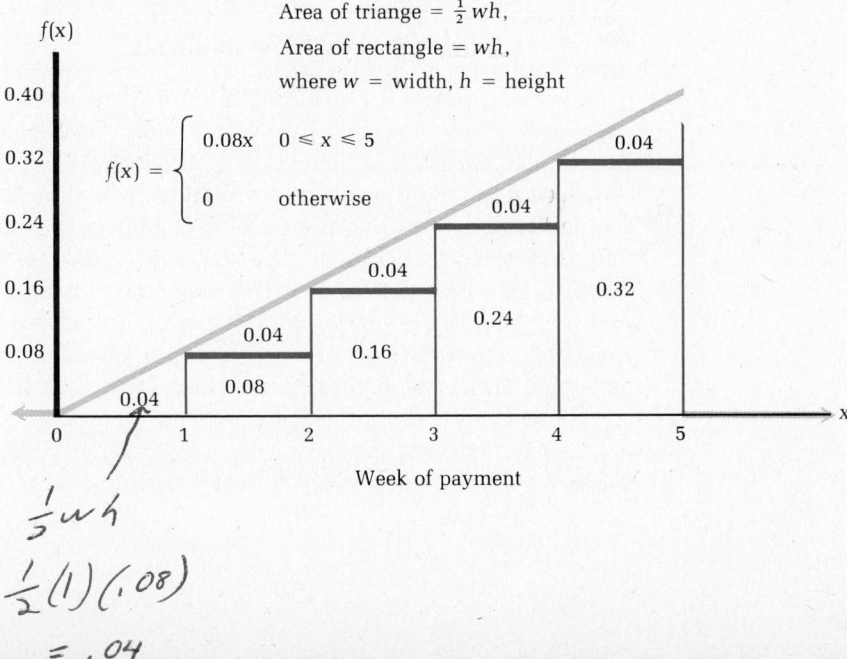

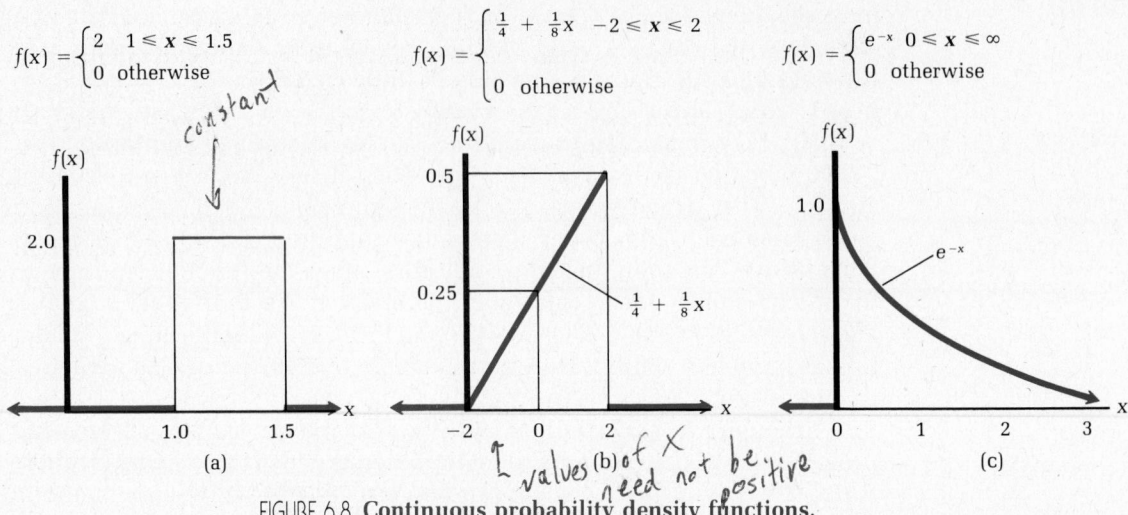

$$f(x) = \begin{cases} 2 & 1 \leqslant x \leqslant 1.5 \\ 0 & \text{otherwise} \end{cases}$$

constant

$$f(x) = \begin{cases} \frac{1}{4} + \frac{1}{8}x & -2 \leqslant x \leqslant 2 \\ 0 & \text{otherwise} \end{cases}$$

$$f(x) = \begin{cases} e^{-x} & 0 \leqslant x \leqslant \infty \\ 0 & \text{otherwise} \end{cases}$$

values of X need not be positive

FIGURE 6.8 **Continuous probability density functions.**

convenient. Fortunately, such areas (probabilities) for commonly used density functions have been calculated and have been listed in tables. Hence, one seldom needs to use integral calculus in solving practical problems.

Examples of Other p.d.f.'s   A number of frequently used probability density functions will be investigated later in this chapter. For now, the diagrams in Fig. 6.8 should suffice to give you some insight into different types of density functions. In the first diagram the density function is seen to be a constant, equal to 2.0 for values between $x = 1.0$ and $x = 1.5$ and equal to zero for all other values of **x**. In this case the random variable **x** might represent the number of bushels (in millions) of wheat the USSR buys from the U.S.A. in a given year. Perhaps the U.S.A. won't sell less than 1.0 million or more than 1.5 million; hence, $\{1.0 \leq \textbf{x} \leq 1.5\}$.

In the second diagram, the function $f(x)$ is the straight line $\frac{1}{4} + \frac{1}{8}x$ for values between $x = -2$ and $x = 2$ (and zero otherwise). The reader should verify that the area under this function is 1.0 This function emphasizes that the values of **x** need not be positive. For instance, a value of $x = -1$ in our book-club example might mean that the customer prepaid (i.e., paid one week before the bill went out). Finally, in the third diagram, $f(x)$ is a decreasing function for x between zero and infinity.*

* In Fig. 6.8(c) the symbol e denotes the same nonrepeating, nonterminating decimal we encountered in Section 5.7 (that is, $e \approx 2.71828$).

This type of function is often used in situations where **x** represents the *time between* certain events. A classic example is the instance in which **x** represents the time interval between the beginning and the end of a service, such as a checkout at a supermarket, or the waiting time for a customer before a service begins, such as waiting in a doctor's office, or waiting in line at an attraction or ride in Disney World. Analysis of such probability density functions is important for improving customer services and for hiring the appropriate number of employees during different periods of the work week.

6.3 SIMILARITIES BETWEEN PROBABILITY CONCEPTS FOR DISCRETE AND CONTINUOUS RANDOM VARIABLES

As we have indicated, the basic difference between a probability mass function and a probability density function is that in the former case probabilities are measured by the *height* of the function, while in the latter case probabilities are measured by *areas* under the function. Most of the probability concepts developed in Chapter 4 are similar for both discrete and continuous random variables. Formal representations of many of the formulas will *look* different, but will not be different in meaning. They look different because wherever a summation occurs in a formula involving probabilities of a discrete random variable, it is replaced in the continuous case by an integral. That is, rather than summing the values representing the heights of a probability mass function, we calculate probabilities by integrating a probability density function. Although we will present the concept of a cumulative distribution function (c.d.f.) for continuous random variables, as well as their mean and variance, we will not present the formulas for a joint distribution, marginal distribution, conditional distribution, independence, and covariance. These formulas, however, can be derived directly from the comparable concepts in Chapter 4.

Cumulative Distribution Function

As before, the function $F(x)$ represents the probability that the random variable **x** assumes a value less than or equal to some specified value, say, b. To calculate $F(b)$ in the continuous case, it is necessary to *integrate* $f(x)$ over the relevant range, rather than to sum discrete probabilities. Since integrating $f(x)$ is equivalent to finding the area under $f(x)$, the **cumulative distribution function $F(x)$** at the value b is defined as follows (see Fig. 6.9):

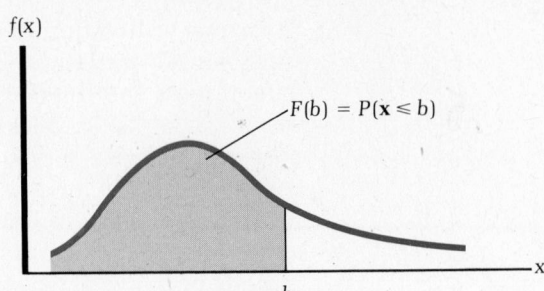

FIGURE 6.9 Illustration of $F(x)$.

Cumulative distribution function:*

$$F(b) = P(x \leq b) = \text{all area under } f(x) \text{ for } x \leq b. \tag{6.2}$$

It is important to keep in mind that while the values of $F(x)$ represent probabilities, the values of $f(x)$ do not represent probabilities. We will not extensively illustrate how to calculate cumulative functions, but rather present a table of values of $F(x)$ derived by summing the probabilities in column 5 of Table 6.2.

Once a cumulative distribution function has been tabled (as in Table 6.3), it can be used to find the probabilities of many events of interest. The following formulas, which will prove especially useful, have been applied to the data in Table 6.3.

1. $P(x \leq b) = F(b)$, by definition of the cumulative distribution function. This gives the probability of observing any value equal to or smaller than a given value b. It is represented by the area to the left of the value b under the density function. Using Table 6.3, $P(x \leq 3) = F(3) = 0.36$. This area is lined in Fig. 6.10.

2. $P(x \geq a) = 1 - P(x < a) = 1 - F(a)$. The area to the right of a value a in the right tail of a distribution may be found using $F(a)$ and the complement rule. For example, $P(x \geq 2) = 1 - F(2) = 1 - 0.16 = 0.84$. This area is shaded in Fig. 6.10.

3. $P(a \leq x \leq b) = F(b) - F(a)$. The probability that x falls between a and b can be found by subtracting the area to the left of a from the

---

* Using calculus, $F(b) = \int_{\infty}^{b} f(x)dx$. Exercise 6.37 asks the reader to verify the formula for $F(x)$ for the three density functions graphed in Fig. 6.8.

TABLE 6.3 **Selected values of $F(x)$ for the example of book-club weekly payments, derived from areas in Fig. 6.7**

x	0	1	2	3	4	5
F(x)	0	0.04	0.16	0.36	0.64	1.00

area to the left of b, to obtain the amount of area between a and b. Using Table 6.3, $P(1 \le x \le 4) = F(4) - F(1) = 0.64 - 0.04 = 0.60$.

This probability is shown in Fig. 6.11 using both the probability density function and the graph of the cumulative distribution function.

> The cumulative distribution is an increasing curve starting at zero and rising to the value 1.0 as more and more probability is accumulated by including larger and larger values of **x**. The *level* of the cumulative function gives the cumulative probability at any value of **x**. The *difference* in the cumulative distribution levels between any two values of **x** gives the probability of the event that **x** lies in that interval.

FIGURE 6.10 **Reproduction of Fig. 6.7.**

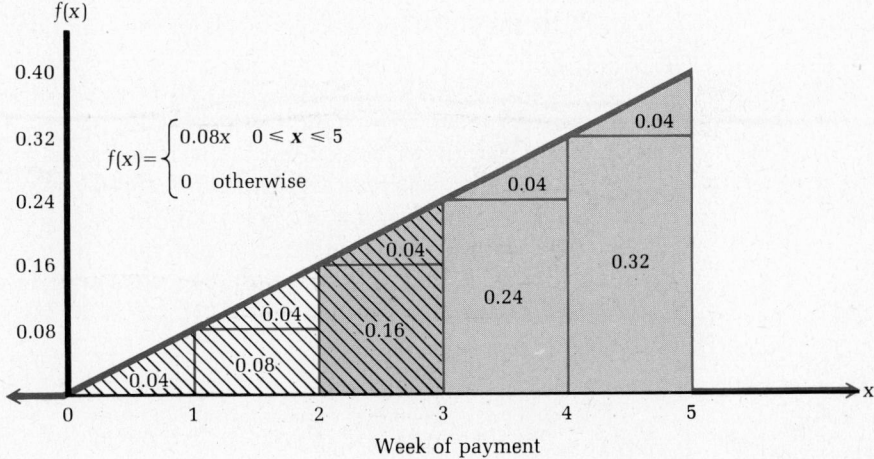

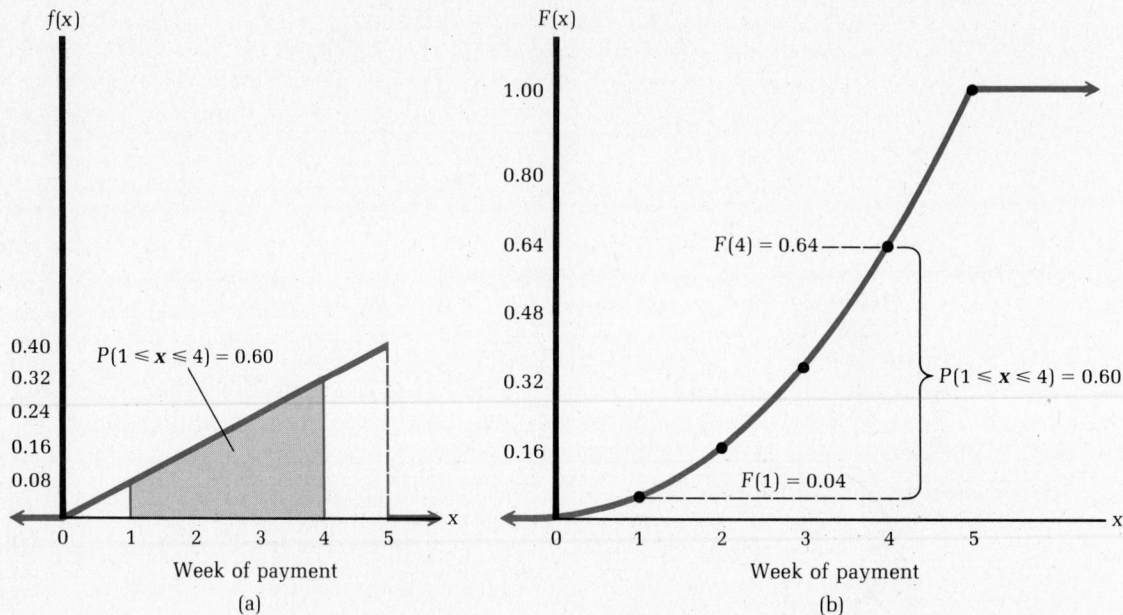

FIGURE 6.11 **Probability density and cumulative distribution functions for week of payment.**

This result is identical to that obtained by finding the area under the density function between the same two values of **x**. In the density function of Fig. 6.11(a) the shaded area gives the probability, $P(1 \leq x \leq 4)$. In the cumulative distribution of Fig. 6.11(b) the probability of this event is given by the difference in the levels of the function, $F(4) - F(1)$.

Mean and Variance*

The summary measures of central location and dispersion are as important in describing a density function as they were in describing a mass function. The mean, which we again denote as $\mu = E[x]$, is our measure of central location. It is the center of gravity, or balance point, of the probability density function. For example, in the book-club example the average payment time can be shown to be $\mu = E[x] = 3\frac{1}{3}$ weeks. That is, the average customer pays the bill $3\frac{1}{3}$ weeks after receiving it. You might picture the book-club p.d.f. (see Fig. 6.10) as balanced on a fulcrum that is located at $x = 3\frac{1}{3}$.

* This section may be omitted without loss of continuity.

The variance and standard deviation of a p.d.f. are denoted by the same symbols used in the discrete case. That is, the variance is $\sigma^2 = V[x]$, and the standard deviation is $\sigma = \sqrt{V[x]}$. For our illustration involving book-club payments, these measures of dispersion can be shown to be:

$$\text{Variance} = V[x] = \sigma^2 = 1.39;$$

$$\text{Standard deviation} = \sigma = \sqrt{V[x]} = \sqrt{1.39} = 1.18.$$

This standard deviation can be interpreted by using the rule of thumb from Chapter 1. For a p.d.f. this rule is:

$\mu \pm 1\sigma$ will contain approximately 68% of the probability (area),

$\mu \pm 2\sigma$ will contain approximately 95% of the probability (area).

Calculating the probability (area) within ($\mu \pm 1\sigma$) and within ($\mu \pm 2\sigma$) may not be an easy task, even with the use of calculus. A clever reader using geometry, however, should be able to verify the probabilities (areas) given below for the book-club example. (*Hint:* Subdivide the area into a rectangle and a triangle.)

Interval	Probability
$\mu \pm 1\sigma = 3\frac{1}{3} \pm 1.18 = 2.15$ to 4.51	0.6287
$\mu \pm 2\sigma = 3\frac{1}{3} \pm 2(1.18) = 0.97$ to 5.69	0.9623

Note how well these calculated probabilities agree with the rule of thumb despite the fact that the p.d.f. is not symmetric.

For the most part, we will not be concerned in this book with the *process* of calculating $E[x]$ and $V[x]$ for continuous functions, although we emphasize again that it is important for the reader to understand the concepts involved. We therefore present below (but do not elaborate on) the formulas for calculating the mean and the variance for a continuous random variable x. The reader should verify that these formulas are the same as those presented in Chapter 4, except for two features. First, the *summation* in the continuous case is represented by an integral sign ($\int$) in substitution for the summation symbol (Σ) used in the discrete case. Second, the probability measures used as *weights* in Formulas (6.3) are areas (height $\times$ width) given by $f(x)dx$. These are applicable for the continuous case in substitution for the height of the probability mass function, $P(x)$, which is used for discrete random variables.

Mean of x:	$E[x] = \mu_x = \int_{-\infty}^{\infty} xf(x)dx;$	
Expectation of $g(x)$:	$E[g(x)] = \int_{-\infty}^{\infty} g(x)f(x)dx;$	**(6.3)**
Expectation of x^2:	$E[x^2] = \int_{-\infty}^{\infty} x^2 f(x)dx;$	
Variance of x:	$V[x] = E[(x - \mu_x)^2] = E[x^2] - (E[x])^2.$	

Define. *Probability density function (p.d.f.), two properties of all probability density functions, cumulative distribution function [F(x)].*

PROBLEMS

6.1 The random variable x = time of arrival of the first customer at a certain store (where x = hours) is defined as:

$$f(x) = \begin{cases} 2x & \text{for } 0 \le x \le 1, \\ 0 & \text{otherwise.} \end{cases}$$

a) Sketch this p.d.f.
b) Show that the total area under $f(x)$ equals 1.0.
c) What is the probability that the first customer will arrive before time $x = \frac{1}{2}$?

6.2 Use Problem 6.1 to answer the following.
a) Verify that x = 0.707 represents the *median* of the distribution. (*Hint:* Half the area lies to the left of the median.)
b) Would you guess that the mean $(E[x])$ of the p.d.f. is larger or smaller than the median? (*Hint:* Remember Chapter 2.)
c) Explain, in words, what significance the mean and median have in this particular example.

6.3 Write down the values of $F(x)$ for the following five values of x, using the function described in Problem 6.1:

x:	0	$\frac{1}{2}$	0.707	1.0	3.7
F(x):	?	?	?	?	?

6.4 A study of the length of 20-meter oil pipeline sections found that they varied from 5 cm too short to 5 cm too long. An expert has used the following p.d.f. to describe the error in the case of a randomly selected pipe section:

$$f(x) = \begin{cases} \frac{1}{10} & \text{for } -5 \leq x \leq 5, \\ 0 & \text{otherwise.} \end{cases}$$

a) Sketch this p.d.f. and show that its area is 1.0.
b) What are the mean and the median length of all pipe sections according to this p.d.f.?
c) What is the probability that a section is more than 3 cm too long? What percent of sections in this population will be more than 2 cm over or under the correct length?

6.5 The cumulative distribution function given below is appropriate for Problem 6.4.

$$F(x) = \begin{cases} 0 & x < -5, \\ \frac{1}{10}x + \frac{1}{2} & -5 \leq x \leq 5, \\ 1.0 & x > 5. \end{cases}$$

a) Sketch this function. What are the values of $F(-5)$ and $F(5)$?
b) Find and interpret the value $F(-2)$.
c) Find the value of $F(3)$. Does the complement of this value agree with your answer to the first part of Problem 6.4(c)?

6.6 Consider the following p.d.f., where x represents the height in inches of lettuce plants one week after planting.
a) Show that the area under this function equals 1.0.
b) What is the probability that a plant will exceed 2 inches?
c) Find $E[x]$ the average height of the plants. (*Hint:* Do not try a formula

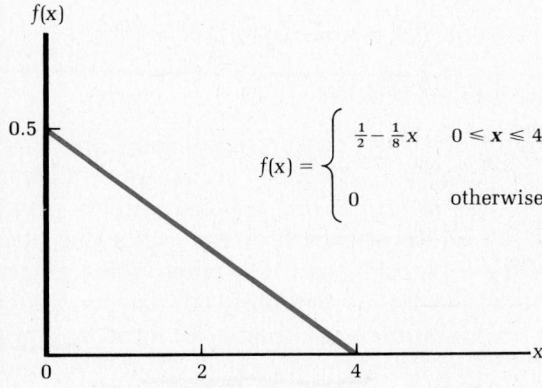

$$f(x) = \begin{cases} \frac{1}{2} - \frac{1}{8}x & 0 \leq x \leq 4 \\ 0 & \text{otherwise} \end{cases}$$

unless you know calculus. Instead, note that the mean of our book-club example, which also had a triangular density function, is two-thirds of the distance from the lower end of the triangle.)

d) For this p.d.f., σ = 0.94. Use this value to find the area between μ − 1σ and μ + 1σ. (*Hint:* Find this area by dividing the interval into a rectangle and a triangle.) Is the area you found close to the 68% rule of thumb? If not, can you offer an explanation?

e) Find the area between μ − 2σ and μ + 2σ. Is this area close to 95%?

f) Find the values of $F(0)$, $F(2)$, $F(4)$, and $F(5.3)$.

6.7 With the normalization of diplomatic relationships between the U.S. and China, numerous business opportunities have opened up. Suppose a U.S. manufacturer has decided to export a certain type of printing calculator to China. This manufacturer estimates that annual demand (d) can be represented by the following p.d.f., where d is in thousands of units:

$$f(d) = \begin{cases} (d - 30)/450 & \text{for } 30 \le d \le 60, \\ 0 & \text{otherwise.} \end{cases}$$

a) Sketch this function and verify that the area under the function equals 1.0.

b) Use the hint in Problem 6.6(c) to find $E[d]$ for this p.d.f. If the net profit is $10 per calculator, what is the expected total net profit for the year?

c) Assume that 60,000 calculators are shipped. What is the probability that there will be an inventory of at least 10,000 units at the end of the year?

d) For this problem, $V[d]$ = 50. What is the variance of total expected annual profit? (*Hint:* Use Rule 4 from Section 4.4.) Using the rule of thumb from Chapter 2, find two values such that the probability is 0.95 that total expected annual profit lies between these two values.

6.4 THE NORMAL DISTRIBUTION

In the eighteenth century, scientists noted a predictable regularity about the frequency with which certain "errors" occur, especially errors of measurement. Suppose, for example, that a blacksmith is supposed to cut a piece of metal to a width of exactly $\frac{5}{16}$ in.; while this blacksmith produces pieces that are $\frac{5}{16}$ in. wide *on the average*, some pieces are in "error" — they are slightly too wide or slightly too narrow. Experiments producing errors of this nature were found to form a symmetrical distribution, originally called the *normal curve of errors*. The continuous probability distribution that such an experiment approximates is usually referred to as the *normal distribution*, or sometimes the *Gaussian distribution*, after an early researcher, Karl Gauss (1755–1855).

The normal distribution is undoubtedly the most widely known and used of all distributions. Many natural phenomena — length, height, and thickness of animals or plants; medical counts of sugar, white blood cells, incidence of inner-ear disease; and behavioral, emotional, or psychological measures of human actions, aptitudes, or abilities — tend to result in normal distributions. The distribution of measured errors — deviations from a specified standard in diameters of pistons, cylinders, or gun barrels, weight of packaged products, and even lengths of yardsticks — also tends to be normal, as does the distribution of the degree of perfection in production processes of many kinds.

Because the normal distribution approximates many natural phenomena so well, it has evolved into a standard of reference for many probability problems. In addition, under certain conditions the binomial and the Poisson distributions can be approximated by the normal distribution. The normal distribution is so important in the theory of statistics that a considerable portion of the sampling, estimation, and hypothesis-testing theory discussed in the remainder of this book is based on the characteristics of this distribution.

Characteristics of the Normal Distribution

The **normal distribution** is a continuous distribution in which x can assume any value between minus infinity and plus infinity $\{-\infty \leq x \leq \infty\}$. Two parameters describe the normal distribution: μ, representing the mean, and σ^2, representing the variance.* A normal distribution with mean μ and variance σ^2 often is denoted by the symbol $N(\mu, \sigma^2)$. The normal density function is a symmetrical, bell-shaped probability density function,† as it appears in the graph in Fig. 6.12.

---

* Beginning students of statistics are sometimes confused by the fact that for the normal distribution the general symbols μ and σ^2 are used to represent the specific parameters of this distribution rather than some different ones such as n and π in the bionomial or λ in the Poisson. This is merely traditional, since the normal is the most commonly used distribution.

† The normal p.d.f. contains two constants: π (where $\pi = 3.14159\ldots$) and e (where $e = 2.71828\ldots$). The normal p.d.f. is given below.

Normal density function, $N(\mu, \sigma^2)$:

$$f(x) = \frac{1}{\sigma\sqrt{2\pi}} e^{-\frac{1}{2}\left(\frac{x-\mu}{\sigma}\right)^2} \qquad \text{for } -\infty \leq x \leq \infty. \tag{6.4}$$

Since π and e are constants, if μ and σ are known, it is possible to evaluate areas under this function by using calculus (integration). Fortunately, such areas (probabilities) have been tabulated for one special case (the standardized normal), so it is not necessary to use calculus.

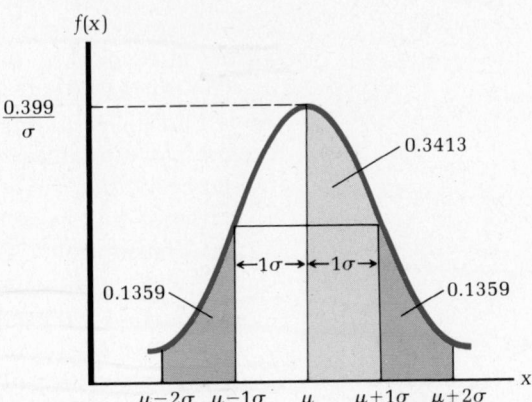

FIGURE 6.12 **Normal distribution with mean μ and standard deviation σ.**

Note that in Fig. 6.12 the area under the curve from μ to μ + 1σ is 0.3413. Thus, $P(\mu \le x \le \mu + 1\sigma) = 0.3413$. By symmetry, $P(\mu - 1\sigma \le x \le \mu + 1\sigma) = 2(0.3413) = 0.6826$. We can also see that $P(\mu + 1\sigma \le x \le \mu + 2\sigma) = 0.1359$; hence

$$P(\mu - 2\sigma \le x \le \mu + 2\sigma) = 0.6826 + 0.1359 + 0.1359 = 0.9544.$$

The rule of thumb we have been using throughout this book is now seen to be based on the normal distribution. The extent to which the intervals we have considered previously have differed from our rule of thumb reflects the fact that these distributions have not been normal distributions.

It is important to remember that all normal distributions have the same bell-shaped curve pictured in Fig. 6.12 regardless of the values of μ and σ. The value of μ indicates where the center of the "bell" lies, while σ represents how spread out (or wide) the distribution is. Note that in Fig. 6.12 the height of the density function at the point $x = \mu$ is 0.399/σ.* In this book, however, we will not be concerned with the height of the density function. In fact, in sketching the normal distribution we often will not indicate any of the values of the vertical axis. Three specific normal distributions, corresponding to σ = 0.5, σ = 1.0, and σ = 1.5, are shown in Fig. 6.13.

Examples of Normal Distributions

Even with the limited information we have presented thus far about the normal distribution we can answer a number of probability questions. The following two examples will serve the reader as a review of that

---

* This fact can be derived from Formula (6.4) by substituting μ for x and observing that $e^0 = 1$, and $1/\sqrt{2\pi} = 0.399$. Thus, if σ = 1.0, then $f(\mu) = 0.399/1.0 = 0.399$. When σ = 0.5, $f(\mu) = 0.399/0.5 = 0.798$, and if σ = 1.5, $f(\mu) = 0.399/1.5 = 0.266$.

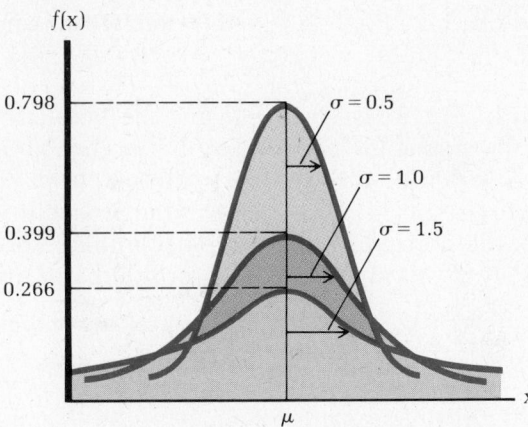

FIGURE 6.13 **Three normal distributions with different standard deviations but the same mean.**

information and as illustrations of the use of the normal distribution in statistical problem-solving.

Example 6.3. (*Unit value of a fund*) The random variable **x** representing the daily change in the unit value of an income fund is normally distributed with mean $\mu_x = 10$ cents and standard deviation $\sigma_x = 0.8$ cents; that is, $N(10, 0.8^2)$. This information is sufficient to completely determine the probability of any event concerning the values of **x**.

For instance, what is the probability that for a randomly selected day the unit value of the fund will change by more than 10 cents? Since the normal distribution is symmetrical, and 10 is the median as well as the mean, the answer is $\frac{1}{2}$. Now, to move to a slightly more difficult question, what is the probability that the unit value change will be less than 9.2 cents? Using Fig. 6.14, we see that 9.2 is the value exactly one standard deviation below the mean (that is, $10.0 - 9.2 = 0.8 = \sigma_x$). The probability $P(\mathbf{x} \le 9.2)$ is represented by the shaded area under the function $f(x)$.

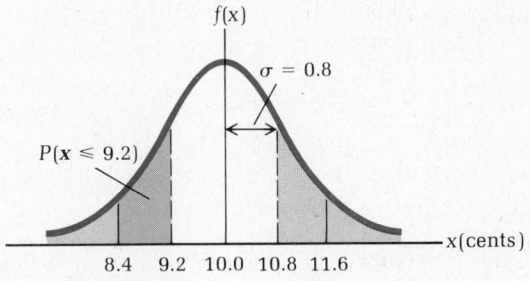

FIGURE 6.14 **Example of normal distribution.**

Unit value change = **x**, $\mu_x = 10.0$, $\sigma_x = 0.8$ cents

The probability $P(x \leq 9.2)$ is thus exactly equivalent to the probability

$$P(x \leq \mu - 1\sigma),$$

as shown in Fig. 6.14. There remains the problem of determining how much of the area of the normal distribution lies to the left of $\mu - 1\sigma$. To calculate $P(x \leq \mu - 1\sigma)$, we first recall that, from Fig. 6.12, $P(\mu - 1\sigma \leq x \leq \mu + 1\sigma) = 2(0.3413) = 0.6826$. If the probability within this interval is 0.6826, the probability of lying outside this interval is $1 - 0.6826 = 0.3174$. Half of this amount (0.1587) would be in the left tail. That is,

$$P(x \leq \mu - 1\sigma) = \tfrac{1}{2}(\text{complement of area within } \mu \pm 1\sigma);$$

$$P(x \leq 9.2) = \tfrac{1}{2}(1 - 0.6826) = \tfrac{1}{2}(0.3174) = 0.1587.$$

Finally, for this same example, suppose that we want to determine the probability that the daily change in unit value is between 11.2 and 12 cents. This probability is given by the area under the curve between 11.2 and 12.0. To find this area using calculus, we would integrate the normal density function [in Formula (6.4)] with $\mu_x = 10$ and $\sigma_x = 0.8$ using as the lower and upper limits of integration, 11.2 and 12.0. Another way to determine this area would be to find a table already calculated for a normal distribution with $\mu = 10$ and $\sigma = 0.8$. We will come back to this problem shortly to reject both these methods and seek an easier way.

Example 6.4. (*Tire life*) Suppose that the random variable y, representing the tread life in miles of a certain new radial tire, is normally distributed with mean $\mu_y = 40{,}000$ miles, and standard deviation $\sigma_y = 3{,}000$ miles [$N(40{,}000, 3000^2)$]. This information is sufficient to determine completely the probability of any event concerning the values of y. For example, $P(y \geq 40{,}000) = \tfrac{1}{2}$, since half of the probability in a normal distribution lies on each side of the mean. Or suppose we calculate the probability that a tire of this model selected at random has a tread life greater than 46,000 miles. Using Fig. 6.15 we see that 46,000 is exactly two standard deviations above the mean $(46{,}000 - 40{,}000 = 6{,}000 = 2\sigma_y)$. The probability $P(y \geq 46{,}000)$ is represented by the shaded area under the function $f(y)$ in Fig. 6.15. The probability $P(y \geq 46{,}000)$ is also equivalent to the $P(x \geq \mu + 2\sigma)$ in the graph of the normal distribution in Fig. 6.12. Since we already know that $P(\mu - 2\sigma \leq x \leq \mu + 2\sigma) = 0.9544$, the value of $P(x \geq \mu + 2\sigma)$ is clearly equal to one-half of the complement of 0.9544. Thus

$$P(y \geq 46{,}000) = \tfrac{1}{2}(1.000 - 0.9544) = \tfrac{1}{2}(0.0456) = 0.0228.$$

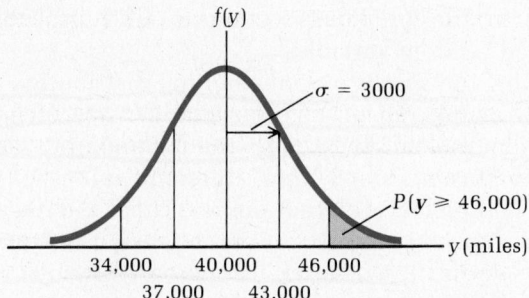

Tread life of tire = y, μ_y = 40,000, σ_y = 3000 miles   FIGURE 6.15 **Tire-life example.**

Finally, we might ask about the probability that tread life, for this example, will fall between 44,500 and 47,500 miles. Again, the answer can be determined in two ways. Using calculus, one could integrate the normal p.d.f. from 44,500 to 47,500 with μ_y = 40,000 and σ_y = 3,000. Or one could use a table of areas already calculated for the precise parameters, μ_y = 40,000 and σ_y = 3,000. Both of these methods are unsatisfactory, however, first because it is too tedious to evaluate a new integral every time one investigates a different set of parameters or new values of the random variable, and secondly because no such tables exist (there obviously cannot be tables listing the *infinite* number of possible values of μ and σ).

6.5 STANDARDIZED NORMAL

Values of x for the normal distribution usually are described in terms of how many standard deviations they are away from the mean. The value x = 200, for example, has little meaning unless we know in what units x was measured (e.g., feet, miles, pounds). On the other hand, the statement that x is one standard deviation larger (or smaller) than the mean can be given a very precise interpretation, as it is always meaningful to talk of x being a certain number of standard deviations above (or below) the mean, no matter what value σ assumes or on what scale the variable x is measured. Now, if x if measured in terms of standard deviations about the mean, it is natural to describe probability values in the same terms — that is, by specifying the probability that x will fall within so many standard deviations of the mean. There are three whole-unit intervals, the first two of which we have referred to often as our "rule of thumb": $\mu \pm 1\sigma$, $\mu \pm 2\sigma$, and $\mu \pm 3\sigma$. Recall that we used the first two of these in the previous section to find probabilities for normally distributed random variables.

Treating the values of x in a normal distribution in terms of standard deviations about the mean has the advantage of permitting all normal distributions to be compared to one common or standard normal distribution. In this standard form, different values of μ and σ no longer generate completely different curves, since x is measured only about μ and all distances away from μ are expressed in terms of multiples of σ. In other words, it is easier to compare normal distributions having different values of μ and σ if these curves are transformed to one common form, which is called the **standardized normal distribution**. The standardized variable represents a new random variable (one we discussed in Chapter 4), namely, $z = (x - \mu)/\sigma$. The standardized variable, by definition, has a mean of zero $(\mu_z = 0)$ and a standard deviation of one $(\sigma_z = 1)$. Note that if the standard deviation is one, the variance must also be one since $\sigma^2 = 1.0$ when $\sigma = 1.0$.

This process of standardization gives a hint about the best method of attack in answering questions concerning a normal probability distribution. Instead of trying to solve directly a probability problem involving a normally distributed random variable x with mean μ and standard deviation σ, an indirect approach is used. We first convert the problem to an equivalent one with a normal variable measured in standard deviation units, called a *standardized normal variable*. A table of standardized normal values (Table III) can then be used to obtain an answer in terms of the converted problem. Finally, by converting back to the original units of measurement for x, we can obtain the answer to the original problem. Figure 6.16 is a schematic outline of this method of solving probability problems.

FIGURE 6.16 **Problem-solving tactic using the standardized normal.**

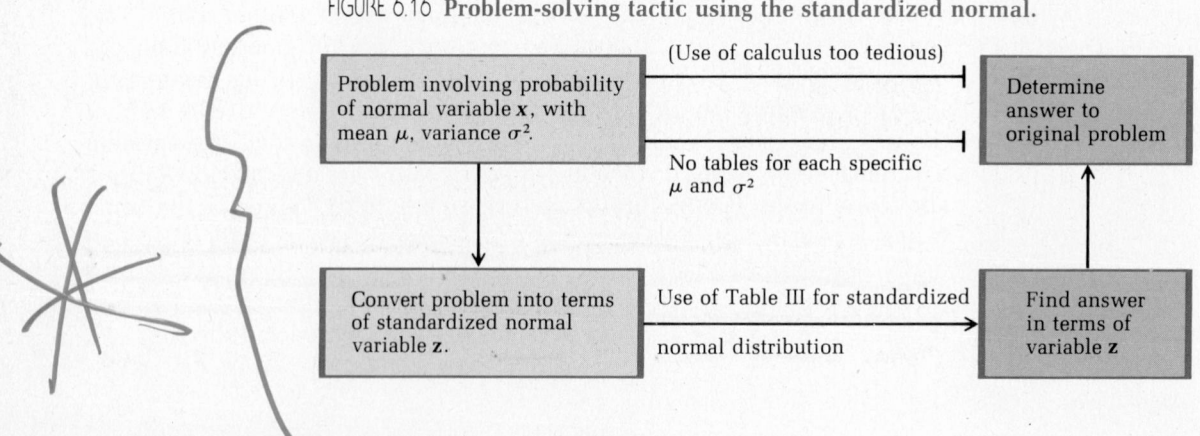

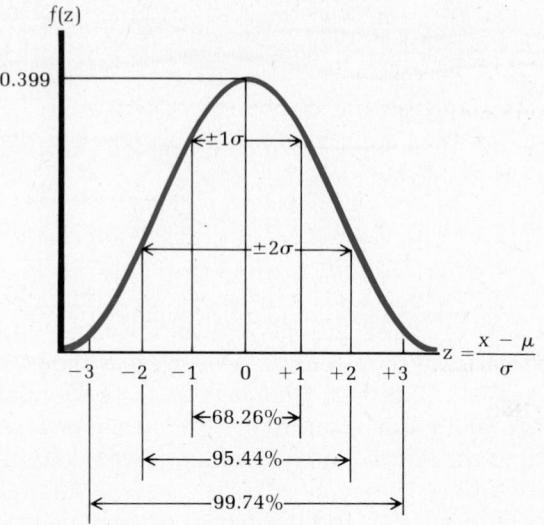

FIGURE 6.17 **Standardized normal distribution.**

We discussed in Section 4.4 the process of transforming a random variable x (whether normally distributed or not) with mean μ and standard deviation σ into a standardized measure with mean zero and standard deviation one. We now add the additional fact that if the original random variable (x) is normally distributed, then the standardized variable z will be normally distributed also. Thus, $z = (x - \mu)/\sigma$ is N(0, 1).

Standardized normal random variable:

$$z = \frac{x - \mu}{\sigma} \text{ is N(0, 1).} \tag{6.5}$$

This function is shown graphically in Fig. 6.17. The reader should compare Fig. 6.17 with Fig. 6.12 and verify that the former is merely a special case of the latter where $\mu = 0$ and $\sigma = 1$.*

The interpretation of z-values is relatively simple — because $\sigma^2 = V[z] = 1.0$, whatever value z has indicates how many standard deviations x is from the mean. For example, if $z = 1.56$, this indicates that the corresponding x-value is exactly 1.56 standard deviations above the mean

---

* The density function for the standardized normal variable z is

$$f(z) = \frac{1}{\sqrt{2\pi}} e^{-\frac{1}{2}z^2} \tag{6.6}$$

of the variable x [i.e., $(x - \mu) = 1.56$]. Similarly, if $z = -2.81$, this means that the comparable value of x falls 2.81 standard deviations below the mean.

Using the Standardized Normal   Consider the two examples in the previous section involving normally distributed random variables, where

x = daily change in unit value of an income fund with $\mu_x = 10$, $\sigma_x = 0.8$;

and

y = tread life of tire in miles with $\mu_y = 40,000$, $\sigma_y = 3,000$.

Some probability questions were suggested there that we did not completely answer. To repeat, what is $P(11.2 \le x \le 12.0)$ and what is $P(44,500 \le y \le 47,500)$? The answer to each question is shown by the shaded areas under the normal curves in Figs. 6.18(a) and (b), respectively. Since we rejected the two proposed direct ways of answering these questions, we proceed now with the indirect approach, using the standard normal distribution.

In transforming the probability $P(11.2 \le x \le 12.0)$ into an equivalent one in standardized normal form, we must apply the transformation $z = (x - \mu)/\sigma$ to each part of the expression in parentheses. The value 11.2 is transformed into its equivalent form by first subtracting $\mu_x = 10.0$, and then dividing the result by $\sigma_x = 0.8$; the value 12.0 is transformed into its equivalent standardized form in exactly the same manner. Finally, we can think of the variable x as being transformed in the same way since the new variable, z, equals $(x - \mu)/\sigma$. Thus,

$$P(11.2 \le x \le 12.0) = P\left(\frac{11.2 - 10.0}{0.8} \le \frac{x - \mu}{\sigma} \le \frac{12.0 - 10.0}{0.8}\right) = P(1.5 \le z \le 2.5).$$

We follow the same process in transforming the probability

$$P(44,500 \le y \le 47,500)$$

into standardized normal form, except that in this case $\mu_y = 40,000$ and $\sigma_y = 3,000$:

$$P(44,500 \le y \le 47,500) = P\left(\frac{44,500 - 40,000}{3,000} \le \frac{y - \mu_y}{\sigma_y} \le \frac{47,500 - 40,000}{3,000}\right)$$

$$= P(1.5 \le z \le 2.5).$$

It is now obvious that we constructed our two unanswered probability questions to show how two diverse problems such as the unit value of a fund and tire life can both be reduced to the identical question in terms of the standardized normal. The fact that these probabilities are equivalent can be seen by comparing Figs. 6.18(a) and (b) with (c).

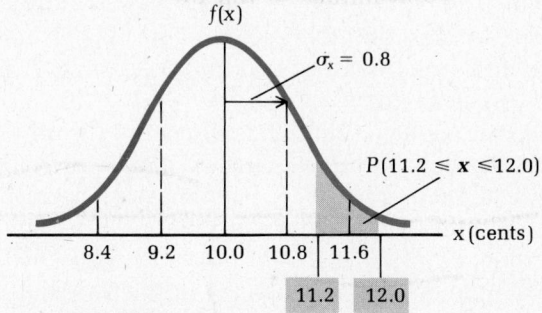

(a) Daily change in unit value of an income fund,
   x; $\mu_x = 10.0$, $\sigma_x = 0.8$

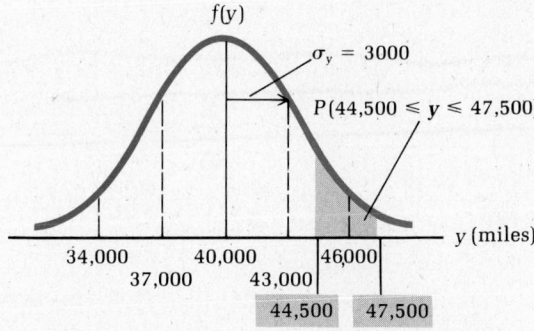

(b) Tread of life of tire, y; $\mu_y = 40,000$, $\sigma_y = 3000$

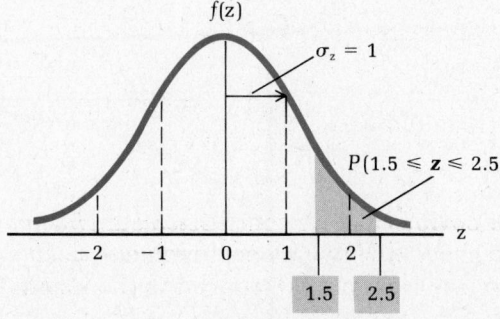

(c) Standardized normal variable z; $\mu_z = 0$, $\sigma_z = 1$

FIGURE 6.18 **Comparative normal distributions.**

Cumulative Distribution of the Standardized Normal

The problem at this point is: How does one evaluate probabilities in standardized form, such as $P(1.5 \leq z \leq 2.5)$? As we indicated previously, there are tables of standardized normal values (called z-values) for this purpose. Table III in Appendix C and on the inside back cover is one such table.

Before we describe the use of Table III, let us investigate $F(z)$, the cumulative distribution function for the variable z. This function, shown in Fig. 6.19, gives $P(z \leq z)$.

Note that we have plotted z-values only from -3 to $+3$, since very little area lies beyond these limits. At $z = 0$ (the mean of z), the value of $F(z)$ must be 0.50, since $z = 0$ represents the median of the z-values. Most of the other values in Fig. 6.19 should be familiar to you by now. For example, $F(-1) = 0.1587$. This value agrees with the one calculated in the example on the daily change in the unit value of an income fund, as we saw then that $P(x \leq \mu - 1\sigma) = 0.1587$. The value $F(-2) = 0.0228$ should also appear familiar, as this is the same value we calculated in the tire-life problem for $P(y \geq \mu + 2\sigma)$. Because of the symmetry of the normal distribution, $F(-2) = 1 - F(2) = P(y \geq \mu + 2\sigma) = 0.0228$.

Since the normal distribution is completely symmetrical, tables of z-values usually include only positive values of z. Thus, the lowest value in Table III is $z = 0$, and the cumulative probability at this point is $F(0) = P(z \leq 0) = 0.50$. Table III gives other values of z, to two decimal points, up to the point $z = 3.49$. The values of z to one decimal are read from the left margin in Table III, while the second decimal is read across the top. The body of the table gives the values of $F(z)$.

As we illustrate the use of Table III, we will consider four basic rules. The reader should try to understand (visualize) these rules, rather than to memorize them.

FIGURE 6.19 **Cumulative z-values.**

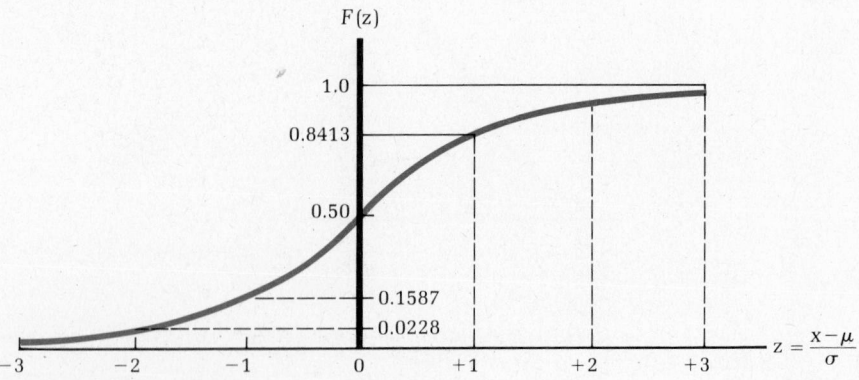

Rule 1. $P(z \leq a)$ is given by $F(a)$ when a is positive.

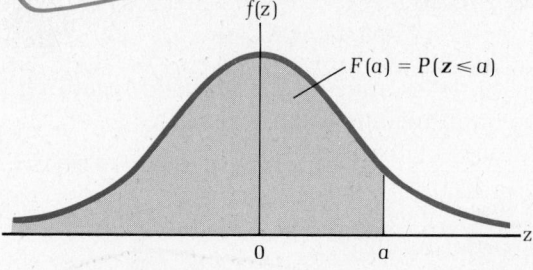

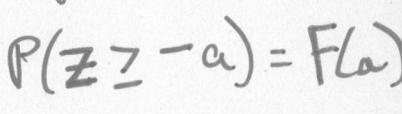

$$P(z \geq -a) = F(a)$$

We can illustrate this rule by determining the probability $P(y \leq 45,000)$ in the tire-life problem:

$$P(y \leq 45,000) = P\left(\frac{y - \mu_y}{\sigma_y} \leq \frac{45,000 - 40,000}{3,000}\right) = P(z \leq 1.67) = F(1.67).$$

The value $z = 1.67$ in Table III yields a cumulative probability of $F(1.67)$ $= 0.9525 = P(y \leq 45,000)$.

Rule 2. $P(z \geq a)$ is given by the complement rule as $1 - F(a)$.

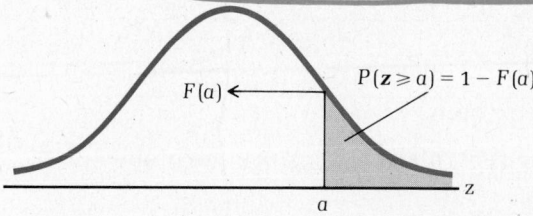

Rule 2 is merely the complement of Rule 1. For example, suppose we calculate $P(z \geq 2.00)$ for our tire example. Since $F(2.00) = 0.9772$,

$$P(z \geq 2.00) = 1 - 0.9772 = 0.0228.$$

This value agrees with the value calculated earlier,

$$P(y \geq \mu + 2\sigma) = 0.0228.$$

Rule 3. $P(z \leq -a)$ is given by $1 - F(a)$, where $-a$ is a negative number.

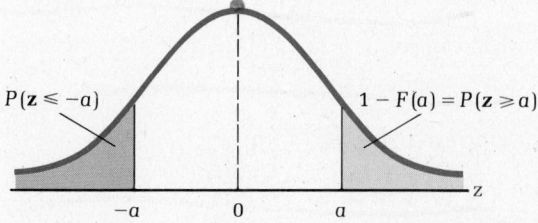

Rule 3 follows directly from Rule 2 because of the symmetry of the normal distribution, for we know that

$$P(z \le -a) = P(z \ge a) = 1 - F(a).$$

For this case, let's return to the problem regarding daily changes in the unit value of an income fund, where

$$P(x \le 9.2) = P(z \le -1.00).$$

Since $F(1.00) = 0.8413$, $P(x \le 9.2) = 1 - 0.8413 = 0.1587$, which agrees with our earlier result.

Rule 4. $P(a \le z \le b)$ is given by $F(b) - F(a)$.

The area under the curve between two points a and b is found by subtracting the area to the left of a, $F(a)$, from the area to the left of b, $F(b)$. This difference gives the area between the values a and b.

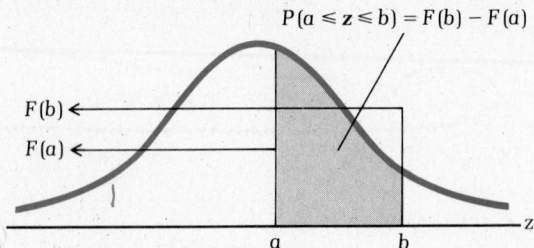

$$P(a \le z \le b) = F(b) - F(a)$$

Using this rule, we can solve the problem with which we began this section:

$$P(1.50 \le z \le 2.50) = F(2.50) - F(1.50).$$

From Table III, $F(2.50) = 0.9938$ and $F(1.50) = 0.9332$. Hence,

$$P(1.50 \le z \le 2.50) = 0.9938 - 0.9332 = 0.0606.$$

In the above example both a and b are positive, which makes calculating $F(b) - F(a)$ quite easy. Suppose, however, that we want to calculate a probability where either a or both a and b are negative. The latter case is fairly simple because, owing to symmetry,

$$P(-a \le z \le -b) = P(b \le z \le a) = F(a) - F(b).$$

As illustrated below,

$$P(-2.50 \le z \le -1.50) = P(1.50 \le z \le 2.50) = 0.0606.$$

Now consider a harder problem:

$$P(-2.00 \le z \le 1.50) = P(z \le 1.50) - P(z \le -2.00).$$

$$P(-a \le z \le b) = F(b) - [1 - F(a)]$$

From Rule 3, $P(z \leq -2.00) = 1 - F(2.00)$; hence,

$$P(-2.00 \leq z \leq 1.50 = F(1.50) - [1 - F(2.00)] = 0.9332 - (1 - 0.9772)$$
$$= 0.9332 - 0.0228 = 0.9104.$$

There are many other types of problems that can be solved using the standardized normal distribution. To illustrate these types of problems, we have included the following two extensions of our tire-life example.

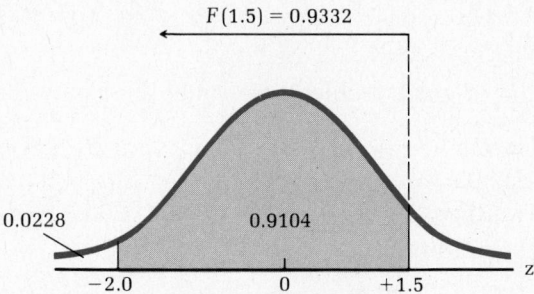

Example 6.5. An owner of a fleet of rental cars uses tires for which the tread life (miles of safe use) is described by the distribution $y \sim N(40,000, 3000^2)$. The owner wishes to establish a policy of replacing tires before they become unsafe or cause downtime for the rental cars. It is decided that all tires should be replaced after a specific number of miles of wear so that, on the average, only two tires out of 100 would wear out prior to replacement. The problem for the owner is to decide on the number of miles (M) at which replacement should occur. We need to find the value M so that $P(y \leq M) = 0.02$.

For this example we know the probability answer (0.02), but we do not know the value of M. To find M, however, we use the same procedure as before, transforming the problem into standardized terms:

$$P(y \leq M) = P\left[z \leq \frac{M - 40,000}{3,000}\right] = 0.02.$$

The probability given in this case is shown by the shaded area in Fig. 6.20. If $P(y \leq M) = 0.02$, then $P(y \geq M) = 1 - 0.02 = 0.98$. Since the value M is smaller than the mean of the distribution, the standardized value corresponding to M will be a negative number. In this type of problem the probability value closest to that desired is located within the table, and then the corresponding z-value is read from the top and left margins. From Table III, the value of z that gives $F(z) = 0.98$ is $z = 2.05$. Remembering that since we want a value below the mean, the *negative* value of z desired in this problem is $z = -2.05$. To convert

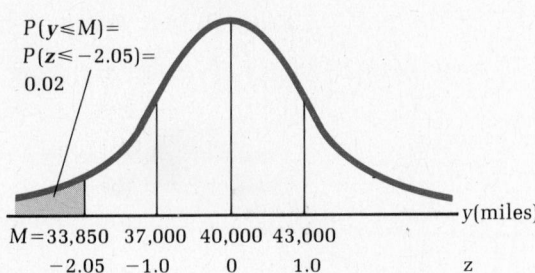

$P(y \leq M) =$
$P(z \leq -2.05) =$
0.02

y(miles)

FIGURE 6.20 **Illustration for Example 6.5.**

$M = 33,850 \quad 37,000 \quad 40,000 \quad 43,000$
$\quad\quad -2.05 \quad -1.0 \quad\quad 0 \quad\quad 1.0 \quad\quad\quad\quad z$

back to the original problem, we solve the formula $z = (M - \mu_y)/\sigma_y$ for M, as follows:

$$M = \mu_y + z\sigma_y.$$

Since $\mu_y = 40,000$, $z = -2.05$, and $\sigma_y = 3,000$, the only unknown value is M. By substitution,

$$M = 40,000 - 2.05(3,000) = 33,850.$$

The probability is 0.02 that a tire lasts less than 33,850 miles. The owner can replace tires when they have been used for 33,850 miles and be confident that only 2% of the tires are apt to cause a problem due to wearing out before replacement.

Our final example in this section involves the solution of a probability problem when both endpoints of the desired interval are unknown. The interval desired may be written as $a \leq y \leq b$, where both a and b are unknown.

Example 6.6. Referring to the tread life of the tires as in Example 6.5, we now consider the view of the manufacturer who may wish to set tread-life specifications for the tires produced. A common specification level is to set limits such that 95% of all tires produced will have a tread life within the **control limits.** To solve this problem, we need to determine two values a and b such that the probability is 0.95 that a randomly selected tire will fall between these values: $P(a \leq y \leq b) = 0.95$. It should be readily apparent that there is an infinitely large number of such intervals, depending on how the values of a and b are selected. If our interval is to include 95% of the area under the curve and exclude 5%, we could exclude all of the 5% above b, or exclude all of the 5% below a, or exclude part of it below a and part above b. In many cases, the best way to split the percentage to be excluded between the two tails will be specified in the problem. If it is not specified, then it is generally agreed that

The best way to split the percentage to be excluded is in a manner that makes the interval from a to b as small as possible. The smallest interval in this case is obtained by excluding equal areas in both the upper and lower tail of the distribution.*

This result follows from the Neyman-Pearson theorem that is proved in more advanced statistics books. It tells us that the best way to split our 5% to be excluded is to have 2.5% in each tail. Let's now use this result to solve the tire-life problem, $P(a \le y \le b) = 0.95$. Since 2.5% is to be excluded above b, we first need to find b so that $P(y \ge b) = 0.025$. Using the standardized transformation,

$$P(y \ge b) = P\left(\frac{y - \mu_y}{\sigma_y} \ge \frac{b - 40,000}{3,000}\right) = 0.025$$

$$= P\left(z \ge \frac{b - 40,000}{3,000}\right) = 0.025.$$

From Table III, $F(1.96) = 0.9750$. Thus, $P(z \ge 1.96) = 1 - 0.9750 = 0.025$, so that $z = 1.96$ is the appropriate value. Now, due to symmetry, if $z = 1.96$ cuts off 2.5% from the upper tail, $-z = -1.96$ cuts off 2.5% from the lower tail; hence, the smallest interval containing 95% of the total area under the curve is

$$P(-1.96 \le z \le 1.96) = 0.95.$$

We now translate these z-values back into the units in our tire-life problem. Let us designate by a the value of y representing the *lower* specification limit of our interval containing 95% of the total area. To find the value of a that corresponds to $z = -1.96$, we first need to substitute the letter a for the symbol y in the standardization formula. That is, when a is substituted for y,

$$z = \frac{y - \mu_y}{\sigma_y} \qquad \text{becomes} \qquad z = \frac{a - \mu_y}{\sigma_y}.$$

The value of a is the only unknown in the latter formula, as $z = -1.96$, $\mu_y = 40,000$, and $\sigma_y = 3000$. Hence we need to solve for a as follows:

$$-1.96 = \frac{a - 40,000}{3000} \Rightarrow a = 40,000 - 1.96(3000),$$

or

$$a = 34,120.$$

* As we will discuss later, this nontechnical statement is always true only for unimodal, symmetrical distributions such as the normal. For other types of distributions, further conditions must be specified.

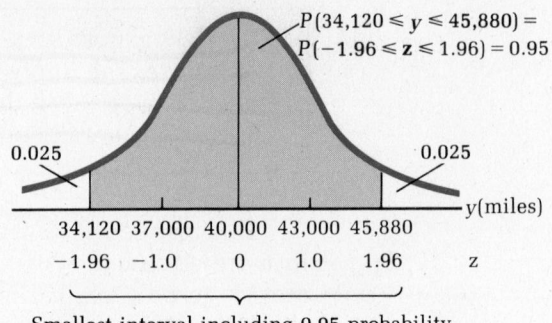

FIGURE 6.21 **Illustration for Example 6.6.**

Smallest interval including 0.95 probability

Similarly, if we let b denote that value of y representing the upper specification limit of our 95% interval, then

$$z = \frac{y - \mu_y}{\sigma_y} \quad \text{becomes} \quad z = \frac{b - \mu_y}{\sigma_y}.$$

The only unknown is b, since $z = 1.96$, $\mu_y = 40{,}000$, and $\sigma_y = 3000$. Hence,

$$1.96 = \frac{b - 40{,}000}{3000} \Rightarrow b = 40{,}000 + 1.96(3000),$$

or

$$b = 45{,}880.$$

The appropriate interval is thus $P(34{,}120 \le y \le 45{,}880) = 0.95$. The reader should verify that 34,120 to 45,880 is the smallest interval possible by trying several other possible splits of the 5% to be excluded. Figure 6.21 shows the normal distribution for this example.

Study Question 6.1: Guarantee Period for Motors
The length of life of an electric motor used in a ceiling fan is approximately normally distributed with a mean of 6.4 years and a standard deviation of 1.1 years.

$N(6.4, 1.1)$

    a) If the fan motor is guaranteed for five years, what is the probability that replacement under the guarantee will be required?

    b) If the manufacturer is willing to replace only 1% of the fan motors, what period of time should be used for the guarantee period?

Answer. Figure 6.22 is helpful in determining the answer.

    a) Let x = length of life in years. To find $P(x \le 5)$, convert to a standardized normal,

$$P(x \leq 5) = P\left[z \leq \frac{(5 - 6.4)}{1.1}\right] = P(z \leq -1.27).$$

Using Table III,

$$P(z \leq -1.27) = 1 - F(1.27)$$
$$= 1 - 0.8980 = 0.1020.$$

About 10% of the fan motors will need replacement under the guarantee.

b) If only 1% of the motors are to be replaced, then $P(x \leq a) = 0.01$. In standardized form,

$$P(x \leq a) = P\left[z \leq \frac{(a - 6.4)}{1.1}\right] = 0.01.$$

From Table III, we find $F(z) = 0.99$ for $z = 2.33$. Since a is smaller than the mean of the distribution, then the negative value of z to be substituted into Formula (6.5) is $z = -2.33$. Thus, $a = 6.4 - 2.33(1.1) = 3.837$. The guarantee period desired is 3.837 years. Since 0.837 years is (0.837)12 months, or about 10 months, the guarantee period should be 3 years and 10 months if only 1% of the fan motors are to be replaced.

The family of probability problems in which the standardized normal z is useful extends even beyond these instances. Many other distributions applying to other types of problems tend to be normal distributions under certain conditions. One example, discussed in the next section, is that of the binomial distribution. Finally, as we will see in the following chapters, the standardized normal distribution is of primary importance in problems of statistical inference dealing with means of samples from a population whose distribution is unknown.

FIGURE 6.22 **Illustration for Study Question 6.1.**

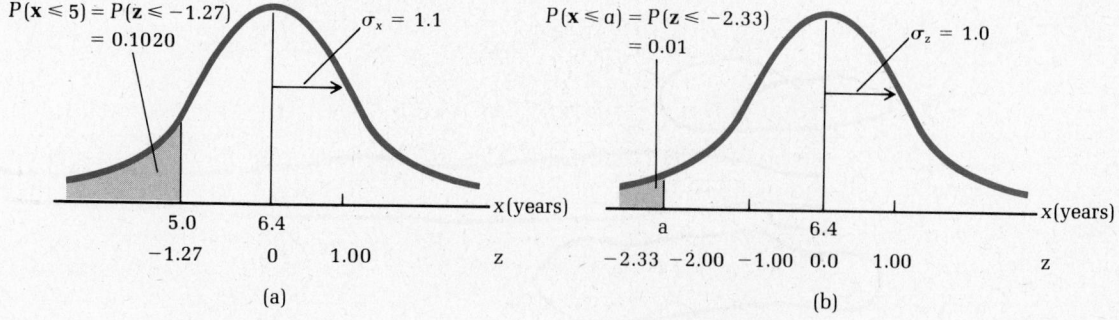

6.6 NORMAL APPROXIMATION TO THE BINOMIAL

In studying the binomial distribution we saw that, when the number of trials n is large, this distribution can be tedious to calculate. When n is not one of the values in Table I, then the binomial formula must be used to determine the exact value of binomial probabilities, and evaluating $_nC_x \, \pi^x(1 - \pi)^{n-x}$ can be burdensome. Similarly, when π involves three or more significant digits (such as $\pi = 0.585$), then we cannot use Table I. The problem is thus: How can one conveniently solve such problems, where Table I is of no help and when evaluating $_nC_x \, \pi^x(1 - \pi)^{n-x}$ is too hard? For example, suppose that the proportion of repeat customers at a K-Mart discount store is $\pi = 0.415$. Then, the probability of a given number of repeat customers out of any randomly selected sample of customers could be described by a random variable with a binomial distribution. Out of $n = 200$ randomly selected customers (that is, the selections are independent), the probability that at least 60 but not more than 80 would be be repeat customers is given by

$$P(60 \leq x \leq 80) = \sum_{x=60}^{80} {}_{200}C_x(0.415)^x \, (0.585)^{200-x}.$$

Rather than solve this type of problem directly, we will use the normal distribution, which may provide a good approximation. Remember that in Fig. 5.4 we saw that when n is as low as 20, the binomial has a fairly symmetrical (bell-shaped) appearance, even when π is not very close to $\frac{1}{2}$. In general, the larger the value of n, and the closer π is to $\frac{1}{2}$, the better the normal will approximate the binomial.

Using the Normal Approximation to the Binomial

When one distribution is used to approximate another, their characteristics must be fairly similar. In particular, the two distributions should have (1) the same mean, (2) the same variance, and (3) a similar shape.

In approximating the binomial by the normal we can ensure that their means are equal by setting μ (the mean of the normal) equal to the value of $n\pi$ (the mean of the binomial distribution we are trying to approximate). That is, we

1. Set $\mu = n\pi$.

To ensure that their variances are equal, we set σ^2 (the variance of the normal) equal to $n\pi(1 - \pi)$ (the variance of the binomial): that is, we

2. Set $\sigma^2 = n\pi(1 - \pi)$

It can be shown that as n gets larger and larger, the shape of the binomial becomes more and more like the normal. In other words,

3. *Binomial → normal as $n → ∞$.*

If n is "large," these conditions ensure that the normal distribution will provide a reasonably good approximation to the binomial. Just how large n needs to be depends on how close π is to $\frac{1}{2}$, and on the precision desired, although fairly good results are usually obtained when $n\pi(1 - \pi) > 3$.

Just as we standardized an x-value in solving problems earlier in this chapter, we again standardize x to approximate the binomial by the normal. In this case, x is standardized by subtracting $\mu = n\pi$ from x, and then dividing this deviation by $\sigma = \sqrt{n\pi(1 - \pi)}$. Thus,

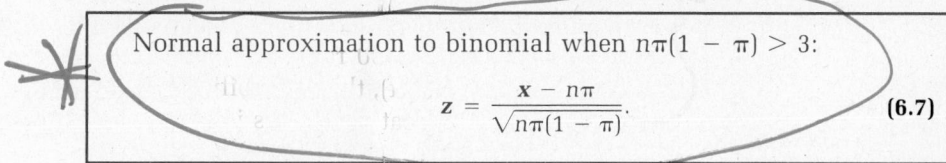

Normal approximation to binomial when $n\pi(1 - \pi) > 3$:

$$z = \frac{x - n\pi}{\sqrt{n\pi(1 - \pi)}}.$$ **(6.7)**

Continuity Correction   One additional factor must be considered in using the normal to approximate the binomial; namely, that a discrete distribution involving only integer values (the binomial) is being approximated by a continuous distribution (the normal) in which x can take on any value between negative and positive infinity. The problem that can arise in this situation is illustrated in Fig. 6.23.

For the binomial "spikes" we see that $P(x \le a)$ and $P(x \ge a + 1)$ will sum to 1.0 whenever a is an integer. But if we sum the *area* under the normal curve corresponding to $P(x \le a)$ and $P(x \ge a + 1)$, this area does *not* sum to 1.0 because the area from a to $(a + 1)$ is missing. The usual way to handle this problem is to *associate one-half of this interval with*

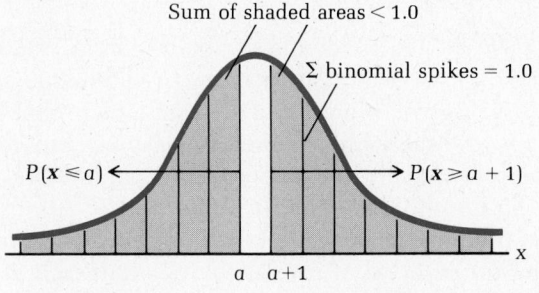

Sum of shaded areas < 1.0

Σ binomial spikes = 1.0

$P(x \le a) \leftarrow$ $\rightarrow P(x \ge a + 1)$

a $a+1$

FIGURE 6.23 Illustration of the need for a continuity correction.

each adjacent integer. The continuous approximation to the probability $P(x \leq a)$ would thus be $P(x \leq a + \frac{1}{2})$, while the continuous approximation to $P(x \geq a + 1)$ would be $P(x \geq a + \frac{1}{2})$. This adjustment is called a **continuity correction**. The best way to remember how to use this correction for continuity is to note that the interval always becomes *larger* when the continuity correction is included.

A simple method for making the correct adjustment begins with rewriting (if necessary) the probability of an event for the binomial random variable x in terms of a *closed interval*; that is, an interval that includes the endpoints as denoted by the use of the symbol "$\leq$" rather than the pure inequality "$<$."

> For the approximation in terms of a continuous random variable, each endpoint of the closed interval is changed by one-half unit so as to make the interval wider.

For example, $P(x \geq 70)$ becomes $P(x \geq 69.5)$, and $P(x \leq 60)$ becomes $P(x \leq 60.5)$. Each of these events was stated originally as a closed interval. If the original event is stated as an open interval, such as $P(20 < x)$, the first step is to rewrite the event for the *discrete* binomial variable as a closed interval, $P(21 \leq x)$. Then the interval is extended to $P(20.5 \leq x)$ for the *continuous* approximation. If there are two endpoints given in the probability problem, both endpoints must be corrected. Thus, $P(50 \leq x \leq 60)$ must be enlarged by one-half unit at each end to become $P(49.5 \leq x \leq 60.5)$. As before, it is very important whether or not the endpoints are included in the original interval because in a binomial problem, $P(50 \leq x \leq 60)$ is quite different from $P(50 < x < 60)$. The latter event does *not* include the values 50 or 60; and so the probability is equivalent to $P(51 \leq x \leq 59)$ for the binomial random variable. When corrected for continuity, this probability becomes $P(50.5 \leq x \leq 59.5)$.

Example 6.7. A statewide survey (Georgia, 1983) found that 64% of all households with annual incomes over $25,000 subscribed to a daily newspaper. Suppose we want to calculate the probability that in a random sample of 100 such households at least 60 and no more than 70 are subscribers to a daily newspaper. The parameters necessary for determining the binomial probability $P(60 \leq x \leq 70)$ are $n = 100$ and $\pi = 0.64$. For the normal approximation we always correct for continuity by extending the interval of interest by one-half unit at either end. Thus, if we extend the interval $60 \leq x \leq 70$, the lower limit becomes 59.5, the upper limit becomes 70.5, and the new probability is

$$P(59.5 \leq x \leq 70.5).$$

The parameters for standardizing this normal probability are $\mu = n\pi = 64$ and $\sigma = \sqrt{n\pi(1 - \pi)} = \sqrt{100(0.64)(0.36)} = 10(0.8)(0.6) = 4.8$. The binomial and its normal approximation are:

Binomial probability:

$$P(60 \leq x \leq 70) = \sum_{x=60}^{70} {}_{100}C_x (0.64)^x (0.36)^{100-x}$$

$$= 0.7397 \quad \text{(from Table I).}$$

Normal approximation:

$$P(59.5 \leq x \leq 70.5) = P\left(\frac{59.5 - n\pi}{\sqrt{n\pi(1 - \pi)}} \leq z \leq \frac{70.5 - n\pi}{\sqrt{n\pi(1 - \pi)}} \right)$$

$$= P\left(\frac{59.5 - 64}{4.8} \leq z \leq \frac{70.5 - 64}{4.8} \right)$$

$$\begin{aligned}
&= P(-0.94 \leq z \leq 1.35) \\
&= F(1.35) - F(-0.94) &&\text{(Rule 4, Section 6.5)} \\
&= F(1.35) - [1 - F(0.94)] &&\text{(Rule 3, Section 6.5)} \\
&= 0.9115 - [1 - 0.8264] &&\text{(from Table III)} \\
&= 0.7379.
\end{aligned}$$

This approximation is very good, as in this case $n\pi(1 - \pi) = 23.04$, which is much larger than the minimum condition $n\pi(1 - \pi) > 3$.

Example 6.8. We want to find the probability of a TV commercial being seen by exactly four out of 12 independent viewers. The probability that any viewer sees the commercial is assumed to be constantly equal to 0.3. Thus, we can find the exact probability using the binomial distribution with $n = 12$ and $\pi = 0.3$. From Table I we get

$$P(x = 4) = {}_{12}C_4(0.30)^4(0.70)^8 = 0.2311.$$

Using the normal approximation, we can approximate $P(x = 4)$ by rewriting this as an interval, $P(4 \leq x \leq 4)$, and making the continuity correction to obtain

$$P(3.5 \leq x \leq 4.5).$$

In this case $\mu = n\pi = 12(0.3) = 3.6$, and $\sigma = \sqrt{n\pi(1 - \pi)} = \sqrt{2.52} = 1.59$.

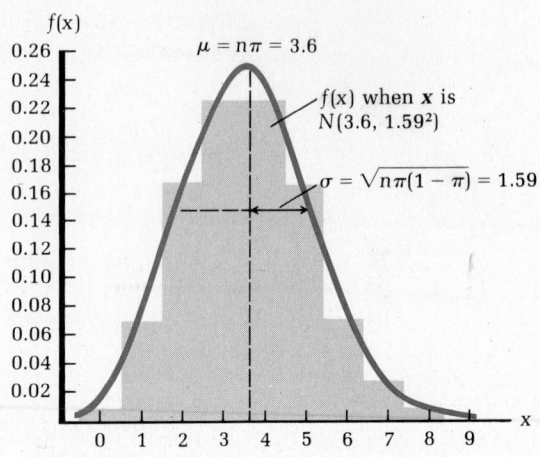

FIGURE 6.24 **Normal approximation to the binomial ($n = 12$, $\pi = 0.30$; $\mu = 3.6$, $\sigma = 1.59$).**

Normal approximation:

$$P(3.5 \le x \le 4.5) = P\left(\frac{3.5 - n\pi}{\sqrt{n\pi(1 - \pi)}} < z < \frac{4.5 - n\pi}{\sqrt{n\pi(1 - \pi)}}\right)$$

$$= P\left(\frac{3.5 - 3.6}{1.59} < z < \frac{4.5 - 3.6}{1.59}\right)$$

$$= P(-0.06 < z < 0.57)$$

$$= F(0.57) - F(-0.06) \qquad \text{(Rule 4)}$$

$$= 0.7157 - [1.0 - F(+0.06)] \qquad \text{(Rule 3)}$$

$$= 0.7157 - 1.0 + 0.5239 = 0.2396.$$

The normal approximation to the binomial is adequate in this case, even though $n\pi(1 - \pi) = 12(0.3)(0.7) = 2.52$ is less than 3. Figure 6.24 gives the histogram for the binomial distribution with $n = 12$, $\pi = 0.30$; superimposed on this histogram is a normal distribution with $\mu = 3.6$ and $\sigma = 1.59$. Notice how good the fit is, despite the small sample size.

In these examples comparing the exact probability of the binomial to the approximation by the normal with a continuity correction, the use of the binomial may seem simpler. The point of these comparisons, however, is that when the value of n is large and is not in Table I, or the value of π has three or more decimal places and is not in Table I, the normal approximation may be used. It will be quite accurate if $n\pi(1 - \pi) > 3$.

Study Question 6.2: Repeat Customers at K-Mart

In the first paragraph of this section an example was suggested to find the probability that at least 60 but no more than 80 out of 200 randomly selected customers at a K-Mart store would be repeat customers.

   a) Explain why the normal distribution might be used to find this probability.
   b) Find the approximate probability using the normal distribution.

Answer
   a) To find $P(60 \leq x \leq 80)$ with $n = 200$ and $\pi = 0.415$, where x has a binomial distribution, the normal approximation may be used because:

1. $n = 200$ is a larger sample size than is included in Table I.
2. $\pi = 0.415$ is not included in Table I since the table only includes two-digit values of π.
3. $n\pi(1 - \pi) = 200(0.415)(0.585) = 48.555$, which greatly exceeds 3.

   b) A continuity correction for the discrete event is used to rewrite the event as $P(59.5 \leq x \leq 80.5)$. The standardization using Formula (6.7) with $n\pi = 200(0.415) = 83$ and $\sqrt{n\pi(1 - \pi)} = \sqrt{48.555} = 6.97$ gives

$$P(59.5 \leq x \leq 80.5) = P\left[\frac{(59.5 - 83)}{6.97} < z < \frac{(80.5 - 83)}{6.97}\right]$$
$$= P(-3.37 < z < -0.36)$$
$$= F(-0.36) - F(-3.37)$$
$$= F(+3.37) - F(+0.36)$$
$$= 0.9996 - 0.6406 = 0.3590.$$

See Fig. 6.25.

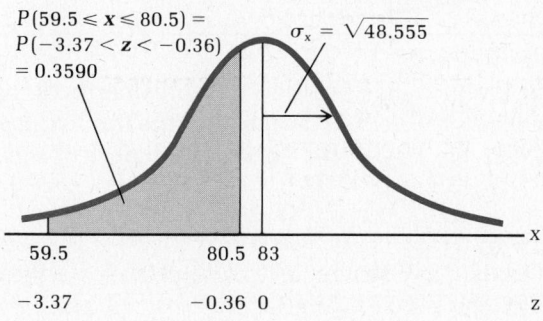

$P(59.5 \leq x \leq 80.5) =$
$P(-3.37 < z < -0.36)$
$= 0.3590$

$\sigma_x = \sqrt{48.555}$

59.5 80.5 83   x

-3.37 -0.36 0   z

FIGURE 6.25 **Illustration for Study Question 6.2.**

Normal Approximation Using Proportions

Recall from Chapter 5 that binomial problems can be phrased in terms of the *proportion* of successes as well as the *number of successes*. For solving problems by the normal approximation method, the following formula using the sample proportion $p = x/n$ is equivalent to Formula (6.7).

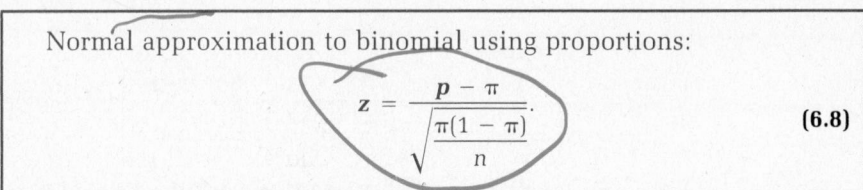

Normal approximation to binomial using proportions:

$$z = \frac{p - \pi}{\sqrt{\dfrac{\pi(1 - \pi)}{n}}}. \qquad (6.8)$$

Formula (6.8) should be recognized as the standardization of the variable $p = x/n$. In Chapter 5 it was shown that the variable p has a mean of $E[p] = \pi$ and a variance of $V[p] = \pi(1 - \pi)/n$.

When using Formula (6.8) to approximate the probability distribution for the proportion of successes, greater accuracy can again be obtained if a correction for continuity is made. As in the previous case for the distribution of the number of successes, x, the event (expressed as a closed interval) for the discrete case must be extended one-half unit in each direction to get the proper event for the approximating continuous random variable. When dealing with the counting variable of the number of successes x, the unit size is one (representing one more occurrence), and so one-half unit is $(\frac{1}{2})1 = \frac{1}{2}$.

When dealing with the proportion of successes (x/n), the unit size is $1/n$ (representing one more occurrence out of n), and so, one-half unit is $\frac{1}{2}(1/n)$. The closed interval expressed in terms of proportions must be extended at each endpoint by the fraction $(1/2n)$ in order to obtain the proper interval for a more accurate normal approximation.

Some practice in using this continuity correction makes the correction more understandable. Let us consider the following events for a binomial random variable x with the specified number of repeated cases n.

1. $P(x < 60)$ with $n = 100$ really means $P(x \le 59)$ for the discrete counting variable x and is extended to $P(x < 59.5)$ by using the continuity correction. $P[p < 0.60]$ with $n = 100$ is similarly rewritten as a closed interval using $p = x/n$,

$$P\left[\frac{x}{n} \le 0.60 - \frac{1}{n}\right] = P\left[\frac{x}{n} \le 0.59\right].$$

This interval is extended for the continuity correction by the amount

$$\frac{1}{2n} = \frac{1}{2(100)} = 0.005,$$

to obtain $P[(x/n) \le 0.595]$. The similarity between the cases for $x =$ (the *number* of successes) and $p = (x/n) =$ (the *proportion* of successes) is quite apparent when $n = 100$. For this one value of n, a unit change in x is 1.0, and the unit change in the proportion is 0.01. Thus, the extension to new endpoints using the continuity correction looks the same except for the decimal location. This similarity is less obvious when the number of cases is not $n = 100$, but it still exists.

2. $P(15 \le x \le 20)$ with $n = 50$ is extended to $P(14.5 \le x - 20.5)$ for the continuity correction. The same event in terms of proportions is

$$P[0.30 \le (p) \le 0.40],$$

since $(15/n) = (15/50) = 0.30$ and $(20/50) = 0.40$. This interval must be extended in each direction by

$$\frac{1}{2n} = \frac{1}{2(50)} = \frac{1}{100} = 0.01.$$

The extended interval is

$$P[0.29 \le p \le 0.41].$$

Again, the limits correspond to those for the event in terms of x since $(14.5/50) = 0.29$ and $(20.5/50) = 0.41$.

These practice items illustrate that there are two ways to make the proper continuity correction when dealing with proportions. The direct way is to extend the closed interval representing the discrete event by the amount $(1/2n)$ in each direction.*

The indirect way is to first rewrite the discrete event in terms of the *number* of successes x and then divide each end point by n to get the proper interval in terms of *proportions*. Actually, problems in terms of $x =$ (the number of successes) or $p =$ (the proportion of successes) can be solved either in terms of x or p, whichever method is most convenient for the decision-maker in the given situation.

---

* When the interval extends to infinity on one side as in practice case 1 above, only the finite end of the interval needs to be extended. The other end is still positive or negative infinity.

Example 6.9. To demonstrate the equivalence of Formulas (6.7) and (6.8), reconsider Example 6.7. Suppose that we wish to know the probability that the *proportion* of newspaper subscribers in a sample of 100 falls between 0.60 and 0.70 inclusive when $\pi = 0.64$. That is, we want to find

$$P(0.60 \leq p \leq 0.70).$$

We have to correct for continuity by enlarging each end of the interval by

$$\frac{1}{2n} = \frac{1}{200} = 0.005$$

at each end. The lower limit becomes 0.595, and the upper limit becomes 0.705. The new probability is

$$P(0.595 \leq \frac{x}{n} \leq 0.705).$$

As shown in Fig. 6.26, this probability can now be standardized by using Formula (6.8), where $\pi = 0.64$ and $\sqrt{\pi(1 - \pi)/n} = \sqrt{(0.64)(0.36)/100} = 0.048$.

$$P\left(\frac{0.595 - 0.640}{0.048} \leq \frac{p - \pi}{\sqrt{\pi(1 - \pi)/n}} \leq \frac{0.705 - 0.640}{0.048}\right)$$

$$= P(-0.94 \leq z \leq 1.35)$$

$$= F(1.35) - F(-0.94)$$

$$= 0.9115 - [1 - F(0.94)] = 0.7379.$$

This result is identical to the previous solution of the equivalent problem. Thus, we have shown that a binomial problem can be solved using either the number of successes [Formula (6.7)] or the proportion of successes [Formula (6.8)].

FIGURE 6.26 **Illustration for Example 6.9.**

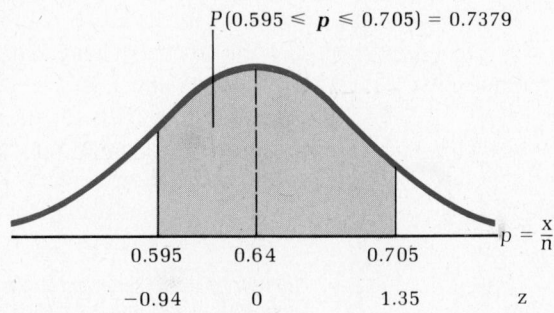

$P(0.595 \leq p \leq 0.705) = 0.7379$

Study Question 6.3: Proportion of Repeat Customers
For the same situation as in Study Question 6.2, show that the same answer is obtained for the corresponding probability expressed in terms of proportions,

$$P\left[\frac{60}{200} \leq p \leq \frac{80}{200}\right] = P[0.30 \leq p \leq 0.40].$$

Answer. Since $n = 200$, the continuity correction uses an extension of the interval in each direction by the amount

$$\frac{1}{2n} = \frac{1}{2(200)} = \frac{1}{400} = 0.0025.$$

The adjusted event is*

$$P[0.30 - 0.0025 \leq p \leq 0.40 + 0.0025] = P[0.2975 \leq p \leq 0.4025].$$

Standardizing according to Formula (6.8) with $\pi = 0.415$ and

$$\sqrt{\frac{\pi(1 - \pi)}{n}} = \sqrt{\frac{(0.415)(0.585)}{200}} = \sqrt{0.001214} = 0.03484,$$

we rewrite

$$P[0.2975 \leq p \leq 0.4025]$$
$$= P\left(\frac{0.2975 - 0.4150}{0.03484} \leq z \leq \frac{0.4025 - 0.4150}{0.03484}\right)$$
$$= P(-3.37 \leq z \leq (-0.36)$$
$$= F(+3.37) - F(+0.36)$$
$$= 0.9996 - 0.6406 = 0.3590.$$

This is the same result as is obtained by using x instead of x/n.

Define. *Gaussian distribution, standardized normal, N(μ, σ^2), F(z), correction for continuity, normal approximation to the binomial.*

PROBLEMS

6.8 Explain what is meant by the phrase "standardization of a variable." Why do we standardize variables?

6.9 Sketch the following.

---

* The limits of this interval are the same values as obtained by adjusting the limits in terms of **x** by one-half unit and dividing by 200 to get (59.5/200) and (80.5/200).

a) The normal density function N(10, 1).

b) The curve N(5, 100).

6.10 Sketch the following.

a) The cumulative distribution function for the p.d.f. given in 6.9(a).

b) The cumulative distribution function for the p.d.f. given in 6.9(b).

6.11 Assume that x is N(15, 100) where x is the change in a commodity price (¢/bushel). Calculate:

a) $P(5 \leq x \leq 25)$.

b) $P(-5 \leq x \leq 35)$.

c) $P(-10 \leq x \leq 35)$.

d) Use your answer to part (b) to determine each of the following:

$$P(x \geq 35), P(x \leq -5), \text{ and } P(x \leq -5 \text{ or } x \geq 35).$$

6.12 Find the following values.

a) The value of b such that $P(z > b) = 0.01$.

b) The value of a such that $P(z < a) = 0.025$.

6.13 Suppose that the number of hours per week of lost work due to illness in a certain automobile assembly plant is approximately normally distributed, with a mean of 60 hours and a standard deviation of 15 hours. For a given week, selected at random, what is the probability that:

a) The number of lost work hours will exceed 85 hours?

b) The number of lost work hours will be between 45 and 55 hours?

c) The number of lost work hours will be exactly 60?

6.14 The average age of state congressmen in 1935 was 49.65 with a standard deviation of 5 years. Assume that their ages follow a normal distribution; what is the probability that a congressman selected at random would be younger than 38 years old?

6.15 A manufacturer of children's clothing knows that the heights of girls in their third year are normally distributed with mean 40 inches and standard deviation 5 inches. If a sweater is designed that will be suitable for anyone in this population with height between 45 and 55 inches, what is the probability that the sweater would fit a randomly selected girl from this population?

6.16 Over the years, the number of breakfasts served per day in the company cafeteria follows a normal distribution with mean 150 and standard deviation 15. What is the probability that the number of breakfasts served on a randomly selected workday will be between 165 and 180?

6.17 If z is a standardized normal variable, what is the probability of obtaining a value of z between -1.28 and $+1.65$?

6.18 For each of the following, find the specified numerical value and illustrate the interval and area involved on a normal distribution sketch (the symbol ~ means "distributed as").
   a) Assuming z is $N(0, 1)$, find $P(1.5 < z < 2.23)$.
   b) Assuming z is $N(0, 1)$, find $P(-1.34 < z < +0.62)$.
   c) For $z \sim N(0, 1)$, find the value of b that yields $P(-0.05 < z < b) = 0.40$.
   d) For $z \sim N(0, 1)$, find the value of b that yields $P(|z| > b) = 0.12$ where $|z|$ denotes the absolute value of z.
   e) For $x \sim N(45, 81)$, find $P(33 < x < 51)$.
   f) For $x \sim N(15, 3.24^2)$, find $P(x > 20)$.
   g) For $x \sim N(100, 400)$, find the value of a that yields $P(x < a) = 0.95$.

6.19 If the income in a community is normally distributed, with a mean of $19,000 and a standard deviation of $2000, what minimum income does a member of this community have to earn in order to be in the top 10%? What is the maximum income one can have and still be in the middle 50%?

6.20 Suppose first that the sales invoices of a certain company have a normal distribution with mean $32 and standard deviation $8. Second, suppose that the service life of telephone poles used by public utility companies is normally distributed with average 15 years and variance 25 years.
   a) Which of these normal distributions has the largest range? (Careful!)
   b) What is the probability that a utility pole selected at random from this latter distribution will have a service life greater than 15 years?
   c) Suppose I observe one utility pole that lasts only 3 years, and I also observe an invoice of $50. Which of these occurrences is the *more* unusual?

6.21 The number of classified ads appearing in a daily newspaper for the sale of used cars is normally distributed with a mean of 100 and standard deviation of 16.
   a) What is the probability that a randomly selected paper will contain more than 140 used car ads?
   b) What is the probability that a paper contains fewer than 80 such ads?

6.22 A traveling circus has found that its average attendance per performance is 6000 people, with a standard deviation of 1500. Assume that attendance is normally distributed.
   a) Suppose a town asks the circus to come, but the only possible site in town holds only 8000 people. What is the probability that this site will not be large enough, based on past experience?
   b) If the circus loses money on 20% of their performances, what attendance must they have to break even for a given performance?

Assume that the profit they make for a given performance depends only on the number of people attending the performance.

6.23 Approximate your answer to Problem 5.13 on page 224 by using the normal distribution.

6.24 Approximate your answer to Problem 5.14(a) on page 225 by using the normal distribution.

6.25 A senator claims that 75% of his constituents favor his voting policies over the past year. In a random sample of 50 of these people, only 50% favored his voting policies. Is this enough evidence to make the senator's claims strongly suspect? Use a normal approximation.

6.26 The manager of a Sears Service fleet estimates that 50% of all local Sears service calls involve 30 minutes or less of on-site work. A randomly selected set of records on 100 recent service calls are examined. Assuming that the manager's estimate is accurate:

a) Use the binomial probability table to determine the probability that at least 55 but no more than 60 of these 100 service calls involved 30 minutes or less work time.

b) Use the normal distribution to approximate this same probability.

6.7   EXPONENTIAL DISTRIBUTION*

Another important continuous distribution, the **exponential distribution,** is closely related to a discrete distribution discussed previously, the Poisson. Both the Poisson and the exponential distributions have many applications in operations research, especially in studies of queueing (waiting-line) theory. These two distributions are related in such applications by the fact that if events (e.g., requests for service, or arrivals) are assumed to occur according to a Poisson probability law, then the exponential distribution can be used to determine the probability distribution of the time that elapses *between* such events. For example, if customers arrive at a bank in accordance with a Poisson distribution, the exponential may be used to determine the probability distribution of the intervals between arrivals. Determination of the time it takes to be serviced (called the service time) in these models is another application of the exponential distribution.

The exponential distribution is a continuous function that has the same parameter, λ, as the Poisson. Lambda, as before, represents the mean rate at which events (arrivals or service completions) occur. Thus, a value of λ = 3.0 may imply that service completions occur, on the average, at

---

* This section may be omitted without loss in continuity.

the rate of 3.0 per minute (or any other time unit). If a telephone line can handle an average of 20 customers per hour, then λ, defined as the mean number of customers being served by the telephone facilities, is $\lambda = 20$ (per hour) or $\lambda = \frac{1}{3}$ (per minute). Similarly, $\lambda = 3.8$ may imply, as it did in Section 5.7, that an average of 3.8 customers arrives at a checkout counter in a supermarket every minute.

The basic assumption underlying the exponential distribution is that the longer the time interval becomes, the less likely it is that the service completion (or the next arrival) will take that long or longer. Suppose that we let the random variable T represent the amount of time between service completions or arrivals. As the value of T becomes larger and larger, the value of $f(T)$ for the exponential becomes smaller and smaller. In fact, as can be seen in the graph of the exponential distribution in Fig. 6.27, $f(T)$ approaches zero as T approaches infinity.

Note that the exponential distribution, similar to the Poisson, assumes a value other than zero only when T is greater than or equal to zero and when λ is greater than zero. The vertical intercept of the function shown in Fig. 6.27 is seen to equal λ, which means that $f(0) = \lambda$. These relationships characterize the exponential distribution, which has the density function:

Exponential distribution:

$$f(T) = \begin{cases} \lambda e^{-\lambda T} & \text{for } 0 \le T \le \infty, \lambda > 0, \\ 0 & \text{otherwise.} \end{cases} \qquad (6.9)$$

FIGURE 6.27 **The exponential distribution:** $f(T) = \lambda e^{-\lambda T}$.

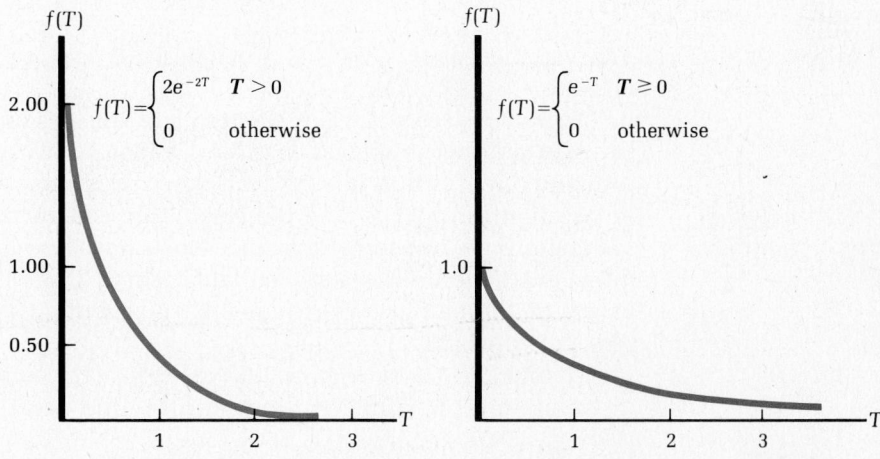

Mean and Variance of the Exponential

Remember that if we interpret λ as the mean arrival (or service) rate, then the exponential gives the probability distribution of the time between arrivals (or between service completions). Thus, it should not be very surprising to learn that the mean of the exponential distribution is $1/\lambda$. For example, suppose that the mean service rate of a cashier in a bank equals one-half customer every minute, or $\lambda = \frac{1}{2}$. Since it takes, on the average, one minute to serve half a customer, it takes two minutes to serve one customer; hence, the mean time between service completions is $1/\lambda = 2$. As was true for the Poisson, the mean and the variance of the exponential are both functions of λ. In this case we could show that the mean and variance of the exponential are:

$$\text{Exponential mean:} \quad \mu = \frac{1}{\lambda};$$

$$\text{Exponential variance:} \quad \sigma^2 = \frac{1}{\lambda^2}. \tag{6.10}$$

Since the exponential and the Poisson distributions can both be applied to problems of arrivals at a service facility, suppose we reconsider the example in Section 5.7, using the exponential function to describe the time between arrivals at a supermarket checkout counter. The mean number of arrivals is $\lambda = 3.8$ per minute, so the mean time between arrivals will be $1/\lambda = 1/3.8 = 0.263$ minutes (or one customer approximately every 16 seconds).

By substituting $\lambda = 3.8$ in Formula (6.9) we get

$$f(T) = 3.8e^{-3.8t}.$$

The variance of this time between arrivals is $1/\lambda^2 = 1/(3.8)^2 = 0.069$ minutes.

Now, suppose we want to calculate the probability that the time between arrivals is greater than one minute, $P(T > 1)$. One procedure utilizing calculus is to integrate the exponential function over the interval in question in order to find the area under the curve. Fortunately, such integrations are not necessary, since tables have been prepared that permit direct evaluation of the exponential function. Table IV in this book gives values of the cumulative exponential distribution $F(T)$ associated with selected values of λT.

To find $P(T > 1)$ when $\lambda = 3.8$, we first use the cumulative exponential distribution table (Table IV) to find $F(1)$. The value of $F(1)$ is found in

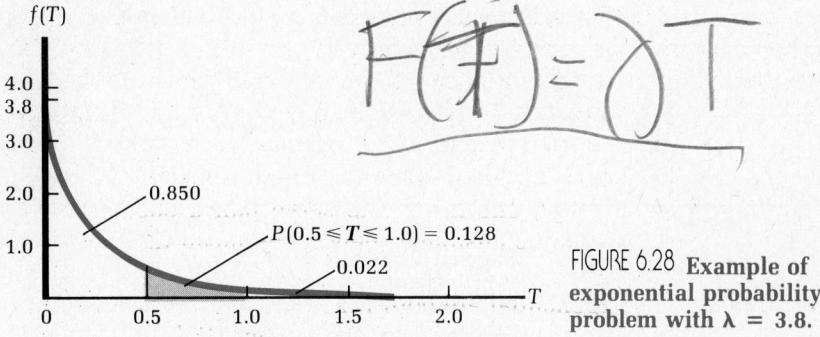

FIGURE 6.28 **Example of exponential probability problem with λ = 3.8.**

the row labeled $\lambda T = 3.8(1) = 3.8$. Since for $\lambda T = 3.8$ the value of $F(1) = 0.978$, we can write $P(T > 1)$ as follows:

$$P(T > 1) = 1.0 - P(T \leq 1) = 1.0 - F(1)$$
$$= 1.0 - 0.978 = 0.022.$$

Similarly, if one wants to determine the probability that an arrival will occur between one-half and one minute when $\lambda = 3.8$, Table IV can be used to find $P(\frac{1}{2} \leq T \leq 1) = F(1.0) - F(0.5)$. We already know that $F(1.0) = 0.978$. The value for $F(0.5)$ is found in Table IV under $\lambda(0.5) = 3.8(0.5) = 1.9$ and equals $F(0.5) = 0.850$. Thus, $F(1.0) - F(0.5) = 0.978 - 0.850 = 0.128$. This example is illustrated in Fig. 6.28.

Calculations of the above nature can be especially useful in the queueing problems mentioned earlier. If, in addition to studying the pattern of arrivals at our supermarket checkout counter, we had also investigated the service time of the cashiers, then we could develop a relationship that would indicate the probability that our cashiers would not be busy for a period of T minutes and the probability that the customers would have to wait more (or less) than T minutes. Ideally, such an investigation could lead to an analysis of the benefits of keeping a customer waiting versus the cost of hiring (or firing) another cashier, the result being a staffing policy designed to balance these costs and benefits. (Too often, it seems, the arrival rate in many supermarkets *exceeds* the service rate for extended periods of time.)

6.8 PROBABILITY DISTRIBUTIONS — SUMMARY

The probability distributions presented in Chapters 5 and 6 are summarized in Table 6.4. The first two are discrete distributions, and the latter three are continuous distributions. Although many practical problems in sta-

TABLE 6.4 **Summary of probability distributions**

Probability Distribution	Parameters	Characteristics	Mass or Density Function Given in Formula	Mean	Variance	Reference Sections	Probability Table
Discrete							
Binomial x^*	$0 \le \pi \le 1$ $n = 0, 1, 2, \ldots$	Skewed unless $\pi = 0.5$, family of distributions	(5.1)	$n\pi$	$n\pi(1 - \pi)$	5.2, 5.3, 5.4	$P(x_{\text{binomial}})$ in Table I
Poisson x	$\lambda > 0$	Skewed positively, family of distributions	(5.6)	λ	λ	5.7	$P(x_{\text{Poisson}})$ in Table II
Continuous							
Normal x	$-\infty < \mu < +\infty$ $\sigma > 0$	Symmetrical, family of distributions	(6.4)	μ	σ^2	6.4	—
Standardized normal z^*	—	Symmetrical, single distribution	(6.6)	0	1	6.5	$F(z)$ in Table III
Exponential T	$\lambda > 0$	Skewed positively, family of distributions	(6.9)	$1/\lambda$	$1/\lambda^2$	6.7	$F(T)$ in Table IV

* The normal approximation to the binomial is presented in Section 6.6.

tistical inference and decision-making can be resolved by using these distributions, they are not the only ones upon which statisticians rely. In the forthcoming chapters of this book we will study three additional continuous distributions, the *t*, the *F*, and the χ^2. Table 6.4 serves as the summary for Chapter 6.

In order to use all these distributions in decision-making about populations, based on sample evidence, we must first be more precise in our study of sampling. In many of our examples, a "sample" or a "random selection" has been mentioned but not formally defined. In Chapter 7, we present the details of sampling and the resulting important probability distributions for sample statistics. These will be used throughout the remainder of this book.

PROBLEMS

6.27 Given the exponential distribution with parameter λ equal to 3.0.
a) Graph the probability density function.
b) What are the mean and the variance of this distribution?

c) What percent of the area of this distribution lies within ± one standard deviation of the mean? Within ± two standard deviations of the mean?

6.28 Describe how the Poisson and the exponential distributions are related. What assumptions underlie these distributions?

6.29 Suppose that a bank can service, on the average, four customers per six-minute period. Assume that the number of customers serviced is Poisson-distributed.
a) What is the probability that this bank will be able to service six or more customers in a six-minute period? (*Hint:* Use the Poisson distribution with $\lambda = 4$.)
b) What is the probability that servicing a customer will take longer than three minutes?
c) What is the probability that servicing a customer will take between two and four minutes?

6.30 A stockbroker has an average of ten customers call between 9:00 and 10:00 each morning that the stock exchange is open. Customers call according to the Poisson distribution.
a) What is the probability that the stockbroker will have exactly ten customers call between these hours on a given morning?
b) What is the probability that the time between consecutive calls will exceed six minutes?
c) What is the probability that the time between consecutive calls will be between three and six minutes?

6.31 Airplanes land at the Purdue University airport at the rate of one every 30 minutes, following a Poisson distribution.
a) What is the probability that the time between arrivals will be less than 15 minutes?
b) What is the probability that the time between arrivals will be greater than three quarters of an hour?

6.32 Suppose that you observe the following service times (in minutes) by a bank teller: 1/2, 1, 1/2, 6, 1, 3.
a) What is the mean service time, given these observations? What is the variance?
b) Graph the probability density function for this application, assuming that times between service completions are exponentially distributed with mean = 2.
c) What is the probability that service will take longer than two minutes? What is $P(1 \leq x \leq 3)$?

6.33 For the exponential distribution, the interval $\mu \pm 1\sigma$ equals $1/\lambda \pm 1(1/\lambda)$, since $\mu = 1/\lambda$ and $\sigma = 1/\lambda$.

a) If $\lambda = 2$, use Table IV to calculate the probability that T falls between $\mu \pm 1\sigma$. Sketch this area on a graph.
b) Repeat part (a) using $\lambda = 4$.
c) Will the probabilities in parts (a) and (b) hold for any positive λ? Why is this probability greater than the rule of thumb of 68%?
d) Repeat parts (a) and (b) for $\mu \pm 2\sigma$.

6.34 Assume that the interarrival time at a tollbooth is exponentially distributed with a mean interarrival time of $\frac{1}{2}$ minute.
a) What is the value of λ for this problem?
b) What is the variance of the interarrival times?
c) What is the probability that the time between two consecutive arrivals will be between 0 and 1 minute?
d) What is $P(T > 2.0)$?

EXERCISES

(*Note:* Exercises 6.35–6.44 require the use of calculus.)

6.35 The cumulative distribution function for Problem 6.1 is

$$F(x) = \begin{cases} 0 & \text{for } x \leq 0, \\ x^2 & 0 \leq x \leq 1, \\ 1 & x \geq 1. \end{cases}$$

a) Sketch this function and the p.d.f., $f(x) = \dfrac{dF(x)}{dx}$.
b) What is the value of $F(\frac{1}{2})$? Does this value agree with $P(x \leq \frac{1}{2})$ calculated in Problem 6.1?
c) Calculate $E[x]$ by evaluating

$$\int_{\text{All } x} xf(x)dx = \int_0^1 2x^2 dx.$$

d) Calculate $V[x]$ by evaluating $E[x^2] - \mu^2$, where

$$E[x^2] = \int_{\text{All } x} x^2 f(x)dx = \int_0^1 2x^3 dx.$$

6.36 Find the following expectations for continuous random variables.
a) Find $E[x]$ for the p.d.f. shown in part (a) of Fig. 6.29 by integrating

$$\int_{\text{All}x} xf(x)dx.$$

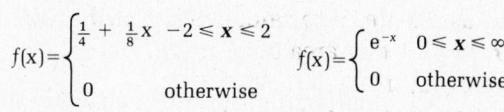

$$f(x)=\begin{cases} 2 & 1 \leq x \leq 1.5 \\ 0 & \text{otherwise} \end{cases}$$

$$f(x)=\begin{cases} \frac{1}{4} + \frac{1}{8}x & -2 \leq x \leq 2 \\ \\ 0 & \text{otherwise} \end{cases}$$

$$f(x)=\begin{cases} e^{-x} & 0 \leq x \leq \infty \\ 0 & \text{otherwise} \end{cases}$$

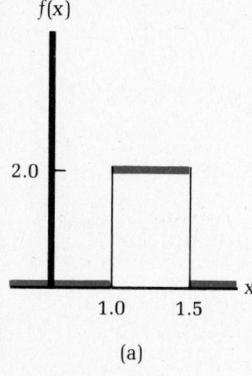

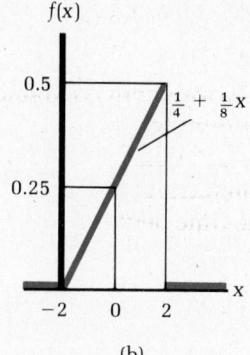

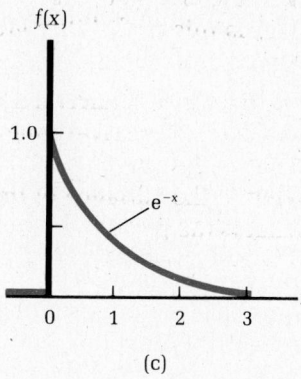

FIGURE 6.29 **Reproduction of Fig. 6.8.**

b) Find $V[x]$ for this same problem by solving $E[x^2] - (E[x])^2$. [See Exercise 6.35 part (d).]

c) Repeat parts (a) and (b) for the p.d.f. in part (b) of Fig. 6.29.

d) Repeat parts (a) and (b) for the p.d.f. in part (c) of Fig. 6.29.

6.37 Find the cumulative distribution function for each p.d.f. shown in Exercise 6.36 by integrating $\int_{-\infty}^{x} f(x)ds$.

a) Verify that for the first graph

$$F(x) = \begin{cases} 0 & x \leq 1, \\ 2x - 2 & 1 \leq x \leq 1.5, \\ 1 & x \geq 1.5. \end{cases}$$

b) Verify that for the second graph

$$F(x) = \begin{cases} 0 & x \leq -2, \\ \frac{1}{16}x^2 + \frac{1}{4}x + \frac{1}{4} & -2 \leq x \leq 2, \\ 1 & x \geq 2. \end{cases}$$

c) Verify that for the third graph

$$F(x) = \begin{cases} 0 & x \leq 0, \\ 1 - e^{-x} & x \geq 0. \end{cases}$$

[Hint: $\int e^{-x}\, dx = -e^{-x}$.]

6.38 Find the mean and the variance of the distribution defined in Problem 6.6.

6.39 The *uniform* or *rectangular* distribution can be defined in terms of its cumulative distribution function, as follows:

$$F(x) = \begin{cases} \dfrac{x-a}{b-a} & \text{for } a \le x \le b, \\ 0 & \text{for } x < a, \\ 1 & \text{for } x > b. \end{cases}$$

a) Derive the uniform density function for $a \le x \le b$ by differentiating $F(x)$ with respect to x.
b) Sketch both the density function and the cumulative function for the uniform distribution.
c) Show that the uniform distribution satisfies the two properties of all probability functions.
d) Find the mean and the variance of this distribution.

6.40 Given the probability density function for the number of hours behind schedule that the Amtrack Silver Comet arrives in New York from Miami,

$$f(x) = \begin{cases} \frac{1}{2}x & 0 \le x \le 2, \\ 0 & \text{otherwise.} \end{cases}$$

a) Determine the cumulative probability function for this problem, and then sketch both the density and the cumulative functions.
b) Show that this function possesses the two properties of a probability density function.
c) What is the probability in a randomly selected trip that the train arrives between 30 and 90 minutes late?
d) Evaluate $F(x)$ at $x = 1$. What probability does $F(1)$ represent?
e) Find the mean and the variance of the random variable x.

6.41 A consulting firm studying the security service for a large production facility has determined that a security guard always falls asleep during the 1:00–2:00 A.M. time period. The following p.d.f. accurately describes the moment the *first* guard falls asleep (x = time, in hours).

$$f(x) = \begin{cases} 3x^2 & 0 \le x \le 1, \\ 0 & \text{otherwise.} \end{cases}$$

a) Sketch this function (plot a few points if you must).
b) Show that the area under the function equals 1.0 by integrating $\int f(x)dx$.
c) Find a formula for $F(x)$. Use this formula to find $F(\frac{1}{4}) = P(x \le \frac{1}{4})$.
d) Calculate $E[x]$ by evaluating $\int xf(x)dx$.
e) Calculate $V[x]$ by evaluating $E[x^2] - \mu^2$. [See Exercise 6.35 part (d).]

6.42 Prove that for the exponential distribution,

$$E[T] = \frac{1}{\lambda} \quad \text{and} \quad V[T] = \frac{1}{\lambda^2}.$$

6.43 Prove the following.
a) The standardized normal density function reaches its maximum height at $z = 0$. (*Hint:* Show that the second derivative is negative.)
b) The points $z = \pm 1$ for the standardized normal density function are inflection points. (*Hint:* Show that the second derivative equals zero.)

6.44 A continuous p.d.f. not presented in this chapter is the *Beta distribution*. This distribution has two parameters, r and n.

$$f(x) = \begin{cases} {}_{n-1}C_{r-1}x^{r-1}(1-x)^{n-r-1} & 0 \le x \le 1, \\ 0 & \text{otherwise.} \end{cases}$$

a) Discuss the similarities and differences between this distribution and the binomial distribution.
b) Graph this distribution for $r = 1, n = 2$.
c) Determine $E[x]$.
d) If $r \le n/2$, will the distribution be positively or negatively skewed?

6.45 Refer to Exercise 2.40 for the Shark Loan Company.
a) Graph the exponential p.d.f. with $\lambda = 0.02$. Compare this graph with the polygon for Exercise 2.40. Do they seem to correspond well?
b) Elaborate on your answer to part (a) by finding $P(0 \le T \le 20)$, $P(20 \le T \le 60)$, and $P(T > 60)$, and then comparing these answers to the table of values given in Exercise 3.50.
c) What are the mean, median, and standard deviation of an exponential distribution with $\lambda = 0.02$? Are these answers consistent with values for Exercise 2.40(b)?

6.46 Sixty percent of all sales at a Gulf Oil Station are charged on credit cards. In a random sample of 200 sales, what is the probability that one-half or more are *cash* sales?

6.47 An auditor reports that 85.2% of the shareholders of a large automobile firm cast votes by proxy at the annual shareholders meeting. What is the probability that a survey of 800 randomly selected shareholders will have 5/6 or fewer who voted by proxy?

6.48 Eighty percent of the professional athletes in a sport favor union representation for bargaining with owners. If ABC Sports contacts 50 of the players at random, what is the probability that more than 90% of these will support the union representation?

6.49 The proportion of buyers of long-term government bonds who sell them prior to maturity is 0.655. In a random sample of 120 buyers, what is the probability that more than 70 will sell before maturity?

6.50 Thirty percent of all the mutual funds are set up to invest in foreign security markets. In a random sample of 40 such funds, what is the probability that more than 15 are set up to invest in foreign security markets?

6.51 A hospital knows that 25% of its bills are paid prior to the second invoice. In a computerized check of 1000 accounts, it is found that 770 bills required two or more statements before payment was received. Would you conclude that the 1000 accounts checked constitutes a random sample from the population of all accounts? Use a probability measure in justifying your answer.

6.52 The table below shows the percent of vehicles exceeding the 55 mph speed limit on Federal highways by state of location of the highway. The

State	Percent of drivers exceeding 55 mph limit	State	Percent of drivers exceeding 55 mph limit
Alabama	39.2	Montana	42.7
Alaska	17.0	Nebraska	39.1
Arizona	49.6	Nevada	51.2
Arkansas	30.0	New Hampshire	39.8
California	45.0	New Jersey	49.5
Colorado	42.7	New Mexico	41.2
Connecticut	44.3	New York	48.3
Delaware	48.9	North Carolina	32.7
Florida	45.7	North Dakota	47.2
Georgia	30.2	Ohio	45.6
Hawaii	43.1	Oklahoma	50.0
Idaho	33.8	Oregon	35.1
Illinois	34.5	Pennsylvania	36.4
Indiana	44.2	Rhode Island	46.3
Iowa	41.4	South Carolina	28.4
Kansas	44.3	South Dakota	37.8
Kentucky	36.8	Tennessee	36.7
Louisiana	43.6	Texas	34.7
Maine	41.6	Utah	47.5
Maryland	44.4	Vermont	50.0
Massachusetts	56.3	Virginia	48.9
Michigan	48.8	Washington	33.1
Minnesota	38.6	West Virginia	18.1
Mississippi	38.0	Wisconsin	33.5
Missouri	47.1	Wyoming	48.4

Source: Federal Highway Administration, 1983.

figures are based on a study using 1800 speed detectors that checked hundreds of thousands of vehicle speeds. The chart heading says percent of "drivers" instead of "vehicles," but this is simply a "jump in bureau-cratic logic and terminology."

a) If the percent specified for Alaska [the state with the lowest percentage of speeders (17.0%)] is correct, what would be the probability of observing 30 or fewer speeders in a random check of 200 vehicles on federal highways in Alaska?

b) Massachusetts wins the booby prize since it has the fewest percentage of drivers obeying the law [largest percentage (56.3%) of speeders]. What would be the probability of observing 100 or fewer speeders in a random check of 200 vehicles on federal highways in Massachusetts?

c) Determine the second best and the second worst states for persons obeying the speed limit on federal highways. For each, find the probability of the same events as in parts (a) and (b), respectively.

d) Find the probability of 60 or fewer speeders for the state you are in (or one designated by the instructor).

6.53 Refer to the age distribution for the United States population given in Problem 4.20 on page 172. If a random selection of 80 persons is taken from this population, what is the probability that:

a) ten or more would be over 65?

b) 15 or fewer would be 14 years old or younger?

c) fewer than five would be in their forties?

USING THE COMPUTER

6.54 Refer to Problem 6.49. Use a computer program to determine the exact probability according to the binomial distribution. How does this answer compare to the approximate answer in Problem 6.49?

6.55 For the situation described in Problem 6.50, use a computer program to determine the exact binomial answer.

6.56 For the hospital accounts in Problem 6.51, use a computer program to determine the exact probability by applying the binomial distribution.

CASE PROBLEMS

6.57 A fruit-packing company in Florida uses sorting machines to separate truckloads of oranges into various size categories. One machine is used to separate Class A fruit from all others. Class A oranges must have a diameter between 7 and 9 cm. To check on the sorting machine, oranges are selected at random from the sorted output stream of Class A fruit and checked for sizing. A "control chart" as shown below is used to keep a record of the test results. The size of each orange checked is plotted as a dot on the chart. If the dot falls within the control limits, then it is presumed that the sorting machine is working properly. If the dot falls outside the limits, or if a series of dots occurs all on the same side of the mean, or if a trend of dots occurs approaching one of the limits, then this indicates that the sorting machine may be "out of control." The process is then halted and the machine adjusted so that it does not select oranges that are either too large or too small. (Note that the rejected fruit proceeds on a different conveyor belt. It is also checked to see whether it contains fruit that *do fall within* the control limits. This result would also indicate a loss of control in the sorting process.)

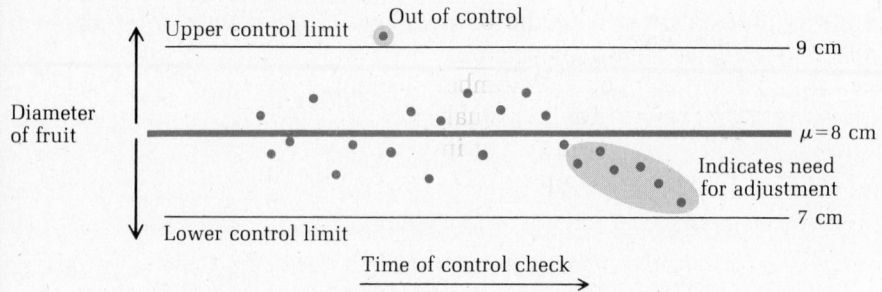

a) If the machine is properly adjusted, the size of Class A oranges selected will be normally distributed with $\mu = 8$ cm. and $\sigma = 0.4$ cm. What is the probability that a single check (using the control chart technique for spotting oranges sized outside the limits) will incorrectly indicate that the process is out of control?

b) Suppose the screening layers within the sorting machine slip so that the machine is now sorting out oranges with $\mu = 7.5$ cm. and $\sigma = 0.6$ cm. What is the probability that an orange randomly selected for the check will be within the control limits and indicate incorrectly that the machine is still sorting properly?

6.58 At the company in Problem 6.57, the Class A fruit also passes through an eye examination for selection of the best quality fruit in appearance. This "Best Quality" fruit is then used in special Sunshine packages that are mailed throughout the country. Usually, about 20% of the Class A sized fruit are selected for these Sunshine packages.

An electronic device can be used to count all the fruit processed at this stage, both the fruit that is selected for the Sunshine packages and the fruit that is not. At some random time within every half hour, the counting device starts and counts 500 oranges. It automatically prints out in the control supervisor's office the number selected for Sunshine packages and the number not. Assuming that the trained selectors are consistent in their judgments, variations from the usual 20% of Best Quality fruit indicate that the particular truckload of fruit being processed had a higher (or lower) percentage of high-quality oranges. The supervisor notes these facts along with the name of the producer and the grove of trees from which the fruit originated. On the other hand, if all the fruit being processed throughout the day is known by the supervisor to be from the same groves, then variations from the usual 20% may indicate some loss of efficiency or change of judgment by the selectors due to monotony or whatever.

a) For a population of 20% Best Quality fruit with perfect judgment by the selectors, what is the probability that in a given control lot of 500 oranges, fewer than 18% of the oranges would be selected as Best Quality fruit?

b) Set up a control chart on the number of oranges in a control lot of 500 that might be selected as Best Quality fruit if 20% of the population is that type. Use control limits that include 96% of all the cases that might occur if the selection process is in control.

GLOSSARY

Probability density function: A rule describing the height of $f(x)$ for a continuous random variable x.

Area under the density function from a to b: The probability measure of the event $P(a \leq x \leq b)$.

Cumulative distribution function $F(x)$: The sum of all the area under the density function to the left of a specified value of the random variable x.

Normal distribution: A symmetrical, bell-shaped continuous probability density function characterized by its two parameters, the mean and the variance.

Standardized normal distribution: A normal distribution with mean = 0 and variance = 1.

Control limits: Upper and lower bounds set on the key measures of a production process, often using the normal distribution, so as to assure some degree of quality control.

Continuity correction: An extension of the interval defining an event in terms of a discrete random variable so that its probability may be more accurately approximated by a continuous probability distribution.

Exponential distribution: A continuous probability density defined for a random variable T by the function,

$$f(T) = \begin{cases} \lambda e^{-\lambda T} & \text{for } 0 \leq T \leq \infty, \lambda > 0, \\ 0 & \text{otherwise.} \end{cases}$$

This distribution is useful for analysis of the time elapsing between events whose occurrence follows a Poisson distribution.

Sampling and
Sampling Distributions

SEVEN

7.1 INTRODUCTION

This chapter begins the task of relating the probability concepts studied in the past four chapters to the objective of statistics stated in Chapter 1: to draw inferences about population parameters on the basis of sample information.

Recall from Chapter 1 that a major portion of statistics is concerned with the problem of estimating population parameters, or testing hypotheses about such parameters. If we could take a "census" (i.e., examine all items in the population), then the value of the population parameters would be known. Unfortunately, a census of a population is usually not feasible because of monetary and/or time limitations. Hence, we must rely on observing a subset (or *sample*) of the items in the population, and use this information to make estimates or test hypotheses about the unknown parameters. The process of making estimates will be covered in Chapter 8, while the subject of hypothesis testing will be described in Chapters 9 and 10. In these subsequent chapters we will usually assume that a sample has been taken. It is therefore important that we describe in this chapter how a sample is taken and what type of information can be drawn from a sample.

There are four basic questions that must be asked about samples and the process of inference:

1. What are the least expensive methods for collecting samples that best ensure that the samples are representative of the parent population?
2. What is the best way to describe sample information usefully and clearly?
3. How does one go about drawing conclusions from samples and making inferences about the population?
4. How reliable are the inferences and conclusions drawn from sample information?

7.2 SAMPLE DESIGNS

By describing various **sample designs**, we will answer first the question of how sample information can be most efficiently collected.

> A sample design is a procedure or plan, specified before any data are collected, for obtaining a sample from a given population.

Nonsampling Errors

The primary requisite for a "good" sample is that it be representative of the population that one is trying to describe. There are, of course, many ways of collecting a "poor" sample. One obvious source of errors of misrepresentation arises when the *wrong population is sampled inadvertently*. The 1936 presidential election poll conducted by the now defunct *Literary Digest* remains a classic example of this problem. The *Literary Digest* predicted, on the basis of a sample of over two million names selected from telephone directories and automobile registrations, that Landon would win an overwhelming victory in the election that year. Instead, Roosevelt won by a substantial margin. The sample collected by the *Digest* apparently represented the population of predominantly middle- and upper-class people who owned cars and telephones; it misrepresented the general electorate, however, and Roosevelt's support came from the lower-income classes, whose opinions were not reflected in the poll.

Another type error known as *response bias* frequently affects results in surveys and public opinion polls. Poorly worded questionnaires or improper interview techniques may elicit responses that do not reflect true opinions. Kinsey's research on sex practices, for example, received widespread criticism for reporting responses to questions to which most people are fairly sensitive. Such responses are, therefore, likely to be distorted from the truth. Similarly, it is amazing how the economic well-being of certain college alumni can vary over the interval between the annual homecoming reunion and the annual fund-raising drive.

These types of error are called **nonsampling errors.** Nonsampling errors include all kinds of "human errors" — mistakes in collecting, analyzing, or reporting data; sampling from the wrong population; and response bias. If the researcher incorrectly adds a column of numbers, this represents a nonsampling error just as much as does the failure of a respondent to provide truthful information on a questionnaire.

Sampling Errors

In addition, even in well-designed and well-executed samples, there are bound to be cases in which the sample does not provide a true representation of the population under study, simply because samples represent only a portion of a population. In such cases the information contained in the sample may lead to incorrect inferences about the parent population; that is, an "error" might be made in estimating the population characteristics based on the sample information. Errors of this nature, representing the differences that can exist between a sample statistic and the population parameter being estimated, are called **sampling errors.** Sampling errors obviously can occur in all data-collection procedures except a complete enumeration of the population (a census).

One primary objective in sample design is to minimize both sampling and nonsampling errors. Errors are costly, not only in terms of the time and money spent in collecting a sample, but also in terms of the potential loss implicit in making a wrong decision on the basis of an incorrect inference from the data. An inaccurate public-opinion survey, for instance, could cost a politician votes if a campaign design is based on inferences from these data. Similarly, investment in real estate or stocks might cause an investor to lose a considerable amount of money if the (sample) information that led to a particular investment proved incorrect.

Note that it is the *decisions* resulting from incorrect inferences that may be costly, not the incorrect inferences themselves; hence, it is customary to refer to one objective of sampling as that of *minimizing the cost of making an incorrect decision* (error). But reducing the costs of making an incorrect decision usually implies increasing the cost of designing and/or collecting the sample. For example, additional effort (or money) devoted to designing a questionnaire, identifying the correct population, or collecting a larger sample usually results in a more representative sample. We can therefore state that the primary objective in sample design is to *balance the costs of making an error and the costs of sampling.*

Designing an optimal sampling procedure may not be easy. One reason is that the elements of a given population may be extremely difficult to locate, gain access to, or even identify. For example, it may be impractical, if not impossible, to identify the population elements of "color television owners" in a particular city in the United States. Another obvious difficulty already mentioned is cost; budget constraints, for example, may force one to collect fewer data or to be less careful about collecting these data than ideal designs would dictate. Also, the costs of making an incorrect decision may be very hard to specify. A discussion of all the problems inherent in sample design, especially those concerned with nonsampling errors and the costs of making an incorrect decision, falls outside the scope of this book. Therefore, we shall concentrate our attention on the problem of determining which sample designs most effectively minimize sampling errors.

Probabilistic Sampling

Probabilistic sampling designs are based primarily on a random selection process. Often, the first criterion for a good sample is that each item in the population under investigation have an *equal and independent chance* to be part of the sample; also, it is often advantageous that each set of n items have an equal probability of being included. Samples in which every possible sample of size n (i.e., every combination of n items from the N in the population) is equally likely are referred to as *simple random* *samples.* These are the types of samples that we have used implicitly throughout our discussion of probability theory to illustrate the use of formulas and probability functions.

Simple random sampling requires that one have access to all items in the population. For a small population of elements that are easy to identify and sample, this procedure normally gives the best results. However, simple random sampling of a large population may be difficult, perhaps even impossible, to implement; at best, it will be quite costly. For this case, a more practical procedure must be designed, even though it also will be more restrictive.

In another popular sampling plan, called **systematic sampling,** a random starting point in the population is selected, and then every *k*th element encountered thereafter becomes an item in the sample. For example, every 200th name in a telephone directory might be called in order to survey public opinion. This method is *not* equivalent to simple random sampling because every set of *n* names does not have an equal probability of being selected. Bias *will* result under systematic sampling if there is a *periodicity* to the elements of the population. For instance, sampling sales in a supermarket every seventh day certainly will result in a sample that represents only the sales of a single day, say Monday, rather than the weekly pattern.

Using a Random Number Table

Designing a sample in which each item in the population has an equal probability of being selected usually requires carefully controlled sampling procedures. The stereotype of drawing slips of paper from a goldfish bowl may satisfy the requirements of a simple random sample, but there is no practical way to be certain of this. The 1969 Selective Service draft lottery was highly criticized for using essentially a ''goldfish bowl'' technique without adequate mixing. A more systematic approach to ensuring randomness is to select a sample with the aid of a table of **random numbers.** In such a table, each digit between 0 and 9 is called a *random digit;* here, the word random implies that all of these digits have the same long-run relative frequency (i.e., the same probability of occurring), and the occurrence or nonoccurrence of any number is independent of the occurrence or nonoccurence of all other numbers, or of all sets of *n* other numbers. In a table of random numbers, random digits are usually combined to form numbers of more than one digit. For example, random digits taken in pairs will result in a set of 100 different numbers (00 to 99), each with a probability of occurring of 1/100, each independent of all other numbers. Likewise, in a table of random numbers consisting of groups of three random digits, each of the 1000 numbers between 000 and 999 will have a probability of occurring of 1/1000 and will be independent of the remaining numbers. Table V in Appendix C is a page of random numbers from a book published by the Rand Corporation, containing one million random digits.*

A table of random numbers can be used in the following manner to select a simple random sample of *n* items from a finite population of size *N*. First, a unique number between 0 and *N* must be assigned to each of the *N* items in the population. The table of random numbers is then consulted. The first *n* numbers encountered (starting at *any* point in the table and moving systematically across rows or down columns) that are less than *N* constitute a set of *n* random numbers. The *n* elements corresponding to these *n* numbers form the random sample.

To illustrate this procedure, we will use Table V to select a sample of four items from a population of 75 elements. A random selection of a starting point in the table is customary; let us arbitrarily start with the number that is tenth from the bottom in the first column, 09237. Since our population has less than 100 elements, we need to look at only two digits of each number. Suppose we use the first two digits. Then the first item in our sample becomes item number 09. Reading down, the next three items are 11, 60, and 71 (we skip 79 because we have only 75 elements in the population). Note that if our sample were to contain five items, the number 09 would have occurred again. This duplication could cause problems, as it may not be possible to sample the same item twice. Its usefulness may be destroyed by the first sample, as would be the case in testing the tread life of a tire or measuring the yield from a new seed variety at an agricultural testing station. For a sample size that is small in relation to the population size, discarding the duplicate item and letting the next element on the list (e.g., item 63) take its place will not seriously distort the usefulness of this method. If an item is discarded, it must be recognized that sampling is now taking place without replacement, rather than with replacement.

Sampling with Prior Knowledge

Two important random sampling plans depend on prior knowledge about the population; stratified sampling and cluster sampling.

Stratified Sampling. The use of **stratified sampling** requies that a population be divided into homogeneous classes or groups, called *strata*. Each stratum is then sampled according to certain specified criteria. The advantage of this procedure is that if homogeneous subsets of the population can be identified, then only a relatively small number of

---

* Each digit in Table V is random; hence, these numbers need not be used in pairs or triplets.

observations is needed to determine the characteristics of each subset. It can be shown that:

> ✂ The optimal method of selecting strata is to find groups with a large variability between strata, but with only a small variability within strata.

We illustrate stratified sampling by considering the task of determining the majority political preference in a given city. Assume that it is known, from previous surveys and elections, that political preferences in this town tend to correspond to various income levels. For instance, upper-income families tend to have similar opinions, as do middle-income and lower-income families. Assume further that in this particular city it is well known that the upper-income families and the lower-income families will have less variability of opinion within their respective groups than will the middle-income group. It may be that upper-income families in general will favor a fiscally conservative candidate, and lower-income families will favor a candidate who promises increased city services, while middle-income families will be less predictable.

A *proportional* stratified sampling plan selects items from each stratum in proportion to the size of that stratum. This procedure ensures that each stratum in the sample is "weighted" by the number of elements it contains. If the category "upper-income families" includes 10% of the voting population, then a proportional stratified sampling plan will randomly select 10% of the sample from this group. Many times, however, a more efficient procedure is to select a *disproportionate* stratified sample. A plan of this nature collects more than a proportionate amount of observations in those strata with the most variability, e.g., the middle-income group in the above example. In other words, by allocating a disproportionate amount of effort (time, money, etc.) to those groups whose opinions are most in doubt, one often obtains a maximum amount of information for a given cost. Similarly, if it is more costly to sample from a particular stratum, one may elect to take fewer items from that stratum.

Cluster Sampling. **Cluster sampling** represents a second important sampling plan in which the population is subdivided into groups in an attempt to design an efficient sample. The subdivisions or classes of the population in this case are called clusters, where each cluster, ideally, has the same characteristics as the parent population. If each cluster is assumed to be representative of the population, then the characteristics of this population can be estimated by (randomly) picking a cluster and then randomly sampling elements from within this cluster. Since clusters contain sampling units that are geographically or physically close together, the cost of sampling is greatly reduced. Sampling within a cluster may take any of the forms already discussed and may even involve sampling from clusters within a cluster (called two-stage cluster sampling). The criterion for the selection of optimal clusters is exactly opposite to that for strata:

> There should be little variability between clusters, but a high variability (e.g., representation of the population) within each cluster.

Cluster sampling can be illustrated by extending our previous example. Assume that we now want to sample political preferences in all cities of the United States rather than just one. In this case a simple random sample would probably be very difficult and expensive, if not impossible, to collect; instead, it may be that a number of cities adequately represent the population of all cities, and it would then be sufficient to sample from just one of these cities. Within the chosen city, one could use simple random sampling, stratified sampling, or systematic sampling, or one could break the city into smaller clusters. In cluster sampling there is always the danger that a cluster is not truly representative of the population; a geographical bias, for example, may exist when one city is used to represent political preferences in all cities of the United States.

Double, Multiple, and Sequential Sampling

One of the most important decisions in any sampling design involves selecting the *size* of the sample. Usually, size is determined in advance of any data collection, but in some circumstances, this may not be the most efficient procedure. Consider the problem of determining whether a shipment of 5000 items meets certain specified standards. It would be too expensive to check all 5000 items for their quality, so a sample is drawn, and each item in the sample is tested for quality. Rather than take one large sample, of perhaps 100 items, a preliminary random sample of 25 items could be drawn and inspected. It may often be unnecessary to examine the remaining 75 items; perhaps the entire lot can be judged on the basis of these 25 items. If a high percentage of the 25 components were defective, the conclusion drawn would probably be that the quality of the entire lot may not be acceptable. A low percentage of defectives may lead to accepting the lot. Values other than these extremes may also lead to acceptance or rejection of the entire lot. Nevertheless, there will usually be a range in which there is doubt about the quality of the entire lot. For example, it may be normal to have zero or one defective in a sample of 25. More than four would indicate too many defectives in the lot. Two or three defectives, however, may lead one to suspect the entire lot, but not necessarily to reject it. An additional sample, perhaps the remaining 75 items, could then be taken, and the lot judged on the basis of all 100 items.

ex. of 2-stage sampling

Samples in which the items are drawn in two different stages, such as in the sequential fashion described above or from a cluster within a cluster, represent a process referred to as *two-stage sampling*. Virtually all important samples, and certainly all large-scale surveys, represent one form or another of multiple-stage sampling, and the sample design is usually not simple to plan. The major advantage of double, multiple, and **sequential sampling** procedures obviously depends on the savings that result when fewer items than usual must be observed. These procedures are especially appropriate when sampling is expensive, as when inspection destroys the usefulness of a valuable item or when travel expenses of the survey team would be high.

Nonprobabilistic Sampling

In some sense, all **nonprobabilistic sampling** procedures represent **judgment samples,** in that they involve the selection of the items in a sample on the basis of the judgment or opinion of one or more persons. Judgment sampling is usually employed when a random sample cannot be taken or is not practical. It may be that there is not enough time or money to collect a random sample; or perhaps the sample represents an exploratory study where randomness is not too important. On the other hand, when the number of population elements is small, the judgment of an expert may be better than random methods in picking a truly representative sample. For example, you are using judgment sampling when you ask a friend's opinion about a movie or about a particular college course. Similarly, "representative" individuals or animals are often chosen to participate in experiments, and accountants frequently select "typical" weeks for auditing accounts.

In **quota sampling,** each person gathering observations is given a specified number of elements to sample. This technique is used often in public-opinion surveys, in which the interviewer is allocated a certain number of people to interview. The decision as to exactly whom to interview is usually left to the individual doing the interviewing, although certain guidelines are almost always established. With well-trained and trustworthy interviewers this procedure can be quite effective and can be carried out at a relatively low cost. Great danger exists, however, that procedures left to the interviewers' judgment and convenience may contain many unknown biases not conducive to a representative sample. Quota sampling is used often to obtain market research data or to survey for political preferences. In some of these situations a quota sample can be thought of as a special form of stratified sampling, in which interviewers are sent out and told to obtain a specified number of interviews from each stratum.

The least representative sampling procedure selects observations on the basis of convenience to the researcher; i.e., a **convenience sample.** "Street-corner surveys," in which the interviewer questions people as they go by, seems to be a favorite method of local TV news reporters for collecting public opinions. This method obviously cannot be considered very likely to yield a representative sample; more often, the results are biased and quite unsatisfactory. Convenience sampling is not widely used in circumstances other than preliminary or exploratory studies, or where representativeness is not a crucial factor.

The following table itemizes the sampling procedures described in Section 7.2. *or designs*

Probabilistic	Nonprobabilistic
Simple random sampling	Judgment sampling
Stratified sampling	Quota sampling
Cluster sampling	Convenience sampling
Multiple/sequential sampling	

7.3   SAMPLE STATISTICS

As we have indicated previously, the usual purpose of sampling is to learn something about the population being sampled. In selecting a sampling design, the primary considerations are the importance of the information to be gathered and the desired degree of accuracy of what is learned about the population. In view of these purposes it is important that we structure the problem of taking a sample and analyzing the sample results in terms of the concepts of probability presented in Chapters 3 through 6.

Assume that we are planning on taking a sample of n observations in order to determine the characteristics of some random variable x. The process of taking a sample from this population can be viewed as an experiment, and the observations that may occur in such an experiment make up the sample space. Suppose we let the random variables x_1, x_2, ..., x_n represent the observations in this sample. That is, the random variable x_1 represents the observation that occurs first in a sample of n observations, x_2 represents the second observation, and so forth. In simple random sampling, every item in the population has an equal chance of being the observation that occurs first, so in this case the sample space for x_1 would be the entire population of x-values. It is important to remember that x_1, x_2, ..., x_n are all *random variables*, and each of these variables has a theoretical probability distribution. Under simple random sampling, the probability distribution of each of the random variables x_1, x_2, ..., x_n will be identical to the distribution of the population random variable x (since the sample space for each one is the entire population of x-values).

Once we have collected a random sample of n observations, we have one value for x_1, one value for x_2, and so forth, with one value for x_n. We now need to learn more about the characteristics of the random variable x (the population) by making use of the sample values of x_1, x_2, ..., x_n. In general, the population parameters of interest are usually those described in Chapters 1 and 2, the most important being the summary measures for central location and dispersion. It is intuitively appealing that the best estimate of a population parameter is given by a comparable sample measure (a sample *statistic*). For example, we will see that the best estimate of the central location of a population is a measure of the central location of a sample; and the best estimate of the population dispersion is a measure of the dispersion of the sample. *Thus, a sample statistic is used as an estimate of a population parameter.*

A **sample statistic** can be defined as a function of some (or all) of the n random variables x_1, x_2, ..., x_n. That is, a sample statistic is a random variable that is based on the sample values of x_1, x_2, ..., x_n. This means that there is a theoretical probability distribution associated with every sample statistic. For example, suppose we let $R = x_{max} - x_{min}$ be the *range* of the values in a sample. In this case, the sample statistic R is a random variable which is a function of only two values in each sample, the largest value (x_{max}) and the smallest value (x_{min}). Since R is a random variable, it has a theoretical probability distribution that we could develop if this statistic were of interest. The method of sampling used will affect the probability distribution of any sample statistic.

Many different sample statistics can be used to estimate the population parameters of interest. Generally, the population parameters of most interest are the mean and variance, since these two measures are so useful in describing a distribution and so necessary in decision-making. Consequently, the most useful sample statistics are the sample mean and the sample variance, which provide the best information about the population mean and variance. As we indicated earlier, there are a number of different sampling procedures that one may use to estimate population parameters. The particular procedure selected will have an effect on one's ability to make inferences about the underlying population. We will assume, at least initially, simple random sampling. In the development to follow, the reader should bear in mind that a similar development could be presented for sample statistics other than the mean and the variance.

Sample Mean

The mean (or average) of a set of observations that represent a sample is calculated in the same manner as demonstrated in Chapter 1 for the mean of a population [Formula (1.1)]: by summing each value of **x** in the sample and then dividing this sum by the number of observations in the sample. The letter n is used to denote the number of observations in the sample, and the **sample mean** is denoted by the symbol $\bar{x}$, which is read "ex-bar."

$$\text{Sample mean:} \quad \bar{x} = \frac{1}{n} \sum_{i=1}^{n} x_i. \tag{7.1}$$

The reader may wish to verify the similarity between Formulas (7.1) and (1.1). They are both averages of a set of numbers. In the case of (7.1), there are only n numbers (the sample size), while for (1.1) there are N numbers (the population size). The x_i's of a sample are a subset of the x_i's of the population.

Example 7.1. The Champaign, Illinois, Chevrolet dealer has ordered a large number of Chevy Vans to be drop-shipped to Elkart, Indiana, where they will be customized. These vans have a list price of $18,500, but each dealer discounts the price down to as low as $14,000 (excluding a trade-in) depending on how hard the customer bargains. The first four vans sold for the following prices (**x** is the price):

$$x: \quad 15,250, \quad 14,500, \quad 14,750, \quad 14,400.$$

The dealer considers these four prices to be a random sample of the selling price for all vans at that dealership during the next six months. The average selling price is

$$\bar{x} = \frac{1}{4}(15,250 + 14,500 + 14,750 + 14,400) = \frac{1}{4}(58,900) = 14,725.$$

The sample mean is $\bar{x}$ = $14,725.
or (avg.)

The Sample
Variance and
Standard
Deviation

Recall we defined a population variance in Chapter 2 as the sum of the squared deviations about μ:

$$\text{Population variance:} \qquad \sigma^2 = \frac{1}{N}\sum_{i=1}^{N}(x_i - \mu)^2.$$

A **sample variance** differs from this formula because we cannot determine the sum of the squared deviations about μ; in most sampling problems, μ is unknown. Instead, we will take the sum of the squared deviations about $\bar{x}$, or $\sum_{i=1}^{n}(x_i - \bar{x})^2$. For a population we divided this sum of squared deviations by N, the population size. *For samples we divide the sum of squared deviations by n − 1.*

The reason for dividing by $(n - 1)$ is that the resulting measure of variability can be shown to provide the *best* estimate of the (unknown) population variance. This fact will be explained in more detail in Section 7.8 and when we discuss estimation procedures in Chapter 8. For now, we merely show how to calculate a sample variance and a sample standard deviation. A sample variance is denoted by the symbol s^2 and is defined as follows:

$$\text{Sample variance:} \qquad s^2 = \frac{1}{n-1}\sum_{i=1}^{n}(x_i - \bar{x})^2. \qquad \textbf{(7.2)}$$

We can use Formula (7.2) to determine the variance of the selling price of the four vans sold by the Chevrolet dealer in Champaign. The steps for this calculation are shown in Table 7.1. Remember that the

TABLE 7.1 **Calculating a variance**

(1)	(2)	(3)	
x (Selling Price)	$(x - \bar{x})$	$(x - \bar{x})^2$	
$15,250	$525	$275,625	
14,500	−225	50,625	$s^2 = \frac{1}{3}(432{,}500)$
14,750	25	625	
14,400	−325	105,625	$= 144{,}166.67$ (dollars squared)
$\sum(x_i - \bar{x}) = 0$		$432{,}500 = \sum(x_i - \bar{x})^2$	

mean of this sample is $\bar{x} = \$14,725$. The second column of Table 7.1 gives the deviation of each x-value about $\bar{x}$. These deviations will always sum to 0. The third column gives the squared deviations about $\bar{x}$. The sum of squared deviations, 432,500, is at the bottom of this column. This sum divided by $n - 1 = 3$ equals the sample variance. That is, $s^2 = 144,166.67$ (dollars squared).

As was the case for a population, the standard deviation is the square root of the variance. A sample standard deviation is represented by the symbol s, where s is defined as follows:

$$\text{Sample standard deviation:} \quad s = \sqrt{s^2}. \tag{7.3}$$

For the example of Chevy vans the standard deviation is

$$s^2 = \sqrt{144,166.67} = 379.69 \text{ (dollars).}$$

Sample Statistics Using Frequencies

Recall from Chapter 2 that data are often presented in the form of a frequency distribution. That is, sometimes a value x_i occurs more than once, and the number of times (the "frequency") this value occurs is denoted as f_i. Formulas (7.1) and (7.2) are really special cases of more general formulas for $\bar{x}$ and s^2 where $f_i = 1$. The general formulas are shown below.

$$\text{Sample mean: } \bar{x} = \frac{1}{n}\sum_{i=1}^{k} x_i f_i.$$

$$\tag{7.4}$$

$$\text{Sample variance: } s^2 = \frac{1}{n-1}\sum_{i=1}^{k}(x_i - \bar{x})^2 f_i.$$

In Formulas (7.4) we assume that the sample consists of n observations but that there are only k *different* values of **x**. The frequency of the first value of x, which is denoted as x_1, is f_1. The frequency of the second value (x_2) is f_2 and so forth, with f_k representing the frequency of the last value (x_k). Thus, the sums in Formulas (7.4) start with $i = 1$ and end with $i = k$.

Before illustrating the use of Formulas (7.4), recall that we developed computational formulas for a variance in Chapter 2 (Formulas 2.6 and 2.10). The same type of computational formula can now be developed for the sample variance in Formula (7.4). The only difference is that the divisor is now $(n - 1)$, so that the old "mean square–square mean" relationship has to be modified slightly.*

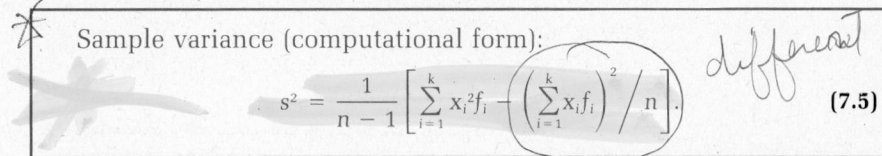

Sample variance (computational form):

$$s^2 = \frac{1}{n-1}\left[\sum_{i=1}^{k} x_i^2 f_i - \left(\sum_{i=1}^{k} x_i f_i\right)^2 \Big/ n\right].$$ (7.5)

different

Example 7.2. Consider the case of a United States Senate committee investigating the number of federal grants awarded for local projects (such as HUD and TOPICS Programs) in cities with populations ranging from 50,000 to 200,000. In an attempt to measure the characteristics of the population in this case (all cities of that size in the United States), ten randomly selected cities were surveyed. Table 7.2 shows the results of this survey (x = number of grants during the past year, f is the frequency of each value of x, and $k = 5$ classes). The sample mean can be calculated by using the information from column (2) into Formula (7.4).

$$\bar{x} = \frac{1}{n}\sum_{i=1}^{5} x_i f_i = \frac{1}{10}(28) = 2.8.$$

The average number of grants in the ten cities sampled is thus 2.8.

TABLE 7.2 **Number of federal grants to cities with populations 50,000–200,000**

(1)	(2)	(3)	(4)	(5)	(6)	(7)	(8)
x	f	xf	$(x - \bar{x})$	$(x - \bar{x})^2$	$(x - \bar{x})^2 f$	x^2	$x^2 f$
1	2	2	-1.8	3.24	6.48	1	2
2	3	6	-0.8	0.64	1.92	4	12
3	1	3	0.2	0.04	0.04	9	9
4	3	12	1.2	1.44	4.32	16	48
5	1	5	2.2	4.84	4.84	25	25
	10	28			17.60		96

* In developing (7.5) from (7.4) the intermediate step is

$$s^2 = \frac{1}{n-1}(\Sigma\, x_i^2 f_i - 2\bar{x}\Sigma f_i x_i + \bar{x}^2 \Sigma f_i) = \frac{1}{n-1}\left[\left(\Sigma\, x_i^2 f_i - \frac{2(\Sigma f_i x_i)^2}{n} + \frac{n(\Sigma f_i x_i)^2}{n^2}\right)\right]$$

where the terms in parentheses represent a simplification of the summation terms in (7.4).

To measure the variance of these data, we can use either Formula (7.4) or (7.5). Using the product of the frequencies times the squared deviations in column (6), we can calculate s^2 as follows:

$$s^2 = \frac{1}{n-1} \sum_{i=1}^{k} (x_i - \bar{x})^2 f_i = \frac{1}{9} (17.60) = 1.956.$$

If the computational Formula (7.5) had been used, only columns (3) and (8) need to be used:

$$\frac{1}{n-1} \left[\sum_{i=1}^{k} x_i^2 f_i - \left(\sum_{i=1}^{k} x_i f_i \right)^2 \bigg/ n \right] = \frac{1}{9} \left[96 - 28^2/10 \right] = 1.956.$$

The sample standard deviation is $s = \sqrt{1.956} = 1.399$. Again, one way to check to see if the result $s = 1.399$ is reasonable is to use our old rule of thumb. About 68% of the sample values should fall within one standard deviation of the mean, $\bar{x} \pm 1s$. In this case the result appears reasonable, since seven of the ten observations lie in the interval $\bar{x} \pm 1s = 2.8 \pm 1.399 = 1.401$ to 4.199.

Study Question 7.1: The Usage of a Student Union Building

A study of the usage of the Penn State University Student Union Building resulted in the following sample data. The variable x represents the number of times per week the Union was used during a one-week period by the 100 students in the survey.

x (Times Used)	Frequency
0	26
1	31
2	19
3	10
4	6
5	3
6	2
7	2
8	1
	n = 100

Find the mean and the variance of this sample. What percent of the sample data lie within two standard deviations of the mean?

Answer. Using Formula (7.4), we get

$$\bar{x} = \frac{1}{100}[0(26) + 1(31) + 2(19) + \cdots + 8(1)] = \frac{1}{100}[172] = 1.72.$$

Using Formula (7.4), we get

$$s^2 = \frac{1}{100 - 1}[(0 - 1.72)^2(26) + (1 - 1.72)^2(31) + \cdots + (8 - 1.72)^2(1)]$$

$$= \frac{1}{99}(306.16) = 3.09 \text{ (visits squared)}.$$

Using Formula (7.5), the computational formula for the sample variance, we get

$$s^2 = \frac{1}{99}[0^2(26) + 1^2(31) + \cdots + 8^2(1) - (172)^2/100]$$

$$= \frac{1}{99}[602 - 295.84] = 3.09 \text{ (visits squared)}.$$

$$s = \sqrt{3.09} = 1.76 \text{ (visits)}.$$

The interval $\bar{x} \pm 2s$ is $1.72 \pm (2)(1.76) = [-1.80$ to $+5.24]$. Since we cannot have a negative number of visits, the interval for practical purposes is [0 to 5.24]. This interval contains the frequencies 26 + 31 + 19 + 10 + 6 + 3 = 95. Thus, 95% of the sample data lies within two standard deviations. This corresponds precisely to the rule of thumb for the percent of values within plus or minus two standard deviations of the mean.

Perhaps at this point we should reiterate that one of our objectives in calculating **sample** means and variances is to be able to make statements about the **population** mean and variance. Since different samples from the same population may have different means and variances, the only way to determine the true population parameters is to enumerate every item in the population (a census). But a census is generally too costly and time-consuming. Thus, we must be content to use *sample statistics to estimate the population parameters and then to make statements about how reliable or accurate such a sample statistic is in describing the population parameter of interest.*

To establish the reliability or accuracy with which a sample statistic describes a population parameter, one must know how probable it is that specific values of this statistic will occur (1) for every possible value of the population parameter and (2) for every possible sample size. To begin our discussion of the reliability and accuracy of a sample, let us suppose that we can take a large number of random samples, all of size n, and then calculate $\bar{x}$ for each of these samples. These values of $\bar{x}$ can be put in the form of a frequency distribution. This frequency distribution will have a certain shape, as well as a mean and a variance. Now, if we take *all possible* samples of size n (and the number of samples may be infinite), and determine $\bar{x}$ for each sample, the resulting distribution is the *probability* distribution of all possible values of $\bar{x}$.

The probability distribution of $\bar{x}$ is called a *sampling distribution*. We can also calculate a sampling distribution for s^2 by considering all possible values of s^2 from samples of a given size n. Such sampling distributions are necessary for making probability statements about the reliability and accuracy of sample statistics, and they will be discussed in detail in the remaining sections of this chapter.

Define. *Sample design, response bias, nonsampling errors, sampling errors, simple random sampling, systematic sampling, stratified sampling, cluster sampling, two-stage sampling, probabilistic sampling, nonprobabilistic sampling, sample statistic, sample mean, sample variance, sample standard deviation.*

PROBLEMS

7.1 Under what conditions is nonprobabilistic sampling more appropriate than probabilistic sampling? Give several examples.

7.2 Distinguish between:
a) Systematic sampling and simple random sampling.
b) Stratified and cluster sampling.
c) Single-stage sampling and multiple-stage sampling.
d) Judgment, quota, and convenience sampling.
e) Random variable, random sample, observations selected "at random."

7.3 In designing a sample survey, what factors are most important in establishing the strata in stratified sampling? The clusters in cluster sampling? How will the cost of sampling affect these decisions?

7.4 A company packages lima bean seeds. Obviously not all the seeds in a given lot will germinate. However, the company does not want to package and present for consumer purchase an excessive number of bad seeds. In the long run, about $\frac{3}{4}$ of the seeds germinate, while $\frac{1}{4}$ do not. Before packaging a new lot, the company would like to be sure that at least $\frac{3}{4}$ of the new seeds will germinate. One clever(?) student says that they could test a random sample of only four seeds, and if three of them grew, they could assume that $\frac{3}{4}$ of all the seeds were good.

a) Do you think that the direct relationship between the probability from the sample and the likelihood of good seeds in the entire lot is perfect, as the student suggests? Explain briefly.

b) Suppose exactly $\frac{3}{4}$ of all the seeds were good; what is the probability that exactly three out of four in a random sample would be good? (Although sampling is without replacement, assume that the number of seeds is very large so that the probability of selecting a good seed, $\frac{3}{4}$, remains the same.)

7.5 Refer once again to **Data Set 1,** containing 78 cities, each with a population between 100,000 and 200,000.

a) Use Table V to select a random sample of five from the population of 78 cities. Specify how you picked the five numbers from Table V.

b) Calculate the mean income for your random sample of cities in part (a). Does your sample mean seem reasonably close to the population mean (which was given in Chapter 1)?

c) Calculate the variance and standard deviation of incomes for your sample of cities. Does the value of s seem reasonably close to σ?

7.6 Use Table V to collect a stratified sample from **Data Set 1.** Stratify the cities by using Moody Ratings, and then take a 20% sample from each stratum (round up to the nearest integer).

a) Determine the sample mean by adding all sample values and dividing by the total n.

b) Find the mean of each stratum.

7.7 Consider as a single population all undergraduate students in your university.

a) Specify exactly how you would go about taking a simple random sample of 50 students. Would a systematic sampling plan be easier in this situation? Would systematic sampling introduce any biases?

b) Specify exactly how you would go about taking a stratified sample, where the strata are the four classes of students (e.g., senior, junior, etc.) and each stratum is sampled in proportion to the number of students in that class.

7.8 Assume that you have been commissioned to design a survey of the age, income, and occupation of the customers who patronize a nationwide chain of stores. Describe how you would proceed with such a study.

7.9 Suppose you consider three George Lucas movies, *Star Wars, The Empire Strikes Back,* and *Raiders of the Lost Ark,* as a sample of top films over the past ten years. These three movies grossed (at the box office) $524, $365, and $224 million, respectively. Find the sample mean and variance. Is this a random sample? Explain.

7.10 Consider the following starting monthly salaries of business majors who recently graduated: $1975, 1990, 2025, 2070, 1940. Find the sample mean and standard deviation.

7.11 An ad in the *Wall Street Journal* reported the following prices for the daily rental of an economy automobile.

	Hertz	Avis
1. Boston	$50	$45
2. Detroit	48	47
3. Kansas City	44	40
4. Los Angeles	42	41
5. Miami	35	32
6. Phoenix	39	40
7. Washington, D.C.	55	54

a) Find the average of these two "samples."
b) Would you expect a "random sample" if Avis paid for the ad?
c) How would you go about taking a random sample in this situation?

7.12 Given the following sample distribution for x = number of soft drink machines needing repair per week at a certain university:

x	Frequency
1	2
2	7
3	10
4	1

find $\bar{x}$ and s.

7.13 The distribution of the number of defects per square yard of a cotton textile is given as follows:

No. of defects (x)	Frequency (f)
0	47
1	33
2	14
3	5
4	1
5	0
Total	100 = n

Find the mean and the standard deviation of this sample distribution.

7.14 Given the following sample distribution by class intervals for the number of hours worked last month by a certain group of business executives; find $\bar{x}$ and s.

Class		Frequency
190–204	197	3
205–219	212	5
220–234	227	9
235–249	242	6
250–264	257	7

0 1 2 3 45 6 7 8 9 10 11 12 13 14

30 = n

7.15 If the weekly wages of 100 workers are grouped into classes of $25 each, the following distribution results:

Wages	f
338–362	4
363–387	15
388–412	20
413–437	30
438–462	15
463–487	10
488–512	6
Total	100

Find $\bar{x}$ for the grouped data, using class marks, 350, 375, 400, . . ., 500.

7.16   A manufacturer of razor blades claims that the product will give, on the average, 15 good shaves. Suppose you have five friends who try using one of these razor blades each. The number of shaves reported by your friends are 12, 16, 8, 14, and 10.
a)   Find the mean and the standard deviation of this sample.
b)   Suggest how you might use this sample evidence to dispute or support the advertiser's claim.

7.17   A fresh-produce distributor has received complaints that bananas have been arriving spoiled at the retail store. The complaint is suspicious, since average delivery time is only 4 days (96 hours) and the bananas are fresh at the time of shipment. The distributor decides to simulate the appropriate conditions by selecting at random a sample of four crates of bananas and measuring the number of hours before spoilage occurs. The results for number of hours, **x**, are given as 106, 102, 104, and 108.
a)   Find the mean hours before spoilage.
b)   Find the standard deviation for **x**.
c)   On the basis of these measures, do you think that many of the bananas may indeed be arriving spoiled, or are you also suspicious of the complaints? Explain.
d)   Find the range of the sample of x-values.
e)   Give one reason why the answer of part (b) is better than that of part (d) as an estimate of dispersion for the entire population of bananas from which the sample was taken.

7.4   SAMPLING DISTRIBUTION OF $\bar{x}$

> The **sampling distribution** of $\bar{x}$ is the probability distribution of **all possible** values of $\bar{x}$ that could occur when a sample (of size n) is taken from some specified parent population.

   Example 7.3. Consider a parent population that has only three values, (1, 2, 3), which occur with equal probability (Fig. 7.1). The parent population is thus **x** = {1, 2, 3}. This population might represent the number of cable sports channels provided by different cable franchises in U.S. cities. The mean of this parent population is easily seen to be μ = 2.0; i.e., the average number of sports channels is 2.0. Now, let us assume that you are not familiar with the parent population, so you decide to take a random sample of size n = 2 of the cable franchises. Your sample of size n = 2 will look like one of the nine ordered pairs

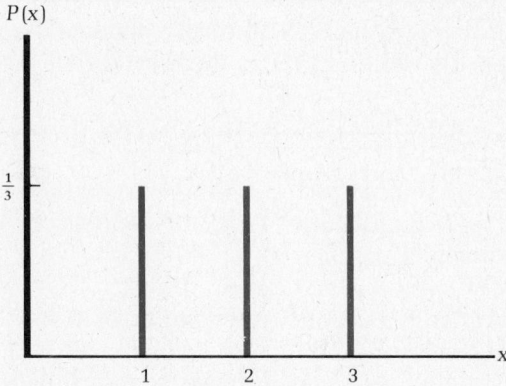

FIGURE 7.1 **Distribution of parent population.**

listed in the left-hand column of Table 7.3. The right-hand column lists the sample mean for each of the nine possible samples.

Each one of the nine samples in column one has the same probability of occurring, $\frac{1}{9}$. This implies that each one of the nine sample means in column two has this same ($\frac{1}{9}$) probability. Now, since only one of the values of $\bar{x}$ in column two equals 1.0, we can write $P(\bar{x} = 1.0) = \frac{1}{9}$. Similarly, there are two instances when $\bar{x}$ equals 1.5; hence $P(\bar{x} = 1.5) = \frac{2}{9}$. A graph (Fig. 7.2) and a table (Table 7.4) show the probabilities associated with all these possible values of $\bar{x}$.

Thus, Fig. 7.2 and Table 7.4 present the sampling distribution of $\bar{x}$ for $n = 2$, when $x = \{1, 2, 3\}$. It should be emphasized at this point that *the sampling distribution of $\bar{x}$ is itself a population.* As such, we are interested in the parameters of this population of $\bar{x}$'s, especially its mean and variance.

TABLE 7.3 **All samples of size $n = 2$ from (1, 2, 3)**

Sample	Sample Mean $\bar{x}$	
(1, 1)	1.0	
(1, 2)	1.5	
(2, 1)	1.5	
(1, 3)	2.0	
(3, 1)	2.0	This is the population of all possible $\bar{x}$'s
(2, 2)	2.0	when the sample size is $n = 2$.
(2, 3)	2.5	
(3, 2)	2.5	
(3, 3)	3.0	

> The symbol $\mu_{\bar{x}}$, which traditionally denotes the mean of the sampling distribution of $\bar{x}$, is the mean of all possible sample means.*

Using the notation of expected values, we can thus write $\mu_{\bar{x}} = E[\bar{x}]$. The variance of this population, which is denoted as $V[\bar{x}] = \sigma_{\bar{x}}^2$, will be discussed shortly.

Mean of $\bar{x}$, or $\mu_{\bar{x}}$ Because you plan to take only *one* sample, of size $n = 2$, you could get a sample mean as low as $\bar{x} = 1.0$ or as high as $\bar{x} = 3.0$ (see Table 7.4). A logical question for a researcher to ask in this situation is what would be the **expected value of $\bar{x}$** in such a situation, or what is $E[\bar{x}] = \mu_{\bar{x}}$? That is, what is the average of the p.m.f. in Table 7.4? The mean of these values is calculated in the same manner in which we calculated a mean in Chapter 4, except that now the random variable is $\bar{x}$, and we denote the mean of this variable as $\mu_{\bar{x}}$.

$$\mu_{\bar{x}} = \Sigma \, \bar{x} \, P(\bar{x}) = (1.0)(\tfrac{1}{9}) + (1.5)(\tfrac{2}{9}) + (2.0)(\tfrac{3}{9}) + 2.5(\tfrac{2}{9}) + (3.0)(\tfrac{1}{9})$$
$$= 2.00.$$

Thus we have shown for this population that $\mu_{\bar{x}} = \mu = 2.00$. The fact that these two means are equal is not a coincidence, as it can be shown that $\mu_{\bar{x}}$ equals μ for *any* parent population and *any* given sample size. That is,

TABLE 7.4 **The sampling distribution of $\bar{x}$**

$\bar{x}$	$P(\bar{x})$
1.0	$\tfrac{1}{9}$
1.5	$\tfrac{2}{9}$
2.0	$\tfrac{3}{9}$
2.5	$\tfrac{2}{9}$
3.0	$\tfrac{1}{9}$
	1.0

* From this point on we will add a subscript to a population parameter or sample statistic whenever it may be unclear which population or sample is being described. For example, s_y refers to the standard deviation of the sample of y-values, while $\mu_{\bar{x}}$ refers to the mean of the population of $\bar{x}$-values. If no subscript is used, such as μ or σ or s, these refer to the distribution of x-values under consideration.

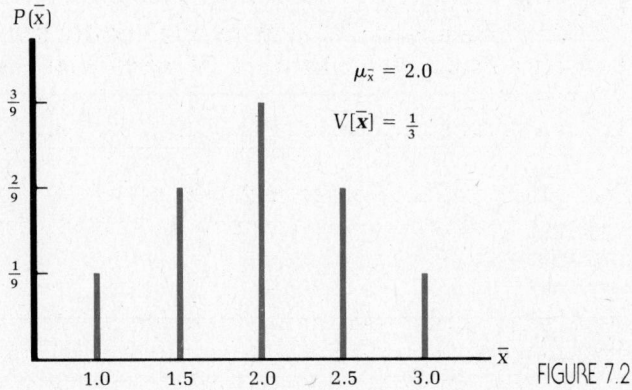

FIGURE 7.2

Expected value of $\bar{x}$:

$$E[\overline{x}] = \mu_{\bar{x}} = \mu, \qquad (7.6)$$

where μ is the mean of the population of x's and $\mu_{\bar{x}}$ is the mean of the population of $\bar{x}$'s.*

The Variance of $\bar{x}$ In addition to knowing the mean of the sampling distribution of $\overline{x}$ for a given sample size n, we also need to know its variance.

The variance of the values of $\overline{x}$ is denoted by either $V[\overline{x}]$ or $\sigma_{\bar{x}}^2$.

---

* Let x_1, x_2, . . ., x_n represent independent random variables corresponding to the n observations in a sample from a population with mean μ_x (i.e., $E[x_i] = \mu$). Now, since $\bar{x}$ $= (1/n)(x_1 + x_2 + \cdots + x_n)$, we can apply the rules of expectation from Section 4.4 as follows:

$$E[\overline{x}] = E\left[\frac{1}{n}(x_1 + x_2 + \cdots + x_n)\right]$$

$$= \frac{1}{n} E[(x_1 + x_2 + \cdots + x_n)] \qquad \text{By Rule 3}$$

$$= \frac{1}{n} \{E[x_1] + E[x_2] + \cdots + E[x_n]\} \qquad \text{By Formula 4.13}$$

$$= \frac{1}{n} (\mu + \mu + \cdots + \mu) = \frac{1}{n} (n\mu) \qquad \text{Since } E[x_i] = \mu$$

$$\mu_{\bar{x}} = \mu.$$

TABLE 7.5 **Calculation of the variance of a distribution of sample means**

(1)	(2)	(3)	(4)	(5)
$\bar{x}$	$P(\bar{x})$	$(\bar{x} - \mu_{\bar{x}})$	$(\bar{x} - \mu_{\bar{x}})^2$	$(\bar{x} - \mu_{\bar{x}})^2 P(\bar{x})$
1.0	$\frac{1}{9}$	-1.0	1.00	$\frac{1}{9}$
1.5	$\frac{2}{9}$	-0.5	0.25	$\frac{2}{36}$
2.0	$\frac{3}{9}$	0	0	0
2.5	$\frac{2}{9}$	0.5	0.25	$\frac{2}{36}$
3.0	$\frac{1}{9}$	1.0	1.00	$\frac{1}{9}$

Mean 2.0 $\qquad\qquad\qquad\qquad\qquad\qquad V[\bar{x}] = \frac{12}{36} = \frac{1}{3}$

The **variance of $\bar{x}$** is defined in the same manner in which we previously defined a variance, namely, as the expected value of the squared deviations of the variable ($\bar{x}$ in this case) about its mean ($\mu_{\bar{x}}$ in this case). Thus,

$$\sigma_{\bar{x}}^2 = V[\bar{x}] = E[(\bar{x} - \mu_{\bar{x}})^2].$$

Suppose that we use the data in Table 7.5 to calculate the variance of the $\bar{x}$'s, or $V[\bar{x}]$. The variance of the $\bar{x}$'s is shown in column 5 to be $\sigma_{\bar{x}}^2 = \frac{1}{3}$; the standard deviation of the $\bar{x}$'s is $\sigma_{\bar{x}} = \sqrt{\frac{1}{3}} = 0.577$. The reader can verify that this standard deviation appears reasonable by noting that $\mu_{\bar{x}} \pm 1\sigma_{\bar{x}} = 2.00 \pm 0.577$ contains about 78% of the probability distribution of $\bar{x}$, which is not too far from the rule of thumb of 68%.

Although we calculated the value of $V[\bar{x}]$ directly in this example, in the many problems in which there is a very large (or infinite) number of values of $\bar{x}$ this approach is impractical, if not impossible. Fortunately, one can calculate $V[\bar{x}]$ without going through this process if one knows the variance of the population from which the samples are drawn (i.e., $V[x]$). The reason for this is that the variance of the random variable $\bar{x}$ is related to the variance of the parent population and to the sample size (n) by a very simple formula, which we will present shortly.

On the basis of intuition, it should appear reasonable that the variance of $\bar{x}$ will always be less than the variance of the parent population (except when $n = 1$), because there is less chance that a sample mean will take on an extreme value than there is that a single value of the parent population will take on an extreme value. In order for a sample mean to have an extremely large value, most or all of the sample items would have to be extremely large values. But we know from our study of probability that the probability of n extremely large values on n repeated draws is much *smaller* than the probability of a single extremely large value on one draw. It would be very unusual in n trials not to draw some middle values or some extremely low values. Such values would balance out the extremely large values and give a less extreme sample mean. Indeed, this intuitive logic is correct. Not only is the variance of $\bar{x}$ always less than or equal to the variance of the parent population, but it can be shown that σ^2 and $\sigma_{\bar{x}}^2$ are very precisely related. *The variance of the mean of a sample of n independent observations is 1/n times the variance of the parent population.**

$$\text{Variance of } \bar{x}: \quad \sigma_{\bar{x}}^2 = \frac{1}{n}\sigma^2. \tag{7.7}$$

When $n = 1$, all samples contain only one observation, and the distributions of x and $\bar{x}$ are identical. That is, $\sigma_{\bar{x}}^2 = \sigma^2/1 = \sigma^2$. As n becomes larger ($n \to \infty$), it is reasonable to expect $\sigma_{\bar{x}}^2$ to become smaller and smaller because the sample means will tend to deviate less and less from the population mean $\mu_{\bar{x}}$. When $n = \infty$ (or for finite populations, when $n = N$), all sample means will equal the population mean and the variance of the $\bar{x}$'s will be zero. To illustrate the relationship described by Formula (7.7), let us return to our example involving the population (1, 2, 3). The variance of this population is:

$$\sigma^2 = \frac{1}{N}\sum (x - \mu_{\bar{x}})^2 = \frac{1}{3}[(1-2)^2 + (2-2)^2 + (3-2)^2] = \frac{2}{3}.$$

Since we know that the variance of this population is $\frac{2}{3}$ and the sample size is $n = 2$, we can calculate $V[\bar{x}]$ using Formula (7.7):

$$\sigma_{\bar{x}}^2 = \frac{1}{n}\sigma^2 = \frac{1}{2}\left(\frac{2}{3}\right) = \frac{1}{3}.$$

This value of $V[\bar{x}]$ is exactly the same number we calculated using Table 7.5.

---

* Let $x_1, x_2, \ldots, x_n$ be independent random variables, each having the same variance (that is, $V[x_i] = \sigma^2$):

$$V[\bar{x}] = V\left[\frac{1}{n}(x_1 + x_2 + \cdots + x_n)\right] \qquad \text{By definition}$$

$$= \left(\frac{1}{n}\right)^2 V[x_1 + x_2 + \cdots + x_n] \qquad \text{By Rule 4 of Section 4.4}$$

$$= \left(\frac{1}{n}\right)^2 \left\{V[x_1] + V[x_2] + \cdots + V[x_n]\right\} \qquad \text{By Formula (4.13)}$$

$$\sigma_{\bar{x}}^2 = \frac{n}{n^2}(\sigma^2) = \frac{1}{n}\sigma^2. \qquad \text{Since } V[x_i] = \sigma^2$$

Standard Error of the Mean

It is customary to call the standard deviation of the $\bar{x}$'s (which is the square root of $V[\bar{x}]$ and is denoted as $\sigma_{\bar{x}}$) the **standard error of the mean.** The word "error" in this context obviously refers to sampling error, as $\sigma_{\bar{x}}$ is a measure of the "standard" (or expected) error when the sample mean is used to obtain information or draw conclusions about the unknown population mean.

$$\text{Standard error of the mean:} \quad \sigma_{\bar{x}} = \sqrt{\frac{\sigma^2}{n}} = \frac{\sigma}{\sqrt{n}}. \qquad (7.8)$$

In the above example the standard error of the mean is

$$\sigma_{\bar{x}} = \sqrt{\frac{\sigma^2}{n}} = \sqrt{\frac{\frac{2}{3}}{2}} = \sqrt{\tfrac{1}{3}} = 0.577.$$

We must emphasize at this point that $\mu_{\bar{x}}$ and $\sigma_{\bar{x}}$ are parameters of the population of sample averages from all conceivable samples of size n, and these population parameters are *unknown* quantities. In fact, the values of μ, $\mu_{\bar{x}}$, σ, and $\sigma_{\bar{x}}$ are usually *all* unknown quantities, which means that the relationship $\mu_{\bar{x}} = \mu$ and $\sigma_{\bar{x}} = \sigma/\sqrt{n}$ cannot be used to solve for the value of one of these quantities. However, knowledge of the fact that such relationships exist is important in determining how far a sample mean can be expected to deviate from the population mean. The advantage of knowing this information is that we can test *hypotheses* about a population by looking at sample results. For example, suppose we had *hypothesized* (but did not know) that our parent population was $x = \{1, 2, 3\}$. If a single sample of size $n = 2$ from the population yielded $\bar{x} = 1.0$, then we might suspect that our assumption about the population $x = \{1, 2, 3\}$ is incorrect. Our knowledge of the sampling distribution for $\bar{x}$ confirms that the $P(\bar{x} = 1.0)$ is only $\tfrac{1}{9}$ for samples of size 2 from this population — not a frequently occurring event. In Chapter 9 we will formally consider this process of testing hypotheses.

Study Question 7.2: Rating the Quality of Restaurants
The Mobil Travel Guide rates restaurants with one to five stars, depending on the quality of the food and service. From one source you hear that the Mobil rating staff gives approximately 20% of the restaurants a one-star rating, 20% a two-star rating, and so forth, with 20% receiving 5 stars. You decide to take a sample of ten randomly selected restaurants and look up the rating of each one.

a) Find the mean and variance of x, where x is the rating.

b) What is meant by the "sampling distribution of $\bar{x}$" for this problem? What mean would you expect for this sampling distribution (sample of size 10) if the source mentioned above is correct? What variance would you expect? What is the standard error of the mean?

c) Based on your answer to part (b), draw a "rough" sketch of the sampling distribution of $\bar{x}$. (We will learn more about sketching this distribution in the next section.)

Answer

a) Using formulas (4.2) and (4.4) from Chapter 4, we get

$$\mu = \sum x_i P(x_i) = 1(0.20) + 2(0.20) + 3(0.20) + 4(0.20) + 5(0.20)$$
$$= 3.0 \text{ stars};$$
$$\sigma^2 = \sum (x_i - \mu)^2 P(x_i)$$
$$= [(1 - 3)^2(0.20) + (2 - 3)^2(0.20) + \cdots + (5 - 3)^2(0.20)]$$
$$= 2.0 \text{ (stars squared)}.$$

b) The sampling distribution of $\bar{x}$ is the probability mass function for the mean of all possible samples of size 10 drawn from the parent population. The mean of the sampling distribution of $\bar{x}$ is the same as the mean of the parent population. Thus, from part (a),

$$\mu_{\bar{x}} = \mu = 3.0 \text{ stars}.$$

The variance of the sampling distribution of $\bar{x}$ is the variance of the parent population divided by n (= 10). Thus,

$$\sigma_{\bar{x}}^2 = \frac{1}{10}(2.0) = 0.20 \text{ (stars squared)}.$$

c) The standard error of the mean is $\sqrt{0.20} = 0.447$ (stars).

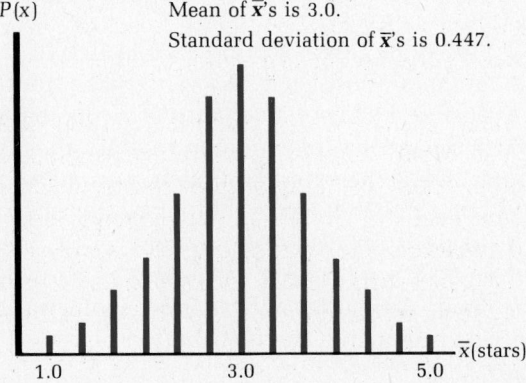

$P(\bar{x})$ Mean of $\bar{x}$'s is 3.0.
Standard deviation of $\bar{x}$'s is 0.447.

1.0   3.0   5.0 $\bar{x}$(stars)

Although we have derived the mean and variance of the $\bar{x}$'s, nothing has been said about the *shape* of the sampling distribution of $\bar{x}$. Recall from Chapter 2 that distributions with the same mean and variance may have distinctly different shapes. It is necessary, therefore, to be more specific about the entire distribution of $\bar{x}$'s. To do so, we will first assume that the parent population is normal and then later drop this assumption.

7.5 SAMPLING DISTRIBUTION OF $\bar{x}$, NORMAL PARENT POPULATION

We already know the mean and variance of the distribution of $\bar{x}$'s, but what is known about its *shape*? It is usually not possible to specify the shape of the $\bar{x}$'s when the parent population is discrete and the sample size is small. However, when the sample is drawn from a parent population (x) that is normally distributed, then the shape of the $\bar{x}$'s can be specified. As you might suspect, in this situation the $\bar{x}$'s are distributed normally. That is,

> The sampling distribution of $\bar{x}$'s drawn from a normal parent population is a normal distribution.

Using the fact that the mean of the $\bar{x}$'s is $\mu_{\bar{x}} = \mu$ [Formula (7.6)] and that the variance of the $\bar{x}$'s is $\sigma_{\bar{x}}^2 = \sigma^2/n$ [Formula (7.7)], we can now specify that the sampling distribution of $\bar{x}$ is $N(\mu_{\bar{x}}, \sigma_{\bar{x}}^2) = N(\mu, \sigma^2/n)$ whenever the parent population is normal. That is, the mean and variance of $\bar{x}$ are $\mu_{\bar{x}}$ and $\sigma_{\bar{x}}^2$ (or μ and σ^2/n), regardless of the shape of the parent population. The new point is that if the population is normal, so is the distribution of $\bar{x}$.

To illustrate this sampling distribution of $\bar{x}$, we will suppose that all possible samples of size $n = 20$ are drawn from a normal population that has a mean $\mu = 50$ and a variance $\sigma^2 = 80$; that is, x is $N(50, 80)$. Because all normal distributions are continuous, an infinite number of different samples of size 20 could be drawn. For any of these samples a mean, $\bar{x}$, could be calculated. Since the population mean is $\mu = 50$, the mean of the $\bar{x}$'s is $\mu_{\bar{x}} = 50$. Similarly, since $\sigma^2 = 80$, the variance of the $\bar{x}$'s is $\sigma_{\bar{x}}^2 = \sigma^2/n = \frac{80}{20} = 4$. Finally, because x is normal, $\bar{x}$ will also be normally distributed. All of this information about $\bar{x}$ can be summarized by the following statement: The distribution of $\bar{x}$ is $N(50, 4)$.

This means that 68.3% of the sample means will fall within plus-or-minus one standard error of the mean $(\sigma_{\bar{x}} = \sqrt{4} = 2)$,

$$\mu \pm 1\sigma_{\bar{x}} = 50 \pm 1(2) = 48 \quad \text{to} \quad 52;$$

95.4% will fall within plus-or-minus two standard errors of the mean,

$$\mu \pm 2\sigma_{\bar{x}} = 50 \pm 2(2) = 46 \quad \text{to} \quad 54;$$

and 99.7% of all sample means will fall within plus-or-minus three standard errors of the mean,

$$\mu \pm 3\sigma_{\bar{x}} = 50 \pm 3(2) = 44 \quad \text{to} \quad 56.$$

Figure 7.3 shows the sampling distribution of $\bar{x}$ for all possible samples of size 20 taken from a population with the distribution $N(50, 80)$.

The following statement summarizes what we now know about the distribution of sample means $(\bar{x})$.

> If the parent population (x) is normally distributed, with mean μ and variance σ^2, then the distribution of $\bar{x}$ for a given sample size n will be
>
> $$N\left(\mu, \frac{\sigma^2}{n}\right).$$

FIGURE 7.3 **Sampling distribution of $\bar{x}$ for samples of $n = 20$ taken from a population with distribution $N(50, 80)$.**

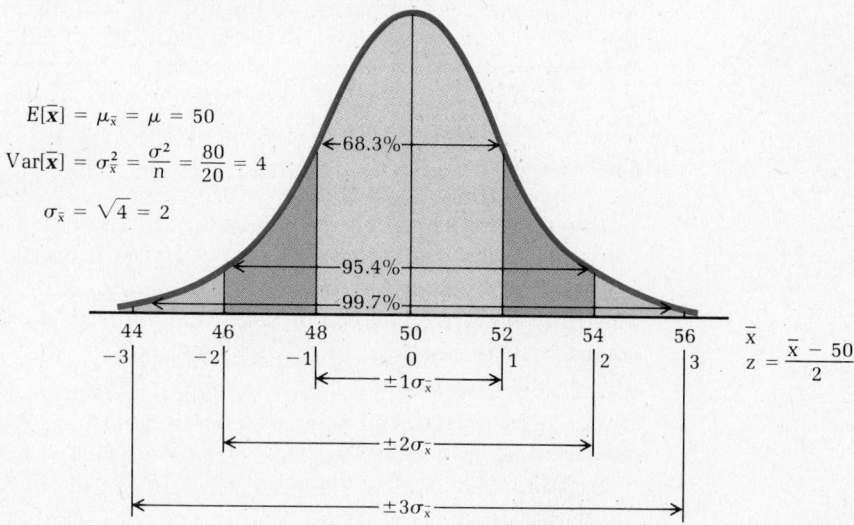

$$E[\bar{x}] = \mu_{\bar{x}} = \mu = 50$$

$$\text{Var}[\bar{x}] = \sigma_{\bar{x}}^2 = \frac{\sigma^2}{n} = \frac{80}{20} = 4$$

$$\sigma_{\bar{x}} = \sqrt{4} = 2$$

$$z = \frac{\bar{x} - 50}{2}$$

The Standardized Form of the Random Variable $\bar{x}$ (σ Known)* In Chapter 6 we saw that it is usually easier to work with the standard normal form of a variable than to leave it in its original units. The same type of transformation that was made on the random variable x at that point can now be made on the random variable $\bar{x}$. Recall that in Section 4.4 the variable x was transformed to its standard normal form by subtracting the mean from each value and then dividing by the standard deviation. The resulting variable, $z = (x - \mu)/\sigma$, was shown to have a mean of zero and a variance of one. Although now we are interested in transforming the variable $\bar{x}$ instead of x, and the standard deviation of this variable is $\sigma/\sqrt{n}$ instead of σ, the **standardization of $\bar{x}$** is accomplished in exactly the same fashion. One simply must take care always to subtract the mean and divide by the standard deviation corresponding to the variable being standardized. The mean and variance of the resulting variable will always be 0 and 1, respectively. Hence, the random variable

$$z = \frac{\bar{x} - \mu_{\bar{x}}}{\sigma_{\bar{x}}} = \frac{\bar{x} - \mu}{\sigma/\sqrt{n}}$$

has a mean of zero and a variance of one. Since we have said that the distribution of the random variable $\bar{x}$ is normal, it follows that the random variable z must also be normally distributed. Thus:

> When sampling from a normal parent population, the distribution of $z = (\bar{x} - \mu)/(\sigma/\sqrt{n})$ will be normal with mean 0 and variance 1. That is: $z = (\bar{x} - \mu)/(\sigma/\sqrt{n})$ is N(0, 1).

The standardized normal form of the variable $\bar{x}$ is shown on the **z**-scale in Fig. 7.3.

The limitations of the preceding discussion should be apparent, for although the normal distribution approximates the probability distribution of many real-world problems, one cannot *always* assume that the parent population is normal. What, for example, will be the shape of the distribution of $\bar{x}$'s when sampling from a highly skewed distribution? We consider this situation in the next section.

---

* Whenever $\bar{x}$ is normal, the distribution of $\bar{x}$ is N(μ, $\sigma/\sqrt{n}$), whether or not σ is known. However, in order to make probability statements about $\bar{x}$, we prefer to standardize this variable, and this standardization requires that we know σ.

7.6 SAMPLING DISTRIBUTION OF $\bar{x}$, POPULATION DISTRIBUTION UNKNOWN, σ KNOWN

When sampling is not from a normal parent population (or when the population is unknown), the size of the sample plays a critical role. When n is small, the shape of the distribution will depend mostly on the shape of the parent population. As n gets large, however, one of the most important theorems in statistical inference states that the shape of the sampling distribution of $\bar{x}$ will become more and more like a *normal distribution, no matter what the shape of the parent population.* This theorem, called the **central limit theorem,** is stated in formal terms below:

> **The central limit theorem:**
> Regardless of the distribution of the parent population (as long as it has a finite mean μ and variance σ^2), the distribution of the means of random samples will approach a normal distribution (with mean μ and variance σ^2/n) as the sample size n goes to infinity.

To summarize this statement and the previous one:

1. When the parent population is normal, the sampling distribution of $\bar{x}$ is exactly normal.
2. When the parent population is not normal (or perhaps unknown), the sampling distribution of $\bar{x}$ is approximately normal as the sample size increases.

We will not prove the central limit theorem, but will merely show, in Fig. 7.4, graphical evidence of its validity. The first row of diagrams in Fig. 7.4 shows four different parent populations. The next three rows show the sampling distribution of $\bar{x}$ for all possible repeated samples of size n = 2, n = 5, and n = 30, respectively, drawn from the populations shown in the first row. Note in the first column that when the parent population is normal, all the sampling distributions are also normal. Also, note that distributions in the same column have the same mean μ, but their variances decrease as $\sqrt{n}$ increases. This agrees with the central limit theorem.

The second column of figures in Fig. 7.4 represents what is called a *uniform (or rectangular) distribution.* We see here that the sampling distribution of $\bar{x}$ is already symmetrical when n = 2, and it is quite

FIGURE 7.4 **Sampling distribution of $\bar{x}$ for various population distributions when $n = 2$, 5, and 30.**

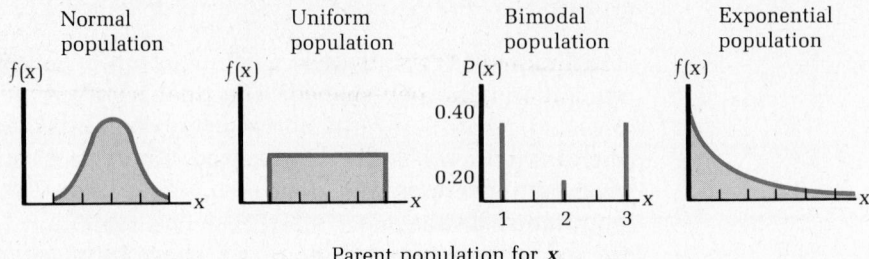

Parent population for **x**

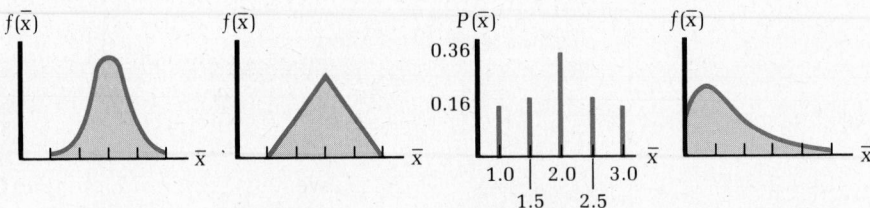

Sampling distribution of **$\bar{x}$** for sample size $n = 2$

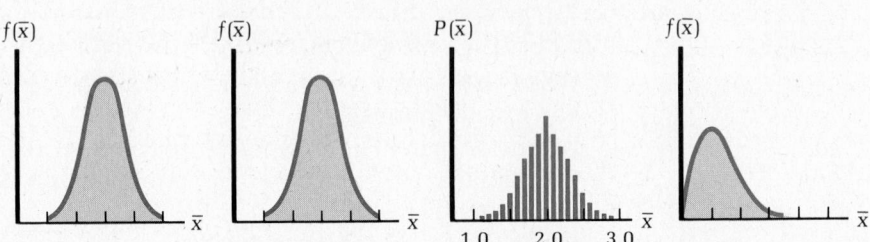

Sampling distribution of **$\bar{x}$** for sample size $n = 5$

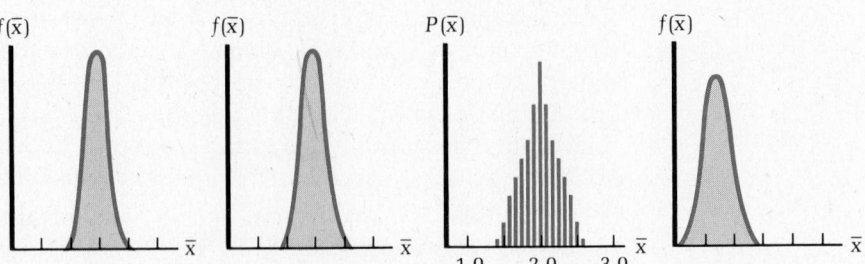

Sampling distribution of **$\bar{x}$** for sample size $n = 30$

normal in appearance when $n = 5$. As we move to the third column of figures, the parent population is now a bimodal distribution with discrete values of x (the central limit theorem applies whether x is discrete or continuous). Again, by $n = 2$ the distribution is symmetrical, and by $n = 5$ it is quite bell-shaped. The final parent population is the highly skewed exponential distribution. Here we see that for $n = 2$ and $n = 5$ the distribution is still fairly skewed, although it becomes more symmetrical as n increases. When $n = 30$, however, even such a skewed parent population results in a symmetrical, bell-shaped distribution for $\bar{x}$ which, by the central limit theorem, we know to be approximately normally distributed.

In general, just how large n needs to be for the sampling distribution of $\bar{x}$ to be a good approximation to the normal depends, as we saw in Fig. 7.4, on the shape of the parent population. Usually the approximation will be quite good if $n \geq 30$, although the third row of Fig. 7.4 demonstrates that satisfactory results are often obtained when n is much smaller.

Example of the Use of the Central Limit Theorem

Example 7.4. A midwestern telephone company recently asked for a rate increase for all residential telephones, including a 25% increase in student phones. To oppose this increase, a group of students decided to investigate the typical phone costs incurred in their town. The information provided by the telephone company was that, for the city as a whole, the average monthly bill was $15.30, with a standard deviation of $4.10. The students, however, were curious as to whether or not dormitory phones incurred similar bills. Since no information was available in this regard, the students decided to take a random sample of $n = 36$, in an attempt to obtain further information.

Now, if the dormitory phone bills come from the same population reported by the telephone company, then we know that the mean of all possible sample means will be $E[\bar{x}] = \mu_{\bar{x}} = \$15.30$, and the standard error of the mean will be $\sigma_{\bar{x}} = \sigma/\sqrt{n} = 4.10/\sqrt{36} = 0.683$. Furthermore, since the sample size is fairly large ($n = 36$), the central limit theorem tells us that the sampling distribution of $\bar{x}$ will be approximately normal [i.e., $\bar{x}$ is $N(\$15.30, 0.683^2)$]. Use of this distribution, shown in Fig. 7.5, allows us to answer a number of different probability questions for the telephone example.

Question 1. Suppose that in the random sample of 36 dormitory residents with phones, we find that the average phone bill is $14.00. A typical question to ask at this point is: What is the probability that a random sample of $n = 36$ will result in an average bill of $14.00 or less, when $\mu_{\bar{x}} = \$15.30$ and $\sigma_{\bar{x}} = 0.683$? Making use of the standard normal transformation, we know that:

$$P(\bar{x} \le \$14.00) = P\left(\frac{\bar{x} - \mu_{\bar{x}}}{\sigma_{\bar{x}}} \le \frac{14.00 - 15.30}{0.683}\right) = P(z \le -1.90).$$

By the central limit theorem, $\bar{x}$ is approximately normally distributed; hence, z is approximately standardized normal and, from Table III in the Appendix,

$$P(z \le -1.90) = F(-1.90) = 1.0 - F(1.90)$$
$$= 1.0 - 0.9713 = 0.0287.$$

The probability that a sample of 36 gives an average no larger than $14.00 is thus 0.0287. The reader should sketch this area on Fig. 7.5.

On the basis of the probability value calculated above, does it appear that dormitory phone bills are part of the same population as residential phone bills in general? We leave such questions concerned with drawing conclusions from sample data for the following chapters, but the reader should keep them in mind to retain a feeling of where we are headed.

Question 2. Rather than finding the probability below a specific value of $\bar{x}$, one often wants to determine values a and b, such that the probability is 0.99 (or some other probability) that the sample mean will fall between these values. Recall that we did a similar calculation in our discussion of the normal distribution in Chapter 6. In the present case we know that when $n = 36$, $\bar{x}$ will be approximately normally distributed, with mean $\mu_{\bar{x}} = \$15.30$, and $\sigma_{\bar{x}} = 4.10/\sqrt{36} = 0.683$.

As before, we want the smallest interval including 99%, which means that we must exclude half of the remaining probability [or $\frac{1}{2}(0.01) = 0.005$] in each tail of the distribution of $\bar{x}$. To do this, let us first see what values of the standardized normal distribution exclude 0.005 in each tail.

FIGURE 7.5 **Sampling distribution of $\bar{x}$ for telephone example.**

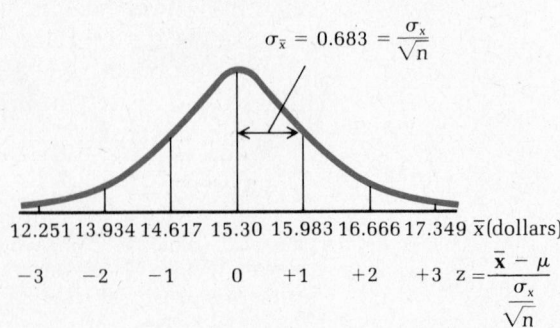

$\sigma_{\bar{x}} = 0.683 = \dfrac{\sigma_x}{\sqrt{n}}$

| 12.251 | 13.934 | 14.617 | 15.30 | 15.983 | 16.666 | 17.349 | $\bar{x}$(dollars) |

| -3 | -2 | -1 | 0 | $+1$ | $+2$ | $+3$ | $z = \dfrac{\bar{x} - \mu}{\frac{\sigma_x}{\sqrt{n}}}$ |

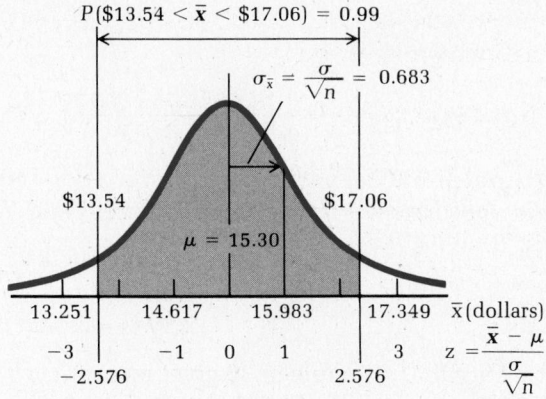

FIGURE 7.6 **Standardized normal form of the sampling distribution of $\bar{x}$, sample mean of monthly phone charges: $\mu = \$15.30$, $\sigma = \$4.10$, $n = 36$.**

From Table III, $F(z) = 0.995$ if $z = 2.576^*$; by symmetry, $F(-2.576) = 1.0 - F(2.576) = 0.005$. Thus,

$$P(-2.576 \leq z \leq 2.576) = 0.99.$$

Finally, we now have to transform the interval $P(-2.576 \leq z \leq 2.576) = 0.99$ into the original units (dollars) by finding values a and b to satisfy $P(a \leq \bar{x} \leq b) = 0.99$. By standardizing the values of a, $\bar{x}$, and b, we get

$$P(a \leq \bar{x} \leq b) = P\left(\frac{a - 15.30}{0.683} \leq z \leq \frac{b - 15.30}{0.683}\right).$$

Thus, $(a - 15.30)/0.683 = -2.576$ and $(b - 15.30)/0.683 = 2.576$. Solving these two equations, we find $a = \$13.54$ and $b = \$17.06$; this means that the appropriate interval is $P(\$13.54 \leq \bar{x} \leq \$17.06)$. A diagram of the values in this example is shown in Fig. 7.6.

Study Question 7.3: Restaurant Quality — continued

We continue Study Question 7.2, in which we were sampling restaurants and recording their Mobil Travel Guide ratings. Now assume that we sample 100 restaurants. Sketch the sampling distribution of $\bar{x}$, and find values of a and b that give the smallest interval such that

$$P(a < \bar{x} < b) = 0.95.$$

Recall that in Study Question 7.2, $\mu = 3.0$ (stars) and $\sigma^2 = 2.0$ (stars squared).

---

* The reader could determine the value 2.576 by looking for $1 - 0.005 = 0.995$ in the body of Table III. The closest values to $F(0.995)$ are $F(0.9949) = 2.57$ and $F(0.9951) = 2.58$. Taking into account the nonlinear shape of the normal curve yields the value $F(0.9950) = 2.576$.

Answer. The mean of $\bar{x}$ is 3.0 (the mean of the original population). The variance of $\bar{x}$ is

$$\sigma_{\bar{x}}^2 = \frac{1}{100}\,(2.0) = 0.020.$$

The standard error of the mean is $\sigma_{\bar{x}} = \sqrt{0.020} = 0.1414$. The shape of the distribution is approximately normal by the central limit theorem (since n is "large").

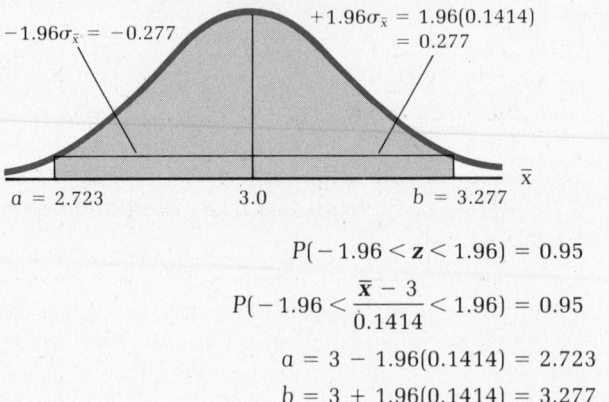

$$P(-1.96 < z < 1.96) = 0.95$$

$$P\left(-1.96 < \frac{\bar{x} - 3}{0.1414} < 1.96\right) = 0.95$$

$$a = 3 - 1.96(0.1414) = 2.723$$

$$b = 3 + 1.96(0.1414) = 3.277$$

7.7 FINITE POPULATION CORRECTION FACTOR

In the standardization for $\bar{x}$ in the previous section, the denominator was $\sigma/\sqrt{n}$. This standard error was calculated under the assumption that sampling occurred either from an infinite population or from a finite population with replacement. But what happens when sampling is *not* of this type — that is, when samples are drawn from a finite population without replacement? In this circumstance the standard error cannot equal $\sigma/\sqrt{n}$; it must be *smaller*. The fact that the standard error must be smaller than $\sigma/\sqrt{n}$ in the case of a finite population should be evident from the logical fact that the standard deviation of the $\bar{x}$'s must approach zero as the sample size n approaches the population size N. That is, if each repeated sample consists of the whole population $(n = N)$, then each sample mean $\bar{x}$ will be identical and equal to the population mean μ. There would be no variation in the values of $\bar{x}$, so $\sigma_{\bar{x}}^2 = 0$. This is not the case for $\sigma/\sqrt{n}$, as it approaches zero as $n \to$ infinity rather than as $n \to N$.

If the sample size is small in relation to the population size, say 10% or less, then Formula (7.8) will be approximately correct even when sampling without replacement. In these cases we usually do not bother with the correction factor. *However, when the sample size is larger than 10% of N, then the denominator of the formula for z must be multiplied by a correction factor.* This correction factor, called the **finite population correction factor,** is defined as follows:

Finite population correction factor:

$$\sqrt{\frac{(N - n)}{(N - 1)}}.$$

Note that this correction factor will always be a number less than 1.0. Multiplying the denominator of (7.8) by this correction factor will decrease the value of the standard error (which is what we wanted). The **z**-standardization, with the finite correction factor included, is given in Formula (7.9).*

$$\text{z-standardization:} \quad z = \frac{\bar{x} - \mu}{\dfrac{\sigma}{\sqrt{n}} \sqrt{\dfrac{(N - n)}{(N - 1)}}}. \tag{7.9}$$

We illustrate the finite population correction factor by assuming in our telephone example that the number of dormitory residents with private phones is 300. Since the sampling of 36 residents was without replacement, and a sample of size $n = 36$ equals 12% of this population $(36/300 = 0.12)$, the finite population correction factor should be used.

We correct our **z** calculation from Example 7.5 as follows:

$$P(\bar{x} \leq 14.00) = P\left(\frac{\bar{x} - \mu_{\bar{x}}}{\dfrac{\sigma}{\sqrt{n}} \sqrt{\dfrac{(N - n)}{(N - 1)}}} \leq \frac{14.00 - 15.30}{\dfrac{4.10}{\sqrt{36}} \sqrt{\dfrac{(300 - 36)}{(300 - 1)}}} \right)$$

$$= P\left(z \leq \frac{-1.30}{0.642} \right).$$

Comparing this result with that on page 346, we see that the denominator has changed from 0.683 to 0.642. Since $-1.30/0.642 = -2.02$, the new probability is

$$P(z \leq -2.02) = F(-2.02) = 1 - F(2.02) = 1 - 0.9783 = 0.0217.$$

* When the population size itself is very small, say $N \leq 30$, then care must be taken in interpreting this formula.

The reader should verify that the finite population correction factor always decreases the value of the uncorrected standard error of the mean.

Define. *Sampling distribution of $\bar{x}$, standardization of $\bar{x}$, central limit theorem, finite population correction factor.*

PROBLEMS

7.18 Given that the balances on Sears charge cards last month is a normally distributed random variable with mean $\mu = 50$ and standard deviation $\sigma = 8$.

a) Find:
$$P(x \geq 40), \quad P(x \leq 54), \quad \text{and} \quad P(44 \leq x \leq 56).$$

b) If a random sample of size $n = 64$ is drawn from this population, find:
$$P(\bar{x} \leq 53), \quad P(\bar{x} \geq 49), \quad \text{and} \quad P(48 \leq \bar{x} \leq 52).$$

c) Sketch the distribution of x and the distribution of $\bar{x}$.

7.19 What is a "sampling distribution"? Why is the knowledge of the sampling distribution of a statistic important to statistical inference?

7.20 State the central limit theorem. Why do you think this theorem is so important to statistical inference?

7.21 A telephone company randomly selected 121 long-distance calls and found that the average length of these calls was 5 minutes. The population standard deviation is 45 seconds.

a) What is the probability that a sample mean will be as large as, or larger than, $\bar{x} = 5$ when the true population mean is $\mu = 4\frac{5}{6}$ minutes? What is the probability that a value will be as small as, or smaller than, $\bar{x} = 5$ when $\mu = 5\frac{1}{5}$?

b) Do your answers to part (a) depend on any assumptions about the distribution of the parent population?

7.22 If the mean of all shoe sizes for 13-year-old boys in the United States is 9 and the variance of these sizes is 1, what percent of this population wears a shoe of size 11 or larger? What is $P(\bar{x} > 11)$ if $n = 16$? Assume that the parent population is normally distributed.

 7.23 Suppose that a random sample is being drawn from a population of executives known to have a mean age of 30, with a standard deviation of 3 years. The population is normally distributed.

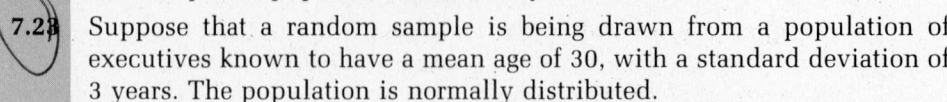
$\mu = 30 \qquad \sigma = 3$

a) What is the probability that a randomly selected executive will be over 35 years of age? What is the probability that the executive will be between 25 and 35?

b) What is the probability, in a sample of 36 executives, that the mean age will exceed 31? What is the probability that the mean age will be less than 30.5? What is $P(29 \leq \bar{x} \leq 31)$?

c) Does your answer to part (a) of this question depend on the assumption that the parent population is normally distributed? What about your answer to part (b)? Explain.

7.24 Funds, Inc., sells bonds maturing in 4, 5, 9, and 10 years. The probability distribution for customers purchasing these bonds is given below:

x	4	5	9	10
P(x)	$\frac{1}{2}$	$\frac{1}{6}$	$\frac{1}{6}$	$\frac{1}{6}$

a) Sketch the probability function and find the mean and the standard deviation.

b) Suppose 115 repeated samples of size $n = 5$ are drawn randomly (with replacement) from this probability distribution. The sample means are calculated and their frequency distribution is given below:

$\bar{x}$	Frequency	$\bar{x}$	Frequency
4.0	2	6.4	15
4.2	6	6.6	6
4.4	2	6.8	2
4.6	1	7.0	3
5.0	2	7.2	5
5.2	15	7.4	7
5.4	12	7.6	8
5.6	5	7.8	1
6.0	3	8.2	2
6.2	17	8.4	1
Total			115

Find the mean and the standard deviation of these values. Compare these values to those defined by the central limit theorem for the distribution of all sample means for samples of size 5.

7.25 Use Table V to collect a random sample of three observations (with replacement) from the population consisting of the digits 0 through 9. Repeat until you have a total of five samples.

a) Calculate $\bar{x}$ for each of your five samples of three observations, and then calculate $\bar{\bar{x}}$, the mean of all five sample means.
b) What is the expected value in the population from which your samples in part (a) were drawn? Is $\bar{\bar{x}}$ reasonably close to $\mu_{\bar{x}}$?
c) Calculate the standard deviation of your five sample means about the grand mean. What is the standard error of the mean in the population from which your samples were drawn? Are the two values reasonably close?

7.26 The five samples you drew in Problem 7.25 represent observations from a population with mean $\mu = 4.5$ and a variance of $\sigma^2 = 8.25$ (i.e., the digits 0, 1, 2, . . ., 9). This population is not normally distributed.

a) Calculate, for each of your five sample means in Problem 7.25, the value of

$$z = \frac{\bar{x} - \mu}{\sigma/\sqrt{n}}.$$

b) Would you expect the distribution of z-values in part (a) to follow a normal distribution? Will these z-values have a mean of zero and a variance of one? If not, explain why not.

7.27 If you repeat Problem 7.25, collecting samples of size 100 rather than of size 3:

a) How will your answers to part (b) of that question change?
b) What is the standard error of the mean for samples of size 100?
c) Will your answer to part (b) in Problem 7.26 change for $n = 100$?

7.28 Collect a simple random sample of size $n = 12$ from the incomes in **Data Set 6** using the random numbers in Table V. If **Data Set 6** is considered a population, the mean and standard deviation are $851.84 and $1042, respectively.

a) Find the mean of your sample. How many standard errors is your value of $\bar{x}$ away from μ (calculate a z-value)? What is the probability of a z-value this far, or farther, from μ?
b) Repeat part (a), using a systematic sample. Start with a randomly selected number less than 14, and then take every 17th number. Does this procedure cause any bias in your sample? Repeat the questions in part (a).
c) Take a stratified sample from **Data Set 6,** using the regions of the United States to stratify the data. Find $\bar{x}$ for this sample.

7.29 Answer parts (a) and (b).

a) What is the "finite population correction," and when is it necessary to apply this factor?

b) If $\sigma_x = 50$, $n = 25$, and $N = 100$, what is the corrected standard error of the mean?

7.30 A company hiring computer programmers has completed a study of 100 randomly selected salary offers, drawn from a population of 500 salary offers. The mean of this sample is $\bar{x} = \$22,985$. What is the probability of a sample mean of \$22,985, or larger, if the population mean is $\mu = \$22,800$ and the population standard deviation is known to be \$1000? Remember to apply the finite population correction.

7.31 A cereal company checks the weight of each lot of 400 boxes of breakfast cereal by randomly checking 64 of the boxes. This particular brand is packed in 20-ounce boxes.

a) Suppose a particular random sample of 64 boxes results in a mean weight of 19.95 ounces. How often will the sample mean be this low, or lower if $\mu = 20$ and $\sigma = 0.10$? Use the finite population correction factor.

b) What is the percentage difference in the standard error after using the finite population correction factor? If it had not been used, what would have been the percentage error in the probability answer?

7.8 SAMPLING DISTRIBUTION OF $\bar{x}$, NORMAL POPULATION, σ UNKNOWN

In Section 7.5 we discussed the importance in problem-solving of using the following standardization:

$$z = \frac{\bar{x} - \mu}{\sigma/\sqrt{n}}$$

Usually, *our objective in using this type of standardization is to determine the probability of observing some specified value of $\bar{x}$, assuming that the population mean is μ, and then to use this probability in making a decision.* This means we have an assumed value of μ to use in the standardization. But what about the value of σ needed in the denominator? What happens if we do not want to (or cannot) assume a value of σ (i.e., if σ is unknown)? In solving a particular problem where σ is unknown, the sample statistic s can be used in place of σ. That is, our standardization now becomes

$$\frac{\bar{x} - \mu}{s/\sqrt{n}}.$$

The substitution of s for σ is reasonable, since we can show* that the expected value of s^2 equals σ^2. That is, $E[s^2] = \sigma^2$. Remember, we are using $n - 1$ in the calculation of s^2. If n had been used in place of $n - 1$, then s^2 would systematically be smaller than the population variance, σ^2.

We have shown previously that, when x is normal, the distribution of

$$\frac{\bar{x} - \mu}{\sigma/\sqrt{n}} \quad \text{is} \quad N(0, 1).$$

Unfortunately, when s is substituted for σ, the resulting distribution is no longer normally distributed, nor is its variance 1.0. Our next task is thus to determine the distribution of the ratio $(\bar{x} - \mu)/(s/\sqrt{n})$. This distribution can be thought of as being generated by the following process:

1. Collect all possible samples of size n from a normal parent population.
2. Calculate $\bar{x}$ and s for each sample.
3. Subtract μ from each value of $\bar{x}$, and then divide this deviation by the appropriate value of $s/\sqrt{n}$. (Remember, s will be usually different for each sample.)

This process will generate an infinite number of values of the random variable

$$\frac{\bar{x} - \mu}{s/\sqrt{n}}.$$

---

* To prove that $E[s^2] = \sigma^2$, we use the rules of expectation in Section 4.4

$$E[s^2] = E\left[\frac{1}{n-1} \sum (x_i - \bar{x})^2\right]$$

$$= \frac{1}{n-1} E\left[\sum \{(x_i - \mu) - (\bar{x} - \mu)\}^2\right] \qquad \begin{array}{l} \text{By rule 3 and because} \\ (x - \bar{x}) = (x - \mu) - (\bar{x} - \mu) \end{array}$$

$$= \frac{1}{n-1} \left\{\sum E[x_i - \mu)^2] - 2E[n(\bar{x} - \mu)(\bar{x} - \mu)] \right. \qquad \begin{array}{l} \text{By expansion of square term,} \\ \text{by Formula (4.13), and} \\ \sum (x_i - \mu)(\bar{x} - \mu) = \end{array}$$

$$\left. + \sum E[(\bar{x} - \mu)^2]\right\} \qquad \qquad n(\bar{x} - \mu)(\bar{x} - \mu).$$

$$= \frac{1}{n-1}\left(\sum \sigma^2 - (2n\sigma^2/n) + \sum \sigma^2/n\right) \qquad \begin{array}{l} \text{Since } \sigma^2 = E[(x - \mu)]^2 \text{ and} \\ \sigma^2/n = E[(\bar{x} - \mu)^2] \end{array}$$

$$= \frac{1}{n-1}(n\sigma^2 - 2\sigma^2 + n\sigma^2/n) \qquad \qquad \text{Since } \sum_{i=1}^{n}(\text{constant}) = n(\text{constant})$$

$$= \frac{1}{n-1}\sigma^2(n-1) \qquad \qquad \text{Collecting terms}$$

$$E[s^2] = \frac{n-1}{n-1}\sigma^2 = \sigma^2.$$

It is not hard to recognize that the mean of this new distribution still equals zero, since the numerator hasn't changed and it was the numerator that made our original standardization have $E[z] = 0$. The variance of $(\bar{x} - \mu)/(s/\sqrt{n})$ is no longer equal to $V[z] = 1.0$; it is larger than 1.0. This is reasonable when one recognizes that with the ratio $(\bar{x} - \mu)/(s/\sqrt{n})$ one more element of uncertainty (the estimator s) has been added to the standardization. The more uncertainty there is, the more spread out the distribution.

Several additional aspects of the distribution of $(\bar{x} - \mu)/(s/\sqrt{n})$ are worth noting. First, we would expect this distribution to be symmetrical, since there is no reason to believe that substituting s for σ will make this distribution skewed either positively or negatively. Second, it should be apparent that the variability of this distribution depends on the size of n, for the sample size affects the reliability with which s estimates σ. When n is large, s will be a good approximation to σ; but when n is small, s may not be very close to σ. This implies that the distribution of $(\bar{x} - \mu)/(s/\sqrt{n})$ is a family of distributions in which variability depends on n.

It should be clear from the above discussion that the distribution of $(\bar{x} - \mu)/(s/\sqrt{n})$ is not normal, but is more spread out than the normal. The distribution of this statistic is called the **t-distribution,** and its random variable is denoted as follows:

t-distribution:

$$t = \frac{\bar{x} - \mu}{s/\sqrt{n}}. \qquad (7.10)$$

The variable t is a continuous random variable. One of the first researchers to work on determining the exact distribution of this random variable was W. S. Gosset, an Irish statistician. However, the Dublin brewery for which Gosset worked did not allow its employees to publish their research; hence, Gosset wrote under the pen name "Student." In honor of Gosset's research, published in 1908, the t-distribution is often referred to as the "Student's t-distribution." It is not clear from historical records whether Gosset enjoyed the product of his employer, as do many modern "students."

Student's
t-distribution   Since the density function for the t-distribution is fairly complex and not of primary importance at this point, we will not present it, but will begin

merely by describing the characteristics of this distribution.* As we indicated previously, the t-distribution depends on the size of the sample. It is customary to describe the characteristics of the t-distribution in terms of the sample size minus one, or $(n - 1)$, as this quantity has special significance.

> The value of $(n - 1)$ is called the number of **degrees of freedom** (abbreviated d.f.) and represents a measure of the number of independent observations in the sample that can be used to estimate the standard deviation of the parent population.

For example, when $n = 1$, there is no way to estimate the population standard deviation; hence there are *no* degrees of freedom $(n - 1 = 0)$. There is one degree of freedom in a sample of $n = 2$, since one observation is now "free" to vary away from the other, and the amount it varies determines our estimate of the population standard deviation. Each additional observation adds one more degree of freedom, so that in a sample of size n there are $(n - 1)$ observations "free" to vary, and hence $(n - 1)$ degrees of freedom. The Greek letter ν (nu) is often used to denote degrees of freedom, where $\nu = n - 1$ in this case.

> A t-distribution is completely described by its one parameter, ν = degrees of freedom. The mean of the t-distribution is zero, $E[t] = 0$. The variance of the t-distribution, when $n \geq 3$, is $V[t] = \nu/(\nu - 2)$.

The last sentence above implies that $V[t] \geq 1.0$ for all sample sizes, in contrast to $V[z]$, which is 1.0 no matter what the sample size. For example, when $\nu = 3$, the variance of the t-distribution is $3/(3 - 2) = 3.0$. The t-distribution with $\nu = 11$ and the standardized normal are contrasted in Fig. 7.7.

For small sample sizes, the t-distribution is seen to be **considerably** more spread out than the normal. When ν is larger, such as $\nu = 30$, then $V[t] = 30/(30 - 2) = 1.07$, which is not much different from $V[z] = 1.0$. In the limit, as $n \to \infty$, the t- and z-distributions are identical. Tables of t-values are usually completely enumerated only for $\nu \leq 30$, because for

---

* Mathematically, the random variable t is defined as a standardized normal variable z divided by the square root of an independently distributed chi-square variable, which has been divided by its degrees of freedom; that is, $t = z/\sqrt{\chi^2/\nu}$. The chi-square distribution is discussed in Section 7.9.

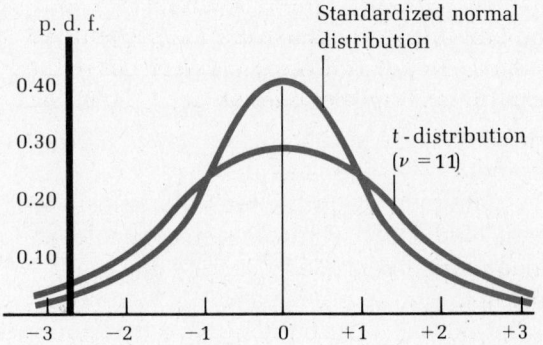

FIGURE 7.7 **The standardized normal and t-distributions compared.**

larger samples the normal gives a very good approximation and is easier to use. For this reason it is customary to speak of the **t**-distribution as applying to "small sample sizes," *even though this distribution holds for any size n.*

Probability questions involving a **t**-distributed random variable can be answered by using the cumulative distribution function, $F(t)$ in Table VI. This table gives the values of **t** for selected values of the cumulative probability $[(F(t) = P(t < t)]$ across the top of the table and for degrees of freedom (ν) down the left margin. Figure 7.8 shows the values of the **t**-distribution for $\nu = 24$ degrees of freedom, taken from Table VI in the Appendix.

Four different values from Table VI in the Appendix are shown in Fig. 7.8:

$$P(t \leq 0.685) = 0.75, \qquad P(t \leq 1.318) = 0.90,$$

and

$$P(t \geq 2.064) = 0.025, \qquad P(t \geq 2.492) = 0.01.$$

FIGURE 7.8 **Various probabilities for the t-distribution for $\nu = 24$ d.f.**

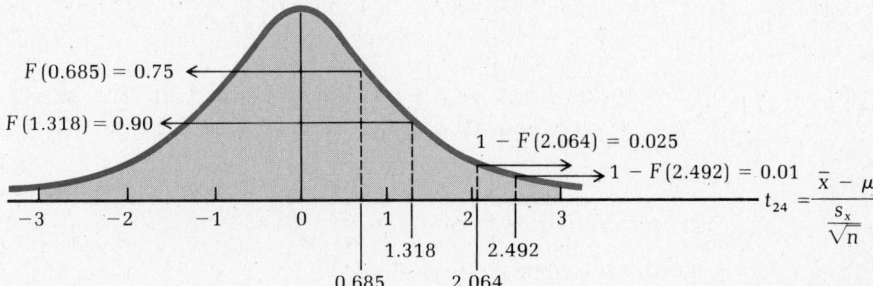

As the latter two values above demonstrate, a probability in the upper tail of the *t*-distribution (beyond one of the cutoff points in Table VI) is obtained by using the complement rule [i.e., using $1 - F(t)$]. A probability value in the lower tail (a negative *t*-value) is determined by changing the sign to positive and using the same procedure described above (because the *t*-distribution is symmetrical).

Table VI gives probabilities for seven selected *t*-values for each degree of freedom. More extensive tables are available, and probabilities may be determined mathematically for any *t*-value.

Examples of the
t-distribution

As with the normal distribution, the *t*-distribution is often used to test an assumption about a population mean based on the standardization of an observed sample mean.

> The *t*-distribution is the appropriate statistic for inference on a population mean whenever the parent population is normally distributed and σ is unknown.

Example 7.5. A small finance company has reported to an auditing firm that its outstanding loans are approximately normally distributed with a mean of $825. The standard deviation is unknown. In an attempt to verify this reported value of $\mu = \$825$, a random sample of 25 accounts was taken. This random sample yields a mean of $\bar{x} = \$780$, with a standard deviation of $s = 105$. The question facing the auditor is how often might one find a sample mean of $780 or lower when the true mean is $825? That is, what is $P(\bar{x} \le \$780)$?

To solve this problem, we would like to standardize the values in the parentheses. But such a standardization requires knowledge of σ. Since we do not know σ, we use a new standardization that follows the *t*-distribution:

$$t = \frac{\bar{x} - \mu}{s/\sqrt{n}}.$$

Because s is only an estimate of σ, the *t*-distribution only *approximately* solves specific problems involving $\bar{x}$ (such as $P(\bar{x} \le \$780)$.

In Example 7.5 we would like to find the probability $P(\bar{x} \le \$780)$. Since $n = 25$, x is normal, and σ is unknown, this probability is approximated by using the *t*-distribution with $n - 1 = 24$ degrees of freedom. Using the *t*-standardization,

$$t = \frac{\bar{x} - \mu}{s/\sqrt{n}} = \frac{780 - 825}{105/\sqrt{25}} = -2.143.$$

The probability $P(t \le -2.143)$ is thus our approximation of the probability $P(\bar{x} \le \$780)$.

Since the *t*-distribution is symmetrical, the probability we want,

$$P(t \le -2.143) = F(-2.143),$$

is equivalent to $1 - F(2.143)$. Because the number 2.143 does not appear in Table VI for $\nu = 24$, the exact value of $F(2.143)$ cannot be determined from this table. However, we can determine between which two probabilities the value $F(2.143)$ lies. From Table VI or Fig. 7.8, $F(2.064) = 0.975$ and $F(2.492) = 0.990$, which means that $F(2.143)$ lies between 0.975 and 0.990. Thus, $1 - F(2.143)$ lies between 0.025 and 0.01, and we can write

$$0.01 < P(t \le -2.143) < 0.025.$$

This result says that a sample mean as low as or lower than \$780 will occur (approximately) between 1% and 2.5% of the time when $\mu = \$825$. Faced with such low probabilities, the auditor might well be concerned with the accuracy of the assumption that $\mu = \$825$.

Suppose that in the above example, instead of the sample results described there, we found the values $\bar{x} = \$842.60$, and $s = 80.0$. For this result we want to determine the probability that $\bar{x}$ is greater than or equal to \$842.60 when $\mu = \$825$. Using the *t*-standardization,

$$t = \frac{\bar{x} - \mu}{s/\sqrt{n}} = \frac{\$842.60 - \$825}{80/\sqrt{25}} = 1.100.$$

From Table VI, $F(1.100)$ lies between $F(0.685) = 0.75$ and $F(1.318) = 0.90$ when $\nu = 24$. Hence,

$$0.25 > P(t \ge 1.100) > 0.10.$$

We see from this result that a sample mean of \$842.60 is fairly probable when $\mu = \$825$ and $n = 25$. These values are shown in Fig. 7.9.

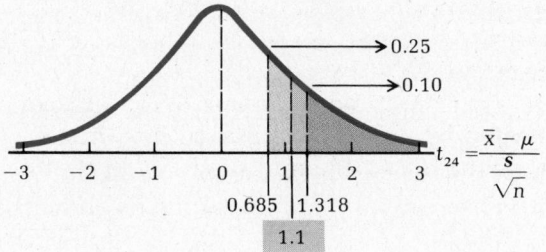

FIGURE 7.9 **The *t*-distribution values for $\nu = 24$.**

As our second example of the use of the *t*-distribution, let us determine an interval (a, b) such that $P(a \le t \le b) = 0.95$, assuming $n - 1 = v = 8$ degrees of freedom. As before, the smallest interval is found by putting half the excluded area, $\frac{1}{2}(0.05) = 0.025$, in each tail of the distribution. For example, we want $P(t \ge b) = 0.025$, which means that, in terms of the cumulative function, we want to find a value t such that $F(t) = 0.975$. From Table VI for $v = 8$, we see that $F(2.306) = 0.975$; hence, $b = 2.306$. Now since the *t*-distribution is symmetrical, the appropriate value for a is merely the negative of the value of b, or $a = -2.306$. Thus,

$$P(-2.306 \le t \le 2.306) = 0.95.$$

Recall, from our previous examples using the standardized normal distribution, that $P(-1.96 \le z \le 1.96) = 0.95$. The critical values for z that exclude 0.025 probability in the upper and lower tails are ± 1.96, as opposed to ± 2.306 for the *t*-distribution with $v = 8$. The difference reflects the fact that the *t*-distribution is more spread out than the **z**-distribution. Note in Table VI that by *increasing* the value of v from 8 to 10, then 20, then 60, then 120, and moving down the column for $F(t) = 0.975$, the critical values for t *decrease* from 2.306 to 2.228, then 2.086, then 2.000, then 1.98, respectively. For larger values of v, the spread of the *t*-distribution closes in to match the spread of the **z**-distribution. Indeed, when $v = \infty$, the critical value for t exactly equals the value for z $(= 1.96)$, as shown by the bottom row in Table VI.

Use of the *t*-distribution When the Population Is Not Normal

It must be emphasized at this point that the *t*-distribution, as well as the chi-square distribution (discussed in the following section), assumes that samples are drawn from a parent population that is normally distributed. Often there is no way to determine the exact distribution of the parent population. In practical problems involving these distributions, the question therefore arises as to just how critical the assumption is that the parent population be exactly normally distributed. Fortunately, the assumption of normality can be relaxed without significantly changing the sampling distribution of the *t*-distribution or the chi-square distribution. Because of this fact these distributions are said to be quite "robust," implying that their usefulness holds up under conditions that do not conform exactly to the original assumptions. The *t*-distribution is much more robust than the chi-square distribution.

We should emphasize again that the *t*-distribution is appropriate whenever **x** is normal and σ is unknown, despite the fact that many t tables do not list values higher than $v = 30$. For practical problems this does not cause many difficulties; as the reader will note, the *t*-values in a given column of Table VI change very little above $\nu = 30$. If the appropriate ν is not in Table VI, we suggest looking at the table entries for ν above and below the one desired.*

> **Study Question 7.4: Waiting Time for Delivery of New Cars**
> Volkswagen dealers have been instructed to quote a 100-day wait for delivery of a new Jetta, ordered from the factory. A random sample of 400 such orders resulted in a mean delivery time of $\overline{x} = 120$ days, with a sample standard deviation of $s = 200$. Approximate the probability that the sample mean will be 120 or larger if μ does, in fact, equal 100 and σ is unknown.

Answer

$$P\left(\frac{\overline{x} - \mu}{s/\sqrt{n}} \geq \frac{120 - 100}{200/\sqrt{400}}\right) = P(t \geq 2.00).$$

Although $\nu = 399$ is not listed in Table VI, by looking at $\nu = 120$ versus $\nu = \infty$ we can easily determine that

$$0.025 > P(t \geq 2.00) > 0.01.$$

7.9 THE SAMPLING DISTRIBUTION OF s^2, NORMAL POPULATION†

The only sampling distribution considered thus far has been that of $\overline{x}$, the sample mean. But in many practical problems we need information about the distribution of the sample variance, s^2. That is, we need to investigate the distribution that consists of all possible values of s^2 calculated from samples of size n. The sampling distribution of s^2 is particularly important in problems concerned with the variability in a random sample. For example, the telephone company may be just as interested in the variance in length of calls in a random sample as they are in the mean length. Or a manufacturer of steel beams may want to

---

* Some texts suggest that the normal distribution be used to approximate the t-distribution when $\nu > 30$, since the t- and z-values will then be quite close (the normal value will be slightly smaller than the exact t-value). Because of this procedure the t-distribution sometimes is referred to *incorrectly* as applying only to "small samples." We prefer to emphasize that the t-distribution is *always* correct whenever σ is unknown and $\mathbf{x}$ is normal.

† This section can be omitted without loss in continuity.

learn just as much about the variance as the mean of tensile strength of the steel beams. The statistician who first worked with the *t*-distribution, W. S. Gosset, was also one of the first to describe the sampling distribution of s^2.

Because s^2 must always be positive, the distribution of s^2 cannot be a normal distribution. Rather, the distribution of s^2 is a unimodal distribution that is *skewed* to the right and looks like the smooth curve in Fig. 7.10. As with the *t*-distribution, sampling is from a normal parent population, and the one parameter is degrees of freedom, ν.

A typical problem in analyzing variances is that of determining the probability that the value of s^2 will be larger (or smaller) than some observed value, given some assumed value of σ^2.

Example 7.6. The variance in the amount of cereal in 16-ounce boxes has been $\sigma^2 = 0.0010$ (ounces squared). What is the probability that a random sample of $n = 21$ cereal boxes will result in a sample variance at least as large as $s^2 = 0.0016$? That is, what is

$$P(s^2 \geq 0.0016),$$

assuming $\nu = n - 1 = 20$ and $\sigma^2 = 0.0010$?

Unfortunately, we cannot solve problems like this one directly but must transform them in a way similar to the standardizations for $\bar{x}$. In this case the transformation is accomplished by multiplying s^2 by $(n - 1)$, and then dividing the product by σ^2. This new random variable is denoted by the symbol χ^2, which is the square of the Greek letter chi. The **chi-square distribution** is a family of positively skewed p.d.f.'s which depend on one parameter, $\nu = n - 1$, which is its degrees of freedom. Thus,

---

Chi-square random variable:

$$\chi^2_{n-1} = \frac{\nu s^2}{\sigma^2} = \frac{(n-1)s^2}{\sigma^2}. \tag{7.11}$$

In words, this formula says the following:

If s^2 is the variance of random samples of size n taken from a normal population having a variance of σ^2, then the variable $(n - 1)s^2/\sigma^2$ has the same distribution as a χ^2-variable with $(n - 1)$ degrees of freedom.

The subscript on the χ^2 symbol in Formula (7.11) merely serves to remind us of the appropriate degrees of freedom.

Although Gosset was unable to prove Formula (7.11) mathematically, he did demonstrate this relationship in his empirical work. Gosset took the heights of 3000 criminals, calculated the value of σ^2 for these heights, and then grouped these heights into 750 random samples of 4. For each of these 750 samples, Gosset, in effect, calculated a value of s^2, multiplied s^2 by $(n - 1) = 3$, and then divided this number by σ^2. The results are plotted in the histogram shown in Fig. 7.10. Note that Gosset's histogram and the chi-square distribution (for $\nu = n - 1 = 3$) superimposed on it are not in perfect agreement, a fact that Gosset attributed to the particular grouping of heights that he used.

Solving a problem involving s^2 by using Formula (7.11) follows essentially the same process used to solve problems involving $\bar{x}$. For example, to solve the cereal problem mentioned earlier, $P(s^2 \geq 0.0016)$, we transform each value in parenthesis as follows:

$$P(s^2 \geq 0.0016) = P\left[\frac{(n - 1)s^2}{\sigma^2} \geq \frac{(20)(0.0016)}{0.0010}\right] = P(\chi^2_{20} \geq 32).$$

FIGURE 7.10 **Chi-square approximation to Gosset's data on the height of criminals.**

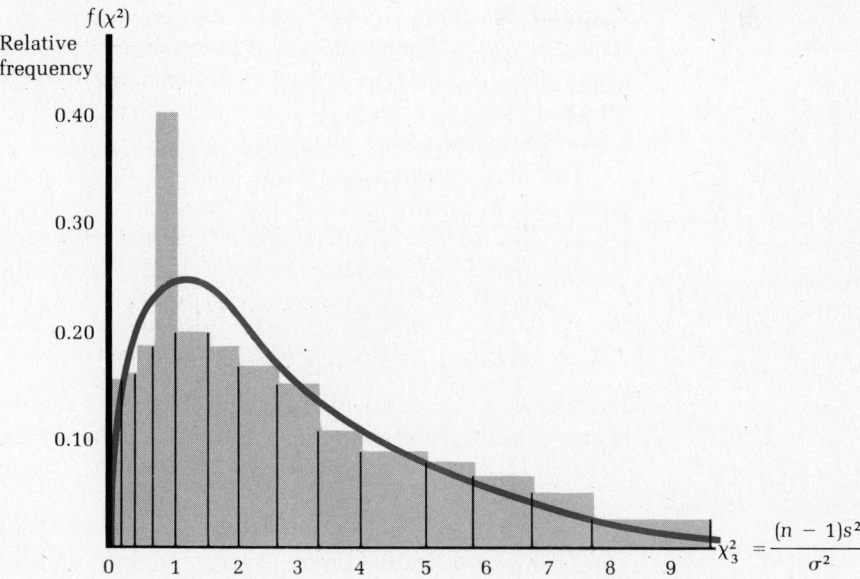

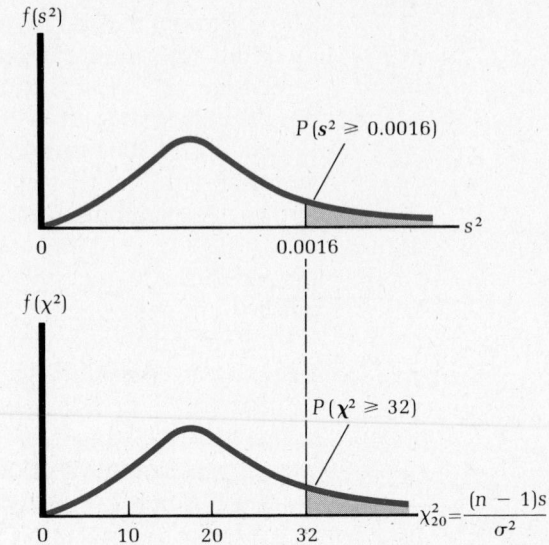

FIGURE 7.11 **Transforming an s²-value into an equivalent χ²-value with $v = n - 1 = 20$.**

The equivalence between $P(s^2 \geq 0.0016)$ and $P(\chi^2_{20} \geq 32)$ is illustrated in Fig. 7.11.

Properties of the χ²-distribution

As shown in Fig. 7.12, the number of degrees of freedom in a χ^2-distribution determines what shape $f(\chi^2)$ will be. When v is small, the shape of the density function is highly skewed to the right. As v gets larger, however, the distribution becomes more and more symmetrical in appearance. Since only squared numbers are involved in calculating χ^2, we know that this variable can never assume a value below zero, but it may take on values up to positive infinity.

The density function for the χ^2-distribution is not of primary importance for our discussion; hence, we will not present its formula, but merely concentrate on its characteristics. The mean and the variance of the chi-square distribution are both related to v as follows:

$$\text{Mean} = E[\chi^2_v] = v;$$

$$\text{Variance} = V[\chi^2_v] = E[(\chi^2_v - v)^2] = 2v.$$

Thus, if we have a chi-square variable with $v = n - 1$ degrees of freedom involved in a problem using random samples of size $n = 19$, then

$$E[\chi^2] = 18, \quad V[\chi^2] = 36, \quad \text{and} \quad \text{standard deviation} = 6.$$

A graph of the chi-square distribution for $n = 19$ ($v = 18$) is shown in Fig. 7.13. Notice in this figure that $\mu = 18 = v$, and the standard deviation

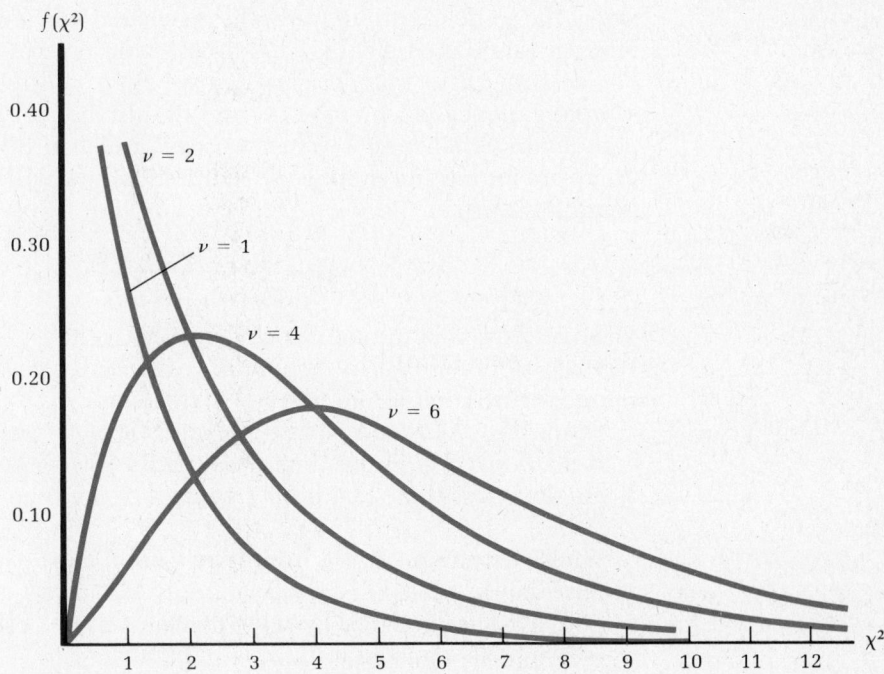

FIGURE 7.12 **The chi-square distribution for various values of ν.**

is $\sigma = \sqrt{2\nu} = \sqrt{36} = 6$. The distribution in Fig. 7.13 is fairly symmetrical in appearance. As ν increases, the χ^2 distribution becomes closer and closer to the normal distribution.

Chi-square Examples   Table VII in Appendix C gives values of the cumulative χ^2-distribution for selected values of ν and gives (at the bottom) a formula for the normal approximation to χ^2, which can be used when $\nu > 30$. To illustrate the

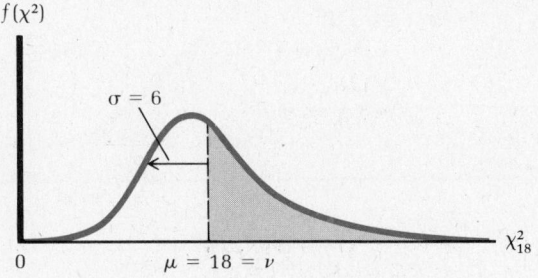

FIGURE 7.13 **Chi-square distribution for $\nu = 18$.**

use of the χ^2-distribution, we will assume that we have taken all possible random samples of size $n = 21$ from some normal parent population. For each of these random samples we then multiply the value of the sample variance (s^2) by $(n - 1)$ and divide the result by the (assumed) population variance (σ^2). When we have finished this hypothetical task (there are an infinite number of such ratios), we will have calculated all possible values of

$$\chi_{20}^2 = \frac{(n - 1)s^2}{\sigma^2} = \frac{(20)s^2}{\sigma^2}.$$

The distribution of the statistic given above is the chi-square distribution. We can use Table VII in Appendix C to graph a few values of the chi-square distribution for 20 degrees of freedom.

From Fig. 7.14 we see that the ratio $(20)s^2/\sigma^2$ will have a value less than 8.26 only 1% of the time, less than 9.59 two and one-half percent of the time, less than 28.4 ninety percent of the time, and so forth.

Study Question 7.5: Variability of Cereal in 16-Ounce Boxes
Use the chi-square distribution to solve the cereal problem in Example 7.6. That is, find $P(s^2 > 0.0016)$ when $n = 21$ and the population variance is assumed to be $\sigma^2 = 0.0010$.

Answer

$$P(s^2 \geq 0.0016) = P\left(\frac{(n - 1)s^2}{\sigma^2} \geq \frac{(20)(0.0016)}{0.0010}\right) = P(\chi_{20}^2 \geq 32.0).$$

FIGURE 7.14 **Chi-square distribution for $\nu = 20$.**

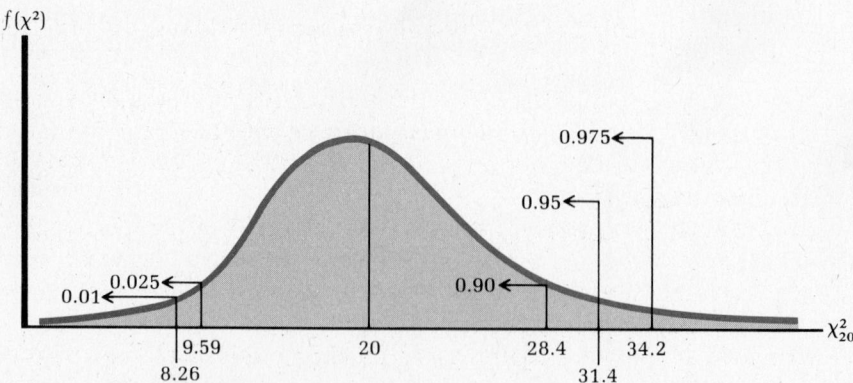

From Fig. 7.14,

$$0.950 < P(\chi^2 \leq 32) < 0.975;$$

thus,

$$0.05 > P(\chi^2 \geq 32.0) = P(s^2 \geq 0.0016) > 0.025.$$

Since a sample variance as high as 0.0016 will occur relatively infrequently when $\sigma^2 = 0.0010$ (less than 5% of the time), we might question this company's statement that $\sigma^2 = 0.0010$.

Define. *Students' t-distribution, sampling distribution of s^2, degrees of freedom, χ^2-distribution.*

PROBLEMS

7.32 Determine, for each of the following cases, whether the *t*-distribution or the standardized normal distribution (or neither) is appropriate for answering probability questions relating to sample means.
a) A small sample from a normal population with known standard deviation.
b) A small sample from a nonnormal population with known standard deviation.
c) A small sample from a normal population with unknown standard deviation.
d) A small sample from a nonnormal population with unknown standard deviation.
e) A large sample from a normal population with unknown standard deviation.
f) A large sample from a nonnormal population with unknown standard deviation.

7.33 Suppose that you collect the following sample of four observations, drawn randomly from a normal population, representing the January heating cost for a 4-bedroom house in Ann Arbor, Michigan: 199, 215, 191, 179. Compute $\bar{x}$.
a) What is the probability of obtaining this $\bar{x}$ or one smaller if the population has mean $\mu = 210$ and unknown variance? What is the probability that $\bar{x}$ is this large or larger if the population has mean $\mu = 180$ and unknown variance?
b) What is the probability of obtaining this $\bar{x}$ or one smaller if the population has mean $\mu = 210$ and a standard deviation of $\sigma = 14$?

What is the probability that $\bar{x}$ is this small or smaller if the population has mean $\mu = 200$ and $\sigma = 10$?

7.34 Answer parts (a) and (b).
  a) Describe the difference between the standardized normal distribution and the t-distribution. Under what conditions can each be used?
  b) Is $P(z \geq 2.0) = 0.0228$ greater than $P(t \geq 2.0)$ for all sample sizes? How do you explain this fact?

7.35 It is suggested that the average weekly wage of student workers is $110. A random sample of 100 students yields the following distribution:

Wages	f
38–62	5
63–87	17
88–112	24
113–137	26
138–162	13
163–187	8
188–212	7
Total	100

  a) Calculate $\bar{x}$ and s^2 using class marks 50, 75, 100, . . ., 200.
  b) How probable is a sample mean this large if $\mu = 110$ and x is normally distributed?
  c) Would your result from part (b) lead you to question the supposition that $\mu = 110$?

7.36 Explain why the standardized normal distribution cannot be used for inferences on the population mean whenever the parent population is normally distributed and σ is unknown. What distribution is appropriate in this circumstance?

7.37 Assume that an economist estimates that the number of gallons of gasoline used monthly by each automobile in the United States is a normally distributed random variable with mean $\mu = 50$ and variance unknown:
  a) Suppose that a sample of nine observations yields a sample variance of $s^2 = 36$. What is the probability that $\bar{x}$ is larger than 54 if $\mu = 50$? What is the probability that $\bar{x}$ is less than 44 if $\mu = 50$? What is the probability that $\bar{x}$ lies between 45 and 55?
  b) How would your answers to the above problem change if $n = 36$ and all else remained the same?

7.38 A professional bowler claims that her bowling scores can be thought of as normally distributed with mean $\mu = 215$ and unknown variance. In her latest performance, the bowler scores 188, 214, and 204.
  a) Calculate $\bar{x}$ and s^2 for this sample.
  b) If these three scores represent a random sample from a normal population with mean $\mu = 215$, what is the probability that $\bar{x}$ will be as low as you calculated it to be in part (a)?
  c) Would you conclude from part (b) that the bowler is "off her game"?

7.39 What is the "sampling distribution of s^2"? How is this distribution related to the chi-square distribution?

7.40 Suppose that you are drawing samples of size $n = 3$ from a normal population with a variance of 8.25. What is the probability that the value of $(n - 1)s^2/\sigma^2$ will exceed 5.99? What is the probability that s^2 will be more than three times as large as σ^2?

7.41 Suppose that a random variable is known to be chi-square-distributed with parameter $\nu = 24$.
  a) What are the mean and the variance of the chi-square distribution for this parameter?
  b) What is the probability that the value of χ^2 will exceed 43.0? What is $P(\chi^2 \geq 33.2)$? What is $P(\chi^2 \geq 9.89)$?
  c) Use your answers to parts (a) and (b) to draw a rough sketch of the chi-square distribution for $\nu = 24$.
  d) Superimpose on your sketch for part (c) a graph of the normal distribution for $\mu = 24$ and $\sigma^2 = 48$. How closely do the two distributions agree?

7.42 A hamburger chain is concerned with the amount of variability in its "quarter-pounder." The amount of meat in these burgers is supposed to have a variance of no more than 0.2 ounces. A random sample of 20 burgers from one chain yields a variance of $s^2 = 0.4$.
  a) What is the probability that a sample variance will equal or exceed 0.4 if it is assumed that $\sigma^2 = 0.2$?
  b) Would you suspect that the meat content of the burgers that this chain is selling varies excessively?

7.43 The Iowa State Extension Bureau considers the usual variance on yield for corn to be 400 (bushels squared) per acre. An agent makes a study of 15 acres selected randomly from one large farm and finds a sample variance of 800. Assuming a normal distribution of yields per acre, is this an unusually high variance? If so, the agent might wish to instruct the farmer on how to get more consistent yields or may wish to further study the underlying reasons for the large variability.

7.44 The Indiana State Tax Board has determined that the usual variance in property-tax assessment for "Type A" houses is 1,000,000 (dollars squared). A random sample of 20 houses in Vermillion County indicated a variance of 600,000. Is this an unusually low variance, assuming a normal distribution of assessments?

USING THE COMPUTER

7.45 Write a computer program that collects random samples from the following *uniform distribution:*

$$f(x) = \begin{cases} 1.0 & 0 \le x \le 1.0, \\ 0 & \text{otherwise.} \end{cases}$$

a) Write the program to collect 100 random samples of size $n = 25$, and calculate $\bar{x}$ and s^2 for each sample.

b) Sketch the distribution of $\bar{x}$, using some convenient class interval for the x's. Compare your result with that predicted by the central limit theorem.

c) For each sample in part (a), calculate $t = (\bar{x} - 0.5)/(s/\sqrt{n})$, and then sketch these 100 t-values. Does the distribution correspond to that given in Table VI for $\nu = 24$?

d) For each sample in part (a), calculate $\chi^2 = 24s^2/\sigma^2$, where $\sigma^2 = \frac{1}{12}$. Sketch this distribution. Does this sketch correspond to the distribution of χ^2_{24}?

7.46 Most computer statistical programs will generate random numbers. Use such a program to generate 20 random numbers, where each random number is drawn from the population of integers between 0 and 500 (include 0 but not 500).

7.47 Many computer statistical programs will provide cumulative probabilities for the distributions discussed in this chapter. Use a computer program to determine the following probabilities.

a) $P(z \le 1.734)$

b) $P(t \le 2.661)$ for 45 d.f.

c) $P(\chi^2 \le 50.00)$ for 35 d.f.

EXERCISES

7.48 Consult a mathematical statistics text to answer the following.

a) Write down the probability density function for the t-distribution and the chi-square distribution. How are these two distributions related?

b) Research the chi-square distribution and explain what it means to say that this distribution is the sum of the squares of a finite number of independent standardized normal random variables.

c) Describe how the finite population correction factor and the hypergeometric distribution are related. See whether you can justify the fact that the correction factor is $\sqrt{(N - n)/(N - 1)}$.

7.49 Prove the following.

a) That $E[s^2] = \sigma^2$ using the fact that the mean of the chi-square distribution is v.

b) That $V[s^2] = 2\sigma^4/v$.

7.50 The auditor's failure to recognize an error in an amount or an error in an internal-control data-processing procedure is described as a

a) Statistical error.

b) Sampling error.

c) Standard error of the mean.

d) Nonsampling error.

7.51 In connection with his review of charges to the plant maintenance account, Mr. John Wilson, CPA, is undecided as to whether to use probability sampling or judgment sampling. As compared to probability sampling, judgment sampling has the primary disadvantage of

a) Providing no known method for making statistical inferences about the population solely from the results of the sample.

b) Not allowing the auditor to select those accounts which he believes should be selected.

c) Requiring that a complete list of all the population elements be compiled.

d) Not permitting the auditor to know which types of items will be included in the sample before the actual selection is made.

7.52 A CPA's client wishes to determine inventory shrinkage by taking a sample of inventory items. If a stratified random sample is to be drawn, the strata should be identified in such a way that

a) The overall population is divided into subpopulations of equal size so that each subpopulation can be given equal weight when estimates are made.

b) Each stratum differs as much as possible with respect to expected shrinkage, but the shrinkages expected for items within each stratum are as close as possible.

c) The sample mean and standard deviation of each individual stratum will be equal to the means and standard deviations of all other strata.

    d) The items in each stratum will follow a normal distribution so that probability theory can be used in making inferences from the sample data.

7.53 In estimating the total value of supplies on repair trucks, Baker Company draws random samples from two equal-sized strata of trucks. The mean value of the inventory stored on the larger trucks (stratum 1) was computed at $1500, with a standard deviation of $250. On the smaller trucks (stratum 2), the mean value of inventory was computed as $500, with a standard deviation of $45. If Baker had drawn an unstratified sample from the entire population of trucks, the expected mean value of inventory per truck would be $1000, and the expected standard deviation would be
    a) Exactly $147.50.
    b) Greater than $250.
    c) Less than $45.
    d) Between $45 and $250, but not $147.50.

7.54 The required size of a statistical sample is influenced by the variability of the items being sampled. The sample standard deviation, a basic measure of variation, is approximately the
    a) Average of the sum of the differences between the individual values and their mean.
    b) Square root of the average determined in (a).
    c) Average of the sum of the squared differences between the individual values and their mean.
    d) Square root of the average determined in (c).

7.55 A student taking statistics suggested that the first ten incomes in **Data Set 2** would constitute a perfectly reasonable "random" sample. Comment on this suggestion. This same student has a personal computer and used a program called Microstat to generate the following data on the first ten incomes. Indicate how the Microstat statistical program calculated each of the following values:

```
        ARITHMETIC MEAN = 24830.00
       SAMPLE STD. DEV. =  2997.61
       SAMPLE VARIANCE = 8985687.45
STD. ERROR OF THE MEAN =   947.93
               MINIMUM = 18878
               MAXIMUM = 28412
                   SUM = 248300.00
         SUM OF SQUARES = 6246160205.99
           DEVIATION SS = 80871187.04
```

CASE PROBLEM

7.56 The main library at your university has asked you to help design a survey of the users of the library. The library staff wants to know who is using it (students, faculty, townspeople), and how often. They also want to know what parts of the library (e.g., periodicals, references, stacks, etc.) these people use. Finally, they want to know something about the students and faculty who are *not* using the library — who are they and why they are not using the library. A questionnaire has been designed. Your task is to gather a random sample consisting of approximately 400 responses to the questionnaire. (*Note:* not everyone who is sent a questionnaire will complete it.) Be very specific as to how you will gather a sample of 400. What might you do to encourage people to respond to the questionnaire? You have a small budget for this study.

GLOSSARY

Table 7.6 gives a summary and the reference sections for probability distributions discussed in this chapter. Figure 7.15 provides a tree diagram

TABLE 7.6 **Summary of sampling distributions**

Random Variable	Situation	Reference Section	Resulting Distribution for Problem-solving	Mean	Variance
$\bar{x}$	Population normal, σ known, sample size n	7.5	$z = \dfrac{\bar{x} - \mu}{\sigma/\sqrt{n}}$	0	1
$\bar{x}$	Population normal, σ unknown, sample size n^*	7.8	$t = \dfrac{\bar{x} - \mu}{s/\sqrt{n}}$	0	$\nu/(\nu - 2)$ (where $\nu = n - 1$)
$\bar{x}$	Population unknown, σ known, n "large"	7.6	$z = \dfrac{\bar{x} - \mu}{\sigma/\sqrt{n}}$	0	1
s^2	Population normal, sample size n	7.9	$\chi^2 = \dfrac{(n - 1)s^2}{\sigma^2}$	ν	2ν (where $\nu = n - 1$)

* If n is "large", $\bar{x}$ will be approximately normally distributed, and s should be close to σ; hence, $(\bar{x} - \mu)/(s/\sqrt{n})$ is approximately $N(0, 1)$.

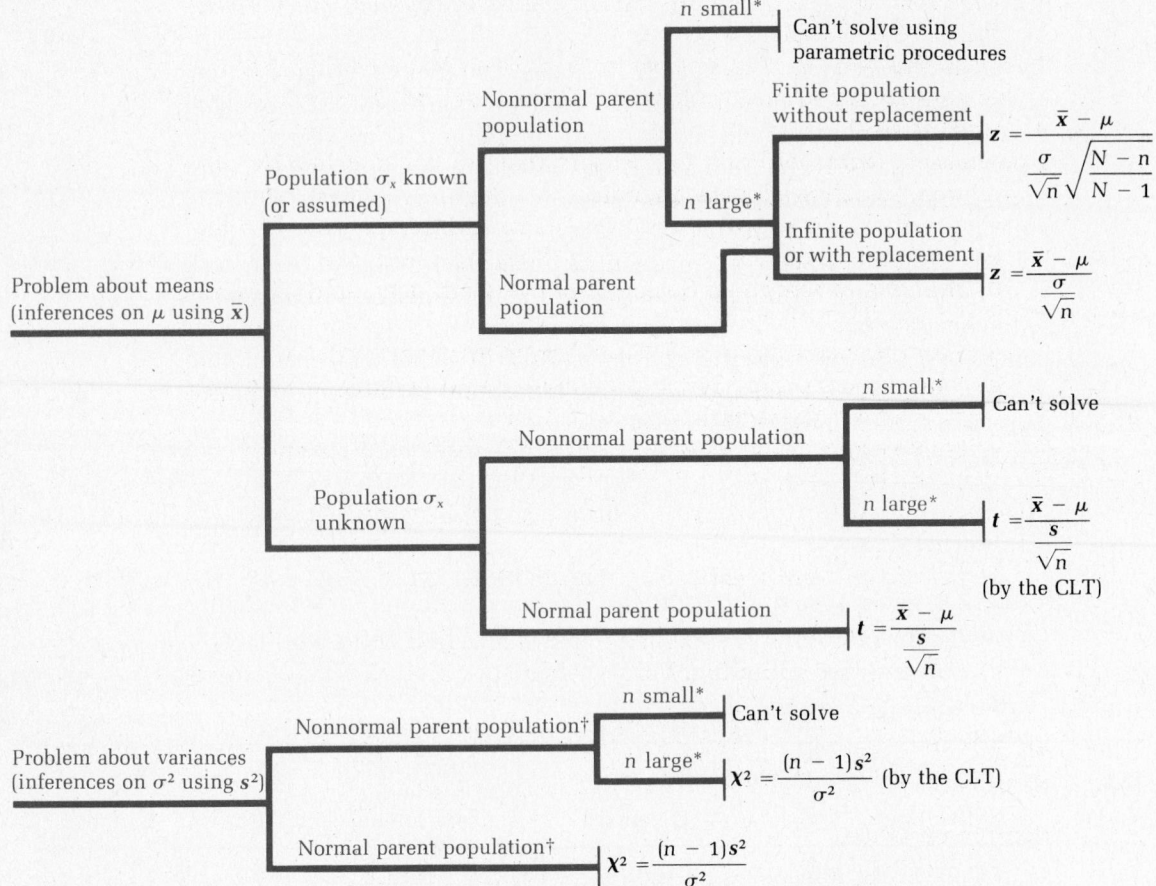

FIGURE 7.15 **Tree diagram for using probability distributions.**

*"Large" and "small" may depend on the accuracy desired and the shape of the parent population. For fairly symmetrical distributions, $n \geq 10$ may be sufficient. In almost all cases, $n \geq 30$ is sufficient for "large."

†Remember, the t and χ^2 are fairly "robust," meaning that they work well, even if the parent population is not exactly normally distributed but has some normal characteristics (unimodal and not badly skewed).

that some students have found useful in deciding when to apply each of these distributions.

Sample design: A plan specified for obtaining a sample before any data are collected.

Sampling and nonsampling errors. Sampling errors are those errors that occur because even a perfectly designed sample may not always represent the population exactly. Nonsampling errors are the "human," or avoidable, errors.

Random number: A number selected from a population in such a way that it has the same probability of occurring as does every other number in the population.

Probabilistic sampling: Sample designs that are based primarily on a random selection process. Includes:

a) **Simple random sampling:** every item and every group of items has the same probability of being in the sample.

b) **Systematic sampling:** Selection of every kth item, starting from a random point.

c) **Stratified sampling:** Selects randomly from layers or strata.

d) **Cluster sampling:** Selects randomly from groups, or clusters, having similar characteristics.

e) **Sequential sampling:** Sample items not taken simultaneously, but sequentially.

Nonprobabilistic sampling: Based primarily on a nonrandom selection process. Includes:

a) **Judgment sampling:** Primary consideration is the judgment of the person in charge.

b) **Quota sampling:** A specified number of values collected.

c) **Convenience sampling:** Values taken according to what is convenient.

Sample statistic: A characteristic of a sample.

Sample mean: $\bar{x} = \dfrac{1}{n}\sum x_i f_i$.

Sample variance:

$$s^2 = \frac{1}{n-1}\sum (x_i - \bar{x})^2 f_i = \frac{1}{n-1}\left[\sum x_i^2 f_i - \frac{(\sum x_i f_i)^2}{n}\right].$$

Sampling distribution: The probability distribution of a sample statistic.

Expected value of $\bar{x}$: $E[\bar{x}] = \mu_{\bar{x}} = \mu$.

Variance of $\bar{x}$: $V[\bar{x}] = \sigma_{\bar{x}}^2 = \sigma^2/n$.

Standard error of the mean: $\sigma_{\bar{x}} = \sigma/\sqrt{n}$.

Standardization of $\bar{x}$: $z = \dfrac{\bar{x} - \mu}{\sigma/\sqrt{n}}$.

Central Limit Theorem: Regardless of the parent population distribution, as n gets larger, the distribution of $\bar{x}$ will become more and more like a normal distribution.

Finite population correction factor: Corrects the standard error of the mean by multiplying by $\sqrt{(N-n)/(N-1)}$ when sampling more than 10% of a finite population of size N without replacement.

Degrees of freedom (v): Number of values in a sample that are "free" to vary when calculating a sample statistic. For example, to calculate s, $v = n - 1$.

t-distribution: A family of symmetrical p.d.f.'s that depend on the parameter v (d.f.) with $E[t] = 0$ and $V[t] = v/(v - 2)$ for $v \geq 3$. Used particularly in probability questions involving the sample mean when sampling from a normal parent population with unknown variance, $t = (\bar{x} - \mu)/(s/\sqrt{n})$. The t approaches the normal z as the sample size gets larger.

Chi-square (χ^2) distribution: A family of positively skewed p.d.f.'s which depend on the parameter v (degrees of freedom) with $E[\chi^2] = v$, $V[\chi^2] = 2v$. Used particularly in probability questions about a sample variance when sampling from a normal parent population, $\chi^2_{v=n-1} = (n - 1)s^2/\sigma^2$.

Estimation

EIGHT

8.1 INTRODUCTION

In the preceding chapters, characteristics of a population and of samples have been measured. Also, the concepts of probability distributions for discrete or continuous random variables have been presented. Our next task is to make use of the knowledge of the probability of sampling statistics so that we might reasonably use sample measures to learn about unknown population measures.

In most statistical studies the population parameters are unknown and must be estimated from a sample because it is impossible or impractical (in terms of time or expense) to look at the entire population. Developing methods for estimating as accurately as possible the value of population parameters is thus an important part of statistical analysis. A firm manufacturing electronic components might wish to investigate the average number of defective units in each batch of 10,000 items without inspecting each and every component before shipment. The economist who wants to determine the mean income of all college graduates will undoubtedly also have to rely on sample information. In these cases the value of a sample statistic, such as the sample mean, must be used as an estimate of the population parameter. If the degree of dispersion of defective electronic components from batch to batch or the variability of income is of interest, then this parameter also must be estimated from the sample data. Our objective in this chapter, which deals with similar estimation problems, is twofold: first, to present criteria for judging how well a given sample statistic estimates the population parameter; and second, to analyze several of the most popular methods for estimating these parameters.

The random variables used to estimate population parameters are called *estimators*, while specific values of these variables are referred to as *estimates* of the population parameters. The random variables $\bar{x}$ and s^2 are thus estimators of the population parameters μ and σ^2. A specific value of $\bar{x}$, such as $\bar{x} = 120$, is an estimate of μ, just as a specific value $s^2 = 237.1$ is an estimate of σ^2.

It is not necessary that an estimate of a population parameter be one single value; instead, the estimate could be a range of values.

> Estimates that specify a single value of the population are called point estimates, while estimates that specify a range of values are called interval estimates.

A **point estimate** for the average income of college graduates may be $42,000, implying that our best estimate of the population mean is $42,000. An **interval estimate** specifies a range of values, say $30,000 to $64,000, indicating that we think the mean income for the population lies in this interval.

The choice of an appropriate point estimator in a given circumstance usually depends on how well the estimator satisfies certain criteria.

The estimators emphasized throughout the remainder of this book are those that have the following four properties of a good estimator.

1. *The property of* **unbiasedness:** On the average, the value of the estimate should equal the population parameter being estimated.
2. *The property of* **efficiency:** The estimator should have a relatively small variance.
3. *The property of* **sufficiency:** The estimator should use all of the information available from the sample.
4. *The property of* **consistency:** The estimator should approach the value of the population parameter with greater probability as the sample size increases.

An estimator is a random variable, since it is the result of a sampling experiment. As a random variable, it has a probability distribution with a specific shape, expected value, and variance. Analysis of these characteristics of the distribution of an estimator permits us to specify desirable properties of the estimator.

8.2 FOUR PROPERTIES OF A "GOOD" ESTIMATOR

Unbiasedness Normally, it is preferable that the expected value of the estimator exactly equal, or fall close to, the true value of the parameter being estimated. If the average value of the estimator does not equal the actual parameter value, the estimator is said to contain a "bias" or to be a "biased estimator." Under ideal conditions an estimator has a bias of zero, in which case it is said to be "unbiased." This property thus can be stated as follows:

> An estimator is said to be unbiased if the expected value of the estimator is equal to the true value of the parameter being estimated. That is,
>
> E[estimator] = population parameter.

∴ E (estimator) − population parameter = 0

Figure 8.1(a) illustrates one unbiased estimator (1) and one biased estimator (2).

In determining a point estimate for the population mean, it is certainly not difficult to construct examples of a biased estimator. Simply using the largest observation in a sample of size $n > 1$ to estimate μ, and ignoring the rest of the observations, will yield an estimate whose expected value is larger than μ. This is obviously a poor choice for estimating the population mean, especially when there is a much more appealing choice, that of using $\bar{x}$. The sample mean is the most widely used estimator of all, for one of its major advantages is that it provides an unbiased estimate of μ. The fact that $E[\bar{x}] = \mu$ was presented in Section 7.4. The parameter most often estimated other than μ is σ^2, the population variance. An unbiased estimator for σ^2 is s^2, since $E[s^2] = \sigma^2$, as we showed in Section 7.8.

As a final example of the property of unbiasedness, consider the problem of estimating π, the population proportion of successes in a binomial distribution. Recall that in Chapter 5 we stated that if a sample yields x successes in n trials, then the ratio $x/n = p$ is an unbiased estimator of π:

$$E[p] = E[x/n] = \frac{1}{n} E[x] = \frac{1}{n} (n\pi) = \pi.$$

The above result implies that if, in a random sample of 100 voters, 60 people indicate that they intend to vote for Candidate A, then $p = 60/100 = 0.60$ is an unbiased estimate of the population proportion of people who would say they intend to vote for Candidate A.

FIGURE 8.1 **Illustration of properties of unbiasedness and efficiency.**

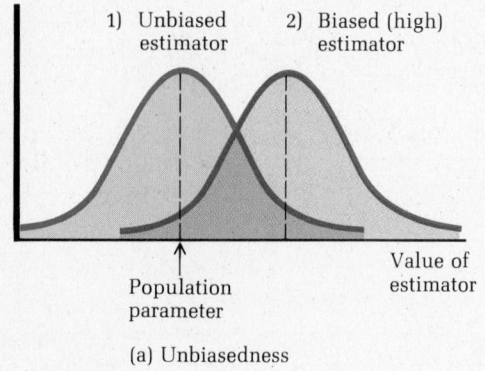

1) Unbiased estimator 2) Biased (high) estimator

Population parameter

Value of estimator

(a) Unbiasedness

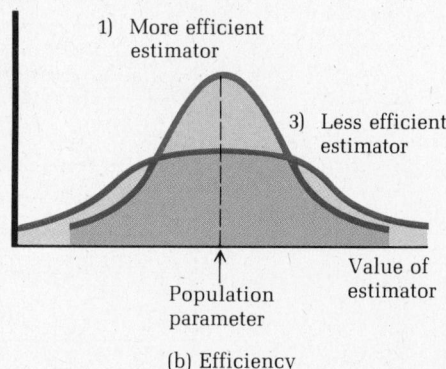

1) More efficient estimator

3) Less efficient estimator

Population parameter

Value of estimator

(b) Efficiency

One weakness of the property of unbiasedness lies in the fact that the criterion requires only that the *average* value of the estimator equal the population parameter. It does not require that most, or even *any*, of the values of the estimator be reasonably close to the population parameter, as would seem desirable in a "good" estimator. For this reason, the property of efficiency is important.

Efficiency
For given repeated samples of size n, it is desirable that an estimator have values that are close to each other. That is, it would be comforting in estimating an unknown parameter to realize that the value you computed on the basis of a particular random sample would not be much different from the value you or anyone else would compute on the basis of another random sample of the same size. *The property of efficiency implies that the variance of the estimator should be small.* However, having a small variance does not make an estimator a good one, unless this estimator is also unbiased. For example, an estimator that always specifies 200 as its estimate of the population parameter will have zero variance. But this estimate will be biased unless the true population parameter happens to equal 200. In other words, a small variance is desirable, but so is unbiasedness.

The property of efficiency of an estimator is defined by comparing its variance to the variance of all other *unbiased* estimators;

> The most efficient estimator among a group of unbiased estimators is the one with the smallest variance.

The most efficient estimator is also called the *best unbiased* estimator, where "best" implies minimum variance. Figure 8.1(b) illustrates the distributions of two different unbiased estimators (labeled 1 and 3) based on samples of the same size. Our definition of efficiency requires that the estimator be *unbiased* and have smaller variance than any other unbiased estimator. Thus, estimator 1 is more efficient than estimator 3.

Relative Efficiency
Since it is generally quite difficult to prove that an estimator is the best among all unbiased ones, the most common approach is to determine the *relative efficiency* of two estimators. Relative efficiency is defined as the ratio of the variances of the two estimators.

> Relative efficiency: $\dfrac{\text{Variance of first estimator}}{\text{Variance of second estimator}}$

As an illustration of the use of relative efficiency, consider the sample mean vs. the sample median as estimators of the mean of a normal population. Both estimators are unbiased when we are sampling from a normal population, since the normal is symmetric. From Section 7.4 we know that the variance of $\bar{x}$ equals σ^2/n. It is also possible to find the variance of an estimator using the sample median to estimate the population mean; this variance is $\pi\sigma^2/2n$. The ratio of these quantities gives their relative efficiency:

$$\frac{V(\text{median})}{V(\bar{x})} = \frac{\pi\sigma^2/2n}{\sigma^2/n} = \frac{\pi}{2} = 1.57.$$

The ratio 1.57 implies that the median is 1.57 times less efficient than the mean in estimating μ. In other words, an estimate based on the median of a sample of 157 observations has the same reliability as an estimate based on the mean of a sample of 100 observations, assuming a normal parent population.

In some problems it is possible to determine precisely the most efficient estimator, that is, the unbiased estimator with the smallest variance. In estimating the mean of a normal population, for example, it can be shown that the variance of any estimator must be greater than or equal to σ^2/n. Since the variance of $\bar{x}$ in this case exactly equals this lower bound (σ^2/n), the sample mean must be the most efficient estimator of μ.

In the design of a sample the most efficient estimator may not always be the best choice because of other factors, such as the time available to collect the sample or the accessibility of the observations. That is, statistical efficiency may have to be sacrificed in order to obtain an estimate in the time allowed; or some other estimator may be less costly to obtain or more meaningful and, therefore, may be preferred over the most efficient one.

A business journal, for example, may publish statements about the managerial competence of various companies in terms of only their ranks relative to each other (e.g., Tandy Corporation ranks third among all retail firms listed in **Data Set 2** in managerial emphasis on new products). Trying to determine the most efficient estimator in this case (for example, the average managerial characteristics) may be difficult, and such an estimator may not be as meaningful as a measure based on the ranked performance.

Sufficiency   Unbiasedness and efficiency are desirable properties for an estimator, particularly when one is dealing with small samples. Another property of interest is *sufficiency*.

> An estimator is said to be sufficient if it uses all the information about the population parameter that the sample can provide.

That is, the sufficient estimator somehow takes into account each of the sample observations, as well as all the information that is provided by these observations. The sample median is not a sufficient estimator because it uses only the *ranking* of the observations to obtain the middle value. The sufficiency property is of importance in that it is a necessary condition for efficiency.

Consistency   Since the distribution of an estimator will change, in general, as the sample size changes, the properties of estimators for large sample sizes (as $n \to \infty$) become important. Properties of estimators based on distributions approached as $n \to \infty$ are called *asymptotic properties*, and these may differ from the finite or small-sample properties. The most important of these asymptotic properties is that of *consistency*, which involves the convergence in probability of the estimator to the population parameter as the size of n increases. Since the topic of probability limits is not presented in this text, we shall define a slightly stronger form of consistency called *mean square consistency*.

> The mean square error of an estimator is defined as the sum of the variance of the estimator plus the square of its bias,
>
> (mean square error) = variance + (bias)^2.
>
> An estimator is said to be mean square consistent if its mean square error approaches zero as the sample size approaches infinity.

To say that the mean square error of an estimator goes to zero as the sample size gets very large means that the probability distribution of the estimator for large samples gets more and more compact (small variance) and is centered more and more closely about the true value of the parameter (small bias), as shown in Fig. 8.2. At the limit of $n = \infty$ the probability distribution of the estimator *degenerates* into a single spike at the true value. That is, the estimator always gives the same value, and that value is the true value. In more symbolic terms,

$$\text{when } n \to \infty, \quad \text{variance} \to 0 \quad \text{and} \quad (\text{bias})^2 \to 0.$$

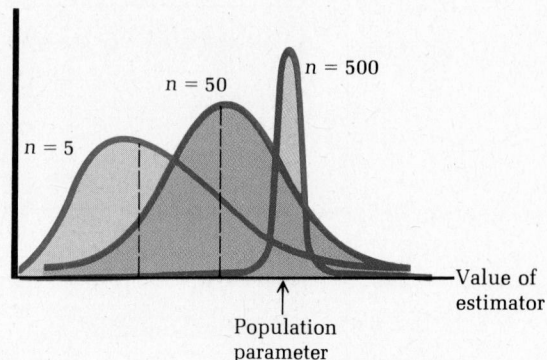

FIGURE 8.2 **Mean square consistency of an estimator.**

Previously, we showed that $\overline{x}$ is an unbiased estimator of the population mean and that p is an unbiased estimator of the population proportion. It is not difficult to show also that both these estimators are consistent as well as unbiased. We shall prove that p is a consistent estimator of π, leaving it to the reader to prove that $\overline{x}$ is also consistent.

$$V(p) = V[x/n] = \frac{1}{n^2} V[x] \qquad \text{(From Section 4.4, Rule 4)}$$

$$= \frac{1}{n^2} n\pi(1 - \pi) \qquad \text{(Since } x \text{ is binomially distributed)}$$

$$= \frac{\pi(1 - \pi)}{n}.$$

Since the value of $\pi(1 - \pi)/n$ approaches zero as n approaches infinity, $V[p] \to 0$. Since p is an unbiased estimator of π for any sample size, $(\text{bias})^2 = 0$. Thus, the mean square error also approaches zero and (p) must be a mean square consistent estimator of π.

While the four properties presented above are certainly all quite desirable, they do not preclude other considerations. We pointed out previously that the inferences (or estimates) made from samples serve as an aid to the process of making decisions and that samples should be drawn with the objective of minimizing the cost of making an incorrect decision (balanced against the cost of sampling). Since one primary purpose in collecting a sample involves estimating parameters, an estimation procedure should be chosen that will minimize the cost (or loss) of making an incorrect estimate from the sample information. This objective is not necessarily incompatible with any of the above properties of good estimators; in fact, in many cases, when these properties are satisfied, the estimator indeed will minimize the cost of making an error.

8.3 ESTIMATING UNKNOWN PARAMETERS

In the 1920's, R. A. Fisher developed the method of **maximum likelihood** as a means of finding estimators that satisfy some (but not necessarily all) of the criteria discussed previously. This method is popular because maximum-likelihood estimators are usually intuitively reasonable, have the property of consistency, and are often approximately normally distributed for large samples. The disadvantage of the method is that maximum-likelihood estimates are not necessarily unbiased for small samples and often involve some fairly complex mathematical derivations.

> The maximum-likelihood method estimates the value of a population parameter by selecting the most likely sample space from which a given sample could have been drawn. In other words, the sample space is selected that would yield the observed sample more frequently than any other sample space. The value of the population parameter corresponding to the generation of this sample space is called the maximum-likelihood estimate. The name *maximum-likelihood* is derived from this process of selecting the most likely sample space.

Example 8.1. The College Placement Center considers its activity to be successful if a graduating senior finds a job as a result of its assistance. In a sample of five graduates, three report finding a job with help from the placement service. Consider the problem of finding the maximum likelihood estimator of the binomial parameter π. The question of interest is, "What sample space (i.e., what binomial population) is most likely to give this particular result; or equivalently, what is the most likely value of π given the observed sample?"

The most likely population parameter can be determined by calculating the probability of obtaining exactly three successes in five trials for all possible values of the population parameter and selecting that value that yields the highest probability. Table 8.1 examines nine possible values of π, indicating for each value the probability of three successes in five trials; for example, if $\pi = \frac{1}{10}$, the appropriate probability is

$$_5C_3\left(\frac{1}{10}\right)^3\left(\frac{9}{10}\right)^2 = 0.0081.$$

The value of π most likely to yield a sample of three successes in five trials, as given by Table 8.1, is $\pi = 0.60$, where the associated

TABLE 8.1 **The probability of three successes in a binomial situation for different values of the parameter** π

Value of π	Probability of Three Successes
0.10	0.0081
0.20	0.0512
0.30	0.1323
0.40	0.2304
0.50	0.3125
0.60	0.3456
0.70	0.3087
0.80	0.2048
0.90	0.0729

probability is 0.3456. The reader will note that this estimate exactly equals the sample proportion $x/n = 3/5 = 0.60$. It is often true that the most likely value for a population parameter is the intuitively appealing one, the corresponding measure of the sample. For example, it can be shown that the maximum-likelihood estimator of a population mean is the sample mean. That is, the value of $\bar{x}$ is the most likely value of μ that can be found based on a sample of size n.

The particular value chosen as most likely for a population parameter is called a *point estimate*. We know that it would be an exceptional coincidence (because of sampling error) if this estimate were identical to the population parameter. Thus, even though the best possible value is used as the point estimate, we should have very little confidence that this value is *exactly* correct. One of the major weaknesses of a point estimate is that it does not permit the expression of any degree of uncertainty about the estimate. The most common way to express uncertainty about an estimate is to define, with a known *probability of error*, an interval or range of values in which the population parameter is *likely* to be. This process is known as *interval estimation*.

Confidence Intervals

You will recall that on a number of occasions thus far we have determined values a and b so that $P(a \le \bar{x} \le b)$ equals some predetermined value. The values a and b were determined from a knowledge about the parent population and its parameters. The interval (a, b) is called a probability interval for $\bar{x}$. For example, if we calculated $P(a \le \bar{x} \le b) = 0.90$, based on a random sample of size n drawn from a population with a known mean μ, we know the random variable $\bar{x}$ will fall in the probability interval (a, b) 90% of the time.

Although it is important to be able to construct probability intervals for $\bar{x}$ based on knowledge of μ, for most practical statistical problems the process must be reversed; i.e., it is μ that is the unknown, and we want to construct a *confidence interval* for μ based on $\bar{x}$. For example, we may want to develop a method for defining an interval based on $\bar{x}$ such that μ is likely to lie in such intervals 90% of the times that the method is used — a 90% confidence interval. This means that, on the average, 90 such intervals out of every 100 calculated on the basis of means of samples of size n will include the population mean μ.

The use of the future tense in explaining a confidence interval is very important because, once such an interval based on a sample is determined, either the true parameter lies in the interval or it does not. The value of μ cannot be said to have a probability of 0.90 of being within the interval because it is not a random variable, but a constant. If it is in a given interval, then the probability that it is in the interval is 1.0; if not, the probability that it is within the interval is 0.0.

Perhaps this concept can be emphasized further by noting that a population parameter, although unknown, is a constant and it does *not* have a probability distribution. Thus, it is improper to make probability statements about values of a population parameter. In finding an interval estimate, the endpoints of the interval are based on sample evidence. They will have different values for each different sample. Thus, these endpoints, or more generally, the intervals themselves, are random variables. Consequently, it is appropriate to make probability statements about the *proportion of intervals* that would include a particular parameter value. But it is *not* appropriate to make probability statements about a parameter.

In order to simplify the language concerning this rather subtle distinction, statisticians use the term *confidence interval* when specifying the upper and lower limits on the likely value of a parameter.

> A 90% confidence interval for a parameter is a shorthand statement for "the probability is 0.90 that the interval to be determined on the basis of the sample evidence would be one that includes the population parameter."

Example 8.2. Consider the following problem in process control. A manufacturer makes large tile pipes; when the production process is working correctly, the interior diameter of the pipe is normally distributed with mean $\mu = 24''$ and standard deviation $\sigma = \frac{1}{4}''$, or $N(24, 0.25^2)$. At random points in time, a sample of four pipe segments is selected from the production process to check on the average diameter of all the pipes in the population being produced. The population parameter being investigated here is μ, and we know that in this case $\bar{x}$ has a normal distribution, since x is normal. Because $(\sigma/\sqrt{n} = (0.25/\sqrt{4}) = 0.125$ is the standard deviation of the $\bar{x}$'s, the distribution of $\bar{x}$ is $N(24, 0.125^2)$.

Figure 8.3 represents the two types of intervals discussed above. This figure shows the mean of 20 different samples (20 dots), each of size $n = 4$. Part (a) of the figure illustrates a probability interval with its center at the population mean, $\mu = 24$ inches, and values $a = 23.755$ and $b = 24.245$, chosen so that, theoretically, 95% of the values of $\bar{x}$ will lie between a and b.

FIGURE 8.3 **Illustration of probability intervals and of confidence intervals for an unbiased estimator with a normal distribution.**

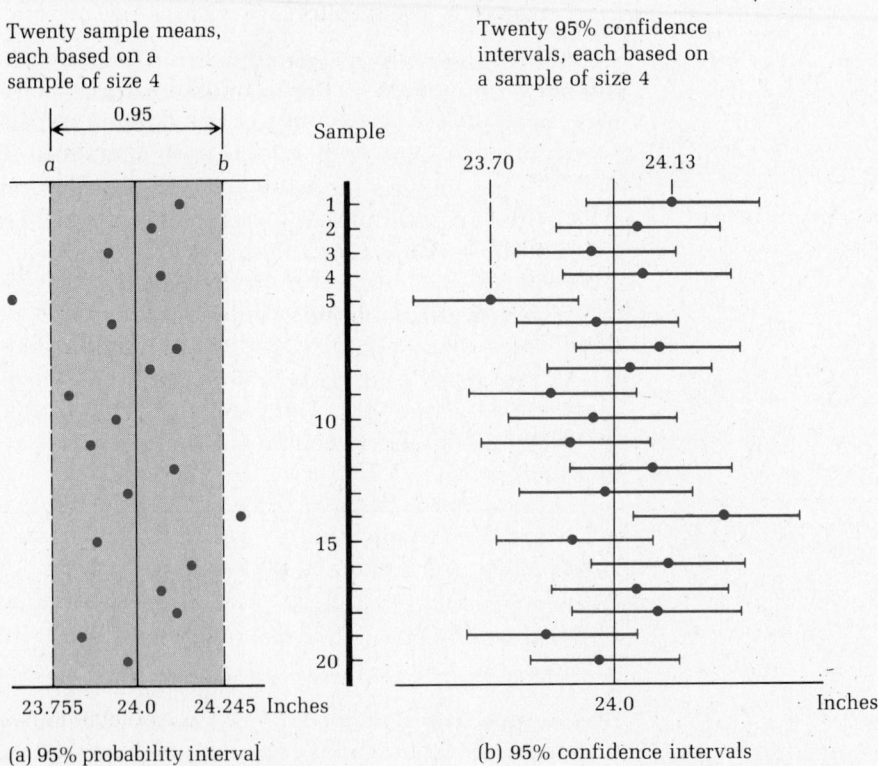

Twenty sample means, each based on a sample of size 4

Twenty 95% confidence intervals, each based on a sample of size 4

(a) 95% probability interval
$P(23.755 < \bar{x} < 24.245) = 0.95$

(b) 95% confidence intervals
$P(\textbf{intervals}$ include $24.0) = 0.95$

the probability that all intervals include μ.

These endpoints are found in the same way as in the probability examples in Chapters 6 and 7. From Table III the values $z = \pm 1.96$ exclude 0.025 in each tail of the normal distribution. With $\mu = 24$ as the center of the probability interval, the endpoints are

$$24 \pm 1.96\,\frac{\sigma}{\sqrt{n}} = 24 \pm 1.96(0.125) = 23.755 \quad \text{and} \quad 24.245.$$

Owing to the uncertainty of sampling, only 18 of 20 rather than 19 of 20 (95%) of these sample means lie between 23.755 and 24.245. However, over all such conceivable sample means with $n = 4$, we know that

$$P(23.755 < \bar{x} < 24.245) = 0.95.$$

In part (b) of Fig. 8.3, the confidence intervals for μ based on each of these 20 samples are shown. The center of each confidence interval is the sample mean $\bar{x}$, shown by the 20 different dots. The endpoints of the intervals are equidistant from these dots as determined by the following equations:

$$\text{upper} = \bar{x} + 1.96(0.125) \quad \text{and} \quad \text{lower} = \bar{x} - 1.96(0.125).$$

Some of the intervals in Fig. 8.3(b) do not include the true value of $\mu = 24$, and some do include it. For example, the first interval is centered at the mean of the first sample, 24.13. The upper and lower confidence limits are $24.13 \pm 1.96(0.125)$, which gives 23.885 and 24.375. Thus, this interval does include the value $\mu = 24$. It makes no sense, therefore, to say that the probability that μ lies in this interval is 0.95. It is a *certainty* (probability $= 1.0$) that 24 lies between 23.885 and 24.375. Similarly, consider the fifth sample with a mean of 23.7. The upper and lower confidence limits using this center value are $23.7 \pm 1.96(0.125)$, which gives 23.455 and 23.945. Again, it is improper to say that the probability that μ lies in this interval is 0.95. Since μ is known to equal 24, we can clearly see that this interval does not include μ. It is *impossible* (probability $= 0.0$) for 24 to be between 23.455 and 23.945.

The concept is the same *when the parameter is unknown.* It is still a constant value, whatever it is, and it either will or will not lie in a given interval. The probability of 0.95 *does not refer to the event that μ is in the interval.* The probability of 0.95 refers to the event that *an interval obtained in this manner would include μ.* That is,

$$P \text{ (interval would include } \mu) = 0.95.$$

This is a probability based on all conceivable repeated samples of four pipe segments from which such intervals could be calculated, not on any one specific interval that has actually been determined.

We express this concept by stating that we are 95% *confident* that the interval covers μ. The term **confidence level** is used when referring to the uncertainty about the likely value of a population parameter. The term *probability* is reserved for statements of uncertainty about random variables. As the discussion above and Fig. 8.3 show, the two concepts are related, but they are significantly different.

Study Question 8.1: Interval Interpretation

Write in symbols the appropriate probability statement that corresponds to each of the following:

a) 90% probability interval for the sample variance s^2 of the incomes of college graduates.
b) 99% confidence interval for the proportion of persons receiving social security payments.
c) 95% confidence interval for the average number of hours worked per week by employees in manufacturing.

Answer
a) $P(a < s^2 < b) = 0.90$.
b) $P(\text{interval would include } \pi) = 0.99$ [not $P(a < \pi < b) = 0.99$].
c) $P(\text{interval would include } \mu) = 0.95$ [not $P(a < \mu < b) = 0.95$].

The Probability of an Error, α   It is often more convenient to refer to the probability that a confidence interval will *not* include the parameter than to express the probability that it will. The former probability is denoted by α (the Greek letter "alpha"). The value of alpha is referred to as the probability of making an error, since it indicates the proportion of times that one will be *incorrect* in assuming that the intervals would contain the population parameter. It is customary to refer to confidence intervals as being of size "$100(1 - \alpha)\%$." Thus, if α is 0.05, then the associated interval is a **$100(1 - \alpha)\%$** or a 95% **confidence interval**; if a 90% confidence interval is specified, then $\alpha = 1.0 - (90/100) = 0.10$. In our previous example, the process-control problem, α equaled 0.05, which means that the probability is 0.05 of making an error in saying that the interval to be calculated will contain the parameter (the process is in control) when in fact it will not (the process needs adjustment). In other words, if we were to repeat the method of determining confidence intervals many times, we would be wrong in only 5% of the cases, on the average, in saying that the intervals include the population parameter.

There is an obvious trade-off between the value of α and the size of the confidence interval: the lower the value of α, the larger the interval must be.* If one need not be very confident that the population parameter will be within the interval, then a relatively small interval will suffice; if one is to be quite confident that the population parameter will be in the interval to be calculated, a relatively large interval will be necessary. The value of α is often set at 0.05 or 0.01, representing 95% and 99% confidence intervals, respectively. This procedure, although widely used, does not necessarily lead to the optimal trade-off between the size of the confidence interval and the risk of making an error.

In general, confidence intervals are constructed on the basis of sample information, so that both changes in α and changes in n (the sample size) affect the size of the interval. The more observations collected, the more confident one can be about the estimate of the population parameter, and thus, the smaller need be the interval to ensure a given level of confidence. Although it usually is desirable to have as small a confidence interval as possible, the optimal interval size must be determined by considering the costs of sampling and the amount of risk of making an error that one wants to assume. We shall return several times to this problem of determining the optimal trade-off between the risks of making an error and the sample size. For now, we merely caution the reader to be aware that the task of determining an "optimal" trade-off may not be an easy one and is often done arbitrarily.

Determining a Confidence Interval

One of the first steps in constructing a confidence interval is to specify the size of the sample and how much confidence one wants to have that the resulting interval is likely to include the population parameter. In other words, both n and α are usually fixed in advance. However, it is possible under certain conditions to consider either n or α as an unknown and to solve for the value of this unknown.

In addition to specifying α in advance, one must also specify how much of the total error α is attributed to the possibility that the true population parameter might be larger than the upper bound of the confidence interval. The remainder of α is attributed to the possibility that the true parameter might be smaller than the lower bound of the interval. As we indicated previously, this split of α is usually obtained by dividing α *equally* between the upper and the lower tails of the distribution. In the case of a confidence interval, however, the decision on how to divide α should depend on how serious or costly it is to make errors on the high side relative to errors on the low side. Since we normally want to avoid expensive errors, α should be divided in such a

---

* We assume here that other factors, such as the sample size, are held constant.

way that expensive errors occur less frequently. Unfortunately, determining the costs of making an error may be quite difficult, so

> the common procedure for determining confidence intervals is the same as for probability intervals — i.e., to exclude half of α (that is, $\alpha/2$) on the high side and half of α on the low side.

Thus, if $\alpha = 0.05$, then $\alpha/2 = 0.025$ is the probability that the upper bound of the confidence interval will be below the true parameter. Also, $\alpha/2 = 0.025$ is the probability that the lower bound will exceed the true parameter. This procedure is based on the assumption that errors on the high side are just as expensive as errors on the low side.

In the above discussion we stated that a given confidence interval will depend on α (and the way α is divided) and on the size of the sample. The other factor that influences the boundaries of a particular confidence interval is the *sampling distribution* of the statistic used to estimate the population parameter. Normally, the procedure for establishing a confidence interval for a population parameter is *first to find a point estimate* of this parameter. The uncertainty of this point estimate is then determined by finding that interval of values about the point estimate that yields the desired degree of confidence, on the basis of the sampling distribution of this statistic. Since different sampling distributions are used for estimating different population parameters, such as the mean, the binomial parameter π, or the variance, we shall describe the process of constructing intervals for each of these cases in separate sections.

8.4 CONFIDENCE INTERVALS FOR μ (σ KNOWN)

In this section a confidence interval for the population parameter μ is constructed, based on a random sample drawn from a normal parent population with *known* standard deviation. The natural sample statistic for estimating μ is $\bar{x}$, the sample mean, for the reasons discussed in Section 8.2. Recall the sampling distribution of $\bar{x}$ under the conditions listed there: the expected value of $\bar{x}$ equals μ, and $\bar{x}$ has a standard deviation of $\sigma\sqrt{n}$. Also recall from page 342 that the variable $z = (\bar{x} - \mu)/(\sigma/\sqrt{n})$ has a standardized normal distribution.

We now introduce a useful notational point. The cumulative probability distribution in Table III gives values of $F(z)$, the area under the curve to the *left* of a point z. That is, if 95% of the area under the curve is to the left of z, then $F(z) = 0.95$.

As an indicator of the proportion of area to the *right* of a point z, we let the symbol z_α represent that point for which the probability of observing values of z greater than z_α is α. By definition, $P(z \geq z_\alpha) = \alpha$, and the cumulative probability at this point is $F(z_\alpha) = 1 - \alpha$.

For example, $F(z_{0.01}) = 0.99$, or $F(z_{0.05}) = 0.95$.

This notation gives us two ways of representing proportions of the total area under a normal probability density function. We can use the cumulative notation $[F(z)]$ for the area to the *left* of a point z or the subscript notation (z_α) for the point z having an area of α to its *right*. The latter is extremely convenient for denoting the area in the extreme tail of a distribution. If we want to exclude 0.01 in the upper tail, the point is denoted by $z_{0.01}$. If the area in the upper tail beyond a certain point is to be 0.05, we denote that point by $z_{0.05}$. Since the normal distribution is symmetric, the negative value ($-z_\alpha$) can similarly denote points in the lower tail of the normal distribution below which a proportion α of the area is excluded. Two such points are shown in Fig. 8.4.

For finding upper and lower bounds of confidence intervals, it is usually convenient to find those points excluding ($\alpha/2$) proportion of the area (probability) in each tail of the normal distribution (so that the total area *excluded* equals α and the area *included* in the interval between the upper and lower limits is ($1 - \alpha$). To do this, let $z_{\alpha/2}$ represent the value for which the probability $P(z \geq z_{\alpha/2}) = \alpha/2$, and let $-z_{\alpha/2}$ equal the point at which $P(z \leq -z_{\alpha/2}) = \alpha/2$. If, for example, $\alpha = 0.05$, the value of $+z_{\alpha/2}$ satisfying $P(z \geq z_{\alpha/2}) = 0.025$ is the same point as $F(z) = 0.975$. From Table III, $z_{\alpha/2} = z_{0.025}$ is seen to be 1.96. The value of $-z_{\alpha/2}$ must be -1.96. The probability that **z** falls between the two limits, -1.96 and $+1.96$, is

$$P(-1.96 \leq \mathbf{z} \leq +1.96) = 1.00 - 0.025 - 0.025 = 0.95,$$

as shown in Fig. 8.5.

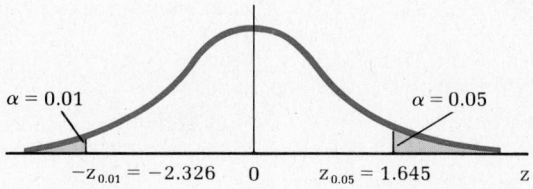

$\alpha = 0.01$

$\alpha = 0.05$

$-z_{0.01} = -2.326 \qquad 0 \qquad z_{0.05} = 1.645 \qquad\qquad z$

FIGURE 8.4 **Values of** $+z_{0.05}$ **and** $-z_{0.01}$.

FIGURE 8.5 **The values of**
±$z_{\alpha/2}$, cutting off a total
area of $\alpha = 0.05$ from the
standardized normal
distribution, leaving an
interval including
100(1 − α) percent = 95%
of the probability.

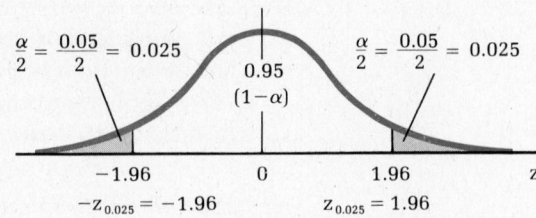

$\dfrac{\alpha}{2} = \dfrac{0.05}{2} = 0.025$ $\qquad$ $\dfrac{\alpha}{2} = \dfrac{0.05}{2} = 0.025$

0.95
(1−α)

−1.96 $\qquad$ 0 $\qquad$ 1.96 $\qquad$ z

$-z_{0.025} = -1.96$ $\qquad$ $z_{0.025} = 1.96$

In more general terms, the probability that **z** falls between the two limits $-z_{\alpha/2}$ and $+z_{\alpha/2}$ can be written as

$$P(-z_{\alpha/2} \leq \mathbf{z} \leq +z_{\alpha/2}) = 1 - \alpha.$$

Note that this interval, $-z_{\alpha/2} \leq \mathbf{z} \leq +z_{\alpha/2}$, is a 100(1 − α)% *probability interval* for **z**, any standardized normal variable. It is also a 100(1 − α)% probability interval for the *particular* standardized normal variable $\mathbf{z} = (\bar{x} - \mu)/(\sigma/\sqrt{n})$. Unfortunately, this is not the interval we originally set out to derive because we wanted a 100(1 − α)% *confidence interval* for μ, not a probability interval for $(\bar{x} - \mu)(\sigma/\sqrt{n})$. However, the difference is not hard to resolve. It is simple to find the confidence limits on μ by rewriting the inequalities in the expression $-z_{\alpha/2} \leq \mathbf{z} \leq +z_{\alpha/2}$ to get:*

100(1 − α)% confidence interval for μ, where σ is known and the parent population is normal:

$$\bar{x} - z_{\alpha/2}\frac{\sigma}{\sqrt{n}} \leq \mu \leq \bar{x} + z_{\alpha/2}\frac{\sigma}{\sqrt{n}}. \qquad (8.1)$$

Example 8.3. For decision-making regarding freight rates, tract maintenance, diesel fuel consumption, etc., a consortium of railroads wishes to estimate with 80% confidence the mean number of freight cars hauled

---

* The solution is

$-z_{\alpha/2} \leq \mathbf{z} \leq z_{\alpha/2}$

$-z_{\alpha/2} \leq \dfrac{\bar{x} - \mu}{\sigma/\sqrt{n}} \leq z_{\alpha/2}$ $\qquad$ By substitution

$-z_{\alpha/2}\dfrac{\sigma}{\sqrt{n}} \leq (\bar{x} - \mu) \leq z_{\alpha/2}\dfrac{\sigma}{\sqrt{n}}$ $\qquad$ By multiplying each term by $\sigma/\sqrt{n}$

$-\bar{x} - z_{\alpha/2}\dfrac{\sigma}{\sqrt{n}} \leq -\mu \leq -x + z_{\alpha/2}\dfrac{\sigma}{\sqrt{n}}$ $\qquad$ By adding $(-\bar{x})$ to each term

$\bar{x} + z_{\alpha/2}\dfrac{\sigma}{\sqrt{n}} \geq \mu \geq x - z_{\alpha/2}\dfrac{\sigma}{\sqrt{n}}.$ $\qquad$ By multiplying each term by (-1), thus changing the direction of both inequalities

per train over a 600-mile segment of track in Wyoming and Nebraska. We assume that the number of cars is normally distributed and that the population variance is known to be 225.

We first obtain a sample of $n = 25$ trains and determine the sample average of $\bar{x} = 107$ cars. Since we want an 80% confidence interval, $\alpha = 0.20$ and the appropriate z-values are $\pm z_{\alpha/2} = \pm z_{0.10} = \pm 1.28$. Substituting these two values, as well as $n = 25$, $\sigma = 15$, and $\bar{x} = 107$ into Formula (8.1), we get the desired 80% confidence interval:

$$\bar{x} - z_{\alpha/2}\frac{\sigma}{\sqrt{n}} \le \mu \le \bar{x} + z_{\alpha/2}\frac{\sigma}{\sqrt{n}},$$

$$107 - (1.28)\frac{15}{\sqrt{25}} \le \mu \le 107 + (1.28)\frac{15}{\sqrt{25}},$$

$$107 - 3.84 \le \mu \le 107 + 3.84,$$

$$103.16 \le \mu \le 110.84.$$

We can be confident that intervals obtained by using this procedure are likely to contain μ 80% of the time. That is, on the average, for 80 out of 100 such samples of size $n = 25$, the intervals calculated in this manner will include the true population mean μ. We do not know, of course, whether the above interval is one of the correct ones or one of the incorrect ones, since μ is unknown. For the 80% confidence interval the probability is $\alpha = 0.20$ that the interval will not include the true mean μ. If one desires a smaller risk of error α, a larger confidence interval must be used.

For example, in order to have $\alpha = 0.01$ (i.e., a 99% confidence interval), the appropriate z-values found in Table III are $z_{\alpha/2} = z_{0.005} = 2.576$ and $-z_{\alpha/2} = -2.576$. The new confidence interval is

$$107 - (2.576)\frac{15}{\sqrt{25}} \le \mu \le 107 + (2.576)\frac{15}{\sqrt{25}},$$

$$107 - 7.728 \le \mu \le 107 + 7.728,$$

$$99.272 \le \mu \le 114.728.$$

Since intervals calculated by using $\alpha = 0.01$ are wider than intervals calculated by using $\alpha = 0.20$, we have greater confidence that the larger interval will include the population parameter μ. We could further increase our confidence and decrease the risk of error α by extending the interval even more. Of course, there is a limit to the usefulness of the interval when it becomes too large. For example, we might have calculated from our sample that the mean number of freight cars almost certainly $(\alpha \to 0.0)$ falls in the interval $27 \le \mu \le 187$, but we could have made such a statement from simple experience without knowing anything about statistical inference. We sample to get useful information that is more precise. To obtain it, we must be willing to subject our conclusions or inferences to a small controlled level of risk α.

Relaxation of the Assumption of Normality for the Population

The relationship expressed in Formula (8.1) depends on the assumptions that σ is known and that the parent population is normal. When these assumptions are valid, Formula (8.1) holds for any sample size, whether n is large or small. But suppose that the parent poulation is *not normal*. In this case, if the sample size n is small, then the distribution of $(\overline{x} - \mu)/(\sigma/\sqrt{n})$ is not normal, and there is no convenient way to determine a confidence interval. On the other hand, when n is large,* we know by the central limit theorem that $(\overline{x} - \mu)/(\sigma/\sqrt{n})$ is *approximately* normally distributed; hence the confidence interval specified by Formula (8.1) is still appropriate.

Example 8.4. Suppose that in Example 8.3 we now drop the assumption of normality, but suppose we increase the sample size to $n = 64$. Since $n > 30$, we can safely rely on the central limit theorem and apply the normal distribution. Let us find a 99% confidence interval if we are again given $\sigma = 15$ and we find a sample mean of $\overline{x} = 107$. The confidence limits are

$$107 - (2.576)\frac{15}{\sqrt{64}} \le \mu \le 107 + (2.576)\frac{15}{\sqrt{64}},$$

$$107 - 4.83 \le \mu \le 107 + 4.83,$$

$$102.17 \le \mu \le 111.83.$$

We have 99% confidence that the interval 102.17 to 111.83 includes the average number of freight cars per train. This interval is smaller than the second one in Example 8.3. Although they have the same level of error, $\alpha = 0.01$, this interval is narrower because it is based on a larger sample size. Figure 8.6 illustrates this 99% confidence interval. Remember that it is based on only a single sample. If many repeated samples were taken, then 99% of the intervals calculated about the different sample means would include the true value of the unknown μ. Whether this one does or does not is unknown. However, we do have a measure of the uncertainty associated with our statement about the likely value of μ.

---

* We repeat that "large" n depends on the shape of the parent population. For symmetric, unimodal populations, n as small as 5 or 10 may be sufficient for a satisfactory approximation. In almost all cases, $n > 30$ is sufficient.

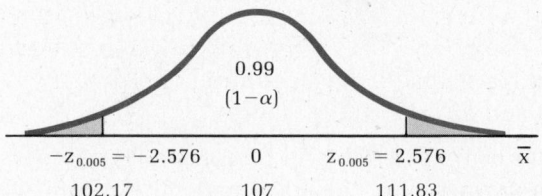

FIGURE 8.6 **Illustration of a 99% confidence interval for Example 8.4 and Study Question 8.2.**

As a final remark about sample sizes, recall that one advantage of a large sample is greater reliability. Hence, the finite population correction factor should be used if the population is finite and the sample size gets so large that it exceeds 10% of the population size. This would modify Formula (8.1) by changing the standard error in the confidence limit from

$$\frac{\sigma}{\sqrt{n}}$$

to

$$\frac{\sigma}{\sqrt{n}}\sqrt{\frac{N-n}{N-1}}.$$

Study Question 8.2: Average Book Expenditure per Pupil
A random sample of 18 out of 145 public schools is taken to find the per-pupil expenditures on books this year. The sample average is $84.60. Assuming a normal population with a standard deviation of $12.36 (determined from a census of schools a few years ago), find a 99% confidence interval for the population mean.

Answer. From Table III the appropriate values of **z** that exclude (α/2) = 0.005 of the distribution are ±2.576. (See Fig. 8.6.) Using Formula (8.1) with σ = 12.36 and $\overline{x}$ = 84.60 plus the finite population correction factor gives

$$84.60 \pm 2.576 \frac{12.36}{\sqrt{18}} \sqrt{\frac{145-18}{145-1}}$$

$$= 84.60 \pm 7.50 \sqrt{0.882}$$

$$= 84.60 \pm 7.05.$$

The upper and lower confidence limits are $77.55 and $91.65.

Define. *Point and interval estimates, unbiasedness, efficiency, sufficiency, consistency, maximum-likelihood estimate, probability interval, confidence interval, α.*

PROBLEMS

8.1 Differentiate between:
a) A point estimate and an interval estimate.
b) Unbiasedness and consistency.

8.2 What are the four properties of a "good estimator?" Explain why each one is important.

8.3 Given a normal parent population, which of the following are unbiased estimators of μ?
a) mean   b) median   c) mode

8.4 Consider the population $x = \{5, 15\}$.
a) Calculate μ, σ^2, and σ for this population.
b) Make a list of the eight possible samples of size $n = 3$, with replacement [that is,

$$(5, 5, 5), \quad (5, 5, 15), \quad (5, 15, 5), \text{ etc.}],$$

and then calculate $\bar{x}$ for each sample.
c) Show from part (b) that $\bar{x}$ is an unbiased estimate of μ (that is, $E[\bar{x}] = \mu$).
d) Calculate s^2 for each sample and then show that $E[s^2] = \sigma^2$.
e) Show that the average of the eight values of s is not equal to σ (that is, $E[s] \neq \sigma$).
f) Calculate the median for each of the 8 samples. Is the average of these medians equal to μ (i.e., is the median an unbiased estimator in this case)?

8.5 Calculate the variance of the median values in Problem 8.4(f). Use this variance and the variance of the values of $\bar{x}$ in Problem 8.4(b) to show that $\bar{x}$ is more efficient than the median as an estimator of μ.

8.6 An accountant selected a random sample of 100 of the commercial accounts in a certain branch bank. The mean balance among these accounts was found to be \$749.13. The accountant then stated that the mean balance for all commercial accounts must be \$749.13, since $\bar{x}$ is an unbiased estimate of μ. Discuss the reasonableness of this assertion.

8.7 Explain, in your own words, how the properties of efficiency and consistency both involve the property of unbiasedness. (*Hint*: Consider unbiasedness in small- and large-size samples respectively.)

8.8 Repeat Problem 8.4(b) using $n = 2$. Compare the case in which $n = 2$ with that in which $n = 3$, and show that the results support the fact that the mean is a consistent estimator.

8.9 Forty percent of the clerks in a department store are part-time workers. Let **x** be the number of part-time workers in a random selection of four clerks.

a) The five possible binomial values of $p = (x/n)$ are 0/4, 1/4, 2/4, 3/4, and 4/4. Calculate $E[p]$ by multiplying each of these five values by the appropriate probabilities in Table I ($n = 4$ and $\pi = 0.40$). Is **p** unbiased (that is, does $E[p] = \pi$)?

b) Calculate the variance of the p-values in part (a). Calculate the variance of **p** for $\pi = 0.40$ and $n = 5$. Does the variance decrease from $n = 4$ to $n = 5$, supporting the fact that **p** is a consistent estimator?

8.10 Find the following values.

a) Find the values of z_α when $P(\mathbf{z} \geq z_\alpha) = 0.025$, and for $P(\mathbf{z} \leq -z_\alpha) = 0.02$.

b) Find the value of $z_{\alpha/2}$ such that $P(-z_{\alpha/2} \leq \mathbf{z} \leq z_{\alpha/2}) = 0.98$.

8.11 Explain, in your own words, under what circumstances **x** does not have to be normally distributed if you wish to calculate a 90% confidence interval for μ.

8.12 When properly adjusted, the period of intense heat applied in a fabricating process is normally distributed with a variance of $\sigma^2 = 0.50$ (seconds)^2. Four random cycles of the process are monitored, and the results are heat periods of 51, 52, 50, and 51 seconds.

a) Find an unbiased estimate of μ.

b) Construct a 95% confidence interval for μ.

8.13 *Forbes* magazine points out in every issue a number of stocks recommended for purchase. A sample of nine recommendations is followed for six months to determine whether these stocks perform better than the overall Dow-Jones index of stocks. The percentage changes above or below the change for the index are -5, 2, -10, 5, 8, 13, 3, -1, and 3.

a) Find the best point estimate of μ (the mean percentage change, net of the index change, for all such recommended stocks).

b) Construct a 90% confidence interval for μ, assuming a normal population and a variance of $\sigma^2 = 40$.

8.14 Find a 90% confidence interval for the mean number of credit sales per week by a Western Auto store. Assume that the population has a standard deviation of 70 and that a sample of 36 weeks yields a sample mean of 950. Does your answer require the assumption that **x** is normally distributed?

8.15 A sample of 36 installment loans for used cars bought in 1982 revealed a mean principal amount of $4528. The standard deviation for the parent population is believed to be $970.

a) Find a 95% confidence interval for the mean amount of all used car loans in 1982.

b) The Motor Vehicle Manufacturers Association reported that the average used car installment loan in 1982 was $4755. Does your confidence interval from part (a) include this value? Explain how your result is consistent with the meaning of a 95% confidence interval.

8.16 A recent survey asked respondents to rate, on a scale from 0 to 100, how good a job they thought the President of the United States had done during the past six months. Assume that the population variance for this survey is known to be $\sigma^2 = 100$. Construct a 95% confidence interval for μ, assuming that a random sample of 256 adults yielded a mean score of 61.0. Is it necessary in this case to assume that the parent population is normal?

8.17 A production assembly process is scheduled as a 20-minute operation. A time study based on 16 randomly selected observation periods (unknown to the employees) shows a sample average of 24.3 minutes. The population standard deviation is $\sigma = 6$ minutes. Find a 90% confidence interval for the population mean time of this assembly operation, assuming that the population is normally distributed.

8.5 CONFIDENCE INTERVALS FOR μ (σ UNKNOWN)

The major assumption specified at the beginning of Section 8.4 was that the population standard deviation σ is known. This assumption may not realistically be applicable to many practical problems. When the mean of the population is unknown and must be estimated, it is unlikely that the standard deviation about that unknown mean will be known. Instead, the population standard deviation often must be estimated on the basis of the sample standard deviation. Under these circumstances it is common to use the t-distributed random variable, $(\bar{x} - \mu)/(s/\sqrt{n})$, with $(n - 1)$ degrees of freedom (assuming that the parent population is normal).

The procedure for determining a $100(1 - \alpha)\%$ confidence interval using the t-distribution is the same as that employed when the normal distribution holds, except that different limits must be used. The limits are found by using t-values from Table VI rather than z-values from Table III. Suppose we let $t_{\alpha/2,\nu}$ represent that value of the t-distribution with $\nu = n - 1$ degrees of freedom which excludes $\alpha/2$ of the probability in the upper tail. Note that a t-value is labeled with *two* subscripts, one to denote the value of $\alpha/2$, the other to denote the degrees of freedom (ν)

because the *t* represents a family of distributions that depend on v. Thus, $t_{0.025,15}$ denotes that value of the *t*-distribution with 15 degrees of freedom that cuts off 0.025 of the area in the upper tail of the distribution. Similarly, $-t_{0.025,15}$ cuts off an area of 0.025 in the lower tail of the *t*-distribution with 15 degrees of freedom. These values are illustrated in Fig. 8.7.

Since each value of $t_{\alpha/2,v}$ cuts off $\alpha/2$ of the *t*-distribution, the area between $-t_{\alpha/2,v}$ and $t_{\alpha/2,v}$ equals $(1 - \alpha/2) - (\alpha/2) = 1 - \alpha$. That is,

$$P\left(-t_{\alpha/2,v} \le \frac{\overline{x} - \mu}{s/\sqrt{n}} \le t_{\alpha/2,v}\right) = 1 - \alpha.$$

Solving the inequalities as before for μ, we obtain the

$100(1 - \alpha)\%$ confidence interval for μ, population normal, σ unknown:

$$\overline{x} - t_{\alpha/2,v}\frac{s}{\sqrt{n}} \le \mu \le \overline{x} + t_{\alpha/2,v}\frac{s}{\sqrt{n}}. \qquad (8.2)$$

Example 8.5. A produce firm in Texas regularly ships fruit and vegetables to a Great Lakes Distribution Center. It uses its own trucks, and each round trip follows an identical route — a distance of more than 1500 miles. Owing to minor variations in each trip, the actual mileage varies. For 10 trips, accurate records are kept on the mileage. The results are given in Table 8.2. On the basis of this sample we wish to find a 99% confidence interval for the mean miles per trip over all such truck shipments.

The sample mean is $(15{,}700/10) = 1570$ miles (see column 1 in Table 8.2). Since the mean is an integer and the number of observations is small, the sample variance is most easily calculated by using Formula (7.2):

$$s^2 = \sum\left(\frac{x_i - \overline{x}^2}{n - 1}\right).$$

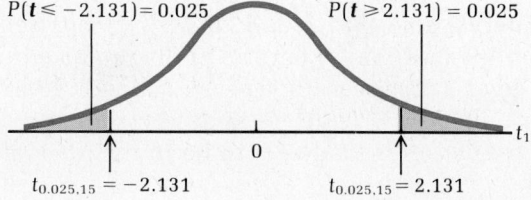

$P(t \le -2.131) = 0.025$ $P(t \ge 2.131) = 0.025$

$t_{0.025,15} = -2.131$ $t_{0.025,15} = 2.131$

FIGURE 8.7 The *t*-distribution for 15 degrees of freedom.

TABLE 8.2 **Truck mileage**

x (miles)	$(x - \bar{x})$	$(x - \bar{x})^2$	
1569	−1	1	
1581	11	121	
1567	−3	9	
1580	10	100	
1571	1	1	
1570	0	0	$\bar{x} = \dfrac{1}{10}15,700 = 1570$
1578	8	64	
1568	−2	4	$s = \sqrt{\dfrac{1}{9}590} = \sqrt{65.56} = 8.10$
1557	−13	169	
1559	−11	121	$s_{\bar{x}} = \dfrac{s}{\sqrt{n}} = \dfrac{8.10}{3.162} = 2.562$
Sum 15,700	0	590	

The sample standard deviation is $s = \sqrt{65.56} = 8.10$, and $(s/\sqrt{n}) = (8.10/\sqrt{10}) = 2.562$.

From Table VI for the *t*-distribution, the critical values, $\pm t_{\alpha/2,\nu}$, for a 99% confidence interval are found. Using the row for $\nu = (n - 1) = 9$ degrees of freedom and the column for $F(t) = 1.0 - \alpha/2 = 1.0 - 0.005 = 0.995$, we obtain $\pm t_{0.005,\,9} = \pm 3.25$; substituting the appropriate values of $\bar{x}$, s, t, and $\sqrt{n}$ into Formula (8.2),

$$\bar{x} - t_{\alpha/2,\nu}\left(\frac{s}{\sqrt{n}}\right) \le \mu \le \bar{x} + t_{\alpha/2,\nu}\left(\frac{s}{\sqrt{n}}\right),$$

the solution is found as follows:

$$1570 - 3.25\left(\frac{8.10}{3.162}\right) \le \mu \le 1570 + 3.25\left(\frac{8.10}{3.162}\right),$$

$$1570 - 3.25(2.562) \le \mu \le 1570 + 3.25(2.562),$$

$$1570 - 8.33 \le \mu \le 1570 + 8.33, \quad \text{and} \quad 1561.67 \le \mu \le 1578.33.$$

The interval from 1561.67 to 1578.33 thus represents a 99% confidence interval for the mean miles per trip of the produce trucks. This statistical work has given a precise method of estimation. It gives us exact knowledge about how often $(\alpha = 0.01)$, if this procedure were repeated over and over, the true mean is *likely not* to lie in the intervals calculated.

We can decrease the size of the interval in two ways, either by allowing a greater chance of error (α) or by expending more time and effort (cost) to increase the sample size n. Let us briefly examine the effects of each alternative. First if we are willing to let α = 0.10 and obtain only a 90% confidence interval, we find in Table VI that $\pm t_{\alpha/2,\nu} = \pm t_{0.05,9} = \pm 1.833$. Substituting the same sample values into Formula (8.2), we obtain the interval

$$1570 - 1.833(2.562) \le \mu \le 1570 + 1.833(2.562),$$
$$1565.304 \le \mu \le 1574.696.$$

As a second alternative, we could take a sample three times larger than before, n = 30, and keep the confidence level at 99%. For comparison purposes, let's assume that the sample of size 30 also yields $\bar{x} = 1570$ and s = 8.10, so the only difference from the original problem is the change in the sample size. The new standard deviation of the sampling distribution for $\bar{x}$ is $(s/\sqrt{n}) = (8.10/\sqrt{30}) = 1.48$. Since n has increased, the degrees of freedom, $\nu = n - 1$, has also increased. Thus, the new critical values are

$$\pm t_{\alpha/2,\nu} = \pm t_{0.005,\,29} = \pm 2.756.$$

The new interval is

$$1570 - 2.756(1.48) \le \mu \le 1570 + 2.756(1.48),$$
$$1565.92 \le \mu \le 1574.08.$$

Clearly, either allowing a *greater* risk of error or incurring a *greater* sampling cost results in a *smaller* confidence interval. Note that each interval estimate is centered at the best point estimate, $\bar{x} = 1570$. The reader may now wish to determine an interval estimate allowing *both* the greater risk of α = 0.10 and the larger sample size, n = 30.

Study Question 8.3: Average Age of Bank Presidents

A sample of the ages of 20 bank presidents is obtained in order to estimate the mean age of the population of nearly a thousand bank presidents. The sample mean and standard deviation are found to be 58 and 8 years, respectively. Find the 95% confidence interval for μ.

Answer. The *t*-distribution with 19 degrees of freedom may be used if we assume that the population of ages is normally distributed. From Table VI the appropriate value of t is $t_{0.025,\,19} = 2.093$. By using Formula (8.2) the upper and lower limits of the confidence interval are

$$\bar{x} \pm t\left(\frac{s}{\sqrt{n}}\right) = 58 \pm 2.093\left(\frac{8}{\sqrt{20}}\right),$$

which gives 54.26 and 61.74.

8.6 CONFIDENCE INTERVALS FOR THE BINOMIAL PARAMETER π, USING THE NORMAL APPROXIMATION

The random variable x/n was introduced earlier as an estimator of π, the population parameter in a binomial distribution. This statistic is denoted by $p = (x/n)$ and is called the *sample proportion*. It can be used to determine confidence intervals for population proportions in applications involving the binomial distribution, such as the proportion of people in a given population who smoke cigarettes, the proportion of voters favoring a certain candidate, or the proportion of defective items resulting from a given production process.

Recall from Chapter 6 that when n is large, the number of successes in n independent Bernoulli trials is approximately normally distributed. Thus, we approximate the number of successes, x, by using the standardized normal variable $z = (x - n\pi)/\sqrt{n\pi(1 - \pi)}$, where $n\pi = E[x]$ and $n\pi(1 - \pi) = V[x]$. Now, if the *number* of successes, x, is normal, the *proportion* of successes in n trials, $p = (x/n)$, must also be normally distributed. Hence, at this point we want to show how the standardized variable z can be used to approximate the *proportion* of successes in n trials in precisely the same manner in which it approximates the *number* of successes.

First, recall that our best estimator of the population proportion π is p, since this estimator has already been shown to be unbiased; that is, $E[p] = \pi$. We also have shown that the variance of p is

$$V[p] = \pi(1 - \pi)/n.$$

Unfortunately, we cannot use this variance to construct a confidence interval because the variance depends on the unknown parameter, π, which we are trying to estimate. The next best thing we can do is to use p, our point estimate of π, in place of π and $1 - p$ in place of $(1 - \pi)$. Thus, our estimate of the variance is:

Estimated variance of the proportion of successes:

$$\frac{p(1 - p)}{n}. \tag{8.3}$$

An approximately normal standardized variable is now obtained by taking the normal variable (p in this case), subtracting its mean ($E[p] = \pi$) and dividing the result by its estimated standard deviation [which is the

square root of the ratio in (8.3)]. The approximate **z**-variable (approximated because an estimated standard deviation was used) is:

Approximately normal standardized variable:

$$z = \frac{p - \pi}{\sqrt{\dfrac{p(1 - p)}{n}}}.$$

(8.4)

Formula (8.4) can now be used to construct a confidence interval in much the same fashion in which the confidence interval for μ was constructed in Section 8.4.* In using the confidence interval below, the reader should remember that we are approximating the binomial distribution by using the normal distribution; hence, it is necessary for n to be reasonably "large." How large n needs to be depends on how close π is to $\frac{1}{2}$. Shortly, we will suggest a procedure for determining whether or not n is large enough that such an approximation will be reasonable.

$100(1 - \alpha)\%$ confidence interval for π:

$$p - z_{\alpha/2}\sqrt{\frac{p(1 - p)}{n}} \leq \pi \leq p + z_{\alpha/2}\sqrt{\frac{p(1 - p)}{n}}$$

(8.5)

Example 8.6. Let us estimate the proportion of families with preschool-age children that own two or more cars. A random sample of n = 144 families shows that x = 48 families have two or more cars. Thus, the best point estimate for the population proportion is the sample proportion

$$p = \frac{48}{144} = \frac{1}{3}.$$

Our best estimate of the population standard deviation is thus

$$\sqrt{\frac{p(1 - p)}{n}} = \sqrt{\frac{(1/3)(2/3)}{144}} = 0.0393.$$

* First, form a $100(1 - \alpha)\%$ confidence interval for $p - \pi$:

$$-z_{\alpha/2}\sqrt{\frac{p(1 - p)}{n}} \leq p - \pi \leq z_{\alpha/2}\sqrt{\frac{p(1 - p)}{n}}.$$

Solving this expression for π, one obtains the desired $100(1 - \alpha)\%$ confidence interval.

We will now use these values and Formula (8.5) to construct a 95% confidence interval for π (remember, $z_{\alpha/2} = 1.96$ for $\alpha/2 = 0.025$):

$$\tfrac{1}{3} - 1.96(0.0393) \le \pi \le \tfrac{1}{3} + 1.96(0.0393),$$
$$0.333 - 0.077 \le \pi \le 0.333 + 0.077,$$
$$0.256 \le \pi \le 0.410.$$

Thus, we have 95% confidence that the interval [0.256 to 0.410] covers the population proportion of families that own two or more cars. We can state that 95% of all such intervals that could be calculated using this procedure (on the basis of repeated samples of size 144) would include the true value of π.

In some applications, especially in product control, a confidence interval for π can be used to find the confidence interval for the *number* of defectives in a given, very large shipping lot.

Example 8.7. Consider the problem of a manufacturer who produces ballpoint pen cartridges. Each shipment includes 10,000 cartridges. The producer desires some control over these shipments, in order to ensure that no shipment will contain an excessive number of defective cartridges. A random sample of 400 cartridges is inspected from a shipping lot of 10,000, and nine defectives ($x = 9$) are found. On the basis of this result, we wish to obtain a 90% confidence interval for the number of defectives in the entire shipment. The random variable x = number of defectives can be approximated by the normal distribution; hence, a 90% confidence interval for the proportion of defectives is obtained by using Formula (8.5). In this case, $n = 400$ and $x = 9$, so $p = 9/400 = 0.0225$. Since $\alpha = 0.10$, $\pm z_{\alpha/2} = \pm z_{0.05} = \pm 1.645$, and the appropriate confidence interval is:

$$0.0225 - 1.645\sqrt{\frac{(0.0225)(0.9775)}{400}} \le \pi \le 0.0225 + 1.645\sqrt{\frac{(0.0225)(0.9775)}{400}},$$
$$0.0225 - 1.645(0.0074) \le \pi \le 0.0225 + 1.645(0.0074),$$
$$0.0103 \le \pi \le 0.0347.$$

Thus, the producer may estimate that the population is likely to contain between 1.03% and 3.47% defectives. More precisely, it is expected that in 90% of such repetitions of this process, the true value of π will lie within the interval calculated.

Since the α used in constructing this confidence interval is rather large, we must assume that the producer will be satisfied with an interval that is correct "only" 90% of the time. If this production process involved $40 stereo cartridges rather than 40¢ ballpoint pen cartridges, then a smaller α-level might be used because errors would be more costly.

In Example 8.7, sampling is from a finite population without replacement, which means that the hypergeometric distribution has to be used to give the theoretically correct probability values. However, the population size is so large ($N = 10,000$) in relation to the sample size ($n = 400$) that any inaccuracy resulting from the use of the binomial distribution is negligible. Of course, in the above calculations we used the normal distribution to approximate the binomial. To check whether this approximation is reasonable, let us recall from Chapter 6 the suggestion that when $n\pi(1 - \pi) > 3$, the approximation of the binomial by the normal should be fairly accurate. For this problem we do not know the exact value of π, but we have a likely value for its *lower* bound, namely, $\pi = 0.0103$ (from the confidence interval). Substituting this value of π into $n\pi(1 - \pi)$ we obtain*

$$np(1-p) > 3$$

$$(400)(0.0103)(0.9897) = 4.08.$$

Since this product is greater than 3, we can consider the approximation acceptable; however, a larger sample will be necessary if greater precision is desired.

To expand on our solution to this cartridge-inspection problem, let us assume that the decision-maker would like to convert the 90% confidence interval from an interval involving proportions to one involving the *number of defectives* in the shipment of size 10,000. If π is the proportion of defectives in the lot of size 10,000, then the number of defectives is $n\pi = 10,000 \pi$. Using the upper and lower limits for π, we conclude, with 90% confidence, that the number of defectives in the shipment is between $10,000(0.0103) = 103$ and $10,000(0.0347) = 347$. If the producer thinks that these are tolerable values, then the lot can be released for shipment. Much has been saved in inspection costs and some quality control has been maintained over the shipment. There is a risk of $\alpha = 0.10$ that such an interval is wrong. Realistically, the producer will be satisfied if the true number of defectives is less than the *lower* bound of 103 and disappointed only if the true number exceeds 347. Hence, the risk is really only $\alpha/2 = 0.05$. In terms of a *one-sided* confidence interval, the producer may have 95% confidence that the

---

* Using the upper bound for π would make $n\pi(1 - \pi)$ even greater. In such cases, always substitute the most extreme value for π, closest to one or to zero, to find the size of $n\pi(1 - \pi)$.

.0255

interval [0 to 347] will include the true number of defectives. Such one-sided intervals are often used, in preference to the two-sided confidence intervals, in similar situations for which the error in one of the directions is unimportant.

Study Question 8.4: Proportion of Defective Lenses

A firm that grinds lenses for eyeglasses wishes to estimate the proportion of lenses that are defective. Over a period of two weeks a random sample of 36 lenses indicates nine that are defective. Find a 98% confidence interval for the true proportion of defective lenses for the population.

Answer. The sample proportion is $p = \frac{9}{36} = 0.25$. We first need to check for the applicability of the normal distribution. We find $np(1 - p) = 36(0.25)(0.75) = 6.75$. Since this value is larger than 3, we use Formula (8.5) with $z_{0.01} = 2.326$ from Table III. The upper and lower confidence limits are

$$p \pm z_{0.01} \sqrt{\frac{p(1 - p)}{n}} = 0.25 \pm 2.326 \sqrt{\frac{(0.25)(0.75)}{36}}$$

$$= 0.25 \pm 2.326(0.072),$$

which gives 0.082 and 0.418. We have 98% confidence that the interval [8.27% to 41.8%] includes the true percentage of defective lenses.

The applicability of the normal distribution should be rechecked by using 0.082, the lower confidence limit for π. The value of $np(1 - p) = 36(0.082)(0.918) = 2.71$. Because 2.71 is less than 3.0, the normal approximation is suspect. A larger sample of lenses should be examined (or the exact binomial distribution could be used) if the firm wishes to estimate π more accurately.

8.7 DETERMINING THE SIZE OF THE SAMPLE (n)

Thus far, we have calculated the width of each confidence interval based on the assumption that the sample size, n, is known. In many practical situations, however, the decision-maker does not know what sample size is optimal. In this situation it is possible for the decision-maker to calculate the optimal sample size, provided that the following two questions can be answered:

1. What level of confidence is desired [i.e., what is the desired value for $100(1 - \alpha)$]?

2. What is the *maximum* difference (labeled D) allowed between the point estimate of the population parameter and the true value of the population parameter?

> D is thus defined as the largest allowable "sampling error" between the estimated and the true values of the population parameter:
>
> $$|\text{estimated value} - \text{true value}| \leq D.$$

We will investigate the process of determining the optimal sample size for two different situations: (1) the case in which the sample will be used to estimate μ and (2) the case in which the sample will be used to estimate π.

Statistical Inference in Relation to μ

Population Normal, σ Known. First, we consider the problem of determining n when the decision-maker wants a $100(1 - \alpha)\%$ confidence interval for μ, given that the parent population has a normal distribution with a known standard deviation. In this case we know that the variable

$$z = \frac{\bar{x} - \mu}{\sigma/\sqrt{n}}$$

is $N(0, 1)$. Now, if the required level of confidence is $1 - \alpha$, then the above equation results in the following $100(1 - \alpha)\%$ interval for $\bar{x} - \mu$:

$$-z_{\alpha/2}\frac{\sigma}{\sqrt{n}} \leq (\bar{x} - \mu) \leq z_{\alpha/2}\frac{\sigma}{\sqrt{n}}. \tag{8.6}$$

Since the normal distribution is symmetric, we can concentrate on the right-hand inequality, $(\bar{x} - \mu) \leq z_{\alpha/2}(\sigma/\sqrt{n})$. This inequality means that the largest value that $\bar{x} - \mu$ can assume is $z_{\alpha/2}(\sigma/\sqrt{n})$. But we also know that our decision-maker says that the largest sampling error allowed for $\bar{x} - \mu$ is some amount D. This maximum allowable error D can be on either side of the true mean. Thus, we set

$$D = |\bar{x} - \mu| = z_{\alpha/2}\frac{\sigma}{\sqrt{n}}.$$

Solving this relationship for n, we obtain the value of n that will ensure with $100(1 - \alpha)\%$ confidence that $|\bar{x} - \mu|$ will be no larger than D.

> Minimum required sample size in estimating the mean:
>
> $$n = \frac{z_{\alpha/2}^2 \sigma^2}{D^2}. \tag{8.7}$$

Example 8.8. We return to the freight car case of Example 8.3. Suppose that we want to find a 95% confidence interval for the mean number of cars such that our sample estimate $(\bar{x})$ and the population mean (μ) differ, either high or low, by no more than five cars; that is,

$$|\bar{x} - \mu| \le D = 5.$$

If we assume, as before, that the parent population is normal and that $\sigma = 15$, how large must n be to satisfy these conditions?

From Table III, $z_{\alpha/2} = 1.96$ when $\alpha/2 = 0.025$. Substituting this value and $D = 5$, $\sigma = 15$ into Formula (8.7), we find the appropriate value for n:

$$n = \frac{(1.96)^2(15)^2}{(5)^2} = 34.57.$$

We always round up in this type of problem to ensure that the sample size is large enough; hence, a random sample of at least 35 trains is needed to ensure that 95% of the time the value of $\bar{x}$ will be within 5 cars of the true population mean, μ.

Population Not Normal, σ Known. If the population is not assumed to be normal but the standard deviation is known, the above method can be used to determine the minimum sample size necessary to satisfy the conditions of confidence and accuracy. By the central limit theorem we know that the distribution of sample means approaches the normal distribution as the sample size increases. Thus, once the necessary sample size is obtained, we can check to see if that size n exceeds 30; and if it does, we may be confident that our method of solution was appropriate.

Population Normal, σ Unknown. If the population is normal but the standard deviation is unknown, then the appropriate statistic to use is the t variable, $t = (\bar{x} - \mu)/(s\sqrt{n})$. Again, the maximum sampling error allowed, $|\bar{x} - \mu| = D$, is specified by the decision-maker. In this case we are stuck for a value of s, since s must be calculated from a sample, and we have not taken a sample yet (the whole purpose is to decide what sample size to take). To make matters even worse, the appropriate t-value to use in calculating a $100(1 - \alpha)\%$ confidence interval is $t_{\alpha/2,\nu}$, which again depends on the unknown sample size. To make a long story short, the solution for n in this case is not a direct process. The interval can be found by a succession of iterative steps, using sequential sampling, but we will not present this method here.

Statistical Inference in Relation to π The size of the sample needed to find a desired confidence interval for the binomial parameter π can be determined if the maximum allowable difference between **p** and π is specified as $D = |p - \pi|$. From Formula (8.4) we know that an approximate **z**-variable involving $p - \pi$ is

$$z = \frac{p - \pi}{\sqrt{\dfrac{p(1 - p)}{n}}}.$$

As in the case with the mean, we can solve this statistic for the unknown value of sample size as follows:

$$z = \frac{(p - \pi)\sqrt{n}}{\sqrt{p(1 - p)}} \qquad \text{so} \qquad \frac{z\sqrt{p(1 - p)}}{(p - \pi)} = \sqrt{n}.$$

By substituting values for the maximum allowable difference, we have $D = |p - \pi|$ and choosing the positive cutoff value $(z_{\alpha/2})$ for a $100(1 - \alpha)\%$ confidence interval, we obtain the **formula for determining the minimum required sampling size:**

Minimum required sample size in estimating a proportion:

$$n = \frac{z_{\alpha/2}^2 p(1 - p)}{D^2}. \qquad (8.8)$$

Thus, we can find n when we know:

$p - \pi$, given by the allowable sampling error D;
the z-value, determined from Table III for a given $(\alpha/2)$ depending on the level of confidence; and
$p(1 - p)$, based on our best guess (p) of a planning value for the unknown proportion.

This last point needs careful consideration. Since we are trying to determine what size sample to take, we obviously have not yet taken a sample or calculated a sample proportion, $p = (x/n)$. We may have some prior information, however, on the possible range of values that would be reasonable for p (or π).

Among the set of values for p that might reasonably be considered, the planning value to use is the one value in this set that is closest to $\frac{1}{2}$. Sometimes, when no prior information about p or π is available, the planning value chosen is exactly $p = \frac{1}{2}$.

The value closest to $\frac{1}{2}$ is chosen because $\frac{1}{2}$ is the proportion between 0 and 1 that maximizes the product, $p(1 - p)$.* Hence, this maximum value of $p(1 - p)$ will give a value of n from Formula (8.8) that is at least as large as needed. By using the planning value of $\frac{1}{2}$, we probably obtain a larger sample size n than is necessary to obtain the desired levels of accuracy (D) and confidence $(1 - \alpha)$.

Example 8.9. Returning to Example 8.6, in which we estimated "the proportion of families owning two or more cars," suppose we wish to estimate 100π within plus or minus three percentage points with 95% confidence. What size sample would be needed?

We know that $z_{\alpha/2} = 1.96$ (since $\alpha = 0.05$) and $D = 0.03$ (since we desire accuracy within three percentage points). Without having any prior planning value for p, we choose $p = \frac{1}{2}$. Using Formula (8.8), we obtain

$$n = \frac{(1.96)^2(\frac{1}{2})(\frac{1}{2})}{(0.03)^2} = \frac{(1.96)^2(\frac{1}{4})}{(0.03)^2} = 1067.1.$$

We may conclude (see Fig. 8.8) that in estimating the desired proportion π, a sample of 1068 families is needed in order to ensure that a sampling error exceeding 0.03 will not occur more than 5% of the time.

Since a normal approximation was used in this binomial problem, we should now check the necessary condition for its applicability, $np(1 - p) > 3$. If the sample size used is $n = 1068$, this condition will hold even for very small values of p, such as 0.01, since $1068(0.01)(0.99) = 10.6 > 3$. The use of the normal approximation is acceptable.

Example 8.10. A survey firm reports a result that is published in a newspaper. (See Fig. 8.9.)

We recognize that the value of 87% is simply a *point estimate*. We do not know how accurate this is or what level of confidence we can have in the published statement. Suppose we wish to repeat the survey and be able to have 98% confidence that the proportion estimated will be within plus or minus 0.03 of the true proportion for the population of all adults with household incomes of $30,000 or more. How large a random sample would we have to take?

For 98% confidence the value of $(\alpha/2)$ is 0.01. From Table III the z-value excluding this area in the tail of the normal distribution is about $z = 2.33$. The allowable difference (sampling error) is $D = (p - \pi) = \pm 0.03$. We can use Formula (8.8) if we substitute a planning value for p. Given the prior information that one point estimate is $p = 0.87$, we can

---

* You may try several values of p, $\{\frac{1}{2}, \frac{1}{3}, \frac{1}{5}, \frac{1}{10}\}$, to convince yourself or use calculus as in Exercise 8.47.

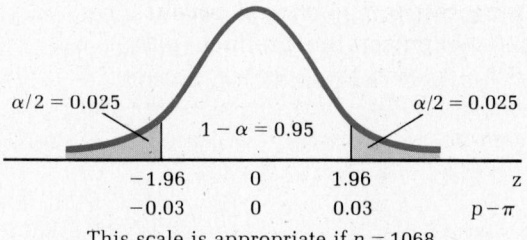

FIGURE 8.8 **Approximate probability distribution for Example 8.9.**

$\alpha/2 = 0.025$

$1 - \alpha = 0.95$

$\alpha/2 = 0.025$

$-1.96 \qquad 0 \qquad 1.96 \qquad\qquad z$

$-0.03 \qquad 0 \qquad 0.03 \qquad\qquad p - \pi$

This scale is appropriate if $n = 1068$.

make a reasonable guess that the proportion will be between 0.80 and 0.99. Thus, let us use the feasible value closest to $\frac{1}{2}$ as our planning value. We choose $p = 0.80$; thus, $(1 - p) = 0.20$. This planning value of 0.80 will result in a smaller sample size than if we choose the maximizing value of $p = (1 - p) = \frac{1}{2}$ (as if we had no prior information). The minimum sample size required is

$$n = \frac{(2.33)^2(0.80)(0.20)}{(0.03)^2}$$

$$= \frac{0.8686}{0.0009} = 965.14.$$

We need survey responses from 966 adults in this population. Since we used a normal approximation to the binomial distribution, we should check the necessary condition for its applicability, $np(1 - p) > 3$. Using $n = 966$, $p = 0.80$, and $(1 - p) = 0.20$, we have

$$966(0.80)(0.20) = 154.56 > 3.$$

The use of the normal approximation is quite acceptable.

Study Question 8.5: Average Commuting Distance
MARTA (Metropolitan Atlanta Rapid Transit Authority) wishes to estimate the *average* number of miles that commuters live from their place of work. The population standard deviation is thought to be

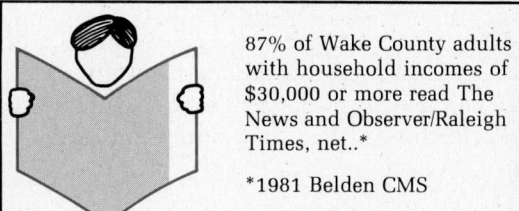

87% of Wake County adults with household incomes of $30,000 or more read The News and Observer/Raleigh Times, net..*

*1981 Belden CMS

FIGURE 8.9 **Survey result. (Source: The *News and Observer*, Raleigh, N.C., October 28, 1983–November 4, 1983.)**

3.5 miles. How large a sample of commuters is needed if 95% confidence is desired that the sample mean will be within plus or minus $\frac{1}{2}$ mile of the population mean?

Answer. Since $\alpha = 0.05$, we use $z_{0.025} = 1.96$ in Formula (8.7) with $\sigma = 3.5$ and $D = |\overline{x} - \mu| = 0.5$:

$$n = \frac{(1.96)^2(3.5)^2}{(0.5)^2} = 188.24.$$

The minimum sample size should be 189 commuters.

Study Question 8.6: Percentage of Public Transit Commuters
MARTA desires to estimate with 99% confidence the *percentage* of commuters who regularly use public transit. They want the estimate to be within plus or minus four percentage points of the true percentage. What size sample should be taken?

Answer. We solve this problem in terms of proportions rather than percentages. Since 90% confidence is desired, $(\alpha/2) = 0.05$; the proper z-value is $z_{0.05} = 1.645$. Formula (8.8) is used with $D = |p - \pi| = 0.04$. A planning value might be used instead of $p = \frac{1}{2}$, since a reasonable guess is that the proportion of commuters using MARTA is surely less than $\frac{1}{3}$. If we arbitrarily select $p = 0.34$ and $(1 - p) = 0.66$, the minimum sample size required is

$$n = \frac{(1.645)^2(0.34)(0.66)}{(0.04)^2}$$

$$= \frac{0.607}{0.0016} = 379.52.$$

MARTA should survey at least 380 commuters.

8.8 CONFIDENCE INTERVAL FOR σ^2*

Under some circumstances it may be desirable to construct a confidence interval for an estimate of an unknown population variance. As we said before, the telephone company is often interested in the *variability* of the length of telephone conversations, and a contractor purchasing steel girders may be interested in the *variance* of their tensile strengths. Or a

---

* This section may be omitted without loss in continuity. It is assumed that the reader has covered Section 7.9.

government economist may be just as concerned about the *variability* of the amount of taxes paid by individuals as about the average tax paid, because the income-redistribution effect of taxation is very important. In such cases it is important to establish limits on just how large or small σ^2 might be, that is, to determine a confidence interval for the population variance.

To construct a **100(1 − α)% confidence interval for σ^2** when sampling from a *normal* population, recall from Section 7.9 that the variable $(n − 1)s^2/\sigma^2$ has a chi-square distribution with $\nu = (n − 1)$ degrees of freedom. Since the values of χ^2 are always positive and the chi-square distribution is not symmetrical, we will *not* be able to use plus and minus values such as $\pm\chi^2_{\alpha/2,\nu}$ as we did with the *t*-distribution. We will need to look up both upper and lower values for the cumulative chi-square distribution, $F(\chi^2)$ as given in Table VII. The value of χ^2 in the left half of the table such that $F(\chi^2) = \alpha/2$ gives the *lower* (left-hand side) cutoff value. The value of χ^2 from the right half of the table such that $F(\chi^2) = 1 − (\alpha/2)$ gives the *upper* cutoff value for the confidence interval. From Table VII, using $\nu = 9$ and $\alpha = 0.05$, we find

$$\chi^2_{upper} = 19.0 \text{ for } \alpha/2 = 0.025$$
$$\chi^2_{lower} = 2.70 \text{ for } F(\chi^2) = 0.025$$

The area of the chi-square distribution lying between these two values must include $(0.975 − 0.025) = 0.95$ of the total area. As shown in Fig. 8.10, these values give us a 95% probability interval for a chi-square

FIGURE 8.10 **The values of χ^2 cutting off a total area of $\alpha = 0.05$ from the chi-square distribution with $\nu = 9$, leaving an interval including 95% of the probability in the middle.**

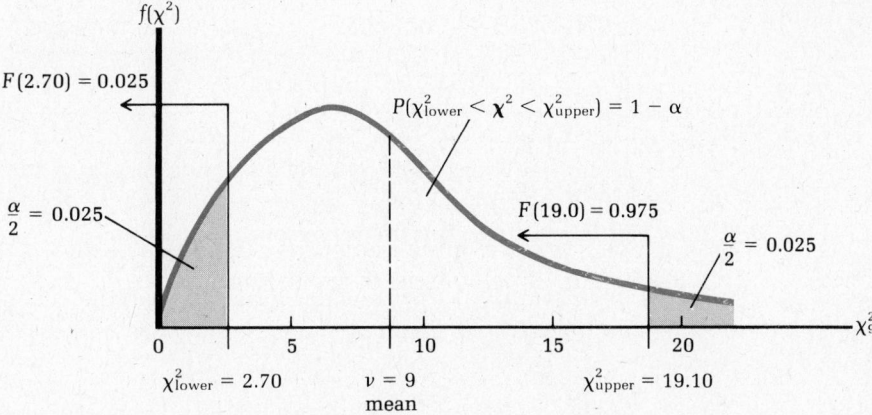

TABLE 8.3 **Summary of random variables and confidence intervals for statistical inference**

Unknown Parameter	Population Characteristics and Other Description	Reference Sections
Mean μ	Population $N(\mu, \sigma^2)$ or population unknown and $n > 30$; σ known	7.5 8.4
Mean μ	Population $N(\mu, \sigma^2)$ σ *unknown*	7.8 8.5
Variance σ^2	Population $N(\mu, \sigma^2)$	7.9 8.8
Proportion π	Repeated independent trials, $n\pi(1 - \pi) > 3$, x = number of successes in n trials	6.6 8.6

distributed random variable. Using this interval and substituting the particular chi-square variable $\chi^2 = (n - 1)s^2/\sigma^2$, we obtain the probability interval

$$P\left[\chi^2_{\text{lower}} \leq \frac{(n - 1)s^2}{\sigma^2} \leq \chi^2_{\text{upper}}\right] = 0.95.$$

Again, solving these inequalities for the unknown parameter σ^2, we obtain:*

$100(1 - \alpha)$ percent confidence interval for σ^2, parent population normal:

$$\frac{(n - 1)s^2}{\chi^2_{\text{upper}}} \leq \sigma^2 \leq \frac{(n - 1)s^2}{\chi^2_{\text{lower}}}. \qquad \textbf{(8.9)}$$

Note that the upper value of χ^2 now appears in the denominator of the *smaller* endpoint for σ^2, while the lower value of χ^2 is in the denominator of the term giving the *larger* endpoint for σ^2.

Example 8.11. Consider again the sample distances of trips for the produce trucks given in Example 8.5. Assume that we are interested in

---

* In this solution, reciprocals of each term are taken to get σ^2 in the numerator. This changes the sense (direction) of the inequalities.

Random Variable Involving the Best Sample Estimator	Formula for $100(1 - \alpha)\%$ Confidence Interval	Reference Formula
$z = \dfrac{(\bar{x} - \mu)}{\sigma/\sqrt{n}}$	$\bar{x} \pm z_{\alpha/2}(\sigma/\sqrt{n})$	(8.1)
$t_{\alpha/2,\nu} = (\bar{x} - \mu)/(s/\sqrt{n})$ where $\nu = n - 1$	$\bar{x} \pm t_{\alpha/2,\nu} (s/\sqrt{n})$	(8.2)
$\chi^2_{\alpha/2,\nu} = \dfrac{(n - 1)s^2}{\sigma^2}$ where $\nu = n - 1$	$\dfrac{(n - 1)s^2}{\chi^2_{upper}} \leq \sigma^2 \leq \dfrac{(n - 1)s^2}{\chi^2_{lower}}$	(8.9)
$z = \dfrac{p - \pi}{\sqrt{\dfrac{\pi(1 - \pi)}{n}}}$	$p \pm z_{\alpha/2} \sqrt{\dfrac{p(1 - p)}{n}}$	(8.5)

estimating the variance of the population, using the same sample of size $n = 10$ reported in Table 8.2. The best point estimate of σ^2 is s^2, which is computed for this sample to be $s^2 = (\frac{1}{9})590 = 65.56$. To achieve an interval estimate for σ^2 with a known level of confidence and a known risk of error, let us compute a 95% confidence interval for σ^2. The values of χ^2 needed here are exactly those used in Fig. 8.10, since $\nu = 9$ and $\alpha = 0.05$. Thus, we substitute into Formula (8.9) the values $\chi^2_{lower} = 2.70$ and $\chi^2_{upper} = 19.0$, along with $n = 10$ and $s^2 = 65.56$. This gives

$$\frac{9(65.56)}{19.0} \leq \sigma^2 \leq \frac{9(65.56)}{2.70},$$

$$31.05 \leq \sigma^2 \leq 218.53.$$

The 95% confidence limits on the population variance are 31.05 and 218.53 (miles)^2.

For interpretation we frequently convert the confidence interval for the variance into one for the standard deviation since we desire a statement in terms of the original units (miles in this case). By taking square roots we get confidence limits on the standard deviation (σ) of 5.57 and 14.78 miles. Note that this interval is *not symmetric* around the point estimate of $s = 8.10$, since the chi-square distribution is not symmetric.

Study Question 8.7: Variance of the Age of Bank Presidents
Determine a 98% confidence interval for the variance of the distribution of ages of bank presidents based on the sample information, $n = 20$ and $s = 8$ years, as given in Study Question 8.3.

Answer. Since $n = 20$, the degrees of freedom are 19 for the random variable $\chi^2 = (n - 1)s^2/\sigma^2$. Since $\alpha = 0.02$, the lower value of χ^2 needed is one such that $F(\chi^2) = 0.01$, and the upper value needed is one such that $F(\chi^2) = 0.99$. From Table VII these values are $\chi^2_{lower} = 7.63$ and $\chi^2_{upper} = 36.2$. Substituting into Formula (8.9) gives

$$\frac{(19)64}{36.2} \leq \sigma^2 \leq \frac{(19)64}{7.63},$$

$$33.59 \leq \sigma^2 \leq 159.37 \text{ (years)}^2.$$

To measure the limits in terms of years, we take the square root of each term to obtain $5.8 \leq \sigma \leq 12.6$ years.

8.9 SUMMARY

Listed in Table 8.3 are the important elements of using probability distributions to find confidence limits or to find the minimum sample size required in an estimation problem.

Define. *Maximum allowable sampling error, minimum required sample size, planning value for* p, χ^2_{lower} *and* χ^2_{upper}.

PROBLEMS

8.18 Suppose that the following nine values represent random observations from a normal parent population of new car sales (daily) by a Ford dealer: 1, 5, 9, 8, 4, 0, 2, 4, 3. Construct a 99% confidence interval for the mean of the parent population.

8.19 A survey of 16 executives selected at random revealed that the average annual consumption of aspirin tablets per executive was 184, with a sample standard deviation of 20. Establish 90% confidence limits for the average annual per capita consumption of aspirin tablets of all executives, assuming that the population is normal.

8.20 Twenty-five small loan applications in a bank were randomly selected for the purpose of determining the average dollar amount requested for each loan. Construct a 95% confidence interval for μ, assuming that the sample mean was $\bar{x} = \$900$ and the sample standard deviation was $\$150$. The population is normally distributed.

8.21 Repeat Problem 8.12(b), but this time assume that the population variance is unknown. How much does the confidence interval change?

8.22 Repeat Problem 8.13(b), assuming that the population variance is unknown.

8.23 A survey of 900 *Wall Street Journal* subscribers indicates that 40% finished at least two years of college. Set 95% confidence limits on the true proportion of all subscribers with this background.

8.24 In order to estimate the percent of all households using a certain detergent, 196 homes were randomly selected. If 108 of these homes use this product, what would be a 99% confidence interval for the percent of this population of households that uses the detergent?

8.25 A television manufacturer would like to know what proportion of television set owners have color sets. In a sample of 100 randomly selected owners, 60% were found to own color sets. Construct a 95% confidence interval for the population proportion of television owners who have color sets.

8.26 The total particle removal (TPR) in a certain cigarette filter can be measured on a smoking machine, using a sample of these cigarettes. The standard deviation for TPR for the population of such cigarettes is 2 mg. What size sample is necessary to estimate with 90% confidence the average TPR for all such cigarettes, within plus or minus 0.4 mg?

8.27 A population of families has an unknown mean income μ; the standard deviation of these incomes is known to be $1000. How large a random sample would be needed to determine the mean income if it is desired that the probability of a sampling error of more than $50 be less than 0.05?

8.28 Suppose you are a state purchasing agent, and you contract with Batpower Company to buy 10,000 batteries according to specifications in the contract. You check 300 batteries and find 42 defective. Use Formula (8.5) to construct a 99% confidence interval. Is your confidence interval compatible with a 10% defective rate for the entire lot of 10,000?

8.29 A supermarket manager wishes to make a sample estimate of the average time a customer spends at the checkout register. It is known from past experience that the standard deviation is $2\frac{1}{2}$ minutes, and the manager would like to estimate the mean checkout time within plus-or-minus $\frac{1}{2}$ minute. If a 99% confidence level is specified, what is the required sample size to obtain this estimate?

8.30 I wish to estimate the proportion of defectives in a large production lot within plus or minus 0.05 of the true proportion, with 90% confidence. From past experience it is believed that the proportion of defectives is about $\pi = 0.02$. How large a sample must be used?

8.31 A sample of size 15 has standard deviation 3. The population is the distance (miles) between home and the work location of commuters (as in Study Question 8.5). Find 90% confidence limits on the true population variance. Assume that the population is normally distributed.

8.32 A manufacturer of steel washers periodically samples the washers produced as a check on the variability of their inside diameter. A sample of size 20 was checked and found to have a standard deviation of 0.002 mm. On the basis of this sample, find a 95% confidence interval for the true variance. Assume that the population is normal.

8.33 Construct a 95% confidence interval for σ^2, based on the data in Problem 8.18.

8.34 Construct a 95% confidence interval for the variance of the bank loans described in Problem 8.20.

8.35 Suppose that the annual earnings of college graduates are normally distributed, with σ = $6000.
a) Based on a sample of n = 16 with $\bar{x}$ = $28,000, find a 98% confidence interval for μ.
b) How many graduates will I need to sample in order to have 98% confidence that the sample mean to be calculated will be within 600 dollars of the true mean?

8.36 Use **Data Set 6** to estimate with 95% confidence the proportion of the head of households who are female in the population of persons over age 54.

8.37 A machine that produces ball bearings is stopped periodically so that the diameter of the bearings produced can be checked for accuracy. In this particular case it is not the mean diameter that is of concern, but the variability of the diameters. Suppose that a sample of size n = 31 is taken and the variance of the diameters of the bearings sampled is found to be 0.94 mm.
a) Construct a 95% confidence interval for σ^2 assuming that the population is normal.
b) Assume that if this machine is working properly, the variance of the bearings produced will be 0.50 mm. Does this sample indicate that the machine is working improperly? Explain.

8.38 Use **Data Set 6** to estimate with 99% confidence the proportion of the head of households who are male in the population of persons over age 54.

8.39 Use **Data Set 4** to estimate with 90% confidence the proportion of doctors with net income exceeding $60,000 in 1980.

8.40 A random sample of 80 highway bridges showed 30 that were unsatisfactory for use by all types of vehicles.

a) Find a 98% confidence interval for the population proportion of unsatisfactory highway bridges.
b) The Federal Highway Administration reported in December 1982 that 44.8% of the nation's bridges were either structurally deficient or functionally obsolete and not satisfactory for use by all types of vehicles. Does your confidence interval in part (a) include this reported population proportion? What does 98% confidence mean in this context?

8.41 A sample of prices of Levis at 24 stores showed a standard deviation of $s = \$2.80$ and a mean of $\bar{x} = \$26.26$. Determine 90% confidence intervals for both the mean and standard deviation (do it for the variance and find the square root) of the population of these prices in all stores. Assume a normal population.

EXERCISES

8.42 Suppose that x_1 and x_2 are independent random variables having the Poisson probability distribution with parameter λ. Show that the mean of these variables is an unbiased estimator of λ.

8.43 If $\hat{\theta}$ is an unbiased estimator of the population parameter θ, under what conditions will $\hat{\theta}^2$ be an unbiased estimator of θ^2?

8.44 Which of the properties of a good estimator does $\bar{x}$ have? Prove as many of these as you can.

8.45 Find the amount of bias that results when the statistic $(1/n) \sum (x_i - \bar{x})^2$ is used to estimate σ^2.

8.46 The Ryder Corporation manufactures a variety of types and sizes of sheet metal. One of their problems has been that of establishing the exact size of the metal plates after they have been cut and stamped, for in some cases it is extremely important that the size of the plate fall within certain tolerance limits. Ryder recently purchased a special gauge that automatically measures the length of the sheet as it passes the gauge. This gauge, however, is subject to random error that has been found to be normally distributed about the true length of the sheet. To compensate for this error, the manufacturers of the gauge designed it so that, instead of producing just one value for the length of the metal passing by, the device actually gives two readings, and these values are independent of each other. Suppose that we let x_1 represent the first estimator of length and x_2 the second.
a) Is $\frac{1}{2}x_1 + \frac{1}{2}x_2$ an unbiased estimator of length?
b) Is $\frac{1}{3}x_1 + \frac{2}{3}x_2$ an unbiased estimator of length?

c) What is the relative efficiency of the estimators in questions (a) and (b)? Which of the two estimators is preferable?

d) Suppose that one of the sheets passing by the gauge is square, and the people at Ryder wish to estimate the area of this sheet. They are unsure whether they should square the two observations first and then average, or average first and then square — i.e., whether they should use

$$\left(\frac{x_1^2 + x_2^2}{2}\right) \quad \text{or} \quad \left(\frac{x_1 + x_2}{2}\right)^2$$

Which method will provide the better estimator?

8.47 Use calculus to show that the maximum value of the function $g(p) = np(1 - p)$ for $0 \le p \le 1$, occurs at the value $p = \frac{1}{2}$.

8.48 Use a mathematical statistics text to find proof that, for x normally distributed:
a) $\bar{x}$ is a maximum likelihood estimate of μ.
b) $(1/n) \Sigma (x_i - \bar{x})^2$ is a maximum likelihood estimate of σ^2.

8.49 If the result obtained from a particular sample will be critical, e.g., the CPA would not be able to render an unqualified opinion (unless every item in the population were examined), which of the following is the most important to the CPA?
a) Size of the population.
b) Estimated occurrence rate.
c) Specified upper precision limit.
d) Specified confidence level.

8.50 From a very large population the auditor selects 400 items at random and finds 16 items in error. The auditor can be 95% confident that the error rate in the population does not exceed:

a) $4\% = \dfrac{16}{400} \times 100$

b) $5.65\% = 1.65 \sqrt{\dfrac{0.04 \times 0.96}{400}} + 0.04$

c) $5.95\% = 1.96 \sqrt{\dfrac{0.04 \times 0.96}{400}} + 0.04$

d) $6\% = 1.65 \sqrt{\dfrac{0.06 \times 0.94}{400}} + 0.04$

e) $6.4\% = 1.96 \sqrt{\dfrac{0.064 \times 0.936}{400}} + 0.04$

8.51 Approximately 5% of the 10,000 homogeneous items included in Barletta's finished-goods inventory are believed to be defective. The CPA examining Barletta's financial statements decides to test this estimated 5% defective rate. The CPA learns by sampling without replacement that a sample of 203 items from the inventory will permit specified reliability (confidence level) of 95% and specified precision (sampling error) of ∓ 0.03. If the specified precision is changed to ∓ 0.06, and the specified reliability remains 95%, the required sample size is:

a) 51   b) 102   c) 406   d) 812

8.52 An auditor wishes to be 95% confident that the true error rate does not exceed 6%. How large a sample must be taken from a very large population if the auditor estimates an error rate of 4%? Select the closest answer.

a) 150   b) 1250   c) 380   d) 450

8.53 Chalmers asks its Certified Public Accountant to estimate the number of the two thousand charge accounts that are delinquent. A sample of 100 accounts reveals that twenty are delinquent. Thus, at 95% confidence the best estimate is that:

a) At least 320 are delinquent.
b) At most 560 are delinquent.
c) Between 320 and 480 are delinquent.
d) Between 240 and 560 are delinquent.
e) Not close to one of the above.

8.54 Refer to Example 1.2 and Table 1.3 on page 12 in Chapter 1 for a sample of ten cities drawn from the population of 78 cities in **Data Set 1.** Use the sample mean and variance to find a 95% confidence interval for the mean income of the population of cities given in **Data Set 1.** (Assume a normal population and use the finite population correction.) Does your interval include the true population mean?

8.55 The average years of experience of a group of 50 young union members is 2.55 with a standard deviation of 0.30 years. Find a 99% confidence interval for the population average.

8.56 The quarterly sales of five different franchises of drive-in restaurants are 170, 160, 140, 180, and 140 (in thousands of dollars), respectively. You wish to make an estimate of the average sales for this quarter, for all the outlets in the entire chain.

a) On the basis of this sample information, can you make an estimate that will have a probability of 1.0 being correct? Why or why not?
b) Make an interval estimate by using the sample mode plus-or-minus $\frac{1}{3}$ its range.
c) Make an interval estimate by using the mean plus-or-minus the standard deviation of the sample.

d) In probability, which of these estimates is better and why, and how could the better one be made even better?

8.57 Suppose that a Senator from California has engaged a consultant to do a public-opinion survey in an effort to determine the percent of the population who favor his stand on a flat-rate income tax. The survey company will conduct a random survey of public opinion at a cost of 35 cents per interview. How much will the survey cost the senator if he insists that 95% of the time the sampling error be less than 5%, and if he has no idea what percent of the population favors his stand?

USING THE COMPUTER

8.58 Assume a normally distributed population and use the sample evidence in **Data Set 6** to find:
a) a 90% confidence interval for the average education level of persons over age 54 in the United States population;
b) a 95% confidence interval for the average monthly income of persons over age 54.

8.59 Near the end of Section 8.3 we mentioned that the size of the error α is always split into two equal parts to form the narrowest interval around a mean that includes $100(1 - \alpha)\%$ of the distribution of values. That is, for $\alpha = 0.10$ we exclude 0.05 at the lower end of the distribution and 0.05 at the upper end. Refer to Problem 8.14 and find anew the 90% confidence intervals if the amount excluded at the lower end is 0.045, 0.040, 0.035, 0.030, ..., 0.010, and 0.005. (The amount excluded at the upper end must be adjusted correspondingly so that each interval includes 90% of the distribution.) Use values from Table III and a computer program to repeat the calculations. Find the width of each interval and show that the smallest width interval is the one determined in Problem 8.14.

8.60 Refer to Problem 8.30 in which a sample size was determined to estimate the proportion of defectives within $D = 0.05$ of the true value allowing for 90% confidence in the interval estimate. Use a computer program to solve for the sample size needed if we wish the estimate to be within plus or minus 0.01, 0.02, 0.03, ..., 0.09, and 0.10 of the true value. Use the same confidence level (90%) throughout. Make a plot of the relation between sample size and the desired difference D.

8.61 Consider the values of taxes for the population of 78 cities in **Data Set 1**. Use a computer program to randomly select a sample of three items from this population (allowing for replacement after each draw). Repeat the process 200 different times, each time calculating and saving the values of the sample mean $\bar{x}$, the sample statistic

$$\hat{x} = \frac{(x_{max} - x_{min})}{2},$$

and the sample variance s^2.

a) Find the average and the standard deviation of the 200 values of sample means. Compare these to the values expected according to the central limit theorem. (The population mean and variance were calculated in Problem 2.28.)

b) Compare the mean and variance of the 200 values of $\hat{x}$ with those for $\bar{x}$. Discuss the results in terms of the properties of unbiasedness, efficiency, and sufficiency for estimators.

c) Repeat the entire process in parts (a) and (b) (called a Monte Carlo experiment) using 200 samples of size 10 each. Compare the values for the mean and variance of $\bar{x}$ between the cases with $n = 3$ and $n = 10$. Discuss the result in terms of the changing variances of the estimators and relate your results to the property of consistency of an estimator.

CASE PROBLEM

8.62 A staff member for a state utilities commission gathers information on the average price of electricity prior to a rate hearing for a particular electric utility. Since there are several hundred different utilities serving thousands of different cities, the staff member selects a random sample of 28 Eastern U.S. cities. The average price per kilowatt hour for residential customers over a 12-month period is reported below.

a) Use this sample to determine 95% confidence intervals for the mean and for the standard deviation of the population of rates, assuming that it is normally distributed. A computer printout of some measures for this sample is given below the listing.

b) Use your own computer program to obtain these same summary statistics. (*Hint:* The measure "VARIATION" is the numerator of the variance, that is, the sum of squared deviations about the mean.)

c) Use a computer program to repeat the calculations needed to find confidence intervals for the mean of the population for values of α equal to 0.10, 0.05, 0.020, 0.01, and 0.005.

d) Use a computer program to solve for the limits of both 90% and 99% confidence intervals for the standard deviation of the population. (Use the positive square roots of the confidence limits for the variance.)

Average Price per Kilowatt Hour for Residential Customers

---

1. Atlanta, GA, 5.83¢
2. Baltimore, MD, 6.77¢
3. Birmingham, AL, 6.32¢
4. Boston, MA, 9.68¢
5. Charlotte, NC, 5.41¢
6. Cincinnati, OH, 5.83¢
7. Cleveland, OH, 8.08¢
8. Columbia, SC, 6.56¢
9. Fairmont, WV, 5.74¢
10. Gulfport, MS, 6.06¢
11. Hartford, CT, 8.62¢
12. Jackson, MS, 6.20¢
13. Miami, FL, 6.91¢
14. Newark, NJ, 10.60¢

15. New Haven, CT, 10.12¢
16. New York, NY, 15.32¢
17. Pensacola, FL, 6.23¢
18. Pittsburgh, PA, 8.36¢
19. Philadelphia, PA, 8.83¢
20. Raleigh, NC, 6.19¢
21. Richmond, VA, 6.65¢
22. Roanoke, VA, 5.25¢
23. St. Petersburg, FL, 7.23¢
24. Savannah, GA, 6.74¢
25. Syracuse, NY, 6.43¢
26. Tampa, FL, 6.83¢
27. Washington, DC, 6.69¢
28. Wheeling, WV, 6.12¢

Computer printout of sample statistics:

```
SUM= 205.60                 SUM OF SQUARES= 1629.362
SAMPLE SIZE= 28             VARIATION= 119.669
MEAN= 7.343                 VARIANCE= 4.432
STANDARD DEVIATION= 2.105
```

GLOSSARY

Point estimate: An estimate of a population parameter that specifies one single value.

Interval estimate: An estimate that specifies a range of values.

Unbiasedness: An unbiased estimator is an estimator that, on the average, equals the parameter being estimated: i.e., E[estimator] = parameter.

Efficiency: An efficient estimator is an unbiased estimator that has a relatively low variance (when compared to other unbiased estimators).

Sufficiency: A sufficient estimator is an estimator that utilizes all the sample information available.

Consistency: A consistent estimator is an estimator with variance and bias (if any) that approach zero as n approaches infinity.

Maximum likelihood: An estimating procedure that selects the most likely population parameter in view of the sample evidence.

$100(1 - \alpha)\%$ confidence interval (C.I.) An interval estimate that will include the population parameter $100(1 - \alpha)\%$ of the time.

$100(1 - \alpha)\%$ C.I. for μ, σ known, normal parent population, or the central limit theorem applies ($n > 30$):

$$\bar{x} \pm z_{\alpha/2} \left(\frac{\sigma}{\sqrt{n}} \right).$$

$100(1 - \alpha)\%$ C.I. for μ, σ unknown, normal parent population:

$$\bar{x} \pm t_{\alpha/2, \nu} \left(\frac{s}{\sqrt{n}} \right).$$

$100(1 - \alpha)\%$ C.I. for π, when $np(1 - p) > 3$:

$$p \pm z_{\alpha/2} \sqrt{\frac{p(1 - p)}{n}}.$$

Formula for determining the minimum required sample size:

$$n = \frac{z_{\alpha/2}^2 \, \sigma^2}{D^2} \qquad \text{for estimating a population mean where } \sigma \text{ is known and } D \text{ is the maximum allowable sampling error,}$$

or

$$n = \frac{z_{\alpha/2}^2 \, p(1 - p)}{D^2} \qquad \text{for estimating a proportion where a planning value is used for } p \text{ (or choose } p = \tfrac{1}{2}\text{).}$$

$100(1 - \alpha)\%$ C.I. for σ^2:

$$\frac{(n - 1)s^2}{\chi_{\text{upper}}^2} \leq \sigma^2 \leq \frac{(n - 1)s^2}{\chi_{\text{lower}}^2}.$$

Hypothesis Testing:
One-sample Tests

NINE

9.1 INTRODUCTION AND BASIC CONCEPTS

The procedures presented in Chapter 8 describe the process of making both point and interval estimates of population parameters. One advantage of using an interval estimate is that it permits the expression of uncertainty about the true value of the population parameter. Another advantage of using confidence intervals is that they serve to test the validity of *assumed values of the population parameters*. Assumptions about population parameters are usually referred to as *statistical hypotheses*. Determining the validity of an assumption of this nature is called the *test of a statistical hypothesis*, or simply *hypothesis testing*.

> The major purpose of hypothesis testing is to choose between two mutually exclusive and exhaustive competing hypotheses about the value of a population parameter.

The process of hypothesis testing brings together many of our previous topics — calculation of sample statistics, random variables, probability distributions, and statistical inference. To illustrate this with a simple example, we will suppose that an engineer in charge of quality control for items produced on an assembly line wishes to choose between the two mutually exclusive and exhaustive hypotheses $\pi > 0.05$ or $\pi \leq 0.05$, where π is the proportion of defective items produced. It may be that the production line must be shut down if the percentage of defectives exceeds 5%. Let us assume that the engineer cannot check every item produced because the cost and time delay would be too expensive. Instead, the engineer decides to take a sample and then use the proportion of defectives in the sample ($p = x/n$) and a knowledge of sampling distributions (i.e., the sampling distribution of p) to decide between the two conflicting hypotheses. In the following section the procedure for constructing such a test of hypotheses is presented. Subsequent sections give specific examples of the use of this procedure in some commonly occurring situations.

Types of Hypotheses

In specifying the conflicting hypotheses about the values that a population parameter might assume, it is convenient to distinguish between *simple hypotheses* and *composite hypotheses*. In a **simple hypothesis,** only one value of the population parameter is specified. If an engineer hypothesizes that the probability of a defective item is $\pi = 0.10$, this represents a simple hypothesis. A financial analyst for McDonald's investigating the hypothesis that the mean income per McDonald's franchise is $\mu =$

$130,000 per month is testing a simple hypothesis. If the exact difference between two population parameters is specified (that is, $\mu_1 - \mu_2 = 0$), this also represents a simple hypothesis. A **composite hypothesis,** on the other hand, specifies not just one value but a *range* of values that the population parameter may assume. The hypotheses $\pi \leq 0.10$, $\mu \neq 100$, and $\mu_1 - \mu_2 \neq 0$ all represent composite hypotheses because more than one value is specified in each case. As you might suspect, assumptions in the form of simple hypotheses are, in general, easier to test than are composite hypotheses. In the former case we need to determine only whether or not the population parameter equals the specified value, while in the latter case it is necessary to determine whether or not the population parameter takes on any one of what may be a very large (or even infinite) number of values.

The two conflicting (i.e., mutually exclusive) hypotheses in a statistical test are normally referred to as the **null hypothesis** and the **alternative hypothesis.** The term "null hypothesis" developed from early work in the theory of hypothesis testing, in which this hypothesis corresponded to a theory about a population parameter that the researcher thought did not represent the true value of the parameter (hence the word "null," which means invalid, void, or amounting to nothing). The *alternative hypothesis* generally specified those values of the parameter that the researcher believed did hold true.

Nowadays, it is generally-accepted common practice *not* to associate any special meaning to the null or alternative hypotheses, but merely to let these terms represent two different assumptions about the population parameter. We shall see in a moment that, for statistical convenience, it may make a difference which hypothesis is called the null and which is called the alternative. It is *most* convenient always to have the null hypothesis be the hypothesis that contains an equal sign, if either one has an equal sign.

The null and alternative hypotheses are distinguished by the use of two different symbols, H_0 representing the null hypothesis and H_a the alternative hypothesis. Suppose, for example, that the automobile industry asserts that new car prices increased only $100 in the last year. You believe the increase was larger than $100. To test whether μ is equal to or greater than 100 you establish the following null and alternative hypotheses:

$$H_0: \mu = 100 \qquad \text{(Null hypothesis);}$$
$$H_a: \mu > 100 \qquad \text{(Alternative hypothesis).}$$

Instead of testing for car price increases over a year's period, you may wish to test for differences between the mean price of two groups of cars at one point in time. In this case the null hypothesis established may be that the two groups have equal means, with the alternative hypothesis that their means are not equal:

$$H_0: \mu_1 - \mu_2 = 0 \quad \text{(Null hypothesis)};$$
$$H_a: \mu_1 - \mu_2 \neq 0 \quad \text{(Alternative hypothesis)}.$$

The null hypothesis and the alternative hypothesis can both be either simple or composite. The simple null hypothesis $H_0: \mu = 100$, for example, may be tested against a simple alternative hypothesis, such as $H_a: \mu = 120$ or $H_a: \mu = 75$; it may be tested against a composite hypothesis, such as $H_a: \mu \neq 100$, $H_a: \mu > 130$, or $H_a: \mu < 75$. Similarly, the composite null hypothesis $H_0: \mu \leq 100$ may be tested against a simple alternative, such as $H_a: \mu = 120$, or against a composite alternative, such as $H_a: \mu > 100$.

Regardless of the form of the two hypotheses, it is extremely important to remember that the true value of the population parameter under consideration *must* be either in the set specified by H_0 or in the set specified by H_a. By testing $H_0: \mu = 100$ against $H_a: \mu = 120$, for example, one is asserting that the true value of μ equals either 100 or 120 and that *no other values are possible*. One means for assuring that either H_0 or H_a contains the true value of the population parameter is to let these two sets be *complementary*. That is, if the null hypothesis is $H_0: \mu = 100$, then the alternative hypothesis will be $H_a: \mu \neq 100$; or if $H_0: \mu \leq 100$, then $H_a: \mu > 100$. From a statistical point of view the easiest form to handle is a simple null hypothesis versus a simple alternative hypothesis. Unfortunately, most real-world problems cannot be stated in this form but instead involve a composite null or a composite alternative hypothesis, or both. If a particular problem cannot be stated as a test between two simple hypotheses, then the next best alternative is to test a simple null hypothesis against a composite alternative. In other words, it is convenient to structure the problem so that the null hypothesis is a simple equality statement.

One- and Two-sided Tests

If one is fortunate enough to be able to construct the test of hypotheses so that the null hypothesis is simple, then the alternative hypothesis may specify one or more values for the population parameter, and these values (or value) may lie entirely above, or entirely below, or on both sides of the value specified by the null hypothesis. A statistical test in which the alternative hypothesis specifies that the population parameter lies entirely above or entirely below the value specified in the null hypothesis is called a **one-sided test;** an alternative hypothesis that specifies that the parameter can lie on either side of the value indicated by H_0 is called a **two-sided test.** Thus, $H_0: \mu = 100$ tested against $H_a: \mu > 100$ is a one-sided test, since H_a specifies that μ lies on one particular side of 100. The same null hypothesis tested against $H_a:\mu \neq 100$ is a two-sided test, since μ can lie on *either* side of 100.

The Form of the Decision Problem

The decision problem that we confront in hypothesis testing is choosing between two mutually exclusive propositions about a population parameter when we are faced with the uncertainty inherent in sampling from a population. The decision-maker has only the sample evidence on which to base the choice of accepting the null hypothesis (which is equivalent to rejecting the alternative hypothesis) or rejecting the null hypothesis (accepting H_a).The standard method of solving this decision problem is, first, to assume that the null hypothesis is true (just as we presume a person's innocence until he or she is proved guilty in a court of law). Then, using the probability theory from Chapters 5, 6, and 7, we can establish the criteria that will be used to decide whether there is sufficient evidence to declare H_0 false. A sample is then taken, the sample evidence is compared to the criteria, and the decision is made whether to accept or reject H_0.

Contrary to practice in a court of law, where innocence is maintained as long as any reasonable doubt about guilt remains, in hypothesis testing we reject H_0 on the basis of only a reasonable doubt about its truth. With such a procedure, the probability value, upon which we base our conclusion that there is reason to doubt the truth of H_0, is critical. Moreover, since the decision to accept or reject H_0 is based on probabilities and not on certainty, there are chances of error in the decision. Specifically, there are two types of potential error:

1. One may decide on the basis of the sample result to reject the null hypothesis when this hypothesis is, in fact, true **(Type I error).**
2. One may decide to accept the null hypothesis when this hypothesis is not true **(Type II error).**

There are four possible situations in hypothesis testing, as shown in Fig. 9.1. This figure presents the basic decision problem in hypothesis testing with reference only to the null hypothesis. A good exercise for the reader would be to construct a similar figure, making reference only to H_a (remember that accepting H_0 implies rejecting H_a, and vice versa).

To illustrate the concept of Type I and II errors, recall our example about the increase in new car prices, where we established the hypotheses $H_0:\mu = 100$ and $H_a:\mu > 100$. Now, suppose that the true mean is actually $\mu = 100$. If we decide (on the basis of some sample evidence) to accept $H_a:\mu > 100$, then a Type I error has been made. Let us consider the

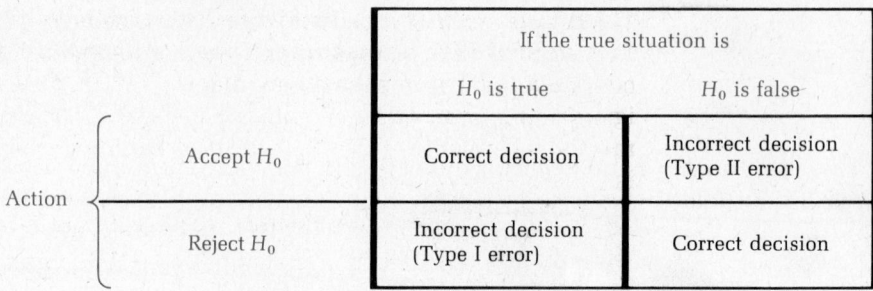

FIGURE 9.1 **The four possible decision outcomes in hypothesis testing.**

opposite situation, where the true value of μ exceeds 100. For example, we might assume that $\mu = 105$. A Type II error is made in this case if we decide to accept the null hypothesis $H_0:\mu = 100$.

Example 9.1. Type I and II errors can be specified for the quality-control problem in Section 5.3. In this problem, defective items occur in a production process with one of two probabilities, $\pi = 0.10$ or $\pi = 0.25$. Suppose we establish the null hypothesis $H_0:\pi = 0.10$ and let the alternative hypothesis be $H_a:\pi = 0.25$. A Type I error is committed if the decision is to accept the alternative hypothesis $H_a:\pi = 0.25$ when the null hypothesis $H_0:\pi = 0.10$ is true. Similarly, a Type II error is committed if $H_0:\pi = 0.10$ is accepted when $H_a:\pi = 0.25$ is true. We reiterate at this point that the above hypotheses are based on the assumption that the true population value of π is either 0.10 or 0.25. By specifying two simple hypotheses we are asserting that no other values are possible.

It should be clear that the probabilities of Type I and Type II errors are conditional probabilities. The former depends on the condition that H_0 is true and the latter on the condition that H_a is true. The probability of a Type I error is commonly denoted by the lowercase Greek letter alpha (α) and is called the **level of significance.** That is,

$$\alpha = \text{Level of significance} = P(\text{Type I error})$$
$$= P(\text{reject } H_0 | H_0 \text{ is true}).$$

The level of significance of a statistical test is comparable to the probability of an error, also called α, discussed in Chapter 8. The value of **(1 − α)** is called a *confidence level* and represents the complement of $P(\text{Type I error})$.

$$(1 - \alpha) = \text{Confidence level} = 1 - P(\text{Type I error})$$
$$= P(\text{accept } H_0 | H_0 \text{ is true}).$$

In constructing a statistical test we obviously would like to have a small probability of making a Type I error; hence, one objective is to construct the test in such a way that α *is small*. This objective, however, ignores the probability of making a Type II error. The probability of making a Type II error — that is, of accepting a false null hypothesis — is usually denoted by the Greek letter beta ($\boldsymbol{\beta}$):

$$\beta = P(\text{Type II error}) = P(\text{accept } H_0 | H_0 \text{ is false}).$$

The complement of this probability is known as the *power* of a statistical test, since it indicates the ability (or "power") of the test to recognize *correctly* that the null hypothesis is false (and hence, that H_0 should be rejected).

$$1 - \beta = \text{power} = P(\text{reject } H_0 | H_0 \text{ is false}).$$

Thus, one always wishes to construct a test that will yield a large power (close to one), or equivalently, a low value of β, when H_0 is false. Figure 9.2 presents the same decision problem shown in Fig. 9.1, except that here we identify the *probability* associated with each of the four cells.

Note that the probability of each decision outcome is a *conditional* probability and that the elements in each column sum to 1.0, since the events with which they are associated are *complements*. By now it should be apparent that α and β need not add to unity, as these two probabilities are not complementary. Thus, a one-unit change in α does not imply a corresponding one-unit change in β, or vice versa. However, α and β are not independent of each other, nor are they independent of the sample size n. When α is lowered, β normally rises, and vice versa (if n remains unchanged). If n is increased, it is possible for both α and β to decrease,

FIGURE 9.2 **The probability of each decision outcome in hypothesis testing.**

		If the true situation is	
		H_0 is true	H_0 is false
Action — Accept H_0		$1 - \alpha$ (Confidence level)	β (beta)
Reject H_0		α (alpha) (Significance level)	$1 - \beta$ (Power of the test)
Sum		1.00	1.00

because the sampling error is potentially decreased. Since increasing n usually costs money, the researcher must decide just how much additional money should be spent on increasing the sample size in order to reduce the sizes of α and β. Such analysis, concerned with balancing the costs of increasing the sample size against the costs of Type I and Type II errors, is a fairly complex subject. We will cover this topic briefly in Section 9.6. Until then, we will assume that the sample size is fixed at some predetermined value n.

9.2 THE STANDARD FORMAT OF HYPOTHESIS TESTING

There are many different population parameters, many different potential forms of hypotheses, and many different sample statistics, random variables, and probability distributions that may be involved in testing hypotheses. It is not, therefore, feasible to catalogue all such tests. However, they all follow a similar procedure, which can be learned and then applied to different situations as they arise. This procedure can be summarized by the following five steps:

1. State the null and alternative hypotheses.
2. Determine the appropriate test statistic.
3. Determine the critical region.
4. Compute the value of the test statistic.
5. Make the statistical decision and interpretation.

We will illustrate this procedure by Example 9.2, which will continue throughout all five steps.

Example 9.2. A financial analyst for McDonald's restaurants has determined that last year the mean monthly income (in thousands of dollars) for a McDonald's franchise was $130. This year, the analyst is concerned that the mean income may be some number other than $130. For the time being, we will assume that this analyst does not know whether μ exceeds 130 or is less than 130. Also, we will assume that monthly incomes are known to be normally distributed with a standard deviation of $\sigma = 5.4$. A random sample of $n = 25$ franchises is proposed to test whether or not the mean is equal to 130. The five steps for performing this test are described below.

Step 1. State the Null and Alternative Hypotheses. In every hypothesis-testing problem the two conflicting hypotheses must be specified clearly. It is usually convenient to formulate the null hypothesis as a simple hypothesis and the alternative hypothesis as a composite hypothesis, although it is not necessary to do so. In any case the two conflicting hypotheses must be mutually exclusive, and they must be formulated so that the true value of the population parameter is included in either the null or the alternative hypothesis (i.e., it is not permissible for *both* hypotheses to be true or both to be false).

For our McDonald's example the parameter in the test is the population mean μ. One hypothesis is that $\mu = 130$, and the other is that $\mu \neq 130$. If we let the simple hypothesis containing the equality statement be H_0, then:

$$\text{Null hypothesis:} \quad H_0 : \mu = 130;$$
$$\text{Alternative hypothesis:} \quad H_a : \mu \neq 130.$$

One of these hypotheses must be true, since the values specified by H_a represent the complement of the value specified by H_0.

Step 2. Determine the Appropriate Test Statistic. The second step in testing hypotheses is to determine which of the random variables that we have studied is appropriate to determine whether we should accept or reject H_0. If the parameter being tested is the population mean, then we know that our best estimate of μ is $\bar{x}$. In testing $H_0 : \mu = 130$ versus $H_a : \mu \neq 130$, we would want to determine how close $\bar{x}$ is to 130. A value of $\bar{x}$ far below or far above 130 would lead us to accept H_a; conversely, a value slightly below, equal to, or slightly above 130 would lead to acceptance of H_0. In order to decide whether $\bar{x}$ is close enough to 130 to accept H_0, first we standardize $\bar{x}$. From the discussion in Chapter 7, we know that if $\bar{x}$ is normal and σ is known, then the standardization of $\bar{x}$ is

$$z = \frac{\bar{x} - \mu_0}{\sigma/\sqrt{n}}.$$

The symbol μ_0 in this standardization is the value of μ specified under the null hypothesis. The random variable z for this example is called the test statistic.

A **test statistic** *is thus a random variable used to determine how close a specific sample result falls to one of the hypotheses being tested.* As we will describe in this chapter, most of the random variables studied thus far can be used as test statistics.

A valid test statistic must satisfy three conditions:

1. Its p.d.f. must be known under the condition that the null hypothesis is true.
2. It must contain the parameter being tested.
3. All of its remaining terms must be known or calculable from the sample.

In our example the distribution of **z** is $N(0, 1)$ when μ is assumed to be $\mu_0 = 130$. Obviously,

$$z = \frac{\bar{x} - \mu}{\sigma/\sqrt{n}}$$

contains the parameter μ. The remaining terms are: σ, which is known to be 5.4, $n = 25$, and $\bar{x}$, which can be calculated from the sample.

Step 3. Determine the Critical Region(s). As we indicated above, certain values of the test statistic lead to acceptance of H_0, while other values lead to the rejection of H_0 (which is equivalent to the acceptance of H_a). In most statistical tests it is important to specify, *before the sample is taken,* exactly which values of the test statistic will lead to rejection of H_0 and which will lead to acceptance of H_0. The former set of values (leading to rejection of H_0) is called the **critical region,** while the latter set (leading to acceptance of H_0) is called the **acceptance region.** The *critical value* is that point which separates the critical region (rejection region) from the acceptance region. When the alternative hypothesis is two-sided (as in our McDonald's example), these regions are characterized as shown in the accompanying diagram.

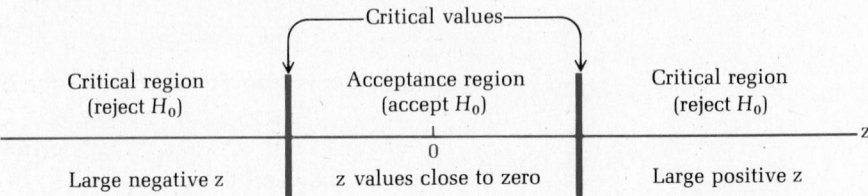

The problem is to determine the *exact* location of the critical values shown in the diagram. These values depend partially on the level of risk of a Type I or Type II error that one is willing to take. For example, the smaller the value of α, the farther outward the critical values in the above diagram will move (thereby making the critical regions smaller). This occurs because when α is small, the decision-maker requires a relatively small critical region (remember, α is the probability that the test statistic will be in the critical region when H_0 is true). Figure 9.3 illustrates the effect of changing the size of α for a given sample size. The size of β affects the critical values in the opposite direction — the smaller the value of β, the more to the *middle* the critical values will move (thereby increasing the size of the critical region). As we indicated previously, the ideal is that both α and β be very small in a given situation. In terms of the critical values, however, the effect of decreasing α is opposite to the

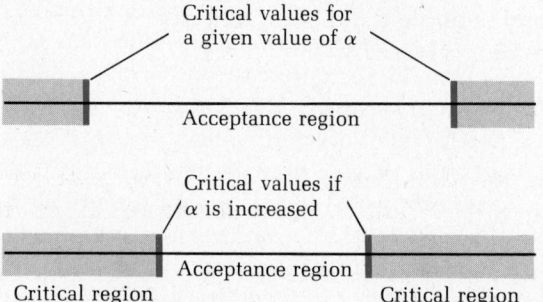

FIGURE 9.3 **Increasing the size of α will move the critical values toward the middle. Since the acceptance region becomes smaller, the value of β becomes smaller.**

effect of decreasing β. It should be clear by now that *decreasing the size of α will increase the size of β*; similarly, if the size of β is decreased, the size of α will increase (assuming that the sample size is fixed).

The traditional method for selecting a critical region is first to establish a value for α and then to choose that critical region that yields the smallest value of β. The rationale behind this procedure is that it is important to establish beforehand the risk that one wants to assume of incorrectly rejecting a true null hypothesis. In other words, the size of the Type I error in this approach is viewed as so much more important than the size of the Type II error that the size of β is considered only after α has been fixed at some predetermined level. The practice of selecting a critical region in this manner stems from the early research on hypothesis testing, in which the null hypothesis usually represented "current opinion" on an issue and the alternative hypothesis represented a viewpoint of the researcher contrary to that commonly accepted. In testing a new drug, such as a cure for cancer, the drug must be assumed to be of no benefit, or even harmful, until it is proved otherwise. The alternative hypothesis is that the drug is indeed beneficial. A most serious Type I error would be made if a harmful drug (H_0 true) were certified as beneficial.

The value of α, or the level of significance, indicates the importance (i.e., "significance") that a researcher attaches to the consequences associated with incorrectly rejecting H_0. Researchers in the social sciences often use a level of significance of $\alpha = 0.05$, indicating that they are willing to accept a 5% chance of being wrong when they reject H_0. For many statistical problems, α is set, rather arbitrarily, at either 0.05 or 0.01. However, in the medical sciences, α is usually set much lower — perhaps as low as 0.005 or 0.001. As we indicated above, medical science has to be very concerned about incorrectly rejecting H_0. Although α is rarely set higher than $\alpha = 0.05$, and values such as $\alpha = 0.025$, $\alpha = 0.01$ and $\alpha = 0.001$ are used frequently, other values may be used. If α is set at some predetermined level, then it is extremely important that this value be specified before any data are collected.

In our McDonald's example, a Type I error occurs when it is concluded that $\mu \neq 130$ when μ is truly 130. Suppose we assume that the researcher uses an $\alpha = 0.05$ level of significance; i.e., this researcher wants to have no more than a 5% chance of rejecting $H_0: \mu = 130$ when this hypothesis is true (a Type I error). This means that the researcher wants the critical region to cut off 5% of the appropriate p.d.f., which from our earlier discussion we know to be the **z**-distribution. When H_a is two-sided, the optimal critical region will cut off $\alpha/2$ of the area in the upper tail and $\alpha/2$ of the area in the lower tail. This is the same procedure we used to construct a $100(1 - \alpha)$% confidence interval. If $\alpha = 0.05$, we know from Table III that the values of **z** that cut off $\alpha/2 = 0.025$ in each tail of the standardized normal distribution are ± 1.96. Figure 9.4 shows the resulting critical regions.

The critical values shown in Fig. 9.4 are expressed in terms of the **z**-distribution. When constructing critical values, we can express these numbers either as a z-value or in terms of $\overline{x}$. The advantage of expressing the critical values in terms of $\overline{x}$ is that it is then possible to compare the sample results directly with these values and to see if the sample result falls in the acceptance region or in the critical regions. Fortunately, it is quite easy to transform a z critical value into its comparable $\overline{x}$ critical value by solving for $\overline{x}$ in the formula that represents the test statistic:

$$z = \frac{\overline{x} - \mu_0}{\sigma/\sqrt{n}}.$$

For our McDonald's example, the value of μ_0 is 130 (the null hypothesis), $n = 25$, and the known value of σ is 5.4. Substituting these values and $z = 1.96$ into this formula, we obtain the $\overline{x}$ critical value for the right-hand tail of the distribution:

$$1.96 = \frac{\overline{x} - 130}{5.4/\sqrt{25}}.$$

Solving for $\overline{x}$, we get

$$\overline{x} = 1.96 \left(\frac{5.4}{5}\right) + 130 = 132.12.$$

Similarly, when the critical value is $z = -1.96$, the appropriate critical value of $\overline{x}$ is derived as follows:

$$-1.96 = \frac{\overline{x} - 130}{5.4/\sqrt{25}} \Rightarrow \overline{x} = -1.96 \left(\frac{5.4}{5}\right) + 130,$$

$$\overline{x} = 127.88.$$

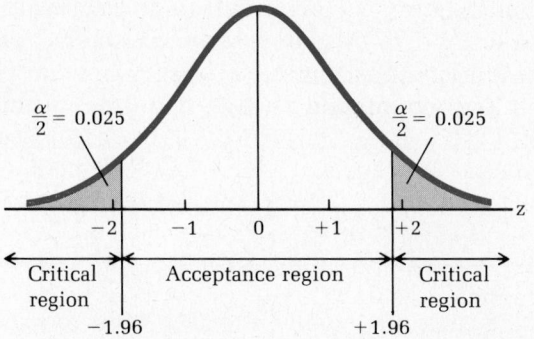

FIGURE 9.4 **Critical regions for testing H_0: $\mu = 130$ against H_a: $\mu \neq 130$ with $\alpha = 0.05$, $\sigma = 5.4$, $n = 25$ (in terms of z).**

We could have saved ourselves some work in the above calculation by recognizing that due to symmetry the lower critical value will be the same distance *below* 130 as the upper critical value is *above* 130 (they are both 2.12 units away from 130). These critical values are shown in Fig. 9.5.

From Fig. 9.5 we know that for random samples of size $n = 25$, 2.5% of the time $\bar{x}$ will be less than 127.88, and 2.5% of the time $\bar{x}$ will be greater than 132.12, assuming that H_0:$\mu = 130$ is true. We must emphasize that Figs. 9.4 and 9.5 are *equivalent* ways of presenting the same critical regions. The only difference is that the former is in terms of the test statistic z, while the latter is in terms of the sample mean itself ($\bar{x}$).

Step 4. Compute the Value of the Test Statistic. Now that we have specified the two conflicting hypotheses, determined the appropriate test statistic, and found the critical region(s), we must see whether the sample result falls in the critical region or in the acceptance region. When the critical values are stated in terms of $\bar{x}$, this process is quite simple. For the most part, however, it will be convenient (and it will help the reader

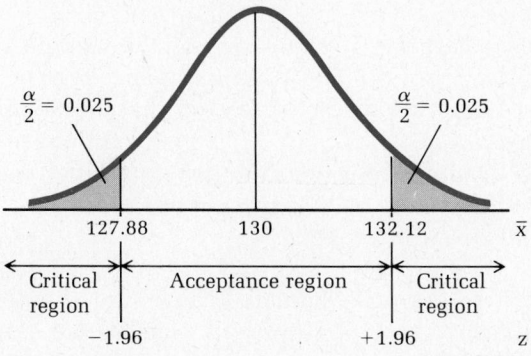

FIGURE 9.5 **Critical regions for testing H_0: $\mu = 130$ against H_a: $\mu \neq 130$ with $\alpha = 0.05$, $\sigma = 5.4$, $n = 25$ (in terms of $\bar{x}$).**

to note the similarities between all problems) to use z-values to denote critical values. To do this, we need to standardize the sample result into its comparable z-value. A value of z calculated on the basis of a sample result is called a **computed z-value,** and is denoted by the symbol z_c.

$$\text{Computed z-value:} \qquad z_c = \frac{\overline{x} - \mu_0}{\sigma/\sqrt{n}}. \tag{9.1}$$

In general, a **computed value** is a value of the test statistic, calculated by using a specific sample result.

To illustrate a computed z-value, we will assume that, in our McDonald's example, the random sample of $n = 25$ resulted in $\overline{x} = 128$. That is, 25 McDonald's franchises were selected at random, and the average monthly income in this sample was 128. When we substitute this value of $\overline{x}$ into our test statistic, we obtain the following computed z-value:

$$z_c = \frac{128 - 130}{5.4/\sqrt{25}} = -1.85.$$

We mention for later use that if the t-variable had been the appropriate test statistic, then we would have calculated the value t_c. Similarly, *computed* values of the chi-square variable will be denoted χ_c^2.

Step 5. Make the Statistical Decision and Conclusion. If the calculated value of the test statistic lies in the critical region, then H_0 is rejected. When the calculated value falls in the acceptance region, then H_0 is accepted. In either case it is important for the researcher to reach a conclusion *in terms of the original problem*, because the results of statistical tests in business, economics, and the social sciences are often presented to and utilized by people who may not understand statistical terminology.

Let us determine whether or not the sample result $\overline{x} = 128$ (or, equivalently, $z_c = -1.85$) leads to acceptance of $H_0:\mu = 130$ or acceptance of $H_a:\mu \neq 130$. From Fig. 9.5 it is clear that this sample result falls in the acceptance region (i.e., above 127.88 for $\overline{x}$, or above -1.96 for z). Thus, we would conclude that the mean may not differ from 130, although we must admit that there is some risk [known as $\beta = P(\text{Type II error})$] that this conclusion is not true.

One-sided Tests For the critical regions calculated above, the alternative hypothesis was two-sided, $H_a:\mu \neq 130$. Now let's change our assumption about this problem by supposing that it is agreed that the mean McDonald's income cannot exceed 130, but could be lower than 130. In this case the appropriate alternative hypothesis is $H_a : \mu < 130$. *Such an alternative hypothesis is legitimate only if one is certain that the population mean cannot exceed 130.*

The only change caused by a one-sided alternative hypothesis is that we now have a single critical region, rather than the two regions shown in Figs. 9.4 and 9.5. The single critical value is found in much the same way as in the two-sided test. The only difference is that all of the probability associated with the error α is cut off from a single end of the distribution. Whether this is the upper or the lower end depends entirely on whether the alternative hypothesis is a more than ($>$) or a less than ($<$) relationship. In our McDonald's example, suppose $\alpha = 0.05$ and we want to find the single value that cuts off 5% of the distribution. Note in Fig. 9.6 that we cut off $\alpha = 0.05$ of the *left-hand* portion of the **z**-distribution, because the values specified by H_a all lie to the *left* of 130 ($\mu < 130$). If the alternative hypothesis had been one-sided on the upper side ($H_a : \mu > 130$), then the critical region would lie entirely in the upper right-hand tail.

The value $z = -1.645$ in Fig. 9.6 was obtained from Table III in Appendix C by interpolating between $z = -1.64$ $[P(z \le -1.64) = 0.0505]$ and $z = -1.65$ $[P(z \le -1.65) = 0.0495]$. The $\bar{x}$-value comparable to $z = -1.645$ is determined as follows:

$$z = \frac{\bar{x} - \mu_0}{\sigma / \sqrt{n}},$$

$$-1.645 = \frac{\bar{x} - 130}{5.4 / \sqrt{25}},$$

$$\bar{x} = -1.645 \left(\frac{5.4}{5} \right) + 130 = 128.22.$$

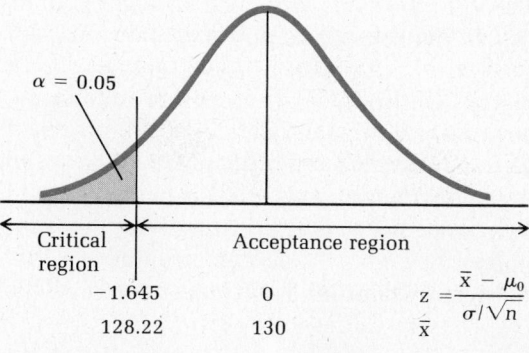

$\alpha = 0.05$

Critical region

-1.645

128.22

0

130

Acceptance region

$z = \dfrac{\bar{x} - \mu_0}{\sigma / \sqrt{n}}$

$\bar{x}$

FIGURE 9.6 **Critical region for testing $H_0 : \mu = 130$ against $H_a : \mu < 130$ with $\alpha = 0.05$, $\sigma = 5.4, n = 25$.**

This critical value of $\bar{x} = 128.22$ is also shown in Fig. 9.6. Note that now the sample value $\bar{x} = 128$ falls in the critical region, as does the z-value of -1.85 (which is less than -1.645).

For the one-sided alternative $H_a:\mu < 130$, we would reject the null hypothesis $H_0:\mu = 130$. Thus, we would conclude that the mean income of McDonald's franchises is probably less than \$130,000 although we admit that there is some risk (no more than $\alpha = 0.05$) that this conclusion is not true. This example was designed to emphasize how important is the selection of the significance level or the type of alternative hypothesis in a statistical test. The more specific one can be in specifying H_a, the more powerful will be the resulting test.

Procedure When H_0 Is Composite

The reader may wonder at this point what happens if the null hypothesis is not simple, but composite. For example, suppose that we wish to test

$$H_0:\mu \geq 130 \qquad \text{versus} \qquad H_a:\mu < 130.$$

For a composite null hypothesis like this, it is impossible to calculate a critical value as we did in Fig. 9.6 because now there is no one value for μ specified under the null hypothesis.

> The common approach to this situation is to construct the critical value(s) by using the most conservative value possible under H_0. The most conservative value is generally the one closest to the alternative hypothesis.

Thus, if the alternative hypothesis is $H_a:\mu < 130$, the closest value specified by the null hypothesis is the value $\mu = 130$. The critical value(s) can now be constructed by treating the null hypothesis as if it were $H_0:\mu = 130$. The resulting critical region will look exactly like that shown in Fig. 9.6. Rejection of H_0 in favor of H_a for this extreme value of μ would certainly lead to the same and even stronger conclusions when the other values of μ in the composite null hypothesis H_0 are used.

Reporting a Probability (p) Value

The five steps outlined above occur in almost all tests of hypotheses, even though the step-by-step details of the process may change from one situation to another. We will illustrate the basic process in a number of examples in this chapter and the following chapter. Before doing so, we should point out that a modification of the steps is often used when it is not possible or desirable to specify the value of α (the level of significance) before taking the sample. This may happen when the decision-maker (say, the manager) is someone other than the person carrying out the research (the statistical analyst). In some cases the decision-maker is not available to specify an α, or perhaps the analyst is writing a report in which each of the various readers may be thought of as potential decision-makers (all with possibly different α's).

When α is not specified, a common procedure is to determine or "report" a probability that depends on the computed z-value (z_c). To illustrate this procedure, we will apply it to our McDonald's example where the hypotheses are

$$H_0{:}\mu = 130 \quad \text{versus} \quad H_a{:}\mu < 130.$$

Recall that the sample result $\bar{x} = 128$ led to a computed z-value of $z_c = -1.85$. *The reported **p-value** is the probability that the random variable **z** would take on a value as extreme as z_c.* For this example the probability is (from Table III)

$$\text{p-value} = P(\mathbf{z} \le z_c) = P(\mathbf{z} \le -1.85) = 1 - 0.9678 = 0.0322.$$

The probability value reported to the decision-maker is thus 0.0322. To a decision-maker who knows little about statistical analysis, we might offer the following statement:

"A sample mean of 128 or lower will occur only 3.22% of the time when the true population mean is 130. Since our sample mean was 128, this result casts serious doubt on the validity of the assumption that the mean is, in fact, 130."

A decision-maker who has set α *higher* than 0.0322 should reject H_0 (because $\bar{x} = 128$ would fall in the critical region). A decision-maker who has set α *lower* than 0.0322 should accept H_0 (because the sample result $\bar{x} = 128$ would fall in the acceptance region). The procedure outlined above is for an alternative hypothesis that is one-sided on the *lower* side of H_0. If H_a is one-sided on the *upper* side of H_0, then the reported p-value is $P(\mathbf{z} \ge z_c)$. Otherwise, the procedures described above do not change. Thus, for one-sided tests about μ, a p-value is determined as follows:

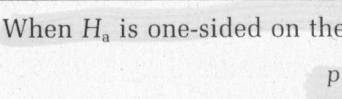

When H_a is one-sided on the lower side,

$$p = P(\mathbf{z} \le z_c).$$

When H_a is one-sided on the upper side,

$$p = P(\mathbf{z} \ge z_c).$$

If the alternative hypothesis is no longer one-sided, but rather two-sided, then the process described above must be modified slightly. Suppose, for instance, in the above example that the alternative hypothesis is changed to $H_a:\mu \neq 130$. This set of alternative values is now *twice* as large as the previous alternative set (which was $H_a:\mu < 130$). Since we now have two critical regions, the probability to be reported must be *twice as large* as in the one-sided case. The p-value for a two-sided alternative must be twice as large as the p-value in the one-sided case, because the p-value in the two-sided case must include both of the one-sided probabilities — that is, $P(\mathbf{z} \leq z_c) + P(\mathbf{z} \geq z_c)$. Thus, the general rule is:

> If H_a is two-sided, then the calculated p-value must be doubled.

Let us now assume that the same sample result, $\bar{x} = 128$, occurs when testing $H_0:\mu = 130$ versus $H_a:\mu \neq 130$. To find the p-value, we must double the probability $P(\mathbf{z} \leq -1.85)$.*

$$2P(\mathbf{z} \leq z_c) = 2P(\mathbf{z} \leq -1.85) = 2(0.0322) = 0.0644.$$

Thus, we would report that, if the null hypothesis is true, a sample result this far away from the hypothesized value of the parameter (either above or below μ) would occur 6.44% of the time. The decision-maker with an α greater than 0.0644 should reject H_0. If α is set at any level of significance below 0.0644, H_0 should be accepted.

To summarize:

> If α is greater than the p-value, reject H_0.
> If α is less than the p-value, accept H_0.

These examples have illustrated the general method of hypothesis testing, which may be applied to many tests. The most common tests of hypotheses involve μ, the population mean. Tests about μ are usually designed to indicate, on the basis of a *single* sample, which of two hypotheses about μ should be rejected. In other circumstances, one may be interested in designing a test to indicate, on the basis of a sample from each of *two different* populations, whether or not these *two* samples were

---

* The reader should always make certain that the probability to be doubled is less than 0.50. It would make no sense to double a probability such as $P(\mathbf{z} \geq -1.85)$; doing so would yield a p-value greater than 1.0.

drawn from populations having equal means. This breakdown between one- and two-sample tests will be a convenient one for us to follow. Some common one-sample tests are discussed in this chapter; two-sample tests are presented in Chapter 10.

Study Question 9.1: Reading Level for a Training Manual

You are in charge of a project to rewrite the training manual for certain RCA assembly line workers in the United States. A previous study indicated that the mean reading level for these workers is normally distributed with a mean of 9.5 (halfway between the ninth and tenth grade) and a population standard deviation of $\sigma = 1.1$. Recent hiring policies have focused on hiring high school graduates, which suggests that the mean reading level may have increased. You take a random sample of 50 of these workers and find $\bar{x} = 9.9$. Report a p-value, assuming that the (population) standard deviation is not changed. Would you accept or reject H_0 using $\alpha = 0.05$?

Answer

1. *Establish the hypotheses:* $H_0: \mu = 9.5$ versus $H_a: \mu > 9.5$ (assuming that μ cannot be less than 9.5).
2. *Determine the test statistic:*

$$z = \frac{\bar{x} - \mu_0}{\sigma/\sqrt{n}}.$$

3. *Determine the critical region:* Since $\alpha = 0.05$, and the alternative hypothesis is one-sided towards the high side, the critical value is $+z_\alpha = +z_{0.05} = +1.645$.
4. *Calculate a test statistic value and report a p-value:*

$$z_c = \frac{9.9 - 9.5}{1.1/\sqrt{50}} = \frac{0.4}{0.1556} = 2.57.$$

$$P(z \geq 2.57) = 0.0051.$$

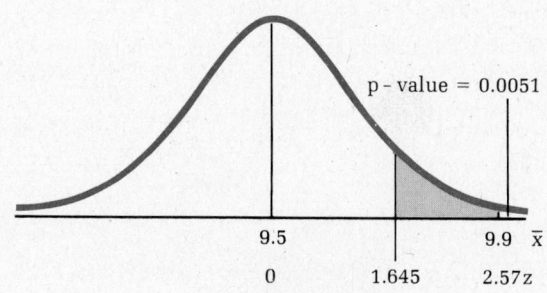

5. *Decision and conclusion:* Since the calculated value ($z_c = 2.57$) falls in the critical region (beyond 1.645), H_0 should be rejected, and H_a should be accepted. The same conclusion (reject H_0) is reached by noting that α is greater than the p-value. We conclude that the mean reading level is probably higher than 9.5, although there is some risk ($p = 0.0051$) that this conclusion is not true.

9.3 ONE-SAMPLE TESTS ON μ

In this section we will discuss tests on the mean of a population, μ. In general, there are two types of tests involving μ, one in which σ is assumed to be known and the other in which σ is assumed to be unknown. In the former case the *z*-distribution is the appropriate test statistic. In the latter case the *t*-distribution is the appropriate test statistic, although the **z** is used commonly even in these cases, provided that n is large (where "large" generally means over 30). In all of our examples in Section 9.2 it was assumed that σ was known; hence we used the **z** test statistic. In this section we will present another example in which σ is known and then move to the situation in which the *t*-distribution is appropriate.

Another Example in Which σ Is Known

Example 9.3. Reconsider Example 7.4 from Section 7.6 in which a sample of 36 dormitory residents was taken to judge whether the average monthly phone charge, claimed to be \$15.30, seemed reasonable for the population of 300 dormitory phone subscribers. The standard deviation for this population was assumed to be $\sigma = \$4.10$. Let us assume that the null hypothesis is to be the simple hypothesis and that the alternative hypothesis is two-sided:

$$H_0{:}\mu = 15.30, \qquad H_a{:}\mu \neq 15.30.$$

From the central limit theorem we know that $\bar{x}$ will be approximately normal; hence, we can again use the standardized normal test statistic $z = (\bar{x} - \mu_0)/(\sigma/\sqrt{n})$, where $\mu_0 = \$15.30$, $\sigma = \$4.10$, and $n = 36$. In this case it is not completely accurate to use a standard error of $\sigma/\sqrt{n}$, since we are sampling without replacement from a *finite* population. Rather, the finite population correction factor, $\sqrt{(N - n)/(N - 1)}$, should be used. The appropriate test statistic is

$$z = \frac{(\bar{x} - \mu_0)}{\left(\dfrac{\sigma}{\sqrt{n}}\right)\sqrt{\dfrac{(N - n)}{(N - 1)}}},$$

where $N = 300$, and all other terms are known or can be obtained from the sample.

The next step is to specify the level of α and find the critical regions. However, for this example we will assume that the researcher does not know the appropriate level of significance set by the decision-maker. Hence, the researcher now proceeds directly to determine the computed value of the test statistic. Assume that a random sample of $n = 36$ yields an average monthly phone bill of $\bar{x} = \$16.90$. The calculated z value is thus:

$$z_c = \frac{\bar{x} - \mu_0}{\left(\frac{\sigma}{\sqrt{n}}\right)\sqrt{\frac{(N-n)}{(N-1)}}} = \frac{\$16.90 - 15.30}{\left(\frac{4.10}{\sqrt{36}}\right)\sqrt{\frac{264}{299}}} = 2.49.$$

The researcher can now report the following p-value:

$$2P(z \geq 2.49) = 2(1 - 0.9936) = 0.0128.$$

Expressed in words that a nonstatistician might understand more readily, this p-value means that only 1.28% of the time will one receive a sample mean as large as $16.90 when $15.30 is the true mean. This result implies that a decision-maker who has an α larger than 0.0128 should reject $H_0: \mu = \$15.30$. If the decision-maker's α is smaller than 0.0128, then he or she should accept the null hypothesis that the true mean is $15.30.

One-sample Test When σ Is Unknown   In many circumstances it is unreasonable to assume that σ is known, for when the mean μ is unknown, the population standard deviation often is unknown also (since σ is a measure based on the size of the squared deviations about μ). And when σ is unknown, the **z** test statistic should no longer be calculated.

Recall from Chapter 7 that, in order to solve problems involving $\bar{x}$ when σ is unknown, we can use the **t**-distribution if the parent population is normal. In our present context this means that if μ_0 is the value of μ specified by the null hypothesis, then when σ is unknown and the population is normal, the appropriate test statistic for tests on μ is

---

Test statistic when σ is unknown:

$$t_{(n-1)} = \frac{\bar{x} - \mu_0}{s/\sqrt{n}}. \tag{9.2}$$

Example 9.4. Suppose that a marketing advisor suggests to the Ford Motor Company that it extend its service guarantee from 12,000 miles to 24,000 miles on transmissions, muffler systems, and brakes. This advisor says the change would make good advertising copy and be relatively costless to Ford Motors because such parts seldom require service during this period anyway. The claim is that an average car will run longer than this before the cost of such repairs exceeds $100.

We will assume that Ford Motors has asked you (as their "expert" on hypothesis testing) to test this claim by sampling a few car owners and checking their service records and to give the company advice on extending its guarantee. Now, suppose that you decide to check the service record of 15 randomly selected Ford owners from a population of several million. You will let the variable x represent the number of miles driven since purchase until the cumulative service repair cost on the parts under study exceeds $100. Ford is interested in determining whether the population mean value (μ) equals 24,000 ($H_0:\mu = 24,000$) or is greater than 24,000 ($H_a:\mu > 24,000$). They use a simple null hypothesis because it is easier to work with than $\mu \leq 24,000$, and if H_0 can be rejected for the simple value 24,000, it will also be rejected for any value less than 24,000. Thus, even if the null hypothesis is $H_0:\mu \leq 24,000$, the test will involve $H_0:\mu = 24,000$. The alternative hypothesis is $H_a:\mu > 24,000$.

In this situation a Type I error occurs if Ford concludes that $\mu > 24,000$ when the null hypothesis ($\mu = 24,000$) is true. Ford might then extend the guarantee policy when it should not do so. A Type II error would occur if $H_0:\mu = 24,000$ were accepted when $\mu > 24,000$. This error might result in Ford's failure to extend the guarantee when it *could* do so.

On the basis of past experience, Ford expects the distribution of x to be normal, but they do not know its standard deviation. The appropriate test statistic has a t-distribution, $t = (\bar{x} - \mu)/(s/\sqrt{n})$. If Ford is willing to accept a risk of $\alpha = 0.025$ of incorrectly rejecting H_0, then the critical region is that 2.5% of the t-distribution that lies in the right-hand tail (since H_a is to the "right" of H_0). The boundary point for the acceptance region is found in Table VI, under the heading 0.975 or $\alpha = 0.025$. The critical t-value for a one-sided test is 2.145, as shown in Fig. 9.7.

FIGURE 9.7 **Critical region for**
$H_0: \mu = 24,000$ against
$H_a: \mu > 24,000$ when σ
is unknown and $n = 15$.

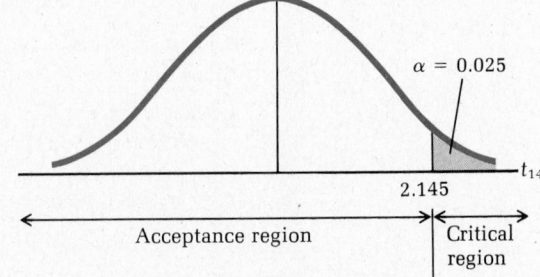

c) Would you accept H_0 or H_a if $\bar{x}$ = $24,300?

d) What p-value would you report?

9.10 You are interested in a site for a new restaurant, and a real estate developer claims that, on the average, male resident students at the university eat at least eight meals per week at establishments located more than one mile (beyond walking distance) from their residences. To test this claim, you randomly select six students, and record the number of times they ate beyond the "one-mile boundary" in one designated week; the results are 6, 5, 7, 4, 8, and 6. Construct a test, at the 0.01 significance level, assuming that σ = 1.5, and that the population is normally distributed.

9.11 An industrial firm that manufactures small battery-powered toys periodically purchases a large number of flashlight batteries for use in the toys. The policy of this company is never to accept a shipment of batteries unless it is possible to reject, at the 0.05 level of significance, the hypothesis that the batteries have a mean life of 50 or fewer hours. The standard deviation of the life of all batteries has typically been 3 hours.

a) What null and alternative hypotheses should be established to implement the company policy?

b) Should the company accept a shipment from which a sample of 64 batteries results in a mean life of 50.5 hours?

c) What is the minimum mean life that this company should accept in a sample of 64 batteries?

9.12 Under what circumstances is the t-distribution appropriate for testing hypotheses on μ?

9.13 Rework Problem 9.3 assuming that σ is unknown and that the population is normal. Calculate s from the four sample values.

9.14 The drive-in window of a First National Bank branch facility in Sarasota, Florida, averaged 24 customers per hour last year. This year the branch manager expects usage to change. Nine observations of usage were taken randomly from the first six months this year: 25, 17, 18, 22, 21, 27, 19, 15, 25.

a) Construct a test assuming that α = 0.05, and that the population is normal. What probability value would you report?

b) What p-value would you report if the manager believed that usage has declined (one-tail test)?

9.15 A power shovel was designed to remove 31.5 cubic feet of earth per scoop. On a test run, some 25 sample scoops were made; the mean of the samples was 29.3 cubic feet. The standard deviation, computed from the sample information, was three cubic feet. Test at the 99% level of confidence whether the design specifications for this equipment should be revised on the basis of the sample information. Describe the two types of error possible in this test. Assume that the population is normal.

9.16 a) The daily output of a certain department within an industrial plant is presumed to be normally distributed and has a scheduled average of 85 units. Twenty-five days are selected at random, and the output for each day is observed. The average output calculated from this sample is 81 units, and the standard deviation is 9 units. Test with 99% confidence whether or not the average output is different from that scheduled.

   b) What p-value would you report?

   c) Explain the meaning of the beta risk for this test.

9.17 A firm that packages deluxe ornamental matches for fireplace use designed a process to place 18 matches in each box. The process was started and allowed to produce 400 boxes. A sample of 16 boxes was then drawn. On the basis of this sample, the number of matches per box averaged 17, while the standard deviation calculated was 2. Would a one-sided test indicate acceptance of the null hypothesis with a mean of 18 if alpha were set at 0.05? Assume that the population is normal.

9.18 Rework Problem 9.10, assuming that σ is unknown and that the population is normal.

9.4 MEASURING β AND THE POWER OF A TEST*

One of the reasons why we have been avoiding discussion of the calculation of β is that the alternative hypothesis is generally a composite hypothesis. This means that we cannot calculate one value for β because there is no one value specified for μ that makes H_0 false. To illustrate this, we again present our test involving telephone charges, in which $H_0:\mu = 15.30$ was tested against $H_a:\mu \neq 15.30$. A Type I error (incorrectly rejecting H_0) in this case is well defined, since we know it will occur only when $\mu = \$15.30$. But a Type II error (incorrectly accepting H_0) can occur for any value of μ not equal to 15.30. It should be obvious that the probability of incorrectly accepting $H_0:\mu = \$15.30$ is much higher when the true value of μ is $\$15.00$ than when the true value of μ is $\$25.00$. In other words, the value of β is different for these two situations.

The different probability values for β that occur when H_a is composite can be presented in a table, graphed, or described by a functional relationship. Often it is more useful to present the values of $(1 - \beta)$.

---

* This section may be omitted without loss in continuity.

A function describing such probabilities is called a *power function*, since it indicates the ability (or "power") of the test to correctly reject a false null hypothesis. In general, test statistics and critical regions having the highest power are preferred. Although it is beyond the scope of this book to examine the concepts involved in finding a power function for most statistical tests, we must emphasize that the tests presented thus far have made use of these concepts in that we have always selected the *most powerful critical region*. The complexity involved in finding the power of a statistical test again emphasizes the rationale for making the null hypothesis a simple test. If H_0 were a composite hypothesis, then we would also have to use a function to describe all the values of α, or be satisfied with just a single value associated with the most conservative value of μ in H_0, as suggested in the preceding section.

Example 9.5. Consider a firm that manufactures rubber bands. Control over the number of rubber bands placed in each box is kept by sampling and testing hypotheses. When the production process is working correctly, the number (x) of good bands placed in each box has a mean of $\mu = 1000$, with a standard deviation of 37.5. This variable x is presumed to have an approximately normal distribution; that is, x is $N(1000, 37.5^2)$.

In this case the company wants to test $H_0{:}\mu = 1000$ against $H_a{:}\mu \neq 1000$, and the appropriate test statistic is $z = (\bar{x} - \mu_0)/(\sigma/\sqrt{n})$. A Type I error occurs whenever the test results suggest that the process is out of control ($\mu \neq 1000$), when it actually is in control ($\mu = 1000$). A Type II error occurs whenever the process is judged to be in control ($\mu = 1000$) and it actually is out of control ($\mu \neq 1000$). In constructing a test of these hypotheses, let us assume that the company periodically selects a random sample of size $n = 9$, and the company policy is to let $\alpha = 0.05$. For these values the critical values are

$$\mu_0 \pm z_{\alpha/2} \frac{\sigma}{\sqrt{n}} = 1000 \pm 1.96 \left(\frac{37.5}{\sqrt{9}} \right) = 1000 \pm 24.5.$$

The acceptance region shown in Fig. 9.8 is [975.5 to 1024.5].

The question we turn to now is how to calculate β for this problem. Since β is a conditional probability that depends on the value of μ, we will assume that $\mu = 990$. We can now write

$$\beta = P(\text{Accept } H_0{:}\mu_0 = 1000|\mu = 990).$$

From Fig. 9.8 we see that H_0 is accepted whenever $\bar{x}$ lies between 975.5 and 1024.5. Hence, $\beta = P(975.5 \leq \bar{x} \leq 1024.5|\mu = 990)$. This probability can be determined by using the same procedure we learned in Chapter 7 in working with $z = (\bar{x} - \mu)/(\sigma/\sqrt{n})$. First, we transform

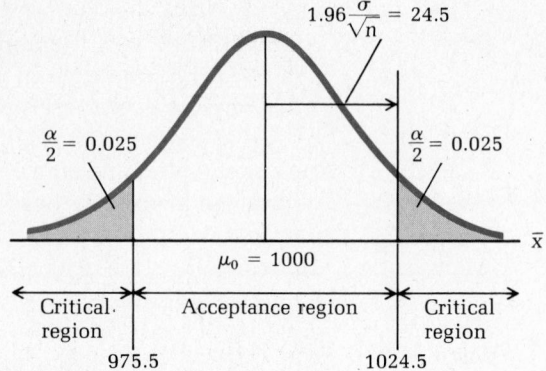

FIGURE 9.8 **Critical region for test on** H_0: $\mu = 1000$ **against** H_a: $\mu \neq 1000$, $\sigma = 37.5$, $n = 9$, and $\alpha = 0.05$.

the problem to standardized normal terms by letting $\mu = 990$, $\sigma = 37.5$, and $\sqrt{n} = \sqrt{9}$, and then we use Table III to find the appropriate probabilities.

$$P(975.5 \leq \bar{x} \leq 1024.5) = P\left(\frac{975.5 - 990}{37.5/\sqrt{9}} \leq \frac{\bar{x} - \mu}{\sigma/\sqrt{n}} \leq \frac{1024.5 - 990}{37.5/\sqrt{9}}\right)$$

$$= P(-1.16 \leq z \leq 2.76) = F(2.76) - F(-1.16)$$

$$= 0.9971 - 0.1230 = 0.8741.$$

Thus, P(Type II error) $= 0.8741$, as shown in Fig. 9.9. This means that when $\mu = 990$, we will *incorrectly* accept H_0:$\mu_0 = 1000$ as being true 87.41% of the time using our test procedure. The *power* of this test is $1 - \beta = 0.1259$, which means that this test will *correctly* recognize this false null hypothesis 12.59% of the time when $\mu = 990$.

Instead of using the value $\mu = 990$ to calculate β, we might have used $\mu = 1010$. These two values of μ are both an equal distance (10 units) away from $\mu_0 = 1000$, so it should not be surprising to learn that

FIGURE 9.9 **Probability of** β **for the critical region shown in Fig. 9.8 if the true mean is** $\mu = 990$.

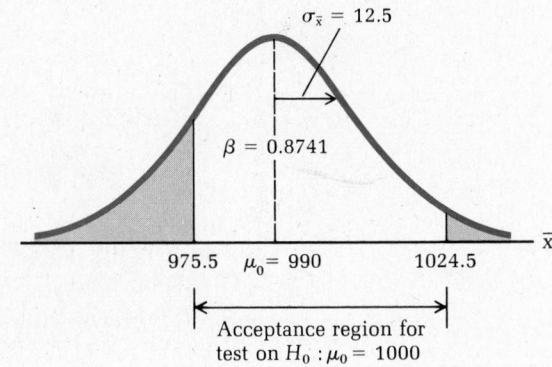

the value of β is the same in both cases (β = 0.8741). Figure 9.10(a) shows the area corresponding to β for μ = 1010, while parts (b) and (c) of this figure show the area for β corresponding to μ = 970 and μ = 950, respectively. The calculation of β when μ = 970 is shown below:

$$P(\text{Type II error}|\mu = 970) = P(975.5 \leq \bar{x} \leq 1024.5|\mu = 970)$$

$$= P\left(\frac{975.5 - 970}{37.5/\sqrt{9}} \leq z \leq \frac{1024.5 - 970}{37.5/\sqrt{9}}\right)$$

$$= P(0.44 \leq z \leq 4.36)$$

$$= F(4.36) - F(0.44) = 1.0000 - 0.6700 = 0.3300.$$

Note that in Fig. 9.10 the size of β decreases as the value of μ gets farther away from μ = 1000. That is, the more incorrect H_0 is, the easier it is to correctly reject it [hence, the higher $(1 - β)$]. This fact is shown in Table 9.1, where we present the value of β and $(1 - β)$ for eight different values of μ. The row corresponding to μ = 1000 is placed in a box to emphasize that this is the one case in which H_0 is true; hence, β is not defined for μ = 1000. Figure 9.11 (on p. 461) is a graph of the power function $(1 - β)$.

In comparing the power functions of a number of different tests, we look for tests where the power function rises quickly as the value of μ differs by small amounts from $μ_0$. The most powerful test would be the one with the steepest ascending power function. In other words, we desire a test such that the probability of recognizing a false null hypothesis increases rapidly, even for rather small differences between the hypothesized value of the parameter and the true value.

The Trade-offs Between α and β We have emphasized that when the sample size is fixed, α and β have an inverse relationship. To illustrate this trade-off, we will use the same production-process example described above, but we now will change α from 0.05 to 0.10. Since α has increased, the acceptance region has become smaller.

The effect of the increase of α should be a reduction of β. Figure 9.12 (on p. 462) shows the new acceptance region, calculated by letting $z_{α/2}$ = $z_{0.05}$ = 1.645. In this situation the null hypothesis is accepted if 979.44 ≤ $\bar{x}$ ≤ 1020.56. The result is that the size of β is reduced from 0.3300 (shown in Table 9.1) to the new value, β = 0.2236. The power of the test has increased correspondingly. These values are shown in Fig. 9.12.

If we calculated additional values of the power function, we would find all of them larger when α = 0.10 than when α = 0.05. As we increase α, we narrow the acceptance region and hence make our test more powerful. Similarly, if we decrease the value of α, then the acceptance region gets larger, β will rise, and the power of the test will drop. Thus, the size of α is related inversely to the size of β and directly to the size

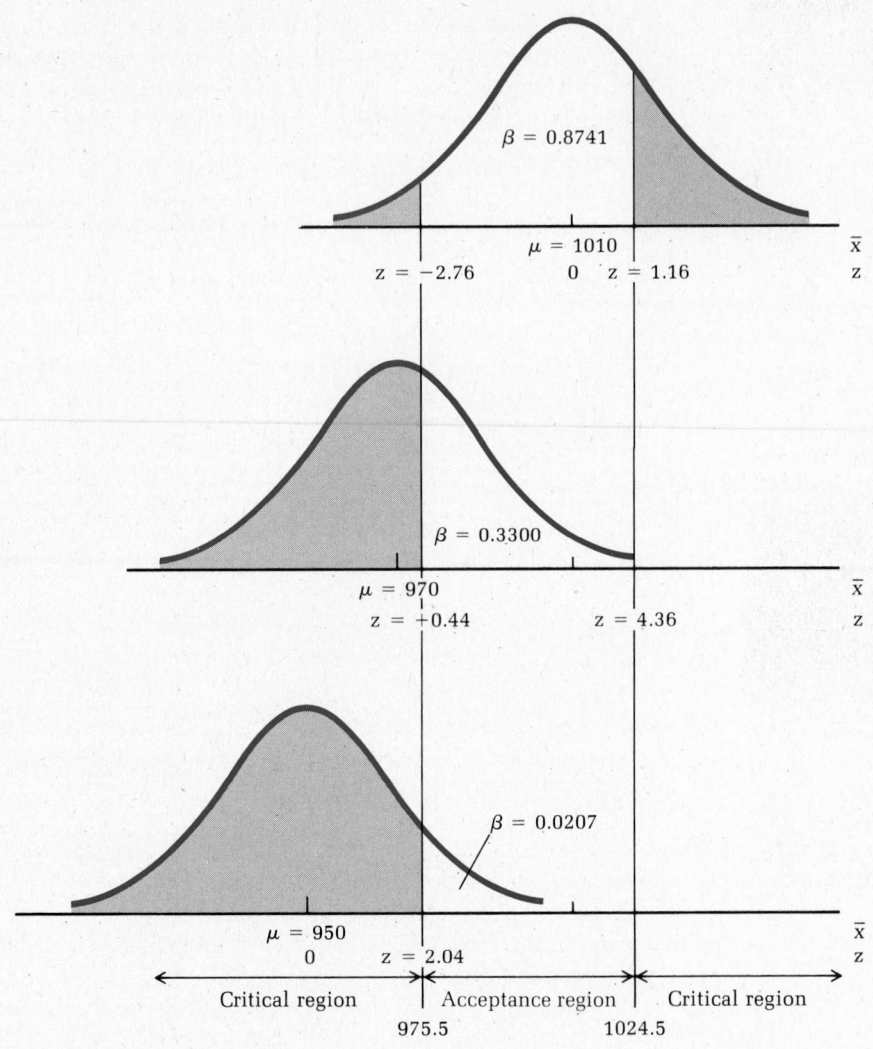

FIGURE 9.10 **Values of β for different μ's, α = 0.05, n = 9, σ = 37.5.**

of the power, but the trade-off is not one-to-one. In this example, α was increased by 0.05 (0.05 to 0.10), but β decreased by more than 0.10 (0.3300 to 0.2236).

Decreasing α and β by Increasing n   Until now our discussion has been based on the assumption that the size of the sample is fixed in advance. If *n* is changed, however, the size of both α and β may be changed because the size of *n* affects the location

TABLE 9.1 Value of β and power for given true values of μ

μ	P(Accept H_0) = β	P(Reject H_0) = Power = 1 − β
950	0.0207	0.9793
970	0.3300	0.6700
980	0.6406	0.3594
990	0.8741	0.1259
1000 .	1 − α = 0.95	α = 0.05
1010	0.8741	0.1259
1020	0.6406	0.3594
1030	0.3300	0.6700
1050	0.0207	0.9793

of the acceptance and critical regions. To illustrate this effect, suppose we return α to its previous level of 0.05 and increase n from 9 to 36. The new critical region for our test, and the determination of β when the true value of μ is 970, are shown in Fig. 9.13.

We see that the increased sample size makes our test more sensitive in distinguishing between H_0 and H_a because the standard error of the mean, $\sigma/\sqrt{n}$, is now half its former value (changing from $37.5/\sqrt{9} = 12.5$ to $37.5/\sqrt{36} = 6.25$). The null hypothesis will be accepted in this test if $987.75 < \bar{x} \le 1012.25$. The probability that H_0 will be accepted given that $\mu = 970$ is now only $\beta = 0.0023$. By comparing Figs. 9.12 and 9.13 we see that we have reduced α from 0.10 to 0.05 and reduced β from

FIGURE 9.11 Graph of the power function.

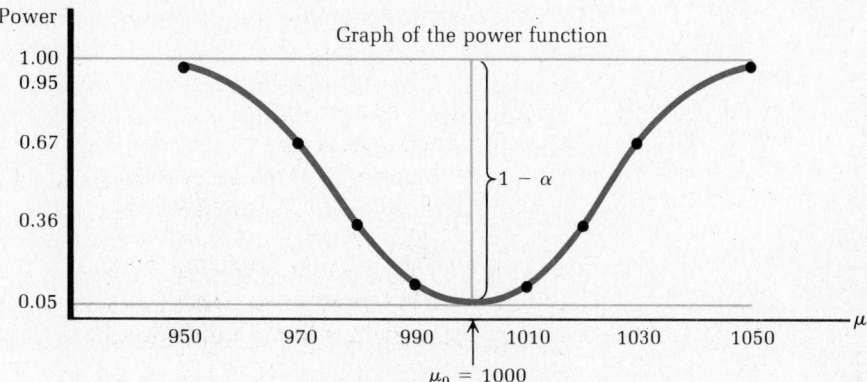

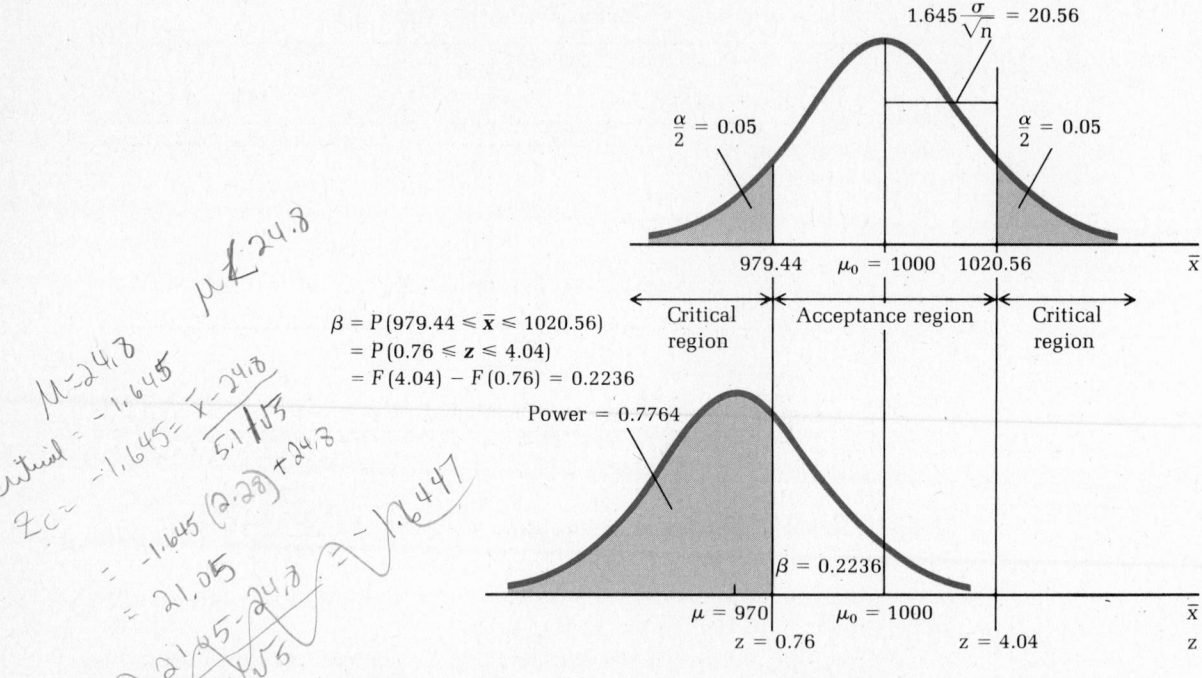

$\beta = P(979.44 \le \overline{x} \le 1020.56)$
$= P(0.76 \le z \le 4.04)$
$= F(4.04) - F(0.76) = 0.2236$

Power = 0.7764

FIGURE 9.12 **Critical region for $H_0 : \mu_0 = 1000$ vs. $H_a : \mu_0 \ne 1000$ given $\sigma = 37.5$, $n = 9$, $\alpha = 0.10$; and the representation of β given that is $\mu = 970$.**

0.2236 to 0.0023 merely by increasing n from 9 to 36. Unfortunately, obtaining larger samples is more time-consuming and is often quite costly, so the researcher is faced with the task of balancing the costs of making incorrect decisions against the costs of sampling. We will return to this consideration in Section 9.6 and in Chapter 11.

Study Question 9.3: Simulation Run-time on a Computer

The systems department of Stanfield Oil Company typically runs a number of large simulation programs on their mainframe computer. The largest of these simulations takes an average of 24.8 minutes of running time, with $\sigma = 5.1$. A manufacturer of a new simulation software package claims that their program will run this simulation at least 20% faster, on the average. You decide to test $H_0 : \mu = 24.80$ versus $H_a : \mu < 24.80$ by using a sample of size $n = 5$ and $\alpha = 0.05$. What is β if the true value of $\mu = 19.50$ and $\sigma = 5.1$?

Answer. The critical value (a) when $\alpha = 0.05$ is derived at the top of page 463.

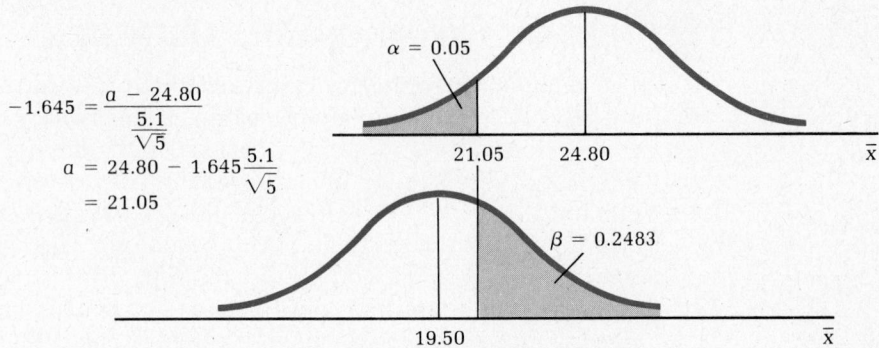

$$-1.645 = \frac{a - 24.80}{\frac{5.1}{\sqrt{5}}}$$

$$a = 24.80 - 1.645\frac{5.1}{\sqrt{5}}$$

$$= 21.05$$

Although H_a is one-sided in this problem, the process of finding β is the same as for a two-sided test — namely, we find the area in the acceptance region, assuming H_a is true. Hence,

$$\beta = P(\bar{x} \geq 21.05 | \mu = 19.50) = P\left(\frac{\bar{x} - \mu}{\sigma/\sqrt{n}} \geq \frac{21.05 - 19.50}{5.1/\sqrt{5}}\right)$$

$$= P(z \geq 0.68) = 0.2483.$$

FIGURE 9.13 **Critical region for the test on H_0: $\mu_0 = 1000$ vs. H_a: $\mu_0 \neq 1000$, $\sigma = 37.5$, $n = 36$, $\alpha = 0.05$; and the representation of β when $\mu = 970$.**

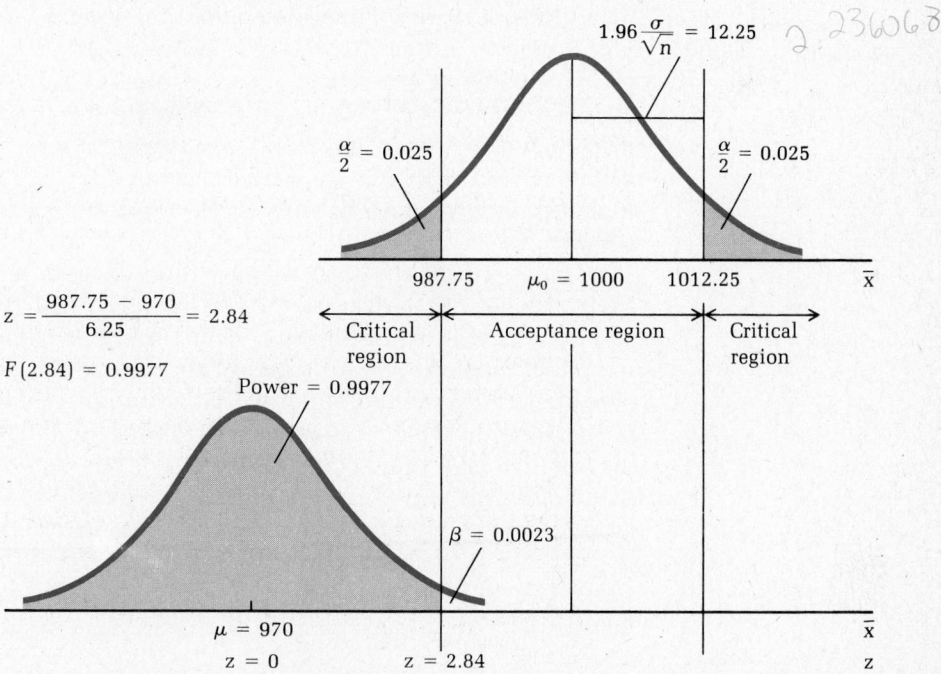

9.5 TEST ON THE BINOMIAL PARAMETER

The population parameter being examined in a test of hypothesis need not always be the population mean μ. In many situations the parameter in question is the *proportion* of observations having a certain attribute. When the observations are independent of one another (i.e., they are randomly selected with replacement) and the attribute of interest either occurs or does not occur in each observation, then the appropriate test statistic follows the *binomial distribution*. A test involving an unknown binomial proportion π may be one-sided or two-sided, and the values for π may range from zero to one. For example, suppose the null hypothesis is

$$H_0 : \pi = \tfrac{1}{2}.$$

This hypothesis may be tested against the two-sided alternative $H_a : \pi \neq \tfrac{1}{2}$, or perhaps against either of the following one-sided alternative hypotheses: $H_a : \pi < \tfrac{1}{2}$ or $H_a : \pi > \tfrac{1}{2}$. As we will demonstrate below, hypotheses involving the binomial parameter π can be tested either by using Table I in Appendix C or by using the normal approximation to the binomial.

Binomial Tests Using Table I

Recall from Chapter 7 that the best estimator of a binomial proportion π is the sample proportion $p = x/n$. If the value of n used in making this estimate is one of the values of n presented in Table I in Appendix C (or available from some other source), then we can test hypotheses about π directly (i.e., without using a normal approximation). The only substantive difference between this approach and our previous tests involving μ is that now we are dealing with a discrete rather than a continuous test statistic.

The one difficulty in working with a discrete test statistic comes in Step 3, where it is necessary to define a critical region cutting off an area of size α. Unfortunately, when discrete probability spikes are involved, there may be no critical value(s) cutting off an amount exactly equal to α. For example, suppose that we are searching for a critical value of the variable x that cuts off exactly 5% of the binomial distribution. It may be that one value of x cuts off 6% of the distribution, and the next value of x cuts off 4%. In these cases the usual procedure is to pick the critical region cutting off the *smaller* area, in order to ensure that the probability of a Type I error is no larger than α. This procedure is equivalent to finding the *extreme value* of x that satisfies the following inequality:

> Procedure for finding the critical region in a binomial problem:
>
> For upper-sided test: $P(x \text{ or more successes}) \leq \alpha$
> For lower-sided test: $P(x \text{ or fewer successes}) \leq \alpha$ **(9.3)**
> For two-sided test: $P(x \text{ or more successes}) \leq \alpha/2$

Example 9.6. Consider again the production example presented in Section 5.4. Recall that in this example a quality-control engineer is going to sample 20 items from a malfunctioning production process to determine whether to accept $H_0 : \pi = 0.10$ (a minor adjustment) or to accept $H_a : \pi = 0.25$ (a major adjustment). Since the alternative hypothesis includes values of π on only one side of the value stated in $H_0 : \pi = 0.10$, we need to establish a single critical region that will cut off a probability of α in the *upper* tail of the binomial distribution (the upper tail is used because 0.25 is larger than the null hypothesis value of 0.10). The appropriate binomial distribution in this case has $n = 20$ and $\pi = 0.10$ (representing the null hypothesis).

Let us assume that α has been set at 0.05 for the problem described above. This means that we want to find the value of x in Table I, under $n = 20$ and $\pi = 0.10$, such that the probability that the true parameter is larger than this value is no greater than 0.05. Looking in Table I, we see that $P(x \geq 9) = 0.0001$. Similarly, $P(x \geq 8) = 0.0005$. Continuing in this fashion, we can calculate that $P(x \geq 5) = 0.0433$. Thus, if our critical value is $x = 5$, the critical region cut off is of size 0.0433. The next value, $x = 4$, cuts off a critical region of size $0.0433 + 0.0898 = 0.1331$, which is too large. Hence, to ensure an α *no larger* than 0.05, $x \geq 5$ is the appropriate critical region. Any sample that results in five or more successes in the 20 trials leads to acceptance of $H_a : \pi = 0.25$. A sample with four or fewer defectives leads to acceptance of $H_0 : \pi = 0.10$. The critical and acceptance regions for this problem are shown in Fig. 9.14(a).

In this example, calculation of the value of β is fairly straightforward, since H_a is a simple alternative hypothesis. Recall that β is the probability that the test statistic falls in the acceptance region when H_a is true. For our problem the acceptance region is $x \leq 4$, and the alternative hypothesis is $H_a : \pi = 0.25$. Hence,

$$\beta = P(x \leq 4 | \pi = 0.25 \text{ and } n = 20)$$
$$= 0.4148 \quad \text{from Table I, as shown in Fig. 9.14(b).}$$

The quality-control engineer thus runs a 41.48% chance of accepting H_0 and making a minor adjustment when H_0 is false and a major adjustment

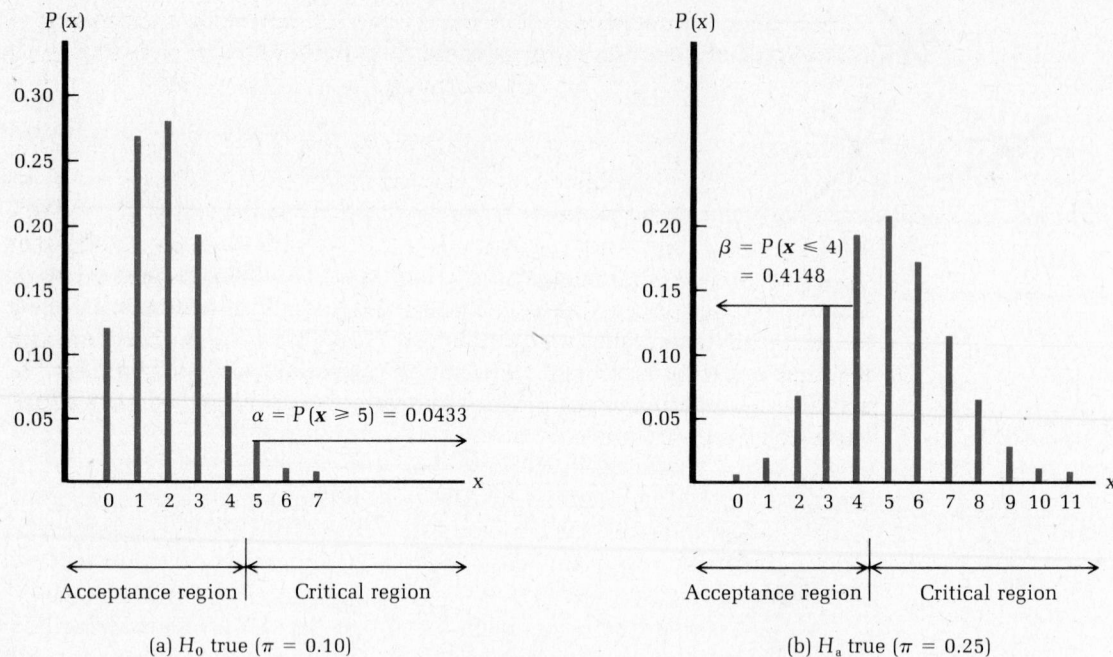

(a) H_0 true ($\pi = 0.10$)

(b) H_a true ($\pi = 0.25$)

FIGURE 9.14 **Critical and acceptance regions for testing H_0: $\pi = 0.10$ versus H_a: $\pi = 0.25$.**

is needed. This β-value is quite large in relation to $\alpha = 0.05$. In Section 9.6 we will discuss how one might go about achieving a balance between α and β by considering the costs of making both Type I and Type II errors.

In the above discussion we assumed that α was known in advance. If it is not possible or desirable to specify α in advance, Table I can also be used to report probability values. For example, suppose that α is not given in the quality-control problem described above, but we know that the sample of $n = 20$ resulted in $x = 6$ defectives. The p-value to be reported is the probability of six *or more** defectives in 20 trials when $\pi = 0.10$ (the null hypothesis):

$$P(x \geq 6 | \pi = 0.10 \text{ and } n = 20) = 0.0114 \qquad \text{(from Table I)}.$$

---

* We must emphasize here that the reported p-value is always the probability of an event that involves a *range* of values and not just a single number. Hence, in this case the probability of six *or more* successes is appropriate. When a p-value is calculated, the range of values used always extends in the same direction as the critical region. Thus, from Fig. 9.14(a) we see that the critical region extends upward in the right-hand tail, so $x \geq 6$ is the correct direction (and $x \leq 6$ is the incorrect direction).

In this case the decision-maker would have to determine whether $p = 0.0114$ is small enough to reject the null hypothesis $H_0: \pi = 0.10$, or if it is large enough to comfortably accept H_0.

Using the Normal Approximation When *n* Is Large
Recall that it is not always convenient to work with binomial tables directly, because the arithmetic may be tedious, or tables may not be available for certain values of π. Fortunately, when the value of n is large and the value of π is not close to either zero or one, then the hypotheses about the binomial parameter π may be tested by using the standardized normal distribution as the appropriate test statistic. An often-used rule of thumb is to assume that the standardized normal approximation can be used when $n\pi(1 - \pi) \geq 3$, where π is the value specified under H_0, and n is the sample size. Letting π_0 represent the null hypothesis value, the appropriate test statistic is:

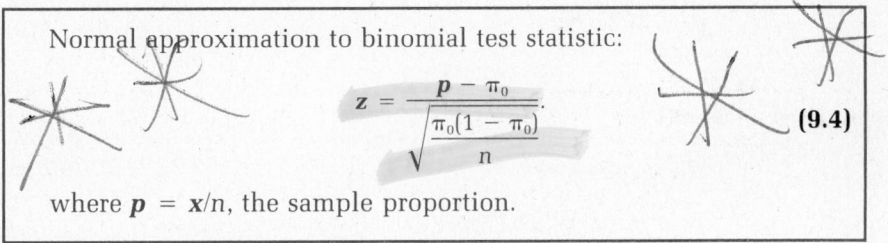

Normal approximation to binomial test statistic:

$$z = \frac{p - \pi_0}{\sqrt{\dfrac{\pi_0(1 - \pi_0)}{n}}}. \qquad (9.4)$$

where $p = x/n$, the sample proportion.

This standardization is exactly like the one described in Section 6.6, Formula (6.8).

Example 9.7. During the 1984 Presidential election campaign, President Reagan wanted an advance indication of whether or not a majority of the general electorate supported his stand on the Equal Rights Amendment (ERA). The hypotheses in this case could have been $H_0: \pi \geq 0.50$ versus $H_a: \pi < 0.50$, where π is the proportion of the electorate supporting Reagan's position. However, recall that composite null hypotheses are somewhat more difficult to work with than simple null hypotheses. Making H_0 simple in this example is quite reasonable, as the concern is whether or not the proportion in favor of the proposal is less than 0.50. Hence, the appropriate hypotheses are

$$H_0: \pi = 0.50 \quad \text{versus} \quad H_a: \pi < 0.50.$$

This change in H_0 does not weaken our test; it only means that an extreme position is taken for H_0. If $\pi_0 = 0.50$ is rejected in favor of $\pi < 0.50$, we are even more confident that other possible values of π, such as $\pi = 0.55$ or $\pi = 0.60$, would similarly be rejected.

Let us assume also that α is specified as 0.01 and that a random sample of 1000 voters is taken. Since $n\pi_0(1 - \pi_0) = 1000(0.50)(0.50) = 250 > 3$, a normal approximation should be quite good. The appropriate normal critical value can be computed by determining from Table III that $z_{0.01} = 2.33$. Since H_a is to the *left* of H_0, we use $-z = -2.33$ in Formula (9.4) in order to solve for the critical value of $p = x/n$:

$$z = \frac{p - \pi_0}{\sqrt{\dfrac{\pi_0(1 - \pi_0)}{n}}},$$

$$-2.33 = \frac{p - 0.50}{\sqrt{\dfrac{(0.50)(0.50)}{1000}}}.$$

Thus,

$$p = 0.50 - 2.33\sqrt{\frac{(0.50)(0.50)}{1000}} = 0.4632.$$

The critical value for p is 0.4632. If desired, this equation could have been solved for x instead of p, since n is known to be 1000. In this case the result would have been $x = 463.2$. Both critical values are shown in Fig. 9.15.

The reader may wonder if a correction for continuity is needed in Formula (9.4) before solving the last problem. The answer is no, because we were not using Formula (9.4) to approximate a *specific* binomial probability. Rather, we were using (9.4) to find the appropriate critical value for p as well as for x.

Now suppose we change our objective somewhat and assume that a sample has been taken and we wish to find z_c. When using the normal

FIGURE 9.15 **Standardized normal approximation to the binomial test statistic.**

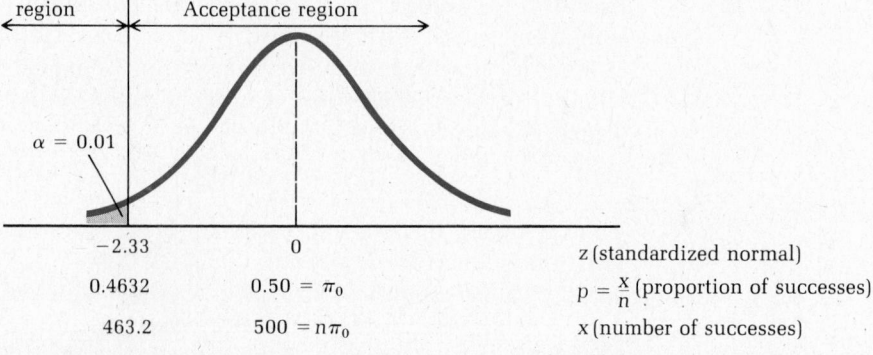

distribution to approximate a specific binomial probability, the correction for continuity should be used for exactness. However, if n is large and π is not close to either 0 or 1.0, the change in the results is not great. In all such problems in this chapter, the reader may presume that the gain in exactness is negligible and would not change the conclusion of the decision-maker.

Completing Example 9.7, 450 out of the 1000 voters surveyed indicated they supported the ERA stand of President Reagan. That is, $x = 450$ and $p = x/n = 450/1000 = 0.45$. This result is clearly in the critical region shown in Fig. 9.15; hence, we reject $H_0:\pi = 0.50$ in favor of $H_a:\pi < 0.50$.

A calculated value of z for this result is

$$z_c = \frac{p - \pi_0}{\sqrt{\dfrac{\pi_0(1 - \pi_0)}{n}}} = \frac{0.45 - 0.50}{\sqrt{\dfrac{(0.50)(0.50)}{1000}}} = -3.16.$$

The reported p-value is thus

$$P(\mathbf{z} \le z_c) = P(\mathbf{z} \le -3.16) = 1 - 0.9992 = 0.0008.$$

We conclude that less than 50% of the voters supported the ERA stand of President Reagan. We admit a risk of 0.08% that this conclusion is wrong.

Study Question 9.4: A Survey to Determine Soup Preference
The fast-food chain RAX is considering substituting Campbell's soup for its own home-made variety (which is more expensive to make). The substitution will be made if RAX is convinced that more than 40% of their soup customers are indifferent or prefer Campbell's soup. A sample of 150 randomly selected soup customers was asked to taste both types (unlabeled) and to indicate their preference (or indifference). Seventy of these people were indifferent or picked Campbell's soup (i.e., $x = 70$). Formulate the appropriate hypotheses and report a p-value. Would you accept H_0 or H_a if $\alpha = 0.05$?

Answer
1. *Establish H_0 and H_a:* $H_0:\pi \le 0.40$ versus $H_a:\pi > 0.40$.
2. *Determine the test statistic:* Since $n\pi_0(1 - \pi_0) = 150(0.4)(0.6) = 36 > 3$, a normal approximation is used.

$$z = \frac{p - \pi_0}{\sqrt{\dfrac{\pi_0(1 - \pi_0)}{n}}}.$$

3. *Determine the critical value:* $z_{0.05} = 1.96$.

4. *Calculate a test statistic value and report a p-value:* Since $p = 70/150 = 0.467$ and $\pi_0 = 0.40$,

$$z_c = \frac{0.467 - 0.40}{\sqrt{\dfrac{0.40(0.60)}{150}}} = 1.67.$$

p-value $= P(z \geq 1.67) = 0.0475.$

5. *Decision and conclusion:* Reject H_0 and accept H_a, since $\alpha \, (= 0.05)$ is greater than the p-value $(= 0.0475)$. Switch to Campbell's soup, although we admit a risk of 4.75% that less than 40% might be indifferent or prefer the Campbell soup.

9.6   BALANCING THE RISKS AND COSTS OF MAKING A WRONG DECISION

We now return to the important problem of how to choose the "best" critical region to weigh the risks and costs associated with making a Type I error against those associated with making a Type II error. As we pointed out in Chapter 7, the objective of sampling can be stated as one of balancing the costs of making an incorrect decision (including sampling costs, which will be considered later). Unfortunately, in many circumstances there may be no easy way even to determine what these costs are, much less to try to balance them. In medical research, for example, it may be difficult if not impossible to assess the costs associated with an incorrect decision involving a new drug or surgical technique. But even if these costs could somehow be assessed, how does one go about balancing costs that may include pain, suffering, and even loss of life? On the other hand, if it is possible to identify the relevant costs and to express them in terms of some comparable basis, such as dollars, then we may be able to balance these costs quite explicitly. The following example describes how to find the critical region by using a process that minimizes the expected cost of making an incorrect decision.

    Example 9.8. Return to the quality-control problem of Section 9.5. It should be noted that, for the first part of this example, we assume that the sample size is fixed at $n = 20$; later we change this assumption and consider a sample of size $n = 50$. Suppose that all the possible costs associated with an incorrect decision (e.g., losses in profit, goodwill) are those shown in Fig. 9.16. A correct decision is assumed to result in no loss in profit or goodwill.

    We can calculate for each possible critical region the expected cost (per sample of 20) that will result if the process is producing defectives

Proportion defectives

		$\pi = 0.10$ H_0 is true	$\pi = 0.25$ H_0 is false
Decision	Accept H_0 make minor adjustment	Correct decision	$200
	Reject H_0 make major adjustment	$500	Correct decision

FIGURE 9.16 **Costs of making an incorrect decision.**

(1) at a rate of 10% or (2) at a rate of 25%. These expected costs are calculated by multiplying the probability of making each type of error by the cost of making that error. We have calculated these values for two critical regions: the value $x \geq 5$ used in Fig. 9.14 and an alternative one, $x \geq 4$, which gives a smaller β at the expense of a larger α.

1. *Critical region $x \geq 4$ ($\alpha = 0.1331$ and $\beta = 0.2251$)**
   a. For $\pi = 0.10$:
      Expected cost = P(Type I error) $\times$ Cost of a Type I error
      $= 0.1331(\$500) = \$66.55.$
   b. For $\pi = 0.25$:
      Expected cost = P(Type II error) $\times$ Cost of a Type II error
      $= 0.2251(\$200) = \$45.02.$
2. *Critical region $x \geq 5$ ($\alpha = 0.0433$ and $\beta = 0.4148$)*
   a. For $\pi = 0.10$:
      Expected cost = P(Type I error) $\times$ Cost of a Type I error
      $= 0.0433(\$500) = \$21.65.$
   b. For $\pi = 0.25$:
      Expected cost = P(Type II error) $\times$ Cost of a Type II error
      $= 0.4148(\$200) = \$82.96.$

The expected costs given above are conditional values, in that each one was calculated on the assumption that either $\pi = 0.10$ or $\pi = 0.25$. In order to determine which of these critical regions is better, we need to know how often the process is expected to produce defectives at a rate of 10%, relative to the number of times it will be producing defectives at a rate of 25%. Suppose that, if an adjustment is required, the probability that it will be a minor adjustment is 0.70, while the probability that it will be a major adjustment is 0.30. The *total* expected costs associated with each of the two critical regions can now be calculated by taking the

---

* These probabilities were given in Table 5.2 of Chapter 5. They can also be calculated from Table I using $n = 20$, $\pi = 0.10$.

product of the expected costs determined above multiplied by the probability that each of these costs will be incurred.

1. *Critical region* x ≥ 4:
   Total expected cost
   = P(Major adjustment needed) × Expected cost of Type II error
   + P(Minor adjustment needed) × Expected cost of Type I error
   = 0.30($45.02) + 0.70($66.55)
   = $60.09.
2. *Critical region* x ≥ 5:
   Total expected cost
   = P(Major adjustment needed) × Expected cost of Type II error
   + P(Minor adjustment needed) × Expected cost of Type I error
   = 0.30($82.96) + 0.70($21.65)
   = $40.04.

Thus, when the process is malfunctioning, the total expected cost for each sample of 20 equals $60.09 if the critical region is x ≥ 4 and $40.04 if the critical region is x ≥ 5. In Problem 9.23 we ask the reader to determine that x ≥ 5 is, in fact, the *optimal* critical region for this problem, with total expected cost smaller than any other critical region.

Changing the Sample Size

Suppose that the size of the above sample could have been increased to n = 50 at a cost of $10. Our discussion of trade-offs between α, β, and n in Section 9.4 suggests that this increase in sample size can lead to a decrease in both α and β if an appropriate critical region is used. The question is whether or not the decreased probability of making an error is worth the increased sampling costs of $10. In order to answer this question, let us select a critical region for the new situation (with n = 50) and then determine α, β and the total expected cost for this critical region. This total expected cost can then be compared to the preceding optimal cost of $40.04.

Since n has increased 2.5 times from 20 to 50, let us arbitrarily try a new critical value that is 2.5 times greater than the initial one (x = 4); that is, x = 10. We leave it as an exercise for the reader to determine if a better critical region than x ≥ 10 could be found, perhaps x ≥ 12 or x ≥ 13 (which are approximately 2.5 times the previous optimal value of x = 5). The probability of observing a specific number of defectives when n = 50 under the two hypotheses, H_0:π = 0.10 and H_a:π = 0.25, is shown in Table 9.2. The probabilities of Type I and Type II errors are seen to be α = 0.0245 and β = 0.1636. Thus, we see that increasing n from 20 to 50 has reduced both α and β.

TABLE 9.2 Determining α and β when $n = 50$ and the critical region is $x \geq 10$

x	Decision	If $\pi = 0.10$, H_0 Is True $P(x) = {}_{50}C_x(0.10)^x(0.90)^{50-x}$		If $\pi = 0.25$, H_a Is True $P(x) = {}_{50}C_x(0.25)^x(0.75)^{50-x}$
0		0.0052		0.0000
1		0.0286		0.0000
2	Accept H_0, make minor adjustment	0.0779		0.0001
.		.	Acceptance region $\beta = 0.1636$	.
.		.		.
.		.		.
8		0.0643		0.0463
9		0.0333		0.0721
10		0.0152		0.0985
11		0.0061		0.1194
12		0.0022		0.1294
.	Reject H_0, make major adjustment	.	$\alpha = 0.0245$ Critical region	.
.		.		.
.		.		.
24		0.0000		0.0002
25		0.0000		0.0001
26–50		0.0000		0.0000
Sum		1.0000		1.0000

Critical region $x \geq 10$ ($\alpha = 0.0245$ and $\beta = 0.1636$)

1. For $p = 0.10$:

   Expected cost = P(Type I error) $\times$ Cost of a Type I error
   $= 0.0245(\$500) = \$12.25$.

2. For $p = 0.25$:

   Expected cost = P(Type II error) $\times$ Cost of a Type II error
   $= 0.1636(\$200) = \$32.72$.

   Total expected cost
   $= P$(Major adjustment needed) $\times$ Expected cost of an error
   $+ P$(Minor adjustment needed) $\times$ Expected cost of an error
   $= 0.30(32.72) + 0.70(12.25) = \$18.39$.

Thus, if we have to choose between a sample of 20 and critical region $x \geq 5$ (with $\alpha = 0.0433$ and $\beta = 0.4148$) in which the costs will average $40.04 and a sample of 50 and critical region $x \geq 10$ (with $\alpha = 0.0245$ and $\beta = 0.1636$) in which the costs will average $18.39 for the incorrect decisions plus $10.00 for the additional observations, it is better to take the larger sample. It may be, of course, that some other critical region will be even better than $x \geq 10$ or that some other sample size gives a lower expected cost. Given information on the cost of all possible sample sizes, the "optimal" sample size and its associated critical region could be determined for this problem. In Chapter 16 we shall return to an extended version of this type of problem and study in more detail the question of sample size.

9.7 ONE-SAMPLE TEST ON σ^2*

Once the procedure for testing hypotheses has been mastered, it can be applied to many other test situations if an appropriate test statistic can be developed. In this section, an example of a test is given, which utilizes a test statistic with a chi-square distribution. Table VII, which defines values of the cumulative chi-square distribution, is used to determine the critical region for this test.

Test on a Population Variance, σ^2

In Section 7.9 we formulated a chi-square random variable,

$$\chi^2_{(n-1)} = \frac{(n-1)s^2}{\sigma^2},$$

for a situation in which a random sample of size n is taken from a normal population with standard deviation σ^2. In Section 8.8 a confidence interval for σ^2 was developed using this variable. We now illustrate the use of the χ^2 variable in testing hypotheses about the unknown population variance σ^2, based on a sample estimator s^2.

Example 9.9. You are considering investing in a franchise for Southern Fried Chicken. So far, you have learned that the monthly profits from such franchises is normally distributed with a mean of $9200. What concerns you now is the variability in monthly profits, as this variability is a measure of the risk that you are assuming. You have decided that if the standard deviation of profits is $800 or more, you do not want to invest. From a statistical point of view we do not test hypotheses about standard deviations, but rather about variances. Therefore, you clarify your position by stating that you will not invest unless we can reject the hypothesis that σ^2 is $800^2 = 640,000$ or more in favor of the hypothesis that σ^2 is less than 640,000. There are several ways in which we could

---

* This section may be omitted without loss of continuity. It is assumed that the reader has covered Section 7.9.

structure the hypotheses in this problem. Perhaps the most convenient is to make H_0 a *simple* hypothesis by taking the most extreme (lowest) value that would cause you not to invest (that is, $\sigma^2 = 640,000$); thus,

$$H_0:\sigma^2 = 640,000.$$

The alternative hypothesis would be the following:

$$H_a:\sigma^2 \lessgtr 640,000.$$

Thus, if H_0 is accepted, you should not invest; if H_a is accepted, you should invest.

For this type of problem the following chi-square test statistic is appropriate.

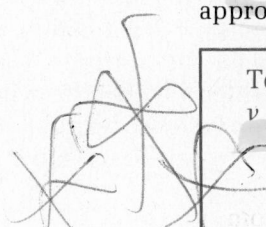

> Test statistic for hypotheses about a population variance for $v = (n - 1)$ d.f.:
>
> $$\chi^2_{(n-1)} = \frac{(n - 1)s^2}{\sigma_0{}^2}. \tag{9.5}$$

In Formula (9.5), $\sigma_0{}^2$ is the hypothesized value of σ^2 when H_0 is true, and s^2 is the sample estimator of the variance based on the random sample of size n.

The next step is to construct the critical region for this test of hypotheses. Since our alternative hypothesis is one-sided to the left of H_0, the appropriate critical region is that $\alpha \times 100$ percent of the values in the left-hand tail of the chi-square distribution. For example, suppose that you decide on a sample of size $n = 12$ (chosen randomly among a set of franchises) and that you set $\alpha = 0.05$. From Table VII the critical value for $v = 11$ is $\chi^2_{11} = 4.57$. The critical region for this example is thus all values of χ^2 less than 4.57, as shown in Fig. 9.17.

Suppose that your sample of $n = 12$ monthly profits yields a sample variance equal to $s^2 = 360,000$. The **computed value of chi-square** is

$$\chi_c{}^2 = \frac{(n - 1)s^2}{\sigma^2} = \frac{11(360,000)}{640,000} = 6.19.$$

The sample result thus falls in the acceptance region. This means that even though the sample variance is much less than the hypothesized value for the population variance, it is not sufficiently smaller for us to reject H_0. Hence, we are wary of an investment in Southern Fried Chicken because it is sufficiently likely that the variance of monthly profits may be as large as 640,000.

The reader should note that, while the standard deviation may be the more easily interpreted measure of risk or variability, the χ^2 test deals with the square of σ, the variance. Similar tests on σ^2 in other situations may be one-sided upper-tail tests or two-sided tests. All of these tests, however, follow the same general procedure. The test statistics and test situations described in this chapter are summarized in Table 9.3.

Study Question 9.5: A Study of the Variance in Gas Mileage

General Motors has developed a new fuel-efficient automobile engine and has already determined average gas mileage estimates for highway driving. Assume that G.M. is now interested in testing hypotheses about the *variability* in MPG (miles per gallon) for the new engine relative to the old one. The engineers are unsure if variability will increase or decrease. The variance of MPG for the previous engine was $\sigma^2 = 3.9$ (MPG squared). In a test of highway driving with a sample of nine of the new engines, the sample variance was $s^2 = 5.1$. Formulate appropriate hypotheses and report a p-value. Would you accept H_0 or H_a if $\alpha = 0.025$?

Answer

1. *Establish the hypotheses:* $H_0: \sigma^2 = 3.9$ versus $H_a: \sigma^2 \neq 3.9$.
2. *Determine the test statistic:*

$$\chi^2 = \frac{(n-1)s^2}{\sigma^2}.$$

FIGURE 9.17 **Critical region for a one-sided chi-square test with $\nu = n - 1 = 11$ and $\alpha = 0.05$.**

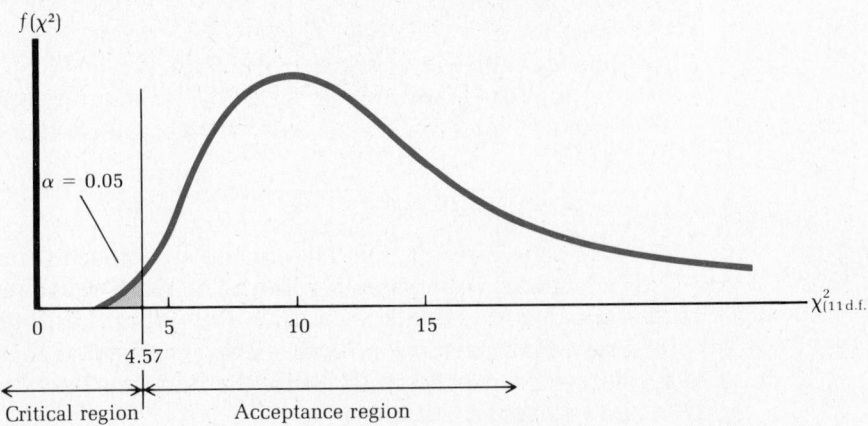

TABLE 9.3 **Summary of one-sample test statistics**

Unknown Parameter	Population Characteristics and Other Description	Reference Section	Test Statistic
Mean μ	Population $N(\mu, \sigma^2)$ σ known	9.2 8.4 7.5	$z = \dfrac{(\bar{x} - \mu_0)}{\dfrac{\sigma}{\sqrt{n}}}$
Mean μ	Population $N(\mu, \sigma^2)$ σ unknown	9.3 8.5 7.8	$t_\nu = \dfrac{(\bar{x} - \mu_0)}{\dfrac{s}{\sqrt{n}}}$ where $\nu = n - 1$
Proportion π	Repeated independent trials $n\pi_0(1 - \pi_0) \geq 3$	9.5 8.6 6.6 5.4	$z = \dfrac{p - \pi_0}{\sqrt{\dfrac{\pi_0(1 - \pi_0)}{n}}}$
Variance σ^2	Population $N(\mu, \sigma^2)$	9.7 8.8 7.9	$\chi_\nu^2 = \dfrac{(n - 1)s^2}{\sigma_0{}^2}$ where $\nu = n - 1$

3. *Determine the critical region:* $\chi^2 \leq 2.18$ and $\chi^2 \geq 17.5$
4. *Calculate a test statistic value and report a p-value:*

$$\chi_c^2 = \frac{(8)(5.1)}{3.9} = 10.46.$$

$2P(\chi^2 \geq 10.46) > 0.20$ (from Table VII, $\nu = 8$, after doubling).

5. *Decision and conclusion:* Do not reject H_0 because α is less than the p-value. The variance from the sample of new engines is not different enough from the previous variance to conclude that the variability in MPG has changed.

PROBLEMS

9.19 Reconsider Problem 9.2, assuming that the true weight of the loaves of bread in this population is 23.90 oz. What is the value of β if $\alpha = 0.01$? What is the power of the test if $\mu = 23.90$? Using words a nonquantitative decision-maker might understand, interpret the meaning of the values of α and β in this problem.

9.20   Use the critical value calculated in Problem 9.3(c).

a)   What is the value of β if the true value of μ is $4900? What is the power of the test?

b)   Repeat part (a), assuming that the true values are $4800, $4700, $4600, and $4500. Construct a graph of the power function, using these values.

9.21   Sketch the power function for Problem 9.8, assuming that the true values of μ are 0.90, 0.95, 1.00, 1.05, and 1.20.

9.22   Return to Problem 9.11, in which the sample size was $n = 64$ and $\alpha = 0.05$.

a)   Find β if $\mu = 51$.

b)   Show that for the hypotheses and critical region presented in part (a), the values of both α and β will decrease if n is increased to 100.

9.23   In the discussion in Section 9.6, we calculated the probability of making an incorrect decision concerning adjustments to a production process. The values of α and β were determined for the critical region $x \geq 4$ and for the critical region $x \geq 5$, assuming a sample size of 20.

a)   Calculate α and β for this problem for the critical region $x \geq 6$.

b)   Calculate the expected cost associated with this critical region when the probability of a defective is 0.10. Do the same thing for the probability of a defective equal to 0.25.

c)   Calculate the total expected cost associated with this critical region, assuming that the probability of a minor adjustment is 0.70 and the probability of a major adjustment is 0.30.

d)   Is the cost that you determined in part (c) better or worse than the cost calculated in Section 9.6 for the critical region $x \geq 5$? Do you think $x \geq 5$ is the best critical region for this sample size? Explain why, and then try to draw a graph relating the location of the critical region to the total expected costs (let the horizontal axis be the lower bound of the critical regions).

9.24   In Section 9.6 it was shown that, for the production process under investigation, a sample size of 50 results in a lower expected cost than a sample size of 20 if the additional observations cost only an extra $10. Suppose that we now have the opportunity to buy 50 more observations (for a total n of 100) for $15 more (i.e., sampling cost of $25). Estimate, as best you can, the optimal critical region for this size of sample. Is the total expected cost in this case lower or higher than the cost when $n = 50$?

9.25   The manager of food services at Rost Labs claims there is more support for the lunch food this year than last year, when 80% of the employees were dissatisfied. A sample of 50 randomly selected employees finds that

20 think the food is satisfactory this year. The others express some dissatisfaction. Test the alternative hypothesis that dissatisfaction has decreased, using $\alpha = 0.01$ and Table I. Repeat the test, using a normal approximation. Report a p-value in both cases.

9.26 At the Capital plant in Seattle, at least two-fifths of the 5500 employees are reported to be 45 years old or older. A random sample of 100 employees finds that 35 are at least 45 years old. Construct a test of the claim at the 0.05 significance level, using both Table I and the normal approximation.

9.27 A national marketing survey found that only one-fifth of all U.S. citizens drink beer on a regular basis. A random sample of 36 residents in Milwaukee found nine who were regular beer drinkers. Test whether or not Milwaukee has a greater than the national proportion of beer drinkers.

9.28 The national proportion of accountants who passed the entire CPA exam on the first attempt is $\frac{1}{3}$. In Oregon last year, 36 people took the test for the first time, and 18 passed. Using $\alpha = 0.05$ is this sufficient evidence to indicate a proportion of first-time passes that is greater than the national proportion?

9.29 Suppose that a supermarket has agreed to advertise through a local newspaper if it can be established that the newspaper's circulation reaches more than 50% of the supermarket's customers.
a) What null and alternative hypotheses should be established in this problem in trying to decide, on the basis of a random sample of customers, whether or not the supermarket should advertise in the newspaper?
b) A sample of size $n = 64$ is collected, and $\alpha = 0.01$. Before a decision should be made to advertise, what number (critical value) is needed of supermarket customers who regularly look at this newspaper's advertisements?

9.30 A nationally known insurance company has been advertising on TV that "9 out of 10 claims are in the return mail two days after receipt." Suppose that you decide to test this assertion and you believe the actual proportion is smaller.
a) What critical region would you establish if $\alpha = 0.05$ and $n = 100$? Use Table I.
b) Would you accept H_0 or H_a if 85 claims were returned within the two days? What p-value would you report?
c) Repeat parts (a) and (b) using a normal approximation.
d) What p-value would you report in part (c) if the sample result found 95 claims settled within two days?

9.31 The telephone company is continually studying the variability in length of phone calls, as well as the average length. Suppose that the national population variance of length of calls is $\sigma^2 = 4$ minutes squared. The telephone company wants to test whether a certain community's calls differ in variability from the national value. The length of calls is assumed to be normally distributed.
   a) What null and alternative hypotheses would you establish for the test described above?
   b) What critical region(s) would you use for this test if $\alpha = 0.05$ and $n = 25$? Assume a normal parent population.
   c) Would you accept or reject H_0 if the sample of $n = 25$ resulted in $s^2 = 3.0$?

9.32 Recent studies of life insurance policies have criticized the industry for the large variability in premiums for what is often very similar coverage. The industry has responded that more standardization has been achieved over the past several years. The variability in yearly premiums for $100,000 in whole life insurance for a 30-year-old male was $\sigma^2 = 900$ (dollars squared) five years ago. A random sample of 15 comparable premiums this year resulted in $s^2 = 700$. Establish appropriate null and alternative hypotheses. Report a p-value, and then determine whether you would accept or reject H_0 if $\alpha = 0.05$. Assume that the parent population is normal.

9.33 The Folbert 100-watt light bulb is known to last an average of 3.0 years, with $\sigma = 1$ (year). A sample of five of Folbert's new improved 100-watt bulbs resulted in lives of 1.3, 4.1, 7.8, 3.4, and 2.9 years.
   a) Write down H_0 and H_a to test the alternative hypothesis that the new variance is larger than the old.
   b) What test statistic is appropriate if the distribution of the life of all 100-watt bulbs is normal?
   c) What critical region is appropriate if $\alpha = 0.05$?
   d) Would you accept H_0 or H_a on the basis of this sample?
   e) What p-value would you report?

9.34 A fast-food chain is considering purchasing a soft-drink machine that automatically fills each cup to the correct level. Previously, employees filled a cup by holding down on a handle. The company has been willing to accept a variance of up to 0.25 (ounces squared) in a 16-ounce cup. Now they are concerned that the variance is significantly larger than 0.25. A random sample of 30 employees, each filling one cup, resulted in $s^2 = 0.45$. Assume that the parent population is normally distributed. Establish appropriate hypotheses and report a p-value. Would you accept H_0 or H_a if $\alpha = 0.025$?

EXERCISES

9.35 A sample survey firm is contracted by an advertising agency to determine whether or not the average income in a certain large metropolitan area exceeds $27,500. The agency wants the results of this survey to reject the null hypothesis $H_0:\mu = \$27,500$ in favor of $H_a:\mu > \$27,500$ at the $\alpha = 0.05$ level of significance when the true mean is as small as $27,600. If the population standard deviation of incomes in this area is assumed to $5000, how large a sample will the survey firm have to take in order to meet the requirements of the advertising agency?

9.36 Suppose that, in Exercise 9.35, the survey firm charges $5 for each observation it collects for the advertising agency. How much more will it cost the agency to be able to reject $H_0:\mu = \$27,500$ at the $\alpha = 0.01$ level rather than at the $\alpha = 0.05$ level?

9.37 Dataland has the local franchise for the Marvel business microcomputer. A shipment of six Marvels has just arrived. In the past, about half of the arriving Marvels have required more than routine adjustment before they were sold. Let $\theta =$ the number of computers in this shipment needing more than routine adjustment. You decide to test $H_0:\theta = 3$ against $H_a:\theta \neq 3$ by inspecting two computers from the shipment. You will accept H_a if both computers need more than routine adjustment or if both need only routine adjustment. Otherwise, you will accept H_0.
a) If sampling occurs with replacement, find the probability of a Type I error. Find the probability of a Type II error, assuming that $\theta = 0$, 1, 2, . . ., 5, or 6.
b) Repeat part (a), assuming that sampling occurs without replacement.

9.38 A *Time* article suggested that the new overseas airfares the past two years may encourage up to a million more visits from the U.S. to Europe per year. A similar article in *Newsweek* suggested the increase may range up to 2 million visits per year. To model this situation, you decide on the following p.d.f.

$$f(x) = \begin{cases} 1/\theta & \text{for } 0 \leq x \leq \theta \text{ (millions)}, \\ 0 & \text{otherwise}. \end{cases}$$

a) You decide to test the null hypothesis $H_0:\theta = 1$ against the alternative hypothesis $H_a:\theta = 2$ by means of a single observation. What are the values of α and β if you select the interval $x \leq 0.5$ as the critical region? Sketch this density function under both the null and alternative hypotheses, and indicate the critical region on this graph.
b) What are the values of α and β if you select $x \leq 0.75$ as the critical region?

c) Which of these two critical regions would be more appropriate if a Type II error is more serious than a Type I error?

9.39 It has been estimated that most families in the United States spend approximately 90% of their yearly income and save no more than 10% of their yearly income. Suppose that a random sample of 100 families with high incomes (exceeding $40,000) shows that 60% of these people save more than 10% of their income.

a) Does this sample support the hypothesis that a majority of families with incomes exceeding $40,000 save more than 10% of their income? What is the null hypothesis in this case? Given these sample results, what is the probability that the null hypothesis is true?

b) Would you conclude from the sample in this problem that families with high incomes will tend to save more than families with more average incomes? Why or why not?

CASE PROBLEM

9.40 The Harlem Globetrotters are trying to decide whether or not to book an appearance in a small town of about 40,000 people. The local spokesperson insists that they will have no trouble filling the 4000-seat gym for the appearance. The Globetrotters, however, have found that in comparable towns the usual attendance is only about 5% of the town's population, which in this case would be 2000 people. If 4000 people attend, the Globetrotters figure that they will earn a profit of about $1200. If only 2000 attend, they will lose about $2000. The Globetrotters decide to use statistics in this case, and let $H_0: \pi = 0.05$ (only 2000 attend) versus $H_a: \pi = 0.10$ (4000 people attend), where π is the proportion of the population that will attend.

a) Set up a table comparable to that in Fig. 9.16, showing each decision and its consequences.

b) Assume that a sample of size $n = 100$ is to be taken to determine how many people in the town say they would attend. What is the appropriate critical region if α is not to exceed 0.03? What is β for this critical region?

c) Calculate the value of α and β if the critical region used is $x \geq 9$, where x is the number of people who say they will attend.

d) Suppose the Globetrotters estimate that there is only one chance in four that H_a is true. Use this information to decide whether the critical region in part (b) or the critical region in part (c) has the smaller total expected cost.

GLOSSARY

Simple hypothesis: A statement that specifies a single value of the population parameter.

Composite hypothesis: A statement that specifies more than one value for the population parameter.

Null and alternative hypotheses: The two mutually exclusive and exhaustive hypotheses about the feasible values of the population parameter.

One-sided test: All values specified by H_a lie to one side of those given in H_0.

Two-sided test: The values of H_a lie on both sides of the values specified in H_0.

Type I error: Rejecting H_0 when H_0 is true.

Type II error: Accepting H_0 when H_0 is false.

α level of significance: Probability of a Type I error.

(1 − α): Confidence level.

β: Probability of a Type II error.

(1 − β): Power of a test.

Test Statistic: The random variable used in a test of hypothesis. It must have a known p.d.f., given that H_0 is true, and contain the parameter being tested: all of its other terms must be either known or calculable from the sample.

Critical region: Values of a test statistic that lead to rejection of H_0.

Acceptance region: Values of a test statistic that lead to acceptance of H_0 (fail to cause rejection of the null hypothesis, based on the sample evidence).

Computed value: A value of the test statistic, calculated by using a specific sample result.

Computed value of z (σ known) for a test on the population mean:

$$z_c = \frac{\bar{X} - \mu_0}{\dfrac{\sigma}{\sqrt{n}}}.$$

p-value: The probability, given that H_0 is true, of observing a sample result more extreme than the one observed or calculated.

Computed value of t (σ unknown) for a test on the population mean:

$$t_c = \frac{\bar{X} - \mu_0}{\dfrac{s}{\sqrt{n}}}.$$

Computed value of z for the normal approximation to a binomial proportion:

$$z_c = \frac{p - \pi_0}{\sqrt{\dfrac{\pi_0(1 - \pi_0)}{n}}}.$$

Chi-square computed value for a test on variance:

$$\chi_c^2 = \frac{(n - 1)s^2}{\sigma_0^2}.$$

Hypothesis Testing: Multi-sample Tests

TEN

10.1 INTRODUCTION

This chapter is a continuation of the presentation on hypothesis testing begun in Chapter 9. The major difference between the two chapters is that, whereas the methods presented in Chapter 9 involved collecting a *single* sample, the methods to be discussed in this chapter all involve collecting *two or more samples*. Fortunately, the procedure for testing hypotheses is substantially the same for multiple samples as it is for a single sample. We must emphasize that neither the listing of multi-sample tests in this chapter nor the listing of single-sample tests in Chapter 9 is meant to be exhaustive. They are intended to illustrate the application of the powerful tool of hypothesis testing to practical problems. Presumably, the reader who can understand and use these particular test statistics will be able to perform similar tests in other situations. Probably more than 100 such test statistics are commonly used in practical applications of statistical methods of hypothesis testing.

10.2 TEST ON THE DIFFERENCE BETWEEN TWO MEANS (σ_1^2 AND σ_2^2 KNOWN)

In Section 9.3 we presented tests about a single population mean μ. The approach outlined there can also be used to test hypotheses about two populations. One quite common test is that for the effect of different treatments on two groups, where one group is a "control" group and the other is given special treatment, such as a new drug, a new approach to learning, or perhaps just a different type of paint or painkiller or razor (remember those ads on television?).

If we designate μ_1 as the mean of one population and μ_2 as the mean of a second, a number of different null and alternative hypotheses are possible. If the null hypothesis is restricted to a simple hypothesis, then the most common form is $H_0: \mu_1 - \mu_2 = 0$, which asserts that the two means are equal. The alternative to this hypothesis might be that μ_1 exceeds μ_2 ($H_a: \mu_1 - \mu_2 > 0$), or that μ_2 exceeds μ_1 ($H_a: \mu_1 - \mu_2 < 0$), or perhaps merely that μ_1 and μ_2 are not equal ($H_a: \mu_1 - \mu_2 \neq 0$). It is also possible to hypothesize that the two means differ by some constant amount k, for which the null hypothesis would be $H_0: \mu_1 - \mu_2 = k$.

As was the case in Chapter 9, an important part of the hypothesis-testing procedure is the specification of the appropriate test statistic. Since the heading of this section indicates that σ_1^2 and σ_2^2 are known, the reader may well guess that the standardized **z**-distribution will again save the day. It does, but we have to specify a new point estimator (to replace $\bar{x}$) and a new standard error (to replace $\sigma/\sqrt{n}$). As with all standardizations, the z-variable in this case takes the following form:

$$z = \frac{\text{point estimator} - \text{hypothesized mean}}{\text{standard error of point estimator}}. \qquad (10.1)$$

When we are testing hypotheses about $(\mu_1 - \mu_2)$, it should not surprise you to learn that the best point estimator of $(\mu_1 - \mu_2)$ is $(\bar{x}_1 - \bar{x}_2)$, representing the difference between the mean of the first sample $(\bar{x}_1)$ and the mean of the second sample $(\bar{x}_2)$. The standard error of $(\bar{x}_1 - \bar{x}_2)$ is denoted by the symbol $\sigma_{\bar{x}_1 - \bar{x}_2}$, and can be shown to be*

$$\sigma_{\bar{x}_1 - \bar{x}_2} = \sqrt{\frac{\sigma_1^2}{n_1} + \frac{\sigma_2^2}{n_2}},$$

where n_1 = sample size from population 1 and n_2 = sample size from population 2, and σ_1^2 and σ_2^2 are (known) variances of the two populations. Finally, it can be shown that if $\bar{x}_1$ and $\bar{x}_2$ are normal, then the distribution of $(\bar{x}_1 - \bar{x}_2)$ will also be normal. Thus, we can write the following test statistic, **the two-sample computed z-value,** assuming that the null hypothesis is some specified value of $(\mu_1 - \mu_2)$:

Two sample z-test statistic for testing $\mu_1 - \mu_2$:

$$z = \frac{(\bar{x}_1 - \bar{x}_2) - (\mu_1 - \mu_2)}{\sqrt{(\sigma_1^2/n_1) + (\sigma_2^2/n_2)}}. \qquad (10.2)$$

Example 10.1. Let us use Formula (10.2) to test hypotheses about the mean starting salaries of college graduates in two cities, New York City (μ_1) and Chicago (μ_2). Assume that we decide to test

$$H_0 : \mu_1 - \mu_2 = 0 \qquad \text{against} \qquad H_a : \mu_1 - \mu_2 \neq 0,$$

---

* The variance of the difference, $V[\bar{x}_1 - \bar{x}_2]$ (or $\sigma_{\bar{x}_1 - \bar{x}_2}^2$) can be derived as follows, assuming that the samples are drawn independently:

$$
\begin{aligned}
V[\bar{x}_1 - \bar{x}_2] &= V[\bar{x}_1] + V[-\bar{x}_2] \\
&= V[\bar{x}_1] + (-1)^2 \, V[+\bar{x}_2] \quad \text{(See Table 4.10)} \\
&= \frac{\sigma_1^2}{n_1} + \frac{\sigma_2^2}{n_2}, \quad \text{(Since } V[\bar{x}] = \sigma^2/n)
\end{aligned}
$$

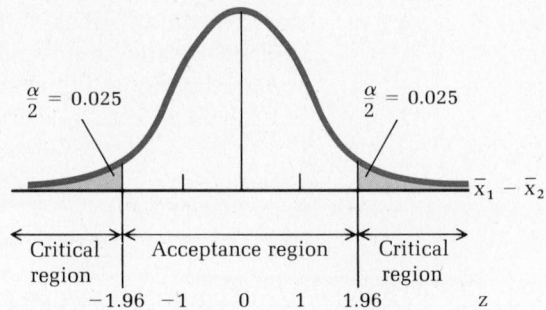

FIGURE 10.1 **Two-sided test on $\mu_1 - \mu_2$.**

using a level of significance of $\alpha = 0.05$. Figure 10.1 (which looks remarkably like Fig. 9.4) shows the critical regions for this test.

Now suppose that a random sample of size $n_1 = 100$ from New York City yields $\bar{x}_1 = \$26,650$, while a random sample of size $n_2 = 60$ from Chicago results in $\bar{x}_2 = \$26,360$. If we assume that the known variances are $\sigma_1^2 = 240,000$ and $\sigma_2^2 = 332,300$, then the computed z_c value is

$$z_c = \frac{(26,650 - 26,360) - (0)}{\sqrt{(240,000/100) + (332,300/60)}} = 3.25.$$

Since this value of z_c exceeds the critical value of 1.96 shown in Fig. 10.1, the null hypothesis must be rejected in favor of the alternative hypothesis. In other words, the difference between these two means appears to be too large to be attributed entirely to chance. If the researcher in this example wants to report a p-value, then the appropriate probability is

$$2P(\mathbf{z} \geq z_c) = 2P(\mathbf{z} \geq 3.25) = 2(1 - 0.9994) = 0.0012.$$

The reported probability is thus 0.0012. For any α larger than 0.0012 the decision-maker should reject H_0. The mean starting salaries of college graduates differ significantly between New York and Chicago.

10.3 TEST ON THE DIFFERENCE BETWEEN TWO MEANS (σ_1^2 AND σ_2^2 UNKNOWN BUT ASSUMED EQUAL)

The two-sample **z**-test described in Section 10.2 is appropriate only when both σ_1^2 and σ_2^2 are known. When σ_1^2 and σ_2^2 are unknown, the **t**-distribution can be applied if both parent populations ($\mathbf{x}_1$ and $\mathbf{x}_2$) are normal. If x_1 and x_2 are not normal, but both n_1 and n_2 are reasonably large (say each ≥ 15), then again the t-distribution can be used. In addition, this two-sample t-test assumes that the variances of the two populations are equal ($\sigma_1^2 = \sigma_2^2$), although there is a t-test, which we shall describe shortly, that does not require this assumption. Fortunately, the t-test is a fairly "robust" distribution (as was pointed out in Section 7.8), so that minor deviations from the above assumptions may not destroy the usefulness of this approach.

Using the t-distribution   It may seem that a t-test for the difference between two means would have the same format as Formula (10.2), with sample variances s_1^2 and s_2^2 substituted for the population variances. However, this is not true, owing to the stipulation that $\sigma_1^2 = \sigma_2^2$. This equality means that both s_1^2 and s_2^2 must represent two estimates of the *same* population variance. In other words, because the two populations are assumed to have the same variance, the two sample variances are merely two separate estimates of this population variance. But if s_1^2 and s_2^2 differ, which of these two values should be used to estimate the unknown population variance? The answer is that a *weighted average* of s_1^2 and s_2^2 is the best estimate and is more reliable than either one alone. The weights applied are the respective degrees of freedom relative to the total number of degrees of freedom. This weighted average is as follows:

Weighted average of s_1^2 and s_2^2:

$$\frac{(n_1 - 1)}{n_1 + n_2 - 2}s_1^2 + \frac{(n_2 - 1)}{n_1 + n_2 - 2}s_2^2 = \frac{(n_1 - 1)s_1^2 + (n_2 - 1)s_2^2}{n_1 + n_2 - 2},$$

where each sample variance has $(n - 1)$ degrees of freedom, and the total number of degrees of freedom is $(n_1 - 1) + (n_2 - 1) = n_1 + n_2 - 2$. The reader should verify that the two "weights" shown above will always sum to 1.0.

Let us now rewrite Formula (10.2), letting σ^2 denote the two equal variances (that is, $\sigma_1^2 = \sigma_2^2 = \sigma^2$). Factoring σ^2 out of the denominator of (10.2) permits us to rewrite Formula (10.2) as follows:

Formula 10.2 assuming that $\sigma_1^2 = \sigma_2^2 = \sigma^2$:

$$\frac{(\bar{x}_1 - \bar{x}_2) - (\mu_1 - \mu_2)}{\sqrt{\sigma^2\left(\frac{1}{n_1} + \frac{1}{n_2}\right)}} = \frac{(\bar{x}_1 - \bar{x}_2) - (\mu_1 - \mu_2)}{\sqrt{\sigma^2\left(\frac{n_1 + n_2}{n_1 n_2}\right)}}.$$

Substituting our weighted-average formula for σ^2 yields the appropriate t-test statistic:

Two-sample t-test statistic for testing $\mu_1 - \mu_2$, assuming equal variances in the normal parent populations:

$$t_{n_1 + n_2 - 2} = \frac{(\bar{x}_1 - \bar{x}_2) - (\mu_1 - \mu_2)}{\sqrt{\left(\dfrac{(n_1 - 1)s_1^2 + (n_2 - 1)s_2^2}{n_1 + n_2 - 2}\right)\left(\dfrac{n_1 + n_2}{n_1 n_2}\right)}} . \qquad \textbf{(10.3)}$$

This t-variable has $(n_1 + n_2 - 2)$ degrees of freedom.

Example 10.2. Formula (10.3) can be illustrated by applying it to Example 10.1, on starting salaries of college graduates in New York City and Chicago. Let us now assume that much smaller samples were taken, namely, $n_1 = 11$ and $n_2 = 9$; that the population variances are unknown but can be assumed to be equal; and that the parent populations are normal. Suppose that the decision-maker has set $\alpha = 0.05$, and established

$$H_0 : \mu_1 - \mu_2 = 0 \qquad \text{versus} \qquad H_a : \mu_1 - \mu_2 \neq 0.$$

The results of the two samples are given below:

Sample 1	Sample 2
$n_1 = 11$	$n_2 = 9$
$\bar{x}_1 = 26{,}600$	$\bar{x}_2 = 26{,}300$
$s_1^2 = 350{,}000$	$s_2^2 = 400{,}000$

Substituting these values into Formula (10.3), we obtain the following computed t-value:

$$t_c = \frac{(26{,}600 - 26{,}300) - (0)}{\sqrt{\left(\dfrac{10(350{,}000) + 8(400{,}000)}{11 + 9 - 2}\right)\left(\dfrac{11 + 9}{(11)(9)}\right)}}$$

$$= \frac{300}{274.22} = 1.09.$$

Since this calculated t-value lies between the two critical values for a two-sided test when $\alpha = 0.05$ and $\nu = 18$ $[t_{0.025, \, 18} = \pm 2.101]$, the decision-maker should accept H_0. The difference of \$300 between $\bar{x}_1$ and $\bar{x}_2$ in these small samples is not large enough to conclude that mean starting salaries differ. The appropriate p-value to be reported has the following form:

$$2P(t \geq t_c) = 2P(t \geq 1.09).$$

This probability cannot be determined exactly, but from Table VI we do know that

$$0.25 > P(t \geq 1.09) > 0.10.$$

Doubling these values, we obtain the expression to be reported:

$$0.50 > 2P(t \geq 1.09) > 0.20.$$

Thus, for any α less than 0.20 the decision-maker should accept H_0.

Again, we must point out that many statistics texts recommend using a normal approximation to the t-distribution when $n_1 + n_2 - 2$ is relatively large (such as ≥ 30). We have not emphasized that process (although it is quite straightforward), but rather remind the reader that the t-distribution is *always* the appropriate distribution when σ_1 and σ_2 (in normal populations) are unknown. If the exact value of $n_1 + n_2 - 2$ for a particular problem cannot be found in Table VI, use the row with the number of degrees of freedom closest to this value.

Study Question 10.1: A Comparison between Two Versions of a Program

An operations research program was written in both FORTRAN and PASCAL for the IBM personal computer. The program written in PASCAL is supposed to run faster, but some experts believe that the running times will be approximately equal. A random sample of fairly large problems was run using each program, with the following results (in minutes). Assume that the populations are normal.

PASCAL	FORTRAN
0.8	3.3
4.4	7.5
1.3	1.3
3.9	6.3
	8.1

a) Establish appropriate null and alternative hypotheses for testing whether the population means differ significantly. Report a p-value. Assume that the population variances are equal.

b) Assume that the population standard deviations are known to be $\sigma_1 = 1.1$ (PASCAL) and $\sigma = 2.3$ (FORTRAN). Test to see whether the sample means are significantly different. Accept or reject H_0 using $\alpha = 0.05$.

Answer

a) H_0: $\mu_1 - \mu_2 = 0$ where μ_1 is PASCAL;
   H_a: $\mu_1 - \mu_2 \neq 0$.

$$\bar{x}_1 = 2.6, \quad s_1{}^2 = 3.29; \qquad \bar{x}_2 = 5.3, \quad s_2{}^2 = 8.42.$$

$$t_c = \frac{(\bar{x}_1 - \bar{x}_2) - (\mu_1 - \mu_2)}{\sqrt{\left(\dfrac{(n_1 - 1)s_1{}^2 + (n_2 - 1)s_2{}^2}{n_1 + n_2 - 2}\right)\left(\dfrac{n_1 + n_2}{n_1 n_2}\right)}}$$

$$= \frac{(2.6 - 5.3) - 0}{\sqrt{\left(\dfrac{(3)(3.29) + (4)(8.42)}{7}\right)\left(\dfrac{4 + 5}{(4)(5)}\right)}} = -1.614.$$

Using Table VI with 7 d.f.,

$$0.10 < 2P(t \leq -1.614) < 0.20.$$

For traditional α-levels ($\alpha \leq 0.10$), we should conclude that the population means for program running time using PASCAL or FORTRAN are perhaps equal.

b)
$$z = \frac{(\bar{x}_1 - \bar{x}_2) - (\mu_1 - \mu_2)}{\sqrt{\dfrac{\sigma_1{}^2}{n_1} + \dfrac{\sigma_2{}^2}{n_2}}} = \frac{2.6 - 5.3}{\sqrt{\dfrac{(1.1)^2}{4} + \dfrac{(2.3)^2}{5}}} = -2.31.$$

The critical values from Table III are $z = \pm 1.96$. Since $z_c = -2.31$ falls in the critical region, we reject H_0 and conclude that the mean running times are significantly different.

10.4   MATCHED PAIRS t-TEST

There is another way to test for significant differences between two samples involving small values of n that does not use the assumption that the variances of the two populations are equal. In this test it is necessary that the observations in the two samples be collected in the form called *matched pairs*. That is, each observation in the one sample must be paired with an observation in the other sample in such a manner that these observations are somehow "matched" or related, in an attempt to eliminate extraneous factors that are not of interest in the test. In our test for differences in starting salaries, for example, the graduates sampled in the New York area may be considerably older than the graduates sampled in the Chicago area, or they may represent a substantially different mix of undergraduate majors. If such differences are not of interest, then they can be systematically eliminated by selecting a sample in which each person in the New York area is carefully matched — in terms of age, sex, undergraduate major, or any other criterion — with a person in the Chicago area. One of the most common methods of forming matched pairs is to let a subject "serve as one's own control," in which case the person is matched with himself or herself at different points in time, or in a "before-and-after" treatment study.

If the observations can be collected in the form of matched pairs, then a *t*-test for differences between the two samples can be constructed on the basis of the *difference score* for each matched pair. This score is calculated by subtracting the score or value associated with the one person or object in each pair from the score of the paired person or object. The *t*-test requires the assumption that these difference scores are normally distributed and independent. If we denote the average difference in scores between the two populations by the capital Greek letter delta Δ, then the hypothesis being tested is $H_0:\Delta = k$ where k is the hypothesized average difference ($k = 0$ in a test of significance). If the values from the two matched samples are denoted by x_i and y_i, and the difference score between matched pairs by $D_i = x_i - y_i$, then the average of D_i is our best estimate of Δ. The sample values of D_i can be used in a test similar to a one-sample test on a mean with σ unknown and the population assumed to be normal. The sample standard deviation of the difference scores, s_D, and the sample mean of the difference scores, $\overline{D}$, are used to form:

Test statistic for matched pairs:

$$t_{n-1} = \frac{\overline{D} - \Delta}{\dfrac{s_D}{\sqrt{n}}}, \qquad (10.4)$$

where n is the number of matched pairs in the two samples, and s_D is computed as follows:

$$s_D = \sqrt{\frac{\sum_{i=1}^{n}(D_i - \overline{D})^2}{n-1}} \quad \text{or} \quad \sqrt{\frac{\sum_{i=1}^{n}D_i^2 - \dfrac{\left(\sum_{i=1}^{n}D_i\right)^2}{n}}{n-1}} \qquad (10.5)$$

Suppose, for example, that the observations in Table 10.1 represent the starting salaries for ten matched pairs from New York City and Chicago. The null and alternative hypotheses to be tested are

$$H_0:\Delta = 0 \qquad \text{versus} \qquad H_a:\Delta \neq 0.$$

TABLE 10.1 **Data for matched-pairs test**

Pair	New York City (x_i)	Chicago (y_i)	$D_i = x_i - y_i$ Difference
1	$ 30,400	$ 30,000	$ 400
2	29,800	29,900	−100
3	29,700	30,000	−300
4	30,500	30,400	100
5	30,600	30,600	0
6	30,100	29,900	200
7	30,300	30,400	−100
8	29,900	29,700	200
9	30,400	30,300	100
10	30,700	30,200	500
Sum	302,400	301,400	1,000
Mean	30,240	30,140	100

From Table 10.1 we know that $\overline{D} = \$100$. By using the ten values of $D_i = x_i - y_i$ in the last column of Table 10.1 and Formula (10.5) for s_D, it is possible to show that $s_D = 240.37$. Substituting these values into Formula (10.4), we obtain the following computed t-value:

$$t_c = \frac{\overline{D} - \Delta}{\dfrac{s_D}{\sqrt{n}}} = \frac{100 - 0}{\dfrac{240.37}{\sqrt{10}}} = 1.32.$$

For $(n - 1) = 9$ degrees of freedom and an α-level of 0.05, the critical values for a two-sided alternative are $t_{0.025,\,9} = \pm 2.262$. Since t_c falls between these values, the decision should be to accept H_0. In other words, the differences in this sample are not large enough to reject the assumption that starting salaries are equal. If we wish to report a p-value, the appropriate probability is

$$2P(t \geq t_c) = 2P(t \geq 1.32).$$

The value of $P(t \geq 1.32)$ is larger than 0.10 and less than 0.25, as shown in Table VI; by doubling these probabilities, we get

$$0.50 > 2P(t \geq 1.32) > 0.20.$$

The statistician now can report that a difference in mean starting salaries as large as $100 will occur relatively frequently (more than 20% of the time) when the two cities do, in fact, have equal starting salaries.

A matched pairs *t*-test generally involves considerably more time and effort than does the use of Formula (10.3) for testing means. This time and effort is necessary, however, if there are systematic differences between the two populations that must be eliminated.

10.5 TEST ON THE DIFFERENCE BETWEEN TWO PROPORTIONS

In Chapter 9 we presented a one-sample test involving the binomial parameter π. The comparable test in this chapter is designed to distinguish between two population proportions, π_1 and π_2. One illustration of this situation involves a politician interested in comparing the proportion of people who intend to vote for him or her in one city relative to the proportion of supporting voters in another city. Or perhaps the politician wants to learn how the proportion in a single city changes over time. A similar example is a business firm interested in comparing, between two time periods, the proportion of units of its product that are defective or in comparing its proportion of defectives to that of another company.

The usual null hypothesis in testing population proportions is that π_1 and π_2 are equal; that is,

$$H_0: \pi_1 - \pi_2 = 0.$$

The alternative hypothesis can take any of the forms used previously, such as

$$H_a: \pi_1 - \pi_2 \neq 0 \quad \text{or} \quad H_a: \pi_1 - \pi_2 > 0 \quad \text{or} \quad H_a: \pi_1 - \pi_2 < 0.$$

The test statistic appropriate in this case is the **z**-distribution, provided that n_1 and n_2 are both sufficiently large. If we let p_1 and p_2 represent the sample proportion from the first and second populations, respectively, then the appropriate formula for z_c is the **computed z-value for the normal approximation to the difference between two proportions:**

Calculated z-value for testing $\pi_1 - \pi_2$:*

$$z_c = \frac{(p_1 - p_2) - (\pi_1 - \pi_2)}{\sqrt{\dfrac{p_1(1 - p_1)}{n_1} + \dfrac{p_2(1 - p_2)}{n_2}}}. \qquad (10.6)$$

* Formula (10.6) could be made more precise by adding a correction for continuity. We will assume that n_1 and n_2 are large enough that this correction changes z_c by a negligible amount.

This test statistic should not be totally unfamiliar, since it merely represents an extension of Formula (9.4) to the two-sample situation.

Example 10.3. An economist is interested in the effects of the recession in 1981–1982 on various industries. In particular, this person is interested in comparing the change in profits from 1981 to 1982 for companies in "retailing (nonfood)" and "banks and bank holding companies." This economist has decided that a listing in the March 14, 1983, issue of *Business Week* containing these data on 65 companies in the first category and 50 in the second category would be a good random sample. For "retailing," 40 of the companies showed an increase in profits, and 25 had a profit decrease. For the "banks and bank holding companies," 36 had a profit increase, and 14 had a profit decrease.

There is no way of knowing whether the *Business Week* listing of companies is representative of all companies in any given category, and it might be possible to find a better sample. Assuming the sample is representative, the economist may wish to test for significant differences in the proportion of companies showing an increase in profits. Let $\pi_1 =$ proportion of "retailing" companies showing an increase, and let $\pi_2 =$ proportion of "banks and bank holding companies" showing an increase. The relevant hypotheses are:

$$H_0: \pi_1 - \pi_2 = 0 \quad \text{versus} \quad H_a: \pi_1 - \pi_2 \neq 0.$$

The sample proportions are

$$p_1 = \frac{x_1}{n_1} = \frac{40}{65} = 0.615 \quad \text{and} \quad p_2 = \frac{x_2}{n_2} = \frac{36}{50} = 0.720.$$

Substituting these values into Formula (10.6) gives z_c:

$$z_c = \frac{(0.615 - 0.720) - (0)}{\sqrt{\dfrac{(0.615)(1 - 0.615)}{65} + \dfrac{(0.720)(1 - 0.720)}{50}}} = \frac{-0.1050}{0.0876} = -1.20.$$

$P(z \leq -1.20) = 1 - 0.8849 = 0.1151$ (from Table III). Because this is a two-tailed test, the **p**-value is doubled and equals $2(0.1151) = 0.2302$. Thus, any usual α-value is less than the p-value, and H_0 should not be rejected. The proportion of companies showing an increase in profits may be the same for "retailing" firms as for "banks and holding" firms.

10.6 TWO-SAMPLE TESTS FOR POPULATION VARIANCES

Two populations with equal variances are called *homoscedastic.** A test for homoscedasticity is important in a number of contexts. For one example, we know that the *t*-test of Section 10.3 requires $\sigma_1^2 = \sigma_2^2$. Or it may be that a quality-control engineer wants to determine whether or not the variance of the quality of the product is changing over time. Similarly, an economist may wish to know whether the variability in incomes or in hours worked differs across two populations. Finally, a financial advisor may wish to investigate the risks inherent in two speculative portfolios by comparing the variance of their likely market value one year from now.

The null hypothesis in testing two population variances is usually

$$H_0: \sigma_1^2 = \sigma_2^2.$$

Any one of a variety of alternative hypotheses can be used, although the most common one is

$$H_a: \sigma_1^2 \neq \sigma_2^2.$$

The sampling distribution for testing hypotheses about two variances is called the **F**-distribution, named in honor of R. A. Fisher, who first studied it in 1924. The **F**-distribution tests the hypothesis $\sigma_1^2 = \sigma_2^2$ by taking the *ratio* of the two sample variances, s_1^2 and s_2^2. Knowledge of the degree to which the ratio s_1^2/s_2^2 differs from 1.0 can be used to test $\sigma_1^2 = \sigma_2^2$. When $\sigma_1^2 = \sigma_2^2$, we would expect the ratio s_1^2/s_2^2 to be close to 1.0. Thus, the more the ratio s_1^2/s_2^2 differs from 1.0, the less confidence we have that $\sigma_1^2 = \sigma_2^2$.

How closely the ratio s_1^2/s_2^2 can be expected to approach 1.0 when $\sigma_1^2 = \sigma_2^2$ depends on the size of the two samples or, more precisely, on the number of degrees of freedom in each sample. We will let $\nu_1 = (n_1 - 1)$ denote the degrees of freedom for the first sample and $\nu_2 = (n_2 - 1)$ denote the degrees of freedom for the second sample. If the samples are drawn from normal parent populations, the following test statistic is used for testing $\sigma_1^2 = \sigma_2^2$:

* This word is derived from two words, *homo* (meaning "the same") and *scedastic* (referring to variability).

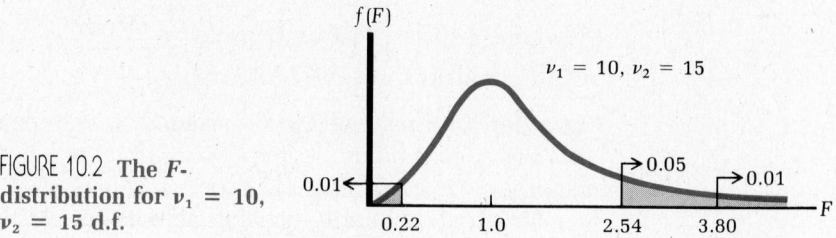

FIGURE 10.2 **The F-distribution for $\nu_1 = 10$, $\nu_2 = 15$ d.f.**

Test statistic for testing $\sigma_1^2 = \sigma_2^2$:

$$F_{\nu_1, \nu_2} = \frac{s_1^2}{s_2^2}.$$ (10.7)

Figure 10.2 shows a typical **F**-distribution; this one represents all possible values of s_1^2/s_2^2 when $\nu_1 = 10$ and $\nu_2 = 15$. Note that the **F**-distribution is always positive or zero and is positively skewed. This is reasonable, since the ratio s_1^2/s_2^2 can never be negative but can assume *any* positive value. The fact that the **F**-distribution looks something like a chi-square distribution is not coincidental, since these distributions are closely related.* Three particular probabilities are indicated in Fig. 10.2, namely, $P(F \geq 2.54) = 0.05$, $P(F \geq 3.80) = 0.01$, and $P(F \leq 0.22) = 0.01$.

Example 10.4. The economist in Example 10.3 is also interested in the variability of price–earnings ratios of firms between various industries. To illustrate the use of the **F**-distribution and Formula (10.7), a random sample of 11 companies was drawn from the *Business Week* list of firms in "miscellaneous manufacturing," and a random sample of 16 companies was drawn from the list of firms in "service industries." The economist desires to test the following hypotheses:

$$H_0: \sigma_1^2 = \sigma_2^2 \quad \text{versus} \quad H_a: \sigma_1^2 \neq \sigma_2^2.$$

The companies sampled and their price–earning ratios are shown in Table 10.2.

The **F**-distribution is appropriate here, assuming the two samples were drawn from normal parent populations. Using the sample variance formula

---

* The **F**-distribution is the ratio of two independent chi-square distributions, each divided by its degrees of freedom.

$$s^2 = \frac{\sum\limits_{i=1}^{n}(x - \bar{x})^2}{n - 1},$$ $V_1 = 5$ $V_2 = 8$

the sample variances are

$$s_1^2 = 59.2546 \quad \text{and} \quad s_2^2 = 16.7292.$$

The appropriate F-distribution for this problem has $v_1 = 11 - 1 = 10$ degrees of freedom, and $v_2 = 16 - 1 = 15$ d.f., which is the distribution shown in Fig. 10.2.

To test the economist's hypotheses about variances, we compute the following value of the F-statistic:

Computed F-value for two variances:

$$F_c = \frac{s_1^2}{s_2^2} = \frac{59.2546}{16.7292} = 3.542.$$

From Fig. 10.2 we see that $P(F \geq F_c) = P(F \geq 3.542)$ is greater than 0.01 but less than 0.05. Hence, we can write

$$0.05 > P(F \geq 3.542) > 0.01.$$

TABLE 10.2 **Sample of companies and their price–earnings (P–E) ratio**

Manufacturing Company	P–E ratio	Service Company	P–E ratio
Corning Glass Works	22	National Education	16
West	14	Amfac	10
Norton	32	Flour	12
Rubbermaid	20	KDI	11
Alleghany	10	Spectro Industries	15
Emhart	7	Premier Industrial	21
Borg-Warner	12	Wetterau	11
Trane	14	Comdisco	20
Penn Central	8	Dynalectron	9
American Standard	25	ARA Services	11
Snap-on Tools	16	IU International	13
		Williams	20
		Nielsen	18
		Manor Care	19
		Kay	14
		Humana	19

Since H_a is two-sided in this example, we double these values, and the reported p-value would be $0.10 > 2P(F \geq 3.542) > 0.02$. Thus, the decision-maker should accept H_0, that the variances of price–earnings ratios are equal for "manufacturing" and "service" industries, if α is lower than 0.02. H_0 should be rejected in favor of a significant difference in these variances if α is higher than 0.10. Since we do not know the exact value of $P(F \geq 3.542)$, we cannot advise the decision-maker what to do if α falls between 0.02 and 0.10.

As has been the case for all the probability distributions studied thus far, the F-distribution has been extensively tabled. Table VIII in Appendix C gives values of the cumulative F-distribution. In the case of the F-distribution the number of values that could be given in a table is so large (because two parameters are involved) that only certain values are listed. First, in most F-tables it is customary only to give values of F that are greater than 1.0. This means that only upper-tail critical regions can be obtained directly from Table VIII. In other words, in order to use Table VIII directly, the value of the sample variance in the numerator of Formula (10.5) must be larger than the value of the sample variance in the denominator. This was the case in the example above, since s_1^2 in the numerator was the larger variance and the calculated F-value exceeded one. If the opposite situation had occurred, so that $s_1^2 < s_2^2$ and hence $F < 1.0$, then the lower-tail critical value for the F-distribution would be used. We will show how to handle this situation shortly.

The other major characteristic of Table VIII is that only two values of the cumulative F-distribution are given. Table VIII(a) shows the critical values of F for the cumulative probability of 0.95 or the α-value of $P(F \geq F) = 0.05$. Table VIII(b) shows the critical values of F for the cumulative probability of 0.99 or the α-value of $P(F \geq F) = 0.01$. To illustrate the use of these tables, we present the hypothesis $H_0 : \sigma_1^2 = \sigma_2^2$, versus the one-sided alternative $H_a : \sigma_1^2 > \sigma_2^2$. Suppose that a random sample of $n_1 = 25$ yields $s_1^2 = 200$, while another sample of $n_2 = 15$ yields $s_2^2 = 75$ (both samples are from normal parent populations). The F-ratio in this case is $F_c = 200/75 = 2.67$, with $25 - 1 = 24$ degrees of freedom in the numerator and $15 - 1 = 14$ degrees of freedom in the denominator. A graph of the F-distribution for 24, 14 d.f. is shown in Fig. 10.3.

From Table VIII(a) the intersection of the column corresponding to $\nu_1 = 24$ and the row corresponding to $\nu_2 = 14$ shows a value of $F_{(24, 14)} = 2.35$. Hence, $P(F \geq 2.35) = 0.05$. Since our observed ratio of $F = 2.67$ is larger than 2.35, we can conclude that $0.05 > P(F_{24, 14} \geq 2.67)$; that is, the probability of drawing two such samples from normal populations

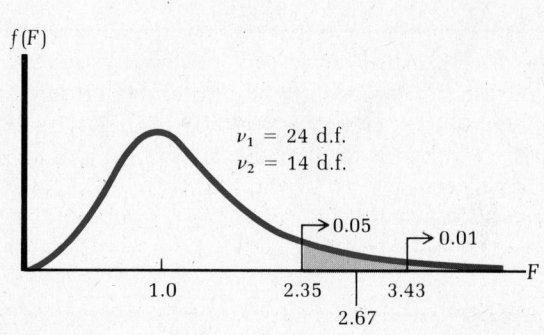

FIGURE 10.3 The F-distribution for 24, 14 d.f.

with the same variance is less than 0.05. Similarly, from Table VIII(b), for 24 and 14 d.f., we find that $P(F \geq 3.43) = 0.01$; this means that $P(F \geq 2.67) > 0.01$ or that the probability is greater than 0.01 that two such samples will be drawn from normal populations whose variances are equal. Putting these results together we can state that

$$0.05 > P(F_{(24, 14)} \geq 2.67) > 0.01,$$

or that a ratio as large as 2.67 or larger will occur between 1% and 5% of the time when the population variances are equal. If our observed ratio had been larger than 3.43, then we would report that the p-value is less than 0.01. If the value of F_c had been less than 2.35, then we would report that the p-value exceeds 0.05.

Example 10.5. Several state legislators are interested in conducting tests involving the variance of incomes across communities. The null hypothesis in this case is that the two variances are equal ($H_0:\sigma_1^2 = \sigma_2^2$), while the alternative hypothesis is that the first community has a smaller variance ($H_a:\sigma_1^2 < \sigma_2^2$). It can be assumed that the two populations are normally distributed and that $\alpha = 0.01$. Random samples of size $n_1 = 11$ and $n_2 = 16$ result in $s_1^2 = (2000)^2$ and $s_2^2 = (2400)^2$. The calculated F-value in this case is

$$F_c = \frac{s_1^2}{s_2^2} = \frac{(2000)^2}{(2400)^2} = 0.69.$$

Since we hypothesized that σ_1^2 is less than σ_2^2, we may use a lower-tail critical value.* To obtain this, we use the following rule:

* Step 2 of the summary procedure below suggests a way of using the upper-tail critical value in all one-sided tests.

A lower-tail critical value of F can always be found by reversing the degrees of freedom of the numerator and the denominator, determining the corresponding value in the upper tail of the F-distribution, and then taking the reciprocal of this number. That is,

$$F_{(\text{lower critical value, } \nu_1, \nu_2)} = \frac{1}{F_{(\text{upper critical value, } \nu_2, \nu_1)}}.$$

As an illustration of the calculation of a lower-tail critical value, recall from Fig. 10.2 that the lower-tail critical value for $\alpha = 0.01$ when $\nu_1 = 10$ and $\nu_2 = 15$ is given as 0.22. This value can be determined by finding first the upper critical value for $\alpha = 0.01$ with the degrees of freedom reversed (that is, 15 for the numerator and 10 for the denominator). From Table VIII(b) we see that $F_{(0.01, 15, 10)} = 4.56$. Hence,

$$F_{(\text{lower critical value, 10, 15})} = \frac{1}{F_{(0.01, 15, 10)}} = \frac{1}{4.56} = 0.22.$$

As Fig. 10.2 illustrates, values of F based on 10 and 15 degrees of freedom will exceed 3.80 one percent of the time and will be less than 0.22 one percent of the time. Since the F-value determined in this example was $F_c = 0.69$, and this value is larger than the critical value of 0.22, the economist cannot reject $H_0:\sigma_1^2 = \sigma_2^2$. The variances of incomes in the two communities may be equal. The reader should verify that the lower critical value for $\alpha = 0.05$ for $\nu_1 = 10$ and $\nu_2 = 15$ is 0.35.

The following steps summarize the procedure described above for testing the equality of two variances $(H_0:\sigma_1^2 = \sigma_2^2)$.

1. If H_a is two-sided $(H_a:\sigma_1^2 \neq \sigma_2^2)$: Calculate the upper critical value, using $\alpha/2$ and Table VIII. Also calculate the lower critical value, using the procedure described above (again using $\alpha/2$ and Table VIII). If s_1^2/s_2^2 falls within the acceptance region, accept H_0. Otherwise, accept H_a. Report the smaller of the two probability values,

$$2P(F \geq s_1^2/s_2^2), \quad \text{and} \quad 2P(F \leq s_1^2/s_2^2).$$

2. If H_a is one-sided (either $H_a:\sigma_1^2 > \sigma_2^2$ or $H_a:\sigma_1^2 < \sigma_2^2$):
   a. Determine whether the ratio of s_1^2 and s_2^2 corresponds to the inequality presented under H_a. For example, if the alternative hypothesis is $H_a:\sigma_1^2 > \sigma_2^2$, then does s_1^2 exceed s_2^2? If s_1^2 and s_2^2 do not have the hypothesized ranking, reject H_a and report a probability value of $p > 0.50$.
   b. If s_1^2 and s_2^2 do have the ranking hypothesized under H_a, then calculate s_1^2/s_2^2 and s_2^2/s_1^2. Let F_c equal the larger of these two

ratios, so that the upper critical value may be used directly from Table VIII, using the d.f. in the numerator and denominator corresponding to the subscripts (on s) in the *larger* ratio.

- Report a p-value of $P(\mathbf{F} \geq F_c)$, and reject H_0 if α is greater than this p-value.
- Accept H_0 if α is less than this p-value.

Study Question 10.2: Quality Control in the Bleaching of Pulp

An article in the *Journal of Quality Technology* reported on the need for quality control in the bleaching of pulp. In some cases the mean effects on pulp brightness of different types of bleach may be equal, but the variabilities differ. In order to guarantee pulp specifications, the company prefers as much uniformity in the pulp brightness as possible. Two chemical bleaches are being considered. The company would like to test the null hypothesis that the use of the two chemicals results in the same variance of brightness, using a two-sided alternative and $\alpha = 0.02$. Two samples of size $n_1 = 11$ and $n_2 = 10$ are taken from pulp treated with these two chemicals. Table 10.3 shows their pulp brightness.

Answer. H_0: $\sigma_1^2 = \sigma_2^2$ versus H_a: $\sigma_1^2 \neq \sigma_2^2$. The sample variances, using

$$s^2 = \frac{\sum_{i=1}^{n} (x_i - \bar{x})^2}{n - 1},$$

TABLE 10.3 **Pulp brightness**

Chemical 1	Chemical 2
78.00	77.20
78.36	74.47
77.54	82.75
77.36	76.21
77.55	82.87
75.91	76.22
78.04	78.06
78.95	76.39
77.15	76.15
77.39	78.05
78.36	

are

$$s_1{}^2 = 0.6405 \qquad s_2{}^2 = 7.9453.$$

$$F_c = \frac{s_1{}^2}{s_2{}^2} = \frac{0.6405}{7.9453} = 0.0806.$$

For $\alpha = 0.02$ the lower critical value for (10, 9) degrees of freedom is found by taking the reciprocal of 4.94 (the upper critical value for (9, 10) d.f. and $\alpha/2 = 0.01$ in Table VIII.

$$\text{Lower critical value} = \frac{1}{4.94} = 0.2024.$$

Since F_c is less than this value, we reject H_0 and conclude that the population variances of brightness using two different chemicals are not equal.

PROBLEMS

10.1 Review the five steps in hypothesis testing from Chapter 9. Are any modifications necessary to apply these steps to two-sample tests?

10.2 Two types of new cars are tested for gas mileage. One group, consisting of 36 cars, averaged 24 miles per gallon of gas, while the other, consisting of 72 cars, averaged 22.5 miles per gallon.
 a) What null and alternative hypotheses would you establish to determine whether or not the mileage differs between the two types of cars?
 b) What test statistic is appropriate if $\sigma_1{}^2 = 1.5$ and $\sigma_2{}^2 = 2.0$?
 c) Construct the appropriate critical values, assuming $\alpha = 0.01$. Would you accept H_0 or H_a?
 d) What p-value would you report if α is not specified?
 e) Is it necessary in this problem to assume that x_1 and x_2 are normally distributed? Explain.

10.3 International Farm Equipment, Inc. is considering purchasing bolts from a different manufacturer. The company being considered claims the "yield point" of its bolt (where the bolt begins to bend under pressure) is significantly higher than that of the bolt currently being used.
 a) What null and alternative hypotheses would you establish in this situation?
 b) What test statistic is appropriate if $\sigma_1{}^2 = 400$, $\sigma_2{}^2 = 800$, and the parent populations are normal?

c) What critical value is appropriate if $\alpha = 0.02$?

d) Assume that the $n_1 = n_2 = 12$ sample values yield the following data on the yield point: $\bar{x}_1 = 370$ and $\bar{x}_2 = 400$. What test conclusion would you reach?

10.4 A commercial airline is interested in determining whether the time is longer for its flights from Indianapolis to New York City than the flight times from New York City to Indianapolis. The airline picks flights that are full and records the following data:

Sample	Sample Size	Mean Time (minutes)	Standard Deviation
Indy–NYC	10	123	$\sqrt{225}$
NYC–Indy	6	108	$\sqrt{185}$

Construct a test using $\alpha = 0.05$. What p-value would you report? Assume normal parent populations.

10.5 Quality Conditioning, Inc. is testing two models of window air conditioners to determine how long the condensers will last under heavy use. The results of the test are as follows:

	Model A	Model B
Number of units tested	8	10
Average time to failure (years)	7.0	5.5
Standard deviation (years)	1.0	$\sqrt{1.7}$

Model A is the more expensive model and is hypothesized to last longer. Formulate the appropriate hypotheses and perform a one-sided test, using $\alpha = 0.01$. Assume that the parent populations are normal.

10.6 All of the staff employees at a firm making microcomputers took a test to determine their familiarity with microcomputers. A sample of nine scores was randomly selected from the set of employees with business degrees, and a sample of four was randomly drawn from the set of employees with liberal arts degrees. The resulting scores are arranged in ascending order:

Business degrees:	65, 68, 72, 75, 82, 85, 87, 91, 95
Liberal arts degrees:	50, 59, 71, 80

a) What assumptions about the parent populations are necessary if we wish to use the *t*-test to test for significant differences between the means of these two groups?

b) Construct such a test at the 0.05 level of significance.

10.7 The speed of an assembly line process is carefully controlled so that each worker has sufficient time (but not too much time) for the assigned task. A time study for one task on an automobile assembly line was conducted by using two workers. At four randomly selected points, each worker was timed for this task. The results, in seconds, are given below. Assume that the populations of times are normally distributed.

Worker A	Worker B
30.7	31.1
31.2	31.2
31.3	31.4
30.9	31.6

On the basis of these times, can you detect, with 99% confidence, any difference between the performance of the two workers?

10.8 An article in the *Journal of the Indiana Dental Association* reported that, in a random sample of 25 entering students each of two consecutive years, the average G.P.A. of the 25 predental majors decreased from 3.28 to 3.20. The standard deviations were 0.33 and 0.36, respectively. Do these G.P.A.'s differ significantly using $\alpha = 0.05$ and assuming normal populations?

10.9 All restaurants are rated for cleanliness and quality by state inspectors. A sample of six restaurants gives the ratings (for two inspectors) shown below. Determine at the $\alpha = 0.05$ level of significance whether the two inspectors differ in their mean rating or whether the differences can be attributed to sampling error. Assume that the parent populations are normal, and use a matched-pairs *t*-test.

Inspector	Restaurants					
	1	2	3	4	5	6
A	99	90	66	75	85	92
B	95	49	48	71	80	93

10.10 The manager of a fleet of automobiles is trying to determine statistically which of two different gasolines is better. This person measures gas mileage (for one car) for eight consecutive tankfuls, using Brands A and B alternately. The mileage difference (B − A) after every two tankfuls is computed. The average difference is 2.5 mpg, and the standard deviation of the differences is s_D = 2.0 mpg. Since the dealer selling Brand A is a friend, the manager will switch to Brand B only if 90% sure that the Brand B mileage will be *at least one* mile per gallon better. What should the manager do? Assume that the D-values are normally distributed.

10.11 The purchasing manager for Foltz, Inc. is replacing the office copying machine with a model that is supposed to be faster for the staff to use. The manager decides to run six major duplicating projects on each machine. Each project on one machine is carefully matched with a project on the other machine, and the difference in times is recorded. The manager finds that the new machine took, on the average, 9.1 minutes less than the old machine, with a standard deviation (of the difference scores) of s_D = 4.4 minutes. Test with 95% confidence whether the manager should switch to the newer machine. Assume that the differences are normally distributed.

10.12 A county agent experiments with eight acres of land. Half the acreage is treated with fertilizer x and half is treated with fertilizer y. The average difference in yield between paired acres is ten bushels. The standard deviation of differences is 4. Would you conclude that there is a significant difference of yield between the two differently-fertilized tracts? You should have 99% confidence if you do find a difference. Assume that the differences in yields are normally distributed.

10.13 Ten male and ten female production line workers were matched according to age and work experience. The number of absent days for each pair (over the past five years) was then recorded.

Pair	Male	$x-\bar{x}_1$		Female	$x-\bar{x}_2$	D	D^2
1	21	8.1		17	6.1	4	16
2	13	.1		15	4.1	−2	4
3	7	−5.9		12	1.1	−5	25
4	18	5.1		9	−1.9	9	81
5	3	−9.9		6	−4.9	−3	9
6	9	−3.9		8	−2.9	1	1
7	24	11.1		10	−.9	14	196
8	8	−4.9		7	−3.9	1	1
9	16	3.1		20	9.1	−4	16
10	10	−2.9		5	−5.1	5	25

$\bar{x}_1 = 12.9$ $\bar{x}_2 = 10.9$ $\bar{D} = 2$

a) Use a matched-pairs t-test to determine whether there is a significant difference between the number of absent days for males and females. Assume that $\alpha = 0.05$.

b) Use Formula (10.3) to determine whether a significant difference exists.

c) Is the p-value for part (a) the same as that for part (b)? Explain why or why not. Which approach is the correct one?

10.14 As part of a study on response and nonresponse biases described in the *Journal of Marketing*, 549 business customers responded to a questionnaire mailed to them concerning the number of telephone lines they have. Personal visits were made to 131 businesses, asking the same question. The mean response to the mail survey was 1.49, with a standard deviation of 0.39. The mean response to the personal visits was 1.54, with $s = 0.56$. Assuming normal populations:

a) Do the variances differ significantly? Let $\alpha = 0.02$.

b) Do the means differ significantly, using $\alpha = 0.05$?

c) Is the answer to question (b) dependent on the answer to (a)? Explain.

10.15 Sixty out of 100 randomly selected shoppers who were classified as having rural backgrounds said they prefer to purchase camera equipment in discount stores. In a comparable study involving 250 shoppers with urban backgrounds, 50% said they prefer the discount stores. Use a two-sided test to determine whether these groups differ in the proportion who prefer discount stores. Use $\alpha = 0.01$.

10.16 Contractor A from Seattle claims to be better at winning major construction contracts than his friend from Portland, Contractor B. They have never bid against one another. In a random sample of 200 projects, Contractor B was the winner 55% of the time. Contractor A was the winner on 65% of 150 projects. Use a one-sided test and $\alpha = 0.05$ to determine whether Contractor A can claim to be better at winning.

10.17 A cereal manufacturer will switch to a new TV advertising campaign if the new campaign will increase, by *at least 0.10*, the proportion of viewers who rate the ad as "highly attractive." In a random sample of 400 viewers, 23% rated the current campaign as "highly attractive." After viewing the new campaign, 35% of a random sample of 100 viewers rated the new campaign as "highly attractive." Would you recommend the company switch if $\alpha = 0.02$?

10.18 A bank is comparing the service given by two of its branches. In one branch, 70% of a random sample of 280 customers indicated that they were satisfied with the services provided. In the other branch, 50% of a random sample of 140 customers indicated that they were satisfied with the services. Would you conclude that the first branch has a significantly higher proportion of satisfied customers? Use $\alpha = 0.01$ and a two-sided test.

10.19 What assumptions are necessary for using the F-test to test the null hypothesis $H_0:\sigma_1^2 = \sigma_2^2$?

10.20 The materials manager for International Farm Equipment, Inc. (see Problem 10.3) is interested in the *variability* of "yield point" for the new bolts, as compared to the variability of the bolts currently being used. Assume that the manager has no idea of the population variances and no idea of which bolt has more variability, but believes that the parent populations can be considered normally distributed.
a)   What null and alternative hypotheses would you establish in this situation?
b)   Assume that a sample of 25 of the new type of bolts yields $s_1^2 = 475$ and a sample of 36 of the old type of bolts yields $s_2^2 = 236$. Assuming that these are random samples, what test conclusion would you reach if $\alpha = 0.01$? What p-value would you report?

10.21 Use an F-test to determine whether or not the assumption of equal variances in Problem 10.6(a) is reasonable. Use $\alpha = 0.02$ and a two-sided alternative hypothesis.

10.22 a)   Sketch the F-distribution for 15 d.f. ($n_1 = 16$) in the numerator and 12 d.f. ($n_2 = 13$) in the denominator.
b)   Two independent samples are drawn from normal populations. The first, of size $n_1 = 16$, results in $s_1^2 = 100$. The second, of size $n_2 = 13$, yields $s_2^2 = 250$. Test to determine whether or not the first has a smaller variance at $\alpha = 0.05$.

10.23 Find the two lower-tail values for the F-distribution excluding 0.01 and 0.05 involving $\nu_1 = 24$ and $\nu_2 = 14$ (see Fig. 10.3).

10.24 A public-policy researcher is studying the variance in the amount of money requested by certain government agencies. The alternative hypothesis is that the variance this year (σ_2^2) is larger than the variance five years ago (σ_1^2). Random samples of size $n_1 = 21$ and $n_2 = 25$ yield variances of $s_1^2 = (67,233)^2$ and $s_2^2 = (37,178)^2$. Assume that the two populations are normally distributed. Make the proper test at $\alpha = 0.01$. What p-value would you report?

10.25 Crafton Leathers of Denver makes leather covers for books. The leather is tested for average strength as well as variability in strength because tears may occur if part of the leather is weak. Two types of leather are tested. The first type, using a random sample of $n_1 = 60$, indicated a strength (before tearing) of 112 (pounds per square inch), with a standard deviation of 6. The second type was tested with a sample of size $n_2 =$

40 and indicated a mean strength of 114, with a standard deviation of 4. Assume that the parent populations are normal.

a) Would you accept or reject the assumption that the two population variances are equal, using a two-sided alternative hypothesis and $\alpha = 0.10$?

b) Would you accept or reject the hypothesis that the two populations have equal means, using $\alpha = 0.01$? Does your answer to part (a) influence your approach to part (b)?

10.26 A sample of 10 rolls of carpet has been found to have an average of 10 flaws per roll, with a standard deviation of 3.2. Another sample of 17 rolls has an average of 20 flaws per roll, with a standard deviation of 3.0. Test, at the 0.05 level of significance, whether the second type can be expected to have an average of *at least* 5 more flaws per roll than the first type. Assume that the populations are normally distributed.

EXERCISES

10.27 Explain why the smallest value in Table VIII is 1.0 despite the fact that s_1^2/s_2^2 can take on values between zero and infinity.

10.28 Go to **Data Set 2** and collect two random samples of sales values. The first sample should be of size $n_1 = 4$ and the second of size $n_2 = 6$. Calculate the sample means and variances. Assume that you do not know that these samples came from the same population.

a) Use a two-sided *F*-test to test for equal variances, setting $\alpha = 0.01$. Are the necessary assumptions for use of the *F*-test met in this case?

b) Use a two-sided *t*-test for equal population means, setting $\alpha = 0.01$. Are the assumptions required for this test met?

10.29 Prove that Formula (10.3) and Formula (10.2) yield identical values of *t* and **z** when $n_1 = n_2$, $s_1^2 = \sigma_1^2$, and $s_2^2 = \sigma_2^2$.

10.30 Information provided by the National Federation of Independent Business Research and Education Foundation compared the standard of living in various cities around the world. Part of their data compared the cost of a commodity basket in Washington and that in Paris, as measured by the minutes of work time (average of manufacturing workers) required to earn enough to purchase the item (after taxes). Use the following data to test whether there is a significant average difference in costs between Washington and Paris for the population of costs of all commodities. Use $\alpha = 0.05$ and a two-sided alternative. Do you see any problems with this comparison?

	Minutes of Work Time	
Commodity	Washington	Paris
Bread, 1 kg	16	18
Hamburger meat, beef, 1 kg	37	80
Sausages, 1 kg	33	75
Sugar, 1 kg	9	9
Butter, 1 kg	55	47
Milk, 1 liter	6	8
Cheese, 1 kg	100	59
Eggs, 10	8	13
Potatoes, 1 kg	7	4
Carrots, 1 kg	11	7
Apples, 1 kg	10	15
Tea, 100 g	10	17
Beer, 1 liter	11	7
Vodka, 0.7 liter	61	107
Cigarettes, 20	9	8

10.31 Consider the incomes information in **Data Set 6** as a sample of $n = 166$ from a normal population. Compare the incomes of males and females in that sample to determine whether there is a significant difference in the population means or variances of incomes. Use $\alpha = 0.01$.

10.32 Use the values in Table VII and VIII to show that $t^2_{(\alpha/2,\nu)} = F_{(\alpha,1,\nu)}$. Try at least three different degrees of freedom and α-levels of both 0.01 and 0.05.

USING THE COMPUTER

10.33 Find (or write) a computer program that will generate random samples, and then generate 100 samples, each of size $n = 10$. Compute the mean and variance of each sample. For parts (a) and (b) below, compare sample 1 with 2, 3 with 4, 5 with 6, and so forth.

a) Determine the variance of the *population* from which you took the 100 samples. Let this variance be both σ_1^2 and σ_2^2 (because you are sampling from the same population). Run 50 **z**-tests to determine whether the means in each pair of samples can be considered significantly different, using $\alpha = 0.05$. How many of the 50 pairs would you expect to have significantly different means? How many did?

b) Repeat part (a), but now assume that you do not know the population variance. Run 50 *t*-tests, using the sample variances and $\alpha = 0.05$. How many pairs were significantly different?

10.34 Use a statistical computer package on the data in Example 10.4 (Table 10.2) to verify the *F*-values presented there.

10.35 Use a statistical computer package on the data in Study Question 10.2 (Table 10.3) to verify the *F*-value presented there.

10.36 Use a statistical computer package on the data in Problem 10.6 to determine whether the sample means differ significantly.

10.37 Use a statistical computer package to verify the answers in the back of the book to Problems 10.9 and 10.13.

CASE PROBLEM

10.38 You are working for the national office of the Chamber of Commerce and have been asked to investigate claims by various regions in the United States that their particular area is a preferred place to live. One continuing battle is between cities east and west of the Mississippi River, each region claiming to be the better place to live. To investigate such claims, assume that you have taken a random sample of cities from both regions. The information in **Data Set 1** is your sample, excluding Hawaii and Alaska (as not being in the continental United States). Divide the sample into those cities east and those west of the Mississippi River, and then run a series of two-sample tests on these data. Prepare a report indicating whether you believe that there is any basis for one region to claim to be a better place to live than the other. Use $\alpha = 0.05$, and report a p-value whenever possible. Assume that the parent populations are normal, whenever necessary.

GLOSSARY

Two-sample computed z-value:

$$z_c = \frac{(\bar{X}_1 - \bar{X}_2) - (\mu_1 - \mu_2)}{\sqrt{(\sigma_1^2/n_1) + (\sigma_2^2/n_2)}}.$$

Two-sample computed *t*-value $(n_1 + n_2 - 2 \text{ d.f.})$

$$t_c = \frac{(\bar{x}_1 - \bar{x}_2) - (\mu_1 - \mu_2)}{\sqrt{\left(\dfrac{(n_1 - 1)s_1^2 + (n_2 - 1)s_2^2}{(n_1 + n_2 - 2)}\right)\left(\dfrac{n_1 + n_2}{n_1 n_2}\right)}}.$$

Computed *t*-value for matched pairs $(n - 1 \text{ d.f.})$:

$$t_c = \frac{\bar{D} - \Delta}{s_D/\sqrt{n}}.$$

Computed *z*-value for normal approximation to the difference between two proportions:

$$z_c = \frac{(p_1 - p_2) - (\pi_1 - \pi_2)}{\sqrt{\dfrac{p_1(1 - p_1)}{n_1} + \dfrac{p_2(1 - p_2)}{n_2}}}.$$

Computed *F*-value for two variances $(n_1 - 1 \text{ and } n_2 - 1 \text{ d.f.})$:

$$F_c = \frac{s_1^2}{s_2^2}.$$

Analysis of Variance

ELEVEN

11.1 INTRODUCTION

The tests of hypotheses in Chapter 10 were designed to test for differences between two population means. Often, practical situations may arise in which we want to compare more than two populations. Comparison of the yields of several varieties of corn plants, the gasoline mileage obtained by four automobiles, and the working hours of five groups of college students are examples of such situations. In these circumstances, one normally does not want to (and usually should not) consider all possible combinations of two populations at a time and test for differences in each pair. Rather, we want to investigate *simultaneously* the differences among the means of all the populations. The method for performing this simultaneous test is called "ANOVA," which is an abbreviation for **analysis of variance.** The essence of ANOVA is that the total amount of variation among categories of data is broken down into two types: that amount which can be attributed to chance and that amount which can be attributed to specified causes. ANOVA tests thus involve a comparison between these amounts.

In general, one can investigate any number of factors that are hypothesized to influence the dependent variable. For example, one may wish to investigate the effect on gasoline mileage (the dependent variable) of such things as the speed of the automobile (factor I), the horsepower of the engine (factor II), and the brand of the car (factor III). In addition, the categories within each of these factors may have a large number of possible values (e.g., there are an infinite number of car speeds we might investigate). It should not be difficult even for the beginning student of ANOVA to see that the relationship among the factors may become quite complex. (For this example, how do horsepower and the speed of an automobile interact in their effect on gasoline mileage?)

In Chapter 7 we introduced the phrase "sample design" to represent the process of designing samples to gain the most precision for a certain level of cost. For ANOVA the comparable process is called "experimental design." In experimental design the statistician is attempting to design an experiment in which the extraneous factors are controlled, so that the factors of interest can be systematically studied. For instance, in the gasoline mileage example mentioned above, the business analyst may use only cars of the same weight so that the weight of the car is not a factor that might contribute to different mileage figures. Similarly, the same type of tires should be used on all cars, unless tires are a factor being studied.

In an ANOVA model, each factor is divided into "levels." For example, the factor "automobile speed" may be divided into four speeds (levels):

25 mph, 35 mph, 45 mph, and 55 mph. Similarly, the factor "automobile brand" might be divided into three categories (levels): General Motors, Ford, and Chrysler. A model with only one factor under study is called a "one-factor model." A "randomized blocks" model is an extension of the one-factor model that permits the analyst to control for an extraneous factor. In our gasoline mileage test, for example, we might want to control for the type of gasoline used. Perhaps three different types could be randomly assigned to each brand of car. The term "randomized blocks" represents the fact that the assignment of gasolines to cars is random. In all cases, ANOVA tests for different effects due to various factors.

11.2 THE ONE-FACTOR MODEL

Example 11.1. Consider the problem of measuring the gasoline mileage (y) of three different brands of compact automobiles. Four cars of each brand are sampled, and each car selected has a standard transmission, four-cylinder engine, and no power equipment. All cars are run on the same trip (city and country driving), using the same drivers, fuel, and tire conditions. In other words, all possible influences except for the brand are controlled as carefully as possible; of course, there may be factors that are not (or cannot be) controlled, such as traffic conditions and weather conditions, but these factors are assumed to be random in their effect. Assume that the sample results for this test are those shown in Table 11.1. (We will return to this example shortly.)

The One-Factor Model   In a one-factor model we will assume that we want to test the null hypothesis that the means of J different populations are all equal. To perform this test, we will take a sample from each of the J populations.

TABLE 11.1 **Gasoline mileage test**

Observa-tion (i)	Brand of Car (Treatment Number, j)			
	1	2	3	
1	28	24	31	
2	25	23	32	
3	27	18	37	
4	28	27	24	
Average	$\bar{y}_1 = 27$	$\bar{y}_2 = 23$	$\bar{y}_3 = 31$	$\bar{y} = 27$

Analysis-of-variance methods test for differences among the means of the populations by examining the amount of variation *within* each of these samples, relative to the amount of variation *between* the samples. For example, in testing for differences in gasoline mileage attributable to the brand of automobile used (the one factor), we could take a sample of J different brands. In ANOVA the J different samples are often called the J "treatments." This term originated from early applications of ANOVA to agricultural problems, where, for example, the amount of crop yielded by a certain type of soil was tested by "treating" the soil with various kinds of fertilizer. The first step in building an ANOVA model is to specify the underlying population relationships. To do this, we will denote the different treatments by the letter j, where $j = 1, 2, 3, \ldots, J$. If we let N_j be the size of the jth population, then the values within the jth population can be denoted as $i = 1, 2, 3, \ldots, N_j$. Assume that y_{ij} represents the ith value of the jth population under investigation. If we now denote the mean value of y in the jth population as μ_j and the mean of all values of y_{ij} in all J columns as μ (or equivalently, μ is the **grand mean** of the values of μ_j), then Table 11.2 represents this situation.

As we indicated above, in ANOVA we are interested in determining the variation within and between the populations. In terms of the variation *within* a given population, we will assume that the values of y_{ij} differ from the mean of this population (μ_j) only because of random effects.

TABLE 11.2

				J Populations (Treatments)					
		1	2	3	$\cdots$	j	$\cdots$	J	
	1	y_{11}	y_{12}	y_{13}	$\cdots$	y_{1j}	$\cdots$	y_{1J}	
	2	y_{21}	y_{22}	y_{23}	$\cdots$	y_{2j}	$\cdots$	y_{2J}	
	3	y_{31}	y_{32}	y_{33}	$\cdots$	y_{3j}	$\cdots$	y_{3J}	
Values within each population	i	y_{i1}	y_{i2}	y_{i3}	$\cdots$	y_{ij}	$\cdots$	y_{iJ}	
Mean of the jth population		μ_1	μ_2	μ_3	$\cdots$	μ_j	$\cdots$	μ_J	μ = Grand mean
Population size		N_1	N_2	N_3	$\cdots$	N_j	$\cdots$	N_J	

That is, there are influences on y_{ij} that are unexplainable (i.e., "random") in terms of our one-factor model. The difference between y_{ij} and μ_j is usually denoted by the symbol ϵ_{ij} (ϵ is the Greek letter epsilon). Thus,

$$\epsilon_{ij} = y_{ij} - \mu_j$$

or

$$y_{ij} = \epsilon_{ij} + \mu_j \tag{11.1}$$

for $j = 1, 2, \ldots, J$ and $i = 1, 2, \ldots, N_j$.

In examining differences *between* populations we will assume that the difference between the mean of the jth population (μ_j) and the grand mean (μ) is attributable to what is called a **treatment effect.** That is, μ_j is not exactly equal to μ because of the effect of the jth treatment. We will label this treatment effect τ_j (τ is the Greek letter tau), where

$$\tau_j = \mu_j - \mu$$

or

$$\mu_j = \tau_j + \mu \tag{11.2}$$

for $j = 1, 2, \ldots, J$.

The one factor ANOVA model can be formulated by substituting Formula (11.2) into Formula (11.1):

One-factor ANOVA model:

$$y_{ij} = \mu + \tau_j + \epsilon_{ij} \qquad \begin{matrix} (j = 1, 2, \ldots, J), \\ (i = 1, 2, \ldots, N_j). \end{matrix} \tag{11.3}$$

This model means that the value of y_{ij} is composed of three components (or effects): a common effect (μ) plus a treatment effect (τ_j) plus a **random-error term** (ϵ_{ij}). The null hypothesis in the one-factor model is that the treatment effects are all zero. That is,

$$H_0: \tau_1 = \tau_2 = \cdots = \tau_J = 0.$$

An equivalent form of this hypothesis is that all the treatment (column) means are equal to the grand mean and equal to each other.

$$H_0: \mu_1 = \mu_2 = \cdots = \mu_J = \mu.$$

We stress that the two null hypotheses stated above are equivalent (as can be seen from the ANOVA model in Formula 11.3). The alternative hypothesis is that not all of the treatment effects are equal to zero, or

$$H_a: \text{at least one } \tau_j \neq 0.$$

To test these hypotheses, we will assume that a sample of size n_j has been taken from each of the J populations. For each sample the mean value is $\bar{y}_j$ (for $j = 1, 2, \ldots, J$). The grand sample mean is $\bar{y}$.

For Example 11.1 the null and alternative hypotheses are

$H_0: \tau_1 = \tau_2 = \tau_3 = 0$ (all three brands have the same gas mileage)
$H_a:$ at least one $\tau_j \neq 0$

If H_0 is true, then the observed differences among $\bar{y}_1$, $\bar{y}_2$, and $\bar{y}_3$ in Table 11.1 can be attributed to random effects and not treatment effects. Note that we can use the column means in Table 11.1 to make estimates of the treatment effects (our estimates are denoted as $\hat{\tau}_j$):

$$\hat{\tau}_1 = \bar{y}_1 - \bar{y} = 27 - 27 = 0,$$

Estimated treatment effects $\hat{\tau}_2 = \bar{y}_2 - \bar{y} = 23 - 27 = -4,$

$$\hat{\tau}_3 = \bar{y}_3 - \bar{y} = 31 - 27 = 4.$$

In effect, the ANOVA test is concerned with determining whether the estimated values of τ_j are large enough to convince us that H_0 is not, in fact, true.

Whenever H_0 is true, we would expect the variability between the J means to be the same as the variability within each sample, since in this case the random effects (ϵ_{ij}) are the only source of variation. If the treatment effects are not all zero, then the variability between samples should be larger than the variability within the samples. Our measure of variability in ANOVA is similar to that used in calculating variances; i.e., first we calculate the sum of the squared deviations about the mean, called the **sum of squares.**

The variation *within* the J samples is calculated by first summing the squared deviations of y_{ij} about $\bar{y}_j$ for each sample; that is, $\sum_{i=1}^{n_j} (y_{ij} - \bar{y}_j)^2$. If we now sum this variation over all J samples, the result is called the **sum of squares within** (abbreviated **SSW**):

$$\text{Sum of squares within:} \quad \text{SSW} = \sum_{j=1}^{J} \sum_{i=1}^{n_j} (y_{ij} - \bar{y}_j)^2. \tag{11.4}$$

We now must find the amount of variation *between* samples, which is called the **sum of squares between (SBB).** In this case we first take the squared deviation of the jth column mean and the grand mean, which is $(\bar{y}_j - \bar{y})^2$. This deviation is multiplied by (i.e., weighted by) the number of observations in the jth sample and summed over all values of j. That is,

$$\text{Sum of squares between:} \quad \text{SSB} = \sum_{j=1}^{J} n_j(\bar{y}_j - \bar{y})^2. \tag{11.5}$$

There is one other variation in ANOVA — the total variation among all observations in the sample. This variation, denoted as **SST (sum of squares total)**, is the sum of squared deviations of all values of y_{ij} about the grand mean $\bar{y}$:

$$\text{Sum of squares total:} \quad \text{SST} = \sum_{j=1}^{J} \sum_{i=1}^{n_j} (y_{ij} - \bar{y})^2.$$

A fundamental equation of ANOVA states that total variation equals the sum of the between and within variations; that is,

$$\text{SST} = \text{SSB} + \text{SSW}.$$

We will illustrate the calculation of these three measures of variation using the data in Table 11.1. First, applying Formula (11.4), we find SSW to be the sum of the squared deviations of the first column (which is 6) plus the sum of squares in column 2 (which is 42) plus the sum of squares in column 3, which is 86). Hence,

$$\text{SSW} = \sum_{i=1}^{4} (y_{i1} - \bar{y}_1)^2 + \sum_{i=1}^{4} (y_{i2} - \bar{y}_2)^2 + \sum_{i=1}^{4} (y_{i3} - \bar{y}_3)^2$$

$$= 6 + 42 + 86 = 134.$$

In using Formula (11.5) to calculate the variation between the column means, we see that $n_1 = n_2 = n_3 = 4$, and

$$\text{SSB} = n_1(\bar{y}_1 - \bar{y})^2 + n_2(\bar{y}_2 - \bar{y})^2 + n_3(\bar{y}_3 - \bar{y})^2$$

$$= 4(0) + 4(16) + 4(16) = 128.$$

Finally, we know that SST = SSB + SSW = 128 + 134 = 262. The reader may wish to verify this value, using Table 11.1 and the formula for SST.

Mean Squares and the ANOVA Table

As shown above, the first step in ANOVA is to calculate SSB and SSW. In order to compare the variability within samples to the variability between samples we need to divide these sums by their respective degrees of freedom (for the same reason that $\Sigma(x_i - \bar{x})^2$ is divided by its d.f. $(n - 1)$, in calculating the sample variance s^2). The d.f. for SSB is always one less than the number of populations, or $J - 1$. Similarly, for SST the number of d.f. is one less than the total sample size, which is $\left(\Sigma_{j=1}^{J} n_j\right) - 1$. For SSW the expression $\left(\Sigma_{j=1}^{J} n_j\right) - J$ gives the degrees of freedom. Note that these d.f. sum in the same manner as do the sums of squares:

Sums of squares: $\quad$ SST $\quad=\quad$ SSB $\quad+\quad$ SSW;

d.f.: $\quad \left(\sum_{j=1}^{J} n_j \right) - 1 = (J - 1) + \left(\sum_{j=1}^{J} n_j \right) - J.$

A sum of squares divided by its degrees of freedom is called a **mean square** (abbreviated MS). Hence,

Mean square between: $\quad$ MSB $= \dfrac{\text{SSB}}{J - 1}$;

$\qquad\qquad\qquad\qquad\qquad\qquad\qquad\qquad\qquad\qquad$ **(11.6)**

Mean square within: $\quad$ MSW $= \dfrac{\text{SSW}}{\left(\sum_{j=1}^{J} n_j \right) - J}$

The various components necessary for ANOVA are usually presented in what is called an "analysis-of-variance table" or "**ANOVA table.**" The general format of such a table is shown in Table 11.3.

We can illustrate this type of table with our gasoline mileage example. These data are shown in Table 11.4.

In ANOVA we test the null hypothesis by comparing the value of MSB to the value of MSW. If the variability between samples (MSB) is small in relation to the variability within samples (MSW), then we should conclude that H_0 cannot be rejected since the differences may simply be due to random causes. On the other hand, if MSB is large in relation to

TABLE 11.3 **Analysis-of-variance table**

Source of Variation	SS	d.f.	MS = SS/d.f.
Between samples (treatments)	$\sum_{j=1}^{J} n_j(\bar{y}_j - \bar{y})^2$	$J - 1$	$\dfrac{\text{SSB}}{(J - 1)}$
Within samples	$\sum_{j=1}^{J} \sum_{i=1}^{n_j} (y_{ij} - \bar{y}_j)^2$	$\sum_{j=1}^{J} n_j - J$	$\dfrac{\text{SSW}}{\left(\sum_{j=1}^{J} n_j \right) - J}$
Total	$\sum_{j=1}^{J} \sum_{i=1}^{n_j} (y_{ij} - \bar{y})^2$	$\left(\sum_{j=1}^{J} n_j \right) - 1$	

TABLE 11.4 ANOVA for gasoline mileage test

Source of Variation	SS	d.f.	MS
Between samples (brands)	128	2	64
Within samples	134	9	14.9
Total	262	11	

MSW, then we must reject H_0 and conclude that the treatment effects are significant. We can determine whether the size of MSB to MSW is large enough to reject H_0 by using a test statistic with an *F*-distribution.

11.3 THE *F*-TEST IN ANOVA

In ANOVA the hypotheses are

$$H_0: \tau_1 = \tau_2 = \cdots = \tau_J = 0$$

versus

$$H_a: \text{at least one } \tau_j \neq 0.$$

The appropriate statistic for testing these hypotheses is the following **F-ratio:**

F-test for ANOVA:

$$F_{(J-1, \, \Sigma n_j - J)} = \frac{\text{MSB}}{\text{MSW}}. \qquad (11.7)$$

Formula (11.7) gives us a method for testing the size of MSB relative to MSW. Note that for this test the critical region lies in the *upper* tail of the *F*-distribution, since H_0 is rejected only for large values of *F*. That is, when MSB is large in relation to MSW, we reject H_0 because it appears that the treatment effects are not all equal to zero. On the other hand, when the treatment effects are all equal to zero (that is, $\mu_1 = \mu_2 = \cdots = \mu_J$), then we expect the ratio of MSB to MSW to be relatively small and H_0 to not be rejected. If the number of treatments (*J*) is equal to 2, then the **F**-test in Formula (11.7) is equivalent to the two-sided **t**-test presented in Chapter 10 for differences between means of two populations.

Using Example 11.1, we can show how to compare MSB and MSW by using the **F**-distribution. First recall, from Table 11.4, that MSB = 64 and MSW = 14.9, and $v_1 = 2$, $v_2 = 9$. The value of F_c is thus

$$F_c = \frac{\text{MSB}}{\text{MSW}} = \frac{64}{14.9} = 4.30.$$

Referring to Table VIII(a) for 2 and 9 degrees of freedom, we see that the critical value for $\alpha = 0.05$ is $F_{(2,\,9)} = 4.26$. Since our calculated value is larger than this number, we conclude that the treatment effects are not all equal to zero; i.e., that a difference does exist in the gas mileage among the three brands of automobiles.

The reader should note that not all samples need to have the same number of observations and that the number of populations (levels) may be two or more. In order to test the null hypothesis that the treatment effects are all equal to zero, it is necessary to make the following two assumptions about the random-error terms:

1. For each sample ($j = 1, 2, \ldots, J$) the random error terms ϵ_{ij} are normally distributed with mean zero and variance σ^2, and the variance is the same for all samples.
2. The random-error terms are independent.

We will presume throughout the examples and problems in this chapter that these ANOVA assumptions are met. Presenting tests of these assumptions is beyond the scope of an introductory book.

Example 11.2. To illustrate ANOVA when the sample sizes are not equal, we present the problem of an agricultural economist who is interested in the yield of fruit from orchards located near each other and similar in all ways except that different treatments of fungicides and pesticides are applied. A random selection of fruit trees is made, and three treatments are used. The appropriate null and alternative hypotheses are

$$H_0: \tau_1 = \tau_2 = \tau_3 = 0;$$

$$H_a: \text{at least one } \tau_j \neq 0.$$

Table 11.5 shows the results of this experiment.

A useful step to reduce computational drudgery in ANOVA is to subtract an arbitrary value from all observations to make the numbers easier to manipulate. (This process does not affect the variations between or within columns, since the same number is subtracted from all y_{ij}.)

TABLE 11.5 **Agricultural experiment yields**

Treatment 1	Treatment 2	Treatment 3
130	126	131
126	127	128
128	129	133
132	124	130
126	126	130
	130	132
	125	
	126	
	128	
	126	

Table 11.6 shows the same data as Table 11.5 after subtracting the arbitrary value 120 from each item. It also shows the sample sums and means and the estimated treatment effects ($\hat{\tau}_j = \bar{y}_j - \bar{y}$) for the new coded data.

While the formulas given previously help describe the different measures used in ANOVA, they are computationally tedious to apply

TABLE 11.6 **Agricultural experiment, using coded yields**

Treatment 1	Treatment 2	Treatment 3	
10	6	11	
6	7	8	
8	9	13	
12	4	10	
6	6	10	
	10	12	
	5		
	6		
	8		
	6		
$n_1 = 5$	$n_2 = 10$	$n_3 = 6$	$n = 21$
$\displaystyle\sum_{i=1}^{5} y_{i1} = 42$	$\displaystyle\sum_{i=1}^{10} y_{i2} = 67$	$\displaystyle\sum_{i=1}^{6} y_{i3} = 64$	$\displaystyle\sum_{j=1}^{3}\sum_{i=1}^{n_j} y_{ij} = 173$
$\bar{y}_1 = 8.4$	$\bar{y}_2 = 6.7$	$\bar{y}_3 = 10.7$	$\bar{y} = 8.2$
$\hat{\tau}_1 = 0.2$	$\hat{\tau}_2 = -1.5$	$\hat{\tau}_3 = 2.5$	

Reject H_0, since $26.56 > 8.02$ (the critical value for $F_{0.01}$ with 2, 9 d.f.). The conclusion is that there is a significant difference between brands. The estimated treatment effects are

$$\hat{\tau}_1 = -2.617, \qquad \hat{\tau}_2 = 4.333, \qquad \hat{\tau}_3 = -1.417.$$

Define. *ANOVA, one-factor model, treatment effect, levels, common effect, random effect, experimental design, randomized blocks model, SSW, SSB, SST, MSB, MSW, F-ratio.*

PROBLEMS

Assume for all problems that the ANOVA assumptions are met.

11.1 Explain in your own words how variances can be used to test for differences in means.

11.2 Describe the assumptions necessary for one-way ANOVA.

11.3 A survey was conducted in five industries to determine whether there are significant differences in the number of executives using electronic mail. The survey was over a three-week period.

		Industry				
		I	II	III	IV	V
Week	1	114	171	147	151	167
	2	120	166	134	179	177
	3	150	143	121	150	199

On the basis of this sample survey, determine, at the $\alpha = 0.05$ level of significance, whether the average number of executives using electronic mail differs among these industries.

11.4 An experiment was designed to test the length of life of light bulbs from three different manufacturers. A random sample of 5 bulbs was selected from each manufacturer, and the life (in hours) of each bulb was recorded.

Manufacturer I: 120, 90, 105, 100, 125
Manufacturer II: 100, 130, 125, 140, 120
Manufacturer III: 110, 75, 100, 90, 100

Use an *F*-test to determine whether or not the life of the light bulbs can be considered different across the three manufacturers. Let $\alpha = 0.05$.

11.5 During the recession in 1982, some workers were not laid off, but rather had to work reduced hours. To study the effect on four industries, consider the following data representing the hours worked over a 14-week period by randomly selected workers in the four industries.

Industry			
A	B	C	D
490	525	475	527
450	506	460	507
478	473	525	492
510	526	420	505
504	502	499	530
482	505	472	555

Determine whether the average hours worked differ significantly (α = 0.01) across the four industries.

11.6 The students in a computer programming course are complaining that significant differences exist between the average final exam grades given out in four sections (A, B, C, D). All four sections took different final exams. Use ANOVA to determine whether the students have a valid complaint if random samples from each section yielded:

Section A: 68, 85, 87, 95, 72, 68, 91, 75, 82
Section B: 59, 50, 80, 71
Section C: 77, 62, 68, 57, 73, 90, 55, 63
Section D: 94, 86, 70, 92

11.7 All restaurants are rated for cleanliness and quality by three state health inspectors. A sample of six restaurants gives the ratings shown below. Determine at the α = 0.05 level of significance whether the inspectors differ significantly in their average rating score, or whether the variation in the average scores can be attributed to sampling error.

Inspector	Restaurant					
	1	2	3	4	5	6
A	99	90	66	75	85	92
B	95	49	48	71	80	93
C	97	62	60	76	90	88

11.8 The information in **Data Set 3** represents the percent elongation of randomly selected pieces of leather. Fifteen pieces of leather were tested by a tannery lab, 15 by a university lab, and 15 by an industrial lab. Test to see whether the sample means differ significantly among labs. Use α = 0.05.

11.9 A study in the *Journal of Quality Technology* reported on the brightness of random samples of pulp after being treated by four different chemicals. Determine whether the average values of brightness differ significantly across chemicals, using α = 0.01.

Chemical 1	Chemical 2	Chemical 3	Chemical 4
77.2	80.5	79.4	78.0
74.5	79.3	78.0	78.3
82.7	81.9	81.5	77.5
76.2	80.3	80.8	77.3
82.8	78.3	80.2	77.5
76.2	81.8	79.0	75.9
78.0	82.7	80.5	78.0
76.3	80.9	78.4	79.4
76.1	79.1	81.7	77.1
78.0	80.0	80.9	77.3

11.10 The Indiana State Tax Board wants to determine whether property taxes have been assessed fairly in five townships in one county in Indiana. The State Tax Board takes a random sample of nine pieces of property in each township and then reassesses each property. Each of the new assessments is divided by the old assessment. Use the following data to determine whether the average ratios (old assessment/new assessment) differ significantly across townships. Use α = 0.01. Write down your null and alternative hypotheses.

Ratio of New Assessment to Old Assessment Township

1	2	3	4	5
1.16	1.01	1.25	1.31	1.15
1.14	1.07	1.21	1.37	1.17
1.17	1.11	1.24	1.25	1.21
1.05	1.15	1.31	1.18	1.12
1.08	1.15	1.25	1.22	1.06
1.12	1.14	1.31	1.14	1.04
1.10	1.28	1.17	1.26	1.16
1.13	1.23	1.13	1.30	1.10
1.11	1.14	1.05	1.29	1.15

11.11 Interpret the following one-way ANOVA computer printout, where the dependent variable is the number of absent days by workers in different job classifications. Indicate what the null and alternative hypotheses might be and the number of observations in each column. What conclusion would you reach? Estimate the treatment effects.

```
------------------------------ANALYSIS OF VARIANCE------------------------------
                         ONE-WAY ANOVA

      GROUP           MEAN        N
        1            3.500       10
        2            6.600       10
        3            7.300       10

GRAND MEAN           5.800       30

------------------------------ANALYSIS OF VARIANCE------------------------------

NUMBER OF CASES:   30                NUMBER OF VARIABLES:   1
                         ONE-WAY ANOVA


                  SUM OF             MEAN
      SOURCE      SQUARES   D.F.    SQUARE    F RATIO
      BETWEEN     81.800      2    40.900    13.305
      WITHIN      83.000     27     3.074
      TOTAL      164.800     29
```

11.4 TWO-FACTOR ANALYSIS OF VARIANCE

Recall from Section 11.1 that some ANOVA models are one-factor models, while others are designed to study more than a single factor. In this section we begin study of the two-factor model.

In a **two-factor model,** two "treatments" are hypothesized to influence the dependent variable. In an agricultural experiment, for example, the dependent variable may be the yield per acre, while the two factors could be (1) the amount of fertilizer and (2) the amount of irrigation used. Similarly, the sales of a new product may depend on (1) its price and (2) the amount of advertising. Finally, the productivity of a worker may depend on (1) wages and (2) skills.

Just as we used a tabular format for the one-factor model, the same approach is useful now. We will call the two treatments "Factor A" and "Factor B." Columns will represent the various levels of Factor A (1, 2,

... j, ..., J), and rows will represent the various levels of Factor B (1, 2, ..., k, ..., K). The resulting matrix is shown in Table 11.8.

Notice in Table 11.8 that there are J levels for Factor A. These J levels are represented by the letter j, where $j = 1, 2, ..., J$. The K levels for Factor B are represented by the letter k, where $k = 1, 2, ..., K$. Finally, within each cell there are n observations. The letter i designates the number of replications, where $i = 1, 2, ..., n$. Thus, y_{ijk} represents the value of the dependent variable corresponding to the ith replication in the jth level of Factor A and the kth level of Factor B.

For the experiment illustrated in Table 11.8 the researcher is interested in three questions:

1. Do the column means differ significantly? If they do, we say that there is a "significant main effect A." A **main effect** is the effect of a single factor (such as A).
2. Do the row means differ significantly? If so, we say there is a "significant main effect B."

TABLE 11.8 **The matrix for a two-factor model**

				Factor A			
		1	2	$\cdots$	j	$\cdots$	J
	1						
	2						
	$\cdot$ $\cdot$ $\cdot$						
Factor B	k				y_{1jk} y_{2jk} y_{3jk} y_{4jk} } *		
	$\cdot$ $\cdot$ $\cdot$						
	K						

* y_{ijk} = values in the body of the table are those of the dependent variable (ith observation in the jth column and kth row)

3. Is there a "significant interaction effect?" An **interaction effect** is a systematic effect due *not* to Factor A or B alone, but rather to a *combination* of a particular level of A with a particular level of B.

If either main effect is significant, or if the interaction effect is significant, the analyst usually wants to make estimates of these effects.

Example 11.3. Return to the study mentioned in Example 11.1, in which the dependent variable is gas mileage (MPG). Assume now that only six-cylinder engines are used, and we now hypothesize that two factors influence MPG: (1) the brand of the car (labeled I, II, and III), and (2) the speed at which it is driven (25, 35, 45, and 55 miles per hour [MPH]). Factor A (brand) thus has three levels ($J = 3$), and Factor B (speed) has four levels ($K = 4$). For each combination of brand and speed there will be four cars tested ($n = 4$). The experimental results of this two-factor ANOVA are given in Table 11.9.

TABLE 11.9 **Results of two-factor MPG test**

		Factor A (Brand)			
		I	II	III	Averages
Factor B (MPH)	25	29.2	29.8	33.7	
		28.6	30.4	34.1	30.4
		28.8	28.5	30.2	
		29.8	30.1	31.6	
	35	23.9	24.7	26.4	
		24.1	26.4	26.2	25.7
		25.5	26.1	27.3	
		24.9	25.2	27.7	
	45	24.4	25.5	24.4	
		20.9	23.7	22.6	23.7
		23.1	23.9	26.3	
		21.6	22.5	25.5	
	55	26.2	28.6	30.1	
		27.7	27.9	29.5	28.6
		25.6	28.0	32.2	
		26.9	29.1	31.4	
Averages		25.7	26.9	28.7	27.1 = Grand mean

For this experiment an EPA officer is interested in the following questions:

1. Are there significant differences in the MPG of the three brands of cars? This is **main effect A.**
2. Are there significant differences in the MPG across the four speeds? This is **main effect B.**
3. Do speed and brand interact in a systematic way that is independent of the two main effects? This is the **interaction effect.**

For the two-factor model the following definitions will be useful.

y_{ijk} = the ith observation in the cell that is the jth level of Factor A and the kth level of Factor B.

μ = the grand mean of all values in the population.

τ_j = the effect of level j of Factor A on y_{ijk}.

λ_k = the effect of level k of Factor B on y_{ijk}.

$(\tau\lambda)_{jk}$ = the interaction effect on y_{ijk} of the jth level of Factor A and the kth level of Factor B.

ϵ_{ijk} = the (random) error of the ith observation in column j and row k.

The two-factor model can be written as follows:

> Two-factor ANOVA model:
>
> $$y_{ijk} = \mu + \tau_j + \lambda_k + (\tau\lambda)_{jk} + \epsilon_{ijk}.$$

This formulation says that each observation in the population is the sum of five components: (1) the grand mean, (2) the effect of Factor A, (3) the effect of Factor B, (4) the interaction effect, and (5) an error term.

TABLE 11.10 **Two-factor components**

Sum of Squares	Abbreviation	d.f.	Mean Square
Columns (τ)	SSC	$J - 1$	$MSC = SSC/(J - 1)$
Rows (λ)	SSR	$K - 1$	$MSR = SSR/(K - 1)$
Interaction ($\tau\lambda$)	SSI	$(J - 1)(K - 1)$	$MSI = SSI/(J - 1)(K - 1)$
Error	SSE	$JK(n - 1)$	$MSE = SSE/JK(n - 1)$
Total	SST	$JKn - 1$	

TABLE 11.11 **ANOVA table for Examples 11.3 and 11.4**

Sum of Squares	SS	d.f.	MS
SSC	72.96	2	36.480
SSR	319.92	3	106.640
SSI	7.84	6	1.307
SSE	45.54	36	1.265
SST	446.26	47	

Sums of Squares in Two-factor ANOVA

The two-factor ANOVA proceeds exactly like one-factor ANOVA, in that the total sum of squares is separated into distinct parts that correspond to the components of y_{ijk} described above.

$$SSTotal = SSColumns + SSRows + SSInteraction + SSError$$

or   **(11.9)**

$$SST = SSC + SSR + SSI + SSE.$$

Table 11.10 lists these four components, the degrees of freedom for each component, and the mean squares (recall that a mean square is a sum of squares divided by its degree of freedom). For most practical problems the sums of squares presented above are calculated by using a computer. In Section 11.6, however, the formulas for determining these sums of squares are presented.

Example 11.4. The sums of squares presented in Table 11.11 are from Example 11.3, in which the dependent variable is MPG and the two factors are (1) the brand of the car and (2) the speed of the car. There are $J = 3$ brands, $K = 4$ speeds, and $n = 4$ replications per cell.

11.5 TESTING HYPOTHESES IN THE TWO-FACTOR MODEL

In order to test hypotheses about the two-factor model the following assumptions are necessary.

1. For each combination of Factors A and B, the random-error terms ϵ_{ijk} are normally distributed with mean zero and variance σ^2. The variance is the same for all combinations jk.
2. The random-error terms are independent.

We will assume throughout this chapter that the ANOVA assumptions are met for all examples and problems. These assumptions can be tested by advanced methods.

There are three sets of hypotheses for a two-factor model.

1. a) H_0: $\tau_1 = \tau_2 = \cdots = \tau_J = 0$. This null hypothesis says that no level of Factor A has any influence on the dependent variable (no main effect A).

   b) H_a: at least one $\tau_j \neq 0$. The alternative hypothesis is that one or more of the levels of Factor A *do* influence the dependent variable (significant main effect A).

2. a) H_0: $\lambda_1 = \lambda_2 = \cdots = \lambda_K = 0$. This null hypothesis says that no level of Factor B has any influence on the dependent variable (no main effect B).

   b) H_a: at least one $\lambda_k \neq 0$. The alternative hypothesis is that one or more of the levels of Factor B *do* influence the dependent variable.

3. a) H_0: $(\tau\lambda)_{jk} = 0$ for all combinations of j and k. This null hypothesis says that there is no interaction effect for any combination of Factor A and Factor B.

   b) H_a: $(\tau\lambda)_{jk} \neq 0$ for at least one combination of j and k. The alternative hypothesis is that there is interaction.

As was the case for the one-way analysis, two-factor ANOVA hypotheses are tested by calculating an *F*-ratio. The three *F*-ratios used for testing the three sets of hypotheses given above are as follows:

---

1. Main effects A:

$$F = \frac{MSC}{MSE}, \qquad \text{with } J - 1, JK(n - 1) \text{ d.f.}$$

2. Main effects B:

$$F = \frac{MSR}{MSE}, \qquad \text{with } K - 1, JK(n - 1) \text{ d.f.}$$

(11.10)

3. Interaction effects:

$$F = \frac{MSI}{MSE}, \qquad \text{with } (J - 1)(K - 1), JK(n - 1) \text{ d.f.}$$

Notice that the denominator in each of these F-ratios is MSE.

If there are significant main effects A, each main effect A can be estimated by taking the difference between the column mean and the grand mean. Significant main effects B can be estimated by taking the difference between the row means and the grand mean.

Example 11.5. We can test hypotheses concerning the effect of brand and speed on mileage using $\alpha = 0.05$ and the data in Examples 11.3 and 11.4. Assume $\alpha = 0.05$.

1. H_0: $\tau_1 = \tau_2 = \tau_3 = 0$ (brand has no influence on gas mileage).
   H_a: at least one $\tau_j \neq 0$ (brand influences MPG).
   Using the mean squares from Example 11.4,

$$F = \frac{\text{MSC}}{\text{MSE}} = \frac{36.480}{1.265} = 28.84 \qquad \text{with 2, 36 d.f.}$$

Table VIII(a) does not list the critical value for 2, 36 d.f., but we know that it must lie between 3.32 (for 2, 30 d.f.) and 3.23 (for 2, 40 d.f.). Since the calculated value of 28.84 is larger than either of these critical values, we reject the null hypothesis and conclude that there are significant main effects A. That is, it appears that car brand *does* influence MPG. A p-value can be reported here by determining $P(F > 28.84)$. Computer programs often give a very precise p-value, and such programs usually label this p-value "significance of F." All we can do using Tables VIII(a) and (b) is note that this probability is less than 0.01. Hence, we report $p < 0.01$. From Table 11.9, the estimated main effects for brand are

$$\hat{\tau}_1 = 25.7 - 27.1 = -1.4;$$

$$\hat{\tau}_2 = 26.9 - 27.1 = -0.2;$$

$$\hat{\tau}_3 = 28.7 - 27.1 = 1.6.$$

(Notice that the sum of the estimated main effects equals zero. This is true only when the sample sizes are equal.)

2. H_0: $\lambda_1 = \lambda_2 = \lambda_3 = \lambda_4 = 0$ (car speed has no influence on MPG).
   H_a: at least one $\lambda_k \neq 0$ (speed influences MPG).

$$F = \frac{\text{MSR}}{\text{MSE}} = \frac{106.64}{1.265} = 84.30 \qquad \text{with 3, 36 d.f.}$$

From Table VIII(a) this F-ratio lies in the critical region; hence, we reject H_0 and conclude that car speeds *do* significantly influence MPG. The p-value to be reported here is $p < 0.01$. The estimated main effects for speed are:

$$\hat{\lambda}_1 = 30.4 - 27.1 = 3.3;$$

$$\hat{\lambda}_2 = 25.7 - 27.1 = -1.4;$$

$$\hat{\lambda}_3 = 23.7 - 27.1 = -3.4;$$

$$\hat{\lambda}_4 = 28.6 - 27.1 = 1.5.$$

Again, the sum of these estimated main effects equals zero.

3. H_0: $(\tau\lambda)_{11} = (\tau\lambda)_{12} = \cdots = (\tau\lambda)_{43} = 0$
   (no interaction effect on MPG between brand and speed).
   H_a: at least one $(\tau\lambda)_{jk} \neq 0$
   (interaction between brand and speed influences MPG).

$$F = \frac{MSI}{MSE} = \frac{1.307}{1.265} = 1.033 \qquad \text{with 6, 36 d.f.}$$

From Table VIII(a) this value of F does not fall in the critical region; hence, we accept the null hypothesis that there is no interaction. The p-value to be reported here is $p > 0.05$.

11.6 CALCULATING THE SUMS OF SQUARES*

When the total sample size in a two-way ANOVA problem is not small, it is not practical to determine the sums of squares by hand calculations. In Section 11.7 we will present a computer output for ANOVA to show how easy it is to interpret. The formulas presented below give the same answers but involve a lot more work.

$$SST = \sum_i \sum_j \sum_k (y_{ijk} - \bar{y})^2.$$

This is the sum of squared deviations of each observation in a cell (y_{ijk}) about the grand sample mean ($\bar{y}$).

$$SSC = Kn \sum_j (\bar{y}_j - \bar{y})^2$$

This sum of squared deviations measures the variability due to differences between the column means ($\bar{y}_j$) and the grand mean ($\bar{y}$). The Kn in the formula assures us that SSC represents the same total number of terms as SST.

$$SSR = Jn \sum_k (\bar{y}_k - \bar{y})^2.$$

---

* This section may be omitted without loss of continuity.

This sum of squared deviations measures the variability due to differences between the row means ($\bar{y}_k$) and the grand mean ($\bar{y}$). The Jn in the formula assures us that SSR represents the same total number of terms as SST.

$$\text{SSI} = n \sum_j \sum_k (\bar{y}_{jk} - \bar{y}_j - \bar{y}_k + \bar{y})^2.$$

This sum of squared deviations measures the variability due to differences between the mean of each cell ($\bar{y}_{jk}$) and the grand mean ($\bar{y}$) after eliminating (subtracting) the effect of both the column mean ($\bar{y}_j$) and the row mean ($\bar{y}_k$).*

$$\text{SSE} = \sum_i \sum_j \sum_k (y_{ijk} - \bar{y}_{jk})^2.$$

This sum of squared deviations measures the (residual) variability between each observation in a cell (y_{ijk}) and the mean of that cell ($\bar{y}_{jk}$).

Example 11.6. We calculate below the five sums of squares using the data given in Examples 11.3 and 11.4 and Table 11.9. Table 11.12 presents the same data as Table 11.9, except that the mean of each cell is also provided. Using the information in Table 11.12 and the formulas for sums of squares, we illustrate the sums of squares in Example 11.4.

$$\text{SST} = (29.2 - 27.1)^2 + (28.6 - 27.1)^2 + \cdots + (31.4 - 27.1)^2$$
$$= 446.26;$$

$$\text{SSC} = (4)(4)[(25.7 - 27.1)^2 + (26.9 - 27.1)^2 + (28.7 - 27.1)^2]$$
$$= 72.96;$$

$$\text{SSR} = (4)(3)[(30.4 - 27.1)^2 + (25.7 - 27.1)^2 + (23.7 - 27.1)^2$$
$$+ (28.6 - 27.1)^2]$$
$$= 319.92;$$

$$\text{SSI} = (4)[(29.1 - 25.7 - 30.4 + 27.1)^2 + (29.7 - 26.9 - 30.4 + 27.1)^2$$
$$+ \cdots + (30.8 - 28.7 - 28.6 + 27.1)^2$$
$$= 7.84;$$

$$\text{SSE} = (29.2 - 29.1)^2 + (28.6 - 29.1)^2 + \cdots + (31.4 - 30.8)^2$$
$$= 45.54.$$

There are computational formulas (which we do not present) that make calculating these sums of squares somewhat easier. As indicated earlier, the easiest method is to use a computer program such as SAS, SPSS, or BMD.

* $\text{SSI} = n \sum_j \sum_k [\bar{y}_{jk} - \bar{y} - (\bar{y}_j - \bar{y}) - (\bar{y}_k - \bar{y})]^2 = n \sum_j \sum_k (\bar{y}_{jk} - \bar{y}_j - \bar{y}_k + \bar{y})^2.$

TABLE 11.12 **Results of two-factor MPG test**

		Factor A (Brand)			
		I	II	III	Averages
Factor B (MPH)	25	29.2	29.8	33.7	
		28.6	30.4	34.1	
		28.8	28.5	30.2	30.4
		29.8	30.1	31.6	
	means	29.1	29.7	32.4	
	35	23.9	24.7	26.4	
		24.1	26.4	26.2	
		25.5	26.1	27.3	25.7
		24.9	25.2	27.7	
	means	24.6	25.6	26.9	
	45	24.4	25.5	24.4	
		20.9	23.7	22.6	
		23.1	23.9	26.3	23.7
		21.6	22.5	25.5	
	means	22.5	23.9	24.7	
	55	26.2	28.6	30.1	
		27.7	27.9	29.5	
		25.6	28.0	32.2	28.6
		26.9	29.1	31.4	
	means	26.6	28.4	30.8	
Averages		25.7	26.9	28.7	$27.1 = \bar{y}$ = Grand mean

11.7 INTERPRETING A COMPUTER OUTPUT

There are a variety of computer programs for ANOVA, most of which differ only slightly in the format of their output. The computer output in Study Question 11.2 illustrates a typical output, this particular one resulting from the program SPSS (Statistical Package for the Social Sciences).

Study Question 11.2: A Pricing Study of Weed Cutters
A study investigated the price of a certain brand of weed cutter. Three cities were considered (City A in the East, City B in the Midwest, and City C in the West). Three types of stores were considered in

each city: department store, hardware store, and garden store. Four observations were taken in ech cell, with the following results (cell values are the observed prices).

	City A	City B	City C
Department store	64, 70, 78, 72	77, 81, 68, 75	56, 62, 63, 60
Hardware store	71, 75, 69, 82	72, 76, 78, 74	62, 65, 61, 59
Garden store	70, 84, 72, 74	69, 77, 73, 79	78, 70, 75, 73

Prepare an analysis of this two-way ANOVA problem using a computer program. State the hypotheses and interpret your output.

Answer. The hypotheses are

1. H_0: $\tau_1 = \tau_2 = \tau_3 = 0$ (no city effect) versus H_a: at least one $\tau_j \neq 0$.
2. H_0: $\lambda_1 = \lambda_2 = \lambda_3 = 0$ (no store effect) versus H_a: at least one $\lambda_k \neq 0$.
3. H_0: $(\tau\lambda)_{jk} = 0$ for all combinations of (j, k) (no interaction effect) versus H_a: $(\tau\lambda)_{jk} \neq 0$ for at least one (j, k) (interaction effect).

The following output is part of that generated by the SPSS program.

```
CITY    CITY A, B OR C
STORE   TYPE OF STORE
------------------------------------------------------------------
                     SUM OF        MEAN              SIGNIFICANCE
SOURCE OF VARIATION  SQUARES  DF   SQUARE     F      OF F
MAIN EFFECTS
   CITY              638      2    319.000    15.27     .001
   STORE             207      2    103.500    4.95      .010
2-WAY INTERACTIONS
   CITY     STORE    285      4    71.25      3.41      .036
RESIDUAL             564      27   20.89                .001
TOTAL                1694     35
```

The conclusions based on the **F**-ratios in this ANOVA analysis are as follows:

1. There is a significant main effect due to city ($F = 15.27$, $p \le 0.001$). That is, prices *do* appear to differ across cities.
2. There is a significant main effect due to store ($F = 4.95$, $p \le 0.001$). That is, prices *do* appear to differ across stores.
3. There is a significant interaction effect ($F = 3.41$, $p = 0.036$). That is, the best type of store to shop for this weed cutter in one city is not necessarily the best type in another city.

Define. *Main effects, interaction effect.*

PROBLEMS

For these problems, assume that the ANOVA assumptions are met.

11.12 Explain why three null hypotheses are needed for two-way ANOVA. Write each of the three null hypotheses.

11.13 Describe a real-world situation in which two-way ANOVA would be useful. Do not use an example presented in the text.

11.14 Describe the assumptions necessary for testing hypotheses for two-way ANOVA.

11.15 What would you conclude if, in a two-way ANOVA test, the *F*-test for one of the main effects equals zero? What would you conclude if the *F*-value for interaction equals 0?

11.16 Return to **Data Set 3,** representing 45 observations on the elongation of leather. Assume that these data came from three different types of leather (I, II, and III). In each column the first five observations came from I, the second five came from II, and the last five came from III. Complete a two-way ANOVA test on these data, using $\alpha = 0.01$. Specify your hypotheses.

11.17 For the experimental data reported in Problem 11.9 the suggestion has been made that pulp brightness may depend on the batch from which each sample was drawn. Use the first nine observations in each column, assuming the first three were from Batch A, the second three from Batch B, and the next three from Batch C. Determine if there are significant main effects (batch or chemical) or significant interaction effects. Let $\alpha = 0.01$.

11.18 Describe, in your own words, why considering main effects alone is not sufficient for two-way ANOVA.

11.19 Floristan, Inc. has run compression tests on three types of chewable pills (to determine the pressure it takes for a pill to crumble). There are three different brands being tested. The results are as follows:

	Type		
	Brand A	Brand B	Brand C
Type I	0.72, 0.58, 0.74, 0.56	0.81, 0.70, 0.64, 0.67	0.68, 0.60, 0.66, 0.61
Type II	0.52, 0.78, 0.56, 0.62	0.64, 0.69, 0.58, 0.67	0.73, 0.55, 0.61, 0.70
Type III	0.68, 0.76, 0.77, 0.71	0.82, 0.80, 0.79, 0.85	0.91, 0.84, 0.82, 0.66

Determine whether there is a significant difference across brands and across types, using $\alpha = 0.05$. Estimate the brand effects and the type effects if they are significant. Is the interaction effect significant?

11.20 Return to the data in Problem 11.10. These data represent the ratio of new assessments to prior assessments for five townships in one county in Indiana. The one-way analysis grouped all nine observations in a single column together. Now we learn that observations 1–3 represented farm property, observations 4–6 represented commercial property, and observations 7–9 represented residential property. Conduct a two-way ANOVA test on these data, using $\alpha = 0.01$. Be sure to specify your hypotheses and interpret your results.

11.21 Three different brands of radial tires were tested to determine how long the tread would last under various temperatures. The tires were tested in dry weather using temperatures of 60°, 70°, and 80°. Use the following data to run a two-factor ANOVA test with $\alpha = 0.01$. Be sure to specify your hypotheses and interpret your results. Entries in the table represent mileage, in thousands of miles.

	Tire		
	A	B	C
80°	46, 49, 49, 48	50, 52, 59, 52	42, 45, 46, 44
70°	48, 50, 50, 51	57, 55, 58, 52	47, 43, 43, 44
60°	44, 42, 45, 44	44, 41, 40, 44	43, 45, 45, 46

11.22 For Problem 11.21 estimate the main effect for each type of tire and for each temperature. Which tire would you buy?

USING THE COMPUTER

11.23 Use a computer statistical package to solve any or all of the following problems.

   a) 11.4   b) 11.5   c) 11.8   d) 11.9   e) 11.10
   f) 11.16   g) 11.17   h) 11.19   i) 11.20   j) 11.21

11.24 For the following computer output, the experiment involves the rating by consumers (of various ages) of different brands of coffee.

```
    CAGE                      CONSUMER AGE CATEGORY
    BRND                      BRAND OF COFFEE

                    SUM OF         MEAN            SIGNIFICANCE
SOURCE OF VARIATION SQUARES DF   SQUARE      F        OF F
MAIN EFFECTS
    CAGE            10.667   2    5.333    1.426      .266
    BRND           354.889   2  177.444   47.436     .001
2-WAY INTERACTIONS
    CAGE    BRND     1.778   4     .444     .119      .974
RESIDUAL            67.333  18    3.741
TOTAL             434.667  26    16.718
```

   a)   How many age categories are there? How many brands? How many replications? What is the total sample size?

   b)   Are the main effects significant? Is there a significant interaction effect? Is the total amount explained significant?

11.25 The output below was generated by a computer program called MICRO-STAT. The dependent variable is the weight loss by men participating in one of four diets. The men are divided into two age groups — under 40 and 40 or older.

```
          ANALYSIS OF VARIANCE
            TWO-WAY ANOVA

        COL        MEAN     N
         1        11.12     8
         2         8.75     8
         3        10.62     8
         4         7.75     8
```

```
                         ROW
                          1        20.25    16
                          2        18.00    16

                CELL   MEANS
                ROW     COL     MEAN     N
                 1       1      12.00     4
                 2       1      10.25     4
                 1       2       9.00     4
                 2       2       8.25     4
                 1       3      11.25     4
                 2       3      10.00     4
                 1       4       8.25     4
                 2       4       7.25     4
              GRAND  MEAN       9.56    32

   SOURCE      SUM OF SQUARES   D.F.    MEAN SQUARE   F-RATIO
    COLS              60          3        20.00       7.49
    ROWS              10          1        10.00       3.75
 INTERACTION           2          3         0.67       0.25
    ERROR             64         24         2.67
    TOTAL            136         31
```

Determine whether there is a significant main effect for rows or columns. Estimate the main effects. Interpret these results in terms of diets and the age of the men.

EXERCISES

11.26 Prove that SST = SSW + SSB for one-way ANOVA.

11.27 Describe the main effects and the interaction effects that might occur in a three-factor ANOVA.

11.28 Make up a problem unlike any in this text for which a three-way ANOVA would be appropriate.

11.29 Consider the two graphs in Fig. 11.1 (on page 546) representing a two-way ANOVA. Each number represents the mean of a cell.
a) Would you guess that in Fig. 11.1(a) there are significant main effects A or B? Would you estimate significant interaction effects? The sample size is 20 for each cell.
b) Repeat the analysis using Fig. 11.1(b).

11.30 Consider the diagram of a two-factor model in Fig. 11.2 (on page 546). Each number represents a cell mean, and each cell contains 50 observa-

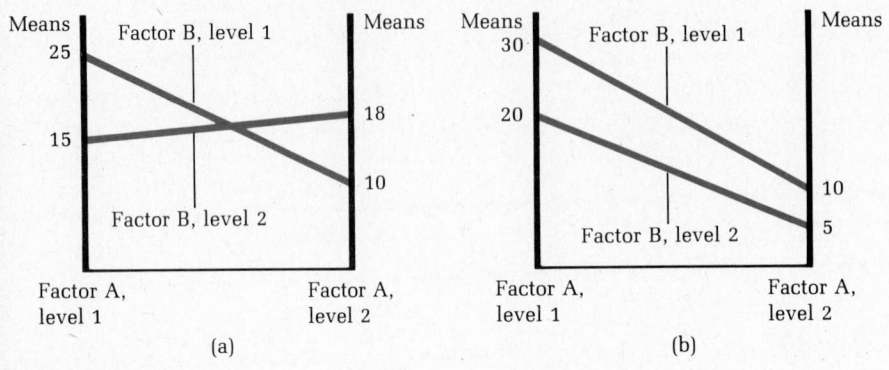

(a) (b)

FIGURE 11.1

tions. From this diagram, would you guess there are significant (a) main effects A, (b) main effects B, or (c) interaction effects?

11.31 An administrator of a medical insurance plan is concerned with the length of time various patients stay in the hospital. To study this situation, the administrator has picked three comparable hospitals and categorized patients in these hospitals as male or female and either under 40 or 40 or older. All patients studied had comparable illnesses. Conduct a three-way analysis of variance on the following data.

Length of Stay in Hospital (Days)			
	Hospital A	Hospital B	Hospital C
Males <40	29, 36, 28,	14, 5, 10,	22, 25, 23,
≥40	35, 33, 38	8, 7, 16	20, 30, 32
Females <40	25, 35, 31,	3, 5, 8,	18, 7, 15,
≥40	32, 26, 34	9, 4, 6	11, 8, 10

FIGURE 11.2 **The matrix for a two-factor model.**

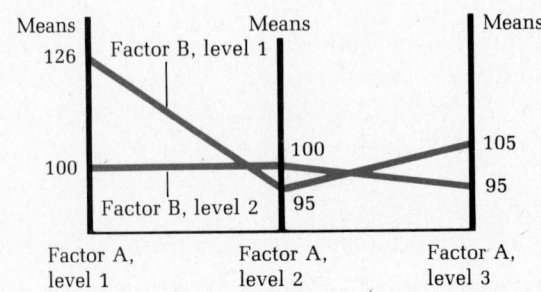

11.32 The National Federation of Independent Business Research and Education Foundations has provided data on the minutes of work time (average of manufacturing workers) required to earn enough income to purchase items in a weekly food basket. Use ANOVA to determine whether the average times in the cities listed below differ at the $\alpha = 0.05$ level of significance.

Commodity	Washington	London	Paris	Munich
Bread, 1 kg	16	16	18	27
Hamburger meat, beef, 1 kg	37	63	80	70
Sausages, 1 kg	33	51	75	75
Sugar, 1 kg	9	11	9	10
Butter, 1 kg	55	50	47	52
Milk, 1 liter	6	9	8	7
Cheese, 1 kg	100	65	59	65
Eggs, 10	8	16	13	12
Potatoes, 1 kg	7	3	4	4
Carrots, 1 kg	11	13	7	10
Apples, 1 kg	10	23	15	15
Tea, 100 g	10	5	17	10
Beer, 1 liter	11	18	7	8
Vodka, 0.7 liter	61	131	107	74
Cigarettes, 20	9	25	8	16

CASE PROBLEM

11.33 **Data Set 1** contains information for 78 cities on income, taxes, Moody rating, and cyclical threat. Suppose you are interested in determining whether a city's income is related to its Moody rating and cyclical threat. Do this by considering cities with only Aa, A, or Baa Moody ratings. Selecting randomly, find nine cities with an Aa rating, three having high cyclical threat, three having moderate cyclical threat, and three having low cyclical threat. Repeat this process for the A Moody rating and for the Baa rating so that you have a total of 27 observations. Record the income level for each of the 27 observations and conduct a two-way ANOVA test. Specify your hypotheses and interpret your results, using $\alpha = 0.05$.

GLOSSARY

Analysis of variance (ANOVA): A method for testing hypotheses about the means of two or more populations.

Grand mean: The mean of all values under investigation.

Treatment effect: An effect associated with a particular population.

Random-error term: A term representing the variability within a column (one-way analysis) or within a cell (two-way analysis).

Sum of squares: A sum of squared deviations about a mean.

SSW: The sum of squares within a column (one-way analysis).

SSB: The sum of squares between columns (one-way analysis).

SST: The sum of squares total: SST = SSW + SSB (one-way analysis).

Mean square: A sum of squares divided by its degrees of freedom.

MSW: Mean square within: $MSW = SSW \left/ \left(\sum\limits_{j=1}^{J} n_j \right) - J \right.$

MSB: Mean square between: MSB = SSB/(J − 1).

F-ratio: F = MSB/MSW; used to test hypotheses of equal means.

ANOVA table: A table showing the sources of variation with sums of squares, degrees of freedom, and mean squares.

Two-factor model: A model of an experiment in which the dependent variable is hypothesized to depend on two variables.

Main effect: An effect associated with a single variable.

Interaction effect: An effect associated with a combination of factors after eliminating the main effects of each separate factor.

SST (two-way analysis): The sum of squares total composed of SSColumns plus SSRows plus SSInteraction plus SSError.

MSC, MSR, MSI, MSE: Mean square columns, rows, interaction, and error.

Simple Regression and Correlation Analysis

TWELVE

12.1 INTRODUCTION

In the past several chapters we have discussed the process of using sample information to make inferences, test hypotheses, or modify beliefs about the characteristics of a population. In this chapter and the next, we turn to a related problem, involving two or more variables — making inferences about how changes in one variable are related to changes in another set of variables. A description of the *nature* of the relationship between two or more variables is called *regression analysis*, while investigation into the *strength* of such relationships is called *correlation analysis*.

Sir Francis Galton, an English expert on heredity in the late 1800's, was one of the first researchers to work with the problem of describing one variable on the basis of one or more other variables. Galton's work centered on the heights of fathers compared to the heights of their sons. He found that there was a tendency toward the mean — both exceptionally short fathers and unusually tall fathers tended to have sons of more average height. Galton said that the heights of the sons "regressed" or reverted to the mean, thus originating the term *regression*. Nowadays the term "regression" more generally means the description of the nature of the relationship between two or more variables.

Regression analysis is concerned with the problem of describing or estimating the value of one variable, called the *dependent* variable, on the basis of one or more other variables, called *independent* or *explanatory* variables.* Suppose, for example, that a business manager is trying to predict sales for next month (the dependent variable) on the basis of indexes of disposable income, price levels, or any of numerous other independent variables, or is trying to predict the performance of one product under certain conditions of stress or at various temperatures. Similarly, this person may be using one or more of a battery of tests to evaluate the ability of prospective employees for new jobs. In these cases, regression analysis is used in an attempt to *predict* or estimate the value of an unknown dependent variable (such as leadership ability) on the basis of the known value of one or more other measured characteristics, which are the given independent variables. In other cases, regression may be used to *describe* the relationship between known values of two or more variables. An economist may use it for this purpose as an aid to understanding the relationship between historical observations over a

---

* This label of dependent and independent variables in a regression model is different from our previous *statistical* definitions of independent and dependent events or of independent random variables.

specified time span, such as the relationship of consumption to current and past levels of income and wealth or the relationship between any one or more of a number of economic indicators and prices, profits, or unemployment.

No matter whether regression analysis is used for descriptive or predictive purposes, one cannot expect to be able to forecast or describe the *exact* value of sales, or profits, or consumption, or any other dependent variable. There may be many factors that could cause variations in the dependent variable, such as fluctuations in the stock market, changes in the weather, a passing fad, or just differences in human ability and motivation. Because of these possible variations, we shall be interested in determining the *average* relationship between the dependent variable and the independent variables. That is, we will want to be able to estimate the mean value of a dependent variable for any given values of the independent variables. Although regression analysis can involve one or more independent variables, in this chapter we will confine our analysis to the case of *simple* linear regression — i.e., only *one* independent variable. *Multiple* linear regression, which involves two or more independent variables, will be presented in Chapter 13.

12.2   THE REGRESSION MODELS

For most regression analysis the average population relationship between the dependent variable (usually denoted by the letter y) and the independent variable (denoted by the letter x) is assumed to be linear. A straight line is used because it is mathematically simple and yet still provides an approximation to the real-world relationship that is sufficient for most practical purposes.*

The Population Regression Model   Since we are interested in determining the mean value of y for a given value x, we are interested in the expectation $\mu_{y \cdot x}$, which is read as "the mean of the y-values for a given x-value." To write down an equation representing the population straight-line relationship between x and the mean of the y-values, called the **population regression line,** we need to know its *slope* and the *y-intercept*. The Greek letter β (beta) is traditionally used to denote the slope, while the letter α (alpha) traditionally represents

---

* The variables y and x may, of course, be transformations of economics or business data, such as $y = $ (change in sales)^2 or $x = $ 1/(interest rate). Thus, theoretically, nonlinear relationships may still be expressed in a linear regression model. See Section 14.6 for further discussion of this point. Also, we shall usually treat the independent variable as a given set of values, not as a random variable.

the y-intercept. The mean value of y for a given value x is denoted by the symbol $\mu_{y \cdot x}$. Thus, the population regression line can be written as follows:

Population regression line:

$$\mu_{y \cdot x} = \alpha + \beta x. \qquad \textbf{(12.1)}$$

To illustrate this population line, we will suppose that y represents the quantity of beef purchased per month by a household and x represents the retail price of beef. The value of $\mu_{y \cdot x}$ is thus the mean quantity of beef purchased per month for some given price of beef. When some particular value of x is specified, it is customary to denote this value as x_i, and to let $\mu_{y \cdot x_i}$ represent the mean of the y-values for the specific value x_i. Thus, x_i in our illustration might be $x_i = \$2.79/\text{lb}$, and

$$\mu_{y \cdot x_i} = \mu_{y \cdot \$2.79} = \alpha + \beta (\$2.79)$$

would be the mean quantity purchased per month when the price is $\$2.79/\text{lb}$. We merely substitute the specific value x_i for x into Formula (12.1).

In addition to estimating the mean value $\mu_{y \cdot x_i}$ we may wish to make statements about a particular value of y for a given value x_i. This ith variable is denoted by y_i. For example, we may want to make a statement about the quantity of beef a household would purchase per month when the price of beef is $x_i = \$2.79/\text{lb}$. As we indicated above, an *observed* value y_i for the given value x_i is usually not equal to $\mu_{y \cdot x_i}$. The difference between y_i and $\mu_{y \cdot x_i}$ depends upon the accuracy of the regression model in depicting the real-world situation and the accuracy with which the variables x and y are measured. It also depends on the predictability of the underlying behavior of the persons, businesses, governments, etc., involved in the model. Any changes in human or institutional behavior could also cause some differences.

The point of the above discussion is that the difference between y_i and $\mu_{y \cdot x_i}$ is the unpredictable element in regression analysis. This difference is usually called the random "error" and is denoted by the symbol epsilon, ϵ_i. That is,

---

Error in the population model:

$$\epsilon_i = y_i - \mu_{y \cdot x_i} \qquad \text{or} \qquad y_i = \mu_{y \cdot x_i} + \epsilon_i. \qquad \textbf{(12.2)}$$

Suppose that the price of beef is $x_i = \$2.79$ and that the average quantity purchased per month by *all* households at this price is

$$\mu_{y \cdot \$2.79} = 5 \text{ lbs.}$$

If the household purchases $y_i = 3.2$ lbs per month, the error in the model in this case would be

$$\epsilon_i = 3.2 - 5.0 = -1.8 \text{ lbs.}$$

Now we can use Formula (12.2) to describe what is called the **population regression model.** This model consists of all the terms that, when added together, sum to y_i. Substituting $y_i = \mu_{y \cdot x_i} + \epsilon_i$ into (12.1), we get

> Population regression model: $y_i = \alpha + \beta x_i + \epsilon_i.$ **(12.3)**

An illustration of this model is shown in Fig. 12.1, in which each dot represents one observation in the population. When values of x and y are plotted in this fashion, the diagram is called a *scatter diagram*. In such a scatter diagram the dependent variable y is plotted on the vertical axis. The model in Fig. 12.1 is a straight line because we are assuming that *linear* regression is appropriate. The point at which this line intersects the vertical axis is called the intercept. The value of the intercept is denoted by the Greek letter alpha (α). The rate of change in the vertical direction for each one-unit change on the x-axis is the slope of the line (denoted by β). For any value of the independent variable (x_i), the corresponding expected value for the dependent variable is $\mu_{y \cdot x_i}$. The

FIGURE 12.1 **The population regression model.**

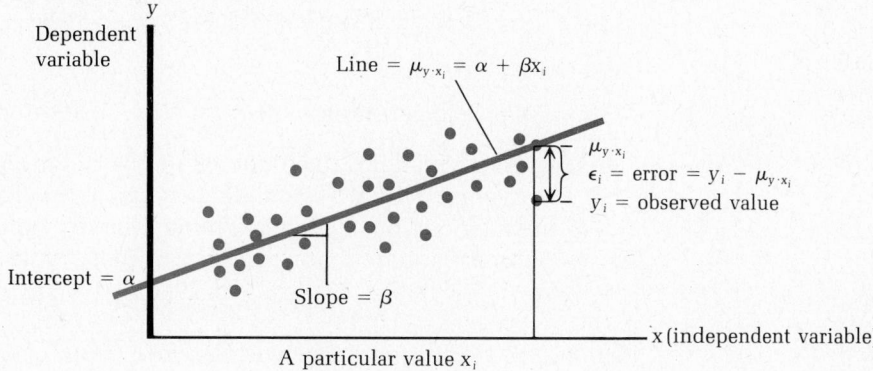

error ϵ_i is the vertical distance measured between the actual point observed (x_i, y_i) and the expected value on the line for the same x_i-coordinate.

To aid our introduction in the use of regression models, let us construct a simple model relating a worker's characteristics as measured by a test score (TEST) to the worker's output on a specific job assignment (OUTPUT). Many electric utility companies are offering customers a discount on the regular rate schedule if they convert to a load control or time-of-day pricing program. To make the conversion, special monitoring and control devices must be installed at the residence. Sometimes this is quite simple; other times it is a rather complex and lengthy installation. The difference depends on the wiring, the location of the main line, and separate devices for electric heating or air-conditioner units and for electric water heaters. Prior to assignment on this type of installation, utility employees or subcontractors must complete a training course and pass an examination. A score of 300 is required to pass; the maximum is 800. The electricians usually require two or three hours to install and check out the new devices at a residence. Thus, it is typical for them to complete at least two, more often three, and sometimes four or more installations in a day.

We wish to examine the relation, if any, between the typical number of installations completed per day (y = OUTPUT) and the training program test results (x = TEST). Observations are taken for a number of electricians over randomly selected days. We expect to find that electricians who score higher on the TEST generally complete a greater number of installations per day. They have demonstrated more knowledge and a higher level of the requisite skills.

Example 12.1. Assume (for the moment) that the population parameters relating OUTPUT (y) to TEST (x) are known quantities. For example, let us assume that $\alpha = 0.95$ and $\beta = 0.0039$. Thus, we have

Population regression line: $\mu_{y \cdot x} = 0.95 + 0.0039x$

and

Population regression model: $y_i = 0.95 + 0.0039x_i + \epsilon_i.$

This regression model is diagrammed in Fig. 12.2, from which we observe that the average OUTPUT for all workers with TEST scores of 550 is 3.095 installations per day. This value is easily derived by substituting $x_i = 550$ into the population regression line, as follows:

$$\mu_{y \cdot 550} = 0.95 + 0.0039(550) = 3.095.$$

If one electrician, Joe Egan, with a TEST score of 550 is selected from

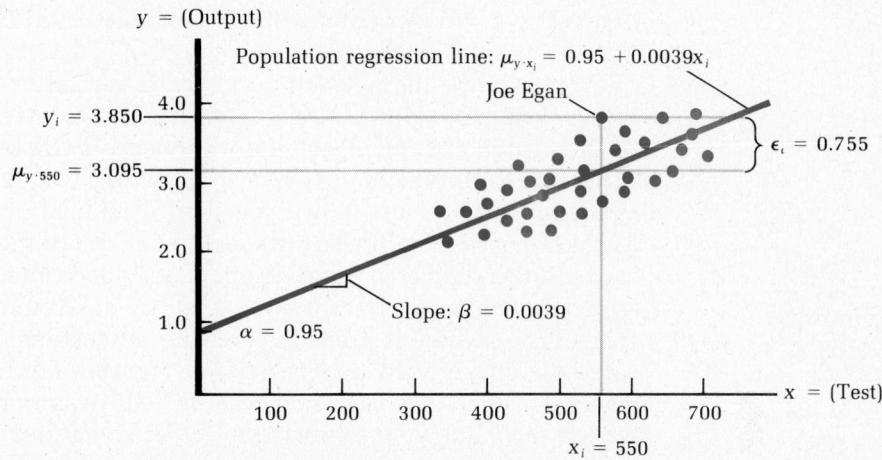

FIGURE 12.2 **Population regression line for TEST–OUTPUT example.**

this population and he has an OUTPUT of $y_i = 3.850$ completed installations per day, the amount of the error ϵ for this observation is

$$\epsilon_i = y_i - \mu_{y \cdot 550} = 3.850 - 3.095 = 0.755.$$

Our assumption that α and β are known is, of course, an unrealistic one. Usually, α and β can only be estimated on the basis of sample data. The following discussion introduces the sample regression model as the basis for estimating α and β.

The Sample Regression Model Following the process we started in Chapter 7, we use sample data to estimate population parameters. In the case of regression analysis the two population parameters to be estimated are α and β. Since α and β are used to determine $\mu_{y \cdot x}$ for a specified value of x, once we have an estimate of α and β we can also derive an estimate of $\mu_{y \cdot x}$ for any specified x-value. The **sample regression line** has the following form:

Sample regression line: $\quad \hat{y} = a + bx.$ **(12.4)**

Let us explore how this sample line relates to the population regression line in Formula (12.1). The sample value of a is our best estimator of α, while the sample value of b is our best estimator of β. Values of a and b, together with a given value of x, yield a predicted value of y, which is denoted $\hat{y}$; this $\hat{y}$-value is our best estimator of the population value $\mu_{y \cdot x}$.

We can add the subscript i to these variables to indicate specific values, just as we did for the population regression line. Thus, if x_i is a specific value of x, the equation for finding $\hat{y}_i$ (which is the best estimate of $\mu_{y \cdot x_i}$ for this value of x) is $\hat{y}_i = a + bx_i$. We can also specify a *sample regression model*, just as we specified a population regression model. Again, we need to define an error term, which in this case is the difference between the predicted value $\hat{y}_i$ and the actual value y_i. Recall that the error term for a population is denoted by ϵ_i. A corresponding English symbol is e_i, which is used to denote our best estimator of the population value ϵ_i. The e_i values in regression analysis are often referred to as *residuals*, since they represent what is "left over," or unexplained, after we use the value $\hat{y}_i$ to estimate the actual value y_i. That is,

$$\text{Residuals:} \quad e_i = y_i - \hat{y}_i \quad \text{or} \quad y_i = \hat{y}_i + e_i.$$

If we use the estimator $\hat{y}_i = y_i - e_i$ in Formula (12.4), we get the **sample regression model:**

$$\text{Sample regression model:} \quad y_i = a + bx_i + e_i. \qquad \textbf{(12.5)}$$

To illustrate the concept of a sample regression model, a group of electricians might be randomly selected, including the one highlighted earlier, Joe Egan. Figure 12.3 shows these sample observations in a scatter diagram; the line drawn through these points is the sample regression line (we will explain later how this line was derived). From Fig. 12.3 we see that

$$a = 0.751 \quad \text{and} \quad b = 0.00435,$$

and we have

$$\text{Sample regression line:} \quad \hat{y} = 0.751 + 0.00435x.$$

Note that, on the basis of our sample regression line, we predict that the mean OUTPUT for all electricians with TEST scores of 550 will be

$$\hat{y}_i = 0.751 + 0.00435(550) = 3.1435.$$

We can also determine the amount of "error" in predicting Joe Egan's OUTPUT by recalling that his actual installation record is $y_i = 3.850$ per day. The value of e_i is therefore

$$e_i = y_i - \hat{y}_i = 3.8500 - 3.1435 = 0.7065.$$

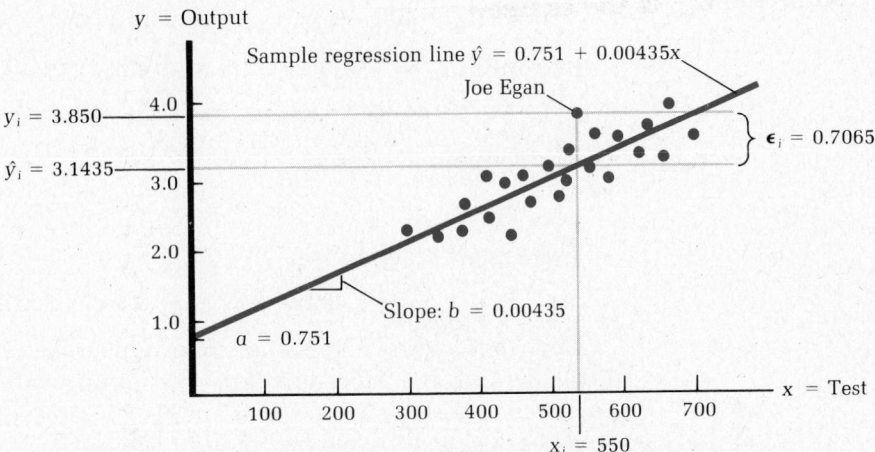

FIGURE 12.3 **Sample scatter diagram of observed values for y and x.**

Thus, the value $a = 0.751$ is an estimate of $\alpha = 0.95$; $b = 0.00435$ is an estimate of $\beta = 0.0039$; and for Joe Egan, the error $e_i = 0.7065$ is an estimate of the true error $\epsilon_i = 0.755$.

Study Question 12.1: Housing Price Population Model

A report by the U.S. Department of Commerce on housing in U.S. cities provides information on many variables related to housing. One part of this report (based on a census of cities) suggests the following population regression model relating the mean price (y) of a housing unit to the median income (x) of households in that city (each measured in thousands of dollars):

$$\mu_{y \cdot x_i} = -10.000 + 5x_i \quad (\$000).$$

A sample of ten cities was taken that included Fort Worth, Texas. The sample regression model based on these ten cities is

$$\hat{y}_i = -8.659 + 4.5404x_i \quad (\$000).$$

For Fort Worth the average housing price is $38,300, and the median income is $11,100. Find both the population model error and the sample model residual for this city.

Answer. Substitute the median income ($11.1 in thousands of dollars) into the population regression model to find the value predicted by the model for the average price of a housing unit:

$$\mu_{y \cdot 11.1} = -10.0 + 5(11.1) = 45.5 \ (\$000) \quad \text{or} \quad \$45,500.$$

Substituting the value $x_i = 11.1$ into the sample model, we obtain

$$\hat{y}_i = -8.659 + 4.5404(11.1) = 41.739 \ (\$000) \quad \text{or} \quad \$41,739.$$

The population error is

$$\epsilon_i = y_i - \mu_{y \cdot 11.1} = 38.3 - 45.5 = -7.2 \ (\$000) \quad \text{or} \quad -\$7200.$$

The sample residual is

$$e_i = y_i - \hat{y}_i = 38.3 - 41.739 = -3.439 \ (\$000) \quad \text{or} \quad -\$3439.$$

Now that we have specified the sample and population regression model, we need a procedure for determining values of **a** and **b** that provide the "best" estimates of α and β. The procedure for finding such estimates is called the *method of least squares*.

12.3 ESTIMATING THE VALUES OF α AND β BY LEAST SQUARES

A first step in finding a sample regression line of best fit is to plot the data in a scatter diagram. Such a plot allows us to visually determine whether a straight-line approximation to the data appears reasonable and to make rough estimates of α and β. Although this approach often yields fairly satisfactory results, there are at least two reasons for having a more systematic approach to finding the "best" straight-line fit to the data. First, different people are likely to find slightly different values for a and b by the freehand drawing method. Second, the freehand estimation procedure provides no way of measuring the sampling errors, which are always important in forming confidence intervals or doing tests of hypotheses on population parameters.

What we need is a mathematical procedure for determining the sample regression line that best fits the sample data. The first step in establishing such a mathematical procedure to obtain the line of best fit is to determine the criterion for defining "best fit." Perhaps the most reasonable criterion is to find values a and b so that the resulting values for $\hat{y}$ (in the equation $\hat{y} = a + bx$) are as close as possible to the observed values y_i. The approach used in Chapter 2 to measure closeness of values to the mean (variance) is the same one we will use now to measure closeness of estimated values to observed values — the sum of the *squared deviations* (this sum is called a *variation*). That is, we will find the line of best fit in regression analysis by determining the values of a and b that minimize the sum of the *squared residuals*. This procedure is known as the *method of least squares*.

There are a number of other criteria that might be used for determining a sample regression model. In some instances when particular distributions are assumed for the random variable ϵ_i, these other criteria are preferable. They often involve a minimization of an *absolute value function* of the deviations rather than the *sum of squares* of deviations. Obviously, different beginning criteria will result in different estimated values in the sample regression equation. In this text we emphasize the curve-fitting criterion of the method of least squares because it is the one most commonly used.

Finding the value of the two unknowns, a and b, that minimizes the sum of squared deviations is a problem that is solvable by calculus.* The reader should take care to understand that the two unknowns are the estimates a and b (not y and x), since it is a and b that must be determined given the sample observations on y_i and x_i. Since the residuals are represented by $e_i = \hat{y}_i - y_i$, the **least-squares estimation method** is defined as follows:

Method of least-squares estimation:

$$\text{Minimize} \sum_{i=1}^{n} e_i^2 = \sum_{i=1}^{n} (y_i - \hat{y}_i)^2.$$

The sample regression line determined by minimizing $\sum e_i^2$ is called *the least-squares regression line.* Since $\hat{y}_i = a + bx_i$, minimizing

$$\sum e_i^2 = \sum (y_i - \hat{y}_i)^2$$

* For convenience, let us denote the function to be minimized as

$$G = \sum_{i=1}^{n} [y_i - a - bx_i]^2.$$

Since this function is to be minimized with respect to a and b, it is necessary to take the partial derivatives of G with respect to these two variables, set each of these partials equal to zero, and then solve the resulting two equations simultaneously. The partial derivatives are

$$\frac{\partial G}{\partial a} = \sum_{i=1}^{n} 2(y_i - a - bx_i)(-1);$$

$$\frac{\partial G}{\partial b} = \sum_{i=1}^{n} 2(y_i - a - bx_i)(-x_i).$$

Setting these equal to zero yields the following two equations (called *the normal equations*), which can be solved to obtain Formula (12.6):

$$\sum_{i=1}^{n} y_i = na + b\sum_{i=1}^{n} x_i;$$

$$\sum_{i=1}^{n} x_i y_i = a\sum_{i=1}^{n} x_i + b\sum_{i=1}^{n} x_i^2.$$

Note also that setting the first partial equal to zero is identical to requiring that the sum of the residuals be zero, since the term in parentheses is the residual $e_i = (y_i - a - bx_i)$.

TABLE 12.2 **Sample points for TEST and OUTPUT and calculations of their means, variations, and covariation**

(1)	(2)	(3)	(4)	(5)	(6)
TEST (x_i)	OUTPUT (y_i)	$(x_i - \bar{x})$	$(y_i - \bar{y})$	$(x_i - \bar{x})(y_i - \bar{y})$	$(x_i - \bar{x})^2$
480	2.70	-60	-0.40	24	3,600
490	2.90	-50	-0.20	10	2,500
510	3.30	-30	$+0.20$	-6	900
510	2.90	-30	-0.20	6	900
530	3.10	-10	0.00	0	100
550	3.00	$+10$	-0.10	-1	100
610	3.20	$+70$	$+0.10$	7	4,900
640	3.70	$+100$	$+0.60$	60	10,000
Sum 4320	24.80	0	0.00	SCxy = 100	SSx = 23,000
Mean $\bar{x}$ = 540	$\bar{y}$ = 3.10				

we get $\hat{y}_i = \bar{y} + b(x_i - \bar{x})$. This means that whenever the given value is $x_i = \bar{x}$, the estimated value is $\hat{y}_i = \bar{y}$. Hence, the population regression line always goes through the point $(\bar{x}, \bar{y})$. Second, in order to minimize $\sum e_i^2$, it is necessary to set $\sum_{i=1}^{n} e_i = 0$ (see the preceding footnote). Thus, the sample regression line passes through the point of averages $(\bar{x}, \bar{y})$ and splits the scatter diagram of observed points so that the positive residuals (underestimates of the true point) always exactly cancel the negative residuals (overestimates of the true points). Such a sample regression line therefore estimates without bias the population regression line.

We will illustrate the technique of finding a least-squares regression line by applying it to our OUTPUT–TEST problem. Suppose that we now use the method of least squares to determine a and b for a random sample of eight observations (i.e., eight electricians).* Columns (1) and (2) in Table 12.2 give the data, ordered from the lowest TEST score to the highest. We will use the rest of the data in Table 12.2 in a moment.

Our first step in analyzing the data in the first two columns of Table 12.2 is to construct a scatter diagram, to see whether the assumption of linearity is a reasonable one in this case. Figure 12.4 indicates that it is.

The sums in columns (5) and (6) of Table 12.2 give the information necessary to calculate the slope. Using Formula (12.8), we can determine b as follows:

---

* For most practical purposes a sample size of eight would not be sufficient. We use small samples here and later only for expositional convenience in illustrating the computations and formulas.

$$b = \frac{SCxy}{SSx} = \frac{\sum\limits_{i=1}^{n} (x_i - \bar{x})(y_i - \bar{y})}{\sum\limits_{i=1}^{n} (x_i - \bar{x})^2}$$

$$= \frac{100}{23,000} = 0.00435.$$

Using this value of b and the means of x and y shown in columns (1) and (2) of Table 12.2, we obtain the following value of a:

$$a = \bar{y} - b\bar{x} = 3.10 - 0.00435(540) = 0.751.$$

Hence, the least-squares regression line for this example is

$$\hat{y} = 0.751 + 0.00435x. \tag{12.9}$$

Figure 12.5 illustrates this sample regression line. Since the line in Fig. 12.5 was determined by the method of least squares, there is no other line that could be drawn so that the sum of the squared residuals between the points and the line (measured in a vertical direction) would be smaller than for this line. The residuals and the estimated values of y_i for all eight sample points are given in Table 12.3. The sum of the residuals in this case (-0.003) differs from zero only because of rounding error.

Figure 12.6 presents a computer printout for the sample regression determined from the data in Table 12.2.

At this time the reader may wish to check his or her understanding of the least-squares procedure by verifying that the point of means $(\bar{x}, \bar{y})$ = (540, 3.1) does lie on the least-squares regression line given in Formula

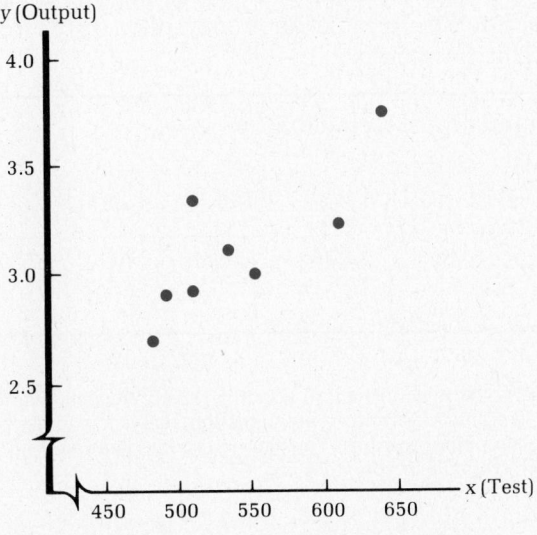

FIGURE 12.4 Scatter diagram for OUTPUT–TEST sample values.

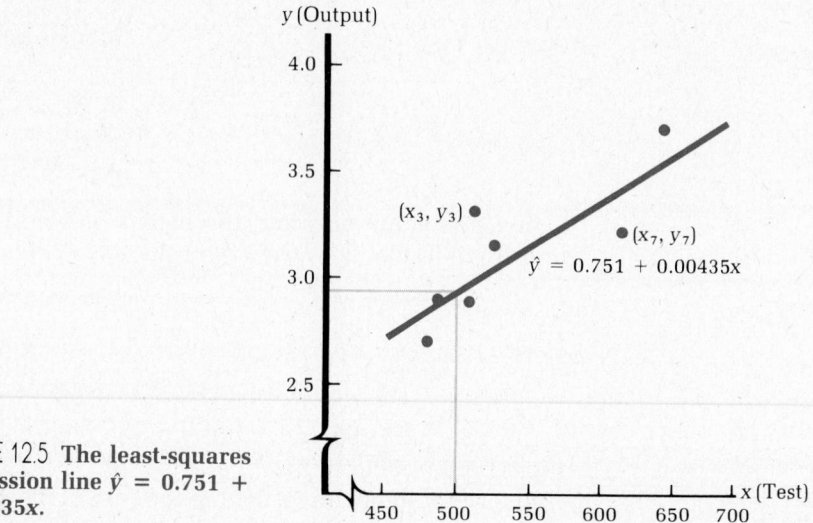

FIGURE 12.5 **The least-squares regression line $\hat{y} = 0.751 + 0.00435x$.**

(12.9). Also, note from Fig. 12.5 that a positive residual such as $e_3 = 0.330$ ($= y_3 - \hat{y}_3$) means that the point (x_3, y_3) lies above the line and, therefore, $\hat{y}_3$ underestimates y_3. On the other hand, a negative residual such as $e_7 = -0.205$ ($= y_7 - \hat{y}_7$) corresponds to an overestimation of y_7 by $\hat{y}_7$, in that the point (x_7, y_7) lies below the regression line.

Further Discussion of the Estimators a and b
Formula (12.8) provides a convenient method for calculating the regression slope b when the values of x and y are integers. When they are not integers, another formula for b may often prove to be computationally easier. This formula is*

Computational formula for b:

$$b = \frac{SCxy}{SSx} = \frac{\displaystyle\sum_{i=1}^{n} x_i y_i - \frac{1}{n}\left(\sum_{i=1}^{n} x_i\right)\left(\sum_{i=1}^{n} y_i\right)}{\displaystyle\sum_{i=1}^{n} x_i^2 - \frac{1}{n}\left(\sum_{i=1}^{n} x_i\right)^2}. \qquad \textbf{(12.10)}$$

* Formula (12.10) is equivalent to Formula (12.8). We also mention that the best way to avoid the computation drudgery in regression analysis is to use one of the numerous "canned" computer programs. You should become familiar with a regression program on a computer available to you.

TABLE 12.3 **Observed, estimated, and residual values for the least-squares regression shown in Fig. 12.5**

x_i	Observed Value (y_i)	Predicted Value $(\hat{y}_i = 0.751 + 0.00435x_i)$	Residual $e_i = (y_i - \hat{y}_i)$
480	2.70	2.839	−0.139
490	2.90	2.883	0.017
510	3.30	2.970	0.330
510	2.90	2.970	−0.070
530	3.10	3.057	0.043
550	3.00	3.144	−0.144
610	3.20	3.405	−0.205
640	3.70	3.535	0.165
Sum 4320	24.80	24.803	−0.003

We point out that since the value of b depends on the relative values of x and y, not on their absolute size, subtracting a constant from each value of x and/or y will not affect the regression slope. The advantage of such subtractions is that the arithmetic of Formula (12.10) will become much easier.

Example 12.2. To illustrate the use of Formula (12.10) and the use of *coded data*, we subtract a convenient number from each value of x and y in our OUTPUT–TEST example (data originally given in Table

FIGURE 12.6 **Computer printout based on the data in Table 12.2.**

```
SAMPLE SIZE= 8
SUM OF X= 4320            SUM OF SQUARES OF X= 2,355,800
SUM OF Y= 24.8            SUM OF SQUARES OF Y= 77.54

MEAN OF X= 540           MEAN OF Y= 3.1

SSx= 23,000              SSy= 0.66
VARIANCE OF X= 3285.7    VARIANCE OF Y= 0.094
STD DEV OF X= 57.32      STD DEV OF Y= 0.3071

SUM OF CROSS-PRODUCTS= 13492      SCxy= 100

SLOPE= 0.00435           INTERCEPT= 0.751
```

TABLE 12.4 **OUTPUT–TEST data repeated, with 500 subtracted from each x-value, and 3.00 subtracted from each y-value**

TEST x	OUTPUT y	xy	x²	y²
−20	−0.30	6.0	400	0.09
−10	−0.10	1.0	100	0.01
10	0.30	3.0	100	0.09
10	−0.10	−1.0	100	0.01
30	0.10	3.0	900	0.01
50	0	0	2,500	0
110	0.20	22.0	12,100	0.04
140	0.70	98.0	19,600	0.49
Sum 320	0.80	132.0	35,800	0.74

12.2). We (arbitrarily) elect to subtract 500 from each value of x and 3.00 from each value of y. The resulting values are shown in Table 12.4.

Using these sums and Formula (12.10), we can calculate b:

$$b = \frac{(132.0) - \frac{1}{8}(320)(0.80)}{(35,800) - \frac{1}{8}(320)^2} = 0.00435.$$

This is the same value of b calculated previously. In using coded data to find the slope b, one must remember to return to the original data in order to calculate the value of the intercept (a) as in Formula (12.8). An incorrect intercept will result unless the original units for the data are used.

Study Question 12.2: Sample Regression Model for Housing Price
Use the sample observations in Table 12.5 to find the sample regression model relating housing price (y) to median income (x) in U.S. cities. (The result should match the sample regression equation given in Study Question 12.1.) Find the slope using both Formulas (12.8) and (12.10). Which way is easier?

Answer. The calculational results (in $000) needed for substitution into Formula (12.8) are

$$\sum x_i = 122.3; \qquad \sum y_i = 468.7;$$
$$\bar{x} = 12.23; \qquad \bar{y} = 46.87;$$
$$SSx = \sum (x_i - \bar{x})^2 = 14.961; \qquad SCxy = \sum (x_i - \bar{x})(y_i - \bar{y}) = 67.929.$$

TABLE 12.5 **Housing price and median income (measured in thousands of dollars)**

Observation	Income	Price	Name
1	12.1	40.1	Albany
2	14.3	53.2	Anaheim
3	12.2	59.1	Boston
4	11.6	31.5	Dallas
5	13.5	46.5	Detroit
6	11.1	38.4	Fort Worth
7	11.0	49.3	Los Angeles
8	10.2	37.9	Memphis
9	13.0	46.8	Minneapolis
10	13.3	65.9	Newark

The values for the slope and intercept are

$$b = \frac{\text{SCxy}}{\text{SSx}} = \frac{67.929}{14.961} = 4.5404;$$

$$a = \bar{y} - b\bar{x} = 46.87 - 4.5404(12.23) = -8.659.$$

In original units, $a = -8.659(\$1000) = -\$8659$. The sample regression model is $\hat{y}_i = -8659 + 4.5405x_i$. The same results are obtained by using Formula (12.10). The covariation is

$$\text{SCxy} = \sum x_i y_i - \frac{1}{n}\left(\sum x_i\right)\left(\sum y_i\right)$$

$$= 5800.13 - \frac{1}{10}(122.3)(468.7) = 67.929.$$

The variation is

$$\text{SSx} = \sum x_i^2 - \frac{1}{n}\left(\sum x_i\right)^2$$

$$= 1510.69 - \frac{1}{10}(122.3)^2 = 14.961.$$

The second method [Formula (12.10)] is easier, since it avoids calculations using the deviations, $(x_i - 12.23)$ and $(y_i - 46.87)$.

Figure 12.7 presents selected parts of two computer printouts for this regression problem. Note how these differ in the print formats and the

FIGURE 12.7 **Computer printout for the housing price regression**

a) SPSS* printout

HOUSING, STUDY QUESTION 12.2

* *

DEPENDENT VARIABLE..   PRICE   AVERAGE HOUSING PRICE

VARIABLE(S) ENTERED ON STEP NUMBER 1..   INC   HOUSEHOLD MEDIAN INCOME

MULTIPLE R   0.55757
R SQUARE   0.31088

STANDARD ERROR   9.24442

----------------- VARIABLES IN THE EQUATION -------------------

VARIABLE   B   STD ERROR B   F

INC   4.5404   2.3900   3.609
(CONSTANT) -8.6591

b) SAS† printout

MODEL: MODEL01   SSE   683.675825   F RATIO   3.61
                          DFE   8   PROB>F   0.0940
DEP VAR: PRICE   MSE   85.459478   R-SQUARE   0.3109
         HOUSING PRICE

DURBIN-WATSON D STATISTIC   =   2.0969

                    PARAMETER   STANDARD
VARIABLE   DF   ESTIMATE   ERROR   T RATIO   PRB>|T|

INTERCEPT   1   -8.659154   29.375650   -0.2948   0.7757
INCOME   1   4.540405   2.390010   1.8997   0.0940

* SPSS is a registered trademark of SPSS, Inc.
† SAS is the registered trademark of SAS Institute Inc., Cary, N.C., 27522, U.S.A.

TABLE 12.6 **Regression model: Terms and symbols**

Term	Population Symbols	Sample Symbols
Model	$y_i = \alpha + \beta x_i + \epsilon_i$	$y_i = a + bx_i + e_i$
Error	ϵ_i (disturbance)	e_i (residual)
Slope	β	b
Intercept	α	a
Equation of line	$\mu_{y \cdot x_i}$	$\hat{y}_i$

selection of statistics reported. As mentioned in Chapter 2, there is a great time saving in using an existing computer program if it provides what is needed. If some specific form of printout or specific statistical measures are desired, a specific computer program may need to be written. The relevant parts of Fig. 12.7 for the current discussion are in color. Some other parts will be referred to later in this chapter.

Table 12.6 summarizes the terms and the symbols used in the regression model.

The least-squares regression line described by Formula (12.9) serves several purposes. First, the regression coefficients provide point estimates of the population parameters, 0.751 being an estimate of the intercept α and 0.00435 an estimate of the slope β. These point estimates serve a variety of research needs. Knowing the regression line also enables us to use the values of $\hat{y}$ to estimate the conditional mean of the dependent variable, $\mu_{y \cdot x}$, for specific values of x. Perhaps most important, the regression line permits prediction of the dependent variable given a value of the independent variable.

Example 12.3. The regression model relating OUTPUT and TEST scores can be used to predict the number of installations per day depending on the TEST scores after the training program (other worker characteristics being ignored). If $x_i = 500$, the best estimate for OUTPUT given by Formula (12.9) is

$$\hat{y}_i = 0.751 + 0.00435(500) = 2.926 \text{ per day.}$$

The slope of the relation, $b = 0.00435$, gives the estimated average change in OUTPUT for a unit change in the TEST scores. An increase in the TEST score of 100 points indicates an increase in installations completed of $0.00435(100) = 0.435$ per day.

Interpretation and Use of a Sample Regression Model

In using a regression line to make predictions about the dependent variable, the amount of uncertainty increases when values of the independent variable fall outside the range of past experience (historical data or sample observations), since it may be that these values cannot be represented by the same equation. The regression equation described above, for example, predicts that the number of completed installations per day of electricians scoring only 100 points on the TEST would be $\hat{y}_i = 0.751 + 0.00435(100) = 1.186$. This is below the practical minimal value for the number of installations completed daily. Moreover, there are no observations of electricians with this low TEST score, since the minimum passing score is 300. There is really no appropriate way of applying this regression equation to predict the OUTPUT when $x_i = 100$. Similarly, the equation would predict an OUTPUT of 5.10 per day by electricians who score 1000 on the TEST:

$$\hat{y}_i = 0.751 + 0.00435(1000) = 5.10.$$

Again, no persons were observed near this TEST score, since the maximum possible is 800.

The point is that special care must be taken in using a regression equation to make predictions. It must be remembered that the equation describes only an average relationship between the variables included in the model. *Other variables not included in the model* may cause deviations and errors from the values predicted by this simple relation. Also, since it is an *average* representation, it may not be accurate for any particular observation. It can be expected to represent only the average relation for values of x and y within the range of the sample data used in the estimation. In the above example the equation should not be used for predictions when the input variable x has values outside the range of about 400–700. The relation may be quite different for especially high or low values of x.

Several aspects of the method of least squares must be emphasized at this point. First, this method is just a curve-fitting technique, and as such it requires no assumptions about the distributions of **x** or **y** or **ε**. It is only when probability statements about the parameters of the population are desired that we need such assumptions because then **a** and **b** become random variables. Economists, for example, use regression analysis in an attempt to form interval estimates and to test various assumptions about population parameters in economic models, such as the marginal propensity to consume, the price elasticity of demand, and the factor shares of labor and capital in production. Also, they study the effect of changes in one variable (e.g., a tax change) on one or more other variables such as employment, consumption, prices, interest rates, or the federal deficit.

Second, the method of least squares can be adapted to apply to nonlinear populations. Although the computations necessary for applying the method of least squares to a nonlinear relationship naturally will differ from those used for linear relationships, the objective in fitting the curve is the same in the two cases — to find the line minimizing the sum of the squared residuals. Nonlinear regression models, which are often quite complex, can be found in more advanced texts on regression analysis.

As we have indicated, the method of least squares is just one curve-fitting technique in which the values of a and b are derived by finding the sample regression line that fits the sample data. The advantage of this approach is that if certain *assumptions* are made about the population, then the resulting estimators a and b can be shown to be unbiased, consistent, and efficient. Furthermore, these assumptions permit us to construct more easily the confidence intervals and to test the hypotheses that are so crucial to regression analysis. Therefore, in every regression-analysis problem the researcher must be satisfied that such assumptions are reasonable.

In Chapter 14 the role of the common assumptions underlying the valuable use of regression analysis will be explained. Also, some tests to examine the validity of the assumptions and some calculational methods to adjust for possible violations of the assumptions will be presented. In the next section we shall give only a brief statement of the assumptions and the derivable properties of the estimators. Following that, we proceed with the mechanics of regression analysis as if the assumptions are presumed to be valid.

12.4 ASSUMPTIONS AND ESTIMATOR PROPERTIES

The assumptions underlying regression analysis are primarily concerned with the random variable ϵ because this variable describes how well $\mu_{y \cdot x_i}$ estimates y_i. Making assumptions about the mean and the variance of ϵ enables us to make deductions about the probability distribution of the random variable e from the sample regression model. In turn, this knowledge allows us to determine the probability distributions of the estimators a for the intercept, b for the slope, and $\hat{y}_i$ for the predicted value of the dependent variable. With such probability distributions known, we can formulate confidence intervals or perform tests of hypotheses to learn about the overall population regression model. Such methods parallel those already presented in Chapters 8–11.

Many possible sets of assumptions could be formulated about the distribution of the variables in the population regression model. Five assumptions are commonly used because they yield estimators possessing desirable properties, and they result in test statistics that follow common distributions (**z**, **t**, **F**). These **five assumptions** of simple linear regression are briefly presented. See Chapter 14 for a more detailed discussion.

The Five Assumptions

Assumption 1. The random variable ϵ *is assumed to be statistically independent of* **x**. This means that the covariance is zero between the independent variable and the corresponding error term at each observation i. This assumption may be violated if the errors are a *percentage* of the values of **x** because of measurement error or if **y** influences **x** as well as being dependent on **x** (two-way causality or simultaneity). This assumption always holds when x is considered to be a set of given values and not a random variable.

Assumption 2. The random variable ϵ *is assumed to be normally distributed.* Figure 12.8 illustrates the meaning of this assumption (and assumptions 3 and 4 as well) by showing the normal distribution of errors ϵ_i about the population regression line.

Assumption 3. The random variable ϵ *is assumed to have a mean of zero; that is,* $E[\epsilon] = 0$. This means that, for a given x_i, the differences between y_i and $\mu_{y \cdot x_i}$ are sometimes positive, sometimes negative, but on the average are zero. Thus, the distribution of ϵ_i about the population regression line $\mu_{y \cdot x_i}$ (as shown in Fig. 12.8) is always centered at the value $\mu_{y \cdot x_i}$ for any given x_i.

FIGURE 12.8 **Normally distributed errors** ϵ_i **about** $\mu_{y \cdot x_i}$ **for any value** x_i **(given that assumptions 3 and 4 also hold).**

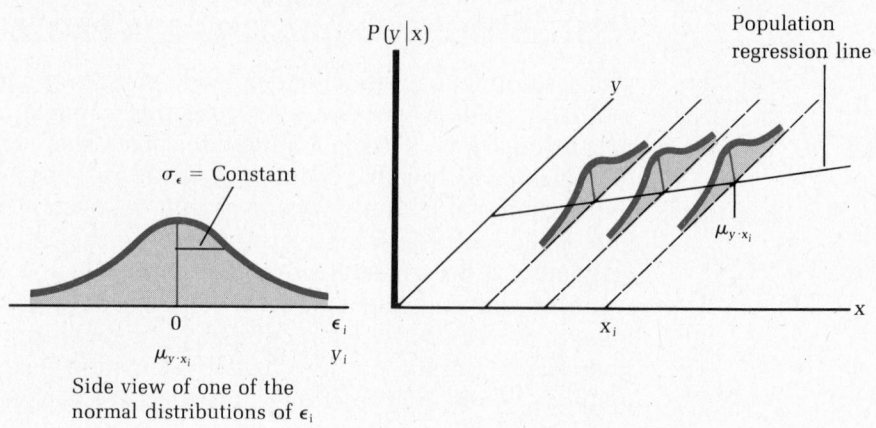

Assumption 4. *The random variables ϵ_i are assumed to have a finite variance σ_ϵ^2 that is constant for all given values of x_i.* This means that the dispersion or variability of points in the population about the population regression line must be constant. In Fig. 12.8 this constant variance of ϵ_i is represented by depicting all the normal distributions about $\mu_{y \cdot x_i}$ as having the same standard deviation. No one distribution is more spread out or more peaked than another for a different value of x. Assumption 4 is violated most often in *cross-sectional* observations of different firms, banks, households, states, countries, etc., measured at the same point of time. It is referred to as the assumption of *homoscedasticity*. Populations that do not have a constant variance are called *heteroscedastic*.

Assumption 5. *Any two errors, ϵ_i and ϵ_t, are assumed to be statistically independent of each other. Since they are normally distributed, this means that their covariance is zero, $C[\epsilon_i, \epsilon_t] = 0$.* This assumption means that the error of one point in the population cannot be related systematically to the error of any other point in the population. In other words, knowledge about the size or sign of one or more errors does not help in predicting the size or sign of any other error. This assumption is violated most commonly in *time-series data* — observations of the same firm, household, state, etc., that are drawn periodically over time. A violation of this assumption is called *autocorrelation*.

Properties of the Regression Coefficients

The good properties of least-squares estimators and the common forms of test statistics that result given these five assumptions account for the widespread use of the least-squares procedure. Given assumption 2, it can be shown that the estimators of α, β, and $\mu_{y \cdot x_i}$ obtained by using the least-squares criterion are normally distributed and are *identical* to the estimators that would result using the principle of maximum likelihood estimation. Such estimators have a number of desirable properties (such as consistency).

A second important result is that, given assumptions 1 and 3, the least-squares estimators can be shown to have the desirable property of unbiasedness. That is, they have an expected value that equals the corresponding population parameter (α, β, or $\mu_{y \cdot x_i}$). Third, given assumptions 4 and 5, the least-squares estimators have the property of efficiency (minimum variance among all unbiased estimators that might be derived).

In summary, these five assumptions are important in allowing us to know the characteristics of the estimators obtained by the simple least-squares fitting rules [Formula (12.8)]. By using these assumptions it is determinable that each estimator (a, b, or $\hat{y}$) is a random variable with a *normal* probability distribution. The means and variances of the estimators can be easily derived by using the rules for expectations (Section 4.4) and the five simplifying assumptions. Examination of these gives us the comforting information that each of these estimators (a, b, or $\hat{y}$) has three desirable properties:

1. correct on the average (unbiasedness);
2. relatively reliable on a single try (efficiency);
3. more and more accurate, on the average, if larger-sized samples are used (consistency).

In Section 12.6 we will make use of this probability knowledge about the estimators in order to make inferences about the population regression model relating variables y and x.

Define. *Independent and dependent variables in a regression model, population and sample regression lines and regression models, residuals, method of least squares, covariance, predicted values $\hat{y}_i$, variation (SSx), covariation (SCxy), five assumptions.*

PROBLEMS

12.1   Explain why a disturbance term ϵ is included in the population regression model.

12.2   Explain what is meant by "desirable properties of the estimator b."

12.3   Suppose that y = average test score on college entrance boards and x = hundreds of dollars of expenditures per pupil in the student's respective high school. Given that a regression of y on x gives $\hat{y} = 320 + 50x$, what is the interpretation of the value 50 and what value would you predict for y if x = 5?

12.4   Given the following data on five observations for the variables y, sales of cordless phones (000), and x, years (with 1983 = 0), find the slope and intercept for the least-squares estimating line, and write the complete estimating equation.

y:	3	19	18	22	23
x:	-2	-1	0	1	2

12.5   A manufacturing firm bases its sales forecast for each year on government estimates for total demand in the industry. The following data give the government estimate for total demand and this firm's sales for the past ten years.

Demand Estimate	Sales
200,000	5,000
220,000	6,000
400,000	12,000
330,000	7,000
210,000	5,000
390,000	10,000
280,000	8,000
140,000	3,000
280,000	7,000
290,000	10,000

a) Draw a scatter diagram and verify that a linear approximation would be appropriate in this problem.
b) Find the least-squares regression line, using Formula (12.10).
c) What sales figure represents the least-squares estimate if the government estimates total demand to be 300,000?

12.6 A study was conducted to determine the relationship (if any) between the number of people in a household (x) and the number of radios in that household (y). The following sample was collected.

people x:	3	1	5	2	4
radios y:	3	2	6	4	5

a) Plot these data on a scatter diagram to verify that none of the five assumptions is obviously violated.
b) Verify that the least-squares regression line is $\hat{y} = 1.3 + 0.9x$, using Formula (12.8). Show that this line goes through the point $(\bar{x}, \bar{y})$.
c) Calculate a $\hat{y}$-value for each x_i. Show that $\Sigma\,(y_i - \hat{y}_i) = 0$ for these values. Find $\Sigma\,(y_i - \hat{y}_i)^2$.
d) If $x_i = 7$, what value would you predict for $\hat{y}_i$?
e) Recalculate the regression line in part (b), using Formula (12.10).

12.7 Recalculate the sample regression line in Problem 12.5 by subtracting 200,000 from each government estimate and 8000 from each sales value. Use Formula (12.10).

12.8 For Problem 12.4, find the regression line $\hat{x} = a + by$, assuming that y is the independent variable. Is this the same line as $\hat{y} = a + bx$? Sketch the two least-squares lines on the same scatter diagram.

12.9 The following data pertain to selling prices and number of pages of new statistics books.

Price	Number of Pages
$25	400
27	600
27	500
25	300
23	400
23	200

Find the regression equation of y (price in dollars) on x (number of pages in hundreds), using the method of least squares.

12.10 The following data on production of spark plugs and average cost were collected.

Average Cost (cents)	Production per Month (000s)
13	25
19	20
40	10
25	20
33	15

a) Find the regression equation of cost (y) on production (x), using the method of least squares.
b) Does the scatter diagram for these observations indicate any possible violations of the five assumptions?
c) What is the value of s_{xy} for these data?
d) Find $\hat{y}$ for each x-value, and then calculate $(y_i - \hat{y}_i)$ for each x-value.

12.11 Consider the following values of x and y.

x:	5	1	7	6	4
y:	22	2	83	38	15

a) Plot the scatter diagram for these data. Which of the five assumptions appears to be violated?
b) Determine the least-squares regression line for these data.

c) Calculate $(y_i - \hat{y}_i)$ for each value of x_i. Is there any pattern to these deviations?

d) What value does the regression line predict if $x_i = 8$? What value would you predict?

12.12 Use the data on housing prices and median income in Table 12.5 and the sample regression line from Study Question 12.2. Find the residuals for each observation. Sum the residuals to see whether they sum to zero. Find the sum of squares of residuals that was minimized by the method of least squares.

12.5 MEASURES OF GOODNESS OF FIT

In this section we will present two measures of goodness of fit. The first is a measure of the *absolute* fit of the sample points to the sample regression line, called the *standard error of the estimate*. The second measure is an index of the *relative* goodness of fit of a sample regression line, called the *coefficient of determination*. Our presentation of these measures will be easier if some of the components of variability in regression analysis are understood first.

Deviations In regression analysis the difference between y_i and the mean of the y-values $(\bar{y})$ is often called the *total deviation of y*; that is, it represents the total amount that the ith observation deviates from the mean of all y-values. By a mathematical identity this total deviation can be written as the *sum* of two other deviations; one is $(y_i - \hat{y}_i)$, and the other is $(\hat{y}_i - \bar{y})$.

You will recognize the first of these two deviations, $(y_i - \hat{y}_i)$, as the residual value e_i discussed in Section 12.4. Since the e_i are the unpredictable (or random) deviations, the term $(y_i - \hat{y}_i)$ is referred to as the *unexplained deviation*. While we cannot explain $(y_i - \hat{y}_i)$, it *is* possible to explain that $\hat{y}_i$ differs from $\bar{y}$ because x_i differs from $\bar{x}$. This deviation $(\hat{y}_i - \bar{y})$ is explained (or accounted for) by the regression line; hence, it is called the *explained deviation*. Putting all this together, we obtain the following relationship:

$$\begin{array}{ccc} \text{Total} & = & \text{Unexplained} \\ \text{deviation} & & \text{deviation} \end{array} + \begin{array}{c} \text{Explained} \\ \text{deviation} \end{array}$$

$$(y_i - \bar{y}) \;\; = \;\; (y_i - \hat{y}_i) \;\; + \;\; (\hat{y}_i - \bar{y}). \tag{12.11}$$

This relationship is illustrated in Fig. 12.9 in the context of our OUTPUT–TEXT example.

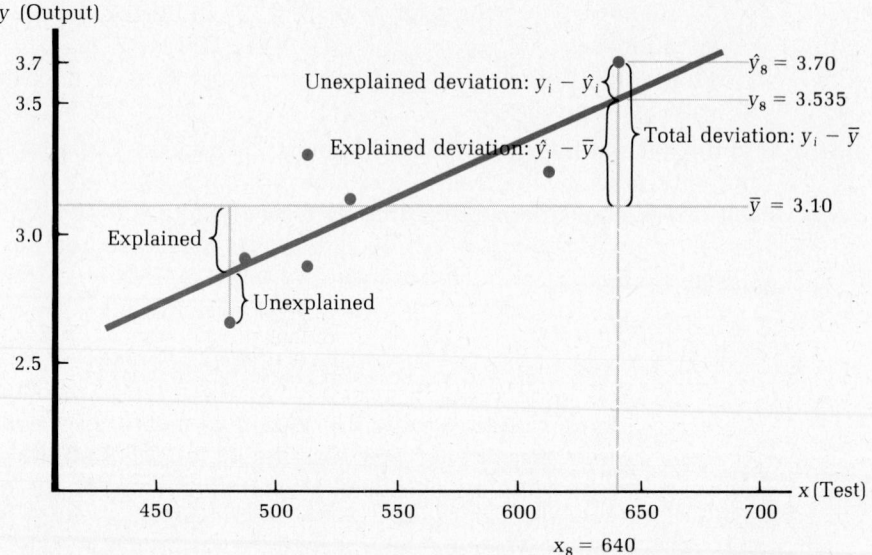

FIGURE 12.9 **Explained and unexplained deviations for $i = 8$ in the OUTPUT– TEST example.**

The deviations emphasized in Fig. 12.9 are for the eighth person in our sample — i.e., the person with a test score of 640 and an output of 3.70 (see Table 12.3). For this person the deviations are

$$
\begin{array}{ccccc}
\text{Total} & = & \text{Unexplained} & + & \text{Explained} \\
\text{deviation} & & \text{deviation} & & \text{deviation} \\
0.600 & = & 0.165 & + & 0.435.
\end{array}
$$

Because the two parts of the total deviation shown in Formula (12.11) are independent, it can be shown that this same relationship holds when we *square* each deviation and sum over all n observations. That is,

$$
\sum_{i=1}^{n} (y_i - \bar{y})^2 = \sum_{i=1}^{n} (y_i - \hat{y}_i)^2 + \sum_{i=1}^{n} (\hat{y}_i - \bar{y})^2.
\tag{12.12}
$$

The left-hand side of Formula (12.12) is referred to as the *total variation,* or as the *sum of squares total* (which is abbreviated as **SST**). The first term on the right is the *unexplained variation,* or equivalently, the *sum of squares error* (**SSE**). You should recognize SSE as Σe_i^2, the term that was minimized in finding the least-squares regression line. The last term in (12.12), which is the sum of squares of the values of $\hat{y}_i$ about

$\overline{y}$, is called the *explained variation*, or the *sum of squares regression* (**SSR**). Thus, we can rewrite (12.12) as follows:

$$
\begin{array}{ccccc}
\text{Total} & = & \text{Unexplained} & + & \text{Explained} \\
\text{variation} & & \text{variation} & & \text{variation}
\end{array}
$$

$$
\sum_{i=1}^{n} (y_i - \overline{y})^2 = \sum_{i=1}^{n} (y_i - \hat{y})^2 + \sum_{i=1}^{n} (\hat{y}_i - \overline{y})^2. \qquad \textbf{(12.13)}
$$

$$
\begin{array}{ccccc}
\text{SST} & = & \text{SSE} & + & \text{SSR.}
\end{array}
$$

The advantage of breaking total variation into these two components is that now we can talk about goodness of fit in terms of the size of SSE. For example, if the line is a perfect fit to the data, then SSE = 0. Usually, however, the line is not a perfect fit; hence, SSE $\neq$ 0.

Calculation of SST, SSR, and SSE   **Example 12.4.** We can calculate SST, SSE, and SSR for our OUTPUT–TEST relation from the data in Tables 12.2 and 12.3. First, SST can be derived by squaring the values in column 4 of Table 12.2. These values are shown in column 1 of Table 12.7. The value of SSE is derived by squaring the errors $e_i = (y_i - \hat{y}_i)$ shown in the final column of Table 12.3. These squares (rounded to three decimals) are shown in column 2 of Table 12.7. Finally, we can calculate

$$
\text{SSR} = \sum_{i=1}^{n} (\hat{y}_i - \overline{y})^2
$$

TABLE 12.7 **Calculation of SST, SSE, and SSR for the OUTPUT–TEST example**

(1)	(2)	(3)	(4)
$(y_i - \overline{y})^2$	$e_i^2 = (y_i - \hat{y}_i)^2$	$(\hat{y}_i - \overline{y})$	$(\hat{y}_i - \overline{y})^2$
0.16	0.019	2.839 − 3.10	0.068
0.04	0.000	2.883 − 3.10	0.047
0.04	0.109	2.970 − 3.10	0.017
0.04	0.005	2.970 − 3.10	0.017
0.00	0.002	3.057 − 3.10	0.002
0.01	0.021	3.144 − 3.10	0.002
0.01	0.042	3.405 − 3.10	0.093
0.36	0.027	3.535 − 3.10	0.189
SST = 0.66	SSE = 0.225		SSR = 0.435

by subtracting $\bar{y} = 3.10$ from each value of $\hat{y}_i$ in column 3 of Table 12.3 and then squaring these differences. These values are shown in column 4 of Table 12.7.

We thus see that

$$SST = SSE + SSR$$

$$0.660 = 0.225 + 0.435.$$

In any regression analysis the components (SSR and SSE) of total variation (SST) need to be determined. They are useful in finding summary measures for the goodness of fit and for aiding in the interpretation of the regression.

Thus, it is convenient to have a simpler way to determine these variation measures that avoids all the calculations used to determine the entries in Table 12.7.

Since SST is simply the measure of the variation to be explained in the dependent variable y, it can be found by using the standard formula for the variation of any variable. Remember that variation is the numerator term in a calculation of variance. Thus, the formula for finding SST = SSy is comparable to the formula for finding SSx.

$$SSy = SST = \sum_{i=1}^{n} y_i^2 - \frac{1}{n}\left(\sum_{i=1}^{n} y_i\right)^2. \qquad \textbf{(12.14)}$$

The amount of SST explained by the regression equation can be determined without first calculating SSE. A roundabout procedure can be used that avoids the calculation of each estimated value $(\hat{y}_i)$. A formula for finding SSR using values already calculated from Formula (12.10) is

$$\text{Explained variation} = SSR = b(SCxy). \qquad \textbf{(12.15)}$$

Once both SST and SSR are found, the unexplained variation SSE is found by subtraction using the relation in Formula (12.13), namely, SSE = SST − SSR.

For the OUTPUT–TEST example the terms needed for finding SST using Formula (12.14) are found directly from the original data in Table

12.2. For $n = 8$ we have $\Sigma y_i = 24.80$, and the sum of squares is $\Sigma y^2 = 77.54$. Thus,

$$\text{SST} = 77.54 - \frac{1}{8}(24.80)^2 = 0.660.$$

The variation explained is easily found by using Formula (12.15). We know that the slope is $b = 0.00435$ and the covariation of x and y was found earlier to be 100.0. Thus,

$$\text{SSR} = 0.00435(100.0) = 0.435.$$

It follows that the sum of squares of the errors is

$$\sum_{i=1}^{8} e^2 = \text{SSE} = \text{SST} - \text{SSR} = 0.660 - 0.435 = 0.225,$$

which is the number determined previously by the direct (but more cumbersome) method shown in Table 12.7.

Our first measure of goodness of fit (the standard error of the estimate) is based on the value of SSE; the second measure (the coefficient of determination) is based on the size of SSR relative to SST. These measures are described below.

Standard Error of the Estimate One of the most useful measures of goodness of fit in regression analysis is called the **standard error of the estimate,** which is denoted by the symbol s_e and defined as follows:

Standard error of estimate:

$$s_e = \sqrt{\frac{1}{n - 2} \sum_{i=1}^{n} (y_i - \hat{y}_i)^2} = \sqrt{\frac{\text{SSE}}{n - 2}}. \qquad \textbf{(12.16)}$$

This sample statistic (s_e) is the standard deviation of the errors (e_i) about the *sample* regression line. The square of s_e represents an unbiased estimate of the variance of the errors (ϵ_i) about the *population* regression line. You may recall from Chapter 8 that an unbiased sample variance is calculated by dividing the sum of squared deviations by the degrees of freedom. The number of degrees of freedom in this case is $n - 2$ because *two* sample statistics (a and b) must be calculated before the value of $\hat{y}_i$ can be computed (since $\hat{y}_i = a + bx_i$). Each of those calculations imposes a linear restriction on the sample values y_i, so that only $n - 2$ of these values are "free" to vary if a and b are determined. Throughout *simple* regression analysis the degrees of freedom are $n - 2$ for any statistics that require use of the residuals (e_i).

Example 12.5. We calculate s_e for the OUTPUT–TEST relation using column 2 of Table 12.7 and find

$$\sum_{i=1}^{8} e_i^2 = SSE = 0.225.$$

Since $n = 8$ for that example, the value of s_e is

$$s_e = \sqrt{\frac{SSE}{n-2}} = \sqrt{\frac{0.225}{6}} = 0.1936.$$

The value of s_e can be interpreted in a manner similar to the sample standard deviation of the values of x about $\bar{x}$. That is, given that assumptions 2, 3, and 4 hold (i.e., the ϵ_i are normal, with mean of zero and a constant variance), then approximately 68% of the sample observations will fall within $\pm 1s_e$ units of the regression line, 95% will fall within $\pm 2s_e$ units of this line, and 99.7% will fall within $\pm 3s_e$ units of it. This information gives a good indication of the fit of the regression line to the sample data. In our example, a range of $\pm 3s_e$ would be

$$\pm 3(0.1936) = \pm 0.5808,$$

which means that the typical sampling error in estimating output on the basis of test scores will be about 0.58 completed installations. This is a rather large potential error, since the average output is 3.10 installations, but we must remember that our sample size was very small ($n = 8$). On the other hand, about two-thirds of the actual values of y will fall within $\pm 1s_e = \pm 0.1936$ installations of the estimated values $\hat{y}$. A band of $\pm 1s_e = \pm 0.1936$ about the regression line is illustrated in Fig. 12.10. In this graph we see that six of the eight "errors" are less than 0.1936.

The Coefficient of Determination

Our second measure of goodness of fit, which is useful in interpreting the *relative* amount of the variation that has been explained by the sample regression line, is called the **coefficient of determination**. This measure, denoted by the symbol r^2, is derived from a commonsense use of the same terms we have been discussing: SST, SSR, and SSE.

Remember from Formula (12.13) that SST = SSE + SSR. Suppose that we divide each term in this equation by SST and note that SST divided by itself equals 1.0. We obtain

$$\frac{SST}{SST} = 1.0 = \frac{SSE}{SST} + \frac{SSR}{SST}.$$

Since the two ratios on the right-hand side of this equation sum to one, they must be a pair of mutually exclusive proportions. As one increases, the other decreases.

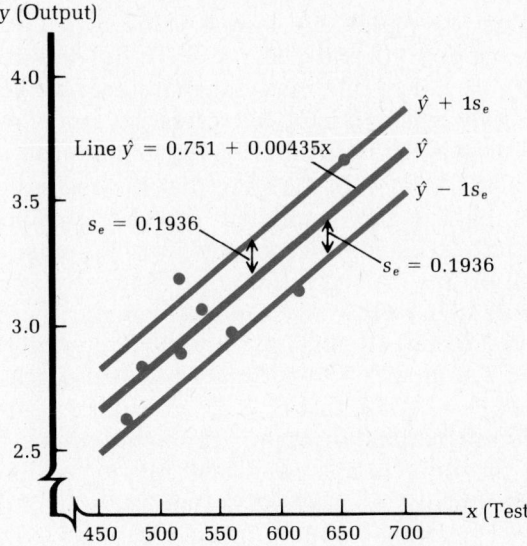

FIGURE 12.10 **A band of one s_e about the regression line.**

Since SSE is the unexplained variation in y, the ratio SSE/SST is the *proportion* of total variation that is unexplained by the regression relation; similarly the ratio SSR/SST is the *proportion* of total variation that is *explained* by the regression line. This last ratio, SSR/SST, is the *relative* measure of goodness of fit we sought and is called the *coefficient of determination.*

Relative measure of goodness of fit, coefficient of determination:

$$r^2 = \frac{\text{SSR}}{\text{SST}} = \frac{\text{Variation explained}}{\text{Total variation}}. \qquad \textbf{(12.17)}$$

If the regression line *perfectly fit* all the sample points, all residuals would be zero. SSE $= \Sigma$ (residuals)^2 would be zero, and SSR would equal SST. In this case,

$$\frac{\text{SSR}}{\text{SST}} = r^2 = 1.0.$$

In other words, a perfect straight-line fit always results in a value of $r^2 = 1$.

As the degree of fit becomes less accurate, less and less of the variation in x is explained by the relation with x (i.e., SSR decreases), which means that r^2 must decrease. The lowest value of r^2 is 0, which will occur whenever SSR = 0 and SSE = SST. By definition this means that $\Sigma (y_i - \hat{y}_i)^2 = \Sigma (y_i - \bar{y})^2$, implying that $\hat{y}_i = \bar{y}$ for all observations. Thus, the case of no explanation by the regression model occurs when the least-squares line $\hat{y}$ is the horizontal line at $\bar{y}$, the mean of y. For a horizontal line the slope is $b = 0$, meaning that the regression model reduces to $\hat{y} = \bar{y} + 0x$. The zero coefficient makes it obvious in this case why **x** has no effect in explaining changes in **y**. Whether an **x**-value is known to be high or low, the corresponding value of **y** is still unpredictable; it may also be high or low and is not systematically related to **x**.

Figure 12.11(a) illustrates a line of perfect fit where SSE = 0 and SSR = SST so that $r^2 = 1.0$. Figure 12.11(b) suggests a case where SSR = 0 and SSE = SST so that $r^2 = 0$. In business applications of regression analysis these extreme cases are usually not found; typically, $0 < r^2 < 1$.

Once the value of r^2 is calculated in a regression analysis, we have a *relative measure of goodness of fit*. For example, if $r^2 = 0.70$, this means that 70% of the total variation in the y-values (SST or SSy) is explained by the regression. Similarly, we know that 30% of the variation in y has *not* been explained.

Example 12.6. Let us calculate r^2 in our OUTPUT–TEST relation. In this case we already know that SSR = 0.435 and SST = 0.660. Hence,

$$r^2 = \frac{SSR}{SST} = \frac{0.435}{0.660} = 0.659.$$

The interpretation of this result is that 65.9% of the total sample variation in OUTPUT is explained by the linear relation of OUTPUT with TEST scores.* The remaining 34.1% of the variation in OUTPUT is still unexplained. Some other worker or job characteristics that are omitted from our regression model could help explain some additional portion of the variation. If these other factors could be measured and included as additional independent variables, we would have a *multiple regression model* (the topic considered in Chapter 13).

Study Question 12.3: Goodness of Fit in the Housing Price Model
Find the goodness-of-fit measures for the regression model relating housing price to income. The data are given in Table 12.5 and Study Question 12.2.

---

* The similarity in size between SST and r^2 is purely coincidental.

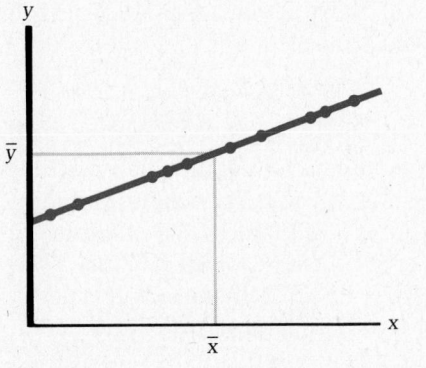
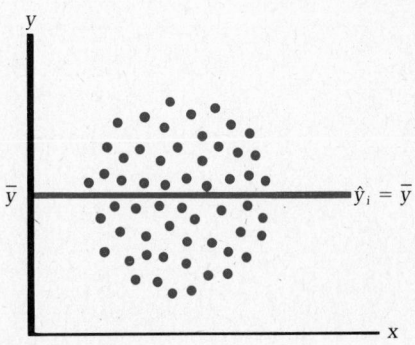

(a) Perfect fit; $r^2 = 1$, $y_i = \hat{y}_i$, $e_i = 0$.   (b) No systematic relation between
y and x; $r^2 = 0$, $\hat{y}_i = \bar{y}$, $b = 0$.

FIGURE 12.11 **Simple regression examples of $r^2 = 1$ and $r^2 = 0$.**

Answer

$$SST = \sum_{i=1}^{10} y_i^2 - \frac{1}{n}\left(\sum_{i=1}^{10} y_i\right)^2$$

$$= 22{,}960.07 - \frac{1}{10}(468.7)^2 = 992.10.$$

$$SSR = b(SCxy) = 4.5404(67.929) = 308.42.$$

$$SSE = SST - SSR = 992.10 - 308.42 = 683.68.$$

The absolute measure of goodness of fit is

$$s_e = \sqrt{\frac{SSE}{n-2}} = \sqrt{\frac{683.68}{8}} = 9.244 \quad (\$000).$$

The relative measure (r^2) is SSR/SST $= 308.42/992.10 = 0.311$.

12.6 CORRELATION ANALYSIS

Although we have presented the relative measure of goodness of fit (r^2) in terms of the regression relationship between **y** and **x,** the strength or closeness of the linear relationship between two variables can be measured *without* estimating the population regression line. The measurement of how well two (or more) variables vary together is called *correlation analysis*.

One measure of the population relationship between two random variables is their covariance,

$$C[\mathbf{x}, \mathbf{y}] = E[(\mathbf{x} - \mu_x)(\mathbf{y} - \mu_y)].$$

Although the covariance has many important statistical uses, this measure in general is *not* a good indicator of the relative strength of the relationship between two variables because its magnitude depends so highly on the *units* used to measure the variables. For example, the covariance between two measures of lengths $\mathbf{x}$ and $\mathbf{y}$ will be $\frac{1}{12}$ as large if $\mathbf{x}$ is scaled in feet than if $\mathbf{x}$ is scaled in inches. For this reason it is necessary to "standardize" the covariance of two variables in order to have a good measure of fit. This standardization is accomplished by dividing $C[\mathbf{x}, \mathbf{y}]$ by σ_x and σ_y. The resulting measure is called the **population correlation coefficient** and is denoted by the Greek letter ρ (rho):

Population correlation coefficient:

$$\rho = \frac{\text{Covariance of } \mathbf{x} \text{ and } \mathbf{y}}{(\text{Std. dev. of } \mathbf{x})(\text{Std. dev. of } \mathbf{y})} = \frac{C[\mathbf{x}, \mathbf{y}]}{\sigma_x \sigma_y}. \qquad \textbf{(12.18)}$$

Three values of ρ serve as benchmarks for interpretation of a correlation coefficient. First, let us consider the population in which the values of $\mathbf{x}$ and $\mathbf{y}$ all fall on a single straight line with a positive slope. In this case, which is referred to as a "perfect positive linear relationship" between $\mathbf{x}$ and $\mathbf{y}$, the value of $C[\mathbf{x}, \mathbf{y}]$ will exactly equal the value of σ_x times σ_y; hence, ρ will equal $+1$.

When the relationship between $\mathbf{x}$ and $\mathbf{y}$ is a perfect *negative* linear relationship, all values of $\mathbf{x}$ and $\mathbf{y}$ lie on a straight line with a negative slope. This situation results in a value of $C[\mathbf{x}, \mathbf{y}]$ that exactly equals $-(\sigma_x)(\sigma_y)$. Thus, in this case ρ will equal -1.

If $\mathbf{x}$ and $\mathbf{y}$ are not linearly related (i.e., if they are independent random variables), then the value of the correlation coefficient will be zero, since in this case $C[\mathbf{x}, \mathbf{y}] = 0$.

Thus, ρ measures the strength of the linear association between $\mathbf{x}$ and $\mathbf{y}$. Values of ρ close to zero indicate a weak relation; values close to $+1.0$ indicate a strong "positive" correlation; and values close to -1.0 indicate a strong "negative" correlation. Figure 12.12 illustrates some representations of values of ρ for selected scatter diagrams.

Note, from Figs. 12.12(b) and 12.12(c), that two populations which appear quite different can have the same correlation coefficient. Figures

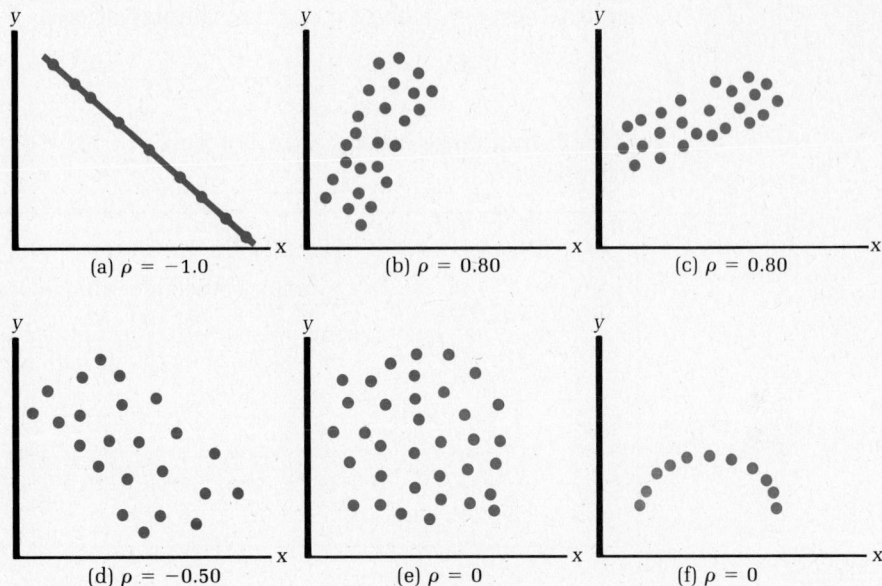

FIGURE 12.12 **The population correlation coefficient.**

12.12(c) and 12.12(d) show the difference between positive and negative correlation. The last two diagrams show different examples of a population with zero correlation. In Fig. 12.12(f), **x** and **y** are related in a nonlinear fashion, yet still $\rho = 0$, which emphasizes the fact that ρ measures the strength of the *linear* relationship.

The Sample Correlation Coefficient As in all estimation problems, we use sample data to estimate the population parameter ρ. In this case the sample statistic is called the **sample correlation coefficient** and denoted by the letter r. The value of r is defined in the same way as ρ, except that we substitute for each population parameter its best estimate based on the sample data. For instance, the best estimate of $C[\mathbf{x},\ \mathbf{y}]$ in Formula (12.18) is the sample covariance, denoted by the symbol s_{xy}, where

$$s_{xy} = \frac{1}{n-1} \sum_{i=1}^{n} (x_i - \bar{x})(y_i - \bar{y}).$$

Similarly, the best estimate of σ_x^2 is the sample variance

$$s_x^2 = \frac{1}{n-1} \sum_{i=1}^{n} (x_i - \bar{x})^2,$$

and the best estimate of σ_y^2 is the sample variance

$$s_y^2 = \frac{1}{n-1} \sum_{i=1}^n (y_i - \bar{y})^2.$$

Substituting these estimates in Formula (12.18) we obtain the following formula for r:

Sample correlation coefficient:

$$r = \frac{s_{xy}}{s_x s_y} = \frac{\text{Covariance of sample values of } x \text{ and } y}{\left(\begin{array}{c}\text{Sample standard} \\ \text{deviation of } x\end{array}\right)\left(\begin{array}{c}\text{Sample standard} \\ \text{deviation of } y\end{array}\right)}$$

$$= \frac{\dfrac{1}{n-1} \sum_{i=1}^n (x_i - \bar{x})(y_i - \bar{y})}{\sqrt{\dfrac{1}{n-1} \sum_{i=1}^n (x_i - \bar{x})^2}\ \sqrt{\dfrac{1}{n-1} \sum_{i=1}^n (y_i - \bar{y})^2}}. \qquad \textbf{(12.19)}$$

A sample correlation coefficient is interpreted in the same manner as ρ, except that it measures the strength of the *sample* data rather than the population values. For example, where $r = \pm 1$, there is a perfect straight-line fit between the sample values of **x** and **y**; hence, they are said to have a perfect correlation. This is the same extreme case as discussed for $r^2 = 1$. At the other extreme, if the sample values of x and y have no relationship, both r and r^2 will be zero.

Example 12.7. Let us determine the sample correlation coefficient for the OUTPUT–TEST relation. The values for these variables are repeated in Table 12.8, followed by the calculations necessary for determining r.

$$r = \frac{\dfrac{1}{n-1} \sum_{i=1}^n (x_i - \bar{x})(y_i - \bar{y})}{\sqrt{\dfrac{1}{n-1} \sum_{i=1}^n (x_i - \bar{x})^2}\ \sqrt{\dfrac{1}{n-1} \sum_{i=1}^n (y_i - \bar{y})^2}} = \frac{100/7}{\sqrt{23,000/7}\ \sqrt{0.66/7}} = 0.8117.$$

The value of the sample correlation coefficient r can also be found by using a simpler calculational formula. If both numerator and denominator in Formula (12.19) are multiplied by $(n - 1)$, the remaining terms are the covariation of x and y in the numerator and the separate variations of x and y in the denominator. In our previous discussion, calculational formulas for covariation and variation were presented. They can also be used here to find

TABLE 12.8 **Intermediate calculations using the OUTPUT–TEST data**

TEST (x_i)	OUTPUT (y_i)	$(x_i - \bar{x})$	$(y_i - \bar{y})$	$(x_i - \bar{x})(y_i - \bar{y})$	$(x_i - \bar{x})^2$	$(y_i - \bar{y})^2$
480	2.70	-60	-0.40	24	3,600	0.16
490	2.90	-50	-0.20	10	2,500	0.04
510	3.30	-30	$+0.20$	-6	900	0.04
510	2.90	-30	-0.20	6	900	0.04
530	3.10	-10	0.00	0	100	0.00
550	3.00	$+10$	-0.10	-1	100	0.01
610	3.20	$+70$	$+0.10$	7	4,900	0.01
640	3.70	$+100$	$+0.60$	60	10,000	0.36
Sum 4320	24.80	0	0.00	100	23,000	0.66

Computational formula for r:

$$r = \frac{SCxy}{\sqrt{(SSx)(SSy)}}$$

$$= \frac{\sum\limits_{i=1}^{n} x_i y_i - \dfrac{1}{n}\left(\sum\limits_{i=1}^{n} x_i\right)\left(\sum\limits_{i=1}^{n} y_i\right)}{\sqrt{\sum\limits_{i=1}^{n} x_i^2 - \dfrac{1}{n}\left(\sum\limits_{i=1}^{n} x_i\right)^2}\sqrt{\sum\limits_{i=1}^{n} y_i^2 - \dfrac{1}{n}\left(\sum\limits_{i=1}^{n} y_i\right)^2}}. \tag{12.20}$$

Example 12.8. We repeat the calculation of the correlation coefficient between OUTPUT and TEST scores using Formula (12.20). The preliminary calculations are:

$$SCxy = 13,492 - \frac{1}{8}(4320)(24.80) = 100.0;$$

$$SSx = 2,355,800 - \frac{1}{8}(4320)^2 = 23,000;$$

$$SSy = 77.54 - \frac{1}{8}(24.80)^2 = 0.660.$$

The sample correlation coefficient is

$$r = \frac{100}{\sqrt{23,000(0.660)}} = 0.8117.$$

The correlation between OUTPUT and TEST in this example is 0.8117, indicating a moderately strong positive linear relationship. This result agrees with our goodness-of-fit analysis of the same data since $(0.8117)^2$ is indeed $r^2 = 0.659$. In fact, we will show in the remainder of this chapter that there are many links between regression and correlation analysis.

Correlation and Regression We can explore the connection between the value of r and the value of the slope b by comparing Formulas (12.8) and (12.20), which are reproduced below:

$$b = \frac{SCxy}{SSx} \quad \text{and} \quad r = \frac{SCxy}{\sqrt{(SSx)(SSy)}}.$$

By multiplying the right-hand side of the equation for r by $1 = SSx/SSx$ and simplifying, we obtain

$$r = \frac{(SCxy)}{\sqrt{(SSx)(SSy)}}\left[\frac{SSx}{SSx}\right],$$

$$r = \frac{SCxy\sqrt{SSx}}{SSx\sqrt{SSy}},$$

$$r = b\frac{\sqrt{SSx}}{\sqrt{SSy}}. \tag{12.21}$$

Since the sums of squares are never negative, the *signs* of r and b will always be the same. That is, a positive correlation must always correspond to a regression line with a positive slope, and a negative r must correspond to a negative slope.

Now consider the connection between the correlation coefficient r and the coefficient of determination r^2. Recall from Formula (12.17) that $r^2 = SSR/SST$ and follow these steps:

$$r^2 = \frac{SSR}{SST} = \frac{b(SCxy)}{SSy},$$

since the explained variation is $SSR = b(SCxy)$ by Formula (12.15), and the total variation (SST) is the variation in the dependent variable y (SSy). Next, substituting the formula for the slope b from Formula (12.8), we obtain

$$r^2 = \frac{SCxy}{SSx}\frac{SCxy}{SSy},$$

$$r^2 = \frac{(SCxy)^2}{(SSx)(SSy)},$$

which is exactly the square of r in Formula (12.20).

The reader can now understand the use of the letter r for the correlation coefficient and the symbol r^2 for the coefficient of determination. The latter is indeed the square of the former. In most cases, r^2 is easier to interpret than r. For instance, if $r = 0.70$, then $r^2 (100) = 49$, so 49% of the sample variation in y has been explained by the regression model. In the OUTPUT–TEST example the correlation coefficient was $r = 0.8117$, which implies that $r^2 = (0.8117) = 0.66$. Thus, 66% of the variation in this sample of completed installations can be explained on the basis of different test scores after the training course. About 34% of the variation in y remains unexplained. Thus, r is an alternate measure of goodness of fit for a regression model.

Interpretation of Correlation Measures

For r to be an unbiased estimator of ρ, the joint distribution of **x** and **y** must be a normal distribution. This means that the value of the correlation coefficient does not depend on which variable is designated **x** and which is designated **y**. The distinction *is* important in regression analysis, however, since the conditional distribution of **y**, given x, results in a different regression line than the conditional distribution of **x**, given y. Formula (12.21) holds only if the numerator is the standard deviation of the *independent* variable.*

A note of caution must be offered to anyone attempting to infer cause and effect from correlation or regression analysis, since a high correlation or a good fit to a regression line does *not* imply that **x** is "causing" **y**. It does not even imply that **x** will provide a good estimate of **y** in the future, or for any other set of sample observations. For example, the weekly Dow-Jones stock index was reported to have a 0.84 correlation with the number of points scored by a New York City basketball team in its weekend game. Also, liquor consumption in the United States is supposed to be highly correlated with teachers' salaries. In this latter case the high correlation undoubtedly results because of the presence of one or more additional influences on both variables, such as increases in the general economic well-being.

The above discussion should not be interpreted to mean that one cannot, or should not, draw inferences or conclusions from regression or correlation analysis, but only that care must be taken in assuming cause and effect. Most colleges, for example, use test scores as one means for estimating academic success; they presumably are basing their opinion

---

* If the independent variable x is not a random variable, but is a *fixed* variable, ρ is not even defined (since the terms $C[x, y]$ and $V[x]$ are zero). Nevertheless, even when x is fixed, r is still a good descriptive statistic for the association between sample values of y and x.

not on the fact that higher SAT scores "cause" higher grades, but rather on the fact that whatever these tests measure (memory, intelligence, vocabulary) *does* have an influence on college grades. As another example, economists make frequent use of regression techniques in attempts to identify potential cause-and-effect relationships, especially those which might prove useful in predicting the future of the economy or the effect of some proposed economic policy.

Define. *Unexplained variation (SSE), explained variation (SSR), total variation (SST), standard error of the estimate (s_e), coefficient of determination (r^2), population correlation coefficient (ρ), sample correlation coefficient (r).*

PROBLEMS

12.13 In a simple regression and correlation analysis based on 72 observations, we find $r = 0.8$ and $s_e = 10$.
a) Find the amount of unexplained variation.
b) Find the proportion of unexplained variation to the total variation.
c) Find the total variation of the dependent variable.

12.14 In a simple regression, explain the importance of r^2 and s_e, and differentiate between them.

12.15 Use the data from the following table to compute the regression equation of sales (**y**) on advertising expenditures (**x**). Then compute a measure that describes the proportion of the variation of sales that is explained by the regression.

Region	Sales, y	Advertising Expense, x ($10,000)
A	31	5
B	40	11
C	25	3
D	30	4
E	20	2
F	34	5

12.16 The least-squares estimating line of the number of motel rooms that are rented (**y**), based on the number of advance reservations made (**x**), for a certain Holiday Inn is $\hat{y} = 26 + (3/4)x$ with an average $\bar{y} = 60$.

a) For a particular night, 60 advance reservations are received. Suppose that the manager needs one maid for each nine rooms that need cleaning the following morning. Advise this manager on the minimum number of maids that should be employed in this particular case, based on your estimate of the number of rooms that will be occupied and will need cleaning.

b) Suppose that, for one day, the number of advance reservations received is 36 and the number of rooms occupied turns out to be 55. Find the total, explained, and unexplained deviations for this case.

12.17 An economist wishes to study the demand relation for a hand calculator over several years. During this time the product has improved somewhat, but its price has fallen considerably. The price per unit (x) and the number of units (in thousands) purchased annually (y) are given below.

Price ($)	120	100	70	50	30	20
Quantity (000)	10	15	20	35	45	55

a) Estimate the linear demand function relating the quantity demanded to the price using the method of least squares.

b) Although price is the independent variable, it is common to graph a demand relation with price on the vertical axis and quantity on the horizontal axis. Following this convention, sketch the observations and the regression line. Interpret the meaning of the values obtained for the estimates of α and β.

c) If the price in another year was $25, what is your estimate of the quantity demanded in that year?

d) Find the proportion of the variation in quantity that is explained by your demand relation.

12.18 We wish to explore the relationship between family monthly food consumption y and family monthly income x, both measured in hundreds of dollars. We are given information for 100 families as follows:

$n = 100$	$\bar{y} = \$6$	$\bar{x} = \$8$
$\Sigma xy = 6000$	$\Sigma y^2 = 4500$	$\Sigma x^2 = 10,000$

a) Find the regression equation $\hat{y} = a + bx$, using the method of least squares.

b) Using the regression equation, make an estimate of consumption for a family with a monthly income of $1500.

c) Compute an absolute measure of goodness of fit of the regression equation and interpret its meaning.

12.19 In a simple regression based on 20 observations it is found that $r^2 = 0.6$ and $s_e{}^2 = 0.81$. Find the total, explained, and unexplained variations.

12.20 Given the following data for quiz scores (y) and class absences (x) for a certain statistics class:

$\Sigma y = 1800$	$\Sigma xy = 4750$	$\Sigma y^2 = 113{,}000$
$\Sigma x = 90$	$n = 30$	$\Sigma x^2 = 400$

a) Find the estimating equation $\hat{y} = a + bx$.
b) Find the coefficient of determination.
c) Determine a student's expected quiz score if this person had six absences; comment on the validity of using the estimating equation for subsequent classes or quizzes.

12.21 In a regression analysis using 16 observations, the explained variation is 40 out of a total variation of 60. Find the standard error of estimate for the regression equation.

12.22 Given the information below for a retail store, compute the measures required:

No. of clerks	x	2	4	6	8	10	12
Daily sales ($000)	y	3	4	4	6	6	7

a) Regression equation of y on x.
b) Coefficient of determination.
c) Standard error of estimate.
d) For the fifth observation, determine the total deviation, the explained deviation, and the unexplained deviation.

12.23 Define or describe briefly each of the following:
a) Covariance.
b) Coefficient of determination.
c) Method of least squares.
d) Normal equations.

12.24 In any simple correlation analysis, state what the logical limits are for values of r^2, and explain why.

12.25 Suppose that we have data on number of sheep x (in millions) and production of wool sweaters y (in thousands) for a certain region of the United Kingdom, as follows:

Year	y	x
1940	2	1
1960	5	4
1980	8	4

a) Find the estimating equation for $\hat{y} = a + bx$, by the method of least squares.

b) Find the sample coefficient of correlation between y and x.

12.26 What is the coefficient of correlation between two variables if:

a) One of the variables is constant?

b) The value of one variable always exceeds the value of the other variable by 100?

c) The unexplained variation is twice the explained variation?

12.27 Suppose that the following three values represent observations for the random variables **x** and **y**.

x	y
3	4
0	2
3	3

a) Compute the sample correlation coefficient.

b) What is the covariance of **x** and **y**? How much of the variability in y is explained by x if the regression model $\hat{y} = a + bx$ is estimated?

12.28 What is the difference between regression analysis and correlation analysis? When should each be used?

12.29 A Peace Corps representative in Chad works with five farmers in a cooperative shop rebuilding small gasoline motors for use in water pumps. She recognizes a difference in the workers' individual ability to learn the new job and to do it properly without supervision. After several weeks she records the following information, where y = average weekly output of correctly rebuilt motors, and x = years of education of each of the five Chadian workers.

x	7	5	6	10	4
y	15	7	10	20	8

a) Find the regression equation $\hat{y} = a + bx$.
b) Find the value of r, using both Formula (12.19) and Formula (12.20).
c) Find SSE and SSR and show that they sum to SST.
d) What percent of the variability in y is explained by the x-values?
e) Show for this data that $r = b\sqrt{SSx}/\sqrt{SSy}$.

12.7 TEST ON THE SIGNIFICANCE OF THE SAMPLE REGRESSION LINE

We have presented a way of estimating the best regression line fitting the linear relation between y and x, and we have discussed measures of the strength of the linear relationship. However, we have not given any rules or guidelines to help determine whether knowledge of the independent variable x is useful in predicting the values of y. Much of our earlier discussion on sampling distributions and inference is again relevant for decision-making based on the results of a regression analysis. The first of several useful methods of inference related to a regression concerns the value of the slope. This matter will be presented in this section. Other special applications of statistical inference in regression will follow.

Any use of inference to learn about a population based on a sample requires knowledge about the probability distribution of the relevant random variables. In regression the random variables of interest are the estimators from the sample model, such as the slope b, or a forecast $\hat{y}_i$, or a measure of fit. The needed probability distributions depend directly on the random variable ϵ_i, representing the errors in the population model. Whatever is known or assumed about the probability distribution of the errors can be translated into information about the probability distribution of the estimators.

In Section 12.4 the common assumptions about the errors ϵ_i were presented. Let us presume that these hold for a regression model. In particular, let us specify that the errors are independent and are normally distributed with a mean of zero and a constant variance of σ_ϵ^2. As suggested in Section 12.4, the probability distribution of the sample estimator for the slope (b), intercept (a), or forecast ($\hat{y}_i$) can be derived. Each of these is found to be normally distributed with mean equal to the respective population parameter (β, α, or $\mu_{y \cdot x_i}$). Also, each has a variance that depends on the unknown variance (σ_ϵ^2) of the errors. Thus, the variance of each of these estimators is also unknown. If we denote these (unknown) variances as σ_b^2 for the slope, σ_a^2 for the intercept, and $\sigma_{\hat{y}}^2$

for the forecast, we can specify the probability distributions of these random variables as shown in Table 12.9.

We must repeat that each of these estimators has a variance that is unknown and that depends on the variance of the population disturbance. In order to make inferences we will follow the familiar procedure of using a sample estimate of this unknown variance. We use the square of the standard error of estimate (s_e^2) to estimate the unknown variance of the population error. Using s_e as a substitute for σ_ϵ, we will compute sample measures of variance for each estimator and denote the corresponding standard deviations by the symbols s_b or s_a. We will substitute these sample standard deviations for the unknown population standard deviations into the standardized forms of the random variables given in Table 12.9. In doing so, we must also recognize that while the probability distribution is normal (denoted by **z**), we must use a substitute distribution (denoted by **t**) that allows for the extra uncertainty in estimating a true variance σ^2 by a sample variance s^2.

Test on the Slope We will follow this procedure of inference in several applications. First, we wish to examine the significance of the relation between the dependent variable **y** and the explanatory variable **x**. Suppose that the population relationship is such that $\beta = 0$. This means that $\alpha = \mu_y - \beta\mu_x = \mu_y - 0$; thus, $\mu_{y \cdot x_i} = \alpha + 0x = \mu_y$, which is simply a horizontal line at the level of $\mu_{y \cdot x_i} = \mu_y$ (similar to Fig. 12.11(b) for the sample regression when $b = 0$). In other words, when there is no systematic relation between **y** and **x** (indicated by a slope of zero such that the term with x in it drops from the model), our best predictor of the expected value of **y** is the mean of **y**. This agrees with our analysis throughout Chapters 7–9 when we emphasized the use of the mean to estimate the level expected for a single variable.

On the other hand, *if β is not equal to zero*, some systematic direct ($\beta > 0$) or inverse ($\beta < 0$) relation does exist between **y** and **x**. In this

TABLE 12.9 **Probability distributions for regression analysis**

Random Variable	Mean	Variance	p.d.f.	Standardized Form
Disturbance, ϵ_i	0	σ_ϵ^2	$N(0, \sigma_\epsilon^2)$	
Slope, **b**	β	σ_b^2	$N(\beta, \sigma_b^2)$	$z = (b - \beta)/\sigma_b$
Intercept, **a**	α	σ_a^2	$N(\alpha, \sigma_a^2)$	$z = (a - \alpha)/\sigma_a$
Forecast, $\hat{y}_i$	$\mu_{y \cdot x_i}$	$\sigma_{\hat{y}_i}^2$	$N(\mu_{y \cdot x_i}, \sigma_{\hat{y}_i}^2)$	$z = (\hat{y}_i - \mu_{y \cdot x_i})/\sigma_{y_i}$

case the term βx in the model does *not* drop out; hence, the changes in x are meaningful in predicting changes in the level of **y**. Thus, to determine whether or not the estimation of the **y**-values is improved by using the regression line, we can test the null hypothesis H_0: $\beta = 0$. Rejecting H_0 is this case means concluding, on the basis of the sample information given, that β does not equal zero and, hence, that the regression line *is* useful in estimating the dependent variable. The alternative hypothesis for this test is usually one-sided. For example, we could use the one-sided alternative that the slope is greater than zero (H_a: $\beta > 0$) or the one-sided alternative that the slope is less than zero (H_a: $\beta < 0$). A two-sided alternative would be to hypothesize merely that the slope does not equal zero (H_a: $\beta \neq 0$). The two-sided test is appropriate only if no *a priori* knowledge or theory is available about the expected direction of the relation between **y** and **x**.

Although the above forms of hypotheses are common, the hypothesized value need not be zero. To illustrate a problem in which β is not assumed to be equal to zero, consider that an economist wishes to test the null hypothesis that the slope of the regression line relating personal income and consumption (slope = marginal propensity to consume) has not increased from some historical value, such as $\beta = 0.80$. The appropriate test is H_0: $\beta = 0.80$ against H_a: $\beta > 0.80$. The assumed value of β in such a test is usually denoted by β_0; the general form of the hypotheses would be

$$H_0: \beta = \beta_0 \quad \text{versus} \quad H_a: \beta > \beta_0.$$

A *t*-test (with $n - 2$ degrees of freedom) for these hypotheses uses the sample estimate b and the standardized form of a test statistic given by Formula (12.22):

Test statistic for inference on the regression slope β:

$$t_{(n-2)} = \frac{b - \beta_0}{s_b}, \qquad \qquad \textbf{(12.22)}$$

This test is very similar to the *t*-test about a population mean, since we are again testing a mean (the slope β in the *average* relation between y and x), the population is assumed to be normal (due to assumption 2 about the normality of the ϵ_i's), and the population standard deviation is unknown. In the present case the sample statistic is **b** (rather than $\overline{x}$), the hypothesized population value is β_0 (rather than μ_0), and the sample standard error is s_b (rather than $s_{\overline{x}}$), where s_b is defined as follows:

> **Estimated standard error of regression coefficient b:**
>
> $$s_b = \frac{s_e}{\sqrt{SSx}} = s_e \sqrt{\frac{1}{\sum_{i=1}^{n} x_i^2 - \frac{1}{n}\left(\sum_{i=1}^{n} x_i^2\right)}}. \qquad (12.23)$$

The value s_b is a measure of the amount of sampling error in the regression coefficient b, just as $s_{\bar{x}}$ was a measure of the sampling error of $\bar{x}$.

We can test the null hypothesis H_0: $\beta = \beta_0$ using Formulas (12.22) and (12.23) and applying the t-distribution with $(n - 2)$ degrees of freedom.

Example 12.9. We can apply Formula (12.22) to our OUTPUT–TEST example. Suppose that the null hypothesis H_0: $\beta = 0$ is tested against H_a: $\beta > 0$ (we use the one-sided test here because we expect electricians with higher test scores, on the average, to complete more installations per day). First we must calculate s_b by substituting into Formula (12.23) the previously determined values

$$s_e = 0.1936 \qquad \text{and} \qquad SSx = 23{,}000;$$

we get

$$s_b = 0.1936 \sqrt{\frac{1}{23{,}000}} = 0.001278.$$

Therefore, the calculated value t_c is

$$t_c = \frac{b - \beta_0}{s_b} = \frac{0.00435 - 0}{0.001278} = 3.404.$$

For $n - 2 = 6$ degrees of freedom the probability that t is larger than 3.404 falls between 0.005 and 0.01 (see Table VI in the Appendix). Thus, it is highly unlikely that a slope of $b = 0.00435$ will occur by chance when $\beta = 0$, and we can conclude that the regression line does seem to improve our ability to estimate the dependent variable (i.e., we reject H_0).

In addition to being able to test hypotheses about β, it is possible to construct a $100(1 - \alpha)\%$ confidence interval for β. Since the regression coefficient b follows a t-distribution with $(n - 2)$ degrees of freedom and standard deviation s_b, the desired interval is:

> **Confidence interval for the regression slope β:**
>
> $$b - t_{(\alpha/2,\, n-2)} s_b \le \beta \le b + t_{(\alpha/2,\, n-2)} s_b. \qquad (12.24)$$

Example 12.10. A 95% confidence interval, for the population slope in the OUTPUT–TEST relation, given that $n = 8$, $t_{(\alpha/2,\, n-2)} = t_{(0.025,6)} = 2.447$, and $s_b = 0.00128$, is found by using Formula (12.24):

$$0.00435 - (2.447)(0.00128) \leq \beta \leq 0.00435 + (2.447)(0.00128),$$
$$0.00122 \leq \beta \leq 0.00748.$$

Thus, based on our sample of eight electricians, an increase in completed installations per day of between 0.122 and 0.748 could be expected for each 100-point increase in test scores. This is rather a wide interval for any precise forecasting of OUTPUT. This degree of uncertainty suggests the need to consider other factors and to take a larger sample of persons.

Test on the Correlation Coefficient

In addition to the t-test presented above for testing H_0: $\beta = 0$, there is an equivalent t-test based on the null hypothesis H_0: $\rho = 0$. In order to test this hypothesis, it is necessary to know the sampling distribution of some random variable involving the sample correlation coefficient r (which is our best estimate of ρ). The following t-distributed random variable, with $(n - 2)$ degrees of freedom, can be used:*

---

t-statistic for test on a correlation coefficient ρ:

$$t_{(n-2)} = \frac{r\sqrt{n - 2}}{\sqrt{1 - r^2}}. \tag{12.25}$$

Example 12.11. The t-statistic in Formula (12.25) can be used to test the null hypothesis of no correlation, H_0: $\rho = 0$. We again use our OUTPUT–TEST example, in which $r = 0.8117$. For the same reason that we used H_a: $\beta > 0$, we now use the alternative hypothesis H_a: $\rho > 0$. To determine the probability that a value such as 0.8117 would occur by chance, given that $\rho = 0$ and $n = 8$, we use Formula (12.25) to obtain

$$t_c = \frac{0.8117\sqrt{8 - 2}}{\sqrt{1 - (0.8117)^2}} = 3.404.$$

Referring to Table VI for 6 degrees of freedom, we find that the probability that t is equal to or larger than 3.404 is between 0.005 and 0.01. (Recall that this probability is the p-value for the test.) It is very unlikely that a

---

* The use of this statistic requires that the combined random variables x and y have a bivariate normal distribution. Although this is not necessarily the case in business and economic applications, the statistic in Formula (12.25) is still useful as an index of association.

sample correlation this high will occur by chance when $\rho = 0$. Thus, we can accept the alternative hypothesis that there is a positive linear relation between y and x. The value of t obtained in this analysis, $t = 3.404$, is *exactly* the same result as that obtained when testing H_0: $\beta = 0$. This agreement between the two is more than mere coincidence, since the outcome of a simple regression analysis and a correlation analysis on the same data must yield identical results when the same hypothesis of *no* relationship between x and y is being tested.*

Finally, we should mention that since the alternative hypothesis in our OUTPUT–TEST example was one-sided, we read the p-value $P(t \geq 3.404)$ directly from Table VI. If the alternative had been two-sided, the probabilities from Table VI would have to be *doubled* to obtain the correct p-value.

Study Question 12.4: Testing the Housing Price Model
Use the regression model relating housing price to income as in Study Question 12.2.

a) Test the significance of the correlation coefficient to see whether income is useful in explaining changes in price.
b) Find a 99% confidence interval on the true slope relating price and income in the population regression model.

Answer
a) Formula (12.25) is used to test the significance of the relation between price and income. Let H_0: $\rho = 0$ and H_a: $\rho > 0$, since a positive relation is expected. Since $r^2 = 0.311$ from Study Question 12.3, its square root is $r = +0.558$. It has a positive sign because the correlation coefficient always has the same sign as the slope.
b. The calculated test statistic is

$$t_c = \frac{r\sqrt{n-2}}{\sqrt{1-r^2}} = \frac{0.558\sqrt{8}}{\sqrt{1-0.311}} = 1.90.$$

From Table VI with 8 degrees of freedom, the p-value for the test is

$$0.025 < P(t > 1.90) < 0.05.$$

---

* These tests are *not* equivalent if the null hypothesis specifies that the slope is equal to some value other than zero, although the previous test on β [Formula (12.22) is still appropriate. In that case the test on β (using Formula (12.22)) is not a test of the significance of the linear relationship, but rather a test on some proposed population parameter β_0. Therefore, such a test would not be equivalent to the t-test in this section for the *significance of ρ*.

This low p-value leads to the conclusion to reject H_0 and accept the alternative hypothesis that income is a useful factor in explaining changes in housing price. However, the amount of unexplained variation is relatively large. This will lead to relatively wide confidence or forecast intervals.

b) A confidence interval on β is found by using Formula (12.24). For 90% confidence and 8 degrees of freedom, the appropriate t-value from Table VI is $t_{0.05,8} = 1.86$. The estimated standard error for the estimate b is $s_b = s_e/\sqrt{SSx}$ from Formula (12.23). Using $SSx = 14.961$ as in Study Question 12.2 and $s_e = 9.244$ from Study Question 12.3, we have

$$s_b = \frac{9.244}{\sqrt{14.961}} = 2.39.$$

The desired limits of the confidence interval are

$$b + ts_b = 4.5404 \pm 1.86(2.39) = 4.5404 \pm 4.4454,$$

which gives 0.095 and 8.986.

Many of these measures used in inference are given in computer outputs of standard regression programs. Figure 12.13 repeats Fig. 12.7 with some of these specific measures highlighted. The reader should find in each printout of Fig. 12.13 the measure of the coefficient of determination, $r^2 = 0.311$, labeled as R-SQUARE. Also, in Fig. 12.13(a) the SPSS program reports the STANDARD ERROR, $s_e = 9.244$. Both printouts give the standard error of the estimate of the slope, $s_b = 2.39$.

Test on the Intercept A test similar to that for the slope can be applied to test hypotheses about the true value of the intercept α in the population model. The appropriate statistic based on the assumptions of Section 12.4 and the distribution as given in Table 12.9 is t-distributed with $n - 2$ degrees of freedom:

---

t-statistic for inference on the intercept α:

$$t_{n-2} = \frac{a - \alpha}{s_a}. \qquad (12.26)$$

The sample standard deviation of the estimator a is found by using Formula (12.27):

a) SPSS output

```
DEPENDENT VARIABLE..    PRICE    AVERAGE HOUSING PRICE

VARIABLE(S) ENTERED ON STEP NUMBER 1..    INC    HOUSEHOLD MEDIAN INCOME


MULTIPLE R         0.55757
R SQUARE           0.31088

STANDARD ERROR     9.24442


----------------- VARIABLE IN THE EQUATION -----------------

VARIABLE      B                 STD ERROR B        F

INC      4.5404                  2.3900         3.609
(CONSTANT) -8.6591
```

b) SAS output

```
MODEL:    MODEL01      SSE   683.675825   F RATIO        3.61
                       DFE          8     PROB>F       0.0940
DEP VAR: PRICE         MSE    85.459478   R-SQUARE     0.3109
         HOUSING PRICE

DURBIN-WATSON D STATISTIC  =  2.0969


                PARAMETER    STANDARD
VARIABLE    DF   ESTIMATE     ERROR      T RATIO    PROB>|T|

INTERCEPT   1   -8.659154   29.375650   -0.2948    0.7757
INCOME      1    4.540405    2.390010    1.8997    0.0940
```

FIGURE 12.13 **SPSS and SAS output for the housing price regression.**

Estimated standard error of the regression intercept a:

$$s_a = s_e \frac{\sqrt{\sum_{i=1}^{n} x_i^2}}{\sqrt{n(SSx)}} = s_e \frac{\sum_{i=1}^{n} x_i^2}{\sqrt{n\left[\sum_{i=1}^{n} x_i^2 - \frac{1}{n}\left(\sum_{i=1}^{n} x_i\right)^2\right]}}. \qquad \textbf{(12.27)}$$

Confidence limits on the true intercept α can also be found by using this same statistic. The endpoints would be $a \pm ts_a$, where the appropriate value of t depends on the level of confidence desired and the degrees of freedom $(n - 2)$. Typically, inference on the intercept is not as common as inference on the slope. The purpose of regression is more to relate the two variables y and x and to determine how changes in x affect changes in y than to determine the base level of y when x = 0. The latter involves extrapolation back to the value x = 0, which is often outside of the meaningful or observed domain of the x-values.

12.8 CONSTRUCTING A FORECAST INTERVAL

One of the important uses of the sample regression line is to obtain forecasts of the dependent variable, given some value of the independent variable. The estimated value $\hat{y}_i = a + bx_i$ is the best estimate we can make of both $\mu_{y \cdot x_i}$ (the mean value of y, given a value x_i) and of y_i (the actual value of y that corresponds to the given value x_i). Forecasts of both types are frequently desired. Economists may wish to forecast the average or expected level of unemployment, given assumed values of independent variables under policy control. From such forecasts they might argue which variables should be affected by policy, by how much, and in what direction, so that a policy goal of 5% unemployed might be expected. The forecast of the actual value of the dependent variable may be desired in other cases, such as predictions of the level of unemployment for the second quarter of the next year, or of the level of the price of General Motors common stock at the end of this year, or of the total sales this year for Sears.

Point Estimates of Forecasts To obtain the best point estimate for forecasts of both the mean value and the actual value of y, the given value of the independent variable (call it x_g) is substituted into the estimating equation to obtain the **forecast value**

$$\hat{y}_g = a + bx_g.$$

Thus, $\hat{y}_g$ is an estimate of both $\mu_{y \cdot x_g}$ and y_g.

Suppose that in our OUTPUT–TEST example we wish to obtain the forecast value for the given test score $x_g = 500$. Using the estimated regression coefficients $a = 0.751$ and $b = 0.00435$, we obtain

$$\hat{y}_g = a + bx_g = 0.751 + 0.00435(500) = 2.926.$$

Thus, our best output estimate for a person who has a score of 500 is $\hat{y}_g = 2.926$.

Similarly, our estimate for the mean output of *all* persons having scores of 500 is also $\hat{y}_g = 2.926$. Although these estimates both equal the same value, we must emphasize that they are interpreted differently. This different interpretation will become important when we investigate the process of making interval estimates. Specifically, we will see that the confidence interval for estimating a single value will necessarily be larger than the confidence interval for estimating the mean value because the former will always have a larger standard error.

Interval Estimates of Forecasts

Recall that an interval estimate is centered, in probability terms, at the values of the point estimate. Then the endpoints of the interval are found by using information about the probability distribution of the point estimator and its standard error. From the above discussion we know that the point estimate for forecasts of both the mean value and the actual value of **y** is always the same value of $\hat{y}_g$. However, the endpoints of interval estimates of these two types of forecasts based on a new extra-sample value x_g will be different because their *standard errors* will be different: they are denoted as $s_{\bar{y} \cdot x}$ for the forecast of the mean value and s_f for the forecast of the actual value of **y**. Each of these is a multiple of the standard error of estimate, s_e, which was used in Section 12.5 for estimating the interval or band around sample values of **y** based on the *original sample values* of **x**. (See Fig. 12.10.)

Let us consider first the interval estimate of the forecast of the actual value of y_g. The appropriate standard error to use for this interval is usually called the **standard error of the forecast,** which we denote by s_f:

Estimated standard error of the forecast:

$$s_f = s_e \sqrt{1 + \frac{1}{n} + \frac{(x_g - \bar{x})^2}{SSx}}. \tag{12.28}$$

Note that s_f will always be larger than s_e, since the term under the square root will always be greater than one. Also, note that s_f depends on the particular value of x_g that is given. The farther the new value x_g is from the mean of the values used in estimating the sample regression line, the less accurate will be the forecasts based on that line. Usually, one must be cautious in making forecasts beyond the range of the observed data. The forecast error gets larger at an increasing rate as $x_g - \bar{x}$ gets larger. Note that the confidence bands in Fig. 12.14 are curved rather than straight lines. Finally, we see that if n is large and if the new sample value of x_g is close to $\bar{x}$ (the mean of the previous sample values), then

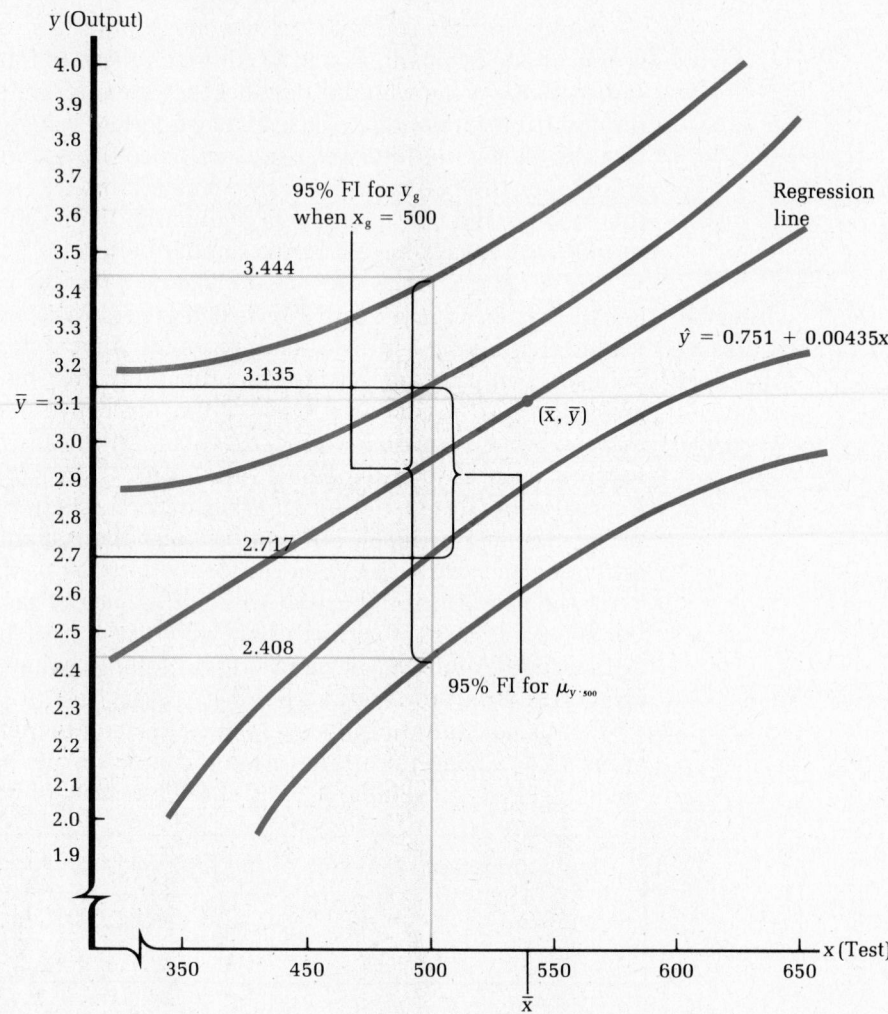

FIGURE 12.14 **Ninety-five-percent forecast interval (FI) for $\mu_{y \cdot x_g}$ (narrow band) and y_g (wide band) in the OUTPUT–TEST example.**

the term under the square root will be close to 1.0; hence, s_e and s_f will be approximately equal. This result should not be too surprising, for we know that the larger the sample and the less a given value x_g deviates from $\bar{x}$, the more faith we have in the sampling results and in the subsequent forecast. The forecast will be most accurate near the point of means $(\bar{x}, \bar{y})$.

We can now use our point estimate $\hat{y}_g$, and the standard error s_f, to construct a $100(1 - \alpha)\%$ confidence interval for y_g. The appropriate test statistic in this case has the t-distribution with $(n - 2)$ degrees of freedom:

Endpoints of a $100(1 - \alpha)\%$ **forecast interval for y_g:**

$$\hat{y}_g \pm t_{(\alpha/2,\, n-2)} s_f. \qquad (12.29)$$

Now we turn to the problem of constructing a forecast interval for $\mu_{y \cdot x_g}$, the *mean* of the *y*-values. In this case the appropriate standard error is denoted by the symbol $s_{\bar{y} \cdot x}$, where

---

Estimated standard error for mean prediction:

$$s_{\bar{y} \cdot x} = s_e \sqrt{\frac{1}{n} + \frac{(x_g - \bar{x})^2}{SSx}}. \qquad (12.30)$$

As was the case for s_f, $s_{\bar{y} \cdot x}$ depends on n, x_g, and s_e. The value of $s_{\bar{y} \cdot x}$, however, will always be smaller than s_f, as seen by comparing positive terms under the square-root sign. Again the appropriate test statistic is the t-distribution, with $(n - 2)$ degrees of freedom. The endpoints of a $100(1 - \alpha)\%$ interval are thus

---

Endpoints for a $100(1 - \alpha)\%$ **forecast interval on $\mu_{y \cdot x_g}$.**

$$\hat{y}_g \pm t_{(\alpha/2;\, n-2)} s_{\bar{y} \cdot x}. \qquad (12.31)$$

Example 12.12. Suppose that we want to construct, on the basis of our sample of $n = 8$, a 95% forecast interval for the output of an electrician with a test score of 500. From Table VI the value of $t_{(0.025,\, 6)} = 2.447$, and we know from our previous analysis that

$$\hat{y}_{500} = 2.926, \quad s_e = 0.1936, \quad \bar{x} = 540, \quad \text{and} \quad SSx = \sum_{i=1}^{8} x_i^2 - \frac{\left(\sum_{i=1}^{8} x_i\right)^2}{n} = 23{,}000.$$

Substituting these values into Formula (12.29) and using the definition of s_f in Formula (12.28), we get the following endpoints for the forecast interval:

$$2.926 \pm 2.447(0.1936)\sqrt{1 + \frac{1}{8} + \left[\frac{(500 - 540)^2}{23,000}\right]}$$

$$= 2.926 \pm 2.447(0.1936)(1.09296)$$

$$= 2.926 \pm 0.518$$

$$= 2.408 \quad \text{and} \quad 3.444.$$

Using this method, we can expect that 95% of the intervals determined by this method will include the true value of the electrician's output. Again, this interval is quite wide, since we have used a very small sample, $n = 8$, which gave us a relatively large standard error (s_e). A narrower interval is obtained if we are predicting a mean value of the dependent variable, $\mu_{y \cdot x_g}$, rather than an individual value y_g. Substituting the appropriate values in Formula (12.31) and using Formula (12.30) for $s_{\bar{y} \cdot x}$, we obtain the following endpoints:

$$2.926 \pm 2.447(0.1936)\sqrt{\frac{1}{8} + \frac{(500 - 540)^2}{23,000}} = 2.926 \pm 2.447(0.1936)(0.4411)$$

$$= 2.926 \pm 0.209.$$

The interval is $(2.717 < \mu_{y \cdot x_g} < 3.135)$.

Study Question 12.5: Forecast for Housing Price
Using the data and results in Study Questions 12.2–12.4, find the 90% forecast interval for the actual housing price in a city given that its median income is $13,000. Repeat for another city with median income of $15,000. Compare the spread of the two intervals.

Answer. A forecast is obtained by substituting the given income value (in $000) into the sample regression equation, $\hat{y} = -8.659 + 4.5404x$.

For $x = 13$:

$$\hat{y} = -8.659 + 4.5404(13) = 50.366.$$

The standard error of the forecast is found by using Formula (12.28):

$$s_f = 9.244\sqrt{1 + \frac{1}{10} + \frac{(13 - 12.23)^2}{14.961}}$$

$$= 9.244\sqrt{1.140} = 9.244(1.068) = 9.873.$$

By using Formula (12.29) and $t_{0.05,8} = 1.860$ from Table VI the limits are

$$50.366 \pm 1.860(9.873),$$

$$50.366 \pm 18.364.$$

Multiplying by 1000 to return to units of dollars, we have the 90% confidence limits on $\hat{y}_{(x=13,000)}$ of $32,002 and $68,730.

For $x = 15$:

$$\hat{y} = -8.659 + 4.5404(15) = 59.447;$$

$$s_f = 9.244\sqrt{1 + \frac{1}{10} + \frac{(15 - 12.23)^2}{14.961}}$$

$$= 9.244\sqrt{1.613} = 9.244(1.270) = 11.740.$$

The limits on $\hat{y}$ are

$$59.477 \pm 1.860(11.740),$$

$$59.447 \pm 21.836.$$

When multiplied by 1000, this gives the endpoints $37,611 and $81,283.

The spread of the two intervals differs owing to the different values of s_f in the two cases. Since s_f depends on the distances that the given values (x_g equal to 13 or 15) are from the mean ($\bar{x} = 12.23$) of the previously observed values of x, the interval is larger for x = 15 than for x = 12. The spread of the first interval is 68,730 − 32,002 = $36,728. The interval width for the case with x = 15,000 is 81,283 − 37,611 = $43,672. The difference in spread is 43,672 − 36,728 = $6,944.

12.9 THE *F*-TEST*

In Section 12.7 we presented some *t*-statistics for testing the significance of the relation between **y** and **x** as expressed by the regression model. There is still another way of testing the null hypothesis $H_0: \beta = 0$, using the measures of unexplained and explained variation. Before the reader bemoans the presentation of one more test to learn, we must point out that the test in this section is particularly important because it can be generalized to problems involving more than just one independent variable (i.e., to the multiple-regression case). This use will be discussed in Chapter 13.

Recall that SST = SSE + SSR. You may recall also that the degrees of freedom associated with SST are $n - 1$ (since only $\bar{y}$ must be calculated before SST can be computed), while the d.f. for SSE are $n - 2$ (both a

---

* It is assumed that the reader has studied the use of an *F*-distributed random variable presented in Section 10.6.

TABLE 12.10 **Analysis-of-variance (ANOVA) table for simple regression**

Source of the Variation	Sum of Squares	Degrees of Freedom	Mean Square
Regression	SSR	1	SSR/1
Error (or residual)	SSE	$n - 2$	SSE/$(n - 2)$
Total	SST	$n - 1$	

and b must be calculated before computing SSE). Since the d.f. for SST must equal the sum of those for SSE and SSR, we see by subtraction that the d.f. for SSR = 1 (because $n - 1 = (n - 2) + 1$). A sum of squares divided by its degrees of freedom is called a **mean square.** The two mean squares we will need are *mean square error* (MSE) and *mean square regression* (MSR):

$$\text{Mean square error:} \quad \text{MSE} = \frac{\text{SSE}}{n - 2} = s_e^2;$$

$$\text{Mean square regression:} \quad \text{MSR} = \frac{\text{SSR}}{1}.$$

It is customary to present information about MSE and MSR in an *analysis-of-variance* (ANOVA) table, as shown in Table 12.10.

One word of caution is necessary here: although the sums of squares and the degrees of freedom are additive, the mean square terms are *not* additive. Note that, in the analysis-of-variance table, no MS term is given in the row labeled "Total." The SST and the degrees of freedom total are given in the table, so it can be verified that elements in the body of the table do sum to these values.

We can use the mean squares to construct a new test on the hypothesis $H_0: \beta = 0$. We recognize that the only way the regression equation can indicate a relatively large amount of variation explained (SSR) is if the one variable (x) doing the explaining has a significant nonzero coefficient. Obversely, if β is not significantly different from zero, then there can be no effect on y of changes in x. In that case the unexplained errors (SSE) would be relatively large. Thus, the measures of SSR and SSE indirectly provide information about the significance of the slope in the relation between y and x. To construct a useful test statistic based on SSE and SSR, we need to adjust them for degrees of freedom. This means that we will use the mean square measures, MSR and MSE, in our new test of $H_0: \beta = 0$. The test statistic is the F-ratio shown in Formula (12.32):

F-statistic for testing the fit of the linear model:

$$F_{(1, n-2 \text{ d.f.})} = \frac{\text{MSR}}{\text{MSE}}.$$

(12.32)

We would reject the null hypothesis of no linear relation between **y** and **x** whenever this **F**-statistic is *larger* than the critical value in Table VIII. Remember that either a positive or a negative value of β can lead to a significant linear relation between **y** and **x**. However, this **F**-test cannot distinguish between $\beta < 0$ and $\beta > 0$ because the values of **F** are always positive. Thus, the alternative hypothesis used in this test is two-sided, H_a: $\beta \neq 0$. That is, the hypotheses are

H_0: no significant relation and $\beta = 0$;

H_a: there is a significant relation between **y** and **x**.

Figure 12.15 illustrates the critical region for the F-test. It has only one section (in the upper tail), even though this is a two-sided test on β.

Clearly, when $\beta \neq 0$, we know that x helps explain changes in y. Correspondingly, we expect the variation explained (SSR) to be large and the variation *not* explained (SSE) to be relatively small. If this effect is significant, the MSR will be large in relation to the MSE. An F-ratio with a large numerator and a small denominator will be a large value and will lie in the critical region for the test. This leads to the correct conclusion that the slope is *not* zero. If MSR is small in relation to MSE, the F-value will be small and will lie in the acceptance region for the test.

Example 12.13. An ANOVA table for regression analysis is constructed for the OUTPUT–TEST example. Recall from Section 12.5 that

$$\text{SST} = 0.660, \quad \text{SSE} = 0.225, \quad \text{and} \quad \text{SSR} = 0.435.$$

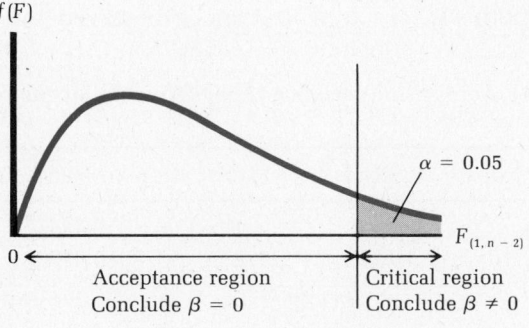

$f(F)$

$\alpha = 0.05$

$F_{(1, n-2)}$

0

Acceptance region
Conclude $\beta = 0$

Critical region
Conclude $\beta \neq 0$

FIGURE 12.15 **The critical region for the analysis-of-variance test on a regression.**

Hence,

$$\text{MSR} = \frac{\text{SSR}}{1} = \frac{0.435}{1} = 0.435 \quad \text{and} \quad \text{MSE} = \frac{\text{SSE}}{n-2} = \frac{0.225}{6} = 0.0375.$$

Table 12.11 is the analysis-of-variance table for this example.

If we choose a significance level of $\alpha = 0.05$, the critical value [from Table VIII(a)] is $F_{(1,6 \text{ d.f.})} = 5.99$. The F-statistic calculated in this example is

$$F_c = \frac{\text{MSR}}{\text{MSE}} = \frac{0.435}{0.0375} = 11.6.$$

Since the calculated F-ratio is larger than the critical value, we reject the null hypothesis and conclude that the linear relationship *does help* explain the variation in OUTPUT.

The F-test in this section is related to the previous t-tests for regression analysis. Both the F- and t-tests will indicate that a significant linear relation exists between the variables y and x. The F-test shows this when a significant amount of variation in y is explained by x. This can occur only if there is a significant correlation between y and x, $\rho \neq 0$, as shown by one t-test [Formula (12.25)] and only if there is a significant slope of the line relating y and x, $\beta \neq 0$, as shown by the other t-test [Formula (12.22)]. Also, we could show that the calculated F-value in Formula (12.32) equals the *square* of the calculated t-values in Formulas (12.22) and (12.25). That is, for these statistics in simple linear regression, $F = t^2$. Theoretically, an F-distributed random variable with 1 and $n - 2$ degrees of freedom (in the numerator and denominator, respectively) is exactly the square of a t-distributed random variable (with $n - 2$ degrees of freedom).

In our OUTPUT–TEST example the t-values were 3.404 for these formulas in Section 12.7. The F-value in this section for the test on β was 11.6, which is the rounded value of $(3.404)^2$.

This same relation between the t- and F-statistics for a test on the null hypothesis, H_0: $\beta = 0$, can be observed for the PRICE–INCOME

TABLE 12.11 **Analysis-of-variance (ANOVA) table for the regression of OUTPUT on TEST**

Source	SS	d.f.	Mean Square
Regression	0.435	1	0.435
Error	0.225	6	0.0375
Total	0.660	7	

regression discussed in the Study Questions in this chapter. Looking back to the computer printout in Fig. 12.13, we note that the SPSS printout gives a value of F associated with the significance test for β: F = 3.609. The SAS printout gives the same value of the F-ratio [Formula (12.32)] for the fit of the model: F RATIO = 3.61. It also gives a value of the t-statistic [Formula (12.22)] associated with the significance test for β; T RATIO = 1.8997. The square of this t-value, $(1.8997)^2 = 3.609$, is the F-value.

Since either a positive or negative t-value would have the same square, the p-value for the t-test would have to be *doubled* to correspond to a two-sided p-value in the F-test. The reader might compare the values from the first column of the F-table (Table VIII), with 1 degree of freedom in the numerator and a significance level of 0.05, to the square of the values in the t-table (Table VI), with a significance level of 0.025. *The F-values are the square of the t-values.*

> We repeat that the F-test on the fit of the simple regression model, the t-test of significance on the slope β, and the t-test on the correlation coefficient ρ are all equivalent tests in simple linear regression. They give the same information, namely, whether or not y and x are significantly linearly related.

In Chapter 13 we will consider a multiple regression model in which several explanatory variables are used to explain changes in y. In that situation, the t-tests will help us learn about the significance of the *individual relation between y and one* of the explanatory variables. The F-test will give us information about the significance of the *overall relation among y and all* the explanatory variables. The advantage of the F-test is that it can be generalized to a test of significance when there is more than one independent variable, while the t-test cannot. The advantage of the t-test is that it can be used to test for values of β other than zero, while the F-test is appropriate only for the null hypothesis $H_0:β = 0$.

12.10 A SAMPLE PROBLEM

Having specified all the concepts and formulas essential for a simple regression and correlation analysis, the best way to review them is to apply them. One of the important decisions faced by business managers is the amount of *investment* they should make in new plant and equipment and in maintenance and repair of existing capital goods. Economists are very interested in the level of aggregate investment over all private business in the United States, since this value is an important factor in determining national income and the potential for growth in an economy.

Suppose that a model is specified in which the dependent variable y is the level of investment. In such a model, one might want to estimate the amount of investment for a *single* firm by analyzing the relationship between investment and one or more independent variables in a sample of firms. On the other hand, one may be more interested in estimating the *aggregate* investment for all firms, using as the sample data a number of past time periods. For this example we choose the latter concept because the data are easily available without a survey of firms. The Department of Commerce and the Federal Reserve Board, among other agencies, report the key monthly, quarterly, or annual economic aggregates for the United States economy.

Any textbook of basic economic principles includes some theoretical relationships between investment and other variables. Generally, it is recognized that the level of investment depends on the availability of funds for investment and on the need for expanding productive capacity. Thus, any variables that reflect these supply or demand factors may be appropriate to explain or predict changes in levels of investment. Such variables as the existing amount of plant and equipment that is depreciating, current and past levels of profits, the interest rate at which funds could be borrowed, indicators of the current general economic conditions, the number of unemployed, etc., may be selected as independent variables to help explain variation in investment.

For simplicity, suppose we specify that the population regression model is $y_i = \alpha + \beta x_i + \epsilon_i$, where x_i represents a composite price index for 500 common stocks during a given time period and y_i represents the amount of aggregate investment *during the following time period*. We might postulate such a relationship because we believe that stock market prices are indicative of the general level of business expectations for the future. For this example we will estimate the population regression line on the basis of 20 quarterly observations. The data, shown in Table 12.12, represent investment measured at an annual rate in billions of dollars. The sample statistics needed for computing the least-squares regression line follow Table 12.12.

We know that the line that provides the least-squares fit to these data has the following slope and intercept [using Formulas (12.10) and (12.8)]:

$$\text{Sample slope:} \quad b = \frac{\text{SCxy}}{\text{SSx}} = \frac{77,626.0}{628,713.46} = 0.12347;$$

$$\text{Sample intercept:} \quad a = \bar{y} - \beta\bar{x} = 88.915 - 0.12347(688.920) = 3.855.$$

TABLE 12.12 **Data for estimating the investment equation**

Observation	Investment y	Stock Index x	Observation	Investment y	Stock Index x
1	62.3	398.4	11	84.3	581.8
2	71.3	452.6	12	85.1	707.1
3	70.3	509.8	13	90.8	776.6
4	68.5	485.4	14	97.9	875.3
5	57.3	445.7	15	108.7	873.4
6	68.8	539.8	16	122.4	943.7
7	72.2	662.8	17	114.0	830.6
8	76.0	620.0	18	123.0	907.5
9	64.3	632.2	19	126.2	905.3
10	77.9	703.0	20	137.0	927.4

Mean of $y = \dfrac{1}{20}\sum_{i=1}^{20} y_i = 88.915$ $\qquad$ Mean of $x = \dfrac{1}{20}\sum_{i=1}^{20} x_i = 688.92$

SST = Variation of y = SSy $\qquad$ Variation of x = SSx

$$= \sum_{i=1}^{20} y_i{}^2 - \frac{1}{n}\left(\sum_{i=1}^{20} y_i\right)^2 \qquad\qquad = \sum_{i=1}^{20} x_i{}^2 - \frac{1}{n}\left(\sum_{i=1}^{20} x_i\right)^2$$

$$= 11{,}485.7. \qquad\qquad\qquad\qquad = 628{,}713.46.$$

Covariation of x and y = SCxy

$$= \sum_{i=1}^{20} x_i y_i - \frac{1}{n}\left(\sum_{i=1}^{20} x_i\right)\left(\sum_{i=1}^{20} y_i\right)$$

$$= 77{,}626.0.$$

The least-squares estimating line is $\hat{y}_i = 3.855 + 0.12347x_i$. The positive value for b confirms our assumption that investment increases when stock prices increase. We see that, for these data, a 10-unit increase in the stock index x in one quarter is associated with an increase in the annual rate of investment during the next quarter of about 1.23 billion dollars. Two computer printouts in Fig. 12.16 provide results for this regression analysis.

To obtain the goodness-of-fit measures, the components of total variation must be found. The total variation in y to be explained is SST = 11,485.7. Its components are found by using Formula (12.15):

Explained variation = SSR = b(SCxy)

$$= 0.12347(77{,}626.0) = 9584.4;$$

Unexplained variation = SSE = SST − SSR

$$= 11{,}485.7 - 9584.4 = 1901.3.$$

a) Microcomputer printout using a BASIC program:

```
Sample size = 20      SUM of x = 13778.4      SUM of y = 1778.3

SCxy = 77,616.0       SSx = 628,713.46       SSy = 11,485.69

MEAN of x = 688.92                  MEAN of y = 88.915

VARIANCE OF x = 33,090.182          VARIANCE of y = 604.510

STD DEV of x = 181.907              STD   DEV of y = 24.587

SLOPE = 0.12347                     y-INTERCEPT = 3.8550

SST = 11,485.7      SSR = 9584.4         SSE = 1901.3

SE = 10.277                         R-SQUARED = 0.8345

SB = 0.01296        T-RATIO = 9.526      F-TEST = 90.74
```

b) SAS program printout:

```
MODEL:    MODELO1         SSE       1901.26    F RATIO        90.74
                          DFE             18   PROB>F        0.0001
DEP VAR: Y                MSE    105.625539    R-SQUARE      0.8345
         INVESTMENT

DURBIN-WATSON D STATISTIC   =   0.7848
```

VARIABLE	DF	PARAMETER ESTIMATE	STANDARD ERROR	T RATIO	PROB>|T|
INTERCEPT	1	3.854980	9.220475	0.4181	0.6808
X1	1	0.123469	0.012962	9.5257	0.0001

FIGURE 12.16 **Computer printouts for a regression using the data in Table 12.12.**

The value SSE $= \Sigma e_i^2 = 1901.3$ can be used to find the standard error of the estimate by using Formula (12.16):

$$s_e = \sqrt{\frac{SSE}{n-2}} = \sqrt{\frac{1901.3}{18}} = 10.277.$$

The reader may wish to check (see Problems 12.64 and 12.65) whether approximately 68% of the data points lie within 10.277 vertical units (billions of dollars) above or below the estimating line.

Our second measure of goodness of fit is the sample coefficient of determination r^2, given by Formula (12.17):

$$r^2 = \frac{\text{Explained variation}}{\text{Total variation}} = \frac{\text{SSR}}{\text{SST}} = \frac{9584.4}{11{,}485.7} = 0.8345.$$

This means that 83.45% of the variation in investment has been explained by the relationship between it and the stock price index.

Any of the tests or confidence intervals on the population parameters, as described in the preceding sections, can be calculated easily by using the information from Fig. 12.16. For example, the test of the significance of the slope parameter involves

$$H_0 : \beta = 0 \qquad \text{versus} \qquad H_a : \beta > 0.$$

The test statistic with a t-distribution and $n - 2 = 18$ degrees of freedom [using Formula (12.22)] is

$$t_{18 \text{ d.f.}} = \frac{b - \beta_0}{s_b},$$

where $\beta_0 = 0$ and $s_b = s_e / \sqrt{\text{SSx}}$. Using a significance level of $\alpha = 0.005$, we find, in Table VI, that the critical region is all values of

$$t > t_{(0.005,\ 18)} = 2.878.$$

The calculated value of s_e is 10.277 and

$$s_b = \frac{10.277}{\sqrt{628{,}713.46}} = 0.01296;$$

thus the calculated value t_c is:

$$t_c = \frac{b - 0}{s_b} = \frac{0.12347}{0.01296} = 9.526.$$

Since $9.526 > 2.878$, we can reject the null hypothesis and conclude that there is a positive linear relationship between current investment and the stock-market index of the previous quarter. If the stock prices do reflect business expectations, then these data support the theory that business firms are more willing to expand their plant and equipment when they foresee "good times" (higher incomes, greater demands, and more potential sales and profits) ahead.

The significance of the positive linear relationship can be found by using the F-test of Section 12.9 and the hypotheses $H_0 : \beta = 0$ and $H_a : \beta \neq 0$. The test statistic is given by the F-ratio in Formula (12.32) with 1 and 18 degrees of freedom. From Table VIII and a significance level of 0.01, the critical value is $F_{(0.01; 1, 18)} = 8.29$. [Note that this is the square of the critical value of the previous one-sided t-test, $(2.878)^2$, using $\alpha = 0.005$.] From Fig. 12.16, SSR = 9584.4, SSE = 1901.3, and $(n - 2) = 18$; hence,

$$MSR = \frac{SSR}{1} = 9584.4 \quad \text{and} \quad MSE = \frac{SSE}{18} = 105.63.$$

The calculated value of the F-statistic is

$$F_c = \frac{MSR}{MSE} = \frac{9584.4}{105.63} = 90.74,$$

which is the square of the calculated t-statistic, $(9.526)^2$, in the previous test. Again, we reject the null hypothesis and conclude that there is a significant linear relation between investment and stock index.

Finally, the regression model can be used to predict investment by using the procedures of Section 12.8. If a quarterly observation for the stock index is given as $x_g = 800$, the best point estimate for the actual value of investment is obtained by substitution into the sample regression equation,

$$\hat{y}_g = a + bx_g = 3.855 + 0.12347(800) = 102.63 \quad (\$billions).$$

To obtain an interval estimate with 90% confidence, Formulas (12.28) and (12.29) are used. The t-value obtained from Table VI is $t_{0.05,18} = 1.734$. The value of the standard deviation for an individual forecast is

$$s_f = s_e \sqrt{1 + \frac{1}{n} + \frac{(x_g - \bar{x})^2}{SSx}}$$

$$= 10.277 \sqrt{1 + \frac{1}{20} + \frac{(800 - 688.92)^2}{628,713.46}}$$

$$= 10.277 \sqrt{1 + 0.05 + 0.0196} = 10.277 \sqrt{1.070}$$

$$= 10.277(1.034) = 10.626.$$

The 90% forecast interval has limits $\hat{y}_g \pm ts_f = 102.63 \pm 1.734(10.626)$, which gives $102.63 + 18.43 = 121.06$ and $102.63 - 18.43 = 84.20$. The width of this interval ($\$84.20$ to $\$121.06$ billion) illustrates the uncertainty involved with predicting investment based on the sample regression model.

Define. *Standard errors: of the slope (s_b), of the intercept (s_a), of the forecast (s_f), of the mean prediction $(s_{\bar{y} \cdot x})$; t-test for β, α, or ρ; forecast or predicted value $(\hat{y}_g)$; MSE, MSR, analysis-of-variance (ANOVA) table.*

PROBLEMS

12.30 In a regression of the amount of sales **y** on the number of customers **x** based on 11 observations, the value of the coefficient of determination is 0.36.

a) Does this indicate a significant correlation between y and x at the 0.05 significance level if proper normality assumptions are made? Let H_a be two-sided.

b) What is the proportion of variation left unexplained in this regression?

12.31 Suppose that the following ten observations were obtained in a survey to determine the relationship between an individual's educational level and this person's salary.

Years of Higher Education	Income
3	$30,000
4	28,000
7	33,000
9	40,000
1	26,000
0	25,000
2	28,000
1	27,000
8	34,000
5	29,000

a) Assuming normal distributions, what is the correlation between years of higher education and income for this sample?

b) Use $\alpha = 0.05$ and your answer to part (a) to test the null hypothesis H_0: $\rho = 0$ against the alternative hypothesis H_a: $\rho > 0$.

12.32 Given a regression equation, $\hat{y} = 14 + 6x$, based on 12 observations, test the hypotheses H_0: $\beta = 0$ versus H_a: $\beta > 0$ using a significance level of 0.05. The standard error of b is $s_b = 1.5$.

12.33 In a correlation between corporate net investment and long-term interest rates, using quarterly observations from the third quarter of 1975 through the fourth quarter of 1984, a correlation coefficient of $+0.60$ is obtained. Determine whether this is a significant positive correlation, using $\alpha = 0.01$, a one-sided alternative hypothesis, and assuming normality.

12.34 Suppose that, in analyzing the relationship between 26 observations of two variables, dividends (y) and profits (x), you find SST equal to 120.0 and SSR equal to 13.2. The slope of the sample regression line is positive. Assume that the populations are normal.

a) What is the coefficient of determination for this problem? What percent of the sample variation in dividends has been explained?

b) Use the t-test described in Section 12.7 to test the null hypothesis H_0: $\rho = 0$ against H_a: $\rho \neq 0$. Can the null hypothesis of no linear correlation be rejected at the 0.05 level of significance?

c) Compute the **F**-value necessary for testing the null and alternative hypotheses equivalent to those in part (b). Is this value of **F** consistent with the **t**-value calculated in part (b)?

12.35 Let **x** represent income payments in Texas (billions of dollars) and let **y** represent retail sales of Texas jewelry stores (millions of dollars). The regression equation is $\hat{y} = 8.505x - 7.41$. The standard error of the estimate is 3.5, and the correlation coefficient is 0.95.

a) For a year in which income payments are $10.0 billion, what is the best estimate of sales in jewelry stores?

b) What proportion of the variation in the retail jewelry sales is explained by the variation in income payments?

c) This correlation indicates that in Texas higher retail jewelry sales cause higher incomes. Comment.

12.36 The following data represent the dollar value of sales and advertising for a retail store.

Advertising, x (in Thousands)	Sales, y (in Thousands)
$600	$5,000
400	4,000
800	7,000
200	3,000
500	6,000

a) Draw the scatter diagram for these data. Fit a line by the freehand method. Does the linear approximation seem appropriate?

b) Find the least-squares regression line.

c) What value for sales would you predict if advertising were $700? What value would you predict if advertising were zero?

d) Given the standard assumptions, construct a 95% confidence interval for the *mean* value of sales when advertising is $500 (i.e., for $\mu_{y\cdot 500}$).

e) Construct a 95% confidence interval for the actual value of sales when advertising is $500.

f) Test the null hypothesis that the slope of the regression line is zero against H_a: $\beta > 0$ using $\alpha = 0.05$.

g) Find the sample correlation coefficient.

h) Assuming normality, test the null hypothesis H_0: $\rho = 0$ against the alternative H_a: $\rho \neq 0$. At what level of significance can H_0 be rejected?

12.37 Given the following least-squares regression line, ANOVA table, and the standard assumptions, define **y** = rental cost ($) of a charter bus and **x** = number of hours rented during the day.

$\hat{y} = 112 + 9.6x$		
Source	SS	d.f.
Regression	144	1
Error	342	38

a) What was the sample size in this problem? What is SST?
b) Use an F-test to accept or reject $H_0: \beta = 0$ versus $H_a: \beta \neq 0$ using $\alpha = 0.05$.
c) Calculate the value of s_b based on the fact that SSx $= 1.5625$.

12.38 Use the value of s_b from Problem 12.37.
a) Construct a t-test to accept or reject $H_0: \beta = 0$ versus $H_a: \beta \neq 0$ using $\alpha = 0.05$. Is your answer consistent with your answer for part (b) of Problem 12.37?
b) Construct a 95% confidence interval for β.
c) Assume, for this problem, that when $x_g = 5$, $s_f = 3.20$ [from Formula (12.28)]. Use this information to construct a 95% confidence interval for y_g.
d) If $s_{\bar{y} \cdot x} = 1.965$ when $x_g = 5$ [from Formula (12.30)], construct a 95% confidence interval for $\mu_{y \cdot x_g}$.

12.39 For the data in Problem 12.36, find s_x, s_y, and s_{xy}. Show that the value of r you calculated for Problem 12.36 equals $s_{xy}/s_x s_y$.

12.40 For $y =$ (delivery time in minutes of pizza orders) and $x =$ (distance in quarter-miles from the pizza shop to the customer) the least-squares regression line fitted to 62 observations yields the equation $\hat{y} = 16.9 + 1.225x$. SST for this sample was determined to be 594, while SSE was found to be 540.
a) Construct an ANOVA table for these values.
b) Find the standard error of b by assuming that SSx $= 36$. Use this information to test the null hypothesis $H_0: \beta = 0$ versus $H_a: \beta \neq 0$ by means of a t-test. Use $\alpha = 0.05$.
c) Test the same relation as in part (b), but this time use an F-test. Are your answers to parts (b) and (c) consistent?
d) Assuming normality, test the null hypothesis $H_0: \rho = 0$ versus $H_a: \rho \neq 0$ at $\alpha = 0.05$. Compare this result to those in parts (b) and (c).

12.41 Use the information provided in Problem 12.40 to answer the following questions.
a) Assume that the given value of x is $x_g = 7$ and $\bar{x} = 10$. Find the standard error of the forecast, s_f. Use this information to construct a 95% forecast interval for y_g.

b) Repeat part (a) for x_g = 8, 9, 10, 11, and 12. Draw a graph similar to Fig. 12.14, illustrating a 95% forecast interval for y_g from x = 7 to x = 12.

c) Find the values of $s_{\bar{y} \cdot x}$ for x = 7 through 12. Draw the 95% forecast interval for $\mu_{y \cdot x_g}$ on your graph from part (b).

EXERCISES

12.42 How would you choose among alternative unbiased estimators of the slope in the population regression model?

12.43 Explain the relation between the t-test on the significance of a slope β and the F-test on the significance of the linear relation between y and x.

12.44 What assumptions about the parent population are necessary to fit a least-squares regression line to a set of observations? What assumptions about the parent population are necessary to make interval estimates on the basis of a least-squares regression line?

12.45 Find the least-squares estimator for β in the function $y = \beta x^3$, based on n sample observations of y and x.

12.46 Use the following data to answer parts (a)–(d).

Age (Years)	Salary ($000)
65	150
70	170
75	160

a) Estimate the salary of a corporate executive who is 71 years old.

b) Estimate the age of an executive whose salary is $153,000.

c) Plot the regression lines you calculated for parts (a) and (b). Why do these lines differ?

d) Find the sample correlation coefficient. Does the value of the correlation coefficient depend on which variable is dependent and which is independent in the regression equation?

12.47 If you used some method other than least-squares to get linear unbiased estimates of the coefficients in a regression model, discuss how your values for s_e and r^2 would compare to those determined by means of a least-squares regression based on the same sample data.

12.48 Derive the normal equations for the least-squares estimation of the function $y = \alpha + \beta x^2$.

12.49 Discuss the following statement: "Cause-and-effect inferences can never be made from regression analysis."

12.50 If it is true that (under the five assumptions) the distribution of the least-square estimator of a coefficient is *normal*, then why does statistical inference on a regression coefficient use the *t*-distribution instead of the *z*-distribution?

12.51 In a regression the estimated value of β is $b = 2.5$ with $s_b = 0.8$. Find a 90% confidence interval on the true parameter β if $n = 22$.

12.52 Given that, for a sample of 17 pairs of observations on **y** and **x**, the total variation is 28,416, the SSR is 7104, and the covariation of x and y is $-42,624$.
  a) Find s_e and r and explain their meaning.
  b) Assuming normality, test the hypothesis that there is no correlation between **y** and **x**. Use a two-sided alternative hypothesis and let $\alpha = 0.10$.

12.53 Define or describe briefly each of the following:
  a) Standard error of the estimate;
  b) Standard error of the forecast;
  c) Standard error of the regression coefficient.

12.54 In a simple regression based on 32 observations, it is found that $r = 0.6$ and $s_e^2 = 100$.
  a) Find SST, SSR, and SSE.
  b) Do an analysis-of-variance test to determine whether the linear relationship is significant at the 0.01 level.

12.55 The number of rooms to be occupied (**y**) in a large hotel is estimated to be $\hat{y} = 10 + 3x$, where **x** is the number of advance guaranteed room reservations. Also, $\bar{y} = 160$ and $\bar{x} = 50$. Explain whether there is any difference in the precision of forecasts ($\hat{y}$) based on this model in the cases where the given values of x_g are 40 and 100.

12.56 Consider a model $y_i = \alpha + \beta x_i + \epsilon_i$, where **y** is the long-term AAA corporate bond yield and x is the income velocity of money,

$$\log (\text{GNP/money supply}).$$

Using quarterly data for over six years, we obtain

$$n = 26 \qquad \Sigma y = 118.27 \qquad \Sigma y^2 = 541.77$$
$$\Sigma xy = 477.05 \qquad \Sigma x = 104.42 \qquad \Sigma x^2 = 420.72$$

  a) Find the least-squares estimates for α and β based on these data. Interpret the meaning of your estimated model by considering the effect on the interest rate of a 0.2-unit decrease in income velocity due to an increased desire by consumers to hold cash.

b) If income velocity is 4.0, find the estimated value for y. If the true interest rate at this level of income velocity is 4.29%, determine the residual e.

c) Compute and interpret the meaning of r^2 and s_e.

12.57 Examine the relation between imports and national income for the United States during the peacetime period, 1955–1965, using the data in the table below:

Year	U.S. Imports y (Billion Dollars)	U.S. National Income x_2 (Billion Dollars)
1955	11.6	331
1956	12.9	351
1957	13.4	366
1958	13.4	368
1959	15.7	400
1960	15.1	414
1961	14.8	427
1962	16.5	458
1963	17.2	482
1964	18.8	517
1965	21.4	559

Source: *International Financial Statistics, Supplement.*

a) By the least-squares method, estimate the model $y_i = \alpha + \beta x_i + \epsilon_i$.

b) Find and interpret the meaning of r^2 and s_e.

c) Test the significance of ρ at the 0.01 level, assuming normal populations.

d) Test at the 0.01 level whether the marginal propensity to import (β) satisfies $(0.02 < \beta < 0.05)$ by making a one-sided test on each endpoint of the interval.

e) Given that national income is 280 for 1951, test whether a level of imports of 10.5 for the same year is consistent with the 1955–1965 experience. Use the 0.05 level of significance.

12.58 A significant change occurred in U.S. federal government expenditures on defense in the period 1940–1948. Use the data below for y = GNP and x = expenditures on national defense, both in billions of dollars.

Year	1940	1941	1942	1943	1944	1945	1946	1947	1948
y	99.7	124.5	157.9	191.6	210.1	211.9	208.5	231.3	257.6
x	1.5	6.1	24.0	63.2	76.8	81.3	43.2	14.4	11.8

a) Estimate the relation $y_i = \alpha + \beta x_i + \epsilon_i$ by the least-squares method.

b) Interpret the meaning of the estimate of β.
c) Determine the residuals for these nine observations.
d) Find and interpret the meaning of r^2 and s_e.
e) By examining these results, discuss the adequacy of this linear representation when enormous structural changes take place. Suggest a better specification of the relation between GNP and defense expenditures for the period 1940–1948.
f) Find the U.S. expenditure on defense and GNP for the current year. Using the relation estimated above, find the residual (unexplained deviation).

12.59 The following data measure y = current corporate investment and x = retained earnings in the previous year.
a) Formulate a linear regression model relating these two variables. Estimate and interpret the meaning of your specification and your results.

y	x	y	x
37.0	16.0	37.3	13.5
30.5	14.2	39.2	16.0
32.5	10.8	44.9	16.6
35.7	16.0	52.0	20.6
34.4	13.2	60.6	25.4

b) Test the hypothesis H_0: $\beta = 1.5$ at the 0.10 significance level against the alternative H_a: $\beta \neq 1.5$.

12.60 Prove that b in Formula (12.10) is equivalent to the b-value in Formula (12.8).

12.61 Prove that the normal equations in the footnote on page 559 do, in fact, lead to the values of a and b in Formula (12.8). Refer to Problem 12.60.

12.62 Using the appropriate definitions, explain why the following equations are correct: SSR = r^2 (SST) and SSE = $(1 - r^2)$(SST). Use these formulas to prove that the F-value in Formula (12.32) is the square of the t-value in Formula (12.25).

12.63 Prove that $r = b(s_x/s_y)$ and r^2 = SSR/SST.

USING THE COMPUTER

12.64 Use the data in Section 12.10. Have a computer program do a plot of investment against stock index. Draw in the sample regression line and two bounding lines parallel to the regression line but a vertical distance of $s_e = 10.28$ units above and below it. Determine what proportion of the 20 observations lie within one standard error of the regression line.

12.65 Use a computer program to recalculate the sample regression line using the same data as in Section 12.10 on investment and stock index. Also, have the list of 20 residuals printed out.
a) Determine what proportion of these values of e_i are smaller in absolute value than s_e.
b) Compare this result to the proportion determined graphically in Problem 12.64.

12.66 Use the observations on sales and assets in **Data Set 2** and make the standard assumptions.
a) Find the least squares regression line between sales (y) and assets (x). Use values in terms of $billions with two decimal places (e.g., Sears sales and assets are 27.36 and 34.51).
b) Test the significance of the slope using a t-test at the 0.01 level.
c) Find a 90% forecast interval for the actual value of sales for a firm with assets of 2.50 ($billion).

12.67 Use the observations in **Data Set 1** on income and taxes.
a) Find the least-squares regression equation between taxes (y) and income (x) and make the standard assumptions.
b) Do an F-test on the significance of the relation using the 0.05 level.
c) Find a 98% confidence interval for the true slope of the relation.

12.68 Refer to **Data Set 4**, which gives 40 observations from a survey of doctors (general practitioners) in private practice. Make the standard assumptions.
a) Do a least-squares regression between the reported annual net income (y) and the average weekly hours worked (x).
b) Find s_e and r^2 and interpret their meaning.
c) Explain why you do or do not think this is a useful model for explaining the different levels of net income of these doctors.

12.69 Refer to **Data Set 5** giving 30 annual observations for 1951–1980 of some economic measures for the United States. We would expect a positive relation between the level of exports and the gross domestic product (GDP).
a) Find the least-squares regression equation between GDP (y) and exports (x).
b) Using a significance level of 0.025 and the standard assumptions, determine whether the change in GDP for a unit change in exports is less than 14.

12.70 Refer to **Data Set 6** taken from a survey of persons over age 54 and make standard assumptions.

a) Find the least-squares regression line using the number of persons in the households as the independent variable (x) to explain the variation in monthly income (y).

b) Test the fit of the relation using an **F**-test with $\alpha = 0.05$.

c) Make an upper-sided **t**-test of significance on the slope β using $\alpha = 0.025$.

d) Compare and interpret the results of the tests in parts (b) and (c).

12.71 Repeat Problem 12.70 using the education level of the person as the independent variable (x).

CASE PROBLEM

12.72 (Highway Safety) The data below give the number of motor vehicle deaths for a recent year and the number of licensed drivers per 10,000 population in the District of Columbia and all states except Hawaii.

OBS	STATE	NUMDEATH	NUMDRVRS
1	AL	968	158
2	AR	640	92
3	CA	4743	952
4	CO	566	109
5	CT	325	167
6	DE	118	30
7	DC	115	35
8	FL	1545	298
9	GA	1302	203
10	IL	2207	544
11	IN	1410	254
12	IA	833	150
13	KS	669	136
14	KY	911	147
15	LA	1037	146
16	ME	196	46
17	MD	616	157
18	MA	766	255
19	MI	2120	403
20	MN	841	189
21	MS	648	85
22	MO	1289	234
23	NB	450	89
24	NH	158	37
25	NJ	1071	329
26	NY	2745	744
27	NC	1580	226

OBS	STATE	NUMDEATH	NUMDRVRS
28	OH	2096	530
29	OK	785	137
30	OR	575	108
31	PA	1889	570
32	RI	100	46
33	SC	870	122
34	TN	1059	177
35	TX	3006	515
36	UT	295	57
37	VT	131	20
38	VA	1050	208
39	WV	467	88
40	WI	1059	207
41	AK	43	11
42	AZ	588	91
43	ID	262	41
44	MT	259	38
45	NE	215	23
46	NM	387	54
47	ND	185	38
48	SD	270	40
49	WA	730	160
50	WY	148	22

a) Find the least-squares regression between the number of deaths (y) and the number of drivers (x).
b) Find the two measures of goodness of fit, s_e and r^2.
c) Assuming normality, do a test of significance on the population correlation coefficient at a level of 0.01.

GLOSSARY

Population regression line [$\mu_{y \cdot x} = \alpha + \beta x$]: For the population, the intercept (α) plus the slope (β) times x equals the mean of the y-values for a given x-value.

Population regression model [$y_i = \alpha + \beta x_i + \epsilon_i$]: An error term ($\epsilon_i$) is added to the regression line to describe the actual value of the ith observation (y_i).

Sample regression line [$\hat{y} = a + bx$]: Estimate of population regression line.

Sample regression model [$y_i = a + bx_i + e_i$]: Estimate of population regression model.

Least-squares estimation method: Process of finding regression coefficients a and b by minimizing $\text{SSE} = \sum_{i=1}^{n} e_i^2 =$ unexplained variation, the sum of squared deviations between the actual and the estimated values of y_i.

Sample Covariance (s_{xy}): Unbiased estimate of $C[\boldsymbol{x}, \boldsymbol{y}]$:

$$s_{xy} = \frac{1}{n-1} \sum_{i=1}^{n} (x_i - \bar{x})(y_i - \bar{y}).$$

Population covariance: $C[\boldsymbol{x}, \boldsymbol{y}] = E[(\boldsymbol{x} - \mu_x)(\boldsymbol{y} - \mu_y)]$; describes how $\boldsymbol{x}$ and $\boldsymbol{y}$ covary in the population.

Variation, covariation:

$$\text{Variation of } x = \text{SSx} = \sum_{i=1}^{n} x_i^2 - \frac{1}{n}\left(\sum_{i=1}^{n} x_i\right)^2;$$

$$\text{Variation of } y = \text{SSy} = \sum_{i=1}^{n} y_i^2 - \frac{1}{n}\left(\sum_{i=1}^{n} y_i\right)^2;$$

$$\text{Covariation of } x \text{ and } y = \text{SCxy} = \sum_{i=1}^{n} x_i y_i - \frac{1}{n}\left(\sum_{i=1}^{n} x_i\right)\left(\sum_{i=1}^{n} y_i\right).$$

These are the sample measures of variance and covariance multiplied by $(n-1)$.

b (least-squares estimate of population slope β):

$$b = \frac{\text{SCxy}}{\text{SSx}}.$$

a (least-squares estimate of population intercept α):

$$a = \bar{y} - b\bar{x}.$$

Five assumptions: The population error terms (ϵ_i) are assumed (1) to be independent of x, (2) to be normally distributed, (3) to have a mean of zero, (4) to have a finite variance (σ_ϵ^2) that is constant, and (5) to be independent of one another.

SST, SSE, SSR: $\text{SST} = $ sum of squares total $= \text{SSy} = \sum_{i=1}^{n} (y_i - \bar{y})^2;$

$$\text{SSE} = \text{sum of squares error} = \sum_{i=1}^{n} e_i^2 = \sum_{i=1}^{n} (y_i - \hat{y}_i)^2;$$

$$\text{SSR} = \text{sum of squares explained by the regression} = \sum_{i=1}^{n} (\hat{y}_i - \bar{y})^2;$$

$$\text{SST} = \text{SSR} + \text{SSE}.$$

Standard error of the estimate (s_e): Standard deviation of sample points about the sample regression line; s_e^2 represents an unbiased estimate of σ_e^2.

Coefficient of determination: r^2 = SSR/SST = explained amount of variation in y relative to the total to be explained; $0 \le r^2 \le 1$.

Population correlation coefficient: $\rho = C[x, y]/\sigma_x\sigma_y$; a measure of the population linear association between x and y; $-1 \le \rho \le 1$.

Sample correlation coefficient: Best estimate of ρ; $r = \dfrac{S_{xy}}{S_x S_y}$ or

$$r = \frac{SCxy}{\sqrt{(SSx)(SSy)}}.$$

Hypothesis of no linear regression: $H_0{:}\beta = 0$.

Standard error of b (s_b): Indicates the uncertainty of the least-squares estimate of β:

$$s_b = s_e \sqrt{\frac{1}{SSx}} = s_e \sqrt{\frac{1}{\sum\limits_{i=1}^{n} x_i^2 - \frac{1}{n}\left(\sum\limits_{i=1}^{n} x_i\right)^2}}.$$

t-statistics for inference on the regression coefficients: $t = (b - \beta)/s_b$ for the slope, and $t = (a - \alpha)/s_a$ for the intercept.

Confidence limits for the regression coefficients: $b \pm t_{(\alpha/2, n-2)}\, s_b$ for the slope, and $a \pm t_{(\alpha/2, n-2)}\, s_a$ for the intercept.

t-test for $H_0{:}\rho = 0$: $t = r\sqrt{n-2}/\sqrt{1 - r^2}$ with $n - 2$ d.f.

Forecast value ($\hat{y}_g$): Obtained by substituting a given value x_g into the estimating equation, $\hat{y}_g = a + bx_g$.

Standard error of the forecast (s_f): A measure of the uncertainty of the least squares forecast $\hat{y}_g$:

$$s_f = s_e \sqrt{1 + \frac{1}{n} + \frac{(x_g - \bar{x})^2}{SSx}}.$$

Forecast interval for y_g: $\hat{y}_g - t_{(\alpha/2, n-2)}\, s_g \le y_g \le \hat{y}_g + t_{(\alpha/2, n-2)}\, s_f$.

Standard error of the mean predicted value ($\mu_{y \cdot x_g}$): A measure of uncertainty for the average forecast given a value x_g:

$$s_{\bar{y} \cdot x} = s_e \sqrt{\frac{1}{n} + \frac{(x_g - \bar{x})^2}{SSx}}.$$

Forecast interval for $\mu_{y \cdot x_g}$:

$$\hat{y}_g - t_{(\alpha/2, n-2)}\, s_{\bar{y} \cdot x} \le \mu_{y \cdot x_g} \le \hat{y}_g + t_{(\alpha/2, n-2)}\, s_{\bar{y} \cdot x}.$$

Mean square: A sum of squares divided by its degrees of freedom. For a simple regression, mean square error MSE = SSE/(n − 2), and mean square regression MSR = SSR/1.

F-statistic for the fit of the linear model: F = MSR/MSE.

Multiple Regression and Correlation Analysis

THIRTEEN

13.1 INTRODUCTION TO MULTIPLE REGRESSION

In Chapter 12 the method of least-squares estimation was found to yield estimates that have the desirable properties of unbiasedness, efficiency, and consistency, given a set of five standard assumptions. Measures of the goodness of fit and methods of statistical inference were discussed for the *simple* linear regression model involving one dependent variable *y* and *one* independent variable *x*. In this chapter we extend the analysis to *multiple* linear regression models involving *two or more* independent or explanatory variables. In the next chapter we will give a more thorough discussion of the underlying assumptions for regression analysis, including some tests for the validity of the assumptions.

The Extended Population Model

In most applications, many factors may be related to the dependent variable, any of which could help explain its variation. Suppose we assume that there are m independent variables and that the population model relating these variables to the dependent variable *y* is given by the following linear model.

Population regression model:

$$y_i = \alpha + \beta_1 x_{i1} + \beta_2 x_{i2} + \beta_3 x_{i3} + \cdots + \beta_m x_{im} + \epsilon_i.$$

As was the case for simple linear regression, the subscript i on each variable represents one of the values in the population. Also, α equals the *y*-intercept, β_1 equals the slope of the relationship between y and x_{i1}, β_2 equals the slope between *y* and x_{i2}, and so forth. The fact that the relationship is linear means that the relationship between *y* and *each one* of the independent variables can be described by a straight line. The conditional mean of the dependent variable is given by the following **population multiple regression equation.**

Population multiple linear regression equation:

$$\mu_{y \cdot x_1, x_2 \ldots x_m} = \alpha + \beta_1 x_1 + \beta_2 x_2 + \ldots + \beta_m x_m. \qquad \textbf{(13.1)}$$

The coefficients $\beta_1, \beta_2, \ldots, \beta_m$ are called **partial regression coefficients,** since they indicate the (partial) influence of each independent variable on **y**, when the influence of all the remaining independent variables is *held constant.*

Example 13.1. Applicants for college admission, for graduate school or law school admission, for jobs, for loans, and so on, always have to fill out some form or present some documented evidence about their qualifications. The appropriate official (school administrator, personnel manager, loan officer, etc.) must somehow weigh the different qualifications and make a judgment about the suitability of the applicant. This involves an estimate of the probability of success, perhaps measured by some subsequent accomplishment.

Suppose the admissions board for a graduate school tries to predict y = grade point average (GPA) expected in graduate school for new enrollees given their individual characteristics. It is common to use several explanatory variables to help make such a prediction. Among these are the UnderGraduate Grades (UGG), the quality of the undergraduate school, the applicant's age, and the scores on standardized Graduate Record Examinations (GRE). Given sufficient historical information on enrollees' characteristics and their eventual graduate-school grade record, a mathematical relation can be determined among these variables. The relation, allowing for uncertainty, is a regression equation that can be used to make predictions for other enrollees.

Assume there are only two explanatory variables in the equation,

$$\mu_{y \cdot x_1, x_2} = \alpha + \beta_1 x_1 + \beta_2 x_2$$

with

$$y = \text{graduate grade point average (GPA)},$$
$$x_1 = \text{graduate record examination scores (GRE)},$$
$$x_2 = \text{undergraduate grade average (UGG)}.$$

Suppose we know that the *population* equation is

$$\mu_{y \cdot x_1, x_2} = -1.75 + 0.005x_1 + 0.70x_2.$$

The value $\beta_1 = 0.005$ in this case indicates that, after eliminating or taking into account the influence on GPA of x_2 (UGG), a one-unit increase in x_1 (GRE) will increase the mean value of y (GPA) by 0.005 units. Similarly, since $\beta_2 = 0.70$, a one-unit increase in x_2 (UGG) will increase the mean GPA by 0.70 units (assuming that the influence of GRE is being held constant). Figure 13.1 is a graph of the plane represented by this multiple regression equation.

Note in Fig. 13.1 that when $x_1 = 0$ and $x_2 = 0$, the regression plane intersects the y-axis at $\alpha = -1.75$. When $x_1 = 800$ and $x_2 = 0$, the value of $\mu_{y \cdot x_1, x_2}$ is 2.25. Similarly, when $x_1 = 800$ and $x_2 = 4.0$, the regression plane yields $\mu_{y \cdot x_1, x_2} = -1.75 + 0.005(800) + 0.70(4.0) = 5.05$.

These extreme points are at the boundaries of the positive coordinates for the multiple regression plane in three-dimensional space. As we saw before for the simple regression model, care must be taken in extending the regression results toward the upper or lower limits of the explanatory

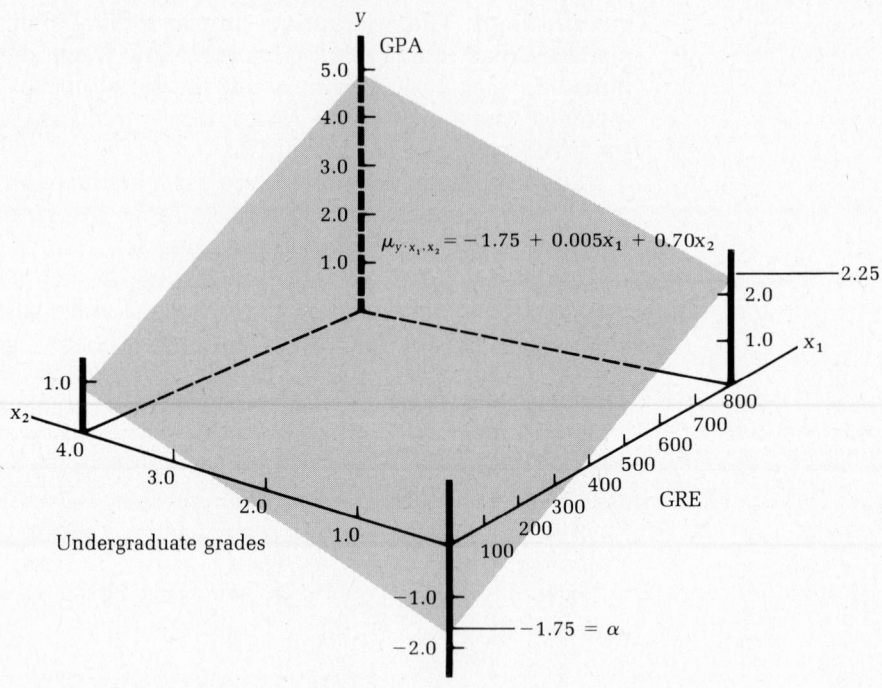

FIGURE 13.1 **The population regression plane $\mu_{y \cdot x_1, x_2} = -1.75 + 0.005x_1 + 0.70x_2$.**

variables. The regression model is the expected or *average* relation and may not be meaningful at the extremes. Clearly, no one enrolled in graduate school could obtain a GPA of -1.75 (which occurs when $x_1 = x_2 = 0$). Making predictions for these low levels of x_1 and x_2 is inappropriate, since the population of graduate school enrollees does not include anyone who has a GRE score of zero and an undergraduate grade point average of zero. The model cannot be linearly extrapolated to the extremes.

The Extended Sample Model

The process of using sample information to estimate the parameters of a multiple linear regression equation involves the same techniques used in the simple linear regression case. Suppose that we have a sample consisting of n observations for each of the variables. The problem is to find the sample regression equation that provides the "best fit" to these data and to use the coefficients of that equation as estimates of the parameters of the population regression equation. For multiple regression the sample equation is

---

Sample multiple regression equation:

$$\hat{y} = a + b_1 x_{i1} + b_2 x_{i2} + \cdots + b_m x_{im}.$$ **(13.2)**

The value of $\hat{y}$ is the estimate of $\mu_{y \cdot x_1, x_2, \ldots, x_m}$; a is the estimate of the intercept α; and b_1, b_2, ..., b_m are the estimates of the partial regression coefficients β_1, β_2, ..., β_m. The multiple regression equation reduces to the simple regression line when $m = 1$ (only one explanatory variable).

13.2 MULTIPLE LEAST-SQUARES ESTIMATION

The least-squares estimates for multiple regression are again based on the principle of minimizing the squared error (i.e., the sum of the squares of the residuals). As before, each residual (e_i) is the difference $e_i = y_i - \hat{y}_i$, where y_i is the observed value and $\hat{y}_i = a + b_1 x_{i1} + b_2 x_{i2} + \cdots + b_m x_{im}$ is the predicted value. For least-squares estimates we want to find the values of a, b_1, b_2, ..., b_m (given observations on y and on the x_j's) that minimize the function

$$G = \sum_{i=1}^{n} e_i^2 = \sum_{i=1}^{n} (y_i - a - b_1 x_{i1} - b_2 x_{i2} - \cdots - b_m x_{im})^2.$$

The procedure for minimizing this function is the same as in the simple linear regression (shown in a footnote in Section 12.3). In this case the result is a set of ($m + 1$) *normal equations* that, when solved simultaneously, yield the ($m + 1$) estimates a, b_1, ..., b_m (see Problem 13.18 for an example when $m = 2$). Although solving for these estimates is not a particularly difficult task, the process usually requires tiresome arithmetic that is prone to computational errors. For this reason, computer programs based on the techniques of matrix algebra are generally employed to calculate the sums, sums of squares, and sums of cross-products of the sample observations and to solve such systems of normal equations. Students who wish to study more advanced methods and applications of multiple regression or correlation analysis in business and economics are well advised to include a course in matrix algebra in their program of study and to become familiar with some standard computer program for regression analysis (such as SPSS or SAS). In this chapter we will emphasize the understanding and interpretation of multiple regression rather than its computational aspects.*

---

* For computational rules and examples see Chapters 9 and 11 of *Introductory Econometrics* by James L. Murphy (Homewood, Ill.: Richard D. Irwin, 1973) or some equivalent-level book.

Example 13.2. We extend the investment example introduced in Section 12.10 by including a second independent variable in our analysis of the dependent variable (investment). Recall that our first independent variable, which we now label x_1, was the *price index* of 500 common stocks. Our second variable, which is denoted by x_2, is the *retained earnings of firms*. Retained earnings are the portion of profits after taxes that is not distributed to owners (stockholders), but is kept within the firm as working capital. Since these retained earnings are often the source of funds used to purchase new land, buildings, and equipment, we presume that a positive relationship exists between x_2 and y. Both current, past, and expected levels of x_2 may influence investment levels. In particular, we will attempt to relate the value of retained earnings (in billions of dollars measured at an annual rate) in one quarter with investment in the following quarter. The 20 observations of x_2 for the example are shown in Table 13.1, along with the corresponding values for y and x_1 that were given in Table 12.12.

Since there are two variables in our model, the population equation to be estimated is

$$\mu_{y \cdot x_1, x_2} = \alpha + \beta_1 x_1 + \beta_2 x_2.$$

If we solve the normal equations using these 20 observations, the following equation is the least-squares regression line:

$$\hat{y} = 1.677 + 0.07856 x_1 + 1.7984 x_2. \tag{13.3}$$

The unexplained variation is now

$$SSE = \sum_{i=1}^{20} e_i^2 = \sum_{i=1}^{20} (y_i - \hat{y}_i)^2 = 1263.77.$$

These and other results (to be used later) are given in Fig. 13.2.

Note how these results compare with those of the analysis involving only x_1 and y, where the regression line was

$$\hat{y} = 3.855 + 0.12347 x_1$$

and the unexplained variation was

$$\sum_{i=1}^{20} e_i^2 = SSE = 1901.3.$$

As suggested by this example, the introduction of a new variable into the sample regression model usually has several effects:

1. The coefficients of previously included variables change.
2. More of the variation of y is explained (SSE gets smaller).

TABLE 13.1 **Data for multiple regression model for investment**

Observation	y_i (Investment)	x_{i1} (Stock Price Index)	x_{i2} (Retained Earnings)
1	62.3	398.4	16.2
2	71.3	452.6	17.4
3	70.3	509.8	14.8
4	68.5	485.4	14.6
5	57.3	445.7	8.2
6	68.8	539.8	14.9
7	72.2	662.8	15.1
8	76.0	620.0	14.3
9	64.3	632.2	10.9
10	77.9	703.0	16.0
11	84.3	581.8	16.2
12	85.1	707.1	16.4
13	90.8	776.6	20.4
14	97.9	875.3	20.5
15	108.7	873.4	26.1
16	122.4	943.7	29.0
17	114.0	830.6	24.6
18	123.0	907.5	27.8
19	126.2	905.3	23.3
20	137.0	927.4	21.6

from Table 12.12

3. The values of *t*- (or *F*-)distributed statistics change.*

Throughout this chapter we explore in depth the causes and the meaning of these changes.

We note that the estimate for the coefficient of x_1 (stock index) changes from 0.12347 to 0.07856 when the variable x_2 (retained earnings) is included in the estimating equation for *y* (investment). That is, a ten-point change in the stock index last quarter is now associated with an increase in investment (annually) of only about $0.79 billion rather than $1.23 billion. The slope between *y* and x_1 has decreased by 36% of its

---

* Change (1) will occur unless the correlation coefficient $r_{x_i x_i} = 0$, where x_i is the included variable and x_j is the new variable. Change (2) occurs unless $r_{x_i x_j} = 1.0$ or -1.0. Change (3) occurs with any change in the model specification or the set of observations.

a) SPSS output

```
DEPENDENT VARIABLE..    Y           INVESTMENT

MULTIPLE R            0.94338
R SQUARE             0.88997
ADJUSTED R SQUARE    0.87703
STANDARD ERROR       8.62203


----------------- VARIABLES IN THE EQUATION ------------------

VARIABLE             B                    STD ERROR B        F

X1          0.7855818D-01                    0.01880      17.461
X2            1.798403                        0.61413       8.575
(CONSTANT)    1.677116


ANALYSIS OF VARIANCE    DF     SUM OF SQUARES     MEAN SQUARE
REGRESSION              2.      10221.91713       5110.95857
RESIDUAL               17.       1263.77127         74.33949

                                                       F
                                                   68.75160
```

b) SAS output

```
MODEL:   MODEL01        SSE      1263.77    F RATIO      68.75
                        DFE          17     PROB>F      0.0001
DEP VAR: Y              MSE    74.339400    R-SQUARE    0.8900
         INVESTMENT

DURBIN-WATSON D STATISTIC   =   0.7836


               PARAMETER     STANDARD
VARIABLE    DF  ESTIMATE       ERROR     T RATIO    PROB>|T|

INTERCEPT    1   1.677130     7.770990    0.2158     0.8317
X1           1   0.078558     0.018800    4.1786     0.0006
X2           1   1.798403     0.614129    2.9284     0.0094
```

FIGURE 13.2 **Computer printout for the investment model.**

previous value. Obviously, the new estimate b_1 must have a different meaning than the estimate b in the simple model. The estimate $b_1 = 0.07856$ is obtained by considering the influence of x_2 on y and its relationship with x_1, as well as the simple influence of x_1 on y.

The technique of multiple regression is similar to a laboratory-controlled experiment in which one independent variable at a time is varied to examine its influence on the dependent variable, while holding all other controlled factors constant. In this case the variables included in the model are the only ones being controlled; other factors are subsumed into the error term.

> The partial regression coefficient measures the influence of one variable on **y** while holding the influence of the other variables constant.*

Thus, b_1 measures the partial effect of changes in last quarter's stock prices on investment as if we had controlled the real world in such a way that the amount of *retained earnings* in the previous quarter was constant. The value of b_1 depends on the selection of the other factors included in the model. If another factor, such as interest rate, were included in addition to (or instead of) retained earnings, then the value of b_1 would change because the controlled environment in which the influence of x_1 is being measured would be different. Only if all the additional explanatory variables includable in the model are independent of x_1 (i.e., have zero covariance with x_1) would the estimate of b_1 remain unchanged when these variables are included.

Similarly, the value of $b_2 = 1.7984$ represents the partial influence of retained earnings on current investment, where the influence of the index of *stock prices* is held constant. Using a familiar term in economics — *ceteris paribus* — (holding other factors constant), the effect of a one-billion-dollar increase in retained earnings is an increase of about $1.8 billion in investment.

Example 13.3. In Chapter 12 several study questions dealt with a simple regression model relating median income (here denoted as x_1) to the average home price (y) in a city. Other factors affecting the price of housing might be included in an extended model. Table 13.2 gives data for an extended model where RENT (x_2) is the average biweekly rental rate of new units and VACANT (x_3) is the percentage of housing units that are vacant. Figure 13.3(a) gives the computer results for the *simple* regression model ($m = 1$), and Fig. 13.3(b) gives the output for the *multiple* regression model ($m = 3$).

Several comparisons between the results of the simple and multiple regression models highlight the three effects listed previously. First, the

* Students with a knowledge of calculus can interpret a simple regression coefficient of x as the derivative dy/dx, whereas the partial regression coefficient of x_1 is the partial derivative, $\partial y/\partial x_1$, obtained by treating every other x_j ($j \neq 1$) as if it were a constant.

coefficient (on the explanatory variable INCOME) changes when other variables are included in the model. In the simple model a change in median income of one dollar leads to a change in housing price of \$4.54 ($b = 4.540$). In other words, a city with a median income \$1000 higher is expected to have housing prices \$4540 higher. Income is the only explanatory variable in the model and is serving as a proxy for many hidden relationships.

When the factors of rent and vacancy rates are included in the multiple regression, the estimated changes are very different. Higher rents indicate a strong housing market and allow correspondingly higher prices for housing units ($b_2 = 164.645 > 0$). Higher vacancy rates indicate a less competitive housing market in which units are more easily found. This puts pressure on housing prices to decline ($b_3 = -293.970 < 0$). The coefficient on INCOME has decreased to a negative value of $b_1 = -0.675$. We see that when more direct factors are included to explain the competitiveness in the housing market, the more indirect factor of income becomes less important. If another factor, such as the average size of the housing unit (square-foot measure) were included, it would probably have an even more direct effect on the housing price. All the coefficients of previously included variables would again change. Thus, it is important for the decision-maker to correctly specify all the relevant factors in a regression model under analysis.

A second change between the results of the simple and multiple regressions is in the amounts of variation unexplained. Referring to Fig. 13.3(a), the *unexplained variation* (SSE) for the simple model is 683.676 (million dollars squared). In the multiple model with two additional

TABLE 13.2 **Data for the housing price regression model**

OBS	INCOME	PRICE	RENT	VACANT	NAME
1	12100	40100	192	40	Albany
2	14300	53200	192	28	Anaheim
3	12200	59100	206	18	Boston
4	11600	31500	115	63	Dallas
5	13500	46500	170	26	Detroit
6	11100	38400	135	52	Fort Worth
7	11000	49300	180	34	Los Angeles
8	10200	37900	106	40	Memphis
9	13000	46800	157	18	Minneapolis
10	13300	65900	241	23	Newark

a) simple regression model [repeat of Fig. 12.7 (b)]

```
MODEL:     MODEL01        SSE    683675825        F RATIO      3.61
                          DFE            8        PROB>F       0.0940
DEP VAR: PRICE            MSE     85459478        R-SQUARE     0.3109
          HOUSING PRICE

DURBIN-WATSON D STATISTIC  =  2.0969


                         PARAMETER     STANDARD
VARIABLE        DF        ESTIMATE       ERROR        T RATIO      PROB>|T|

INTERCEPT       1        -8659.15      29375.65      -0.2948       0.7757
INCOME          1         4.540405      2.390010      1.8997       0.0940
```

b) multiple regression model

```
MODEL:     MODEL02        SSE    125308751        F RATIO     13.83
                          DFE            6        PROB>F       0.0042
DEP VAR: PRICE            MSE     20884792        R-SQUARE     0.8737
          HOUSING PRICE

DURBIN-WATSON D STATISTIC  =  1.7725


                         PARAMETER     STANDARD
VARIABLE        DF        ESTIMATE       ERROR        T RATIO      PROB>|T|

INTERCEPT       1        37290.06      20800.91       1.7927       0.1232
INCOME          1        -0.675160      1.553683     -0.4346       0.6791
RENT            1       164.645394     52.806723      3.1179       0.0206
VACANT          1      -293.970271    144.214994     -2.0384       0.0876
```

FIGURE 13.3 **Computer output for the housing price models using SAS.**

variables helping to explain the variation in housing price, the unexplained variation is reduced to SSE = 125.309 (million dollars squared).

Looking at the relative measure of goodness of fit, $R^2 = SSR/SST$, we note its increase from 0.31 in the simple model to 0.87 in the multiple model. Income alone explained 31% of the variation in housing price, whereas income, rent, and vacancy rate together explained 87% of the variation in housing price.

Finally, the values of *F*-statistics for the overall fit of the model and of *t*-statistics for the significance of individual coefficients of each explanatory variable are also shown in Fig. 13.3. A comparison quickly reveals that the F-values have changed and the t-value for the variable INCOME has changed. In the following sections of this chapter, more explanation is given of the meaning and the use of these test statistics and goodness-of-fit measures.

13.3 COMMON ASSUMPTIONS AND GOODNESS-OF-FIT MEASURES

As in the case of simple regression, some goodness-of-fit measures are needed to judge how well the multiple regression equation fits the observed data. Again, an absolute measure and a relative measure are common; they have an interpretation completely analogous to those discussed in Section 12.5. Before presenting these measures, we must again present the assumptions (about the errors ϵ_i) that are necessary for interpreting these measures.

Assumptions for the Multiple Regression Model

Again we must emphasize that the least-squares procedure does not require *any* assumptions about the population, since this procedure is merely a curve-fitting technique. However, in order to be able to test the goodness of fit of a sample regression equation, it is once more necessary to make certain assumptions about the error term (ϵ) in the population regression model. The first five of these assumptions are parallel to those specified in Section 12.4 for the simple regression model. We repeat them below for the multiple regression case:

Assumption 1. *The error term* ϵ *is independent of each of the m independent variables* $x_1, x_2, \ldots, x_m$.

Assumption 2. *The errors* ϵ_1 *for all possible sets of given values,* $x_1, x_2, \ldots, x_m$, *are normally distributed.*

Assumption 3. *The expected value of the errors is zero for all possible sets of given values,* $x_1, x_2, \ldots, x_m$. *That is,* $E[\epsilon_i] = 0$ *for* $i = 1, 2, \ldots, n$.

Assumption 4. *The variance of the errors is finite and is the same for all possible sets of given values,* $x_1, x_2, \ldots x_m$. *That is,* $V[\epsilon_i] = \sigma_\epsilon^2$ *is a constant for* $i = 1, 2, \ldots, n$.

Assumption 5. *Any two errors* ϵ_i *and* ϵ_t *are independent; i.e., their covariance is zero,* $C[\epsilon_i, \epsilon_t] = 0$ *for* $i \neq t$.

In addition to these five assumptions, two additional conditions are necessary to obtain least-squares estimates in the multiple regression equation.

Condition 1. *None of the independent variables is an exact linear combination of the other independent variables.* This means that no one variable x_j is an exact multiple of any other independent variable. Further, if $m \geq 2$, this assumption means that no one variable x_j can be written as

$$x_j = a_1x_1 + a_2x_2 + \cdots + a_{j-1}x_{j-1} + a_{j+1}x_{j+1} + \cdots + a_mx_m,$$

where the a's are constants. This assumption is a weak condition, since it requires only that the variables not be *perfectly* related to each other in a linear function. In practice, the independent variables often are partially linearly related to each other, or related to each other in some nonlinear way. Although least-squares estimates can be calculated in these situations, problems do arise in their interpretation.

Condition 2. *The number of observations (n) must exceed the number (m + 1) of coefficients being estimated; that is, $n > m + 1$.* Since there are $m + 1$ coefficients to be estimated in the multiple regression equation, the number of degrees of freedom is $n - (m + 1)$. This condition merely specifies that there be at least one degree of freedom. In practice, the sample size must be quite a bit larger than $m + 1$ in order to obtain meaningful information about the underlying relation.

Standard Error of Estimate

The **standard error of the estimate** for the multiple regression equation is defined just as it is for simple regression by

$$s_e = \sqrt{\frac{\text{unexplained variation}}{\text{degrees of freedom}}}.$$

However, since $(m + 1)$ parameters must be estimated before a residual from the multiple regression equation can be calculated, the degrees of freedom in this statistic are $n - (m + 1)$. Thus, we have

Standard error of estimate in multiple regression:

$$s_e = \sqrt{\frac{\text{SSE}}{n - m - 1}} = \sqrt{\frac{1}{n - m - 1}\sum_{i=1}^{n} e_i^2}. \qquad \textbf{(13.4)}$$

As before, we know that about 68% of all sample points should lie within one standard error of the estimated values of y_i; about 95% should lie within two standard errors.

Example 13.4. For our multiple regression example for investment the value of $\sum e_i^2 = 1263.77$, $m = 2$ (two independent variables), and $n = 20$ (see Fig. 13.2). Thus,

$$s_e = \sqrt{\frac{1263.77}{20 - 2 - 1}} = \sqrt{\frac{1263.77}{17}} = \$8.62 \text{ billion.}$$

Comparing this value of s_e with that obtained by using the simple regression model (Fig. 12.16), where the standard error was \$10.277 billion, we observe that the value of s_e has decreased. Since the amount of variation explained in a regression model (SSR) can never be reduced by the addition of another variable, the variation unexplained (SSE) can never be increased, so s_e will usually decrease. If a weakly related independent variable is added, however, the reduction in unexplained variation could be so small that it would not compensate for the loss of one degree of freedom due to its inclusion. In this case, s_e would increase when the extra variable is included. This is a signal that the new variable should be reconsidered and possibly omitted from the equation.

Multiple Coefficient of Determination

For the multiple regression model the relative measure of goodness of fit is designated by the symbol R^2, to differentiate it from the simple coefficient of determination r^2. This **multiple coefficient of determination,** R^2, is the ratio of the variation explained by the multiple regression equation (SSR) to the total variation of y (SST). The only difference between R^2 and r^2 is that, in the multiple case, the explained variation results from m independent variables rather than from only a single independent variable. It is customary to write the multiple coefficient of determination as $R^2_{y \cdot x_1, x_2, \ldots, x_m}$, where the dependent variable is specified *before* the dot and the independent variables are listed *after* the dot.

Multiple coefficient of determination:

$$R^2_{y \cdot x_1, x_2, \ldots, x_m} = \frac{\text{Variation explained by all } x_j\text{'s (SSR)}}{\text{Total variation of } y \text{ (SST)}}. \qquad \textbf{(13.5)}$$

Example 13.5. We can calculate R^2 for the multiple regression model on investment (Example 13.2 and Fig. 13.2). With x_1 and x_2 in the analysis we found that SSE $= 1263.77$. From Fig. 12.16 we know that the total variation in y is

$$\text{SST} = \sum_{i=1}^{20} (y_i - \bar{y})^2 = 11,485.7.$$

Since the explained variation due to regression (SSR) equals the difference between the total variation and the unexplained variation, we know that

$$SSR = SST - SSE$$
$$= 11,485.70 - 1263.77$$
$$= 10,221.93.$$

Therefore,

$$R^2_{y \cdot x_1, x_2} = \frac{10,221.93}{11,485.70} = 0.8900.$$

This means that 89% of the variation in investment is explained by the linear relationship between investment, stock prices, and retained earnings. In comparing the value of $R^2 = 0.8900$ to the value $r^2 = 0.8345$ obtained from the simple model (using stock prices alone), we see that the addition of variable x_2 to the analysis explains an additional 5.55% of the variation in investment. Since the explained variation (SSR) can never be decreased by the addition of another independent variable, R^2 always will either increase or remain the same as more variables are included in the model.

The fact that x_1 explains 83.45% of the variability in y and x_2 explains only an additional 5.55% *does not imply that stock prices (x_1) are better predictors of investment than are retained earnings (x_2).* If retained earnings had been the variable considered first and then controlled during the addition of stock prices to the analysis, then retained earnings would appear to explain the greater share of total variation. By reversing the order it can be shown that x_2 alone would explain 77.7% of the variation in y and the addition of x_1 would explain an extra 11.3%, giving the same joint total explained as before, 89%.

Remember that a single variable in a model may serve as a proxy for the influence of other related variables not explicitly included. When one of these other related variables is included, the two variables share the explanatory role. Each will have its separate role, and each will still share some explanatory power of other nonincluded variables to which it is linearly related. When a third or fourth variable is included, similar results occur. Separate effects of each explanatory variable are partially distinguished, and, collectively, all included variables may still share some role as a proxy for other relevant variables that are not yet included. The analyst must interpret the statistical results accordingly. As an aid for interpretation, tests of hypothesis may be used to determine which variable is the most (or least) influential. However, the analyst is still responsible for the specification of the cause-and-effect nature of the relationships among the variables. The statistical regression results show only *association, not causal linkages.*

Adjusted Coefficient of Determination

The coefficient of determination R^2 can never decrease as another variable is added to the multiple regression model. Even if the new variable is irrelevant and has a coefficient of zero, the new R^2 would be no lower than the old R^2. If the new variable has just a small effect, SSR would be a little larger, and the new R^2 would be higher than before. This effect differs from that on the absolute measure of goodness of fit, s_e. Recall that when a new variable is largely irrelevant, the reduction in unexplained variation (SSE gets a little smaller) does not always make s_e smaller. The difference is due to the fact that s_e takes into account the degrees of freedom in the model, but R^2 does not.

In order to have corresponding goodness-of-fit measures, most analysts prefer to compute an **adjusted coefficient of determination** rather than the standard R^2. The adjusted R^2 is often denoted by the symbol R-bar-squared, $\overline{R}^2$. This is a rather poor symbol since an overbar usually denotes an average of a sample statistic or the complement of an event, neither of which is relevant in this case. We will denote the adjusted coefficient of determination by R^2_{adj}, which clearly identifies its meaning. R^2_{adj} is adjusted for the degrees of freedom in the estimating equation. This avoids the upward bias in the unadjusted R^2 when the number of explanatory variables in the model is large in relation to the sample size. The adjusted measure allows a fairer comparison between models of the same dependent variable that have a different number of explanatory variables or a different number of observations. We obtain the adjusted measure by rewriting the numerator for R^2 as

$$R^2 = \text{SSR/SST} = (1 - \text{SSE})/\text{SST}$$

and adjusting for the degrees of freedom by dividing SSE by $n - m - 1$ and dividing SST by $n - 1$. A convenient form for the answer is

Adjusted coefficient of determination:

$$R^2_{\text{adj}} = 1 - (1 - R^2)\left[\frac{n - 1}{n - m - 1}\right]. \qquad \textbf{(13.6)}$$

Without such an adjustment the coefficient of determination can be made arbitrarily close to unity simply by increasing the number of explanatory variables. Just as two observation points can be fit perfectly by a straight line (using one explanatory variable), three observation points can be fit perfectly by a plane (using two explanatory variables). Four observations could be fit perfectly by using three variables; five observations could be fit perfectly by using four variables, and so on. In general, n observations could be fit perfectly by using $m = n - 1$ explanatory variables. Each separate variable provides another dimension that can contribute to the amount of variation in y explained by the regression equation. Each addition can increase the numerator (SSR) of R^2. For the adjusted measure, however, the extra variation explained is offset by the loss of one extra degree of freedom in the denominator term $(n - m - 1)$.

For a numerical comparison, suppose two regression equations (A and B), are determined, each based on 20 observations. Let equation A have two explanatory variables and a value of $R^2 = 0.80$; let equation B have six explanatory variables and a value of $R^2 = 0.82$. The adjusted values of R^2_{adj} would be

$$1 - (1 - 0.80)\frac{19}{17} = 0.776 \quad \text{for equation A,}$$

$$1 - (1 - 0.82)\frac{19}{13} = 0.737 \quad \text{for equation B.}$$

Note that R^2_{adj} will always be smaller than the unadjusted R^2. Considering the number of variables included, equation A has the relatively better fit.

Study Question 13.1: Multiple Regression Fit for Housing Price

Using the computer output in Fig. 13.3, find the adjusted coefficient of determination for the simple and multiple regression equations. Discuss the results.

Answer. The simple model has $n = 10$, $m = 1$, and $R^2 = 0.31$. The adjusted measure is

$$R^2_{adj} = 1 - (1 - 0.31)\frac{9}{8} = 0.224.$$

For the multiple model, $n = 10$, $m = 3$, and $R^2 = 0.87$. The adjusted value is

$$R^2_{adj} = 1 - (1 - 0.87)\frac{9}{6} = 0.805.$$

The increase in explanatory power indicates that the contribution of the two extra variables, rent and vacancy rate, is worthwhile in the model. They explain more than enough extra variation to offset the loss of the two degrees of freedom.

The Coefficient of Multiple Correlation

Multiple linear correlation bears the same relationship to simple linear correlation as multiple linear regression does to simple linear regression: It represents an extension of the techniques for handling the relationship among *more than two* variables. In multiple linear correlation the objective is to estimate the *strength* of the relationship between a variable y and a group of m other variables $x_1, x_2, \ldots, x_m$. The measure usually used for this purpose is called the **multiple correlation coefficient** and is denoted by the symbol $R_{y \cdot x_1, x_2, \ldots, x_m}$. This measure can be interpreted in much the same manner as r, since a multiple linear correlation coefficient represents the simple linear correlation coefficient between the sample values of y and estimates of these values provided by the multiple regression equation. However, the value of R is never negative, but rather $0 \le R \le 1$. This is so because the sign of R does *not* indicate the slope of the regression equation, since it is not possible to indicate *all* the signs of the regression coefficients that relate y to the variables $x_1, x_2, \ldots, x_m$ by a *single* plus or minus sign. As we indicated above, the square of the multiple correlation coefficient (R^2) indicates the proportion of the total variation in y accounted for by the regression equation.

For our investment example the value of R is the square root of $R^2 = 0.89$:

$$R_{y \cdot x_1, x_2} = \sqrt{R^2_{y \cdot x_1, x_2}} = \sqrt{0.89} = 0.943.$$

Partial Correlation Coefficient

The value of R measures the degree of association between the variable y and *all* of the variables $x_1, x_2, \ldots,$ and x_m. One may, however, be more interested in the degree of association between y and *one* of the variables $x_1, x_2, \ldots,$ or x_m, *with the linear effect of all the other explanatory variables removed*. A measure of the strength of the relationship between the dependent variable and one explanatory variable, with the linear effect of the rest of the variables eliminated, is called a *partial correlation coefficient*. A partial correlation coefficient is analogous to a partial regression coefficient, in that all other factors are "held constant." Simple correlation, on the other hand, ignores the effect of all other variables, even though these variables might be quite strongly related to the dependent variable y, or to the explanatory variable x, or to one another.

Partial correlation measures the strength of the relationship between y and a single independent variable by considering the *relative* amount that the unexplained variation is reduced by including this variable in the regression equation. We might want to calculate the partial correlation between y and x_2, when the linear effect of x_1 is held constant (i.e., eliminated). This partial correlation is denoted by the symbol $r_{y,x_2 \cdot x_1}$, where the variables *before the dot* indicate those for which correlation is being measured (y and x_2) and the variable(s) *after the dot* indicate those with influence held constant (x_1). For instance, in the investment example, $r_{y,x_2 \cdot x_1}$ would be a measure of the strength of the relationship between investment (y) and retained earnings (x_2), with the influence of stock prices (x_1) held constant.

As before, the *square* of a corelation coefficient is usually easier to interpret than the coefficient itself. In the case of a partial correlation coefficient, this square is called a **partial coefficient of determination.** The partial coefficient of determination measures the *additional* proportion of the unexplained variation in y that is explained by the variable that is *not* being held constant.

Partial coefficient of determination:

$$r_{y,x_2 \cdot x_1}^2 = \frac{\left(\begin{array}{l}\text{Extra variation in } y \text{ explained} \\ \text{by the additional influence of } x_2\end{array}\right)}{\text{Variation in } y \text{ unexplained by } x_1 \text{ alone}}. \qquad \textbf{(13.7)}$$

Example 13.6. Figure 13.4 illustrates the determination of the value of $r_{y,x_2 \cdot x_1}^2$ for our investment equation. The total variation in y (investment) to be explained is

$$\sum_{i=1}^{20} (y_i - \bar{y})^2 = 11,485.7,$$

FIGURE 13.4 **The elements of variation used in a partial coefficient of determination, $r_{y,x_2 \cdot x_1}^2$ for the investment example.**

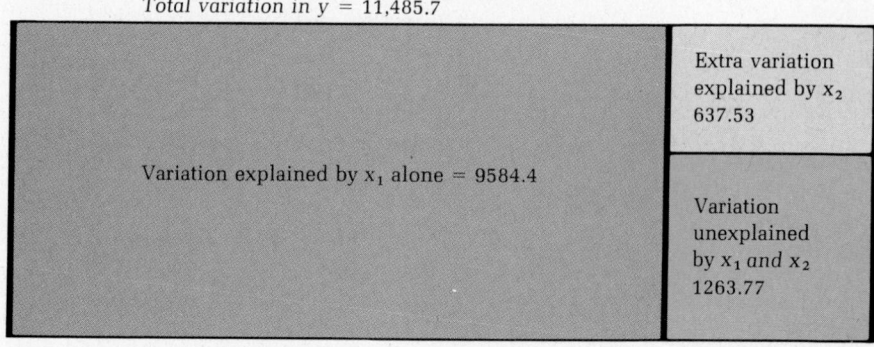

Total variation in y = 11,485.7

Variation explained by x_1 alone = 9584.4

Extra variation explained by x_2 637.53

Variation unexplained by x_1 and x_2 1263.77

Variation unexplained by x_1 alone = 1901.3

represented by the area of the entire rectangle. Based on the simple relationship between y and x_1 (stock prices), the amount of unexplained variation when x_1 is the only independent variable is SSE = 1901.3. The denominator of Formula (13.7) is thus 1901.3. Now, recall from Fig. 13.2 that the amount of unexplained variation with both x_1 and x_2 in the analysis is 1263.77. Thus, the *extra* amount of variation explained by adding x_2 to the analysis is

$$1901.3 - 1263.77 = 637.53,$$

which is the value needed for the numerator of Formula (13.7). The proportion of previously unexplained variation in investment that is explained by the addition of retained earnings x_2 is

$$r^2_{y,x_2 \cdot x_1} = \frac{637.53}{1901.3} = 0.335.$$

The square root of this value gives the partial correlation coefficient,

$$r_{y,x_2 \cdot x_1} = \sqrt{0.335} = 0.579,$$

between investment and retained earnings when stock prices are held constant.

Such partial coefficients of correlation or partial coefficients of determination can be extended to more than two explanatory variables. If a third variable is included, or a group of new variables, the partial coefficient of determination measures the *additional* proportion of the *previously unexplained* variation in y that is explained by the newly included variables. For each such case, all that is needed to find the value of the partial coefficient of determination is the amount of variation left unexplained at each step. If the variables already included in the model are designated as group A and the newly added variables are designated as group B, then

Multiple partial coefficient of determination:

$$r^2_{y,B \cdot A} = \frac{\left[\begin{array}{l} \text{(Variation unexplained by group A)} \\ - \text{(Variation unexplained by groups A and B)} \end{array} \right]}{\text{Variation unexplained by the variables in group A}}. \tag{13.8}$$

The numerator in Formula (13.8) is the extra variation explained by the variable or variables in group B.

Study Question 13.2: Partial Correlations in the Housing Price Model
In Example 13.3 the multiple regression model for explaining housing price utilized three explanatory variables: income, rent, and vacancy rates. Suppose each of these variables is added one by one into the model. After including only x_1 = income the unexplained variation from Fig. 13.3(a) is SSE = 683.676 million. After including the two variables, x_1 and x_2 = rent, the unexplained variation is 212.088 million (not previously shown). Finally, when all three variables are included, x_1, x_2, and x_3 = vacancy rate, SSE from Fig. 13.3(b) is 125.309 million. Find the following partial coefficients of determination and interpret their meaning:

a) $r^2_{y,x_2 \cdot x_1}$;
b) $r^2_{y,x_3 \cdot x_1 x_2}$;
c) $r^2_{y,x_2 x_3 \cdot x_1}$.

Answer

a) $r^2_{y,x_2 \cdot x_1} = \dfrac{(\text{SSE with only } x_1) - (\text{SSE with } x_1 \text{ and } x_2)}{\text{SSE with only } x_1}$

$= \dfrac{683.676 - 212.088}{683.676} = 0.690.$

Rent explains 69% of the residual variation in housing price that was not explained by income.

b) $r^2_{y,x_3 \cdot x_1 x_2} = \dfrac{(\text{SSE with } x_1 \text{ and } x_2) - (\text{SSE with all three})}{\text{SSE with } x_1 \text{ and } x_2}$

$= \dfrac{212.088 - 125.309}{212.088} = 0.409.$

The vacancy rate explains 40.9% of the residual variation in housing price that was not explained by income and rent.

c) $r^2_{y,x_2 x_3 \cdot x_1} = \dfrac{(\text{SSE with only } x_1) - (\text{SSE with all three})}{\text{SSE with only } x_1}$

$= \dfrac{683.676 - 125.309}{683.676} = 0.817.$

The addition of the two variables, rent and vacancy rate, explain 81.7% of the residual variation in housing price that was not explained by income.

Define. *Population and sample multiple regression models, partial regression coefficient b_j, multiple coefficient of correlation (R), multiple coefficient of determination (R^2), adjusted R^2, partial coefficients of determination.*

PROBLEMS

13.1 Discuss the usefulness and value of the extension of regression analysis to include more than one explanatory factor.

13.2 Explain the difference in meaning between the simple regression coefficient in a simple regression analysis and a partial regression coefficient in a multiple regression analysis.

13.3 Figure 13.5 is a computer printout using the variable measures in **Data Set 4.**
   a) Use these results to compare the multiple regression to the simple regression of Problem 12.68.
   b) Interpret the meaning of the measures of goodness of fit for the multiple regression.

FIGURE 13.5 **Output of multiple regression for net income of doctors.**

```
DEPENDENT VARIABLE..      INC       ANNUAL NET INCOME $000

----------------- VARIABLES IN THE EQUATION -------------------

VARIABLE            B                    STD ERROR B        F

                                           0.47649        30.945
HRS            2.650621                    0.20689        46.487
FEE            1.410629                    0.10610         5.500
EXPS           0.2488212
(CONSTANT)    -107.9707

                  MULTIPLE R          0.89897
                  R SQUARE            0.80815
                  ADJUSTED R SQUARE   0.79216
                  STANDARD ERROR      8.08833

ANALYSIS OF VARIANCE    DF      SUM OF SQUARES     MEAN SQUARE
REGRESSION               3.       9920.91564       3306.97188
RESIDUAL                36.       2355.15660         65.42102

                                                        F
                                                     50.54907
```

c) Find and interpret the partial coefficient of determination, $r^2_{y,x_2,x_3 \cdot x_1}$, where x_1 = HRS, x_2 = FEE, and x_3 = EXPS.

13.4 In a multiple regression analysis of changes in annual average U.S. interest rates (y) on three explanatory variables $(x_1, x_2,$ and $x_3)$, the following results are found:

$$\sum_{i=1}^{n} (y_i - \bar{y})^2 = 600, \qquad \sum_{i=1}^{n} e_i^2 = 150,$$

and the variation explained by x_1 and x_2 is 350.
a) Find the multiple coefficient of determination, and explain its meaning.
b) Find $r^2_{y,x_3 \cdot x_1 x_2}$, and interpret its meaning.

13.5 Suppose the variation in y is 500 units and the model

$$\hat{y} = a + b_1 x_1 + b_2 x_2$$

leaves 240 units unexplained (based on 15 observations). Extending the model to include variable x_3 explains 80 more units of variation in y. Find $R^2_{y \cdot x_1 x_2 x_3}$ and $r^2_{y,x_3 \cdot x_1 x_2}$.

13.6 Suppose that in a multiple regression of y (profits) on three types of expenses, $x_1, x_2,$ and x_3, we obtain SST = 1000 and SSE = 200; the variation explained by only x_2 and x_3 is 400. Find $R^2_{y \cdot x_1 x_2 x_3}$ and $r^2_{y,x_1 \cdot x_2 x_3}$.

13.7 Discuss whether each of the following statements is true or false.
a) If $s_e = s_y$, then $b = 0$.
b) If $R_{y \cdot x_1 x_2 x_3} = 1$, then $r_{y,x_1 \cdot x_2 x_3} = 0$.
c) If $R_{y \cdot x_1 x_2 x_3} = R_{y \cdot x_1 x_2}$, then $r_{y,x_3 \cdot x_1 x_2} = 0$.
d) $R^2_{y \cdot x_1 x_2 x_3} \geq R^2_{y \cdot x_1 x_2}$.
e) $r^2_{y,x_1} + r^2_{y,x_2} = R^2_{y \cdot x_1 x_2}$.

13.8 In a multiple regression of y (sales) on three characteristics of retail outlets, $x, z,$ and w, the total variation is 200, the residual variation is 20, and the variation explained by only variables z and w is 120 units.
a) Find $R^2_{y \cdot x, z, w}$.
b) Find $r^2_{y,x \cdot zw}$.

13.9 Given a multiple regression model, $\hat{y} = a + b_1 x_1 + b_2 x_2 + b_3 x_3$ based on 24 observations on each variable, suppose that the total variation, SST, equals 300, the unexplained variation is 60, and the amount of variation explained by variables x_1 and x_2 together is 160.
a) Calculate the value of the multiple coefficient of determination and interpret its meaning.
b) Prepare a diagram similar to Fig. 13.4 to explain the meaning and value of $r^2_{y,x_3 \cdot x_1 x_2}$.

13.4   ANALYSIS-OF-VARIANCE TESTS*

A variety of test procedures involving the multiple correlation coefficient and the parameters of the multiple regression model have been developed. Not all will be discussed here, since the complexity of many of them is better handled in a more advanced text.† The primary questions of interest in a multiple linear relationship usually concern the goodness of fit and the significance of the partial regression parameters.

Analysis-of-Variance Test

The test of the significance of the entire multiple linear regression is equivalent to the test of the significance of the simple linear relationship. Hence, the same type of **ANOVA (analysis-of-variance) table** and an **F**-distributed statistic can be utilized (see Table 12.10 and Formula (12.32)). In simple linear regression we tested the null hypothesis $H_o: \beta = 0$ (the hypothesis of no linear association between y and x). In multiple linear regression we test the null hypothesis of no linear association between y and *all* the explanatory variables $x_j, j = 1, 2, \ldots, m$. We use the following hypotheses:

H_o: the x_j are *not* linearly related to y;

H_a: the x_j as a group *are* linearly related to y.

If the linear regression equation of Formula (13.2) fits the data well, the amount of variation in y that is explained (SSR) should be large in relation to the amount of variation that is left unexplained (SSE). If each of these amounts of variation is divided by its degrees of freedom, then a mean square is obtained. The ratio of the mean square explained (MSR) to the mean square unexplained (MSE) has an **F**-distribution. In multiple regression, $(m + 1)$ parameters are estimated on the basis of n observations, so the unexplained variation will have $n - (m + 1)$ degrees of freedom. The degrees of freedom for the explained variation equal the number of independent variables (m) included in the model to do the "explaining." Total variation always has $(n - 1)$ degrees of freedom. Table 13.3 is the analysis-of-variance table for multiple linear regression, analogous to Table 12.10 for simple regression analysis.

The appropriate statistic to test the significance of the entire multiple regression equation follows an **F**-distribution with m and $(n - m - 1)$ degrees of freedom:

---

* It is assumed that the reader of this section has studied Section 12.9 concerning the **F**-distributed statistic for ANOVA in regression analysis.

† See James L. Murphy, *Introductory Econometrics* (Homewood, Ill.: Richard D. Irwin, 1973), Chapter 11.

TABLE 13.3 **Analysis-of-variance (ANOVA) table for multiple regression**

Source of the Variation	Sum of Squares	Degrees of Freedom	Mean Square
Multiple regression	SSR	m	SSR/m = MSR
Residual	SSE	$n - m - 1$	SSE/$(n - m - 1)$ = MSE
Total	SST	$n - 1$	

F-statistic for fit of the multiple regression model:

$$F_{(m, n-m-1)} = \frac{\text{SSR}/m}{\text{SSE}/(n - m - 1)} = \frac{\text{MSR}}{\text{MSE}}. \qquad \textbf{(13.9)}$$

Example 13.7. We apply this *F*-test to our investment equation for which the computer output is repeated in Fig. 13.6. Since there are $m = 2$ independent variables, we are testing H_0: x_1 and x_2 are not linearly related to y versus H_a: they are. From Fig. 13.6 we get the sums of squares SSR = 10,221.92 and SSE = 1263.77. By addition, SST = 11,485.69.

In this example, $n = 20$ and $m = 2$. From the analysis-of-variance table (Table 13.4), we find the calculated value of F to be

$$F_c = \frac{\text{MSR}}{\text{MSE}} = \frac{5110.96}{74.34} = 68.75.$$

This value far exceeds the critical value (from Table VIII(b)) for $\alpha = 0.01$ with 2 and 17 d.f., which is

$$F_{(2,17)} = 6.11.$$

TABLE 13.4 **Analysis-of-variance table for the multiple regression of investment on stock prices and retained earnings**

Source	SS	d.f.	MS
Regression	SSR = 10,221.92	$m = 2$	MSR = 5110.96
Error	SSE = 1263.77	$n - m - 1 = 17$	MSE = s_e^2 = 74.34
Total	SST = 11,485.69	$n - 1 = 19$	

FIGURE 13.6 **Computer printout for the investment regression.**

a) SPSS output

DEPENDENT VARIABLE..   Y   INVESTMENT

```
MULTIPLE R           0.94338
R SQUARE             0.88997
ADJUSTED R SQUARE    0.87703
STANDARD ERROR       8.62203
```

```
----------------- VARIABLES IN THE EQUATION -----------------

VARIABLE          B                   STD ERROR B       F

X1          0.7855818D-01                 0.01880     17.461
X2          1.798403                      0.61413      8.575
(CONSTANT)  1.677116
```

```
ANALYSIS OF VARIANCE    DF        SUM OF SQUARES     MEAN SQUARE
REGRESSION              2.          10221.91713      5110.95857
RESIDUAL               17.           1263.77127        74.33959
                                                          F
                                                       68.75160
```

b) SAS output

```
                        SSE     1263.77     F RATIO      68.75
                        DFE          17     PROB>F      0.0001
DEP VAR: Y              MSE    74.339400    R-SQUARE     0.8900
       INVESTMENT

DURBIN-WATSON D STATISTIC  =  0.7836
```

```
                    PARAMETER    STANDARD
VARIABLE      DF    ESTIMATE      ERROR      T RATIO    PROB>|T|

INTERCEPT      1    1.677130     7.770990    0.2158     0.8317
X1             1    0.078558     0.018800    4.1786     0.0006
X2             1    1.798403     0.614129    2.9284     0.0094
```

We conclude that the null hypothesis of no linear relationship can be rejected. Thus, *stock prices* and *retained earnings* do appear to have a significant linear association with investment.

Study Question 13.3: *F*-test for the Housing Price Model

Use the housing price model, the results of Study Question 12.3, and the computer printout in Fig. 13.3 to do an *F*-test on the linear relation between housing price and the three variables, income, rent, and vacancy rate.

Answer. This printout does not give the total variation, SST, but it was found in Study Question 12.3 to be 992.10 ($million)^2. The printout does give the unexplained variation, SSE = 125.31 ($million)^2 and the associated degrees of freedom (6). This gives a mean square error of MSE = SSE/6 = 20.885 ($million)^2. By subtraction the explained variation due to the $m = 3$ variables in the equation is

$$SSR = SST - SSE = 992.10 - 125.31 = 866.79 \quad (\$million)^2.$$

The mean square explained due to the regression is

$$MSR = \frac{SSR}{m} = \frac{866.79}{3} = 288.930.$$

Using Formula (13.9), the value of the *F*-statistic for this sample equation is

$$F_{(3,6)} = \frac{MSR}{MSE} = \frac{288.930}{20.885} = 13.83.$$

This is larger than the critical value, $F_{0.01} = 9.78$, in Table VIII for 3 and 6 degrees of freedom. The conclusion is to reject the null hypothesis of no linear relation and to argue that the sample model indicates that the three variables together do have a significant linear association with y.

The printout in Fig. 13.7 repeats Fig. 13.3(b). It gives this same value for the F-RATIO of 13.83. It also gives a p-value for this calculated test statistic of p-value = PROB > F = 0.0042. That is,

$$P(F_{3,6} > 13.83) = 0.0042.$$

Test on a Subgroup of Variables   Sometimes a hypothesis needs to be tested regarding the linear relation between y and a *subset* of all the explanatory variables. This subset of variables may be those that are subject to policy manipulation, or they may be all the same type of economic or business measures, such as a set of expenditure class measures, a set of interest rate measures, or a set

```
MODEL:                          SSE    125308751    F RATIO      13.83
                                DFE            6    PROB>F       0.0042
DEP VAR: PRICE                  MSE     20884792    R-SQUARE     0.8737
         HOUSING PRICE

DURBIN-WATSDON D STATISTIC  =  1.7725


                         PARAMETER     STANDARD
VARIABLE         DF       ESTIMATE       ERROR      T RATIO    PROB>|T|

INTERCEPT         1       37290.06     20800.91     1.7927      0.1232
INCOME            1       -0.675160     1.553683   -0.4346      0.6791
RENT              1      164.645394    52.806723    3.1179      0.0206
VACANT            1     -293.970271   144.214994   -2.0384      0.0876
```

FIGURE 13.7 **Multiple regression results for the housing price model.**

of demographic measures. We denote the number of these variables of special interest by the letter J. We wish to develop a test to determine whether these J variables together are significantly related to y *given the other variables included in the model*. That is, for the model $y = \alpha + \beta_1 x_1 + \cdots + \beta_m x_m$, suppose there are $(m - J)$ variables that we definitely wish to include in the equation and J variables that are to be tested for their joint contribution. An analysis-of-variance type test can be used to examine the amount of *extra* variation in y that the J variables explain relative to the variation left unexplained by all m variables. The hypotheses to be tested are

H_0: the joint contribution of the J explanatory variables is *not* significant;

H_a: the group of J variables do contribute significantly to the explanation of the variation in y.

An appropriate test statistic is based on the comparison between the amount of unexplained variation (SSE) when *all* the variables are included in the model and the amount of unexplained variation when the group of J variables is *not included*.*

We label the latter sum of squares as SSE_S for the unexplained variation in the "shorter" or "smaller" form of the model (including only $m - J$ variables). The F-ratio is

---

* This concept is similar to that of a partial coefficient of correlation when the variables in group B are the J variables of special interest and group A includes the other $(m - J)$ variables. A similar test would involve the null hypothesis $H_0:r_{y,B \cdot A} = 0$.

> For a test on the significance of a subgroup
> of J variables in a multiple regression:
> $$F_{(J, n-m-1)} = \frac{(SSE_S - SSE)/J}{SSE/(n-m-1)}.$$ **(13.10)**

Example 13.8. For the housing price model with results in Fig. 13.7, use Formula (13.10) to test the joint significance of the two variables, rent and vacancy rate. The interpretation of this test parallels the discussion on partial coefficients of determination in Study Question 13.2. There are $m = 3$ variables in the complete model, $J = 2$ variables to be jointly considered as a subgroup, and $m - J = 1$ variable in the "shorter" model. We have already determined that the unexplained variation in the shorter model with INCOME as the only explanatory variable is 683.676 million, now denoted as SSE_S. The unexplained variation in the complete model with all three explanatory variables (including the $J = 2$ added variables) is SSE $= 125.309$. The hypotheses are

H_0: the variables RENT and VACANT are *not* jointly significant in the model including the independent variable INCOME.

H_a: RENT and VACANT do contribute significantly to the *extra* explanation of the variation in *y*.

If the null is rejected, this indicates that the two extra variables are useful in the model.

For our sample the number of observations is $n = 10$, so we shall use the *F*-distributed random variable with $J = 2$ and $n - m - 1 = 10 - 3 - 1 = 6$ degrees of freedom. The calculated value using Formula (13.10) is

$$F_c = \frac{(683.676 - 125.309)/2}{125.309/6} = \frac{279.184}{20.885} = 13.37.$$

This is larger than the critical value, $F_{0.01} = 10.92$, in Table VIII for 2 and 6 degrees of freedom. We conclude that rent and vacancy rate are jointly significant in this multiple regression model.

13.5 TESTS ON PARAMETERS

In the previous section we dealt with tests related to the overall fit and the joint explanation of variables in a multiple regression model. In addition to knowing whether or not a significant amount of variation in *y* has been explained, the important questions of statistical inference on the parameters in the model must be asked. Which of the coefficients is significant? What is the confidence interval on the unknown variance of the disturbances in the model? What are the confidence limits on the coefficient associated with the most critical explanatory variable (most critical meaning the one of special interest for policy purposes, for decision-making, for forecasting, or for theoretical cause-and-effect relationships)?

Examining the Size of the Variance of the Disturbances*

Since the true distributions of the estimators of the coefficients in the model depend on the variance of the disturbances, σ_ϵ^2 (refer to Table 12.9), we first present a method for obtaining a confidence interval on the size of this parameter. The resulting confidence limits also serve as a guide to the accuracy of the model, since they enable us to put bounds on the typical size of the error σ_ϵ.

If the model fits well, the variance of the errors about the regression equation should be relatively small (in comparison to the variance in the dependent variable *y*). That is, the "clear channel" representation of the relation among *y* and the *x*'s is not drowned out by the "static and random noise" due to the disturbance term (the errors due to mismeasurement or misspecification or behavioral changes).

The best estimate of the variance of the disturbance term (σ_ϵ^2) is given by the mean square error (s_e^2). Moreover, the distribution of a test statistic involving these terms has a known distribution given the assumptions underlying our regression model. The formula is similar to that presented in Chapters 7 and 8 for the variance of a population, except that the degrees of freedom are $n - m - 1$, not $n - 1$ (where *m* is the number of explanatory variables in the model).

Chi-square statistic for inference on the variance of the disturbance:

$$\chi^2_{(n-m-1)} = \frac{(n - m - 1)s_e^2}{\sigma_\epsilon^2}.$$

(13.11)

This statistic can be used to test hypotheses about particular values of the variance of the disturbances, usually based on previous empirical studies. More frequently, it is used to set confidence limits on the size

---

* This discussion assumes that Section 7.9 on the chi-square random variable has been studied.

of this variance of errors for the particular regression model. As such, the limits give a guide to the goodness of fit of the model and to the likely range of values for the unknown error ϵ_i. To find the confidence limits, two values must be obtained from the chi-square table (Table VII in the Appendix) for $n - m - 1$ degrees of freedom and the $100(1 - \alpha)\%$ level of confidence. The χ^2_{upper} value should *exclude* $100(\alpha/2)\%$ of the *upper tail* of the relevant distribution; the χ^2_{lower} value should *exclude* the same percent of the *lower tail*, leaving $100(1 - \alpha)\%$ in the middle. The confidence limits are

---

Confidence limits for σ_ϵ^2:

$$\frac{(n - m - 1)s_e^2}{\chi^2_{\text{upper}}} < \sigma_\epsilon^2 < \frac{(n - m - 1)s_e^2}{\chi^2_{\text{lower}}}. \qquad \textbf{(13.12)}$$

Example 13.9. We can use Formula (13.12) to find the 95% confidence interval on the variance of the disturbances in the regression model for investment. Figure 13.6 provides the results of the estimation of investment in terms of stock price index and retained earnings. We used those results previously to find $s_e^2 = (1263.77/17) = 74.34$. The values of n and m are $n = 20$ and $m = 2$, so $n - m - 1 = 17$. For $(\alpha/2) = 0.025$ we look in Table VII for the chi-square values in the row for 17 degrees of freedom and the columns for 0.025 and 0.975 to obtain $\chi^2_{\text{lower}} = 7.56$ and $\chi^2_{\text{upper}} = 30.19$, respectively. The 95% confidence limits on σ_ϵ^2 are

$$\frac{17(74.34)}{30.19} = 41.86 \quad \text{and} \quad \frac{17(74.34)}{7.56} = 167.17.$$

By using square roots, the typical size of the error has limits

$$6.47 < \sigma_\epsilon < 12.93.$$

Note that these limits are not equally distant from the standard error of estimate, $s_e = 8.62$, because the chi-square distribution is not symmetrical.

Tests on a Particular Parameter   To determine the significance of an individual coefficient (β_j) in the regression model, a test similar to that for the slope in the simple regression equation is used. The null hypothesis H_0: $\beta_j = 0$ means that the variable x_j has no significant linear relationship with y, *when the effect of the other independent variables is held constant.* The best linear unbiased estimator of β_j is the sample partial regression coefficient b_j. Under assumption 2 that the unknown disturbances are normally distributed, the test for this null hypothesis follows the *t*-distribution with $(n - m - 1)$ degrees of freedom, as given in Formula (13.13):

---

t-statistic for inference on a partial regression coefficient β_j:

$$t_{(n-m-1)} = \frac{b_j - \beta_j}{s_{b_j}}.$$

(13.13)

Here s_{b_j} is the estimated standard error of the estimator b_j. Calculation of s_{b_j} is quite tedious, but its value is readily available in the computer output of any standard regression analysis program.

For a test of significance, $\beta_j = 0$ is substituted in Formula (13.13). Thus, the determination of t in a practical application is accomplished simply by forming the ratio of the coefficient to its estimated standard error. When the calculated value of t exceeds the critical value, $t_{(\alpha, n-m-1)}$ determined from Table VI, the null hypothesis of no significance can be rejected. It is then concluded that the variable x_j does have an important influence on the dependent variable y, after accounting for the influence of all other independent variables included in the model. Analysts usually report such *t*-ratios for tests of significance in any discussion of multiple regression results.

Example 13.10. In the investment model of Example 13.2 and Fig. 13.6, the estimated standard errors of the coefficients b_1 and b_2 of the variables x_1 (stock prices) and x_2 (retained earnings) are

$$s_{b_1} = 0.0188 \quad \text{and} \quad s_{b_2} = 0.6141,$$

respectively. Since $n = 20$ and $m = 2$ in this case, the critical value for a one-sided test on either coefficient (using a significance level of $\alpha = 0.01$) is

$$t_{(\alpha, n-m-1)} = t_{(0.01, 17)} = 2.567.$$

Thus, the critical region for a one-sided test when $H_0:\beta_1 = 0$ (or $H_0:\beta_2 = 0$) includes *all values of t that exceed* 2.567. We choose a one-sided upper-tail test because our *a priori* theoretical propositions were that both x_1 and x_2 were positively related to y.

The value of b_1 was 0.07856; hence for the test on β_1,

$$t_c = \frac{b_1}{s_{b_1}} = \frac{0.07856}{0.0188} = 4.179.$$

The value of b_2 was 1.7984, so for the test on the significance of β_2,

$$t_c = \frac{b_2}{s_{b_2}} = \frac{1.7984}{0.6141} = 2.929.$$

These t-values are shown in the SAS output of Fig. 13.6(b) in the column headed "T RATIO." In Fig. 13.5(a) the t-ratios are not given. The SPSS program reports the square of the t-ratio in the column headed "F." For the coefficient b_1 or x_1 the square root of the F-value, $\sqrt{17.461}$, is 4.18, which is the *t*-ratio. Similarly, for b_2 the square root of the F-value of 8.575 is the t-value, 2.93.*

We repeat that it is standard operating procedure in any multiple regression analysis to report the coefficients and their t-values for tests of significance. This allows a quick check to determine whether any variable is *not* contributing significantly to the explanation of the variation in **y**. The t-values also quickly reveal which variable has the most significant coefficient in terms of having the greatest t-value in absolute size. For the investment regression we conclude that both variables, x_1 = stock prices and x_2 = retained earnings, are significantly related to **y** = investment. The variable x_1 is the more influential of the two, since it has the higher t-value.

However, these are not the only t-values that may be of interest to a decision-maker. Previous regression results may have already shown which variables tend to have significant coefficients. For example, we know that the level of income is important in explaining the amount of household expenditures. However, we may not know exactly the value of the coefficient (β_j, which is the marginal propensity to consume) relating income and expenditures for a particular group of households. We may wish to determine whether the coefficient for households in rural areas, or those of a certain ethnic group, or those which have only a single adult is similar to the coefficient that has been determined for some other group or for the whole population. In such a case we would do a test of hypothesis using Formula (13.13) with the value of β_j set to the previously accepted value. For example, if a population of households is thought to have a marginal propensity to consume of $\beta_j = 0.8$, the null hypothesis to test based on a sample of households would be $H_0 : \beta_j = 0.8$.

In many cases of applied regression analysis it is also desirable to find an interval estimate for the partial slope β_j rather than simply the

---

* See Problem 13.16 for another explanation of this comparison between the *t*- and **F**-values in tests of significance for regression coefficients.

point estimate b_j. Formula (13.13) can be used in the usual way to find $100(1 - \alpha)\%$ confidence limits on β_j. These would be

---

$100(1 - \alpha)\%$ confidence limits on β_j:

$$b_j \pm t_{(\alpha/2, n-m-1)}s_{b_j}. \qquad \textbf{(13.14)}$$

Study Question 13.4: *t*-test for the Housing Price Model
Use the housing price model and the regression results shown in Fig. 13.3(b) or Fig. 13.7.

a) Interpret the meaning of the individual *t*-ratios for the coefficients of each included variable.
b) Find and interpret the meaning of a 90% confidence interval for the coefficient of the variable that is most influential in explaining changes in the variation of ***y***.
c) Do the results show any cause and effect among the variables?

Answer

a) The estimated equation and the corresponding *t*-values (given below each coefficient) are.

PRICE = 37,290 − 0.675 (INCOME)
(1.79)   (−0.43)

+ 164.65 (RENT) − 293.97 (VACANT)
(3.12)   (−2.04)

The coefficient for INCOME is *not* significant for a significance level of 0.05 and a critical value from Table VI of $t_{0.05,6}$ = 1.943. The coefficient for VACANT is significantly negative. The most influential variable is RENT, which has a significantly positive coefficient and has the largest absolute value of the *t*-ratios.

b) The 90% confidence interval on β_2 associated with the variable RENT is found by using Formula (13.14), the *t*-value of 1.943, and the standard error for the estimator from Fig. 13.7 of s_{b_2} = 52.81. The limits are

164.65 ± 1.943(52.81),   which gives   62.04   and   267.26.

Based on the sample regression results, a $1 change in biweekly rent (assuming no change in income or vacancy rates) indicates a change in the average housing price of $62.04 to $267.26. A different set of sample observations would lead to a different estimate and a different confidence interval. Theoretically,

90% of such confidence intervals would include the true value of the slope (β_2).

c) Whether or not there is any cause and effect between rent and housing price is not determinable from these statistical results. The analysis gives information only on the linear association among these variables. The *analyst* specifies the cause and effect linkage by designating rent as an explanatory (causal) variable that affects the dependent variable, housing price. In an alternative model another analyst might have these causal roles reversed.

Forecasting Based on the Regression Model

Once we have found that the regression equation has a significant fit and have determined which coefficients are significant, we can proceed to use the equation for determining point forecasts. In doing so, we must remember that the sample model gives results for only one set of data. Even if it has a high level of fit, it is not necessarily true that its predictions will be accurate for other situations. If there is some change in the underlying behavior or in some legal, social, political, regulatory, economic, or military factor (and so forth), the mathematical mechanism described by the equation may not hold. This makes it difficult to predict into the future using a model based on data from the past. The equation is most accurate near the point of means for the given variables and for no changes in the environmental or business conditions surrounding the time or place setting in which the data were gathered.

However, the objective information of point forecasts is not to be dismissed. Forecasts may provide the decision-maker with insights just as worthwhile as those obtained from subjective experience or from discussion with "experts." Usually, the best that can be done is to courageously calculate forecasts under the assumption that conditions do not change substantially. To do this, new values for the explanatory variables are substituted into the sample regression equation, and the predicted value of $\hat{y}$ is calculated.

Example 13.11. Returning to the investment model, suppose new values for stock prices and retained earnings are projected for a future quarter, and we think that the investment equation in Fig. 13.6 is appropriate. The *forecasted* level of investment is found by substituting the new values into the equation. Let x_{g1} (stock price index) be 950 and x_{g2} (retained earnings) be 25. The forecasted value is

$$\hat{y}_g = a + b_1 x_{g1} + b_2 x_{g2}$$
$$= 1.6771 + 0.07856(950) + 1.7984(25) = 121.27.$$

The estimated level of investment for the next quarter is $121.27 billion.

It is important to recognize that we have presented only a point estimate for the forecast $\hat{y}$. The computation of *interval* forecasts with a stated level of confidence (or of error) is quite cumbersome for the multiple regression model. Since this computation is best presented by using matrix operations, it is not described in this text.

Define. *F-tests on significance, subgroup test, confidence interval on* σ_ϵ^2, *t-tests on regression coefficients, point forecasts.*

PROBLEMS

13.10 In multiple regression analysis:
a) What measures are used to determine whether the equation fits the data well and may be useful for forecasting?
b) How can you determine which of the explanatory factors included in the model has the most significance in explaining the variation of the dependent variable y?

13.11 The following results are given for a multiple regression analysis, for y = tax revenue using 53 observations (standard errors are in parenthesis).

$$\hat{y} = \underset{(1.5)}{6} + \underset{(2)}{3x_1} + \underset{(4)}{10x_2} - \underset{(0.8)}{4x_3}.$$

a) What value of y would you predict if $x_1 = -1$, $x_2 = 3$, and $x_3 = 2$?
b) Calculate the values of the *t*-statistic for one-sided tests of the significance of each individual estimate of the regression coefficients, and find the critical value for such tests using a significance level of 0.05.
c) Determine which independent variable is most important and which is least important for explaining the variation in the dependent variable.
d) Suppose that x_1, x_2, and x_3 are policy variables that can be manipulated. If x_1 and x_2 are increased by 20 units each while x_3 is increased by 50 units, what is your best estimate of the change in tax revenue?

13.12 Given the following information on a linear multiple-regression model:

y = average yield in bushels of corn per acre on an Iowa farm;

x_1 = amount of summer rainfall, District 3 weather station, Iowa;

x_2 = average daily use in machine hours of tractors on the farm;

x_3 = amount of fertilizer, type XS80, used per acre.

The sample includes observations for ten crop years.

Results:

$\hat{y} = 16 + 75x_1 + 6x_2 + 48x_3$ Regression equation
    (10)   (25)   (4)   (8)   Standard errors of regression coefficients

$n = 10,$ $s_e = 20$ bushels, $s_y = 40$ bushels, $r^2_{y,x_1 \cdot x_2 x_3} = 0.60.$

Answer parts (a) through (f):

a) What are the degrees of freedom for t-distributed test statistics for regression?

b) Explain which variable appears to be the most important in explaining the variation of yield.

c) From the regression results, is it proper to argue that more machine hours of tractor use causes more yield or that more yield requires more machine hours of tractor use? Explain.

d) Find the coefficient of multiple correlation, $R^2_{y \cdot x_1 x_2 x_3}$.

e) Account for the different values of

$$R^2_{y \cdot x_1 x_2 x_3} \quad \text{and} \quad r^2_{y,x_1 \cdot x_2 x_3}$$

by explaining the different meanings of the two coefficients.

f) Determine a 90% confidence interval on σ_ϵ.

13.13 Using 12 weekly observations, a model to estimate tourism revenue, $y = \alpha + \beta_1 x_1 + \beta_2 x_2 + \beta_3 x_3 + \beta_4 x_4$, is estimated by the method of least squares. Here SST $= 400$, SSE $= 170$, and the amount of variation explained jointly by x_1, x_2, and x_3 is 200.

a) Find $r^2_{y,x_4 \cdot x_1 x_2 x_3}$ and explain what it means.

b) Do an ANOVA test with $\alpha = 0.05$ to determine whether this linear relationship is significant.

13.14 In a multiple regression to explain monthly new car sales by a dealer, based on 40 observations, the following results are obtained:

$$\hat{y} = 10 + 4x_1 + 6x_2 - 2x_3$$

with standard errors: (1.2)   (5.0)   (0.4)

a) Explain the meaning of the coefficient for the variable x_2, which measures the number of full-time salespeople.

b) Using some test statistic, explain which of the independent variables is the most significant.

c) Explain one probable effect of dropping variable x_2 from the regression model and reestimating.

d) What value of y would you predict if $x_1 = 4$, $x_2 = 1$, and $x_3 = 2$?

13.15 Consider a linear-regression model, $y = \alpha + \beta_1 x_1 + \beta_2 x_2 + \epsilon$, where

y = learning by grade 12, as measured by an academic test score composite, with mean 300 and standard deviation 150, for the entire population of twelfth-graders;

x_1 = school expenditures per pupil during three years of high school (in hundreds of dollars);

x_2 = an index of socioeconomic status of the individual, with mean 10 and standard deviation 2, for the entire population of twelfth-graders.

Based on a sample of 25 twelfth-grade-level individuals who were arrested on drug possession charges, the following results are obtained. Analyze, interpret, and explain these data in the way you think most appropriate and meaningful.

Variable	Mean	Standard Deviation
y	306.67	175.98
x_1	12.58	9.31
x_2	11.17	8.95

Correlations:

$$r_{yx_1} = 0.83; \qquad r_{yx_2} = 0.35; \qquad r_{x_1x_2} = 0.10.$$

Coefficient	Estimate	Standard Error	t-Value
a	10.16	11.90	0.85
b_1	17.60	0.62	28.30
b_2	4.30	2.90	1.48

Multiple $R = 0.92$; $\qquad s_e = 3.015$.

Analysis of Variance	SS	d.f.	Mean Square
Regression	1090	2	545.00
Residual	200	22	9.09

13.16 Using the results for the investment model given in Fig. 12.16 and Fig. 13.2 and using the *F*-test for a subgroup of coefficients [Formula (13.10)], test the significance of the contribution of the single variable x_2 = retained earnings. Treat it as a subgroup of size $J = 1$. Compare the result to the *t*-test for β_2.

13.17 Explain how the use of the *t*-distribution differs from the use of the *F*-distribution in testing hypotheses in multiple linear regression.

13.18 In a multiple regression problem the following data are used:

y	x_1	x_2	x_1^2	x_2^2	x_1y	x_2y	x_1x_2	y^2
9	3	2	9	4	27	18	6	81
10	4	3	16	9	40	30	12	100
2	1	2	1	4	2	4	2	4
9	2	3	4	9	18	27	6	81
20	5	5	25	25	100	100	25	400
Σ 50	15	15	55	51	187	179	51	666
μ 10	3	3						

a) The normal equations for two independent variables are

$$\Sigma y = na + b_1 \Sigma x_1 + b_2 \Sigma x_2,$$
$$\Sigma x_1 y = a \Sigma x_1 + b_1 \Sigma x_1^2 + b_2 \Sigma x_1 x_2,$$
$$\Sigma x_2 y = a \Sigma x_2 + b_1 \Sigma x_1 x_2 + b_2 \Sigma x_2^2.$$

Find a, b_1, and b_2.

b) Find SSE, SSR, and SST. Use this information to calculate s_e and R^2.

c) Determine a 90% confidence interval on σ_ϵ.

d) If $r_{y,x_1}^2 = 136.9/166$, and $r_{y,x_2}^2 = 140.167/166$, find $r_{y,x_1 \cdot x_2}^2$ and $r_{y,x_2 \cdot x_1}^2$.

e) Test the null hypothesis of no linear association using the **F**-test. Use $\alpha = 0.05$ and include the ANOVA table for this problem.

13.19 A stenographic pool supervisor wishes to use the intermediate results provided below to determine a regression equation that can predict the total typing hours, y, for report drafts. She uses as independent variables the number of words in the draft, x_1 (in tens of thousands) and an index x_2 for level of difficulty on a scale of 1 (least difficult) to 5 (most difficult).

$$n = 25, \quad \Sigma y = 200, \quad \Sigma x_1 = 100, \quad \Sigma x_2 = 75,$$
$$\Sigma x_1 y = 1000, \quad \Sigma x_2 y = 800, \quad \Sigma x_1^2 = 600,$$
$$\Sigma x_2^2 = 325, \quad \Sigma y^2 = 3800, \quad \Sigma x_1 x_2 = 200.$$

a) Calculate the coefficients a, b_1, and b_2 for the estimated regression equation. *Note:* Solve the normal equations as in Problem 13.18(a).

b) Explain the meaning of the values obtained for b_1 and b_2.

c) Calculate and interpret R^2.

d) Test for the significance of the individual coefficients, using an appropriate one-tailed test and $\alpha = 0.05$.

e) Determine a 90% confidence interval on σ_ϵ^2.

13.20 Suppose that, in a multiple regression problem, the ANOVA table is as follows:

Source	SS	d.f.
Regression	36	2
Error	64	32

a) How many independent variables are there? What is the sample size?
b) What is the value of the multiple correlation coefficient R? What percent of the variability in y is explained by the independent variables?
c) Test the null hypothesis that there is no linear regression. Use a two-sided alternative hypothesis and let $\alpha = 0.05$.
d) Find the value of $r^2_{y,x_2 \cdot x_1}$ given that the unexplained variation in a simple regression with x_1 alone is 80.
e) Calculate the standard error of the estimate.

13.21 During the summer of 1985, ten State University students were hired by Disney World as entertainers. Before being hired, each student was given two different aptitude tests. They were then given three days of training, after which they were rated by a committee. The results were as follows:

Test I (Score x_1)	Test II (Score x_2)	Rating (y)
74	40	91
59	41	72
83	45	95
76	43	90
69	40	82
88	47	98
71	37	80
69	36	75
61	34	74
70	37	79

a) Calculate a, b_1, and b_2 in the equation $\hat{y} = a + b_1 x_1 + b_2 x_2$. [Hint: See Problem 13.18, part (a) or use a computer.]
b) How would you interpret b_1? How would your answer differ if you had estimated the equation $\hat{y} = a + b_1 x_1$?
c) Calculate SSR and SST for part (a).
d) Use your results from part (c) to test the hypothesis of no linear regression.
e) Determine a 90% confidence interval on σ_ϵ^2.

13.6 DUMMY VARIABLES IN REGRESSION ANALYSIS

Thus far, the variables we have used in regression problems have been "quantitative variables," which means that they represent variables that are either measured or counted. In some types of problems it is desirable to use another type of variable called a *qualitative variable*, which merely indicates whether or not an object belongs to a particular category or possesses a particular quality. For example, in a regression analysis in which the dependent variable is the consumption expenditures of families in the United States, one may be interested in relating *y* not only to family income (x_1) but also to whether or not the family lives in an urban or rural community (x_2). The variable x_1 is a quantitative variable (it measures income), while the variable x_2 is a qualitative variable (it indicates whether or not the family is classified as rural or urban). To use such a variable in regression analysis, we might let $x_2 = 0$ if the family lives in a rural community and let $x_2 = 1$ if they live in an urban community. A variable such as x_2 is often called a **dummy variable.**

The introduction of a dummy variable does not change the multiple regression process described thus far. That is, all computations are made in the same way as for a regression analysis involving only quantitative variables. One characteristic of the addition of a dummy variable, x_2, is that we know that its value in the regression equation is either zero or one. Hence, we can write two regression equations, one using $x_2 = 0$ and the other using $x_2 = 1$. To illustrate this, we present the following least-squares regression line where x_2 = dummy variable:

$$\hat{y} = a + b_1 x_1 + b_2 x_2.$$

If $x_2 = 1$, then substituting $x_2 = 1$ into this equation yields

$$E[\hat{y} \mid x_2 = 1] = a + b_1 x_1 + b_2(1) = (a + b_2) + b_1 x_1.$$

Since $x_2 = 1$ indicates an urban family, this equation represents the regression line for urban families. If we substitute $x_2 = 0$ in the original regression line, we get the regression line for rural families:

$$E[\hat{y} \mid x_2 = 0] = a + b_1 x_1 + b_2(0) = a + b_1 x_1.$$

Thus, we have derived two regression lines from the original regression model, as shown in Fig. 13.8.

In this example the distinction between rural and urban families shifts the regression intercept from a to $(a + b_2)$. (Our graph shows a positive value for b_2.) Note that the slope of both straight lines is the same (b_1).

If one wishes to allow for a different slope in the relation between consumption and income for rural versus urban families, the specification

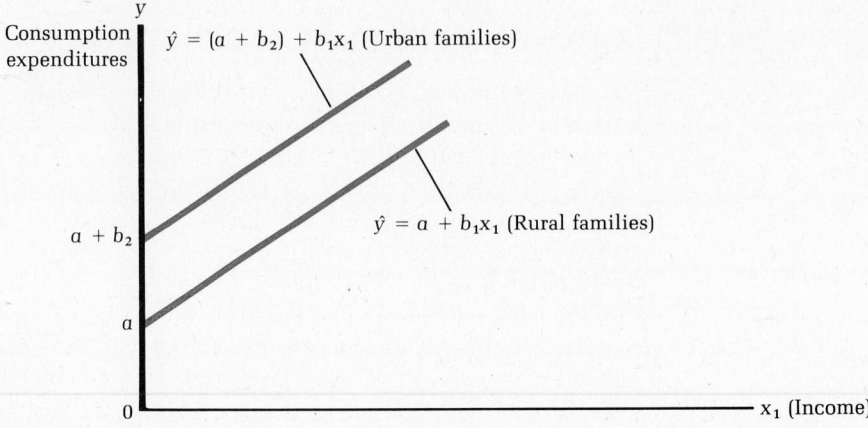

FIGURE 13.8 **Two regression lines resulting from the use of a dummy variable.**

of the model that includes the dummy variable would be different. We would then specify the regression model as

$$\hat{y} = a + (b + cx_2)x_1,$$

where x_2 = dummy variable. Then, if $x_2 = 1$ for an urban family, the line is

$$E[\hat{y} \mid x_2 = 1] = a + (b + c)x_1 \quad \text{with a slope of } (b + c).$$

When $x_2 = 0$ for a rural family, the line is

$$E[\hat{y} \mid x_2 = 0] = a + bx_1 \quad \text{with a slope of } b.$$

A positive value of c would indicate that urban families have a higher propensity to consume out of extra income received than do rural families, who would have a higher propensity to save extra income. A negative value of c would give evidence of the converse. In both cases the intercept is the same value a. Figure 13.9 illustrates the situation of a dummy slope variable. The reader should recognize that dummy variables may be used to allow for both different intercepts and different slopes in the same model.*

An Example Using a Single Dummy Variable   To illustrate the use of dummy variables, we will present two examples: one involving a single dummy variable and a second example involving three dummy variables. In each example, dummy variables will be used

---

* A model allowing for both different intercepts and slopes due to the urban/rural distinction would be $\hat{y} = a + (b + c)x_1 + dx_2$. For $x_2 = 1$ the urban equation is $\hat{y} = (a + d) + (b + c)x_1$. For $x_2 = 0$ the rural equation is $\hat{y} = a + bx_1$.

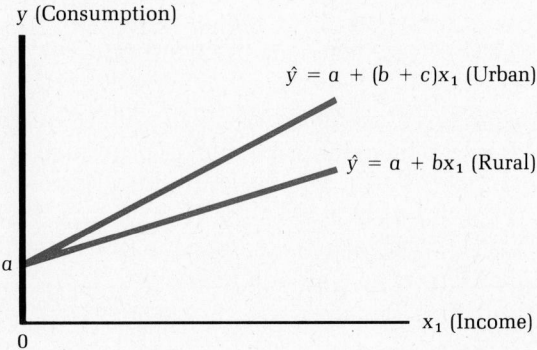

FIGURE 13.9 **Two regression lines resulting from the use of a dummy slope variable.**

for intercepts, since the algebra is simpler. Dummy variables used for different slopes would be treated similarly. The data for these examples are presented in Table 13.5.

Regression models are often used on historical data to learn about the theoretical relations among economic variables. Generalizations are often inferred that help predict future changes or effects. Table 13.5 presents quarterly data, measured at an annual rate, on retail sales (in

TABLE 13.5 **Data for regression model on retail sales**

	Quarter	Retail Sales, y	GNP, x_1	Price Increase Variable, x_2	Quarter Variable x_3	x_4	x_5
1972	1	978	1112.5	0	1	0	0
	2	1123	1143.0	0	0	1	0
	3	1125	1169.3	0	0	0	1
	4	1260	1204.7	0	0	0	0
1973	1	1121	1248.9	0	1	0	0
	2	1275	1277.9	0	0	1	0
	3	1257	1308.9	0	0	0	1
	4	1381	1344.0	1	0	0	0
1974	1	1172	1358.8	1	1	0	0
	2	1368	1383.8	1	0	1	0
	3	1382	1416.3	1	0	0	1
	4	1454	1430.9	1	0	0	0
1975	1	1260	1416.6	1	1	0	0
	2	1462	1440.9	1	0	1	0

Source: *Survey of Current Business.*

millions of dollars) as the dependent variable (y) and gross national product (in \$billions) between 1972 and mid-1975 as x_1.

Example 13.12. Suppose that we want to investigate the effect on retail sales of the huge oil price increase initiated by the OPEC countries in October 1973. To do this, we introduce the dummy variable x_2, and let $x_2 = 1$ for any period after the price increase and $x_2 = 0$ before the price increase. A least-squares regression line using these variables yields (the standard errors are in parentheses)

$$\hat{y} = -330.29 + 1.2346x_1 - 42.456x_2.$$
$$\phantom{\hat{y} = -330.29 + }(0.4122)(89.61)$$

By substituting $x_2 = 0$ into this equation we get the regression equation for the period before the price increase:

$$\hat{y} = -330.29 + 1.2346x_1 - 42.456(0)$$
$$= -330.29 + 1.2346x_1.$$

Substituting $x_2 = 1$ yields the equation for the period after the price increase:

$$\hat{y} = -330.29 + 1.2346x_1 - 42.456(1)$$
$$= -372.75 + 1.2346x_1.$$

The short-run impact of the oil price increase, as represented by these data, was to dampen retail sales by about 42 million dollars per year. Perhaps a shift in sales from large expensive cars to cheaper gas-saving cars accounts for much of this.

As is the case with all regression variables, we are interested in whether or not the coefficient of a dummy variable differs significantly from zero. In the present example we might have hypothesized that the sign of the coefficient b_2 will be negative due to a shift from "gas-guzzlers" to "gas-sippers"; i.e., we might be testing

$$H_0: \beta_2 = 0 \qquad \text{versus} \qquad H_a: \beta_2 < 0.$$

The calculated value t_c for these hypotheses is

$$t_c = \frac{b_2}{s_{b_2}} = \frac{-42.456}{89.61} = -0.474.$$

Since the value $t_c = -0.474$ is not in the critical region for

$$(n - m - 1) = (14 - 2 - 1) = 11 \text{ d.f.}$$

for any reasonable α, we must accept the null hypothesis $H_0: \beta_2 = 0$. Therefore, our conclusion must be that the price increase did not significantly affect retail sales. The size of the apparent change in sales is not uncommon even during periods of no change in oil prices.

An Example Using Multiple Dummy Variables   **Example 13.13.** Again, we will use Table 13.5 to illustrate how two or more dummy variables can be used simultaneously. Suppose we decide that there may be consistent differences in retail sales related to the quarters of the year (winter, spring, summer, fall). To include the quarter of the year as a variable in the problem, we must add *three* dummy variables to the analysis, as shown in the final three columns of Table 13.5. If $x_3 = 1$ (and $x_4 = x_5 = 0$), this indicates the first (or winter) quarter; when $x_4 = 1$ (and $x_3 = x_5 = 0$), this indicates the second (or spring) quarter; for the third (or summer) quarter, $x_5 = 1$ (and $x_3 = x_4 = 0$). Note that we only need *three* dummy variables to indicate *four* quarters because the fourth quarter (fall) is designated by the absence of a 1 in the x_3, x_4, and x_5 columns (i.e., $x_3 = x_4 = x_5 = 0$).

> If the model includes an intercept term a, the number of dummy variables needed to specify h different categories or levels is $h - 1$.

Thus, to indicate four different quarters, three dummy variables are required. Also, to indicate two different categories (such as rural versus urban or before OPEC price change versus after), only one dummy variable is needed.

The least-squares regression equation for the data in Table 13.5 (omitting variable x_2) is given below (with standard errors in parentheses).

$$\hat{y} = 76.022 + 0.972x_1 - 191.115x_3 - 43.295x_4 - 82.770x_5.$$
$$\quad\quad\quad (0.0503) \quad (15.614) \quad\quad (15.487) \quad\quad (16.598)$$

When the appropriate values of x_3, x_4, and x_5 are substituted, the above equation yields the four different regression lines shown in Fig. 13.10. For example, the equation for the first quarter is derived by setting $x_3 = 1$, $x_4 = 0$, and $x_5 = 0$:

$$\hat{y} = 76.022 + 0.972x_1 - 191.115(1) - 43.295(0) - 82.770(0)$$

$$= -115.093 + 0.972x_1.$$

The values of $\hat{y}$ for the other three quarters are

$$\hat{y} = 32.727 + 0.972x_1 \text{ (second quarter),}$$

$$\hat{y} = -6.748 + 0.972x_1 \text{ (third quarter),}$$

$$\hat{y} = 76.022 + 0.972x_1 \text{ (fourth quarter).}$$

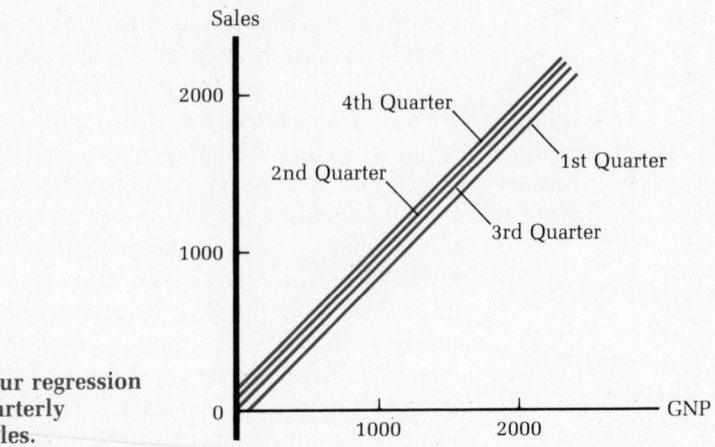

FIGURE 13.10 **Four regression lines using quarterly dummy variables.**

Testing the Joint Effect of a Subgroup of Dummy Variables*

From Fig. 13.10 we see that the regression lines do appear to differ from quarter to quarter. At this point we could use a t-test to determine whether each of the coefficients b_3, b_4, and b_5 is significantly different from zero. Perhaps a more meaningful test, however, would be to test the explanatory contribution of all three dummy variables simultaneously, as follows:

H_0: the joint effect of the dummy variables is not significant

versus

H_a: the dummy variables as a group do contribute to the explanation of the variation in y.

A test statistic useful in this circumstance is the F-test in Formula (13.10). It requires the amount of unexplained variation (SSE) when all the variables are in the equation and the amount of unexplained variation when the dummy variables are not included.

Example 13.14. For the retail sales data in Table 13.5 we could investigate the joint effect of the quarterly dummy variables, x_3, x_4, and x_5. Figure 13.11 provides a computer printout of the results of the complete and the "shorter" models, including or excluding the three dummy variables, respectively. The unexplained variation in the shorter model is $SSE_S = 75{,}955.7$; for the complete model we have $SSE = 3691.5$. In this case the number of variables in the subgroup is $J = 3$; the number of explanatory variables in the complete model is $m = 4$; and the number

* This section requires that the reader has studied the use of the F-distribution and the F-test in Section 13.4.

of observations is $n = 14$. Thus, $(n - m - 1) = (14 - 4 - 1) = 9$. Substituting these values into Formula (13.10) yields

$$F_c = \frac{(75{,}955.7 - 3{,}691.5)/3}{3691.5/9} = \frac{24{,}088.1}{410.2} = 58.7.$$

Since this value of F_c exceeds the critical value for $\alpha = 0.01$ shown in Table VIII(b) of $F_{(3,9)} = 6.99$, we can reject the null hypothesis that seasonal factors do not affect retail sales and conclude that the quarterly dummy variables are useful in explaining variation in retail sales.

Define. *Dummy variable for intercept, dummy variable for slope.*

FIGURE 13.11 **Computer printout for the retail sales models.**

```
                                                GNP = X2
                                                Q1  = X3
                                                Q2  = X4
                                                Q3  = X5

DEPENDENT VARIABLE..    SALES       RETAIL SALES

VARIABLE(S)ENTERED ON STEP NUMBER   1..     GNP

MUTIPLE R            0.84359   VARIABLE        B      STD ERROR B      F
R SQUARE            0.71165    GNP        1.064442       0.19560     29.616
ADJUSTED R SQUARE   0.68765    (CONSTANT) -129.6420
STANDARD ERROR     79.55907

ANALYSIS OF VARIANCE   DF      SUM OF SQUARES         MEAN SQUARE      F
REGRESSION             1.       187455.68491        187455.68491   29.61551
RESIDUAL              12.        75955.74366          6329.64530

* * * * * * * * * * * * * * * * * * * * * * * * * * * * * * * * * * * * *

VARIABLE(S) ENTERED ON STEP NUMBER  2..    Q3        THIRD QUARTER
                                           Q1        FIRST QUARTER
                                           Q2        SECOND QUARTER

                               VARIABLE        B      STD ERROR B      F
MULTIPLE R          0.99297
R SQUARE            0.98599    GNP        0.9716888      0.05031    372.99
ADJUSTED SQUARE     0.97976    Q3         -82.76965     16.59757     24.86
STANDARD ERROR     20.25250    Q1        -191.1151      15.61405    149.81
                              Q2          .-43.29506    15.48683      7.81
                              (CONSTANT)  76.02249


ANALYSIS OF VARIANCE   DF      SUM OF SQUARES         MEAN SQUARE      F
REGRESSION             4.       259719.95483         64929.98871   158.30260
RESIDUAL               9.         3691.47374           410.16375
```

PROBLEMS

13.22 Let y = individual income for persons selected from among full-time workers in manufacturing, and let x = age. A simple regression model is written $y = \alpha + \beta x + \epsilon$.

a) Suppose that I wish to include in the model the factor of sex. Specify and interpret the dummy variable to be included in order to differentiate levels of income depending on sex as well as on age.

b) Suppose that now I wish to allow for different impacts of age on income, depending on whether or not the person completed college. Specify a dummy slope variable to be added to the model, and explain the separate regression lines that can be derived.

c) Make a sketch with income and age on the axes, and illustrate the different potential regression lines you have implied in parts (a) and (b).

d) Finally, add a set of dummy variables to the model to allow for different income levels for five different areas of the country: northeast, midwest, southeast, southwest, and west. In your model, specify the difference in the intercepts for females in the northeast compared to males in the west.

13.23 Lifetime earnings are explained in a human capital model by the characteristics of the individual, such as the level of schooling attained. Suppose that five such levels are distinguished in the available data: high school dropout, high school graduate, college graduate, master's degree or equivalent, and doctoral or other professional degree requiring at least three years of postgraduate work. To use the level of schooling as an explanatory variable in a regression model, specify the number of dummy variables you would use. Define them, and make a list of their values for each level of education described.

13.24 Refer to **Data Set 6** for survey data on persons over age 54. Included is a variable identifying the region of the country of the respondent. Suppose that regional differences are thought to be one of the factors determining the monthly income of the respondent.

a) Explain how to define dummy variables to represent these different regions.

b) Specify a model in which the regional effect changes the *level* of monthly income.

c) Specify a model in which the regional effect changes the *impact of education* on monthly income.

USING THE COMPUTER

13.25 A firm producing detergent has done a market analysis trying to improve its ability to predict annual sales of detergent in particular market areas. Four explanatory variables were measured, including population, unemployment rate, advertising expenditures in the area, and the number of competitors in the market. Observations on 30 market areas are given in Table 13.6.

TABLE 13.6

	Population	Unemployment Rate	Advertising Expense	Competition	Sales (lbs)
1.	7,500,000	5.1	59,000	0	5,170,000
2.	8,710,000	6.3	62,500	1	5,780,000
3.	10,000,000	4.7	61,000	1	4,840,000
4.	7,450,000	5.4	61,000	1	6,000,000
5.	8,670,000	5.4	6,100	1	6,000,000
6.	11,000,000	7.2	12,500	1	6,120,000
7.	13,180,000	5.8	35,800	1	6,400,000
8.	13,810,000	5.8	59,900	1	7,100,000
9.	14,430,000	6.2	57,200	2	8,500,000
10.	10,000,000	5.5	35,800	1	7,500,000
11.	13,210,000	6.8	27,900	1	9,300,000
12.	17,100,000	6.2	24,100	2	8,800,000
13.	15,120,000	6.3	27,700	2	9,960,000
14.	18,700,000	5.0	24,000	3	9,830,000
15.	20,200,000	5.5	57,200	3	10,120,000
16.	15,000,000	5.8	44,300	3	10,700,000
17.	17,600,000	7.1	49,200	4	10,450,000
18.	19,800,000	7.5	23,000	4	11,320,000
19.	14,400,000	8.2	62,700	2	11,870,000
20.	20,350,000	7.8	55,800	2	11,910,000
21.	18,900,000	6.2	50,000	3	12,600,000
22.	21,600,000	7.1	47,600	4	12,600,000
23.	25,250,000	4.0	43,500	4	14,240,000
24.	27,500,000	4.2	55,900	5	14,410,000
25.	21,000,000	7.0	51,200	4	13,730,000
26.	19,700,000	6.4	76,600	3	13,730,000
27.	24,150,000	5.0	63,000	3	13,800,000
28.	17,650,000	8.5	68,100	4	14,920,000
29.	22,300,000	7.1	74,400	5	15,280,000
30.	24,000,000	8.0	70,100	5	14,410,000

a) Use a computer program to find the sample regression equation for sales in terms of the four explanatory variables. (For better computational accuracy, code population and sales in millions and code advertising in thousands of dollars.)

b) Use tests to determine the significance of each coefficient and of the overall fit of the model.

c) Find a 90% confidence interval on the variance of the disturbance σ_ϵ^2.

d) Find a forecast of sales for the Atlanta market area if the values of the explanatory variables are specified to be $x_1 = 9.66$ million people, $x_2 = 6.4\%$ unemployed, $x_3 = 35$ thousand dollars, and $x_4 = 2$ competitors.

13.26 Refer to **Data Set 4** for sample observations on the variables: a doctor's net income, hours worked, office fee, and office expenses.

a) Estimate the sample regression equation for a doctor's income based on the other three variables. Compare your results to those given in Problem 13.3.

b) Test the significance of the overall fit of the equation.

c) Find a 95% confidence interval for the partial regression coefficient of the variable "office fee."

d) Do a test to determine the significance of the contribution of the two variables, office fee and office expenses.

13.27 Refer to **Data Set 5** to estimate a model explaining U.S. imports in terms of the gross domestic product, the population, and the level of exports.

a) Formulate the desired model and hypothesize the sign of the respective coefficients of the explanatory variables. [*Hint:* Exports are a component of U.S. production and provide for jobs and income for U.S. residents. With more income they may afford to buy more imports (as well as more of other products). Thus we expect a positive relation with $\beta_3 > 0$.]

b) Use a computer to estimate the complete model and to estimate a model using only gross domestic product as a single explanatory variable. Discuss the significance of the coefficients in both models.

c) Do a test to determine the significance of the contribution in the extended model of the two extra variables, population and level of exports.

d) For the simple model, find a 98% confidence interval on σ_ϵ^2, the variance of the disturbance term.

13.28 Use the survey data in **Data Set 6.**

a) Estimate a regression model for the dependent variable y = monthly income on the explanatory variables: years of education (x_1), number of persons in the household (x_2), and a dummy variable for the sex of the respondent (x_3).

b) Test the significance of the coefficient for the dummy variable at the 0.05 level.

c) Explain the meaning of the coefficient b_3 for the dummy variable.

13.29 Refer to **Data Set 1** and formulate a model explaining taxes in terms of income and the cyclical-threat variable.

a) Define two dummy variables to represent the three levels of cyclical threat.

b) Use a computer to estimate the model by the method of least squares.

c) Interpret the results of the regression analysis using *t*-tests and an *F*-test.

d) Suggest how many dummy variables would be needed to represent the variable, Moody Rating. Define the values for these dummy variables for the first five observations.

13.30 Reformulate, estimate, and analyze the results of the model as in Problem 13.28(a) except that the region of the respondent is included rather than the sex of the respondent. Assign region 1 as the base region. Refer to Problem 13.24(b) on the specification of regional dummy variables.

CASE PROBLEMS

13.31 As part of an economic study on development, it is desired to estimate a regression explaining literacy rates for population groups in different regions of countries throughout the world. Some explanatory variables may be quantitative, such as newspaper circulation, availability of radios or televisions, school enrollment, or the like. Other variables may not be measurable or may be qualitative. Hoping to represent different levels of some of these other variables, the economist categorizes the state of economic development of each region into one of these four classes:

> 1 = rapidly developing with sustained growth;
>
> 2 = some current growth;
>
> 3 = stagnant but with the prospect of soon experiencing growth;
>
> 4 = not developing and with little prospect of growth soon.

a) Write a model using three dummy variables, G_1, G_2, and G_3, to represent the four states of growth (letting development group 4 be the base group represented by all zeros), and use x_1 to denote school enrollment as a percent of people aged 5–19 and x_2 to denote the number of radios and televisions per thousand people.

TABLE 13.7 **Summary table (R² = 0.283, $\bar{y}$ = 59.297, SST = 73,875.877, n = 79)**

Variable	Coefficient	Standard Error
x_1	1.017	0.125
x_2	0.022	0.023
G_1	21.220	8.235
G_2	16.321	5.353
G_3	9.417	3.985
Intercept =	−4.55	

Data source: *Literacy Codebook*, Louis Harris Political Data Center, University of North Carolina, Chapel Hill.

b) Interpret the results of the regression using the summary table of output, Table 13.7. Use tests on the significance of the coefficients and on the fit of the model.

c) Write the equations for regions with development status 1 and for regions with development status 3 and interpret the meaning of the difference between the equations.

13.32 Problem 12.72 (Highway Safety) gave data for a simple regression on the number of highway deaths in terms of the number of drivers in 49 states and the District of Columbia. Below is a measure on another potential explanatory variable, the density of the area as defined by the number of persons per square mile. Include it in the model and reestimate the sample regression equation. Compare the results of the simple and multiple regression equations.

OBS	STATE	DENSITY	OBS	STATE	DENSITY	OBS	STATE	DENSITY
1	AL	64.0	18	MA	655.0	35	TX	37.0
2	AR	34.0	19	MI	137.0	36	UT	10.0
3	CA	100.0	20	MN	43.0	37	VT	42.0
4	CO	17.0	21	MS	46.0	38	VA	100.0
5	CT	518.0	22	MO	63.0	39	WV	77.0
6	DE	226.0	23	NB	18.4	40	WI	72.0
7	DC	12524.0	24	NH	67.0	41	AK	0.0
8	FL	91.0	25	NJ	807.0	42	AZ	12.0
9	GA	68.0	26	NY	350.0	43	ID	8.0
10	IL	180.0	27	NC	93.0	44	MT	4.0
11	IN	129.0	28	OH	237.0	45	NE	2.0
12	IA	49.0	29	OK	34.0	46	NM	7.0
13	KS	27.0	30	OR	18.0	47	ND	9.0
14	KY	76.0	31	PA	252.0	48	SD	9.0
15	LA	72.0	32	RI	812.0	49	WA	43.0
16	ME	31.0	33	SC	79.0	50	WY	3.0
17	MD	314.0	34	TN	85.0			

GLOSSARY

Population multiple regression equation: $\mu_{y \cdot x_1 x_2 \ldots x_m} = \alpha + \beta_1 x_1 + \beta_2 x_2 + \cdots + \beta_m x_m$.

Partial regression coefficient: The coefficient of x_j in a multiple regression model that gives the change in y for a unit change in x_j holding constant the linear effect on y of all other explanatory variables in the model.

Sample multiple regression equation: $\hat{y}_i = a + b_1 x_{i1} + b_2 x_{i2} + \cdots + b_m x_{im}$ for observations $i = 1, 2, \ldots, n$.

Standard error of the estimate; (s_e): Absolute measure of the typical size of the residual in the sample model:

$$s_e = \sqrt{\frac{SSE}{n - m - 1}}.$$

Multiple coefficient of determination (R^2)**:** Relative measure of fit for the entire model: $R^2 = SSR/SST$.

Adjusted coefficient of determination: Relative measure of fit adjusted for degrees of freedom:

$$R_{adj}^2 = 1 - (1 - R^2)\left[\frac{n - 1}{n - m - 1}\right].$$

Multiple correlation coefficient: Index of linear association among y and two or more explanatory variables, $R_{y \cdot x_1, x_2, x_3, \ldots, x_m}$.

Partial coefficients of determination: Relative measures of the extra variation explained by a group A of variables out of the variation previously unexplained by another group B of variables:

$$r_{yA \cdot B}^2 = \frac{\text{Extra variation in } y \text{ explained by adding group A}}{\text{Variation in } y \text{ unexplained by group B alone}}.$$

ANOVA tests in multiple regression: Tests using an F-distributed random variable to determine the overall contribution of all or of a subgroup of explanatory variables.

Chi-square statistic: For a confidence interval on the variance of a disturbance term in a multiple regression model:

$$\chi^2 = \frac{(n - m - 1)s_e^2}{\sigma_\epsilon^2}$$

with $n - m - 1$ degrees of freedom.

t-test on partial regression coefficients: $t = \dfrac{(b_j - \beta_j)}{s_{b_j}}$ with $n - m - 1$ degrees of freedom.

Dummy variable: A variable that reflects qualitative data by assigning either zero or one as the value of the variable.

Econometric Analysis

FOURTEEN

14.1 INTRODUCTION

In regression analysis a sample regression equation is estimated on the basis of data on a dependent variable y and a set of explanatory variables, $x_1, x_2, \ldots, x_m$. The significance of the association between y and the explanatory variables has been examined by using various test statistics. The interpretations and conclusions that can be drawn from the regression model depend on the values of the estimates and on the outcome of such tests.

While the use of the method of least squares to find the estimates is merely a technical process, the use of test statistics and methods of inference require knowledge of the probability distribution associated with the estimators and test statistics (which are random variables). Our previous discussion in conjunction with Table 12.9 indicated that these probability distributions depend on the probability distribution of the disturbance term (ϵ_i) in the regression model. When information is provided, *or assumed*, about the characteristics of the random variable ϵ_i across all observations $i = 1, 2, \ldots, n$, properties of the least-squares estimators and various test statistics can be derived.

Such derivations are not our purpose in this text, but we stated in Sections 12.4 and 13.3 the common assumptions and conditions underlying the least-squares regression analysis. We also specified the importance of these assumptions in terms of the properties of the least-squares estimators. We collect all these materials together again, and expand some of them, in the next section. In subsequent sections of this chapter, particular assumptions or conditions will be studied more carefully. We will discuss some situations in which our simple analysis (as done in Chapters 12 and 13) is not the most appropriate because of potential violations of an assumption or condition. The *effect* of the violation on our previous methods and results will be explained. We will consider some methods of *detection* of such potential violations and briefly examine a possible *remedy* for the situation.

This material is commonly included in textbooks on **econometrics,** which present statistical estimation and testing procedures for economics and finance (or other areas of business and social sciences) using the framework of the linear regression model. In scientific and engineering fields, similar methods are studied under the heading of "residual analysis" in texts on linear and nonlinear models. In the sections of this chapter we will simplify this material and relate it to the regression analysis of Chapters 12 and 13. Students may follow their interests in topics of econometrics in subsequent courses. Familiarity with and use of a computer would be essential in such courses.

Four particular violations of the "common" assumptions are studied in this chapter. When the explanatory variables are linearly related to each other, the violation is called *multicollinearity*. This problem is discussed in Section 14.3. If the disturbance terms are linearly related with each other, the problem is called *autocorrelation*. If the variance of the disturbance term in the model is not constant across observations, the violation is called *heteroscedasticity*. These situations are discussed in Sections 14.4 and 14.5, respectively. Section 14.6 considers some situations for which the true relation between the dependent and the explanatory variable(s) is *nonlinear* and not well represented by direct application of the *linear* regression model. In the final section, 14.7, we give a checklist for the preparation of a research report or term paper using a regression model.

14.2 THE "COMMON" ASSUMPTIONS AND CONDITIONS

Five assumptions for simple linear regression were presented in Section 12.4. These were generalized to the multiple regression case in Section 13.3, wherein two extra conditions were included as well. We repeat this listing below and add one other obvious condition which is appropriate if we are to directly apply our methods of Chapters 12 and 13 to any practical case of estimation and testing of the linear regression model. After the listing, more explanation about these items is given. Later sections of this chapter deal extensively with some particular items from this list.

Assumption 1. *The error term ϵ is independent of each of the m independent variables, $x_1, x_2, \ldots, x_m$.*

Assumption 2. *The errors ϵ_i for all possible sets of given values $x_1, x_2, \ldots, x_m$ are normally distributed.*

Assumption 3. *The expected value of the errors is zero for all possible sets of given values $x_1, x_2, \ldots, x_m$. That is, $E[\epsilon_i] = 0$ for $i = 1, 2, \ldots, n$.*

Assumption 4. *The variance of the errors is finite and is the same for all possible sets of given values $x_1, x_2, \ldots, x_m$. That is, $V[\epsilon_i] = \sigma_\epsilon^2$ is a constant for $i = 1, 2, \ldots, n$.*

Assumption 5. *Any two errors ϵ_i and ϵ_t are independent; i.e., their covariance is zero, $C[\epsilon_i, \epsilon_t] = 0$ for $i \neq t$.*

Condition 1. *None of the independent variables is an exact linear combination of the other independent variables.*

Condition 2. *The number of observations (n) must exceed the number (m + 1) of coefficients being estimated; that is, n > m + 1.*

Condition 3. *The true relation between the variables denoted by **y** and **x** in the model is a "straight-line" (linear) relation.*

Correlation Between x_j and the Disturbance ϵ

The first assumption was used in the previous presentation on least-squares estimation. It concerns the independence between the explanatory variables and the disturbance term in the same observation period. This means that the covariance between the values of an explanatory variable and the corresponding error terms is zero, $C[\epsilon_i, x_{ij}] = 0$. This assumption will be true necessarily when x is a *fixed* variable with values known in advance, rather than a *random* variable with values drawn from an underlying sampling distribution. When x is a fixed variable, it must be independent of the random variable ϵ, since the covariance of a random variable and a constant is always zero. The constant has no variation from its fixed values. When **x** is a random variable, this assumption may be violated, and many of our previous results are *not* true.

A violation of assumption 1 most often results from either measurement error or simultaneity between **y** and x_j. Let us first consider the problem arising from **simultaneity** when the underlying theory suggests not only a causal relation from the variable x_j affecting **y**, but also from **y** to x_j. Such a two-way causal ordering cannot be adequately reflected in a single-equation model. Instead, a set of simultaneous equations is needed in which both **y** and x_j are *jointly* dependent variables based on other explanatory variables and one or more disturbance terms.

Using the implication symbol ($\rightarrow$) for direction of causality, we denote the two-way relationship by $y \leftrightarrow x_j$ in contrast to the single-equation model having $y \leftarrow x_j$. Consider a simple regression model, $y = \alpha + \beta x + \epsilon$, where both x and ϵ are used to determine y; $(x, \epsilon) \rightarrow y$. If **y** also is a cause of **x**, so that $y \rightarrow x$, then $\epsilon \rightarrow y \rightarrow x$. A dependency is created between the disturbance term ϵ and the explanatory variable **x**. In this case of simultaneity it is no longer valid to assume that $C[x, \epsilon] = 0$.

Example 14.1. A typical simultaneous relation between two variables involves the relation between **x** = national income and **y** = consumption expenditures. Methods of determining national accounts prescribe that national income is determined by summing the important types of expenditures in the economy (because in any transaction what one agent spends is income for another agent). Thus, $y \rightarrow x$, since consumption expenditures (as well as investment expenditures, government expenditures, and foreign expenditures on our exports, etc.) is a component of national income:

National income = Consumption + Investment + Government + Net exports.

On the other hand, a simple model to determine the level of consumption expenditures is theoretically specified to include national income as an explanatory factor:

$$\text{Consumption} = \alpha + \beta(\text{National income}) + \epsilon,$$

which means that $y \leftarrow x$. The two considerations together give $y \leftrightarrow x$. This simultaneity means that in the consumption function the disturbance ϵ will be related to the income variable in violation of assumption 1.

Another common problem resulting in a violation of assumption 1 is **error in measurement** of the explanatory variable. If the variable x_j is incorrectly measured, say by a constant percentage, as in a 1% error in measurement, then for larger values of x_j, the size of the error, $\epsilon = 0.01x_j$, would also be larger. The correlation between x_j and ϵ will not be zero, especially if the error-in-measurement component dominates the other components of the overall disturbance.

Example 14.2. Let y be aggregate consumption expenditures and x be national income measured over the years 1950–1985, and suppose the measurement error is a percentage of the value of x. Since these values have increased by more than a factor of 10 (but less than 100) since 1950, it is likely that the size of the typical errors of measurement are changed by one order of magnitude (one decimal place). Thus, the random variable is larger in 1985 than it was in 1950. In this case the probability of observing larger-sized errors increases as the size of the variable x increases, as shown in Fig. 14.1. Also, the variance of the errors is changing, a violation of assumption 4.

Other violations of assumption 1 may occur when an important variable is omitted from the regression analysis.

Example 14.3. Let us consider the problem of estimating demand for U.S. compact cars, where the quantity demanded is y and the price of compacts is x. For simplicity, suppose that we assume that the only variable of importance omitted from this model is the price of the substitute good, import compacts. If the price of U.S. compacts increases, we would expect a lower demand for U.S. compacts, assuming that all other factors are equal. But all other factors are not equal, since demand also depends on the price of imports. If, as the price of U.S. compacts increases, it becomes more and more difficult to predict demand (i.e., the errors increase because we do not know what will happen to the price of imports), then assumption 1 is violated. Figure 14.2 illustrates this situation by a diagram showing errors on the vertical axis.

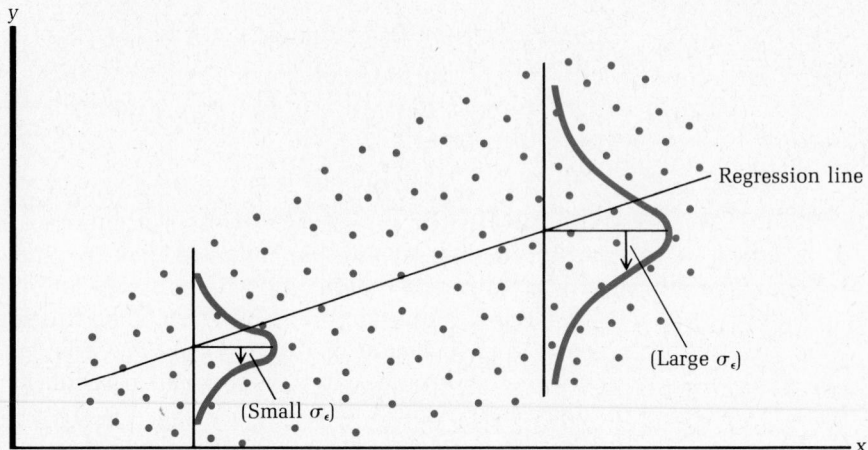

FIGURE 14.1 **Violation of assumption 1 (and assumption 4).**

Many other examples can be cited in which behavior is fairly exact for moderate values of the independent variables but erratic for extreme high or low values of **x**. These also correspond to violations of assumption 1.

Example 14.4. Suppose that **y** is investment expenditures by firms and **x** is annual growth in sales. If sales growth is 5–10%, firms might make corresponding investment expenditures to replace worn-out equipment and buy some new goods to allow for some expansion of production.

FIGURE 14.2 **Illustration of how larger values of x may lead to larger errors, a violation of assumption 1.**

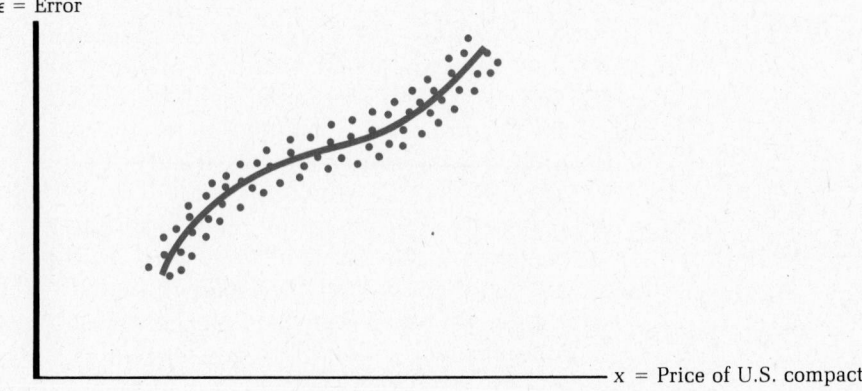

This behavioral response would be quite consistent across firms. However, suppose that sales growth for a group of firms was 75–100%. More variation in response could be expected. Some firms might feel very optimistic and make large investment expenditures to double their output. Others might be very cautious and feel that the sales growth was a one-time increase. They might save the extra revenues temporarily and not expand at all. They might not even replace what wears out, and instead, use the current sales figures as motivation to sell out at a good price. Large variations in investment decisions could also be expected in response to a sudden downturn indicated by a negative growth in sales. Thus, the errors ϵ would be quite large in estimating investment at a high (or low) level of sales growth because the behavior predicted in the model is not systematic under these circumstances. The errors ϵ and the sales growth x are not independent because the relation fits much better (small ϵ) in the range of x where investment behavior is consistent and fits much worse (large ϵ) in the ranges of x where firms make widely different decisions on investment expenditures. Figure 14.3 represents this situation.

All these cases of potential violations of assumption 1 have quite serious implications for our analysis. When assumption 1 is violated, the primary effect is that our estimators, a for the intercept α, b_j for the slope coefficients β_j, and s_e^2 for the variance of the disturbance σ_ϵ^2, are all *biased*. This also affects the correctness of the *t*- and *F*-distributed test statistics that we presented in Chapters 12 and 13. In practice, nearly every model relating economic or business variables will involve some extent of mismeasurement, simultaneity, or changing behavior that may cause a violation of assumption 1. When the specified relation among y and $x_1, x_2, \ldots, x_m$ is relatively strong and these potential violations are

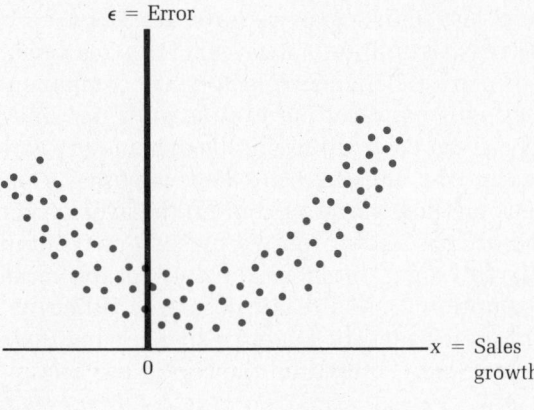

FIGURE 14.3 **Illustration of errors dependent on sales growth, a violation of assumption 1.**

minor, the extent of the bias in our estimators may not be worth worrying about. In cases in which the problem is potentially severe, a partial remedy is often obtained by using a two-stage method of estimation. We do not pursue this topic further in this text, but interested readers can consult textbooks in econometrics under the topics of "instrumental variable estimation" and "simultaneity."

Normal Distribution of ϵ with Mean Zero

Assumptions 2 and 3 are generally not violated in a well-specified model for which a full range of values is available for the measures of the variables. Errors in processes, errors in nature, deviation in measures of behavior, and other disturbances tend to be normally distributed. Specific errors caused by wars, floods, elections, diseases, or other "shocks" are not. All such error components, as well as other errors due to systematic business, economic, and noneconomic factors not explicitly included in the model, are blotted together in the disturbance term ϵ. Since ϵ is a composite of so many factors and since many of these factors are unrelated to each other, it is reasonable to assume that many of them act to offset each other. Therefore, large values of ϵ are much less likely to occur than small values, giving a bell-shaped distribution of errors. Indeed, when *many independent* factors act together to determine a random variable, a form of the *central limit theorem* guarantees that their joint effect produces a normally distributed random variable. Consequently, when the important explanatory factors are included in the model and *many other linearly independent* factors are components of the error term, it is reasonable to expect *normally distributed errors*.

The value of assumption 2 (as stated in Section 12.7) is that the distributions of the estimators for the coefficients in the model depend on the probability distribution of ϵ. Thus, if assumption 2 holds, these estimators will be normally distributed. Also, the implications of the normal distribution for ϵ make it proper to develop and use the *t*- and *F*-distributed test statistics as we have described.

Similarly, assumption 3 is generally reasonable for the regression model. If many independent factors are components of the disturbance term, they will be offsetting to a large degree and quite unpredictable. Thus, for a given set of values for the explanatory variables, the differences between the true and the estimated values of y ought to be sometimes positive, sometimes negative, but on the average zero. If the data are not truncated or censored or limited by some maximum or minimum bound so that the full range of potential values for the variables can be observed, then assumption 2 should not pose any difficulty. Both assumptions 2 and 3 are represented in Fig. 14.4 by showing the distribution of any ϵ_i to be normal and centered on the regression line.

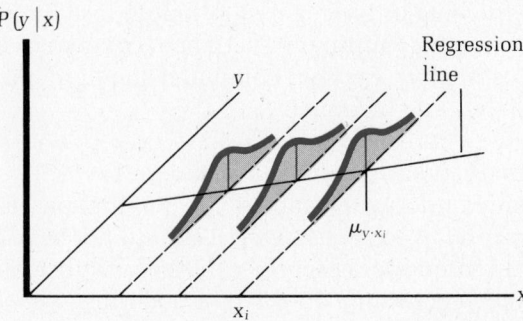

FIGURE 14.4 **Normally distributed errors ϵ_i about $\mu_{y \cdot x_i}$ for any value x_i (given that assumptions 3 and 4 also hold).**

Assumption 3 is important because it establishes the estimability of the intercept α. Along with assumption 1 it is required in order to establish that the least-squares estimators of the coefficients are *unbiased*.

Constant Variance   We specify in assumption 4 that the dispersion or variability of points in the population about the true regression equation must be constant. In Fig. 14.4 this constant variance of ϵ_i is represented by depicting all the normal distributions about $\mu_{y \cdot x_i}$ as having the same standard deviation. No one distribution is more spread out or more compact than another for a different value of x.

Assumption 4 is violated most often in data measured at the same point of time (*cross-sectional data*). For example, in a study relating certain variables across the United States, assumption 4 might be violated because of differing state legal codes, climate, or political interests. Similarly, a study relating educational attainment and household income might be affected by differing races or locations (urban, suburban, rural).

We point out that when assumption 1 is violated because of proportional errors in measuring x, assumption 4 (constant variance) will also be violated. Thus, Fig. 14.1 is also an illustration of the violation of assumption 4, because the distribution of errors is more spread out (i.e., larger variances) for higher values of x than for lower values of x. Usually, assumption 4 is referred to as the assumption of *homoscedasticity*.

The importance of assumption 4 is that it allows us to estimate only one variance of the disturbance rather than many different levels of variance across observations. Since the disturbance variance (σ_ϵ^2) is a term in the specification of the probability distribution of each least-squares estimator or of a forecast based on these estimators (refer to table 12.9), it is convenient to have one representation for this value rather than many. If assumption 4 does not hold and we fail to utilize the information about the changing variance of ϵ, the least-squares estimators of the coefficients in the regression model lose the desirable property of *efficiency* (having minimum variance compared to any other linear unbiased estimator). Further, computed standard errors for the estimated coefficients will be incorrect.

Independence of the Disturbances

If each observation on values of y and x_j, $j = 1, 2, \ldots, m$, is to be used for maximum information about the population regression model, the "noise" (errors) in each observation should not be related. Otherwise, the relationship among our observed values is unduly affected in a nonrandom way by some continuing effects of a one-time "shock" or the temporary effect of an excluded variable. This problem of carry-over effects from one error to the next tends to occur in *time-series* data, especially when the time intervals are short.

If some underlying factors not specified in the model exert an influence on the fit of the model over several time periods, the disturbances tend to be correlated to each other. Consider a change in corporate tax laws that might affect both the amount of investment (due to investment tax credit or depreciation write-offs) and the amount of retained earnings (due to taxes on profits). This legal factor may not be represented in the model, but its effect may be seen in the errors of the regression equation. The average relationship estimated may give values too high before the tax-law change and too low afterwards. The residuals would then tend to be all negative for observations taken before the tax change and all positive for observations made after the change. Thus, the residuals would not be occurring at random but would systematically be related to each other; this problem is called *autocorrelation*.

Example 14.5. Suppose we are studying the demand for automobiles and we have collected data on sales and economic factors of demand over time. If we have weekly observations, we would have to include in our model variables representing rebates, special financing arrangements, or other marketing features that are introduced and withdrawn, causing changes in weekly sales. If we use annual data, we might assume that these minor variations balance out over the year and are represented well enough by a measure of annual marketing and advertising expenses. The errors ϵ_i from annual data are not as likely to be related to each other, owing to the continuing influence of a one-time "shock," as are the errors from weekly data.

Suppose a safety defect for an automobile is announced, and cautious buyers delay purchases of that automobile or buy another brand. The effect could decrease sales of the automobile over *several* weeks. Our model would tend to overpredict during these successive weeks because of the negative value of the disturbance terms. Suppose, after several weeks, another announcement proclaims that further tests indicate that the safety defect is not widespread and no recalls are needed. At the same time a consumer magazine rates this automobile as one of the "best buys" of all new cars. Sales may pick up and exceed the predicted value from our model for several weeks. The successive positive disturbances are affected by these factors that are *not* included in the model. Assumption 5 is violated since the errors are correlated with previous values rather than being independent of them. Figure 14.5 indicates the situation of dependent, nonrandom disturbances in a simple graph of the values of ϵ over time.

Autocorrelation can also be related to some of the same causes as error in measurement or heteroscedasticity. First, suppose that one explanatory variable is measured with error and is available only annually, whereas the other explanatory variables are measured monthly. If we interpolate within the year to approximate a series of monthly values for the annually observed variable, it is likely that we will also apportion a related share of its error of measurement into the successive monthly values. This would introduce autocorrelation into the disturbances.

Second, cross-sectional data that lead to heteroscedasticity may also lead to a violation of assumption 5 called *spatial autocorrelation*. Many of the same excluded factors may be influencing the error term over different observations. This is particularly true, for example, if the cross-sections are regions such as states and the variables are aggregates of individual measures of economic activity. The state boundaries determine to which aggregate a certain individual measure belongs (such as persons included in a census), but these state boundaries are politically or geographically determined. Economic activity on both sides of the bound-

FIGURE 14.5 **Time-sequence plots of autocorrelated errors ϵ_t.**

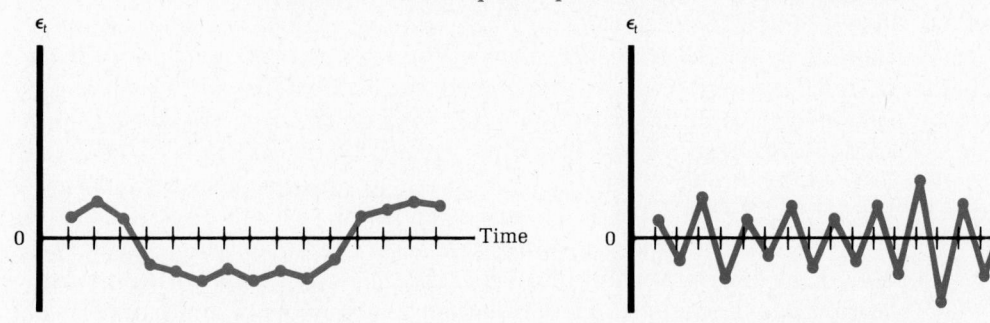

(a) Direct dependence   (b) Oscillating pattern

ary may be affected to a significant extent by the same underlying factors, such as the weather, the quality of the land, the education and culture and productivity of the workers, and so on. Since such common factors are absorbed by the error term, autocorrelation is likely to result among errors for states in the same geographic region.

Conditions 1, 2, and 3   These final conditions about the regression analysis are required in order for our least-squares statistics to have the meaningful interpretations that we gave them in Chapters 12 and 13. Condition 1 requiring linear independence among the explanatory variables is necessary in order for our calculations of estimates to be defined. If it were violated and there existed a perfect linear dependency among the explanatory variables, we would be trying to perform calculations that are essentially the same as dividing a number by zero. Even a "near violation" of condition 1 causes difficulty in distinguishing the separate effects on y of the included explanatory variables. This problem, called *multicollinearity*, is discussed in Section 14.3.

Condition 2, that $n > m + 1$, is essential in order to have positive degrees of freedom in our test statistics. No meaningful conclusions can be drawn from our model unless the results are based on a sufficient number of sample observations.

Finally, condition 3 requires that our model specifies a linear relation between y and x_j. If the variables that are represented by these measures of y and x_j do not have a linear relation, we face an obvious problem of misspecification. This may produce rather unreliable results. The statistical methods of regression analysis are only as good as the data and the specification of the model allow them to be. If the true relation among y and x_j is nonlinear, a transformation of variables might be employed before using the linear model. We examine some examples of such transformations in Section 14.6.

Properties of the Regression Coefficients   As we indicated previously, the five assumptions presented above provide a rationale for the widespread use of the least-squares procedure. Given assumption 2, it can be shown that the estimators of α, β, and $\mu_{y \cdot x}$ obtained by using the least-squares criterion are *identical* to the estimators that would result from using the principle of maximum likelihood estimation. (Refer to Section 8.3.) Such estimators have a number of desirable properties (such as consistency).

A second important result related to the least-squares estimators is called the **Gauss–Markov theorem.** This classical result of linear estimation was formulated by the German mathematician and astronomer, Karl F. Gauss (1777–1855), in his early works published in 1807 and

1821. Since these involved applications in physics and planetary motion, they generally remained unknown to social scientists and businessmen until they were restated in a more modern context by A. A. Markov in 1912, in a study of linear processes. In the 1930's the work of Markov was extended and applied directly to least-squares estimation in several ways, and the Gauss–Markov Theorem assumed the identity it has today:

> Gauss–Markov Theorem: If assumptions 1, 3, 4, and 5 hold true, then the estimators of α, β and $\mu_{y \cdot x}$ determined by the least-squares criterion are Best Linear Unbiased Estimators (BLUE).

In the above context the term *linear* means that the estimators are straight-line functions of the values of the dependent variable y. They are *unbiased* because their expected value is equal to the population value (given that assumptions 1 and 3 are true). They are *best* in the sense of being *efficient* (if assumptions 4 and 5 are true). That is, the least-squares estimators have a variance smaller than that of any other linear unbiased estimator. Thus, the importance of the Gauss–Markov theorem is that if assumptions 1, 3, 4, and 5 hold, the least-squares estimators have the desirable properties of unbiasedness and efficiency.

Define. *Assumptions for multiple regression, econometrics, measurement error, simultaneity, spatial autocorrelation, Gauss–Markov theorem, times-series or cross-sectional data.*

PROBLEMS

14.1 Explain why a disturbance term ϵ is included in the population regression model.

14.2 Explain what is meant by "best" in a best linear unbiased estimator (BLUE).

14.3 Consider which assumption(s) may be violated in each of the following cases for a simple model of the form $y = \alpha + \beta x + \epsilon$.
a) y and x are both growing over time, and the error in measurement of x is a constant 3% of the size of x.
b) x measures unemployment and y measures the change in average wages for quarterly observations from 1960–1970. During 1962–1965 there are externally controlled wage and price guidelines so that the model consistently overpredicts wages during this period.

c) The specified model is erroneous, and the true form of the relation between y and x is similar to the right half of a convex (with respect to x) parabola. (*Hint:* Draw a scatter diagram of such a parabolic relation and draw a straight line through it representing the best linear fit. Examine the signs of successive residuals.)

14.4 Consider a model specifying annual aggregate consumption dependent on disposable personal income and a disturbance term, as in Consumption $= \alpha + \beta$ (income) $+ \epsilon$.
   a) For assumptions 1–5, discuss the implication of each on the underlying economic environment in which this model is presumed to hold.
   b) Criticize one of the assumptions and suggest a reason why it may impose an invalid background condition.

14.5 Consider a model specifying quarterly corporate dividends dependent on total corporate profits in the preceding four quarters and a disturbance term. Answer parts (a) and (b) of Problem 14.4 in this context.

14.6 Give an argument that explains why any one of the standard assumptions for regression analysis would be violated, in each of the following situations, for a simple model of the form $y = \alpha + \beta x + \epsilon$. Also, suggest how the violation of this assumption would affect the properties of the ordinary least-squares (OLS) estimators.
   a) y measures wealth of an individual and x measures this person's age; $V[y]$ increases with age.
   b) Observations on y and x are daily stock averages and volume of trading, respectively.

14.7 Explain the meaning of each of the following assumptions in which ϵ is a random term in a linear-regression model. Give an example of some specified model that might violate each assumption, and explain why.
   a) $C[\epsilon_i, \epsilon_t] = 0$ for $i \neq t$.
   b) $V[\epsilon_i] \neq \sigma_\epsilon^2$ for all i.

14.8 For the model specified in Problem 13.15 on academic test scores, select one of the assumptions 1–5 of Section 14.2 and express its meaning in terms of the model. Suggest some real situation for which the assumption would probably be violated.

14.9 Repeat Problem 14.8 for the model on corn yield specified in Problem 13.12.

14.3 MULTICOLLINEARITY

We now consider special problems that arise when one of the conditions specified in Section 14.2 is violated. We first consider the violation or near violation of condition 1, which specifies that none of the independent variables can be an exact linear combination of the other independent variables. If the independent variables, $x_1, x_2, \ldots, x_m$ are perfectly linearly related to each other, they are linearly *dependent*. In this case, no estimates of the partial regression coefficients can be obtained, since the normal equations will not be solvable; that is, the method of least squares breaks down and no estimates can be calculated. Perfect dependence seldom occurs in practice because most investigators are careful not to include in the regression model two or more explanatory variables that represent the same influence on the dependent variable *y*. Indeed, even if an investigator did accidentally include two or more such variables, it is unlikely that the *sample* observations representing measures of these variables would be perfectly related because some slight errors of measurement and sampling are almost inevitable.

Sometimes, however, special problems do occur when two or more of the independent variables are strongly (but not perfectly) related to one another. This situation is known as **multicollinearity.** When multicollinearity occurs, it is possible to calcualte least-squares estimates, but difficulty arises in the interpretation of the separate effects of each explanatory variable.

Example 14.6. In our investment example (sections 13.2 and 13.3), the variable x_2 (retained earnings) was correlated with the stock price index (x_1). By using x_1 alone, 83.45% of the variation in *y* is explained; by using x_2 alone, 77.7% of the variation in *y* is explained. However, by using both x_1 and x_2, the combined explained variation is 89% of the total variation. Thus, there is considerable *overlap* in the explanatory roles of the variables x_1 and x_2, probably since both react to other economic, political, and social factors within the society. Precisely distinguishing the separate influences of the two variables is the problem caused by multicollinearity. In this example we realize that there is some collinearity because of the large correlation between x_1 and x_2 (the simple correlation between the two independent variables can be shown to be $r_{x_1 x_2} = 0.8158$), but this may or may not constitute a serious multicollinearity problem.

Detection of a Multicollinearity Problem

From the above discussion we see that a high correlation between any pair of explanatory variables x_j and x_k may be used to help identify multicollinearity. It is possible, however, for all independent variables to have relatively small *mutual* correlations and yet to have some multicollinearity among three or more of them. Sometimes it is possible to detect these higher-order associations by using a multiple correlation coefficient that deals only with the explanatory variables. Suppose that we use the symbol R_j to denote the multiple correlation coefficient of variable x_j with all the other $(m - 1)$ independent variables, $x_1, x_2, \ldots, x_{j-1}, x_{j+1}, \ldots,$ x_m. Such a measure could be determined for each of the independent variables. Generally, if one or more of these values, $R_1, R_2, \ldots, R_j, \ldots,$ R_m, is approximately the same size as the multiple correlation coefficient $R_{y \cdot x_1 \ldots x_m}$, then multicollinearity is a problem. In other words, if the strength of the association among any of the independent variables is approximately as great as the strength of their combined linear association with the dependent variable, then the amount of overlapping influence may be substantial enough to make the interpretation of the separate influences difficult and imprecise.

Example 14.7. Consider a model with four independent variables,

$$y = \alpha + \beta_1 x_1 + \beta_2 x_2 + \beta_3 x_3 + \beta_4 x_4 + \epsilon.$$

The multiple correlation coefficient for this model is

$$R_{y \cdot x_1 x_2 x_3 x_4} = 0.90.$$

To check for multicollinearity, one would first calculate the six simple correlations between pairs of independent variables

$$r_{x_1 x_2}, \quad r_{x_1 x_3}, \quad r_{x_1 x_4}, \quad r_{x_2 x_3}, \quad r_{x_2 x_4}, \quad r_{x_3 x_4}.$$

If one of these is close to unity, then imprecise estimation will result. The next step would be to calculate the multiple correlation coefficients of each explanatory variable with the other three, that is,

$$R_{x_1 \cdot x_2 x_3 x_4}, \quad R_{x_2 \cdot x_1 x_3 x_4}, \quad R_{x_3 \cdot x_1 x_2 x_4}, \quad \text{and} \quad R_{x_4 \cdot x_1 x_2 x_3}.$$

If any of these are as large as $R_{y \cdot x_1 x_2 x_3 x_4} = 0.90$, then the problem of multicollinearity may be substantial. If the number of observations is quite small, these comparisons may be made by using adjusted R measures (analogous to the adjusted R^2 measures in Section 13.3), which are corrected for the different number of variables involved. We do not present any statistical method for testing whether these values indicate high multicollinearity or not. Since this multicollinearity is a property of the sample observtions, no inference about the population is needed.

Study Question 14.1: Multicollinearity in the Housing Price Model
Examine the extent of multicollinearity in the data for the multiple regression model for housing price (Table 13.2 and Fig. 13.3),

$$\text{PRICE} = \alpha + \beta_1(\text{INCOME}) + \beta_2(\text{RENT}) + \beta_3(\text{VACANT}) + \epsilon.$$

Answer. The value of the multiple correlation coefficient for the model is

$$R = \sqrt{R^2} = \sqrt{0.8737} = 0.935.$$

The mutual correlation coefficients among all the variables are given below (note the symmetry of correlations between any pair of variables):

	PRICE	INCOME	RENT	VACANT
PRICE	1.00000	0.55757	0.88652	−0.80947
INCOME	0.55757	1.00000	0.61351	−0.56950
RENT	0.88652	0.61351	1.00000	−0.67098
VACANT	−0.80947	−0.56950	−0.67098	1.00000

None of these is close to unity (positive or negative). The largest (in absolute value) correlation coefficient between any two explanatory variables is $r_{RENT,VACANT} = -0.67$.

The next step is to relate each x_j with the other two explanatory variables using a computer program for multiple regression or correlation. It is found that the multiple correlation coefficients of each explanatory variable with the other two are:

$$R_{INCOME \cdot x_2 x_3} = 0.649;$$

$$R_{RENT \cdot x_1 x_3} = 0.727;$$

$$R_{VACANT \cdot x_1 x_2} = 0.700.$$

None of these is as large as $R_{y \cdot x_1 x_2 x_3} = 0.935$. Multicollinearity is probably not a serious problem for this estimation.

Effects of Multicollinearity

When multicollinearity occurs, the least-squares estimates are still unbiased and efficient. The problem is that the estimated standard error of the coefficient (say, s_{b_j} for the coefficient b_j) tends to be inflated. This standard error tends to be larger than it would be in the absence of multicollinearity because the estimates are very sensitive to any changes in the sample observations or in the model specification. In other words, including or excluding a particular variable or certain observations may greatly change the estimated partial coefficient. When s_{b_j} is larger than it should be, the t-value for testing the significance of β_j is smaller than it should be [Formula (13.13)]. Thus, one is likely to conclude that a variable x_j is not important in the relationship when it really is.

> When the presence of multicollinearity is quite severe, we have less confidence in the estimates of the coefficients. They are prone to have excessively large variances and are not precise in distinguishing the separate effects on **y** of the individual explanatory variables.

If the purpose of the model is *forecasting* values for the dependent variable **y** based on new observations of the explanatory variables, the multicollinearity problem may not need any drastic correction. If the multicollinearity can be expected to continue, forecasts are not seriously disturbed, since the individual estimates of the coefficients are unbiased. Further, the forecasts are not severely upset by minor changes in the specification among sets of collinear variables. For example, if some excluded variable should be in the true specification, but it is highly correlated with the set of included variables, then its omission is not serious in terms of forecasting. Although its absence introduces a specification bias in the estimated coefficients, the combined effect on the collinear variables would be relatively neutral. Thus, forecasts would not be significantly affected.

To repeat this point in a slightly different way, the effect of severe multicollinearity may be to increase s_{b_j} so much that no coefficient b_j is significantly different from zero. Yet the joint effect of all the explanatory variables in the model is highly significant. The model may have a high value of R^2 based on the sample observations. This high degree of fit indicates that the estimated values will be very close to the observed values within the sample. If this multicollinearity continues for new observations and the specification is not changed, the model will also give a close fit for these new sample values. Forecasts based on them will be close to the actual values.

Correction for Multicollinearity

The primary problem of multicollinearity is that the values of b_j are quite imprecise. Unfortunately, there is no one best remedy for this problem in all cases, nor even a consistent ranking of possible remedies that should be attempted. With some skill and a lot of luck, one of the following alternatives might provide more precise estimates of the desired coefficients.

Changing the Specification. One common procedure is to select the independent variable *most seriously involved* in the multicollinearity and remove it from the model. The difficulty with this approach is that the model now may not correctly represent the population relationship, and all estimated coefficients would contain a *specification bias*. It would be better to try to replace the multicollinear variable with another that is less collinear but may still measure the same theoretical construct.

Example 14.8. If the theoretical variable "business expectations" is measured by a stock price index that is highly collinear with retained earnings, then it may be possible to replace the stock index with some other measure, perhaps an index of business expectations obtained by surveying executives in the 500 largest corporations. In this way the multicollinearity may be reduced while the theoretical base for the model is still retained. Of course, the change in variables is useful only if the new variable is less collinear with the other explanatory variables than was the original variable.

A second way to change the specification is to express all the important interrelations among the explanatory variables as separate equations in the specification. The model-builder has to specify a number of the variables (equal to the number of equations in the model) as jointly dependent. The coefficients can be reestimated in the context of a simultaneous equations model. The formulation, identification, and estimation of such models and their unique problems are topics in econometrics not treated in this book.

Transformation or Aggregation of Variables. Sometimes the problem of multicollinearity is resolved by making suitable changes in the definitions of the variables in the model. Two popular suggestions are *aggregations* and *transformations* of variables. An aggregation follows some rule for combining several variables into one *composite variable*. A transformation follows a rule for creating a new variable (call it x^*) as a function of current or past values of one of the given variables.

Transformations that are commonly used are ordinary first differences or logarithmic first differences. For a variable x these are represented by the transformation rules, $x_t^* = x_t - x_{t-1}$ and $x_t^* = \ln(x_t/x_{t-1}) = \ln(x_t) - \ln(x_{t-1})$, respectively, for observations $t = 2, 3, \ldots, n$. The error terms in the model must also be transformed accordingly. The assumptions for least-squares estimation from Section 14.2 must apply to the transformed variables and error terms. These do not automatically hold true even if they were true for the model before the transformation.

The logarithmic first difference is often used to eliminate the effect of trends and cycles in a time series. To the extent that the explanatory variables have trends and cyclical components in common, this transformation helps to reduce multicollinearity.

Such transformations are also useful when forecasts are to be made based on new observations of the explanatory variables. If a growth trend occurs, new values would tend to be larger than any previously observed values. Forecast intervals would be excessively large owing to the large deviation of the new given value from the sample mean of the previous observations. (Refer to Section 12.8.) However, the size of the first difference or of the logarithmic first difference is probably within the range of previous experience of such differences. Thus, the standard error for the forecast of the difference would not be exaggerated, and the confidence interval would not be unduly wide.

The type of aggregation of variables that is most common is a grouping of collinear variables into a composite index that allows a similar interpretation. (Index numbers are discussed in Section 15.6). For example, four separate interest rate variables that are highly correlated with each other may be replaced by some single weighted composite of these variables. The total effect of the interest rate variables on the dependent variable may still be reflected by the coefficient of this single variable, and the multicollinearity in the model may be eliminated.

Forming a composite in this way is fruitful only if the variables included in the composite have some useful *combined* interpretation. The meaning of the composite will be unclear if too many diverse factors are involved. Statistically, the formation of a composite is most useful if the included variables are highly correlated with each other and each has a low correlation with the remaining explanatory variables not included within the composite.

Improvements in the Data or the Calculations. Very frequently, multicollinearity may occur as a result of data that are limited in coverage and do not adequately represent the domain of the variables being sampled. If additional data could be acquired, it is possible that more independent variation would be observed. Thereby, the multicollinearity would be reduced. The new data may be obtained simply by increasing the sample size. If this is not possible within the restraints of the variable definitions, model specification, and purpose of the analysis, an independent study may be done on a suitable submodel for which other data can be used. On the basis of this submodel, one or more of the coefficients of some collinear variables in the original model may be approximated by these so-called **extraneous estimates.** By using these extraneous estimates, the *other* coefficients in the original model may be estimated from the original data under conditions of reduced multicollinearity.

Example 14.9. Suppose the model $y = \alpha + \beta_1 x_1 + \beta_2 x_2 + \beta_3 x_3 + \epsilon$ is to be estimated, but x_2 and x_3 are highly correlated. If independent data are available that provide evidence on the relation between x_3 and the dependent variable y, an extraneous estimate of β_3 may be obtained, say $\hat{\beta}_3$. The model can be rewritten with a revised dependent variable and error term:

$$y^* = (y - \hat{\beta}_3 x_3) = \alpha + \beta_1 x_1 + \beta_2 x_2 + \epsilon^*.$$

The remaining coefficients, β_1 and β_2, can be estimated on the basis of the original data.

The use of extraneous estimates creates some other questions of interpretation and validity. More of the econometric literature on extraneous estimates should be studied before the reader uses this approach.

When multicollinearity is a problem, intermediate calculations used in multiple regression computer programs (to find determinants and inverses of matrices) are subject to roundoff error. These errors affect the calculations of the estimates (b_j) and their standard errors (s_{b_j}), the standard error of estimate (s_e), and the statistics for testing significance. Consequently, when a particular estimation of a model seems to involve multicollinearity, we should try to make the calculations of these inverses as precise as possible.†

14.4 AUTOCORRELATION

Assumption 5 in the list of "common" assumptions states that each disturbance is independent of each other; that is, $C[\epsilon_i \epsilon_t] = 0$, for $i \neq t$. If the disturbances tend to be correlated with each other, this assumption is violated. This situation is known as **autocorrelation** and is a frequently occurring problem.

Effect of Autocorrelation

As stated in Section 14.2, assumption 5 is crucial (along with assumption 4) for obtaining least-squares estimates of the coefficients that are *efficient*. If either or both of these assumptions (4 and 5) are violated, the estimators calculated by the method of least squares would not have the smallest possible variance. Some *other* unbiased estimator that uses *more information* would be the efficient one. Also, s_e^2 would no longer be an unbiased estimate of the variance of the disturbance (σ_ϵ^2). Thus, s_{b_j}, the estimated standard errors of the coefficients, would not be correct, and tests of hypotheses or confidence intervals based on these will not be correct.

Detection of Autocorrelation

The most frequently encountered form of autocorrelation is the linear association of successive residuals. If we denote a residual at time period t by e_t and the previous residual by e_{t-1}, first-order autocorrelation refers to the simple linear correlation of e_t with e_{t-1} over the entire set of observations, $t = 2, 3, 4, \ldots, n$. A measure of this correlation is given by the correlation coefficient between these two variables, $r_{e_t e_{t-1}}$. A geometric representation can be obtained by making a scatter diagram of the points corresponding to each pair (e_t, e_{t-1}). Figure 14.6 illustrates

---

† In using a computer for the calculations the program should be written in double precision with built-in checks for small determinants.

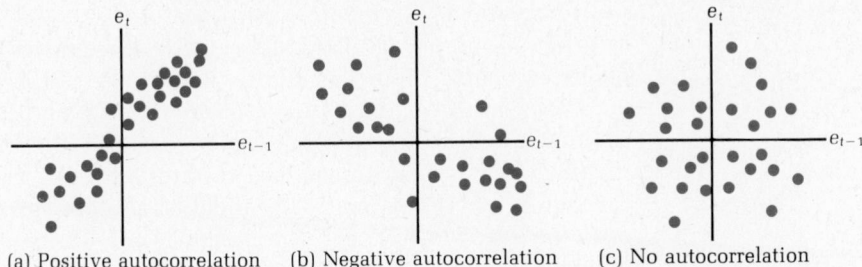

(a) Positive autocorrelation   (b) Negative autocorrelation   (c) No autocorrelation

FIGURE 14.6 **Plots of successive residuals.**

three cases: positive autocorrelation (a), negative autocorrelation (b), and no autocorrelation (c). When the points are predominantly in the positive quadrants (a), this means that successive residuals tend to have the same sign. If most points lie in the negative quadrants (b), then successive residuals tend to have opposite signs. If the scatter of points is spread over all quadrants (c), successive residuals tend to be independent.

Example 14.10. The residuals from our investment example are given in Table 14.1. A plot of e_t against e_{t-1} tends to look like Fig. 14.6(a), indicating positive autocorrelation. The reader can make such a sketch and note that the signs of the residuals tend to be grouped over time. The first group of five are positive residuals; the second group are mostly negative until the final four residuals, which are all positive. Thus, the least-squares estimates for this model, as given in Formula (13.3), probably are not efficient owing to the problem of autocorrelation.

Study Question 14.2: Residual Analysis in the Housing Price Model Make a plot of e_t against e_{t-1} as in Fig. 14.6 using the residuals in Table 14.2 from the housing price model (data and regression results given in Table 13.2 and Fig. 13.3(b), respectively). YHAT is the predicted value of price, and E is the residual. Interpret the meaning of the plot in terms of possible autocorrelation.

Answer. The plot in Fig. 14.7 is similar to Fig. 14.6(c), indicating no autocorrelation.

Although autocorrelation clearly exists in both Fig. 14.6(a) and Fig. 14.6(b), it is generally difficult to determine whether autocorrelation is present merely by using a scatter diagram. Hence, we need a test statistic to determine whether or not to accept the null hypothesis of independence

TABLE 14.1 **Residuals from the investment model**

SEQNUM	OBSERVED Y	PREDICTED Y	RESIDUAL
1	62.3	62.1	0.2
2	71.3	68.5	2.8
3	70.3	68.3	2.0
4	68.5	66.1	2.4
5	57.3	51.4	5.9
6	68.8	70.9	−2.1
7	72.2	80.9	−8.7
8	76.0	76.1	−0.1
9	64.3	70.9	−6.6
10	77.9	85.7	−7.8
11	84.3	76.5	7.8
12	85.1	86.7	−1.6
13	90.8	99.4	−8.6
14	97.9	107.3	−9.4
15	108.7	117.2	−8.5
16	122.4	128.0	−5.6
17	114.0	111.2	2.8
18	123.0	123.0	0.0
19	126.2	114.7	11.5
20	137.0	113.4	23.6

TABLE 14.2 **Residuals for housing model**

OBS	PRICE	YHAT	E
1	40100	46279.7	−6180
2	53200	56268.6	−3069
3	59100	46733.8	12366
4	31500	44009.5	−12510
5	46500	52636.3	−6136
6	38400	41739.3	−3339
7	49300	41285.3	8015
8	37900	37653.0	247
9	46800	50366.1	−3566
10	65900	51728.2	14172

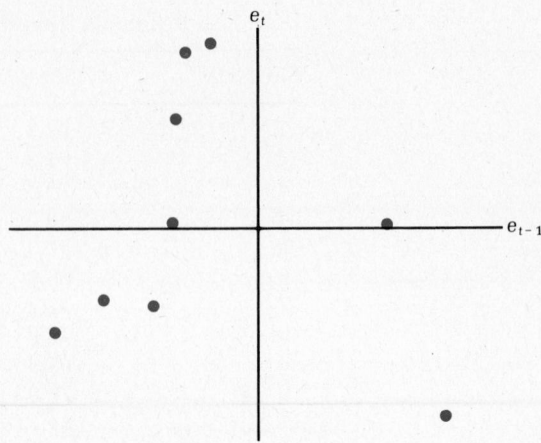

FIGURE 14.7 **Plot of successive residuals from Table 14.2.**

(no autocorrelation) among successive error terms. The test used most often for this purpose is called the Durbin–Watson test.

The Durbin– Watson Test

The **Durbin–Watson** (D–W) **test** is designed to test the null hypothesis that there is no first-order autocorrelation among the error terms. The alternative hypothesis is that first-order autocorrelation does exist. To be more precise, let us suppose that the relationship between the population errors ϵ_t and ϵ_{t-1} can be expressed as follows:

First-order autoregressive model of the errors:

$$\epsilon_t = \rho\epsilon_{t-1} + v_t,$$ (14.1)

where ρ is the population autocorrelation coefficient between ϵ_t and ϵ_{t-1}. The v_t are the error terms, and they satisfy assumptions 1–5 as applied to this model. When $\rho = 0$, no autocorrelation exists; the farther ρ is away from zero toward $+1.0$ or -1.0, the greater the autocorrelation.

The test statistic for autocorrelation is the value of d determined by the following equation:

Durbin–Watson statistic:

$$d = \frac{\sum_{t=2}^{n}(e_t - e_{t-1})^2}{\sum_{t=1}^{n}e_t^2}.$$ (14.2)

The following examples will demonstrate how to use Table X and Fig. 14.8 to detect the problem of autocorrelation.

Example 14.11. Suppose that we suspect the presence of positive autocorrelation in a particular regression problem involving $m = 3$ independent variables, $n = 45$ observations, and a calculated d-value, from Formula (14.2), of $d_c = 1.31$. The hypotheses are:

$$H_0: \text{no autocorrelation } (d = 2);$$

$$H_a: \text{positive autocorrelation } (d < 2).$$

Using the left side of Table X for $\alpha = 0.05$, we find $d_L = 1.38$ and $d_U = 1.67$. Since our computed value d_c is below d_L, we conclude that positive autocorrelation is a problem. We have in our model a significant violation of assumption 5.

Example 14.12. Suppose that we suspect the presence of negative autocorrelation in a particular regression problem where $m = 4$ independent variables, $n = 70$, $d_c = 2.94$, and $\alpha = 0.01$. The hypotheses are:

$$H_0: \text{no autocorrelation } (d = 2);$$

$$H_a: \text{negative autocorrelation } (d > 2).$$

Using the right side of Table X for $\alpha = 0.01$, we find $d_L = 1.34$ and $d_U = 1.58$. Since we are testing for negative autocorrelation and Table X gives values only for the test on positive autocorrelation, we must transform the d-statistic, using the property of symmetry. We find that the transformed critical values are $4 - d_L = 2.66$ and $4 - d_U = 2.42$. Since our computed value $d_c = 2.94$ lies above $4 - d_L$, we conclude that a significant problem of negative autocorrelation exists.

Most commonly, prior to calculating d from Formula (14.2) or before looking at a plot of successive residuals as in Fig. 14.6, it is not known whether to be suspicious of positive or negative autocorrelation (although positive correlation occurs much more frequently in business and economic applications of regression analysis). In this case, we really are using a two-sided test and should realize that *the proper significance level is found by doubling the values of 0.05 or 0.01 given in Table X.*

FIGURE 14.8 **Alternative conclusions based on the Durbin–Watson d-statistic.**

Positive autocorrelation	Don't know	No autocorrelation	Don't know	Negative autocorrelation
0	d_L d_U	2	$4 - d_U$ $4 - d_L$	4

Finally, recent research on the distribution of d and on alternate new statistics for detecting autocorrelation indicate that the inconclusive region in the D–W test may usually be reduced in the direction of d_U. That is, a single critical value separating the no-autocorrelation region from the positive-autocorrelation region moves closer to d_U as the collinearity increases among the explanatory variables in the model (and toward $4 - d_U$ for the negative autocorrelation test). Therefore, current users of the d-statistic would use the d_U- and d_L-values as indexes of the severity of the problem, replacing the original conclusions in Fig. 14.8 as follows:

$d < d_L$:	serious problem of positive autocorrelation that requires correction.
$d_L < d < d_U$:	weaker problem of positive autocorrelation for which a correction is probably worthwhile.
$d_U < d < 4 - d_U$:	no problem of autocorrelation worth correcting.
$4 - d_U < d < 4 - d_L$:	weaker problem of negative autocorrelation for which correction is probably worthwhile.
$4 - d_L < d$:	serious problem of negative autocorrelation that requires correction.

Example 14.13. Suppose that we wish to test for autocorrelation in a particular regression problem with $m = 2$ independent variables, $n = 100$, and $d_c = 1.60$. Using the table for $\alpha = 0.01$, we find $d_c > d_U = 1.58$. Thus, we accept the condition of no autocorrelation (along with the possibility of some unknown Type II error that we are accepting this when it is false). Using the table for $\alpha = 0.05$, we find that $d_c < d_L = 1.63$. In this case we would conclude that positive autocorrelation is a problem (accepting a potential Type I error of 0.10, since we must double the α-value in a two-sided test for which we did not know *a priori* whether the computed d_c would lie above or below the value 2.0). In this example the test conclusion is critically affected by the choice of the significance level $\alpha = 0.01$ or 0.05.

Study Question 14.3: Autocorrelation Test in the Investment Model
Compute and interpret the Durbin–Watson d-statistic for the investment model using a significance level of 0.05 (residuals given in Table 14.1).

Answer. By using Formula (14.2) the value of d is 0.784. By using Table X for $m = 2$ explanatory variables and $n = 20$ observations, the lower critical value is $d_L = 1.10$. Thus, the null hypothesis of no autocorrelation is rejected. The conclusion is that positive autocorrelation is a problem in this investment model.

Correction for Autocorrelation   Sometimes the problem of autocorrelation can be corrected by improving the specification of the model. This is especially true if the cause of the autocorrelation is the significant role of an *excluded* variable that has a strong cyclical pattern. Inclusion of such a variable or a transformation of included variables may often be effective. A commonly used transformation is suggested among the following statistical remedy.

Recall that the basic problem to be corrected is the inefficiency of the ordinary least squares (OLS) estimators of the coefficients in the model and incorrect standard errors of these estimators. An estimating procedure exists that also gives linear unbiased estimates and in which the variance of the estimators is smaller than that of OLS estimators. This procedure corrects for violations of assumption 5 by using a more complete estimating procedure, called **generalized least squares (GLS),** which explicitly uses in the calculation information about the variances and covariances of the error terms ϵ_i. This information is usually determined from an analysis of the residuals e_i obtained from a first OLS estimation of the regression model. The purpose in using this information is to generate a new model situation in which the new error terms are free of the violations of assumption 5.

For example, if the problem is a first-order positive autocorrelation of the errors, a method is needed whereby the data or the model can be transformed so that the revised error terms are free of autocorrelation. The model can be reestimated in terms of the transformed data. Estimators that are more efficient and that are still unbiased and consistent can be obtained in this way. The four steps for this practical remedy in the case of autocorrelation are:

1. Determine the residuals from the first estimation of the model and use the Durbin–Watson test to detect first-order autocorrelation.
2. Estimate the autocorrelation coefficient ρ using these residuals. Call this estimate $\hat{\rho}$.
3. Transform all the original data (including the intercept) according to the same autocorrelation pattern uncovered among the residuals in step 2. Call the transformed observations y^* for the dependent variable and x_j^* for each explanatory variable ($j = 1, 2, \ldots, m$).
4. Reestimate the model

$$y^* = \alpha(1 - \rho) + \beta_1 x_1^* + \beta_2 x_2^* + \cdots + \beta_m x_m^* + \epsilon^*,$$

using the transformed data (with $n - 1$ observations, since the first observation is lost in the transformation process).

There are several methods for finding the estimate of ρ needed in step 2. The population autocorrelation coefficient (ρ) is defined by the relation among the disturbances in Formula (14.1):

$$\epsilon_t = \rho \epsilon_{t-1} + \nu_t.$$

The estimate of ρ from the sample information is defined by the same relation among the residuals:

$$e_t = \hat{\rho} e_{t-1} + \text{errors}.$$

Thus, $\hat{\rho}$ can be found as the least-squares regression coefficient in the simple model relating current residuals e_t to their previous values e_{t-1}. It could also be determined from the serial correlation coefficient, $r_{e_t e_{t-1}}$. Both of these measures are related to the size of the squared differences between e_t and e_{t-1}, which is the numerator term in Formula (14.2). By algebraic manipulation and use of the definitions of correlation and regression coefficients (which are not necessary to recite here), a relation can also be found between the desired estimate $\hat{\rho}$ and the Durbin–Watson statistic d. For sufficiently large samples, the following approximation holds:

Approximation of the autocorrelation coefficient in terms of the Durbin–Watson statistic:

$$\hat{\rho} \simeq \tfrac{1}{2}(2 - d). \tag{14.3}$$

Since step 1 requires computation of d, the simplest and quickest way to find $\hat{\rho}$ for step 2 is to use Formula (14.3).

We find the transformed data in step 3 for observations $t = 2, 3, \ldots,$ n, for all variables in the model according to the following rule:

$$\text{(Transformed value)}_t = \text{(Original value)}_t - \hat{\rho}\text{(original value)}_{t-1}. \tag{14.4}$$

In the usual least-squares regression the correct values associated with the intercept are 1.0 for every observation. In the revised equation with transformed variables the correct values associated with the intercept would be $1 - \hat{\rho}$ for every observation. If it is easiest to use a standard least-squares regression program and inconvenient to have the program revise the intercept, the program can still be used. However, to determine the correct value of a and to make inference about α, the reported value of a and of its standard error (s_a) must be multiplied by the factor $1/(1 - \hat{\rho})$.

Whereas the initial disturbances violated assumption 5, the disturbances in the transformed model of step 4 are free of the first-order autocorrelation based on the coefficient $\hat{\rho}$. They are more independent than the original disturbances and may satisfy assumption 5. The Durbin–Watson statistic (d), based on the residuals from the transformed model, may serve as an index of the independence of the disturbances.

While these four steps give a rather simplified and modified version of a complete generalized least-squares estimation, this method usually does provide a worthwhile improvement in the efficiency of the estimators. It has the advantage of requiring only ordinary least-squares computations.

Example 14.14. Since the d-value of the Durbin–Watson statistic in the investment model (refer to Study Question 14.3) is $d = 0.784$, which indicates positive autocorrelation, the four-step remedy for autocorrelation should be applied. Step 1 gives the value of $\boldsymbol{d}$. In step 2, the approximate value of $\hat{\rho}$ is found by using Formula (14.3):

$$\hat{\rho} = \tfrac{1}{2}(2 - 0.784) = 0.608.$$

Step 3 requires transformation of the observations for $\boldsymbol{y} =$ investment, $x_1 =$ stock price, $x_2 =$ retained earnings, and the intercept. We will not transform the intercept but will correct its value after doing the estimation.

The other observations are transformed according to Formula (14.4) to obtain the values of y^*, x_1^*, and x_2^* as shown in Table 14.3. The value used for $\hat{\rho}$ is 0.608. For example, the new observation for the dependent variable in period nine is

$$y_9^* = y_9 - 0.608y_8 = 64.3 - 0.608(76.0) = 18.09.$$

The computer printout of the least-squares estimation for the revised model is given in Fig. 14.9. The output for the original model was given in Fig. 13.2.

The estimated value of the intercept (a) is obtained by multiplying the reported value for the intercept by the factor $1/(1 - \hat{\rho})$. That is, $a = 7.69/(1 - 0.608) = 19.62$. The new estimates $b_1^* = 0.061$ and $b_2^* = 1.637$ are preferred to the simple least-squares estimators $(b_1 = 0.0786$ and $b_2 = 1.798)$. This method, which makes use of the extra information about the autocorrelation pattern, is expected to give better estimates. If such information is not used (as in the ordinary least-squares case without the transformation), the estimators cannot have the desirable property of efficiency. We note that the Durbin–Watson statistic is $d = 1.106$ for the residuals from the transformed data estimation. This value is closer to 2.0 than the original value $(d = 0.784)$, indicating that the disturbances for the revised model are more independent than those in the original model. However, this remedy was not sufficient to remove the autocor-

TABLE 14.3 Original and transformed observations for the investment model

Observation	Y	X1	X2	Y*	X1*	X2*
1	62.3	398.4	16.2	—	—	—
2	71.3	452.6	17.4	33.4216	210.373	7.5504
3	70.3	509.8	14.8	26.9496	234.619	4.2208
4	68.5	485.4	14.6	25.7576	175.442	5.6016
5	57.3	445.7	8.2	15.6520	150.577	−0.6768
6	68.8	539.8	14.9	33.9616	268.814	9.9144
7	72.2	662.8	15.1	30.3696	334.602	6.0408
8	76.0	620.0	14.3	32.1024	217.018	5.1192
9	64.3	632.2	10.9	18.0920	255.240	2.2056
10	77.9	703.0	16.0	38.8056	318.622	9.3728
11	84.3	581.8	16.2	36.9368	154.376	6.4720
12	85.1	707.1	16.4	33.8456	353.366	6.5504
13	90.8	776.6	20.4	39.0592	346.683	10.4288
14	97.9	875.3	20.5	42.6936	403.127	8.0968
15	108.7	873.4	26.1	49.1768	341.218	13.6360
16	122.4	943.7	29.0	56.3104	412.673	13.1312
17	114.0	830.6	24.6	39.5808	256.830	6.9680
18	123.0	907.5	27.8	53.6880	402.495	12.8432
19	126.2	905.3	23.3	51.4160	353.540	6.3976
20	137.0	927.4	21.6	60.2704	376.978	7.4336

FIGURE 14.9 Least-squares estimation results for the transformed investment data of Table 14.3.

```
MODEL:    MODEL01            SSE    851.687239    F RATIO      17.59
                            DFE            16    PROB>F      0.0001
DEP VAR: Y*                 MSE     53.230452    R-SQUARE    0.6874

DURBIN-WATSON D STATISTIC =      1.1061


                 PARAMETER    STANDARD
VARIABLE    DF    ESTIMATE      ERROR    T RATIO    PROB>|T|

INTERCEPT    1    7.690440    6.110537    1.2586     0.2262
X1*          1    0.061199    0.026578    2.3026     0.0351
X2*          1    1.636893    0.630229    2.5973     0.0194
```

relation among disturbances. In many applications it will work quite well, especially if the technique is applied iteratively by repeating steps 2–4, using the *most recently obtained value* of d to transform the *original data*. The reader might try (as in Problem 14.40) a second iteration for the investment case using the revised value of $d = 1.106$ and the revised estimate, $\hat{\rho} = \frac{1}{2}(2 - 1.106)$.

14.5 HETEROSCEDASTICITY

Referring to the disturbance terms in the regression model, **heteroscedasticity** defines the condition where the variance of ϵ is not constant across all observations, $i = 1, 2, \ldots, n$. In this section we consider the violation of assumption 4 of Section 14.2, which states the desired condition of constant variance, $V[\epsilon_i] = \sigma_\epsilon^2$.

Usually, the assumption of constant variance is not seriously violated when using economic or business data *measured over time* unless some significant structural change occurred to affect the observations, such as a new law, a war, a revolution, or some natural disaster. More often, the problem of heteroscedasticity arises when cross-sectional data, *at a given point in time*, is used, such as employment or production data across firms, or tax and revenue data across states. In these cases the disturbances may not have constant variances because of differing factors related to the size or the legal code of the different cross-sectional entities. For example, large corporations have different structures and operate under different tax laws than do small business firms. Thus, one would expect a specified model to represent one of these types better than the other. The variance of disturbances for the one type that it fits best will be smaller than the variance of disturbances for observations of the other type.

Also, as was mentioned in Examples 14.2 and 14.3, the violation of assumption 4 is not always independent of the violation of assumption 1. Errors in measurement may exist, for example, as a large component of the disturbance term. If there are changes in measurement procedures so that some observations have significantly more accuracy than others, the variance of the disturbance term will be smaller for the subset of observations that are measured with the greater accuracy.

Effect of Heteroscedasticity

When only assumption 4 is violated, the distribution and expectations of the least-squares estimators b_j of the coefficients β_j do not change. They are still linear and unbiased estimators with the property of consistency. The problem is that if the variance changes for different observations, we are not making use of all the information. This is always an indication that the estimators are not efficient. That is, $V[b_j]$ (where the estimators b_j are obtained by the least-squares estimators) are greater than variances of b_j^* determined by some other estimating procedure that uses the additional information about the changing variance of the disturbance term. Moreover, the estimated standard errors of the estimates and the calculated values of test statistics are incorrect. Thus, the effect of a violation of assumption 4 is basically the same as that for autocorrelation (violation of assumption 5) reported in the last section. We will proceed to show that methods of detection and correction for this violation parallel the presentation in the last section. The detection of heteroscedasticity is aided by plots using the residuals and by a rather simple test using an F-distributed statistic. The correction is again a variation of generalized least squares by which information about the changing variance is incorporated into the estimation process.

Plots to Detect Heteroscedasticity

Sometimes, it is suspected that a population regression model may fit better for some subset of observations and fit worse for another subset (or have a gradation of fit across multiple subsets of the observations). For instance, suppose there are three distinct subsets of observations for which the variance of the disturbances differs. Figure 14.10 illustrates the situation for the three groups I, II, and III.

Detection of such differences in $V[\epsilon_i]$ cannot be made by using ϵ_i directly, since these are unknown. Instead, it is common to make plots of the residuals e_i to detect any signs of possible heteroscedasticity. If the

FIGURE 14.10 **Change in** $V(\epsilon_i)$ **among three groups of observations.**

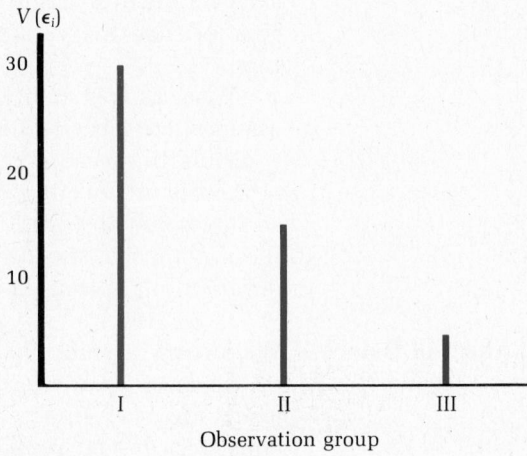

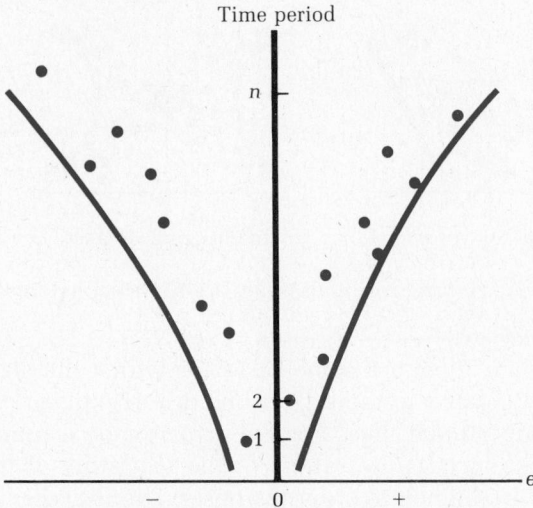

FIGURE 14.11 **Residual plot against time.**

observations are time-series data (periodic over time), a useful sketch for detecting heteroscedasticity plots the values of the residuals against time.

For the residuals plotted in Fig. 14.11 there seems to be an indication of an increasing variance over time, indicated by the $\vee$-shape of the bounding lines. A changing variance would also be indicated if the bounding lines are approximately $\wedge$, an inverted V; if they widened and narrowed in the shape of an egg timer or a football; or if they had any systematic pattern other than parallel lines. This plot may also reveal a linear or second-degree relation between the residuals and time. This indicates that a variable representing time, say t, t^2, or preferably, some excluded variable with a definite time trend should be included as an explanatory variable in the model.

If the observation groups are not consecutive, similar information is obtained by plotting the residuals against the estimated values of the dependent variable, $\hat{y}$. The interpretation is similar.

For example, the V-shaped slope of the boundary lines for the scatter of points in Fig. 14.12(a) suggests an increasing variance of the residuals as the value $\hat{y}$ increases. Such a plot may indicate that the fit of the model is not uniform and that the disturbances may not have a constant variance. A changing variance could also be indicated if the boundary lines approximated an inverted V or if they were close together at some points and wider apart at others, as in Fig. 14.12(b). Assumption 4 of constant variance does *not* seem to be violated if the boundary lines are approximately parallel, as in Fig. 14.12(c).

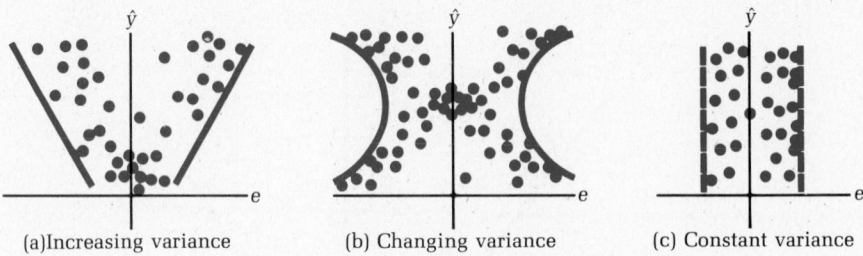

(a)Increasing variance   (b) Changing variance   (c) Constant variance

FIGURE 14.12 **Plotting residuals against ŷ to detect heteroscedasticity.**

Finally, there are some cases for which the size of the disturbance might be related to the size of one of the explanatory variables (such as with proportional measurement error) or be a function of one of these variables (such as the square or the logarithm of the variable). In such cases it is common to order the observations according to the size of that explanatory variable (smallest to largest) and make a plot of the residuals against the values of that variable x_j (just as in Fig. 14.11, in which the variable was time). The same guidelines for interpretation apply.

Example 14.15. Consider a simple model that relates defense expenditures to gross national product (GNP) in the United States during 1940–1948 ($n = 9$, as first given in Problem 12.58). We define y = GNP and x = defense expenditures. This is quite clearly an incomplete model, since many other factors are important in determining GNP. Also, defense expenditures will vary considerably depending on the level of military involvement, independent of the total goods and services produced. Thus, we should examine this model to see whether the varying background conditions cause a severe problem of heteroscedasticity.

Table 14.4 gives the data and the results for the least-squares regression of this model. The observations have been ordered according to the size of x. [Defense expenditures range from about 1.5% of GNP in 1940 ($i = 1$) to over 38% in 1945 ($i = 6$). For comparison, in the United States in 1984 the ratio was 6.1%.] For this sample regression we note that the value of R^2 is only $(0.3849)^2 = 0.148$. Only about 15% of the variation in GNP is explained in this model. The other 85% remains unexplained. Also, the slope coefficient appears to be insignificant, since its t-ratio is only

$$t = b/s_b = 0.631/0.572 = 1.10$$

(but this t-value may be incorrect if assumption 4 does not hold). Since we suspect a problem of heteroscedasticity, we could plot the values of

TABLE 14.4 **Results of GNP–defense expenditure model**

Year	Observation	y	x	$\hat{y}$	e	Group	s_e
1940	1	99.7	1.5	166.463	−66.763		
1941	2	124.5	6.1	169.367	−44.867	I	33.315
1948	9	257.6	11.8	172.965	84.635		
1947	8	231.3	14.4	174.606	56.694		
1942	3	157.9	24.0	180.666	−22.766		
1946	7	208.5	43.2	192.787	15.713	II	26.375
1943	4	191.6	63.2	205.412	−13.812		
1944	5	210.1	76.8	213.997	−3.897	III	
1945	6	211.9	81.3	216.838	−4.938		0.736

y = GNP
x = defense expenditures
$\hat{y} = 165.516 + 0.63127x$
　　$(26.513)\ (0.57208)$

$r = 0.3849$
$s_e = 50.4878$

the residuals against the estimated values of $\hat{y}$, as shown in Fig. 14.13. The plot indicates a decreasing variance of residuals about the estimating equation as the size of the estimated value increases.

Another way to detect a change in residual variance involves grouping the observations according to the size of x. Table 14.4 presents a grouping for example only, since the number of observations is so small. Group I

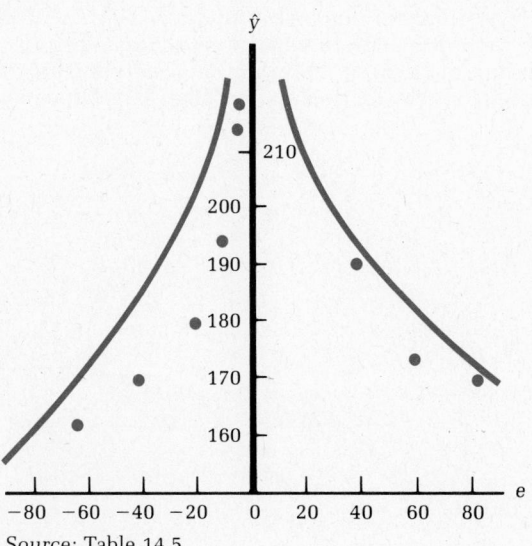

FIGURE 14.13 **Residual plot against estimated $\hat{y}$ for GNP–defense expenditure model.**

Source: Table 14.5

includes the four smallest values of x, group II includes the next three larger, and group III has the two largest. A plot of the calculated variance of e_i within each of these subgroups resembles Fig. 14.10. Such a plot indicates that assumption 4 may be violated. Another representation of the problem is shown in Fig. 14.14.

A Test for Hetero-scedasticity

To test for differences in variance between two groups, one might consider using the F-distributed ratio for a two-sample test as in Section 10.6. That test on differences between variances uses the statistic

$$F_{(n_1 - 1, n_2 - 1)} = \frac{s_1^2}{s_2^2} = \frac{SSx_1/(n_1 - 1)}{SSx_2/(n_2 - 1)},$$

where the sums of squares of deviations in the numerator and denominator are independent. However, in this case for differences in the variances between two subsets of residuals, the condition of independence would *not* be met if the two subsets of residuals come from the *same* regression equation. Each residual in either subgroup would depend on the same estimated values of the coefficients b_j, which depend in turn on *all* the observations.

To satisfy the independence condition, we must find the variance of the subgroups of residuals from *separate* regressions based on the corresponding subgroups of observations. If there are n_A observations in

FIGURE 14.14 **Example of heteroscedasticity. As in the example problem with results in Table 14.4, heteroscedasticity occurs when the variance of the disturbance term changes. This case shows diminishing $V(\epsilon)$ for larger values of x. The normal distribution of ϵ becomes less dispersed for larger x.**

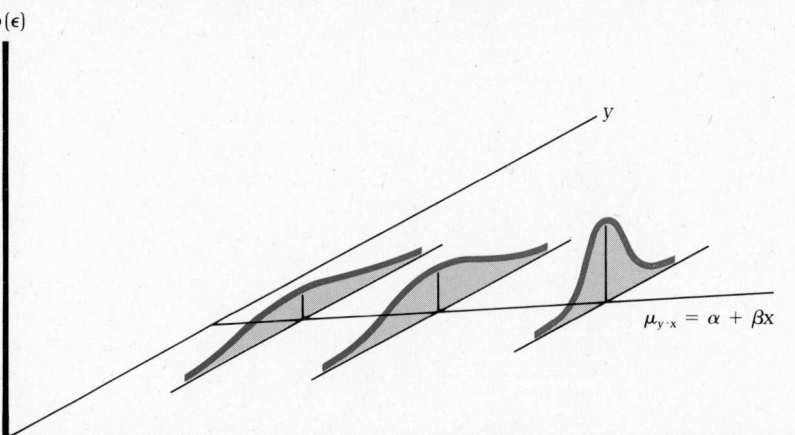

one subgroup and an additional n_B observations in the other, the sums of squares of residuals obtained from separate regressions on the group A data and on the group B data would be independent. To test the hypotheses,

H_0: constant variance of ϵ_i;

H_a: heteroscedasticity of the disturbances.

The ratio appropriate for an *F*-distributed test statistic is

---

F-test for heteroscedasticity:

$$F_{(n_A - m - 1, n_B - m - 1)} = \frac{(SSE)_A/(n_A - m - 1)}{(SSE)_B/(n_B - m - 1)}. \qquad \textbf{(14.5)}$$

The terms in the ratio are the mean square errors (MSE) from the separate regressions (see Section 13.4). If the calculated *F*-value is in the upper or lower critical region, we reject the null hypothesis of homoscedasticity. We conclude in a two-sided test that the variance of the disturbance term is different between subgroup A and subgroup B. A one-sided alternative hypothesis together with the upper-tail critical region may be used when the subgroup expected to have the larger $V[\epsilon_i]$ is designated as subgroup A in the numerator of Formula (14.5). This test is named the **Goldfeld–Quandt** (G–Q) **test** after two economists at Princeton University, who first introduced it in 1965. The critical regions are determined by using the standard *F*-table.

Example 14.16. Consider a model explaining a firm's level of employment based on four explanatory variables measuring particular firm characteristics. The model is estimated on the basis of data from the annual U.S. Census of Manufacturers, Bureau of the Census, Department of Commerce, for 68 firms. The cross-sectional sample includes 44 firms in the food industry and 24 firms in the primary metals industry. It is suspected that the variance of the errors may be different in the two separate industries. The food industry is denoted as subgroup A with $n_A = 44$, and the primary metals industry is subgroup B with $n_B = 24$. The null hypothesis is $H_0: V[\epsilon]_A = V[\epsilon]_B$ against a one-sided alternative, $H_a: V[\epsilon]_A > V[\epsilon]_B$. The degrees of freedom are $44 - 4 - 1 = 39$ and $24 - 4 - 1 = 19$. The null hypothesis H_0 will be rejected if the calculated *F*-value exceeds the critical value from Table VIII of $F_{(0.05;39,19)} = 2.02$.

Two regressions are determined, one for each subgroup of data. The sum of squares of errors for each regression is $(SSE)_A = 0.90888$ and

$(SSE)_B = 0.25047$. The calculated value of the test statistic using Formula (14.5) is

$$F_c = \frac{(0.90888/39)}{(0.25047/19)} = \frac{0.0233}{0.01318} = 1.77.$$

Assumption 4 of constant variance is *not* rejected.

Sometimes, separate subgroups of the data are not so obvious, and the test is to be applied in general to determine whether $V[\epsilon_i]$ is increasing, decreasing, or constant over the complete set of observations (ordered by time or by size of $\hat{y}$ or by size of some x_j). In this situation it is recommended that the data be separated into *three* groups with numbers of observations n_A, n_M, and n_B. The G–Q test statistic (14.5) can be used on the subgroups A and B, excluding the middle n_M observations. This disuse of some of the data tends to make the test less powerful because some sample information is not used. However, comparing more widely separated observations has the opposite effect of making the test more powerful because it tends to make the difference between $(SSE)_A$ and $(SSE)_B$ larger. Research studies indicate that a good trade-off between these competing uses of the data often occurs when the middle group of n_M observations includes about 20% of the observations. Thus, this method of ordering the observations and excluding about 20% of the middle observations to form subgroups A and B is quite commonly and successfully used.

Study Question 14.4: Heteroscedasticity Test in the GNP–Defense Expenditures Model

Do a Goldfeld–Quandt test for heteroscedasticity on the data and results of Table 14.4. Order the observations by the size (smallest to largest) of x = defense expenditures. Let group A be the one with larger expected $V[\epsilon]$ and use a one-sided test with a significance level of 0.05.

Answer. Separate the observations in Table 14.4 to get two groups, each of four observations, leaving out one observation in the middle. Group A includes the observations with the smallest four values of x (from the early and postwar period) and the largest $V[\epsilon_i]$ based on Figs. 14.13 and 14.14. Group B includes the observations for years 1943–1946 with the largest four values of x. The excluded middle value is for $i = 3$ (1942). A regression based on group A gives a sum of squares of residuals of $(SSE)_A = 2522.54$. For group B, $(SSE)_B = 248.45$. These results are shown in Fig. 14.15. The calculated value of the test statistic using Formula (14.5) is

$$F_c = \frac{2522.54/2}{248.45/2} = 10.15.$$

```
                GROUP A DATA
       DEPENDENT VARIABLE Y

       VARIABLE        COEFFICIENT     STD. ERROR
          X             12.4809         3.54347
        CONST           72.8115        34.8118

       SUM SQUARE       STD ERROR       MULT CORR
        2522.54          35.5143         .927992

       ROW    OBSERVED      ESTIMATED      DEVIATION
        1       99.7         91.5328        8.16716
        2      124.5        148.945       -24.4449
        3      257.6        220.086        37.514
        4      231.3        252.536       -21.2363


                GROUP B DATA
       DEPENDENT VARIABLE Y

       VARIABLE        COEFFICIENT     STD. ERROR
          X              .134466         .376073
        CONST          196.633         25.4846

       SUM SQUARE       STD ERROR        MULT CORR
        248.452          11.1457          .245077

       ROW    OBSERVED      ESTIMATED      DEVIATION
        1      208.5        202.442        6.05763
        2      191.6        205.132       -13.5317
        3      210.1        206.960        3.13958
        4      211.9        207.566        4.22449
```

FIGURE 14.15 Computer printout of subgroup regressions.

The critical value from Table VIII is 19.0 for $4 - 1 - 1 = 2$ degrees of freedom in both numerator and denominator and for a significance level of 0.05. Thus, the test does not reject the null hypothesis of constant variance. Even though the plots indicate a problem, the number of observations is so small that the test does not give a significant result of heteroscedasticity.

Correction for Hetero-scedasticity Suppose the data are determined to have subgroups for which the variances of the corresponding disturbance terms are different. Then, if the variances of the disturbance terms within each subgroup can be assumed to be equal, the problem of heteroscedasticity can be avoided by determining separate estimations for the subgroups of data within which assumption

4 is valid. Of course, the estimates of the coefficients based on the separate subgroups of observations may then differ.

As an alternative, a separate dummy variable may be used for each subgroup. (See Section 13.6. The number of dummy variables required would be one fewer than the number of subgroups.) The dummy variables might serve as a proxy for some of the underlying causes of the heteroscedasticity, thereby partially decreasing the differences in variance of the disturbance terms among the subgroups. This use of dummy variables underlies a more complex method of estimation known as the *covariance method*.

If the variance of the disturbance term is continually changing for each different observation, the procedure of **weighted least squares** is appropriate. To obtain better estimates than the simple least-squares estimates, the observations for which the disturbance variance is small should be given larger weights in the estimation, and the observations for which the disturbance variance is large should be given smaller weights. Ordinary least squares (OLS) without explicit weights presumes that each observation is equally important in estimating the "true" relation. However, the "true" relation is more easily determined when the level of disturbance "noise" (variation) is small. Consequently, to obtain the most accurate estimation of this relation, more importance should be given to observations for which $V[\epsilon_i]$ is small. Observations for which $V[\epsilon_i]$ is large should be deemphasized.

In weighted least squares this differential treatment is accomplished by dividing each observation (for every variable) by some measure that is hoped to correspond to the size of the standard deviation of the disturbance for that observation, $\sqrt{V[\epsilon_i]}$. A very common weighting scheme assumes that $V[\epsilon_i]$ is proportional to the square of one explanatory variable. Thus, the standard error of ϵ_i for observation i would be proportional to x_{ij} for some j, perhaps because x_j is thought to have a systematic error of measurement. The mathematical formulation of this weighting scheme is a special case of the method of generalized least squares, which was also used in the remedy for autocorrelation. The transformation to be used on all observations of all variables is as follows:

Heteroscedasticity remedy if $V[\epsilon_i]$ is proportional to x_{ij}^2:

$$(\text{Transformed value})_i = \frac{(\text{Original value})_i}{x_{ij}}. \qquad \textbf{(14.6)}$$

Another common procedure is to estimate the size of $V[\epsilon_j]$ for separate subgroups of the observations based on $s_e{}^2$ for each subgroup. Then the original observations can be weighted inversely according to the standard error of estimate for the subgroup to which they belong. Either of these weighting methods gives a more efficient estimator than the use of least squares on the original data. The *weighted least-squares* estimator can be determined by making a transformation of each observation for each variable and then repeating least squares on the transformed data. Finally, the new residuals from this second least-squares estimation should be subjected to analysis such as the Goldfeld–Quandt test to check that heteroscedasticity has been significantly reduced. That is, the process follows steps similar to that for correcting for autocorrelation (Section 14.4). More sophisticated detection and correction procedures for special problems of heteroscedasticity and autocorrelation are beyond the level of this text. The interested reader should refer to textbooks and research publications in econometrics.

14.6 USE OF LINEAR REGRESSION FOR NONLINEAR RELATIONS

Condition 3 in Section 14.2 made clear again that we have been dealing throughout Chapters 12, 13, and 14 with a *linear* regression model. Any student who has studied relations among economic or business variables knows that these are not always linear. (Recall the graphs used in lectures or textbooks that used curved lines, not straight ones.) Thus, it is fair to ask how appropriate the methods of linear regression are when many of the underlying relations are actually nonlinear.

First, although a relation may be nonlinear over its full range, when we consider a segment of the overall curve, it is often approximately correct to assume a straight line. A downward-sloping demand schedule for, say, gasoline (petrol) may be nonlinear. However, over a range of values commonly occurring in the world market, such as a price of 75¢ to $3.50 per gallon, a linear approximation is quite accurate. We need not worry about the fact that the quantity demanded would surely decrease at a nonlinear rate if the price per gallon increased to $10.

A second reason that we extensively study the linear model is that we can convert many nonlinear relations among variables into linear relations among **transformations of those variables.** That is, the model can be made linear among the measures y and x_j, but these measures are not the values of the theoretical variables being studied. They may be *nonlinear functions* of the underlying variables. The observations y_i may be the reciprocal or the logarithm of an economic variable. Second- and higher-order relations, square roots, or exponential transformations may also be included. A few examples of such transformations and their uses can be listed.

Higher-order Transformations The linear model can represent a higher-order relation. A complete second-order model with two independent variables Z and W might be represented as

$$y = \alpha + \sum_{j=1}^{5} \beta_j x_j + \epsilon,$$

where $x_1 = Z$, $x_2 = W$, $x_3 = Z^2$, $x_4 = W^2$, and $x_5 = ZW$. Such a model allows for nonlinear, second-degree curves (parabolic or hyperbolic) including an interaction term (ZW). However, the analysis involves only a linear model in terms of the observations of y and x_j. Third-, fourth-, or higher-order models can be developed similarly.

One particular use of such models is in forecasting and in fitting series of values over time. The use of powers of t = time as values of x_j, such as $x_1 = t$, $x_2 = t^2$, $x_3 = t^3$, etc., allows for nonlinear trends (see Section 15.3) to be built into the forecasting model.

Reciprocal Transformations Often the theoretical relation between two variables may be nonlinear and contain the implication of an asymptotic level on one variable for extreme values of the other. An example in economics is the Keynesian liquidity trap described by the relation $y = \alpha + (\beta/z)$, where y is investment (expenditure for plant and equipment) and z is the interest rate. Figure 14.16(a) depicts such a relation of a negative slope (for all values of z) that decreases in absolute value as z increases. Thus, investment approaches the asymptotic level given by the value α. If β is negative, y approaches the asymptote α from below with positive but

FIGURE 14.16 **Nonlinear functions with asymptotes.**

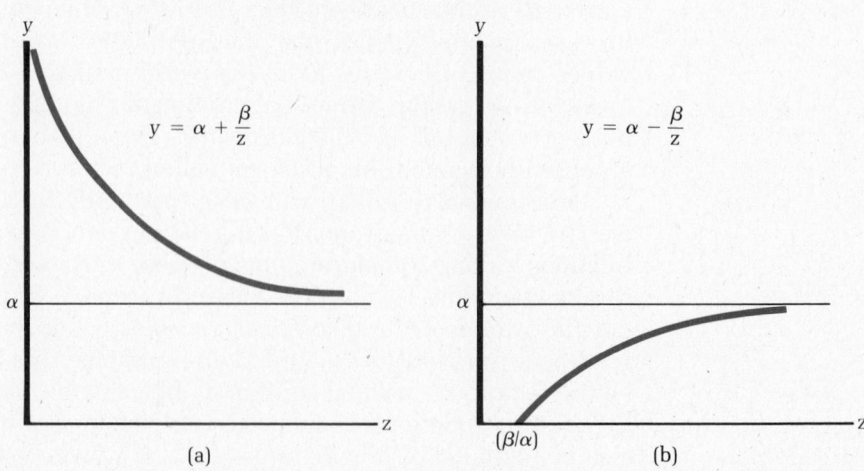

(a)   (b)

TABLE 14.5 **Example values of investment (y) and interest rate (I)**

y	∞	45	25	15	13	10	9	7	6	5
I	0	1	2	4	5	8	10	20	40	∞
x	∞	1	0.5	0.25	0.20	0.125	0.10	0.05	0.025	0

decreasing slope as in Fig. 14.16(b). For such cases the simple transformation of variable using the reciprocal, $x = 1/z$, provides the linear model $y = \alpha + \beta x$ with constant slope β and intercept α.

Example 14.17. Suppose the true relation for a particular industry is $y = 5 + (40/I)$, where y is investment and I is the interest rate. Using the data in Table 14.5, plots of this relation and of the relation, $y = 5 + 40x$, where $x = 1/I$, are shown in Fig. 14.17(a) and Fig. 14.17(b), respectively. Use of the reciprocal transformation allows estimation of the linear model to learn about a nonlinear relation.

Logarithmic Transformations on y and x Many theoretical relations between economic or business variables may be expressed in multiplicative models rather than additive ones. They have the form $y = \alpha x_1^{\beta_1} x_2^{\beta_2} x_3^{\beta_3}$. This is a common representation for production functions where y is output and the different x_j are input factors (labor, machines, management). Also, economists frequently are interested in the values of the elasticity of a relation rather than the slope of the function. The slope is the relative *unit* change in y for a *unit* change in x and is easily measured by β in the linear model. The **elasticity**

FIGURE 14.17 **Investment–interest rate relations.**

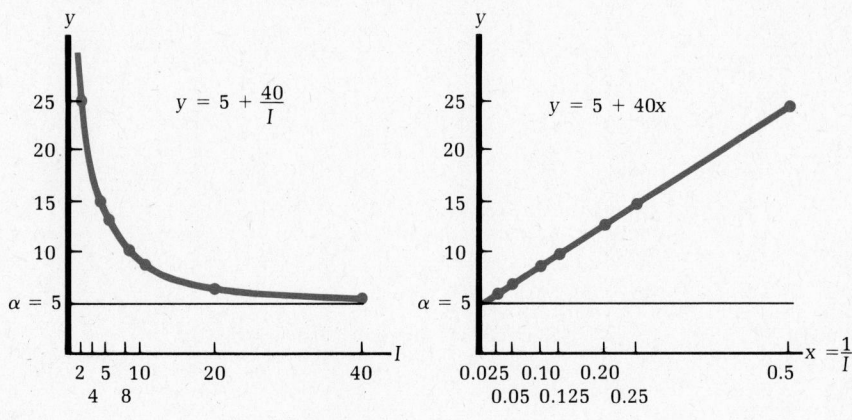

(denoted by the Greek letter eta, η) is the relative *percentage* change in y for a 1% change in x. It is easily measured by β_j in a multiplicative model. Without variable transformations the linear regression cannot adequately treat the multiplicative model and measures of elasticity.

In the model $y = \alpha + \beta^* x$, the slope is β^*, a constant. The elasticity is $\eta = \beta^*(x/y)$, and it changes all along the line as values of x and y change. If the theoretical relation suggests a *constant* rather than a changing elasticity, a logarithmic transformation on both variables, y and x, may be applied. The model obtained is linear in the logs, $(\ln y) = \alpha + \beta(\ln x)$. Such a specification really comes from an original multiplicative model, $y = \lambda x^\beta$ where $\ln \lambda = \alpha$. This double-log transformation corresponds to a model with a constant elasticity of y with respect to x (given by β). Depending on the size of this elasticity, various nonlinear curves as illustrated in Fig. 14.18 may be represented by a linear model.

Example 14.18. The well-known Cobb–Douglas production function has the form $Q = \lambda L^{\beta_1} K^{\beta_2}$, where Q is output, L is labor, and K is capital (building and equipment). If the double-log transformation is used, the model becomes linear, $y = \alpha + \beta_1 x_1 + \beta_2 x_2$, where $y = \ln Q$, $x_1 = \ln L$, $x_2 = \ln K$, and $\alpha = \ln \lambda$.

Logarithmic Transformation on x Only

Some nonlinear relations between economic or business variables may be represented in a linear model if a semi-log transformation is used. The model, $y = \alpha + \beta(\ln x)$, has a changing slope given by (β/x), which decreases as x increases. It also has a changing elasticity given by $\eta = (\beta/y)$, which decreases as y increases.

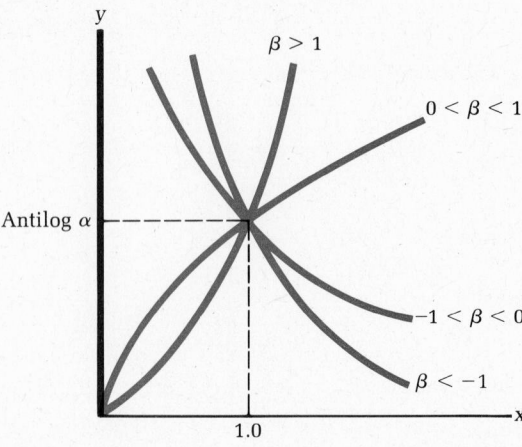

FIGURE 14.18 **Double-log transformation** $\ln y = \alpha + \beta \ln x$.

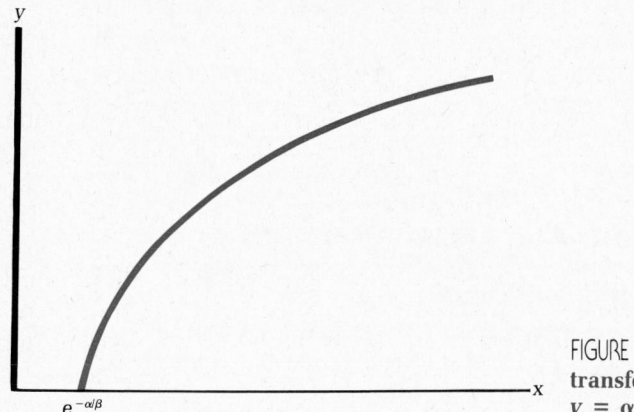

FIGURE 14.19 **Semi-log transformation** $y = \alpha + \beta \ln x$.

Example 14.19. Consider a model where y = output of wheat and x = expected price of wheat. The semi-log model may be appropriate for this situation, represented in Fig. 14.19. No wheat would be produced for sale unless the price were above some minimal level ($e^{-\alpha/\beta}$). Also, the percentage increase in wheat produced is limited at high output levels by production constraints, such as the available amount of cultivated land. Thus, the elasticity is decreasing as output increases, and the slope is decreasing as price increases.

The inverse of the semi-log function (here we reverse the symbols for y and x from those used above) has the form $y = \alpha\beta^x$, which is often used to represent a variable that has a constant rate of growth (β) over time. This so-called *exponential model* has frequent uses for estimating nonlinear trends (see Section 15.3) or compound interest at a fixed rate over x years. Such a function is shown in Fig. 14.20.

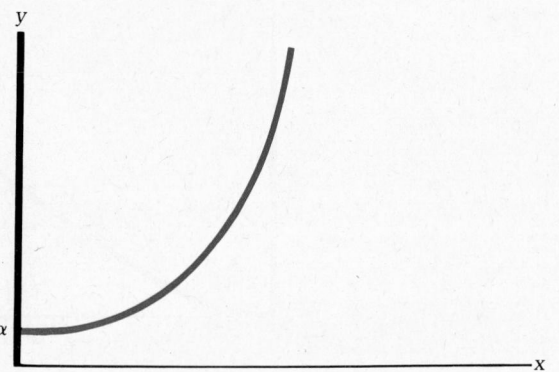

FIGURE 14.20 **Exponential model** $y = \alpha\beta^x$.

your propositions in step 6. Interpret these results to see whether a more detailed analysis of this model is worthwhile.

11. Complete any other useful analysis of the regression results, including tests of any remaining hypotheses suggested in step 6. These may involve computing forecasts or making comparisons of results from different regressions for subgroups of the data or for different specifications of the set of explanatory variables.

12. Examine the correlation coefficients among the explanatory variables for detection of multicollinearity. Examine plots and tests of residuals for detection of autocorrelation or heteroscedasticity.

Phase IV:
Interpretation
and Revision

13. If one or more of the problems in step 12 are detected, a reestimation of the model may be needed. Do so, using additional data or a revised specification, probably involving a transformation of the original variables.

14. If part of the analysis suggests the need for another statistical result that you did not compute the first time, or the need for a different regression, do the extra procedure to obtain what is needed.

Phase V:
Interpretation
and Conclusion

15. Compile a detailed list of each result with its separate meaning. From this, formulate the interpretation of the complete set of results. Relate the individual and collective results to the purpose of your project. Understand which results contribute to your conclusions and which make it dubious or ambiguous.

16. Write a report including the following:
    a) Statement of the purpose of the project.
    b) Statement of the model(s) and its relevance to the issue.
    c) Definition of variables and source of their statistical measures detailing the units and cases being used in each regression.
    d) Hypotheses to be tested, forecasts to be calculated, and their relevance to the issue.
    e) Summary of results, including any residual analysis and revised estimations.
    f) Conclusions based on the results and their overall bearing on the issue raised in item (a).

    Use the computer output as an appendix to your paper, and clearly mark the crucial results referred to in your written report. It is often convenient to write the formulas and calculated values of the test statistics on the computer output as well.

Try to write parts (a) and (b) of the report on about one page. Items (c) and (d) may require more pages, depending on the number of variables and regressions involved. A reasonable limit is three pages. Item (e) will probably correspond in length to items (c) and (d) together. Two pages should suffice for item (f). Thus, a typical research report may be concisely written in about ten pages or less, plus computer output. In the context of a term paper the instructor may request some longer detail on a particular part of the report. In the context of a job, if the report is especially relevant, containing important and unambiguous results, the supervisor who requested it may ask for an expanded version and a presentation to a policy or review group.

Define. *Multicollinearity; composite variable; extraneous estimate; respecification; autocorrelation; Durbin–Watson test; generalized least squares; transformation of variable; heteroscedasticity; Goldfeld–Quandt test; weighted least squares; nonlinear relations; reciprocal, double-log, semi-log, and exponential transformations; elasticity; prior analysis in a research project.*

PROBLEMS

14.10 Explain the meaning of multicollinearity, and specify one of its effects that you think is important.

14.11 Suppose that the values of **y** are related to both variables x and w. The observations for y, x, and w are:

y	x	w
1.0	1.00	5.0
2.0	1.44	3.5
3.0	1.96	3.0
4.0	3.24	4.0
5.0	4.00	1.0
6.0	7.84	2.0

a) Plot the relationship between y and x, and between y and w. Is the relationship approximately linear in both cases? If not, what would be the problem in fitting an equation of the form $\hat{y} = a + bx + cw$?

    b) Find the simple correlation coefficient of variables x and w. Do you think multicollinearity might be a problem in using x and w as copredictors of y?

14.12 Given the residuals below for a regression of y = consumption and x = income over ten time periods, plot e_t against time and plot e_t againet e_{t-1}. Interpret the plots as indicators of possible autocorrelation.

Year	e_t	Year	e_t
1975	−0.4	1980	+0.3
1976	−0.1	1981	+1.2
1977	−0.1	1982	+0.6
1978	−0.8	1983	−0.1
1979	+0.4	1984	−1.0

14.13 For the residuals in Problem 14.12, do a Durbin–Watson test for autocorrelation.

14.14 Use the residuals from the regression model for imports in Problem 12.57. Make a plot of e against $\hat{y}$. Calculate the Durbin–Watson d-statistic. Interpret the results in terms of possible violations of assumptions 4 and 5.

14.15 Repeat Problem 14.14 using the residuals from:
a) the simple regression model for investment (see Fig. 12.16);
b) the multiple regression model for investment (see Table 14.1).

14.16 The application of OLS treats all observations as equally important. State one situation in which this may be an inappropriate procedure, and explain the general principle or method of a better procedure.

14.17 Consider a simple model, $y_t = \alpha + \beta x_t + \epsilon_t$, for which it is known that $\epsilon_t = 0.3\epsilon_{t-1} + v_t$ where the v_t are normally and independently distributed with constant variance and mean zero.
a) Explain the problem of using ordinary least squares in this situation.
b) Construct the appropriate expression that will minimize the sum of squares, if the variables are transformed to correct for the problem. (*Hint*: Let the new variables be $y_t^* = y_t - 0.3y_{t-1}$ and $x_t^* = x_t - 0.3x_{t-1}$.)

14.18 Repeat Problem 14.14 using the residuals from the simple regression model of sales on GNP based on the data in Table 13.5. The following table gives the values of y, $\hat{y}$, and e.

SEQNUM	Observed Sales	Predicted Sales	Residual
1	978.000	1054.550	−76.550
2	1123.000	1087.015	35.985
3	1125.000	1115.010	9.990
4	1260.000	1152.691	107.309
5	1121.000	1199.740	−78.740
6	1275.000	1230.608	44.392
7	1257.000	1263.606	−6.606
8	1381.000	1300.968	80.032
9	1172.000	1316.722	−144.722
10	1368.000	1343.333	24.667
11	1382.000	1377.927	4.073
12	1454.000	1393.468	60.532
13	1260.000	1378.247	−118.247
14	1462.000	1404.113	57.887

14.19 Answer parts (a) and (b).

a) Suppose an individual's personal income tax liability T is related to personal adjusted gross income I by the model, $T = \alpha I^{\beta+1}(10)^\epsilon$. Determine a representation of this theory that allows estimation of α and β as parameters in the simple linear model.

b) Let E denote hours of work per capita per week, and let I denote per capita national income in the model, $E = \alpha I^\beta \epsilon$. Sketch the relation between E and I. Determine a representation of this theory that allows estimation of α and β as parameters in the simple linear model.

14.20 Given the following values of x and y:

x	1.00	1.44	1.96	3.24	4.00	7.84
y	1.0	2.0	3.0	4.0	5.0	6.0

a) Plot these six values of x and y on a graph, and then make a freehand estimate of the curve relating the two variables. Would a linear function be appropriate in this circumstance? What type of relationship to the values of x does y appear to have?

b) Transform the variable x into a new variable by taking the square root of x, and then plot this new variable against y. Is this relationship approximately linear?

c) Use the transformation in part (b) to establish a least-squares regression line for the relationship between **y** and $\sqrt{x}$. Calculate a list of the residuals.

d) Find the sample correlation coefficient for the original data and then find it for the transformed data. Explain how the different values give a hint to the best-fitting form of model relating **y** to **x**.

14.21 The following data represent the growth pattern of a certain plant life, where x is in months and **y** is in inches.

x	1	2	3	4	5	6	7
y	0.80	1.10	1.70	2.60	3.80	5.70	8.50

a) Find the least-squares equation relating x and **y**, of the form $\hat{y} = ab^x$. (Take the logarithm of both sides of this equation, letting $\log \hat{y} = \log a + x \log b$.)

b) Plot the original data and your least-squares estimate, and then use this sketch to find the error of prediction for these seven observations.

14.22 Determine the least-squares estimate for the following data, assuming that $\hat{y} = ax^b$ (let $\log \hat{y} = \log a + b \log x$). Plot the original data and the least-squares estimate on graph paper, and compute the residuals $e_i = y_i - \hat{y}_i$. Find s_e using Formula (12.16).

x	1	2	3	4	5
y	1.0	2.1	4.3	8.1	13.0

Determine the least-squares estimate using the line $\hat{y} = a + bx$ and find the residuals. By comparing s_e for both forms of the estimation, determine which model specification provides the best fit.

14.23 The following ten observations represent the price movement of a certain common stock over a ten-year period.

x (Year)	y (Price)	x (Year)	y (Price)
1	100	6	35
2	120	7	60
3	75	8	75
4	50	9	80
5	40	10	70

a) Sketch the relationship between x and y. What type of function does this relationship seem to follow for the given ten years?
b) Use the method of least squares to fit the equation $\hat{y} = a + bx$.
c) Determine the residuals for these ten observations, and check to see whether autocorrelation may be a problem in this estimation. Relate this result to your answer to part (a).

EXERCISES

14.24 A study was made of 53 countries to determine whether the formal character of a country's political constitution has a systematic impact on decentralization of public revenues. The following regression results were obtained:

$$\hat{y} = \underset{(12.1)}{96} - \underset{(-1.3)}{1.21x_1} - \underset{(-2.3)}{0.004x_2} - \underset{(-5.5)}{0.6x_3} - \underset{(-4.7)}{15.9x_4},$$
$$R^2 = 0.65$$

where

y is central government share of total public revenues, expressed as a percentage,
x_1 is the natural logarithm of population size in thousands,
x_2 is per-capita income in 1965 U.S. dollars,
x_3 is Social Security contributions as a percentage of total public revenue,
x_4 is 1 for countries with a federal constitution and 0 otherwise.

The values in parentheses are t-ratios of the regression estimates to their standard errors.
a) Interpret the meaning of the coefficient of x_4 in descriptive terms.
b) Using a 1% level of significance, test the hypothesis that the formal character of a country's constitution affects the proportion of public revenue that the central government obtains against the hypothesis that it does not.
c) Using a 5% level of significance and the statistic

$$F = \frac{R^2/m}{(1 - R^2)/(n - m - 1)},$$

which is equal algebraically to

$$F = \frac{SSR/m}{SSE/(n - m - 1)},$$

test the null hypothesis of no linear relationship.

TABLE 14.6 **Regression Results for** y = **imports**

Row	Observed	Estimated	Deviation
1	7.2	7.2822	−0.0822
2	8.2	8.6568	−0.4568
3	10.3	10.1508	0.1491
4	9.7	10.0910	−0.3910
5	12.1	11.7046	0.3954
6	15.1	14.3342	0.7658
7	15.8	15.3501	0.4499
8	16.6	16.4856	0.1144
9	16.1	16.3661	−0.2661
10	17.9	18.3980	−0.4980
11	19.8	19.7128	0.0872
12	20.7	20.9678	−0.2678

d) an interpretation of the results of parts (a)–(c) in terms of possible violations of assumption 4 or 5.

14.28 Repeat Exercise 14.27 using Table 14.7, based on a model with y = ln (imports) and x = ln (domestic price) for textiles over an eight-year period.

14.29 Repeat Exercise 14.27 using Table 14.8, based on a model with y = annual corporate profit before taxes and x = average monthly wholesale sales for a 16-year period.

14.30 Repeat Exercise 14.27 for Table 14.9, based on a model with y = net income earned from direct investment in Canada by U.S. firms and x = imports into the United States from Canada over a ten-year period.

TABLE 14.7 **Regression Results for** y = **ln (imports)**

Row	Observed	Estimated	Deviation
1	7.96	7.7391	0.2209
2	7.79	7.9512	−0.1612
3	7.73	8.2718	−0.5418
4	8.33	8.2718	0.0582
5	8.94	8.7037	0.2363
6	8.96	8.8124	0.1476
7	9.98	9.5823	0.3977
8	10.16	10.4798	−0.3198

TABLE 14.8 **Regression Results for** y **= corporate profit**

Row	Observed	Estimated	Deviation
1	16.8	17.7977	−0.9977
2	15.3	17.3958	−2.0958
3	20.4	18.9900	1.4100
4	24.4	20.1957	4.2043
5	21.1	20.4368	0.6632
6	21.4	20.7986	0.6014
7	18.4	20.7182	−2.3182
8	25.0	21.9239	3.0761
9	23.5	22.7544	0.7456
10	22.9	22.7143	0.1857
11	18.3	22.4195	−4.1195
12	25.4	23.9601	1.4399
13	23.0	24.0003	−1.0003
14	21.7	24.2548	−2.5548
15	24.7	24.9649	−0.2649
16	26.7	25.6749	1.0251

14.31 A model to explain the level of imports of a country over time uses 60 quarterly observations on imports and on these explanatory variables: disposable income, government expenditures, money stock, and interest rate. Analysis of the residuals gives a Durbin–Watson statistic of d = 1.156.

a) Is autocorrelation a problem?

TABLE 14.9 **Regression Results for** y **= foreign investment income**

Row	Observed	Eesimated	Deviation
1	24	20.4888	3.5112
2	22	22.8432	−0.8432
3	21	25.1976	−4.1976
4	24	24.0204	0.0204
5	29	31.0835	−2.0835
6	33	32.2607	0.7393
7	34	33.4379	0.5621
8	34	32.2607	1.7393
9	35	35.7923	−0.7923
10	36	34.6151	1.3849

b) Estimate a value of $\hat{\rho}$ that could be used to transform the data for reestimation.

c) A second estimation using the transformed data provides a d-value of 1.813. Explain what improvement has been made.

USING THE COMPUTER

14.32 Refer to the data for a model on job ratings in Problem 13.21(b). Use the residuals from regressions on two subgroups of this data to check for a violation of assumption 4 by making a Goldfeld–Quandt test. Order the observations according to the size of $\hat{y}$.

14.33 Using the residuals from the import model in Problem 12.57, do an appropriate plot to detect possible heteroscedasticity. Order the observations by time and run two regressions on subgroups of the data to make a Goldfeld–Quandt test.

14.34 Repeat Problem 14.33 using the education–income data from Problem 12.31 and the model income = α + β(educ). Order the observations by size of $\hat{y}$.

14.35 Return to the data set and results in Table 13.2 and Fig. 13.3(a) for the housing model.

a) Run a computer program for the least-squares regression that provides a list of residuals. Also, have the computer make a plot of e_t against $\hat{y}_t$ for the detection of heteroscedasticity.

b) Order the data according to the variable VACANT and do two regressions on subgroups of data to make a Goldfeld–Quandt (G–Q) test. Interpret the results.

14.36 Answer parts (a), (b), and (c).

a) Repeat Problem 14.35(a) using the data and model in Problem 13.25 for detergent sales.

b) Order the observations by size of population and do a G–Q test.

c) Repeat part (b) ordering the observations by the size of advertising expense.

14.37 Answer parts (a) and (b).

a) Repeat Problem 14.35(a) using **Data Set** 1 and the model in Problem 12.67 for taxes.

b) Order the data by the size of $\hat{y}$ and do a G–Q test.

14.38 Answer parts (a) and (b).

a) Repeat Problem 14.35(a) using **Data Set 2** and the model in Problem 12.66 for sales.

b) Order the data by size of $\hat{y}$ and do a G–Q test.

14.39 Answer parts (a) and (b).

a) Repeat Problem 14.35(a) using **Data Set 1** and the model in Problem 13.29 for taxes including dummy variables.

b) Order the data by the size of $\hat{y}$ and do a G–Q test.

14.40 Refer to Table 14.3 for the original and transformed data used in the investment model.

a) Repeat steps 2–4 of the correction process for autocorrelation, beginning with an estimated value of $d = 1.106$.

b) Compare your regression results to those in Fig. 14.9.

c) Examine the value of the d-statistic based on your regression. Does it differ from the previous value enough, say $|d - 1.106| > 0.05$, to warrant another iteration of the process?

14.41 Use **Data Set 5** and the model in Problem 12.69 for exports. Run a computer program for the least-squares regression that provides a list of the residuals and do a Durbin–Watson test. Also, have the computer make appropriate plots to examine for possible violations of assumption 4 or 5. Order the observations by time and run regressions for the Goldfeld–Quandt test. Interpret the results of your plots and test.

14.42 Use **Data Set 5** and the expanded model in Problem 13.27 for imports.

a) Repeat the residual analysis suggested in Problem 14.41.

b) Use the d-value to estimate the autocorrelation coefficient. Make a transformation of variables as in Formula (14.4) and reestimate the model. Repeat the residual analysis and interpret the results to examine the effect of the transformation on potential violations of assumptions 4 and 5.

c) Compare and interpret the results of the "before-and-after" regressions, including consideration of the properties of the estimators.

14.43 Use **Data Set 6** to regress income on years of education and on the number of persons in the household.

a) Have the computer find the OLS estimation and the OLS residuals.

b) Obtain three plots of residuals versus $\hat{y}$, x_1, or x_2 in order to check for possible heteroscedasticity.

c) Divide the data by the variable SEX into two natural groups. Make a Goldfeld–Quandt test for heteroscedasticity.

d) Explain whether a transformation of variable and reestimation might be appropriate. If so, specify the transformed values of all variables for observations 2 and 3.

14.44 For **Data Set 6** and the same model as in Problem 14.43:
  a) Divide the data by the variable REGION into four groups and run four separate regressions. Find s_e for the OLS regression on each region.
  b) Make a G–Q test between the pair of regions with the largest difference in the respective values of s_e. If heteroscedasticity is indicated, repeat the test for the pair of regions with the next largest difference in values of s_e. Continue examining pairs of regions until you are satisfied that you have identified any violations of assumption 4.
  c) Make a transformation of variables by dividing each observation by the value of s_e for its respective region. Reestimate the model using the transformed data and compare your results to the original estimation [Problem 14.43(a)] in terms of both the values and the properties of the estimates.
  d) Compare the results of the reestimated model in part (c) to the estimation of the same relation including dummy variables for the regions as in Problem 13.30.

CASE PROBLEMS

14.45 (Highway Safety) Using the model and data in Problem 12.72 for highway deaths:
  a) Obtain the least-squares regression results including a list of residuals and a plot of residuals versus $\hat{y}$.
  b) Order the observations used in part (a) by the size of the population density given in Problem 13.32, and do a G–Q test omitting the middle 20% of the observations.
  c) Include the variable "population density" in the model and repeat the residual analysis of parts (a) and (b).

14.46 (Personal project) Follow the steps in Section 14.7 to develop your own model, estimate it, test it, and write a report on your findings.

GLOSSARY

Econometrics: A study of methods of statistical analysis of economic models.

Simultaneity: Two-way causal relation among variables in a model.

Error in measurement: Inaccuracies in the values of the explanatory variable.

Gauss–Markov Theorem: Theorem developed by K. F. Gauss and A. A. Markov which says that the least-squares estimators of the intercept and the slope in the population regression line are the best linear unbiased estimators (BLUE).

Multicollinearity: A condition in which two or more of the independent variables are strongly (but not perfectly) related to one another in a linear relationship.

Extraneous estimate: The value of a coefficient in a model that is obtained from a result external to the estimation of the model.

Autocorrelation: There is a correlation among the error terms.

Durbin–Watson test: A test to detect autocorrelation.

Generalized least squares (GLS): Estimation method based on the least-squares principle that incorporates into the estimation information about the variance and covariance of the disturbance terms.

Heteroscedasticity: The variance of the error terms is not constant.

Goldfeld–Quandt test: A test to detect heteroscedasticity.

Weighted least squares: A special case of generalized least squares to correct for changing variance of the disturbances.

Transformation of variables: Algebraic changes in the definitions of y and x so that the linear model can better represent an underlying nonlinear relation or so that the underlying assumptions for multiple regression are better satisfied.

Elasticity: The percentage change in y for a 1% change in x.

Time Series and Index Numbers

FIFTEEN

15.1 INTRODUCTION TO TIME SERIES

In Chapter 12 we studied methods for describing the nature of the relationship between two variables. In this chapter we turn to a subset of this type of problem in which the independent variable under investigation is time.

Recording observations of a variable that is a function of time results in a set of numbers called a **time series.** Most data in business and economic publications take the form of a time series — e.g., the monthly sales receipts in a retail store, the annual Gross National Product (GNP) of the United States, and indexes of consumer and wholesale prices, to name just a few. The analysis of time-series data in such circumstances usually focuses on two types of problems:

1. Attempting to estimate the factors (or components, as they are called) that produce the pattern in the series; and
2. Using these estimates in forecasting the future behavior of the series.

In this chapter we shall concentrate our attention mainly on estimating the components of the time series, rather than studying the forecasting implications provided by these estimates. Our approach will emphasize economic time series because of their central importance in the planning function performed by many businesses and government agencies.

Components of a Time Series

In general, the fluctuations in an economic time series are assumed to result from four different components: trend (T), seasonal variation (S), cyclical variation (C), and irregular or random variation (I). **Trend** is the long-term movement in a time series. (GNP, for example, has grown at a rate of approximately 3–4% a year over the past 20 years. The tendency toward a decreasing work week and increasing price levels over the past several decades also illustrates long-term movements or trends.) **Seasonal variation** represents fluctuations that repeat themselves within a fixed period of one year. Many economic series have seasonal highs or lows due to changes in the supply of certain factors (youth employment in the summer, food harvests in the fall), in demand for certain factors (ski equipment in the winter, toys before Christmas, gardening supplies in the spring), or in marketing factors (seasonal changes in clothing, new car models in the fall). The **cyclical variation** of a time series represents a pattern repeated over time periods of differing length, usually longer than one year. (Business cycles, with their stages of prosperity, recession, and recovery, are important examples of such cyclical movements.)

The movements in a time series generated by trend, seasonal variation, and cyclical variation are assumed to be based on systematic causes; that is, these movements do not occur merely by chance, but reflect factors that have a more or less regular influence. Exactly the opposite hold true for random or **irregular variation,** which is, by definition, fluctuation that is unpredictable or takes place at various points in time, by chance or randomly. (Floods, strikes, and fads illustrate the irregular component of a time series.) Figure 15.1 presents a graphical view of the four components of a time series. In each case the dependent variable **y** is expressed as a function of the independent variable t (time).

The Time-Series Model

Now that we have specified the components of a time series, the problem becomes one of estimating each of these components for a given series. That is, we want to be able to estimate what portions of the value of **y** for any given year are attributable respectively to trend, seasonal factors, cyclical factors, or random or irregular variation. In order to separate these values, we must make some assumptions about how these compo-

FIGURE 15.1 **The four components of a time series.**

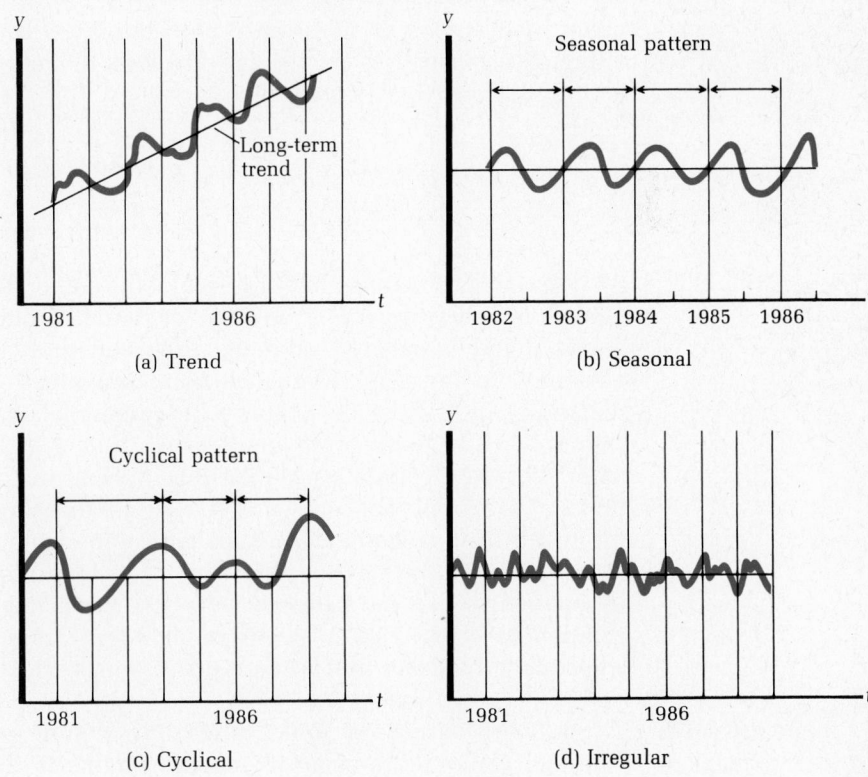

(a) Trend

(b) Seasonal

(c) Cyclical

(d) Irregular

nents are related in the population under investigation; these assumptions are referred to as the *time-series model*.

Time-series models usually fall into one of two categories, depending on whether their components are expressed as sums or products. The first of these, called the **additive model**, assumes that the value of y equals the *sum* of the four components, or that $y = T + S + C + I$. By assuming that the components of a time series are additive we are, in effect, assuming that these components are independent of one another. Thus, for example, trend can affect neither seasonal nor cyclical variation, nor can these components affect trend. The other major type of relationship between the components expresses y in the form $y = T \times S \times C \times I$ and is called the **multiplicative model**. A model of this form assumes that the four components are related to one another, yet still allows for the components to result from different basic causes. Note that one can transform a multiplicative model into a linear (i.e., additive) model by taking the logarithm of both sides,

$$\log y = \log T + \log S + \log C + \log I.$$

Other models exist in addition to the additive and multiplicative ones, although these models usually take the form of combinations of additive and multiplicative elements, such as

$$y = S + T \times C \times I$$

or

$$y = C + T \times S \times I.$$

For the purpose of estimating each of the components of a time series, models normally treat S, C, and I as deviations from the trend. In other words, trend is usually estimated first, and the variation that can be attributed to trend is eliminated from the values of y. The variation remaining in y must be due to either seasonal, cyclical, or irregular factors. Each of these components of the time series can be isolated by other statistical techniques. While some of these methods are excessively tedious, the basic concepts are similar to the simple methods to be discussed in this chapter. Once all the components of a time series are estimated, then forecasts of the value of the time series at some future point in time can be made by first estimating the value of the trend component at that point and then modifying this trend value by an adjustment that takes into account the seasonal and cyclical components.

Some Purposes and Problems of Forecasts

The primary purpose of forecasting future values of a time series is to facilitate planning. A business manager wants to forecast the trend in sales in order to make long-range planning decisions about investment in more plant capacity and new equipment. Or there may be a need to forecast cyclical movements in order to take advantage of lower interest-rate periods to conduct a bond sale or of a period of high investor expectations to release a new issue of common stocks. Seasonal variation is important for short-run planning of inventories and employment levels, as the manager needs to be prepared for periods of high demand for certain products and services. As consumers, we recognize these seasonal components also and plan to make purchases at times of special sales when prices are lower. Of course, the marketing experts use the seasonal components to plan advertising campaigns to entice buyers to purchase during the high season when the product or service is most desirable. We are sure that any salesman would prefer to handle ski equipment in the fall and winter and air conditioners in the spring and summer, rather than vice versa.

The most obvious problem inherent in forecasting future values of a time series is the potential size of the (unpredictable) irregular component. This component is a random variable whose size depends upon a large number of independent factors that affect the economic variable y. Psychological and sociological variables of individual and group behavior, as well as other economic and business considerations, can affect the forecast. In addition, the irregular component may consist of one single occurrence in the time period being forecast, such as a flood, a major political event, or an energy crisis. Neither the size nor the direction of the irregular component can be predicted.

There is also an important problem in trying to forecast the more regular parts of the time series: the trend, cyclical, and seasonal components. In forecasting, it is necessary to assume that no change occurs in the fundamental causes underlying these regular patterns. For this reason, forecasts far beyond the range of presently observable values of the time series are always very dubious. In most cases this means that the forecaster must not try to predict very far into the future, for fear of being greatly embarrassed.

15.2 LINEAR TREND

The first step in analyzing a time series is usually estimation of the trend component T. As was true in regression analysis, the first decision usually must be whether or not the trend can be assumed to be linear. Several linear methods will be discussed briefly before we discuss the methods for estimating trend when the relationship is not linear.

The linear trend is written $y = a + bx$, where x is a measure of time. Often a graph of the time-series data indicates quite well whether or not this linear relationship provides a good approximation to the long-term movement of the series. If a linear relationship is appropriate, then there are several methods for roughly approximating T. A fairly accurate approximation can often be obtained by merely drawing the line that, by freehand estimation, seems to represent best the long-run movement of the points. A more systematic approach is to use what is called the **method of semi-averages.** In this approach the data are divided into two equal parts, one representing the values associated with the first half of the years under investigation and the second representing the remaining years. The average value of the independent (time) and dependent variables is calculated for each of these parts, and the points representing these averages are connected by a straight line representing the trend line. For data containing an odd number of observations, the middle observation may be left out when dividing the data into two equal parts. Similarly, it may be advisable to eliminate one or two observations when calculating the mean value of **y** if these observations are clearly atypical of the rest of the series and if their inclusion will disturb the whole trend line.

The method of least squares, developed in Chapter 12, represents the most popular method of fitting a trend line to time-series data. Recall that in order to determine the values of a and b in a least-squares analysis, it is necessary to solve the following two normal equations:

$$\sum_{i=1}^{n} y_i = na + b \sum_{i=1}^{n} x_i,$$

$$\sum_{i=1}^{n} x_i y_i = a \sum_{i=1}^{n} x_i + b \sum_{i=1}^{n} x_i^2.$$

(15.1)

We will describe the use of these equations shortly.

Scaling and Interpreting the Time Variable

In any time-series analysis it is important to define carefully the units of the time variable x and to scale this variable so that it is easy to manipulate. Since time is continuous, it really makes little difference if the units used to express time are years, months, weeks, days, or any other desirable period. Also, because the point in time that is selected as $x = 0$ has no influence on the analysis, any point in time can be assigned this value. For whatever period is used, however, it usually is convenient to let $x = 0$ represent the *middle* of that period. For example, if x is in months, then $x = 0$ would be the middle of one of the months; similarly, if x is in periods six months long (half-years), then $x = 0$ would represent the middle of this period (i.e., after three months). A simple coding rule used often in assigning the values of x is:

1. If the number of time periods is odd, let x be in the same units as the observed time periods (years, months, etc.) and assign x = 0 to that time period falling in the exact center. Then let time periods before x = 0 be denoted by . . ., −3, −2, −1, and future time periods be denoted by +1, +2, +3, ...
2. If the number of time periods is even, let x be in units one-half as large as the observed time periods (half-years, half-months, etc.), and assign x = 0 to the midpoint in time between the two middle observations. Then denote time periods before x = 0 as . . ., −5, −3, −1, and denote future periods as +1, +3, +5, ...

This coding procedure has the advantage that the mean of the x-values will always be $\bar{x}$ = 0 and also that the middle of each time period is represented by an integer value of x. This makes the interpretation and use of the trend equation simpler. We will illustrate both of these two types of scaling.

Example 15.1. First, suppose that the time-series data we have available concerns the variable y = days of sick leave by all employees in a firm, measured over the six-month period shown in Table 15.1. Since the number of time periods is even, we use coding procedure 2.

The units of x in Table 15.1 are expressed in units of half-months, with x = 0 corresponding to the date, midnight May 31, 1984. The values of x now represent the number of half-months before or after the end of May 1984. For example, the value x = 5 represents August 15, 1984, which is five half-months after May 31. Note that the sum of the x-values is zero, which means that $\bar{x}$ = 0. To forecast a trend value for November, the value x = 11 would be substituted into the trend equation. To forecast a trend value at the end of the year (December 31, 1984), the value x = 14 would be used.

TABLE 15.1 **Monthly observations of days of sick leave**

Days of Sick Leave	Time Period (1984)	Value of x
16	March	−5
17	April	−3
18	May	−1
20	June	+1
18	July	+3
24	August	+5

The lower line in Fig. 15.4 represents the same data shown in quarterly magnitudes. That is, the values represented by circles are one-fourth the size of the values represented by squares. Note that these circle values are plotted at the middle of each quarter (e.g., Feb. 15, May 15, Aug. 15, and Nov. 15), and thus no quarterly value falls at the same point in time as do the yearly values (July 1).

There are three basic ways in which to translate one trend line into another, each following a simple rule.

Rule 1. *Changing magnitudes of the series* (y): Multiply both coefficients a and b by the ratio of the size of the new magnitude for y to the size of the old magnitude for y.

Rule 2. *Changing time units of* (x): Multiply the slope coefficient b by the ratio of the size of the new unit for x to the size of the original unit for x.

Rule 3. *Changing the origin point in time:* Substitute x + t into the equation and solve for a new intercept, where t is the number of x-units desired (positive or negative) to move the origin (forward or backward in time).

Example 15.4. In reducing annual magnitudes to quarterly magnitudes for the trend equation $\hat{y} = a + bx = 9.4 + 3.5x$, where x is in years with origin at July 1, 1982, it is necessary to multiply both a and b

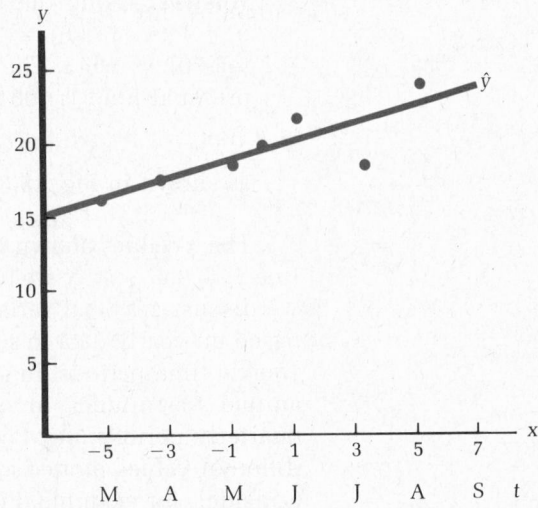

FIGURE 15.3 **Trend line for data of Table 15.1.**

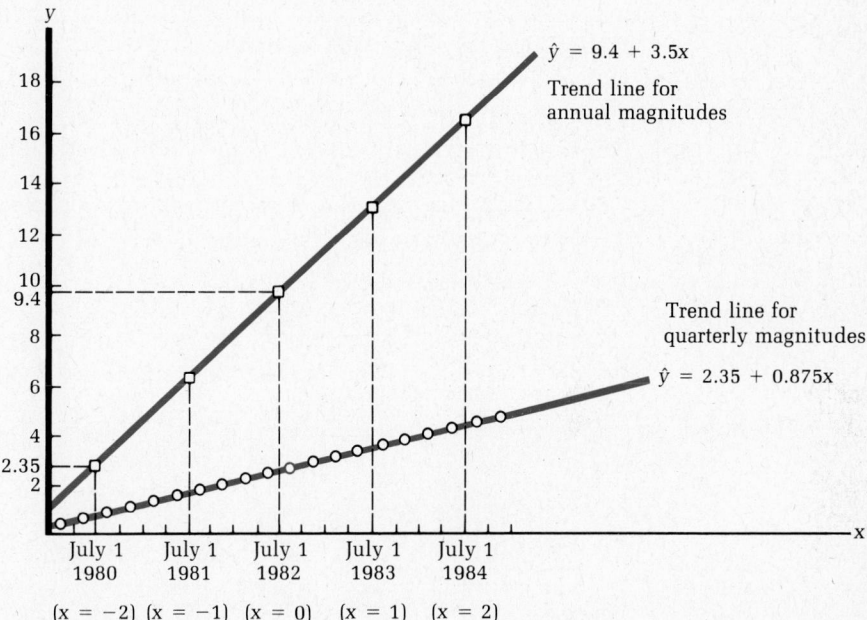

FIGURE 15.4 **Annual (□) versus quarterly (○) magnitudes used to plot a trend line.**

by the ratio $\frac{1}{4}$. This follows rule 1, since a quarter is one-fourth of a year. We obtain

$$\hat{y} = \tfrac{1}{4}(9.4 + 3.5x) = 2.35 + 0.875x.$$

This equation gives quarterly magnitudes, but the values of x are still measured in years ($x = 1$ is one year), and the origin remains at July 1 as shown in the lower line of Fig. 15.4.

To obtain quarterly magnitudes with x measured in quarters, we use rule 2 and multiply the slope coefficient b by $\frac{1}{4}$. This yields

$$\hat{y} = 2.35 + \tfrac{1}{4}(0.875x) = 2.35 + 0.21875x.$$

where $x = 0$ at July 1, 1982, and $x = 1$ is one quarter later, October 1, 1982. This line is the same as the lower line in Fig. 15.4 with the scale for x changed so that each unit of x is one quarter (shown by the tick marks on the x-scale) rather than one year. If we wish to have the quarterly magnitudes centered at the middle of a quarter, we need to shift the origin of the line in quarterly units ($\hat{y} = 2.35 + 0.21875x$) one-half quarter to the right from July 1 to August 15. Using rule 3, we add $\frac{1}{2}$ to x in the equation above. The equation is

$$\hat{y} = 2.35 + 0.21875(x + \tfrac{1}{2}) = 2.46 + 0.21875x.$$

This equation is again represented by the lower line in Fig. 15.4 except that the integer values of x (in quarters) are now located exactly on the circles shown on the line. The colored circle is now the origin point (x = 0 at August 15, 1982). Note that all three of these steps in converting the trend line could be combined if the latter equation is the desired one. The combined change beginning with the original trend line for annual magnitudes, $\hat{y} = a + bx$, would be

$$\hat{y} = \left(\frac{a}{4}\right) + \left(\frac{b}{16}\right)\left(x + \frac{1}{2}\right) = \left(\frac{a}{4} + \frac{b}{32}\right) + \left(\frac{b}{16}\right)x.$$

For our example, a = 9.4 and b = 3.5. Hence, the resulting equation is

$$\hat{y} = \frac{9.4}{4} + \frac{3.5}{32} + \left(\frac{3.5}{16}\right)x$$

$$= 2.46 + 0.21875x.$$

Changes in trend equations from annual magnitudes to monthly, or from monthly to quarterly, can be done following the same logical processes.

Study Question 15.2: Quarterly Trend Line for Days of Sick Leave
Change the trend equation in Study Question 15.1 to one in quarterly magnitudes and quarterly time units with origin at mid–first quarter, 1984.

Answer. The trend equation in monthly units and magnitudes with origin at June 1, 1984, is

$$\hat{y} = 18.83 + 0.643x.$$

To change to quarterly from monthly magnitudes, both coefficients must be multiplied by $\frac{3}{1}$. To change to quarterly from monthly units, the coefficient of x must be multiplied by $\frac{3}{1}$. To move the origin back 3.5 months to mid-February 1982, the term (x − 3.5) is substituted for x in the trend equation. The revised trend line desired is

$$\hat{y} = 3[18.83 + 3(0.643)(x - 3.5)],$$

$$\hat{y} = (56.490 - 20.255) + 5.79x,$$

$$\hat{y} = 36.235 + 5.79x.$$

A special problem arises when data are analyzed for a product or service that is produced for only a fraction of a year in each year. For example, sugar beet–processing plants operate for about four months, starting in September of each year, and all sugar-refining processes shut down completely when the last beets are processed around the beginning of the following calendar year. When a trend line is being plotted for monthly production of sugar from sugar beets, the x-values must be expressed in months, but there will be only four nonzero values of x observed in each year. Problem 15.4 provides the reader with an opportunity to work an example of this type.

15.3   NONLINEAR TRENDS

The problem of fitting a trend line to a nonlinear time series is essentially the same problem we mentioned in Chapter 12 concerning nonlinear regression — that of finding an equation that best describes the relationship between an independent variable (time, in this case) and the dependent variable (the time-series values). As is true in fitting a regression line, it is not sufficient merely to find an equation that provides a good fit to the data; it also is necessary to find a model that is justifiable in terms of the underlying economic nature of the series. In estimating the trend in a time series, there are a number of nonlinear equations that can be justified under a wide variety of circumstances.

Exponential Curve   Time series are often used to describe data that increase or decrease at a constant proportion over time, such as population growth, the sales of a new product, or the spread of a highly communicable disease. Data taking this form can be approximated by an equation referred to as the **exponential curve:**

$$\text{Exponential curve:} \quad y = ab^x. \qquad (15.3)$$

The form of the exponential curve depends on the values of a and b. If b is between zero and one, then the value of y will decrease as x increases. When b is larger than one, y will increase as x increases. The value of a gives the y-intercept of the curve, as shown in Fig. 15.5.

As seen in Section 14.6, we can transform the exponential curve into a linear relationship by taking the logarithm of both sides of Formula (15.3):

$$\log y = \log (ab^x) = \log a + x \log b.$$

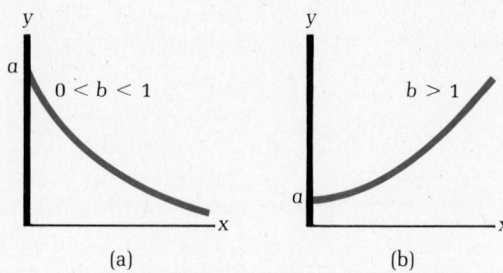

FIGURE 15.5 **The exponential curve** $y = ab^x$.

(a)

(b)

Our model is now linear, and the least-squares approach can be used to find the line of best fit.

Example 15.5. Consider the profits data given in Table 15.3 and graphed in Fig. 15.6. Again, the values of x have been specified so that $\Sigma x_i = 0$. From Fig. 15.6 we see that profits from 1980 to 1984 were not linear and that an equation of the type shown in Fig. 15.5(b) might be reasonable. To use least-squares regression analysis to find the values of a and b in the equation $y = ab^x$, it is necessary to substitute log a for a, log b for b, and log y for y in the normal equations. Since $\Sigma x_i = 0$, the appropriate equations are thus

Least-squares formula for an exponential curve when $\overline{x} = 0$:

$$\log a = \frac{\sum_{i=1}^{n} \log y_i}{n}, \qquad \log b = \frac{\sum_{i=1}^{n} x_i \log y_i}{\sum_{i=1}^{n} x_i^2}. \qquad (15.4)$$

To solve these equations, we need to transform the data in Table 15.3 by finding the logarithm of y and finding $x \log_{10} y$ (given in Table 15.4).

TABLE 15.3 **Profits**

Year	x	y
1980	−2	$1
1981	−1	3
1982	0	6
1983	1	14
1984	2	41

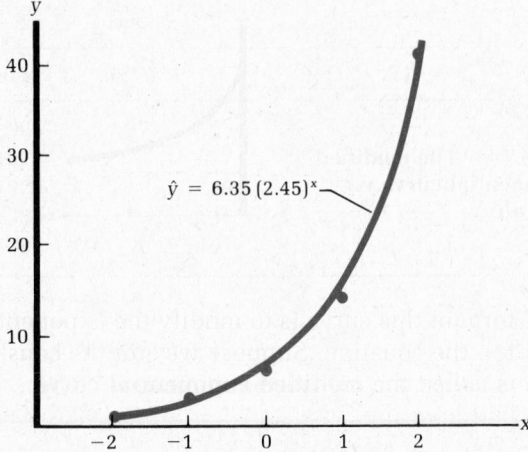

FIGURE 15.6 **Profits from Table 15.3.**

We can now solve for a and b. Substituting the values calculated in Table 15.4 into Formula (15.4) yields

$$\log a = 0.8028, \quad \log b = 0.3895.$$

Taking the antilog of these values yields the least-squares estimates $a = 6.35$ and $b = 2.45$. Thus, the exponential trend equation is

$$\hat{y} = (6.35)(2.45)^x.$$

Using this equation to forecast profits for 1985 ($x = 3$) yields $(6.35)(2.45)^3 = 93.38$. The fit provided by this equation for all values of x from -2 to $+2$ is shown in Fig. 15.6.

Modified Exponential Curve In a number of circumstances it is desirable to allow for more flexibility in deciding on the position of the trend line than is provided by the exponential curve. One way to accomplish this objective without altering

TABLE 15.4 **Profits**

x	y	$\log_{10} y$	$x \log_{10} y$	x^2
-2	1	0.000	0.000	4
-1	3	0.477	-0.477	1
0	6	0.778	0.000	0
1	14	1.146	1.146	1
2	41	1.613	3.226	4
Sum		4.014	3.895	10

The procedure just described for fitting a trend line to a set of observations is called the *three-point method*. When more than just a small number of observations is involved, it is customary to apply this method by dividing the relevant years into three equal periods. The mean value of y for each of these periods is used for each of the three points, rather than the value of y from a single year. In either case the three-point method should be viewed as providing only an approximation to the more precise fitting obtainable by the method of nonlinear least squares (which is not presented here).

Logistic Curve There are a number of additional curves used to estimate trend in a time series, two of which are suitable for mention here. The first is known as a **logistic curve** and is defined by the following equation:

$$\text{Logistic curve:} \qquad y = \frac{1}{c + ab^x}. \qquad\qquad \textbf{(15.6)}$$

Note that the logistic curve is just the reciprocal of the modified exponential curve. Its rate of growth or decline is relatively rapid at first but slows down in the later stages of the series, as shown in Fig. 15.9. Bacterial growth or sales increases for a new company sometimes exhibit such a pattern over time. Solving for the values of a, b, and c in a logistic curve presents the same problem as solving for these values in the modified exponential curve. The same approach described previously, using average points for three subgroups of the time-series values to establish three equations in three unknowns, can be used to determine a logistic curve by letting $1/y$ be the dependent variable, rather than y. The resulting equation, $1/y = c + ab^x$, has the same form as the modified exponential.

FIGURE 15.9 **The logistic curve $y = 1/(c + ab^x)$.**

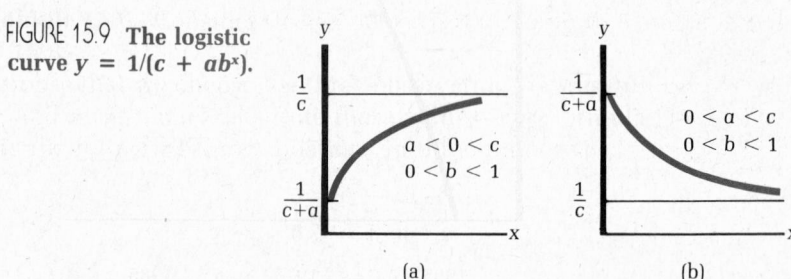

(a) $\qquad\qquad$ (b)

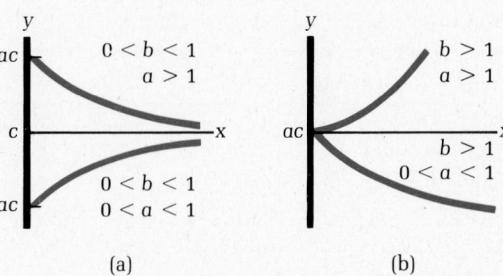

FIGURE 15.10 **The Gompertz curve** $y = ca^{b^x}$.

Gompertz Curve

The final trend equation we shall discuss is called the **Gompertz curve**, named after Benjamin Gompertz, who used the curve in the early 1800's in work concerning mortality tables. This curve is similar to the exponential curve, except that the constant a is raised to the b^x power instead of to the x power:

$$\text{Gompertz curve:} \quad y = ca^{b^x}. \qquad (15.7)$$

When the value of b in a Gompertz curve is between zero and one, the power to which a is raised will approach zero as x increases; hence, the value of y will become closer and closer to c, as shown in part (a) of Fig. 15.10. When the value of b is greater than one, the curve will either increase without bound (when $a > 1$) or approach zero (when $0 < a < 1$) as x gets larger and larger, as shown in part (b) of Fig. 15.10. The Gompertz curve can be fitted to time-series data in essentially the same fashion as the modified exponential curve. Taking the logarithm of both sides of Formula (15.7), we obtain

$$\log y = \log c + (b^x) \log a. \qquad (15.8)$$

Formula (15.8) is a special form of the modified exponential curve, with unknowns $\log a$, b, and $\log c$, instead of a, b, and c.

The problem of deciding which of the many available nonlinear equations to use in estimating trend in a given circumstance is often a difficult one. It is not unusual, in fitting the commonly used mathematical curves to a set of time-series observations, to find that two or more equations provide approximately the same closeness of fit. Thus, for the purpose of merely describing the data there is little to choose among these curves. The problem arises when such curves are used to predict future values of the time series (i.e., extrapolations into the future) because

TABLE 15.6 **Maximum annual social security tax**

Year	Tax	Year	Tax
1959	288	1974	1544
1962	300	1977	1930
1965	348	1980	3175
1968	686	1983	4784
1971	811	1986	6306

the curves tend to diverge rather quickly. Unacceptably large divergences may result from even a small extrapolation. Thus, as we pointed out earlier in this chapter, it is not sufficient merely to find a trend line providing a "good fit" to the data. It is necessary to fit a curve that can be theoretically justified by a general assessment of the underlying nature of the series. In other cases, no curve may fit well because there may be no single persistent relationship between the dependent variable and time.

FIGURE 15.11 **Plot of social security tax values.**

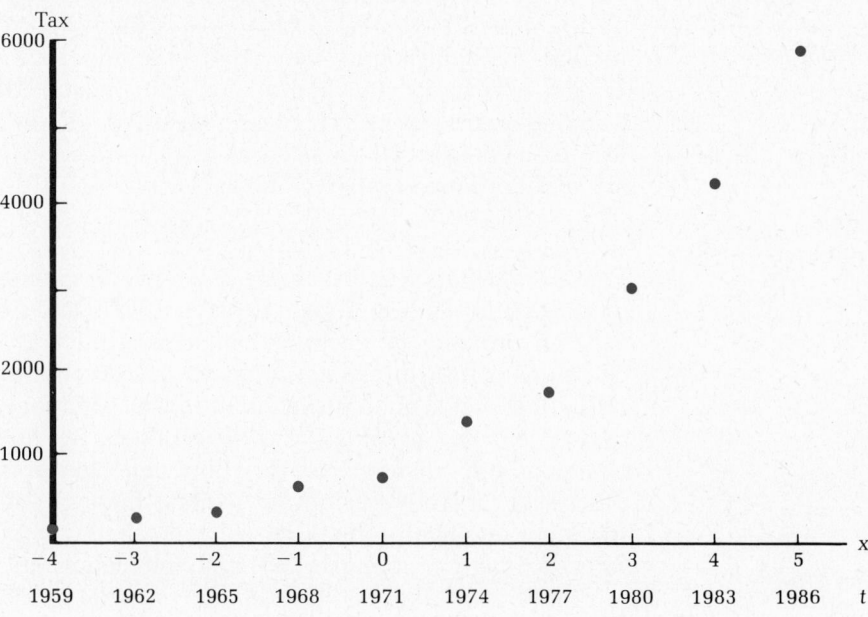

Study Question 15.3: Nonlinear Trends for Social Security Tax
Use the values in Table 15.6 for the maximum individual annual social security tax (employer and employee contributions) for the years 1959–1986. Let x be in units of 3 years with x = 0 at mid-1971, so x = 1 at mid-1974. Plot the tax values. Suggest which nonlinear curve given in this section might best represent the trend in maximum social security tax.

Answer. A plot of the maximum social security tax values for these years is shown in Fig. 15.11. The two nonlinear functions that might best fit these data are the exponential curve as in Formula (15.3) and Fig. 15.5(b) and the Gompertz curve as in Formula (15.8) and Fig. 15.10(b) with $b > 1$ and $a > 1$.

15.4 MOVING AVERAGES TO SMOOTH A TIME SERIES

In the discussion thus far, we have assumed that a trend line can be calculated without first removing, or at least minimizing, the effect of seasonal, cyclical, and random movements in the series. In some circumstances, however, it may be easier to estimate trend if the effects of these fluctuations are removed from the data. Methods for removing these effects are usually referred to as smoothing techniques.

The Method of Moving Averages

The most commonly used method of smoothing data is called the **method of moving averages.** A moving average is actually a series of averages, where each average is the mean value of the time series over a fixed interval of time and where all possible averages of this time length are included in the analysis. A 12-month moving average, for example, must include the mean value for each 12-month period in the series. These averages represent a new series that has been smoothed to eliminate fluctuations that occur within a 12-month period. Since a seasonal pattern will repeat itself every 12 months, a 12-month moving average will reduce fluctuations caused by the seasons of the year. Note that a 12-month moving average will also tend to eliminate any other fluctuations with a pattern that repeats itself over an interval of less than a year's duration, such as daily or weekly patterns. Similarly, a five-year moving average could be used to reduce a pattern or cycle that repeats itself every five years.

Example 15.7. To illustrate the process of calculating a moving average, we will use this approach to smooth the data in Table 15.7. These data appear to fluctuate in a cyclical pattern that repeats itself every five years. In calculating a five-year moving average, we first must determine the mean value for the initial five years, 1970–1974. This mean value, which equals $(1/5)(2 + 4 + 5 + 7 + 8) = 5.2$, is "centered" on (i.e., placed in the middle of) the five years being averaged, 1972. Similarly, the next moving average, 6.0, is computed from the values corresponding to 1971 through 1975 and centered in the year 1973. This process continues until the last observation is included; the last moving average is 17.2, and this value is centered at the year 1982. The moving average values, when compared to the original values, tend to reduce the variation and represent a smoothed version of the time series in which the cyclical component has been reduced. If the observation units were one quarter of a year or less, the moving average technique would smooth out seasonal variations also. The comparison between the original time series and its representation by the moving average values is shown in Fig. 15.12.

This moving average procedure gives equal weights to all five observations in calculating each mean value. Sometimes, one may wish to increase the relative importance of one or more observations by using a **weighted moving average.** To calculate a weighted moving average, each observation being averaged is given a weight that reflects its relative importance.

Example 15.8. In a five-year weighted moving average, for example, the weights might be 1, 2, 3, 2, 1, based on the assumption that the middle value in a series of observations should have the largest weight and the first and fifth observations should have the smallest weights. Using this weighting system on the data in Table 15.7, we obtain a weighted moving average centered at 1972 equal to

$$\frac{1(2) + 2(4) + 3(5) + 2(7) + 1(8)}{1 + 2 + 3 + 2 + 1} = 5.22.$$

TABLE 15.7 **Profits (millions of dollars)**

Year	y	Centered M.A.	Year	y	Centered M.A.
1970	2		1978	13	11.4
1971	4		1979	14	12.6
1972	5	5.2	1980	11	14.0
1973	7	6.0	1981	14	15.4
1974	8	6.8	1982	18	17.2
1975	6	8.0	1983	20	
1976	8	9.2	1984	23	
1977	11	10.4			

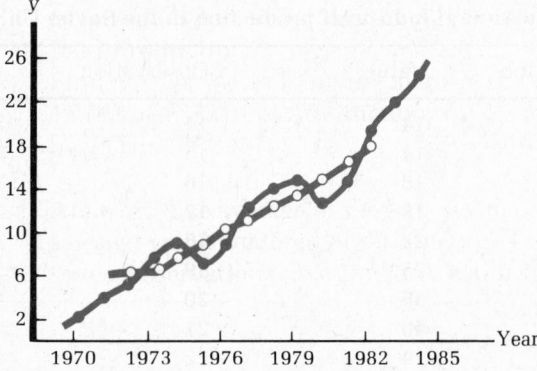

FIGURE 15.12 **Values of annual profits (-●-) and five-period moving average values (-○-) from Table 15.7.**

The second weighted moving average would be centered in 1973 and equal to

$$\frac{1(4) + 2(5) + 3(7) + 2(8) + 1(6)}{1 + 2 + 3 + 2 + 1} = 5.67.$$

By continuing this process we could derive the entire series for the weights 1, 2, 3, 2, 1. Had we used some other weighting system, an entirely different moving average would be determined. In general, the weights used depend on the degree to which the analyst wishes to emphasize particular values.

The Use of Moving Averages for Smoothing   It is important to note that by smoothing a time series we have not solved the problem of estimating the trend component for that series. Smoothing the series merely serves to eliminate some of the variability not attributable to trend, in the hope that the trend component can be more easily identified.

    Although the use of a moving average may help to identify trend, a moving average method has several weaknesses as a smoothing device. First of all, this method is often only partially successful in removing all the effects of S, C, and I from y when determining T, because C and I usually do not have regular fluctuations. In addition, the moving average method tends to introduce spurious cyclical movements into the data being smoothed, so that an analyst who tries to remove cyclical effects from data may, in fact, introduce a nonexistent cycle.

    A final problem with the use of the moving average is the arbitrary choice of its length, denoted by h, which is the number of consecutive values used in the averages. The larger the value of h, the more the moving average smooths out the original data, but the greater is $(h - 1)$, the number of total observations at the beginning and end of the data for

$$\text{Seasonally adjusted value} = \frac{\text{Original value} \times 100}{\text{Seasonal index}}. \qquad \textbf{(15.9)}$$

Example 15.9.   We will assume that bicycle sales for a given manufacturer have averaged 50,000 units a month for the past five years. However, the average sales in each month are not always equal to 50,000. In February, for example, sales over the past five years have averaged 30,000 units. Similarly, May has averaged 50,000 units, and December, 80,000 units. Since February has averaged only 60% of the overall average sales of 50,000, the seasonal index for February is $S_{\text{Feb.}} = 60.0$. The indexes for May and December would be $S_{\text{May}} = 100.0$ and $S_{\text{Dec.}} = 160$.

Formula (15.9) is used to adjust values of bicycle sales. Assume that the actual sales for February and December in a given year were 32,000 and 84,000, respectively. Adjusting these values, we obtain:

$$\text{Adjusted February sales} = \frac{32,000 \times 100}{60} = 53,333;$$

$$\text{Adjusted December sales} = \frac{84,000 \times 100}{160} = 52,500.$$

Note how this seasonal adjustment makes the comparison of sales between the two months very easy. Here we see that February sales were slightly better than December sales on a seasonally adjusted basis. Because the average seasonal index for these two months exceeds $100[(60 + 160)/2 = 110]$, their total adjusted values (105,833) must be less than the total sales that actually occurred (116,000). If a seasonal index has been correctly formulated, the adjusted total for 12 months will always equal the actual total over all 12 months.

Ratio-to-Trend Method

In order to determine seasonal index numbers, it is necessary to estimate the seasonal component of a time series. Suppose that a given time series can be represented by the multiplicative model $y = T \times S \times C \times I$. One method for estimating the seasonal component in this model is called the **ratio-to-trend method.** We estimate S by removing trend from the series without attempting to remove cyclical and irregular variation. Assume that a value of T has been calculated for each monthly value of y in the series. Trend can be eliminated by dividing y by these monthly trend values, $y/T = S \times C \times I$; the remaining fluctuations are assumed to represent, primarily, seasonal variation.

Example 15.10. We illustrate the ratio-to-trend method using the data in Table 15.10, which represent the monthly sales in a department store over the three-year period from 1982 to 1984.

The trend component of these observations can be estimated by fitting a least-squares regression line to the data. Rather than fit a line to all 36 points, we can estimate the trend line by using just the three monthly averages shown in the last column of Table 15.10 as follows:

Year	x	y	x^2	xy
1982	-1	73.0	1	-73.0
1983	0	86.8	0	0.0
1984	1	99.5	1	99.5
Sum	0	259.3	2	26.5

Since $\Sigma x_i = 0$, we can use the reduced form of the normal equations presented in Formula (15.2):

$$a = \sum_{i=1}^{n} y_i/n \quad \text{and} \quad b = \sum_{i=1}^{n} x_i y_i \bigg/ \sum_{i=1}^{n} x_i^2.$$

Substituting the appropriate values into these equations, we obtain a value of a equal to $259.3/3 = 86.43$ and a value of b equal to $26.5/2 = 13.25$. These values determine the following trend line for monthly sales with x = years and x = 0 at mid-1983:

$$\hat{y} = 86.43 + 13.25x.$$

Since we want to estimate monthly trend changes with the origin at mid-July 1983, we follow the rules of Section 15.2 to adjust the trend equation. We multiply the slope by $\frac{1}{12}$ and substitute $(x + \frac{1}{2})$ for x. The resulting equation is

TABLE 15.10 **Monthly sales**

Year	Jan.	Feb.	Mar.	Apr.	May	June	July	Aug.	Sept.	Oct.	Nov.	Dec.	Monthly Average
1982	67	71	72	73	71	70	67	64	66	74	82	99	73.0
1983	80	86	89	89	84	83	79	76	77	87	98	114	86.8
1984	92	98	101	103	96	96	89	87	90	99	112	131	99.5

$$\hat{y} = 86.43 + (\tfrac{1}{12})13.25(x + \tfrac{1}{2}),$$

$$\hat{y} = 86.98 + 1.104x \quad (x = \text{months}; x = 0 \text{ at mid-July 1983}).$$

This monthly trend equation indicates that y will increase 1.104 each month, accumulating an annual increase of 13.25 as in the annual trend equation. These monthly trend values are shown in Table 15.11.

We have now determined a value of T for each month in the series. The next step is to divide each month's sales value shown in Table 15.10 by the corresponding monthly trend value given in Table 15.11, and multiply by 100. The results of this computation are shown in the first three rows of Table 15.12. Since there are three different index numbers for each month in Table 15.12, we combine these values by taking their average, as shown in the bottom row of Table 15.12. The values shown in the bottom row of Table 15.12 are the monthly seasonal index values and may be used to deseasonalize observations, as discussed before. The deseasonalized data can be more accurately examined for trend and cycles than the original data, since any confusion of seasonal movements is eliminated.

A final step that is sometimes necessary in the construction of seasonal indexes is called *leveling the index*. The need for leveling may arise from the construction of seasonal indexes by either the ratio-to-moving-average method (which will be discussed in the next section) or the ratio-to-trend method. For example, in the ratio-to-trend method of constructing the index, raw seasonal index values are obtained by "averaging" the ratio-to-trend values for each quarter or month as the case may be. This averaging process is done without a restriction as to what the average of these "averages" must be over the entire year. However, the average of these "averages" or new seasonal indexes, must be 100 if deseasonalizing the series is to alter only the pattern but not the level of the raw data. For example, if the average over the year of the raw seasonal indexes were 90, the use of the raw seasonal indexes would raise the average level of the deseasonalized series by $100[(100/90) - 1]\%$ or about 11% above the average level of the raw data series. Clearly, this is an unintended

TABLE 15.11 **Monthly trend (rounded to one decimal)**

Year	Jan.	Feb.	Mar.	Apr.	May	June	July	Aug.	Sept.	Oct.	Nov.	Dec.
1982	67.1	68.2	69.3	70.4	71.5	72.6	73.7	74.8	75.9	77.0	78.1	79.3
1983	80.4	81.5	82.6	83.7	84.8	85.9	87.0	88.1	89.2	90.3	91.4	92.5
1984	93.6	94.7	95.8	96.9	98.0	99.1	100.2	101.3	102.4	103.5	104.6	105.7

TABLE 15.12 **Seasonal index numbers**

Year	Jan.	Feb.	Mar.	Apr.	May	June	July	Aug.	Sept.	Oct.	Nov.	Dec.
1982	99.9	104.1	103.9	103.7	99.3	96.4	90.9	85.6	87.0	96.1	105.0	124.8
1983	99.5	105.5	107.7	106.3	99.1	96.6	90.8	86.3	86.3	96.3	107.2	123.2
1984	98.3	103.5	105.4	106.3	98.0	96.9	88.8	85.9	87.9	95.7	107.1	123.9
Average	99.2	104.4	105.7	105.4	98.8	96.6	90.2	85.9	87.1	96.0	106.4	124.0

result of deasonalizing the series. The seasonal index in Table 15.12 averaged 100; hence, leveling was not necessary in this case.

In order to level an index, one finds the average of the raw seasonal indexes over the year and divides that average value into each raw seasonal index or "average" for each month or quarter and multiplies by 100. The effect of this computation is to increase or decrease all values of the raw seasonals in the same proportion and to make the leveled index average exactly 100 over the year. Use of the leveled index to deseasonalize a series alters the pattern within the year and tends to reduce monthly distortions in the level of the index.

Perhaps Fig. 15.13 will help summarize some of the material in this section. Fig. 15.13(a) shows the original sales data from Table 15.10 and the trend component of these data from Table 15.11. It is apparent that a pattern of monthly changes exist, having a low point in August and a high point in December. This pattern is reflected in the seasonal index from Table 15.12 that is shown in Fig. 15.13(b).

Ratio-to-Moving-Average Method

The ratio-to-trend procedure we have just described produces a seasonal index that still contains C and I. Although the process is considerably more cumbersome, there is a way to calculate an index, called the **ratio-to-moving-average method,** in which these fluctuations have been removed. The first step in this approach is to smooth the data by using a 12-month moving average. If we disregard the irregular component, the causes and occurrences of which are unknown, the smoothed series will contain fluctuations attributable only to T and C, since a 12-month moving average will remove seasonal variations. In terms of the multiplicative model we have, in effect, divided y by S, so the new series is $y/S = T \times C$. If the *original* time-series values, y, are now divided by this newly calculated series containing only T and C multiplied by 100, the result is $y(100)/(T \times C) = (T \times S \times C)/(T \times C) = S$. Thus, by a rather roundabout route, we have isolated S and determined a seasonal index

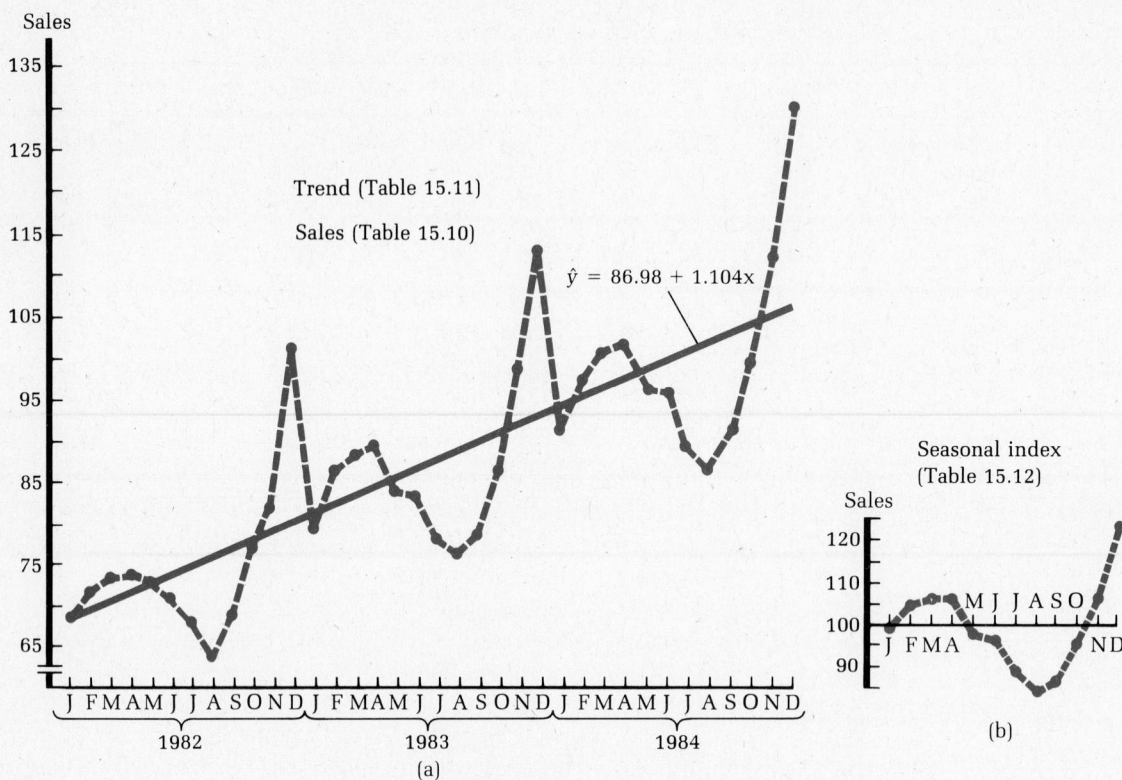

FIGURE 15.13 **Observations, trend, and seasonal index for sales from Tables 15.10 to 15.12.**

in which the variations attributable to T and C have been removed. To illustrate how this process works, we again use the data of Table 15.10.

Example 15.11. First, a 12-month moving average is taken over all months in the series. This moving average is shown in columns 3, 6, and 9 of Table 15.13. Now, to associate the moving-average values with the fifteenth rather than the first day of each month, these values are "centered" by taking the average of each two adjacent months. The centered moving-average values are shown in columns 4, 7, and 10 and represent $T \times C$ and some parts of I.

We have now eliminated S and some remaining parts of I from the series. To find a seasonal index, we must divide the original time-series values (sales) in column (2) of Table 15.13 by the 12-month centered

TABLE 15.13 **Original and moving average (M.A.) values for sales**

(1)	(2)	(3)	(4)	(2)	(3)	(4)	(2)	(3)	(4)
Month	1982 Sales	12-month M.A.	Centered 12-month M.A.	1983 Sales	12-month M.A.	Centered 12-month M.A.	1984 Sales	12-month M.A.	Centered 12-month M.A.
Jan.	67			80	81.3	80.8	92	93.9	93.5
Feb.	71			86	82.3	81.8	98	94.8	94.4
Mar.	72			89	83.2	82.8	101	95.9	95.4
Apr.	73			89	84.3	83.8	103	96.9	96.4
May	71			84	85.6	85.0	96	98.1	97.5
June	70	73.0		83	86.8	86.2	96	99.5	98.8
July	67	74.1	73.6	79	87.8	87.3	89		
Aug.	64	75.3	74.7	76	88.8	88.3	87		
Sept.	66	76.8	76.1	77	89.8	89.3	90		
Oct.	74	78.1	77.5	87	91.0	90.4	99		
Nov.	82	79.2	78.7	98	92.0	91.5	112		
Dec.	99	80.3	79.8	114	93.1	92.6	131		

moving-average values in column (4) and multiply by 100. The result of this computation, shown in Table 15.14, is two index numbers for each month of the year.

Since these index numbers may differ, some irregular component variation I is still included. By averaging the monthly $S \times I$ estimates for each calendar month, some more of the irregular component is eliminated. In a long time series with at least five values of $S \times I$ for each month, this averaging virtually isolates the pure seasonal index component S, with T, C, and I removed. The averages of these two values are the

TABLE 15.14 **Seasonal index numbers**

Year	Jan.	Feb.	Mar.	Apr.	May	June	July	Aug.	Sept.	Oct.	Nov.	Dec.
1982							91.0	85.7	86.7	95.5	104.2	124.1
1983	99.0	105.1	107.5	106.2	98.8	96.3	90.5	86.1	86.2	96.2	107.1	123.1
1984	98.4	103.8	105.9	106.8	98.5	97.2						
Average	98.7	104.5	106.7	106.5	98.7	96.8	90.8	85.9	86.5	95.9	105.7	123.6

15.4 A study is being made to determine the growth of annual honey production (y) over time (x) measured in years before and after 1980. The following data are given ($x = 0$ is 1980):

x	−2	−1	0	1	2
y	6	9	12	11	15

a) Find the regression equation of y on x.
b) Find the estimated value of honey production for 1983.

15.5 The value of building permits in a certain town over an eight-year period is given below.

x (year)	Value (thousands)	x (year)	Value (thousands)
1976	$300	1980	$310
1977	150	1981	490
1978	210	1982	380
1979	400	1983	400

a) Plot the above data and make a freehand estimate of the trend line.
b) Use the method of semi-averages to construct a trend line.
c) Use the method of least squares to determine a trend line.
d) Compare your estimates of the trend line for parts (a), (b), and (c). What value would you estimate for 1984 under each of these methods?
e) Find the least-squares regression line for quarterly magnitudes, with x measured in years. Shift the origin one-half quarter to the right.
f) Find the trend line, using annual values reported quarterly.

15.6 The following values represent sales data for the years 1975–1980.

Year	Sales (units)
1975	18,000
1976	19,000
1977	23,000
1978	24,000
1979	26,000
1980	28,000

a) Plot the values and then estimate a linear trend line by the freehand method.

b) Use the method of semi-averages to estimate a trend line.
c) Construct a least-squares regression line to estimate trend.
d) Find the least-squares regression line for quarterly magnitudes, with x measured in years. Shift the origin one-half unit to the left.
e) Find the trend line, using annual values reported quarterly.

15.7 The sales of a new product had the following growth pattern:

x (year)	Sales (thousands)	x (year)	Sales (thousands)
1	1.6	4	4.6
2	2.7	5	5.1
3	3.9	6	5.4

a) Fit a Gompertz curve to these data.
b) Fit a logistic curve.
c) Graph both of the curves constructed in parts (a) and (b), and then indicate which model appears to give the better fit.

15.8 Refer to the social security tax values in Table 15.6 and the plot in Fig. 15.11.
a) Fit an exponential curve to these data.
b) Fit a Gompertz curve to these data using three subgroups of data, each with three values, to determine the averages for the three-point estimating procedure.

15.9 Find a three-year moving average for the following data.

Year	Sales (thousands)
1972	$18
1973	20
1974	22
1975	19
1976	21
1977	24
1978	21
1979	23
1980	27

15.10 Given the following amounts of money (to the nearest thousand dollars) gambled and lost each year by a certain businessman during his vacations in Las Vegas or Atlantic City:

Year	Amount	Year	Amount
1976	2	1981	23
1977	7	1982	29
1978	5	1983	68
1979	16	1984	2
1980	12		

Find the four-period moving average for the amounts lost.

15.11 Use the table below to answer parts (a) and (b).
  a) Compute the trend equation for the following series by the method of least squares.
  b) Compare the trend value for 1980 with the three-period moving average value for 1980.

Year	Tons	Year	Tons
1975	30	1979	51
1976	44	1980	68
1977	50	1981	65
1978	42		

15.12 Answer parts (a)–(e).
  a) State two reasons for estimating the seasonal component of a time series.
  b) State two reasons for estimating the trend equation for a time series.
  c) State two disadvantages of the use of a (simple) moving average as a fit of trend.
  d) Describe one advantage and one disadvantage of using a moving-average smoothing method in time-series analysis.
  e) Explain the difference between cyclical and seasonal variations in a time series.

15.13 Assume that the trend line (annual total equation) for suits is $\hat{y} = 3600 + 480x$ with origin at October, 1981. The seasonal index for April is 80. Estimate the seasonally adjusted output for April, 1985.

15.14 The operating season for a certain tomato cannery is from June to October. Suppose that the following observations represent monthly sales, in thousands, for this cannery from 1979 to 1981.

Year	June	July	August	September	October
1979	75	86	102	105	90
1980	83	89	110	115	92
1981	84	95	113	118	89

a) Use the ratio-to-trend method to find a seasonal index for sales for the months June to October.

b) Find a seasonal index using the ratio-to-moving-average method, using a five-month moving average.

c) Assume that the multiplicative model $y = T \times S \times C \times I$ holds and that there is no irregular variation. Decompose the index for August of 1980 into the component parts T, S, and C, using your answer to part (a).

d) Repeat the above process, using your answer to part (b).

15.15 Explain how to find the cyclical component of a time series.

15.16 Find the cyclical component of the time series on industrial production in the Soviet Union (data given in Table 15.8).

15.17 The Business Research Department of the Carolina Corporation forecasts sales for next year of $12 million, based on a trend projection. It is expected that no sharp cyclical fluctuations will occur during the year, that the effect of trend *within* the year will be negligible, and that the past pattern of quarterly seasonal variation will continue. The pattern is as follows:

Quarter	1st	2nd	3rd	4th
Seasonal index	130	90	75	105

Prepare a forecast of quarterly sales from the above information for the first and second quarters of next year.

15.18 In finding the cyclical component of a time series, explain how to obtain C once the $(C \times I)$ component has been isolated.

15.19 Answer parts (a) and (b).

a) The unadjusted sales index of the C-B Company is 102 for January 1984. The seasonally adjusted index for the same month is 133. Find the seasonal index for January.

b) The annual sales for 1986 are forecast to be $240,000. The seasonal index for March is computed to be 90. Give a reasonable forecast of the sales for March 1986.

15.20 The index of seasonal variation for cement production for selected months is 60 for January, 70 for March, 122 for August, and 100 for November.
   a) In which of these months is cement production usually the greatest?
   b) In which of these months is the production most typical of the monthly average?
   c) ction in a certain region increased from 6,060,000 cubic yards of cement in January 1984 to 11,590,000 cubic yards of cement in August 1984. Determine the percentage change in cement production, allowing for seasonal variation.

15.21 Using the data for quarterly values at annual levels of GNP in Table 13.5 (page 673):
   a) Find the trend line in quarterly magnitudes with time units of one-half quarter and origin at October 1, 1973.
   b) Construct a quarterly seasonal index using the ratio-to-trend method.

15.22 Assume that you have been given the following quarterly seasonal index.

Quarter	1st	2nd	3rd	4th
Seasonal index	90	115	95	108

Note that these seasonal values do not sum to 100. Prepare a new seasonal index by leveling these values so that the sum equals 100.

15.23 Consider the following monthly data representing female employment levels for the two-year period 1979–1980 (in millions).

Month	Year 1979	1980
Jan.	22.1	22.9
Feb.	21.9	22.3
Mar.	22.6	23.0
Apr.	23.4	23.9
May	24.5	25.0
June	26.0	26.5
July	26.0	26.6
Aug.	25.9	25.7
Sept.	25.7	25.9
Oct.	25.4	25.7
Nov.	24.6	24.1
Dec.	24.1	24.6

a) Plot the above data, letting $x = 0$ represent January 1, 1980.
b) Use the method of least squares to determine a trend line.
c) Construct a seasonal index using the ratio-to-trend method.
d) Find a seasonal index using the ratio-to-moving-average method, based on a five-month moving average.

15.6 INDEX NUMBERS

Earlier in this chapter, index numbers were used to express the seasonal components of a time series. Our objective at that point and in the following discussion is to develop a measure that summarizes the characteristics of large masses of data. An index number accomplishes this purpose by aggregating information into a single measure that permits comparisons to be easily made. Although index numbers are used in many areas of the behavioral and social sciences, their main application involves describing business and economic activity, such as changes in prices, production, wages, and employment, over a period of time.

An **index number** is simply the ratio of two numbers expressed as a percentage. The denominator is the value in a selected time period, known as the *base* period. The numerator is the value for the period (*i*) of interest. The ratio is multiplied by 100 to put it in percentage terms. Formula (15.10) provides the definition of an index number:

$$(\text{Index number})_i = 100 \left[\frac{\text{Value in period } i}{\text{Value in base period}} \right]. \tag{15.10}$$

Example 15.12. Consider the data first given in Fig. 2.4 and repeated in the second column of Table 15.15 for the price in cents of gasoline (average of regular and unleaded pump price, self-service) on Easter in

TABLE 15.15 **Pump prices of gasoline (cents/gallon)**

Year	Price	Index (1978 = 100)	Index (1980 = 100)
1978	63	100.0	51.6
1979	78	123.8	63.9
1980	122	193.7	100.0
1981	139	220.6	113.9
1982	124	196.8	101.6
1983	117	185.7	95.9

Source: AAA—Carolina Motor Club

North Carolina for six successive years. If the year 1978 is chosen as the base year, the index number for gas price in 1983 is 100(117/63) = 185.7. This indicates an 85.7% increase in price for 1983 relative to the base year 1978. Other values of the index are computed the same way and are shown in the third column of Table 15.15. If a different base year had been selected, say 1980, the index for each year would change to reflect the percentage change of a given year relative to 1980. As shown in the final column of Table 15.15, the index for 1983 with base year 1980 is 100(117/122) = 95.9. This indicates a 4.1% decrease in price for 1983 relative to 1980. When examining any reports or arguments using index numbers, it is important to know the base year so that appropriate comparative statements can be made.

Uses of Index Numbers

The primary purposes of an index number are to provide a value useful for comparing magnitudes of aggregates of related variables to each other and to measure the changes in these magnitudes over time. Consequently, many different index numbers have been developed for special uses. Let us briefly mention some of their common uses.

First, index numbers are useful summary measures for policy guides. The Federal Reserve Board may use index numbers on interest rates, employment, or consumer credit as inputs to discussions on appropriate open-market transactions. Presidential advisors may use price and income indexes to set wage and price guidelines.

Second, many index numbers have been developed as indicators of business conditions, including the *Forbes*, *Fortune*, or *Business Week* indexes. The Federal Reserve System, the Bureau of Labor Statistics, and the Commerce Department all publish various index numbers for this same purpose.

Also, some of these indexes are commonly used for comparing changes among different sectors of the economy. Growth in the agricultural or mining sector might be compared to growth in the manufacturing sector. Levels of state and local government expenditures might be analyzed and compared among regions by using index numbers.

A fourth use of certain special indexes, such as wage, productivity, and cost-of-living indexes, is in wage contracts and labor–management bargaining. Management often likes to tie wage increases to productivity increases, while labor unions like to relate the need for wage increases to cost-of-living increases. Similar relations among indexes are used in escalator clauses to adjust insurance coverage, change retirement and social security benefits, etc.

Finally, a fifth and very common use of an index number is as a deflator. Certain measures of economic activity are divided by price or cost indexes and multiplied by 100 in order to obtain the *real* or constant dollar value of these measures. That is, an adjustment is made for the changing value of the dollar, so that more meaningful comparisons can be made over time.

Using an Index as a Deflator   The use of an index as a *deflator* is so common that it merits special attention. Since the base value of any index number is 100, the real value is obtained by the following rule:

$$\text{Real value} = \frac{(\text{Nominal value}) \times 100}{\text{Index number}}. \qquad \textbf{(15.11)}$$

Example 15.13. Suppose that a person's income increases from $10,000 to $15,000 over a given period, while the consumer price index (C.P.I.) increases from 100 to 130. The *nominal* increase in income of $5,000 is offset by general inflation indicated by the 30% increase in the C.P.I. If this index is assumed to be relevant to the consumer purchases of such a person, it could be used to "deflate" the income increase and to find the *real* increase in income.

The real income at the beginning and at the end of the period being studied, respectively, is:

$$\frac{10{,}000 \times 100}{100} = \$10{,}000 \qquad \text{(Beginning real income)},$$

$$\frac{15{,}000 \times 100}{130} = \$11{,}538 \qquad \text{(Ending real income)}.$$

With the extra $5000 income this person could buy only an extra $1538 worth of goods and services because prices increased.

Real income is usually called the "purchasing power" of the money income. In comparing incomes, wages, or rents of individuals, or gross national product, or personal income per capita of different countries, the use of an appropriate deflator is common practice. In this way, the real value is more easily recognized.

Example 15.14. Suppose that a state government allocated $25 million for highway construction in 1978, when costs of labor, materials, land, equipment, etc., were measured by a construction cost index of 125 (relative to a base period equal to 100, in 1975). Suppose that in 1985 some highway projects receive funding of $30 million. However, the index of costs in 1985 has risen to 180. We find the real value of the

TABLE 15.16 **Supermarket survey: Food price data**

Item	Sept. 29, 1981, Prices	Sept. 14, 1982, Prices	June 14, 1983, Prices	Sept. 13, 1983, Prices
Meats				
Bacon, 1 lb.	1.89	2.68	1.90	2.03
Frankfurters, 1 lb.	1.86	2.07	1.88	1.85
Pork loin chops, 1 lb.	2.25	2.71	2.84	2.55
Ground beef, 1 lb.	1.56	1.67	1.63	1.57
Sirloin steak, 1 lb.	3.19	3.45	3.49	3.12
Boneless rump roast, 1 lb.	3.07	3.09	2.83	2.91
Whole fryers, 1 lb.	0.63	0.73	0.65	0.83
Chunk light tuna, $6\frac{1}{2}$-oz. can	0.86	0.81	0.84	0.75

Example 15.15. Suppose we use the price data in the newspaper survey shown in Table 15.16 to compute a simple aggregate price index. We use prices on September 29, 1981, as the base period and compute the index for prices on September 13, 1983. The sum of the prices for "meats" on September 13, 1983, is $\Sigma p_2 = \$15.61$ (the subscript 2 indicates two years after the base period). The sum of the prices on September 29, 1981, is $\Sigma p_0 = \$15.31$. Substitution into Formula (15.12) gives

$$P_2 = 100 \frac{\sum p_2}{\sum p_0} = 100 \frac{15.61}{15.31} = 102.0.$$

This index indicates that meat prices in 1983 were 2.0% higher than in 1981.

The simple aggregate price index has two main disadvantages. First, it is sensitive to the units of measurement for each commodity. For example, if three-pound packages of ground beef were used as the commodity instead of one-pound packages, the price for ground beef would be higher in each year. The ground beef item would have a greater influence in the aggregate measure. For instance, suppose the tuna price in Table 15.16 were changed to the equivalent price for one pound of tuna (since all other items are quoted in terms of one pound). The price for one pound would be $2.12 in 1981, and the price would be $1.85 in 1983. If these larger prices were used, the effect of the decrease in tuna price would have a greater influence in the index. Recomputing the index number for 1983 relative to 1981 would give

$$P_2 = 100 \frac{16.71}{16.57} = 100.8.$$

If this index were being used in a cost-of-living adjustment for welfare benefits, the increase of 0.8% instead of an increase of 2.0% would be very significant to the total government budget.

Second, the index in Formula (15.12) fails to consider the relative importance of the commodities. That is, this price index is formulated under the assumption that each commodity is used equally as much. Thus, if persons typically use more than one pound of ground beef for every pound of pork loin chops, or if persons use more than one pound of whole fryers (chicken) for every pound of sirloin steak, this index would be incorrect. The actual price aggregate that would be appropriate should take into account the differing quantities of the items used.

The first disadvantage can be overcome merely by changing to a *simple average of price relatives* index. As the name suggests, this index equals the average of all price relatives. Since $\Sigma(p_i/p_0)$ equals the sum of these price relatives and N equals the total number of commodities, then

$$\text{Simple average of price relatives:} \quad P_i = \frac{100 \sum \dfrac{p_i}{p_0}}{N}. \qquad \textbf{(15.13)}$$

Example 15.16. To find the simple price relative index for September 1982 or 1983 relative to September 1981 for the meat prices in Table 15.16, we first find each price relative, p_1/p_0 and p_2/p_0 for each item. These are shown in Table 15.17.

TABLE 15.17 **Price relatives for prices in Table 15.16**

Item	p_1/p_0	p_2/p_0
Bacon	1.42	1.07
Frankfurters	1.11	0.99
Pork loin chops	1.20	1.13
Ground beef	1.07	1.01
Sirloin steak	1.08	0.98
Rump roast	1.01	0.95
Fryers	1.16	1.32
Tuna	0.94	0.87
Sum	8.99	8.32

The index computed by Formula (15.13) for these eight items for 1983 is

$$P_2 = 100 \, \frac{8.32}{8} = 104.$$

This index would be unaffected by changes in units of measurement for a particular commodity, since the units cancel out in each calculation of the price relative prior to summing and computing the index. However, this index still equally weights each price relative.

Weighted Price Indexes

Weighted index numbers overcome the second disadvantage of the simple indexes. They permit consideration of the relative importance of the commodities in the market basket, which is usually measured in terms of the total amount of money spent on each commodity during a year. The product of the price of a commodity and the quantity consumed in a given year represents the total amount of money consumers spend on that particular commodity. If q_i represents the quantity consumed in year i, then $p_0 q_0$ equals the total amount spent on a particular commodity in the base year, and $p_i q_i$ represents the amount spent some other year. A *weighted average of price relatives* index weights the various price relatives in a market basket by the total amount spent on that commodity. This index may take on two different forms, depending on whether base-year weights ($p_0 q_0$) or the weights of some given year ($p_i q_i$) are used in constructing the index. Whichever weighting system is applied, it must be used for all values of the index being constructed.

Weighted average of price relatives:

Base-year weights:

$$P_i = \frac{100 \sum \left(\frac{p_i}{p_0} p_0 q_0 \right)}{\sum p_0 q_0};$$

Given-year weights:

$$P_i = \frac{100 \sum \left(\frac{p_i}{p_0} p_i q_i \right)}{\sum p_i q_i}.$$

(15.14)

A weighted average of price relatives index can be constructed from the data in Table 15.16 if the quantities purchased for each commodity are known. To illustrate the use of Formula (15.14), let us consider another subset of commodities with prices and quantities as shown in Table 15.18.

TABLE 15.18 **Price and quantity data**

	Quantities		Prices	
Commodity	1981	1984	1981	1984
Milk (qt.)	30	35	0.60	0.75
Bread (loaf)	25	20	0.60	0.80
Cheese (4 oz.)	20	30	0.40	0.45
Margarine (lb.)	10	5	0.55	0.65
Oranges (doz)	15	20	1.80	1.95

Example 15.17. The data in Table 15.18 can be used to determine a weighted average of price relatives. Consider 1981 as the base period indicated by the subscript zero. The weighted price relative for milk using base-year weights of $p_0 q_0 = 30(0.60) = \$18.00$ would be

$$\frac{p_3}{p_0}\, p_0 q_0 = \frac{0.75}{0.60}(\$18.00) = 1.25(\$18.00) = \$22.50.$$

The weighted price relative values given in Table 15.19 are calculated in the same fashion.

We can now use this information to calculate the two types of weighted average of price relatives by using Formula (15.14). Using base-year weights $p_0 q_0$,

$$\frac{100 \sum \left[\dfrac{p_3}{p_0}\, p_0 q_0 \right]}{\sum p_0 q_0} = 100\,\frac{\$87.25}{\$73.50} = 118.7.$$

TABLE 15.19 **Weighted price relative values for the data in Table 15.18**

Commodity	Base-Year Weights $\dfrac{p_3}{p_0}\, p_0 q_0$	Given-Year Weights $\dfrac{p_3}{p_0}\, p_3 q_3$
Milk	$22.50	$ 32.81
Bread	20.00	21.33
Cheese	9.00	15.19
Margarine	6.50	3.84
Oranges	29.25	42.25
Total	$87.25	$115.42

Using given-year weights p_3q_3,

$$\frac{100\sum\left[\dfrac{p_3}{p_0}p_3q_3\right]}{\sum p_3q_3} = 100\,\frac{\$115.42}{\$98.00} = 117.8.$$

In this example the two methods give results that happen to be quite close together.

A popular means of constructing a weighted price index does not employ weighted price relatives, but rather weights each price directly by multiplying it by the quantity of that commodity consumed in either the base year or some other year. The value p_iq_0, for example, represents the price of a commodity in year i weighted by the quantity of the commodity consumed in the base year. The total theoretical value of the commodities in year i is thus $\sum p_iq_0$. If we now take the ratio of this value to the actual value of these goods in the base year, $\sum p_0q_0$, the resulting index is called a **Laspeyres price index:**

$$\text{Laspeyres price index:} \quad LP_i = \frac{100\sum p_iq_0}{\sum p_0q_0}. \tag{15.15}$$

If, instead of q_0, the quantity q_i consumed in the given year i is used to weight prices, the resulting index is called a **Paasche price index:**

$$\text{Paasche price index:} \quad PP_i = \frac{100\sum p_iq_i}{\sum p_0q_i}. \tag{15.16}$$

Note that the Laspeyres price index is equivalent to the weighted average of price relatives index using base-year weights, since

$$\frac{100\sum\left[\dfrac{p_i}{p_0}p_0q_0\right]}{\sum p_0q_0} = \frac{100\sum p_iq_0}{\sum p_0q_0}.$$

Example 15.18. The Laspeyres and Paasche price indexes can be constructed from the data in Table 15.20:

TABLE 15.20 **Prices weighted by quantities as given in Table 15.18**

	Base Year Quantity Weights		Year 3 Quantity Weights	
Commodity	p_0q_0	p_3q_0	p_0q_3	p_3q_3
Milk	$18.00	$22.50	$21.00	$26.25
Bread	15.00	20.00	12.00	16.00
Cheese	8.00	9.00	12.00	13.50
Margarine	5.50	6.50	2.75	3.25
Oranges	27.00	29.25	36.00	39.00
Total	$73.50	$87.25	$83.75	$98.00

$$\textit{Laspeyres price index:} \qquad \frac{100\sum p_3q_0}{\sum p_0q_0} = 100\,\frac{\$87.25}{\$73.50} = 118.7;$$

$$\textit{Paasche price index:} \qquad \frac{100\sum p_3q_3}{\sum p_0q_3} = 100\,\frac{\$98.00}{\$83.75} = 117.0.$$

Since construction of the Paasche index requires determination of new weights each year, while the Laspeyres index does not, the Laspeyres index is used much more often. Furthermore, the Laspeyres index has the added advantage that indexes obtained from this formula may be compared from year to year, while indexes obtained by using the Paasche formula can be compared easily only with the base year. Both indexes, however, tend to reflect a slight bias when reporting price changes. Under the usual conditions of a downward-sloping demand schedule, when people tend to purchase more of low-priced items and less of high-priced items, the numerator of the Laspeyres index will be somewhat higher than it should be, resulting in an overestimation of price increases. At the same time, the numerator of the Paasche index will tend to be lower than it should be, resulting in an underestimation of price increases.

15.8 ECONOMIC INDEXES AND THEIR LIMITATIONS

We have presented just a brief introduction to the topic of index numbers. In practice, the process of constructing and updating an index can become quite involved. Before leaving the subject, we shall describe a number of the more widely used indexes and some of their limitations.

The Consumer Price Index (C.P.I.) and the Producer Price Index (P.P.I.), both published by the Department of Labor, Bureau of Labor Statistics, are the two best-known price indexes. These two indexes represent excellent examples of attempts to summarize large masses of data in a single price index. The C.P.I. is based primarily on 265 different items in 68 separate expenditure classes (foods, fuels, apparel, etc.), which are priced throughout each month. The C.P.I. is a modified Laspeyres index with 1967 as the base year. It represents average changes in prices paid by consumers in retail markets and represents about 80% of the total noninstitutional civilian population of the United States. Half of these are wage-earners and clerical workers, but also included are salaried workers, self-employed, retired, and unemployed persons. It does not include farm families. It is compiled from a survey of such persons in 85 urban areas chosen to represent all towns with a population over 2500. Persons are selected based on a probability sample from the 1980 Census of Population.

The graph of the Consumer Price Index for the years 1975 through 1983 is shown in Fig. 15.14. Note that the vertical scale is a ratio rather than an arithmetic scale. This means that equal distances between any two points A and B on the vertical scale ($A < B$) represent an equal ratio (B/A) rather than an equal difference ($B - A$) between the values at those points. In other words, equal vertical distances represent equal percentage changes. The same size absolute level changes are represented by smaller and smaller distances as the level increases.

The Producer Price Index involves about 26,000 price quotations for that Tuesday during the week that contains the thirteenth day of the month. These prices are gathered by mail questionnaire for approximately 3400 commodities. This index gives an indication of prices received in primary markets (not retail) of the United States by producers in all stages of processing. It includes components for price movements of goods in all mining and manufacturing categories and will eventually include 6000 separate industries from beet sugar production and boat building to poultry dressing and pesticide manufacturing. A graph of some components of the Producers Price Index and the P.P.I. for total finished goods (seasonally adjusted) as shown in Fig. 15.15.

There are two major economic quantity indexes: (1) the *Index of Industrial Production* (I.I.P.), published by the Federal Reserve Board, and (2) the Export and Import Indexes, published by the U.S. Department of Commerce. The Export and Import Indexes calculate quantity changes in both exports and imports. The I.I.P., which is a *weighted average of relative quantity* index, measures changes in manufacturing output.

The limitations of economic indexes follow directly from the problems suggested earlier in the construction of an index. Since the useful and

Index 1967 = 100 (ratio scale)

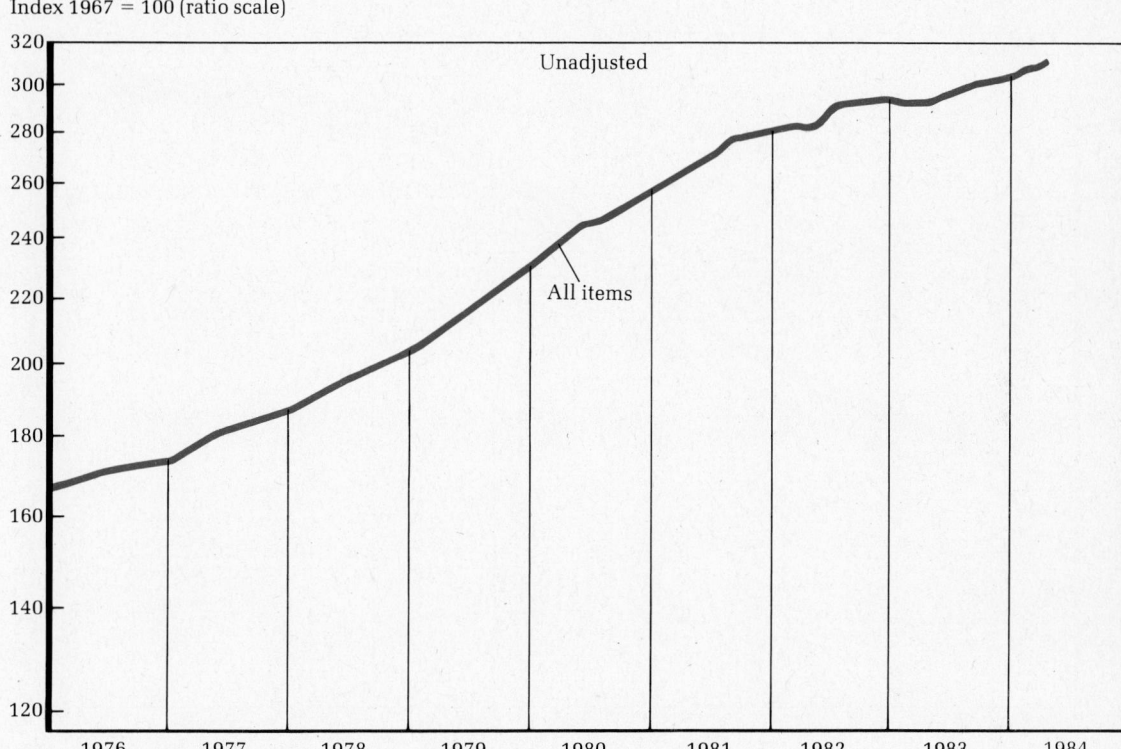

Source: Department of Labor, Council of Economic Advisers

FIGURE 15.14 **Consumer Price Index (C.P.I.).**

meaningful application of an index often depends on what year is selected as the base, it is important to use as a base a period with "normal" or "average" economic activity. Sometimes the base-year value can be the average price or quantity of several years rather than a single year.

Both the C.P.I. and the P.P.I. have 1967 as the current base year. The base can be changed only when a major revision of the indexes occurs, currently about every 10–12 years. The cost and time involved in such a major revision is quite significant. For example, since the C.P.I. was first formulated in 1919, it has undergone major revisions in 1940, 1953, 1964, and 1978. The last three of these have taken three, five, and eight years and have cost $4 million, $6.5 million, and $50 million, respectively. Thus, the 1978 revision began in 1970 and used the base year 1967. Since 1978, it has been a government policy to do continuing sample surveys and partial updates of the information used in the C.P.I. so that it is kept

Index, 1967 = 100 (ratio scale)

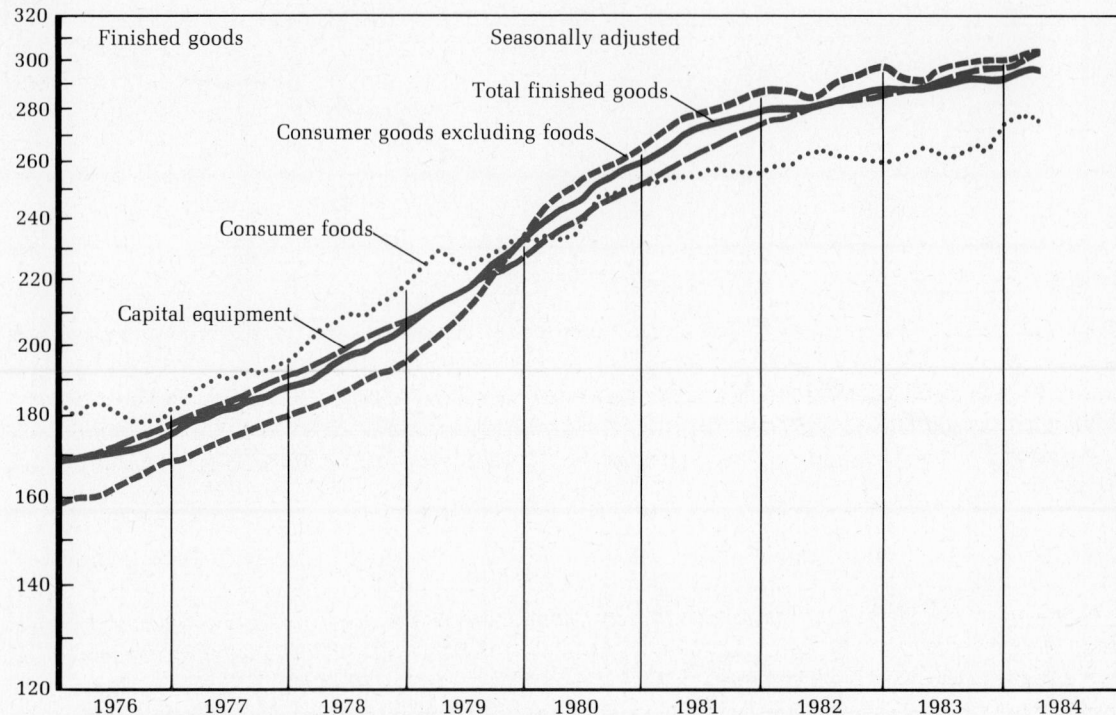

Source: Department of Labor, Council of Economic Advisers

FIGURE 15.15 **Producer Price Index (P.P.I.).**

useful between major revisions. Because of the sampling error involved, about three years of consecutive data are needed before the updated market basket of goods can be determined with enough statistical accuracy. The next major revision of the C.P.I. is scheduled for 1987.

Exactly what items are included in the index also has an important bearing on the validity of the index. In the case of the C.P.I., besides the primary items, there are hundreds of specific items whose price and quantity need to be determined and updated. Census information is used to determine the geographic sample areas based on population shifts. Thus, as population growth occurs faster in the West and South, new spending patterns will emerge in the index as more persons from these areas will be included in the sample.

In addition, two major surveys help provide information on prices and quantities. To provide an accurate list of the marketplace to be sampled and to know where consumers buy items, the Point-of-Purchase Survey is conducted. Particular items selected in the market basket must conform to detailed specifications (variety, brand, size, special features, etc.) that are basically the same across the country, although the final selection of items reported are store-specific and depend on local sales information. The reporting stores (including about 2300 food stores, 18,000 rental units, and 22,000 others in many categories) are determined from this Point-of-Purchase Survey of 23,000 families in the United States. These families are asked for information on the name, location, and amount spent in retail stores for many different categories of goods and services. This survey is updated by a continuing survey of one-fifth of the sampling units each year. Thus, in a five-year cycle the entire sample has been repeated.

The weights (quantities) used in the C.P.I. are based on information from the Consumer Expenditure Survey, most recently conducted in 1972–1973 as part of the major revision of 1978. This was a sample of 20,000 families in 216 geographic areas across the country using quarterly interviews. Since it is often difficult to recall expenditures on minor or everyday items, the Survey also included a sample of 20,000 families who kept a one-week diary of all expenditures for each of two selected weeks. To update this information, the Continuing Survey covers 85 geographic sampling units and includes quarterly interviews for five consecutive quarters with 6000 households. Also, 4800 households are asked each year to keep and submit two one-week diaries of expenditures. These surveys help to keep the index more current, even though it is scaled for a base year of 1967. For example, among the over 250 items in the "general" or "other" category (not food, apparel, transportation, housing, energy, or some other major category), the Continuing Surveys have allowed recent changes such as from the former item "piano lessons, organs" to the new item "fees for lessons — golf, swimming, tennis, piano, etc." and from "movie admissions" to "admissions to movies, concerts, theaters, etc.," new items that reflect current life-styles. Also, diesel fuel and gasohol were first included in the motor fuels component beginning in September 1981. An important revision in the treatment of housing prices occurred in January 1983, which treats costs of home ownership in terms of equivalent monthly costs (like rental housing) instead of as an investment-type expenditure.

In the case of the Producers Price Index, seasonal adjustment factors are recalculated annually. The items and industries covered are revised semiannually. It is common for over 100 new items to be included and as many others to be dropped. In July 1982, 162 new commodities were added.

These indexes try to take into account changes in quality as well. In October 1982 the P.P.I. adjusted its component for passenger cars, for example. Of the average producer price increase per car in 1983 of $215.55, it was determined that nearly half of this, $107.66, was due to quality improvements. The quality changes were split about evenly between those for fuel economy or emission controls and those for improved warranties or corrosion protection.

Even with such attention, the indexes are still open to question because of rapid changes in technology, quality, and products. In 1985 the C.P.I. still did not include the large amounts of expenditures on computers, printers, software, video games, and the like. Since, over a period of time, some items fall out of use completely, and others appear that had no earlier counterpart, it is difficult, if not impossible, to compare the prices of many of today's goods with those of an earlier period. For example, it is unrealistic to compare the price of an old icebox with the price of today's modern refrigerator, and the price of a color television set cannot be compared with the price of an article that was not on the market 50 years ago.

This inability to compare goods, and consequently prices, over time has led to charges that price indexes exaggerate the real increase in prices and that the C.P.I., in particular, exaggerates the change in the cost of living because the indexes do not sufficiently take into account the improvement in the quality of goods and the worth of these quality increases to consumers. The economist Lloyd G. Reynolds suggested the following type of comparison to illustrate this problem. Give a family a 1965 Sears Roebuck Catalog, a 1985 Sears Catalog, and $1000 and allow them to make up an order list from either the 1965 or the 1985 catalog, but not from both. Most families would probably use the 1985 catalog, which must mean that they consider the higher 1985 prices more than offset by new and improved quality products. This implies that there was no real increase in consumer prices between 1965 and 1985, even though the C.P.I. indicated a sizeable increase.

Both the consumer and the producer price indexes are available in seasonally adjusted or unadjusted form. The seasonally adjusted indexes reveal more clearly underlying cyclical trends and are most useful in regression analysis involving other quantities that are seasonally adjusted. Unadjusted data are of primary interest to users who need information on the actual dollar value of transactions, such as marketing specialists, purchasing agents, and commodity traders. Unadjusted indexes are also used generally to escalate contracts such as purchase agreements and real-estate leases. The Bureau of Labor Statistics revises the seasonal adjustment factors for these indexes annually.

Because there are so many difficulties in constructing meaningful price indexes, they should be used only as guides and indicators of price movements and should not be quoted as indisputable facts. Also, one should remember that they represent prices to some "average" person with "average" tastes and preferences. Whether or not they are relevant to a particular person or group must always be questioned before they are applied.

Define. *Index number, deflator, real income, price relative, weighted price index, Laspeyres index, Paasche index, base year, consumer and producer price indexes.*

PROBLEMS

15.24 Go to a library and find the current value of the *Consumer Price Index* (C.P.I.) and the *Producer Price Index* (P.P.I.).
   a) Determine how the value of these indexes has changed over the past year, as well as over the past ten years. How has the composition of the items included in these indexes changed over the past ten years?
   b) Find as many examples as you can from the news media illustrating current uses of these indexes, (e.g., labor–management negotiations, inflation reports, etc.).

15.25 Suppose that a budget request for a new university building was $3.5 million in 1980, and a similar request is $4.5 million in 1985. Also, an index of building and construction costs (assumed to be applicable to this situation) with base year 1977 = 100 is equal to 95 in 1980 and 140 in 1985. Compare the relative real value of the building that could have resulted from the two budget requests.

15.26 The Bureau of Labor Statistics Consumer Price Index for services increased from 107 to 115 during a certain period.
   a) If a consumer budgeted $20 per month for services at the beginning of this period, how much should be budgeted for the same level of services at the end of the period?
   b) Suppose a person's salary increased from $800 to $852 per month during this period. What is the real change experienced in purchasing power for services?

15.27 In the past year the GNP of a nation has risen from $200 billion to $212 billion, which represents a 6% growth rate. However, the price index used to calculate the national product has also risen from 125 to 130.

What is the real growth rate of this nation's GNP after accounting for inflation?

15.28 If an index of money wages of workers (1967 = 100) was 250 in 1980 and an appropriate index of living costs (1967 = 100) was 200 in the same year, what has been the percent increase from 1967 to 1980 in:
a) money wages of workers?
b) real wages of workers?

15.29 Suppose that the average beginning salary for business graduates has increased from $22,000 to $25,000 over a period of years when the consumer price index increased from 100 to 120. What is the change in the "real" value of beginning salaries?

15.30 Given below are data for the average expenditures on new cars.

Average expenditure for new cars (U.S. Bureau of Economic Analysis)	
1982	$9963
1981	8717
1980	7526
1979	6861
1978	6382

a) Convert the data to index numbers using 1978 as the base year.
b) Repeat part (a) using 1980 as the base year.
c) Using the index numbers from part (a), determine whether a buyer spending $7000 in 1979 or a buyer spending $10,000 in 1982 got "more" car for the money.
d) Repeat part (c), using the index numbers from part (b). Compare the results of parts (c) and (d).

15.31 The table below gives salaries in 1973 and 1983 for selected state employees in North Carolina.

Employee	1973 Salary	1983 Salary
Secretary	$ 6,888	$11,004
Manager	11,376	17,880
Janitor	6,000	9,672
Teacher	13,120	21,088
Governor	38,500	57,864

a) If 1973 is chosen as the base period, the cost-of-living index for 1983 is 224. Determine the real value of the 1983 salaries in terms of 1973 dollars.

b) If 1983 is chosen as the base period, what would be the value of the cost-of-living index for 1973?

15.32 Suppose that the market basket values for 1980 and 1982 were observed as given below.

Item	1980		1983	
	Price	Quantity	Price	Quantity
Bus rides	0.30	100	0.50	50
Hamburger (lb.)	1.00	25	1.40	30
Shirts	10.00	4	15.00	3
Tennis balls (can)	2.50	1	2.00	2

Construct the following:
a) price relatives for each commodity;
b) a simple aggregate price index;
c) a simple average of price relatives index;
d) a weighted average of price relatives index; using both base-year and given-year weights;
e) a Laspeyres and a Paasche price index.

15.33 Repeat Problem 15.32 for the following market basket values that were observed in 1955 and 1956:

Item	1955		1956	
	Price	Quantity	Price	Quantity
Milk	15¢ qt.	25 qt.	15¢ qt.	20 qt.
Eggs	50¢ doz.	10 doz.	45¢ doz.	15 doz.
Bread	15¢ loaf	30 loaves	20¢ loaf	35 loaves

15.34 Given the following data for price (p) and quantity (q) for vegetables:

Item	p (1982)	p (1983)	q (1982)	q (1983)
Lettuce (head)	0.57	0.86	8	9
Tomatoes (lb.)	0.59	0.70	12	14
Onions (3 lb.)	0.93	1.09	3	4
Potatoes (10 lb.)	1.88	2.67	4	2

a) Find the simple index of price relatives for 1983 using 1982 as the base year.
b) Construct a Laspeyres price index for 1983 vegetable prices.
c) Construct a Paasche price index for 1983.
d) Explain the difference between the index in part (a) and those in parts (b) and (c).

15.35 Given the following data on monthly energy costs for a household:

Item	1975		1985	
	p	q	p	q
Electricity	6	30	7	40
Natural gas	8	10	12	9
Gasoline	6	5	11	4

a) Compute a weighted aggregate Laspeyres price index using 1975 as the base year.
b) If a household spent $5000 for energy in 1975 and $6000 in 1985, explain in which year they would have consumed more units of energy.

15.36 Given the following historical data on monthly purchases by the average midwestern farm family:

Commodity	1950		1960	
	p	q	p	q
Eggs (doz.)	0.40	10	0.60	9
Sugar (lb.)	0.10	35	0.20	30
Butter (lb.)	0.50	5	0.40	6

a) Compute a weighted aggregate Laspeyres price index, using 1950 as the base year.
b) Assume that your index applied in general for all foods. Also assume that a certain family spends $1200 for food in 1950 and $1750 in 1960. In which year would they have had more to eat for their money?

15.37 Suppose that price and quantity data (in relevant units) for sales of major appliances are collected in order to construct a consumer durable-goods price index. From the data, determine a Laspeyres price index for 1981 relative to the base period, 1984, and interpret its meaning.

Item	1981		1984	
	p	*q*	*p*	*q*
Range	7.5	8	8	12
Refrigerator	8	10	8.8	12
Air conditioner	1	6	2	15

15.38 The following data on student expenses is dug up by the campus newspaper for an editorial on the "good old days."

Item	Lunch	Gasoline	Movie
1960			
Price (cents)	30	25	50
Quantity	6	1	4
1964			
Price (cents)	50	30	90
Quantity	6	2	2
1966			
Price (cents)	60	35	100
Quantity	6	3	3

a) Compute the Laspeyres price index for the three years, using 1960 as the base.

b) Assuming that these data are representative of all commodities and all students, determine the real level of living, relative to 1960, of students who spent $500 per semester in 1960, $600 in 1964, and $700 in 1966.

EXERCISES

15.39 Describe the additive and the multiplicative models used in time-series analysis. Which of these models do you think is more realistic for most economic time series? Explain why. Give examples where each model would be appropriate.

15.40 Assume that the sales volume in a certain industry can be described by the multiplicative model $y = T \times S \times C \times I$. One month last year, the trend estimate of sales was 44,000 units, and actual sales were 55,000 units. If we assume that the seasonal index was S = 95, and the index for cyclical movement was C = 119, what index value must be associated with the irregular ent, I?

15.41 The estimate of trend accounted for $180,000 of a department store's sales last October. Assuming a multiplicative model, no irregular variation, and a cyclical index of 110, find the seasonal index for this month. Actual sales were $210,000.

15.42 Given a trend equation, $\hat{y} = 37.50 + 6x$ with origin at July 1, 1985, and x in units of one year, where y is truck sales in thousands, convert the equation to monthly units with origin at March 1, 1987.

15.43 Given the following trend equation: $\hat{y} = 137.50 + 8x$. Origin is July 1, 1985; x is expressed in units of one year; y is fruit sales in thousands. Find the monthly trend value for February 15, 1987.

15.44 A producer of one-man portable helicopters had sales over the five years, 1976–1980, of 1, 2, 3, 5, and 9 units, respectively.
a) Find the trend line for sales, letting x = 0 represent 1978.
b) Find the standard error of estimate for this trend line, and explain its meaning.
c) What is your estimate for sales in 1982?

15.45 A company has determined a seasonal index and a trend line for their monthly sales. The seasonal index for December is 140. The trend line for monthly sales is $\hat{y} = 163{,}250 + 4{,}520x$, with x in units of months, and origin at mid-April 1984. Forecast company sales for December 1986.

15.46 Given the following data for sales of boating supplies:

1984 Quarter	Actual Sales	Trend Values	Seasonal Index
1	100,000	90,000	80
2	150,000	95,000	130
3	120,000	100,000	110
4	110,000	105,000	80

a) Give one representation of the trend equation for sales of boating supplies.
b) Find seasonally adjusted sales for the four quarters of 1984.
c) Assuming no change in the trend or seasonal pattern and assuming that other factors remain constant, forecast second-quarter sales for 1986.

15.47 The following data are the means of ratios of original data to the 12-month moving averages for the sales of a retail store. The data cover a period of ten years.

Month	Means of Ratios
Jan.	56
Feb.	60
Mar.	100
Apr.	110
May	105
June	102
July	80
Aug.	72
Sept.	88
Oct.	105
Nov.	120
Dec.	145
Total	1143

a) Compute the index of seasonal variation from these ratios for the months of March, April, and August. Be sure to adjust so that the indexes average 100.

b) Suppose that the total sales for next year are estimated in December of this year at 120 million. What would be the best estimate of sales for April and August?

15.48 Given the following information:

Year	Import Price, y	Quantity Imported, x
1977	2	6
1978	3	5
1979	6	4
1980	5	5
1981	4	7
1982	3	10
1983	5	9
1984	7	7
1985	8	8
1986	7	9

a) Suppose that the trend line for import price is $\hat{y} = 2.8 + 0.5x$, where $x = 0$ for 1977. Is the import price for these years above or below the trend estimates?

b) Do you think it would be a good idea to remove seasonal variation from this data, as well as trend, before studying the cyclical relatives? Give a reason.

c) Find the values of the three-year moving average of quantity imported for the years 1979 and 1982.

15.49 The secular trend of sales for the Jones Department Store is accurately described by the equation $\hat{y} = 120,000 + 1000x$, where x represents a period of one month and has a value of zero in December 1984. The seasonal indexes for the company's sales are:

1984											
J	F	M	A	M	J	J	A	S	O	N	D
100	80	90	120	115	95	75	70	90	95	120	150

a) Ignoring cyclical and random influences, forecast sales for February 1986, May 1989, and December 1987.
b) What factors could cause these estimates to be incorrect?
c) What may be done to compensate for inaccuracies as they become apparent?

15.50 In the library, find a ten-year time series on annual household income for the United States, a region, your state, or for some occupation, race, or sex subgroup. Find a time series on consumer prices that is relevant for this group of households. Calculate the adjusted annual household income, corrected for price changes, and interpret your results in terms of the growth of real income over the period.

15.51 Answer parts (a) and (b) about the Laspeyres price index.
a) Suggest two important practical difficulties in determining a Laspeyres price index.
b) Explain how a Laspeyres price index differs from a simple arithmetic average of price relatives.

USING THE COMPUTER

15.52 Use the annual values for imports in **Data Set 5.**
a) Find a trend line for imports.
b) Fit an exponential trend to the data for imports.
c) Which of the two trends gives the better approximation?

15.53 Answer parts (a), (b), and (c).
a) Work part (a) of Exercise 14.21.
b) Fit a modified exponential curve to the data in (a).

c) Does your answer to part (a) or part (b) provide a better fit to the data? Explain why one model is better than the other.

15.54 Answer parts (a) and (b).
a) Fit an exponential curve of the form $y = ab^x$ to the data on population in **Data Set 5.**
b) Plot this time series and the curve you calculated above on a graph. What value would you predict for population in 1982?

15.55 Using the library, find the price and quantity sold of shares of ten selected stocks on the last day of the previous 40 weeks. Using one week as the base period, program the computer to find:
a) simple price index of the stocks;
b) Laspeyres price index of these stocks.
c) Find the Dow-Jones stock index at week-end for these same weeks and, using the same base period, construct an index of the Dow-Jones index to compare with your index in part (b).
d) Write a program to find a four-week moving average of your index.

15.56 Answer parts (a) and (b).
a) Write a computer program to determine seasonally adjusted monthly values for a time series. Follow the pattern as presented in conjunction with Tables 15.10 through 15.14 including options for a trend line or moving average smoothing. Include a check and process for leveling, if necessary.
b) Using a monthly series over at least five years, demonstrate how your program works.

GLOSSARY

Time series: Periodic observations of a variable that is a function of time.
Trend (T): Long-term movement in a time series.
Seasonal variation (S): Fluctuations repeated over a period of one year.
Cyclical variation (C): Pattern repeated over periods of varying lengths, usually longer than one year.
Irregular variation (I): Unpredictable or random fluctuations.
Additive model: $y = T + S + C + I$.
Multiplicative model: $y = T \times S \times C \times I$.
Method of semi-averages: Division of data into two parts with a trend line connecting the average value of each of the two groups.
Reduced equations: Normal equations from regression, simplified by choosing x so that $\Sigma x_i = 0$.

Exponential curve: $y = ab^x$.

Modified exponential curve: $y = c + ab^x$.

Logistic curve: $y = 1/(c + ab^x)$.

Gompertz curve: $y = ca^{b^x}$.

Method of moving averages: A series of averages in which each average is the mean value over an interval of time of fixed length centered at the midpoint of each interval.

Weighted moving average: A moving average in which each observation is given a weight that reflects its relative importance.

Seasonal index: A number that expresses the value of the seasonal fluctuation during a period of time.

Ratio-to-trend method: Method for estimating S by dividing both sides of $y = T \times S \times C \times I$ by T. Does not eliminate $C \times I$.

Ratio-to-moving average method: A method for estimating S by first isolating $T \times C$ and then dividing $T \times S \times C$ by $T \times C$.

Index number: A number that relates the values of a particular aggregate to its value in a selected base period.

Price relative: The ratio of the price of a certain commodity in a given period to the price of that commodity in some base year.

Market basket: The group of commodities selected to represent the typical purchases of an "average" person.

Laspeyres price index: A price index constructed by weighting each price by the quantity consumed in the base year.

Paasche price index: A price index constructed by weighting each price by the quantity consumed in year i.

Statistical
Decision Theory

SIXTEEN

16.1 INTRODUCTION TO A DECISION PROBLEM

The focus of this chapter, as the title implies, is on the process of making decisions from a statistical point of view. Decision-making in this context is often referred to as *decision-making under uncertainty* because the consequences or payoffs resulting from each decision are assumed not to be known (in advance) with certainty. As you might suspect, there is also a set of techniques concerned with *decision-making under certainty*, in which consequences of a decision are assumed to be known (in advance) with certainty. Most real-world decisions generally involve some element of uncertainty; hence, it is convenient to have a formal procedure for analyzing each possible action a decision-maker might take in a given situation, and for selecting the best action.

The origins of statistical decision theory are relatively recent, dating back to the early 1950's. Since that time, this branch of statistics has grown rapidly in popularity, with a corresponding development of the theory and its applications. Because much of the analysis of statistical decision theory centers around a formula first published in 1763 by the Reverend Thomas Bayes (Bayes' rule), this approach is often referred to as the "Bayesian" approach. In fact, there is considerable debate among statisticians about the appropriateness of the Bayesian approach compared to the "classical" approach to statistics (i.e., traditional procedures for sampling, estimation, and hypothesis-testing). We will not enter into this debate here but instead will present both the advantages and disadvantages of statistical decision theory.

In analyzing a decision-making problem it is necessary to be able to specify exactly what **actions** (or alternatives) are available. We will label actions as a_1, a_2, a_3, ... In addition, we assume that each action yields a *payoff* or some type of consequence that depends on the value of a random variable called the **state of nature**. States of nature will be labeled as θ_1, θ_2, θ_3, . . . (θ is the Greek letter "theta").

Example 16.1. Suppose that you are considering buying 100 shares of one of four common stocks (actions a_1, a_2, a_3, or a_4), each of which costs $10 now. You intend to sell your stock at the end of one year. If you could somehow foresee the future and *know* that one year from now the prices of these stocks would be $15, $11, $8, and $10, respectively, then your decision would be an easy one — buy the first stock (action a_1). Action a_1 yields a profit of $500 ($5 profit on each of 100 shares); a_2 gives a payoff of $100; a_3 results in a profit of $-$200 (a loss); and a_4 produces zero profit. This situation represents decision-making under certainty, since there is no uncertainty about what state of nature (i.e., what set of prices) will occur a year from now.

Instead of knowing what prices will be in one year, you probably can only guess what the prices might be on the basis of your impression of the economy in general, your knowledge of various industries and firms within these industries, or perhaps merely a hot tip from a friend. There may be many different states of nature, each yielding a different set of payoffs for the various actions you could take. Thus, your problem is really one of decision-making under uncertainty.

A Decision Problem under Uncertainty

To extend the stock problem to include uncertainty, suppose that you decide that there are three possible states of nature (θ_1, θ_2, and θ_3). For instance, you might decide that stock prices one year hence are directly related to the stability of the economy during the year. In this case, θ_1 might correspond to a mild recession, θ_2 to a stable economy, and θ_3 to a mild expansion. [Other states are also possible (e.g., a depression), but for convenience we will assume that there are only three.] Suppose that for θ_1 the prices a year from now will be those given previously ($15, $11, $8, and $10); for θ_2 the prices will be $5, $12, $12, and $13; and for θ_3 they will be $17, $11, $15, and $15. The payoffs that these prices reflect can be expressed in what is called a **payoff table,** as shown in Table 16.1.

Dominated actions. No one action from this payoff table is obviously the "best" one. Action a_1 yields the largest payoff *if* θ_1 or θ_3 occurs, while a_4 is optimal if θ_2 occurs. Note that a_3 can never be the optimal action because a_4 always results in a payoff at least as large as, or larger than, a_3 no matter *what* state of nature occurs. When θ_1 occurs, a_4 yields $0 and a_3 yields only $-$200; for θ_2, a_4 results in a payoff of $300 compared to only $200 for a_3; in θ_3, both actions yield the same payoff, $500. An

TABLE 16.1 **Payoff table for stock example**

		States of Nature		
		θ_1	θ_2	θ_3
	a_1	$500	$-$500	$700
Actions	a_2	100	200	100
	a_3	$-$200	200	500
	a_4	0	300	500

action such as a_3 in this case, which is no better than some other action no matter what state of nature occurs, is said to be a **dominated action.** Thus, a_3 could be dropped from the decision problem, since it can never be the optimal action.

16.2 EXPECTED MONETARY VALUE CRITERION

We would like to establish a decision criterion that not only takes into account all of the values in the payoff table, but also considers their *relative likelihood.* Fortunately, there is a procedure for accomplishing this, called the **Expected Monetary Value criterion.**

In order to be able to use the Expected Monetary Value (EMV) criterion, it is necessary to know (or be able to determine) the probability of each state of nature. If there is considerable "objective" evidence (e.g., historical data) or a theoretical basis for assigning probabilities, then this task may be a fairly easy one. The difficulty in many real-world problems is that there may be little or no historical data and no theoretical basis to use in making probability assessments. The answer to the question of how to assign probabilities in these circumstances is not an easy one. Bayesian statisticians usually suggest that, in assessing the *subjective probability* of an event, the decision-maker should ask, "What odds would make me exactly indifferent between the two sides of an even bet?"*

Example 16.2. At what odds would you consider it a "fair" bet (i.e., you would be indifferent between the two sides of a bet) if you were asked to participate in a bet in which the two sides are (1) the prime interest rate will be less than 10% next January, or (2) the prime rate will equal or exceed 10% next January? Suppose you say that 4:1 odds against the rate's being less than 10% represents "fair" odds (that is, you would be willing to take either side of the bet at these odds). By definition, your subjective probability that the rate will be less than 10% is $\frac{1}{5}$, or 0.20. In a decision-making context, one could use this approach to assess the probability of each state of nature. One must be careful, of course, to see that the sum of these probabilities equals one.

You should recall from the material on expectations in Section 4.3 that an expected value is merely the mean (or arithmetic average) of a random variable. As we indicated previously, such an expectation cal-

---

* Odds represent the *ratio* of the probabilities representing two mutually exclusive events. In betting, odds represent an allowance for the differing risks assumed by the bettors — the greater the risk, the greater the odds.

culated in decision theory is generally referred to as an *expected monetary value* (or *EMV*). To illustrate the calculation of EMV's, let us suppose that, in the stock example, the probabilities of our three states of nature are

$$P(\theta_1) = 0.30, \qquad P(\theta_2) = 0.60, \qquad \text{and} \qquad P(\theta_3) = 0.10.$$

The EMV of actions a_1, a_2, a_3, and a_4 is obtained by multiplying each payoff by its probability of occurrence, and then summing these values:

$$\text{EMV}(a_1) = \$500(0.30) \quad - \$500(0.60) + \$700(0.10) = -\$80;$$

$$\text{EMV}(a_2) = \$100(0.30) \quad + \$200(0.60) + \$100(0.10) = \$160;$$

$$\text{EMV}(a_3) = -\$200(0.30) + \$200(0.60) + \$500(0.10) = \$110;$$

$$\text{EMV}(a_4) = \$0(0.30) \qquad + \$300(0.60) + \$500(0.10) = \$230.$$

> Under the EMV criterion the decision-maker selects the alternative that will yield the highest expected monetary value.

For this example, action a_4 results in the highest EMV, with an average payoff of $230. (If the three states of nature had been assigned probabilities other than 0.30, 0.60, and 0.10, then some other action might have been the optimal decision. For example, you should verify that 0.40, 0.20, and 0.40 lead to action a_1 as the optimal EMV.) No matter what values $P(\theta_1)$, $P(\theta_2)$, and $P(\theta_3)$ take on, however, a_3 can never yield the largest EMV because it is a *dominated action*.

The Effect of Risk on the Optimal Decision

The EMV criterion itself suffers from one major weakness, namely, that it considers only the expected or mean profit and does not take into account the variance in the payoffs. If the variance is fairly constant across the relevant alternatives, this weakness probably will not cause any problems; but when the variability is large, the EMV criterion may indicate an action that will not be the most preferred for some people.

Example 16.3. Suppose that you must choose between two stocks (a_1 and a_2) and that there are only two possible states of nature (θ_1 and θ_2), each having the *same* probability,

$$P(\theta_1) = 0.50 = P(\theta_2).$$

Table 16.2 indicates the relative payoffs for these data. Even though the EMV of a_2 is ten times as large as that of a_1, most people (including the authors) would select a_1 if forced to pick between the two stocks because

TABLE 16.2 **Example of decision affected by risk**

		States of Nature		
		θ_1	θ_2	EMV
Actions	a_1	−$50	$100	25
	a_2	10,500	−10,000	250
Probability		0.50	0.50	

they cannot afford to risk losing $10,000. Some people might prefer a_2 over a_1, which merely illustrates the fact that the value of a dollar is not necessarily the same for one person as for some other person; neither does the value of a dollar necessarily *remain the same* to one person over time. We will see later in this chapter (Section 16.7) that it is possible to take the *value* of money into account in decision-making situations by using the expected utility criterion.

Our decision situations thus far have been based on the assumption that a single decision is to be made for the payoffs involved. This may not be the case for an executive who regularly makes decisions involving relatively large amounts of money or a stockbroker who is investing continually in the stock market. In such cases a decision-maker may be less concerned about the variance in payoffs for any one decision because he or she knows that, over a large number of decisions, gains should offset losses.

16.3 PERKINS PLASTICS — AN EXAMPLE

To illustrate the process involved in calculating EMV's in a more complicated setting, we present the following example involving a small plastics firm:

Example 16.4. Perkins Plastics has had adhesion problems in its experiments with chrome plating on a plastic butterfly valve because of irregularities in the electric flow during the plating process. On the basis of historical data, management knows that approximately 70% of the time the current is fairly uniform, in which case 90% of each batch of 1000 valves produced will be good and only 10% will be defective. The other 30% of the time, when the current is somewhat irregular, only 60% of the valves are good and 40% are defective.

Unfortunately, there is no way the engineers at Perkins Plastics can determine how good the current flow is without testing each item in the batch. All they know is that either 90% or 60% of the valves in each batch will be good.

Perkins Plastics has several alternative ways to handle each batch. One alternative is to send the batch directly to the next operation (assembly) and hope for the best; their records shows that when they do this they incur costs of delay and adjustment of about $1000 for each batch in which 90% of the valves are good and $4000 cost for those in which 60% are good. Another alternative for Perkins Plastics is to rework the entire batch. This process ensures that the batch will be sufficiently free from defects that no delay and adjustment costs occur; however, this reworking costs $2000.

The decision facing Perkins Plastics at this point is whether they should send each batch directly to assembly or rework it. The relevant data are shown in Table 16.3. Note in Table 16.3 that the optimal decision is for Perkins to send each batch to assembly, as this action has a higher EMV than does the rework action.

Another way to systematically display the information in a decision problem is to use a **tree diagram** such as the one shown in Fig. 16.1. Just as we explained in Section 3.2, the tree diagram shows the steps of the problem. The first set of "branches" of the tree represents the decision-maker's possible *actions*, and the second set represents the various *states of nature*. The circled value represents the EMV that results from the decision to send the batch directly to assembly. Nonoptimal branches on a decision tree are usually marked with the symbol ⅄, as shown on the rework branch. The symbol □ on the decision tree indicates a point at which the decision-maker has to select between alternatives; the symbol ○ indicates a point at which selection between branches is made by "nature" (that is, in a probabilistic manner). The decision tree in Fig. 16.1 shows the same optimal decision, "assembly," as does Table 16.3.

TABLE 16.3 **Payoff table for Perkins Plastics**

	States of Nature			
	90% Good	60% Good	EMV	Optimal
Actions { Assembly	−$1000	−$4000	−$1900	←
Rework	−$2000	−$2000	−$2000	
Probability	0.70	0.30		

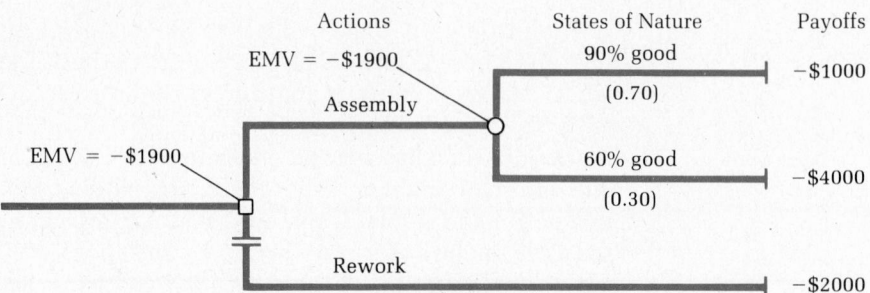

FIGURE 16.1 **Tree diagram for Perkins Plastics, no sampling information.**

Thus far we have assumed that a decision-maker arrives at a probability value for each state of nature via a personal assessment of the situation; this assessment can be based on a large variety of factors, such as available historical data, personal experience in similar situations, or just "gut" feelings. In many circumstances, however, it is desirable to have more information about the probability of each state of nature before attempting to make a decision. Most people gather information of this type almost daily: We ask our friends about places to eat, or live, or courses to take; we read consumer reports before making major purchases; and we study the stock market before investing. In a very real sense, you could say that we are *gathering sample evidence* about the relevant states of nature.

In our analysis of decisions we would like to be able to formally incorporate additional (sample) information into the process. Additional information is usually not free, however; if nothing else, it takes time and effort merely to gather and interpret this information. Thus, our decision process should not only be able to incorporate new information, but it should also be able to indicate how *much* additional information it is worthwhile to collect.

Our first step in evaluating information will be to consider the effect of sample information on the decision-maker's evaluation of the relative likelihood of each state of nature. We will then turn to the more general question of *how much* information should be collected.

Formulating a Bayesian Problem

We will illustrate Bayes' rule by assuming that Perkins Plastics has recently learned that they can use a device in their plating operations that is capable of testing a sample of valves from each batch. Perkins is currently considering testing a *single valve* from the current batch (larger samples will be considered later). Perkins believes that determining whether one valve, randomly selected from a batch, is good or defective might help them estimate P(90% good) and P(60% good). Better estimates of these probabilities will, presumably, improve their ability to select between "assembly" and "rework."

The description of the Perkins Plastics problem gave the following two probabilities:

$$P(90\% \text{ good}) = 0.70 \quad \text{and} \quad P(60\% \text{ good}) = 0.30.$$

These two probabilities are called **prior probabilities.** They represent the probabilities of the two states of nature *before* any sample information is seen. The purpose of using Bayes' rule is to revise these prior probabilities in the light of (or given) the various possible sample outcomes. These revised probabilities are called **posterior probabilities.**

In the Perkins example there are two possible sample outcomes: either one good valve is drawn (G) or one defective value is drawn (D). The posterior probabilities for Perkins are thus

$$P(90\% \text{ good}|G) \quad \text{and} \quad P(90\% \text{ good}|D)$$
$$P(60\% \text{ good}|G) \quad \text{and} \quad P(60\% \text{ good}|D).$$

Note that while we had *two* prior probabilities, there are *four* posterior probabilities. This occurs because each of the two prior probabilities must be reevaluated in the light of both possible results, G and D.

Study Question 16.1: Cost Estimate of Sewage Treatment Facility

The city of Bedford is trying to estimate the cost of a new sewage treatment facility. A major factor in the cost is the amount of rock (limestone) found at the site. If the city estimates a normal amount of rock and the amount is found to be excessive, the penalty to the city in time lost, legal battles, etc., will be $20,000. The penalty for estimating an excessive amount when it is really normal will be

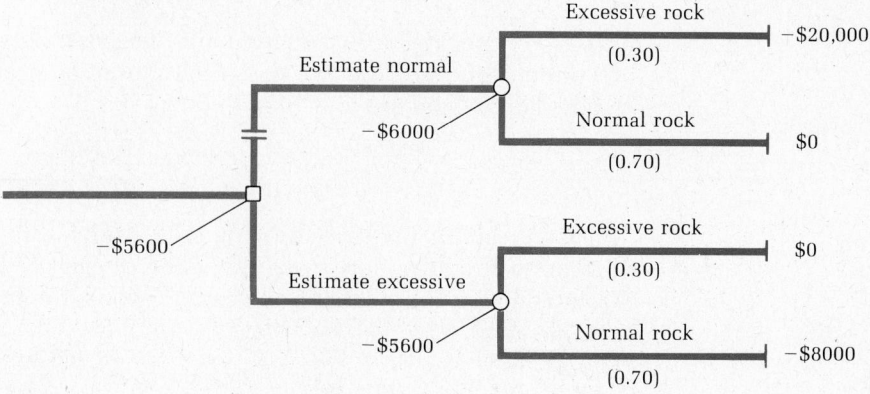

$8000. If they estimate correctly, there is no penalty. The city estimates the probability of normal rock to be 0.70 and the probability of excessive rock to be 0.30. What is the best decision to make based on this information? Draw the decision tree.

Answer. The optimal decision is to estimate excessive rock. The decision tree is shown on page 821.

16.4 THE REVISION OF PROBABILITIES

The general formula for **Bayes' rule** that was given in Chapter 3 is presented below, using the terminology of this chapter. The sums in these formulas include all possible states of nature.

Bayes' Rule:

P(state of nature|sample)

$$= \frac{P(\text{state of nature})P(\text{sample}|\text{state of nature})}{\Sigma \, P(\text{state of nature})P(\text{sample}|\text{state of nature})}$$

(16.1)

or

$$\text{Posterior probability} = \frac{(\text{Prior probability})(\text{likelihood})}{\Sigma \, (\text{Prior probability})(\text{likelihood})}.$$

The second equation in Formula (16.1) clearly shows that the calculation of a posterior probability involves prior probabilities and likelihoods. A **likelihood** indicates how "likely" each sample outcome is, given the various states of nature. Thus, in this context a likelihood is defined as follows:

Likelihood: P(sample|state of nature).

In our Perkins Plastics case there are two possible sample results [good (G) or defective (D)] and two possible states of nature (90% good and 60% good). Thus, there are four likelihoods:

P(G|90% good)   and P(D|90% good)

P(G|60% good)   and P(D|60% good).

Since our sample involves drawing only a single valve from a large batch, it is not difficult to determine the value of each of the four likelihoods. For example, *given that* 90% of a batch is good, the probability of drawing a single good valve is 0.90. That is,

P(G|90% good) = 0.90.

The complement of this probability is another likelihood,

$$P(D|90\% \text{ good}) = 0.10.$$

By similar reasoning,

$$P(G|60\% \text{ good}) = 0.60 \quad \text{and} \quad P(D|60\% \text{ good}) = 0.40.$$

We now have all the information necessary to calculate the four posterior probabilities in our Perkins Plastics example. Suppose that we now assume that a sample of one of Perkins' valves resulted in a good valve. Thus, we want to use Bayes' rule to determine the two posteriors, $P(90\% \text{ good}|G)$ and $P(60\% \text{ good}|G)$. The first of these two values is calculated below, using Formula (16.1).

$$P(90\% \text{ good}|G) = \frac{P(90\% \text{ good})P(G|90\% \text{ good})}{P(90\% \text{ good})P(G|90\% \text{ good}) + P(60\% \text{ good})P(G|60\% \text{ good})}$$

$$= \frac{(0.70)(0.90)}{(0.70)(0.90) + (0.30)(0.60)} = \frac{0.63}{0.81} = 0.7778.$$

The posterior probability $P(60\% \text{ good}|G)$ is the complement of this value — that is, $P(60\% \text{ good}|G) = 1 - 0.7778 = 0.2222$.

We have just calculated the two posteriors for the case in which the sample was a good valve. To complete our statistical decision theory analysis, we also need to calculate the two posteriors for the case in which the sample results in a defective valve. Rather than use Formula (16.1) explicitly to calculate these two posteriors, we now present a tabular procedure that is often a more convenient format for calculating posteriors. The reader should keep in mind that this process is exactly equivalent to using Formula (16.1). In the tabular approach, each possible sample result is treated separately. Hence, Table 16.4 is relevant only for the sample result "one defective."

TABLE 16.4 **Sample result — One defective**

(1) States of Nature	(2) Prior	(3) Likelihood	(4) Joint Probability = (Prior)(Likelihood)	(5) Posterior
90% good	0.70	0.10	0.07	0.07/0.19 = 0.3684
60% good	0.30	0.40	0.12	0.12/0.19 = 0.6316
Marginal probability = Σ(prior)(likelihood) =			0.19 = P(1D)	

The first three columns in this table merely represent the information already known — namely, the states of nature, the priors, and the likelihoods. Each value in column (4) represents the numerator of the formula for Bayes' rule. This numerator is called a joint probability and is always the product [prior · likelihood]. The sum of column (4), which is Σ(prior)(likelihood), represents the denominator of the formula for Bayes' rule (called a marginal probability). Finally, dividing each value in column (4) by the sum of the values in column (4), we obtain the posterior probabilities given in column (5).

Marginal Probabilities. In the process of making decisions on the basis of posterior probabilities, we will need to determine how likely it is that each sample result will occur. In the Perkins Plastics case, we thus need to know $P(G)$ and $P(D)$. Marginal probabilities are always easy to calculate once Bayes' rule has been used, as each value of Σ(prior) (likelihood) is a marginal probability. Thus, from our two Bayesian calculations thus far, we can determine that

$$P(G) = \Sigma(\text{prior})(\text{likelihood}) = 0.81$$

and

$$P(D) = \Sigma(\text{prior})(\text{likelihood}) = 0.19.$$

In other words, a good valve will be drawn 81% of the time, while a defective valve will be drawn 19% of the time.

Scheme for Revising Probabilities. Bayes' rule thus provides us with a means for revising probabilities in the light of sample information. The prior probabilities represent a state of uncertainty before any sample

FIGURE 16.2 **The revision of probabilities.**

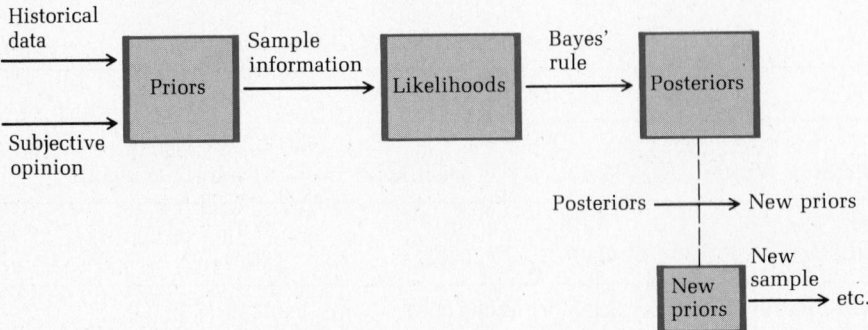

evidence is seen, while the posterior probabilities represent the state of uncertainty *after* a particular sample has been seen. It is important to emphasize that the terms prior and posterior probabilities relate only to a particular sample. A decision-maker may want to consider taking a second sample after observing the result of the first sample. The result of the first sample at that point represents "historical data"; hence, the posterior probabilities from the first sample become prior probabilities for the second sample. A diagram of this relationship appears in Fig. 16.2.

16.5 THE VALUE OF INFORMATION ($n = 1$)

One of the most important decisions in all statistical decision theory problems is whether or not gathering sample information is worthwhile. The advantage of having sample information is that we can look at the results of the sample and, in light of this information, make the optimal decision. The disadvantage of gathering sample information is that the information is usually not free. Fortunately, the methods of statistical decision theory provide us with a procedure for determining whether the advantages of gathering sample information outweigh the disadvantages.

In our Perkins Plastics example, the decision about gathering sample information involves whether the company should rent the testing device. We will assume that the cost for this device, including its rent and all labor involved, is $5 for each valve tested. Our objective is to decide whether a sample of one valve ($n = 1$) is worth $5 (larger samples will be considered later). To make this decision, we will determine the EMV after both possible sample results (G and D), using the posterior probabilities calculated in Section 16.4. This type of analysis is referred to as *preposterior analysis*, since we are looking at the posterior probabilities before we have even decided to sample.

The Decision Tree

Recall that in our original decision problem in Section 16.3 a tree diagram was useful. A tree diagram is also useful at this point, except that now we must expand the tree shown in Fig. 16.1 to include a branch (a decision) that represents "gathering a sample of size $n = 1$." The resulting decision tree is presented in Fig. 16.3.

The sequence of actions and states of nature in a decision tree must always be arranged in exactly the same order in which they occur. In this case the first decision is whether to send the valves to assembly, to rework them, or to sample ($n = 1$). *If the sample branch is followed, then the results of the sample must appear next on the decision tree.* Our

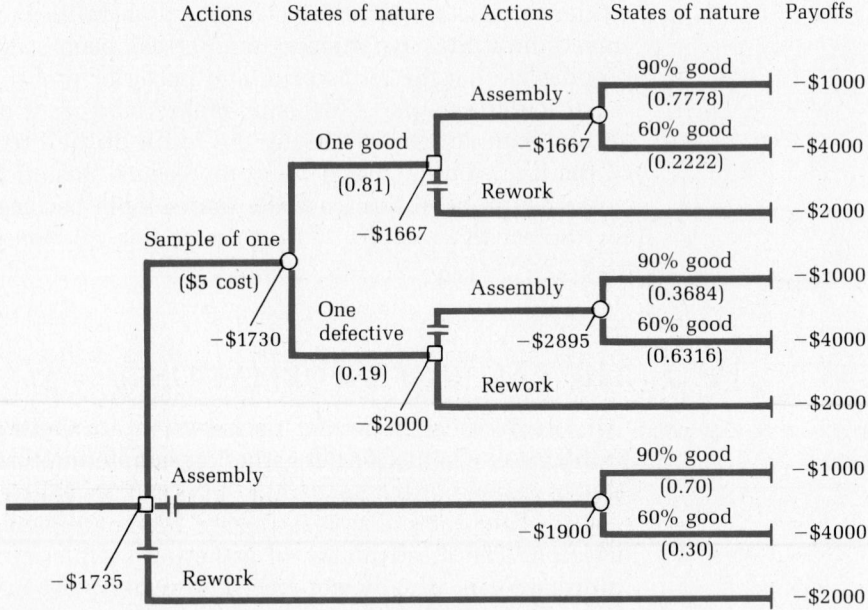

FIGURE 16.3 **Tree diagram for sample of one.**

sample results are either "one good" or "one defective." Note that the probabilities presented below these results are the same marginal probabilities calculated in Section 16.4,

$$P(G) = 0.81 \quad \text{and} \quad P(D) = 0.19.$$

After observing a sample outcome, the decision-maker will have the alternative of deciding on the same actions that were outlined in the original statement of the problem. In Fig. 16.3 the actions presented after the sample outcomes are the original choices: either send the valves to assembly or rework them. Finally, our decision tree indicates that if we send the batch to assembly, we will find that the state of nature is, in reality, either 90% good or 60% good. Note that the probabilities at the end of the tree (0.7778, 0.2222, 0.3684, and 0.6316) are the posterior probabilities calculated in Section 16.4. The payoffs (losses) given in the original problem are listed at the end of the tree, and the circled values are EMV's.

Calculation of the EMV's in a decision tree usually starts with the branches at the right-hand margin and proceeds toward the left (this is called **backwards induction**). For example, the expected cost of −$1667 is derived from multiplying the posterior probability $P(90\% \text{ good}|G) =$

0.7778 times the cost of a 90% batch, $-\$1000$, and adding this to $P(60\%$ good$|G) = 0.2222$ times the cost of a 60% batch, $-\$4000$; that is,

$$-\$1667 = (0.7778)(-\$1000) + (0.2222)(-\$4000).$$

After a sample of one good valve, the optimal action is to send directly to assembly (at an expected value of $-\$1667$), rather than to rework (at a cost of \$2000). If the sample valve is *defective*, however, the best strategy is to rework (at a cost of \$2000) rather than send to assembly at an expected value of $-\$2895$; that is,

$$(0.3684)(-\$1000) + (0.6316)(-\$4000) = -\$2895.$$

We now know what cost to expect after each possible sample result. We also know how often each possible result will occur; that is, $P(G) = 0.81$ and $P(D) = 0.19$. Putting this information together, we now can say that 81% of the time the cost will be \$1667, and 19% of the time the cost will be \$2000. Thus, the expected value of the sample branch equals the sum of these two expected values times the probability that they will occur, or

$$(0.81)(-\$1667) + (0.19)(-\$2000) = -\$1730.$$

Subtract from this value the \$5 cost of sampling, and the total EMV is $-\$1735$.

Evaluating the Results   It is now evident, from our decision tree, that the "sample of one" branch (with its EMV of $-\$1735$) is a better choice than the next best alternative, which is to send to assembly (EMV $= -\$1900$). In statistical decision theory there are two important measures that indicate by how much sample information increases expected profits or reduces expected costs. One of these measures is designed to *include* the cost of the sample itself, while the other *excludes* sampling costs. For instance, if sample costs are not included in the Perkins Plastics case, then the value of the sampling information (i.e., the testing device) is the difference between $-\$1900$ (the optimal payoff before sampling) and $-\$1730$ (the optimal payoff after sampling). This difference is called the *expected value of sample information* **(EVSI),** and is defined as follows:

EVSI = EMV (optimal after sample, excluding sampling costs)
    $-$ EMV (optimal before sample).   **(16.2)**

In the case of Perkins Plastics,

$$\text{EVSI} = -\$1730 - (-\$1900) = \$170.$$

The value of EVSI can be thought of as the maximum amount the decision-maker should pay for the sample information. Thus, Perkins Plastics should pay no more than $170 for a sample of one, since they cannot expect to save more than this amount (on the average) from the single observation.

When the cost of sampling is known, it is useful in decision theory analysis to include this cost in calculating the *net* savings to the decision-maker. This value is called the *expected net gain from sampling* **(ENGS),** which can be defined as follows:

$$\text{ENGS} = \text{EMV (optimal after sample, including sampling costs)} - \text{EMV (optimal before sample).}$$ **(16.3)**

For Perkins Plastics the after-sample EMV is −$1730 less the $5 sampling cost, or −$1735. Hence,

$$\text{ENGS} = -\$1735 - (-\$1900) = \$165.$$

It is not difficult to see that ENGS and EVSI differ by the cost of the sample, and EVSI is the larger of the two — that is,

$$\text{ENGS} = \text{EVSI} - \text{cost of sampling.}$$

Study Question 16.2: A Study of the Cost of Testing for Rock

The city of Bedford (see Study Question 16.1) is considering drilling a single hole to test for rock. The likelihood of this test indicating "normal" or "excessive" rock is

		State of Nature	
		Normal	Excessive
Test results	No rock	0.90	0.30
	Rock	0.10	0.70

Complete the decision tree started in Study Question 16.1, assuming that the sample costs $1000. Calculate ENGS and EVSI. What decision should Bedford make?

Answer. The optimal decision is to take the sample of size $n = 1$. (See Fig. 16.4.)

Sample Result	States of Nature	Prior	Likelihood	Joint	Posterior
Rock	excessive rock	0.30	0.70	0.21	0.75
	normal rock	0.70	0.10	0.07	0.25
			$P(\text{rock}) =$	0.28	
No rock	excessive rock	0.30	0.30	0.09	0.125
	normal rock	0.70	0.90	0.63	0.875
			$P(\text{no rock}) =$	0.72	

From Formula (16.2),

$$\text{EVSI} = -\$2360 - (-\$5600) = \$3240.$$

From Formula (16.3),

$$\text{ENGS} = -\$3360 - (-\$5600) = \$2240.$$

FIGURE 16.4 **Tree diagram for Bedford rock.**

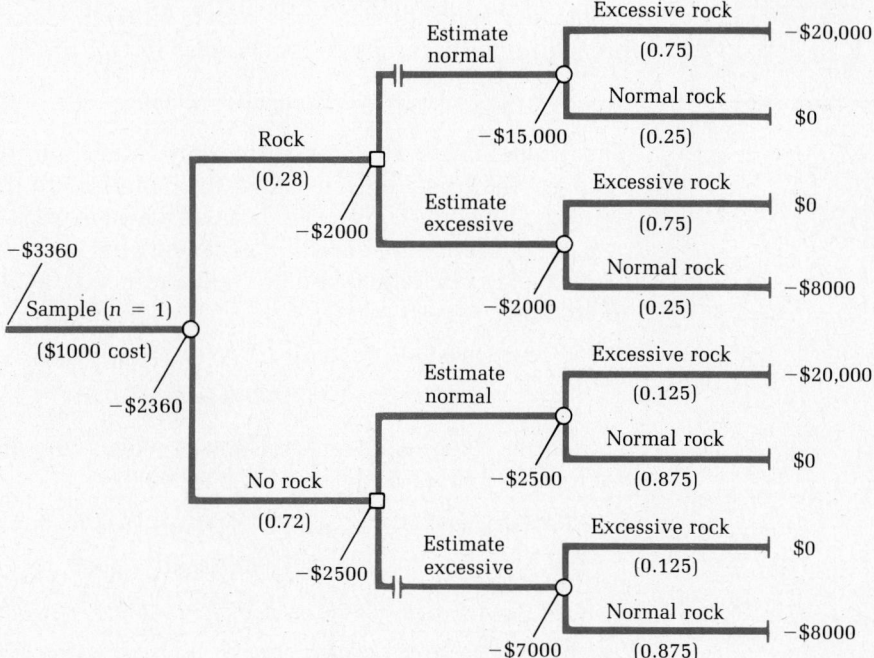

16.6   ANALYSIS FOR LARGER SAMPLE SIZES

If a sample of size one saves \$165, a logical question is whether or not we can do even better with a larger sample, perhaps $n = 2$, or $n = 3$ or more. Fortunately, the process of analyzing these larger samples is very similar to the one carried out for $n = 1$. We will complete the process for $n = 2$ below, assuming that testing this additional sample valve will cost Perkins another \$5.

To begin our analysis, we first need to determine what sample outcomes are possible. When drawing two valves, we could receive: (1) two good [2G]; (2) one good, one defective [1G, 1D]; or (3) two defective [2D]. Since there are three different sample outcomes, we now have the following *six* posterior probabilities to calculate:

$$P(90\% \text{ good}|2G), \quad P(90\% \text{ good}|1G, 1D), \quad P(90\% \text{ good}|2D)$$

and

$$P(60\% \text{ good}|2G), \quad P(60\% \text{ good}|1G, 1D), \quad P(60\% \text{ good}|2D).$$

As before, we must determine the likelihood corresponding to each one of these posteriors. For example, the first likelihood, $P(2G|90\% \text{ good})$ is determined by noting that if the two draws are independent and the probability of finding a good valve on each draw is 0.90,* then the probability of finding two good valves in two draws is $(0.90)^2$; that is,

$$P(2G|90\% \text{ good}) = (0.90)(0.90) = 0.81.$$

The reader may recall a standard formula and a routine process for finding such probabilities. Indeed, when the samples are drawn independently and the probability of success is a constant (as we assumed here, $P(\text{good})$ = 0.90), the *binomial distribution* can be used to calculate the likelihoods. Thus, looking in Table I under $n = 2$ and $\pi = 0.90$, we find the following likelihoods:

$$P(2G|90\% \text{ good}) = 0.81, \quad P(1G, 1D|90\% \text{ good}) = 0.18, \quad \text{and}$$
$$P(2D|90\% \text{ good}) = 0.01.$$

To find the likelihoods for the batch in which 60% of the values are good, we look in Table I under $n = 2$, $\pi = 0.60$:

$$P(2G|60\% \text{ good}) = 0.36, \quad P(1G, 1D|60\% \text{ good}) = 0.48, \quad \text{and}$$
$$P(2D|60\% \text{ good}) = 0.16.$$

---

* We will assume that the number of valves per batch is large enough (1000 items) that the probability of finding a good valve changes very little from one draw to the next.

It will be possible to calculate the likelihoods for all of the discrete Bayesian problems discussed in the remainder of this book by using Table I.

We are now ready to calculate the three marginal probabilities and the six posteriors, using the tabular format presented in Section 16.4. The values obtained are shown in Table 16.5.

Note that in Table 16.5 the three marginal probabilities sum to 1.0, as they must [$P(2G) = 0.675$, $P(1G, 1D) = 0.270$, $P(2D) = 0.055$]. The six posterior probabilities are shown in the last column.

Our next step in the decision analysis is to draw the decision tree. This tree should have four initial branches, corresponding to the four actions "assembly," "rework," "sample of one," and "sample of two." Because the first three of these branches were given in Fig. 16.3, we present in Fig. 16.5 only the new branch, that of "sample of two."

The reader should verify that the marginal and posterior probabilities given in Fig. 16.4 correspond to those of Table 16.5. The EMV's are determined as before, by backwards induction. Note that the optimal decision is to send the valves to assembly only after a sample of two good valves — otherwise, the optimal decision is to rework the valves. The total EMV of this "sample of two" branch is $-\$1649$, excluding the $10 cost. A summary of the EMV's is given in Table 16.6.

Our final step in the decision analysis is to calculate EVSI and ENGS. The value of EVSI indicates how much better $n = 2$ is than the optimal action before sampling (which was to send the valves to assembly at an expected value of $-\$1900$).

$$\text{EVSI}(n = 2) = \text{EMV}(\text{optimal for } n = 2) - \text{EMV}(\text{optimal before sampling})$$
$$= -\$1649 - (-\$1900) = \$251.$$

TABLE 16.5 **Probabilities for the Perkins Plastics example ($n = 2$)**

Sample	State of Nature	Prior	Likelihood	Joint	Posterior
2 good	90% batch	0.70	0.81	0.567	0.567/0.675 = 0.840
	60% batch	0.30	0.36	0.108	0.108/0.675 = 0.160
		1.00	Marginal = 0.675		1.000
1 good,	90% batch	0.70	0.18	0.126	0.126/0.270 = 0.467
1 defective	60% batch	0.30	0.48	0.144	0.144/0.270 = 0.533
		1.00	Marginal = 0.270		1.000
2 defective	90% batch	0.70	0.01	0.007	0.007/0.055 = 0.127
	60% batch	0.30	0.16	0.048	0.0048/0.055 = 0.873
		1.00	Marginal = 0.055		1.000

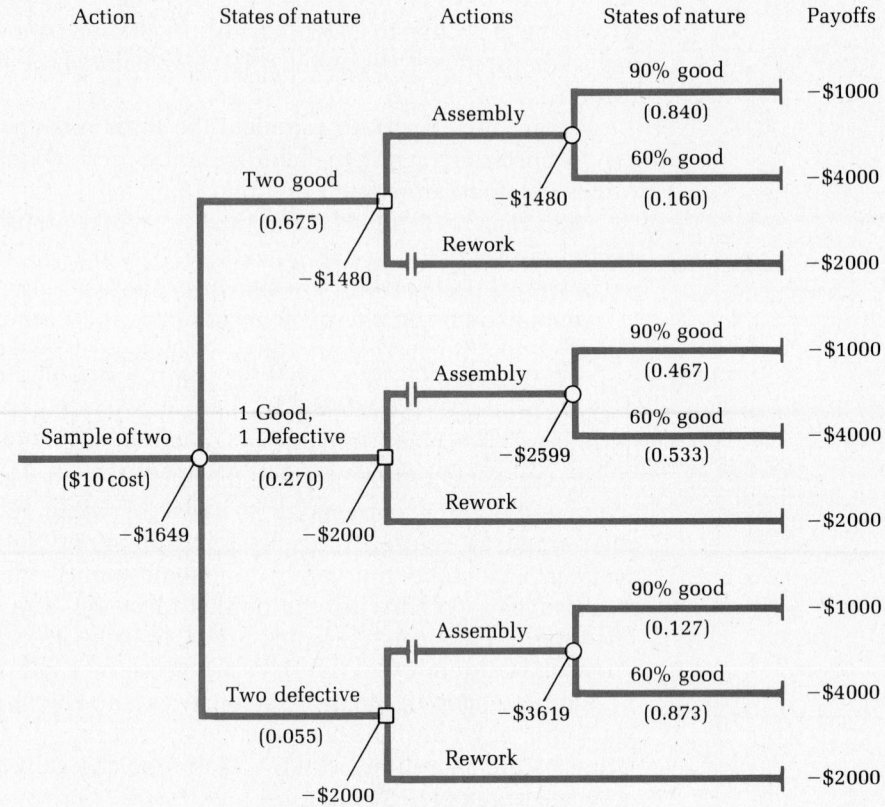

FIGURE 16.5 Tree diagram for $n = 2$ based on Table 16.5.

The value $251 represents the maximum amount Perkins Plastics should pay for a sample of size two. To calculate ENGS, we must subtract the $10 sampling cost from $251. That is,

$$\text{ENGS}(n = 2) = \text{EVSI}(n = 2) - \text{cost of sample}(n = 2)$$
$$= \$251 - \$10 = \$241.$$

Since ENGS($n = 1$) was $165 and ENGS($n = 2$) is $241, a sample of size two is better than a sample of size one.

Samples of Size $n > 2$. It should be clear by now that we can continue this process of analyzing larger and larger samples and that the best sample size is the one giving the largest ENGS. Although the calculations become increasingly tedious as the sample size gets larger, it is often

TABLE 16.6 **Summary of decision analysis for** $n = 2$ **from Fig. 16.4**

Sample Results	Marginal Probability	Optimal Action	EMV	(EMV) × (Marginal prob.)
2 good values	0.675	Assembly	−$1480	−$ 999
1 good, 1 defective	0.270	Rework	−$2000	−$ 540
2 defective	0.055	Rework	−$2000	−$ 110
			Total EMV =	−$1649

relatively easy to program these calculations on a computer. If this is done, then computer costs must be added to the analysis. At this point it would be feasible but tedious for the reader to calculate ENGS for the Perkins Plastics problem for $n = 3$. However, we do advise the reader to calculate the marginal and posterior probabilities for $n = 3$, which should be checked by referring to Table 16.7. The ENGS for $n = 3$ is $265.70.

In Table 16.8 the values of ENGS and EVSI for $n = 1, 2, \ldots, 26$, are given under the assumption that each additional sample observation costs an extra $5. From Table 16.8 we see that $n = 20$ is the optimal sample

TABLE 16.7 **Probabilities for Perkins Plastics example** ($n = 3$)

Sample	State of Nature	Prior	Likelihood	Joint	Posterior
3G	90% good	0.70	0.729	0.5103	0.8873
	60% good	0.30	0.216	0.0648	0.1127
				Marginal = 0.5751	
2G, 1D	90% good	0.70	0.243	0.1701	0.5676
	60% good	0.30	0.432	0.1296	0.4324
				Marginal = 0.2997	
1G, 2D	90% good	0.70	0.027	0.0189	0.1795
	60% good	0.30	0.288	0.0864	0.8205
				Marginal = 0.1053	
3D	90% good	0.70	0.001	0.0007	0.0352
	60% good	0.30	0.064	0.0192	0.9648
				Marginal = 0.0199	

TABLE 16.8 **Values of EVSI and ENGS for selected sample sizes**

Sample Size	EVSI	Sample Cost	ENGS	Sample Size	EVSI	Sample Cost	ENGS
1	$170.00	$ 5	$165.00	14	$494.53	$ 70	$424.53
2	251.00	10	241.00	15	506.82	75	431.82
3	280.70	15	265.70	16	513.03	80	433.03
4	281.51	20	261.51	17	514.30	85	429.30
5	340.80	25	315.80	18	523.77	90	433.77
6	380.05	30	350.05	19	533.60	95	438.60
7	400.04	35	365.04	20	539.21	100	439.21
8	405.35	40	365.35	21	541.33	105	436.33
9	423.85	45	378.85	22	543.92	110	433.92
10	450.49	50	400.49	23	551.80	115	436.80
11	451.96	55	406.96	24	556.66	120	436.66
12	472.33	60	412.33	25	559.01	125	434.01
13	479.94	65	414.94	26	559.26	130	429.26

for Perkins Plastics.* For other problems the optimal size could be very large. Or it may be that all values of ENGS are negative, implying that the decision-maker should not sample at all. In other instances it may be better to take a sample, observe the results of this sample, and then decide whether or not to stop sampling or to continue with further observations. A discussion of such *stopping rules* is beyond the scope of this book but can be found in reference 20 at the end of this book.

Study Question 16.3: The Cost of Testing for Rock When $n = 2$
Extend Study Question 16.2 by assuming that the city now has the option to drill twice for rock. The two drillings are independent and will cost a total of $1200. Determine whether $n = 2$ is better than $n = 1$, and calculate ENGS.

Answer. A sample of $n = 2$ is better than $n = 1$. The problem is solved below in tabular form. The reader may wish to draw the decision tree.

* The decision rule for $n = 20$ (which is not shown here) is to rework if the number of defectives is 5 or larger. Otherwise, the batch is sent to assembly.

Sample Result	State of Nature	Prior	Likelihood	Joint	Posterior
Both rock	excessive	0.30	0.490	0.147	0.995
	normal	0.70	0.010	0.007	0.045
			P(both rock) $= 0.154$		
One rock, One no rock	excessive	0.30	0.420	0.126	0.500
	normal	0.70	0.180	0.126	0.500
		P(1 rock, 1 no rock) $= 0.252$			
Both no rock	excessive	0.30	0.090	0.027	0.045
	normal	0.70	0.810	0.567	0.955
			P(both no rock) $= 0.594$		

Decision Table:	Payoff if City Estimates	
Sample Results:	Excessive	Normal
Both rock	$0.955(0) +$ $0.045(-8000) = -360$	$0.955(-20,000) +$ $0.045(0) = -19,100$
1 rock, 1 no rock	$0.500(-8000) +$ $0.500(0) = -4000$	$0.500(0) +$ $0.500(-20,000) =$ $-10,000$
Both no rock	$0.045(0) +$ $0.955(-8000) =$ -7640	$0.045(-20,000) +$ $0.955(0) = -900$

A summary of the EMV's is given in Table 16.9.

$$\text{EVSI}(n = 2) = -\$1598 - (-\$5600) = \$4002;$$

$$\text{ENGS}(n = 2) = \$4002 - \$1200 = \$2802.$$

TABLE 16.9 **Summary of decision analysis for Study Question 16.3**

Sample Results	Marginal Probability	Optimal Action	EMV	(EMV) × (Marginal Probability)
Both rock	0.154	Est. excessive	-360	-55.40
1 rock, 1 no rock	0.252	Est. excessive	-4000	-1008.00
Both no rock	0.594	Est. normal	-900	-534.60
		Total EMV $= -1598.00$		

Define. *Decision-making under uncertainty, states of nature, dominated actions, EMV criterion, prior probability, posterior probability, likelihoods, Bayes' rules, preposterior analysis, backwards induction, EVSI, ENGS.*

PROBLEMS

16.1 What are the disadvantages of the EMV criterion?

16.2 The Koseman Company is considering adding a new boiler to its factory in an attempt to avoid costly delays in case one of the present boilers must shut down for repairs. The company has determined that the following payoff table is appropriate for its present time horizon (5 years).

	States of Nature		
	No Repairs	Minor Repairs	Major Repairs
Actions { Do not add boiler	$0	−$ 4,000	−$15,000
Add new boiler	−$10,000	−$10,000	−$10,000
Probability	0.20	0.30	0.50

Find the optimal action using the EMV criterion.

16.3 Draw the decision tree for Problem 16.2, indicating the optimal action by EMV.

16.4 A toy manufacturer is considering introducing a novely item in time for the Christmas season. Because of a distribution agreement, the number of items produced must be either 1000, 5000, or 10,000 units. These units can be produced either by a labor-intensive process that involves a fixed cost of $2000 plus a variable cost of $1.50 per unit or by a capital-intensive process involving fixed costs of $5000 and a variable cost of $1.00 per unit. The company sells this novelty item for $3.00 per unit. Their current estimates are that the probability of selling only 1000 units is $\frac{1}{6}$, the probability of selling 5000 units is $\frac{1}{2}$, and the probability of selling 10,000 units is $\frac{1}{3}$. Unsold units have no salvage value. The company is trying to decide whether to produce 1000, 5000, or 10,000 units.
a) Find the optimal action, using the EMV criterion.
b) Draw the decision tree, indicating the optimal action under EMV.

16.5 A lab test for diabetes has been shown to correctly identify the presence of this disease in 80% of all people who are diabetics. Thirty percent of the time, however, the test will indicate diabetes in someone who does not have this disease. If 10% of a given population has diabetes, what is the probability that a person whose lab test indicates diabetes actually has the disease?

16.6 Professor Ward Edwards of the University of Southern California conducted an experiment in which he asked college students to estimate the probability that a given sample of green and red balls came from one of two urns. Urn 1 contained 70 red balls and 30 green, while Urn 2 contained 70 green and 30 red balls. At the beginning of the experiment, one of these urns was selected at random, and then samples were drawn from this urn by randomly selecting a ball, noting its color, and then replacing the ball. The subjects did not know which urn had been selected.

a) Suppose that one red ball is drawn. Without working it out, what is your guess as to the posterior value $P(\text{Urn 1}|\text{One red})$?

b) Suppose that a sample of ten balls is drawn, resulting in seven red and three green. Without working it out, what is your guess as to the value of $P(\text{Urn 1}|7R, 3G)$?

c) In Edwards' experiments, a typical subject guessed that the probability in part (a) was about 0.60, and most estimated that the probability in a question similar to part (b) was less than 0.80. Use Bayes' rule to calculate the actual posterior values for parts (a) and (b), and then assess how well you and Dr. Edwards' subjects did in estimating these probabilities. [Hint: Table I can be used to calculate the four likelihoods, $P(\text{One red}|\text{Urn 1})$, $P(\text{One red}|\text{Urn 2})$, $P(7 \text{ red}, 3 \text{ green}|\text{Urn 1})$, and $P(7 \text{ red}, 3 \text{ green}|\text{Urn 2})$.]

16.7 A company can ship some equipment either by sea or by air. There is a possibility of a strike affecting either type of shipment. The cost matrix, including shipment and delay costs, is given below.

	Strike (B_1)	No Strike (B_2)
Ship by air	4000	3000
Ship by sea	6000	1000

a) If the probability of a strike is 0.4, what are the expected costs of each method of shipment?

b) Suppose that some inside informer suggests that a strike will occur and that the accuracy of this rumor (R) is given by the following likelihoods:

$$P(R|B_1) = 0.8, \quad \text{and} \quad P(R|B_2) = 0.3.$$

Find the revised probability of a strike, given this extra information [find $P(B_1|R)$].

c) Using the revised probability, find the best choice of shipment according to the expected monetary value criterion.

16.8 Suppose that we receive a concession to sell popcorn at football games. We must decide whether to build one booth on the "Home" side or to build two booths, one each on the "Home" and "Visitors" sides of the stadium. If the games attract large crowds of visitors, it would be better to have two booths, but their cost and the cost of equipment within them would be a considerable expense. The payoff matrix is determined to be:

Action		Capacity Crowds	Regular "Home" Crowd
A_1	Build one booth	$350	$300
A_2	Build two booths	500	200

a) Suppose that we consider the probability of capacity crowds to be 0.4 and the probability of regular-sized "home" crowds to be 0.6. Which action is "better"?

b) Suppose that a preseason forecast predicts a much improved team and preseason ticket sales are up by 30%. From previous experience we determine that such situations have preceded games with capacity crowds four out of ten times and have preceded games with regular crowds in two out of ten cases — i.e., the likelihoods are P(up 30%|cap.) = $\frac{4}{10}$ and P(up 30%|reg.) = $\frac{2}{10}$. Find the revised probability of the two different-sized crowds, and determine which action is better in light of the new information.

16.9 A corporation considers two levels of investment in a real-estate development, a low participation (A_1) or a high participation (A_2). Two states of nature are deemed possible, a partial success (B_1) or a complete success (B_2). The payoff matrix is estimated to be:

	B_1	B_2
A_1	−200	400
A_2	−500	1000

a) How large does the prior probability of B_1 have to be in order to make action A_1 the better choice?

b) Suppose that the states of nature are presumed initially to occur with probabilities $P(B_1) = 0.4$, $P(B_2) = 0.6$. Then a more careful study is made, which leads to the conclusion that the project will be only a partial success. In previous relevant studies, this same conclusion was obtained in eight out of ten cases when similar projects were partial successes. Also, this conclusion was obtained in four out of 12 cases when similar projects were *complete* successes. Thus, the likelihoods are $P(\text{study says partial}|B_1) = \frac{8}{10}$ and $P(\text{study says partial}|B_2) = \frac{4}{12}$. Find the revised probabilities of the states of nature, and determine which investment level is appropriate.

16.10 Suppose that you are trying to choose between these investments (a_1, a_2, a_3), where the payoff table (in dollars) is as follows.

		States of Nature		
		θ_1	θ_2	θ_3
	a_1	0	0	1400
Action	a_2	500	500	500
	a_3	400	100	900
Probability		0.30	0.30	0.40

What is the optimal action under EMV?

16.11 Joe Doakes is considering flying from New York City to Boston in the hopes of making an important sale to P. J. Bety, president of NOCO, Inc. If Joe makes this sale, he will earn a commission of $1100. Unfortunately, Joe figures that there is a 50–50 chance that Bety will be called out of town at the last moment and he will have no chance at a sale. Even if he goes to see Bety, Joe estimates that he has only one chance in five of making the sale. The trip will cost Joe $100, whether or not he gets to see Bety.

a) Draw the tree diagram for Joe, and determine whether Joe should fly to Boston or not.

b) Joe was heard to remark, "I'd give my right arm to know if Bety will be in town." How much does he value his right arm?

c) Suppose an information service offers to tell Joe, before he decides to fly, whether or not they think Bety will be in town. The record of this company is such that if they say Bety will be in, the probability that he will, in fact, be in is 0.70; i.e., the posterior probability is $P(\text{in}|\text{say in}) = 0.70$. If they say he will be out, they will be correct 90% of the time; i.e., $P(\text{out}|\text{say out}) = 0.90$. If this service costs $10, and Joe figures that the probability that they will say Bety is in is 0.50, should he buy the service? Draw the tree diagram. Find ENGS.

16.12 Answer parts (a) and (b).
  a) Can EVSI ever assume a negative value? Explain.
  b) What will be the value of EVSI if, no matter what sample result is observed, the same decision is optimal after sampling as was optimal before sampling?

16.13 The Dixon Corporation makes picture tubes for a large television manufacturer. Dixon is concerned because approximately 30% of their tubes have been defective. When the television manufacturer encounters a defective tube, Dixon is charged a $20 penalty cost (to pay for repairs and lost time). One way Dixon can avoid this penalty cost is to reexamine and fix each defective tube before shipping. This would cost an extra $7 per tube. Or they can rent a testing device that costs $1 for each tube tested. Since this device is not infallible, its effectiveness was tested by running through it a large number of tubes, some known to be good and others known to be defective. The results of this study determined the following likelihoods.

		State of Tube	
		Good	Defective
Test results	Good	0.75	0.20
	Def.	0.25	0.80
		1.00	1.00

Draw the decision tree for Dixon, assuming that they must decide between shipping directly, reexamining each tube, or testing each tube. Calculate ENGS and EVSI.

16.14 The Techno Corporation is considering making either minor or major repairs to a malfunctioning production process. When the process is malfunctioning, the percentage of defective items produced seems to be a constant, with either $\pi = 0.10$ (indicating minor repairs necessary) or $\pi = 0.25$ (indicating major repairs necessary). Defective items are produced randomly, and there is no way Techno can tell for sure whether the machine needs minor or major repairs. If minor repairs are made when $\pi = 0.25$, the probability of a defective is reduced to 0.05. If minor repairs are made when $\pi = 0.10$ or major repairs are made when $\pi = 0.10$ or $\pi = 0.25$, then the proportion of defectives is reduced to zero. Techno has recently received an order for 1000 items. This item yields then a profit of $0.50 per unit, except that they have to pay a $2.00

penalty cost for each item found defective. Major repairs to the process cost $100, while minor repairs cost $60. No adjustment can be made to the production process once a run has started. Prior to starting the run, however, Techno can sample items from a "trial" run, at a cost of $1.00 per item. The prior probabilities are $P(\text{major}) = 0.3$, $P(\text{minor}) = 0.7$.

a)   Find the optimal action for Techno if they are trying to decide between not sampling at all, and sampling one item. Draw the decision tree.

b)   Find the optimal action for Techno if they are willing to consider a sample of either one or two items. Draw the decision tree. Calculate ENGS and EVSI.

16.15   Handballs produced by a certain company are considered defective if they do not bounce at least 42 inches when dropped from a height of six feet. In the past, about 40% of all balls shipped are later found to be defective. If the company ships a defective ball, they incur costs (lost goodwill, returns, etc.) of $0.20 per ball. Instead of shipping directly, however, the company can vacuum-seal each ball at a cost of $0.10 per ball. This ensures that each ball will be good. The company is also considering testing each ball by dropping it *twice* from a height of six feet. A good ball will always bounce at least 42 inches; a defective will bounce 42 inches or more half of the time, with each bounce independent of all others. This testing procedure costs $0.02 per ball. Draw the decision tree for this company, calculate ENGS and EVSI, and indicate the optimal action for the company.

16.16   A university is trying to decide whether to schedule its June commencement indoors or outdoors. If they schedule it outdoors and it rains, the change of plans and move indoors will cost the university an extra $1000. On the other hand, if the decision is to hold commencement indoors and it does not rain, the extra cost to the university will be $300 (mostly lighting and air conditioning). The probability of rain in June is 0.20.

a)   Find the optimal action. Draw the decision tree.

b)   A local expert has promised to forecast the weather on commencement day (rain or no rain) for $100. This person is known to forecast according to the two likelihoods $P(\text{predicts rain}|\text{will rain}) = 0.70$ and $P(\text{predict no rain}|\text{will not rain}) = 0.80$. Draw the decision tree and calculate EVSI and ENGS.

16.17   Some decision-theory texts emphasize a measure called *the expected value of perfect information (EVPI)*. This measure indicates the average payoff advantage expected under the assumption that the decision-maker knows in advance what state of nature will occur (i.e., perfect information). For example, in Table 16.2 on page 818, the optimal action is a_2 if θ_1 is going to occur; if θ_2 is going to occur, then action a_1 is optimal. Since

$P(a_1) = P(a_2) = 0.50$, and the two optimal payoffs are \$10,500 and \$100, the decision-maker's payoff under perfect information would be

$$0.50(\$10,500) + 0.50(\$100) = \$5300.$$

To determine EVPI, we need to know how much *better off* the decision maker is with perfect information. Without perfect information, the best action was a_2, and the EMV was \$250. Hence,

$$\text{EVPI} = \text{EMV}\left(\begin{array}{c}\text{optimal with perfect} \\ \text{information}\end{array}\right) - \text{EMV}\left(\begin{array}{c}\text{optimal without perfect} \\ \text{information}\end{array}\right)$$

$$= \$5300 - \$250 = \$5050.$$

a) Find EVPI for Problem 16.2.
b) Find EVPI for part (a) of Problem 16.7.
c) Find EVPI for Problem 16.10.

16.18 One interesting property of Bayes' rule is that when $n > 1$, probabilities may be revised after *each observation* or after *each group* of observations. For example, in Section 16.6 we calculated the posterior probability $P(90\% \text{ good}|1G, 1D) = 0.467$. This probability could have been calculated by assuming that the good valve was received on the first sample and the defective valve on the second sample. The posteriors $P(90\% \text{ good}|1G)$ and $P(60\% \text{ good}|1G)$ become the priors for calculating the new posteriors, which are determined after seeing the second valve (a defective).

a) Show that the two-phase method described above yields the same value as $P(90\% \text{ good}|1G, 1D)$.
b) Show that the above posterior, when acting as the prior for a sample of one more valve (another good), yields the posterior for the sample (G, D, G) of $P(90\% \text{ good}|2G, 1D) = 0.568$.

16.7 UTILITY ANALYSIS*

As we pointed out earlier, the EMV criterion suffers from the weakness that it fails to take into account the variability in profits of a decision. As early as the eighteenth century, Daniel Bernoulli investigated the fact that, for most people, the value of a payoff does not always vary proportionally with its dollar amount. Bernoulli's work can be considered as perhaps the first stage in the development of a method permitting measurement of *relative* values in a decision-making context. This method was developed by the late John von Neumann, a mathematician, and Oskar Morgenstern, an economist, and was first published in 1944 in

---

* This section may be omitted without loss in continuity.

their now classic book, *The Theory of Games and Economic Behavior.* Their method measures relative values using an index or scale of "utility," called a **utility function.**

A Utility Scale It is important to point out at this time that a utility scale is *unique to the individual* for whom it is constructed, and it is not meaningful to compare the values on one person's scale with the values on any other person's scale. We must mention also that, although the examples given below involve only monetary payoffs or consequences, nonmonetary factors can be taken into account as well.

A utility index, as determined by the von Neumann–Morgenstern approach, is measured on an **interval scale.** This type of scale is characterized by its lack of a predetermined zero-point (i.e., no specified origin) and the fact that the units of measurement can be selected arbitrarily (for example, Centigrade and Fahrenheit temperature scales both represent interval measurement). It is because of this arbitrary choice of origin and unit that one cannot make interpersonal comparisons of utility.

The von Neumann–Morgenstern approach to determining a utility function is to ascertain the utility for a number of points between two values, and then use these points as the basis for sketching a continuous function over the entire range. Finding the utility for given dollar values is accomplished by asking the decision-maker to indicate whether alternative I or II is more attractive for certain values of A, B, and C (where A, B, and C are dollar values such that $\$A > \$B > \$C$):

Alternative I: Receive $\$B$ for certain;

Alternative II: Receive $\$A$ with probability π,

Receive $\$C$ with probability $1 - \pi$.

Alternative II is sometimes referred to as the **standard lottery,** while Alternative I is called the **certainty equivalent.** Suppose that we denote the utility of Alternative I to the decision-maker as $U(\$B)$ and denote the expected utility for Alternative II as $\pi U(\$A) + (1 - \pi)U(\$C)$. If the decision-maker is indifferent between these two alternatives, then

$$U(\$B) = \pi\, U(\$A) + (1 - \pi)U(\$C).$$

This equation is the basis from which a von Neumann–Morgenstern utility function is constructed.

Constructing a Utility Function **Example 16.5.** Construct a utility function for the decision-maker in the Perkins Plastics example that will associate a utility value for profits ranging from $-\$5000$ to $\$5000$. In constructing a utility scale, two points must be assigned arbitrarily. Any dollar value can be assigned any utility value, as long as the higher dollar value is assigned the higher utility (we assume that everyone prefers more money to less). Let us rather arbitrarily set

$$U(\$0) = 0 \quad \text{and} \quad U(\$5000) = 100.$$

The unit of measurement in utility is called a **utile,** so $0 has a value of 0 utiles, and $5000 has a value of 100 utiles.

There are a number of ways we can use these two values to determine additional points on the utility function. In one method the value of B is the decision variable. For example, we might let $A = \$5000$, $C = \$0$, and $\pi = \frac{1}{2}$ and ask the decision-maker what value of B makes the following two alternatives equally attractive:

> *Alternative I:* Receive $B for certain;
>
> *Alternative II:* Receive $5000 with probability $\pi = \frac{1}{2}$,
>
> Receive $0 with probability $1 - \pi = \frac{1}{2}$.

Assume that our decision-maker says that the two alternatives are equally attractive when $B = \$1000$. The utility associated with $1000 can now be calculated as follows:

$$U(\$1000) = \tfrac{1}{2}U(\$5000) + \tfrac{1}{2}U(\$0)$$

$$= \tfrac{1}{2}(100) + \tfrac{1}{2}(0)$$

$$= 50.$$

Now we have three points on the utility curve (counting the original two points).

To determine a fourth point, we can use a second method in which the value of C is the unknown value. Let $A = \$1000$, $B = \$0$, and $\pi = \frac{1}{2}$, and ask the decision-maker to choose between the following alternatives:

> *Alternative I:* Receive $0 for certain;
>
> *Alternative II:* Receive $1000 with probability $\pi = \frac{1}{2}$,
>
> Receive $C with probability $1 - \pi = \frac{1}{2}$.

Assume that the decision-maker is indifferent when $C = -\$1500$. Then

$$U(\$0) = \tfrac{1}{2}U(\$1000) + \tfrac{1}{2}U(-\$1500),$$

$$0 = \tfrac{1}{2}(50) + \tfrac{1}{2}U(-\$1500),$$

$$U(-\$1500) = -50.$$

This result gives a fourth point on the utility curve.

Although it is usually convenient to let either A, B, or C be the value the decision-maker must adjust to the point of indifference and to let π

$= \frac{1}{2}$ (the subjective appraisal of Alternative II is easier with 50–50 odds), we can formulate a third method in which π is the decision variable. Let $A = \$0$, $B = -\$1500$, and $C = -\$5000$. The two alternatives are

> *Alternative I:*   Lose \$1500 for certain;
>
> *Alternative II:*   Receive \$0 with probability π,
>
>   Lose \$5000 with probability $1 - \pi$.

If our decision-maker is indifferent when $\pi = 0.75$, then

$$U(-\$1500) = (0.75)U(\$0) + (0.25)U(-\$5000),$$
$$-50 = (0.75)(0) + (0.25)U(-\$5000),$$
$$U(-\$5000) = -200.$$

    The above examples illustrate three variations on the process of determining points on a utility function. Once a sufficient number of such points have been calculated to ensure that the function is accurately represented, then the utility function can be drawn by sketching a line between the points. We show, in Fig. 16.6, what the function for Perkins Plastics might look like when it is completed (the five points already calculated are marked with the symbol ●).

The Effect of Risk on the Utility Function   Note several interesting characteristics about this function. First, the slope of the curve for most positive values is *concave* in shape, meaning that the decision-maker is a **risk-avoider** in this region. That is, if two alternatives have equal EMV's, then the decision-maker will prefer the alternative with the *lower* variability in payoff. This fact can be seen by our decision-maker's answer to the first set of alternatives presented. At that time, the decision-maker indicated indifference between receiving \$1000 for sure and gambling for stakes of \$0 and \$5000 at 50–50 odds. Note that this gamble has an EMV of \$2500. The decision-maker's answer

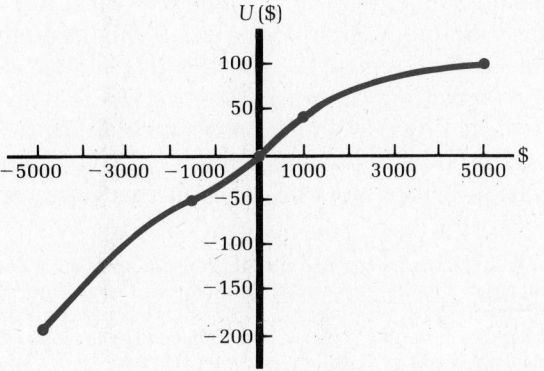

FIGURE 16.6 **Utility function for the decision-maker of Perkins Plastics.**

thus implies that any amount above $1000, received with certainty, is preferable to the gamble. In other words, our decision-maker would rather have, say, $1100 for sure than take the risk that the gamble might result in a payoff of only $0. Hence, for dollar values between $1000 and $5000 this decision-maker can be classified as a "risk-avoider." Perhaps Fig. 16.7, which is an enlarged view of the decision-maker's utility function between $0 and $5000, will help explain why the function between $1000 and $5000 represents risk avoidance.

The dashed line in this figure (the "gamble line") represents a standard lottery where $A = \$5000$ and $C = \$0$. When $\pi = \frac{1}{2}$, then the point a, which is halfway between the endpoints of the gamble line, represents the expected value of the gamble. We see that the EMV at point a is $2500, and the expected utility is 50 utiles. Point b represents the utility received by the decision-maker for $1000 received with certainty. Thus,

$$U(\$1000) = U(\text{Gamble}) = 50 \text{ utiles},$$

which is the answer that this person indicated in response to our first set of alternatives.

Note from the diagram that our decision-maker's utility for $2500 received with certainty is 80 utiles (point c). One might ask at this time what value of π would make this decision-maker indifferent between the standard lottery and the certainty of receiving $2500. As shown by point d on the gamble line, it requires a gamble with an EMV of $4000 to yield the 80 utiles that the certainty of $2500 yields. Thus, the value of π has to be 0.80, since

$$0.80(\$5000) + 0.20(\$0) = \$4000.$$

For payoffs from about $-\$1500$ to $1000 we see in Fig. 16.6 that this decision-maker is a **risk-taker,** since the function is convex in shape in this region.* The answer to our second set of alternatives illustrates this fact. Recall that our second set of alternatives involved a gamble between $-\$1500$ and $1000, with $\pi = \frac{1}{2}$. The EMV of this gamble is thus $-\$250$. Since the certainty equivalent is $0 in this case, the decision-maker is indicating a willingness to take the risk of the gamble whenever the amount received for certain is less than $0. For example, suppose that this person is given a choice between receiving $-\$100$ for sure (i.e., a $100 loss) or taking a gamble between $-\$1500$ and $1000 at 50–50 odds. Our decision-maker is a risk-taker in this range and would prefer the

---

* Concave from below means that the slope of the function is decreasing as the amount of dollars increases. That is, the second derivative of the function is negative. Its shape is rounded like a mountain top. A convex function has a second derivative that is positive; thus, its shape is more like a valley or a soup bowl. The slope of a convex function is increasing as the amount of dollars increases.

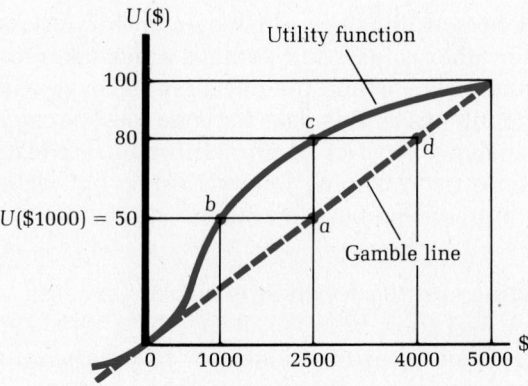

FIGURE 16.7 **A utility function for a risk-avoider.**

gamble, even though its average loss of $\frac{1}{2}(\$-1500) + \frac{1}{2}(\$1000) = -\$250$ is worse than the certain loss of $-\$100$. Finally, we see that for large losses our decision-maker is again a *risk-avoider*, since the utility function is concave in shape in negative regions of the function. This fact is illustrated by the answers to our third set of alternatives.

Had our decision-maker's function been a straight line over part of its range (i.e., linear in shape), then this person would have been classified as **risk-neutral** in these portions of the utility function. That is, the gamble line and the utility function would be the same line; hence, this person would select the alternative yielding the highest EMV. The following table summarizes the three categories often used to distinguish decision-makers.

Category	Utility Function Shape	Description
1. Risk-taker	Convex (slope increasing)	If a gamble has the same EMV as a dollar amount to be received with certainty, a *risk-taker* will always prefer the gamble.
2. Risk-neutral	Straight line (slope constant)	A person who is *risk-neutral* will always select that alternative (gamble or certainty) with the highest EMV.
3. Risk-avoider	Concave (slope decreasing)	If a gamble has the same EMV as a dollar amount to be received with certainty, a *risk-avoider* will always prefer the certainty.

As indicated in Fig. 16.6, most utility functions are not entirely convex, concave, or linear over the entire range of dollar values. Rather, a typical person might be a risk-avoider for certain dollar values, risk-neutral for other values, and perhaps a risk-taker for part of the curve. A utility function in which the decision-maker is willing to take risks for small amounts but avoids risks for large losses or gains, is perhaps typical of many people. Most of us are willing to risk losing small amounts in poker games or by buying lottery tickets, but we avoid large losses by insuring our cars, homes, and businesses.

Maximizing Expected Utility

Constructing a utility function is not an easy task, as we have seen. For important decisions, however, it may be a very worthwhile task, in that the substitution of utility values for monetary values may well change the optimal decision from one action to another.

Example 16.6. We have reproduced, in Fig. 16.8, the Perkins Plastics problem for $n = 1$ (see Figs. 16.1 and 16.3). The final number at the end

FIGURE 16.8 **Utility analysis for Perkins Plastics ($n = 1$).**

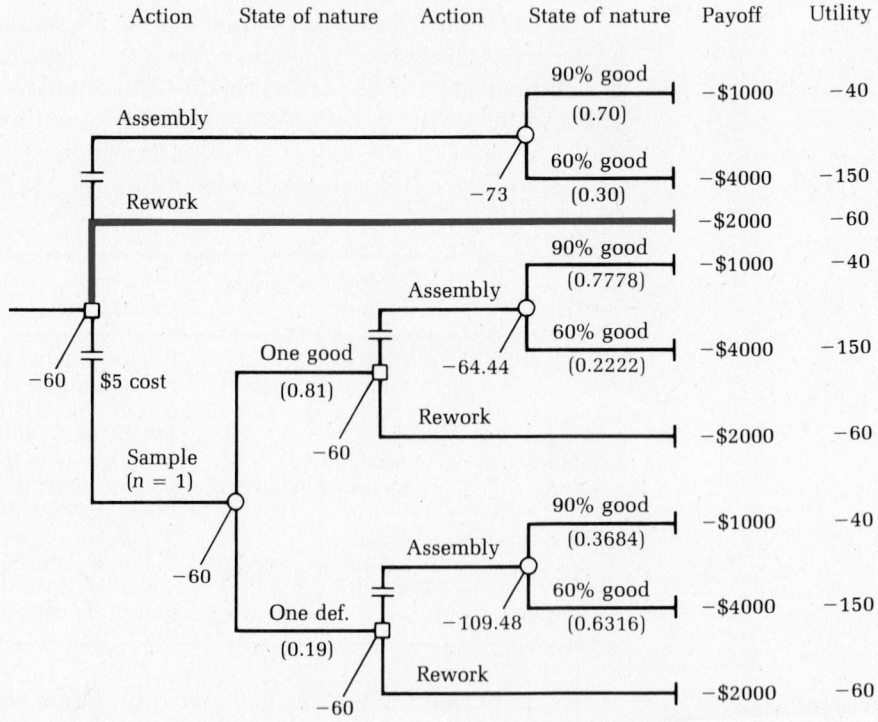

of each branch is the appropriate utility value taken from Fig. 16.6 (that is,

$$-\$4000 = -150 \text{ utiles}, \quad -\$2000 = -60 \text{ utiles}, \quad \text{and} \quad -\$1000 = -40 \text{ utiles}).$$

The analysis is carried out in terms of expected utilities (instead of the expected monetary values used in Figs. 16.1 and 16.3).

The tree diagram in Fig. 16.8 indicates the effect of risk on the Perkins Plastics decision when $n = 1$. By looking at the sample branch we see that *both* sample results lead to a decision to rework. Since this is the same decision that is optimal without taking the sample, the decision-maker need not bother taking the sample. In other words, the sample is worthless, and the value of EVSI must be zero. *EVSI will always equal zero if the sample branch cannot possibly lead to a different solution from that which was optimal before the sample.* Of course, the fact that a sample of size $n = 1$ is not advantageous does not mean that larger samples would also have no value.

Study Question 16.4: Utility Analysis in Bedford Rock Case

Subtract the sample cost ($1000) from each dollar value at the end of the decision tree in Study Question 16.2. Replace these dollar values with utilities, and then determine the optimal action. Use the following information about utilities, and indicate whether the person is a risk-taker, a risk-avoider, or risk-neutral.

$U(\text{cost of } \$21,000) = -100, \quad U(\text{cost of } \$20,000) = 0,$

$U(\text{cost of } \$9000) = 750, \quad U(\text{cost of } \$1000) = 950,$

$U(\text{cost of } \$0) = 1000.$

The decision-maker is indifferent between I and II, where

> *Alternative I:* $8000 cost for sure;
>
> *Alternative II:* $20,000 cost at $\pi = 0.30$, and $0 at $1 - \pi = 0.70$.

Answer. Expected utilities are shown in the tree diagram in Fig. 16.9 (sample costs are included in the payoffs on the right). The utility of a cost of $8000 = 0.70U(0) + 0.30U(-\$20,000) = 0.70(1000) + 0.30(0) = 700$. The optimal decision is to sample because the expected utility of the "sample branch" (841.5) is higher than the expected utility of the "do not sample" branch (700). The utility function, determined by graphing the points given above, is that of a risk avoider. (The curve is concave from below.) The indifference relationship given also indicates a risk-avoider.

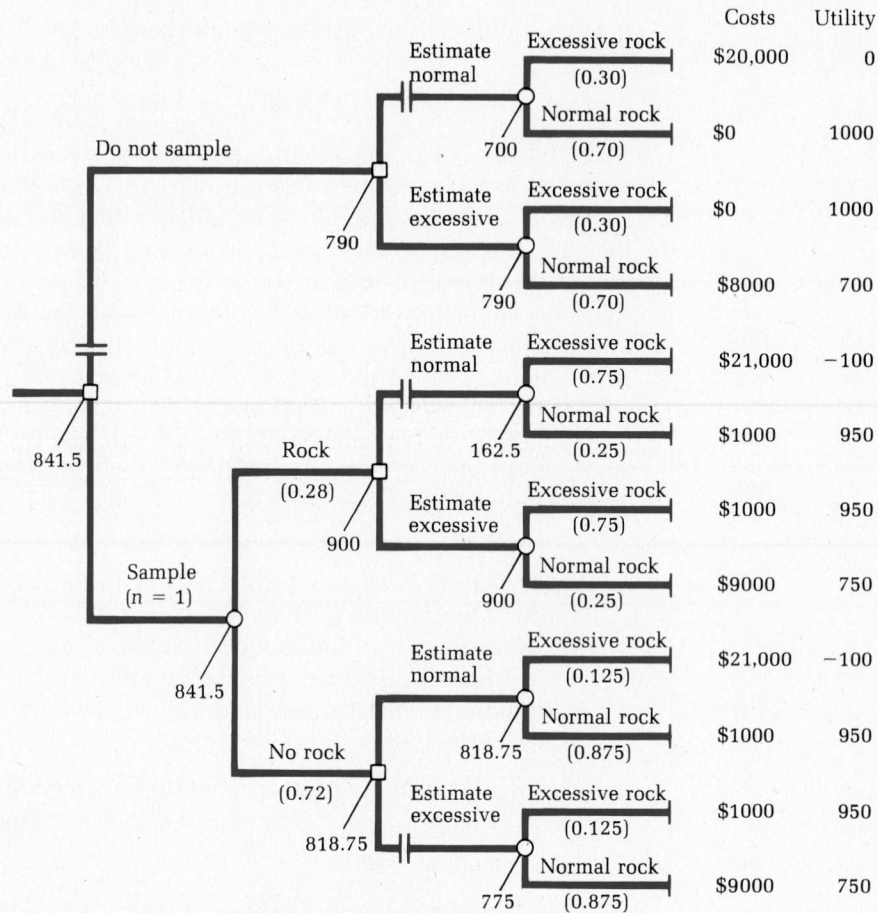

FIGURE 16.9 **Utility analysis for Bedford rock.**

16.8 DECISION ANALYSIS FOR CONTINUOUS FUNCTIONS*

Thus far, only discrete functions have been used in our decision-theory analysis. That is, the number of actions have been discrete sets, as have the states of nature, the prior probabilities, the sampling distribution, the likelihoods, and the posterior probabilities. Although most real-world problems involve only discrete functions, the number of alternatives in

---

* This section may be omitted without loss of continuity.

many cases is so large that a continuous function is much easier to handle. We will see in this section that decision analysis theory for continuous functions is a direct extension of the theory for discrete functions.

Example 16.7. A decision-maker is faced with a situation in which one of the variables is too large to handle in discrete form. Perhaps the president of a company is trying to estimate what sales might be for a new product under a number of different assumptions about its price. Or a book club might be trying to determine whether or not to acquire the rights to a new book by estimating the percent of its members who will purchase this book. In both of these examples it may be possible to collect sample information, and the result of the sample could be any one of a large number of outcomes. The tree diagram in Fig. 16.10 represents what the book club's decision problem might look like. The fans (⬅) in this diagram represent variables involving a large number of outcomes or alternatives.

FIGURE 16.10 **Tree diagram for book club.**

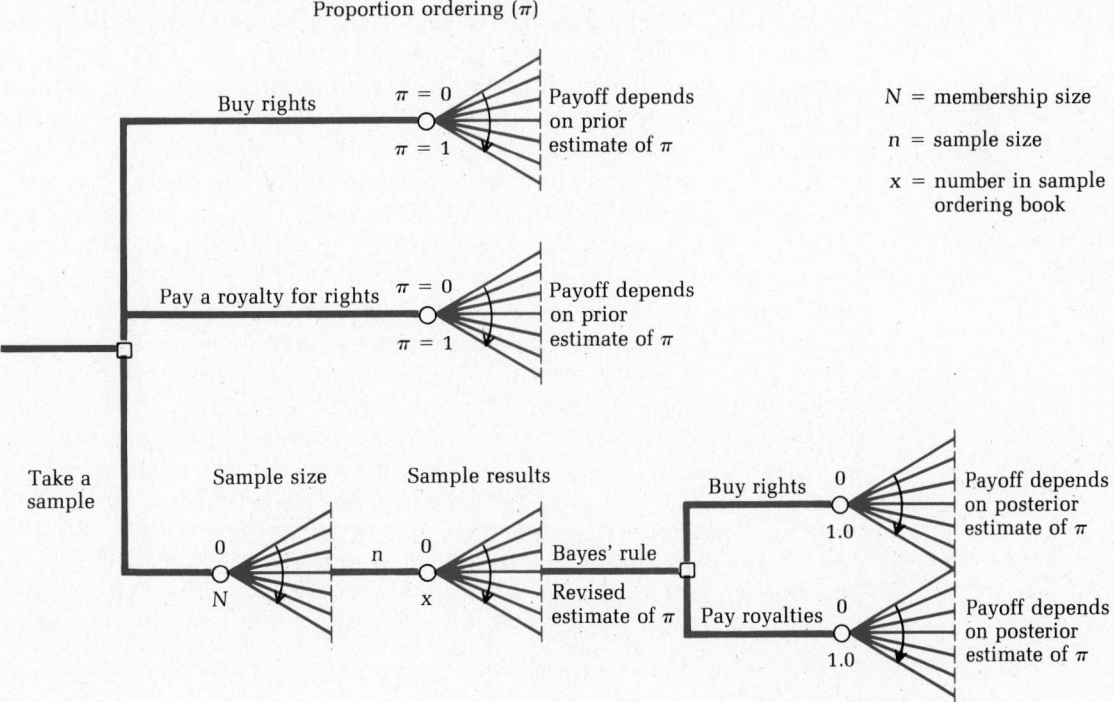

The final branch in Fig. 16.10 represents a random sample of the book club's members. This potential action for the book club could be used if the club decided to conduct a sample to try to estimate how many members intend to purchase the book. Clearly, the sample size (n) must be less than or equal to the number of members in the club (N). The proportion of members in this sample who indicate that they would buy the book provides the basis for revising (via Bayes' rule) the decision-maker's prior probability distribution into a posterior distribution. The posterior distribution is then used (in the same manner as the prior) to decide whether to buy the rights or to pay royalties. Before taking the sample, the decision-maker will want to decide whether or not any sample size leads to a positive ENGS and, if more than one sample size does, which will be the optimal sample size. This is exactly the same process we carried out with the Perkins Plastics example. We will not attempt to exhaust all possible aspects of the analysis of our book-club example because doing so involves several concepts beyond the scope of this chapter. However, Exercise 16.30 at the end of this chapter encourages the reader to carry out several additional steps in the analysis of the book-club example.

To begin an analysis of a decision situation such as that shown in Fig. 16.10, we must assume that the decision-maker can express the prior probabilities in the form of a probability density function. Although theoretically this density function can assume any shape, we will see that the process of revising these probabilities in light of the sample information becomes quite complicated unless the prior distribution either is normally distributed or follows the beta distribution.* Limiting the prior distribution in this way is not as restrictive as it may seem, for these two distributions have been shown to be appropriate in many different situations. It is interesting to note that if a decision-maker's prior distribution is relatively flat, this means that the decision-maker has little or no knowledge about the relative likelihood of the various states of nature. Such a prior distribution is called a "diffuse" prior.

Let us illustrate the assessment of a prior probability by assuming that the decision-maker in our book-club example has indicated that a normal prior is appropriate. Let us assume also that the decision-maker is indifferent, at 50–50 odds, when betting that the proportion (π) of book club members who will order the book is either (1) less than or equal to 0.129 or (2) more than 0.129. In addition, this person says that there is only one chance in 20 that the proportion of sales will be larger than

---

* The beta distribution is a continuous function that is closely related to the binomial distribution.

0.162. These values are consistent with a (prior) normal distribution having a mean of 0.129 and a standard deviation of $\sigma = 0.02$. This standard deviation was calculated by noting that the estimate of one chance in 20 corresponds to the ninety-fifth percentile, for which the standardized normal equivalent is $F(z) = 1.645$ (see Table III). Solving

$$z = \frac{x - \mu}{\sigma},$$

where $x = 0.162$, $\mu = 0.129$, and $z = 1.645$, we obtain the value $\sigma = 0.02$. The decision-maker's prior distribution is thus normally distributed, with a mean of 0.129 and $\sigma = 0.02$, or $N(0.129, 0.02^2)$.

Our next step in analyzing the book-club tree diagram in Fig. 16.8 is to incorporate payoffs into the analysis. For this example, suppose that buying the rights to the book costs \$12,000; if royalties are paid, the company must pay \$1000 for each 1% of the membership that orders the book. The revenue to the company is \$120,000π if they buy the rights and \$20,000π if they pay royalties. (Note that the difference in these revenues is the \$1000 royalty cost per 1%.) Fixed costs to the company are \$2000 in either case. These costs and revenues, including the fixed cost of \$2000, are reflected in the following two payoff functions:

$$\text{Action } a_1: \quad \text{Buy rights} \quad -\$14{,}000 + \$120{,}000\pi$$

$$\text{Action } a_2: \quad \text{Pay royalties} \quad -\$2000 + \$20{,}000\pi$$

By setting these two functions equal and solving for π, we can determine the breakeven value of π — that value at which the expected cost of the two actions is exactly equal. In our example the breakeven value is $\pi_b = 0.12$, which means that if less than 12% order the book, action a_2 is better, while if more than 12% order, action a_1 is better. At 12% the actions a_1 and a_2 have the same expected cost. Since our payoff functions are both linear, it is not difficult to prove that in deciding between these two actions we need only compare the mean of the decision-maker's prior distribution with π_b. Since the prior mean (0.129) exceeds $\pi_b (= 0.120)$, the optimal action is to buy the rights. The expected profit for this action is $-\$14{,}000 + 120{,}000(0.129) = \$1480$. We might note at this point that our decision tree might have had a branch that said, "Do not print book." If this branch had an EMV $= 0$, the action "buy rights" is clearly better for the estimated $\pi = 0.129$, since its EMV $= \$1480$. Had the estimated π been 0.10 or less, both actions a_1 and a_2 would have negative EMV's; hence, "Do not print" would have been better.

Let us assume that the decision-maker in Fig. 16.8 has decided on the upper branch (buy the rights) and is now faced with the problem of

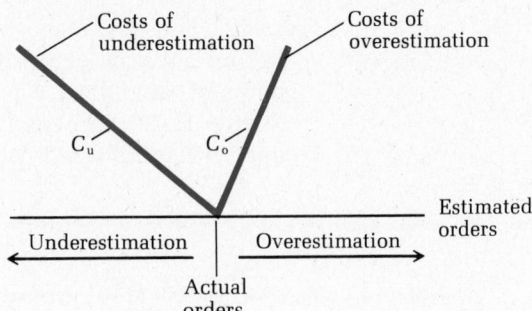

FIGURE 16.11 **Cost of overestimating or underestimating orders.**

deciding how many books to print on the initial production run, a decision that must be made before the orders begin coming in. Ideally, the company would like to print exactly enough books to cover the orders they will receive. If they overestimate or underestimate the number of orders, they will incur additional costs, as shown in Fig. 16.11. The optimal value to estimate in this situation depends on the value of c_u (cost of underestimation) and c_0 (cost of overestimation), as well as on the decision-maker's probability distribution of the anticipated orders. *The optimal estimate for minimizing expected costs is that value of the decision variable which corresponds to the following cumulative probability.*†

Value of cumulative probability that minimizes expected costs:

$$\frac{c_u}{c_u + c_0}. \qquad (16.4)$$

For our example, we will suppose that $c_u = \$0.50$ and $c_0 = \$0.75$. Thus, the optimal value of the decision-maker's prior distribution of orders is, from Formula (16.4),

$$\frac{0.50}{0.50 + 0.75} = 0.40$$

This means that if we denote the optimal number of books to print as x^*, then we need to solve the expression $P(x \le x^*) = 0.40$ for x^*. To do this, first recall that the decision-maker's prior distribution was determined to

† Proof of this fact can be found in most operations research texts.

be normally distributed, with $\mu = 0.129$ and $\sigma = 0.02$. This information can be used to standardize $P(\boldsymbol{x} \leq x^*) = 0.40$ as follows:

$$P(\boldsymbol{x} \leq x^*) = P\left(\frac{\boldsymbol{x} - \mu}{\sigma} \leq \frac{x^* - 0.129}{0.02}\right) = 0.40,$$

or

$$P\left(\boldsymbol{z} \leq \frac{x^* - 0.129}{0.02}\right) = 0.40.$$

From Table III in Appendix C we know that

$$P(\boldsymbol{x} \leq -0.25) = 0.40,$$

which means (from these two equations) that

$$-0.25 = \frac{x^* - 0.129}{0.02},$$

$$x^* = 0.129 + 0.02(-0.25) = 0.124.$$

The optimal number for the decision-maker to print is thus 12.4% of the club's membership.

16.9 BAYES' RULE FOR CONTINUOUS FUNCTIONS*

If a decision-maker wants to gather additional (sample) information, then Bayes' rule is again the means for transforming prior probabilities into posterior probabilities. Bayes' rule for continuous functions follows the same form as for discrete functions, except that the continuous case involves integrating a continuous density function rather than summing a discrete probability function (refer to Formula (16.1) in Section 16.4).† The random variables in the continuous case can, at least theoretically, be any proper probability distributions. However, integration of the denominator of Bayes' rule is quite difficult unless the likelihood function is a beta distribution and sampling is from a binomial distribution, or the likelihood function is normally distributed and sampling is from a normal

---

* This section may be omitted without loss of continuity.

† If we let $f(\theta)$ be the prior density function, $f(x|\theta)$ represent the likelihood function, x be the sample result, and $f(\theta|x)$ be the posterior density function, then Bayes' rule is

| Bayes' rule for continuous random variables: | $f(\theta|x) = \dfrac{f(\theta)f(x|\theta)}{\int f(\theta)f(x|\theta)d\theta}$. |

distribution. When the prior is a beta distribution and the sampling is from a binomial distribution, the posterior distribution will also be a beta distribution. Since the beta distribution has not been discussed in this book, we will not attempt to illustrate how priors can be revised in this fashion (although the process is not a difficult one). Rather, we turn to a more thorough analysis of the case in which $f(\theta)$ and the sampling distribution are both normal.

> When the prior is normal and sampling is from a normal distribution, then the posterior distribution will also be normal.

Furthermore, if the prior distribution has a mean μ_0 and a variance σ_0^2, and a sample of size n with sample mean $\bar{x}$ is taken from a normal distribution with variance σ^2, then the posterior distribution will have a mean μ_1 and a variance σ_1^2, as follows:

For normal distributions:

Posterior mean:
$$\mu_1 = \frac{\mu_0\sigma^2 + n\bar{x}\sigma_0^2}{\sigma^2 + n\sigma_0^2};$$
(16.6)

Posterior variance:
$$\sigma_1^2 = \frac{\sigma^2\sigma_0^2}{\sigma^2 + n\sigma_0^2}.$$
(16.7)

These formulas merely represent the process of taking a weighted average of the prior and sample evidence. The posterior mean μ_1 will always lie between the prior mean μ_0 and the sample mean $\bar{x}$. In addition, the posterior variance will always be smaller than the prior variance.* The more **diffuse** (i.e., flat) the decision-maker's **prior** distribution, the more the posterior distribution will depend on the sample data.

Example 16.8. Assume that a company is attempting to forecast sales of their product in a new area. The decision-maker's prior distribution for sales is normally distributed with a mean of $\mu_0 = 2000$ and a variance of $\sigma_0^2 = 200^2$. We will assume that the decision-maker has taken a random sample from ten other (comparable) areas and found $\bar{x} = 1800$. We will assume also that these ten samples came from a normally distributed

---

* This result holds only for the normal process being discussed and not for revising a beta prior by sampling from a binomial distribution.

population with variance $\sigma^2 = 400^2$. The posterior values are computed from Eqs. (16.6) and (16.7) to be

Posterior mean:
$$\mu_1 = \frac{\mu_0\sigma^2 + n\bar{x}\sigma_0^2}{\sigma^2 + n\sigma_0^2}$$

$$= \frac{2000(400)^2 + 10(1800)(200)^2}{(400)^2 + 10(200)^2} = 1857;$$

Posterior variance:
$$\sigma_1^2 = \frac{\sigma^2\sigma_0^2}{\sigma^2 + n\sigma_0^2}$$

$$= \frac{(400)^2(200)^2}{(400)^2 + 10(200)^2} = 106.9^2.$$

Note that the posterior mean (1857) lies between the prior mean (2000) and the sample mean (1800). The posterior variance $(106.9)^2$ is smaller than the prior variance (200^2) and smaller than the variance of the population from which the sample was drawn (400^2).

As in our book-club example, the decision-maker can now use the mean of the probability distribution (in this case the posterior rather than the prior distribution) to calculate the EMV's and to determine the breakeven value of the mean (μ_b) at which the expected costs are equal. The decision about which of two or more actions minimizes expected costs is similar to that of our prior analysis: If $\mu_1 > \mu_b$ one action is taken, while if $\mu_1 < \mu_b$ the other action is taken. (When $\mu_1 = \mu_b$, the actions result in the same EMV.)

Loss Functions

In many statistical decision theory problems, **loss functions** are somewhat more convenient for determining optimal actions than are the profit functions we have used thus far. In this context a loss is generally defined to be an opportunity loss. Thus, we must specify, for each possible state of nature, a function that describes the loss a decision-maker incurs by not making the optimal decision. A loss function can have any form, although linear functions are often used because they are fairly easy to manipulate and because they are appropriate in many different situations. For example, we will see below that the linear payoff functions for our book-club example translate into the two linear loss functions graphed in Fig. 16.12.

Let us determine the decision-maker's opportunity loss from Fig. 16.10. If the true π is less than 0.12 and decision a_2 (pay royalties) is made, then there is no loss, since this is the correct decision. However, if $\pi > 0.12$, then decision a_2 is incorrect and the decision-maker incurs a loss that depends on the value of π. For instance, suppose that $\pi = 0.13$ (see Fig. 16.12). The opportunity loss is the difference between the

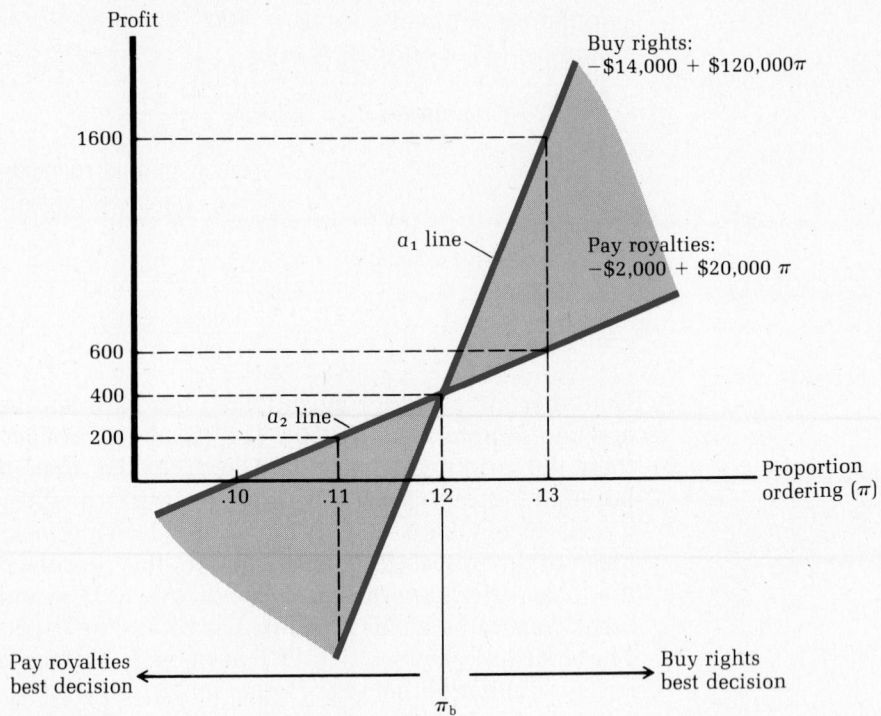

FIGURE 16.12 **Payoff functions for book club.**

EMV of the optimal decision [EMV(a_1) = $1600] and the EMV of the incorrect decision [EMV(a_2) = $600], which is $1600 − $600 = $1000. With a little knowledge of algebra the reader should be able to verify that the opportunity loss when π = 0.11 is also $1000, only this time a_2 is the better decision. Thus, in Fig. 16.12, opportunity loss is given by the difference between the higher and the lower line (the shaded areas). Figure 16.13 presents the opportunity loss for this problem.

We will see shortly how the linear loss function can be especially helpful in decision-theory analysis. A "quadratic loss function," which is another type of loss function used in decision-making problems, is diagrammed in Fig. 16.14. There, the decision-maker's loss is given by the *square* of the difference between the estimated value (a) and the true value (θ). If we let $l(a, \theta)$ represent the loss incurred when $a \neq \theta$, then the quadratic loss function is $l(a, \theta) = (a − \theta)^2$. A quadratic loss function is popular not only because squared errors are appropriate in some circumstances, but because it is mathematically convenient — it can be differentiated easily using calculus.

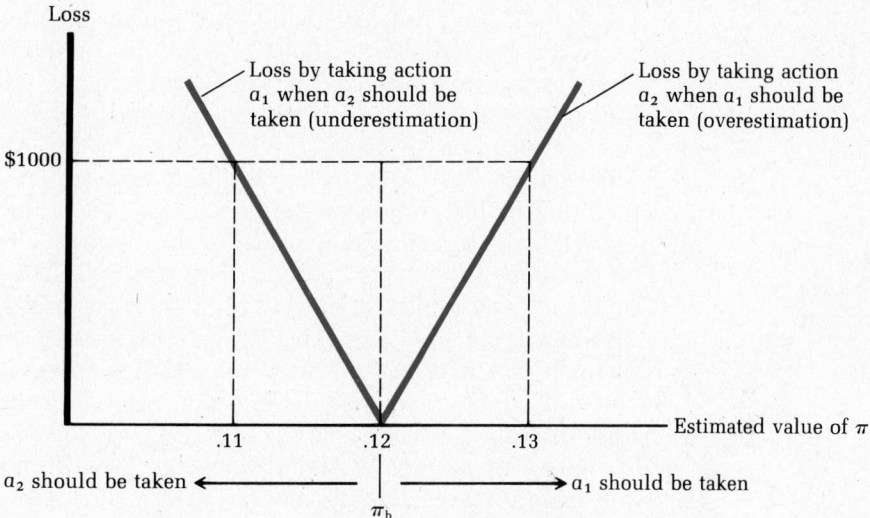

FIGURE 16.13 **Opportunity loss function.**

Unit Normal Linear Loss Integral

When the loss function is linear and the decision-maker's probability assessment is normal, the calculation of expected losses can be aided by the use of a table called the **unit normal linear loss integral.** We present below a very brief description of how this table works and how it is used to calculate EVSI.

Let us assume that in our sales-forecasting example the breakeven point between two actions is sales of 1900 units, which we denote as μ_b

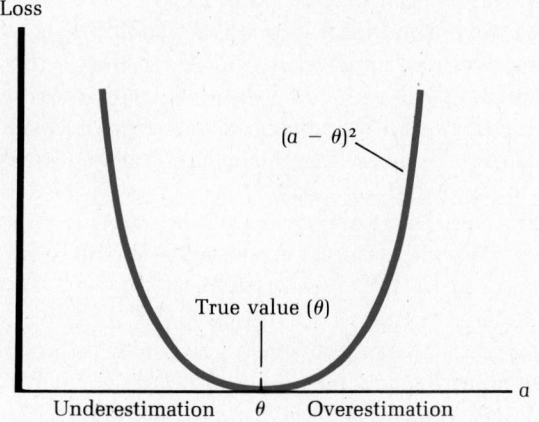

FIGURE 16.14 **Quadratic loss function.**

= 1900. If the prior distribution has a mean (μ_0) less than 1900, action a_1 will be taken; if $\mu_0 > 1900$, then action a_2 will be taken. Since in our sales-forecasting example the prior was normally distributed with mean $\mu_0 = 2000$, action a_2 is optimal. Now let us assume that the loss function for action a_2 is as shown in Fig. 16.15, which also graphs the prior distribution. The expected loss resulting from action a_2, denoted as $\text{EL}(a_2)$, is found by (essentially) weighting each value of the function $l(a_2, \mu)$ by its relative frequency (the normal prior). If we let s be the absolute value of the slope of the loss function, then this expected loss is calculated by multiplying s times the integral of the normal prior function from minus infinity up to μ_b.* The expected loss for a_1 is determined in the same manner. Calculating these integrals, which are necessary for finding $\text{EL}(a_1)$ and $\text{EL}(a_2)$, is much easier if one uses a table of the unit normal linear loss integral.

Actually, we do not need to find $\text{EL}(a_1)$ and $\text{EL}(a_2)$ in this case because we have already determined that action a_2 is better than a_1, since μ_0 exceeds μ_b. The advantage of the unit normal linear loss table is that it simplifies a related calculation — that of EVSI. The formula for calculating EVSI is

$$\text{EVSI} = s\sigma_D L_N(D), \qquad \textbf{(16.8)}$$

where

$$\sigma_D = \sqrt{\frac{n(\sigma_0^2)^2}{\sigma^2 + n\sigma_0^2}}, \qquad D = \left| \frac{\mu_b - \mu_0}{\sigma_D} \right|,$$

s is the absolute value of the slope of either $l(a_2, \mu)$ or $l(a_1, \mu)$, assuming that both have equal slopes,† and $L_N(D)$ is a value (that depends on D) from the unit normal linear loss table (Table IX in Appendix C). The term σ_D in the expression for EVSI essentially indicates the amount the decision-maker's variance is reduced by the sample information — i.e., it is the square root of the difference between the prior variance and the posterior variance, $\sqrt{\sigma_0^2 - \sigma_1^2}$, while D is a standardized measure of the difference between μ_b and μ_0.

---

* If the density function is labeled $f(\mu)$, then this integral is

$$\text{EL}(a_2) = s \int_{-\infty}^{\mu_b} (\mu_b - \mu)f(\mu)\, d\mu.$$

† In terms of our linear payoff functions, $s = |s_1 - s_2|$ where s_1 and s_2 are the slopes of the two payoff functions.

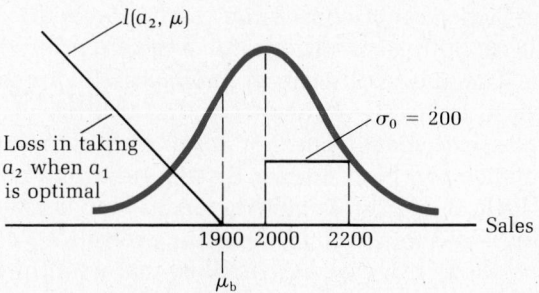

FIGURE 16.15 **Loss function** $l(a_2, \mu)$**.**

Example 16.9. Let us assume that in our sales-forecasting problem both $l(a_2, \mu)$ and $l(a_1, \mu)$ have a slope whose absolute value is $s = 25$. Recall that the prior variance is $\sigma_0^2 = 200^2$, the variance of the population from which the sample was drawn is $\sigma^2 = 400^2$, and $\mu_b = 1900$, $\mu_0 = 2000$. Using these values, we can now calculate σ_D and D:

$$\sigma_D = \sqrt{\frac{n(\sigma_0^2)^2}{\sigma^2 + n\sigma_0^2}} = \sqrt{\frac{10(200^2)^2}{400^2 + (10)200^2}} = 169.03,$$

$$D = \left| \frac{\mu_b - \mu_0}{\sigma_D} \right| = \left| \frac{1900 - 2000}{169.03} \right| = 0.59.$$

Since σ_D^2 measures the reduction in variance from the prior to the posterior, we could have found σ_D as follows:

$$\sigma_D = \sqrt{\sigma_0^2 - \sigma_1^2} = \sqrt{(200)^2 - (106.9)^2} = 169.03.$$

From Table IX, and the fact that $D = 0.59$, we find that $L_N(D) = L_N(0.59) = 0.1714$. The value of EVSI is thus

$$\text{EVSI} = s\sigma_D L_N(D) = 25(169.03)(0.1714) = \$724.29.$$

A sample of $n = 10$ thus yields an expected savings of $724.29 (excluding sample costs). To determine the optimal sample size, the decision-maker would need to calculate ENGS for all possible values of n and then select the largest positive value of ENGS.

16.10 BAYESIAN ANALYSIS: ADVANTAGES AND DISADVANTAGES

Most procedures normally associated with classical statistics, such as point and interval estimation, hypothesis testing, and regression analysis also can be accomplished from a Bayesian point of view, although the two approaches differ considerably. The Bayesian approach is designed to result in optimal decisions for a given prior distribution and loss function. The major criticism of the Bayesian approach is that it requires a number of subjective evaluations, the validity of which is questioned by the classical statistician. For instance, how reasonable is it to ask a decision-maker to form a prior distribution for a set of events of which one has little or no prior knowledge? And even if one has prior knowledge, is it really valid to ascertain the prior probability distribution by asking questions about alternatives (gambles) that would never have to be faced in real life? Also, how is it possible for a decision-maker to formulate a loss function for events when he or she may have no idea of the consequences of a wrong decision or may not be able to express the losses in monetary terms (consider the surgeon trying to decide on an operation that may cost the patient's life)?

The Bayesian answer to these questions is that often a decision-maker is making a number of similar evaluations in classical statistics and may not even be aware of it. For example, in hypothesis-testing, the classical statistician is assuming, in effect, a flat (diffuse) prior and basing all decisions on the sample evidence and a *quite subjective* value of the risk of making a Type I error (α).

Despite the obvious advantages of statistical decision theory as an aid to the decision-making process, the number of businesses that have even experimented with its use remains quite small. Many companies simply have not been exposed to this "new" technique, while others have tried it and found it too time-consuming and/or costly to add to their decision-making process. On the other hand, a number of major companies, such as DuPont, Pillsbury, General Electric, and the Ford Motor Company, have tried decision-theory analysis, and most often the users are pleased with it. Just how great an impact this approach will have on decision-making in the future is a question that cannot be answered at this time.

Define. *Utility function, interval scale, standard lottery, certainty equivalent, utiles, risk-avoider, risk-taker, risk-neutral, diffuse prior, linear loss function, quadratic loss function.*

PROBLEMS

16.19 Suppose that $U(\$500) = 100$ and $U(\$100) = 50$. If a decision-maker expresses indifference between a gamble when $500 occurs with probability $\frac{1}{2}$, $100 occurs with probability $\frac{1}{2}$, and $200 occurs for certain, find $U(\$200)$. Is this person risk-taking or risk-avoiding?

16.20 Suppose that a decision-maker has expressed an indifference between receiving B for sure and a 50–50 gamble between A and C for each of the following values:

A	C	B
$ 10	−$ 5	$ 0
10	− 10	− 5
20	− 5	10
50	− 10	10
100	0	20

a) Let $U(\$10) = 10$ and $U(0) = 0$ and then find the utility for $-\$5$, $-\$10$, $\$20$, $\$50$, and $\$100$.

b) Sketch this person's utility function. Can you classify this person as a risk-taker, risk-neutral, or a risk-avoider?

16.21 Sketch a utility function for a person who is, simultaneously, a risk-avoider for dollar values between $2000 and $1000 at $\pi = \frac{1}{2}$ and a risk-taker between $2000 and $0 at $\pi = \frac{1}{2}$.

16.22 A business executive has asked your advice on the following decision. The executive can either take $50 for certain or participate in a venture that gives an equal chance of winning $100, $40, or $0.

a) What decision should you recommend (i.e., to participate in the venture or not) if the executive wants to maximize expected earnings?

b) What decision should you recommend if the executive wants to maximize expected utility and is indifferent between two cases of equal chances of A and C, or B for certain, as follows:

	A	B	C
Case 1	100	40	0
Case 2	100	50	40

c) Sketch the utility function. Does the executive appear to be a risk-taker, risk-neutral, or a risk-avoider?

16.23 Attempt to construct your own utility function for money for dollar values between $-\$500$ and $+\$1500$.

16.24 A decision-maker considers the utility function $U(m) = m^{1/2}$, where m = money and $0 \leq m \leq 1600$.

a) Sketch this function.

b) Does this function represent a risk-taker, risk-neutral, or a risk-avoider?

c) Use this utility function to find the action that maximizes expected utility in Exercise 16.10. Can you guess, before calculating EU, which action will be optimal? Explain.

d) Will your answer to part (c) change if the utility function $U(m) = 100 + 10m^{1/2}$ is used instead of $U(m) = m^{1/2}$? Explain.

16.25 Redo the Perkins Plastics problem from this chapter for $n = 2$ (see Fig. 16.4), letting $U(-\$1000) = -100$, $U(-\$2000) = -300$, and $U(-\$4000) = -1000$, and find the action that maximizes expected utility.

16.26 Rework Problem 16.14, letting $U(m) = m^{1/2}$, where $m = $ money, and find the optimal action by maximizing expected utility.

16.27 Suppose that the decision-maker for the problem represented by Fig. 16.10 is attempting to assess the prior probability distribution of π_0, the proportion of customers who will buy the book. This person decides that the chances are only one out of four that π will be less than 0.10 and the chances are four out of five that π will not be greater than 0.14. Assuming that the prior is normal, find its mean and variance.

16.28 A food manufacturer is trying to determine the mean weight of its boxes of breakfast cereal. The company considers the weight to be normally distributed with a standard deviation of 0.4, and its prior distribution is normal with a mean of 16.2 ounces and a standard deviation of 0.2. Find the posterior distribution if $n = 100$ and $\bar{x} = 16.0$.

16.29 The owner of a local fabric store is trying to prepare an order for a certain type of very expensive material, based on the mean number of yards sold during each six-month period. The owner can sell this material on consignment (action a_1) or purchase it outright (action a_2). The payoffs for these two actions are ($x = $ number of yards sold) as follows:

$$\text{Action } a_1: \quad -\$100 + 5x;$$

$$\text{Action } a_2: \quad -\$1290 + 15x.$$

a) What is the breakeven value of μ? What action would you select if $\mu_0 = 120$ yards and $\sigma_0^2 = 25$ yards, and the prior is normally distributed?

b) The owner feels that the cost of overestimating the size of the order is four times as much as the cost of underestimating. What size order should be placed?

c) Assume that the owner takes a sample of the sales of four comparable fabric stores and finds that sales are 120, 112, 122, and 118 yards. If it is assumed that the sample came from a normal distribution with a variance of 20, what is the posterior distribution?

d) What action should be taken on the basis of the posterior distribution?

What size order should be placed on the basis of the posterior distribution, assuming the same costs as in part (b)?

e) Construct two graphs, one showing the loss function if a_1 is taken incorrectly $[l(a_1, \mu)]$ and the other showing the loss function if a_2 is taken incorrectly $[l(a_2, \mu)]$.

f) Find EVSI for the sample of four in part (c).

EXERCISES

16.30 Return to the book-club example of Section 16.8. Assume that the decision-maker has taken a sample of size $n = 10$ and four of these ten book-club members indicate that they would buy the book.

a) Use *discrete* decision analysis to revise the decision-maker's prior. To do this, you should graph the cumulative prior, then divide the horizontal axis into ten intervals so that each interval contains 10% of the area. Let the midpoints of the ten intervals be the π values used to calculate the likelihoods where each π value has a prior of 0.10. The sample result of four of ten and Table I in Appendix C will give you ten posterior values. Plot these posterior values and fit (sketch) the normal distribution they seem to approximate.

b) Read reference 20 at the end of this book on the use of the beta distribution as a prior and binomial sampling; then try to rework the entire problem using what you have learned.

16.31 A procedure for calculating EVSI, equivalent to that presented in Section 16.5, is to focus *only* on those sample results that lead to a decision *different* from the optimal decision without sample information. The expected value of the sample information depends only on how much additional profit (on the average) is earned because of this change in decision. Thus, one first must calculate how much more expected profit the new decision yields over the old (using the posterior probabilities), and then multiply this value by the (marginal) probability of observing the sample result(s) that lead to a new decision.

a) Note that for the data given in Fig. 16.3 the previously optimal decision (shown in Fig. 16.1 to be to *send the batch to assembly*) is changed to *rework* only after observance of a defective valve. Since the expected value of sending the batch to assembly after such a sample is $-\$2895$ and reworking costs are only \$2000, the decision to rework saves \$895. Verify that this savings, multiplied times the probability of observing one defective valve, equals the EVSI for $n = 1$.

b)   Verify by the above method that the EVSI for Fig. 16.4 is $251.

16.32   Read enough of a reference on Bayesian analysis so that you can describe what is meant by a "natural conjugate prior."

16.33   As an exercise in assessing subjective probabilities, try to construct a probability distribution representing your estimate of the number of checks processed each day by one of the major banks in Boston (this bank has six branch offices in the Boston area). For example, to find the mean of your distribution, you might ask yourself what value of x would make you indifferent between the following two bets at 50–50 odds; Bet I: no. of checks ≥ x and Bet II: no. of checks < x. It might be interesting also to assess your 0.01 and 0.99 fractiles (the 0.01 fractile is the value of x that you think makes Bet I 99 times as likely to be correct as Bet II; for the 0.99 fractile, Bet II must be 99 times as likely as Bet I). Check your answers against the true value given in the back of the book to see how good your estimate is. Does the true value fall between your 0.01 and 0.99 fractiles?

USING THE COMPUTER

16.34   Return to Problem 16.14.
   a)   Prepare a flowchart designed to find the optimal sample size for Techno. This flow chart should have a subroutine for generating binomial probabilities, and it should print out the action Techno should take (major or minor repairs) for each possible sample result using the optimal sample size.
   b)   Write and run the computer program for part (a).

16.35   For the Perkins Plastics problem (see Table 16.7):
   a)   Draw the decision tree and find EVSI and ENGS for n = 3.
   b)   Prepare a flowchart for a computer program designed to solve the Perkins Plastics problem for 0 ≤ n ≤ 30 (see Table 16.8).
   c)   Write and run the computer program for part (b).

16.36   The values of ENGS in Table 16.8 were calculated on a computer by calculating first the value for n = 1, then the value for n = 2, and so forth, up to n = 26.
   a)   In writing a computer program to find the optimal sample size, why is it not possible to program the computer to stop as soon as ENGS begins to decrease? (*Hint:* See Table 16.8 for n = 3, n = 4.)
   b)   In Table 16.8, why does EVSI increase only a small amount for some

values of n (for example, $n = 3$ to $n = 4$), while it increases a large amount for other values (for example, $n = 4$ to $n = 5$)?

c) Design a decision rule for stopping a computer program that is calculating ENGS for successive sample sizes [keeping in mind your answer to part (a)].

CASE PROBLEM

16.37 The Delaney-Bryce Corporation is a major manufacturer of specialized soap and detergent products. It currently controls 31 subsidiary companies that manufacture disinfecting detergent powder primarily for use by hospitals, linen suppliers, diaper services, and other large institutional laundry facilities. Each of the 31 subsidiaries sells in its own region, and together they serve a large portion of the United States.

Delaney-Bryce established the Ohio Valley Detergent Corporation in Cincinnati last year. Since that time, Ohio Valley has captured a larger market share in each of the three quarters its plant has been in operation. The directors expect that the company will have reached maturity sometime in the next three years and that the rapid growth in sales it has been experiencing during the present start-up period will begin to level off. The warehouse that Ohio Valley has been using for the past year is rapidly becoming inadequate to serve the company's growing sales volume. The directors, knowing that such rapid changes in requirements would occur in the company's first stages, leased the present warehouse facilities for only 18 months. This lease will expire soon, and the directors and officers now wish to negotiate another. Now that Ohio Valley is approaching maturity, they wish to acquire warehouse space for a period of three years. Leasing facilities on this long-term basis will save the company money both as a result of lower monthly rent payments and by avoiding the need to regularly renegotiate lease terms.

There are only two warehouse facilities in Cincinnati that the directors of Ohio Valley feel may be adequate. Both contain the necessary equipment and other features that the company's operation requires. The location of each warehouse is also suitable to the directors. But the sizes of the facilities differ, one being 16,500 square feet, the other being 21,000 square feet. The decision must be made, then, as to which of these two different-sized warehouses Ohio Valley Detergent Corporation should lease in order to minimize its expected cost. But before such a decision can be made it will be necessary for the directors to have some reliable prediction of the level of sales the company can expect to maintain over the period covered by the lease. Kenneth Rein, a member of the board, has predicted that over the next three years Ohio Valley will sell about 10.83 million pounds of detergent annually and that this prediction of sales comes from a normal distribution with a standard deviation of 1.18 million pounds. The 16,500-square-foot warehouse will hold a maximum of 1,835,000 pounds of detergent. Likewise, the 21,000-square-foot warehouse can be used to store at most 2,300,000 pounds.

The company plans to keep on hand at any one time a two-month supply of its product. This means that if Ohio Valley should sell exactly the predicted amount of 10.83 million pounds, it would want always to keep in storage $(1/6)(10.83) = 1,805,000$ pounds of detergent. Note that, for this prediction for two months of sales, the standard deviation is 196,667 pounds, which is one-sixth of the error associated with the prediction of full-year sales (that is, $1/6 \times 1,180,000$).

In addition to this information on warehouse utilization, Rein has given you the following guidelines concerning the costs involved in leasing each of the two warehouses available. As Ohio Valley is most concerned here with avoiding unnecessary expenses, Rein tells you to consider that, for this decision process, the cost will be zero if the company leases the smaller warehouse and, for the duration of the lease, requires no more than the space that the smaller warehouse can provide. The cost is also assumed to be zero if Ohio Valley leases the larger facility and requires over the years more space than the smaller warehouse could have provided. If the company leases the smaller warehouse and sales are at a higher level than can be supplied by this facility, high-cost short-term facilities will have to be leased to supplement the main warehouse. Rein estimates that this added cost, combined with costs of reduced efficiency due to the resulting lack of centralization, will be approximately $500,000 over the entire period of the lease. If the company leases the larger warehouse and sales over the lease years prove to be low enough that it actually needs only the smaller warehouse, the extra expense will be $325,000 over the life of the lease (lease terms prohibit subleasing of unused space).

Ohio Valley has recently learned that they can purchase a sample survey for $5000. This survey's outcomes will be either "favorable" (meaning large sales) or "unfavorable" (meaning moderate sales). Judging from past records, Ohio Valley estimates that if sales $\leq 1,835,000$ is the true state of nature, the survey will result in the "unfavorable" outcome about 77% of the time. Conversely, if sales $> 1,835,000$ is the true state of nature, the survey will result in the "favorable" outcome about 66% of the time. On the basis of this information, draw the decision tree, and calculate EVSI and ENGS.

GLOSSARY

Actions: The choices available to the decision-maker.

States of nature: The possible conditions (or "states") that influence the choice of an action in a decision situation.

Payoff table: A table that gives all the possible consequences (or payoffs) to the decision-maker that would result from each combination of action and state of nature.

Dominated action: An action with payoffs no better than the payoffs of some other action, no matter what state of nature occurs.

EMV criterion: Maximization of expected monetary value.

Tree diagram: A design for systematically presenting the important features of the decision problem.

Prior probability: A probability determined before any sample information is seen.

Posterior probability: A revised probability determined in light of sample information.

Bayes' rule: A formula for transforming a prior probability into a posterior probability:

$$\text{Posterior} = \frac{(\text{prior})(\text{likelihood})}{\Sigma(\text{priors})(\text{likelihoods})}.$$

Likelihood: The probability that a specified sample result will take place, given that a particular state of nature is true.

Backwards induction: Process of determining EMV on a decision tree, proceeding from right to left.

EVSI: Expected value of sample information.

ENGS: Expected net gain from sampling.

Utility function: A description of the relationship between various dollar amounts and the index used to measure the value to the decision-maker of these dollars.

Interval scale: A measurement or index in which the origin and units are not predetermined, but the size of the interval must be constant.

Standard lottery: A gamble between A with probability π and C with probability $1 - \pi$, in which $A > C$.

Certainty equivalent: The amount of money (B) that leaves the decision-maker indifferent to a given standard lottery.

Utiles: The units used to measure utility.

Risk-avoider: A decision-maker who, for certain gambles, will prefer a dollar amount received with certainty over a gamble, even though the latter has a higher EMV.

Risk-taker: A decision-maker who, in certain circumstances, prefers a gamble with EMV lower than the alternative amount that could be received with certainty.

Risk-neutral: A decision-maker who neither takes nor avoids risks — i.e., a person who maximizes EMV, since the utility function is a straight line.

Diffuse prior: A relatively flat prior distribution.

Loss function: A function $l(a, \theta)$ specifying the loss under action a when the actual state of nature is θ.

Unit normal linear loss integral: A table of values that facilitates calculation of certain EMV's for continuous function decision problems.

Nonparametric
Statistics

SEVENTEEN

17.1 INTRODUCTION

The statistical tests considered thus far have specified certain properties of the parent population that must hold before these tests can be used. A *t*-test, for example, requires that the observations come from a normal population; and if this test is used in testing for differences between means, the two populations must have equal variances. Although these tests are quite "robust," in the sense that the tests are still useful when the assumptions about the parent population are not exactly fulfilled, there are still many circumstances when the researcher cannot or does not want to make such assumptions. The statistical methods appropriate in these circumstances are called *nonparametric tests* because they do not depend on any assumptions about the parameters of the distribution of the parent population.

Measurement

Nonparametric tests do not require assumptions about the parameters of the parent population, nor do they require a **level of measurement** as strong as that necessary for parametric tests. By "measurement" we mean the process of assigning numbers to objects or observations; the level of measurement depends on how the numbers are assigned. The measurement of quantifiable information usually takes place on one of four levels, depending on the strength of the underlying scaling procedure used. The four major levels of measurement are represented by nominal, ordinal, interval, and ratio scales.

The weakest type of measurement is given by a **nominal scale,** which merely sorts objects into categories according to some distinguishing characteristic and gives each category a "name" (hence nominal). Since classification on a nominal scale does not depend on the label or symbol assigned to each category, these symbols may be interchanged without affecting the information given by the scale. Classifying automobiles by brands constitutes a nominal scale, as does distinguishing Republican from Democratic voters or apples from oranges. In most nominal measurement, one is concerned with the number (or frequency) of observations falling in each of the categories.

An **ordinal scale** offers the next highest level of measurement and expresses the relationship of order. Objects in an ordinal scale are characterized by relative rank so that a typical relationship is expressed in terms such as "higher," "greater," or "preferred to." Only the relations "greater than," "less than," or "equal to" have meaning in ordinal measurement. When a football team is "ranked" nationally, for example, the measurement used is an ordinal scale if it is impossible (or meaningless) to say how *much* better or worse this team is compared to others.

this entire group from the lowest number to the highest number. If the null hypothesis that the two samples were drawn from the sample population is true, the observations from the two samples will be fairly well scattered throughout this ranking of both groups. If the two samples do not come from identical populations, the observations of one sample will tend to be bunched together at the low end of the rankings, at the high end of the rankings, or in the middle of the rankings. Such patterns can be detected by calculating a value of **U**, which is the statistic for the Mann–Whitney test. The statistic **U** is calculated by counting the number of times the scores from one sample precede each score in the other sample. If the count is quite large or quite small in relation to the value expected under the null hypothesis, then the two samples may not be randomly interspersed. This result indicates that one set of observations may have come from a different population than the other.

To calculate the value of the statistic **U** for any data set, suppose we let T_1 represent the total number of times an observation in sample 1 precedes each value in sample 2. Similarly, let T_2 represent the total number of times an observation in sample 2 precedes each observation in sample 1. Because the process of calculating T_1 and T_2 can become quite tedious, there is a formula that makes the calculations much easier. If we let n_1 and n_2 be the two sample sizes, r_1 = the sum of the ranks of all values from sample 1, and r_2 = sum of the ranks from sample 2, we use the following:

Mann–Whitney *U*-statistic:

$$T_1 = n_1 n_2 + \frac{n_1(n_1 + 1)}{2} - r_1$$

and   (17.1)

$$T_2 = n_1 n_2 - T_1.$$

We should point out that for these formulas it makes no difference which sample is labeled 1 and which one is labeled 2.

The value of the Mann–Whitney statistic is defined to be the *minimum* of the two values, $\{T_1, T_2\}$. Defining it this way means that the more similar the two samples are, the higher will be the value of **U**. Hence, we reject H_0 when **U** is small. Since the value of **U** depends only on the ranks of the scores in the two groups, it is possible to determine the probability of various values of **U**. Table XI in Appendix C presents critical values of the Mann–Whitney statistic for small samples.

Example 17.1. To illustrate the Mann–Whitney U-test, we use the data on pulp brightness from Chapter 10. Recall from Table 10.3 (which is reproduced in Table 17.1 with the observations for each chemical ordered from lowest to highest) that a random sample of size $n_1 = 11$ is taken for Chemical 1, and a sample of size $n_2 = 10$ is taken for Chemical 2. The pulp brightnesses are shown below.

The null hypothesis is that the two samples were drawn from the same population in regard to pulp brightness. The alternative hypothesis is that they were drawn from different populations. To calculate T_1, focus on each observation for Chemical 2 and count the number of observations from Chemical 1 *lower than* this value. For example, the smallest observation for Chemical 2 is 74.47, and no values of Chemical 1 are lower than this number. If we focus on the next smallest Chemical 2 value (76.15), we find one Chemical 1 value (75.91) smaller than this number. The same result is true for the next three values of Chemical 2. For the final Chemical 2 value (82.87), there are 11 Chemical 1 values smaller. The sum of these numbers is the value of T_1:

$$T_1 = 0 + 1 + 1 + 1 + 1 + 2 + 8 + 8 + 11 + 11 = 44.$$

To complete the Mann–Whitney Test, we also need to calculate T_2, which is the total number of times a value from sample 2 precedes each value in sample 1. A good exercise for the reader is to verify that

$$T_2 = 66.$$

For the pulp problem,

$$U = \min\{44,66\} = 44.$$

From Table XI for $n_1 = 11$ and $n_2 = 10$, the critical value for $\alpha = 0.05$ is seen to be 26. This means that for any value of U less than or equal to 26, the null hypothesis should be rejected, since $P(U \le 26) = 0.05$. Our observed value of 44 is greater than 26. Hence, we do not reject H_0 and instead conclude that the samples could have come from the same population.

TABLE 17.1 **Sample of pulp brightness (Table 10.3, with ordered data)**

Chemical 1
75.91, 77.15, 77.36, 77.39, 77.54, 77.55, 78.00, 78.04, 78.36, 78.36, 78.95

Chemical 2
74.47, 76.15, 76.21, 76.22, 76.39, 77.20, 78.05, 78.06, 82.75, 82.87

TABLE 17.2 **Ranks derived from Table 17.1**

Value	74.47	75.91	76.15	76.21	76.22	76.39	77.15	77.20	77.36	77.39	77.54
Chemical	2	1	2	2	2	2	1	2	1	1	1
Ranks	1	2	3	4	5	6	7	8	9	10	11
Value		77.55	78.00	78.04	78.05	78.06	78.36	78.36	78.95	82.75	82.87
Chemical		1	1	1	2	2	1	1	1	2	2
Ranks		12	13	14	15	16	17	18	19	20	21

Suppose we use Formula (17.1) to determine T_1 and T_2. Table 17.2 gives the necessary ranks. The sum of the ranks associated with Chemical 1 in Table 17.2 is

$$r_1 = 2 + 7 + 9 + 10 + 11 + 12 + 13 + 14 + 17 + 18 + 19 = 132.$$

This means that

$$T_1 = (11)(10) + \frac{(11)(11 + 1)}{2} - 132 = (110 - 66) - 132 = 44.$$

and

$$T_2 = (11)(10) - 44 = 66.$$

This verifies our earlier result.

Table XI gives critical values up to $n_1 = n_2 = 20$. When n_1 or n_2 is larger than 20 and the two sample sizes are not too different in size, the sampling distribution of U can be approximated with the following *normal* statistic:

Normal approximation for the Mann–Whitney test:

$$z = \frac{U - E[U]}{\sigma_U},$$

where

$$E[U] = \frac{n_1(n_2)}{2} \qquad \qquad \textbf{(17.2)}$$

and

$$\sigma_U = \sqrt{\frac{n_1 n_2 (n_1 + n_2 + 1)}{12}}.$$

When ties occur across samples in the Mann–Whitney test, they are treated by assigning the *average* of the ranks of those observations that are tied. In the pulp brightness example the observations corresponding to ranks 17 and 18 are identical. In this case, both observations would be given a rank of 17.5, which is the average of the ranks 17 and 18.

The Wald–Wolfowitz Runs Test

Another test that can be used in place of the *t*-test for independent samples is the **Wald–Wolfowitz runs test.** Although this test is not as powerful as the Mann–Whitney *U*-test, it is useful in some situations for which that test may not be appropriate. The null hypothesis in this test is the same as in the Mann–Whitney test — namely that the two samples were drawn from the same population. The alternative hypothesis is that the populations differ in some respect.

To test for differences between two samples, the observations are placed in a single group and then ranked (just as they were in the Mann–Whitney test). The number of runs in this ranking can now be counted, where a run is a sequence of the ranked observations all of which came from the same sample. An indication of whether or not the two samples came from the same population is given by the total number of runs. If the number of runs is not particularly large, or not particularly small, this means that the ranks corresponding to the samples are randomly intermixed; hence, it is reasonable to accept H_0 that they came from the same population. A small number of runs will occur whenever there is some systematic difference between the two samples. For example, if the ranks corresponding to one sample are consistently lower than those for the other sample, this suggests that the central location of the two samples differs. Similarly, if one sample has a smaller *spread* than the other sample, the ranks corresponding to this sample will bunch in the center of the array, resulting in a low number of runs. If there is a systematic alternating pattern to the data, the number of runs will be large, indicating that the null hypothesis of randomness should be rejected.

When ties occur in this test, the usual procedure is to assign ranks so as to make the number of runs as large as possible (i.e., ranks are assigned in a manner least favorable to rejecting H_0).

Table XII in Appendix C presents critical values (r) for the Wald–Wolfowitz runs test. The values in Table XII are lower-tail critical values only (when the number of runs is expected to be low). When the test is two-sided, the upper critical value is related to the lower critical value (r) by the following relationship:

Upper critical value: $\quad n_1 + n_2 - r.$

As the examples below will illustrate, the Wald–Wolfowitz test can be used with two-sample data (Example 17.2) or with certain data representing only a single sample (Example 17.3).

Example 17.2. As illustration of a two-sample Wald–Wolfowitz runs test, consider once again the data in Example 17.1. As in Table 17.2, we arrange all 21 of the observations in order from the lowest number to the highest. The number of runs in Table 17.3 is shown below to be 9. From Table XII we see that the critical region for $\alpha = 0.05$, when $n_1 = 11$ and $n_2 = 10$ is $r \leq 6$. (In this problem we are interested only in the lower critical value, since an alternating pattern to the data would have no meaning.) Because the sample result does not fall in the critical region, the null hypothesis that these two samples of pulp brightness were drawn from the same population is accepted.

Sometimes the observations in a single sample can be classified into one of two categories. For example, a single sample of average (daily) price changes on the New York Stock Exchange (NYSE) might result in each day's being classified as "average price increases" or "average price does not increase." Similarly, in looking at a sequence of customers in a store, we might classify them as "male" or "female." In using the Wald–Wolfowitz test for such *one-sample* problems, it is necessary for the sample to fall into some natural sequence such as day 1, day 2, etc. for the NYSE and customer 1, customer 2, etc. for people in a store.

Example 17.3. In our discussion on regression analysis we indicated that examining the residuals is one method for testing for autocorrelation. If successive residuals tend to have the same sign or systematically alternate in sign, this indicates that autocorrelation may be a problem. The null and alternative hypotheses in this situation are

TABLE 17.3 **Number of runs derived from Table 17.1**

Value	74.47	75.91	76.15	76.21	76.22	76.39	77.15	77.20	77.36	77.39	77.54
Chemical	2	1	2	2	2	2	1	2	1	1	1
Run	1	2			3		4	5		6	

Value		77.55	78.00	78.04	78.05	78.06	78.36	78.36	78.95	82.75	82.87
Chemical		1	1	1	2	2	1	1	1	2	2
Run		6 (continued)			7		8			9	

H_0: Residuals independent (random),

H_a: Residuals autocorrelated (positively or negatively).

A nonparametric way of examining the residuals for autocorrelation is to look at the list of residuals for runs of plus ($+$) and minus ($-$) signs. To do this, we repeat (in Table 17.4) the residuals for the model in Problem 14.18 (based on the data in Table 13.5).

Let n_1 = the number of positive signs and n_2 = the number of negative signs. From Table 17.4, $n_1 = 9$ and $n_2 = 5$, and the number of runs is ten. The lower-tail critical value from Table XII is $r = 3$, which means that the upper-tail critical value is

$$n_1 + n_2 - r = 9 + 5 - 3 = 11.$$

Thus, H_0 is rejected whenever the number of runs is three or fewer or 11 or more. Our result, which was ten runs, means that we cannot reject the null hypothesis that the pattern of positive or negative signs is random.

Table XII presents critical values only for small values of n_1 and n_2. When both sample sizes are fairly large (e.g., greater than 19), the following normal approximation can be used.

Standardization of r for runs test:

$$z = \frac{r - E[r]}{\sigma_r},$$

where

$$E[r] = \frac{2n_1 n_2}{n_1 + n_2} + 1 \qquad \textbf{(17.3)}$$

and

$$\sigma_r = \sqrt{\frac{2n_1 n_2 (2n_1 n_2 - n_1 - n_2)}{(n_1 + n_2)^2 (n_1 + n_2 - 1)}}.$$

The Matched-Pairs Sign Test

The **matched-pairs sign test** is an example of a nonparametric test that may be used instead of the t-test for matched-pairs samples (see Section 10.4). It is designed to determine whether significant differences exist between two populations based on two samples that are related in such a manner that each observation from one sample can be matched with a specific observation from the other sample. For example, one may wish to study the behavior of carefully matched workers under two wage-incentive plans. Or the attitudes of wives may be contrasted with the attitudes of their husbands. Another common example is the "before-

TABLE 17.4 **The residuals from Problem 14.18**

Observation	Residual	Sign	Run No.
1	−76.550	−	1
2	35.985	+ ⎫	
3	9.990	+ ⎬	2
4	107.309	+ ⎭	
5	−78.740	−	3
6	44.392	+	4
7	−6.606	−	5
8	80.032	+	6
9	−144.722	−	7
10	24.667	+ ⎫	
11	4.073	+ ⎬	8
12	60.532	+ ⎭	
13	−118.247	−	9
14	57.887	+	10

and-after'' effect of a treatment on individuals or objects. Consumers are frequently asked to make ''before-and-after'' judgments, such as rating breakfast cereals before and after tasting each brand. Another illustration would be measuring the productivity of an employee before and after a special training course.

In the sign test the two values in each ''pair'' are compared. If the sample 1 value is larger than the sample 2 value, this pair is given a plus (+) sign. If the sample 1 value is smaller than the sample 2 value, this pair is given a minus sign (−). Usually, the null hypothesis is that the two samples were drawn from populations with the same central tendency as measured by the median. The alternative hypothesis is that they differ. These hypotheses can be tested via the binomial distribution by specifying a value of the binomial parameter π.

Example 17.4. A questionnaire is administered to nine women working in executive positions and to their husbands to determine whether differences exist in the typical number of hours they spend at work (per week). The null hypothesis is that the sample was drawn from a population in which the median number of hours worked by a woman and her husband do not differ. This is equivalent to the null hypothesis H_0: $\pi = 0.50$. The alternative hypothesis is that either the husbands or the wives work more hours: H_a: $\pi \neq 0.50$. Table 17.5 gives the data appropriate for use in the sign test.

TABLE 17.5 **Number of hours worked in matched-pairs samples**

Sample	Wife's Hours	Husband's Hours	Sign
1	51	45	+
2	56	44	+
3	38	40	−
4	44	41	+
5	55	52	+
6	40	35	+
7	65	59	+
8	48	42	+
9	58	46	+

In using the sign test the only relevant fact about these matched hours is whether the wife's hours are higher or lower than the husband's hours. The *t*-test from Chapter 10 cannot be used unless the hours are given (as in Table 17.5) and the additional assumption of normality of the populations is made.

If the null hypothesis is true, then $\pi = \frac{1}{2}$; that is, half of the signs should be positive in the entire population of couples. We must find the probability that the sample distribution of signs would occur if $\pi = \frac{1}{2}$ and compare this to a significance level, say $\alpha = 0.05$. Since we are not hypothesizing whether the husbands or the wives will have the higher hours, this is an example of a two-sided test, and we must double the probability value obtained from Appendix C. If the doubled probability value is *less* than α, then we *reject* the null hypothesis and conclude that there is a significant difference in the central location of the distributions of husbands' and wives' hours. Let x = number of positive signs. For this example, x = 8. From Table I,

$$P(x \geq 8 | n = 9, \pi = 0.50) = 0.0196.$$

Because H_a is two-sided, we double this value. Thus, the p-value is

$$2P(x \geq 8) = 2(0.0196) = 0.0392.$$

Since $0.0392 < \alpha = 0.05$, the null hypothesis is rejected. If the alternative hypothesis for this problem had been a one-sided test (e.g., if it had been predicted that the wives would have higher hours), then H_0 could be rejected at the 0.0196 level of significance or higher.

Example 17.5. As in the binomial test, the null hypothesis in the sign test need not specify that $\pi = \frac{1}{2}$. Consider a problem in which

Product A is compared with Product B, and suppose that we asked each of ten people interviewed to rate these two products on a scale of 100. We might hypothesize that the probability of A being preferred to B is not $\frac{1}{2}$, but some other value, say $\frac{3}{4}$ [that is, $P(A > B) = \frac{3}{4}$]. The alternative to this hypothesis may be that $P(A > B) < \frac{3}{4}$. The sample results of the ten interviews given in Table 17.6 show five positive signs.

Under the null hypothesis with $n = 10$ and $\pi = \frac{3}{4}$, the probability of five or fewer positives is (from Table I):

$$P(x \leq 5) = 0.0781.$$

It is not possible, on the basis of this sample, to reject the null hypothesis $H_0 : \pi = \frac{3}{4}$ at conventional levels of significance such as $\alpha = 0.01$ or 0.05. We conclude that it remains an acceptable view that $\frac{3}{4}$ of the population prefer product A to B. Note that a *t*-test and the individual scores themselves should be used here unless interval measurement is assumed.

Use of Normal Approximation for Large Samples

When the number of matched pairs n is large and the hypothesized value of π is not extremely close to 0 or 1, then the normal approximation to the binomial may be applied to this sign test (as discussed in Section 5.4). The mean and variance of a binomial random variable are $\mu = n\pi$ and $\sigma^2 = n\pi(1 - \pi)$. Thus, an approximately standardized normal variable may be determined when $n\pi(1 - \pi) \geq 3$ by

$$z = \frac{x - n\pi}{\sqrt{n\pi(1 - \pi)}},$$

where x is the number of positive signs.

TABLE 17.6 **Scaled values of preference for two products A and B**

Consumer	Product A Score	Product B Score	Sign
1	75	58	+
2	85	92	−
3	61	69	−
4	55	50	+
5	82	71	+
6	88	84	+
7	45	78	−
8	90	79	+
9	63	69	−
10	71	80	−

Example 17.6. Suppose that we test whether $\frac{3}{4}$ of the population prefers product A to B by asking $n = 180$ consumers to rate each product on a scale of 100. The comparative results contain 120 positive signs. Because $n\pi(1 - \pi) \doteq 180(\frac{3}{4})(\frac{1}{4}) = 33.7573 > 3$, we may use the normal approximation. Substituting $n\pi = 180(\frac{3}{4}) = 135$, we calculate

$$z_c = \frac{x - n\pi}{\sqrt{n\pi(1 - \pi)}} = \frac{120 - 135}{\sqrt{33.75}} = -2.58.$$

Since the probability $P(z \leq -2.58) = 0.0049$ is smaller than $\alpha = 0.01$, we reject the null hypothesis and conclude on the basis of this larger sample that less than $\frac{3}{4}$ of the population prefer product A to B.

Define. *Level of measurement; ratio, interval, ordinal, and nominal scales; nonparametric tests; Mann–Whitney test; Wald–Wolfowitz runs test.*

PROBLEMS

17.1 Identify the level of measurement required for the following tests:
a) the binomial test
b) the Mann–Whitney U-test
c) the sign test

17.2 What is the "power of a test"? Explain why nonparametric tests are generally less powerful than parametric tests.

17.3 Identify each of the following numbers as representing measurement on nominal, ordinal, interval, or ratio scales.
a) The number of shares traded in the NYSE on a given day.
b) The numbers on football players' jerseys.
c) A listing of the top 500 companies in the United States according to total assets.
d) Social Security numbers.
e) The order in which five candidates for election finished in a primary election.

17.4 Using the Mann–Whitney U-test, test for significant differences between the populations represented by the sample data given in the first two columns in **Data Set 3.** Let $\alpha = 0.05$. Be sure to specify your null and alternative hypotheses in advance.

17.5 From **Data Set 1** draw a random sample of twenty cities, ten having an income over \$25,000 and another ten having an income of less than \$25,000. Use a Mann–Whitney U-test on the *taxes* from these two samples to see whether the populations differ. State your null and alternative hypotheses and let $\alpha = 0.05$.

17.3 GOODNESS-OF-FIT TESTS

The tests presented thus far represent nonparametric procedures designed to see how closely two samples correspond to one another in order to test the hypothesis that they come from the same population. In many statistical problems the researcher is interested in another, similar problem, that of determining how closely sample observations fit a theoretical population. In this section we will present two tests designed for this purpose, called *goodness-of-fit tests*.

The One-sample Chi-Square Test

Recall that when the set of outcomes in an experiment can be divided into two categories (such as a success or a failure, make a sale or not, male or female, own stock or not), the appropriate test statistic is the binomial variable. When more than two categories or classes of outcomes are involved, then the appropriate statistic is the chi-square variable. Although the **chi-square test** also can be used when there are only two categories, the binomial is preferred in this case because it is more powerful.

The chi-square variable is used in cases with more than two categories to test how closely a set of *observed* frequencies corresponds to a given set of *expected* frequencies. The expected frequencies can be thought of as the average number of values expected to fall in each category, based on some theoretical probability distribution. For example, one probability distribution that is often useful is one in which all expected frequencies in the various categories will be equal. The observed frequencies can be thought of as a sample of values from some probability distribution. The chi-square variable can be used to test our hypotheses about the expected frequencies by determining whether the observed and expected frequencies are close enough for us to conclude that they came from the same probability distribution. For this reason the test is called a "goodness-of-fit" test.

Assume that there are k categories ($k > 1$) and that the *expected* frequency in each of these categories is denoted as $E_1, E_2, \ldots, E_k$, or equivalently, E_i ($i = 1, 2, \ldots, k$). Similarly, the k *observed* frequencies will be denoted as $O_1, O_2, \ldots, O_k$, or O_i ($i = 1, 2, \ldots, k$). To test the goodness of fit of the observed frequencies (O_i) to the expected frequencies (E_i), we use the following chi-square variable with $\nu = k - 1$ degrees of freedom.

Chi-square goodness-of-fit statistic:

$$\chi^2_{(k-1)} = \sum_{i=1}^{k} \frac{(O_i - E_i)^2}{E_i}. \tag{17.4}$$

Formula (17.4) measures the goodness of fit between the values of O_i and E_i as follows: When the fit is good (that is, O_i and E_i are generally close), then the numerator of (17.4) will be relatively small, and hence the value of χ^2 will be small. Conversely, if O_i and E_i are not close, then the numerator of (17.4) will be relatively large, and the value of χ^2 will be large also. Note that this implies that the chi-square formula (17.4) is always a one-sided test, using the right-hand tail of the distribution. In other words, since *both* positive and negative differences between E_i and O_i become positive when squared, the critical region for chi-square tests must lie in the upper (positive) tail of the χ^2-distribution. For example, suppose that in a particular problem involving 16 categories the fit between the 16 values of O_i and E_i from formula (17.4) yields $\chi^2 = 25.0$. From Table VII in the row corresponding to $k - 1 = 15$ d.f., we find that $P(\chi^2 \geq 25) = 0.05$. Thus, at any $\alpha > 0.05$ level of significance, we can reject the null hypothesis about the expected values.

Example 17.7. Suppose that an automobile dealer trying to arrange vacations for the sales personnel decides to test the (null) hypothesis that sales of new cars were equally distributed over the first six months of last year. The expected frequency for this hypothesis thus specifies that $E_1 = E_2 = \cdots = E_6$. The alternative hypothesis is that sales were not equally distributed over the six months. If the dealer sold 150 new cars in this period, the expected frequency under the null hypothesis would be 25 cars sold in each month. The observed sales are given in Table 17.7.

The null and alternative hypotheses are

$$H_0: E_1 = E_2 = \cdots = E_6 = 25;$$

$$H_a: \text{The frequencies are not all equal.}$$

The chi-square statistic for this example has $k - 1 = 5$ degrees of freedom. If we arbitrarily let $\alpha = 0.025$, the appropriate critical region, shown in Fig. 17.1, is obtained from Table VII in the row $\nu = 5$. From

TABLE 17.7 **Monthly new car sales**

	Months						
	Jan.	Feb.	Mar.	Apr.	May	June	Total
Expected sales (E_i)	25	25	25	25	25	25	150
Observed sales (O_i)	27	18	15	24	36	30	150

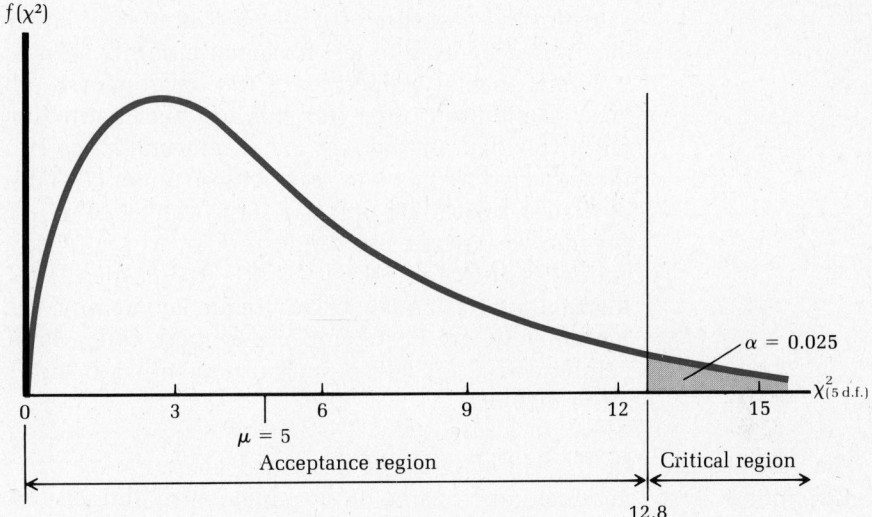

FIGURE 17.1 **Critical region for a goodness-of-fit test, $\nu = 5$, $\alpha = 0.025$.**

this figure we see that the null hypothesis will be rejected in favor of the alternative hypothesis of unequal frequencies in monthly sales if the calculated value of χ^2 exceeds 12.8.

The value of χ^2 can now be calculated as follows:

$$\chi_c^2 = \frac{(27 - 25)^2}{25} + \frac{(18 - 25)^2}{25} + \frac{(15 - 25)^2}{25}$$

$$+ \frac{(24 - 25)^2}{25} + \frac{(36 - 25)^2}{25} + \frac{(30 - 25)^2}{25}$$

$$= 12.0.$$

Thus, at the significance level $\alpha = 0.025$, we fail to reject the null hypothesis that all monthly sales are equal (i.e., deviations from monthly sales of 25 are due to random occurrences). However, from Table VII, note that for $k - 1 = 5$ degrees of freedom and $\alpha = 0.05$, the critical value for the test would be 11.1. Therefore, if $\alpha = 0.05$ had been selected as the level of significance for rejecting H_0, the null hypothesis would have been rejected. In this case the choice of the α-level is crucial to the decision. The costs of having too many or too few salespeople on hand in a given month should be given more consideration before α is set at an arbitrary level. Also, a larger number of past months may be sampled, if the sales pattern is presumed not to have changed. For example, the sales for the past three years in the months of January, February, March, etc., might be used to test for equal monthly sales.

Two special properties of the chi-square goodness-of-fit test merit special attention. First, for this test the distinction between one-sided and two-sided alternatives is not relevant, since H_a merely specifies that the expected frequencies are not those under H_0. The chi-square goodness-of-fit test rejects H_0 only for large values of χ^2. Hence, in reporting a p-value we always use the form $P(\chi^2 > \chi_c^2)$. A second property of this goodness-of-fit test is that $\Sigma(O_i - E_i)^2/E_i$ may not closely follow the χ^2 distribution if the expected frequency in any cell is less than 5. In problems where $E_i < 5$ for one or more cells, the usual procedure is to combine adjacent cells in such a manner that the new expected frequencies all exceed 5.

The Two-sample Chi-Square Test for Independence

In the chi-square test described above, a set of values was tested for goodness of fit using only a single attribute. At this time we extend that analysis by assuming that two attributes are under investigation and that we want to determine whether or not these attributes are independent. For example, instead of investigating car sales relative to the single attribute "month of the year," we may wish to construct a test to determine whether the attribute "car model" (such as sedans versus hardtops) and the attribute "months of the year" are independent in their effect on sales. Similarly, in the supermarket example in Section 5.7 (Example 5.11), we might have been interested in determining whether or not the pattern of arrivals is independent of the attribute "days of the week." For such examples there is no general "theory" available to use in determining the expected frequency for each category. However, we can use the observed data to calculate expected frequencies under the assumption that the null hypothesis (of independence) is true.

The one-sample chi-square test illustrated above can be generalized to include problems involving any number of categories for the two attributes. Let us designate the two attributes as A and B, where attribute A is assumed to have r categories ($r > 1$) and attribute B is assumed to have k categories ($k > 1$). Furthermore, assume that the total number of observations in the problem is labeled n. A representation of these n observations in matrix form is shown in Fig. 17.2, where O_{ij} represents the observation in the ith row and the jth column. A matrix in the form of Fig. 17.2 is called a *contingency table*.

The dots in the column and row totals in the matrix indicate that these numbers represent the sum of a particular set of values. For example, the number $O_{.1}$ represents the sum down the rows of all the observed values in the first column, while $O_{1.}$ represents the sum across the

Attribute B

	1	2	3	$\cdots$	j	$\cdots$	k	Totals
1	O_{11}	O_{12}	O_{13}	$\cdots$	O_{1j}	$\cdots$	O_{1k}	$O_{1\cdot}$
2	O_{21}	O_{22}	O_{23}	$\cdots$	O_{2j}	$\cdots$	O_{2k}	$O_{2\cdot}$
3	O_{31}	O_{32}	O_{33}	$\cdots$	O_{3j}	$\cdots$	O_{3k}	$O_{3\cdot}$
$\vdots$	$\vdots$	$\vdots$	$\vdots$		$\vdots$		$\vdots$	$\vdots$
i	O_{i1}	O_{i2}	O_{i3}	$\cdots$	O_{ij}	$\cdots$	O_{ik}	$O_{i\cdot}$
$\vdots$	$\vdots$	$\vdots$	$\vdots$		$\vdots$		$\vdots$	$\vdots$
r	O_{r1}	O_{r2}	O_{r3}	$\cdots$	O_{rj}	$\cdots$	O_{rk}	$O_{r\cdot}$
Totals	$O_{\cdot 1}$	$O_{\cdot 2}$	$O_{\cdot 3}$	$\cdots$	$O_{\cdot j}$	$\cdots$	$O_{\cdot k}$	$O_{\cdot\cdot}=n$

Attribute A

FIGURE 17.2 **Contingency table.**

columns of all the observed frequencies in the first row. The symbol $O_{\cdot\cdot}$ represents the sum over all rows and columns; hence, $O_{\cdot\cdot}$ must equal n, the total number of observations.

Calculating the expected frequency E_{ij} for each cell in a contingency table involves multiplying the *proportion* of the total number of observations falling in the jth category for Attribute B (which is $O_{\cdot j}/n$) times the *number* of observations falling in the ith category of Attribute A (which is $O_{i\cdot}$).

Expected frequency in ith row, jth column:*

$$E_{ij} = \left(\frac{O_{\cdot j}}{n}\right)(O_{i\cdot}) = \frac{O_{i\cdot}O_{\cdot j}}{n}. \qquad (17.5)$$

As we mentioned earlier, the expected frequency should be five or more for each cell in a chi-square goodness-of-fit test. When this is not the case, adjacent cells should be combined.

Once the expected frequency for each of the cells in the contingency table is obtained [using Formula (17.5)], the χ^2 statistic for testing

---

* This expectation is a direct result of the relationship presented in Chapter 3, which says that two discrete events A_i and B_j are independent if and only if

$$P(A_i \cap B_j) = P(A_i)P(B_j).$$

Since our estimates of $P(A_i)$ and $P(B_j)$ are $O_{i\cdot}/n$ and $O_{\cdot j}/n$, respectively, the product $(O_{i\cdot}/n)(O_{\cdot j}/n)$ is our estimate of the joint probability. Multiplying this product by the total number of observations (n), we obtain Formula (17.5).

independence between the effects of two attributes can be determined by the following formula:

Two-attribute χ^2 statistic

$$\chi^2 = \sum_{i=1}^{r} \sum_{j=1}^{k} \frac{(O_{ij} - E_{ij})^2}{E_{ij}}.$$
(17.6)

The number of degrees of freedom for this χ^2-statistic can be determined by noting that, in calculating the expected frequency for each cell, we must assume that the marginal totals ($O_{i.}$ and $O_{.j}$) are fixed quantities. This means that one degree of freedom is lost for each row and each column, so that the total number of degrees of freedom is $(r - 1)(k - 1)$.

Example 17.8. We will apply Formula 17.6 to the problem of trying to determine whether the prices of certain stocks on the New York Stock Exchange are independent of the industry to which they belong. Assume that four categories of industries are investigated (labeled I, II, III, and IV) and that stock prices in these industries are classified into one of three categories ("high-priced," "middle-priced," or "low-priced"). The data from such an analysis might look like the values shown in Table 17.8, where the expected values are in the upper left of each cell, and the observed values are in the lower right.

To illustrate the calculation of expected frequencies, note that the expected frequency of high-priced stocks in Industry I is found by multiplying the proportion of stock in Industry I to the total number of observations, which is 40/130, by the number of observations in the high-priced category (45). The resulting product is

$$\frac{40}{130} 45 = 13.8,$$

which is shown in the first cell. Similarly, the expected frequency for high-priced stocks in Industry II is $(30/130)(45) = 10.4$. Note that, for each row and column, the sum of the expected frequencies must be the same as the sum of the observed frequencies. The number of degrees of freedom for this problem is $(r - 1)(k - 1) = (3)(2) = 6$, and the calculated value of χ_c^2 is

$$\chi_c^2 = \frac{(15 - 13.8)^2}{13.8} + \frac{(8 - 10.4)^2}{10.4} + \cdots + \frac{(11 - 6.7)^2}{6.7}$$

$$= 6.825$$

TABLE 17.8 **Frequencies for the stock example**

E_{ij} / O_{ij}					
			Industry		
Stock prices	I	II	III	IV	Total
High	13.8 / 15	10.4 / 8	8.7 / 10	12.1 / 12	45
Medium	18.5 / 20	13.8 / 16	11.5 / 12	16.2 / 12	60
Low	7.7 / 5	5.8 / 6	4.8 / 3	6.7 / 11	25
Total	40	30	25	35	130

To be significant at the 0.05 level, the value of χ^2 has to be greater than 12.6 for 6 degrees of freedom (see Table VII). Since the computed value $\chi_c^2 = 6.825$ is less than this value, the null hypothesis cannot be rejected at the 0.05 level of significance. Thus, we conclude that the price of stocks is independent of the industry associated with that stock.

The Kolmogorov–Smirnov Test

We showed above how the chi-square test can be used to measure goodness of fit when the data are in nominal form (e.g., categories). When the data are in at least *ordinal* form, then the **Kolmogorov–Smirnov test** can be used. This test has the advantage over the chi-square test in that it is generally more powerful, it is easier to compute, and it does not require a minimum expected frequency in each cell.

The Kolmogorov-Smirnov (K–S) test involves a comparison between the theoretical and sample *cumulative* relative frequency distributions. To make this comparison, the data are put into classes (or categories) that have been arrayed from the lowest to the highest class. Suppose we use the symbol F_i to denote the cumulative relative frequency for each category of the theoretical distribution and S_i to denote the comparable value for the sample frequency. The K–S test is based on the maximum value of the absolute difference between F_i and S_i. Denoting this statistic as **D**, we have

$$\text{Statistic for K–S test:} \quad \boldsymbol{D} = \text{Max}_i |F_i - S_i|. \qquad \textbf{(17.7)}$$

The decision to reject the null hypothesis (that the sample and theoretical distributions are equal) is based on the value of $\boldsymbol{D}$. The larger the value of $\boldsymbol{D}$, the more confidence we have that H_0 is false. Note that this is a one-tailed test, since the value of $\boldsymbol{D}$ is always positive, and we reject H_0 for large values of $\boldsymbol{D}$. Table XIII in Appendix C gives the critical values for various probability values.

Example 17.9. Once again consider the supermarket data from Chapter 5. In Table 17.9 we repeat the data from Table 5.5, showing the relative frequencies for both the observed and theoretical Poisson distributions. Table 17.9 also shows the cumulative frequencies and $|F_i - S_i|$.

From the last column in Table 17.9 we see that the maximum value of $|F_i - S_i|$ is $D = 0.0365$. Since the sample size is $n = 100$ (see page 237 in Chapter 5), the last row of Table XIII in Appendix C gives the appropriate critical value of $\boldsymbol{D}$. For $\alpha = 0.01$ the critical value is $1.63/\sqrt{n} = 1.63/\sqrt{100} = 0.163$. Because $D = 0.0365$ is less than the critical value, we do not reject H_0. That is, the agreement between the observed

TABLE 17.9 **Supermarket data from Table 5.5 for K–S test**

Arrivals	Observed Relative Frequency	Cumulative Relative Frequency (S_i)	Theoretical Relative Frequency	Cumulative Relative Frequency (F_i)	$|F_i - S_i|$
0	0.010	0.010	0.0224	0.0224	0.0124
1	0.080	0.090	0.0850	0.1074	0.0174
2	0.190	0.280	0.1615	0.2689	0.0111
3	0.230	0.510	0.2046	0.4735	0.0365
4	0.170	0.680	0.1944	0.6679	0.0121
5	0.150	0.830	0.1477	0.8156	0.0144
6	0.080	0.910	0.0936	0.9092	0.0008
7	0.030	0.940	0.0508	0.9600	0.0200
8	0.030	0.970	0.0241	0.9841	0.0141
9	0.020	0.990	0.0102	0.9943	0.0043
10	0.010	1.000	0.0039	0.9982	0.0018
11	0.000	1.000	0.0013	0.9995	0.0005
12	0.000	1.000	0.0004	0.9999	0.0001
13	0.000	1.000	0.0001	1.0000	0.0000

and the theoretical values is sufficiently close for us to believe that they came from the same distribution.

The K–S test uses the *ordinal* nature of the classes, while the chi-square test makes use of only *nominal* properties of the data. We should also point out that the K–S test can be used for testing goodness of fit between two *sample* cumulative relative frequency distributions. In this case the procedure is exactly the same as before, except that the statistic **D** has a different distribution (which we do not present).

17.4 NONPARAMETRIC MEASURES OF CORRELATION

All the correlation measures presented in Chapters 12 and 13 have been based on measurements of variables for which a mean, variance, and covariance can be determined. Sometimes, it is desirable to be able to calculate correlations among variables when such measures are not obtainable. In general, the determination of means, variances, and covariances requires *interval measurement*, which means that the difference (i.e., interval) between any two observations must be meaningful. Frequently, data may be observed that have only *ordinal measurement*. In such cases, only the *relative* ranking of any two observations has meaning. For example, a stock analyst may list a ranking of the ten best common stocks for purchase by investors interested primarily in safety and income. The rank of any two stocks in such a list has meaning, but the difference between ranks does not. For example, we know that stock 4 is ranked better than stock 7 and stock 2 is ranked higher than stock 5. However, we do *not* know whether the difference in desirability between stocks 4 and 7 is identical to the difference between stocks 2 and 5, even though this difference is three rank positions in both instances. Now, if one had two such rankings of stocks (by different analysts), a measure of correlation between the two rank orderings might be desired. In such a situation the previous correlation measures are not appropriate because of the ordinal nature of the data. Fortunately, there are other measures of correlation, called nonparametric measures, that can be used.

Spearman's Rank Correlation Coefficient

Research published by C. Spearman in 1904 led to the development of what is perhaps the most widely used nonparametric measure of correlation. This measure, usually denoted either by r_s or by the Greek word *rho*, has thus become known as **Spearman's rho.** Spearman's rank correlation coefficient r_s is very similar to the ordinary correlation coefficient we have studied thus far, except that now ranks are used as the data. A perfect positive correlation ($r_s = +1$) means that the two samples rank each object identically, while a perfect negative correlation ($r_s = -1$) means that the ranks of the two samples have an exactly *inverse* relationship. Values of r_s between -1 and $+1$ denote less than perfect correlation. To measure corelation by Spearman's method, we first take the difference between the rank of an object in one sample and its rank in the second sample, and we then square this difference. If this squared difference is denoted as d_i^2 for the ith pair of observations, then the sum of these squared differences over a set of n pairs of observations is

$$\sum_{i=1}^{n} d_i^2.$$

The value of r_s is derived from Σd_i^2 as follows:

Spearman's rank correlation coefficient:

$$r_s = 1 - \frac{6 \sum_{i=1}^{n} d_i^2}{n^3 - n}. \tag{17.8}$$

Example 17.10. To illustrate Formula (17.8), suppose two investment services are asked to rate five different money (growth) funds. We label the growth funds A, B, C, D, E and assume that the first service rates the funds as $A > B > C > D > E$, while the second rates them as $A > C > E > B > D$, as shown in Table 17.10. We see in Table 17.10 that $\Sigma d_i^2 = 10$. Thus, the rank correlation between the two service ratings is

$$r_s = 1 - \frac{6(10)}{5^3 - 5} = 1 - \frac{60}{120} = 0.50.$$

In order to test the significance of a given value of r_s, it is necessary to determine the probability that this given value of r_s will occur under

TABLE 17.10 **Calculating Spearman's rho**

Fund	Service 1	Service 2	d_i	d_i^2
A	1	1	0	0
B	2	4	-2	4
C	3	2	1	1
D	4	5	-1	1
E	5	3	2	4
	$n = 5$			Sum $= 10$

the null hypothesis. This probability depends on the number of permutations of the two variables that give rise to the particular value of r_s. Tables are available that give the critical values of r_s for small values of n. We will not present these tables in this text, but they are readily available. (See, for example, reference 6.)

When n is large $(n \geq 10)$, the significance of an obtained value of r_s under the null hypothesis can be determined from the following *t*-variable:

$$\text{Test statistic for Spearman's rho:} \quad t = \frac{r_s\sqrt{n-2}}{\sqrt{1-r_s^2}}. \qquad (17.9)$$

This statistic can be shown to follow the *t*-distribution with $(n - 2)$ degrees of freedom. Formula (17.9) is identical to Formula (12.25).

Example 17.11. Suppose a company owns a large number of different McDonald's franchises in Texas. This company is interested in the rank correlation between sales and advertising for each franchise. A sample of size $n = 11$ is taken, and Spearman's rho is calculated to be $r_s = 0.755$. In this case the computed value t_c is

$$t_c = \frac{0.755\sqrt{11-2}}{\sqrt{1-0.755^2}} = 3.454.$$

From the *t*-table in Appendix C this value is seen to be significant at the 0.005 level of significance. We can, with a high degree of confidence, reject the null hypothesis that there is no correlation in the population — i.e., we can reject $H_0: \rho = 0$. Note that we have assumed that a one-tailed test is appropriate in this example. That is, the alternative hypothesis is $H_a: \rho > 0$. If a two-tailed test had been used (i.e., $H_a: \rho \neq 0$), the significance level would be $2(0.005) = 0.01$ rather than 0.005.

Kendall's Correlation Coefficient
An alternative to Spearman's rho for determining a rank correlation is to calculate Kendall's correlation coefficient. This statistic, developed by the statistician M. G. Kendall, is denoted by the Greek letter τ (tau) and called **Kendall's tau.** Although Kendall's tau is suitable for determining the rank correlation of the same type of data for which Spearman's rho is useful, the two methods employ different techniques for determining this correlation, so their values will not usually be the same. Spearman's rho is perhaps more widely used, but Kendall's tau has the advantage of being generalizable to a partial correlation coefficient, and the distribution of tau more rapidly approaches a normal distribution.

The rank correlation coefficient τ is determined by first calculating an index that indicates how the ranks of one set of observations, *taken two at a time*, differ from the ranks of the other set of observations. The easiest way to determine the value of this index is to arrange the two sets of rankings so that one of them, say the first sample, is in ascending order, from the lowest score (rank) to the highest score (rank). The other set, representing the second sample, will not be in ascending order unless the ranks of the two samples agree perfectly. Now, consider all possible combinations of the n ranks in this second sample, taken two at a time (i.e., all pairs); assign a value of $+1$ to each pair in which the two ranks are in the same (ascending) *order* as they are in the first sample, and assign -1 to each pair in which the two ranks are *not* in the same order as they are in the first sample. The sum of these $+1$ and -1 values is an indication of how well the second set of rankings agrees with the first set. Since there are $_nC_2$ combinations of n objects taken two at a time, this sum (or index) can assume any value between $+ _nC_2$ and $- _nC_2$. Kendall's tau is defined as the ratio of the computed value of this index to the maximum value it can assume (which is $_nC_2$).

Kendall's rank correlation coefficient:

$$\tau = \frac{\text{Computed index}}{\text{Maximum index}}. \qquad \textbf{(17.10)}$$

Note that when there is perfect positive correlation, τ will equal $+1$, since the computed index and the maximum index will both equal $_nC_2$. If there is a perfect negative correlation, the computed index will equal $- _nC_2$, and τ will equal -1.

Example 17.12. The value of Kendall's tau can be determined for the set of data in Table 17.10, pertaining to the rank correlation between mutual funds rated by two investment services. Let us use the ratings by Service 1 as the base for comparison, since these ranks are already in ascending order. Now the ratings for Service 2 in Table 17.10 must be compared, two at a time, in order to determine the number of pairs in the correct order $(+)$ and the number not in correct order $(-)$. First Fund A is compared with each of the four other funds. Since Fund A is ranked ahead of Fund B by Service 2, we score a $+1$ for the A–B comparison. Similarly, Service 2 ranks Fund A ahead of Funds C, D, and E; hence, we score a $+1$ for each of the comparisons A–C, A–D, and A–E. Now we must compare Fund B with the other three funds (C, D, and E). We see

TABLE 17.11 **Computations for Kendall's tau using the data in Table 17.10**

Pair	Value	Pair	Value	Pair	Value
A vs B	+1	B vs C	−1	C vs E	+1
A vs C	+1	B vs D	+1	D vs E	−1
A vs D	+1	B vs E	−1		
A vs E	+1	C vs D	+1		

Computed index = Sum of values = 4

that B is ahead of C in Service 1 rankings, but the ordering is reversed for Service 2. Thus, the B–C comparison is given a −1 score. All such paired comparisons for this example are shown in Table 17.11.

The maximum index in this example is the number of paired comparisons, which is

$$_nC_2 = {}_5C_2 = 10.$$

The computed index is the number of +1 scores (7) minus the number of −1 scores (3), which is

$$7 - 3 = 4.$$

Thus, Kendall's tau is

$$\tau = \frac{4}{10} = 0.40.$$

Note that Kendall's tau (0.40) is less than the comparable value of Spearman's rho (0.50). Both coefficients, however, utilize the same amount of information about the association between two variables, and for a given set of observations both can be used to test the null hypothesis that two variables are unrelated in the population. For small samples, tables are available for determining the probability of a given value of τ or r_s under this null hypothesis. For large samples, methods of statistical inference involving r_s and τ can be constructed utilizing the t-distribution and the normal distribution, respectively. We presented the t-statistic for Spearman's rho earlier. The comparable statistic for Kendall's tau is the following standardized **z**-statistic:

Standardized **z**-value for Kendall's tau: $z = \dfrac{\tau - \mu_\tau}{s_\tau},$ **(17.11)** where μ_τ is assumed to be zero under the null hypothesis, and

$$s_\tau = \sqrt{\frac{2(2n+5)}{9n(n-1)}}.$$

Example 17.13. Consider once again the McDonald's franchises (Example 17.11) and assume that the calculated value of Kendall's tau is $\tau = 0.527$. The standard deviation for a sample of $n = 11$ is

$$s_\tau = \sqrt{\frac{2(2 \times 11 + 5)}{9 \times 11(11-1)}} = 0.234.$$

The computed standardized normal value is thus

$$z_c = \frac{0.527}{0.234} = 2.252.$$

Since $P(z \geq 2.252) = 0.0122$, we can reject H_0: $\rho = 0$ when $\alpha > 0.0122$ for a one-sided test and when $\alpha > 2(0.0122) = 0.0244$ for a two-sided test.

Define. *Goodness of fit, observed and theoretical frequencies, nonparametric correlation, Spearman's rho, Kendall's tau.*

PROBLEMS

17.14 What is meant by the phrase "goodness-of-fit test"? How is the chi-square distribution used to make this test? How does a one-sample test differ from a two-sample test?

17.15 Certain industries are often criticized for having hired less than a proportional number of members of minority groups. Suppose you are interested in students with an M.B.A. degree, and you find that the recipients of M.B.A.'s are 20% females, 10% male minorities, and 70% white males. In one of the industries criticized, a random sample of 1000 executive positions resulted in the following breakdown:

White Males	Women	Minority Males
800	150	50

a) Calculate the expected frequency for each cell, using the population proportions 0.70, 0.20, and 0.10. Use the chi-square test to determine whether the observed and expected frequencies are close enough for the null hypothesis to be accepted. Use $\alpha = 0.01$. State your null and alternative hypotheses.

b) What p-value would you report?

17.16 In one of his classic experiments on heredity, Gregor Mendel observed the color of the plants bred from a purple-flowered and a white-flowered hybrid. Out of 929 plants observed, 705 had a purple flower, and 224 had a white flower. Using the chi-square statistic, test the hypothesis that the probability of observing a purple-flowered plant is $\frac{3}{4}$. State H_0 and H_a.

17.17 A Sears store has four different entrances. The store manager is trying to determine whether there is a difference in the number of customers coming into the store through these entrances. The manager establishes the null hypothesis that one-fourth of all customers will use each entrance. A random sample of 200 customers resulted in the following data.

Entrance:	I	II	III	IV
Customers:	75	40	30	55

Use a chi-square test and $\alpha = 0.05$ to decide whether the null hypothesis should be accepted or rejected. State H_0 and H_a.

17.18 A cafeteria proposes to serve four main entrees. For planning purposes the manager expects that the proportions of each that will be selected by the customers will be:

Selection	Hot Dogs and Chili	Roast Beef	Steak	Fish
Proportion	0.20	0.50	0.20	0.10

Of the first 50 customers, 15 select hot dogs and chili, 20 select roast beef, five select steak, and ten select fish. The manager wonders whether to revise the preparation schedule or whether this deviation from the expectations is merely chance variation that should balance out overall. Make an appropriate test, at the 0.01 level of significance, on which to base your advice to this manager.

17.19 A company making cardboard boxes of a variety of shapes has been working three shifts for the past four months. The plant manager is interested in determining whether the number of packaging errors that occur in a given week is related to the shift or to the sex of the worker. The plant has approximately the same number of male and female workers on each shift. The packaging errors below were recorded over a two-week period.

	7 A.M.–3 P.M.	3 P.M.–11 P.M.	11 P.M.–7 A.M.
Males	15	5	10
Females	5	10	15

a) Determine the expected frequency in each cell. What null and alternative hypotheses are being tested here?
b) Would you accept H_0 or H_a if $\alpha = 0.05$?
c) What p-value would you report?

17.20 A marketing advisor was asked to rate various brands of jeans on color and style. Each brand was rated I, II, or III according to color and rated A or B according to style. The frequencies of classifications were as follows:

		Color	
	I	II	III
Style A	20	15	5
Style B	10	20	10

a) Use a chi-square test to determine whether or not these data indicate independence between style and color. Use $\alpha = 0.025$.
b) What p-value would you report?

17.21 Fifty apple trees near Bellingham, Washington, were treated with one of two new types of insect spray. Each tree was rated at the end of the season as either having a "normal" amount of insects or being "insect free." The results are as follows:

	Normal	Insect Free
Spray I	9	16
Spray II	1	24

a) What null and alternative hypotheses should be tested here? What level of α would you recommend?
b) Can H_0 be rejected if $\alpha = 0.01$?

17.22 In an experiment on economic behavior, the price decisions of various producers are observed. For each decision the producer's profit position in the previous period is known. Consider the following price decisions by 100 different producers.

Action	Compared to Previous Profit		
	Profits Increased	Profits Same	Profits Decreased
Raise price	12	5	20
Price same	15	16	2
Lower price	8	4	18

Test at the $\alpha = 0.05$ level whether the price actions of these producers are independent of their previous profit positions.

17.23 In a study on new automobile purchases, it was suggested that the color of car a person picks is not independent of the amount of optional equipment purchased. The data given below report on two color selections (white and black) and three levels of optional equipment (I = none, II = $1–$600, and III = over $600). Use these data and a chi-square test for the null hypothesis that color is independent of the optional equipment selected.

		Color	
		White	Black
Equipment	I	14	26
	II	14	6
	III	30	10

17.24 Use the K–S test to measure the goodness of fit of the data in Problem 5.46 to a Poisson distribution with $\lambda = 0.7$. Is H_0 accepted or rejected if $\alpha = 0.05$?

17.25 A study was recently completed to determine whether or not the *order* in which a person's name appears on a political ballot has any influence on that person's chances of being elected. Ninety-two elections were observed, each having four candidates. The results are shown below.

	Position on Ballot				
	1	2	3	4	Total
No. of wins	29	21	17	25	92

a) Use the K–S test to examine the relationship between these data and the distribution one would expect if the probability of winning were equal for all four positions. Is H_0 accepted or rejected? Let $\alpha = 0.05$.

b) Use a chi-square test to accomplish the same purpose as in part (a).

17.26 One study by a major airline indicated that the number of passengers requesting the smoking section on domestic flights follows a binomial distribution with $\pi = 0.30$. The data from this study included a random sample of 50 passengers selected from each of 100 different flights.

No. of People Requesting Smoking	Frequency
9	5
10	5
11	6
12	10
13	12
14	11
15	13
16	12
17	8
18	6
19	6
20	3
21	2
22	1

$$n = 100$$

Use the K–S test to compare these data with the binomial distribution for $n = 50$ and $\pi = 0.30$. State H_0 and H_a and let $\alpha = 0.01$.

17.27 Five microcomputers have been rated by two different computer magazines. Each magazine rated the computers on a scale from 0 to 50. Compute and interpret Spearman's rho and Kendall's tau.

Microcomputer	Magazine I	Magazine II
1	25	15
2	39	22
3	21	30
4	48	12
5	8	10

17.28 Compute Spearman's rho and Kendall's tau between the first two columns in **Data Set 3**.

17.29 Use the data in Table 17.5 to find
a) Spearman's rho.
b) Kendall's tau.

17.30 Find the rank correlation for the data in Problem 17.10 using either Spearman's rho or Kendall's tau.

17.31 Use the data in Problem 17.12 to calculate
a) Kendall's tau.
b) Spearman's rho.

17.32 Determine Kendall's tau and Spearman's rho for the salary data in Problem 17.13.

17.33 A group of workers are scored on their ability to perform two sets of tasks emphasizing strength and coordination.
a) Using the data below, compute and compare the values of Spearman's rho and Kendall's tau. Interpret your results.
b) Calculate the *t*-statistics for Spearman's rho. Can you reject H_0 on the basis of this statistic? Use a two-sided test and $\alpha = 0.05$.

Worker	Task 1	Task 2
1	32	25
2	37	31
3	49	45
4	51	40
5	65	33
6	66	73
7	82	72
8	86	80
9	94	60
10	95	69

17.34 Two groups of students decided to rate 11 different professors. The two rankings are as follows:

Professor	Group I	Group II
Marketing Prof.	9	7
Economics Prof.	3	2
Statistics Prof.	1	1
Accounting Prof.	6	5
Finance Prof.	4	3
Law Prof.	11	11
Psychology Prof.	10	9
History Prof.	7	10
Calculus Prof.	5	8
Biology Prof.	2	4
English Prof.	8	6

a) Calculate Kendall's tau and Spearman's rho.
b) Test the significance of your results in part (a) by calculating t for Spearman's rho and z for Kendall's tau. Use a one-sided alternative and $\alpha = 0.01$.

EXERCISES

17.35 Return to the residuals in Table 17.4. Calculate a rank correlation measure using the following pairs of residuals: 1–2, 2–3, 3–4, . . ., 13–14.

17.36 Consult a text that presents nonparametric statistics and read about the contingency coefficient C. Describe how this measure differs from Spearman's rho and Kendall's tau.

17.37 Show that Spearman's rho is the rank–order equivalent of the Pearson product–moment correlation coefficient.

USING THE COMPUTER

17.38 Find a computer program that calculates nonparametric statistics. Solve the following problems using this program.
a) Problem 17.34.
b) Problem 17.21.
c) Problem 17.20.

17.39 Write a computer program that will determine Spearman's rho for a set of data with ten observations. Test your program using the data in Problem 17.33.

CASE PROBLEM

17.40 In Chapter 10, Problem 10.38, the case problem was to consider **Data Set 1**, a sample of cities from both east and west of the Mississippi River. At that time you were to run a series of parametric tests contrasting the two regions and prepare a report indicating whether you believe there is any basis for one region to claim to be a better place to live than the other. Redo that report now, using only nonparametric statistics. Use as many of the tests in this chapter as possible.

GLOSSARY

Levels of measurement:

    Nominal: Categorize data by "names" only.

    Ordinal: Scale has the property of order.

    Interval: Scale has order plus a constant interval.

    Ratio: Scale has order, a constant interval, plus a unique zero-point (making ratio statements meaningful).

Parametric versus nonparametric tests: Parametric tests generally require a measurement level of at least an interval scale and some assumption about the underlying distribution, such as the normality of the parent population. Nonparametric tests require no such assumptions.

Mann–Whitney U-test: A nonparametric test to determine whether or not two samples were drawn from the same population.

Wald–Wolfowitz runs test: A nonparametric test to determine whether or not two samples were drawn from the same population.

Matched-pairs sign test: An ordinal test involving paired samples and information on whether an object's rating is larger (+) or smaller (−) than the rating of its paired object.

Chi-square test: A test to determine the goodness of fit between a single sample and a theoretical population (one-sample test) or to determine whether two attributes are dependent or independent (two-sample test).

Kolmorogov–Smirnov test: A goodness-of-fit test when the data are in at least ordinal form.

Spearman's rho (r_s): A nonparametric measure of correlation based on ranks.

Kendall's tau (τ): A nonparametric measure of correlation based on ranks.

Data Sets

APPENDIX A

DATA SET 1 **Household income, Moody rating, cyclical threat, and taxes for all 78 U.S. cities with a population between 100,000 and 200,000**

City, State	Income	Moody Rating	Cyclical Threat	Taxes
1 Abilene, TX	$24,985	A1	Low	$192
2 Albany, GA	20,009	A	Low	931
3 Alexandria, LA	18,878	Baa	Moderate	475
4 Altoona, PA	20,104	Baa	High	625
5 Amarillo, TX	28,388	Aa	Low	214
6 Anchorage, AK	44,175	A1	High	2,844
7 Anderson, IN	24,349	A	High	688
8 Anniston, AL	18,168	Baa	High	920
9 Asheville, NC	20,966	A1	High	1,301
10 Atlantic City, NJ	23,525	Baa	Low	680
11 Battle Creek, MI	25,048	Aa	High	1,238
12 Bay City, MI	24,379	A1	High	1,151
13 Billings, MT	26,943	A	Low	1,954
14 Biloxi-Gulfport, MS	19,305	Baa	Low	761
15 Bloomington-Normal, IL	25,040	Aa	Low	870
16 Boise City, ID	30,691	Aa	High	2,207
17 Bradenton, FL	25,291	A	Low	200
18 Brockton, MA	26,090	A	Moderate	1,441
19 Cedar Rapids, IA	28,412	Aaa	High	1,977
20 Champaign-Urbana, IL	22,721	Aa	Low	797
21 Columbia, MO	23,695	Aaa	Low	1,244
22 Danbury, CT	33,518	Aa	High	420
23 Decatur, IL	26,749	A	High	928
24 Eau Claire, WI	20,493	Aa	Low	1,860
25 Fall River, MA–RI	21,295	Baa	High	1,151
26 Fayetteville-Springdale, AR	22,035	A1	High	1,069
27 Florence, AL	21,884	A1	High	918
28 Fort Collins, CO	24,905	Aa	Moderate	1,670
29 Gadsden, AL	20,928	Baa	High	991
30 Gainesville, FL	22,991	A1	Low	189
31 Galveston–Texas City, TX	27,146	Baa	Low	203
32 Grand Forks, ND–MN	22,010	Aa	Low	1,618
33 Greenley, CO	23,325	Aa	Moderate	1,535
34 Green Bay, WI	23,614	Aa	Moderate	2,230
35 Jackson, MI	24,176	A1	Moderate	1,193
36 Kankakee, IL	25,699	A1	High	886
37 Kenosha, WI	26,568	A1	High	2,593
38 Kokomo, IN	28,793	A1	High	803
39 Lafayette, LA	30,119	A	Low	982
40 Lafayette, IN	23,115	Aa	Moderate	651
41 Lake Charles, LA	24,154	Baa	Moderate	716

(handwritten annotations: "credit risk", "1 aa = highest")

City, State	Income	Moody Rating	Cyclical Threat	Taxes
42 Lawton, OK	17,531	A1	Low	520
43 Lincoln, NE	26,922	Aa	Low	997
44 Lynchburg, VA	22,683	Aa	High	1,224
45 Manchester, NH	25,456	A1	High	0
46 Mansfield, OH	23,369	A1	High	524
47 Monroe, LA	20,920	Baa	Moderate	567
48 Muncie, IN	21,457	Aa	High	604
49 Muskegon, MI	21,346	A	High	986
50 Nashua, NH	25,032	Aa	High	314
51 New Bedford, MA	21,314	Baa	High	1,152
52 New Britain, CT	25,344	A1	Moderate	361
53 Norwalk, CT	33,518	Aa	High	420
54 Odessa, TX	29,209	A	Low	214
55 Portland, ME	23,906	Aaa	Moderate	1,572
56 Pueblo, CO	24,316	A	Moderate	1,623
57 Racine, WI	25,977	A1	High	2,512
58 Reno, NV	38,686	A1	Low	230
59 St. Cloud, MN	19,661	A1	Moderate	2,209
60 St. Joseph, MO	21,746	A1	Moderate	1,103
61 Santa Cruz, CA	26,414	A	Moderate	2,386
62 Sioux City, IA	25,612	Aa	Moderate	1,677
63 Sioux Falls, SD	26,436	Aa	Low	364
64 Springfield, IL	28,669	Aa	Low	990
65 Springfield, OH	22,901	A1	High	772
66 Stamford, CT	33,518	Aaa	Moderate	420
67 Terre Haute, IN	22,073	Aa	High	629
68 Texarkana, TX–AR	21,354	A	Moderate	170
69 Topeka, KS	25,620	Aa	Moderate	1,880
70 Tuscaloosa, AL	20,820	A	Moderate	1,030
71 Tyler, TX	27,383	A1	Moderate	203
72 Waco, TX	24,168	A1	Moderate	192
73 Waterloo–Cedar Falls, IA	26,430	Aa	High	1,769
74 Wheeling, WV	24,370	A1	Moderate	1,105
75 Wichita Falls, TX	26,606	A1	Low	203
76 Williamsport, PA	22,680	A	High	695
77 Wilmington, NC	21,060	A1	High	1,308
78 Yakima, WA	25,380	A1	Low	277

Source: Moody's Investors Service, *Moody's Bond Record*, April 1981, The Bureau of Economic Analysis, Regional Economic Projections, "County and Metropolitan Area Personal Income," Survey of Current Business, 1981; Commerce Clearing House, State Tax Handbook

1-5 =35
5-10 = 10
10-15 = 2
15-20 = 2

DATA SET 2   **1981 Sales and assets of the 50 largest retailing companies (in thousands of dollars)**

Company	Sales	Assets
1. Sears Roebuck	$27,357,400	$34,509,400
2. Safeway Stores	16,580,318	3,690,404
3. K Mart	16,527,012	6,673,004
4. J. C. Penney	11,860,169	6,216,000
5. Kroger	11,266,520	2,405,290
6. F. W. Woolworth	7,223,404	3,141,965
7. Lucky Stores	7,201,404	1,524,444
8. American Stores	7,096,590	1,356,328
9. Federated Department Stores	7,067,673	4,096,877
10. Great Atlantic & Pacific Tea	6,989,529	1,308,983
11. Winn-Dixie Stores	6,200,167	924,776
12. Montgomery Ward	5,742,491	4,116,593
13. Southland	5,693,636	1,677,791
14. Jewel Companies	5,107,614	1,379,871
15. Household Merchandising	5,079,932	1,354,299
16. Dayton Hudson	4,942,859	2,555,168
17. Grand Union	3,626,231	781,449
18. Albertson's	3,480,570	709,847
19. May Department Stores	3,413,204	2,387,583
20. Supermarkets General	2,999,379	363,777
21. AAR Services	2,915,876	1,137,778
22. Carter Hawley Hale Stores	2,870,735	1,741,722
23. Allied Stores	2,760,867	2,179,328
24. Melville	2,760,842	1,134,254
25. Associated Dry Goods	2,751,200	1,557,478
26. R.H. Macy	2,656,689	1,479,467
27. Dillon Companies	2,494,577	497,581
28. McDonalds	2,477,229	2,899,322
29. Rapid-American	2,457,140	1,567,444
30. Wal-Mart	2,449,997	937,513
31. Stop & Shop Companies	2,168,148	468,578
32. Marriott	2,000,314	1,454,876
33. Signor	1,835,363	495,216
34. Zayre	1,797,139	643,444
35. Jack Eckerd	1,752,550	643,935
36. Walgreen	1,743,471	521,041
37. Tandy	1,691,373	936,545
38. Fisher Foods	1,492,709	222,299
39. Giant Food	1,483,476	339,542
40. Waldbaum	1,375,787	240,964
41. Revco D.S.	1,310,404	447,652

(continued)

Company	Sales	Assets
42. Mercantile Stores	$1,269,491	$711,370
43. First National Supermarkets	1,230,173	194,981
44. Pantry Pride	1,225,263	223,169
45. Marshall Field	1,193,961	680,758
46. Pneumo	1,093,611	370,716
47. U.S. Shoe	1,087,982	519,993
48. Scoa Industries	1,057,573	373,080
49. Thrifty	1,054,418	352,774
50. Service Merchandise	1,027,093	453,555

Source: *Fortune* magazine

2.2094×10^8

DATA SET 3 Leather elongation study
Percent elongation of leather

(A random sample of $n = 45$, 15 from each of three labs)

Sample	Tannery Lab	University Lab	Industrial Lab
1	21	23	25
2	20	25	33
3	22	25	30
4	20	29	31
5	23	24	27
6	21	28	33
7	22	22	25
8	15	20	29
9	10	10	14
10	19	14	26
11	18	19	25
12	15	20	28
13	18	16	22
14	18	19	28
15	20	22	24
Total	282	316	400
Mean	18.8	21.1	26.7
Variance	11.42	26.11	22.66
Standard Deviation	3.38	5.11	4.76

DATA SET 4 **Hours, income, fees, and expenses from survey of doctors**

OBS: **Number of doctor in survey**
HRS: **Reported weekly hours worked**
INC: **Reported annual net income of doctors**
FEE: **Average fee charged by doctor for office visit**
EXPS: **Average annual operating expense**

OBS	HRS	INC	FEE	EXPS
1	48.2	62000	20.43	55700
2	48.4	57900	22.15	51000
3	47.6	57900	17.40	45600
4	46.7	75700	32.87	26400
5	44.4	50200	18.77	34200
6	47.8	49900	23.55	37300
7	47.7	62200	19.41	57900
8	47.6	66400	18.95	51700
9	46.6	57400	22.24	47300
10	45.2	51800	21.78	35000
11	45.3	56600	26.12	64800
12	47.9	94700	43.90	79300
13	52.0	96000	33.07	69300
14	50.4	91800	34.03	67000
15	50.4	46300	18.56	33300
16	50.8	78100	33.07	57500
17	51.3	94400	37.02	58400
18	52.5	93200	34.40	64700
19	50.6	95900	26.89	58900
20	50.1	97800	30.10	81400
21	53.0	67300	16.38	62600
22	54.4	98600	22.36	61300
23	49.0	62900	20.06	48900
24	56.8	97300	29.73	61200
25	49.5	66900	21.89	55500
26	52.2	96400	30.88	70400
27	49.4	87100	34.57	63700
28	51.9	77100	18.48	57900
29	56.2	106000	24.97	92200
30	53.3	71800	20.47	86500
31	55.6	91500	27.71	44100
32	50.7	71800	18.56	71800
33	51.2	99500	29.60	66400
34	51.0	71300	22.00	63400
35	49.3	89600	29.94	59600
36	50.5	62800	21.54	62700
37	56.9	86100	27.59	67500
38	55.3	95100	27.71	73000
39	50.4	101200	40.09	89400
40	49.1	64100	26.87	64200

n = 40

Source: *14th Survey of Physicians*, American Medical Association, March 1980.

DATA SET 5 **Annual aggregate economic data for United States**

OBS: Observation number
GDP: Gross domestic product
EXP: Level of exports
IMP: Level of imports
POP: Population size

OBS	GDP	EXP	IMP	POP
1	328.7	15.04	11.92	154.88
2	345.7	15.21	11.71	157.55
3	364.6	15.78	11.85	160.18
4	364.5	15.11	11.14	163.03
5	397.3	15.56	12.49	165.93
6	418.5	19.10	13.99	168.90
7	440.5	20.87	14.62	171.98
8	446.6	17.92	14.62	174.88
9	484.6	17.64	17.01	177.83
10	502.9	20.60	16.37	180.68
11	520.7	21.04	15.94	183.69
12	560.5	21.71	17.78	186.54
13	591.8	23.39	18.62	189.24
14	632.3	26.65	20.30	191.89
15	685.2	27.53	23.19	194.30
16	750.3	30.43	27.74	196.56
17	793.7	31.62	28.74	198.71
18	866.7	34.64	35.32	200.71
19	937.1	38.01	38.31	202.68
20	985.4	43.22	42.43	203.81
21	1068.5	44.13	48.34	206.22
22	1175.0	49.76	58.86	208.23
23	1310.4	71.34	73.58	209.86
24	1414.4	98.51	108.00	211.39
25	1531.9	107.59	103.39	213.56
26	1697.5	115.34	129.90	215.15
27	1894.5	121.21	157.56	216.88
28	2126.2	143.66	183.09	218.23
29	2370.1	181.80	218.93	220.10
30	2576.6	220.71	253.00	227.64

n = 30

Source: International Financial Statistics, *Yearbook of IMF* U.S. data, 1951–1980

DATA SET 6 U.S. Department of Agriculture survey on food consumption for the elderly

Sample of *n* = 166. The variables for Data Set 6 are:

REGION Section of the U.S. (1 = northeast, 2 = central, 3 = south, 4 = west)
AGEYRS Age in years of head of household
NUMINHSE Number of persons living in household
INCMON Monthly income $ of household
HHSEX Sex of head of household (1 = male, 0 = female)
EDUC Years of education of head of household (17 = 17 or more years)

OBS	REGION	AGEYRS	NUMINHSE	INCMON	HHSEX	EDUC
1	1	73	2	608	1	8
2	1	64	2	1369	1	9
3	3	64	1	508	0	7
4	2	73	1	1218	0	9
5	3	77	1	104	0	4
6	1	86	1	200	0	4
7	1	60	2	4034	1	12
8	1	62	3	400	1	8
9	2	64	1	187	0	10
10	2	63	1	1238	0	12
11	4	71	1	648	0	12
12	3	77	1	417	0	7
13	3	77	1	380	0	13
14	3	77	1	204	0	14
15	2	68	2	801	1	16
16	1	67	1	272	0	8
17	3	57	3	600	1	8
18	3	67	2	858	1	12
19	1	59	2	1325	1	12
20	3	56	2	1465	1	12
21	2	65	5	1910	1	12
22	3	79	2	555	1	3
23	4	57	5	5400	1	12
24	2	79	1	187	0	8
25	2	57	2	667	0	13
26	3	78	1	304	1	7
27	4	56	2	1070	1	12
28	3	73	1	344	0	8
29	2	68	1	762	1	12
30	2	60	2	474	0	10
31	1	56	1	456	0	6
32	2	59	2	320	0	10
33	2	68	2	725	1	8
34	1	56	2	445	0	14

OBS	REGION	AGEYRS	NUMINHSE	INCMON	HHSEX	EDUC
35	1	64	2	1429	0	12
36	3	59	3	1412	1	12
37	1	84	1	245	0	12
38	1	67	1	319	0	8
39	3	55	3	302	0	11
40	2	56	1	2042	0	16
41	4	62	2	556	1	12
42	3	74	2	300	1	7
43	1	79	2	387	1	7
44	3	69	1	204	0	12
45	1	56	3	825	1	12
46	2	69	2	318	1	7
47	3	72	2	394	1	8
48	4	74	2	970	1	9
49	3	68	1	270	1	8
50	1	72	2	606	1	12
51	3	63	1	185	0	8
52	2	70	1	179	1	8
53	3	72	2	500	0	10
54	4	76	1	302	0	14
55	2	64	4	1618	1	8
56	1	68	1	248	1	14
57	3	62	2	2500	1	17
58	1	64	2	462	0	8
59	3	60	2	1376	1	17
60	3	68	2	668	1	11
61	2	55	1	933	0	12
62	3	72	2	675	1	4
63	3	56	2	1332	0	5
64	1	63	1	220	0	10
65	2	68	2	830	1	12
66	3	56	2	466	0	8
67	4	61	2	1908	1	14
68	4	71	1	370	1	14

(continued)

OBS	REGION	AGEYRS	NUMINHSE	INCMON	HHSEX	EDUC
69	1	88	2	1280	1	12
70	2	64	2	225	1	12
71	3	73	1	359	0	12
72	4	60	2	542	1	12
73	3	74	2	600	1	6
74	2	65	3	628	1	7
75	1	75	2	490	0	9
76	1	83	1	468	0	16
77	1	69	2	546	1	6
78	1	70	1	355	0	10
79	1	69	1	412	1	8
80	2	56	1	9900	0	12
81	2	58	4	2167	1	12
82	2	55	3	1695	1	12
83	2	63	3	375	1	8
84	2	69	1	404	0	7
85	3	64	2	1011	1	9
86	3	66	1	184	1	8
87	3	73	3	905	1	9
88	1	85	1	276	0	6
89	3	62	2	833	1	12
90	2	61	2	1000	1	8
91	1	77	1	316	0	3
92	2	68	1	2300	1	17
93	2	70	1	238	0	10
94	3	56	1	159	0	4
95	4	55	3	141	1	17
96	2	82	2	353	1	12
97	4	75	2	554	1	14
98	2	64	2	517	1	7
99	2	75	1	223	0	8
100	2	56	2	1700	1	12
101	2	55	2	1218	1	12
102	4	63	1	850	0	12
103	1	59	4	1110	1	12
104	3	79	2	207	1	6
105	4	65	1	575	0	11
106	4	65	2	1344	0	17
107	1	67	7	942	1	8
108	1	59	2	1100	1	12
109	2	66	1	481	1	8
110	2	58	2	252	1	8
111	3	70	2	344	1	8

OBS	REGION	AGEYRS	NUMINHSE	INCMON	HHSEX	EDUC
112	3	66	1	150	1	8
113	3	90	2	200	1	6
114	2	62	2	505	1	10
115	3	64	2	349	1	4
116	1	61	1	192	0	9
117	4	65	2	797	1	9
118	3	57	3	3400	1	17
119	1	63	2	902	1	12
120	1	63	2	801	1	12
121	1	83	1	198	0	8
122	1	72	1	427	1	6
123	2	63	2	1330	1	12
124	3	85	2	1539	1	14
125	4	57	4	3035	1	12
126	3	59	2	320	1	7
127	1	56	1	1250	1	12
128	2	58	1	575	0	12
129	4	73	2	359	1	12
130	1	56	1	3186	1	14
131	1	59	4	2004	0	9
132	1	56	2	2100	1	12
133	3	55	2	260	1	12
134	2	56	1	521	0	12
135	2	61	2	750	1	8
136	4	62	1	0	0	14
137	1	56	5	1310	1	17
138	2	63	1	311	1	12
139	2	75	2	211	0	8
140	2	75	3	814	0	12
141	1	80	2	419	1	8
142	2	75	2	1043	1	8
143	4	68	2	549	1	10
144	1	79	2	422	1	7
145	1	58	2	1541	1	10
146	1	86	1	268	0	8
147	3	69	2	697	1	12
148	3	56	8	672	1	6
149	2	59	2	336	1	11
150	1	71	1	427	0	6
151	2	77	2	882	0	6
152	2	57	2	2085	1	16
153	4	73	1	265	0	11
154	3	67	3	973	1	12

(continued)

OBS	REGION	AGEYRS	NUMINHSE	INCMON	HHSEX	EDUC
155	2	73	2	478	1	8
156	4	74	1	677	0	11
157	3	74	2	367	0	6
158	1	83	2	370	1	0
159	1	70	2	271	1	12
160	2	62	2	1905	1	11
161	2	55	3	616	1	3
162	2	80	2	450	1	9
163	2	55	5	2225	1	12
164	3	57	2	537	0	12
165	2	58	3	1200	1	12
166	2	65	2	720	1	12

Summary Measures

Number in Household

NUMINHSE	FREQUENCY	CUM FREQ	PERCENT	CUM PERCENT
1	58	58	34.940	34.940
2	82	140	49.398	84.337
3	15	155	9.036	93.373
4	5	160	3.012	96.386
5	4	164	2.410	98.795
7	1	165	0.602	99.398
8	1	166	0.602	100.000

Years of Education

EDUC	FREQUENCY	CUM FREQ	PERCENT	CUM PERCENT
0	1	1	0.602	0.602
3	3	4	1.807	2.410
4	5	9	3.012	5.422
5	1	10	0.602	6.024
6	11	21	6.627	12.651
7	11	32	6.627	19.277
8	32	64	19.277	38.554
9	10	74	6.024	44.578
10	10	84	6.024	50.602
11	7	91	4.217	54.819
12	52	143	31.325	86.145
13	2	145	1.205	87.349
14	10	155	6.024	93.373
16	4	159	2.410	95.783
17	7	166	4.217	100.000

Sex of Head of Household

HHSEX	FREQUENCY	CUM FREQ	PERCENT	CUM PERCENT
0	61	61	36.747	36.747
1	105	166	63.253	100.000

Region Code

REGION	FREQUENCY	CUM FREQ	PERCENT	CUM PERCENT
1	46	46	27.711	27.711
2	53	99	31.928	59.639
3	46	145	27.711	87.349
4	21	166	12.651	100.000

VARIABLE	N	MEAN	STANDARD DEVIATION	MINIMUM VALUE	MAXIMUM VALUE	STD ERROR OF MEAN
REGION	166	2.2530120	1.001131	1.00000000	4.000000	0.0777028
AGEYRS	166	66.6265060	8.608961	55.00000000	90.000000	0.6681849
NUMINHSE	166	1.9397590	1.071384	1.00000000	8.000000	0.0831555
INCMON	166	851.8433735	1042.908613	0.00000000	9900.000000	80.9454068
HHSEX	166	0.6325301	0.483575	0.00000000	1.000000	0.0375327
EDUC	166	10.0783133	3.251090	0.00000000	17.000000	0.2523335

Subscripts,
Summations,
Variables, and
Functions

APPENDIX B

SUBSCRIPTS AND SUMMATIONS

Throughout this book we use certain symbols to distinguish between the numbers in a set of data and to indicate the sum of such numbers. For example, we may wish to distinguish between the monthly sales of a certain business and then sum these monthly sales to get the yearly sales. To do this, suppose that we let the symbol x denote the monthly sales of this firm. Furthermore, we will add a subscript to this symbol to denote which month is being represented. Thus, x_1 = sales in first month, x_2 = sales in second month, and so forth, with x_{12} = sales in the twelfth month. That is, if sales in the sixth month were 120 units, then we would write $x_6 = 120$. The notation x_i thus stands for "sales in the ith month," where i can be any number from 1 to 12; that is, $i = 1, 2, \ldots, 12$. The dots in this last expression are used to indicate "and so on."

Now assume that we want to sum the sales for all 12 months in a year, which is

$$x_1 + x_2 + \cdots + x_{12}.$$

Another way of writing this sum is to use the Greek letter Σ (capital sigma). This symbol is read as "take the sum of." At the bottom of this Σ sign we usually place the first value of i that is to be included in the sum. The last value of i to be summed is usually placed at the top of the sum sign. Thus,

$$\sum_{i=1}^{12} x_i$$

is read as "sum the values of x_i starting from $i = 1$ and ending with $i = 12$." That is,

$$\sum_{i=1}^{12} x_i = x_1 + x_2 + \cdots + x_{12}.$$

Similarly, suppose that we want the sum of only the last seven months in the year. This sum is written as follows:

$$\sum_{i=6}^{12} x_i = x_6 + x_7 + \cdots + x_{12}.$$

In statistics we often will not know in advance what the final value in a summation will be. For example, we know that we want to sum a set of sales values, but we do not know how many values there are to be summed. To designate this situation, we will let the symbol n represent the last number in the sum (where n can be any integer value, such as 1, 2, 3, \ldots). The notation

$$\sum_{i=1}^{n} x_i = x_1 + x_2 + \cdots + x_n$$

is thus read as "the sum of n numbers, where the first number is x_1, the second is x_2, and the last is x_n." In summing monthly sales over a year, we would thus let $n = 12$, so that $\Sigma_{i=1}^n x_i = \Sigma_{i=1}^{12} x_i$.

Perhaps we should mention that in some chapters in this book we have sometimes omitted the limits of summation and simply written Σx_i. This notation should be interpreted to mean "sum all relevant values of x_i." In these instances we have made sure that the reader always knows what the relevant values of x_i are. Also, we might point out that the choice of symbols in designating a sum of numbers is often quite arbitrary. For example, we might have used the letter y to denote monthly sales (instead of x) and used the letter j as a subscript (instead of i). In this case $\Sigma_{j=1}^{12} y_j$ would denote the sum of the twelve monthly values.

Double summations In a number of chapters in this book we have found it convenient to use *two* subscripts instead of just one. In these instances the first subscript indicates one characteristic under study, and the second subscript indicates some other characteristic. For example, suppose that we let $x_{ij} =$ sales in the ith month by the jth salesman. The notation $x_{6,2} = 15$ would indicate that in the sixth month ($i = 6$), salesman number 2 ($j = 2$) sold 15 units. Using the same procedure as described above, we can denote the total sales over 12 months by the jth salesman as the sum of x_{1j} (sales in the 1st month by the jth salesman) plus $x_{2j}, \ldots$, plus $x_{12,j}$ (sales in the 12th month by the jth salesman). That is,

$$\text{Total sales by salesman j:} \quad \sum_{i=1}^{12} x_{ij} = x_{1j} + x_{2j} + \cdots + x_{12,j}.$$

Another example of a similar type of sum is the sum of sales in the ith month (where i is some number between 1 and 12) over all the salesmen in the company. If we let $m =$ total number of salesmen, then this sum is x_{i1} (sales in month i by salesman #1) plus $x_{i2}, \ldots$, plus x_{im} (sales in month i by salesman m). That is,

$$\text{Total sales in month i:} \quad \sum_{j=1}^{m} x_{ij} = x_{i1} + x_{i2} + \cdots + x_{im}.$$

Finally, we might wish to sum over all months ($i = 1, 2, \ldots, 12$) and all salesmen ($j = 1, 2, \ldots, m$). This sum could be written as:

Total sales over all months and all salesmen:

$$\sum_{\text{All } j} \sum_{\text{All } i} x_{ij} = \left\{ \begin{array}{l} x_{11} + x_{12} + \cdots + x_{1m} \\ + x_{21} + x_{22} + \cdots + x_{2m} \\ \quad \cdot \\ \quad \cdot \\ \quad \cdot \\ + x_{12,1} + x_{12,2} + \cdots + x_{12,m} \end{array} \right\}.$$

VARIABLES AND FUNCTIONS

Variables
Variables and the relationship between variables represent an important part of statistics. Hence, it is important that we define these concepts carefully.

A variable is a quantity that may assume any one of a set of values. For example, we might describe the worth of a common stock by the variable "current worth on the stock market." The values of this variable are the different prices the stock can assume. Or we might be interested in describing how well a specific brand of alkaline battery works by defining the variable "the length of time before failure when in constant use." The values of this variable are the various times it might take before the battery fails.

Variables are often classified according to whether their values are *discrete* or *continuous*. The values of a discrete variable are individually distinct, that is, they are separable from one another. The price of a common stock, for instance, represents a discrete variable because the prices a stock can assume are all separate values, distinguishable from one another. The following examples also represent discrete variables:

1. the number of defectives in a production lot,
2. the amount of advertising expenditure a certain company plans for next year,
3. the amount of federal income tax owed by an individual.

Most discrete variables represent some quantity that can be "counted."

The values of a *continuous* variable are not separable from one another; each value is immediately adjacent to and indistinguishable from the next. Quantities that are *measured* are usually continuous variables; for example, measures of time, weight, length, and area typically represent continuous variables. Thus, in our earlier example the time it takes a battery to fail represents a continuous random variable. There are always an infinite number of values of a continuous variable.* The following variables also are continuous:

1. the percentage increase in the consumer price index last month,
2. the amount of gasoline available in the United States next year,
3. the quality of the air in Los Angeles yesterday, measured in a way so as to include all numbers from 0 to 100.

One of the practical difficulties with continuous variables is that the devices used to measure such variables usually are read only in a discrete manner. For example, the variable "amount of gasoline needed to fill a

---

* The number of values of a discrete variable may be either finite or infinite.

car" is clearly a continuous random variable, since this amount may be *any* value between zero and the capacity of the gas tank. From a *practical* point of view, however, this variable is discrete because most gas pumps cannot be read (at least accurately) beyond a few decimal points (usually 1/10 of a gallon). *For most statistical analysis it makes little difference if we treat such variables as discrete or continuous, although a continuous variable is often easier to manipulate than is a discrete variable with many different values.*

Functions   If a unique value of some variable y is associated with every possible value of another variable x, then the variable y is said to be "a function of" the variable x. To illustrate a functional relationship, we will let x represent the number of gallons of gasoline you purchase at a service station and let y be the amount of money you must pay for this gasoline. In this case, y is a function of x [written $y = f(x)$] because the exact (unique) amount (y) you will be charged for every possible gasoline purchase (x) is known (assuming the price doesn't change before you get there).

There are three commonly used methods for describing a functional relationship: (1) a table, (2) a graph, and (3) an equation. As we will illustrate below, the first two of these methods work well for discrete functions, while the latter two work well for continuous functions.

Discrete Functions. By a discrete function we mean the function in any situation where x is a discrete variable. If x is discrete, then y must be discrete as well. To illustrate a discrete function, we propose that the Environmental Protection Agency (EPA) is testing a new car to determine its gas mileage (y) at various speeds (x). This car was tested at $x = 10$, 20, 30, 40 and 50 miles per hour (MPH). The miles per gallon (MPG) at these speeds were $y = 21.6, 26.1, 27.8, 25.3$, and 19.5 respectively. This information is shown below.

Miles per hour (x)	Miles per gallon [$y = f(x)$]
$x = 10$	$y = f(10) = 21.6$
$x = 20$	$y = f(20) = 26.1$
$x = 30$	$y = f(30) = 27.8$
$x = 40$	$y = f(40) = 25.3$
$x = 50$	$y = f(50) = 19.5$

Note that the variable x is discrete, since all possible values of this variable are distinguishable from one another — that is, they are individually distinct. It is important to understand the symbolic notation in

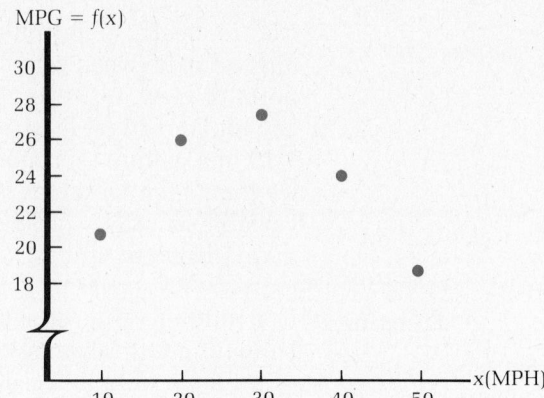

FIGURE B.1 **Graph of the function relating** x = MPH **and** Y = MPG.

writing functions. For example, the notation $f(10) = 21.6$ means that when $x = 10$, the value of $f(x)$ is $y = 21.6$. Similarly, $f(50) = 19.5$ means that $y = 19.5$ when $x = 50$. Figure B.1 is a graph of the function relating MPH (x) and MPG (y).

We must resist the temptation to connect the points in Fig. B.1 with a line, since such a line might incorrectly lead a viewer to assume that the function is defined for speeds other than $x = 10, 20, 30, 40,$ and 50 MPH. It may be possible to define a function that relates additional values of x to y, but in this example the function is defined only for five x-values. When the number of x-values is large, a formula is often useful to describe a functional relationship. Chapter 4 gives several examples of such formulas.

Continuous Functions. When the random variable x is continuous, then the functional relationship between x and y usually must be expressed as a formula or in a graph. Consider a simple example, in which the variable x is temperature measured on the Fahrenheit scale and the variable y is temperature measured on the centigrade scale. For converting values from the Fahrenheit scale (x) to the centigrade scale (y), the following functional relationship is used:*

$$y = \frac{5}{9}x - \frac{160}{9}.$$

---

* We could have written this formula as

$$f(x) = \frac{5}{9}(x - 32).$$

This relationship represents a function because a unique value of y is specified for each value of x. The function is continuous, since the values of x are indistinguishable. Now suppose that we want to graph this function. First, we recognize that it is a straight line, since the exponent of the variable x is 1. To graph a straight line, we need only two points. The easiest two points to take are usually the one where x = 0 and the one where y = 0. When x = 0,

$$y = \frac{5}{9}(0) - \frac{160}{9} = -17.78.$$

Similarly, when y = 0 we can solve for x as follows:

$$0 = \frac{5}{9}x - \frac{160}{9},$$

$$\frac{5}{9}x = \frac{160}{9},$$

so

$$x = \frac{160}{9} \cdot \frac{9}{5} = \frac{160}{5} = 32.$$

We now have two points on our function, $(0, -17.78)$ and $(32, 0)$. This function is graphed in Fig. B.2 by connecting these two points.

From either the straight line in Fig. B.2 or the function itself we can solve for any additional point. For example, most of us are familiar with

FIGURE B.2 **A graph of** $y = f(x) = \dfrac{5}{9}x - \dfrac{160}{9}.$

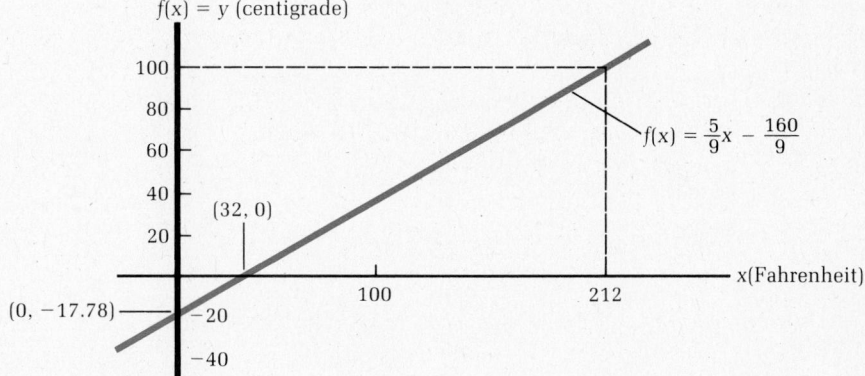

the boiling point of water at 212 degrees Fahrenheit, $x = 212$. The comparable value of y is $f(212)$:

$$y = f(212) = \frac{5}{9}(212) - \frac{160}{9},$$

or

$$y = f(212) = 100,$$

which is the centigrade temperature for the boiling point of water. We could have solved for any one of the infinite number of different y-values in a similar manner.

Tables of
Functions

APPENDIX C

Table I gives values of the binomial mass function defined by

$$P(x) = {}_nC_x \, \pi^x(1 - \pi)^{n-x}$$

$$= \frac{n!}{x!(n - x)!} \, \pi^x(1 - \pi)^{n-x}.$$

This is the probability of exactly x successes in n independent Bernoulli trials with probability of success on a single trial equal to π. The values of x at the left of any section are to be used in conjunction with the values of π at the top of that section; the values of x at the right of any section are to be used in conjunction with the values of π at the bottom of that section.

   Example: To evaluate P(x) for n = 5, x = 3, and π = 0.83, locate the section of the table for n = 5, the column for π = 0.83, and the row for x = 3, and read

$$P(x) = 0.1652.$$

TABLE I **Binomial distribution ($n = 1$, $n = 2$)**

						$n = 1$							
x	π	01	02	03	04	05	06	07	08	09	10		
0		9900	9800	9700	9600	9500	9400	9300	9200	9100	9000		1
1		0100	0200	0300	0400	0500	0600	0700	0800	0900	1000		0
		99	98	97	96	95	94	93	92	91	90	π	x
x	π	11	12	13	14	15	16	17	18	19	20		
0		8900	8800	8700	8600	8500	8400	8300	8200	8100	8000		1
1		1100	1200	1300	1400	1500	1600	1700	1800	1900	2000		0
		89	88	87	86	85	84	83	82	81	80	π	x
x	π	21	22	23	24	25	26	27	28	29	30		
0		7900	7800	7700	7600	7500	7400	7300	7200	7100	7000		1
1		2100	2200	2300	2400	2500	2600	2700	2800	2900	3000		0
		79	78	77	76	75	74	73	72	71	70	π	x
x	π	31	32	33	34	35	36	37	38	39	40		
0		6900	6800	6700	6600	6500	6400	6300	6200	6100	6000		1
1		3100	3200	3300	3400	3500	3600	3700	3800	3900	4000		0
		69	68	67	66	65	64	63	62	61	60	π	x
x	π	41	42	43	44	45	46	47	48	49	50		
0		5900	5800	5700	5600	5500	5400	5300	5200	5100	5000		1
1		4100	4200	4300	4400	4500	4600	4700	4800	4900	5000		0
		59	58	57	56	55	54	53	52	51	50	π	x

		n = 2									
x	π	01	02	03	04	05	06	07	08	09	10	
0		9801	9604	9409	9216	9025	8836	8649	8464	8281	8100	2
1		0198	0392	0582	0768	0950	1128	1302	1472	1638	1800	1
2		0001	0004	0009	0016	0025	0036	0049	0064	0081	0100	0
		99	98	97	96	95	94	93	92	91	90	π x
x	π	11	12	13	14	15	16	17	18	19	20	
0		7921	7744	7569	7396	7225	7056	6889	6724	6561	6400	2
1		1958	2112	2262	2408	2550	2688	2822	2952	3078	3200	1
2		0121	0144	0169	0196	0225	0256	0289	0324	0361	0400	0
		89	88	87	86	85	84	83	82	81	80	π x
x	π	21	22	23	24	25	26	27	28	29	30	
0		6241	6084	5929	5776	5625	5476	5329	5184	5041	4900	2
1		3318	3432	3542	3648	3750	3848	3942	4032	4118	4200	1
2		0441	0484	0529	0576	0625	0676	0729	0784	0841	0900	0
		79	78	77	76	75	74	73	72	71	70	π x
x	π	31	32	33	34	35	36	37	38	39	40	
0		4761	4624	4489	4356	4225	4096	3969	3844	3721	3600	2
1		4278	4352	4422	4488	4550	4608	4662	4712	4758	4800	1
2		0961	1024	1089	1156	1225	1296	1369	1444	1521	1600	0
		69	68	67	66	65	64	63	62	61	60	π x
x	π	41	42	43	44	45	46	47	48	49	50	
0		3481	3364	3249	3136	3025	2916	2809	2704	2601	2500	2
1		4838	4872	4902	4928	4950	4968	4982	4992	4998	5000	1
2		1681	1764	1849	1936	2025	2116	2209	2304	2401	2500	0
		59	58	57	56	55	54	53	52	51	50	π x

TABLE I   **Binomial distribution ($n = 3$, $n = 4$)**

						$n = 3$							

x	π	01	02	03	04	05	06	07	08	09	10		
0		9703	9412	9127	8847	8574	8306	8044	7787	7536	7290		3
1		0294	0576	0847	1106	1354	1590	1816	2031	2236	2430		2
2		0003	0012	0026	0046	0071	0102	0137	0177	0221	0270		1
3		0000	0000	0000	0001	0001	0002	0003	0005	0007	0010		0
		99	98	97	96	95	94	93	92	91	90	π	x

x	π	11	12	13	14	15	16	17	18	19	20		
0		7050	6815	6585	6361	6141	5927	5718	5514	5314	5120		3
1		2614	2788	2952	3106	3251	3387	3513	3631	3740	3840		2
2		0323	0380	0441	0506	0574	0645	0720	0797	0877	0960		1
3		0013	0017	0022	0027	0034	0041	0049	0058	0069	0080		0
		89	88	87	86	85	84	83	82	81	80	π	x

x	π	21	22	23	24	25	26	27	28	29	30		
0		4930	4746	4565	4390	4219	4052	3890	3732	3579	3430		3
1		3932	4014	4091	4159	4219	4271	4316	4355	4386	4410		2
2		1045	1133	1222	1313	1406	1501	1597	1693	1791	1890		1
3		0093	0106	0122	0138	0156	0176	0197	0220	0244	0270		0
		79	78	77	76	75	74	73	72	71	70	π	x

x	π	31	32	33	34	35	36	37	38	39	40		
0		3285	3144	3008	2875	2746	2621	2500	2383	2270	2160		3
1		4428	4439	4444	4443	4436	4424	4406	4382	4354	4320		2
2		1989	2089	2189	2289	2389	2488	2587	2686	2783	2880		1
3		0298	0328	0359	0393	0429	0467	0507	0549	0593	0640		0
		69	68	67	66	65	64	63	62	61	60	π	x

x	π	41	42	43	44	45	46	47	48	49	50		
0		2054	1951	1852	1756	1664	1575	1489	1406	1327	1250		3
1		4282	4239	4191	4140	4084	4024	3961	3894	3823	3750		2
2		2975	3069	3162	3252	3341	3428	3512	3594	3674	3750		1
3		0689	0741	0795	0852	0911	0973	1038	1106	1176	1250		0
		59	58	57	56	55	54	53	52	51	50	π	x

						$n = 4$							
x	π	01	02	03	04	05	06	07	08	09	10		
0		9606	9224	8853	8493	8145	7807	7481	7164	6857	6561		4
1		0388	0753	1095	1416	1715	1993	2252	2492	2713	2916		3
2		0006	0023	0051	0088	0135	0191	0254	0325	0402	0486		2
3		0000	0000	0001	0002	0005	0008	0013	0019	0027	0036		1
4		0000	0000	0000	0000	0000	0000	0000	0000	0001	0001		0
		99	98	97	96	95	94	93	92	91	90	π	x
x	π	11	12	13	14	15	16	17	18	19	20		
0		6274	5997	5729	5470	5220	4979	4746	4521	4305	4096		4
1		3102	3271	3424	3562	3685	3793	3888	3970	4039	4096		3
2		0575	0669	0767	0870	0975	1084	1195	1307	1421	1536		2
3		0047	0061	0076	0094	0115	0138	0163	0191	0222	0256		1
4		0001	0002	0003	0004	0005	0007	0008	0010	0013	0016		0
		89	88	87	86	85	84	83	82	81	80	π	x
x	π	21	22	23	24	25	26	27	28	29	30		
0		3895	3702	3515	3336	3164	2999	2840	2687	2541	2401		4
1		4142	4176	4200	4214	4219	4214	4201	4180	4152	4116		3
2		1651	1767	1882	1996	2109	2221	2331	2439	2544	2646		2
3		0293	0332	0375	0420	0469	0520	0575	0632	0693	0756		1
4		0019	0023	0028	0033	0039	0046	0053	0061	0071	0081		0
		79	78	77	76	75	74	73	72	71	70	π	x
x	π	31	32	33	34	35	36	37	38	39	40		
0		2267	2138	2015	1897	1785	1678	1575	1478	1385	1296		4
1		4074	4025	3970	3910	3845	3775	3701	3623	3541	3456		3
2		2745	2841	2933	3021	3105	3185	3260	3330	3396	3456		2
3		0822	0891	0963	1038	1115	1194	1276	1361	1447	1536		1
4		0092	0105	0119	0134	0150	0168	0187	0209	0231	0256		0
		69	68	67	66	65	64	63	62	61	60	π	x
x	π	41	42	43	44	45	46	47	48	49	50		
0		1212	1132	1056	0983	0915	0850	0789	0731	0677	0625		4
1		3368	3278	3185	3091	2995	2897	2799	2700	2600	2500		3
2		3511	3560	3604	3643	3675	3702	3723	3738	3747	3750		2
3		1627	1719	1813	1908	2005	2102	2201	2300	2400	2500		1
4		0283	0311	0342	0375	0410	0448	0488	0531	0576	0625		0
		59	58	57	56	55	54	53	52	51	50	π	x

TABLE I Binomial distribution ($n = 5$, $n = 6$)

$n = 5$

x	π	01	02	03	04	05	06	07	08	09	10	
0		9510	9039	8587	8154	7738	7339	6957	6591	6240	5905	5
1		0480	0922	1328	1699	2036	2342	2618	2866	3086	3280	4
2		0010	0038	0082	0142	0214	0299	0394	0498	0610	0729	3
3		0000	0001	0003	0006	0011	0019	0030	0043	0060	0081	2
4		0000	0000	0000	0000	0000	0001	0001	0002	0003	0004	1
		99	98	97	96	95	94	93	92	91	90	π x

x	π	11	12	13	14	15	16	17	18	19	20	
0		5584	5277	4984	4704	4437	4182	3939	3707	3487	3277	5
1		3451	3598	3724	3829	3915	3983	4034	4069	4089	4096	4
2		0853	0981	1113	1247	1382	1517	1652	1786	1919	2048	3
3		0105	0134	0166	0203	0244	0289	0338	0392	0450	0512	2
4		0007	0009	0012	0017	0022	0028	0035	0043	0053	0064	1
5		0000	0000	0000	0001	0001	0001	0001	0002	0002	0003	0
		89	88	87	86	85	84	83	82	81	80	π x

x	π	21	22	23	24	25	26	27	28	29	30	
0		3077	2887	2707	2536	2373	2219	2073	1935	1804	1681	5
1		4090	4072	4043	4003	3955	3898	3834	3762	3685	3601	4
2		2174	2297	2415	2529	2637	2739	2836	2926	3010	3087	3
3		0578	0648	0721	0798	0879	0962	1049	1138	1229	1323	2
4		0077	0091	0108	0126	0146	0169	0194	0221	0251	0283	1
5		0004	0005	0006	0008	0010	0012	0014	0017	0021	0024	0
		79	78	77	76	75	74	73	72	71	70	π x

x	π	31	32	33	34	35	36	37	38	39	40	
0		1564	1454	1350	1252	1160	1074	0992	0916	0845	0778	5
1		3513	3421	3325	3226	3124	3020	2914	2808	2700	2592	4
2		3157	3220	3275	3323	3364	3397	3423	3441	3452	3456	3
3		1418	1515	1613	1712	1811	1911	2010	2109	2207	2304	2
4		0319	0357	0397	0441	0488	0537	0590	0646	0706	0768	1
5		0029	0034	0039	0045	0053	0060	0069	0079	0090	0102	0
		69	68	67	66	65	64	63	62	61	60	π x

x	π	41	42	43	44	45	46	47	48	49	50	
0		0715	0656	0602	0551	0503	0459	0418	0380	0345	0313	5
1		2484	2376	2270	2164	2059	1956	1854	1755	1657	1562	4
2		3452	3442	3424	3400	3369	3332	3289	3240	3185	3125	3
3		2399	2492	2583	2671	2757	2838	2916	2990	3060	3125	2
4		0834	0902	0974	1049	1128	1209	1293	1380	1470	1562	1
5		0116	0131	0147	0165	0185	0206	0229	0255	0282	0312	0
		59	58	57	56	55	54	53	52	51	50	π x

x	π	01	02	03	04	05	06	07	08	09	10		
0		9415	8858	8330	7828	7351	6899	6470	6064	5679	5314		6
1		0571	1085	1546	1957	2321	2642	2922	3164	3370	3543		5
2		0014	0055	0120	0204	0305	0422	0550	0688	0833	0984		4
3		0000	0002	0005	0011	0021	0036	0055	0080	0110	0146		3
4		0000	0000	0000	0000	0001	0002	0003	0005	0008	0012		2
5		0000	0000	0000	0000	0000	0000	0000	0000	0000	0001		1
		99	98	97	96	95	94	93	92	91	90	π	x

x	π	11	12	13	14	15	16	17	18	19	20		
0		4970	4644	4336	4046	3771	3513	3269	3040	2824	2621		6
1		3685	3800	3888	3952	3993	4015	4018	4004	3975	3932		5
2		1139	1295	1452	1608	1762	1912	2057	2197	2331	2458		4
3		0188	0236	0289	0349	0415	0486	0562	0643	0729	0819		3
4		0017	0024	0032	0043	0055	0069	0086	0106	0128	0154		2
5		0001	0001	0002	0003	0004	0005	0007	0009	0012	0015		1
6		0000	0000	0000	0000	0000	0000	0000	0000	0000	0001		0
		89	88	87	86	85	84	83	82	81	80	π	x

x	π	21	22	23	24	25	26	27	28	29	30		
0		2431	2252	2084	1927	1780	1642	1513	1393	1281	1176		6
1		3877	3811	3735	3651	3560	3462	3358	3251	3139	3025		5
2		2577	2687	2789	2882	2966	3041	3105	3160	3206	3241		4
3		0913	1011	1111	1214	1318	1424	1531	1639	1746	1852		3
4		0182	0214	0249	0287	0330	0375	0425	0478	0535	0595		2
5		0019	0024	0030	0036	0044	0053	0063	0074	0087	0102		1
6		0001	0001	0001	0002	0002	0003	0004	0005	0006	0007		0
		79	78	77	76	75	74	73	72	71	70	π	x

x	π	31	32	33	34	35	36	37	38	39	40		
0		1079	0989	0905	0827	0754	0687	0625	0568	0515	0467		6
1		2909	2792	2673	2555	2437	2319	2203	2089	1976	1866		5
2		3267	3284	3292	3290	3280	3261	3235	3201	3159	3110		4
3		1957	2061	2162	2260	2355	2446	2533	2616	2693	2765		3
4		0660	0727	0799	0873	0951	1032	1116	1202	1291	1382		2
5		0119	0137	0157	0180	0205	0232	0262	0295	0330	0369		1
6		0009	0011	0013	0015	0018	0022	0026	0030	0035	0041		0
		69	68	67	66	65	64	63	62	61	60	π	x

x	π	41	42	43	44	45	46	47	48	49	50		
0		0422	0381	0343	0308	0277	0248	0222	0198	0176	0156		6
1		1759	1654	1552	1454	1359	1267	1179	1095	1014	0937		5
2		3055	2994	2928	2856	2780	2699	2615	2527	2436	2344		4
3		2831	2891	2945	2992	3032	3065	3091	3110	3121	3125		3
4		1475	1570	1666	1763	1861	1958	2056	2153	2249	2344		2
5		0410	0455	0503	0554	0609	0667	0729	0795	0864	0937		1
6		0048	0055	0063	0073	0083	0095	0108	0122	0138	0156		0
		59	58	57	56	55	54	53	52	51	50	π	x

$n = 7$

x	π	01	02	03	04	05	06	07	08	09	10	
0		9321	8681	8080	7514	6983	6485	6017	5578	5168	4783	7
1		0659	1240	1749	2192	2573	2897	3170	3396	3578	3720	6
2		0020	0076	0162	0274	0406	0555	0716	0886	1061	1240	5
3		0000	0003	0008	0019	0036	0059	0090	0128	0175	0230	4
4		0000	0000	0000	0001	0002	0004	0007	0011	0017	0026	3
5		0000	0000	0000	0000	0000	0000	0000	0001	0001	0002	2
		99	98	97	96	95	94	93	92	91	90	π x

x	π	11	12	13	14	15	16	17	18	19	20	
0		4423	4087	3773	3479	3206	2951	2714	2493	2288	2097	7
1		3827	3901	3946	3965	3960	3935	3891	3830	3756	3670	6
2		1419	1596	1769	1936	2097	2248	2391	2523	2643	2753	5
3		0292	0363	0441	0525	0617	0714	0816	0923	1033	1147	4
4		0036	0049	0066	0086	0109	0136	0167	0203	0242	0287	3
5		0003	0004	0006	0008	0012	0016	0021	0027	0034	0043	2
6		0000	0000	0000	0000	0001	0001	0001	0002	0003	0004	1
		89	88	87	86	85	84	83	82	81	80	π x

x	π	21	22	23	24	25	26	27	28	29	30	
0		1920	1757	1605	1465	1335	1215	1105	1003	0910	0824	7
1		3573	3468	3356	3237	3115	2989	2860	2731	2600	2471	6
2		2850	2935	3007	3067	3115	3150	3174	3186	3186	3177	5
3		1263	1379	1497	1614	1730	1845	1956	2065	2169	2269	4
4		0336	0389	0447	0510	0577	0648	0724	0803	0886	0972	3
5		0054	0066	0080	0097	0115	0137	0161	0187	0217	0250	2
6		0005	0006	0008	0010	0013	0016	0020	0024	0030	0036	1
7		0000	0000	0000	0000	0001	0001	0001	0001	0002	0002	0
		79	78	77	76	75	74	73	72	71	70	π x

x	π	31	32	33	34	35	36	37	38	39	40	
0		0745	0672	0606	0546	0490	0440	0394	0352	0314	0280	7
1		2342	2215	2090	1967	1848	1732	1619	1511	1407	1306	6
2		3156	3127	3088	3040	2985	2922	2853	2778	2698	2613	5
3		2363	2452	2535	2610	2679	2740	2793	2838	2875	2903	4
4		1062	1154	1248	1345	1442	1541	1640	1739	1838	1935	3
5		0286	0326	0369	0416	0466	0520	0578	0640	0705	0774	2
6		0043	0051	0061	0071	0084	0098	0113	0131	0150	0172	1
7		0003	0003	0004	0005	0006	0008	0009	0011	0014	0016	0
		69	68	67	66	65	64	63	62	61	60	π x

x	π	41	42	43	44	45	46	47	48	49	50	
0		0249	0221	0195	0173	0152	0134	0117	0103	0090	0078	7
1		1211	1119	1032	0950	0872	0798	0729	0664	0604	0547	6
2		2524	2431	2336	2239	2140	2040	1940	1840	1740	1641	5
3		2923	2934	2937	2932	2918	2897	2867	2830	2786	2734	4
4		2031	2125	2216	2304	2388	2468	2543	2612	2676	2734	3
5		0847	0923	1003	1086	1172	1261	1353	1447	1543	1641	2
6		0196	0223	0252	0284	0320	0358	0400	0445	0494	0547	1
7		0019	0023	0027	0032	0037	0044	0051	0059	0068	0078	0
		59	58	57	56	55	54	53	52	51	50	π x

x	π	01	02	03	04	05	06	07	08	09	10	
0		9227	8508	7837	7214	6634	6096	5596	5132	4703	4305	8
1		0746	1389	1939	2405	2793	3113	3370	3570	3721	3826	7
2		0026	0099	0210	0351	0515	0695	0888	1087	1288	1488	6
3		0001	0004	0013	0029	0054	0089	0134	0189	0255	0331	5
4		0000	0000	0001	0002	0004	0007	0013	0021	0031	0046	4
5		0000	0000	0000	0000	0000	0000	0001	0001	0002	0004	3
		99	98	97	96	95	94	93	92	91	90	π	x

x	π	11	12	13	14	15	16	17	18	19	20	
0		3937	3596	3282	2992	2725	2479	2252	2044	1853	1678	8
1		3892	3923	3923	3897	3847	3777	3691	3590	3477	3355	7
2		1684	1872	2052	2220	2376	2518	2646	2758	2855	2936	6
3		0416	0511	0613	0723	0839	0959	1084	1211	1339	1468	5
4		0064	0087	0115	0147	0185	0228	0277	0332	0393	0459	4
5		0006	0009	0014	0019	0026	0035	0045	0058	0074	0092	3
6		0000	0001	0001	0002	0002	0003	0005	0006	0009	0011	2
7		0000	0000	0000	0000	0000	0000	0000	0000	0001	0001	1
		89	88	87	86	85	84	83	82	81	80	π	x

x	π	21	22	23	24	25	26	27	28	29	30	
0		1517	1370	1236	1113	1001	0899	0806	0722	0646	0576	8
1		3226	3092	2953	2812	2670	2527	2386	2247	2110	1977	7
2		3002	3052	3087	3108	3115	3108	3089	3058	3017	2965	6
3		1596	1722	1844	1963	2076	2184	2285	2379	2464	2541	5
4		0530	0607	0689	0775	0865	0959	1056	1156	1258	1361	4
5		0113	0137	0165	0196	0231	0270	0313	0360	0411	0467	3
6		0015	0019	0025	0031	0038	0047	0058	0070	0084	0100	2
7		0001	0002	0002	0003	0004	0005	0006	0008	0010	0012	1
8		0000	0000	0000	0000	0000	0000	0000	0000	0001	0001	0
		79	78	77	76	75	74	73	72	71	70	π	x

x	π	31	32	33	34	35	36	37	38	39	40	
0		0514	0457	0406	0360	0319	0281	0248	0218	0192	0168	8
1		1847	1721	1600	1484	1373	1267	1166	1071	0981	0896	7
2		2904	2835	2758	2675	2587	2494	2397	2297	2194	2090	6
3		2609	2668	2717	2756	2786	2805	2815	2815	2806	2787	5
4		1465	1569	1673	1775	1875	1973	2067	2157	2242	2322	4
5		0527	0591	0659	0732	0808	0888	0971	1058	1147	1239	3
6		0118	0139	0162	0188	0217	0250	0285	0324	0367	0413	2
7		0015	0019	0023	0028	0033	0040	0048	0057	0067	0079	1
8		0001	0001	0001	0002	0002	0003	0004	0004	0005	0007	0
		69	68	67	66	65	64	63	62	61	60	π	x

x	π	41	42	43	44	45	46	47	48	49	50	
0		0147	0128	0111	0097	0084	0072	0062	0053	0046	0039	8
1		0816	0742	0672	0608	0548	0493	0442	0395	0352	0312	7
2		1985	1880	1776	1672	1569	1469	1371	1275	1183	1094	6
3		2759	2723	2679	2627	2568	2503	2431	2355	2273	2187	5
4		2397	2465	2526	2580	2627	2665	2695	2717	2730	2734	4
5		1332	1428	1525	1622	1719	1816	1912	2006	2098	2187	3
6		0463	0517	0575	0637	0703	0774	0848	0926	1008	1094	2
7		0092	0107	0124	0143	0164	0188	0215	0244	0277	0312	1
8		0008	0010	0012	0014	0017	0020	0024	0028	0033	0039	0
		59	58	57	56	55	54	53	52	51	50	π	x

TABLE I Binomial distribution ($n = 9$, $n = 10$)

						$n = 9$						
x π	01	02	03	04	05	06	07	08	09	10		
0	9135	8337	7602	6925	6302	5730	5204	4722	4279	3874	9	
1	0830	1531	2116	2597	2985	3292	3525	3695	3809	3874	8	
2	0034	0125	0262	0433	0629	0840	1061	1285	1507	1722	7	
3	0001	0006	0019	0042	0077	0125	0186	0261	0348	0446	6	
4	0000	0000	0001	0003	0006	0012	0021	0034	0052	0074	5	
5	0000	0000	0000	0000	0000	0001	0002	0003	0005	0008	4	
6	0000	0000	0000	0000	0000	0000	0000	0000	0000	0001	3	
	99	98	97	96	95	94	93	92	91	90	π	x
x π	11	12	13	14	15	16	17	18	19	20		
0	3504	3165	2855	2573	2316	2082	1869	1676	1501	1342	9	
1	3897	3884	3840	3770	3679	3569	3446	3312	2169	3020	8	
2	1927	2119	2295	2455	2597	2720	2823	2908	2973	3020	7	
3	0556	0674	0800	0933	1069	1209	1349	1489	1627	1762	6	
4	0103	0138	0179	0228	0283	0345	0415	0490	0573	0661	5	
5	0013	0019	0027	0037	0050	0066	0085	0108	0134	0165	4	
6	0001	0002	0003	0004	0006	0008	0012	0016	0021	0028	3	
7	0000	0000	0000	0000	0000	0001	0001	0001	0002	0003	2	
	89	88	87	86	85	84	83	82	81	80	π	x
x π	21	22	23	24	25	26	27	28	29	30		
0	1199	1069	0952	0846	0751	0665	0589	0520	0458	0404	9	
1	2867	2713	2558	2404	2253	2104	1960	1820	1685	1556	8	
2	3049	3061	3056	3037	3003	2957	2899	2831	2754	2668	7	
3	1891	2014	2130	2238	2336	2424	2502	2569	2624	2668	6	
4	0754	0852	0954	1060	1168	1278	1388	1499	1608	1715	5	
5	0200	0240	0285	0335	0389	0449	0513	0583	0657	0735	4	
6	0036	0045	0057	0070	0087	0105	0127	0151	0179	0210	3	
7	0004	0005	0007	0010	0012	0016	0020	0025	0031	0039	2	
8	0000	0000	0001	0001	0001	0001	0002	0002	0003	0004	1	
	79	78	77	76	75	74	73	72	71	70	π	x
x π	31	32	33	34	35	36	37	38	39	40		
0	0355	0311	0272	0238	0207	0180	0156	0135	0117	0101	9	
1	1433	1317	1206	1102	1004	0912	0826	0747	0673	0605	8	
2	2576	2478	2376	2270	2162	2052	1941	1831	1721	1612	7	
3	2701	2721	2731	2729	2716	2693	2660	2618	2567	2508	6	
4	1820	1921	2017	2109	2194	2272	2344	2407	2462	2508	5	
5	0818	0904	0994	1086	1181	1278	1376	1475	1574	1672	4	
6	0245	0284	0326	0373	0424	0479	0539	0603	0671	0743	3	
7	0047	0057	0069	0082	0098	0116	0136	0158	0184	0212	2	
8	0005	0007	0008	0011	0013	0016	0020	0024	0029	0035	1	
9	0000	0000	0000	0001	0001	0001	0001	0002	0002	0003	0	
	69	68	67	66	65	64	63	62	61	60	π	x
x π	41	42	43	44	45	46	47	48	49	50		
0	0087	0074	0064	0054	0046	0039	0033	0028	0023	0020	9	
1	0542	0484	0431	0383	0339	0299	0263	0231	0202	0176	8	
2	1506	1402	1301	1204	1110	1020	0934	0853	0776	0703	7	
3	2442	2369	2291	2207	2119	2027	1933	1837	1739	1641	6	
4	2545	2573	2592	2601	2600	2590	2571	2543	2506	2461	5	
5	1769	1863	1955	2044	2128	2207	2280	2347	2408	2461	4	
6	0819	0900	0983	1070	1160	1253	1348	1445	1542	1641	3	
7	0244	0279	0318	0360	0407	0458	0512	0571	0635	0703	2	
8	0042	0051	0060	0071	0083	0097	0014	0132	0153	0176	1	
9	0003	0004	0005	0006	0008	0009	0011	0014	0016	0020	0	
	59	58	57	56	55	54	53	52	51	50	π	x

						$n = 10$						
x	π	01	02	03	04	05	06	07	08	09	10	
0		9044	8171	7374	6648	5987	5386	4840	4344	3894	3487	10
1		0914	1667	2281	2770	3151	3438	3643	3777	3851	3874	9
2		0042	0153	0317	0519	0746	0988	1234	1478	1714	1937	8
3		0001	0008	0026	0058	0105	0168	0248	0343	0452	0574	7
4		0000	0000	0001	0004	0010	0019	0033	0052	0078	0112	6
5		0000	0000	0000	0000	0001	0001	0003	0005	0009	0015	5
6		0000	0000	0000	0000	0000	0000	0000	0000	0001	0001	4
		99	98	97	96	95	94	93	92	91	90	π	x

x	π	11	12	13	14	15	16	17	18	19	20	
0		3118	2785	2484	2213	1969	1749	1552	1374	1216	1074	10
1		3854	3798	3712	3603	3474	3331	3178	3017	2852	2684	9
2		2143	2330	2496	2639	2759	2856	2929	2980	3010	3020	8
3		0706	0847	0995	1146	1298	1450	1600	1745	1883	2013	7
4		0153	0202	0260	0326	0401	0483	0573	0670	0773	0881	6
5		0023	0033	0047	0064	0085	0111	0141	0177	0218	0264	5
6		0002	0004	0006	0009	0012	0018	0024	0032	0043	0055	4
7		0000	0000	0000	0001	0001	0002	0003	0004	0006	0008	3
8		0000	0000	0000	0000	0000	0000	0000	0000	0001	0001	2
		89	88	87	86	85	84	83	82	81	80	π	x

x	π	21	22	23	24	25	26	27	28	29	30	
0		0947	0834	0733	0643	0563	0492	0430	0374	0326	0282	10
1		2517	2351	2188	2030	1877	1730	1590	1456	1330	1211	9
2		3011	2984	2942	2885	2816	2735	2646	2548	2444	2335	8
3		2134	2244	2343	2429	2503	2563	2609	2642	2662	2668	7
4		0993	1108	1225	1343	1460	1576	1689	1798	1903	2001	6
5		0317	0375	0439	0509	0584	0664	0750	0839	0933	1029	5
6		0070	0088	0109	0134	0162	0195	0231	0272	0317	0368	4
7		0011	0014	0019	0024	0031	0039	0049	0060	0074	0090	3
8		0001	0002	0002	0003	0004	0005	0007	0009	0011	0014	2
9		0000	0000	0000	0000	0000	0000	0001	0001	0001	0001	1
		79	78	77	76	75	74	73	72	71	70	π	x

x	π	31	32	33	34	35	36	37	38	39	40	
0		0245	0211	0182	0157	0135	0115	0098	0084	0071	0060	10
1		1099	0995	0898	0808	0725	0649	0578	0514	0456	0430	9
2		2222	2107	1990	1873	1757	1642	1529	1419	1312	1209	8
3		2662	2644	2614	2573	2522	2462	2394	2319	2237	2150	7
4		2093	2177	2253	2320	2377	2424	2461	2487	2503	2508	6
5		1128	1229	1332	1434	1536	1636	1734	1829	1920	2007	5
6		0422	0482	0547	0616	0689	0767	0849	0934	1023	1115	4
7		0108	0130	0154	0181	0212	0247	0285	0327	0374	0425	3
8		0018	0023	0028	0035	0043	0052	0063	0075	0090	0106	2
9		0002	0002	0003	0004	0005	0006	0008	0010	0013	0016	1
10		0000	0000	0000	0000	0000	0000	0000	0001	0001	0001	0
		69	68	67	66	65	64	63	62	61	60	π	x

x	π	41	42	43	44	45	46	47	48	49	50	
0		0051	0043	0036	0030	0025	0021	0017	0014	0012	0010	10
1		0355	0312	0273	0238	0207	0180	0155	0133	0114	0098	9
2		1111	1017	0927	0843	0763	0688	0619	0554	0494	0439	8
3		2058	1963	1865	1765	1665	1654	1464	1364	1267	1172	7
4		2503	2488	2462	2427	2384	2331	2271	2204	2130	2051	6
5		2087	2162	2229	2289	2340	2383	2417	2441	2456	2461	5
6		1209	1304	1401	1499	1596	1692	1786	1878	1966	2051	4
7		0480	0540	0604	0673	0746	0824	0905	0991	1080	1172	3
8		0125	0147	0171	0198	0229	0263	0301	0343	0389	0439	2
9		0019	0024	0029	0035	0042	0050	0059	0070	0083	0098	1
10		0001	0002	0002	0003	0003	0004	0005	0006	0008	0010	0
		59	58	57	56	55	54	53	52	51	50	π	x

TABLE I Binomial distribution ($n = 20$)

$n = 20$

x π	01	02	03	04	05	06	07	08	09	10	
0	8179	6676	5438	4420	3585	2901	2342	1887	1516	1216	20
1	1652	2725	3364	3683	3774	3703	3526	3282	3000	2702	19
2	0159	0528	0988	1458	1887	2246	2521	2711	2828	2852	18
3	0010	0065	0183	0364	0596	0860	1139	1414	1672	1901	17
4	0000	0006	0024	0065	0133	0233	0364	0523	0703	0898	16
5	0000	0000	0002	0009	0022	0048	0088	0145	0222	0319	15
6	0000	0000	0000	0001	0003	0008	0017	0032	0055	0089	14
7	0000	0000	0000	0000	0000	0001	0002	0005	0011	0020	13
8	0000	0000	0000	0000	0000	0000	0000	0001	0002	0004	12
9	0000	0000	0000	0000	0000	0000	0000	0000	0000	0001	11
	99	98	97	96	95	94	93	92	91	90	π x

x π	11	12	13	14	15	16	17	18	19	20	
0	0972	0776	0617	0490	0388	0306	0241	0189	0148	0115	20
1	2403	2115	1844	1595	1368	1165	0986	0829	0693	0576	19
2	2822	2740	2618	2466	2293	2109	1919	1730	1545	1369	18
3	2093	2242	2347	2409	2428	2410	2358	2278	2175	2054	17
4	1099	1299	1491	1666	1821	1951	2053	2125	2168	2182	16
5	0435	0567	0713	0868	1028	1189	1345	1493	1627	1746	15
6	0134	0193	0266	0353	0454	0566	0689	0819	0954	1091	14
7	0033	0053	0080	0115	0160	0216	0282	0360	0448	0545	13
8	0007	0012	0019	0030	0046	0067	0094	0128	0171	0222	12
9	0001	0002	0004	0007	0011	0017	0026	0038	0053	0074	11
10	0000	0000	0001	0001	0002	0004	0006	0009	0014	0020	10
11	0000	0000	0000	0000	0000	0001	0001	0002	0003	0005	9
12	0000	0000	0000	0000	0000	0000	0000	0000	0001	0001	8
	89	88	87	86	85	84	83	82	81	80	π x

x π	21	22	23	24	25	26	27	28	29	30	
0	0090	0069	0054	0041	0032	0024	0016	0014	0011	0008	20
1	0477	0392	0321	0261	0211	0170	0137	0109	0087	0068	19
2	1204	1050	0910	0783	0669	0569	0480	0403	0336	0278	18
3	1920	1777	1631	1484	1339	1199	1065	0940	0823	0716	17
4	2169	2131	2070	1991	1897	1790	1675	1553	1429	1304	16
5	1845	1923	1979	2012	2023	2013	1982	1933	1868	1789	15
6	1226	1356	1478	1589	1686	1768	1833	1879	1907	1916	14
7	0652	0765	0883	1003	1124	1242	1356	1462	1558	1643	13
8	0282	0351	0429	0515	0609	0709	0815	0924	1034	1144	12
9	0100	0132	0171	0217	0271	0332	0402	0479	0563	0654	11
10	0029	0041	0056	0075	0099	0128	0163	0205	0253	0308	10
11	0007	0010	0015	0022	0030	0041	0055	0072	0094	0120	9
12	0001	0002	0003	0005	0008	0011	0015	0021	0029	0039	8
13	0000	0000	0001	0001	0002	0002	0003	0005	0007	0010	7
14	0000	0000	0000	0000	0000	0000	0001	0001	0001	0002	6
	79	78	77	76	75	74	73	72	71	70	π x

x	π	31	32	33	34	35	36	37	38	39	40	
0		0006	0004	0003	0002	0002	0001	0001	0001	0001	0000	20
1		0054	0042	0033	0025	0020	0015	0011	0009	0007	0005	19
2		0229	0188	0153	0124	0100	0080	0064	0050	0040	0031	18
3		0619	0531	0453	0383	0323	0270	0224	0185	0152	0123	17
4		1181	1062	0947	0839	0738	0645	0559	0482	0412	0350	16
5		1698	1599	1493	1384	1272	1161	1051	0945	0843	0746	15
6		1907	1881	1839	1782	1712	1632	1543	1447	1347	1244	14
7		1714	1770	1811	1836	1844	1836	1812	1774	1722	1659	13
8		1251	1354	1450	1537	1614	1678	1730	1767	1790	1797	12
9		0750	0849	0952	1056	1158	1259	1354	1444	1526	1597	11
10		0370	0440	0516	0598	0686	0779	0875	0974	1073	1171	10
11		0151	1188	0231	0280	0336	0398	0467	0542	0624	0710	9
12		0051	0066	0085	0108	0136	0168	0206	0249	0299	0355	8
13		0014	0019	0026	0034	0045	0058	0074	0094	0118	0146	7
14		0003	0005	0006	0009	0012	0016	0022	0029	0038	0049	6
15		0001	0001	0001	0002	0003	0004	0005	0007	0010	0013	5
16		0000	0000	0000	0000	0000	0001	0001	0001	0002	0003	4
		69	68	67	66	65	64	63	62	61	60	π x

x	π	41	42	43	44	45	46	47	48	49	50	
1		0004	0003	0002	0001	0001	0001	0001	0000	0000	0000	19
2		0024	0018	0014	0011	0008	0006	0005	0003	0002	0002	18
3		0100	0080	0064	0051	0040	0031	0024	0019	0014	0011	17
4		0295	0247	0206	0170	0139	0113	0092	0074	0059	0046	16
5		0656	0573	0496	0427	0365	0309	0260	0217	0180	0148	15
6		1140	1037	0936	0839	0746	0658	0577	0501	0432	0370	14
7		1585	1502	1413	1318	1221	1122	1023	0925	0830	0739	13
8		1790	1768	1732	1683	1623	1553	1474	1388	1296	1201	12
9		1658	1707	1742	1763	1771	1763	1742	1708	1661	1602	11
10		1268	1359	1446	1524	1593	1652	1700	1734	1755	1762	10
11		0801	0895	0991	1089	1185	1280	1370	1455	1533	1602	9
12		0417	0486	0561	0642	0727	0818	0911	1007	1105	1201	8
13		0178	0217	0260	0310	0366	0429	0497	0572	0653	0739	7
14		0062	0078	0098	0122	0150	0183	0221	0264	0314	0370	6
15		0017	0023	0030	0038	0049	0062	0078	0098	0121	0148	5
16		0004	0005	0007	0009	0013	0017	0022	0028	0036	0046	4
17		0001	0001	0001	0002	0002	0003	0005	0006	0008	0011	3
18		0000	0000	0000	0000	0000	0000	0001	0001	0001	0002	2
		59	58	57	56	55	54	53	52	51	50	π x

TABLE I Binomial distribution (n = 50)

n = 50

x π	01	02	03	04	05	06	07	08	09	10	
0	6050	3642	2181	1299	0769	0453	0266	0155	0090	0052	50
1	3056	3716	3372	2706	2025	1447	0999	0672	0443	0286	49
2	0756	1858	2555	2762	2611	2262	1843	1433	1073	0779	48
3	0122	0607	1264	1842	2199	2311	2219	1993	1698	1386	47
4	0015	0145	0459	0902	1360	1733	1963	2037	1973	1809	46
5	0001	0027	0131	0346	0658	1018	1359	1629	1795	1849	45
6	0000	0004	0030	0108	0260	0487	0767	1063	1332	1541	44
7	0000	0001	0006	0028	0086	0195	0363	0581	0828	1076	43
8	0000	0000	0001	0006	0024	0067	0147	0271	0440	0643	42
9	0000	0000	0000	0001	0006	0020	0052	0110	0203	0333	41
10	0000	0000	0000	0000	0001	0005	0016	0039	0082	0152	40
11	0000	0000	0000	0000	0000	0001	0004	0012	0030	0061	39
12	0000	0000	0000	0000	0000	0000	0001	0004	0010	0022	38
13	0000	0000	0000	0000	0000	0000	0000	0001	0003	0007	37
14	0000	0000	0000	0000	0000	0000	0000	0000	0001	0002	36
15	0000	0000	0000	0000	0000	0000	0000	0000	0000	0001	35
	99	98	97	96	95	94	93	92	91	90	π x

x π	11	12	13	14	15	16	17	18	19	20	
0	0029	0017	0009	0005	0003	0002	0001	0000	0000	0000	50
1	0182	0114	0071	0043	0026	0016	0009	0005	0003	0002	49
2	0552	0382	0259	0172	0113	0073	0046	0029	0018	0011	48
3	1091	0833	0619	0449	0319	0222	0151	0102	0067	0044	47
4	1584	1334	1086	0858	0661	0496	0364	0262	0185	0128	46
5	1801	1674	1493	1286	1072	0869	0687	0530	0400	0295	45
6	1670	1712	1674	1570	1419	1242	1055	0872	0703	0554	44
7	1297	1467	1572	1606	1575	1487	1358	1203	1037	0870	43
8	0862	1075	1262	1406	1493	1523	1495	1420	1307	1169	42
9	0497	0684	0880	1068	1230	1353	1429	1454	1431	1364	41
10	0252	0383	0539	0713	0890	1057	1200	1309	1376	1398	40
11	0113	0190	0293	0422	0571	0732	0894	1045	1174	1271	39
12	0045	0084	0142	0223	0328	0453	0595	0745	0895	1033	38
13	0016	0034	0062	0106	0169	0252	0356	0478	0613	0755	37
14	0005	0012	0025	0046	0079	0127	0193	0277	0380	0499	36
15	0002	0004	0009	0018	0033	0058	0095	0146	0214	0299	35
16	0000	0001	0003	0006	0013	0024	0042	0070	0110	0164	34
17	0000	0000	0001	0002	0005	0009	0017	0031	0052	0082	33
18	0000	0000	0000	0001	0001	0003	0007	0012	0022	0037	32
19	0000	0000	0000	0000	0000	0001	0002	0005	0009	0016	31
20	0000	0000	0000	0000	0000	0000	0001	0002	0003	0006	30
21	0000	0000	0000	0000	0000	0000	0000	0000	0001	0002	29
22	0000	0000	0000	0000	0000	0000	0000	0000	0000	0001	28
	89	88	87	86	85	84	83	82	81	80	π x

x	π	21	22	23	24	25	26	27	28	29	30	
1		0001	0001	0000	0000	0000	0000	0000	0000	0000	0000	49
2		0007	0004	0002	0001	0001	0000	0000	0000	0000	0000	48
3		0028	0018	0011	0007	0004	0002	0001	0001	0000	0000	47
4		0088	0059	0039	0025	0016	0010	0006	0004	0002	0001	46
5		0214	0152	0106	0073	0049	0033	0021	0014	0009	0006	45
6		0427	0322	0238	0173	0123	0087	0060	0040	0027	0018	44
7		0713	0571	0447	0344	0259	0191	0139	0099	0069	0048	43
8		1019	0865	0718	0583	0463	0361	0276	0207	0152	0110	42
9		1263	1139	1001	0859	0721	0592	0476	0375	0290	0220	41
10		1377	1317	1226	1113	0985	0852	0721	0598	0485	0386	40
11		1331	1351	1332	1278	1194	1089	0970	0845	0721	0602	39
12		1150	1238	1293	1311	1294	1244	1166	1068	0957	0838	38
13		0894	1021	1129	1210	1261	1277	1261	1215	1142	1050	37
14		0628	0761	0891	1010	1110	1186	1233	1248	1233	1189	36
15		0400	0515	0639	0766	0888	1000	1094	1165	1209	1223	35
16		0233	0318	0417	0529	0648	0769	0885	0991	1080	1147	34
17		0124	0179	0249	0334	0432	0540	0655	0771	0882	0983	33
18		0060	0093	0137	0193	0264	0348	0444	0550	0661	0772	32
19		0027	0044	0069	0103	0148	0206	0277	0360	0454	0558	31
20		0011	0019	0032	0050	0077	0112	0159	0217	0288	0370	30
21		0004	0008	0014	0023	0036	0056	0084	0121	0168	0227	29
22		0001	0003	0005	0009	0016	0026	0041	0062	0090	0128	28
23		0000	0001	0002	0004	0006	0011	0018	0029	0045	0067	27
24		0000	0000	0001	0001	0002	0004	0008	0013	0021	0032	26
25		0000	0000	0000	0000	0001	0002	0003	0005	0009	0014	25
26		0000	0000	0000	0000	0000	0001	0001	0002	0003	0006	24
27		0000	0000	0000	0000	0000	0000	0000	0001	0001	0002	23
28		0000	0000	0000	0000	0000	0000	0000	0000	0000	0001	22
		79	78	77	76	75	74	73	72	71	70	π	x

TABLE I   Binomial distribution ($n = 50$, cont.)

					$n = 50$						

x π	31	32	33	34	35	36	37	38	39	40	
4	0001	0000	0000	0000	0000	0000	0000	0000	0000	0000	46
5	0003	0002	0001	0001	0000	0000	0000	0000	0000	0000	45
6	0011	0007	0005	0003	0002	0001	0001	0000	0000	0000	44
7	0032	0022	0014	0009	0006	0004	0002	0001	0001	0000	43
8	0078	0055	0037	0025	0017	0011	0007	0004	0003	0002	42
9	0164	0120	0086	0061	0042	0029	0019	0013	0008	0005	41
10	0301	0231	0174	0128	0093	0066	0046	0032	0022	0014	40
11	0493	0395	0311	0240	0182	0136	0099	0071	0050	0035	39
12	0719	0604	0498	0402	0319	0248	0189	0142	0105	0076	38
13	0944	0831	0717	0606	0502	0408	0325	0255	0195	0147	37
14	1121	1034	0933	0825	0714	0607	0505	0412	0330	0260	36
15	1209	1168	1103	1020	0923	0819	0712	0606	0507	0415	35
16	1188	1202	1189	1149	1088	1008	0914	0813	0709	0606	34
17	1068	1132	1171	1184	1171	1133	1074	0997	0906	0808	33
18	0880	0976	1057	1118	1156	1169	1156	1120	1062	0987	32
19	0666	0774	0877	0970	1048	1107	1144	1156	1144	1109	31
20	0463	0564	0670	0775	0875	0956	1041	1098	1134	1146	30
21	0297	0379	0471	0570	0673	0776	0874	0962	1035	1091	29
22	0176	0235	0306	0387	0478	0575	0676	0777	0873	0959	28
23	0096	0135	0183	0243	0313	0394	0484	0580	0679	0778	27
24	0049	0071	0102	0141	0190	0249	0319	0400	0489	0584	26
25	0023	0035	0052	0075	0106	0146	0195	0255	0325	0405	25
26	0010	0016	0025	0037	0055	0079	0110	0150	0200	0259	24
27	0004	0007	0011	0017	0026	0039	0058	0082	0113	0154	23
28	0001	0003	0004	0007	0012	0018	0028	0041	0060	0084	22
29	0000	0001	0002	0003	0005	0008	0012	0019	0029	0043	21
30	0000	0000	0001	0001	0002	0003	0005	0008	0013	0020	20
31	0000	0000	0000	0000	0001	0001	0002	0003	0005	0009	19
32	0000	0000	0000	0000	0000	0000	0001	0001	0002	0003	18
33	0000	0000	0000	0000	0000	0000	0000	0000	0001	0001	17
	69	68	67	66	65	64	63	62	61	60	π x

		n = 50								
x π	41	42	43	44	45	46	47	48	49	50	
8	0001	0001	0000	0000	0000	0000	0000	0000	0000	0000	42
9	0003	0002	0001	0001	0000	0000	0000	0000	0000	0000	41
10	0009	0006	0004	0002	0001	0001	0001	0000	0000	0000	40
11	0024	0016	0010	0007	0004	0003	0002	0001	0001	0000	39
12	0054	0037	0026	0017	0011	0007	0005	0003	0002	0001	38
13	0109	0079	0057	0040	0027	0018	0012	0008	0005	0003	37
14	0200	0152	0113	0082	0059	0041	0029	0019	0013	0008	36
15	0334	0264	0204	0155	0116	0085	0061	0043	0030	0020	35
16	0508	0418	0337	0267	0207	0158	0118	0086	0062	0044	34
17	0706	0605	0508	0419	0339	0269	0209	0159	0119	0087	33
18	0899	0803	0703	0604	0508	0420	0340	0270	0210	0160	32
19	1053	0979	0893	0799	0700	0602	0507	0419	0340	0270	31
20	1134	1099	1044	0973	0588	0795	0697	0600	0506	0419	30
21	1126	1137	1126	1092	1030	0967	0884	0791	0695	0598	29
22	1031	1086	1119	1131	1119	1086	1033	0963	0880	0788	28
23	0872	0957	1028	1082	1115	1126	1115	1082	1029	0960	27
24	0682	0780	0872	0956	1026	1079	1112	1124	1112	1080	26
25	0493	0587	0684	0781	0873	0956	1026	1079	1112	1123	25
26	0329	0409	0497	0590	0687	0783	0875	0957	1027	1080	24
27	0203	0263	0333	0412	0500	0593	0690	0786	0877	0960	23
28	0116	0157	0206	0266	0336	0415	0502	0596	0692	0788	22
29	0061	0086	0118	0159	0208	0268	0338	0417	0504	0598	21
30	0030	0044	0062	0087	0119	0160	0210	0270	0339	0419	20
31	0013	0020	0030	0044	0063	0088	0120	0161	0210	0270	19
32	0006	0009	0014	0021	0031	0044	0063	0088	0120	0160	18
33	0002	0003	0006	0009	0014	0021	0031	0044	0063	0087	17
34	0001	0001	0002	0003	0006	0009	0014	0020	0030	0044	16
35	0000	0000	0001	0001	0002	0003	0005	0009	0013	0020	15
36	0000	0000	0000	0000	0001	0001	0002	0003	0005	0006	14
37	0000	0000	0000	0000	0000	0000	0001	0001	0002	0003	13
38	0000	0000	0000	0000	0000	0000	0000	0000	0001	0001	12
	59	58	57	56	55	54	53	52	51	50	π x

TABLE | Binomial distribution ($n = 100$)

					$n = 100$						
x π	01	02	03	04	05	06	07	08	09	10	
0	3660	1326	0476	0169	0059	0021	0007	0002	0001	0000	100
1	3697	2707	1471	0703	0312	0131	0053	0021	0008	0003	99
2	1849	2734	2252	1450	0812	0414	0198	0090	0039	0016	98
3	0610	1823	2275	1973	1396	0864	0486	0254	0125	0059	97
4	0149	0902	1706	1994	1781	1338	0888	0536	0301	0159	96
5	0029	0353	1013	1595	1800	1639	1283	0895	0571	0339	95
6	0005	0114	0496	1052	1500	1657	1529	1233	0895	0596	94
7	0001	0031	0206	0589	1060	1420	1545	1440	1188	0889	93
8	0000	0007	0074	0285	0649	1054	1352	1455	1366	1148	92
9	0000	0002	0023	0121	0349	0687	1040	1293	1381	1304	91
10	0000	0000	0007	0046	0167	0399	0712	1024	1243	1319	90
11	0000	0000	0002	0016	0072	0209	0439	0728	1006	1199	89
12	0000	0000	0000	0005	0028	0099	0245	0470	0738	0988	88
13	0000	0000	0000	0001	0010	0043	0125	0276	0494	0743	87
14	0000	0000	0000	0000	0003	0017	0058	0149	0304	0513	86
15	0000	0000	0000	0000	0001	0006	0025	0074	0172	0327	85
16	0000	0000	0000	0000	0000	0002	0010	0034	0090	0193	84
17	0000	0000	0000	0000	0000	0001	0004	0015	0044	0106	83
18	0000	0000	0000	0000	0000	0000	0001	0006	0020	0054	82
19	0000	0000	0000	0000	0000	0000	0000	0002	0009	0026	81
20	0000	0000	0000	0000	0000	0000	0000	0001	0003	0012	80
21	0000	0000	0000	0000	0000	0000	0000	0000	0001	0005	79
22	0000	0000	0000	0000	0000	0000	0000	0000	0000	0002	78
23	0000	0000	0000	0000	0000	0000	0000	0000	0000	0001	77
	99	98	97	96	95	94	93	92	91	90	π x

x	π	11	12	13	14	15	16	17	18	19	20	
						n = 100						
1		0001	0000	0000	0000	0000	0000	0000	0000	0000	0000	99
2		0007	0003	0001	0000	0000	0000	0000	0000	0000	0000	98
3		0027	0012	0005	0002	0001	0000	0000	0000	0000	0000	97
4		0080	0038	0018	0008	0003	0001	0001	0000	0000	0000	96
5		0189	0100	0050	0024	0011	0005	0002	0001	0000	0000	95
6		0369	0215	0119	0063	0031	0015	0007	0003	0001	0001	94
7		0613	0394	0238	0137	0075	0039	0020	0009	0004	0002	93
8		0881	0625	0414	0259	0153	0086	0047	0024	0012	0006	92
9		1112	0871	0632	0430	0276	0168	0098	0054	0029	0015	91
10		1251	1080	0860	0637	0444	0292	0182	0108	0062	0034	90
11		1265	1205	1051	0849	0640	0454	0305	0194	0118	0069	89
12		1160	1219	1165	1025	0838	0642	0463	0316	0206	0128	88
13		0970	1125	1179	1130	1001	0827	0642	0470	0327	0216	87
14		0745	0954	1094	1143	1098	0979	0817	0641	0476	0335	86
15		0528	0745	0938	1067	1111	1070	0960	0807	0640	0481	85
16		0347	0540	0744	0922	1041	1082	1044	0941	0798	0638	84
17		1212	0364	0549	0742	0908	1019	1057	1021	0924	0789	83
18		0121	0229	0379	0557	0739	0895	0998	1033	1000	0909	82
19		0064	0135	0244	0391	0563	0736	0882	0979	1012	0981	81
20		0032	0074	0148	0258	0402	0567	0732	0870	0962	0993	80
21		0015	0039	0084	0160	0270	0412	0571	0728	0859	0946	79
22		0007	0019	0045	0094	0171	0282	0420	0574	0724	0849	78
23		0003	0009	0023	0052	0103	0182	0292	0427	0576	0720	77
24		0001	0004	0011	0027	0058	0111	0192	0301	0433	0577	76
25		0000	0002	0005	0013	0031	0064	0119	0201	0309	0439	75
26		0000	0001	0002	0006	0016	0035	0071	0127	0209	0317	74
27		0000	0000	0001	0003	0008	0018	0040	0076	0134	0217	73
28		0000	0000	0000	0001	0004	0009	0021	0044	0082	0141	72
29		0000	0000	0000	0000	0002	0004	0011	0024	0048	0088	71
30		0000	0000	0000	0000	0001	0002	0005	0012	0027	0052	70
31		0000	0000	0000	0000	0000	0001	0002	0006	0014	0029	69
32		0000	0000	0000	0000	0000	0000	0001	0003	0007	0016	68
33		0000	0000	0000	0000	0000	0000	0000	0001	0003	0008	67
34		0000	0000	0000	0000	0000	0000	0000	0001	0002	0004	66
35		0000	0000	0000	0000	0000	0000	0000	0000	0001	0002	65
36		0000	0000	0000	0000	0000	0000	0000	0000	0000	0001	64
		89	88	87	86	85	84	83	82	81	80	π x

TABLE I **Binomial distribution ($n = 100$, cont.)**

$n = 100$

x π	21	22	23	24	25	26	27	28	29	30	
7	0001	0000	0000	0000	0000	0000	0000	0000	0000	0000	93
8	0003	0001	0001	0000	0000	0000	0000	0000	0000	0000	92
9	0007	0003	0002	0001	0000	0000	0000	0000	0000	0000	91
10	0018	0009	0004	0002	0001	0000	0000	0000	0000	0000	90
11	0038	0021	0011	0005	0003	0001	0001	0000	0000	0000	89
12	0076	0043	0024	0012	0006	0003	0001	0001	0000	0000	88
13	0136	0082	0048	0027	0014	0007	0004	0002	0001	0000	87
14	0225	0144	0089	0052	0030	0016	0009	0004	0002	0001	86
15	1343	0233	0152	0095	0057	0033	0018	0010	0005	0002	85
16	0484	0350	0241	0159	0100	0061	0035	0020	0011	0006	84
17	0636	0487	0356	0248	0165	0106	0065	0038	0022	0012	83
18	0780	0634	0490	0361	0254	0171	0111	0069	0041	0024	82
19	0895	0772	0631	0492	0365	0259	0177	0115	0072	0044	81
20	0963	0881	0764	0629	0493	0369	0264	0182	0120	0076	80
21	0975	0947	0869	0756	0626	0494	0373	0269	0186	0124	79
22	0931	0959	0932	0858	0749	0623	0495	0376	0273	0190	78
23	0839	0917	0944	0919	0847	0743	0621	0495	0378	0277	77
24	0716	0830	0905	0931	0906	0837	0736	0618	0496	0380	76
25	0578	0712	0822	0893	0918	0894	0828	0731	0615	0496	75
26	0444	0579	0708	0814	0883	0906	0883	0819	0725	0613	74
27	0323	0448	0580	0704	0806	0873	0896	0873	0812	0720	73
28	0224	0329	0451	0580	0701	0799	0864	0886	0864	0804	72
29	0148	0231	0335	0455	0580	0697	0793	0855	0876	0856	71
30	0093	0154	0237	0340	0458	0580	0694	0787	0847	0868	70
31	0056	0098	0160	0242	0344	0460	0580	0691	0781	0840	69
32	0032	0060	0103	0165	0248	0349	0462	0579	0688	0776	68
33	0018	0035	0063	0107	0170	0252	0352	0464	0579	0685	67
34	0009	0019	0037	0067	0112	0175	0257	0356	0466	0579	66
35	0005	0010	0021	0040	0070	0116	0179	0261	0359	0468	65
36	0002	0005	0011	0023	0042	0073	0120	0183	0265	0362	64
37	0001	0003	0006	0012	0024	0045	0077	0123	0187	0268	63
38	0000	0001	0003	0006	0013	0026	0047	0079	0127	0191	62
39	0000	0001	0001	0003	0007	0015	0028	0049	0082	0130	61
40	0000	0000	0001	0002	0004	0008	0016	0029	0051	0085	60
41	0000	0000	0000	0001	0002	0004	0008	0017	0031	0053	59
42	0000	0000	0000	0000	0001	0002	0004	0009	0018	0032	58
43	0000	0000	0000	0000	0000	0001	0002	0005	0010	0019	57
44	0000	0000	0000	0000	0000	0000	0001	0002	0005	0010	56
45	0000	0000	0000	0000	0000	0000	0000	0001	0003	0005	55
46	0000	0000	0000	0000	0000	0000	0000	0001	0001	0003	54
47	0000	0000	0000	0000	0000	0000	0000	0000	0001	0001	53
48	0000	0000	0000	0000	0000	0000	0000	0000	0000	0001	52
	79	78	77	76	75	74	73	72	71	70	π x

x	π	31	32	33	34	35	36	37	38	39	40	
15		0001	0001	0000	0000	0000	0000	0000	0000	0000	0000	85
16		0003	0001	0001	0000	0000	0000	0000	0000	0000	0000	84
17		0006	0003	0002	0001	0000	0000	0000	0000	0000	0000	83
18		0013	0007	0004	0002	0001	0000	0000	0000	0000	0000	82
19		0025	0014	0008	0004	0002	0001	0000	0000	0000	0000	81
20		0046	0027	0015	0008	0004	0002	0001	0001	0000	0000	80
21		0079	0049	0029	0016	0009	0005	0002	0001	0001	0000	79
22		0127	0082	0051	0030	0017	0010	0005	0003	0001	0001	78
23		0194	0131	0085	0053	0032	0018	0010	0006	0003	0001	77
24		0280	0198	0134	0088	0055	0033	0019	0011	0006	0003	76
25		0382	0283	0201	0137	0090	0057	0035	0020	0012	0006	75
26		0496	0384	0286	0204	0140	0092	0059	0036	0021	0012	74
27		0610	0495	0386	0288	0207	0143	0095	0060	0037	0022	73
28		0715	0608	0495	0387	0290	0209	0145	0097	0062	0038	72
29		0797	0710	0605	0495	0388	0292	0211	0147	0098	0063	71
30		0848	0791	0706	0603	0494	0389	0294	0213	0149	0100	70
31		0860	0840	0785	0702	0601	0494	0389	0295	0215	0151	69
32		0833	0853	0833	0779	0698	0599	0493	0390	0296	0217	68
33		0771	0827	0846	0827	0774	0694	0597	0493	0390	0297	67
34		0683	0767	0821	0840	0821	0769	0691	0595	0492	0391	66
35		0578	0680	0763	0816	0834	0816	0765	0688	0593	0491	65
36		0469	0578	0678	0759	0811	0829	0811	0761	0685	0591	64
37		0365	0471	0578	0676	0755	0806	0824	0807	0757	0682	63
38		0272	0367	0472	0577	0674	0752	0802	0820	0803	0754	62
39		0194	0275	0369	0473	0577	0672	0749	0799	0816	0799	61
40		0133	0197	0277	0372	0474	0577	0671	0746	0795	0812	60
41		0087	0136	0200	0280	0373	0475	0577	0670	0744	0792	59
42		0055	0090	0138	0203	0282	0375	0476	0576	0668	0742	58
43		0033	0057	0092	0141	0205	0285	0377	0477	0576	0667	57
44		0019	0035	0059	0094	0143	0207	0287	0378	0477	0576	56
45		0011	0020	0036	0060	0096	0045	0210	0289	0380	0478	55
46		0006	0011	0021	0037	0062	0098	0147	0211	0290	0381	54
47		0003	0006	0012	0022	0038	0063	0099	0149	0213	0292	53
48		0001	0003	0007	0012	0023	0039	0064	0101	0151	0215	52
49		0001	0002	0003	0007	0013	0023	0040	0066	0102	0152	51
50		0000	0001	0002	0004	0007	0013	0024	0041	0067	0103	50
51		0000	0000	0001	0002	0004	0007	0014	0025	0042	0068	49
52		0000	0000	0000	0001	0002	0004	0008	0014	0025	0042	48
53		0000	0000	0000	0000	0001	0002	0004	0008	0015	0026	47
54		0000	0000	0000	0000	0000	0001	0002	0004	0008	0015	46
55		0000	0000	0000	0000	0000	0000	0001	0002	0004	0008	45
56		0000	0000	0000	0000	0000	0000	0000	0001	0002	0004	44
57		0000	0000	0000	0000	0000	0000	0000	0001	0001	0002	43
58		0000	0000	0000	0000	0000	0000	0000	0000	0001	0001	42
59		0000	0000	0000	0000	0000	0000	0000	0000	0000	0001	41
		69	68	67	66	65	64	63	62	61	60	π x

TABLE I   **Binomial distribution ($n = 100$, cont.)**

	$n = 100$										
x π	41	42	43	44	45	46	47	48	49	50	
23	0001	0000	0000	0000	0000	0000	0000	0000	0000	0000	77
24	0002	0001	0000	0000	0000	0000	0000	0000	0000	0000	76
25	0003	0002	0001	0000	0000	0000	0000	0000	0000	0000	75
26	0007	0003	0002	0001	0000	0000	0000	0000	0000	0000	74
27	0013	0007	0004	0002	0001	0000	0000	0000	0000	0000	73
28	0023	0013	0007	0004	0002	0001	0000	0000	0000	0000	72
29	0039	0024	0014	0008	0004	0002	0001	0000	0000	0000	71
30	0065	0040	0024	0014	0008	0004	0002	0001	0001	0000	70
31	0102	0066	0041	0025	0014	0008	0004	0002	0001	0001	69
32	0152	0103	0067	0042	0025	0015	0008	0004	0002	0001	68
33	0218	0154	0104	0068	0043	0026	0015	0008	0004	0002	67
34	0298	0219	0155	0105	0069	0043	0026	0015	0009	0005	66
35	0391	0299	0220	0156	0106	0069	0044	0026	0015	0009	65
36	0491	0391	0300	0221	0157	0107	0070	0044	0027	0016	64
37	0590	0490	0391	0300	0222	0157	0107	0070	0044	0027	63
38	0680	0588	0489	0391	0301	0222	0158	0108	0071	0045	62
39	0751	0677	0587	0489	0391	0301	0223	0158	0108	0071	61
40	0796	0748	0675	0586	0488	0391	0301	0223	0159	0108	60
41	0809	0793	0745	0673	0584	0487	0391	0301	0223	0159	59
42	0790	0806	0790	0743	0672	0583	0487	0390	0301	0223	58
43	0740	0787	0804	0788	0741	0670	0582	0486	0390	0301	57
44	0666	0739	0785	0802	0786	0739	0669	0581	0485	0390	56
45	0576	0666	0737	0784	0800	0784	0738	0668	0580	0485	55
46	0479	0576	0665	0736	0782	0798	0783	0737	0667	0580	54
47	0382	0480	0576	0065	0736	0781	0797	0781	0736	0666	53
	59	58	57	56	55	54	53	52	51	50	π x

					n = 100						
x π	41	42	43	44	45	46	47	48	49	50	
48	0293	0383	0480	0577	0665	0735	0781	0797	0781	0735	52
49	0216	0295	0384	0481	0577	0664	0735	0780	0796	0780	51
50	0153	0218	0296	0385	0482	0577	0665	0735	0780	0796	50
51	0104	0155	0219	0297	0386	0482	0578	0665	0735	0780	49
52	0068	0105	0156	0220	0298	0387	0483	0578	0665	0735	48
53	0043	0069	0106	0156	0221	0299	0388	0483	0579	0666	47
54	0026	0044	0070	0107	0157	0221	0299	0388	0484	0580	46
55	0015	0026	0044	0070	0108	0158	0222	0300	0389	0485	45
56	0008	0015	0027	0044	0071	0108	0158	0222	0300	0390	44
57	0005	0009	0016	0027	0045	0071	0108	0158	0223	0301	43
58	0002	0005	0009	0016	0027	0045	0071	0108	0159	0223	42
59	0001	0002	0005	0009	0016	0027	0045	0071	0109	0159	41
60	0001	0001	0002	0005	0009	0016	0027	0045	0071	0108	40
61	0000	0001	0001	0002	0005	0009	0016	0027	0045	0071	39
62	0000	0000	0001	0001	0002	0005	0009	0016	0027	0045	38
63	0000	0000	0000	0001	0001	0002	0005	0009	0016	0027	37
64	0000	0000	0000	0000	0001	0001	0002	0005	0009	0016	36
65	0000	0000	0000	0000	0000	0001	0001	0002	0005	0009	35
66	0000	0000	0000	0000	0000	0000	0001	0001	0002	0005	34
67	0000	0000	0000	0000	0000	0000	0000	0001	0001	0002	33
68	0000	0000	0000	0000	0000	0000	0000	0000	0001	0001	32
69	0000	0000	0000	0000	0000	0000	0000	0000	0000	0001	31
	59	58	57	56	55	54	53	52	51	50	π x

From Robert O. Schlaifer, *Analysis of Decisions Under Uncertainty* (Preliminary Edition, Volume II). New York: McGraw-Hill Book Company, 1967. Reprinted by permission of the Harvard Business School. Copyright © 1967 by the President and Fellows of Harvard College.

Table II gives the probability of exactly x successes, for various values of λ, as defined by the Poisson mass function.

$$P(x) = \frac{e^{-\lambda}\lambda^x}{x!}$$

Examples: If $\lambda = 1.5$, then $P(2) = 0.2510$, $P(3) = 0.1255$.

TABLE II **Poisson distribution ($\lambda = 0.1$ to $\lambda = 4.0$)**

Poisson Probabilities

λ

x	0.1	0.2	0.3	0.4	0.5	0.6	0.7	0.8	0.9	1.0
0	.9048	.8187	.7408	.6703	.6065	.5488	.4966	.4493	.4066	.3679
1	.0905	.1637	.2222	.2681	.3033	.3293	.3476	.3595	.3659	.3679
2	.0045	.0164	.0333	.0536	.0758	.0988	.1217	.1438	.1647	.1839
3	.0002	.0011	.0033	.0072	.0126	.0198	.0284	.0383	.0494	.0613
4	.0000	.0001	.0002	.0007	.0016	.0030	.0050	.0077	.0111	.0153
5	.0000	.0000	.0000	.0001	.0002	.0004	.0007	.0012	.0020	.0031
6	.0000	.0000	.0000	.0000	.0000	.0000	.0001	.0002	.0003	.0005
7	.0000	.0000	.0000	.0000	.0000	.0000	.0000	.0000	.0000	.0001

λ

x	1.1	1.2	1.3	1.4	1.5	1.6	1.7	1.8	1.9	2.0
0	.3329	.3012	.2725	.2466	.2231	.2019	.1827	.1653	.1496	.1353
1	.3662	.3614	.3543	.3452	.3347	.3230	.3106	.2975	.2842	.2707
2	.2014	.2169	.2303	.2417	.2510	.2584	.2640	.2678	.2700	.2707
3	.0738	.0867	.0998	.1128	.1255	.1378	.1496	.1607	.1710	.1804
4	.0203	.0260	.0324	.0395	.0471	.0551	.0636	.0723	.0812	.0902
5	.0045	.0062	.0084	.0111	.0141	.0176	.0216	.0260	.0309	.0361
6	.0008	.0012	.0018	.0026	.0035	.0047	.0061	.0078	.0098	.0120
7	.0001	.0002	.0003	.0005	.0008	.0011	.0015	.0020	.0027	.0034
8	.0000	.0000	.0001	.0001	.0001	.0002	.0003	.0005	.0006	.0009
9	.0000	.0000	.0000	.0000	.0000	.0000	.0001	.0001	.0001	.0002

	λ									
x	2.1	2.2	2.3	2.4	2.5	2.6	2.7	2.8	2.9	3.0
0	.1225	.1108	.1003	.0907	.0821	.0743	.0672	.0608	.0550	.0498
1	.2572	.2438	.2306	.2177	.2052	.1931	.1815	.1703	.1596	.1494
2	.2700	.2681	.2652	.2613	.2565	.2510	.2450	.2384	.2314	.2240
3	.1890	.1966	.2033	.2090	.2138	.2176	.2205	.2225	.2237	.2240
4	.0992	.1082	.1169	.1254	.1336	.1414	.1488	.1557	.1622	.1680
5	.0417	.0476	.0538	.0602	.0668	.0735	.0804	.0872	.0940	.1008
6	.0146	.0174	.0206	.0241	.0278	.0319	.0362	.0407	.0455	.0504
7	.0044	.0055	.0068	.0083	.0099	.0118	.0139	.0163	.0188	.0216
8	.0011	.0015	.0019	.0025	.0031	.0038	.0047	.0057	.0068	.0081
9	.0003	.0004	.0005	.0007	.0009	.0011	.0014	.0018	.0022	.0027
10	.0001	.0001	.0001	.0002	.0002	.0003	.0004	.0005	.0006	.0008
11	.0000	.0000	.0000	.0000	.0000	.0001	.0001	.0001	.0002	.0002
12	.0000	.0000	.0000	.0000	.0000	.0000	.0000	.0000	.0000	.0001

	λ									
x	3.1	3.2	3.3	3.4	3.5	3.6	3.7	3.8	3.9	4.0
0	.0450	.0408	.0369	.0334	.0302	.0273	.0247	.0224	.0202	.0183
1	.1397	.1304	.1217	.1135	.1057	.0984	.0915	.0850	.0789	.0733
2	.2165	.2087	.2008	.1929	.1850	.1771	.1692	.1615	.1539	.1465
3	.2237	.2226	.2209	.2186	.2158	.2125	.2087	.2046	.2001	.1954
4	.1734	.1781	.1823	.1858	.1888	.1912	.1931	.1944	.1951	.1954
5	.1075	.1140	.1203	.1264	.1322	.1377	.1429	.1477	.1522	.1563
6	.0555	.0608	.0662	.0716	.0771	.0826	.0881	.0936	.0989	.1042
7	.0246	.0278	.0312	.0348	.0385	.0425	.0466	.0508	.0551	.0595
8	.0095	.0111	.0129	.0148	.0169	.0191	.0215	.0241	.0269	.0298
9	.0033	.0040	.0047	.0056	.0066	.0076	.0089	.0102	.0116	.0132
10	.0010	.0013	.0016	.0019	.0023	.0028	.0033	.0039	.0045	.0053
11	.0003	.0004	.0005	.0006	.0007	.0009	.0011	.0013	.0016	.0019
12	.0001	.0001	.0001	.0002	.0002	.0003	.0003	.0004	.0005	.0006
13	.0000	.0000	.0000	.0000	.0001	.0001	.0001	.0001	.0002	.0002
14	.0000	.0000	.0000	.0000	.0000	.0000	.0000	.0000	.0000	.0001

TABLE II **Poisson distribution (λ = 4.1 to λ = 8.0)**

	λ									
x	4.1	4.2	4.3	4.4	4.5	4.6	4.7	4.8	4.9	5.0
0	.0166	.0150	.0136	.0123	.0111	.0101	.0091	.0082	.0074	.0067
1	.0679	.0630	.0583	.0540	.0500	.0462	.0427	.0395	.0365	.0337
2	.1393	.1323	.1254	.1188	.1125	.1063	.1005	.0948	.0894	.0842
3	.1904	.1852	.1798	.1743	.1687	.1631	.1574	.1517	.1460	.1404
4	.1951	.1944	.1933	.1917	.1898	.1875	.1849	.1820	.1789	.1755
5	.1600	.1633	.1662	.1687	.1708	.1725	.1738	.1747	.1753	.1755
6	.1093	.1143	.1191	.1237	.1281	.1323	.1362	.1398	.1432	.1462
7	.0640	.0686	.0732	.0778	.0824	.0869	.0914	.0959	.1002	.1044
8	.0328	.0360	.0393	.0428	.0463	.0500	.0537	.0575	.0614	.0653
9	.0150	.0168	.0188	.0209	.0232	.0255	.0280	.0307	.0334	.0363
10	.0061	.0071	.0081	.0092	.0104	.0118	.0132	.0147	.0164	.0181
11	.0023	.0027	.0032	.0037	.0043	.0049	.0056	.0064	.0073	.0082
12	.0008	.0009	.0011	.0014	.0016	.0019	.0022	.0026	.0030	.0034
13	.0002	.0003	.0004	.0005	.0006	.0007	.0008	.0009	.0011	.0013
14	.0001	.0001	.0001	.0001	.0002	.0002	.0003	.0003	.0004	.0005
15	.0000	.0000	.0000	.0000	.0001	.0001	.0001	.0001	.0001	.0002

	λ									
x	5.1	5.2	5.3	5.4	5.5	5.6	5.7	5.8	5.9	6.0
0	.0061	.0055	.0050	.0045	.0041	.0037	.0033	.0030	.0027	.0025
1	.0311	.0287	.0265	.0244	.0225	.0207	.0191	.0176	.0162	.0149
2	.0793	.0746	.0701	.0659	.0618	.0580	.0544	.0509	.0477	.0446
3	.1348	.1293	.1239	.1185	.1133	.1082	.1033	.0985	.0938	.0892
4	.1719	.1681	.1641	.1600	.1558	.1515	.1472	.1428	.1383	.1339
5	.1753	.1748	.1740	.1728	.1714	.1697	.1678	.1620	.1632	.1606
6	.1490	.1515	.1537	.1555	.1571	.1584	.1594	.1656	.1605	.1606
7	.1086	.1125	.1163	.1200	.1234	.1267	.1298	.1301	.1353	.1377
8	.0692	.0731	.0771	.0810	.0849	.0887	.0925	.0926	.0998	.1033
9	.0392	.0423	.0454	.0486	.0519	.0552	.0586	.0662	.0654	.0688
10	.0200	.0220	.0241	.0262	.0285	.0309	.0334	.0359	.0386	.0413
11	.0093	.0104	.0116	.0129	.0143	.0157	.0173	.0190	.0207	.0225
12	.0039	.0045	.0051	.0058	.0065	.0073	.0082	.0092	.0102	.0113
13	.0015	.0018	.0021	.0024	.0028	.0032	.0036	.0041	.0046	.0052
14	.0006	.0007	.0008	.0009	.0011	.0013	.0015	.0017	.0019	.0022
15	.0002	.0002	.0003	.0003	.0004	.0005	.0006	.0007	.0008	.0009
16	.0001	.0001	.0001	.0001	.0001	.0002	.0002	.0002	.0003	.0003
17	.0000	.0000	.0000	.0000	.0000	.0001	.0001	.0001	.0001	.0001

					λ				
x	6.1	6.2	6.3	6.4	6.5	6.6	6.7	6.8	6.9	7.0
0	.0022	.0020	.0018	.0017	.0015	.0014	.0012	.0011	.0010	.0009
1	.0137	.0126	.0116	.0106	.0098	.0090	.0082	.0076	.0070	.0064
2	.0417	.0390	.0364	.0340	.0318	.0296	.0276	.0258	.0240	.0223
3	.0848	.0806	.0765	.0726	.0688	.0652	.0617	.0584	.0552	.0521
4	.1294	.1249	.1205	.1162	.1118	.1076	.1034	.0992	.0952	.0912
5	.1579	.1549	.1519	.1487	.1454	.1420	.1385	.1349	.1314	.1277
6	.1605	.1601	.1595	.1586	.1575	.1562	.1546	.1529	.1511	.1490
7	.1399	.1418	.1435	.1450	.1462	.1472	.1480	.1486	.1489	.1490
8	.1066	.1099	.1130	.1160	.1188	.1215	.1240	.1263	.1284	.1304
9	.0723	.0757	.0791	.0825	.0858	.0891	.0923	.0954	.0985	.1014
10	.0441	.0469	.0498	.0528	.0558	.0588	.0618	.0649	.0679	.0710
11	.0245	.0265	.0285	.0307	.0330	.0353	.0377	.0401	.0426	.0452
12	.0124	.0137	.0150	.0164	.0179	.0194	.0210	.0227	.0245	.0264
13	.0058	.0065	.0073	.0081	.0089	.0098	.0108	.0119	.0130	.0142
14	.0025	.0029	.0033	.0037	.0041	.0046	.0052	.0058	.0064	.0071
15	.0010	.0012	.0014	.0016	.0018	.0020	.0023	.0026	.0029	.0033
16	.0004	.0005	.0005	.0006	.0007	.0008	.0010	.0011	.0013	.0014
17	.0001	.0002	.0002	.0002	.0003	.0003	.0004	.0004	.0005	.0006
18	.0000	.0001	.0001	.0001	.0001	.0001	.0001	.0002	.0002	.0002
19	.0000	.0000	.0000	.0000	.0000	.0000	.0000	.0001	.0001	.0001

					λ				
x	7.1	7.2	7.3	7.4	7.5	7.6	7.7	7.8	7.9	8.0
0	.0008	.0007	.0007	.0006	.0006	.0005	.0005	.0004	.0004	.0003
1	.0059	.0054	.0049	.0045	.0041	.0038	.0035	.0032	.0029	.0027
2	.0208	.0194	.0180	.0167	.0156	.0145	.0134	.0125	.0116	.0107
3	.0492	.0464	.0438	.0413	.0389	.0366	.0345	.0324	.0305	.0286
4	.0874	.0836	.0799	.0764	.0729	.0696	.0663	.0632	.0602	.0573
5	.1241	.1204	.1167	.1130	.1094	.1057	.1021	.0986	.0951	.0916
6	.1468	.1445	.1420	.1394	.1367	.1339	.1311	.1282	.1252	.1221
7	.1489	.1486	.1481	.1474	.1465	.1454	.1442	.1428	.1413	.1396
8	.1321	.1337	.1351	.1363	.1373	.1382	.1388	.1392	.1395	.1396
9	.1042	.1070	.1096	.1121	.1144	.1167	.1187	.1207	.1224	.1241
10	.0740	.0770	.0800	.0829	.0858	.0887	.0914	.0941	.0967	.0993
11	.0478	.0504	.0531	.0558	.0585	.0613	.0640	.0667	.0695	.0722
12	0.283	.0303	.0323	.0344	.0366	.0388	.0411	.0434	.0457	.0481
13	.0154	.0168	.0181	.0196	.0211	.0227	.0243	.0260	.0278	.0296
14	.0078	.0086	.0095	.0104	.0113	.0123	.0134	.0145	.0157	.0169
15	.0037	.0041	.0046	.0051	.0057	.0062	.0069	.0075	.0083	.0090
16	.0016	.0019	.0021	.0024	.0026	.0030	.0033	.0037	.0041	.0045
17	.0007	.0008	.0009	.0010	.0012	.0013	.0015	.0017	.0119	.0021
18	.0003	.0003	.0004	.0004	.0005	.0006	.0006	.0007	.0008	.0009
19	.0001	.0001	.0001	.0002	.0002	.0002	.0003	.0003	.0003	.0004
20	.0000	.0000	.0001	.0001	.0001	.0001	.0001	.0001	.0001	.0002
21	.0000	.0000	.0000	.0000	.0000	.0000	.0000	.0000	.0001	.0001

TABLE II Poisson distribution ($\lambda = 8.1$ to $\lambda = 20$)

					λ					
x	8.1	8.2	8.3	8.4	8.5	8.6	8.7	8.8	8.9	9.0
0	.0003	.0003	.0002	.0002	.0002	.0002	.0002	.0002	.0001	.0001
1	.0025	.0023	.0021	.0019	.0017	.0016	.0014	.0013	.0012	.0011
2	.0100	.0092	.0086	.0079	.0074	.0068	.0063	.0058	.0054	.0050
3	.0269	.0252	.0237	.0222	.0208	.0195	.0183	.0171	.0160	.0150
4	.0544	.0517	.0491	.0466	.0443	.0420	.0398	.0377	.0357	.0337
5	.0882	.0849	.0816	.0784	.0752	.0722	.0692	.0663	.0635	.0607
6	.1191	.1160	.1128	.1097	.1066	.1034	.1003	.0972	.0941	.0911
7	.1378	.1358	.1338	.1317	.1294	.1271	.1247	.1222	.1197	.1171
8	.1395	.1392	.1388	.1382	.1375	.1366	.1356	.1344	.1332	.1318
9	.1256	.1269	.1280	.1290	.1299	.1306	.1311	.1315	.1317	.1318
10	.1017	.1040	.1063	.1084	.1104	.1123	.1140	.1157	.1172	.1186
11	.0749	.0776	.0802	.0828	.0853	.0878	.0902	.0925	.0948	.0970
12	.0505	.0530	.0555	.0579	.0604	.0629	.0654	.0679	.0703	.0728
13	.0315	.0334	.0354	.0374	.0395	.0416	.0438	.0459	.0481	.0504
14	.0182	.0196	.0210	.0225	.0240	.0256	.0272	.0289	.0306	.0324
15	.0098	.0107	.0116	.0126	.0136	.0147	.0158	.0169	.0182	.0194
16	.0050	.0055	.0060	.0066	.0072	.0079	.0086	.0093	.0101	.0109
17	.0024	.0026	.0029	.0033	.0036	.0040	.0044	.0048	.0053	.0058
18	.0011	.0012	.0014	.0015	.0017	.0019	.0021	.0024	.0026	.0029
19	.0005	.0005	.0006	.0007	.0008	.0009	.0010	.0011	.0012	.0014
20	.0002	.0002	.0002	.0003	.0003	.0004	.0004	.0005	.0005	.0006
21	.0001	.0001	.0001	.0001	.0001	.0002	.0002	.0002	.0002	.0003
22	.0000	.0000	.0000	.0000	.0001	.0001	.0001	.0001	.0001	.0001

					λ					
x	9.1	9.2	9.3	9.4	9.5	9.6	9.7	9.8	9.9	10
0	.0001	.0001	.0001	.0001	.0001	.0001	.0001	.0001	.0001	.0000
1	.0010	.0009	.0009	.0008	.0007	.0007	.0006	.0005	.0005	.0005
2	.0046	.0043	.0040	.0037	.0034	.0031	.0029	.0027	.0025	.0023
3	.0140	.0131	.0123	.0115	.0107	.0100	.0093	.0087	.0081	.0076
4	.0319	.0302	.0285	.0269	.0254	.0240	.0226	.0213	.0201	.0189
5	.0581	.0555	.0530	.0506	.0483	.0460	.0439	.0418	.0398	.0378
6	.0881	.0851	.0822	.0793	.0764	.0736	.0709	.0682	.0656	.0631
7	.1145	.1118	.1091	.1064	.1037	.1010	.0982	.0955	.0928	.0901
8	.1302	.1286	.1269	.1251	.1232	.1212	.1191	.1170	.1148	.1126
9	.1317	.1315	.1311	.1306	.1300	.1293	.1284	.1274	.1263	.1251
10	.1198	.1210	.1219	.1228	.1235	.1241	.1245	.1249	.1250	.1251
11	.0991	.1012	.1031	.1049	.1067	.1083	.1098	.1112	.1125	.1137
12	.0752	.0776	.0799	.0822	.0844	.0866	.0888	.0908	.0928	.0948
13	.0526	.0549	.0572	.0594	.0617	.0640	.0662	.0685	.0707	.0729
14	.0342	.0361	.0380	.0399	.0419	.0439	.0459	.0479	.0500	.0521
15	.0208	.0221	.0235	.0250	.0265	.0281	.0297	.0313	.0330	.0347
16	.0118	.0127	.0137	.0147	.0157	.0168	.0180	.0192	.0204	.0217
17	.0063	.0069	.0075	.0081	.0088	.0095	.0103	.0111	.0119	.0128
18	.0032	.0035	.0039	.0042	.0046	.0051	.0055	.0060	.0065	.0071
19	.0015	.0017	.0019	.0021	.0023	.0026	.0028	.0031	.0034	.0037
20	.0007	.0008	.0009	.0010	.0011	.0012	.0014	.0015	.0017	.0019
21	.0003	.0003	.0004	.0004	.0005	.0006	.0006	.0007	.0008	.0009
22	.0001	.0001	.0002	.0002	.0002	.0002	.0003	.0003	.0004	.0004
23	.0000	.0001	.0001	.0001	.0001	.0001	.0001	.0001	.0002	.0002
24	.0000	.0000	.0000	.0000	.0000	.0000	.0000	.0001	.0001	.0001

x	11	12	13	14	15	16	17	18	19	20
0	.0000	.0000	.0000	.0000	.0000	.0000	.0000	.0000	.0000	.0000
1	.0002	.0001	.0000	.0000	.0000	.0000	.0000	.0000	.0000	.0000
2	.0010	.0004	.0002	.0001	.0000	.0000	.0000	.0000	.0000	.0000
3	.0037	.0018	.0008	.0004	.0002	.0001	.0000	.0000	.0000	.0000
4	.0102	.0053	.0027	.0013	.0006	.0003	.0001	.0001	.0000	.0000
5	.0224	.0127	.0070	.0037	.0019	.0010	.0005	.0002	.0001	.0001
6	.0411	.0255	.0152	.0087	.0048	.0026	.0014	.0007	.0004	.0002
7	.0646	.0437	.0281	.0174	.0104	.0060	.0034	.0018	.0010	.0005
8	.0888	.0655	.0457	.0304	.0194	.0120	.0072	.0042	.0024	.0013
9	.1085	.0874	.0661	.0473	.0324	.0213	.0135	.0083	.0050	.0029
10	.1194	.1048	.0859	.0063	.0486	.0341	.0230	.0150	.0095	.0058
11	.1194	.1144	.1015	.0844	.0663	.0496	.0355	.0245	.0164	.0106
12	.1094	.1144	.1099	.0984	.0829	.0661	.0504	.0368	.0259	.0176
13	.0926	.1056	.1099	.1060	.0956	.0814	.0658	.0509	.0378	.0271
14	.0728	.0905	.1021	.1060	.1024	.0930	.0800	.0655	.0514	.0387
15	.0534	.0724	.0885	.0989	.1024	.0992	.0906	.0786	.0650	.0516
16	.0367	.0543	.0719	.0866	.0960	.0992	.0963	.0884	.0772	.0646
17	.0237	.0383	.0550	.0713	.0847	.0934	.0963	.0936	.0863	.0760
18	.0145	.0256	.0397	.0554	.0706	.0830	.0909	.0936	.0911	.0844
19	.0084	.0161	.0272	.0409	.0557	.0699	.0814	.0887	.0911	.0888
20	.0046	.0097	.0177	.0286	.0418	.0559	.0692	.0798	.0866	.0888
21	.0024	.0055	.0109	.0191	.0299	.0426	.0560	.0684	.0783	.0846
22	.0012	.0030	.0065	.0121	.0204	.0310	.0433	.0560	.0676	.0769
23	.0006	.0016	.0037	.0074	.0133	.0216	.0320	.0438	.0559	.0669
24	.0003	.0008	.0020	.0043	.0083	.0144	.0226	.0328	.0442	.0557
25	.0001	.0004	.0010	.0024	.0050	.0092	.0154	.0237	.0336	.0446
26	.0000	.0002	.0005	.0013	.0029	.0057	.0101	.0164	.0246	.0343
27	.0000	.0001	.0002	.0007	.0016	.0034	.0063	.0109	.0173	.0254
28	.0000	.0000	.0001	.0003	.0009	.0019	.0038	.0070	.0117	.0181
29	.0000	.0000	.0001	.0002	.0004	.0011	.0023	.0044	.0077	.0125
30	.0000	.0000	.0000	.0001	.0002	.0006	.0013	.0026	.0049	.0083
31	.0000	.0000	.0000	.0000	.0001	.0003	.0007	.0015	.0030	.0054
32	.0000	.0000	.0000	.0000	.0001	.0001	.0004	.0009	.0018	.0034
33	.0000	.0000	.0000	.0000	.0000	.0001	.0002	.0005	.0010	.0020
34	.0000	.0000	.0000	.0000	.0000	.0000	.0001	.0002	.0006	.0012
35	.0000	.0000	.0000	.0000	.0000	.0000	.0000	.0001	.0003	.0007
36	.0000	.0000	.0000	.0000	.0000	.0000	.0000	.0001	.0002	.0004
37	.0000	.0000	.0000	.0000	.0000	.0000	.0000	.0000	.0001	.0002
38	.0000	.0000	.0000	.0000	.0000	.0000	.0000	.0000	.0000	.0001
39	.0000	.0000	.0000	.0000	.0000	.0000	.0000	.0000	.0000	.0001

From *Handbook of Probability and Statistics* by R. S. Burington and D. C. May, Jr. Copyright 1953 by McGraw-Hill, Inc. Used with permission of McGraw-Hill Book Company.

TABLE III Cumulative standardized normal distribution $F(z)$

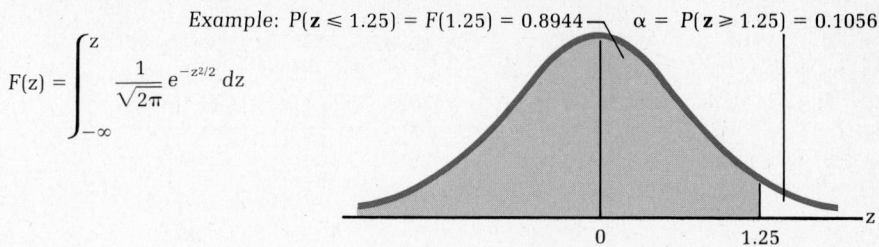

Example: $P(z \leqslant 1.25) = F(1.25) = 0.8944$ $\alpha = P(z \geqslant 1.25) = 0.1056$

$$F(z) = \int_{-\infty}^{z} \frac{1}{\sqrt{2\pi}} e^{-z^2/2}\, dz$$

z	.00	.01	.02	.03	.04	.05	.06	.07	.08	.09
.0	.5000	.5040	.5080	.5120	.5160	.5199	.5239	.5279	.5319	.5359
.1	.5398	.5438	.5478	.5517	.5557	.5596	.5636	.5675	.5714	.5753
.2	.5793	.5832	.5871	.5910	.5948	.5987	.6026	.6064	.6103	.6141
.3	.6179	.6217	.6255	.6293	.6331	.6368	.6406	.6443	.6480	.6517
.4	.6554	.6591	.6628	.6664	.6700	.6736	.6772	.6808	.6844	.6879
.5	.6915	.6950	.6985	.7019	.7054	.7088	.7123	.7157	.7190	.7224
.6	.7257	.7291	.7324	.7357	.7389	.7422	.7454	.7486	.7517	.7549
.7	.7580	.7611	.7642	.7673	.7704	.7734	.7764	.7794	.7823	.7852
.8	.7881	.7910	.7939	.7967	.7995	.8023	.8051	.8078	.8106	.8133
.9	.8159	.8186	.8212	.8238	.8264	.8289	.8315	.8340	.8365	.8389
1.0	.8413	.8438	.8461	.8485	.8508	.8531	.8554	.8577	.8599	.8621
1.1	.8643	.8665	.8686	.8708	.8729	.8749	.8770	.8790	.8810	.8830
1.2	.8849	.8869	.8888	.8907	.8925	.8944	.8962	.8980	.8997	.9015
1.3	.9032	.9049	.9066	.9082	.9099	.9115	.9131	.9147	.9162	.9177
1.4	.9192	.9207	.9222	.9236	.9251	.9265	.9279	.9292	.9306	.9319
1.5	.9332	.9345	.9357	.9370	.9382	.9394	.9406	.9418	.9429	.9441
1.6	.9452	.9463	.9474	.9484	.9495	.9505	.9515	.9525	.9535	.9545
1.7	.9554	.9564	.9573	.9582	.9591	.9599	.9608	.9616	.9625	.9633
1.8	.9641	.9649	.9656	.9664	.9671	.9678	.9686	.9693	.9699	.9706
1.9	.9713	.9719	.9726	.9732	.9738	.9744	.9750	.9756	.9761	.9767
2.0	.9772	.9778	.9783	.9788	.9793	.9798	.9803	.9808	.9812	.9817
2.1	.9821	.9826	.9830	.9834	.9838	.9842	.9846	.9850	.9854	.9857
2.2	.9861	.9864	.9868	.9871	.9875	.9878	.9881	.9884	.9887	.9890
2.3	.9893	.9896	.9898	.9901	.9904	.9906	.9909	.9911	.9913	.9916
2.4	.9918	.9920	.9922	.9925	.9927	.9929	.9931	.9932	.9934	.9936
2.5	.9938	.9940	.9941	.9943	.9945	.9946	.9948	.9949	.9951	.9952
2.6	.9953	.9955	.9956	.9957	.9959	.9960	.9961	.9962	.9963	.9964
2.7	.9965	.9966	.9967	.9968	.9969	.9970	.9971	.9972	.9973	.9974
2.8	.9974	.9975	.9976	.9977	.9977	.9978	.9979	.9979	.9980	.9981
2.9	.9981	.9982	.9982	.9983	.9984	.9984	.9985	.9985	.9986	.9986
3.0	.9987	.9987	.9987	.9988	.9988	.9989	.9989	.9989	.9990	.9990
3.1	.9990	.9991	.9991	.9991	.9992	.9992	.9992	.9992	.9993	.9993
3.2	.9993	.9993	.9994	.9994	.9994	.9994	.9994	.9995	.9995	.9995
3.3	.9995	.9995	.9995	.9996	.9996	.9996	.9996	.9996	.9996	.9997
3.4	.9997	.9997	.9997	.9997	.9997	.9997	.9997	.9997	.9997	.9998

TABLE IV Cumulative exponential distribution, $F(T) = 1 - e^{-\lambda T}$

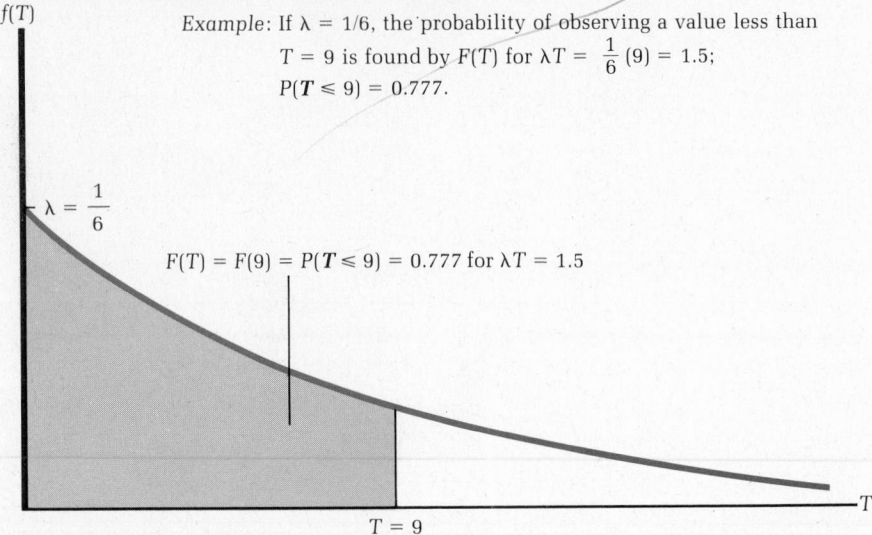

Example: If $\lambda = 1/6$, the probability of observing a value less than $T = 9$ is found by $F(T)$ for $\lambda T = \frac{1}{6}(9) = 1.5$; $P(T \leq 9) = 0.777$.

$F(T) = F(9) = P(T \leq 9) = 0.777$ for $\lambda T = 1.5$

λT	$F(T)$	λT	$F(T)$	λT	$F(T)$	λT	$F(T)$
0.0	0.000	2.5	0.918	5.0	0.9933	7.5	0.99945
0.1	0.095	2.6	0.926	5.1	0.9939	7.6	0.99950
0.2	0.181	2.7	0.933	5.2	0.9945	7.7	0.99955
0.3	0.259	2.8	0.939	5.3	0.9950	7.8	0.99959
0.4	0.330	2.9	0.945	5.4	0.9955	7.9	0.99963
0.5	0.393	3.0	0.950	5.5	0.9959	8.0	0.99966
0.6	0.451	3.1	0.955	5.6	0.9963	8.1	0.99970
0.7	0.503	3.2	0.959	5.7	0.9967	8.2	0.99972
0.8	0.551	3.3	0.963	5.8	0.9970	8.3	0.99975
0.9	0.593	3.4	0.967	5.9	0.9973	8.4	0.99978
1.0	0.632	3.5	0.970	6.0	0.9975	8.5	0.99980
1.1	0.667	3.6	0.973	6.1	0.9978	8.6	0.99982
1.2	0.699	3.7	0.975	6.2	0.9980	8.7	0.99983
1.3	0.727	3.8	0.978	6.3	0.9982	8.8	0.99985
1.4	0.753	3.9	0.980	6.4	0.9983	8.9	0.99986
1.5	0.777	4.0	0.982	6.5	0.9985	9.0	0.99989
1.6	0.798	4.1	0.983	6.6	0.9986	9.1	0.99989
1.7	0.817	4.2	0.985	6.7	0.9988	9.2	0.99990
1.8	0.835	4.3	0.986	6.8	0.9989	9.3	0.99991
1.9	0.850	4.4	0.988	6.9	0.9990	9.4	0.99992
2.0	0.865	4.5	0.989	7.0	0.9991	9.5	0.99992
2.1	0.878	4.6	0.990	7.1	0.9992	9.6	0.99993
2.2	0.889	4.7	0.991	7.2	0.9993	9.7	0.99994
2.3	0.900	4.8	0.992	7.3	0.9993	9.8	0.99994
2.4	0.909	4.9	0.993	7.4	0.9993	9.9	0.99995

TABLE V **Random digits**

07018	31172	12572	23968	55216	85366	56223	09300	94564	18172
52444	65625	97918	46794	62370	59344	20149	17596	51669	47429
72161	57299	87521	44351	99981	55008	93371	60620	66662	27036
17918	75071	91057	46829	47992	26797	64423	42379	91676	75127
13623	76165	43195	50205	75736	77473	07268	31330	07337	55901
27426	97534	89707	97453	90836	78967	00704	85734	21776	85764
96039	21338	88169	69530	53300	29895	71507	28517	77761	17244
68282	98888	25545	69406	29470	46476	54562	79373	72993	98998
54262	21477	33097	48125	92982	98382	11265	25366	06636	25349
66290	27544	72780	91384	47296	54892	59168	83951	91075	04724
53348	39044	04072	62210	01209	43999	54952	68699	31912	09317
34482	42758	40128	48436	30254	50029	19016	56837	05206	33851
99268	98715	07545	27317	52459	75366	43688	27460	65145	65429
95342	97178	10401	31615	95784	77026	33087	65961	10056	72834
38556	60373	77935	64608	28949	94764	45312	71171	15400	72182
39159	04795	51163	84475	60722	35268	05044	56420	39214	89822
41786	18169	96649	92406	42773	23672	37333	85734	99886	81200
95627	30768	30607	89023	60730	31519	53462	90489	81693	17849
98738	15548	42263	79489	85118	97073	01574	57310	59375	54417
75214	61575	27805	21930	94726	39454	19616	72239	93791	22610
73904	89123	19271	15792	72675	62175	48746	56084	54029	22296
33329	08896	94662	05781	59187	53284	28024	45421	37956	14252
66364	94799	62211	37539	80172	43269	91133	05562	82385	91760
68349	16984	86532	96186	53893	48268	82821	19526	63257	14288
19193	99621	66899	12351	72438	99839	24228	32079	53517	18558
09237	23489	19172	80439	76263	98918	59330	20121	89779	58862
11007	77008	27646	82072	28048	41589	70883	72035	81800	50296
60622	25875	26446	25738	32962	24266	26814	01194	48587	93319
79973	26895	65304	34978	43053	28951	22676	05303	39725	60054
71080	74487	83196	61939	05045	20405	69324	80823	20905	68727
09923	36773	21247	54735	68996	16937	18134	51873	10973	77090
63094	85087	94186	67793	18178	82224	17069	87880	54945	73489
34968	76028	54285	90845	35464	68076	15868	70063	26794	81386
99696	78454	21700	12301	88832	96796	59341	16136	01803	17537
55282	61051	97260	89829	69121	86547	62195	72492	33536	60137

From RAND Corporation, *A Million Random Digits*. By permission.

TABLE VI Cumulative t-distribution F(t)

$$F(t) = \int_{-\infty}^{t} \frac{\left(\dfrac{\nu-1}{2}\right)!}{\left(\dfrac{\nu-2}{2}\right)!\,\sqrt{\pi n}\left(1 + \dfrac{t^2}{\nu}\right)^{(\nu+1)/2}}\, dt$$

$f(t)$

$F(t) = P(t_{19} \le 2.093)$
$= 0.975$

$\alpha = 0.025$

$t_{19\,\text{d.f.}}$

Example; $n = 20$, $\nu = 19$

F(t)	.75	.90	.95	.975	.99	.995	.9995
ν (α)	(.25)	(.10)	(.05)	(.025)	(.01)	(.005)	(.0005)
1	1.000	3.078	6.314	12.706	31.821	63.657	636.619
2	.816	1.886	2.920	4.303	6.965	9.925	31.598
3	.765	1.638	2.353	3.182	4.541	5.841	12.941
4	.741	1.533	2.132	2.776	3.747	4.604	8.610
5	.727	1.476	2.015	2.571	3.365	4.032	6.859
6	.718	1.440	1.943	2.447	3.143	3.707	5.959
7	.711	1.415	1.895	2.365	2.998	3.499	5.405
8	.706	1.397	1.860	2.306	2.896	3.355	5.041
9	.703	1.383	1.833	2.262	2.821	3.250	4.781
10	.700	1.372	1.812	2.228	2.764	3.169	4.587
11	.697	1.363	1.796	2.201	2.718	3.106	4.437
12	.695	1.356	1.782	2.179	2.681	3.055	4.318
13	.694	1.350	1.771	2.160	2.650	3.012	4.221
14	.692	1.345	1.761	2.145	2.624	2.977	4.140
15	.691	1.341	1.753	2.131	2.602	2.947	4.073
16	.690	1.337	1.746	2.120	2.583	2.921	4.015
17	.689	1.333	1.740	2.110	2.567	2.898	3.965
18	.688	1.330	1.734	2.101	2.552	2.878	3.922
19	.688	1.328	1.729	2.093	2.539	2.861	3.883
20	.687	1.325	1.725	2.086	2.528	2.845	3.850
21	.686	1.323	1.721	2.080	2.518	2.831	3.819
22	.686	1.321	1.717	2.074	2.508	2.819	3.792
23	.685	1.319	1.714	2.069	2.500	2.807	3.767
24	.685	1.318	1.711	2.064	2.492	2.797	3.745
25	.684	1.316	1.708	2.060	2.485	2.787	3.725
26	.684	1.315	1.706	2.056	2.479	2.779	3.707
27	.684	1.314	1.703	2.052	2.473	2.771	3.690
28	.683	1.313	1.701	2.048	2.467	2.763	3.674
29	.683	1.311	1.699	2.045	2.462	2.756	3.659
30	.683	1.310	1.697	2.042	2.457	2.750	3.646
40	.681	1.303	1.684	2.021	2.423	2.704	3.551
60	.679	1.296	1.671	2.000	2.390	2.660	3.460
120	.677	1.289	1.658	1.980	2.358	2.617	3.373
$\infty(z_\alpha)$	.674	1.282	1.645	1.960	2.326	2.576	3.291

* This table is abridged from the "Statistical Tables" of R. A. Fisher and Frank Yates published by Oliver & Boyd, Ltd., Edinburgh and London, 1938. It is here published with the kind permission of the authors and their publishers.

TABLE VII **Cumulative chi-square distribution**

$$F(\chi^2) = \int_0^{\chi^2} \frac{\chi^{(\nu-2)/2}\,e^{-\chi/2}\,d\chi}{2^{\nu/2}[(\nu-2)/2]!}$$

Example: $P(\chi^2_{19} \le 30.1)$ for d.f. = 19

$P(\chi^2 \le 30.1) = F(30.1) = 0.950$

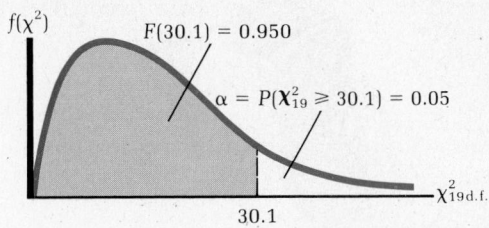

$F(\chi^2)$	.005	.010	.025	.050	.100	.900	.950	.975	.990	.995
ν (α)	(.995)	(.990)	(.975)	(.950)	(.900)	(.100)	(.050)	(.025)	(.010)	(.005)
1	$.0^4393$	$.0^3157$	$.0^3982$	$.0^2393$	0.158	2.71	3.84	5.02	6.63	7.88
2	.0100	.0201	.0506	.103	.211	4.61	5.99	7.38	9.21	10.6
3	.0717	.115	.216	.352	.584	6.25	7.81	9.35	11.3	12.8
4	.207	.297	.484	.711	1.06	7.78	9.49	11.1	13.3	14.9
5	.412	.554	.831	1.15	1.61	9.24	11.1	12.8	15.1	16.7
6	.676	.872	1.24	1.64	2.20	10.6	12.6	14.4	16.8	18.5
7	.989	1.24	1.69	2.17	2.83	12.0	14.1	16.0	18.5	20.3
8	1.34	1.65	2.18	2.73	3.49	13.4	15.5	17.5	20.1	22.0
9	1.73	2.09	2.70	3.33	4.17	14.7	16.9	19.0	21.7	23.6
10	2.16	2.56	3.25	3.94	4.87	16.0	18.3	20.5	23.2	25.2
11	2.60	3.05	3.82	4.57	5.58	17.3	19.7	21.9	24.7	26.8
12	3.07	3.57	4.40	5.23	6.30	18.5	21.0	23.3	26.2	28.3
13	3.57	4.11	5.01	5.89	7.04	19.8	22.4	24.7	27.7	29.8
14	4.07	4.66	5.63	6.57	7.79	21.1	23.7	26.1	29.1	31.3
15	4.60	5.23	6.26	7.26	8.55	22.3	25.0	27.5	30.6	32.8
16	5.14	5.81	6.91	7.96	9.31	23.5	26.3	28.8	32.0	34.3
17	5.70	6.41	7.56	8.67	10.1	24.8	27.6	30.2	33.4	35.7
18	6.26	7.01	8.23	9.39	10.9	26.0	28.9	31.5	34.8	37.2
19	6.84	7.63	8.91	10.1	11.7	27.2	30.1	32.9	36.2	38.6
20	7.43	8.26	9.59	10.9	12.4	28.4	31.4	34.2	37.6	40.0
21	8.03	8.90	10.3	11.6	13.2	29.6	32.7	35.5	38.9	41.4
22	8.64	9.54	11.0	12.3	14.0	30.8	33.9	36.8	40.3	42.8
23	9.26	10.2	11.7	13.1	14.8	32.0	35.2	38.1	41.6	44.2
24	9.89	10.9	12.4	13.8	15.7	33.2	36.4	39.4	43.0	45.6
25	10.5	11.5	13.1	14.6	16.5	34.4	37.7	40.6	44.3	46.9
26	11.2	12.2	13.8	15.4	17.3	35.6	38.9	41.9	45.6	48.3
27	11.8	12.9	14.6	16.2	18.1	36.7	40.1	43.2	47.0	49.6
28	12.5	13.6	15.3	16.9	18.9	37.9	41.3	44.5	48.3	51.0
29	13.1	14.3	16.0	17.7	19.8	39.1	42.6	45.7	49.6	52.3
30	13.8	15.0	16.8	18.5	20.6	40.3	43.8	47.0	50.9	53.7
z_α	-2.576	-2.326	-1.960	-1.645	-1.282	$+1.282$	$+1.645$	$+1.960$	$+2.326$	$+2.576$

NOTE: For $\nu > 30$ (i.e., for more than 30 degrees of freedom) take

$$\chi^2 = \nu\left[1 - \frac{2}{9\nu} + z_x\sqrt{\frac{2}{9\nu}}\right]^2 \quad \text{or} \quad \chi^2 = \tfrac{1}{2}[z_x + \sqrt{(2\nu-1)}]^2$$

according to the degree of accuracy required. z_α is the standardized normal deviate corresponding to the α level of significance, and is shown in the bottom line of the table.

This table is abridged from "Tables of percentage points of the incomplete beta function and of the chi-square distribution," *Biometrika*. Vol. 32 (1941). Reprinted with permission of its author, Catherine M. Thompson, and the editor of *Biometrika*.

Table VIII(a) gives the critical values of the F distribution for a cumulative probability of 0.95 ($\alpha = 0.05$). The probability (α) represents the area exceeding the value of $F_{0.05,\nu_1,\nu_2}$, as shown by the shaded area in the figure below.

Example: If $\nu_1 = 15$ (d.f. for the numerator), and $\nu_2 = 20$, then the critical value cutting off 0.05 is 2.20. $P(F \geq 2.20) = 0.05$, $P(F \leq 2.20) = 0.95$.

TABLE VIII(a) **Cumulative F-distribution of 0.95 ($\alpha = 0.05$)**

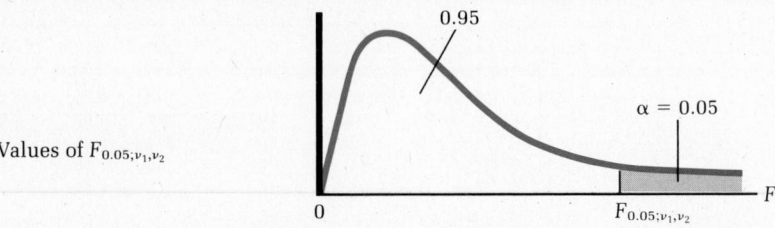

Values of $F_{0.05;\nu_1,\nu_2}$

		ν_1 = Degrees of freedom for numerator							
	1	2	3	4	5	6	7	8	9
1	161	200	216	225	230	234	237	239	241
2	18.5	19.0	19.2	19.2	19.3	19.3	19.4	19.4	19.4
3	10.1	9.55	9.28	9.12	9.01	8.94	8.89	8.85	8.81
4	7.71	6.94	6.59	6.39	6.26	6.16	6.09	6.04	6.00
5	6.61	5.79	5.41	5.19	5.05	4.95	4.88	4.82	4.77
6	5.99	5.14	4.76	4.53	4.39	4.28	4.21	4.15	4.10
7	5.59	4.74	4.35	4.12	3.97	3.87	3.79	3.73	3.68
8	5.32	4.46	4.07	3.84	3.69	3.58	3.50	3.44	3.39
9	5.12	4.26	3.86	3.63	3.48	3.37	3.29	3.23	3.18
10	4.96	4.10	3.71	3.48	3.33	3.22	3.14	3.07	3.02
11	4.84	3.98	3.59	3.36	3.20	3.09	3.01	2.95	2.90
12	4.75	3.89	3.49	3.26	3.11	3.00	2.91	2.85	2.80
13	4.67	3.81	3.41	3.18	3.03	2.92	2.83	2.77	2.71
14	4.60	3.74	3.34	3.11	2.96	2.85	2.76	2.70	2.65
15	4.54	3.68	3.29	3.06	2.90	2.79	2.71	2.64	2.59
16	4.49	3.63	3.24	3.01	2.85	2.74	2.66	2.59	2.54
17	4.45	3.59	3.20	2.96	2.81	2.70	2.61	2.55	2.49
18	4.41	3.55	3.16	2.93	2.77	2.66	2.58	2.51	2.46
19	4.38	3.52	3.13	2.90	2.74	2.63	2.54	2.48	2.42
20	4.35	3.49	3.10	2.87	2.71	2.60	2.51	2.45	2.39
21	4.32	3.47	3.07	2.84	2.68	2.57	2.49	2.42	2.37
22	4.30	3.44	3.05	2.82	2.66	2.55	2.46	2.40	2.34
23	4.28	3.42	3.03	2.80	2.64	2.53	2.44	2.37	2.32
24	4.26	3.40	3.01	2.78	2.62	2.51	2.42	2.36	2.30
25	4.24	3.39	2.99	2.76	2.60	2.49	2.40	2.34	2.28
30	4.17	3.32	2.92	2.69	2.53	2.42	2.33	2.27	2.21
40	4.08	3.23	2.84	2.61	2.45	2.34	2.25	2.18	2.12
60	4.00	3.15	2.76	2.53	2.37	2.25	2.17	2.10	2.04
120	3.92	3.07	2.68	2.45	2.29	2.18	2.09	2.02	1.96
∞	3.84	3.00	2.60	2.37	2.21	2.10	2.01	1.94	1.88

ν_2 = Degrees of freedom for denominator

		10	12	15	20	24	30	40	60	120	∞
		\multicolumn{10}{c}{ν_1 = Degrees of freedom for numerator}									
	1	242	244	246	248	249	250	251	252	253	254
	2	19.4	19.4	19.4	19.4	19.5	19.5	19.5	19.5	19.5	19.5
	3	8.79	8.74	8.70	8.66	8.64	8.62	8.59	8.57	8.55	8.53
	4	5.96	5.91	5.86	5.80	5.77	5.75	5.72	5.69	5.66	5.63
	5	4.74	4.68	4.62	4.56	4.53	4.50	4.46	4.43	4.40	4.37
	6	4.06	4.00	3.94	3.87	3.84	3.81	3.77	3.74	3.70	3.67
	7	3.64	3.57	3.51	3.44	3.41	3.38	3.34	3.30	3.27	3.23
	8	3.35	3.28	3.22	3.15	3.12	3.08	3.04	3.01	2.97	2.93
	9	3.14	3.07	3.01	2.94	2.90	2.86	2.83	2.79	2.75	2.71
	10	2.98	2.91	2.85	2.77	2.74	2.70	2.66	2.62	2.58	2.54
	11	2.85	2.79	2.72	2.65	2.61	2.57	2.53	2.49	2.45	2.40
	12	2.75	2.69	2.62	2.54	2.51	2.47	2.43	2.38	2.34	2.30
	13	2.67	2.60	2.53	2.46	2.42	2.38	2.34	2.30	2.25	2.21
	14	2.60	2.53	2.46	2.39	2.35	2.31	2.27	2.22	2.18	2.13
	15	2.54	2.48	2.40	2.33	2.29	2.25	2.20	2.16	2.11	2.07
	16	2.49	2.42	2.35	2.28	2.24	2.19	2.15	2.11	2.06	2.01
	17	2.45	2.38	2.31	2.23	2.19	2.15	2.10	2.06	2.01	1.96
	18	2.41	2.34	2.27	2.19	2.15	2.11	2.06	2.02	1.97	1.92
	19	2.38	2.31	2.23	2.16	2.11	2.07	2.03	1.98	1.93	1.88
	20	2.35	2.28	2.20	2.12	2.08	2.04	1.99	1.95	1.90	1.84
	21	2.32	2.25	2.18	2.10	2.05	2.01	1.96	1.92	1.87	1.81
	22	2.30	2.23	2.15	2.07	2.03	1.98	1.94	1.89	1.84	1.78
	23	2.27	2.20	2.13	2.05	2.01	1.96	1.91	1.86	1.81	1.76
	24	2.25	2.18	2.11	2.03	1.98	1.94	1.89	1.84	1.79	1.73
	25	2.24	2.16	2.09	2.01	1.96	1.92	1.87	1.82	1.77	1.71
	30	2.16	2.09	2.01	1.93	1.89	1.84	1.79	1.74	1.68	1.62
	40	2.08	2.00	1.92	1.84	1.79	1.74	1.69	1.64	1.58	1.51
	60	1.99	1.92	1.84	1.75	1.70	1.65	1.59	1.53	1.47	1.39
	120	1.91	1.83	1.75	1.66	1.61	1.55	1.50	1.43	1.35	1.25
	∞	1.83	1.75	1.67	1.57	1.52	1.46	1.39	1.32	1.22	1.00

ν_2 = Degrees of freedom for denominator

Tables VIII(a) and (b) from M. Merrington and C. M. Thompson, "Tables of percentage points of the inverted beta (F) distribution." *Biometrica*, Vol. 33 (1943) by permission of the *Biometrica* Trustees.

Table VIII(b) gives the critical values of the **F** distribution for a cumulative probability of 0.99 ($\alpha = 0.01$). The probability (α) represents the area exceeding the value of $F_{0.01,v_1,v_2}$, as shown by the shaded area in the figure below.

Examples: If $v_1 = 15$ (representing the greater mean square) and $v_2 = 20$, then the critical value for $\alpha = 0.01$ is 3.09. $P(F \geq 3.09) = 0.01$, $P(F \leq 3.09) = 0.99$.

TABLE VIII(b) **Cumulative F-distribution of 0.99 ($\alpha = 0.01$)**

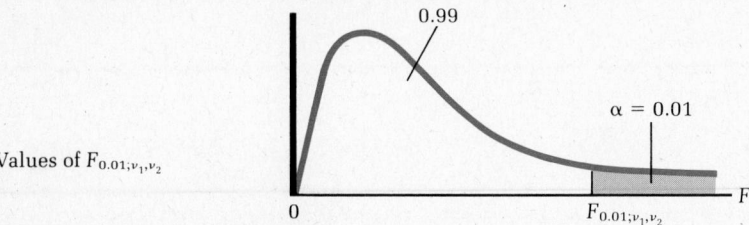

Values of $F_{0.01;v_1,v_2}$

		v_1 = Degrees of freedom for numerator							
	1	2	3	4	5	6	7	8	9
1	4,052	5,000	5,403	5,625	5,764	5,859	5,928	5,982	6,023
2	98.5	99.0	99.2	99.2	99.3	99.3	99.4	99.4	99.4
3	34.1	30.8	29.5	28.7	28.2	27.9	27.7	27.5	27.3
4	21.2	18.0	16.7	16.0	15.5	15.2	15.0	14.8	14.7
5	16.3	13.3	12.1	11.4	11.0	10.7	10.5	10.3	10.2
6	13.7	10.9	9.78	9.15	8.75	8.47	8.26	8.10	7.98
7	12.2	9.55	8.45	7.85	7.46	7.19	6.99	6.84	6.72
8	11.3	8.65	7.59	7.01	6.63	6.37	6.18	6.03	5.91
9	10.6	8.02	6.99	6.42	6.06	5.80	5.61	5.47	5.35
10	10.0	7.56	6.55	5.99	5.64	5.39	5.20	5.06	4.94
11	9.65	7.21	6.22	5.67	5.32	5.07	4.89	4.74	4.63
12	9.33	6.93	5.95	5.41	5.06	4.82	4.64	4.50	4.39
13	9.07	6.70	5.74	5.21	4.86	4.62	4.44	4.30	4.19
14	8.86	6.51	5.56	5.04	4.70	4.46	4.28	4.14	4.03
15	8.68	6.36	5.42	4.89	4.56	4.32	4.14	4.00	3.89
16	8.53	6.23	5.29	4.77	4.44	4.20	4.03	3.89	3.78
17	8.40	6.11	5.19	4.67	4.34	4.10	3.93	3.79	3.68
18	8.29	6.01	5.09	4.58	4.25	4.01	3.84	3.71	3.60
19	8.19	5.93	5.01	4.50	4.17	3.94	3.77	3.63	3.52
20	8.10	5.85	4.94	4.43	4.10	3.87	3.70	3.56	3.46
21	8.02	5.78	4.87	3.37	4.04	3.81	3.64	3.51	3.40
22	7.95	5.72	4.82	4.31	3.99	3.76	3.59	3.45	3.35
23	7.88	5.66	4.76	4.26	3.94	3.71	3.54	3.41	3.30
24	7.82	5.61	4.72	4.22	3.90	3.67	3.50	3.36	3.26
25	7.77	5.57	4.68	4.18	3.86	3.63	3.46	3.32	3.22
30	7.56	5.39	4.51	4.02	3.70	3.47	3.30	3.17	3.07
40	7.31	5.18	4.31	3.83	3.51	3.29	3.12	2.99	2.89
60	7.08	4.98	4.13	3.65	3.34	3.12	2.95	2.82	2.72
120	6.85	4.79	3.95	3.48	3.17	2.96	2.79	2.66	2.56
∞	6.63	4.61	3.78	3.32	3.02	2.80	2.64	2.51	2.41

v_2 = Degrees of freedom for denominator

		ν_1 = Degrees of freedom for numerator								
		10	12	15	20	24	30	40	60	120	∞
	1	6,056	6,106	6,157	6,209	6,235	6,261	6,287	6,313	6,339	6,366
	2	99.4	99.4	99.4	99.4	99.5	99.5	99.5	99.5	99.5	99.5
	3	27.2	27.1	26.9	26.7	26.6	26.5	26.4	26.3	26.2	26.1
	4	14.5	14.4	14.2	14.0	13.9	13.8	13.7	13.7	13.6	13.5
	5	10.1	9.89	9.72	9.55	9.47	9.38	9.29	9.20	9.11	9.02
	6	7.87	7.72	7.56	7.40	7.31	7.23	7.14	7.06	6.97	6.88
	7	6.62	6.47	6.31	6.16	6.07	5.99	5.91	5.82	5.74	5.65
	8	5.81	5.67	5.52	5.36	5.28	5.20	5.12	5.03	4.95	4.86
	9	5.26	5.11	4.96	4.81	4.73	4.65	4.57	4.48	4.40	4.31
	10	4.85	4.71	4.56	4.41	4.33	4.25	4.17	4.08	4.00	3.91
	11	4.54	4.40	4.25	4.10	4.02	3.94	3.86	3.78	3.69	3.60
	12	4.30	4.16	4.01	3.86	3.78	3.70	3.62	3.54	3.45	3.36
	13	4.10	3.96	3.82	3.66	3.59	3.51	3.43	3.34	3.25	3.17
	14	3.94	3.80	3.66	3.51	3.43	3.35	3.27	3.18	3.09	3.00
	15	3.80	3.67	3.52	3.37	3.29	3.21	3.13	3.05	2.96	2.87
	16	3.69	3.55	3.41	3.26	3.18	3.10	3.02	2.93	2.84	2.75
	17	3.59	3.46	3.31	3.16	3.08	3.00	2.92	2.83	2.75	2.65
	18	3.51	3.37	3.23	3.08	3.00	2.92	2.84	2.75	2.66	2.57
	19	3.43	3.30	3.15	3.00	2.92	2.84	2.76	2.67	2.58	2.49
	20	3.37	3.23	3.09	2.94	2.86	2.78	2.69	2.61	2.52	2.42
	21	3.31	3.17	3.03	2.88	2.80	2.72	2.64	2.55	2.46	2.36
	22	3.26	3.12	2.98	2.83	2.75	2.67	2.58	2.50	2.40	2.31
	23	3.21	3.07	2.93	2.78	2.70	2.62	2.54	2.45	2.35	2.26
	24	3.17	3.03	2.89	2.74	2.66	2.58	2.49	2.40	2.31	2.21
	25	3.13	2.99	2.85	2.70	2.62	2.53	2.45	2.36	2.27	2.17
	30	2.98	2.84	2.70	2.55	2.47	2.39	2.30	2.21	2.11	2.01
	40	2.80	2.66	2.52	2.37	2.29	2.20	2.11	2.02	1.92	1.80
	60	2.63	2.50	2.35	2.20	2.12	2.03	1.94	1.84	1.73	1.60
	120	2.47	2.34	2.19	2.03	1.95	1.86	1.76	1.66	1.53	1.38
	∞	2.32	2.18	2.04	1.88	1.79	1.70	1.59	1.47	1.32	1.00

ν_2 = Degrees of freedom for denominator

TABLE IX Unit normal linear loss integral $L_N(D)$

D	.00	.01	.02	.03	.04	.05	.06	.07	.08	.09
.0	.3989	.3940	.3890	.3841	.3793	.3744	.3697	.3649	.3602	.3556
.1	.3509	.3464	.3418	.3373	.3328	.3284	.3240	.3197	.3154	.3111
.2	.3069	.3027	.2986	.2944	.2904	.2863	.2824	.2784	.2745	.2706
.3	.2668	.2630	.2592	.2555	.2518	.2481	.2445	.2409	.2374	.2339
.4	.2304	.2270	.2236	.2203	.2169	.2137	.2104	.2072	.2040	.2009
.5	.1978	.1947	.1917	.1887	.1857	.1828	.1799	.1771	.1742	.1714
.6	.1687	.1659	.1633	.1606	.1580	.1554	.1528	.1503	.1478	.1453
.7	.1429	.1405	.1381	.1358	.1334	.1312	.1289	.1267	.1245	.1223
.8	.1202	.1181	.1160	.1140	.1120	.1100	.1080	.1061	.1042	.1023
.9	.1004	.09860	.09680	.09503	.09328	.09156	.08986	.08819	.08654	.08491
1.0	.08332	.08174	.08019	.07866	.07716	.07568	.07422	.07279	.07138	.06999
1.1	.06862	.06727	.06595	.06465	.06336	.06210	.06086	.05964	.05844	.05726
1.2	.05610	.05496	.05384	.05274	.05165	.05059	.04954	.04851	.04750	.04650
1.3	.04553	.04457	.04363	.04270	.04179	.04090	.04002	.03916	.03831	.03748
1.4	.03667	.03587	.03508	.03431	.03356	.03281	.03208	.03137	.03067	.02998
1.5	.02931	.02865	.02800	.02736	.02674	.02612	.02552	.02494	.02436	.02380
1.6	.02324	.02270	.02217	.02165	.02114	.02064	.02015	.01967	.01920	.01874
1.7	.01829	.01785	.01742	.01699	.01658	.01617	.01578	.01539	.01501	.01464
1.8	.01428	.01392	.01357	.01323	.01290	.01257	.01226	.01195	.01164	.01134
1.9	.01105	.01077	.01049	.01022	$.0^2 9957$	$.0^2 9698$	$.0^2 9445$	$.0^2 9198$	$.0^2 8957$	$.0^2 8721$
2.0	$.0^2 8491$	$.0^2 8266$	$.0^2 8046$	$.0^2 7832$	$.0^2 7623$	$.0^2 7418$	$.0^2 7219$	$.0^2 7024$	$.0^2 6835$	$.0^2 6649$
2.1	$.0^2 6468$	$.0^2 6292$	$.0^2 6120$	$.0^2 5952$	$.0^2 5788$	$.0^2 5628$	$.0^2 5472$	$.0^2 5320$	$.0^2 5172$	$.0^2 5028$
2.2	$.0^2 4887$	$.0^2 4750$	$.0^2 4616$	$.0^2 4486$	$.0^2 4358$	$.0^2 4235$	$.0^2 4114$	$.0^2 3996$	$.0^2 3882$	$.0^2 3770$
2.3	$.0^2 3662$	$.0^2 3556$	$.0^2 3453$	$.0^2 3352$	$.0^2 3255$	$.0^2 3159$	$.0^2 3067$	$.0^2 2977$	$.0^2 2889$	$.0^2 2804$
2.4	$.0^2 2720$	$.0^2 2640$	$.0^2 2561$	$.0^2 2484$	$.0^2 2410$	$.0^2 2337$	$.0^2 2267$	$.0^2 2199$	$.0^2 2132$	$.0^2 2067$

D	.00	.01	.02	.03	.04	.05	.06	.07	.08	.09
2.5	$.0^{2}2004$	$.0^{2}1943$	$.0^{2}1883$	$.0^{2}1826$	$.0^{2}1769$	$.0^{2}1715$	$.0^{2}1662$	$.0^{2}1610$	$.0^{2}1560$	$.0^{2}1511$
2.6	$.0^{2}1464$	$.0^{2}1418$	$.0^{2}1373$	$.0^{2}1330$	$.0^{2}1288$	$.0^{2}1247$	$.0^{2}1207$	$.0^{2}1169$	$.0^{2}1132$	$.0^{2}1095$
2.7	$.0^{2}1060$	$.0^{2}1026$	$.0^{3}9928$	$.0^{3}9607$	$.0^{3}9295$	$.0^{3}8992$	$.0^{3}8699$	$.0^{3}8414$	$.0^{3}8138$	$.0^{3}7870$
2.8	$.0^{3}7611$	$.0^{3}7359$	$.0^{3}7115$	$.0^{3}6879$	$.0^{3}6650$	$.0^{3}6428$	$.0^{3}6213$	$.0^{3}6004$	$.0^{3}5802$	$.0^{3}5606$
2.9	$.0^{3}5417$	$.0^{3}5233$	$.0^{3}5055$	$.0^{3}4883$	$.0^{3}4716$	$.0^{3}4555$	$.0^{3}4398$	$.0^{3}4247$	$.0^{3}4101$	$.0^{3}3959$
3.0	$.0^{3}3822$	$.0^{3}3689$	$.0^{3}3560$	$.0^{3}3436$	$.0^{3}3316$	$.0^{3}3199$	$.0^{3}3087$	$.0^{3}2978$	$.0^{3}2873$	$.0^{3}2771$
3.1	$.0^{3}2673$	$.0^{3}2577$	$.0^{3}2485$	$.0^{3}2396$	$.0^{3}2311$	$.0^{3}2227$	$.0^{3}2147$	$.0^{3}2070$	$.0^{3}1995$	$.0^{3}1922$
3.2	$.0^{3}1852$	$.0^{3}1785$	$.0^{3}1720$	$.0^{3}1657$	$.0^{3}1596$	$.0^{3}1537$	$.0^{3}1480$	$.0^{3}1426$	$.0^{3}1373$	$.0^{3}1322$
3.3	$.0^{3}1273$	$.0^{3}1225$	$.0^{3}1179$	$.0^{3}1135$	$.0^{3}1093$	$.0^{3}1051$	$.0^{3}1012$	$.0^{4}9734$	$.0^{4}9365$	$.0^{4}9009$
3.4	$.0^{4}8666$	$.0^{4}8335$	$.0^{4}8016$	$.0^{4}7709$	$.0^{4}7413$	$.0^{4}7127$	$.0^{4}6852$	$.0^{4}6587$	$.0^{4}6331$	$.0^{4}6085$
3.5	$.0^{4}5848$	$.0^{4}5620$	$.0^{4}5400$	$.0^{4}5188$	$.0^{4}4984$	$.0^{4}4788$	$.0^{4}4599$	$.0^{4}4417$	$.0^{4}4242$	$.0^{4}4073$
3.6	$.0^{4}3911$	$.0^{4}3755$	$.0^{4}3605$	$.0^{4}3460$	$.0^{4}3321$	$.0^{4}3188$	$.0^{4}3059$	$.0^{4}2935$	$.0^{4}2816$	$.0^{4}2702$
3.7	$.0^{4}2592$	$.0^{4}2486$	$.0^{4}2385$	$.0^{4}2287$	$.0^{4}2193$	$.0^{4}2103$	$.0^{4}2016$	$.0^{4}1933$	$.0^{4}1853$	$.0^{4}1776$
3.8	$.0^{4}1702$	$.0^{4}1632$	$.0^{4}1563$	$.0^{4}1498$	$.0^{4}1435$	$.0^{4}1375$	$.0^{4}1317$	$.0^{4}1262$	$.0^{4}1208$	$.0^{4}1157$
3.9	$.0^{4}1108$	$.0^{4}1061$	$.0^{4}1016$	$.0^{5}9723$	$.0^{5}9307$	$.0^{5}8908$	$.0^{5}8525$	$.0^{5}8158$	$.0^{5}7806$	$.0^{5}7469$
4.0	$.0^{5}7145$	$.0^{5}6835$	$.0^{5}6538$	$.0^{5}6253$	$.0^{5}5980$	$.0^{5}5718$	$.0^{5}5468$	$.0^{5}5227$	$.0^{5}4997$	$.0^{5}4777$
4.1	$.0^{5}4566$	$.0^{5}4346$	$.0^{5}4170$	$.0^{5}3985$	$.0^{5}3807$	$.0^{5}3637$	$.0^{5}3475$	$.0^{5}3319$	$.0^{5}3170$	$.0^{5}3027$
4.2	$.0^{5}2891$	$.0^{5}2760$	$.0^{5}2635$	$.0^{5}2516$	$.0^{5}2402$	$.0^{5}2292$	$.0^{5}2188$	$.0^{5}2088$	$.0^{5}1992$	$.0^{5}1901$
4.3	$.0^{5}1814$	$.0^{5}1730$	$.0^{5}1650$	$.0^{5}1574$	$.0^{5}1501$	$.0^{5}1431$	$.0^{5}1365$	$.0^{5}1301$	$.0^{5}1241$	$.0^{5}1183$
4.4	$.0^{5}1127$	$.0^{5}1074$	$.0^{5}1024$	$.0^{6}9756$	$.0^{6}9296$	$.0^{6}8857$	$.0^{6}8437$	$.0^{6}8037$	$.0^{6}7655$	$.0^{6}7290$
4.5	$.0^{6}6942$	$.0^{6}6610$	$.0^{6}6294$	$.0^{6}5992$	$.0^{6}5704$	$.0^{6}5429$	$.0^{6}5167$	$.0^{6}4917$	$.0^{6}4679$	$.0^{6}4452$
4.6	$.0^{6}4236$	$.0^{6}4029$	$.0^{6}3833$	$.0^{6}3645$	$.0^{6}3467$	$.0^{6}3297$	$.0^{6}3135$	$.0^{6}2981$	$.0^{6}2834$	$.0^{6}2694$
4.7	$.0^{6}2560$	$.0^{6}2433$	$.0^{6}2313$	$.0^{6}2197$	$.0^{6}2088$	$.0^{6}1984$	$.0^{6}1884$	$.0^{6}1790$	$.0^{6}1700$	$.0^{6}1615$
4.8	$.0^{6}1533$	$.0^{6}1456$	$.0^{6}1382$	$.0^{6}1312$	$.0^{6}1246$	$.0^{6}1182$	$.0^{6}1122$	$.0^{6}1065$	$.0^{6}1011$	$.0^{7}9588$
4.9	$.0^{7}9096$	$.0^{7}8629$	$.0^{7}8185$	$.0^{7}7763$	$.0^{7}7362$	$.0^{7}6982$	$.0^{7}6620$	$.0^{7}6276$	$.0^{7}5950$	$.0^{7}5640$

Examples: $L_N(-D) = D + L_N(D)$; $L_N(3.57) = 0.0^{4}4417 = 0.00004417$; $L_N(-3.57) = 3.57004417$.

From Robert O. Schlaifer, *Probability and Statistics for Business Decisions.* New York: McGraw-Hill Book Company, 1959. Reprinted by permission of the Harvard Business School. Copyright © 1959 by the President and Fellows of Harvard College.

TABLE X **The Durbin–Watson d-statistic**
Significance points of d_L and d_U: α = 0.05

n	m = 1		m = 2		m = 3		m = 4		m = 5	
	d_L	d_U	d_L	d_U	d_L	d_U	d_L	d_U	d_L	d_U
15	1.08	1.36	0.95	1.54	0.82	1.75	0.69	1.97	0.56	2.21
16	1.10	1.37	0.98	1.54	0.86	1.73	0.74	1.93	0.62	2.15
17	1.13	1.38	1.02	1.54	0.90	1.71	0.78	1.90	0.67	2.10
18	1.16	1.39	1.05	1.53	0.93	1.69	0.82	1.87	0.71	2.06
19	1.18	1.40	1.08	1.53	0.97	1.68	0.86	1.85	0.75	2.02
20	1.20	1.41	1.10	1.54	1.00	1.68	0.90	1.83	0.79	1.99
21	1.22	1.42	1.13	1.54	1.03	1.67	0.93	1.81	0.83	1.96
22	1.24	1.43	1.15	1.54	1.05	1.66	0.96	1.80	0.86	1.94
23	1.26	1.44	1.17	1.54	1.08	1.66	0.99	1.79	0.90	1.92
24	1.27	1.45	1.19	1.55	1.10	1.66	1.01	1.78	0.93	1.90
25	1.29	1.45	1.21	1.55	1.12	1.66	1.04	1.77	0.95	1.89
26	1.30	1.46	1.22	1.55	1.14	1.65	1.06	1.76	0.98	1.88
27	1.32	1.47	1.24	1.56	1.16	1.65	1.08	1.76	1.01	1.86
28	1.33	1.48	1.26	1.56	1.18	1.65	1.10	1.75	1.03	1.85
29	1.34	1.48	1.27	1.56	1.20	1.65	1.12	1.74	1.05	1.84
30	1.35	1.49	1.28	1.57	1.21	1.65	1.14	1.74	1.07	1.83
31	1.36	1.50	1.30	1.57	1.23	1.65	1.16	1.74	1.09	1.83
32	1.37	1.50	1.31	1.57	1.24	1.65	1.18	1.73	1.11	1.82
33	1.38	1.51	1.32	1.58	1.26	1.65	1.19	1.73	1.13	1.81
34	1.39	1.51	1.33	1.58	1.27	1.65	1.21	1.73	1.15	1.81
35	1.40	1.52	1.34	1.58	1.28	1.65	1.22	1.73	1.16	1.80
36	1.41	1.52	1.35	1.59	1.29	1.65	1.24	1.73	1.18	1.80
37	1.42	1.53	1.36	1.59	1.31	1.66	1.25	1.72	1.19	1.80
38	1.43	1.54	1.37	1.59	1.32	1.66	1.26	1.72	1.21	1.79
39	1.43	1.54	1.38	1.60	1.33	1.66	1.27	1.72	1.22	1.79
40	1.44	1.54	1.39	1.60	1.34	1.66	1.29	1.72	1.23	1.79
45	1.48	1.57	1.43	1.62	1.38	1.67	1.34	1.72	1.29	1.78
50	1.50	1.59	1.46	1.63	1.42	1.67	1.38	1.72	1.34	1.77
55	1.53	1.60	1.49	1.64	1.45	1.68	1.41	1.72	1.38	1.77
60	1.55	1.62	1.51	1.65	1.48	1.69	1.44	1.73	1.41	1.77
65	1.57	1.63	1.54	1.66	1.50	1.70	1.47	1.73	1.44	1.77
70	1.58	1.64	1.55	1.67	1.52	1.70	1.49	1.74	1.46	1.77
75	1.60	1.65	1.57	1.68	1.54	1.71	1.51	1.74	1.49	1.77
80	1.61	1.66	1.59	1.69	1.56	1.72	1.53	1.74	1.51	1.77
85	1.62	1.67	1.60	1.70	1.57	1.72	1.55	1.75	1.52	1.77
90	1.63	1.68	1.61	1.70	1.59	1.73	1.57	1.75	1.54	1.78
95	1.64	1.69	1.62	1.71	1.60	1.73	1.58	1.75	1.56	1.78
100	1.65	1.69	1.63	1.72	1.61	1.74	1.59	1.76	1.57	1.78

Significance points of d_L and d_U: $\alpha = 0.01$

n	m = 1		m = 2		m = 3		m = 4		m = 5	
	d_L	d_U	d_L	d_U	d_L	d_U	d_L	d_U	d_L	d_U
15	0.81	1.07	0.70	1.25	0.59	1.46	0.49	1.70	0.39	1.96
16	0.84	1.09	0.74	1.25	0.63	1.44	0.53	1.66	0.44	1.90
17	0.87	1.10	0.77	1.25	0.67	1.43	0.57	1.63	0.48	1.85
18	0.90	1.12	0.80	1.26	0.71	1.42	0.61	1.60	0.52	1.80
19	0.93	1.13	0.83	1.26	0.74	1.41	0.65	1.58	0.56	1.77
20	0.95	1.15	0.86	1.27	0.77	1.41	0.68	1.57	0.60	1.74
21	0.97	1.16	0.89	1.27	0.80	1.41	0.72	1.55	0.63	1.71
22	1.00	1.17	0.91	1.28	0.83	1.40	0.75	1.54	0.66	1.69
23	1.02	1.19	0.94	1.29	0.86	1.40	0.77	1.53	0.70	1.67
24	1.04	1.20	0.96	1.30	0.88	1.41	0.80	1.53	0.72	1.66
25	1.05	1.21	0.98	1.30	0.90	1.41	0.83	1.52	0.75	1.65
26	1.07	1.22	1.00	1.31	0.93	1.41	0.85	1.52	0.78	1.64
27	1.09	1.23	1.02	1.32	0.95	1.41	0.88	1.51	0.81	1.63
28	1.10	1.24	1.04	1.32	0.97	1.41	0.90	1.51	0.83	1.62
29	1.12	1.25	1.05	1.33	0.99	1.42	0.92	1.51	0.85	1.61
30	1.13	1.26	1.07	1.34	1.01	1.42	0.94	1.51	0.88	1.61
31	1.15	1.27	1.08	1.34	1.02	1.42	0.96	1.51	0.90	1.60
32	1.16	1.28	1.10	1.35	1.04	1.43	0.98	1.51	0.92	1.60
33	1.17	1.29	1.11	1.36	1.05	1.43	1.00	1.51	0.94	1.59
34	1.18	1.30	1.13	1.36	1.07	1.43	1.01	1.51	0.95	1.59
35	1.19	1.31	1.14	1.37	1.08	1.44	1.03	1.51	0.97	1.59
36	1.21	1.32	1.15	1.38	1.10	1.44	1.04	1.51	0.99	1.59
37	1.22	1.32	1.16	1.38	1.11	1.45	1.06	1.51	1.00	1.59
38	1.23	1.33	1.18	1.39	1.12	1.45	1.07	1.52	1.02	1.58
39	1.24	1.34	1.19	1.39	1.14	1.45	1.09	1.52	1.03	1.58
40	1.25	1.34	1.20	1.40	1.15	1.46	1.10	1.52	1.05	1.58
45	1.29	1.38	1.24	1.42	1.20	1.48	1.16	1.53	1.11	1.58
50	1.32	1.40	1.28	1.45	1.24	1.49	1.20	1.54	1.16	1.59
55	1.36	1.43	1.32	1.47	1.28	1.51	1.25	1.55	1.21	1.59
60	1.38	1.45	1.35	1.48	1.32	1.52	1.28	1.56	1.25	1.60
65	1.41	1.47	1.38	1.50	1.35	1.53	1.31	1.57	1.28	1.61
70	1.43	1.49	1.40	1.52	1.37	1.55	1.34	1.58	1.31	1.61
75	1.45	1.50	1.42	1.53	1.39	1.56	1.37	1.59	1.34	1.62
80	1.47	1.52	1.44	1.54	1.42	1.57	1.39	1.60	1.36	1.62
85	1.48	1.53	1.46	1.55	1.43	1.58	1.41	1.60	1.39	1.63
90	1.50	1.54	1.47	1.56	1.45	1.59	1.43	1.61	1.41	1.64
95	1.51	1.55	1.49	1.57	1.47	1.60	1.45	1.62	1.42	1.64
100	1.52	1.56	1.50	1.58	1.48	1.60	1.46	1.63	1.44	1.65

SOURCE: Reproduced by permission of the editor and authors, from J. Durbin and G. S. Watson, "Testing for serial correlation in least squares regression, (II)," *Biometrika*, **38**, 1951, pp. 159–178.

TABLE XI   **Critical values of r in the runs test**

Given in the body of Table XI are various critical values of r for various values of n_1 and n_2. For the Wald–Wolfowitz two-sample runs test, any value of r that is equal to or smaller than that shown in Table XI is significant at the 0.05 level.

n_1 \ n_2	2	3	4	5	6	7	8	9	10	11	12	13	14	15	16	17	18	19	20
2											2	2	2	2	2	2	2	2	2
3				2	2	2	2	2	2	2	2	2	3	3	3	3	3	3
4			2	2	2	3	3	3	3	3	3	3	3	4	4	4	4	4
5		2	2	3	3	3	3	3	4	4	4	4	4	4	4	5	5	5
6	2	2	3	3	3	3	4	4	4	4	5	5	5	5	5	5	6	6
7	2	2	3	3	3	4	4	5	5	5	5	5	6	6	6	6	6	6
8	2	3	3	3	4	4	5	5	5	6	6	6	6	6	7	7	7	7
9	2	3	3	4	4	5	5	5	6	6	6	7	7	7	7	8	8	8
10	2	3	3	4	5	5	5	6	6	7	7	7	7	8	8	8	8	9
11	2	3	4	4	5	5	6	6	7	7	7	8	8	8	9	9	9	9
12	2	2	3	4	4	5	6	6	7	7	7	8	8	8	9	9	9	10	10
13	2	2	3	4	5	5	6	6	7	7	8	8	9	9	9	10	10	10	10
14	2	2	3	4	5	5	6	7	7	8	8	9	9	9	10	10	10	11	11
15	2	3	3	4	5	6	6	7	7	8	8	9	9	10	10	11	11	11	12
16	2	3	4	4	5	6	6	7	8	8	9	9	10	10	11	11	11	12	12
17	2	3	4	4	5	6	7	7	8	9	9	10	10	11	11	11	12	12	13
18	2	3	4	5	5	6	7	8	8	9	9	10	10	11	11	12	12	13	13
19	2	3	4	5	6	6	7	8	8	9	10	10	11	11	12	12	13	13	13
20	2	3	4	5	6	6	7	8	9	9	10	10	11	12	12	13	13	13	14

Adapted from Frieda S. Swed and C. Eisenhart, "Tables for testing randomness of grouping in a sequence of alternatives." *Ann. Math. Statist.*, Vol. 14 (1943), pp. 83–86, with the kind permission of the authors and publisher.

TABLE XII **Critical values of *T* for the Wilcoxon matched-pairs signed-ranks test**

	Level of Significance for One-Tailed Test		
	.025	.01	.005
n	Level of Significance for Two-Tailed Test		
	.05	.02	.01
6	0	—	—
7	2	0	—
8	4	2	0
9	6	3	2
10	8	5	3
11	11	7	5
12	14	10	7
13	17	13	10
14	21	16	13
15	25	20	16
16	30	24	20
17	35	28	23
18	40	33	28
19	46	38	32
20	52	43	38
21	59	49	43
22	66	56	49
23	73	62	55
24	81	69	61
25	89	77	68

Adapted from Table I of F. Wilcoxon, *Some Rapid Approximate Statistical Procedures*. New York: American Cyanamid Company, 1949, p. 13. Reproduced with the permission of the American Cyanamid Company.

TABLE XIII **Critical values of D in the Kolmogorov–Smirnov one-sample test**

Sample Size (n)	Level of Significance for D = Maximum $\|F_i - S_i\|$				
	.20	.15	.10	.05	.01
1	.900	.925	.950	.975	.995
2	.684	.726	.776	.842	.929
3	.565	.597	.642	.708	.828
4	.494	.525	.564	.624	.733
5	.446	.474	.510	.565	.669
6	.410	.436	.470	.521	.618
7	.381	.405	.438	.486	.577
8	.358	.381	.411	.457	.543
9	.339	.360	.388	.432	.514
10	.322	.342	.368	.410	.490
11	.307	.326	.352	.391	.468
12	.295	.313	.338	.375	.450
13	.284	.302	.325	.361	.433
14	.274	.292	.314	.349	.418
15	.266	.283	.304	.338	.404
16	.258	.274	.295	.328	.392
17	.250	.266	.286	.318	.381
18	.244	.259	.278	.309	.371
19	.237	.252	.272	.301	.363
20	.231	.246	.264	.294	.356
25	.21	.22	.24	.27	.32
30	.19	.20	.22	.24	.29
35	.18	.19	.21	.23	.27
Over 35	$\dfrac{1.07}{\sqrt{n}}$	$\dfrac{1.14}{\sqrt{n}}$	$\dfrac{1.22}{\sqrt{n}}$	$\dfrac{1.36}{\sqrt{n}}$	$\dfrac{1.63}{\sqrt{n}}$

Adapted from F. J. Massey, Jr., "The Kolmogorov–Smirnov test for goodness of fit." *J. Amer. Statist. Ass.*, Vol. 46 (1951), p. 70, with the kind permission of the author and publisher.

BIBLIOGRAPHY

Extensive tables of the normal, t, chi-square, and F distributions are found in

1. Pearson, E.S. and H.O. Hartley, *Biometrika Tables for Statisticians*, Vol. 1. New York: John Wiley and Sons, 1968.

Binomial probabilities for $n = 50$ to $n = 100$ are found in

2. Romig, H.G., *50–100 Binomial Tables*. New York: John Wiley and Sons, 1953.

Poisson probability tables are found in

3. Molina, E.C., *Poisson's Exponential Binomial Limit*. New York: D. Van Nostrand, 1943.

More detailed treatments of mathematical probability distributions are found in

4. DeGroot, M.H., *Probability and Statistics*. Reading, MA: Addison-Wesley, 1975.
5. Hogg, R.V. and A.T. Craig, *Introduction to Mathematical Statistics*, 4th ed. New York: Macmillan, 1978.

The first widely recognized treatment of nonparametric statistics is in

6. Siegel, S., *Nonparametric Statistics for the Behavioral Sciences*. New York: McGraw-Hill, 1956.

A more current source is

7. Noether, G.E., *Introduction to Statistics: A Nonparametric Approach*, 2nd ed. Boston: Houghton Mifflin, 1976.

General texts on analysis of variance and experimental design are

8. Anderson, V.C. and R.A. McLean, *Design of Experiments: A Realistic Approach*. New York: Marcel Dekker, 1974.
9. Snedecor, G.W. and W.G. Cochran, *Statistical Methods*, 7th ed. Ames, IA: Iowa University Press, 1980.

Some readings that illustrate some uses or misuses of statistical analysis are

10. Huff, D., *How to Lie with Statistics*. New York: Norton, 1954.
11. Mansfield, E. (ed.), *Statistics for Business and Economics, Readings and Cases*, 2nd ed. New York: W.W. Norton, 1983.

12. J. Tanur et al. (eds.), *Statistics: A Guide to the Unknown*, 2nd ed. San Francisco: Holden-Day, 1978.

Textbooks on econometric methods are

13. Kennedy, P., *A Guide to Econometrics*. Cambridge, MA: MIT Press, 1979.
14. Mirer, Thad W., *Economic Statistics and Econometrics*. New York: Macmillan, 1983.
15. Murphy, J. L., *Introductory Econometrics*. Homewood, IL: Richard D. Irwin, 1973.

Other textbooks that give complementary treatments of many of the topics in this book are

16. Hamburg, M., *Basic Statistics*, 2nd ed. New York: Harcourt Brace Jovanovich, 1979.
17. Harnett, D.L., *Statistical Methods*, 3rd ed. Reading, MA: Addison-Wesley, 1982.
18. Plane, D.R. and E.B. Opperman, *Statistics for Management Decisions*. Dallas: Business Publication, Inc., 1977.
19. Summers, G.W. and W. Peters, *Basic Statistics in Business and Economics*, 3rd ed. Belmont, CA: Wadsworth, 1981.
20. Winkler, R.L., *Introduction to Bayesian Inference and Decision*. New York: Holt, Rinehart, and Winston, 1972.
21. Winkler, R.L. and W.L. Hays, *Statistics: Probability, Inference, and Decision*, 2nd ed. New York: Holt, Rinehart, and Winston, 1975.
22. Wonnacott, T.H. and R.J. Wonnacott, *Introductory Statistics for Business and Economics*, 3rd ed. New York: John Wiley and Sons, 1984.

CHAPTER 1

1.5 a) $\mu = \$4,418,828$, $\pi = 25/50 =$

1.7

Class	f
0– 300	
300– 600	
600– 900	
900–120	
1200–	
15	

ANSWERS

0.50   b) $\bar{x}$ = \$4,286,860, p = 6/12 = 0.50

	f/n	Cum. Freq.	Cum. Rel. Freq.
13	0.167	13	0.167
10	0.128	23	0.295
14	0.179	37	0.474
17	0.218	54	0.692
1500 6	0.077	60	0.769
00–1800 7	0.090	67	0.859
1800–2100 4	0.051	71	0.910
2100–2400 4	0.051	75	0.962
2400–2700 2	0.026	77	0.987
2700–3000 1	0.013	78	1.000
	1.000		

1.13

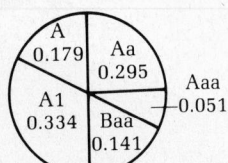

1.17 b) μ = \$2,132,008   d) Percent > \$25,000 = 75%, Percent ≤ \$26,000 = 56.25%

CHAPTER 2

2.3 Average percent decrease is $\dfrac{100[5(10) + 3(25)]}{5(45) + 3(85)} = \dfrac{100(125)}{480} = 26.04\%$.

2.5 a) Median is 150.5th value, which is 28.5.   b) Mode = 25   c) Mean = 9200/300 = 30.67

2.7 a) Median is 50.5th value, which is 1; mode = 0   b) μ = 80/100 = 0.8

2.9 Using class marks of 5, 10, and 15, μ = 8.5.

2.11 a) Median = \$61,250; $\bar{x}$ = 2,399,000/40 = \$59,975. Negative skewness.   b) $\bar{x}$ = \$59,750.

2.15 $\sigma^2 = \dfrac{306,500}{300} - (30.67)^2 = 81.02$

2.17 a) $\sigma = \sqrt{3.4} = 1.844$

b) $\mu \pm 1\sigma$ = 15.156 to 18.844. The included values are 16 and 18, which occur 100(16/30) = 53% of the time.

$\mu \pm 2\sigma$ = 17 ± 2(1.844) is the interval 13.312 to 20.688, which includes 100% of the distribution.

2.19 $\sigma^2 = 15.25$

2.21 a) $\sigma^2 = 0.443/6 = 0.0738$
b) $\sigma = \sqrt{0.0738} = 0.272$
$\mu \pm 1\sigma = 1.07 \pm 0.272$ is the interval 0.798 to 1.342, which includes 3 of 6 for a proportion included of 0.50.

2.23 a) $\mu = 20/5 = 4; \sigma = \sqrt{5.6} = 2.37$ b) $\mu = 28/7 = 4; \sigma = \sqrt{5.14} = 2.27$
c) $\mu = 28/7 = 4; \sigma > 2.37$ because items -1 and 9 have larger than average deviations from the mean.

2.25 $\mu = 166/10 = 16.6$; mode $= 14$; median $= 14$; 60% mid-range $= 19 - 12 = 7$;
$\sigma = \sqrt{70.04} = 8.37$

2.29 $\mu = 81.91; \sigma^2 = 137.085$

2.31 a) Model is $26,400; median is halfway between the eighth and ninth values, which is $25,900.
b) $\bar{x} = 412,500/16 = 25,781.25$ using midpoints and having grouping error.

2.33 a) $\mu = \$18,986.50; \sigma^2 = 23,214,515.25; \sigma = \$4818.14$; median $= \$17,885$
b) The distribution for Oldberry has the smaller mean but larger variance, so it is more variable. The regional distribution has greater positive skewness.

2.39 We assume class marks of 10 for "under 20" and 70 for "60 and over." For those who liked the movie, $\mu = 24.91$ and $\sigma^2 = 308.58$. For those who disliked the movie, $\mu = 33.33$ and $\sigma^2 = 411.33$. The movie appeals more to younger people.

2.41 c) $\mu = 225.25$
d) $\sigma = \sqrt{31,370.44} = 177.12$
$\mu \pm 1\sigma = 48.13$ to 402.37, which includes about 70% of the population (interpolating within classes).
$\mu \pm 2\sigma = 0$ to 579.49, which includes about 95.5%.
e) Median $= 190.05$

2.43 Answer is b, standard deviation.

2.45 For income, $\mu \pm 1\sigma = \$77,515 \pm 17,518.61$ includes $100(22/40) = 55\%$ of the values. For expenses, $\mu \pm 1\sigma = \$59,975 \pm 14,822.46$ includes $100(29/40) = 72.5\%$ of the values.

2.47 $\mu = 20,605/105 = 196.2381; \sigma^2 = 245.132; \sigma = 15.66$

CHAPTER 3

3.1 a) Finite, discrete
b) $P(A) = 0.167, P(B) = 0.167, P(C) = 0.167, P(D) = 0.50$. These are subjective probabilities.

3.3 a) Infinite, discrete b) Infinite, discrete c) Finite, discrete d) Infinite, continuous
e) Infinite, continuous

3.5 $P(\text{win}) = 1501/50,000 = 0.003002$

3.7 $P(\text{low threat and Moody rating} \geq \text{Åa}) = 9/78 = 0.1154$

3.9 a) 360 workers b) $P(\text{Black}) = 70/360 = 0.1944$ c) $P(\text{over 50}) = 95/360 = 0.2639$

3.11 a) $(2)(2) \cdots (2) = 2^9 = 512$ combinations, P(one try) = 1/512   b) P(one try) = 1/9

3.13 $_8C_0 + {}_8C_1 + \cdots + {}_8C_8 = 256$

3.15 $3! = 6$

3.17 a) $_{10}P_{10} = 3,628,000$ ways   b) $_{10}C_3 = 120$ combinations

3.23 a) P(≤30 ∩ female) = P(≤30)P(female|≤30) = (1/2)(1/2) = 1/4   b) Dependence
   c) P(female ∩ ≤30) = 1/4, P(≤50) = 3/4, P(≤|female) = 4/7
   d) P(female) + P(>50) − P(female ∩ >50) = 7/16 + 1/4 − 1/8 = 9/16

3.25 a) P(G ∩ M) = 0.12   b) P(G ∪ M) = 0.78

c)

	M	N	C	
G	0.12	0.30	0.18	0.60
E	0.18	0.10	0.12	0.40
	0.30	0.40	0.30	

   d) P(M|G) = 0.20 ≠ P(M) = 0.30; not independent

3.27 a) P(#6 ∩ #6) = (1/6)(1/6) = 1/36   b) P(#6 ∪ #6) = 1/6 + 1/6 − 1/36 = 11/36
   c) P(different) = 1 − P(same) = 1 − 6/36 = 5/6

3.29 a) P(male) = 150/250 = 0.60   b) P(>150 lb) = 130/250 = 0.52   c) P(>67 in.) = 170/150 =
   0.68   d) P(male ∩ ≤67 in.) = 0.04   e) P(female|≥67 in.) = 0.1765

3.31 a) P(G|M) = 0.12/(0.12 + 0.18) = 0.40   b) P(female|≤30) = 0.25/(0.25 + 0.25) = 0.50

3.33 a) P(≥10%) = (1/3)(1/3) + (2/3)(1/5) = 11/45   b) P(best| ≥ 10%) = 5/11

3.35 a) P(pass) = 0.42   b) P(correctly|pass) = 3/7

3.37 a) P(≥60) = 0.46 + 0.18 = 0.64   b) P(≥70|S) = 0.06/0.19 = 0.3158

c)

	<50	50–59	60–69	≥70	
L	0.030	0.1500	0.2300	0.09	0.50
M	0.035	0.0775	0.0975	0.04	0.25
S	0.050	0.0600	0.0800	0.06	0.25
	0.115	0.2875	0.4075	0.19	1.000

3.39 a) Using Formula (3.13): P(neither) = P(fiscal incorrect) P(monetary incorrect) = (0.20)(0.20) =
   0.04; P(both) = P(fiscal correct)P(monetary correct) = (0.80)(0.80) = 0.64; P(only 1) =
   P(fiscal correct)P(monetary incorrect) + P(fiscal incorrect)P(monetary correct) =
   (0.80)(0.20) + (0.20)(0.80) = 0.32.
   b) P(only 1|stable) = 0.2564, P(both|stable) = 0.7253, P(neither|stable) = 0.0183; 0.2564 +
   0.7253 + 0.0183 = 1.000

3.43 a) P(W ∩ >90) = 1/4   b) P(>90|W) = 1/2   c) P(W|>90) = 1/3

3.45 μ = \$370.33, P(≥1 below average) = 1/3

3.47 a) $P(S \cap \leq 1) = P(S)P(\leq 1|S) = 0.02$ b) $P(\leq 1|ISF) = 0.20$
     c) $P(ISF|\leq 1) = 0.05 \neq P(ISF) = 0.01$; not independent
         $P(\leq 1|\text{student}) = 1/3 \neq P(\leq 1) = 0.04$; not independent

3.49 $P(\text{both same} \cup \text{at least one } 0) = 0.87$

3.53 a) $P(\geq 25,000 \cup \geq Aa) = 46/78$ b) $P(\geq 25,000 \cup \geq Aa) = 15/78$ c) $P(LCT|\geq Aa) = 1/3$
     d) $P(LCT \cap \geq Aa) = 9/78$

CHAPTER 4

4.1 The c.m.f. is a step function with values equal to the sum of the p.m.f. for all values equal to or smaller than the one being considered.

4.3 a) $E[\mathbf{x}] = 123/12 = 10.25$ b) $E[\mathbf{x}^2] = 1647/12 = 137.25$; $V[\mathbf{x}] = E[\mathbf{x}^2] - (E[\mathbf{x}])^2 = 32.1875$

4.5 a) There are 20 sample pairs with sums from 3 to 9.   b) $E[\mathbf{x}] = 60/10 = 6.0$
     c) $V[\mathbf{x}] = \Sigma(x - \mu)^2 P(x) = 30/10 = 3.0$; $\sigma_x = 1.732$
     d) Add five more sample pairs to part (a).

4.7 a) $E[\mathbf{x}] = \sum_{i=1}^{6} x(\tfrac{1}{2})^x = 1.875$

     b) $E[\mathbf{x}^2] = 4.969$; $V[\mathbf{x}] = 1.398$ by Formula (4.4). Using Formula (4.6), $V[\mathbf{x}] = E[\mathbf{x}]^2 - (1.875)^2$
        $= 1.453$. The answers differ because of the truncation to values $x \leq 6$.

4.9 a) $E[\mathbf{x}] = 1950/10 = 195$ b) $V[\mathbf{x}] = E[\mathbf{x} - 195]^2 = 100$; $\sigma = 10$
     c) Eight values or 80% lie between 185 and 205. All values lie between 175 and 215.

4.11 c) $E[\mathbf{x}] = 2.571$; $E[\mathbf{x}]^2 = 7.0$; $V[\mathbf{x}] = 7.0 - (2.571)^2 = 0.39$

4.13 b) $E[\mathbf{x}] = 6.0$; $V[\mathbf{x}] = 12$

4.15 b) The student will earn \$65 or less if sales are $x \leq 5$.
         $P(x \leq 5) = (1/2) + 0 + (1/4) + (1/8) + (1/16) + (1/32) = 31/32$
     c) $E[\mathbf{x}] = \Sigma xP(x) = 1 + 2 + 2 + \cdots + 2 + \cdots = \infty$

4.17 a) $E[\mathbf{x}] = 20,000$; $E[\mathbf{y}] = 20,000$ b) Same as part (a)
     c) $V[\mathbf{x}] = E[\mathbf{x} - 20,000]^2 = 200,000,000$; $V[\mathbf{y}] = 66,666,666$; $V[\mathbf{x}/10,000] = 2$;
        $V[\mathbf{x}]/10,000 = 20,000$

$$V\left[\frac{\mathbf{x}}{10,000}\right] = \frac{1}{(10,000)^2} V[\mathbf{x}].$$

4.19 b) Use class marks of 1500, 4000, 6000, 8500, 11,000, 13,500, and 35,000. $\mu = 14,050.5$;
        $\sigma^2 = 137,296,700$; $\sigma = 11,717.37$.

4.23 a) Let $\mathbf{y} = -2500 + 0.001\mathbf{x}$; $E[\mathbf{y}] = 2$ b) $E[\mathbf{x}]$ $\dfrac{E[\mathbf{y}] - (-2500)}{0.001} = 2,502,000$
     c) $V[\mathbf{y}] = 780/4 = 195$; $V[\mathbf{x}] = (1000)^2 V[\mathbf{y}] = 195,000,000$

4.27 a) $E[\mathbf{x}] + E[\mathbf{y}] = 2.4 + 6.0 = 8.4 = E[\mathbf{x} + \mathbf{y}]$
     b) $E[\mathbf{x}]^2 = 7.6$; $V[\mathbf{x}] = 1.84$; $E[\mathbf{y}]^2 = 42$; $V[\mathbf{y}] = 6.0$; $V[\mathbf{x}] + V[\mathbf{y}] = 1.84 + 6.0 = 7.84$;
        $V[\mathbf{x} + \mathbf{y}] = 78.40 - 70.56 = 7.84$

4.29 a) $E[xy] = 10.25$

b) $E[x + y] = \dfrac{107 + 41}{20} = 7.4; E[x - y] = \dfrac{107 - 41}{20} = 3.3$

c) $C[x, y] - E[x]E[y] = -0.72$

d) $V[x] = 14.23; V[y] = 0.65; V[x + y] = 14.23 + 0.65 + 2(-0.72) = 13.44;$
$V[x - y] = 16.32$

4.31 b) $E[x] = 2.0; E[x]^2 = 5.0; V[x] = 1.0$ c) $E[y] = 0; E[y]^2 = 4.0; V[y] = 4.0$

d) $E[2x - 4] = 2E[x] - E[4] = 4.0 - 4.0 = 0; V[2x - 4] = 4V[x] + 0 = 4$

4.33 a) Joint probability table, $P(x, y)$:

		x					
		1	2	3	4	5	6
	1	1/36	0	0	0	0	0
	2	1/36	1/30	0	0	0	0
	3	1/36	1/30	1/24	0	0	0
y	4	1/36	1/30	1/24	1/18	0	0
	5	1/36	1/30	1/24	1/18	1/12	0
	6	1/36	1/30	1/24	1/18	1/12	1/6

b) $P(y = 0|x = 3) = P(y = 1|x = 3) = P(y = 2|x = 3) = 0; P(y = 3|x = 3) = P(y = 4|x = 3)$

$= P(y = 5|x = 3) = P(y = 6|x = 3) = \dfrac{1/24}{4/24} = \dfrac{1}{4}$ c) $\Sigma y P(y) = 4.75$

4.37 $E[x] = 7.2; E[x]^2 = 54.4; V[x] = 2.56; E[y] = 4.3; E[y]^2 = 20.2; V[y] = 1.71; E[xy] = 30.8;$
$C[x, y] = 30.8 - 7.2(4.3) = -0.16$

4.39 $\mu = 200/10 = 20; \sigma^2 = 100$

4.41 Profit $= 0.03x$. Since $E[x] = 5.64, E[0.03x] = 0.03(5.64) = 0.1692. E[(0.03x)^2] = 0.04169$
$V[0.03x] = 0.01306; \sigma_{profit} = 0.1143$

4.43 $\mu = 2.37; \sigma^2 = 7.57 - 5.62 = 1.95; \sigma = 1.4$

4.45 a) $E[x] = 1.87; E[x]^2 = 4.21; V[x] = 0.71; E[y] = 2.59; E[y]^2 = 7.75; V[y] = 1.04$

b) $E[xy] = 5.08; C[x, y] = 5.08 - 1.87(2.59) = 0.24$ c) Dependent

4.47 $E[sales] = 6$ boxes; $V[sales] = 12.0$. Thus, $E[profit] = (\$10)6 = \$60;$
$V[profit] = (\$10)^2(12) = 1200.$

CHAPTER 5

5.1 a) Skewed right b) $E[x] = 2.40, \sigma^2 = 1.44, \sigma = 1.20$ c) $P(x \geq 4|n = 6, \pi = 0.40) = 0.1792$

5.3 $P(x = 2|n = 4, \pi = 0.20) = 0.1536$

5.5 b) $P(x = 7) = 0.0079, P(x \geq 7) = 0.0086$

5.7 a) $p = 28/165 = 0.1687$, est. of underpaid $= 0.1697(22,395) = 3800; p = 15/165 = 0.11,$
est. of overpaid $= 2463$ b) $3800(\$10.20) - 2463(\$1.81) = \$34,301.97$

5.9 a) $P(x \geq 12|n = 20, \pi = 0.50) = 0.2517$ b) In advance, $P(5 \text{ heads}) = (1/2)^5$

5.11 a) $P(x = 3|n = 6, \pi = 0.25) = 0.1318$ b) $P(x \geq 3|n = 6, \pi = 0.25) = 0.1694$
   c) $P(x < 3|n = 6, \pi = 0.25) = 0.9624$ d) $P(2 \leq x \leq 4|n = 6, \pi = 0.25) = 0.4614$
   e) $E[x] = 1.50$, $V[x] = 1.125$

5.13 $P(x \geq 13|n = 6, \pi = 0.25) = 0.0867$. Probably should not dispute claim on the basis of this sample.

5.15 $P(x \geq 67|n = 100, \pi = 0.50) = 0.0004$. Do not support.

5.17 b) $P(x \geq 2|n = 4, \pi = 0.25) = 0.2617$

5.19 a) $P(x \leq 12|n = 20, \pi = 0.67) = 0.3267$, conclude not different.
   b) $P(x \leq 8|n = 20, \pi = 0.67) = 0.0118$, surprising.

5.21 a) $\dfrac{_4C_3 \, _4C_2}{_{52}C_5} = 0.00000923$ b) $\dfrac{_4C_4 \, _4C_1}{_{52}C_5} = 0.00000154$ c) $\dfrac{_4C_4 \, _{48}C_1}{_{52}C_5} = 0.000018$

5.23 a) $\dfrac{_5C_3 \, _5C_3}{_{10}C_6} = 0.47619$ b) $\dfrac{_4C_4 \, _5C_2}{_{10}C_6} + \dfrac{_5C_5 \, _5C_1}{_{10}C_6} = 0.2619$

5.25 $\dfrac{_4C_3 \, _{17}C_1}{_{20}C_4} = 0.0132$

5.29 $P(x = 1|n = 3, \pi = 0.40) = 0.4320$. Compares favorably with answer of 0.4438 in Problem 5.20.

5.31 $P(x = 3|n = 4, \pi = 0.20) = 0.0256$. Since $n = 4$ is 20% of $N = 20$, this number is not a good approximation to Problem 5.25 answer (0.0132).

5.33 $P(x = 10|\lambda = 8.5) = 0.1104$

5.35 $P(x = 2|\lambda = 2.3) = 0.2652$

5.37 a) $P(0 \leq x \leq 2) = 0.9197$, $P(0 \leq x \leq 3) = 0.9801$. The first one does not compare favorably; the second one does.

5.39 a) $P(x = 3|\lambda = 3) = 0.2240$ b) $P(x = 6) = 0.1606$
   c) The longer the time period, the longer will be the list of events that could take place. Note that the variance increases as $\lambda = 3$, $\sigma^2 = 3$ goes to $\lambda = 6$, $\sigma^2 = 6$.

5.41 a) $P(2 \text{ of A}, 4 \text{ of B}, 1 \text{ of C}) = 0.0326$ b) $P(3 \text{ of O}, 2 \text{ of A}, 1 \text{ of AB}) = 0.0437$

5.43 $P(x \geq 1|n = 4, \pi = 1/12) = 1 - P(x = 0) = 1 - 0.7061 = 0.2939$

5.51 $P(x = 5|n = 10, \pi = 0.08) = 0.0005$, $V[\text{binomial}] = 0.736$;
   $P(x = 5|\lambda = 0.80) = 0.0012$, $V[\text{Poisson}] = 0.80$

5.55 $P(x = 5|n = 2000, \pi = 0.001) = 0.0526$

5.57 $P(x_1 = 65, x_2 = 35) = 0.00104$

CHAPTER 6

6.1 b) The area under $f(x)$ is a triangle. Calculate the area by using the formula

$$A = \frac{1}{2}(\text{base})(\text{height}) = \frac{1}{2}(1)(2) = 1.$$

Alternatively, using calculus: $A = \int_0^1 f(x)dx = \int_0^1 2x\,dx = [x^2]_0^1 = 1 - 0 = 1.$

c) $P\left(0 \le x \le \dfrac{1}{2}\right) =$ Area under $f(x)$ between $x = 0$ and $x = \dfrac{1}{2}$. Again, the area is a triangle,

with base $= \dfrac{1}{2}$ and height $= f\left(\dfrac{1}{2}\right) = 1$:

$$A = \frac{1}{2}\,(\text{base})(\text{height}) = \frac{1}{2}\left(\frac{1}{2}\right)(1) = \frac{1}{4}.$$

6.3 $F(0) = 0;\ F\left(\dfrac{1}{2}\right) = \left(\dfrac{1}{4}\right);\ F(0.707) = \dfrac{1}{2},\ F(1) = F(3.7) = 1$

6.5   a) $F(-5) = 0;\ F(5) = 1$ b) $F(-2) = 0.30$ c) $F(3) = 0.80;$ complement $= 1 - 0.80 = 0.20.$

6.7   b) Mean is two thirds of the way from 30 to 60; $\mu = E[d] = 50(= \$50,000)$
$E[10d] = 10E[d] = 10(50) = 500$
Expected net profit is $500,000

c) $P(\text{inventory of} > 10,000) = P(d > 50)$
At $d = 50$, height of $f(d)$ is $(50 - 30)/450 = 2/45.$

Area of triangle is $P(d < 50) = \dfrac{1}{2}(20)(2/45) = 20/45 = 4/9$

d) $V[10d] = 10^2 V[d] = 100(50) = 5000$, but d is in units of 1000. Hence, $V[\text{net profit}] = 1000^2 V[10d] = 10^6(5,000) = 5 \times 10^9;\ \sigma = \$70,711;\ \mu \pm 2\sigma = \$500,000 \pm 2(70,711) = \$358,578$ to $\$641,422$

6.11 a) $P(5 \le x \le 25) = P\left(\dfrac{5 - 15}{10} \le \dfrac{x - \mu}{\sigma} \le \dfrac{25 - 15}{10}\right) = 0.6826$

b) $P(-5 \le x \le 35) = P\left(\dfrac{-5 - 15}{10} \le \dfrac{x - \mu}{\sigma} \le \dfrac{35 - 15}{20}\right) = 0.9544$

c) $P(-10 \le x \le 35) = P\left(\dfrac{-10 - 15}{10} \le \dfrac{x - \mu}{\sigma} \le \dfrac{35 - 15}{10}\right) = 0.9710$

d) $P(x \ge 35) = 1 - F(2.0) = 1 - 0.9772 = 0.0228$
$P(x \le -5) = F(-2.0) = 1 - 0.9772 = 0.0228$
$P(x \le -5 \text{ or } x \ge 35) = P(x \le -5) + P(x \ge 35) = 0.0228 + 0.0228 = 0.0456$

6.13 a) $P(x \ge 85) = P\left(\dfrac{x - \mu}{\sigma} \ge \dfrac{85 - 60}{15}\right) = P(z \ge 1.67) = 0.0475$

b) $P(45 \le x \le 55) = P\left(\dfrac{45 - 60}{15} \le \dfrac{x - \mu}{\sigma} \le \dfrac{55 - 60}{15}\right) = P(-1 \le z \le -0.33) = 0.2120$

c) $P(x = 60) = 0$

6.15 $P(45 \le x \le 55) = P\left(\dfrac{45 - 40}{5} \le \dfrac{x - \mu}{\sigma} \le \dfrac{55 - 40}{5}\right) = P(1 \le z \le 3) = 0.1574$

6.17 $P(-1.28 \le z \le 1.65) = F(1.65) - F(-1.28) = F(1.65) - [1 - F(1.28)] = 0.8502$

6.19 $P(x \le a) = 0.90 = P\left(\dfrac{x - \mu}{\sigma} \le \dfrac{a - 19,000}{2,000}\right)$

$P(z \leq 1.282) = 0.90$; hence, $\dfrac{a - 19{,}000}{2{,}000} = 1.282$, or $a = \$21{,}564$

$P(x \geq b) = 0.25 = P\left(\dfrac{x - \mu}{\sigma} \geq \dfrac{b - 19{,}000}{2{,}000}\right); \; P(z > 0.675) = 0.25$

Thus, $\dfrac{b - 19{,}000}{2{,}000} = 0.675$, or $b = \$20{,}350$.

6.21 a) $P(x \geq 140) = P\left(\dfrac{x - \mu}{\sigma} \geq \dfrac{140 - 100}{16}\right) = P(z \geq 2.50) = 1 - F(2.50) = 1 - 0.9938 = 0.0062$

b) $P(x \leq 80) = P\left(\dfrac{x - \mu}{\sigma} \leq \dfrac{80 - 100}{16}\right) = P(z \leq -1.25) = F(-1.25) = 1 - 0.8944 = 0.1056$

6.23 $n\pi = 20(0.80) = 16$; $n\pi(1 - \pi) = 20(0.80)(0.20) = 3.2$; $\sqrt{n\pi(1 - \pi)} = \sqrt{3.2} = 1.79$. Using the normal approximation, $N(n\pi, n\pi(1 - \pi)) = N(16, 3.2)$, corrected for continuity,

$P(x \leq 13.5) = P\left(\dfrac{x - n}{\sqrt{n\pi(1 - \pi)}} \leq 13.5\right) = P\left(z \leq \dfrac{-2.5}{1.79}\right) = P(z \leq -1.40) = F(-1.40) =$
$1 - 0.9192 = 0.0808.$

6.25 $\sqrt{\pi(1 - \pi)/n} = \sqrt{(0.75)(0.25)/50} = 0.061$. Using the normal approximation, $N(\pi, \pi(1 - \pi)/n) = N(0.75, 0.061^2)$, correcting for continuity $P(p \leq 0.51) =$

$P\left(\dfrac{p - \pi}{\sqrt{\pi(1 - \pi)/n}} \leq \dfrac{0.51 - 0.75}{0.061}\right) = P\left(z \leq \dfrac{-0.24}{0.061}\right) = P(z \leq -3.93).$

Since $P(z \leq -3.93) < 0.00005$ (i.e., it is not shown on Table III), we would doubt the senator's claim.

6.27 b) $\mu = 1/\lambda = \dfrac{1}{3}$; $V[T] = 1/\lambda^2 = \dfrac{1}{9}$

c) $\mu \pm \sigma$ is $\dfrac{1}{3} \pm \dfrac{1}{3}$ or the interval 0 to $\dfrac{2}{3}$, $P\left(0 \leq T \leq \dfrac{2}{3}\right) = F(T) = 0.865$ using $\lambda T = 3\left(\dfrac{2}{3}\right) = 2.$

$\mu \pm 2$ is $\dfrac{1}{3} \pm \dfrac{2}{3}$ or the interval $-\dfrac{1}{3}$ to 1, $P(0 \leq T \leq 1.0) = F(1) = 0.950$ using $\lambda T = 3(1) = 3$
(Note: $T < 0$ is not defined.)

6.29 a) $\lambda = 4$ per 6 min; $P(x \geq 6) = 0.2148$ from Table II.

b) $P(T \geq 3) = 1 - F(3)$, where $\lambda = \dfrac{2}{3}$ per min.

F(3) is found in Table IV using $\lambda T = \left(\dfrac{2}{3}\right)(3) = 2$; $F(3) = 0.865$.

$P(T \geq 3) = 1 - 0.865 = 0.135$

c) $P(2 \leq T \leq 4)$. Use the same approach as in part (b), where $\lambda = \dfrac{2}{3}$ customer.

$P(2 \leq T \leq 4) = F(4) - F(2)$

For F(4), $\lambda T = \left(\dfrac{2}{3}\right)(4) = \dfrac{8}{3} \cong 2.7$ For F(2), $\lambda T = \left(\dfrac{2}{3}\right)(2) = \dfrac{4}{3} \cong 1.33$

$P(2 \leq T \leq 4) = F(4) - F(2) = 0.933 - 0.727 = 0.206$ (using Table IV)

6.31 a) $P\left(T \leq \frac{1}{4}\right) = F\left(\frac{1}{4}\right)$; for $\lambda T = 2\left(\frac{1}{4}\right) = \frac{1}{2}$, $F\left(\frac{1}{4}\right) = 0.393$

b) $P\left(T \geq \frac{3}{4}\right) = 1 - F\left(\frac{3}{4}\right)$; for $\lambda T = 2\left(\frac{3}{4}\right) = \frac{6}{4} = 1.5$, $F\left(\frac{3}{4}\right) = 0.777$;

$1 - F\left(\frac{3}{4}\right) = 1 - 0.777 = 0.223$

6.33 a) $P(0 \leq T \leq 1.0) = F(1.0) - F(0)$ for $\lambda = 2$; for $\lambda T = 2(1) = 2$, $F(1) = 0.865$
$P(0 \leq T \leq 1.0) = F(1.0) - F(0) = 0.865 - 0 = 0.865$

b) For $\lambda T = (4)\left(\frac{1}{2}\right) = 2$, $F\left(\frac{1}{2}\right) = 0.865$

$P\left(0 \leq T \leq \frac{1}{2}\right) = F\left(\frac{1}{2}\right) - F(0) = 0.865 - 0 = 0.865$

c) Yes, $P(0 \leq T \leq \mu + \lambda) = 0.865$ for any $\lambda > 0$. This probability exceeds 68% because the distribution is skewed.

d) We solve the problem below for any λ:
$P(\mu - 2\sigma \leq T \leq \mu + 2\sigma) = P(0 \leq T \leq 3/\lambda)$; for $T = 3/\lambda$, $\lambda T = 3.0$ and $F(3/\lambda) = 0.950$.
Therefore, $P(0 \leq T \leq 3/\lambda) = F(3/\lambda) - F(0) = 0.950 - 0 = 0.950$.

6.35 b) $F\left(\frac{1}{2}\right) = \left(\frac{1}{2}\right)^2 = \frac{1}{4}$ c) $E[\boldsymbol{x}] = \mu = \int_0^1 2x^2\, dx = \frac{2}{3}$

d) $E[\boldsymbol{x}^2] = \frac{1}{2}$; $V[\boldsymbol{x}] = E[\boldsymbol{x}^2] - \mu^2 = \frac{9}{18} - \frac{8}{18} = \frac{1}{18}$

6.37 a) $\int_1^x 2dx = [2x]_1^x = 2x - 2$ for $1 \leq \boldsymbol{x} \leq 1.5$

b) $\int_{-2}^x \left(\frac{1}{4} + \left(\frac{1}{8}\right)x\right) dx = \left[\left(\frac{1}{4}\right)x + \left(\frac{1}{16}\right)x^2\right]_{-2}^x = \left[\left(\frac{1}{4}\right)x + \left(\frac{1}{16}\right)x^2\right)\right] - \left[\frac{-2}{4} + \frac{(-2)^2}{16}\right] =$

$\left(\frac{1}{16}\right)x^2 + \left(\frac{1}{4}\right)x + \frac{1}{4}$

c) $\int_0^x e^{-x}\, dx = [-e^{-x}]_0^x = -e^{-x} + (e^0) = 1 - e^{-x}$

6.39 a) $f(x) = 1/(b - a)$ for $a \leq \boldsymbol{x} \leq b$ d) $E[\boldsymbol{x}] = \mu = (b + a)/2$; $V[\boldsymbol{x}] = (b - a)^2/12$

6.41 b) $\int_0^1 f(x)\, dx = \int_0^1 3x^2\, dx = [x^3]_0^1 = 1.0$

c) $F(x) = \int_{-\infty}^x f(x)\, dx = [x^3]_0^x = x^3$ $P\left(\boldsymbol{x} \leq \frac{1}{4}\right) = F\left(\frac{1}{4}\right) = \left(\frac{1}{4}\right)^3 = \frac{1}{64}$

d) $E[\boldsymbol{x}] = \int_0^1 x\, f(x)\, dx = \int_0^1 x(3x^2)\, dx = \int_0^1 3x^3\, dx = \left[\frac{3x^4}{4}\right]_0^1 = \frac{3}{4}$

e) $V[\boldsymbol{x}] = E[\boldsymbol{x}^2] - (E[\boldsymbol{x}])^2 = \frac{3}{5} - \left(\frac{3}{4}\right)^2 = \frac{3}{5} - \frac{9}{16} = \frac{3}{80}$

6.43 a) First derivative of $(1/\sqrt{2\pi})\, e^{(-1/2)z^2}$ is $(1/\sqrt{2\pi})e^{(-1/2)z^2}(-z)$. This derivative will equal zero only when $z = 0$.

b) Second derivative is $-z[(1/\sqrt{2\pi})\, e^{(-1/2)z^2}(-z)] + [(1/\sqrt{2\pi})\, e^{(-1/2)z^2}(-1)]$. This derivative will equal zero only when $z = \pm 1$.

6.45 b) $P(20 \leq T \leq 60) = F(60) - F(20) = 0.369$. $P(T \geq 60) = 1 - F(60) = 0.301$; compares well with Problem 3.50.

6.47 $P\left(p \le 0.833 + \dfrac{1}{2n}\right) = P(p \le 0.834) = P\left[z \le \dfrac{0.834 - 0.852}{\sqrt{0.852(0.148)/800}}\right] = P(z \le -1.43) = 0.0764$

6.49 $P(x_{\text{binomial}} \ge 71) \simeq P(x_{\text{normal}} \ge 70.5) = P\left[z \ge \dfrac{70.5 - 120(0.655)}{\sqrt{120(0.655)(0.345)}}\right] = P(z \ge -1.56) = 0.9406$

6.51 $P(x_{\text{binomial}} \le 230) \simeq P(x_{\text{normal}} \le 230.5) = P\left[z \le \dfrac{230.5 - 1000(0.25)}{\sqrt{1000(0.25)(0.75)}}\right] = P(z \le -1.42) = 0.0778$

6.53 a) From Problem 4.20, $\pi = 0.113$ and $n = 80$.

$P(x_{\text{binomial}} \ge 10) \simeq P(x_{\text{normal}} \ge 9.5) = P\left[z \ge \dfrac{9.5 - 80(0.113)}{\sqrt{80(0.113)(0.887)}}\right] = P(z \ge 0.16) = 0.4364$

b) $\pi = 0.081 + 0.074 + 0.072 = 0.227$

$P(x_{\text{binomial}} \le 15) \simeq P(x_{\text{normal}} \le 15.5) = P\left[z \le \dfrac{-2.66}{3.747}\right] = 0.7611$

c) $\pi = 0.052 + 0.048 = 0.10$

$P(x_{\text{binomial}} \le 4) \simeq P(x_{\text{normal}} \le 4.5) = P\left[z \le \dfrac{-3.5}{2.683}\right] = 0.0968$

6.55 $\displaystyle\sum_{x=16}^{40} P(x) = 0.1152$

6.57 a) $P(x > 9) + P(x < 7)$ using $\mu = 8$ and $\sigma = 0.4$ is $P(z > 2.5) + P(z < -2.5) = 2(0.0062) = 0.0124$.   b) $P(7 \le x \le 9)$ using $\mu = 7.5$ and $\sigma = 0.6$ is $P(-0.833 \le z \le 2.5) = 0.7905$.

CHAPTER 7

7.9 $\bar{x} = \$371$ million, $s^2 = \$22{,}527$ million^2, $s = \$150{,}090$

7.11 a) $\bar{x}_{\text{Hertz}} = \$44.71$, $\bar{x}_{\text{Avis}} = \$42.71$

7.13 $\bar{x} = 0.80$, $s^2 = 0.8687$, $s = 0.932$

7.15 $\bar{x} = 422.75$

7.17 a) $\bar{x} = 105$ b) $s^2 = 6.67$; $s = 2.58$ c) More suspicious, since $\bar{x} = 105$ is large in relation to $\mu = 96$.   d) Range $= |108 - 102| = 6$ e) Range considers only highest and lowest values.

7.21 a) $P(\bar{x} \ge 5) = P\left(\dfrac{\bar{x} - \mu}{s/\sqrt{n}} \ge \dfrac{5 - 4.833}{0.75/\sqrt{121}}\right) = P(t \ge 2.44)$

Using the *t*-distribution with $\nu = 120$, $0.01 \ge P(t \ge 2.44) > 0.005$. Since n is large, *z* can be used to approximate *t*, and we have $P(z \ge 2.44) = 1 - F(2.44) = 0.0073$,

$P(\bar{x} \le 5) = P\left(t \le \dfrac{5 - 5.2}{0.75/11}\right) = P(t \le -2.93)$, which is less than 0.005.

Using *z*, $P(z \le -2.93) = 1 - F(2.93) = 0.0017$.

7.23 a) $P(x \ge 35) = 0.0475$; $P(25 \le x \le 35) = 0.9050$
b) $P(\bar{x} \ge 31) = 0.0228$; $P(29 \le \bar{x} \le 31) = 0.9544$

7.25 b) $\mu = \left(\dfrac{1}{10}\right)[0 + 1 + 2 + \cdots + 9] = \left(\dfrac{1}{10}\right)(45) = 4.5$

7.27 a) $E[\overline{x}] = \mu$ remains the same. $V[\overline{x}] = \sigma^2/n$ becomes smaller as n changes from 3 to 100. So the interpretation of reasonably close will differ.

b) $\sigma_{\overline{x}} = \sigma/\sqrt{n} = \sqrt{8.25}/\sqrt{100} = 0.2872$

c) Due to the CLT, $\mathbf{z}$-values now should approximate a normal distribution, since n is large.

7.29 b) $\sigma_{\overline{x}}^2 = \dfrac{\sigma_x^2}{n}\left(\dfrac{N - n}{N - 1}\right) = 75.8$, so $\sigma_{\overline{x}} = 8.704$

7.31 a) $\sigma_{\overline{x}} = \dfrac{0.10}{8}\sqrt{\dfrac{400 - 64}{399}} = 0.0115$; $P(\overline{x} \leq 119.995) \cong 0.3336$

b) The standard error is 8% less when using the correction. $P(\mathbf{z} \leq -0.40) = 0.3446$ with the correction factor.

7.33 $\overline{x} = 784/4 = 196$, $s^2 = 684/3$, $s = 15.1$

a) $P(\overline{x} \leq 196 | \mu = 210) = P(t \leq -1.85)$, $0.05 \leq P(t \leq -1.85) \leq 0.10$;
$P(\overline{x} \geq 196 | \mu = 180) = P(t \geq 2.12)$, $0.10 > P(t \geq 2.12) > 0.05$

b) $P(\overline{x} \leq 196 | \mu = 210, \sigma = 14) = P(\mathbf{z} \leq -2) = 0.0228$,
$P(\overline{x} \leq 196 | \mu = 200, \sigma = 10) = P(\mathbf{z} \leq -0.80) = 0.2119$

7.35 a) $\overline{x} = 119.25$, $s^2 = 1513.32$

b) $n = 100$, $s = 38.90$; $P(\overline{x} \geq 119.25) = P(t \geq 2.378)$ is between 0.01 and 0.005. (Check $v = 60$, $v = 120$.)

7.37 a) With $s = 6$, $n = 9$, d.f. $= 8$, $P(\overline{x} \geq 54) = P(t \geq 2)$, which is between 0.025 and 0.05.
$P(x \leq 44) = P(t \leq -3)$, which is between 0.005 and 0.01.
$P(45 \leq \overline{x} \leq 55) = P(-2.5 \leq t \leq 2.5)$, which is between 0.95 and 0.98.

b) All t-values are doubled, since the sample size increases by a factor of 4. $P(t \geq 4) \cong 0$,
$P(t \leq -6) \cong 0$, $P(-5 \leq t \leq 5) \cong 1.0$

7.41 a) $E(\chi^2) = v = n - 1 = 24$, $V[\chi^2] = 2v = 48$

b) $P(\chi^2 > 42.98) = 1 - F(42.98) = 0.01$; $P(\chi^2 > 33.2) = 1 - F(33.2) = 0.10$;
$P(\chi^2 \geq 9.89) = 1 - F(9.89) = 0.995$

7.43 $P(s^2 \geq 800 | \sigma^2 = 400) = P(\chi_{14}^2 \geq 28)$ is between 0.025 and 0.01.

7.51 The correct answer is (a).

7.53 The correct answer is (b).

CHAPTER 8

8.3 Each of the estimators is unbiased.

8.5 $V[\mathbf{med}] = 25$; $V(\overline{x}) = 8.34$

8.9 a) $E[\mathbf{p}] = \pi = 0.4$, demonstrating that $\mathbf{p}$ is unbiased   b) $V[\mathbf{p}] = E[\mathbf{p}^2] - (E[\mathbf{p}])^2 = 0.06$

8.13 a) $\overline{x}$ is best estimate of μ, $\overline{x} = 2.0$ b) 90% C.I. for μ is $-1.47 \leq \mu \leq 5.47$

8.15 a) 95% CI for μ is $4528 \pm 1.96 \dfrac{970}{\sqrt{36}}$ or $\$4211.13 \le \mu \le \$4844.87$

8.17 90% C.I. for μ is $21.833 \le \mu \le 26.768$

8.19 90% C.I. for μ is $75.235 \le \mu \le 92.765$

8.21 95% C.I. for μ is $49.701 \le \mu \le 52.299$ [changes by more than $\dfrac{1}{2}$ second at each end].

8.23 99% C.I. for π is $0.358 < \pi < 0.442$

8.25 95% C.I. for π is $0.504 \le \pi \le 0.696$

8.27 $n = (1.96)^2(1000)^2/50^2 = 1536.64$; a sample of 1537 is necessary.

8.29 166 observations are necessary.

8.31 $5.32 \le \sigma^2 \le 19.17$

8.33 $4.114 \le \sigma^2 \le 33.027$

8.35 a) A 98% C.I. for μ is $24,505 \le \mu \le \$31,495$ b) 543 observations are necessary.

8.37 a) $6.00 \le \sigma^2 \le 16.79$ b) $P\left(\dfrac{vs^2}{\sigma^2} \ge 70.5\right) < 0.005$ This probability is low enough to assert that the machine is working improperly.

8.39 $p = 32/40 = 0.80$ and $n = 40$. A 90% CI for π is $0.80 + 1.645 \sqrt{\dfrac{0.80(0.20)}{40}}$; $0.696 \le \pi \le 0.904$

8.41 A 90% CI for μ using $t_{0.05,24} = 1.711$ is $26.26 \pm 1.711\dfrac{2.80}{\sqrt{24}}$ or $25.28 \le \mu \le 27.24$.

A 90% CI for σ^2 is $\dfrac{23(2.80)^2}{35.2} \le \sigma^2 \le \dfrac{23(2.80)^2}{13.1}$. Using square roots of each term, $2.26 \le \sigma \le 3.71$.

8.49 Answer is item (d).

8.51 Answer is item (a).

8.53 Answer is item (d).

8.55 Interpolating within Table VI, $t_{0.005,49} = 2.683$. A 99% CI for μ is $2.55 \pm 2.683\dfrac{0.30}{\sqrt{50}}$ or $2.44 \le \mu \le 2.66$.

8.57 Use a planning value of $p = \frac{1}{2}$ and $z_{0.025} = 1.96$; $n = \dfrac{(1.96)^2(\frac{1}{2})(\frac{1}{2})}{(0.05)^2} = 384.16$. Use $n = 385$ at a cost of $385(\$0.35) = \$134.75$.

8.59

Lower Prob.	Upper Prob.	Interval Width	Lower Prob.	Upper Prob.	Interval Width
0.050	0.050	38.38	0.025	0.075	39.66
0.045	0.055	38.43	0.020	0.080	40.35
0.040	0.060	38.57	0.015	0.085	41.33
0.035	0.065	38.79	0.010	0.090	42.77
0.030	0.070	39.16	0.005	0.095	45.32

CHAPTER 9

9.3 a) H_0: μ = \$5000 vs. H_a: μ < \$5000
Type I: reject μ = \$5000 when μ is, in fact, equal to \$5000.
Type II: accept μ = \$5000 when μ is, in fact, less than \$5000.

b) Use $z = \dfrac{\bar{x} - \mu_0}{\sigma/\sqrt{n}}$ c) $\bar{x} \geq$ \$4588 is acceptance region

d) Accept H_0; $P\left(z \leq \dfrac{4650 - 5000}{500/2}\right) = 0.0808$ e) $2P(z \leq -1.40) = 2(0.0808) = 0.1616$

9.5 H_0: μ = \$22,000 vs. H_a: μ < \$22,000; $z \leq -1.645$ is the critical region. Since $z_c = -2.50$ is less than -1.645, we reject H_0 and conclude that the average income in this rural county does seem to be less than \$22,000.

9.7 $z_c = -2.71$; $P(z \leq -2.71) = 0.0034$; $2P(z \leq -2.71) = 2(0.0034) = 0.0068$

9.9 b) $\bar{x} \leq$ \$24,467.10 is the critical region.   c) Reject H_0 d) $P(\bar{x} \leq 24,300) = P(z \leq -10) \cong 0$

9.11 a) H_0: $\mu \leq 50$ vs. H_a: $\mu > 50$ b) $z_c = 1.333$; $z_{0.05} = 1.645$; accept H_0.

c) $\bar{x} = 1.645\left(\dfrac{3}{8}\right) + 50 = 50.617$ hours

9.13 a) H_0: μ = 5000 vs. H_a: $\mu < 5000$ b) $t = \dfrac{\bar{x} - \mu_0}{s/\sqrt{n}}$

c) Critical region: $t \leq -2.353$; $\bar{x}$ = \$4650; s^2 = 196,666; $t_c = -1.578$
d) Reject H_a and accept H_0.   e) $0.25 > P(t \leq -1.578) > 0.10$

9.15 H_0: μ = 31.5 vs. H_a: $\mu < 31.5$; $t_{0.01} = -2.492$; $t_c = -3.667$; reject H_0.

9.17 H_0: μ = 18 vs. H_a: $\mu < 18$; $-t_{0.05,15} = -1.753$; $t_c = -2.00$; reject H_0.

9.19 The acceptance region is $\bar{x} \geq 23.94$, $\beta = P(\bar{x} \geq 23.94 | \mu_a = 23.90) = 0.0418$.
Power = $1 - \beta = 0.9582$.

9.21 $\beta(0.90) = 0.0075$, $\beta(0.95) = 0.1200$, $\beta(1.00) = 0.5319$, $\beta(1.05) = 0.9082$, $\beta(1.20) = 0.5139$

9.23 a) $\alpha = 0.0114$; $\beta = 0.7171$
b) $E[\text{cost}|\pi = 0.10]$ is $0.0114(500) = \$5.70$. $E[\text{cost}|\pi = 0.25]$ is $0.7171(200) = \$143.42$.
c) TEC = \$43.03   d) $x \geq 5$ is best C.R.

9.25 H_0: π = 0.80 vs. H_a: $\pi < 0.80$
$P(x \leq 3 | n = 50, \pi = 0.80) = 0.0009$
$z_c = -3.53$; $P(z \leq -3.53) \cong 0$

9.27 H_0: π = 0.20 vs. H_a: $\pi > 0.20$; $z_c = 0.7462$; do not reject H_0.

9.29 a) H_a: $\pi > 0.50$ vs. H_0: π = 0.50 (use conservative H_0.)   b) x = 42 customers

9.31 a) H_0: σ^2 = 4 vs. H_a: $\sigma^2 \neq 4$;   b) Acceptance region is $12.4 \leq \chi^2 \leq 39.4$.
c) χ^2 = 18; do not reject H_0.

9.33 a) H_0: σ^2 = 1 vs. H_a: $\sigma^2 > 1$ b) χ_c^2 = 23.26   c) Critical region is $\chi_4^2 \geq 9.49$
d) Reject H_0 e) $P(\chi_4^2 \geq 23.26) < 0.005$

9.35 a)

	$\pi = 0.05$ H_0 true	$\pi = 0.10$ H_0 is false
Accept H_0 Do not play	Correct decision	Miss opportunity to earn $1200
Reject H_0 Do play	Lose $2000	Correct decision

b) $P(x \geq 10|\pi = 0.05) = 0.0281$; critical region is $x \geq 10$. $\beta = P(x \leq 9|\pi = 0.10) = 0.4513$

c) $a = P(x \geq 9|\pi = 0.05) = 0.630$; $\beta = P(x \leq 8|\pi = 0.10) = 0.3839$

d) The critical region of $x \geq 10$ has the smaller total expected cost ($196.44 vs. $209.67).

9.37 The extra cost is $5(542 - 271) = $1355.

CHAPTER 10

10.3 a) $H_0: \mu_1 \geq \mu_2$ vs. $H_a: \mu_1 < \mu_2$. We must adjust H_0 to $H_0: \mu_1 - \mu_2 = 0$.

b) Use z for the difference between two sample means.

c) $z_{.02} = -2.06$ d) $z_c = -3$; reject H_0.

10.5 $t_c = 2.677$; since 2.677 exceeds critical value of 2.583, we reject H_0.

10.7 $\bar{x}_1 = 31.025$; $s_1^2 = 0.0758$; $\bar{x}_2 = 31.325$; $s_2^2 = 0.0492$; $t_c = -1.695$; since $t_c = -1.695$ is $> t_{0.005,6} = -3.707$, accept $H_0: \mu_1 - \mu_2 = 0$.

10.9 $H_0: \Delta = 0$ $H_a: \Delta > 0$; $\bar{\Delta} = 9.1$, $s_D = 4.4$

$$t_c = \frac{9.1 - 0}{4.4/\sqrt{6}} = 5.07;$$ Critical value is $t_{0.05,5} = 2.015$.

Reject H_0 and switch to the new machine.

10.13 $H_0: \mu_M - \mu_F = 0$ vs. $H_a: \mu_M - \mu_F \neq 0$

$\Delta = -3.9$, $s_D = 8,13$, $t_c = -1.52$

Critical values are $t_{0.025,9} = \pm 2.262$; accept H_0.

10.15 $H_0: \pi_1 - \pi_2 = 0$ vs. $H_a: \pi_1 - \pi_2 \neq 0$

$z_{0.005} = \pm 2.575$; $t_c = 1.715$; do not reject H_0.

10.19 $H_0: \pi_2 - \pi_1 = 0.10$ vs. $H_a: \pi_2 - \pi_1 > 0.10$

$z_c = 0.384$; $z_{0.02} = 2.056$; do not reject H_0.

10.21 $F_c = \dfrac{s_A^2}{s_B^2} = \dfrac{110.25}{174} = 0.634$

Accept $H_0: \sigma_A^2 = \sigma_B^2$, since $F_c = 0.634$ exceeds the lower critical value of 0.132.

Report $2P(F \leq 0.634) > 0.10$.

10.23 Approximating (14, 24) by (15, 24), we get 0.474 and 0.346 as the two lower critical values.

10.25 a) $t_c = -1.85$. Since critical values are (approximately) $t = \pm 1.671$, reject the assumption.

b) Accept the assumption.

10.31 $H_0: \mu_1 - \mu_2 = 0$ vs. $H_a: \mu_1 - \mu_2 \neq 0$, where μ_1 is males; $\bar{x}_1 = 975.91$, $n_1 = 105$, $s_1 = 865.73$, $\bar{x}_2 = 638.28$, $n_2 = 61$, $s_2 = 1272.62$, $t_c = 2.03$; accept H_0. $H_0: = \sigma_1^2 - \sigma_2^2 = 0$ vs. $H_a: \sigma_1^2 - \sigma_2^2 \neq 0$, $F_c = 1.469$; accept H_0.

CHAPTER 11

11.3 C.F. $= 39015$, $\Sigma y_{ij}^2 = 359,345$, SST $= 320,330$, SSB $= 317,820$,

$$F_c = \frac{317820/4}{2510/10} = 316.55; \text{ reject } H_0.$$

11.5 Rather than using the original data, it is easier to solve this problem if some constant, say 400, is subtracted from each value.
C.F. $= 223,880$; SST $= 20,166$; SSB $= 7,124$; SSW $= 13,042$; $F_c = 3.64$; accept H_0.

11.7 C.F. $= 111,392$; SST $= 4472$; SSB $= 420.33$; SSW $= 4051.67$; $F_c = 0.78$; accept H_0.

11.9 $H_0: \tau_1 = \tau_2 = \tau_3 = \tau_4 = 0$ vs. $H_a:$ at least one $\tau_j \neq 0$; C.F. $= 249,561.01$; SST $= 249,736.83 -$ C.F. $= 175.82$; SSW $= 109.94$; MSB $= 21.96$; MSW $= 18.32$; $F_c = 1.198$; $F_{0.01,3,6} = 9.78$, so accept H_0.

11.11 $H_0: \tau_1 = \tau_2 = \tau_3 = 0$; absenteeism does not depend on job classification. $H_a:$ at least one $\tau_j \neq 0$. Thirty observations in each column. Reject H_0.
$\hat{\tau}_1 = -2.3$, $\hat{\tau}_2 = 0.8$, $\hat{\tau}_3 = 1.5$

11.17

Source	SS	d.f.	MS	F
Columns	21.29	3	7.10	1.70
Rows	0.28	2	0.14	0.03
Interaction	45.56	6	7.59	1.82
Error	100.18	24	4.17	
Total	167.31	35		

11.19 C.F. $= 17.40$

Source	SS	d.f.	MS	F
Columns	0.020	2	0.0100	1.75
Rows	0.149	2	0.0745	13.07
Interaction	0.006	4	0.0015	0.26
Error	0.155	27	0.0057	
Total	0.330	35		

Only the row effect is significant. $\hat{\lambda}_1 = -0.031$, $\hat{\lambda}_2 = -0.057$, $\hat{\lambda}_3 = 0.089$

11.21 $H_0: \tau_1 = \tau_2 = \tau_3 = 0$ vs. $H_a:$ at least one $\tau_j \neq 0$; $H_0: \lambda_1 = \lambda_2 = \lambda_3 = 0$ vs. $H_a:$ at least one $\lambda_k \neq 0$; $H_0: (\tau\lambda)_{jk} = 0$ for all j, k vs. $H_a:$ at least one $(\tau\lambda)_{jk} \neq 0$, C.F. $= 80,561$

Source	SS	d.f.	MS	F
Columns	210.75	2	105.4	23.7
Rows	260.42	2	130.2	29.2
Interaction	218.58	4	54.6	12.3
Error	120.25	27	4.5	
Total	810.00	35		

Reject all three H_0's. Durability depends on temperature, brand of tire, and their interaction.

11.27 Three possible main effects and four reasonable interaction effects.

11.29 a) Significant main effects A, but not B, and significant interaction effects.
   b) Significant main effects A and perhaps B, but no interaction effects.

CHAPTER 12

12.3 50 is the rate of change of y with respect to x (the slope). That is, a one-unit change in x will result in 50 units of change in y. $g = 320 + 50(5) = 570$.

12.5 a) A linear approximation seems appropriate. b) $\hat{y} = -920 + 0.03x$ c) $\hat{y} = 8,080$ for $x = 300,000$

12.7 $b = 0.03$

12.9 $\hat{y} = 21.0 + 0.01x$

12.11 a) Relationship does not appear to be linear and may lead to a violation of Assumptions 3 and 5.
   b) $\hat{y} = -21.175 + 11.56x$

   c)

$(y - \hat{y})$
-14.625
11.615
23.255
-10.185
-10.065

   The sign of the deviations seems to be alternating somewhat.
   d) For $x = 8$, $\hat{y} = -21.175 + 11.56(8) = 71.305$. Guess would be approximately $\hat{y} = 125$.

12.13 a) SSE = 7000 b) $r^2 = 0.64$; 36% is unexplained. c) SST = 19,444.4

12.15 $\hat{y} = 20 + 2x$; $r^2 = 0.826$

12.17 a) $b = -3400/7750 = -0.439$; $a = 30 - (-0.439)65 = 58.535$; $\hat{y} = 58.535 - 0.439x$
   b) α is the intercept on the dependent variable axis. β is the slope of the demand function.
   c) $\hat{y} = 58.535 - 0.439(25) = 47.56$ (thousand calculators)
   d) SSR $= (-0.439)(-3400) = 1492.6$; proportion of variation explained is
   $R^2 = 1492.6/1600 = 0.933$.

12.19 $SSE = 14.58$; $SST = 36.45$; $SSR = 21.87$

12.21 $s_e = 1.195$

12.25 a) $\hat{y} = 0.5 + 1.5x$ b) $SST = 18$; $SSR = 13.5$; $r = \sqrt{0.75} = 0.866$

12.27 a) $r = 0.866$ b) $s_{xy} = 1.50$; $r^2 = 0.75$; thus, 75% is explained.

12.29 a) $\hat{y} = -2.464 + 2.26x$ b) $r = 0.960$
   c) $SSE = \Sigma(y - \hat{y})^2 = 9.33$; $SSR = \Sigma(\hat{y} - \overline{y})^2 = 108.28$; $SST = SSE + SSR = 117.61$
   d) $R^2 = SSR/SST = 0.918$; 91.8% of the variation is explained.
   e) $r = \sqrt{0.918} = 0.958$ from part (d)
   $$r = \frac{b\sqrt{SSx}}{\sqrt{SSy}} = \frac{2.26\sqrt{21.2}}{\sqrt{118}} = 0.958$$

12.31 a) $r = \dfrac{119,000}{\sqrt{90}\sqrt{1.84 \times 10^8}} = 0.925$
   b) $t_c = \dfrac{0.925\sqrt{8}}{\sqrt{0.145}} = 6.87$. Since $t_{0.05,8} = 1.860$, reject H_0.

12.33 $H_0: \rho = 0$ vs. $H_a: \rho > 0$; $t_c = 4.5$; reject H_0.

12.35 a) $\hat{y} = -7.41 + 8.505(10) = \$77.64$ million in sales
   b) 90.25% of variation in sales is explained by variation in income.
   c) Demand theory would suggest that higher income implies higher sales, rather than the other way around.

12.37 a) $n = 40$; $SST = 486$ b) $F_c = 16$. Since F_c exceeds $F_{0.05,1,40} = 4.08$, we reject H_0.
   c) $s_e = 3$; $s_b = 2.4$

12.39 $s_x = 223.60$, $s_y = 1581.14$, $s_{xy} = 325,000$, $r = 0.92$

12.41 a) $s_f = 3.376$; $18.723 \le y_g \le 32.227$

b)

x	$\hat{y}$	Interval
8	26.70	20.31 to 33.07
9	27.925	21.79 to 34.06
10	29.15	23.10 to 35.20
11	30.375	24.24 to 36.51
12	31.60	25.21 to 37.99

c)

x	$s_{\overline{y}\cdot x}$	Interval
7	1.548	22.38 to 28.57
8	1.070	24.56 to 28.84
9	0.629	26.67 to 29.18
10	0.381	28.38 to 29.91
11	0.629	29.12 to 31.63
12	1.070	30.38 to 33.74

12.45 $b = \dfrac{\Sigma yx^3}{\Sigma x^6}$

12.47 SSE would be greater and r^2 less for any method other than OLS.

12.49 One should be very careful in making "cause-and-effect" inferences; the causal relation is part of the specification.

12.51 $1.12 \le \beta \le 3.88$

12.55 Would expect precision of forecast when $x = 40$ to be better than precision when $x = 100$ because the former value of x is closer to the mean of $\bar{x} = 50$.

12.57 a) $\hat{y} = -0.841 + 0.03853x$

b) $r^2 = 78.012/81.065 = 0.962$; 96.2% of variation explained; $s_e = \sqrt{3.053/9} = 0.58$

c) Comparing $t_{0.01,9} = 2.821$ with $t_c = \dfrac{0.981\sqrt{9}}{\sqrt{1 - 0.962}} = 15.1$, we accept H_a: $\rho > 0$.

d) For H_a: $\beta \ge 0.02$, $t_c = 7.28$; for H_a: $\beta \le 0.05$, $t_c = -4.53$. Each H_a holds, so $0.02 \le \beta \le 0.05$.

e) $\hat{y} = -0.841 + 0.03853(280) = 9.94$; $s_f = 0.5825\sqrt{1.49} = 0.71$. Comparing $t_{0.025,9} = 2.262$

with $t_c = \dfrac{9.94 - 10.5}{0.71} = -0.79$, we accept H_0 that the 1951 observation is consistent

with the model.

12.59 a) $\hat{y} = 5.635 + 2.143x$

b) Comparing $t_{0.05,8} = 1.860$ with $t_c = \dfrac{2.143 - 1.5}{0.2827} = 2.27$, we reject H_0 and conclude that

the slope differs from 1.5.

12.65 The number of residuals smaller than $|10.28|$ is 13.

12.67 a) taxes $= 665.105 + 0.0136(\text{income})$ b) $F_{0.05;1,76} = 3.98$; $F_c = \dfrac{266,797/1}{34,719,045/76} = 0.58$.

Accept H_0 of an insignificant relation.

c) Using $t_{0.01,76} = 2.381$ and $s_b = 0.0178$, the 98% CI for β is $0.0136 \pm 2.381(0.0178)$ or from -0.0288 to 0.0560.

12.69 a) GDP $= 328.52 + 11.52(\text{exports})$

b) Comparing $t_{0.025,28} = -2.048$ with $t_c = \dfrac{11.52 - 14}{0.478} = -5.188$, we accept H_a that the

slope is less than 14.

12.71 a) income $= -212.042 + 105.562(\text{educ})$ b) $F_c = 19.92$

c) $t_c = \dfrac{105.562}{23.654} = 4.46$; conclude that $\beta > 0$.   d) F_c in part (b) is the square of t_c in part (c).

CHAPTER 13

13.3 a), b) Variation explained has increased from 40.8% to 79.2%. s_e has decreased from 13.65 to 8.088. The slope coefficient relating income to hours has decreased from 3.6847 to 2.6506.

c) $r^2_{yx_2x_3 \cdot x_1} = \dfrac{7084.6 - 2355.2}{7084.6} = 0.667$

13.5 $R^2_{y \cdot x1x2x3} = 0.68$; $r^2_{yx3 \cdot x1x2} = 0.333$

13.7 a) True b) False; all remaining variation is always explained. c) True d) True
e) False; true only if $r_{x1x2} = 0$; in general, $r^2_{yx1} + r^2_{yx2} \geq R^2_{y \cdot x1x2}$.

13.9 a) $R^2 = 0.80$ b) $r^2_{yx3 \cdot x1x2} = 0.571$

13.11 a) $\hat{y} = 6 + 3(-1) + 10(3) - 4(2) = 25$ b) $t_1 = 1.5$, $t_2 = 2.5$, $t_3 = -5$
c) x_3 most and x_1 least important d) 60

13.13 a) $r^2_{yx4 \cdot x1x2x3} = 0.15$ b) $F_c = 2.368$.

13.19 a) Solving yields $b_1 = 4$, $b_2 = 6$, and $a = -26$ c) $R_2 = 0.909$
d) $t_1 = \dfrac{b_1 - \beta_0}{s_{b_1}} = \dfrac{4}{0.302} = 13.25$;
reject H_0: $\beta_1 = 0$. $t_2 = \dfrac{b_2 - \beta_0}{s_{b_2}} = \dfrac{6}{0.427} = 14.05$; reject H_0: $\beta_2 = 0$.
e) $\dfrac{22(9.12)}{33.9} \leq \sigma^2_\epsilon \leq \dfrac{22(9.12)}{12.3}$ $5.92 \leq \sigma^2_\epsilon \leq 16.31$ (hours)^2

13.21 a) $b_1 = 0.7905$; $b_2 = 0.5323$; $a = 5.39$; $\hat{y} = 5.39 + 0.7905x_1 + 0.5323x_2$
c) $SSR = 700.37$; $SST = 770.4$; $SSE = 70.03$
d) $F_c = \dfrac{700.37/2}{70.4/7} = 35.0$. This exceeds $F_{0.05;2,7} = 4.74$, so conclude that x_1 and x_2 are linearly related to y.
e) $\dfrac{SSE}{14.1} \leq \sigma^2_\epsilon \leq \dfrac{SSE}{2.17}$
$4.97 \leq \sigma^2_\epsilon \leq 32.27$

13.23 Use four dummy variables with values of 0, except let $x_1 = 1$ for high school graduates, $x_2 = 1$ for college graduates, $x_3 = 1$ for master's degree, and $x_4 = 1$ for doctoral level.

13.25 a) Sales $= -1.791 + 0.365(\text{Pop}) + 0.540(\text{Unem}) + 0.022(\text{Adex}) + 0.612(\text{Comp})$
b) $t_1 = 4.18$; $t_2 = 2.67$; $t_3 = 1.77$; $t_4 = 1.78$
c) $\dfrac{25(1.39)}{37.7} \leq \sigma^2_\epsilon \leq \dfrac{34.75}{14.6}$
$0.92 \leq \sigma^2_\epsilon \leq 2.38$

13.27 b) imports $= 87.415 + 0.070(\text{GDP}) - 0.676(\text{pop}) + 0.619(\text{exports})$, with $t_1 = 6.01$, $t_2 = -5.41$, and $t_3 = 5.87$. All coefficients are significant. Imports $= -39.449 + 0.102(\text{GDP})$ with t-ratio $= 25.5$.
c) $SSE = 509.208$ and $SSE_S = 5350.845$.
$F_{0.05;2,26} = 3.38$; $F_c = \dfrac{(5350.845 - 509.208)/2}{509.208/26} = 123.606$.
The two extra variables make a significant joint contribution.
d) $\dfrac{28(191.10)}{48.3} \leq \sigma^2_\epsilon \leq \dfrac{5350.8}{13.6}$
$110.78 \leq \sigma^2_\epsilon \leq 393.44$

13.29 a) Let the base level be low cyclical threat. Let MOD = 1 if moderate and HIGH = 1 if high.
b) Tax = 275.209 + 0.017(income) + 453.034(MOD) + 391.371(HIGH)
c) $t_1 = 1.0$; $t_2 = 2.33$; $t_3 = 2.18$; $t_{0.05,74} = 1.668$. The dummy variables have significant coefficients. $F_c = 2.41$ compared to $F_{0.05;3,74} = 2.75$, so the entire relation is not significant.
d) Use four dummy variables with values of 0, except $D_1 = 1$ if the rating is A, $D_2 = 1$ if the rating is A1, $D_3 = 1$ if the rating is Aa, and $D_4 = 1$ if the rating is Aaa.

13.31 a) $y = \alpha + \beta_1 x_1 + \beta_2 x_2 + \beta_3 G_1 + \beta_4 G_2 + \beta_5 G_3 + \epsilon$
b) 28.3% of the variation is explained. $t_{0.05,73} = 1.668$ (interpolating within Table VI) compared to $t_1 = 8.136$ (significant), $t_2 = 0.957$ (not significant), $t_3 = 2.577$ (significant), $t_4 = 3.049$ (significant), and $t_5 = 2.363$ (significant). $F_{0.05;5,73} = 2.35$ (by interpolation) compared to

$$F_c = \frac{SSR/5}{SSE/73} = \frac{4181.375}{780.397} = 5.358.$$

The joint linear relation is significant.
c) The intercept for development status 1 is 16.67; for status 3 the intercept is 4.867. The difference is 11.803% more literacy within status 1 countries.

CHAPTER 14

14.1 Specification and measurement error and changes in behavior

14.3 a) Assumptions 1 and 4 b) Assumption 5

14.11 a) Not a linear relationship. b) $r_{xw} = -11.50/17.97 = -0.640$

14.13 Use the lowest size n in Table X. Critical values for $\alpha = 0.01$ are $d_L = 0.81$ and $d_U = 1.07$.
$d = \dfrac{4.50}{3.88} = 1.16$, giving an indication of possible positive autocorrelation.

14.15 a) $d = 0.785$ lies below d_L and indicates positive autocorrelation.
b) $d = 0.784$, which is below $d_L = 0.86$ for $\alpha = 0.01$; positive autocorrelation exists.

14.21 a) $\log \hat{y} = \log a + (\log b)x$; $\log b = 0.1735$; $\log a = -0.2861$. Using antilogs, $\hat{y} = (0.517)(1.491)^x$.
b) $\{y - \hat{y}\} = \{0.03, -0.05, -0.01, 0.05, -0.01, 0.02, 0.03\}$

14.23 a) The relationship is roughly parabolic.
b) $b = \dfrac{-262.5}{82.5} = -3.18$; $a = 70.5 - (-3.18)(5.5) = 88$; $\hat{y} = 88 - 3.18x$
c) The first two residuals are positive, the next five negative, and the last three positive, indicating positive autocorrelation.

14.25 a) Since $d = 1.1$, which is less than $d_L = 1.14$ for $n = 26$, $m = 3$, and $\alpha = 0.05$, we conclude that positive autocorrelation is present.
b) In the presence of autocorrelation the usual t and F tests are suspect and not reliable.

14.27 c) $d = 1.39$, which is near the value of d_U for $n = 15$.
d) Autocorrelation is probably not a serious problem.

14.29 c) $d = 2.06$, indicating no autocorrelation.

14.31 a) Since $d_L = 1.28$ for $n = 60$, $m = 4$, and $\alpha = 0.01$, the d-value of 1.156 indicates positive autocorrelation.
b) $\hat{p} = \frac{1}{2}(2 - d) = 0.42$
c) $d = 1.813$ indicates that the problem of autocorrelation has probably been corrected.

14.33 Use $n_A = 5$ and $n_B = 4$ with group A being the more recent time periods. $SSE_A = 0.271$ and $SSE_B = 0.071$. Comparing $F_{0.05;3,2} = 19.2$ with $F_c = 2.534$, we accept H_0 that there is no heteroscedasticity.

14.35 a) Plot $\hat{y}$ on the vertical axis and e on the horizontal axis.
b) Group A has observations 1–4, and group B has observations 7–10.
Comparing $F_{0.05;2,2} = 19.0$ with

$$F_c = \frac{225.87/2}{42.53/2} = 5.31,$$

we conclude that there is no heteroscedasticity.

14.37 a) Order the observations by the size of $\hat{y}$.
b) Let group A include data points 48–78 and group B include items 1–31.
Comparing $F_{0.05;30,30} = 1.84$ with

$$F_c = \frac{23,324,818/29}{6,142,589/29} = 3.797,$$

we see that no heteroscedasticity is indicated.

14.39 a) Order the observations by $\hat{y}$.
b) Exclude the middle $0.20(78) = 16$ observations, denoting items 48–78 by group A and items 1–31 by group B. Comparing $F_{0.05;30,30} = 1.84$ with

$$F_c = \frac{19,848,497/28}{6,545,730/28} = 3.03,$$

we conclude that heteroscedasticity may be present.

14.41 The D–W statistic is $d = 0.3599$, which is below $d_L = 1.35$ for $m = 1$, $n = 30$, and $\alpha = 0.05$. Reject H_0 and conclude that positive autocorrelation exists. Excluding the six middle observations and denoting items 19–30 as group A and items 1–12 as group B, we find $SSE_A = 97,308.6$ and $SSE_B = 13,209.6$. Comparing $F_{0.05;10,10} = 2.98$ to $F_c = 7.37$, we also find a problem of heteroscedasticity.

14.43 a) Income $= -624.57 + 233.38(\text{persons}) + 101.58(\text{educ})$
c) Let the 61 females be group A and the 105 males be group B. Comparing $F_{0.05;60,80} = 1.53$ with

$$F_c = \frac{93,426,289/58}{55,104,710/102} = 2.98,$$

we conclude that the variance of disturbances is larger for females.
d) For males, divide each observation of each variable by $s_e = 735.01$; similarly, for females divide by 1269.17.

Obs.	Y^*	X_1^*	X_2^*
2	1.86	0.0027	0.012
3	0.16	0.00079	0.0032

14.45 a) Order the observations by density;

$$\text{deaths} = 107.029 + 4.306(\text{drivers}).$$

b) Let observations 31–50 be group A and items 1–20 be group B:

$$F_{0.05;18,18} = 2.22 \quad \text{and} \quad F_c = \frac{2,305,701/18}{122,800/18} = 18.78.$$

Heteroscedasticity exists.

c) Deaths $= 117.71 + 4.29(\text{drivers}) - 0.0205(\text{density})$. Using the same groupings of observations as in part (b),

$$F_{0.05;17,17} = 2.28 \quad \text{and} \quad F_c = \frac{2,278,093/17}{106,203/17} = 21.45.$$

Heteroscedasticity exists in the multiple model as well, with $V[\epsilon_i]$ possibly related to $(\text{density})^2$.

CHAPTER 15

15.3 a) \$300/year   b) $x = 10$; $\hat{y}_{1983} = 19,500$; income is \$500 below trend.

15.5 b) $\hat{y} = 330 + 16.25x$ c) $\hat{y} = 330 + 15.47x$

d) $\hat{y}_{1984}$ values using $x = 9$ in equations from (b) and (c) are \$476.25 and \$469.23, respectively.

e) $\hat{y} = 330\left(\frac{1}{4}\right) + 15.47\left(\frac{1}{4}\right)\left(\frac{2}{1}\right)\left(x + \frac{1}{8}\right)$; $\hat{y} = 83.467 + 7.735x$

f) Use the equation in part (c) in annual magnitudes and x in half-years:
$\hat{y} = 330 + 15.47(\frac{1}{2})x = 330 + 7.735x.$

15.7 Use values of $x = -1, -0.5, 0, 0.5, 1, 1.5$.

a) Use $\log \hat{y} = \log c + b^x \log a$, and three-point method. $\hat{y} = (5.715)(0.682)^{0.298x}$.

b) $\dfrac{1}{y} = c + ab^{x'}$ and three-point method

$\hat{y} = 0.1842 + (0.0722)(0.1038)^{x'}.$

c) The two fits are about the same.

15.9

Year	1972	1973	1974	1975	1976	1977	1978	1979	1980
Sales	18	20	22	19	21	24	21	23	27
M.A.		20	20.33	20.67	21.33	22	22.67	23.67	

15.11 $y = 50 + 5.5x$ $y_{1980} = 50 + 5.5(2) = 61.0$

$$\text{M.A.}_{1980} = \frac{51 + 68 + 65}{3} = \frac{184}{3} = 61.33$$

15.13 Since $\hat{y} = 3600 + 480x$ is for annual trend, to get equation for months, divide b by $12 \rightarrow \hat{y} = 3600 + 40x$. Since $x = 0$ for October 1981, $x = 42$ for April 1985, and $\hat{y} = 3600 + 40(42) = 5280$ is trend value for April 1985. Seasonally adjusted figure is $5280 \times 0.80 = 4224$.

15.17 Quarterly average = \$3 million; 1st quarter = \$3.9 million; 2nd quarter = \$2.7 million

15.19 a) $S_{\text{Jan}} = 133/102 = 130.4$

b) Monthly average sales = \$240,000/12 = \$20,000. Adjusted sales for March = $20,000(0.9) =$ \$18,000.

15.21 a) $\hat{y} = 1105.1 + 26.52x$ for x in quarters, $x = 0$ at mid-fourth quarter, 1971, from regressing GNP on $t = 1, 2, \ldots, 14$. Adjustment gives $\hat{y} = 1105.1(\frac{1}{4}) + 26.52(\frac{1}{4})(\frac{1}{2})(x + 15)$; $\hat{y} = 326.0 + 3.315x$.

b) Use the original trend line; find $y/\hat{y}$, and level the index to get $S_1 = 0.99425$, $S_2 = 0.99525$, $S_3 = 1.00425$, and $S_4 = 1.00625$.

15.23 b) $y = 24.52 - 0.085x$

c) Trend values (where $x = 0$ is Jan. 1, 1980)

Year	Jan	Feb	Mar	Apr	May	June	July	Aug	Sept	Oct	Nov	Dec
1979	23.54	23.63	23.71	23.80	23.88	23.97	24.05	24.14	24.22	24.31	24.39	24.48
1980	24.56	24.65	24.73	24.82	24.90	24.99	25.07	25.16	25.24	25.33	25.41	25.50

Seasonal index numbers

	Jan	Feb	Mar	Apr	May	June	July	Aug	Sept	Oct	Nov	Dec
Ave.	0.936	0.916	0.942	0.973	1.015	1.073	1.071	1.047	1.043	1.030	0.979	0.975

d) Dividing original data by the 5-month M.A.

	Jan	Feb	Mar	Apr	May	June	July	Aug	Sept	Oct	Nov	Dec
Ave.	0.979	0.961	0.970	0.990	1.000	1.036	1.022	0.995	1.016	1.012	0.944	1.004

15.25 Using 1977 dollars, get \$3.68 million building in 1980 and \$3.21 million in 1985. Get \$0.47 million more building in 1980.

15.27 First year real value is 160. Next year is 163.1. Percent change in real value is $100\left(\dfrac{3.1}{160}\right) = 1.94\%$ increase.

15.29 Decrease in real income is $\$20,833.33 - 22,000 = \$1166.67$.

15.31 a) All employees had a real decline in income.

Employee	Real Value
Secretary	$ 4913
Manager	7982
Janitor	4318
Teacher	9414
Governor	25832

b) $100(100/224) = 44.6$

15.33 a) Price relatives are 1.0 for milk, 0.9 for eggs, and 1.33 for bread.

b) $I = 100\left(\dfrac{15 + 45 + 20}{15 + 50 + 15}\right) = 100$ c) $I = 100\left(\dfrac{1.0 + 0.9 + 1.33}{3}\right) = 107.67$

d) Using 1955 weights, $I_n = 100\left(\dfrac{14.25}{13.25}\right) = 107.5$ Using 1956 weights,

$I_n = 100\left(\dfrac{18.405}{16.75}\right) = 109.9$

e) $LP_{56} = 100\left(\dfrac{14.25}{13.25}\right) = 107.5$

$PP_{56} = 100\left(\dfrac{16.75}{15.75}\right) = 106.3$

15.35 a) $LP = 100\left(\dfrac{385}{290}\right) = 133$

b) For 1975, real value $= 100\left(\dfrac{5000}{100}\right) = \$5000$. For 1985, real value $= 100\left(\dfrac{6000}{133}\right) = \$4511.28$.

15.37 $LP = 100\left(\dfrac{201}{231.6}\right) = 86.79$. Prices in 1981 were 13.21% lower than in 1984.

15.41 Using a multiplicative model, $Y = 210,000 = 180,000(S)(1.10)$; $S = 1.06$.

15.43 $\hat{y} = 137.50 + (8/12)x$ with $x = 0$ at July 1, 1985. For February 15, 1987, set $x = 19.5$; $\hat{y} = 150.5$

15.45 For December 1986, set $x = 32$; $\hat{y} = 307.890$. Seasonally adjusted value is $\dfrac{307,890(140)}{100} = \$431,046$.

15.47 a) Average monthly ratio is $1143/12 = 95.25$. $S_{March} = 105$; $S_{April} = 115.5$; $S_{August} = 75.6$.
b) $10 million average per month; seasonally adjusted values are April = $11.55 million and August = $7.56 million.

15.49 a) February 1986 $= \hat{y} = 120,000 + 1000(14)$; seasonally adjusted value is $\dfrac{134,000(80)}{100} = 107,200$; May 1989 forecast ($x = 53$) $= 173,000\dfrac{115}{100} = 198,950$; December 1987 forecast ($x = 36$) $= 234,000$

15.53 a) See the answer to Problem 14.21.

b) Let x = − 1, 0, +1 for the second, fourth, and sixth values.

$$\hat{y} = -0.32 + 2.92(2.07)^x.$$

c) Exponential curve seems to give the better fit.

CHAPTER 16

16.3

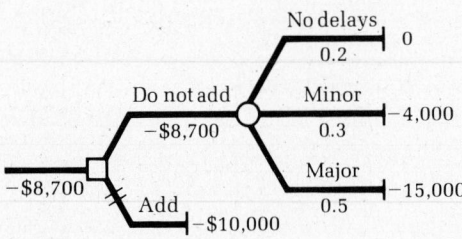

16.5 $P(D|\text{test } +) = 8/35$

16.7 a) $E[\text{air}] = 3400$, $E[\text{sea}] = 3000$ b) $P(B_1|R) = 0.64$

c) Best choice air: EMV[air] = 3640; EMV[sea] = 4200

16.9 a) Any value of $P(B_1) > \dfrac{2}{3}$ will make A_1 best.

b) $P(\text{partial}|x) = 0.615$; EMV[$A_1$] = \$31.00; EMV[A_2] = \$77.50

16.11 a)

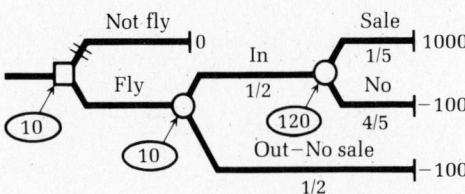

b)

16.13   16.15

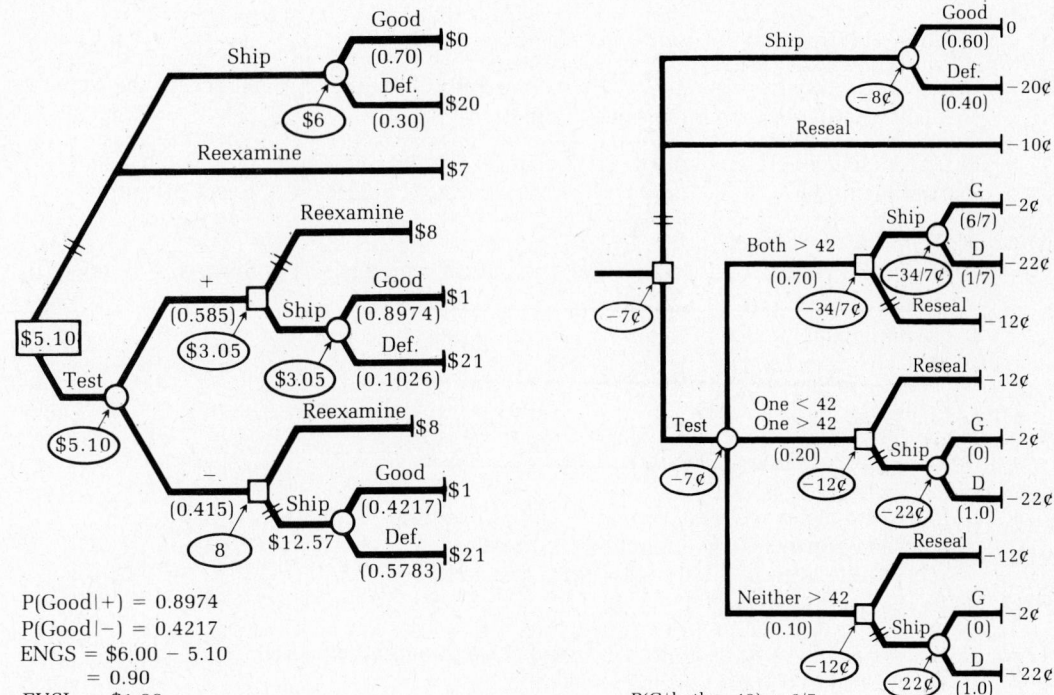

P(Good|+) = 0.8974
P(Good|−) = 0.4217
ENGS = $6.00 − 5.10
     = 0.90
EVSI = $1.90

P(G|both > 42) = 6/7

16.17 a) EVPI = $2500   b) EVPI = $800   c) EVPI = $300

16.19 U(200) = 75. Person is risk avoiding, since EMV (gamble) = $300, which exceeds the $200 for certain.

16.25 The EU of sampling branch is −262.20. Using EU leads to the same decision as using EMV in this case.

16.27 σ^2 = 0.0264, μ = 0.118

16.29 a) μ_b = 119; since μ_0 = 120, optimal action is a_2.
   b) x^* = 115.8 is optimal order.   c) μ_1 = 118 1/3; σ_1^2 = 4.167
   d) Since μ_1 = 118⅓ < 119 = μ_b (breakeven), the owner should select action a_1. x^* = 116.67 is optimal order.

16.31 EVSI = −1620 − (−1900) = $280; ENGS = $280 − 15 = $265

16.35 Number of checks processed daily is very close to 600,000.

16.37 ENGS = $60,199; EVSI = $65,199

CHAPTER 17

17.1 a) Nominal b) Ordinal c) Ordinal

17.3 a) Ratio b) Nominal c) Ratio d) Nominal e) Ordinal

17.7 Critical region for $\alpha = 0.05$, $n_A = 10$, $n_B = 10$ is $r \leq 6$. Since $r = 11$, accept the hypothesis that both samples are from the same population.

17.9 H_0: Price changes are random H_a: Price changes are not random.
Critical region for $\alpha = 0.05$, $n_I = 14$, $n_N = 9$ is $r \leq 7$. Since $r = 7$, reject the null.

17.13 H_0: $\pi = 1/2$ vs. H_a: $\pi \neq 1/2$
At $\alpha = 0.05$, with $n = 9$ (due to a tie), the critical region is $x \geq 6$. Since $x = 6$, reject H_0.

17.15 a)

White males	Women	Minorities
700	200	100
800	150	50

H_0: White males = 70%; Women = 20%; Minorities = 10%.
H_a: The frequencies are different from these.
$\chi_c^2 = 51.79$. With $\alpha = 0.01$, $\chi_2^2 = 9.21$; reject H_0.
b) $P(\chi_2^2 \geq 51.79) \leq 0.005$

17.17 H_0: $E_1 = E_2 = E_3 = E_4 = 50$ vs. H_a: frequencies do not all equal 50.
$\chi_c^2 = 23$. With $\alpha = 0.05$, $\chi_3^2 = 7.81$; reject H_0.
c) $0.01 < P(\chi_2^2 \geq 7.67) \leq 0.025$

17.19 a)

	7–3		3–11		11–7		
	E	O	E	O	E	O	
Males	10	15	7.5	5	12.5	10	30
Females	10	5	7.5	10	12.5	15	30
	20		15		25		

H_0: Errors are independent of shift and sex.
H_a: Errors are not independent of shift and sex.
b) $\chi_c^2 = 7.67$. With $\alpha = 0.05$, $\chi_2^2 = 5.99$; reject H_0. c) $0.01 \leq P(\chi_2^2 \geq 7.67) \leq 0.025$

17.21 a) H_0: The degree of infestation and type of spray are independent vs. H_a: They are not independent.
$\chi_c^2 = 8$. An $\alpha = 0.05$ would be reasonable.
b) With $\alpha = 0.01$, $\chi_1^2 = 6.63$; H_0 would be rejected.

17.23

	White		Black			
	E	O	E	O		
I	23.2	14	16.8	26	40	
II	11.6	14	8.4	6	20	$\chi_c^2 = 11.39$
III	23.2	30	16.8	10	30	
	58		42		100	

$P(\chi_2 \geq 11.39) \leq 0.005$; since the p-value is small, H_a would be accepted for most α-levels.

17.25 a) $D = \text{Max} |F_i - S_i| = 0.065$. For $\alpha = 0.05$, $1.36/\sqrt{92} = 0.142$, accept H_0.

b) $H_0: E_1 = E_2 = E_3 = E_4 = 23$ H_a: The frequencies are not all equal. $\chi_c^2 = 3.48$.
For $\alpha = 0.05$, $\chi_3^2 = 7.81$; accept H_0.

17.27 $r_s = 1 - \dfrac{6(18)}{120} = 0.1, \tau = \dfrac{2}{10} = 0.20$

17.29 $r_s = 1 - \dfrac{6(12)}{720} = 0.90, \tau = \dfrac{29}{36} = 0.8055$

17.31 a) $\tau = \dfrac{22}{45} = 0.488$ b) $r_s = 1 - \dfrac{6(56)}{990} = 0.661$

17.33 a) H_0: No correlation between test scores.
H_a: Correlation is not equal to zero.

$$r_s = 1 - \frac{6(40)}{990} = 0.76 \qquad \tau = \frac{23}{45} = 0.51$$

b) $t_c = 0.76 \dfrac{\sqrt{8}}{\sqrt{0.422}} = 3.31$, $t_{0.05,9} = \pm 2.262$, reject H_0.

INDEX

Acceptance region, 438
Actions, 814, 869
Additive probability, 108
Aggregation of variables, 703
Alpha (α) error, in confidence interval, 390
Alternative hypothesis, 431
Analysis of variance, 516, 548
Analysis of variance table, in regression, 610
Analysis of variance tests, in regression, 654
ANOVA table, 548
Assumptions in regression, 572, 642, 687
Autocorrelation, 694, 695, 705, 712

Backwards induction, 826, 829
Base year, 787
Basic counting rule, 90
Basic definitions, 103
Bayes' rule, 123, 822, 869
Bimodal distribution, 68
Binomial distribution, 204, 245, A-24–A-45
Binomial formula, 245
Binomial parameters, 214, 245
Bivariate probability functions, 178
BLUE, 697

Calculating a sample mean, 12
Calculating population parameters, 8
Census, 14, 29
Central limit theorem, 343, 375
Central location, 33
Certainty equivalent, 843, 869
Chi-square (χ^2) distribution, 376
Chi-square test, 887, 907
Chi-square test on σ_ϵ^2, 660
Class marks, 18, 29
Cluster sampling, 317, 375
c.m.f., 153
Coefficient of determination, 582, 644, 646, 649, 650
Combinations, 97
Combined random variables, 178
Composite hypothesis, 431
Composite variable, 703
Computed F-value for two variances, 499, 513
Computed t-value for matched pair, 513
Computed value, 442
Computed value of chi-square, 475

Computed z-value, 442, 487, 512, 513
Conditional probability, 106
Conditional probability function, 180
Confidence interval, 386
    for binomial parameter, π, 405
    for expected prediction ($\mu_{y \cdot xg}$), 607
    for μ (σ known), 394
    for μ (σ unknown), 401
    for regression forecast, 607
    for regression intercept, 604
    for regression slope, 599, 664
    for variance of disturbance in regression, 661
    for variance σ^2, 414
Consistency, 383
Consumer Price Index (CPI), 798
Continuity correction, 285, 310
Control limits, 308
Convenience sample, 320, 375
Correlation analysis, 550, 585
Correlation coefficient, 587, 600, 648
    population, 586
Counting variable, 193
Covariance, 185
    population, 560
    sample, 560
Covariation (SCxy), 561
Critical region, 438
Cross-sectional data, 693
Cumulative chi-square distribution, A-57
Cumulative distribution function, 260
Cumulative exponential distribution, A-54
Cumulative F-distribution, A-58–A-61
Cumulative frequency, 20, 29
Cumulative histogram, 21, 29
Cumulative mass function, 153
Cumulative relative frequency, 21, 29
Cumulative standardized normal distribution, 276, A-53
Cumulative t-distribution, A-56
Cyclical variation, 750, 780

Deciles, 67
Decision-making under uncertainty (or risk), 28
Deflator, 789

Degrees of freedom, 376
Dependent variable, 550
Descriptive statistics, 2, 28
Deseasonalized data, 773, 774, 777
Deviation, 48
    in regression, 561, 578
Dispersion, 46
Distribution of parent population, 333
Dominated action, 816, 869
Dummy variables, 671
Durbin–Watson d-statistic, A-64
Durbin–Watson test, 708

Econometrics, 686
Economic index numbers, 797
Efficiency, 381
Elasticity, 727
EMV criterion, 869
ENGS, 828, 869
Engel's Law, 731
Estimator, 378
    properties of, 379
Estimation
    least squares, 558
    maximum likelihood, 385
    three-point method, 766
Event, 86
EVSI, 827, 869
Exhaustive outcomes, 85
Expectation rules, 173
Expectations of a binomial proportion, 220, 245
Expected value
    of function of a random variable, 162, 184, 188, 264
    of random variable, 160, 262
    of $\bar{x}$, 334, 375
Experiment, 83
Explanatory variable, 550
Exponential curve, 761, 812
    modified, 763
Exponential distribution, 296, 310
Exponential mean, 298
Exponential variance, 298
Extraneous estimates, 704

F-distribution, 498, 499
F-ratio, 536, 537, 548
F-test, 609, 655, 659, 721, 739
Finite population correction factor, 349, 375
First differences of observations, 703
Forecasting using regression model, 665

Forecast interval, 607
Forecasts, purposes and problems, 752
Frequency distribution, 6, 17, 28
Frequency polygon, 19, 29
Frequency table, 17
Functions, A-19
  continuous, A-20
  discrete, A-19

Galton, Sir Francis, 550
Gauss, Karl F., 696
Gauss–Markov theorem, 697
Generalized least squares, 711
Goldfeld–Quandt test, 721
Gompertz curve, 767, 812
Gossett, W. S., 71
Grand mean, 518, 548

Heteroscedasticity, 715, 720
Histogram, 19, 29
Homoscedasticity, 693
Hypergeometric distribution, 226, 245
Hypergeometric p.m.f., 226, 245

Independence, 112
  of random variables, 181
Independent variable, 550
Index
  Consumer Price, 798
  economic, 797
  price, 791, 794, 796
  seasonal, 773
Index leveling, 776
Index numbers, 787, 788, 812
Indicator variable, 192
Inductive statistics, 3
Integral sign, 251
Interaction effect, 532, 534, 548
Intercept of regression line, 560, 602, 603, 604
Interquartile range, 67
Interval estimates, 378, 386
Interval measurement, 873
Interval scale, 843, 869
Irregular variation, 751

Joint probability, 108
Joint probability function, 179
Judgment sampling, 319, 375

Kendall's tau, 897
Kolmogorov–Smirnov test, 893, 907
Kurtosis, 70

Laspeyres price index, 796, 812
Least squares
  assumptions, 572, 642
  for exponential curve, 762
  generalized, 711
  predicted values, 556
  reduced equations for trend, 756
  weighted, 724
Least squares estimation, multiple regression, 635
Least squares estimation model, 558
Least squares regression line, 559
  intercept of, 560
  slope of, 560
Least squares trend, 756
Leveling an index, 776
Level of measurement, 872
Level of significance, 434
Likelihood, 869
Linear transformations, 175
Logistic curve, 766, 812
Loss functions, 857

MAD, 50
Main effect, 532, 534, 548
Mann–Whitney U-test, 874, 907
Marginal probability, 120, 824
Marginal probability function, 180
Market basket, 791, 801, 812
Markov, A.A., 697
Matched-pairs sign test, 880, 907
Maximum allowable sampling error (D), 409
Maximum likelihood estimation, 385
Mean
  for frequency distribution, 41
  of the Poisson distribution, 235
  of population, 37
Mean absolute deviation (MAD), 50
Mean and variance, of the Poisson distribution, 246
Mean square, 548
Mean square consistency, 383
Mean square error, 383
  in regression, 610
Mean square regression, 610
Measurement error, 689
Measures of goodness of fit, 577
Median, 35
Method of moving averages, 812
Method of semi-averages, 754
Mid-range, 48

Minimum required sample size, 409, 411
Mode, 34
Modified exponential curve, 812
Moving average, 769
  weighted, 770
MSB, 548
MSE, 610
MSR, 610
MSW, 548
Multicollinearity, 696, 698
Multiple correlation coefficient, 648
Multiple regression equation, 632, 635
Mutually exclusive outcomes, 85

n factorial, 95
Nominal, 907
Nominal scale, 872
Nominal value, 789
Nonlinear relations, 725
Nonprobabilistic sampling, 319, 375
Nonsampling errors, 313
Normal approximation to binomial, 284
  using proportions, 290
Normal distribution, 266
  of errors in regression, 692
Normal equations, 559, 635
Null hypothesis, 431

Objective probability, 86
Ogive, 21, 29
Ordinal scale, 872, 907

p-value, 445
Paasche price index, 796, 812
parameters, 5, 28
partial regression coefficient, 639
payoff table, 815, 869
p.d.f., 248
Percentiles, 67
Permutations, 96
p.m.f., 151
Point estimates, 378, 386
Poisson distributions, 231, 246, A-46–A-52
Population, 4, 28, 327
Population mean, 8, 28
Population proportion, 9, 29
Posterior probabilities, 821, 869
Price index, 791
  Laspeyres, 796, 812
  Paasche, 796, 812
  weighted, 794

Price relatives, 791, 812
Prior, 856
Prior analysis, in a research project, 732
Prior probabilities, 821, 869
Probabilistic sampling, 314, 375
Probability density functions, 248
Probability distribution, 148
Probability interval, 387
Probability mass function, 151
Probability model, 151
Probability of an event, 86, 92
Probability of the complement, 104
Producer Price Index, 800
Properties, 253
Purchasing power, 789

Quartiles, 67
Quota sampling, 319, 375

Random-error term, 519, 548
Random number, 375
Random variable, 144
Range, 47
Ratio scales, 873, 907
Ratio-to-moving average method, 777, 812
Ratio-to-trend method, 774, 812
Real value, 789
Regression analysis, 550
    multiple, 632
    tests, 596, 609
Regression line
    population, 552, 553
    sample, 555, 556
Regression model
    population, 553
    sample, 556
Relative efficiency, 381
Relative frequency, 18, 29
Research report writing, 732
Residual, in sample regression, 556
Respecification, 702, 732
Revision of probabilities, 824
Risk-avoider, 845, 869
Risk-neutral, 847
Risk-taker, 846, 869
Rule of thumb, 57

Sample, 10, 29, 327
Sample designs, 312, 374
Sample mean, 12, 29, 322, 375
Sample proportion, 13, 29
Sample size determination, 408

Sample statistic, 11, 29, 321, 375
Sample variance, 323, 375
Sampling and nonsampling errors, 374
Sampling distribution, 375
Sampling error, 13, 29, 313
Scaling, of time variable, 754
Scatter diagram, 553
SCxy, 561
Seasonal index, 773, 812
Seasonal variation, 750
Sequential sampling, 375
Simple hypothesis, 430
Simple random sampling, 315, 375
Simultaneity, 688
Skewness, 70
Slope of regression line, 560
    confidence interval on, 599
    estimated standard error of, 599
    test on, 597, 662
Spearman's rho, 895, 907
SSB, 548
SSE, 579
SSR, 579
SST, 548, 579
SSW, 548
SSx, 561
Standard deviation
    of population, 56
    of random variable, 164
Standard error
    of estimate, 581, 643
    of the mean, 338, 375
    of the mean prediction ($\mu_{y \cdot x_g}$), 607
    of regression coefficient, 599
    of regression forecast ($\hat{y}$), 605
    of regression intercept (a), 603
Standardization of $\bar{x}$, 342, 375
Standardized normal distribution, 271
Standardized normal variable, 273
Standardized variable, 175
Standard lottery, 843, 869
State of nature, 814, 869
Statistical inference, 3
Statistical terms, 14
Stratified sampling, 316, 375
Subjective probability, 87
Sufficiency, 382
Subscripts, A-16
Summations, A-16
    double, A-17
Sum of squares, 548

Sum of squares error, 578
Symmetric distribution, 68
Systematic sampling, 315, 375

t-distribution, 355, 376, 899
t-statistic, 899
t-test, 878, 883, 889
t-test for α, regression intercept, 602
t-test for β, regression slope, 598, 662
t-test for ρ, correlation coefficient, 600
t-variable, 897
Test statistic, 437
Three point method, 766
Time-series components, 750
Time-series data, 694
Time-series model, 751
    additive, 752
    multiplicative, 752
Transformation of variables, 703, 725
Treatment effect, 519, 548
Tree diagram, 819, 869
Trend, 750
    linear, 753
    method of semi-averages, 754
    nonlinear, 761
    using moving averages, 771
Two-factor components, 535
Two-factor model, 548
Type I error, 433
Type II error, 433

Unbiasedness, 379
Unit normal linear loss integral, 859, A-62
Universe, 4
Utile, 844, 869
Utility function, 843, 869

Variability, 63
Variables, A-18
Variance
    for frequency distribution, 59
    of the Poisson distribution, 235
    of population, 50
    of random variable, 164, 264
    of weighted sum of combined random variables, 188
    of $\bar{x}$, 336, 375

Variation
  cyclical, 750
  explained in regression (SSR),
    580, 649
  irregular, 751
  sample (SSx), 561
  seasonal, 750

total (SST), 579
unexplained (SSE), 579, 649

Wald–Wolfowitz runs test, 878,
  907
Weighted average, 39
Weighted least squares, 724

Weighted moving average, 770, 812
Weighted price index, 794

z-statistic, 899

GLOSSARY OF SYMBOLS

GENERAL

x, y, z	variables
i, j	indexes used on variables
a, b, c, k	constants
f, g, h	functions

MATHEMATICAL

$\leq$	less than or equal to
$\geq$	greater than or equal to
$|a|$	absolute value of a
$y = f(x)$	y is a function of x
Σ	summation sign (capital sigma)
∞	infinity sign
$\int$	integral sign
$\sqrt{}$	square root sign

CHAPTER 1

μ	population mean
$\bar{x}$	sample mean
π	population proportion
p	sample proportion
f_i	frequency of observations in the ith class
N	population size
n	sample size

CHAPTER 2

σ^2	population variance
σ	population standard deviation
w_i	weight assigned to value x_i
R	range

CHAPTER 3

$P(E_i)$	probability of event i
N	total number of sample points
n_i	number of outcomes in step i
$n!$	n factorial $= n(n-1)\ldots 1$
$_nP_x$	permutations of n objects taken x at a time
$_nC_x$	combinations of n objects taken x at a time
$P(\bar{A})$	P(complement of A)
$P(A|B)$	P(event A given event B)
$P(A \cup B)$	P(event A or B or both)
$P(A \cap B)$	P(event A and event B)

CHAPTER 4

$P(x)$	probability of the value x
$F(x)$	cumulative probability of the occurrence of values $\leq x$
p.m.f.	probability mass function
c.m.f.	cumulative mass function
$E[x]$	expected value of x
$C[x, y]$	covariance of x and y
$V[x]$	variance of x

CHAPTER 5

π	probability of success on a Bernoulli trial
n	number of trials
p	sample proportion
q	$1 - p$
λ	Poisson parameter (mean arrival rate)

CHAPTER 6

p.d.f.	probability density function
c.d.f.	cumulative density function
$N(\mu, \sigma^2)$	normally distributed, with mean μ, variance σ^2
z	standardized normal variable
T	exponential random variable
ν, or d.f.	degrees of freedom
t	Student's t random variable

CHAPTER 7

s^2, s	sample variance, standard deviation
$\mu_{\bar{x}} = E[\bar{x}]$	mean of the $\bar{x}$'s
$V[\bar{x}] = \sigma_{\bar{x}}$	standard deviation of the $\bar{x}$'s
$s/\sqrt{n}$	standard error of the means
$V[z], V[t]$	variance of z, t
χ_ν^2	chi-square variable with ν d.f.

CHAPTER 8

α	probability of an error
D	maximum allowable difference

GLOSSARY OF SYMBOLS

(continued)

CHAPTER 11

τ_j	jth treatment effect of factor A
SSB, SSW	sum of squares between, within
λ_k	k treatment effect of factor B
$(\tau\lambda)_{ij}$	interaction effect in cell i, j
ϵ_{ij}	error term in cell i, j
O_{ijk}	ith observation in cell j, k
E_{ijk}	expected frequency

CHAPTER 9

H_0, H_a	null, alternative hypotheses
μ_0, μ_a	value of μ specified by H_0 or H_a
α	level of significance [P(Type I Error)]
β	P(Type II Error)
z_c, t_c, χ_c^2	computed value of z, t, χ^2
$z_{\alpha/2}$	value of z cutting off $\alpha/2$ in upper tail
$t_{\alpha/2,\nu}$	value of t cutting off $\alpha/2$ in upper tail with ν d.f.

CHAPTER 12

α, β	population intercept, slope
$\mu_{y\cdot x}$	population mean of y given x
ϵ_i	ith value of population error
$\hat{y}_g$	estimated value of y given x_g
a, b	sample intercept, slope
SSx	sample variation of x
SCxy	sample covariation of x, y
s_{xy}	sample covariance of x, y
s_x^2	sample variance
s_e	standard error of the estimate
r^2	sample coefficient of determination
r	sample correlation coefficient
SST, SSR, SSE	total, explained by regression, and unexplained (error) variation
ρ	population correlation coefficient
MSE	mean square of the errors

CHAPTER 10

$\sigma_{\bar{x}_1 \cdot \bar{x}_2}$	standard error of $(\bar{x}_1 - \bar{x}_2)$
D_i	value of ith difference score
$\overline{D}$	average of difference scores
$\triangle$	hypothesized mean of D's
F_{ν_1,ν_2}	F-distribution variable with ν_1, ν_2 d.f.